THE FAMINE IMMIGRANTS

Lists of Irish Immigrants
Arriving at the Port of New York,
1846-1851

CHILDREN OF THE FAMINE

Illustrated London News, May 10, 1851.

EMIGRANTS ON THE QUAY AT CORK, 1851.

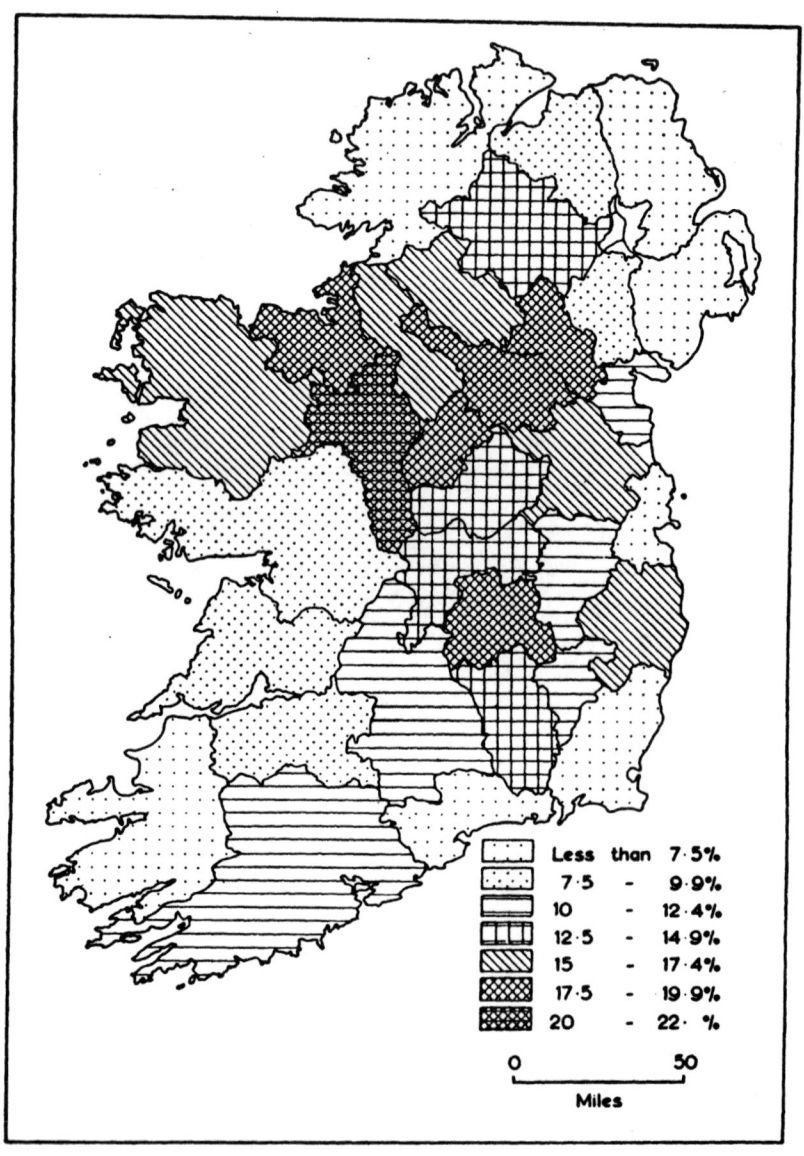

Less than	7·5%
7·5 -	9·9%
10 -	12·4%
12·5 -	14·9%
15 -	17·4%
17·5 -	19·9%
20 -	22· %

0   50

Miles

EMIGRATION DURING THE FAMINE, 1846-1851,
AS A PERCENTAGE OF THE POPULATION IN 1841

From "The Regional Pattern of Emigration During the Great Irish Famine, 1846-1851," by S. H. Cousens, in *Transactions and Papers of the Institute of British Geographers*, No. 28, 1960. Reprinted with permission.

THE FAMINE IMMIGRANTS

Lists of Irish Immigrants
Arriving at the Port of New York,
1846-1851

Ira A. Glazier
Editor

Michael Tepper
Associate Editor

Volume I
January 1846 - June 1847

CLEARFIELD

Reprinted for
Clearfield Company, Inc. by
Genealogical Publishing Co., Inc.
Baltimore, Maryland
2000, 2003

PREFACE

The blight that struck the Irish potato crop during the winter of 1845-46 brought ruin to tens of thousands of tenant farmers and rural laborers and reduced almost all of Ireland to poverty. Dependent on the potato not only as the staple of his diet but as a means of barter and paying rent, the Irish peasant was forever at the mercy of his crop; yet accustomed as he was to the natural cycles of bounty and dearth, nothing could have prepared him for the calamity of the Great Potato Famine. When the blight struck it brought total destruction to the primitive agrarian economy of the island. There was no means of counteracting it, no known chemical agent that could retard it; nor was there an alternative crop that could be quickly sown and harvested.

At the time — despite the abolition of the vicious Penal Laws — very few Irish farmers owned their own land or held title to their cottages and cabins, and when the crop failed they had no means whatever of satisfying their remorseless landlords or the hated "gombeen man," the ubiquitous money lender. Rents and obligations soon fell into arrears, and before long there were wholesale evictions throughout the length and breadth of Ireland. Thousands of families were thrown on the meagre resources of local jurisdictions or roamed the countryside in desperate search of food. For many of these wretched cottiers — homeless now and without any means of sustenance, in dread of the hunger which claimed the lives of a million of their countrymen — the choice was painfully clear: quit Ireland or perish. Of necessity, therefore, hundreds of thousands chose to leave, and during the epochal period from 1846 to 1851 more than a million men, women, and children immigrated to the United States and Canada, mostly through the port of New York.

Who they were precisely, who they came with, and when they arrived are questions of the utmost importance to demographers, social historians, and genealogists. Happily, answers to these questions can be found in an invaluable series of port arrival records known as Customs Passenger Lists. These lists are unpublished, however, and only partially indexed, and are therefore well out of the reach of the average researcher, the more so since they are not classified by nationality. To bring those dealing with Irish immigrants within range of the researcher, *The Famine Immigrants* — of which this forms the first volume — offers an enumeration of all Irish passengers arriving between 1846 and 1851 at the port of New York by name, by ship, and by date of arrival. Answers regarding the identity of the Famine immigrants, therefore, are not only possible to find, they are now at hand; and the full extent of this remarkable migration, the first mass movement of a single people to the United States, is now within view.

FOREWORD

When legislation was enacted in March of 1819 regulating passenger ships arriving at American ports, hardly anyone in Congress could have foreseen the magnitude of immigration to the United States a quarter-century later. In 1820, for instance, the first year in which official passenger lists were kept, roughly 10,000 passengers arrived at Atlantic and Gulf Coast ports from abroad; but by 1846, the first year of the Irish Potato Famine, the number of arrivals at the port of New York alone reached nearly 100,000, and at the same port, just five years later, the number swelled to 300,000. Events in Europe and opportunities in America were contributing factors, of course, but the catastrophe in Ireland was the chief cause of this dramatic increase in immigration. Although there were men in government at that time who might be credited with visionary thinking, it is doubtful that any of them could have predicted the upheaval in Ireland or the phenomenon of mass migration.

Still, the law passed in 1819 was farsighted if not visionary. While it did not foresee the vast migrations of the nineteenth and early twentieth centuries, it almost certainly paved the way, for it had as its object the safety and well-being of in-coming passengers, regardless of their number. It was, moreover, a timely piece of legislation, for passengers were being crammed into ships' holds like so much cargo, with little thought given to their comfort or their chances of survival. On the voyage itself, provisions, sanitation, and ventilation were generally inadequate, and in their weakened states many hundreds of passengers succumbed to disease. In the year 1817, it was said, one-fifth of the passengers died before reaching their port of destination.

By 1818 the situation was critical enough to be taken up by the House Committee on Commerce and Manufactures. In December of that year, Representative Thomas Newton of Virginia, the Committee chairman, expressed the concern of the Committee by introducing a bill to curb the abuses of the so-called immigrant trade. This bill, enacted into law less than three months later, was designed to regulate passenger ships entering American ports from abroad, and by so doing to assure ships' passengers a sufficiency of provisions and alleviate overcrowding, its key provision being to fix the limit of two passengers for every five tons of burden. Specific quantities of food and drink were also provided for in this legislation and so the plight of in-coming passengers was at least partially redressed. The way was now clear for a relatively safe it not altogether comfortable voyage, and the basis for the administrative control of immigration was in place, the first such controls ever imposed.

Throughout the century legislation was enacted which modified the regulatory powers of the 1819 act, in some cases providing for specific allocations of space for each passenger or changing the proportions to one passenger for every two tons of burden, while in other cases demanding specific procedures for ventilation and sanitation or requiring increased rations. But the act of 1819, called *An Act to Regulate Passenger Ships and Vessels,* continued to be the foundation for all subsequent legislation, and such modifications as resulted from later amendments only strengthened the humanitarian intent of the original statute.

By a happy stroke, one of the provisions of the act which remained intact throughout the century was that requiring masters of vessels arriving at American ports from abroad to submit a list of passengers to the collector of the customs district in which the ship arrived. This provision was scrupulously honored and became the basis for one of the largest bodies of records of the entire nineteenth century — our Customs Passenger Lists. Under Section 4 of the 1819 act, ships' captains were required to submit lists designating the name, age, and occupation of all passengers, the name of the country to which they belonged and the name of the country of which they intended becoming inhabitants, together with the name of the ship, its port or place of embarkation, and the date of its arrival in port, the salient features of which have been incorporated in this present work.* These lists were filed with the customs collectors, who in turn were required to deliver, "quarter yearly," copies of the lists to the Secretary of State, by whom statements on immigration were to be laid before Congress at every session.

---

*During the period of heaviest emigration from Ireland the task of preparing the passenger lists seems to have fallen to the passenger brokers. The calling of the roll, a ceremony often performed while the emigrant ship was being towed into the wind, was undertaken by the passenger broker's clerk from the rail above the quarter-deck. From this elevation he was able to verify the passenger list and at the same time have the passengers pass in review before the watchful eyes of the ship's medical officer. *See illustration p. 363B.*

FOREWORD

The original passenger lists were kept under the authority of the Bureau of Customs at the various ports of entry, while copies of the lists, as well as abstracts, or consolidated quarterly reports, were maintained by the State Department, presumably until 1874, when an act of Congress repealed the provision of the 1819 statute requiring customs collectors to send copies of the passenger lists to the Secretary of State and directed instead that they send only statistical reports on passenger arrivals to the Secretary of the Treasury. All the Customs Passenger Lists — originals, copies, and abstracts — were eventually acquired by the National Archives in Washington, D.C., where they remained until 1977, when, for reasons of space, they were transferred to Temple University's National Immigration Archives, located at the Balch Institute in Philadelphia.

Owing, no doubt, to the magnitude of the passenger arrival records they have never before been published, nor for that matter have they been fully indexed (indexes to passenger arrival records at the port of New York, for example, extend only to 1846), and only recently has an attempt been made to reproduce the data in these lists systematically, port by port, in a series of publications designed to cover passenger arrivals at the five major ports of entry up to the end of the nineteenth century, with New York arrivals only to 1846. (This project is still in its infancy, however.) This present listing of the Famine immigrants, a joint undertaking by Temple University's National Immigration Archives and the Genealogical Publishing Company, is intended to cover ground not specifically envisioned as part of this other series while yet being parallel with it, but differing in one major respect; namely, that it deals with a single category of immigrants — a single nationality — rather than the aggregate body of immigrant arrivals at a given port. Of course the records of such a group as the Famine immigrants are compassable in book form, while records pertaining to all immigrant arrivals at the port of New York are almost certainly not. But in this case necessity is truly the mother of invention, for what has been distilled here for purposes of expedience is no less than a directory of refugees from the historic Irish Famine, a rich and singularly cohesive body of information that cannot fail to extend the very bounds of knowledge and stir the imagination of the descendants of the Famine immigrants themselves.

M.H.T.

INTRODUCTION

The passenger list data which appear in this volume are from the original ship manifest schedules on deposit in the National Immigration Archives in the Balch Institute in Philadelphia. The NIA contains one of the largest collections of manuscript data on European Immigration in the Western Hemisphere—U.S. ships' passenger lists from 1820 to the period preceding the First World War. The documents have been transferred from the National Archives (Record Group 36 - Customs) to Temple University for research on European immigration to the U.S.

We have begun to index records for the New York arrivals, 1846–1896, as part of a major research on trans-Atlantic migration. The data-base will serve as an index and a finding aid to the manuscripts, and computer tapes of the index will be deposited with the National Archives.

The manifests make it possible to reconstruct in great detail population flows from the major European sender countries to the U.S. during several decades and to identify the towns, regions, and families most affected by these flows at different periods of time. They are an invaluable source for demographic, genealogical, socio-economic, and medical characteristics of emigrant populations and their antecedents.

The present volume is the first in a series on the Famine Immigrants and contains nominative data on the 86,222 passengers who immigrated to New York between January 1, 1846 and June 31, 1847. The Famine immigration holds special interest for historians and demographers as it was the first mass immigration to the U.S. Although it has been the subject of a vast literature in the past, its significance for the history of Irish population studies has been re-evaluated in recent works by Irish historians and demographers. Questions, however, about various aspects of the Famine immigration remain. It is our hope that in presenting these lists of Irish immigrants to the general public, it may stimulate further research on the history of Irish population and migration in the nineteenth century.

Sources

There are two primary statistical sources on Irish immigration to the U.S. in the first half of the nineteenth century. The first contains the annual estimates of the Commissioners General of Emigration of the U.K. based on the official records of Irish and English outports since 1825 and the record of arrivals at Quebec since 1828 (Table 1, columns 1 and 2).* These show the total number of Irish immigrants to overseas destinations—destinations, that is, other than Great Britain. The second is based on U.S. materials collected since 1820 by customs officials at the major ports of entry from ships' passenger lists (Table 1, column 5). These data were compiled on a quarterly basis and incorporated into the annual reports of the Secretary of State to the U.S. Congress.

Both the British and American series in Table 1 present formidable statistical problems because of serious omissions and are not easily reconciled. The estimates of the Emigration Commissioners involved some "informed guesswork" in the pre-Famine period, as they recorded not only movements from Irish ports but two-thirds of the total number of emigrants who embarked from Liverpool. This was necessary because British customs could not distinguish between Irish who were native born and lived in Ireland and those who resided abroad (in England) at the time of emigration. The estimating procedures, moreover, changed in the 1840s when the proportion of Irish was increased to nine-tenths of the departures from Liverpool and again in 1851 when it changed to seventeen-twentieths. In addition, the British source made inadequate allowance for Irish subjects who embarked from English ports other than Liverpool (London, Bristol, etc.) or via the Clyde from Glasgow. British data also did not include the Irish who re-emigrated from Canada to the U.S., variously estimated at between forty and sixty percent of the total immigration to British North America.

The U.S. data also suffered from serious *lacunae*.[1] The quarterly data from the major ports were not always included in the annual reports of the Secretary of State, so the official estimates were incomplete. Moreover, individuals in the U.S. passenger lists were classified by country and last place of residence. An Irish emigrant proceeding to New York from London, Liverpool, or Glasgow might therefore be classified as a citizen of England, Great Britain, Scotland, or Wales and designated as Irish only if he came directly from an Irish port. The Irish, however, emigrating directly from Irish ports, constituted only about a quarter of the total flow to the U.S.

*For Table 1, see p. xxi.

Although both statistical series show similar long-run trends, significant differences are all too evident. U.S. totals are higher than the U.K. totals between 1830 and 1845 but lower in the years of the Famine migration, with the exception of the year 1851. Both series understate the actual flow of Irish immigration to the U.S. A cross-check of the U.S. returns against the passenger list data in the NIA, it is hoped, will eventually resolve some of the inconsistencies. Estimates of Irish immigration to the U.S. in Tables 2 and 3,* however, are based on the official returns of the U.K. Commissioners General of Emigration.

Historical Background of the Famine

Irish population grew rapidly during the first half of the nineteenth century as a result of early marriage, high birth rates, and declining mortality. Growth meant a persistent surplus of births over deaths and large-scale exodus, the natural response of a traditional society to over-population, which gave Irish population history its unique character in the nineteenth century. The population of Ireland declined from 8.3 or 8.4 million to 6.5 million between 1841 and 1851.[2] In the Famine period, 1846-1851, between 600,000 and 800,000 died of disease and starvation and close to one million emigrated overseas. However, the Famine was not a true watershed in Irish social and economic history. Irish population grew at an annual rate of 1.3% in the 1820s, but at only 0.5% in the 1830s. That there would be a decline in population in the years after the Famine was already evident from the slower rate of natural increase in the 1830s, which was caused by emigration (40,000-50,000 annually between 1821 and 1845), increased celibacy, later age at marriage, and lower fertility. The Famine, then, has been given more credit than it deserves· in the history of population change, and its relative impact has been moderate compared to earlier demographic crises in Irish history.[3] It continues to fascinate, nevertheless, because of its intense human drama and its appalling Malthusian character.

Emigration in the pre-Famine period was closely related to Ireland's economic backwardness and the leisurely pace of industrialization and urbanization. It was generally favored as a means of relieving population pressures in the pre-Famine period. However, the complaint was frequently made that, "The present migration does not relieve us from those classes that it would be most desirable to part with . . . the voluntary emigrants, for the most part, consisted of families possessing capital, whilst our paupers

*For Tables 2 and 3, see pp. xxii and xxiii.

remain at home . . . ."[4] The general view expressed in the literature is that compared to Famine emigration and post-Famine emigration, the pre-Famine movement was of a more affluent and voluntary nature. According to Adams, the Irish preferred to emigrate in families.[5] Famine and post-Famine migration, on the other hand, is seen as being dominated by the movement of individuals. Yet, in a study of 700 emigrants on ships from Londonderry to New York in 1830-1831, sex ratios were skewed in favor of the males, the 15-20 age cohort was dominant for both male and female, and the number of children was small, all findings which are inconsistent with the idea of family migration in the pre-Famine period.[6]

Pre-Famine migration was highly localized, and came from the northeast of Ireland, particularly Ulster and the neighboring counties of Connaught and Leinster. The northeast was an industrial region (Belfast) and was open to communications with outside areas. Emigration from Ulster occurred because of the contraction and collapse of the Irish linen industry.[7] But the Gaelic-speaking regions in the more remote areas in the south and west were cut off, geographically and linguistically, from these movements. Thus emigration in the pre-Famine period did not reflect widespread variations in income levels and agricultural conditions that deteriorated as one moved from east to west.

Cousens' study of pauperism and emigration in the Famine period shows that the heaviest emigration was from north-central and northwest Ireland[8] (Map p. 222 C). These were areas in which small tenants and rate payers predominated — the social and occupational groups which had the highest propensity to emigrate and the least reason to stay. The area of lowest emigration was in the south of Ireland, a region of extreme destitution which also had the highest concentration of agricultural laborers. But emigration from the northeast was also very low, as this was the most prosperous and urbanized region in the country. Thus, in the Famine period, emigration at the lowest level of Irish society was impossible for want of material resources while at the highest level it was unnecessary.

Character and Timing of the Famine Migration

Historians have been prone to exaggerate the backwardness of Irish agriculture in the nineteenth century. On the eve of the Great Famine perhaps ten or eleven percent of the agricultural land in use in Ireland was under potato cultivation. This provided in normal years for an average daily male consumption of about four kilos.[9] It is estimated that the potato accounted for less than one-fourth of the total agricultural output in the mid-1840s.[10] Agriculture underwent a sharp rise in output at the end of the eighteenth century. And in the 1820s, with the opening of steam navigation between Ireland and England, Irish agriculture benefitted from English demand for Irish meat and dairy products. Pasture farming and grazing grew rapidly in this period. But Irish industry, despite the abundant labor supply in the country, was slow to take advantage of the technological revolution that was transforming British industry because it lacked natural resources. Thus a weakening industrial base coincided with a period of increasing unreliability of the potato and created a precarious balance between population and subsistence. Agriculture remained highly labor intensive and depended on the potato for low labor costs before the Famine, but it was unable to adjust to the exogenous shocks of the potato blight.[11]

The *modus operandi* governing the Famine migration was both simple and straightforward — emigration in the current year depended on the harvest of the preceding year.[12] It took then two additional years for the "chain effects" that followed emigration to be felt at the local level. The "chain effects" were associated with family remittances and pre-paid fares. According to contemporary sources, between one-quarter and three-quarters of the Irish who emigrated from Liverpool in the Famine years had their passages pre-paid.[13] Remittances were sent back by the family members who had emigrated in earlier years. The extent of remittance payments depended on the strength of the family relationship as well as on the opportunities for employment and savings in the immigrant community in the new country.

The chronology of the Famine hardly bears repeating. There was a very slight rise in emigration after the initial crop failure of 1845. Table 2 shows a heavy exodus (autumn) after the potato blight of 1846 when 106,000 took flight to avoid starvation and disease. In 1847, the first year of mass emigration, 206,000 emigrated, though the blight was neither as wide-spread nor as devastating as in 1845 or 1846. This was followed by a sharp decline in the emigration tide in late 1847 and mid-1848. A secondary wave was nonetheless inevitable because of family remittances. The harvest of 1848, however, was disasterous as the potato crop failed throughout Ireland, and a new wave of emigration erupted in the autumn and winter of 1848. It swept unchecked through 1849 and 1850 despite the fact that the harvests in those years were a partial success. However, a rise in the poor rate, high rents, evictions, and falling incomes pushed emigration to over 200,000 in

1849 and 1850. The Famine migration climaxed in 1851 when over a quarter of a million Irish immigrated to North America (Table 2).

In the 1820s more than half of the emigrant passenger trade from Ireland came from Irish ports while the remainder came from Liverpool. New York received over half the total amount of Irish immigration to the U.S. in this period. Steerage fares between Liverpool and New York underwent substantial reduction between 1842 and 1851, however, falling from about £5 per passenger in 1842 to £3 or £4 in 1851, or from about one-half to one-third of the annual earnings of a pre-Famine laborer. During the early decades of the nineteenth century emigrant passengers formed "human ballast" for ships on the return voyage to New York and Canada. In the 1840s Liverpool emerged as the leading commercial center in the import of cotton, flaxseed, and timber from the U.S. and Canada, and the Liverpool-New York route became the main artery of trans-Atlantic commerce. Emigration now followed the established lines of trans-Atlantic trade, and Liverpool, offering cheaper fares and more regular service to the U.S., effectively eclipsed competition from the Irish ports and prepared the way for the Famine migration.

Liverpool ships averaged between four and five hundred passengers on the trans-Atlantic routes and weighed about three hundred tons.[14] In the 1840s, the U.S. began to build ships specially designed for the emigrant trade because of its demonstrated potential for large profits. English ships were larger but less well suited to emigrant passengers as they were basically built to carry timber. According to British estimates, U.S. ships had captured about seventy-five percent of the emigrant trade by 1851. New York received about seventy percent of the total number of Irish who immigrated to the U.S. between 1848 and 1851 (Table 3, column 1). These estimates of the Commissioners of Emigration of the Port of New York, however, in Table 3, appear to understate the actual numbers.

Conclusion

Researchers in the emigration field generally rely on aggregate statistics to explain the development, extent, and characteristics of migration. With nominative data from the passenger lists, however, it is now possible to disaggregate and to study emigration at the level of the individual and of the family. With new techniques of record linkage we are able to follow emigrants from their place of origin to place of destination and to focus on behavioral and structural aspects of the process.[15]

INTRODUCTION

Who then were the Famine immigrants? From where did they come? To what social and economic strata did they belong? How did their demographic conditions and social and economic status change in the new urban, industrial areas of the U.S.? These, to be sure, are questions for future research. The reader, however, will find some of the answers in this book.

The editor would like to express his appreciation to the students and staff at NIA who worked with great energy, intelligence, and dedication in the preparation of this volume. A special debt is owed to the archivist, Stephanie Morris, and to the associate editor, Michael Tepper. Without the heroic efforts of all the members of the group this project could never have been brought to fruition.

I.A.G.

FOOTNOTES

1. E. P. Hutchinson, "Notes on Immigration Statistics of the United States," *Journal of the American Statistical Association* 53 (1958):963-1025.
2. C. O'Grada, "The Population of Ireland 1700-1900: A Survey," *Annales De Demographie Historique,* 1979, p. 291.
3. *Second Report from the Select Committee of the House of Lords on Colonization from Ireland* (P. P. H. C., 1847-1848, XVII), 301 (evidence of Edward Wakefield).
4. *Commissioners of Inquiry into the state of law and practice in respect to the occupation of land in Ireland,* 1847, Part I, p. 567 (Devon Commission).
5. W. F. Adams, *Ireland and Irish Emigration to the New World from 1815 to the Famine* (New Haven, 1932).
6. Deirdre Mageean, "Pre and Post Famine Migration Families: Patterns and Change" (Paper presented to the annual meeting of the Social Science History Association, Nashville, Tennessee, October 1981.) Also, Mageean, "Ulster Emigration to Philadelphia 1847-1865: A Preliminary Analysis Using the Passenger Lists," in I. A. Glazier and L. de Rosa, eds., *History, Models and Methods in Migration Research, Papers Presented to the Eighth International Economic History Congress,* Budapest, 1982 (Forthcoming).
7. Brenda Collins, "Proto-Industrialization and Pre-Famine Emigration," *Social History* 7 (1982).
8. S. H. Cousens, "The Regional Patterns of Emigration During the Great Irish Famine, 1846-1851," *Transactions and Papers of the Institute of British Geographers,* No. 28, 1960; Cousens, "The Regional Variations in Emigration from Ireland Between 1821 and 1841," *Transactions and Papers of the Institute of British Geographers,* No. 36-37, 1965.
9. P. M. A. Bourke, "The Use of the Potato in Pre-Famine Ireland," *Journal of Statistical and Social Inquiry Society of Ireland,* XXI, 1967-68, cited in O'Grada, *op. cit.*
10. O'Grada, *op. cit.,* p. 290.
11. O'Grada, *op. cit.,* pp. 290-291.
12. Oliver Mac Donagh, "The Irish Famine Emigration to the United States," *Perspectives in American History* 10 (1976):406.
13. *Report from the Select Committee on the Passengers Act* (P. P. H. C., 1851, XIX, No. 632), 295; *Ninth General Report of the Colonial Land and Emigration Commissioners,* H. C., 1849, XXII, No. 932), 1-2.
14. Report from the Select Committee on the Passengers Act, *ibid.*
15. Walter Kamphoefner, *Westfalen in der Neuen Welt, Eine Sozialgeschichte der Auswanderung im 19 Jahr hundert* (Münster, 1982). Also papers of Robert Swierenga, "Dutch International Migration and Occupational Change: A Structural Analysis of Multinational Linked Files," and Lynn Lees, "The Irish Transatlantic Migration System in the Nineteenth Century," in Glazier and de Rosa, *op. cit.*

Table 1
Irish Emigration from U.K. by Destination 1825-1845 *(in thousands)*

	Official Irish Statistics—Irish Emigrants to:				Official U.S. Statistics
Year	U.S.	British North America (Canada)	Other Countries	Total Irish Overseas Emigrants	Irish Immigration to U.S.
1825	4.3	7.0	0.1	11.4	4.8
1826	5.4	10.6	0.1	16.1	5.4
1827	10.3	9.2	0.1	19.6	9.7
1828	7.5	6.8	—	14.3	12.5
1829	9.5	7.9	0.1	17.5	7.4
1830	12.4	19.8	0.1	32.3	2.7
1825-30	49.4	61.3	0.5	111.2	42.5
1831	13.2	42.2	0.4	55.8	5.8
1832	14.6	39.1	1.0	54.7	12.4
1833	n.a.	n.a.	n.a.	27.6	8.6
1834	n.a.	n.a.	n.a.	44.0	24.4
1835	13.0	9.8	0.1	22.9	20.9
1831-35	40.8	91.1	1.5	205.0	72.1
1836	n.a.	n.a.	n.a.	42.7	30.5
1837	21.7	23.8	0.7	46.2	28.5
1838	n.a.	n.a.	n.a.	13.3	12.6
1839	n.a.	n.a.	n.a.	32.8	23.9
1840	n.a.	n.a.	n.a.	54.9	39.4
1836-40	21.7	23.8	0.7	189.9	134.9
1841	3.9	24.0	4.5	32.4	37.7
1842	6.1	33.4	1.0	40.5	51.3
1843	23.4	13.5	0.6	37.5	19.6
1844	37.2	16.4	0.6	54.2	33.5
1845	50.2	24.7		74.9	44.8
1841-45	120.8	112.0	6.7	239.5	186.9

Columns 1-4, *Commission on Emigration and Other Population Problems: Reports* (Dublin, 1956), 314.
Column 5, *Historical Statistics of the United States* (Washington, 1960), 49;
William J. Bromwell, *History of Immigration to the United States* (New York, 1856).
Column 3, "Other Countries" are Australia and New Zealand.

Table 2

Estimated Irish Overseas Emigration from the U.K. by Destination 1846-1851
(thousands and percentage of total)

Irish Emigrants to:

Year	U.S.		British North America (Canada)		Other Countries		Total Number of Irish Emigrants to U.S.	Irish Emigrants
	(1)	(2)	(3)	(4)	(5)	(6)	(7)	(8)
		percent		*percent*		*percent*		
1846	68	(64.2)	38	(35.8)	—	—	106	51.7
1847	117	(54.4)	97	(45.1)	1	(0.5)	215	105.5
1848	154	(86.5)	23	(12.9)	1	(0.6)	178	112.9
1849	177	(82.7)	31	(14.5)	6	(2.8)	214	159.3
1850	181	(86.6)	24	(11.5)	4	(1.9)	209	164.0
1851	216	(86.4)	29	(11.6)	5	(2.0)	250	221.2
Total 1846– 1851	913	(77.9)	242	(20.6)	17	(1.5)	1172	814.6

Column 1-7, Census of Ireland, 1851, Part VI, General Report (Parliamentary Papers, H.C., 1856, XXXI), iv.
Column 8, Historical Statistics of the United States (Washington, 1960), 49.

Table 3

Irish Emigration to the U.S. by Port of Embarkation 1846-1851 (Adjusted) (thousands)

Year	London (1)	Liverpool (2)	Glasgow (3)	Other U.K. (4)	Irish Ports (5)	Total Irish Emigration to U.S. (6)	Irish Immigrants to New York (7)	New York as a Percentage of Total U.S. (8) (6-7)
							Irish Immigration to New York	
1846	2.9	57.6	0.4	0.1	7.0	68	—	—
1847	1.0	87.2	1.1	4.3	24.5	118	52.9	44.8
1848	6.0	108.0	2.0	—	38.0	154	98.0	63.6
1849	7.9	125.0	2.0	—	43.0	177	112.5	63.5
1850	5.3	140.9	3.0	3.5	31.3	184	117.6	63.9
1851	8.6	166.0	3.0	—	38.4	216	163.3	75.6

Columns 1-6 are from the annual reports of the Colonial Land and Emigration Commissioners: *Seventh Report, CLEC* (P. P. H. C., 1847, XXXIII, No. 809), 131; *Eighth Report, CLEC* (P. P. H. C., 1847-48, XXVI, No. 961), 1; *Ninth Report, CLEC* (P. P. H.C., 1849, XXII, No. 1082), 1; *Tenth Report, CLEC* (P. P. H. C., 1850, XXIII, No. 1204), 55; *Eleventh Report, CLEC* (P. P. H. C., 1851, XXII, No. 1383), 333; *Twelfth Report, CLEC* (P. P. H. C., 1852, XVIII, No. 1499), 161.

Column 7 is from *New York Commissioners of Emigration: Reports and Laws 1847-1860*, Table A (New York, 1860), 288.

1847 includes only months from May 5 to December 31, 1847.

Column 1 has been adjusted by a factor of .57 to show the Irish component in the total number of embarkations from the port of London. Column 2 by a factor ranging from .85 to .90, and Column 3 by a factor of .33.

ILLUSTRATIONS

KEY

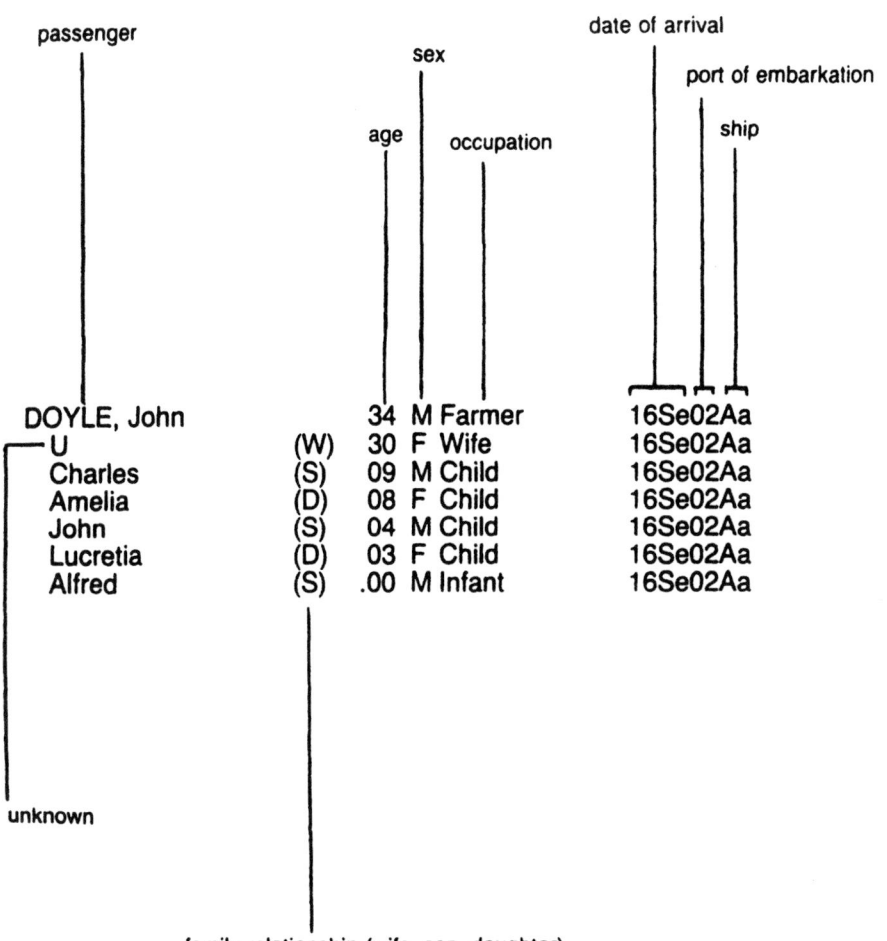

passenger

sex

date of arrival

port of embarkation

age   occupation   ship

DOYLE, John		34	M	Farmer	16Se02Aa
U	(W)	30	F	Wife	16Se02Aa
Charles	(S)	09	M	Child	16Se02Aa
Amelia	(D)	08	F	Child	16Se02Aa
John	(S)	04	M	Child	16Se02Aa
Lucretia	(D)	03	F	Child	16Se02Aa
Alfred	(S)	.00	M	Infant	16Se02Aa

unknown

family relationship (wife, son, daughter)

Also *A* aunt; *B* brother; *C* cousin; *F* stepdaughter; *G* stepson;
H husband; *L* in-law; *M* mother; *N* niece/nephew; *O* widow/widower;
P father; *R* relative; *T* sister; *Y* grandparent; *Z* grandchild.

AA	GARRICK	CS	AGNES	FM	OCEAN-QUEEN
AB	NIAGARA	CT	PHILADELPHIA	FN	WASHINGTON
AC	JOHN-R.SKIDDY	CU	FRANCIS	FO	EVANDER
AD	QUINCY	CV	ANTARCTIC	FP	LORD-ASHBURTON
AE	THETIS	CW	PATRICK-HENRY	FQ	EMMANUEL
AF	BALTIMORE	CX	JAVA	FR	WAVE
AG	MARGARET-JANE	CY	GREAT-WESTERN	FS	GEORGIA
AH	SARACEN	CZ	CRISTOVAL-COLON	FT	ARVUM
AI	EMPIRE	DA	CHARLOTTE	FU	HELEN-THOMPSON
AJ	OXFORD	DB	ANN-HARLEY	FV	LETITIA-HEYES
AK	ROCHESTER	DC	NORTH-BEND	FW	LIBERTY
AL	SWITZERLAND	DD	ANN-LOUISA	FX	TAROLINTA
AM	CORNELIA	DE	GLAMIS-CASTLE	FY	PLATO
AN	NEW-YORK-PACKET	DF	SEA-KING	FZ	MESSENGER
AO	MONTEZUMA	DG	GLADIATOR	GA	COSMO
AP	VIRGINIAN	DH	CLARISSA	GB	HENRIETTA-MARY
AQ	HYDER-ALI	DI	VENICE	GC	ALVERTON
AR	COLUMBUS	DJ	ORPHAN	GD	HAYTI
AS	WATERLOO	DK	WAGRAM	GE	ENVOY
AT	MUDARA	DL	AMETHYST	GF	SILAS-HOLMES
AU	QUEBEC	DM	RAPPAHANOCK	GG	CHAOS
AV	ST.GEORGE	DN	JUNIUS	GH	HANNAH-SPRAGUE
AW	ADAM-CARR	DO	SHERIDAN	GI	BRUTUS
AX	FIDELIA	DP	SHANANGA	GJ	WILLIAM-CAULDWELL
AY	VICTORIA	DQ	ACADIA	GK	DIADEM
AZ	GRANDEE	DR	EXCHANGE	GL	ELIZABETH
BA	TORONTO	DS	PANTHEA	GM	QUEEN-VICTORIA
BB	MASSACHUSETTS	DT	MEDIATOR	GN	CORNET
BC	HOTTINGUER	DU	BELFAST	GO	PERSEVERANCE
BD	ASHBURTON	DV	JANE	GP	CLARENCE
BE	HUGUENOT	DW	RELIANCE	GQ	HANNAH-KERR
BF	ROSCIUS	DX	MACEDONIA	GR	CATHERINE
BG	SEA	DY	SOUTHERNER	GS	MACON
BH	HENDRIK-HUDSON	DZ	AGNES-GILMORE	GT	SARDINIA
BI	EUROPE	EA	CAMBRIDGE	GU	EMILY
BJ	PACIFIC	EB	THOMAS	GV	GRAMPION
BK	NEW-YORK	EC	ATLAS	GW	WARD-CHIPMAN
BL	WELLINGTON	ED	ETRURIA	GX	MARY-BROUGHTON
BM	OHIO	EF	OTTAWA	GY	ANAHUAC
BN	PRINCE-ALBERT	EG	GONDOLA	GZ	ALMANDRALNA
BO	LIVERPOOL	EH	JOHN-CLARK	HA	HENRY-PRATT
BP	SHAKESPEARE	EI	ARABELLA	HB	ROBERT-PARKS
BQ	HUDSON	EJ	MONTEZUMA	HC	MARMION
BR	WESTMINSTER	EK	ANN-ELIZABETH	HD	ROBERT-BRUCE
BS	SAMUEL-HICKS	EL	NEW-HAMPSHIRE	HE	NEW-ORLEANS
BT	KALAMAZOO	EM	HECLA	HF	INDEPENDENCE
BU	ST.JAMES	EN	MAINE	HG	ENGLAND
BV	SHENANDOAH	EP	REGULUS	HI	CONSTITUTION
BW	ST.PATRICK	EQ	JOHN-ROBERT	HJ	DORCAS
BX	SIDDONS	ER	LAUREL	HK	AMERICAS
BY	ADELAIDE	ES	LADY-HUNTLEY	HL	MADRAS
BZ	YORKSHIRE	ET	AVOLA	HM	GREENOCK
CA	FREDONIA	EU	AVALANCHE	HN	JOSEPH-CUNARD
CB	FINLAND	EV	LOUISA	HO	KATE
CC	KESTREL	EW	ALBATROSS	HP	GREAT-BRITAIN
CD	STEPHEN-WHITNEY	EX	BROOKSBY	HQ	CHUSAN
CE	METEOR	EY	BROOM	HR	MERSEY
CF	JOHN-BARING	EZ	CHOCTAW	HS	POLAND
CG	NORTHUMBERLAND	FA	ESPINDOLA	HT	CROTON
CH	CHARLES-HUMBERTON	FB	BALTIC	HU	MANCHESTER
CI	LADY-SALE	FC	PLANTER	HV	SCOTIA
CJ	FAIR-FIELD	FD	SOUTH-CAROLINA	HW	ANN-STILLE
CK	PETER-HATTRICK	FE	ISABELLA	HX	HAMPDEN
CL	DEVONSHIRE	FF	RAMMOHURN-ROY	IA	COLLOONEY
CM	ADIRONDACK	FG	HELEN	IB	NORMAL
CN	QUEEN-OF-THE-WEST	FH	MARY-HARRINGTON	IC	HENRY
CO	HENRY-CLAY	FI	HARRIET-AND-JESSIE	ID	CHESTER
CP	A.LAWRENCE	FJ	ARABIAN	IE	COLLECTOR
CQ	NONANTUM	FK	JOHN-GARROW	IF	AURELIUS
CR	BROTHERS	FL	ALERT	IG	MAYFIELD

IH	LADY-MARY	KZ	AILSA	NQ	LOUISIANA
IJ	CORSAIR	LA	ABBY-PRATT	NR	H.PATTERSON
IK	CASPIAN	LB	JUNO	NS	IOWA
IL	PRATENCOLE	LC	AERIAL	NT	BURNHOLM
IM	VERONICA	LD	MAY-T.RUNDLET	NU	ARCHIMEDES
IN	PANAMA	LE	GASPER	NV	REPUBLIC
IO	RAPID	LF	RICHARD-WATSON	NW	CLIFTON
IP	MARGARET-EVANS	LG	ZENOBIA	NX	FAGAN-BEALAC
IQ	NICHOLAS-BIDDLE	LH	LEVERETT	NY	ASHLAND
IR	ROBERT-A.PARKE	LI	TASSIE	NZ	DIANA
IS	SEA-OF-NEW-YORK	LJ	COXON	OA	ELLERSLIE
IT	LUCONIA	LK	ONEIDA	OB	AGILE
IU	JOHN-CADMUS	LM	F.MATHEWS	OC	SYMMETRY
IV	CAROLINA	LN	CARTHAGE	OD	DEFENSE
IW	GENERAL-MARION	LO	JAMES-REDDON	OE	HIGHLAND-MARY
IX	SWAN	LP	FALCON	OF	JANE-AND-BARBARA
IY	BRILLIANT	LQ	THARTUS	OG	ROGER-STEWART
IZ	DOLPHIN	LR	DIPLOMA	OH	MARION
JA	BURLINGTON	LS	AGINA	OI	AYRSHIRE
JB	HARRIET	LT	FLORA	OJ	JOHN-BRIGHT
JC	VERMONT	LU	KENSINGTON	OK	IMPERIAL
JD	ELEUTHERIA	LV	ABERFOIL	OL	MARY-MORRIS
JE	NARTISKA	LW	WINDSOR-CASTLE	OM	CUSHLAMACHREE
JF	GENERAL-GRANT	LX	JAMES	ON	UNDINE
JG	SIR-C.CAMPBELL	LY	ANGORA	OO	ROYAL-SOVEREIGN
JH	FOAM	LZ	TONQUIN	OP	LORD-DUFFERIN
JI	ST.MARGARET	MA	ROSE	OQ	BARLOW
JJ	CLAUSMAN	MB	ORIZABA	OR	JOHN-RAVENEL
JK	WALPOLE	MC	SARAH-BOYDE	OS	FONS
JL	JOHN-W.CARTER	MD	BAVARIA	OT	OSCEOLA
JM	EDWARD-KOPPICH	ME	FRANKLIN	OU	MEG-LEE
JN	ELIZABETH-DENISON	MF	TENNESSEE	OV	ALBION
JO	CHRISTIANA	MG	HINDOSTAN	OW	ZANONI
JP	JOSEPH-ATKINS	MH	GOLCONDA	OX	COURTNEY
JQ	MILLICETE	MI	CALYPSO	OY	HARMONY
JR	FRANCONIA	MJ	MORGIANA	OZ	COMPTON
JS	UNITED-KINGDOM	MK	SHAMROCK	PA	DROMAHAIR
JT	GLOBE	ML	METOKA	PB	HIBERNIA
JU	GAZELLE	MM	ALICE-MARIA	PC	W.WARD
JV	ANDREW-KING	MN	FANNY	PD	SPEED
JW	PONTIAC	MO	VICTOR	PE	HINDOO
JX	OCEAN	MP	ROSCINE	PF	FLORIDIAN
JY	PRINCE-HENRY	MQ	VERONA	PG	FRIENDSHIP
JZ	MIRACLE	MR	ROBINSON	PH	WALKELLA
KA	AFFGHAN	MS	HECTOR	PI	HEATHER-BELL
KB	ABEONA	MT	MONTEREY	PJ	SEVEN-LASS
KC	CHARLEMAGNE	MU	SIR-ROBERT-PEEL	PK	YOUNG-QUEEN
KD	HOWARD	MV	SPARTAN	PL	ROSE-STANDISH
KE	ELSINORE	MW	BARRINGTON	PM	ANNAMARIA
KF	YUCATAN	MX	GIPSY	PN	DOWNS
KG	TERESA-JANE	MY	ATLANTIC	PO	COMMERCE
KH	SALLY-ANN	MZ	LEILA	PP	COOLOCK
KI	ISLAN	NA	HENRY-HOBBS	PQ	EMBLEM
KJ	YUMCHI	NB	LA-GRANGE	PR	LONDON
KK	LADY-OF-THE-LAKE	NC	FRANCIS-WATTS	PS	VICTORY
KL	HYNDERFORD	ND	FEROZEPORE	PT	NACOOCHEE
KM	GLENMORE	NE	ARCOLE	PU	EMIGRANT
KN	COLONIST	NF	SIBERIA	PV	ADAM-WRIGHT
KO	INDIANA	NG	UNCAS	PW	WILLIAM-CARSON
KP	SARAH-SANDS	NH	PAOLI	PX	D.B.
KQ	JOSEPHINE	NI	PRINCE-DE-JOINVILLE	PY	CHARLES
KR	WRENHAM	NJ	EARL-DUNHAM	PZ	ELLEN
KS	TALLEYRAND	NK	CHRISAN	QA	DRYDEN
KT	ELIZA	NL	ATLANTA	QB	OLINDER
KU	NEW-WORLD	NM	ELISA-ANN	QC	JANE-E.WILLIAMS
KV	MARY-H.KENDALL	NN	LORD-FITZGERALD	QD	HELENA
KW	CEYLON	NO	MONTICELLO	QE	E.CHURCHILL
KX	ADAM-LODGE	NP	PELTONA	QF	HERMANN
KY	BIRKINHEAD				

PORTS OF EMBARKATION
With Code Numbers

00 UNKNOWN	31 LIVERPOOL, LONDONDERRY	61 NEW-RUSH
01 LONDONDERRY	32 DROGHEDA	62 SAVANILLA
02 LIVERPOOL	33 LIMERICK	63 MANILA
03 QUEENSTOWN	34 SYDNEY, CAPE-BRETON	64 ST.MICHAELS
04 GLASGOW	35 BLACK-RIVER	65 MARANHAM
05 HAVRE	36 PUERTO-CABELLO	66 NEWCASTLE
06 HAVANA	37 HULL	67 RIO-HACHA
07 BELFAST	38 VERA-CRUZ	68 GREENOCK
08 MOVILLE	39 GUAYAMA,P.R.	69 CAMPECHE
09 SOUTHAMPTON	40 ST.VINCENT	70 SAVANNA-LA-MAR, JAMAICA
10 NUEVITAS	41 ELEUTHERA	71 YOUGHALL
11 GALWAY	42 FALMOUTH	72 CARBONEAR-NF.
12 LAGUNA	43 PICTOU,N.S.	73 ST.CROIX
13 RIO-DE-JANIERO	44 NEWPORT,WALES	74 TRINIDAD DE CUBA
14 CORK	45 GLASGOW,FAYAL	75 BERMUDA
15 DEMERARA	46 FAYAL	76 TAMPICO
16 WATERFORD	47 TORQUAY	77 ST.JOHN,CAPE NF.
17 TRINIDAD	48 COLON,R.C.	78 MARSEILLES
18 BRISTOL	49 VALPARAISO,CHILE	79 ST.JOHNS,N.B.
19 NEWRY	50 BELIZE	80 CADIZ
20 DUBLIN	51 PRINCE-EDWARD-ISLAND	81 PUERTO-CABELLO
21 LONDON	52 NASSAU,ELEUTHERA	82 DONEGAL
22 HALIFAX	53 TRALEE	83 ST.CROIX-VIA-TURKS-IS.
23 KINGSTON	54 MADEIRA	84 SANTO-DOMINGO
24 TURKS-ISLAND	55 LISBON	85 ST.ANNS-BAY-JAMAICA
25 LIVERPOOL,QUEENSTOWN	56 MATANZAS	86 ST.JOHNS-NF.
26 GLASGOW,LARNE	57 YARMOUTH,N.S.	87 MALAGA-AND-GIBRALTER
27 GLASGOW,MOVILLE	58 SAGUA-LA-GRANDE	88 PENZANCE
28 SLIGO	59 DUNDEE	89 CALAIS
29 BARROW,DUBLIN	60 KILRUSH	90 BREMEN, SOUTHAMPTON
30 HAITI		

LIST OF OCCUPATIONS
With Code Letters

AY-LT	ARMY LIEUTENANT
AY-LTCOL	ARMY LT.COLONEL
AY-OFF	ARMY OFFICER
BFCR	BIRD FANCIER
BLKP	BLOCK PRINTER
BLWMKR	BELLOWS MAKER
BRF	BRASS FOUNDER
BTMKR-SH	BOOT-SHOE MAKER
CBTMKR	CABINET MAKER
CHTMR	COACH TRIMMER
CHWKR	CLOTH WORKER
CLCP	CALICO PRINTER
CLFN	CLOTH FINISHER
CMAGT	COMMISSION AGENT
CNF	CONFECTIONER
CRPM	CARPET MAKER
CST	CORSET STAY MAKER
CTLH	CATTLE HERDER
CTNSP	COTTON SPINNER
CUOF	CUSTOMS OFFICIAL
DIACTR	DIAMOND CUTTER
ENGD	ENGINE DRIVER
FLABR	FARM LABORER
FLAXDR	FLAX DRESSER
FMR-FSHM	FARMER-FISHERMAN
FRNGMR	FRINGE MAKER
FSVNT	FARM SERVANT
FWKR	FACTORY WORKER
GDNR	GARDNER/GROWER
HRSDLR	HORSE DEALER
HRSM	HARNESS MAKER
HTLKPR	HOTEL KEEPER
IRNMLDR	IRON MOULDER
ISB	IRON SHIP BUILDER
LABR-MNR	LABORER MINER
LABRW	LABORER'S WIFE
LAD	LAUNDRY WORKER
LDPR	LINEN DRAPER
LNBL	LINEN BLEACHER
LRFH	LEATHER FINISHER
LRFHM	MOROCCO FINISHER
MCTR	MARBLE CUTTER
MNFTR	MANUFACTURER
MNRE	MINE ENGINEER
MTMKR	MANTEAU MAKER
MUSDLR	MUSIC DEALER
NVOF	NAVAL OFFICER
PLGMKR	PLOUGH MAKER
PMBR-GZR	PLUMBER-GLAZIER
POST	POST OFFICER
PPSTR	PAPER STAINER
PROF-LIT	PROFESSOR OF LITERATURE
PTMKR	PATTERN MAKER
RE-MERCY	SISTER OF MERCY
SCER	SCAFFOLD ERECTOR
SCHM	SCHOOL MASTER
SCHMS	SCHOOL MISTRESS
SLT-PLST	SLATER-PLASTERER
SPRNTR	SILK PRINTER
STB	STONE BREAKER
STCTR	STONE CUTTER
STDLR	STONE DEALER
STHMKR	STARCH MAKER
STNSP	COTTON SPINNER
SVNT-NRS	SERVANT-NURSE
TBCMCHT	TOBACCO MERCHANT
TNR-CUR	TANNER-CURRIER
WI	WIDOW WIDOWER
WI-SVNT	WIDOW SERVANT
WLMCHT	WOOL MERCHANT
WLS	WOOL SPINNER
WMCHT	WINE MERCHANT

THE FAMINE IMMIGRANTS

Lists of Irish Immigrants
Arriving at the Port of New York,
1846-1851

MARGARET-JANE 12 JANUARY 1846

From SYDNEY,Cape-Breton

NAMES OF PASSENGERS		AGE	SEX	OCCUPATIONS	DATE PORT SHIP
SOMER, John		17	M	Tailor	12Ja34Ag

EMPIRE 15 JANUARY 1846

From Liverpool

NAMES OF PASSENGERS		AGE	SEX	OCCUPATIONS	DATE PORT SHIP
LOCKE, Ellen		44	F	Weaver	15Ja02AI
Catherine		22	F	Weaver	15Ja02AI
SHERIDAN, Mary		18	F	Weaver	15Ja02AI
MCNAMEE, Arthur		20	M	Laborer	15Ja02AI
SHERIDAN, Jno.		22	M	Laborer	15Ja02AI
Margt.		20	F	Laborer	15Ja02AI
FARRELL, Christopher		20	M	Laborer	15Ja02AI
WELSH, Thomas		31	M	Weaver	15Ja02AI
SMYTH, Pat		21	M	Laborer	15Ja02AI
BOURKE, Ellen		25	F	Servant	15Ja02AI
MCGOVERN, Bridget		21	F	Servant	15Ja02AI
SMYTH, Mary		20	F	Servant	15Ja02AI
WALSH, Anne		20	F	Servant	15Ja02AI
FARREL, Francis		31	M	Shoemaker	15Ja02AI
LYNCH, Michl.		18	M	Laborer	15Ja02AI
GALIGAN, Pat		38	M	Laborer	15Ja02AI
SHEAL, Peter		20	M	Laborer	15Ja02AI
COAN, Mary		20	F	Servant	15Ja02AI
DOUGLASS, Saml.		00	M	Farmer	15Ja02AI
Jno.		24	M	Farmer	15Ja02AI
Saml.		20	M	Farmer	15Ja02AI
Margt.		20	F	Farmer	15Ja02AI
Catherine		20	F	Farmer	15Ja02AI
Samuel		06	M	Child	15Ja02AI
Susan		03	F	Child	15Ja02AI
Mary-Jane		.00	F	Infant	15Ja02AI
LYONS, Patt		20	M	Tailor	15Ja02AI
KELLY, John		39	M	Tanner	15Ja02AI
Mary	(W)	34	F	Wife	15Ja02AI
CASEY, Johanna		30	F	Mtmkr	15Ja02AI
James	(S)	04	M	Child	15Ja02AI
FARRELL, Patrick		21	M	Laborer	15Ja02AI
MCKIERNAN, Redmond		16	M	Laborer	15Ja02AI
Bridget		15	F	Servant	15Ja02AI
PORT, Feilx		19	M	Laborer	15Ja02AI
MCANTEE, Mary		21	F	Servant	15Ja02AI
WELSH, Robert		45	M	Laborer	15Ja02AI
NELSON, Susan		20	F	Servant	15Ja02AI
TWEEDY, Wm.		29	M	Weaver	15Ja02AI
MOORE, Wm.		00	M	Farmer	15Ja02AI
DAVIS, Mary		00	F	Servant	15Ja02AI
MCCABE, Ann		35	F	Servant	15Ja02AI
Margaret	(D)	08	F	Child	15Ja02AI
Jane	(D)	13	F	Servant	15Ja02AI
William	(S)	06	M	Child	15Ja02AI
MCNAME, Charles		20	M	Laborer	15Ja02AI
SMYTH, Jno.		19	M	Laborer	15Ja02AI
BROOKS, James		20	M	Laborer	15Ja02AI
MCCANNA, Phil		21	M	Tbcmcht	15Ja02AI
KELLY, Thomas		20	M	Laborer	15Ja02AI
IRVIN, John		27	M	Mechanic	15Ja02AI
Anne	(W)	22	F	Wife	15Ja02AI
CAIRNS, Pat		40	M	Engineer	15Ja02AI
CAIRNS, Mary-Anne	(W)	39	F	Wife	15Ja02AI
James	(S)	07	M	Child	15Ja02AI
Julia	(D)	05	F	Child	15Ja02AI
Pat	(S)	02	M	Child	15Ja02AI
Mary-Anne	(D)	.00	F	Infant	15Ja02AI
KELLY, Anne		25	F	Servant	15Ja02AI
BYRNES, Rose		40	F	Servant	15Ja02AI
Michl.	(S)	18	M	Servant	15Ja02AI
Byrne.	(S)	15	M	Laborer	15Ja02AI
James	(S)	12	M	Laborer	15Ja02AI
Ellen	(D)	10	F	Servant	15Ja02AI
JIROUN, Judy		18	F	Servant	15Ja02AI
KUFFE, Michl.		18	M	Laborer	15Ja02AI
WOODS, Bridget		18	F	Servant	15Ja02AI
MULHOLLAND, Henry		20	M	Laborer	15Ja02AI
MCDONALD, James		25	M	Laborer	15Ja02AI
CLARKE, Bridget		20	F	Servant	15Ja02AI
SCALEY, Michl.		20	M	Farmer	15Ja02AI
LARED, Jno.		20	M	Laborer	15Ja02AI

OXFORD 16 JANUARY 1846

From Liverpool

NAMES OF PASSENGERS		AGE	SEX	OCCUPATIONS	DATE PORT SHIP
JEBB, Mary-Anne		15	F	None	16Ja02AJ
James		13	M	None	16Ja02AJ
Thomas		17	M	None	16Ja02AJ
KELLY, Bridget		17	F	None	16Ja02AJ
KANE, Bridget		60	F	None	16Ja02AJ
CONLOA, Catherine		25	F	None	16Ja02AJ
DUNNIGAN, Mary		20	F	None	16Ja02AJ
DOWD, Jane		22	F	None	16Ja02AJ
RILEY, Anne		35	F	None	16Ja02AJ
Catherine	(D)	09	F	Child	16Ja02AJ
LAUL, Robt.		28	M	None	16Ja02AJ
COFFEE, David		18	M	None	16Ja02AJ
DOWYEN, John		20	M	None	16Ja02AJ
OHARE, U		43	M	None	16Ja02AJ
JERRITT, Wm.		35	M	None	16Ja02AJ
MCFATRICK, Alexandria		21	M	None	16Ja02AJ
U	(W)	25	F	Wife	16Ja02AJ
SIMMONS, Eliza		17	F	None	16Ja02AJ
Mary		18	F	None	16Ja02AJ
DELANY, Martin		20	M	None	16Ja02AJ
ROSE, Mathew		35	M	None	16Ja02AJ
Mary		34	F	None	16Ja02AJ
RILEY, Michl.		29	M	None	16Ja02AJ
MCCABE, Michl.		21	M	None	16Ja02AJ
BONNER, Pathk.		23	M	None	16Ja02AJ
RILEY, Rose		37	F	None	16Ja02AJ
KELLY, Margaret		20	F	None	16Ja02AJ
MCLAUGHLIN, Anne		16	F	None	16Ja02AJ
CONNYAN, B.		28	M	None	16Ja02AJ
CONNISKY, B.		25	M	None	16Ja02AJ
RILEY, John		20	M	None	16Ja02AJ
CONNELLY, Catherine		20	F	None	16Ja02AJ
CRONICAN, Mary		20	F	None	16Ja02AJ
SEXTON, John		37	M	None	16Ja02AJ
DONNELLY, Jorena		18	F	None	16Ja02AJ
MCCARTY, Pathk.		30	M	Iron Worker	16Ja02AJ
MCLYONS, Pathk.		28	M	Iron Worker	16Ja02AJ
CLARENDON, Wm.		21	M	Iron Worker	16Ja02AJ
BRYANS, James		25	M	Shoemaker	16Ja02AJ
MCFINEGAN, Catherine		18	F	None	16Ja02AJ
LYNCH, John		25	M	None	16Ja02AJ
MCCANNON, Margaret		27	F	None	16Ja02AJ
MCBRYAN, Anne		19	F	None	16Ja02AJ
LAYLAN, Pathk.		45	M	None	16Ja02AJ
RIGNEY, Martin		23	M	None	16Ja02AJ

NAMES OF PASSENGERS		AGE	SEX	OCCUPATIONS	DATE PORT SHIP
BENNETT, Mary		20	F	None	16Ja02AJ
WILLICON, Thomas		40	M	None	16Ja02AJ
MCBRIAR, Thomas		22	M	None	16Ja02AJ
RYAN, John		25	M	None	16Ja02AJ
MCKEOWN, Anne		20	F	None	16Ja02AJ
ONEILL, Catherine		19	F	None	16Ja02AJ
Bridget		19	F	None	16Ja02AJ
FORLEY, Jone		30	M	None	16Ja02AJ
SCOTT, Mary		24	F	None	16Ja02AJ
BAGLAN, Bridget		26	F	None	16Ja02AJ
COREY, Mary		19	F	None	16Ja02AJ
CARTY, Kate		21	F	None	16Ja02AJ
RILEY, James		42	F	None	16Ja02AJ
FOLEY, John		26	F	None	16Ja02AJ
BURNS, Catherine		28	F	None	16Ja02AJ
John	(S)	05	M	Child	16Ja02AJ
GARTY, Thomas		23	M	None	16Ja02AJ
KANE, Eliza		22	F	None	16Ja02AJ
Mary		22	F	None	16Ja02AJ
HEFFERMAN, Anne		21	F	None	16Ja02AJ
KANE, Barnard		27	M	Shoemaker	16Ja02AJ
John		33	M	None	16Ja02AJ
BROCK, Pathk.		24	M	None	16Ja02AJ
WELSH, B.		18	F	Dressmaker	16Ja02AJ

NAMES OF PASSENGERS		AGE	SEX	OCCUPATIONS	DATE PORT SHIP
JONES, Mary-Ann	(D)	06	F	Child	16Ja02Ak
Sarah	(D)	04	F	Child	16Ja02Ak
Hannah	(D)	01	F	Child	16Ja02Ak
CROPPER, James		35	M	Molder	16Ja02Ak
COPELAND, John		15	M	Joiner	16Ja02Ak
KINCAN, Cath.		24	F	None	16Ja02Ak
SMITH, C.		35	M	Laborer	16Ja02Ak
MCMANUS, J.		30	M	Coachman	16Ja02Ak
GIBNEY, Owen		30	M	Laborer	16Ja02Ak
DARSEY, Thos.		20	M	Laborer	16Ja02Ak
Mgt.		25	F	None	16Ja02Ak
CONWAY, John		27	M	Laborer	16Ja02Ak
KARIN, Pat.		20	M	Laborer	16Ja02Ak
WILSON, John		25	M	Laborer	16Ja02Ak
CONNAH, Jos.		18	M	Laborer	16Ja02Ak
CASKEY, Rebec.		50	F	Laborer	16Ja02Ak
HARGRAVES, R.		23	M	Printer	16Ja02Ak
COLLARY, M.		20	F	None	16Ja02Ak
BYRNE, James		45	M	Merchant	16Ja02Ak
DOUGLAS, E.M.Mrs.		00	F	None	16Ja02Ak
James	(S)	06	M	Child	16Ja02Ak

CORNELIA 26 JANUARY 1846

From Liverpool

NAMES OF PASSENGERS		AGE	SEX	OCCUPATIONS	DATE PORT SHIP
BURRELL, Edward		31	M	Laborer	26Ja02Am
BERRYMAN, Elizabeth		24	F	None	26Ja02Am
Richd.	(S)	03	M	Child	26Ja02Am
RILEY, William		26	M	Laborer	26Ja02Am
FOSTER, George		25	M	Laborer	26Ja02Am
Rachel		24	F	None	26Ja02Am
Saml.		23	M	Laborer	26Ja02Am
Sarah		19	F	None	26Ja02Am
GOODMAN, Thomas		23	M	Laborer	26Ja02Am
WALDON, Daniel		24	M	Laborer	26Ja02Am
ROACH, Jane		29	F	None	26Ja02Am
Johnson	(S)	04	M	Child	26Ja02Am
JOHNSON, Jane		60	F	None	26Ja02Am
ROBERTS, Thos.		30	M	Laborer	26Ja02Am
WALFORD, Chas.		24	M	Laborer	26Ja02Am
Sarah	(W)	20	F	Wife	26Ja02Am
Sarah	(D)	01	F	Child	26Ja02Am
BACKLEY, Robt.		28	M	Laborer	26Ja02Am
Elizabeth	(D)	04	F	Child	26Ja02Am
MARSH, Francis		38	M	None	26Ja02Am
LOLLIS, Pat.		52	M	Laborer	26Ja02Am
RUTHERFORD, Jane		22	F	None	26Ja02Am
VERNON, Arthur-C.		34	M	None	26Ja02Am
FARR, W.A.		24	M	None	26Ja02Am

ROCHESTER 16 JANUARY 1846

From Liverpool

NAMES OF PASSENGERS		AGE	SEX	OCCUPATIONS	DATE PORT SHIP
SPROOL, Eliza		17	F	None	16Ja02Ak
Henry-W.		15	M	Baker	16Ja02Ak
MCALLISTER, Archd.		25	M	Gdnr	16Ja02Ak
KEDLING, Mark		25	M	Carpenter	16Ja02Ak
MCCANN, Paul		18	M	Baker	16Ja02Ak
TALKINGTON, Wm.		25	M	Joiner	16Ja02Ak
Sarah		22	F	None	16Ja02Ak
Sarah		60	F	None	16Ja02Ak
STEVENSON, Mary		60	F	None	16Ja02Ak
FISHER, John		35	M	Clergyman	16Ja02Ak
HAGAN, Mark		35	M	Agent	16Ja02Ak
Mary		16	F	None	16Ja02Ak
Ellen		13	F	None	16Ja02Ak
MCDONALD, James		20	M	Servant	16Ja02Ak
WALKER, Jas.		19	M	Laborer	16Ja02Ak
MCGANNON, Bel.		27	F	Servant	16Ja02Ak
THOMPSON, Fanny		30	F	Baker	16Ja02Ak
Wm.		13	M	Baker	16Ja02Ak
David		11	M	Baker	16Ja02Ak
Eliza		10	F	Child	16Ja02Ak
Femy.		05	F	Child	16Ja02Ak
MOULD, Benj.		17	M	Potter	16Ja02Ak
John		13	M	Potter	16Ja02Ak
MCKIGNEY, Wm.		13	M	Child	16Ja02Ak
Jane		11	F	None	16Ja02Ak
CRAWFORD, Ann		26	F	None	16Ja02Ak
CORN, John		18	M	Laborer	16Ja02Ak
MCKEE, John		13	M	Laborer	16Ja02Ak
MCLAUGHLIN, Benjm.		22	M	Laborer	16Ja02Ak
Mary		19	F	None	16Ja02Ak
PRIOR, Rose		20	F	None	16Ja02Ak
DHAGAN, Nancy		20	F	None	16Ja02Ak
GILLARHAN, Ann		18	F	None	16Ja02Ak
BRYAN, Wm.		26	M	Laborer	16Ja02Ak
JONES, Tutar		40	M	Joiner	16Ja02Ak
Eliz.	(W)	39	F	Wife	16Ja02Ak
Eliz.	(D)	17	F	None	16Ja02Ak
Lem.	(S)	12	M	None	16Ja02Ak
Amos	(S)	10	M	Child	16Ja02Ak
Benjn.	(S)	08	M	Child	16Ja02Ak

NEW-YORK-PACKET 26 JANUARY 1846

From Halifax

NAMES OF PASSENGERS	AGE	SEX	OCCUPATIONS	DATE PORT SHIP
QUIN, Thomas-D.	35	M	Merchant	26Ja22An
HACKETT, James	28	M	Clerk	26Ja22An

NAMES OF PASSENGERS	AGE	SEX	OCCUPATIONS	DATE PORT SHIP

VIRGINIAN 29 JANUARY 1846

From Liverpool

NAMES OF PASSENGERS	AGE	SEX	OCCUPATIONS	DATE PORT SHIP
NUTTY, James	45	M	Unknown	29Ja02Ap
Bridget (D)	07	F	Domestic	29Ja02Ap
LAUGHTON, Wm.H.	20	M	Joiner	29Ja02Ap
NEAL, James	30	M	Laborer	29Ja02Ap
BRANAGAN, Ann	25	F	Domestic	29Ja02Ap
FARRELLY, Ann	22	F	Domestic	29Ja02Ap
HALFPENNY, Ellen	20	F	Dressmaker	29Ja02Ap
MCEROY, Jane	26	F	Domestic	29Ja02Ap
LENNAN, Biddy	20	F	Domestic	29Ja02Ap
HEALY, John	21	M	Laborer	29Ja02Ap
Catherine (W)	20	F	Wife	29Ja02Ap
MURPHY, Pattk.	21	M	Laborer	29Ja02Ap
DUFFY, Mary	21	F	Domestic	29Ja02Ap
WILSON, Robt.	24	M	Draper	29Ja02Ap
CONNALLY, John	21	M	Laborer	29Ja02Ap
LERY, Edward	25	M	Joiner	29Ja02Ap
MCELROY, Chas.	20	M	Laborer	29Ja02Ap
SCOTT, Robt.J.	25	M	Merchant	29Ja02Ap
JOHNSON, David	22	M	Laborer	29Ja02Ap
MCFARLANE, Wm.	20	M	Laborer	29Ja02Ap
MALONY, Dennis	25	M	Tailor	29Ja02Ap
HARE, Pattk.	40	M	Shoemaker	29Ja02Ap
John	19	M	Shoemaker	29Ja02Ap
Rose	20	F	Domestic	29Ja02Ap
HARREY, John	19	M	Laborer	29Ja02Ap
WARD, Cathe.	26	F	Domestic	29Ja02Ap
Bridget	15	F	Domestic	29Ja02Ap
Cathe.	12	F	Domestic	29Ja02Ap
FITZSIMONS, Ann	22	F	Domestic	29Ja02Ap
James	20	M	Tailor	29Ja02Ap
LOGAN, Wm.	25	M	Laborer	29Ja02Ap
Mary (W)	23	F	Wife	29Ja02Ap
KELLY, James	30	M	Weaver	29Ja02Ap
KEENAN, Pattk.	22	M	Laborer	29Ja02Ap
KELGAN, Luke	24	M	Shoemaker	29Ja02Ap
TAGGART, John	26	M	Laborer	29Ja02Ap
MALLON, Joel	30	M	None	29Ja02Ap
Catherine	24	F	Domestic	29Ja02Ap
MCCOURT, Pattk.	21	M	Laborer	29Ja02Ap
WELDERS, Thos.	20	M	Laborer	29Ja02Ap
LENNON, Cathe.	20	F	Hatter	29Ja02Ap
SHEA, Margt.	18	F	Lady	29Ja02Ap
DRISCOLL, Ann	46	F	Domestic	29Ja02Ap
PARK, Allex	22	M	Weaver	29Ja02Ap
MASON, Saml.	20	M	Laborer	29Ja02Ap
KEIRNAN, Mary	21	F	Domestic	29Ja02Ap
MURRAY, John	22	M	Stone Mason	29Ja02Ap
FOX, Francis	27	M	Laborer	29Ja02Ap
Mary (W)	21	F	Wife	29Ja02Ap
Sarah	20	F	Domestic	29Ja02Ap
WISELEY, Mary	19	F	Domestic	29Ja02Ap
GANIGAN, Ann	19	F	Domestic	29Ja02Ap
ROBERTS, Betty-Jane	38	F	Domestic	29Ja02Ap
Isaac (S)	08	M	Child	29Ja02Ap
WATERS, Wm.	28	M	Laborer	29Ja02Ap
Ann	21	F	Domestic	29Ja02Ap
REILY, James	55	M	Laborer	29Ja02Ap
Margt.	46	F	Domestic	29Ja02Ap
Julia	13	F	Domestic	29Ja02Ap
ERSKIN, Margt.	25	F	Domestic	29Ja02Ap
DONALLY, Margt.	20	F	Wife	29Ja02Ap
CONWAY, Wm.	35	M	Laborer	29Ja02Ap
Ann (W)	30	F	Wife	29Ja02Ap
John (S)	09	M	Child	29Ja02Ap
Cathe.	20	F	Domestic	29Ja02Ap
CONWAY, Eliza	07	F	Child	29Ja02Ap
Pattk.	05	M	Child	29Ja02Ap
James	03	M	Child	29Ja02Ap
MCCURLEY, Ellen	22	F	Domestic	29Ja02Ap
MALONE, Mary	20	F	Domestic	29Ja02Ap
CASEMENT, Wm.	17	M	Clerk	29Ja02Ap
FOSTER, John	26	M	Gdnr	29Ja02Ap
Martha (W)	27	F	Wife	29Ja02Ap
DONAHY, Wm.	18	M	Weaver	29Ja02Ap
NESTOR, Wm.	30	M	Laborer	29Ja02Ap
Bridget	14	F	Domestic	29Ja02Ap
Mary	13	F	Domestic	29Ja02Ap
KERWAN, Margt.	24	F	Domestic	29Ja02Ap
DERLEN, Ann	21	F	Domestic	29Ja02Ap
DOWD, Mathew	25	M	Tailor	29Ja02Ap
Ann (W)	27	F	Wife	29Ja02Ap
SULLIVAN, Timothy	36	M	Weaver	29Ja02Ap
CLARK, John	07	M	Child	29Ja02Ap
CRANESEY, Cathe.Ann	21	F	Domestic	29Ja02Ap
WEBB, Richd.	20	M	Laborer	29Ja02Ap
SUMMERS, Ellen	21	F	Domestic	29Ja02Ap
COOK, Wm.	30	M	Shopkeeper	29Ja02Ap
BRIEN, John	12	M	Child	29Ja02Ap
Ann	10	F	Child	29Ja02Ap
CASEY, Margt.	19	F	Domestic	29Ja02Ap
RICHARDSON, Eliza	17	F	Domestic	29Ja02Ap
Ellen	13	F	Domestic	29Ja02Ap
MULLIGAN, Francis	26	M	Plasterer	29Ja02Ap
Martha (W)	21	F	Wife	29Ja02Ap
Ann (D)	01	F	Child	29Ja02Ap
Ellen (D)	03	F	Child	29Ja02Ap
MAHONE, Conrad	22	M	Laborer	29Ja02Ap
FLEMING, Elizh.	21	F	Domestic	29Ja02Ap
MCCLUSKEY, Rosanna	21	F	Domestic	29Ja02Ap
Mary	18	F	Domestic	29Ja02Ap
MCCABE, Daniel	30	M	Tailor	29Ja02Ap
REILLY, John	21	M	Laborer	29Ja02Ap
James	05	M	Child	29Ja02Ap
DOYL, Mary	20	F	Domestic	29Ja02Ap
MURRAY, Mary	21	F	Domestic	29Ja02Ap
LERNARD, Ann	17	F	Domestic	29Ja02Ap
PIGOTT, James	24	M	Farmer	29Ja02Ap
QUAID, Mathew	26	M	Laborer	29Ja02Ap
BRENNAN, James	34	M	Laborer	29Ja02Ap
WOOD, Mary	40	F	Wife	29Ja02Ap
WOODS, Pattk.	10	M	Child	29Ja02Ap
Margt.	08	F	Child	29Ja02Ap
Ellen	06	F	Child	29Ja02Ap
MATHEWS, John	30	M	Laborer	29Ja02Ap

HYDER-ALI 02 FEBRUARY 1846

From Black-River

NAMES OF PASSENGERS	AGE	SEX	OCCUPATIONS	DATE PORT SHIP
OGELBY, Robert	30	M	Merchant	02Fe35Aq

COLUMBUS 02 FEBRUARY 1846

From Liverpool

NAMES OF PASSENGERS	AGE	SEX	OCCUPATIONS	DATE PORT SHIP
CARROLL, Patrick	54	M	Laborer	02Fe02Ar
Ann (W)	50	F	Wife	02Fe02Ar
Wm. (S)	11	M	Laborer	02Fe02Ar

NAMES OF PASSENGERS		AGE	SEX	OCCUPATIONS	DATE PORT SHIP
LOCHLIN, Edwd.		20	M	Laborer	02Fe02Ar
RYAN, Esther		35	F	Laborer	02Fe02Ar
CARREGAN, Mary		26	F	None	02Fe02Ar
CURRAN, Bernard		31	M	Laborer	02Fe02Ar
DILLON, Luke		35	M	Laborer	02Fe02Ar
REGAN, Cornelius		30	M	Laborer	02Fe02Ar
Elizabeth		26	F	None	02Fe02Ar
MOORE, Wm.		30	M	Laborer	02Fe02Ar
Harriet	(W)	29	F	Wife	02Fe02Ar
Fanny	(D)	11	F	None	02Fe02Ar
Ann	(D)	09	F	Child	02Fe02Ar
Isballa	(D)	07	F	Child	02Fe02Ar
Wm.	(S)	05	M	Child	02Fe02Ar
John	(S)	04	M	Child	02Fe02Ar
Mary	(D)	02	F	Child	02Fe02Ar
CLARK, Patrick		26	M	None	02Fe02Ar
CARROLL, James		30	M	None	02Fe02Ar
CLARK, Mary		25	F	None	02Fe02Ar
MELDON, Mary		28	F	None	02Fe02Ar
BROUGHTEN, George		30	M	Laborer	02Fe02Ar
FERRILL, Patrick		24	M	Laborer	02Fe02Ar
OBRIEN, Ellen		22	F	None	02Fe02Ar
REGAN, Ellen		03	F	Child	02Fe02Ar
SMITRE, Catherine		28	F	None	02Fe02Ar
BAKER, Saml.		44	M	Laborer	02Fe02Ar
MABRIN, Moses		24	M	Laborer	02Fe02Ar
GORGAN, Winney		20	F	Laborer	02Fe02Ar
MOORE, Harriett		04	F	Child	02Fe02Ar
MURRAY, Joseph		30	M	None	02Fe02Ar
RYAN, Esther		00	F	None	02Fe02Ar

WATERLOO 05 FEBRUARY 1846

From Liverpool

NAMES OF PASSENGERS		AGE	SEX	OCCUPATIONS	DATE PORT SHIP
DOUGLAS, David		24	M	Mnftr	05Fe02As

MUDARA 07 FEBRUARY 1846

From Havana

NAMES OF PASSENGERS		AGE	SEX	OCCUPATIONS	DATE PORT SHIP
BRACKINGRIDGE, Frances		40	M	Doctor	07Fe06At

ST.GEORGE 18 FEBRUARY 1846

From Liverpool

NAMES OF PASSENGERS		AGE	SEX	OCCUPATIONS	DATE PORT SHIP
MURTHA, Brian		26	M	Laborer	18Fe02Av
Margaret		30	F	None	18Fe02Av
BISSETT, Wm.		23	M	Laborer	18Fe02Av
DAVNEY, James		42	M	Laborer	18Fe02Av
MCALLISTER, James		21	M	Laborer	18Fe02Av
MCINTYRE, Alex		22	M	Laborer	18Fe02Av
Ellen		40	F	None	18Fe02Av
LANAN, Edward		20	M	Laborer	18Fe02Av
POWER, Edmund		23	M	Laborer	18Fe02Av
William		30	M	Laborer	18Fe02Av

NAMES OF PASSENGERS		AGE	SEX	OCCUPATIONS	DATE PORT SHIP
HIGGINS, Mary		20	F	None	18Fe02Av
MCGARY, Rose		21	F	None	18Fe02Av
BRADY, Cathe.		20	F	None	18Fe02Av
FERGUSON, Ellen		20	F	None	18Fe02Av
HEALY, Mary		40	F	None	18Fe02Av
Jeremiah	(S)	11	M	None	18Fe02Av
John	(S)	13	M	None	18Fe02Av
Honara	(D)	20	F	None	18Fe02Av
Julia		50	F	None	18Fe02Av
OBREN, Jeremiah		20	M	Shoemaker	18Fe02Av
MADDEN, Mary		20	F	None	18Fe02Av
DONALLY, Cath.		25	F	None	18Fe02Av
Julia		22	F	None	18Fe02Av
SEDDEN, Thomas		26	M	Laborer	18Fe02Av
CURRY, Hugh		30	M	Laborer	18Fe02Av
DAVISON, Eliza		20	F	None	18Fe02Av
CROSS, Stafford		19	M	Laborer	18Fe02Av
MORGAN, Elizabeth		50	F	Laborer	18Fe02Av
Robert-A.		32	M	Laborer	18Fe02Av
Elizabeth		26	F	None	18Fe02Av
Robert		10	M	Child	18Fe02Av
Thomas		08	M	Child	18Fe02Av
WINTER, Mangin		22	M	Laborer	18Fe02Av
Matthew	(S)	.06	M	Infant	18Fe02Av
HUES, Sarah		20	F	None	18Fe02Av
CULLEN, Philip		20	M	Laborer	18Fe02Av
GILL, Micheal		30	M	Laborer	18Fe02Av
Ellen	(W)	30	F	Wife	18Fe02Av
Mary	(D)	02	F	Child	18Fe02Av
Andrew	(S)	.05	M	Infant	18Fe02Av
MULROY, James		20	M	Tool Maker	18Fe02Av
GILL, Thomas		20	M	Laborer	18Fe02Av
WARD, Mary		18	F	None	18Fe02Av
WHILEHAN, Bridget		20	F	Servant	18Fe02Av
HEANY, Bridget		20	F	Servant	18Fe02Av
MAXWELL, John		20	M	Laborer	18Fe02Av
LING, Martha		19	M	Laborer	18Fe02Av
CORRAGAN, Judy		19	F	Laborer	18Fe02Av
GORMIN, James		40	M	Laborer	18Fe02Av
SEDDIN, Thomas		27	M	Laborer	18Fe02Av
MCMAHON, Phillp		30	M	Laborer	18Fe02Av
Mary	(W)	30	F	Wife	18Fe02Av
Mary	(D)	13	F	None	18Fe02Av
Eliza	(D)	11	F	None	18Fe02Av
Joseph	(S)	09	M	Child	18Fe02Av
Ann	(D)	04	F	Child	18Fe02Av
Cathrine	(D)	02	F	Child	18Fe02Av
TATE, Saml.		25	M	Porter	18Fe02Av
FOWLEY, John		40	M	Laborer	18Fe02Av
Eliza	(W)	34	F	Wife	18Fe02Av
DALEY, James		20	M	Laborer	18Fe02Av
BRADY, Matthew		25	M	Laborer	18Fe02Av
DONALLY, Thomas		21	M	Laborer	18Fe02Av
WALLERS, Thomas		20	M	Laborer	18Fe02Av
BRADY, Ellen		.00	F	Infant	18Fe02Av
MCNAMARRA, Peter		20	M	Laborer	18Fe02Av
MURY, Wm.J.		40	M	Farmer	18Fe02Av

ADAM-CARR 19 FEBRUARY 1846

From Glasgow

NAMES OF PASSENGERS		AGE	SEX	OCCUPATIONS	DATE PORT SHIP
LOGAN, John		21	M	Ctnsp	19Fe04Aw

NAMES OF PASSENGERS		AGE	SEX	OCCUPATIONS	DATE PORT SHIP

FIDELIA 23 FEBRUARY 1846

From Liverpool

NAMES OF PASSENGERS		AGE	SEX	OCCUPATIONS	DATE PORT SHIP
CANTRALL, Eliza		48	F	None	23Fe02Ax
CRAWFORD, John		30	M	Laborer	23Fe02Ax
CROSBY, Thomas		25	M	Laborer	23Fe02Ax
William		23	M	Laborer	23Fe02Ax
FARRELL, Catherine		32	F	None	23Fe02Ax
Ann	(D)	05	F	Child	23Fe02Ax
GRIBBON, Richard		28	M	Laborer	23Fe02Ax
Mary	(W)	28	F	Wife	23Fe02Ax
Ann	(D)	03	F	Child	23Fe02Ax
Thomas	(S)	01	M	Child	23Fe02Ax
CARROLL, Mary		24	F	None	23Fe02Ax
Hannah	(D)	03	F	Child	23Fe02Ax
Henry	(S)	02	M	Child	23Fe02Ax
CASSIDY, Mary		60	F	None	23Fe02Ax
ASKEW, Ellen		22	F	None	23Fe02Ax
Margaret	(D)	02	F	Child	23Fe02Ax
CREIGHTON, Mary		22	F	None	23Fe02Ax
CROSBY, John		32	M	Laborer	23Fe02Ax
Eliza	(W)	30	F	Wife	23Fe02Ax
Patrick	(S)	14	M	None	23Fe02Ax
Ann	(D)	07	F	None	23Fe02Ax
MULVANNY, Patrick		25	M	Clcp	23Fe02Ax
JONES, Thomas		24	M	Servant	23Fe02Ax
CONNALL, Anthony		26	M	Grocer	23Fe02Ax
REGAN, John		34	M	Tailor	23Fe02Ax
Catherine	(W)	29	F	Wife	23Fe02Ax
William	(S)	05	M	Child	23Fe02Ax
Mary	(D)	03	F	Child	23Fe02Ax
Peter	(S)	01	M	Child	23Fe02Ax
HINES, Edward		25	M	Tinsmith	23Fe02Ax
Catherine	(W)	22	F	Wife	23Fe02Ax
John	(S)	05	M	Child	23Fe02Ax
Martin	(S)	02	M	Child	23Fe02Ax
MONAGHAN, Betty		50	F	None	23Fe02Ax
Catherine		35	F	None	23Fe02Ax
MACDONNELL, Eliza		32	F	None	23Fe02Ax
Anny	(D)	02	F	Child	23Fe02Ax
RYAN, Catherine		32	F	None	23Fe02Ax
MARR, Margaret		22	F	None	23Fe02Ax
MCGROTTY, Henry		70	M	Farmer	23Fe02Ax
Sarah	(W)	65	F	Wife	23Fe02Ax
Cuningham		27	M	Farmer	23Fe02Ax
James		21	M	Farmer	23Fe02Ax
Sarah		18	F	None	23Fe02Ax
William		17	M	Farmer	23Fe02Ax
LAIN, Dorah		50	F	None	23Fe02Ax
OWENS, Patrick		28	M	Farmer	23Fe02Ax
REID, George		45	M	Weaver	23Fe02Ax
Frances	(W)	40	F	Wife	23Fe02Ax
Frances	(D)	05	F	Child	23Fe02Ax
OCONNELL, Daniel		25	M	Baker	23Fe02Ax
RYLEY, Catherine		17	F	None	23Fe02Ax
FARRELL, Mary		16	F	None	23Fe02Ax
Bridgett		14	F	None	23Fe02Ax
CRAYTON, Eliza		28	F	None	23Fe02Ax
Catherine		30	F	None	23Fe02Ax
MOORE, Mary-Agnes		34	F	None	23Fe02Ax
Edward	(S)	05	M	Child	23Fe02Ax
DELANY, Catherine		18	F	None	23Fe02Ax
MACEVER, Arther		65	M	Hatter	23Fe02Ax
Arther		23	M	Laborer	23Fe02Ax
RAFTRY, William		16	M	None	23Fe02Ax
MULLIGAN, Peter		24	M	Laborer	23Fe02Ax
Mary		20	F	None	23Fe02Ax
GANNON, Peter		22	M	Laborer	23Fe02Ax

NAMES OF PASSENGERS		AGE	SEX	OCCUPATIONS	DATE PORT SHIP
FISHER, Margaret		23	F	None	23Fe02Ax
Ann		20	F	None	23Fe02Ax
HAYDON, Mary		21	F	None	23Fe02Ax
COLLINS, John		32	M	Laborer	23Fe02Ax
Mary		28	F	None	23Fe02Ax
GRAY, Ellen		21	F	None	23Fe02Ax
MACEIGHTON, Rosana		50	F	None	23Fe02Ax
BLAIR, Mary		25	F	None	23Fe02Ax
OWENS, Catherine		21	F	None	23Fe02Ax
BAILEY, Valentine		27	M	Printer	23Fe02Ax
FLARGHTY, William		24	M	Laborer	23Fe02Ax
NEDWEIGHAN, Thomas		37	M	Laborer	23Fe02Ax
Margt.		28	F	None	23Fe02Ax
MACQUEEN, George		21	M	Laborer	23Fe02Ax
CRAYTON, Patrick		21	M	Laborer	23Fe02Ax
DUFFIN, Peter		25	M	Laborer	23Fe02Ax
Bridgett		24	F	None	23Fe02Ax
ILAND, Catherine		23	F	None	23Fe02Ax
WHALING, Lawrence		26	M	Plasterer	23Fe02Ax
Marla	(W)	20	F	Wife	23Fe02Ax
Michael	(S)	01	M	Child	23Fe02Ax
FITZIMONS, Hugh		21	M	Laborer	23Fe02Ax
BURKE, Thomas		22	M	Laborer	23Fe02Ax
HAYES, Mary		20	F	Dressmaker	23Fe02Ax

GRANDEE 02 MARCH 1846

From Halifax

NAMES OF PASSENGERS		AGE	SEX	OCCUPATIONS	DATE PORT SHIP
CAHILL, J.		48	M	Merchant	02Mr22Az
DELANEY, P.		28	M	Merchant	02Mr22Az

TORONTO 04 MARCH 1846

From London

NAMES OF PASSENGERS		AGE	SEX	OCCUPATIONS	DATE PORT SHIP
RILEY, Henry		32	M	Wmcht	04Mr21Ba
Eliza		23	F	None	04Mr21Ba
WILSON, William		25	M	None	04Mr21Ba

MASSACHUSETTS 05 MARCH 1846

From Liverpool

NAMES OF PASSENGERS		AGE	SEX	OCCUPATIONS	DATE PORT SHIP
GLEASON, Mary		21	F	None	05Mr02Bb
GRAY, William		24	M	Draper	05Mr02Bb
MONTJOY, George		17	M	Watchmaker	05Mr02Bb
LAGAN, Patrick		26	M	Grocer	05Mr02Bb
DAVIS, James		26	M	Stone Mason	05Mr02Bb
Susan	(W)	22	F	Wife	05Mr02Bb

5

HOTTINGUER 06 MARCH 1846

From Liverpool

NAMES OF PASSENGERS		AGE	SEX	OCCUPATIONS	DATE PORT SHIP
KEATING, Thomas		20	M	Laborer	06Mr02Bc
HOREY, James		27	M	Laborer	06Mr02Bc
KERNAN, Robert		47	M	Laborer	06Mr02Bc
Robert	(S)	13	M	Laborer	06Mr02Bc
Mary-Jane	(D)	09	F	Child	06Mr02Bc
BOYD, Mary		25	F	Servant	06Mr02Bc
Jane		18	F	Servant	06Mr02Bc
CARTER, Eliza		18	F	Servant	06Mr02Bc
HOLTIN, Bridget		19	F	Servant	06Mr02Bc
KNOWLAND, Robert		37	M	Pmbr-Gzr	06Mr02Bc
Margaret	(D)	05	F	Child	06Mr02Bc
BARKER, Elizabeth		29	F	Servant	06Mr02Bc
Anne	(D)	03	F	Child	06Mr02Bc
Eliza	(D)	.00	F	Infant	06Mr02Bc
ENGLISH, William		26	M	Laborer	06Mr02Bc
Ann		36	F	None	06Mr02Bc
GEARNY, Thomas		23	M	Laborer	06Mr02Bc
John		17	M	Laborer	06Mr02Bc
HOGG, William		26	M	Clerk	06Mr02Bc
Mary		26	F	None	06Mr02Bc

ASHBURTON 07 MARCH 1846

From Liverpool

NAMES OF PASSENGERS		AGE	SEX	OCCUPATIONS	DATE PORT SHIP
JOHNSON, Wm.		41	M	Clerk	07Mr02Bd
FAIRFIELD, Mike		21	M	Smith	07Mr02Bd
ROSS, John		36	M	Butcher	07Mr02Bd
GORMLEY, Bernard		24	M	Cooper	07Mr02Bd
MCMARREY, John		20	M	None	07Mr02Bd
CONNELL, Patrick		35	M	None	07Mr02Bd
TONNER, Pat.		30	M	None	07Mr02Bd
GILLIGAN, Mike		17	M	None	07Mr02Bd
GAFFSEY, John		23	M	None	07Mr02Bd
ROWAN, Francis		25	M	None	07Mr02Bd
QUEEN, Mike		20	M	None	07Mr02Bd
KERNAN, Bernard		25	M	None	07Mr02Bd
WAYNE, Jas.		23	M	None	07Mr02Bd
STANTON, Pat.		50	M	None	07Mr02Bd
PENNEY, Andrew		23	M	None	07Mr02Bd
SHIELDS, James		19	M	None	07Mr02Bd
BURNS, Thos.		26	M	Clerk	07Mr02Bd
KELLY, Mike		20	M	Stctr	07Mr02Bd
NANGLE, Peter		28	M	Tailor	07Mr02Bd
ARMSTRONG, John		35	M	None	07Mr02Bd
NANGLE, Mary		22	F	None	07Mr02Bd
Marg.	(D)	01	F	Child	07Mr02Bd
SCULLION, Oliver		20	M	Weaver	07Mr02Bd
REYNOLDS, Francis		21	M	None	07Mr02Bd
WAYNE, Ellen		20	F	None	07Mr02Bd
SHARDIN, Bernard		26	M	None	07Mr02Bd
Ann		22	F	None	07Mr02Bd
KEGGIN, James		19	M	None	07Mr02Bd
SHIERDON, Edw.		23	M	None	07Mr02Bd
MULLIGAN, John		25	M	Farmer	07Mr02Bd
Marg.	(W)	24	F	Wife	07Mr02Bd
John	(S)	02	M	Child	07Mr02Bd
MCMANUS, Francis		18	M	None	07Mr02Bd
TAYLEY, John		21	M	Shopkeeper	07Mr02Bd
KOUGH, John		00	M	Blacksmith	07Mr02Bd
MCKERING, Pat		45	M	None	07Mr02Bd
DURNEY, Pat		26	M	None	07Mr02Bd
LOYD, Mat		23	M	None	07Mr02Bd
MILES, Pat		33	M	None	07Mr02Bd
HALPIN, Pat		23	M	None	07Mr02Bd
WILLIAMS, Jas.		24	M	Stctr	07Mr02Bd
MORN, Pat		40	M	Stctr	07Mr02Bd
SULLIVAN, Wm.		22	M	None	07Mr02Bd
WATERS, Jas.		24	M	None	07Mr02Bd
KING, Mary		24	F	None	07Mr02Bd
LYNCH, Biddy		22	F	None	07Mr02Bd
Marg.		18	F	None	07Mr02Bd
REDDIHAN, Ellen		16	F	None	07Mr02Bd
SLATTERY, Wm.		20	M	Butcher	07Mr02Bd
RILEY, Marg.		16	F	None	07Mr02Bd
COLES, Catherine		17	F	None	07Mr02Bd
BURNS, Biddy		21	F	None	07Mr02Bd
CAMRON, Mary		22	F	None	07Mr02Bd
BROOKS, Edwd.		18	M	None	07Mr02Bd
MORRIS, Mary		20	F	None	07Mr02Bd
DUFFEY, John		25	M	None	07Mr02Bd
Ann		25	F	None	07Mr02Bd
MOSSON, Jas.		21	M	None	07Mr02Bd
MCLAUGHLIN, Sarah		16	F	None	07Mr02Bd
Marg.		08	F	Child	07Mr02Bd
MARTIN, Pat		24	M	None	07Mr02Bd
HOY, James		32	M	None	07Mr02Bd
BROWN, Biddy		40	F	None	07Mr02Bd
Thos.	(S)	13	M	None	07Mr02Bd
Ann	(D)	13	F	None	07Mr02Bd
BUTLER, Lucy		09	F	Child	07Mr02Bd
FITZPATRICK, Martin		00	M	None	07Mr02Bd
NARYLE, Thos.		24	M	None	07Mr02Bd
ONEIL, Owen		28	M	None	07Mr02Bd
WILSON, E.		21	U	None	07Mr02Bd
J.		20	U	None	07Mr02Bd

ROSCIUS 07 MARCH 1846

From Liverpool

NAMES OF PASSENGERS		AGE	SEX	OCCUPATIONS	DATE PORT SHIP
MCCRAE, James		34	M	Butcher	07Mr02Bf
M.Anne	(D)	11	F	None	07Mr02Bf
READE, Margt.		15	F	None	07Mr02Bf
WELSH, John		22	M	Butcher	07Mr02Bf
Jane	(W)	20	F	Wife	07Mr02Bf
KENNEDY, James		37	M	Cooper	07Mr02Bf
MCINTIRE, William		25	M	Coachman	07Mr02Bf
Mary	(W)	23	F	Wife	07Mr02Bf
Cathe.	(D)	04	F	Child	07Mr02Bf
Michl.	(S)	02	M	Child	07Mr02Bf
John	(S)	01	M	Child	07Mr02Bf
FARRELL, William		24	M	Weaver	07Mr02Bf
Biddy	(W)	24	F	Wife	07Mr02Bf
BRYAN, Michl.		20	M	Agent	07Mr02Bf
Mary		18	F	None	07Mr02Bf
LENNOX, William		25	M	Dealer	07Mr02Bf
HUDSON, George		25	M	Surveyor	07Mr02Bf
HART, William		22	M	Surveyor	07Mr02Bf
DANFORD, Henry		22	M	Victualler	07Mr02Bf
MCCLURE, John		25	M	Factor	07Mr02Bf
SMITH, William		17	M	Laborer	07Mr02Bf
MARSTON, John		21	M	Clerk	07Mr02Bf
RICHARDSON, John		22	M	Silversmith	07Mr02Bf
Robert		21	M	Silversmith	07Mr02Bf
GERMAN, William		22	M	Silversmith	07Mr02Bf
DILLON, Thomas		20	M	Clerk	07Mr02Bf
MCCLURE, John		20	M	Laborer	07Mr02Bf

NAMES OF PASSENGERS	A G E	S E X	OCCUPATIONS	DATE PORT SHIP	NAMES OF PASSENGERS	A G E	S E X	OCCUPATIONS	DATE PORT SHIP
MCCARTHY, Danl.	66	M	Laborer	07Mr02Bf	MILLER, Elizabeth	12	F	Printer	09Mr21Bh
CORBITT, Thomas	35	M	Gunsmith	07Mr02Bf	Anna	10	F	Printer	09Mr21Bh
GOODISON, Jane	30	F	None	07Mr02Bf	MARK, Caroline	23	F	Clerk	09Mr21Bh
LUCE, Eliza	18	F	Dressmaker	07Mr02Bf					
BRADY, Eliza	18	F	Dressmaker	07Mr02Bf					
JERMAN, Kate	27	F	None	07Mr02Bf					
Kate	13	F	None	07Mr02Bf					
Anne	11	F	None	07Mr02Bf					
HURST, Margt.	18	F	Servant	07Mr02Bf		EUROPE 09 MARCH 1846			
MAHON, Martin	30	M	Laborer	07Mr02Bf					
Mary (W)	30	F	Wife	07Mr02Bf		From Liverpool			
Margt. (D)	13	F	None	07Mr02Bf					
Richd. (S)	10	M	Child	07Mr02Bf					
John (S)	08	M	Child	07Mr02Bf					
William (S)	08	M	Child	07Mr02Bf	CALDWELL, Jno.	16	M	Laborer	09Mr02Bl
Dorothe (D)	06	F	Child	07Mr02Bf	MULVANEY, Peter	28	M	Laborer	09Mr02Bl
Eliza (D)	02	F	Child	07Mr02Bf	BURN, Bridget	20	F	Spinster	09Mr02Bl
KELCH, Thomas	24	M	Laborer	07Mr02Bf	GALLAGER, Mary	20	F	Spinster	09Mr02Bl
Anne (W)	25	F	Wife	07Mr02Bf	GERTY, Mary	23	F	Spinster	09Mr02Bl
U (D)	.00	F	Infant	07Mr02Bf	BOLEN, Rose	20	F	Spinster	09Mr02Bl
KAYLS, Margt.	23	F	Dressmaker	07Mr02Bf	Maria	24	F	Spinster	09Mr02Bl
CALLERY, James	19	M	Laborer	07Mr02Bf	DELANEY, Jane	25	F	Spinster	09Mr02Bl
KELCH, Mary	25	F	Cook	07Mr02Bf	BANNIGAN, Willm.	30	M	Laborer	09Mr02Bl
KELLY, Bridget	18	F	Dressmaker	07Mr02Bf	Patk.	23	M	Laborer	09Mr02Bl
MURRAY, Margt.	20	F	Dressmaker	07Mr02Bf	GARTLAND, Jno.	26	M	Weaver	09Mr02Bl
CALLAGHAN, Anne	22	F	Lad	07Mr02Bf	MAVOCY, James	20	M	Laborer	09Mr02Bl
FEONE, Cathe.	24	F	Lad	07Mr02Bf	FARLEY, Willm.	21	M	Nail Maker	09Mr02Bl
MCGOVERN, Mary	22	F	Lad	07Mr02Bf	NICHOLSON, Thos.	20	M	Surveyor	09Mr02Bl
WARD, Thomas	22	M	Laborer	07Mr02Bf	LYNCH, Philip	18	M	Laborer	09Mr02Bl
OBRIEN, John	19	M	Laborer	07Mr02Bf	Jno.	10	M	Laborer	09Mr02Bl
MOORE, John	25	M	Coachman	07Mr02Bf	Patk.	08	M	Child	09Mr02Bl
HOGAN, John	20	M	Laborer	07Mr02Bf	James	07	M	Child	09Mr02Bl
BRYAN, Anne	34	F	None	07Mr02Bf	BYRNES, Chrlsr.	17	M	Laborer	09Mr02Bl
Bridget (D)	15	F	None	07Mr02Bf	MCKEOWN, Patk.	25	M	Laborer	09Mr02Bl
RILEY, Cathe.	21	F	Servant	07Mr02Bf	HART, Jno.	19	M	Laborer	09Mr02Bl
DOLAN, Margt.	16	F	Servant	07Mr02Bf	MCHUGH, Cathne.	25	F	Spinster	09Mr02Bl
Cathe.	12	F	Servant	07Mr02Bf	ODONNELL, Jno.	27	F	Laborer	09Mr02Bl
Mary	21	F	Servant	07Mr02Bf	OHARA, Willm.	14	M	Laborer	09Mr02Bl
MCKENNY, Felix	30	M	Gdnr	07Mr02Bf	MONEY, Hannah	17	F	Spinster	09Mr02Bl
FLOOD, Joseph	22	M	Carpenter	07Mr02Bf	OHARA, Jane	14	F	Spinster	09Mr02Bl
					WICKHAM, Richd.	23	M	Laborer	09Mr02Bl
					Jno.	23	M	Laborer	09Mr02Bl
					MARES, Maria	30	F	Spinster	09Mr02Bl
					FENERAW, Margt.	22	F	Spinster	09Mr02Bl
	SEA 09 MARCH 1846				MCNAMOE, Judy	25	F	Spinster	09Mr02Bl
					MURRAY, Mary	22	F	Spinster	09Mr02Bl
	From Liverpool				LAWLER, David	26	M	Laborer	09Mr02Bl
					MARTIN, Michl.	25	M	Laborer	09Mr02Bl
					CONNER, Margt.	18	F	Spinster	09Mr02Bl
					CARSON, Willm.	24	M	Cooper	09Mr02Bl
					HEAT, Cathne.	18	F	Spinster	09Mr02Bl
LAWLER, John	22	M	Laborer	09Mr02Bg	REYNOLDS, Jno.	30	M	Laborer	09Mr02Bl
JUDGE, Mary	28	F	Servant	09Mr02Bg	SHEELAM, Jeremiah	19	M	Laborer	09Mr02Bl
WHITE, Ellen	20	F	Servant	09Mr02Bg	ROACHE, Thos.	24	M	Spinner	09Mr02Bl
					CADEN, Patk.	21	M	Laborer	09Mr02Bl
					FITZPATRICK, Hugh	20	M	Laborer	09Mr02Bl
					CARROLL, Michl.	30	M	Laborer	09Mr02Bl
					MULHOLLAND, James	24	M	Roller	09Mr02Bl
					CRAWE, Thos.	25	M	Weaver	09Mr02Bl
	HENDRIK-HUDSON 09 MARCH 1846				CAVANNAH, Willm.	25	M	Tailor	09Mr02Bl
					Eliza	24	F	None	09Mr02Bl
	From London				FLYNN, Fras.	20	M	Laborer	09Mr02Bl
					AHERN, John	18	M	Shoemaker	09Mr02Bl
					CONNER, Ann	15	F	Spinster	09Mr02Bl
					GRAY, U	09	F	Child	09Mr02Bl
ERFORD, Jane	25	F	Broker	09Mr21Bh	HARDY, Cathne.	40	F	Spinster	09Mr02Bl
PERRY, Susan-J.	23	F	Broker	09Mr21Bh	Anne (D)	.00	F	Infant	09Mr02Bl
WHITWAY, Mary-Ann	22	F	Broker	09Mr21Bh	Mary (D)	06	F	Child	09Mr02Bl
MONTEGUE, Edward-C.	28	M	Gentleman	09Mr21Bh	MCGOVERN, James	20	M	Mason	09Mr02Bl
COLLINS, John	29	M	Gentleman	09Mr21Bh					
MARSH, Alfred	28	M	Brazier	09Mr21Bh					
ALLEN, George-C.	27	M	Farmer	09Mr21Bh					
MILLER, James	35	M	Printer	09Mr21Bh					
Emily	21	F	Printer	09Mr21Bh					
John	13	M	Printer	09Mr21Bh					

NAMES OF PASSENGERS	AGE	SEX	OCCUPATIONS	DATE PORT SHIP
PACIFIC 09 MARCH 1846				
From Liverpool				
IRR, Robert	25	M	Gdnr	09Mr02BJ
DEAMOND, Jacob	19	M	Tailor	09Mr02BJ
EMMET, John	17	M	Laborer	09Mr02BJ
PORTLAND, James	27	M	Laborer	09Mr02BJ
FAGAN, Thomas	25	M	Farmer	09Mr02BJ
PORTLAND, Thomas	33	M	Farmer	09Mr02BJ
NOLAND, John	23	M	Plasterer	09Mr02BJ
Ellen (W)	21	F	Wife	09Mr02BJ
James (S)	.07	M	Infant	09Mr02BJ
MCBEAKE, John	30	M	Tailor	09Mr02BJ
BRADLEY, Hugh	20	M	Thief	09Mr02BJ
MORIN, John	22	M	Laborer	09Mr02BJ
CONNOR, Patrick	21	M	Laborer	09Mr02BJ
MALLOY, Patrick	27	M	Laborer	09Mr02BJ
HABERLY, Mrgaret	30	F	Servant	09Mr02BJ
DEMPSEY, John	29	M	Unknown	09Mr02BJ
Thomas	26	M	Unknown	09Mr02BJ
Ann	20	F	Unknown	09Mr02BJ
Christin	27	F	Unknown	09Mr02BJ
AMBY, Michal	26	M	Laborer	09Mr02BJ
MCCORMIC, Michl.	55	M	Laborer	09Mr02BJ
MCGUIRE, Henry	14	M	None	09Mr02BJ
MASTER, John	21	M	Carpenter	09Mr02BJ
MANGLEY, Mary	30	F	Servant	09Mr02BJ
Micheal	24	M	Laborer	09Mr02BJ
POORE, Philip	22	M	Laborer	09Mr02BJ
PAITON, Mary	20	F	Servant	09Mr02BJ
FOX, Mary	18	F	Servant	09Mr02BJ
Ann	07	F	Child	09Mr02BJ
MALIN, James	72	M	None	09Mr02BJ
Margaret (W)	40	F	Wife	09Mr02BJ
Ann (D)	10	F	Child	09Mr02BJ
MCGOVERN, Parker	22	M	Laborer	09Mr02BJ
LUNCH, Michael	28	M	Shepherd	09Mr02BJ
NANGLE, Edward	.08	M	Infant	09Mr02BJ
RAYDE, Mary	19	F	Servant	09Mr02BJ
MCGRATH, James	26	M	Weaver	09Mr02BJ
RANE, Peter	27	M	Miner	09Mr02BJ
YOUNG, Joseph	22	M	Saddler	09Mr02BJ
Ann (W)	20	F	Wife	09Mr02BJ
JORDAN, William	19	M	Shopman	09Mr02BJ
MONTGOMERY, Ann	30	F	Servant	09Mr02BJ
FARRELL, Patrick	25	M	Laborer	09Mr02BJ
CARLIN, Margaret	40	F	Servant	09Mr02BJ
Bartholomew (S)	17	M	Laborer	09Mr02BJ
LISNON, James	21	M	Laborer	09Mr02BJ
FARRELL, John	18	M	Laborer	09Mr02BJ
HANFORD, Andrew	18	M	Laborer	09Mr02BJ
DILLON, Pat	24	M	Laborer	09Mr02BJ
BURK, Robert	23	M	Butcher	09Mr02BJ
NEW-YORK 13 MARCH 1846				
From Liverpool				
FINIGHRTY, Bryan	21	M	Farmer	13Mr02Bk
BUTLER, James	21	M	Unknown	13Mr02Bk
MCDONALD, Wm.	25	M	Unknown	13Mr02Bk
U (W)	21	F	Wife	13Mr02Bk

NAMES OF PASSENGERS	AGE	SEX	OCCUPATIONS	DATE PORT SHIP
RUSH, Fras.	24	U	Unknown	13Mr02Bk
MCCABE, Edwd.	21	M	Unknown	13Mr02Bk
LARKIN, Pat	19	M	Unknown	13Mr02Bk
FASLAY, John	20	M	Unknown	13Mr02Bk
GRAHAM, Pat	24	M	Unknown	13Mr02Bk
Biddy	23	F	Unknown	13Mr02Bk
FARLEY, Margt.	23	F	Unknown	13Mr02Bk
SMITH, John	20	M	Unknown	13Mr02Bk
KENEDY, John	21	M	Unknown	13Mr02Bk
Margt.	20	F	Unknown	13Mr02Bk
MCCARTHY, Danl.	12	M	Unknown	13Mr02Bk
MEYERS, U-Mrs.	34	F	Unknown	13Mr02Bk
Ellen (D)	09	F	Child	13Mr02Bk
U	04	U	Child	13Mr02Bk
BANNON, Danl.	24	M	Unknown	13Mr02Bk
GLANON, Patk.	21	M	Unknown	13Mr02Bk
BRANLEY, John	21	M	Unknown	13Mr02Bk
SHATWELL, Fln	20	M	Unknown	13Mr02Bk
METTLEY, Ann	30	F	Unknown	13Mr02Bk
HINDS, Mary	18	F	Unknown	13Mr02Bk
STANTON, George	06	M	Child	13Mr02Bk
SAXON, H.	24	U	Unknown	13Mr02Bk
FRENCH, W.	24	U	Unknown	13Mr02Bk
TENNAN, Pat	21	M	Unknown	13Mr02Bk
FERNAN, Bridget	60	F	Unknown	13Mr02Bk
BOKNAN, Mary	20	F	Unknown	13Mr02Bk
CLYNE, Owen	19	M	Unknown	13Mr02Bk
MICHEL, Mary	20	F	Unknown	13Mr02Bk
CUMMINS, Edwd.	30	M	Unknown	13Mr02Bk
KEARNEY, John	23	M	Unknown	13Mr02Bk
FLYNN, Bryan	26	M	Unknown	13Mr02Bk
GLANCY, Frans.	27	U	Unknown	13Mr02Bk
SCANLON, Cath.	13	F	Unknown	13Mr02Bk
BRADY, Owen	19	M	Unknown	13Mr02Bk
GLANCY, Ann	20	F	Unknown	13Mr02Bk
CONLAN, Brigt.	20	F	Unknown	13Mr02Bk
MAHON, Rose	20	F	Unknown	13Mr02Bk
EVANS, John	20	M	Unknown	13Mr02Bk
BRADY, Thos.	21	M	Unknown	13Mr02Bk
GIBNEY, John	21	M	Unknown	13Mr02Bk
BRADY, Mary	18	F	Unknown	13Mr02Bk
KILROY, Michl.	22	M	Unknown	13Mr02Bk
MURPHY, U	24	M	Unknown	13Mr02Bk
MCCABE, Alex	28	M	Unknown	13Mr02Bk
GRANT, John	18	M	Unknown	13Mr02Bk
DOGHERTY, John	42	M	Unknown	13Mr02Bk
Thomas (S)	16	M	Unknown	13Mr02Bk
Maria (D)	15	F	Unknown	13Mr02Bk
CONNOR, Mary	20	F	Unknown	13Mr02Bk
MURREY, Thos.	21	M	Unknown	13Mr02Bk
GALAGHER, John	19	M	Unknown	13Mr02Bk
Ann	17	F	Unknown	13Mr02Bk
FAGAN, Mary	17	F	Unknown	13Mr02Bk
CARR, Thomas	30	M	Unknown	13Mr02Bk
CONNOR, Frans.	18	M	Unknown	13Mr02Bk
CANE, Philip	18	M	Unknown	13Mr02Bk
REYNOLDS, Edwd.	17	M	Unknown	13Mr02Bk
KENEDY, Pat	24	M	Unknown	13Mr02Bk
Winney	20	F	Unknown	13Mr02Bk
MCTEAGUE, Michl.	20	M	Unknown	13Mr02Bk
HOGG, James	17	M	Unknown	13Mr02Bk
Isabella	19	F	Unknown	13Mr02Bk
John	04	M	Child	13Mr02Bk
Jane-Eliza	02	F	Child	13Mr02Bk
KENEDY, Danl.	40	M	Unknown	13Mr02Bk
Catha.	37	F	Unknown	13Mr02Bk
Thos.	27	M	Unknown	13Mr02Bk
FLYNN, Pat	20	M	Unknown	13Mr02Bk
KENEDY, Dennis	11	M	Unknown	13Mr02Bk
Danl.	09	M	Child	13Mr02Bk
Timo.	07	M	Child	13Mr02Bk
CASSEDY, John	63	M	Unknown	13Mr02Bk
KENEDY, John	03	M	Child	13Mr02Bk
Ellen	01	F	Child	13Mr02Bk
GRAY, Michl.	47	M	Unknown	13Mr02Bk

NAMES OF PASSENGERS		AGE	SEX	OCCUPATIONS	DATE PORT SHIP
GRAY, U	(W)	47	F	Wife	13Mr02Bk
Michl.		30	M	Unknown	13Mr02Bk
Pat		07	M	Child	13Mr02Bk
Cathn.		07	F	Child	13Mr02Bk
DEVINE, Cecelia		19	F	Unknown	13Mr02Bk
GRAY, Pat		22	M	Unknown	13Mr02Bk
Owen		18	M	Unknown	13Mr02Bk
Peter		15	M	Unknown	13Mr02Bk
DYNAN, Peter		17	M	Unknown	13Mr02Bk
Rose		18	F	Unknown	13Mr02Bk
Biddy		13	F	Unknown	13Mr02Bk
INGLSBY, Ann		24	F	Unknown	13Mr02Bk
KIERNAN, Pebby		23	U	Unknown	13Mr02Bk
BAXTER, Pat		20	M	Unknown	13Mr02Bk
MEALY, Pebby		20	U	Unknown	13Mr02Bk
CONROY, Michl.		21	M	Unknown	13Mr02Bk
MCGUINESS, Frans.		35	M	Unknown	13Mr02Bk
DONALLY, James		30	M	Unknown	13Mr02Bk
MCGINN, Julia		17	F	Unknown	13Mr02Bk
MCDERMOTT, Backl.		24	U	Unknown	13Mr02Bk
GRANT, L.		32	U	Unknown	13Mr02Bk
BRADY, Pat		20	M	Unknown	13Mr02Bk
Pat		18	M	Unknown	13Mr02Bk
MCDERMETT, James		20	M	Unknown	13Mr02Bk
MURREY, Mich.		20	M	Unknown	13Mr02Bk
PEHALIGAN, Thos.		22	M	Unknown	13Mr02Bk
WATSON, J.		20	U	Unknown	13Mr02Bk
CUDDY, Pat		20	M	Unknown	13Mr02Bk
LABLEY, John		14	M	Unknown	13Mr02Bk
Brady		07	M	Child	13Mr02Bk
Thos.		06	M	Child	13Mr02Bk
FARREL, James		20	M	Unknown	13Mr02Bk
HARVEY, Thos.		26	M	Unknown	13Mr02Bk
GALAGHER, Tins		21	U	Unknown	13Mr02Bk
MORRIS, James		18	M	Unknown	13Mr02Bk
KENNY, Pat		16	M	Unknown	13Mr02Bk
John		20	M	Unknown	13Mr02Bk
Ann		16	F	Unknown	13Mr02Bk
MCCABE, John		17	M	Unknown	13Mr02Bk
Mary		13	F	Unknown	13Mr02Bk
MCGUIRE, Margt.		13	F	Unknown	13Mr02Bk
GILL, Cath.		14	F	Unknown	13Mr02Bk
MORRIS, Biddy		15	F	Unknown	13Mr02Bk
KENEDY, Cath.		16	F	Unknown	13Mr02Bk
KEASON, Cath.		15	F	Unknown	13Mr02Bk
KELLY, Sarah		19	F	Unknown	13Mr02Bk
ROGERS, W.		00	U	Unknown	13Mr02Bk
Died-At-Sea					
CAIN, Mary		20	F	Unknown	13Mr02Bk
CURRAN, Margt.		19	F	Unknown	13Mr02Bk
BRAMOCK, Wm.		19	M	Unknown	13Mr02Bk
Mary		24	F	Unknown	13Mr02Bk
BRANLEY, John		21	M	Unknown	13Mr02Bk
BROGAN, Mary		22	F	Unknown	13Mr02Bk
MCCAMN, Cath.		20	F	Unknown	13Mr02Bk
DOGHERTY, John		20	M	Unknown	13Mr02Bk
FINIGAN, Owen		20	M	Unknown	13Mr02Bk
Owen		21	M	Unknown	13Mr02Bk
Owen		20	M	Unknown	13Mr02Bk
BRADY, James		20	M	Unknown	13Mr02Bk
FLOOD, Pat		20	M	Unknown	13Mr02Bk
TRUCAN, Mary		16	F	Unknown	13Mr02Bk
CORCORAN, Fras.		24	M	Unknown	13Mr02Bk
MURPHEY, Peter		27	M	Unknown	13Mr02Bk
James		27	M	Unknown	13Mr02Bk
MCNELLY, Pat		47	M	Unknown	13Mr02Bk
MCCABE, Ann		29	F	Unknown	13Mr02Bk
MURPHEY, James		05	M	Child	13Mr02Bk
MCLANE, W.		24	U	Unknown	13Mr02Bk
Eliza		27	F	Unknown	13Mr02Bk
QUILLIAN, Mary		14	F	Unknown	13Mr02Bk
CASSEDY, U		22	F	Unknown	13Mr02Bk
THILY, Cath.		19	F	Unknown	13Mr02Bk
Julia		15	F	Unknown	13Mr02Bk
DELANEY, Pat		23	M	Unknown	13Mr02Bk

NAMES OF PASSENGERS		AGE	SEX	OCCUPATIONS	DATE PORT SHIP
PELAN, James		20	M	Unknown	13Mr02Bk
DUGNAN, Ann		17	F	Unknown	13Mr02Bk
CONNOR, Pat		17	M	Unknown	13Mr02Bk
AGNUS, Lucy		20	F	Unknown	13Mr02Bk
SILK, Stephen		19	M	Unknown	13Mr02Bk
BOHM, Brigt.		14	F	Unknown	13Mr02Bk
ROONEY, Mary		21	F	Unknown	13Mr02Bk
James	(S)	03	M	Child	13Mr02Bk
MOORAN, U		15	M	Unknown	13Mr02Bk
CRAN, James		40	M	Unknown	13Mr02Bk

OHIO 13 MARCH 1846

From Liverpool

NAMES OF PASSENGERS		AGE	SEX	OCCUPATIONS	DATE PORT SHIP
LODER, Benjamine		30	M	Watchmaker	13Mr02Bm
HALL, Ann-Mrs.		37	F	None	13Mr02Bm
Frances	(D)	05	F	Child	13Mr02Bm
Thomas	(S)	.02	M	Infant	13Mr02Bm
MCDEVITT, Sarah		34	F	Servant	13Mr02Bm
MCKENNA, Ellen		17	F	Servant	13Mr02Bm
SMITH, Jane		18	F	Servant	13Mr02Bm
MCELROY, Ellen-Mrs.		51	F	Servant	13Mr02Bm
Sally	(D)	14	F	Servant	13Mr02Bm
John	(S)	19	M	Butcher	13Mr02Bm
William		15	M	Butcher	13Mr02Bm
Charles	(S)	12	M	Butcher	13Mr02Bm
KELLY, Patt		22	M	Laborer	13Mr02Bm
TEARNEY, Patt		19	M	Laborer	13Mr02Bm
CRUMNEY, William		19	M	Laborer	13Mr02Bm

PRINCE-ALBERT 13 MARCH 1846

From London

NAMES OF PASSENGERS		AGE	SEX	OCCUPATIONS	DATE PORT SHIP
MAHONEY, Robert		25	M	Gentleman	13Mr21Bn
HALL, Thomas		30	M	Gentleman	13Mr21Bn
WILSON, Edward		19	M	Gentleman	13Mr21Bn
LEWISSON, Fredk.		18	M	Gentleman	13Mr21Bn
CORNABY, John		55	M	Gentleman	13Mr21Bn
LUCAS, William		32	M	Farmer	13Mr21Bn
Robert		22	M	Carpenter	13Mr21Bn
Frances		28	F	None	13Mr21Bn
Frances		03	F	Child	13Mr21Bn
PETTIT, John		22	M	Laborer	13Mr21Bn
CROCK, George		39	M	Merchant	13Mr21Bn
BRETT, George		18	M	Laborer	13Mr21Bn
DYKE, John		21	M	Baker	13Mr21Bn
ANDREWS, Frederick		20	M	Farmer	13Mr21Bn
ELY, Thomas		20	M	Laborer	13Mr21Bn
KENNEDY, Alice		44	F	None	13Mr21Bn
Jane	(D)	11	F	None	13Mr21Bn
HAMILTON, Ands.		21	M	Farmer	13Mr21Bn
ANDREWS, Thomas		43	M	Farmer	13Mr21Bn
ELY, Thomas		21	M	Farmer	13Mr21Bn
MILLS, William		19	M	Chair Maker	13Mr21Bn
COOK, John		22	M	Laborer	13Mr21Bn
CHAY, Margaret		23	F	None	13Mr21Bn
Mary	(D)	01	F	Child	13Mr21Bn
Died-At-Sea					
BARNARD, Alfred		21	M	Clerk	13Mr21Bn
MILLER, Albert		47	M	Carpenter	13Mr21Bn
MCDONNOR, Hugh		30	M	Tailor	13Mr21Bn

9

NAMES OF PASSENGERS		AGE	SEX	OCCUPATIONS	DATE PORT SHIP
JACOBS, Kenny		50	M	Merchant	13Mr21Bn
ROBERTSON, Thomas		36	M	Carpenter	13Mr21Bn
RICE, John		34	M	Farmer	13Mr21Bn
WHITTENHAM, Samuel		28	M	Carpenter	13Mr21Bn
HEALY, George		33	M	Farmer	13Mr21Bn
SMITH, Benjamin		09	M	Child	13Mr21Bn
RILEY, Richard		43	M	Printer	13Mr21Bn
DUNSTON, Thomas		24	M	Farmer	13Mr21Bn
WILLIAMSON, William		40	M	Clerk	13Mr21Bn
COOK, Thomas		24	M	Hatter	13Mr21Bn
EASTMEAD, Charles		25	M	Carpenter	13Mr21Bn
SOUTHON, Thomas		25	M	Farmer	13Mr21Bn
Caleb		18	M	Farmer	13Mr21Bn
CLARK, William		66	M	Gentleman	13Mr21Bn
BORGHARDT, John		27	M	Furrier	13Mr21Bn
Eliza	(W)	27	F	Wife	13Mr21Bn
Eliza	(D)	02	F	Child	13Mr21Bn
Ruth	(D)	01	F	Child	13Mr21Bn
COLLINS, Maria		26	F	None	13Mr21Bn
James	(S)	09	M	Child	13Mr21Bn
Samuel	(S)	01	M	Child	13Mr21Bn
BEADLE, Henry		38	M	Waterman	13Mr21Bn
LUCAS, Albert		.00	M	Infant	13Mr21Bn
Born-At-Sea					

LIVERPOOL 13 MARCH 1846

From Liverpool

NAMES OF PASSENGERS		AGE	SEX	OCCUPATIONS	DATE PORT SHIP
EGAN, Michl.		29	M	Mason	13Mr02Bo
U	(W)	24	F	Wife	13Mr02Bo
U		19	F	None	13Mr02Bo
Bridget	(D)	.10	F	Infant	13Mr02Bo
SHIELDS, Anne		37	F	Wife	13Mr02Bo
Patt	(S)	10	M	Child	13Mr02Bo
Michl.	(S)	07	M	Child	13Mr02Bo
Margt.Ann	(D)	05	F	Child	13Mr02Bo
Elizbth.	(D)	02	F	Child	13Mr02Bo
Julia	(D)	.10	F	Infant	13Mr02Bo
LEES, James		26	M	Miner	13Mr02Bo
ARGRAMS, John		36	M	Weaver	13Mr02Bo
Faithful	(S)	08	M	Child	13Mr02Bo
HAVEN, Richd.		30	M	Laborer	13Mr02Bo
MCGUIGANN, Thomas		31	M	Shoemaker	13Mr02Bo
Anne	(W)	29	F	Wife	13Mr02Bo
Anne	(D)	.10	F	Infant	13Mr02Bo
BARNET, Aron		21	M	Laborer	13Mr02Bo
U	(W)	21	F	Wife	13Mr02Bo
COATE, Chas.		20	M	Laborer	13Mr02Bo
MINNIS, Robt.		45	M	Weaver	13Mr02Bo
KELLY, Elizebth.		18	F	Servant	13Mr02Bo
MCCALL, Margt.		18	F	Servant	13Mr02Bo
FRYERS, Danl.		36	M	Blacksmith	13Mr02Bo
SMYTH, Geo.		38	M	Weaver	13Mr02Bo
HENSEY, James		23	M	Laborer	13Mr02Bo
RICHEY, Thos.		24	M	Laborer	13Mr02Bo
FULLEY, John		23	M	Laborer	13Mr02Bo
CONNELLY, Patt		19	M	Laborer	13Mr02Bo
KELLY, Mary		19	F	Servant	13Mr02Bo
DONNELLY, Mary		19	F	Servant	13Mr02Bo
MCDERMOTTE, Cathe.		28	F	Servant	13Mr02Bo
HENEGAN, Bridget		20	F	Servant	13Mr02Bo
MCCARN, Jno.		28	M	Laborer	13Mr02Bo
DOONAN, Michl.		20	M	Farmer	13Mr02Bo
CARROLL, Mary		28	F	Servant	13Mr02Bo
MAHON, Michl.		18	M	Laborer	13Mr02Bo
MCFARLANE, Lakey		28	M	Laborer	13Mr02Bo
Biddy	(W)	21	F	Wife	13Mr02Bo
KINN, Jno.		20	M	Laborer	13Mr02Bo

NAMES OF PASSENGERS		AGE	SEX	OCCUPATIONS	DATE PORT SHIP
KINN, Mary		16	F	Servant	13Mr02Bo
RILEY, Cathe.		20	F	Servant	13Mr02Bo
Anne		21	F	Servant	13Mr02Bo
LEECH, Wm.		34	M	Baker	13Mr02Bo
BRIDGEMAN, Mark		25	M	Upholsterer	13Mr02Bo
U	(W)	20	F	Wife	13Mr02Bo
HEALEY, Martin		22	M	Laborer	13Mr02Bo
BYRNE, Patt		25	M	Laborer	13Mr02Bo
CONWAY, Michl.		21	M	Laborer	13Mr02Bo
MCDONNELL, Michl.		22	M	Laborer	13Mr02Bo
KEALEY, Jno.		23	M	Laborer	13Mr02Bo
RUSSELL, Robert		27	M	Watchmaker	13Mr02Bo
U	(W)	20	F	Wife	13Mr02Bo
Jane		19	F	Servant	13Mr02Bo
WHELAN, Patt		26	M	Laborer	13Mr02Bo
BOYLE, Danl.		45	M	Laborer	13Mr02Bo
Saml.		43	M	Laborer	13Mr02Bo
Wm.		16	M	Laborer	13Mr02Bo
Biddy		13	F	Laborer	13Mr02Bo
Richard		10	M	Laborer	13Mr02Bo
Barney		07	M	Child	13Mr02Bo
Jane		05	F	Child	13Mr02Bo
MCKANN, Michl.		23	M	Laborer	13Mr02Bo
POWLEY, Cathe.		30	F	Servant	13Mr02Bo
John	(S)	07	M	Child	13Mr02Bo
James	(S)	03	M	Child	13Mr02Bo
THANNON, Michl.		11	M	Laborer	13Mr02Bo
MCLAUGHLIN, Isabella		20	F	Servant	13Mr02Bo
MCQUINEY, Thomas		20	M	Laborer	13Mr02Bo
Anne		18	F	Servant	13Mr02Bo
MINTON, Bernrd		18	M	Laborer	13Mr02Bo
REYNOLDS, Pat		20	M	Laborer	13Mr02Bo
MCGUINEY, Bridget		18	F	Servant	13Mr02Bo
MCGANN, Owen		18	M	Laborer	13Mr02Bo
KENNEDAY, Bernard		49	M	Weaver	13Mr02Bo
Mary	(W)	30	F	Wife	13Mr02Bo
John	(S)	08	M	Child	13Mr02Bo
Donald	(S)	01	M	Child	13Mr02Bo
MCMURRAY, Eliza		17	F	Servant	13Mr02Bo
Rose		18	F	Servant	13Mr02Bo
Anne		19	F	Servant	13Mr02Bo
CONNER, Cathe.		21	F	Servant	13Mr02Bo
Bridget		23	F	Servant	13Mr02Bo
LAWLES, Bridget		30	F	Servant	13Mr02Bo
Margt.	(D)	08	F	Child	13Mr02Bo
WUNE, John		25	M	Carpenter	13Mr02Bo
KELLY, Patt		19	M	Laborer	13Mr02Bo
MCNALLY, Homer		22	M	Servant	13Mr02Bo
SMYTH, Anne		24	F	Servant	13Mr02Bo
Mary		21	F	Servant	13Mr02Bo
MCWILLIAMS, Pat		30	M	Farmer	13Mr02Bo
Cathe.	(W)	25	F	Wife	13Mr02Bo
REDFERIN, Frances		20	F	None	13Mr02Bo
MELLIN, Thomas		20	M	Laborer	13Mr02Bo
MCKINN, Biddy		18	F	Servant	13Mr02Bo
MCELAIN, Rosey		15	F	Servant	13Mr02Bo
MCGUIGAN, Patt		20	M	Weaver	13Mr02Bo
MCKIVER, Matthew		21	M	Laborer	13Mr02Bo
Margt.	(D)	01	F	Child	13Mr02Bo
Died-At-Sea					
MCGRATH, Philip		50	M	Shoemaker	13Mr02Bo
Christy	(S)	17	M	Laborer	13Mr02Bo
Cathe.	(D)	13	F	Servant	13Mr02Bo
MATHAN, Hugh		16	M	Laborer	13Mr02Bo
Biddy		10	F	Servant	13Mr02Bo
QUINN, Edward		27	M	Laborer	13Mr02Bo
REYNOLDS, John		20	M	Laborer	13Mr02Bo
MAKIN, Anne		23	F	Servant	13Mr02Bo
Pat	(S)	01	M	Child	13Mr02Bo
MCALISTER, Mary		52	F	Servant	13Mr02Bo
Sarah	(D)	25	F	Servant	13Mr02Bo
Rindale		21	M	Laborer	13Mr02Bo
Hugh	(S)	13	M	Laborer	13Mr02Bo
NUGENT, Mary		25	F	Cnf	13Mr02Bo
Margt.	(D)	08	F	Child	13Mr02Bo

NAMES OF PASSENGERS	AGE	SEX	OCCUPATIONS	DATE PORT SHIP
BURKE, Geo.	35	M	Plasterer	13Mr02Bo
TONNEY, Michl.	25	M	Bricklayer	13Mr02Bo
CRAMER, Thomas	25	M	Laborer	13Mr02Bo
CALAGHAN, Rose	20	F	Servant	13Mr02Bo
WATERS, Ellen	20	F	Servant	13Mr02Bo
MASTRESON, Bernard	20	M	Servant	13Mr02Bo
Mary	18	F	Servant	13Mr02Bo
HANIGAN, Peter	25	M	Laborer	13Mr02Bo
CALAGHAN, James	24	M	Laborer	13Mr02Bo
SMYTH, Mary	20	F	Servant	13Mr02Bo
BRADY, Mary	22	F	Servant	13Mr02Bo
MALINE, Michl.	25	M	Laborer	13Mr02Bo
HARDIN, Francis	25	M	Laborer	13Mr02Bo
CONDUE, Wm.	25	M	Laborer	13Mr02Bo
CONNELL, John	30	M	Laborer	13Mr02Bo
MCCARTY, Dennis	25	M	Laborer	13Mr02Bo
TULLY, Michl.	16	M	Laborer	13Mr02Bo
MCGREEVEY, Mary	25	F	Servant	13Mr02Bo
BRADY, Michl.	22	M	Laborer	13Mr02Bo
HARRINGTON, Thos.	25	M	Plasterer	13Mr02Bo
FAYING, Pat	20	M	Plasterer	13Mr02Bo
TREIMER, Thos.	20	M	Smith	13Mr02Bo
SEPHTIN, James	19	M	Laborer	13Mr02Bo
MAGINNESS, Felix	50	M	Farmer	13Mr02Bo
DONNELLY, Thos.	26	M	Servant	13Mr02Bo
WARD, Francis	20	M	Laborer	13Mr02Bo
CULLEN, Cathe.	20	F	Servant	13Mr02Bo
REYNOLDS, Biddy	19	F	Servant	13Mr02Bo
EGAN, Biddy	18	F	Servant	13Mr02Bo
HAGAN, Owen	20	M	Laborer	13Mr02Bo
LEAVEY, Michl.	19	M	Laborer	13Mr02Bo
BREMAN, Anne	20	F	Servant	13Mr02Bo
SMYTH, Patt	21	M	Laborer	13Mr02Bo
GILCHRIST, John	20	M	Laborer	13Mr02Bo
Anne	17	F	Laborer	13Mr02Bo
Thomas	20	M	Laborer	13Mr02Bo
NOLLEY, William	20	M	Laborer	13Mr02Bo
DOUGHERTY, Peter	20	M	Laborer	13Mr02Bo
MCGRANN, Mary	20	F	Servant	13Mr02Bo
CONROY, Anne	18	F	Servant	13Mr02Bo
HEALEY, Cathe.	30	F	Servant	13Mr02Bo
NOTLEY, Cathe.	04	F	Child	13Mr02Bo
EARLEY, Biddy	20	F	Servant	13Mr02Bo
GILCHRIST, James	20	M	Laborer	13Mr02Bo
DUFFEY, Bernard	24	M	Laborer	13Mr02Bo
MCLAUGHLIN, Patt	24	M	Laborer	13Mr02Bo
WARD, Patt	20	M	Laborer	13Mr02Bo
BYRNE, Anne	20	F	Servant	13Mr02Bo
CANTIN, John-I.	18	M	Brick Maker	13Mr02Bo
LYNCH, Michl.	20	M	Laborer	13Mr02Bo
CAFFERTY, James	26	M	Laborer	13Mr02Bo
Mary (W)	20	F	Wife	13Mr02Bo
CLARKE, Cathe.	23	F	Servant	13Mr02Bo
GREGAN, John	20	M	Laborer	13Mr02Bo
MCCORMICK, Pat	20	M	Laborer	13Mr02Bo
ROGAN, Anne	17	F	Servant	13Mr02Bo
MCGAY, Bridget	24	F	Servant	13Mr02Bo
FANNELL, Thos.	21	M	Joiner	13Mr02Bo
Michl.	20	M	Joiner	13Mr02Bo
MEREDITH, Elizth.	27	F	Housekeeper	13Mr02Bo
ONEIL, Cathe.	21	F	Dressmaker	13Mr02Bo
BUCKLEY, John	39	M	Mason	13Mr02Bo
Ellen (W)	30	F	Wife	13Mr02Bo
Ellen (D)	12	F	None	13Mr02Bo
Elizth. (D)	10	F	None	13Mr02Bo
John (S)	08	M	Child	13Mr02Bo
Margt. (D)	05	F	Child	13Mr02Bo
Died-At-Sea				
Wm. (S)	03	M	Child	13Mr02Bo
Chrisn. (S)	01	M	Child	13Mr02Bo
BRENAN, Mary	18	F	Servant	13Mr02Bo
Cathe.	17	F	Servant	13Mr02Bo
MULVEY, Cathe.	17	F	Servant	13Mr02Bo
MARKEY, Mary	18	F	Servant	13Mr02Bo
QUIGLEY, Bridget	22	F	Servant	13Mr02Bo
GILLIGAN, John	22	M	Laborer	13Mr02Bo
Anne	17	F	Servant	13Mr02Bo
Cathe.	13	F	Servant	13Mr02Bo
CONNERTON, Winney	17	F	Servant	13Mr02Bo
BRADLEY, Key	20	M	Machinist	13Mr02Bo
Wm.	25	M	Carpenter	13Mr02Bo
CARROLL, Danl.	25	M	Laborer	13Mr02Bo
CAULFIELD, Margt.	20	F	Servant	13Mr02Bo
BANAGHAN, Patt	18	M	Laborer	13Mr02Bo
Bridget	20	F	Servant	13Mr02Bo
LOUGH, James	26	M	Laborer	13Mr02Bo
KELLY, Margt.	25	F	Servant	13Mr02Bo
HANLEY, Hugh	20	M	Laborer	13Mr02Bo
MOOLAHAN, Margt.	25	F	Servant	13Mr02Bo
BRENNAN, Bridget	20	F	Servant	13Mr02Bo
WATSON, Margt. •	25	F	Servant	13Mr02Bo
BOLGER, David	22	M	Servant	13Mr02Bo
MURPHY, Martin	25	M	Servant	13Mr02Bo
LENNIN, Michl.	18	M	Servant	13Mr02Bo
BINNEY, Martin	26	M	Tailor	13Mr02Bo
WELSH, Thomas	23	M	Farmer	13Mr02Bo
KANE, Michl.	25	M	Laborer	13Mr02Bo
MANGAN, John	20	M	Laborer	13Mr02Bo
HEALEY, Stephen	13	M	Laborer	13Mr02Bo
LEWIS, Wm.	30	M	Upholsterer	13Mr02Bo
CAMPION, Benjn.	24	M	Upholsterer	13Mr02Bo
CARRIGAN, Michl.	20	M	Laborer	13Mr02Bo
Patt	21	M	Laborer	13Mr02Bo
MORAN, Martin	20	M	Laborer	13Mr02Bo
GARRY, Patt	22	M	Laborer	13Mr02Bo
GROGAN, Anne	20	F	Servant	13Mr02Bo
BROGAN, Thomas	22	M	Laborer	13Mr02Bo
U (W)	20	F	Wife	13Mr02Bo
DARNIN, John	20	M	Laborer	13Mr02Bo
NEWMAN, Michl.	25	M	Laborer	13Mr02Bo
SPELMAN, Elizth.	25	F	Wife	13Mr02Bo
Matthew	12	M	None	13Mr02Bo
Judy	09	F	Child	13Mr02Bo
Patt	21	M	Servant	13Mr02Bo
RUSH, Thomas	20	M	Laborer	13Mr02Bo
TURNAN, Thoms.	20	M	Laborer	13Mr02Bo
MORAN, Thomas	20	M	Laborer	13Mr02Bo
ROSS, Thoms.	20	M	Laborer	13Mr02Bo
TIERNAN, James	20	M	Laborer	13Mr02Bo
SMYTH, Mary	19	F	Servant	13Mr02Bo
Margt.	19	F	Servant	13Mr02Bo
FERGUSON, John	14	M	Laborer	13Mr02Bo
MAHEY, Wm.	50	M	Farmer	13Mr02Bo
Sarah (W)	40	F	Wife	13Mr02Bo
Patt (S)	12	M	Child	13Mr02Bo
James (S)	07	M	Child	13Mr02Bo
Robert (S)	04	M	Child	13Mr02Bo
BRADY, Jane	20	F	Servant	13Mr02Bo
LEA, Pat	25	M	Laborer	13Mr02Bo
ONEIL, Hugh	40	M	Laborer	13Mr02Bo
MCCOURT, Dennis	26	M	Laborer	13Mr02Bo
Cathe. (W)	26	F	Wife	13Mr02Bo
Mary (D)	06	F	Child	13Mr02Bo
Patt (S)	03	M	Child	13Mr02Bo
Bridget (D)	01	F	Child	13Mr02Bo
THIGLAS, Esther	27	F	Servant	13Mr02Bo
HORAM, Michl.	20	M	Carpenter	13Mr02Bo
KELLY, Martin	25	M	Servant	13Mr02Bo
MCCULLOUGH, Wm.	12	M	Servant	13Mr02Bo
John	13	M	Servant	13Mr02Bo
Mary-Anne	20	F	Servant	13Mr02Bo
FARLEY, John	30	M	Farmer	13Mr02Bo
FAULKNER, Charles	20	M	Blacksmith	13Mr02Bo
GREY, Margt.	16	F	Servant	13Mr02Bo
FLINN, Anne	16	F	Servant	13Mr02Bo
FAULKNER, Laurence	11	M	Servant	13Mr02Bo
NICKLE, Alexr.	20	M	Laborer	13Mr02Bo
U (W)	20	F	Wife	13Mr02Bo
LANE, David	20	M	Laborer	13Mr02Bo
U (W)	20	F	Wife	13Mr02Bo

NAMES OF PASSENGERS		AGE	SEX	OCCUPATIONS	DATE PORT SHIP
SCALLY, Thomas		18	M	Laborer	13Mr02Bo
HANLEY, Bridget		20	F	Servant	13Mr02Bo
DALEY, Cathe.		18	F	Servant	13Mr02Bo
CARROLL, Mary		30	F	Servant	13Mr02Bo
SEYERS, Geoe.		25	M	Miner	13Mr02Bo
MONTGOMERY, Robt.		21	M	Miner	13Mr02Bo
WARD, Andr.		20	M	Farmer	13Mr02Bo

SHAKESPEARE 14 MARCH 1846

From Liverpool

NAMES OF PASSENGERS		AGE	SEX	OCCUPATIONS	DATE PORT SHIP
TRAINER, John		22	M	Bricklayer	14Mr02Bp
MCGUIRE, Hugh		15	M	None	14Mr02Bp
James		13	M	None	14Mr02Bp
Mary		13	F	None	14Mr02Bp
GIBBONS, Elizabeth		29	F	Spinster	14Mr02Bp
LANEGHAN, Thomas		17	M	Spinner	14Mr02Bp
CALLAGHAN, Jas.		29	M	Shoemaker	14Mr02Bp
Ellen	(W)	25	F	Wife	14Mr02Bp
Thos.	(S)	.00	M	Infant	14Mr02Bp
ROURK, James		24	M	Laborer	14Mr02Bp
HACKEL, Michael		24	M	Laborer	14Mr02Bp
WELSH, Redmond		30	M	Laborer	14Mr02Bp
Thomas		27	M	Laborer	14Mr02Bp
MCNENORMION, James		21	M	Laborer	14Mr02Bp
MOORE, Mary		50	F	Spinster	14Mr02Bp
SCAHILL, Michael		26	M	Laborer	14Mr02Bp
U	(W)	25	F	Wife	14Mr02Bp
DOOLAN, Martin		20	M	Laborer	14Mr02Bp
CONNELL, Pat		20	M	Laborer	14Mr02Bp
DONAHOO, Geo.		20	M	Laborer	14Mr02Bp
Dolly		21	F	Spinster	14Mr02Bp
CONNOLLY, Biddy		20	F	Spinster	14Mr02Bp
HANLEY, Thomas		22	M	Laborer	14Mr02Bp
MCCARTNEY, Pat		40	M	Musician	14Mr02Bp
DURNIN, Michael		30	M	Laborer	14Mr02Bp
BOYLE, Peter		30	M	Laborer	14Mr02Bp
CONNELL, Wm.		24	M	Laborer	14Mr02Bp
ROWLAND, Wm.		21	M	Laborer	14Mr02Bp
FOSTER, Robt.		24	M	Laborer	14Mr02Bp
MCKAY, Peter		19	M	Engineer	14Mr02Bp
CONWAY, Pat		21	M	Laborer	14Mr02Bp
U	(W)	20	F	Wife	14Mr02Bp
Pat	(S)	03	M	Child	14Mr02Bp
U		.00	U	Infant	14Mr02Bp
Died-At-Sea					
HODGES, John		32	M	Steward	14Mr02Bp
U	(W)	32	F	Wife	14Mr02Bp
Wm.		16	M	None	14Mr02Bp
Margt.	(D)	13	F	None	14Mr02Bp
Rachel	(D)	10	F	Child	14Mr02Bp
MURRAY, Mary		20	F	Spinster	14Mr02Bp
Wm.		17	M	Laborer	14Mr02Bp
MCLAUGHLIM, Jas.		20	M	Fisherman	14Mr02Bp
ELLANT, Pat		30	M	Laborer	14Mr02Bp
MURPHY, Pat		26	M	Miner	14Mr02Bp
Ann		24	F	None	14Mr02Bp
Elizabeth		29	F	None	14Mr02Bp
DALEY, Margt.		20	F	Spinster	14Mr02Bp
DOOLAN, Ann		23	F	Spinster	14Mr02Bp
DUCK, Catharine		23	F	Spinster	14Mr02Bp
MARTIN, Mary-Mrs.		25	F	Spinster	14Mr02Bp
BYRNES, Eliza		23	F	Spinster	14Mr02Bp
OHARA, Mary		18	F	Spinster	14Mr02Bp
Cath.		24	F	Spinster	14Mr02Bp
MULLIGAN, Cath.		16	F	Spinster	14Mr02Bp
KELLY, Luke		45	M	None	14Mr02Bp
HEGAN, Andrew		24	M	Laborer	14Mr02Bp
HEGAN, Cath.		16	F	Spinster	14Mr02Bp
Mary		13	F	Spinster	14Mr02Bp
Michael		11	M	None	14Mr02Bp
BRYAN, James		26	M	Laborer	14Mr02Bp
FLANAGHAN, Christr.		20	M	Hrsdlr	14Mr02Bp
EGAN, Jas.		25	M	Laborer	14Mr02Bp
CUNLIFFE, Thos.		30	M	Laborer	14Mr02Bp
REILLY, Peter		26	M	Shoemaker	14Mr02Bp
Cath.		20	F	Shoemaker	14Mr02Bp
MARTIN, Mary		25	F	Spinster	14Mr02Bp
REILLY, John		22	M	Laborer	14Mr02Bp
Michael		23	M	Laborer	14Mr02Bp
CLARKE, Rich.		26	M	Farmer	14Mr02Bp
U	(W)	20	F	Wife	14Mr02Bp
U		.00	U	Infant	14Mr02Bp
DALTON, Thos.		40	M	Laborer	14Mr02Bp
U	(W)	45	F	Wife	14Mr02Bp
Owen	(S)	13	M	None	14Mr02Bp
U		.00	U	Infant	14Mr02Bp
CONNOR, Michael		27	M	None	14Mr02Bp
THOMPSON, John		28	M	None	14Mr02Bp
GORMAN, Geo.		22	M	None	14Mr02Bp
Ann		20	F	None	14Mr02Bp
KELLY, Mary		40	F	Spinster	14Mr02Bp
U		.00	U	Infant	14Mr02Bp
U		.00	U	Infant	14Mr02Bp
CORCORAN, Cath.		20	F	Spinster	14Mr02Bp
MCKAY, Pat		22	M	Smith	14Mr02Bp
CULLEN, Jas.		20	M	Coachman	14Mr02Bp
CULBY, Thos.		18	M	Groom	14Mr02Bp
MCDONALD, Mary		20	F	Spinster	14Mr02Bp
HENRY, Lawrence		26	M	Pigmkr	14Mr02Bp
RYAN, U-Mrs.		31	F	Spinster	14Mr02Bp
CONNOR, Phelim		24	M	Laborer	14Mr02Bp
LINCH, Bridget		23	F	Spinster	14Mr02Bp
LONGBY, Geo.		18	M	Laborer	14Mr02Bp
SMITH, Duncan		16	M	Laborer	14Mr02Bp
MULILY, John		18	M	Laborer	14Mr02Bp

JOHN-R.SKIDDY 16 MARCH 1846

From Liverpool

NAMES OF PASSENGERS		AGE	SEX	OCCUPATIONS	DATE PORT SHIP
ROBINSON, John		25	M	Farmer	16Mr02Ac
CAVENAGH, Michel		25	M	Farmer	16Mr02Ac
BURK, Rich.		22	M	Farmer	16Mr02Ac
FAHY, James		28	M	Farmer	16Mr02Ac
MALONEY, Mich.		35	M	None	16Mr02Ac
DIMOND, Andrew		24	M	None	16Mr02Ac
Anna		18	F	None	16Mr02Ac
BRUNKER, B.		34	M	Grocer	16Mr02Ac
BENDEN, E.		37	M	Grocer	16Mr02Ac
CULLIGAN, E.		21	M	Laborer	16Mr02Ac
Mary		20	F	Laborer	16Mr02Ac
HAMMON, Patt		45	M	Gdnr	16Mr02Ac
BURNES, Peter		58	M	Farmer	16Mr02Ac
TYRELL, Robt.		20	M	Shoemaker	16Mr02Ac
ONEIL, Hugh		20	M	Weaver	16Mr02Ac
NUGENT, Ann		18	F	Dressmaker	16Mr02Ac
Eliza		14	F	None	16Mr02Ac
CHRONSON, Alex		60	M	None	16Mr02Ac
Died-At-Sea					
OBRIEN, Edw.		34	M	None	16Mr02Ac
Cath.	(W)	28	F	Wife	16Mr02Ac
Wm.W.	(S)	10	M	Child	16Mr02Ac
Henry-K.	(S)	08	M	Child	16Mr02Ac
Anna	(D)	06	F	Child	16Mr02Ac
Mary	(D)	04	F	Child	16Mr02Ac
Edw.	(S)	02	M	Child	16Mr02Ac

NAMES OF PASSENGERS		AGE	SEX	OCCUPATIONS	DATE PORT SHIP
HICKMAN, Wm.		36	M	None	16Mr02Ac
Eliza		30	F	None	16Mr02Ac
John		16	M	None	16Mr02Ac
Wm.		12	M	None	16Mr02Ac
BISHOP, Edw.		18	M	Farmer	16Mr02Ac
ROBINSON, Thos.		32	M	Farmer	16Mr02Ac
Eliza		28	F	None	16Mr02Ac
STEVENS, Mary		18	F	Dressmaker	16Mr02Ac
PATTERSON, Sarah		35	F	None	16Mr02Ac
John	(S)	11	M	None	16Mr02Ac
Thos.	(S)	09	M	Child	16Mr02Ac
Jas.	(S)	07	M	Child	16Mr02Ac
Hugh	(S)	05	M	Child	16Mr02Ac
Mary-Jane	(D)	03	F	Child	16Mr02Ac
AGAN, Patt		26	M	Laborer	16Mr02Ac
Lucy		20	F	None	16Mr02Ac
Thos.		40	M	None	16Mr02Ac
LAWDER, John		30	M	Laborer	16Mr02Ac
MCDEEN, Redman		23	M	None	16Mr02Ac
TINNUE, Thos.		30	M	None	16Mr02Ac
COBIN, Cath.		19	F	Servant	16Mr02Ac
LAKIE, Cath.		45	F	None	16Mr02Ac
ROCK, Patt		12	M	Laborer	16Mr02Ac
CROSIN, Henry		20	M	Laborer	16Mr02Ac
CRONE, John		45	M	Laborer	16Mr02Ac
Mary		15	F	None	16Mr02Ac
DONEVON, Patt		23	M	Laborer	16Mr02Ac
BOHAN, Thos.		20	M	None	16Mr02Ac
Cath.		15	F	Servant	16Mr02Ac
HESTAN, Cath.		23	F	Servant	16Mr02Ac
MCGUIRE, Bridget		21	F	Servant	16Mr02Ac
CARL, Joseph		20	M	Laborer	16Mr02Ac
FARL, Frank		18	M	Laborer	16Mr02Ac
NOLAND, Brien		20	M	Laborer	16Mr02Ac
DUFFEE, Owen		25	M	Laborer	16Mr02Ac
LARLEY, Betty		20	F	Servant	16Mr02Ac
FLIN, Mary		30	F	Servant	16Mr02Ac
KIM, Mary		20	F	Servant	16Mr02Ac
DONEGAN, Bridget		25	F	Servant	16Mr02Ac
DILLON, Edw.		30	M	Clergyman	16Mr02Ac
MCNALLY, Mary		21	F	Servant	16Mr02Ac
TINNEY, Mary		15	F	Servant	16Mr02Ac
MCDURMONT, Thos.		23	M	Laborer	16Mr02Ac
Jane		23	F	None	16Mr02Ac
MATTHUES, Barney		27	M	Laborer	16Mr02Ac
GARVY, Jas.		24	M	Laborer	16Mr02Ac
MORRIS, Wm.		21	M	Laborer	16Mr02Ac
MAHER, Mich.		21	M	Laborer	16Mr02Ac
BURNES, Pattr.		30	M	Laborer	16Mr02Ac
TEAVEN, Andy		25	M	Laborer	16Mr02Ac
LYONS, Thos.		24	M	Laborer	16Mr02Ac
REYOLDS, Eliza		22	F	Servant	16Mr02Ac
JORDAN, Biddy		18	F	Servant	16Mr02Ac
MCHALAN, Mary		20	F	Servant	16Mr02Ac
HAGAN, Biddy		19	F	Servant	16Mr02Ac
GAHAN, Rose		18	F	Servant	16Mr02Ac
COSGAN, Wm.		25	M	Laborer	16Mr02Ac
RATICAN, Ned		23	M	Laborer	16Mr02Ac
Julia		18	F	None	16Mr02Ac
CARRY, Thos.		12	M	Laborer	16Mr02Ac
MITCHEL, Sarah		20	F	Servant	16Mr02Ac
DAILEY, Mary		20	F	Servant	16Mr02Ac
BURNES, Mary		21	F	Servant	16Mr02Ac
CONE, Nancy		22	F	Servant	16Mr02Ac
ROCK, Biddy		25	F	Servant	16Mr02Ac
WALIN, Winna		60	F	None	16Mr02Ac
Eliza		25	F	None	16Mr02Ac
Winna		60	F	None	16Mr02Ac
KERRITY, Thos.		22	M	Laborer	16Mr02Ac
CLINCH, Patt		21	M	Blacksmith	16Mr02Ac
RILEY, Cornelius		18	M	Laborer	16Mr02Ac
GREENWAY, John		24	M	Laborer	16Mr02Ac
Hannah	(W)	23	F	Wife	16Mr02Ac
Mary	(D)	03	F	Child	16Mr02Ac
PANTLAIN, Jane		21	F	Servant	16Mr02Ac
GREENWAY, Sarah		.06	F	Infant	16Mr02Ac
				Died-At-Sea	
FLOOD, Thos.		25	M	Blacksmith	16Mr02Ac
NELLY, Nell		26	M	Laborer	16Mr02Ac
HIGGINS, Dan		18	M	Laborer	16Mr02Ac
Eliza		09	F	Child	16Mr02Ac
CROW, John		22	M	Laborer	16Mr02Ac
KELLY, Mich		25	M	Laborer	16Mr02Ac
MANNUM, Jas.		21	M	Laborer	16Mr02Ac
COFF, Nancy		24	F	Servant	16Mr02Ac
MURRY, Cath.		22	F	Servant	16Mr02Ac
KENNEDY, John		27	M	Laborer	16Mr02Ac
KERNAN, Patt		48	M	None	16Mr02Ac
COMMICK, Francis		27	M	Laborer	16Mr02Ac
RILEY, Owen		15	M	Laborer	16Mr02Ac
RYAN, Mich.		18	M	Laborer	16Mr02Ac
MCCOMMICK, John		26	M	Laborer	16Mr02Ac
Margreat		25	F	None	16Mr02Ac
SMITH, Wm.		32	M	Laborer	16Mr02Ac
WHITEHEAD, Jas.		21	M	Laborer	16Mr02Ac
HAILEY, John		40	M	Laborer	16Mr02Ac
HARLAND, Thos.		30	M	Laborer	16Mr02Ac
COOK, John		16	M	Laborer	16Mr02Ac
FILIN, John		15	M	Laborer	16Mr02Ac
Cath.		11	F	None	16Mr02Ac
MOOHAN, Ann		23	F	Servant	16Mr02Ac
ROLK, Thomas		21	M	Laborer	16Mr02Ac
COIN, John		20	M	None	16Mr02Ac
FAHIE, Ann		24	F	Servant	16Mr02Ac
MCKEE, Mary		20	F	Servant	16Mr02Ac
SMITH, Terry		20	M	Laborer	16Mr02Ac
MCGUIRE, Patt		21	M	Laborer	16Mr02Ac
FAGAN, Jas.		37	M	Laborer	16Mr02Ac
KINNEY, Thos.		27	M	Laborer	16Mr02Ac
FLANAGAN, Mich.		23	M	Laborer	16Mr02Ac
DORAN, Francis		22	M	Laborer	16Mr02Ac
COLAVAN, John		38	M	Laborer	16Mr02Ac
Mary		20	F	None	16Mr02Ac
ROSS, Mich.		19	M	Laborer	16Mr02Ac
CASSIDY, Mich.		57	M	Groom	16Mr02Ac
Nicholas		20	M	Laborer	16Mr02Ac
WELDEN, James		27	M	Laborer	16Mr02Ac
MILLER, Wm.		24	M	Butcher	16Mr02Ac
DORAN, Tim		24	M	Butcher	16Mr02Ac
Eliza		24	F	None	16Mr02Ac
MCSEASIER, Mary		18	F	Servant	16Mr02Ac
BAXTER, Ellen		20	F	Servant	16Mr02Ac
NOLAND, Ann		13	F	Servant	16Mr02Ac
CARAH, Mary		15	F	Servant	16Mr02Ac
SCHELEN, Ellen		16	F	Servant	16Mr02Ac
Mary		12	F	Servant	16Mr02Ac
RING, Dan		31	M	Laborer	16Mr02Ac
LAWRENCE, John		21	M	Laborer	16Mr02Ac
BOYD, Sarah		70	F	None	16Mr02Ac
				Died-At-Sea	
FARLAN, Eliza		26	F	None	16Mr02Ac
Mich.	(S)	07	M	Child	16Mr02Ac
Rose-Ann	(D)	05	F	Child	16Mr02Ac
Eliza	(D)	02	F	Child	16Mr02Ac
BARNAM, Wm.		30	M	Carpenter	16Mr02Ac
LOGAN, Mich.		20	M	Laborer	16Mr02Ac
COURIE, Patt		20	M	Shoemaker	16Mr02Ac
MCMANUS, Andrew		40	M	Laborer	16Mr02Ac
MCGUIRE, John		30	M	Laborer	16Mr02Ac
Mary	(W)	26	F	Wife	16Mr02Ac
Thos.	(S)	02	M	Child	16Mr02Ac
MCVEA, Ellen		22	F	Servant	16Mr02Ac
CHRONSON, Margreat		60	F	None	16Mr02Ac
Eliza		25	F	None	16Mr02Ac
John		25	M	None	16Mr02Ac
HAGGET, James		23	M	Blacksmith	16Mr02Ac
GRIMES, Alex		19	M	Laborer	16Mr02Ac
ANDERSON, Wm.		22	M	Weaver	16Mr02Ac
DONEGAN, John		20	M	Laborer	16Mr02Ac
FEATHERSON, Wm.		16	M	Laborer	16Mr02Ac

13

NAMES OF PASSENGERS		AGE	SEX	OCCUPATIONS	DATE PORT SHIP
CLARK, John		22	M	Laborer	16Mr02Ac
HIGGINS, Barney		25	M	Laborer	16Mr02Ac
Margreat		20	F	None	16Mr02Ac
Sarah		19	F	None	16Mr02Ac
CROHAN, Peter		28	M	Laborer	16Mr02Ac
Ann		19	F	None	16Mr02Ac
Mary		24	F	None	16Mr02Ac
Margreat		18	F	None	16Mr02Ac
MCDURMONT, Luke		35	M	Laborer	16Mr02Ac
MCFERNAN, Patt		28	M	Tailor	16Mr02Ac
MCKERNAN, Patt		24	M	Laborer	16Mr02Ac
WARD, John		28	M	Weaver	16Mr02Ac
DERLAIN, John		25	M	Weaver	16Mr02Ac
CONRAY, Patt		24	M	Laborer	16Mr02Ac
BROWN, Mich.		20	M	Laborer	16Mr02Ac
CONRAY, Rose		18	F	Servant	16Mr02Ac
MCGRAW, Ellen		21	F	Servant	16Mr02Ac
MURRY, Jas.		20	M	Laborer	16Mr02Ac
CARTBUCK, Jas.		20	M	Laborer	16Mr02Ac
BILLEN, Mich.		17	M	Laborer	16Mr02Ac
BOYD, Mary		28	F	None	16Mr02Ac
Mary-Jane	(D)	10	F	Child	16Mr02Ac
PATTERSON, John		40	M	Weaver	16Mr02Ac

HUDSON 19 MARCH 1846

From Glasgow

NAMES OF PASSENGERS		AGE	SEX	OCCUPATIONS	DATE PORT SHIP
CONALLY, Frances		27	M	Mechanic	19Mr04Bq
Margaret	(W)	28	F	Lady	19Mr04Bq
Charls	(S)	.06	M	Infant	19Mr04Bq
Mary	(D)	06	F	Child	19Mr04Bq
DOUARTY, John		45	M	Laborer	19Mr04Bq

WESTMINSTER 24 MARCH 1846

From London

NAMES OF PASSENGERS		AGE	SEX	OCCUPATIONS	DATE PORT SHIP
PAREDISE, Maria		40	F	None	24Mr21Br
SARGENT, Robert		53	M	Iron Monger	24Mr21Br
Mary		33	F	Iron Monger	24Mr21Br
POWELL, John-W.		10	M	Child	24Mr21Br
Henry		08	M	Child	24Mr21Br
BRYDGES, William		30	M	Artist	24Mr21Br
BRIDGE, Thos.W.		22	M	None	24Mr21Br
BENJAMIN, Leon		22	M	None	24Mr21Br
RISINGHAM, Arthur		23	M	Engineer	24Mr21Br
MATHIE, John		22	M	Farmer	24Mr21Br
DALLAWAY, John		27	M	Saddler	24Mr21Br
CHAPMAN, Thos.		40	M	Farmer	24Mr21Br
AUSTIN, John		27	M	Shoemaker	24Mr21Br
Mary		30	F	None	24Mr21Br
TAYLOR, Dinah		07	F	Child	24Mr21Br
CARTER, John		29	M	Farmer	24Mr21Br
Emma	(W)	25	F	Wife	24Mr21Br
Emma-E.	(D)	05	F	Child	24Mr21Br
LYONS, Abraham		00	M	Cook	24Mr21Br
SYMONS, Henry		30	M	Baker	24Mr21Br
KOEN, Michael		24	M	Clerk	24Mr21Br
EADE, Daniel		23	M	Farmer	24Mr21Br
HART, Alfred		13	M	Farmer	24Mr21Br

SAMUEL-HICKS 24 MARCH 1846

From Liverpool

NAMES OF PASSENGERS		AGE	SEX	OCCUPATIONS	DATE PORT SHIP
MURPHY, Wm.		30	M	Laborer	24Mr02Bs
GETTY, John		45	M	Laborer	24Mr02Bs
CAIN, Michael		27	M	Laborer	24Mr02Bs
MCCABE, John		22	M	Laborer	24Mr02Bs
FUNNY, Thomas		23	M	Laborer	24Mr02Bs
MCDONALD, John		22	M	Laborer	24Mr02Bs
REGAN, Wm.		27	M	Laborer	24Mr02Bs
ARMSTRONG, Edward		28	M	Laborer	24Mr02Bs
COULTER, Alexander		22	M	Laborer	24Mr02Bs
Ellen		25	F	Servant	24Mr02Bs
KELLY, Ally		24	F	Servant	24Mr02Bs
Biddy		20	F	Servant	24Mr02Bs
BURNS, Peter		21	M	Servant	24Mr02Bs
HIGGINS, James		22	M	Farmer	24Mr02Bs
ALONE, Robert		21	M	Farmer	24Mr02Bs
GARTNEY, Philip		25	M	Farmer	24Mr02Bs
Rose		16	F	Farmer	24Mr02Bs
MCGREGOR, Owen		24	M	Blacksmith	24Mr02Bs

KALAMAZOO 24 MARCH 1846

From Liverpool

NAMES OF PASSENGERS		AGE	SEX	OCCUPATIONS	DATE PORT SHIP
MCCABE, Ann		30	F	None	24Mr02Bt
SUTTON, Benn.		30	M	Farmer	24Mr02Bt
GALLAGER, Thos.		31	M	Laborer	24Mr02Bt
BOOTH, Edwin		19	M	Laborer	24Mr02Bt
GANNON, Patk.		22	M	Laborer	24Mr02Bt
KELLY, Thos.		23	M	Laborer	24Mr02Bt
WARR, John		20	M	Laborer	24Mr02Bt
LENNON, Chs.		20	M	Laborer	24Mr02Bt
Mary		20	F	Laborer	24Mr02Bt
NULTY, John		20	M	Laborer	24Mr02Bt
Cath.		21	F	Laborer	24Mr02Bt
DOLANAN, Eliz.		40	F	Laborer	24Mr02Bt
CHRISTAL, Hugh		31	M	Laborer	24Mr02Bt
REDICAN, Patk.		20	M	Laborer	24Mr02Bt
LEVERY, Patrick		30	M	Laborer	24Mr02Bt
DEVLIN, James		31	M	Laborer	24Mr02Bt
Hannah		27	F	Laborer	24Mr02Bt
Bridget		29	F	Laborer	24Mr02Bt
Mary-Ann		06	F	Child	24Mr02Bt
John		04	M	Child	24Mr02Bt
Margaret		.00	F	Infant	24Mr02Bt
KELLY, Matthew		29	M	Laborer	24Mr02Bt
MARTIN, Thos.		21	M	Laborer	24Mr02Bt
BLAKE, John		21	M	Carpenter	24Mr02Bt
TULLY, Mary		19	F	None	24Mr02Bt
CLARK, Mary		19	F	None	24Mr02Bt
DURYER, Patk.		20	M	Laborer	24Mr02Bt
TAYLOR, Edwd.		20	M	Laborer	24Mr02Bt
Benj.		20	M	Laborer	24Mr02Bt
WILSON, Thos.		20	M	Laborer	24Mr02Bt
SULLIVAN, Mary		30	F	Laborer	24Mr02Bt
Honor	(D)	06	F	Child	24Mr02Bt
MONOGHAN, Mary		20	F	Laborer	24Mr02Bt
DEMPEY, Alice		20	F	Laborer	24Mr02Bt
MURRAY, Michl.		13	M	Laborer	24Mr02Bt
MAKIN, James		22	M	Laborer	24Mr02Bt

NAMES OF PASSENGERS	A G E	S E X	OCCUPATIONS	DATE PORT SHIP	NAMES OF PASSENGERS	A G E	S E X	OCCUPATIONS	DATE PORT SHIP
MAKIN, Ellen	19	F	Laborer	24Mr02Bt	FEENEY, Michl.	18	M	Laborer	24Mr02Bt
MAHON, Patk.	22	M	Laborer	24Mr02Bt	Cath.	16	F	Laborer	24Mr02Bt
DORAN, Jno.	20	M	Laborer	24Mr02Bt	OCONELL, John	20	M	Laborer	24Mr02Bt
James	20	M	Laborer	24Mr02Bt	MCDERMOT, Peter	20	M	Laborer	24Mr02Bt
KELLY, Wm.	20	M	Laborer	24Mr02Bt	BARDEN, Mary	20	F	Laborer	24Mr02Bt
GARRATY, Thos.	20	M	Laborer	24Mr02Bt	KILKENNY, James	20	M	Laborer	24Mr02Bt
DONOHUE, Henry	28	M	Laborer	24Mr02Bt	BOHARA, John	20	M	Laborer	24Mr02Bt
NORTON, Michl.	20	M	Laborer	24Mr02Bt	DULLON, James	20	M	Laborer	24Mr02Bt
Martin	20	M	Laborer	24Mr02Bt	U (W)	20	F	Wife	24Mr02Bt
SULLY, Mary	20	F	Laborer	24Mr02Bt	BENLY, Michl.	20	M	Laborer	24Mr02Bt
JOLLY, Wm.	30	M	Laborer	24Mr02Bt	LEWIS, Jos.	20	M	Laborer	24Mr02Bt
JONES, Wm.	30	M	Laborer	24Mr02Bt	Mary	30	F	Laborer	24Mr02Bt
PRIOR, Eugene	17	M	Laborer	24Mr02Bt	MCCABE, Owen	20	M	Laborer	24Mr02Bt
MORGAN, Patk.	22	M	Laborer	24Mr02Bt	EVANS, Margt.	25	F	Laborer	24Mr02Bt
SOMMERVILLE, Rich.	34	M	Farmer	24Mr02Bt	FARRAHY, Biddy	12	F	Laborer	24Mr02Bt
BAGSTER, Patk.	25	M	Laborer	24Mr02Bt	CLARK, John	20	M	Farmer	24Mr02Bt
DILLON, James	23	M	Laborer	24Mr02Bt	KEENAN, John	25	M	Laborer	24Mr02Bt
Laurence	19	M	Laborer	24Mr02Bt	CONNELLY, Patk.	20	M	Laborer	24Mr02Bt
YORK, Thos.	23	M	Laborer	24Mr02Bt	SHERDON, Andrew	20	M	Laborer	24Mr02Bt
Cornl.	25	M	Laborer	24Mr02Bt	REILY, Mary	20	F	Laborer	24Mr02Bt
EARLY, James	25	M	Laborer	24Mr02Bt	KELLY, James	26	M	Laborer	24Mr02Bt
Ann	20	F	Laborer	24Mr02Bt	U (W)	26	F	Wife	24Mr02Bt
CLINES, Margt.	18	F	Laborer	24Mr02Bt	ROSTEFF, Wm.	26	M	Laborer	24Mr02Bt
CASSIDY, James	27	M	Laborer	24Mr02Bt	MILLS, Thos.	20	M	Laborer	24Mr02Bt
GARNER, Ed.	18	M	Laborer	24Mr02Bt	GAY, Robt.	60	M	Laborer	24Mr02Bt
GANNON, Michl.	20	M	Laborer	24Mr02Bt	ALLAN, George	21	M	Laborer	24Mr02Bt
Ann	20	F	Laborer	24Mr02Bt	WATERS, George	21	M	Laborer	24Mr02Bt
FITZSIMMONS, Biddy	20	F	Laborer	24Mr02Bt	KELLETT, Soln.	20	M	Laborer	24Mr02Bt
KING, Mary	50	F	Laborer	24Mr02Bt	DALEY, James	20	M	Laborer	24Mr02Bt
HELPEN, Sarah	20	F	Laborer	24Mr02Bt	DUNN, Edward	13	M	Laborer	24Mr02Bt
FARRELL, Patk.	19	M	Laborer	24Mr02Bt	CARROLL, Bridget	17	F	Laborer	24Mr02Bt
FOLEY, Corn.	22	M	Laborer	24Mr02Bt	BEHIN, Margt.	18	F	Laborer	24Mr02Bt
MCCALL, Patricia	22	F	Laborer	24Mr02Bt	Bridget	26	F	Laborer	24Mr02Bt
FARRELL, Mich.	20	M	Laborer	24Mr02Bt	Mary	30	F	Laborer	24Mr02Bt
MURPHY, John	18	M	Laborer	24Mr02Bt	MAHONY, Wm.	40	M	Laborer	24Mr02Bt
BERREN, Thos.	20	M	Laborer	24Mr02Bt	Ann	30	F	Laborer	24Mr02Bt
Bridget	20	F	Laborer	24Mr02Bt	SUSCOM, John	20	M	Farmer	24Mr02Bt
MCREYNOULDS, James	21	M	Laborer	24Mr02Bt	Francis	20	U	Farmer	24Mr02Bt
SPENCER, Andrew	30	M	Laborer	24Mr02Bt	COULON, Michl.	20	M	Laborer	24Mr02Bt
DUKE, Ann	25	F	Laborer	24Mr02Bt	U (W)	20	F	Wife	24Mr02Bt
CALLAGER, Clarissa	20	F	Laborer	24Mr02Bt	REILLY, Michl.	20	M	Laborer	24Mr02Bt
Ann	18	F	Laborer	24Mr02Bt	BRADY, Jas.	20	M	Laborer	24Mr02Bt
JONES, Richd.	40	M	Laborer	24Mr02Bt	HUGES, Michl.	20	M	Laborer	24Mr02Bt
THURSTON, George	14	M	Farmer	24Mr02Bt	Cath.	20	F	Laborer	24Mr02Bt
Robt.	12	M	Farmer	24Mr02Bt	Margt.	20	F	Laborer	24Mr02Bt
HUBEN, Wm.	21	M	Farmer	24Mr02Bt	TIPPIN, Mary	26	F	Laborer	24Mr02Bt
COCKLEY, Mich.	20	M	Laborer	24Mr02Bt	Ann	24	F	Laborer	24Mr02Bt
GRIFFIN, John	30	M	Laborer	24Mr02Bt	Thos.	19	M	Laborer	24Mr02Bt
Wm.	30	M	Laborer	24Mr02Bt	PINK, Edmund	22	M	Laborer	24Mr02Bt
MCDONALD, Frank	30	M	Laborer	24Mr02Bt	MANN, Richd.	38	M	Farmer	24Mr02Bt
Jno.	20	M	Laborer	24Mr02Bt	U (W)	37	F	Wife	24Mr02Bt
HEALY, James	20	M	Laborer	24Mr02Bt	John (S)	17	M	Farmer	24Mr02Bt
MCGAVRY, Thos.	20	M	Laborer	24Mr02Bt	Wm. (S)	15	M	Farmer	24Mr02Bt
NARRY, Thos.	20	M	Laborer	24Mr02Bt	Sarah (D)	11	F	Farmer	24Mr02Bt
ECLESTON, John	30	M	Farmer	24Mr02Bt	Elizabeth (D)	03	F	Child	24Mr02Bt
U (W)	30	F	Wife	24Mr02Bt	George (S)	.00	M	Infant	24Mr02Bt
James	30	M	Farmer	24Mr02Bt	MCCABE, Francis	19	M	Farmer	24Mr02Bt
YATES, James	30	M	Farmer	24Mr02Bt	JOHNSON, Wm.	21	M	Farmer	24Mr02Bt
U (W)	20	F	Wife	24Mr02Bt	CRON, Michl.	23	M	Laborer	24Mr02Bt
Thos.	20	M	Farmer	24Mr02Bt	ELWOOD, Patk.	21	M	Laborer	24Mr02Bt
Jas.	21	M	Farmer	24Mr02Bt	BEARD, Ellen	35	F	Laborer	24Mr02Bt
CONNORS, Dennis	22	M	Laborer	24Mr02Bt	POWER, John	20	M	Laborer	24Mr02Bt
COLLINS, Francis	25	M	Laborer	24Mr02Bt	SMITH, Wm.	20	M	Laborer	24Mr02Bt
ELLIS, James	20	M	Laborer	24Mr02Bt	FARELLY, John	24	M	Laborer	24Mr02Bt
Ellis	18	M	Laborer	24Mr02Bt	Ellen	20	F	Laborer	24Mr02Bt
FENTON, John	17	M	Laborer	24Mr02Bt	Jas.	08	M	Child	24Mr02Bt
MCKEON, John	20	M	Laborer	24Mr02Bt	MOORE, Robt.	20	M	Laborer	24Mr02Bt
MCCORMICK, Patk.	20	M	Laborer	24Mr02Bt	BEGLEY, Patk.	20	M	Laborer	24Mr02Bt
COCHLIN, Catha.	20	F	Laborer	24Mr02Bt	KELLAR, Julia	30	F	Laborer	24Mr02Bt
RIEHON, Bridget	22	F	Laborer	24Mr02Bt	BARRY, John	20	M	Mechanic	24Mr02Bt
MINN, Margt.	21	F	Laborer	24Mr02Bt	KELLAR, Mary-Ann	.00	F	Infant	24Mr02Bt
MCSARRY, Ally	20	F	Laborer	24Mr02Bt	John	00	M	Unknown	24Mr02Bt
HOWARTH, John	20	M	Laborer	24Mr02Bt	CLARK, Abel	20	M	Mechanic	24Mr02Bt
Ann	18	F	Laborer	24Mr02Bt	BRADLY, Wm.	20	M	Mechanic	24Mr02Bt
FEENEY, Michl.	20	M	Laborer	24Mr02Bt	James	20	M	Mechanic	24Mr02Bt

NAMES OF PASSENGERS		AGE	SEX	OCCUPATIONS	DATE PORT SHIP
OHARA, Susanna		20	F	Mechanic	24Mr02Bt
SHERIDAN, Wm.		25	M	Mechanic	24Mr02Bt
LALLY, Jno.		30	M	Mechanic	24Mr02Bt
MIGGINS, Lewis		20	M	Laborer	24Mr02Bt
U	(W)	20	F	Wife	24Mr02Bt
HENDERSON, Thos.		25	M	Servant	24Mr02Bt
U	(W)	20	F	Wife	24Mr02Bt
Bridget		19	F	None	24Mr02Bt
MILDMAY, Peter		30	M	Laborer	24Mr02Bt
BURK, Bartley		25	M	Laborer	24Mr02Bt
FINALLY, Thos.		19	M	Laborer	24Mr02Bt
MONOLON, Mary		22	F	Laborer	24Mr02Bt
SMITH, Maria		22	F	Laborer	24Mr02Bt
ADLER, John		54	M	Farmer	24Mr02Bt
U	(W)	50	F	Wife	24Mr02Bt
Sarah	(D)	14	F	None	24Mr02Bt
David	(S)	23	M	Farmer	24Mr02Bt
Rebecca	(D)	19	F	Farmer	24Mr02Bt
John	(S)	26	M	Farmer	24Mr02Bt
Ann	(D)	20	F	Farmer	24Mr02Bt
BAY, Dennis		22	M	Farmer	24Mr02Bt
QUINN, Peter		21	M	Farmer	24Mr02Bt
HAGAN, John		30	M	Farmer	24Mr02Bt
Mary		20	F	Farmer	24Mr02Bt
WRIGHT, James		23	M	Farmer	24Mr02Bt
THOMPSON, Wm.		20	M	Soldier	24Mr02Bt
BUGNALL, Cathn.		20	F	None	24Mr02Bt
CRINGLE, Mary		20	F	None	24Mr02Bt
Bridget		12	F	None	24Mr02Bt
John		10	M	Child	24Mr02Bt
SMITH, John		47	M	Laborer	24Mr02Bt
Wm.		26	M	Laborer	24Mr02Bt
JOHNSON, W.		20	U	Laborer	24Mr02Bt
HUGHES, Patrick		36	M	Laborer	24Mr02Bt
U	(W)	32	F	Wife	24Mr02Bt
John	(S)	06	M	Child	24Mr02Bt
James	(S)	04	M	Child	24Mr02Bt
Mary	(D)	.00	F	Infant	24Mr02Bt
BYRNE, Thos.		18	M	Laborer	24Mr02Bt
STEWART, Ann		18	F	Laborer	24Mr02Bt
THOMPSON, John		23	M	Laborer	24Mr02Bt
MCDERMOT, Bernan		20	M	Laborer	24Mr02Bt
BRADY, Margt.		20	F	Laborer	24Mr02Bt
SHAW, Mary		20	F	Laborer	24Mr02Bt
MCCABE, Bridget		18	F	Laborer	24Mr02Bt
HOPKINS, John		38	M	Laborer	24Mr02Bt
Martha	(D)	15	F	None	24Mr02Bt
Nancy	(D)	10	F	None	24Mr02Bt
Elizabeth	(D)	09	F	Child	24Mr02Bt
William	(S)	09	M	Child	24Mr02Bt
Alexr.	(S)	07	M	Child	24Mr02Bt
James	(S)	05	M	Child	24Mr02Bt
Margt.	(D)	.00	F	Infant	24Mr02Bt
MCKERRY, Thos.		20	M	Laborer	24Mr02Bt
FARRELL, Thos.		20	M	Laborer	24Mr02Bt
ENNIS, Jane		20	F	Laborer	24Mr02Bt
GREGORY, Bridget		20	F	Laborer	24Mr02Bt
Ellen		20	F	Laborer	24Mr02Bt
FOX, Cathn.		22	F	Laborer	24Mr02Bt
FARRELL, Thos.		24	M	Laborer	24Mr02Bt
BIENNON, Mary		19	F	Laborer	24Mr02Bt
DARVIN, Peter		20	M	Laborer	24Mr02Bt
MURTOGH, Michl.		24	M	Laborer	24Mr02Bt
DARMODY, Peter		30	M	Laborer	24Mr02Bt
GORMBY, Martin		21	M	Laborer	24Mr02Bt
GILLICK, Patk.		23	M	Laborer	24Mr02Bt
MCGINNIS, Patk.		25	M	Laborer	24Mr02Bt
COLLINS, James		22	M	Laborer	24Mr02Bt
GILLICK, Patk.		20	M	Laborer	24Mr02Bt
REILLY, Ellen		20	F	Laborer	24Mr02Bt
CARR, Rose		23	F	Laborer	24Mr02Bt
RUDDER, Margt.		40	F	Laborer	24Mr02Bt
COOK, Philip		18	M	Mechanic	24Mr02Bt
SMITH, Cathr.		30	F	None	24Mr02Bt
MCDERMOT, Michl.		30	M	Laborer	24Mr02Bt

NAMES OF PASSENGERS		AGE	SEX	OCCUPATIONS	DATE PORT SHIP
AYLWORTH, Wm.		30	M	Laborer	24Mr02Bt
SMITH, Michl.		30	M	Laborer	24Mr02Bt
ROACH, James		20	M	Laborer	24Mr02Bt
KING, Wm.		20	M	Laborer	24Mr02Bt
KINSELLAN, Wm.		20	M	Laborer	24Mr02Bt
U	(W)	20	F	Wife	24Mr02Bt
RUSSELL, Wm.		38	M	Farmer	24Mr02Bt
U	(W)	35	F	Wife	24Mr02Bt
Thos.	(S)	16	M	Farmer	24Mr02Bt
Charles	(S)	11	M	Farmer	24Mr02Bt
Henry	(S)	06	M	Child	24Mr02Bt
Betsy	(D)	.00	F	Infant	24Mr02Bt
Mary-Ann	(D)	.00	F	Infant	24Mr02Bt
CUNNINGHAM, Michl.		20	M	Laborer	24Mr02Bt
CALSILL, John		20	M	None	24Mr02Bt
ENGLAND, George		40	M	Farmer	24Mr02Bt
U	(W)	40	F	Wife	24Mr02Bt
John	(S)	09	M	Child	24Mr02Bt
Mary	(D)	03	F	Child	24Mr02Bt
Jane	(D)	.00	F	Infant	24Mr02Bt
Wm.	(S)	.00	M	Infant	24Mr02Bt

SHENANDOAH 27 MARCH 1846

From Liverpool

NAMES OF PASSENGERS		AGE	SEX	OCCUPATIONS	DATE PORT SHIP
BROWN, Frederick		21	M	Jeweller	27Mr02Bv
DONOHOE, Matthew		19	M	Laborer	27Mr02Bv
GRADY, Michael		25	M	Laborer	27Mr02Bv
Catherine		23	F	Laborer	27Mr02Bv
CURRANS, Thomas		23	M	Clerk	27Mr02Bv
BIGLEY, John		47	M	Cooper	27Mr02Bv
Catherine	(W)	36	F	Wife	27Mr02Bv
John	(S)	18	M	Cooper	27Mr02Bv
James	(S)	16	M	Cooper	27Mr02Bv
Mary	(D)	13	F	None	27Mr02Bv
Michael	(S)	07	M	Child	27Mr02Bv
Catherine	(D)	02	F	Child	27Mr02Bv
James	(S)	01	M	Child	27Mr02Bv
Margaret	(D)	.10	F	Infant	27Mr02Bv
MCGUIRE, John		20	M	Laborer	27Mr02Bv
KIRK, Edward		20	M	Walter	27Mr02Bv
MCGRADE, Michael		18	M	Laborer	27Mr02Bv
NEWMAN, John		20	M	Laborer	27Mr02Bv
CAIRNS, James		18	M	Laborer	27Mr02Bv
William		20	M	Laborer	27Mr02Bv
CASEY, John		22	M	Laborer	27Mr02Bv
MORNERN, John		30	M	Laborer	27Mr02Bv
BYRNES, Thomas		20	M	Laborer	27Mr02Bv
COOLEY, Dennis		25	M	Shoemaker	27Mr02Bv
CHEEVERS, Patrick		24	M	Shoemaker	27Mr02Bv
FORLE, Michael		20	M	Shoemaker	27Mr02Bv
SPONE, Daniel		20	M	Laborer	27Mr02Bv
HART, Thomas		25	M	Laborer	27Mr02Bv
CASSIDY, Patrick		16	M	Laborer	27Mr02Bv
GRADY, Michael		19	M	Laborer	27Mr02Bv
ONEILL, Frederick		17	M	Laborer	27Mr02Bv
John		16	M	Laborer	27Mr02Bv
MCKOY, Patrick		28	M	Blacksmith	27Mr02Bv
LAWRIE, Michael		18	M	Laborer	27Mr02Bv
SIMS, Thos.		20	M	Laborer	27Mr02Bv
CONNOR, Patrick		20	M	Laborer	27Mr02Bv
SWEENEY, Thomas		25	M	Coachman	27Mr02Bv
WHEELAND, B.		25	M	Laborer	27Mr02Bv
MCKOY, Patrick		18	M	Laborer	27Mr02Bv
CASEY, James		26	M	Laborer	27Mr02Bv
MARTIN, Thomas		20	M	Laborer	27Mr02Bv
GRINDON, Owen		24	M	Laborer	27Mr02Bv
MCGRATH, Andrew		22	M	Laborer	27Mr02Bv

NAMES OF PASSENGERS	A G E	S E X	OCCUPATIONS	DATE PORT SHIP	NAMES OF PASSENGERS	A G E	S E X	OCCUPATIONS	DATE PORT SHIP
CREMONT, John	20	M	Laborer	27Mr02Bv	MORRIS, Biddy	17	F	Servant	27Mr02Bv
AGAR, William	20	M	Laborer	27Mr02Bv	MCFEE, Jane	20	F	Servant	27Mr02Bv
BOYLE, Michael	25	M	Laborer	27Mr02Bv	SHERIDAN, Sarah	25	F	Servant	27Mr02Bv
Ann	20	F	Laborer	27Mr02Bv	CASEY, Catherine	20	F	Servant	27Mr02Bv
CASEY, Bartley	25	M	Laborer	27Mr02Bv	CONNOR, Patrick	20	M	Laborer	27Mr02Bv
CONNOR, Patrick	25	M	Laborer	27Mr02Bv	MULHOORN, Ann	24	F	Servant	27Mr02Bv
COSTON, Thomas	23	M	Laborer	27Mr02Bv	MORTON, Ann	17	F	Servant	27Mr02Bv
Mary	23	F	Laborer	27Mr02Bv	KELLY, Edward	12	M	Laborer	27Mr02Bv
DUNN, William	30	M	Laborer	27Mr02Bv	TOOMES, Owen	28	M	Laborer	27Mr02Bv
Margaret	18	F	Servant	27Mr02Bv	COGAN, Peter	22	M	Laborer	27Mr02Bv
CALLOGHAN, Thomas	30	M	Laborer	27Mr02Bv	DONALD, George	19	M	Laborer	27Mr02Bv
CHEEVERS, James	25	M	Laborer	27Mr02Bv	BUCHANON, Michael	30	M	Laborer	27Mr02Bv
Catherine	15	F	Servant	27Mr02Bv	Mary (W)	32	F	Wife	27Mr02Bv
Ann	20	F	Servant	27Mr02Bv	Thomas (S)	05	M	Child	27Mr02Bv
May	18	F	Servant	27Mr02Bv	INGOLDSBY, John	25	M	Laborer	27Mr02Bv
HORAN, Timothy	19	M	Laborer	27Mr02Bv	QUINN, James	25	M	Laborer	27Mr02Bv
DUFFY, George	25	M	Laborer	27Mr02Bv	CUMBERFORD, James	25	M	Laborer	27Mr02Bv
Bridget	25	F	Laborer	27Mr02Bv	LEIGH, Thomas	23	M	Laborer	27Mr02Bv
CRUNEY, Matthew	17	M	Laborer	27Mr02Bv	FARRALL, James	20	M	Laborer	27Mr02Bv
KELLY, Patrick	20	M	Laborer	27Mr02Bv	BALSTON, James	25	M	Laborer	27Mr02Bv
DONOLLY, Patrick	20	M	Shoemaker	27Mr02Bv	FARRALL, John	22	M	Laborer	27Mr02Bv
CONNOR, James	25	M	Laborer	27Mr02Bv	KENNEDY, James	20	M	Laborer	27Mr02Bv
CALLOM, John	24	M	Laborer	27Mr02Bv	HALL, Richard	19	M	Laborer	27Mr02Bv
HONNATY, Owen	21	M	Laborer	27Mr02Bv	Morld	24	F	Servant	27Mr02Bv
COLMAN, Patrick	18	M	Laborer	27Mr02Bv	Betsy	17	F	Servant	27Mr02Bv
JENNINGS, Thomas	25	M	Laborer	27Mr02Bv	Margaret	11	F	Servant	27Mr02Bv
Margaret	25	F	Laborer	27Mr02Bv	MACAULAY, John	23	M	Baker	27Mr02Bv
DREW, Barnard	38	M	Laborer	27Mr02Bv	BRANAGAN, Patrick	19	M	Laborer	27Mr02Bv
Ellen (W)	35	F	Wife	27Mr02Bv	TRACEY, Patrick	15	M	Painter	27Mr02Bv
Michael (S)	13	M	Laborer	27Mr02Bv	CARTER, Jerrard	32	M	Laborer	27Mr02Bv
Mary (D)	10	F	Child	27Mr02Bv	ALDWELL, Francis	30	M	Shoemaker	27Mr02Bv
Thomas (S)	07	M	Child	27Mr02Bv	CLARK, Lawrence	27	M	Laborer	27Mr02Bv
SMITH, Lawrence	58	M	Laborer	27Mr02Bv	Margaret (W)	23	F	Wife	27Mr02Bv
SULLILEY, John	28	M	Laborer	27Mr02Bv	Thomas (S)	.03	M	Infant	27Mr02Bv
DEGAN, Hannah	20	F	Servant	27Mr02Bv	CARTY, Owen	23	M	Gdnr	27Mr02Bv
Ann	20	F	Servant	27Mr02Bv	PARRY, Patrick	23	M	Laborer	27Mr02Bv
LEE, Jane	20	F	Servant	27Mr02Bv	FERRAND, Patrick	21	M	Laborer	27Mr02Bv
MCCARL, Peter	25	M	Laborer	27Mr02Bv	Mary	55	F	None	27Mr02Bv
COONEY, James	26	M	Laborer	27Mr02Bv	Eliza	14	F	None	27Mr02Bv
SMITH, Thomas	17	M	Laborer	27Mr02Bv	CASEY, Catherine	17	F	Servant	27Mr02Bv
CONWAY, Michael	32	M	Laborer	27Mr02Bv	MACAULAY, Mary	30	F	Servant	27Mr02Bv
HART, Michael	20	M	Laborer	27Mr02Bv	FORLEN, Bridget	16	F	Servant	27Mr02Bv
SMITH, Thomas	17	M	Laborer	27Mr02Bv	LAWLEY, Maria	16	F	Servant	27Mr02Bv
COGAN, John	30	M	Stone Mason	27Mr02Bv	BAGLEY, Alice	16	F	Servant	27Mr02Bv
COX, Joseph	20	M	Laborer	27Mr02Bv	LYNCH, Bridgett	17	F	Servant	27Mr02Bv
CONWAY, Catherine	20	F	Servant	27Mr02Bv	JENNER, Jane	23	F	Servant	27Mr02Bv
COSTELEE, Catherine	20	F	Servant	27Mr02Bv	DONNOR, Mary	19	F	Servant	27Mr02Bv
GREEN, Eliza	21	F	Servant	27Mr02Bv	GRAY, Mary	19	F	Servant	27Mr02Bv
GOFF, Margaret	20	F	Servant	27Mr02Bv	RILEY, Ann	16	F	Servant	27Mr02Bv
DONOVAN, Michael	18	M	Laborer	27Mr02Bv	CONNOR, Mary	17	F	Servant	27Mr02Bv
NORRIS, Biddy	23	F	Servant	27Mr02Bv	MCROE, Cathr.	20	F	Servant	27Mr02Bv
KELLY, Catherine	20	F	Servant	27Mr02Bv	FARMER, Biddy	22	F	Servant	27Mr02Bv
WARD, Ellen	38	F	Servant	27Mr02Bv	Ann	16	F	Servant	27Mr02Bv
DALY, Joahnna	20	F	Servant	27Mr02Bv	CORBY, Madge	18	F	Servant	27Mr02Bv
SHIELDS, Biddy	20	F	Servant	27Mr02Bv	COX, Sally	19	F	Servant	27Mr02Bv
COONEY, Catherine	20	F	Servant	27Mr02Bv	GONBY, Margaret	20	F	Servant	27Mr02Bv
COLMAN, Timothy	20	M	Laborer	27Mr02Bv	LLOYD, Jane	20	F	Servant	27Mr02Bv
WORTH, Richard	20	M	Laborer	27Mr02Bv	REYNOLDS, Ruth	21	F	Servant	27Mr02Bv
DOGHERTY, Edward	21	M	Laborer	27Mr02Bv	OLDWELL, Betsy	12	F	Servant	27Mr02Bv
WATTS, John	22	M	Laborer	27Mr02Bv	WORD, Ellen	22	F	Servant	27Mr02Bv
CASEY, Richard	20	M	Laborer	27Mr02Bv	MARTIN, Rose	12	F	Servant	27Mr02Bv
AGAR, Mary	16	F	Servant	27Mr02Bv	Ann	40	F	Servant	27Mr02Bv
GOODEN, John	25	M	Laborer	27Mr02Bv	JARVIS, Francis	17	F	Servant	27Mr02Bv
Judith (W)	30	F	Wife	27Mr02Bv	MARTIN, Catherine	21	F	Servant	27Mr02Bv
Patrick (S)	03	M	Child	27Mr02Bv	FARLAND, Ann	18	F	Servant	27Mr02Bv
DONOLLY, Mary	23	F	Servant	27Mr02Bv	MCQUILLAM, Mary	19	F	Servant	27Mr02Bv
RYAN, Mary	25	F	Servant	27Mr02Bv	MACILROY, Alice	18	F	Servant	27Mr02Bv
HURSLEY, Catherine	18	F	Servant	27Mr02Bv	MURPHY, Susan	16	F	Servant	27Mr02Bv
MCNEIL, Peter	22	M	Stationer	27Mr02Bv	MCCLORTY, Rose	22	F	Servant	27Mr02Bv
Bridget (W)	21	F	Wife	27Mr02Bv	Mary	20	F	Servant	27Mr02Bv
WARD, Catherine	20	F	Servant	27Mr02Bv	FLANAGAN, Kitty	17	F	Servant	27Mr02Bv
WELSH, James	20	M	Laborer	27Mr02Bv	GOODEN, Catherine	17	F	Servant	27Mr02Bv
MCCARN, Ruth	20	F	Servant	27Mr02Bv	Bridgett	20	F	Servant	27Mr02Bv
GREGORY, Mary	20	F	Servant	27Mr02Bv	MONAGHAN, Ann	19	F	Servant	27Mr02Bv
GEE, Mary	20	F	Servant	27Mr02Bv					

ST.PATRICK 27 MARCH 1846

From Liverpool

NAMES OF PASSENGERS		AGE	SEX	OCCUPATIONS	DATE PORT SHIP
CAIRNS, James		42	M	Shoemaker	27Mr02Bw
Catherine	(W)	40	F	Wife	27Mr02Bw
Alexander	(S)	13	M	None	27Mr02Bw
Hannah	(D)	10	F	Child	27Mr02Bw
Margaret	(D)	07	F	Child	27Mr02Bw
Christy	(S)	05	M	Child	27Mr02Bw
James	(S)	03	M	Child	27Mr02Bw
John	(S)	.00	M	Infant	27Mr02Bw
NICKELSON, William		20	M	Weaver	27Mr02Bw
Mary-J.	(W)	19	F	Wife	27Mr02Bw
John	(S)	.00	M	Infant	27Mr02Bw
CAYTON, Pat		30	M	Laborer	27Mr02Bw
HODGSON, Thomas		30	M	Laborer	27Mr02Bw
GERTY, Michael		37	M	Laborer	27Mr02Bw
CONLON, Pat		30	M	Laborer	27Mr02Bw
Bridget		30	F	None	27Mr02Bw
WHITE, Henry		23	M	Laborer	27Mr02Bw
GEELAN, Francis		20	M	Laborer	27Mr02Bw
Pat		22	M	Laborer	27Mr02Bw
TIMMONS, Anne		21	F	None	27Mr02Bw
Margaret		20	F	None	27Mr02Bw
CARTAN, Pat		21	M	Laborer	27Mr02Bw
CALLAN, Bernard		20	M	Laborer	27Mr02Bw
MONAGHAN, Michael		18	M	Laborer	27Mr02Bw
CONNALY, Michael		19	M	Laborer	27Mr02Bw
Mary		18	F	None	27Mr02Bw
GIVEN, Mary		28	F	None	27Mr02Bw
CAROLIN, John		23	M	None	27Mr02Bw
Peter		20	M	None	27Mr02Bw
LYNCH, James		20	M	None	27Mr02Bw
MCCONRAE, Michael		25	M	None	27Mr02Bw
LYNCH, Brian		21	M	None	27Mr02Bw
Lawrence		20	M	None	27Mr02Bw
MCVAY, James		20	M	None	27Mr02Bw
CLARKE, Thomas		25	M	Coachman	27Mr02Bw
RILEY, Thomas		20	M	Laborer	27Mr02Bw
MCKANE, Anne		25	F	None	27Mr02Bw
COOKE, John		25	M	Laborer	27Mr02Bw
MCNAMEE, Ellen		18	F	None	27Mr02Bw
SHERIDAN, Bridget		21	F	None	27Mr02Bw
CARTY, Jane		25	F	None	27Mr02Bw
KELLY, Mary		21	F	None	27Mr02Bw
MCGOWAN, Catherine		28	F	None	27Mr02Bw
NASH, Thomas		06	M	Child	27Mr02Bw
HARAN, James		21	M	Laborer	27Mr02Bw
MADIGAN, James		21	M	Laborer	27Mr02Bw
CARTAN, Pat		18	M	Laborer	27Mr02Bw
Mary		22	F	None	27Mr02Bw
RANAGHAN, Pat		26	M	Laborer	27Mr02Bw
WALL, Matthew		24	M	Laborer	27Mr02Bw
SHANLEY, Thomas		21	M	Laborer	27Mr02Bw
Pat		20	M	Laborer	27Mr02Bw
Ellen		18	F	None	27Mr02Bw
FLAGHERTY, Ann		18	F	None	27Mr02Bw
MULVEHILL, William		21	M	Laborer	27Mr02Bw
RUSSELL, John		24	M	Laborer	27Mr02Bw
GILLEN, John		24	M	Laborer	27Mr02Bw
KELLY, John		32	M	Laborer	27Mr02Bw
MCLEAN, Joseph		20	M	Laborer	27Mr02Bw
NAUGHTEN, Martin		25	M	Shepherd	27Mr02Bw
HARTFORD, Ann		20	F	None	27Mr02Bw
Catherine		20	F	None	27Mr02Bw
RING, Mary		20	F	None	27Mr02Bw
FERRARD, Margaret		20	F	None	27Mr02Bw
MURPHY, Catherine		22	F	None	27Mr02Bw
MURPHY, James		22	M	Laborer	27Mr02Bw
DONNELLY, Peter		25	M	Laborer	27Mr02Bw
MCVEUGH, Mary		19	F	None	27Mr02Bw
MCGUFFIE, James		20	M	Laborer	27Mr02Bw
DOUGLASS, William		20	M	Laborer	27Mr02Bw
MCGUFFIE, William		12	M	None	27Mr02Bw
DOWNEY, William		24	M	Laborer	27Mr02Bw
Nancy		20	F	None	27Mr02Bw
Mary		18	F	None	27Mr02Bw
BOYLE, Pat		18	M	Laborer	27Mr02Bw
REYNOLDS, Henry		20	M	Laborer	27Mr02Bw
MCGUIRE, James		13	M	None	27Mr02Bw
RILEY, Bridget		20	F	None	27Mr02Bw
COX, Margaret		18	F	None	27Mr02Bw
RILEY, Mary		18	F	None	27Mr02Bw
MULLIGAN, Catharine		17	F	None	27Mr02Bw
DONNELLY, Eliza		13	F	None	27Mr02Bw
HOGAN, Mary		20	F	None	27Mr02Bw
Eliza		17	F	None	27Mr02Bw
GUINCHAN, Michael		17	M	Laborer	27Mr02Bw
CLARKE, Margaret		20	F	None	27Mr02Bw
MCMANUS, Edward		25	M	Laborer	27Mr02Bw
MCTHALEY, James		58	M	Laborer	27Mr02Bw
Thomas	(S)	18	M	Laborer	27Mr02Bw
Catherine	(D)	14	F	None	27Mr02Bw
SHANLEY, Thomas		20	M	Laborer	27Mr02Bw
BARDEN, Pat		20	M	Laborer	27Mr02Bw
KINGSLEY, James		27	M	Mason	27Mr02Bw
KERAGHAN, Ellen		18	F	None	27Mr02Bw
CONLEY, Michael		18	M	Laborer	27Mr02Bw
CURLEY, Ellen		12	F	None	27Mr02Bw
BRIGHOUSE, Samuel		39	M	Miner	27Mr02Bw
Elizabeth	(W)	40	F	Wife	27Mr02Bw
Mary	(D)	12	F	None	27Mr02Bw
Esther	(D)	04	F	Child	27Mr02Bw
BRADLEY, Thomas		18	M	Laborer	27Mr02Bw
CAROL, Ellen		20	F	None	27Mr02Bw
RICHIE, Andrew		40	M	Mnre	27Mr02Bw
U	(W)	35	F	Wife	27Mr02Bw
Margaret	(D)	06	F	Child	27Mr02Bw
Charles	(S)	07	M	Child	27Mr02Bw
Anne	(D)	.00	F	Infant	27Mr02Bw
MCMANUS, Peter		20	M	Laborer	27Mr02Bw
MCGEE, William		26	M	Tanner	27Mr02Bw
BRANAN, Edward		28	M	Laborer	27Mr02Bw
TRAINER, James		21	M	Laborer	27Mr02Bw
MURPHY, James		21	M	Laborer	27Mr02Bw
DEVINE, John		21	M	Weaver	27Mr02Bw
EGAN, Bridget		24	F	None	27Mr02Bw
Catherine		22	F	None	27Mr02Bw
SCULLY, William		32	M	Laborer	27Mr02Bw
Mary		24	F	None	27Mr02Bw
DOLAN, Michael		20	M	Laborer	27Mr02Bw
Catherine		17	F	None	27Mr02Bw
MCCAHEY, John		25	M	Laborer	27Mr02Bw
HANLAN, Michael		27	M	Laborer	27Mr02Bw
WALSH, Edward		27	M	Tailor	27Mr02Bw
HACKETT, Peter		26	M	Laborer	27Mr02Bw
HEFFERIN, Pat		29	M	Laborer	27Mr02Bw
QUINN, Anne		32	F	None	27Mr02Bw
RILEY, Mary		18	F	None	27Mr02Bw
SMYTH, Margaret		17	F	None	27Mr02Bw
ROURKE, Peter		34	M	Laborer	27Mr02Bw
DOLAN, John		25	M	Mason	27Mr02Bw
GALLAGHER, Rose		18	F	None	27Mr02Bw
BRADY, Mary		18	F	None	27Mr02Bw
GRIBBON, John		38	M	Laborer	27Mr02Bw
Elizabeth	(W)	29	F	Wife	27Mr02Bw
Pat	(S)	11	M	None	27Mr02Bw
John	(S)	09	M	Child	27Mr02Bw
Rosey	(D)	06	F	Child	27Mr02Bw
Mary	(D)	03	F	Child	27Mr02Bw
SHERIDAN, Farroll		25	M	Laborer	27Mr02Bw
WARD, James		21	M	Laborer	27Mr02Bw
RENNY, James		20	M	Laborer	27Mr02Bw

NAMES OF PASSENGERS		AGE	SEX	OCCUPATIONS	DATE PORT SHIP
ONEILL, James		23	M	Laborer	27Mr02Bw
RENNY, Kitty		23	F	None	27Mr02Bw
KENNEDY, Mary		23	F	None	27Mr02Bw
QUINN, Michael		20	M	Laborer	27Mr02Bw
ROURKE, Pat		20	M	Laborer	27Mr02Bw
Sarah		21	F	None	27Mr02Bw
HUNTER, James		20	M	Weaver	27Mr02Bw
CARROLL, Thomas		21	M	Laborer	27Mr02Bw
Mary	(W)	23	F	Wife	27Mr02Bw
Fanny	(D)	.00	F	Infant	27Mr02Bw
Died-At-Sea					
HART, James		33	M	Laborer	27Mr02Bw
Mary		12	F	None	27Mr02Bw
MANGAN, Thomas		28	M	Laborer	27Mr02Bw
Nancy	(W)	24	F	Wife	27Mr02Bw
Ellen	(D)	02	F	Child	27Mr02Bw
Thomas	(S)	.00	M	Infant	27Mr02Bw
CARROLL, Martin		20	M	None	27Mr02Bw
BOYLE, Ellen		11	F	None	27Mr02Bw
Edward		13	M	None	27Mr02Bw
MCKANE, Frank		35	M	Laborer	27Mr02Bw
KENNEDY, Mary		18	F	None	27Mr02Bw
DOLAN, Bridget		18	F	None	27Mr02Bw
DONNELLY, Mary		03	F	Child	27Mr02Bw
William		.00	M	Infant	27Mr02Bw
MORAN, Bridget		22	F	None	27Mr02Bw
TULLY, Mary		20	F	None	27Mr02Bw
SHANLY, Ellen		19	F	None	27Mr02Bw
HENRY, Anne		20	F	None	27Mr02Bw
WARD, Francis		20	M	Laborer	27Mr02Bw
BAIRNE, Bridget		20	F	None	27Mr02Bw
KILLENY, Lawrence		24	M	Laborer	27Mr02Bw
FLOOD, Thomas		25	M	Laborer	27Mr02Bw
U	(W)	20	F	Wife	27Mr02Bw
DOYLE, John		28	M	Laborer	27Mr02Bw
OBRIEN, Thomas		29	M	Clfn	27Mr02Bw
CROW, Michael		23	M	Blacksmith	27Mr02Bw
ELLWOOD, Pat		21	M	Laborer	27Mr02Bw
MCLARN, Michael		40	M	Laborer	27Mr02Bw
MCCONNELL, Dennis		30	M	Naller	27Mr02Bw
Bridget		24	F	None	27Mr02Bw
Margaret		30	F	None	27Mr02Bw
Mary		10	F	None	27Mr02Bw
Bridget		08	F	Child	27Mr02Bw
Margaret		05	F	Child	27Mr02Bw
Mary		02	F	Child	27Mr02Bw
BILLINGTON, Ernest		26	M	Miner	27Mr02Bw
Charles		36	M	Blacksmith	27Mr02Bw
U	(W)	32	F	Wife	27Mr02Bw
Elizabeth	(D)	13	F	None	27Mr02Bw
Sarah	(D)	11	F	None	27Mr02Bw
Ernest	(S)	.00	M	Infant	27Mr02Bw
BURGES, Joseph		28	M	Miner	27Mr02Bw
U	(W)	26	F	Wife	27Mr02Bw
Fredrick	(S)	05	M	Child	27Mr02Bw
Margaret	(D)	02	F	Child	27Mr02Bw
Died-At-Sea					
Phelix	(S)	.00	M	Infant	27Mr02Bw
ROWNEY, William		20	M	Miner	27Mr02Bw
DONNELLY, Martin		25	M	Shoemaker	27Mr02Bw
BOURKE, Thomas		40	M	Wheelwright	27Mr02Bw
DONNELLY, Thomas		50	M	Laborer	27Mr02Bw
Mary		30	F	None	27Mr02Bw
BOURKE, Biddy		35	F	None	27Mr02Bw
MCLAUGHLIN, John		35	M	Laborer	27Mr02Bw
BARRETT, William		30	M	Laborer	27Mr02Bw
HAGAN, Letita		50	F	None	27Mr02Bw
BOYLAN, Pat		18	M	Bookkeeper	27Mr02Bw
Mary		20	F	None	27Mr02Bw
BEAN, Richard		35	M	Engineer	27Mr02Bw
U	(W)	26	F	Wife	27Mr02Bw
OBRIEN, Bridget		17	F	None	27Mr02Bw
SULLIVAN, John		18	M	Laborer	27Mr02Bw
MURPHY, John		20	M	Laborer	27Mr02Bw
GILMOUR, John		21	M	Laborer	27Mr02Bw
MAHAN, John		21	M	Laborer	27Mr02Bw
MARTIN, James		30	M	Laborer	27Mr02Bw
U	(W)	25	F	Wife	27Mr02Bw
Thomas	(S)	02	M	Child	27Mr02Bw
Peter	(S)	.00	M	Infant	27Mr02Bw
WALSH, Julia		20	F	None	27Mr02Bw
MANGAN, Catherine		10	F	None	27Mr02Bw
NEALE, John		25	M	Laborer	27Mr02Bw
WHITAKER, Joseph		09	M	Child	27Mr02Bw
Anne		07	F	Child	27Mr02Bw
RILLEY, Lawrence		20	M	Laborer	27Mr02Bw
GALLAGHER, John		20	M	Laborer	27Mr02Bw
MCALARNEY, Peter		18	M	Laborer	27Mr02Bw
MCENTIRE, Mary		20	F	None	27Mr02Bw
SMYTH, Catherine		21	F	None	27Mr02Bw
FOY, Mary		18	F	None	27Mr02Bw
GALLAGHER, Pat		21	M	Laborer	27Mr02Bw
BOHEN, Andrew		20	M	Laborer	27Mr02Bw
MOFFITT, Catherine		18	F	None	27Mr02Bw
CARNEN, Anne		18	F	None	27Mr02Bw
DONNELLY, Mary		19	F	None	27Mr02Bw
MCCARTY, Mary		20	F	None	27Mr02Bw
MCGLOUGHLIN, John		21	M	Laborer	27Mr02Bw
FANNAN, Pat		18	M	Laborer	27Mr02Bw
REYNOLDS, Pat		20	M	Laborer	27Mr02Bw
MOFFITT, John		20	M	Laborer	27Mr02Bw
GRANEN, Michael		24	M	Miner	27Mr02Bw
FOY, John		23	M	Laborer	27Mr02Bw
WHEELAN, James		20	M	Laborer	27Mr02Bw
Rosey		18	F	None	27Mr02Bw
KEENAN, James		28	M	Laborer	27Mr02Bw
Ellen		24	F	None	27Mr02Bw
RILEY, Bridget		18	F	None	27Mr02Bw
MCGUINISS, Bridget		18	F	None	27Mr02Bw
Biddy		16	F	None	27Mr02Bw
MCKANA, Betsy		18	F	None	27Mr02Bw
COLLINS, Mary		20	F	None	27Mr02Bw
HOY, Anne		40	F	None	27Mr02Bw
Bridget	(D)	13	F	None	27Mr02Bw
Anne	(D)	11	F	None	27Mr02Bw
BRIEN, Michael		21	M	Laborer	27Mr02Bw
TAMMANY, John		22	M	Laborer	27Mr02Bw
HENDERSON, Anne		20	F	None	27Mr02Bw
MORRISON, John		30	M	Laborer	27Mr02Bw
CUMIN, Ellen		18	F	None	27Mr02Bw
CARROLL, Bridget		18	F	None	27Mr02Bw
MCAVOY, Rose		16	F	None	27Mr02Bw
FOX, Mary		18	F	None	27Mr02Bw
SMYTH, Mary		17	F	None	27Mr02Bw
BYRNE, Anne		18	F	None	27Mr02Bw
PLUNKET, Catherine		17	F	None	27Mr02Bw
DIVINE, Mary		19	F	None	27Mr02Bw
DOUGHERTY, Bridget		18	F	None	27Mr02Bw
CORBLIS, Peggy		17	F	None	27Mr02Bw
MURRAY, Pat		21	M	Laborer	27Mr02Bw
LEVAN, John		20	M	Laborer	27Mr02Bw
MEATH, Christopher		21	M	Laborer	27Mr02Bw
WILSON, James		19	M	Laborer	27Mr02Bw
GANLY, Matthew		26	M	Laborer	27Mr02Bw
HEALY, Honorah		24	F	None	27Mr02Bw
CONBRY, Mary		23	F	None	27Mr02Bw
RATAGAN, Charles		20	M	Laborer	27Mr02Bw
CONLAN, Pat		24	M	Laborer	27Mr02Bw
GAHERTY, Pat		20	M	Laborer	27Mr02Bw
CONBRY, Bridget		20	F	None	27Mr02Bw
TAMMINY, Margaret		24	F	None	27Mr02Bw
MCCARTER, Eliza		24	F	None	27Mr02Bw
MCCUE, Anne		24	F	None	27Mr02Bw
WHEELAN, Catherine		20	F	None	27Mr02Bw
GALL, Bridget		17	F	None	27Mr02Bw
ROE, Pat		25	M	Laborer	27Mr02Bw
KELLY, John		24	M	Laborer	27Mr02Bw
CONNELL, James		26	M	Laborer	27Mr02Bw
MCCONNELL, Mary		22	F	None	27Mr02Bw
KELLY, Catherine		21	F	None	27Mr02Bw

NAMES OF PASSENGERS		AGE	SEX	OCCUPATIONS	DATE PORT SHIP	NAMES OF PASSENGERS		AGE	SEX	OCCUPATIONS	DATE PORT SHIP
REYNOLDS, Mary-A.		20	F	None	27Mr02Bw	BONSALL, Wm.	(S)	03	M	Child	28Mr02Bx
CUSACK, Mary		19	F	None	27Mr02Bw	John	(S)	.00	M	Infant	28Mr02Bx
OBRIEN, Bernard		20	M	Laborer	27Mr02Bw	WILLIAMS, Rich		40	M	Laborer	28Mr02Bx
Honorah		20	F	None	27Mr02Bw	MURPHY, Arthur		31	M	Laborer	28Mr02Bx
HART, Alice		18	F	None	27Mr02Bw	WALSH, Peter		20	M	Laborer	28Mr02Bx
Jane		16	F	None	27Mr02Bw	BRADY, Mary		20	F	Laborer	28Mr02Bx
MCCORMICK, Bernard		20	M	Laborer	27Mr02Bw	Cathe.		20	F	Laborer	28Mr02Bx
COMISKEY, Pat		18	M	Laborer	27Mr02Bw	DEGNAN, Tiddy		40	M	Laborer	28Mr02Bx
DEGNAN, Francis		20	M	Laborer	27Mr02Bw	Margret	(W)	37	F	Laborer	28Mr02Bx
HARVEY, Michael		22	M	Laborer	27Mr02Bw	Mary	(D)	02	F	Child	28Mr02Bx
CONLAN, Bernard		18	M	Laborer	27Mr02Bw	Cathe.	(D)	.00	F	Infant	28Mr02Bx
BRENAN, Pat		70	M	Laborer	27Mr02Bw	CONRAY, Cathe.		23	F	Laborer	28Mr02Bx
Died-At-Sea						MEIGHAN, Anne		25	F	Laborer	28Mr02Bx
Ellen	(W)	60	F	Wife	27Mr02Bw	Hannah		23	F	Laborer	28Mr02Bx
Michael	(S)	20	M	Laborer	27Mr02Bw	BOONEY, Dennis		24	M	Farmer	28Mr02Bx
MULLALY, Peter		19	M	Laborer	27Mr02Bw	DENNIS, Eduard		25	M	Farmer	28Mr02Bx
DUNAGHY, Hugh		26	M	Laborer	27Mr02Bw	CRENNAN, Peter		22	M	Farmer	28Mr02Bx
MASON, Thomas		25	M	Laborer	27Mr02Bw	Thom.		20	M	Farmer	28Mr02Bx
WHITE, Michael		60	M	Laborer	27Mr02Bw	SWEENY, Patt		29	M	Farmer	28Mr02Bx
BRADY, Biddy		19	F	None	27Mr02Bw	Sarah		36	F	Farmer	28Mr02Bx
MASON, Daniel		22	M	Laborer	27Mr02Bw	Thomas		22	M	Farmer	28Mr02Bx
COSTELLO, James		13	M	None	27Mr02Bw	CONNAY, Betsey		13	F	Farmer	28Mr02Bx
Andrew		11	M	None	27Mr02Bw	BARLOW, Thos.		20	M	Farmer	28Mr02Bx
MILLER, James		23	M	Laborer	27Mr02Bw	SIMMONS, Henry		36	M	Farmer	28Mr02Bx
WHEETLY, James		16	M	Shoemaker	27Mr02Bw	MCARDLE, Thos.		31	M	Farmer	28Mr02Bx
MACKEE, John		20	M	Laborer	27Mr02Bw	Anne		21	F	Farmer	28Mr02Bx
Felix		18	M	Laborer	27Mr02Bw	THOMAS, Susan		18	F	Farmer	28Mr02Bx
FOY, James		20	M	Laborer	27Mr02Bw	Thomas		24	M	Farmer	28Mr02Bx
SMYTH, Thomas		24	M	Laborer	27Mr02Bw	James		26	M	Farmer	28Mr02Bx
CAMPBELL, Michael		20	M	Shoemaker	27Mr02Bw	ODONNELL, Michl.		26	M	Farmer	28Mr02Bx
BYRNE, Anne		20	F	None	27Mr02Bw	BOWCOCK, Ifourd		22	U	Farmer	28Mr02Bx
MCREYNOLDS, Samuel		20	M	Weaver	27Mr02Bw	Fanny	(D)	02	F	Child	28Mr02Bx
Antony		18	M	Weaver	27Mr02Bw	READON, John		42	M	Farmer	28Mr02Bx
COYLE, James		21	M	Laborer	27Mr02Bw	DROYLE, Anne		09	F	Child	28Mr02Bx
Bridget		19	F	None	27Mr02Bw	Mary		08	F	Child	28Mr02Bx
REDLEY, Mary		19	F	None	27Mr02Bw	DONEGHAR, Pat		27	M	Farmer	28Mr02Bx
SULLIVAN, Florence		30	M	Laborer	27Mr02Bw	U	(W)	25	F	Wife	28Mr02Bx
DIVINE, Henry		18	M	Weaver	27Mr02Bw	Bridget		20	F	Farmer	28Mr02Bx
MCGROYNE, Anne		18	F	None	27Mr02Bw	HORAN, Awen		20	M	Farmer	28Mr02Bx
REILLY, James		25	M	Laborer	27Mr02Bw	BALAND, Honora		20	F	Farmer	28Mr02Bx
Catherine		22	F	None	27Mr02Bw	SULAREN, Bridget		20	F	Farmer	28Mr02Bx
FLANIGAN, Mary		18	F	None	27Mr02Bw	DRULLY, Michl.		20	M	Farmer	28Mr02Bx
REILLY, Catherine		.00	F	Infant	27Mr02Bw	U	(W)	20	F	Wife	28Mr02Bx
MCQUILLAN, John		20	M	Laborer	27Mr02Bw	CREAGHAN, Michl.		21	M	Laborer	28Mr02Bx
LAWRENCE, Mary		18	F	None	27Mr02Bw	FLANAGAN, Daniel		20	M	Laborer	28Mr02Bx
OCONNOR, Thomas		29	M	Laborer	27Mr02Bw	CHOOT, Bridget		20	F	Laborer	28Mr02Bx
John		20	M	Shoemaker	27Mr02Bw	RILLUN, Mary		18	F	Laborer	28Mr02Bx
FITZGERALD, Margaret		22	F	None	27Mr02Bw	LALLEY, Thos.		24	M	Laborer	28Mr02Bx
HIGGINS, Kate		12	F	None	27Mr02Bw	STEELE, Daniel		20	M	Farmer	28Mr02Bx
FITZGERALD, Thomas		.00	M	Infant	27Mr02Bw	BREMON, Thos.		20	M	Farmer	28Mr02Bx
HANLON, Edward		26	M	Laborer	27Mr02Bw	KELLEN, Henry		19	M	Farmer	28Mr02Bx
Margaret		22	F	None	27Mr02Bw	KELLY, Mary		18	F	Farmer	28Mr02Bx
GIBNEY, Biddy		26	F	None	27Mr02Bw	KENWITH, Peggy		18	F	Farmer	28Mr02Bx
Mary		13	F	None	27Mr02Bw	BRADY, Michl.		20	M	Farmer	28Mr02Bx
James		05	M	Child	27Mr02Bw	LEE, Bridget		25	F	Farmer	28Mr02Bx
Margery		02	F	Child	27Mr02Bw	KELLY, Corneilous		20	M	Farmer	28Mr02Bx
HANLY, Catherine		.00	F	Infant	27Mr02Bw	RELLY, Patrick		20	M	Farmer	28Mr02Bx
CAHILL, Mary		20	F	None	27Mr02Bw	DALTON, Ellen		21	F	Farmer	28Mr02Bx
MCGRATH, Pat		35	M	Laborer	27Mr02Bw	FARRELL, Eliza		20	F	Farmer	28Mr02Bx
ONEILL, Frances		20	F	None	27Mr02Bw	CLARK, Margret		19	F	Farmer	28Mr02Bx
SMITH, Terence		21	M	Laborer	27Mr02Bw	PAPPARD, Jno.		48	M	Farmer	28Mr02Bx
KELLY, John		20	M	Laborer	27Mr02Bw	Bridget		28	F	Farmer	28Mr02Bx
						Margret		12	F	Farmer	28Mr02Bx
						Mary		11	F	Farmer	28Mr02Bx
						Patt		09	M	Child	28Mr02Bx
						James		.00	M	Infant	28Mr02Bx
						DOONAN, John		20	M	Farmer	28Mr02Bx
SIDDONS 28 MARCH 1846						STANTON, John		24	M	Laborer	28Mr02Bx
						BREAN, Timothy		18	M	Laborer	28Mr02Bx
From Liverpool						HORAN, Ellen		20	F	Laborer	28Mr02Bx
						CUMELL, Judy		19	F	Laborer	28Mr02Bx
						HESLIND, Thos.		22	M	Laborer	28Mr02Bx
						RILEY, James		22	M	Farmer	28Mr02Bx
BONSALL, Wm.		20	M	Farmer	28Mr02Bx	KYLE, Patrick		23	M	Farmer	28Mr02Bx
U	(W)	20	F	Wife	28Mr02Bx	MADDIN, Michael		26	M	Farmer	28Mr02Bx

NAMES OF PASSENGERS		AGE	SEX	OCCUPATIONS	DATE PORT SHIP
MADDIN, Alice	(W)	21	F	Wife	28Mr02Bx
Thomas	(S)	.00	M	Infant	28Mr02Bx
CARROLL, Maria		03	F	Child	28Mr02Bx
HACKIN, Jno.		18	M	Farmer	28Mr02Bx
Bridget		20	F	Farmer	28Mr02Bx
GILLHOOLEY, Jno.		20	M	Farmer	28Mr02Bx
REGAN, Martha		18	F	Farmer	28Mr02Bx
FOX, Rose		19	F	Farmer	28Mr02Bx
RAGAN, Bridget		20	F	Farmer	28Mr02Bx
MURING, Anne		19	F	Farmer	28Mr02Bx
GALLAGHER, Mary		20	F	Farmer	28Mr02Bx
CARROLL, Mary		20	F	Farmer	28Mr02Bx
PRUNTY, Patt		27	M	Laborer	28Mr02Bx
RILLY, Bryan		24	M	Laborer	28Mr02Bx
HUGHES, Patt		24	M	Laborer	28Mr02Bx
QUINN, Lance.		20	M	Laborer	28Mr02Bx
LENNAN, Jno.		20	M	Laborer	28Mr02Bx
CAVANAGH, Jno.		20	M	Laborer	28Mr02Bx
KENNY, Michl.		29	M	Laborer	28Mr02Bx
HAGAN, Michl.		18	M	Laborer	28Mr02Bx
STEWART, Pat		20	M	Laborer	28Mr02Bx
HUGHES, Jno.		25	M	Farmer	28Mr02Bx
REYNOLDS, Edwd.		24	M	Farmer	28Mr02Bx
KENNEY, Bridget		20	F	Farmer	28Mr02Bx
GORMAN, Paddy		20	M	Farmer	28Mr02Bx
MULLOY, Mary		20	F	Farmer	28Mr02Bx
GOONEY, Bridget		20	F	Farmer	28Mr02Bx
MURPHY, Bessy		18	F	Farmer	28Mr02Bx
Marget		17	F	Farmer	28Mr02Bx
KENNY, Cath.		13	F	Farmer	28Mr02Bx
MAHON, Mary		16	F	Farmer	28Mr02Bx
Sally		13	F	Farmer	28Mr02Bx
KENNY, Michl.		20	M	Farmer	28Mr02Bx
DOLAN, Mary		30	F	Farmer	28Mr02Bx
John	(S)	07	M	Child	28Mr02Bx
Thomas	(S)	.00	M	Infant	28Mr02Bx
GAMMON, James		20	M	Farmer	28Mr02Bx
Cath.		20	F	Farmer	28Mr02Bx
CLARK, John		20	M	Farmer	28Mr02Bx
CONWAY, Hugh		18	M	Farmer	28Mr02Bx
DEGNAN, Patt		20	M	Farmer	28Mr02Bx
Cath.		03	F	Child	28Mr02Bx
CONWAY, Cath.		10	F	Child	28Mr02Bx
RILLY, Jno.		20	M	Farmer	28Mr02Bx
HANOWAY, Marget		20	F	Farmer	28Mr02Bx
Marget	(D)	.00	F	Infant	28Mr02Bx
FALAN, Patt		25	M	Laborer	28Mr02Bx
TIERNAN, Lance.		18	M	Laborer	28Mr02Bx
Thos.		18	M	Laborer	28Mr02Bx
CRAY, Andrew		30	M	Laborer	28Mr02Bx
Thomas		35	M	Laborer	28Mr02Bx
DOMELY, Thos.		25	M	Laborer	28Mr02Bx
FLYNCH, Patt		13	M	Laborer	28Mr02Bx
MALLOW, James		24	M	Laborer	28Mr02Bx
CAFFERY, Mahew		23	M	Laborer	28Mr02Bx
Thomas		21	M	Laborer	28Mr02Bx
MURPHEY, John		20	M	Laborer	28Mr02Bx
RILLY, Mary		18	F	Laborer	28Mr02Bx
SMYTH, Biddy		17	F	Laborer	28Mr02Bx
Kitty		16	F	Laborer	28Mr02Bx
WARD, Wm.		22	M	Farmer	28Mr02Bx
BERNUCHAM, Jno.		22	M	Farmer	28Mr02Bx
KEAN, John		21	M	Farmer	28Mr02Bx
Michl.		20	M	Farmer	28Mr02Bx
HUGH, Michl.M.		21	M	Farmer	28Mr02Bx
KEAN, John		22	M	Farmer	28Mr02Bx
Honoreth		20	F	Farmer	28Mr02Bx
RUSH, Ellen		20	F	Farmer	28Mr02Bx
NOON, Honorah		26	F	Farmer	28Mr02Bx
QUIENS, Mary		24	F	Farmer	28Mr02Bx
SPUR, Francis		20	M	Farmer	28Mr02Bx
CARTY, Morris		24	M	Farmer	28Mr02Bx
LYNCH, Bryen		34	M	Farmer	28Mr02Bx
QUILLEN, James		20	M	Farmer	28Mr02Bx
COOKE, James		20	M	Farmer	28Mr02Bx
RILLY, Harriet		24	F	Farmer	28Mr02Bx
Cath.		24	F	Farmer	28Mr02Bx
MCTRIMAN, Miles		40	M	Farmer	28Mr02Bx
DONOHAL, Michl.		24	M	Farmer	28Mr02Bx
Mary		24	F	Farmer	28Mr02Bx
HAGAN, James		20	M	Farmer	28Mr02Bx
DOHERTY, James		20	M	Farmer	28Mr02Bx
Margt.		20	F	Farmer	28Mr02Bx
LYNCH, William		20	M	Farmer	28Mr02Bx
DUFFY, James		20	M	Farmer	28Mr02Bx
KELLY, Hugh		36	M	Farmer	28Mr02Bx
JONES, Thos.		24	M	Farmer	28Mr02Bx
KEIGHEY, Michl.		20	M	Farmer	28Mr02Bx
CALY, James		21	M	Farmer	28Mr02Bx
Bridget		12	F	Farmer	28Mr02Bx
MCGUIRE, John		27	M	Farmer	28Mr02Bx
Mary		20	F	Farmer	28Mr02Bx
SMITH, Edward		25	M	Farmer	28Mr02Bx
Wm.		10	M	Child	28Mr02Bx
Kity		09	F	Child	28Mr02Bx
WOODS, Bridget		35	F	Farmer	28Mr02Bx
Rose		12	F	Farmer	28Mr02Bx
Eliza		09	F	Child	28Mr02Bx
SMYTH, Patt		21	M	Farmer	28Mr02Bx
Mary		22	F	Farmer	28Mr02Bx
KELLY, Margret		19	F	Farmer	28Mr02Bx
DEVINE, Mary		21	F	Farmer	28Mr02Bx
MULLOWLEY, Maria		21	F	Farmer	28Mr02Bx
DOOLAY, Bessy		21	F	Farmer	28Mr02Bx
SMITH, Cath.		24	F	Farmer	28Mr02Bx
TORDICK, Christy		20	M	Farmer	28Mr02Bx
FALIN, Tomas		20	M	Laborer	28Mr02Bx
MORRIS, Barnard		25	M	Laborer	28Mr02Bx
WARD, Mary		20	F	Laborer	28Mr02Bx
CLEAIGE, Anne		20	F	Laborer	28Mr02Bx
FAHER, Mary		20	F	Laborer	28Mr02Bx
LANGAN, Jno.		30	M	Laborer	28Mr02Bx
MORGAN, David		21	M	Laborer	28Mr02Bx
CAIN, Danl.		26	M	Laborer	28Mr02Bx
CILBERSEY, James		26	M	Laborer	28Mr02Bx
MILLS, James		26	M	Laborer	28Mr02Bx
ENNIS, Edward		30	M	Laborer	28Mr02Bx
CRAWFORD, James		50	M	Laborer	28Mr02Bx
ENNIS, Mary		30	F	Laborer	28Mr02Bx
Cath.		13	F	Laborer	28Mr02Bx
CRAWFORD, Mary		30	F	Laborer	28Mr02Bx
MILLS, James		20	M	Farmer	28Mr02Bx
HUETS, Dolly		22	F	Farmer	28Mr02Bx
ENNIS, Mary		10	F	Child	28Mr02Bx
Marsella		08	F	Child	28Mr02Bx
James		06	M	Child	28Mr02Bx
James		06	M	Child	28Mr02Bx
JOHNSTON, Biddy		20	F	Farmer	28Mr02Bx
HOOSE, Cath.		20	F	Farmer	28Mr02Bx
KERRY, James		30	M	Farmer	28Mr02Bx
MCGUIRE, Pat		20	M	Farmer	28Mr02Bx
MULLORY, Pat		17	M	Farmer	28Mr02Bx
Michl.		15	M	Farmer	28Mr02Bx
Mary		12	F	Farmer	28Mr02Bx
MCCUIE, Anne		18	F	Farmer	28Mr02Bx
MCLAUGHLIN, Cath.		20	F	Farmer	28Mr02Bx
BIGGIN, Elizth.		20	F	Farmer	28Mr02Bx
Margery		18	F	Farmer	28Mr02Bx
SHUR, Patt		18	M	Farmer	28Mr02Bx
MCCARMA, James		20	M	Farmer	28Mr02Bx
HUGHES, Bernard		20	M	Farmer	28Mr02Bx
Nancy		18	F	Farmer	28Mr02Bx
Hannah		45	F	Farmer	28Mr02Bx
Michl.		21	M	Farmer	28Mr02Bx
HANATTY, Sarah		18	F	Farmer	28Mr02Bx
AITEILL, John		25	M	Farmer	28Mr02Bx
Ellen	(W)	20	F	Wife	28Mr02Bx
Rose	(D)	.00	F	Infant	28Mr02Bx
MURPHY, Wm.		28	M	Farmer	28Mr02Bx
DEMPSEY, James		28	M	Farmer	28Mr02Bx

NAMES OF PASSENGERS	AGE	SEX	OCCUPATIONS	DATE PORT SHIP
LACEY, John	28	M	Farmer	28Mr02Bx
CROSLEY, Mary	18	F	Farmer	28Mr02Bx
MCPHILIP, Margt.	20	F	Farmer	28Mr02Bx
CLARKE, Anne	20	F	Farmer	28Mr02Bx
RACKEY, Cath.	18	F	Farmer	28Mr02Bx
FITZSIMONS, Bridget	18	F	Farmer	28Mr02Bx
CULLEN, Thos.	19	M	Farmer	28Mr02Bx
CLARKE, Hugh	20	M	Farmer	28Mr02Bx
FALLOW, John	26	M	Farmer	28Mr02Bx
BONES, Margt.	18	F	Farmer	28Mr02Bx
DALTON, Mary	20	F	Farmer	28Mr02Bx
POWDERLAY, Bridget	21	F	Farmer	28Mr02Bx
MCAVOY, Judy	19	F	Farmer	28Mr02Bx
LINCHIN, Thos.	19	M	Farmer	28Mr02Bx
CAMPBELL, Jno.	21	M	Farmer	28Mr02Bx
NAUGHTEN, Thos.	23	M	Farmer	28Mr02Bx
BOYLE, James	26	M	Farmer	28Mr02Bx
SMALL, Patt	31	M	Farmer	28Mr02Bx
MELET, Michl.	27	M	Farmer	28Mr02Bx
MARAN, Cathe.	20	F	Farmer	28Mr02Bx
LOGULD, Patt	36	M	Farmer	28Mr02Bx
BEGLEY, John	26	M	Farmer	28Mr02Bx
MOORE, John	26	M	Farmer	28Mr02Bx
MCQUIGN, Rose	20	F	Farmer	28Mr02Bx
SAYMON, Wm.	20	M	Farmer	28Mr02Bx
FLEING, Laurence	23	M	Farmer	28Mr02Bx
DAVIS, Paul	22	M	Farmer	28Mr02Bx
COHILL, Patt	40	M	Farmer	28Mr02Bx
CASEY, James	28	M	Farmer	28Mr02Bx
Mary (W)	28	F	Wife	28Mr02Bx
Cath. (D)	09	F	Child	28Mr02Bx
Patt (S)	05	M	Child	28Mr02Bx
Anne (D)	03	F	Child	28Mr02Bx
James (S)	.00	M	Infant	28Mr02Bx
HORSE, Edwd.	25	M	Farmer	28Mr02Bx
COOPER, Jno.	25	M	Farmer	28Mr02Bx
MCGUIRE, Jno.	30	M	Farmer	28Mr02Bx
Patt	28	M	Farmer	28Mr02Bx
CONLEY, Biddey	20	F	Farmer	28Mr02Bx
COURTNEY, Cath.	20	F	Farmer	28Mr02Bx
GORMAN, Biddy	20	F	Farmer	28Mr02Bx
EWING, Wm.	30	M	Farmer	28Mr02Bx
MCINTRIE, Jno.	22	M	Farmer	28Mr02Bx
Bridget	20	F	Farmer	28Mr02Bx
CULLINAN, Peter	20	M	Farmer	28Mr02Bx
CATRAGE, Sarah	19	F	Farmer	28Mr02Bx
CARROLL, Mathew	78	M	Farmer	28Mr02Bx
MOORE, Martin	27	M	Farmer	28Mr02Bx
U (W)	28	F	Wife	28Mr02Bx
Saul (S)	04	M	Child	28Mr02Bx
RIGNEY, Michl.	20	M	Farmer	28Mr02Bx
Morgan	18	M	Farmer	28Mr02Bx
MORIAGHAN, James	10	M	Farmer	28Mr02Bx
DEVENNY, John	20	M	Farmer	28Mr02Bx
RIGNEY, Maria	18	F	Farmer	28Mr02Bx
KENNERY, Mary	18	F	Farmer	28Mr02Bx
MCNEELTY, Edward	19	M	Farmer	28Mr02Bx
ONEILL, Alice	21	F	Farmer	28Mr02Bx
MCCREMRA, Rose	20	F	Farmer	28Mr02Bx
HICKEY, Anne	20	F	Farmer	28Mr02Bx
BYRNE, Nancy	23	F	Farmer	28Mr02Bx
MITCHELL, Peter	25	M	Farmer	28Mr02Bx
U (W)	24	F	Wife	28Mr02Bx
DOOLEY, John	20	M	Farmer	28Mr02Bx
MACKILKEMY, Dennis	32	M	Farmer	28Mr02Bx
GAGHAN, John	22	M	Farmer	28Mr02Bx
FLANAGUN, Hn.	25	M	Farmer	28Mr02Bx
Ellen	22	F	Farmer	28Mr02Bx
SWEENY, Mary	20	F	Farmer	28Mr02Bx
Owen	21	M	Farmer	28Mr02Bx
QUINN, Mary	22	F	Farmer	28Mr02Bx
BEAMAN, Jas.	35	M	Farmer	28Mr02Bx
CAMBALAY, John	40	M	Farmer	28Mr02Bx
Ellen	40	F	Farmer	28Mr02Bx
RICE, Mary	20	F	Farmer	28Mr02Bx

NAMES OF PASSENGERS	AGE	SEX	OCCUPATIONS	DATE PORT SHIP
PORTER, Isaiah	20	M	Farmer	28Mr02Bx
Eliza	40	F	Farmer	28Mr02Bx
BURKE, Pat	30	M	Farmer	28Mr02Bx
HADDY, John	26	M	Farmer	28Mr02Bx
MADDEN, Thos.	20	M	Farmer	28Mr02Bx
HEESON, Martin	18	M	Farmer	28Mr02Bx
BRYAN, James	20	M	Farmer	28Mr02Bx
QUGLEY, Mary	20	F	Farmer	28Mr02Bx
CONLEY, Bryan	21	M	Farmer	28Mr02Bx
MACK, Thos.	21	M	Farmer	28Mr02Bx
DOYLE, Thos.	25	M	Farmer	28Mr02Bx
DOOLEY, William	20	M	Farmer	28Mr02Bx
SULVAN, John	20	M	Farmer	28Mr02Bx
GRADY, Pat	25	M	Farmer	28Mr02Bx
GREGORY, Biddy	31	F	Farmer	28Mr02Bx
MCGOWAN, Jno.	30	M	Farmer	28Mr02Bx
DENLAN, Patt	25	M	Farmer	28Mr02Bx
QUINN, Jno.	25	M	Farmer	28Mr02Bx
BUTHER, Jno.	22	M	Farmer	28Mr02Bx
KELLY, Biddy	22	F	Farmer	28Mr02Bx
CLARKE, Malach	21	M	Farmer	28Mr02Bx
BLAKE, Donald	23	M	Farmer	28Mr02Bx
KERNAGHAN, James	19	M	Farmer	28Mr02Bx
LAVEY, Wm.	25	M	Farmer	28Mr02Bx
DUFFEY, Maria	20	F	Farmer	28Mr02Bx
FARREL, Anne	18	F	Farmer	28Mr02Bx
Mary	16	F	Farmer	28Mr02Bx
CARRD, Jno.	18	M	Farmer	28Mr02Bx
KILLEN, Mary	18	F	Farmer	28Mr02Bx
KENNY, Jno.	30	M	Farmer	28Mr02Bx
HOPKINS, James	21	M	Farmer	28Mr02Bx
JEITE, Cath.	20	F	Farmer	28Mr02Bx
HOPKINS, Mary	24	F	Farmer	28Mr02Bx
MANGAN, Kitty	17	F	Farmer	28Mr02Bx
BROIAN, Barney	25	M	Farmer	28Mr02Bx
BADY, Jno.	20	M	Farmer	28Mr02Bx
MCDONELL, Mathew	25	M	Farmer	28Mr02Bx
MEHAN, Ellen	24	F	Farmer	28Mr02Bx
Mary	18	F	Farmer	28Mr02Bx
JOLE, Philip	30	M	Farmer	28Mr02Bx
CORWRAN, Thomas	20	M	Farmer	28Mr02Bx
MUNROE, Henry	26	M	Farmer	28Mr02Bx
RODDY, Bridget	20	F	Farmer	28Mr02Bx
CONLEY, Pat	24	M	Farmer	28Mr02Bx
JAMES, U-Mrs.	40	F	Farmer	28Mr02Bx
Wm. (S)	13	M	Farmer	28Mr02Bx

ADELAIDE 30 MARCH 1846

From Havana

NAMES OF PASSENGERS	AGE	SEX	OCCUPATIONS	DATE PORT SHIP
LEES, Wm.	38	M	Merchant	30Mr06By

YORKSHIRE 02 APRIL 1846

From Liverpool

NAMES OF PASSENGERS	AGE	SEX	OCCUPATIONS	DATE PORT SHIP
WARD, Ann	23	F	Spinster	02Ap02Bz
Bridget	18	F	Spinster	02Ap02Bz
MULLIGAN, Ellen	28	F	Spinster	02Ap02Bz
KELLY, Bridget	16	F	Spinster	02Ap02Bz
MONE, Marseilla	17	F	Spinster	02Ap02Bz
MCNAMEE, Patk.	18	M	Farmer	02Ap02Bz

NAMES OF PASSENGERS	AGE	SEX	OCCUPATIONS	DATE PORT SHIP
MCNAMEE, James	19	M	Farmer	02Ap02Bz
LEAVY, Thos.	27	M	Tanner	02Ap02Bz
CALLAGHAN, Ewd.	45	M	Laborer	02Ap02Bz
Bernard	22	M	Laborer	02Ap02Bz
Ann	22	F	Spinster	02Ap02Bz
ENGLISH, Thos.	16	M	Farmer	02Ap02Bz
HARTY, Mary	20	F	Spinster	02Ap02Bz
DONAGHY, Owen	16	M	Farmer	02Ap02Bz
MORRIS, Pat	20	M	Farmer	02Ap02Bz
KELLY, Patk.	18	M	Farmer	02Ap02Bz
REEL, James	18	M	Farmer	02Ap02Bz
LARKIN, Bridget	18	F	Spinster	02Ap02Bz
Alley	17	F	Spinster	02Ap02Bz
Alley	20	F	Spinster	02Ap02Bz
LAWLESS, Ann	22	F	Spinster	02Ap02Bz
MCNAMEE, Alice	16	F	Spinster	02Ap02Bz
LOYE, Mary	15	F	Spinster	02Ap02Bz
MCABE, Michael	17	M	Farmer	02Ap02Bz
DONOGHY, James	16	M	Farmer	02Ap02Bz
FLINN, Bridget	17	F	Spinster	02Ap02Bz
KARRAN, Mary	18	F	Spinster	02Ap02Bz
Catherine	17	F	Spinster	02Ap02Bz
DONNELLY, Bridget	15	F	Spinster	02Ap02Bz
Ann	13	F	Spinster	02Ap02Bz
HARVEY, Chas.	20	M	Farmer	02Ap02Bz
MURTAGH, John	20	M	Farmer	02Ap02Bz
MCKEEVER, Pat	19	M	Farmer	02Ap02Bz
FEGAN, John	16	M	Farmer	02Ap02Bz
BURNS, Michael	18	M	Laborer	02Ap02Bz
BEGLEY, Pat	17	M	Laborer	02Ap02Bz
Mary	17	F	Spinster	02Ap02Bz
ARMSTRONG, Ann	18	F	Spinster	02Ap02Bz
DUNCAN, Jane	20	F	Spinster	02Ap02Bz
MCKEEVER, Mary	18	F	Spinster	02Ap02Bz
MONE, Bridget	17	F	Spinster	02Ap02Bz
GILCOT, Ann	20	F	Spinster	02Ap02Bz
GILL, Bridget	20	F	Spinster	02Ap02Bz
DOWD, Bridget	16	F	Spinster	02Ap02Bz
MURRY, Bridget	16	F	Spinster	02Ap02Bz
MARTIN, Mary-Ann	18	F	Spinster	02Ap02Bz
RIELEY, Ann	16	F	Spinster	02Ap02Bz
MARTIN, Jane	14	F	Spinster	02Ap02Bz
Cathine	12	F	Spinster	02Ap02Bz
Patk.	10	M	Laborer	02Ap02Bz
DALY, Bridget	18	F	Spinster	02Ap02Bz
SMITH, Michael	18	M	Laborer	02Ap02Bz
DELANEY, Ewd.	20	M	Laborer	02Ap02Bz
Chas.	19	M	Laborer	02Ap02Bz
CORRAN, Mary	20	F	Spinster	02Ap02Bz
SMITH, Ann	20	F	Spinster	02Ap02Bz
COYLE, Catherine	19	F	Spinster	02Ap02Bz
MCCALL, Ann	23	F	Spinster	02Ap02Bz
MCCONE, Matthew	17	M	Laborer	02Ap02Bz
BROWN, Pat	17	M	Laborer	02Ap02Bz
FARLEY, John	17	M	Laborer	02Ap02Bz
FLOOD, Margaret	30	F	Spinster	02Ap02Bz
MCCONE, Eliza	18	F	Spinster	02Ap02Bz
FORBY, Catherine	17	F	Spinster	02Ap02Bz
MCKENNA, Mary	26	F	Spinster	02Ap02Bz
RIELEY, Ann	20	F	Spinster	02Ap02Bz
DONOHUE, Philip	20	M	Laborer	02Ap02Bz
COYLE, Dennis	20	M	Shoemaker	02Ap02Bz
LYNCH, John	22	M	Laborer	02Ap02Bz
CASHELS, Catherine	19	F	Spinster	02Ap02Bz
Margaret	22	F	Spinster	02Ap02Bz
KUSIC, Betsy	18	F	Spinster	02Ap02Bz
Catherine	13	F	Spinster	02Ap02Bz
SMITH, Thos.	25	M	Laborer	02Ap02Bz
MCGAVENY, Thos.	20	M	Hatter	02Ap02Bz
GAFFENEY, Philip	25	M	Laborer	02Ap02Bz
SMITH, Patk.	17	M	Laborer	02Ap02Bz
MCCONNOR, Catherine	18	F	Spinster	02Ap02Bz
DONOHOE, Rosy	20	F	Spinster	02Ap02Bz
Mary	20	F	Spinster	02Ap02Bz
SMITH, Ann	21	F	Spinster	02Ap02Bz
SMITH, Susan	18	F	Spinster	02Ap02Bz
Mary	12	F	Spinster	02Ap02Bz
BRADY, Mary	18	F	Spinster	02Ap02Bz
ARESDLE, Cathrine	19	F	Spinster	02Ap02Bz
MCGAVENA, Mary	20	F	Spinster	02Ap02Bz
CULLIVAN, Mary	21	F	Spinster	02Ap02Bz
DONAHOE, Cathrine	15	F	Spinster	02Ap02Bz
BRADY, Ann	23	F	Spinster	02Ap02Bz
MARTIN, Mary	20	F	Spinster	02Ap02Bz
BRADY, Margaret	10	F	Spinster	02Ap02Bz
SMITH, Cathrine	24	F	Spinster	02Ap02Bz
OCONNELL, Bridget	34	F	Spinster	02Ap02Bz
CONLAN, Bridget	18	F	Spinster	02Ap02Bz
CLINTON, Cathrine	20	F	Spinster	02Ap02Bz
OCONNELL, James	.00	M	Infant	02Ap02Bz
Morris	30	M	Laborer	02Ap02Bz
FINEGAN, James	22	M	Laborer	02Ap02Bz
Pat	20	M	Laborer	02Ap02Bz
GALE, Michael	30	M	Laborer	02Ap02Bz
GALLAGHER, Elizabeth	52	F	Spinster	02Ap02Bz
Cathrine	20	F	Spinster	02Ap02Bz
Ann	16	F	Spinster	02Ap02Bz
DOLTON, Ellen	18	F	Spinster	02Ap02Bz
GALLAGHER, John	24	M	Laborer	02Ap02Bz
Michael	17	M	Laborer	02Ap02Bz
Lawrence	13	M	Laborer	02Ap02Bz
COSTERLA, John	23	M	Laborer	02Ap02Bz
FLOYD, John	40	M	Butcher	02Ap02Bz
GELLOCK, Thos.	40	M	Laborer	02Ap02Bz
CALHAN, James	24	M	Blacksmith	02Ap02Bz
LYNCH, James	22	M	Laborer	02Ap02Bz
FEGAN, Thos.	33	M	Laborer	02Ap02Bz
Mary	30	F	Spinster	02Ap02Bz
KENNY, Cathrine	18	F	Spinster	02Ap02Bz
Daniel	55	M	Laborer	02Ap02Bz
Bridget	54	F	Spinster	02Ap02Bz
Malachi	12	M	Laborer	02Ap02Bz
Daniel	09	M	Child	02Ap02Bz
MALEY, Patk.	22	M	Laborer	02Ap02Bz
KENNEDY, Margaret	24	F	Spinster	02Ap02Bz
Bridget	20	F	Spinster	02Ap02Bz
NORTON, Bridget	20	F	Spinster	02Ap02Bz
Oney	23	F	Spinster	02Ap02Bz
KANE, Mary	24	F	Spinster	02Ap02Bz
HANLEY, Mary	20	F	Spinster	02Ap02Bz
MCMANUS, Mary	20	F	Spinster	02Ap02Bz
CONGOVE, Oney	25	F	Spinster	02Ap02Bz
COMUSKY, Owen	26	M	Laborer	02Ap02Bz
KENNY, Wm.	25	M	Laborer	02Ap02Bz
MCLOUGHLIN, Teddy	24	M	Laborer	02Ap02Bz
HAGGERTY, Michael	21	M	Laborer	02Ap02Bz
FLINN, John	24	M	Shepherd	02Ap02Bz
ROCK, James	20	M	Laborer	02Ap02Bz
COMUSKY, Mary	19	F	Spinster	02Ap02Bz
TEARNEY, Cathrine	18	F	Spinster	02Ap02Bz
DUFFY, Cathrine	12	F	Spinster	02Ap02Bz
MURRY, Ann	60	F	Spinster	02Ap02Bz
BURK, Cathrin	22	F	Spinster	02Ap02Bz
MCDONALD, Eliza	22	F	Spinster	02Ap02Bz
LENOARD, Mary	18	F	Spinster	02Ap02Bz
DIVINE, Mary-Ann	10	F	Spinster	02Ap02Bz
QUIGLY, Ann	16	F	Spinster	02Ap02Bz
DIVINE, James	19	M	Farmer	02Ap02Bz
LEONARD, James	19	M	Farmer	02Ap02Bz
MCGOWAN, Michael	20	M	Farmer	02Ap02Bz
SAPPERSON, Thos.	20	M	Farmer	02Ap02Bz
RIELEY, Ann	18	F	Spinster	02Ap02Bz
KEAL, Mary	20	F	Spinster	02Ap02Bz
SMITH, Ann	16	F	Spinster	02Ap02Bz
Cathrine	22	F	Spinster	02Ap02Bz
FARLEY, Chas.	49	M	Farmer	02Ap02Bz
MCMANUS, Thos.	26	M	Farmer	02Ap02Bz
MCCOY, Pat	24	M	Farmer	02Ap02Bz
FOX, James	26	M	Farmer	02Ap02Bz
MCBRIDE, Nancy	28	F	Spinster	02Ap02Bz

NAMES OF PASSENGERS		AGE	SEX	OCCUPATIONS	DATE PORT SHIP
MCBRIDE, Bridget		26	F	Spinster	02Ap02Bz
SHORT, Ann		27	F	Spinster	02Ap02Bz
HUGHES, Ewd.		19	M	Mason	02Ap02Bz
John		21	M	Mason	02Ap02Bz
WOODS, Pat		32	M	Laborer	02Ap02Bz
CONNELLY, Patrick		15	M	Laborer	02Ap02Bz
FINEGAN, Cathrine		25	F	Spinster	02Ap02Bz
BANNON, Cathrine		25	F	Spinster	02Ap02Bz
CORRON, Cele		19	F	Spinster	02Ap02Bz
BANNON, James		06	M	Child	02Ap02Bz
Michael		03	M	Child	02Ap02Bz
Mary-Ann		.00	F	Infant	02Ap02Bz
DONAHUE, John		26	M	Laborer	02Ap02Bz
DEGNAN, Michael		26	M	Laborer	02Ap02Bz
MCGUIRE, Peter		17	M	Laborer	02Ap02Bz
SMITH, Cathrine		25	F	Spinster	02Ap02Bz
BRADY, Cathrine		25	F	Spinster	02Ap02Bz
LYNCH, Mary		19	F	Spinster	02Ap02Bz
SAXTON, Thomas		19	M	Laborer	02Ap02Bz
Terrence		22	M	Laborer	02Ap02Bz
BRADY, Bridget		20	F	Spinster	02Ap02Bz
Rose		20	F	Spinster	02Ap02Bz
SMITH, Judy		20	F	Spinster	02Ap02Bz
DONAHUE, John		23	M	Laborer	02Ap02Bz
BRADY, Matthew		25	M	Laborer	02Ap02Bz
GREENAN, Bernard		22	M	Laborer	02Ap02Bz
MCANALLY, Patk.		25	M	Laborer	02Ap02Bz
Died-At-Sea					
MORRIS, Thos.		18	M	Laborer	02Ap02Bz
REILY, Terrence		18	M	Laborer	02Ap02Bz
HACKET, Mary		52	F	Spinster	02Ap02Bz
CALLAGHAN, Bridget		20	F	Spinster	02Ap02Bz
RYNALDS, Nevin		20	F	Spinster	02Ap02Bz
CONWAY, Nicholas		27	M	Laborer	02Ap02Bz
LODGE, James		22	M	Laborer	02Ap02Bz
BRADY, Edward		25	M	Laborer	02Ap02Bz
DANIEL, John		21	M	Tanner	02Ap02Bz
Isaac		18	M	Tanner	02Ap02Bz
MOUSLEY, Sarah		54	F	Spinster	02Ap02Bz
Ann		21	F	Spinster	02Ap02Bz
Joseph		09	M	Child	02Ap02Bz
Elizabeth		32	F	Child	02Ap02Bz
Sarah-A.		06	F	Child	02Ap02Bz
Emma		04	F	Child	02Ap02Bz
Richard		02	M	Child	02Ap02Bz
MITCHEL, Cathrine		20	F	Spinster	02Ap02Bz
DEVANEY, Cathrine		20	F	Spinster	02Ap02Bz
BROADBENT, Betty		20	F	Spinster	02Ap02Bz
Thos.	(S)	02	M	Child	02Ap02Bz
Joseph	(S)	.00	M	Infant	02Ap02Bz
ROE, U-Mrs.		30	F	Spinster	02Ap02Bz
BROE, U-Mrs.		30	F	Spinster	02Ap02Bz
MOUSLEY, Richard		23	M	Ctnsp	02Ap02Bz
Wm.		29	M	Twister	02Ap02Bz
DOUGHERTY, Francis		18	M	Laborer	02Ap02Bz
REELY, John		20	M	Laborer	02Ap02Bz
HAYS, Thos.		28	M	Shoemaker	02Ap02Bz
HAYSE, Cathrine		24	F	Spinster	02Ap02Bz
HAYS, Richard-J.		.00	M	Infant	02Ap02Bz
BUCKLY, Elizabeth		28	F	Spinster	02Ap02Bz
CONNON, Thos.		26	M	Laborer	02Ap02Bz
BRIT, Bernard		35	M	Laborer	02Ap02Bz
SYLBY, John		23	M	Laborer	02Ap02Bz
HALEY, Cathrine		20	F	Spinster	02Ap02Bz
FARRELL, Ann		17	F	Spinster	02Ap02Bz
GRANGER, Thos.		36	M	Engineer	02Ap02Bz
Wm.		28	M	Baker	02Ap02Bz
STATHUM, Jonathan		45	M	Mctr	02Ap02Bz
HUSTER, Ann		28	F	Spinster	02Ap02Bz
Thos.	(S)	08	M	Child	02Ap02Bz
Mary	(D)	06	F	Child	02Ap02Bz
Eliza	(D)	01	F	Child	02Ap02Bz
JACKSON, Matilda		22	F	Spinster	02Ap02Bz
GRIFFEN, Wm.		28	M	Laborer	02Ap02Bz
BASKE, Andrew		50	M	Mason	02Ap02Bz
LEDDY, Pat.		30	M	Laborer	02Ap02Bz
CALLAGHAN, Cathrine		19	F	Spinster	02Ap02Bz
LEDDY, Ann		19	F	Spinster	02Ap02Bz
BODE, Rosy		15	F	Spinster	02Ap02Bz
DAILEY, Mary		28	F	Spinster	02Ap02Bz
Ann	(D)	05	F	Child	02Ap02Bz
John	(S)	.00	M	Infant	02Ap02Bz
JOKES, Elizabeth		26	F	Spinster	02Ap02Bz
Henry	(S)	06	M	Child	02Ap02Bz
Wm.	(S)	04	M	Child	02Ap02Bz
HEARY, Bridget		18	F	Spinster	02Ap02Bz
Mary		13	F	Spinster	02Ap02Bz
REILEY, Rose		30	F	Spinster	02Ap02Bz
Lawrence	(S)	03	M	Child	02Ap02Bz
Cathrine	(D)	05	F	Child	02Ap02Bz
GANYAN, Thos.		12	M	None	02Ap02Bz
BRINE, Pat		20	M	Laborer	02Ap02Bz
FLOOD, John		20	M	Laborer	02Ap02Bz
HELO, Henry		30	M	Cooper	02Ap02Bz
BRINE, Ellen		20	F	Spinster	02Ap02Bz
LYNCH, Nancy		20	F	Spinster	02Ap02Bz
MCMAHON, Bridget		20	F	Spinster	02Ap02Bz
SHOFREY, Ann		22	F	Spinster	02Ap02Bz
Cathrine		17	F	Spinster	02Ap02Bz
Bess		20	F	Spinster	02Ap02Bz
KELLOT, Jane		17	F	Spinster	02Ap02Bz
GROWNEY, Margaret		18	F	Spinster	02Ap02Bz
KING, Philip		18	M	Laborer	02Ap02Bz
CLARK, Philip		18	M	Laborer	02Ap02Bz
GLENNON, Pat.		21	M	Laborer	02Ap02Bz
CLARK, Sarah		21	F	Spinster	02Ap02Bz
LEE, Betsy		23	F	Spinster	02Ap02Bz
CLARK, Mary		19	F	Spinster	02Ap02Bz
SMITH, Sarah		14	F	Spinster	02Ap02Bz
Ann		13	F	Spinster	02Ap02Bz
Mary		18	F	Spinster	02Ap02Bz
ROGERS, Ann		20	F	Spinster	02Ap02Bz
Bridget		13	F	Spinster	02Ap02Bz
LYNCH, Bridget		13	F	Spinster	02Ap02Bz
BRIDE, Bridget		18	F	Spinster	02Ap02Bz
ROGERS, Mary		16	F	Spinster	02Ap02Bz
GILLALAN, Isabella		18	F	Spinster	02Ap02Bz
BURNS, Jane		20	F	Spinster	02Ap02Bz
Margaret		18	F	Spinster	02Ap02Bz
Betsy		20	F	Spinster	02Ap02Bz
ROGERS, Mary		20	F	Spinster	02Ap02Bz
GILLEN, Isabella		20	F	Spinster	02Ap02Bz
PIDGEON, Pat		30	M	Laborer	02Ap02Bz
HANRETTY, James		20	M	Laborer	02Ap02Bz
LYNCH, Abby		30	F	Tailor	02Ap02Bz
MCCALL, Nancy		60	F	Spinster	02Ap02Bz
SMITH, Ann		17	F	Spinster	02Ap02Bz
LENON, Ann		25	F	Spinster	02Ap02Bz
LYNCH, Margaret		25	F	Spinster	02Ap02Bz
CLARK, Thos.		25	M	Shoemaker	02Ap02Bz
CASSIDY, Philip		26	M	Laborer	02Ap02Bz
MCABE, Pat		25	M	Laborer	02Ap02Bz
FAHY, Philip		20	M	Laborer	02Ap02Bz
BOYLE, Joseph		58	M	Baker	02Ap02Bz
Margaret	(W)	60	F	Wife	02Ap02Bz
READY, John		25	M	Carpenter	02Ap02Bz
GAFFERTY, James		20	M	Laborer	02Ap02Bz
CORRIGAN, Philip		20	M	Laborer	02Ap02Bz
FITZSUMONS, John		20	M	Laborer	02Ap02Bz
Died-At-Sea					
MCCANN, Ann		20	F	Spinster	02Ap02Bz
HANN, Margaret		20	F	Spinster	02Ap02Bz
BROGAN, Rose		25	F	Spinster	02Ap02Bz
SMITH, Ann		22	F	Spinster	02Ap02Bz
WINTER, Michael		22	M	Laborer	02Ap02Bz
DARBY, Pat		17	M	Smith	02Ap02Bz
SHOUGHNESS, Pat		25	M	Laborer	02Ap02Bz
DOWDLE, James		26	M	Laborer	02Ap02Bz
MCCREADY, Mary-A.		13	F	None	02Ap02Bz
Jane		24	F	Spinster	02Ap02Bz

24

NAMES OF PASSENGERS		AGE	SEX	OCCUPATIONS	DATE PORT SHIP
MCCREADY, James		18	M	Laborer	02Ap02Bz
BURK, Francis		21	M	Laborer	02Ap02Bz
HENRY, Ewel		22	M	Laborer	02Ap02Bz
BURK, Mary		18	F	Spinster	02Ap02Bz
ONEIL, Michael		17	M	Laborer	02Ap02Bz
PARKER, Patk.		18	M	Gdnr	02Ap02Bz
Mary		20	F	Spinster	02Ap02Bz
LYNCH, Judy		20	F	Spinster	02Ap02Bz
MATTHEWS, Bridget		23	F	Spinster	02Ap02Bz
NONAN, Michael		01	M	Child	02Ap02Bz
MATHEWS, Eliza		01	F	Child	02Ap02Bz
MCDERMOT, Patk.		20	M	Laborer	02Ap02Bz
Patk.		27	M	Carpenter	02Ap02Bz
COX, Owen		25	M	Laborer	02Ap02Bz
FARLEY, Margaret		20	F	Spinster	02Ap02Bz
CLARKE, Ann		22	F	Spinster	02Ap02Bz
TYE, Ann		20	F	Spinster	02Ap02Bz
GLANCY, Ann		21	F	Spinster	02Ap02Bz
FITZSUMMON, Margaret		30	F	Spinster	02Ap02Bz
PHILIPS, Thos.		70	M	Laborer	02Ap02Bz
Patk.		31	M	Laborer	02Ap02Bz
Ellen		16	F	Spinster	02Ap02Bz
WHYBORN, David		41	M	Laborer	02Ap02Bz
Sarah	(W)	40	F	Wife	02Ap02Bz
David	(S)	10	M	Child	02Ap02Bz
Sarah	(D)	02	F	Child	02Ap02Bz
POWELL, Cathrine		40	F	Spinster	02Ap02Bz
Ellen	(D)	10	F	Child	02Ap02Bz
Mary	(D)	06	F	Child	02Ap02Bz
Patk.	(S)	02	M	Child	02Ap02Bz
CLARK, Ellen		30	F	Spinster	02Ap02Bz
Ann	(D)	11	F	Spinster	02Ap02Bz
Peter	(S)	09	M	Child	02Ap02Bz
Margaret	(D)	07	F	Child	02Ap02Bz
Ellen	(D)	05	F	Child	02Ap02Bz
John	(S)	02	M	Child	02Ap02Bz
CONNELLY, Cathrine		22	F	Spinster	02Ap02Bz
Cathrine	(D)	01	F	Child	02Ap02Bz
LARKIN, Mary		18	F	Spinster	02Ap02Bz
GARRET, Cathrine		19	F	Spinster	02Ap02Bz
NEWMAN, Mary		22	F	Spinster	02Ap02Bz
FARREL, Rosy		16	F	Spinster	02Ap02Bz
HAREY, Essey		16	F	Spinster	02Ap02Bz
DAILEY, Mary		24	F	None	02Ap02Bz
DUFFY, Margaret		26	F	Spinster	02Ap02Bz
Jane		12	F	None	02Ap02Bz
Michael		02	M	Child	02Ap02Bz
Thos.		01	M	Child	02Ap02Bz
WELSH, Pat		23	M	Laborer	02Ap02Bz
DERBY, John		23	M	Laborer	02Ap02Bz
JENT, Wm.		24	M	Laborer	02Ap02Bz
SLATTERDY, Patk.		25	M	Laborer	02Ap02Bz
HANIGAN, Cathrine		19	F	Laborer	02Ap02Bz
MURY, Bridget		20	F	Spinster	02Ap02Bz
MURRY, Patk.		17	M	Laborer	02Ap02Bz
HICKEY, Patk.		24	M	Laborer	02Ap02Bz
DAVIDSON, Eliza		24	F	Spinster	02Ap02Bz
Jane	(D)	07	F	Child	02Ap02Bz
MCGARRY, Francis		49	M	Carpenter	02Ap02Bz
Jenette	(W)	49	F	Spinster	02Ap02Bz
Anthony	(S)	08	M	Child	02Ap02Bz
Elizabeth	(D)	20	F	Spinster	02Ap02Bz
Jenette	(D)	18	F	Spinster	02Ap02Bz
Cathrine	(D)	10	F	None	02Ap02Bz
HAGGERTY, Chas.		21	M	Laborer	02Ap02Bz
STEPHENSON, Andrew		20	M	Laborer	02Ap02Bz
ONEIL, Mary		18	F	Dressmaker	02Ap02Bz
OBRIEN, Ellen		24	F	Spinster	02Ap02Bz
MCABE, Margaret		17	F	Spinster	02Ap02Bz
BRADY, Mary		20	F	Spinster	02Ap02Bz
BURKE, Patk.		24	M	Carpenter	02Ap02Bz
MCGERNEY, Terrence		20	M	Laborer	02Ap02Bz
KERRAN, Nancy		37	F	Spinster	02Ap02Bz
Pat	(S)	09	M	Child	02Ap02Bz
Margaret	(D)	05	F	Child	02Ap02Bz
KERRAN, Mary	(D)	01	F	Child	02Ap02Bz
DUFFY, Ann		20	F	Spinster	02Ap02Bz
MALON, Wm.		69	M	Hatter	02Ap02Bz
Mary	(W)	58	F	Wife	02Ap02Bz
Jane	(D)	24	F	Spinster	02Ap02Bz
Ellen	(D)	19	F	Spinster	02Ap02Bz
CANNON, U		19	F	None	02Ap02Bz
ROE, John		09	M	Child	02Ap02Bz
Michael		07	M	Child	02Ap02Bz
REILY, Patk.		19	M	Laborer	02Ap02Bz
U, U		.00	U	Infant	02Ap02Bz
Born-At-Sea					

FREDONIA 04 APRIL 1846

From Liverpool

NAMES OF PASSENGERS		AGE	SEX	OCCUPATIONS	DATE PORT SHIP
REILLY, Thomas		24	M	Laborer	04Ap02Ca
Mathew		22	M	Laborer	04Ap02Ca
Cornelius		25	M	Laborer	04Ap02Ca
GRAHAGAN, Patrick		30	M	Laborer	04Ap02Ca
EVANS, Thomas		44	M	Weaver	04Ap02Ca
Mary	(W)	43	F	Wife	04Ap02Ca
Anne	(D)	21	F	None	04Ap02Ca
John	(S)	16	M	None	04Ap02Ca
Mary	(D)	13	F	None	04Ap02Ca
Thomas	(S)	06	M	Child	04Ap02Ca
FIRTH, David		22	M	Clfn	04Ap02Ca
DEVINE, Mary		20	F	Servant	04Ap02Ca
BEWSHER, John		35	M	Shoemaker	04Ap02Ca
Jane	(W)	35	F	Wife	04Ap02Ca
Anne	(D)	16	F	None	04Ap02Ca
Martha	(D)	13	F	None	04Ap02Ca
Elizabeth	(D)	11	F	Child	04Ap02Ca
William	(S)	10	M	Child	04Ap02Ca
Thomas	(S)	07	M	Child	04Ap02Ca
Margaret	(D)	06	F	Child	04Ap02Ca
John	(S)	04	M	Child	04Ap02Ca
Jane	(D)	01	F	Child	04Ap02Ca
POTTS, William		35	M	Laborer	04Ap02Ca
Eunice		35	F	Laborer	04Ap02Ca
MENNELL, John		41	M	Farmer	04Ap02Ca
COWAN, James		40	M	Slater	04Ap02Ca
HOPKINS, Thomas		38	M	Laborer	04Ap02Ca
Anna	(W)	40	F	Wife	04Ap02Ca
Rheuben	(S)	09	M	Child	04Ap02Ca
Walter	(S)	06	M	Child	04Ap02Ca
Herbert	(S)	04	M	Child	04Ap02Ca
MORGAN, Mary		20	F	Servant	04Ap02Ca
Rose		18	F	Servant	04Ap02Ca
SOROHAN, William		40	M	Laborer	04Ap02Ca
Eliza		38	F	Laborer	04Ap02Ca
MCKENNA, James		24	M	Laborer	04Ap02Ca
Bridget		23	F	Laborer	04Ap02Ca
WHITE, John		40	M	Laborer	04Ap02Ca
WOODRUFFE, Nathaniel		34	M	Mason	04Ap02Ca
Anne	(W)	36	F	Wife	04Ap02Ca
Betsy	(D)	08	F	Child	04Ap02Ca
Ellen	(D)	05	F	Child	04Ap02Ca
William	(S)	03	M	Child	04Ap02Ca
Sophia	(D)	01	F	Child	04Ap02Ca
U		.00	U	Infant	04Ap02Ca
Born-At-Sea					
MCELLORY, Edward		22	M	Laborer	04Ap02Ca
MILNOR, George		25	M	Ctnsp	04Ap02Ca
REILLY, Mary		18	F	Domestic	04Ap02Ca
MCIVER, John		24	M	Laborer	04Ap02Ca
MANGAN, Pat.		27	M	Bricklayer	04Ap02Ca
RUSSELL, Edward		21	M	Laborer	04Ap02Ca

NAMES OF PASSENGERS		AGE	SEX	OCCUPATIONS	DATE PORT SHIP	NAMES OF PASSENGERS		AGE	SEX	OCCUPATIONS	DATE PORT SHIP
GIBBON, Thomas		27	M	Farrier	04Ap02Ca	DOWD, George-W.		42	M	Sailor	04Ap02Ca
LARKIN, Mary		24	F	Domestic	04Ap02Ca	FOWLER, William		29	M	Miller	04Ap02Ca
IGOE, John		24	M	Laborer	04Ap02Ca	Mary	(W)	28	F	Wife	04Ap02Ca
MURRY, Catherine		20	F	Domestic	04Ap02Ca	James	(S)	06	M	Child	04Ap02Ca
MURTHA, Bernard		31	M	Laborer	04Ap02Ca	George	(S)	04	M	Child	04Ap02Ca
THORNTON, James		24	M	Miller	04Ap02Ca	Thomas	(S)	.06	M	Infant	04Ap02Ca
BRANNICK, Michael		25	M	Laborer	04Ap02Ca	Eliza	(D)	03	F	Child	04Ap02Ca
DEVINE, Conner		21	M	Laborer	04Ap02Ca	VALENTINE, Jane		27	F	Servant	04Ap02Ca
HENNAN, Hugh		30	M	Laborer	04Ap02Ca	ADAMS, John		22	M	Farmer	04Ap02Ca
Mary	(W)	29	F	Wife	04Ap02Ca	WILSON, William		45	M	Maker	04Ap02Ca
James	(S)	05	M	Child	04Ap02Ca	Elizabeth	(W)	44	F	Wife	04Ap02Ca
Catherine	(D)	02	F	Child	04Ap02Ca	Elizabeth	(D)	10	F	Child	04Ap02Ca
Ellen		32	F	None	04Ap02Ca	William	(S)	13	M	None	04Ap02Ca
Alice		20	F	None	04Ap02Ca	Isabella	(D)	03	F	Child	04Ap02Ca
Henry		13	M	None	04Ap02Ca	JOHNSON, William		30	M	Irnmldr	04Ap02Ca
Mary		07	F	Child	04Ap02Ca	STAFFORD, Patrick		23	M	Laborer	04Ap02Ca
MCGOVERN, Anne		24	F	Domestic	04Ap02Ca	CLANCEY, James		19	M	Laborer	04Ap02Ca
PEDDOW, James		25	M	Farmer	04Ap02Ca	GORDON, James		20	M	Laborer	04Ap02Ca
Eliza	(W)	22	F	Wife	04Ap02Ca	RODDER, John		27	M	Miner	04Ap02Ca
Elizabeth	(D)	.04	F	Infant	04Ap02Ca	BARNETT, John		24	M	Miner	04Ap02Ca
Richard		20	M	Weaver	04Ap02Ca	PHILLIPS, Joseph		25	M	Miner	04Ap02Ca
MCANENY, Mathew		26	M	Servant	04Ap02Ca	STEVENS, Thomas		27	M	Farmer	04Ap02Ca
MARSDEN, Berry		17	M	Servant	04Ap02Ca	James		65	M	Farmer	04Ap02Ca
MATIER, William		22	M	Laborer	04Ap02Ca	Henry		20	M	Farmer	04Ap02Ca
MCARDLE, Hugh		21	M	Laborer	04Ap02Ca	John		24	M	Tailor	04Ap02Ca
DILWORTH, James		44	M	Weaver	04Ap02Ca	Jane		18	F	None	04Ap02Ca
KERR, Rebecka		50	F	None	04Ap02Ca	Lydia		16	F	None	04Ap02Ca
Patrick	(S)	18	M	None	04Ap02Ca	Sarah		23	F	None	04Ap02Ca
James	(S)	11	M	Child	04Ap02Ca	PIERCE, John		18	M	Farmer	04Ap02Ca
GRENCAR, Mary		21	F	Domestic	04Ap02Ca	Sarah		16	F	None	04Ap02Ca
MCCABE, John		18	M	Bleacher	04Ap02Ca	Jane		15	F	None	04Ap02Ca
Catherine		16	F	None	04Ap02Ca	Anne		14	F	None	04Ap02Ca
MCATTAMARY, John		22	M	Farmer	04Ap02Ca	Mellon		12	F	None	04Ap02Ca
Mary	(W)	20	F	Wife	04Ap02Ca	HENWOOD, William		27	M	Tailor	04Ap02Ca
Ally	(D)	.03	F	Infant	04Ap02Ca	SAMBLER, Benja.		22	M	Tailor	04Ap02Ca
MAGLONE, Edward		25	M	Laborer	04Ap02Ca	FETHERSTON, Michael		25	M	Laborer	04Ap02Ca
CARTY, Bernard		25	M	Laborer	04Ap02Ca	CONLY, Patrick		22	M	Laborer	04Ap02Ca
Bridget		32	F	None	04Ap02Ca	SWEENY, Pat		23	M	Laborer	04Ap02Ca
Thomas	(S)	01	M	Child	04Ap02Ca	MCGANN, Margaret		25	F	Servant	04Ap02Ca
Mary		56	F	None	04Ap02Ca	CONREY, Bridget		20	F	Servant	04Ap02Ca
GRADY, Ellen		20	F	Servant	04Ap02Ca	HEAGIN, Mary		20	F	Servant	04Ap02Ca
DALEY, Anne		21	F	Servant	04Ap02Ca	SWEENY, Thomas		21	M	Laborer	04Ap02Ca
DILLAN, Rose		20	F	Servant	04Ap02Ca	KILPATRICK, James		21	M	Laborer	04Ap02Ca
KANNY, Ellen		26	F	Servant	04Ap02Ca	Ellen		20	F	None	04Ap02Ca
MCDONOUGH, Michael		25	M	Laborer	04Ap02Ca	HACKETT, Dennis		20	M	Laborer	04Ap02Ca
Anne		23	F	None	04Ap02Ca	COLMAN, Thomas		19	M	Laborer	04Ap02Ca
BUTLER, Tobias		32	M	Laborer	04Ap02Ca	BERNARD, Michael		24	M	Laborer	04Ap02Ca
Anty	(W)	30	F	Wife	04Ap02Ca	GOLDING, Bridget		21	F	Servant	04Ap02Ca
Thomas	(S)	02	M	Child	04Ap02Ca	GAVAN, Mary		30	F	Servant	04Ap02Ca
Mary	(D)	.03	F	Infant	04Ap02Ca	Patrick		21	M	Laborer	04Ap02Ca
DUFFIE, Rose-Ann		21	F	Servant	04Ap02Ca	Michael		19	M	Laborer	04Ap02Ca
HACKETT, John		27	M	Servant	04Ap02Ca	Thomas		18	M	Laborer	04Ap02Ca
JOHNSTON, John		36	M	Shoemaker	04Ap02Ca	John		15	M	Laborer	04Ap02Ca
Eliza	(W)	30	F	Wife	04Ap02Ca	Biddy		14	F	Servant	04Ap02Ca
John	(S)	10	M	Child	04Ap02Ca	KILLEN, John		23	M	Laborer	04Ap02Ca
Eliza	(D)	01	F	Child	04Ap02Ca	Mary		20	F	None	04Ap02Ca
James	(S)	08	M	Child	04Ap02Ca	BOYLE, Daniel		23	M	Trader	04Ap02Ca
Saul	(S)	07	M	Child	04Ap02Ca	CLAVE, Robert		64	M	Weaver	04Ap02Ca
William	(S)	05	M	Child	04Ap02Ca	Died-At-Sea					
Mary-Ann	(D)	04	F	Child	04Ap02Ca	Janet	(W)	54	F	Wife	04Ap02Ca
CONNILL, Catherine		24	F	Servant	04Ap02Ca	Alexander	(S)	25	M	Laborer	04Ap02Ca
HACKETT, Ellen		21	F	Servant	04Ap02Ca	Elizabeth	(D)	28	F	None	04Ap02Ca
MCCORNICK, Catherine		40	F	Servant	04Ap02Ca	William	(S)	19	M	Laborer	04Ap02Ca
MARTIN, Libby		35	F	Servant	04Ap02Ca	Mary	(D)	17	F	None	04Ap02Ca
BOYLE, Michael		21	M	Servant	04Ap02Ca	Hawthorne	(S)	13	M	None	04Ap02Ca
DOOLING, John		23	M	Gdnr	04Ap02Ca	Janet	(D)	09	F	Child	04Ap02Ca
MCWADE, John		26	M	Trader	04Ap02Ca	William	(S)	02	M	Child	04Ap02Ca
Mary		48	F	Servant	04Ap02Ca	Elizabeth	(D)	02	F	Child	04Ap02Ca
KELLY, Ellen		18	F	Servant	04Ap02Ca	CRAWFORD, Catherine		21	F	Servant	04Ap02Ca
STEVENS, Sarah		18	F	Servant	04Ap02Ca	MARHE, Michael		24	M	Blacksmith	04Ap02Ca
MCWADE, Bridget		28	F	Servant	04Ap02Ca	MCCANN, Michael		24	M	Laborer	04Ap02Ca
MCCORMICK, Bridget		18	F	Servant	04Ap02Ca	Ann	(W)	26	F	Wife	04Ap02Ca
CANNON, Rose		18	F	Servant	04Ap02Ca	John	(S)	02	M	Child	04Ap02Ca
CONEY, William		30	M	Laborer	04Ap02Ca	ROGUSON, Michael		18	M	Laborer	04Ap02Ca
KILPATRICK, Robert		18	M	Laborer	04Ap02Ca	CUNNINGHAM, William		18	M	Laborer	04Ap02Ca

26

NAMES OF PASSENGERS		AGE	SEX	OCCUPATIONS	DATE PORT SHIP
GOODWIN, Pat		25	M	Laborer	04Ap02Ca
Ellen		30	F	None	04Ap02Ca
KELLY, Margaret		22	F	Servant	04Ap02Ca
CARROLL, Catherine		19	F	Servant	04Ap02Ca
KELLY, Sally		35	F	Servant	04Ap02Ca
Bridget	(D)	05	F	Child	04Ap02Ca
Mary	(D)	03	F	Child	04Ap02Ca
CANE, Biddy		25	F	Servant	04Ap02Ca
INGHAM, Thomas		19	M	Servant	04Ap02Ca
ONEIL, John		19	M	Servant	04Ap02Ca
KIERNEY, Charles		19	M	Packer	04Ap02Ca
MILLEGAN, Edward		24	M	Laborer	04Ap02Ca
MOON, Philip		24	M	Laborer	04Ap02Ca
TAFE, Thomas		24	M	Laborer	04Ap02Ca
DORSEY, Michael		24	M	Laborer	04Ap02Ca

STEPHEN-WHITNEY 06 APRIL 1846

From Liverpool

NAMES OF PASSENGERS		AGE	SEX	OCCUPATIONS	DATE PORT SHIP
MAHON, James		55	M	Laborer	06Ap02Cd
Anne	(W)	55	F	Wife	06Ap02Cd
John	(S)	20	M	Laborer	06Ap02Cd
Joseph	(S)	18	M	Laborer	06Ap02Cd
James	(S)	15	M	Laborer	06Ap02Cd
Margaret	(D)	11	F	Child	06Ap02Cd
Madge	(D)	13	F	None	06Ap02Cd
LEVIY, Mary		19	F	None	06Ap02Cd
MAGAN, Catherine		17	F	None	06Ap02Cd
FLANNIGAN, Catherine		17	F	None	06Ap02Cd
REARSTON, Mary		15	F	None	06Ap02Cd
FINNEN, Bridget		19	F	None	06Ap02Cd
MCCORMAC, Anne		16	F	None	06Ap02Cd
BURNS, Nancy		17	F	None	06Ap02Cd
HANNISON, Anne		20	F	None	06Ap02Cd
FINNEN, Thomas		27	M	Laborer	06Ap02Cd
DOYLE, Anne		28	F	None	06Ap02Cd
CONNOR, Mary		20	F	None	06Ap02Cd
SHERDAN, Anne		20	F	None	06Ap02Cd
DOYLAN, Bridget		22	F	None	06Ap02Cd
HANEY, Patrick		19	M	Laborer	06Ap02Cd
BURNS, Patrick		21	M	Carpenter	06Ap02Cd
DONOHOE, Thomas		21	M	Servant	06Ap02Cd
REYNOLDS, Patrick		38	M	Laborer	06Ap02Cd
GILRAINE, Anne		20	F	None	06Ap02Cd
MURRAY, Mary		18	F	None	06Ap02Cd
BOYLEN, Rose		18	F	None	06Ap02Cd
SMITH, Rose		18	F	None	06Ap02Cd
Mary		16	F	None	06Ap02Cd
SHANKEY, Margaret		16	F	None	06Ap02Cd
Thomas		22	M	Laborer	06Ap02Cd
MALONE, Mary		21	F	None	06Ap02Cd
GOOD, Margaret		12	F	None	06Ap02Cd
GAVAN, Mary		20	F	None	06Ap02Cd
KEEGAN, Anne		18	F	None	06Ap02Cd
WALLACE, Mary		21	F	None	06Ap02Cd
SMITH, Edward		20	M	Laborer	06Ap02Cd
LYNCH, Patrick		18	M	Laborer	06Ap02Cd
MALOY, John		22	M	Laborer	06Ap02Cd
Luke		16	M	Laborer	06Ap02Cd
BRADY, Philim		25	M	Tailor	06Ap02Cd
Patrick	(S)	04	M	Child	06Ap02Cd
MALAGEN, Anne		18	F	None	06Ap02Cd
FLANNIGAN, Anne		18	F	None	06Ap02Cd
MULDOON, Mary		20	F	None	06Ap02Cd
Martin		21	M	Laborer	06Ap02Cd
KENAN, Margaret		18	F	None	06Ap02Cd
BOYLAN, Margaret		15	F	None	06Ap02Cd
Micheal		20	M	Weaver	06Ap02Cd
SHEILDS, Terrence		19	M	Gdnr	06Ap02Cd
Mary		20	F	None	06Ap02Cd
MCANULTY, Patrick		20	M	Carpenter	06Ap02Cd
Connie		18	M	Laborer	06Ap02Cd
GALLAGHER, Patrick		18	M	Laborer	06Ap02Cd
Bridget		20	F	None	06Ap02Cd
MULLAN, Catherine		20	F	None	06Ap02Cd
QUINN, Mary		20	F	None	06Ap02Cd
ODONNELL, Isabella		18	F	None	06Ap02Cd
MAGEE, John		21	M	Laborer	06Ap02Cd
Rose		17	F	None	06Ap02Cd
Catharine		60	F	None	06Ap02Cd
CARR, Peter		20	M	Shepherd	06Ap02Cd
TURNER, Patrick		21	M	Laborer	06Ap02Cd
MOORHEAD, William		20	M	Gameskeeper	06Ap02Cd
Mary		26	F	None	06Ap02Cd
MAGHER, Mary		28	F	None	06Ap02Cd
DELMOODIE, Catharine		20	F	None	06Ap02Cd
DOMLEY, Ellen		26	F	None	06Ap02Cd
MANION, Bridget		20	F	None	06Ap02Cd
CURN, John		24	M	Laborer	06Ap02Cd
MANION, Daniel		42	M	Laborer	06Ap02Cd
Keiran		22	M	Laborer	06Ap02Cd
DEEGAN, Kitty		21	F	None	06Ap02Cd
BURN, Dorothea		23	F	None	06Ap02Cd
KELLY, Catharine		22	F	None	06Ap02Cd
DUNN, Micheal		35	M	Laborer	06Ap02Cd
HORN, Patrick		30	M	Laborer	06Ap02Cd
HALL, Stewart		35	M	Laborer	06Ap02Cd
MULROONEY, William		22	M	Coach Maker	06Ap02Cd
MAGRATH, Laurence		22	M	Groom	06Ap02Cd
MULLIGAN, Margaret		14	F	None	06Ap02Cd
STAKEN, Sally		18	F	None	06Ap02Cd
LYON, James		27	M	Stctr	06Ap02Cd
MAGRATH, Bridget		18	F	None	06Ap02Cd
MCQUAID, Catherine		16	F	None	06Ap02Cd
FOSTER, Hugh		30	M	Laborer	06Ap02Cd
Alice	(W)	20	F	Wife	06Ap02Cd
Catharine	(D)	.02	F	Infant	06Ap02Cd
KURAN, Catharine		20	F	Dressmaker	06Ap02Cd
HAGAN, John		20	M	Laborer	06Ap02Cd
HORN, Edward		25	M	Laborer	06Ap02Cd
KENNEDY, Thomas		26	M	Laborer	06Ap02Cd
WADE, James		20	M	Laborer	06Ap02Cd
DOYLE, Margaret		25	F	None	06Ap02Cd
Catharine		20	F	None	06Ap02Cd
MCGLOUGHLAN, Mary		20	F	None	06Ap02Cd
Bridget		18	F	None	06Ap02Cd
RILIY, Anne		18	F	None	06Ap02Cd
MAHAN, Margaret		16	F	None	06Ap02Cd
SMITH, Thomas		31	M	Painter	06Ap02Cd
Anne	(W)	22	F	Wife	06Ap02Cd
Margaret	(D)	01	F	Child	06Ap02Cd
MCANULTY, Patrick		26	M	Laborer	06Ap02Cd
SHANLEY, Edward		22	M	Laborer	06Ap02Cd
MALEY, Mary		26	F	None	06Ap02Cd
FITZGERALD, Mary		20	F	None	06Ap02Cd
FLYNN, Jeremiah		20	M	Laborer	06Ap02Cd
David		19	M	Laborer	06Ap02Cd
FLANNIGAN, Mary		18	F	None	06Ap02Cd
Rose		25	F	None	06Ap02Cd
James		24	M	Laborer	06Ap02Cd
Marianne		02	F	Child	06Ap02Cd
MGINNISS, Edward		16	M	Stableman	06Ap02Cd
Rose		14	F	None	06Ap02Cd
FLANNIGAN, Bridget		20	F	None	06Ap02Cd
Mary		18	F	None	06Ap02Cd
CASSIDY, John		27	M	Laborer	06Ap02Cd
LOUGHNAN, Micheal		23	M	Laborer	06Ap02Cd
MCANALLY, Mary		16	F	None	06Ap02Cd
GONAHMON, Patrick		25	M	Laborer	06Ap02Cd
MULLIGAN, Catharine		24	F	Laborer	06Ap02Cd
MAGRATH, Thomas		22	M	Laborer	06Ap02Cd
GAHERTY, John		27	M	Laborer	06Ap02Cd
FLEMING, John		23	M	Laborer	06Ap02Cd

NAMES OF PASSENGERS		AGE	SEX	OCCUPATIONS	DATE PORT SHIP
FLEMING, Judith	(W)	20	F	Wife	06Ap02Cd
Mary	(D)	.02	F	Infant	06Ap02Cd
KENAN, Patrick		35	M	Laborer	06Ap02Cd
Bryan		20	M	Carpenter	06Ap02Cd
Thomas		19	M	Laborer	06Ap02Cd
LYNAH, Micheal		28	M	Laborer	06Ap02Cd
MALIN, Margaret		26	F	None	06Ap02Cd
DELANY, Martha		22	F	None	06Ap02Cd
KINKEAD, Joseph		19	M	Laborer	06Ap02Cd
Rebecca		17	F	None	06Ap02Cd
LAIRD, Mary		19	F	None	06Ap02Cd
MCDONNELL, Patrick		16	M	Fwkr	06Ap02Cd
FLANNAGAN, Bridget		45	F	None	06Ap02Cd
CONOLEY, Patrick		28	M	Laborer	06Ap02Cd
MALEY, John		22	M	Laborer	06Ap02Cd
MALADY, Peter		17	M	Laborer	06Ap02Cd
MAXWELL, Patrick		21	M	Laborer	06Ap02Cd
FAULL, Martin		18	M	Laborer	06Ap02Cd
DALY, William		24	M	Laborer	06Ap02Cd
Bridget		16	F	None	06Ap02Cd
MANING, Micheal		13	M	None	06Ap02Cd
William		11	M	Child	06Ap02Cd
Ellen		09	F	Child	06Ap02Cd
Johannah		06	F	Child	06Ap02Cd
FLANNIGAN, Daniel		28	M	Laborer	06Ap02Cd
Jane	(W)	27	F	Wife	06Ap02Cd
Eliza	(D)	.00	F	Infant	06Ap02Cd
MALLOY, Bridget		20	F	None	06Ap02Cd
DELANY, Micheal		24	M	Laborer	06Ap02Cd
SHANLEY, Micheal		14	M	None	06Ap02Cd
Anne		08	F	Child	06Ap02Cd
DIFFERY, Annie		18	F	None	06Ap02Cd
MURRAY, Thomas		12	M	None	06Ap02Cd
John		10	M	Child	06Ap02Cd
Mary		07	F	Child	06Ap02Cd
Micheal		04	M	Child	06Ap02Cd
TODERIM, William		24	M	Laborer	06Ap02Cd
JACKSON, John		20	M	Laborer	06Ap02Cd
MORIN, Patrick		24	M	Laborer	06Ap02Cd
FLANNIGAN, Micheal		21	M	Laborer	06Ap02Cd
KERNAN, Charles		28	M	Laborer	06Ap02Cd
FEENY, Madge		20	F	None	06Ap02Cd
DAVIES, Micheal		20	M	Laborer	06Ap02Cd
EARLY, Mabel		17	F	Laborer	06Ap02Cd
DELMOODIE, John		25	M	Laborer	06Ap02Cd
HALPIN, John		33	M	Carpenter	06Ap02Cd
MCKEOWN, Anne		23	F	None	06Ap02Cd
CARL, Dominic		35	M	Laborer	06Ap02Cd
DELMOODIE, Catharine		12	F	None	06Ap02Cd
COURTENAY, James		19	M	Laborer	06Ap02Cd
MARTIN, John		27	M	Laborer	06Ap02Cd
TOONEY, John		12	M	Laborer	06Ap02Cd
MCKEEVER, Robert		20	M	Laborer	06Ap02Cd
HESLIN, Mary		20	F	None	06Ap02Cd
HALPIN, Bridget		26	F	None	06Ap02Cd
MULLIGAN, Judith		18	F	None	06Ap02Cd
FEGAN, Mary		20	F	None	06Ap02Cd
FARELL, Bridget		16	F	None	06Ap02Cd
SHERIDAN, Micheal		19	M	Laborer	06Ap02Cd
John		25	M	Laborer	06Ap02Cd
FARLEY, Judith		20	F	None	06Ap02Cd
HART, Mary		19	F	None	06Ap02Cd
FARLEY, John		27	M	Laborer	06Ap02Cd
Jane		19	F	None	06Ap02Cd
BILMAN, John		28	M	Laborer	06Ap02Cd
FITZSUMMONS, Bridget		22	F	Laborer	06Ap02Cd
BROWN, Bridget		19	F	Laborer	06Ap02Cd
SHERDAN, Mary		10	F	Laborer	06Ap02Cd
LYNCH, Barclay		20	M	Laborer	06Ap02Cd
COHIG, Patrick		18	M	Laborer	06Ap02Cd
SHERDAN, Phillp		20	M	Laborer	06Ap02Cd
DAGMAN, John		25	M	Laborer	06Ap02Cd
KANE, Anne		25	F	None	06Ap02Cd
Mary		17	F	None	06Ap02Cd
BOGIE, Anne		13	F	None	06Ap02Cd
KELLY, Patrick		24	M	Laborer	06Ap02Cd
GRADY, Thomas		25	M	Laborer	06Ap02Cd
TALBOT, George		30	M	Shoemaker	06Ap02Cd
MCANALLY, Rose		20	F	None	06Ap02Cd
CONOLEY, Catharine		20	F	None	06Ap02Cd
KEIRAN, Bessie		18	F	None	06Ap02Cd
KARRY, Patrick		22	M	Laborer	06Ap02Cd
CAREY, Patrick		30	M	Laborer	06Ap02Cd
OWENS, Thomas		26	M	Laborer	06Ap02Cd
DAY, Bridget		30	F	None	06Ap02Cd
Marianne	(D)	02	F	Child	06Ap02Cd
HEAD, James		23	M	Laborer	06Ap02Cd
Catharine		21	F	None	06Ap02Cd
DOWNIE, John		24	M	Laborer	06Ap02Cd
BLAKE, Patrick		23	M	Carpenter	06Ap02Cd
DAW, Alice		17	F	None	06Ap02Cd
RODDY, John		20	M	Laborer	06Ap02Cd
BLAKE, Margaret		17	F	None	06Ap02Cd
CONNOR, Mary		22	F	None	06Ap02Cd
WILSON, Joseph		26	M	Laborer	06Ap02Cd
BRADY, James		25	M	Laborer	06Ap02Cd
CAUFIELD, Thomas		21	M	Laborer	06Ap02Cd
REYNOLDS, Thomas		23	M	Laborer	06Ap02Cd
MAGRATH, Cicely		16	F	None	06Ap02Cd
BURN, Ellenor		18	F	None	06Ap02Cd
CARLISQUE, Bridget		18	F	None	06Ap02Cd
Micheal		20	M	Laborer	06Ap02Cd
MULVEHAN, Thomas		21	M	Laborer	06Ap02Cd
DOOLAN, Edward		21	M	Laborer	06Ap02Cd
BYRON, Martin		24	M	Laborer	06Ap02Cd
Peggy		22	F	None	06Ap02Cd
FAGHEY, Bridget		18	F	None	06Ap02Cd
KELLY, Daniel		45	M	Laborer	06Ap02Cd
Rose		18	F	None	06Ap02Cd
STOCKMAN, Bridget		40	F	None	06Ap02Cd
John		21	M	Shoemaker	06Ap02Cd
CALLEN, Mary		19	F	None	06Ap02Cd
ROE, Bridget		19	F	None	06Ap02Cd
RODGERS, Bridget		19	F	None	06Ap02Cd
RYAL, William		28	M	Butcher	06Ap02Cd
COMESQUE, Jane		28	F	None	06Ap02Cd
BLACK, Rose		18	F	None	06Ap02Cd
MCEVOY, Susan		20	F	None	06Ap02Cd
MCCORMAC, James		35	M	Laborer	06Ap02Cd
NOULAN, Andrew		28	M	Laborer	06Ap02Cd
MOORE, James		23	M	Laborer	06Ap02Cd
LAYO, John		20	M	Laborer	06Ap02Cd
KALEY, Richard		27	M	Laborer	06Ap02Cd
HAYS, Thomas		20	M	Laborer	06Ap02Cd
QUIGLEY, Mary		24	F	None	06Ap02Cd
RILEY, Mary		25	F	None	06Ap02Cd
MURRAY, Bernard		22	M	Laborer	06Ap02Cd
MINAH, Bridget		25	F	None	06Ap02Cd
William		26	M	Laborer	06Ap02Cd
CONLAGHAN, Mary		27	F	None	06Ap02Cd
KINNEY, Anne		21	F	None	06Ap02Cd
BOLEYN, Mary		20	F	None	06Ap02Cd
HUSFAGAN, Mary		22	F	None	06Ap02Cd
CLAFFEY, Catharine		20	F	None	06Ap02Cd
HIGGINS, Anne		22	F	None	06Ap02Cd
RIGNEY, Bernard		28	M	Laborer	06Ap02Cd
MALLOY, Kieran		24	M	Laborer	06Ap02Cd
RIGNEY, Mary		30	F	None	06Ap02Cd
FLYNN, Peter		19	M	Laborer	06Ap02Cd
FALLEN, James		25	M	Laborer	06Ap02Cd
FAGHEY, John		22	M	Laborer	06Ap02Cd
DONLAN, Patrick		19	M	Laborer	06Ap02Cd
HUSSEY, Patrick		28	M	Laborer	06Ap02Cd
MCDERMOTT, Andrew		24	M	Laborer	06Ap02Cd
BYRON, John		29	M	Laborer	06Ap02Cd
DOCKRY, John		28	M	Laborer	06Ap02Cd
BURN, John		23	M	Laborer	06Ap02Cd
HAYS, Micheal		46	M	Laborer	06Ap02Cd
Mary	(W)	43	F	Wife	06Ap02Cd
Bridget	(D)	18	F	None	06Ap02Cd

NAMES OF PASSENGERS		AGE	SEX	OCCUPATIONS	DATE PORT SHIP
HAYS, Margaret	(D)	16	F	None	06Ap02Cd
John	(S)	13	M	None	06Ap02Cd
Micheal	(S)	11	M	None	06Ap02Cd
Mary	(D)	09	F	Child	06Ap02Cd
Laurence	(S)	07	M	Child	06Ap02Cd
Kennedy	(S)	05	M	Child	06Ap02Cd
Patrick	(S)	03	M	Child	06Ap02Cd
KINNEY, Bridget		28	F	None	06Ap02Cd
FLANNAGAN, Bridget		21	F	None	06Ap02Cd
MEHAN, Bridget		23	F	None	06Ap02Cd
HAGAN, Bridget		24	F	None	06Ap02Cd
QUINN, Catharine		19	F	None	06Ap02Cd
Mary		23	F	None	06Ap02Cd
COCHRAN, Johannah		22	F	None	06Ap02Cd
Catharine		18	F	None	06Ap02Cd
ROACH, Bridget		18	F	None	06Ap02Cd
John		25	M	Laborer	06Ap02Cd
LOGAN, James		24	M	Laborer	06Ap02Cd
William		20	M	Laborer	06Ap02Cd
BRADISH, Patrick		25	M	Jockey	06Ap02Cd
NORID, John		23	M	Servant	06Ap02Cd
KINCHELLA, Terrence		25	M	Laborer	06Ap02Cd
HERON, Micheal		24	M	Laborer	06Ap02Cd
HORN, John		22	M	Laborer	06Ap02Cd
DOYLE, Patrick		26	M	Laborer	06Ap02Cd
HARRON, Micheal		23	M	Laborer	06Ap02Cd
RYAN, Thomas		25	M	Clerk	06Ap02Cd
BUCKLEY, Charles		23	M	Laborer	06Ap02Cd
BOYLAN, Anne		20	F	None	06Ap02Cd
MAGRATH, Mary		16	F	None	06Ap02Cd
WARD, Ann		22	F	None	06Ap02Cd
COCHRAN, James		30	M	Laborer	06Ap02Cd
HOPE, Andrew		21	M	Laborer	06Ap02Cd
HALIAN, Elisha		18	F	None	06Ap02Cd
FARELL, Anne		23	F	None	06Ap02Cd
CARLING, Catharine		14	F	None	06Ap02Cd
ELLIOTT, James		22	M	Laborer	06Ap02Cd
CULLAGHAN, Thomas		19	M	Laborer	06Ap02Cd
CARLING, James		19	M	Blacksmith	06Ap02Cd
ROORKE, Rose		19	F	None	06Ap02Cd
CARL, Margaret		18	F	None	06Ap02Cd
HART, Bridget		20	F	None	06Ap02Cd
MCSHANE, Peter		19	M	Laborer	06Ap02Cd
FLINN, Bryan		20	M	Laborer	06Ap02Cd
LYNCH, Patrick		24	M	Weaver	06Ap02Cd
WHITE, James		15	M	None	06Ap02Cd
KELLY, William		22	M	Tailor	06Ap02Cd
BURNS, Edward		32	M	Laborer	06Ap02Cd
Patack	(S)	.07	M	Infant	06Ap02Cd
Betty	(W)	22	F	Wife	06Ap02Cd
FITZSUMMON, Catharine		22	F	None	06Ap02Cd
WHITE, Susan		14	F	None	06Ap02Cd
MCCOLOUGH, Irvine		25	M	Laborer	06Ap02Cd
Jane		20	F	None	06Ap02Cd
WATTERS, Alice		20	F	None	06Ap02Cd
KELLY, Daniel		48	M	Merchant	06Ap02Cd
Eliza	(W)	40	F	Wife	06Ap02Cd
Catharine	(D)	17	F	None	06Ap02Cd
KEENAN, Mary		22	F	None	06Ap02Cd
MURPHY, Nancy		18	F	None	06Ap02Cd
Patrick		19	M	Laborer	06Ap02Cd
MARKEY, Margaret		19	F	None	06Ap02Cd
MCLAINE, Rosey		18	F	None	06Ap02Cd
FANNET, Anne		23	F	None	06Ap02Cd
KELLY, Catharine		14	F	None	06Ap02Cd
CARLAN, Owen		21	M	Laborer	06Ap02Cd
BRADY, Margaret		20	F	None	06Ap02Cd

METEOR 06 APRIL 1846

From Liverpool

NAMES OF PASSENGERS		AGE	SEX	OCCUPATIONS	DATE PORT SHIP
CONNER, Bridget		20	F	Laborer	06Ap02Ce
FARREL, Edward		20	M	Laborer	06Ap02Ce
KELLY, Margaret		39	F	Laborer	06Ap02Ce
Eliza	(D)	12	F	Laborer	06Ap02Ce
MULREDY, Anthony		30	M	Farmer	06Ap02Ce
Rose		25	F	Farmer	06Ap02Ce
WARDEN, Phillip		24	M	Farmer	06Ap02Ce
MCKEVER, James		21	M	Farmer	06Ap02Ce
CAFFNY, Phillip		22	M	Farmer	06Ap02Ce
FARLY, Owen		22	M	Farmer	06Ap02Ce
DUNIVAN, Betsey		15	F	None	06Ap02Ce
DOLAND, Catherine		16	F	None	06Ap02Ce
MALARDY, Anthony		09	M	Child	06Ap02Ce
MALADY, Bridget		18	F	None	06Ap02Ce
RILEY, James		26	M	Farmer	06Ap02Ce
MCCAY, Anne		17	F	None	06Ap02Ce
MCCANT, John		30	M	Carpenter	06Ap02Ce
Eliza	(W)	25	F	Wife	06Ap02Ce
John-Jr.	(S)	07	M	Child	06Ap02Ce
James	(S)	04	M	Child	06Ap02Ce
MANN, John		26	M	Blacksmith	06Ap02Ce
FLOOD, James		21	M	Laborer	06Ap02Ce
FANNING, James		22	M	Laborer	06Ap02Ce
GILL, John		22	M	Laborer	06Ap02Ce
ROONEY, John		20	M	Laborer	06Ap02Ce
CONNER, Bridget		20	F	Laborer	06Ap02Ce
EDWARDS, Mary		33	F	Laborer	06Ap02Ce
James	(S)	02	M	Child	06Ap02Ce
Catherine	(D)	01	F	Child	06Ap02Ce
MALOY, Anne		14	F	Laborer	06Ap02Ce
ONEAL, Anne		14	F	Laborer	06Ap02Ce
NOLAN, Brian		40	M	Laborer	06Ap02Ce
KELLY, Patrick		24	M	Laborer	06Ap02Ce
FENEY, Mary		25	F	Laborer	06Ap02Ce
MCGOWAN, Betsey		22	F	Laborer	06Ap02Ce
WHITE, Thomas		30	M	Weaver	06Ap02Ce
MARTER, William		20	M	Shoemaker	06Ap02Ce
GUNSLINER, Michael		30	M	Laborer	06Ap02Ce
Bridget	(W)	24	F	Wife	06Ap02Ce
Margaret	(D)	.10	F	Infant	06Ap02Ce
RILEY, Alexander		20	M	Laborer	06Ap02Ce
MARR, John		40	M	Laborer	06Ap02Ce
MULVY, Margaret		20	F	Laborer	06Ap02Ce
MAHAN, Mary		21	F	Laborer	06Ap02Ce
MARHAN, Biddy		23	F	Laborer	06Ap02Ce
MAHAN, Michael		39	M	Laborer	06Ap02Ce
CONNER, John		48	M	Laborer	06Ap02Ce
PATTERSON, Allexander		27	M	Laborer	06Ap02Ce
BOVILLE, Richard		22	M	Laborer	06Ap02Ce
Rachel	(W)	19	F	Wife	06Ap02Ce
U	(D)	.00	F	Infant	06Ap02Ce
Born-At-Sea		Died-At-Sea			
MCCOLAGH, Andrew		17	M	Laborer	06Ap02Ce
MORRISON, John		22	M	Laborer	06Ap02Ce
KALLS, William		19	M	Laborer	06Ap02Ce
MCMANN, Thomas		23	M	Laborer	06Ap02Ce
SULIVAN, James		19	M	Laborer	06Ap02Ce
CLARY, Thomas		25	M	Laborer	06Ap02Ce
DUGAN, Richard		20	M	Laborer	06Ap02Ce
Julia		19	F	Laborer	06Ap02Ce
MALONE, Bridget		21	F	Laborer	06Ap02Ce
MCGINN, Juda		20	M	Laborer	06Ap02Ce
FINIGIN, Mary		25	F	Laborer	06Ap02Ce
NERNEY, Bridget		20	F	Laborer	06Ap02Ce
Ellen		18	F	Laborer	06Ap02Ce

NAMES OF PASSENGERS	A G E	S E X	OCCUPATIONS	DATE PORT SHIP
DONLAY, Peter	21	M	Laborer	06Ap02Ce
TUNY, Gilbert	24	M	Butcher	06Ap02Ce
CALSTON, Charles	24	M	Laborer	06Ap02Ce
KIENIN, Partrick	31	M	Laborer	06Ap02Ce
FOX, Thomas	25	M	Carpenter	06Ap02Ce
CARLE, Ann	24	F	Dressmaker	06Ap02Ce
GOWAN, Owen	32	M	Laborer	06Ap02Ce
CASSADAY, Barnard	30	M	Laborer	06Ap02Ce
Mary (W)	25	F	Wife	06Ap02Ce
Michael (S)	02	M	Child	06Ap02Ce
FALLAN, Daniel	20	M	Laborer	06Ap02Ce
TIE, John	20	M	Laborer	06Ap02Ce
MILLER, William	21	M	Laborer	06Ap02Ce
Catherine	26	F	Wife	06Ap02Ce
James	05	M	Child	06Ap02Ce
CALAHAN, Catherine	18	F	Laborer	06Ap02Ce
MCCOWN, Mary	22	F	Laborer	06Ap02Ce
LEONARD, John	26	M	Laborer	06Ap02Ce
LENARD, Ann-Jane	19	F	Laborer	06Ap02Ce
MAHAN, Partrick	22	M	Laborer	06Ap02Ce
FARREL, Margaret	17	F	Laborer	06Ap02Ce
MELLALY, Ellen	17	F	Laborer	06Ap02Ce
HAY, Betsey	17	F	Laborer	06Ap02Ce
HEGAN, Bridget	17	F	Laborer	06Ap02Ce
FURGERSON, Innis	27	M	Stctr	06Ap02Ce
JIMERSON, Alexander	23	M	Weaver	06Ap02Ce
Fanny	24	F	Weaver	06Ap02Ce
MARTIN, Catherine	18	F	Laborer	06Ap02Ce
CONNER, John	25	M	Laborer	06Ap02Ce
Betsey	20	F	Laborer	06Ap02Ce
CONNIGHTON, Dennis	22	M	Laborer	06Ap02Ce
CANIGAN, Mary	20	F	Laborer	06Ap02Ce
HILLIARD, Mary	22	F	Dressmaker	06Ap02Ce
COX, James	24	M	Laborer	06Ap02Ce
FEANEY, Thomas	20	M	Laborer	06Ap02Ce
LEASON, Bridget	20	F	Laborer	06Ap02Ce
MCGOVERN, Mary	16	F	Laborer	06Ap02Ce
KERR, Michael	31	M	Laborer	06Ap02Ce
Maryann (W)	23	F	Wife	06Ap02Ce
James (S)	03	M	Child	06Ap02Ce
DONALD, Robert	25	M	Farmer	06Ap02Ce
FENEY, Bridget	25	F	None	06Ap02Ce
CAFFRY, Ann	20	F	None	06Ap02Ce
GRAY, Mary	20	F	None	06Ap02Ce
MULDRANE, Thomas	19	M	Laborer	06Ap02Ce
WHELEOR, Margaret	19	F	None	06Ap02Ce
Rosey	19	F	None	06Ap02Ce
HAGETT, Ann	25	F	None	06Ap02Ce
MCGUIRE, Mary	20	F	None	06Ap02Ce
MANN, Bridget	16	F	None	06Ap02Ce
BYRNE, Michael	28	M	None	06Ap02Ce
KING, Richard	20	M	None	06Ap02Ce
MARTIN, Owen	26	M	None	06Ap02Ce
QUIN, Henry	30	M	None	06Ap02Ce
GARITY, Martin	21	M	None	06Ap02Ce
BANUN, John	26	M	None	06Ap02Ce
CONALLY, Mary	21	F	None	06Ap02Ce
MULVY, Mary	20	F	None	06Ap02Ce
RILEY, Catherine	22	F	None	06Ap02Ce
James	20	M	None	06Ap02Ce
Maryann	20	F	None	06Ap02Ce
ONEAL, Charles	20	M	Carpenter	06Ap02Ce
STEVENSON, John	20	M	Laborer	06Ap02Ce
DELANEY, Michael	25	M	Laborer	06Ap02Ce
Ann	21	F	Laborer	06Ap02Ce
MURRAY, Eliza	30	F	Laborer	06Ap02Ce
Ann (D)	07	F	Child	06Ap02Ce
MCCANN, John	26	M	Laborer	06Ap02Ce
Sarah	20	F	Laborer	06Ap02Ce
MCGOWAN, Mary	19	F	Laborer	06Ap02Ce
DAILEY, Henry	20	M	Weaver	06Ap02Ce
CONLIN, Francis	32	M	Weaver	06Ap02Ce
PARKER, Edward	30	M	Laborer	06Ap02Ce
HILON, Partrick	30	M	Mason	06Ap02Ce
ROACH, William	24	M	Clerk	06Ap02Ce
FLEMING, Elizabeth	24	F	None	06Ap02Ce
KEHO, Mary	25	F	None	06Ap02Ce
MURRY, Owen	22	M	Carpenter	06Ap02Ce
Margaret	20	F	Carpenter	06Ap02Ce
PRUNTY, Mary	19	F	Laborer	06Ap02Ce
GILLMURRY, Catherine	16	F	Laborer	06Ap02Ce
MCCANN, Mary	19	F	Laborer	06Ap02Ce
ROLL, Mary	20	F	Laborer	06Ap02Ce
MARTIN, Julia	16	F	Laborer	06Ap02Ce
MCGUIRE, Phill	22	M	Laborer	06Ap02Ce
CONNWAY, Thomas	24	M	Laborer	06Ap02Ce
SULIVAN, Daniel	45	M	Sawer	06Ap02Ce
AGAN, Mary	18	F	None	06Ap02Ce
GRAGAN, John	30	M	Farmer	06Ap02Ce
RUNEY, Brian	18	M	Shoemaker	06Ap02Ce
James	20	M	Baker	06Ap02Ce
MURRY, Margaret	20	F	None	06Ap02Ce
CONNER, Francis	18	M	Laborer	06Ap02Ce
Peter	15	M	Tailor	06Ap02Ce
John	14	M	Laborer	06Ap02Ce
GOWAN, Mary	30	F	Laborer	06Ap02Ce
MCMULLIN, John	19	M	Laborer	06Ap02Ce
CARN, Margaret	20	F	Laborer	06Ap02Ce
SHAUGHNESSY, Margaret	25	F	Laborer	06Ap02Ce
MEIHAN, Richard	26	M	Laborer	06Ap02Ce
James	20	M	Laborer	06Ap02Ce
Mary	20	F	Laborer	06Ap02Ce
Ann	20	F	Laborer	06Ap02Ce
COLLINS, Mary	20	F	Laborer	06Ap02Ce
LINES, Partrick	24	M	Laborer	06Ap02Ce
ROWAN, Partrick	28	M	Laborer	06Ap02Ce
CONARTY, Martin	23	M	Laborer	06Ap02Ce
RILEY, Christopher	20	M	Groom	06Ap02Ce
MCCUE, James	30	M	Laborer	06Ap02Ce
MORN, Partrick	30	M	Laborer	06Ap02Ce
ROACH, Catherine	20	F	Laborer	06Ap02Ce
MEEHAN, John	19	M	Laborer	06Ap02Ce
Nancy	25	F	Laborer	06Ap02Ce
BYRNE, Peter	25	M	Clerk	06Ap02Ce
RILEY, Susan	17	F	Laborer	06Ap02Ce
HAGER, Catherine	17	F	Laborer	06Ap02Ce

JOHN-BARING 08 APRIL 1846

From Liverpool

NAMES OF PASSENGERS	A G E	S E X	OCCUPATIONS	DATE PORT SHIP
SOMERS, John	40	M	Laborer	08Ap02Cf
Rose (W)	36	F	Wife	08Ap02Cf
Cathn. (D)	11	F	Laborer	08Ap02Cf
Thos. (S)	08	M	Child	08Ap02Cf
MURPHY, Saml.	27	M	Cooper	08Ap02Cf
MCCLAIRE, Robt.	21	M	Carpenter	08Ap02Cf
COUGHLIN, Eliza	20	F	Laborer	08Ap02Cf
Cathn.	20	F	Laborer	08Ap02Cf
Maria	20	F	Laborer	08Ap02Cf
CONNELL, Eliza	20	F	Laborer	08Ap02Cf
DORAN, Jas.	40	M	Laborer	08Ap02Cf
CASY, Thos.	20	M	Carpenter	08Ap02Cf
RILEY, Richd.	20	M	None	08Ap02Cf
MAXWELL, Danl.	28	M	None	08Ap02Cf
FARRELS, Jno.	30	M	None	08Ap02Cf
PARKS, Saml.	21	M	Cooper	08Ap02Cf
TOLON, Wm.	30	M	None	08Ap02Cf
Ellen	30	F	None	08Ap02Cf
MCKER, Brady	18	F	None	08Ap02Cf
NOWLAN, Matilda	28	F	None	08Ap02Cf
REILY, Mary	20	F	None	08Ap02Cf
MCDONNELL, Ellen	20	F	None	08Ap02Cf
Mary	20	F	None	08Ap02Cf

NAMES OF PASSENGERS		AGE	SEX	OCCUPATIONS	DATE PORT SHIP
COLAHAN, Jane		11	F	Child	08Ap02Cf
Cathn.		12	F	None	08Ap02Cf
LYNCH, Cathn.		20	F	None	08Ap02Cf
REER, Mary		20	F	None	08Ap02Cf
CRONON, Owin		20	M	None	08Ap02Cf
Tunis		20	M	None	08Ap02Cf
Margt.		18	F	None	08Ap02Cf
MCDONNELL, Michl.		20	M	Ctnsp	08Ap02Cf
Margt.		20	F	None	08Ap02Cf
REILY, Patt		20	M	Carpenter	08Ap02Cf
CONALY, John		20	M	None	08Ap02Cf
Michl.		20	M	None	08Ap02Cf
BRENAN, Jas.		20	M	None	08Ap02Cf
CALLIN, Michl.		20	M	Tnr-Cur	08Ap02Cf
ROGAN, Jas.		20	M	None	08Ap02Cf
GANTRY, Jas.		20	M	None	08Ap02Cf
MERRIS, Jas.		20	M	None	08Ap02Cf
Tim		20	M	Shoemaker	08Ap02Cf
QUIN, Anaty.		20	M	None	08Ap02Cf
U-Mrs.		30	F	Wife	08Ap02Cf
Bartty		26	M	None	08Ap02Cf
MCKENRY, Jane		20	F	None	08Ap02Cf
QUINN, Cathn.		09	F	Child	08Ap02Cf
Mary		.00	F	Infant	08Ap02Cf
Edwd.		.00	M	Infant	08Ap02Cf
MURPHY, Charles		25	M	None	08Ap02Cf
Jno.		20	M	None	08Ap02Cf
KEARNEY, Patt		21	M	None	08Ap02Cf
DORNOTT, Robt.		20	M	None	08Ap02Cf
FINALY, Margt.		20	F	None	08Ap02Cf
SHORTLE, Robt.		30	M	None	08Ap02Cf
U	(W)	30	F	Wife	08Ap02Cf
John	(S)	.00	M	Infant	08Ap02Cf
JOHNSON, Cathn.		20	F	None	08Ap02Cf
FOX, Alley		20	F	None	08Ap02Cf
LEYNERD, Brady		20	F	None	08Ap02Cf
MCMAHAN, Margt.		20	F	None	08Ap02Cf
DALY, Cathn.		20	F	None	08Ap02Cf
DOLAN, John		21	M	None	08Ap02Cf
HARNY, Mary		19	F	None	08Ap02Cf
HANTY, Rose		40	F	None	08Ap02Cf
BEEMAN, Thos.		20	M	Tnr-Cur	08Ap02Cf
HOY, Bernard		20	M	None	08Ap02Cf
MCCORMECK, Peter		20	M	None	08Ap02Cf
KIERNAN, Ellen		20	F	None	08Ap02Cf
FARRELL, Patt		20	M	None	08Ap02Cf
MONAGAN, Ann		20	F	None	08Ap02Cf
DUFFY, Ann		20	F	None	08Ap02Cf
KENRY, Michl.		20	M	None	08Ap02Cf
U	(W)	20	F	Wife	08Ap02Cf
DUGAN, Patt		21	M	None	08Ap02Cf
REILY, Ellen		21	F	None	08Ap02Cf
RUER, Jno.		24	M	None	08Ap02Cf
ONEIL, Denis		22	M	None	08Ap02Cf
MCKENNEN, Francis		21	M	Flaxdr	08Ap02Cf
CON, Ellen		19	F	None	08Ap02Cf
CROEWE, John		24	M	None	08Ap02Cf
FARRELLS, Patt		20	M	None	08Ap02Cf
MARLEY, Margth.		20	F	None	08Ap02Cf
FLYNN, Mary		25	F	None	08Ap02Cf
DEVLIN, Cathn.		23	F	None	08Ap02Cf
RYAN, Michl.		25	M	Flaxdr	08Ap02Cf
DONAGHY, Michl.		26	M	Flaxdr	08Ap02Cf
Jane		20	F	None	08Ap02Cf
MORISY, Martin		20	M	None	08Ap02Cf
BRONAN, Patt		20	M	Carpenter	08Ap02Cf
Jas.		20	M	Carpenter	08Ap02Cf
MCGARN, Jas.		24	M	None	08Ap02Cf
KURNAN, Patt		00	M	None	08Ap02Cf
JOHNSON, Cathn.		20	F	None	08Ap02Cf
Henry	(S)	01	M	Child	08Ap02Cf
MULLEN, Brady		18	F	None	08Ap02Cf
PARSONS, Margt.		17	F	None	08Ap02Cf
DONOHOE, Michl.		22	M	None	08Ap02Cf
KARN, Maria		19	F	None	08Ap02Cf
CONARTY, Maria		20	F	None	08Ap02Cf
FARRELL, Margt.		20	F	None	08Ap02Cf
DELAHUNT, Brigt.		20	F	None	08Ap02Cf
JOHNSON, Geo.		20	M	None	08Ap02Cf
DEGNAN, Mary		20	F	None	08Ap02Cf
COSTILON, Anne		20	F	None	08Ap02Cf
ZONG, Eliza		20	F	None	08Ap02Cf
Tunis		20	M	None	08Ap02Cf
FLATERTY, Patt		20	M	None	08Ap02Cf
HORR, Francis		20	M	Flaxdr	08Ap02Cf
Brian		20	M	None	08Ap02Cf
COLWELL, Wm.		20	M	None	08Ap02Cf
MCINNESS, Phillp		20	M	None	08Ap02Cf
MURAN, Michl.		20	M	None	08Ap02Cf
HURSON, Jno.		20	M	None	08Ap02Cf
Mary		20	F	None	08Ap02Cf
SMITH, Brady		18	F	None	08Ap02Cf
Mary		18	F	None	08Ap02Cf
Cathn.		17	F	None	08Ap02Cf
MIE, Jno.		30	M	None	08Ap02Cf
DELANY, Jas.		24	M	None	08Ap02Cf
MARTIN, Michl.		20	M	None	08Ap02Cf
GUFFY, Patt		26	M	None	08Ap02Cf
MONAGHN, Michl.		20	M	None	08Ap02Cf
KEATING, Patt		19	M	None	08Ap02Cf
KELLY, Jas.		24	M	None	08Ap02Cf
U-Mrs.		40	F	Wife	08Ap02Cf
Jody		20	M	Cooper	08Ap02Cf
Patt		20	M	Cooper	08Ap02Cf
Margt.		19	F	None	08Ap02Cf
Anren		17	M	Cooper	08Ap02Cf
Charles		18	M	Baker	08Ap02Cf
Jas.		07	M	Child	08Ap02Cf
Judy		09	F	Child	08Ap02Cf
Michl.		21	M	None	08Ap02Cf
IRTMAN, Patt		20	M	None	08Ap02Cf
MORAN, Michl.		20	M	None	08Ap02Cf
KELLY, John		24	M	None	08Ap02Cf
LUMPERT, Mary		19	F	None	08Ap02Cf
FANNER, Mary		21	F	None	08Ap02Cf
Mary		20	F	None	08Ap02Cf
SHURP, Mary		20	F	None	08Ap02Cf
MCGUNYS, Hugh		18	M	None	08Ap02Cf
CAHILL, Michl.		18	M	None	08Ap02Cf
MCCORMICK, Cathn.		20	F	None	08Ap02Cf
MCDANELL, Mary		20	F	None	08Ap02Cf
LEARY, Anne		20	F	None	08Ap02Cf
WALSH, Judy		20	F	None	08Ap02Cf
DAVY, Brady		20	F	None	08Ap02Cf
KEARNY, Maria		20	F	None	08Ap02Cf
QUIRNER, Maria		20	F	None	08Ap02Cf
MAY, Patt		25	M	None	08Ap02Cf
Margt.		20	F	None	08Ap02Cf
Michl.		22	M	None	08Ap02Cf
BRADY, Michl.		20	M	None	08Ap02Cf
KELLY, Cathn.		20	F	None	08Ap02Cf
MAY, Mary		20	F	None	08Ap02Cf
Batty		20	F	None	08Ap02Cf
MCKUGH, Anne		20	F	None	08Ap02Cf
Mary		21	F	None	08Ap02Cf
CORCERAN, Thos.		24	M	None	08Ap02Cf
MAY, Betty		20	F	None	08Ap02Cf
BRINON, Mathew		30	M	None	08Ap02Cf
Edwd.		28	M	None	08Ap02Cf
CORAN, Michl.		20	M	None	08Ap02Cf
MCDONAGH, Cathn.		18	F	None	08Ap02Cf
CORTOWAL, Cath.		20	F	None	08Ap02Cf
KERSHAW, Thos.		22	M	Whitesmith	08Ap02Cf
U	(W)	25	F	Wife	08Ap02Cf
MCGLAUGHLIN, Rose		18	F	None	08Ap02Cf
OLIVER, John		42	M	None	08Ap02Cf
Eliza	(W)	40	F	Wife	08Ap02Cf
Harnetty	(S)	10	M	Child	08Ap02Cf
Margt.	(D)	05	F	Child	08Ap02Cf
INGERSOL, Anne		19	F	None	08Ap02Cf

NAMES OF PASSENGERS	A G E	S E X	OCCUPATIONS	DATE PORT SHIP
SHANNON, Patt	32	M	Tailor	08Ap02Cf
KIGTEN, Brdgt.	20	F	Servant	08Ap02Cf
COFFIELD, Jos.	24	M	Tailor	08Ap02Cf
MCDERMITT, Michl.	20	M	None	08Ap02Cf
DAVIS, Jas.	20	M	None	08Ap02Cf
U (W)	20	F	Wife	08Ap02Cf
MARTIN, Jas.	20	M	None	08Ap02Cf
CARNY, Patt	20	M	None	08Ap02Cf
JITTIA, Mary	20	F	None	08Ap02Cf
KEATING, Mary	20	F	None	08Ap02Cf
Peggy	20	F	None	08Ap02Cf
CONNER, Mary	20	F	None	08Ap02Cf
HUFFY, Brady	18	F	None	08Ap02Cf
Margt.	20	F	None	08Ap02Cf
TAYLER, Jas.	40	M	None	08Ap02Cf
Mary (W)	37	F	Wife	08Ap02Cf
Margtt. (D)	12	F	None	08Ap02Cf
Eliza (D)	10	F	Child	08Ap02Cf
Anne (D)	08	F	Child	08Ap02Cf
John (S)	06	M	Child	08Ap02Cf
Jane (D)	04	F	Child	08Ap02Cf
Mary (D)	.00	F	Infant	08Ap02Cf

NORTHUMBERLAND 09 APRIL 1846

From London

NAMES OF PASSENGERS	A G E	S E X	OCCUPATIONS	DATE PORT SHIP
TAYLOR, William	60	M	Medical	09Ap21Cg
Elizabeth (W)	54	F	Wife	09Ap21Cg
Amelia (D)	18	F	None	09Ap21Cg
Emma (D)	16	F	None	09Ap21Cg
William (S)	13	M	None	09Ap21Cg
HANCOCK, Edward-Chads	22	M	Gentleman	09Ap21Cg
Barbara	21	F	None	09Ap21Cg
GOPSILL, John	28	M	Farmer	09Ap21Cg
Elizabeth-Mary (W)	22	F	Wife	09Ap21Cg
John-B. (S)	01	M	Child	09Ap21Cg
HUGGINS, Edward-Henry	36	M	Mariner	09Ap21Cg
Sarah	33	F	None	09Ap21Cg
POTTER, George	53	M	Merchant	09Ap21Cg
HARBOTTLE, John	41	M	Merchant	09Ap21Cg
BACKER, George	30	M	Engineer	09Ap21Cg
Elizabeth	30	F	None	09Ap21Cg
STUART, Hugh	25	M	Baker	09Ap21Cg
LOFT, William	17	M	Farmer	09Ap21Cg
GURNEY, John	38	M	Surgeon	09Ap21Cg
GILBERT, William	21	M	Clerk	09Ap21Cg
CROMWELL, George	32	M	Painter	09Ap21Cg
JONES, Peter	40	M	Packer	09Ap21Cg
HARTLEY, Hartley	47	M	Farmer	09Ap21Cg
RATCLIFF, Abel	34	M	Carpenter	09Ap21Cg
Azerath (W)	36	F	Wife	09Ap21Cg
Caroline-Ann (D)	09	F	Child	09Ap21Cg
LACEY, Joseph	31	M	Wheelwright	09Ap21Cg
Sarah	63	F	None	09Ap21Cg
DONOVAN, Dennis	23	M	Farrier	09Ap21Cg
YOUNGMANN, George	22	M	Bootmaker	09Ap21Cg
YOUNGMAN, Mary	54	F	None	09Ap21Cg
Caroline (D)	16	F	None	09Ap21Cg
James (S)	10	M	None	09Ap21Cg
Emily (D)	19	F	None	09Ap21Cg
PETERS, Nathaniel-J.	20	M	Shoemaker	09Ap21Cg
GALLEZ, Peter	22	M	Carpenter	09Ap21Cg
FOREAU, Daniel	19	M	Farmer	09Ap21Cg
DELARUE, Massy	20	M	Tailor	09Ap21Cg
Willm.	20	M	None	09Ap21Cg
HUMPHRIES, James	41	M	Painter	09Ap21Cg
DELAY, Patrick	15	M	None	09Ap21Cg
YOUNG, Charles	25	M	Tea Dealer	09Ap21Cg

NAMES OF PASSENGERS	A G E	S E X	OCCUPATIONS	DATE PORT SHIP
YOUNG, John	25	M	Farmer	09Ap21Cg
NICHOLDS, John	30	M	Goldbeater	09Ap21Cg
GILBERT, Henry	38	M	Saddler	09Ap21Cg
ADMONDS, Benjamen	12	M	Baker	09Ap21Cg
John	10	M	Baker	09Ap21Cg

DEVONSHIRE 10 APRIL 1846

From Liverpool

NAMES OF PASSENGERS	A G E	S E X	OCCUPATIONS	DATE PORT SHIP
WILLARD, P.C.	32	M	Farmer	10Ap02CI
KEARNS, Thomas	30	M	Laborer	10Ap02CI
FOLEY, Mary	20	F	Servant	10Ap02CI
MCKEARNIN, Mary	18	F	Servant	10Ap02CI
MCCARTY, Catherine	17	F	Servant	10Ap02CI
MCCUE, John	19	M	Laborer	10Ap02CI
MCGUIRE, John	28	M	Laborer	10Ap02CI
CORLEY, Pat.	32	M	Laborer	10Ap02CI
Ann (D)	02	F	Child	10Ap02CI
MASON, Wm.	21	M	Laborer	10Ap02CI
MARTIN, Honora	19	F	Servant	10Ap02CI
NOLAN, Mollcan	18	M	Laborer	10Ap02CI
GRIFFIN, Michael	18	M	Laborer	10Ap02CI
Mary	20	F	Servant	10Ap02CI
LEEDS, Andrew	17	M	Laborer	10Ap02CI
DOWDE, James	27	M	Laborer	10Ap02CI
MCMANNUS, Thomas	22	M	Laborer	10Ap02CI
DEGNAN, John	25	M	Laborer	10Ap02CI
CONNOUGHT, Mary	20	F	Servant	10Ap02CI
QUINN, Bridget	18	F	Servant	10Ap02CI
FLANIGAN, Mary	17	F	Servant	10Ap02CI
MEE, Bridget	17	F	Servant	10Ap02CI
DOLAN, Margaret	20	F	Servant	10Ap02CI
MCGARVIN, Ann	16	F	Servant	10Ap02CI
MCBRINE, Jane	20	F	Servant	10Ap02CI
MCGARVIN, Elen	16	F	Servant	10Ap02CI
BRADY, Mary	16	F	Servant	10Ap02CI
BENTLEY, John	32	M	Tailor	10Ap02CI
PILHEE, Charles	31	M	Laborer	10Ap02CI
HENRY, William	26	M	Laborer	10Ap02CI
DAVIDSON, Elizabeth	16	F	Dressmaker	10Ap02CI
MITCHEL, Elenor	17	F	Servant	10Ap02CI
THOMAS, Margaret	24	F	Servant	10Ap02CI
HENSLEY, Margaret	16	F	Dressmaker	10Ap02CI
SMITH, Martha	16	F	Servant	10Ap02CI
MILLER, Sarah-A.	16	F	Servant	10Ap02CI
HANSLEY, Robert	21	M	Laborer	10Ap02CI
MOURN, Michael	28	M	Laborer	10Ap02CI
VINEY, George	33	M	Laborer	10Ap02CI
ROACH, Mary	18	F	Servant	10Ap02CI
CANTWELL, Mary	16	F	Servant	10Ap02CI
CLARK, Mary	19	F	Servant	10Ap02CI
FOGERTY, Thomas	18	M	Laborer	10Ap02CI
John	17	M	Laborer	10Ap02CI
DOYLE, Willey	36	M	Laborer	10Ap02CI
BETTRIGE, John	34	M	Laborer	10Ap02CI
KAYHO, Paul	19	M	Laborer	10Ap02CI
MCDONALD, Chas.	20	M	Servant	10Ap02CI
LEONARD, Bridget	18	F	Servant	10Ap02CI
DONAHOE, Mary	18	F	Servant	10Ap02CI
MCGUIRE, Mary	19	F	Servant	10Ap02CI
RILEY, Mary	19	F	Servant	10Ap02CI
SHERIDAN, Mary	19	F	Servant	10Ap02CI
RILEY, Mary	28	F	Servant	10Ap02CI
MCDONALD, James	20	M	Laborer	10Ap02CI
MANERING, James	28	M	Servant	10Ap02CI
Margaret	26	F	Servant	10Ap02CI
BRABERSON, Chas.	25	M	Farmer	10Ap02CI
Henry	28	M	Farmer	10Ap02CI

NAMES OF PASSENGERS	A G E	S E X	OCCUPATIONS	DATE PORT SHIP	NAMES OF PASSENGERS	A G E	S E X	OCCUPATIONS	DATE PORT SHIP
HARDING, Michael	50	M	Farmer	10Ap02CI	MCDONALD, Pat	21	M	Laborer	10Ap02CI
MILLER, Susan	18	F	Servant	10Ap02CI	LASTRANGE, Mary	18	F	Servant	10Ap02CI
LAULER, Catherine	17	F	Servant	10Ap02CI	ROWLAND, Mercy	22	F	Servant	10Ap02CI
GOSS, Margaret	16	F	Servant	10Ap02CI	GIBBIN, Pat	23	M	Laborer	10Ap02CI
MCGOOKIN, Patrick	22	M	Laborer	10Ap02CI	MICKELHILL, Michael	17	M	Laborer	10Ap02CI
WILLIAMS, Wm.	20	M	Laborer	10Ap02CI	FLANAGAN, Michael	21	M	Laborer	10Ap02CI
SWEENEY, Pat	20	M	Laborer	10Ap02CI	COVEY, Helen	14	F	Servant	10Ap02CI
VALANTINE, Peter	18	M	Laborer	10Ap02CI	LINCH, Susan	16	F	Servant	10Ap02CI
DEERING, James	20	M	Laborer	10Ap02CI	Margaret	18	F	Servant	10Ap02CI
DAILEY, Thos.	35	M	Laborer	10Ap02CI	RILEY, James	30	M	Servant	10Ap02CI
CLAREY, John	20	M	Laborer	10Ap02CI	Betsey	20	F	Servant	10Ap02CI
MALEY, James	19	M	Laborer	10Ap02CI	BEARD, Eliza	20	F	Servant	10Ap02CI
KANE, Pat	19	M	Laborer	10Ap02CI	FARLEY, Bridget	16	F	Servant	10Ap02CI
DROMGOOLD, Judy	18	F	Servant	10Ap02CI	Bridget	19	F	Servant	10Ap02CI
HOMES, Mary	20	F	Servant	10Ap02CI	SMITH, Edward	20	M	Servant	10Ap02CI
KEW, Margaret	16	F	Servant	10Ap02CI	POLEND, Hugh	29	M	Laborer	10Ap02CI
RILEY, Danl.	19	M	Laborer	10Ap02CI	BOOGY, Martin	25	M	Laborer	10Ap02CI
GAFNEY, Peter	20	M	Laborer	10Ap02CI	GORY, Thomas	28	M	Laborer	10Ap02CI
DALE, Andrew	21	M	Laborer	10Ap02CI	HAVANAH, Mary	18	F	Servant	10Ap02CI
KAINE, Patrick	24	M	Laborer	10Ap02CI	WHALIN, Eliza	19	F	Servant	10Ap02CI
MURRY, Thos.	20	M	Laborer	10Ap02CI	LAMB, Julia	19	F	Servant	10Ap02CI
SHELDIN, Robert	18	M	Laborer	10Ap02CI	COCHRANE, James	25	M	Laborer	10Ap02CI
CORMICK, Thos.	20	M	Laborer	10Ap02CI	DAGGIN, William	22	M	Laborer	10Ap02CI
NOOLAN, Catharine	18	F	Servant	10Ap02CI	LINNEN, Pat	22	M	Laborer	10Ap02CI
FALLEN, Edward	18	M	Laborer	10Ap02CI	MARK, Pat	20	M	Servant	10Ap02CI
GIBNEY, Ann	19	F	Servant	10Ap02CI	LENNON, Pat	22	M	Servant	10Ap02CI
MURRY, Mary	16	F	Servant	10Ap02CI	DEGNON, Margaret	14	F	Servant	10Ap02CI
GAINES, Ann	16	F	Servant	10Ap02CI	Honora	15	F	Servant	10Ap02CI
BIRD, Michael	30	M	Laborer	10Ap02CI	KELLERAN, Bridget	18	F	Servant	10Ap02CI
BRINE, Bartlett	22	M	Laborer	10Ap02CI	LINCH, James	20	M	Servant	10Ap02CI
HARMON, Arthur	20	M	Laborer	10Ap02CI	Ann	20	F	Servant	10Ap02CI
WHALEN, Joseph	21	M	Laborer	10Ap02CI	BOWNAN, Mercia	18	F	Servant	10Ap02CI
Laurence	20	M	Laborer	10Ap02CI	LEONARD, Anna	18	F	Servant	10Ap02CI
TOOLE, Martin	21	M	Laborer	10Ap02CI	CAUDRY, Ann	16	F	Servant	10Ap02CI
CONOLY, Wm.	30	M	Laborer	10Ap02CI	DOLAN, Helen	17	F	Servant	10Ap02CI
MCCLINTOCK, William	20	M	Laborer	10Ap02CI	Ann	16	F	Servant	10Ap02CI
WOODS, James	22	M	Laborer	10Ap02CI	TURLEY, Mary	19	F	Servant	10Ap02CI
MURPHY, Michael	28	M	Laborer	10Ap02CI	Rosey	17	F	Servant	10Ap02CI
RILEY, Ann	16	F	Milliner	10Ap02CI	FANNON, Jane	20	F	Servant	10Ap02CI
CULVIN, Ann	18	F	Dressmaker	10Ap02CI	BRENON, Patrick	24	M	Laborer	10Ap02CI
RILEY, Pat	19	M	Servant	10Ap02CI	CAREY, James	18	M	Laborer	10Ap02CI
DENPSEY, Mary	19	F	Servant	10Ap02CI	MOREY, John	20	M	Laborer	10Ap02CI
Edward	21	M	Servant	10Ap02CI	BRADY, Phillip	20	M	Laborer	10Ap02CI
LORINER, Michael	24	M	Laborer	10Ap02CI	HENESEY, Charles	18	M	Laborer	10Ap02CI
MURPHY, Margaret	25	F	Servant	10Ap02CI	OHARA, Patrick	18	M	Laborer	10Ap02CI
Catharine	16	F	Servant	10Ap02CI	DONOHER, John	18	M	Laborer	10Ap02CI
HICKEY, Catharine	21	F	Servant	10Ap02CI	GOTREY, Catharine	25	F	Servant	10Ap02CI
FARRELL, Margaret	18	F	Servant	10Ap02CI	HENRY, Mary	20	F	Servant	10Ap02CI
CALOLA, Margaret	20	F	Servant	10Ap02CI	HERVES, Helen	17	F	Servant	10Ap02CI
HANLEY, Ann	16	F	Servant	10Ap02CI	TELLEY, Rosa	20	F	Servant	10Ap02CI
SHIELDS, Ann	20	F	Servant	10Ap02CI	JONES, Thomas	21	M	Laborer	10Ap02CI
WELDEN, James	18	M	Laborer	10Ap02CI	HALPIN, Bridget	19	F	Servant	10Ap02CI
WILDER, Pat	22	M	Laborer	10Ap02CI	SMITH, Helen	19	F	Servant	10Ap02CI
WELDEN, Jane	16	F	Servant	10Ap02CI	GARAGIN, Mary	17	F	Servant	10Ap02CI
MCCORMICK, Mary	20	F	Servant	10Ap02CI	DUFFEE, Margaret	20	F	Servant	10Ap02CI
Kitty	18	F	Servant	10Ap02CI	TRACY, James	30	M	Laborer	10Ap02CI
DOWD, Biddy	16	F	Servant	10Ap02CI	Catharine (W)	29	F	Wife	10Ap02CI
LOW, Mary	18	F	Servant	10Ap02CI	Sarah (D)	03	F	Child	10Ap02CI
MURRY, Dennis	20	M	Laborer	10Ap02CI	Thomas (S)	01	M	Child	10Ap02CI
LOWE, Thomas	20	M	Laborer	10Ap02CI	PURDY, Patrick	24	M	Laborer	10Ap02CI
DOWD, Thomas	18	M	Laborer	10Ap02CI	ROONEY, Catharine	15	F	Servant	10Ap02CI
MCGUIRE, Sisily	18	F	Servant	10Ap02CI	Eliza	18	F	Servant	10Ap02CI
SCANLIN, Michael	30	M	Laborer	10Ap02CI	Pat	18	M	Laborer	10Ap02CI
WELCH, Thomas	21	M	Laborer	10Ap02CI	REED, Mary	17	F	Servant	10Ap02CI
GALLIGHER, John	18	M	Laborer	10Ap02CI	FARLAND, Michael	20	M	Laborer	10Ap02CI
GORMELY, Thomas	25	M	Laborer	10Ap02CI	ROWLAN, John	16	M	Laborer	10Ap02CI
BATICAN, Michael	23	M	Laborer	10Ap02CI	REYNOLDS, Mathew	22	M	Laborer	10Ap02CI
DILLAN, Thomas	40	M	Courier	10Ap02CI	HAGGERTY, Mary	50	F	Servant	10Ap02CI
GRIFFITH, Morgan	30	M	Weaver	10Ap02CI	CORCLE, Mary	19	F	Servant	10Ap02CI
HIND, Daniel	40	M	Laborer	10Ap02CI	CASEDY, Margaret	19	F	Servant	10Ap02CI
TERRY, James	16	M	Laborer	10Ap02CI	BIRD, John	20	M	Laborer	10Ap02CI
MOORE, Pat	18	M	Laborer	10Ap02CI	Pat	18	M	Laborer	10Ap02CI
CUSACK, Edward	17	M	Laborer	10Ap02CI	HARY, Niel	20	M	Laborer	10Ap02CI
DIVINE, Mathew	25	M	Laborer	10Ap02CI	LINCH, Hugh	18	M	Laborer	10Ap02CI
FEATHERSON, Hugh	27	M	Laborer	10Ap02CI	CALIVAN, James	21	M	Laborer	10Ap02CI

NAMES OF PASSENGERS		AGE	SEX	OCCUPATIONS	DATE PORT SHIP
CALIVAN, James		20	M	Laborer	1CAp02CI
GARATY, Pat		22	M	Laborer	1CAp02CI
LARKIN, John		20	M	Laborer	1CAp02CI
MALOY, Ann		16	F	Servant	10Ap02CI
DUNLEYLEE, Bridget		18	F	Servant	10Ap02CI
GARATY, Catharine		17	F	Servant	10Ap02CI
DUFFY, Mary		19	F	Servant	10Ap02CI
RAFFERTY, Ann		25	F	Servant	10Ap02CI
ODONEL, Betsey		22	F	Servant	10Ap02CI
REILEY, Helen		23	F	Servant	10Ap02CI
LEONARD, Mary		36	F	Servant	10Ap02CI
Thomas	(S)	13	M	Laborer	1CAp02CI
Bridget	(D)	10	F	None	10Ap02CI
William	(S)	07	M	Child	1CAp02CI
Mary	(D)	05	F	Chilc	1CAp02CI
BRINE, Olly		18	F	Servent	10Ap02CI
HUGHES, Ann		22	F	Servant	10Ap02CI
MCKEARN, Mary		20	F	Servant	10Ap02CI
KELLY, Helen		18	F	Servant	10Ap02CI
HANLEY, Naby		20	F	Servant	10Ap02CI
CASEY, Mary		15	F	Servant	10Ap02CI
CLINCH, Biddy		20	F	Servant	10Ap02CI
HUGHES, John		20	M	Mason	10Ap02CI
EGNEW, John		20	M	Servant	10Ap02CI
HIGGINS, Mary		18	F	Servant	10Ap02CI
Mary		13	F	Servant	10Ap02CI
COONIER, Mary		19	F	Servant	10Ap02CI
DAVIS, Michael		30	M	Laborer	1CAp02CI
MCCORMICK, William		20	M	Laborer	1CAp02CI
SLAN, Patrick		19	M	Laborer	10Ap02CI
KENNEDY, Dennis		40	M	Slater	10Ap02CI
Pat.		18	M	Slater	10Ap02CI
BOYLE, Peter		20	M	Laborer	10Ap02CI
REYNOLDS, Barney		22	M	Laborer	10Ap02CI
WILSON, Peter		19	M	Laborer	10Ap02CI
FARLEE, Michael		17	M	Laborer	1CAp02CI
COLLINS, Kitty		18	F	Servant	10Ap02CI
KANE, Anna		18	F	Servant	10Ap02CI
DIVINE, Mary		18	F	Servant	10Ap02CI
MCBRADY, Hugh		24	M	Laborer	10Ap02CI
DOWD, James		20	M	Laborer	10Ap02CI
LEE, Hugh		24	M	Laborer	10Ap02CI
Anna		22	F	Servant	10Ap02CI
Miles		12	M	Laborer	10Ap02CI
Edward		14	M	Laborer	10Ap02CI
MCGATHEN, Larry		21	M	Laborer	10Ap02CI
BALOLEY, James		21	M	Laborer	10Ap02CI
BRAWLEY, Susan		21	F	Laborer	10Ap02CI
MCMERRYMAN, Rosa		20	F	Servant	10Ap02CI
CREED, Bridget		21	F	Servant	10Ap02CI
LINCH, Peter		17	M	Laborer	10Ap02CI
MCLEAGUE, James		24	M	Laborer	10Ap02CI
Mary		20	F	Servent	10Ap02CI
Hugh		19	M	Laborer	10Ap02CI
Mary		17	F	Servant	10Ap02CI
MCGORBIN, Mary		21	F	Servant	10Ap02CI
FOX, Mary		21	F	Servant	10Ap02CI
Jane		24	F	Servant	10Ap02CI
HAMMOND, John		18	M	Laborer	10Ap02CI
CLARK, Rosa		20	F	Servant	10Ap02CI
SHIELDS, Michael		19	M	Laborer	10Ap02CI
RILEY, Edward		20	M	Laborer	10Ap02CI
FACKLAND, Bernard		24	N	Laborer	10Ap02CI
HARTIN, Pat.		20	M	Laborer	10Ap02CI
SMITH, Harry		20	M	Laborer	10Ap02CI
DIGNAL, Mary		20	F	Servent	10Ap02CI
FARREL, Margaret		20	F	Servant	10Ap02CI
RILEY, Catharine		18	F	Servant	10Ap02CI

ADIRONDACK 11 APRIL 1846

From Cork

NAMES OF PASSENGERS		AGE	SEX	OCCUPATIONS	DATE PORT SHIP
TRACEY, John		56	M	Mechanic	11Ap14Cm
Mary-Ann	(W)	55	F	Wife	11Ap14Cm
STOKES, Jane		30	F	None	11Ap14Cm
Mary-Ann	(D)	08	F	Chila	11Ap14Cm
TRACEY, Mary-Ann		26	F	None	11Ap14Cm
THOMPSON, Hannah		46	F	None	11Ap14Cm
LOMBARD, Margaret		28	F	None	11Ap14Cm
BURNS, Bridget		20	F	None	11Ap14Cm
Joanna		15	F	None	11Ap14Cm
TOBIN, Morris		20	M	Laborer	11Ap14Cm
Joanna		30	F	None	11Ap14Cm
Mary		25	F	None	11Ap14Cm
CARROLL, Mary		21	F	None	11Ap14Cm
WELSH, James		27	M	Laborer	11Ap14Cm
Bridget		27	F	None	11Ap14Cm
MURPHY, Bridget		25	F	None	11Ap14Cm
Edwd.		17	M	Laborer	11Ap14Cm
Michael		C1	M	Child	11Ap14Cm
OREILLY, Pat.		21	M	Carpenter	11Ap14Cm
PARKER, Thos.		40	M	Laborer	11Ap14Cm
DWYER, Danl.		24	M	Laborer	11Ap14Cm
Mary	(W)	25	F	Wife	11Ap14Cm
Hannah	(D)	01	F	Child	11Ap14Cm
MOUNTAIN, Mary		19	F	None	11Ap14Cm
GRAY, James		25	M	Laborer	11Ap14Cm
MCSHENEDY, Jno.		26	M	Laborer	11Ap14Cm
CONDIN, Pat.		30	M	Gdnr	11Ap14Cm
Catherire	(W)	25	F	Wife	11Ap14Cm
Mary-Ann	(D)	03	F	Child	11Ap14Cm
John	(S)	01	M	Child	11Ap14Cm
CONNELL, Charles		23	M	Laborer	11Ap14Cm
Margaret		24	F	None	11Ap14Cm
FLYNN, Mary		23	F	None	11Ap14Cm
LYONS, Mary		23	F	None	11Ap14Cm
LEAHY, Wm.		25	M	Farmer	11Ap14Cm
TWOHY, James		24	M	Carpenter	11Ap14Cm
KELLAHER, Lawrence		23	M	Laborer	11Ap14Cm
Mary		19	F	None	11Ap14Cm
EARRY, Thos.		19	M	Laborer	11Ap14Cm
MURPHY, John		26	M	Shoemaker	11Ap14Cm
Mary		16	F	None	11Ap14Cm
SCANLEN, John		20	M	None	11Ap14Cm
TWISS, Henrietta		18	F	None	11Ap14Cm
GREEN, Wm.		30	M	Shoemaker	11Ap14Cm
Catherire	(W)	28	F	Wife	11Ap14Cm
Rebecca	(D)	09	F	Child	11Ap14Cm
Mary	(D)	C7	F	Child	11Ap14Cm
John	(S)	05	M	Child	11Ap14Cm
Elizabeth	(D)	01	F	Child	11Ap14Cm
KELLAHER, Norah		22	F	None	11Ap14Cm
Joanna		21	F	None	11Ap14Cm
COLBERT, James		26	M	Laborer	11Ap14Cm
MCCARTHY, Margaret		29	F	None	11Ap14Cm
Mary	(D)	10	F	None	11Ap14Cm
CROWLEY, John		30	M	Gdnr	11Ap14Cm
MCGRATH, Edwd.		28	M	Laborer	11Ap14Cm
Ellen		30	F	None	11Ap14Cm
HEMPSEY, Margaret		20	F	None	11Ap14Cm
MCCOXEN, Eliza		19	F	None	11Ap14Cm
HALEY, Thos.		22	M	Accountant	11Ap14Cm
KNOWLES, Wm.		28	M	Laborer	11Ap14Cm
KEEFE, David		39	M	Laborer	11Ap14Cm
WELSH, Michael		26	M	Laborer	11Ap14Cm
SHEE, Richd.		20	M	Laborer	11Ap14Cm
OWEN, Pat.		24	M	Laborer	11Ap14Cm

34

NAMES OF PASSENGERS	A G E	S E X	OCCUPATIONS	DATE PORT SHIP	NAMES OF PASSENGERS	A G E	S E X	OCCUPATIONS	DATE PORT SHIP
BONHIG, Timothy	24	M	Laborer	11Ap14Cm	CARROLL, John	(S) .06	M	Infant	11Ap14Cm
Hannah	27	F	None	11Ap14Cm	KENNEDY, Charles	32	M	Surgeon	11Ap14Cm
SULLIVAN, Catherine	30	F	None	11Ap14Cm	SHEA, Harriet	30	F	None	11Ap14Cm
COLLIGHAN, Henry	22	M	Gdnr	11Ap14Cm	Mary-Ann	(D) .08	F	Infant	11Ap14Cm
TARRANT, Sarah	21	F	None	11Ap14Cm	LYNCH, Michael	22	M	Laborer	11Ap14Cm
DEENAN, Mary	20	F	None	11Ap14Cm	SCANLIN, John	23	M	Laborer	11Ap14Cm
MAHONEY, Catherine	20	F	None	11Ap14Cm	LANTCN, Norah	24	F	None	11Ap14Cm
PIGOT, Mary	29	F	None	11Ap14Cm	GAMBLE, Mary	22	F	None	11Ap14Cm
BRIAN, Timothy	18	M	Laborer	11Ap14Cm	RYAN, Mary	23	F	None	11Ap14Cm
CONNOR, Catherine	19	F	None	11Ap14Cm	DALY, Mary	17	F	None	11Ap14Cm
MCCARTHY, Justin	26	M	Smith	11Ap14Cm	Betty	18	F	None	11Ap14Cm
HART, Margaret	21	F	None	11Ap14Cm	FLEMING, Cathe.	20	F	None	11Ap14Cm
BERRY, Fanny	21	F	None	11Ap14Cm	DONOVAN, Thos.	21	M	Laborer	11Ap14Cm
MCCARTHY, John	20	M	Laborer	11Ap14Cm	OBRIEN, Dennis	31	M	Laborer	11Ap14Cm
Dennis	26	M	Laborer	11Ap14Cm	Catherine	(W) 28	F	Wife	11Ap14Cm
Joanna	25	F	None	11Ap14Cm	Honora	(M) 50	F	None	11Ap14Cm
Mary	27	F	None	11Ap14Cm	Ann	(D) 03	F	Child	11Ap14Cm
Margaret	40	F	None	11Ap14Cm	Mary	(D) 01	F	Child	11Ap14Cm
Florence	.06	F	Infant	11Ap14Cm	COLEMAN, Ellen	50	F	None	11Ap14Cm
WREN, John	23	M	Gameskeeper	11Ap14Cm	Peggy	(D) 20	F	None	11Ap14Cm
FORAN, Edwd.	35	M	Laborer	11Ap14Cm	Catherine	(D) 21	F	None	11Ap14Cm
LONG, Thos.	30	M	Tanner	11Ap14Cm	Joanna	(D) 12	F	None	11Ap14Cm
COLLINS, John	22	M	Laborer	11Ap14Cm	May	(D) 11	F	None	11Ap14Cm
DONNAVAN, Dennis	22	M	Laborer	11Ap14Cm	Patrick	(S) 10	M	None	11Ap14Cm
COTTER, Thos.	35	M	Laborer	11Ap14Cm	Dennis	(S) 13	M	None	11Ap14Cm
DILL, Betsey	20	F	None	11Ap14Cm	CURRAN, Pat.	27	M	Carpenter	11Ap14Cm
LEARY, Thos.	24	M	Laborer	11Ap14Cm	QUINLAN, Elizth.	64	F	None	11Ap14Cm
HARRINGTON, Mary	20	F	None	11Ap14Cm	CAREY, Mary	14	F	None	11Ap14Cm
WREN, Margaret	24	F	None	11Ap14Cm	HOOLAHAN, Norah	12	F	None	11Ap14Cm
John	(S) 01	M	Child	11Ap14Cm	CARY, Cathe.	08	F	Child	11Ap14Cm
BROWN, James	50	M	Shoemaker	11Ap14Cm	HOOLAHAN, Cathe.	05	F	Child	11Ap14Cm
Michael	(S) 01	M	Child	11Ap14Cm	LANE, David	14	M	None	11Ap14Cm
FITZPATRICK, Pat	24	M	Laborer	11Ap14Cm	John	12	M	None	11Ap14Cm
Matthew	22	M	Laborer	11Ap14Cm	HARRINGTON, Matthew	19	M	None	11Ap14Cm
Jeremiah	25	M	None	11Ap14Cm	Joanna	30	F	None	11Ap14Cm
John	18	M	None	11Ap14Cm	Mary	(D) 06	F	Child	11Ap14Cm
Jeremiah	08	M	Child	11Ap14Cm	Philip	(S) 04	M	Child	11Ap14Cm
Margaret	20	F	None	11Ap14Cm	ROOING, Joanna	30	F	None	11Ap14Cm
Mary	24	F	None	11Ap14Cm	BARRY, Ann	19	F	None	11Ap14Cm
Catherine	10	F	None	11Ap14Cm	CONDEN, John	30	M	Farmer	11Ap14Cm
Helen	20	F	None	11Ap14Cm	LANE, Dennis	30	M	Farmer	11Ap14Cm
Mary	60	F	None	11Ap14Cm	Timothy	18	M	Farmer	11Ap14Cm
Catherine	30	F	None	11Ap14Cm	BARRY, Michael	12	M	None	11Ap14Cm
CROTTY, Wm.	21	M	Laborer	11Ap14Cm	SHERLOCK, Thos.	20	M	Laborer	11Ap14Cm
GLEESON, Michael	22	M	Laborer	11Ap14Cm	SULLIVAN, John	20	M	Laborer	11Ap14Cm
LINEHAN, Richd.	22	M	Laborer	11Ap14Cm	Corn.	20	M	Laborer	11Ap14Cm
GRIFFEN, John	19	M	Laborer	11Ap14Cm	FORD, Patrick	22	M	Laborer	11Ap14Cm
Margaret	24	F	None	11Ap14Cm	HIGGINS, Margaret	18	F	None	11Ap14Cm
Joanna	10	F	None	11Ap14Cm	Eliza	16	F	None	11Ap14Cm
GUINESS, Honora	20	F	None	11Ap14Cm					
GOGGIN, Thos.	20	M	Laborer	11Ap14Cm					
WELSH, Joanna	24	F	None	11Ap14Cm					
MULHEARY, Catherine	20	F	None	11Ap14Cm					
FITZGERALD, Elizabeth	23	F	None	11Ap14Cm					
DARRAN, Martha	21	F	None	11Ap14Cm	QUEEN-OF-THE-WEST 11 APRIL 1846				
Mary-Ann	20	F	None	11Ap14Cm					
Anastasia	50	F	None	11Ap14Cm	From Liverpool				
George	24	M	Chtmr	11Ap14Cm					
George-Jr.	.06	M	Infant	11Ap14Cm					
TOOMEY, Thos.	27	M	Laborer	11Ap14Cm					
MCOBOY, Lawrence	17	M	Laborer	11Ap14Cm	MILLS, John	21	M	Laborer	11Ap02Cn
SHORT, Augustine	23	M	Laborer	11Ap14Cm	EARLY, Luke	24	M	Laborer	11Ap02Cn
DALY, Cathe.	22	F	None	11Ap14Cm	Mary	24	F	None	11Ap02Cn
BARRY, Cathe.	19	F	None	11Ap14Cm	KENNEDY, Owen	24	M	Laborer	11Ap02Cn
DALY, Ellen	23	F	None	11Ap14Cm	CONLON, Margaret	20	F	None	11Ap02Cn
AHERN, Corns.	40	M	Butcher	11Ap14Cm	NEARY, Bridget	20	F	None	11Ap02Cn
DESMOND, Dennis	29	M	Laborer	11Ap14Cm	BOYLE, Bridget	18	F	None	11Ap02Cn
KEANE, Joanna	20	F	None	11Ap14Cm	MCCAVEN, James	20	M	Laborer	11Ap02Cn
FLEMING, Catherine	20	F	None	11Ap14Cm	Mary	20	F	None	11Ap02Cn
SHEA, John	22	M	Laborer	11Ap14Cm	NEWCOMBE, Rose	18	F	None	11Ap02Cn
BARRY, David	24	M	Laborer	11Ap14Cm	MCGAHEN, Mary	16	F	None	11Ap02Cn
DRISCOLL, Dennis	22	M	Laborer	11Ap14Cm	TRAYNOR, Mary	20	F	None	11Ap02Cn
Ellen	00	F	None	11Ap14Cm	MURTHA, Owen	20	M	Laborer	11Ap02Cn
CARROLL, Edwd.	28	M	Carpenter	11Ap14Cm	CUNNINGHAM, Pat	18	M	Laborer	11Ap02Cn
Joanna	(W) 20	F	Wife	11Ap14Cm	KELLY, Richard	23	M	Laborer	11Ap02Cn

NAMES OF PASSENGERS		AGE	SEX	OCCUPATIONS	DATE PORT SHIP
KELLY, Ann		22	F	None	11Ap02Cn
NEWCOMBE, Bernard		23	M	Laborer	11Ap02Cn
DOWNEY, Martha		13	F	Laborer	11Ap02Cn
MCILROY, Margaret		20	F	None	11Ap02Cn
MCMEEHAN, Mary		20	F	None	11Ap02Cn
CUNNINGHAM, Edwd.		15	M	Laborer	11Ap02Cn
SCANLAN, Margaret		25	F	None	11Ap02Cn
WHITEHEAD, Charles		40	M	Blacksmith	11Ap02Cn
CAHAN, Michael		21	M	Laborer	11Ap02Cn
SMITH, Maria		22	F	None	11Ap02Cn
Bridget	(D)	02	F	Child	11Ap02Cn
CROSSIN, Michael		21	M	Laborer	11Ap02Cn
Catherine		21	F	None	11Ap02Cn
RILEY, Edwd.		29	M	Laborer	11Ap02Cn
DOOLAN, Michael		22	M	Laborer	11Ap02Cn
BENNETT, Thos.		20	M	Rope Maker	11Ap02Cn
DOORLEY, Catherine		10	F	None	11Ap02Cn
CLARKE, Patrick		20	M	Laborer	11Ap02Cn
GILLICK, Bridget		20	F	None	11Ap02Cn
SHERIDAN, Judy		20	F	None	11Ap02Cn
KELLY, Catherine		18	F	None	11Ap02Cn
SWEENY, Margaret		15	F	None	11Ap02Cn
HARRINGTON, Patrick		21	M	Laborer	11Ap02Cn
NOOLAN, James		23	M	Laborer	11Ap02Cn
MOONEY, Bernard		18	M	Mason	11Ap02Cn
DEVLIN, Bridget		26	F	None	11Ap02Cn
Catherine	(D)	03	F	Child	11Ap02Cn
CAREY, Patrick		21	M	Laborer	11Ap02Cn
STANS, Bernard		19	M	Laborer	11Ap02Cn
NESBITT, Charles		22	M	Gameskeeper	11Ap02Cn
MITCHELL, Isabella		11	F	None	11Ap02Cn
RILEY, Catherine		12	F	None	11Ap02Cn
MCCAFFEY, Ellen		32	F	None	11Ap02Cn
SEXTON, Michael		12	M	None	11Ap02Cn
SMALL, Mary		22	F	None	11Ap02Cn
Mary	(D)	01	F	Child	11Ap02Cn
TIGHE, Ann		34	F	None	11Ap02Cn
Bernard	(S)	11	M	Child	11Ap02Cn
Maria	(D)	09	F	Child	11Ap02Cn
Matthew	(S)	07	M	Child	11Ap02Cn
GLASGOW, Margaret		25	F	None	11Ap02Cn
Catherine	(D)	02	F	Child	11Ap02Cn
FAGAN, Margaret		12	F	None	11Ap02Cn
MCANALLY, Catherine		19	F	None	11Ap02Cn
SMITH, Thos.		21	M	Laborer	11Ap02Cn
Susan		18	F	None	11Ap02Cn
FLOOD, Bridget		18	F	None	11Ap02Cn
MCDOWELL, Robt.		32	M	Farmer	11Ap02Cn
Margaret	(W)	36	F	Wife	11Ap02Cn
John	(S)	09	M	Child	11Ap02Cn
Jane	(D)	07	F	Child	11Ap02Cn
Robert	(S)	05	M	Child	11Ap02Cn
Margaret	(D)	03	F	Child	11Ap02Cn
WALLS, Thos.		50	M	Butcher	11Ap02Cn
Bridget	(W)	48	F	Wife	11Ap02Cn
Patrick	(S)	13	M	None	11Ap02Cn
Thomas	(S)	11	M	None	11Ap02Cn
Margaret	(D)	06	F	Child	11Ap02Cn
Catherine	(D)	08	F	Child	11Ap02Cn
Bridget	(D)	04	F	Child	11Ap02Cn
MCKANN, John		25	M	Laborer	11Ap02Cn
DONNELLY, Michael		50	M	Laborer	11Ap02Cn
Mary	(W)	40	F	Wife	11Ap02Cn
Eliza	(D)	12	F	None	11Ap02Cn
Susan	(D)	04	F	Child	11Ap02Cn
Ellen	(D)	10	F	Child	11Ap02Cn
James	(S)	08	M	Child	11Ap02Cn
Pat	(S)	06	M	Child	11Ap02Cn
GRADY, Harriet		13	F	None	11Ap02Cn
Lucy		06	F	Child	11Ap02Cn
BOYD, Jane		30	F	None	11Ap02Cn
Ezekiel	(S)	10	M	Child	11Ap02Cn
ATKINSON, Rhody		18	M	Blacksmith	11Ap02Cn
Rosey		13	F	None	11Ap02Cn
Susan		10	F	None	11Ap02Cn

NAMES OF PASSENGERS		AGE	SEX	OCCUPATIONS	DATE PORT SHIP
MCGEE, Joseph		18	M	Laborer	11Ap02Cn
DONOHOE, Mary		18	F	None	11Ap02Cn
KELLY, Ann		17	F	None	11Ap02Cn
MALLON, James		22	M	Laborer	11Ap02Cn
GRIFFIN, Bridget		35	F	None	11Ap02Cn
MCCARTHY, James		30	M	Laborer	11Ap02Cn
Ann	(W)	30	F	Wife	11Ap02Cn
Timothy	(S)	02	M	Child	11Ap02Cn
MCAULIFF, Timothy		21	M	Laborer	11Ap02Cn
CALLAGHAN, Ann		20	F	None	11Ap02Cn
MCCARTHY, Thos.		03	M	Child	11Ap02Cn
KEARY, Ellen		27	F	None	11Ap02Cn
Letitia	(D)	06	F	Child	11Ap02Cn
John	(S)	04	M	Child	11Ap02Cn
FARLEY, Margaret		16	F	None	11Ap02Cn
FLINN, Jane		19	F	None	11Ap02Cn
BURN, Peggy		24	F	None	11Ap02Cn
NUGENT, Catherine		19	F	None	11Ap02Cn
KELLY, Michail		26	M	Btmkr-Shmk	11Ap02Cn
Barbara	(W)	28	F	Wife	11Ap02Cn
John	(S)	01	M	Child	11Ap02Cn
STEWART, Ellen		20	F	None	11Ap02Cn
DONOGHOE, Mary		20	F	None	11Ap02Cn
Margaret		18	F	None	11Ap02Cn
GREGORY, Rebecca		20	F	None	11Ap02Cn
PATTERSON, Hannah		28	F	None	11Ap02Cn
SHANNON, Patrick		21	M	Laborer	11Ap02Cn
GRIFFIN, Michail		20	M	Laborer	11Ap02Cn
Ann		18	F	None	11Ap02Cn
SCANLAN, Patrick		20	M	Farmer	11Ap02Cn
LYNCH, Patrick		21	M	Laborer	11Ap02Cn
DONOHOE, Patrick		19	M	Laborer	11Ap02Cn
CASEY, Brian		25	M	Carpenter	11Ap02Cn
RILEY, Felix		17	M	Laborer	11Ap02Cn
KELLY, John		20	M	Laborer	11Ap02Cn
RILEY, John		17	M	Laborer	11Ap02Cn
MONAGHAN, Mary		20	F	None	11Ap02Cn
RILEY, Ann		16	F	None	11Ap02Cn
DUFF, Margaret		70	F	None	11Ap02Cn
DEVLIN, Mark		18	M	Laborer	11Ap02Cn
CHATTAN, Catherine-M.L		15	F	None	11Ap02Cn
CORNWALL, John		27	M	Laborer	11Ap02Cn
NOONAN, Patrick		26	M	Laborer	11Ap02Cn
SULLIVAN, Ellen		26	F	None	11Ap02Cn
HALLIRAY, Honora		20	F	None	11Ap02Cn
BUCKLEY, Johanna		20	F	None	11Ap02Cn
MCABER, Catherine		19	F	None	11Ap02Cn
BROWN, Thos.		25	M	Laborer	11Ap02Cn
NOONAN, James		24	M	Laborer	11Ap02Cn
BRIDGAN, Ann		18	F	None	11Ap02Cn
BATTERSBY, John		13	M	Laborer	11Ap02Cn
MCANASTY, Ann		20	F	None	11Ap02Cn
GARTLAN, Judy		18	F	None	11Ap02Cn
CORRIGAN, Thomas		47	M	Laborer	11Ap02Cn
Judith	(W)	47	F	Wife	11Ap02Cn
Ann	(D)	13	F	None	11Ap02Cn
FARLEY, Mary		16	F	None	11Ap02Cn
CORRIGAN, Bridget		12	F	None	11Ap02Cn
Judith		10	F	None	11Ap02Cn
Thomas		08	M	Laborer	11Ap02Cn
Rose		06	F	Child	11Ap02Cn
GARTLAN, Ann		20	F	None	11Ap02Cn
DELANY, Michael		25	M	Laborer	11Ap02Cn
RILEY, James		18	M	Laborer	11Ap02Cn
DONOHOE, James		30	M	Farmer	11Ap02Cn
DOONEY, Ann		28	F	None	11Ap02Cn
DONOHGO, Ann		08	F	Child	11Ap02Cn
Thomas		07	M	Child	11Ap02Cn
John		02	M	Child	11Ap02Cn
HUGHES, Mary		20	F	None	11Ap02Cn
BRADLEY, Eliza		21	F	None	11Ap02Cn
MCCANN, Margaret		20	F	None	11Ap02Cn
OWENS, Bridget		30	F	None	11Ap02Cn
FERGUSON, Alexander		25	M	Saddler	11Ap02Cn

NAMES OF PASSENGERS	AGE	SEX	OCCUPATIONS	DATE PORT SHIP	NAMES OF PASSENGERS	AGE	SEX	OCCUPATIONS	DATE PORT SHIP
FERGUSON, Mary (W)	23	F	Wife	11Ap02Cn	NORRIS, Patrick	30	M	Laborer	11Ap02Cn
James (S)	01	M	Child	11Ap02Cn	HUGHES, Mary	20	F	None	11Ap02Cn
CORRIGAN, Peter	18	M	Laborer	11Ap02Cn	SEALLY, Mary	18	F	None	11Ap02Cn
Alexander	18	M	Laborer	11Ap02Cn	FARLEY, Peter	25	M	Laborer	11Ap02Cn
GUSLIN, Catherine	18	F	None	11Ap02Cn	COONEY, Catherine	20	F	None	11Ap02Cn
DOHERTY, Margery	20	F	None	11Ap02Cn	MCNEAL, Mary	20	F	None	11Ap02Cn
HART, Wm.	30	M	Laborer	11Ap02Cn	MCAVOY, David	20	M	Laborer	11Ap02Cn
LYNCH, Patrick	29	M	Mechanic	11Ap02Cn	LALLY, Kean	32	M	Bricklayer	11Ap02Cn
DONNELLY, Margaret	20	F	None	11Ap02Cn	MCLEN, John	22	M	Laborer	11Ap02Cn
MCDOWNEY, James	18	M	Mechanic	11Ap02Cn	SILNER, Wirney	20	F	None	11Ap02Cn
Mary	17	F	None	11Ap02Cn	LARKIN, Ann	16	F	None	11Ap02Cn
MCGUIRE, Ann	07	F	Child	11Ap02Cn	LALLY, Bidy	20	F	None	11Ap02Cn
Owen (P)	40	M	Laborer	11Ap02Cn	DOLAN, Bridget	18	F	None	11Ap02Cn
MCKIRNAN, Rosey	20	F	None	11Ap02Cn	HORAN, Mary	21	F	None	11Ap02Cn
Peggy	18	F	None	11Ap02Cn	CORCORRAN, Bess.	20	F	None	11Ap02Cn
GALLAGHER, Bidy	20	F	None	11Ap02Cn	EYRNE, William	20	M	Laborer	11Ap02Cn
Rosey	18	F	None	11Ap02Cn	Michael	22	M	Laborer	11Ap02Cn
NAUGHTIN, Matthew	20	M	Laborer	11Ap02Cn	Catherine	18	F	None	11Ap02Cn
Thomes	18	M	Laborer	11Ap02Cn	MURRAY, Rose	23	F	None	11Ap02Cn
LUNNEN, Mark	21	M	Laborer	11Ap02Cn	Mary (D)	06	F	Child	11Ap02Cn
MCDONNEL, John	21	M	Laborer	11Ap02Cn	MCGEE, Mary	20	F	None	11Ap02Cn
Mary	21	F	None	11Ap02Cn	MULLEN, Catherine	18	F	None	11Ap02Cn
BLAKE, Mary	17	F	None	11Ap02Cn	MCCARTY, Margaret	19	F	None	11Ap02Cn
MCCOOK, Bridget	18	F	None	11Ap02Cn	Sarah	17	F	None	11Ap02Cn
KELLY, Mary	21	F	None	11Ap02Cn	Mary	21	F	None	11Ap02Cn
MURPHY, Catherine	17	F	None	11Ap02Cn	MCCALIE, Rosanna	18	F	None	11Ap02Cn
MCKEOWN, Mary	22	F	None	11Ap02Cn	DARBY, Ann	17	F	None	11Ap02Cn
FLEMING, Michael	12	M	Laborer	11Ap02Cn	CALLAGHAN, Sarah	19	F	None	11Ap02Cn
KILLEEN, Margaret	17	F	None	11Ap02Cn	WARD, John	18	M	Laborer	11Ap02Cn
DALY, Margaret	18	F	None	11Ap02Cn	CARTLIN, Hugh	18	M	Tailor	11Ap02Cn
GANNON, Catherine	17	F	None	11Ap02Cn	DORDEY, Bridget	13	F	None	11Ap02Cn
FULLON, Ann	18	F	None	11Ap02Cn	KENNEDY, Wm.	25	M	Laborer	11Ap02Cn
MCLOUGHLIN, Michael	20	M	Laborer	11Ap02Cn	Eliza-Jane	25	F	None	11Ap02Cn
FOLEY, Thos.	22	M	Mason	11Ap02Cn	SMITH, John	20	M	Weaver	11Ap02Cn
Patrick	20	M	Mason	11Ap02Cn	MORROW, Ann	20	F	None	11Ap02Cn
PAYLE, Elizabeth	19	F	None	11Ap02Cn	HENRY, Ellen	22	F	None	11Ap02Cn
NORTON, Winifred	17	F	None	11Ap02Cn	MORROW, Margaret	22	F	None	11Ap02Cn
HOARE, James	22	M	Laborer	11Ap02Cn	ALEXANDER, Robert	22	M	Laborer	11Ap02Cn
Ann	17	F	None	11Ap02Cn	GILL, Thomas	19	M	Laborer	11Ap02Cn
Betsey	20	F	None	11Ap02Cn	SPELECEY, Patrick	18	M	Laborer	11Ap02Cn
CUNNANE, Ellen	18	F	None	11Ap02Cn	MAXWELL, Margaret	21	F	None	11Ap02Cn
KELLY, Bernard	22	M	Laborer	11Ap02Cn	COMBE, Edward	18	M	Tailor	11Ap02Cn
QUIGLEY, Michail	22	M	Laborer	11Ap02Cn	DAVIES, Thomas	31	M	Joiner	11Ap02Cn
CONROY, Ann	30	F	None	11Ap02Cn	DONNELLY, Barney	40	M	Mechanic	11Ap02Cn
FINNERAN, William	20	M	Laborer	11Ap02Cn	KANE, Bernard	20	M	Laborer	11Ap02Cn
CONNAUGHTY, Bridget	19	F	None	11Ap02Cn	DONNELLY, Joseph	20	M	Laborer	11Ap02Cn
BRANNIN, William	28	M	Laborer	11Ap02Cn	GROOMBY, Joseph	20	M	Turner	11Ap02Cn
CONNOR, Patrick	20	M	Laborer	11Ap02Cn	DONNELLY, James	20	M	Laborer	11Ap02Cn
MCENREE, Catherine	14	F	None	11Ap02Cn	MCALTER, Francis	20	M	Laborer	11Ap02Cn
SMITH, Bridget	22	F	None	11Ap02Cn	MACKIE, W.H.	25	M	Laborer	11Ap02Cn
WHELAN, Bridget	22	F	None	11Ap02Cn	KERLING, Mary	25	F	None	11Ap02Cn
PURCELL, Martin	22	M	Laborer	11Ap02Cn	MULTON, Peter	18	M	Laborer	11Ap02Cn
FELLON, Patrick	21	M	Laborer	11Ap02Cn	FITZPATRICK, John	20	M	Laborer	11Ap02Cn
Bridget	20	F	None	11Ap02Cn	CASSIDY, John	20	M	Laborer	11Ap02Cn
MCCARLEY, Eliza	26	F	None	11Ap02Cn	MARTIN, Ann	20	F	None	11Ap02Cn
MCNOLTY, Wm.	26	M	Shoemaker	11Ap02Cn	ROONEY, John	23	M	Laborer	11Ap02Cn
James	24	M	Shoemaker	11Ap02Cn	BULGER, Ellen	20	F	None	11Ap02Cn
HUNE, Mary	17	F	None	11Ap02Cn	BYRNES, Rose	20	F	None	11Ap02Cn
GARTY, Bernard	16	M	Laborer	11Ap02Cn	BRANNIN, Mary	20	F	None	11Ap02Cn
CONNAUGHTON, Mary	20	F	None	11Ap02Cn	Mary	20	F	None	11Ap02Cn
MCMULLEN, Michl.	30	M	Gentleman	11Ap02Cn	CUNANE, Michael	25	M	Laborer	11Ap02Cn
Mary	20	F	None	11Ap02Cn	DROUGHT, Edward	20	M	Laborer	11Ap02Cn
MEAGHER, Thomas	23	M	Laborer	11Ap02Cn	James	24	M	Laborer	11Ap02Cn
BRISLIN, Charles	20	M	Laborer	11Ap02Cn	ROSNEY, James	25	M	Laborer	11Ap02Cn
James	20	M	Laborer	11Ap02Cn	DELANEY, Patrick	24	M	Laborer	11Ap02Cn
SWEENEY, John	24	M	Laborer	11Ap02Cn	GLENNON, John	20	M	Laborer	11Ap02Cn
Susan	28	F	None	11Ap02Cn	DROUGHT, Ellen	20	F	None	11Ap02Cn
MURPHY, John	22	M	Shoemaker	11Ap02Cn	HEALY, Betsy	24	F	None	11Ap02Cn
TAFFE, Catherine	20	F	None	11Ap02Cn	MURRAY, Mary	20	F	None	11Ap02Cn
Ann	18	F	None	11Ap02Cn	RIGNEY, Mary	20	F	None	11Ap02Cn
MONOGHAN, Mary	20	F	None	11Ap02Cn	DUNN, Sally	16	F	None	11Ap02Cn
CUNNURK, John	20	M	Tailor	11Ap02Cn	GILL, Edward	27	M	Joiner	11Ap02Cn
MCCALIE, Patrick	20	M	Laborer	11Ap02Cn	KELLY, William	25	M	Shoemaker	11Ap02Cn
MCCARRALL, John	22	M	Laborer	11Ap02Cn	QUALTHROUGH, Joseph	20	M	Miller	11Ap02Cn
HENRY, James	27	M	Laborer	11Ap02Cn	MOORE, Thos.	25	M	Shoemaker	11Ap02Cn

NAMES OF PASSENGERS	A G E	S E X	OCCUPATIONS	DATE PORT SHIP	NAMES OF PASSENGERS	A G E	S E X	OCCUPATIONS	DATE PORT SHIP
QUALTHROUGH, Thomas	28	M	Blacksmith	11Ap02Cn	FOLEY, Mary	28	F	None	11Ap02Cn
GILL, Joseph	27	M	Laborer	11Ap02Cn	LENEHAN, Ellen	26	F	None	11Ap02Cn
DOWD, Peter	20	M	Laborer	11Ap02Cn	EGAN, Mark	25	M	Laborer	11Ap02Cn
BRADY, Bernard	20	M	Miller	11Ap02Cn	Larry	19	M	Laborer	11Ap02Cn
ELLIOTT, Edward	30	M	Carpenter	11Ap02Cn	LENEHAN, Patrick	32	M	Laborer	11Ap02Cn
MCALLINAY, Hugh	20	M	Printer	11Ap02Cn	FITZGERALD, Thos.	25	M	Laborer	11Ap02Cn
DUFFY, Catherine	18	F	None	11Ap02Cn	MORGAN, Thos.	21	M	Laborer	11Ap02Cn
MURRAY, Mary	16	F	None	11Ap02Cn	JONES, Mary-Ann	19	F	None	11Ap02Cn
HUGHES, John	18	M	Butcher	11Ap02Cn	BARKEY, Betty	40	F	None	11Ap02Cn
COLEMAN, Thos.	20	M	Laborer	11Ap02Cn	Ann (D)	13	F	None	11Ap02Cn
CARROLL, Ann	28	F	None	11Ap02Cn	Ellen (D)	12	F	None	11Ap02Cn
LAWLER, James	27	M	Farmer	11Ap02Cn	Patrick (S)	11	M	None	11Ap02Cn
Margaret (W)	25	F	Wife	11Ap02Cn	James (S)	09	M	Child	11Ap02Cn
Bridget (D)	02	F	Child	11Ap02Cn	MCGEOGH, Michael	24	M	Laborer	11Ap02Cn
Michael (S)	01	M	Child	11Ap02Cn	MCGENITY, Nancy	24	F	None	11Ap02Cn
DOYLE, William	25	M	Farmer	11Ap02Cn	MCMAHON, Ann	28	F	None	11Ap02Cn
YOUNG, James	20	M	Tailor	11Ap02Cn	CONLON, Rosey	20	F	None	11Ap02Cn
OWENS, James	22	M	Laborer	11Ap02Cn	COWEN, Mary	20	F	None	11Ap02Cn
Mary	20	F	None	11Ap02Cn	MCALLISON, Eliza	22	F	None	11Ap02Cn
NOWLIN, Allen	20	M	Laborer	11Ap02Cn	MULLEN, Bernard	22	M	Farmer	11Ap02Cn
KEY, Margaret	20	F	None	11Ap02Cn	Rosanna	20	F	None	11Ap02Cn
DOYLE, Winney	17	F	None	11Ap02Cn	ROSE, James	19	M	Laborer	11Ap02Cn
NOWLIN, Catherine	20	F	None	11Ap02Cn	KELLY, John	20	M	Laborer	11Ap02Cn
MURPHY, Ann	20	F	None	11Ap02Cn	JONES, Jonah	16	M	Laborer	11Ap02Cn
MORAN, Catherine	17	F	None	11Ap02Cn	COLLINS, Johannah	50	F	None	11Ap02Cn
SHERIDAN, Thos.	27	M	Cork Cutter	11Ap02Cn	MULLERICK, Michael	20	M	Laborer	11Ap02Cn
HALLIGAN, Matthew	30	M	Merchant	11Ap02Cn	Mary	19	F	None	11Ap02Cn
JOYCE, Thomas	20	M	Laborer	11Ap02Cn	RILEY, John	18	M	Butcher	11Ap02Cn
KELLY, Patrick	20	M	Weaver	11Ap02Cn	CAROLIN, James	16	M	Blacksmith	11Ap02Cn
CONNOR, Patrick	20	M	Laborer	11Ap02Cn	QUIN, Charles	21	M	Laborer	11Ap02Cn
TIGHT, James	20	M	Weaver	11Ap02Cn	COLLINS, John	25	M	Laborer	11Ap02Cn
PADDEEN, Kitty	20	F	None	11Ap02Cn	MCNEILL, Alexander	10	M	Laborer	11Ap02Cn
GRADY, Patrick	20	M	Laborer	11Ap02Cn	Mary	05	F	Child	11Ap02Cn
KING, Honora	20	F	None	11Ap02Cn	John	03	M	Child	11Ap02Cn
KEAGHER, Ann	20	F	None	11Ap02Cn	CURTIN, Mary	60	F	None	11Ap02Cn
MOORE, Biddy	18	F	None	11Ap02Cn	Eliza (D)	23	F	None	11Ap02Cn
DONNELAN, Patrick	20	M	Laborer	11Ap02Cn	Cornelius (S)	24	M	Laborer	11Ap02Cn
TIERNAN, James	18	M	Laborer	11Ap02Cn	Jeremiah (S)	20	M	Laborer	11Ap02Cn
LEESON, Patrick	21	M	Laborer	11Ap02Cn	REARDON, Julia	30	F	None	11Ap02Cn
TURNER, William	18	M	Laborer	11Ap02Cn	Julia (D)	05	F	Child	11Ap02Cn
Catherine	16	F	None	11Ap02Cn	Mary (D)	02	F	Child	11Ap02Cn
CLOGHER, Mary	21	F	None	11Ap02Cn	NEEHAN, James	19	M	Laborer	11Ap02Cn
KEELY, Ann	20	F	None	11Ap02Cn	RYAN, James	26	M	Laborer	11Ap02Cn
BRADY, Thos.	21	M	Laborer	11Ap02Cn	Jane	24	F	None	11Ap02Cn
SHEILDS, Matthias	18	M	Laborer	11Ap02Cn	MALLON, James	08	M	Shoemaker	11Ap02Cn
REILLY, Francis	18	M	Laborer	11Ap02Cn	RILEY, Rose	18	F	None	11Ap02Cn
Patrick	20	M	Laborer	11Ap02Cn	Mary	13	F	None	11Ap02Cn
MURRAY, Patrick	20	M	Laborer	11Ap02Cn	Jane	11	F	None	11Ap02Cn
BARRY, John	28	M	Laborer	11Ap02Cn	CAULIFFE, Catherine	30	F	None	11Ap02Cn
MASTERSON, Thos.	25	M	Laborer	11Ap02Cn	CAREY, Patrick	21	M	Butcher	11Ap02Cn
RILEY, Edward-C.	20	M	Laborer	11Ap02Cn	MCDONNELL, John	20	M	Servant	11Ap02Cn
DOWE, Thomas	25	M	Laborer	11Ap02Cn	SEYMOUR, Morris-B.	30	M	Merchant	11Ap02Cn
MURPHY, Daniel	60	M	Laborer	11Ap02Cn					
ATKINSON, Isabella	22	F	None	11Ap02Cn					
ROGERS, Peggy	19	F	None	11Ap02Cn					
CONNER, Margaret	17	F	None	11Ap02Cn					
SHERIDAN, Edward	22	M	Laborer	11Ap02Cn					
Catherine	21	F	None	11Ap02Cn	HENRY-CLAY 15 APRIL 1846				
BRADY, John	20	M	Laborer	11Ap02Cn					
Catherine	18	F	None	11Ap02Cn	From Liverpool				
CUNNINGHAM, Richard	20	M	Shoemaker	11Ap02Cn					
BOURKE, Patrick	30	M	Coachman	11Ap02Cn					
ROBINSON, George	20	M	Joiner	11Ap02Cn					
Robert	18	M	Joiner	11Ap02Cn	CUNNINGHAM, Letitia	09	F	Child	15Ap02Co
NCLEAN, Gilbert	18	M	Servant	11Ap02Cn	DUMELY, Mary-A.	24	F	None	15Ap02Co
COOGAN, Patrick	30	M	Laborer	11Ap02Cn	BOYLAN, Thos.	21	M	Farmer	15Ap02Co
MCCORMICK, Cornelius	34	M	Laborer	11Ap02Cn	PORTER, Hugh	19	M	None	15Ap02Co
BRADY, Daniel	40	M	Laborer	11Ap02Cn	MCMONDAY, Wm.	24	M	None	15Ap02Co
MCBRIDE, Richard	26	M	Farmer	11Ap02Cn	FLINN, Michael	19	M	Laborer	15Ap02Co
MOORE, Mary	24	F	None	11Ap02Cn	BORK, Ann	20	F	None	15Ap02Co
MCBRIDE, Neil	20	M	Laborer	11Ap02Cn	DONALD, Peggy	21	F	Laborer	15Ap02Co
BURKE, Mary-Ann	21	F	None	11Ap02Cn	OBRIEN, Terenc	24	M	Farmer	15Ap02Co
QUIGLEY, Philip	25	M	Carpenter	11Ap02Cn	WARD, Margt.	09	F	Child	15Ap02Co
REGAN, Mary	20	F	None	11Ap02Cn	SAVAGE, Eliza	08	F	Child	15Ap02Co
Mary	21	F	None	11Ap02Cn	GANTT, Geo.	54	M	Butcher	15Ap02Co

NAMES OF PASSENGERS		AGE SEX EX	OCCUPATIONS	DATE PORT SHIP
GANTT, Jane	(W)	31 F	Wife	15Ap02Co
Wm.F.	(S)	01 M	Child	15Ap02Co
WHITCOME, John		22 M	Farmer	15Ap02Co
ODONNELL, Danl.		30 M	Farmer	15Ap02Co
MCGORMACK, Patt		30 M	Farmer	15Ap02Co
Bridget		30 F	Farmer	15Ap02Co
ROONEY, John		27 M	Farmer	15Ap02Co
WAUGH, Mary		30 F	Farmer	15Ap02Co
DIGNAL, John		14 M	Farmer	15Ap02Co
LIND, Hannah		18 F	Farmer	15Ap02Co
SHERIDEN, John		20 M	Laborer	15Ap02Co
SMITH, Phillip		18 M	Laborer	15Ap02Co
John		16 M	None	15Ap02Co
COYRN, Mary		20 F	None	15Ap02Co
SMITH, Biddy		18 F	None	15Ap02Co
Eliza		18 F	None	15Ap02Co
LANGTON, Thos.		22 M	Carpenter	15Ap02Co
FLYN, Pat		20 M	Groom	15Ap02Co
DONOHOE, Thos.		21 M	Farmer	15Ap02Co
HANLEY, Ann		20 F	None	15Ap02Co
GRUER, Cath.		19 F	None	15Ap02Co
CLYLL, Cath.		22 F	None	15Ap02Co
CORR, Bridgt.		24 F	None	15Ap02Co
CUNNIGHAM, Marry		24 F	None	15Ap02Co
GRACE, Celia		20 F	None	15Ap02Co
RILEY, Michl.		30 M	Farmer	15Ap02Co
DORAN, Jno.		25 M	Farmer	15Ap02Co
ROCHELL, Wm.		29 M	Farmer	15Ap02Co
HANLON, Thos.		24 M	Farmer	15Ap02Co
MCCLOUD, Thos.		25 M	None	15Ap02Co
GRAY, Margt.		21 F	None	15Ap02Co
RAY, Sarah		20 F	None	15Ap02Co
BELL, Chas.		23 M	None	15Ap02Co
MCCULLOGH, Eliza		21 F	None	15Ap02Co
MCKENNA, Jas.		21 M	None	15Ap02Co
Eliza		20 F	None	15Ap02Co
MULDRICK, Jas.		24 M	Schm	15Ap02Co
MCCHIVERS, David		20 M	Carpenter	15Ap02Co
HARR, Wm.John		21 M	None	15Ap02Co
HOLENS, David		19 M	None	15Ap02Co
WILLSON, Saml.		29 M	None	15Ap02Co
Letitia	(W)	25 F	Wife	15Ap02Co
Elizabh.	(D)	08 F	Child	15Ap02Co
Wm.John	(S)	02 M	Child	15Ap02Co
MARTIN, Alexn.		20 M	None	15Ap02Co
Ewd.		16 M	None	15Ap02Co
CORMICK, Michl.		25 M	None	15Ap02Co
NILL, Jane		23 F	None	15Ap02Co
OBRIEN, Jno.		20 M	Laborer	15Ap02Co
ODONELY, Peter		40 M	Laborer	15Ap02Co
MORAN, Wm.		21 M	Farmer	15Ap02Co
Michail		20 M	None	15Ap02Co
CUMING, Maria		17 F	None	15Ap02Co
CANTWELL, Ellen		18 F	None	15Ap02Co
LIND, Adam		17 M	Farmer	15Ap02Co
RYAN, Thos.		20 M	Laborer	15Ap02Co
FAYAN, Michl.		38 M	None	15Ap02Co
FALLON, Thos.		26 M	None	15Ap02Co
Mary		34 F	None	15Ap02Co
Bridgt.		18 F	None	15Ap02Co
Ann		16 F	None	15Ap02Co
LANAN, Peter		25 M	Farmer	15Ap02Co
DOLAN, Robt.		20 M	None	15Ap02Co
Patt		22 M	None	15Ap02Co
Mary		27 F	None	15Ap02Co
FLANAGAN, John		22 M	None	15Ap02Co
Malichi		22 M	None	15Ap02Co
Cathn.		21 F	None	15Ap02Co
CORMAN, Winif.		18 F	None	15Ap02Co
Margt.		22 F	None	15Ap02Co
MALARGHAN, Celia		20 F	None	15Ap02Co
KILORAN, Patt		25 M	None	15Ap02Co
Hinafd.		22 F	None	15Ap02Co
RENOLDS, Pat		24 M	Tanner	15Ap02Co
HINOHER, Michl.		24 M	None	15Ap02Co

NAMES OF PASSENGERS		AGE SEX EX	OCCUPATIONS	DATE PORT SHIP
CONNOR, Barnard		21 M	None	15Ap02Co
Jas.		24 M	None	15Ap02Co
Kelley		22 M	None	15Ap02Co
David		.11 M	Infant	15Ap02Co
HARRISON, Geo.		23 M	Farmer	15Ap02Co
Ellenor		24 F	None	15Ap02Co
THARNOR, Peter		24 M	Farmer	15Ap02Co
KEARN, Mary		21 F	None	15Ap02Co
FOX, Ellen		24 F	None	15Ap02Co
FERUSON, Maggy		21 F	None	15Ap02Co
RUSHWORTH, Geo.		20 M	Coalman	15Ap02Co
Jas.		20 M	None	15Ap02Co
John		19 M	None	15Ap02Co
Ann		27 F	None	15Ap02Co
CARMICHEL, Jas.		22 M	None	15Ap02Co
CHARLES, Geo.		28 M	Farmer	15Ap02Co
MCMARTIN, Alexn.		33 M	None	15Ap02Co
BURNS, Bridget		19 F	None	15Ap02Co
CATHEL, John		22 M	Rope Maker	15Ap02Co
Jane		19 F	None	15Ap02Co
CARIGAN, Hen.		25 M	None	15Ap02Co
BOLSTON, Ann		25 F	None	15Ap02Co
HAGAN, Jane		12 F	None	15Ap02Co
GRAHAM, John		35 M	None	15Ap02Co
RICE, Mary-A.		27 F	None	15Ap02Co
WARD, Ann		35 F	None	15Ap02Co
MORTON, Alexn.		27 M	None	15Ap02Co
COUSIE, Michl.		25 M	Laborer	15Ap02Co
HENLEY, Pat		24 M	None	15Ap02Co
HUGHS, Mary		21 F	None	15Ap02Co
GILLARTIN, Cath.		24 F	None	15Ap02Co
Bridgt.		22 F	None	15Ap02Co
LAMB, Michl.		45 M	Laborer	15Ap02Co
GEOGAN, Jas.		21 M	None	15Ap02Co
MCCABE, Jas.		20 M	None	15Ap02Co
SCANNEY, Bridget		24 F	None	15Ap02Co
CLAM, Michael		25 M	None	15Ap02Co
SMITH, Amy		21 F	None	15Ap02Co
NOUGHTON, Ellen		20 F	None	15Ap02Co
Ann		21 F	None	15Ap02Co
KENNY, Mary		20 F	None	15Ap02Co
THOMPSON, John		22 M	Miller	15Ap02Co
HALL, Saml.		25 M	None	15Ap02Co
GALLIGHER, Jas.		28 M	None	15Ap02Co
HUGHS, Mary		23 F	None	15Ap02Co
CONDAN, Danl.		24 M	None	15Ap02Co
OBRIEN, Wm.		17 M	None	15Ap02Co
RILLEY, Bryen		30 M	None	15Ap02Co
HANIGAN, Michl.		22 M	Farmer	15Ap02Co
Mary	(W)	25 F	Wife	15Ap02Co
Pat	(S)	.03 M	Infant	15Ap02Co
GARNER, John		12 M	None	15Ap02Co
TINNS, Mary		32 F	None	15Ap02Co
KELLEY, Ester		25 F	None	15Ap02Co
DUN, Cath.		21 F	None	15Ap02Co
MOT, John		28 M	None	15Ap02Co
HIPASON, Joseph		42 M	Farmer	15Ap02Co
CLARK, Mary-A.		40 F	None	15Ap02Co
NILO, Jane		30 F	None	15Ap02Co
Wm.	(S)	08 M	Child	15Ap02Co

A.LAWRENCE 17 APRIL 1846

From Liverpool

NAMES OF PASSENGERS		AGE SEX EX	OCCUPATIONS	DATE PORT SHIP
FITZSIMONS, Thomas		22 M	Laborer	17Ap02Cp
TALENT, John		36 M	Laborer	17Ap02Cp
MCCUNE, Elizabeth		18 F	Laborer	17Ap02Cp
WALSH, Michl.		19 M	Laborer	17Ap02Cp

NAMES OF PASSENGERS		AGE	SEX	OCCUPATIONS	DATE PORT SHIP	NAMES OF PASSENGERS		AGE	SEX	OCCUPATIONS	DATE PORT SHIP
SHANLEY, Michl.		23	M	Laborer	17Ap02Cp	FANNER, Thomas		40	M	Weaver	17Ap02Cp
MALONE, Mary		21	F	Laborer	17Ap02Cp	Margt.	(D)	18	F	Laborer	17Ap02Cp
MCIVER, Bridget		28	F	Laborer	17Ap02Cp	Susan	(D)	14	F	Laborer	17Ap02Cp
MALONE, Thomas		18	F	Laborer	17Ap02Cp	CORSSIN, James		22	M	Cooper	17Ap02Cp
BOSWORTH, Mary		40	F	Laborer	17Ap02Cp	MCDONNELL, Ann		20	F	Laborer	17Ap02Cp
MURPHE, Michl.		35	M	Laborer	17Ap02Cp	BRADY, Judy		24	F	Laborer	17Ap02Cp
PACKENHAM, John		25	M	Laborer	17Ap02Cp	FAY, Judy		20	F	Laborer	17Ap02Cp
Mary		19	F	Laborer	17Ap02Cp	OWENS, Michl.		28	M	Laborer	17Ap02Cp
MCCABE, James		21	M	Laborer	17Ap02Cp	KELLEY, John		25	M	Laborer	17Ap02Cp
RUSH, Ann		25	F	Laborer	17Ap02Cp	BRANNER, Cathn.		24	F	Laborer	17Ap02Cp
DEGNAN, Patt		27	M	Laborer	17Ap02Cp	Ann		20	F	Laborer	17Ap02Cp
FARRELLY, Mary		20	F	Laborer	17Ap02Cp	Thomas		21	M	Laborer	17Ap02Cp
BROADRECK, Patt		20	M	Laborer	17Ap02Cp	DUNNE, Peter		21	M	Laborer	17Ap02Cp
MULHCAM, Patt		22	M	Laborer	17Ap02Cp	WHILAND, John		28	M	Laborer	17Ap02Cp
GARAGAN, Cathn.		20	F	Laborer	17Ap02Cp	Ellen	(W)	26	F	Wife	17Ap02Cp
HALL, Thomas		21	M	Laborer	17Ap02Cp	Michl.	(S)	03	M	Child	17Ap02Cp
MULLOVY, Patt		21	M	Laborer	17Ap02Cp	Mary	(D)	01	F	Child	17Ap02Cp
Hannah		18	F	Laborer	17Ap02Cp	CURTES, Ann		50	F	Laborer	17Ap02Cp
MCGRATH, Michl.		22	M	Laborer	17Ap02Cp	DELANEY, John		22	M	Laborer	17Ap02Cp
GATH, Eliza		18	F	Laborer	17Ap02Cp	MAHONY, John		25	M	Laborer	17Ap02Cp
FINEGAN, Martin		25	M	Laborer	17Ap02Cp	Ellen		20	F	Laborer	17Ap02Cp
Michl.		22	M	Laborer	17Ap02Cp	MOORE, Sally		22	F	Laborer	17Ap02Cp
KENADY, John		18	M	Laborer	17Ap02Cp	Margt.		20	F	Laborer	17Ap02Cp
TAGLE, Peggy		20	F	Laborer	17Ap02Cp	CUNINGHAM, Mary		21	F	Laborer	17Ap02Cp
MCLANE, John		26	M	Laborer	17Ap02Cp	SEALES, Cathn.		24	F	Laborer	17Ap02Cp
COX, James		22	M	Laborer	17Ap02Cp	STONE, Christy		26	M	Laborer	17Ap02Cp
JOHNSTON, James		16	M	Laborer	17Ap02Cp	John		28	M	Laborer	17Ap02Cp
CODDEN, Patt		21	M	Laborer	17Ap02Cp	Julia		27	F	Laborer	17Ap02Cp
DELANEY, Eliza		20	F	Laborer	17Ap02Cp	Rose		05	F	Child	17Ap02Cp
HEARY, Patt		20	M	Laborer	17Ap02Cp	Christy		03	M	Child	17Ap02Cp
MILLER, Mary		20	F	Laborer	17Ap02Cp	U		.06	M	Infant	17Ap02Cp
MATHEWS, Mathew		45	M	Laborer	17Ap02Cp	MURRY, Francis		21	M	Laborer	17Ap02Cp
James	(S)	18	M	Laborer	17Ap02Cp	MUNDY, John		23	M	Clerk	17Ap02Cp
Margt.	(D)	23	F	Laborer	17Ap02Cp	REILLY, John		24	M	Laborer	17Ap02Cp
Clara	(D)	11	F	Laborer	17Ap02Cp	FARRELL, John		13	M	Laborer	17Ap02Cp
CLARK, John		24	M	Laborer	17Ap02Cp	CONNELLY, Berry		20	M	Laborer	17Ap02Cp
Cathn.	(D)	02	M	Child	17Ap02Cp	GAFFNEY, Michl.		21	M	Laborer	17Ap02Cp
U	(D)	.06	M	Infant	17Ap02Cp	GALLIGAN, Ann		16	F	Laborer	17Ap02Cp
Mathew		09	M	Child	17Ap02Cp	SMITH, Bartley		16	F	Laborer	17Ap02Cp
CARVEY, William		22	M	Laborer	17Ap02Cp	WHETOGEN, George		27	M	Laborer	17Ap02Cp
RONAN, Thomas		23	M	Hatter	17Ap02Cp	ROACH, Ellen		10	F	Laborer	17Ap02Cp
SWEENEY, James		24	M	Laborer	17Ap02Cp	LYNON, Mary		21	F	Laborer	17Ap02Cp
FITZPATRICK, Michl.		16	M	Laborer	17Ap02Cp	Cathn.	(D)	02	F	Child	17Ap02Cp
MCGUIRE, James		22	M	Laborer	17Ap02Cp	CONNER, John		22	M	Laborer	17Ap02Cp
GALAPER, Bridget		23	F	Laborer	17Ap02Cp	MULVEY, Patt		21	M	Laborer	17Ap02Cp
GRAGAN, Mary		16	F	Laborer	17Ap02Cp						
SWEENEY, Ann		22	F	Laborer	17Ap02Cp						
FITZPATRICK, Mary		13	F	Laborer	17Ap02Cp						
TUITE, Cath.		20	F	Laborer	17Ap02Cp						
HARTLEY, Mary		60	F	Laborer	17Ap02Cp						
Maria		15	F	Laborer	17Ap02Cp	NONANTUM 18 APRIL 1846					
MURPHY, Jane		20	F	Laborer	17Ap02Cp						
MCDERMOT, Rose		20	F	Laborer	17Ap02Cp	From Liverpool					
DELANEY, John		24	M	Laborer	17Ap02Cp						
HUGHES, John		26	M	Laborer	17Ap02Cp						
CARLAND, James		21	M	Laborer	17Ap02Cp						
COLLINS, Mathew		20	M	Laborer	17Ap02Cp	RYAN, John		18	M	Laborer	18Ap02Cq
GALLEGAN, Patt		32	M	Laborer	17Ap02Cp	SMITH, John		23	M	Laborer	18Ap02Cq
Mary		26	F	Laborer	17Ap02Cp	JOHNSTON, Alice		24	F	None	18Ap02Cq
TIMMINGS, John		21	M	Laborer	17Ap02Cp	MCVALTY, Patk.		18	M	Laborer	18Ap02Cq
BRADLEY, Ann		30	F	Laborer	17Ap02Cp	Cornelius		14	M	None	18Ap02Cq
FARRELLY, Ann		17	F	Laborer	17Ap02Cp	VAUGH, James		30	M	Laborer	18Ap02Cq
KANE, Grace		35	F	Laborer	17Ap02Cp	JOHNSTON, James		18	M	Laborer	18Ap02Cq
CONNER, Cathn.		18	F	Laborer	17Ap02Cp	GAHARAN, Thos.		20	M	Laborer	18Ap02Cq
MULLEN, Cathn.		22	F	Laborer	17Ap02Cp	GILLOM, James		20	M	Laborer	18Ap02Cq
THOMPSON, Rebecca		16	F	Laborer	17Ap02Cp	COX, Jas.		20	M	Laborer	18Ap02Cq
MCFEELY, Mary		22	F	Laborer	17Ap02Cp	WARD, John		18	M	Laborer	18Ap02Cq
Margt.		19	F	Laborer	17Ap02Cp	SCALLY, Michl.		18	M	Laborer	18Ap02Cq
DONAHUE, Cilely		06	F	Child	17Ap02Cp	CONNOLLY, Christy		18	M	Laborer	18Ap02Cq
MCCARTENEY, Ann		35	F	Laborer	17Ap02Cp	FARRELL, Thos.		18	M	Laborer	18Ap02Cq
MULHENY, Thomas		20	M	Laborer	17Ap02Cp	BRADY, Patk.		28	M	Laborer	18Ap02Cq
DOWD, Cathn.		20	F	Laborer	17Ap02Cp	CONNOR, James		19	M	Laborer	18Ap02Cq
KEENA, Dolly		35	F	Laborer	17Ap02Cp	CASEY, Patk.		18	M	Laborer	18Ap02Cq
Owen	(S)	11	M	Laborer	17Ap02Cp	SALMON, Ann		19	F	None	18Ap02Cq
KELLEY, Hugh		21	M	Laborer	17Ap02Cp	CASEY, Biddy		19	F	None	18Ap02Cq

40

NAMES OF PASSENGERS		AGE	SEX	OCCUPATIONS	DATE PORT SHIP
BARLOW, Mary		19	F	None	18Ap02Cq
CASEY, Biddy-Jr.		19	F	None	18Ap02Cq
GRADY, Mary		19	F	None	18Ap02Cq
CASEY, Susan		19	F	None	18Ap02Cq
COX, James		20	M	Laborer	18Ap02Cq
KENNY, Andw.		20	M	Laborer	18Ap02Cq
NOWLAN, Thos.		20	M	Laborer	18Ap02Cq
MCGRATH, Jim		19	M	Laborer	18Ap02Cq
DWYER, Michl.		20	M	Laborer	18Ap02Cq
DUNFEY, Thos.		30	M	Laborer	18Ap02Cq
HOGG, Stephen		40	M	Laborer	18Ap02Cq
MORGAN, Kitty		25	F	None	18Ap02Cq
CLARKE, Michl.		22	M	Laborer	18Ap02Cq
MONKS, Mary		28	F	None	18Ap02Cq
DUNFEY, Thos.		.00	M	Infant	18Ap02Cq
Died-At-Sea					
REYNOLDS, Peter		40	M	Farmer	18Ap02Cq
DOGHERTY, Max		21	M	Laborer	18Ap02Cq
MCGRATH, John		20	M	Laborer	18Ap02Cq
LARKIN, Pat		52	M	Laborer	18Ap02Cq
LEONARD, Thos.		20	M	Laborer	18Ap02Cq
CUFF, Denis		20	M	Laborer	18Ap02Cq
PATRICK, Christfr.		20	M	Laborer	18Ap02Cq
MCGRATH, James		20	M	Laborer	18Ap02Cq
Mary		23	F	None	18Ap02Cq
DONOHOE, Thos.		30	M	Laborer	18Ap02Cq
GILLELAM, John		29	M	Laborer	18Ap02Cq
Teressa		18	F	None	18Ap02Cq
CURTIS, James		25	M	Laborer	18Ap02Cq
Ellen		23	F	None	18Ap02Cq
RILEY, Mary		21	F	None	18Ap02Cq
Thos.		21	M	Laborer	18Ap02Cq
REARDON, Thos.		24	M	Laborer	18Ap02Cq
SMITH, Owen		21	M	Laborer	18Ap02Cq
Peter		25	M	Laborer	18Ap02Cq
Mary		13	F	None	18Ap02Cq
HARVEY, John		25	M	Farmer	18Ap02Cq
James		22	M	Farmer	18Ap02Cq
Hugh		20	M	Farmer	18Ap02Cq
David		16	M	Farmer	18Ap02Cq
Ford		18	M	Farmer	18Ap02Cq
Mary		45	F	None	18Ap02Cq
Mary-Jr.		23	F	None	18Ap02Cq
DICK, John		25	M	Laborer	18Ap02Cq
DONOVAN, Patt		26	M	Laborer	18Ap02Cq
Bridget		28	F	None	18Ap02Cq
RUDE, Patt		40	M	Laborer	18Ap02Cq
Mary	(D)	13	F	None	18Ap02Cq
Biddy	(D)	12	F	None	18Ap02Cq
MCENRUE, Ellen		22	F	None	18Ap02Cq
MACGUINESS, Mary		23	F	None	18Ap02Cq
DONOHOE, Mary		20	F	None	18Ap02Cq
NEARNY, Thos.		23	M	Laborer	18Ap02Cq
MCNAMARA, Patt.		26	M	Laborer	18Ap02Cq
NEARNY, U-Mrs.		22	F	None	18Ap02Cq
MCNAMARA, U-Mrs.		21	F	None	18Ap02Cq
TYLER, John		22	M	Laborer	18Ap02Cq
CORSYM, Bridget		22	F	None	18Ap02Cq
DONNELLY, Patt		24	M	Laborer	18Ap02Cq
MULLONY, Cormack		20	M	Laborer	18Ap02Cq
MANION, Patt		24	M	Laborer	18Ap02Cq
MCGURRELL, Patt		24	M	Laborer	18Ap02Cq
LANNON, Thomas		26	M	Laborer	18Ap02Cq
Ellen		24	F	None	18Ap02Cq
DUNN, John		28	M	Laborer	18Ap02Cq
U	(W)	25	F	Wife	18Ap02Cq
James	(S)	.00	M	Infant	18Ap02Cq
CUDDY, Mary		24	F	None	18Ap02Cq
COMER, James		27	M	Laborer	18Ap02Cq
TARBET, Peter		16	M	Laborer	18Ap02Cq
APPLETON, William		17	M	Laborer	18Ap02Cq
Andw.		13	M	None	18Ap02Cq
MCBRIDE, Michl.		19	M	Laborer	18Ap02Cq
BRYAN, Hugh		20	M	Laborer	18Ap02Cq
DEGNAN, Patt		21	M	Laborer	18Ap02Cq
PRIOR, Cathn.		21	F	None	18Ap02Cq
MCCARTNEY, Margt.		22	F	None	18Ap02Cq
Mary	(D)	03	F	Child	18Ap02Cq
CAMPBELL, James		25	M	Laborer	18Ap02Cq
NOONAN, John		24	M	Laborer	18Ap02Cq
GAFNEY, James		18	M	Laborer	18Ap02Cq
TOMEY, Michl.		18	M	Laborer	18Ap02Cq
CALLIN, Bridget		13	F	Laborer	18Ap02Cq
LIRJUNE, James		30	M	Laborer	18Ap02Cq
Honora		28	F	None	18Ap02Cq
GRAY, Thomas		26	M	Laborer	18Ap02Cq
LEWIS, Phillip		20	M	Laborer	18Ap02Cq
QUINN, Patt		20	M	Laborer	18Ap02Cq
ARMSTRONG, Bratan---		19	F	None	18Ap02Cq
LATIMER, Elizabeth		19	F	None	18Ap02Cq
MCMUNCOS, Margt.		19	F	None	18Ap02Cq
MURPHY, Thomas		24	M	Farmer	18Ap02Cq
SHUAR, Cornelius		19	M	Laborer	18Ap02Cq
FURRELLY, James		21	M	Laborer	18Ap02Cq
MURPHY, Michl.		22	M	Laborer	18Ap02Cq
QUIG, Manus		24	M	Laborer	18Ap02Cq
DRUMMOND, Danl.		27	M	Laborer	18Ap02Cq
MCANNALLY, John		20	M	Laborer	18Ap02Cq
HEMPHILL, Joseph		16	M	Laborer	18Ap02Cq
MCKEIREN, Elizabeth		16	F	None	18Ap02Cq
GILS, Margarett		18	F	None	18Ap02Cq
MARTIN, James		19	M	Laborer	18Ap02Cq
CLERK, James		20	M	Laborer	18Ap02Cq
RULLY, Joseph		22	M	Laborer	18Ap02Cq
John		22	M	Laborer	18Ap02Cq
U	(W)	22	F	Wife	18Ap02Cq
ROURKE, Michl.		20	M	Laborer	18Ap02Cq
FALLON, Thomas		18	M	Laborer	18Ap02Cq
MCCULLOUGH, Burney		20	M	Laborer	18Ap02Cq
MCGEE, Margt.		18	F	None	18Ap02Cq
Cathn.		16	F	None	18Ap02Cq
RULLY, Cathn.		20	F	None	18Ap02Cq
MCADAM, Chas.		20	M	Laborer	18Ap02Cq
RULLY, John		30	M	Laborer	18Ap02Cq
U	(W)	20	F	Wife	18Ap02Cq
Miles		30	M	Laborer	18Ap02Cq
MORROW, Ann		18	F	None	18Ap02Cq
WHITE, Sally		19	F	None	18Ap02Cq
MCINTRSSE, Mary		16	F	None	18Ap02Cq
BOYLE, John		18	M	Laborer	18Ap02Cq
MCKENNA, Mary		18	F	Laborer	18Ap02Cq
GINTY, Francis-C.		18	M	Laborer	18Ap02Cq
CONWAY, Michl.		20	M	Laborer	18Ap02Cq
RULLY, Mary		22	F	None	18Ap02Cq
GUINAN, Betty		18	F	None	18Ap02Cq
RULLY, Biddy		18	F	None	18Ap02Cq
KENNALLY, James		21	M	Laborer	18Ap02Cq
Margt.		21	F	None	18Ap02Cq
GARRITY, Thomas		24	M	Laborer	18Ap02Cq
TUFFE, Margt.		19	F	None	18Ap02Cq
WATERS, Ann		22	F	None	18Ap02Cq
LOGAN, Mary		30	M	Laborer	18Ap02Cq
CULCANNON, Martin		25	M	Laborer	18Ap02Cq
MCDARMOTH, Patt		18	M	Laborer	18Ap02Cq
ODOWD, Michl.		18	M	Laborer	18Ap02Cq
RIDDINGTON, Patt		20	M	Laborer	18Ap02Cq
MALLEN, Michl.		21	M	Laborer	18Ap02Cq
GALLAGHER, Thos.		20	M	Laborer	18Ap02Cq
Ellen	(W)	19	F	Wife	18Ap02Cq
Margt.	(D)	.00	F	Infant	18Ap02Cq
CONNELL, Edwd.		30	M	Laborer	18Ap02Cq
SHAW, John		28	M	Laborer	18Ap02Cq
MULHAY, John		28	M	Laborer	18Ap02Cq
FONDAY, James		22	M	Laborer	18Ap02Cq
HINCY, Jas.		30	M	Laborer	18Ap02Cq
LEONARD, Michl.		20	M	Laborer	18Ap02Cq
Cathn.		40	F	Laborer	18Ap02Cq
Ann		19	F	None	18Ap02Cq
Richard		20	M	Laborer	18Ap02Cq
LAMB, Patt		20	M	Laborer	18Ap02Cq

41

NAMES OF PASSENGERS		A G E	S E X	OCCUPATIONS	DATE PORT SHIP	NAMES OF PASSENGERS		A G E	S E X	OCCUPATIONS	DATE PORT SHIP
BLYTH, Rosay		20	M	Laborer	18Ap02Cq	PARKS, James		33	M	Carpenter	23Ap19Cr
GRAY, C.		20	M	Laborer	18Ap02Cq	ORORKE, John		37	M	Blacksmith	23Ap19Cr
SMITH, Mary		30	F	Laborer	18Ap02Cq	HAUGHEY, Patrick		40	M	Farmer	23Ap19Cr
DONNELLY, Francis		24	M	Laborer	18Ap02Cq	Margt.		33	F	Spinster	23Ap19Cr
MCQUAID, Francis		24	M	Laborer	18Ap02Cq	Ann		27	F	Spinster	23Ap19Cr
HUGHS, Edwd.		22	M	Laborer	18Ap02Cq	James		1C	M	Child	23Ap19Cr
WALLRY, Licy		20	F	None	18Ap02Cq	Patrick		14	M	Child	23Ap19Cr
MARKEY, Mary		05	F	Child	18Ap02Cq	Arthur		15	M	Child	23Ap19Cr
John		04	M	Child	18Ap02Cq	Mary		16	F	Child	23Ap19Cr
STENTSTON, Mary		22	F	None	18Ap02Cq	MCCRUM, Rober+		43	M	Farmer	23Ap19Cr
BELL, Arthur		20	M	Laborer	18Ap02Cq	Ann	(W)	35	F	Wife	23Ap19Cr
MCILHATTAN, Michl.		25	M	Laborer	18Ap02Cq	ROGAN, Patrick		38	M	Laborer	23Ap19Cr
MCQUADE, John		18	M	Laborer	18Ap02Cq	Hugh		36	M	Laborer	23Ap19Cr
HAYES, Michl.		20	M	Laborer	18Ap02Cq	KEARNEY, James		37	M	Laborer	23Ap19Cr
Nancy	(W)	21	F	Wife	18Ap02Cq	Elizabeth	(W)	38	F	Wife	23Ap19Cr
Margt.	(D)	04	F	Child	18Ap02Cq	MCCANN, Mary-A.		36	F	Spinster	23Ap19Cr
James	(S)	03	M	Child	18Ap02Cq	Margt.		35	F	Spinster	23Ap19Cr
KERNNAN, Thomas		25	M	Laborer	18Ap02Cq	MCKENNA, John		34	M	Farmer	23Ap19Cr
DORNEY, Edmond		25	M	Laborer	18Ap02Cq	Margt.	(W)	28	F	Wife	23Ap19Cr
ALAIRN, Peggy		22	F	None	18Ap02Cq	Catherine		20	F	None	23Ap19Cr
MCARTNEY, Bety		24	F	Laborer	18Ap02Cq	Mary		18	F	None	23Ap19Cr
MORAN, Farrell		22	M	Laborer	18Ap02Cq	Charles		15	M	None	23Ap19Cr
SMITH, Bricget		13	F	None	18Ap02Cq	Bessy		14	F	None	23Ap19Cr
CADDEN, Francis		28	M	Laborer	18Ap02Cq	DONAGHY, James		30	M	Farmer	23Ap19Cr
LAGHEY, Thos.		23	M	Laborer	18Ap02Cq	Mary	(W)	28	F	Wife	23Ap19Cr
Mary		21	F	None	18Ap02Cq	MAGIN, Patrick		40	M	Farmer	23Ap19Cr
CRAMM, Pat		22	M	Laborer	18Ap02Cq	NERRAL, Robert		38	M	Carpenter	23Ap19Cr
Owen		23	M	Laborer	18Ap02Cq	CAMPBELL, Mary		34	F	Spinster	23Ap19Cr
BYRNE, Ch.		27	M	Laborer	18Ap02Cq	MAGEE, Catherire		32	F	Spinster	23Ap19Cr
KILKENNY, Mary		22	F	None	18Ap02Cq	CUSKER, Hugh		37	M	Laborer	23Ap19Cr
HUTTON, Ben		25	M	Laborer	18Ap02Cq	HUGHES, John		39	M	Shoemaker	23Ap19Cr
DONOHOE, Edwd.		23	M	Laborer	18Ap02Cq	EARLEY, Catherine		31	F	Spinster	23Ap19Cr
KENNAN, Rose		50	F	None	18Ap02Cq	DOYLE, Ann		29	F	Spinster	23Ap19Cr
Francis	(S)	18	M	None	18Ap02Cq	MCSORLEY, Rosanna		32	F	Spinster	23Ap19Cr
Edwd.	(S)	16	M	None	18Ap02Cq	HACKETT, John		38	M	Mechanic	23Ap19Cr
KELLY, Cathn.		20	F	None	18Ap02Cq	DONNELLY, John		36	M	Laborer	23Ap19Cr
KENNA, Cathn.		14	F	None	18Ap02Cq	Mary		26	F	Spinster	23Ap19Cr
BRADY, Judy		20	F	None	18Ap02Cq	KEENAN, James		27	M	Fsvnt	23Ap19Cr
RULLY, Biddy		19	F	None	18Ap02Cq	NILLAN, Susana		21	F	Servant	23Ap19Cr
CASEY, Johane		20	F	None	18Ap02Cq	DONNELLY, Cathrine		37	F	Spinster	23Ap19Cr
PIERSON, John		40	M	Laborer	18Ap02Cq	HART, Patrick		25	M	Laborer	23Ap19Cr
Martha	(W)	42	F	Wife	18Ap02Cq	CONNOLLY, John		28	M	Laborer	23Ap19Cr
John	(S)	13	M	None	18Ap02Cq	ALLEN, Joseph		29	M	Farmer	23Ap19Cr
Martha	(D)	11	F	None	18Ap02Cq	RAFFERTY, Susana		1C	F	Child	23Ap19Cr
Sarah	(D)	09	F	Child	18Ap02Cq	MAGEE, Sarah		30	F	Spinster	23Ap19Cr
Edward	(S)	07	M	Child	18Ap02Cq	Mary		33	F	Spinster	23Ap19Cr
POTTER, William		34	M	None	18Ap02Cq	MCSORLEY, Bicdy		28	F	Spinster	23Ap19Cr
Margt.	(W)	30	F	Wife	18Ap02Cq	RAFFERTY, Ann		29	F	Spinster	23Ap19Cr
William	(S)	03	M	Child	18Ap02Cq	MCFARLANE, Sarah		28	F	Spinster	23Ap19Cr
Margt.	(D)	.00	F	Irfant	18Ap02Cq	MCGERRITY, Mary		22	F	Spinster	23Ap19Cr
Thomas		30	M	None	18Ap02Cq	ALLEN, Joseph		3C	M	Laborer	23Ap19Cr
						MCCARVER, Mich.		31	M	Servant	23Ap19Cr
						Jane	(W)	30	F	Wife	23Ap19Cr
						FLANIGAN, James		27	M	Laborer	23Ap19Cr
						KING, James		25	M	Farmer	23Ap19Cr
						Mary		09	F	Child	23Ap19Cr
BROTHERS 23 APRIL 1846						MCKEVITT, Cathrine		30	F	Spinster	23Ap19Cr
						Mary	(D)	.10	F	Infant	23Ap19Cr
From Newry						PARRTRIDGE, Ewd.		31	M	Laborer	23Ap19Cr
						BOYLE, John		35	M	Laborer	23Ap19Cr
						HILL, John		37	M	Bricklayer	23Ap19Cr
						MCSHANE, Bern		38	M	Carpenter	23Ap19Cr
MCGRATH, Michael		31	M	Laborer	23Ap19Cr	MINNIS, Rose		35	F	Spinster	23Ap19Cr
Owen		28	M	Laborer	23Ap19Cr	MARKEY, Ann		28	F	Spinster	23Ap19Cr
Sarah	(W)	26	F	Wife	23Ap19Cr	MCDONNELL, Catherine		29	F	Spinster	23Ap19Cr
Michael	(S)	07	M	Child	23Ap19Cr	KEENAN, Biddy		32	F	Spinster	23Ap19Cr
MCMURRAY, Davia		40	M	Farmer	23Ap19Cr	Serah		35	F	Spinster	23Ap19Cr
Eliza	(W)	35	F	Wife	23Ap19Cr	MCKOWN, Patrick		34	M	Laborer	23Ap19Cr
Anne-Jane	(D)	08	F	Chilc	23Ap19Cr	GRIBBEN, Matthew		35	M	Farmer	23Ap19Cr
DORAN, Ann		26	F	Spinster	23Ap19Cr	Betty	(W)	30	F	Wife	23Ap19Cr
Mary		25	F	Spinster	23Ap19Cr	John		28	M	Farmer	23Ap19Cr
Alice		39	F	Wi	23Ap19Cr	Wm.		25	M	Farmer	23Ap19Cr
KILLEEN, Mary		38	F	Spinster	23Ap19Cr	Peter		3C	M	Farmer	23Ap19Cr
HENNING, John		42	M	Farmer	23Ap19Cr	Mary	(W)	27	F	Wife	23Ap19Cr
Serah	(W)	34	F	Wife	23Ap19Cr	Mary	(D)	08	F	Chila	23Ap19Cr

NAMES OF PASSENGERS		AGE	SEX	OCCUPATIONS	DATE PORT SHIP
FRAY, Biddy		33	F	Spinster	23Ap19Cr
KING, Peter		30	M	Laborer	23Ap19Cr
CARVILL, Robert		34	M	Laborer	23Ap19Cr
MURPHY, Edwd.		35	M	Laborer	23Ap19Cr
KING, Catherine		36	F	Servant	23Ap19Cr
MOHAN, Owen		36	M	Farmer	23Ap19Cr
Mary	(W)	34	F	Wife	23Ap19Cr
Ann	(D)	10	F	Child	23Ap19Cr
Mary	(D)	08	F	Child	23Ap19Cr
SHILLON, Biddy		30	F	Spinster	23Ap19Cr
TRIMBBEL, Wm.		38	M	Farmer	23Ap19Cr
FARRELL, Peter		39	M	Laborer	23Ap19Cr
James		43	M	Laborer	23Ap19Cr
KELLY, Patrick		42	M	Farmer	23Ap19Cr
STEWART, David		28	M	Quarryman	23Ap19Cr
KENNEY, Henry		27	M	Farmer	23Ap19Cr
Mary		25	F	Spinster	23Ap19Cr
Biddy		28	F	Spinster	23Ap19Cr
ROGAN, James		30	M	Farmer	23Ap19Cr
GRIMES, James		32	M	Laborer	23Ap19Cr
QUEN, James		33	M	Laborer	23Ap19Cr
DEVLIN, Mary		34	F	Spinster	23Ap19Cr
BURKE, Rose		35	F	Spinster	23Ap19Cr
GIBSON, Sarah-A.		35	F	Wi	23Ap19Cr
FRAZER, Margt.		24	F	Spinster	23Ap19Cr
GIBSON, Eliza		22	F	Spinster	23Ap19Cr
Alex		10	M	Child	23Ap19Cr
BAITTEN, Robert		26	M	Farmer	23Ap19Cr
ARMSTRONG, Wm.		27	M	Farmer	23Ap19Cr
Sarah	(W)	28	F	Wife	23Ap19Cr
MCCOURT, James		30	M	Laborer	23Ap19Cr
GARLAND, Brian		30	M	Blacksmith	23Ap19Cr
ROONEY, Ann		33	F	Spinster	23Ap19Cr
NESBIT, Hamilton		34	M	Farmer	23Ap19Cr
MALLAGH, John		31	M	Laborer	23Ap19Cr
Terence		28	M	Laborer	23Ap19Cr
MURPHY, Edwd.		29	M	Farmer	23Ap19Cr
FEARON, Ann		35	F	Spinster	23Ap19Cr
DOWNEY, Mary		31	F	Spinster	23Ap19Cr
BOYLE, Catherine		33	F	Spinster	23Ap19Cr
MORGAN, Biddy		29	F	Spinster	23Ap19Cr
TREANOR, Mary		28	F	Spinster	23Ap19Cr
BOYLE, Patrick		34	M	Laborer	23Ap19Cr
MCARDLE, Mary		36	F	Spinster	23Ap19Cr
GARVEY, Margt.		31	F	Spinster	23Ap19Cr
MCCANBLY, Mark		30	M	Laborer	23Ap19Cr
GRIMES, Mary-A.		31	F	Spinster	23Ap19Cr
COPELAND, Wm.		36	M	Farmer	23Ap19Cr
STRAIN, Mary		37	F	Spinster	23Ap19Cr
EASTWOOD, Robert		29	M	Farmer	23Ap19Cr
MCCLURY, Robert		26	M	Farmer	23Ap19Cr
Wm.		24	M	Farmer	23Ap19Cr
MILLS, Betty		24	F	Spinster	23Ap19Cr
MORGAN, Michl.		25	M	Laborer	23Ap19Cr
STEEN, Mary		27	F	Spinster	23Ap19Cr
CONNOR, Cathrine		30	F	Spinster	23Ap19Cr
HALLIGAN, Biddy		28	F	Spinster	23Ap19Cr
HOEY, Rose		24	F	Spinster	23Ap19Cr
MULIGAN, Owen		25	M	Farmer	23Ap19Cr
Biddy	(W)	21	F	Wife	23Ap19Cr
THACKEY, Ann		30	F	Servant	23Ap19Cr
HOEY, Cathrine		28	F	Servant	23Ap19Cr
HOUSELY, James		26	M	Carpenter	23Ap19Cr
WOODS, Ann		32	F	Spinster	23Ap19Cr
DONNELLY, Patrick		30	M	Laborer	23Ap19Cr
DONNOLLY, Margt.		26	F	Wife	23Ap19Cr
MOONEN, Mary		30	F	Spinster	23Ap19Cr
CONNOR, Thos.		31	M	Laborer	23Ap19Cr
CALLAN, Ann		33	F	Spinster	23Ap19Cr
WOODS, Peter		29	M	Laborer	23Ap19Cr
PASSMORE, Lucinda		10	F	Child	23Ap19Cr
Mary-Ann		14	F	Child	23Ap19Cr
FARRELL, Ann		30	F	Spinster	23Ap19Cr
Mary		31	F	Spinster	23Ap19Cr
MCFADEN, Cathrine		28	F	Spinster	23Ap19Cr

NAMES OF PASSENGERS		AGE	SEX	OCCUPATIONS	DATE PORT SHIP
QUEN, Cathrine		27	F	Spinster	23Ap19Cr
MOORE, Robert		25	M	Laborer	23Ap19Cr
TRAINOR, Bernd.		28	M	Cooper	23Ap19Cr
LAPPIN, John		31	M	Laborer	23Ap19Cr
STEEL, Sarah		34	F	Spinster	23Ap19Cr
MURPHY, Robt.		35	M	Farmer	23Ap19Cr
Jane	(W)	30	F	Wife	23Ap19Cr
Matthew		20	M	None	23Ap19Cr
Ann		18	F	None	23Ap19Cr
Margt.		17	F	None	23Ap19Cr
George		16	M	None	23Ap19Cr
GRIMES, George		28	M	Laborer	23Ap19Cr
CONROY, Mary		30	F	Spinster	23Ap19Cr
JUDGE, Roseana		31	F	Spinster	23Ap19Cr
SIMPSON, Robt.		40	M	Farmer	23Ap19Cr
Mary	(W)	37	F	Wife	23Ap19Cr
MALONE, Patrick		38	M	Laborer	23Ap19Cr
ROONEY, Patrick		22	M	Laborer	23Ap19Cr
COLLINS, Mary-A.		23	F	Spinster	23Ap19Cr
ROACH, John		21	M	Farmer	23Ap19Cr
Mary-Jane	(W)	18	F	Wife	23Ap19Cr
MCCUDDEN, Mary		22	F	Spinster	23Ap19Cr
CAMPBELL, Wm.		23	M	Laborer	23Ap19Cr
DULLION, James		24	M	Laborer	23Ap19Cr
ROGAN, James		26	M	Laborer	23Ap19Cr
CUNNOUGHA, Terence		28	M	Laborer	23Ap19Cr
BURNS, Brian		29	M	None	23Ap19Cr
Ann		32	F	None	23Ap19Cr
DORAN, Cathrine		33	F	None	23Ap19Cr
FERAN, John		24	M	None	23Ap19Cr
QUEN, John		25	M	None	23Ap19Cr
MCKEVITT, Julia		26	F	Spinster	23Ap19Cr
BURDEN, James		24	M	None	23Ap19Cr

OXFORD 25 APRIL 1846

From Liverpool

NAMES OF PASSENGERS		AGE	SEX	OCCUPATIONS	DATE PORT SHIP
MCCHENACG, Mary		40	F	None	25Ap02Aj
MCGRATH, Patk.		22	M	Hrsm	25Ap02Aj
JAMISON, David		20	M	Laborer	25Ap02Aj
GASTON, James		21	M	Weaver	25Ap02Aj
AGIN, Patk.		24	M	Laborer	25Ap02Aj
MCNAMARA, Patk.		26	M	Laborer	25Ap02Aj
SEWAL, Francis		19	M	Butcher	25Ap02Aj
Francis		24	M	Laborer	25Ap02Aj
KELLY, Thos.		25	M	Laborer	25Ap02Aj
HEWES, Timothy		26	M	Laborer	25Ap02Aj
LOGAN, Patk.		25	M	Laborer	25Ap02Aj
Bridt.		21	F	None	25Ap02Aj
FEENEY, Bridt.		21	F	None	25Ap02Aj
HEWES, Ann		37	F	None	25Ap02Aj
BODKIN, Mary		17	F	None	25Ap02Aj
LEONARD, Mary		15	F	None	25Ap02Aj
FARLEY, Ellen		23	F	None	25Ap02Aj
MURVEY, Marie		22	F	None	25Ap02Aj
GARTIN, Alice		20	F	None	25Ap02Aj
MASCHON, Ann		19	F	None	25Ap02Aj
LARY, Nancy		16	F	None	25Ap02Aj
CRIMMING, John		40	M	Wheelwright	25Ap02Aj
Ellen	(D)	10	F	None	25Ap02Aj
Eliza	(W)	35	F	Wife	25Ap02Aj
Mary	(D)	04	F	Child	25Ap02Aj
Willm.	(S)	01	M	Child	25Ap02Aj
GREGORY, John		25	M	Shoemaker	25Ap02Aj
Rebecca		18	F	None	25Ap02Aj
MACKEY, Eliza-A.		15	F	None	25Ap02Aj
MCCORMICK, Thos.		25	M	Laborer	25Ap02Aj
Catherine		18	F	None	25Ap02Aj

NAMES OF PASSENGERS		AGE	SEX	OCCUPATIONS	DATE PORT SHIP
RILEY, Catherine		21	F	Laborer	25Ap02AJ
BRISLEY, John		29	M	Laborer	25Ap02AJ
LILLY, James		20	M	Laborer	25Ap02AJ
Catherine		15	F	Laborer	25Ap02AJ
HANNING, Margaret		21	F	Laborer	25Ap02AJ
Hannah		20	F	Laborer	25Ap02AJ
ELLIS, Mary		13	F	Laborer	25Ap02AJ
NOLAN, Mary		03	F	Child	25Ap02AJ
SULLIVAN, Dennis		22	M	Tailor	25Ap02AJ
RILEY, Patrick		29	M	Laborer	25Ap02AJ
Rosa		27	F	None	25Ap02AJ
GRAN, James		34	M	Laborer	25Ap02AJ
MURPHY, John		32	M	Laborer	25Ap02AJ
HERLIAN, Patrick		23	M	Laborer	25Ap02AJ
CRIMMINGS, John		13	M	Laborer	25Ap02AJ
BUCKLEY, Mary		20	F	None	25Ap02AJ
SIMMS, Norah		27	F	None	25Ap02AJ
MCCAMBRAY, Norah		20	F	None	25Ap02AJ
BOLAND, John		24	M	Laborer	25Ap02AJ
GLEASON, Michl.		31	M	Laborer	25Ap02AJ
KENNEDY, Dennis		24	M	Laborer	25Ap02AJ
QUIN, John		30	M	Laborer	25Ap02AJ
RIAN, Eliza		22	F	Laborer	25Ap02AJ
POW, Biddy		16	F	None	25Ap02AJ
RIAN, Anna		17	F	None	25Ap02AJ
CARNEY, John		21	M	Laborer	25Ap02AJ
MCLOCRAN, Patk.		22	M	Laborer	25Ap02AJ
Philip		20	M	Laborer	25Ap02AJ
DOUGHERTY, John		20	M	Laborer	25Ap02AJ
LUNCH, Catherine		18	F	Laborer	25Ap02AJ
Catherine		20	F	Laborer	25Ap02AJ
MORSE, Catherine		18	F	Laborer	25Ap02AJ
FORD, John		21	M	Laborer	25Ap02AJ
DEVINE, George		24	M	Laborer	25Ap02AJ
MCGOVERAN, Frank		25	M	Laborer	25Ap02AJ
PURCELL, Patrick		30	M	Laborer	25Ap02AJ
Anna	(W)	30	F	Wife	25Ap02AJ
Philip	(S)	06	M	Child	25Ap02AJ
Thos.	(S)	04	M	Child	25Ap02AJ
Patrick	(S)	03	M	Child	25Ap02AJ
Margaret	(D)	07	F	Child	25Ap02AJ
Mary	(D)	01	F	Child	25Ap02AJ
DUGGAN, Richard		25	M	Laborer	25Ap02AJ
HOGAN, Michael		20	M	Laborer	25Ap02AJ
HATY, James		20	M	Laborer	25Ap02AJ
BURKE, Edwd.		20	M	Laborer	25Ap02AJ
CAMPTON, Thomas		21	M	Laborer	25Ap02AJ
PURCELL, James		20	M	Laborer	25Ap02AJ
WHILAN, John		20	M	Laborer	25Ap02AJ
LESTER, Thos.		20	M	Clerk	25Ap02AJ
WELSH, Michael		19	M	Shoemaker	25Ap02AJ
FLAHERTY, Cornelius		22	M	Farmer	25Ap02AJ
LESTER, Bridget		17	F	None	25Ap02AJ
DALEY, Julia		20	F	None	25Ap02AJ
HOGAN, Anna		14	F	Laborer	25Ap02AJ
ANDERSON, John		19	M	Laborer	25Ap02AJ
William		22	M	Laborer	25Ap02AJ
MAHALPY, Hance		25	M	Laborer	25Ap02AJ
DAVISON, Samuel		27	M	Laborer	25Ap02AJ
HOGAN, Bridget		20	F	None	25Ap02AJ
FLAHARTY, Bridget		05	F	Child	25Ap02AJ
CARR, Martha		20	F	None	25Ap02AJ
HEWS, Mary		18	F	None	25Ap02AJ
MCFREE, David		19	M	Laborer	25Ap02AJ
CLIFFORD, Thomas		19	M	Laborer	25Ap02AJ
Thomas		13	M	Laborer	25Ap02AJ
MARTEN, James		19	M	Weaver	25Ap02AJ
MACK, John		27	M	Carpenter	25Ap02AJ
Bessy		28	F	None	25Ap02AJ
Ann		17	F	None	25Ap02AJ
Margt.		18	F	None	25Ap02AJ
CARROLL, Thomas		18	M	Laborer	25Ap02AJ
MURRIER, Daniel		22	M	Laborer	25Ap02AJ
MCLOCRAN, Margaret		22	F	None	25Ap02AJ
GRIMM, Maria		20	F	None	25Ap02AJ
FLOOD, Mathew		30	M	Laborer	25Ap02AJ
Alla		31	F	None	25Ap02AJ
MOODIE, Patrick		18	M	Painter	25Ap02AJ
KELLY, Mary		33	F	None	25Ap02AJ
LESTRAIN, Bridget		14	F	None	25Ap02AJ
SALMON, Watt		18	M	Laborer	25Ap02AJ
Mary		16	F	None	25Ap02AJ
MARDY, James		17	M	Laborer	25Ap02AJ
CUNNINGHAM, Catherine		25	F	None	25Ap02AJ
Ann	(D)	03	F	Child	25Ap02AJ
Michael	(S)	02	M	Child	25Ap02AJ
CRAWFORD, James		17	M	Laborer	25Ap02AJ
BUCKLEY, Andy		26	M	Laborer	25Ap02AJ
RILEY, Ann		27	F	None	25Ap02AJ
Biddy		25	F	None	25Ap02AJ
HANNAN, Patrick		22	M	Laborer	25Ap02AJ
Catherine		19	F	None	25Ap02AJ
DOLAN, Ann		22	F	None	25Ap02AJ
MOONEY, Honor		22	F	None	25Ap02AJ
GANNON, Margaret		28	F	None	25Ap02AJ
Michael	(S)	04	M	Child	25Ap02AJ
John	(S)	08	M	Child	25Ap02AJ
WELSH, Catherine		19	F	None	25Ap02AJ
KENNEDY, Bridget		17	F	None	25Ap02AJ
GARNLEY, Patrick		20	M	None	25Ap02AJ
COX, Thomas		30	M	Clerk	25Ap02AJ
MCGUINNIS, Willm.		19	M	Laborer	25Ap02AJ
HARRISON, Andrew		21	M	None	25Ap02AJ
NAYLUS, James		12	M	None	25Ap02AJ
Michael		09	M	Child	25Ap02AJ
MCLOCHRAN, Catherine		26	F	None	25Ap02AJ
Patrick		20	M	None	25Ap02AJ
MCLOCHRIN, Thomas		29	M	None	25Ap02AJ
John		19	M	None	25Ap02AJ
Biddy		09	F	Child	25Ap02AJ
GREEN, Mary		23	F	None	25Ap02AJ
FOX, Rosanna		21	F	None	25Ap02AJ
CANE, Rose		25	F	None	25Ap02AJ
Eliza		22	F	None	25Ap02AJ
HINNISS, Mary		16	F	None	25Ap02AJ
DOUGLAS, Robt.		21	M	Gdnr	25Ap02AJ
DOYLE, John		26	M	Laborer	25Ap02AJ
USHER, Thomas		24	M	None	25Ap02AJ
DORSEY, William		24	M	None	25Ap02AJ
MAYERS, Michael		25	M	None	25Ap02AJ
MCFADDON, Edwd.		20	M	None	25Ap02AJ
LETTICE, Andrew		21	M	None	25Ap02AJ
Died-At-Sea					
CASEY, Patrick		20	M	None	25Ap02AJ
HAGAN, Peter		21	M	None	25Ap02AJ
MCDONALD, George		23	M	None	25Ap02AJ
MCDERMOTH, Ann		19	F	None	25Ap02AJ
FARROLL, Edward		22	M	Stctr	25Ap02AJ
DALEY, Elizabeth		19	F	None	25Ap02AJ
CALLAHAN, Sarah		20	F	None	25Ap02AJ
MULLEN, Bridget		25	F	None	25Ap02AJ
BREELY, Jane		25	F	None	25Ap02AJ
GILLIAN, Jane		45	F	None	25Ap02AJ
ALWELL, James		55	M	Laborer	25Ap02AJ
Anna	(W)	55	F	Wife	25Ap02AJ
Patrick	(S)	16	M	None	25Ap02AJ
Margaret	(D)	14	F	None	25Ap02AJ
Phillp	(S)	12	M	Laborer	25Ap02AJ
HILLS, George		49	M	Tailor	25Ap02AJ
Jane	(W)	44	F	Wife	25Ap02AJ
Rosanna	(D)	25	F	None	25Ap02AJ
Eliza	(D)	22	F	None	25Ap02AJ
Nahey	(D)	20	F	None	25Ap02AJ
Marla	(D)	14	F	None	25Ap02AJ
Margaret	(D)	10	F	None	25Ap02AJ
Grace	(D)	06	F	Child	25Ap02AJ
Robert	(S)	08	M	Child	25Ap02AJ
HANNON, Mary-Ann		20	F	None	25Ap02AJ
MANNA, Michael		16	M	None	25Ap02AJ
DARVIN, John		19	M	Laborer	25Ap02AJ

NAMES OF PASSENGERS	AGE	SEX	OCCUPATIONS	DATE PORT SHIP
SHELLY, Judy	16	F	None	25Ap02AJ
CARROLL, John	24	M	Laborer	25Ap02AJ
FORGHERTY, Michael	22	M	Laborer	25Ap02AJ
James	26	M	Laborer	25Ap02AJ
PURCELL, Edward	25	M	Laborer	25Ap02AJ
FORGHERTY, Catherine	23	F	None	25Ap02AJ
MCGUIRE, Timothy	25	M	Laborer	25Ap02AJ
TIRE, Teddy	33	M	Laborer	25Ap02AJ
MURTIGH, William	26	M	Laborer	25Ap02AJ
FORD, Thomas	22	M	Laborer	25Ap02AJ
MULVI, Eliza	22	F	None	25Ap02AJ
YOUNG, Maria	23	F	None	25Ap02AJ
MCILLVAY, Catherine	20	F	None	25Ap02AJ
BURNS, Mary	18	F	None	25Ap02AJ
DOUGHERTY, Harry	40	M	Weaver	25Ap02AJ
DUNN, John	25	M	None	25Ap02AJ
GOCHOVAN, Timothy	27	M	Laborer	25Ap02AJ
DELANY, John	22	M	Laborer	25Ap02AJ
DUNNOIS, John	20	M	Laborer	25Ap02AJ
MECHAN, John	24	M	Shoemaker	25Ap02AJ
CASSIAN, Patrick	24	M	Laborer	25Ap02AJ
DEGNON, Sylvester	22	M	Laborer	25Ap02AJ
CLIBBON, William	25	M	Farmer	25Ap02AJ
GUINAN, William	30	M	Laborer	25Ap02AJ
RIGNEY, Martin	22	M	Laborer	25Ap02AJ
Mary	20	F	None	25Ap02AJ
Judy	14	F	None	25Ap02AJ
WHITE, Johanna	18	F	None	25Ap02AJ
RILEY, Biddy	27	F	None	25Ap02AJ
Margaret (D)	01	F	Child	25Ap02AJ
MARSARTON, John	18	M	Laborer	25Ap02AJ
SHORT, John	38	M	Laborer	25Ap02AJ
CARON, Brian	23	M	Laborer	25Ap02AJ
RILEY, Patrick	18	M	Laborer	25Ap02AJ
CANNA, Elizabeth	20	F	None	25Ap02AJ
HANLIN, Bridget	20	F	None	25Ap02AJ
CLARKIN, Margaret	16	F	None	25Ap02AJ
MASTERTON, Mary	15	F	None	25Ap02AJ
RILEY, Edward	18	M	Laborer	25Ap02AJ
WARD, Michael	19	M	Laborer	25Ap02AJ
CAFFERY, Peter	22	M	Laborer	25Ap02AJ
CLERKIN, Thomas	29	M	Laborer	25Ap02AJ
CAFFERY, Mary	26	F	None	25Ap02AJ
Peggy	18	F	None	25Ap02AJ
CONLY, Isabella	16	F	None	25Ap02AJ
ANDERSON, Sarah	20	F	None	25Ap02AJ
BRADY, Fanny	13	F	None	25Ap02AJ
MUNDY, Ann	25	F	None	25Ap02AJ
GARRETT, Ellen	13	F	None	25Ap02AJ
DOWD, Biddy	26	F	None	25Ap02AJ
James	31	M	Laborer	25Ap02AJ
MORRIS, Thomas	17	M	Laborer	25Ap02AJ
HETTELL, Daniel	30	M	Laborer	25Ap02AJ
MCCANNON, James	21	M	Laborer	25Ap02AJ
MASTERTON, Patrick	22	M	Laborer	25Ap02AJ
LOONEY, Thomas	17	M	Laborer	25Ap02AJ
BRADY, Peter	20	M	Laborer	25Ap02AJ
MCMANN, Bridget	20	F	None	25Ap02AJ
Ann	18	F	None	25Ap02AJ
QUIN, Ann	20	F	None	25Ap02AJ
KIMMIS, Martha	20	F	None	25Ap02AJ
MCGAFFERAY, John	24	M	Laborer	25Ap02AJ
MCGONAL, Patrick	20	M	Blacksmith	25Ap02AJ
GILLIN, James	20	M	Laborer	25Ap02AJ
GRENAN, Hugh	24	M	Cooper	25Ap02AJ
WHALAN, Mary	21	F	None	25Ap02AJ
FARROLL, Nabby	18	F	None	25Ap02AJ
GRENAN, Mary	14	F	None	25Ap02AJ
DELANEY, Mary	23	F	None	25Ap02AJ
BRADY, Barney	23	M	Laborer	25Ap02AJ
LEDDY, Philip	25	M	Carpenter	25Ap02AJ
James	23	M	Laborer	25Ap02AJ
BRADY, Biddy	21	F	None	25Ap02AJ
MURTER, Bessy	16	F	None	25Ap02AJ
SHERDAN, Anny	13	F	None	25Ap02AJ
BRADY, Mary	17	F	None	25Ap02AJ
Biddy	18	F	None	25Ap02AJ
Philip	22	M	Laborer	25Ap02AJ
BURNS, Philip	20	M	Laborer	25Ap02AJ
Mary	18	F	None	25Ap02AJ
MALONE, Margaret	20	F	None	25Ap02AJ
HART, Ellen	22	F	None	25Ap02AJ
Judy	24	F	None	25Ap02AJ
BREENAN, Mary	20	F	None	25Ap02AJ
COCHRAN, Patrick	16	M	Laborer	25Ap02AJ
Michael	22	M	Laborer	25Ap02AJ
GALLAGAN, Daniel	14	M	Laborer	25Ap02AJ
HASLEN, Biddy	16	F	Laborer	25Ap02AJ
NEWMAN, Octavius	24	M	Clerk	25Ap02AJ
MOSELEY, Mary-Ann	24	F	None	25Ap02AJ
Sarah-Jane	26	F	None	25Ap02AJ

PATRICK-HENRY 25 APRIL 1846

From Liverpool

NAMES OF PASSENGERS	AGE	SEX	OCCUPATIONS	DATE PORT SHIP
NEWMAN, Michael	16	M	Student	25Ap02Cw
MARTIN, John	21	M	Laborer	25Ap02Cw
MCGARAHAN, Ann	20	F	Servant	25Ap02Cw
MCKAAIN, Ann	21	F	Servant	25Ap02Cw
MINARY, John	27	M	Laborer	25Ap02Cw
MCKENNA, James	26	M	Farmer	25Ap02Cw
Catharine	21	F	None	25Ap02Cw
BIRCH, John	38	M	Upholsterer	25Ap02Cw
CANTWELL, John	30	M	Farmer	25Ap02Cw
Mary	26	F	None	25Ap02Cw
WATSON, William	26	M	Mason	25Ap02Cw
MASSEY, Thomas	23	M	Farmer	25Ap02Cw
OHARA, Patrick	24	M	Gdnr	25Ap02Cw
BELL, William	25	M	Laborer	25Ap02Cw
MALCOLMSON, Joseph	20	M	Laborer	25Ap02Cw
MCKAY, James	18	M	Farmer	25Ap02Cw
KIRKPATRICK, Robert	26	M	Farmer	25Ap02Cw
STEWART, John	21	M	Farmer	25Ap02Cw
OHARA, Thomas	19	M	Farmer	25Ap02Cw
STEWART, Margarett	19	F	None	25Ap02Cw
WATSON, Elisa	29	F	None	25Ap02Cw
Mary-A.	18	F	None	25Ap02Cw
STEWART, Anne	20	F	None	25Ap02Cw
KIRKPATRICK, Anne	21	F	None	25Ap02Cw
DOHERTY, Mary	20	F	None	25Ap02Cw
MULLEN, Catharine	17	F	None	25Ap02Cw
FLOOD, Patrick	19	M	Laborer	25Ap02Cw
COTTON, Thomas	21	M	Laborer	25Ap02Cw
DRURY, Patrick	20	M	Laborer	25Ap02Cw
CAVENEY, Bridget	21	F	None	25Ap02Cw
BERN, Mary	20	F	None	25Ap02Cw
BURKE, Bridget	20	F	None	25Ap02Cw
OBRIEN, Michael	20	M	Seaman	25Ap02Cw
MULVEY, Patrick	22	M	Laborer	25Ap02Cw
Mary	26	F	None	25Ap02Cw
WHEELAHAN, Michael	22	M	Laborer	25Ap02Cw
KERR, James	21	M	Laborer	25Ap02Cw
MCFADDEN, Cornelius	22	M	Laborer	25Ap02Cw
DUNNE, James	23	M	Laborer	25Ap02Cw
MCONDLE, Owen	22	M	Laborer	25Ap02Cw
ROONEY, Margarett	18	F	None	25Ap02Cw
LYNCH, John	22	M	Laborer	25Ap02Cw
Died-At-Sea				
MCDONNELL, John	21	M	Laborer	25Ap02Cw
CUNNINGHAM, Thomas	21	M	Laborer	25Ap02Cw
BRIEN, Michael	19	M	Laborer	25Ap02Cw
GREEN, James	20	M	Laborer	25Ap02Cw
CONNOR, Mary	18	F	None	25Ap02Cw

NAMES OF PASSENGERS	A G E	S E X	OCCUPATIONS	DATE PORT SHIP
DOYLE, Omy	20	M	Laborer	25Ap02Cw
NOLAN, Patrick	30	M	Laborer	25Ap02Cw
GILTHORPE, James	21	M	Cbtmkr	25Ap02Cw
WATSON, Andrew	20	M	Baker	25Ap02Cw
COONAN, Martin	21	M	Laborer	25Ap02Cw
John	21	M	Laborer	25Ap02Cw
CAHIL, Thomas	22	M	Laborer	25Ap02Cw
KNAGY, Henry	20	M	Laborer	25Ap02Cw
CURREN, Mary	21	F	None	25Ap02Cw
MCKOWN, Patrick	20	M	Laborer	25Ap02Cw
LENNAN, Owen	24	M	Laborer	25Ap02Cw
CLARK, Ann	19	F	None	25Ap02Cw
Margarett	18	F	None	25Ap02Cw
FANEGAN, Anne	19	F	None	25Ap02Cw
TREANOR, John	24	M	Laborer	25Ap02Cw
MALLEN, Toll	26	M	Miller	25Ap02Cw
CAMPBELL, Patt	23	M	Laborer	25Ap02Cw
ROURKE, John	27	M	Laborer	25Ap02Cw
MORGAN, Bridget	20	F	Servant	25Ap02Cw
MURPHY, Michael	24	M	Millwright	25Ap02Cw
MCQUILLAN, Bryan	36	M	Laborer	25Ap02Cw
U (W)	25	F	Wife	25Ap02Cw
Mary	21	F	None	25Ap02Cw
Margarett (D)	01	F	Child	25Ap02Cw
Ann	19	F	None	25Ap02Cw
MCGILL, Alice	20	F	Servant	25Ap02Cw
COLEMAN, Thomas	20	M	Laborer	25Ap02Cw
Mary	20	F	None	25Ap02Cw
WOOD, Ann	22	F	None	25Ap02Cw
MARKEY, Thomas	26	M	Laborer	25Ap02Cw
MCGOWEN, Bessie	16	F	None	25Ap02Cw
FITZPATRICK, Jane	25	F	None	25Ap02Cw
NEVILLE, Mary	20	F	None	25Ap02Cw
CLARK, Peter	24	M	Laborer	25Ap02Cw
Judeth	20	F	None	25Ap02Cw
WALSH, John	26	M	Laborer	25Ap02Cw
COCKRAIN, Elisabeth	20	F	Dressmaker	25Ap02Cw
LAHY, William	36	M	Farmer	25Ap02Cw
U (W)	34	F	Wife	25Ap02Cw
William	21	M	Farmer	25Ap02Cw
Mary	24	F	None	25Ap02Cw
James	19	M	None	25Ap02Cw
John	09	M	Child	25Ap02Cw
Elisabeth	11	F	None	25Ap02Cw
Mary	19	F	None	25Ap02Cw
ACHESON, Margarett	20	F	None	25Ap02Cw
Alice	19	F	None	25Ap02Cw
CHAMBERS, Isabella	07	F	Child	25Ap02Cw
LENAHAN, Mary	20	F	None	25Ap02Cw
WILEY, Isabella	09	F	Child	25Ap02Cw
MCFARLAND, John	20	M	Plumber	25Ap02Cw
DOBSON, Mathew	21	M	Peddler	25Ap02Cw
DOLAN, Patrick	21	M	Laborer	25Ap02Cw
SMITH, Patt	22	M	Laborer	25Ap02Cw
WALLEY, Phillip	21	M	Clerk	25Ap02Cw
FERVIN, John	19	M	Laborer	25Ap02Cw
KOUGH, Susan	18	F	None	25Ap02Cw
FAIOLIN, Catherine	20	F	None	25Ap02Cw
KERR, James	20	M	Clfn	25Ap02Cw
CORMALY, James	25	M	Laborer	25Ap02Cw
LEPHAM, Sam	23	M	Laborer	25Ap02Cw
SANDS, Joseph	30	M	Baker	25Ap02Cw
FARRELLY, Mathias	16	M	Laborer	25Ap02Cw
BOYLAN, Ann	16	F	None	25Ap02Cw
LYNCH, Owen	16	M	Laborer	25Ap02Cw
CAMPBELL, Ann	22	F	None	25Ap02Cw
FARRELLY, Anne	30	F	None	25Ap02Cw
Cornelius	15	M	Laborer	25Ap02Cw
Daniel	20	M	Laborer	25Ap02Cw
Philip	09	M	Child	25Ap02Cw
MCPHILLIPS, Mary	20	F	None	25Ap02Cw
TRAINOR, Mary	20	F	None	25Ap02Cw
CAMPBELL, Laurence	24	M	Laborer	25Ap02Cw
FARRELL, Michael	25	M	Laborer	25Ap02Cw
DUNNE, John	24	M	Laborer	25Ap02Cw

NAMES OF PASSENGERS	A G E	S E X	OCCUPATIONS	DATE PORT SHIP
WALSH, Julia	22	F	None	25Ap02Cw
MOONY, Catharine	20	F	None	25Ap02Cw
WARD, Patrick	25	M	Laborer	25Ap02Cw
Owen	20	M	Laborer	25Ap02Cw
Ann	48	F	None	25Ap02Cw
Ann	18	F	None	25Ap02Cw
Margarett	14	F	None	25Ap02Cw
George	12	M	None	25Ap02Cw
John	10	M	Child	25Ap02Cw
Laurence	08	M	Child	25Ap02Cw
Phillip	05	M	Child	25Ap02Cw
MCKANNA, Henry	30	M	Laborer	25Ap02Cw
CARNEY, John	26	M	Gdnr	25Ap02Cw
FARRILY, Patrick	20	M	Laborer	25Ap02Cw
REILEY, James	17	M	Laborer	25Ap02Cw
HOEY, Owen	20	M	Gdnr	25Ap02Cw
MORGAN, James	21	M	Laborer	25Ap02Cw
EBBITT, Betty	22	F	None	25Ap02Cw
KEARNY, Thomas	26	M	Blacksmith	25Ap02Cw
ECKERSLY, James	21	M	Cobbler	25Ap02Cw
MURRAY, Henry	28	M	Bookmaker	25Ap02Cw
CARR, James	21	M	Laborer	25Ap02Cw
RODGERS, Thomas	30	M	Laborer	25Ap02Cw
GOGGINS, Michael	22	M	Laborer	25Ap02Cw
GAFFNEY, Phillip	21	M	Laborer	25Ap02Cw
FLAHERTY, Mary	30	F	None	25Ap02Cw
MCGOWEN, Thomas	28	M	Cooper	25Ap02Cw
GREEN, Benjamin	40	M	Clfn	25Ap02Cw
BLAKE, James	34	M	Laborer	25Ap02Cw
BRADY, Ellen	14	F	None	25Ap02Cw
SMITH, Bridget	22	F	None	25Ap02Cw
Bridget	18	F	None	25Ap02Cw
FITZPATRICK, Bridget	18	F	None	25Ap02Cw
SHIELDS, Catharine	20	F	None	25Ap02Cw
GAFFNEY, John	24	M	Laborer	25Ap02Cw
BRADY, Rose	20	F	None	25Ap02Cw
MCKOWN, Mary	20	F	Carpenter	25Ap02Cw
OHARA, John	23	M	Laborer	25Ap02Cw
MCLAUGHLIN, John	25	M	Laborer	25Ap02Cw
RILEY, Ann	19	F	None	25Ap02Cw
Ellen	18	F	None	25Ap02Cw
MCLAUGHLIN, Catharine	20	F	None	25Ap02Cw
MORRISON, David	22	M	Laborer	25Ap02Cw
FINNAN, Bridget	19	F	None	25Ap02Cw
GAFFEY, Mary	20	F	None	25Ap02Cw
MCGIVNEY, Ellen	19	F	None	25Ap02Cw
WARD, William	22	M	Laborer	25Ap02Cw
KIERNAN, Ellen	21	F	None	25Ap02Cw
CARNEY, Thos.	22	M	Blacksmith	25Ap02Cw
Mary	18	F	None	25Ap02Cw
FAHELLY, Mary	21	F	None	25Ap02Cw
Thomas (S)	04	M	Child	25Ap02Cw
Elizabeth (D)	02	F	Child	25Ap02Cw
RYAN, Mary	18	F	None	25Ap02Cw
CASY, Mary	22	F	None	25Ap02Cw
MCKOWAN, Susan	21	F	None	25Ap02Cw
CASEY, Timothy	22	M	Mason	25Ap02Cw
Margarett	19	F	None	25Ap02Cw
MULLALY, Catharine	20	F	None	25Ap02Cw
SHORT, Edward	28	M	Laborer	25Ap02Cw
John (S)	07	M	Child	25Ap02Cw
Patrick (S)	06	M	Child	25Ap02Cw
Catharine (D)	03	F	Child	25Ap02Cw
MCDONNELL, Owen	25	M	Laborer	25Ap02Cw
MCGUIRE, Thomas	24	M	Laborer	25Ap02Cw
Bridget	21	F	None	25Ap02Cw
CONOLY, Mary	21	F	None	25Ap02Cw
LOGAN, Mary	03	F	Child	25Ap02Cw
CASEY, Ann	20	F	None	25Ap02Cw
FARRELLY, Bridget	21	F	None	25Ap02Cw
May	14	F	None	25Ap02Cw
Thomas	10	M	Laborer	25Ap02Cw
Died-At-Sea				
LARKEN, U-Mrs.	30	F	None	25Ap02Cw
John (S)	09	M	Child	25Ap02Cw

NAMES OF PASSENGERS		AGE	SEX	OCCUPATIONS	DATE PORT SHIP	NAMES OF PASSENGERS		AGE	SEX	OCCUPATIONS	DATE PORT SHIP
LARKEN, James	(S)	07	M	Child	25Ap02Cw						
Rosey	(D)	05	F	Child	25Ap02Cw						
Patrick	(S)	03	M	Child	25Ap02Cw						
MULLEN, John		27	M	Laborer	25Ap02Cw						
MCMANUS, John		30	M	Laborer	25Ap02Cw	**JAVA 27 APRIL 1846**					
James		12	M	Laborer	25Ap02Cw						
CAULFIELD, Julia		20	F	None	25Ap02Cw	From Liverpool					
ONEIL, Catharine		09	F	Child	25Ap02Cw						
RILEY, Bridget		36	F	None	25Ap02Cw						
REILEY, James		09	M	Child	25Ap02Cw	GRANT, Daniel		22	M	Laborer	27Ap02Cx
KILLROY, Bridgett		20	F	Servant	25Ap02Cw	BERNETT, Michael		20	M	Laborer	27Ap02Cx
GILROY, Ann		20	F	Servant	25Ap02Cw	GRAWEY, Dav.		24	M	Laborer	27Ap02Cx
GLINN, James		26	M	Laborer	25Ap02Cw	WALSH, David		23	M	Laborer	27Ap02Cx
LAVENY, Christianne		19	F	None	25Ap02Cw	PROEKE, Catherin		21	F	None	27Ap02Cx
MADDEN, Bernard		20	M	Laborer	25Ap02Cw	DELAWORTH, Jas.		22	M	Laborer	27Ap02Cx
GILL, Bernard		21	M	Laborer	25Ap02Cw	Sarah		21	F	None	27Ap02Cx
FAY, Margarett		16	F	None	25Ap02Cw	Margaret		18	F	None	27Ap02Cx
KERGAN, Mary		19	F	None	25Ap02Cw	MCJOHATTON, Edwd.		25	M	Laborer	27Ap02Cx
Anne		16	F	None	25Ap02Cw	Michl.		20	M	Laborer	27Ap02Cx
HAMILTON, Mary		21	F	Shoe Binder	25Ap02Cw	MONAGHAN, Rose		28	F	None	27Ap02Cx
Matilda		19	F	Shoe Binder	25Ap02Cw	JEFFERY, Edwd.		24	M	Laborer	27Ap02Cx
SHERIDAN, Ann		21	F	None	25Ap02Cw	Rose		16	F	None	27Ap02Cx
THOMPSON, Rosanna		21	F	None	25Ap02Cw	ROACH, Wm.		27	M	Farmer	27Ap02Cx
MELLON, Robert		20	M	Laborer	25Ap02Cw	Sarah	(W)	25	F	Wife	27Ap02Cx
MORRISON, David		70	M	Laborer	25Ap02Cw	Sarah-Jane	(D)	04	F	Child	27Ap02Cx
SHANNON, William		21	M	Laborer	25Ap02Cw	Mary	(D)	.00	F	Infant	27Ap02Cx
LENNON, Peter		26	M	Laborer	25Ap02Cw	Hugh		31	M	Laborer	27Ap02Cx
MCCASSIN, Patt		21	M	Laborer	25Ap02Cw	SMITH, Eliza		26	F	None	27Ap02Cx
DUFFEE, Patrick		26	M	Laborer	25Ap02Cw	Matt		17	M	Laborer	27Ap02Cx
Patt		19	M	Laborer	25Ap02Cw	HARSALE, Eliza		26	F	None	27Ap02Cx
Mary		16	F	None	25Ap02Cw	Jane		22	F	None	27Ap02Cx
KELLEY, Thomas		26	M	Laborer	25Ap02Cw	DORAGH, Danl.		20	M	Laborer	27Ap02Cx
Bridget		20	F	None	25Ap02Cw	HUGHES, Edward		40	M	Laborer	27Ap02Cx
MAHONE, Peter		20	M	Laborer	25Ap02Cw	CARLIN, Patrick		24	M	Laborer	27Ap02Cx
MCMAHONE, Michael		26	M	Laborer	25Ap02Cw	DALAWORTH, John		55	M	Laborer	27Ap02Cx
Patrick		24	M	Laborer	25Ap02Cw	DONAVIN, Morris		20	M	Laborer	27Ap02Cx
Alice		20	F	None	25Ap02Cw	Mary		23	F	None	27Ap02Cx
RYAN, John		22	M	Laborer	25Ap02Cw	DEMEORID, Malter		21	M	None	27Ap02Cx
MCQUADE, James		22	M	Laborer	25Ap02Cw	John		20	M	None	27Ap02Cx
TRACY, Edward		22	M	Laborer	25Ap02Cw	STANTON, John		22	M	None	27Ap02Cx
FEELY, Mary		20	F	Laborer	25Ap02Cw	HUGHES, Ellen		18	F	None	27Ap02Cx
JOHNSON, Matilda		16	F	Dressmaker	25Ap02Cw	RING, Wm.		22	M	None	27Ap02Cx
MCGAUGHEY, Isabella		21	F	Dressmaker	25Ap02Cw	BROMFIELD, James		24	M	Farmer	27Ap02Cx
SMALL, A.		25	F	Schm	25Ap02Cw	Catharine	(W)	22	F	Wife	27Ap02Cx
SMITH, Hugh		26	M	Laborer	25Ap02Cw	Bridget	(D)	.00	F	Infant	27Ap02Cx
Bridget		26	F	None	25Ap02Cw	SHEKAN, Patk..		23	M	Laborer	27Ap02Cx
MURRAY, Ann		18	F	None	25Ap02Cw	COFFIN, John		19	M	None	27Ap02Cx
MONEGHAN, Mary		25	F	None	25Ap02Cw	Ellen		20	F	None	27Ap02Cx
BRADY, Thomas		18	M	Laborer	25Ap02Cw	HENERY, Margaret		40	F	None	27Ap02Cx
SMITH, Ellen		.06	F	Infant	25Ap02Cw	Mary		20	F	None	27Ap02Cx
RYAN, Michael		20	M	Laborer	25Ap02Cw	COLLINS, Johanna		20	F	None	27Ap02Cx
BURKE, Mary		20	F	None	25Ap02Cw	LYONS, Patk.		22	M	None	27Ap02Cx
HARLIN, James		18	M	Shoemaker	25Ap02Cw	HONE, Mary		18	F	None	27Ap02Cx
CASEY, Ann		18	F	None	25Ap02Cw	REEVE, Margaret		30	F	None	27Ap02Cx
GRIMES, Ann		20	F	None	25Ap02Cw	Patrick	(S)	.00	M	Infant	27Ap02Cx
MALLEN, Michael		25	M	Laborer	25Ap02Cw	KANE, Edward		24	M	None	27Ap02Cx
MADGE, Peter		22	M	Laborer	25Ap02Cw	MCKEA, John		23	M	None	27Ap02Cx
CAULFIELD, Ann		22	F	None	25Ap02Cw	CLEARY, Mary		20	F	None	27Ap02Cx
DONOHUE, Bridget		20	F	None	25Ap02Cw	BOYLE, Ann		20	F	None	27Ap02Cx
GILROY, Catharine		20	F	None	25Ap02Cw	MOREGAN, Felix		30	M	Laborer	27Ap02Cx
DALTON, Lawrence		29	M	Laborer	25Ap02Cw	MCNAMARA, Thomas		22	M	Laborer	27Ap02Cx
TULLY, Ann		18	F	None	25Ap02Cw	Margaret		20	F	None	27Ap02Cx
LYNCH, Judith		18	F	None	25Ap02Cw	HALPER, Michael		08	M	Child	27Ap02Cx
FLOOD, Mary		18	F	None	25Ap02Cw	HANEGAN, Charles		25	M	None	27Ap02Cx
LYONS, Patrick		19	M	Laborer	25Ap02Cw	STUART, James		22	M	None	27Ap02Cx
SMITH, Laurence		21	M	Laborer	25Ap02Cw	MARTIN, Owen		20	M	None	27Ap02Cx
NANERY, Patt		23	M	Laborer	25Ap02Cw	MURRAY, Michael		20	M	None	27Ap02Cx
MCKENNA, Ross		21	M	Laborer	25Ap02Cw	WILBROOK, Thomas		66	M	None	27Ap02Cx
						ELSE, Stephen		31	M	None	27Ap02Cx
						SHAPSHELL, Thomas		31	M	None	27Ap02Cx
						Steadman		28	M	None	27Ap02Cx
						Charles		26	M	None	27Ap02Cx
						HILE, Elizabeth		20	F	None	27Ap02Cx
						DALTON, Robert		30	M	Laborer	27Ap02Cx

NAMES OF PASSENGERS	AGE	SEX	OCCUPATIONS	DATE PORT SHIP	NAMES OF PASSENGERS	AGE	SEX	OCCUPATIONS	DATE PORT SHIP
CORMACK, Ellen	21	F	None	27Ap02Cx	MCGORMAN, Chas.	28	M	None	27Ap02Cx
GILIREN, Ellen	27	F	None	27Ap02Cx	John	26	M	None	27Ap02Cx
BRANT, Fanny	27	F	None	27Ap02Cx	FRIN, John	20	M	None	27Ap02Cx
MOGORICK, Bruand	26	M	None	27Ap02Cx	TURNER, John	28	M	None	27Ap02Cx
FLINN, Bruand	25	M	Farmer	27Ap02Cx	CANAVAN, Michael	19	M	None	27Ap02Cx
MURRAY, Christopher	25	M	Farmer	27Ap02Cx	LEE, James	21	M	None	27Ap02Cx
MAGEE, Patrick	25	M	None	27Ap02Cx	QUINN, Mary	20	F	None	27Ap02Cx
CAMPBELL, Jane	19	F	None	27Ap02Cx	GUIGHAN, Mary	22	F	None	27Ap02Cx
GARTAN, James	19	M	None	27Ap02Cx	MULLEN, Patrick	20	M	None	27Ap02Cx
CALLAGHER, Mary	19	F	None	27Ap02Cx	U (W)	28	F	Wife	27Ap02Cx
MCCONNELL, Catharine	19	F	None	27Ap02Cx	FLANIGAN, Michael	30	M	None	27Ap02Cx
RAFFERTY, Mary	19	F	None	27Ap02Cx	GILLONEY, John	24	M	None	27Ap02Cx
CAMPBELL, Ally	19	F	None	27Ap02Cx	KEEGAN, Maria	18	F	None	27Ap02Cx
CAVANAGH, Margaret	19	F	None	27Ap02Cx	LANGHAN, Margaret	55	F	None	27Ap02Cx
BRODEGAN, Kitty	19	F	None	27Ap02Cx	DURGAN, James	19	M	None	27Ap02Cx
BRINNAN, Patk.	25	M	None	27Ap02Cx	HEYSHAM, Wm.	25	M	None	27Ap02Cx
MCDONALD, Patk.	20	M	None	27Ap02Cx	MULLEN, Thomas	28	M	None	27Ap02Cx
HARLEY, Ann	30	F	None	27Ap02Cx	Bridget	18	F	None	27Ap02Cx
MCINTEGART, Jas.	19	M	None	27Ap02Cx	DRINITY, Ann	16	F	None	27Ap02Cx
MCKENNA, Patk.	19	M	None	27Ap02Cx	SHEARDEN, Felax	17	M	None	27Ap02Cx
MCINTEGART, Catharine	19	F	None	27Ap02Cx	HERNAN, Pat	18	M	None	27Ap02Cx
BAGLEY, Ann	19	F	None	27Ap02Cx	FORGAT, John	20	M	None	27Ap02Cx
FITZPATRICK, Edward	22	M	None	27Ap02Cx	REDMOND, James	30	M	None	27Ap02Cx
MALONE, James	20	M	None	27Ap02Cx	Ellen	24	F	None	27Ap02Cx
MCGUIRE, Pat	21	M	None	27Ap02Cx	LEVI, Wm.	28	M	None	27Ap02Cx
FREHILL, Patt	20	M	None	27Ap02Cx	FARLEY, Owen	20	M	None	27Ap02Cx
KERNAHAN, Peter	20	M	None	27Ap02Cx	CAFFEY, Mary	18	F	None	27Ap02Cx
MALOREE, Nicholas	30	M	None	27Ap02Cx	GUFFREY, Ann	19	F	None	27Ap02Cx
HARE, Michael	29	M	None	27Ap02Cx	MCCAFFREY, Judy	23	F	None	27Ap02Cx
Ann	21	F	None	27Ap02Cx	Catharine	21	F	None	27Ap02Cx
HIGHLAND, Bess	19	F	None	27Ap02Cx	CREED, Phillip	30	M	None	27Ap02Cx
FLOOD, Mary	19	F	None	27Ap02Cx	MONAGHAN, James	29	M	None	27Ap02Cx
KENNEDY, Ann	19	F	None	27Ap02Cx	SULLIVAN, Thos.	28	M	None	27Ap02Cx
BYRNE, Edward	25	M	None	27Ap02Cx	CHRISTTERSON, Thos.	35	M	None	27Ap02Cx
KOGHAN, Christopher	21	M	Farmer	27Ap02Cx	LOUGHAN, Thos.	30	M	None	27Ap02Cx
Michael	19	M	None	27Ap02Cx	James	29	M	None	27Ap02Cx
FIGHE, John	20	M	None	27Ap02Cx	DONALD, Bedy	24	F	None	27Ap02Cx
GANNON, John	20	M	None	27Ap02Cx	May	20	F	None	27Ap02Cx
KEEGAN, Michael	20	M	None	27Ap02Cx	Thomas	.00	M	Infant	27Ap02Cx
OWENS, Wm.	20	M	None	27Ap02Cx	KENNEY, Mary	25	F	None	27Ap02Cx
CRANER, Rose	18	F	None	27Ap02Cx	FANNALL, Mary	20	F	None	27Ap02Cx
LEVY, Pat	27	M	None	27Ap02Cx	BARLOW, Wm.	25	M	None	27Ap02Cx
Ann	23	F	None	27Ap02Cx	LERNNON, Ann	12	F	None	27Ap02Cx
GAYNOR, George	13	M	None	27Ap02Cx	Catherine	13	F	None	27Ap02Cx
MORAN, Ann	25	F	None	27Ap02Cx	BRINE, Timothy	12	M	None	27Ap02Cx
GILLIGAN, Ann	18	F	None	27Ap02Cx	CUNAN, Margaret	22	F	None	27Ap02Cx
CAFFEE, Mary	18	F	None	27Ap02Cx	SLEIGHT, John	20	M	None	27Ap02Cx
KEEGAN, Catharine	20	F	None	27Ap02Cx	Elizabeth	31	F	None	27Ap02Cx
KENNIGAN, Ellen	18	F	None	27Ap02Cx	John	70	M	None	27Ap02Cx
TURNNONS, Francis	20	M	None	27Ap02Cx	Ann	07	F	Child	27Ap02Cx
Bartte.	21	M	None	27Ap02Cx	Susan	04	F	Child	27Ap02Cx
LOUGHLEN, Matthew	20	M	None	27Ap02Cx	MCANALHY, John	27	M	None	27Ap02Cx
TYRALL, James	21	M	None	27Ap02Cx	REGNEY, James	24	M	None	27Ap02Cx
BRADY, Fanny	13	F	None	27Ap02Cx	NELSON, Jonah	42	M	None	27Ap02Cx
LAGHAN, Michael	29	M	None	27Ap02Cx	QUAYLE, Wm.	22	M	None	27Ap02Cx
COYLE, Hugh	25	M	None	27Ap02Cx	CRONELLY, Wm.	20	M	None	27Ap02Cx
CRAMAN, John	18	M	None	27Ap02Cx	SWEENEY, Jane	20	F	None	27Ap02Cx
COYLE, Anne	18	F	None	27Ap02Cx	MALRANY, Patt	23	M	None	27Ap02Cx
WARD, Richard	19	M	None	27Ap02Cx	MCGUIER, Terance	22	M	None	27Ap02Cx
DORNELD, Ellen-G.	19	F	None	27Ap02Cx	NASH, Bridget	19	F	None	27Ap02Cx
GILLERIOT, Ann	19	F	None	27Ap02Cx	MILLER, Mary-A.	18	F	None	27Ap02Cx
SMITH, Hugh	22	M	None	27Ap02Cx	John	13	M	None	27Ap02Cx
CLARKE, Archibald	30	M	None	27Ap02Cx	Wm.	12	M	None	27Ap02Cx
MCDONNALL, Edward	21	M	None	27Ap02Cx	MATHER, Francis	26	M	None	27Ap02Cx
REYNOLD, Alexander	22	M	None	27Ap02Cx	FARLEY, Mary	20	F	None	27Ap02Cx
MARTEN, Jas.	21	M	None	27Ap02Cx	KERN, Margaret	20	F	None	27Ap02Cx
Michael	23	M	None	27Ap02Cx	CUNNINGHAM, Charles	20	M	None	27Ap02Cx
DUMODY, John	20	M	None	27Ap02Cx					
Jane	19	F	None	27Ap02Cx					
GASSNEY, Pat	25	M	None	27Ap02Cx					
CONEGAN, Mary	21	F	None	27Ap02Cx					
MULVAREY, Francis	20	M	None	27Ap02Cx					
SMITH, Ellen	19	F	None	27Ap02Cx					
COSTELL, Jas.	30	M	None	27Ap02Cx					
RIELLY, Margaret	18	F	None	27Ap02Cx					

GREAT-WESTERN 28 APRIL 1846

From Liverpool

NAMES OF PASSENGERS	AGE	SEX	OCCUPATIONS	DATE PORT SHIP
FLETCHER, Robert	25	M	Physician	28Ap02Cy
Ann	22	F	None	28Ap02Cy
THOMPSON, G.H.	26	M	Merchant	28Ap02Cy
AULD, Jno.	32	M	Merchant	28Ap02Cy
PATTERSON, J.	28	M	Merchant	28Ap02Cy
LYSAGHT, Thos.	46	M	Gentleman	28Ap02Cy
URE, Thos.	31	M	Merchant	28Ap02Cy
SPEIRS, John	34	M	Merchant	28Ap02Cy
FORBES, Wm.	30	M	Merchant	28Ap02Cy
DOWIE, Jas.	18	M	Merchant	28Ap02Cy
WADDLE, Thos.	48	M	Merchant	28Ap02Cy
WATSON, George-D.	40	M	Merchant	28Ap02Cy
JONES, H.N.	39	M	Merchant	28Ap02Cy
RICHARDSON, Thos.	27	M	Merchant	28Ap02Cy

SEA-KING 29 APRIL 1846

From Liverpool

NAMES OF PASSENGERS		AGE	SEX	OCCUPATIONS	DATE PORT SHIP
MCCULLOUGH, U	(W)	40	F	Wife	29Ap02Df
Mary	(D)	18	F	Unknown	29Ap02Df
Wm.	(S)	16	M	Unknown	29Ap02Df
John	(S)	12	M	Unknown	29Ap02Df
Grace	(D)	10	F	Unknown	29Ap02Df
Robert	(S)	08	M	Child	29Ap02Df
James	(S)	05	M	Child	29Ap02Df
U		.00	U	Infant	29Ap02Df
GLENN, Samul		28	M	Unknown	29Ap02Df
MCCAHY, James		20	M	Unknown	29Ap02Df
GREER, James		19	M	Unknown	29Ap02Df
CADOCK, James		24	M	Unknown	29Ap02Df
Prudence		20	F	Unknown	29Ap02Df
LITTLE, Andrew		40	M	Unknown	29Ap02Df
GRINDY, James		32	M	Unknown	29Ap02Df
U	(W)	30	F	Wife	29Ap02Df
Eliza	(D)	07	F	Child	29Ap02Df
Martin-James	(S)	05	M	Child	29Ap02Df
Dorethy	(D)	03	F	Child	29Ap02Df
CARTER, Catherine		17	F	None	29Ap02Df
CONNELL, George		21	M	Unknown	29Ap02Df
FITZSIMMONS, James		20	M	Unknown	29Ap02Df
MCBRIDE, Andrew		25	M	Unknown	29Ap02Df
MURPHEY, Joseph		26	M	Unknown	29Ap02Df
U	(W)	24	F	Wife	29Ap02Df
U		.00	U	Infant	29Ap02Df
Auty		16	F	Unknown	29Ap02Df
FARRELLY, James		20	M	Unknown	29Ap02Df
LOFTUS, Bryan		40	M	Unknown	29Ap02Df
PRATT, Joseph		30	M	Unknown	29Ap02Df
MULLINAMORE, James		22	M	Unknown	29Ap02Df
MCLAUGHLIN, Bryan		36	M	Unknown	29Ap02Df
U	(W)	30	F	Wife	29Ap02Df
Anne	(D)	14	F	None	29Ap02Df
Patrick	(S)	07	M	Child	29Ap02Df
Patrick		23	M	Unknown	29Ap02Df
RILEY, Mary		18	F	Unknown	29Ap02Df
LYNCH, Rose		21	F	Unknown	29Ap02Df
GARTLAND, Thomas		22	M	Unknown	29Ap02Df
KEELAN, Terence		30	M	Unknown	29Ap02Df

NAMES OF PASSENGERS		AGE	SEX	OCCUPATIONS	DATE PORT SHIP
DOWDALE, Jane		20	F	Unknown	29Ap02Df
MCDONNELL, James		21	M	Unknown	29Ap02Df
FITZHARRIS, John		25	M	Unknown	29Ap02Df
RYAN, John		21	M	Unknown	29Ap02Df
CLANNY, James		22	M	Unknown	29Ap02Df
MULLOY, Wm.		24	M	Unknown	29Ap02Df
BURKE, Richard		23	M	Unknown	29Ap02Df
BRYAN, Margt.		21	F	Unknown	29Ap02Df
MCNULTY, Danl.		20	M	Unknown	29Ap02Df
RYAN, Patk.		42	M	Unknown	29Ap02Df
John	(S)	11	M	Unknown	29Ap02Df
DALRUNTY, Stephen		21	M	Unknown	29Ap02Df
GARTLAND, James		29	M	Unknown	29Ap02Df
MCLAUGHLIN, Patt		15	M	Unknown	29Ap02Df
QUIGLEY, Bridget		20	F	Unknown	29Ap02Df
MCMORROW, Thos.		24	M	Unknown	29Ap02Df
GEGAN, Saml.		24	M	Unknown	29Ap02Df
MEATH, Anne		21	F	Unknown	29Ap02Df
MCNULTY, Wm.		24	M	Unknown	29Ap02Df
MCATEER, Catherine		21	F	Unknown	29Ap02Df
Ellen		29	F	Unknown	29Ap02Df
CARNEY, Patk.		21	M	Unknown	29Ap02Df
Thomas		20	M	Unknown	29Ap02Df
FOSTER, John		20	M	Unknown	29Ap02Df
Robert		21	M	Unknown	29Ap02Df
ROBINSON, Wm.		16	M	Unknown	29Ap02Df
CONEITY, Mary		16	F	Unknown	29Ap02Df
CLARKE, Mary		20	F	Unknown	29Ap02Df
ARMSTRONG, Mary		20	F	Unknown	29Ap02Df
CLARKE, Bridget		15	F	Unknown	29Ap02Df
GRANT, Michl.		16	M	Unknown	29Ap02Df
RILEY, Thos.		20	M	Unknown	29Ap02Df
GOODWIN, Catherine		20	F	Unknown	29Ap02Df
FITZPATRICK, Martin		22	M	Unknown	29Ap02Df
Mary		20	F	Unknown	29Ap02Df
Ellen		60	F	Unknown	29Ap02Df
Julia		25	F	Unknown	29Ap02Df
FOLEY, John		27	M	Unknown	29Ap02Df
MOYLAN, Michl.		20	M	Unknown	29Ap02Df
U	(W)	40	F	Wife	29Ap02Df
Mary		25	F	Unknown	29Ap02Df
Julia		18	F	Unknown	29Ap02Df
FITZPATRICK, Patt		20	M	Unknown	29Ap02Df
Danl.		18	M	Unknown	29Ap02Df
BREEN, Wm.		25	M	Unknown	29Ap02Df
DALY, Judith		19	F	Unknown	29Ap02Df
WALSH, John		25	M	Unknown	29Ap02Df
BOURKE, Wm.		25	M	Unknown	29Ap02Df
CLEMENTS, Henry		20	M	Unknown	29Ap02Df
HILLIARD, Henry		55	M	Unknown	29Ap02Df
SCALLY, Mary		25	F	Unknown	29Ap02Df
MARKEY, Jane		25	F	Unknown	29Ap02Df
MCGEE, Michl.		25	M	Unknown	29Ap02Df
FARRELLY, Saml.		25	M	Unknown	29Ap02Df
TURLEY, Margt.		20	F	Unknown	29Ap02Df
DUDMEDER, George		22	M	Unknown	29Ap02Df
MACCORMICK, Catherine		21	F	Unknown	29Ap02Df
DOYLE, Ellen		20	F	Unknown	29Ap02Df
MCLEAN, Mary		20	F	Unknown	29Ap02Df
HOWARD, Thos.		25	M	Unknown	29Ap02Df
LAVERY, Patt		30	M	Unknown	29Ap02Df
TYZE, James		20	M	Unknown	29Ap02Df
GARLANY, John		16	M	Unknown	29Ap02Df
CONNOR, Mary		26	F	Unknown	29Ap02Df
SEAGRAVE, Mary		26	F	Unknown	29Ap02Df
SMITH, Richard		26	M	Unknown	29Ap02Df
Margaret		25	F	Unknown	29Ap02Df
GILMORE, Mary		29	F	Unknown	29Ap02Df
MOORE, Bridget		23	F	Unknown	29Ap02Df
CONNOLLY, Margt.		23	F	Unknown	29Ap02Df
HALLORAN, Edwd.		27	M	Unknown	29Ap02Df
LAVERY, Timothy		27	M	Unknown	29Ap02Df
SHEA, Catherine		23	F	Unknown	29Ap02Df
FITZGERALD, Margt.		20	F	Unknown	29Ap02Df
MAHER, Andrew		27	M	Unknown	29Ap02Df

NAMES OF PASSENGERS		AGE	SEX	OCCUPATIONS	DATE PORT SHIP	NAMES OF PASSENGERS		AGE	SEX	OCCUPATIONS	DATE PORT SHIP
MAHER, Ellen		17	F	Unknown	29Ap02Df	CONNOUGHTON, Honor		23	F	None	30Ap02Dl
CAFFREY, Patt		27	M	Unknown	29Ap02Df	MCDANIEL, Thos.		22	M	Laborer	30Ap02Dl
Catherine		18	F	Unknown	29Ap02Df	NORTON, Biddy		22	F	Laborer	30Ap02Dl
Bernard		21	M	Unknown	29Ap02Df	GALLGHER, Mary		23	F	Laborer	30Ap02Dl
TUITE, Micheal		19	M	Unknown	29Ap02Df	TALLON, Sally		22	F	Laborer	30Ap02Dl
Bernard		18	M	Unknown	29Ap02Df	DERVIN, Mathew		25	M	Tanner	30Ap02Dl
CORSCADEN, Thos.		21	M	Unknown	29Ap02Df	Mary		21	F	None	30Ap02Dl
FARRON, Mary		19	F	Unknown	29Ap02Df	CASSIDY, Cath.		20	F	None	30Ap02Dl
Bridget		10	F	Child	29Ap02Df	MCGOWAN, Cath.		19	F	None	30Ap02Dl
John		09	M	Child	29Ap02Df	HOPKINS, Hugh		20	M	Laborer	30Ap02Dl
DOGHERTY, Patt		20	M	Unknown	29Ap02Df	MCMASTER, Wm.		25	M	None	30Ap02Dl
MCCARRON, Rose		20	F	Unknown	29Ap02Df	MCMANELON, John		21	M	None	30Ap02Dl
MCNABB, Mary		21	F	Unknown	29Ap02Df	CRANFORD, James		19	M	None	30Ap02Dl
Owen		20	M	Unknown	29Ap02Df	ALLEN, Eliza		20	F	None	30Ap02Dl
NUGENT, Thos.		48	M	Unknown	29Ap02Df	Rebecca		30	F	None	30Ap02Dl
RAFFERTY, Betty		32	F	Unknown	29Ap02Df	Robert		30	M	None	30Ap02Dl
DALY, Betty		21	F	Unknown	29Ap02Df	LYNARD, Jas.		18	M	None	30Ap02Dl
MCGOVERN, John		33	M	Unknown	29Ap02Df	Wm.		07	M	Child	30Ap02Dl
KIRK, Thomas		26	M	Unknown	29Ap02Df	CRISLEY, John		29	M	None	30Ap02Dl
AYLWARD, Martin		26	M	Unknown	29Ap02Df	LANE, James		20	M	None	30Ap02Dl
KILLY, Ellen		10	F	Child	29Ap02Df	COONEY, Mich.		27	M	Farmer	30Ap02Dl
DOORLY, Mary		39	F	Unknown	29Ap02Df	Rodger		23	M	None	30Ap02Dl
John	(S)	09	M	Child	29Ap02Df	KELLY, Sarah		27	F	None	30Ap02Dl
HUGHES, Michl.		21	M	Unknown	29Ap02Df	CONNER, Mary		23	F	None	30Ap02Dl
Peter		26	M	Unknown	29Ap02Df	CASEY, Edward		28	M	None	30Ap02Dl
MCFADDEN, Hannah		20	F	Unknown	29Ap02Df	EAGAN, Mary		19	F	None	30Ap02Dl
MCGINLEY, Cornelius		23	M	Unknown	29Ap02Df	Peter		21	M	None	30Ap02Dl
WOODS, Bridget		21	F	Unknown	29Ap02Df	LOGAN, John		40	M	None	30Ap02Dl
MURRAY, John		25	M	Unknown	29Ap02Df	REGAN, Mary		30	F	None	30Ap02Dl
COSGROVE, Anne		21	F	Unknown	29Ap02Df	WALSH, Patt		19	M	Farmer	30Ap02Dl
FARLEY, Patt		37	M	Unknown	29Ap02Df	ONNORD, Maurice		32	M	None	30Ap02Dl
U	(W)	36	F	Wife	29Ap02Df	HOUND, Mary		18	F	None	30Ap02Dl
Philip	(S)	13	M	Unknown	29Ap02Df	BLENETT, Cath.		19	F	None	30Ap02Dl
Anne	(D)	11	F	Unknown	29Ap02Df	SCANLEN, Biddy		17	F	None	30Ap02Dl
CARTER, Mary		18	F	Unknown	29Ap02Df	DEMPSEY, Dennis		27	M	Tanner	30Ap02Dl
Mary		04	F	Child	29Ap02Df	James		25	M	None	30Ap02Dl
FITZSIMONS, Mary		22	F	Unknown	29Ap02Df	Cath.		20	F	None	30Ap02Dl
Ann		20	F	Unknown	29Ap02Df	Julia		19	F	None	30Ap02Dl
MCCLUSKEY, John		20	M	Unknown	29Ap02Df	NEAL, Julia		19	F	None	30Ap02Dl
MCGAHON, Hugh		21	M	Unknown	29Ap02Df	DEMPSEY, Ann		17	F	None	30Ap02Dl
TRACY, Margt.		31	F	Unknown	29Ap02Df	John		20	M	Laborer	30Ap02Dl
MANUS, Lucy		17	F	Unknown	29Ap02Df	CATER, John		15	M	None	30Ap02Dl
Mary-Anne		15	F	Unknown	29Ap02Df	CONNER, Honor		20	F	None	30Ap02Dl
James		07	M	Child	29Ap02Df	Peggy		19	F	None	30Ap02Dl
MULLINAMORE, Anne		21	F	Unknown	29Ap02Df	KENNEDY, James		25	M	None	30Ap02Dl
MCKAFFREY, Alexr.		20	M	Unknown	29Ap02Df	CONDON, Michael		24	M	Farmer	30Ap02Dl
Anne		18	F	Unknown	29Ap02Df	MCGRATH, Patt		26	M	None	30Ap02Dl
OBRIEN, Catherine		20	F	Unknown	29Ap02Df	QUINN, Cath.		23	F	None	30Ap02Dl
DONLAN, Patk.		21	M	Unknown	29Ap02Df	MALAEDY, Cath.		27	F	None	30Ap02Dl
HANLON, Wm.		30	M	Unknown	29Ap02Df	CONLAN, Mary		26	F	None	30Ap02Dl
U	(W)	26	F	Wife	29Ap02Df	DOYLE, Mary		22	F	None	30Ap02Dl
U		.00	U	Infant	29Ap02Df	QUENY, Elenor		19	F	None	30Ap02Dl
FREEHILL, Elen		19	U	Unknown	29Ap02Df	GIBSON, Sandy		28	M	Laborer	30Ap02Dl
RILEY, Elen		20	F	Unknown	29Ap02Df	LYNON, Margaret		22	F	None	30Ap02Dl
MCGOVERN, Anne		20	F	Unknown	29Ap02Df	BARRET, Ellen		20	F	None	30Ap02Dl
EGAN, Wm.		51	M	Unknown	29Ap02Df	GATELY, Margaret		20	F	None	30Ap02Dl
BLAKE, Richard		29	M	Unknown	29Ap02Df	DONOHUGH, Bridget		18	F	None	30Ap02Dl
GREMDLY, Emily		02	F	Child	29Ap02Df	HAMILTON, Pattrick		30	M	Tanner	30Ap02Dl
HANLON, Mary		02	F	Child	29Ap02Df	Jane		22	F	None	30Ap02Dl
						Mary		20	F	None	30Ap02Dl
						NEILLY, Mary		25	F	None	30Ap02Dl
						QUINN, James		23	M	None	30Ap02Dl
						JOHNSON, Robert		26	M	Laborer	30Ap02Dl
						MCKINNY, Ellis		20	M	None	30Ap02Dl
						CRANLEY, Daniel		24	M	None	30Ap02Dl
						CONNER, Cath.		25	F	None	30Ap02Dl
		VENICE 30 APRIL 1846				DOHERTY, Ellen		25	M	None	30Ap02Dl
						LEAHY, Simon		25	M	None	30Ap02Dl
		From Liverpool				Margaret		19	F	None	30Ap02Dl
						MCTEEGUE, James		27	M	None	30Ap02Dl
MURPHEY, Cath.		22	F	None	30Ap02Dl	KELLY, Charles		20	M	None	30Ap02Dl
MCELROY, Thomas		21	M	Laborer	30Ap02Dl	MALONY, John		20	M	Tanner	30Ap02Dl
KELLY, Martin		30	M	Tanner	30Ap02Dl	MURPHEY, Edward		20	M	None	30Ap02Dl
CROSBY, Bridget		26	F	None	30Ap02Dl	MULROY, John		22	M	None	30Ap02Dl
CONNOUGHTON, Pat		25	M	None	30Ap02Dl	BUCK, Pat		20	M	None	30Ap02Dl

NAMES OF PASSENGERS		A G E	S E X	OCCUPATIONS	DATE PORT SHIP	NAMES OF PASSENGERS		A G E	S E X	OCCUPATIONS	DATE PORT SHIP
CAIN, Thos.		21	M	None	30Ap02DI	BROGAN, Hugh		25	M	Sailor	30Ap02DI
John		20	M	None	30Ap02DI	GALLAGHER, Dennis		22	M	Blacksmith	30Ap02DI
SKIHAN, Wm.		19	M	None	30Ap02DI	GALBRAITH, Samuel		18	M	Laborer	30Ap02DI
QUIGLEY, Bridget		20	F	None	30Ap02DI	DONELLY, Mary		22	F	None	30Ap02DI
CONLAN, Wm.		25	M	None	30Ap02DI	MCGLACHY, Ellen		26	F	None	30Ap02DI
GALVIN, Edward		20	M	Farmer	30Ap02DI	OWEN, Michael		21	M	None	30Ap02DI
KENE, Patt		18	M	None	30Ap02DI	CAULFIELD, Thos.		19	M	None	30Ap02DI
LOURY, Biddy		12	F	None	30Ap02DI	John		21	M	None	30Ap02DI
GILLIGAN, Mary		19	F	None	30Ap02DI	MCKINNEY, Thos.		45	M	Weaver	30Ap02DI
CONWAY, Mary		20	F	None	30Ap02DI	KANE, Richard		24	M	Laborer	30Ap02DI
LOURY, John		08	M	Child	30Ap02DI	SHINE, Judy		20	F	None	30Ap02DI
MOORE, Patt		22	M	None	30Ap02DI	Cath.		21	F	None	30Ap02DI
Biddy		30	F	None	30Ap02DI	RIELY, Bridget		26	F	None	30Ap02DI
TINNATY, Cath.		20	F	None	30Ap02DI	MCINTIRE, Cella		19	F	None	30Ap02DI
HORAN, Michael		20	M	None	30Ap02DI	TURNEY, Rosy		20	F	None	30Ap02DI
MCKENA, James		20	M	Laborer	30Ap02DI	CONNER, Jane		20	F	None	30Ap02DI
BOYD, David		76	M	None	30Ap02DI	BRETT, Wm.		27	M	None	30Ap02DI
Died-At-Sea						JUDY, Michael		24	M	None	30Ap02DI
Andrew		37	M	None	30Ap02DI	SULLIVAN, Patt		26	M	None	30Ap02DI
Cath.		40	F	None	30Ap02DI	KNIGHT, Emella		22	F	None	30Ap02DI
John		01	M	Child	30Ap02DI	TREHEARY, Mary		21	F	None	30Ap02DI
Died-At-Sea						MURREY, Mary		15	F	None	30Ap02DI
James		01	M	Child	30Ap02DI	NAGLE, James		21	M	None	30Ap02DI
HOPKINS, Patt		24	M	Tanner	30Ap02DI	WEND, Michael		18	M	None	30Ap02DI
CAVELLY, Nelly		21	F	None	30Ap02DI	KEEFE, Daniel		26	M	None	30Ap02DI
Cath.		22	F	None	30Ap02DI	RAGAN, Thos.		24	M	Laborer	30Ap02DI
MCKINNEY, John		24	M	None	30Ap02DI	KEEFE, Bessy		19	F	None	30Ap02DI
Mary		24	F	None	30Ap02DI	FITZPATRICK, Cath.		19	F	None	30Ap02DI
William		21	M	None	30Ap02DI	NOLEN, Bridget		32	F	None	30Ap02DI
REYNOLDS, Ellen		25	F	None	30Ap02DI	Patrick	(S)	10	M	Child	30Ap02DI
BRENNAN, Michael		20	M	Farmer	30Ap02DI	Cathrine	(D)	08	F	Child	30Ap02DI
SHORTAL, Brian		22	M	Cbtmkr	30Ap02DI	Mary	(D)	04	F	Child	30Ap02DI
NOLAN, James		24	M	Laborer	30Ap02DI	LECKER, Neal		60	M	None	30Ap02DI
MCMANUS, Thos.		20	M	Laborer	30Ap02DI	Mary		20	F	None	30Ap02DI
James		18	M	None	30Ap02DI	Ellen		23	F	None	30Ap02DI
Ann		25	F	None	30Ap02DI	Mary		04	F	None	30Ap02DI
GRIMES, Ann		40	F	None	30Ap02DI	GELFRIN, Ann		20	F	None	30Ap02DI
Mary	(D)	06	F	Child	30Ap02DI	GELCHRIST, Alex		26	M	None	30Ap02DI
John	(S)	03	M	Child	30Ap02DI	Wm.		10	M	None	30Ap02DI
Margaret	(D)	10	F	Child	30Ap02DI	Ann		21	F	None	30Ap02DI
LENNOX, James		24	M	Tanner	30Ap02DI	CAMPBELL, Jane		20	F	None	30Ap02DI
RUSH, Nancy		21	F	None	30Ap02DI	KENNA, James		20	M	None	30Ap02DI
BYRNES, Margaret		21	F	None	30Ap02DI	WALSH, Patrick		50	M	None	30Ap02DI
MCDONELL, Edward		20	M	None	30Ap02DI	John	(S)	27	M	None	30Ap02DI
Patt		21	M	None	30Ap02DI	Patt	(S)	25	M	None	30Ap02DI
MCADAM, James		21	M	None	30Ap02DI	Hannah	(W)	50	F	Wife	30Ap02DI
HENNLER, Wm.		22	M	None	30Ap02DI	Mary	(D)	27	F	None	30Ap02DI
Margaret		21	F	None	30Ap02DI	DOLAN, Nancy		21	F	None	30Ap02DI
Cath.		18	F	None	30Ap02DI	John	(S)	04	M	Child	30Ap02DI
HAGAN, Thomas		30	M	None	30Ap02DI	Patrick	(S)	03	M	Child	30Ap02DI
MULLALY, John		19	M	None	30Ap02DI	LOFTUS, Thomas		27	M	None	30Ap02DI
MULROY, James		19	M	None	30Ap02DI	KELLY, Patt		19	M	None	30Ap02DI
LENGUIG, Mary		22	F	None	30Ap02DI	HUGHES, John		25	M	None	30Ap02DI
SULLIVAN, Edward		17	M	None	30Ap02DI	Frank		30	M	None	30Ap02DI
STRONG, John		24	M	Baker	30Ap02DI	U	(W)	26	F	Wife	30Ap02DI
TULLY, Patt		21	M	Laborer	30Ap02DI	Ellen	(D)	06	F	Child	30Ap02DI
HANEHAN, Patt		28	M	None	30Ap02DI	MCCABE, Cath.		20	F	None	30Ap02DI
WALSH, Julia		20	F	None	30Ap02DI	Wm.		30	M	None	30Ap02DI
HONELL, Bridget		25	F	None	30Ap02DI	WATERS, Bridget		12	F	None	30Ap02DI
KEEFE, Mary		23	F	None	30Ap02DI	COCHRAN, Robert		28	M	Blacksmith	30Ap02DI
DALEY, Mary		21	F	None	30Ap02DI	Jane		24	F	None	30Ap02DI
MITCHELL, Cath.		21	F	None	30Ap02DI	Elizabeth		18	F	None	30Ap02DI
COLTHER, Patt		22	M	None	30Ap02DI	Daniel		02	M	Child	30Ap02DI
James		20	M	None	30Ap02DI	PETTERSON, Robert		24	M	Laborer	30Ap02DI
CAVENEH, Michael		26	M	None	30Ap02DI	Margaret		22	F	None	30Ap02DI
CALLAHER, Judith		40	F	None	30Ap02DI	MULVOY, Mary		42	F	None	30Ap02DI
Biddy	(D)	07	F	Child	30Ap02DI	RIDER, James		43	M	None	30Ap02DI
CAVENEH, Cath.		06	F	Child	30Ap02DI	U	(W)	44	F	Wife	30Ap02DI
DALEY, James		29	M	None	30Ap02DI	FAGAN, B.		45	U	None	30Ap02DI
CONSTANT, Peter		21	M	Shoemaker	30Ap02DI	MALHAUL, John		46	M	None	30Ap02DI
Frances		20	F	None	30Ap02DI	LEIGH, Edward		27	M	None	30Ap02DI
Ellen		19	F	None	30Ap02DI	NELLY, Patt		20	M	None	30Ap02DI
TUERRY, Terrence		20	M	None	30Ap02DI	MCGRATH, Owen		21	M	None	30Ap02DI
Eliza		21	F	None	30Ap02DI	LYNCH, Ellen		21	F	None	30Ap02DI
DORNMAN, Hugh		18	M	Wool Comber	30Ap02DI	RILLY, Margaret		26	F	None	30Ap02DI

51

NAMES OF PASSENGERS		A G E	S E X	OCCUPATIONS	DATE PORT SHIP	NAMES OF PASSENGERS		A G E	S E X	OCCUPATIONS	DATE PORT SHIP
MORAN, John		25	M	None	30Ap02Di	FAGAN, Christ		19	M	Laborer	01Ma02Dj
DARVIN, Luke		23	M	None	30Ap02Di	GRAHAM, James		22	M	Laborer	01Ma02Dj
MCGUIRE, Hugh		21	M	None	30Ap02Di	SHERIDAN, Ally		19	F	Laborer	01Ma02Dj
MCCARTHY, Patrick		21	M	None	30Ap02Di	Biddy		19	F	Laborer	01Ma02Dj
MCMAINS, Anne		25	F	None	30Ap02Di	FANNEL, James		19	M	Laborer	01Ma02Dj
GILCHREST, William		25	M	None	30Ap02Di	WALTON, Eliza		19	F	Laborer	01Ma02Dj
Eliza	(W)	20	F	Wife	30Ap02Di	DALY, James		19	M	Laborer	01Ma02Dj
James	(S)	04	M	Child	30Ap02Di	LESTER, George		21	M	Laborer	01Ma02Dj
						RYAN, William		31	M	Laborer	01Ma02Dj
						REILLY, James		22	M	Laborer	01Ma02Dj
						MEE, Thomas		26	M	Laborer	01Ma02Dj
						FARRELL, John		46	M	Laborer	01Ma02Dj
ORPHAN 01 MAY 1846						Mary	(W)	40	F	Wife	01Ma02Dj
						Bridget	(D)	20	F	Laborer	01Ma02Dj
From Liverpool						May	(D)	18	F	Laborer	01Ma02Dj
						Jane	(D)	15	F	Laborer	01Ma02Dj
						John	(S)	12	M	Laborer	01Ma02Dj
						Alice	(D)	06	F	Child	01Ma02Dj
						Ann	(D)	04	F	Child	01Ma02Dj
KEATING, James		21	M	Laborer	01Ma02Dj	Cath.	(D)	.00	F	Infant	01Ma02Dj
CLARK, David		25	M	Laborer	01Ma02Dj	NEIL, Thomas		21	M	Laborer	01Ma02Dj
Ann	(W)	20	F	Wife	01Ma02Dj	BROOKE, J.H.		25	M	Laborer	01Ma02Dj
June	(D)	.05	F	Infant	01Ma02Dj	U	(W)	22	F	Wife	01Ma02Dj
MURPHY, David		22	M	Laborer	01Ma02Dj	KENNEDY, Robt.		24	M	Laborer	01Ma02Dj
Cath.		19	F	Laborer	01Ma02Dj	Eliza	(W)	21	F	Wife	01Ma02Dj
Tim		25	M	Laborer	01Ma02Dj	Isabella	(D)	05	F	Child	01Ma02Dj
MCKENNA, Margt.		35	F	Laborer	01Ma02Dj	WALLACE, Rob.		21	M	Laborer	01Ma02Dj
SHANY, Margt.		20	F	Laborer	01Ma02Dj	DONOHOE, Ann		16	F	Laborer	01Ma02Dj
MCRUDDEN, Margt.		20	F	Laborer	01Ma02Dj	OBRIEN, Letitia		22	F	Laborer	01Ma02Dj
KELLY, Dennis		26	M	Laborer	01Ma02Dj	FLANAGAN, Mary		20	F	Laborer	01Ma02Dj
John		33	M	Laborer	01Ma02Dj	OATES, Eliza		18	F	Laborer	01Ma02Dj
DOLAN, Michl.		26	M	Laborer	01Ma02Dj	MULLERS, Niel		25	M	Laborer	01Ma02Dj
U	(W)	20	F	Wife	01Ma02Dj	KENIMAN, John		20	M	Laborer	01Ma02Dj
COFFEY, Morris		22	M	Laborer	01Ma02Dj	Mary		30	F	Laborer	01Ma02Dj
MAGINNIS, Martin		24	M	Laborer	01Ma02Dj	BRACKEN, Ann		20	F	Laborer	01Ma02Dj
U	(W)	21	F	Wife	01Ma02Dj	MARTIN, Mary		17	F	Laborer	01Ma02Dj
TRACEY, Thomas		22	M	Laborer	01Ma02Dj	HALPIN, Christopher		21	M	Laborer	01Ma02Dj
James		15	M	Laborer	01Ma02Dj	CATHERWOOD, Andrew		21	M	Laborer	01Ma02Dj
KEOGHAN, Mich.		26	M	Laborer	01Ma02Dj	NEIL, Mary		30	F	Laborer	01Ma02Dj
MORGAN, Mary		18	F	Laborer	01Ma02Dj	MACOM, Simon		25	M	Laborer	01Ma02Dj
Pat		07	M	Child	01Ma02Dj	U	(W)	25	F	Wife	01Ma02Dj
CAWLIN, Bridget		24	F	Laborer	01Ma02Dj	Letitia	(D)	03	F	Child	01Ma02Dj
BRANNAN, Bridget		20	F	Laborer	01Ma02Dj	U	(D)	.00	F	Infant	01Ma02Dj
NOLAN, Rose		20	F	Laborer	01Ma02Dj	GALLAGHER, Saml.		25	M	Laborer	01Ma02Dj
BUTTERLY, Edw.		28	M	Laborer	01Ma02Dj	James		20	M	Laborer	01Ma02Dj
SMITH, Owen		50	M	Laborer	01Ma02Dj	RAMP, James		40	M	Laborer	01Ma02Dj
Ann	(W)	45	F	Wife	01Ma02Dj	BROWN, Soapy		30	F	Laborer	01Ma02Dj
Patk.	(S)	25	M	Laborer	01Ma02Dj	SPEIR, Alexander		19	M	Laborer	01Ma02Dj
Owen	(S)	20	M	Laborer	01Ma02Dj	MURPHY, James		25	M	Laborer	01Ma02Dj
Mary	(D)	17	F	Laborer	01Ma02Dj	Cath		20	F	Laborer	01Ma02Dj
William	(S)	14	M	Laborer	01Ma02Dj	John		22	M	Laborer	01Ma02Dj
Michael		35	M	Laborer	01Ma02Dj	John		20	M	Laborer	01Ma02Dj
May	(W)	30	F	Wife	01Ma02Dj	Pat		21	M	Laborer	01Ma02Dj
Cath.	(D)	05	F	Child	01Ma02Dj	BANNON, Pat		25	M	Laborer	01Ma02Dj
Andrew	(S)	03	M	Child	01Ma02Dj	Kit		23	F	Laborer	01Ma02Dj
James	(S)	01	M	Child	01Ma02Dj	Ann		25	F	Laborer	01Ma02Dj
LUDLOW, Brigelt		21	F	Laborer	01Ma02Dj	May	(D)	.00	F	Infant	01Ma02Dj
HOEY, Bridget		20	F	Laborer	01Ma02Dj	VANCE, Eliza		30	F	Laborer	01Ma02Dj
CARLETON, Chr.		35	M	Laborer	01Ma02Dj	MCGUKIN, Eliza		25	F	Laborer	01Ma02Dj
Caroline	(W)	35	F	Wife	01Ma02Dj	HALL, James		30	M	Laborer	01Ma02Dj
James	(S)	18	M	Laborer	01Ma02Dj	BRADY, James		25	M	Laborer	01Ma02Dj
Ann	(D)	10	F	Laborer	01Ma02Dj	Cath.		22	F	Laborer	01Ma02Dj
ELLIOTT, Thomas		20	M	Laborer	01Ma02Dj	SMITH, May		20	F	Laborer	01Ma02Dj
RYAN, William		25	M	Laborer	01Ma02Dj	MCCALL, Margt.		20	F	Laborer	01Ma02Dj
BISBY, Margt.		19	F	Laborer	01Ma02Dj	MCCANN, Hugh		09	M	Child	01Ma02Dj
GARDNER, William		21	M	Laborer	01Ma02Dj	Margt.		04	F	Child	01Ma02Dj
Eliza		17	F	Laborer	01Ma02Dj	SMITH, John		24	M	Laborer	01Ma02Dj
ROMUS, Eliza		21	F	Laborer	01Ma02Dj	KELLY, Michl.		22	M	Laborer	01Ma02Dj
Hannah		19	F	Laborer	01Ma02Dj	HALPIN, Patt		24	M	Laborer	01Ma02Dj
FITZWILLIAM, Danl.		40	M	Laborer	01Ma02Dj	SMITH, Ann		24	F	Laborer	01Ma02Dj
FENNAY, Rich.		20	M	Laborer	01Ma02Dj	Eliza	(D)	07	F	Child	01Ma02Dj
DEVLIN, Bessy		19	F	Laborer	01Ma02Dj	BRICK, William		30	M	Laborer	01Ma02Dj
FOULD, Margt.		19	F	Laborer	01Ma02Dj	EACH, George		19	M	Laborer	01Ma02Dj
CASSIDY, Mary		19	F	Laborer	01Ma02Dj	Miles		19	M	Laborer	01Ma02Dj
FLAHERTY, Margt.		19	F	Laborer	01Ma02Dj	WALSH, Patt		20	M	Laborer	01Ma02Dj

| --- | --- | --- | --- | --- |
WALSH, Peter	18	M	Laborer	01Ma02DJ
FUNNIGAN, Peter	17	M	Laborer	01Ma02DJ
KEENAN, Alice	22	F	Laborer	01Ma02DJ
MCDONNELL, Bridget	18	F	Laborer	01Ma02DJ
FARLEY, Mary	15	F	Laborer	01Ma02DJ
DUFFY, Mary	20	F	Laborer	01Ma02DJ
LEAHY, Mary	18	F	Laborer	01Ma02DJ
CALLANS, James	20	M	Laborer	01Ma02DJ
DUFFY, Peter	16	M	Laborer	01Ma02DJ
MANIEN, Margt.	18	F	Laborer	01Ma02DJ
BOYLE, May	20	F	Laborer	01Ma02DJ
FREEMAN, Pat	19	M	Laborer	01Ma02DJ
MCKEON, Nancy	20	F	Laborer	01Ma02DJ
MCCALL, Peter	20	M	Laborer	01Ma02DJ
FINNIGAN, Alice	21	F	Laborer	01Ma02DJ
CONNOLLY, Mary	20	F	Laborer	01Ma02DJ
MCMAHON, Mary	20	F	Laborer	01Ma02DJ
DUFFY, Cath.	20	F	Laborer	01Ma02DJ
CONNELLON, Owen	24	M	Laborer	01Ma02DJ
HENY, James	20	M	Laborer	01Ma02DJ
Eliza	17	F	Laborer	01Ma02DJ
MCGANEA, James	48	M	Laborer	01Ma02DJ
May (W)	40	F	Wife	01Ma02DJ
Ellen (D)	12	F	Laborer	01Ma02DJ
John (S)	10	M	Laborer	01Ma02DJ
Mary (D)	06	F	Child	01Ma02DJ
HARVEY, Bridget	15	F	Laborer	01Ma02DJ
NALLY, John	25	M	Laborer	01Ma02DJ
MCKAY, Michl.	25	M	Laborer	01Ma02DJ
MCGRATH, Margt.	21	F	Laborer	01Ma02DJ
BYRNE, Mary	20	F	Laborer	01Ma02DJ
MALIN, Owen	22	M	Laborer	01Ma02DJ
LAVEY, John	28	M	Laborer	01Ma02DJ
GRADY, Thomas	28	M	Laborer	01Ma02DJ
HORAN, Patrick	28	M	Laborer	01Ma02DJ
May	26	F	Laborer	01Ma02DJ
BODDY, Mich.	27	M	Laborer	01Ma02DJ
Bridget	21	F	Laborer	01Ma02DJ
EARS, Fanny	27	F	Laborer	01Ma02DJ
HALERAN, David	25	M	Laborer	01Ma02DJ
FARRELL, Patrick	27	M	Laborer	01Ma02DJ
KENNEDY, Laurence	25	M	Laborer	01Ma02DJ
REYNOLDS, John	25	M	Laborer	01Ma02DJ
Cath. (W)	24	F	Wife	01Ma02DJ
Ellen (D)	.00	F	Infant	01Ma02DJ
MCNAMEE, Philip	27	M	Laborer	01Ma02DJ
U (W)	20	F	Wife	01Ma02DJ
FALLON, Pat	25	M	Laborer	01Ma02DJ
MCGRATH, John	35	M	Laborer	01Ma02DJ
FORD, George	25	M	Laborer	01Ma02DJ
REYNOLDS, Thomas	21	M	Laborer	01Ma02DJ
Hugh	20	M	Laborer	01Ma02DJ
MULLIGAN, Francis	21	M	Laborer	01Ma02DJ
MILTON, Bridget	20	F	Laborer	01Ma02DJ
COWLEY, Peter	28	M	Laborer	01Ma02DJ
Ann	20	F	Laborer	01Ma02DJ
SERGEANT, Saml.	30	M	Laborer	01Ma02DJ
WILKINS, Edw.	20	M	Laborer	01Ma02DJ
CROW, Joseph	21	M	Laborer	01Ma02DJ
HASTINGS, Saml.	31	M	Laborer	01Ma02DJ
IRONS, George	22	M	Laborer	01Ma02DJ
Wm.	17	M	Laborer	01Ma02DJ
BENDLEY, Danl.	40	M	Laborer	01Ma02DJ
Edwd.	35	M	Laborer	01Ma02DJ
Charles	25	M	Laborer	01Ma02DJ
Rory	20	M	Laborer	01Ma02DJ
Biddy	18	F	Laborer	01Ma02DJ
Mary	16	F	Laborer	01Ma02DJ
MARTIN, William	20	M	Laborer	01Ma02DJ
COWL, Sarah	25	F	Laborer	01Ma02DJ
May	20	F	Laborer	01Ma02DJ
MCBRIDE, Rose	21	F	Laborer	01Ma02DJ
MATCHER, Sarah	18	F	Laborer	01Ma02DJ
Nancy	16	F	Laborer	01Ma02DJ
MOFFATT, Sarah	23	F	Laborer	01Ma02DJ
NUGENT, Susan	21	F	Laborer	01Ma02DJ
BAKER, James	18	M	Laborer	01Ma02DJ
FANNER, Frederick	13	M	Laborer	01Ma02DJ
Eliza	12	F	Laborer	01Ma02DJ
GILMER, John	30	M	Laborer	01Ma02DJ
U (W)	26	F	Wife	01Ma02DJ
John (S)	08	M	Child	01Ma02DJ
Margt. (D)	06	F	Child	01Ma02DJ
Charles (S)	04	M	Child	01Ma02DJ
Wm. (S)	02	M	Child	01Ma02DJ
Sarah (D)	.00	F	Infant	01Ma02DJ
GRIER, James	30	M	Laborer	01Ma02DJ
MCGIVER, Heny.	15	M	Laborer	01Ma02DJ
SAVAGE, Chas.	25	M	Laborer	01Ma02DJ
CARROLE, Pat	23	M	Laborer	01Ma02DJ
BRIEN, John	21	M	Laborer	01Ma02DJ
SHEAN, Jenny	20	F	Laborer	01Ma02DJ
CARROLL, James	19	M	Laborer	01Ma02DJ
CROSS, William	22	M	Laborer	01Ma02DJ
MILLER, William	26	M	Laborer	01Ma02DJ
HUNT, Mary	22	F	Laborer	01Ma02DJ
DOWNES, Margt.	20	F	Laborer	01Ma02DJ
DEHAN, May	17	F	Laborer	01Ma02DJ
MILLER, U-Mrs.	24	F	Wife	01Ma02DJ
FARRELL, Arthur	20	M	Laborer	01Ma02DJ
Margt.	25	F	Laborer	01Ma02DJ
Cath.	20	F	Laborer	01Ma02DJ
COLLINS, Richd.	22	M	Laborer	01Ma02DJ
Jane	50	F	Laborer	01Ma02DJ
BUNTING, Bridget	20	F	Laborer	01Ma02DJ
FARRELL, Mary-W.	10	F	Laborer	01Ma02DJ
MANION, Thomas	25	M	Laborer	01Ma02DJ
Bridget	24	F	Laborer	01Ma02DJ
MOORE, Margt.	24	F	Laborer	01Ma02DJ
LAWLER, Thomas	20	M	Laborer	01Ma02DJ
KENNEDY, Pat	21	M	Laborer	01Ma02DJ
MURRAY, May	27	F	Laborer	01Ma02DJ
KINSLEY, May	20	F	Laborer	01Ma02DJ
DONNELAN, John	29	M	Laborer	01Ma02DJ
May (W)	25	F	Wife	01Ma02DJ
Margt. (D)	03	F	Child	01Ma02DJ
Mah. (D)	.00	F	Infant	01Ma02DJ
HALLERAN, Dennis	20	M	Laborer	01Ma02DJ
Kitty	20	F	Laborer	01Ma02DJ
KENNEDY, Lema	20	F	Laborer	01Ma02DJ
EASCON, Jane	19	F	Laborer	01Ma02DJ
Geo.	21	M	Laborer	01Ma02DJ
FARRELL, Pat	23	M	Laborer	01Ma02DJ
MCCRACKIN, John	20	M	Laborer	01Ma02DJ
Thos.	22	M	Laborer	01Ma02DJ
MAYAN, Rose	40	F	Laborer	01Ma02DJ
Susan (D)	13	F	Laborer	01Ma02DJ
James (S)	11	M	Laborer	01Ma02DJ
John (S)	09	M	Child	01Ma02DJ
David (S)	07	M	Child	01Ma02DJ
May (D)	06	F	Child	01Ma02DJ
Betsey (D)	05	F	Child	01Ma02DJ
MCKARBE, Pat	50	M	Laborer	01Ma02DJ
Ellen (D)	20	F	Laborer	01Ma02DJ
Margt. (D)	12	F	Laborer	01Ma02DJ
DONOHUE, Honora	30	F	Laborer	01Ma02DJ
Bridget	12	F	Laborer	01Ma02DJ

JUNIUS 01 MAY 1846

From Liverpool

| LYONS, Dennis | 23 | M | Laborer | 01Ma02Dn |
| Marcilla | 30 | F | None | 01Ma02Dn |

NAMES OF PASSENGERS		AGE	SEX	OCCUPATIONS	DATE PORT SHIP
DOYLE, James		20	M	Laborer	01Ma02Dn
NOBLE, Sally		20	F	None	01Ma02Dn
MOURNE, John		28	M	Laborer	01Ma02Dn
MCCORMACK, Christn.		51	M	Laborer	01Ma02Dn
Ann		21	F	None	01Ma02Dn
Christian		.00	M	Infant	01Ma02Dn
Helen		15	F	None	01Ma02Dn
Margaret		13	F	None	01Ma02Dn
FARRELL, Patt		27	M	Laborer	01Ma02Dn
Margt.	(W)	27	F	Wife	01Ma02Dn
Patt	(S)	.00	M	Infant	01Ma02Dn
CASEY, Ann		42	F	None	01Ma02Dn
Cathn.	(D)	20	F	None	01Ma02Dn
Mary	(D)	18	F	None	01Ma02Dn
Biddy	(D)	13	F	None	01Ma02Dn
HANLON, Mary		19	F	None	01Ma02Dn
Mary		20	F	None	01Ma02Dn
MCCORMACK, Ann		18	F	None	01Ma02Dn
SULLIVAN, Dennis		27	M	Laborer	01Ma02Dn
Dennis		24	M	Laborer	01Ma02Dn
Jeremiah		20	M	Laborer	01Ma02Dn
FARRELL, Dennis		20	M	Laborer	01Ma02Dn
CONNOR, Michl.		20	M	Laborer	01Ma02Dn
CASEY, Jeremiah		20	M	Laborer	01Ma02Dn
MCMAHON, Mary		30	F	None	01Ma02Dn
SULLIVAN, Florence		24	F	None	01Ma02Dn
WHITE, William		19	M	Laborer	01Ma02Dn
REILLY, Dorothy		21	F	None	01Ma02Dn
RYAN, William		22	M	Laborer	01Ma02Dn
COONEY, Lawrence		25	M	Laborer	01Ma02Dn
BUTLER, William		30	M	Laborer	01Ma02Dn
HEGAN, Thomas		27	M	Laborer	01Ma02Dn
CARS, Michael		25	M	Laborer	01Ma02Dn
MADDEN, Walter		30	M	Laborer	01Ma02Dn
U	(W)	25	F	Wife	01Ma02Dn
Richard	(S)	05	M	Child	01Ma02Dn
Alice	(D)	.00	F	Infant	01Ma02Dn
WALSH, John		30	M	Laborer	01Ma02Dn
Johanna		20	F	None	01Ma02Dn
Died-At-Sea					
Mary		14	F	None	01Ma02Dn
Patt		13	M	None	01Ma02Dn
MACK, Mary		25	F	None	01Ma02Dn
HANLIN, John		28	M	Laborer	01Ma02Dn
CLAREY, Mary		18	F	None	01Ma02Dn
Ellen		19	F	None	01Ma02Dn
CREED, Mary		13	F	None	01Ma02Dn
CLANCEY, James		30	M	Laborer	01Ma02Dn
BARRY, Timothy		21	M	Laborer	01Ma02Dn
Honora		18	F	None	01Ma02Dn
Nancy		19	F	None	01Ma02Dn
WALSH, Bill		20	M	Laborer	01Ma02Dn
NOLAN, Timothy		20	M	Laborer	01Ma02Dn
BURK, William		35	M	Laborer	01Ma02Dn
KENNEDY, Thomas		30	M	Laborer	01Ma02Dn
MYERS, Margt.		40	F	None	01Ma02Dn
James	(S)	12	M	None	01Ma02Dn
Mary	(D)	10	F	None	01Ma02Dn
John	(S)	07	M	Child	01Ma02Dn
WALSH, Michael		30	M	Laborer	01Ma02Dn
CONWAY, Wm.		06	M	Child	01Ma02Dn
SULLIVAN, Cathn.		24	F	None	01Ma02Dn
SPELMAN, Mary		24	F	None	01Ma02Dn
BEATTY, Michael		09	M	Child	01Ma02Dn
Patt		31	M	Laborer	01Ma02Dn
Mary		11	F	None	01Ma02Dn
FLYNN, William		21	M	Laborer	01Ma02Dn
DERVAN, James		24	M	Laborer	01Ma02Dn
MONAGHAN, Matt		25	M	Laborer	01Ma02Dn
Ann	(W)	24	F	Wife	01Ma02Dn
Thomas	(S)	03	M	Child	01Ma02Dn
John	(S)	.00	M	Infant	01Ma02Dn
TEGAR, Patt		16	M	Laborer	01Ma02Dn
CONLAN, James		30	M	Laborer	01Ma02Dn
ONEIL, John		30	M	Laborer	01Ma02Dn

NAMES OF PASSENGERS		AGE	SEX	OCCUPATIONS	DATE PORT SHIP
GALLAGHER, James		25	M	Laborer	01Ma02Dn
NELY, Cathn.		20	F	None	01Ma02Dn
GLYNN, Bicdy		18	F	None	01Ma02Dn
CLOUGHESY, Biody		23	F	None	01Ma02Dn
Thomas		20	M	Laborer	01Ma02Dn
HALLERAN, Michael		21	M	Laborer	01Ma02Dn
COLLINS, Fergus		21	M	Laborer	01Ma02Dn
BOYLAN, John		21	M	Laborer	01Ma02Dn
REILLY, Hugh		14	M	Laborer	01Ma02Dn
NEIGH, Patrick		40	M	Farmer	01Ma02Dn
U	(W)	39	F	Wife	01Ma02Dn
Ann	(D)	12	F	None	01Ma02Dn
Biddy	(D)	09	F	Child	01Ma02Dn
Cathrn.	(D)	07	F	Child	01Ma02Dn
Patt	(S)	05	M	Child	01Ma02Dn
DOWLING, Edward		22	M	Laborer	01Ma02Dn
Thomas		20	M	Laborer	01Ma02Dn
BECKETT, Maria		19	F	None	01Ma02Dn
DOYLE, Biddy		19	F	None	01Ma02Dn
BARRY, Ann		35	F	None	01Ma02Dn
CONLAN, Thomas		28	M	Laborer	01Ma02Dn
MASTERSON, Patt		21	M	Laborer	01Ma02Dn
DARBY, Marcus		28	M	Laborer	01Ma02Dn
Jemima		26	F	None	01Ma02Dn
BOOTH, Mary-Jane		18	F	None	01Ma02Dn
WALES, Ann		30	F	None	01Ma02Dn
MCCOLLOM, Bridget		24	F	None	01Ma02Dn
BOOTH, Robert		37	M	Laborer	01Ma02Dn
QUIN, Michael		20	M	Laborer	01Ma02Dn
DAVIDSON, Thomas		20	M	Laborer	01Ma02Dn
EVANS, William		19	M	Laborer	01Ma02Dn
MCCORMACK, Rose		22	F	None	01Ma02Dn
Ellen		18	F	None	01Ma02Dn
MCNAMEE, William		19	M	Laborer	01Ma02Dn
Thomas		18	M	Laborer	01Ma02Dn
FARRADAY, Bill		30	M	Laborer	01Ma02Dn
JOHNSTON, James		27	M	Laborer	01Ma02Dn
MCCRACKEN, Wm.		17	M	Laborer	01Ma02Dn
GORDON, Samuel		17	M	Laborer	01Ma02Dn
U, U		.00	U	Infant	C1Ma02Dn
Born-At-Sea					

SHANANGA C1 MAY 1846

From Liverpool

NAMES OF PASSENGERS		AGE	SEX	OCCUPATIONS	DATE PORT SHIP
RITCHIE, John		26	M	Farmer	01Ma02Dp
Sarah		26	F	Farmer	01Ma02Dp
PIERCE, Margaret		23	F	Wife	01Ma02Dp
Catherine	(D)	02	F	Child	01Ma02Dp
MCGARTH, Catherine		60	F	Mother	01Ma02Dp
Owen		50	M	Father	01Ma02Dp
Catherine		15	F	Child	01Ma02Dp
QUIGLEY, Bridget		17	F	Servant	C1Ma02Dp
MCGARTH, James		08	M	Child	01Ma02Dp
Catherine		05	F	Child	01Ma02Dp
FOLLON, James		28	M	Laborer	01Ma02Dp
COLLON, Michael		28	M	Tailor	01Ma02Dp
DOLAN, Peter		22	M	Laborer	01Ma02Dp
MCENEFF, Mary		20	F	Servant	C1Ma02Dp
Rose		17	F	Servant	01Ma02Dp
DIVINE, Ann		18	F	Servant	01Ma02Dp
MCENEFF, Michael		16	M	Laborer	01Ma02Dp
HCGLYNN, Ann		15	F	Servant	C1Ma02Dp
MCGLIN, Mary		17	F	Servant	C1Ma02Dp
NCKENNA, Bicdy		20	F	Servant	C1Ma02Dp
Patrick		21	M	Laborer	01Ma02Dp
Edward		20	M	Laborer	01Ma02Dp
BARLOW, Owen		18	M	Laborer	01Ma02Dp

NAMES OF PASSENGERS	AGE	SEX	OCCUPATIONS	DATE PORT SHIP	NAMES OF PASSENGERS	AGE	SEX	OCCUPATIONS	DATE PORT SHIP
SHERRY, Patrick	18	M	Laborer	01Ma02Dp	DOLAN, Ann	17	F	Servant	01Ma02Dp
ERWIN, James	35	M	Gdnr	01Ma02Dp	HANLEY, Lawrence	20	M	Laborer	01Ma02Dp
CROW, Joseph	20	M	Laborer	01Ma02Dp	Ann	20	F	Laborer	01Ma02Dp
NORRIS, John	20	M	Laborer	01Ma02Dp	MCGANLEY, Margaret	25	F	Servant	01Ma02Dp
MCCAUGHLEY, James	21	M	Laborer	01Ma02Dp	BROGAN, Peter	18	M	Laborer	01Ma02Dp
DANLEY, James	20	M	Farmer	01Ma02Dp	CUSACK, Bartholomy	60	M	Father	01Ma02Dp
DOLAN, Patrick	26	M	Tailor	01Ma02Dp	MCGRANE, Thomas	25	M	Laborer	01Ma02Dp
Bridget	24	F	Tailor	01Ma02Dp	HANN, Michael	24	M	Laborer	01Ma02Dp
Catherine	23	F	Servant	01Ma02Dp	MANGHAN, Pat	39	M	Butcher	01Ma02Dp
MURRAY, Mary	21	F	Servant	01Ma02Dp	U (W)	35	F	Wife	01Ma02Dp
Bridget	19	F	Servant	01Ma02Dp	MURRAY, Harriet	17	F	Dressmaker	01Ma02Dp
FOX, John	21	M	Laborer	01Ma02Dp	GILLIODY, Pat	18	M	Laborer	01Ma02Dp
MCSORLEY, Patrick	22	M	Shoemaker	01Ma02Dp	GARVIN, Mary	21	F	Servant	01Ma02Dp
James	30	M	Shoemaker	01Ma02Dp	CONNER, Ann	19	F	Servant	01Ma02Dp
BARLOW, Allice	40	F	Servant	01Ma02Dp	EAGAN, Ellen	21	F	Servant	01Ma02Dp
Henry (S)	14	M	Servant	01Ma02Dp	KENNEDY, Ann	24	F	Servant	01Ma02Dp
James (S)	10	M	Servant	01Ma02Dp	MULARDINE, Maria	20	F	Servant	01Ma02Dp
John (S)	09	M	Child	01Ma02Dp	BLYTHE, William	25	M	Farmer	01Ma02Dp
GAHAGAN, Catherine	16	F	Servant	01Ma02Dp	GIBSON, William	20	M	Painter	01Ma02Dp
BROGHAN, James	24	M	Laborer	01Ma02Dp	MAGARRY, John	24	M	Laborer	01Ma02Dp
GALLES, Ann	19	F	Servant	01Ma02Dp	FERRELL, Forkney	27	M	Laborer	01Ma02Dp
MCGOWAN, Mary	16	F	Servant	01Ma02Dp	KELLEY, Thomas	23	M	Laborer	01Ma02Dp
EARLY, Mary	17	F	Servant	01Ma02Dp	Pat	20	M	Laborer	01Ma02Dp
MCKENNA, Barnard	43	M	Laborer	01Ma02Dp	MURRAY, Ann	22	F	Servant	01Ma02Dp
Mary	40	F	Servant	01Ma02Dp	COOLEY, Margaret	22	F	Servant	01Ma02Dp
Betsey	20	F	Servant	01Ma02Dp	MCNAINARRA, John	17	M	Servant	01Ma02Dp
Peter	18	M	Laborer	01Ma02Dp	CONLEY, Michael	29	M	Servant	01Ma02Dp
Sally	14	F	Servant	01Ma02Dp	COONEY, Barney	35	M	Shepherd	01Ma02Dp
Ann	15	F	Servant	01Ma02Dp	MCCABE, Mary	24	F	Servant	01Ma02Dp
John	12	M	Servant	01Ma02Dp	DEVANEY, Pat	21	M	Laborer	01Ma02Dp
Margaret	11	F	Servant	01Ma02Dp	CONNAUGHTON, Pat	20	M	Laborer	01Ma02Dp
Pat	09	M	Child	01Ma02Dp	HOGG, Thomas	20	M	Laborer	01Ma02Dp
Lawrance	03	M	Child	01Ma02Dp	John	20	M	Laborer	01Ma02Dp
Barnard	.00	M	Infant	01Ma02Dp	IGOE, Michael	20	M	Laborer	01Ma02Dp
John	20	M	Laborer	01Ma02Dp	BRISLAND, James	30	M	Quarryman	01Ma02Dp
KEAGAN, Hugh	22	M	Laborer	01Ma02Dp	Ann	26	F	None	01Ma02Dp
Robert-H.	08	M	Child	01Ma02Dp	BARRY, Alexander	36	M	Mnftr	01Ma02Dp
GIBBON, John	24	M	Child	01Ma02Dp	Mary (W)	38	F	Wife	01Ma02Dp
ROACH, Gerrard	44	M	Farmer	01Ma02Dp	Matilda (D)	15	F	None	01Ma02Dp
Ann	40	F	Farmer	01Ma02Dp	Alexander (S)	11	M	None	01Ma02Dp
NEALLY, Ann	16	F	Servant	01Ma02Dp	William (S)	09	M	Child	01Ma02Dp
MCGUIN, Catherine	20	F	Servant	01Ma02Dp	Nancy (D)	07	F	Child	01Ma02Dp
COLLIN, Charles	40	M	Laborer	01Ma02Dp	Samuel (S)	03	M	Child	01Ma02Dp
CASSIDY, Joseph	25	M	Laborer	01Ma02Dp	Matilda (D)	.00	F	Infant	01Ma02Dp
--ILEY, Francis	28	M	Laborer	01Ma02Dp	HOLLAND, John	28	M	Fisherman	01Ma02Dp
MCELROY, Patrick	25	M	Laborer	01Ma02Dp	CLEARY, William	29	M	Fisherman	01Ma02Dp
Catherine	20	F	Servant	01Ma02Dp	CAMPBELL, Mary	40	F	Mother	01Ma02Dp
LOUGHER, John	25	M	Farmer	01Ma02Dp	Mary (D)	18	F	Servant	01Ma02Dp
Patt	17	M	Farmer	01Ma02Dp	Bridget (D)	16	F	Servant	01Ma02Dp
Ally	21	F	Farmer	01Ma02Dp	Francis (S)	20	M	Laborer	01Ma02Dp
Mary	50	F	Farmer	01Ma02Dp	Ann (D)	08	F	Child	01Ma02Dp
HART, Joseph	18	M	Farmer	01Ma02Dp	Ellen	04	F	Child	01Ma02Dp
CARDLE, John	21	M	Farmer	01Ma02Dp	DOLAN, Mary	16	F	Servant	01Ma02Dp
MALANY, Honorra	21	F	Servant	01Ma02Dp	GALLAGIN, Ann	17	F	Servant	01Ma02Dp
CASSIDY, Thomas	20	M	Laborer	01Ma02Dp	BRANNAN, Catherin	16	F	Servant	01Ma02Dp
FINNERTY, James	30	M	Laborer	01Ma02Dp	PUFFETT, Maria	17	F	Servant	01Ma02Dp
WELCH, Thomas	21	M	Laborer	01Ma02Dp	CAMPBELL, Catherine	16	F	Servant	01Ma02Dp
QUINN, Catherine	20	F	Servant	01Ma02Dp	HALL, James	35	M	Grocer	01Ma02Dp
MARTIN, Owen	21	M	Laborer	01Ma02Dp	Margaret (W)	28	F	Wife	01Ma02Dp
Ann	18	F	Servant	01Ma02Dp	John (S)	03	M	Child	01Ma02Dp
Francis	08	F	Child	01Ma02Dp	FISHER, Mary	21	F	Servant	01Ma02Dp
Sally	04	F	Child	01Ma02Dp					
Mary	.00	F	Infant	01Ma02Dp					
MCGUIRE, John	18	M	Laborer	01Ma02Dp					
GIRNEY, Mary-Ann	18	F	Servant	01Ma02Dp					
Sally	21	F	Servant	01Ma02Dp					
DATLEY, Elizabeth	20	F	Servant	01Ma02Dp					
HACKETT, Peter	18	M	Servant	01Ma02Dp	PANTHEA 04 MAY 1846				
Roger	16	M	Servant	01Ma02Dp					
Peter	17	M	Servant	01Ma02Dp	From Liverpool				
MCCABE, Ellen	20	F	Servant	01Ma02Dp					
MCGIRNEY, Owen	18	M	Farmer	01Ma02Dp					
CONLIN, Pat	09	M	Child	01Ma02Dp	OBRINE, Susan	22	F	Servant	04Ma02Ds
Terence	06	M	Child	01Ma02Dp	HENRRETTE, Catharine	13	F	Servant	04Ma02Ds
BANAGHAN, Ally	16	F	Servant	01Ma02Dp	SHADWELL, John	28	M	Farmer	04Ma02Ds

NAMES OF PASSENGERS		AGE	SEX	OCCUPATIONS	DATE PORT SHIP
SHADWELL, Maria		25	F	None	04Ma02Ds
HIGGINS, Patrick		22	M	Farmer	04Ma02Ds
SIGGIN, Jane		25	F	None	04Ma02Ds
LEWIS, Edward		15	M	None	04Ma02Ds
SHADWELL, Ellzea		10	F	None	04Ma02Ds
SCALLY, Owen		28	M	Weaver	04Ma02Ds
Cathrine	(W)	24	F	Wife	04Ma02Ds
Cath.	(D)	07	F	Child	04Ma02Ds
John	(S)	03	M	Child	04Ma02Ds
Patrick	(S)	03	M	Child	04Ma02Ds
Mary	(D)	.06	F	Infant	04Ma02Ds
BOYLE, Hugh		19	M	Carpenter	04Ma02Ds
PAUL, Charles		16	M	None	04Ma02Ds
TOOEY, Hughe		17	M	None	04Ma02Ds
GALLAGHAN, Sarah		20	F	None	04Ma02Ds
SWEENY, Rosanna		20	F	None	04Ma02Ds
HALY, Elizebeth		19	F	None	04Ma02Ds
DONAVEN, Patk.		23	M	None	04Ma02Ds
KILLIAN, Patk.		18	M	None	04Ma02Ds
DUNNODY, Bridget		17	F	None	04Ma02Ds
CAILEN, Ann		22	F	None	04Ma02Ds
GILLERLAND, Mary		18	F	None	04Ma02Ds
LAKINS, Catha.		08	F	Child	04Ma02Ds
GANNON, Bryan		21	M	Farmer	04Ma02Ds
WARD, Patk.		20	M	Farmer	04Ma02Ds
BRANNIN, Thos.		20	M	Farmer	04Ma02Ds
MCGEE, James		21	M	Farmer	04Ma02Ds
BURNS, Owen		30	M	Farmer	04Ma02Ds
MCELVEY, Patk.		52	M	Farmer	04Ma02Ds
HALY, Ann		18	F	None	04Ma02Ds
ODONNALL, Margrt.		20	F	None	04Ma02Ds
MCELVEY, Cathrine		50	F	None	04Ma02Ds
John	(S)	20	M	Painter	04Ma02Ds
Charles	(S)	18	M	Painter	04Ma02Ds
Jane	(D)	14	F	None	04Ma02Ds
KELLY, Mary		18	F	None	04Ma02Ds
RILEY, Michel		21	M	Laborer	04Ma02Ds
Mary		12	F	None	04Ma02Ds
SHAW, Robert		18	M	None	04Ma02Ds
Charlotte		19	F	None	04Ma02Ds
MCCORLEY, Domick		22	M	Farmer	04Ma02Ds
Margret	(M)	50	F	None	04Ma02Ds
Mary	(T)	27	F	None	04Ma02Ds
Bridget	(T)	18	F	None	04Ma02Ds
Margret	(T)	15	F	None	04Ma02Ds
Peter	(B)	16	M	None	04Ma02Ds
ROXBOROUGH, John		22	M	None	04Ma02Ds
LOVE, Dorthe		16	F	None	04Ma02Ds
ARMSTRONG, Patk.		19	M	Laborer	04Ma02Ds
FITZSIMMONS, Patk.		16	M	Laborer	04Ma02Ds
Peter		13	M	Laborer	04Ma02Ds
HAYDEN, William		18	M	Laborer	04Ma02Ds
Eliz.		17	F	None	04Ma02Ds
VILLY, John		19	M	None	04Ma02Ds
CALLAN, Patk.		15	M	None	04Ma02Ds
MAHON, Rose		18	F	None	04Ma02Ds
KINSILLA, Eilz.		18	F	None	04Ma02Ds
COLLINS, James		21	M	Farmer	04Ma02Ds
WOODFIELD, John		54	M	Farmer	04Ma02Ds
MASDEN, George		25	M	Farmer	04Ma02Ds
BARNS, Cornelius		11	M	Farmer	04Ma02Ds
DEGAN, John		24	M	Farmer	04Ma02Ds
MCCUE, Mary		20	F	None	04Ma02Ds
LEONARD, Maria		21	F	None	04Ma02Ds
POWELL, Thomas		30	M	Farmer	04Ma02Ds
Mary		29	F	None	04Ma02Ds
MCELVEY, Patk.		25	M	None	04Ma02Ds
BATLEY, Jane		23	F	None	04Ma02Ds
ODONALD, Francis		34	M	Laborer	04Ma02Ds
LAKINS, Ann		20	F	None	04Ma02Ds
DOBSON, John		45	M	Farmer	04Ma02Ds
CARRAK, Bridget		19	F	None	04Ma02Ds
COONIN, Maria		20	F	None	04Ma02Ds
BOYLE, Betty		24	F	None	04Ma02Ds
BATLY, Margret		21	F	None	04Ma02Ds
RILEY, John		24	M	Laborer	04Ma02Ds
BRADY, Bridget		21	F	None	04Ma02Ds
MCDONOUGH, John		24	M	Tailor	04Ma02Ds
MCNATTY, John		23	M	Tailor	04Ma02Ds
COLLINS, Michil		21	M	Farmer	04Ma02Ds
LOVE, William		24	M	Farmer	04Ma02Ds
Sarah		30	F	None	04Ma02Ds
BRACK, Martha		25	F	None	04Ma02Ds
Johnson		15	M	None	04Ma02Ds
Matlidia		17	F	None	04Ma02Ds
MCNEAL, Hector		24	M	Farmer	04Ma02Ds
DEVINE, Thomas		60	M	Farmer	04Ma02Ds
Mary	(W)	55	F	Wife	04Ma02Ds
Daniel	(S)	21	M	Farmer	04Ma02Ds
Francis	(S)	19	M	Farmer	04Ma02Ds
Mary	(D)	15	F	None	04Ma02Ds
WHITE, Thomas		24	M	Laborer	04Ma02Ds
HIGGINS, Thomas		35	M	Laborer	04Ma02Ds
TIGH, Patk.		24	M	Laborer	04Ma02Ds
HARKINS, Rose		34	F	None	04Ma02Ds
BARRAN, Patk.		34	M	Mason	04Ma02Ds
LAWLESS, James		24	M	Mason	04Ma02Ds
CUNIFF, John		30	M	Mason	04Ma02Ds
Ann		28	F	None	04Ma02Ds
CARLYON, James		29	M	Farmer	04Ma02Ds
TOEY, William		24	M	Farmer	04Ma02Ds
Mary-Ann		23	F	None	04Ma02Ds
CHAPMAN, John		23	M	Laborer	04Ma02Ds
WOODWARD, Sarah		56	F	None	04Ma02Ds
DAYLY, Michel		24	M	Farmer	04Ma02Ds
MCCALL, Ann		24	F	None	04Ma02Ds
MULLIGAN, Mary		20	F	None	04Ma02Ds
SMITH, Julia		21	F	None	04Ma02Ds
WELCH, Ann		21	F	None	04Ma02Ds
TARRAN, Mary		20	F	None	04Ma02Ds
GALLAGHER, Wm.		25	M	Farmer	04Ma02Ds
SYER, Beddy		24	F	None	04Ma02Ds
HAYDEN, John		60	M	Farmer	04Ma02Ds
FOLEY, Bridget		50	F	None	04Ma02Ds
HAYDEN, Margret		16	F	None	04Ma02Ds
BRENNEN, Elizebeth		30	F	None	04Ma02Ds
KELLY, Mary		31	F	None	04Ma02Ds
OHANA, Cathrine		30	F	None	04Ma02Ds
MORAN, Patk.		31	M	Farmer	04Ma02Ds
NEALY, Michal		24	M	Farmer	04Ma02Ds
OHARRAN, Thomas		22	M	Farmer	04Ma02Ds
KELLY, John		22	M	Farmer	04Ma02Ds
BARMAN, Mary		27	F	None	04Ma02Ds
CARNEY, Michal		42	M	Laborer	04Ma02Ds
Mary		38	F	None	04Ma02Ds
CONNELL, John		22	M	Tailor	04Ma02Ds
SHEAN, Thomas		20	M	Tailor	04Ma02Ds
KELLARKEN, Ellen		20	F	None	04Ma02Ds
HOGAN, Patk.		24	M	Weaver	04Ma02Ds
DONAHUE, John		22	M	Weaver	04Ma02Ds
MCGRAGLE, Michel		25	M	Weaver	04Ma02Ds
SHEAN, Beddy		19	F	None	04Ma02Ds
MULLANY, John		20	M	Mason	04Ma02Ds
BRISMAHON, Coels		20	M	Mason	04Ma02Ds
CUNNINGHAM, John		19	M	Laborer	04Ma02Ds
MCKENNA, John		24	M	Laborer	04Ma02Ds
Peter		20	M	Laborer	04Ma02Ds
John		22	M	Laborer	04Ma02Ds
SHANY, Owen		20	M	Laborer	04Ma02Ds
MULLEN, Peggy		28	F	None	04Ma02Ds
GANNON, Rhoden		21	F	None	04Ma02Ds
BYRNS, Patk.		24	M	Farmer	04Ma02Ds
James		22	M	Farmer	04Ma02Ds
LEONARD, Domineck		27	M	Farmer	04Ma02Ds
MARTIN, Mary		40	F	None	04Ma02Ds
MUGAN, Patk.		26	M	None	04Ma02Ds
FAGAN, Michal		26	M	None	04Ma02Ds
MANGY, Laurance		22	M	None	04Ma02Ds
SIMMENDS, Martin		28	M	None	04Ma02Ds
ROONEY, Michell		25	M	Hatter	04Ma02Ds

NAMES OF PASSENGERS		AGE	SEX	OCCUPATIONS	DATE PORT SHIP
MADDEN, Honora		21	F	None	04Ma02Ds
MULLENS, Ann		32	F	None	04Ma02Ds
Patk.		15	M	None	04Ma02Ds
QUIN, Denis		24	M	Baker	04Ma02Ds
James		27	M	Baker	04Ma02Ds
MALLY, Catharine		17	F	None	04Ma02Ds
MAGENT, Ann		16	F	None	04Ma02Ds
LAUGHLEN, David		31	M	Farmer	04Ma02Ds
GINLEY, Ellen		17	F	None	04Ma02Ds
Jane		16	F	None	04Ma02Ds
OBRINE, Elizth.		30	F	None	04Ma02Ds
LEARY, John		08	M	Child	04Ma02Ds
ONEAL, Michal		25	M	Farmer	04Ma02Ds
Mary		22	F	None	04Ma02Ds
TURNAN, Ann		22	F	None	04Ma02Ds
MURORAN, Ellen		22	F	None	04Ma02Ds
NOUGHTON, Patk.		25	M	Laborer	04Ma02Ds
CORLY, Patk.		22	M	Laborer	04Ma02Ds
DATY, Nicholes		31	M	Laborer	04Ma02Ds
Mary		27	F	None	04Ma02Ds
MORATY, Mathew		28	M	Farmer	04Ma02Ds
KELLY, James		36	M	Farmer	04Ma02Ds
CONNELL, Michel		28	M	Farmer	04Ma02Ds
KILKENNY, Patk.		26	M	Farmer	04Ma02Ds
MCGRAY, John		27	M	Farmer	04Ma02Ds
FITZPATRICK, Michal		31	M	Farmer	04Ma02Ds
Kate	(W)	30	F	Wife	04Ma02Ds
Bridget	(D)	03	F	Child	04Ma02Ds
Thomas	(S)	.02	M	Infant	04Ma02Ds
MALLONE, Biddy		29	F	None	04Ma02Ds
ROBERTS, Julia		34	F	None	04Ma02Ds
FLYNN, John		30	M	Farmer	04Ma02Ds
Andrew		35	M	Farmer	04Ma02Ds
COURTNEY, Hughe		70	M	Farmer	04Ma02Ds
Owen	(S)	35	M	Farmer	04Ma02Ds
Ann	(D)	25	F	None	04Ma02Ds
Patk.	(S)	24	M	Farmer	04Ma02Ds
MCKENNA, John		24	M	Farmer	04Ma02Ds
BYRNES, Mary		23	F	None	04Ma02Ds
MCCANNON, Mary		23	F	None	04Ma02Ds
HENRRATH, Cath.		22	F	None	04Ma02Ds
COSTELLO, Bryan		30	M	Farmer	04Ma02Ds
Cath.	(W)	29	F	Wife	04Ma02Ds
Mary	(D)	04	F	Child	04Ma02Ds
John	(S)	02	M	Child	04Ma02Ds
GARATTY, Catharine		55	F	None	04Ma02Ds
Died-At-Sea					
MORAN, Peter		24	M	Laborer	04Ma02Ds
CLARK, Mary		22	F	None	04Ma02Ds
Ann		24	F	None	04Ma02Ds
CONLON, James		30	M	Farmer	04Ma02Ds
MCDANIEL, Patk.		24	M	Farmer	04Ma02Ds
Cathrina		60	F	None	04Ma02Ds
MCANANY, Margt.		20	F	None	04Ma02Ds
LUKAS, Charles		40	M	Farmer	04Ma02Ds
WALLIS, Honora		24	F	None	04Ma02Ds
ANAN, James		40	M	Farmer	04Ma02Ds
Sarah	(W)	40	F	Wife	04Ma02Ds
Mary	(D)	23	F	None	04Ma02Ds
John	(S)	14	M	None	04Ma02Ds
BOYLE, Charles		25	M	None	04Ma02Ds
Ellen	(W)	23	F	Wife	04Ma02Ds
Charles	(S)	.04	M	Infant	04Ma02Ds
WELSH, Cath.		17	F	None	04Ma02Ds
MCQUILLEN, Peggy		42	F	None	04Ma02Ds
James	(S)	16	M	None	04Ma02Ds
Patrick	(S)	.04	M	Infant	04Ma02Ds
Sarah	(D)	14	F	None	04Ma02Ds
Margt.	(D)	12	F	None	04Ma02Ds
Rhoda	(D)	08	F	Child	04Ma02Ds
Peter	(S)	05	M	Child	04Ma02Ds
CARR, John		30	M	Farmer	04Ma02Ds
Bridget		28	F	None	04Ma02Ds
MCGERGH, Mary		22	F	Servant	04Ma02Ds
CARR, William		22	M	Gdnr	04Ma02Ds

NAMES OF PASSENGERS		AGE	SEX	OCCUPATIONS	DATE PORT SHIP
CARR, Teresa	(W)	21	F	None	04Ma02Ds
Wm.	(S)	03	M	Child	04Ma02Ds
Mary	(D)	.04	F	Infant	04Ma02Ds

MEDIATOR 04 MAY 1846

From London

CLERK, Young		26	M	Unknown	04Ma21Dt
Mary-W.	(W)	23	F	Wife	04Ma21Dt
Johnathan	(S)	01	M	Child	04Ma21Dt
SHEEN, Edward		30	M	Laborer	04Ma21Dt
OLEARY, Ann		32	F	Servant	04Ma21Dt

BELFAST 05 MAY 1846

From St.Vincent

RICHARDS, James		31	M	Gentleman	05Ma40Du
HENDERSON, Jane		25	F	None	05Ma40Du

JANE 05 MAY 1846

From Liverpool

MADDEN, Patrick		28	M	Laborer	05Ma02Dv
DONOHUE, John		22	M	Unknown	05Ma02Dv
ROARKE, Edward		20	M	Unknown	05Ma02Dv
HIGGINS, Margt.		20	F	Unknown	05Ma02Dv
CONWAY, Bridget		19	F	Unknown	05Ma02Dv
COONEY, Bridget		30	F	Unknown	05Ma02Dv
KILREA, Bridget		22	F	Unknown	05Ma02Dv
CLARKE, Patrick		36	M	Unknown	05Ma02Dv
MAHON, Thomas		40	M	Unknown	05Ma02Dv
MCDONNELL, Wm.		22	M	Unknown	05Ma02Dv
MASTERSON, Rose		20	F	Unknown	05Ma02Dv
CORCORAN, Micheal		20	M	Unknown	05Ma02Dv
MCNEILL, Francis		21	M	Unknown	05Ma02Dv
SMITH, John		24	M	Unknown	05Ma02Dv
James		16	M	Unknown	05Ma02Dv
MORAN, Patk.		20	M	Unknown	05Ma02Dv
CANE, Peter		22	M	Unknown	05Ma02Dv
REILLY, Margt.		19	F	Unknown	05Ma02Dv
CANE, Margaret		22	F	Unknown	05Ma02Dv
TORPY, John		21	M	Unknown	05Ma02Dv
Margt.		20	F	Unknown	05Ma02Dv
Conner		19	M	Unknown	05Ma02Dv
FLANNIGAN, John		16	M	Unknown	05Ma02Dv
MCCABE, Bessy		19	F	Unknown	05Ma02Dv
MURPHEY, Mary		18	F	Unknown	05Ma02Dv
CARTER, Mary		20	F	Unknown	05Ma02Dv
DOLAN, Mary		26	F	Unknown	05Ma02Dv
MCKEERNEN, Patk.		21	M	Unknown	05Ma02Dv
SHEEHAN, Owen		20	M	Unknown	05Ma02Dv
SHEENAN, Mary		30	F	Unknown	05Ma02Dv
U	(D)	.02	F	Infant	05Ma02Dv
REILLY, Phillip		20	M	Unknown	05Ma02Dv

NAMES OF PASSENGERS	A G E	S E X	OCCUPATIONS	DATE PORT SHIP	NAMES OF PASSENGERS	A G E	S E X	OCCUPATIONS	DATE PORT SHIP
BRENNAN, Wm.	21	M	Unknown	05Ma02Dv	GAINOR, Rose	11	F	Unknown	05Ma02Dv
BAXTER, Maria	21	F	Unknown	05Ma02Dv	MARTIN, Ellen	30	F	Unknown	05Ma02Dv
MCGRATH, Bessy	20	F	Unknown	05Ma02Dv	James (S)	06	M	Child	05Ma02Dv
MAHON, Catherine	18	F	Unknown	05Ma02Dv	MCDONNALD, Augustin	20	M	Unknown	05Ma02Dv
DOBSON, Thos.	21	M	Unknown	05Ma02Dv	MURPHEY, Mathew	27	M	Unknown	05Ma02Dv
GARLAND, Bridget	24	F	Unknown	05Ma02Dv	REILLY, Michl.	40	M	Unknown	05Ma02Dv
TRAINOR, Michl.	34	M	Unknown	05Ma02Dv	Thos.	21	M	Unknown	05Ma02Dv
GRAY, Jas.	30	M	Unknown	05Ma02Dv	NICKSON, J.J.	24	M	Unknown	05Ma02Dv
James	25	M	Unknown	05Ma02Dv	MCLEAN, Chas.	16	M	Unknown	05Ma02Dv
MURPHEY, Robt.	25	M	Unknown	05Ma02Dv	BREEN, James	20	M	Unknown	05Ma02Dv
Letty	20	F	Unknown	05Ma02Dv	MYLS, Geo.	21	M	Unknown	05Ma02Dv
DUFFY, Mary	23	F	Unknown	05Ma02Dv	MILLS, Eliza	19	F	Unknown	05Ma02Dv
Betty	26	F	Unknown	05Ma02Dv	HEARY, Peter	26	M	Unknown	05Ma02Dv
CALAHON, James	20	M	Unknown	05Ma02Dv	WALSH, Patk.	20	M	Unknown	05Ma02Dv
MCLEAVY, Peter	27	M	Unknown	05Ma02Dv	KILLY, John	21	M	Unknown	05Ma02Dv
Ellen	45	F	Unknown	05Ma02Dv	TRACY, Bridget	19	F	Unknown	05Ma02Dv
Catherine	22	F	Unknown	05Ma02Dv	CRESSWELL, Henry	16	M	Unknown	05Ma02Dv
MARLEY, John	02	M	Child	05Ma02Dv	DELANEY, Nicholas	00	M	Unknown	05Ma02Dv
MCAVEENY, Anne	19	F	Unknown	05Ma02Dv	MCGUIRE, Owen	23	M	Unknown	05Ma02Dv
CARROLL, Alice	18	F	Unknown	05Ma02Dv	BURKE, Peter	40	M	Unknown	05Ma02Dv
CLARKE, Francis	24	M	Unknown	05Ma02Dv	HOBAN, Edwd.	36	M	Unknown	05Ma02Dv
MORAN, James	26	M	Unknown	05Ma02Dv	MCGINNESS, Elen	26	F	Unknown	05Ma02Dv
U (W)	24	F	Wife	05Ma02Dv	KELLY, Edwd.	19	M	Unknown	05Ma02Dv
BYRNE, Amelia	20	F	Unknown	05Ma02Dv	DONALD, John	22	M	Unknown	05Ma02Dv
DUFFY, James	22	M	Unknown	05Ma02Dv	HINES, Chas.	22	M	Unknown	05Ma02Dv
KELLY, Jas.	25	M	Unknown	05Ma02Dv	GRAY, Danl.	16	M	Unknown	05Ma02Dv
U (W)	24	F	Wife	05Ma02Dv	Catherine	15	F	Unknown	05Ma02Dv
Patk. (S)	03	M	Child	05Ma02Dv	MURTAGH, Margt.	15	F	Unknown	05Ma02Dv
Owen (S)	01	M	Child	05Ma02Dv	MCGRATH, Danl.	24	M	Unknown	05Ma02Dv
JUDGE, John	21	M	Unknown	05Ma02Dv	KILFOYLE, Mary	20	F	Unknown	05Ma02Dv
REILY, Patk.	20	M	Unknown	05Ma02Dv	FAHEY, Michl.	26	M	Unknown	05Ma02Dv
Owen	19	M	Unknown	05Ma02Dv	SHEEL, Cathe.	20	F	Unknown	05Ma02Dv
JUDGE, John	19	M	Unknown	05Ma02Dv	Peter	24	M	Unknown	05Ma02Dv
GALAGHER, Martin	22	M	Unknown	05Ma02Dv	HARDYMAN, Thos.	20	M	Unknown	05Ma02Dv
JUDGE, Bridget	22	F	Unknown	05Ma02Dv	CORMER, Jas.	20	M	Unknown	05Ma02Dv
CASEY, Mary	20	F	Unknown	05Ma02Dv	GARATY, Michl.	22	M	Unknown	05Ma02Dv
HENSON, Patrick	19	M	Unknown	05Ma02Dv	GREEVE, Jas.	20	M	Unknown	05Ma02Dv
MURPHEY, Edwd.	21	M	Unknown	05Ma02Dv	KEARNEY, Martin	20	M	Unknown	05Ma02Dv
KENEDY, Patk.	20	M	Unknown	05Ma02Dv	MCCONNELL, Jas.	26	M	Unknown	05Ma02Dv
MURPHEY, Mary	32	F	Unknown	05Ma02Dv	Sarah (W)	26	F	Wife	05Ma02Dv
HENSON, Ann	19	F	Unknown	05Ma02Dv	John (S)	04	M	Child	05Ma02Dv
CARBERY, Ann	30	F	Unknown	05Ma02Dv	U (S)	.00	M	Infant	05Ma02Dv
HUESTON, Stephen	32	M	Unknown	05Ma02Dv	U (S)	.00	M	Infant	05Ma02Dv
Mary	11	F	Unknown	05Ma02Dv	HURST, Ann	25	F	Unknown	05Ma02Dv
ROBERTS, John	30	M	Unknown	05Ma02Dv	COYLE, Rose	16	F	Unknown	05Ma02Dv
GRUMLY, Michl.	21	M	Unknown	05Ma02Dv	MCCABE, Rose	16	F	Unknown	05Ma02Dv
Anne	19	F	Unknown	05Ma02Dv	RAFFERTY, John	25	M	Unknown	05Ma02Dv
Mary	13	F	Unknown	05Ma02Dv	REYNOLDS, Patk.	24	M	Unknown	05Ma02Dv
Mary	22	F	Unknown	05Ma02Dv	REILLY, Alice	20	F	Unknown	05Ma02Dv
HUGHES, Betty	20	F	Unknown	05Ma02Dv	MCCABE, Mary-Ann	17	F	Unknown	05Ma02Dv
GRIMLEY, James	19	M	Unknown	05Ma02Dv	FORHILL, Thos.	20	M	Unknown	05Ma02Dv
BRANNIGAN, Catherine	22	F	Unknown	05Ma02Dv	OKANE, Bernard	22	M	Unknown	05Ma02Dv
CHURCHILL, John	21	M	Unknown	05Ma02Dv	BERGAN, Daniel	20	M	Unknown	05Ma02Dv
MURRAY, Michl.	26	M	Unknown	05Ma02Dv	CONNIELL, Patk.	25	M	Unknown	05Ma02Dv
MORRISON, John	30	M	Unknown	05Ma02Dv	COSTELLO, Catherine	23	F	Unknown	05Ma02Dv
Michl.	25	M	Unknown	05Ma02Dv	DEMOND, U-Mrs.	25	F	Unknown	05Ma02Dv
CLEMENTS, Patk.	24	M	Unknown	05Ma02Dv	Patrick	25	M	Unknown	05Ma02Dv
FITZPATRICK, Ann	21	F	Unknown	05Ma02Dv	DELAVEY, Bridget	02	F	Child	05Ma02Dv
DEVERY, Catherine	32	F	Unknown	05Ma02Dv	Catherine (M)	24	F	Unknown	05Ma02Dv
MCDONALD, Peter	06	M	Child	05Ma02Dv	FITZPATRICK, Bernd.	02	M	Child	05Ma02Dv
MULLIN, John	22	M	Unknown	05Ma02Dv	U-Mrs. (M)	25	F	Unknown	05Ma02Dv
ARTH, Judith	24	F	Unknown	05Ma02Dv	U (T)	.00	F	Infant	05Ma02Dv
KEELAN, Patk.	25	M	Unknown	05Ma02Dv	HINES, James	24	M	Unknown	05Ma02Dv
GARGIN, Ann	23	F	Unknown	05Ma02Dv	Fanny	30	F	Unknown	05Ma02Dv
MCGRATH, Ann	20	F	Unknown	05Ma02Dv	VERLIE, Anne	22	F	Unknown	05Ma02Dv
CLINTON, Mary	35	F	Unknown	05Ma02Dv	KEARNS, John	20	M	Unknown	05Ma02Dv
QUINN, Patk.	30	M	Unknown	05Ma02Dv	CONATY, Ellen	25	F	Unknown	05Ma02Dv
MURPHEY, Francis	23	M	Unknown	05Ma02Dv	REILLY, Catherine	20	F	Unknown	05Ma02Dv
Ann	20	F	Unknown	05Ma02Dv	SHENDON, Bridgit	20	F	Unknown	05Ma02Dv
MCGRAVE, Patrick	19	M	Unknown	05Ma02Dv	MULLIN, Mary	20	F	Unknown	05Ma02Dv
BRADY, Char.	24	M	Unknown	05Ma02Dv	TEEMALTY, Mary	20	F	Unknown	05Ma02Dv
POWDERLY, Maggy	17	F	Unknown	05Ma02Dv	CARROLL, James	20	M	Unknown	05Ma02Dv
MCGUIRE, Catherine	24	F	Unknown	05Ma02Dv	FITZGERALD, John	36	M	Unknown	05Ma02Dv
BOYLAN, Laurence	21	M	Unknown	05Ma02Dv	BUCHANAN, Jos.	29	M	Unknown	05Ma02Dv
GAINOR, Ann	17	F	Unknown	05Ma02Dv	WOODS, Henry	21	M	Unknown	05Ma02Dv

BUCHANAN, John	21	M	Unknown	05Ma02Dv	MORRISON, U-Mrs.	40	F	None	06Ma02Dw
MULLIN, Mathew	24	M	Unknown	05Ma02Dv	MCAVERY, Jane	30	F	None	06Ma02Dw
U (W)	27	F	Wife	05Ma02Dv	GALLAGHER, Jane	20	F	Spinster	06Ma02Dw
COONEY, John	27	M	Unknown	05Ma02Dv	MULLAVAN, Phil.	27	M	Laborer	06Ma02Dw
MOHILL, U-Mrs.	19	F	Unknown	05Ma02Dv	Mary	16	F	None	06Ma02Dw
MAGAN, Bernard	27	M	Unknown	05Ma02Dv	CONWAY, Phil.	25	M	None	06Ma02Dw
Thos.	15	M	Unknown	05Ma02Dv	FALNEY, Edw.	25	M	None	06Ma02Dw
BYRNE, Patk.	05	M	Child	05Ma02Dv	SMITH, Jas.	23	M	None	06Ma02Dw
Jane	21	F	Unknown	05Ma02Dv	FOX, Jas.	25	M	None	06Ma02Dw
MARTIN, Thos.	19	M	Unknown	05Ma02Dv	Patk.	20	M	None	06Ma02Dw
Catherine	45	F	Unknown	05Ma02Dv	LARKIN, Jno.	21	M	None	06Ma02Dw
DUFFY, Mary	20	F	Unknown	05Ma02Dv	MORAN, Danl.	21	M	None	06Ma02Dw
DUGAN, Henry	30	M	Unknown	05Ma02Dv	GALLAGHER, Jno.	20	M	None	06Ma02Dw
CADWELL, Arthur	40	M	Unknown	05Ma02Dv	LARKIN, Ann	20	F	Spinster	06Ma02Dw
KERNEY, John	20	M	Unknown	05Ma02Dv	MORAN, Jas.	20	M	Laborer	06Ma02Dw
HEADRIN, U-Mrs.	20	F	Unknown	05Ma02Dv	MOONAN, Biddy	20	F	Spinster	06Ma02Dw
WALSH, Catherine	22	F	Unknown	05Ma02Dv	COOLOHAN, Ann	27	F	Spinster	06Ma02Dw
BRENNAN, Maria	23	F	Unknown	05Ma02Dv	REYNOLDS, Barney	20	M	Laborer	06Ma02Dw
LEONARD, Thos.	22	M	Unknown	05Ma02Dv	RYAN, Jas.	20	M	Laborer	06Ma02Dw
HANLEY, Michl.	23	M	Unknown	05Ma02Dv	SMITH, Ann	20	F	Spinster	06Ma02Dw
MCGRAY, Mary	23	F	Unknown	05Ma02Dv	ARMSTRONG, Jas.	23	M	Laborer	06Ma02Dw
DEALY, Patk.	23	M	Unknown	05Ma02Dv	KEEFE, Judith	25	F	Spinster	06Ma02Dw
FLYNNE, Jos.	23	M	Unknown	05Ma02Dv	LOGAN, Thos.	20	M	Laborer	06Ma02Dw
EGESTON, Patrick	22	M	Unknown	05Ma02Dv	DOYLE, Sarah	50	F	Wife	06Ma02Dw
HAVERTY, John	22	M	Unknown	05Ma02Dv	Jno. (S)	21	M	None	06Ma02Dw
MCFEE, Thos.	20	M	Unknown	05Ma02Dv	Stephen (S)	14	M	None	06Ma02Dw
CONWAY, Mathew	26	M	Unknown	05Ma02Dv	Bernard (S)	01	M	Child	06Ma02Dw
HEALY, Michl.	20	M	Unknown	05Ma02Dv	WISELEY, Jas.	16	M	Laborer	06Ma02Dw
CORRY, Stephen	22	M	Unknown	05Ma02Dv	Esther	20	F	Spinster	06Ma02Dw
U (W)	25	F	Wife	05Ma02Dv	MCCABE, Patk.	20	M	Laborer	06Ma02Dw
HEALY, Michl.	20	M	Unknown	05Ma02Dv	FARRELL, Cathe.	21	F	Spinster	06Ma02Dw
DEALY, Hugh	20	M	Unknown	05Ma02Dv	KELLY, Jas.	25	M	Laborer	06Ma02Dw
PARR, Wm.	20	M	Unknown	05Ma02Dv	RILEY, Winifred	18	F	Spinster	06Ma02Dw
BRODRICK, Cathe.	20	F	Unknown	05Ma02Dv	OHARA, Bernard	25	M	Laborer	06Ma02Dw
LARKIN, Bridget	25	F	Unknown	05Ma02Dv	Jane	40	F	Wi	06Ma02Dw
MULVEHILL, U	20	F	Unknown	05Ma02Dv	CONLEY, Margaret	16	F	Spinster	06Ma02Dw
MAHON, Thos.	21	M	Unknown	05Ma02Dv	DOYLE, Cathe.	20	F	Spinster	06Ma02Dw
SHEIL, Thos.	19	M	Unknown	05Ma02Dv	LANNON, Sarah	09	F	Child	06Ma02Dw
MCDONOUGH, Andrew	30	M	Unknown	05Ma02Dv	CULLEN, Margt.	20	F	Spinster	06Ma02Dw
DOUD, Mary	21	F	Unknown	05Ma02Dv	CAVANAUGH, Margt.	20	F	Spinster	06Ma02Dw
SCALLY, Mary	30	F	Unknown	05Ma02Dv	CONWAY, Bridget	21	F	Spinster	06Ma02Dw
GAVIGAN, Mary	04	F	Child	05Ma02Dv	HANLON, Jno.	18	M	Laborer	06Ma02Dw
BRENNAN, Owen	22	M	Unknown	05Ma02Dv	Patk.	20	M	Laborer	06Ma02Dw
CRAVEN, Thos.	27	M	Unknown	05Ma02Dv	RILEY, Bridget	25	F	Spinster	06Ma02Dw
KEALEY, Patrick	26	M	Unknown	05Ma02Dv	MCGUIRE, Margt.	21	F	Spinster	06Ma02Dw
Mary	44	F	Unknown	05Ma02Dv	GHAN, Celia	20	F	Spinster	06Ma02Dw
MCAVOY, Patk.	19	M	Unknown	05Ma02Dv	LYNN, Michl.	18	M	Laborer	06Ma02Dw
MCDONALD, James	04	M	Child	05Ma02Dv	DONOHUE, Edw.	20	M	Laborer	06Ma02Dw
MCCARTON, Michl.	27	M	Unknown	05Ma02Dv	KEEFE, Arthur	30	M	Laborer	06Ma02Dw
MCCABE, Ann	00	F	Unknown	05Ma02Dv	MCSWEENEY, Johannah	40	F	Wife	06Ma02Dw
CAMPBILL, Roseann	27	F	Unknown	05Ma02Dv	KEEFE, Mary-Ann	06	F	Child	06Ma02Dw
MCCABE, Catherine	20	F	Unknown	05Ma02Dv	MARAGH, Honorah	20	F	Spinster	06Ma02Dw
CAMPBELL, Julia	22	F	Unknown	05Ma02Dv	Johannah	11	F	Spinster	06Ma02Dw
KELLY, James	20	M	Unknown	05Ma02Dv	HOPKINS, Francis	21	M	Laborer	06Ma02Dw
BRAHON, John	24	M	Unknown	05Ma02Dv	Jno.	20	M	Laborer	06Ma02Dw
HARNEY, Ann	26	F	Unknown	05Ma02Dv	DUIGNAN, Thos.	10	M	Laborer	06Ma02Dw
Thos.	25	M	Unknown	05Ma02Dv	REILLY, Bridget	20	F	Spinster	06Ma02Dw
SHENDON, Jas.	02	M	Child	05Ma02Dv	MCCABE, Felix	21	M	Laborer	06Ma02Dw
BELLON, Robt.	21	M	Unknown	05Ma02Dv	Cathe.	18	F	None	06Ma02Dw
MCGOVERN, Mary	24	F	Unknown	05Ma02Dv	CALWELL, Susan	18	F	Spinster	06Ma02Dw
					FAGAN, Margt.	10	F	Spinster	06Ma02Dw
					HAYES, Jno.	14	M	Laborer	06Ma02Dw
					HESHAN, Ally	30	F	Wife	06Ma02Dw
					Thomas (S)	02	M	Child	06Ma02Dw
					Jno. (S)	.00	M	Infant	06Ma02Dw
RELIANCE 06 MAY 1846					MCCARTHY, Jno.	20	M	Laborer	06Ma02Dw
					DOHERTY, Susan	20	F	Spinster	06Ma02Dw
From Liverpool					COSTIGAN, Cathe.	25	F	Wife	06Ma02Dw
					Michel (S)	02	M	Child	06Ma02Dw
					LONOGAN, Bridget	20	F	Spinster	06Ma02Dw
					COWLEY, Bridget	29	F	Spinster	06Ma02Dw
BRADY, Eliza	20	F	Spinster	06Ma02Dw	CORRIGAN, Owen	10	M	None	06Ma02Dw
POUTING, Patk.	30	M	Laborer	06Ma02Dw	COX, Michl.	54	M	Laborer	06Ma02Dw
U (W)	18	F	Wife	06Ma02Dw	Ann (W)	54	F	Wife	06Ma02Dw
COLLINS, Jno.	19	M	None	06Ma02Dw	Patk. (S)	20	M	None	06Ma02Dw

NAMES OF PASSENGERS		AGE	SEX	OCCUPATIONS	DATE PORT SHIP
CONLEY, Mary		18	F	Spinster	06Ma02Dw
MCGUIRE, Jas.		21	M	Laborer	06Ma02Dw
CORCORAN, Alice		14	F	Spinster	06Ma02Dw
GAYER, Jno.		21	M	Laborer	06Ma02Dw
Judy		21	F	Laborer	06Ma02Dw
GIBBON, Domnick		20	M	Laborer	06Ma02Dw
BARDIS, Ann		20	F	Spinster	06Ma02Dw
MORGAN, Biddy		20	F	Spinster	06Ma02Dw
HERLEY, Betty		19	F	Spinster	06Ma02Dw
DILLON, Jas.		30	M	Laborer	06Ma02Dw
Cathe.		32	F	Laborer	06Ma02Dw
Ellen		28	F	Spinster	06Ma02Dw
JOHNSON, Mary		20	F	Spinster	06Ma02Dw
ONEILL, Chas.		32	M	Laborer	06Ma02Dw
DONNOLLY, Chas.		20	M	Laborer	06Ma02Dw
Alice		18	F	None	06Ma02Dw
AVERY, Wm.		24	M	None	06Ma02Dw
MCEILLARD, Ally		20	F	Spinster	06Ma02Dw
HEUGHES, Peggy		20	F	Spinster	06Ma02Dw
ONEILL, Jas.		17	M	Laborer	06Ma02Dw
Margaret		29	F	Spinster	06Ma02Dw
Mary		25	F	Spinster	06Ma02Dw
HAGAN, Jno.		20	M	Laborer	06Ma02Dw
HUGHES, Peter		20	M	Laborer	06Ma02Dw
GIBBIN, Bridget		25	F	Spinster	06Ma02Dw
MORAN, Jas.		20	M	Laborer	06Ma02Dw
WATSON, Wm.		40	M	Laborer	06Ma02Dw
Danl.		30	M	Laborer	06Ma02Dw
SHANKS, Ann		30	F	Spinster	06Ma02Dw
MCMANUS, James		20	M	Laborer	06Ma02Dw
GIFFIS, Jane		40	F	Wife	06Ma02Dw
Mary	(D)	16	F	None	06Ma02Dw
Susan	(D)	13	F	None	06Ma02Dw
Dorothy	(D)	12	F	None	06Ma02Dw
Jane	(D)	10	F	None	06Ma02Dw
Ellen	(D)	06	F	Child	06Ma02Dw
Ann	(D)	08	F	Child	06Ma02Dw
BRUCE, Wm.		25	M	Laborer	06Ma02Dw
U	(W)	20	F	Wife	06Ma02Dw
Richard		24	M	Laborer	06Ma02Dw
Isaac		28	M	Laborer	06Ma02Dw
MORRIS, Lues		24	U	None	06Ma02Dw
GALBRAITH, Rosetta		30	F	Spinster	06Ma02Dw
FOOLEY, Margt.		20	F	Spinster	06Ma02Dw
MCCULLOGH, Jno.		19	M	Laborer	06Ma02Dw
WHRIGHT, Jas.		50	M	Farmer	06Ma02Dw
Cathe.	(W)	45	F	Wife	06Ma02Dw
Eliza	(D)	19	F	Farmer	06Ma02Dw
Mary	(D)	17	F	Farmer	06Ma02Dw
Sophia	(D)	13	F	Farmer	06Ma02Dw
Martha	(D)	07	F	Child	06Ma02Dw
Caroline	(D)	04	F	Child	06Ma02Dw
FARRELL, Patrick		40	M	Laborer	06Ma02Dw
Cathe.		24	F	Laborer	06Ma02Dw
Jane		18	F	Laborer	06Ma02Dw
Cathe.		46	F	Laborer	06Ma02Dw
Thos.		20	M	Laborer	06Ma02Dw
Eliza		10	F	Child	06Ma02Dw
Jas.		09	M	Child	06Ma02Dw
DUFF, Patk.		20	M	Laborer	06Ma02Dw
NUNN, Maria		20	F	Spinster	06Ma02Dw
RYAN, Denis		20	M	Laborer	06Ma02Dw
REYNOLDS, Michl.		20	M	None	06Ma02Dw
LODGE, Michl.		25	M	None	06Ma02Dw
FLATLEY, Bessy		18	F	Spinster	06Ma02Dw
CAVENEY, Ellen		20	F	Spinster	06Ma02Dw
FOLEY, Bridget		18	F	Spinster	06Ma02Dw
FLATLEY, Wm.		25	M	Laborer	06Ma02Dw
KELLY, Michel		20	M	Laborer	06Ma02Dw
Jno.		13	M	Laborer	06Ma02Dw
MORLAN, Peter		30	M	Laborer	06Ma02Dw
DAY, Dennis		27	M	Laborer	06Ma02Dw
COGHLAN, Henry		09	M	Child	06Ma02Dw
GLENDON, Jas.		19	M	Laborer	06Ma02Dw
SCALLY, Jas.		20	M	Laborer	06Ma02Dw
JOHNSON, Patk.		20	M	Laborer	06Ma02Dw
CANNON, Richd.		26	M	Laborer	06Ma02Dw
SMITH, Thoms.		25	M	Laborer	06Ma02Dw
SWEENEY, Patk.		20	M	Laborer	06Ma02Dw
Jas.		15	M	None	06Ma02Dw
WELSH, Mary		22	F	Spinster	06Ma02Dw
Ellen		22	F	None	06Ma02Dw
BRYAN, Jno.		40	M	Laborer	06Ma02Dw
Mary		30	F	None	06Ma02Dw
Michel		19	M	Laborer	06Ma02Dw
Jas.		18	M	Laborer	06Ma02Dw
Bridget		09	F	Child	06Ma02Dw
Ellen		11	F	None	06Ma02Dw
CROAK, John		36	M	None	06Ma02Dw
U	(W)	30	F	Wife	06Ma02Dw
ENGLISH, Mary		60	F	Wi	06Ma02Dw
CROAK, Cathe.		12	F	Laborer	06Ma02Dw
Judith		09	F	Child	06Ma02Dw
Anthony		08	M	Child	06Ma02Dw
Ellen		07	F	Child	06Ma02Dw
Patk.		03	M	Child	06Ma02Dw
Philip		.00	M	Infant	06Ma02Dw
HUTCHINSON, Robt.		28	M	Laborer	06Ma02Dw
Mary-Ann	(W)	24	F	Wife	06Ma02Dw
NAGLE, Jno.		24	M	Laborer	06Ma02Dw
Michl.		26	M	Laborer	06Ma02Dw
Johanna		23	F	Spinster	06Ma02Dw
ODONNELL, Daniel		30	M	Laborer	06Ma02Dw
MCALLEER, Ann		25	F	Spinster	06Ma02Dw
Cathe.		30	F	Spinster	06Ma02Dw
MULLEN, Peter		30	M	Laborer	06Ma02Dw
HANNAN, Thomas		25	M	Laborer	06Ma02Dw
ARCHER, U-Mrs.		42	F	Wife	06Ma02Dw
WHELAN, Mary		30	F	Spinster	06Ma02Dw
MULLEN, Ellen		30	F	Spinster	06Ma02Dw
DORAN, Ellen		25	F	Spinster	06Ma02Dw
Margaret	(D)	02	F	Child	06Ma02Dw
Margt.		11	F	None	06Ma02Dw
MARTN, Danl.		23	M	Laborer	06Ma02Dw
DELANEY, Michl.		25	M	Laborer	06Ma02Dw
REYNOLDS, Tedy		22	M	Laborer	06Ma02Dw
HARRISON, Thos.		24	M	Laborer	06Ma02Dw
ONEILL, Patk.		22	M	Laborer	06Ma02Dw
HARRISON, Margaret		24	F	Spinster	06Ma02Dw
ONEIL, Biddy		23	F	Spinster	06Ma02Dw
DONLAN, Margaret		20	F	Spinster	06Ma02Dw
GALLAGHER, Mary		19	F	Spinster	06Ma02Dw
CONNOLLY, Bridget		21	F	Spinster	06Ma02Dw
KENNEDY, Mary		20	F	Spinster	06Ma02Dw
Cathe.		23	F	Spinster	06Ma02Dw
KELLY, Darby		24	F	Spinster	06Ma02Dw
GALLAGHER, Ellen		18	F	Spinster	06Ma02Dw
WHELAN, Mary		19	F	Spinster	06Ma02Dw
TRACY, Patk.		22	M	Laborer	06Ma02Dw
Peggy		20	F	None	06Ma02Dw
MULLIGAN, Bridget		25	F	Spinster	06Ma02Dw
INGLESBY, Jno.		18	M	Laborer	06Ma02Dw
FEY, Bridget		18	F	Spinster	06Ma02Dw
FLYNN, Jas.		20	M	Laborer	06Ma02Dw
LONDON, Pat		25	M	None	06Ma02Dw
MAHONEY, Chas.		28	M	None	06Ma02Dw
BARRETT, Cathe.		20	F	Spinster	06Ma02Dw
KEEFE, And.		06	M	Laborer	06Ma02Dw
Hannah		.00	F	Infant	06Ma02Dw
MCCLOGHEY, Thos.		26	M	Laborer	06Ma02Dw
HANNAN, Patk.		20	M	None	06Ma02Dw
SCOTT, Richd.		20	M	None	06Ma02Dw
ORPEN, Jno.		20	M	None	06Ma02Dw
DALTON, Luke		20	M	None	06Ma02Dw
MATHEWS, Owen		25	M	None	06Ma02Dw
MURRAY, Wm.		25	M	None	06Ma02Dw
ELLIOTTS, Wm.		24	M	None	06Ma02Dw
MURRAY, Biddy		20	F	Spinster	06Ma02Dw
NOWLAN, Jas.		20	M	Laborer	06Ma02Dw
MCDONALD, Thos.		20	M	Laborer	06Ma02Dw

NAMES OF PASSENGERS	AGE	SEX	OCCUPATIONS	DATE PORT SHIP
KING, Bridget	20	F	Spinster	06Ma02Dw
DONOHUE, Jno.	20	M	Laborer	06Ma02Dw
U (W)	20	F	Wife	06Ma02Dw
CORCORAN, Jas.	30	M	Laborer	06Ma02Dw
CREVAN, Jno.	30	M	Laborer	06Ma02Dw
MATHEWS, Mary	21	F	Spinster	06Ma02Dw
MCGUINDS, Rose	21	F	Spinster	06Ma02Dw
WENBY, Sarah	30	F	Spinster	06Ma02Dw
HANLY, Rodger	20	M	Laborer	06Ma02Dw
BERT, Michl.	40	M	Laborer	06Ma02Dw
MCCONNELL, Patk.	25	M	Laborer	06Ma02Dw
Bridget (W)	20	F	Wife	06Ma02Dw
Susan	19	F	Spinster	06Ma02Dw
Wm.	25	M	Laborer	06Ma02Dw
OHARA, Jas.	30	M	Laborer	06Ma02Dw
GARTLIN, Patk.	20	M	Laborer	06Ma02Dw
RYAN, Dean	25	M	Laborer	06Ma02Dw
HEFFIN, Jno.	20	M	Laborer	06Ma02Dw
READY, Jno.	21	M	Laborer	06Ma02Dw
WATSON, Michl.	20	M	Laborer	06Ma02Dw
CAVANAUGH, Jas.	24	M	Laborer	06Ma02Dw
FOGARTY, Mary	21	F	Spinster	06Ma02Dw
BEGGAN, Margt.	20	F	Spinster	06Ma02Dw
MCDONNELL, Peggy	25	F	Spinster	06Ma02Dw
HAUGHLIN, Mary	15	F	Spinster	06Ma02Dw
PURCELL, Caroline	20	F	Spinster	06Ma02Dw
LOUGHLIN, Ellen	18	F	Spinster	06Ma02Dw
MCGUIRE, Geo.	24	M	Laborer	06Ma02Dw
JOHNSON, Jas.	54	M	Farmer	06Ma02Dw
U (W)	52	F	Wife	06Ma02Dw
Geo. (S)	20	M	None	06Ma02Dw
Jno. (S)	18	M	None	06Ma02Dw
Eliza (D)	16	F	None	06Ma02Dw
Thos. (S)	14	M	None	06Ma02Dw
Jas. (S)	12	M	None	06Ma02Dw
Maria (D)	10	F	None	06Ma02Dw
Joseph (S)	08	M	Child	06Ma02Dw
Jonas (S)	06	M	Child	06Ma02Dw
Sarah (D)	04	F	Child	06Ma02Dw
Timothy (S)	02	M	Child	06Ma02Dw
DOGHERTY, Biddy	24	F	Spinster	06Ma02Dw
Eliza	22	F	Spinster	06Ma02Dw
DEVLIN, Sarah	18	F	Spinster	06Ma02Dw
Maria	16	F	Spinster	06Ma02Dw
COOK, Thos.	40	M	Laborer	06Ma02Dw
U (W)	38	F	Wife	06Ma02Dw
James (S)	16	M	None	06Ma02Dw
Sarah (D)	14	F	None	06Ma02Dw
Jos. (S)	12	M	None	06Ma02Dw
Geo. (S)	10	M	None	06Ma02Dw
Samuel (S)	08	M	Child	06Ma02Dw
Mathew	06	M	Child	06Ma02Dw
Jno.	04	M	Child	06Ma02Dw
FLYNN, Cathe.	20	F	Spinster	06Ma02Dw
CONLAN, Biddy	20	F	Spinster	06Ma02Dw
SMITH, Sarah	21	F	Spinster	06Ma02Dw
JOHNSON, Nora	19	F	Spinster	06Ma02Dw
COOK, Maria	20	F	Spinster	06Ma02Dw
HANLAN, Maria	19	F	Spinster	06Ma02Dw

MACEDONIA 07 MAY 1846

From Liverpool

NAMES OF PASSENGERS	AGE	SEX	OCCUPATIONS	DATE PORT SHIP
BRADLEY, John	21	M	Cbtmkr	07Ma02Dx
ROBINSON, William	21	M	Cbtmkr	07Ma02Dx
QUINN, Jane	46	F	None	07Ma02Dx
Cormack	21	M	None	07Ma02Dx
QUINN, Patrick	16	M	None	07Ma02Dx
John	10	M	None	07Ma02Dx
Thomas	23	M	None	07Ma02Dx
DUFFEY, John	22	M	Laborer	07Ma02Dx
Patrick	30	M	Laborer	07Ma02Dx
CLARK, Ann	27	F	Servant	07Ma02Dx
Bridg	18	F	Servant	07Ma02Dx
Peggy	19	F	Servant	07Ma02Dx
BRENNEN, Patrick	20	M	Laborer	07Ma02Dx
KELLEY, James	21	M	Laborer	07Ma02Dx
LEE, Martin	21	M	Laborer	07Ma02Dx
GALLAGHER, John	35	M	Laborer	07Ma02Dx
Marey	32	F	Laborer	07Ma02Dx
NOON, Bridget	18	F	Servant	07Ma02Dx
FLANAGAN, James	32	M	Laborer	07Ma02Dx
GRIFFIN, Thomas	30	M	Laborer	07Ma02Dx
SMITH, Patrick	25	M	Laborer	07Ma02Dx
Marey (W)	26	F	Laborer	07Ma02Dx
John (S)	01	M	Child	07Ma02Dx
FALLON, Jane	19	F	Servant	07Ma02Dx
LANE, Judy	23	F	Servant	07Ma02Dx
FARRELL, Thomas	25	M	Laborer	07Ma02Dx
CRONEN, Marey	24	F	Servant	07Ma02Dx
LAVENDOR, John	19	M	Laborer	07Ma02Dx
LAVENDER, Catherine	19	F	Laborer	07Ma02Dx
SHIRKETT, Marey	27	F	Servant	07Ma02Dx
FEENEY, Marey	16	F	Servant	07Ma02Dx
BYRNE, Marey	24	F	Servant	07Ma02Dx
SMITH, Bernard	30	M	Cooper	07Ma02Dx
Phillip	32	M	Laborer	07Ma02Dx
GAFFNEY, James	25	M	Laborer	07Ma02Dx
MCGUIRE, James	25	M	Laborer	07Ma02Dx
SHANNAHAN, Ann	19	F	House Maid	07Ma02Dx
CARROLL, Michael	24	M	Laborer	07Ma02Dx
SHEEKERN, Mary	18	F	Servant	07Ma02Dx
HIGGINS, John	20	M	Laborer	07Ma02Dx
HANLEY, Honor	28	F	Servant	07Ma02Dx
TRACEY, Bridget	17	F	Servant	07Ma02Dx
MCGUIRE, Mary	20	F	Servant	07Ma02Dx
BARCALAY, Dorothy	20	F	Servant	07Ma02Dx
KEENAN, Mary	23	F	Servant	07Ma02Dx
HENREY, Thomas	35	M	Laborer	07Ma02Dx
EGAN, David	26	M	Butcher	07Ma02Dx
COYLE, Stephen	26	M	Servant	07Ma02Dx
KELLEY, William	20	M	Baker	07Ma02Dx
HORAN, James	20	M	Turner	07Ma02Dx
BYRNE, Terrance	22	M	Laborer	07Ma02Dx
GRABTON, Michael	22	M	Laborer	07Ma02Dx
Winiferd	17	F	Servant	07Ma02Dx
KEARNEY, John	22	M	Servant	07Ma02Dx
SHANNON, Patrick	20	M	Laborer	07Ma02Dx
KEARNEY, Thomas	20	M	Laborer	07Ma02Dx
CARROLL, Bridget	25	F	House Maid	07Ma02Dx
DUFFEY, John	20	M	Laborer	07Ma02Dx
GREENE, John	23	M	Laborer	07Ma02Dx
RILEY, Mary	23	F	House Maid	07Ma02Dx
COLGAN, Bernard	32	M	Laborer	07Ma02Dx
MCGUIRE, Michael	30	M	Laborer	07Ma02Dx
MOLADY, Patrick	26	M	Laborer	07Ma02Dx
HANLEY, Bridget	26	F	Wife	07Ma02Dx
Martin (S)	03	M	Child	07Ma02Dx
John (S)	05	M	Child	07Ma02Dx
SINNOTT, Eliza	25	F	Servant	07Ma02Dx
MOORE, Mary-Ann	22	F	Dressmaker	07Ma02Dx
HOWLAN, James	35	M	Shoemaker	07Ma02Dx
HAYDEN, James	44	M	Laborer	07Ma02Dx
LEARY, Paul	25	M	Laborer	07Ma02Dx
MURPHEY, Laurance	18	M	Laborer	07Ma02Dx
MCGUIRE, Bridget	24	F	House Maid	07Ma02Dx
WARD, Patrick	34	M	Laborer	07Ma02Dx
TYRELL, James	20	M	Laborer	07Ma02Dx
LAMBERT, Joseph	26	M	Mason	07Ma02Dx
LAWLER, Mary	19	F	House Maid	07Ma02Dx
BURKE, Bernard	20	M	Laborer	07Ma02Dx
DAILEY, Jane	19	F	House Maid	07Ma02Dx

NAMES OF PASSENGERS	A G E	S E X	OCCUPATIONS	DATE PORT SHIP
DELAP, Peter	18	M	Laborer	07Ma02Dx
Charles	20	M	Laborer	07Ma02Dx
LYNCH, Judy	26	F	House Maid	07Ma02Dx
Catherine	17	F	House Maid	07Ma02Dx
Catherine	18	F	House Maid	07Ma02Dx
WELCH, Patrick	20	M	Laborer	07Ma02Dx
George	19	M	Laborer	07Ma02Dx
GLYNN, Bridget	19	F	Servant	07Ma02Dx
KENEDAY, Thomas	26	M	Laborer	07Ma02Dx
ONEALE, Patrick	26	M	Laborer	07Ma02Dx
Catherin (W)	26	F	Wife	07Ma02Dx
Michael	21	M	Laborer	07Ma02Dx
Phelam	23	M	Laborer	07Ma02Dx
LINNON, Elen	22	F	Housekeeper	07Ma02Dx
REYNALDS, William	28	M	Shoemaker	07Ma02Dx
GILLASFER, Juda	27	F	House Maid	07Ma02Dx
WILLIAMS, Henrey	25	M	Carver	07Ma02Dx
Mary (W)	20	F	Wife	07Ma02Dx
KEOUGH, Patrick	34	M	Laborer	07Ma02Dx
BRODEN, Mary	22	F	House Maid	07Ma02Dx
HARNEY, John	20	M	Groom	07Ma02Dx
TULEY, John	24	M	Laborer	07Ma02Dx
MAGAN, Andrew	21	M	Laborer	07Ma02Dx
NAUGHTON, Michal	21	M	Laborer	07Ma02Dx
SHEINAN, Michal	22	M	Laborer	07Ma02Dx
Mary	20	F	House Maid	07Ma02Dx
GATLEY, Bridget	20	F	House Maid	07Ma02Dx
SHANHUSSEY, Mary	18	F	House Maid	07Ma02Dx
MORAN, Mary	20	F	House Maid	07Ma02Dx
MURPHEY, Hugh	26	M	Servant	07Ma02Dx
MULRANON, Thomas	20	M	Laborer	07Ma02Dx
Catherin	21	F	House Maid	07Ma02Dx
NAUGHTON, Bridget	28	F	House Maid	07Ma02Dx
SHEIGHHAN, Bridget	26	F	House Maid	07Ma02Dx
SIMMONS, Phillip	18	M	Laborer	07Ma02Dx
MCCAHILL, John	20	M	Carpenter	07Ma02Dx
DANNING, John	19	M	Laborer	07Ma02Dx
LYNCH, James	21	M	Laborer	07Ma02Dx
FITZIMONSS, Catherin	18	F	House Maid	07Ma02Dx
FITTZIMMONS, Rose	16	F	House Maid	07Ma02Dx
LYNCH, Bridget	20	F	House Maid	07Ma02Dx
GULSHANNON, John	22	M	Laborer	07Ma02Dx
Mary	15	F	House Maid	07Ma02Dx
WALCH, John	22	M	Laborer	07Ma02Dx
MARTIN, John	22	M	Laborer	07Ma02Dx
MACCALL, James	20	M	Laborer	07Ma02Dx
MCCONAHEE, Margaret	19	F	Dressmaker	07Ma02Dx
GULSHANNON, Bridget	20	F	House Maid	07Ma02Dx
BRADEY, Mary	16	F	House Maid	07Ma02Dx
CANLON, Nancy	14	F	House Maid	07Ma02Dx
RODDEN, Mary	17	F	House Maid	07Ma02Dx
BURKE, James	26	M	Laborer	07Ma02Dx
HICKEY, John	24	M	Farmer	07Ma02Dx
Peggy	21	F	Housekeeper	07Ma02Dx
CORR, Phillip	26	M	Laborer	07Ma02Dx
Thomas	20	M	Laborer	07Ma02Dx
Mary-D.	45	F	Housekeeper	07Ma02Dx
Mary	17	F	Housekeeper	07Ma02Dx
COMMOFORD, John	24	M	Farmer	07Ma02Dx
Anne	20	F	House Maid	07Ma02Dx
LYNCH, Thomas	20	M	Farmer	07Ma02Dx
TORNEY, Peter	36	M	Farmer	07Ma02Dx
Ellen	13	F	House Maid	07Ma02Dx
SMITH, Catherin	23	F	House Maid	07Ma02Dx
Catherin-P.	20	F	House Maid	07Ma02Dx
GILLOCK, Ann	13	F	Dressmaker	07Ma02Dx
Mary	16	F	Dressmaker	07Ma02Dx
SMITH, Ann	20	F	House Maid	07Ma02Dx
GAUGHF, Catherine	19	F	House Maid	07Ma02Dx
HUSSEY, Peter	28	M	Farmer	07Ma02Dx
REILEY, Margaret	18	F	House Maid	07Ma02Dx
Bridget	12	F	House Maid	07Ma02Dx
FAGAN, Bridget	18	F	House Maid	07Ma02Dx
FITZSIMMONS, James	25	M	Farmer	07Ma02Dx
GILROY, Margaret	15	F	House Maid	07Ma02Dx

NAMES OF PASSENGERS	A G E	S E X	OCCUPATIONS	DATE PORT SHIP
GILROY, Bridget	18	F	House Maid	07Ma02Dx
FLINN, Mary	16	F	House Maid	07Ma02Dx
REILEY, Peggy	20	F	House Maid	07Ma02Dx
FINNEGAN, Miles	25	M	Shoemaker	07Ma02Dx

SHERIDAN 07 MAY 1846

From Liverpool

NAMES OF PASSENGERS	A G E	S E X	OCCUPATIONS	DATE PORT SHIP
STOOKER, Thos.	26	M	Laborer	07Ma02Do
MCEVOY, Jas.	22	M	Laborer	07Ma02Do
BANNON, Cathn.	21	F	Servant	07Ma02Do
MULLIGAN, Patt	20	M	Laborer	07Ma02Do
Mary	22	F	Unknown	07Ma02Do
WOODS, John	56	M	Farmer	07Ma02Do
John	22	M	Farmer	07Ma02Do
MCADAM, Patt	24	M	Laborer	07Ma02Do
MCGINNIS, Jas.	25	M	Laborer	07Ma02Do
BRADY, Ellen	21	F	Servant	07Ma02Do
MCATEE, Rose	21	F	Servant	07Ma02Do
WHITE, Thos.	20	M	Laborer	07Ma02Do
NEAL, Hugh	23	M	Laborer	07Ma02Do
CORREY, Cathn.	19	F	Servant	07Ma02Do
GERETY, Bridget	20	F	Servant	07Ma02Do
CONNOR, Jas.	32	M	Laborer	07Ma02Do
Cath.	32	F	Unknown	07Ma02Do
DONNELL, Mich.	25	M	Laborer	07Ma02Do
MCCARTY, Hannah	18	F	Servant	07Ma02Do
MCKINNON, Mary	23	F	Servant	07Ma02Do
Sarah	22	F	Servant	07Ma02Do
CASKVIEW, Margt.	18	F	Servant	07Ma02Do
LYNN, John	20	M	Laborer	07Ma02Do
ASBORN, Francis	21	M	Laborer	07Ma02Do
HOUGHSTON, Alex.	20	M	Laborer	07Ma02Do
KERRY, Alexn.	19	M	Laborer	07Ma02Do
MCKINNON, Anthy.	20	M	Laborer	07Ma02Do
CARTER, Charles	20	M	Laborer	07Ma02Do
DEVLIN, Susan	20	F	Servant	07Ma02Do
MCCLUSKEY, Bridget	25	F	Servant	07Ma02Do
KILEY, John	22	M	Laborer	07Ma02Do
Mary	24	F	Unknown	07Ma02Do
GARVEY, Bernard	18	M	Laborer	07Ma02Do
KENNEDY, Jas.	20	M	Laborer	07Ma02Do
MCEVOY, Margt.	19	F	Unknown	07Ma02Do
CANFIELD, Anthy.	25	M	Unknown	07Ma02Do
STOCK, Thos.	26	M	Unknown	07Ma02Do
HOWARD, Margt.	22	F	Unknown	07Ma02Do
GLYNN, Morris	24	M	Unknown	07Ma02Do
Bessey	21	F	Unknown	07Ma02Do
MCANNLLY, Owen	19	M	Unknown	07Ma02Do
MCARDALE, Patt	21	M	Unknown	07Ma02Do
Margt.	19	F	Unknown	07Ma02Do
MCADAM, Danl.	19	M	Unknown	07Ma02Do
HAND, John	18	M	Unknown	07Ma02Do
DONOHUE, Andrew	25	M	Unknown	07Ma02Do
U (W)	24	F	Unknown	07Ma02Do
FITZPATRICK, Bridget	19	F	Unknown	07Ma02Do
OKEEFE, U-Mrs.	27	F	Unknown	07Ma02Do
Bridget	18	F	Unknown	07Ma02Do
ROACH, Mary	18	F	Unknown	07Ma02Do
CALLAHAN, John	25	M	Unknown	07Ma02Do
HUTCHINSON, Robert	23	M	Unknown	07Ma02Do
GRAY, John	25	M	Unknown	07Ma02Do
NEIL, Thos.	20	M	Unknown	07Ma02Do
MOONEY, Francis	23	M	Unknown	07Ma02Do
BRENNAN, John	20	M	Unknown	07Ma02Do
DUGAN, Wm.	24	M	Unknown	07Ma02Do
MCGINNIS, Patt	20	M	Unknown	07Ma02Do
FARNHAM, Neal	23	M	Unknown	07Ma02Do

NAMES OF PASSENGERS		AGE	SEX	OCCUPATIONS	DATE PORT SHIP
YOUNG, Bridget		20	F	Unknown	07Ma02Do
POLLOCK, Nancy		20	F	Unknown	07Ma02Do
MCKENNON, Alexn.		19	M	Unknown	07Ma02Do
U-Mrs.		32	F	Unknown	07Ma02Do
Sarah-Jane	(D)	08	F	Child	07Ma02Do
Mary	(D)	04	F	Child	07Ma02Do
PATTON, David		26	M	Unknown	07Ma02Do
U	(W)	25	F	Unknown	07Ma02Do
Ann	(D)	04	F	Child	07Ma02Do
Jas.	(S)	02	M	Child	07Ma02Do
U		.09	U	Infant	07Ma02Do
HUMPHREYS, Edwd.		28	M	Unknown	07Ma02Do
KANE, Neal		22	M	Shoemaker	07Ma02Do
Mary-Ann		19	F	Unknown	07Ma02Do
Margt.		17	F	Unknown	07Ma02Do
MORAN, Thos.		18	M	Laborer	07Ma02Do
MCDERMOTT, Patt		20	M	Laborer	07Ma02Do
DOHERTY, Michl.		21	M	Laborer	07Ma02Do
SCUNLIN, Patt		31	M	Laborer	07Ma02Do
Mary		19	F	Servant	07Ma02Do
MCBREADY, Charles		16	M	Laborer	07Ma02Do
CALLAHAN, Jas.		20	M	Laborer	07Ma02Do
MOORE, Geo.		21	M	Clerk	07Ma02Do
ELLIOTT, Wm.		20	M	Laborer	07Ma02Do
Henry		19	M	Laborer	07Ma02Do
VEITCH, Jas.		21	M	Carpenter	07Ma02Do
SHELLY, Michl.		20	M	Carpenter	07Ma02Do
KING, Wm.		24	M	Carpenter	07Ma02Do
MCMANNERY, Patt		24	M	Laborer	07Ma02Do
CRAUFORD, John		20	M	Farmer	07Ma02Do
WILLIS, Joseph		21	M	Laborer	07Ma02Do
DALTON, Richd.		21	M	Laborer	07Ma02Do
QUINN, Mary		19	F	Unknown	07Ma02Do
LENDELL, Geo.		22	M	Laborer	07Ma02Do
HUGHES, Thos.		22	M	Laborer	07Ma02Do
CULLEN, Michl.		22	M	Laborer	07Ma02Do
John		25	M	Laborer	07Ma02Do
HEMPSTELL, Dani.		24	M	Laborer	07Ma02Do
U	(W)	24	F	Unknown	07Ma02Do
U		.06	U	Infant	07Ma02Do
BYRNN, John		21	M	Laborer	07Ma02Do
Margt.		25	F	Unknown	07Ma02Do
CAVANAH, Jas.		20	M	Laborer	07Ma02Do
U		24	M	Laborer	07Ma02Do
WALSH, Margt.		17	F	Unknown	07Ma02Do
HANLON, John		44	M	Laborer	07Ma02Do
Cathn.		36	F	Unknown	07Ma02Do
BRADLEY, Michl.		21	M	Nailer	07Ma02Do
David		22	M	Clerk	07Ma02Do
WALSH, Patt		20	M	Laborer	07Ma02Do
MCKYAN, Bridget		19	F	Unknown	07Ma02Do
DYERS, Margt.		21	F	Unknown	07Ma02Do
ANDERSON, Ann		20	F	Unknown	07Ma02Do
CHRISTY, Robert		21	M	Laborer	07Ma02Do
ELLIOTT, Thos.		00	M	Laborer	07Ma02Do
DAYLEY, Andrew		00	M	Widr	07Ma02Do
CARROLL, Peter		00	M	Laborer	07Ma02Do
CALERMAN, Walter		00	M	Laborer	07Ma02Do
BYRNN, Simon		00	M	Laborer	07Ma02Do
IVERS, Wm.		00	M	Laborer	07Ma02Do
GARVREY, Judy		00	F	Unknown	07Ma02Do
BRADY, Thos.		00	M	Laborer	07Ma02Do
REILEY, Mathew		00	M	Laborer	07Ma02Do
MURRY, Thos.		00	M	Laborer	07Ma02Do
Andrew		00	M	Laborer	07Ma02Do
Hugh		00	M	Laborer	07Ma02Do
Ellen		00	F	Unknown	07Ma02Do
MCGOLDRICK, Rodger		00	M	Laborer	07Ma02Do
MCQUADE, Jas.		00	M	Laborer	07Ma02Do
RYANS, Corneilus		23	M	Laborer	07Ma02Do
GORMLY, Arthur		19	M	Laborer	07Ma02Do
John		20	M	Laborer	07Ma02Do
MCHUGH, Alice		20	F	Unknown	07Ma02Do
TIERNEY, Jas.		22	M	Laborer	07Ma02Do
MAHER, Richd.		24	M	Laborer	07Ma02Do
MAHER, Margt.		21	F	Unknown	07Ma02Do
MALLEY, Thos.		21	M	Laborer	07Ma02Do
FITZPATRICK, John		21	M	Laborer	07Ma02Do
PURRELL, Philip		22	M	Laborer	07Ma02Do
Bridget		20	F	Unknown	07Ma02Do
WHEELON, Henry		22	M	Laborer	07Ma02Do
Michl.		23	M	Laborer	07Ma02Do
Mary		19	F	Unknown	07Ma02Do
SMITH, Andrew		40	M	Laborer	07Ma02Do
U	(W)	40	F	Unknown	07Ma02Do
Daniel	(S)	20	M	Laborer	07Ma02Do
Cathn.	(D)	01	F	Child	07Ma02Do
HALTON, Ellen		17	F	Unknown	07Ma02Do
HIGGINS, Jane		17	F	Unknown	07Ma02Do
EGAN, Thos.		24	M	Laborer	07Ma02Do
Honora		20	F	Unknown	07Ma02Do
LAFERTY, Patt		22	M	Laborer	07Ma02Do
James		23	M	Laborer	07Ma02Do
TAYLOR, David		28	M	Laborer	07Ma02Do
WILSON, Jane		38	F	Unknown	07Ma02Do
TULLEY, Mary		20	F	Unknown	07Ma02Do
KELLY, Margt.		18	F	Unknown	07Ma02Do
HENRY, Paul		27	M	Laborer	07Ma02Do
MCCLUSKEY, Jas.		24	M	Laborer	07Ma02Do
MELLEN, Thos.		21	M	Laborer	07Ma02Do
Ann		19	F	Unknown	07Ma02Do
FAULKNER, John		24	M	Laborer	07Ma02Do
U	(W)	24	F	Laborer	07Ma02Do
U		.09	U	Infant	07Ma02Do
HOLLINGS, John		22	M	Laborer	07Ma02Do
Mary		30	F	Unknown	07Ma02Do
MCBRIDE, Alice		19	F	Unknown	07Ma02Do
Bridget		20	F	Unknown	07Ma02Do
KINGSLEY, Charles		21	M	Laborer	07Ma02Do
DAVIES, Charles		27	M	Laborer	07Ma02Do
Henry		19	M	Laborer	07Ma02Do
MCNULTY, Jeramiah		27	M	Laborer	07Ma02Do
Cathn.	(W)	23	F	Unknown	07Ma02Do
U		.06	U	Infant	07Ma02Do
BURNTON, John		20	M	Laborer	07Ma02Do
MURRY, John		23	M	Laborer	07Ma02Do
Mary	(W)	21	F	Unknown	07Ma02Do
U		.04	U	Infant	07Ma02Do
NEAVEN, Jas.		27	M	Laborer	07Ma02Do
FANNESSY, Edwd.		25	M	Laborer	07Ma02Do
SAVAGE, Mary		30	F	Unknown	07Ma02Do
Wm.	(S)	12	M	Unknown	07Ma02Do
HARRINGTON, John		20	M	Laborer	07Ma02Do
LENAHAN, Charles		24	M	Laborer	07Ma02Do
WHELHAN, Wm.		26	M	Laborer	07Ma02Do
CHIFFERS, Michl.		25	M	Laborer	07Ma02Do
GREENE, Thos.		25	M	Laborer	07Ma02Do
Arthur		20	M	Laborer	07Ma02Do
GAY, Charles		24	M	Stone Mason	07Ma02Do
RAIL, Mary		20	F	Servant	07Ma02Do
HOWARD, John		21	M	Laborer	07Ma02Do
DONLAN, Bridget		17	F	Unknown	07Ma02Do
MCGEE, Patt		20	M	Laborer	07Ma02Do
RAFFERTY, Mary		19	F	Unknown	07Ma02Do
FINNALLY, John		20	M	Laborer	07Ma02Do
MCBRIDE, Patt		18	M	Laborer	07Ma02Do
Ann		22	F	Unknown	07Ma02Do
Mary		21	F	Unknown	07Ma02Do
MCMAHON, Patt		20	M	Laborer	07Ma02Do
MCQUERK, Hugh		22	M	Laborer	07Ma02Do
Patt		25	M	Laborer	07Ma02Do
Cathn.		00	F	Unknown	07Ma02Do
Margt.		00	F	Unknown	07Ma02Do
Ester		00	F	Unknown	07Ma02Do
HORNER, Jas.		00	M	Unknown	07Ma02Do
RYANS, Cath.		00	F	Unknown	07Ma02Do
BOYLAN, Alice		00	F	Unknown	07Ma02Do
FOGERTY, John		00	M	Unknown	07Ma02Do
MCNEILTY, Rose		00	F	Unknown	07Ma02Do
RODGERS, Cath.		00	F	Unknown	07Ma02Do

NAMES OF PASSENGERS	AGE	SEX	OCCUPATIONS	DATE PORT SHIP	NAMES OF PASSENGERS	AGE	SEX	OCCUPATIONS	DATE PORT SHIP
RODGERS, Alice	00	F	Unknown	07Ma02Do	MONAGHAN, Ann	09	F	Child	07Ma02Dz
ONEIL, Cath.	00	F	Unknown	07Ma02Do	REILLEY, Owen	30	M	Laborer	07Ma02Dz
Patt	00	M	Unknown	07Ma02Do	DWER, Wm.	26	M	Laborer	07Ma02Dz
Ann	00	F	Unknown	07Ma02Do	HALL, Mary	23	F	Unknown	07Ma02Dz
Alice	00	F	Unknown	07Ma02Do	TRACY, Patrick	30	M	Laborer	07Ma02Dz
James	00	M	Unknown	07Ma02Do	HALL, Catherine	20	F	Unknown	07Ma02Dz
John	00	M	Unknown	07Ma02Do	MURTAGH, Catherine	20	F	Unknown	07Ma02Dz
DUFFEY, Bridget	00	F	Unknown	07Ma02Do	BRADY, Rose	18	F	Unknown	07Ma02Dz
MCADAM, Mary	00	F	Unknown	07Ma02Do	KELLY, Susan	28	F	Unknown	07Ma02Dz
MCMANNER, Michl.	00	M	Unknown	07Ma02Do	CONNELL, James	19	M	Laborer	07Ma02Dz
FITZPATRICK, Cathn.	00	F	Unknown	07Ma02Do	MAGNESS, Peter	20	M	Laborer	07Ma02Dz
GALLAGER, Margt.	00	F	Unknown	07Ma02Do	BOYLE, John	18	M	Laborer	07Ma02Dz
HURAN, Mary	29	F	Servant	07Ma02Do	Michl.	19	M	Laborer	07Ma02Dz
Edwd.	06	M	Child	07Ma02Do	Ann	19	F	Unknown	07Ma02Dz
Francis	07	M	Child	07Ma02Do	MCDONNELL, John	20	M	Laborer	07Ma02Dz
ROONEY, John	40	M	Farmer	07Ma02Do	Anthony	18	M	Laborer	07Ma02Dz
MOORAN, Wm.	18	M	Miner	07Ma02Do	Bernard	10	M	Laborer	07Ma02Dz
TWEEDY, Mary	22	F	Unknown	07Ma02Do	Judy	13	F	Unknown	07Ma02Dz
Mary	21	F	Unknown	07Ma02Do	HATTERY, James	21	M	Laborer	07Ma02Dz
BOHAN, Peter	00	M	Miner	07Ma02Do	Martin	30	M	Laborer	07Ma02Dz
RUSSELL, Ann	56	F	Unknown	07Ma02Do	COSGROVE, Judith	20	F	Unknown	07Ma02Dz
DONNELLY, Bridget	21	F	Unknown	07Ma02Do	RAFFERTY, Allice	18	F	Unknown	07Ma02Dz
MCBRIDE, Peter	18	M	Laborer	07Ma02Do	CONNELLY, Patrick	20	M	Laborer	07Ma02Dz
Jane	21	F	Unknown	07Ma02Do	Thos.	18	M	Laborer	07Ma02Dz
Bernard	18	M	Laborer	07Ma02Do	Esther	16	F	Unknown	07Ma02Dz
U-Mrs.	40	F	Unknown	07Ma02Do	MCILHONE, Anne	24	F	Unknown	07Ma02Dz
MCALEER, Ann	21	F	Unknown	07Ma02Do	CALAGHAN, Anne	21	F	Unknown	07Ma02Dz
JOHNSON, Mary	19	F	Unknown	07Ma02Do	Elizabeth	19	F	Unknown	07Ma02Dz
GAHERTY, Cathn.	20	F	Unknown	07Ma02Do	REILEY, Samuel	20	M	Laborer	07Ma02Dz
MCEVOY, Bridget	19	F	Unknown	07Ma02Do	MCILROY, John	20	M	Laborer	07Ma02Dz
MCCARTY, Ann	19	F	Unknown	07Ma02Do	MCALEER, Patrick	20	M	Laborer	07Ma02Dz
MCGUARTY, Mary	22	F	Unknown	07Ma02Do	SHEA, Catherine	20	F	Unknown	07Ma02Dz
KEENNAN, Michl.	36	M	Laborer	07Ma02Do	GURNLEY, Ellen	19	F	Unknown	07Ma02Dz
OBRIEN, Margt.	20	F	Servant	07Ma02Do	HAY, Catherine	17	F	Unknown	07Ma02Dz
MCBRIDE, Geo.	20	M	Unknown	07Ma02Do	CALLENAN, Betty	17	F	Unknown	07Ma02Dz
HUSTLEY, Ann	19	F	Servant	07Ma02Do	MINCHIN, Michl.	28	M	Laborer	07Ma02Dz
DOWN, Mary	18	F	Servant	07Ma02Do	MALONEY, J.	22	M	Laborer	07Ma02Dz
CLUSKEY, John	31	M	Unknown	07Ma02Do	WALSH, Thomas	20	M	Laborer	07Ma02Dz
NEILSON, Kenedy	20	M	Unknown	07Ma02Do	MOSLEY, Ellen	20	F	Unknown	07Ma02Dz
BIRD, Patt	18	M	Unknown	07Ma02Do	AHERN, Richard	24	M	Laborer	07Ma02Dz
MCCANN, Christopher	18	M	Unknown	07Ma02Do	PEAL, Patrick	20	M	Laborer	07Ma02Dz
FORSYTH, Rose	18	F	Servant	07Ma02Do	AHERN, Cathn.	21	F	Unknown	07Ma02Dz
BOYD, Jas.	25	M	Unknown	07Ma02Do	LEHAM, Johanna	21	F	Unknown	07Ma02Dz
HICKS, Ann	16	F	Servant	07Ma02Do	LEAHEY, Jerah.	24	M	Laborer	07Ma02Dz
BRADSLEY, Ann	20	F	Servant	07Ma02Do	BRODERICK, John	22	M	Laborer	07Ma02Dz
MALEADY, Mary	18	F	Servant	07Ma02Do	Michael	28	M	Laborer	07Ma02Dz
FARLEY, Alice	11	F	Child	07Ma02Do	TRACY, Jeramiah	28	M	Laborer	07Ma02Dz
KENNAN, Mary	20	F	Servant	07Ma02Do	BARRETT, Ellen	24	F	Unknown	07Ma02Dz
BROOPHNY, Ann	20	F	Servant	07Ma02Do	HIGGINS, Dennis	25	M	Laborer	07Ma02Dz
LAW, Betty	20	F	Servant	07Ma02Do	HAVERLY, Honorah	20	F	Unknown	07Ma02Dz
MCDONNALD, Ann	20	F	Servant	07Ma02Do	KILLY, Martin	20	M	Laborer	07Ma02Dz
John	20	M	Unknown	07Ma02Do	MONAGHAN, Catherine	20	F	Unknown	07Ma02Dz
Whinney	20	M	Unknown	07Ma02Do	KILLY, Anne	18	F	Unknown	07Ma02Dz
MOORE, Cath.	20	F	Servant	07Ma02Do	MCNOOKIN, Patk.	20	M	Laborer	07Ma02Dz
BROCKLEY, Mary	20	F	Servant	07Ma02Do	GALLIGAN, Thos.	24	M	Laborer	07Ma02Dz
MOORE, Wm.	20	M	Unknown	07Ma02Do	John	20	M	Laborer	07Ma02Dz
LINAHAN, Mary	46	F	Servant	07Ma02Do	Daniel	18	M	Laborer	07Ma02Dz
Daniel (S)	13	M	Unknown	07Ma02Do	SMITH, Mary	20	F	Unknown	07Ma02Dz
John (S)	14	M	Unknown	07Ma02Do	MCLAUGHLIN, Catherine	20	F	Unknown	07Ma02Dz
HAVANAH, Francis	25	M	Unknown	07Ma02Do	GREFFIN, James	18	M	Laborer	07Ma02Dz
Cath.	20	F	Servant	07Ma02Do	Mary	20	F	Unknown	07Ma02Dz
					Ellen	16	F	Unknown	07Ma02Dz

AGNES-GILMORE 07 MAY 1846

From Liverpool

CAMBRIDGE 08 MAY 1846

From Liverpool

NAMES OF PASSENGERS	AGE	SEX	OCCUPATIONS	DATE PORT SHIP
MONAGHAN, Patrick	40	M	Laborer	07Ma02Dz
Bridget	26	F	Unknown	07Ma02Dz
Patrick	13	M	Laborer	07Ma02Dz
NEWBIGGEN, David	46	M	Gentleman	08Ma02Ea
BELLAIES, Maria	25	F	Unknown	08Ma02Ea

64

NAMES OF PASSENGERS		AGE	SEX	OCCUPATIONS	DATE PORT SHIP
LYONS, Lewis		46	M	Merchant	08Ma02Ea
MCKENZIE, Joseph		28	M	Merchant	08Ma02Ea
PELAN, James		60	M	Laborer	08Ma02Ea
Margt.	(W)	58	F	None	08Ma02Ea
Mary	(D)	23	F	None	08Ma02Ea
John	(S)	18	M	Laborer	08Ma02Ea
AIKEN, James		30	M	Carpenter	08Ma02Ea
MCCORKILL, Wm.		25	M	Laborer	08Ma02Ea
HICKEY, Wm.		24	M	Cooper	08Ma02Ea
HANLEY, Bridget		18	F	None	08Ma02Ea
Jane		20	F	None	08Ma02Ea
GILLESPIE, George		26	M	Laborer	08Ma02Ea
COLLINS, Bridget		20	F	None	08Ma02Ea
KENNEDY, Mary		20	F	None	08Ma02Ea
COYNE, Richd.		21	M	Laborer	08Ma02Ea
WEST, Ellen		20	F	None	08Ma02Ea
LYNCH, Margt.		21	F	None	08Ma02Ea
MCDERMOTT, Wm.		30	M	Laborer	08Ma02Ea
Mary		29	F	None	08Ma02Ea
DUFFY, Cathn.		20	F	None	08Ma02Ea
SULLIVAN, Cathn.		21	F	None	08Ma02Ea
MOSS, Francis		21	M	Laborer	08Ma02Ea
MARROW, Thos.		30	M	Laborer	08Ma02Ea
BOYLE, Cathn.		21	F	None	08Ma02Ea
BAEFF, Bridget		21	F	None	08Ma02Ea
DELLANY, Jas.		21	M	Farmer	08Ma02Ea
Cathn.		25	F	None	08Ma02Ea
MADDEN, Simon		21	M	Laborer	08Ma02Ea
BARRY, Biddy		04	F	Child	08Ma02Ea
DONELLY, Francis		21	M	Carpenter	08Ma02Ea
DIVINE, Timothy		18	M	Laborer	08Ma02Ea
RODDY, Edwd.		19	M	Laborer	08Ma02Ea
DEGAFNEY, Ann		20	F	None	08Ma02Ea
RILEY, Andw.		21	M	Laborer	08Ma02Ea
GARRITY, Bridget		20	F	None	08Ma02Ea
SULLIVAN, Judy		50	F	None	08Ma02Ea
Died-At-Sea					
GILLIWAN, Mary		20	F	None	08Ma02Ea
SPENCER, Thos.		21	M	Cooper	08Ma02Ea
PENN, Thos.		21	M	Laborer	08Ma02Ea
MCCARTY, Timothy		24	M	Shoemaker	08Ma02Ea
CLOWSER, Thos.		25	M	Laborer	08Ma02Ea
KENNEDY, Jane		21	F	None	08Ma02Ea
HALPIN, Hannah		21	F	None	08Ma02Ea
GUINN, Jane		30	F	None	08Ma02Ea
Hugh	(S)	.07	M	Infant	08Ma02Ea
LOYS, James		30	M	Laborer	08Ma02Ea
Mary		40	F	None	08Ma02Ea
RUDDY, Patk.		19	M	Laborer	08Ma02Ea
MCKINNA, Judith		20	F	None	08Ma02Ea
Jane		18	F	None	08Ma02Ea
GUINN, Margt.		22	F	None	08Ma02Ea
MCLAUGHLIN, Thos.		20	M	Laborer	08Ma02Ea
Henry		17	M	Laborer	08Ma02Ea
COOK, Betsey		21	F	None	08Ma02Ea
MCLAUGHLIN, Owen		35	M	Laborer	08Ma02Ea
Ellen		18	F	None	08Ma02Ea
Edwd.		13	M	None	08Ma02Ea
KENNEY, Peter-M.		25	M	Laborer	08Ma02Ea
GUINN, John		23	M	Laborer	08Ma02Ea
LOY, Chas.		21	M	Laborer	08Ma02Ea
WALDEN, Mary		18	F	None	08Ma02Ea
MCCABE, Hy.		05	M	Child	08Ma02Ea
LARRY, John		29	M	Laborer	08Ma02Ea
SUMSEIZE, Wm.		45	M	Laborer	08Ma02Ea
Henry	(S)	16	M	Laborer	08Ma02Ea
John	(S)	14	M	Laborer	08Ma02Ea
Henry	(S)	12	M	Laborer	08Ma02Ea
Edwd.		31	M	Laborer	08Ma02Ea
Mary		40	F	None	08Ma02Ea
STOCKFORD, Jas.		30	M	Laborer	08Ma02Ea
Ann	(W)	30	F	None	08Ma02Ea
John	(S)	10	M	None	08Ma02Ea
CUNNINGHAM, Thos.		21	M	Laborer	08Ma02Ea
Bridget		20	F	None	08Ma02Ea
WELDON, Mary		21	F	None	08Ma02Ea
MORAN, Alice		21	F	None	08Ma02Ea
RYAN, Mary		20	F	None	08Ma02Ea
MURPHY, Cathn.		20	F	None	08Ma02Ea
FANEN, Ann		19	F	None	08Ma02Ea
GUINN, Francis		27	M	Laborer	08Ma02Ea
BRADY, Thos.		24	M	Laborer	08Ma02Ea
ONEILL, Bridget		20	F	None	08Ma02Ea
RIELLY, Bridget		21	F	None	08Ma02Ea
MCINTER, Michl.		50	M	Laborer	08Ma02Ea
BRADY, Mary		24	F	None	08Ma02Ea
LYNCH, Luke		21	M	Laborer	08Ma02Ea
Bridget		24	F	None	08Ma02Ea
CONWAY, John		24	M	Laborer	08Ma02Ea
William		22	M	Laborer	08Ma02Ea
Matthew		21	M	Laborer	08Ma02Ea
KERR, Patk.		17	M	Laborer	08Ma02Ea
MORGAN, John		20	M	Laborer	08Ma02Ea
DALEY, Cathn.		21	F	None	08Ma02Ea
MITCHELL, Margt.		21	F	None	08Ma02Ea
KIERNAN, Patk.		20	M	Laborer	08Ma02Ea
LINDSEY, Robt.		25	M	Laborer	08Ma02Ea
WRIGHT, Adam		26	M	Laborer	08Ma02Ea
MUIR, John		20	M	Laborer	08Ma02Ea
REILLY, Patrick		29	M	Laborer	08Ma02Ea
DONNELY, John		45	M	Laborer	08Ma02Ea
MULLEN, Edwd.		32	M	Laborer	08Ma02Ea
Rose		28	F	None	08Ma02Ea
LYNCH, Margt.		21	F	None	08Ma02Ea
GIBSON, Robert		19	M	Laborer	08Ma02Ea
MAY, Patrick		27	M	Laborer	08Ma02Ea
Ann	(W)	25	F	Wife	08Ma02Ea
Michl.	(S)	10	M	Laborer	08Ma02Ea
Edwd.	(S)	08	M	Child	08Ma02Ea
Bridget	(D)	01	F	Child	08Ma02Ea
HERBERT, Michl.		37	M	Laborer	08Ma02Ea
Ann		36	F	None	08Ma02Ea
GLEASON, Nancy		21	F	None	08Ma02Ea
DONOHOE, Fras.		24	M	Laborer	08Ma02Ea
Bridget		24	F	None	08Ma02Ea
MCLAUGHLIN, W.		50	F	None	08Ma02Ea
Mary		30	F	None	08Ma02Ea
GUINN, Michl.		30	M	Laborer	08Ma02Ea
Jane		32	F	None	08Ma02Ea
HUGHES, Bridget		18	F	None	08Ma02Ea
GUINN, Bernard		55	M	Shoemaker	08Ma02Ea
Bernard	(S)	20	M	Laborer	08Ma02Ea
Thos.	(S)	16	M	None	08Ma02Ea
Elizth.	(W)	55	F	None	08Ma02Ea
Margt.	(D)	12	F	None	08Ma02Ea
Mary	(D)	06	F	Child	08Ma02Ea
STROTHERS, Thos.		19	M	Laborer	08Ma02Ea
GRIMES, Elizth.		24	F	None	08Ma02Ea
HART, Elizth.		16	F	None	08Ma02Ea
DOUGHERTY, John		21	M	Laborer	08Ma02Ea
SMITH, Robt.		23	M	Cutler	08Ma02Ea
OMEARA, Ellen		20	F	None	08Ma02Ea
DUFFY, Michl.		29	M	Laborer	08Ma02Ea
DOLAN, Bridget		40	F	None	08Ma02Ea
John	(S)	14	M	None	08Ma02Ea
Peggy	(D)	12	F	None	08Ma02Ea
Mary	(D)	10	F	None	08Ma02Ea
Thos.	(S)	02	M	Child	08Ma02Ea
CONNOR, Jas.		22	M	Laborer	08Ma02Ea
KILLAGER, Mary		16	F	None	08Ma02Ea
HEADON, Ellen		30	F	None	08Ma02Ea
BRADY, Ellen		21	F	None	08Ma02Ea
MCMANUS, Edwd.		18	M	Barber	08Ma02Ea
Cathn.		13	F	None	08Ma02Ea
MCCARRON, Nancy		20	F	None	08Ma02Ea
CORMICK, Bernard		40	M	Laborer	08Ma02Ea
Bridget		50	F	None	08Ma02Ea
Dennis		03	M	Child	08Ma02Ea
John		.08	M	Infant	08Ma02Ea
BURNS, Bridget		31	F	None	08Ma02Ea

NAMES OF PASSENGERS		AGE	SEX	OCCUPATIONS	DATE PORT SHIP
KILMORRY, Michl.		50	M	Laborer	08Ma02Ea
Julia	(W)	40	F	None	08Ma02Ea
William	(S)	18	M	Laborer	08Ma02Ea
Patk.	(S)	15	M	Laborer	08Ma02Ea
Michl.	(S)	11	M	Laborer	08Ma02Ea
Mary	(D)	08	F	Child	08Ma02Ea
GUINN, Mary		21	F	None	08Ma02Ea
MURRAY, Marcella		20	F	None	08Ma02Ea
BARRY, Michl.		30	M	Laborer	08Ma02Ea
Sarah		30	F	None	08Ma02Ea
CAMPBELL, Mary		21	F	None	08Ma02Ea
WARD, John		50	M	Laborer	08Ma02Ea
Died-At-Sea					
Mary		50	F	Wife	08Ma02Ea
MCGIVERN, Ann		20	F	None	08Ma02Ea
GILL, Danl.		31	M	Laborer	08Ma02Ea
DILLON, Edwd.		24	M	Laborer	08Ma02Ea
Mary		18	F	None	08Ma02Ea
MCCABE, Richd.		40	M	Laborer	08Ma02Ea
Cathn.	(W)	35	F	None	08Ma02Ea
William	(S)	18	M	Laborer	08Ma02Ea
James	(S)	11	M	Laborer	08Ma02Ea
Sarah	(D)	18	F	None	08Ma02Ea
GURGSON, Mary		48	F	None	08Ma02Ea
Thos.	(S)	22	M	Laborer	08Ma02Ea
James	(S)	11	M	Laborer	08Ma02Ea
RIELLY, Bridget		18	F	None	08Ma02Ea
Philip		01	M	Child	08Ma02Ea
SMITH, Matthew		20	M	Laborer	08Ma02Ea
WOODFIELD, Elizth.		34	F	None	08Ma02Ea
Ann		20	F	None	08Ma02Ea
Elizth.		18	F	None	08Ma02Ea
BRADY, Mary		18	F	None	08Ma02Ea
CULLEY, Wm.		25	M	Laborer	08Ma02Ea
CULLY, Elizth.		18	F	None	08Ma02Ea
AFTEN, Margt.		20	F	None	08Ma02Ea
MCGUIRE, Edwd.		20	M	Laborer	08Ma02Ea
CORCORAN, Peter		20	M	Laborer	08Ma02Ea
KANE, Ann		30	F	None	08Ma02Ea
Francis	(S)	07	M	Child	08Ma02Ea
MOLLAGHTEY, Lawce.		25	M	Laborer	08Ma02Ea
MAHEN, Owen		24	M	Laborer	08Ma02Ea
MURPHY, Biddy		06	F	Child	08Ma02Ea
CULLEN, Margt.		12	F	None	08Ma02Ea
Julia		10	F	None	08Ma02Ea
CORCORAN, Ann		18	F	None	08Ma02Ea
FARREL, Thos.		25	M	Laborer	08Ma02Ea
Ann		20	F	None	08Ma02Ea
KING, Chas.		20	M	Laborer	08Ma02Ea
BYRN, Pat		21	M	Laborer	08Ma02Ea
Cathn.		15	F	None	08Ma02Ea
MURPHY, Anastasia		20	F	None	08Ma02Ea
COYNE, Elizth.		20	F	None	08Ma02Ea
MULLIGAN, Bridget		20	F	None	08Ma02Ea
HUGHES, Patrick		20	M	Laborer	08Ma02Ea
MCLAGHLIN, Ellen		21	F	None	08Ma02Ea
RYAN, Cathn.		14	F	None	08Ma02Ea
LEONARD, Patk.		25	M	Laborer	08Ma02Ea
FITZPATRICK, Honor		21	F	None	08Ma02Ea
NANGLE, Thos.		20	M	Laborer	08Ma02Ea
MCCORMICK, Michl.		17	M	Laborer	08Ma02Ea
MEEHAN, Bernard		24	M	Laborer	08Ma02Ea
MULLEN, Cath.		20	F	None	08Ma02Ea
MCCABE, Sally		13	F	None	08Ma02Ea
GARDNER, Mary		20	F	None	08Ma02Ea
MCCARTNEY, Horatio		20	M	Laborer	08Ma02Ea
DUNN, John		20	M	Laborer	08Ma02Ea
KILKENNY, Peter		24	M	Laborer	08Ma02Ea
Bridget		11	F	None	08Ma02Ea
NEEVE, Bridget		30	F	None	08Ma02Ea
Mary	(D)	10	F	None	08Ma02Ea
Bridget	(D)	04	F	Child	08Ma02Ea
LYNCH, Cath.		20	F	None	08Ma02Ea
FOLEY, Bridget		21	F	None	08Ma02Ea
BRADY, Ann		18	F	None	08Ma02Ea
JAMIESON, Mary		20	F	None	08Ma02Ea
KIERNAN, Mary		18	F	None	08Ma02Ea
RIELLY, Michl.		22	M	Laborer	08Ma02Ea
NOLAN, John		20	M	Laborer	08Ma02Ea
Bernard		25	M	Laborer	08Ma02Ea
RILEY, Ann		30	F	None	08Ma02Ea
FAGAN, Mary		11	F	None	08Ma02Ea
DUNN, Thos.		26	M	Laborer	08Ma02Ea
Julia	(W)	24	F	None	08Ma02Ea
Sarah	(D)	.06	F	Infant	08Ma02Ea
MULLEN, Rose		16	F	None	08Ma02Ea
RIELLY, Honour		21	F	None	08Ma02Ea
MCGARRY, Mary		12	F	None	08Ma02Ea
CURRAN, Bridget		18	F	None	08Ma02Ea
BYRNES, Patk.		36	M	Laborer	08Ma02Ea
Cathn.		30	F	None	08Ma02Ea
MANSFIELD, Thos.		17	M	None	08Ma02Ea
John		15	M	None	08Ma02Ea
MCDERMOTT, Ann		25	F	None	08Ma02Ea
BOWEN, Thos.		26	M	Laborer	08Ma02Ea
FOLEY, Pat		40	M	Laborer	08Ma02Ea
Margt.	(W)	35	F	None	08Ma02Ea
John	(S)	07	M	Child	08Ma02Ea
Joanna	(D)	04	F	Child	08Ma02Ea
Michl.	(S)	.05	M	Infant	08Ma02Ea
MURRAY, Julia		21	F	None	08Ma02Ea
ANDERSON, Eliza		13	F	None	08Ma02Ea
DUNN, Patk.		30	M	Laborer	08Ma02Ea
MCMANORNY, Martha		30	F	None	08Ma02Ea
MCCANN, Mary		20	F	None	08Ma02Ea
MCLAUGHLAN, Pat		23	M	Lab/rer	08Ma02Ea
Marcella		25	F	None	08Ma02Ea
GALLIGAN, Pat		22	M	Laborer	08Ma02Ea
MCBRIDE, Pat		20	M	Laborer	08Ma02Ea
RIELLY, Wm.		24	M	Laborer	08Ma02Ea
KIERNAN, Jas.		20	M	Laborer	08Ma02Ea
BRIENS, Pat		10	M	None	08Ma02Ea
FITZPATRICK, Cath.		25	F	None	08Ma02Ea
GILLISPIE, Cathn.		25	F	None	08Ma02Ea
MITCHELL, Michl.		20	M	Laborer	08Ma02Ea
HAGERTY, Wm.		25	M	Laborer	08Ma02Ea
BROWN, Bridget		18	F	None	08Ma02Ea
MCATEAR, Betsey		19	F	None	08Ma02Ea
MOHONY, Michl.		19	M	Laborer	08Ma02Ea
Nancy		20	F	None	08Ma02Ea
CONNAN, Patk.		19	M	Laborer	08Ma02Ea
Cathn.		20	F	None	08Ma02Ea
REAL, Michl.		02	M	Child	08Ma02Ea
GARRITY, Margt.		20	F	None	08Ma02Ea
Ann		11	F	None	08Ma02Ea
REILLY, Bridget		21	F	None	08Ma02Ea
CASSIDY, Joseph		20	M	Laborer	08Ma02Ea

SARACEN 08 MAY 1846

From Glasgow

NAMES OF PASSENGERS		AGE	SEX	OCCUPATIONS	DATE PORT SHIP
MARNEY, Michel		40	M	Tailor	08Ma04Ah
Saley	(W)	42	F	Unknown	08Ma04Ah
Timothy	(S)	16	M	Unknown	08Ma04Ah
Mary	(D)	14	F	Unknown	08Ma04Ah
John	(S)	07	M	Child	08Ma04Ah
Michel	(S)	04	M	Child	08Ma04Ah
CASTLE, Elizabeth		21	F	Servant	08Ma04Ah
MONIGHIN, Catharine		22	F	Dressmaker	08Ma04Ah

66

ROCHESTER 08 MAY 1846

From Liverpool

NAMES OF PASSENGERS	AGE	SEX	OCCUPATIONS	DATE PORT SHIP
RAIKES, Francis	24	M	Gentleman	08Ma02Ak
STEVENSON, Benjm.	24	M	Speculator	08Ma02Ak
PULLEN, Richd.	24	M	Butcher	08Ma02Ak
FARMER, Thos.	42	M	Farmer	08Ma02Ak
ORME, John	40	M	Merchant	08Ma02Ak
Anna	35	F	None	08Ma02Ak
BRADY, Cath.	18	F	Servant	08Ma02Ak
HENAN, James	28	M	Tailor	08Ma02Ak
HERITICH, Fanny	18	F	None	08Ma02Ak
MURRAY, Ann	23	F	Servant	08Ma02Ak
John	20	M	Laborer	08Ma02Ak
CANNON, Pat	23	M	Laborer	08Ma02Ak
KAIN, Pat.	21	M	Laborer	08Ma02Ak
HANNARTY, John	18	M	Laborer	08Ma02Ak
HALPIN, Bridget	18	F	Servant	08Ma02Ak
FITZPATRICK, Thos.	28	M	Laborer	08Ma02Ak
Mgt.	16	F	Servant	08Ma02Ak
BYRNE, Rodger	32	M	Laborer	08Ma02Ak
LAMON, S.	19	M	Farmer	08Ma02Ak
BATH, Robt.	48	M	Porter	08Ma02Ak
Sarah	53	F	None	08Ma02Ak
BROUGHTON, Ed.	31	M	Laborer	08Ma02Ak
NEIL, Pat.	27	M	Laborer	08Ma02Ak
WOOLLAHAN, J.	23	M	Laborer	08Ma02Ak
Mary	25	F	Servant	08Ma02Ak
CORDY, Ellen	23	F	Servant	08Ma02Ak
DOUGLASS, Mary	18	F	Servant	08Ma02Ak
DUNFEY, Cath.	18	F	Servant	08Ma02Ak
Thos.	20	M	Laborer	08Ma02Ak
WATERS, Pat.	26	M	Farmer	08Ma02Ak
HITCHY, Mary	26	F	Servant	08Ma02Ak
DUNN, Mgt.	25	F	Servant	08Ma02Ak
KATAN, Pat.	20	M	Laborer	08Ma02Ak
CLARY, Pat	24	M	Laborer	08Ma02Ak
NUGENT, Ed.	21	M	Laborer	08Ma02Ak
OLLERHAN, Mary	18	F	Servant	08Ma02Ak
HUGHES, Wm.	42	M	Farmer	08Ma02Ak
Eliz. (W)	40	F	None	08Ma02Ak
Thos. (S)	22	M	Farmer	08Ma02Ak
Mary (D)	19	F	None	08Ma02Ak
Hugh (S)	17	M	Farmer	08Ma02Ak
John (S)	15	M	Farmer	08Ma02Ak
Wm. (S)	09	M	Child	08Ma02Ak
Martha (D)	07	F	Child	08Ma02Ak
WILLIAM, David	23	M	Farmer	08Ma02Ak
ROEN, Mgt.	15	F	Servant	08Ma02Ak
CONNELLY, Mgt.	17	F	Servant	08Ma02Ak
CONNOR, Thos.	25	M	Laborer	08Ma02Ak
Jane	26	F	Servant	08Ma02Ak
MCGUIRE, Stev.	26	M	Laborer	08Ma02Ak
GILROY, John	20	M	Laborer	08Ma02Ak
James	23	M	Laborer	08Ma02Ak
Pat	15	M	Laborer	08Ma02Ak
Ann	46	F	Servant	08Ma02Ak
Mgt.	25	F	Servant	08Ma02Ak
MCGUIRE, Rose	18	F	Servant	08Ma02Ak
Mary	18	F	Servant	08Ma02Ak
Mary	20	F	Servant	08Ma02Ak
DOWD, Pat	20	M	Laborer	08Ma02Ak
MURPHY, Biddy	20	F	Servant	08Ma02Ak
DUGAN, Thos.	20	M	Laborer	08Ma02Ak
MURPHY, Rose	20	F	Servant	08Ma02Ak
MELLOY, Susan	20	F	Servant	08Ma02Ak
Ellen	19	F	Servant	08Ma02Ak
GRAHAM, Wm.	20	M	Laborer	08Ma02Ak
CONNOR, James	24	M	Laborer	08Ma02Ak
NULTY, John	22	M	Laborer	08Ma02Ak
MURRAY, Robt.	25	M	Laborer	08Ma02Ak
FITZSOMERS, Thos.	27	M	Laborer	08Ma02Ak
Mary	20	F	Servant	08Ma02Ak
MELLOY, Philip	21	M	Farmer	08Ma02Ak
Wm.	25	M	Farmer	08Ma02Ak
James	15	M	Farmer	08Ma02Ak
GILSHIN, Pat	22	M	Laborer	08Ma02Ak
NAVIN, Bridget	15	F	Servant	08Ma02Ak
FORD, Mary	20	F	Servant	08Ma02Ak
KNOWLAN, Mary	21	F	Servant	08Ma02Ak
CONWAY, Thos.	17	M	Laborer	08Ma02Ak
FARL, And.	25	M	Laborer	08Ma02Ak
BLYAN, Thos.	23	M	Laborer	08Ma02Ak
QUINN, Mich.	20	M	Laborer	08Ma02Ak
BRADRICK, Ann	20	F	Servant	08Ma02Ak
MURPHY, Hy.	19	M	Farmer	08Ma02Ak
KANE, John	24	M	Laborer	08Ma02Ak
NONAN, James	22	M	Tailor	08Ma02Ak
QUINN, Pat	28	M	Shoemaker	08Ma02Ak
SCOTT, Cath.	30	F	Servant	08Ma02Ak
HATTY, Mich.	19	M	Farmer	08Ma02Ak
MOLE, Wm.	32	M	Cbtmkr	08Ma02Ak
Mary	32	F	None	08Ma02Ak
George	30	M	Silversmith	08Ma02Ak
Mary (D)	09	F	Child	08Ma02Ak
Caroline (D)	07	F	Child	08Ma02Ak
Wm. (S)	04	M	Child	08Ma02Ak
Walter (S)	.04	M	Infant	08Ma02Ak
WILSON, John	25	M	Potter	08Ma02Ak
Mary (W)	21	F	None	08Ma02Ak
Mary-Jane (D)	01	F	Child	08Ma02Ak
MURPHY, Frank	21	M	Currier	08Ma02Ak
Wm.	38	M	Laborer	08Ma02Ak
DURMODY, Ann	23	F	None	08Ma02Ak
WILLIAMS, W.	26	M	Servant	08Ma02Ak
COWAN, Pat.	21	M	Merchant	08Ma02Ak
CLAGAN, Esther	20	F	Servant	08Ma02Ak
FOY, Mary	18	F	Servant	08Ma02Ak
SPENCER, Jos.	36	M	Engineer	08Ma02Ak
MCLELLAN, Peter	23	M	Farmer	08Ma02Ak
PLUNKET, James	18	M	Farmer	08Ma02Ak
LYON, John	20	M	Farmer	08Ma02Ak
HAVY, James	23	M	Laborer	08Ma02Ak
NOLAN, Mich.	20	M	Butcher	08Ma02Ak
BYRNE, Geo.	28	M	Bricklayer	08Ma02Ak
Sarah	25	F	None	08Ma02Ak
ROE, Pat	22	M	Farmer	08Ma02Ak
ARMSTRONG, Maria	22	F	None	08Ma02Ak
MCDERMOT, Hugh	25	M	Laborer	08Ma02Ak
DOYLE, Mich.	26	M	Spinner	08Ma02Ak
ODONOUGH, Johannah	18	F	None	08Ma02Ak
FITZGERALD, Hannah	19	F	None	08Ma02Ak
CLEARY, Pat	13	M	None	08Ma02Ak
DENSMORE, Pat.	30	M	Laborer	08Ma02Ak
DUGAN, Ed.	20	M	Laborer	08Ma02Ak
MAGEE, John	22	M	Laborer	08Ma02Ak
COYLE, John	22	M	Laborer	08Ma02Ak
MAGEE, Morris	21	M	Laborer	08Ma02Ak
GALLAHAN, Chas.	22	M	Laborer	08Ma02Ak
HERITICK, Chas.	23	M	Laborer	08Ma02Ak
MCHUGH, J.	20	M	Laborer	08Ma02Ak
FERRY, John	20	M	Laborer	08Ma02Ak
GALLAHAN, Chas.	22	M	Laborer	08Ma02Ak
SWEENY, Doty	16	F	Unknown	08Ma02Ak
HARKIN, Ed.	21	M	Laborer	08Ma02Ak
GALLAHAN, James	18	M	Laborer	08Ma02Ak
PERRIN, Wm.	20	M	Laborer	08Ma02Ak
MCFAGAN, Ellen	19	F	Servant	08Ma02Ak
BOYLE, Ann	22	F	Servant	08Ma02Ak
MCGINLEY, Fanny	30	F	Servant	08Ma02Ak
MCNULTY, Pat	25	M	Laborer	08Ma02Ak
WAGGIN, Sophia	18	F	Servant	08Ma02Ak
MCAULIS, Alex	68	M	Millwright	08Ma02Ak

NAMES OF PASSENGERS		AGE	SEX	OCCUPATIONS	DATE PORT SHIP
FINCH, Rach.		16	F	Servant	08Ma02Ak
Mary		15	F	Servant	08Ma02Ak
MCKINLEY, Mary		21	F	Servant	08Ma02Ak
COBURN, Alex.		20	M	Laborer	08Ma02Ak
BENNETT, Sm.		48	M	Brf	08Ma02Ak
Sarah		47	F	None	08Ma02Ak
PERRY, Sam.		24	M	Wire Drawer	08Ma02Ak
Ann		26	F	None	08Ma02Ak
SHORTLE, Wm.		28	M	Laborer	08Ma02Ak
KELLY, James		30	M	Laborer	08Ma02Ak
CONNELLY, James		26	M	Laborer	08Ma02Ak
KELLY, Ann		19	F	Servant	08Ma02Ak
OVINGTON, Mgt.		18	F	Servant	08Ma02Ak
BRIDGE, John		37	M	Blacksmith	08Ma02Ak
Jane	(W)	36	F	None	08Ma02Ak
Wm.	(S)	04	M	Child	08Ma02Ak
Mary	(D)	02	F	Child	08Ma02Ak
PURCEL, Mich.		30	M	Laborer	08Ma02Ak
LAHY, James		26	M	Laborer	08Ma02Ak
BERGEN, Mich.		25	M	Laborer	08Ma02Ak
Biddy		22	F	Servant	08Ma02Ak
CONWAY, John		26	M	Laborer	08Ma02Ak
DWIRE, Pat.		25	M	Laborer	08Ma02Ak
RILEY, Pat.		23	M	Laborer	08Ma02Ak
DULAN, John		22	M	Laborer	08Ma02Ak
CONNOR, Eliza		17	F	Servant	08Ma02Ak
CLASSEY, Judy		22	F	Servant	08Ma02Ak
FOX, Nancy		20	F	Servant	08Ma02Ak
RONEY, Sarah		19	F	Servant	08Ma02Ak
WILLIAMS, Kitty		26	F	Servant	08Ma02Ak
DOYLE, Cath.		18	F	Servant	08Ma02Ak
RYEN, Judy		25	F	Servant	08Ma02Ak
CAMPHIN, Mgt.		25	F	Servant	08Ma02Ak
HULS, Hermon		23	M	Merchant	08Ma02Ak
MAHA, Mich.		26	M	Laborer	08Ma02Ak
HOWLAND, John		25	M	Laborer	08Ma02Ak
Ann		23	F	Servant	08Ma02Ak
NUGENT, Ann		28	F	Servant	08Ma02Ak
Kate		24	F	Servant	08Ma02Ak
LAHAN, Kate		19	F	Servant	08Ma02Ak
MCGOVERN, Owen		32	M	Laborer	08Ma02Ak
Pat		23	M	Laborer	08Ma02Ak
James		23	M	Laborer	08Ma02Ak
DWIRE, John		24	M	Butcher	08Ma02Ak
Mgt.		25	F	None	08Ma02Ak
Mgt.		22	F	None	08Ma02Ak
Julia	(D)	01	F	Child	08Ma02Ak
HAGAN, Mich.		22	M	Laborer	08Ma02Ak
Mary	(W)	19	F	None	08Ma02Ak
Maria	(D)	01	F	Child	08Ma02Ak
PARKER, James		33	M	Qmagt	08Ma02Ak
DARGAN, Pat.		23	M	Laborer	08Ma02Ak
Ellen	(W)	23	F	None	08Ma02Ak
Mary	(D)	.04	F	Infant	08Ma02Ak
HICKIE, Pat		22	M	Laborer	08Ma02Ak
CRANY, Pat		23	M	Laborer	08Ma02Ak
NEIL, James		27	M	Laborer	08Ma02Ak
SHARP, John		25	M	Laborer	08Ma02Ak
Alex		20	M	Laborer	08Ma02Ak
MCRAIG, Mary		19	F	Servant	08Ma02Ak
MCMULLEN, James		24	M	Carpenter	08Ma02Ak
DILLON, John		24	M	Weaver	08Ma02Ak
MCCORMICK, Mgt.		24	F	Servant	08Ma02Ak
Martha		18	F	Servant	08Ma02Ak
MCNEIL, James		18	M	Fiddler	08Ma02Ak
ROBERTS, David		34	M	Farmer	08Ma02Ak
Mgt.	(W)	38	F	None	08Ma02Ak
John	(S)	13	M	None	08Ma02Ak
Jane	(D)	11	F	None	08Ma02Ak
Robt.	(S)	08	M	Child	08Ma02Ak
Phoebe	(D)	03	F	Child	08Ma02Ak
Wm.	(S)	.09	M	Infant	08Ma02Ak
HIGANBOTTOM, Mary		39	F	None	08Ma02Ak
Eliz.	(D)	16	F	None	08Ma02Ak
Saml.	(S)	14	M	None	08Ma02Ak
HIGANBOTTOM, John	(S)	06	M	Child	08Ma02Ak
DOWNY, John		26	M	Laborer	08Ma02Ak
JOYL, Maria		22	F	Servant	08Ma02Ak
DOCHERTY, Pat		20	M	Laborer	08Ma02Ak
MARA, Nancy		28	F	Servant	08Ma02Ak
SULLIVAN, John		20	M	Servant	08Ma02Ak
SHOYLE, D.		25	M	Servant	08Ma02Ak
CRONNIN, Pat.		20	M	Laborer	08Ma02Ak
LONG, James		20	M	Laborer	08Ma02Ak
MARRIN, Thos.		21	M	Laborer	08Ma02Ak
Francis		18	M	Laborer	08Ma02Ak
COLEMAN, Alice		19	F	Servant	08Ma02Ak
HAPIN, Mary		21	F	Servant	08Ma02Ak
MURRAY, Ann		24	F	Servant	08Ma02Ak
MOORE, James		22	M	Laborer	08Ma02Ak
SCOTT, Ann		31	F	None	08Ma02Ak
LONG, James		28	M	Wheelwright	08Ma02Ak
Wm.		20	M	Wheelwright	08Ma02Ak
Mgt.		32	F	None	08Ma02Ak
Ed.		18	M	None	08Ma02Ak
Letitia		16	F	None	08Ma02Ak
HOLLAND, B.		30	M	Laborer	08Ma02Ak
MULLEN, Biddy		26	F	Servant	08Ma02Ak
HUGHES, Mich.		20	M	Mason	08Ma02Ak
MCCARTNEY, Ann		30	F	Servant	08Ma02Ak
HOLLAND, Owen		25	M	Coach Maker	08Ma02Ak
HANLIN, Mich.		23	M	Laborer	08Ma02Ak
MCNULTY, Pat		30	M	Laborer	08Ma02Ak
OLLAHAN, John		26	M	Laborer	08Ma02Ak
Bridget		30	F	Servant	08Ma02Ak
CRAWLY, Ellen		30	F	Servant	08Ma02Ak
RILEY, Ann		17	F	Servant	08Ma02Ak
Bridget		22	F	Servant	08Ma02Ak
Mgt.		20	F	Servant	08Ma02Ak
LYNCH, Ann		25	F	Servant	08Ma02Ak
FAGAN, Mary		22	F	Servant	08Ma02Ak
FITZPATRICK, Ed.		37	M	Laborer	08Ma02Ak
DARDES, Pat		25	M	Laborer	08Ma02Ak
LAWLESS, Pat		23	M	Laborer	08Ma02Ak
DARDES, Bridget		20	F	Servant	08Ma02Ak
JUTE, Mary		22	F	Servant	08Ma02Ak
CALLAHAN, Mary		22	F	Servant	08Ma02Ak
SIMONS, Betsey		22	F	Servant	08Ma02Ak
KAZAN, Jane		23	F	Servant	08Ma02Ak
EDGAR, Saml.		21	M	Carpenter	08Ma02Ak
BATZ, James		20	M	Gdnr	08Ma02Ak
HOUSTON, Thos.		21	M	Carpenter	08Ma02Ak
Janet		11	F	None	08Ma02Ak
Wm.		09	M	Child	08Ma02Ak
MCLEOD, Wm.		20	M	Merchant	08Ma02Ak
DOUGLASS, Isaiah		28	M	Weaver	08Ma02Ak
Ellen		68	F	None	08Ma02Ak
Joseph		08	M	Child	08Ma02Ak
FARLEY, Mich.		40	M	Worm Cutter	08Ma02Ak

THOMAS 11 MAY 1846

From Liverpool

NAMES OF PASSENGERS		AGE	SEX	OCCUPATIONS	DATE PORT SHIP
DARCEY, Hugh		20	M	Laborer	11Ma02Eb
TIGHE, Peter		21	M	Unknown	11Ma02Eb
GAGHIRON, Ann		18	F	Dressmaker	11Ma02Eb
DARCEY, Mary		18	F	Dressmaker	11Ma02Eb
SILVER, Margaret		19	F	Dressmaker	11Ma02Eb
JUDGE, Michael		20	M	Laborer	11Ma02Eb
BYRNE, Charles		20	M	Tailor	11Ma02Eb
WARD, Ann		18	F	Spinster	11Ma02Eb
REYNOLDS, Ann		18	F	Spinster	11Ma02Eb
WARD, Bridget		18	F	Spinster	11Ma02Eb

68

NAMES OF PASSENGERS		AGE	SEX	OCCUPATIONS	DATE PORT SHIP	NAMES OF PASSENGERS		AGE	SEX	OCCUPATIONS	DATE PORT SHIP
CARTER, Thomas		20	M	Laborer	11Ma02Eb	FARRELL, John		30	M	Laborer	11Ma02Eb
Francis		22	M	Laborer	11Ma02Eb	MURRAY, Patrick		24	M	Laborer	11Ma02Eb
Ann		18	F	Spinster	11Ma02Eb	HARRELL, Jas.		22	M	Laborer	11Ma02Eb
MULVEY, Michael		25	M	Laborer	11Ma02Eb	MCGINNIS, John		26	M	Shoemaker	11Ma02Eb
TIGHE, John		20	M	Laborer	11Ma02Eb	COLEMAN, Patrick		23	M	Laborer	11Ma02Eb
OBRIEN, James		20	M	Laborer	11Ma02Eb	ROGAN, Richd.		30	M	Laborer	11Ma02Eb
OROARKE, Michael		22	M	Laborer	11Ma02Eb	GLEESON, John		36	M	Laborer	11Ma02Eb
KILCRAN, Mary		20	F	Spinster	11Ma02Eb	Catharine		30	F	Spinster	11Ma02Eb
MAGUIRE, Mary		20	F	Spinster	11Ma02Eb	MCLAUGHLIN, John		17	M	Carpenter	11Ma02Eb
KANE, Margt.		20	F	Spinster	11Ma02Eb	FLANEGAN, Martin		30	M	Laborer	11Ma02Eb
REYNOLDS, Winfred		25	F	Spinster	11Ma02Eb	MURRAY, John		25	M	Laborer	11Ma02Eb
Jane	(D)	02	F	Child	11Ma02Eb	MCGOVERAN, Kate		19	F	Spinster	11Ma02Eb
HEANEY, Patrick		20	M	Laborer	11Ma02Eb	Rosa		23	F	Spinster	11Ma02Eb
KANE, John		18	M	Baker	11Ma02Eb	FEARON, Catherine		16	F	Spinster	11Ma02Eb
ROBINSON, Samuel		35	M	Shoemaker	11Ma02Eb	Patrick		02	M	Child	11Ma02Eb
BOHEN, Catharine		11	F	Spinster	11Ma02Eb	REILLY, Biddy		17	F	Spinster	11Ma02Eb
TEA, Julia		40	F	Spinster	11Ma02Eb	BLAKELY, Margaret		25	F	Dressmaker	11Ma02Eb
WELSH, Mary		35	F	Spinster	11Ma02Eb	MCKEWON, Biddy		16	F	Spinster	11Ma02Eb
SHANDY, Ellen		20	F	Spinster	11Ma02Eb	LOYD, Julia		17	F	Spinster	11Ma02Eb
HAZELTON, Benj.		29	M	Laborer	11Ma02Eb	FAHY, Lawrence		30	M	Stctr	11Ma02Eb
Jane		29	F	Spinster	11Ma02Eb	HORAN, Michael		25	M	Laborer	11Ma02Eb
STEWART, Margaret		18	F	Spinster	11Ma02Eb	OHARA, Thomas		21	M	Laborer	11Ma02Eb
GALLAGHER, Daniel		30	M	Weaver	11Ma02Eb	FAHY, Margaret		50	F	Spinster	11Ma02Eb
Katharine	(W)	28	F	Spinster	11Ma02Eb	MARA, Catharine		18	F	Spinster	11Ma02Eb
Eliza	(D)	02	F	Child	11Ma02Eb	MCDERMOTT, Ellen		21	F	Dressmaker	11Ma02Eb
MCGLOWN, Bernard		35	M	Laborer	11Ma02Eb	KELLY, Kate		25	F	Spinster	11Ma02Eb
RAFFERTY, Francis		20	M	Laborer	11Ma02Eb	TULLY, Ann		20	F	Spinster	11Ma02Eb
Peter		22	M	Laborer	11Ma02Eb	LALLY, Martin		21	M	Laborer	11Ma02Eb
Rose		50	F	Spinster	11Ma02Eb	HOLEHAN, Thomas		21	M	Laborer	11Ma02Eb
Ann		19	F	Spinster	11Ma02Eb	BRANTY, Alexander		23	M	Laborer	11Ma02Eb
CARNAN, James		20	M	Laborer	11Ma02Eb	CONLAN, Bridget		25	F	Spinster	11Ma02Eb
BRADY, Patrick		21	M	Laborer	11Ma02Eb	MULLIGAN, Ann		22	F	Spinster	11Ma02Eb
DONOGHUE, Hugh		24	M	Laborer	11Ma02Eb	BOHAN, Thomas		32	M	Laborer	11Ma02Eb
MEMNON, Mary		20	F	Spinster	11Ma02Eb	Margaret		30	F	Spinster	11Ma02Eb
SMITH, Thomas		20	M	Laborer	11Ma02Eb	DONEGAN, James		22	M	Laborer	11Ma02Eb
BRAY, Thomas		20	M	Laborer	11Ma02Eb	REYNOLDS, Thomas		25	M	Laborer	11Ma02Eb
GAGHNEY, Wm.		20	M	Baker	11Ma02Eb	MULLIGAN, Michael		24	M	Laborer	11Ma02Eb
COONEY, John		35	M	Laborer	11Ma02Eb	DONEGAN, Margaret		15	F	Spinster	11Ma02Eb
Margaret		40	F	Spinster	11Ma02Eb	LOBBY, Bridget		16	F	Spinster	11Ma02Eb
DONAGHOE, Catharine		18	F	Spinster	11Ma02Eb	BRADY, Andrew		40	M	Laborer	11Ma02Eb
BOYLE, Peter		30	M	Laborer	11Ma02Eb	KELLY, Eliza		25	F	Dressmaker	11Ma02Eb
DAILY, Thomas		25	M	Laborer	11Ma02Eb	BRADY, Ellen		40	F	Spinster	11Ma02Eb
MCSWEEGAN, Patrick		20	M	Laborer	11Ma02Eb	Kate	(D)	14	F	Dressmaker	11Ma02Eb
GRAY, Mary		24	F	Dressmaker	11Ma02Eb	Andrew	(S)	16	M	Laborer	11Ma02Eb
Mary-A.		.10	F	Infant	11Ma02Eb	REILLY, Mary		39	F	Dressmaker	11Ma02Eb
BRADDLEY, Margaret		19	F	Spinster	11Ma02Eb	BRADY, Michael		12	M	None	11Ma02Eb
MCSWEEGAN, Rose		14	F	Spinster	11Ma02Eb	Mary		16	F	Spinster	11Ma02Eb
REILLY, Thomas		20	M	Laborer	11Ma02Eb	Edward		11	M	None	11Ma02Eb
Wm.		18	M	Laborer	11Ma02Eb	FLOYD, Ann		32	F	Spinster	11Ma02Eb
Thomas		22	M	Tailor	11Ma02Eb	MURPHY, Kate		22	F	Spinster	11Ma02Eb
TIERNAN, Felix		45	M	Shoemaker	11Ma02Eb	HAGGERTY, Kate		20	F	Spinster	11Ma02Eb
Felix		22	M	Laborer	11Ma02Eb	MCGINTY, Ann		18	F	Spinster	11Ma02Eb
MCKEWON, Patrick		20	M	Laborer	11Ma02Eb	QUIN, James		32	M	Laborer	11Ma02Eb
TIERNAN, Bridget		25	F	Spinster	11Ma02Eb	ODONNELL, Patrick		25	M	Laborer	11Ma02Eb
Bridget-Jr.		18	F	Spinster	11Ma02Eb	HAGGERTY, Thomas		22	M	Laborer	11Ma02Eb
Margaret		18	F	Spinster	11Ma02Eb	MCKEARN, Phillip		30	M	Shoemaker	11Ma02Eb
MCGOVERN, Catharine		23	F	Spinster	11Ma02Eb	MCGINTY, James		20	M	Laborer	11Ma02Eb
SMITH, Michael		22	M	Laborer	11Ma02Eb	SWEENY, James		20	M	Laborer	11Ma02Eb
CRONAN, Andrew		33	M	Laborer	11Ma02Eb	RESLAND, Andr.		20	M	Laborer	11Ma02Eb
KING, John		21	M	Laborer	11Ma02Eb	DREW, Daniel		25	M	Laborer	11Ma02Eb
BOYLAN, John		21	M	Shoemaker	11Ma02Eb	CAGHEL, Wm.		25	M	Laborer	11Ma02Eb
SMITH, Moses		30	M	Laborer	11Ma02Eb	BROOKS, John		21	M	Laborer	11Ma02Eb
Elizabeth	(W)	28	F	Spinster	11Ma02Eb	Michael		20	M	Laborer	11Ma02Eb
Maria	(D)	05	F	Child	11Ma02Eb	DOOLAN, Peter		18	M	Laborer	11Ma02Eb
William	(S)	03	M	Child	11Ma02Eb	GILLIAN, Robt.		38	M	Laborer	11Ma02Eb
Theophilus	(S)	01	M	Child	11Ma02Eb	CONLON, Edwd.		22	M	Laborer	11Ma02Eb
GUNN, Bernard		27	M	Laborer	11Ma02Eb	MURPHY, James		20	M	Laborer	11Ma02Eb
MCTEAGUE, Stephen		28	M	Weaver	11Ma02Eb	Patrick		18	M	Laborer	11Ma02Eb
KENNEDY, Francis		22	M	Laborer	11Ma02Eb	STOWE, Owen		19	M	Laborer	11Ma02Eb
FAHY, Patrick		20	M	Laborer	11Ma02Eb	DEFEVRE, Michael		40	M	Laborer	11Ma02Eb
BOYLE, John		30	M	Laborer	11Ma02Eb	Ann	(W)	45	F	Spinster	11Ma02Eb
GUNN, Mary		23	F	Spinster	11Ma02Eb	Ellen	(D)	07	F	Child	11Ma02Eb
RUXTON, Nora		19	F	Spinster	11Ma02Eb	John	(S)	05	M	Child	11Ma02Eb
KEARNS, Catharine		17	F	Spinster	11Ma02Eb	James	(S)	02	M	Child	11Ma02Eb
HARRELL, Mary		24	F	Dressmaker	11Ma02Eb	DAILY, John		30	M	Laborer	11Ma02Eb

NAMES OF PASSENGERS		AGE	SEX	OCCUPATIONS	DATE PORT SHIP
CAMPBELL, John		25	M	Laborer	11Ma02Eb
MOONEY, Owen		19	M	Laborer	11Ma02Eb
FINNEGAN, John		32	M	Laborer	11Ma02Eb
CALL, James		18	M	Laborer	11Ma02Eb
MCGRAIN, Mary		25	F	Spinster	11Ma02Eb
MCBRIDE, Kate		30	F	Spinster	11Ma02Eb
Alice		20	F	Dressmaker	11Ma02Eb
FITZPATRICK, Rose		22	F	Spinster	11Ma02Eb
FINNEGAN, Kate		22	F	Spinster	11Ma02Eb
ADAMS, Mary		22	F	Spinster	11Ma02Eb
MCGRAIL, Mary		35	F	Spinster	11Ma02Eb
CALLAGHAN, Ellen		16	F	Dressmaker	11Ma02Eb
MCGRAIL, Mary		06	F	Child	11Ma02Eb
Michael		30	M	Tailor	11Ma02Eb
Ann	(W)	21	F	Spinster	11Ma02Eb
Patrick	(S)	02	M	Child	11Ma02Eb
CONNER, James		30	M	Laborer	11Ma02Eb
RATICAN, Thomas		32	M	Laborer	11Ma02Eb
GLENN, James		31	M	Laborer	11Ma02Eb
John		26	M	Laborer	11Ma02Eb
PORTLAND, Charles		22	M	Shoemaker	11Ma02Eb
BOHAN, Michael		25	M	Laborer	11Ma02Eb
CANNING, Michael		20	M	Laborer	11Ma02Eb
BOHAN, James		25	M	Laborer	11Ma02Eb
HOUSTON, Francis		22	M	Laborer	11Ma02Eb
James		20	M	Laborer	11Ma02Eb
MOHY, John		22	M	Laborer	11Ma02Eb
CARROLL, Dennis		30	M	Laborer	11Ma02Eb
QUIN, James		28	M	Laborer	11Ma02Eb
GROWNEY, John		20	M	Laborer	11Ma02Eb
CRAIG, Francis		25	M	Laborer	11Ma02Eb
MCLOUGHLIN, Michael		31	M	Laborer	11Ma02Eb
CONLAN, Patrick		25	M	Laborer	11Ma02Eb
Jas.		23	M	Laborer	11Ma02Eb
FARRELL, James		22	M	Laborer	11Ma02Eb
Kate		19	F	Spinster	11Ma02Eb
HUSTON, Mary		20	F	Spinster	11Ma02Eb
MASTON, Mary		24	F	Spinster	11Ma02Eb
PURCELL, Peggy		25	F	Spinster	11Ma02Eb
HANLEY, Alice		20	F	Spinster	11Ma02Eb
COX, Bridget		22	F	Spinster	11Ma02Eb
LITTLE, Ellen		24	F	Spinster	11Ma02Eb
FLEMING, Christopher		24	M	Laborer	11Ma02Eb
MCCANNING, Michael		24	M	Laborer	11Ma02Eb
DAVIS, Thomas		24	M	Mechanic	11Ma02Eb
MOONEY, Edward		22	M	Laborer	11Ma02Eb
BRIAN, Ann		20	F	Spinster	11Ma02Eb
DOYLE, Michael		30	M	Laborer	11Ma02Eb
Catharine	(W)	28	F	Spinster	11Ma02Eb
Michael	(S)	02	M	Child	11Ma02Eb
CROLLY, Thomas		37	M	Laborer	11Ma02Eb
Johanna		44	F	Spinster	11Ma02Eb
GRACE, Patrick		21	M	Laborer	11Ma02Eb
BOTTOMER, Catherine		21	F	Spinster	11Ma02Eb
Julia		19	F	Spinster	11Ma02Eb
CONNOR, Michael		19	M	Laborer	11Ma02Eb
GRACE, Julia		22	F	Spinster	11Ma02Eb
CONNOR, John		18	M	Laborer	11Ma02Eb
COCKLEY, Timothy		21	M	Laborer	11Ma02Eb
BUTTLER, Ellen		18	F	Spinster	11Ma02Eb
KEEFFE, Joseph		24	M	Laborer	11Ma02Eb
Patrick		20	M	Laborer	11Ma02Eb
MURPHY, George		22	M	Laborer	11Ma02Eb
GOVEREIGN, John		28	M	Laborer	11Ma02Eb
KEEFFE, Kate		22	F	Spinster	11Ma02Eb
SULLIVAN, Mary		24	F	Spinster	11Ma02Eb
HOLMES, Andrew		35	M	Laborer	11Ma02Eb
Mary	(W)	35	F	Spinster	11Ma02Eb
Eliza	(D)	05	F	Child	11Ma02Eb
Ann	(D)	03	F	Child	11Ma02Eb
John	(S)	01	M	Child	11Ma02Eb
Sarah	(D)	09	F	Child	11Ma02Eb
Elizabeth		27	F	Dressmaker	11Ma02Eb
KENNY, Biddy		26	F	Spinster	11Ma02Eb
JOYCE, Bridget		35	F	Spinster	11Ma02Eb

NAMES OF PASSENGERS		AGE	SEX	OCCUPATIONS	DATE PORT SHIP
WATSON, Alexn.		24	M	Laborer	11Ma02Eb
Henry		22	M	Carpenter	11Ma02Eb
MULROONEY, Mary		24	F	Spinster	11Ma02Eb
KILLMARTON, William		26	M	Laborer	11Ma02Eb
DILLON, Barthw.		22	M	Laborer	11Ma02Eb
MAHON, Francis		27	M	Laborer	11Ma02Eb
HAZELTON, Ben		.08	M	Infant	11Ma02Eb
DUFFY, Patrick		21	M	Laborer	11Ma02Eb
Died-At-Sea					

WAVE 11 MAY 1846

From Dublin

NAMES OF PASSENGERS		AGE	SEX	OCCUPATIONS	DATE PORT SHIP
HORAN, Peter		30	M	Laborer	11Ma20Fr
HALL, U		20	F	Laborer	11Ma20Fr
TYGUE, Mary		20	F	Laborer	11Ma20Fr
Ann		22	F	Laborer	11Ma20Fr
CARROLL, Ann		20	F	Laborer	11Ma20Fr
FITZSIMONS, Ann		20	F	Laborer	11Ma20Fr
Ann		20	F	Laborer	11Ma20Fr
MAGRATH, Pattk.		50	M	Unknown	11Ma20Fr
U	(W)	45	F	Unknown	11Ma20Fr
Luke	(S)	24	M	Unknown	11Ma20Fr
Mary	(D)	23	F	Unknown	11Ma20Fr
Eliza	(D)	18	F	Unknown	11Ma20Fr
Christy	(S)	20	M	Unknown	11Ma20Fr
Matty	(S)	14	M	Unknown	11Ma20Fr
John	(S)	17	M	Unknown	11Ma20Fr
Catharine	(D)	20	F	Unknown	11Ma20Fr
GORMAN, Patrick		20	M	Unknown	11Ma20Fr
TWOOMY, Patt		20	M	Unknown	11Ma20Fr
FAY, U		20	M	Unknown	11Ma20Fr
FENLON, Andrew		22	M	Unknown	11Ma20Fr
ATENDITH, U		30	M	Unknown	11Ma20Fr
Ann		25	F	Unknown	11Ma20Fr
WILLIS, Jane		23	F	Unknown	11Ma20Fr
WADE, Mary		16	F	Unknown	11Ma20Fr
SHERIDAN, Margt.		21	F	Unknown	11Ma20Fr
GANHAN, Cathne.		21	F	Unknown	11Ma20Fr
WILLIS, Bell		25	F	Unknown	11Ma20Fr
SHORT, Mary		24	F	Unknown	11Ma20Fr
CONNAUGHT, Bridget		26	F	Unknown	11Ma20Fr
PHELAN, Mary		20	F	Unknown	11Ma20Fr
SEALLY, U		25	M	Unknown	11Ma20Fr
U	(W)	30	F	Unknown	11Ma20Fr
BOOKER, Thomas		22	M	Unknown	11Ma20Fr
DOOLEY, Patrick		18	M	Unknown	11Ma20Fr
MULLEN, Sarah		20	F	Unknown	11Ma20Fr
Ann		18	F	Unknown	11Ma20Fr
MCQUILLEN, Ann		20	F	Unknown	11Ma20Fr
HUNT, Michael		21	M	Unknown	11Ma20Fr
Mary		19	F	Unknown	11Ma20Fr
CONNAUGHTON, Thomas		11	M	Unknown	11Ma20Fr
KEARY, Thomas		30	M	Unknown	11Ma20Fr
John		28	M	Unknown	11Ma20Fr
Edward		26	M	Unknown	11Ma20Fr
BRYAN, Mary		25	F	Unknown	11Ma20Fr
DOOLEY, Dorah		20	F	Unknown	11Ma20Fr
BRYAN, Ann		20	F	Unknown	11Ma20Fr
DAY, Martin		26	M	Unknown	11Ma20Fr
RYAN, Timothy		19	M	Unknown	11Ma20Fr
KELLY, U-Mrs.		50	F	Unknown	11Ma20Fr
Patrick	(S)	28	M	Unknown	11Ma20Fr
James	(S)	26	M	Unknown	11Ma20Fr
Margaret	(D)	22	F	Unknown	11Ma20Fr
Honor	(D)	15	F	Unknown	11Ma20Fr
FOGARTY, Julia		20	F	Unknown	11Ma20Fr
MAHER, Michael		20	M	Unknown	11Ma20Fr

NAMES OF PASSENGERS	AGE	SEX	OCCUPATIONS	DATE PORT SHIP	NAMES OF PASSENGERS	AGE	SEX	OCCUPATIONS	DATE PORT SHIP
MENTON, Michael	20	M	Unknown	11Ma20Fr	MORAN, John	22	M	Unknown	11Ma20Fr
FEANET, Michael	30	M	Unknown	11Ma20Fr	LYONS, Sally	20	F	Unknown	11Ma20Fr
FARRELL, Ann	20	F	Unknown	11Ma20Fr	MCDONNELL, Biddy	22	F	Unknown	11Ma20Fr
DILLON, Honor	60	F	Unknown	11Ma20Fr	PARKINSON, Mary	20	F	Unknown	11Ma20Fr
Timothy (S)	30	M	Unknown	11Ma20Fr	CARROLL, John	20	M	Unknown	11Ma20Fr
Margaret (D)	20	F	Unknown	11Ma20Fr	MURPHY, Peter	18	M	Unknown	11Ma20Fr
MONAGHAN, Julia	06	F	Child	11Ma20Fr	MCGRA, Rose	.09	F	Infant	11Ma20Fr
HOLDEN, Eliza	20	F	Unknown	11Ma20Fr	COOLEEN, Morgan	25	M	Unknown	11Ma20Fr
MASON, John	30	M	Unknown	11Ma20Fr	CRENEN, Cathnr.	20	F	Unknown	11Ma20Fr
Mary	28	F	Unknown	11Ma20Fr	GARLEY, Mary-S.	20	F	Unknown	11Ma20Fr
MCCABE, Andrew	25	M	Unknown	11Ma20Fr	KAVANAGH, Pat	22	M	Unknown	11Ma20Fr
Fanny	16	F	Unknown	11Ma20Fr	Ellen	20	F	Unknown	11Ma20Fr
Mary	12	F	Unknown	11Ma20Fr	RIELLY, Cathne.	20	F	Unknown	11Ma20Fr
DALY, Patrick	30	M	Unknown	11Ma20Fr	ROURKE, Mary-A.	20	F	Unknown	11Ma20Fr
MCCABE, Thomas	20	M	Unknown	11Ma20Fr	SWEENEY, Thomas	21	M	Unknown	11Ma20Fr
Barney	20	M	Unknown	11Ma20Fr	COY, Thomas	28	M	Unknown	11Ma20Fr
MURRAY, James	28	M	Unknown	11Ma20Fr	Patrick	06	M	Child	11Ma20Fr
DEMPSEY, Alley	18	F	Unknown	11Ma20Fr	HUGHES, U-Mrs.	26	F	Unknown	11Ma20Fr
GILGRIST, Patt	25	M	Unknown	11Ma20Fr	Anthony (S)	02	M	Child	11Ma20Fr
Betty	39	F	Unknown	11Ma20Fr	John (S)	01	M	Child	11Ma20Fr
John	18	M	Unknown	11Ma20Fr	CULLEN, Ann	16	F	Unknown	11Ma20Fr
Bridget	16	F	Unknown	11Ma20Fr	SORATHAN, Eliza	20	F	Unknown	11Ma20Fr
MCCABE, Patt	20	M	Unknown	11Ma20Fr	SHEERAN, John	26	M	Unknown	11Ma20Fr
DOYLE, Ann	20	F	Unknown	11Ma20Fr	LUKE, James	20	M	Unknown	11Ma20Fr
BRADY, Cathne.	20	F	Unknown	11Ma20Fr	SHEERAN, Mary	20	M	Unknown	11Ma20Fr
TULLY, Cathne.	20	F	Unknown	11Ma20Fr	GIBBONS, Thomas	22	M	Unknown	11Ma20Fr
MASTERSON, John	20	M	Unknown	11Ma20Fr	JORDAN, Martin	20	M	Unknown	11Ma20Fr
U (W)	20	F	Unknown	11Ma20Fr	KERRIGAN, John	20	M	Unknown	11Ma20Fr
CULLEN, Ellen	20	F	Unknown	11Ma20Fr	CONDRAN, Judy	21	F	Unknown	11Ma20Fr
FARRELL, James	24	M	Unknown	11Ma20Fr	Catharin	20	F	Unknown	11Ma20Fr
BRENNAN, Margt.	25	F	Unknown	11Ma20Fr	KANE, Patrick	20	M	Unknown	11Ma20Fr
CRANEY, Patk.	24	M	Unknown	11Ma20Fr	MELLIA, William	21	M	Unknown	11Ma20Fr
FLATTERY, John	22	M	Unknown	11Ma20Fr	BRYAN, James	24	M	Unknown	11Ma20Fr
CONWAY, Ann	18	F	Unknown	11Ma20Fr	John	22	M	Unknown	11Ma20Fr
ROURKE, Cathne.	24	F	Unknown	11Ma20Fr	Margaret	17	F	Unknown	11Ma20Fr
NEWMAN, John	24	M	Unknown	11Ma20Fr	BROWN, George	24	M	Unknown	11Ma20Fr
FLYNN, Patt	27	M	Unknown	11Ma20Fr	WALSH, John	24	M	Unknown	11Ma20Fr
LARKIN, Ann	20	F	Unknown	11Ma20Fr	BYRNE, James	20	M	Unknown	11Ma20Fr
Sarah	22	F	Unknown	11Ma20Fr	LEOH, John	24	M	Unknown	11Ma20Fr
EAGAN, Margaret	12	F	Unknown	11Ma20Fr	Michael	20	M	Unknown	11Ma20Fr
HOGAN, Patrick	20	M	Unknown	11Ma20Fr	DEVEREAUX, John	27	M	Unknown	11Ma20Fr
DOWD, Biddy	22	F	Unknown	11Ma20Fr	NEVILL, John	24	M	Unknown	11Ma20Fr
SMALL, Julia	24	F	Unknown	11Ma20Fr	BRYNE, Honor	20	F	Unknown	11Ma20Fr
KEALEY, Thomas	26	M	Unknown	11Ma20Fr	Johnny	22	M	Unknown	11Ma20Fr
BYRNE, George	33	M	Unknown	11Ma20Fr	RYAN, Catharine	18	F	Unknown	11Ma20Fr
U (W)	30	F	Unknown	11Ma20Fr	DINNEEN, Daniel	24	M	Unknown	11Ma20Fr
George (S)	07	M	Child	11Ma20Fr	TEERNEY, Catharine	20	F	Unknown	11Ma20Fr
Martin (S)	11	M	Unknown	11Ma20Fr	FOX, Tim	28	M	Unknown	11Ma20Fr
BUGGY, Cathrn.	20	F	Unknown	11Ma20Fr	Bridget (W)	24	F	Unknown	11Ma20Fr
DUNN, Martin	20	M	Unknown	11Ma20Fr	John (S)	03	M	Child	11Ma20Fr
GILLIGAN, Thomas	28	M	Unknown	11Ma20Fr	MURPHY, Essey	22	F	Unknown	11Ma20Fr
JOHNSTON, Biddy	20	F	Unknown	11Ma20Fr	HIGGINS, Susan	20	F	Unknown	11Ma20Fr
PARKER, Henry	26	M	Unknown	11Ma20Fr	QUINNINGAN, Mat.	28	M	Unknown	11Ma20Fr
DRUMMOND, John	20	M	Unknown	11Ma20Fr	FAHEY, Pat.	28	M	Unknown	11Ma20Fr
CULLEN, Edward	26	M	Unknown	11Ma20Fr	Mary	18	F	Unknown	11Ma20Fr
James	20	M	Unknown	11Ma20Fr	MALLOY, Onny	20	M	Unknown	11Ma20Fr
HALPHIN, William	24	M	Unknown	11Ma20Fr	KELLY, Michael	30	M	Unknown	11Ma20Fr
KAVANAGH, Cathrn.	50	F	Unknown	11Ma20Fr	Ellen (W)	30	F	Unknown	11Ma20Fr
Thomas (S)	25	M	Unknown	11Ma20Fr	James (S)	03	M	Child	11Ma20Fr
MCMANUS, Margt.	18	F	Unknown	11Ma20Fr	MCCORMACK, Biddy	20	F	Unknown	11Ma20Fr
REILLY, Patrick	18	M	Unknown	11Ma20Fr	BRACKEN, Pat.	24	M	Unknown	11Ma20Fr
KILLEN, George	18	M	Unknown	11Ma20Fr	HACKET, Michl.	20	M	Unknown	11Ma20Fr
BAXTER, John	25	M	Unknown	11Ma20Fr	KEEGAN, Peter	22	M	Unknown	11Ma20Fr
MCMANUS, Bernard	23	M	Unknown	11Ma20Fr	CAULFIELD, Pat	28	M	Unknown	11Ma20Fr
BRADY, Charles	21	M	Unknown	11Ma20Fr	KELLY, Thomas	26	M	Unknown	11Ma20Fr
KELLEGHER, Margt.	20	F	Unknown	11Ma20Fr	Mary	20	F	Unknown	11Ma20Fr
SMITH, Margaret	20	F	Unknown	11Ma20Fr	Bridget	18	F	Unknown	11Ma20Fr
Margaret	18	F	Unknown	11Ma20Fr	FARRELLY, Martha	24	F	Unknown	11Ma20Fr
MCATEER, Margt.	20	F	Unknown	11Ma20Fr	Richard	07	M	Child	11Ma20Fr
FARLEY, Ann	13	F	Unknown	11Ma20Fr	HUGHES, Joseph	26	M	Unknown	11Ma20Fr
MCCAULEY, Jane	26	F	Unknown	11Ma20Fr	MORAN, Matt	22	M	Unknown	11Ma20Fr
Ann	26	F	Unknown	11Ma20Fr	MURPHY, Mary	20	F	Unknown	11Ma20Fr
Phillip	18	M	Unknown	11Ma20Fr	WALSH, Mary	20	F	Unknown	11Ma20Fr
DARLINGTON, Thomas	30	M	Unknown	11Ma20Fr					
TAYLOR, James	30	M	Unknown	11Ma20Fr					

ATLAS 11 MAY 1846

From Liverpool

NAMES OF PASSENGERS		AGE	SEX	OCCUPATIONS	DATE PORT SHIP
RIDGWAY, George-Newsom		33	M	Army	11Ma02Ec
GRAY, Joseph		28	M	Bkp	11Ma02Ec
Mary		25	F	Spinster	11Ma02Ec
Matilda		27	F	Spinster	11Ma02Ec
Rebecca		23	F	Spinster	11Ma02Ec
Elizabeth		22	F	Spinster	11Ma02Ec
MCNAMEE, James		20	M	Laborer	11Ma02Ec
LIVINGSTON, James		19	M	Spinner	11Ma02Ec
MCGUINEAS, Pat.		22	M	Spinner	11Ma02Ec
BRADLEY, Elen		24	F	Spinster	11Ma02Ec
MASTERSON, Mary		60	F	WI	11Ma02Ec
MCNANIS, Andrew		23	M	Laborer	11Ma02Ec
John		13	M	Laborer	11Ma02Ec
James		09	M	Child	11Ma02Ec
Andrew		16	M	Laborer	11Ma02Ec
MCNAMEE, Catharine		26	F	Spinster	11Ma02Ec
HUGHES, Ann		50	F	WI	11Ma02Ec
Andrea		35	F	Spinster	11Ma02Ec
William		11	M	Unknown	11Ma02Ec
KANE, John		29	M	Laborer	11Ma02Ec
MCCAFFERY, John		23	M	Laborer	11Ma02Ec
Eliza		20	F	Spinster	11Ma02Ec
DRUMOND, Ann		21	F	Spinster	11Ma02Ec
CURLY, Peggy		23	F	Spinster	11Ma02Ec
BRADLEY, Catharine		23	F	Spinster	11Ma02Ec
LOVE, Alexander		24	M	Laborer	11Ma02Ec
MCGREHAM, Frances		23	M	Weaver	11Ma02Ec
BENSON, Samuel		26	M	Laborer	11Ma02Ec
James		18	M	Laborer	11Ma02Ec
WATTS, Samuele		21	M	Laborer	11Ma02Ec
HAGGIN, James		36	M	Laborer	11Ma02Ec
FORD, Michal		45	M	Laborer	11Ma02Ec
BARRY, William		30	M	Laborer	11Ma02Ec
FENIS, John		20	M	Laborer	11Ma02Ec
BARRY, Catharine		30	F	Wife	11Ma02Ec
Bridget	(D)	11	F	Unknown	11Ma02Ec
Ellen	(D)	09	F	Child	11Ma02Ec
Mary	(D)	06	F	Child	11Ma02Ec
John	(S)	02	M	Child	11Ma02Ec
Thos.	(S)	.06	M	Infant	11Ma02Ec
RYAN, Timothy		32	M	Laborer	11Ma02Ec
SMITH, William		21	M	Laborer	11Ma02Ec
BALLING, Mary		25	F	WI	11Ma02Ec
GRAHAM, Elizabeth		34	F	Wife	11Ma02Ec
Hester	(D)	06	F	Child	11Ma02Ec
Benjamin	(S)	04	M	Child	11Ma02Ec
Nancy	(D)	01	F	Child	11Ma02Ec
MOONEY, Elin		20	F	Spinster	11Ma02Ec
BROWNING, Eliza		32	F	Wife	11Ma02Ec
WOODBOURNE, Isabella		21	F	Spinster	11Ma02Ec
FOREGRAM, Jane		20	F	Spinster	11Ma02Ec
GRAHAM, Eliza		25	F	Spinster	11Ma02Ec
GETTY, Rachel		16	F	Spinster	11Ma02Ec
MADDEN, Jane		19	F	Spinster	11Ma02Ec
ROUKE, Catharine		19	F	Spinster	11Ma02Ec
William		23	M	Laborer	11Ma02Ec
SMITH, Mary		16	F	Spinster	11Ma02Ec
TOSSING, Martha		50	F	Wife	11Ma02Ec
HEALY, Margrat		19	F	Spinster	11Ma02Ec
Catharina		25	F	Spinster	11Ma02Ec
GAMBLE, Nancy		19	F	Spinster	11Ma02Ec
PICKINGS, Ralph		28	M	Laborer	11Ma02Ec
Margret		21	F	Spinster	11Ma02Ec
FRELFORD, Fanny		20	F	Spinster	11Ma02Ec
CASEY, Peter		20	M	Laborer	11Ma02Ec
DONAHOE, Margrat		17	F	Spinster	11Ma02Ec
GAFFNEY, Terance		20	M	Laborer	11Ma02Ec
Mary		17	F	Spinster	11Ma02Ec
MCEVOY, Joseph		22	M	Laborer	11Ma02Ec
BACON, Samuel		47	M	Laborer	11Ma02Ec
Rosanna	(W)	47	F	Wife	11Ma02Ec
Margrat	(D)	18	F	Spinster	11Ma02Ec
Sarah	(D)	12	F	Unknown	11Ma02Ec
Nancy	(D)	15	F	Unknown	11Ma02Ec
George	(S)	12	M	Unknown	11Ma02Ec
Elizabeth	(D)	10	F	Unknown	11Ma02Ec
Henry	(S)	04	M	Unknown	11Ma02Ec
MCGUGAN, John		27	M	Carpenter	11Ma02Ec
Ann	(W)	26	F	Wife	11Ma02Ec
KENAN, Thomas		26	M	Laborer	11Ma02Ec
Nancy	(W)	20	F	Wife	11Ma02Ec
GUNNINGS, Martin		28	M	Carpenter	11Ma02Ec
Mary		17	F	Spinster	11Ma02Ec
DOOLEY, James		26	M	Laborer	11Ma02Ec
HOLEOWAY, James		66	M	Shoemaker	11Ma02Ec
COLLINS, James		22	M	Laborer	11Ma02Ec
KINNY, Michael		29	M	Laborer	11Ma02Ec
MORRISON, Michael		29	M	Laborer	11Ma02Ec
BOTHERICK, John		23	M	Laborer	11Ma02Ec
Mary		25	F	Spinster	11Ma02Ec
LAUGHTON, Biddey		25	F	Spinster	11Ma02Ec
CLARK, Edwards		17	M	Laborer	11Ma02Ec
DUNEGAN, Timothy		29	M	Laborer	11Ma02Ec
WEIR, William		20	M	Laborer	11Ma02Ec
BARNET, Abraham		22	M	Laborer	11Ma02Ec
DELEANY, Thomas		31	M	Laborer	11Ma02Ec
Mary		30	F	Laborer	11Ma02Ec
HUGHES, James		24	M	Laborer	11Ma02Ec
HANDY, James		50	M	Laborer	11Ma02Ec
Jane	(W)	46	F	Wife	11Ma02Ec
William	(S)	18	M	Unknown	11Ma02Ec
James	(S)	17	M	Unknown	11Ma02Ec
Jane	(D)	15	F	Unknown	11Ma02Ec
Richard	(S)	13	M	Unknown	11Ma02Ec
John	(S)	11	M	Unknown	11Ma02Ec
Thomas	(S)	07	M	Child	11Ma02Ec
Henry	(S)	05	M	Child	11Ma02Ec
Alexander	(S)	02	M	Child	11Ma02Ec
FORESTER, Michal		70	M	Laborer	11Ma02Ec
CONDEY, Margret		50	F	Wife	11Ma02Ec
James	(S)	16	M	Unknown	11Ma02Ec
Margaret	(D)	11	F	Unknown	11Ma02Ec
GILPIN, Elizabeth		17	F	Spinster	11Ma02Ec
CONWAY, James		60	M	Shoemaker	11Ma02Ec
Bridget	(W)	47	F	Wife	11Ma02Ec
John	(S)	22	M	Shoemaker	11Ma02Ec
Patrick	(S)	20	M	Shoemaker	11Ma02Ec
Catharine	(D)	17	F	Unknown	11Ma02Ec
James	(S)	12	M	Unknown	11Ma02Ec
Margret	(D)	09	F	Child	11Ma02Ec
Mary	(D)	04	F	Child	11Ma02Ec
KEATING, Thos.		21	M	Laborer	11Ma02Ec
DUNAHOE, Patrick		20	M	Laborer	11Ma02Ec
Cornelius		19	M	Laborer	11Ma02Ec
SPLADES, Daniel		20	M	Laborer	11Ma02Ec
Julia		25	F	Spinster	11Ma02Ec
FINNEY, Mary		25	F	Spinster	11Ma02Ec
Catharine		28	F	Spinster	11Ma02Ec
CUMMINGS, Ann		23	F	Spinster	11Ma02Ec
ASHERTON, Mary		57	F	WI	11Ma02Ec
FITZPATRICK, Barry		19	M	Laborer	11Ma02Ec
Mary	(M)	50	F	WI	11Ma02Ec
Rose	(T)	13	F	Unknown	11Ma02Ec
MARTIN, Owen		33	M	Laborer	11Ma02Ec
GIBBONS, Charles		20	M	Laborer	11Ma02Ec
JACOBS, Samuel		25	M	Laborer	11Ma02Ec
Jane	(W)	26	F	Wife	11Ma02Ec
LEHEANEY, James		22	M	Laborer	11Ma02Ec
Bridget		24	F	Wife	11Ma02Ec
ODONNALLY, John		26	M	Laborer	11Ma02Ec

NAMES OF PASSENGERS		AGE	SEX	OCCUPATIONS	DATE PORT SHIP
ODONNALLY, Thomas		22	M	Laborer	11Ma02Ec
Hugh		24	M	Laborer	11Ma02Ec
John		10	M	Unknown	11Ma02Ec
TIERNAN, Edward		35	M	Unknown	11Ma02Ec
Eliza	(W)	26	F	Unknown	11Ma02Ec
Mary	(D)	05	F	Child	11Ma02Ec
James	(S)	01	M	Child	11Ma02Ec
GARDNER, Michal		30	M	Laborer	11Ma02Ec
BRIGHT, Mary		21	F	Spinster	11Ma02Ec
WHITE, Martin		26	M	Laborer	11Ma02Ec
Catharine		24	F	Spinster	11Ma02Ec
CROUGHAN, Mary		23	F	Spinster	11Ma02Ec
HEFFERNAN, Patrick		20	M	Laborer	11Ma02Ec
DUNN, Pierce		20	M	Laborer	11Ma02Ec
HOGAN, John		27	M	Laborer	11Ma02Ec
Ann	(W)	25	F	Wife	11Ma02Ec
WHITNEY, Rose		24	F	Spinster	11Ma02Ec
FEHELY, Elln		16	F	Spinster	11Ma02Ec
WILLIAM, Williams		20	M	Laborer	11Ma02Ec
KELLY, Barney		27	M	Laborer	11Ma02Ec
TWOMY, James		27	M	Laborer	11Ma02Ec
MORRISEY, Thos.		39	M	Laborer	11Ma02Ec
BUCKLEY, Michael		20	M	Laborer	11Ma02Ec
LONAGIN, John		20	M	Laborer	11Ma02Ec
FITZGIBBONS, Gerard		25	M	Laborer	11Ma02Ec
MCANN, James		21	M	Laborer	11Ma02Ec
MCNAMEE, James		17	M	Laborer	11Ma02Ec
DUNAHOE, Francis		19	M	Laborer	11Ma02Ec
MAGEE, Bridget		20	F	Spinster	11Ma02Ec
KELLAM, Kitty		20	F	Spinster	11Ma02Ec
MCALEAR, Edward		18	M	Laborer	11Ma02Ec
Sarah		20	F	Spinster	11Ma02Ec
KELLY, John		25	M	Shoemaker	11Ma02Ec
Betsey	(W)	26	F	Wife	11Ma02Ec
Margrat	(D)	04	F	Child	11Ma02Ec
Alice	(D)	.06	F	Infant	11Ma02Ec
MCLAUGHLIN, Barney		23	M	Laborer	11Ma02Ec
Ann		19	F	Spinster	11Ma02Ec
BOUHAN, Timothy		28	M	Laborer	11Ma02Ec
Peter		25	M	Laborer	11Ma02Ec
CUNNIFF, James		13	M	Laborer	11Ma02Ec
MCKINEY, Mary		21	F	Spinster	11Ma02Ec
NOTCHFORD, Mary		19	F	Spinster	11Ma02Ec
Patrick		21	M	Laborer	11Ma02Ec
Michal		16	M	Laborer	11Ma02Ec
MCEVOY, Margrat		45	F	Wi	11Ma02Ec
James	(S)	17	M	Laborer	11Ma02Ec
Patrick	(S)	15	M	Laborer	11Ma02Ec
Mary	(D)	19	F	Spinster	11Ma02Ec
LYNCH, Ann		20	F	Spinster	11Ma02Ec
HOLLAND, Michal		20	M	Laborer	11Ma02Ec
CUFF, James		18	M	Laborer	11Ma02Ec
Ann		23	F	Spinster	11Ma02Ec
BLACK, Catharine		18	F	Spinster	11Ma02Ec
CAFFERY, Bridget		17	F	Spinster	11Ma02Ec
DEVINE, Mary		18	F	Spinster	11Ma02Ec
CLARK, Thos.Jas.		11	M	Unknown	11Ma02Ec
MCDOWELL, Robert		18	M	Carpenter	11Ma02Ec
CONNER, Thomas		21	M	Laborer	11Ma02Ec
Patrick		28	M	Laborer	11Ma02Ec
BROFFY, Thomas		.06	M	Infant	11Ma02Ec
Mary		25	F	Spinster	11Ma02Ec
DONLAN, Mary		23	F	Spinster	11Ma02Ec
WHITE, Ann		19	F	Spinster	11Ma02Ec
Mary		22	F	Spinster	11Ma02Ec
DONLEY, Mary		22	F	Spinster	11Ma02Ec
Ann		24	F	Spinster	11Ma02Ec
GLASS, Niel		21	M	Tailor	11Ma02Ec
Elizabeth		18	F	Spinster	11Ma02Ec
MCCAUGHAN, John		21	M	Laborer	11Ma02Ec
MCCALE, Archibald		22	M	Laborer	11Ma02Ec
Nancy		20	F	Spinster	11Ma02Ec
COURTNEY, Michal		22	M	Laborer	11Ma02Ec
SHIRLIN, Patrick		22	M	Laborer	11Ma02Ec
BURNS, Hugh		21	M	Laborer	11Ma02Ec
KENNAN, John		21	M	Laborer	11Ma02Ec
ROGERS, James		18	M	Laborer	11Ma02Ec
OROAK, John		24	M	Laborer	11Ma02Ec
Ann		19	F	Spinster	11Ma02Ec
MULVEY, John		18	M	Laborer	11Ma02Ec
Mary		22	F	Spinster	11Ma02Ec
BRYAN, Bridget		26	F	Spinster	11Ma02Ec
BRYNE, Bridget		18	F	Spinster	11Ma02Ec
HANNEN, Daniele		02	M	Child	11Ma02Ec
RYAN, James		65	M	Laborer	11Ma02Ec
DUNN, Catharine		08	F	Child	11Ma02Ec
OBRIAN, Jeremiah		24	M	Laborer	11Ma02Ec
DESMOND, Patrick		26	M	Laborer	11Ma02Ec
ROBB, William		40	M	Laborer	11Ma02Ec
Mary	(W)	38	F	Wife	11Ma02Ec
MCLAUGHLIN, Charles		35	M	Laborer	11Ma02Ec
DOOLAN, Ally		25	F	Spinster	11Ma02Ec
FOX, Mary		22	F	Spinster	11Ma02Ec
HARMAN, Elln		27	F	Wife	11Ma02Ec
Martha	(D)	06	F	Child	11Ma02Ec
PAUL, John		20	M	Laborer	11Ma02Ec
MCKINEY, James		45	M	Laborer	11Ma02Ec
Catharine	(W)	40	F	Wife	11Ma02Ec
Frances	(S)	13	M	Unknown	11Ma02Ec
Catharine	(D)	12	F	Unknown	11Ma02Ec
Michal	(S)	10	M	Unknown	11Ma02Ec
Rosanna	(D)	05	F	Child	11Ma02Ec
MCGOUGHLEY, Biddy		15	F	Unknown	11Ma02Ec
QULTING, Thomas		22	M	Laborer	11Ma02Ec
MCCABE, Julia		14	F	Spinster	11Ma02Ec
HUSSEY, Martin		20	M	Laborer	11Ma02Ec
HURLEY, Thomas		21	M	Laborer	11Ma02Ec
GUNN, Mallcia		23	M	Laborer	11Ma02Ec
MCGANN, Catharine		22	F	Spinster	11Ma02Ec
HUGHES, Bridget		21	F	Spinster	11Ma02Ec
GROGAN, Mary		17	F	Spinster	11Ma02Ec
GILLIGAN, Mary-Ann		20	F	Spinster	11Ma02Ec
MOORE, Margret		17	F	Spinster	11Ma02Ec
THOMPSON, Jane		20	F	Spinster	11Ma02Ec
MILAND, Julia		25	F	Spinster	11Ma02Ec
MADDAN, Julia		12	F	Spinster	11Ma02Ec
LARKIN, Catharine		20	F	Spinster	11Ma02Ec
REYNOLDS, James		25	M	Spinner	11Ma02Ec
OMARA, James		20	M	Spinner	11Ma02Ec

GEORGIA 11 MAY 1846

From Liverpool

NAMES OF PASSENGERS		AGE	SEX	OCCUPATIONS	DATE PORT SHIP
FARRELL, Edward		20	M	Gdnr	11Ma02Fs
Michael		20	M	Gdnr	11Ma02Fs
TRACY, Patt		25	M	Laborer	11Ma02Fs
CONALY, Michael		25	M	Laborer	11Ma02Fs
CUFF, James		25	M	Laborer	11Ma02Fs
BIRMINGHAM, Michael		25	M	Laborer	11Ma02Fs
HANLEY, Frances		25	M	Laborer	11Ma02Fs
DOLAN, Patt		25	M	Laborer	11Ma02Fs
CLANCY, John		25	M	Laborer	11Ma02Fs
CURRON, Owen		40	M	Laborer	11Ma02Fs
Patt		20	M	Laborer	11Ma02Fs
MAHAN, Rose		20	F	Servant	11Ma02Fs
OATS, Mary		20	F	Servant	11Ma02Fs
DOLAN, Mary		25	F	Servant	11Ma02Fs
CLIFFORD, Catharine		30	F	Servant	11Ma02Fs
MCKENNA, Mary		30	F	Servant	11Ma02Fs
LYNCH, Rose		30	F	Servant	11Ma02Fs
KIRVIN, Mary		65	F	Servant	11Ma02Fs
Patt	(H)	65	M	Laborer	11Ma02Fs
COLE, George		25	M	Laborer	11Ma02Fs

NAMES OF PASSENGERS		AGE	SEX	OCCUPATIONS	DATE PORT SHIP	NAMES OF PASSENGERS		AGE	SEX	OCCUPATIONS	DATE PORT SHIP
ROGAN, James		25	M	Laborer	11Ma02Fs	RANGAN, John		20	M	Laborer	11Ma02Fs
CASGA, John		25	M	Laborer	11Ma02Fs	CLORREN, James		30	M	Laborer	11Ma02Fs
NORRIS, Thomas		40	M	Laborer	11Ma02Fs	Cath.		30	F	Laborer	11Ma02Fs
Michael	(S)	03	M	Child	11Ma02Fs	EAGAN, Kernan		20	M	Laborer	11Ma02Fs
Biddy	(W)	40	F	Laborer	11Ma02Fs	DOYLE, Cath.		25	F	Servant	11Ma02Fs
Betsy	(D)	02	F	Child	11Ma02Fs	MCLOUGHTON, Cath.		25	F	Servant	11Ma02Fs
Mary	(D)	01	F	Child	11Ma02Fs	WHELDEN, Conner		25	M	Laborer	11Ma02Fs
KING, Ann		20	F	Servant	11Ma02Fs	HOREN, Erny.		20	M	Laborer	11Ma02Fs
KANON, Ann		20	F	Servant	11Ma02Fs	DONNELY, Michael		25	M	Laborer	11Ma02Fs
LOUGHRY, France		30	M	Tailor	11Ma02Fs	John		20	M	Laborer	11Ma02Fs
Mary	(W)	30	F	Unknown	11Ma02Fs	KELLY, Thomas		25	M	Laborer	11Ma02Fs
Elizabeth	(D)	.10	F	Infant	11Ma02Fs	LYNCH, Patt		20	M	Laborer	11Ma02Fs
STOKER, Wm.		25	M	Clerk	11Ma02Fs	STANTON, John		20	M	Laborer	11Ma02Fs
RANKIN, John		25	M	Clerk	11Ma02Fs	RYAN, James		30	M	Laborer	11Ma02Fs
LOUGHRY, Patt		25	M	Laborer	11Ma02Fs	Briget		25	F	Laborer	11Ma02Fs
EAGAN, Michael		35	M	Laborer	11Ma02Fs	DAIN, Michael		28	M	Laborer	11Ma02Fs
S.	(W)	35	F	Laborer	11Ma02Fs	Cath.		30	F	Servant	11Ma02Fs
Mary	(D)	.10	F	Infant	11Ma02Fs	LYONS, Marcela		25	F	Servant	11Ma02Fs
WILSON, James		45	M	Porter	11Ma02Fs	Dennis		25	M	Laborer	11Ma02Fs
Ellen		20	F	Seamstress	11Ma02Fs	DOYLE, James		18	M	Laborer	11Ma02Fs
ELLIOT, Mary		25	F	Seamstress	11Ma02Fs	CURRAN, Mary		35	F	Servant	11Ma02Fs
STEWARD, John		30	M	Laborer	11Ma02Fs	KENON, John		30	M	Laborer	11Ma02Fs
DAHLY, Michael		30	M	Laborer	11Ma02Fs	EARLY, Patt		25	M	Laborer	11Ma02Fs
TRERINGTON, Patt		30	M	Laborer	11Ma02Fs	HYDE, James		30	M	Laborer	11Ma02Fs
BYRN, Sylvester		30	M	Laborer	11Ma02Fs	MCNULTY, Charle		18	M	Laborer	11Ma02Fs
GORRAKIN, Peter		50	M	Farmer	11Ma02Fs	MULCOY, Patt		20	M	Laborer	11Ma02Fs
Patt	(S)	20	M	Farmer	11Ma02Fs	GAUGHRAN, Patt		25	M	Laborer	11Ma02Fs
Hugh	(S)	22	M	Farmer	11Ma02Fs	LYNCH, Patt		20	M	Laborer	11Ma02Fs
Michael	(S)	24	M	Farmer	11Ma02Fs	FETHERSTON, Darly		20	M	Laborer	11Ma02Fs
Mary	(W)	51	F	Farmer	11Ma02Fs	FEENY, Patt		25	M	Laborer	11Ma02Fs
Nancy	(D)	20	F	Farmer	11Ma02Fs	MCGOWEN, John		40	M	Laborer	11Ma02Fs
Rose	(M)	75	F	Farmer	11Ma02Fs	Died-At-Sea					
MANN, Rose		20	F	Servant	11Ma02Fs	Jane	(W)	35	F	Unknown	11Ma02Fs
SMITH, James		30	M	Servant	11Ma02Fs	Wm.	(S)	10	M	Unknown	11Ma02Fs
FOX, Ally		30	F	Servant	11Ma02Fs	Thompson	(S)	08	M	Child	11Ma02Fs
GLANCY, Ann		20	F	Servant	11Ma02Fs	Allen	(S)	06	M	Child	11Ma02Fs
GUNSHANNON, Kitty		20	F	Servant	11Ma02Fs	Mary	(D)	05	F	Child	11Ma02Fs
GORMON, Cath.		20	F	Servant	11Ma02Fs	Elizabeth	(D)	04	F	Child	11Ma02Fs
BIRMINGHAM, Cath.		20	F	Servant	11Ma02Fs	ONEILL, U		35	M	Farmer	11Ma02Fs
QUIN, Charles		30	M	Laborer	11Ma02Fs	HIGGINS, Petter		30	M	Farmer	11Ma02Fs
BYRNE, Christy		30	M	Laborer	11Ma02Fs	LEE, James		30	M	Farmer	11Ma02Fs
MAGUIRE, U		20	M	Laborer	11Ma02Fs	GIFNEY, Richard		20	M	Farmer	11Ma02Fs
FAGAN, Michael		25	M	Laborer	11Ma02Fs	WHELDEN, Any.		25	M	Servant	11Ma02Fs
DONAHUE, Cath.		30	F	Servant	11Ma02Fs	MURPHY, Michael		30	M	Laborer	11Ma02Fs
MCVOY, Mary		25	F	Servant	11Ma02Fs						
FORRESTER, Mary		30	F	Servant	11Ma02Fs						
CONNER, Jane		30	F	Servant	11Ma02Fs						
CROUGHTON, Eliza		10	F	Unknown	11Ma02Fs						
HOGG, Bridget		30	F	Servant	11Ma02Fs						
MCGUIRE, Margaret		30	F	Servant	11Ma02Fs	OTTAWA 12 MAY 1846					
NOON, Wm.		20	M	Servant	11Ma02Fs	From Liverpool					
CONAUGHTON, Patt		20	M	Servant	11Ma02Fs						
HANLEY, Dan		25	M	Servant	11Ma02Fs						
BOYED, Margaret		25	F	Servant	11Ma02Fs						
HOREN, James		30	M	Laborer	11Ma02Fs						
Mary		30	F	Laborer	11Ma02Fs	REILY, U-Mrs.		50	F	Dressmaker	12Ma02Ef
SMITH, Andrew		22	M	Laborer	11Ma02Fs	Bidena	(D)	16	F	Dressmaker	12Ma02Ef
BRODY, Mary		20	F	Servant	11Ma02Fs	Sarah	(D)	29	F	Dressmaker	12Ma02Ef
DONLEY, Mary		18	F	Servant	11Ma02Fs	Catharine	(D)	20	F	Dressmaker	12Ma02Ef
SMITH, Bridget		20	F	Servant	11Ma02Fs	Mary	(D)	18	F	Dressmaker	12Ma02Ef
MCQUIRK, Owen		40	M	Laborer	11Ma02Fs	WILSON, David		25	M	Laborer	12Ma02Ef
Cathn.	(W)	40	F	Laborer	11Ma02Fs	Catharine		24	F	Unknown	12Ma02Ef
Mary	(D)	10	F	Unknown	11Ma02Fs	SMITH, Andrew		19	M	Unknown	12Ma02Ef
Ally	(D)	06	F	Child	11Ma02Fs	James		21	M	Unknown	12Ma02Ef
Peggy	(D)	05	F	Child	11Ma02Fs	Adam		17	M	Unknown	12Ma02Ef
MANAHON, John		19	M	Laborer	11Ma02Fs	DUNLOP, John		21	M	Unknown	12Ma02Ef
CLARRIN, U		20	M	Laborer	11Ma02Fs	MONTGOMERY, John		20	M	Unknown	12Ma02Ef
LAWLER, Christy		25	M	Laborer	11Ma02Fs	HOPPER, George		20	M	Unknown	12Ma02Ef
Wineford		25	F	Laborer	11Ma02Fs	Margt.		20	F	Unknown	12Ma02Ef
LONDON, Mary		25	F	Servant	11Ma02Fs	Jane		16	F	Unknown	12Ma02Ef
ROAKE, Rose		25	F	Servant	11Ma02Fs	Barbara		14	F	Unknown	12Ma02Ef
MORIARTY, Briget		20	F	Servant	11Ma02Fs	Betty-Sally		09	F	Child	12Ma02Ef
HIGENS, Briget		30	F	Servant	11Ma02Fs	Brown		11	M	Unknown	12Ma02Ef
HOUGHLIN, Rose		25	F	Servant	11Ma02Fs	CAULFIELD, James		30	M	Unknown	12Ma02Ef
CONDRON, James		20	M	Laborer	11Ma02Fs	KILKERTIN, Mary		15	F	Unknown	12Ma02Ef

74

NAMES OF PASSENGERS		AGE	SEX	OCCUPATIONS	DATE PORT SHIP	NAMES OF PASSENGERS		AGE	SEX	OCCUPATIONS	DATE PORT SHIP
BELL, Judy		40	F	Unknown	12Ma02Ef	NELSON, Phebe		23	F	Unknown	12Ma02Ef
Isabella	(D)	04	F	Child	12Ma02Ef	DALTON, Peter		30	M	Unknown	12Ma02Ef
John	(S)	09	M	Child	12Ma02Ef	U	(W)	30	F	Unknown	12Ma02Ef
Andrew	(S)	03	M	Child	12Ma02Ef	Catharine	(D)	04	F	Child	12Ma02Ef
MCADOO, Henry		25	M	Unknown	12Ma02Ef	Michael	(S)	02	M	Child	12Ma02Ef
SCOTT, U-Mrs.		50	F	Unknown	12Ma02Ef	Thomas	(S)	.00	M	Infant	12Ma02Ef
Jane	(D)	16	F	Unknown	12Ma02Ef	GUNNIE, James		20	M	Unknown	12Ma02Ef
John	(S)	13	M	Unknown	12Ma02Ef	MAGUIRE, Michal		33	M	Unknown	12Ma02Ef
Mary	(D)	11	F	Unknown	12Ma02Ef	DRONE, Thomas		18	M	Unknown	12Ma02Ef
Mary	(D)	03	F	Child	12Ma02Ef	Caroline		17	F	Unknown	12Ma02Ef
CHADWICK, John		30	M	Unknown	12Ma02Ef	DUNNSDY, Francis		18	M	Unknown	12Ma02Ef
U	(W)	56	F	Unknown	12Ma02Ef	RODGERS, James		22	M	Unknown	12Ma02Ef
HENRY, John		23	M	Unknown	12Ma02Ef	Elizabeth		19	F	Unknown	12Ma02Ef
MARKAY, Bridget		22	F	Unknown	12Ma02Ef	MORRISON, Wm.		26	M	Unknown	12Ma02Ef
RAMSAY, John		21	M	Unknown	12Ma02Ef	Jane	(W)	25	F	Unknown	12Ma02Ef
MCGURK, Patt		24	M	Unknown	12Ma02Ef	James	(S)	02	M	Child	12Ma02Ef
DEVINE, Mary		21	F	Unknown	12Ma02Ef	Agnes	(D)	.00	F	Infant	12Ma02Ef
COLLINS, Daniel		22	M	Unknown	12Ma02Ef	MURRAY, Patt		25	M	Unknown	12Ma02Ef
WALL, John		18	M	Unknown	12Ma02Ef	CASEY, John		30	M	Unknown	12Ma02Ef
FINN, Michal		25	M	Unknown	12Ma02Ef	NOWLAN, Bridget		19	F	Unknown	12Ma02Ef
DARRY, Michal		22	M	Unknown	12Ma02Ef	HANCOCK, Mary		36	F	Unknown	12Ma02Ef
Cornelius		24	M	Unknown	12Ma02Ef	John	(S)	12	M	Unknown	12Ma02Ef
HARDMAN, Michal		18	M	Unknown	12Ma02Ef	James	(S)	08	M	Unknown	12Ma02Ef
BYRNES, Edwd.		20	M	Unknown	12Ma02Ef	Maria	(D)	06	F	Unknown	12Ma02Ef
SULLIVAN, David		21	M	Unknown	12Ma02Ef	Charles	(S)	04	M	Unknown	12Ma02Ef
SEXTON, David		30	M	Unknown	12Ma02Ef	Harriet	(D)	.00	F	Infant	12Ma02Ef
CURRAN, Patrick		25	M	Unknown	12Ma02Ef	COGAN, Joseph		26	M	Unknown	12Ma02Ef
BOGART, Dnl.		24	M	Unknown	12Ma02Ef	BEGLY, Daniel		30	M	Unknown	12Ma02Ef
MCGUIRE, John		22	M	Unknown	12Ma02Ef	CALLAGHAN, John		24	M	Unknown	12Ma02Ef
RATTIGAN, James		24	M	Unknown	12Ma02Ef	CONNOR, Thomas		32	M	Unknown	12Ma02Ef
Rose		21	F	Unknown	12Ma02Ef	KELLION, James		27	M	Unknown	12Ma02Ef
Anna		20	F	Unknown	12Ma02Ef	Cathrn.		25	F	Unknown	12Ma02Ef
CROFT, George		41	M	Unknown	12Ma02Ef	HEALY, Della		24	F	Unknown	12Ma02Ef
U	(W)	45	F	Unknown	12Ma02Ef	CARLEY, John		23	M	Unknown	12Ma02Ef
Wm.	(S)	19	M	Unknown	12Ma02Ef	James		22	M	Unknown	12Ma02Ef
Anne	(D)	13	F	Unknown	12Ma02Ef	FARMER, Edward		22	M	Unknown	12Ma02Ef
James	(S)	11	M	Unknown	12Ma02Ef	DOYLE, Archibald		35	M	Unknown	12Ma02Ef
John	(S)	07	M	Child	12Ma02Ef	MATHEW, John		21	M	Unknown	12Ma02Ef
Mary	(D)	06	F	Child	12Ma02Ef	MCCARROL, James		21	M	Unknown	12Ma02Ef
U	(D)	02	F	Child	12Ma02Ef	Rosey		20	F	Unknown	12Ma02Ef
U	(D)	.00	F	Infant	12Ma02Ef	MAGRATH, Francis		22	M	Unknown	12Ma02Ef
DANNILLON, James		25	M	Unknown	12Ma02Ef	Ann		20	F	Unknown	12Ma02Ef
NOLAN, Patt		20	M	Unknown	12Ma02Ef	Fanny		18	F	Unknown	12Ma02Ef
FERRY, Mary		19	F	Unknown	12Ma02Ef	BURN, Owen		30	M	Unknown	12Ma02Ef
MCQUAID, Ellen		20	F	Unknown	12Ma02Ef	KEARNY, Rose		18	F	Unknown	12Ma02Ef
LOVE, Mary		19	F	Unknown	12Ma02Ef	DONOHOE, Michael		26	M	Unknown	12Ma02Ef
FORREST, John		40	M	Unknown	12Ma02Ef	Judy		26	F	Unknown	12Ma02Ef
Nancy	(W)	40	F	Unknown	12Ma02Ef	GOULDING, Richard		24	M	Unknown	12Ma02Ef
Mary-Ann	(D)	22	F	Unknown	12Ma02Ef	Richd.		22	M	Unknown	12Ma02Ef
Robert	(S)	18	M	Unknown	12Ma02Ef	OLEARY, Joseph		28	M	Unknown	12Ma02Ef
Jane	(D)	16	F	Unknown	12Ma02Ef	NEVIN, Edward		28	M	Unknown	12Ma02Ef
MULLEN, John		22	M	Unknown	12Ma02Ef	RYAN, James		28	M	Unknown	12Ma02Ef
GALAGHER, Catharine		23	F	Unknown	12Ma02Ef	Mary		29	F	Unknown	12Ma02Ef
HENESY, Bridget		16	F	Unknown	12Ma02Ef	DALTON, Mary		23	F	Unknown	12Ma02Ef
MCDONALD, James		22	M	Unknown	12Ma02Ef	REGAN, Michal		18	M	Unknown	12Ma02Ef
MCCLUSKY, James		20	M	Unknown	12Ma02Ef	BLAKELY, Geo.		28	M	Unknown	12Ma02Ef
Nancy		23	F	Unknown	12Ma02Ef	Ann		18	F	Unknown	12Ma02Ef
John		22	M	Unknown	12Ma02Ef	BAXTER, Mary		19	F	Unknown	12Ma02Ef
Mary		.00	F	Infant	12Ma02Ef	JUDGE, Patt		20	M	Unknown	12Ma02Ef
MURPHY, Patt		28	M	Unknown	12Ma02Ef	COYNE, Biddy		20	F	Unknown	12Ma02Ef
KEATING, Mich.		20	M	Unknown	12Ma02Ef	BROWN, Mary		20	F	Unknown	12Ma02Ef
HOLAHAN, Michael		19	M	Unknown	12Ma02Ef	GOHAN, Peggy		20	F	Unknown	12Ma02Ef
DOHERTY, Wm.		24	M	Unknown	12Ma02Ef	TRACEY, Thomas		26	M	Unknown	12Ma02Ef
Catharine		20	F	Unknown	12Ma02Ef	Mary		60	F	Unknown	12Ma02Ef
ROACH, Johanah		20	F	Unknown	12Ma02Ef	HEATON, Mary		60	F	Unknown	12Ma02Ef
COLEMAN, Morris		24	M	Unknown	12Ma02Ef	Kerwin		30	M	Unknown	12Ma02Ef
FLYN, Mary-A.		21	F	Unknown	12Ma02Ef	Barney		16	M	Unknown	12Ma02Ef
COLEMAN, James		22	M	Unknown	12Ma02Ef	KELLY, Patt		28	M	Unknown	12Ma02Ef
CARSON, John		45	M	Unknown	12Ma02Ef	Bridget		19	F	Unknown	12Ma02Ef
Thomas	(S)	20	M	Unknown	12Ma02Ef	MOORE, Michal		34	M	Unknown	12Ma02Ef
Eliza-Ann	(D)	18	F	Unknown	12Ma02Ef	DOOLEY, Mary		20	F	Unknown	12Ma02Ef
Agness	(D)	16	F	Unknown	12Ma02Ef	ENGLISH, Catharine		24	F	Unknown	12Ma02Ef
John	(S)	13	M	Unknown	12Ma02Ef	FARINSH, Maria		24	F	Unknown	12Ma02Ef
Jane	(D)	09	F	Child	12Ma02Ef	Catharine		22	F	Unknown	12Ma02Ef
Elizabeth	(D)	07	F	Child	12Ma02Ef	MCDERMOTT, Maria		18	F	Unknown	12Ma02Ef

NAMES OF PASSENGERS		AGE	SEX	OCCUPATIONS	DATE PORT SHIP
HENRY, Elizabeth		22	F	Unknown	12Ma02Ef
MORGAN, Thomas		22	M	Unknown	12Ma02Ef
KEGAN, John		21	M	Unknown	12Ma02Ef
MORGAN, Cella		20	F	Unknown	12Ma02Ef
FLYN, Judy		19	F	Unknown	12Ma02Ef
BOYLAN, Cathrn.		20	F	Unknown	12Ma02Ef
HORAN, Wm.		23	M	Unknown	12Ma02Ef
MORRIS, John		20	M	Unknown	12Ma02Ef
CONDY, Winnifred		19	F	Unknown	12Ma02Ef
LAWLER, Thomas		23	M	Unknown	12Ma02Ef
Mary		23	F	Unknown	12Ma02Ef
DUNN, Ann		20	F	Unknown	12Ma02Ef
COSTELLO, James		25	M	Unknown	12Ma02Ef
MITCHEL, Thomas		27	M	Unknown	12Ma02Ef
SHANE, Michl.		19	M	Unknown	12Ma02Ef
Cathrn.		19	F	Unknown	12Ma02Ef
HALFPENNY, Michl.		18	M	Unknown	12Ma02Ef
MORAN, Arthur		26	M	Unknown	12Ma02Ef
Rose		20	F	Unknown	12Ma02Ef
Cathrn.		20	F	Unknown	12Ma02Ef
Elizabeth		23	F	Unknown	12Ma02Ef
HUGHES, Edward		33	M	Unknown	12Ma02Ef
Jane	(W)	21	F	Unknown	12Ma02Ef
Jane	(D)	.00	F	Infant	12Ma02Ef
HENERY, Jane		23	F	Unknown	12Ma02Ef
BRINAN, Patt		20	M	Unknown	12Ma02Ef
ONEIL, Jane		19	F	Unknown	12Ma02Ef
CONNOLLY, Francis		36	M	Unknown	12Ma02Ef
Sally	(W)	30	F	Unknown	12Ma02Ef
Mary	(D)	12	F	Unknown	12Ma02Ef
Peter	(S)	10	M	Unknown	12Ma02Ef
Joseph	(S)	06	M	Child	12Ma02Ef
Rose	(D)	.00	F	Infant	12Ma02Ef
MCCANN, Patt		30	M	Unknown	12Ma02Ef
CARR, Bessy		30	F	Unknown	12Ma02Ef
BARKEY, Catharin		16	F	Unknown	12Ma02Ef
MCCANNA, Rose		30	F	Unknown	12Ma02Ef
HUGHES, John		22	M	Unknown	12Ma02Ef
Mary		18	F	Unknown	12Ma02Ef
MACKLIN, Mary		20	F	Unknown	12Ma02Ef
Mary		18	F	Unknown	12Ma02Ef
CONNOLLY, Mary		19	F	Unknown	12Ma02Ef
FISHER, Mary		18	F	Unknown	12Ma02Ef
MCBRIDE, Edward		16	M	Unknown	12Ma02Ef
DUFFY, Mary		18	F	Unknown	12Ma02Ef
DONNOLLY, Owen		19	M	Unknown	12Ma02Ef
HUGHES, Mary-A.		19	F	Unknown	12Ma02Ef
COLE, Wm.		33	M	Unknown	12Ma02Ef
BRADY, Ann		40	F	Unknown	12Ma02Ef
Patt		28	M	Unknown	12Ma02Ef
Thomas		26	M	Unknown	12Ma02Ef
John		21	M	Unknown	12Ma02Ef
Mary		23	F	Unknown	12Ma02Ef
Biddy		18	F	Unknown	12Ma02Ef
Michael		12	M	Unknown	12Ma02Ef
Owen		11	M	Unknown	12Ma02Ef
LADY, Patt		24	M	Unknown	12Ma02Ef
KELLY, Mary		20	F	Unknown	12Ma02Ef
RALL, Patt		40	M	Unknown	12Ma02Ef
Mary	(D)	11	F	Unknown	12Ma02Ef
Phillip	(S)	09	M	Child	12Ma02Ef
Bridget	(D)	07	F	Child	12Ma02Ef
Thomas	(S)	05	M	Child	12Ma02Ef
James	(S)	03	M	Child	12Ma02Ef
GILL, Martin		25	M	Unknown	12Ma02Ef
Thomas		23	M	Unknown	12Ma02Ef
MCMAHON, Michal		32	M	Unknown	12Ma02Ef
Catharin	(W)	30	F	Unknown	12Ma02Ef
Patt	(S)	10	M	Unknown	12Ma02Ef
Jane	(D)	10	F	Unknown	12Ma02Ef
Ann	(D)	03	F	Child	12Ma02Ef
Catharin	(D)	.00	F	Infant	12Ma02Ef
FINNIGAN, Phillip		21	M	Unknown	12Ma02Ef
COLLINS, Bernard		28	M	Unknown	12Ma02Ef
DUFFY, Mary		22	F	Unknown	12Ma02Ef

NAMES OF PASSENGERS		AGE	SEX	OCCUPATIONS	DATE PORT SHIP
DUFFY, Catharin		19	F	Unknown	12Ma02Ef
Mary		22	F	Unknown	12Ma02Ef
CARROL, Mary		19	F	Unknown	12Ma02Ef
JONES, Maurice		20	M	Unknown	12Ma02Ef
EVANS, David		21	M	Unknown	12Ma02Ef
GOSS, Jane		18	F	Unknown	12Ma02Ef
LANE, Wm.		35	M	Unknown	12Ma02Ef
Ruth		25	F	Unknown	12Ma02Ef
Rushton		09	M	Child	12Ma02Ef
Ralf		07	M	Child	12Ma02Ef
Amelia		03	F	Child	12Ma02Ef
Sarah		.00	F	Infant	12Ma02Ef
REDFERN, John		20	M	Unknown	12Ma02Ef
MEDEWORTH, Mark		36	M	Unknown	12Ma02Ef
HARRIS, Morgan		20	M	Unknown	12Ma02Ef
CAMPBELL, Joseph		19	M	Unknown	12Ma02Ef
LEFFERMAN, Thomas		30	M	Unknown	12Ma02Ef
Ann		27	F	Unknown	12Ma02Ef
MCLAUGHLIN, Oawrence		18	M	Unknown	12Ma02Ef
Bridget		23	F	Unknown	12Ma02Ef
Mary		20	F	Unknown	12Ma02Ef
WATSON, Ann		21	F	Unknown	12Ma02Ef
CASEDY, Patt		19	M	Unknown	12Ma02Ef
FLANIGAN, Martin		04	M	Child	12Ma02Ef
WALDRON, Edward		25	M	Unknown	12Ma02Ef
Mary		22	F	Unknown	12Ma02Ef
HARLEY, James		21	M	Unknown	12Ma02Ef
STETSON, Thomas		25	M	Unknown	12Ma02Ef
MCGORMAN, Charles		28	M	Unknown	12Ma02Ef
John		13	M	Unknown	12Ma02Ef
PRIOR, John		30	M	Unknown	12Ma02Ef
TURNER, John		28	M	Unknown	12Ma02Ef
CANNON, Richard		12	M	Unknown	12Ma02Ef
FEE, James		08	M	Child	12Ma02Ef
BEATTY, Patt		30	M	Unknown	12Ma02Ef
Mary		12	F	Unknown	12Ma02Ef
QUIN, Mary		20	F	Unknown	12Ma02Ef
QUIGIN, Mary		22	F	Unknown	12Ma02Ef
WALLIN, Cath.		16	F	Unknown	12Ma02Ef
PLUMTREE, Thomas		39	M	Unknown	12Ma02Ef
Elizabeth		45	F	Unknown	12Ma02Ef
Susan		21	F	Unknown	12Ma02Ef
Ann		18	F	Unknown	12Ma02Ef
Charlotte		04	F	Child	12Ma02Ef
Joseph		03	M	Child	12Ma02Ef

JOHN-CLARK 14 MAY 1846

From Liverpool

NAMES OF PASSENGERS		AGE	SEX	OCCUPATIONS	DATE PORT SHIP
SHEILDS, Mary		40	F	Wife	14Ma02Eh
SHEEHEY, Edward		07	M	Child	14Ma02Eh
John	(B)	09	M	Child	14Ma02Eh
TENNIN, John		20	M	Laborer	14Ma02Eh
REARDON, John		22	M	Laborer	14Ma02Eh
FOLEY, Timothy		25	M	Laborer	14Ma02Eh
SCULLY, Michl.		30	M	Laborer	14Ma02Eh
Mark		25	M	Laborer	14Ma02Eh
Charles		.00	M	Infant	14Ma02Eh
MURPHY, Henna		20	F	Servant	14Ma02Eh
ROCHE, Margaret		20	F	Servant	14Ma02Eh
MURPHY, Daniel		15	M	Servant	14Ma02Eh
Henna		20	F	Servant	14Ma02Eh
KALACHY, Kelly		20	M	Servant	14Ma02Eh
WALCH, Mary		20	F	Servant	14Ma02Eh
DUGGAN, Timothy		25	M	Laborer	14Ma02Eh
RICKLEY, Pat		20	M	Laborer	14Ma02Eh
CANNON, Julia		18	F	Servant	14Ma02Eh
DUGGAN, Mary		50	F	Servant	14Ma02Eh

NAMES OF PASSENGERS		AGE	SEX	OCCUPATIONS	DATE PORT SHIP
WARD, James		05	M	Child	14Ma02Eh
HARRINGTON, Tinney		24	U	Servant	14Ma02Eh
FITZGERALD, Alice		20	F	Servant	14Ma02Eh
SHANAHAN, John		43	M	Laborer	14Ma02Eh
MCFARLAND, Saml.		20	M	Laborer	14Ma02Eh
FATE, William		35	M	Laborer	14Ma02Eh
BELL, George		25	M	Laborer	14Ma02Eh
MCCORMICK, Michl.		25	M	Laborer	14Ma02Eh
GIVEN, John-D.		30	M	Laborer	14Ma02Eh
DUGGAN, Mary		30	F	Laborer	14Ma02Eh
WARD, Jas.		05	M	Child	14Ma02Eh
GALLAGHER, Bridget		19	F	Servant	14Ma02Eh
GOODWIN, Jas.		18	M	Servant	14Ma02Eh
Robt.		18	M	Servant	14Ma02Eh
Rose		20	M	Servant	14Ma02Eh
AICHER, U		42	M	Laborer	14Ma02Eh
DALEY, Pat		19	M	Laborer	14Ma02Eh
COSTELLO, Martin		28	M	Laborer	14Ma02Eh
DOUGHLIN, Pat		22	M	Laborer	14Ma02Eh
DONNELLY, Peggy		23	F	Servant	14Ma02Eh
BOYLAN, Mary		18	F	Servant	14Ma02Eh
KEAN, John		25	M	Laborer	14Ma02Eh
Cathe.		19	F	Servant	14Ma02Eh
BRENNAN, John		30	M	Servant	14Ma02Eh
GILMARTIN, Wm.		28	M	Servant	14Ma02Eh
KEAN, Biddy		18	F	Servant	14Ma02Eh
HEALY, Jas.		20	M	Laborer	14Ma02Eh
DANDERELETT, Pat		23	M	Laborer	14Ma02Eh
Margaret		18	F	Servant	14Ma02Eh
NUGENT, Ann		18	F	Servant	14Ma02Eh
CANNON, Michl.		28	M	Laborer	14Ma02Eh
MCBRIDE, Connel		18	M	Laborer	14Ma02Eh
GREEN, Hugh		22	M	Laborer	14Ma02Eh
GLASSY, James		23	M	Laborer	14Ma02Eh
HALL, John		18	M	Laborer	14Ma02Eh
Rachel		59	F	Servant	14Ma02Eh
Rachel		20	F	Servant	14Ma02Eh
MCVEIGH, Henry		20	M	Laborer	14Ma02Eh
FALONER, James		24	M	Laborer	14Ma02Eh
MOHER, John		22	M	Laborer	14Ma02Eh
DWYER, Pat		22	M	Laborer	14Ma02Eh
BOLGEN, Jas.		22	M	Laborer	14Ma02Eh
SHANAHAN, Timothy		26	M	Laborer	14Ma02Eh
DEVLIN, John		20	M	Laborer	14Ma02Eh
Bridget	(W)	21	F	Wife	14Ma02Eh
MARLIN, Pat		20	M	Laborer	14Ma02Eh
CASSEDY, Peggy		20	F	Servant	14Ma02Eh
HENRY, Simon		23	M	Servant	14Ma02Eh
MASTERSON, Margaret		30	F	Servant	14Ma02Eh
BRANIFF, Danl.		20	M	Laborer	14Ma02Eh
HIGGINS, Michl.		23	M	Laborer	14Ma02Eh
Bridget	(W)	20	F	Wife	14Ma02Eh
TAYLER, James		25	M	Laborer	14Ma02Eh
Catherin	(W)	26	F	Wife	14Ma02Eh
MCADAM, Cath.		22	F	Servant	14Ma02Eh
Mary		21	F	Servant	14Ma02Eh
CURRAN, Cathrn.		18	F	Servant	14Ma02Eh
OATES, James		25	M	Laborer	14Ma02Eh
DAILEY, John		20	F	Laborer	14Ma02Eh
DONOHUE, Michl.		30	M	Laborer	14Ma02Eh
FEIGHEY, John		23	M	Laborer	14Ma02Eh
Catherin		26	F	Servant	14Ma02Eh
TENNIEN, Mary		20	F	Servant	14Ma02Eh
SULLIVAN, Timothy		22	M	Laborer	14Ma02Eh
Danl.		40	M	Laborer	14Ma02Eh
CROONAN, Pat		11	M	Unknown	14Ma02Eh
Margaret		20	F	Laborer	14Ma02Eh
FIELDS, Richd.		18	M	Laborer	14Ma02Eh
Jane		34	F	Unknown	14Ma02Eh
Samuel	(B)	13	M	Unknown	14Ma02Eh
Thomas	(B)	12	M	Unknown	14Ma02Eh
Alexr.	(B)	09	M	Child	14Ma02Eh
Isabella	(T)	04	F	Child	14Ma02Eh
William	(B)	15	M	Unknown	14Ma02Eh
MCLEAN, Ana		20	F	Servant	14Ma02Eh
MCLEAN, Susan		21	F	Servant	14Ma02Eh
MCCULLEN, Mary		19	F	Servant	14Ma02Eh
FLANAGHAN, Ally		14	F	Servant	14Ma02Eh
CARROLL, May		30	F	Servant	14Ma02Eh
John	(S)	06	M	Child	14Ma02Eh
James	(S)	03	M	Child	14Ma02Eh
Richd.	(S)	.00	M	Infant	14Ma02Eh
MCCANEN, Hugh		22	M	Servant	14Ma02Eh
DUFFY, Ann		20	F	Servant	14Ma02Eh
RILY, Ellen		20	F	Servant	14Ma02Eh
CONNALY, Ann		29	F	Servant	14Ma02Eh
Mary		18	F	Servant	14Ma02Eh
DUGAN, Jeremiah		15	M	Laborer	14Ma02Eh
Cornelius		10	M	Unknown	14Ma02Eh
John		09	M	Child	14Ma02Eh
John		20	M	Laborer	14Ma02Eh
May		17	F	Laborer	14Ma02Eh
KELLY, Thomas		25	M	Laborer	14Ma02Eh
DRADY, Jane		.00	F	Infant	14Ma02Eh
Maria		22	F	Servant	14Ma02Eh
KENNEDY, Owen		32	M	Laborer	14Ma02Eh
CONLON, Bidy		22	F	Servant	14Ma02Eh
CONLEN, Pat		20	M	Laborer	14Ma02Eh
MERROW, Pat		25	M	Laborer	14Ma02Eh
William		21	M	Laborer	14Ma02Eh
LEROHAN, Bridget		20	F	Servant	14Ma02Eh
FLINN, Ann		20	F	Servant	14Ma02Eh
GOOD, Hannah		20	F	Servant	14Ma02Eh
FLANAGAN, Owen		18	M	Servant	14Ma02Eh
HORN, David		25	M	Servant	14Ma02Eh
Eliza		18	F	Servant	14Ma02Eh
WHITNEY, Bridget		06	F	Child	14Ma02Eh
Ann		08	F	Child	14Ma02Eh
QUIN, Phelim		20	M	Servant	14Ma02Eh
Ann		15	F	Servant	14Ma02Eh
TOOHILL, Rose		20	F	Servant	14Ma02Eh
WREN, Mary		20	F	Servant	14Ma02Eh
RYAN, Pat		40	M	Laborer	14Ma02Eh
Cathn.	(W)	40	F	Wife	14Ma02Eh
Catherin	(D)	11	F	Unknown	14Ma02Eh
FLANAGAN, Mary		10	F	Unknown	14Ma02Eh
LAVERTY, Simon		13	M	Laborer	14Ma02Eh
BIRMINGHAM, W.		10	M	Unknown	14Ma02Eh
U	(M)	36	F	Unknown	14Ma02Eh
William	(B)	07	M	Child	14Ma02Eh
Martin	(B)	05	M	Child	14Ma02Eh
Daniel	(B)	03	M	Child	14Ma02Eh
Thomas	(B)	.00	M	Infant	14Ma02Eh
Bridget		11	F	Unknown	14Ma02Eh
Michael		18	M	Unknown	14Ma02Eh
GILES, David		25	M	Laborer	14Ma02Eh
Geo.		20	M	Unknown	14Ma02Eh
Margaret		20	F	Unknown	14Ma02Eh
CARMICAN, Pat		25	M	Laborer	14Ma02Eh
COSTELLO, Thos.		20	M	Laborer	14Ma02Eh
FARRELL, Peter		20	M	Laborer	14Ma02Eh
PARDY, John		20	M	Laborer	14Ma02Eh
WALLACE, Henry		20	M	Laborer	14Ma02Eh
WALCH, Michl.		25	M	Laborer	14Ma02Eh
GREEN, Pat		20	M	Laborer	14Ma02Eh
COSTELLO, Danl.		20	M	Laborer	14Ma02Eh
KELLY, Mary		20	F	Servant	14Ma02Eh
CODY, Martha		20	F	Servant	14Ma02Eh
FEHAN, Bridget		20	F	Servant	14Ma02Eh
MCALTOY, John		25	M	Servant	14Ma02Eh
GRADY, John		25	M	Laborer	14Ma02Eh
U	(W)	20	F	Wife	14Ma02Eh
Pat	(S)	.00	M	Infant	14Ma02Eh
CARROL, Pat		25	M	Laborer	14Ma02Eh
MCCANNES, Catherine		18	F	Servant	14Ma02Eh
DAVIDSON, Mary		21	F	Servant	14Ma02Eh
Catherine		26	F	Servant	14Ma02Eh
CRAVEN, Pat		20	M	Servant	14Ma02Eh
WALES, Margret		18	F	Servant	14Ma02Eh
CHURCH, John		40	M	Laborer	14Ma02Eh

NAMES OF PASSENGERS		AGE	SEX	OCCUPATIONS	DATE PORT SHIP
CRASSY, Joseph		25	M	Laborer	14Ma02Eh
RAFFERTY, John		35	M	Laborer	14Ma02Eh
Mary	(W)	30	F	Wife	14Ma02Eh
DOOLEY, Catherin		18	F	Servant	14Ma02Eh
CROSSY, Cathrn.		20	F	Servant	14Ma02Eh
BELL, Margaret		36	F	Wife	14Ma02Eh
Eliza	(D)	12	F	Unknown	14Ma02Eh
Mary	(D)	12	F	Unknown	14Ma02Eh
William	(S)	11	M	Unknown	14Ma02Eh
John	(S)	08	M	Child	14Ma02Eh
Jane	(D)	05	F	Child	14Ma02Eh
Margaret	(D)	.00	F	Infant	14Ma02Eh
HUGHES, Eduard		20	M	Laborer	14Ma02Eh
MCBENNETT, Michl.		20	M	Laborer	14Ma02Eh
DOWNES, Michl.		28	M	Laborer	14Ma02Eh
FORE, Mary		30	F	Servant	14Ma02Eh
MURRAY, Ellen		34	F	Servant	14Ma02Eh
John		23	M	Servant	14Ma02Eh
KEARNS, Mary		19	F	Servant	14Ma02Eh
BAMBRICK, John		23	M	Laborer	14Ma02Eh
BROWN, John		23	M	Laborer	14Ma02Eh
TIERNEY, Mary		06	F	Child	14Ma02Eh
HURLEY, Stephen		24	M	Laborer	14Ma02Eh
HAGAN, Thomas		30	M	Laborer	14Ma02Eh
HANNEY, James		20	M	Laborer	14Ma02Eh
WALKER, Mary		12	F	Servant	14Ma02Eh
ROOKE, Cathn.		25	F	Servant	14Ma02Eh
GORE, Cathrn.		24	F	Servant	14Ma02Eh
MURPHY, Mary		05	F	Child	14Ma02Eh
FLEMMING, H.		22	F	Servant	14Ma02Eh
LANGTON, James		22	M	Servant	14Ma02Eh
CONNOR, Rose		19	F	Servant	14Ma02Eh
MANGEN, Mary		16	F	Servant	14Ma02Eh
DALY, Ann		30	F	Servant	14Ma02Eh
Ann		08	F	Child	14Ma02Eh
Margaret		.00	F	Infant	14Ma02Eh
DELLARD, Mary		20	F	Servant	14Ma02Eh
DOWNES, Pat		20	M	Servant	14Ma02Eh
Ann		18	F	Servant	14Ma02Eh
EGAN, Michl.		25	M	Servant	14Ma02Eh
Peter		20	M	Servant	14Ma02Eh
BRESLIN, Mathew		20	M	Servant	14Ma02Eh
Ann		11	F	Unknown	14Ma02Eh
WALKER, Hannah		18	F	Laborer	14Ma02Eh
Ann		18	F	Servant	14Ma02Eh
BEALEY, Thomas		22	M	Laborer	14Ma02Eh
FURLEY, Joseph		20	M	Laborer	14Ma02Eh
YOUNGHALL, Thomas		30	M	Laborer	14Ma02Eh
MCINTOSH, William		40	M	Laborer	14Ma02Eh
Wm.		26	M	Laborer	14Ma02Eh
Margaret		40	F	Laborer	14Ma02Eh
Margaret		20	F	Laborer	14Ma02Eh
DOHERTY, Bridget		20	F	Servant	14Ma02Eh
RILEY, Cathn.		13	F	Servant	14Ma02Eh
TWEED, Eliza		30	F	Servant	14Ma02Eh
MCAFEE, May		42	F	Servant	14Ma02Eh
Mary		14	F	Servant	14Ma02Eh
HALL, Charles		25	M	Servant	14Ma02Eh
GILL, Ann		21	F	Servant	14Ma02Eh
Michael		19	M	Servant	14Ma02Eh
DOYLE, James		32	M	Servant	14Ma02Eh
Bridget	(W)	28	F	Servant	14Ma02Eh
John	(S)	.00	M	Infant	14Ma02Eh
Hugh	(S)	.00	M	Infant	14Ma02Eh
MULLAN, Mathias		20	M	Laborer	14Ma02Eh
KELLY, Mary		20	F	Servant	14Ma02Eh
FARREL, Jenny		26	F	Servant	14Ma02Eh
PRIOR, Rose		20	F	Servant	14Ma02Eh
HEROHAN, Bridget		18	F	Servant	14Ma02Eh
MCCAGNE, John		27	M	Servant	14Ma02Eh
MCNALLY, Margy.		22	F	Servant	14Ma02Eh
MULLEN, Mary		22	F	Servant	14Ma02Eh
BARTLETT, John		25	M	Laborer	14Ma02Eh
SMITH, Dennis		00	M	Laborer	14Ma02Eh
MCGEE, James		26	M	Laborer	14Ma02Eh
MCCROCK, Charly		26	M	Laborer	14Ma02Eh
Margaret		22	F	Servant	14Ma02Eh
RIDGE, Fergus		20	M	Laborer	14Ma02Eh
MCCARTHER, Thomas		20	M	Laborer	14Ma02Eh
Pat		27	M	Laborer	14Ma02Eh
GILL, Ben		22	M	Laborer	14Ma02Eh
WHEELEN, Mary		23	F	Servant	14Ma02Eh
HYNES, Bridget		17	F	Servant	14Ma02Eh
BRIGHT, Daniel		20	M	Servant	14Ma02Eh
MULLEN, Pat		27	M	Servant	14Ma02Eh
WALL, Cathn.		20	F	Servant	14Ma02Eh
FARRELL, Dara		20	M	Laborer	14Ma02Eh
MCCOONEY, Bernd.		27	M	Laborer	14Ma02Eh
ONEILL, Owen		27	M	Laborer	14Ma02Eh
GRECIAN, John		20	M	Laborer	14Ma02Eh
JACKSON, Wm.		20	M	Laborer	14Ma02Eh
DELACY, Wm.		28	M	Laborer	14Ma02Eh
MOORE, Paul		21	M	Laborer	14Ma02Eh
CARROLL, Ellen		18	F	Servant	14Ma02Eh
MURPHY, Peter		20	M	Servant	14Ma02Eh
Ann		18	F	Servant	14Ma02Eh
MOORE, Morris		20	M	Laborer	14Ma02Eh
HELERTY, Hey		17	U	Laborer	14Ma02Eh
COXE, Thos.		20	M	Laborer	14Ma02Eh
John		28	M	Laborer	14Ma02Eh
DALY, Honora		30	F	Servant	14Ma02Eh
BENNETT, Ann		18	F	Servant	14Ma02Eh
CONEGALL, Mary		22	F	Servant	14Ma02Eh
MILLER, Jane		40	F	Servant	14Ma02Eh
Elizabeth		20	F	Servant	14Ma02Eh
FAULKNER, Mary		30	F	Servant	14Ma02Eh
Wm.		26	M	Servant	14Ma02Eh
Elizabeth		24	F	Servant	14Ma02Eh
CAHILL, Daniel		12	M	Laborer	14Ma02Eh
HUNTER, Saml.		20	M	Laborer	14Ma02Eh
Jane		21	F	Laborer	14Ma02Eh
MCDERMOTT, Mathew		28	M	Laborer	14Ma02Eh
DIVER, Pat		21	M	Laborer	14Ma02Eh
Michl.		26	M	Laborer	14Ma02Eh
Martin		22	M	Laborer	14Ma02Eh
DONOHUE, J.		11	M	Unknown	14Ma02Eh
ONEILL, Danl.		18	M	Laborer	14Ma02Eh
Mary		15	F	Servant	14Ma02Eh
WHELAN, Pat		26	M	Servant	14Ma02Eh
WABAH, Jane		21	F	Servant	14Ma02Eh
POWERS, Jane		24	F	Servant	14Ma02Eh
WELCH, Lena		21	F	Servant	14Ma02Eh
RYAN, Nancy		22	F	Servant	14Ma02Eh
WELCH, James		.00	M	Infant	14Ma02Eh
Pat		14	M	Unknown	14Ma02Eh
Ephraim		18	M	Unknown	14Ma02Eh
Jane		20	F	Unknown	14Ma02Eh
DAWSON, Michl.		26	M	Laborer	14Ma02Eh
COXE, Thomas		25	M	Laborer	14Ma02Eh
Peter		24	M	Laborer	14Ma02Eh
CALEN, Peter		16	M	Laborer	14Ma02Eh
RAFFERTY, Danl.		17	M	Laborer	14Ma02Eh
Margaret		18	F	Servant	14Ma02Eh
MITCHELL, Hanna		19	F	Servant	14Ma02Eh
WARD, Cathn.		21	F	Servant	14Ma02Eh
SWIFT, John		18	M	Laborer	14Ma02Eh
GOREN, Edwd.		20	M	Laborer	14Ma02Eh
MURPHY, John		20	M	Laborer	14Ma02Eh
WILLEN, Henry		28	M	Laborer	14Ma02Eh
MCCULLOUGH, Mary		18	F	Laborer	14Ma02Eh
Mary		20	F	Laborer	14Ma02Eh
WILLIAMS, Ellen		19	F	Laborer	14Ma02Eh

ARABELLA 14 MAY 1846

From Liverpool

NAMES OF PASSENGERS	AGE	SEX	OCCUPATIONS	DATE PORT SHIP
FARRELL, James	22	M	Laborer	14Ma02EI
CUGAN, Honora	19	F	Servant	14Ma02EI
MARTIN, Peter	20	M	Laborer	14Ma02EI
DUFFY, Peter	26	M	Laborer	14Ma02EI
BURKE, Ellen	16	F	Laborer	14Ma02EI
COX, Ann	20	F	Laborer	14Ma02EI
CAHILL, Paddy	70	M	Laborer	14Ma02EI
Ellen	27	F	Laborer	14Ma02EI
Bridget	21	F	Laborer	14Ma02EI
POLAND, Catherine	20	F	Laborer	14Ma02EI
CARGILL, James	70	M	Farmer	14Ma02EI
Isabella	37	F	Farmer	14Ma02EI
William	20	M	Farmer	14Ma02EI
Henry	17	M	Farmer	14Ma02EI
James	12	M	Farmer	14Ma02EI
Hugh	.00	M	Infant	14Ma02EI
Matty	18	M	Farmer	14Ma02EI
Mary-Jane	16	F	Farmer	14Ma02EI
Elizabeth	10	F	Farmer	14Ma02EI
HEANEY, Jane	25	F	Farmer	14Ma02EI
CAMPBELL, Mary	20	F	Farmer	14Ma02EI
RICE, Isabella	26	F	Farmer	14Ma02EI
Robert	20	M	Farmer	14Ma02EI
Sarah-Ann (D)	.00	F	Infant	14Ma02EI
LLOYD, U	25	M	Laborer	14Ma02EI
U (W)	20	F	Laborer	14Ma02EI
Francis (S)	06	M	Child	14Ma02EI
HOPKIN, Mary-Ann	20	F	Unknown	14Ma02EI
John (S)	02	M	Child	14Ma02EI
Died-At-Sea				
JONES, Henry	25	M	Farmer	14Ma02EI
William (S)	02	M	Child	14Ma02EI
Henry (S)	.00	M	Infant	14Ma02EI
U (W)	25	F	Wife	14Ma02EI
DONAHUE, William	26	M	Farmer	14Ma02EI
MANSON, Thomas	20	M	Laborer	14Ma02EI
Richard	23	M	Laborer	14Ma02EI
Margaret	26	F	Laborer	14Ma02EI
Bartley	20	M	Laborer	14Ma02EI
ENGLISH, Peggy	24	F	Laborer	14Ma02EI
PRENDERGRAST, John	30	M	Laborer	14Ma02EI
ARGUS, Robert	30	M	Laborer	14Ma02EI
HAGGERTY, John	22	M	Laborer	14Ma02EI
Patrick	20	M	Laborer	14Ma02EI
TRACY, Timothy	22	M	Laborer	14Ma02EI
MURRAY, Peter	25	M	Laborer	14Ma02EI
GILLON, Mary	20	F	Laborer	14Ma02EI
CLARK, Hugh	20	M	Laborer	14Ma02EI
REILLY, Margaret	20	F	Laborer	14Ma02EI
SEXTON, Bridget	20	F	Laborer	14Ma02EI
COONEY, Dafney	21	M	Laborer	14Ma02EI
Mary	13	F	Laborer	14Ma02EI
SMITH, Ann	18	F	Laborer	14Ma02EI
LOFTUS, Patrick	30	M	Laborer	14Ma02EI
FLAHERTY, Mary	30	F	Laborer	14Ma02EI
DOOHAN, Anthony	30	M	Laborer	14Ma02EI
LOFTUS, Daniel	30	M	Laborer	14Ma02EI
LANGAN, Sarah	25	F	Laborer	14Ma02EI
CLASKY, Nancy	28	F	Servant	14Ma02EI
LINSKY, Patrick	36	M	Laborer	14Ma02EI
CRAIG, Edward	20	M	Laborer	14Ma02EI
MCANDER, James	30	M	Laborer	14Ma02EI
Died-At-Sea				
MURPHY, Thomas	20	M	Laborer	14Ma02EI
MCANDER, Patrick	20	M	Laborer	14Ma02EI

NAMES OF PASSENGERS	AGE	SEX	OCCUPATIONS	DATE PORT SHIP
FITZPATRICK, James	28	M	Laborer	14Ma02EI
BALL, Simeon	24	M	Laborer	14Ma02EI
COLTON, John	24	M	Laborer	14Ma02EI
MCGUIRE, Richard	24	M	Laborer	14Ma02EI
BOLD, Arthur	24	M	Laborer	14Ma02EI
DONAHUE, John	20	M	Laborer	14Ma02EI
Margaret	20	F	Laborer	14Ma02EI
Bridget	18	F	Laborer	14Ma02EI
Died-At-Sea				
Ann	13	F	Laborer	14Ma02EI
ROURKE, Biddy	20	F	Laborer	14Ma02EI
MCBRIEN, Judy	18	F	Laborer	14Ma02EI
GALLAHON, Thomas	22	M	Laborer	14Ma02EI
HARGRAVE, Edward	20	M	Laborer	14Ma02EI
DOWD, John	20	M	Laborer	14Ma02EI
Bridget	20	F	Laborer	14Ma02EI
COYLE, Rose	20	F	Laborer	14Ma02EI
Mary	18	F	Laborer	14Ma02EI
MCGUIRE, Phillip	23	M	Laborer	14Ma02EI
HARMON, Thomas	25	M	Laborer	14Ma02EI
CALLAHAN, Mathew	17	M	Laborer	14Ma02EI
JOHNSON, James	25	M	Laborer	14Ma02EI
FINNAGAN, Margaret	20	F	Laborer	14Ma02EI
FERGUSON, Samuel	22	M	Farmer	14Ma02EI
Joseph	25	M	Farmer	14Ma02EI
Mary	19	F	Farmer	14Ma02EI
BROWN, John	20	M	Laborer	14Ma02EI
Mary (W)	20	F	Laborer	14Ma02EI
Thomas (S)	02	M	Child	14Ma02EI
William (S)	.00	M	Infant	14Ma02EI
CARLISLE, Edward	23	M	Laborer	14Ma02EI
MCCUE, John	25	M	Laborer	14Ma02EI
BLIGH, John	32	M	Laborer	14Ma02EI
SWEENEY, Ann	22	F	Laborer	14Ma02EI
CONNOR, Margaret	20	F	Laborer	14Ma02EI
MCCALL, Betty	20	F	Laborer	14Ma02EI
GRUNNERTY, Catherine	30	F	Laborer	14Ma02EI
DUFFY, Sylvester	30	M	Laborer	14Ma02EI
CALLON, William	18	M	Laborer	14Ma02EI
REILLY, James	26	M	Laborer	14Ma02EI
Ann	20	F	Laborer	14Ma02EI
GORDON, Biddy	26	F	Laborer	14Ma02EI
DONOHUE, Ann	20	F	Laborer	14Ma02EI
DONNELL, Isaket	20	M	Laborer	14Ma02EI
U (W)	20	F	Laborer	14Ma02EI
LAWLER, John	64	M	Laborer	14Ma02EI
Ann (W)	54	F	Laborer	14Ma02EI
William (S)	22	M	Laborer	14Ma02EI
Anty. (S)	22	M	Laborer	14Ma02EI
Bridget (D)	16	F	Laborer	14Ma02EI
MAHER, Mary	34	F	Laborer	14Ma02EI
BULGER, Larin	24	M	Laborer	14Ma02EI
MCCABE, John	18	M	Laborer	14Ma02EI
MCAVERY, Thomas	35	M	Laborer	14Ma02EI
U (W)	28	F	Laborer	14Ma02EI
James (S)	07	M	Laborer	14Ma02EI
STRAM, Bridget-L.	25	F	Laborer	14Ma02EI
Catherine	20	F	Laborer	14Ma02EI
NALLY, Margaret	18	F	Laborer	14Ma02EI
QUILT, Bessy	18	F	Laborer	14Ma02EI
FLOYD, Cornelius	20	M	Laborer	14Ma02EI
BURKE, Mary	18	F	Laborer	14Ma02EI
DUNN, Patrick	24	M	Laborer	14Ma02EI
Margaret	21	F	Laborer	14Ma02EI
GEGAN, Michael	25	M	Laborer	14Ma02EI
FLOWN, Mathew	19	M	Laborer	14Ma02EI
WHELAN, Dolly	20	F	Laborer	14Ma02EI
GEGAN, Mary	20	F	Laborer	14Ma02EI
Mary (D)	.00	F	Infant	14Ma02EI
MANGHAN, Patrick	20	M	Laborer	14Ma02EI
RYAN, Michael	20	M	Laborer	14Ma02EI
DAUGHENY, Ellen	21	F	Laborer	14Ma02EI
CONNELL, Bridget	20	F	Laborer	14Ma02EI
MULLAWLEY, Owen	20	M	Laborer	14Ma02EI
Bridget	20	F	Laborer	14Ma02EI

NAMES OF PASSENGERS	AGE	SEX	OCCUPATIONS	DATE PORT SHIP	NAMES OF PASSENGERS	AGE	SEX	OCCUPATIONS	DATE PORT SHIP
CARROLL, Patrick	22	M	Laborer	14Ma02EI	CAFFREY, Owen	16	M	Laborer	14Ma02EI
MCDONNELL, John	18	M	Laborer	14Ma02EI	KENNEDY, John	20	M	Laborer	14Ma02EI
DAVIS, Mark	20	M	Laborer	14Ma02EI	Margaret (W)	20	F	Laborer	14Ma02EI
DUPRE, Isaac	20	M	Laborer	14Ma02EI	Bridget (D)	.00	F	Infant	14Ma02EI
WARD, James	24	M	Laborer	14Ma02EI	BRINE, Mary	20	F	Laborer	14Ma02EI
KELLY, John	24	M	Laborer	14Ma02EI	MALALAND, James	20	M	Laborer	14Ma02EI
CARBARY, Thomas	20	M	Laborer	14Ma02EI	DOWNS, Louis	21	M	Laborer	14Ma02EI
HINCHY, John	20	M	Laborer	14Ma02EI	Mary	17	F	Laborer	14Ma02EI
COLEMAN, Michael	20	M	Laborer	14Ma02EI	DOWNEY, John	30	M	Laborer	14Ma02EI
CARROLL, William	29	M	Laborer	14Ma02EI	Michael	20	M	Laborer	14Ma02EI
BOLAND, Catherine	20	F	Laborer	14Ma02EI	Sally	30	F	Laborer	14Ma02EI
MINTHA, Ann	20	F	Laborer	14Ma02EI	CAFFERY, Sarah	25	F	Laborer	14Ma02EI
MCLOUGHLIN, John	25	M	Laborer	14Ma02EI	CONNOR, John	27	M	Laborer	14Ma02EI
Timothy	25	M	Laborer	14Ma02EI	Died-At-Sea				
POLAND, James	26	M	Laborer	14Ma02EI	CAFFERTY, Patrick	25	M	Laborer	14Ma02EI
BRACKEN, Dennis	24	M	Laborer	14Ma02EI	METCALF, Francis	20	M	Laborer	14Ma02EI
FLYNN, Mary	20	F	Laborer	14Ma02EI	REILLY, James	23	M	Laborer	14Ma02EI
CORLEY, Patrick	24	M	Laborer	14Ma02EI	KEENAN, Francis	20	M	Laborer	14Ma02EI
RODGERS, James	30	M	Laborer	14Ma02EI	MURRAY, Michael	28	M	Laborer	14Ma02EI
CURLEY, Patrick	20	M	Laborer	14Ma02EI	HUEY, David	24	M	Laborer	14Ma02EI
CLELAND, James	23	M	Laborer	14Ma02EI	DENISINORE, Samuel	23	M	Laborer	14Ma02EI
GAFFEY, William	12	M	Laborer	14Ma02EI	GILMORE, James	18	M	Laborer	14Ma02EI
MCKEON, Michl.	24	M	Laborer	14Ma02EI	ROSS, Andy	20	M	Laborer	14Ma02EI
MURRAY, Michl.	20	M	Laborer	14Ma02EI	JOHNSON, William	18	M	Laborer	14Ma02EI
KEARNS, Mary	20	F	Laborer	14Ma02EI	DAVIS, Sarah	21	F	Laborer	14Ma02EI
MORRIS, Mary	20	F	Servant	14Ma02EI	DOHERTY, William	22	M	Laborer	14Ma02EI
Margaret	20	F	Servant	14Ma02EI	REILLY, Biddy	20	F	Laborer	14Ma02EI
MCKUSKER, Elizabeth	20	F	Servant	14Ma02EI	DENNISON, Catherine	20	F	Laborer	14Ma02EI
Catherine	20	F	Servant	14Ma02EI	Mary	20	F	Laborer	14Ma02EI
LAWLER, Patrick	40	M	Laborer	14Ma02EI	MGIORNEY, James	20	M	Laborer	14Ma02EI
U (W)	35	F	Laborer	14Ma02EI	BRADY, Hugh	20	M	Laborer	14Ma02EI
KENNY, Margaret	25	F	Laborer	14Ma02EI	HART, Patrick	20	M	Laborer	14Ma02EI
LAWLER, Joseph	.00	M	Infant	14Ma02EI	MCGUIRE, Mary	20	F	Laborer	14Ma02EI
FALLON, John	19	M	Laborer	14Ma02EI	LINSKY, James	20	M	Laborer	14Ma02EI
SMITH, Peter	19	M	Laborer	14Ma02EI	Bridget	20	F	Laborer	14Ma02EI
RYAN, Ann	20	F	Laborer	14Ma02EI	OLIVER, Patrick	04	M	Child	14Ma02EI
MCMANUS, Owen	26	M	Laborer	14Ma02EI	GALLAHER, Thomas	06	M	Child	14Ma02EI
MCCABE, Michael	21	M	Laborer	14Ma02EI	GILLISPIE, Sarah	.00	F	Infant	14Ma02EI
GAHEN, Margaret	25	F	Laborer	14Ma02EI	MCGUIRE, James	20	M	Laborer	14Ma02EI
MONOHAN, Michael	33	M	Laborer	14Ma02EI	MORAN, Patrick	20	M	Laborer	14Ma02EI
SHAW, Patrick	28	M	Laborer	14Ma02EI	Christy	20	M	Laborer	14Ma02EI
TYGHE, Danl.	23	M	Laborer	14Ma02EI	REILLY, John	20	M	Laborer	14Ma02EI
ELLIOTT, John	40	M	Laborer	14Ma02EI	MURPHY, Barney	20	M	Laborer	14Ma02EI
MILLS, Bridget	13	F	Laborer	14Ma02EI	CURTIS, James	20	M	Laborer	14Ma02EI
FENNAUGHTY, Thomas	25	M	Laborer	14Ma02EI	SIMONS, Patrick	20	M	Laborer	14Ma02EI
MALONE, Mary	20	F	Laborer	14Ma02EI	LONDIGAN, Mary	20	F	Laborer	14Ma02EI
MURRAY, Phillip	20	M	Laborer	14Ma02EI	HINCH, John	20	M	Laborer	14Ma02EI
SMITH, John	20	M	Laborer	14Ma02EI	MCDERMOTT, Ann	25	F	Laborer	14Ma02EI
MCQUADE, Patrick	20	M	Laborer	14Ma02EI	BRADLEY, Edward	20	M	Laborer	14Ma02EI
SMITH, Ellen	20	F	Laborer	14Ma02EI	TUMERSEY, Edward	35	M	Laborer	14Ma02EI
MCPHILLIPS, Nelly	20	F	Laborer	14Ma02EI	MCGUINESS, Jane	23	F	Laborer	14Ma02EI
MCLEAKY, Catherine	20	F	Laborer	14Ma02EI	FLYNN, Andrew	30	M	Laborer	14Ma02EI
PROCTOR, Mary-Ann	20	F	Laborer	14Ma02EI	MUMFORD, Jane	20	F	Laborer	14Ma02EI
PLEXINE, Bridget	20	F	Laborer	14Ma02EI	FARELL, Edward	20	M	Laborer	14Ma02EI
MCGARVEY, Brian	20	M	Laborer	14Ma02EI	MARTIN, Bartho.	25	M	Laborer	14Ma02EI
KELLY, Thomas	20	M	Laborer	14Ma02EI					
Mary	20	F	Laborer	14Ma02EI					
SMITH, Lavinia	20	F	Laborer	14Ma02EI					
MITCHELL, Brian	20	M	Laborer	14Ma02EI					
SAVAGE, Mary	20	F	Laborer	14Ma02EI					
Bridget	20	F	Laborer	14Ma02EI	**MONTEZUMA 15 MAY 1846**				
KINSELLER, Bridget	20	F	Laborer	14Ma02EI					
CASSIDY, Patrick	20	M	Laborer	14Ma02EI	From Liverpool				
KELLY, Margaret	20	F	Laborer	14Ma02EI					
GILTHARAN, Patrick	20	M	Laborer	14Ma02EI					
Mary	18	F	Laborer	14Ma02EI					
CAROLLY, Mary	20	F	Laborer	14Ma02EI	JONES, Richard	28	M	Merchant	15Ma02Ao
CONOLLY, Mary	20	F	Laborer	14Ma02EI	MCGUIRE, Burrill	24	M	Farmer	15Ma02Ao
RUSH, Margaret	20	F	Laborer	14Ma02EI	RYMER, Henry	25	M	Gentleman	15Ma02Ao
GILLON, Margaret	20	F	Servant	14Ma02EI	OCONNER, Mary-Agnes-Sr	31	F	Re-Mercy	15Ma02Ao
MCCORMICK, Dennis	20	M	Laborer	14Ma02EI	MAHER, Mary-Angelo-Sr.	43	F	Re-Mercy	15Ma02Ao
Ann	20	F	Laborer	14Ma02EI	HORCAN, Mary-Austin-Sr	24	F	Re-Mercy	15Ma02Ao
MCKENNA, Thomas	24	M	Laborer	14Ma02EI	ODONNELLY, Mary-Minach	35	F	Re-Mercy	15Ma02Ao
Died-At-Sea					BYRNE, Mary-Cammilles-	23	F	Re-Mercy	15Ma02Ao
LAHEY, Isabella	16	F	Laborer	14Ma02EI	HARE, Mary-Vincent-Sr.	24	F	Re-Mercy	15Ma02Ao

NAMES OF PASSENGERS		AGE	SEX	OCCUPATIONS	DATE PORT SHIP	NAMES OF PASSENGERS		AGE	SEX	OCCUPATIONS	DATE PORT SHIP
BREEN, Mary-Teresa-Sr.		33	F	Re-Mercy	15Ma02Ao	DAVIES, John		26	M	Laborer	15Ma02Ao
TRIPPET, Jno.Rev.		47	M	Clergyman	15Ma02Ao	CARROLL, Mary-Ann		21	F	Laborer	15Ma02Ao
POTTS, Jno.		42	M	Gentleman	15Ma02Ao	Margt.		20	F	Laborer	15Ma02Ao
RINTOAL, U		27	F	Lady	15Ma02Ao	CORBIT, Daniel		29	M	Laborer	15Ma02Ao
BYRNE, Mariann		23	F	Servant	15Ma02Ao	Owen		29	M	Laborer	15Ma02Ao
BRADY, Bridget		21	F	Servant	15Ma02Ao	CORBEY, Philip		29	M	Laborer	15Ma02Ao
HERVEST, E.		29	U	Farmer	15Ma02Ao	Philip		29	M	Laborer	15Ma02Ao
GODMAN, John		28	M	Farmer	15Ma02Ao	HOGAN, Jeremiah		25	M	Laborer	15Ma02Ao
Joseph		19	M	Farmer	15Ma02Ao	KELLY, James		24	M	Laborer	15Ma02Ao
PORTER, Henry		18	M	Farmer	15Ma02Ao	SOUTHMIETH, Jno.		21	M	Laborer	15Ma02Ao
DEACON, James		25	M	Servant	15Ma02Ao	SLATERY, Mary		20	F	Laborer	15Ma02Ao
BROWN, Ellen		27	F	Servant	15Ma02Ao	Jane		20	F	Laborer	15Ma02Ao
MAGUIRE, John		27	M	Laborer	15Ma02Ao	WELSH, Thomas		24	M	Laborer	15Ma02Ao
SHERIDAN, Patt		18	M	Laborer	15Ma02Ao	CONOLY, Elizabeth		24	F	Laborer	15Ma02Ao
TAYLOR, Mary-A.		24	F	Laborer	15Ma02Ao	SMYTH, James		25	M	Laborer	15Ma02Ao
SIMONS, Thos.Rev.		44	M	Clergyman	15Ma02Ao	Mary		20	F	Laborer	15Ma02Ao
Thomas	(S)	11	M	None	15Ma02Ao	GANNON, Mary		18	F	Laborer	15Ma02Ao
Jno.Amos	(S)	10	M	None	15Ma02Ao	REILLY, Bryan		25	M	Shoemaker	15Ma02Ao
Jane-Olivia	(D)	05	F	Child	15Ma02Ao	Mary		24	F	Shoemaker	15Ma02Ao
Charles-Yerks	(S)	03	M	Child	15Ma02Ao	MCQUILLIN, Mary		20	F	Servant	15Ma02Ao
QUOLAHAN, Margaret		45	F	Laborer	15Ma02Ao	MCGEEHAN, Patrick		19	M	Carpenter	15Ma02Ao
GORMLEY, Margt.		17	F	Laborer	15Ma02Ao	Rosannah		18	F	Dressmaker	15Ma02Ao
Michael		14	M	Laborer	15Ma02Ao	MCDOOGAN, Jane		18	F	Dressmaker	15Ma02Ao
Michael		10	M	Child	15Ma02Ao	WITHERLY, U-Mrs.		30	F	Dressmaker	15Ma02Ao
Malachi		07	M	Child	15Ma02Ao	U		28	F	Dressmaker	15Ma02Ao
KELLY, Michael		30	M	Blacksmith	15Ma02Ao	COOK, Jno.		20	M	Farmer	15Ma02Ao
MEE, Catherine		20	F	Laborer	15Ma02Ao	MULVEY, Biddy		29	F	Farmer	15Ma02Ao
WARD, Mary		21	F	Laborer	15Ma02Ao	OBYRNE, James		29	M	Shoemaker	15Ma02Ao
EARLY, Thos.		21	M	Laborer	15Ma02Ao	WEDMAN, Catherin		25	F	Shoemaker	15Ma02Ao
Mary		20	F	Laborer	15Ma02Ao	ROWLEY, Henry		28	M	Grocer	15Ma02Ao
DOUGHERTY, Catherine		19	F	Laborer	15Ma02Ao	BROGAN, Mary		24	F	Servant	15Ma02Ao
BOYLAN, Jno.		18	M	Laborer	15Ma02Ao	COURK, Jno.		20	M	Laborer	15Ma02Ao
DURMODY, Mary		15	F	Laborer	15Ma02Ao	CALAGHAN, Michael		29	M	Laborer	15Ma02Ao
BRADLEY, Betsey		21	F	Laborer	15Ma02Ao	MUCHELSGE, David		28	M	Laborer	15Ma02Ao
SMITH, Catherine		24	F	Laborer	15Ma02Ao	FROST, Eduard		36	M	Laborer	15Ma02Ao
ROONEY, Bridget		21	F	Laborer	15Ma02Ao	Elizabeth		52	F	Laborer	15Ma02Ao
ADSPEN, Sarah		20	F	Laborer	15Ma02Ao	SKINNER, Mary		20	F	Laborer	15Ma02Ao
RIDDLE, Sarah		20	F	Laborer	15Ma02Ao	NEILL, James		21	M	Laborer	15Ma02Ao
HEAKY, Biddy		25	F	Laborer	15Ma02Ao	BYRNES, Mary		22	F	Laborer	15Ma02Ao
SCOTT, Biddy		24	F	Laborer	15Ma02Ao	JUSTLECSON, Mary		25	F	Laborer	15Ma02Ao
LAWLER, Jno.		25	M	Laborer	15Ma02Ao	Robert		19	M	Laborer	15Ma02Ao
HERNIN, Jno.		29	M	Mason	15Ma02Ao	John		14	M	Laborer	15Ma02Ao
CONNERSON, Jno.		25	M	Clerk	15Ma02Ao	Hannah		06	F	Child	15Ma02Ao
SCOTT, Alex.		29	M	Tailor	15Ma02Ao	Thomas		04	M	Child	15Ma02Ao
FISHER, William		14	M	Clerk	15Ma02Ao	SWEENEY, Timothy		21	M	Laborer	15Ma02Ao
HAMPTON, Edward		24	M	Chemist	15Ma02Ao	HARTWELL, Ellen		21	F	Laborer	15Ma02Ao
WOODS, Joseph		19	M	Spinner	15Ma02Ao	PARRY, John		22	M	Laborer	15Ma02Ao
MAKIN, Mary		17	F	Spinner	15Ma02Ao	Margt.	(D)	.00	F	Infant	15Ma02Ao
MORAN, Patt		28	M	Laborer	15Ma02Ao	LOCKWOOD, John		28	M	Carpenter	15Ma02Ao
BOHAN, Michael		28	M	Laborer	15Ma02Ao	DALTON, Thomas		09	M	Child	15Ma02Ao
HARGADEN, Mary		24	F	Laborer	15Ma02Ao	MCLAUGHLIN, Mary		18	F	Laborer	15Ma02Ao
MAHAR, Thos.		20	M	Laborer	15Ma02Ao	MCCAFFREY, Patt		40	M	Laborer	15Ma02Ao
Thos.		22	M	Laborer	15Ma02Ao	HUSTON, Robert		20	M	Laborer	15Ma02Ao
RYAN, Maria		45	F	Laborer	15Ma02Ao	FOX, Jno.		21	M	Tailor	15Ma02Ao
SHEARMAN, Joseph		21	M	Laborer	15Ma02Ao	CANLAHAN, Patt		20	M	Laborer	15Ma02Ao
SCALLY, Mary		22	F	Laborer	15Ma02Ao	Mary		18	F	Laborer	15Ma02Ao
DEKIN, Thomas		22	M	Laborer	15Ma02Ao	Mary		20	F	Laborer	15Ma02Ao
RYAN, John		21	M	Laborer	15Ma02Ao	Sabina		16	F	Laborer	15Ma02Ao
Wm.		27	M	Laborer	15Ma02Ao	William		20	M	Laborer	15Ma02Ao
WHELAN, Eliza		20	F	Laborer	15Ma02Ao	Salina		06	F	Child	15Ma02Ao
FLANIGAN, Catherine		21	F	Laborer	15Ma02Ao	ROCH, Ellen		31	F	Laborer	15Ma02Ao
BUTLER, Patt		21	M	Farmer	15Ma02Ao	CAREY, Daniel		19	M	Laborer	15Ma02Ao
PAYNE, Thomas		24	M	Farmer	15Ma02Ao	MCDONOUGH, Ann		21	F	Laborer	15Ma02Ao
HENGAN, Patt		20	M	Farmer	15Ma02Ao	EAGAN, Anthony		21	M	Laborer	15Ma02Ao
KEYTON, Ann		21	F	Farmer	15Ma02Ao	FALLON, William		20	M	Laborer	15Ma02Ao
CAVENAGH, Ann		16	F	Farmer	15Ma02Ao	SHEERAN, Ann		20	F	Laborer	15Ma02Ao
CONOUGHTON, Cella		18	F	Farmer	15Ma02Ao	KELLY, Robert		21	M	Laborer	15Ma02Ao
CORR, Thomas		15	M	Printer	15Ma02Ao	BRADY, Ally		00	F	Laborer	15Ma02Ao
CALLAGHAN, Daniel		24	M	Carpenter	15Ma02Ao	MCGLINSKEY, John		18	M	Farmer	15Ma02Ao
GILMORE, Catherine		25	F	Servant	15Ma02Ao	FURY, Catherine		09	F	Child	15Ma02Ao
CAREY, Mary		17	F	Servant	15Ma02Ao	MCFREMICK, John		20	M	Laborer	15Ma02Ao
SHIELDS, Rose		21	F	Servant	15Ma02Ao	GISH, Mary-Ann		17	F	Laborer	15Ma02Ao
GETTIN, Andrew		21	M	Farmer	15Ma02Ao	MCGEEHAN, Edward		24	M	Laborer	15Ma02Ao
HERBBOTSON, Wm.		26	M	Miller	15Ma02Ao	HIGGINS, James		50	M	Laborer	15Ma02Ao
GILLARN, Michael		24	M	Shepherd	15Ma02Ao	Mary	(W)	45	F	Wife	15Ma02Ao

81

NAMES OF PASSENGERS		AGE	SEX	OCCUPATIONS	DATE PORT SHIP
HIGGINS, Ellen	(D)	25	F	Laborer	15Ma02Ao
HARMAN, James		18	M	Laborer	15Ma02Ao
SWAN, Ellen		18	F	Laborer	15Ma02Ao
FORAN, Mary		24	F	Laborer	15Ma02Ao
WHELAN, Honor		16	F	Laborer	15Ma02Ao
COX, George		20	M	Laborer	15Ma02Ao
GALLAGHAN, Catherine		60	F	Laborer	15Ma02Ao
Charles		16	M	Laborer	15Ma02Ao
RYAN, Charles		24	M	Laborer	15Ma02Ao
Susan		26	F	Laborer	15Ma02Ao
TIMMANY, Owen		18	M	Watchmaker	15Ma02Ao
MCGUIRE, Ann		10	F	Servant	15Ma02Ao
FITZPATRICK, Mary		20	F	Servant	15Ma02Ao
Samuel		04	M	Child	15Ma02Ao
RAFTEN, James		50	M	Laborer	15Ma02Ao
Mary		50	F	Laborer	15Ma02Ao
SPALLON, Mary		18	F	Laborer	15Ma02Ao
RAFTEN, Jno.		14	M	Laborer	15Ma02Ao
Michael		12	M	Laborer	15Ma02Ao
DENNING, Elizabeth		24	F	Laborer	15Ma02Ao
CAMPBELL, Bridget		18	F	Laborer	15Ma02Ao
CARRIGAN, Miles		20	M	Laborer	15Ma02Ao
EARLY, Thaddy		25	M	Laborer	15Ma02Ao
Mary		08	F	Child	15Ma02Ao
Michael		06	M	Child	15Ma02Ao
MCMANUS, Mary		51	F	Laborer	15Ma02Ao
Margt.		40	F	Laborer	15Ma02Ao
Michael		14	M	Laborer	15Ma02Ao
CALLAGHAN, Catherin		05	F	Child	15Ma02Ao
GIBSON, Frank		20	M	Laborer	15Ma02Ao
ARMSTRONG, Patt		21	M	Laborer	15Ma02Ao
CAMPBELL, Andrew		19	M	Laborer	15Ma02Ao
BURKES, Peter		28	M	Laborer	15Ma02Ao
CASSIDY, Ann		21	F	Laborer	15Ma02Ao
HIGGINS, Michael		18	M	Laborer	15Ma02Ao
OBYRNE, Mary		13	F	Laborer	15Ma02Ao
MCCARTY, John		18	M	Laborer	15Ma02Ao
Catherin		03	F	Child	15Ma02Ao
OBRIEN, Ann		21	F	Laborer	15Ma02Ao
FITZSIMMONS, Mary		20	F	Laborer	15Ma02Ao
Ann		18	F	Laborer	15Ma02Ao
CLARK, Mary		17	F	Laborer	15Ma02Ao
Patt		11	M	None	15Ma02Ao
Margt.		10	F	None	15Ma02Ao
WHELEGHAN, Jane		13	F	Laborer	15Ma02Ao
CORR, Patt		27	M	Farmer	15Ma02Ao
BRICKERTON, Charles		18	M	Carpenter	15Ma02Ao
BRANAGAN, Catherin		30	F	Servant	15Ma02Ao
Ann	(D)	03	F	Child	15Ma02Ao
Margt.	(D)	04	F	Child	15Ma02Ao
LANGTREE, Mary		09	F	Child	15Ma02Ao
DEACON, Catherin		29	F	Servant	15Ma02Ao
John		28	M	Shoemaker	15Ma02Ao
FEHERY, Catherine		29	F	Laborer	15Ma02Ao
Bridget	(D)	02	F	Child	15Ma02Ao
Marla	(D)	.00	F	Infant	15Ma02Ao
MULLANSSY, Mary		00	F	Laborer	15Ma02Ao
James		00	M	Laborer	15Ma02Ao
Mary		10	F	Child	15Ma02Ao
Margt.		08	F	Child	15Ma02Ao
Ellen		05	F	Child	15Ma02Ao
Edward		02	M	Child	15Ma02Ao
MULLIN, Ann		20	F	Laborer	15Ma02Ao
CARROLL, Mary		20	F	Laborer	15Ma02Ao
HERRICK, Mary		30	F	Laborer	15Ma02Ao
DERMODY, Wm.		07	M	Child	15Ma02Ao
MAHARTY, John		17	M	Laborer	15Ma02Ao
KEENAN, Bridget		17	F	Laborer	15Ma02Ao
DONNOVAN, Martin		20	M	Laborer	15Ma02Ao
KEEGAN, Cecilia		18	F	Laborer	15Ma02Ao
GARRICK, John		06	M	Child	15Ma02Ao
MCWEENEY, Betsey		20	F	Laborer	15Ma02Ao
TOOLE, Susan		19	F	Laborer	15Ma02Ao
MCMANUS, Francis		18	M	Laborer	15Ma02Ao
REILLY, Laurain		20	M	Farmer	15Ma02Ao
REILLY, Michael		19	M	Farmer	15Ma02Ao
BEGLEY, Ellen		12	F	Laborer	15Ma02Ao
SHERIDAN, Jno.		29	M	Laborer	15Ma02Ao
HAGAN, Peter		20	M	Laborer	15Ma02Ao
MURRY, John		28	M	Laborer	15Ma02Ao
OWENS, James		26	M	Laborer	15Ma02Ao
HINSON, Mary		21	F	Laborer	15Ma02Ao
BRADY, Honey		18	F	Laborer	15Ma02Ao
MCQUADE, Catherine		20	F	Laborer	15Ma02Ao
KILRED, Bridget		20	F	Laborer	15Ma02Ao
MCALEAR, Robt.		23	M	Farmer	15Ma02Ao
Harriet	(W)	23	F	Wife	15Ma02Ao
Catherin	(D)	05	F	Child	15Ma02Ao
Jno.	(S)	03	M	Child	15Ma02Ao
Thomas	(S)	.00	M	Infant	15Ma02Ao
TOFFY, Betsey		20	F	Laborer	15Ma02Ao
DONNELLY, Jane		25	F	Laborer	15Ma02Ao
CLUSKY, Alice		18	F	Laborer	15Ma02Ao
BYRNES, Margt.		25	F	Laborer	15Ma02Ao
MULLIGAN, Rose		24	F	Laborer	15Ma02Ao
MURPHY, Cecila		12	F	Laborer	15Ma02Ao
Teresa		12	F	Laborer	15Ma02Ao
CAIN, Michael		25	M	Laborer	15Ma02Ao
MAHONY, Jno.		21	M	Laborer	15Ma02Ao
MCGIERVEY, Patt		08	M	Child	15Ma02Ao
James		39	M	Laborer	15Ma02Ao
Mary		25	F	Laborer	15Ma02Ao
SHEARMAN, John		26	M	Laborer	15Ma02Ao
Mary		24	F	Laborer	15Ma02Ao
Judith		29	F	Laborer	15Ma02Ao
FOLEY, Thomas		40	M	Laborer	15Ma02Ao
William	(S)	20	M	Laborer	15Ma02Ao
Catherin	(D)	18	F	Laborer	15Ma02Ao
Cornelius	(S)	13	M	Laborer	15Ma02Ao
WILSON, Mary		18	F	Laborer	15Ma02Ao
SHEHAN, Eliza		21	F	Laborer	15Ma02Ao
MCGRAW, Matilda		26	F	Laborer	15Ma02Ao
William		30	M	Weaver	15Ma02Ao
HEDLEY, Jno.		29	M	Laborer	15Ma02Ao
ODONNELL, Jno.		20	M	Laborer	15Ma02Ao
PRENDERNILLI, Maurice		25	M	Gdnr	15Ma02Ao
CRONIN, Patt		10	M	Laborer	15Ma02Ao
MCCOY, Ann		19	F	Laborer	15Ma02Ao
Bridget		17	F	Laborer	15Ma02Ao
MULLIN, Jane		18	F	Laborer	15Ma02Ao
PERRY, Sarah		26	F	Laborer	15Ma02Ao
NOON, Bridget		24	F	Laborer	15Ma02Ao
DOLAN, Ann		26	F	Laborer	15Ma02Ao
BEATTY, Jno.		19	F	Laborer	15Ma02Ao
REILLY, Dennis		28	M	Blacksmith	15Ma02Ao
MCCARTY, Margt.		06	F	Servant	15Ma02Ao
STORY, Teresa		18	F	Servant	15Ma02Ao
COOGAN, Thomas		40	M	Groom	15Ma02Ao
Patt		29	M	Laborer	15Ma02Ao
Ann		19	F	Laborer	15Ma02Ao
SAVAGE, Michael		12	M	Laborer	15Ma02Ao
DONOHOE, Patt		25	M	Laborer	15Ma02Ao
LYNCH, Jeremiah		21	M	Laborer	15Ma02Ao
MURPHY, Margaret		18	F	Laborer	15Ma02Ao
TOOLE, Jno.		21	M	Clerk	15Ma02Ao
MCMAHAN, Margt.		18	F	Spinner	15Ma02Ao
MCCOURT, Rosannah		19	F	Spinner	15Ma02Ao
MCGUINESS, Ellen		18	F	Spinner	15Ma02Ao
MURRY, Ellen		19	F	Spinner	15Ma02Ao
CRAIG, Jno.		34	M	Spinner	15Ma02Ao
TOWHILL, Ellen		18	F	Servant	15Ma02Ao
COLLINS, Elizabeth		20	F	Servant	15Ma02Ao
BIGLEY, John		20	M	Servant	15Ma02Ao
MCARDLE, Patt		22	M	Laborer	15Ma02Ao
WRIGHT, Geo.		50	M	Weaver	15Ma02Ao
Ann	(W)	48	F	Wife	15Ma02Ao
George	(S)	20	M	Weaver	15Ma02Ao
Mary	(D)	13	F	Weaver	15Ma02Ao
John	(S)	10	M	Weaver	15Ma02Ao
Joseph	(S)	08	M	Child	15Ma02Ao

NAMES OF PASSENGERS		AGE	SEX	OCCUPATIONS	DATE PORT SHIP
WRIGHT, Eliza	(D)	05	F	Child	15Ma02Ao
CASEY, Michael		20	M	Laborer	15Ma02Ao
HOWARD, Elizabeth		21	F	Servant	15Ma02Ao
MCKILLIGART, Mary		20	F	Servant	15Ma02Ao
COOK, Grace		21	F	Servant	15Ma02Ao
KELLY, Jno.		20	M	Laborer	15Ma02Ao
NEILL, Rose		20	F	Laborer	15Ma02Ao
DOYLE, Honoro		22	F	Laborer	15Ma02Ao
BRADY, Bridget		21	F	Laborer	15Ma02Ao
MARTIN, Owen		18	M	Laborer	15Ma02Ao
Ann		17	F	Laborer	15Ma02Ao
WARD, Hugh		18	M	Laborer	15Ma02Ao
BOYLE, Patt		20	M	Weaver	15Ma02Ao
MOBRIEN, James		21	M	Laborer	15Ma02Ao
FLANAGAN, Patt		21	M	Coachman	15Ma02Ao
U, U		21	U	Laborer	15Ma02Ao
ROBERTS, Michael		25	M	Laborer	15Ma02Ao
Mary		20	F	Laborer	15Ma02Ao
SMITH, John		20	M	Laborer	15Ma02Ao
MOORE, Elizabeth		21	F	Laborer	15Ma02Ao
FINNIGAN, Jane		19	F	Laborer	15Ma02Ao
DURMODY, Catherine		15	F	Laborer	15Ma02Ao
BOHAN, Jno.		24	M	Laborer	15Ma02Ao
GOUGLIN, Rosannah		12	F	Laborer	15Ma02Ao
BRICARDY, Thomas		22	M	Laborer	15Ma02Ao
Henry		23	M	Laborer	15Ma02Ao
Bridget		24	F	Laborer	15Ma02Ao
William		.00	M	Infant	15Ma02Ao
CONDON, Mary		16	F	Laborer	15Ma02Ao
CONLAN, Betsey		21	F	Laborer	15Ma02Ao
Catherine		19	F	Laborer	15Ma02Ao
GRAY, Patrick		18	M	Laborer	15Ma02Ao
MCCABE, Edward		21	M	Laborer	15Ma02Ao
MANTON, Thomas		24	M	Laborer	15Ma02Ao
BRISLLY, Hannah		18	F	Laborer	15Ma02Ao
MCDERMOTT, Eliza		18	F	Dressmaker	15Ma02Ao
DERBY, Ann		24	F	Dressmaker	15Ma02Ao
REYNOLDS, Jno.		20	M	Laborer	15Ma02Ao
MURPHY, Catherine		20	F	Laborer	15Ma02Ao
CARR, Bridget		24	F	Laborer	15Ma02Ao
FARRELL, Bridget		24	F	Laborer	15Ma02Ao

LETITIA-HEYES 15 MAY 1846

From Liverpool

NAMES OF PASSENGERS		AGE	SEX	OCCUPATIONS	DATE PORT SHIP
GALLAGHAN, Ellen		23	F	Dressmaker	15Ma02Fv
STACK, John		30	M	Weaver	15Ma02Fv
SIMM, James		54	M	Weaver	15Ma02Fv
John		31	M	Weaver	15Ma02Fv
U	(W)	58	F	Weaver	15Ma02Fv
U	(W)	38	F	Weaver	15Ma02Fv
Margret		05	F	Child	15Ma02Fv
GILBERT, Peggy		20	F	Unknown	15Ma02Fv
MCMENOMY, Pat		22	M	Servant	15Ma02Fv
MCCUNARY, Margret		18	F	Servant	15Ma02Fv
BRENNAN, Patt		23	M	Servant	15Ma02Fv
GALVIN, Pat		20	M	Servant	15Ma02Fv
NELSON, Micheal		19	M	Servant	15Ma02Fv
MCILRAINE, Peter		21	M	Servant	15Ma02Fv
COSGRAVE, Ann		18	F	Servant	15Ma02Fv
KELLY, James		20	M	Laborer	15Ma02Fv
JEBB, Wm.		10	M	Child	15Ma02Fv
WILLIAMSON, Mary		23	F	Dressmaker	15Ma02Fv
HYLAND, Thomas		20	M	Farmer	15Ma02Fv
MUNRO, John		21	M	Farmer	15Ma02Fv
MCGRATH, Jeremiah		24	M	Farmer	15Ma02Fv
FARLEY, Pat		20	M	Farmer	15Ma02Fv
HEGAN, Pat		38	M	Farmer	15Ma02Fv

NAMES OF PASSENGERS		AGE	SEX	OCCUPATIONS	DATE PORT SHIP
HEGAN, U	(W)	36	F	Farmer	15Ma02Fv
Michael	(S)	11	M	Farmer	15Ma02Fv
Pat	(S)	09	M	Child	15Ma02Fv
CONROY, John		20	M	Farmer	15Ma02Fv
MORRISON, John		21	M	Farmer	15Ma02Fv
WATSON, William		30	M	Farmer	15Ma02Fv
TRAPP, James		24	M	Shoemaker	15Ma02Fv
U	(W)	24	F	Servant	15Ma02Fv
Mary		19	F	Servant	15Ma02Fv
BURKE, Pat		24	M	Servant	15Ma02Fv
KELLY, Micheal		18	M	Servant	15Ma02Fv
MELLON, Ann		20	F	Servant	15Ma02Fv
COLLINTINE, John		17	M	Servant	15Ma02Fv
LARKIN, John		22	M	Servant	15Ma02Fv
DELHAN, William		19	M	Servant	15Ma02Fv
HICKEY, Micl.		20	M	Servant	15Ma02Fv
LANG, Lawrence		24	M	Servant	15Ma02Fv
RYAN, Mary		18	F	Servant	15Ma02Fv
DURNAN, James		26	M	Servant	15Ma02Fv
Jane		24	F	Dressmaker	15Ma02Fv
LESLIE, Thomas		13	M	Servant	15Ma02Fv
LYNCH, William		21	M	Unknown	15Ma02Fv
MCCORMICK, Samuel		21	M	Unknown	15Ma02Fv
MCDONOUGH, Thomas		35	M	Shoemaker	15Ma02Fv
MARE, James		25	M	Farmer	15Ma02Fv
RIELLY, John		20	M	Farmer	15Ma02Fv
Margret		16	F	Farmer	15Ma02Fv
Bridget		18	F	Farmer	15Ma02Fv
Thomas		22	M	Farmer	15Ma02Fv
LAHEY, Margt.		18	F	Farmer	15Ma02Fv
FLOOD, David		24	M	Blacksmith	15Ma02Fv
CUSACK, Mary		20	F	Blacksmith	15Ma02Fv
FLOOD, Tom		20	M	Blacksmith	15Ma02Fv
Bridget		20	F	Servant	15Ma02Fv
Bridget		11	F	Child	15Ma02Fv
RODGERS, Henry		25	M	Servant	15Ma02Fv
U	(W)	22	F	Servant	15Ma02Fv
LEECH, Martha		17	F	Servant	15Ma02Fv
Eliza		19	F	Servant	15Ma02Fv
WINCHESTER, William		31	M	Servant	15Ma02Fv
U	(W)	20	F	Servant	15Ma02Fv
COALTER, Charles		25	M	Servant	15Ma02Fv
EDEW, Wm.		30	M	Servant	15Ma02Fv
GALLAGHER, Pat		22	M	Servant	15Ma02Fv
FOLEY, James		24	M	Unknown	15Ma02Fv
Bridget		24	F	Dressmaker	15Ma02Fv
WILKINS, Joseph		26	M	Unknown	15Ma02Fv
SMITH, Sarah		38	F	Unknown	15Ma02Fv
Mary	(D)	20	F	Unknown	15Ma02Fv
John	(S)	18	M	Unknown	15Ma02Fv
Ann	(D)	00	F	Unknown	15Ma02Fv
Elizabeth	(D)	16	F	Unknown	15Ma02Fv
Mary	(D)	13	F	Unknown	15Ma02Fv
Enna	(D)	12	F	Unknown	15Ma02Fv
Charles	(S)	10	M	Farmer	15Ma02Fv
Sarah	(D)	06	F	Child	15Ma02Fv
Samuel	(S)	04	M	Child	15Ma02Fv
James	(S)	02	M	Child	15Ma02Fv
Edward	(S)	.00	M	Infant	15Ma02Fv
James		36	M	Farmer	15Ma02Fv
Mary	(W)	31	F	Farmer	15Ma02Fv
George	(S)	10	M	Farmer	15Ma02Fv
Charles	(S)	05	M	Child	15Ma02Fv
James	(S)	03	M	Child	15Ma02Fv
Martha	(D)	.00	F	Infant	15Ma02Fv
BANNAN, Michael		21	M	Unknown	15Ma02Fv
LYNCH, Cath.		18	F	Unknown	15Ma02Fv
WARD, John		28	M	Servant	15Ma02Fv
RIELL, Bathonemy		30	M	Servant	15Ma02Fv
Ann	(W)	28	F	Servant	15Ma02Fv
Helena	(D)	05	F	Child	15Ma02Fv
Mary-Ann	(D)	03	F	Child	15Ma02Fv
Sarah	(D)	.00	F	Infant	15Ma02Fv
MCGRATH, Michal		24	M	Servant	15Ma02Fv
KENEDY, James		25	M	Servant	15Ma02Fv

83

NAMES OF PASSENGERS	AGE	SEX	OCCUPATIONS	DATE PORT SHIP
MCCORT, Bridget	25	F	Servant	15Ma02Fv
ONEIL, James	24	M	Servant	15Ma02Fv
LULEY, Richard	25	M	Servant	15Ma02Fv
CASHEN, Pat	20	M	Servant	15Ma02Fv
CLEAREY, Mich.	25	M	Servant	15Ma02Fv
Joseph	20	M	Servant	15Ma02Fv
RYAN, John	22	M	Servant	15Ma02Fv
FLOOD, Michal	22	M	Servant	15Ma02Fv
QUINLAN, John	20	M	Servant	15Ma02Fv
Bridgit	18	F	Milliner	15Ma02Fv
DWIRE, Thomas	28	M	Servant	15Ma02Fv
LAMPIERE, Bridget	28	F	Dressmaker	15Ma02Fv
REMBLE, Honorah	20	F	Dressmaker	15Ma02Fv
LEDDY, Margret	22	F	Dressmaker	15Ma02Fv
LENAGHAN, Mary	23	F	Dressmaker	15Ma02Fv
KEOGHE, Pat	34	M	Laborer	15Ma02Fv
KEATING, Thomas	23	M	Laborer	15Ma02Fv
MUELLORY, William	30	M	Laborer	15Ma02Fv
DONELLY, Pat	30	M	Laborer	15Ma02Fv
CARROLE, Thomas	30	M	Laborer	15Ma02Fv
GALLANCEY, Rose	20	F	Laborer	15Ma02Fv
HALLEGAN, William	28	M	Laborer	15Ma02Fv
Ann	30	F	Servant	15Ma02Fv
Bridgit	28	F	Servant	15Ma02Fv
Maurice (S)	08	M	Child	15Ma02Fv
Mary (D)	03	F	Child	15Ma02Fv
DUNN, Edward	27	M	Servant	15Ma02Fv
RIVELLE, Kitty	25	F	Servant	15Ma02Fv
GLESON, Ann	25	F	Servant	15Ma02Fv
TYSON, John	20	M	Servant	15Ma02Fv

PLATO 15 MAY 1846

From Liverpool

NAMES OF PASSENGERS	AGE	SEX	OCCUPATIONS	DATE PORT SHIP
LENOX, William	21	M	Laborer	15Ma02Fy
Andrew	29	M	Laborer	15Ma02Fy
CARNEY, William	22	M	Laborer	15Ma02Fy
OWENS, Michl.	25	M	Laborer	15Ma02Fy
FOLMSON, Geo.	18	M	Laborer	15Ma02Fy
CASEY, Patrick	25	M	Laborer	15Ma02Fy
MCGOWAN, Thos.	50	M	Laborer	15Ma02Fy
James	40	M	Laborer	15Ma02Fy
TIERNAN, Patrick	19	M	Laborer	15Ma02Fy
DOHERTY, William	18	M	Laborer	15Ma02Fy
CORBETT, Luke	15	M	Laborer	15Ma02Fy
Michl.	15	M	Laborer	15Ma02Fy
Thomas	15	M	Laborer	15Ma02Fy
Laurence	10	M	Laborer	15Ma02Fy
ASHBURN, John	24	M	Laborer	15Ma02Fy
BROWER, Andrew	17	M	Laborer	15Ma02Fy
MCGALLAHER, Robt.	28	M	Laborer	15Ma02Fy
LENOX, Christan	30	F	Laborer	15Ma02Fy
Eliza (D)	10	F	Laborer	15Ma02Fy
Mary (D)	07	F	Child	15Ma02Fy
Christan (D)	04	F	Child	15Ma02Fy
GUIN, Mary	40	F	Laborer	15Ma02Fy
CORBETT, Sarah	41	F	Laborer	15Ma02Fy
BROWER, Sarah	45	F	Laborer	15Ma02Fy
OWENS, Ellen	28	F	Laborer	15Ma02Fy
Ally	23	F	Laborer	15Ma02Fy
DOHERTY, Rebeca	21	F	Laborer	15Ma02Fy
MCGOVERN, Robt.	26	M	Laborer	15Ma02Fy
LOVE, Bridget	16	F	Laborer	15Ma02Fy
Rebeca	19	F	Laborer	15Ma02Fy
MOORE, Margt.	20	F	Laborer	15Ma02Fy
HOUSE, Mary	20	F	Laborer	15Ma02Fy
DUFFY, Ellen	22	F	Laborer	15Ma02Fy
CASEY, Bridgit	25	F	Laborer	15Ma02Fy

NAMES OF PASSENGERS	AGE	SEX	OCCUPATIONS	DATE PORT SHIP
CASEY, Ellen (D)	.05	F	Infant	15Ma02Fy

MESSENGER 15 MAY 1846

From Torquay

NAMES OF PASSENGERS	AGE	SEX	OCCUPATIONS	DATE PORT SHIP
FERNEUX, Henry	21	M	Cooper	15Ma47Fz
HAMBLING, William	25	M	Fisherman	15Ma47Fz
SPRAGUE, George	18	M	Fisherman	15Ma47Fz
WILLIAMS, John	19	M	Fisherman	15Ma47Fz

HENRIETTA-MARY 15 MAY 1846

From Liverpool

NAMES OF PASSENGERS	AGE	SEX	OCCUPATIONS	DATE PORT SHIP
WHITE, Ann	30	F	Farmer	15Ma02Gb
Michl. (S)	.03	M	Infant	15Ma02Gb
Mary (D)	.00	F	Infant	15Ma02Gb
Patrick (H)	30	M	Farmer	15Ma02Gb
MCBRIDE, Elizth.	25	F	Farmer	15Ma02Gb
KILKELLY, James	30	M	Farmer	15Ma02Gb
OHEARN, John	30	M	Farmer	15Ma02Gb
NUGENT, Patrick	23	M	Laborer	15Ma02Gb
U (W)	23	F	Unknown	15Ma02Gb
Margt.	25	F	Dressmaker	15Ma02Gb
COUGHLIN, Patk.	28	M	Laborer	15Ma02Gb
DOWD, John	26	M	Laborer	15Ma02Gb
GROGAHAN, Thos.	25	M	Laborer	15Ma02Gb
CAVANAGH, Michl.	20	M	Laborer	15Ma02Gb
BARRY, Bridget	19	F	Laborer	15Ma02Gb
Margt.	16	F	Laborer	15Ma02Gb
ONEILL, Mary	16	F	Laborer	15Ma02Gb
CLIFF, Mary	18	F	Laborer	15Ma02Gb
RYAN, Michl.	25	M	Laborer	15Ma02Gb
VERDON, Jno.	20	M	Laborer	15Ma02Gb
Cathe. (W)	20	F	Laborer	15Ma02Gb
BOWDAN, Patk.	20	F	Laborer	15Ma02Gb
Bridget	20	F	Laborer	15Ma02Gb
FLYNN, Dennis	21	M	Laborer	15Ma02Gb
Bridget	18	F	Laborer	15Ma02Gb
SHALLY, Felix	18	M	Laborer	15Ma02Gb
MCCAHILL, Francis	16	M	Shoemaker	15Ma02Gb
SHAIKEY, Mary	14	F	Shoemaker	15Ma02Gb
ONEILL, Wm.	25	M	Shoemaker	15Ma02Gb
Ellen (W)	22	F	Shoemaker	15Ma02Gb
Timothy (S)	.04	M	Infant	15Ma02Gb
HUGHES, Anne	20	F	Shoemaker	15Ma02Gb
ONEILL, Owen	40	M	Shoemaker	15Ma02Gb
MEGARD, Manus	40	M	Shoemaker	15Ma02Gb
ROACH, Jas.	29	M	Shoemaker	15Ma02Gb
HOLLERAN, Hugh	26	M	Shoemaker	15Ma02Gb
MCCABE, Patk.	22	M	Shoemaker	15Ma02Gb
WHELAND, Wm.	23	M	Shoemaker	15Ma02Gb
MCGUIRE, Bernd.	16	M	Shoemaker	15Ma02Gb
SHANNON, Patk.	22	M	Shoemaker	15Ma02Gb
DAILY, Patk.	25	M	Shoemaker	15Ma02Gb
KENNY, Bridget	45	F	Shoemaker	15Ma02Gb
Jas.	18	M	Weaver	15Ma02Gb
John	16	M	Weaver	15Ma02Gb
Sarah	13	F	Weaver	15Ma02Gb
Eliza	03	F	Child	15Ma02Gb
GAYNOR, Betty	30	F	Weaver	15Ma02Gb
ROURKE, Martin	25	M	Weaver	15Ma02Gb

NAMES OF PASSENGERS		AGE	SEX	OCCUPATIONS	DATE PORT SHIP
KENNEDY, Wm.		24	M	Weaver	15Ma02Gb
BRENNAN, John		27	M	Weaver	15Ma02Gb
Ellen		26	F	Weaver	15Ma02Gb
ROGERS, Ann		23	F	Weaver	15Ma02Gb
KELLY, Clara		24	F	Weaver	15Ma02Gb
WHELAN, John		23	M	Weaver	15Ma02Gb
COMONS, Wm.		26	M	Weaver	15Ma02Gb
NAYLOR, Joseph		30	M	Weaver	15Ma02Gb
Wm.		26	M	Weaver	15Ma02Gb
MORSE, Joshua		30	M	Weaver	15Ma02Gb
KELLY, Mary		25	F	Weaver	15Ma02Gb
SHANE, Alice		18	F	Weaver	15Ma02Gb
MURPHY, Patk.		40	M	Weaver	15Ma02Gb
Margt.	(W)	35	F	Weaver	15Ma02Gb
Mathew	(S)	11	M	Child	15Ma02Gb
Mary	(D)	07	F	Child	15Ma02Gb
Jas.	(S)	04	M	Child	15Ma02Gb
Bernard	(S)	02	M	Child	15Ma02Gb
BROWN, Jas.		35	M	Weaver	15Ma02Gb
MCGRATH, John		25	M	Weaver	15Ma02Gb
VALE, John		30	M	Weaver	15Ma02Gb
COLEMAN, Ellen		22	F	Weaver	15Ma02Gb
BARNETT, Michl.		25	M	Weaver	15Ma02Gb
Margt.		22	F	Weaver	15Ma02Gb
CAMMERON, John		24	M	Weaver	15Ma02Gb
FARLEY, Master		24	M	Weaver	15Ma02Gb
DONOHUE, Joseph		25	M	Weaver	15Ma02Gb
MCGOWAN, Margt.		28	F	Spinster	15Ma02Gb
BANNON, Isaac		30	M	Weaver	15Ma02Gb
DAVIS, Wm.		32	M	Weaver	15Ma02Gb
GUNNING, Wm.		26	M	Weaver	15Ma02Gb
Sarah		22	F	Weaver	15Ma02Gb
Jas.		12	M	Weaver	15Ma02Gb
SALLY, Timothy		25	M	Weaver	15Ma02Gb
Hannah		20	F	Weaver	15Ma02Gb
MONAGHAN, Bridget		07	F	Child	15Ma02Gb
LYONS, Hannah		22	F	Weaver	15Ma02Gb
KELLY, Mary		22	F	Weaver	15Ma02Gb
MURRAY, Seline		19	F	Weaver	15Ma02Gb
SERIN, Mary		18	F	Weaver	15Ma02Gb
DONALDSON, Richd.		23	M	Weaver	15Ma02Gb
READY, Michl.		30	M	Weaver	15Ma02Gb
LYONS, Cathe.		25	F	Weaver	15Ma02Gb
COLLINS, Patk.		30	M	Tailor	15Ma02Gb
HICKEY, Patk.		40	M	Tailor	15Ma02Gb
Patk.	(S)	17	M	Tailor	15Ma02Gb
Ellen	(D)	12	F	None	15Ma02Gb
Mary	(D)	10	F	None	15Ma02Gb
PENDERGAST, Edwd.		30	M	Tailor	15Ma02Gb
DOWGAN, Michl.		28	M	Tailor	15Ma02Gb
CASEY, Tim.		32	M	Tailor	15Ma02Gb
KING, John		25	M	Tailor	15Ma02Gb
AHERN, Patk.		24	M	Tailor	15Ma02Gb
Cathe.		18	F	Tailor	15Ma02Gb
BAKER, Martha		19	F	Tailor	15Ma02Gb
CONLAN, Margt.		16	F	Tailor	15Ma02Gb
MCLOUGHLIN, Michl.		40	M	Tailor	15Ma02Gb
Bridget	(W)	40	F	Tailor	15Ma02Gb
Patk.	(S)	20	M	Tailor	15Ma02Gb
Francis	(S)	20	M	Tailor	15Ma02Gb
Michl.	(S)	16	M	Tailor	15Ma02Gb
Jas.	(S)	14	M	Tailor	15Ma02Gb
Mary	(D)	11	F	None	15Ma02Gb
Margt.	(D)	.00	F	Infant	15Ma02Gb
Michl.		40	M	Weaver	15Ma02Gb
John		20	M	Weaver	15Ma02Gb
Patk.		20	M	Weaver	15Ma02Gb
MCDERMOTT, Michl.		24	M	Weaver	15Ma02Gb
Margt.		20	F	Weaver	15Ma02Gb
CLARKE, Mary		20	F	Weaver	15Ma02Gb
HAYDEN, Francis		20	M	Weaver	15Ma02Gb
Bridget		20	F	Weaver	15Ma02Gb
MCLOUGHLIN, Matilda		20	F	Weaver	15Ma02Gb
BERNE, Mary		20	F	Weaver	15Ma02Gb
DUFFY, Mary		20	F	Weaver	15Ma02Gb
BURKE, John		20	M	Weaver	15Ma02Gb
BROWN, Maurice		17	M	Weaver	15Ma02Gb
MCQUINN, Thos.		35	M	Weaver	15Ma02Gb
BLUTE, John		30	M	Weaver	15Ma02Gb
BLERY, Wm.		28	M	Weaver	15Ma02Gb
MCLEAN, Edwd.		20	M	Weaver	15Ma02Gb
RYAN, Pierce		40	M	Weaver	15Ma02Gb
EAGAN, Judy		26	F	Weaver	15Ma02Gb
RYAN, Mary		30	F	Weaver	15Ma02Gb
Cathe.	(D)	10	F	Child	15Ma02Gb
Thos.	(S)	08	M	Child	15Ma02Gb
Cathe.	(D)	10	F	Child	15Ma02Gb
Maurice	(S)	04	M	Child	15Ma02Gb
FLYNN, Patk.		20	M	Weaver	15Ma02Gb
Michl.		20	M	Weaver	15Ma02Gb
WHELAN, Eliza		21	F	Weaver	15Ma02Gb
DOWD, Thos.		20	M	Weaver	15Ma02Gb
Patk.		20	M	Weaver	15Ma02Gb
QUINLAN, John		19	M	Weaver	15Ma02Gb
EGAN, Michl.		19	M	Weaver	15Ma02Gb
MORRISSY, Patk.		30	M	Shoemaker	15Ma02Gb
DOWD, Mary		18	F	Shoemaker	15Ma02Gb
Bridget		20	F	Shoemaker	15Ma02Gb
GIBBINS, Bridget		20	F	Shoemaker	15Ma02Gb
Bridget		20	F	Shoemaker	15Ma02Gb
CORBETT, Cathe.		20	F	Shoemaker	15Ma02Gb
GIBBINS, Jane		15	F	Shoemaker	15Ma02Gb
STOOR, Fredk.		50	M	Shoemaker	15Ma02Gb
Jas.	(S)	20	M	Shoemaker	15Ma02Gb
MCGANN, Andrew		20	M	Shoemaker	15Ma02Gb
CARROLL, Thos.M.		20	M	Shoemaker	15Ma02Gb
BURNES, Bridgt.		20	F	Shoemaker	15Ma02Gb
MCNEESNY, Ann		20	F	Shoemaker	15Ma02Gb
FITZSIMMONS, Margt.		20	F	Shoemaker	15Ma02Gb
CARROLL, Cathe.		20	F	Shoemaker	15Ma02Gb
MCDONNELL, Patk.		26	M	Shoemaker	15Ma02Gb
MEYERS, John		18	M	Shoemaker	15Ma02Gb
MCDONNELL, Michl.		20	M	Shoemaker	15Ma02Gb
MCLEAN, Danl.		20	M	Shoemaker	15Ma02Gb
MULHOLLAND, Sarah		21	F	Shoemaker	15Ma02Gb
RICE, Henry		20	M	Shoemaker	15Ma02Gb
Mary		22	F	Shoemaker	15Ma02Gb
ONEILL, Hugh		21	M	Shoemaker	15Ma02Gb
Susan		18	F	Shoemaker	15Ma02Gb
MCALMOUNT, Jas.		16	M	Shoemaker	15Ma02Gb
CORNING, Edw.		34	M	Shoemaker	15Ma02Gb
DOLAN, John		20	M	Shoemaker	15Ma02Gb
Rose		16	F	Shoemaker	15Ma02Gb
MCGUIRE, Bridget		19	F	Shoemaker	15Ma02Gb
KELLY, Ellen		25	F	Shoemaker	15Ma02Gb
FARRELL, Patk.		20	M	Shoemaker	15Ma02Gb
HUGHES, Henry		19	M	Shoemaker	15Ma02Gb
Phillip		19	M	Stctr	15Ma02Gb
SHERRY, Margt.		17	F	Unknown	15Ma02Gb
LAUGHRAN, Ellen		17	F	Dressmaker	15Ma02Gb
MCMAHON, Jas.		30	M	Tailor	15Ma02Gb
WOOD, Geo.		18	M	Tailor	15Ma02Gb
Eliza		30	F	Tailor	15Ma02Gb
ROACH, John		19	M	Tailor	15Ma02Gb
Margt.		20	F	Tailor	15Ma02Gb
BASHBY, Thos.		25	M	Tailor	15Ma02Gb
KELLY, Wm.		22	M	Tailor	15Ma02Gb
BOLE, Thos.		21	M	Tailor	15Ma02Gb
WARWICK, Peter		13	M	Tailor	15Ma02Gb
DIXON, Thos.		25	M	Tailor	15Ma02Gb
FLYNN, Thos.		26	M	Tailor	15Ma02Gb
CAINS, John		24	M	Tailor	15Ma02Gb
HENEHAN, Patk.		18	M	Tailor	15Ma02Gb
STAPLETON, Jane		20	F	Tailor	15Ma02Gb
CAPES, James		25	M	Tailor	15Ma02Gb
DRUM, Maurice		22	M	Tailor	15Ma02Gb
RYAN, Cathe.		20	F	Tailor	15Ma02Gb
CARROLL, Cathe.		20	F	Tailor	15Ma02Gb
KELLY, Terry		55	M	Tailor	15Ma02Gb
Mary	(W)	44	F	Tailor	15Ma02Gb

NAMES OF PASSENGERS		AGE	SEX	OCCUPATIONS	DATE PORT SHIP
KELLY, Michl.	(S)	24	M	Tailor	15Ma02Gb
Bartley	(S)	20	M	Tailor	15Ma02Gb
Cath.	(D)	15	F	Tailor	15Ma02Gb
Danl.	(S)	22	M	Tailor	15Ma02Gb
GUNNING, David		25	M	Carpenter	15Ma02Gb
John		24	M	Carpenter	15Ma02Gb
KELLY, Maurcie		25	M	Carpenter	15Ma02Gb
COLE, Danl.		30	M	Carpenter	15Ma02Gb
Ellen		25	F	Carpenter	15Ma02Gb
CASSIDY, Mary		23	F	Carpenter	15Ma02Gb
COLLWILL, Jas.		30	M	Carpenter	15Ma02Gb
CULLEN, Thos.		22	M	Carpenter	15Ma02Gb
COLLWILL, Wm.		30	M	Carpenter	15Ma02Gb
Andress	(W)	25	F	Carpenter	15Ma02Gb
Jas.	(S)	.00	M	Infant	15Ma02Gb
KEATON, Patk.		28	M	Carpenter	15Ma02Gb
DWYER, Walter		22	M	Carpenter	15Ma02Gb
NEALL, Wm.		23	M	Carpenter	15Ma02Gb
Bridget		23	F	Carpenter	15Ma02Gb
COFFEE, Mary		21	F	Carpenter	15Ma02Gb
DAILEY, Judy		21	F	Carpenter	15Ma02Gb
KELLY, Nancy		22	F	Carpenter	15Ma02Gb
DARCY, Mathew		22	M	Carpenter	15Ma02Gb
MURPHY, Jas.		20	M	Carpenter	15Ma02Gb
SALLY, Cathe.		20	F	Carpenter	15Ma02Gb
FITZPATRICK, Ellen		21	F	Carpenter	15Ma02Gb
COSTIGAN, John		23	M	Carpenter	15Ma02Gb
DONNELLY, Margt.		22	F	Carpenter	15Ma02Gb
Phebeus		55	F	Carpenter	15Ma02Gb
MCGANN, Thos.		27	M	Carpenter	15Ma02Gb
BOWDEN, Wm.		25	M	Carpenter	15Ma02Gb
Bridget		20	F	Carpenter	15Ma02Gb
Edward		19	M	Carpenter	15Ma02Gb
Mary		22	F	Carpenter	15Ma02Gb
CARROLL, John		20	M	Tailor	15Ma02Gb
SMITH, Danl.		18	M	Tailor	15Ma02Gb
RYAN, Danl.		19	M	Tailor	15Ma02Gb
MARK, Cathe.		17	F	Dressmaker	15Ma02Gb
CRAWLEY, Jas.		28	M	Dressmaker	15Ma02Gb
LADEN, Jno.		22	M	Dressmaker	15Ma02Gb
HEGAN, Jno.		20	M	Dressmaker	15Ma02Gb
LARON, Thos.		20	M	Dressmaker	15Ma02Gb
LEADEN, Susan		22	F	Dressmaker	15Ma02Gb
TIERNAN, Nancy		22	F	Dressmaker	15Ma02Gb
BRADLEY, John		20	M	Dressmaker	15Ma02Gb
MCGULLEN, Nancy		20	F	Dressmaker	15Ma02Gb
ARMSTRONG, Patk.		25	M	Dressmaker	15Ma02Gb
KENDEIGAN, Patk.		20	M	Laborer	15Ma02Gb
Mary		18	F	Laborer	15Ma02Gb
Bridget		16	F	Laborer	15Ma02Gb
KNAUGHTON, Mary		19	F	Laborer	15Ma02Gb
KING, John		40	M	Laborer	15Ma02Gb
Cath.	(W)	37	F	Laborer	15Ma02Gb
Margt.	(D)	06	F	Child	15Ma02Gb
Hannah	(D)	04	F	Child	15Ma02Gb
MCGEE, Thos.		38	M	Laborer	15Ma02Gb
Sarah	(W)	38	F	Laborer	15Ma02Gb
John	(S)	06	M	Child	15Ma02Gb
Saul	(S)	04	M	Child	15Ma02Gb
Sarah	(D)	02	F	Child	15Ma02Gb
MERCER, Mary		27	F	Laborer	15Ma02Gb
CONNOLLY, Margt.		22	F	Laborer	15Ma02Gb
BELFORD, Henry		16	M	Laborer	15Ma02Gb
Rose		14	F	Laborer	15Ma02Gb
POWER, Margt.		19	F	Laborer	15Ma02Gb
NICHOLS, Isaac		50	M	Laborer	15Ma02Gb
Esther	(W)	55	F	Laborer	15Ma02Gb
Jane	(D)	27	F	Laborer	15Ma02Gb
Isaac	(S)	21	F	Laborer	15Ma02Gb
Emma	(D)	16	F	Laborer	15Ma02Gb
MCGURK, Thos.		25	M	Laborer	15Ma02Gb
LYONS, Luke		45	M	Laborer	15Ma02Gb
Nancy		40	F	Laborer	15Ma02Gb
BARRELL, Nancy		30	F	Laborer	15Ma02Gb
MCKINZY, Jas.		24	M	Laborer	15Ma02Gb
CANNRONAN, Timothy		20	M	Laborer	15Ma02Gb
MARTIN, Mariah		20	F	Laborer	15Ma02Gb
REILY, Anne		27	F	Laborer	15Ma02Gb
Jas.	(S)	08	M	Child	15Ma02Gb
Mary-A.	(D)	06	F	Child	15Ma02Gb
MCGAURIN, Jas.		25	M	Laborer	15Ma02Gb
MCMANUS, Mary		22	F	Laborer	15Ma02Gb
HARNEY, Michl.		30	M	Laborer	15Ma02Gb
Darby		25	M	Laborer	15Ma02Gb
Thos.		18	M	Laborer	15Ma02Gb
Wm.		17	M	Laborer	15Ma02Gb
Mary		20	F	Laborer	15Ma02Gb
Ellen		11	F	None	15Ma02Gb
LONDERGAN, Jas.		22	M	Laborer	15Ma02Gb
Honor		20	F	Laborer	15Ma02Gb
SHELLY, Thos.		19	M	Laborer	15Ma02Gb
BYRNE, Peter		20	M	Laborer	15Ma02Gb
Michl.		30	M	Laborer	15Ma02Gb
CAMPBELL, Bridget		20	F	Laborer	15Ma02Gb
CARROLL, Thos.		30	M	Laborer	15Ma02Gb
MCKENNA, Conr.		20	M	Laborer	15Ma02Gb
Julia		18	F	Laborer	15Ma02Gb
CONVERY, Matilda		11	F	None	15Ma02Gb
John		09	M	Child	15Ma02Gb
WALDRON, John		22	M	Laborer	15Ma02Gb
BURNS, John		19	M	Laborer	15Ma02Gb
Maria		17	F	Laborer	15Ma02Gb
Jane		08	F	Child	15Ma02Gb
Henry		05	M	Child	15Ma02Gb
MURPHY, Peter		25	M	Laborer	15Ma02Gb
Ellen		22	F	Laborer	15Ma02Gb
Thos.		11	M	Laborer	15Ma02Gb
CARROLL, John		19	M	Laborer	15Ma02Gb
MCORMICK, Wm.		21	M	Laborer	15Ma02Gb
MOORE, James		25	M	Laborer	15Ma02Gb
John		21	M	Laborer	15Ma02Gb
FOSTER, John		23	M	Laborer	15Ma02Gb
MCFARLAND, U		22	U	Laborer	15Ma02Gb

VIRGINIAN 15 MAY 1846

From Liverpool

NAMES OF PASSENGERS		AGE	SEX	OCCUPATIONS	DATE PORT SHIP
RILEY, Mary		20	F	Domestic	15Ma02Ap
FITZPATRICK, Rose		20	F	Domestic	15Ma02Ap
ROURK, Biddy		18	F	Domestic	15Ma02Ap
GOUGH, Catherine		19	F	Domestic	15Ma02Ap
Bridget		16	F	Domestic	15Ma02Ap
HEALY, William		20	M	Laborer	15Ma02Ap
SWEENEY, Thomas		24	M	Laborer	15Ma02Ap
RILEY, Thos.		18	M	Laborer	15Ma02Ap
GOODWIN, Nick		28	M	Laborer	15Ma02Ap
FOULEY, James		18	M	Laborer	15Ma02Ap
DOEHARTY, Edward		18	M	Laborer	15Ma02Ap
MCGOOKIN, Thomas		24	M	Laborer	15Ma02Ap
Susanna		20	F	Domestic	15Ma02Ap
ROURK, Catherine		16	F	Domestic	15Ma02Ap
ARMSTRONG, Betsey		19	F	Domestic	15Ma02Ap
MCCABE, Biddy		20	F	Domestic	15Ma02Ap
GUNNE, Edward		27	M	Weaver	15Ma02Ap
Alex	(B)	35	M	Weaver	15Ma02Ap
James	(F)	60	M	Weaver	15Ma02Ap
Bridget		35	F	Domestic	15Ma02Ap
Margaret		04	F	Child	15Ma02Ap
Mary		11	F	Domestic	15Ma02Ap
Mary	(M)	55	F	Domestic	15Ma02Ap
KEARNAN, Thos.		22	M	Laborer	15Ma02Ap
DUFFY, John		22	M	Clerk	15Ma02Ap
Margaret		18	F	Domestic	15Ma02Ap

| --- | --- | --- | --- | --- | --- | --- | --- | --- | --- |
KEARNAN, Margret	20	F	Domestic	15Ma02Ap	NERISS, Thomas	24	M	Hrsm	15Ma02Ap
LOWE, Thos.	21	M	Laborer	15Ma02Ap	BRINON, John	20	M	Laborer	15Ma02Ap
WILSON, John	30	M	Laborer	15Ma02Ap	MCDERMOTT, Thomas	19	M	Laborer	15Ma02Ap
FAGEN, Wm.	23	M	Laborer	15Ma02Ap	HICKS, John	23	M	Laborer	15Ma02Ap
FAGAN, Ann	20	F	Domestic	15Ma02Ap	LAUGHLIN, Patrick	26	M	Laborer	15Ma02Ap
LYONS, Thos.	23	M	Laborer	15Ma02Ap	SCOTT, Edward	25	M	Laborer	15Ma02Ap
CASTLAND, Daniel	23	M	Laborer	15Ma02Ap	MCGIVEN, Mick	20	M	Laborer	15Ma02Ap
DONLAN, Mick	22	M	Laborer	15Ma02Ap	Patrick	16	M	Laborer	15Ma02Ap
RYAN, John	17	M	Laborer	15Ma02Ap	Hugh	22	M	Laborer	15Ma02Ap
SWEENY, Patrick	30	M	Laborer	15Ma02Ap	Pat	14	M	Laborer	15Ma02Ap
LANING, Patrick	28	M	Laborer	15Ma02Ap	KILLASE, Patrick	19	M	Laborer	15Ma02Ap
U, Thomas	22	M	Laborer	15Ma02Ap	MCGIVEN, Thomas	24	M	Laborer	15Ma02Ap
RYAN, Johannah	22	F	Domestic	15Ma02Ap	Owen	26	M	Laborer	15Ma02Ap
SWEENY, Catherine	29	F	Domestic	15Ma02Ap	DERWIN, Biddy	19	F	Domestic	15Ma02Ap
CONDON, Mary	26	F	Domestic	15Ma02Ap	GOODLICK, Mary	18	F	Domestic	15Ma02Ap
Alice	18	F	Domestic	15Ma02Ap	RAKILL, Mary	20	F	Domestic	15Ma02Ap
GORDON, Batley	40	M	Laborer	15Ma02Ap	MCGIVEN, Thomas	19	M	Laborer	15Ma02Ap
Michel	36	M	Laborer	15Ma02Ap	BRADY, Patrick	21	M	Laborer	15Ma02Ap
REED, Wm.	22	M	Laborer	15Ma02Ap	MCGIVEN, Patrick	28	M	Laborer	15Ma02Ap
CASKAN, Eliza	18	F	Domestic	15Ma02Ap	John	20	M	Laborer	15Ma02Ap
DAY, Patrick	48	M	Clerk	15Ma02Ap	Patrick	24	M	Laborer	15Ma02Ap
Catherine (W)	44	F	Domestic	15Ma02Ap	Ann	26	F	Domestic	15Ma02Ap
Mary (D)	14	F	Domestic	15Ma02Ap	Catherine	16	F	Domestic	15Ma02Ap
Catherine (D)	12	F	Domestic	15Ma02Ap	Mary	14	F	Domestic	15Ma02Ap
Patrick (S)	08	M	Child	15Ma02Ap	CUNNIF, John	24	M	Laborer	15Ma02Ap
Eliza (D)	10	F	Domestic	15Ma02Ap	Patrick	19	M	Laborer	15Ma02Ap
MARKE, Patrick	35	M	Laborer	15Ma02Ap	SHIELDS, Thomas	17	M	Laborer	15Ma02Ap
DUNCAN, Michel	22	M	Laborer	15Ma02Ap	MCGOUGH, Patrick	18	M	Laborer	15Ma02Ap
BRADBURN, Patrick	22	M	Laborer	15Ma02Ap	CAMEL, Thomas	22	M	Laborer	15Ma02Ap
CASEY, Bridget	27	F	Domestic	15Ma02Ap	Catherine	21	F	Domestic	15Ma02Ap
MAXWELL, Robert	15	M	Unknown	15Ma02Ap	Bridget	14	F	Domestic	15Ma02Ap
James	18	M	Laborer	15Ma02Ap	RILEY, Margret	26	F	Domestic	15Ma02Ap
George	20	M	Laborer	15Ma02Ap	MCGOUGH, Rose	20	F	Domestic	15Ma02Ap
MCMULLIN, Jane	22	F	Domestic	15Ma02Ap	BURRIS, Catherine	25	F	Domestic	15Ma02Ap
MAXWELL, George	50	M	Weaver	15Ma02Ap	DALEY, Mary	15	F	Servant	15Ma02Ap
Margret (W)	50	F	Wife	15Ma02Ap	MICHAL, Catherine	14	F	Servant	15Ma02Ap
Jane (D)	09	F	Child	15Ma02Ap	MULLOY, Judy	16	F	Servant	15Ma02Ap
Margret (D)	14	F	Unknown	15Ma02Ap	CAUGHLIN, Maria	29	F	Servant	15Ma02Ap
Joseph (S)	07	M	Child	15Ma02Ap	SKELLEY, William	30	M	Carpenter	15Ma02Ap
Alan (S)	24	M	Laborer	15Ma02Ap	Catherin (W)	26	F	Wife	15Ma02Ap
Margret (L)	26	F	Wife	15Ma02Ap	HAPENNY, James	23	M	Laborer	15Ma02Ap
John (S)	02	M	Child	15Ma02Ap	CAMEL, John	24	M	Laborer	15Ma02Ap
SHYAN, Jane	23	F	Laborer	15Ma02Ap	CONLIN, James	20	M	Laborer	15Ma02Ap
FINERTY, John	21	M	Laborer	15Ma02Ap	FARWIN, James	18	M	Laborer	15Ma02Ap
DUNCAN, Thomas	22	M	Laborer	15Ma02Ap	MARVIN, James	31	M	Laborer	15Ma02Ap
SHYAN, Thomas	24	M	Laborer	15Ma02Ap	Margret (W)	31	F	Wife	15Ma02Ap
John	23	M	Tailor	15Ma02Ap	James (S)	11	M	None	15Ma02Ap
HUGES, Peter	26	M	Laborer	15Ma02Ap	Mary (D)	09	F	Child	15Ma02Ap
HAMMOND, Wm.	23	M	Laborer	15Ma02Ap	John (S)	06	M	Child	15Ma02Ap
HAGAN, Henry	26	M	Laborer	15Ma02Ap	Francis (S)	03	M	Child	15Ma02Ap
KING, Denis	49	M	Laborer	15Ma02Ap	MCGOUGH, Mary	17	F	Servant	15Ma02Ap
WILEY, Ann	21	F	Domestic	15Ma02Ap	HIGGINS, Thomas	23	M	Shoemaker	15Ma02Ap
MCALLISTER, Fabes	27	F	Domestic	15Ma02Ap	MUNDY, Dennis	23	M	Unknown	15Ma02Ap
MCKENNY, Mary	23	F	Domestic	15Ma02Ap	Ann (W)	23	F	Wife	15Ma02Ap
Eliza	29	F	Domestic	15Ma02Ap	BOYLE, James	20	M	Laborer	15Ma02Ap
LISTON, John	23	M	Laborer	15Ma02Ap	BURNS, Patrick	22	M	Laborer	15Ma02Ap
BURKE, Thomas	24	M	Laborer	15Ma02Ap	CUMMIN, Michel	21	M	Laborer	15Ma02Ap
CASSIDY, Thomas	18	M	Laborer	15Ma02Ap	ROONEY, Margret	27	F	Servant	15Ma02Ap
COYLE, Thomas	20	M	Laborer	15Ma02Ap	Margret	04	F	Child	15Ma02Ap
CASSIDY, Ann	16	F	Domestic	15Ma02Ap	CROGAN, Margret	26	F	Dressmaker	15Ma02Ap
COYLE, Sarah	24	F	Domestic	15Ma02Ap	Ann-Mary	03	F	Child	15Ma02Ap
RIGBY, Mary	13	F	Domestic	15Ma02Ap	DEVER, William	20	M	Laborer	15Ma02Ap
CODY, Sandy	19	M	Laborer	15Ma02Ap	Patrick	19	M	Laborer	15Ma02Ap
MALONY, Thomas	20	M	Laborer	15Ma02Ap	MANALISS, Patrick	20	M	Laborer	15Ma02Ap
NEELE, Wm.	48	M	Laborer	15Ma02Ap	SMITH, Peter	26	M	Weaver	15Ma02Ap
MALONEY, Patrick	22	M	Miner	15Ma02Ap	Ellen	03	F	Child	15Ma02Ap
MOORE, William	28	M	Laborer	15Ma02Ap	MCCABE, Frank	21	M	Laborer	15Ma02Ap
KELLEY, John	20	M	Shoemaker	15Ma02Ap	MUNDY, Alex	20	M	Laborer	15Ma02Ap
Michel	20	M	Shoemaker	15Ma02Ap	CAMEL, Charles	22	M	Laborer	15Ma02Ap
KENWICK, John	20	M	Shoemaker	15Ma02Ap	MCGLINACH, Isabel	21	F	Dressmaker	15Ma02Ap
CORDEY, Susan	22	F	Domestic	15Ma02Ap	HARKEL, Sally	21	F	Servant	15Ma02Ap
Margret	22	F	Domestic	15Ma02Ap	KENNEDY, Mary	19	F	Servant	15Ma02Ap
GARRICAN, Mary	19	F	Domestic	15Ma02Ap	MAHON, Nancy	19	F	Servant	15Ma02Ap
FLANNEL, Biddy	21	F	Domestic	15Ma02Ap	HERBERSTON, Jamson	51	M	Weaver	15Ma02Ap
DERR, William	23	M	Laborer	15Ma02Ap	James (S)	10	M	Child	15Ma02Ap

NAMES OF PASSENGERS		AGE	SEX	OCCUPATIONS	DATE PORT SHIP
HERBERSTON, Francis(S)		16	M	Unknown	15Ma02Ap
HAGIN, John		19	M	Weaver	15Ma02Ap
DUFFIN, Sarah-Ann		25	F	Servant	15Ma02Ap
LEFERTY, Mary		21	F	Servant	15Ma02Ap
WALL, Mary		26	F	Servant	15Ma02Ap
SLANE, Mary		19	F	Servant	15Ma02Ap
Nancy		16	F	Servant	15Ma02Ap
MUNN, John		28	M	Laborer	15Ma02Ap
Mary		30	F	Servant	15Ma02Ap
ROGERS, Bridget		17	F	Servant	15Ma02Ap
MELANE, Rose		18	F	Dressmaker	15Ma02Ap
ROONEY, Susanna		20	F	Servant	15Ma02Ap
MCPEEK, Maria		19	F	Servant	15Ma02Ap
DAVISON, William		19	M	Laborer	15Ma02Ap
HERBSON, John		19	M	Laborer	15Ma02Ap
MURRY, Henery		18	M	Laborer	15Ma02Ap
MCQUILLAN, Henery		08	M	Child	15Ma02Ap
Robert		16	M	Child	15Ma02Ap
WARD, Alice		21	F	Servant	15Ma02Ap
Mary		17	F	Servant	15Ma02Ap
MARTIN, Isabel		19	F	Servant	15Ma02Ap
BRAKEY, William		55	M	Laborer	15Ma02Ap
Margaret	(W)	47	F	Wife	15Ma02Ap
MAGOON, Thomas		28	M	Weaver	15Ma02Ap
Bridget	(W)	27	F	Wife	15Ma02Ap
John	(S)	.02	M	Infant	15Ma02Ap
HERBERSON, Ann		22	F	Servant	15Ma02Ap
LOUGHRAN, Mary-Ann		16	F	Servant	15Ma02Ap
CAHELY, Patrick		42	M	Clerk	15Ma02Ap
BAGLEY, Peter		19	M	Clerk	15Ma02Ap
DAVISON, James		18	M	Laborer	15Ma02Ap
GAY, Edward		26	M	Farmer	15Ma02Ap
BOLD, William		19	M	Printer	15Ma02Ap
STEWARD, John		25	M	Farmer	15Ma02Ap
KELLEY, Daniel		23	M	Laborer	15Ma02Ap
RYAN, Marshall		22	M	Laborer	15Ma02Ap
MORRISS, Rachel-Virgin		.00	F	Infant	15Ma02Ap
Born-At-Sea		Died-At-Sea			
LOUGHRAN, William		00	M	Unknown	15Ma02Ap
CORBIT, William		00	M	Unknown	15Ma02Ap
Eliza		00	F	Unknown	15Ma02Ap
Ellen		00	F	Unknown	15Ma02Ap
LOMBARD, Anna		00	F	Unknown	15Ma02Ap

ELIZABETH 16 MAY 1846

From Liverpool

NAMES OF PASSENGERS		AGE	SEX	OCCUPATIONS	DATE PORT SHIP
TRAYNOR, Ann		21	F	Seamstress	16Ma02GI
HUGHES, May		20	F	Spinster	16Ma02GI
CONELY, Ann		22	F	Servant	16Ma02GI
Margaret		18	F	Servant	16Ma02GI
HUGHES, Henry		24	M	Farmer	16Ma02GI
SMITH, John		23	M	Farmer	16Ma02GI
DECOURSEY, John		30	M	Tailor	16Ma02GI
Henry	(S)	10	M	Child	16Ma02GI
NEAVIN, Ann		20	F	Tailor	16Ma02GI
CONNOLLY, Mary		20	F	Servant	16Ma02GI
DOLAN, William		21	M	Laborer	16Ma02GI
CARTY, James		20	M	Laborer	16Ma02GI
GALLAGHER, Ann		16	F	Servant	16Ma02GI
KENNEDY, Louisa		12	F	Servant	16Ma02GI
Lawe.		26	M	Surgeon	16Ma02GI
MURRAY, Thomas		60	M	Land Agent	16Ma02GI
Ann	(W)	50	F	Wife	16Ma02GI
Mary	(D)	21	F	Unknown	16Ma02GI
John	(S)	20	M	Laborer	16Ma02GI
Thomas	(S)	17	M	Laborer	16Ma02GI
Patrick	(S)	14	M	Laborer	16Ma02GI

NAMES OF PASSENGERS		AGE	SEX	OCCUPATIONS	DATE PORT SHIP
MURRAY, Lawrence	(S)	11	M	Child	16Ma02GI
James	(S)	07	M	Child	16Ma02GI
Bryan	(S)	05	M	Child	16Ma02GI
COX, James		27	M	Shoemaker	16Ma02GI
Ann	(W)	27	F	Wife	16Ma02GI
John	(S)	07	M	Child	16Ma02GI
William	(S)	02	M	Child	16Ma02GI
MCHUGH, John		21	M	Laborer	16Ma02GI
RIELY, Edward		22	M	Laborer	16Ma02GI
MEALEY, Thomas		30	M	Shoemaker	16Ma02GI
Mary	(W)	25	F	Wife	16Ma02GI
HORSE, Hugh		16	M	Shoemaker	16Ma02GI
MEALY, John		09	M	Child	16Ma02GI
James	(B)	06	M	Child	16Ma02GI
Thomas	(B)	04	M	Child	16Ma02GI
MCSHANE, John		26	M	Tailor	16Ma02GI
CARR, Franics		25	M	Tailor	16Ma02GI
Frances		30	F	Shoemaker	16Ma02GI
Mary	(W)	30	F	Wife	16Ma02GI
Mary	(D)	03	F	Child	16Ma02GI
U	(D)	.03	F	Infant	16Ma02GI
MCLAUGHLIN, James		22	M	Farmer	16Ma02GI
COSTIGAN, James		24	M	Blacksmith	16Ma02GI
OHARRA, Thomas		33	M	Laborer	16Ma02GI
LYNCH, Judy		23	F	Servant	16Ma02GI
CORMICK, Judy		19	F	Servant	16Ma02GI
FLYNN, Patrick		21	M	Laborer	16Ma02GI
U	(W)	20	F	Wife	16Ma02GI
MCBRIDE, Danl.		39	M	Carpenter	16Ma02GI
U	(W)	36	F	Wife	16Ma02GI
Mary	(D)	16	F	Servant	16Ma02GI
Margaret	(D)	14	F	Servant	16Ma02GI
Cathrn.	(D)	12	F	Servant	16Ma02GI
James	(S)	10	M	None	16Ma02GI
Elena	(D)	08	F	Servant	16Ma02GI
Jane	(D)	06	F	Child	16Ma02GI
Ann	(D)	04	F	Child	16Ma02GI
Archibald	(S)	02	M	Child	16Ma02GI
Daniel	(S)	01	M	Child	16Ma02GI
MCCLARTY, Daniel		16	M	Laborer	16Ma02GI
CAMPBELL, Patk.		21	M	Flaxdr	16Ma02GI
CUNNINGHAM, John		23	M	Flaxdr	16Ma02GI
Cathrn.	(W)	19	F	Wife	16Ma02GI
DAILEY, Bridget		20	F	Servant	16Ma02GI
Margaret		19	F	Servant	16Ma02GI
LOUTH, Cathrn.		21	F	Servant	16Ma02GI
RYAN, James		24	M	Laborer	16Ma02GI
U	(W)	24	F	Wife	16Ma02GI
PENNEFATHER, James		24	M	Laborer	16Ma02GI
U	(W)	24	F	Wife	16Ma02GI
John	(S)	01	M	Child	16Ma02GI
KENNA, Mary		20	F	Servant	16Ma02GI
FANNING, Cathrn.		19	F	Servant	16Ma02GI
GORMAN, Cathrn.		19	F	Servant	16Ma02GI
GALLAHER, Thos.		20	M	Laborer	16Ma02GI
KEARNEY, Kean		20	M	Laborer	16Ma02GI
SCOTT, John		20	M	Laborer	16Ma02GI
Margaret		21	F	Servant	16Ma02GI
Ann		06	F	Child	16Ma02GI
Cathrn.		22	F	Servant	16Ma02GI
DUFFY, Patk.		19	M	Laborer	16Ma02GI
FRIELL, Patrick		20	M	Laborer	16Ma02GI
TOOLE, John		20	M	Laborer	16Ma02GI
MEALEY, Edmond		23	M	Laborer	16Ma02GI
MCNAMARA, Patk.		23	M	Laborer	16Ma02GI
DAVITT, Neppy		16	F	Servant	16Ma02GI
MCDONALD, James		18	M	Laborer	16Ma02GI
TOOLE, Thomas		28	M	Laborer	16Ma02GI
MCCABE, John		25	M	Weaver	16Ma02GI
RIELY, Thos.		26	M	Laborer	16Ma02GI
CONNORY, William		25	M	Laborer	16Ma02GI
MCKINTY, Patk.		19	M	Laborer	16Ma02GI
Sarah		21	F	Servant	16Ma02GI
KEENAN, Mary		21	F	Servant	16Ma02GI
OHARA, Mary		55	F	Servant	16Ma02GI

NAMES OF PASSENGERS	AGE	SEX	OCCUPATIONS	DATE PORT SHIP
OHARA, Martin	36	M	Laborer	16Ma02GI
Charles	24	M	Laborer	16Ma02GI
MCCAVAGH, John	18	M	Laborer	16Ma02GI
OHARA, Ann	22	F	Servant	16Ma02GI
Margt.	21	F	Servant	16Ma02GI
Elena	18	F	Servant	16Ma02GI
COLEMAN, Margt.	16	F	Servant	16Ma02GI
WALSH, Anne	18	F	Servant	16Ma02GI
DUFF, John	22	M	Laborer	16Ma02GI
Rose	19	F	Servant	16Ma02GI
MCSHANE, James	22	M	Laborer	16Ma02GI
MELVIN, Margt.	22	F	Servant	16Ma02GI
COYLE, Ann	55	F	Servant	16Ma02GI
Patrick (S)	20	M	Shoemaker	16Ma02GI
Hugh (S)	19	M	Laborer	16Ma02GI
Stephen (S)	18	M	Laborer	16Ma02GI
Denis (S)	13	M	Laborer	16Ma02GI
MCBRIDE, Daniel	29	M	Laborer	16Ma02GI
SHEVLIN, James	20	M	Laborer	16Ma02GI
SHIELL, James	20	M	Laborer	16Ma02GI
BOYCE, Neill	22	M	Laborer	16Ma02GI
DOHERTY, Robt.	22	M	Farmer	16Ma02GI
MCDEVITT, Chas.	22	M	Farmer	16Ma02GI
BRYAN, James	30	M	Laborer	16Ma02GI
KANE, Abigall	20	F	Servant	16Ma02GI
MULLCAHEY, William	29	M	Laborer	16Ma02GI
Johanna (W)	27	F	Servant	16Ma02GI
Cathrn. (D)	05	F	Child	16Ma02GI
CORBITT, William	23	M	Laborer	16Ma02GI
FARRELL, Cathrn.	23	F	Servant	16Ma02GI
BARRY, Johanna	23	F	Servant	16Ma02GI
MORRISS, Alice	20	F	Servant	16Ma02GI
GINIVAN, Margt.	20	F	Servant	16Ma02GI
MURRAY, Mary	20	F	Dressmaker	16Ma02GI
FITZGERALD, Margt.	20	F	Dressmaker	16Ma02GI
MCVEAGH, Patk.	20	M	Farmer	16Ma02GI
BOYLE, Henry	22	M	Laborer	16Ma02GI
BARLOW, Patt.	15	M	Laborer	16Ma02GI
MCGUIGAN, Mary	21	F	Dressmaker	16Ma02GI
DOOLL, George	21	M	Joiner	16Ma02GI
NOWLAN, Patt.	23	M	Laborer	16Ma02GI
Francis	20	F	Servant	16Ma02GI
Mathew	23	M	Gdnr	16Ma02GI
FLYNN, Denis	28	M	Laborer	16Ma02GI
David	22	M	Laborer	16Ma02GI
MURRAY, John	19	M	Laborer	16Ma02GI
SEXTON, Anastla	24	F	Servant	16Ma02GI
TRAINOR, John	28	M	Servant	16Ma02GI
CUNNINGHAM, Patt.	26	M	Coachman	16Ma02GI
TREANOR, Cathrn.	20	F	Servant	16Ma02GI
MCKENNA, Ann	25	F	Servant	16Ma02GI
BRIAN, Jeremiah	27	M	Laborer	16Ma02GI
CLEARY, Elena	22	F	Servant	16Ma02GI
DONOHOE, John	32	M	Weaver	16Ma02GI
Edwd.	22	M	Weaver	16Ma02GI
Alice	20	F	Servant	16Ma02GI
Thomas	24	M	Laborer	16Ma02GI
Mary	40	F	Servant	16Ma02GI
Ann	20	F	Servant	16Ma02GI
SULLIVAN, Honora	17	F	Servant	16Ma02GI
BULL, Daniel	15	M	Servant	16Ma02GI
MULGRAVE, John	19	M	Tailor	16Ma02GI
RYAN, John	19	F	Servant	16Ma02GI
TRAYNOR, James	26	M	Laborer	16Ma02GI
MCMAHON, Peter	24	M	Shoemaker	16Ma02GI
Bridget	19	F	Servant	16Ma02GI
REDDINGTON, Bridget	22	F	Servant	16Ma02GI
GRAY, Mary	24	F	Dressmaker	16Ma02GI
MCLAUGHLIN, James	16	M	Servant	16Ma02GI
Margery	11	F	Servant	16Ma02GI
CARR, Patt	21	M	Laborer	16Ma02GI
Nancy	11	F	Servant	16Ma02GI
BURNS, Bridget	19	F	Servant	16Ma02GI
DUGGAN, Mary	19	F	Servant	16Ma02GI
HAGERTY, Mary	20	F	Servant	16Ma02GI
DORAN, Margt.	21	F	Servant	16Ma02GI
HAGERTY, Ellen	21	F	Servant	16Ma02GI
CARR, Patt	21	M	Laborer	16Ma02GI
GILLESPIE, Sarah	21	F	Servant	16Ma02GI
BURNS, Thos.	24	M	Laborer	16Ma02GI
MCCAULEY, James	22	M	Laborer	16Ma02GI
MCSHANE, Bridget	21	F	Servant	16Ma02GI
CARR, Condy	21	M	Laborer	16Ma02GI
BURNS, Elen	21	F	Servant	16Ma02GI
Mary	20	F	Servant	16Ma02GI
KANE, Eliza	24	F	Wife	16Ma02GI
Mary (D)	06	F	Child	16Ma02GI
Patk. (S)	02	M	Child	16Ma02GI
MCLAUGHLIN, John	21	M	Laborer	16Ma02GI
HAMMILL, James	19	M	Laborer	16Ma02GI
HAGERTY, Patk.	21	M	Laborer	16Ma02GI
KEEGAN, James	20	M	Laborer	16Ma02GI
HARNEY, Mary	20	F	Servant	16Ma02GI
RIELEY, Bridget	18	F	Servant	16Ma02GI
Betty	17	F	Servant	16Ma02GI
NOLAN, Michael	24	M	Laborer	16Ma02GI
CARRAKY, Denis	24	M	Laborer	16Ma02GI
CARTY, James	24	M	Laborer	16Ma02GI
GRAHAM, Thos.	23	M	Shoemaker	16Ma02GI
Peter	13	M	Laborer	16Ma02GI
MCDERMOTT, Luke	18	M	Laborer	16Ma02GI
Rose	04	F	Child	16Ma02GI
Ann	07	F	Child	16Ma02GI
BOYLAN, Bridget	15	F	Servant	16Ma02GI
NEVLIN, William	46	M	Weaver	16Ma02GI
Francis (W)	40	F	Wife	16Ma02GI
Cathrn. (D)	16	F	Servant	16Ma02GI
William (S)	10	M	Weaver	16Ma02GI
Martha (D)	07	F	Child	16Ma02GI
TOOLE, Thomas	21	M	Laborer	16Ma02GI
GREELEY, John	20	M	Laborer	16Ma02GI
DEVIN, Patt	21	M	Laborer	16Ma02GI
BOYLAN, John	22	M	Laborer	16Ma02GI
OHARE, Peter	23	M	Laborer	16Ma02GI
RIELY, Hugh	22	M	Laborer	16Ma02GI
GARTLAND, Nicholas	23	M	Weaver	16Ma02GI
MULROY, Nicholas	20	M	Laborer	16Ma02GI
DARCY, Cathrn.	20	F	Servant	16Ma02GI
GARTLAND, Cathrn.	19	F	Servant	16Ma02GI
CLINTON, Bessy	19	F	Servant	16Ma02GI
CAMPBELL, Ann	18	F	Servant	16Ma02GI
NEILE, Ann	20	F	Servant	16Ma02GI
MAGEE, Mary	20	F	Servant	16Ma02GI
FITZPATRICK, Rose	20	F	Servant	16Ma02GI
GAMMON, Peter	21	M	Laborer	16Ma02GI
RIELEY, Peter	22	M	Laborer	16Ma02GI
MURPHY, John	30	M	Laborer	16Ma02GI
RIELY, John	22	M	Laborer	16Ma02GI
MILODY, Thos.	24	M	Laborer	16Ma02GI
PERRY, Margt.	20	F	Dressmaker	16Ma02GI
BYRNE, Bryan	24	M	Laborer	16Ma02GI
HANNON, Richard	19	M	Laborer	16Ma02GI
LAPAN, Thos.	18	M	Laborer	16Ma02GI
Margt.	19	F	Servant	16Ma02GI
DOONAN, Jane	18	F	Servant	16Ma02GI

QUEEN-VICTORIA 16 MAY 1846

From St.Vincent

NAMES OF PASSENGERS	AGE	SEX	OCCUPATIONS	DATE PORT SHIP
NEWTON, J.G.	50	M	None	16Ma40Gm
Edw. (S)	20	M	None	16Ma40Gm
Augustus (S)	18	M	None	16Ma40Gm
U (D)	30	F	None	16Ma40Gm

NAMES OF PASSENGERS		A G E	S E X	OCCUPATIONS	DATE PORT SHIP	NAMES OF PASSENGERS		A G E	S E X	OCCUPATIONS	DATE PORT SHIP
NEWTON, Caroline	(D)	20	F	None	16Ma40Gm	MARTIN, Cathne.		17	F	Spinster	18Ma02Ay
Georgiana	(D)	17	F	None	16Ma40Gm	RIALLEY, Rosanah		30	F	Wife	18Ma02Ay
TUCKER, U		19	F	None	16Ma40Gm	CUNAN, Margt.		25	F	House Maid	18Ma02Ay
LOVE, John		20	M	None	16Ma40Gm	RUSSELL, Ann		23	F	House Maid	18Ma02Ay
U		20	M	None	16Ma40Gm	HALLIGAN, James		27	M	Laborer	18Ma02Ay
PLAIN, Pauline		45	F	None	16Ma40Gm	DEVIN, John		20	M	Laborer	18Ma02Ay
BALT, Charles		30	M	None	16Ma40Gm	ALLEN, Pat		25	M	Laborer	18Ma02Ay
CORWIN, Noel		14	M	None	16Ma40Gm	DUGGAN, Thomas		21	M	Laborer	18Ma02Ay
BALT, Rich.		09	M	Child	16Ma40Gm	MCCREADY, Thomas		23	M	Joiner	18Ma02Ay
SOLISTRY, James		30	M	None	16Ma40Gm	KELLY, Peter		25	M	Laborer	18Ma02Ay
						GRADY, Joseph		26	M	Farmer	18Ma02Ay
						William		30	M	Farmer	18Ma02Ay
						DAVIDSON, Richard		22	M	Weaver	18Ma02Ay
						Ann	(W)	25	F	Wife	18Ma02Ay
						MCDONNELL, Dominick		22	M	Laborer	18Ma02Ay
VICTORIA 18 MAY 1846						RIELLY, Charles		23	M	Laborer	18Ma02Ay
						CONNOLLY, Dennis		24	M	Farmer	18Ma02Ay
From Liverpool						Catharin	(W)	22	F	Wife	18Ma02Ay
						BYRNE, John		26	M	Farmer	18Ma02Ay
						Hugh		36	M	Farmer	18Ma02Ay
						SAMPSON, Christopher		36	M	Weaver	18Ma02Ay
HENNESSY, Michael		50	M	Farmer	18Ma02Ay	MCDONNELL, Edward		29	M	Carpenter	18Ma02Ay
RYAN, Margt.		21	F	Dressmaker	18Ma02Ay	MCGRATH, Robert		32	M	Laborer	18Ma02Ay
RILEY, Mary		18	F	Cst	18Ma02Ay	RUSSELL, Thomas		18	M	Weaver	18Ma02Ay
Catherine		16	F	Spinster	18Ma02Ay	BELL, John		16	M	Weaver	18Ma02Ay
KIRBY, Simon		28	M	Chandler	18Ma02Ay	BARR, Joseph		22	M	Laborer	18Ma02Ay
MANSON, Martin		27	M	Laborer	18Ma02Ay	HENDERSON, James		21	M	Laborer	18Ma02Ay
Susan	(W)	24	F	Wife	18Ma02Ay	Eliza		16	F	Spinster	18Ma02Ay
Bridget	(D)	01	F	Child	18Ma02Ay	KENNY, Mary		22	F	Spinster	18Ma02Ay
CONNORS, David		26	M	Laborer	18Ma02Ay	Catharine		20	F	Spinster	18Ma02Ay
COMB, William		28	M	Laborer	18Ma02Ay	HINSON, Mary		18	F	Spinster	18Ma02Ay
Honora	(W)	24	F	Wife	18Ma02Ay	LENNY, Mary		20	F	House Maid	18Ma02Ay
LANNON, Mary		19	F	Spinster	18Ma02Ay	John		56	M	Weaver	18Ma02Ay
Hugh		21	M	Laborer	18Ma02Ay	Patrick		25	M	Laborer	18Ma02Ay
QUINN, Mary		18	F	Spinster	18Ma02Ay	John		20	M	Laborer	18Ma02Ay
MCDERMOND, James		27	M	Laborer	18Ma02Ay	LYNCH, James		30	M	Laborer	18Ma02Ay
DOUGAN, Michael		27	M	Laborer	18Ma02Ay	Bridget	(W)	25	F	Wife	18Ma02Ay
SCULLY, Wm.		26	M	Laborer	18Ma02Ay	Elizabeth	(D)	07	F	Child	18Ma02Ay
DUNN, Thomas		18	M	Laborer	18Ma02Ay	KELLY, Mathew		32	M	Laborer	18Ma02Ay
COSTELLO, Bridget		17	F	Spinster	18Ma02Ay	MORGAN, James		34	M	Laborer	18Ma02Ay
MORAN, Elizabeth		20	F	Spinster	18Ma02Ay	James		30	M	Laborer	18Ma02Ay
HARRINGTON, Mary		24	F	Spinster	18Ma02Ay	BYRNE, Peter		28	M	Laborer	18Ma02Ay
COX, Catherine		22	F	Spinster	18Ma02Ay	NELLAN, Michael		20	M	Laborer	18Ma02Ay
HENSON, John		23	M	Laborer	18Ma02Ay	HUSSEY, Edward		24	M	Groom	18Ma02Ay
HENRY, Michael		20	M	Laborer	18Ma02Ay	RENNOLDS, Michael		28	M	Laborer	18Ma02Ay
James		12	M	Laborer	18Ma02Ay	LEE, Barclay		21	M	Laborer	18Ma02Ay
MORAN, Cathrne.		20	F	Spinster	18Ma02Ay	SCOTT, William		30	M	Laborer	18Ma02Ay
HYNES, Ann		20	F	Spinster	18Ma02Ay	EARLY, James		21	M	Dressmaker	18Ma02Ay
KELLY, Mary		19	F	Spinster	18Ma02Ay	REYNOLDS, James		18	M	Spinner	18Ma02Ay
HARRINGTON, Ann		19	F	Spinster	18Ma02Ay	TURNBULL, Mary		17	F	Spinster	18Ma02Ay
SULLIVAN, Ellen		30	F	Spinster	18Ma02Ay	FLYNN, Bridget		18	F	Spinster	18Ma02Ay
Johanna		18	F	Spinster	18Ma02Ay	MALONEY, Wm.		25	M	Laborer	18Ma02Ay
WALSH, Maurice		21	M	Carpenter	18Ma02Ay	MORAN, William		26	M	Laborer	18Ma02Ay
MAHN, Ann		18	F	Spinster	18Ma02Ay	NAGLE, Hannah		20	F	Dressmaker	18Ma02Ay
Margaret		16	F	Spinster	18Ma02Ay	KEEFE, Johannah		20	F	Dressmaker	18Ma02Ay
WHEELER, Eliza		20	F	Cnf	18Ma02Ay	Margaret		22	F	Dressmaker	18Ma02Ay
LYONS, Mary		19	F	Spinster	18Ma02Ay	KAVANNAGH, John		20	M	Teacher	18Ma02Ay
QUINN, Michael		25	M	Laborer	18Ma02Ay	KELLAHER, Michael		20	M	Laborer	18Ma02Ay
MARNEY, John		22	M	Laborer	18Ma02Ay	MURPHY, Daniel		20	M	Laborer	18Ma02Ay
WALSH, John		22	M	Laborer	18Ma02Ay	KAVANAUGH, Cathnr.		22	F	Dressmaker	18Ma02Ay
QUINN, William		21	M	Laborer	18Ma02Ay	CONNOR, James		25	M	Shoemaker	18Ma02Ay
WALSH, Bridget		25	F	House Maid	18Ma02Ay	KENNEDY, Jeremiah		25	M	Laborer	18Ma02Ay
RYAN, Mary		26	F	House Maid	18Ma02Ay	CONNOR, John		20	M	Laborer	18Ma02Ay
ROSS, Mary		18	F	House Maid	18Ma02Ay	GRIFFIN, Patrick		19	M	Laborer	18Ma02Ay
COMMINS, Cathne.		22	F	Spinster	16Ma02Ay	BOYD, James		30	M	Laborer	18Ma02Ay
Jane		19	F	Spinster	18Ma02Ay	SHERARD, James		22	M	Laborer	18Ma02Ay
KENNEDY, Cathne.		25	F	Spinster	18Ma02Ay	FULLEN, Robert		19	M	Laborer	18Ma02Ay
LOUREY, Pat		35	M	Tailor	18Ma02Ay	CHERRY, Mary		26	F	Seamstress	18Ma02Ay
GIBBONS, Thomas		20	M	Baker	18Ma02Ay	HENRY, George		26	M	Laborer	18Ma02Ay
QUINN, Patt		20	M	Tailor	18Ma02Ay	YOUNG, David		22	M	Clerk	18Ma02Ay
LANNON, Ann		26	F	Spinster	18Ma02Ay	QUINN, Robt.		26	M	Painter	18Ma02Ay
CUNNINGHAM, Margt.		18	F	Spinster	18Ma02Ay	GLEESON, Thomas		25	M	Laborer	18Ma02Ay
MCDONALD, Rose		19	F	Spinster	18Ma02Ay	TOOHEY, James		30	M	Laborer	18Ma02Ay
MCCAULLEE, Cathne.		19	F	Spinster	18Ma02Ay	DONNELLY, Ellen		18	F	Wife	18Ma02Ay
MCDONNELL, Mary		18	F	Spinster	18Ma02Ay	MCFATRIDGE, James		37	M	Farmer	18Ma02Ay

NAMES OF PASSENGERS		AGE	SEX	OCCUPATIONS	DATE PORT SHIP
CURRY, James		22	M	Shoemaker	18Ma02Ay
GILMORE, Robert		38	M	Farmer	18Ma02Ay
NALLELY, Bridget		18	F	Nurse	18Ma02Ay
DAVIS, Ellen		16	F	Dressmaker	18Ma02Ay
FARELL, Ann		18	F	Spinster	18Ma02Ay
CONNORS, James		17	M	Butler	18Ma02Ay
CANNOVAN, Jane		38	F	Weaver	18Ma02Ay
ROGERS, James		23	M	Weaver	18Ma02Ay
MACAULLY, Dennis		33	M	Weaver	18Ma02Ay
MAGUIRE, Catharin		23	F	Spinster	18Ma02Ay
DONNELLY, Mary		20	F	Dressmaker	18Ma02Ay
ROGERS, Margaret		20	F	Dressmaker	18Ma02Ay
DONNELLY, Thomas		11	M	Child	18Ma02Ay
DEVINE, Bridget		25	F	Spinster	18Ma02Ay
Johanna		20	F	Spinster	18Ma02Ay
DWYER, James		30	M	Farmer	18Ma02Ay
BALLANEY, Patt		28	M	Laborer	18Ma02Ay
GODFREY, John		20	M	Laborer	18Ma02Ay
GAMBLE, James		20	M	Laborer	18Ma02Ay
TODD, Ellen		35	F	Wi	18Ma02Ay
HEANEY, Margaret		30	F	Spinster	18Ma02Ay
ROONEY, Mary		19	F	Spinster	18Ma02Ay
SULLIVAN, Ann		23	F	House Maid	18Ma02Ay
RICKARD, Patk.		22	M	Laborer	18Ma02Ay
James		18	M	Laborer	18Ma02Ay
FEGAN, Mary		23	F	Spinster	18Ma02Ay
GILLIGAN, Cathne.		23	F	Lad	18Ma02Ay
LEONARD, Cathne.		36	F	Wife	18Ma02Ay
MORAN, Thomas		22	M	Laborer	18Ma02Ay
DUMFEY, Edward		23	M	Gdnr	18Ma02Ay
PICKARD, Michael		24	M	Laborer	18Ma02Ay
Ann		23	F	House Maid	18Ma02Ay
COMMING, Ann		26	F	Spinster	18Ma02Ay
REGAN, Mary		20	F	Spinster	18Ma02Ay
MURRAY, John		25	M	Laborer	18Ma02Ay
CLARK, John		30	M	Laborer	18Ma02Ay
DORNAN, Elizth.		25	F	Spinster	18Ma02Ay
HALFPENCE, Mary		60	F	Cook	18Ma02Ay
NEVILLE, George		18	M	Laborer	18Ma02Ay
James		20	M	Laborer	18Ma02Ay
THOMPSON, Charles		23	M	Laborer	18Ma02Ay
MOONEY, Edward		25	M	Laborer	18Ma02Ay
REGAN, Julia		25	F	Dressmaker	18Ma02Ay
PATTON, Sarah		19	F	Nurse	18Ma02Ay
Cathne.		17	F	House Maid	18Ma02Ay
ALEXANDER, Sarah		25	F	House Maid	18Ma02Ay
OBRIEN, Michl.		30	M	Laborer	18Ma02Ay
DESMOND, Michl.		26	M	Laborer	18Ma02Ay
HEIRNE, Mich.		23	M	Laborer	18Ma02Ay
WALSH, Michl.		27	M	Laborer	18Ma02Ay
HANNAHAN, John		28	M	Laborer	18Ma02Ay
RYAN, Michael		28	M	Laborer	18Ma02Ay
MCCARTY, Pat		25	M	Laborer	18Ma02Ay
CALLAHAN, Dennis		25	M	Laborer	18Ma02Ay
DONOVAN, Jeremiah		25	M	Laborer	18Ma02Ay
FARRELL, Andrew		35	M	Laborer	18Ma02Ay
Alice	(W)	33	F	Wife	18Ma02Ay
James	(S)	15	M	Single	18Ma02Ay
Ellen	(D)	10	F	Child	18Ma02Ay
Patrick	(S)	02	M	Child	18Ma02Ay
ROURKE, James		20	M	Laborer	18Ma02Ay
SHERDON, Barry		19	M	Laborer	18Ma02Ay
MCGARLAND, John		22	M	Laborer	18Ma02Ay
Mary		40	F	Wife	18Ma02Ay
FITZPATRICK, Jane		20	F	Spinster	18Ma02Ay
CASEY, Bridget		38	F	Wife	18Ma02Ay
OWEN, Rose		55	F	Wi	18Ma02Ay
FEENAN, Ellen		25	F	Lady'S Maid	18Ma02Ay
WELDAN, Cathne.		26	F	Seamstress	18Ma02Ay
TURNAN, Maria		30	F	Spinster	18Ma02Ay
Maria		16	F	Spinster	18Ma02Ay
DUGAN, Michael		35	M	Coachman	18Ma02Ay
John		32	M	Laborer	18Ma02Ay
James		25	M	Laborer	18Ma02Ay
WELDAN, John		28	M	Laborer	18Ma02Ay

NAMES OF PASSENGERS		AGE	SEX	OCCUPATIONS	DATE PORT SHIP
LAWLER, Thomas		22	M	Laborer	18Ma02Ay
Jeremiah		20	M	Laborer	18Ma02Ay
WALSH, Phillip		25	M	Laborer	18Ma02Ay
FARRELL, John		23	M	Tailor	18Ma02Ay
CONNOR, Michael		26	M	Laborer	18Ma02Ay
MATHEW, Thomas		26	M	Laborer	18Ma02Ay
BULGER, Isaac		20	M	Laborer	18Ma02Ay
DOOLAN, Maurice		30	M	Laborer	18Ma02Ay
ODONNELL, William		48	M	Farmer	18Ma02Ay
Margaret	(W)	38	F	Wife	18Ma02Ay
John	(S)	17	M	Laborer	18Ma02Ay
Patt	(S)	09	M	Child	18Ma02Ay
William	(S)	07	M	Child	18Ma02Ay
Alice		23	F	Seamstress	18Ma02Ay
Mary	(D)	21	F	Spinster	18Ma02Ay
Margaret	(D)	18	F	Spinster	18Ma02Ay
Honora		09		Child	18Ma02Ay
Johanna		01		Child	18Ma02Ay
GEARY, Margaret		23	F	Spinster	18Ma02Ay
NOLAND, Thomas		54	M	Farmer	18Ma02Ay
George	(S)	23	M	Farmer	18Ma02Ay
Thomas	(S)	21	M	Farmer	18Ma02Ay
Silvester	(S)	14	M	Single	18Ma02Ay
Eleanor	(W)	50	F	Wife	18Ma02Ay
Mary	(D)	18	F	Spinster	18Ma02Ay
FEEHAN, Mathew		21	M	Farmer	18Ma02Ay
Bridget		20	F	Dairymaid	18Ma02Ay
NEILL, Thomas		22	M	Shoemaker	18Ma02Ay
HORAN, James		20	M	Laborer	18Ma02Ay
FARRELL, James		30	M	Laborer	18Ma02Ay
HELEY, Philip		28	M	Laborer	18Ma02Ay
HEIES, Cathne.		20	F	House Maid	18Ma02Ay
BALLADY, Mary		22	F	Cook	18Ma02Ay
TREASAY, Cathne.		20	F	House Maid	18Ma02Ay
MAQUILLAN, Mary		19	F	Spinster	18Ma02Ay
HENRY, Jane		17	F	Nurse	18Ma02Ay

CORNET 18 MAY 1846

From Liverpool

NAMES OF PASSENGERS		AGE	SEX	OCCUPATIONS	DATE PORT SHIP
RIELLY, Patt		21	M	Laborer	18Ma02Gn
FINERAN, Ann		21	F	None	18Ma02Gn
MARTIN, Cathn.		23	F	None	18Ma02Gn
Ellen		28	F	None	18Ma02Gn
LEARY, Mary		16	F	None	18Ma02Gn
FOLEY, Martin		30	M	Laborer	18Ma02Gn
U	(W)	20	F	None	18Ma02Gn
RYAN, Thos.		29	M	Laborer	18Ma02Gn
WALLACE, John		29	M	Laborer	18Ma02Gn
MALONEY, Saml.		24	M	Laborer	18Ma02Gn
COLLENTON, John		23	M	Laborer	18Ma02Gn
CLASFRY, Wm.		24	M	Laborer	18Ma02Gn
QUINN, John		27	M	Laborer	18Ma02Gn
KEENAN, James		46	M	Laborer	18Ma02Gn
Maurice	(S)	20	M	Laborer	18Ma02Gn
James	(S)	17	M	Laborer	18Ma02Gn
Dennis	(S)	14	M	Laborer	18Ma02Gn
Ally	(W)	50	F	None	18Ma02Gn
SHAUGHNESY, Thos.		23	M	Laborer	18Ma02Gn
Mary		26	F	None	18Ma02Gn
HEACHMAN, John		21	M	Laborer	18Ma02Gn
CALLAGHAN, Mary		23	F	None	18Ma02Gn
RUNGROSS, Mary		17	F	None	18Ma02Gn
DOWNEY, James		20	M	Laborer	18Ma02Gn
MCGOWAN, Mickl.		26	M	Laborer	18Ma02Gn
KEOGH, Wm.		26	M	Laborer	18Ma02Gn
GREEN, Mickl.		24	M	Laborer	18Ma02Gn
CRAVEN, Patr.		24	M	Laborer	18Ma02Gn

NAMES OF PASSENGERS		A G E	S E X	OCCUPATIONS	DATE PORT SHIP
COYNE, Mary		20	F	None	18Ma02Gn
SHAUGHNESSY, Betty		22	F	None	18Ma02Gn
TYERALL, John		26	M	Laborer	18Ma02Gn
ROONEY, Biddy		16	F	None	18Ma02Gn
MORAN, Mary		20	F	None	18Ma02Gn
FINERTY, Mary		20	F	None	18Ma02Gn
KELERY, Kitty		20	F	None	18Ma02Gn
CANNON, Mary		20	F	None	18Ma02Gn
COYNE, Mary		19	F	None	18Ma02Gn
MURRAY, Robt.		25	M	Laborer	18Ma02Gn
MONTGOMERY, Thos.		20	M	Laborer	18Ma02Gn
BOYLAN, Biddy		19	F	None	18Ma02Gn
CANNON, James		28	M	Laborer	18Ma02Gn
U	(W)	27	F	None	18Ma02Gn
KANE, Mary		30	F	None	18Ma02Gn
LINTON, Margt.		16	F	None	18Ma02Gn
Charlotte		14	F	None	18Ma02Gn
SMITH, John		20	M	Laborer	18Ma02Gn
FOGARTY, John		26	M	Laborer	18Ma02Gn
FINN, Patrick		22	M	Laborer	18Ma02Gn
SHEEHAN, Ellen		25	F	None	18Ma02Gn
KELLY, Margt.S.		20	F	None	18Ma02Gn
GUBBINS, Wm.		50	M	Laborer	18Ma02Gn
RYAN, Joseph		20	M	Laborer	18Ma02Gn
KERRIGAN, Dennis		20	M	Laborer	18Ma02Gn
POSSER, Patrick		41	M	Laborer	18Ma02Gn
Thomas	(S)	11	M	Child	18Ma02Gn
MALONY, Patt		40	M	Laborer	18Ma02Gn
U	(W)	40	F	None	18Ma02Gn
John	(S)	28	M	Laborer	18Ma02Gn
Andy	(S)	21	M	Laborer	18Ma02Gn
Patt	(S)	19	M	Laborer	18Ma02Gn
William	(S)	17	M	Laborer	18Ma02Gn
Nancy	(D)	15	F	None	18Ma02Gn
Michael	(S)	11	M	Child	18Ma02Gn
DONNELL, Nancy		20	F	None	18Ma02Gn
CLARY, Edw.		27	M	Laborer	18Ma02Gn
CATEN, Patt		18	M	Laborer	18Ma02Gn
RYAN, Mary		20	F	None	18Ma02Gn
ODONNELL, Richd.		21	M	Laborer	18Ma02Gn
WALSH, Thomas		28	M	Laborer	18Ma02Gn
COLLINS, Bridget		16	F	None	18Ma02Gn
FLYNN, Elizabeth		20	F	None	18Ma02Gn
BRANNAN, Mary		20	F	None	18Ma02Gn
ENNIS, Patrick		22	M	Laborer	18Ma02Gn
Elizabeth		22	F	None	18Ma02Gn
COONEY, Thomas		20	M	Laborer	18Ma02Gn
CANSKY, Julia		20	F	None	18Ma02Gn
LYNANE, Ann		20	F	None	18Ma02Gn
DALY, Thomas		18	M	Laborer	18Ma02Gn
BRACKEN, Thomas		18	M	Laborer	18Ma02Gn
HAY, James		18	M	Laborer	18Ma02Gn
CAHILL, Peter		18	M	Laborer	18Ma02Gn
MURPHY, Samuel		25	M	Laborer	18Ma02Gn
MALONNE, Patt		25	M	Laborer	18Ma02Gn
BRIEN, Laurence		20	M	Laborer	18Ma02Gn
CONDREN, Patt		26	M	Laborer	18Ma02Gn
KILEY, James		21	M	Laborer	18Ma02Gn
NEVILLE, John		21	M	Laborer	18Ma02Gn
OBRIEN, Mich.		24	M	Laborer	18Ma02Gn
CASEY, Mich.		22	M	Laborer	18Ma02Gn
Thomas		21	M	Laborer	18Ma02Gn
COLLINS, Mich.		21	M	Laborer	18Ma02Gn
MAHONY, Ellen		20	F	None	18Ma02Gn
BRADY, Maria		06	F	Child	18Ma02Gn
WARREN, Peter		28	M	Laborer	18Ma02Gn
MORRIS, Cath.		21	F	None	18Ma02Gn
ASHTON, Thos.		16	M	Laborer	18Ma02Gn
ROBINSON, John		18	M	Laborer	18Ma02Gn
WILSON, Charles		17	M	Laborer	16Ma02Gn
LETTICE, Julia		20	F	None	18Ma02Gn
SLEVIN, Thos.		22	M	Laborer	16Ma02Gn
MCCABE, Alice		18	F	None	18Ma02Gn
MCARDLE, Michl.		22	M	Laborer	18Ma02Gn
GAFFNEY, Timothy		30	M	Laborer	18Ma02Gn

NAMES OF PASSENGERS		A G E	S E X	OCCUPATIONS	DATE PORT SHIP
RIFF, Connor		30	M	Laborer	18Ma02Gn
Michl.		23	M	Laborer	18Ma02Gn
Henry		18	M	Laborer	18Ma02Gn
Thos.		25	M	Laborer	18Ma02Gn
Ann		22	F	None	18Ma02Gn
KELLY, Bridget		23	F	None	18Ma02Gn
MURRAY, Susan		25	F	None	18Ma02Gn
KENNA, Mary		19	F	None	18Ma02Gn
NEILAND, John		20	M	Laborer	18Ma02Gn
U	(W)	21	F	None	18Ma02Gn
FITZPATRICK, Mary		25	F	None	18Ma02Gn
Julia		19	F	None	18Ma02Gn
LESTRANGE, John		23	M	Laborer	18Ma02Gn
FOGARTY, Mary		20	F	None	18Ma02Gn
BURKE, Judy		20	F	None	18Ma02Gn
MORRIS, Mary		16	F	None	18Ma02Gn
MAHON, Mary		16	F	None	18Ma02Gn
SHEEHAN, Patt		26	M	Laborer	18Ma02Gn
MURPHY, Mary		22	F	None	18Ma02Gn
SHEEHAN, Cath.		20	F	None	18Ma02Gn
DUGGAN, Mary		18	F	None	18Ma02Gn
MCLEAN, Dennis		28	M	Laborer	18Ma02Gn
U	(W)	26	F	None	18Ma02Gn
BANNON, Biddy		12	F	None	18Ma02Gn
CASHION, Mickl.		40	M	Laborer	18Ma02Gn
John	(S)	15	M	Laborer	18Ma02Gn
HORIBSTER, John		25	M	Laborer	18Ma02Gn
PHELAN, Edw.		24	M	Laborer	18Ma02Gn
GALLAGHER, Christy		29	M	Laborer	18Ma02Gn
U	(W)	20	F	None	18Ma02Gn
NOONEY, Thomas		29	M	Laborer	18Ma02Gn
COLLINS, Patt		25	M	Laborer	18Ma02Gn
SEXTON, Patt		24	M	Laborer	18Ma02Gn
Mary		23	F	None	18Ma02Gn
COYNE, Bridget		18	F	None	18Ma02Gn
SCALLY, Peggy		19	F	None	18Ma02Gn
MULLIGAN, Ann		09	F	Child	18Ma02Gn
DONOHOE, Patt		25	M	Laborer	18Ma02Gn
CONROY, James		24	M	Laborer	18Ma02Gn
GALLIGAR, John		22	M	Laborer	18Ma02Gn
EARLY, Cathn.		19	F	None	18Ma02Gn
REYNOLDS, Cathn.		17	F	None	18Ma02Gn
MCCABE, John		28	M	Laborer	18Ma02Gn
MATHEWS, Patt		24	M	Laborer	18Ma02Gn
MCCABE, Maria		20	F	None	18Ma02Gn
FLYNN, John		28	M	Laborer	18Ma02Gn
HANNA, Elizabeth		20	F	None	18Ma02Gn
CONNOR, Margt.		08	F	Child	18Ma02Gn
James		04	M	Child	18Ma02Gn
MCLOUGHLIN, Bessy		28	F	None	18Ma02Gn
LESTRANGE, Thos.		28	M	Laborer	18Ma02Gn
Margt.	(W)	24	F	None	18Ma02Gn
John	(S)	.00	M	Infant	18Ma02Gn
HANES, Susan		24	F	None	18Ma02Gn
QUINN, Chas.		20	M	None	18Ma02Gn
MURPHY, Ellen		20	F	None	18Ma02Gn
Ann		18	F	None	18Ma02Gn
CONNELLY, Sarah		16	F	None	18Ma02Gn
YORKEY, James		19	M	Laborer	18Ma02Gn
SHERIDAN, Robt.		34	M	Laborer	18Ma02Gn
U	(W)	28	F	None	18Ma02Gn
SMITH, Ann		27	F	None	18Ma02Gn
MOFFITT, James		22	M	Laborer	18Ma02Gn
Eliza		25	F	None	18Ma02Gn
JARVIN, Jane		19	F	None	18Ma02Gn
NESBITT, Dorcas		30	F	None	18Ma02Gn
MCCABE, Bernard		20	M	Laborer	18Ma02Gn
DEVLIN, James		20	M	Laborer	18Ma02Gn
John		20	M	Laborer	18Ma02Gn
LYNCH, Peter		18	M	Laborer	18Ma02Gn
Terence		17	M	Laborer	18Ma02Gn
DOWD, Terence		20	M	Laborer	18Ma02Gn
Bridget		18	F	None	18Ma02Gn
KIRGBY, Peggy		16	F	None	18Ma02Gn
MCGUIRE, Margt.		18	F	None	18Ma02Gn

NAMES OF PASSENGERS	A G E	S E X	OCCUPATIONS	DATE PORT SHIP
BANNON, Biddy	16	F	None	18Ma02Gn
HUTCHINSON, Hannah	16	F	None	18Ma02Gn
PAUL, Wm.	24	M	Laborer	18Ma02Gn
U (W)	25	F	None	18Ma02Gn
James (S)	.00	M	Infant	18Ma02Gn
PIERCE, Henry	20	M	Laborer	18Ma02Gn
LESTRANGE, Bridget	35	F	None	18Ma02Gn
Michl. (S)	.00	M	Infant	18Ma02Gn
COGNE, Philip	40	M	Laborer	18Ma02Gn
Margaret (W)	40	F	None	18Ma02Gn
Mary (D)	20	F	None	18Ma02Gn
Cath. (D)	18	F	None	18Ma02Gn
Ann (D)	17	F	None	18Ma02Gn
Wm. (S)	15	M	Laborer	18Ma02Gn
Jane (D)	09	F	Child	18Ma02Gn
Elizabeth (D)	07	F	Child	18Ma02Gn
Philip (S)	05	M	Child	18Ma02Gn
MURRAY, Cath.	13	F	None	18Ma02Gn
BURKE, John	25	M	Laborer	18Ma02Gn
Bridget	20	F	None	18Ma02Gn
CONNELL, Mary	22	F	None	18Ma02Gn
HART, Sarah	30	F	None	18Ma02Gn
HENRY, Bridget	24	F	None	18Ma02Gn
GRAY, Cath.	20	F	None	18Ma02Gn
DONLAN, Ellen	10	F	Child	18Ma02Gn
ROCHDALE, John	20	M	Laborer	18Ma02Gn
ROLAND, Mich.	20	M	Laborer	18Ma02Gn
DEVITT, Mary	21	F	None	18Ma02Gn
NEELY, John	25	M	Laborer	18Ma02Gn
Hill	22	M	Laborer	18Ma02Gn
TURNER, Jane	20	F	None	18Ma02Gn
Nancy	18	F	None	18Ma02Gn
CONNER, John	20	M	Laborer	18Ma02Gn
ONEILE, Susan	22	F	None	18Ma02Gn
Elizabeth	24	F	None	18Ma02Gn
CONNER, Wm.	45	M	Laborer	18Ma02Gn
Bridget (D)	22	F	None	18Ma02Gn
Cath. (D)	18	F	None	18Ma02Gn
John (S)	16	M	None	18Ma02Gn
Martin (S)	13	M	None	18Ma02Gn
May (D)	11	F	Child	18Ma02Gn
READBY, Francis	19	M	Laborer	18Ma02Gn
MITCHELL, Margt.	20	F	None	18Ma02Gn
MILLEN, Ann	22	F	None	18Ma02Gn
KELLY, Mickl.	20	M	Laborer	18Ma02Gn
FARLEY, Peter	25	M	Laborer	18Ma02Gn
OLIVER, Joseph	45	M	Laborer	18Ma02Gn
Mary (W)	45	F	None	18Ma02Gn
Mary (D)	13	F	None	18Ma02Gn
Joseph (S)	08	M	Child	18Ma02Gn
MCCALLUM, Ellen	30	F	None	18Ma02Gn
MCCRACKEN, John	20	M	Laborer	18Ma02Gn
BRADY, Hugh	22	M	Laborer	18Ma02Gn
GALLAGHER, Phillllp	20	M	Laborer	18Ma02Gn
REILLY, Judy	20	F	None	18Ma02Gn
LYNCH, Maria	13	F	None	18Ma02Gn
MADDEN, James	20	M	Laborer	18Ma02Gn
FOX, Patt	22	M	Laborer	18Ma02Gn
MADDEN, Thomas	24	M	Laborer	18Ma02Gn
MARTIN, Bridget	18	F	None	18Ma02Gn
Ellz.	13	F	None	18Ma02Gn
CROOK, Edward	24	M	Laborer	18Ma02Gn
WALSH, James	22	M	Laborer	18Ma02Gn
NOON, Anthony	21	M	Laborer	18Ma02Gn
MURPHY, Francis	21	M	Laborer	18Ma02Gn
CLARKE, Thomas	20	M	Laborer	18Ma02Gn
MULLOY, John	20	M	Laborer	18Ma02Gn
MANLEY, John	20	M	Laborer	18Ma02Gn
BEST, Andrew	20	M	Laborer	18Ma02Gn
Patt	20	M	Laborer	18Ma02Gn
HOLMES, John	20	M	Laborer	18Ma02Gn
NOON, Bridget	20	F	None	18Ma02Gn
GRADY, Peggy	20	F	None	18Ma02Gn
HOLMES, Cath.	20	F	None	18Ma02Gn
REYNOLDS, Mary	19	F	None	18Ma02Gn
BOYLE, Mary	22	F	None	18Ma02Gn
GILMARTIN, Mary	21	F	None	18Ma02Gn
KERRON, Bridget	20	F	None	18Ma02Gn
Phiobe	18	F	None	18Ma02Gn
HOPE, John	25	M	Laborer	18Ma02Gn
RODGERS, Pat	24	M	Laborer	18Ma02Gn
RAFFERTY, Wm.	21	M	Laborer	18Ma02Gn
MCMULLIN, James	18	M	Laborer	18Ma02Gn
WARD, Wm.	18	M	Laborer	18Ma02Gn
RAFFERTY, Teresa	22	F	Laborer	18Ma02Gn
MCCANDLE, Ann	21	F	Laborer	18Ma02Gn
KEARNY, Ann	20	F	Laborer	18Ma02Gn
LYNCH, Mathew	24	M	Laborer	18Ma02Gn
Mary	22	F	None	18Ma02Gn
GLYNN, Bicdy	20	F	None	18Ma02Gn
MCANEENY, Cath.	22	F	None	18Ma02Gn
CURRAN, Bridget	20	F	None	18Ma02Gn
Mary	28	F	None	18Ma02Gn
HANLEY, Anthony	24	M	Laborer	18Ma02Gn
THOMAS, Peter	35	M	Laborer	18Ma02Gn
U (W)	35	F	None	18Ma02Gn
Wm. (S)	10	M	Child	18Ma02Gn
John (S)	07	M	Child	18Ma02Gn
Hannah (D)	03	F	Child	18Ma02Gn
Peter (S)	.00	M	Infant	18Ma02Gn
DAVIDSON, John	20	M	Laborer	18Ma02Gn
CONDON, Wm.	20	M	Laborer	18Ma02Gn
HARRIGAN, Peter	22	M	Laborer	18Ma02Gn
BOWYER, Mary	21	F	Unknown	18Ma02Gn

PERSEVERANCE 18 MAY 1846

From Dublin

NAMES OF PASSENGERS	A G E	S E X	OCCUPATIONS	DATE PORT SHIP
ARCHBOLD, Christe	20	M	Laborer	18Ma20Go
CASHEN, Pat	22	M	Laborer	18Ma20Go
MARRINAN, Ann	24	F	Servant	18Ma20Go
GRAHAM, U-Mrs.	21	F	Servant	18Ma20Go
ARCHBOLD, John	22	M	Laborer	18Ma20Go
MORGAN, James	19	M	Laborer	18Ma20Go
MCNULTY, Charles	24	M	Laborer	18Ma20Go
MITCHELTON, Sarah	40	F	Wife	18Ma20Go
DOWLING, Marie	20	F	Servant	18Ma20Go
MCPARLIN, John	20	M	Laborer	18Ma20Go
Rose	16	F	Servant	18Ma20Go
FITZPATRICK, Ann	22	F	Servant	18Ma20Go
HAY, U	22	F	Lady'S Maid	18Ma20Go
Jane	20	F	Lady'S Maid	18Ma20Go
SPENCER, U	25	M	Clerk	18Ma20Go
MONKS, Laurence	22	M	Butcher	18Ma20Go
GALOGHLIN, Jos.	22	M	Tailor	18Ma20Go
BAKER, Christopher	18	M	Tailor	18Ma20Go
CUMMING, Richd.	20	M	Clerk	18Ma20Go
LYNN, Ann	20	F	Wife	18Ma20Go
FLOOD, Eliza	22	F	Dressmaker	18Ma20Go
MORRISON, James	25	M	Weaver	18Ma20Go
CARROLIN, Rose	30	F	Weaver	18Ma20Go
LEONARD, Julia	20	F	Laborer	18Ma20Go
LAWLESS, John	30	M	Laborer	18Ma20Go
U (W)	25	F	Wife	18Ma20Go
Peter (S)	02	M	Child	18Ma20Go
Catharine (D)	01	F	Child	18Ma20Go
RIDDLE, Wm.	25	M	Carpenter	18Ma20Go
FLYNN, Mary	20	F	Servant	18Ma20Go
DOYLE, Ann	22	F	Servant	18Ma20Go
COSTELLO, Michael	25	M	Servant	18Ma20Go
CULLIN, Bridge	20	F	Servant	18Ma20Go
MAGUIRE, Patrick	30	M	Laborer	18Ma20Go
BYRNE, Peter	25	M	Laborer	18Ma20Go

NAMES OF PASSENGERS		AGE	SEX	OCCUPATIONS	DATE PORT SHIP
CAUFIELD, Cathne.		17	F	Seamstress	18Ma20Go
MAXWELL, John		26	M	Carpenter	18Ma20Go
U	(W)	20	F	Wife	18Ma20Go
FLANNIGAN, Joseph		20	M	Laborer	18Ma20Go
FENERAL, James		26	M	Laborer	18Ma20Go
SHANNON, Edward		24	M	Laborer	18Ma20Go
CAROLIN, Bridget		18	F	Servant	18Ma20Go
NOON, Mark		23	M	Carpenter	18Ma20Go
CLOONE, John		21	M	Carpenter	18Ma20Go
FINNIGAN, Cathne.		22	F	Servant	18Ma20Go
CARROLL, Bessy		17	F	Servant	18Ma20Go
Sally		15	F	Servant	18Ma20Go
SHARP, William		20	M	Baker	18Ma20Go
LYONS, Michael		25	M	Laborer	18Ma20Go
KENNY, Peter		24	M	Laborer	18Ma20Go
FARRELLY, A.		25	F	Wife	18Ma20Go
Mary-Ann	(D)	02	F	Child	18Ma20Go
HALLIGAN, Cathrn.		20	F	Seamstress	18Ma20Go
KILLIEN, Michl.		50	M	Laborer	18Ma20Go
Bridget	(M)	80	F	None	18Ma20Go
REGAN, Jas.		24	M	Servant	18Ma20Go
Bridget	(W)	22	F	Servant	18Ma20Go
Thomas	(S)	02	M	Child	18Ma20Go
KENNY, Pat		21	M	Laborer	18Ma20Go
MALONE, Mary		20	F	Servant	18Ma20Go
HANBURY, Thos.		30	M	Blacksmith	18Ma20Go
RYAN, Thos.		26	M	Laborer	18Ma20Go
Ellen	(W)	20	F	Wife	18Ma20Go
NYSELL, Peter		27	M	Butler	18Ma20Go
SWEETMAN, Mary		20	F	Servant	18Ma20Go
CREATION, Pat		24	M	Laborer	18Ma20Go
GOUGH, Pat		18	M	Laborer	18Ma20Go
STOKES, James		21	M	Laborer	18Ma20Go
HUGHES, Richard		18	M	Laborer	18Ma20Go
RAIL, John		21	M	Laborer	18Ma20Go
Mary	(W)	18	F	Wife	18Ma20Go
TRAINER, John		20	M	Carpenter	18Ma20Go
GILL, Bessy		19	F	Wife	18Ma20Go
RYAN, Patrick		19	M	Butcher	18Ma20Go
CUNNINGHAM, Margt.		20	F	Servant	18Ma20Go
BURK, Francis		25	M	Laborer	18Ma20Go
FEGAN, Ann		20	F	Servant	18Ma20Go
MAGUIRE, Julia		20	F	Servant	18Ma20Go
Manilla		21	F	Servant	18Ma20Go
DOOLEY, Pat		27	M	Tailor	18Ma20Go
MAGRETT, Margt.		18	F	Servant	18Ma20Go
FEHALLY, Margt.		20	F	Servant	18Ma20Go
GERAGHTY, Margt.		21	F	Servant	18Ma20Go
LONG, Patrick		20	M	Baker	18Ma20Go
CLABBY, Mary		20	F	Dressmaker	18Ma20Go
MOORE, John		25	M	Cooper	18Ma20Go
GAGHAGAN, Margt.		20	F	Servant	18Ma20Go
KELLY, Ann		20	F	Servant	18Ma20Go
FARRELL, Mary		20	F	Servant	18Ma20Go
AYRES, Eliza		20	F	Servant	18Ma20Go
MCCORMACK, Michl.		24	M	Barber	18Ma20Go
Tessy	(W)	18	F	Wife	18Ma20Go
COLLINS, Mary-Ann		24	F	Servant	18Ma20Go
SANFORD, U-Mrs.		20	F	Servant	18Ma20Go
NEWMAN, Patk.		24	M	Walter	18Ma20Go
KELLY, Mary		21	F	Seamstress	18Ma20Go
DUNCAN, Patt		18	M	Laborer	18Ma20Go
BRAHAM, Mary		20	F	Servant	18Ma20Go
DOYLE, William		18	M	Laborer	18Ma20Go
MCCABE, Patt		20	M	Laborer	18Ma20Go
MONAGHAN, Bridget		20	F	Spinster	18Ma20Go
SHERIDAN, Henry		20	M	Spinner	18Ma20Go
MCSOLLOUGH, Michl.		25	M	Blacksmith	18Ma20Go
BURKE, Julia		20	F	Spinster	18Ma20Go
KENNY, Bridget		22	F	Spinster	18Ma20Go
MALEY, John		24	M	Servant	18Ma20Go
MCCABE, Bridget		22	F	Servant	18Ma20Go
MCCUE, Ann		20	F	Servant	18Ma20Go
WHITE, Henry		50	M	Laborer	18Ma20Go
Ellen		20	F	Servant	18Ma20Go
CARTY, Margt.		19	F	Servant	18Ma20Go
COSGILL, Patt		25	M	Laborer	18Ma20Go
GRADY, Michael		23	M	Laborer	18Ma20Go
DEMPSEY, Mary		20	F	Servant	18Ma20Go
GLENNIN, Margt.		21	F	Servant	18Ma20Go
PENDER, Mary		21	F	Servant	18Ma20Go
BUTLER, John		25	M	Watchmaker	18Ma20Go
Patt		22	M	Laborer	18Ma20Go
EGAN, Winiford		20	M	Laborer	18Ma20Go
TREACY, Mary		20	F	House Maid	18Ma20Go
DEEGAN, Mary		20	F	House Maid	18Ma20Go
KENNY, Cathne.		20	F	House Maid	18Ma20Go
WALSH, Michael		27	M	Laborer	18Ma20Go
LYONS, John		22	M	Laborer	18Ma20Go
GATSBY, John		09	M	Child	18Ma20Go
CUNNINGHAM, Patt		24	M	Laborer	18Ma20Go
BURK, Thomas		22	M	Laborer	18Ma20Go
MCAVOCK, Richie		20	M	Laborer	18Ma20Go
KENNY, John		27	M	Laborer	18Ma20Go
CONLON, William		20	M	Laborer	18Ma20Go
MCNULTY, Sally		24	F	Servant	18Ma20Go
TYGUE, Mary		26	F	Servant	18Ma20Go
MULLALLY, Watt		20	M	Laborer	18Ma20Go
NEWMAN, Peter		20	M	Laborer	18Ma20Go
WINEN, Thos.		53	M	Laborer	18Ma20Go
Eliza	(W)	50	F	Servant	18Ma20Go
Francis	(S)	24	M	Cooper	18Ma20Go
Bridget	(D)	18	F	Servant	18Ma20Go
Onney	(D)	18	F	Servant	18Ma20Go
Barney	(S)	26	M	Baker	18Ma20Go
Ellen	(D)	16	F	Servant	18Ma20Go
Ann	(D)	09	F	Child	18Ma20Go
REILLY, Cathn.		20	F	Servant	18Ma20Go
Michael		15	M	Laborer	18Ma20Go
LOWE, Ann		18	F	Wife	18Ma20Go
LEIBY, Mary		20	F	Servant	18Ma20Go
DUFFY, Bridget		20	F	Servant	18Ma20Go
MURRAY, Cathn.		18	F	Servant	18Ma20Go
BRADY, Catherine		20	F	Servant	18Ma20Go
DERMODY, Geo.		24	M	Cbtmkr	18Ma20Go
Patt		22	M	Cbtmkr	18Ma20Go
U	(W)	25	F	Wife	18Ma20Go
Thomas		20	M	Servant	18Ma20Go
BURKE, James		20	M	Laborer	18Ma20Go
CONNOLLY, John		30	M	Laborer	18Ma20Go
RENNOLDS, Owen		24	M	Laborer	18Ma20Go
KING, Ann		28	F	House Maid	18Ma20Go
REILLY, Bridget		18	F	House Maid	18Ma20Go
HEGAN, Cathn.		20	F	House Maid	18Ma20Go
REYNOLDS, Mary		20	F	House Maid	18Ma20Go
HAY, John		20	M	Watchmaker	18Ma20Go
Cathne.		25	F	Wife	18Ma20Go
JORDAN, Mary		20	F	Servant	18Ma20Go
GARDNER, Richd.		40	M	Laborer	18Ma20Go
U	(W)	46	F	Wife	18Ma20Go
Robert	(S)	03	M	Child	18Ma20Go
WEBB, U-Mrs.		60	F	Wife	18Ma20Go
HOPKINS, Jas.		24	M	Shoemaker	18Ma20Go
PENDER, Thomas		24	M	Shoemaker	18Ma20Go
MCNALLY, Terence		20	M	Laborer	18Ma20Go
Patt		22	M	Laborer	18Ma20Go
WHITNEY, Michael		20	M	Laborer	18Ma20Go
DWYER, Richd.		20	M	Laborer	18Ma20Go
SWEETMAN, Michael		20	M	Laborer	18Ma20Go
KELLY, Rose		20	F	Servant	18Ma20Go
FLYNN, Sally		22	F	Servant	18Ma20Go
BYRNE, Edward		20	M	Laborer	18Ma20Go
DUNN, Patt		20	M	Laborer	18Ma20Go
FLEMMON, John		34	M	Laborer	18Ma20Go
ONEILL, Cathne.		20	F	Servant	18Ma20Go
BRUANYHAND, Geo.		20	M	Laborer	18Ma20Go
COLLIGAN, Barny		20	M	Laborer	18Ma20Go
REILLY, Edward		22	M	Laborer	18Ma20Go
MCKENNAN, Biddy		20	F	House Maid	18Ma20Go
GAFNEY, James		20	M	Baker	18Ma20Go

NAMES OF PASSENGERS	A G E	S E X	OCCUPATIONS	DATE PORT SHIP
BOYD, U	20	F	Servant	18Ma20Go
CASEY, Ann	20	F	Servant	18Ma20Go
MURRAY, Margt.	24	F	Servant	18Ma20Go
MILLER, Margt.	20	F	Servant	18Ma20Go
MCDONALD, Pat	20	M	Baker	18Ma20Go
WIELON, Ann	20	F	Wife	18Ma20Go
MILLER, Ann	20	F	Servant	18Ma20Go
DALY, Bessy	24	F	Servant	18Ma20Go
FLATTERY, Cathne.	20	F	Servant	18Ma20Go
KELLY, John	20	M	Farmer	18Ma20Go
FOX, Ann	20	F	Servant	18Ma20Go
FITZPATRICK, John	25	M	Laborer	18Ma20Go
LOWE, Michael	20	M	Laborer	18Ma20Go
CARTLEY, Ann	20	F	Servant	18Ma20Go
FEGAN, Mary	20	F	Servant	18Ma20Go
BYRNE, Pat	25	M	Blacksmith	18Ma20Go
MCCORMICK, Cathne.	20	F	Servant	18Ma20Go
BURK, John	26	M	Farmer	18Ma20Go
Sally (W)	22	F	Wife	18Ma20Go
James	20	M	Laborer	18Ma20Go
SULLIVAN, Michl.	24	M	Laborer	18Ma20Go
John	20	M	Laborer	18Ma20Go
BUTLER, Saml.	22	M	Laborer	18Ma20Go
WALL, Mary	16	F	House Maid	18Ma20Go
FOLEY, Sally	27	F	Cook	18Ma20Go

CLARENCE 19 MAY 1846

From Galway

NAMES OF PASSENGERS	A G E	S E X	OCCUPATIONS	DATE PORT SHIP
FLANIGAN, Mary	27	F	Wife	19Ma11Gp
John	00	M	None	19Ma11Gp
Kate	06	F	Child	19Ma11Gp
MAGUIRE, Peter	47	M	None	19Ma11Gp
Mary	40	F	Spinster	19Ma11Gp
DOMADY, Thomas	36	M	Laborer	19Ma11Gp
GALVIN, Ellen	42	F	Spinster	19Ma11Gp
DILLON, William	36	M	Laborer	19Ma11Gp
HUGHES, James	54	M	Laborer	19Ma11Gp
CARRICK, Patrick	41	M	Laborer	19Ma11Gp
Catherine (W)	40	F	Wife	19Ma11Gp
TIERNEY, Martin	22	M	Laborer	19Ma11Gp
WALTERS, Matthew	30	M	Laborer	19Ma11Gp
DOOLARTY, Patrick	26	M	Laborer	19Ma11Gp
CREW, John	39	M	Laborer	19Ma11Gp
WARD, James	21	M	Laborer	19Ma11Gp
Mary	20	F	Servant	19Ma11Gp
HEAGANY, Owen	39	M	Laborer	19Ma11Gp
NEILAN, James	27	M	Laborer	19Ma11Gp
PRENDERGAST, Patrick	42	M	Laborer	19Ma11Gp
Ellen (W)	17	F	Wife	19Ma11Gp
FARRELL, Martin	42	M	Laborer	19Ma11Gp
CONNER, Thomas	36	M	Laborer	19Ma11Gp
DUANE, John	37	M	Laborer	19Ma11Gp
Mary (W)	32	F	Wife	19Ma11Gp
Bridget (D)	08	F	Child	19Ma11Gp
Mary (D)	06	F	Child	19Ma11Gp
Judy (D)	04	F	Child	19Ma11Gp
John (S)	02	F	Child	19Ma11Gp
HEAGANY, John	49	M	Mason	19Ma11Gp
Margaret (W)	47	F	Wife	19Ma11Gp
Mary (D)	23	F	None	19Ma11Gp
John (S)	20	M	None	19Ma11Gp
James (S)	18	M	None	19Ma11Gp
Judy (D)	16	F	None	19Ma11Gp
COST, Patrick	47	M	Laborer	19Ma11Gp
Betty (W)	46	F	Wife	19Ma11Gp
Kate (D)	10	F	Child	19Ma11Gp
LYNCH, Patrick	48	M	Carpenter	19Ma11Gp
MANGHAN, Patrick	40	M	Laborer	19Ma11Gp
KELLY, Catherine	18	F	Spinster	19Ma11Gp
BEAMAN, Biddy	38	F	Wi	19Ma11Gp
FEENEY, John	19	M	Servant	19Ma11Gp
Catherine (W)	19	F	Wife	19Ma11Gp
MAHONY, Bridget	27	F	Spinster	19Ma11Gp
Ellen	25	F	Spinster	19Ma11Gp
LEONARD, Catharine	18	F	Spinster	19Ma11Gp
FORD, Malachi	38	M	Laborer	19Ma11Gp
MCMAHON, John	39	M	Laborer	19Ma11Gp
HARE, Jane	27	F	Spinster	19Ma11Gp
OBRIEN, James	36	M	Laborer	19Ma11Gp
MCDONNELL, Mary	27	F	Wife	19Ma11Gp
DARCY, Darby	40	M	Laborer	19Ma11Gp
FLAHERTY, Michael	43	M	Laborer	19Ma11Gp
NEVIN, John	21	M	Laborer	19Ma11Gp
CAHILAN, John	36	M	Laborer	19Ma11Gp
WARD, Mary	27	F	Spinster	19Ma11Gp
CALLAGHY, Patrick	46	M	Laborer	19Ma11Gp
CARTY, Thomas	41	M	Laborer	19Ma11Gp
FLEMMING, Thomas	38	M	Laborer	19Ma11Gp
Catherine	37	F	Spinster	19Ma11Gp
LAWLESS, Biddy	42	F	Spinster	19Ma11Gp
BRODERICK, Kittty	61	F	Wife	19Ma11Gp
BURKE, Bridget	18	F	Spinster	19Ma11Gp
Margaret	19	F	Spinster	19Ma11Gp
FLEMMING, Michael	47	M	Laborer	19Ma11Gp
Mary (W)	40	F	Wife	19Ma11Gp
Mary (D)	07	F	Child	19Ma11Gp
Patt (S)	09	M	Child	19Ma11Gp
CANNON, John	40	M	Laborer	19Ma11Gp
LALLEY, Mary	21	F	Spinster	19Ma11Gp
FINEGAN, John	27	M	Laborer	19Ma11Gp
Michael	30	M	Laborer	19Ma11Gp
OBRIEN, Mary	16	F	Spinster	19Ma11Gp
COPPINGER, John	30	M	Carpenter	19Ma11Gp
KEHILL, John	41	M	Laborer	19Ma11Gp
HARDIMAN, Mary	60	F	None	19Ma11Gp
CARRICK, Bridget	27	F	Spinster	19Ma11Gp
FINEGAN, Mary	26	F	Spinster	19Ma11Gp
PLEESE, Catherine	21	F	Spinster	19Ma11Gp
Margaret	20	F	Spinster	19Ma11Gp
FLAHERTY, John	40	M	Laborer	19Ma11Gp
KENNY, Ann	25	F	Spinster	19Ma11Gp
SILVER, Ann	27	F	Spinster	19Ma11Gp
CONNELLY, Pat	36	M	Laborer	19Ma11Gp
RAFTERY, Nancy	24	F	Spinster	19Ma11Gp
MANNION, Michael	32	M	Tailor	19Ma11Gp
Mary (W)	28	F	Wife	19Ma11Gp
MURRAY, John	46	M	Laborer	19Ma11Gp
BURNS, Mary	25	F	Spinster	19Ma11Gp
DARCY, Mary	39	F	Wife	19Ma11Gp
KEALY, Mary	23	F	Spinster	19Ma11Gp
BOYLE, Biddy	27	F	Spinster	19Ma11Gp
BUTLER, Michael	40	M	Laborer	19Ma11Gp
FLEMMING, Michael	50	M	Laborer	19Ma11Gp
HYNES, Thomas	27	M	Laborer	19Ma11Gp
MCDERMOT, William	37	M	Laborer	19Ma11Gp
HANE, Pat	21	M	Laborer	19Ma11Gp
GLYNN, John	19	M	Laborer	19Ma11Gp
QUIN, John	32	M	Laborer	19Ma11Gp

SARDINIA 20 MAY 1846

From Liverpool

NAMES OF PASSENGERS	A G E	S E X	OCCUPATIONS	DATE PORT SHIP
BREADY, Rose	21	F	Servant	20Ma02Gt
BAGHT, James	30	M	Carpenter	20Ma02Gt
CAUGHLIN, Carney	16	M	Laborer	20Ma02Gt

NAMES OF PASSENGERS		AGE	SEX	OCCUPATIONS	DATE PORT SHIP
MCGRATH, Charles		20	M	Laborer	20Ma02Gt
GROGGAN, James		24	M	Laborer	20Ma02Gt
MULLEN, Mary		22	F	Servant	20Ma02Gt
MCCOURT, Mary		27	F	Servant	20Ma02Gt
MCGUSGAN, Sarah		29	F	Servant	20Ma02Gt
Mary	(D)	01	F	Child	20Ma02Gt
KELLY, Richard		25	M	Laborer	20Ma02Gt
DUGHAN, Michael		24	M	Laborer	20Ma02Gt
MCELROY, Mary		20	F	Laborer	20Ma02Gt
Margaret		21	F	Laborer	20Ma02Gt
Kitty		18	F	Laborer	20Ma02Gt
John		01	M	Child	20Ma02Gt
RILLEY, Ervin		66	M	Laborer	20Ma02Gt
GLYNN, Patrick		21	M	Laborer	20Ma02Gt
MCCLARRIN, William		21	M	Laborer	20Ma02Gt
MOGAN, Edward		18	M	Laborer	20Ma02Gt
MULLEN, Sally		24	F	Servant	20Ma02Gt
MCGAUGHF, Henry		24	M	Laborer	20Ma02Gt
HOGAN, James		21	M	Laborer	20Ma02Gt
MCGAUGHF, Hugh		20	M	Laborer	20Ma02Gt
CASEY, Bridget		17	F	Laborer	20Ma02Gt
MCMAHON, Judeth		20	F	Laborer	20Ma02Gt
LANGSTON, Daniel		40	M	Laborer	20Ma02Gt
Mary		40	F	Laborer	20Ma02Gt
BAYLESS, Joseph		39	M	Laborer	20Ma02Gt
HURTILL, William		28	M	Laborer	20Ma02Gt
Sarah		36	F	Laborer	20Ma02Gt
ELROY, John		26	M	Laborer	20Ma02Gt
BEW, Lancalat		09	M	Child	20Ma02Gt
KENNY, Michael		23	M	Laborer	20Ma02Gt
Ann		22	F	Laborer	20Ma02Gt
GILLAGEN, Rosey		18	F	Laborer	20Ma02Gt
KELLY, Hugh		22	M	Laborer	20Ma02Gt
CLEARY, Susan		21	F	Laborer	20Ma02Gt
KELLY, Biddy		19	F	Laborer	20Ma02Gt
JORDAN, Margrate		18	F	Laborer	20Ma02Gt
YOUNGS, Andrew		30	M	Laborer	20Ma02Gt
BRANNON, Hugh		25	M	Laborer	20Ma02Gt
LANGUE, John		20	M	Laborer	20Ma02Gt
MCLEVITT, Eliza		12	F	Laborer	20Ma02Gt
FERRY, Catherine		28	F	Laborer	20Ma02Gt
BARNES, Fanny		18	F	Laborer	20Ma02Gt
GALLAGHER, Ann		23	F	Laborer	20Ma02Gt
MCNELLIS, Ann		14	F	Laborer	20Ma02Gt
GASTAN, Biddy		24	F	Laborer	20Ma02Gt
GALLAGHER, Margrate		23	F	Laborer	20Ma02Gt
HART, John-Harris		40	M	Laborer	20Ma02Gt
U	(W)	40	F	Wife	20Ma02Gt
Mariah	(D)	10	F	Child	20Ma02Gt
Mary	(D)	08	F	Child	20Ma02Gt
Fredrick	(S)	03	M	Child	20Ma02Gt
Elizabeth	(D)	.06	F	Infant	20Ma02Gt
COLWELL, Thomas		29	M	Laborer	20Ma02Gt
MCCULLACK, William		20	M	Laborer	20Ma02Gt
CAUSLEY, Alexander		24	M	Laborer	20Ma02Gt
CALWELL, Andrew		20	M	Laborer	20Ma02Gt
COWETT, Robert		18	M	Laborer	20Ma02Gt
NICHOLSON, Patt.		20	M	Laborer	20Ma02Gt
MCELROY, Mary		20	F	Laborer	20Ma02Gt
KENNY, Dennis		24	M	Laborer	20Ma02Gt
GILL, Elenor		10	F	Child	20Ma02Gt
COLLINS, John		35	M	Laborer	20Ma02Gt
HILL, U		50	M	Doctor	20Ma02Gt
Robert	(S)	24	M	Laborer	20Ma02Gt
MCCLELAND, U-Mrs.		30	F	Laborer	20Ma02Gt
Mary	(D)	13	F	Laborer	20Ma02Gt
Robert	(S)	03	M	Child	20Ma02Gt
Jane	(D)	01	F	Child	20Ma02Gt
KENNY, Catherine		23	F	Servant	20Ma02Gt
GALLAGHER, Mary		18	F	Servant	20Ma02Gt
KENNY, Dennis		21	M	Servant	20Ma02Gt
MCGRATH, Margrate		26	F	Servant	20Ma02Gt
KELLY, Thomas		37	M	Servant	20Ma02Gt
Rose		20	F	Servant	20Ma02Gt
POWELL, John		30	M	Servant	20Ma02Gt
MULLEN, Ellin		28	F	Servant	20Ma02Gt
COONEY, Catherine		26	F	Servant	20Ma02Gt
IRWIN, Mary		25	F	Servant	20Ma02Gt
GILHENY, Catherine		20	F	Servant	20Ma02Gt
GAMBLE, James		21	M	Servant	20Ma02Gt
REILLY, John		22	M	Servant	20Ma02Gt
LIDDY, Budann		18	F	Servant	20Ma02Gt
MCFADDEN, Mary		26	F	Servant	20Ma02Gt
LYNCH, Patt		22	M	Servant	20Ma02Gt
Thomas		13	M	Child	20Ma02Gt
HAYES, Frances		18	M	Laborer	20Ma02Gt
MEANS, Thomas		50	M	Laborer	20Ma02Gt
U	(W)	54	F	Wife	20Ma02Gt
Thomas	(S)	21	M	Laborer	20Ma02Gt
Robert	(S)	19	M	Laborer	20Ma02Gt
James	(S)	16	M	Laborer	20Ma02Gt
Margrate	(D)	15	F	Laborer	20Ma02Gt
Addam	(S)	09	M	Child	20Ma02Gt
Sarah	(D)	11	F	Child	20Ma02Gt
Thompson	(S)	07	M	Child	20Ma02Gt
LINN, Michael		40	M	Laborer	20Ma02Gt
Isabella	(W)	29	F	Laborer	20Ma02Gt
Mary	(D)	02	F	Child	20Ma02Gt
Julia	(D)	.04	F	Infant	20Ma02Gt
DONLEY, Patt		50	M	Laborer	20Ma02Gt
Mary		54	F	Laborer	20Ma02Gt
CAMPBELL, Mary		21	F	Laborer	20Ma02Gt
MAHER, Mary		13	F	Laborer	20Ma02Gt
DELLIN, Brady		24	M	Laborer	20Ma02Gt
KELPATRICK, Ann		21	F	Laborer	20Ma02Gt
MCSARELY, Catherine		24	F	Laborer	20Ma02Gt
GROGEHAN, Thomas		24	M	Laborer	20Ma02Gt
MCGUSKER, Thomas		29	M	Laborer	20Ma02Gt
WADDE, Ellin		20	F	Laborer	20Ma02Gt
MCCAUGHERY, Terrence		21	M	Laborer	20Ma02Gt
Bernard		13	M	Laborer	20Ma02Gt
HOLMES, Anna		40	F	Laborer	20Ma02Gt
Ann	(D)	20	F	Laborer	20Ma02Gt
Jane	(D)	12	F	Laborer	20Ma02Gt
Robert	(S)	09	M	Child	20Ma02Gt
James	(S)	06	M	Child	20Ma02Gt
William	(S)	04	M	Child	20Ma02Gt
DONELY, Mary		20	F	Servant	20Ma02Gt
MCCAUGHEY, Francis		26	M	Servant	20Ma02Gt
MCELROY, James		24	M	Servant	20Ma02Gt
KENNY, Moses		26	M	Laborer	20Ma02Gt
Margrate		40	F	Laborer	20Ma02Gt
Frances		13	M	Laborer	20Ma02Gt
MCKEVVER, Catherine		30	F	Laborer	20Ma02Gt
CARNES, John		17	M	Laborer	20Ma02Gt
MCKENNY, Mary		30	F	Laborer	20Ma02Gt
Catherine	(D)	04	F	Child	20Ma02Gt
Margrate	(D)	02	F	Child	20Ma02Gt
Charles	(S)	03	M	Child	20Ma02Gt
MCGUIRE, Rose		18	F	Laborer	20Ma02Gt
GUSKIN, Bridget		15	F	Laborer	20Ma02Gt
RUDER, Mary		20	F	Laborer	20Ma02Gt
KANE, Mary		17	F	Laborer	20Ma02Gt
WHITE, Edwin		24	M	Laborer	20Ma02Gt
MURPHY, Hugh		22	M	Laborer	20Ma02Gt
LINCH, James		21	M	Laborer	20Ma02Gt
BAILE, Hanna		20	F	Laborer	20Ma02Gt
MCGINLEY, Ellin		18	F	Laborer	20Ma02Gt
DUGHAN, Catherine		17	F	Laborer	20Ma02Gt
MCGINLEY, Ellin		06	F	Child	20Ma02Gt
MCCLUSKEY, Dan		22	M	Laborer	20Ma02Gt
LAFFERTY, Ann		18	F	Laborer	20Ma02Gt
JAMERSON, William		39	M	Laborer	20Ma02Gt
MEIRE, Agnis		25	M	Laborer	20Ma02Gt
JAMERISON, Agnis		13	M	Laborer	20Ma02Gt
Jannett		09	F	Child	20Ma02Gt
Mary		06	F	Child	20Ma02Gt
Marian		04	F	Child	20Ma02Gt
Jane		03	F	Child	20Ma02Gt
Eliza-Hill		.05	F	Infant	20Ma02Gt

NAMES OF PASSENGERS	AGE	SEX	OCCUPATIONS	DATE PORT SHIP
MCBRIDE, Mary	24	F	Servant	20Ma02Gt
CONNOR, Ellen	21	F	Servant	20Ma02Gt
MULLIGAN, John	20	M	Laborer	20Ma02Gt
MARSHAW, Catherine	35	M	Servant	20Ma02Gt
George (S)	04	M	Child	20Ma02Gt
Jake (S)	12	M	Servant	20Ma02Gt
Ann (D)	10	F	Child	20Ma02Gt
BAGLEY, Mary-Ann	20	F	Servant	20Ma02Gt
William	16	M	Servant	20Ma02Gt
RYERRATEN, Michal	26	M	Servant	20Ma02Gt
Ellin	21	F	Servant	20Ma02Gt
MCDONALD, Catherine	21	F	Servant	20Ma02Gt
MCDONNELD, John	18	M	Servant	20Ma02Gt
Ellner	19	F	Servant	20Ma02Gt
DOYLE, Catherine	40	F	Servant	20Ma02Gt
Patt (S)	13	M	Servant	20Ma02Gt
John (S)	12	M	Servant	20Ma02Gt
Peter	08	M	Child	20Ma02Gt
Phelix (S)	07	M	Child	20Ma02Gt
Hugh (S)	04	M	Child	20Ma02Gt
Catherine (D)	10	F	Child	20Ma02Gt
James (S)	02	M	Child	20Ma02Gt
Susan (D)	.03	F	Infant	20Ma02Gt
MULLEN, Richard	40	M	Laborer	20Ma02Gt
Bernard	40	M	Laborer	20Ma02Gt
RUSSELL, Patt	22	M	Laborer	20Ma02Gt
COWEN, Mary	18	F	Laborer	20Ma02Gt
SCALLY, Thomas	24	M	Laborer	20Ma02Gt
James	21	M	Laborer	20Ma02Gt
MURPHEY, Mary	18	F	Servant	20Ma02Gt
DAVELIN, Martin	29	M	Laborer	20Ma02Gt
Ann	18	F	Servant	20Ma02Gt
DUFFEY, Michael	19	M	Laborer	20Ma02Gt
GALLEN, Edward	24	M	Laborer	20Ma02Gt
HART, Mary	24	F	Laborer	20Ma02Gt

EMILY 20 MAY 1846

From St.Croix

NAMES OF PASSENGERS	AGE	SEX	OCCUPATIONS	DATE PORT SHIP
FRANKLIN, Jane-Lady	50	F	None	20Ma73Gu
C.J.	24	F	None	20Ma73Gu
Mary	48	F	None	20Ma73Gu
WOOD, U	60	M	None	20Ma73Gu
PETRIE, U	24	M	None	20Ma73Gu
BROWN, U	40	M	Merchant	20Ma73Gu
OLIVER, U	35	M	Merchant	20Ma73Gu

LIBERTY 21 MAY 1846

From Cork

NAMES OF PASSENGERS	AGE	SEX	OCCUPATIONS	DATE PORT SHIP
BRIEN, Michael	32	M	Laborer	21Ma14Fw
COTTY, Patrick	28	M	Laborer	21Ma14Fw
HALLERHAN, William	26	M	Laborer	21Ma14Fw
COTTY, Robert	20	M	Laborer	21Ma14Fw
CASHMAN, Mary	15	F	None	21Ma14Fw
HALLERHAN, John	27	M	None	21Ma14Fw
CARROLL, Ellen	25	F	None	21Ma14Fw
BARRETT, Mary	24	F	None	21Ma14Fw
MCCARTHY, David	26	M	Laborer	21Ma14Fw
Ellen	24	F	None	21Ma14Fw
Catherine	22	F	None	21Ma14Fw
TOLIN, John	20	M	Laborer	21Ma14Fw
HENESEY, Michael	25	M	Laborer	21Ma14Fw
MCCARTHY, Michael	28	M	Laborer	21Ma14Fw
Mary	20	F	None	21Ma14Fw
COLEMAN, Maurice	22	M	None	21Ma14Fw
HAFFY, Mallck	22	M	None	21Ma14Fw
CONNELLY, Michael	30	M	None	21Ma14Fw
BRIEN, Catharine	30	F	None	21Ma14Fw
OWNES, Martin	22	M	None	21Ma14Fw
BRIEN, Dennis	20	M	None	21Ma14Fw
HENESEY, James	55	M	Laborer	21Ma14Fw
Ellen (W)	55	F	Wife	21Ma14Fw
John (S)	24	M	Laborer	21Ma14Fw
James (S)	22	M	Laborer	21Ma14Fw
Michael (S)	21	M	Laborer	21Ma14Fw
William (S)	16	M	Laborer	21Ma14Fw
Betty (D)	22	F	Laborer	21Ma14Fw
GLEASON, Patrick	28	M	Farmer	21Ma14Fw
Mary	28	F	None	21Ma14Fw
LEARY, Michael	28	M	Laborer	21Ma14Fw
William	26	M	Laborer	21Ma14Fw
COTTER, Mary	24	F	Dressmaker	21Ma14Fw
REARDON, John	42	M	Servant	21Ma14Fw
FITZPATRICK, Dennis	30	M	None	21Ma14Fw
STACK, Patrick	30	M	None	21Ma14Fw
HURLEY, Margaret	20	F	Milliner	21Ma14Fw
FABIN, Ellen	20	F	Milliner	21Ma14Fw
CONNELL, William	21	M	Clerk	21Ma14Fw
MURPHY, Cornelius	17	M	Engineer	21Ma14Fw
CALLAHAN, John	20	M	Wheelwright	21Ma14Fw
Mary	25	F	Wheelwright	21Ma14Fw
DEADY, John	30	M	Laborer	21Ma14Fw
Elizabeth	18	F	Dressmaker	21Ma14Fw
John	16	M	Carpenter	21Ma14Fw
MAHONEY, Ellen	18	F	Servant	21Ma14Fw
JORDAN, James	28	M	None	21Ma14Fw
WILLIAMS, Francis	25	M	None	21Ma14Fw
Patrick	06	M	Child	21Ma14Fw
Thomas	03	M	Child	21Ma14Fw
Richard	36	M	Laborer	21Ma14Fw
MANNING, Daniel	40	M	Laborer	21Ma14Fw
GOING, Jeremiah	23	M	Watchmaker	21Ma14Fw
ODONNELL, Edmund	24	M	Laborer	21Ma14Fw
MULLANPHY, David	23	M	Laborer	21Ma14Fw
BROWN, John	22	M	Laborer	21Ma14Fw
Margaret	24	F	Laborer	21Ma14Fw
JOHNSTON, George	26	M	Coachman	21Ma14Fw
WATTS, Patrick	32	M	Laborer	21Ma14Fw
CONEHAN, Michael	25	M	Laborer	21Ma14Fw
GOODY, William	22	M	Laborer	21Ma14Fw
HENNESEY, Elizabeth	22	F	Servant	21Ma14Fw
CASEY, Dennis	25	M	Sawer	21Ma14Fw
SULLIVAN, Darby	25	M	Laborer	21Ma14Fw
MURPHY, Johanna	21	F	None	21Ma14Fw
SHEEHY, Eliza	22	F	Dressmaker	21Ma14Fw
FLEMING, Catherine	18	F	Dressmaker	21Ma14Fw
SHEA, Margaret	18	F	Dressmaker	21Ma14Fw
Catherine	20	F	Dressmaker	21Ma14Fw
HICKSON, Ann	20	F	Dressmaker	21Ma14Fw
MAYBERRY, Francis	20	M	None	21Ma14Fw
FOLEY, Timothy	20	M	Coachman	21Ma14Fw
CONNELLY, Mary	21	F	Servant	21Ma14Fw
FERRY, Johanna	21	F	Milliner	21Ma14Fw
IRVIN, Margaret	22	F	None	21Ma14Fw
RYAN, Timothy	26	M	Laborer	21Ma14Fw
CAHILL, Thomas	25	M	Farmer	21Ma14Fw
COGHLAN, John	21	M	Farmer	21Ma14Fw
LEAHY, John	27	M	Laborer	21Ma14Fw
AHERN, John	27	M	Laborer	21Ma14Fw
DALY, Maurice	21	M	Laborer	21Ma14Fw
Maurice	60	M	Carpenter	21Ma14Fw
DENNIEN, Bridget	50	F	None	21Ma14Fw
DALY, Mary	18	F	None	21Ma14Fw
William	12	M	None	21Ma14Fw
WALSH, Catherine	20	F	None	21Ma14Fw

NAMES OF PASSENGERS		A G E	S E X	OCCUPATIONS	DATE PORT SHIP	NAMES OF PASSENGERS		A G E	S E X	OCCUPATIONS	DATE PORT SHIP
RIORDAN, Michael		22	M	Laborer	21Ma14Fw	SEXTON, Bridget		21	F	None	21Ma14Fw
DALY, Eliza		20	F	Laborer	21Ma14Fw	CRONIN, Michael		32	M	Laborer	21Ma14Fw
STEWART, George		23	M	Surveyor	21Ma14Fw	GALVIN, Mary		20	F	None	21Ma14Fw
MCAULIFFE, John		29	M	Laborer	21Ma14Fw	BUCKLY, Thomas		18	M	Victualler	21Ma14Fw
CONNER, Dennis		28	M	Laborer	21Ma14Fw	COTTON, Johannah		25	F	None	21Ma14Fw
FLOOD, Ellen		25	F	Cnf	21Ma14Fw	THOMAS, Ron		21	M	None	21Ma14Fw
Catherine		24	F	Dressmaker	21Ma14Fw	EAGER, Edward		19	M	Mason	21Ma14Fw
FAGAN, George		60	M	Farmer	21Ma14Fw	COGHLAN, Catharine		25	F	Dressmaker	21Ma14Fw
Mary	(W)	58	F	None	21Ma14Fw	John		30	M	Laborer	21Ma14Fw
Thomas	(S)	21	M	None	21Ma14Fw	CUMMINS, Dennis		25	M	Laborer	21Ma14Fw
Dorah	(D)	19	F	None	21Ma14Fw	SHEEHAN, Patrick		25	M	Laborer	21Ma14Fw
George	(S)	17	M	None	21Ma14Fw	CROWLEY, Mary		18	F	None	21Ma14Fw
William	(S)	14	M	None	21Ma14Fw	OKEEFE, Laurence		30	M	Laborer	21Ma14Fw
Mary	(D)	12	F	None	21Ma14Fw	MCCARTHY, Mary		22	F	None	21Ma14Fw
Anne	(D)	10	F	Child	21Ma14Fw	DONNOVAN, James		21	M	Laborer	21Ma14Fw
GOOD, William		21	M	Farmer	21Ma14Fw	CONNELLY, Daniel		24	M	Laborer	21Ma14Fw
LORDAN, Mary		40	F	None	21Ma14Fw	MCCARTHY, Patrick		27	M	Laborer	21Ma14Fw
COGHLAN, Catherine		11	F	Child	21Ma14Fw	KEEFFE, Mary		30	F	None	21Ma14Fw
DOWNING, Margaret		18	F	None	21Ma14Fw	Ellen		20	F	None	21Ma14Fw
CALLAGHAN, Johanna		22	F	Dressmaker	21Ma14Fw	Ellen		20	F	None	21Ma14Fw
DEMPSEY, Nelly		25	F	Servant	21Ma14Fw	Mary		20	F	None	21Ma14Fw
DALY, Timothy		28	M	Laborer	21Ma14Fw	John		.08	M	Infant	21Ma14Fw
COLLINS, John		28	M	Laborer	21Ma14Fw	KEARNEY, Johanna		20	F	None	21Ma14Fw
Catharine		25	F	Laborer	21Ma14Fw	NEIL, Owen		20	M	Laborer	21Ma14Fw
BRIAN, John		70	M	Laborer	21Ma14Fw	BRIEN, James		25	M	Laborer	21Ma14Fw
Jeremiah		23	M	Laborer	21Ma14Fw	MURRY, Timothy		22	M	Laborer	21Ma14Fw
Timothy		13	M	Laborer	21Ma14Fw	BARRETT, Peter		22	M	Laborer	21Ma14Fw
Patrick		10	M	Child	21Ma14Fw	HOOLEY, Thomas		20	M	Laborer	21Ma14Fw
Margaret		50	F	Laborer	21Ma14Fw	CLEARY, Michael		22	M	Laborer	21Ma14Fw
Norry		22	F	Laborer	21Ma14Fw	CALLAHAN, Thomas		31	M	Weaver	21Ma14Fw
Margaret		13	F	Laborer	21Ma14Fw	Mary		28	F	Servant	21Ma14Fw
Mary		11	F	Child	21Ma14Fw	John		26	M	Wheelwright	21Ma14Fw
SULLIVAN, Norry		25	F	Servant	21Ma14Fw	Catharine		22	F	None	21Ma14Fw
CONNELL, Honora		26	F	Servant	21Ma14Fw	Daniel		01	M	Child	21Ma14Fw
OBRIAN, Mary		21	F	Servant	21Ma14Fw	SHEEHAN, Judy		30	F	Servant	21Ma14Fw
MCDONNELL, William		24	M	Laborer	21Ma14Fw	DONNOVAN, Mary		21	F	None	21Ma14Fw
MURPHY, Mary		17	F	None	21Ma14Fw	DALY, Patrick		20	M	Coachman	21Ma14Fw
WALSH, Patrick		44	M	Laborer	21Ma14Fw	Johanna		20	F	Coachman	21Ma14Fw
SHERIDAN, John		18	M	Laborer	21Ma14Fw	MCCARTHY, Thomas		23	M	Coachman	21Ma14Fw
DALY, Dan		24	M	Laborer	21Ma14Fw	Margaret		21	F	None	21Ma14Fw
KEEFE, Dan		23	M	Shoemaker	21Ma14Fw	SHINE, Michael		22	M	None	21Ma14Fw
Margaret		18	F	Servant	21Ma14Fw	Thomas		24	M	Seedman	21Ma14Fw
LEARY, Anne		20	F	None	21Ma14Fw	MALONE, Thomas		30	M	Laborer	21Ma14Fw
NORRIS, Ketty		21	F	None	21Ma14Fw	Bridget		20	F	None	21Ma14Fw
MURPHY, Jeremiah		17	M	Farmer	21Ma14Fw	FITZGERALD, Catharine		22	F	None	21Ma14Fw
John		15	M	Farmer	21Ma14Fw	SHANAHAN, James		23	M	None	21Ma14Fw
FORD, Batt		25	M	None	21Ma14Fw	LINIHAN, David		28	M	None	21Ma14Fw
HOBART, Frank		25	M	Laborer	21Ma14Fw	CONNOR, Margaret		25	F	Servant	21Ma14Fw
SWEENEY, Cornellus		30	M	Laborer	21Ma14Fw	KELEHER, Ellen		21	F	None	21Ma14Fw
DAY, Francis		20	M	Laborer	21Ma14Fw	CREEDON, Mary		23	F	None	21Ma14Fw
HAYES, Michael		23	M	Laborer	21Ma14Fw	HOOLIHAN, Betty		21	F	None	21Ma14Fw
Catharine		25	F	Laborer	21Ma14Fw	DRISCOL, Florence		32	F	None	21Ma14Fw
DONOGHUE, Jeremiah		24	M	Laborer	21Ma14Fw	DONNOVAN, Michael		22	M	None	21Ma14Fw
MCCARTHY, Timothy		25	M	Laborer	21Ma14Fw	LEE, Thomas		28	M	Laborer	21Ma14Fw
CULLAAM, Thomas		25	M	Laborer	21Ma14Fw	DEMPSEY, James		22	M	None	21Ma14Fw
LONG, Michael		24	M	Laborer	21Ma14Fw	LENON, Richard		23	M	Gdnr	21Ma14Fw
KELCHER, Anastasy		22	F	None	21Ma14Fw	STACKPOLE, Eliza		26	F	None	21Ma14Fw
DAHID, Jeremiah		30	M	Laborer	21Ma14Fw	Bridget		24	F	None	21Ma14Fw
Mary		20	F	Laborer	21Ma14Fw	ROURK, Johanna		20	F	None	21Ma14Fw
Margaret		30	F	Laborer	21Ma14Fw	Sarah		17	F	Dressmaker	21Ma14Fw
KEELY, Margaret		20	F	Laborer	21Ma14Fw	DOODY, Eliza		20	F	None	21Ma14Fw
Daniel		30	M	Laborer	21Ma14Fw	HEAFY, Ellen		20	F	None	21Ma14Fw
HURLEY, Thomas		24	M	Laborer	21Ma14Fw	CAVIN, Cornellus		30	M	Laborer	21Ma14Fw
CADIGAN, Edmund		19	M	None	21Ma14Fw	AHERN, Catharine		50	F	None	21Ma14Fw
Michael		20	M	None	21Ma14Fw	Mary	(D)	25	F	None	21Ma14Fw
KELLY, Edmund		20	M	None	21Ma14Fw	NEVILLE, Mary		25	F	Dressmaker	21Ma14Fw
LEARY, Daniel		30	M	None	21Ma14Fw	Fanny		23	F	Dressmaker	21Ma14Fw
LOYNS, Mary		26	F	Servant	21Ma14Fw	AHERN, Edmund		22	M	Seaman	21Ma14Fw
DENEHY, Patrick		21	M	None	21Ma14Fw	QUIRKE, Catherin		25	F	None	21Ma14Fw
DWYER, Henry		21	M	Smith	21Ma14Fw	WALSH, Mary		25	F	None	21Ma14Fw
Mary		50	F	None	21Ma14Fw	BARRY, Ellen		26	F	Servant	21Ma14Fw
SHAW, Mary		30	F	None	21Ma14Fw	Mary		24	F	Servant	21Ma14Fw
Jerry		40	M	Laborer	21Ma14Fw	MCCREAL, James		25	M	Laborer	21Ma14Fw
Mary		28	F	Laborer	21Ma14Fw	WALSH, Ellen		23	F	None	21Ma14Fw
COTTERAL, Honora		23	F	Laborer	21Ma14Fw	CURTIN, Mary		25	F	None	21Ma14Fw

NAMES OF PASSENGERS	AGE	SEX	OCCUPATIONS	DATE PORT SHIP
QUINLAN, Mary	18	F	None	21Ma14Fw
DONDON, Ellen	21	F	None	21Ma14Fw
AHERN, John	20	M	Seaman	21Ma14Fw
BARRY, Richard	25	M	Farmer	21Ma14Fw
DRISCOLL, Thomas	26	M	Laborer	21Ma14Fw
BRIEN, Michael	27	M	Laborer	21Ma14Fw
HARRIGAN, Tade	26	M	Laborer	21Ma14Fw
CREENA, John	25	M	Laborer	21Ma14Fw
HADNETT, Ellen	20	F	Milliner	21Ma14Fw
DALY, Patrick	30	M	None	21Ma14Fw
SPILLAN, Daniel	23	M	None	21Ma14Fw
BARNETT, Peter	23	M	Laborer	21Ma14Fw
CONNOLLY, Mary	22	F	None	21Ma14Fw
LYNCH, John	22	M	Laborer	21Ma14Fw
BARRITT, Mary	22	F	None	21Ma14Fw
RYAN, Michael	21	M	None	21Ma14Fw
CARROLL, Michael	23	M	Laborer	21Ma14Fw
CLEARY, Thomas	22	M	Laborer	21Ma14Fw
CONNOR, John	22	M	Laborer	21Ma14Fw
Michael	22	M	Laborer	21Ma14Fw
MAHONY, Michael	22	M	Laborer	21Ma14Fw
CALLAHAN, Michael	22	M	Laborer	21Ma14Fw
MAHONEY, Michael	23	M	Laborer	21Ma14Fw
CAVANNAGH, Patrick	21	M	Shoemaker	21Ma14Fw
QUILE, Michael	24	M	Weaver	21Ma14Fw
HOOLIHAN, John	35	M	Weaver	21Ma14Fw
MURPHY, Dennis	30	M	Laborer	21Ma14Fw
CASTIGAN, John	30	M	Laborer	21Ma14Fw
SULLIVAN, Michael	30	M	Laborer	21Ma14Fw
WILLIAM, Margaret	58	F	None	21Ma14Fw
CROONIN, Con	60	M	None	21Ma14Fw
COGHLAN, John	30	M	Laborer	21Ma14Fw
Catherine	30	F	Laborer	21Ma14Fw
James	28	M	Laborer	21Ma14Fw
Julia	25	F	Laborer	21Ma14Fw
Timothy	23	F	Laborer	21Ma14Fw
Michael	06	M	Child	21Ma14Fw
Mary	02	F	Child	21Ma14Fw
Timothy	01	M	Child	21Ma14Fw

GRAMPION 22 MAY 1846

From Liverpool

NAMES OF PASSENGERS		AGE	SEX	OCCUPATIONS	DATE PORT SHIP
NICHOLSON, William		20	M	Farmer	22Ma02Gv
HAUGHURY, Cathe.		50	F	None	22Ma02Gv
Margt.	(D)	13	F	None	22Ma02Gv
Frances	(D)	12	F	None	22Ma02Gv
MCMANUS, Andw.		18	M	Laborer	22Ma02Gv
BUCKLEY, Patk.		20	M	Laborer	22Ma02Gv
Ellen		20	F	Laborer	22Ma02Gv
MURPHY, Thomas		20	M	Laborer	22Ma02Gv
FALLON, John		32	M	Laborer	22Ma02Gv
Bridget	(W)	32	F	Wife	22Ma02Gv
Richard	(S)	13	M	Laborer	22Ma02Gv
Ann	(D)	12	F	Laborer	22Ma02Gv
Martin	(S)	10	M	Child	22Ma02Gv
LYNAN, Ellen		19	F	Servant	22Ma02Gv
HUGHES, Michl.		40	M	Farmer	22Ma02Gv
Ann	(W)	36	F	None	22Ma02Gv
Patk.	(S)	20	M	None	22Ma02Gv
Barney	(S)	17	M	None	22Ma02Gv
Alice	(D)	13	F	None	22Ma02Gv
Ann	(D)	12	F	None	22Ma02Gv
Mary	(D)	11	F	Child	22Ma02Gv
MCCANN, Charley		20	M	Laborer	22Ma02Gv
Alice		23	F	Laborer	22Ma02Gv
GREENE, Cathe.		20	F	Servant	22Ma02Gv
KENNEDY, Michl.		21	M	Laborer	22Ma02Gv

NAMES OF PASSENGERS		AGE	SEX	OCCUPATIONS	DATE PORT SHIP
CASY, John		21	M	Laborer	22Ma02Gv
BURKE, Edwd.		28	M	Laborer	22Ma02Gv
LANCY, Hugh		23	M	Laborer	22Ma02Gv
Margt.		20	F	Laborer	22Ma02Gv
REED, James		21	M	Laborer	22Ma02Gv
U	(W)	20	F	Wife	22Ma02Gv
RICHARDS, Jane		20	F	Laborer	22Ma02Gv
MCKENNA, John		20	M	Laborer	22Ma02Gv
MURPHY, James		20	M	Laborer	22Ma02Gv
HAZELTON, John		20	M	Laborer	22Ma02Gv
NEALE, Robt.		20	M	Laborer	22Ma02Gv
James		20	M	Laborer	22Ma02Gv
MCLAUGHLIN, Michl.		20	M	Laborer	22Ma02Gv
DUNLOP, Wm.		25	M	Laborer	22Ma02Gv
CURRAGH, Sarah		20	F	Servant	22Ma02Gv
FITZSIMMONS, Cathe.		18	F	Servant	22Ma02Gv
EVANS, Thomas		36	M	Laborer	22Ma02Gv
FENNESY, Pierce		30	M	Laborer	22Ma02Gv
CARNEY, Danl.		20	M	Laborer	22Ma02Gv
BRIAN, Thos.		25	M	Laborer	22Ma02Gv
CARNEY, Biddy		20	F	Servant	22Ma02Gv
BRIEN, Kitty		.00	F	Infant	22Ma02Gv
LENAHAN, Ann		24	F	Servant	22Ma02Gv
MCHUGH, Michl.		23	M	Servant	22Ma02Gv
GILLAN, Michl.		20	M	Servant	22Ma02Gv
MCGURK, Arthur		20	M	Servant	22Ma02Gv
BURRETS, Thos.		40	M	Servant	22Ma02Gv
GRAHAN, Patk.		30	M	Servant	22Ma02Gv
BEATY, Wm.		23	M	Servant	22Ma02Gv
JANE, Ann		23	F	Servant	22Ma02Gv
BERGIN, Patk.		27	M	Servant	22Ma02Gv
Thos.		28	M	Servant	22Ma02Gv
Patk.		21	M	Servant	22Ma02Gv
HUGHES, Edwd.		22	M	Servant	22Ma02Gv
CURRY, Michl.		20	M	Servant	22Ma02Gv
CASEY, Jno.		35	M	Servant	22Ma02Gv
U	(W)	35	F	Wife	22Ma02Gv
CAULEY, Peggy		20	F	Servant	22Ma02Gv
Rose		20	F	Servant	22Ma02Gv
HAMMOND, Eliza		20	F	Servant	22Ma02Gv
COCHLIN, Michl.		20	M	Servant	22Ma02Gv
BRANNAN, Michl.		20	M	Servant	22Ma02Gv
DEVERAUX, Bridgt.		20	F	Servant	22Ma02Gv
SWANOLS, John		30	M	Servant	22Ma02Gv
Mary		30	F	Servant	22Ma02Gv
SMITH, John		20	M	Servant	22Ma02Gv
MCCARTY, Danl.		28	M	Servant	22Ma02Gv
U	(W)	20	F	Wife	22Ma02Gv
BARRY, Patk.		18	M	Servant	22Ma02Gv
DONNEVAN, Denis		27	M	None	22Ma02Gv
WHITE, John		24	M	None	22Ma02Gv
DONOVAN, Mary		20	F	None	22Ma02Gv
HARRINGTON, Mark		24	M	None	22Ma02Gv
Mary		18	F	None	22Ma02Gv
SULLIVAN, Michl.		22	M	None	22Ma02Gv
LYNCH, Daniel		28	M	None	22Ma02Gv
Judith		24	F	None	22Ma02Gv
BRENNAN, James		17	M	None	22Ma02Gv
MADDEN, Morgan		25	M	None	22Ma02Gv
Patk.		20	M	None	22Ma02Gv
Johanna		20	F	None	22Ma02Gv
TIERNAN, Wm.		20	M	None	22Ma02Gv
DOOLAN, Wm.		13	M	None	22Ma02Gv
LENAHAN, John		18	M	None	22Ma02Gv
CLEARY, Morris		20	M	None	22Ma02Gv
ROACHE, Thomas		20	M	None	22Ma02Gv
SULLIVAN, John		20	M	None	22Ma02Gv
DALTON, Margt.		20	F	None	22Ma02Gv
MORGAN, Margt.		20	F	None	22Ma02Gv
DOOLY, Patk.		20	M	None	22Ma02Gv
SHIELDS, Domnick		21	M	None	22Ma02Gv
KEEGAN, Bridgt.		21	F	None	22Ma02Gv
Cathe.		18	F	None	22Ma02Gv
SLATTERY, Denis		26	M	None	22Ma02Gv
BOYD, Ann		12	F	None	22Ma02Gv

NAMES OF PASSENGERS	AGE	SEX	OCCUPATIONS	DATE PORT SHIP	NAMES OF PASSENGERS	AGE	SEX	OCCUPATIONS	DATE PORT SHIP
BEGLEY, Mary	18	F	None	22Ma02Gv	RIELY, Jerry	20	M	Laborer	22Ma02Gv
MCBARRY, Charles	14	M	None	22Ma02Gv	Ellen	20	F	Laborer	22Ma02Gv
HAGAN, John	21	M	None	22Ma02Gv	ROWLEY, John	20	M	Laborer	22Ma02Gv
TENPENY, James	26	M	None	22Ma02Gv	HARE, Ellnor	20	F	Laborer	22Ma02Gv
CROWLEY, Johanna	19	F	None	22Ma02Gv	WADE, Anthony	20	M	Laborer	22Ma02Gv
CORMICK, Bridgt.	29	F	None	22Ma02Gv	CUNNINGHAM, Thomas	20	M	Laborer	22Ma02Gv
PARRY, Michl.	20	M	None	22Ma02Gv	REDMOND, John	20	M	Laborer	22Ma02Gv
Wm.	06	M	Child	22Ma02Gv	MURRAY, Ellen	20	F	Laborer	22Ma02Gv
Mary	04	F	Child	22Ma02Gv	MCCAULEY, Anthony	20	M	Mechanic	22Ma02Gv
Griffith	03	M	Child	22Ma02Gv	WADE, Henry	20	M	Mechanic	22Ma02Gv
Robert	.00	M	Infant	22Ma02Gv	SMITH, Bessy	20	F	Mechanic	22Ma02Gv
Catherine	30	F	None	22Ma02Gv	CLIFF, Michl.	20	M	Mechanic	22Ma02Gv
TRANER, John	22	M	None	22Ma02Gv	IRWIN, Margh.	20	F	Servant	22Ma02Gv
Frances	31	F	None	22Ma02Gv	CAVANAGH, Thomas	40	M	Farmer	22Ma02Gv
HOLLAND, John	20	M	None	22Ma02Gv	MALONE, James	20	M	Farmer	22Ma02Gv
MILNER, John	18	M	None	22Ma02Gv	Mary	20	F	Servant	22Ma02Gv
HARVEY, Francis	18	M	Laborer	22Ma02Gv	HORAN, Martin	20	M	Servant	22Ma02Gv
HOLLAND, Mary	48	F	Servant	22Ma02Gv	U (W)	20	F	Servant	22Ma02Gv
SEATON, Morris	20	F	Servant	22Ma02Gv	HARDY, John	40	M	Servant	22Ma02Gv
SLEVEGG, James	20	M	Servant	22Ma02Gv	Thomas	20	M	Servant	22Ma02Gv
Jeremiah	20	M	Servant	22Ma02Gv	Margh.	18	F	Servant	22Ma02Gv
CREENAGE, Cathe.	20	F	Servant	22Ma02Gv	James	16	M	Servant	22Ma02Gv
MINER, Peter	20	M	Servant	22Ma02Gv	Peggy	30	F	Servant	22Ma02Gv
Patk.	06	M	Child	22Ma02Gv	BYRNE, Garrit	20	M	Servant	22Ma02Gv
Ellen	04	F	Child	22Ma02Gv	FITZPATRICK, John	20	M	Laborer	22Ma02Gv
DAY, Thomas	49	M	Servant	22Ma02Gv	WALSH, Mathew	20	M	Laborer	22Ma02Gv
ROCHE, John	30	M	Servant	22Ma02Gv	SLEERA, Michl.	20	M	Laborer	22Ma02Gv
SULLIVAN, Elizabeth	30	F	Servant	22Ma02Gv	Nancy	20	F	Laborer	22Ma02Gv
OHARA, John	30	M	Servant	22Ma02Gv	SPENCE, Rose	15	F	Laborer	22Ma02Gv
SHEPPARD, Wm.	23	M	Servant	22Ma02Gv	Mary	13	F	Laborer	22Ma02Gv
Johanna	21	F	Servant	22Ma02Gv	BRADY, Thomas	16	M	Laborer	22Ma02Gv
PRICE, Frances	20	M	Servant	22Ma02Gv	REGAN, John	20	M	Laborer	22Ma02Gv
Margt.	20	F	Servant	22Ma02Gv	GANNAN, Patk.	20	M	Laborer	22Ma02Gv
Cassidy	20	M	Servant	22Ma02Gv	Ann	25	F	Laborer	22Ma02Gv
Cathe.	30	F	Servant	22Ma02Gv	WILSON, Mary	19	F	Laborer	22Ma02Gv
Betsy	20	F	Servant	22Ma02Gv	HEARN, John	18	M	Laborer	22Ma02Gv
WRIGHT, Bridget	20	F	Servant	22Ma02Gv	REDDINGTON, Sarah	21	F	Laborer	22Ma02Gv
GILLAN, Bridget	20	F	Servant	22Ma02Gv	CHOTTER, Mary	21	F	Laborer	22Ma02Gv
SULLIVAN, John	28	M	Servant	22Ma02Gv	CONNOR, Thomas	26	M	Laborer	22Ma02Gv
KEEFE, Margt.	20	F	Servant	22Ma02Gv	MCDONALD, Pat	20	M	Laborer	22Ma02Gv
CHAMBERS, James	28	M	Servant	22Ma02Gv	MARTIN, Mary	20	F	Laborer	22Ma02Gv
PUDEL, Michl.	20	M	Servant	22Ma02Gv	BOHAN, Ellen	20	F	Laborer	22Ma02Gv
Thomas	18	M	Servant	22Ma02Gv	KELLY, James	20	M	Laborer	22Ma02Gv
COOLAHAN, Ann	21	F	Servant	22Ma02Gv	U (W)	20	F	Laborer	22Ma02Gv
NEWCOMB, Thomas	30	M	Servant	22Ma02Gv	Rose-Ann (D)	03	F	Child	22Ma02Gv
Michl.	26	M	Servant	22Ma02Gv	Fanny (D)	.00	F	Infant	22Ma02Gv
Martin	20	M	Servant	22Ma02Gv	CASSIDY, Owen	20	M	Farmer	22Ma02Gv
Mary	18	F	Servant	22Ma02Gv	BRANNON, Ann	20	F	Servant	22Ma02Gv
Mary	25	F	Servant	22Ma02Gv	VAUGHAN, Peter	20	M	Servant	22Ma02Gv
DALY, Owen	40	M	Servant	22Ma02Gv	Margt.	18	F	Servant	22Ma02Gv
Ann	28	F	Servant	22Ma02Gv	HARA, John	20	M	Servant	22Ma02Gv
Cathe.	23	F	Servant	22Ma02Gv	Bridget	36	F	Servant	22Ma02Gv
FLAHERTY, Patk.	25	M	Servant	22Ma02Gv	James	10	M	Child	22Ma02Gv
Sally	20	F	Servant	22Ma02Gv	Thomas	06	M	Child	22Ma02Gv
DORAN, John	20	M	Servant	22Ma02Gv	CONNOLLY, Michl.	30	M	Servant	22Ma02Gv
FLAHERTY, Martin	.00	M	Infant	22Ma02Gv	Peter	26	M	Servant	22Ma02Gv
WINN, Cathe.	20	F	Servant	22Ma02Gv	FLANAGAN, John	24	M	Servant	22Ma02Gv
SULLIVAN, John	20	M	Servant	22Ma02Gv	HILL, Bridgt.	20	F	Servant	22Ma02Gv
NEWHAN, Wm.	20	M	Servant	22Ma02Gv	THOMPSON, Mary	19	F	Servant	22Ma02Gv
DORLING, Wm.	20	M	Servant	22Ma02Gv	DOHERTY, Henry	31	M	Servant	22Ma02Gv
LENAHAN, John	20	M	Laborer	22Ma02Gv	CASEY, John	25	M	Servant	22Ma02Gv
CLEARY, Maurice	20	M	Laborer	22Ma02Gv	MAHON, John	25	M	Laborer	22Ma02Gv
ROACHE, Thomas	20	M	Laborer	22Ma02Gv	MCGOWAN, Michl.	25	M	Laborer	22Ma02Gv
DOOLAN, Thomas	20	M	Laborer	22Ma02Gv	ROPER, Brien	20	M	Laborer	22Ma02Gv
KEEFE, David	20	M	Laborer	22Ma02Gv	CLANCY, Terence	20	M	Laborer	22Ma02Gv
SULLIVAN, Richd.	20	M	Laborer	22Ma02Gv	MARSHALL, John	20	M	Laborer	22Ma02Gv
MACK, Thos.	20	M	Laborer	22Ma02Gv	COONEY, Robert	20	M	Laborer	22Ma02Gv
RYAN, Thos.	20	M	Laborer	22Ma02Gv	Jane	20	F	Laborer	22Ma02Gv
CONNER, Michl.	20	M	Laborer	22Ma02Gv	JOHNSON, Robert	20	M	Laborer	22Ma02Gv
U (W)	20	F	Wife	22Ma02Gv	CLARKE, Patk.	26	M	Laborer	22Ma02Gv
LYNCH, John	20	M	Laborer	22Ma02Gv	SLURAN, Michl.	22	M	Laborer	22Ma02Gv
Mary	20	F	Laborer	22Ma02Gv	HANEY, Chris.	20	M	Laborer	22Ma02Gv
BURKE, Garrick	20	M	Laborer	22Ma02Gv	MCGRATH, John	36	M	Laborer	22Ma02Gv
ROCHE, John	20	M	Laborer	22Ma02Gv	DUFF, James	30	M	Laborer	22Ma02Gv
Abby	20	F	Laborer	22Ma02Gv	LALLY, Margt.	26	F	Laborer	22Ma02Gv

NAMES OF PASSENGERS		AGE	SEX	OCCUPATIONS	DATE PORT SHIP
SLURAN, John		20	M	Laborer	22Ma02Gv
DEVLIN, Margt.		23	F	Laborer	22Ma02Gv
SLURAN, Mary		24	F	Laborer	22Ma02Gv
Biddy		22	F	Laborer	22Ma02Gv
Cathe.		20	F	Laborer	22Ma02Gv
Ann		18	F	Laborer	22Ma02Gv
Mary		16	F	Laborer	22Ma02Gv
FREELAN, John		23	M	Laborer	22Ma02Gv
BOHAN, Biddy		18	F	Laborer	22Ma02Gv
Mary		20	F	Laborer	22Ma02Gv
CONNER, Margt.		18	F	Laborer	22Ma02Gv
COFFREY, Mary		20	F	Laborer	22Ma02Gv
COURTNEY, Ann		23	F	Laborer	22Ma02Gv
KEARNY, Owen		20	M	Laborer	22Ma02Gv
BANNAN, John		20	M	Laborer	22Ma02Gv
GORDAN, Peter		20	M	Laborer	22Ma02Gv
MACKEN, Mary		20	F	Laborer	22Ma02Gv
FALLAN, Michl.		10	M	Child	22Ma02Gv
MCNAMARA, Michl.		25	M	Laborer	22Ma02Gv
Bridget		20	F	Laborer	22Ma02Gv
TAYLOR, Wm.		40	M	Seaman	22Ma02Gv
U	(W)	35	F	Wife	22Ma02Gv
Wm.	(S)	05	M	Child	22Ma02Gv
Mary	(D)	03	F	Child	22Ma02Gv

CHARLOTTE 21 MAY 1846

From Dublin

NAMES OF PASSENGERS		AGE	SEX	OCCUPATIONS	DATE PORT SHIP
DOWNEY, Lawrence		20	M	Laborer	21Ma20Da
FOLEY, John		24	M	Laborer	21Ma20Da
U	(W)	20	F	Wife	21Ma20Da
Bridget	(D)	.00	F	Infant	21Ma20Da
DWYER, Patt		34	M	Laborer	21Ma20Da
WILSON, Edward		28	M	Laborer	21Ma20Da
Eliza	(W)	20	F	Wife	21Ma20Da
BYRNE, Wm.		30	M	Servant	21Ma20Da
Ann	(D)	11	F	Servant	21Ma20Da
BOURKE, William		25	M	Farmer	21Ma20Da
U	(W)	20	F	Wife	21Ma20Da
Patt		30	M	Farmer	21Ma20Da
MEIGHAN, John		28	M	Farmer	21Ma20Da
Ann		08	F	Child	21Ma20Da
John		24	M	Laborer	21Ma20Da
WHELAN, Martin		20	M	Laborer	21Ma20Da
Margret	(W)	22	F	Wife	21Ma20Da
MEIGHAN, Bridget		22	F	Servant	21Ma20Da
KELLY, John		20	M	Laborer	21Ma20Da
HANNAHAN, Mary		20	F	Servant	21Ma20Da
CURREY, Mary		20	F	Servant	21Ma20Da
MCGIFF, Barney		20	M	Laborer	21Ma20Da
Betty	(W)	20	F	Wife	21Ma20Da
GEERY, Thomas		25	M	Mason	21Ma20Da
BRENAN, Daniel		22	M	Mason	21Ma20Da
Bridget	(W)	22	F	Wife	21Ma20Da
James	(S)	.00	M	Infant	21Ma20Da
SHORTAL, Nicholas		24	M	Laborer	21Ma20Da
Anty	(W)	20	F	Wife	21Ma20Da
DUNN, William		26	M	Laborer	21Ma20Da
KERAVAN, James		22	M	Laborer	21Ma20Da
FOGARTY, Micheal		18	M	Laborer	21Ma20Da
WALSH, Mary		20	F	Seamstress	21Ma20Da
MURRAY, Ellen		30	F	Seamstress	21Ma20Da
Ann		11	F	Seamstress	21Ma20Da
HEAVAN, Bridget		20	F	Servant	21Ma20Da
CAULY, James		22	M	Laborer	21Ma20Da
BLAKE, Daniel		20	M	Laborer	21Ma20Da
KENEDY, Mary		20	F	Servant	21Ma20Da
KANE, Mary		20	F	Servant	21Ma20Da

NAMES OF PASSENGERS		AGE	SEX	OCCUPATIONS	DATE PORT SHIP
HOGAN, M.		25	U	Servant	21Ma20Da
HARFORD, Patt		30	M	Laborer	21Ma20Da
MCCABE, Patt		26	M	Laborer	21Ma20Da
Bridget	(W)	24	F	Wife	21Ma20Da
Ann	(D)	.09	F	Infant	21Ma20Da
CAHILL, Patt		26	M	Clerk	21Ma20Da
DONELLY, William		24	M	Clerk	21Ma20Da
LAHAN, Michael		16	M	Laborer	21Ma20Da
CONDRON, Bridget		20	F	Servant	21Ma20Da
WALSH, Catherine		20	F	Servant	21Ma20Da
FARRELL, Eliza		20	F	Servant	21Ma20Da
FLYNN, Luke		24	M	Laborer	21Ma20Da
CONNOR, Patt		30	M	Laborer	21Ma20Da
Margret	(W)	28	F	Wife	21Ma20Da
Micheal	(S)	03	M	Child	21Ma20Da
John	(S)	01	M	Child	21Ma20Da
CLUSKEY, Thomas		26	M	Laborer	21Ma20Da
Bessy	(W)	22	F	Wife	21Ma20Da
NULTY, Peter		28	M	Laborer	21Ma20Da
BLACKBURN, John		24	M	Laborer	21Ma20Da
Richd.		22	M	Laborer	21Ma20Da
CONNOR, Thomas		26	M	Laborer	21Ma20Da
Mary	(W)	20	F	Wife	21Ma20Da
LEONARD, Hugh		20	M	Laborer	21Ma20Da
SMITH, Ann		17	F	Seamstress	21Ma20Da
BURKE, Patt		30	M	Mason	21Ma20Da
REILY, Bridget		20	F	Servant	21Ma20Da
FINEGAN, Catherine		19	F	Servant	21Ma20Da
CONNOLLY, Rose		40	F	Servant	21Ma20Da
Mary	(D)	16	F	Servant	21Ma20Da
Rose	(D)	14	F	Servant	21Ma20Da
Margret	(D)	12	F	Servant	21Ma20Da
James	(S)	10	M	Child	21Ma20Da
LEE, Barthol.		24	M	Laborer	21Ma20Da
TWEE, Mary		15	F	Servant	21Ma20Da
SMITH, Bridget		24	F	Servant	21Ma20Da
FRENCH, Kate		03	F	Child	21Ma20Da
COX, Thomas		20	M	Servant	21Ma20Da
ELLIOT, Eliza		20	F	Servant	21Ma20Da
Pheby		18	F	Servant	21Ma20Da
ARMSTRONG, Jane		20	F	Servant	21Ma20Da
HEWETT, Bessey		20	F	Servant	21Ma20Da
HEFFERNAN, Patt		20	M	Laborer	21Ma20Da
NOWD, Andrew		22	M	Laborer	21Ma20Da
RAPHEL, William		21	M	Laborer	21Ma20Da
SCOTT, Patt		22	M	Laborer	21Ma20Da
GAFNEY, Patt		20	M	Laborer	21Ma20Da
MAGRATH, Robert		17	M	Laborer	21Ma20Da
HARRINGTON, Eliza		25	F	Servant	21Ma20Da
MAGRATH, William		28	M	Laborer	21Ma20Da
CARTY, U-Mrs.		34	F	Seamstress	21Ma20Da
David	(S)	11	M	Child	21Ma20Da
BRADY, U		30	M	Mechanic	21Ma20Da
U	(W)	20	F	Wife	21Ma20Da
Mary		20	F	Seamstress	21Ma20Da
MURPHY, James		20	M	Laborer	21Ma20Da
MCGINLEY, John		24	M	Laborer	21Ma20Da
Eliza	(W)	20	F	Servant	21Ma20Da
John	(S)	02	M	Child	21Ma20Da
RATTIGAN, U		27	M	Laborer	21Ma20Da
DOWLING, Thomas		26	M	Laborer	21Ma20Da
Richard		24	M	Laborer	21Ma20Da
Biddy		20	F	Servant	21Ma20Da
DUNPHY, Jos.		24	M	Laborer	21Ma20Da
LANNAN, Thomas		21	M	Laborer	21Ma20Da
KELLY, Peter		20	M	Laborer	21Ma20Da
WALACE, John		20	M	Laborer	21Ma20Da
BURKE, Tim		18	M	Laborer	21Ma20Da
GORDEN, Bridget		16	F	Servant	21Ma20Da
MCDONELL, Timy.		22	M	Laborer	21Ma20Da
DUNIGAN, John		20	M	Laborer	21Ma20Da
BURKE, Patt		25	M	Laborer	21Ma20Da
MCDONNELL, Charles		26	M	Laborer	21Ma20Da
Bridget		22	F	Seamstress	21Ma20Da
FOSSET, Hannah		22	F	Seamstress	21Ma20Da

Name	Rel	Age	Sex	Occupation	Date/Port/Ship
FOSSET, Elijha		20	F	Seamstress	21Ma20Da
KENEDY, Patt		25	M	Laborer	21Ma20Da
MAHON, Matt		25	M	Laborer	21Ma20Da
NEANY, James		25	M	Laborer	21Ma20Da
KELLEGHER, Mary		20	F	Servant	21Ma20Da
Patt		20	M	Laborer	21Ma20Da
CHAMBERS, John		24	M	Laborer	21Ma20Da
Jahn	(W)	21	F	Wife	21Ma20Da
BRADY, Peter		25	M	Laborer	21Ma20Da
QUIRK, James		25	M	Laborer	21Ma20Da
Emily		20	F	Wife	21Ma20Da
TRAPP, Sarah		21	F	Servant	21Ma20Da
Louisa		19	F	Servant	21Ma20Da
DONELLY, Thomas		20	M	Laborer	21Ma20Da
LEATHDUM, Jane		20	F	Servant	21Ma20Da
REILY, Catherine		20	F	Servant	21Ma20Da
KEOGHER, Patt		22	M	Laborer	21Ma20Da
Catherine	(W)	20	F	Wife	21Ma20Da
BYRNE, James		26	M	Laborer	21Ma20Da
WHELAN, Michael		24	M	Laborer	21Ma20Da
COADY, James		20	M	Laborer	21Ma20Da
MOORE, Honora		20	F	Seamstress	21Ma20Da
BRENNAN, John		20	M	Laborer	21Ma20Da
HOHER, Thomas		18	M	Laborer	21Ma20Da
RYAN, Catherine		21	F	Servant	21Ma20Da
DONELLY, Judy		20	M	Laborer	21Ma20Da
SMALLEN, Patt		21	M	Laborer	21Ma20Da
Ann	(W)	30	F	Servant	21Ma20Da
Christy	(S)	02	M	Child	21Ma20Da
CREANER, Mary		20	F	Servant	21Ma20Da
CORCORAN, Micheal		22	M	Laborer	21Ma20Da
COSTELLO, Patt		20	M	Laborer	21Ma20Da
CARTEN, U		26	F	Servant	21Ma20Da
MURRAY, Thomas		21	M	Laborer	21Ma20Da
DULHANTY, U-Mrs.		25	F	Servant	21Ma20Da
U		20	F	Servant	21Ma20Da
DOYLE, Bridget		20	F	Servant	21Ma20Da
BYRNE, Mallachy		30	M	Laborer	21Ma20Da
Stephen		07	M	Child	21Ma20Da
TEENYAN, James		29	M	Laborer	21Ma20Da
Maria		09	F	Child	21Ma20Da
BOYLE, John		45	M	Laborer	21Ma20Da
CARBERRY, John		25	M	Laborer	21Ma20Da
FLYNN, Mary		18	F	Servant	21Ma20Da
GORE, James		20	M	Laborer	21Ma20Da
CANNON, James		22	M	Laborer	21Ma20Da
Maria		20	F	Servant	21Ma20Da
MAHER, Margret		20	F	Servant	21Ma20Da
MCDERMOTT, Mary		60	F	Servant	21Ma20Da
James	(S)	16	M	Laborer	21Ma20Da
Hugh	(S)	24	M	Laborer	21Ma20Da
Bridget	(D)	14	F	Seamstress	21Ma20Da
FLYNN, Mary		20	F	Seamstress	21Ma20Da
LYNCH, James		24	M	Laborer	21Ma20Da
HINEY, James		26	M	Laborer	21Ma20Da
GEHARTY, Micheal		20	M	Laborer	21Ma20Da
Ellen		18	F	Servant	21Ma20Da
FARRELL, Biddy		20	F	Servant	21Ma20Da
HEFERNAN, James		20	M	Laborer	21Ma20Da
GILLOIGHTY, Bridget		20	F	Servant	21Ma20Da
EAGAN, John		22	M	Laborer	21Ma20Da
HERNAN, Ellen		20	F	Servant	21Ma20Da
BURKE, Thomas		22	M	Laborer	21Ma20Da
SHORTE, William		25	M	Laborer	21Ma20Da
NEVAN, William		18	M	Laborer	21Ma20Da
Ellen		20	F	Seamstress	21Ma20Da
DAY, John		25	M	Laborer	21Ma20Da
BREEN, James		25	M	Laborer	21Ma20Da
CORCORAN, James		25	M	Laborer	21Ma20Da
MURPHY, Thomas		22	M	Laborer	21Ma20Da
MARAH, John		25	M	Laborer	21Ma20Da
Bridget		24	F	Servant	21Ma20Da
Ellen		21	F	Servant	21Ma20Da
Catherine		20	F	Servant	21Ma20Da
MARSHALL, Edwd.		22	M	Laborer	21Ma20Da
CONWAY, Thomas		21	M	Laborer	21Ma20Da
KELLY, William		20	M	Laborer	21Ma20Da
REANEY, Edward		20	M	Laborer	21Ma20Da
Jane		18	F	Servant	21Ma20Da
BRENAN, U		20	F	Servant	21Ma20Da
Martin		18	F	Carpenter	21Ma20Da
DOODY, John		20	M	Laborer	21Ma20Da
HESHAL, Onney		20	M	Laborer	21Ma20Da
LAWLER, Thomas		22	M	Laborer	21Ma20Da
July		20	F	Servant	21Ma20Da
FRANE, Danil		20	M	Laborer	21Ma20Da
HERNAN, James		22	M	Laborer	21Ma20Da
U-Mrs.		40	F	Servant	21Ma20Da
DALEY, Micheal		45	M	Laborer	21Ma20Da
BRENAN, Mary		21	F	Servant	21Ma20Da
DALEY, William		22	M	Laborer	21Ma20Da
Mary		18	F	Servant	21Ma20Da
DELANCY, Andrew		26	M	Laborer	21Ma20Da
DANIEL, George		20	M	Laborer	21Ma20Da
DENAN, Nicholas		25	M	Laborer	21Ma20Da
FENERTY, Edward		20	M	Laborer	21Ma20Da
GAFFENY, Bridget		22	F	Seamstress	21Ma20Da
FENERTY, Ellen		16	F	Seamstress	21Ma20Da
KEENAN, Patt		32	M	Laborer	21Ma20Da
Onony	(W)	30	F	Seamstress	21Ma20Da
Patt	(S)	09	M	Child	21Ma20Da
Joseph	(S)	07	M	Child	21Ma20Da
Micheal	(S)	05	M	Child	21Ma20Da
John	(S)	01	M	Child	21Ma20Da
Ann		20	F	Servant	21Ma20Da
Ann		20	F	Servant	21Ma20Da
REILY, Mary		20	F	Servant	21Ma20Da
CONNORS, Thomas		00	M	Laborer	21Ma20Da
CAHILL, Ellen		00	F	Servant	21Ma20Da

HENRY-PRATT 23 MAY 1846

From Liverpool

Name	Rel	Age	Sex	Occupation	Date/Port/Ship
MELTON, Joshua		40	M	Laborer	23Ma02Ha
Sarah	(W)	40	F	Wife	23Ma02Ha
Mary-Ellen	(D)	03	F	Child	23Ma02Ha
FINNOCK, John		25	M	Farmer	23Ma02Ha
Ann		25	F	Unknown	23Ma02Ha
Ann		03	F	Child	23Ma02Ha
Margt.Ann		13	F	Unknown	23Ma02Ha
Jane		11	F	Child	23Ma02Ha
Olivia		29	F	Unknown	23Ma02Ha
Sampson		10	M	Child	23Ma02Ha
Olivia-Ann		03	F	Child	23Ma02Ha
DUGGAN, Mgt.		20	F	Servant	23Ma02Ha
HARLEY, Mary		19	F	Servant	23Ma02Ha
TERRELL, Samuel		22	M	Laborer	23Ma02Ha
James		25	M	Laborer	23Ma02Ha
MATTHEWS, Wm.		24	M	Laborer	23Ma02Ha
JOLLY, Mary-A.		22	F	Servant	23Ma02Ha
DECORDY, Archbld.		62	M	Servant	23Ma02Ha
Ann	(W)	60	F	Servant	23Ma02Ha
NORRISON, Mary-A.		30	F	Servant	23Ma02Ha
MCGRATH, John		30	M	Servant	23Ma02Ha
U	(W)	25	F	Wife	23Ma02Ha
James	(S)	09	M	Child	23Ma02Ha
HORAN, Michael		21	M	Servant	23Ma02Ha
BURNS, John		25	M	Servant	23Ma02Ha
CURA, James		32	M	Servant	23Ma02Ha
U	(W)	25	F	Wife	23Ma02Ha
John	(S)	08	M	Child	23Ma02Ha
Bill	(S)	07	M	Child	23Ma02Ha
Mary	(D)	02	F	Child	23Ma02Ha

NAMES OF PASSENGERS		AGE	SEX	OCCUPATIONS	DATE PORT SHIP
CURA, John		24	M	Servant	23Ma02Ha
STUART, Geo.		18	M	Shoemaker	23Ma02Ha
BOURK, Martin		20	M	Shoemaker	23Ma02Ha
LOVE, Margaret		18	F	Servant	23Ma02Ha
MCSHELIS, Bee		18	F	Servant	23Ma02Ha
DIVINE, Margaret		18	F	Servant	23Ma02Ha
WHITLEY, Patk.		18	M	Servant	23Ma02Ha
John		20	M	Servant	23Ma02Ha
KEOW, John		20	M	Servant	23Ma02Ha
MCCONLY, Margt.		50	F	Servant	23Ma02Ha
CAULY, Eliza		22	F	Laborer	23Ma02Ha
Hugh		22	M	Laborer	23Ma02Ha
Robert		26	M	Laborer	23Ma02Ha
MAGUIRE, Catherine		20	F	Laborer	23Ma02Ha
HURLY, Patk.		27	M	Laborer	23Ma02Ha
COLLINS, Patk.		20	M	Laborer	23Ma02Ha
MEADE, Margt.		24	F	Laborer	23Ma02Ha
ODONNELL, Johanna		24	F	Laborer	23Ma02Ha
REGAN, Mary		20	F	Laborer	23Ma02Ha
CONNOLLY, Paul		30	M	Laborer	23Ma02Ha
HENESSY, Richd.		20	M	Servant	23Ma02Ha
Cathe.		20	F	Servant	23Ma02Ha
John		20	M	Servant	23Ma02Ha
CARBOTT, Richd.		30	M	Servant	23Ma02Ha
U	(W)	20	F	Wife	23Ma02Ha
Michl.	(S)	.00	M	Infant	23Ma02Ha
ODONNELL, Ellen		20	F	Servant	23Ma02Ha
Danl.		20	M	Servant	23Ma02Ha
HART, Pat.		30	M	Servant	23Ma02Ha
CONWAY, Mary		20	F	Servant	23Ma02Ha
FLOOD, Phoebe		20	F	Servant	23Ma02Ha
LEVY, Margt.		20	F	Servant	23Ma02Ha
HART, Dennis		28	M	Servant	23Ma02Ha
James		25	M	Servant	23Ma02Ha
DONOVAN, Daniel		24	M	Servant	23Ma02Ha
DENIGAN, Michl.		26	M	Servant	23Ma02Ha
GILL, Bee		18	F	Servant	23Ma02Ha
JONES, Mary		20	F	Servant	23Ma02Ha
FITZPATRICK, Michl.		22	M	Farmer	23Ma02Ha
MCCARTY, Ally		23	F	Servant	23Ma02Ha
HANNA, John		25	M	Servant	23Ma02Ha
ODONNELL, Alice		22	F	Servant	23Ma02Ha
Honora		21	F	Servant	23Ma02Ha
BARRETT, Edward		24	M	Servant	23Ma02Ha
Patk.		26	M	Servant	23Ma02Ha
MEHAN, James		24	M	Servant	23Ma02Ha
TRACY, Mary		20	F	Servant	23Ma02Ha
CANTWELL, John		20	M	Servant	23Ma02Ha
Ann		30	F	Servant	23Ma02Ha
Sarah		30	F	Servant	23Ma02Ha
Cromie		.00	F	Infant	23Ma02Ha
CASTIGAN, Jas.		24	M	Servant	23Ma02Ha
DUGGAN, Conls.		30	M	Servant	23Ma02Ha
Ellen	(W)	26	F	Servant	23Ma02Ha
Cath.	(D)	.00	F	Infant	23Ma02Ha
ROPER, Ann		50	F	Servant	23Ma02Ha
Ann	(D)	13	F	Servant	23Ma02Ha
Hugh	(F)	84	M	Servant	23Ma02Ha
John	(S)	20	M	Servant	23Ma02Ha
James	(S)	27	M	Servant	23Ma02Ha
RYAN, Wm.		20	M	Servant	23Ma02Ha
MCCLATCHY, Jno.		16	M	Weaver	23Ma02Ha
KERNAN, Wm.		26	M	Servant	23Ma02Ha
BRYAN, John		21	M	Servant	23Ma02Ha
HALLIGAN, John		21	M	Farmer	23Ma02Ha
Sarah		21	F	Farmer	23Ma02Ha
SMITH, Mary		20	F	Farmer	23Ma02Ha
Ann		18	F	Farmer	23Ma02Ha
BRADY, John		26	M	Farmer	23Ma02Ha
CURRAGH, Ellen		21	F	Servant	23Ma02Ha
COLLINS, Margt.		33	F	Servant	23Ma02Ha
Pat	(S)	08	M	Child	23Ma02Ha
Peter	(S)	06	M	Child	23Ma02Ha
Wm.	(S)	.00	M	Infant	23Ma02Ha
HART, Ellen		20	F	Servant	23Ma02Ha
CUNNINGHAM, Ann		20	F	Farmer	23Ma02Ha
RILEY, Cath.		17	F	Farmer	23Ma02Ha
CULLINAN, Honora		16	F	Servant	23Ma02Ha
DONOODN, Thimothy		19	M	Servant	23Ma02Ha
HART, Julia		22	F	Servant	23Ma02Ha
MULLANE, Dennis		23	M	Servant	23Ma02Ha
DALEY, Eliza		24	F	Servant	23Ma02Ha
GALLAGHER, Margt.		19	F	Servant	23Ma02Ha
COLLINS, Patk.		26	M	Servant	23Ma02Ha
TEIGH, Hugh		18	M	Servant	23Ma02Ha
MCAVENEY, Edwd.		22	M	Servant	23Ma02Ha
BRIEN, Margt.		26	F	Servant	23Ma02Ha
KENT, Danl.		24	M	Servant	23Ma02Ha
LANDAS, Mary		20	F	Servant	23Ma02Ha
DUGGAN, Florence		25	F	Servant	23Ma02Ha
CORBETT, Peggy		25	F	Servant	23Ma02Ha
CLIFFORD, Nancy		29	F	Servant	23Ma02Ha
HEALY, Bridget		22	F	Servant	23Ma02Ha
LENAHAN, Ellen		24	F	Servant	23Ma02Ha
Cath.		18	F	Servant	23Ma02Ha
MCCOOL, Bridget		18	F	Servant	23Ma02Ha
CALLINAN, Cath.		25	F	Servant	23Ma02Ha
NEAL, Michl.		30	M	Weaver	23Ma02Ha
BUTTON, Thomas		30	M	Servant	23Ma02Ha
GIBBIN, Cath.		30	F	Servant	23Ma02Ha
Mary	(D)	11	F	Child	23Ma02Ha
Thos.	(S)	09	M	Child	23Ma02Ha
HENNESSY, Ellen		18	F	Servant	23Ma02Ha
HAMILTON, Pat		28	M	Servant	23Ma02Ha
DONOHOE, Richd.		10	M	Child	23Ma02Ha
Cath.		08	F	Child	23Ma02Ha
MCCABE, Phillp		17	M	Servant	23Ma02Ha
MILLERD, Pat		30	M	Servant	23Ma02Ha
Ann		30	F	Servant	23Ma02Ha
CARTY, John		18	M	Laborer	23Ma02Ha
QUINN, Patk.		20	M	Laborer	23Ma02Ha
CAROLIN, Richard		25	M	Laborer	23Ma02Ha
COYLE, Cath.		18	F	Servant	23Ma02Ha
FETLEY, Cath.		19	F	Servant	23Ma02Ha
Josiah	(S)	07	M	Child	23Ma02Ha
Eliza	(D)	03	F	Child	23Ma02Ha
ASHTON, John		30	M	Laborer	23Ma02Ha
SHEAN, Thos.		33	M	Laborer	23Ma02Ha
MACKEY, Owen		25	M	Laborer	23Ma02Ha
CURREY, Patk.		21	M	Laborer	23Ma02Ha
WHELAN, John		20	M	Servant	23Ma02Ha
BRIEN, Ellen		13	F	Servant	23Ma02Ha
Mary		12	F	Servant	23Ma02Ha
LEARY, Danl.		33	M	Servant	23Ma02Ha
U	(W)	36	F	Servant	23Ma02Ha
ROURKE, Andrew		24	M	Servant	23Ma02Ha
Ellen		40	F	Servant	23Ma02Ha
MULVEY, Tedy		20	M	Servant	23Ma02Ha
Esther		20	F	Servant	23Ma02Ha
FARRELL, Thos.		18	M	Servant	23Ma02Ha
MAHON, Ann		20	F	Servant	23Ma02Ha
OCONNOR, Richd.		18	M	Servant	23Ma02Ha
MCLOUGHLIN, Ellen		20	F	Servant	23Ma02Ha
FARRELL, Margt.		19	F	Servant	23Ma02Ha
Ann		17	F	Servant	23Ma02Ha
LAMPBELL, Joseph		20	M	Servant	23Ma02Ha
SHIELDS, Owen		21	M	Servant	23Ma02Ha
KELLY, Francis		21	M	Servant	23Ma02Ha
Mary		18	F	Servant	23Ma02Ha
KENNEDY, Ann		30	F	Servant	23Ma02Ha
DIVINE, Margt.		18	F	Servant	23Ma02Ha
OULAS, Margaret		20	F	Servant	23Ma02Ha
SULLIVAN, Margt.		21	F	Servant	23Ma02Ha
MURPHY, Margt.		21	F	Servant	23Ma02Ha
CANOLLY, Cath.		20	F	Servant	23Ma02Ha
KAVANAUGH, Mary		21	F	Servant	23Ma02Ha
RAFERTY, Susan		21	F	Servant	23Ma02Ha
Michl.		08	M	Child	23Ma02Ha
TOMMEY, Francis		20	M	Weaver	23Ma02Ha
HOEY, Bridget		18	F	Weaver	23Ma02Ha

NAMES OF PASSENGERS		AGE	SEX	OCCUPATIONS	DATE PORT SHIP
MCGRATH, Patk.		40	M	Servant	23Ma02Ha
U	(W)	30	F	Servant	23Ma02Ha
HESINE, Edw.		30	M	Servant	23Ma02Ha
U	(W)	25	F	Servant	23Ma02Ha
SCOTT, Thos.		20	M	Servant	23Ma02Ha
CONNOR, John		20	M	Servant	23Ma02Ha
WOODS, John		20	M	Servant	23Ma02Ha
James		18	M	Servant	23Ma02Ha
HENN, Jno.		34	M	Servant	23Ma02Ha
BIRCH, Eliza		66	F	Servant	23Ma02Ha
HENN, Mary		39	F	Servant	23Ma02Ha
Eliza	(D)	13	F	Servant	23Ma02Ha
Ellen	(D)	11	F	Child	23Ma02Ha
Mary	(D)	05	F	Child	23Ma02Ha
Mark	(S)	.00	M	Infant	23Ma02Ha
MCGUIRE, John		24	M	Servant	23Ma02Ha
MCINTIRE, Thos.		30	M	Servant	23Ma02Ha
CANNING, John		40	M	Servant	23Ma02Ha
ONEILL, Ellen		20	F	Servant	23Ma02Ha
HONEYMAN, Ellen		18	F	Servant	23Ma02Ha
GAORA, Ellen		20	F	Servant	23Ma02Ha
LAFFLERS, Thos.		30	M	Farmer	23Ma02Ha
FERGUSON, Wm.		16	M	Servant	23Ma02Ha
DAVIS, Geo.		22	M	Servant	23Ma02Ha
DUNRY, Mary		20	F	Servant	23Ma02Ha
HUNTER, James		18	M	Servant	23Ma02Ha
KILBRIDE, Mary-D.		14	F	Servant	23Ma02Ha
FARLEY, Bridget		18	F	Servant	23Ma02Ha
MARTIN, Esther		21	F	Servant	23Ma02Ha
GREEN, Thos.		30	M	Servant	23Ma02Ha
BOWRMANN, James		30	M	Servant	23Ma02Ha
FITZPATRICK, Jno.		18	M	Servant	23Ma02Ha
KEENAN, Bridgt.		25	F	Servant	23Ma02Ha
Peter		20	M	Servant	23Ma02Ha
KELLY, Thos.		20	M	Servant	23Ma02Ha
WOOD, James		20	M	Servant	23Ma02Ha
TIGHE, Cath.		18	F	Servant	23Ma02Ha
SCANLAN, Cath.		32	F	Servant	23Ma02Ha
CANNING, Bridgt.		40	F	Servant	23Ma02Ha
Mary	(D)	13	F	Servant	23Ma02Ha
Joseph	(S)	12	M	Servant	23Ma02Ha
J.E.	(S)	08	M	Child	23Ma02Ha
Charles	(S)	04	M	Child	23Ma02Ha
ONEILL, James		20	M	Servant	23Ma02Ha
HUTCHINSON, James		18	M	Servant	23Ma02Ha
DAILING, U		30	M	Unknown	23Ma02Ha
U	(W)	21	F	Wife	23Ma02Ha
KIRBY, U		50	M	Unknown	23Ma02Ha
U	(W)	40	F	Wife	23Ma02Ha
Mgt.	(D)	17	F	Unknown	23Ma02Ha
Elizabeth	(D)	12	F	Unknown	23Ma02Ha
GUNN, Thos.		40	M	Unknown	23Ma02Ha
BELL, Thos.		45	M	Unknown	23Ma02Ha
ANDERSON, Thos.		32	M	Unknown	23Ma02Ha
KIRBY, E.		15	M	Unknown	23Ma02Ha

ROBERT-PARKS 25 MAY 1846

From Liverpool

NAMES OF PASSENGERS		AGE	SEX	OCCUPATIONS	DATE PORT SHIP
AUSTIN, Anne		51	F	Farmer	25Ma02Hb
WILKINSON, Robert		20	M	Farmer	25Ma02Hb
MCKESSER, Saml.		17	M	Farmer	25Ma02Hb
HARRIS, Geo.		24	M	Farmer	25Ma02Hb
GOIN, Henry		28	M	Physician	25Ma02Hb
John		30	M	Farmer	25Ma02Hb
Richard		27	M	Farmer	25Ma02Hb
Catherine		18	F	Laborer	25Ma02Hb
SLAVER, Francis		21	M	Servant	25Ma02Hb
SLAVER, Catherine		20	F	Laborer	25Ma02Hb
KEARNEY, Margaret		25	F	Laborer	25Ma02Hb
GLOSHEE, William		26	M	Laborer	25Ma02Hb
SHEA, Mary		27	F	Laborer	25Ma02Hb
BOYER, William		19	M	Laborer	25Ma02Hb
KILLBRIDE, Catherine		20	F	Laborer	25Ma02Hb
Bridget		25	F	Laborer	25Ma02Hb
BOYER, Margaret		17	F	Laborer	25Ma02Hb
Honora		21	F	Laborer	25Ma02Hb
ROBINSON, John		21	M	Druggist	25Ma02Hb
SOMERVILLE, William		19	M	Draper	25Ma02Hb
DERMEDDY, Patrick		20	M	Laborer	25Ma02Hb
KENNEDY, Pat		20	M	Servant	25Ma02Hb
DERMEDY, Sally		20	F	Milliner	25Ma02Hb
DERMIDY, James		20	M	Farmer	25Ma02Hb
GRIFFIN, Joseph		24	M	Laborer	25Ma02Hb
LANG, James		22	M	Laborer	25Ma02Hb
MCCLARY, Mary		15	F	Laborer	25Ma02Hb
DOUGLASS, Isabella		18	F	Laborer	25Ma02Hb
CAMPBELL, Mary		10	F	Child	25Ma02Hb
CARROLL, Wm.		20	M	Laborer	25Ma02Hb
KILLCARROLL, Mary		18	F	Laborer	25Ma02Hb
DEA, Michael		25	M	Laborer	25Ma02Hb
BARRY, Wm.		20	M	Laborer	25Ma02Hb
DWYER, John		22	M	Servant	25Ma02Hb
WHALEN, Thos.		24	M	Servant	25Ma02Hb
MORAN, Mary		28	F	Servant	25Ma02Hb
KILLCUDDY, Margaret		24	F	Servant	25Ma02Hb
SULLIVAN, James		21	M	Servant	25Ma02Hb
GUIRRIN, James		20	M	Servant	25Ma02Hb
SMITH, Pat		30	M	Servant	25Ma02Hb
MATTHEWS, Hugh		19	M	Servant	25Ma02Hb
GALLIGHER, John		25	M	Servant	25Ma02Hb
CAFFREY, Sally		19	F	Servant	25Ma02Hb
MASTERTON, Matthew		25	M	Servant	25Ma02Hb
MORLEY, James		20	M	Servant	25Ma02Hb
Alexander		18	M	Servant	25Ma02Hb
JAMIESON, Sarah		24	F	Servant	25Ma02Hb
Ann		10	F	Child	25Ma02Hb
DAVISON, David		19	M	Servant	25Ma02Hb
HANNAH, Rose		22	F	Laborer	25Ma02Hb
BOYLAN, Patrick		20	M	Laborer	25Ma02Hb
REILLY, Robert		20	M	Laborer	25Ma02Hb
MURPHY, Ellen		17	F	Laborer	25Ma02Hb
COLLINS, Judy		18	F	Laborer	25Ma02Hb
TOOLE, Ann		36	F	Laborer	25Ma02Hb
Biddy	(D)	11	F	Child	25Ma02Hb
Peter	(S)	09	M	Child	25Ma02Hb
CUDDY, Batt		38	M	Servant	25Ma02Hb
Mike	(S)	12	M	Servant	25Ma02Hb
William	(S)	08	M	Child	25Ma02Hb
Mary	(D)	13	F	Servant	25Ma02Hb
KEEFE, Pat		30	M	Servant	25Ma02Hb
LYNCH, John		30	M	Miller	25Ma02Hb
CORRIS, John		30	M	Servant	25Ma02Hb
WELCH, Peter		30	M	Servant	25Ma02Hb
MAHON, Biddy		21	F	Servant	25Ma02Hb
Margaret		18	F	Servant	25Ma02Hb
QUINLAN, John		20	M	Mason	25Ma02Hb
SLATTERY, Simon		20	M	Servant	25Ma02Hb
HANNEGAN, Harry		17	M	Servant	25Ma02Hb
PATTERSON, Alexander		23	M	Printer	25Ma02Hb
CLARK, Thomas		20	M	Weaver	25Ma02Hb
TAILOR, Ambrose		21	M	Weaver	25Ma02Hb
ADAMS, James		21	M	Weaver	25Ma02Hb
Margaret		21	F	Servant	25Ma02Hb
CLARK, Sarah-J.		19	F	Servant	25Ma02Hb
TAYLOR, Ann		25	F	Servant	25Ma02Hb
WOODS, Ann		25	F	Servant	25Ma02Hb
MURRAY, Eliza		25	F	Servant	25Ma02Hb
MCCARTNEY, Michael		20	M	Servant	25Ma02Hb
GILLESPIE, Bridget		29	F	Servant	25Ma02Hb
Margaret		26	F	Farmer	25Ma02Hb
MORA, Michael		21	M	Servant	25Ma02Hb
Mary		22	F	Servant	25Ma02Hb

NAMES OF PASSENGERS	AGE	SEX	OCCUPATIONS	DATE PORT SHIP
RYAN, Larry	22	M	Servant	25Ma02Hb
CONDON, Ellen	21	F	Servant	25Ma02Hb
FINN, Bridgette	21	F	Servant	25Ma02Hb
CROW, Mary	20	F	Servant	25Ma02Hb
SWEENEY, Joseph	30	M	Farmer	25Ma02Hb
POWER, John	21	M	Mason	25Ma02Hb
MORRISON, James	20	M	Laborer	25Ma02Hb
BAILEY, Henry	24	M	Laborer	25Ma02Hb
MORFAT, Catharine	22	F	Laborer	25Ma02Hb
MCBRIDE, Edward	30	M	Laborer	25Ma02Hb
Rose	25	F	Laborer	25Ma02Hb
WARD, Michael	24	M	Laborer	25Ma02Hb
John	22	M	Laborer	25Ma02Hb
MOONEY, Rose	23	F	Laborer	25Ma02Hb
ROCH, Mary	24	F	Laborer	25Ma02Hb
CLARK, Bridget	21	F	Servant	25Ma02Hb
MILLIGAN, John	25	M	Servant	25Ma02Hb
MCKEW, Catharine	20	F	Servant	25Ma02Hb
NUGENT, Biddy	12	F	Servant	25Ma02Hb
DONNELLY, Biddy	17	F	Servant	25Ma02Hb
MAUD, Magnis	25	M	Servant	25Ma02Hb
MONTRITH, James	20	M	Servant	25Ma02Hb
DOAK, Joseph	20	M	Servant	25Ma02Hb
MOORE, Catharine	20	F	Servant	25Ma02Hb
SCANLON, Owen	20	M	Laborer	25Ma02Hb
Catharine	30	F	Servant	25Ma02Hb
NOLAND, Wm.	22	M	Servant	25Ma02Hb
Richd.	20	M	Servant	25Ma02Hb
KINSOLA, Patrick	39	M	Laborer	25Ma02Hb
Sarah	30	F	Laborer	25Ma02Hb
Pat	36	M	Laborer	25Ma02Hb
STAUNTON, Pat	25	M	Laborer	25Ma02Hb
KERVEY, Honora	20	F	Laborer	25Ma02Hb
HOWELL, E.Mrs.	30	F	Laborer	25Ma02Hb
Biddy (D)	09	F	Child	25Ma02Hb
HAZARD, Margaret	20	F	Laborer	25Ma02Hb
MONEGAN, Barnard	20	M	Laborer	25Ma02Hb
CARROLL, Biddy	19	F	Laborer	25Ma02Hb
HARGAN, Ellen	19	F	Laborer	25Ma02Hb
Margaret	19	F	Laborer	25Ma02Hb
KERRIGAN, Catherine	19	F	Laborer	25Ma02Hb
BOYLAN, Rose	30	F	Laborer	25Ma02Hb
RILEY, John	35	M	Laborer	25Ma02Hb
MCKUSKAR, James	38	M	Laborer	25Ma02Hb
Margaret (W)	34	F	Laborer	25Ma02Hb
John (S)	12	M	Laborer	25Ma02Hb
MCCUSKER, Rose	09	F	Child	25Ma02Hb
Mary (T)	04	F	Child	25Ma02Hb
Henry (B)	.00	M	Infant	25Ma02Hb
MCCAUGHAY, John	18	M	Servant	25Ma02Hb
Anne	13	F	Servant	25Ma02Hb
Maria	11	F	Child	25Ma02Hb
Pat	09	M	Child	25Ma02Hb
WILKINSON, John	30	M	Weaver	25Ma02Hb
Eliza (W)	24	F	Servant	25Ma02Hb
Nancy (D)	.00	F	Infant	25Ma02Hb
MARKS, Mary-J.	20	F	Locksmith	25Ma02Hb
MALONEY, Matthew	30	M	Laborer	25Ma02Hb
RYAN, Dennis	25	M	Shoemaker	25Ma02Hb
LYONS, Cornelius	25	M	Farmer	25Ma02Hb
GRADY, William	30	M	Servant	25Ma02Hb
Margaret	19	F	Servant	25Ma02Hb
STORAN, Pat	50	M	Servant	25Ma02Hb
Michael	18	M	Servant	25Ma02Hb
HOGAN, Michael	23	M	Servant	25Ma02Hb
Johanna	24	F	Servant	25Ma02Hb
DOREY, John	25	M	Laborer	25Ma02Hb
BUCK, Mary-Ann	40	F	Laborer	25Ma02Hb
Eliza-J. (D)	18	F	Laborer	25Ma02Hb
Richard (S)	16	M	Laborer	25Ma02Hb
George (S)	12	M	Laborer	25Ma02Hb
William-J. (S)	13	M	Laborer	25Ma02Hb
John (S)	10	M	Child	25Ma02Hb
Mary-Ann (D)	08	F	Child	25Ma02Hb
ANDERSON, Margaret	18	F	Joiner	25Ma02Hb
ANDERSON, Elizabeth	20	F	Shoemaker	25Ma02Hb
DEHAN, Mary	19	F	Shoemaker	25Ma02Hb
MCMAHON, Edward	24	M	Shoemaker	25Ma02Hb
CLANCY, Michael	34	M	Shoemaker	25Ma02Hb
REARDON, Pat	24	M	Farmer	25Ma02Hb
DEVINE, Daniel	21	M	Laborer	25Ma02Hb
OBRIEN, Luke	21	M	Laborer	25Ma02Hb
Thomas	15	M	Laborer	25Ma02Hb
HAYES, James	20	M	Laborer	25Ma02Hb
KENNEDY, John	25	M	Lrfh	25Ma02Hb
COLBER, Margaret	22	F	Lrfh	25Ma02Hb
MADDEN, Francis	22	M	Lrfh	25Ma02Hb
GUINIS, Mary	18	F	Lrfh	25Ma02Hb
BURNS, John	22	M	Lrfh	25Ma02Hb
LYNCH, Ally	20	F	Servant	25Ma02Hb
Bridget	19	F	Servant	25Ma02Hb
Lawrance	23	M	Servant	25Ma02Hb
FARLEY, Rose	21	F	Servant	25Ma02Hb
Mary	20	F	Servant	25Ma02Hb
FARONES, Christie	24	M	Servant	25Ma02Hb
Bridget	20	F	Servant	25Ma02Hb
MURTOUGH, Ellen	20	F	Laborer	25Ma02Hb
COYLE, Ann	20	F	Laborer	25Ma02Hb
BURNS, Thomas	17	M	Laborer	25Ma02Hb
COWAN, Samuel	28	M	Laborer	25Ma02Hb
Elizabeth	38	F	Laborer	25Ma02Hb
Martha	20	F	Clerk	25Ma02Hb
LITTLE, Mary	20	F	Laborer	25Ma02Hb
WHALEN, John	20	M	Laborer	25Ma02Hb
MARGHER, Kitty	22	F	Laborer	25Ma02Hb
ONEIL, Hannah	20	F	Servant	25Ma02Hb
GLOSHER, William	.00	M	Infant	25Ma02Hb
DONNELLAN, Sally	17	F	Servant	25Ma02Hb
Died-At-Sea				
U, U	.00	U	Infant	25Ma02Hb
Born-At-Sea				

MARMION 25 MAY 1846

From Liverpool

NAMES OF PASSENGERS	AGE	SEX	OCCUPATIONS	DATE PORT SHIP
MESCOCK, W.M.	29	M	Gentleman	25Ma02Hc
RUTHERFORD, J.	35	M	Merchant	25Ma02Hc
PHITTS, Catherine	29	F	None	25Ma02Hc
James (S)	06	M	Child	25Ma02Hc
Maria (D)	02	F	Child	25Ma02Hc
EBBOTT, Etty	35	F	None	25Ma02Hc
Sarah (D)	07	F	Child	25Ma02Hc
BRADLEY, Michael	22	M	Farmer	25Ma02Hc
Mary	24	F	None	25Ma02Hc
MURPHY, Hannah	29	F	None	25Ma02Hc
BRADLEY, Betsey	21	F	None	25Ma02Hc
GILLHOOLY, Patrick	25	M	Laborer	25Ma02Hc
Mary	28	F	None	25Ma02Hc
WALSH, John	16	M	Laborer	25Ma02Hc
Bridget	17	F	Servant	25Ma02Hc
BARKER, Sally	17	F	Servant	25Ma02Hc
FLANNAGAN, Francis	24	M	Blacksmith	25Ma02Hc
KIRK, Ellen	16	F	Servant	25Ma02Hc
Catherine	18	F	Servant	25Ma02Hc
MULLIN, John	18	M	Laborer	25Ma02Hc
MCAHANY, Mary	18	F	Servant	25Ma02Hc
NEIL, Henry	25	M	Servant	25Ma02Hc
BRENNAN, James	12	M	Servant	25Ma02Hc
DUNN, Judy	18	F	Servant	25Ma02Hc
CORMICK, Mary	16	F	Servant	25Ma02Hc
BROGAN, Patrick	24	M	Servant	25Ma02Hc
CARLOT, Robert	50	M	Joiner	25Ma02Hc
COWELL, John	40	M	Joiner	25Ma02Hc

NAMES OF PASSENGERS		AGE	SEX	OCCUPATIONS	DATE PORT SHIP
COWELL, Ann	(W)	30	F	None	25Ma02Hc
Robert	(S)	02	M	Child	25Ma02Hc
John	(S)	01	M	Child	25Ma02Hc
KEARN, William		07	M	Child	25Ma02Hc
SMITH, Philip		20	M	Laborer	25Ma02Hc
MURRAY, Hester		21	F	Servant	25Ma02Hc
Margaret		18	F	Servant	25Ma02Hc
MAGUIRE, Anne		20	F	Servant	25Ma02Hc
MCGUINESS, Philip		24	M	Laborer	25Ma02Hc
KING, Charles		22	M	Laborer	25Ma02Hc
WICKLEY, Francis		24	M	Laborer	25Ma02Hc
DUNN, James		20	M	Laborer	25Ma02Hc
MCKEON, Patrick		29	M	Laborer	25Ma02Hc
MORAN, Thomas		24	M	Laborer	25Ma02Hc
COUGHLAN, Mary		18	F	Servant	25Ma02Hc
FLYNN, Thomas		20	M	Laborer	25Ma02Hc
MCPORTER, Biddy		16	F	Servant	25Ma02Hc
CRAMER, Patrick		17	M	Laborer	25Ma02Hc
Bridget		16	F	Servant	25Ma02Hc
GRIMES, Michael		16	M	Laborer	25Ma02Hc
Margaret		18	F	Servant	25Ma02Hc
SMITH, Thomas		20	M	Shoemaker	25Ma02Hc
MORTON, Ambrose		22	M	Laborer	25Ma02Hc
Mary		21	F	Servant	25Ma02Hc
DORIM, John		20	M	Painter	25Ma02Hc
STAUNTEN, Patrick		19	M	Gdnr	25Ma02Hc
Fanny		18	F	Servant	25Ma02Hc
DONOHUE, John		26	M	Laborer	25Ma02Hc
MOLESEGTSEY, Rodney		26	M	Laborer	25Ma02Hc
RYAN, Thomas		25	M	Laborer	25Ma02Hc
Patrick		26	M	Laborer	25Ma02Hc
CORBEN, Ann		24	F	Servant	25Ma02Hc
RYAN, Catherine		24	F	Servant	25Ma02Hc
MCPARTLAND, Owen		25	M	Laborer	25Ma02Hc
Mary		24	F	None	25Ma02Hc
MCCARRY, Mary		19	F	Servant	25Ma02Hc
CAIN, John		28	M	Laborer	25Ma02Hc
Bridget		26	F	None	25Ma02Hc
MORAN, Ann		16	F	Servant	25Ma02Hc
MCMAHON, Catherine		20	F	Servant	25Ma02Hc
MCFADDAN, John		20	M	Slater	25Ma02Hc
REID, Samuel		29	M	Weaver	25Ma02Hc
TIERNEY, Hugh-Michael		20	M	Laborer	25Ma02Hc
CAMPBELL, Margaret		20	F	Dressmaker	25Ma02Hc
Agnes		22	F	Dressmaker	25Ma02Hc
HENEY, Mary		20	F	Servant	25Ma02Hc
DOHERTY, Biddy		20	F	Servant	25Ma02Hc
MCDONAL, Terence		21	M	Laborer	25Ma02Hc
CASEY, Patrick		20	M	Laborer	25Ma02Hc
MAUGER, Honer		20	F	Servant	25Ma02Hc
HORAN, Thomas		21	M	Laborer	25Ma02Hc
Michael		20	M	Laborer	25Ma02Hc
BURKE, Thomas		20	M	Laborer	25Ma02Hc
BYRAN, Honer		25	F	Servant	25Ma02Hc
CASEY, Bridget		60	F	None	25Ma02Hc
Mary	(D)	27	F	None	25Ma02Hc
Margaret	(D)	16	F	None	25Ma02Hc
David	(S)	21	M	None	25Ma02Hc
GANNON, James		21	M	Smith	25Ma02Hc
IGO, Edward		27	M	Smith	25Ma02Hc
ILINN, John		30	M	Smith	25Ma02Hc
Catherin		30	F	None	25Ma02Hc
Nancy		26	F	Servant	25Ma02Hc
Ellen		30	F	Servant	25Ma02Hc
IRELAND, Richard		28	M	Laborer	25Ma02Hc
BOGGS, John		20	M	Shopman	25Ma02Hc
BOYD, John		48	M	Weaver	25Ma02Hc
JORDAN, Mary		22	F	Servant	25Ma02Hc
MCMANUS, Alice		30	F	Servant	25Ma02Hc
Biddy		17	F	Servant	25Ma02Hc
GARTEN, Pat		21	M	Tailor	25Ma02Hc
Rice		19	F	Servant	25Ma02Hc
CONOLLY, James		21	M	Laborer	25Ma02Hc
DOYLE, Mary		21	F	Servant	25Ma02Hc
Biddy		17	F	Servant	25Ma02Hc
KEEGAN, Patrick		25	M	Laborer	25Ma02Hc
DOWD, John		21	M	Laborer	25Ma02Hc
CONOLLY, Michael		28	M	Laborer	25Ma02Hc
CARTY, Thomas		25	M	Laborer	25Ma02Hc
HUGHES, John		25	M	Laborer	25Ma02Hc
Mary		25	F	Laborer	25Ma02Hc
LALY, Ellen		22	F	Servant	25Ma02Hc
BRISTOW, Margaret		50	F	None	25Ma02Hc
Charles		15	M	Laborer	25Ma02Hc
SAUL, James		22	M	Laborer	25Ma02Hc
TRACY, Edward		35	M	Laborer	25Ma02Hc
TIERNEY, Daniel		26	M	Laborer	25Ma02Hc
OCALLAGHAN, Thomas		26	M	Laborer	25Ma02Hc
FOGARTY, Judy		22	F	Servant	25Ma02Hc
RYAN, Bridget		23	F	Servant	25Ma02Hc
HAGAN, John		30	M	Laborer	25Ma02Hc
Judy		26	F	None	25Ma02Hc
BRIEN, Thomas		28	M	Laborer	25Ma02Hc
HORROGAN, Bridget		21	F	Servant	25Ma02Hc
GAUGHRAN, Bridget		20	F	Servant	25Ma02Hc
CORNAR, Thomas		24	M	Weaver	25Ma02Hc
MCDONELL, Daniel		22	M	Weaver	25Ma02Hc
WOODLOCK, Pat		24	M	Farmer	25Ma02Hc
Michael		22	M	Farmer	25Ma02Hc
George		20	M	Farmer	25Ma02Hc
COLEMAN, Biddy		20	F	Servant	25Ma02Hc
MCGUIGGAN, Michael		21	M	Groom	25Ma02Hc
Susan		18	F	Dressmaker	25Ma02Hc
LONG, Catherine		21	F	Servant	25Ma02Hc
MAGUIRE, Anne		21	F	Servant	25Ma02Hc
KEEGAN, Michael		55	M	Grocer	25Ma02Hc
Margaret	(W)	39	F	None	25Ma02Hc
Mary	(D)	22	F	None	25Ma02Hc
Catherine	(D)	20	F	None	25Ma02Hc
Ann	(D)	17	F	None	25Ma02Hc
LOUGHLIN, James		40	M	Shoemaker	25Ma02Hc
Catherine		20	F	None	25Ma02Hc
MAHONY, Dennis		58	M	Laborer	25Ma02Hc
Jerry		29	M	Laborer	25Ma02Hc
MARTIN, Esther		30	F	Cook	25Ma02Hc
HEENAN, Michal		24	M	Blacksmith	25Ma02Hc
DOOLAN, James		20	M	Laborer	25Ma02Hc
GLANNAN, Maria		23	F	Servant	25Ma02Hc
MCGOWRAN, Alice		20	F	Servant	25Ma02Hc
WELSH, Betsey		20	F	Servant	25Ma02Hc
ODONNELL, Dormack		27	M	Tailor	25Ma02Hc
QUINN, Margaret		20	F	Dressmaker	25Ma02Hc
MILLER, Peter		27	M	Farmer	25Ma02Hc
Mary		22	F	None	25Ma02Hc
HANAGAN, Patrick		20	M	Laborer	25Ma02Hc
GALLAGHER, Thomas		20	M	Laborer	25Ma02Hc
QUIGG, Charles		22	M	Laborer	25Ma02Hc
HIRNAY, Rose		50	F	Dressmaker	25Ma02Hc
Rose		18	F	Dressmaker	25Ma02Hc
Sarah		17	F	Dressmaker	25Ma02Hc
Margaret-Ann		15	F	Dressmaker	25Ma02Hc
DALY, James		30	M	Seaman	25Ma02Hc
Rose		27	F	None	25Ma02Hc
HEFFRON, Rose		50	F	None	25Ma02Hc
MCKEON, Owen		24	M	Laborer	25Ma02Hc
KIENAY, William		24	M	Jobber	25Ma02Hc
RUSH, Edward		22	M	Laborer	25Ma02Hc
MCCAB, James		14	M	Laborer	25Ma02Hc
CESEY, John		24	M	Laborer	25Ma02Hc
KANE, Margaret		17	F	Servant	25Ma02Hc
QUINN, Bridget		17	F	Servant	25Ma02Hc
MULHIAL, Mary		17	F	Servant	25Ma02Hc
TOBIN, Moses		19	M	Butcher	25Ma02Hc
KELLY, Thomas		27	M	Farmer	25Ma02Hc
FURLONG, James		12	M	Farmer	25Ma02Hc
TOBIN, Mary		21	F	Dressmaker	25Ma02Hc
GILDAY, John		35	M	Laborer	25Ma02Hc
Nancy		26	F	Servant	25Ma02Hc
HINSON, Martin		30	M	Laborer	25Ma02Hc
CAUTLER, Ellen		18	F	Servant	25Ma02Hc

NAMES OF PASSENGERS	A G E	S E X	OCCUPATIONS	DATE PORT SHIP	NAMES OF PASSENGERS	A G E	S E X	OCCUPATIONS	DATE PORT SHIP
DONOHUE, Anastatia	20	F	Servant	25Ma02Hc					
MULCHY, Mary	17	F	Servant	25Ma02Hc					
FOLEY, Abby	21	F	Servant	25Ma02Hc					
HELY, Helen	20	F	Servant	25Ma02Hc					
Catherine	19	F	Servant	25Ma02Hc					
Mary	20	F	Servant	25Ma02Hc	INDEPENDENCE 26 MAY 1846				
SHEA, Johanna	17	F	Servant	25Ma02Hc					
MANNIX, Mary	24	F	Servant	25Ma02Hc	From Liverpool				
OHARA, Bridget	21	F	Servant	25Ma02Hc					
KELLY, Philip	22	M	Laborer	25Ma02Hc					
KIERNAN, Bryan	20	M	Laborer	25Ma02Hc	OREILLY, U	29	F	None	26Ma02Hf
MOORE, Michael	20	M	Tailor	25Ma02Hc	HAND, James	46	M	Laborer	26Ma02Hf
LAFFEY, Thomas	20	M	Laborer	25Ma02Hc	NEVIN, Thomas	30	M	Farmer	26Ma02Hf
NUNN, Anne	18	F	Servant	25Ma02Hc	BAMBRICK, Patrick	28	M	Farmer	26Ma02Hf
MCDONOHUE, Helen	18	F	Servant	25Ma02Hc	MCDONNELL, Patk.	25	M	Farmer	26Ma02Hf
LOUGHLIN, Ann	08	F	Child	25Ma02Hc	BYRNE, Mag.	24	F	None	26Ma02Hf
MURRAY, Edward	20	M	Laborer	25Ma02Hc	MOORE, Mary	26	F	None	26Ma02Hf
CULAGHAN, John	24	M	Laborer	25Ma02Hc	QUIRK, Mary	26	F	None	26Ma02Hf
OWEN, James	21	M	Laborer	25Ma02Hc	FITZGERALD, Mary	25	F	None	26Ma02Hf
Catherine	18	F	Servant	25Ma02Hc	DUFFY, Eliz.	25	F	None	26Ma02Hf
KELLY, William	24	M	Laborer	25Ma02Hc	KERR, Kate	25	F	None	26Ma02Hf
Bridget	21	F	Servant	25Ma02Hc	FINLAN, Michael	36	M	Laborer	26Ma02Hf
WYNN, Roger	20	M	Laborer	25Ma02Hc	SOMERS, Pat	23	M	Laborer	26Ma02Hf
KENEDY, Philip	22	M	Laborer	25Ma02Hc	SHIELS, John	26	M	Farmer	26Ma02Hf
Mary	18	F	Servant	25Ma02Hc	FUNSTON, George	21	M	Tanner	26Ma02Hf
CULLEN, John	18	M	Baker	25Ma02Hc	COLESTON, Jane	18	F	None	26Ma02Hf
Alice	16	F	Servant	25Ma02Hc	HERNE, Eliza	20	F	None	26Ma02Hf
GREEN, Michael	21	M	Laborer	25Ma02Hc	WILSON, John	22	M	Saddler	26Ma02Hf
Patrick	30	M	Laborer	25Ma02Hc	TOOLE, Peter	21	M	Laborer	26Ma02Hf
CUSICK, Bernard	22	M	Laborer	25Ma02Hc	RICHARDSON, Alex	25	M	Laborer	26Ma02Hf
SHANNON, Catherine	20	F	Servant	25Ma02Hc	HAMILTON, George	60	M	Laborer	26Ma02Hf
MULLIGAN, Ann	17	F	Servant	25Ma02Hc	GILCHRIST, John	22	M	Baker	26Ma02Hf
DOBBIN, Joseph	24	M	Laborer	25Ma02Hc	Jane	22	F	None	26Ma02Hf
KILFEATHER, Margaret	60	F	None	25Ma02Hc	WILSON, Mary	30	F	None	26Ma02Hf
CRUIT, Michael	24	M	Tailor	25Ma02Hc	MALABREY, James	17	M	Laborer	26Ma02Hf
SMITH, William-M.	20	M	Farmer	25Ma02Hc	SULLIVAN, Pat	30	M	Laborer	26Ma02Hf
DELANEY, Dennis	30	M	Laborer	25Ma02Hc	Bid	24	F	None	26Ma02Hf
LOUGHLIN, Mary	21	F	None	25Ma02Hc	SERODDY, Matth.	22	M	None	26Ma02Hf
CASHIN, Catherine	18	F	Servant	25Ma02Hc	COOEY, John	19	M	None	26Ma02Hf
CARLIN, Edward	20	M	Laborer	25Ma02Hc	MCCORMICK, John	12	M	None	26Ma02Hf
EARLY, Michael	24	M	Laborer	25Ma02Hc	Dan	10	M	Child	26Ma02Hf
Catherine	20	F	Servant	25Ma02Hc	CURREY, James	26	M	None	26Ma02Hf
ROKE, Patrick	40	M	Laborer	25Ma02Hc	PARKER, Campbell	23	M	Farmer	26Ma02Hf
FLINN, Michael	10	M	Child	25Ma02Hc	HANNAH, Joseph	23	M	Tailor	26Ma02Hf
Ben	09	M	Child	25Ma02Hc	MARTIN, Thomas	29	M	Storekeeper	26Ma02Hf
FITZPATRICK, Hugh	16	M	Laborer	25Ma02Hc	WARD, Bridget	17	F	None	26Ma02Hf
REYNOLDS, Mary	18	F	Servant	25Ma02Hc	BOYLAN, Michael	16	M	None	26Ma02Hf
CONRAN, Julia	20	F	Servant	25Ma02Hc	MCDONALD, James	22	M	None	26Ma02Hf
Helen	20	F	Servant	25Ma02Hc	CLEARY, James	31	M	Laborer	26Ma02Hf
NOLAN, William	20	M	Laborer	25Ma02Hc	MCELROY, Bernard	23	M	Laborer	26Ma02Hf
SMITH, Anne	16	F	Servant	25Ma02Hc	CLEARY, Brid.	19	F	None	26Ma02Hf
CONNELL, Catherine	20	F	Servant	25Ma02Hc	KEARNEN, Ellen	20	F	None	26Ma02Hf
POWELL, Rose-Anne	12	F	Servant	25Ma02Hc	CASSIDY, Mary	21	F	None	26Ma02Hf
KEEGAN, Christian	24	F	Servant	25Ma02Hc	MCCAFFREY, Rose	09	F	Child	26Ma02Hf
MCHENRY, Mary	15	F	Servant	25Ma02Hc	KEELAHAN, Dan.	30	M	Laborer	26Ma02Hf
CANE, Henry	23	M	Seaman	25Ma02Hc	HARRIGAN, Dan	20	M	Laborer	26Ma02Hf
Francis	12	M	Seaman	25Ma02Hc	Dennis	24	M	Laborer	26Ma02Hf
BYRNE, Honora	22	F	Servant	25Ma02Hc	SULLIVAN, Dennis	24	M	Blacksmith	26Ma02Hf
MCDERMOTT, Essy	21	F	Servant	25Ma02Hc	CAVANAH, Dennis	24	M	Laborer	26Ma02Hf
BRENNAN, Mary	19	F	Servant	25Ma02Hc	MCCARTHY, Mary	22	F	None	26Ma02Hf
DUFFY, Mary	18	F	Servant	25Ma02Hc	Kate	20	F	None	26Ma02Hf
Bridget	19	F	Servant	25Ma02Hc	DALY, John	30	M	None	26Ma02Hf
KEEGAN, Catherine	44	F	Servant	25Ma02Hc	MALONE, John	23	M	None	26Ma02Hf
Mary (D)	12	F	Servant	25Ma02Hc	Bridget	30	F	None	26Ma02Hf
Patrick (S)	08	M	Child	25Ma02Hc	DALY, Bridget	24	F	None	26Ma02Hf
OBRIEN, Ellen	24	F	None	25Ma02Hc	GOULD, William	31	M	Laborer	26Ma02Hf
					William	24	M	Laborer	26Ma02Hf
					TOBIN, John	22	M	Laborer	26Ma02Hf
					KENNEDY, William	23	M	Laborer	26Ma02Hf
					RYAN, John	26	M	Laborer	26Ma02Hf
					TOBIN, Mathew	24	M	Laborer	26Ma02Hf
					Mary	22	F	Laborer	26Ma02Hf
					THOMPSON, Andrew	20	M	Laborer	26Ma02Hf
					WOODSIDE, James	20	M	Laborer	26Ma02Hf
					THOMPSON, Margaret	22	F	Laborer	26Ma02Hf

NAMES OF PASSENGERS	AGE	SEX	OCCUPATIONS	DATE PORT SHIP
HUNTERS, Eliza	21	F	Laborer	26Ma02Hf
MULROONEY, Brody	28	M	Laborer	26Ma02Hf
MASON, Robert	25	M	Laborer	26Ma02Hf
ADAM, James	24	M	Laborer	26Ma02Hf
MULROONEY, Margaret	23	F	Laborer	26Ma02Hf
MAGRATH, Michael	12	M	Laborer	26Ma02Hf
SAVAGE, John	30	M	Laborer	26Ma02Hf
Mary (W)	28	F	Laborer	26Ma02Hf
Catharine (D)	08	F	Child	26Ma02Hf
Michael (S)	06	M	Child	26Ma02Hf
Anne (D)	04	F	Child	26Ma02Hf
John (S)	02	M	Child	26Ma02Hf
MCCARTNEY, Bernard	19	M	Laborer	26Ma02Hf
KINLEY, Eliza	20	F	Laborer	26Ma02Hf
Catharine	13	F	Laborer	26Ma02Hf
CUNNINGHAM, Benjamin	22	M	Laborer	26Ma02Hf
DOOGAN, John	22	M	Laborer	26Ma02Hf
GRIFFIN, Pat	24	M	Carpenter	26Ma02Hf
CARNEY, John	24	M	Blacksmith	26Ma02Hf
SHEA, Thomas	21	M	Laborer	26Ma02Hf
KEVELING, Catharine	19	F	Laborer	26Ma02Hf
MCCANN, Jane	19	F	Laborer	26Ma02Hf
MURPHY, Timothy	22	M	Bootmaker	26Ma02Hf
SULIVAN, Mary	21	F	None	26Ma02Hf
SAKELY, Julia	20	F	None	26Ma02Hf
GILLAN, Samuel	28	M	Bookkeeper	26Ma02Hf
DREW, Cornelius	18	M	None	26Ma02Hf
FITZPATRICK, Jeremiah	20	M	Bookkeeper	26Ma02Hf
OHARE, Daniel	22	M	None	26Ma02Hf
CLARK, Eliza	19	F	None	26Ma02Hf
HEFRAN, Thomas	24	M	Laborer	26Ma02Hf
Jane	23	F	None	26Ma02Hf
HICKEY, Martin	26	M	None	26Ma02Hf
Edward	60	M	None	26Ma02Hf
WARREN, U-Mrs.	26	F	None	26Ma02Hf
Thom. (S)	05	M	Child	26Ma02Hf
John (S)	.09	M	Infant	26Ma02Hf
MCDEVITTE, Edward	21	M	Servant	26Ma02Hf
CRILLY, John	25	M	Laborer	26Ma02Hf
SHANNON, James	22	M	Laborer	26Ma02Hf
CUMMINGS, John	30	M	Laborer	26Ma02Hf
U (W)	22	F	None	26Ma02Hf
REID, John	22	M	Weaver	26Ma02Hf
BARRY, Thom.	21	M	Weaver	26Ma02Hf
LAWRENSON, Pat.	19	M	Spinner	26Ma02Hf
KENNY, Thom.	22	M	Weaver	26Ma02Hf
CAVANAH, James	26	M	Weaver	26Ma02Hf
U (W)	24	F	Weaver	26Ma02Hf
Mary (D)	01	F	Child	26Ma02Hf
Pat	20	M	Weaver	26Ma02Hf
John	20	M	Weaver	26Ma02Hf
MCCORMICK, Bernard	18	M	Laborer	26Ma02Hf
MCCAHAN, Mary	20	F	None	26Ma02Hf
Mary	10	F	Child	26Ma02Hf
GRAHAM, Pat	26	M	Carpenter	26Ma02Hf
FLINN, James	35	M	Laborer	26Ma02Hf
JOHNSON, Peter	30	M	Mason	26Ma02Hf
Alice	24	F	None	26Ma02Hf
MATHEWS, Ann	30	F	None	26Ma02Hf
IRVING, William	37	M	Laborer	26Ma02Hf
Margaret (W)	35	F	None	26Ma02Hf
Flora (D)	17	F	None	26Ma02Hf
Elizabeth (D)	09	F	Child	26Ma02Hf
Mary-Jane (D)	06	F	Child	26Ma02Hf
Anne (D)	02	F	Child	26Ma02Hf
EAGER, Thomas	28	M	Mason	26Ma02Hf
Jane	27	F	None	26Ma02Hf
GREEGAN, James	27	M	Laborer	26Ma02Hf
MURPHY, Jeremiah	34	M	Shoemaker	26Ma02Hf
Margaret	30	F	None	26Ma02Hf
MCCABE, Terrence	19	M	Nailer	26Ma02Hf
OCONNOR, James	19	M	Bookmaker	26Ma02Hf
SEICE, M.J.	20	U	None	26Ma02Hf
MOONY, Michael	27	M	Laborer	26Ma02Hf
KENNAH, Pat.	30	M	Laborer	26Ma02Hf
MORRIS, Thom.	28	M	Laborer	26Ma02Hf
MOONY, Bridget	22	F	None	26Ma02Hf
MORRIS, Mary	25	F	None	26Ma02Hf
SMITH, U-Mrs.	50	F	None	26Ma02Hf
MEEHAN, Sarah	21	F	None	26Ma02Hf
MURPHY, U	32	F	None	26Ma02Hf
QUINN, Andy	20	M	None	26Ma02Hf
BOWLAN, Dennis	31	M	None	26Ma02Hf
BRYAN, James	21	M	None	26Ma02Hf
REILLY, Mary	19	F	None	26Ma02Hf
DORAN, John	23	M	Laborer	26Ma02Hf
NOLAN, Silvester	25	M	Laborer	26Ma02Hf
QUINN, Laurence	30	M	Servant	26Ma02Hf
BYRNN, Thom.	25	M	None	26Ma02Hf
GILMARTIN, J.	35	M	Tailor	26Ma02Hf
Hannah (W)	30	F	None	26Ma02Hf
Mary (D)	09	F	Child	26Ma02Hf
Ellen (D)	06	F	Child	26Ma02Hf
Mary (D)	04	F	Child	26Ma02Hf
Ann (D)	01	F	Child	26Ma02Hf
GARDEN, Ann	19	F	None	26Ma02Hf
ROONEY, Kate	19	F	None	26Ma02Hf
GILMARTIN, Tom	21	M	Farmer	26Ma02Hf
ROURKE, David	22	M	Gdnr	26Ma02Hf
GORMLEY, Edward	26	M	Gdnr	26Ma02Hf
HERMAN, Wm.	17	M	Laborer	26Ma02Hf
SHERIDAN, B.	24	U	None	26Ma02Hf
KEHILL, A.	22	U	None	26Ma02Hf
Kate	20	F	None	26Ma02Hf
BEATTY, Charles	24	M	Laborer	26Ma02Hf
Kate	22	F	None	26Ma02Hf
FARRELL, M.	10	U	Child	26Ma02Hf
KELLY, John	20	M	Laborer	26Ma02Hf
HART, James	22	M	Laborer	26Ma02Hf
MCGOWEN, Peter	25	M	Laborer	26Ma02Hf
Brid.	33	F	None	26Ma02Hf
Mary	14	F	None	26Ma02Hf
KOWSHAW, Ellen	22	F	None	26Ma02Hf
CUNNINGHAM, Mary	22	F	None	26Ma02Hf
DEVINE, Thomas	21	M	Farmer	26Ma02Hf
BOYLE, James	23	M	Laborer	26Ma02Hf
MOONEY, Bid.	21	F	Laborer	26Ma02Hf
KEENAN, John	22	M	None	26Ma02Hf
Bridget	21	F	None	26Ma02Hf
MCCULLOGH, Kate	25	F	None	26Ma02Hf
KENNEDY, Martin	24	M	Laborer	26Ma02Hf
DEVEREUX, John	22	M	Steward	26Ma02Hf
U (W)	21	F	None	26Ma02Hf
CULLAN, Richard	22	M	Laborer	26Ma02Hf
MOORE, Michael	30	M	Mason	26Ma02Hf
Mary	20	F	None	26Ma02Hf
John	.03	M	Infant	26Ma02Hf
Biddy	12	F	None	26Ma02Hf
Biddy	50	F	None	26Ma02Hf
John	60	M	None	26Ma02Hf
BERNAN, Hugh	22	M	Laborer	26Ma02Hf
CASSADY, Michael	20	M	Laborer	26Ma02Hf
Rose	20	F	None	26Ma02Hf
ODONNEL, John	24	M	Laborer	26Ma02Hf
Catharine	19	F	None	26Ma02Hf
BRENNAN, Daniel	22	M	None	26Ma02Hf
Catharine	22	F	None	26Ma02Hf
BRADY, George	24	M	Shopkeeper	26Ma02Hf
SHIELD, Eleanor	19	F	None	26Ma02Hf
MCBIRENEY, Lucy	14	F	None	26Ma02Hf
LASTY, Patrick	21	M	Laborer	26Ma02Hf
James	27	M	Laborer	26Ma02Hf
MCCORMICK, Owen	30	M	Laborer	26Ma02Hf
BARRON, Michael	34	M	Laborer	26Ma02Hf
MACCASTOR, Eliza	20	F	None	26Ma02Hf
CASSIDY, Bernard	27	M	Farmer	26Ma02Hf
Sarah	21	F	None	26Ma02Hf
CURLY, Michael	23	M	Farmer	26Ma02Hf
RALEIGH, Alice	18	F	None	26Ma02Hf
DONAGAN, Edward	22	M	Farmer	26Ma02Hf

NAMES OF PASSENGERS	AGE	SEX	OCCUPATIONS	DATE PORT SHIP
DONOLLY, James	20	M	Weaver	26Ma02Hf
Mary	22	F	None	26Ma02Hf
HILL, Michael	25	M	Carpenter	26Ma02Hf
MOORE, William	27	M	Laborer	26Ma02Hf
Catherine	27	F	None	26Ma02Hf
CAISY, James	22	M	Laborer	26Ma02Hf
MAHONY, Jeremiah	27	M	Weaver	26Ma02Hf
BUCK, Thomas	18	M	Bookkeeper	26Ma02Hf
CANTY, Jeremiah	24	M	Weaver	26Ma02Hf
MALRONY, Rain	40	M	Weaver	26Ma02Hf
DONALDSON, William	24	M	Silk Weaver	26Ma02Hf
HAN, Pat	15	M	None	26Ma02Hf
CAMPBELL, Bridget	20	F	None	26Ma02Hf
LOGAN, Ann	20	F	None	26Ma02Hf
CASSIDY, Charles	22	M	Weaver	26Ma02Hf
KAIRNS, James	28	M	Blacksmith	26Ma02Hf
HARTS, Catherine	22	F	None	26Ma02Hf
RALAHAN, Thomas	30	M	Laborer	26Ma02Hf
ALEXANDER, Jane	23	F	None	26Ma02Hf
SMITH, Ellen	20	F	None	26Ma02Hf
LYNCH, Catherine	19	F	None	26Ma02Hf

ENGLAND 26 MAY 1846

From Liverpool

NAMES OF PASSENGERS	AGE	SEX	OCCUPATIONS	DATE PORT SHIP
MCCOURTY, James	20	M	Laborer	26Ma02Hg
KELLY, John	20	M	Laborer	26Ma02Hg
Marla	20	F	Servant	26Ma02Hg
COSTELLO, Mechall	20	M	Laborer	26Ma02Hg
Mary	20	F	Servant	26Ma02Hg
KELLY, Mary	20	F	Servant	26Ma02Hg
LANGAN, Frank	28	M	Laborer	26Ma02Hg
Mary (W)	26	F	Servant	26Ma02Hg
Biddy (D)	04	F	Child	26Ma02Hg
Mary (D)	02	F	Child	26Ma02Hg
Edward (S)	.00	M	Infant	26Ma02Hg
Ellnor	20	F	Servant	26Ma02Hg
CREOGAN, Margaret	15	F	Servant	26Ma02Hg
MALLON, James	25	M	Laborer	26Ma02Hg
MCDONALD, John	18	M	Laborer	26Ma02Hg
BURNS, James	20	M	Laborer	26Ma02Hg
CONNERY, John	20	M	Laborer	26Ma02Hg
WATKIN, Patrick	28	M	Laborer	26Ma02Hg
Biddy	26	F	Servant	26Ma02Hg
MCKEEGAN, Nancy	17	F	Servant	26Ma02Hg
MCCULLOCK, Catherine	16	F	Servant	26Ma02Hg
Biddy	18	F	Servant	26Ma02Hg
MANUS, Thomas	25	M	Laborer	26Ma02Hg
MCGONNEY, John	20	M	Laborer	26Ma02Hg
MULLIGAN, John	20	M	Laborer	26Ma02Hg
CONNOLLY, John	13	M	Laborer	26Ma02Hg
CROAK, John	36	M	Laborer	26Ma02Hg
U	30	F	Servant	26Ma02Hg
ENGLISH, Nancy	00	F	Servant	26Ma02Hg
CROAK, Catherine	12	F	Servant	26Ma02Hg
Judith	09	F	Child	26Ma02Hg
Anthony	08	M	Child	26Ma02Hg
Ellen	07	F	Child	26Ma02Hg
Patrick	03	M	Child	26Ma02Hg
Phillip	.00	M	Infant	26Ma02Hg
REGAN, David	26	M	Laborer	26Ma02Hg
KAVANNAH, Patrick	21	M	Coachman	26Ma02Hg
BARRY, Ann	26	F	Servant	26Ma02Hg
DOOLAN, Patrick	08	M	Child	26Ma02Hg
BARRY, Mary	23	F	Servant	26Ma02Hg
TALLON, Bryan	17	M	Laborer	26Ma02Hg
MCELIOT, Bernard	20	M	Laborer	26Ma02Hg
DEADISS, Patrick	30	M	Laborer	26Ma02Hg

NAMES OF PASSENGERS	AGE	SEX	OCCUPATIONS	DATE PORT SHIP
LAWLESS, Patrick	20	M	Laborer	26Ma02Hg
FEADY, Michel	20	M	Laborer	26Ma02Hg
DAIDLESS, Bridget	20	F	Servant	26Ma02Hg
TUITE, Mary	20	F	Servant	26Ma02Hg
COLLEHAN, Mary	20	F	Servant	26Ma02Hg
SIMMINS, Betsey	20	F	Servant	26Ma02Hg
KEEGON, Jenny	20	F	Servant	26Ma02Hg
CUSTAN, James	20	M	Laborer	26Ma02Hg
TAYLOR, Thomas	20	M	Laborer	26Ma02Hg
KERR, Ellin	20	F	Servant	26Ma02Hg
GRAHAM, George	20	M	Laborer	26Ma02Hg
GILLON, Biddy	20	F	Servant	26Ma02Hg
Samuel	20	M	Laborer	26Ma02Hg
LANAN, Patrick	20	M	Laborer	26Ma02Hg
MCAIDLE, Thomas	20	M	Laborer	26Ma02Hg
MURPHY, Mary	20	F	Servant	26Ma02Hg
MCSHEEN, Rose	20	F	Servant	26Ma02Hg
SMITH, Mary	20	F	Servant	26Ma02Hg
MCGINN, Mary	30	F	Servant	26Ma02Hg
C., U	20	M	Laborer	26Ma02Hg
U, U	20	M	Laborer	26Ma02Hg
KEENA, Patrick	20	M	Laborer	26Ma02Hg
MURDA, Lawrence	20	M	Laborer	26Ma02Hg
REED, U	26	M	Laborer	26Ma02Hg
KEOGH, Michel	20	M	Laborer	26Ma02Hg
KILBRIDE, Michel	43	M	Silk Dyer	26Ma02Hg
Ellin	18	F	Servant	26Ma02Hg
Betsey	24	F	Servant	26Ma02Hg
BRADY, James	24	M	Laborer	26Ma02Hg
BRYAN, Silvester	20	M	Miner	26Ma02Hg
BROWN, Thomas	.00	M	Infant	26Ma02Hg
REILEY, John	25	M	Miner	26Ma02Hg
PREEDY, Judy	24	F	Servant	26Ma02Hg
Bridget	20	F	Servant	26Ma02Hg
DELANY, Patrick	20	M	Laborer	26Ma02Hg
Judy	20	F	Servant	26Ma02Hg
FITZMORE, Ellen	18	F	Servant	26Ma02Hg
TAYLOR, John	40	M	Laborer	26Ma02Hg
Mary	50	F	None	26Ma02Hg
DUFF, Patrick	20	M	Brick Maker	26Ma02Hg
Bridget	20	F	Servant	26Ma02Hg
Thomas	20	M	Laborer	26Ma02Hg
WHELAND, John	20	M	Laborer	26Ma02Hg
MAHER, Kitty	20	F	Servant	26Ma02Hg
REILLY, Biddy	04	F	Child	26Ma02Hg
Ann (M)	26	F	Servant	26Ma02Hg
CASSEY, Martin	26	M	Laborer	26Ma02Hg
U, Anthony	30	M	Laborer	26Ma02Hg
KEEGAN, Edward	20	M	Laborer	26Ma02Hg
RIELLY, Margaret	20	F	Servant	26Ma02Hg
FAGAN, Mary	20	F	Servant	26Ma02Hg
LYNCH, Honora	25	F	Servant	26Ma02Hg
FITZPATRICK, Edward	31	M	Laborer	26Ma02Hg
MCCOURT, Bernard	20	M	Laborer	26Ma02Hg
MONAGHAN, James	50	M	Laborer	26Ma02Hg
James (S)	19	M	Laborer	26Ma02Hg
KEEFE, James	19	M	Laborer	26Ma02Hg
GAFFER, Patrick	20	M	Laborer	26Ma02Hg
RYAN, James	30	M	Laborer	26Ma02Hg
GILLEGAN, Ellin	20	F	Servant	26Ma02Hg
KEAN, Ellin	19	F	Servant	26Ma02Hg
FELLAN, James	20	M	Laborer	26Ma02Hg
BROPHY, Bridget	23	F	Servant	26Ma02Hg
MCGRAGH, Catherine	20	F	Servant	26Ma02Hg
DUNN, Eliza	20	F	Servant	26Ma02Hg
BURNS, Catherine	20	F	Servant	26Ma02Hg
CUSHION, Patrick	20	M	Laborer	26Ma02Hg
HIGGINS, William	26	M	Laborer	26Ma02Hg
MITCHELL, Essey	20	F	Servant	26Ma02Hg
TYNAN, Catherine	20	F	Servant	26Ma02Hg
GRADY, Sally	19	F	Servant	26Ma02Hg
Timothy	20	M	Laborer	26Ma02Hg
WINN, John	21	M	Laborer	26Ma02Hg
REYNOLDS, Patrick	21	M	Laborer	26Ma02Hg
HANLEY, Mary	20	F	Servant	26Ma02Hg

NAMES OF PASSENGERS	AGE	SEX	OCCUPATIONS	DATE PORT SHIP
MCCALE, Thomas	31	M	Laborer	26Ma02Hg
REILLY, James	19	M	Laborer	26Ma02Hg
Ann	17	F	Laborer	26Ma02Hg
SIMMON, John	24	M	Laborer	26Ma02Hg
Bridget	20	F	Servant	26Ma02Hg
Mary	20	F	Servant	26Ma02Hg
Catherine	05	F	Child	26Ma02Hg
Ellnor	.00	F	Infant	26Ma02Hg
CHARLES, Andrew	40	M	Laborer	26Ma02Hg
Elizabeth	31	F	Servant	26Ma02Hg
SIMMON, Thomas	25	M	Laborer	26Ma02Hg
REILLY, Mary	13	F	None	26Ma02Hg
William	11	M	Child	26Ma02Hg
John	09	M	Child	26Ma02Hg
CARROLE, Andrew	21	M	Laborer	26Ma02Hg
CARLAND, Mary	21	F	Servant	26Ma02Hg
Ann	21	F	Servant	26Ma02Hg
CLARK, Margaret	23	F	Servant	26Ma02Hg
Daffney	22	M	Laborer	26Ma02Hg
BURN, Mary	20	F	Servant	26Ma02Hg
MCLANNY, Michael	20	M	Laborer	26Ma02Hg
CONINSKY, Thomas	20	M	Laborer	26Ma02Hg
REYNOLDS, Patrick	20	M	Laborer	26Ma02Hg
WINTER, Mary	50	F	Laborer	26Ma02Hg
DUEY, Mary	12	F	Child	26Ma02Hg
Danl.	12	M	Child	26Ma02Hg
CLARY, Michael	20	M	Laborer	26Ma02Hg
Joseph	20	M	Laborer	26Ma02Hg
LAHY, Richard	20	M	Laborer	26Ma02Hg
KNIGHT, Hannah	20	F	Servant	26Ma02Hg
LAWFER, Bridget	20	F	Servant	26Ma02Hg
RYAN, John	20	M	Laborer	26Ma02Hg
FLOOD, Michael	20	M	Laborer	26Ma02Hg
GRAHAM, Eliza	20	F	Servant	26Ma02Hg
BOLAN, Michael	23	M	Laborer	26Ma02Hg
LAFFREY, Henry	36	M	Weaver	26Ma02Hg
NOLAN, Michael	22	M	Blacksmith	26Ma02Hg
BURN, Thomas	26	M	Tailor	26Ma02Hg
CONOLLY, Catherine	25	F	Servant	26Ma02Hg
FINN, Catherine	20	F	Servant	26Ma02Hg
BAILIE, John	43	M	Laborer	26Ma02Hg
DOYLE, John	21	M	Laborer	26Ma02Hg
REYNOLDS, Hugh	20	M	Laborer	26Ma02Hg
Catherine	20	F	Servant	26Ma02Hg
BANNING, Patrick	21	M	Laborer	26Ma02Hg
BAKER, Margaret	24	F	Servant	26Ma02Hg
BANNON, James	23	M	Laborer	26Ma02Hg
EDGAR, Samuel	21	M	Laborer	26Ma02Hg
BEATY, James	20	M	Laborer	26Ma02Hg
HUSTON, Thomas	21	M	Laborer	26Ma02Hg
FEENEY, Catherine	22	F	Servant	26Ma02Hg
HAGAN, Cella	20	F	Servant	26Ma02Hg
BURN, Thomas	20	M	Shoemaker	26Ma02Hg
BRENNON, Ellen	20	F	Servant	26Ma02Hg
HUSTON, William	09	M	Child	26Ma02Hg
Janet	11	F	Child	26Ma02Hg
BEATTIE, Matthew	20	M	Laborer	26Ma02Hg
WALSH, Ellen	20	F	Servant	26Ma02Hg
WOODLOCK, Bridget	20	F	Servant	26Ma02Hg
MARTIN, Nancy	20	F	Servant	26Ma02Hg
FENISY, Edward	20	M	Laborer	26Ma02Hg
DRADDY, Charles	20	M	Stone Mason	26Ma02Hg
CLIFFORD, John	20	M	Laborer	26Ma02Hg
CARROLL, Anthony	20	M	Laborer	26Ma02Hg
KENNEDY, Edward	20	M	Tailor	26Ma02Hg
CONNOR, William	20	M	Laborer	26Ma02Hg
HUGHES, Thomas	54	M	Laborer	26Ma02Hg
HARMON, Patrick	20	M	Laborer	26Ma02Hg
FITZGERALD, Hannah	20	F	Servant	26Ma02Hg
MCCLOUD, William	20	M	Laborer	26Ma02Hg
MCQUADE, James	20	M	Laborer	26Ma02Hg
DEVINE, Sally	20	F	Servant	26Ma02Hg
MCKENNA, Margaret	20	F	Servant	26Ma02Hg
MCCARTHY, Mary-Ann	21	F	Dressmaker	26Ma02Hg
Margaret	19	F	Dressmaker	26Ma02Hg
DUANE, Dennis	24	M	Flabr	26Ma02Hg
SULLIVAN, Daniel	20	M	Flabr	26Ma02Hg
BAGLEY, Marie	36	F	Servant	26Ma02Hg
FERRINS, Daniel	30	M	Laborer	26Ma02Hg
TRAYNOR, Thomas	20	M	Laborer	26Ma02Hg
MCCAFFREY, John	28	M	Laborer	26Ma02Hg
MCGEE, U	28	M	Laborer	26Ma02Hg
CLARK, Patrick	20	M	Laborer	26Ma02Hg
U (W)	18	F	Servant	26Ma02Hg
BAKER, Mary	28	F	Servant	26Ma02Hg
KEONE, Mary	16	F	Servant	26Ma02Hg
John	13	M	Child	26Ma02Hg
Matthew	10	M	Child	26Ma02Hg
Thomas	11	M	Child	26Ma02Hg
BURKE, Thomas	20	M	Laborer	26Ma02Hg
MCCALE, Patrick	40	M	Laborer	26Ma02Hg
U (W)	30	F	Servant	26Ma02Hg
Mary (D)	.00	F	Infant	26Ma02Hg
BANNON, Peter	20	M	Laborer	26Ma02Hg
LERNNON, Patrick	30	M	Laborer	26Ma02Hg
OBRIEN, Catherine	20	F	Servant	26Ma02Hg
CALL, Margaret	20	F	Servant	26Ma02Hg
BRAGGAN, Bridget	20	F	Servant	26Ma02Hg
MODERWAY, Anthony	20	M	Weaver	26Ma02Hg
FITZPATRICK, Edward	20	M	Laborer	26Ma02Hg
MCLEAD, Margaret	20	F	Servant	26Ma02Hg
MCNULTY, Bridget	20	F	Servant	26Ma02Hg
ROPER, Hugh	54	M	Laborer	26Ma02Hg
John (S)	20	M	Laborer	26Ma02Hg
ONEILL, John	30	M	Laborer	26Ma02Hg
ROPER, Ann	30	F	Servant	26Ma02Hg
MCDERMOTT, Michael	20	M	Laborer	26Ma02Hg
DOONAN, Patrick	24	M	Laborer	26Ma02Hg
Martin	20	M	Laborer	26Ma02Hg
Michael	22	M	Laborer	26Ma02Hg
HAGAN, Patrick	20	M	Laborer	26Ma02Hg
MORAPHY, Michael	23	M	Laborer	26Ma02Hg
FEEHY, John	26	M	Laborer	26Ma02Hg
RENAN, John	23	M	Laborer	26Ma02Hg
QUILLAN, Patrick	30	M	Laborer	26Ma02Hg
DUNN, John	26	M	Laborer	26Ma02Hg
Richard	36	M	Laborer	26Ma02Hg
MYER, Michael	30	M	Laborer	26Ma02Hg
DEVINE, Thomas	20	M	Laborer	26Ma02Hg
SULLIVAN, Ann	24	F	Servant	26Ma02Hg
CURTY, William	25	M	Laborer	26Ma02Hg
HUGHES, Ellen	19	F	Servant	26Ma02Hg
MORRIS, Honra	20	F	Servant	26Ma02Hg
RONEY, Mary	20	F	Servant	26Ma02Hg
OEARA, Patrick	21	M	Laborer	26Ma02Hg
HEARN, John	22	M	Laborer	26Ma02Hg
TOBIN, Michael	18	M	Trade Man	26Ma02Hg
OEGAN, Bridget	25	F	Servant	26Ma02Hg
CONOLLY, William	19	M	Laborer	26Ma02Hg
ROPER, James	27	M	Laborer	26Ma02Hg
CROWNEY, Hugh	20	M	Laborer	26Ma02Hg
MCGINN, Thomas	28	M	Laborer	26Ma02Hg
MCDONALD, Patrick	30	M	Shoemaker	26Ma02Hg
U (W)	25	F	Servant	26Ma02Hg
Catherine (D)	05	F	Child	26Ma02Hg
Bernard (S)	04	M	Child	26Ma02Hg
WALSH, Owen	24	M	Laborer	26Ma02Hg
Ellen	17	F	Servant	26Ma02Hg
Bridget	15	F	Servant	26Ma02Hg
REILLY, Edward	26	M	Laborer	26Ma02Hg
CAREY, Patrick	18	M	Laborer	26Ma02Hg
MATTHEWS, Bridget	20	F	Servant	26Ma02Hg
CALLEN, Jane	20	F	Servant	26Ma02Hg
MARTIN, Bridget	20	F	Servant	26Ma02Hg
COWLEY, John-B.	17	M	Physician	26Ma02Hg
OBRIEN, Michael	20	M	Laborer	26Ma02Hg
DAILEY, Thomas	21	M	Laborer	26Ma02Hg
PROCTER, Thomas	20	M	Laborer	26Ma02Hg
CONOLLY, Alice	20	F	Servant	26Ma02Hg
JENNER, Joseph	48	M	Farmer	26Ma02Hg

NAMES OF PASSENGERS		AGE	SEX	OCCUPATIONS	DATE PORT SHIP	NAMES OF PASSENGERS	AGE	SEX	OCCUPATIONS	DATE PORT SHIP
JENNER, U	(W)	39	F	Farmer	26Ma02Hg	CORDSWAIN, Mary	18	F	None	28Ma11Ho
OBRIEN, Thomas		28	M	Laborer	26Ma02Hg	John	19	M	None	28Ma11Ho
U	(W)	26	F	Servant	26Ma02Hg	COLEMAN, Peter	25	M	Laborer	28Ma11Ho
Thomas	(S)	03	M	Child	26Ma02Hg	Sebrina	17	F	Spinster	28Ma11Ho
Martha	(D)	.00	F	Infant	26Ma02Hg	GREELY, Dennis	27	M	Laborer	28Ma11Ho
DONOHUE, Julia		26	F	Servant	26Ma02Hg	BURKE, Dennis	24	M	Laborer	28Ma11Ho
Thomas	(H)	23	M	Laborer	26Ma02Hg	SURLEY, John	27	M	Laborer	28Ma11Ho
Edward	(S)	.00	M	Infant	26Ma02Hg	CAYSAIN, John	23	M	Laborer	28Ma11Ho
STEPHENSON, Martha		42	F	Servant	26Ma02Hg	TOOL, Mary	29	F	Spinster	28Ma11Ho
George	(H)	40	M	Laborer	26Ma02Hg	May	24	F	Spinster	28Ma11Ho
Susan	(D)	18	F	Servant	26Ma02Hg	KEENAN, Barth.	39	M	Laborer	28Ma11Ho
Michael	(S)	06	M	Laborer	26Ma02Hg	WALSH, Michael	20	M	Laborer	28Ma11Ho
Judy	(D)	13	F	Child	26Ma02Hg	MCDONOUGH, Jeremiah	27	M	Laborer	28Ma11Ho
Edward	(S)	11	M	Child	26Ma02Hg	GALLAHER, Nancy	23	F	Spinster	28Ma11Ho
William	(S)	09	M	Child	26Ma02Hg	SWEENEY, Nelly	21	F	Spinster	28Ma11Ho
Peter	(S)	07	M	Child	26Ma02Hg	BURKE, Thomas	31	M	Laborer	28Ma11Ho
Ann	(D)	05	F	Child	26Ma02Hg	Mary	19	F	Spinster	28Ma11Ho
Margaret	(D)	03	F	Child	26Ma02Hg	CONOLLY, Mary	24	F	Spinster	28Ma11Ho
Thomas	(S)	.00	M	Infant	26Ma02Hg	Margaret	27	F	Spinster	28Ma11Ho
HENDERSON, Edward		30	M	Laborer	26Ma02Hg	KERNS, Ellen	20	F	Spinster	28Ma11Ho
						REAY, Darley	21	M	Laborer	28Ma11Ho
						INNS, Michael	29	M	Laborer	28Ma11Ho
						FLANAGAN, Michael	21	M	Laborer	28Ma11Ho
						GRUFFIN, Bartholomew	28	M	Laborer	28Ma11Ho
						SMITH, Margrett	25	F	Spinster	28Ma11Ho
	KATE 28 MAY 1846					REDDINGTON, Michael	24	M	Laborer	28Ma11Ho
						WHITE, Michael	23	M	Laborer	28Ma11Ho
	From Galway					William	29	M	Laborer	28Ma11Ho
						RYAN, Michael	27	M	Laborer	28Ma11Ho
						HYNES, Biddy	19	F	Spinster	28Ma11Ho
						BURKE, Judy	25	F	Spinster	28Ma11Ho
DEELY, William		25	M	Laborer	28Ma11Ho	MINTAM, Patrick	40	M	Laborer	28Ma11Ho
Mary		20	F	Spinster	28Ma11Ho	Mary	19	F	Spinster	28Ma11Ho
Dennis		18	M	Laborer	28Ma11Ho	STANINTON, John	31	M	Laborer	28Ma11Ho
Margrett		19	F	Spinster	28Ma11Ho	WALSH, Patrick	24	M	Laborer	28Ma11Ho
Mary		20	F	Spinster	28Ma11Ho	FAHY, Patrick	29	M	Laborer	28Ma11Ho
MCGOWAN, Morgan		30	M	Laborer	28Ma11Ho	Nelly	20	F	Spinster	28Ma11Ho
Patrick		21	M	Laborer	28Ma11Ho	MOONEY, Margrett	25	F	Spinster	28Ma11Ho
FORD, L.		38	M	Laborer	28Ma11Ho	Bridget	29	F	Spinster	28Ma11Ho
Martin		20	M	Laborer	28Ma11Ho	Bridget	21	F	Spinster	28Ma11Ho
GEOHAGAN, John		19	M	Laborer	28Ma11Ho	DILLON, Catharine	25	F	Spinster	28Ma11Ho
NORMAN, James		33	M	Laborer	28Ma11Ho					
GLEESON, Mary		17	F	Spinster	28Ma11Ho					
Sally		20	F	Spinster	28Ma11Ho					
FAHY, Mary		30	F	Spinster	28Ma11Ho					
FARSEE, Nicholas		25	M	Laborer	28Ma11Ho	GREAT-BRITAIN 29 MAY 1846				
Catharin		19	F	Spinster	28Ma11Ho					
CONNOR, Michael		31	M	Laborer	28Ma11Ho	From Liverpool				
GUTREY, Ctharin		22	F	None	28Ma11Ho					
Bridget		37	F	None	28Ma11Ho					
DONOHUE, Pat		21	M	Laborer	28Ma11Ho	RICHARDSON, Willm.	41	M	Tourist	29Ma02Hp
SHIELDS, Tom		33	M	Laborer	28Ma11Ho	COLLINS, William	46	M	Tourist	29Ma02Hp
MURRAY, Tom		27	M	Laborer	28Ma11Ho	WHITAKER, C.Mrs.	22	F	Lady	29Ma02Hp
FEENEY, Thomas		23	M	Laborer	28Ma11Ho					
Mary		17	F	Spinster	28Ma11Ho					
COOK, Bridget		24	F	Spinster	28Ma11Ho					
CALLAHAN, John		21	M	Laborer	28Ma11Ho					
GLYNN, John		27	M	Laborer	28Ma11Ho	JANE 29 MAY 1846				
KELLY, John		23	M	Laborer	28Ma11Ho					
Pat		21	M	Laborer	28Ma11Ho	From Liverpool				
MCGOUGHAN, Pat		29	M	Laborer	28Ma11Ho					
HEALY, Thomas		30	M	Laborer	28Ma11Ho					
HANNON, Andrew		40	M	Laborer	28Ma11Ho	SHEVLIN, Phillip	18	M	Farmer	29Ma02Dv
LYAN, Mary		20	F	Spinster	28Ma11Ho	Jane	16	F	Unknown	29Ma02Dv
NEWMAN, Mary		23	F	Spinster	28Ma11Ho	MCCARTY, Floranc	27	M	Unknown	29Ma02Dv
SEALHY, Marie		18	F	Spinster	28Ma11Ho	Mary	23	F	Unknown	29Ma02Dv
LAFFY, Patrick		34	M	Laborer	28Ma11Ho	LAVINS, William	20	M	Unknown	29Ma02Dv
LAMBE, Homer		23	M	Laborer	28Ma11Ho	DONLAN, Margret	22	F	Unknown	29Ma02Dv
HAYNES, Michael		24	M	Laborer	28Ma11Ho	JACKSON, James	24	M	Unknown	29Ma02Dv
GIBSON, John		15	M	Laborer	28Ma11Ho	HANNARAY, Owen	23	M	Unknown	29Ma02Dv
MAHER, Anna		25	F	Spinster	28Ma11Ho	QUILLAN, Mies.	21	M	Unknown	29Ma02Dv
CORDSWAIN, Matty		45	M	Laborer	28Ma11Ho					
Biddy		31	F	Spinster	28Ma11Ho					
Michael		24	M	None	28Ma11Ho					
Mary		21	F	None	28Ma11Ho					

111

NAMES OF PASSENGERS		AGE	SEX	OCCUPATIONS	DATE PORT SHIP
BELL, John		30	M	Unknown	29Ma02Dv
U	(W)	27	F	Unknown	29Ma02Dv
George	(S)	06	M	Child	29Ma02Dv
KINGSBURY, John		24	M	Unknown	29Ma02Dv
U	(W)	21	F	Unknown	29Ma02Dv
Abby	(D)	.00	F	Infant	29Ma02Dv
MURRAY, Patt		28	M	Unknown	29Ma02Dv
NAUGHTON, Patt		26	M	Unknown	29Ma02Dv
MANNEY, Owen		21	M	Unknown	29Ma02Dv
MULLEN, Catherin		20	F	Unknown	29Ma02Dv
DUNKIN, James		21	M	Unknown	29Ma02Dv
MULLENY, Rose		20	F	Unknown	29Ma02Dv
MCGRATH, Ellen		19	F	Unknown	29Ma02Dv
EVENS, Margret		20	F	Unknown	29Ma02Dv
COFFREY, James		26	M	Unknown	29Ma02Dv
U	(W)	25	F	Unknown	29Ma02Dv
Bridget	(D)	.00	F	Infant	29Ma02Dv
BRESLAND, Neal		24	M	Unknown	29Ma02Dv
OGARA, Hugh		28	M	Unknown	29Ma02Dv
MCGIVELY, Mary		19	F	Unknown	29Ma02Dv
OSBOURNE, Bess		20	F	Unknown	29Ma02Dv
LESLIE, Hannah		19	F	Unknown	29Ma02Dv
SHAKESHAFT, John		45	M	Unknown	29Ma02Dv
FARRELL, John		26	M	Unknown	29Ma02Dv
GOLLIHER, Hugh		20	M	Unknown	29Ma02Dv
HAMILTON, Patt		20	M	Unknown	29Ma02Dv
MCHUGH, Charles		22	M	Unknown	29Ma02Dv
SCALLY, Thomas		19	M	Unknown	29Ma02Dv
FAGAN, James		24	M	Unknown	29Ma02Dv
Mary		20	F	Unknown	29Ma02Dv
EVANS, John		30	M	Unknown	29Ma02Dv
Jane		25	F	Unknown	29Ma02Dv
Martha		04	F	Child	29Ma02Dv
Nancy		01	F	Child	29Ma02Dv
MCCLELLAND, William		26	M	None	29Ma02Dv
John		27	M	None	29Ma02Dv
James		20	M	None	29Ma02Dv
MILLER, James		19	M	None	29Ma02Dv
CLARK, Rochal		20	F	None	29Ma02Dv
HANIHAN, John		30	M	None	29Ma02Dv
Mary		40	F	None	29Ma02Dv
Patt		01	M	Child	29Ma02Dv
NELAN, Francis		28	M	None	29Ma02Dv
BESWICK, Patrick		30	M	None	29Ma02Dv
BUCKLY, Edward		24	M	None	29Ma02Dv
LEE, William		24	M	None	29Ma02Dv
DUMPHY, James		26	M	None	29Ma02Dv
Bridget		26	F	None	29Ma02Dv
NOWLAN, William		24	M	None	29Ma02Dv
U	(W)	22	F	None	29Ma02Dv
BELL, John		03	M	Child	29Ma02Dv
BULGER, Michael		00	M	Unknown	29Ma02Dv
Ann		00	F	Unknown	29Ma02Dv
FLENIGAN, Michael		00	M	Unknown	29Ma02Dv
ROBINSON, John		00	M	Unknown	29Ma02Dv
Ann		00	F	Unknown	29Ma02Dv
KANE, John		00	M	Unknown	29Ma02Dv
U	(W)	00	F	Unknown	29Ma02Dv
MORGAN, Benj.		26	M	Unknown	29Ma02Dv
U	(W)	26	F	Unknown	29Ma02Dv
David	(S)	08	M	Child	29Ma02Dv
Jacob	(S)	07	M	Child	29Ma02Dv
Mary	(D)	04	F	Child	29Ma02Dv
Jane	(D)	02	F	Child	29Ma02Dv
LUCIE, Michael		24	M	Unknown	29Ma02Dv
KERWIN, May		30	F	Unknown	29Ma02Dv
Thomas	(S)	12	M	Unknown	29Ma02Dv
Patrick	(S)	10	M	Child	29Ma02Dv
James	(S)	08	M	Child	29Ma02Dv
Charles	(S)	06	M	Child	29Ma02Dv
Owen	(S)	05	M	Child	29Ma02Dv
John	(S)	02	M	Child	29Ma02Dv
BRIEN, Thomas		30	M	Unknown	29Ma02Dv
Rosey	(D)	12	F	Unknown	29Ma02Dv
Maria	(D)	10	F	Child	29Ma02Dv
BRIEN, Mary	(D)	09	F	Child	29Ma02Dv
Bridget	(D)	05	F	Child	29Ma02Dv
John	(S)	07	M	Child	29Ma02Dv
CUNNINGHAM, John		27	M	Unknown	29Ma02Dv
Margret	(W)	21	M	Unknown	29Ma02Dv
Mary	(D)	02	F	Child	29Ma02Dv
HAUGHAGAN, Mary		11	F	Child	29Ma02Dv
KANE, Patt		21	M	Unknown	29Ma02Dv
U	(W)	20	F	Unknown	29Ma02Dv
MCCALLISTER, George		36	M	Unknown	29Ma02Dv
U	(W)	34	F	Unknown	29Ma02Dv
Rachel		13	F	Unknown	29Ma02Dv
Margt.	(D)	10	F	Child	29Ma02Dv
John	(S)	08	M	Child	29Ma02Dv
MOLLOY, James		35	M	Unknown	29Ma02Dv
U	(W)	30	F	Unknown	29Ma02Dv
Patt	(S)	04	M	Child	29Ma02Dv
Timothy	(S)	08	M	Child	29Ma02Dv
Betty	(D)	06	F	Child	29Ma02Dv
HUGHES, James		30	M	Unknown	29Ma02Dv
GRAHAM, Francis		18	M	Unknown	29Ma02Dv
FEGAN, James		16	M	Unknown	29Ma02Dv
FOGARTY, Patrick		10	M	Child	29Ma02Dv
Mary		06	F	Child	29Ma02Dv
BRESLIN, James		36	M	Unknown	29Ma02Dv
George	(S)	13	M	Unknown	29Ma02Dv
Mary	(D)	09	F	Child	29Ma02Dv
Rosey	(D)	08	F	Child	29Ma02Dv
Margret	(D)	05	F	Child	29Ma02Dv
MCDEVITT, Alexn.		19	M	Unknown	29Ma02Dv
CANON, Rose		28	F	Unknown	29Ma02Dv
MCARDLE, Ann		22	F	Unknown	29Ma02Dv
BRETT, Margret		27	F	Unknown	29Ma02Dv
LOGAN, James		40	M	Unknown	29Ma02Dv
Alice		36	F	Unknown	29Ma02Dv
BURK, James		35	M	Unknown	29Ma02Dv
LOGAN, Peter		17	M	Unknown	29Ma02Dv
Mary		13	F	Unknown	29Ma02Dv
Benjm.		10	M	Child	29Ma02Dv
Hugh		08	M	Child	29Ma02Dv
SHARKEY, Ann		25	F	Unknown	29Ma02Dv
BOYLE, Catherine		23	F	Unknown	29Ma02Dv
CURREN, Elizabeth		17	F	Unknown	29Ma02Dv
HUGHES, Thomas		20	M	Unknown	29Ma02Dv
MCMANUS, Jas.		20	M	Unknown	29Ma02Dv
BOYLE, Patt		46	M	Unknown	29Ma02Dv
U	(W)	40	F	Unknown	29Ma02Dv
John	(S)	15	M	Unknown	29Ma02Dv
Patt	(S)	12	M	Unknown	29Ma02Dv
Thimothy	(S)	10	M	Child	29Ma02Dv
Mary	(D)	01	F	Child	29Ma02Dv
Jane	(D)	04	F	Child	29Ma02Dv
MCAULEY, John		22	M	Unknown	29Ma02Dv
U	(W)	20	F	Unknown	29Ma02Dv
MCMANUS, Ellen		20	F	Unknown	29Ma02Dv
EMERSON, Neptune		25	M	Unknown	29Ma02Dv
KAIN, Alice		18	F	Unknown	29Ma02Dv
MCGEOUGH, Jane		24	F	Unknown	29Ma02Dv
SMITH, Geo.		38	M	Unknown	29Ma02Dv
U	(W)	36	F	Unknown	29Ma02Dv
John	(S)	13	M	Unknown	29Ma02Dv
George	(S)	12	M	Unknown	29Ma02Dv
Mary	(D)	06	F	Child	29Ma02Dv
James	(S)	01	M	Child	29Ma02Dv
HUGHES, Morgan		24	M	Unknown	29Ma02Dv
U	(W)	22	F	Unknown	29Ma02Dv
John	(S)	01	M	Infant	29Ma02Dv
OWENS, Mary		18	F	Unknown	29Ma02Dv
CASSIDY, John		20	M	Unknown	29Ma02Dv
FLANNIGAN, Thomas		20	M	Unknown	29Ma02Dv
GANTY, Catherine		20	F	Unknown	29Ma02Dv
MCELROY, Ann		18	F	Unknown	29Ma02Dv
CASSIDY, Martha		18	F	Unknown	29Ma02Dv
SAVAGE, Micheal		21	M	Unknown	29Ma02Dv
John		49	M	Unknown	29Ma02Dv

| --- | --- | --- | --- | --- | --- | --- | --- | --- | --- | --- | --- |
SAVAGE, Mary		21	F	Unknown	29Ma02Dv	BOYD, Nancy	(W)	23	F	None	30Ma02Hq
ANDREWS, Catherine		17	F	Unknown	29Ma02Dv	Elizabeth	(D)	.00	F	Infant	30Ma02Hq
KELLY, Ann		21	F	Unknown	29Ma02Dv	MCGINAGH, William		24	M	Servant	30Ma02Hq
KERR, Martha		21	F	Unknown	29Ma02Dv	FOSSIT, Charles		27	M	None	30Ma02Hq
Bryan		25	M	Unknown	29Ma02Dv	CAHILL, James		26	M	None	30Ma02Hq
SMITH, Kitty		18	F	Unknown	29Ma02Dv	Nancy	(W)	25	F	None	30Ma02Hq
SAVAGE, Patt		30	M	Unknown	29Ma02Dv	Johanna	(D)	.00	F	Infant	30Ma02Hq
PRATT, Henry		11	M	Child	29Ma02Dv	TALBOT, Patrick		20	M	None	30Ma02Hq
U-Mrs.		32	F	None	29Ma02Dv	MATHEWS, Mary		20	F	None	30Ma02Hq
Ellen		50	F	None	29Ma02Dv	ALENESEY, James		43	M	Farmer	30Ma02Hq
George		10	M	Child	29Ma02Dv	U	(W)	35	F	None	30Ma02Hq
Mary		06	F	Child	29Ma02Dv	Margret		22	F	None	30Ma02Hq
Henry	(B)	04	M	Child	29Ma02Dv	Mary		20	F	None	30Ma02Hq
DALY, Thimothy		30	M	None	29Ma02Dv	John		19	M	None	30Ma02Hq
U	(W)	28	F	None	29Ma02Dv	Patrick		15	M	None	30Ma02Hq
John	(S)	01	M	Child	29Ma02Dv	James		13	M	None	30Ma02Hq
MOONEY, James		12	M	None	29Ma02Dv	Dennis		10	M	Child	30Ma02Hq
Peter		10	M	Child	29Ma02Dv	Alley		08	F	Child	30Ma02Hq
Alex		06	M	Child	29Ma02Dv	Ellen		04	F	Child	30Ma02Hq
HIGGINS, Michae		27	M	None	29Ma02Dv	Margret		.00	F	Infant	30Ma02Hq
CORCORAN, Owen		17	M	None	29Ma02Dv	HENELTY, James		33	M	Carpenter	30Ma02Hq
CONNOR, Ann		18	F	None	29Ma02Dv	DARCY, Dominick		21	M	Servant	30Ma02Hq
HOPKINS, Marla		11	F	Child	29Ma02Dv	Michael		20	M	None	30Ma02Hq
HAMPSON, Eliza		18	F	None	29Ma02Dv	MCCABE, Catherine		19	F	None	30Ma02Hq
WALSH, John		24	M	None	29Ma02Dv	MCCAFFREY, Margret		19	F	None	30Ma02Hq
MCDONNELL, William		22	M	None	29Ma02Dv	SULLIVAN, Mary		24	F	None	30Ma02Hq
DOLAN, Michael		30	M	None	29Ma02Dv	BYRNE, Micheal		26	M	Laborer	30Ma02Hq
SHEEAN, John		27	M	None	29Ma02Dv	CASEY, Patrick		25	M	None	30Ma02Hq
BRIEN, Thomas		30	M	None	29Ma02Dv	LESLIS, Thomas		25	M	None	30Ma02Hq
HAGANS, John		22	M	None	29Ma02Dv	Catherine		30	F	Dressmaker	30Ma02Hq
CERRARSKY, Mary		20	F	None	29Ma02Dv	CONELLY, Danlal		24	M	Servant	30Ma02Hq
GILLESPIE, Styles		24	M	None	29Ma02Dv	HARNAN, Bernard		25	M	None	30Ma02Hq
Connor		19	M	None	29Ma02Dv	U	(W)	22	F	None	30Ma02Hq
FISHER, Ellen		24	F	None	29Ma02Dv	WALSH, John		26	M	Farmer	30Ma02Hq
NAUGHTON, Jane		36	F	None	29Ma02Dv	Michael		22	M	None	30Ma02Hq
Mary	(D)	09	F	Child	29Ma02Dv	Patrick		20	M	None	30Ma02Hq
Oney	(D)	06	F	Child	29Ma02Dv	HOLDHAN, Patrick		50	M	None	30Ma02Hq
Ann	(D)	03	F	Child	29Ma02Dv	Patrick		10	M	Child	30Ma02Hq
James	(S)	01	M	Child	29Ma02Dv	Mary		20	F	None	30Ma02Hq
HORN, John		21	M	Unknown	29Ma02Dv	CANNON, Thomas		20	M	Laborer	30Ma02Hq
KEVIN, John		21	M	Unknown	29Ma02Dv	MCCABE, Owen		25	M	None	30Ma02Hq
MILLER, Samuel		30	M	Unknown	29Ma02Dv	Patrick		28	M	None	30Ma02Hq
U	(W)	28	F	Unknown	29Ma02Dv	HENRY, Bryne		45	M	None	30Ma02Hq
ROBERTS, Samuel		04	M	Child	29Ma02Dv	HEADLY, John		35	M	None	30Ma02Hq
Jane		01	F	Child	29Ma02Dv	Bryne		26	M	None	30Ma02Hq
GILLEECE, John		21	M	Unknown	29Ma02Dv	Michael		24	M	None	30Ma02Hq
MCPARTLAND, Cath.		20	F	Unknown	29Ma02Dv	Mark		22	M	None	30Ma02Hq
WALKER, James		21	M	Unknown	29Ma02Dv	MCKENDREW, Jas.		20	M	None	30Ma02Hq
CLARK, William		24	M	Unknown	29Ma02Dv	MCLAUGHLIN, Martin		36	M	None	30Ma02Hq
Eliza		21	F	Unknown	29Ma02Dv	DRAROND, John		26	M	None	30Ma02Hq
SHEEHAN, Dennis		13	M	Unknown	29Ma02Dv	GREEN, Jane		40	F	Dressmaker	30Ma02Hq
MEGGERTON, Ann		12	F	Unknown	29Ma02Dv	Edward	(S)	10	M	Child	30Ma02Hq
FOYLE, William		20	M	Unknown	29Ma02Dv	MURTHA, Patrick		20	M	Servant	30Ma02Hq
Margaret		17	F	Unknown	29Ma02Dv	Thomas		16	M	Servant	30Ma02Hq
LAUGHLIN, Hugh		40	M	Unknown	29Ma02Dv	BYRNES, Mary		20	F	Milliner	30Ma02Hq
Susanna		53	F	Unknown	29Ma02Dv	CONNELL, Betty		20	F	Dressmaker	30Ma02Hq
MULLEN, James		12	M	Unknown	29Ma02Dv	BURN, Margaret		19	F	Farmer	30Ma02Hq
Jane		10	F	Unknown	29Ma02Dv	HEALY, Bridget		12	F	Milliner	30Ma02Hq
Janet		06	F	Unknown	29Ma02Dv	CANSTERY, Mary		12	F	Milliner	30Ma02Hq
						DANGHER, Mary		12	F	Milliner	30Ma02Hq
						CANSTERY, Thomas		10	M	Child	30Ma02Hq
						MCLAUGHLIN, Mary		50	F	None	30Ma02Hq
						COCHERAN, Bridget		22	F	None	30Ma02Hq
						BLACK, Susan		20	F	None	30Ma02Hq
CHUSAN 30 MAY 1846						RIELLY, John		40	M	Farmer	30Ma02Hq
						Mary		40	F	None	30Ma02Hq
From Liverpool						BURNS, Peter		19	M	None	30Ma02Hq
						KILCULLEN, Leila		50	F	None	30Ma02Hq
						Mary		20	F	Dressmaker	30Ma02Hq
						CONLAN, Patrick		19	M	Servant	30Ma02Hq
SCAMLIN, Biddy		25	F	Dressmaker	30Ma02Hq	DOYLE, Catherine		18	F	None	30Ma02Hq
Jane		21	F	None	30Ma02Hq	MCLAUGHLIN, Biddy		40	F	None	30Ma02Hq
Susan		19	F	None	30Ma02Hq	KENNEDY, John		25	M	None	30Ma02Hq
Jane		18	F	None	30Ma02Hq	KELLY, James		18	M	None	30Ma02Hq
BOYD, Samuel		24	M	Farmer	30Ma02Hq	DUGGAN, John		32	M	None	30Ma02Hq

NAMES OF PASSENGERS		AGE	SEX	OCCUPATIONS	DATE PORT SHIP
STEWART, William		20	M	None	30Ma02Hq
REILLY, Catherine		22	F	Servant	30Ma02Hq
Patrick		23	M	None	30Ma02Hq
MERGAN, James		24	M	None	30Ma02Hq
FARRELL, Ann		25	F	None	30Ma02Hq
LENNIN, Ann		26	F	None	30Ma02Hq
BEGGEY, Patrick		25	M	None	30Ma02Hq
CLARK, John		26	M	None	30Ma02Hq
DOWING, John		27	M	None	30Ma02Hq
Edward		24	M	None	30Ma02Hq
MANSFIELD, William		24	M	None	30Ma02Hq
BARNET, Catherine		25	F	None	30Ma02Hq
CROWE, Mary		25	F	None	30Ma02Hq
BARNET, William		23	M	None	30Ma02Hq
BIRGUGER, Johanna		31	F	Dressmaker	30Ma02Hq
MANNING, Wilgam		25	F	None	30Ma02Hq
HAFFIN, Maria		20	F	None	30Ma02Hq
EBITTS, John		25	M	Servant	30Ma02Hq
FANER, Micheal		20	M	None	30Ma02Hq
CAMPBELL, John		40	M	None	30Ma02Hq
Rachel	(W)	35	F	None	30Ma02Hq
John	(S)	05	M	Child	30Ma02Hq
Jas.	(S)	.00	M	Infant	30Ma02Hq
EDWARDS, David		58	M	Servant	30Ma02Hq
Ellen	(W)	60	F	None	30Ma02Hq
Ann	(D)	13	F	None	30Ma02Hq
KEENAN, Felix		34	M	None	30Ma02Hq
PHELAN, Catherine		23	F	None	30Ma02Hq
Ann		21	F	None	30Ma02Hq
COLLINS, Thimothy		22	M	None	30Ma02Hq
HEAGAN, John		50	M	None	30Ma02Hq
Margaret	(W)	50	F	None	30Ma02Hq
Nicholas	(S)	24	M	None	30Ma02Hq
William	(S)	18	M	None	30Ma02Hq
Ellen	(D)	13	F	None	30Ma02Hq
Mathew	(S)	12	M	None	30Ma02Hq
Fanney	(D)	09	F	Child	30Ma02Hq
PIERCE, Michael		46	M	Unknown	30Ma02Hq
Catherine		32	F	Unknown	30Ma02Hq
Margret		35	F	Unknown	30Ma02Hq
Elizabeth		07	F	Child	30Ma02Hq
BARRY, Nicholas		04	M	Child	30Ma02Hq
POTTS, William		02	M	Child	30Ma02Hq
JORDEN, Patrick		.00	M	Infant	30Ma02Hq
FLYNN, Micheal		35	M	None	30Ma02Hq
MARSHALL, John		27	M	None	30Ma02Hq
Jane		25	F	None	30Ma02Hq
William		37	M	None	30Ma02Hq
John		23	M	None	30Ma02Hq
Nancy		27	F	None	30Ma02Hq
James		10	M	Child	30Ma02Hq
Samuel		08	M	Child	30Ma02Hq
Rechl.		06	F	Child	30Ma02Hq
KELLY, Mary		03	F	Child	30Ma02Hq
HAGAN, Patrick		02	M	Child	30Ma02Hq
CAHILL, Phillip		.00	M	Infant	30Ma02Hq
U-Mrs.		24	F	None	30Ma02Hq
BURKE, Patt		29	M	None	30Ma02Hq
MCGERRY, Lace		22	M	None	30Ma02Hq
CONNOR, James		22	M	None	30Ma02Hq
MACGINN, Jane		21	F	None	30Ma02Hq
MCCULLIN, Jas.		24	M	None	30Ma02Hq
FRENT, Jas.		50	M	None	30Ma02Hq
MURPHY, Jane		29	F	None	30Ma02Hq
James	(S)	08	M	Child	30Ma02Hq
John	(S)	06	M	Child	30Ma02Hq
MARSHALL, James		04	M	Child	30Ma02Hq
MURPHY, Patrick		04	M	Child	30Ma02Hq
RELHERAN, William		27	M	None	30Ma02Hq
Jane		25	F	None	30Ma02Hq
MURPHY, Ann		21	F	None	30Ma02Hq

MERSEY 30 MAY 1846

From Liverpool

NAMES OF PASSENGERS		AGE	SEX	OCCUPATIONS	DATE PORT SHIP
DOUGHERTY, James		20	M	Laborer	30Ma02Hr
BOLES, Thos.		25	M	Laborer	30Ma02Hr
Ellen		20	F	Spinster	30Ma02Hr
BLAIR, Lucy		20	F	Spinster	30Ma02Hr
MILLER, Peter		27	M	Laborer	30Ma02Hr
Mary-Ann		22	F	None	30Ma02Hr
KIRK, John		35	M	Laborer	30Ma02Hr
CARROLL, Chas.		25	M	Laborer	30Ma02Hr
COFFEY, Wm.		26	M	Laborer	30Ma02Hr
BLAKE, Nancy		26	F	Laborer	30Ma02Hr
Mary		24	F	Laborer	30Ma02Hr
FITZGERALD, Judith		28	F	Laborer	30Ma02Hr
LENEHAN, Chas.		22	M	Laborer	30Ma02Hr
GALVIN, Wm.		26	M	Laborer	30Ma02Hr
WALSH, Jas.		25	M	Laborer	30Ma02Hr
Mary		20	F	Laborer	30Ma02Hr
MCCORMACK, Jas.		21	M	Laborer	30Ma02Hr
Chas.		20	M	Laborer	30Ma02Hr
KEHOE, Michl.		21	M	Laborer	30Ma02Hr
GARVEY, Patk.		20	M	Laborer	30Ma02Hr
MCCORMACK, Cathe.		18	F	Laborer	30Ma02Hr
DANN, Rose		20	F	Laborer	30Ma02Hr
GAFFNEY, Pat		40	M	Laborer	30Ma02Hr
LEE, Brian		30	M	Laborer	30Ma02Hr
LYNCH, Mary		25	F	Laborer	30Ma02Hr
MASTERSON, Anne		24	F	Laborer	30Ma02Hr
MALONY, Pat.		22	M	Laborer	30Ma02Hr
HOPKINS, Maria		22	F	Laborer	30Ma02Hr
GREALY, Ellen		18	F	Laborer	30Ma02Hr
JUDE, Bridget		20	F	Laborer	30Ma02Hr
HENRY, Cathe.		16	F	Laborer	30Ma02Hr
HALWELL, Mary		22	F	Laborer	30Ma02Hr
BYRNE, Edwd.		27	M	Laborer	30Ma02Hr
MURPHY, Pat		22	M	Laborer	30Ma02Hr
MILLER, Jas.		40	M	Laborer	30Ma02Hr
Joseph	(S)	15	M	Laborer	30Ma02Hr
Alice	(D)	10	F	Child	30Ma02Hr
MIDGLY, Alice		23	F	Laborer	30Ma02Hr
Mary		25	F	Laborer	30Ma02Hr
HAINES, Wm.		25	M	Laborer	30Ma02Hr
Hande.		00	F	Laborer	30Ma02Hr
BOTTOMLY, John		25	M	Laborer	30Ma02Hr
Susan		32	F	Laborer	30Ma02Hr
Mary		38	F	Laborer	30Ma02Hr
Nathn.		03	M	Child	30Ma02Hr
Nathn.		27	M	Laborer	30Ma02Hr
JORDAN, Thos.		40	M	Laborer	30Ma02Hr
Margt.		45	F	Laborer	30Ma02Hr
John		13	M	Laborer	30Ma02Hr
LEARY, John		11	M	Child	30Ma02Hr
MORGAN, Mary		20	F	Laborer	30Ma02Hr
COLEMAN, Ann		18	F	Laborer	30Ma02Hr
MCCLARKE, Betsy		18	F	Laborer	30Ma02Hr
HANAH, Bridget		20	F	Laborer	30Ma02Hr
MILLER, Rachl.		18	F	Laborer	30Ma02Hr
BOYLE, John		32	M	Laborer	30Ma02Hr
Mary	(W)	30	F	Laborer	30Ma02Hr
Mary	(D)	.00	F	Infant	30Ma02Hr
FITZGERALD, Wm.		24	M	Laborer	30Ma02Hr
MCCORMACK, Mary		27	F	Laborer	30Ma02Hr
RAY, Wm.		18	M	Laborer	30Ma02Hr
LAVERTY, Mary		30	F	Laborer	30Ma02Hr
DONNELLY, Francis		27	M	Laborer	30Ma02Hr
JUDE, John		30	M	Laborer	30Ma02Hr
MCGUIRE, Mathew		45	M	Laborer	30Ma02Hr

NAMES OF PASSENGERS		A G E	S E X	OCCUPATIONS	DATE PORT SHIP	NAMES OF PASSENGERS		A G E	S E X	OCCUPATIONS	DATE PORT SHIP
MCGUIRE, Elizth.	(W)	45	F	Laborer	30Ma02Hr	FITZGERALD, Thos.		30	M	Laborer	30Ma02Hr
Thos.	(S)	21	M	Laborer	30Ma02Hr	Alice		30	F	Laborer	30Ma02Hr
Bridget	(D)	19	F	Laborer	30Ma02Hr	Stephen		00	M	Laborer	30Ma02Hr
Francis	(S)	16	M	Laborer	30Ma02Hr	DOOLY, Anne		30	F	Laborer	30Ma02Hr
Mary	(D)	11	F	Child	30Ma02Hr	DAWSON, Margt.		24	F	Laborer	30Ma02Hr
Mathew	(S)	08	M	Child	30Ma02Hr	Mary-Anne		18	F	Laborer	30Ma02Hr
Eliza	(D)	04	F	Child	30Ma02Hr	KELLY, Anne		20	F	Laborer	30Ma02Hr
DUNN, Mathew		26	M	Laborer	30Ma02Hr	BRENNAN, Margt.		21	F	Laborer	30Ma02Hr
Patk.		26	M	Laborer	30Ma02Hr	HENNISY, John		24	M	Laborer	30Ma02Hr
John		14	M	Laborer	30Ma02Hr	SULLIVAN, John		20	M	Laborer	30Ma02Hr
Cathe.		21	F	Laborer	30Ma02Hr	RYAN, Bridget		41	F	Laborer	30Ma02Hr
Cathe.		50	F	Laborer	30Ma02Hr	HENNESSY, Judith		24	F	Laborer	30Ma02Hr
Mary		16	F	Laborer	30Ma02Hr	CORMACK, Cathe.		30	F	Laborer	30Ma02Hr
CRAWLY, Anne		18	F	Laborer	30Ma02Hr	CARROLL, Jane		15	F	Laborer	30Ma02Hr
Mary		20	F	Laborer	30Ma02Hr	Mary		16	F	Laborer	30Ma02Hr
MCCANN, Geo.		17	M	Laborer	30Ma02Hr	MURRAY, Bridget		20	F	Laborer	30Ma02Hr
Judith		20	F	Laborer	30Ma02Hr	BRENNAN, Mary		20	F	Laborer	30Ma02Hr
FLEMMING, Cath.		20	F	Laborer	30Ma02Hr	Ellen		18	F	Laborer	30Ma02Hr
MONAGHAN, Thos.		20	M	Laborer	30Ma02Hr	DYE, Andrew		20	M	Laborer	30Ma02Hr
MARTIN, Anne		22	F	Laborer	30Ma02Hr	MACK, Mary		21	F	Laborer	30Ma02Hr
CRIGHTON, Alice		21	F	Laborer	30Ma02Hr	SULLIVAN, Ellen		22	F	Laborer	30Ma02Hr
RICHEY, Eliza		20	F	Laborer	30Ma02Hr	MASTERSON, Patk.		35	M	Laborer	30Ma02Hr
MONTGOMERY, Mary		21	F	Laborer	30Ma02Hr	Bridget		30	F	Laborer	30Ma02Hr
DOWDALL, Anne		20	F	Laborer	30Ma02Hr	DONAHUE, James		40	M	Laborer	30Ma02Hr
DUNN, Margt.		19	F	Laborer	30Ma02Hr	HALLAHAN, James		28	M	Laborer	30Ma02Hr
BRYAN, Jas.		30	M	Laborer	30Ma02Hr	THOMPSON, Robt.		36	M	Laborer	30Ma02Hr
BARRY, Michl.		29	M	Laborer	30Ma02Hr	BARR, Johanna		21	F	Laborer	30Ma02Hr
Patrick		28	M	Laborer	30Ma02Hr	BRAY, Joseph		20	M	Laborer	30Ma02Hr
Jas.		25	M	Laborer	30Ma02Hr	BOLES, Thomas		40	M	Laborer	30Ma02Hr
Mary		32	F	Laborer	30Ma02Hr	HUGHES, Michl.		30	M	Laborer	30Ma02Hr
Bridget		55	F	Laborer	30Ma02Hr	MCKENNA, Hugh		24	M	Laborer	30Ma02Hr
MCCARTY, Mary		06	F	Child	30Ma02Hr	GURNER, Charles		24	M	Laborer	30Ma02Hr
LYNCH, Bridget		.00	F	Infant	30Ma02Hr	ROACH, David		21	M	Laborer	30Ma02Hr
MCMURREY, Francis		30	M	Laborer	30Ma02Hr	QUIN, Mary		22	F	Laborer	30Ma02Hr
Anne		22	F	Laborer	30Ma02Hr	CALLAHAN, Patrick		21	M	Laborer	30Ma02Hr
GALLAGHER, Peter		18	M	Laborer	30Ma02Hr	OKEEFE, William		20	M	Laborer	30Ma02Hr
John		16	M	Laborer	30Ma02Hr	COWLAN, Redmd.		40	M	Laborer	30Ma02Hr
Jas.		20	M	Laborer	30Ma02Hr	Johanna	(W)	40	F	Laborer	30Ma02Hr
Mary		18	F	Laborer	30Ma02Hr	Bridget	(D)	18	F	Laborer	30Ma02Hr
SMITH, Patk.		55	M	Laborer	30Ma02Hr	William	(S)	13	M	Laborer	30Ma02Hr
Wm.		19	M	Laborer	30Ma02Hr	Henry	(S)	12	M	Laborer	30Ma02Hr
MADDEN, Mary		24	F	Laborer	30Ma02Hr	CONLAN, John		06	M	Child	30Ma02Hr
REILY, Bridget		24	F	Laborer	30Ma02Hr	Kate		04	F	Child	30Ma02Hr
DILLON, Bridget		18	F	Laborer	30Ma02Hr	MCCARTY, Owen		20	M	Laborer	30Ma02Hr
GRAHAM, Pat		20	M	Laborer	30Ma02Hr	Jeremiah		18	M	Laborer	30Ma02Hr
DILLON, John		26	M	Laborer	30Ma02Hr	MALONE, John		20	M	Laborer	30Ma02Hr
CONNOR, John		24	M	Laborer	30Ma02Hr	BAGLEY, Danl.		21	M	Laborer	30Ma02Hr
Cathe.		26	F	Laborer	30Ma02Hr	SHEEHAN, Cornelius		22	M	Laborer	30Ma02Hr
DOWD, John		30	M	Laborer	30Ma02Hr	CALLAHAN, John		22	M	Laborer	30Ma02Hr
LYNCH, Patk.		25	M	Laborer	30Ma02Hr	Patk.		23	M	Laborer	30Ma02Hr
FITZSIMMONS, Patk.		24	M	Laborer	30Ma02Hr	LEHARAN, Ellen		24	F	Laborer	30Ma02Hr
COMLY, Patk.		26	M	Laborer	30Ma02Hr	LYONS, Timothy		18	M	Laborer	30Ma02Hr
DWIRY, Patk.		23	M	Laborer	30Ma02Hr	Mary		22	F	Laborer	30Ma02Hr
Mary		16	F	Laborer	30Ma02Hr	MCCARTY, Betsey		13	F	Laborer	30Ma02Hr
Margt.		25	F	Laborer	30Ma02Hr	WALSH, Mary		18	F	Laborer	30Ma02Hr
WARD, Owen		21	M	Laborer	30Ma02Hr	BAKER, John		25	M	Laborer	30Ma02Hr
FORD, Patk.		30	M	Laborer	30Ma02Hr	CALAHAN, Michl.		22	M	Laborer	30Ma02Hr
MCMANUS, Jane		18	F	Laborer	30Ma02Hr	FARRELL, James		20	M	Laborer	30Ma02Hr
CONNOLLY, Lawrence		20	M	Laborer	30Ma02Hr	LOWREY, Michl.		20	M	Laborer	30Ma02Hr
BARRY, Thos.		30	M	Laborer	30Ma02Hr	MARTIN, Mathew		26	M	Laborer	30Ma02Hr
Wm.		30	M	Laborer	30Ma02Hr	LYONS, Michl.		25	M	Laborer	30Ma02Hr
Patk.		09	M	Child	30Ma02Hr	John		24	M	Laborer	30Ma02Hr
SLAVEN, Patk.		26	M	Laborer	30Ma02Hr	Cathe.		.00	F	Infant	30Ma02Hr
GLOVER, Margt.		24	F	Laborer	30Ma02Hr	William		18	M	Laborer	30Ma02Hr
Edwd.	(S)	.00	M	Infant	30Ma02Hr	MASTERSON, Geo.		20	M	Laborer	30Ma02Hr
Died-At-Sea						Margt.		18	F	Laborer	30Ma02Hr
BRYAN, Owen		27	M	Laborer	30Ma02Hr	LORD, Mary-Ann		13	F	Laborer	30Ma02Hr
HOGAN, Thos.		30	M	Laborer	30Ma02Hr	Eliza		17	F	Laborer	30Ma02Hr
Hanah		25	F	Laborer	30Ma02Hr	BROPHEY, Patk.		24	M	Laborer	30Ma02Hr
Mcmichl., Jas.		27	M	Laborer	30Ma02Hr	MURPHY, James		25	M	Laborer	30Ma02Hr
Jane		26	F	Laborer	30Ma02Hr	CONNOLLY, Ellen		20	F	Laborer	30Ma02Hr
MCMAHON, David		28	M	Laborer	30Ma02Hr	CARROLL, James		25	M	Laborer	30Ma02Hr
BATES, John		20	M	Laborer	30Ma02Hr	MORAN, William		25	M	Laborer	30Ma02Hr
Susan		03	F	Child	30Ma02Hr	CADDY, Anthony		26	M	Laborer	30Ma02Hr
CATER, Jane		00	F	Laborer	30Ma02Hr	Bridget		24	F	Laborer	30Ma02Hr

NAMES OF PASSENGERS	A G E	S E X	OCCUPATIONS	DATE PORT SHIP
MULLEN, Mary	13	F	Laborer	30Ma02Hr
MCKEON, Rose	12	F	Laborer	30Ma02Hr
CALLAGHAN, Cornelius	32	M	Laborer	30Ma02Hr
John	28	M	Laborer	30Ma02Hr
OHARA, John	26	M	Laborer	30Ma02Hr
BRYAN, Michl.	28	M	Laborer	30Ma02Hr
MALONE, Jerry	28	M	Laborer	30Ma02Hr
Michl.	26	M	Laborer	30Ma02Hr
Patt.	28	M	Laborer	30Ma02Hr
Ellen	21	F	Laborer	30Ma02Hr
LYONS, Patt	30	M	Laborer	30Ma02Hr
KELLY, Patrick	23	M	Laborer	30Ma02Hr
RYAN, Peter	28	M	Laborer	30Ma02Hr
HEALEY, James	23	M	Laborer	30Ma02Hr
QUINN, Ellen	35	F	Laborer	30Ma02Hr
Mary	23	F	Laborer	30Ma02Hr
Hannah	28	F	Laborer	30Ma02Hr
Edwd.	06	M	Child	30Ma02Hr
CONDON, William	23	M	Laborer	30Ma02Hr
CLARKE, Georg.	23	M	Laborer	30Ma02Hr
TOOMEY, Mary	20	F	Laborer	30Ma02Hr
DONOVAN, Michl.	23	M	Laborer	30Ma02Hr
MCDONNELL, Patrick	20	M	Laborer	30Ma02Hr
TRAENOR, Johanna	26	F	Laborer	30Ma02Hr
DILLON, Margt.	13	F	Laborer	30Ma02Hr
RIELLY, Thomas	03	M	Laborer	30Ma02Hr
FOSTER, Dorathy	25	F	Laborer	30Ma02Hr
Hanna	11	F	Child	30Ma02Hr
William	04	M	Child	30Ma02Hr
John	.00	M	Infant	30Ma02Hr
Harriet	20	F	Laborer	30Ma02Hr
James	18	F	Laborer	30Ma02Hr
ROBERTSON, Susan	12	F	Laborer	30Ma02Hr
BELL, Abraham	20	M	Laborer	30Ma02Hr
MURRAY, Rose	20	F	Laborer	30Ma02Hr
COURSEY, Ann	21	F	Laborer	30Ma02Hr
MCMANUS, John	24	M	Laborer	30Ma02Hr
CROW, Barnaba	22	F	Laborer	30Ma02Hr
Unity	27	F	Laborer	30Ma02Hr
CROTHERS, Joseph	27	M	Laborer	30Ma02Hr
MCDONOUGH, Matt	40	M	Laborer	30Ma02Hr
DALEY, Bridget	13	F	Laborer	30Ma02Hr
CAVANAGH, Ellen	20	F	Laborer	30Ma02Hr
KELLY, Thomas	34	M	Laborer	30Ma02Hr
James	30	M	Laborer	30Ma02Hr
Michl.	27	M	Laborer	30Ma02Hr
Jane	24	F	Laborer	30Ma02Hr
Mary	22	F	Laborer	30Ma02Hr
HURLEY, William	26	M	Laborer	30Ma02Hr
LANAHAN, Susan	18	F	Laborer	30Ma02Hr
MURRAY, Martin	26	M	Laborer	30Ma02Hr
Sarah	30	F	Laborer	30Ma02Hr
Margt.	13	F	Laborer	30Ma02Hr
DUFFY, Hugh	20	M	Laborer	30Ma02Hr
MURRAY, Alex.	22	M	Laborer	30Ma02Hr
LORIN, John	30	M	Laborer	30Ma02Hr
RIED, Ann	16	F	Laborer	30Ma02Hr
CORRIGAN, John	30	M	Laborer	30Ma02Hr
RIED, Domnick	24	M	Laborer	30Ma02Hr
GILL, Cathe.	18	F	Laborer	30Ma02Hr
NOLAN, David	40	M	Laborer	30Ma02Hr

ALHAMBRA 01 JUNE 1846

From Dublin

NAMES OF PASSENGERS	A G E	S E X	OCCUPATIONS	DATE PORT SHIP
COSTIGAN, Patt	20	M	Tailor	01Ju20EJ
CONWAY, Cathrine	30	F	Servant	01Ju20EJ
QUINN, Bridget	20	F	Servant	01Ju20EJ

NAMES OF PASSENGERS	A G E	S E X	OCCUPATIONS	DATE PORT SHIP
HALMOND, Mary	20	F	Servant	01Ju20EJ
LANNENRY, Bridget	25	F	Servant	01Ju20EJ
LAMANIS, John	20	M	Laborer	01Ju20EJ
U	20	M	Laborer	01Ju20EJ
WHELAN, Michal	20	M	Laborer	01Ju20EJ
Rale	20	M	Laborer	01Ju20EJ
CUFF, Julia	20	F	Servant	01Ju20EJ
MADDEN, Bridget	40	F	None	01Ju20EJ
Thomas	25	M	Laborer	01Ju20EJ
John	13	M	Laborer	01Ju20EJ
Julia	30	F	Servant	01Ju20EJ
Ellen	20	F	Servant	01Ju20EJ
Mary	21	F	Servant	01Ju20EJ
Susan	07	F	Child	01Ju20EJ
Michal	18	M	Laborer	01Ju20EJ
KERSHAW, William	25	M	Laborer	01Ju20EJ
Thomas	20	M	Laborer	01Ju20EJ
William	06	M	Child	01Ju20EJ
HAND, Mary	20	F	Servant	01Ju20EJ
LEONARD, Sarah	50	F	Servant	01Ju20EJ
Hugh	(S) 12	M	Child	01Ju20EJ
CAREY, Bridget	20	F	Servant	01Ju20EJ
DUME, Michal	22	F	Servant	01Ju20EJ
LYONS, Catharine	27	F	Servant	01Ju20EJ
DOWLLY, Mary	20	F	Servant	01Ju20EJ
ONEAL, Julia	11	F	Child	01Ju20EJ
FARRELLY, Bridget	20	F	Servant	01Ju20EJ
FELLEM, Thomas	28	M	Servant	01Ju20EJ
MCDONAL, Michal	28	M	Laborer	01Ju20EJ
GALIVAN, John	25	M	Laborer	01Ju20EJ
Cathrine	50	F	Servant	01Ju20EJ
Cathrine	20	F	Servant	01Ju20EJ
DINNING, Margret	21	F	Servant	01Ju20EJ
NANTON, Patt	24	M	Laborer	01Ju20EJ
HARDEMAN, Thomas	20	M	Laborer	01Ju20EJ
RELLY, Mary	20	F	Servant	01Ju20EJ
MALONE, Marten	24	M	Laborer	01Ju20EJ
WHILE, Patt	24	M	Laborer	01Ju20EJ
WOODS, Mary	20	F	Servant	01Ju20EJ
ADEMS, Ellen	21	F	Servant	01Ju20EJ
HUMPHRY, Mary	22	F	Servant	01Ju20EJ
TRACY, Ester	24	F	Servant	01Ju20EJ
RYLEY, Cathrine	20	F	Servant	01Ju20EJ
HAGEN, Mary	20	F	Servant	01Ju20EJ
TERRILL, Bridget	20	F	Servant	01Ju20EJ
DOYLE, Patt	20	M	Cooper	01Ju20EJ
Mary	11	F	Child	01Ju20EJ
FOX, Edward	20	M	Laborer	01Ju20EJ
CATTICKS, Ann	24	F	Servant	01Ju20EJ
HIGHS, Roas	20	F	Laborer	01Ju20EJ
MCGURSEN, Patt	24	M	Laborer	01Ju20EJ
MONIGLSS, Patt	23	M	Laborer	01Ju20EJ
BOYD, Patt	22	M	Laborer	01Ju20EJ
Ann	20	F	Servant	01Ju20EJ
FREASY, Martin	20	M	Laborer	01Ju20EJ
TERRELL, John	20	M	Carpenter	01Ju20EJ
BROPHY, Judy	24	F	None	01Ju20EJ
KAVANAGH, Mary	19	F	None	01Ju20EJ
YOUNG, Emiley	24	F	Servant	01Ju20EJ
MCGREEDY, Patt	30	M	Servant	01Ju20EJ
Peter	20	M	Servant	01Ju20EJ
James	22	M	Farmer	01Ju20EJ
Ann	19	F	Farmer	01Ju20EJ
RILLEY, Ally	26	F	Farmer	01Ju20EJ
Michal	(S) .00	M	Infant	01Ju20EJ
HERIGH, Marton	20	M	None	01Ju20EJ
SLATERY, John	50	M	None	01Ju20EJ
Dolly	(W) 40	F	Seamstress	01Ju20EJ
Bridget	(D) 16	F	Laborer	01Ju20EJ
John	(S) 12	M	Laborer	01Ju20EJ
Patt	(S) 09	M	Child	01Ju20EJ
EAGEN, Julia	17	F	None	01Ju20EJ
BERREL, Edward	20	M	Servant	01Ju20EJ
FANOUEL, Michal	55	M	Laborer	01Ju20EJ
Mary	(W) 50	F	Wife	01Ju20EJ

NAMES OF PASSENGERS		A G E	S E X	OCCUPATIONS	DATE PORT SHIP	NAMES OF PASSENGERS		A G E	S E X	OCCUPATIONS	DATE PORT SHIP
FANOUEL, Patt	(S)	12	M	None	01Ju20EJ	CONNOR, Morris		26	M	Laborer	01Ju20EJ
REYNOLD, Cathrine		20	F	None	01Ju20EJ	U	(W)	25	F	Wife	01Ju20EJ
HERSOM, Thomas		20	M	None	01Ju20EJ	John	(S)	08	M	Child	01Ju20EJ
KERNEY, Patt		20	M	None	01Ju20EJ	Catherine	(D)	02	F	Child	01Ju20EJ
ALERDON, John		23	M	Servant	01Ju20EJ	MCDONALD, John		24	M	Laborer	01Ju20EJ
DEREAN, George		25	M	Carpenter	01Ju20EJ	REY, Ann		26	F	Laborer	01Ju20EJ
MONAHAM, James		27	M	Carpenter	01Ju20EJ	DONAHER, John		23	M	Laborer	01Ju20EJ
MOONEY, Thomas		24	M	Servant	01Ju20EJ	RYAN, Patt		26	M	Laborer	01Ju20EJ
FERRELL, Margret		20	F	Servant	01Ju20EJ	Roady		23	M	Laborer	01Ju20EJ
MCNAMARE, William		24	M	Servant	01Ju20EJ	Thomas		21	M	Laborer	01Ju20EJ
William		20	M	Servant	01Ju20EJ	Caherine		18	F	Laborer	01Ju20EJ
FAGEN, U		40	F	WI	01Ju20EJ	CORBURN, Ann		19	F	Laborer	01Ju20EJ
Mary		21	F	Laborer	01Ju20EJ	KELLY, Margaret		17	F	Laborer	01Ju20EJ
BRACKEN, U		36	F	WI-Svnt	01Ju20EJ	CAFFRY, Michael		00	M	Unknown	01Ju20EJ
Patt		20	M	Servant	01Ju20EJ	LYONS, Patrick		18	M	Laborer	01Ju20EJ
Dolly		21	F	Servant	01Ju20EJ	FARREL, Catherine		21	F	Laborer	01Ju20EJ
LANLYN, John		21	M	Farmer	01Ju20EJ	RIELY, Bridget		20	F	Laborer	01Ju20EJ
GALLAGER, U		43	F	WI	01Ju20EJ	PHELAN, James		23	M	Laborer	01Ju20EJ
Hellena	(D)	20	F	None	01Ju20EJ	MALEY, Pat		22	M	Laborer	01Ju20EJ
Ann	(D)	16	F	Servant	01Ju20EJ	William		24	M	Laborer	01Ju20EJ
Mary	(D)	13	F	Servant	01Ju20EJ	MORN, Charles		25	M	Laborer	01Ju20EJ
CROWLEY, John		38	M	Servant	01Ju20EJ	BIRNINGHAM, John		24	M	Laborer	01Ju20EJ
William		38	M	Servant	01Ju20EJ	BURKE, Matthew		25	M	Laborer	01Ju20EJ
Christopher		20	M	Laborer	01Ju20EJ	WHEELER, Marton		28	M	Laborer	01Ju20EJ
Catherine		18	F	Laborer	01Ju20EJ	Ellen	(W)	28	F	Wife	01Ju20EJ
Ann		16	F	Laborer	01Ju20EJ	Samuel	(S)	04	M	Child	01Ju20EJ
MORAN, James		20	M	Laborer	01Ju20EJ	James	(S)	02	M	Child	01Ju20EJ
LYNCH, Ann		22	F	Laborer	01Ju20EJ	SULLIVAN, John		29	M	Laborer	01Ju20EJ
HELY, Bridget		20	F	Laborer	01Ju20EJ	Salay	(W)	30	F	Wife	01Ju20EJ
BODRICK, Ann		02	F	Child	01Ju20EJ	Edward	(S)	03	M	Child	01Ju20EJ
LAWLESS, James		21	M	Laborer	01Ju20EJ	Mary	(D)	11	F	Laborer	01Ju20EJ
BYNE, James		22	M	Laborer	01Ju20EJ	WRIGHT, George		24	M	Laborer	01Ju20EJ
MARAN, James		22	M	Laborer	01Ju20EJ	JUFT, Samuel		.00	M	Infant	01Ju20EJ
HENY, Michal		24	M	Laborer	01Ju20EJ	FOX, Edward		20	M	Laborer	01Ju20EJ
DANLEN, Thomas		26	M	Laborer	01Ju20EJ	GROGAN, George		22	M	Laborer	01Ju20EJ
BRINE, Mary		22	F	Laborer	01Ju20EJ	Sally		21	F	Laborer	01Ju20EJ
Beddy		20	F	Laborer	01Ju20EJ	DARDIS, Edward		24	M	Laborer	01Ju20EJ
Margret		18	F	Laborer	01Ju20EJ	John	(S)	03	M	Child	01Ju20EJ
QUINN, Mary		20	F	Laborer	01Ju20EJ	Mary	(D)	.00	F	Infant	01Ju20EJ
MCLAUGHLIN, James		26	M	Laborer	01Ju20EJ						
Mary		32	F	Laborer	01Ju20EJ						
Patt		14	M	Laborer	01Ju20EJ						
Catherine		24	F	Laborer	01Ju20EJ						
MCCAFFRY, Patt		26	M	Laborer	01Ju20EJ	GARRICK 01 JUNE 1846					
DORAN, U		20	M	Laborer	01Ju20EJ						
MCGUINN, Bernard		21	M	Laborer	01Ju20EJ	From Liverpool					
HESLAN, Thomas		26	M	Laborer	01Ju20EJ						
FORD, May		21	F	Laborer	01Ju20EJ						
MCCONALD, William		25	M	Laborer	01Ju20EJ						
John		22	M	Laborer	01Ju20EJ	SULLEVAN, Mary		17	F	Servant	01Ju02Aa
BRANAN, Richard		21	M	Laborer	01Ju20EJ	BOOK, Ellen		18	F	Servant	01Ju02Aa
ONEALE, John		22	M	Laborer	01Ju20EJ	LARVIN, James		19	M	Laborer	01Ju02Aa
TREACY, Mary		20	F	Laborer	01Ju20EJ	DUFFY, Patrick		30	M	Laborer	01Ju02Aa
Maluchy		22	M	Laborer	01Ju20EJ	Catherin		20	F	None	01Ju02Aa
SCOT, Richard		24	M	Laborer	01Ju20EJ	HANLEY, Bridget		20	F	Servant	01Ju02Aa
BRENEN, John		24	M	Laborer	01Ju20EJ	LARKIN, Martin		20	M	Laborer	01Ju02Aa
HOLTON, John		21	M	Laborer	01Ju20EJ	SCULLY, Thomas		30	M	Laborer	01Ju02Aa
Catherine		23	F	Laborer	01Ju20EJ	MURRY, Patrick		19	M	Laborer	01Ju02Aa
LONDOL, Ann		20	F	Laborer	01Ju20EJ	JOICE, John		14	M	Laborer	01Ju02Aa
MULVERY, Margaret		40	F	Laborer	01Ju20EJ	HOWETT, Elizabeth		18	F	Servant	01Ju02Aa
Patrick	(S)	12	M	Laborer	01Ju20EJ	BRAN, Elizth.		20	F	Servant	01Ju02Aa
Francis	(S)	10	M	Laborer	01Ju20EJ	KELLY, Bridget		20	F	Servant	01Ju02Aa
Mary	(D)	07	F	Child	01Ju20EJ	REILLY, Barn.		18	M	Servant	01Ju02Aa
Margaret	(D)	03	F	Child	01Ju20EJ	HONEYMAN, Ellen		19	F	Servant	01Ju02Aa
MCNULLY, Maller		25	M	Laborer	01Ju20EJ	GILLAHER, Ellen		15	F	Servant	01Ju02Aa
FLANIGAN, Patt		34	M	Laborer	01Ju20EJ	CASIDY, Mary		16	F	Servant	01Ju02Aa
Bridget		17	F	Laborer	01Ju20EJ	Ellen		14	F	Servant	01Ju02Aa
WELSH, Bridget		17	F	Laborer	01Ju20EJ	CASSIDY, Andrew		50	M	Laborer	01Ju02Aa
MULRAY, Mary		20	F	Laborer	01Ju20EJ	WREN, Michl.		22	M	Laborer	01Ju02Aa
CASTEL, Patt		30	M	Laborer	01Ju20EJ	COCHRAN, James		26	M	Laborer	01Ju02Aa
CULLEN, Ellen		20	F	Laborer	01Ju20EJ	Michl.		22	M	Laborer	01Ju02Aa
TOLL, Michal		23	M	Laborer	01Ju20EJ	GREY, Patrick		14	M	Hawker	01Ju02Aa
FOLY, Tim		20	F	Laborer	01Ju20EJ	DEVILING, Dennis		16	M	Laborer	01Ju02Aa
BYRNE, Mary		20	F	Laborer	01Ju20EJ	MCNELLY, Barnet		20	M	Laborer	01Ju02Aa
Ann		18	F	Laborer	01Ju20EJ						

NAMES OF PASSENGERS	A G E	S E X	OCCUPATIONS	DATE PORT SHIP	NAMES OF PASSENGERS	A G E	S E X	OCCUPATIONS	DATE PORT SHIP
MCNELLY, Mary	17	F	Servent	01Ju02Aa	FALLY, Wm.	30	M	Carpenter	01Ju02Aa
GUNNING, Thimothy	25	M	Labcrer	01Ju02Aa	Catherne (W)	22	F	Wife	01Ju02Aa
Elizth.	24	F	None	01Ju02Aa	Margret (D)	01	F	Child	01Ju02Aa
KILLDUFF, James	21	M	Laborer	01Ju02Aa	TAIL, Joanna	26	F	Servent	01Ju02Aa
Denniss	13	M	Labcrer	01Ju02Aa	FALLY, Patrick	16	M	Laborer	01Ju02Aa
Tim	15	M	Laborer	01Ju02Aa	Thos.	26	M	Laborer	01Ju02Aa
GIFFIN, John	26	M	Laborer	01Ju02Aa	CAMPELL, Peter	22	M	Laborer	01Ju02Aa
Mary	22	F	Servent	01Ju02Aa	MCCART, James	19	M	Laborer	01Ju02Aa
MOOR, Martha	19	F	Servent	01Ju02Aa	PROUDFOOT, Patk.	21	M	Latcrer	01Ju02Aa
MCNELLY, Elizth.	17	F	Servent	01Ju02Aa	LAWLESS, Michl.	18	M	Laborer	01Ju02Aa
BURNS, Cathrn.	18	F	Servent	01Ju02Aa	CARDEN, Wm.	09	M	Child	01Ju02Aa
KILLDUFF, Sarah	20	F	Servent	01Ju02Aa	CALESBY, Jes.	25	M	Laborer	01Ju02Aa
FANNING, Cathrn.	20	F	Servent	01Ju02Aa	MCHANUS, Patrick	20	M	Laborer	01Ju02Aa
FLEMING, Jane	20	F	Servent	01Ju02Aa	MCNANNA, Ralph	30	M	Cbtmkr	01Ju02Aa
FEGGIN, Mary	21	F	Servent	01Ju02Aa	Francis	19	M	Clerk	01Ju02Aa
KILROY, Cathrn.	19	F	Servent	01Ju02Aa	MCCROGEN, Thos.	19	M	Grocer	01Ju02Aa
BRICKINGS, Michl.	26	M	Blacksmith	01Ju02Aa	LFANE, Thomltry	30	M	Cooper	01Ju02Aa
Mary (W)	21	F	Wife	01Ju02Aa	Mary	24	F	None	01Ju02Aa
Michl. (S)	01	M	Child	01Ju02Aa	CARROL, Mary	23	F	Servent	01Ju02Aa
MCLACKEN, Nary	22	F	Servent	01Ju02Aa	Thos.	25	M	Laborer	01Ju02Aa
KELLY, Mary	16	F	Servent	01Ju02Aa	KEARN, John	34	M	Laborer	01Ju02Aa
BURNS, Margret	18	F	Servent	01Ju02Aa	Cathrn.	24	F	None	01Ju02Aa
Patrick	21	M	Laborer	01Ju02Aa	COONER, John	18	M	Laborer	01Ju02Aa
Margret	19	F	Servent	01Ju02Aa	MOYLES, Mathes.	23	M	Laborer	01Ju02Aa
MCHENLY, Mary	13	F	Servent	01Ju02Aa	MCCORMICK, Thos.	26	M	Laborer	01Ju02Aa
Ann	11	F	Servent	01Ju02Aa	MURPHY, Mary	18	F	Servent	01Ju02Aa
BURNS, James	27	M	Laborer	01Ju02Aa	MACAN, Ann	18	F	Servent	01Ju02Aa
Ann	22	F	None	01Ju02Aa	DAREY, Ann	17	F	Servent	01Ju02Aa
MURPHY, John	27	M	Labcrer	01Ju02Aa	BURNS, Mary	18	F	Servant	01Ju02Aa
Isabella (W)	25	F	Wife	01Ju02Aa	MCCAN, Patk.	20	M	Laborer	01Ju02Aa
Wm. (S)	01	M	Child	01Ju02Aa	ROX, Michl.	20	M	Laborer	01Ju02Aa
NAY, Goward	23	M	Laborer	01Ju02Aa	MCCHIN, James	20	M	Laborer	01Ju02Aa
Michl.	21	M	Laborer	01Ju02Aa	CARTY, Martin	18	M	Labcrer	01Ju02Aa
MURTHAGH, James	18	M	Labcrer	01Ju02Aa	HARKIN, Patrick	22	M	Laborer	01Ju02Aa
Andrew	25	M	Laborer	01Ju02Aa	JOHNSTON, Michl.	22	M	Laborer	01Ju02Aa
Roger	14	M	Laborer	01Ju02Aa	DUFFY, Cathrn.	23	F	Servant	01Ju02Aa
Mary	20	F	Servent	01Ju02Aa	MOOR, Patk.	30	M	Laborer	01Ju02Aa
Bricget	49	F	Servent	01Ju02Aa	GORDON, Patk.	30	M	Laborer	01Ju02Aa
DONOHOE, John	25	M	Tailor	01Ju02Aa	MILL, Michl.	20	M	Laborer	01Ju02Aa
MULIGAN, Patrick	23	M	Labcrer	01Ju02Aa	WHITE, Jane	18	F	Servant	01Ju02Aa
MURPHY, Thos.	35	M	Laborer	01Ju02Aa	Mary	24	F	Servant	01Ju02Aa
MCDONALD, Charls	21	M	Carpenter	01Ju02Aa	ONEIL, Nany	20	F	Servent	01Ju02Aa
AKEN, James	21	M	Labcrer	01Ju02Aa	SULIVAN, Thos.	18	M	Shoemaker	01Ju02Aa
ROX, Edward	17	M	Laborer	01Ju02Aa	JONES, Wm.	52	M	Farmer	01Ju02Aa
MURPHY, Mary	18	F	Servent	01Ju02Aa	MURTHGA, Bartl.	20	M	Laborer	01Ju02Aa
KARY, Ann	16	F	Servent	01Ju02Aa	MICHELVAIN, Eliza	20	F	Servant	01Ju02Aa
CORMACK, Elizth.	16	F	Servent	01Ju02Aa	Sarah	20	F	Servant	01Ju02Aa
COGHAN, Byron	35	M	Labcrer	01Ju02Aa	SMITH, Fanny	20	F	Servant	01Ju02Aa
Mary (W)	30	F	Servent	01Ju02Aa	MCFAGIN, Mary	18	F	Servant	01Ju02Aa
Micheal (S)	10	M	Servent	01Ju02Aa	CHESEON, Mary	35	F	Dressmaker	01Ju02Aa
Thos. (S)	03	M	Child	01Ju02Aa	MONDAY, Hugh	07	M	Child	01Ju02Aa
Mary (D)	10	F	Servent	01Ju02Aa	TELFORD, John	26	M	Laborer	01Ju02Aa
GLADSEY, John	35	M	Tinsmith	01Ju02Aa	Mary (W)	26	F	Wife	01Ju02Aa
Ann (D)	06	F	Child	01Ju02Aa	James (S)	03	M	Child	01Ju02Aa
Bricget (D)	02	F	Child	01Ju02Aa	Mary (D)	01	F	Child	01Ju02Aa
Margret (D)	04	F	Child	01Ju02Aa	TORLEY, James	30	M	Laborer	01Ju02Aa
ANDERSON, Mary	27	F	House Maid	01Ju02Aa	SURY, John	18	M	Mason	01Ju02Aa
ROBERTSON, Mary	48	F	House Maid	01Ju02Aa	WELCH, John	25	M	Laborer	01Ju02Aa
LYNCH, Mary	25	F	Servent	01Ju02Aa	MURPHY, Patrick	16	M	Laborer	01Ju02Aa
HEAD, Eliza	21	F	Servent	01Ju02Aa	BELCH, John	21	M	Laborer	01Ju02Aa
MORN, Cathrn.	16	F	Servent	01Ju02Aa	OCONNELL, Corneals.	24	M	Laborer	01Ju02Aa
HEAD, Thos.	18	M	Labcrer	01Ju02Aa	FITZGERRALD, Margret	30	F	Stalr	01Ju02Aa
FLANARY, Winfred	23	M	Servent	01Ju02Aa	Michl. (S)	12	M	None	01Ju02Aa
MORRISON, Michl.	26	M	Laborer	01Ju02Aa	Joseph (D)	09	M	Child	01Ju02Aa
Mary	30	F	Servent	01Ju02Aa	Jane	32	F	None	01Ju02Aa
CHRISTY, Michl.	26	M	Labcrer	01Ju02Aa	WILKINSON, Alexd.	20	M	Carpenter	01Ju02Aa
MCKIE, Michl.	22	M	Labcrer	01Ju02Aa	HORANS, Mary-Ann	24	F	House Maid	01Ju02Aa
Jane	23	F	Servent	01Ju02Aa	COMMERTON, Patk.	50	M	Weaver	01Ju02Aa
CONARGHTY, Ann	14	F	Servant	01Ju02Aa	HENRY, John	28	M	Laborer	01Ju02Aa
TRANING, Wm.A.	24	M	Engraver	01Ju02Aa	REILLY, John	16	M	Laborer	01Ju02Aa
GALFORD, James	24	M	Shoemaker	01Ju02Aa	BYRON, James	30	M	Laborer	01Ju02Aa
BEST, Robert	20	M	Laborer	01Ju02Aa	MULLYAN, John	32	M	Laborer	01Ju02Aa
OBRYEN, Jane	20	F	Servent	01Ju02Aa	NEWTON, Wm.	24	M	Spinner	01Ju02Aa
GRAHM, Rose	16	F	Servent	01Ju02Aa	SMITH, Joseph	23	M	Shoemaker	01Ju02Aa
MCMALL, Bessy	04	F	Child	01Ju02Aa	WORTHINGTON, Thos.	29	M	Butcher	01Ju02Aa

NAMES OF PASSENGERS		AGE	SEX	OCCUPATIONS	DATE PORT SHIP	NAMES OF PASSENGERS		AGE	SEX	OCCUPATIONS	DATE PORT SHIP
CAHILL, Thos.		24	M	Smith	01Ju02Aa	JACKSON, Mary		59	F	Servant	01Ju02Aa
BATTEN, Joseph		17	M	Clerk	01Ju02Aa	Stephen		17	M	Farmer	01Ju02Aa
DEAMOND, James		17	M	Clerk	01Ju02Aa	MCROIL, George		10	M	Farmer	01Ju02Aa
STONES, S.		32	M	Founder	01Ju02Aa	CAR, Barhy		28	M	Laborer	01Ju02Aa
Ann	(W)	30	F	Wife	01Ju02Aa	Fanny	(W)	28	F	Wife	01Ju02Aa
John	(S)	13	M	None	01Ju02Aa	Wm.	(S)	02	M	Child	01Ju02Aa
David	(S)	09	M	Child	01Ju02Aa	BARTLOW, Wm.		12	M	None	01Ju02Aa
Saml.	(S)	06	M	Child	01Ju02Aa	BURGESS, Saml.		21	M	Laborer	01Ju02Aa
Elizth.	(D)	02	F	Child	01Ju02Aa	ELLIOTT, James		30	M	Laborer	01Ju02Aa
Joane	(D)	12	F	Child	01Ju02Aa	Emma		19	F	None	01Ju02Aa
HUNTER, Richard		60	M	Farmer	01Ju02Aa	LEVERTON, Marianna		35	F	Servant	01Ju02Aa
Jane		60	F	None	01Ju02Aa	Emily	(D)	12	F	Servant	01Ju02Aa
James		20	M	Farmer	01Ju02Aa	Stephen	(S)	10	M	Servant	01Ju02Aa
Adam		15	M	Farmer	01Ju02Aa	GIGG, Wm.		22	M	Currier	01Ju02Aa
Andrews		15	M	Farmer	01Ju02Aa	Merla	(W)	23	F	Wife	01Ju02Aa
Thos.		13	M	Farmer	01Ju02Aa	Henry	(S)	03	M	Child	01Ju02Aa
LEWET, Robt.		25	M	Miner	01Ju02Aa	JONES, Henry		23	M	Wheelwright	01Ju02Aa
BROWN, Jonathan		25	M	Miner	01Ju02Aa	Mary		20	F	None	01Ju02Aa
BAKER, Wm.		35	M	Miner	01Ju02Aa	BROOK, Wm.		21	M	Grocer	01Ju02Aa
Sarah		62	F	None	01Ju02Aa	GOULDING, Patrick		24	M	Merchant	01Ju02Aa
BROWELL, John		34	M	Miner	01Ju02Aa	CONNERS, Richd.		40	M	Shepherd	01Ju02Aa
Christiana		30	F	None	01Ju02Aa	LUNEDER, John		24	M	Cooper	01Ju02Aa
CROSSGROVES, Thos.		30	M	Miner	01Ju02Aa	Georgianna		24	F	None	01Ju02Aa
Ellen	(W)	27	F	Wife	01Ju02Aa	Jane		20	F	None	01Ju02Aa
Elizth.	(D)	05	F	Child	01Ju02Aa	SMITH, John		20	M	Laborer	01Ju02Aa
Isabella	(D)	06	F	Child	01Ju02Aa	MCCHAN, John		20	M	Laborer	01Ju02Aa
Thos.	(S)	01	M	Child	01Ju02Aa	MARRIAN, James		24	M	Laborer	01Ju02Aa
BORDEN, Wm.		37	M	Miner	01Ju02Aa	MCGULLISON, Danl.		25	M	Laborer	01Ju02Aa
REED, Thomas		23	M	Miner	01Ju02Aa	WARD, Patrick		19	M	Laborer	01Ju02Aa
WILSON, Thomas		41	M	Miner	01Ju02Aa	DOLIN, Andrew		19	M	Laborer	01Ju02Aa
ORDEN, Robert		19	M	Miner	01Ju02Aa	COSSRONE, Thos.		22	M	Laborer	01Ju02Aa
BRIEN, Thomas		30	M	Laborer	01Ju02Aa	HOARNE, Bicy		17	F	Servant	01Ju02Aa
Peter		25	M	Laborer	01Ju02Aa	MURRAY, Cathrn.		18	F	Servant	01Ju02Aa
SULIVAN, Lawrie		25	M	Laborer	01Ju02Aa	HENRY, Henry		16	M	Laborer	01Ju02Aa
DIAMOND, Bessy		20	F	Servant	01Ju02Aa	MANN, Margret		27	F	Dressmaker	01Ju02Aa
Anne		23	F	Servant	01Ju02Aa	CONSK, Elizth.		24	F	Servant	01Ju02Aa
MCCAN, John		25	M	Baker	01Ju02Aa	Rose		16	F	Servant	01Ju02Aa
Catherine		21	F	None	01Ju02Aa	BUTLER, Cathrn.		20	F	Servant	01Ju02Aa
REILLY, Thomas		23	M	Laborer	01Ju02Aa	RICE, Owen		22	M	Laborer	01Ju02Aa
CONNIEKS, Abraham		25	M	Laborer	01Ju02Aa	Henry		18	M	Laborer	01Ju02Aa
JACKSON, James		30	M	Miner	01Ju02Aa	GLANCEY, John		19	M	Laborer	01Ju02Aa
Helen	(D)	04	F	Child	01Ju02Aa	DANLEY, Susan		19	F	Servant	01Ju02Aa
Lousira	(D)	03	F	Child	01Ju02Aa	MCLOUIS, Mary		18	F	Servant	01Ju02Aa
Henry	(S)	01	M	Child	01Ju02Aa	KENNY, Ann		15	F	Servant	01Ju02Aa
Carten	(W)	25	F	Wife	01Ju02Aa	MCGOWAN, Peter		20	M	Laborer	01Ju02Aa
CHAPPLE, Edward		29	M	Miner	01Ju02Aa	MCLOUDEY, Patrick		20	M	Laborer	01Ju02Aa
Caroline	(W)	27	F	Wife	01Ju02Aa	MCQUINLY, John		20	M	Laborer	01Ju02Aa
Wilim.	(S)	05	M	Child	01Ju02Aa	FALKARD, Charles		21	M	Laborer	01Ju02Aa
Andrew	(S)	01	M	Child	01Ju02Aa	KENNY, Patk.		21	M	Laborer	01Ju02Aa
BENSON, Hery		30	M	Miner	01Ju02Aa	CLARK, Barny		22	M	Laborer	01Ju02Aa
Marianna	(W)	25	F	Wife	01Ju02Aa	MCGINNISS, B.		23	M	Laborer	01Ju02Aa
Edwin	(S)	03	M	Child	01Ju02Aa	CHAMBERS, Mary		18	F	Servant	01Ju02Aa
Marianna	(D)	01	F	Child	01Ju02Aa	MCARNEY, Ann		27	F	Servant	01Ju02Aa
HELEN, Mary		12	F	None	01Ju02Aa	GAFF, John		25	M	Laborer	01Ju02Aa
ROWIE, John		30	M	Miner	01Ju02Aa	THOMPSON, John		27	M	Laborer	01Ju02Aa
Mary		36	F	None	01Ju02Aa	BURNS, Thos.		22	M	Painter	01Ju02Aa
FAY, James		45	M	Miner	01Ju02Aa	Sarah		20	F	None	01Ju02Aa
CHAPPEL, Henry		23	M	Miner	01Ju02Aa	MOLOCK, Bricget		30	F	Servant	01Ju02Aa
ARTHUR, Wm.		25	M	Miner	01Ju02Aa	MOOR, Andrew		24	M	Laborer	01Ju02Aa
Edwin		23	M	Miner	01Ju02Aa	Jane		21	F	None	01Ju02Aa
ROSS, Robert		28	M	Farmer	01Ju02Aa	PHILAN, Wm.		21	M	Clerk	01Ju02Aa
FOREST; John		38	M	Clerk	01Ju02Aa	Mary-Ann		20	F	None	01Ju02Aa
Ann	(W)	24	F	Wife	01Ju02Aa	HORNE, Patrick		26	M	Servant	01Ju02Aa
Sarah	(S)	01	F	Child	01Ju02Aa	FRUALL, John		40	M	Sailor	01Ju02Aa
MCALUNS, Patrick		06	M	Child	01Ju02Aa	MEEHAN, Mary		25	F	Servant	01Ju02Aa
MCCANN, Patrick		24	M	Baker	01Ju02Aa	MCLOUGHLIN, S.		24	M	Servant	01Ju02Aa
Margret	(W)	21	F	Wife	01Ju02Aa	DAY, Ann		18	F	None	01Ju02Aa
John	(S)	03	M	Child	01Ju02Aa	BELEK, Thos.		24	M	Laborer	01Ju02Aa
Marianna	(D)	01	F	Child	01Ju02Aa	MALONE, Thos.		21	M	Laborer	01Ju02Aa
NICHOL, Andrew		22	M	Joiner	01Ju02Aa	DUFFY, John		20	M	Laborer	01Ju02Aa
BARRONS, George		25	M	Painter	01Ju02Aa	DIAMOND, Mary		20	F	Laborer	01Ju02Aa
CROTHILL, Brian		29	M	Grocer	01Ju02Aa	QUINORL, Betty		24	F	None	01Ju02Aa
PIERCE, Eliza		18	F	Servant	01Ju02Aa	MURRY, Isabela		25	F	None	01Ju02Aa
MURPHY, Ellen		16	F	Servant	01Ju02Aa	CRUISE, John		18	M	Laborer	01Ju02Aa
HUDSON, George		52	M	Farmer	01Ju02Aa	Ellen		20	F	Servant	01Ju02Aa

NAMES OF PASSENGERS	AGE	SEX	OCCUPATIONS	DATE PORT SHIP
CUFF, James	40	M	Laborer	01Ju02Aa
NEWLAN, John	28	M	Groom	01Ju02Aa
Mary	21	F	None	
KEADHER, Wm.	30	M	Stctr	01Ju02Aa
Margret	27	F	None	01Ju02Aa
PODDER, Julia	18	F	Servant	01Ju02Aa
David	25	M	Gdnr	01Ju02Aa
Mary	21	F	None	01Ju02Aa
DAVIDSON, Wm.	32	M	Teacher	01Ju02Aa
Agnes	27	F	None	01Ju02Aa
James	40	M	Mason	01Ju02Aa
Jane	37	F	None	01Ju02Aa
Robert	08	M	Child	01Ju02Aa
Andrew	07	M	Child	01Ju02Aa
Isabella	04	F	Child	01Ju02Aa
Christian	03	M	Child	01Ju02Aa
William	01	M	Child	01Ju02Aa
ORBY, Wm.	30	M	Laborer	01Ju02Aa
Mary (W)	23	F	Wife	01Ju02Aa
Patrick (S)	01	M	Child	01Ju02Aa
SHEA, Frank	26	M	Servant	01Ju02Aa
Julia	24	F	Servant	01Ju02Aa
TOBAN, Cathrn.	29	F	Dressmaker	01Ju02Aa
DONOLY, Biddy	20	F	Servant	01Ju02Aa
GALAKER, Kitty	16	F	Servant	01Ju02Aa
BERRY, Patrick	25	M	Laborer	01Ju02Aa
MCGRETEN, John	51	M	Laborer	01Ju02Aa
MCDONALL, James	31	M	Laborer	01Ju02Aa
BLACKBURN, Richard	24	M	Farmer	01Ju02Aa
Matilda-H.	27	F	None	01Ju02Aa

MAINE 01 JUNE 1846

From Liverpool

NAMES OF PASSENGERS	AGE	SEX	OCCUPATIONS	DATE PORT SHIP
REYNOLDS, Edward	20	M	Laborer	01Ju02En
Died-At-Sea				
GILLROY, Michael	18	M	Laborer	01Ju02En
GANNING, John	24	M	Laborer	01Ju02En
CORNELIILS, John	24	M	Laborer	01Ju02En
HAGEN, Mary	23	F	None	01Ju02En
MANN, James	19	M	Laborer	01Ju02En
John	20	M	Laborer	01Ju02En
KAIN, Joseph	31	M	Carpenter	01Ju02En
John	27	M	Carpenter	01Ju02En
Anne	26	F	None	01Ju02En
Joseph-Jr.	03	M	Child	01Ju02En
MATHEW, Thomas	34	M	Laborer	01Ju02En
BRADY, Mary	21	F	None	01Ju02En
SMITH, Ellen	17	F	None	01Ju02En
Mary	18	F	None	01Ju02En
CONELL, Mary	19	F	None	01Ju02En
MAGUIRE, Edward	29	M	Farmer	01Ju02En
SMITH, Peter	27	M	Farmer	01Ju02En
DONOCHE, Owen	30	M	Farmer	01Ju02En
BRADY, James	21	M	Farmer	01Ju02En
NELSON, Bernard	20	M	Farmer	01Ju02En
BRADY, Edward	19	M	Farmer	01Ju02En
FARDY, Michael	44	M	Farmer	01Ju02En
Thomas	21	M	Farmer	01Ju02En
John	13	M	Farmer	01Ju02En
Elvie	19	F	None	01Ju02En
Anne	15	F	None	01Ju02En
Catherine	12	F	None	01Ju02En
Sisley	07	F	Child	01Ju02En
Patrick	30	M	Farmer	01Ju02En
Catharine	20	F	None	01Ju02En
Marie	06	F	Child	01Ju02En
Anne	05	F	Child	01Ju02En
FARDY, John	01	M	Child	01Ju02En
Died-At-Sea				
MILKENE, Catharine	25	F	None	01Ju02En
ROWLEY, Anne	21	F	None	01Ju02En
KALLARGH, John	26	M	Laborer	01Ju02En
CARLES, David	35	M	Laborer	01Ju02En
DOWNEY, James	22	M	Laborer	01Ju02En
MULLAN, Mathew	28	M	Weaver	01Ju02En
MCGRANE, Patrick	30	M	Laborer	01Ju02En
MCCORMICK, John	25	M	Laborer	01Ju02En
Jane	30	F	None	01Ju02En
Thomas	03	M	Child	01Ju02En
Lawrence	20	M	None	01Ju02En
Catharine	01	F	Child	01Ju02En
Marie	14	F	None	01Ju02En
Thomas	13	M	None	01Ju02En
MOWBRAY, Margaret	50	F	None	01Ju02En
Margaret-Jr. (D)	16	F	None	01Ju02En
Thomas-H. (S)	09	M	Child	01Ju02En
MITCHELL, James	35	M	Grocer	01Ju02En
HAWTHORN, David	12	M	None	01Ju02En
DEVLIN, Hugh	21	M	Farmer	01Ju02En
ELEXANDER, Samuel	22	M	Farmer	01Ju02En
MOWBRAY, Oliver	25	M	Wimcht	01Ju02En
CAVNAUGH, Thomas	22	M	Laborer	01Ju02En
CASTLE, Catharine	20	F	None	01Ju02En
MCLAULIN, Bridget	60	F	None	01Ju02En
KING, Bridget	12	F	None	01Ju02En
NICHOLS, Patrick	30	M	None	01Ju02En
GILLHOULEY, John	25	M	Farmer	01Ju02En
FALLEN, Bridget	20	F	None	01Ju02En
GILLHUNEY, Anne	20	F	None	01Ju02En
HALEY, Owen	24	M	Farmer	01Ju02En
BATES, Charles	22	M	Grocer	01Ju02En
MCCONELL, Oliver	22	M	Farmer	01Ju02En
MCCABE, Joseph	22	M	Carpenter	01Ju02En
BATES, Ruth	20	F	None	01Ju02En
ERICE, Nancy	20	F	None	01Ju02En
HILL, Elviebeth	30	F	None	01Ju02En
MASTERSON, James	26	M	Weaver	01Ju02En
FANNER, Henry	26	M	Weaver	01Ju02En
DERMONT, Michael	26	M	Laborer	01Ju02En
HALFPENY, James	26	M	Laborer	01Ju02En
MCANROE, Anne	21	F	None	01Ju02En
CARLL, Mary	26	F	None	01Ju02En
MCANROE, James	01	M	Child	01Ju02En
MCLAULIN, Domnick	35	M	Farmer	01Ju02En
COSTELOW, John	28	M	Laborer	01Ju02En
CLANLIN, Patrick	25	M	Laborer	01Ju02En
MORIN, Michael	45	M	Laborer	01Ju02En
CUNINGHAM, John	22	M	Laborer	01Ju02En
MARTIN, Patrick	21	M	Laborer	01Ju02En
CAMPBELL, Patrick	26	M	Laborer	01Ju02En
Mary	56	F	None	01Ju02En
Catherine	18	F	None	01Ju02En
MARKY, Jane	30	F	None	01Ju02En
KELLY, Margaret	30	F	None	01Ju02En
Bridget (D)	01	F	Child	01Ju02En
TOOLE, Elizabeth (W)	22	F	Wife	01Ju02En
Patrick (S)	04	M	Child	01Ju02En
HUDSON, Michael	28	M	Laborer	01Ju02En
John	48	M	Laborer	01Ju02En
HENRY, John	28	M	Laborer	01Ju02En
DARVILLE, Patrick	23	M	Laborer	01Ju02En
BANHEUTER, Patrick	22	M	Laborer	01Ju02En
CAIN, Nancy	20	F	None	01Ju02En
KILLEEN, James	21	M	Laborer	01Ju02En
GILLIGHEN, Michael	22	M	Laborer	01Ju02En
HALLIGEN, William	23	M	Laborer	01Ju02En
WILSON, Daniel	17	M	Laborer	01Ju02En
WILLIAMS, William	40	M	Laborer	01Ju02En
Bridget (W)	30	F	Wife	01Ju02En
Ellen (D)	10	F	None	01Ju02En
Bridget (D)	07	F	Child	01Ju02En
DENAHOE, Catharine	09	F	Child	01Ju02En

NAMES OF PASSENGERS		AGE	SEX	OCCUPATIONS	DATE PORT SHIP
WILSON, David		19	M	None	01Ju02En
William		36	M	Fisherman	01Ju02En
William-Jr.		21	M	Fisherman	01Ju02En
PARKE, John		19	M	Farmer	01Ju02En
WILSON, Catharine		55	F	None	01Ju02En
ASEDELL, John		28	M	Weaver	01Ju02En
David		19	M	Farmer	01Ju02En
Mary		32	F	None	01Ju02En
Mary-J.		10	F	None	01Ju02En
Mary-A.		02	F	Child	01Ju02En
KINARY, Mary		12	F	None	01Ju02En
KEEHAGEN, Martin		28	M	Tailor	01Ju02En
MARTIN, Peter		26	M	Laborer	01Ju02En
FAGEN, Thomas		24	M	Laborer	01Ju02En
KEEHAGEN, Michael		15	M	Laborer	01Ju02En
KILLEEN, Margaret	(D)	16	F	None	01Ju02En
Hanah	(D)	18	F	None	01Ju02En
MANION, Ellinor		21	F	None	01Ju02En
SLAVIN, Ellen		21	F	None	01Ju02En
BRANAN, Mary		18	F	None	01Ju02En
Catharine		17	F	None	01Ju02En
MAHAN, Margaret		18	F	None	01Ju02En
HAGEN, Mary		25	F	None	01Ju02En
FANEN, Malachy		10	M	None	01Ju02En
Margaret		08	F	Child	01Ju02En
DOUGHETY, James		30	M	Laborer	01Ju02En
Patrick		26	M	Laborer	01Ju02En
KELLY, Patrick		24	M	Laborer	01Ju02En
FAGEN, John		19	M	Laborer	01Ju02En
Mary	(M)	53	F	None	01Ju02En
Michael		21	M	Laborer	01Ju02En
Mathew		10	M	Laborer	01Ju02En
Jane		25	F	None	01Ju02En
KILROY, Mathias		40	M	Laborer	01Ju02En
Bridget	(W)	42	F	Wife	01Ju02En
Hanah	(D)	12	F	None	01Ju02En
Mary	(D)	10	F	None	01Ju02En
Michael	(S)	08	M	Child	01Ju02En
John	(S)	06	M	Child	01Ju02En
Mathew	(S)	03	M	Child	01Ju02En
Died-At-Sea					
Sarah	(D)	01	F	Child	01Ju02En
MANNAN, John		21	M	None	01Ju02En
COSTELOW, Mary		18	F	None	01Ju02En
COYLA, Dafna		25	F	None	01Ju02En
KEELEN, Mary		18	F	None	01Ju02En
DONOLY, Mary		32	F	None	01Ju02En
OBRIEN, Isabella		32	F	None	01Ju02En
Mary	(D)	12	F	None	01Ju02En
Catharine	(D)	10	F	None	01Ju02En
John	(S)	06	M	Child	01Ju02En
Sarah	(D)	03	F	Child	01Ju02En
Susan	(D)	02	F	Child	01Ju02En
ORR, Thomas		20	M	Carpenter	01Ju02En
CAMPBELL, Thomas		19	M	Laborer	01Ju02En
MCFLINN, Edward		17	M	Laborer	01Ju02En
Arthur		26	M	Laborer	01Ju02En
CUNINGHAM, James		19	M	Laborer	01Ju02En
MCCIUGH, William		19	M	Laborer	01Ju02En
MINOR, Anne	(W)	21	F	Wife	01Ju02En
Ellen	(D)	01	F	Child	01Ju02En
MCGARDE, Anne		20	F	None	01Ju02En
MCQUILLEN, Catharine		18	F	None	01Ju02En
DONOLLE, Margaret		19	F	None	01Ju02En
TRAINER, Rosana		20	F	None	01Ju02En
MCQUILLIN, Mary		22	F	None	01Ju02En
THORNTON, James		20	M	Laborer	01Ju02En
Patrick		40	M	Laborer	01Ju02En
Mary		35	F	None	01Ju02En
John		01	M	Child	01Ju02En
VAUGHAN, James		25	M	Laborer	01Ju02En
Patrick		24	M	Laborer	01Ju02En
Catharine		30	F	None	01Ju02En
Thomas		06	M	Child	01Ju02En
John		03	M	Child	01Ju02En

NAMES OF PASSENGERS		AGE	SEX	OCCUPATIONS	DATE PORT SHIP
LAUDA, Adam		25	M	Laborer	01Ju02En
DONEGAN, Michael		17	M	Laborer	01Ju02En
MCCORMICK, Patrick		20	M	Laborer	01Ju02En
HADEN, Patrick		25	M	Laborer	01Ju02En
Michael		22	M	Laborer	01Ju02En
MCADAM, Andr.		28	M	Laborer	01Ju02En
GROGEN, Bernard		20	M	Carpenter	01Ju02En
MCADAM, Mary		22	F	None	01Ju02En
GLESHAN, Michael		25	M	Shoemaker	01Ju02En
MCCAINE, James		26	M	Laborer	01Ju02En
MCCAN, Patrick		26	M	Laborer	01Ju02En
MCARDLE, Mary		18	F	None	01Ju02En
BRANIGAN, Catherine		17	F	None	01Ju02En
HANA, Catherine		20	F	None	01Ju02En
EIGEN, John		32	M	Laborer	01Ju02En
FITZSIMONS, Peter		23	M	Weaver	01Ju02En
GATELY, Winow		24	F	None	01Ju02En
MANIN, Elvia		22	F	None	01Ju02En
GAFNY, Michael		32	M	Laborer	01Ju02En
JUDGE, Thomas		23	M	Laborer	01Ju02En
WELCH, Patrick		28	M	Blacksmith	01Ju02En
CURABY, Thomas		25	M	Laborer	01Ju02En
BRANAN, Thomas		21	M	Laborer	01Ju02En
RATCHFORD, John		26	M	Laborer	01Ju02En
James		20	M	Laborer	01Ju02En
KELLY, Joseph		25	M	Laborer	01Ju02En
HALEY, James		25	M	Laborer	01Ju02En
CAIN, Michael		26	M	Laborer	01Ju02En
HAAR, Mark		30	M	Laborer	01Ju02En
Mary		22	F	None	01Ju02En
CONNER, Margaret		30	F	None	01Ju02En
MCKIM, Margaret		21	F	None	01Ju02En
Bridget		17	F	None	01Ju02En
LYME, Margaret		21	F	None	01Ju02En
HALEY, Hanah		30	F	None	01Ju02En
FLANIGEN, Juda		35	F	None	01Ju02En
GALLIGHER, Daniel		30	M	Tailor	01Ju02En
WALKER, Stephen		22	M	Laborer	01Ju02En
James		20	M	Weaver	01Ju02En
Catherine		20	F	None	01Ju02En
ROWAN, Samuel		23	M	Weaver	01Ju02En
MCKEE, Dianah		18	F	None	01Ju02En
GALLGHER, Margaret		22	F	None	01Ju02En

JOHN-ROBERT 01 JUNE 1846

From Liverpool

NAMES OF PASSENGERS		AGE	SEX	OCCUPATIONS	DATE PORT SHIP
DEVLIN, Andrew		25	M	Laborer	01Ju02Eq
TOMARRY, Edward		25	M	Laborer	01Ju02Eq
Susan		19	F	Laborer	01Ju02Eq
MOONEY, Mary-Ann		20	F	Laborer	01Ju02Eq
HARRISON, Edward		30	M	Laborer	01Ju02Eq
Ellen		20	F	Laborer	01Ju02Eq
RIVETS, Mary-Ann		36	F	Laborer	01Ju02Eq
BOYCE, John		30	M	Laborer	01Ju02Eq
Robert		20	M	Laborer	01Ju02Eq
KIM, Denis		25	M	Laborer	01Ju02Eq
GALBRAITH, William		28	M	Laborer	01Ju02Eq
Sarah		28	F	Laborer	01Ju02Eq
Martha		58	F	Laborer	01Ju02Eq
Mary		30	F	Laborer	01Ju02Eq
Martha		02	F	Child	01Ju02Eq
Ann		.06	F	Infant	01Ju02Eq
RUSSELL, William		21	M	Laborer	01Ju02Eq
CAMPBELL, Robert		18	M	Laborer	01Ju02Eq
HEAREY, Daniel		27	M	Laborer	01Ju02Eq
Ann	(W)	25	F	Wife	01Ju02Eq
James	(S)	03	M	Child	01Ju02Eq

NAMES OF PASSENGERS		AGE	SEX	OCCUPATIONS	DATE PORT SHIP
HEAREY, Grace	(D)	02	F	Child	01Ju02Eq
ORR, James		40	M	Laborer	01Ju02Eq
James	(S)	20	M	Laborer	01Ju02Eq
John	(S)	18	M	Laborer	01Ju02Eq
Nancy	(D)	17	F	Laborer	01Ju02Eq
REGAN, John		23	M	Laborer	01Ju02Eq
Martha		20	F	Laborer	01Ju02Eq
Joseph		20	M	Laborer	01Ju02Eq
MCKAY, John		20	M	Laborer	01Ju02Eq
PATTERSON, James		28	M	Laborer	01Ju02Eq
Ellizabeth		25	F	Laborer	01Ju02Eq
Joseph		26	M	Laborer	01Ju02Eq
John		05	M	Child	01Ju02Eq
James		04	M	Child	01Ju02Eq
Joseph		01	M	Child	01Ju02Eq
DOGHERTY, Charlotte		20	F	Laborer	01Ju02Eq
JAMISON, Hannah		20	F	Laborer	01Ju02Eq
SCOTT, John		22	M	Laborer	01Ju02Eq
BENNETT, Arthur		25	M	Laborer	01Ju02Eq
Margaret		18	F	Laborer	01Ju02Eq
Martha		17	F	Laborer	01Ju02Eq
Hugh		01	M	Child	01Ju02Eq
James		18	M	Laborer	01Ju02Eq
DILLON, Robert		30	M	Laborer	01Ju02Eq
Agnes		29	F	Laborer	01Ju02Eq
MURPHY, Hugh		28	M	Laborer	01Ju02Eq
Mary		20	F	Laborer	01Ju02Eq
DONALDSON, Elizabeth		24	F	Laborer	01Ju02Eq
BENNETT, Sarah		09	F	Child	01Ju02Eq
SCULLEN, James		24	M	Laborer	01Ju02Eq
Biddy	(W)	20	F	Wife	01Ju02Eq
Jane	(D)	.00	F	Infant	01Ju02Eq
Michael		20	M	Laborer	01Ju02Eq
Elizabeth		20	F	Laborer	01Ju02Eq
AGNEW, Robert		22	M	Laborer	01Ju02Eq
TAGGART, Archibald		21	M	Laborer	01Ju02Eq
BANLAY, Ann-J.		20	F	Laborer	01Ju02Eq
Mary		14	F	Laborer	01Ju02Eq
JACKSON, Hugh		22	M	Laborer	01Ju02Eq
DINSMORE, Henry		25	M	Laborer	01Ju02Eq
HASKETT, William		26	M	Laborer	01Ju02Eq
WALLACE, Elizth.		22	F	Laborer	01Ju02Eq
CULLY, Biddy		40	F	Laborer	01Ju02Eq
William	(S)	11	M	Laborer	01Ju02Eq
GLOVER, John		20	M	Laborer	01Ju02Eq
GRAHAM, William		22	M	Laborer	01Ju02Eq
MATHEWS, Thomas		35	M	Laborer	01Ju02Eq
BRADLEY, William		40	M	Laborer	01Ju02Eq
John		20	M	Laborer	01Ju02Eq
Sarah		17	F	Laborer	01Ju02Eq
COCKPRANE, James		46	M	Laborer	01Ju02Eq
Betty		29	F	Laborer	01Ju02Eq
Robert		17	M	Laborer	01Ju02Eq
AGNEW, William		20	M	Laborer	01Ju02Eq
CASSADY, Francis		40	M	Laborer	01Ju02Eq
Sarah		25	F	Laborer	01Ju02Eq
GRAY, Hugh		33	M	Laborer	01Ju02Eq
Ann		29	F	Laborer	01Ju02Eq
MCEVERY, P.		18	M	Laborer	01Ju02Eq
KILLEN, Ann		40	F	Laborer	01Ju02Eq
MCCULLOGH, Betty		20	F	Laborer	01Ju02Eq
Rebecca		14	F	Laborer	01Ju02Eq
COLLIER, Thos.		32	M	Laborer	01Ju02Eq
Ann-Jane	(W)	30	F	Wife	01Ju02Eq
Thomas	(S)	.06	M	Infant	01Ju02Eq
HILL, Hugh		31	M	Laborer	01Ju02Eq
Ann-Jane	(W)	23	F	Wife	01Ju02Eq
E.J.	(D)	08	F	Child	01Ju02Eq
Joseph	(S)	06	M	Child	01Ju02Eq
MURPHY, Joseph		25	M	Laborer	01Ju02Eq
Jane	(W)	28	F	Wife	01Ju02Eq
Fanny	(D)	08	F	Child	01Ju02Eq
Margaret	(D)	06	F	Child	01Ju02Eq
Jane	(D)	04	F	Child	01Ju02Eq
Sarah	(D)	.02	F	Infant	01Ju02Eq
NEILLY, Mary		30	F	Laborer	01Ju02Eq
KANE, Cathne.		21	F	Laborer	01Ju02Eq
MCCANN, Nancy		25	F	Laborer	01Ju02Eq
GIBSON, Robert		24	M	Laborer	01Ju02Eq
JOHNSTON, John		24	M	Laborer	01Ju02Eq
MULLIGAN, Jane		22	F	Laborer	01Ju02Eq
AGNEW, Robert		26	M	Laborer	01Ju02Eq
MCMASTER, Thomas		21	M	Laborer	01Ju02Eq
CAMPBELL, Hugh		21	M	Laborer	01Ju02Eq
May	(W)	21	F	Wife	01Ju02Eq
John	(S)	01	M	Child	01Ju02Eq
LAMB, Danl.		36	M	Laborer	01Ju02Eq
Mary-Ann		28	F	Laborer	01Ju02Eq
MONTGOMERY, Rebecca		19	F	Laborer	01Ju02Eq
STEPHENSON, Mary-Ann		18	F	Laborer	01Ju02Eq
KENNEDY, Rose		21	F	Laborer	01Ju02Eq
James	(S)	01	M	Child	01Ju02Eq
DURHAM, Richard		21	M	Laborer	01Ju02Eq
NEILL, F.Ann		21	F	Laborer	01Ju02Eq
DURHAM, Thomas		21	M	Laborer	01Ju02Eq
MCQUILKAN, Henry		21	M	Laborer	01Ju02Eq
William		19	M	Laborer	01Ju02Eq
ADAMS, Robert		60	M	Laborer	01Ju02Eq
Margaret		30	F	Laborer	01Ju02Eq
DALEY, Thomas		19	M	Laborer	01Ju02Eq
HIGGINS, Charles		18	M	Laborer	01Ju02Eq
MCNALLY, Cathne.		18	F	Laborer	01Ju02Eq
AGNEW, John		18	M	Laborer	01Ju02Eq
Rose	(W)	20	F	Wife	01Ju02Eq
Mary-Ann	(D)	.07	F	Infant	01Ju02Eq
LYONS, Joseph		21	M	Laborer	01Ju02Eq
FULTON, Joseph		26	M	Laborer	01Ju02Eq
DONNELLY, James		24	M	Laborer	01Ju02Eq
MCBRIDE, Henry		30	M	Laborer	01Ju02Eq
GORMLEY, Henry		28	M	Laborer	01Ju02Eq
DALEY, Michl.		19	M	Laborer	01Ju02Eq
John		21	M	Laborer	01Ju02Eq
TAGGART, Mary		24	F	Laborer	01Ju02Eq
MCSHANE, Mary		21	F	Laborer	01Ju02Eq
CONROY, John		26	M	Laborer	01Ju02Eq
MURRAY, Patrick		22	M	Laborer	01Ju02Eq
MCHENRY, Joseph		25	M	Laborer	01Ju02Eq
ALISON, Margt.		17	F	Laborer	01Ju02Eq
WALLACE, Sarah		19	F	Laborer	01Ju02Eq
BYRNE, Wm.		20	M	Laborer	01Ju02Eq
MURPHY, James		26	M	Laborer	01Ju02Eq
DOYLE, Mary		30	F	Laborer	01Ju02Eq
ROWE, Maria		30	F	Laborer	01Ju02Eq
THOMPSON, Rebecca		20	F	Laborer	01Ju02Eq
DAVIS, Amelia		20	F	Laborer	01Ju02Eq
COULTER, John		25	M	Laborer	01Ju02Eq
Elizabeth		27	F	Laborer	01Ju02Eq
TAYLOR, Valentine		38	M	Laborer	01Ju02Eq
CABET, James		17	M	Laborer	01Ju02Eq
MOLLOY, Patrick		13	M	Laborer	01Ju02Eq
Michael		13	M	Laborer	01Ju02Eq
Mary		12	F	Laborer	01Ju02Eq
LONG, Ann-Jane		19	F	Laborer	01Ju02Eq
CUNAY, Martha		66	F	Laborer	01Ju02Eq
John		40	M	Laborer	01Ju02Eq
Mary		40	F	Laborer	01Ju02Eq
Sarah		19	F	Laborer	01Ju02Eq
Joseph		17	M	Laborer	01Ju02Eq
MCKAY, Thos.		15	M	Laborer	01Ju02Eq
CUNAY, William		14	M	Laborer	01Ju02Eq
Eliza		12	F	Laborer	01Ju02Eq
Thos.		10	M	Laborer	01Ju02Eq
Mary-Jane		09	F	Child	01Ju02Eq
Samuel		07	M	Child	01Ju02Eq
COLEMAN, Agnes		04	F	Child	01Ju02Eq
Margaret		50	F	Laborer	01Ju02Eq
Robert		26	M	Laborer	01Ju02Eq
CUNAY, Jane		25	F	Laborer	01Ju02Eq
Jane		23	F	Laborer	01Ju02Eq
Henry		24	M	Laborer	01Ju02Eq

NAMES OF PASSENGERS		AGE	SEX	OCCUPATIONS	DATE PORT SHIP
CUNAY, Agnes		21	F	Laborer	01Ju02Eq
Ellen		19	F	Laborer	01Ju02Eq
Charlotte		16	F	Laborer	01Ju02Eq
Sarah		13	F	Laborer	01Ju02Eq
Nancy		13	F	Laborer	01Ju02Eq
William		10	M	Laborer	01Ju02Eq
Martha		05	F	Child	01Ju02Eq
KEATING, Thomas		20	M	Laborer	01Ju02Eq
CURREN, Andrew		20	M	Laborer	01Ju02Eq
CARSON, Thomas		50	M	Laborer	01Ju02Eq
Mary	(W)	50	F	Wife	01Ju02Eq
Francis	(S)	18	M	Laborer	01Ju02Eq
Daniel	(S)	14	M	Laborer	01Ju02Eq
Isabella	(D)	13	F	Laborer	01Ju02Eq
Patrick	(S)	08	M	Child	01Ju02Eq
Jane	(D)	10	F	Child	01Ju02Eq
TOBIAS, Thomas		50	M	Laborer	01Ju02Eq
John		17	M	Laborer	01Ju02Eq
Elizabeth		13	F	Laborer	01Ju02Eq
GUTTREE, Ann-Jane		18	F	Laborer	01Ju02Eq
TOBIAS, Daniel		11	M	Laborer	01Ju02Eq
Mary-Jane		09	F	Child	01Ju02Eq
PRITCHARD, Thomas		28	M	Laborer	01Ju02Eq
Sally		24	F	Laborer	01Ju02Eq
Robert		18	M	Laborer	01Ju02Eq
James		.00	M	Infant	01Ju02Eq
MORELAND, William		20	M	Laborer	01Ju02Eq
DOUGHTY, John		18	M	Laborer	01Ju02Eq
NEILSON, Nathl.		18	M	Laborer	01Ju02Eq

FIDELIA 01 JUNE 1846

From Liverpool

NAMES OF PASSENGERS		AGE	SEX	OCCUPATIONS	DATE PORT SHIP
FALLEN, Edward		40	M	Laborer	01Ju02Ax
DUNN, Thos.		35	M	Laborer	01Ju02Ax
RYAN, Thos.		25	M	Laborer	01Ju02Ax
MCCARTY, Jas.		21	M	Laborer	01Ju02Ax
FARRAL, Edward		36	M	Laborer	01Ju02Ax
Cathe.	(W)	29	F	Wife	01Ju02Ax
Bryan	(S)	10	M	Child	01Ju02Ax
MANNINGTON, Matthew		28	M	Laborer	01Ju02Ax
MCCARTY, Judy		19	F	Laborer	01Ju02Ax
FALREY, Morris		22	M	Laborer	01Ju02Ax
DOWNEY, Margt.		18	F	Laborer	01Ju02Ax
HANAN, Jno.		23	M	Laborer	01Ju02Ax
GAGAN, Henry		21	M	Laborer	01Ju02Ax
NIXON, Cathe.		23	F	Laborer	01Ju02Ax
RUSH, Mary		26	F	Laborer	01Ju02Ax
Jno.	(S)	05	M	Child	01Ju02Ax
COLIGHAN, Mary		21	F	Laborer	01Ju02Ax
MANASIAN, Michl.		23	M	Musician	01Ju02Ax
MCDURMOT, Eliza		26	F	Laborer	01Ju02Ax
CARMIT, Michl.		25	M	Laborer	01Ju02Ax
GROGAN, Ellen		55	F	Laborer	01Ju02Ax
Mary		20	F	Laborer	01Ju02Ax
DALTON, Edwd.		00	M	Laborer	01Ju02Ax
MCBORLEY, Cathe.		20	F	Laborer	01Ju02Ax
MCCABE, Mary		45	F	Laborer	01Ju02Ax
Mary	(D)	18	F	Laborer	01Ju02Ax
Margt.	(D)	09	F	Child	01Ju02Ax
Thos.	(S)	01	M	Child	01Ju02Ax
KAGLIN, Mary		17	F	Laborer	01Ju02Ax
FITZGERALD, Margt.		28	F	Laborer	01Ju02Ax
KINNEN, Robt.		21	M	Laborer	01Ju02Ax
FIELD, Christn.		25	M	Baker	01Ju02Ax
BRODY, Betty		40	F	Laborer	01Ju02Ax
GARETY, Peter		16	M	Laborer	01Ju02Ax
MOORE, Bridget		21	F	Laborer	01Ju02Ax

NAMES OF PASSENGERS		AGE	SEX	OCCUPATIONS	DATE PORT SHIP
CARR, Cathe.		23	F	Laborer	01Ju02Ax
HAGAN, Danl.		20	M	Laborer	01Ju02Ax
TRACY, Patt		09	M	Child	01Ju02Ax
DEA, Jno.		29	M	Laborer	01Ju02Ax
Bridget		25	F	Laborer	01Ju02Ax
Margt.		20	F	Laborer	01Ju02Ax
HYMAN, Henry		30	M	Laborer	01Ju02Ax
MULLIGAN, Thos.		13	M	Tanner	01Ju02Ax
HUGHES, Thos.		40	M	Painter	01Ju02Ax
Jane	(W)	37	F	Wife	01Ju02Ax
Jno.	(S)	17	M	None	01Ju02Ax
James	(S)	13	M	None	01Ju02Ax
Marion	(D)	08	F	Child	01Ju02Ax
Thos.	(S)	04	M	Child	01Ju02Ax
KELLY, James		28	M	Laborer	01Ju02Ax
Joseph		25	M	Laborer	01Ju02Ax
PRATT, Thos.		19	M	Laborer	01Ju02Ax
CHARTERS, Mary		23	F	Laborer	01Ju02Ax
David	(S)	01	M	Child	01Ju02Ax
GAFFENY, Viney		17	M	Laborer	01Ju02Ax
STAFFORD, Wm.		21	M	Laborer	01Ju02Ax
Cathe.		18	F	Laborer	01Ju02Ax
FITZSIMMONS, Jno.		22	M	Laborer	01Ju02Ax
MURPHY, Barnard		25	M	Laborer	01Ju02Ax
DONOLLY, Eliza		22	F	Laborer	01Ju02Ax
CARLIN, Mary		22	F	Laborer	01Ju02Ax
MEA, Jno.		23	M	Laborer	01Ju02Ax
Mary	(W)	22	F	Wife	01Ju02Ax
James	(S)	.07	M	Infant	01Ju02Ax
HAGEN, Jno.		00	M	Laborer	01Ju02Ax
BRYAN, Michl.		20	M	Laborer	01Ju02Ax
Patt		17	M	Laborer	01Ju02Ax
CARLEY, Jno.		17	M	Laborer	01Ju02Ax
BURN, Frank		22	M	Laborer	01Ju02Ax
FINN, Patt		21	M	Laborer	01Ju02Ax
BROPHY, Martin		21	M	Laborer	01Ju02Ax
CARROL, Judy		17	F	Laborer	01Ju02Ax
DELAY, Mary		16	F	Laborer	01Ju02Ax
CASSIDAY, Jno.		19	M	Laborer	01Ju02Ax
AGEN, Jno.		19	M	Laborer	01Ju02Ax
Ann		21	F	Laborer	01Ju02Ax
WELSH, Patt		25	M	Laborer	01Ju02Ax
KEIGAN, Barney		21	M	Laborer	01Ju02Ax
KAIGAN, Jno.		21	M	Laborer	01Ju02Ax
DOWLING, James		20	M	Laborer	01Ju02Ax
RAMSBOTTOM, Jno.		19	M	Laborer	01Ju02Ax
DANE, Thim		21	M	Laborer	01Ju02Ax
KALBORD, Bridget		17	F	Laborer	01Ju02Ax
WELSH, Mary-A.		18	F	Laborer	01Ju02Ax
WALL, Mary		16	F	Laborer	01Ju02Ax
KARAS, Mary		16	F	Laborer	01Ju02Ax
PENDERGAST, Susan		19	F	Laborer	01Ju02Ax
B.		15	F	Laborer	01Ju02Ax
MCDONALD, Cathe.		20	F	Laborer	01Ju02Ax
CONWAY, Jno.		24	M	Sawer	01Ju02Ax
MATTHEWS, Judy		21	F	Sawer	01Ju02Ax
Ann		19	F	Sawer	01Ju02Ax
MOLLYN, Margt.		20	F	Sawer	01Ju02Ax
MCDONALD, Jno.		21	M	Mason	01Ju02Ax
Jane		20	F	Mason	01Ju02Ax
Edwd.		09	M	Child	01Ju02Ax
MATTHEWS, Jno.		17	M	Laborer	01Ju02Ax
CARLEY, Jane		22	F	Laborer	01Ju02Ax
CARMEN, Danl.		24	M	Laborer	01Ju02Ax
Biddy		20	F	Laborer	01Ju02Ax
QUINN, Mary		15	F	Laborer	01Ju02Ax
Micl.		12	M	Laborer	01Ju02Ax
DUKE, Jno.		13	M	Laborer	01Ju02Ax
Eliza		10	F	Laborer	01Ju02Ax
FAGAN, Mic.		18	M	Laborer	01Ju02Ax
SMITH, Kate		25	F	Tailor	01Ju02Ax
MCCARROL, Mary		22	F	Tailor	01Ju02Ax
GARETY, Michl.		15	M	Tailor	01Ju02Ax
MARTIN, Rose		21	F	Tailor	01Ju02Ax
OHALLORAN, Ann		19	F	Tailor	01Ju02Ax

NAMES OF PASSENGERS		AGE	SEX	OCCUPATIONS	DATE PORT SHIP
ONIELL, Margt.		21	F	Tailor	01Ju02Ax
Bridget		14	F	Tailor	01Ju02Ax
MCKANOR, Barnard		24	M	Tailor	01Ju02Ax
Ann		23	F	Tailor	01Ju02Ax
BAYLEY, Wm.		19	M	Tailor	01Ju02Ax
Robt.		22	M	Tailor	01Ju02Ax
HORN, Thos.		22	M	Boatmaker	01Ju02Ax
Biddy		23	F	Boatmaker	01Ju02Ax
DAVISON, Joseph		18	M	Laborer	01Ju02Ax
MORRIS, James		20	M	Weaver	01Ju02Ax
Kate		20	F	Weaver	01Ju02Ax
ANDERSON, Elizth.		21	F	Weaver	01Ju02Ax
MCGOAY, Teddy		32	M	Laborer	01Ju02Ax
James	(S)	07	M	Child	01Ju02Ax
FARROL, Tim		16	M	Laborer	01Ju02Ax
GANNON, Bridget		27	F	Laborer	01Ju02Ax
Judy		40	F	Laborer	01Ju02Ax
James		03	M	Child	01Ju02Ax
Christn.		02	M	Child	01Ju02Ax
Marla		.06	F	Infant	01Ju02Ax
GIDNEY, Jno.		20	M	Laborer	01Ju02Ax
RUDY, Pat		28	M	Laborer	01Ju02Ax
Margt.		32	F	Laborer	01Ju02Ax
KALEY, Wm.		27	M	Carpenter	01Ju02Ax
CONNELL, Mary		25	F	Carpenter	01Ju02Ax
Marla	(D)	02	F	Child	01Ju02Ax
MCCAFFERY, Mary		12	F	Carpenter	01Ju02Ax
HARVEY, Hugh		24	M	Laborer	01Ju02Ax
Mary		19	F	Laborer	01Ju02Ax
OBRIAN, Danl.		19	M	Laborer	01Ju02Ax
Ellen		17	F	Laborer	01Ju02Ax
Jane		16	F	Laborer	01Ju02Ax
DAGHON, Ellen		13	F	Laborer	01Ju02Ax
FARNON, Mary		20	F	Laborer	01Ju02Ax
GARVEN, Kate		21	F	Laborer	01Ju02Ax
Honr.		12	F	Laborer	01Ju02Ax
CALLERY, Mary		15	F	Laborer	01Ju02Ax
FIELDING, Bridget		18	F	Laborer	01Ju02Ax
MURPHY, Biddy		16	F	Laborer	01Ju02Ax
DUNNIGAN, Kate		19	F	Laborer	01Ju02Ax
CUNNINGHAM, Mary		23	F	Laborer	01Ju02Ax
MOLYN, Mary		14	F	Laborer	01Ju02Ax
DUGAN, Jane		21	F	Laborer	01Ju02Ax
LOGAN, Mary		16	F	Laborer	01Ju02Ax
SMITH, Hester		25	F	Laborer	01Ju02Ax
Alexr.	(S)	05	M	Child	01Ju02Ax
Page-Jane	(D)	.03	F	Infant	01Ju02Ax
Basey-Ann	(D)	01	F	Child	01Ju02Ax
GAHAGEN, Pat		25	M	Laborer	01Ju02Ax
Peter		60	M	Laborer	01Ju02Ax
HARVEY, Ann		16	F	Laborer	01Ju02Ax
DORLEY, Ann		15	F	Laborer	01Ju02Ax
VALENTINE, Saml.		25	M	Laborer	01Ju02Ax
FAGEN, Matthew		24	M	Laborer	01Ju02Ax
Biddy		18	F	Laborer	01Ju02Ax
KENNEDY, Jno.		22	M	Laborer	01Ju02Ax
DAKERY, Jno.		22	M	Laborer	01Ju02Ax
FURNON, Jas.		37	M	Laborer	01Ju02Ax
Dany		26	M	Laborer	01Ju02Ax
Mary	(D)	02	F	Child	01Ju02Ax
Margt.	(D)	06	F	Child	01Ju02Ax
FLANNAGIN, Mary		18	F	Laborer	01Ju02Ax
HADEN, Ann		18	F	Laborer	01Ju02Ax
DUFFY, Mic.		26	M	Laborer	01Ju02Ax
LANNEN, Bridget		25	F	Laborer	01Ju02Ax
GAHAGEN, Mary		15	F	Laborer	01Ju02Ax
LANNEN, Ann		16	F	Laborer	01Ju02Ax
Ellen		16	F	Laborer	01Ju02Ax
DALTON, Vina		20	F	Laborer	01Ju02Ax
FLINN, Biddy		20	F	Laborer	01Ju02Ax
QUINN, Mary		14	F	Laborer	01Ju02Ax
Mic.		11	M	Laborer	01Ju02Ax
FAY, Philip		23	M	Laborer	01Ju02Ax
CLARK, Kate		20	F	Laborer	01Ju02Ax
BRANNON, Rose		16	F	Laborer	01Ju02Ax
DUFFY, Biney		15	F	Laborer	01Ju02Ax
DOLEN, Margt.		18	F	Laborer	01Ju02Ax
HACKETT, Michl.		22	M	Laborer	01Ju02Ax
GOHERTY, Julia		18	F	Laborer	01Ju02Ax
Kate		12	F	Laborer	01Ju02Ax
Pat		07	M	Child	01Ju02Ax
SMITH, James		25	M	Carpenter	01Ju02Ax
SULLIVAN, Kate		24	F	Laborer	01Ju02Ax
SMITH, Sarah		04	F	Child	01Ju02Ax
BALLARD, Robert		24	M	Shoemaker	01Ju02Ax
MCGAN, Cathe.		18	F	Shoemaker	01Ju02Ax
WHITTLE, Margt.		22	F	Shoemaker	01Ju02Ax
QUEENE, Peter		51	M	Weaver	01Ju02Ax
Cathe.	(W)	51	F	Wife	01Ju02Ax
Michl.	(S)	20	M	Weaver	01Ju02Ax
Mary	(D)	20	F	Weaver	01Ju02Ax
Anthony	(S)	12	M	Weaver	01Ju02Ax
Ann	(D)	14	F	Weaver	01Ju02Ax
Jno.	(S)	10	M	Weaver	01Ju02Ax
DILLON, Ann		18	F	Weaver	01Ju02Ax
BYRNE, Jno.		28	M	Laborer	01Ju02Ax
Judy		30	F	Laborer	01Ju02Ax
Kate		18	F	Laborer	01Ju02Ax
Bridget		20	F	Laborer	01Ju02Ax
BOYLE, Tarence		02	M	Child	01Ju02Ax
DANENEY, Judy		18	F	Laborer	01Ju02Ax
SMITH, Cathe.		18	F	Laborer	01Ju02Ax
LERING, Jno.		26	M	Laborer	01Ju02Ax
Nanny		18	F	Laborer	01Ju02Ax
SULLIVAN, Jane		19	F	Laborer	01Ju02Ax
MAGEY, Alexr.		30	M	Laborer	01Ju02Ax
PORTER, Susan		19	F	Laborer	01Ju02Ax
CARIN, Micl.		23	M	Laborer	01Ju02Ax
Mary	(W)	22	F	Wife	01Ju02Ax
Pat	(S)	01	M	Child	01Ju02Ax
JORDAN, Nancy		28	F	Laborer	01Ju02Ax
ROGERS, Rose		11	F	Laborer	01Ju02Ax
BOHEN, Cathe.		50	F	Laborer	01Ju02Ax
Biddy		15	F	Laborer	01Ju02Ax
CLANCY, Mary		18	F	Laborer	01Ju02Ax
HURLEY, Jno.		09	M	Child	01Ju02Ax
MALONEY, Edwd.		19	M	Stctr	01Ju02Ax
Danl.		60	M	Stctr	01Ju02Ax
Jane		16	F	Stctr	01Ju02Ax
FLINN, Patt		20	M	Laborer	01Ju02Ax
KELLY, Jno.		24	M	Laborer	01Ju02Ax
CONISK, Margt.		20	F	Laborer	01Ju02Ax
CAREY, Mary		20	F	Laborer	01Ju02Ax
DORAN, Mary		21	F	Laborer	01Ju02Ax
BOHEN, Betty		20	F	Laborer	01Ju02Ax
MORAN, Eliza		18	F	Laborer	01Ju02Ax
HOY, Matthew		25	M	Laborer	01Ju02Ax
MCSOREY, Cathe.		60	F	Laborer	01Ju02Ax
Ann		30	F	Laborer	01Ju02Ax
CONWAY, Ann		17	F	Laborer	01Ju02Ax
BARRETT, Jno.		25	M	Laborer	01Ju02Ax
BURKE, Mary		20	F	Laborer	01Ju02Ax
DUFFY, Biddy		19	F	Laborer	01Ju02Ax
MARTIN, Hugh		32	M	Laborer	01Ju02Ax
MCGUIRE, Margt.		17	F	Laborer	01Ju02Ax
GLISON, Rody		20	F	Laborer	01Ju02Ax
WELIN, Mary		38	F	Laborer	01Ju02Ax
GLESON, Jane		26	F	Laborer	01Ju02Ax
MARTIN, Eliza		21	F	Laborer	01Ju02Ax
SCOTT, Margt.		70	F	Laborer	01Ju02Ax
HARVEY, Mary		25	F	Laborer	01Ju02Ax
MCCAFFERY, Margt.		24	F	Laborer	01Ju02Ax
CANAGEN, Margt.		24	F	Laborer	01Ju02Ax
SMITH, Daffeney		22	F	Laborer	01Ju02Ax
BOGEY, Jane		20	F	Laborer	01Ju02Ax
Eliza	(D)	02	F	Child	01Ju02Ax
HALTON, Mary		20	F	Laborer	01Ju02Ax
SHERIDAN, Cathe.		20	F	Laborer	01Ju02Ax
HARVEY, Thos.		23	M	Laborer	01Ju02Ax
Sally		19	F	Laborer	01Ju02Ax

NAMES OF PASSENGERS		AGE	SEX	OCCUPATIONS	DATE PORT SHIP	NAMES OF PASSENGERS		AGE	SEX	OCCUPATIONS	DATE PORT SHIP
HANDLEY, Bridget		27	F	Laborer	01Ju02Ax	WARD, Mary		22	F	None	01Ju02Ax
Michl.	(S)	03	M	Child	01Ju02Ax	BEATTIE, Letitia		24	F	None	01Ju02Ax
Niels	(S)	01	M	Child	01Ju02Ax	HAGAN, Jno.		40	M	None	01Ju02Ax
HEARNE, Jane		25	F	Laborer	01Ju02Ax	MALOY, Mary		35	F	None	01Ju02Ax
Mary	(D)	04	F	Child	01Ju02Ax	GREEN, Eliza		43	F	None	01Ju02Ax
Eliza	(D)	02	F	Child	01Ju02Ax	Jane	(D)	14	F	None	01Ju02Ax
FLINN, Ellen		26	F	Laborer	01Ju02Ax	Elizabeth	(D)	08	F	Child	01Ju02Ax
DAVINE, Jno.		26	M	Laborer	01Ju02Ax	Emma	(D)	07	F	Child	01Ju02Ax
Mary	(D)	02	F	Child	01Ju02Ax	THORNTON, Mary-Ann		19	F	None	01Ju02Ax
BRING, Jno.		20	M	Blacksmith	01Ju02Ax						
SWEENEY, Jno.		25	M	Laborer	01Ju02Ax						
COURNAN, Dennis		50	M	Laborer	01Ju02Ax						
Honore	(W)	40	F	Wife	01Ju02Ax						
Humphrey	(S)	18	M	Laborer	01Ju02Ax	LADY-HUNTLEY 01 JUNE 1846					
Bridget	(D)	16	F	Laborer	01Ju02Ax						
Edwd.	(S)	12	M	Laborer	01Ju02Ax	From Liverpool					
LALE, Edward		23	M	Laborer	01Ju02Ax						
MONAHAN, Margt.		20	F	Laborer	01Ju02Ax						
MURPHY, James		21	M	Laborer	01Ju02Ax	BROWN, Margt.		50	F	None	01Ju02Es
BOYLE, Cathe.		20	F	Laborer	01Ju02Ax	James		30	M	Laborer	01Ju02Es
SANDERSON, Wm.		23	M	Laborer	01Ju02Ax	James-Jr.		35	M	Laborer	01Ju02Es
BRANNEN, Ellen		18	F	Laborer	01Ju02Ax	Ann		22	F	None	01Ju02Es
Margt.		10	F	Laborer	01Ju02Ax	CLEARY, James		22	M	Laborer	01Ju02Es
CARROL, Judy		16	F	Laborer	01Ju02Ax	Mary		20	F	None	01Ju02Es
COLLINS, Jno.		30	M	Shoemaker	01Ju02Ax	SMITH, Cathr.		25	F	None	01Ju02Es
COOK, Honore		30	F	Shoemaker	01Ju02Ax	Owen		20	M	Laborer	01Ju02Es
Bridget	(D)	05	F	Child	01Ju02Ax	MEEHAN, Dennis		20	M	Laborer	01Ju02Es
MCCAGEY, Ann		40	F	Shoemaker	01Ju02Ax	Cathr.		23	F	None	01Ju02Es
MCCANNA, Brigt.		23	F	Shoemaker	01Ju02Ax	Nancy		20	F	None	01Ju02Es
BOYLEN, Audey		50	M	Shoemaker	01Ju02Ax	KIERNAN, John		22	M	Laborer	01Ju02Es
Biddy	(W)	48	F	Wife	01Ju02Ax	MAXWELL, Mary		25	F	None	01Ju02Es
Philip	(S)	20	M	Shoemaker	01Ju02Ax	FITZSIMMONS, Rosey		20	F	None	01Ju02Es
DONOHOU, Cathe.		16	F	Shoemaker	01Ju02Ax	CULLERY, Bartley		21	M	Laborer	01Ju02Es
MCCOANEN, Chas.		65	M	Laborer	01Ju02Ax	BRADLEY, Biddy		22	F	None	01Ju02Es
Mary		55	F	None	01Ju02Ax	CULLY, Mary		21	F	None	01Ju02Es
MOORE, Thomas		30	M	Mason	01Ju02Ax	HART, Niell		23	M	Laborer	01Ju02Es
CARROM, James		25	M	Laborer	01Ju02Ax	Thos.		20	M	Laborer	01Ju02Es
Richl.		22	M	None	01Ju02Ax	MOGHAN, Edwd.		24	M	Laborer	01Ju02Es
CARFIELD, Jno.		22	M	None	01Ju02Ax	DENNAN, John		25	M	Laborer	01Ju02Es
Cathe.		20	F	None	01Ju02Ax	KENNEDY, John		22	M	Laborer	01Ju02Es
Joana.		23	F	None	01Ju02Ax	DALTON, Richd.		25	M	Laborer	01Ju02Es
GRINNEN, Jno.		23	M	None	01Ju02Ax	DILLON, Richd.		30	M	Laborer	01Ju02Es
DONOHEU, Joseph		21	M	None	01Ju02Ax	RENKINS, Biddy		21	F	None	01Ju02Es
MOORE, Jno.		18	M	None	01Ju02Ax	FEEHAN, Margt.		21	F	None	01Ju02Es
Margt.		20	F	None	01Ju02Ax	PENDER, Margt.		21	F	None	01Ju02Es
DUNN, Edwd.		11	M	None	01Ju02Ax	HORAN, Larry		20	M	Laborer	01Ju02Es
Wm.		10	M	None	01Ju02Ax	TOLIEN, John		25	M	Laborer	01Ju02Es
Cathe.		14	F	None	01Ju02Ax	SHARLOW, Richd.		22	M	Laborer	01Ju02Es
PURSEL, Pat		28	M	None	01Ju02Ax	CONNOR, James		20	M	Laborer	01Ju02Es
Cathe.		21	F	None	01Ju02Ax	WILLIS, James		20	M	Laborer	01Ju02Es
Margt.		23	F	None	01Ju02Ax	DARCY, Mary		13	F	None	01Ju02Es
ROFTER, Jno.		24	M	None	01Ju02Ax	MCBRINE, Ellen		17	F	None	01Ju02Es
HACKETT, Bridget		26	F	None	01Ju02Ax	MCGUIRE, Cathr.		17	F	None	01Ju02Es
HASEY, Bridget		30	F	None	01Ju02Ax	ONCALL, Margt.		17	F	None	01Ju02Es
HAFSED, David		24	M	None	01Ju02Ax	RYAN, Martin		20	M	Laborer	01Ju02Es
Ellen		16	F	None	01Ju02Ax	NOWLAN, Thos.		22	M	Laborer	01Ju02Es
BRASSEL, Dennis		20	M	None	01Ju02Ax	Michl.		20	M	Laborer	01Ju02Es
Cathe.		22	F	None	01Ju02Ax	RYAN, Thos.		20	M	Laborer	01Ju02Es
MCLAGLIN, Margt.		23	F	None	01Ju02Ax	BOGAN, Bessey		20	F	None	01Ju02Es
Cathe.	(D)	.04	F	Infant	01Ju02Ax	Moore		30	M	Laborer	01Ju02Es
CONERY, Sarah		20	F	None	01Ju02Ax	GERAGHTY, James		20	M	Laborer	01Ju02Es
HAND, Michl.		20	M	None	01Ju02Ax	Bessey		19	F	None	01Ju02Es
MCCANNAN, Pat		20	M	None	01Ju02Ax	MURRAY, Michl.		25	M	Laborer	01Ju02Es
SMITH, Saml.		26	M	None	01Ju02Ax	Cathr.		25	F	None	01Ju02Es
OMALEY, Susan		19	F	None	01Ju02Ax	ROONEY, Nick		19	M	Laborer	01Ju02Es
KAGAN, Jno.		19	M	Mason	01Ju02Ax	FARNAN, Anthony		19	M	Laborer	01Ju02Es
BAKENGALL, Lucy		22	F	Mason	01Ju02Ax	HANIN, Bryan		20	M	Laborer	01Ju02Es
KRANTZ, Maria		28	F	Mason	01Ju02Ax	FAY, James		20	M	Laborer	01Ju02Es
Geo.Wm.	(S)	04	M	Child	01Ju02Ax	FARRELL, Pat		20	M	Laborer	01Ju02Es
OCONNER, Jas.		02	M	Child	01Ju02Ax	BOGOT, Peter		20	M	Laborer	01Ju02Es
DUNCAN, Thos.		01	M	Child	01Ju02Ax	Biddy		20	F	None	01Ju02Es
SOMMERVILLE, Susan		00	F	None	01Ju02Ax	NUGENT, Ann		20	F	None	01Ju02Es
ROBINSON, Irene		00	F	None	01Ju02Ax	HUGHS, Anny		20	F	None	01Ju02Es
RAGAN, Mary		35	F	None	01Ju02Ax						
GAGAN, Thos.		18	M	None	01Ju02Ax						

NAMES OF PASSENGERS		AGE	SEX	OCCUPATIONS	DATE PORT SHIP
CRENA, Nora		19	F	None	01Ju02Es
FLYNN, John		20	M	Laborer	01Ju02Es
MCCAFFE, U		20	M	Laborer	01Ju02Es
BAWN, Pat		22	M	Laborer	01Ju02Es
BUCKLEY, Ellen		20	F	None	01Ju02Es
MAHAN, John		38	M	Laborer	01Ju02Es
LYON, Pat		25	M	Laborer	01Ju02Es
RYAN, Ann		20	F	None	01Ju02Es
MEALE, James		23	M	Laborer	01Ju02Es
JONES, John		27	M	Laborer	01Ju02Es
Charlotte	(W)	26	F	Wife	01Ju02Es
Charlotte-Jr.	(D)	06	F	Child	01Ju02Es
Samuel	(S)	04	M	Child	01Ju02Es
John	(S)	.00	M	Infant	01Ju02Es
FLANAGAN, Bryan		62	M	Laborer	01Ju02Es
Margaret	(W)	52	F	Wife	01Ju02Es
Judy	(D)	24	F	None	01Ju02Es
James	(S)	22	M	Laborer	01Ju02Es
John	(S)	20	M	Laborer	01Ju02Es
Ellen	(D)	17	F	None	01Ju02Es
Michl.	(S)	12	M	Laborer	01Ju02Es
Mary	(D)	08	F	Child	01Ju02Es
GAVIN, Biddy		20	F	None	01Ju02Es
Maria		20	F	None	01Ju02Es
FERNY, Mary		22	F	None	01Ju02Es
CASEY, Biddy		22	F	None	01Ju02Es
FLANAGAN, Margaret		C6	F	Child	01Ju02Es
HAPELTON, Jane		20	F	None	01Ju02Es
CONNOR, Biddy		40	F	None	01Ju02Es
MILEY, Edward		25	M	Laborer	01Ju02Es
RYAN, Mick		25	M	Laborer	01Ju02Es
U	(W)	24	F	Wife	01Ju02Es
Mary	(D)	.00	F	Infant	01Ju02Es
FINERTY, Dart		24	M	Laborer	01Ju02Es
GORDEN, Pat		00	M	None	01Ju02Es
REILLY, Michel		24	M	Laborer	01Ju02Es
DOWNEY, Michl.		25	M	Laborer	01Ju02Es
REILLY, Cathr.		18	F	None	01Ju02Es
FINERTY, Margt.		18	F	None	01Ju02Es
DRENNAN, Thos.		22	M	Laborer	01Ju02Es
CONWAY, Margt.		23	F	None	01Ju02Es
BRENNAN, James		24	M	Laborer	01Ju02Es
Dennis		20	M	Laborer	01Ju02Es
Mick		23	M	Laborer	01Ju02Es
CANAVAN, John		30	M	Laborer	01Ju02Es
GILLIGAN, John		22	M	Laborer	01Ju02Es
Mary		20	F	None	01Ju02Es
NORTON, Thomas		20	M	Laborer	01Ju02Es
MCKANE, Herbert		20	M	Laborer	01Ju02Es
CAGAN, Margt.		16	F	None	01Ju02Es
ROCHE, Margt.		15	F	None	01Ju02Es
CANERGHA, Margret		18	F	None	01Ju02Es
Cathrine		16	F	None	01Ju02Es
KELROY, Ann		18	F	None	01Ju02Es
CURLEY, Biddy		30	F	None	01Ju02Es
MCDERNOT, Biddy		30	F	None	01Ju02Es
KELLY, Kernan		21	M	Laborer	01Ju02Es
CARROL, Thos.		23	M	Laborer	01Ju02Es
Jeremiah		24	M	Laborer	01Ju02Es
HAPLES, Richd.		17	M	Laborer	01Ju02Es
DUGAN, Margrt.		17	F	None	01Ju02Es
MURRAY, Pat		24	M	Laborer	01Ju02Es
BOYD, James		33	M	Laborer	01Ju02Es
DEVEREUX, Ellen		46	F	None	01Ju02Es
ROCHE, John-R.		30	M	Laborer	01Ju02Es
GAFFNEY, John		30	M	Laborer	01Ju02Es
DEMPSY, Betty		24	F	None	01Ju02Es
MURVES, Ally		30	F	None	01Ju02Es
Johanna		27	F	None	01Ju02Es
MORGAN, Mary		30	F	None	01Ju02Es
Thos.	(S)	07	M	Child	01Ju02Es
Pat	(S)	05	M	Child	01Ju02Es
Cathr.	(D)	05	F	Child	01Ju02Es
KELLY, Mary		21	F	None	01Ju02Es
NIXON, Will		21	M	Laborer	01Ju02Es
MCGRANE, Pat		24	M	Laborer	01Ju02Es
Ann	(W)	24	F	Wife	01Ju02Es
Bicdy	(D)	.00	F	Infant	01Ju02Es
COLLINS, Richd.		24	M	Laborer	01Ju02Es
CUDDLE, Pat		24	M	Laborer	01Ju02Es
HEALY, Edward		27	M	Laborer	01Ju02Es
DOLAN, James		21	M	Laborer	01Ju02Es
FARREL, James		21	M	Laborer	01Ju02Es
MURPHY, Thos.		27	M	Laborer	01Ju02Es
ONIEL, Michl.		21	M	Laborer	01Ju02Es
Mary		19	F	None	01Ju02Es
ENGLISH, Pat		27	M	Laborer	01Ju02Es
Margret		24	F	None	01Ju02Es
MARICN, Pat		27	M	Laborer	01Ju02Es
CONLIN, P.		26	M	Laborer	01Ju02Es
CARLEY, Pat		24	M	Laborer	01Ju02Es
HENRY, Ella		20	F	None	01Ju02Es
EGAN, Marie		20	F	None	01Ju02Es
KENNEDY, Cathr.		40	F	None	01Ju02Es
BORLAND, Archy		24	M	Laborer	01Ju02Es
SHANLY, Bicdy		20	F	None	01Ju02Es
BRAKTT, Will		24	M	Laborer	01Ju02Es
WELSH, John		22	M	Laborer	01Ju02Es
KENNEDY, James		24	M	Laborer	01Ju02Es
MCQUADE, Margt.		20	F	None	01Ju02Es
CHRISTIAN, Biddy		20	F	None	01Ju02Es
DOYLE, Bicdy		19	F	None	01Ju02Es
Ellen		19	F	None	01Ju02Es
SMITH, Biddy		18	F	None	01Ju02Es
HENRY, Pat		13	M	Laborer	01Ju02Es
MCGLOVER, Allice		20	F	None	01Ju02Es
WALSH, Bessy		17	F	None	01Ju02Es
FARRELL, James		24	M	Laborer	01Ju02Es
Ann		20	F	None	01Ju02Es
RIED, John		21	M	Laborer	01Ju02Es
MILEY, John		21	M	Laborer	01Ju02Es
MCPENNY, Ann		16	F	None	01Ju02Es
DONELLY, Harry		18	M	Laborer	01Ju02Es
TEASDALE, John		20	M	Laborer	01Ju02Es
NICHOLDSON, U		30	M	Laborer	01Ju02Es
U	(W)	25	F	Wife	01Ju02Es
U		.00	U	Infant	01Ju02Es
OCONNOR, Michl.		30	M	Laborer	01Ju02Es
SWEENY, Thos.		24	M	Laborer	01Ju02Es
GREENALGH, Saml.		27	M	Laborer	01Ju02Es
WINTER, Jane		18	F	None	01Ju02Es
MCCARTY, Will		18	M	Laborer	01Ju02Es
MCLORAN, Margret		17	F	None	01Ju02Es
Eliza-Jane		05	F	Child	01Ju02Es
MATTHEWS, Robert		40	M	Laborer	01Ju02Es
Rossy		35	F	None	01Ju02Es
MCTREIY, John		26	M	Laborer	01Ju02Es
MCMAN, James		40	M	Laborer	01Ju02Es
Michel.		20	M	Laborer	01Ju02Es
CUMINS, Peter		22	M	Laborer	01Ju02Es
Cath.D.		24	F	None	01Ju02Es
DEMPSY, Allas		20	F	None	01Ju02Es
EGDGAN, Pat		30	M	Laborer	01Ju02Es
James		20	M	Laborer	01Ju02Es
FLANAGAN, Christ.		29	M	Laborer	01Ju02Es
Ann		24	F	Laborer	01Ju02Es
FLEMING, John		18	M	Laborer	01Ju02Es
PARKER, Edw.		22	M	Laborer	01Ju02Es
BAYNOR, John		31	M	Laborer	01Ju02Es
WYNN, Pat		28	M	Laborer	01Ju02Es
GLEESON, Laurence		36	M	Laborer	01Ju02Es
FLEMING, Anne		20	F	Laborer	01Ju02Es

WATERLOO 01 JUNE 1846

From Liverpool

NAMES OF PASSENGERS	Rel	AGE	SEX	OCCUPATIONS	DATE PORT SHIP
BARR, U		28	M	Clergyman	01Ju02As
U	(W)	24	F	Wife	01Ju02As
SLACK, Thomas		32	M	Servant	01Ju02As
GORMAN, Ellen		30	F	Servant	01Ju02As
Mary		28	F	Servant	01Ju02As
MCCABE, Bridget		26	F	Servant	01Ju02As
GORBEY, Jas.		05	M	Child	01Ju02As
John		05	M	Child	01Ju02As
Thomas	(P)	30	M	Blacksmith	01Ju02As
MCDERMOT, Jas.		24	M	Laborer	01Ju02As
NOLAN, Michael		28	M	Laborer	01Ju02As
SMALL, Hannah		30	F	Servant	01Ju02As
MCCANN, Patk.		33	M	Laborer	01Ju02As
Ellen	(W)	24	F	Wife	01Ju02As
James	(S)	05	M	Child	01Ju02As
John	(S)	01	M	Child	01Ju02As
Patrick	(S)	02	M	Child	01Ju02As
Arthur		20	M	Laborer	01Ju02As
TORRENCE, Patrick		20	M	Laborer	01Ju02As
U	(W)	20	F	Wife	01Ju02As
MURNEN, Rose		22	F	Servant	01Ju02As
OHARA, Cormick		27	M	Laborer	01Ju02As
Margt.	(W)	20	F	Wife	01Ju02As
LOUGHTEN, Michael		30	M	Laborer	01Ju02As
U	(W)	30	F	Wife	01Ju02As
Cath.		25	F	None	01Ju02As
Mary		02	F	Child	01Ju02As
MULLIGAN, Cath.		30	F	None	01Ju02As
DOYLE, Michael		35	M	Farmer	01Ju02As
Cath.	(W)	30	F	Wife	01Ju02As
Biddy	(D)	10	F	Child	01Ju02As
Molly	(D)	08	F	Child	01Ju02As
Rose	(D)	07	F	Child	01Ju02As
Cath.	(D)	03	F	Child	01Ju02As
Margt.	(D)	01	F	Child	01Ju02As
FITZSIMMONS, Thos.		30	M	Carpenter	01Ju02As
DALY, Jas.		30	M	Carpenter	01Ju02As
CARLEY, Michael		35	M	Laborer	01Ju02As
NUGENT, Thos.		28	M	Laborer	01Ju02As
HAILFORD, Bryan		28	M	Laborer	01Ju02As
RILEY, Ann		25	F	Servant	01Ju02As
FITZSIMMONS, Ann		25	F	Servant	01Ju02As
Michael		32	M	Laborer	01Ju02As
LYONS, Nancy		28	F	Servant	01Ju02As
LYNCH, Rose		28	F	Servant	01Ju02As
CASSIDY, Michl.		28	M	Laborer	01Ju02As
BEHM, Wm.		27	M	Laborer	01Ju02As
Margaret		17	F	Servant	01Ju02As
PRICE, Rose		21	F	Servant	01Ju02As
MULCAHY, Margt.		20	F	Servant	01Ju02As
SULLIVAN, Cath.		20	F	Servant	01Ju02As
DELMUR, Jas.		24	M	Laborer	01Ju02As
DAVIS, Margt.		46	F	Servant	01Ju02As
BUCKLEY, Benj.		40	M	Farmer	01Ju02As
Thomas		30	M	Farmer	01Ju02As
John		18	M	Farmer	01Ju02As
FITZSIMMONS, Margt.		18	F	Servant	01Ju02As
FEARL, Nicholas		25	M	Servant	01Ju02As
OBRIEN, Harriet		21	F	Servant	01Ju02As
CONWAY, Loughton		24	M	Coach Maker	01Ju02As
DUNN, Edward		22	M	Laborer	01Ju02As
WHALEN, Cath.		26	F	Servant	01Ju02As
Betty		20	F	Servant	01Ju02As
MCCONGHAN, Thos.		24	M	Farmer	01Ju02As
THOMPSON, Matth.		25	M	Laborer	01Ju02As
THOMPSON, U	(W)	20	F	Wife	01Ju02As
GURNEY, Ann		27	F	Servant	01Ju02As
CARNEY, Jas.		27	M	Laborer	01Ju02As
Ellen	(W)	20	F	Wife	01Ju02As
WHALEN, Wm.		18	M	Laborer	01Ju02As
MAGE, Wm.		60	M	Laborer	01Ju02As
Thomas	(S)	22	M	Laborer	01Ju02As
John	(S)	24	M	Laborer	01Ju02As
Samuel	(S)	18	M	Laborer	01Ju02As
Jane	(D)	19	F	Laborer	01Ju02As
Isabella	(W)	50	F	Wife	01Ju02As
James	(S)	13	M	Laborer	01Ju02As
William	(S)	11	M	Laborer	01Ju02As
Irwin	(S)	09	M	Child	01Ju02As
ORR, Matt		19	M	Laborer	01Ju02As
WHITE, John		20	M	Farmer	01Ju02As
James		25	M	Farmer	01Ju02As
MCPHILLIPS, James		25	M	Laborer	01Ju02As
ROHN, Eliza		18	F	Servant	01Ju02As
TRAINER, Nancy		24	F	Servant	01Ju02As
MCGAHEY, Mary		16	F	Servant	01Ju02As
CONALLY, Bridget		20	F	Servant	01Ju02As
MCCEARNEY, James		24	M	Shoemaker	01Ju02As
DUFFEY, Mary		19	F	Servant	01Ju02As
MCCARMA, John		22	M	Laborer	01Ju02As
Hugh		15	M	Laborer	01Ju02As
BREMAN, Hugh		26	M	Laborer	01Ju02As
MURPHY, Michl.		20	M	Laborer	01Ju02As
MCGUIRE, John		20	M	Laborer	01Ju02As
FEGAN, John		30	M	Blacksmith	01Ju02As
MCCADY, Patk.		20	M	Laborer	01Ju02As
SHEEHAN, Jas.		22	M	Laborer	01Ju02As
SKIDDY, Michl.		23	M	Laborer	01Ju02As
KELLEY, Phil.		23	M	Laborer	01Ju02As
KEDDAN, Michl.		26	M	Laborer	01Ju02As
BRADY, Edwd.		20	M	Laborer	01Ju02As
KELLY, Patt.		20	M	Farmer	01Ju02As
RUSSEL, Honora		17	F	Servant	01Ju02As
MENAHAN, Joshua		20	M	Laborer	01Ju02As
LITTLETON, John		20	M	Laborer	01Ju02As
DOUGHERTY, Johanna		21	F	Servant	01Ju02As
WARD, Wm.		28	M	Laborer	01Ju02As
MCCALLISTER, James		24	M	Laborer	01Ju02As
Hugh		19	M	Laborer	01Ju02As
CROOKSHANK, Margt.		23	F	Servant	01Ju02As
DONALLY, Wm.		30	M	Laborer	01Ju02As
U	(W)	30	F	Wife	01Ju02As
Thos.		17	M	None	01Ju02As
Nicholas		32	M	Laborer	01Ju02As
Mary		25	F	None	01Ju02As
John		11	M	None	01Ju02As
Bridget		06	F	Child	01Ju02As
BLAKE, Rose		12	F	Servant	01Ju02As
SANFORD, Mary		18	F	Servant	01Ju02As
DUGAN, Wm.		30	M	Laborer	01Ju02As
SALOR, Michael		61	M	Laborer	01Ju02As
Ann		21	F	None	01Ju02As
Bridget		07	F	Child	01Ju02As
MCEEHELL, Jas.		22	M	Farmer	01Ju02As
QUIGLEY, Mary		20	F	Servant	01Ju02As
FITZSIMMONS, Ann		18	F	Servant	01Ju02As
Michael		17	M	Servant	01Ju02As
BANAHER, Bridget		20	F	Servant	01Ju02As
Catherine		20	F	Servant	01Ju02As
FOWLER, Thomas		33	M	Laborer	01Ju02As
Patrick		22	M	Laborer	01Ju02As
SWIFT, Thomas		25	M	Laborer	01Ju02As
WHITE, Thomas		22	M	Painter	01Ju02As
MCINTOSH, Henry		40	M	Carpenter	01Ju02As
BUCKLEY, Thaddeus		33	M	Laborer	01Ju02As
Patrick		35	M	Laborer	01Ju02As
KIVE, Richard		40	M	Laborer	01Ju02As
DEE, Thomas		24	M	Laborer	01Ju02As
DANIEL, Margaret		20	F	Servant	01Ju02As
RYAN, William		23	M	Servant	01Ju02As

NAMES OF PASSENGERS		AGE	SEX	OCCUPATIONS	DATE PORT SHIP	NAMES OF PASSENGERS		AGE	SEX	OCCUPATIONS	DATE PORT SHIP
RYAN, Edward		26	M	Servant	01Ju02As						
STAPLETON, Roger		22	M	Laborer	01Ju02As						
MARA, Ellen		23	F	Servant	01Ju02As						
Catherine		19	F	Servant	01Ju02As						
BURKE, Mary		25	F	Servant	01Ju02As						
MULNIX, Matilda		20	F	Servant	01Ju02As		BROOKSBY 01 JUNE 1846				
GENDERS, Francis		30	M	Laborer	01Ju02As						
FLOOD, Patrick		17	M	Laborer	01Ju02As		From Glasgow				
BLAKE, Mary		20	F	Servant	01Ju02As						
SHERIDAN, Phelix		22	M	Laborer	01Ju02As						
Ellen	(W)	24	F	Wife	01Ju02As	POURIL, Peter		37	M	Laborer	01Ju04Ex
SHEA, Patrick		20	M	Laborer	01Ju02As	MCDONALD, Stewart		25	M	Weaver	01Ju04Ex
Betty	(W)	19	F	Wife	01Ju02As	POURIL, Jane		25	F	None	01Ju04Ex
MOORE, Cath.		38	F	Servant	01Ju02As	MCDONALD, Margt.		30	F	Wife	01Ju04Ex
OHARA, Charles		25	M	Laborer	01Ju02As	Jane		49	F	WI	01Ju04Ex
FOY, Peter		24	M	Laborer	01Ju02As	BALFOUR, Wm.		33	M	Farmer	01Ju04Ex
DOLAN, Patrick		24	M	Laborer	01Ju02As	C.	(W)	28	F	Wife	01Ju04Ex
DILLAN, Michael		24	M	Laborer	01Ju02As	Henry	(S)	06	M	Child	01Ju04Ex
DEVLIN, Margaret		20	F	Servant	01Ju02As	William	(S)	02	M	Child	01Ju04Ex
Mary		18	F	Servant	01Ju02As	Robt.	(S)	.11	M	Infant	01Ju04Ex
HEALY, Mary		24	F	Servant	01Ju02As	MCGOWN, Lachn.		39	M	Farmer	01Ju04Ex
MONEY, John		21	M	Laborer	01Ju02As	U		39	F	Wife	01Ju04Ex
MCGLYNN, Ann		20	F	Servant	01Ju02As	James	(S)	13	M	None	01Ju04Ex
MCCABE, Hugh		38	M	Butcher	01Ju02As	Cathe.	(D)	12	F	None	01Ju04Ex
Mary	(W)	28	F	Wife	01Ju02As	Alexr.	(S)	09	M	Child	01Ju04Ex
John	(S)	07	M	Child	01Ju02As	Margt.	(D)	07	F	Child	01Ju04Ex
Mary-Ellen	(D)	05	F	Child	01Ju02As	ELLIS, James		25	M	Farmer	01Ju04Ex
Catharine	(D)	03	F	Child	01Ju02As	MIKLEJOHN, U-Mrs.		45	F	WI	01Ju04Ex
Ann-Eliza	(D)	.00	F	Infant	01Ju02As	Mary	(D)	22	F	None	01Ju04Ex
DONOHUE, Ann		14	F	Servant	01Ju02As	Agnes	(D)	19	F	None	01Ju04Ex
MCCABE, Eliza		30	F	Servant	01Ju02As	MILLER, Alexr.		35	M	Farmer	01Ju04Ex
ROGERS, Margt.		24	F	Servant	01Ju02As	Janet	(W)	29	F	Wife	01Ju04Ex
GREEN, Patrick		24	M	Laborer	01Ju02As	Cath.	(D)	08	F	Child	01Ju04Ex
DAVIS, James		40	M	Laborer	01Ju02As	Janet	(D)	06	F	Child	01Ju04Ex
FOGARTY, Andrew		26	M	Laborer	01Ju02As	George	(S)	04	M	Child	01Ju04Ex
MURRAN, James		36	M	Laborer	01Ju02As	Walter	(S)	.11	M	Infant	01Ju04Ex
DUNN, Charles		28	M	Laborer	01Ju02As	DYSART, Margt.Mrs.		45	F	WI	01Ju04Ex
CONALLY, Michael		26	M	Laborer	01Ju02As	Ann	(D)	14	F	None	01Ju04Ex
BROUGHAM, John		26	M	Laborer	01Ju02As	Cath.	(D)	09	F	Child	01Ju04Ex
DOLAN, Ann		20	F	Wife	01Ju02As	James	(S)	06	M	Child	01Ju04Ex
MCDAVID, Hugh		22	M	Laborer	01Ju02As	MCLEAN, Alexr.		50	M	Farmer	01Ju04Ex
ALLEN, Robert		21	M	Laborer	01Ju02As	Janet	(W)	45	F	Wife	01Ju04Ex
MCGORMIS, Dennis		18	M	Laborer	01Ju02As	Mary	(D)	24	F	None	01Ju04Ex
Mary	(W)	16	F	Wife	01Ju02As	Isabella	(D)	22	F	None	01Ju04Ex
GORMAN, Margaret		16	F	Servant	01Ju02As	Janet	(D)	20	F	None	01Ju04Ex
MCCALLY, John		19	M	Laborer	01Ju02As	Jane	(D)	16	F	None	01Ju04Ex
St.Johns-PLACE, Charle		25	M	Laborer	01Ju02As	Alexr.	(S)	13	M	None	01Ju04Ex
John		22	M	Laborer	01Ju02As	Agnes	(D)	10	F	None	01Ju04Ex
MCGOWAN, Margaret		28	F	Servant	01Ju02As	MCLEOD, Isabella		30	F	Wife	01Ju04Ex
Mary		24	F	Servant	01Ju02As	HENDERSON, Thos.		56	M	Farmer	01Ju04Ex
FOLEY, Margaret		12	F	Servant	01Ju02As	Barbara	(W)	53	F	Wife	01Ju04Ex
JOYCE, Patrick		35	M	Farmer	01Ju02As	Barbarra	(D)	23	F	None	01Ju04Ex
REGAN, William		24	M	Farmer	01Ju02As	INNES, Harriot		25	F	N	01Ju04Ex
REILLY, William		24	M	Farmer	01Ju02As	HENDERSON, Geo.		19	M	Son	01Ju04Ex
MUNAGAN, Patrick		23	M	Laborer	01Ju02As	Wm.		12	M	Son	01Ju04Ex
JOYCE, John		25	M	Shopkeeper	01Ju02As	David		06	M	Child	01Ju04Ex
U	(W)	26	F	Wife	01Ju02As	Alexr.		09	M	Child	01Ju04Ex
Biddy	(D)	04	F	Child	01Ju02As	DUNLOP, Jno.		27	M	Laborer	01Ju04Ex
Patrick	(S)	03	M	Child	01Ju02As	MCKIMON, Jno.		52	M	Farmer	01Ju04Ex
LYNCH, James		17	M	Laborer	01Ju02As	Margt.	(W)	54	F	Wife	01Ju04Ex
LAFFERTY, Ann		27	F	Servant	01Ju02As	James	(S)	20	M	None	01Ju04Ex
LANGAN, Catharine		20	F	Servant	01Ju02As	Alexr.	(S)	16	M	None	01Ju04Ex
MCDAVID, Hugh		22	M	Farmer	01Ju02As	Andrew	(S)	11	M	None	01Ju04Ex
MCBRIDE, Jas.		50	M	Farmer	01Ju02As	Janet	(D)	25	F	None	01Ju04Ex
Bridget	(W)	45	F	Wife	01Ju02As	Agnes	(D)	22	F	None	01Ju04Ex
Patrick	(S)	22	M	Farmer	01Ju02As	Elizabeth	(D)	19	F	None	01Ju04Ex
Margaret	(W)	16	F	Wife	01Ju02As	MORE, Robt.		39	M	Farmer	01Ju04Ex
Sarah	(D)	12	F	None	01Ju02As	Helen	(W)	37	F	Wife	01Ju04Ex
HALFORD, Catharine		18	F	Servant	01Ju02As	Margt.	(D)	15	F	None	01Ju04Ex
MARTIN, James		18	M	Laborer	01Ju02As	U	(S)	13	M	None	01Ju04Ex
TRACLE, Edward		22	M	Laborer	01Ju02As	Eliz.	(D)	11	F	None	01Ju04Ex
GALLAGHER, Fanny		18	F	Servant	01Ju02As	Cath.	(D)	09	F	Child	01Ju04Ex
SHUMAN, Bart.		30	M	Laborer	01Ju02As	Jno.	(S)	07	M	Child	01Ju04Ex
Schan		25	M	Laborer	01Ju02As	Agnes	(D)	05	F	Child	01Ju04Ex
						Robt.	(S)	03	M	Child	01Ju04Ex

NAMES OF PASSENGERS		AGE	SEX	OCCUPATIONS	DATE PORT SHIP
MORE, May	(D)	.10	F	Infant	01Ju04Ex
SMITH, Andr.		45	M	Farmer	01Ju04Ex
Agnes	(T)	36	F	None	01Ju04Ex
JOHNSON, Eliza.		17	F	Spinster	01Ju04Ex
SMITH, David		15	M	Son	01Ju04Ex
Geo.		13	M	Son	01Ju04Ex
Andr.		07	M	Child	01Ju04Ex
Wm.		05	M	Child	01Ju04Ex
CAMPBELL, Robt.Mrs.		36	F	Wife	01Ju04Ex
Christina	(D)	02	F	Child	01Ju04Ex
Colin	(S)	04	M	Child	01Ju04Ex
Wm.	(S)	09	M	Child	01Ju04Ex
Robt.	(S)	20	M	None	01Ju04Ex
STRANG, Robt.		30	M	Merchant	01Ju04Ex
U	(W)	26	F	Wife	01Ju04Ex
TOMY, Jno.		25	M	Laborer	01Ju04Ex
Ellen		30	F	Wife	01Ju04Ex
HILL, Alexr.		12	M	N	01Ju04Ex
James		11	M	N	01Ju04Ex
THOMAS, James		70	M	Farmer	01Ju04Ex
Janet	(D)	19	F	None	01Ju04Ex
MCCULLOCH, James		26	M	Servant	01Ju04Ex
Bridget	(W)	24	F	Wife	01Ju04Ex
PARKER, Wm.		21	M	Laborer	01Ju04Ex
SIMPSON, Jno.		30	M	Weaver	01Ju04Ex
WARDE, Bernard		46	M	Laborer	01Ju04Ex
Patrick		21	M	Laborer	01Ju04Ex
GRINDLY, James		40	M	Laborer	01Ju04Ex
FOAL, Jane		40	F	Spinster	01Ju04Ex
MCDONALD, Mary		19	F	Spinster	01Ju04Ex
ANKIN, James		27	M	Grocer	01Ju04Ex
Margt.	(W)	33	F	Wife	01Ju04Ex
Wm.	(S)	04	M	Child	01Ju04Ex
BROWN, Margt.		24	F	Spinster	01Ju04Ex
HOWIESON, Jno.		27	M	Laborer	01Ju04Ex
SINCLAIR, Jno.		30	M	Laborer	01Ju04Ex
INNES, Janie		19	F	Wife	01Ju04Ex
FLYNN, Mary		18	F	Sister	01Ju04Ex
BARCLAY, Lachn.		50	M	Gdnr	01Ju04Ex
Margt.	(W)	46	F	Wife	01Ju04Ex
David	(S)	13	M	None	01Ju04Ex
Alexr.	(S)	08	M	Child	01Ju04Ex
Louis	(S)	06	M	Child	01Ju04Ex
Archd.	(S)	03	M	Child	01Ju04Ex
MCCOMBIE, Jno.		54	M	Servant	01Ju04Ex
EDDIR, James		30	M	Servant	01Ju04Ex
RAE, Jno.Mrs.		46	F	Farmer	01Ju04Ex
EDDIR, Jno.		28	M	Farmer	01Ju04Ex
U	(W)	22	F	Wife	01Ju04Ex
THOMPSON, Jessie		18	F	Spinster	01Ju04Ex
CRAIGN, Catharine		19	F	Spinster	01Ju04Ex
BARCLAY, Jane		22	F	Spinster	01Ju04Ex
ROSS, Ann		35	F	Spinster	01Ju04Ex
MIKHEARN, Jno.		30	M	Laborer	01Ju04Ex
BRAE, Jno.		32	M	Preacher	01Ju04Ex
Susannah	(W)	33	F	Wife	01Ju04Ex
Theophilus	(D)	05	F	Child	01Ju04Ex
Ann	(D)	04	F	Child	01Ju04Ex
Susana	(D)	01	F	Child	01Ju04Ex
MCMASTER, Robt.		16	M	Clerk	01Ju04Ex
WILSON, James		42	M	Laborer	01Ju04Ex
REID, Thos.		20	M	Clerk	01Ju04Ex
STRAIN, James		26	M	Tailor	01Ju04Ex
HARLEY, Michael		25	M	Cooper	01Ju04Ex
GALLOWAY, Jno.		39	M	Laborer	01Ju04Ex
ONEIL, Felix		19	M	Porter	01Ju04Ex
ARTHUR, Jno.		21	M	Laborer	01Ju04Ex
RANKUN, U-Mrs.		40	F	WI	01Ju04Ex
Helen	(D)	19	F	None	01Ju04Ex
KENNEDY, James		22	M	Unknown	01Ju04Ex
HENDERSON, U-Mrs.		30	F	None	01Ju04Ex
Adam	(S)	11	M	None	01Ju04Ex
Cath.	(D)	09	F	Child	01Ju04Ex
Alice	(D)	06	F	Child	01Ju04Ex
Magt.	(D)	04	F	Child	01Ju04Ex

NAMES OF PASSENGERS		AGE	SEX	OCCUPATIONS	DATE PORT SHIP
IRVIN, Wm.		30	M	Shoemaker	01Ju04Ex
WILSON, Wm.		22	M	Dyer	01Ju04Ex
BLAIR, Sarah		55	F	Bootblack	01Ju04Ex
Robt.		31	M	Laborer	01Ju04Ex
Saml.		17	M	Laborer	01Ju04Ex
Sarah	(D)	13	F	None	01Ju04Ex
SHAW, Ann		25	F	Wife	01Ju04Ex
HAUGHERTON, Margt.		17	F	Spinster	01Ju04Ex
Marg.		22	F	Spinster	01Ju04Ex
FLYNN, Rose		24	F	Spinster	01Ju04Ex
RAMSAY, Sarah		22	F	Spinster	01Ju04Ex
Balthia		20	F	Spinster	01Ju04Ex
WHITE, Mary		25	F	Spinster	01Ju04Ex
WARD, Robt.		25	M	Laborer	01Ju04Ex
BROLLEY, Leah-Jane		20	F	Spinster	01Ju04Ex
LONG, Jno.		30	M	Laborer	01Ju04Ex
U	(W)	24	F	Wife	01Ju04Ex
HOWARD, Jno.		21	M	Laborer	01Ju04Ex
MCBRIDE, James		23	M	Laborer	01Ju04Ex
U-Mrs.	(M)	60	F	WI	01Ju04Ex
Sarah	(T)	14	F	None	01Ju04Ex
Alexr.	(B)	34	M	Laborer	01Ju04Ex
WALLACE, Jno.		30	M	Merchant	01Ju04Ex
PIERSTON, Matthew		20	M	Unknown	01Ju04Ex

BROOM 01 JUNE 1846

From Liverpool

NAMES OF PASSENGERS		AGE	SEX	OCCUPATIONS	DATE PORT SHIP
KELLY, John		25	M	Laborer	01Ju02Ey
Mary		20	F	Laborer	01Ju02Ey
SMITH, John-Duncan		44	M	Laborer	01Ju02Ey
DUNLOP, David		19	M	Laborer	01Ju02Ey
ANDREWS, Mary		21	F	Laborer	01Ju02Ey
Elizabeth		19	F	Laborer	01Ju02Ey
ARCHIBALD, Martha		21	F	Laborer	01Ju02Ey
PAUL, Sarah		22	F	Laborer	01Ju02Ey
RACE, James		17	M	Laborer	01Ju02Ey
MURPHY, Mary		19	F	Laborer	01Ju02Ey
HEALY, Winney		17	F	Laborer	01Ju02Ey
BOSTICK, Robert		20	M	Laborer	01Ju02Ey
KING, Lawrence		30	M	Laborer	01Ju02Ey
ROWE, Dennis		30	M	Laborer	01Ju02Ey
DUGAN, Thomas		26	M	Laborer	01Ju02Ey
MCLEAN, James		24	M	Laborer	01Ju02Ey
CONOLLY, Thomas		28	M	Laborer	01Ju02Ey
DOLAN, Nicholas		29	M	Laborer	01Ju02Ey
DAWGAN, Mary		24	F	Laborer	01Ju02Ey
BOYLE, Bridget		22	F	Laborer	01Ju02Ey
MCGEE, Patrick		22	M	Laborer	01Ju02Ey
MOORAN, Pattrick		22	M	Laborer	01Ju02Ey
JOYCE, Thomas		21	M	Laborer	01Ju02Ey
WILD, Jacob		26	M	Laborer	01Ju02Ey
FRITS, Abraham		24	M	Laborer	01Ju02Ey
DUGAN, Henry		20	M	Laborer	01Ju02Ey
Biddy		22	F	Laborer	01Ju02Ey
PINDER, Ellen		20	F	Laborer	01Ju02Ey
FARREL, Ellen		15	F	Laborer	01Ju02Ey
LYONS, Josiah		29	M	Laborer	01Ju02Ey
Catherina		19	F	Laborer	01Ju02Ey
Mary		32	F	Laborer	01Ju02Ey
Thomas		16	M	Laborer	01Ju02Ey
Mary-Jane		25	F	Laborer	01Ju02Ey
KERNEY, Hugh		24	M	Laborer	01Ju02Ey
LANAN, Lark		40	M	Laborer	01Ju02Ey
Honora		21	F	Wife	01Ju02Ey
Matilda		.00	F	Infant	01Ju02Ey
VESTIGNEY, Johanna		48	F	Laborer	01Ju02Ey
Erving	(S)	11	M	Laborer	01Ju02Ey

NAMES OF PASSENGERS		AGE	SEX	OCCUPATIONS	DATE PORT SHIP
BENORING, Jaobain		48	M	Laborer	01Ju02Ey
NOLAN, William		35	M	Laborer	01Ju02Ey
WALL, Ernent		37	U	Laborer	01Ju02Ey
STUKENLAN, Charles		30	M	Laborer	01Ju02Ey
TURPING, Thmothy		30	M	Laborer	01Ju02Ey
Dennis		22	M	Laborer	01Ju02Ey
Mary		25	F	Laborer	01Ju02Ey
Daniel		10	M	Laborer	01Ju02Ey
Catherne		14	F	Laborer	01Ju02Ey
TALBOT, Charles		28	M	Laborer	01Ju02Ey
MCSHIMLY, Thomas		25	M	Laborer	01Ju02Ey
MCKINNA, Owen		20	M	Laborer	01Ju02Ey
JUDGE, Bryan		26	M	Laborer	01Ju02Ey
Ann		21	F	Laborer	01Ju02Ey
Micheal		20	M	Laborer	01Ju02Ey
KELLY, Bryan		14	M	Laborer	01Ju02Ey
BLOCK, Samuel		21	M	Laborer	01Ju02Ey
COLGNON, Dennis		22	M	Laborer	01Ju02Ey
STURSHAM, Johanna		24	F	Laborer	01Ju02Ey
SUDGESAMON, John		22	M	Laborer	01Ju02Ey
Mary		25	F	Laborer	01Ju02Ey
ANGLS, John		24	M	Laborer	01Ju02Ey
DUNSHORT, John		26	M	Laborer	01Ju02Ey
QURDM, John		23	M	Laborer	01Ju02Ey
KINMIS, John		26	M	Laborer	01Ju02Ey
JORDAN, Mary		23	F	Laborer	01Ju02Ey
BATDIGE, Echanus		30	M	Laborer	01Ju02Ey
Sophia		24	F	Laborer	01Ju02Ey
Sopher		22	U	Laborer	01Ju02Ey
MCFIE, Alex		20	M	Laborer	01Ju02Ey
FRASER, John		22	M	Laborer	01Ju02Ey
Donald		60	M	Laborer	01Ju02Ey
U	(W)	60	F	Wife	01Ju02Ey
Ann		30	F	Laborer	01Ju02Ey
Agnes		26	F	Laborer	01Ju02Ey
Catherine		20	F	Laborer	01Ju02Ey
Jane		70	F	Laborer	01Ju02Ey
Margaret		20	F	Laborer	01Ju02Ey
Duncan		03	M	Child	01Ju02Ey
BRYANT, John		21	M	Laborer	01Ju02Ey
BAKER, Seath		19	M	Laborer	01Ju02Ey
KEENAN, Ellen		18	F	Laborer	01Ju02Ey
HANE, Patrick		19	M	Laborer	01Ju02Ey
HARDIMAN, Catherine		18	F	Laborer	01Ju02Ey
MONAGHAN, Mary		18	F	Laborer	01Ju02Ey
HARDINAN, Bridget		15	F	Laborer	01Ju02Ey
Mary		20	F	Laborer	01Ju02Ey
QUINN, James		22	M	Laborer	01Ju02Ey
BRIDGEMAN, Thomas		26	M	Laborer	01Ju02Ey
GALAGHER, Francis		24	M	Laborer	01Ju02Ey
MCIILROY, Catherine		25	F	Laborer	01Ju02Ey
MCGIWN, Thomas		25	M	Laborer	01Ju02Ey
MCMANNIS, William		28	M	Laborer	01Ju02Ey
CASSIDY, James		26	M	Laborer	01Ju02Ey
GORMLY, Mary		30	F	Laborer	01Ju02Ey
CASSIDY, George		21	M	Laborer	01Ju02Ey
MCGAN, Mathew		19	M	Laborer	01Ju02Ey
GALLAGHER, George		19	M	Laborer	01Ju02Ey
HASTINGS, William		50	M	Laborer	01Ju02Ey
U	(W)	40	F	Wife	01Ju02Ey
James		29	M	Laborer	01Ju02Ey
William		20	M	Laborer	01Ju02Ey
Susan		17	F	Laborer	01Ju02Ey
Jane		14	F	Laborer	01Ju02Ey
Joseph		05	M	Child	01Ju02Ey
Margret		03	F	Child	01Ju02Ey
BLORSNEY, Henry		13	M	Laborer	01Ju02Ey
DIRE, Mary		22	F	Laborer	01Ju02Ey
DONLY, Helen		20	F	Laborer	01Ju02Ey
MCLOCHLIN, Thomas		21	M	Laborer	01Ju02Ey
RUSSEL, William		19	M	Laborer	01Ju02Ey
JAMESON, Mary		22	F	Laborer	01Ju02Ey
Margret		21	F	Laborer	01Ju02Ey
DUNERDEN, Margret		20	F	Laborer	01Ju02Ey
Jane		18	F	Laborer	01Ju02Ey
MCLAUGHLIN, U-Mrs.		40	F	Laborer	01Ju02Ey
BURK, Patt		24	M	Laborer	01Ju02Ey
RYAN, Thomas		24	M	Laborer	01Ju02Ey
DONOVAN, Dennis		27	M	Laborer	01Ju02Ey
RYAN, Micheal		22	M	Laborer	01Ju02Ey
James		20	M	Laborer	01Ju02Ey
BRYAN, Mary		21	F	Laborer	01Ju02Ey
RYAN, Johanna		12	F	Laborer	01Ju02Ey
MOON, Edward		22	M	Laborer	01Ju02Ey
RYAN, Micheal		21	M	Laborer	01Ju02Ey
NOORE, Marla		20	F	Laborer	01Ju02Ey
Eliza		19	F	Laborer	01Ju02Ey
TRONY, Michael		18	M	Laborer	01Ju02Ey
WAR, John		27	M	Laborer	01Ju02Ey
CARROLL, Mathew		25	M	Laborer	01Ju02Ey
KELLY, Edward		22	M	Laborer	01Ju02Ey
FLYNN, James		28	M	Laborer	01Ju02Ey
Margret		24	F	Laborer	01Ju02Ey
CARTY, William		21	M	Laborer	01Ju02Ey
GALLAGHER, Patt		20	M	Laborer	01Ju02Ey
MCGRATH, John		19	M	Laborer	01Ju02Ey
Bridget		19	F	Laborer	01Ju02Ey
BRODY, James		20	M	Laborer	01Ju02Ey
EGAN, Patt		20	M	Laborer	01Ju02Ey
CORINGEN, Patt		20	M	Laborer	01Ju02Ey
HUGHIE, James		20	M	Laborer	01Ju02Ey
MCGRATH, Thomas		28	M	Laborer	01Ju02Ey
Mary		14	F	Laborer	01Ju02Ey
WATSON, Thomas		31	M	Laborer	01Ju02Ey
WRIGHT, William		60	M	Laborer	01Ju02Ey
James	(S)	25	M	Laborer	01Ju02Ey
Thomas	(S)	21	M	Laborer	01Ju02Ey
Catherine	(W)	60	F	Wife	01Ju02Ey
Sarah	(D)	25	F	Laborer	01Ju02Ey
Kitty	(D)	20	F	Laborer	01Ju02Ey
WATSON, Edward		25	M	Laborer	01Ju02Ey
BANCE, William		25	M	Laborer	01Ju02Ey
PAGAN, Ann		20	F	Laborer	01Ju02Ey
KELLY, Eliza		24	F	Laborer	01Ju02Ey
PERCIVAL, Thomas		30	M	Laborer	01Ju02Ey
Hannagh		23	F	Laborer	01Ju02Ey
MONAGHER, Thomas		20	M	Laborer	01Ju02Ey
Mary		22	F	Laborer	01Ju02Ey
BRADY, James		28	M	Laborer	01Ju02Ey
Mary		11	F	Laborer	01Ju02Ey
BARRY, Catherine		20	F	Laborer	01Ju02Ey
WALSH, John		23	M	Laborer	01Ju02Ey
DERR, Biddy		21	F	Laborer	01Ju02Ey
WALSH, Catherine		16	F	Laborer	01Ju02Ey
Dennis		12	M	Laborer	01Ju02Ey
GROONE, John		22	M	Laborer	01Ju02Ey
CALLAGHAN, Thomas		40	M	Laborer	01Ju02Ey
Bridget	(D)	20	F	Laborer	01Ju02Ey
Margret	(D)	17	F	Laborer	01Ju02Ey
Dennis	(S)	13	M	Laborer	01Ju02Ey
Ellen	(D)	12	F	Laborer	01Ju02Ey
Marry	(D)	08	F	Child	01Ju02Ey
Thomas	(S)	05	M	Child	01Ju02Ey
MOLAN, Michael		20	M	Laborer	01Ju02Ey
DUFFY, Christian		22	M	Laborer	01Ju02Ey
James		21	M	Laborer	01Ju02Ey
MULLIGAN, Micheal		21	M	Laborer	01Ju02Ey
FITZPATRICK, Mary		20	F	Laborer	01Ju02Ey
CURRAN, Susan		20	F	Laborer	01Ju02Ey
KELLY, John		35	M	Laborer	01Ju02Ey
WHELAN, Thomas		28	M	Laborer	01Ju02Ey
MARTIN, Patt		33	M	Laborer	01Ju02Ey
SANLER, William		29	M	Laborer	01Ju02Ey
WALSH, John		26	M	Laborer	01Ju02Ey
COGGAN, Johanna		19	F	Laborer	01Ju02Ey
CUMMINS, James		30	M	Laborer	01Ju02Ey
DENLAM, William		20	M	Laborer	01Ju02Ey
MACK, Mary		19	F	Laborer	01Ju02Ey
FARREL, Patt		19	M	Laborer	01Ju02Ey
BRAHAM, Dan		21	M	Laborer	01Ju02Ey

NAMES OF PASSENGERS		AGE	SEX	OCCUPATIONS	DATE PORT SHIP
HANLEY, John		20	M	Laborer	01Ju02Ey
HUGHES, Mary		25	F	Laborer	01Ju02Ey
QUINN, Mary		19	F	Laborer	01Ju02Ey
CLARK, Margret		19	F	Laborer	01Ju02Ey
Mary		19	F	Laborer	01Ju02Ey
CAREY, Charles		15	M	Laborer	01Ju02Ey
HIND, Cathn.		24	F	Laborer	01Ju02Ey
MOORE, Patt		23	M	Laborer	01Ju02Ey
Caslohr		22	M	Laborer	01Ju02Ey
CARTY, Patt		20	M	Laborer	01Ju02Ey
SEXTON, Thomas		20	M	Laborer	01Ju02Ey
CAROWN, Mary		20	F	Laborer	01Ju02Ey
FYE, Thomas		23	M	Laborer	01Ju02Ey
Bridget		24	F	Laborer	01Ju02Ey
REILLY, Catherne		20	F	Laborer	01Ju02Ey
MAHER, Margret		01	F	Child	01Ju02Ey
GAVIN, Ann		10	F	Child	01Ju02Ey
MABODY, Rose		21	F	Laborer	01Ju02Ey
John		06	M	Child	01Ju02Ey
FARRELL, Catherine		04	F	Child	01Ju02Ey
BOHEWN, James		19	M	Laborer	01Ju02Ey
Anthony		27	M	Laborer	01Ju02Ey
JOHNSTON, Mary		25	F	Laborer	01Ju02Ey
MCDONNAGH, Mary		25	F	Laborer	01Ju02Ey
FALLEN, Michael		20	M	Laborer	01Ju02Ey
Mary		18	F	Laborer	01Ju02Ey
DWYRE, Biddy		19	F	Laborer	01Ju02Ey
DUNN, Mary		20	F	Laborer	01Ju02Ey
MCCANN, Jabella		24	F	Laborer	01Ju02Ey
DONELLY, Patrick		30	M	Laborer	01Ju02Ey
Sally		20	F	Laborer	01Ju02Ey
DOYLE, Lewis		22	M	Laborer	01Ju02Ey
BARRET, Michael		50	M	Laborer	01Ju02Ey
Mary		40	F	Laborer	01Ju02Ey
John		24	M	Laborer	01Ju02Ey
Michael		24	M	Laborer	01Ju02Ey
Mary		08	F	Child	01Ju02Ey
Martin		06	M	Chelne	01Ju02Ey
Ann		02	F	Child	01Ju02Ey
BRANNAN, Mary		24	F	Laborer	01Ju02Ey
BARRY, Philip		55	M	Laborer	01Ju02Ey
MILLOR, Thomas		26	M	Laborer	01Ju02Ey
PRIESTNALL, Thomas		23	M	Laborer	01Ju02Ey
LEVI, M.		27	M	Laborer	01Ju02Ey
BRIGNELL, Ann		31	F	Laborer	01Ju02Ey
HALL, Mary		30	F	Laborer	01Ju02Ey
Joseph	(S)	08	M	Child	01Ju02Ey
MALLOY, Gerald		30	M	Laborer	01Ju02Ey
BRADY, Bernard		18	M	Laborer	01Ju02Ey
BOUKE, Hyancinth		29	F	Laborer	01Ju02Ey
Ann		20	F	Laborer	01Ju02Ey
CONNISKY, Marie		19	F	Laborer	01Ju02Ey
Barthy	(D)	02	F	Child	01Ju02Ey
SWEENEY, Ann		19	F	Laborer	01Ju02Ey
KEATIN, Ellen		17	F	Laborer	01Ju02Ey
TOLIN, Mary		28	F	Laborer	01Ju02Ey
KEATNY, Catherine		25	F	Laborer	01Ju02Ey
GORMAN, Bridget		20	F	Laborer	01Ju02Ey
DWYRE, John		27	M	Laborer	01Ju02Ey
DOYLE, Patrick		18	M	Laborer	01Ju02Ey
MALONEY, John		21	M	Laborer	01Ju02Ey
BRISLIN, Catherine		24	F	Laborer	01Ju02Ey
FAULKNER, Elizabeth		25	F	Laborer	01Ju02Ey
DONOVAN, Ellen		20	F	Laborer	01Ju02Ey
MULLIN, Catherine		20	F	Laborer	01Ju02Ey
Sarah		21	F	Laborer	01Ju02Ey
MADDEN, Mary		18	F	Laborer	01Ju02Ey
CRWAN, Mary-Ann		18	F	Laborer	01Ju02Ey
NORTON, John		24	M	Laborer	01Ju02Ey
MULLIN, Martin		26	M	Laborer	01Ju02Ey
SHERIDAN, John		35	M	Laborer	01Ju02Ey
FARREL, Micheal		19	M	Laborer	01Ju02Ey
COOK, John		20	M	Laborer	01Ju02Ey
SMITH, Bernard		18	M	Laborer	01Ju02Ey
MCCABE, Patt		17	M	Laborer	01Ju02Ey
MCGALIN, Rose		21	F	Laborer	01Ju02Ey
SMITH, Bridget		19	F	Laborer	01Ju02Ey
Connor		21	F	Laborer	01Ju02Ey
WICKS, Edward		22	M	Laborer	01Ju02Ey
MORTON, Ellen		22	F	Laborer	01Ju02Ey
WOODS, Michael		24	M	Laborer	01Ju02Ey
Susan		21	F	Laborer	01Ju02Ey
MCGUNNAGH, James		22	M	Laborer	01Ju02Ey
BRANNIGAN, Thomas		40	M	Laborer	01Ju02Ey
U	(W)	35	F	Wife	01Ju02Ey
Elizabeth	(D)	01	F	Child	01Ju02Ey
KEENAN, Edward		21	M	Laborer	01Ju02Ey
MCDONAGH, William		35	M	Laborer	01Ju02Ey
Bridget	(W)	32	F	Wife	01Ju02Ey
Edward	(S)	.00	M	Infant	01Ju02Ey
Francis	(S)	12	M	Laborer	01Ju02Ey
Joseph	(S)	09	M	Child	01Ju02Ey
COLLINS, Edward		28	M	Laborer	01Ju02Ey
CASEY, Michael		22	M	Laborer	01Ju02Ey
CAMERY, James		26	M	Laborer	01Ju02Ey
GUGG, James		29	M	Laborer	01Ju02Ey
FLANNIGAN, Martin		24	M	Laborer	01Ju02Ey
EGAN, Catherne		19	F	Laborer	01Ju02Ey
MOWRAN, Bess		20	F	Laborer	01Ju02Ey
MCCARTY, Ellen		18	F	Laborer	01Ju02Ey
MCGRATH, William		30	M	Laborer	01Ju02Ey
CARNEY, Margret		25	F	Laborer	01Ju02Ey
SHERIDAN, John		13	M	Laborer	01Ju02Ey
WILD, Samuel		22	M	Laborer	01Ju02Ey
COOKINGHAM, Samuel		35	M	Laborer	01Ju02Ey
MURRAY, Thomas		21	M	Laborer	01Ju02Ey
Mary		66	F	Laborer	01Ju02Ey
Thomas		60	M	Laborer	01Ju02Ey
WALSH, Michael		20	M	Laborer	01Ju02Ey
GORDAN, Peter		30	M	Laborer	01Ju02Ey
MURRAY, Mary		20	F	Laborer	01Ju02Ey
Ellen		21	F	Laborer	01Ju02Ey
Cathelne		10	F	Laborer	01Ju02Ey
Catherne		08	F	Child	01Ju02Ey
KINNY, James		02	M	Child	01Ju02Ey
FLYNN, John		10	M	Laborer	01Ju02Ey
SCARLICK, Mary		17	F	Laborer	01Ju02Ey
MORNAN, Alice		20	F	Laborer	01Ju02Ey
LONG, Mathew		20	M	Laborer	01Ju02Ey
SHERMAN, Andrew		30	M	Laborer	01Ju02Ey
U	(W)	24	F	Wife	01Ju02Ey
George	(S)	01	M	Child	01Ju02Ey
Elizabeth	(D)	.00	F	Infant	01Ju02Ey
MCGUNY, Thomas		40	M	Laborer	01Ju02Ey
Patrick		20	M	Laborer	01Ju02Ey
Catherin		18	F	Laborer	01Ju02Ey
HY, Patrick		20	M	Laborer	01Ju02Ey
Margret		17	F	Laborer	01Ju02Ey
QUNN, Burney		19	F	Laborer	01Ju02Ey
RAFFERDY, Mary		20	F	Laborer	01Ju02Ey
GLESAN, William		21	M	Laborer	01Ju02Ey
BODAN, Mathew		22	M	Laborer	01Ju02Ey
MCCULIGAN, John		26	M	Laborer	01Ju02Ey
HALPIN, Mck		24	M	Laborer	01Ju02Ey
QUILLAN, John		20	M	Laborer	01Ju02Ey
DORGAN, Fredrick		19	M	Laborer	01Ju02Ey
QURNNING, John		18	M	Laborer	01Ju02Ey
SMITH, John		18	M	Laborer	01Ju02Ey
GLESSEY, Micheal		19	M	Laborer	01Ju02Ey
CLARK, Mary		20	F	Laborer	01Ju02Ey
William		21	M	Laborer	01Ju02Ey
Ann		20	F	Laborer	01Ju02Ey

NAMES OF PASSENGERS		AGE	SEX	OCCUPATIONS	DATE PORT SHIP
RICE, Michael		25	M	Laborer	01Ju02Fa
John		17	M	Laborer	01Ju02Fa
READ, John		21	M	Laborer	01Ju02Fa
SHIRE, Margt.		21	F	Laborer	01Ju02Fa
MCARDLE, Owen		56	M	Laborer	01Ju02Fa
Mary		37	F	Laborer	01Ju02Fa
Owen		19	M	Laborer	01Ju02Fa
Phillp		15	M	Laborer	01Ju02Fa
Mary		13	F	Laborer	01Ju02Fa
Thomas		06	M	Child	01Ju02Fa
STOKES, James		23	M	Laborer	01Ju02Fa
SAVAGE, Alice		23	F	Laborer	01Ju02Fa
CORALON, Thomas		19	M	Laborer	01Ju02Fa
MATHEWS, John		21	M	Laborer	01Ju02Fa
Thomas		26	M	Laborer	01Ju02Fa
HUGHES, James		20	M	Laborer	01Ju02Fa
BYRNE, Owen		20	M	Laborer	01Ju02Fa
FITZIMMONS, James		16	M	Laborer	01Ju02Fa
RODDY, Pat		26	M	Laborer	01Ju02Fa
DONNELLY, James		25	M	Laborer	01Ju02Fa
SMITH, Michael		20	M	Laborer	01Ju02Fa
MCBRIDE, Michael		20	M	Laborer	01Ju02Fa
Michael		20	M	Laborer	01Ju02Fa
QUIGLEY, John		19	M	Laborer	01Ju02Fa
Mary		20	F	Laborer	01Ju02Fa
MCBRIDE, Thomas		23	M	Laborer	01Ju02Fa
CARROLL, Patrick		26	M	Laborer	01Ju02Fa
NEARY, Catherine		24	F	Laborer	01Ju02Fa
MAGEE, Barnard		20	M	Laborer	01Ju02Fa
MALONE, Lawrence		25	M	Laborer	01Ju02Fa
Catherine		24	F	Laborer	01Ju02Fa
THORNTON, Rose		20	F	Laborer	01Ju02Fa
SAVEN, John		21	M	Laborer	01Ju02Fa
Sarah	(W)	19	F	Wife	01Ju02Fa
Maria	(D)	.00	F	Infant	01Ju02Fa
KILBRIDE, Martin		22	M	Laborer	01Ju02Fa
SNAIGHT, Michael		30	M	Laborer	01Ju02Fa
ROONEY, Lackey		30	M	Laborer	01Ju02Fa
ROGAN, Owen		21	M	Laborer	01Ju02Fa
COSTELLO, Richard		24	M	Laborer	01Ju02Fa
PADDEN, Patrick		24	M	Laborer	01Ju02Fa
OHEAR, Peter		19	M	Laborer	01Ju02Fa
SMITH, James		24	M	Laborer	01Ju02Fa
MILLER, John		28	M	Laborer	01Ju02Fa
MONAGHAN, Richard		26	M	Laborer	01Ju02Fa
Pheebe		26	F	Laborer	01Ju02Fa
COGAN, Mary		24	F	Laborer	01Ju02Fa
WILLIS, Catherine		25	F	Laborer	01Ju02Fa
MONGIN, Mary		24	F	Laborer	01Ju02Fa
TAFFEY, Bridget		23	F	Laborer	01Ju02Fa
MURTAGH, Mary		26	F	Laborer	01Ju02Fa
FALOON, Ann		21	F	Laborer	01Ju02Fa
COGAN, Mary		25	F	Laborer	01Ju02Fa
MORAN, John		20	M	Laborer	01Ju02Fa
LATEY, Joseph		30	M	Laborer	01Ju02Fa
U	(W)	25	F	Wife	01Ju02Fa
Mary-Ann	(D)	09	F	Child	01Ju02Fa
Fanny	(D)	07	F	Child	01Ju02Fa
Hessey	(D)	02	F	Child	01Ju02Fa
CONNOR, Thomas		23	M	Laborer	01Ju02Fa
Patrick		25	M	Laborer	01Ju02Fa
MULGAN, Mary		28	F	Laborer	01Ju02Fa
Judy		33	F	Laborer	01Ju02Fa
COSTELLO, Martin		22	M	Laborer	01Ju02Fa
KELLY, Patrick		27	M	Laborer	01Ju02Fa
MCGOVEN, James		28	M	Laborer	01Ju02Fa
U	(W)	26	F	Wife	01Ju02Fa
NOONAN, Michael		30	M	Laborer	01Ju02Fa
CLIFFORD, John		22	M	Laborer	01Ju02Fa
BRYAN, Edwd.		20	M	Laborer	01Ju02Fa
WHEELAN, John		21	M	Laborer	01Ju02Fa
MORAS, Thomas		23	M	Laborer	01Ju02Fa
JONES, Danl.		23	M	Laborer	01Ju02Fa
MCSHANE, Patrick		22	M	Laborer	01Ju02Fa
CARRON, John		24	M	Laborer	01Ju02Fa
CARROLL, Catherine		20	F	Laborer	01Ju02Fa
CANTON, James		20	M	Laborer	01Ju02Fa
DUFFY, Thomas		20	M	Laborer	01Ju02Fa
HEARTY, John		22	M	Laborer	01Ju02Fa
CONNELLY, Alice		16	F	Laborer	01Ju02Fa
MCKDOAN, Patrick		16	M	Laborer	01Ju02Fa
WHITE, Pat		26	M	Laborer	01Ju02Fa
MITCHELL, Thomas		26	M	Laborer	01Ju02Fa
KENNEDY, Michael		22	M	Laborer	01Ju02Fa
OBRIAN, Fergus		21	M	Laborer	01Ju02Fa
CANTON, Pat		28	M	Laborer	01Ju02Fa
OGARA, Thomas		24	M	Laborer	01Ju02Fa
ROGERS, Martin		23	M	Laborer	01Ju02Fa
BELL, Mary-Ann		25	F	Laborer	01Ju02Fa
MCKEE, Eliza		24	F	Laborer	01Ju02Fa
DALEY, Mary		20	F	Laborer	01Ju02Fa
FINNEGAN, John		25	M	Laborer	01Ju02Fa
BAYLAN, Owen		40	M	Laborer	01Ju02Fa
Bridget	(W)	40	F	Wife	01Ju02Fa
Mary	(D)	16	F	Laborer	01Ju02Fa
Bridget	(D)	15	F	Laborer	01Ju02Fa
Catherine	(D)	13	F	Laborer	01Ju02Fa
Bessy	(D)	10	F	Laborer	01Ju02Fa
CASSADAY, Catherine		30	F	Laborer	01Ju02Fa
MARTIN, Patrick		30	M	Laborer	01Ju02Fa
Bridget	(W)	28	F	Wife	01Ju02Fa
John	(S)	.00	M	Infant	01Ju02Fa
MOONEY, George		45	M	Laborer	01Ju02Fa
Catherine	(W)	45	F	Wife	01Ju02Fa
James	(S)	20	M	Laborer	01Ju02Fa
Bridget	(D)	16	F	Laborer	01Ju02Fa
John	(S)	13	M	Laborer	01Ju02Fa
Patrick	(S)	12	M	Laborer	01Ju02Fa
Peter	(S)	07	M	Child	01Ju02Fa
Sylvester	(S)	05	M	Child	01Ju02Fa
Ann	(D)	02	F	Child	01Ju02Fa
LAMB, Judith		17	F	Laborer	01Ju02Fa
BOYLE, Bridget		22	F	Laborer	01Ju02Fa
CARROLL, James		21	M	Laborer	01Ju02Fa
MANGAN, Michael		24	M	Laborer	01Ju02Fa
HUFF, Abraham		26	M	Laborer	01Ju02Fa
GLENON, Tom		25	M	Laborer	01Ju02Fa
GARRATY, Ann		20	F	Laborer	01Ju02Fa
HOLLAGAN, David		21	M	Laborer	01Ju02Fa
BARR, Nathaniel		21	M	Laborer	01Ju02Fa
SHARPLES, Charles		18	M	Laborer	01Ju02Fa
HART, Peter		25	M	Laborer	01Ju02Fa
SCHWEETZER, Moritz		42	M	Laborer	01Ju02Fa
Dorathea	(W)	42	F	Wife	01Ju02Fa
Henrietta	(D)	18	F	Laborer	01Ju02Fa
Julian	(D)	13	F	Laborer	01Ju02Fa
UKNMACHER, Joseph		29	M	Laborer	01Ju02Fa
Ennostine-Hersch	(W)	28	F	Wife	01Ju02Fa
Julius	(S)	02	M	Child	01Ju02Fa
Rosalie	(D)	.00	F	Infant	01Ju02Fa
COWLEY, Edward		25	M	Laborer	01Ju02Fa
SHAMEY, Thomas		20	M	Laborer	01Ju02Fa
MCDERMOTT, Biddy		28	F	Laborer	01Ju02Fa
SCALLY, Owen		34	M	Laborer	01Ju02Fa
GALLAGHER, James		26	M	Laborer	01Ju02Fa
BURKE, Edward		26	M	Laborer	01Ju02Fa
SCALLY, Mary		30	F	Laborer	01Ju02Fa
George	(S)	12	M	Laborer	01Ju02Fa
Biddy	(D)	10	F	Laborer	01Ju02Fa
MOLEY, Anne		22	F	Laborer	01Ju02Fa

NAMES OF PASSENGERS		AGE	SEX	OCCUPATIONS	DATE PORT SHIP
MAHER, Ellen		19	F	Laborer	01Ju02Fa
BURKE, Margt.		22	F	Laborer	01Ju02Fa
FALONE, Ellen		23	F	Laborer	01Ju02Fa
QUIRK, Patt		20	M	Laborer	01Ju02Fa
Mary		25	F	Laborer	01Ju02Fa
RULRY, Danl.		22	M	Laborer	01Ju02Fa
BLYTHE, Mary		18	F	Laborer	01Ju02Fa
SPANN, Biddy		20	F	Laborer	01Ju02Fa
QUIRK, Margt.		21	F	Laborer	01Ju02Fa
FITZGERRALD, Thomas		30	M	Laborer	01Ju02Fa
GLYNN, Nicholas		38	M	Laborer	01Ju02Fa
GRATY, Mary		20	F	Laborer	01Ju02Fa
LEE, Bridget		20	F	Laborer	01Ju02Fa
MICHIN, Nelly		20	F	Laborer	01Ju02Fa
FOSTER, John		35	M	Laborer	01Ju02Fa
Margaret	(W)	30	F	Wife	01Ju02Fa
Margaret	(D)	09	F	Child	01Ju02Fa
Catherine	(D)	07	F	Child	01Ju02Fa
John	(S)	05	M	Child	01Ju02Fa
Jane	(D)	02	F	Child	01Ju02Fa
Thomas	(S)	.00	M	Infant	01Ju02Fa
COURY, Jane		18	F	Laborer	01Ju02Fa
DOUGHERTY, Patt		25	M	Laborer	01Ju02Fa
MANEY, Jane		22	F	Laborer	01Ju02Fa
CASEY, John		30	M	Laborer	01Ju02Fa
KELLY, John		18	M	Laborer	01Ju02Fa
Edward		22	M	Laborer	01Ju02Fa
CASEY, Mary		18	F	Laborer	01Ju02Fa
CARLIN, Margt.		18	F	Laborer	01Ju02Fa
CONLIN, Margt.		18	F	Laborer	01Ju02Fa
LEDGRINTCH, James		27	M	Laborer	01Ju02Fa
Patt		20	M	Laborer	01Ju02Fa
CUNNINGHAM, Peter		18	M	Laborer	01Ju02Fa
Rose		16	F	Laborer	01Ju02Fa
CLARKE, Ellen		18	F	Laborer	01Ju02Fa
MEHIN, James		20	M	Laborer	01Ju02Fa
JOYCE, Hannah		20	F	Laborer	01Ju02Fa
MURRAY, Lack		20	U	Laborer	01Ju02Fa
MORTOUGH, Cathe.		18	F	Laborer	01Ju02Fa
BOLAND, Ellen		20	F	Laborer	01Ju02Fa
WALTERS, Melmouth		24	U	Laborer	01Ju02Fa
WHITTY, Thomas		28	M	Laborer	01Ju02Fa
MADDOCK, John		24	M	Laborer	01Ju02Fa
FLANAGAN, Pat		35	M	Laborer	01Ju02Fa
Mary		28	F	Laborer	01Ju02Fa
SMITH, Philip		30	M	Laborer	01Ju02Fa
Elizth.		25	F	Laborer	01Ju02Fa
MARTIN, Mary		20	F	Laborer	01Ju02Fa
DUNN, James		20	M	Laborer	01Ju02Fa
MOON, Epaminondis		22	U	Laborer	01Ju02Fa
DAVIES, Edward		36	M	Laborer	01Ju02Fa
Margaret		38	F	Laborer	01Ju02Fa
BROCK, William		26	M	Laborer	01Ju02Fa
DOLAN, James		28	M	Laborer	01Ju02Fa
DONLAN, John		18	M	Laborer	01Ju02Fa
DOLAN, Mary		25	F	Laborer	01Ju02Fa
CURLEY, Owen		28	M	Laborer	01Ju02Fa
MULDY, Patt		22	M	Laborer	01Ju02Fa
Maty		20	M	Laborer	01Ju02Fa
KEHO, Peter		20	M	Laborer	01Ju02Fa
Mary		20	F	Laborer	01Ju02Fa
RYAN, Robert		21	M	Laborer	01Ju02Fa
LANAN, Watt		25	M	Laborer	01Ju02Fa
CONDRAN, Patt		22	M	Laborer	01Ju02Fa
CARRIGAN, Martin		20	M	Laborer	01Ju02Fa
DARMODY, Catherine		20	F	Laborer	01Ju02Fa
MANIFOLD, Richard		24	M	Laborer	01Ju02Fa
MORAN, Edward		25	M	Laborer	01Ju02Fa
CONDON, Gannet		21	M	Laborer	01Ju02Fa
KELENEY, Michael		24	M	Laborer	01Ju02Fa
WILSON, Thomas		25	M	Laborer	01Ju02Fa
MCLARNON, Thomas		50	M	Laborer	01Ju02Fa
Catherine	(W)	50	F	Wife	01Ju02Fa
Bernard	(S)	22	M	Laborer	01Ju02Fa
Mary	(D)	20	F	Laborer	01Ju02Fa
MCLARNON, Teresa	(D)	18	F	Laborer	01Ju02Fa
Patrick	(S)	16	M	Laborer	01Ju02Fa
Francis	(S)	14	M	Laborer	01Ju02Fa
Thomas	(S)	12	M	Laborer	01Ju02Fa
Henry	(S)	10	M	Laborer	01Ju02Fa
DAW, Peter		24	M	Laborer	01Ju02Fa
James		22	M	Laborer	01Ju02Fa
WHITE, Thomas		24	M	Laborer	01Ju02Fa
QUINN, Nicholas		48	M	Laborer	01Ju02Fa
AUTEY, James		28	M	Laborer	01Ju02Fa
Elizabeth	(W)	32	F	Wife	01Ju02Fa
Mary-Ann	(D)	02	F	Child	01Ju02Fa
LEONARD, John		20	M	Laborer	01Ju02Fa
Catherine		16	F	Laborer	01Ju02Fa
SLAVIN, Felix		20	M	Laborer	01Ju02Fa
MULLIN, John		25	M	Laborer	01Ju02Fa
Danl.		21	M	Laborer	01Ju02Fa
MCCARN, Mary		19	F	Laborer	01Ju02Fa
SHENY, Mary		22	F	Laborer	01Ju02Fa
HAMILL, Bill		20	M	Laborer	01Ju02Fa
SHENY, Margt.		19	F	Laborer	01Ju02Fa
RILEY, John		40	M	Laborer	01Ju02Fa
FRAINE, Patrick		22	M	Laborer	01Ju02Fa
MEGRATH, Francis		18	M	Laborer	01Ju02Fa
Barnard		22	M	Laborer	01Ju02Fa
BORDON, James		23	M	Laborer	01Ju02Fa
KELLY, Pat		19	M	Laborer	01Ju02Fa
MCDONE, Pat		20	M	Laborer	01Ju02Fa
TURNER, Wm.		66	M	Laborer	01Ju02Fa
CKHILL, Pat		32	M	Laborer	01Ju02Fa
HAFRON, Darby		24	M	Laborer	01Ju02Fa
CDIHON, James		20	M	Laborer	01Ju02Fa
HOOFRON, Henry		25	M	Laborer	01Ju02Fa
BRITT, Thomas		28	M	Laborer	01Ju02Fa
DORIN, Thomas		22	M	Laborer	01Ju02Fa
CAMPIN, Nancy		40	F	Laborer	01Ju02Fa
Pagy	(D)	13	F	Laborer	01Ju02Fa
Ann	(D)	15	F	Laborer	01Ju02Fa
Catherine	(D)	11	F	Laborer	01Ju02Fa
HALMALRAY, Mary		19	F	Laborer	01Ju02Fa
LINCH, Pat		20	M	Laborer	01Ju02Fa
CONNLY, Wm.		24	M	Laborer	01Ju02Fa
MCGRAFF, Mary		26	F	Laborer	01Ju02Fa
HANECY, Brigget		22	F	Laborer	01Ju02Fa
HAMILTON, Eliza		20	F	Laborer	01Ju02Fa
HEGANS, Catharin		20	F	Laborer	01Ju02Fa
Mary	(D)	.00	F	Infant	01Ju02Fa
COLIGAN, Cath.		20	F	Laborer	01Ju02Fa
HASE, Feby		40	F	Laborer	01Ju02Fa
Gee	(S)	20	M	Laborer	01Ju02Fa
Ann	(D)	16	F	Laborer	01Ju02Fa
Absolem	(S)	14	M	Laborer	01Ju02Fa
Manasah	(S)	12	M	Laborer	01Ju02Fa
Ephragm	(S)	10	M	Laborer	01Ju02Fa
Cyrus	(S)	07	M	Child	01Ju02Fa
Daniel	(S)	03	M	Child	01Ju02Fa
MURRY, James		49	M	Laborer	01Ju02Fa

MARY-HARRINGTON 02 JUNE 1846

From Londonderry

NAMES OF PASSENGERS		AGE	SEX	OCCUPATIONS	DATE PORT SHIP
KERRIGAN, Hugh		30	M	Laborer	02Ju01Fh
FERGUSON, Chas.		20	M	Spinner	02Ju01Fh
SCOTT, Thomas		40	M	Laborer	02Ju01Fh
Nancy	(W)	35	F	Wife	02Ju01Fh
Hannah	(D)	07	F	Child	02Ju01Fh
Martha	(D)	05	F	Child	02Ju01Fh
Mary-J.	(D)	02	F	Child	02Ju01Fh

NAMES OF PASSENGERS		AGE	SEX	OCCUPATIONS	DATE PORT SHIP
GEE, Mary-M.		18	F	Spinster	02Ju01Fh
LAVERTY, Medina		13	M	Spinner	02Ju01Fh
MCCORMICK, Sally		30	F	Spinster	02Ju01Fh
WILLIAMS, Eliz.		21	F	Spinster	02Ju01Fh
Mary		19	F	Spinster	02Ju01Fh
PATTON, Arthur		34	M	Farmer	02Ju01Fh
Margt.	(W)	32	F	Wife	02Ju01Fh
James	(S)	07	M	Child	02Ju01Fh
CHAMBERS, Betty		12	F	Spinster	02Ju01Fh
Sophia		09	F	Child	02Ju01Fh
MCCREEDY, Jane		28	F	Spinster	02Ju01Fh
PATTON, Jas.		12	M	Laborer	02Ju01Fh
ORR, Robert		26	M	Laborer	02Ju01Fh
MCDERMOTT, Jno.		10	M	Child	02Ju01Fh
Sally	(M)	33	F	Wi	02Ju01Fh
LOUGHREA, Thomas		11	M	None	02Ju01Fh
GILDEA, Margt.		22	F	Spinster	02Ju01Fh
QUINN, Biddy		13	F	Spinster	02Ju01Fh
DIVENNY, James		24	M	Mason	02Ju01Fh
CASSIDY, Cath.		10	F	Child	02Ju01Fh
WILSON, Matilda		52	F	Wife	02Ju01Fh
PEOPLES, Jane		13	F	Spinster	02Ju01Fh
DUFFY, James		27	M	Farmer	02Ju01Fh
Mary		34	F	Spinster	02Ju01Fh
Cath.		12	F	Spinster	02Ju01Fh
MCLOUGHLIN, Martha		48	F	Spinster	02Ju01Fh
HASLETT, Wm.		37	M	Farmer	02Ju01Fh
Sarah	(M)	65	F	Wife	02Ju01Fh
Died-At-Sea					
Jane	(D)	17	F	Spinster	
Isabella	(D)	14	F	Spinster	
CANNON, Jas.		29	M	Laborer	02Ju01Fh
Wm.	(S)	11	M	None	02Ju01Fh
MCGLINCHY, Wm.		32	M	Spinner	02Ju01Fh
MCCLOSKEY, Cath.		12	F	Spinster	02Ju01Fh
MCCALLUM, Eleanor		18	F	Spinster	02Ju01Fh
Denis		10	M	Child	02Ju01Fh
MCARTER, Jno.		27	M	Blacksmith	02Ju01Fh
BOWEN, Anne		07	F	Child	02Ju01Fh
GORMLEY, James		37	M	Farmer	02Ju01Fh
Margt.		10	F	Child	02Ju01Fh
Eliz.		19	F	Spinster	02Ju01Fh
DENSIMORE, Mary		12	F	Spinster	02Ju01Fh
BRADLEY, Susanna		18	F	Spinster	02Ju01Fh
MCCAFFERTY, Hannah		10	F	Child	02Ju01Fh
KERRIGAN, Jas.		35	M	Shoemaker	02Ju01Fh
MCCOLLIM, Chas.		10	M	Child	02Ju01Fh
Cath.	(M)	29	F	Wife	02Ju01Fh
HUGHES, Eliz.		29	F	Wife	02Ju01Fh
Mary	(D)	07	F	Child	02Ju01Fh
DUFFY, Francis		34	M	Farmer	02Ju01Fh
Anne	(W)	26	F	Wife	02Ju01Fh
Isa.	(D)	05	F	Child	02Ju01Fh
CANNON, Danl.		26	M	Butcher	02Ju01Fh
HARKIN, Eliz.		12	F	Spinster	02Ju01Fh
CONAHAN, Manus		10	M	Child	02Ju01Fh
DIVENNY, Elianor		22	F	Dressmaker	02Ju01Fh
GALLAGHER, Robt.		13	M	Laborer	02Ju01Fh
MALLON, Mary		24	F	Spinster	02Ju01Fh
PORTER, Jane		09	F	Child	02Ju01Fh
MCGRYOR, Matilda		17	F	Spinster	02Ju01Fh
BISHOP, Martha		13	F	Spinster	02Ju01Fh
DOUGLAS, Geo.		54	M	Farmer	02Ju01Fh
U	(W)	48	F	Wife	02Ju01Fh
Jno.	(S)	24	M	Farmer	02Ju01Fh
Rosanna	(D)	22	F	Farmer	02Ju01Fh
James	(S)	13	M	Farmer	02Ju01Fh
George	(S)	18	M	Farmer	02Ju01Fh
William	(S)	10	M	Child	02Ju01Fh
Frederick	(S)	07	M	Child	02Ju01Fh
OCAM, Mary		21	F	Spinster	02Ju01Fh
HOPPER, Martha		13	F	Spinster	02Ju01Fh
ALCOON, Mary-Anne		24	F	Spinster	02Ju01Fh
MCKEEVER, Rosanna		31	F	Spinster	02Ju01Fh
AUGHRY, Jane		12	F	Spinster	02Ju01Fh
MARSHALL, Martha		10	F	Child	02Ju01Fh
MADDEN, Jno.		17	M	Laborer	02Ju01Fh
Eliza		13	F	Spinster	02Ju01Fh
WATTS, Robert		24	M	Farmer	02Ju01Fh
HALL, John		13	M	Laborer	02Ju01Fh
BOWEN, Alxr.		47	M	Laborer	02Ju01Fh
MCCAFFRAY, Anthony		30	M	Farmer	02Ju01Fh
Mary	(W)	28	F	Wife	02Ju01Fh
James	(S)	12	M	None	02Ju01Fh
Rose	(D)	10	F	Child	02Ju01Fh
Alexr.	(S)	07	M	Child	02Ju01Fh
Anthony	(S)	03	M	Child	02Ju01Fh
MCFALL, Rebecca		25	F	Spinster	02Ju01Fh
PARKHILL, William		32	M	Farmer	02Ju01Fh
Margt.	(D)	10	F	Child	02Ju01Fh
MCCLOSKEY, Mary		25	F	Spinster	02Ju01Fh
Edwd.		19	M	Laborer	02Ju01Fh
Robert		13	M	Laborer	02Ju01Fh
Grace		11	F	None	02Ju01Fh
Hannah		09	F	Child	02Ju01Fh
DOGHERTY, Mary		30	F	Wife	02Ju01Fh
Hammond	(S)	10	M	Child	02Ju01Fh
Emily	(D)	08	F	Child	02Ju01Fh
Robert-John	(S)	06	M	Child	02Ju01Fh
TAYLOR, Jno.		24	M	Laborer	02Ju01Fh
ALLEN, Robert		25	M	Laborer	02Ju01Fh
DOGHERTY, Eliz.		21	F	Spinster	02Ju01Fh
ORR, Esther		13	F	Spinster	02Ju01Fh
ALLEN, Saml.		25	M	Mason	02Ju01Fh
MCCANN, Mi.		27	M	Farmer	02Ju01Fh
BARR, Patk.		10	M	Child	02Ju01Fh
EATON, Sarah		17	F	Spinster	02Ju01Fh
MCHUGH, Matt.		12	M	Laborer	02Ju01Fh
MCCLINTOCK, Danl.		50	M	Farmer	02Ju01Fh
Mary	(W)	42	F	Wife	02Ju01Fh
Martha	(D)	13	F	Spinster	02Ju01Fh
Alexander	(S)	18	M	Farmer	02Ju01Fh
James	(S)	11	M	None	02Ju01Fh
Jane	(D)	04	F	Child	02Ju01Fh
MCCAM, Margt.		19	F	Dressmaker	02Ju01Fh
MILES, Cath.		13	F	Dressmaker	02Ju01Fh
PARK, Eliza		40	F	Spinster	02Ju01Fh
DOGHERTY, Sarah		12	F	None	02Ju01Fh
MAILEY, James		27	M	Farmer	02Ju01Fh
Margt.		15	F	Spinster	02Ju01Fh
WADE, Susan		09	F	Child	02Ju01Fh
LOUTHER, Mary		24	F	Spinster	02Ju01Fh
MCNAMEE, Rebecca		13	F	Spinster	02Ju01Fh
Eleanor		19	F	Spinster	02Ju01Fh
MCLOUGHLIN, Bernard		24	M	Carpenter	02Ju01Fh
EMLENSON, Jas.		13	M	Laborer	02Ju01Fh
ROBINSON, Martha		19	F	Spinster	02Ju01Fh
GALLAGHER, Patk.		25	M	Farmer	02Ju01Fh
SMITH, Susan		11	F	None	02Ju01Fh
DEVLIN, Eleanor		27	F	Spinster	02Ju01Fh
MCCONAGHY, Anne		22	F	Spinster	02Ju01Fh
MARSHALL, Margt.		60	F	Spinster	02Ju01Fh
Died-At-Sea					
Sarah		25	F	Spinster	02Ju01Fh
MCBAY, James		27	M	Mason	02Ju01Fh
Margt.		19	F	Spinster	02Ju01Fh
KELLY, Jane		13	F	Spinster	02Ju01Fh
PERRY, Robt.		24	M	Farmer	02Ju01Fh
HASSIN, Mary		17	F	Spinster	02Ju01Fh
WILSON, Sarah		10	F	Child	02Ju01Fh
DUNBAR, Jane		26	F	Spinster	02Ju01Fh
QUIN, Ellen		13	F	Spinster	02Ju01Fh
KAIN, Betty		17	F	Spinster	02Ju01Fh
MCCLOSKY, Nancy		23	F	Spinster	02Ju01Fh
FANEN, Anne		26	F	Spinster	02Ju01Fh
MCCLOSKY, Ann		12	F	None	02Ju01Fh
DEVINE, Robt.		22	M	Farmer	02Ju01Fh
Margt.		09	F	Child	02Ju01Fh
GALLGHER, Jas.		17	M	Laborer	02Ju01Fh
HASSAN, Wm.		13	M	Laborer	02Ju01Fh

NAMES OF PASSENGERS		AGE	SEX	OCCUPATIONS	DATE PORT SHIP
KAIN, Biddy		13	F	Spinster	02Ju01Fh
KIRK, Nancy		09	F	Child	02Ju01Fh
KELLY, Mary		10	F	Child	02Ju01Fh
Cath.		15	F	Spinster	02Ju01Fh
BLACK, Jane		17	F	Spinster	02Ju01Fh
Margt.		19	F	Spinster	02Ju01Fh
MCAWARD, Chas.		26	M	Mason	02Ju01Fh
WETHERELL, Hannah		32	F	Spinster	02Ju01Fh
BOUVAIN, James		60	M	Farmer	02Ju01Fh
Jane	(W)	54	F	Wife	02Ju01Fh
Jane	(D)	15	F	Spinster	02Ju01Fh
Mary	(D)	09	F	Child	02Ju01Fh
Mitchell	(S)	07	M	Child	02Ju01Fh
Margt.	(D)	03	F	Child	02Ju01Fh
TROM, Jno.		13	M	Laborer	02Ju01Fh
FLANAGAN, Jno.		32	M	Farmer	02Ju01Fh
Alice	(W)	31	F	Wife	02Ju01Fh
Bridget	(D)	14	F	Spinster	02Ju01Fh
Bridget	(D)	10	F	Child	02Ju01Fh
Mary	(D)	08	F	Child	02Ju01Fh
Cath.	(D)	05	F	Child	02Ju01Fh
BOYLE, Con.		13	M	Laborer	02Ju01Fh

JOHN-GARROW 02 JUNE 1846

From Liverpool

NAMES OF PASSENGERS		AGE	SEX	OCCUPATIONS	DATE PORT SHIP
FARRELL, Anne		21	F	Laborer	02Ju02Fk
COLLINS, James		25	M	Laborer	02Ju02Fk
ROCHE, Ellen		35	F	Laborer	02Ju02Fk
JOYCE, Pat		30	M	Laborer	02Ju02Fk
ROGAN, William		24	M	Laborer	02Ju02Fk
KEILLEY, Will		29	M	Laborer	02Ju02Fk
SWINNON, Pat		23	M	Laborer	02Ju02Fk
JOYCE, John		26	M	Laborer	02Ju02Fk
U	(W)	26	F	Wife	02Ju02Fk
Biddy	(D)	04	F	Child	02Ju02Fk
Pat	(S)	.00	M	Infant	02Ju02Fk
SHEERAN, Bart.		30	M	Mechanic	02Ju02Fk
Johanna	(W)	25	F	Wife	02Ju02Fk
FALVEY, Dennis		25	M	Laborer	02Ju02Fk
MCARDLE, John		37	M	Mechanic	02Ju02Fk
Helen	(W)	27	F	Wife	02Ju02Fk
Oswald	(S)	07	M	Child	02Ju02Fk
Maurice	(S)	05	M	Child	02Ju02Fk
BELLE, Robert		50	M	Laborer	02Ju02Fk
Esther	(D)	18	F	Servant	02Ju02Fk
Mary	(W)	50	F	Wife	02Ju02Fk
Eliza	(D)	13	F	Servant	02Ju02Fk
Ellen	(D)	07	F	Child	02Ju02Fk
Margt.	(D)	07	F	Child	02Ju02Fk
William	(S)	03	M	Child	02Ju02Fk
SHERIDAN, Pat		20	M	Laborer	02Ju02Fk
KEARNEY, Cath.		16	F	Servant	02Ju02Fk
Ellen		26	F	Servant	02Ju02Fk
Nicholas		06	M	Child	02Ju02Fk
Aleen		.00	U	Infant	02Ju02Fk
MCKENNA, Mary		27	F	Servant	02Ju02Fk
WHITTLE, Jas.		21	M	Laborer	02Ju02Fk
MUNDY, James		37	M	Laborer	02Ju02Fk
AULTS, Eder		20	M	Laborer	02Ju02Fk
MCDERMOTH, Jas.		18	M	Laborer	02Ju02Fk
HUGHES, Pat		17	M	Laborer	02Ju02Fk
ONEIL, Mary		25	F	Servant	02Ju02Fk
CANNON, Mary		20	F	Servant	02Ju02Fk
MCJUDE, Anne		18	F	Servant	02Ju02Fk
MANNING, Anne		18	F	Servant	02Ju02Fk
MCAULEY, Anne		18	F	Servant	02Ju02Fk
CAMPLE, Ellen		20	F	Servant	02Ju02Fk

NAMES OF PASSENGERS		AGE	SEX	OCCUPATIONS	DATE PORT SHIP
MCCUSKER, Sally		19	F	Servant	02Ju02Fk
MCCULLICK, Cath.		03	F	Child	02Ju02Fk
Ellen		11	F	Servant	02Ju02Fk
CONNOLLY, Edwd.		25	M	Laborer	02Ju02Fk
BARRAN, Hugh		20	M	Laborer	02Ju02Fk
MORRIS, Ellis		38	M	Laborer	02Ju02Fk
Will		30	M	Laborer	02Ju02Fk
Thos.		03	M	Child	02Ju02Fk
Margt.		.00	F	Infant	02Ju02Fk
Morris		26	M	Laborer	02Ju02Fk
Ellen		23	F	Servant	02Ju02Fk
Evan		32	M	Laborer	02Ju02Fk
U	(W)	29	F	Wife	02Ju02Fk
THICKENS, John		39	M	Laborer	02Ju02Fk
U	(W)	30	F	Wife	02Ju02Fk
JONES, Mary		20	F	Servant	02Ju02Fk
David	(S)	.00	M	Infant	02Ju02Fk
POSEL, Jean		23	M	Laborer	02Ju02Fk
JONES, James		30	M	Laborer	02Ju02Fk
CRISE, Maria		13	F	Servant	02Ju02Fk
Alice		13	F	Servant	02Ju02Fk
PARRY, Cath.		32	F	Servant	02Ju02Fk
Will	(S)	06	M	Child	02Ju02Fk
Mary	(D)	02	F	Child	02Ju02Fk
Eliza	(D)	.00	F	Infant	02Ju02Fk
Griffith	(S)	.00	M	Infant	02Ju02Fk
PINGUERRY, Simeon		47	M	Laborer	02Ju02Fk
U	(W)	40	F	Wife	02Ju02Fk
John	(S)	13	M	Laborer	02Ju02Fk
Jas.	(S)	13	M	Laborer	02Ju02Fk
Benj.	(S)	11	M	Laborer	02Ju02Fk
Anne	(D)	09	F	Servant	02Ju02Fk
Liman	(S)	06	M	Child	02Ju02Fk
MORRIS, Evan		20	M	Laborer	02Ju02Fk
PARY, Daniel		27	M	Laborer	02Ju02Fk
SAMUEL, Richard		26	M	Laborer	02Ju02Fk
JONES, Ellis		38	M	Laborer	02Ju02Fk
U	(W)	33	F	Wife	02Ju02Fk
Ellis	(S)	05	M	Child	02Ju02Fk
Evder	(S)	04	M	Child	02Ju02Fk
John	(S)	.00	M	Infant	02Ju02Fk
James	(S)	13	M	Laborer	02Ju02Fk
Jane	(D)	15	F	Servant	02Ju02Fk
John	(S)	13	M	Laborer	02Ju02Fk
William	(S)	18	M	Mechanic	02Ju02Fk
JEFFREYS, John		35	M	Laborer	02Ju02Fk
U	(W)	33	F	Wife	02Ju02Fk
Howell	(S)	12	M	Laborer	02Ju02Fk
Thos.	(S)	10	M	Laborer	02Ju02Fk
Evan	(S)	09	M	Child	02Ju02Fk
Mary	(D)	06	F	Child	02Ju02Fk
Cath.	(D)	.00	F	Infant	02Ju02Fk
BAXTER, John		30	M	Laborer	02Ju02Fk
SCOTT, Belle		29	F	Servant	02Ju02Fk
LYNCH, Mary		30	F	Servant	02Ju02Fk
KEIRNAN, Mary		23	F	Servant	02Ju02Fk
MCMURRAY, Eleanor		28	F	Servant	02Ju02Fk
Mary	(D)	12	F	Servant	02Ju02Fk
Eliza	(D)	06	F	Child	02Ju02Fk
Francis	(S)	09	F	Servant	02Ju02Fk
Michael	(H)	30	M	Laborer	02Ju02Fk
GRUBBINS, Alice		40	F	Servant	02Ju02Fk
John		20	M	Laborer	02Ju02Fk
BANNIN, Eliza		19	F	Servant	02Ju02Fk
BYNNES, Will		30	M	Laborer	02Ju02Fk
THOMPSON, John		30	M	Laborer	02Ju02Fk
KEENAN, Mick		30	M	Laborer	02Ju02Fk
Mary		25	F	Servant	02Ju02Fk
Tom		.00	M	Infant	02Ju02Fk
Mickey		12	M	None	02Ju02Fk
DAGNAM, Mary		19	F	Servant	02Ju02Fk
MCTEA, Mary		20	F	Servant	02Ju02Fk
FLYM, Jas.		16	M	Laborer	02Ju02Fk
MULLAN, Rossy		12	F	Servant	02Ju02Fk
MURRAY, John		50	M	Laborer	02Ju02Fk

NAMES OF PASSENGERS		AGE	SEX	OCCUPATIONS	DATE PORT SHIP
MURRAY, Bella		13	F	Servant	02Ju02Fk
BRADY, Barnard		30	M	Laborer	02Ju02Fk
Biddy	(W)	30	F	Servant	02Ju02Fk
Biddy	(D)	13	F	Servant	02Ju02Fk
Ansy	(D)	12	F	Servant	02Ju02Fk
Jas.	(S)	08	M	Child	02Ju02Fk
Annie	(D)	.00	F	Infant	02Ju02Fk
Thos.		38	M	Laborer	02Ju02Fk
KEALY, Thos.		58	M	Laborer	02Ju02Fk
Mary		23	F	Servant	02Ju02Fk
REILLEY, U-Mrs.		40	F	Servant	02Ju02Fk
Biddy		30	F	Servant	02Ju02Fk
BRAMIN, Owen		27	M	Laborer	02Ju02Fk
Cath.	(W)	28	F	Wife	02Ju02Fk
PAGAN, Terrey		40	M	Laborer	02Ju02Fk
BRANNIN, Thomas		20	M	Laborer	02Ju02Fk
KELLY, Will		20	M	Laborer	02Ju02Fk
Cath.		18	F	Servant	02Ju02Fk
Betty		13	F	Servant	02Ju02Fk
Jas.		08	M	Child	02Ju02Fk
Bella		06	F	Child	02Ju02Fk
Mary		40	F	Servant	02Ju02Fk
MORRISON, Dennis		17	M	Laborer	02Ju02Fk
WALSH, Will		35	M	Laborer	02Ju02Fk
Nancy		30	F	Servant	02Ju02Fk
JEFFREY, Mick		18	M	Laborer	02Ju02Fk
Will		20	M	Laborer	02Ju02Fk
MORRIS, Nancy		13	F	Servant	02Ju02Fk
DENNY, Ellen		18	F	Servant	02Ju02Fk
TORMEY, Mick		27	M	Laborer	02Ju02Fk
Margt.	(W)	20	F	Wife	02Ju02Fk
John	(S)	.00	M	Infant	02Ju02Fk
Biddy	(D)	.00	F	Infant	02Ju02Fk
ROGERS, Cormick		32	M	Laborer	02Ju02Fk
HUSSEY, Cella		23	F	Servant	02Ju02Fk
RAFFERTY, Mary		18	F	Servant	02Ju02Fk
SWEENY, Biddy		22	F	Servant	02Ju02Fk
BRILLEY, Martin		22	M	Laborer	02Ju02Fk
MAHONY, Tom		21	M	Laborer	02Ju02Fk
CRANAN, Cornia		21	M	Laborer	02Ju02Fk
BROWNE, Handen		24	F	Servant	02Ju02Fk
GILLSEN, Will		42	M	Laborer	02Ju02Fk
Eliza	(W)	40	F	Wife	02Ju02Fk
Will	(S)	17	M	Laborer	02Ju02Fk
Edwd.	(S)	11	M	Laborer	02Ju02Fk
Francis	(S)	08	M	Child	02Ju02Fk
FARMAN, Jas.		28	M	Laborer	02Ju02Fk
MCKENNY, Jas.		19	M	Laborer	02Ju02Fk
DUFFEY, Mary		20	F	Servant	02Ju02Fk
REILLY, Ellen		30	F	Servant	02Ju02Fk
MCCHARTY, Mary		20	F	Servant	02Ju02Fk
BANKE, Mary		18	F	Servant	02Ju02Fk
GARVER, Mary		23	F	Servant	02Ju02Fk
VAUGHEY, Richd.		26	M	Laborer	02Ju02Fk
BILLARD, Sarah		21	F	Servant	02Ju02Fk
MCDANDED, Mary		30	F	Servant	02Ju02Fk
HANDEN, Pat		06	M	Child	02Ju02Fk
Margt.		09	F	Child	02Ju02Fk
KELLY, Thomas		26	M	Laborer	02Ju02Fk
MCDONALD, Manus		25	M	Laborer	02Ju02Fk
HIGGINS, Martha		25	F	Servant	02Ju02Fk
CARTIN, James		30	M	Laborer	02Ju02Fk
SMITH, Thomas		44	M	Laborer	02Ju02Fk
U	(W)	40	F	Wife	02Ju02Fk
SHERRIT, Henry		33	M	Laborer	02Ju02Fk
U	(W)	26	F	Wife	02Ju02Fk
SMITH, John		39	M	Laborer	02Ju02Fk
Mary	(D)	02	F	Child	02Ju02Fk
WIGGINS, John		21	M	Laborer	02Ju02Fk
CUMBERLAND, Jane		30	F	Servant	02Ju02Fk
CUMMINS, Timothy		23	M	Laborer	02Ju02Fk
PARKER, Hugh		22	M	Laborer	02Ju02Fk
Morris		24	M	Laborer	02Ju02Fk
WISEMAN, Edwd.		18	M	Laborer	02Ju02Fk
COLLINS, Richd.		26	M	Laborer	02Ju02Fk
LANG, Jeremiah		28	M	Laborer	02Ju02Fk
MONAGHAN, John		26	M	Laborer	02Ju02Fk
SILLY, Mich		26	M	Laborer	02Ju02Fk
Bess	(W)	27	F	Wife	02Ju02Fk
DEMPSY, John		20	M	Laborer	02Ju02Fk
RENELL, Will		36	M	Laborer	02Ju02Fk
FOY, Mary		20	F	Servant	02Ju02Fk
MANNEY, James		28	M	Laborer	02Ju02Fk
CORKERINE, Mike		27	M	Laborer	02Ju02Fk
MCCARTY, Jerry		30	M	Laborer	02Ju02Fk
U	(W)	26	F	Wife	02Ju02Fk
Mary	(D)	.00	F	Infant	02Ju02Fk
DALY, Nicholls		22	M	Laborer	02Ju02Fk
LARKIN, Bridget		23	F	Servant	02Ju02Fk
Ellen		22	F	Servant	02Ju02Fk
BURKE, Cella		24	F	Servant	02Ju02Fk
WHITE, Ellen		20	F	Servant	02Ju02Fk
KELLY, Pat		21	M	Laborer	02Ju02Fk
MADDON, U		24	M	Laborer	02Ju02Fk
BLEGDUE, James		24	M	Laborer	02Ju02Fk
PACKHAM, John		27	M	Laborer	02Ju02Fk
U	(W)	23	F	Wife	02Ju02Fk
Martha	(D)	.00	F	Infant	02Ju02Fk
Henry	(S)	.00	M	Infant	02Ju02Fk
DOUGHERTY, Mary		22	F	Servant	02Ju02Fk
HUGHS, Ann		24	F	Servant	02Ju02Fk
JASKEN, John		30	M	Laborer	02Ju02Fk
Isabella		16	F	Servant	02Ju02Fk
James		13	M	Servant	02Ju02Fk
Barbara		12	F	Servant	02Ju02Fk
George		10	M	Servant	02Ju02Fk
Valentine		09	M	Child	02Ju02Fk
JACKENS, Martha		23	F	Servant	02Ju02Fk

ALERT 02 JUNE 1846

From Cork

NAMES OF PASSENGERS		AGE	SEX	OCCUPATIONS	DATE PORT SHIP
DWYER, Alley		27	F	Laborer	02Ju14Fl
Cathne.		25	F	Laborer	02Ju14Fl
MCAULIFFE, Jeremiah		22	M	Laborer	02Ju14Fl
BENKE, William		23	M	Laborer	02Ju14Fl
Mathew		25	M	Laborer	02Ju14Fl
MORESSEY, Thos.		23	M	Laborer	02Ju14Fl
FITZGERALD, James		25	M	Laborer	02Ju14Fl
CALLAGHAN, Cathne.		25	F	Laborer	02Ju14Fl
BUCKLEY, Corns.		25	M	Laborer	02Ju14Fl
LUOOME, William		18	M	Laborer	02Ju14Fl
SHAHAN, Michael		21	M	Laborer	02Ju14Fl
SWEENEY, Danl.		20	M	Laborer	02Ju14Fl
WARREN, John		21	M	Laborer	02Ju14Fl
BIRMINGHAM, Cathne.		21	F	Laborer	02Ju14Fl
BURKE, Mary		02	F	Child	02Ju14Fl
MCCARTHY, Danl.		45	M	Laborer	02Ju14Fl
FITZGERALD, James		21	M	Laborer	02Ju14Fl
MOYMAHER, Mary		22	F	Servant	02Ju14Fl
LUOMMY, John		22	M	Servant	02Ju14Fl
WHITE, John		30	M	Servant	02Ju14Fl
Margt.		23	F	Servant	02Ju14Fl
CATHEY, Cathne.		23	F	Servant	02Ju14Fl
LYONS, Bridget		21	F	Servant	02Ju14Fl
Cathne.		21	F	Servant	02Ju14Fl
KELLY, Mary		26	F	Servant	02Ju14Fl
DONOVAN, Ceon		27	F	Servant	02Ju14Fl
HARNIGER, Honora		22	F	Servant	02Ju14Fl
LYNCH, Timothy		30	M	Servant	02Ju14Fl
HERLIHY, Francis		29	M	Servant	02Ju14Fl
Mary	(W)	24	F	Wife	02Ju14Fl
Patrick	(S)	07	M	Child	02Ju14Fl

NAMES OF PASSENGERS		AGE	SEX	OCCUPATIONS	DATE PORT SHIP
HERLIHY, Daniel	(S)	06	M	Child	02Jul4FI
FLOOD, Ellen		25	F	Servant	02Jul4FI
SULLIVAN, Bridget		18	F	Servant	02Jul4FI
MEAL, Quenie		30	F	Servant	02Jul4FI
HALLESSEY, Julia		25	F	Servant	02Jul4FI
SHELTON, Mary		20	F	Servant	02Jul4FI
SULLIVAN, Patk.		30	M	Servant	02Jul4FI
LEARY, Michael		30	M	Servant	02Jul4FI
SHEA, Daniel		24	M	Servant	02Jul4FI
Ellen		16	F	Servant	02Jul4FI
SINEHEN, Danl.		24	M	Laborer	02Jul4FI
KELLEHE, Patt		22	M	Laborer	02Jul4FI
RERDEN, Daniel		20	M	Laborer	02Jul4FI
HOGAN, Timothy		20	M	Laborer	02Jul4FI
BUCKLEY, Patrick		24	M	Laborer	02Jul4FI
MCCARTHY, Margt.		40	F	Laborer	02Jul4FI
John	(S)	09	M	Child	02Jul4FI
MAHONY, Danl.		26	M	Laborer	02Jul4FI
Kitty		26	F	Laborer	02Jul4FI
CONDON, William		18	M	Laborer	02Jul4FI
BUCKLEY, John		24	M	Laborer	02Jul4FI
Cathne.		50	F	Laborer	02Jul4FI
ROURKE, Dennis		19	M	Laborer	02Jul4FI
Ellen		30	F	Laborer	02Jul4FI
Michael		07	M	Child	02Jul4FI
SCANLON, Richard		20	M	Laborer	02Jul4FI
CALLAHAN, Richd.		22	M	Laborer	02Jul4FI
CONNER, Johanna		25	F	Laborer	02Jul4FI
Mary		23	F	Laborer	02Jul4FI
SEALEY, Cathne.		20	F	Laborer	02Jul4FI
MCCARTY, Daniel		20	M	Servant	02Jul4FI
BRODERICK, John		26	M	Servant	02Jul4FI
Ellen		24	F	Servant	02Jul4FI
BARRELL, Corneleous		30	M	Servant	02Jul4FI
Peggy		28	F	Servant	02Jul4FI
CARTIN, Lenloth		26	M	Servant	02Jul4FI
CONNOR, Onlan		26	M	Servant	02Jul4FI
WALSH, James		20	M	Servant	02Jul4FI
SULLIVAN, Curly		30	M	Servant	02Jul4FI
CONLEY, Barara		25	M	Servant	02Jul4FI
REORDON, John		22	M	Servant	02Jul4FI
MOONAN, John		26	M	Servant	02Jul4FI
Ellen		22	F	Servant	02Jul4FI
MCENINEY, Thos.		24	M	Servant	02Jul4FI
MILLANE, Corns.		30	M	Servant	02Jul4FI
SULLIVAN, Jeremiah		22	M	Laborer	02Jul4FI
MCCARTHEY, Michl.		26	M	Laborer	02Jul4FI
CONNOLLY, Patrick		24	M	Laborer	02Jul4FI
BRADLEY, Dennis		25	M	Laborer	02Jul4FI
Cathne.		30	F	Laborer	02Jul4FI
HODENELL, James		25	M	Laborer	02Jul4FI
BUCKLEY, Patrick		30	M	Laborer	02Jul4FI
Peggy	(W)	24	F	Wife	02Jul4FI
Kitty	(D)	01	F	Child	02Jul4FI
COURTNEY, Michl.		18	M	Laborer	02Jul4FI
Dennis		17	M	Laborer	02Jul4FI
SLATTY, Patrick		18	M	Laborer	02Jul4FI
MURPHY, Martin		26	M	Laborer	02Jul4FI
John		23	M	Laborer	02Jul4FI
CLIFFORD, Lael		28	M	Laborer	02Jul4FI
PENHOKE, Michael		25	M	Laborer	02Jul4FI
CONNOR, John		24	M	Laborer	02Jul4FI
LOONLEY, Martin		28	M	Laborer	02Jul4FI
CONNELLY, John		20	M	Laborer	02Jul4FI
Mary		21	F	Laborer	02Jul4FI
COGLAN, Richard		23	M	Laborer	02Jul4FI
AHERNE, Mary		50	F	Laborer	02Jul4FI
MURPHY, Kitty		26	F	Laborer	02Jul4FI
AHERN, Ellen		22	F	Laborer	02Jul4FI
Johanna		20	F	Laborer	02Jul4FI
Kitty		22	F	Laborer	02Jul4FI
Maurice		09	M	Child	02Jul4FI
Honora		08	F	Child	02Jul4FI
Corneleus		05	M	Child	02Jul4FI
DESMORE, Margt.		22	F	Laborer	02Jul4FI
DESMORE, William		20	M	Laborer	02Jul4FI
Margaret		13	F	Laborer	02Jul4FI
COGHLAN, Matt		24	M	Laborer	02Jul4FI
KENNY, Patrick		28	M	Laborer	02Jul4FI
BUCKLEY, Thomas		50	M	Servant	02Jul4FI
Mary	(W)	43	F	Wife	02Jul4FI
Daniel	(S)	22	M	Servant	02Jul4FI
Ellen	(D)	20	F	Servant	02Jul4FI
Peter	(S)	19	M	Servant	02Jul4FI
Bartholemew	(S)	17	M	Servant	02Jul4FI
Johannah	(D)	15	F	Servant	02Jul4FI
John	(S)	06	M	Child	02Jul4FI
TUOMAY, Betty		48	F	Servant	02Jul4FI
Johannah	(D)	11	F	Servant	02Jul4FI
Ellen	(D)	04	F	Child	02Jul4FI
RIORDEN, John		26	M	Servant	02Jul4FI
QUALE, John		30	M	Servant	02Jul4FI
GERALD, Julia		48	F	Servant	02Jul4FI
GARATY, Jas.		43	M	Servant	02Jul4FI
LENEGAN, Thos.		45	M	Servant	02Jul4FI
OCONNOR, Patrick		34	M	Servant	02Jul4FI
RIORDAN, Henry		30	M	Servant	02Jul4FI
SHEA, M.		32	F	Servant	02Jul4FI
Cathne.		23	F	Servant	02Jul4FI
LAWLESS, Patt		18	M	Servant	02Jul4FI
CANTY, Cathne.		18	F	Servant	02Jul4FI
COLEHUNY, Margt.		38	F	Servant	02Jul4FI
SAPLE, Ellen		18	F	Servant	02Jul4FI
MOUNG, John		30	M	Servant	02Jul4FI

WASHINGTON 02 JUNE 1846

From Liverpool

NAMES OF PASSENGERS		AGE	SEX	OCCUPATIONS	DATE PORT SHIP
JACKSON, Francis		21	M	Laborer	02Ju02Fn
James		23	M	Laborer	02Ju02Fn
U	(W)	21	F	Wife	02Ju02Fn
MARRIOTT, Francis		36	M	Laborer	02Ju02Fn
Maria	(W)	35	F	Wife	02Ju02Fn
Osborne-Wm.	(S)	09	M	Child	02Ju02Fn
Louisa	(D)	06	F	Child	02Ju02Fn
DAVIS, Mathew-O.		25	M	Laborer	02Ju02Fn
FOGARTY, Michl.		25	M	Laborer	02Ju02Fn
Jane	(W)	26	F	Wife	02Ju02Fn
Michl.	(S)	03	M	Child	02Ju02Fn
Mary	(D)	02	F	Child	02Ju02Fn
MCCORMACK, John		33	M	Laborer	02Ju02Fn
Cathne.	(W)	32	F	Wife	02Ju02Fn
MUDDLE, John		21	M	Laborer	02Ju02Fn
BOURNE, Joseph		21	M	Laborer	02Ju02Fn
GRUENAN, Mary		21	F	Servant	02Ju02Fn
MARROW, Mary		18	F	Servant	02Ju02Fn
MCBENNETT, Kitty		20	F	Servant	02Ju02Fn
BARRON, Margt.		15	F	Servant	02Ju02Fn
CRAIG, John		38	M	Laborer	02Ju02Fn
THOMPSON, Richd.R.		25	M	Laborer	02Ju02Fn
Anna	(W)	23	F	Wife	02Ju02Fn
U	(D)	.00	F	Infant	02Ju02Fn
FOWLER, Ramsey		26	M	Laborer	02Ju02Fn
ELLIOTT, Benjn.		26	M	Laborer	02Ju02Fn
PROCTOR, U-Mrs.		26	F	Servant	02Ju02Fn
HOGAN, Pat		64	M	Farmer	02Ju02Fn
James		25	M	Farmer	02Ju02Fn
Margt.		23	F	Servant	02Ju02Fn
Pat		21	M	Farmer	02Ju02Fn
HACKETT, Edwd.		28	M	Farmer	02Ju02Fn
Mary	(W)	28	F	Wife	02Ju02Fn
Thomas		28	M	Laborer	02Ju02Fn
RYAN, Daniel		42	M	Laborer	02Ju02Fn

NAMES OF PASSENGERS		AGE	SEX	OCCUPATIONS	DATE PORT SHIP
THEIR, Geo.		42	M	Laborer	02Ju02Fn
Mary-Ann	(D)	18	F	Servant	02Ju02Fn
Charles	(S)	17	M	Tailor	02Ju02Fn
Harriott	(D)	15	F	Dressmaker	02Ju02Fn
James	(S)	08	M	Child	02Ju02Fn
Henry	(S)	06	M	Child	02Ju02Fn
MCLAUGHLIN, Ester		50	F	Servant	02Ju02Fn
John		26	M	Laborer	02Ju02Fn
Ann	(W)	24	F	Wife	02Ju02Fn
John	(S)	06	M	Child	02Ju02Fn
CUNNINGHAM, Pat		20	M	Laborer	02Ju02Fn
MURRAY, Ann		22	F	Servant	02Ju02Fn
HANLAN, Luke		25	M	Laborer	02Ju02Fn
MOLLOY, Hugh		20	M	Tailor	02Ju02Fn
SCRENEY, Pat		26	M	Tailor	02Ju02Fn
Susan	(W)	26	F	Wife	02Ju02Fn
HOSEY, Pat		32	M	Laborer	02Ju02Fn
LUGHEY, John		26	M	Laborer	02Ju02Fn
LIVINGSTON, Ellen		40	F	Spinster	02Ju02Fn
Maria	(D)	20	F	Servant	02Ju02Fn
Sarah	(D)	18	F	Servant	02Ju02Fn
MADDEN, John		20	M	Laborer	02Ju02Fn
FARRELLY, Andrew		15	M	Laborer	02Ju02Fn
MCGOVENS, John		20	M	Laborer	02Ju02Fn
Ann		19	F	Servant	02Ju02Fn
Cathne.		18	F	Servant	02Ju02Fn
ROCKS, James		20	M	Tailor	02Ju02Fn
Ann	(W)	22	F	Wife	02Ju02Fn
HOPE, Thomas		40	M	Laborer	02Ju02Fn
DUFFY, Thomas		24	M	Laborer	02Ju02Fn
SHERIDAN, Laurence		21	M	Laborer	02Ju02Fn
MCDADE, John		21	M	Laborer	02Ju02Fn
MATHER, Thomas		30	M	Laborer	02Ju02Fn
Jonathan		19	M	Laborer	02Ju02Fn
PHILLIPS, Mary		30	F	Servant	02Ju02Fn
JOLLY, Moses		20	M	Laborer	02Ju02Fn
FLYNN, Martin		16	M	Laborer	02Ju02Fn
MCMULLEN, Thomas		65	M	Laborer	02Ju02Fn
Betty	(W)	65	F	Wife	02Ju02Fn
Alexr.	(S)	30	M	Laborer	02Ju02Fn
Thomas	(S)	27	M	Laborer	02Ju02Fn
Robert	(S)	21	M	Laborer	02Ju02Fn
Mary	(D)	24	F	Servant	02Ju02Fn
MCCONAGHEY, Wm.		25	M	Laborer	02Ju02Fn
Isabella		25	F	Servant	02Ju02Fn
PURCELL, Isabella		38	F	Servant	02Ju02Fn
REYNOLDS, John		25	M	Laborer	02Ju02Fn
CODY, James		21	M	Laborer	02Ju02Fn
POWER, John		21	M	Laborer	02Ju02Fn
RYAN, John		21	M	Laborer	02Ju02Fn
MAHER, James		22	M	Laborer	02Ju02Fn
COMMONS, Allice		19	F	Servant	02Ju02Fn
Dorah		18	F	Servant	02Ju02Fn
QUINLAN, Judy		19	F	Servant	02Ju02Fn
COMMONS, Mary		23	F	Servant	02Ju02Fn
HORAN, Norey		20	F	Servant	02Ju02Fn
MAHER, Mary		19	F	Servant	02Ju02Fn
MCCONNELL, Randell		20	M	Laborer	02Ju02Fn
SWEENEY, John		20	M	Laborer	02Ju02Fn
Sarah	(W)	16	F	Wife	02Ju02Fn
MCDONNELL, James		20	M	Laborer	02Ju02Fn
FLEMING, Wm.		20	M	Laborer	02Ju02Fn
Isabella	(W)	18	F	Wife	02Ju02Fn
CODY, Edward		28	M	Laborer	02Ju02Fn
U	(W)	28	F	Wife	02Ju02Fn
Oliver	(S)	01	M	Child	02Ju02Fn
DWYER, Richd.		24	M	Laborer	02Ju02Fn
LANDREGAN, David		24	M	Laborer	02Ju02Fn
Pat		26	M	Laborer	02Ju02Fn
MURPHY, Allice		20	F	Servant	02Ju02Fn
Catharine		17	F	Servant	02Ju02Fn
COLEMAN, Mary		20	F	Servant	02Ju02Fn
HART, Felix		24	M	Tailor	02Ju02Fn
U	(W)	22	F	Wife	02Ju02Fn
Catharine		21	F	Servant	02Ju02Fn
NEALE, Garrett		19	M	Laborer	02Ju02Fn
MCCARTNEY, Felix		26	M	Laborer	02Ju02Fn
FARRESSY, John		25	M	Laborer	02Ju02Fn
Ellen	(W)	25	F	Wife	02Ju02Fn
MURPHY, John		23	M	Laborer	02Ju02Fn
Margt.	(W)	31	F	Wife	02Ju02Fn
BROWN, Michl.		24	M	Tailor	02Ju02Fn
CALLAGHAN, John		33	M	Tailor	02Ju02Fn
BURK, Pat		31	M	Tailor	02Ju02Fn
RYAN, Judy		24	F	Servant	02Ju02Fn
LOUGHNAN, Mary		21	F	Servant	02Ju02Fn
PETUS, Mary		30	F	Servant	02Ju02Fn
Bridget		26	F	Servant	02Ju02Fn
HINAH, Pat		24	M	Laborer	02Ju02Fn
FOGARTY, Margt.		21	F	Servant	02Ju02Fn
HOGAN, Mathew		19	M	Servant	02Ju02Fn
FITZGERALD, Ellen		24	F	Cook	02Ju02Fn
HERAGHTY, Pat		24	M	Laborer	02Ju02Fn
BRADY, Jane		19	F	Servant	02Ju02Fn
FINAN, Jane		19	F	Servant	02Ju02Fn
GILMOUR, Cathne.		20	F	Servant	02Ju02Fn
MCGOWAN, Ann		20	F	Servant	02Ju02Fn
SPELLANE, Pat		30	M	Tailor	02Ju02Fn
U	(W)	26	F	Wife	02Ju02Fn
Catharine	(D)	02	F	Child	02Ju02Fn
CANNON, Wm.		30	M	Laborer	02Ju02Fn
BLOOMER, John		20	M	Laborer	02Ju02Fn
SKIFFINGTON, Mary		20	F	Milliner	02Ju02Fn
Mary		20	F	Milliner	02Ju02Fn
HUGHES, Ann		25	F	Servant	02Ju02Fn
WELSH, Connor		21	M	Laborer	02Ju02Fn
RYAN, Thomas		20	M	Laborer	02Ju02Fn
FAHEY, Ann		30	F	Servant	02Ju02Fn
FEGAN, Thos.		42	M	Laborer	02Ju02Fn
U	(W)	40	F	Wife	02Ju02Fn
FAGAN, Danl.		13	M	Tailor	02Ju02Fn
Jane		11	F	None	02Ju02Fn
John		08	M	Child	02Ju02Fn
Sally		06	F	Child	02Ju02Fn
Pat		01	M	Child	02Ju02Fn
REGAN, Thos.		26	M	Laborer	02Ju02Fn
Sally	(W)	24	F	Wife	02Ju02Fn
OBRIEN, Jeremiah		36	M	Laborer	02Ju02Fn
U	(W)	34	F	Wife	02Ju02Fn
Mary	(D)	08	F	Child	02Ju02Fn
Jerry	(S)	06	M	Child	02Ju02Fn
Sally	(D)	.00	F	Infant	02Ju02Fn
MCNULLY, Terence		40	M	Laborer	02Ju02Fn
Mary	(W)	38	F	Wife	02Ju02Fn
Elizabeth	(D)	13	F	Servant	02Ju02Fn
Ann	(D)	10	F	Child	02Ju02Fn
Eleanor	(D)	06	F	Child	02Ju02Fn
CARROLL, Patt		22	M	Laborer	02Ju02Fn
NEALON, Patt		26	M	Laborer	02Ju02Fn
CARROLL, Margt.		21	F	Servant	02Ju02Fn
DONOHOE, Honor		25	F	Servant	02Ju02Fn
WESTINGTON, U		24	M	Clerk	02Ju02Fn
DOWD, Bernard		24	M	Laborer	02Ju02Fn
Bridget	(W)	20	F	Wife	02Ju02Fn
BURRELL, James		40	M	Laborer	02Ju02Fn
U	(W)	38	F	Wife	02Ju02Fn
Henry	(S)	13	M	None	02Ju02Fn
Joseph	(S)	10	M	Child	02Ju02Fn
John	(S)	07	M	Child	02Ju02Fn
Margt.	(D)	04	F	Child	02Ju02Fn
Mary	(D)	01	F	Child	02Ju02Fn
KENEDY, James		24	M	Laborer	02Ju02Fn
SHEEHAN, Patt		22	M	Laborer	02Ju02Fn
ROCKETT, James		22	M	Laborer	02Ju02Fn
ANDERSON, Wm.		24	M	Laborer	02Ju02Fn
CONWAY, Danl.		20	M	Laborer	02Ju02Fn
LLOYD, Daniel		26	M	Laborer	02Ju02Fn
U	(W)	22	F	Wife	02Ju02Fn
WILLIAMS, Thos.		38	M	Laborer	02Ju02Fn
U	(W)	38	F	Wife	02Ju02Fn

NAMES OF PASSENGERS		A G E	S E X	OCCUPATIONS	DATE PORT SHIP	NAMES OF PASSENGERS		A G E	S E X	OCCUPATIONS	DATE PORT SHIP
WILLIAMS, John	(S)	12	M	None	02Ju02Fn	SMITH, Hugh		08	M	Child	02Ju02Fn
William	(S)	10	M	Child	02Ju02Fn	Jane		04	F	Child	02Ju02Fn
Thomas	(S)	07	M	Child	02Ju02Fn	SHEA, Jane		16	F	Servant	02Ju02Fn
Mary	(D)	03	F	Child	02Ju02Fn	Isabella		12	F	None	02Ju02Fn
Henry	(S)	01	M	Child	02Ju02Fn	Cathne.		08	F	Child	02Ju02Fn
REDDY, Pat		24	M	Laborer	02Ju02Fn	John		04	M	Child	02Ju02Fn
KEEFE, Judith		22	F	Servant	02Ju02Fn	GROGAN, Ann		22	F	Servant	02Ju02Fn
Ann		20	F	Servant	02Ju02Fn	MCKEOWN, Ann		23	F	Servant	02Ju02Fn
DUNFIELD, Mary		20	F	Servant	02Ju02Fn	FARRELLY, Bessy		26	F	Servant	02Ju02Fn
MULLOWNEY, Anty		22	F	Servant	02Ju02Fn	REILLY, U-Widow		34	F	Servant	02Ju02Fn
WHITE, Mary		24	F	Servant	02Ju02Fn	James	(S)	11	M	None	02Ju02Fn
ONEILL, Feilx		39	M	Laborer	02Ju02Fn	Pat	(S)	06	M	Child	02Ju02Fn
Jane	(W)	38	F	Wife	02Ju02Fn	MCNULTY, Margt.		10	F	Child	02Ju02Fn
Mary	(D)	13	F	None	02Ju02Fn	Jane		07	F	Child	02Ju02Fn
Timothy	(S)	10	M	Child	02Ju02Fn	OHARA, Terence		32	M	Laborer	02Ju02Fn
Dennis	(S)	08	M	Child	02Ju02Fn	Cathne.	(W)	30	F	Wife	02Ju02Fn
Barney	(S)	03	M	Child	02Ju02Fn	John	(S)	10	M	Child	02Ju02Fn
Felix	(S)	01	M	Child	02Ju02Fn	BENKE, Margt.		12	F	None	02Ju02Fn
MORGAN, Henry		28	M	Laborer	02Ju02Fn	MOLLOY, Geo.		30	M	Tailor	02Ju02Fn
Mary	(W)	28	F	Wife	02Ju02Fn	Kitty	(W)	28	F	Wife	02Ju02Fn
Thomas	(S)	06	M	Child	02Ju02Fn	Winnefred	(D)	06	F	Child	02Ju02Fn
Mary	(D)	02	F	Child	02Ju02Fn	John	(S)	04	M	Child	02Ju02Fn
DURKER, John		26	M	Laborer	02Ju02Fn	Henry	(S)	02	M	Child	02Ju02Fn
John		24	M	Laborer	02Ju02Fn	HANNAN, Cathne.		20	F	Servant	02Ju02Fn
John		23	M	Laborer	02Ju02Fn	BUCHANAN, Mary		25	F	Servant	02Ju02Fn
HOWLEY, Jas.		26	M	Laborer	02Ju02Fn	HOLLY, John		24	M	Farmer	02Ju02Fn
OHARA, Thomas		26	M	Laborer	02Ju02Fn	MONEEGHAN, U-Mrs.		24	F	Milliner	02Ju02Fn
KILCAULEY, Cathne.		22	F	Servant	02Ju02Fn	MCINTYRE, Ann		21	F	Milliner	02Ju02Fn
MCHALE, Richd.		22	M	Laborer	02Ju02Fn	MCARDLE, Ellen		26	F	Servant	02Ju02Fn
KERRIGAN, Ellen		22	F	Servant	02Ju02Fn						
RICKARD, Margt.		19	F	Servant	02Ju02Fn						
HOWARD, Cathne.		30	F	Servant	02Ju02Fn						
TOBIN, David		21	M	Laborer	02Ju02Fn						
FEGAN, Thomas		20	M	Laborer	02Ju02Fn						
Richard		19	M	Laborer	02Ju02Fn		VICTORIA 02 JUNE 1846					
COMMIS, Alice		19	F	Servant	02Ju02Fn						
Dorah		18	F	Servant	02Ju02Fn		From London					
PERRY, U-Mrs.		30	F	Servant	02Ju02Fn						
BRIEN, Margt.		22	F	Servant	02Ju02Fn						
MCGAHAN, Mary		21	F	Servant	02Ju02Fn						
DIERY, Rose		20	F	Servant	02Ju02Fn	BEDDONE, Patience	(D)	22	F	Lady	02Ju21Ay
MCKENNA, Ellen		20	F	Servant	02Ju02Fn	SHERLOCK, Robert-H.		50	M	Gentleman	02Ju21Ay
FEENEY, Thomas		36	M	Baker	02Ju02Fn	Anne-I.	(D)	20	F	Lady	02Ju21Ay
Sally	(W)	34	F	Wife	02Ju02Fn	PURCELL, Ellen		22	F	Lady	02Ju21Ay
James	(S)	12	M	None	02Ju02Fn						
Henry	(S)	10	M	Child	02Ju02Fn						
Mary	(D)	07	F	Child	02Ju02Fn						
Pat	(S)	04	M	Child	02Ju02Fn						
Margt.	(D)	01	F	Child	02Ju02Fn		EMMANUEL 03 JUNE 1846					
MCLAUGHLIN, U-Widow		40	F	Cook	02Ju02Fn						
Rose	(D)	18	F	Servant	02Ju02Fn		From Liverpool					
Mary	(D)	12	F	None	02Ju02Fn						
Pat	(S)	08	M	Child	02Ju02Fn						
DWYER, Jas.		12	M	None	02Ju02Fn						
Mary		06	F	Child	02Ju02Fn	GORMLY, James		23	M	Laborer	03Ju02Fq
ODONNELL, John		30	M	Farmer	02Ju02Fn	Jane		21	F	Spinster	03Ju02Fq
HARVEY, John		35	M	Farmer	02Ju02Fn	SHEEN, Timothy		30	M	Laborer	03Ju02Fq
GERRARD, Edwd.		25	M	Farmer	02Ju02Fn	DONNOLLY, Nicholas		25	M	Laborer	03Ju02Fq
James		20	M	Farmer	02Ju02Fn	BROWN, Wm.		25	M	Laborer	03Ju02Fq
Mary		18	F	Servant	02Ju02Fn	CURREN, Thos.		21	M	Laborer	03Ju02Fq
MCGINNISS, Biddy		22	F	Servant	02Ju02Fn	Mathew		22	M	Laborer	03Ju02Fq
BROWN, George		16	M	Tailor	02Ju02Fn	Bridget		20	F	Spinster	03Ju02Fq
Mary		13	F	None	02Ju02Fn	HARCORT, Bessy		25	F	Spinster	03Ju02Fq
FERRISON, Jane		10	F	Child	02Ju02Fn	CUMSKEY, Pat		26	M	Laborer	03Ju02Fq
Margaret		04	F	Child	02Ju02Fn	SEALLY, Luke		27	M	Laborer	03Ju02Fq
GERRARD, Mary		55	F	Cook	02Ju02Fn	KELLY, Mary		25	F	Spinster	03Ju02Fq
Edward		25	M	Tailor	02Ju02Fn	HOBAN, Pat		27	M	Cobbler	03Ju02Fq
MORGAN, Henry		30	M	Tailor	02Ju02Fn	SULLIVAN, Micheal		21	M	Clogger	03Ju02Fq
WILLIAMS, Mary		12	F	None	02Ju02Fn	SHACKELTON, Thos.		17	M	Clogger	03Ju02Fq
George		10	M	Child	02Ju02Fn	ONEAL, Jane		20	F	Spinster	03Ju02Fq
William		06	M	Child	02Ju02Fn	CAMPBELL, Owen		22	M	Laborer	03Ju02Fq
MORGAN, Mary		13	F	None	02Ju02Fn	DEENEN, Pat		24	M	Laborer	03Ju02Fq
POTTER, James		32	M	Laborer	02Ju02Fn	Catherine		11	F	None	03Ju02Fq
SMITH, Hugh		12	M	None	02Ju02Fn	REDFARN, Mark		22	M	Laborer	03Ju02Fq
Mary		10	F	Child	02Ju02Fn						

NAMES OF PASSENGERS		AGE	SEX	OCCUPATIONS	DATE PORT SHIP
MCCORN, Catherine		20	F	Spinster	03Ju02Fq
TRANNER, Margaret		25	F	Spinster	03Ju02Fq
MCCROAN, Elizabeth		17	F	Spinster	03Ju02Fq
WOODS, John		20	M	Laborer	03Ju02Fq
CARNON, John		20	M	Laborer	03Ju02Fq
Catherine		19	F	Spinster	03Ju02Fq
FAGAN, Mary		20	F	Spinster	03Ju02Fq
FOSTER, John		30	M	Laborer	03Ju02Fq
PRAT, Catherine		20	F	None	03Ju02Fq
WELSH, Mathew		24	M	Laborer	03Ju02Fq
CANAGHAN, Pat		22	M	Laborer	03Ju02Fq
MULLEN, Pat		22	M	Laborer	03Ju02Fq
HARCY, John		21	M	Laborer	03Ju02Fq
RORK, James		45	M	Coachman	03Ju02Fq
Bessy	(W)	40	F	Wife	03Ju02Fq
FORD, Biddy		27	F	Spinster	03Ju02Fq
MCPHILLIP, Sally		17	F	Spinster	03Ju02Fq
SHANNON, Biddy		20	F	Spinster	03Ju02Fq
MCMAHON, Biddy		20	F	Spinster	03Ju02Fq
James		19	M	Laborer	03Ju02Fq
ROONEY, Owen		20	M	Whitesmith	03Ju02Fq
BRINAN, John		20	M	Laborer	03Ju02Fq
Mary		19	F	Spinster	03Ju02Fq
GORDON, Peter		28	M	Blacksmith	03Ju02Fq
Mary	(W)	20	F	Wife	03Ju02Fq
BOYD, James		33	M	Laborer	03Ju02Fq
CARNEGIE, David		20	M	Mechanic	03Ju02Fq
John		22	M	Mechanic	03Ju02Fq
BILL, David		30	M	Weaver	03Ju02Fq
Mary	(W)	30	F	Wife	03Ju02Fq
RANSEY, James		30	M	Weaver	03Ju02Fq
FINNERON, Andrew		40	M	Laborer	03Ju02Fq
Anne	(W)	26	F	Wife	03Ju02Fq
NAUGHTON, Mary		19	F	Spinster	03Ju02Fq
Bridget		17	F	Spinster	03Ju02Fq
MCADAM, Hugh		20	M	Baker	03Ju02Fq
BOYLE, James		24	M	Laborer	03Ju02Fq
GIBBON, Rose		20	F	Spinster	03Ju02Fq
MCALRONE, Biddy		21	F	Spinster	03Ju02Fq
HENLY, Michl.		19	M	Laborer	03Ju02Fq
CALRO, Anne		19	F	Spinster	03Ju02Fq
SHEAL, Biddy		19	F	Spinster	03Ju02Fq
MCCABE, Sally		23	F	Spinster	03Ju02Fq
CASEY, Catherine		20	F	Spinster	03Ju02Fq
GAINES, Catherine		30	F	Wife	03Ju02Fq
Bridget	(D)	09	F	Child	03Ju02Fq
Mary	(D)	08	F	Child	03Ju02Fq
Micheal	(S)	06	M	Child	03Ju02Fq
Pat	(S)	03	M	Child	03Ju02Fq
MCCARTHY, Catherine		30	F	Spinster	03Ju02Fq
WIOLY, Margaret		22	F	Spinster	03Ju02Fq
DUFF, Sally		26	F	Spinster	03Ju02Fq
CASTELO, Catherine		20	F	Spinster	03Ju02Fq
CASHEN, John		25	M	Laborer	03Ju02Fq
COMEFORD, John		22	M	Laborer	03Ju02Fq
FOGARTY, Jeremiah		22	M	Laborer	03Ju02Fq
BERGIN, Pat		22	M	Laborer	03Ju02Fq
DRENAN, Anne		16	F	Spinster	03Ju02Fq
ALWELL, Pat		40	M	Laborer	03Ju02Fq
Jane	(W)	38	F	Wife	03Ju02Fq
Phillip	(S)	13	M	None	03Ju02Fq
Bridget	(D)	11	F	None	03Ju02Fq
Rosey	(D)	09	F	Child	03Ju02Fq
Peggy	(D)	07	F	Child	03Ju02Fq
John	(S)	05	M	Child	03Ju02Fq
Jane	(D)	.00	F	Infant	03Ju02Fq
OWEN, John		28	M	Laborer	03Ju02Fq
Catherine		20	F	Spinster	03Ju02Fq
CORMICK, Pat		21	M	Laborer	03Ju02Fq
RYAN, Hannah		20	F	Spinster	03Ju02Fq
OCONNOR, Robt.		30	M	Laborer	03Ju02Fq
MCGRADE, Bernard		54	M	Laborer	03Ju02Fq
Charles	(S)	24	M	Laborer	03Ju02Fq
Owen	(S)	21	M	Laborer	03Ju02Fq
Anne	(D)	26	F	Spinster	03Ju02Fq
MCGRADE, Margaret	(D)	21	F	Spinster	03Ju02Fq
Susan	(D)	22	F	Spinster	03Ju02Fq
Mary	(D)	23	F	Spinster	03Ju02Fq
John	(S)	13	M	Laborer	03Ju02Fq
MCALEAR, Pat		25	M	Laborer	03Ju02Fq
ROACHFORT, Michl.		26	M	Laborer	03Ju02Fq
LYNAN, Thos.		22	M	Laborer	03Ju02Fq
GILL, John		23	M	Laborer	03Ju02Fq
DUFFIE, Ellen		22	F	Spinster	03Ju02Fq
BARDON, Margaret		20	F	Spinster	03Ju02Fq
CAIN, John		28	M	Laborer	03Ju02Fq
LAMB, John		24	M	Laborer	03Ju02Fq
FARREL, Thos.		24	M	Laborer	03Ju02Fq
Catherine	(W)	40	F	Wife	03Ju02Fq
CARNEY, John		20	M	Laborer	03Ju02Fq
Catherine		15	F	Spinster	03Ju02Fq
KELLY, William		23	M	Laborer	03Ju02Fq
KEENAN, Mary		18	F	Spinster	03Ju02Fq
KELLY, Ann		24	F	Spinster	03Ju02Fq
SCALEN, Margaret		24	F	Spinster	03Ju02Fq
KENNADY, Wirney		25	F	Spinster	03Ju02Fq
CARR, Owen		30	M	Laborer	03Ju02Fq
Mary	(D)	07	F	Child	03Ju02Fq
MCDONALD, Thos.		26	M	Laborer	03Ju02Fq
MEIRTON, Barnerd		21	M	Laborer	03Ju02Fq
MORRIS, Bridget		19	F	Spinster	03Ju02Fq
STAUNTON, Catherine		16	F	Spinster	03Ju02Fq
DOYLE, Mary		17	F	Spinster	03Ju02Fq
James		26	M	Laborer	03Ju02Fq
GILHOOLY, James		20	M	Laborer	03Ju02Fq
Jane		23	F	Spinster	03Ju02Fq
WYNN, Miles		23	M	Laborer	03Ju02Fq
HANEY, Anne		20	F	Spinster	03Ju02Fq
MCCORMICK, Thos.		28	M	Laborer	03Ju02Fq
CANNON, Wirney		20	F	Spinster	03Ju02Fq
Ciceley		21	F	Spinster	03Ju02Fq
CALAGHN, Sally		30	F	Spinster	03Ju02Fq
Ellin		25	F	Spinster	03Ju02Fq
MCCANAGHAN, Conely		26	M	Laborer	03Ju02Fq
GIBBON, Micheal		25	M	Laborer	03Ju02Fq
John		23	M	Laborer	03Ju02Fq
CONNOLLY, William		40	M	Laborer	03Ju02Fq
Margaret	(W)	40	F	Wife	03Ju02Fq
Phillm		60	M	Laborer	03Ju02Fq
Anne		03	F	Child	03Ju02Fq
Mary		.00	F	Infant	03Ju02Fq
MCGEE, Paddy		25	M	Laborer	03Ju02Fq
Mary	(W)	24	F	Wife	03Ju02Fq
Pat	(S)	.00	M	Infant	03Ju02Fq
MURPHY, James		25	M	Laborer	03Ju02Fq
HERK, Dinnis		24	M	Laborer	03Ju02Fq
HAMPTON, John		16	M	Laborer	03Ju02Fq
TORDOFF, Edwd.		24	M	Schm	03Ju02Fq
Sarrah	(W)	24	F	Wife	03Ju02Fq
HOWARD, Juble		39	M	Wheelwright	03Ju02Fq
Mary	(W)	38	F	Wife	03Ju02Fq
Alice		43	F	None	03Ju02Fq
John	(S)	11	M	None	03Ju02Fq
Jane	(D)	13	F	None	03Ju02Fq
James	(S)	08	M	Child	03Ju02Fq
Franise	(D)	06	F	Child	03Ju02Fq
Rubir	(S)	03	M	Child	03Ju02Fq
Anne	(D)	10	F	Child	03Ju02Fq
HARRISON, Wirny		16	F	Spinster	03Ju02Fq
TERNON, Winny		17	F	Spinster	03Ju02Fq
DANIEL, Rose		15	F	Spinster	03Ju02Fq
TERNEY, Thos.		30	M	Merchant	03Ju02Fq
Frances	(D)	07	F	Child	03Ju02Fq
Mary		20	F	Spinster	03Ju02Fq
Rose		18	F	Spinster	03Ju02Fq
MILLIGAN, Andrew		20	M	Laborer	03Ju02Fq
FLANAGHAN, Pat		30	M	Laborer	03Ju02Fq
JONES, Benjamin		50	M	Carpenter	03Ju02Fq
CLOTHIER, Edward		37	M	Laborer	03Ju02Fq
MCMEVEN, Thos.		20	M	Laborer	03Ju02Fq

NAMES OF PASSENGERS		AGE	SEX	OCCUPATIONS	DATE PORT SHIP
KNOX, Wm.		19	M	None	03Ju02Fq
DUNN, John		26	M	None	03Ju02Fq

HELEN-THOMPSON 03 JUNE 1846

From Liverpool

NAMES OF PASSENGERS		AGE	SEX	OCCUPATIONS	DATE PORT SHIP
MCKEON, John		23	M	Laborer	03Ju02Fu
DOLAN, Thos.		40	M	Laborer	03Ju02Fu
BLAKE, Patk.		28	M	Laborer	03Ju02Fu
MCGRALE, Peter		23	M	Laborer	03Ju02Fu
MALONE, Margt.		20	F	Spinster	03Ju02Fu
WARD, Thos.		30	M	Laborer	03Ju02Fu
U	(W)	30	F	Wife	03Ju02Fu
DICKEY, James		21	M	Laborer	03Ju02Fu
MULDOON, Mary		19	F	Spinster	03Ju02Fu
THOMPSON, Eliza		20	F	Spinster	03Ju02Fu
FIELD, Mary		18	F	Spinster	03Ju02Fu
DOONAN, Margt.		17	F	Spinster	03Ju02Fu
FARREL, Margt.		18	F	Spinster	03Ju02Fu
COHENCY, Margt.		18	F	Spinster	03Ju02Fu
MARTIN, Ann		20	F	Spinster	03Ju02Fu
HOGAN, Michl.		26	M	Laborer	03Ju02Fu
U	(W)	25	F	Wife	03Ju02Fu
DOLEN, Jno.		12	M	None	03Ju02Fu
Patk.		18	M	Laborer	03Ju02Fu
Sally		18	F	None	03Ju02Fu
Jane		41	F	None	03Ju02Fu
Joseph		24	M	None	03Ju02Fu
NOWLAN, James		36	M	Laborer	03Ju02Fu
PRUE, David		18	M	Laborer	03Ju02Fu
HIGGINS, Ann		20	F	Spinster	03Ju02Fu
RODDY, Jno.		20	M	Laborer	03Ju02Fu
FITZPATRICK, Flora		30	F	None	03Ju02Fu
MURRAY, Michl.		20	M	Laborer	03Ju02Fu
COX, Stepn.		20	M	Laborer	03Ju02Fu
KEARNEY, James		21	M	Laborer	03Ju02Fu
MCGRALE, Margt.		20	F	Spinster	03Ju02Fu
DONNELLY, Betty		20	F	Spinster	03Ju02Fu
MALINE, Jno.		18	M	Spinster	03Ju02Fu
MALIN, Margt.		18	F	Spinster	03Ju02Fu
ROURKE, Jno.		30	M	Laborer	03Ju02Fu
Ann	(W)	21	F	Wife	03Ju02Fu
Patk.	(S)	.00	M	Infant	03Ju02Fu
DOWE, Mary		18	F	Spinster	03Ju02Fu
BYRNE, Henry		25	M	Laborer	03Ju02Fu
Alice		25	F	None	03Ju02Fu
FALLOW, Winfred		21	F	Spinster	03Ju02Fu
RATIGAN, Michl.		20	M	Laborer	03Ju02Fu
MAHER, Jno.		20	M	Laborer	03Ju02Fu
FARREL, Michl.		25	M	Laborer	03Ju02Fu
HAGAN, Timothy		20	M	Laborer	03Ju02Fu
BUSH, Ellen		20	F	Spinster	03Ju02Fu
GATELY, Jno.		35	M	Laborer	03Ju02Fu
Patk.		18	M	Laborer	03Ju02Fu
Honora		18	F	Spinster	03Ju02Fu
CORBETT, Honor		15	F	Spinster	03Ju02Fu
COLLINS, Patk.		18	M	Laborer	03Ju02Fu
RILEY, James		22	M	Laborer	03Ju02Fu
HARROD, U		40	M	Farmer	03Ju02Fu
SMITHMEN, U		20	M	Clerk	03Ju02Fu
MCGOVERN, Jas.		20	M	Laborer	03Ju02Fu
Cath.		20	F	None	03Ju02Fu
MCGRADY, Cath.		20	F	Spinster	03Ju02Fu
FLAGGHERTY, Sally		20	F	Spinster	03Ju02Fu
FOX, Betty		60	F	None	03Ju02Fu
Nora	(D)	26	F	None	03Ju02Fu
Cathe.	(D)	25	F	None	03Ju02Fu
BENDER, Ann		27	F	Carpenter	03Ju02Fu
DANCE, Geo.		23	M	Farmer	03Ju02Fu
ROCHE, Michl.		26	M	Blacksmith	03Ju02Fu
BRICKMAN, Henry		26	M	Brewer	03Ju02Fu
DAVENBECK, Jacob		36	M	Farmer	03Ju02Fu
HOYLE, Richd.		21	M	Smith	03Ju02Fu
BEE, Jacob		11	M	None	03Ju02Fu
Henry		12	M	None	03Ju02Fu
ZIMMERMAN, Eliza		23	F	Spinster	03Ju02Fu
CONNOR, Martha		11	F	Laborer	03Ju02Fu
SMITH, Chas.		26	M	Laborer	03Ju02Fu
Fredk.		25	M	Laborer	03Ju02Fu
FELSWYGER, Henry		23	M	Farmer	03Ju02Fu
CORP, Chas.		20	M	Rope Maker	03Ju02Fu
Ann		18	F	None	03Ju02Fu
Affey		13	U	None	03Ju02Fu
BOLE, Barbara		23	F	None	03Ju02Fu
STENLOW, Debora		21	F	None	03Ju02Fu
BUCKLEY, Patk.		25	M	Farmer	03Ju02Fu
U	(W)	24	F	Wife	03Ju02Fu
Michl.	(S)	06	M	Child	03Ju02Fu
Kelly		05	U	Child	03Ju02Fu
Bridget	(D)	02	F	Child	03Ju02Fu
FITZPATRICK, Michl.		22	M	Laborer	03Ju02Fu
MELIA, Patrick		20	M	Laborer	03Ju02Fu
HANLON, Jno.		23	M	Laborer	03Ju02Fu
LOUGHLAN, Thos.		20	M	None	03Ju02Fu
CRAWLEY, Mary		23	F	Spinster	03Ju02Fu
Wm.	(S)	02	M	Child	03Ju02Fu
Thos.	(S)	.00	M	Infant	03Ju02Fu
CAHITY, Mary		20	F	None	03Ju02Fu
SMITH, Jno.		20	M	Laborer	03Ju02Fu
BERGEN, Jas.		22	M	Laborer	03Ju02Fu
Harry		20	M	Laborer	03Ju02Fu
MCGAVNEY, Ann		21	F	Spinster	03Ju02Fu
Rose		20	F	Spinster	03Ju02Fu
DEVENE, Philip		25	M	Laborer	03Ju02Fu
Peter		20	M	Laborer	03Ju02Fu
BRENNAN, Thos.		23	M	Laborer	03Ju02Fu
Eliza		20	F	Laborer	03Ju02Fu
BRYAN, Patk.		34	M	Laborer	03Ju02Fu
ROURKE, Thos.		16	M	None	03Ju02Fu
Mary		13	F	None	03Ju02Fu
COONAN, Patk.		18	M	Laborer	03Ju02Fu
HAWLEY, Ann		18	F	Spinster	03Ju02Fu
ROURKE, Julia		18	F	Spinster	03Ju02Fu
HORAN, Mary		16	F	Spinster	03Ju02Fu
WHEALAN, Wm.		30	M	Laborer	03Ju02Fu
Michl.		27	M	Laborer	03Ju02Fu
Patk.		27	M	None	03Ju02Fu
DEGAN, Jno.		60	M	Laborer	03Ju02Fu
Jno.		25	M	Laborer	03Ju02Fu
TRACEY, Peter		27	M	Laborer	03Ju02Fu
MORIS, James		28	M	Laborer	03Ju02Fu
NAUGHTON, Dennis		25	M	Laborer	03Ju02Fu
DALEY, Ellen		18	F	Spinster	03Ju02Fu
KELLY, Mary		25	F	Spinster	03Ju02Fu
STAKER, Jno.		69	M	Farmer	03Ju02Fu
Ann	(W)	45	F	Wife	03Ju02Fu
Francis	(S)	28	M	None	03Ju02Fu
Jno.	(S)	25	M	None	03Ju02Fu
Jos.	(S)	16	M	None	03Ju02Fu
Louis	(S)	12	M	None	03Ju02Fu
Benjn.F.	(S)	08	M	Child	03Ju02Fu
HYSLOP, Hannah		19	F	None	03Ju02Fu
SWETZLER, Philip		29	M	Farmer	03Ju02Fu
WALTER, Rob		25	M	None	03Ju02Fu
Cathe.		19	F	None	03Ju02Fu
STAGER, Mary		26	F	None	03Ju02Fu
SWEEL, Philip		22	M	None	03Ju02Fu
SUNDAY, Jno.		25	M	Laborer	03Ju02Fu
DONNELLY, Michl.		26	M	None	03Ju02Fu
U	(W)	21	F	Wife	03Ju02Fu
CARTY, Jas.		25	M	None	03Ju02Fu
DONNELLY, Maria		20	F	Spinster	03Ju02Fu
Johannah		20	F	Spinster	03Ju02Fu

NAMES OF PASSENGERS		AGE	SEX	OCCUPATIONS	DATE PORT SHIP
POWER, Patk.		28	M	Laborer	03Ju02Fu
U	(W)	30	F	Wife	03Ju02Fu
MURPHY, Jno.		28	M	Laborer	03Ju02Fu
U	(W)	24	F	Wife	03Ju02Fu
MCCARTHY, Michl.		25	M	Carpenter	03Ju02Fu
ROGERS, Peter		23	M	Laborer	03Ju02Fu
BURKE, Jas.		22	M	Laborer	03Ju02Fu
DEVISE, Jno.		20	M	Laborer	03Ju02Fu
FLYNN, Val		21	M	Laborer	03Ju02Fu
NOWLEN, Jno.		21	M	Yeoman	03Ju02Fu
FITZGERALD, Michl.		21	M	Yeoman	03Ju02Fu
Patk.		18	M	Yeoman	03Ju02Fu
Mary		18	F	None	03Ju02Fu
Honora		50	F	None	03Ju02Fu
REAL, Thos.		25	M	Laborer	03Ju02Fu
Cathe.		20	F	Laborer	03Ju02Fu
SHEEPAWN, Louis		25	M	Laborer	03Ju02Fu
GARTHWATES, Jno.		25	M	Laborer	03Ju02Fu
Frances	(W)	28	F	Wife	03Ju02Fu
Jno.	(S)	03	M	Child	03Ju02Fu
Wm.	(S)	02	M	Child	03Ju02Fu
Mary	(D)	.00	F	Infant	03Ju02Fu
CLARKE, Bernard		20	M	Laborer	03Ju02Fu
Cathe.		20	F	Laborer	03Ju02Fu
GANAUER, Cathe.		20	F	Laborer	03Ju02Fu
ROCHE, Jno.		20	M	Laborer	03Ju02Fu
QUANLEN, Wm.		20	M	Laborer	03Ju02Fu
FLYNN, Michl.		35	M	Laborer	03Ju02Fu
U	(W)	30	F	Wife	03Ju02Fu
Jno.	(S)	02	M	Child	03Ju02Fu
Martin	(S)	04	M	Child	03Ju02Fu
REILLY, Rose		30	F	Servant	03Ju02Fu
Ann		32	F	Servant	03Ju02Fu
GREEN, Cathe.		18	F	None	03Ju02Fu
KEARNEY, Jas.		30	M	Servant	03Ju02Fu
LYONS, Roger		25	M	None	03Ju02Fu
DAFFNEY, Bricget		25	F	Servant	03Ju02Fu
FITZPATRICK, Michl.		18	M	Servant	03Ju02Fu
REILLY, Fanny		18	F	Servant	03Ju02Fu
MCGUIRE, Mary		25	F	Servant	03Ju02Fu
DOLEN, Ellen		25	F	Servant	03Ju02Fu
QUEEN, Edmond		20	M	Laborer	03Ju02Fu
MCCANA, Mary		20	F	Servant	03Ju02Fu

HAYTI 04 JUNE 1846

From Haiti

| HEARN, John | | 50 | M | Merchant | 04Ju30Gd |
| U | (W) | 45 | F | Wife | 04Ju30Gd |

ENVOY 04 JUNE 1846

From Liverpool

JONES, Philip		30	M	Farmer	04Ju02Ge
Calvin		27	M	Farmer	04Ju02Ge
KINSELLA, James		20	M	Farmer	04Ju02Ge
FITZSIMONS, James		20	M	Farmer	04Ju02Ge
HANNAN, Sally		20	F	Servant	04Ju02Ge
WILSON, Martha		20	F	Servant	04Ju02Ge
PARKER, Saml.		20	M	Mechanic	04Ju02Ge
Mary-Jane		20	F	None	04Ju02Ge

NAMES OF PASSENGERS		AGE	SEX	OCCUPATIONS	DATE PORT SHIP
JOHNSON, Wm.		20	M	None	04Ju02Ge
MCGEE, Ann		20	F	Servant	C4Ju02Ge
CORAN, Eilza		20	F	Servant	04Ju02Ge
Ann		18	F	Servant	C4Ju02Ge
NEIL, Mary		21	F	Servant	04Ju02Ge
MCKINNAN, Patk.		21	M	Laborer	04Ju02Ge
MARKEE, Patk.		21	M	Laborer	04Ju02Ge
MCGINN, Patk.		21	M	Laborer	04Ju02Ge
MCNEIL, John		25	M	Laborer	04Ju02Ge
U		23	F	None	04Ju02Ge
MURRAY, Cathe.		20	F	None	04Ju02Ge
NAIL, Mathew		30	M	Farmer	04Ju02Ge
Mary		24	F	None	04Ju02Ge
DEVINE, Gregory		21	M	Laborer	04Ju02Ge
FLAHERTY, John		21	M	Laborer	04Ju02Ge
MEEHAN, James		21	M	Laborer	04Ju02Ge
CONNELL, James		21	M	Mechanic	04Ju02Ge
COCHRAN, Michl.		21	M	Mechanic	04Ju02Ge
SULLIVAN, Dan.		20	M	Mechanic	04Ju02Ge
FLINN, Dinis		20	M	Mechanic	04Ju02Ge
SULLIVAN, Hellen		18	F	None	04Ju02Ge
MCCARTY, Peggy		18	F	None	04Ju02Ge
HORGAN, Cathe.		20	F	Servant	04Ju02Ge
DENNIS, James		20	M	Laborer	04Ju02Ge
MCCALLEM, Eliza		20	F	Servant	04Ju02Ge
KINSELLA, Ann-Jane		20	F	Servant	04Ju02Ge
DENNIS, Sorale		20	F	Servant	04Ju02Ge
HUGHES, Ann		20	F	Servant	04Ju02Ge
MCEWEN, James		30	M	Farmer	04Ju02Ge
James	(S)	09	M	Child	04Ju02Ge
Mary	(D)	07	F	Child	04Ju02Ge
Catherine	(W)	28	F	Wife	04Ju02Ge
MCCUE, Hellen		20	F	Servant	04Ju02Ge
ROACH, John		26	M	Farmer	04Ju02Ge
Eilza		23	F	None	04Ju02Ge
REILLY, James		21	M	Farmer	04Ju02Ge
BYRNE, Margt.		20	F	Servant	C4Ju02Ge
ROACH, Mary		20	F	Servant	04Ju02Ge
SHEEN, Nichl.		25	M	Laborer	04Ju02Ge
Hellen	(W)	22	F	Wife	04Ju02Ge
Biddy	(D)	.00	F	Infant	C4Ju02Ge
DENOHY, Margt.		21	F	Servant	04Ju02Ge
MCGINNES, Margt.		21	F	Servant	C4Ju02Ge
POLLOCK, Patt		20	M	Mechanic	04Ju02Ge
FLINN, Michl.		20	M	Mechanic	04Ju02Ge
KENNY, Michl.		21	M	Mechanic	04Ju02Ge
DONAHY, Pat		22	M	Mechanic	04Ju02Ge
MCGINNIS, James		24	M	Mechanic	04Ju02Ge
Thomas		21	M	Mechanic	04Ju02Ge
REGAN, John		21	M	Mechanic	04Ju02Ge
BRYAN, Cathe.		20	F	Servant	04Ju02Ge
Mary		20	F	Servant	C4Ju02Ge
BRASSER, Ann		20	F	Servant	04Ju02Ge
SMOLLEN, Ann		20	F	Servant	04Ju02Ge
BRYAN, Conn.		21	M	Laborer	04Ju02Ge
HANSEAD, Cathe.		20	F	Servant	C4Ju02Ge
MCMULLEN, Dan		27	M	Farmer	04Ju02Ge
Cathe.	(W)	24	F	Wife	04Ju02Ge
Bricget	(D)	.00	F	Infant	04Ju02Ge
MADDEN, Bicdy		20	F	Servant	C4Ju02Ge
BURK, Patk.		24	M	Servant	04Ju02Ge
Margt.		20	F	Servant	C4Ju02Ge
DEMPSEY, Ann		20	F	Servant	C4Ju02Ge
GRENAN, Rosy		20	F	Servant	04Ju02Ge
CUSACK, Biddy		21	F	Servant	04Ju02Ge
REGAN, Cathe.		.00	F	Irfant	C4Ju02Ge
FARRELL, Cathe.		21	F	Servant	04Ju02Ge
HINES, Bicdy		21	F	Servant	04Ju02Ge
Susan		19	F	Servant	C4Ju02Ge
Mary		18	F	Servant	04Ju02Ge
MARTIN, Ellen		20	F	Servant	04Ju02Ge
LILLY, Ann		20	F	Servant	04Ju02Ge
TUMBLIN, Cathe.		20	F	Servant	04Ju02Ge
BEATTY, Mary-Ann		20	F	Servant	C4Ju02Ge
MCAVENIE, Maria		20	F	Servant	04Ju02Ge

NAMES OF PASSENGERS		AGE	SEX	OCCUPATIONS	DATE PORT SHIP
HANLY, Owen		21	M	Laborer	04Ju02Ge
MOLONY, Arthur		21	M	Mechanic	04Ju02Ge
PARRY, Edwd.		21	M	Mechanic	04Ju02Ge
IGO, Owen		20	M	Laborer	04Ju02Ge
FOY, John		28	M	Laborer	04Ju02Ge
Mary	(W)	23	F	Servant	04Ju02Ge
Edwd.	(S)	.00	M	Infant	04Ju02Ge
REILLY, Owen		21	M	Farmer	04Ju02Ge
Mary		19	F	Servant	04Ju02Ge
MCCANN, Wm.		20	M	Farmer	04Ju02Ge
COWDAL, Wm.		22	M	Farmer	04Ju02Ge
SMITH, Thos.		22	M	Farmer	04Ju02Ge
MCCAIL, Pat		22	M	Farmer	04Ju02Ge
MCMANUS, Thos.		23	M	Farmer	04Ju02Ge
REILLY, Luke		21	M	Farmer	04Ju02Ge
Bessey		19	F	Servant	04Ju02Ge
Cathe.		17	F	Servant	04Ju02Ge
MACKIE, Biddy		21	F	Servant	04Ju02Ge
Nancy		18	F	Servant	04Ju02Ge
SHORT, Susan		18	F	Servant	04Ju02Ge
DORAN, Alice		18	F	Servant	04Ju02Ge
KELLY, Ann		18	F	Servant	04Ju02Ge
FLINN, James		23	M	Farmer	04Ju02Ge
MCGRAW, Pat		23	M	Farmer	04Ju02Ge
MCADAM, Mary		21	F	Servant	04Ju02Ge
KERR, Wm.		20	M	Servant	04Ju02Ge
FEENEY, Cathe.		20	F	Servant	04Ju02Ge
TROY, Ellen		20	F	Servant	04Ju02Ge
GUNN, Danl.		26	M	Farmer	04Ju02Ge
Margt.	(W)	25	F	Wife	04Ju02Ge
Mary	(D)	.00	F	Infant	04Ju02Ge
MOFFAT, Michl.		23	M	Painter	04Ju02Ge
ALECE, John		24	M	Mechanic	04Ju02Ge
BARRY, Mary		20	F	Servant	04Ju02Ge
HOLLAND, Danl.		21	M	Clerk	04Ju02Ge
MCCARTY, Michl.		24	M	Farmer	04Ju02Ge
Danl.		22	M	Farmer	04Ju02Ge
REILLY, James		22	M	Farmer	04Ju02Ge
HOLLAN, Patk.		22	M	Farmer	04Ju02Ge
MURRAY, Wm.		24	M	Farmer	04Ju02Ge
Cathe.		20	F	Servant	04Ju02Ge
KELLY, John		26	M	Mechanic	04Ju02Ge
U	(W)	24	F	Wife	04Ju02Ge
PATHAN, Cathe.		21	F	Servant	04Ju02Ge
BYRNE, Margt.		21	F	Servant	04Ju02Ge
HUNT, Thomas		20	M	Laborer	04Ju02Ge
PAINTER, Michl.		20	M	Mechanic	04Ju02Ge
FARRELL, Pat		20	M	Mechanic	04Ju02Ge
Lucy		18	F	Servant	04Ju02Ge
MITCHELL, James		20	M	Carpenter	04Ju02Ge
MARKIE, Biddy		38	F	None	04Ju02Ge
Bitty		13	F	None	04Ju02Ge
Wm.		38	M	Farmer	04Ju02Ge
Mary		10	F	None	04Ju02Ge
Biddy		06	F	Child	04Ju02Ge
COLLINS, Mary		20	F	Servant	04Ju02Ge
CARSEN, Martha		20	F	Servant	04Ju02Ge
PARKINSON, Susan		.00	F	Infant	04Ju02Ge
Saml.	(P)	25	M	Farmer	04Ju02Ge
U	(M)	23	F	None	04Ju02Ge
MCAVOY, Mary		20	F	Servant	04Ju02Ge
DEMPSEY, Biddy		21	F	Servant	04Ju02Ge
CRAYNOR, Margt.		21	F	Servant	04Ju02Ge
PERRY, Wm.		24	M	Carpenter	04Ju02Ge
DEMPSEY, Thomas		23	M	Farmer	04Ju02Ge
ONEIL, Feilx		23	M	Farmer	04Ju02Ge
MCVICAR, James		23	M	Farmer	04Ju02Ge
REGAN, Timothy		26	M	Farmer	04Ju02Ge
Mary	(W)	24	F	Wife	04Ju02Ge
Helen	(D)	.00	F	Infant	04Ju02Ge
MURPHY, Margt.		20	F	Servant	04Ju02Ge
MURRAY, John		26	M	Farmer	04Ju02Ge
Timothy	(S)	.00	M	Infant	04Ju02Ge
Johanna	(W)	23	F	Wife	04Ju02Ge
PEGAN, Denis		21	M	Farmer	04Ju02Ge

NAMES OF PASSENGERS		AGE	SEX	OCCUPATIONS	DATE PORT SHIP
WALKER, Margt.		20	F	Servant	04Ju02Ge
MCCULLOUGH, Margt.		20	F	Servant	04Ju02Ge
TUCKER, Cathe.		20	F	Servant	04Ju02Ge
DUNN, Wm.		28	M	Farmer	04Ju02Ge
David	(S)	07	M	Child	04Ju02Ge
Margt.	(D)	05	F	Child	04Ju02Ge
Jane	(W)	27	F	Wife	04Ju02Ge
Mary-Jane	(D)	03	F	Child	04Ju02Ge
James	(S)	.00	M	Infant	04Ju02Ge
WHEATAN, John		24	M	Mechanic	04Ju02Ge
CAMPBELL, Thos.		21	M	Mechanic	04Ju02Ge
CORRIGAN, Bernd.		24	M	Mechanic	04Ju02Ge
COGAN, Thos.		21	M	Laborer	04Ju02Ge
CANTELL, John		24	M	Mechanic	04Ju02Ge
FENESLEY, James		23	M	Mechanic	04Ju02Ge
CORRAGAN, Judy		20	F	Servant	04Ju02Ge
MULVIHOL, John		21	M	Laborer	04Ju02Ge
SCANLIN, James		20	M	Laborer	04Ju02Ge
FOROHY, John		20	M	Laborer	04Ju02Ge
LEURY, Pat		21	M	Laborer	04Ju02Ge
MESCOL, Mary		20	F	Servant	04Ju02Ge
BRADY, Bridget		20	F	Servant	04Ju02Ge
DELANY, Thos.		22	M	Laborer	04Ju02Ge
CONLY, Mary		21	F	Servant	04Ju02Ge
CONLIN, Cathe.		20	F	Servant	04Ju02Ge
Ann		18	F	Servant	04Ju02Ge
POSTLN, Thos.		22	M	Tailor	04Ju02Ge
DAVIS, Abraham		23	M	Mechanic	04Ju02Ge
MCCOLGAN, Cathe.		24	F	Servant	04Ju02Ge
Michl.		22	M	Farmer	04Ju02Ge
FOACH, Patk.		21	M	Farmer	04Ju02Ge
DUNN, Denis		21	M	Farmer	04Ju02Ge
ARMSTRONG, Margt.		22	F	Servant	04Ju02Ge
WHELAN, Julia		21	F	Servant	04Ju02Ge
BRYAN, Mary		20	F	Servant	04Ju02Ge
SHORKIT, Pat		21	M	Farmer	04Ju02Ge
CUMMINS, Tim		21	M	Farmer	04Ju02Ge
MULLIGAN, James		23	M	Farmer	04Ju02Ge
MCCAHEY, George		22	M	Farmer	04Ju02Ge
KEAN, James		21	M	Farmer	04Ju02Ge
ARKINS, James		18	M	Farmer	04Ju02Ge
Susanna		16	F	Servant	04Ju02Ge
KERR, Mary		20	F	Servant	04Ju02Ge
CLOSAN, Mary		20	F	Servant	04Ju02Ge
SMITH, Richd.		24	M	Laborer	04Ju02Ge
Cathe.		22	F	None	04Ju02Ge
DORNAN, James		21	M	None	04Ju02Ge
FLINN, Mary		.00	F	Infant	04Ju02Ge
SMITH, Richd.		23	M	Farmer	04Ju02Ge
WHEELAN, George		29	M	Farmer	04Ju02Ge
Ann	(W)	28	F	Wife	04Ju02Ge
George	(S)	06	M	Child	04Ju02Ge
Wm.	(S)	03	M	Child	04Ju02Ge
Mary-Ann	(D)	.00	F	Infant	04Ju02Ge
MULLAN, Hugh		36	M	None	04Ju02Ge
Ann	(W)	33	F	Wife	04Ju02Ge
Cathe.	(D)	14	F	None	04Ju02Ge
John	(S)	08	M	Child	04Ju02Ge
Michl.	(S)	04	M	Child	04Ju02Ge
BURN, Paul		23	M	None	04Ju02Ge
NOWLAN, Garrol		20	M	None	04Ju02Ge
BURN, Rosey		18	F	None	04Ju02Ge
KELLY, Ellen		18	F	None	04Ju02Ge
LOYD, Ml.		20	M	None	04Ju02Ge
ALLEN, John		20	M	None	04Ju02Ge
Ann		20	F	None	04Ju02Ge
Martha		20	F	None	04Ju02Ge

NAMES OF PASSENGERS	AGE	SEX	OCCUPATIONS	DATE PORT SHIP
ANAHUAC 04 JUNE 1846				
From Rio-De-Janiero				
HUTTON, Hugh	45	M	Gentleman	04Jul3Gy
Mary	40	F	Lady	04Jul3Gy
ALMANDRALNA 05 JUNE 1846				
From VALPARAISO,Chile				
CARR, John	47	M	Butler	05Ju49Gz
MESSENGER 05 JUNE 1846				
From Liverpool				
SEALY, Cathr.	18	F	Spinster	05Ju02Fz
FITZGERALD, Michl.	35	M	Laborer	05Ju02Fz
Mary (W)	35	F	Spinner	05Ju02Fz
Ellen (D)	07	F	Child	05Ju02Fz
Patk. (S)	05	M	Child	05Ju02Fz
Mary (D)	02	F	Child	05Ju02Fz
Michl. (S)	.00	M	Infant	05Ju02Fz
SMITH, Richd.	22	M	Laborer	05Ju02Fz
WHALAN, John	30	M	Spinner	05Ju02Fz
CORNIN, Mary	20	F	Laborer	05Ju02Fz
FITZK, Edwd.	19	M	Laborer	05Ju02Fz
CURRIN, Anne	21	F	Laborer	05Ju02Fz
LOCHRY, Danl.	20	M	Laborer	05Ju02Fz
Michl.	25	M	Laborer	05Ju02Fz
FLINN, Danl.	32	M	Laborer	05Ju02Fz
LUDEN, Jas.	24	M	Laborer	05Ju02Fz
Bridgt.	40	F	Laborer	05Ju02Fz
REYNOLDS, Anne	25	F	Laborer	05Ju02Fz
HANAGHY, Pat	22	M	Laborer	05Ju02Fz
BRET, Pat	21	M	Laborer	05Ju02Fz
BULGER, Margt.	19	F	Laborer	05Ju02Fz
KING, May	18	F	Laborer	05Ju02Fz
SOGHIN, Pat	25	M	Laborer	05Ju02Fz
INGLISH, Jos.	20	M	Laborer	05Ju02Fz
MAHAN, Peter	20	M	Laborer	05Ju02Fz
REILY, Elzth	16	F	Laborer	05Ju02Fz
GOVERN, Bridgt.	18	F	Laborer	05Ju02Fz
MCCARTEY, Mary	17	F	Laborer	05Ju02Fz
DONELY, Rosan	20	F	Farmer	05Ju02Fz
GILCRIST, Anne	16	F	Farmer	05Ju02Fz
CONWAY, Rose	20	F	Farmer	05Ju02Fz
NEWTON, Wm.	25	M	Farmer	05Ju02Fz
WARD, Owen	25	M	Farmer	05Ju02Fz
TAYLOR, Wm.	20	M	Farmer	05Ju02Fz
Mary	25	F	Farmer	05Ju02Fz
SLATER, Margt.	40	F	Farmer	05Ju02Fz
MCCUE, Pat	19	M	Farmer	05Ju02Fz
Mary	18	F	Farmer	05Ju02Fz
TAYLOR, Wm.	22	M	Farmer	05Ju02Fz
Jane	19	F	Farmer	05Ju02Fz

NAMES OF PASSENGERS	AGE	SEX	OCCUPATIONS	DATE PORT SHIP
LYONS, Anne	17	F	Farmer	05Ju02Fz
MALY, Hana	24	F	Farmer	05Ju02Fz
SEDWICH, Wm.	40	M	Farmer	05Ju02Fz
FLINN, Pat	47	M	Farmer	05Ju02Fz
DOLAN, Andrew	23	M	Farmer	05Ju02Fz
KENEDY, Melachi	45	M	Farmer	05Ju02Fz
CARLTON, John	22	M	Farmer	05Ju02Fz
CONNY, Michl.	19	M	Farmer	05Ju02Fz
CARRIGAN, Wm.	24	M	Farmer	05Ju02Fz
BAILY, Wm.	34	M	Farmer	05Ju02Fz
CASEY, Pat	30	M	Farmer	05Ju02Fz
SMITH, Pat	28	M	Farmer	05Ju02Fz
KEHOE, Brigt.	22	F	Farmer	05Ju02Fz
U, Wm.	20	M	Farmer	05Ju02Fz
CURRIN, Thos.	30	M	Farmer	05Ju02Fz
KELBAN, Barny	25	M	Farmer	05Ju02Fz
Margt.	22	F	Farmer	05Ju02Fz
Bridgt.	22	F	Farmer	05Ju02Fz
MCSHERRY, John	18	M	Farmer	05Ju02Fz
KILROSS, Mary	19	F	Farmer	05Ju02Fz
Hugh	24	M	Farmer	05Ju02Fz
FULTON, James	27	M	Farmer	05Ju02Fz
Josephene	22	F	Farmer	05Ju02Fz
DUNLOP, Susan	26	F	Farmer	05Ju02Fz
U	24	F	Farmer	05Ju02Fz
Fredrick	09	M	Child	05Ju02Fz
Francis	11	M	None	05Ju02Fz
SHATON, Shedwick	21	M	Farmer	05Ju02Fz
Mark	22	M	Farmer	05Ju02Fz
Joseph	25	M	Farmer	05Ju02Fz
SHILLINGER, F.	39	U	Farmer	05Ju02Fz
U-Mrs.	50	F	Farmer	05Ju02Fz
Polly	50	F	Farmer	05Ju02Fz
Sebastian	05	M	Child	05Ju02Fz
Cestel	04	M	Child	05Ju02Fz
Fidel	11	M	None	05Ju02Fz
Josephene	18	F	Farmer	05Ju02Fz
Edder	17	U	Farmer	05Ju02Fz
REILY, Pat	20	M	Farmer	05Ju02Fz
Michl.	22	M	Farmer	05Ju02Fz
DERMOTT, Bryan	21	M	Farmer	05Ju02Fz
GROLER, John	50	M	Laborer	05Ju02Fz
Sabina (W)	40	F	Wife	05Ju02Fz
Edwd. (S)	20	M	Laborer	05Ju02Fz
Earnest (S)	18	M	Laborer	05Ju02Fz
Paulina (D)	06	F	Child	05Ju02Fz
SHERIFF, Gabriel	44	M	Laborer	05Ju02Fz
Barbara (W)	40	F	Wife	05Ju02Fz
Lorien	09	U	Child	05Ju02Fz
Reinhart (S)	08	M	Child	05Ju02Fz
Chilian	04	U	Child	05Ju02Fz
RAMDRE, Joseph	24	M	Laborer	05Ju02Fz
Barbara	22	F	Laborer	05Ju02Fz
France	26	U	Laborer	05Ju02Fz
BROW, Jacob	30	M	Laborer	05Ju02Fz
Eliza (W)	25	F	Wife	05Ju02Fz
Carl (S)	05	M	Child	05Ju02Fz
SULLIVAN, Michl.	20	M	Laborer	05Ju02Fz
PETERS, Wm.	27	M	Laborer	05Ju02Fz
Elizth. (W)	27	F	Wife	05Ju02Fz
Geo. (S)	.00	M	Infant	05Ju02Fz
MURY, Alexr.	22	M	Shoemaker	05Ju02Fz
REILY, Barry	30	M	Weaver	05Ju02Fz
Hugh (S)	.00	M	Infant	05Ju02Fz
MURY, Alexr.	22	M	Weaver	05Ju02Fz
HARTZ, Edwd.	30	M	Weaver	05Ju02Fz
COLLINS, John	25	M	Weaver	05Ju02Fz
HARTZ, Mary	17	F	Weaver	05Ju02Fz
Nora	13	F	Weaver	05Ju02Fz
COOPER, Johanna	14	F	Weaver	05Ju02Fz
MOLD, Pat	24	M	Weaver	05Ju02Fz
TRINAN, Thos.	22	M	Weaver	05Ju02Fz
MAHON, Bridget	40	F	Weaver	05Ju02Fz
SHANLAN, Thos.	21	M	Weaver	05Ju02Fz
FLEMING, Edwd.	28	M	Weaver	05Ju02Fz

NAMES OF PASSENGERS		AGE	SEX	OCCUPATIONS	DATE PORT SHIP	NAMES OF PASSENGERS		AGE	SEX	OCCUPATIONS	DATE PORT SHIP
RYAN, John		25	M	Weaver	05Ju02Fz	SENAHAN, John		25	M	Farmer	05Ju02Fz
HASET, Pat		22	M	Weaver	05Ju02Fz	Brigt.		30	F	Farmer	05Ju02Fz
DORAN, Walter		40	M	Weaver	05Ju02Fz	CAMNON, Cathr.		21	F	Farmer	05Ju02Fz
SHEHAN, Margt.		24	F	Weaver	05Ju02Fz	CRAUTERS, Michl.		21	M	Farmer	05Ju02Fz
Elizth.		17	F	Weaver	05Ju02Fz	FEARL, Mary		20	F	Farmer	05Ju02Fz
NOONAN, Jno.		35	M	Weaver	05Ju02Fz	CAVER, Edwd.		23	M	Farmer	05Ju02Fz
SHEHAND, Dani.		25	M	Weaver	05Ju02Fz	LIONS, Cathr.		19	F	Farmer	05Ju02Fz
SINCONEY, Dani.		25	M	Weaver	05Ju02Fz	OWENS, Mary		10	F	Farmer	05Ju02Fz
SEAN, Jas.		23	M	Weaver	05Ju02Fz	SULLIVAN, Margt.		25	F	Farmer	05Ju02Fz
SENAHAN, Pat		36	M	Weaver	05Ju02Fz	MAYAN, Lawrence		24	M	Farmer	05Ju02Fz
MORGAN, Morgan		36	M	Weaver	05Ju02Fz	DEMPSY, Mary		28	F	Farmer	05Ju02Fz
Pat		30	M	Weaver	05Ju02Fz	Susan		25	F	Farmer	05Ju02Fz
Johana		24	F	Weaver	05Ju02Fz	MARA, Cathr.		20	F	Farmer	05Ju02Fz
WELSH, Pat		20	M	Weaver	05Ju02Fz	LIONS, Bend.		25	M	Farmer	05Ju02Fz
Ellen		18	F	Weaver	05Ju02Fz	SEALY, Michl.		21	M	Farmer	05Ju02Fz
Eliza		24	F	Weaver	05Ju02Fz	SULLIVAN, Jno.		22	M	Farmer	05Ju02Fz
BROWN, John		22	M	Weaver	05Ju02Fz	HARTSEL, U		40	M	Farmer	05Ju02Fz
SULLIVAN, E.		27	U	Weaver	05Ju02Fz	U	(W)	46	F	Wife	05Ju02Fz
Jno.		20	M	Weaver	05Ju02Fz	Johana	(D)	22	F	Farmer	05Ju02Fz
BOLES, Tim		24	M	Weaver	05Ju02Fz	Carrol	(D)	18	F	Farmer	05Ju02Fz
BRYAN, Ellen		23	F	Weaver	05Ju02Fz	Cath.	(D)	16	F	Farmer	05Ju02Fz
CUNAHAN, Ellen		27	F	Weaver	05Ju02Fz	Wm.	(S)	08	M	Child	05Ju02Fz
GALLAWAY, E.		27	U	Weaver	05Ju02Fz	Se--Rs		09	U	Child	05Ju02Fz
Johana		27	F	Weaver	05Ju02Fz	Henry	(S)	06	M	Child	05Ju02Fz
Julia		14	F	Weaver	05Ju02Fz	Caroline	(D)	04	F	Child	05Ju02Fz
MURPHY, Pat		22	M	Weaver	05Ju02Fz	Albert	(S)	03	M	Child	05Ju02Fz
Jno.		26	M	Weaver	05Ju02Fz	DEMPSY, Michl.		32	M	Farmer	05Ju02Fz
GALVAN, Mary		26	F	Weaver	05Ju02Fz	Matilda	(W)	31	F	Wife	05Ju02Fz
MAHONY, Florence		21	F	Weaver	05Ju02Fz	Jason	(S)	09	M	Child	05Ju02Fz
Michl.		18	M	Weaver	05Ju02Fz	KEFT, Lovery		40	M	Farmer	05Ju02Fz
LONG, Thos.		21	M	Weaver	05Ju02Fz	BRENARD, Tonfield		30	M	Farmer	05Ju02Fz
Jno.		21	M	Weaver	05Ju02Fz	Zester		21	M	Farmer	05Ju02Fz
CORCORAN, Mary		16	F	Weaver	05Ju02Fz	THESEL, Men		30	M	Farmer	05Ju02Fz
DUGAN, Hanna		26	F	Weaver	05Ju02Fz	MARSEL, L.		61	M	Farmer	05Ju02Fz
Bridget		26	F	Weaver	05Ju02Fz	Rosallen	(D)	08	F	Child	05Ju02Fz
CASSIDY, M.		37	U	Weaver	05Ju02Fz	Sysmator		04	U	Child	05Ju02Fz
MCDOWL, Thos.		21	M	Farmer	05Ju02Fz	Grason	(S)	.00	M	Infant	05Ju02Fz
FITZ, Dani.		31	M	Farmer	05Ju02Fz	LABOR, Mihan		38	M	Farmer	05Ju02Fz
HARLY, U-Mrs.		30	F	Farmer	05Ju02Fz	Cordwise		03	M	Child	05Ju02Fz
CLEEK, G.		23	U	Farmer	05Ju02Fz	Yrbal		32	U	Farmer	05Ju02Fz
CARTHY, Amy		20	F	Farmer	05Ju02Fz	Tonny		40	M	Farmer	05Ju02Fz
DEVINE, Bridgt.		17	F	Farmer	05Ju02Fz	Anton		20	M	Farmer	05Ju02Fz
Margt.		20	F	Farmer	05Ju02Fz	Paloza		32	M	Farmer	05Ju02Fz
Mary		21	F	Farmer	05Ju02Fz	TOMPSON, Ann		25	F	Farmer	05Ju02Fz
CROLE, Pigy		20	F	Farmer	05Ju02Fz	Wm.	(S)	08	M	Child	05Ju02Fz
DONOVAN, Julia		24	F	Farmer	05Ju02Fz	Johnson	(S)	07	M	Child	05Ju02Fz
Johana		24	F	Farmer	05Ju02Fz						
STET, John		25	M	Farmer	05Ju02Fz						
CLAY, Josh.		25	M	Farmer	05Ju02Fz						
BALDON, John		30	M	Farmer	05Ju02Fz						
Johana	(W)	25	F	Wife	05Ju02Fz						
Edwd.	(S)	08	M	Child	05Ju02Fz						
Jas.	(S)	.00	M	Infant	05Ju02Fz	NEW-YORK-PACKET 06 JUNE 1846					
HATON, Jno.		24	M	Farmer	05Ju02Fz						
MURY, Jno.		22	M	Farmer	05Ju02Fz	From Halifax					
CONNELL, Richd.		22	M	Farmer	05Ju02Fz						
MAHONY, Jno.		20	M	Farmer	05Ju02Fz						
MURPHY, Nancy		20	F	Farmer	05Ju02Fz	JUGLIS, John		23	M	Gentleman	06Ju22An
SURET, Betsy		15	F	Farmer	05Ju02Fz	CONLY, Morris		40	M	Laborer	06Ju22An
MURY, Jno.		21	M	Farmer	05Ju02Fz	Mary	(W)	30	F	Wife	06Ju22An
MURPHY, Nora		20	F	Farmer	05Ju02Fz	Joanna	(D)	05	F	Child	06Ju22An
Jno.		22	M	Farmer	05Ju02Fz	John	(S)	03	M	Child	06Ju22An
Cathn.		21	F	Farmer	05Ju02Fz	Mary	(D)	01	F	Child	06Ju22An
SLEETER, Ellen		21	F	Farmer	05Ju02Fz						
DONOHUE, Julia		15	F	Farmer	05Ju02Fz						
CUNNIFF, Mary		25	F	Farmer	05Ju02Fz						
PLUNKETT, Michl.		20	M	Farmer	05Ju02Fz						
CHAMBERS, Mary		21	F	Farmer	05Ju02Fz						
Eliza		18	F	Farmer	05Ju02Fz						
BRADY, Edwd.		20	M	Farmer	05Ju02Fz						
BRATON, C.		20	U	Farmer	05Ju02Fz						
Cath.		16	F	Farmer	05Ju02Fz						
GLINN, Margt.		20	F	Farmer	05Ju02Fz						
HORNET, Edwd.		32	M	Farmer	05Ju02Fz						
Ellen	(D)	04	F	Child	05Ju02Fz						

NAMES OF PASSENGERS		A G E	S E X	OCCUPATIONS	DATE PORT SHIP	NAMES OF PASSENGERS		A G E	S E X	OCCUPATIONS	DATE PORT SHIP
						RAILEY, Mary		23	F	House Maid	09Ju02Ab
						MOWAN, Catherine		20	F	House Maid	09Ju02Ab
						JOHNSON, Peter		21	M	Laborer	09Ju02Ab
NIAGARA 09 JUNE 1846						ORAILLY, Charles		19	M	Laborer	09Ju02Ab
						MCGOVAN, Patrick		14	M	Laborer	09Ju02Ab
From Liverpool						LUNNAY, Ellen		20	F	Dressmaker	09Ju02Ab
						FARRALL, Mary		16	F	House Maid	09Ju02Ab
						RAILLY, Bridget		16	F	House Maid	09Ju02Ab
						COGARVIN, Patrick		29	M	Laborer	09Ju02Ab
						MADAGIN, William		20	M	Laborer	09Ju02Ab
COONEY, Patrick		25	M	Laborer	09Ju02Ab	COGLIN, Patrick		40	M	Carpenter	09Ju02Ab
REILY, Bridget		22	F	House Maid	09Ju02Ab	WELSH, Michael		23	M	Carpenter	09Ju02Ab
MCCABE, Ellen		16	F	House Maid	09Ju02Ab	CRATAN, William		46	M	Laborer	09Ju02Ab
NULTY, Letty		30	F	House Maid	09Ju02Ab	Lucy	(W)	30	F	Wife	09Ju02Ab
QUINN, Sarah		19	F	House Maid	09Ju02Ab	GIBLIN, Catherine		12	F	Domestic	09Ju02Ab
MCMANOMAN, Francis		21	M	Laborer	09Ju02Ab	REYNOLDS, Catherine		15	F	Domestic	09Ju02Ab
GORMIN, Daniel		19	M	Laborer	09Ju02Ab	MILLMORE, Mary		24	F	House Maid	09Ju02Ab
RORKE, Francis		25	M	Laborer	09Ju02Ab	GIBLIN, James		46	M	Laborer	09Ju02Ab
MCCRY, Eliza		16	F	House Maid	09Ju02Ab	Bridget	(W)	23	F	Wife	09Ju02Ab
MCGANNIS, Mary		16	F	House Maid	09Ju02Ab	KENEDY, Mary		20	F	House Maid	09Ju02Ab
MCPICK, Mary		18	F	House Maid	09Ju02Ab	PATTISON, Robert		20	M	Laborer	09Ju02Ab
MOORE, Barnard		23	M	Laborer	09Ju02Ab	Mary	(W)	20	F	Wife	09Ju02Ab
Ann	(W)	26	F	Wife	09Ju02Ab	HALPIN, Owen		25	M	Butcher	09Ju02Ab
HURSAN, John		18	M	Laborer	09Ju02Ab	ROGAN, Thomas		21	M	Farmer	09Ju02Ab
MCDUGIN, Cormick		22	M	Laborer	09Ju02Ab	BLAKE, James		28	M	Laborer	09Ju02Ab
RAILEY, Patrick		12	M	Laborer	09Ju02Ab	COONEY, Bridget		30	F	House Maid	09Ju02Ab
CORNHY, Bridget		30	F	Dressmaker	09Ju02Ab	SHAILE, Owan		35	M	Farmer	09Ju02Ab
MIGGIN, Michael		08	M	None	09Ju02Ab	William		52	M	Laborer	09Ju02Ab
KELLY, Bridget		18	F	Nurse	09Ju02Ab	Catherine		11	F	Domestic	09Ju02Ab
MONNIHIN, Ann		22	F	House Maid	09Ju02Ab	CARRIHIN, Bridget		10	F	House Maid	09Ju02Ab
DUNNIHOE, Ellen		20	F	House Maid	09Ju02Ab	JORDAN, Mary		22	F	House Maid	09Ju02Ab
FARRALL, Rosa		30	F	Domestic	09Ju02Ab	MCGURIL, Ann		15	F	House Maid	09Ju02Ab
MILLIGAN, Patrick		.10	M	Infant	09Ju02Ab	ARLY, Anthony		35	M	Farmer	09Ju02Ab
LAURICE, Mary		14	F	House Maid	09Ju02Ab	Mary	(W)	30	F	Wife	09Ju02Ab
DOWNLAN, Sally		20	F	House Maid	09Ju02Ab	Bridget	(D)	.06	F	Infant	09Ju02Ab
MULLOY, Thomas		30	M	Farmer	09Ju02Ab	NALLIN, Hannah		19	F	Domestic	09Ju02Ab
Margaret	(W)	24	F	Wife	09Ju02Ab	CRAUGHWAL, Owan		24	M	Farmer	09Ju02Ab
NATALY, William		19	M	Jockey	09Ju02Ab	CARROLL, Thos.		28	M	Farmer	09Ju02Ab
CONNERTY, Bridget		80	F	Mother	09Ju02Ab	LOFTUS, James		26	M	Farmer	09Ju02Ab
Mary	(D)	33	F	House Maid	09Ju02Ab	WILSH, Ann		28	F	House Maid	09Ju02Ab
Bridget	(D)	34	F	House Maid	09Ju02Ab	LOFTUS, Margaret		06	F	Child	09Ju02Ab
GALLIAGAN, Catherine		19	F	House Maid	09Ju02Ab	Ann		01	F	Infant	09Ju02Ab
GAFFANY, Ellen		18	F	House Maid	09Ju02Ab	MONIGHIN, Ann		26	F	House Maid	09Ju02Ab
NAILE, John		19	M	Laborer	09Ju02Ab	Sally		30	F	House Maid	09Ju02Ab
HALEY, James		23	M	Laborer	09Ju02Ab	Mary		06	F	Child	09Ju02Ab
FLINN, James		30	M	Laborer	09Ju02Ab	WILLS, Patrick		06	M	Child	09Ju02Ab
BOYLIN, Peggy		24	F	House Maid	09Ju02Ab	DOWNES, Tanand		35	M	Laborer	09Ju02Ab
MCCINNA, Mary		16	F	House Maid	09Ju02Ab	DAREY, Owen		22	M	Laborer	09Ju02Ab
COLLON, Ann		17	F	House Maid	09Ju02Ab	MCQUINEA, Margaret		20	F	House Maid	09Ju02Ab
WHITNEY, Mehll		13	M	Laborer	09Ju02Ab	MCGUINIA, Mary		18	F	House Maid	09Ju02Ab
LAWLIS, Mary		25	F	House Maid	09Ju02Ab	GIENOR, Catherine		28	F	House Maid	09Ju02Ab
LANCTIN, Peggy		25	F	House Maid	09Ju02Ab	FLANNAGAN, Margaret		20	F	House Maid	09Ju02Ab
FLYNN, Margaret		17	F	House Maid	09Ju02Ab	CAMPBELL, Owan		25	M	Laborer	09Ju02Ab
RAILY, Ann		50	F	Mother	09Ju02Ab	WHITNEY, James		27	M	Laborer	09Ju02Ab
Francis	(S)	20	M	Laborer	09Ju02Ab	MCKEON, Jane		24	F	House Maid	09Ju02Ab
Edward	(S)	17	M	Laborer	09Ju02Ab	LEDDY, Margaret		13	F	House Maid	09Ju02Ab
Betsy	(D)	12	F	Domestic	09Ju02Ab	Ellen		14	F	House Maid	09Ju02Ab
Peter	(S)	11	M	None	09Ju02Ab	COIL, Margaret		30	F	Wife	09Ju02Ab
BARNETT, Robt.		21	M	Laborer	09Ju02Ab	Andrew	(S)	03	M	Child	09Ju02Ab
MORIN, James		21	M	Laborer	09Ju02Ab	Grace	(D)	05	F	Child	09Ju02Ab
BALKIN, John		35	M	Laborer	09Ju02Ab	KORAN, Mary		22	F	Mother	09Ju02Ab
RAILEY, James		24	M	Laborer	09Ju02Ab	Samuel	(S)	03	M	Child	09Ju02Ab
CRATAN, Barnard		22	M	Laborer	09Ju02Ab	LEE, Thomas		29	M	Laborer	09Ju02Ab
Patrick		12	M	Laborer	09Ju02Ab	CULLIGAN, Patrick		15	M	Tailor	09Ju02Ab
Philip		10	M	Laborer	09Ju02Ab	MCQUIDE, Thomas		20	M	Laborer	09Ju02Ab
William		02	M	Laborer	09Ju02Ab	HANDERSON, Robert		19	M	Laborer	09Ju02Ab
GALLAGAN, Ann		16	F	House Maid	09Ju02Ab	MCDAVIT, Rosa		21	F	Led	09Ju02Ab
Margaret		17	F	House Maid	09Ju02Ab	Sarah		19	F	Nurse	09Ju02Ab
GALVIN, Mary		20	F	House Maid	09Ju02Ab	BADLY, Susan		19	F	House Maid	09Ju02Ab
CAMPBELL, Catherine		28	F	House Maid	09Ju02Ab	MCRATH, James		30	M	Butcher	09Ju02Ab
MCSHEANE, Bridget		23	F	House Maid	09Ju02Ab	GAUGHIN, Catherine		36	F	Wife	09Ju02Ab
Hugh		17	M	Laborer	09Ju02Ab	John	(S)	18	M	Laborer	09Ju02Ab
Arthur		14	M	Laborer	09Ju02Ab	James	(S)	14	M	Laborer	09Ju02Ab
TOBYNE, Patrick		40	M	Blwmkr	09Ju02Ab	Anthony	(S)	10	M	Laborer	09Ju02Ab
QUAGLEY, Ann		20	F	House Maid	09Ju02Ab	FLANAGAN, James		29	M	Shoemaker	09Ju02Ab

NAMES OF PASSENGERS	A G E	S E X	OCCUPATIONS	DATE PORT SHIP	NAMES OF PASSENGERS	A G E	S E X	OCCUPATIONS	DATE PORT SHIP
GIBLIN, John	19	M	Laborer	09Ju02Ab	MCDONALD, Judy	23	F	Wife	09Ju02Ab
YOUNG, Robert	25	M	Bleacher	09Ju02Ab					
MCCURDY, Alexander	18	M	Coachman	09Ju02Ab					
CARMODY, Dennis	20	M	Laborer	09Ju02Ab					
Theresa (W)	22	F	Wife	09Ju02Ab					
MCRATH, Alexander	18	M	Farmer	09Ju02Ab					
MORELAND, John	26	M	Laborer	09Ju02Ab	KESTREL 09 JUNE 1846				
MCFARLAND, John	18	M	Farmer	09Ju02Ab					
MCLANE, John	25	M	Unknown	09Ju02Ab	From Liverpool				
GARRATY, Alice	25	F	House Maid	09Ju02Ab					
Jane	21	F	House Maid	09Ju02Ab					
KNOX, John	25	M	Farmer	09Ju02Ab					
Sarah (W)	24	F	Wife	09Ju02Ab	WHEDLEY, Mary	21	F	Servant	09Ju02Cc
George (S)	02	M	Child	09Ju02Ab	BANNAN, Jane	22	F	Servant	09Ju02Cc
GLENN, Margaret	20	F	House Maid	09Ju02Ab	MCKANE, Patrick	24	M	Laborer	09Ju02Cc
DOGHERTY, George	22	M	Laborer	09Ju02Ab	REILLY, Bridget	21	F	Servant	09Ju02Cc
MCKEON, Thomas	27	M	Blacksmith	09Ju02Ab	DOYLE, Margaret	21	F	Servant	09Ju02Cc
Margaret	18	F	Domestic	09Ju02Ab	COX, Catherine	20	F	Servant	09Ju02Cc
BARRETT, James	23	M	Laborer	09Ju02Ab	MCQUILLAN, Bridget	21	F	Servant	09Ju02Cc
ROOK, Martin	21	M	Laborer	09Ju02Ab	EAGAN, Patrick	24	M	Laborer	09Ju02Cc
KELLY, James	20	M	Laborer	09Ju02Ab	Martin	24	M	Laborer	09Ju02Cc
MCDONALD, Randall	30	M	Laborer	09Ju02Ab	DARBY, John	23	M	Laborer	09Ju02Cc
MURPHY, Nancy	23	F	Wife	09Ju02Ab	DOLAN, Pat	24	M	Laborer	09Ju02Cc
HANIGHAN, Patrick	45	M	Laborer	09Ju02Ab	GARVIE, Ann	24	F	Seamstress	09Ju02Cc
Bridget	20	F	House Maid	09Ju02Ab	DOLAN, Mary	16	F	Seamstress	09Ju02Cc
LALLY, John	23	M	Laborer	09Ju02Ab	SAVAGE, Thos.	30	M	Laborer	09Ju02Cc
HANIGHAN, Anthony	19	M	Laborer	09Ju02Ab	GROVES, Neal	22	M	Laborer	09Ju02Cc
Mary	14	F	Domestic	09Ju02Ab	MCGRANE, Bessey	24	F	Servant	09Ju02Cc
Nancy	21	F	Domestic	09Ju02Ab	KELLY, Emily	17	F	Servant	09Ju02Cc
BARRATT, Dominic	25	M	Laborer	09Ju02Ab	HAISLAND, Sarah	25	F	Servant	09Ju02Cc
Thomas (S)	.08	M	Infant	09Ju02Ab	GIBBONS, Rebecca	19	F	Servant	09Ju02Cc
LOFTUS, Judy	21	F	Domestic	09Ju02Ab	HENNESSEY, John	24	M	Laborer	09Ju02Cc
Patrick	25	M	Laborer	09Ju02Ab	NOWLAN, Thos.	30	M	Laborer	09Ju02Cc
BARRATT, Henry	25	M	Farmer	09Ju02Ab	GOWAN, Thomas	22	M	Laborer	09Ju02Cc
PARDON, Thos.	20	M	Laborer	09Ju02Ab	DUNN, Michael	24	M	Laborer	09Ju02Cc
BARRATT, Nancy	33	F	Wife	09Ju02Ab	PRESTON, U-Mr.	22	M	Clerk	09Ju02Cc
CONNELL, James	35	M	Traveller	09Ju02Ab	U (W)	21	F	Wife	09Ju02Cc
PARDON, Michael	18	M	Farmer	09Ju02Ab	FLANAGAN, Pat.	23	M	Laborer	09Ju02Cc
SHIELDS, Henry	24	M	Farmer	09Ju02Ab	COMMISKEY, Betty	22	F	Servant	09Ju02Cc
PARDON, Ann	11	F	Child	09Ju02Ab	HANLEY, James	20	M	Laborer	09Ju02Cc
STEWART, William	22	M	Carpenter	09Ju02Ab	EVANS, Michael	39	M	Laborer	09Ju02Cc
MORIN, Margaret	50	F	Mother	09Ju02Ab	GEMMELL, James	40	M	Laborer	09Ju02Cc
LAUGHLAN, Mary	15	F	Domestic	09Ju02Ab	Martha (W)	35	F	Wife	09Ju02Cc
Margaret	14	F	Domestic	09Ju02Ab	Jane (D)	13	F	Child	09Ju02Cc
William	19	M	Clerk	09Ju02Ab	James (S)	10	M	Child	09Ju02Cc
John-James	20	M	Clerk	09Ju02Ab	John (S)	06	M	Child	09Ju02Cc
GRAYHAM, Archibald	21	M	Laborer	09Ju02Ab	Mary (D)	.10	F	Infant	09Ju02Cc
SINCLAIR, Henry	26	M	Laborer	09Ju02Ab	NOONAN, Patt.	27	M	Laborer	09Ju02Cc
Mary (W)	24	F	Wife	09Ju02Ab	FITZPATRICK, John	24	M	Laborer	09Ju02Cc
NARILLE, Bridget	20	F	House Maid	09Ju02Ab	DUFFY, Michl.	29	M	Laborer	09Ju02Cc
MCGURK, Mary	14	F	House Maid	09Ju02Ab	U (W)	28	F	Wife	09Ju02Cc
SKELLY, John	26	M	Laborer	09Ju02Ab	John (S)	07	M	Child	09Ju02Cc
DENNISH, Patrick	24	M	Laborer	09Ju02Ab	BURNS, Bridget	18	F	Servant	09Ju02Cc
MORIN, Daniel	23	M	Laborer	09Ju02Ab	CONNORS, Mary	17	F	Servant	09Ju02Cc
MCBRIDE, Mary	18	F	House Maid	09Ju02Ab	MCKENNA, Mary	30	F	Servant	09Ju02Cc
MCSWEGGIN, Margery	19	F	House Maid	09Ju02Ab	Sally (D)	10	F	Child	09Ju02Cc
MCANENEY, Mary	20	F	House Maid	09Ju02Ab	Robert (S)	06	M	Child	09Ju02Cc
GARNON, Dominick	28	M	Gdnr	09Ju02Ab	John (S)	02	M	Child	09Ju02Cc
Ann (W)	26	F	Wife	09Ju02Ab	John	26	M	Laborer	09Ju02Cc
MCALLAAR, John	19	M	Clerk	09Ju02Ab	U (W)	25	F	Wife	09Ju02Cc
MCCULLOCK, Patrick	16	M	Tailor	09Ju02Ab	KEENAN, Thomas	24	M	Farmer	09Ju02Cc
WHITNEY, Onar	20	F	House Maid	09Ju02Ab	GRIBBON, John	22	M	Farmer	09Ju02Cc
KELLY, Bridget	20	F	House Maid	09Ju02Ab	MCGARRY, Michl.	24	M	Farmer	09Ju02Cc
HANEY, Margaret	16	F	House Maid	09Ju02Ab	CLARK, Martin	20	M	Farmer	09Ju02Cc
ROGERS, Rosa	20	F	House Maid	09Ju02Ab	KELLY, Bryan	21	M	Farmer	09Ju02Cc
CARR, Bridget	19	F	House Maid	09Ju02Ab	Pat	22	M	Farmer	09Ju02Cc
WHITNEY, John	22	M	Teacher	09Ju02Ab	BUCHANAN, Norman	34	M	Farmer	09Ju02Cc
Catherine (M)	40	F	Mother	09Ju02Ab	U (W)	30	F	Wife	09Ju02Cc
Miles (B)	13	M	Child	09Ju02Ab	Robert (S)	12	M	Child	09Ju02Cc
ROGERS, Thomas	20	M	Nail Maker	09Ju02Ab	Margaret (D)	10	F	Child	09Ju02Cc
GOULDRICK, Michael	50	M	Laborer	09Ju02Ab	John (S)	06	M	Child	09Ju02Cc
Died-At-Sea					Norman (S)	04	M	Child	09Ju02Cc
PARDAN, Michael	18	M	Laborer	09Ju02Ab	Mary (D)	01	F	Child	09Ju02Cc
GALLAGAN, Catherine	20	F	House Maid	09Ju02Ab	LYONS, Dennis	25	M	Laborer	09Ju02Cc
BLAKE, Catherine	30	F	House Maid	09Ju02Ab	DWYER, John	24	M	Laborer	09Ju02Cc

NAMES OF PASSENGERS		AGE	SEX	OCCUPATIONS	DATE PORT SHIP	NAMES OF PASSENGERS		AGE	SEX	OCCUPATIONS	DATE PORT SHIP
EAGAN, Francis		20	M	Laborer	09Ju02Cc	GLADDEN, Fred	(S)	01	M	Child	09Ju02Cc
MACKAY, James		20	M	Laborer	09Ju02Cc	MALLOY, George		28	M	Laborer	09Ju02Cc
Ellen		16	F	None	09Ju02Cc	U	(W)	27	F	None	09Ju02Cc
MCKENNA, John		30	M	None	09Ju02Cc	Jane	(D)	08	F	Child	09Ju02Cc
John		11	M	Child	09Ju02Cc	Robert	(S)	04	M	Child	09Ju02Cc
Ann		20	F	None	09Ju02Cc	REDFORD, William		28	M	Laborer	09Ju02Cc
Mary		21	F	None	09Ju02Cc	U	(W)	26	F	Wife	09Ju02Cc
DUNNE, Arthur		21	M	Laborer	09Ju02Cc	Ruth-Ann	(D)	01	F	Child	09Ju02Cc
DOGHERTY, Catherine		22	F	Unknown	09Ju02Cc	MCKAY, John		20	M	Laborer	09Ju02Cc
HAMILTON, Ann		30	F	Unknown	09Ju02Cc	SMITH, Phillip		21	M	Laborer	09Ju02Cc
George	(H)	30	M	Laborer	09Ju02Cc	CREASE, Bridget		20	F	None	09Ju02Cc
Jane	(D)	10	F	Child	09Ju02Cc	JAMISON, Thomas		23	M	Laborer	09Ju02Cc
James	(S)	04	M	Child	09Ju02Cc	Sarah	(W)	20	F	None	09Ju02Cc
John	(S)	02	M	Child	09Ju02Cc	John	(S)	01	M	Child	09Ju02Cc
Eliza	(D)	01	F	Child	09Ju02Cc	MCGROLTY, Hugh		23	M	Laborer	09Ju02Cc
MAHON, Patt.		28	M	Laborer	09Ju02Cc	Ann	(W)	22	F	None	09Ju02Cc
U	(W)	28	F	Wife	09Ju02Cc	MULVANEY, Jane		20	F	None	09Ju02Cc
Sally	(D)	06	F	Child	09Ju02Cc	SAWYER, George		10	M	Child	09Ju02Cc
Thimothy	(S)	04	M	Child	09Ju02Cc	Jane	(T)	08	F	Child	09Ju02Cc
NEAL, Alice		18	F	None	09Ju02Cc	GAVEN, Catherine		25	F	None	09Ju02Cc
SMITH, Ann		18	F	None	09Ju02Cc	EVANS, Mary		24	F	None	09Ju02Cc
ROBINSON, Joseph		32	M	Laborer	09Ju02Cc	DEACON, Michael		27	M	Laborer	09Ju02Cc
CRONE, Charles		42	M	Laborer	09Ju02Cc	Jane		25	F	None	09Ju02Cc
BYRNE, William		21	M	Laborer	09Ju02Cc	WALSH, Patt		20	M	Laborer	09Ju02Cc
SHEHAN, Daniel		30	M	Laborer	09Ju02Cc	Jane		48	F	None	09Ju02Cc
MATHEWS, John		26	M	Laborer	09Ju02Cc	Eliza		48	F	None	09Ju02Cc
Mary		24	F	Unknown	09Ju02Cc	William		38	M	Laborer	09Ju02Cc
COUGHAN, Patt.		40	M	Laborer	09Ju02Cc	Joseph		12	M	Laborer	09Ju02Cc
MCNULTY, Terence		32	M	Laborer	09Ju02Cc	Ann		10	F	Child	09Ju02Cc
U	(W)	30	F	Wife	09Ju02Cc	CAMPBELL, Hugh		08	M	Child	09Ju02Cc
John	(S)	10	M	Child	09Ju02Cc	ONEILL, Jas.		03	M	Child	09Ju02Cc
Patt	(S)	06	M	Child	09Ju02Cc	MCQUADE, Ellen		10	F	Child	09Ju02Cc
Thimothy	(S)	04	M	Child	09Ju02Cc	Edward		07	M	Child	09Ju02Cc
Sally	(D)	02	F	Child	09Ju02Cc	MCNEAL, Margaret		24	F	None	09Ju02Cc
JONES, John		34	M	Laborer	09Ju02Cc	Catherine		08	F	Child	09Ju02Cc
Mary	(W)	30	F	Servant	09Ju02Cc	DONNELLY, Bridget		24	F	None	09Ju02Cc
Jane	(D)	08	F	Child	09Ju02Cc	MCNEIL, Daniel		07	M	Child	09Ju02Cc
William	(S)	06	M	Child	09Ju02Cc	DONNELLY, Ann		25	M	Laborer	09Ju02Cc
George	(S)	03	M	Child	09Ju02Cc	HART, Ellen		25	F	Servant	09Ju02Cc
KENNY, James		22	M	Servant	09Ju02Cc	HUGHES, James		30	M	Servant	09Ju02Cc
Ann		20	F	Servant	09Ju02Cc	CULLEN, Henry		34	M	Servant	09Ju02Cc
DALTON, James		21	M	Servant	09Ju02Cc	JOHNSON, Edward		26	M	Servant	09Ju02Cc
Bess		20	F	Servant	09Ju02Cc	BYRNE, Ann		30	F	Servant	09Ju02Cc
Cathr.		19	F	Servant	09Ju02Cc	CULLEN, Cath.		27	F	Servant	09Ju02Cc
KELLEY, Michael		21	M	Servant	09Ju02Cc	HUTCHINSON, John		28	M	Servant	09Ju02Cc
HUGHS, Eliza		18	F	Servant	09Ju02Cc	GALE, Ann		20	F	Servant	09Ju02Cc
NOWLAN, Eliza		30	F	Servant	09Ju02Cc	CARROLL, Peter		21	M	Servant	09Ju02Cc
SCALLY, Pat		28	M	Servant	09Ju02Cc	Bryan		30	M	Servant	09Ju02Cc
CROKER, Patt		27	M	Servant	09Ju02Cc	Rose		25	F	Servant	09Ju02Cc
U	(W)	27	F	Servant	09Ju02Cc	WALSH, John		60	M	Servant	09Ju02Cc
Bridget	(D)	07	F	Child	09Ju02Cc	Mary	(W)	55	F	Servant	09Ju02Cc
John	(S)	01	M	Child	09Ju02Cc	Thimothy	(S)	20	M	Servant	09Ju02Cc
SAWYER, James		40	M	Servant	09Ju02Cc	Biddy	(D)	24	F	Servant	09Ju02Cc
U	(W)	38	F	Servant	09Ju02Cc	Michael	(S)	20	M	Servant	09Ju02Cc
Henry	(S)	13	M	Child	09Ju02Cc	John	(S)	18	M	Servant	09Ju02Cc
Joseph	(S)	10	M	Child	09Ju02Cc	TREANOR, Arthur		24	M	Servant	09Ju02Cc
Mary	(D)	01	F	Child	09Ju02Cc	MYLES, John		24	M	Servant	09Ju02Cc
WALKER, William		20	M	Servant	09Ju02Cc	DONNELLY, Mary		19	F	Servant	09Ju02Cc
LANCASTER, Thomas		25	M	Servant	09Ju02Cc	MCGRATH, Cath.		20	F	Servant	09Ju02Cc
BARNWELL, Henry		22	M	Laborer	09Ju02Cc	GILLISPIE, Frans.		24	M	Servant	09Ju02Cc
CLARK, James		24	M	Laborer	09Ju02Cc	WALSH, John		18	M	Servant	09Ju02Cc
CASSERLY, Thomas		26	M	Laborer	09Ju02Cc	SWEENEY, Wm.J.		20	M	Servant	09Ju02Cc
SHORT, Nicholas		33	M	Laborer	09Ju02Cc	HARDOVAN, Jas.		26	M	Servant	09Ju02Cc
RACZEY, Henry		32	M	Laborer	09Ju02Cc	DEACON, Michael		26	M	Servant	09Ju02Cc
Sarah	(W)	30	F	Wife	09Ju02Cc	MCGARN, Mary		26	F	Servant	09Ju02Cc
Robert	(S)	13	M	Child	09Ju02Cc	DAILEY, John		29	M	Servant	09Ju02Cc
Henry	(S)	12	M	Laborer	09Ju02Cc	Ann		27	F	Servant	09Ju02Cc
Eliza	(D)	08	F	Child	09Ju02Cc	Barnard		26	M	Servant	09Ju02Cc
Andrew	(S)	06	M	Child	09Ju02Cc	FANNING, Jas.		30	M	Servant	09Ju02Cc
FRANKLIN, William		25	M	Laborer	09Ju02Cc	BRADLEY, Robert		20	M	Servant	09Ju02Cc
U	(W)	20	F	Wife	09Ju02Cc	MCCLURE, Jas.		20	M	Servant	09Ju02Cc
Jessy	(M)	45	F	None	09Ju02Cc	Joseph		18	M	Servant	09Ju02Cc
LYNCH, Bridget		20	F	None	09Ju02Cc	KEARNEY, Thomas		19	M	Servant	09Ju02Cc
GLADDEN, George		22	M	Laborer	09Ju02Cc	HUGHES, Rose		36	F	Servant	09Ju02Cc
U	(W)	21	F	Wife	09Ju02Cc	KING, Margaret		18	F	Servant	09Ju02Cc

NAMES OF PASSENGERS	AGE	SEX	OCCUPATIONS	DATE PORT SHIP
LYNNE, Jane	19	F	Servant	09Ju02Cc
MCBIRDE, Patt.	22	M	Servant	09Ju02Cc
MONAGHAN, Patt.	18	M	Servant	09Ju02Cc
Terence	21	M	Servant	09Ju02Cc
SLAVIN, Bridget	20	F	Servant	09Ju02Cc
MULLIN, Edward	35	M	Servant	09Ju02Cc
U (W)	32	F	Servant	09Ju02Cc
Mary (D)	12	F	Child	09Ju02Cc
Kitty (D)	10	F	Child	09Ju02Cc
Jane (D)	08	F	Child	09Ju02Cc
Rose-Ann (D)	04	F	Child	09Ju02Cc
Patt. (S)	01	M	Child	09Ju02Cc
MCGOVERN, Michael	25	M	Servant	09Ju02Cc
Bridget (W)	24	F	Servant	09Ju02Cc
Martin (S)	06	M	Child	09Ju02Cc
CANLIN, Bridget	24	F	Servant	09Ju02Cc
DOGGET, Margaret	26	F	Laborer	09Ju02Cc
GALLAGHER, James	21	M	Laborer	09Ju02Cc
LOURAND, James	26	M	Laborer	09Ju02Cc
REILLEY, Margaret	20	F	Laborer	09Ju02Cc
CONLEY, Bridget	18	F	Laborer	09Ju02Cc
MCGAHAN, Ann	23	F	Laborer	09Ju02Cc
MURRAY, Patt.	24	M	Laborer	09Ju02Cc
KELLY, Bridget	26	F	Laborer	09Ju02Cc
CALIHAIN, Margt.	24	F	Laborer	09Ju02Cc
Eleanor	20	F	Laborer	09Ju02Cc
ONEIL, John	30	M	Laborer	09Ju02Cc
BRADLEY, John	23	M	Laborer	09Ju02Cc
MCCALLOWAY, Terence	18	M	Laborer	09Ju02Cc
HUGHES, James	30	M	Laborer	09Ju02Cc
MCLURGGAN, John	27	M	Laborer	09Ju02Cc
CLEARY, Thos.	23	M	Laborer	09Ju02Cc
Mary	26	F	Laborer	09Ju02Cc
STAPPLETON, Bridget	20	F	Laborer	09Ju02Cc
CLEARY, Margt.	40	F	Laborer	09Ju02Cc
MCBRIAN, Thomas	20	M	Laborer	09Ju02Cc
REILLY, Mary	28	F	Laborer	09Ju02Cc
MCKANE, Cathr.	22	F	Laborer	09Ju02Cc
BRADY, Bridget	21	F	Laborer	09Ju02Cc
MANGAN, Jas.	30	M	Laborer	09Ju02Cc
SHERIDAN, Rosey	23	F	Laborer	09Ju02Cc
MCLOUGHLIN, John	20	M	Laborer	09Ju02Cc
CORLICK, Biddy	17	F	Laborer	09Ju02Cc
SULLIVAN, Jas.	20	M	Laborer	09Ju02Cc
PATTERSON, Jas.	20	M	Laborer	09Ju02Cc
MAGUNNESS, Ann	20	F	Laborer	09Ju02Cc
Mary	09	F	Child	09Ju02Cc
FISHER, Cath.	20	F	Laborer	09Ju02Cc
DOWNEY, Andrew	60	M	Laborer	09Ju02Cc
GILLTRAP, Mary-A.	20	F	Laborer	09Ju02Cc
GARDNER, Bridget	17	F	Laborer	09Ju02Cc
HANDLAN, Mary	22	F	Laborer	09Ju02Cc
MCMANUS, Bridgt.	20	F	Laborer	09Ju02Cc
MCHUGHES, Cathn.	19	F	Laborer	09Ju02Cc
MULLIGAN, U	60	F	WI	09Ju02Cc
Phillip (S)	23	M	Laborer	09Ju02Cc
Biddy (D)	20	F	Laborer	09Ju02Cc
WEILLY, Margret	16	F	Laborer	09Ju02Cc
BRADY, Thomas	13	M	Laborer	09Ju02Cc
Margret	10	F	Laborer	09Ju02Cc
CADDEN, Ross	18	F	Laborer	09Ju02Cc
REILLY, Ann	21	F	Laborer	09Ju02Cc
Rose	12	F	Laborer	09Ju02Cc
BARNS, Betty	26	F	Laborer	09Ju02Cc
Mary-Ann	05	F	Child	09Ju02Cc
BURROW, John	78	M	Laborer	09Ju02Cc
John	14	M	Laborer	09Ju02Cc
Sarah	30	F	Laborer	09Ju02Cc
GIBBONS, William	22	M	Laborer	09Ju02Cc
REILLY, Daniel	24	M	Laborer	09Ju02Cc
BONER, Michael	19	M	Laborer	09Ju02Cc
DUFFEY, Thomas	23	M	Laborer	09Ju02Cc
Michael	21	M	Laborer	09Ju02Cc
Mary	17	F	Laborer	09Ju02Cc
Bridget	11	F	Child	09Ju02Cc
DUFFEY, Ellen	09	F	Child	09Ju02Cc
Mary	07	F	Child	09Ju02Cc
Peggy	08	F	Child	09Ju02Cc
KENNEDY, Mary	22	F	Laborer	09Ju02Cc
FITZPATRICK, Rose	20	F	Laborer	09Ju02Cc
Eliza	19	F	Laborer	09Ju02Cc
SHIELDS, Eliza	20	F	Laborer	09Ju02Cc
SAUL, E	00	M	Laborer	09Ju02Cc
U (W)	00	F	Unknown	09Ju02Cc
Edward (S)	10	M	Child	09Ju02Cc
Emily (D)	02	F	Child	09Ju02Cc
George (S)	.09	M	Infant	09Ju02Cc

CHARLES-HUMBERTON 13 JUNE 1846

From Liverpool

NAMES OF PASSENGERS	AGE	SEX	OCCUPATIONS	DATE PORT SHIP
HINNEY, Thos.	20	M	Farmer	13Ju02Ch
EGAN, Cath.	20	F	Unknown	13Ju02Ch
REILLY, Brian	30	M	Farmer	13Ju02Ch
MORAN, Cath.	08	F	Child	13Ju02Ch
HAMILTON, Jno.	30	M	Farmer	13Ju02Ch
KEATING, Robt.	27	M	Farmer	13Ju02Ch
CLIFFORD, Pat	20	M	Farmer	13Ju02Ch
Jno.	20	M	Farmer	13Ju02Ch
ATTISON, Jas.	20	M	Farmer	13Ju02Ch
HINDY, Edwd.	20	M	Farmer	13Ju02Ch
KUNHAN, Mic.	21	M	Farmer	13Ju02Ch
Rosey	17	F	Unknown	13Ju02Ch
DENON, Rosey	13	F	Unknown	13Ju02Ch
Mary	20	F	Unknown	13Ju02Ch
COWRY, Mic.	18	M	Farmer	13Ju02Ch
H----OSY, Nancy	12	F	Unknown	13Ju02Ch
DONLY, Ant.	12	M	Farmer	13Ju02Ch
MULLIN, Mic.	21	M	Farmer	13Ju02Ch
PALE, Wm.	19	M	Farmer	13Ju02Ch
Ann	13	F	Unknown	13Ju02Ch
MURPHY, Jas.	26	M	Farmer	13Ju02Ch
Mary	28	F	Unknown	13Ju02Ch
CONGAN, Wm.	20	M	Farmer	13Ju02Ch
MILLIGAN, David	30	M	Farmer	13Ju02Ch
Pat	20	M	Farmer	13Ju02Ch
Brid.	20	F	Farmer	13Ju02Ch
CALLIGAN, Mic.	20	M	Farmer	13Ju02Ch
SHEAN, Dennis	20	M	Farmer	13Ju02Ch
Ellen	22	F	Unknown	13Ju02Ch
MORTON, Alice	20	F	Unknown	13Ju02Ch
MALTON, Frank	20	M	Farmer	13Ju02Ch
MORTON, Grace	20	F	Unknown	13Ju02Ch
Ellen	20	F	Unknown	13Ju02Ch
Thos.	11	M	Child	13Ju02Ch
LINCH, Jno.	60	M	Farmer	13Ju02Ch
Eliz.	40	F	Unknown	13Ju02Ch
LYNCH, Michl.	60	M	Farmer	13Ju02Ch
Mary (W)	40	F	Unknown	13Ju02Ch
Richd. (S)	17	M	Farmer	13Ju02Ch
Barth. (S)	13	M	Farmer	13Ju02Ch
Cath. (D)	11	F	Child	13Ju02Ch
Jno. (S)	09	M	Child	13Ju02Ch
Wm. (S)	05	M	Child	13Ju02Ch
Pk. (S)	07	M	Child	13Ju02Ch
WHITE, Terrence	20	M	Farmer	13Ju02Ch
HART, Jno.	21	M	Farmer	13Ju02Ch
JUDGE, Mic.	22	M	Farmer	13Ju02Ch
MCDONNELL, Pk.	23	M	Farmer	13Ju02Ch
DERNON, Eliza	20	F	Unknown	13Ju02Ch
Wm.	20	M	Farmer	13Ju02Ch
TRACY, Law.	20	M	Farmer	13Ju02Ch
GREEN, Danl.	20	M	Farmer	13Ju02Ch

NAMES OF PASSENGERS		AGE	SEX	OCCUPATIONS	DATE PORT SHIP
FOX, Jas.		22	M	Farmer	13Ju02Ch
DOON, Wm.		17	M	Farmer	13Ju02Ch
COLLINS, Chris		16	M	Farmer	13Ju02Ch
DORN, Corn.		23	M	Farmer	13Ju02Ch
SHEA, Jas.		60	M	Farmer	13Ju02Ch
Pat		50	M	Farmer	13Ju02Ch
Danl.		20	M	Farmer	13Ju02Ch
Mic.		20	M	Farmer	13Ju02Ch
Jno.		11	M	Farmer	13Ju02Ch
Biddy		13	F	Unknown	13Ju02Ch
Ally		09	F	Child	13Ju02Ch
Martin		26	M	Farmer	13Ju02Ch
OSBORNE, Mary		23	F	Unknown	13Ju02Ch
TIRRELL, Pierce		30	M	Farmer	13Ju02Ch
U	(W)	30	F	Unknown	13Ju02Ch
Jno.	(S)	07	M	Child	13Ju02Ch
Cath.	(D)	05	F	Child	13Ju02Ch
Pat.	(S)	.00	M	Infant	13Ju02Ch
TYNALD, Jno.		20	M	Farmer	13Ju02Ch
FLEMMING, Mary		20	F	Unknown	13Ju02Ch
MOHN, Edwd.		24	M	Farmer	13Ju02Ch
SHEA, Mary		30	F	Unknown	13Ju02Ch
LUCAS, Thos.		20	M	Farmer	13Ju02Ch
CALLANAN, Hy		30	M	Farmer	13Ju02Ch
RYAN, Jno.		30	M	Farmer	13Ju02Ch
COLLINS, Brid.		45	F	Unknown	13Ju02Ch
SWEENY, Danl.		30	M	Farmer	13Ju02Ch
Julia		25	F	Unknown	13Ju02Ch
NOLAN, Edwd.		20	M	Farmer	13Ju02Ch
WALSH, Richd.		27	M	Farmer	13Ju02Ch
FORREST, Isaac		20	M	Farmer	13Ju02Ch
LAWLESS, Nich.		13	M	Farmer	13Ju02Ch
MILLICAMP, Jno.		40	M	Farmer	13Ju02Ch
BYRNE, Judith		22	F	Unknown	13Ju02Ch
DIGGIN, Jno.		25	M	Farmer	13Ju02Ch
Thos.		20	M	Farmer	13Ju02Ch
Ann		60	F	Unknown	13Ju02Ch
Peggy		26	F	Unknown	13Ju02Ch
CAVANNAH, Chas.		20	M	Farmer	13Ju02Ch
Geo.		18	M	Farmer	13Ju02Ch
SOLODY, Jane		20	F	Unknown	13Ju02Ch
TUMEGAN, Cath.		18	F	Unknown	13Ju02Ch
HANNAGAN, Ann		20	F	Unknown	13Ju02Ch
NULTY, Brid.		22	F	Unknown	13Ju02Ch
BRANNAN, Rose		22	F	Unknown	13Ju02Ch
DIGNAN, Cath.		.00	F	Infant	13Ju02Ch
FLANNAGAN, Pk.		50	M	Farmer	13Ju02Ch
U	(W)	40	F	Unknown	13Ju02Ch
Wm.	(S)	22	M	Farmer	13Ju02Ch
Martin	(S)	15	M	Farmer	13Ju02Ch
Jno.	(S)	13	M	Farmer	13Ju02Ch
Ann	(D)	11	F	Unknown	13Ju02Ch
Brid.	(D)	09	F	Child	13Ju02Ch
MYERS, Margt.		20	F	Unknown	13Ju02Ch
GLEASON, Nancy		20	F	Unknown	13Ju02Ch
TAYLOR, Jos.		27	M	Farmer	13Ju02Ch
BURKE, Mick		31	M	Farmer	13Ju02Ch
Rose		27	F	Unknown	13Ju02Ch
DAVIS, Robt.		45	M	Farmer	13Ju02Ch
Eliza	(W)	50	F	Unknown	13Ju02Ch
Robt.	(S)	24	M	Farmer	13Ju02Ch
Benj.	(S)	22	M	Farmer	13Ju02Ch
Edwd.	(S)	17	M	Farmer	13Ju02Ch
Eliza		16	F	Unknown	13Ju02Ch
SHERIDAN, Eliza		18	F	Unknown	13Ju02Ch
CATING, Mic.		29	M	Farmer	13Ju02Ch
Ellen	(W)	29	F	Unknown	13Ju02Ch
MEHAN, And.		50	M	Farmer	13Ju02Ch
Ann	(W)	50	F	Unknown	13Ju02Ch
Ann	(D)	12	F	Unknown	13Ju02Ch
Andrew	(S)	12	M	Unknown	13Ju02Ch
CARLAN, Ann		30	F	Unknown	13Ju02Ch
DUNN, Birn		30	M	Farmer	13Ju02Ch
CARROLL, Thos.		40	M	Farmer	13Ju02Ch
U.	(W)	35	F	Unknown	13Ju02Ch
CARROLL, Jno.	(S)	08	M	Child	13Ju02Ch
Mary	(D)	10	F	Child	13Ju02Ch
KUGAN, Jno.		26	M	Farmer	13Ju02Ch
Mic.		30	M	Farmer	13Ju02Ch
Brid.		20	F	Unknown	13Ju02Ch
DALTON, Jno.		30	M	Farmer	13Ju02Ch
LUTLIFF, Jno.		24	M	Farmer	13Ju02Ch
CRAWFORD, Jno.		24	M	Farmer	13Ju02Ch
BURNS, Chas.		25	M	Farmer	13Ju02Ch
DOYLE, Ford		20	M	Farmer	13Ju02Ch
BRADLEY, Cath.		23	F	Unknown	13Ju02Ch
Eliza.		25	F	Unknown	13Ju02Ch
SMITH, Thos.		20	M	Farmer	13Ju02Ch
CONOVON, Brid.		20	F	Unknown	13Ju02Ch
Edwd.		20	M	Farmer	13Ju02Ch
Cath.		10	F	Child	13Ju02Ch
CALLAHAN, Mic.		30	M	Farmer	13Ju02Ch
Rose		20	F	Unknown	13Ju02Ch
MCCABE, Mary		26	F	Unknown	13Ju02Ch
ROBINSON, Fred		30	M	Farmer	13Ju02Ch
BROPHY, Danl.		27	M	Farmer	13Ju02Ch
PROISU, John		26	M	Farmer	13Ju02Ch
WELSH, Pk.		24	M	Farmer	13Ju02Ch
FOX, Ellen		30	F	Unknown	13Ju02Ch
STILL, Wm.		22	M	Farmer	13Ju02Ch
MAHONY, Jno.		19	M	Farmer	13Ju02Ch
BYRNE, Jas.		20	M	Farmer	13Ju02Ch
PAINE, Wm.		20	M	Farmer	13Ju02Ch
U		21	F	Unknown	13Ju02Ch
KEATING, Wm.		27	M	Farmer	13Ju02Ch
HIRAN, Pk.		33	M	Farmer	13Ju02Ch
Brid.	(W)	30	F	Unknown	13Ju02Ch
Ellen	(D)	08	F	Child	13Ju02Ch
CORGAN, Wm.		18	M	Farmer	13Ju02Ch
Thos.		20	M	Farmer	13Ju02Ch
Ann		20	F	Unknown	13Ju02Ch
Mary		18	F	Unknown	13Ju02Ch
KELLY, Mary		18	F	Unknown	13Ju02Ch
DEMPSEY, Brid.		18	F	Unknown	13Ju02Ch
BYRNE, Thos.		27	M	Farmer	13Ju02Ch
TURNER, Frank		50	M	Farmer	13Ju02Ch
Wm.	(S)	25	M	Farmer	13Ju02Ch
Eliza.	(D)	18	F	Unknown	13Ju02Ch
Ellen	(D)	12	F	Unknown	13Ju02Ch
Frank	(S)	10	M	Child	13Ju02Ch
Eliza	(D)	20	F	Unknown	13Ju02Ch
BOYNE, Saml.		35	M	Farmer	13Ju02Ch
ELLIS, Wm.		29	M	Farmer	13Ju02Ch
OWEN, Richd.		20	M	Farmer	13Ju02Ch
Jane		18	F	Unknown	13Ju02Ch
FITZGERALD, Richd.		20	M	Farmer	13Ju02Ch
U	(W)	20	F	Unknown	13Ju02Ch
HORGAN, Mary		20	F	Unknown	13Ju02Ch
ODONNELL, Judith		20	F	Unknown	13Ju02Ch
OBRIEN, Pat.		30	M	Farmer	13Ju02Ch
BAGOT, Malaca		30	M	Farmer	13Ju02Ch
BRIGGS, Wm.		30	M	Farmer	13Ju02Ch
Mary	(W)	30	F	Unknown	13Ju02Ch
Mary		20	F	Unknown	13Ju02Ch
Wm.		.00	M	Infant	13Ju02Ch
James		02	M	Child	13Ju02Ch
Sarah		.00	F	Infant	13Ju02Ch
LOUGHTON, Margaret		13	F	Unknown	13Ju02Ch
TURNAN, Dennis		27	M	Farmer	13Ju02Ch
GLEASON, Brid.		20	F	Unknown	13Ju02Ch
HERN, Wm.		30	M	Farmer	13Ju02Ch
U	(W)	30	F	Unknown	13Ju02Ch
Isab.		21	F	Unknown	13Ju02Ch
Don.		26	M	Farmer	13Ju02Ch
WATSON, Ann		13	F	Unknown	13Ju02Ch
OWEN, Hugh		21	M	Farmer	13Ju02Ch
MONAGHAN, Jno.		21	M	Farmer	13Ju02Ch
Pk.		21	M	Farmer	13Ju02Ch
MCGINNIS, Mary		18	F	Unknown	13Ju02Ch
Mary		12	F	Unknown	13Ju02Ch

NAMES OF PASSENGERS		A G E	S E X	OCCUPATIONS	DATE PORT SHIP
CONLON, Owen		20	M	Farmer	13Ju02Ch
DORINGDALE, Nancy		30	F	Unknown	13Ju02Ch
GLENNING, Wm.		24	M	Farmer	13Ju02Ch
Jno.		24	M	Farmer	13Ju02Ch
MALLIN, Nathl.		28	M	Farmer	13Ju02Ch
Brid.		13	F	Unknown	13Ju02Ch
Ann		13	F	Unknown	13Ju02Ch
SPEARMAN, Margt.		18	F	Unknown	13Ju02Ch
CURRY, Rose		19	F	Unknown	13Ju02Ch
GALLAGHER, Ann		19	F	Unknown	13Ju02Ch
CANNELL, Rob.		20	M	Farmer	13Ju02Ch
SCOTT, Pk.		20	M	Farmer	13Ju02Ch
HAMMOND, Biddy		13	F	Unknown	13Ju02Ch
LINSEY, Thos.		20	M	Farmer	13Ju02Ch
COLLINS, Pk.		20	M	Farmer	13Ju02Ch
SHIELDS, Pk.		20	M	Farmer	13Ju02Ch
GROGAN, Jno.		30	M	Farmer	13Ju02Ch
U-Mrs.		20	F	Wife	13Ju02Ch
Emma		12	F	Unknown	13Ju02Ch
Mary		06	F	Child	13Ju02Ch
Robt.		.00	M	Infant	13Ju02Ch
MURPHY, Jas.		40	M	Farmer	13Ju02Ch
Emma	(W)	36	F	Unknown	13Ju02Ch
Julia	(D)	04	F	Child	13Ju02Ch
Mary-Ann	(D)	.00	F	Infant	13Ju02Ch
BOYDE, Jno.		40	M	Farmer	13Ju02Ch
DEALE, Mary		22	F	Unknown	13Ju02Ch
Jno.	(S)	06	M	Child	13Ju02Ch
Mary	(D)	04	F	Child	13Ju02Ch
Thos.	(S)	02	M	Child	13Ju02Ch
MURPHY, Martin		20	M	Farmer	13Ju02Ch
Petro		16	M	Farmer	13Ju02Ch
Ellen		12	F	Unknown	13Ju02Ch
James		07	M	Child	13Ju02Ch
LYNN, James		40	M	Farmer	13Ju02Ch
Mary		29	F	Unknown	13Ju02Ch

LADY-SALE 15 JUNE 1846

From Liverpool

NAMES OF PASSENGERS		A G E	S E X	OCCUPATIONS	DATE PORT SHIP
MCDONALD, Noah		22	M	Laborer	15Ju02CI
U	(W)	20	F	Laborer	15Ju02CI
MOOR, John		22	M	Laborer	15Ju02CI
WILSON, Robert		25	M	Laborer	15Ju02CI
MCGEE, Sally		45	F	Laborer	15Ju02CI
ROSS, Mary		47	F	Laborer	15Ju02CI
LYNN, Henry		20	M	Laborer	15Ju02CI
COCKLIN, Danl.		19	M	Laborer	15Ju02CI
CALLAN, Owen		23	M	Laborer	15Ju02CI
U	(W)	22	F	Laborer	15Ju02CI
BOYLE, Mary		22	F	Laborer	15Ju02CI
MCPEAKE, U-Mrs.		22	F	Laborer	15Ju02CI
FISK, Thomas		30	M	Farmer	15Ju02CI
Mary	(W)	30	F	Unknown	15Ju02CI
George	(S)	.00	M	Infant	15Ju02CI
HEVERIN, Wm.		21	M	Farmer	15Ju02CI
FITZGERALD, James		21	M	Farmer	15Ju02CI
HANNON, John		20	M	Farmer	15Ju02CI
LENNAN, Wm.		30	M	Farmer	15Ju02CI
Honora		26	F	Unknown	15Ju02CI
SHEA, Margt.		25	F	Unknown	15Ju02CI
Mary		20	F	Unknown	15Ju02CI
CARTY, Cath.		40	F	Unknown	15Ju02CI
Wm.	(S)	10	M	Child	15Ju02CI
Martin	(S)	06	M	Child	15Ju02CI
Cath.	(D)	02	F	Child	15Ju02CI
SULLIVAN, Patk.		20	M	Farmer	15Ju02CI
SHEA, Honora		20	F	Unknown	15Ju02CI

NAMES OF PASSENGERS		A G E	S E X	OCCUPATIONS	DATE PORT SHIP
BRENNAN, Denis		30	M	Farmer	15Ju02CI
DOYLE, Cornelius		30	M	Farmer	15Ju02CI
Julia		20	F	Unknown	15Ju02CI
SLUNTON, Mary		20	F	Unknown	15Ju02CI
Biddy		20	F	Unknown	15Ju02CI
SHEA, Darby		20	M	Farmer	15Ju02CI
CONWELL, Maurice		30	M	Farmer	15Ju02CI
Mary		30	F	Unknown	15Ju02CI
Julia		20	F	Unknown	15Ju02CI
Bridget		05	F	Child	15Ju02CI
Martha		.00	F	Infant	15Ju02CI
SHEA, M.		20	F	Unknown	15Ju02CI
Bridget		20	F	Unknown	15Ju02CI
SHAUNAHAN, Danl.		20	M	Farmer	15Ju02CI
CORMELL, Timy.		30	M	Farmer	15Ju02CI
BARRY, Michl.		20	M	Farmer	15Ju02CI
HOGAN, John		40	M	Farmer	15Ju02CI
U	(W)	40	F	Unknown	15Ju02CI
Stephen	(S)	.00	M	Infant	15Ju02CI
Michael	(S)	.00	M	Infant	15Ju02CI
KELLY, Mary		30	F	Unknown	15Ju02CI
Ellen		20	F	Unknown	15Ju02CI
CONWAY, Mary		50	F	Unknown	15Ju02CI
REDDY, Thomas		30	M	Farmer	15Ju02CI
NEIL, Mary		20	F	Unknown	15Ju02CI
DONOVAN, Danl.		20	M	Farmer	15Ju02CI
MCCARTHY, John		20	M	Farmer	15Ju02CI
ROONEY, Mary		24	F	Unknown	15Ju02CI
IRWIN, Ann		20	F	Unknown	15Ju02CI
MORRAN, Michl.		34	M	Farmer	15Ju02CI
Ann		30	F	Unknown	15Ju02CI
FINNERAN, James		19	M	Farmer	15Ju02CI
Ann		22	F	Unknown	15Ju02CI
ROCHE, Henry		20	M	Farmer	15Ju02CI
FINERTY, Judith		20	F	Unknown	15Ju02CI
RYNE, Michl.		20	M	Farmer	15Ju02CI
Cath.		20	F	Unknown	15Ju02CI
MCCARTHY, Michl.		25	M	Farmer	15Ju02CI
Danl.		20	M	Farmer	15Ju02CI
CONNELL, Bln.		40	M	Farmer	15Ju02CI
CURRAN, James		35	M	Farmer	15Ju02CI
Mary		30	F	Unknown	15Ju02CI
DOWNEY, Danl.		25	M	Farmer	15Ju02CI
CURRAN, Mary		03	F	Child	15Ju02CI
Thomas	(B)	.00	M	Infant	15Ju02CI
DUGGAN, Cors.		22	M	Farmer	15Ju02CI
MURPHY, Cors.		45	M	Farmer	15Ju02CI
Ellen	(W)	40	F	Unknown	15Ju02CI
Denis		25	M	Farmer	15Ju02CI
Cornelius	(S)	22	M	Farmer	15Ju02CI
John	(S)	13	M	Farmer	15Ju02CI
Jounnah	(S)	10	M	Child	15Ju02CI
Mary	(D)	08	F	Child	15Ju02CI
Brian	(S)	.00	M	Infant	15Ju02CI
MCNULTY, James		25	M	Farmer	15Ju02CI
Margt.		26	F	Unknown	15Ju02CI
BOYD, Bridgt.		30	F	Unknown	15Ju02CI
CONNOLLY, Thos.		20	M	Farmer	15Ju02CI
EGAN, Elizth.		20	F	Unknown	15Ju02CI
OHORA, Edwd.		11	M	Child	15Ju02CI
KELLY, Patk.		20	M	Farmer	15Ju02CI
CONNOLLY, Patk.		35	M	Farmer	15Ju02CI
ROBINSON, Chas.		20	M	Farmer	15Ju02CI
BRODIN, Cath.		20	F	Unknown	15Ju02CI
WARROW, Wm.		31	M	Farmer	15Ju02CI
Harlett		19	F	Unknown	15Ju02CI
Arthur		40	M	Mechanic	15Ju02CI
Thomas		27	M	Mechanic	15Ju02CI
Eliza		.00	F	Infant	15Ju02CI
GREENAN, Richd.		20	M	Unknown	15Ju02CI
KENNEDY, Thos.		16	M	Laborer	15Ju02CI
John		19	M	Laborer	15Ju02CI
COONEY, Jane		27	F	Laborer	15Ju02CI
DUNN, Julia		30	F	Laborer	15Ju02CI
Wm.		13	M	Laborer	15Ju02CI

NAMES OF PASSENGERS	AGE	SEX	OCCUPATIONS	DATE PORT SHIP	NAMES OF PASSENGERS	AGE	SEX	OCCUPATIONS	DATE PORT SHIP
DUNN, John	11	M	Child	15Ju02CI	RUSSEL, U-Mrs.	20	F	Laborer	15Ju02CI
Mary	09	F	Child	15Ju02CI	MCENNIS, Ann	50	F	Laborer	15Ju02CI
Jane	07	F	Child	15Ju02CI	John	06	M	Child	15Ju02CI
CORMICK, John	19	M	Child	15Ju02CI	Nelly	05	F	Child	15Ju02CI
ONEILL, Patk.	33	M	Carpenter	15Ju02CI	Andw.	04	M	Child	15Ju02CI
CARROLL, Sally	24	F	Servant	15Ju02CI	Isabella	.00	F	Infant	15Ju02CI
FALLAN, Mary	11	F	Unknown	15Ju02CI	Alex	.00	M	Infant	15Ju02CI
DALEY, Philip	09	M	Servant	15Ju02CI	WILLIAMS, Wm.	25	M	Servant	15Ju02CI
WILLIAMS, Thos.	22	M	Mechanic	15Ju02CI	HUGHES, Wm.	20	M	Laborer	15Ju02CI
DONOHAN, Ellen	28	F	Servant	15Ju02CI	Wm.	18	M	Laborer	15Ju02CI
CONNOR, Barbara	20	F	Unknown	15Ju02CI	Thos.	13	M	Laborer	15Ju02CI
GRAY, James	20	M	Farmer	15Ju02CI	Margt.	40	F	Laborer	15Ju02CI
MEDBITT, Isabella	30	F	Servant	15Ju02CI	Mary	10	F	Child	15Ju02CI
WALSH, John	20	M	Laborer	15Ju02CI	Margt.	08	F	Child	15Ju02CI
MURPHY, Patk.	27	M	Laborer	15Ju02CI	Ann	05	F	Child	15Ju02CI
BROWN, Ellen	30	F	Laborer	15Ju02CI	Hugh	04	M	Child	15Ju02CI
Wm. (S)	05	M	Child	15Ju02CI	Eliz	.00	F	Infant	15Ju02CI
MCGUIRE, Wm.	24	M	Laborer	15Ju02CI	Ellen	.00	F	Infant	15Ju02CI
KING, Saml.	28	M	Laborer	15Ju02CI	CONWAY, Pat	20	M	Laborer	15Ju02CI
Jane	20	F	Laborer	15Ju02CI	DEMPSEY, Thos.	20	M	Farmer	15Ju02CI
Andrew	37	M	Laborer	15Ju02CI	U (W)	20	F	Unknown	15Ju02CI
GAHAN, Michl.	33	M	Laborer	15Ju02CI	Jas.	21	M	Farmer	15Ju02CI
COLLINS, James	10	M	Child	15Ju02CI	Margt.	20	F	Unknown	15Ju02CI
Ann	27	F	Laborer	15Ju02CI	Bridget	21	F	Unknown	15Ju02CI
DEVLIN, Arthur	25	M	Laborer	15Ju02CI	Michl.	20	M	Farmer	15Ju02CI
COLLINS, Mary-Ann	23	F	Laborer	15Ju02CI	Michl.	.00	M	Infant	15Ju02CI
MCCULLEN, Bridget	12	F	Laborer	15Ju02CI	ARCH, John	20	M	Farmer	15Ju02CI
LITTLE, Matilda	23	F	Laborer	15Ju02CI	U (W)	21	F	Unknown	15Ju02CI
STEVENS, Mary-Ann	12	F	Laborer	15Ju02CI	Jeffrey (S)	.00	M	Infant	15Ju02CI
William	08	M	Child	15Ju02CI	Michl.	30	M	Farmer	15Ju02CI
COREY, Bernard	20	M	Laborer	15Ju02CI	Wm.	20	M	Farmer	15Ju02CI
Thomas	20	M	Laborer	15Ju02CI	Ellen	20	F	Unknown	15Ju02CI
Cath.	20	F	Servant	15Ju02CI	Pat	22	M	Farmer	15Ju02CI
COLT, Bridget	20	F	Servant	15Ju02CI	MEAY, Jas.	21	M	Farmer	15Ju02CI
HUTTON, Ron	20	M	Servant	15Ju02CI	U (W)	20	F	Farmer	15Ju02CI
GAFFNEY, Cathl.	20	F	Servant	15Ju02CI	John (S)	.00	M	Infant	15Ju02CI
BRIERLY, Ann	22	F	Servant	15Ju02CI	CRAWFORD, Thos.	40	M	Farmer	15Ju02CI
MCGWIN, Thos.	27	M	Farmer	15Ju02CI	U (W)	40	F	Unknown	15Ju02CI
CONROY, Patk.	20	M	Farmer	15Ju02CI	Margt. (D)	17	F	Unknown	15Ju02CI
CONWAY, Thomas	30	M	Farmer	15Ju02CI	Pat	15	M	Farmer	15Ju02CI
BROPHY, Wm.	24	M	Farmer	15Ju02CI	John	12	M	Farmer	15Ju02CI
James	30	M	Farmer	15Ju02CI	Wm.	10	M	Child	15Ju02CI
MEATH, Wm.	12	M	Farmer	15Ju02CI	Jas.	05	M	Child	15Ju02CI
CONNOLLY, Mary	05	F	Child	15Ju02CI	Cath.	05	F	Child	15Ju02CI
BYRNE, Denis	27	M	Mechanic	15Ju02CI	Philip	.00	M	Infant	15Ju02CI
Cath. (W)	26	F	Unknown	15Ju02CI	BRODERICK, Mary	20	F	Unknown	15Ju02CI
Michl. (S)	07	M	Child	15Ju02CI	CONWAY, Mary	20	F	Laborer	15Ju02CI
TAYLOR, Wm.	13	M	Unknown	15Ju02CI	MORRIS, Jas.	36	M	Laborer	15Ju02CI
MCELLIOTT, Richd.	30	M	Miner	15Ju02CI	Ann (W)	36	F	Unknown	15Ju02CI
MCCARTHY, Thos.	30	M	Laborer	15Ju02CI	May (D)	15	F	Unknown	15Ju02CI
HORN, Fredk.R.	50	M	Farmer	15Ju02CI	Jane (D)	15	F	Unknown	15Ju02CI
EINICK, Michl.	10	M	Child	15Ju02CI	Jane (D)	11	F	Child	15Ju02CI
OBRIEN, Barnd.	34	M	Farmer	15Ju02CI	Ellz. (D)	09	F	Child	15Ju02CI
COSTELLO, Thos.	30	M	Farmer	15Ju02CI	TAYLOR, Thos.	12	M	Farmer	15Ju02CI
GALLAGHER, Stephen	13	M	Farmer	15Ju02CI	MORRIS, Thos.	06	M	Child	15Ju02CI
LYNCH, Robt.	45	M	Farmer	15Ju02CI	HUMPHREY, Ellz.	20	F	Unknown	15Ju02CI
Mary-Ann (W)	40	F	Unknown	15Ju02CI	TRAYNOR, Thos.	50	M	Farmer	15Ju02CI
Elizabeth (D)	08	F	Child	15Ju02CI	Mary (W)	50	F	Unknown	15Ju02CI
James (S)	06	M	Child	15Ju02CI	Frances (D)	17	F	Unknown	15Ju02CI
Robert (S)	04	M	Child	15Ju02CI	Mary (D)	18	F	Unknown	15Ju02CI
GAFNY, Nancy	17	F	Unknown	15Ju02CI	Alice (D)	25	F	Unknown	15Ju02CI
GORGROW, Rose	17	F	Unknown	15Ju02CI	Rose (D)	.00	F	Infant	15Ju02CI
KELLY, Richd.	22	M	Farmer	15Ju02CI	Pat (S)	30	M	Farmer	15Ju02CI
CUNNIFF, G.	25	M	Farmer	15Ju02CI	MCCULLEN, Betsey	25	F	Unknown	15Ju02CI
KNIGHT, Jane	29	F	Unknown	15Ju02CI	MCANDREW, Jane	25	F	Unknown	15Ju02CI
HELEHEN, Wm.	46	M	Farmer	15Ju02CI	FAY, John	34	M	Farmer	15Ju02CI
WOTRAN, Robt.	18	M	Farmer	15Ju02CI	May (W)	30	F	Unknown	15Ju02CI
MOONEY, Peter	60	M	Farmer	15Ju02CI	Emily (D)	11	F	Child	15Ju02CI
MCARDLE, Peter	.00	M	Infant	15Ju02CI	FITZPATRICK, Biddy	40	F	Unknown	15Ju02CI
MCGUITY, Fras.	25	M	Farmer	15Ju02CI	Margt. (D)	17	F	Unknown	15Ju02CI
U (W)	20	F	Unknown	15Ju02CI	Arthur (S)	15	M	Farmer	15Ju02CI
Bridget (D)	05	F	Child	15Ju02CI	U	12	M	Farmer	15Ju02CI
CONWAY, Owen	20	M	Laborer	15Ju02CI	Wm.	26	M	Farmer	15Ju02CI
RUSSEL, Andw.	30	M	Laborer	15Ju02CI	MCCANN, Pat	.00	M	Infant	15Ju02CI
Jas.	13	M	Laborer	15Ju02CI	HOPKINS, Margt.	20	F	Unknown	15Ju02CI

NAMES OF PASSENGERS	AGE	SEX	OCCUPATIONS	DATE PORT SHIP
WATERSON, Cath.	26	F	Unknown	15Ju02CI
BOYLAN, Ann	20	F	Unknown	15Ju02CI
MCGURLY, Cath.	.00	F	Infant	15Ju02CI
M-----, Cath.	19	F	Unknown	15Ju02CI
Rose	17	F	Unknown	15Ju02CI
MILIHILL, Robt.	20	M	Farmer	15Ju02CI
MCGUIRE, Ann	20	F	Unknown	15Ju02CI
MCDONNOTT, Cath.	20	F	Unknown	15Ju02CI
DUFFEY, Ann	20	F	Unknown	15Ju02CI
MURRAY, Barry	20	M	Farmer	15Ju02CI
OBRIEN, Wm.	30	M	Farmer	15Ju02CI
WALSH, Mary	25	F	Unknown	15Ju02CI
BRYAN, Cathe.	04	F	Child	15Ju02CI
Michl.	.00	M	Infant	15Ju02CI

HOTTINGUER 15 JUNE 1846

From Liverpool

NAMES OF PASSENGERS		AGE	SEX	OCCUPATIONS	DATE PORT SHIP
TIMS, Robert		46	M	Gunsmith	15Ju02Bc
Rebecca	(W)	40	F	None	15Ju02Bc
Sarah	(D)	14	F	None	15Ju02Bc
William	(S)	14	M	None	15Ju02Bc
Elisa	(D)	08	F	Child	15Ju02Bc
Mary-A.	(D)	04	F	Child	15Ju02Bc
Fanny	(D)	.00	F	Infant	15Ju02Bc
LATTIMER, John		04	M	Child	15Ju02Bc
Mary-A.	(M)	30	F	None	15Ju02Bc
SLOAN, John		20	M	Laborer	15Ju02Bc
BAKER, Ellen		16	F	Servant	15Ju02Bc
MCCLOLAN, Jane		19	F	Servant	15Ju02Bc
LOVE, Jane		20	F	Servant	15Ju02Bc
MCMINUS, Pat		20	M	Laborer	15Ju02Bc
COSTILO, Michael		25	M	Laborer	15Ju02Bc
James		17	M	Laborer	15Ju02Bc
KING, George		26	M	Servant	15Ju02Bc
MORGIN, Owin		20	M	Laborer	15Ju02Bc
MCANTAW, Matthew		20	M	Laborer	15Ju02Bc
MOUBRY, James		22	M	Laborer	15Ju02Bc
Robert		23	M	Laborer	15Ju02Bc
MCDARELEN, Dennis		21	M	Laborer	15Ju02Bc
COCKLIN, John		28	M	Servant	15Ju02Bc
Mary		30	F	None	15Ju02Bc
FRY, Edward		25	M	Carpenter	15Ju02Bc
Elizabeth		20	F	None	15Ju02Bc
CLARK, Margret		21	F	Servant	15Ju02Bc
MULIGAN, Bridget		20	F	Servant	15Ju02Bc
MASTERSON, Mary		18	F	Servant	15Ju02Bc
CLARK, Thomas		20	M	Servant	15Ju02Bc
Matthew		20	M	Servant	15Ju02Bc
FORBES, Pat		30	M	Servant	15Ju02Bc
Mary		20	F	Servant	15Ju02Bc
Mary		40	F	Servant	15Ju02Bc
KELLEY, Armony		21	F	Servant	15Ju02Bc
GANTLEY, Pat		20	M	Servant	. 15Ju02Bc
LANGIN, Rogerd		26	M	Servant	15Ju02Bc
SHANNON, Carson		20	M	Servant	15Ju02Bc
MCGLINN, John		28	M	Servant	15Ju02Bc
KNOX, Christiana		29	F	Servant	15Ju02Bc
ADAMSON, John		22	M	Servant	15Ju02Bc
MUSTER, Sarah		27	F	Servant	15Ju02Bc
MAGGIN, Robert		28	M	Servant	15Ju02Bc
MCPHILLIP, James		24	M	Servant	15Ju02Bc
COFFY, Edward		29	M	Servant	15Ju02Bc
DANIN, Thomas		12	M	Servant	15Ju02Bc
Catherine		10	F	Child	15Ju02Bc
MCPHILLIP, Elizabeth		20	F	Servant	15Ju02Bc
WARK, Martha		20	F	Servant	15Ju02Bc
Mary-J.		19	F	Servant	15Ju02Bc

NAMES OF PASSENGERS		AGE	SEX	OCCUPATIONS	DATE PORT SHIP
MURPHY, Thomas		20	M	Laborer	15Ju02Bc
Ann	(W)	21	F	None	15Ju02Bc
MCDONNAL, Owen		25	M	Laborer	15Ju02Bc
Peggy	(W)	30	F	None	15Ju02Bc
GAFFRY, Pat		30	M	Laborer	15Ju02Bc
DOLAN, John		35	M	Laborer	15Ju02Bc
MCDARNAL, Peter		25	M	Laborer	15Ju02Bc
BROWN, Robert		28	M	Laborer	15Ju02Bc
DIGNIN, Mary		20	F	Servant	15Ju02Bc
CANTWELL, Elisa		20	F	Servant	15Ju02Bc
MCARDLE, Catherine		20	F	Servant	15Ju02Bc
MACK, Julia		28	F	Servant	15Ju02Bc
BANN, Elisa		40	F	Servant	15Ju02Bc
Isaac	(S)	20	M	Servant	15Ju02Bc
Isabella	(D)	18	F	Servant	15Ju02Bc
William	(S)	13	M	Servant	15Ju02Bc
Ursella	(D)	10	F	Child	15Ju02Bc
Samuel	(S)	09	M	Child	15Ju02Bc
Ephraigm	(S)	07	M	Child	15Ju02Bc
HOLMES, John		20	M	Laborer	15Ju02Bc
KENNEDY, Robert		30	M	Draper	15Ju02Bc
JOHNSTON, James		23	M	Saddler	15Ju02Bc
SINCLAIR, John		21	M	Weaver	15Ju02Bc
CLARK, James		21	M	Weaver	15Ju02Bc
GOOLRY, Mary		19	F	Servant	15Ju02Bc
DALE, Jane		20	F	Servant	15Ju02Bc
MCGRIFFIN, Isabella		19	F	Servant	15Ju02Bc
KENNEDY, Jane		21	F	Servant	15Ju02Bc
HAGAN, Thomas		14	M	Shoemaker	15Ju02Bc
SHEPPARD, John		24	M	Servant	15Ju02Bc
DARLIN, John		20	M	Servant	15Ju02Bc
HANRY, Susan		24	M	Servant	15Ju02Bc
MALONE, Catherine		09	F	Child	15Ju02Bc
Ann-Jane		04	F	Child	15Ju02Bc
DODD, Robert		20	M	Servant	15Ju02Bc
GARNETT, William		32	M	Servant	15Ju02Bc
KELANY, Catherine		20	F	Servant	15Ju02Bc
Margaret		24	F	Servant	15Ju02Bc
CUNNINGHAM, Bridget		20	F	Servant	15Ju02Bc
MCALWAA, Thomas		26	M	Servant	15Ju02Bc
MEKIN, James		25	M	Servant	15Ju02Bc
SUNNY, Bryan		30	M	Servant	15Ju02Bc
MASTERSON, Patrick		25	M	Servant	15Ju02Bc
MORRISEY, Edward		25	M	Servant	15Ju02Bc
Edward		27	M	Servant	15Ju02Bc
CALATEN, John		27	M	Servant	15Ju02Bc
HARIGAN, Jeremiah		27	M	Servant	15Ju02Bc
WARD, Bryne		18	M	Servant	15Ju02Bc
Owen		18	M	Servant	15Ju02Bc
KERNAN, Gurns		18	M	Servant	15Ju02Bc
CONNER, Pat		25	M	Servant	15Ju02Bc
LEONARD, Owen		25	M	Servant	15Ju02Bc
KALAHAN, Phil		25	M	Servant	15Ju02Bc
SMITH, John		25	M	Servant	15Ju02Bc
Catherine		21	F	Servant	15Ju02Bc
HERBERT, William		18	M	Servant	15Ju02Bc
Catherine		13	F	Child	15Ju02Bc
GLEASON, Thomas		32	M	Servant	15Ju02Bc
KENNY, Maria		21	F	Servant	15Ju02Bc
GALLA, Mary		19	F	Servant	15Ju02Bc
DOYLE, James		32	M	Servant	15Ju02Bc
FLANARY, Michael		20	M	Servant	15Ju02Bc
CASEY, Pat		24	M	Blacksmith	15Ju02Bc
RYAN, Pat		33	M	Shoemaker	15Ju02Bc
HOGAN, Timothy		30	M	Laborer	15Ju02Bc
Mary	(W)	26	F	None	15Ju02Bc
John	(S)	.00	M	Infant	15Ju02Bc
KENNEDY, Mary		17	F	None	15Ju02Bc
HUNTER, James		25	M	Carpenter	15Ju02Bc
Susan	(W)	29	F	None	15Ju02Bc
Ellen	(D)	.00	F	Infant	15Ju02Bc
Samuel		19	M	Carpenter	15Ju02Bc
BENNETT, John		45	M	Smith	15Ju02Bc
James		42	M	Smith	15Ju02Bc
James		22	M	Smith	15Ju02Bc

NAMES OF PASSENGERS	AGE	SEX	OCCUPATIONS	DATE PORT SHIP	NAMES OF PASSENGERS	AGE	SEX	OCCUPATIONS	DATE PORT SHIP
BENNETT, Jane	45	F	None	15Ju02Bc	COONEY, John	20	M	Child	15Ju02Bc
Edward	03	M	Child	15Ju02Bc	DUFT, Bridget	20	F	Child	15Ju02Bc
HAMLEY, Ellen	19	F	None	15Ju02Bc	FITZPATRICK, Nancy	20	F	Child	15Ju02Bc
James	21	M	Smith	15Ju02Bc	DALY, Bryne	20	M	Child	15Ju02Bc
Samuel	18	M	Smith	15Ju02Bc	Peggy	20	F	Child	15Ju02Bc
Margaret	33	F	None	15Ju02Bc	SMITH, Peter	24	M	Laborer	15Ju02Bc
SALES, James	24	M	Laborer	15Ju02Bc	CLARK, Gurns	20	M	Laborer	15Ju02Bc
MOORE, James	25	M	Laborer	15Ju02Bc	QUILLIN, Rose	20	F	Servant	15Ju02Bc
RYAN, Mary	06	F	Child	15Ju02Bc	WELSH, Michael	20	M	Servant	15Ju02Bc
CRANFIELD, Mary	24	F	Servant	15Ju02Bc	Elisa	20	F	Servant	15Ju02Bc
Ann	24	F	Servant	15Ju02Bc	CONNER, Ellen	20	F	Servant	15Ju02Bc
HUNTER, John	20	M	Carpenter	15Ju02Bc	KATON, Pat	30	M	Laborer	15Ju02Bc
KOA, Arthur	20	M	Carpenter	15Ju02Bc	MALONE, John	30	M	Laborer	15Ju02Bc
WALLIS, Stephen	17	M	Painter	15Ju02Bc	MCKEY, Henry	30	M	Laborer	15Ju02Bc
KELLERY, John	12	M	Child	15Ju02Bc	MALONE, Nancy	25	F	Servant	15Ju02Bc
COX, Thomas	20	M	Laborer	15Ju02Bc	Alley	24	F	Servant	15Ju02Bc
George	25	M	Carpenter	15Ju02Bc	HANLIN, Margaret	17	F	Servant	15Ju02Bc
Harriet	21	F	None	15Ju02Bc	FITZGARRALD, John	30	M	Laborer	15Ju02Bc
Catherine	18	F	None	15Ju02Bc	FITZPATRICK, John	22	M	Laborer	15Ju02Bc
KENSULER, Margaret	20	F	None	15Ju02Bc	GRIFFIN, Dan	30	M	Laborer	15Ju02Bc
MCWADE, Charles	39	M	Laborer	15Ju02Bc	MCDONNAL, John	20	M	Laborer	15Ju02Bc
John	30	M	Laborer	15Ju02Bc	Ellen	56	F	Laborer	15Ju02Bc
Felix	20	M	Laborer	15Ju02Bc	LONG, Thomas	30	M	Laborer	15Ju02Bc
MCCOSTER, Ellen	26	F	Servant	15Ju02Bc	DAVIS, Dennis	35	M	Laborer	15Ju02Bc
Mary	20	F	Servant	15Ju02Bc	John	19	M	Servant	15Ju02Bc
GIVIN, Jane	18	F	Servant	15Ju02Bc	Mary	20	F	Servant	15Ju02Bc
HENIGHAN, John	24	M	Servant	15Ju02Bc	DRUMMING, Mary	20	F	Servant	15Ju02Bc
KALAGHIN, Biddy	18	F	Servant	15Ju02Bc	COLLINS, Anna	18	F	Servant	15Ju02Bc
Sarah	18	F	Servant	15Ju02Bc	FINGLETON, William	30	M	Laborer	15Ju02Bc
Biddy	20	F	Servant	15Ju02Bc	SARLOV, Edward	25	M	Laborer	15Ju02Bc
KELSH, James	30	M	Cicp	15Ju02Bc	HERD, James	26	M	Laborer	15Ju02Bc
BUSHWELL, Tempest	21	M	Cicp	15Ju02Bc	WARD, Thomas	27	M	Laborer	15Ju02Bc
MCKANOR, Elisabeth	26	F	Servant	15Ju02Bc	Ann	22	F	Servant	15Ju02Bc
Sarah	24	F	Servant	15Ju02Bc	WARRINT, Catherine	22	F	Servant	15Ju02Bc
Nancy	20	F	Servant	15Ju02Bc	KENOY, John	28	M	Servant	15Ju02Bc
COCARIN, Alexander	22	M	Servant	15Ju02Bc	Gerry	20	M	Servant	15Ju02Bc
WATT, Thomas	29	M	Servant	15Ju02Bc	Mary	23	F	Servant	15Ju02Bc
CANELL, James	25	M	Servant	15Ju02Bc	Esther	30	F	Servant	15Ju02Bc
POKE, James	19	M	Servant	15Ju02Bc	MADDEN, Mary	21	F	Servant	15Ju02Bc
BAILEY, Henry	25	M	Servant	15Ju02Bc	BURNS, Biddy	22	F	Servant	15Ju02Bc
MAGGHIN, Joseph	28	M	Laborer	15Ju02Bc	BRANIN, Catherine	19	F	Servant	15Ju02Bc
GALLY, Catherine	24	F	Servant	15Ju02Bc	MOONES, Catherine	19	F	Servant	15Ju02Bc
DUNN, Mary	06	F	Child	15Ju02Bc	WAVERLY, Ann	19	F	Servant	15Ju02Bc
Lawrence	08	M	Servant	15Ju02Bc	GOULDIN, John	50	M	Servant	15Ju02Bc
MCCABES, Pat	25	M	Servant	15Ju02Bc	Catherine (W)	48	F	Servant	15Ju02Bc
KENNY, Bridget	20	F	Servant	15Ju02Bc	James (S)	15	M	Servant	15Ju02Bc
Peter	25	M	Servant	15Ju02Bc	DWYRE, John	26	M	Servant	15Ju02Bc
HUGHES, Christopher	20	M	Servant	15Ju02Bc	Joanna	17	F	Servant	15Ju02Bc
BAGNAN, Richard	04	M	Child	15Ju02Bc	Catherine	60	F	Unknown	15Ju02Bc
MOOTY, Margaret	21	F	Servant	15Ju02Bc	John (P)	60	M	Unknown	15Ju02Bc
GLEASON, Tom	25	M	Servant	15Ju02Bc	MINS, John	21	M	Servant	15Ju02Bc
MANAGIN, Dennis	27	M	Servant	15Ju02Bc	Francis	20	M	Laborer	15Ju02Bc
MALONEY, Mary	30	F	Servant	15Ju02Bc	MENTEITH, Steward	22	M	Laborer	15Ju02Bc
Bessy	28	F	Servant	15Ju02Bc	BROWN, Patrick	29	M	Laborer	15Ju02Bc
MCKANE, Ann	14	F	Servant	15Ju02Bc	GALVIN, William	22	M	Laborer	15Ju02Bc
Phil	14	M	Servant	15Ju02Bc	KEARNEY, James	22	M	Laborer	15Ju02Bc
Anna	60	F	Servant	15Ju02Bc	GALLEY, James	20	M	Laborer	15Ju02Bc
MANOGIN, Dan	21	M	Servant	15Ju02Bc	CAFFREY, Thomas	25	M	Laborer	15Ju02Bc
GLEASON, Mat	19	M	Servant	15Ju02Bc	GANNEY, James	20	M	Laborer	15Ju02Bc
Mary	40	F	Servant	15Ju02Bc	Burnett	40	M	Laborer	15Ju02Bc
Pat (S)	12	M	Child	15Ju02Bc	Pat	14	M	Laborer	15Ju02Bc
Biddy (D)	06	F	Child	15Ju02Bc	MURRAY, Antony	46	M	Laborer	15Ju02Bc
Elisa (D)	04	F	Child	15Ju02Bc	MCGOUGH, Mary	20	F	Servant	15Ju02Bc
Mary (D)	02	F	Child	15Ju02Bc	HALIGHIN, Mary	19	F	Servant	15Ju02Bc
Ellen (D)	.00	F	Infant	15Ju02Bc	GARVEY, Catherine	16	F	Servant	15Ju02Bc
BRANIN, Pat	36	M	Servant	15Ju02Bc	FINNIGAN, Mary	18	F	Servant	15Ju02Bc
KANE, John	31	M	Servant	15Ju02Bc	MCGINN, James	18	M	Servant	15Ju02Bc
CLEARY, Thomas	32	M	Servant	15Ju02Bc	Pat	16	M	Servant	15Ju02Bc
DIVING, James	17	M	Servant	15Ju02Bc	GARTLIN, Pat	18	M	Servant	15Ju02Bc
COLLINS, Joanna	21	F	Servant	15Ju02Bc	MCGINN, Mary	40	F	Servant	15Ju02Bc
DIVING, Julia	20	F	Servant	15Ju02Bc	Mary	18	F	Servant	15Ju02Bc
MURPHY, Biddy	21	F	Servant	15Ju02Bc	FINIGAN, Bridget	20	F	Servant	15Ju02Bc
CARTY, Catherine	16	F	Servant	15Ju02Bc	HILCRAN, James	23	M	Laborer	15Ju02Bc
BURNS, Catherine	21	F	Servant	15Ju02Bc	TEMPLE, John	22	M	Laborer	15Ju02Bc
SCANDLIN, Mary	03	F	Child	15Ju02Bc	DAVIS, Thomas	20	M	Laborer	15Ju02Bc

154

NAMES OF PASSENGERS	AGE	SEX	OCCUPATIONS	DATE PORT SHIP
FITZPATRICK, Bryne	22	M	Laborer	15Ju02Bc
SHARR, Cornelius	24	M	Laborer	15Ju02Bc
MANNING, Thomas	24	M	Laborer	15Ju02Bc
Michael	18	M	Laborer	15Ju02Bc
Catherine	18	F	Servant	15Ju02Bc
MADDEN, John	28	M	Laborer	15Ju02Bc
Mary	24	F	Laborer	15Ju02Bc
MCKAY, John	25	M	Laborer	15Ju02Bc
Ann	27	F	Laborer	15Ju02Bc
HEARLY, Dennis	23	M	Laborer	15Ju02Bc
LINCH, Michael	23	M	Laborer	15Ju02Bc
DOLAN, Pat	23	M	Laborer	15Ju02Bc
FITZPATRICK, John	25	M	Laborer	15Ju02Bc
RILEY, Rose	16	F	Servant	15Ju02Bc
MCGOULDIN, Ellen	17	F	Servant	15Ju02Bc
DOLAN, Catherine	20	F	Servant	15Ju02Bc
RAFFERTY, Catherine	18	F	Servant	15Ju02Bc
DUNN, Michael	25	M	Laborer	15Ju02Bc
MOORE, Ganton	20	M	Servant	15Ju02Bc
HOGAN, John	19	M	Servant	15Ju02Bc
CARTLERS, Pat	23	M	Servant	15Ju02Bc
MCKEARN, William	38	M	Servant	15Ju02Bc
GUILFOULE, John	25	M	Laborer	15Ju02Bc
Mary	25	F	Laborer	15Ju02Bc
DONALLY, Gurns	50	M	Laborer	15Ju02Bc
Peggy	48	F	Laborer	15Ju02Bc
CAVENOR, Michael	15	M	Laborer	15Ju02Bc
GREENON, Michael	20	M	Laborer	15Ju02Bc
James	19	M	Laborer	15Ju02Bc
SMITH, Catherine	20	F	Servant	15Ju02Bc
HANARY, Margaret	25	F	Servant	15Ju02Bc
MEKIN, Ann	25	F	Servant	15Ju02Bc
CAVENOR, Catherine	14	F	Servant	15Ju02Bc
RIORDIN, Dennis	20	M	Servant	15Ju02Bc
Ellen	20	F	Servant	15Ju02Bc
HAYS, John	28	M	Servant	15Ju02Bc
KALAHER, Mary	20	F	Servant	15Ju02Bc
MCCAFFREY, Catherine	21	F	Servant	15Ju02Bc
BOYLIN, Margaret	18	F	Servant	15Ju02Bc
DINKIN, Sarah	19	F	Servant	15Ju02Bc
THORNTON, Barney	35	M	Laborer	15Ju02Bc
MARTIN, James	22	M	Laborer	15Ju02Bc
MCGOULSTIN, Pat	18	M	Laborer	15Ju02Bc
THORNTON, Hugh	24	M	Laborer	15Ju02Bc
William	28	M	Laborer	15Ju02Bc
Peter	19	M	Laborer	15Ju02Bc
Braney	18	M	Laborer	15Ju02Bc
DOOLEY, Matthew	25	M	Laborer	15Ju02Bc
MCDIERMONT, Michael	23	M	Laborer	15Ju02Bc
LOYDEN, William	20	M	Laborer	15Ju02Bc
KELLY, Michael	28	M	Laborer	15Ju02Bc
HICKEY, William	35	M	Laborer	15Ju02Bc
DESMOND, Timothy	24	M	Laborer	15Ju02Bc
GEMMY, Dennis	20	M	Laborer	15Ju02Bc
MCCARHAL, John	20	M	Laborer	15Ju02Bc
MCGUINTY, John	27	M	Laborer	15Ju02Bc
GRECOR, John	55	M	Laborer	15Ju02Bc
Richie	19	M	Laborer	15Ju02Bc
Leticia	40	F	Laborer	15Ju02Bc
MCGIM, Michael	20	M	Laborer	15Ju02Bc
GORMAN, Dennis	20	M	Laborer	15Ju02Bc
JOICE, Morris	26	M	Laborer	15Ju02Bc
MCGINN, James	24	M	Laborer	15Ju02Bc
John	22	M	Laborer	15Ju02Bc
MCKAMOR, Owen	23	M	Laborer	15Ju02Bc
MARRAH, Phil	30	M	Laborer	15Ju02Bc
Catherine	29	F	None	15Ju02Bc
MCKANON, Bridget	25	F	Servant	15Ju02Bc
HOLLAND, Rose	20	F	Servant	15Ju02Bc
MCCARON, Ann	20	F	Servant	15Ju02Bc
LEYDON, Farral	31	M	Servant	15Ju02Bc
GODD, Jane	50	F	None	15Ju02Bc
LOURY, Margaret	23	F	Servant	15Ju02Bc
FERGUSON, Thomas	28	M	Mnftr	15Ju02Bc
Isabella	28	F	None	15Ju02Bc

PETER-HATTRICK 15 JUNE 1846

From Liverpool

NAMES OF PASSENGERS	AGE	SEX	OCCUPATIONS	DATE PORT SHIP
FIELD, Margaret	26	F	Servant	15Ju02Ck
MURPHY, Michael	21	M	Blacksmith	15Ju02Ck
MCDERMOTT, Catherine	23	F	Servant	15Ju02Ck
GILLAN, Patrick	22	M	Farmer	15Ju02Ck
Bridget	20	F	Servant	15Ju02Ck
LAMAND, James	19	M	Laborer	15Ju02Ck
GAFFNEY, Margaretta	18	F	Servant	15Ju02Ck
Mary	22	F	Servant	15Ju02Ck
DARSEY, Catherine	18	F	Servant	15Ju02Ck
MCKANNALEY, Barney	35	M	Servant	15Ju02Ck
QUINN, Cornelius	28	M	Tailor	15Ju02Ck
Julia	21	F	Servant	15Ju02Ck
WENSLEY, William	26	M	Farmer	15Ju02Ck
Mary (W)	24	F	Farmer	15Ju02Ck
Robert (S)	01	M	Child	15Ju02Ck
SHANNON, Mary	17	F	Dressmaker	15Ju02Ck
BRANNAN, Peter	28	M	Farmer	15Ju02Ck
RING, John	28	M	Farmer	15Ju02Ck
BRANNAN, Margarett	02	F	Servant	15Ju02Ck
GLEESON, Ellen	22	F	Servant	15Ju02Ck
HEARN, Margarett	26	F	Servant	15Ju02Ck
KENNEDY, James	21	M	Carpenter	15Ju02Ck
LANE, Francis	25	M	Laborer	15Ju02Ck
DUFFY, Peter	20	M	Farmer	15Ju02Ck
SMALLEN, William	28	M	Laborer	15Ju02Ck
Betsey (W)	26	F	None	15Ju02Ck
Anne (D)	08	F	Child	15Ju02Ck
Mary-Ann (D)	04	F	Child	15Ju02Ck
Died-At-Sea				
Elizabeth (D)	.01	F	Infant	15Ju02Ck
CANLEY, Peter	19	M	Laborer	15Ju02Ck
Patrick	46	M	Laborer	15Ju02Ck
GRAHAM, Mary	23	F	Servant	15Ju02Ck
HAAY, Hugh	25	M	Farmer	15Ju02Ck
CANROY, Thomas	22	M	Laborer	15Ju02Ck
GANNON, Thomas	35	M	Laborer	15Ju02Ck
FINNERAN, Mary	23	F	Servant	15Ju02Ck
GANNON, Jane	23	F	Servant	15Ju02Ck
LYDIATE, Richard	61	M	Shoemaker	15Ju02Ck
Horinda	16	F	Servant	15Ju02Ck
LEADBETTER, Edward	47	M	Weaver	15Ju02Ck
MCARDLE, Henry	24	M	Whitesmith	15Ju02Ck
Alice	22	F	Whitesmith	15Ju02Ck
LEADBETTER, Ellen	17	F	Servant	15Ju02Ck
OBRIAN, Johanah	25	F	Servant	15Ju02Ck
Ellen	23	F	Servant	15Ju02Ck
FITZGERALD, Mary	22	F	Servant	15Ju02Ck
CASEY, Anne	20	F	Servant	15Ju02Ck
EUGAN, Mary	18	F	Servant	15Ju02Ck
CANNELL, David	20	M	Laborer	15Ju02Ck
DALEY, Catherine	19	F	Servant	15Ju02Ck
MCCANVEL, Betsey-Ann	28	F	Dressmaker	15Ju02Ck
James	05	M	Child	15Ju02Ck
ROBINSON, Michael	21	M	Laborer	15Ju02Ck
FARRELL, Elizabeth	22	F	Servant	15Ju02Ck
REDENAN, Ann	19	F	Servant	15Ju02Ck
CAHY, John	17	M	Laborer	15Ju02Ck
James (B)	11	M	Laborer	15Ju02Ck
Margarett (T)	09	F	Child	15Ju02Ck
BRANNAN, Anto	18	F	Servant	15Ju02Ck
BALL, Bridget	22	F	Servant	15Ju02Ck
Mary	24	F	Servant	15Ju02Ck
FITZPATTRICK, Owen	21	M	Laborer	15Ju02Ck
CALLAHAN, James	20	M	Laborer	15Ju02Ck
Fanny	14	F	Servant	15Ju02Ck

NAMES OF PASSENGERS	AGE	SEX	OCCUPATIONS	DATE PORT SHIP
SHERIDIN, Susan	13	F	Servant	15Ju02Ck
CLARK, Susan	20	F	Servant	15Ju02Ck
FALSEY, Michael	63	M	Mason	15Ju02Ck
Thomas	25	M	Mason	15Ju02Ck
Michael	23	M	Mason	15Ju02Ck
Daniel	18	M	Mason	15Ju02Ck
Ellen	20	F	None	15Ju02Ck
PAYNE, Ann	32	F	Wife	15Ju02Ck
MCGAVEREN, Margarett	20	F	Servant	15Ju02Ck
KILLEY, Frances	20	F	Dressmaker	15Ju02Ck
PURVIS, Nancy	20	F	Servant	15Ju02Ck
MCLAUGHLIN, Patrick	20	M	Carpenter	15Ju02Ck
MCGUIRE, Thomas	21	M	Laborer	15Ju02Ck
BOYLE, Charles	22	M	Nail Maker	15Ju02Ck
RILEY, Ann	17	F	Servant	15Ju02Ck
KEGAN, Bridget	50	F	Lady	15Ju02Ck
FLANNAGAN, Bryan	28	M	Laborer	15Ju02Ck
WHEELEN, Ellen	22	F	Servant	15Ju02Ck
DUCK, Ann	18	F	Servant	15Ju02Ck
KENNEDY, Ann	18	F	Servant	15Ju02Ck
BRANNAN, Ellen	12	F	Servant	15Ju02Ck
OBRIAN, Ann	18	F	Servant	15Ju02Ck
BANNAN, Margarett	17	F	Servant	15Ju02Ck
KILHEIDE, Mary	21	F	Servant	15Ju02Ck
MCKENAN, Mary	23	F	Servant	15Ju02Ck
TRAINER, Bridget	24	F	Dressmaker	15Ju02Ck
MOLANE, Daniel	23	M	Laborer	15Ju02Ck
Debby	18	F	None	15Ju02Ck
MULGROO, Patrick	20	M	Laborer	15Ju02Ck
Margaret	16	F	Servant	15Ju02Ck
RAGAN, James	20	M	Laborer	15Ju02Ck
MCMAHAN, Hugh	20	M	Laborer	15Ju02Ck
SMITH, Peter	22	M	Miller	15Ju02Ck
Owen	24	M	Miller	15Ju02Ck
Judith	18	F	Servant	15Ju02Ck
GILLIGAN, Edward	20	M	Laborer	15Ju02Ck
BRADY, Peter	20	M	Laborer	15Ju02Ck
SARAHAN, Phillip	25	M	Laborer	15Ju02Ck
SLAYMAN, John	33	M	Laborer	15Ju02Ck
Elizabeth	20	F	Laborer	15Ju02Ck
SWEENEY, John	20	M	Laborer	15Ju02Ck

EUROPE 15 JUNE 1846

From Liverpool

NAMES OF PASSENGERS	AGE	SEX	OCCUPATIONS	DATE PORT SHIP
CUFF, Michael	21	M	Laborer	15Ju02BI
MCHUGH, Sarah	22	F	Laborer	15Ju02BI
LONE, John	24	M	Laborer	15Ju02BI
BAUNON, Peter	20	M	Laborer	15Ju02BI
BRYNE, Peter	20	M	Laborer	15Ju02BI
REEFFE, Michael	24	M	Laborer	15Ju02BI
DUNN, Robert	22	M	Laborer	15Ju02BI
DEAN, Patt	22	M	Laborer	15Ju02BI
HAGAN, Michael	36	M	Laborer	15Ju02BI
DALTON, Margret	22	F	Laborer	15Ju02BI
MAHON, Patt	20	M	Laborer	15Ju02BI
MACORMICK, John	20	M	Laborer	15Ju02BI
MURRY, Daniel	20	M	Laborer	15Ju02BI
MCELROY, Biddy	18	F	Laborer	15Ju02BI
Nancy	20	F	Laborer	15Ju02BI
RELLY, Biddy	20	F	Laborer	15Ju02BI
MARTIN, Nicholas	18	M	Laborer	15Ju02BI
GIBSON, Samuel	18	M	Laborer	15Ju02BI
Mary-Ann	25	F	Laborer	15Ju02BI
BEHENEY, Catherine	21	F	Laborer	15Ju02BI
FEGAN, Catherine	23	F	Laborer	15Ju02BI
COOK, Charles	25	M	Laborer	15Ju02BI
James	25	M	Laborer	15Ju02BI

NAMES OF PASSENGERS	AGE	SEX	OCCUPATIONS	DATE PORT SHIP
COOK, Samuel	24	M	Laborer	15Ju02BI
LYNCH, John	13	M	Laborer	15Ju02BI
Catherine	10	F	Laborer	15Ju02BI
MCDONALD, Rose	16	F	Laborer	15Ju02BI
SMITH, Catherine	06	F	Child	15Ju02BI
CASSIDY, Mary	18	F	Laborer	15Ju02BI
GRAVE, John	16	M	Laborer	15Ju02BI
MCGLAUGHLIN, Biddy	19	F	Laborer	15Ju02BI
BLOOM, Robert	18	M	Laborer	15Ju02BI
RELLY, Patrick	40	M	Laborer	15Ju02BI
Biddy (W)	36	F	Laborer	15Ju02BI
Anne (D)	10	F	Laborer	15Ju02BI
Mary (D)	03	F	Child	15Ju02BI
MCTULOCK, Eliza	18	F	Laborer	15Ju02BI
FARRELL, Thomas	27	M	Laborer	15Ju02BI
CAMPBELL, Anthony	23	M	Laborer	15Ju02BI
Peggy	22	F	Laborer	15Ju02BI
DEVITT, John	20	M	Laborer	15Ju02BI
Elizabeth	18	F	Laborer	15Ju02BI
MCDERMOTT, Biddy	13	F	Laborer	15Ju02BI
MCCARTY, James	60	M	Laborer	15Ju02BI
BOLTON, Bridget	30	F	Laborer	15Ju02BI
Thomas	.07	M	Infant	15Ju02BI
FLYN, James	18	M	Laborer	15Ju02BI
BOHEN, Ellen	20	F	Laborer	15Ju02BI
REILLY, Mary	12	F	Laborer	15Ju02BI
CUNNINGHAM, Bessy	20	F	Laborer	15Ju02BI
Margaret	02	F	Child	15Ju02BI
COX, Catherine	05	F	Child	15Ju02BI
JOHNSIN, Christopher	66	M	Laborer	15Ju02BI
Thomas	25	M	Laborer	15Ju02BI
Mary	17	F	Laborer	15Ju02BI
MCNABB, Ellen	60	F	Laborer	15Ju02BI
Ellen	24	F	Laborer	15Ju02BI
Peter	20	M	Laborer	15Ju02BI
Thomas	18	M	Laborer	15Ju02BI
DONELAN, Rose	56	F	Laborer	15Ju02BI
James	54	M	Laborer	15Ju02BI
Thomas	11	M	Laborer	15Ju02BI
ROARKE, Catherine	10	F	Laborer	15Ju02BI
BESTICK, Eluand	23	F	Laborer	15Ju02BI
HOWELL, Rose	20	F	Laborer	15Ju02BI
MURPHY, Catherine	14	F	Laborer	15Ju02BI
Patt	11	M	Laborer	15Ju02BI
CLARKEN, Thomas	20	M	Laborer	15Ju02BI
Owen	21	M	Laborer	15Ju02BI
Maria	18	F	Laborer	15Ju02BI
CULLEN, Mary	18	F	Laborer	15Ju02BI
HAMILTON, Mary	17	F	Laborer	15Ju02BI
MCELRATH, John	22	M	Laborer	15Ju02BI
DONAGHY, John	20	M	Laborer	15Ju02BI
DONOVAN, Daniel	13	M	Laborer	15Ju02BI
COLLINS, Jeremiah	30	M	Laborer	15Ju02BI
SWEENEY, John	15	M	Laborer	15Ju02BI
CASSIDY, Thomas	17	M	Laborer	15Ju02BI
MCKENNA, Anne	25	F	Laborer	15Ju02BI
John	12	M	Laborer	15Ju02BI
KELLY, Patt	20	M	Laborer	15Ju02BI
John	23	M	Laborer	15Ju02BI
CANNALLY, Michael	29	M	Laborer	15Ju02BI
MURREY, Thomas	18	M	Laborer	15Ju02BI
BRYNE, James	20	M	Laborer	15Ju02BI
Michl.	24	M	Laborer	15Ju02BI
WILSON, John	60	M	Laborer	15Ju02BI
GORMAN, Jas.	24	M	Laborer	15Ju02BI
James	22	M	Laborer	15Ju02BI
SAVAGE, Eliza	18	F	Laborer	15Ju02BI
FINIGAN, Mary	17	F	Laborer	15Ju02BI
COYLE, Alice	02	F	Child	15Ju02BI
MCCANN, Charles	18	M	Laborer	15Ju02BI
MURAW, William	30	M	Laborer	15Ju02BI
DONAGLE, Pattrick	17	M	Laborer	15Ju02BI
BILINGTON, George	40	M	Laborer	15Ju02BI
U-Mrs. (W)	42	F	Laborer	15Ju02BI
William (S)	12	M	Laborer	15Ju02BI

NAMES OF PASSENGERS		AGE	SEX	OCCUPATIONS	DATE PORT SHIP
BILINGTON, Henry	(S)	10	M	Laborer	15Ju02BI
David	(S)	08	M	Child	15Ju02BI
Edwin	(S)	06	M	Child	15Ju02BI
SULIVAN, Daniel		20	M	Laborer	15Ju02BI
CLARK, Mary		20	F	Laborer	15Ju02BI
FEENY, Anne		20	F	Laborer	15Ju02BI
FLAVOR, John		21	M	Laborer	15Ju02BI
GREEN, Biddy		19	F	Laborer	15Ju02BI
CLARKE, Charles		24	M	Laborer	15Ju02BI
MCGORWN, Anne		18	F	Laborer	15Ju02BI
MUIAGLE, Biddy		20	F	Laborer	15Ju02BI
MCGUINE, Mary		20	F	Laborer	15Ju02BI
FINIGAN, Biddy		20	F	Laborer	15Ju02BI
FRANKLIN, John		78	M	Laborer	15Ju02BI
BOLTON, U-Mrs.		34	F	Laborer	15Ju02BI
BILLING, Geo.		01	M	Child	15Ju02BI
BOLTON, William		40	M	Laborer	15Ju02BI
Thomas	(B)	50	M	Laborer	15Ju02BI
William	(P)	74	M	Laborer	15Ju02BI
William		12	M	Laborer	15Ju02BI
Thos.		08	M	Child	15Ju02BI
Henry		06	M	Child	15Ju02BI
Henry		17	M	Laborer	15Ju02BI
HOLMES, Martha		22	F	Laborer	15Ju02BI
NALLY, William		03	M	Child	15Ju02BI
ROURKE, Biddy		20	F	Laborer	15Ju02BI
GREEN, Margret		18	F	Laborer	15Ju02BI
FYNALL, Thomas		27	M	Laborer	15Ju02BI
Catherine		20	F	Laborer	15Ju02BI
DOLAN, Patrick		24	M	Laborer	15Ju02BI
Margt.		24	F	Laborer	15Ju02BI
BAIL, William		21	M	Laborer	15Ju02BI
MIDDLETON, Robt.		25	M	Laborer	15Ju02BI
SWEENEY, Bridget		20	F	Laborer	15Ju02BI
REYNOLDS, Jane		19	F	Laborer	15Ju02BI
HAWLEY, Elisa		15	F	Laborer	15Ju02BI
KNIHAN, Edward		20	M	Laborer	15Ju02BI
MCGARRY, Thos.		20	M	Laborer	15Ju02BI
DUNN, Mary		18	F	Laborer	15Ju02BI
FURNER, John		56	M	Laborer	15Ju02BI
SEFFNADGE, Thos.		50	M	Laborer	15Ju02BI
MCPHELON, Hugh		12	M	Laborer	15Ju02BI
BESSON, Bernard		50	M	Laborer	15Ju02BI
U-Mrs.		48	F	Laborer	15Ju02BI
BESUDEN, Martin		20	M	Laborer	15Ju02BI
MCCUE, Teddy		19	M	Laborer	15Ju02BI
CARROLL, Catherine		18	F	Laborer	15Ju02BI
AMBROSE, Joshua		23	M	Laborer	15Ju02BI
LEADER, Timothy		30	M	Laborer	15Ju02BI
MCCARTY, Mary		12	F	Laborer	15Ju02BI
GOLDING, Anne		22	F	Laborer	15Ju02BI
Patt		21	M	Laborer	15Ju02BI
CONALLY, Sarah		23	F	Laborer	15Ju02BI
TYNAN, Owen		19	M	Laborer	15Ju02BI
KEEFFE, Joshua		16	M	Laborer	15Ju02BI
KELLY, John		26	M	Laborer	15Ju02BI
FRARER, Elisa		30	F	Laborer	15Ju02BI
Frances		05	F	Child	15Ju02BI
Robert		02	M	Child	15Ju02BI
MUHANY, Henry		25	M	Laborer	15Ju02BI
CARDERL, Henry		20	M	Laborer	15Ju02BI
FEENY, Patt		23	M	Laborer	15Ju02BI
Mary		22	F	Laborer	15Ju02BI
MUFLY, Patrick		20	M	Laborer	15Ju02BI
LAWBER, Finton		25	M	Laborer	15Ju02BI
MOORE, Luke		40	M	Laborer	15Ju02BI
GOLDNICK, Fredrick		20	M	Laborer	15Ju02BI
WILLIAMS, Anne		56	F	Laborer	15Ju02BI
GIBSON, John		30	M	Laborer	15Ju02BI
READEN, Eliza		19	F	Laborer	15Ju02BI
SHARAGAN, Margret		40	F	Laborer	15Ju02BI
David	(S)	11	M	Laborer	15Ju02BI
John	(S)	.06	M	Infant	15Ju02BI
MAHON, Bridget		70	F	Laborer	15Ju02BI
MCDERMOTT, Mary		54	F	Laborer	15Ju02BI
MCDERMOTT, Margret		10	F	Laborer	15Ju02BI
James		13	M	Laborer	15Ju02BI
ONEIL, Ann		24	F	Laborer	15Ju02BI
STANLEY, James		23	M	Laborer	15Ju02BI
LYNCH, John		21	M	Laborer	15Ju02BI
SHACLETER, Eliza		20	F	Laborer	15Ju02BI
MCKEON, Mary		17	F	Laborer	15Ju02BI
DAVITT, Patt		25	M	Laborer	15Ju02BI
COSACK, James		30	M	Laborer	15Ju02BI
MCCUSAN, Thos.		31	M	Laborer	15Ju02BI
GILLEGAN, Bd.		20	F	Laborer	15Ju02BI
KNICKAN, Margret		19	F	Laborer	15Ju02BI
KELLIGAN, Owen		61	M	Laborer	15Ju02BI
U	(W)	60	F	Laborer	15Ju02BI
Matthew	(S)	21	M	Laborer	15Ju02BI
Mary	(D)	19	F	Laborer	15Ju02BI
WALSH, Geo.		21	M	Laborer	15Ju02BI
LINSEY, John		21	M	Laborer	15Ju02BI
SHEILS, Patrick		25	M	Laborer	15Ju02BI
GALLAGHER, John		16	M	Laborer	15Ju02BI
Margret		19	F	Laborer	15Ju02BI
MCCULLOUGH, Magt.		11	F	Laborer	15Ju02BI
MCLOUGHLIN, John		12	M	Laborer	15Ju02BI
RENNICK, James		18	M	Laborer	15Ju02BI
LEONARD, Patrick		19	M	Laborer	15Ju02BI
MAETEN, Julia		18	F	Laborer	15Ju02BI
REILY, Jane		15	F	Laborer	15Ju02BI
MCCABE, John		17	M	Laborer	15Ju02BI
DUFFY, Beyon		11	M	Laborer	15Ju02BI
CRANERN, Michael		14	M	Laborer	15Ju02BI
CONROY, Timothy		13	M	Laborer	15Ju02BI
Catherine		11	F	Laborer	15Ju02BI
MUFLY, Peter		21	M	Laborer	15Ju02BI
FOX, Ann		21	F	Laborer	15Ju02BI
REYNOLDS, Francis		24	M	Laborer	15Ju02BI
MCHUGH, Catherine		25	F	Laborer	15Ju02BI
MORNEL, Margret		27	F	Laborer	15Ju02BI
ARRENEY, Catherine		03	F	Child	15Ju02BI
SHERIDEN, Ellen		50	F	Laborer	15Ju02BI
COYLE, Alice		26	F	Laborer	15Ju02BI
MCGOWN, Betty		12	F	Laborer	15Ju02BI
CONOR, Mary		19	F	Laborer	15Ju02BI
DONAVAN, John		21	M	Laborer	15Ju02BI
HUSSY, Patt		20	M	Laborer	15Ju02BI
MCWILLIAMS, William		27	M	Laborer	15Ju02BI
CONNOR, Ann		19	F	Laborer	15Ju02BI
BLOOMER, Margret		18	F	Laborer	15Ju02BI
MCCORMIC, Mary		24	F	Laborer	15Ju02BI
MAXWELL, Timothy		14	M	Laborer	15Ju02BI
FARRELL, Eliza		16	F	Laborer	15Ju02BI
MCEUTRIE, Ann		14	F	Laborer	15Ju02BI
SHAWLY, Maria		12	F	Laborer	15Ju02BI
COSTELLO, Margret		18	F	Laborer	15Ju02BI
HENLEY, William		61	M	Laborer	15Ju02BI
STAFFORD, Ellen		19	F	Laborer	15Ju02BI
MULDOON, Patrick		20	M	Laborer	15Ju02BI
MCGIRR, Ann		12	F	Laborer	15Ju02BI
Edward		10	M	Laborer	15Ju02BI
Ellen		01	F	Child	15Ju02BI
CONNOR, Mary		30	F	Laborer	15Ju02BI
Margret	(D)	05	F	Child	15Ju02BI
Mary	(D)	04	F	Child	15Ju02BI
FIRMORY, Bridget		.05	F	Infant	15Ju02BI
MURPHY, Mary		15	F	Laborer	15Ju02BI
Died-At-Sea					
ODONNALL, Patt		25	M	Laborer	15Ju02BI
Martha		09	F	Child	15Ju02BI
ROY, John		40	M	Laborer	15Ju02BI
KEENAN, U		03	M	Child	15Ju02BI
WILSON, J.		02	M	Child	15Ju02BI

NAMES OF PASSENGERS	A G E	S E X	OCCUPATIONS	DATE PORT SHIP

ROSCIUS 15 JUNE 1846

From Liverpool

NAMES OF PASSENGERS		A G E	S E X	OCCUPATIONS	DATE PORT SHIP
SHIRR, Peter		50	M	Unknown	15Ju02Bf
Elizabeth	(D)	16	F	Spinster	15Ju02Bf
Ann	(D)	18	F	Spinster	15Ju02Bf
MCWHARTER, Andrew		35	M	Laborer	15Ju02Bf
COLLINS, William		19	M	Merchant	15Ju02Bf
ONEIL, Mary		16	F	Spinster	15Ju02Bf
Bridget		20	F	Spinster	15Ju02Bf
Ann		19	F	Spinster	15Ju02Bf
DELANY, Sarah		15	F	Spinster	15Ju02Bf
BRENIMAN, William		21	M	Laborer	15Ju02Bf
Catherine	(W)	18	F	Spinster	15Ju02Bf
FAGHY, Patrick		20	M	Laborer	15Ju02Bf
HANAN, Ellen		23	F	Spinster	15Ju02Bf
LOLY, Martin		20	M	Laborer	15Ju02Bf
MAURICE, John		36	M	Laborer	15Ju02Bf
Margret	(D)	12	F	Spinster	15Ju02Bf
Michael	(S)	10	M	Unknown	15Ju02Bf
James		23	M	Laborer	15Ju02Bf
Margret		22	F	Spinster	15Ju02Bf
COCHRAN, Sarah		24	F	Spinster	15Ju02Bf
FARRELL, Rose		20	F	Spinster	15Ju02Bf
OBRIEN, Mary		20	F	Spinster	15Ju02Bf
KEELY, Rosetta		20	F	Hatter	15Ju02Bf
MAVERHILL, John		19	M	Laborer	15Ju02Bf
MURPHY, Michael		24	M	Laborer	15Ju02Bf
KEARY, John		25	M	Laborer	15Ju02Bf
LAMB, Owen		35	M	Laborer	15Ju02Bf
EUSTICE, Bridget		19	F	Spinster	15Ju02Bf
PERRYMAN, Jeremiah		30	M	Laborer	15Ju02Bf
DOERING, Jane		17	F	Spinster	15Ju02Bf
PHAGAN, Julia		20	F	Spinster	15Ju02Bf
MURDOCK, Bridget		30	F	Spinster	15Ju02Bf
Elizabeth		17	F	Spinster	15Ju02Bf
LINEHAN, Elizabeth		26	F	Spinster	15Ju02Bf
Margret	(D)	07	F	Child	15Ju02Bf
Eliza	(D)	01	F	Child	15Ju02Bf
BRYAN, Margret		26	F	Dressmaker	15Ju02Bf
John		42	M	Laborer	15Ju02Bf
KEENAN, Patrick		23	M	Laborer	15Ju02Bf
MINES, Neal		17	M	Laborer	15Ju02Bf
BAYLE, John		34	M	Joiner	15Ju02Bf
PERRYMAN, Cathrine		52	F	Spinster	15Ju02Bf
William	(S)	26	M	Laborer	15Ju02Bf
Ann	(D)	23	F	Spinster	15Ju02Bf
Mary	(D)	21	F	Spinster	15Ju02Bf
Charles	(S)	18	M	Blacksmith	15Ju02Bf
Catharine	(D)	15	F	Spinster	15Ju02Bf
FRAZER, Elizabeth		17	F	Spinster	15Ju02Bf
NENON, John		13	M	Laborer	15Ju02Bf
REARDAN, James		20	M	Laborer	15Ju02Bf
DORLY, John		30	M	Blacksmith	15Ju02Bf
Mary	(W)	25	F	Spinster	15Ju02Bf
Catharine	(D)	03	F	Child	15Ju02Bf
Francis	(S)	01	M	Child	15Ju02Bf
Agness		18	F	Spinster	15Ju02Bf
MCCULLY, Owen		21	M	Shoemaker	15Ju02Bf
HANDRIN, Leroy		29	M	Laborer	15Ju02Bf
Ellen	(W)	24	F	Spinster	15Ju02Bf
FLINN, Timothy		21	M	Carpenter	15Ju02Bf
BORING, Thomas		26	M	Laborer	15Ju02Bf
Winfred		26	F	Spinster	15Ju02Bf
FITZMORRIS, Thomas		54	M	Laborer	15Ju02Bf
Margret	(W)	54	F	Spinster	15Ju02Bf
Mathew	(S)	23	M	Laborer	15Ju02Bf
Dennis	(S)	17	M	Laborer	15Ju02Bf

NAMES OF PASSENGERS		A G E	S E X	OCCUPATIONS	DATE PORT SHIP
FITZMORRIS, Norris	(S)	22	M	Laborer	15Ju02Bf
Ellen	(D)	20	F	Spinster	15Ju02Bf
Margret	(D)	18	F	Spinster	15Ju02Bf
MURPHY, Patrick		26	M	Laborer	15Ju02Bf
PURCELL, Edmund		24	M	Laborer	15Ju02Bf
MAHONY, Bartolomew		28	M	Tailor	15Ju02Bf
PEARSE, Michael		30	M	Mason	15Ju02Bf
Catherine	(W)	24	F	Spinster	15Ju02Bf
Ann	(D)	06	F	Child	15Ju02Bf
Mary	(D)	.03	F	Infant	15Ju02Bf
COLLINS, James		24	M	Farmer	15Ju02Bf
Mary		22	F	Spinster	15Ju02Bf
KING, Roddy		26	M	Laborer	15Ju02Bf
Bridget		23	F	Spinster	15Ju02Bf
HARRINGTON, Daniel		35	M	Merchant	15Ju02Bf
NEAGLE, Margret		24	F	Spinster	15Ju02Bf
STILNE, Johanna		18	F	Spinster	15Ju02Bf
FLING, Ellen		22	F	Spinster	15Ju02Bf
SHERDIN, James		24	M	Merchant	15Ju02Bf
FITZGERALD, Alexr.		28	M	Laborer	15Ju02Bf
HAYE, Bryen		24	M	Laborer	15Ju02Bf
DONELY, William		28	M	Laborer	15Ju02Bf
Catharine	(W)	28	F	Dressmaker	15Ju02Bf
BARRINGTON, Nicholas		24	M	Laborer	15Ju02Bf
EASAK, Joseph		23	M	Painter	15Ju02Bf
BURNS, John		22	M	Mason	15Ju02Bf
DONUHY, John		30	M	Laborer	15Ju02Bf
CASEY, Ellen		22	F	Spinster	15Ju02Bf
OWEN, Michel		25	M	Laborer	15Ju02Bf
Margret		21	F	Spinster	15Ju02Bf
KELLY, William		14	M	Laborer	15Ju02Bf
PHAGAN, Elizabeth		18	F	Spinster	15Ju02Bf
KING, Mary		18	F	Spinster	15Ju02Bf
KEARL, Julia		20	F	Spinster	15Ju02Bf
HINES, Mathew		27	M	Tailor	15Ju02Bf
SMITH, Ann		19	F	Dressmaker	15Ju02Bf
Catharine		17	F	Spinster	15Ju02Bf
BINNY, Ann		24	F	Spinster	15Ju02Bf
SOMERS, Johanna		20	F	Spinster	15Ju02Bf
STEWART, William		16	M	Laborer	15Ju02Bf
George-S.		14	M	Laborer	15Ju02Bf
DOUGHERTY, Patrick		20	M	Laborer	15Ju02Bf
MCANULLY, Patrick		21	M	Laborer	15Ju02Bf
Patrick		21	M	Laborer	15Ju02Bf
APPY, Patrick		26	M	Laborer	15Ju02Bf
ELLIGETT, Mary		15	F	Spinster	15Ju02Bf
KULE, Lucy		11	F	Spinster	15Ju02Bf
ELLIGETT, Catharine		10	F	Spinster	15Ju02Bf
DUFFY, James		22	M	Engraver	15Ju02Bf
MELLAN, Thomas		26	M	Laborer	15Ju02Bf
PADLOUR, Daniel		48	M	Farmer	15Ju02Bf
Thomas		19	M	Farmer	15Ju02Bf
NOLEN, Patrick		38	M	Farmer	15Ju02Bf
DAVIS, Edmund		19	M	Carpenter	15Ju02Bf
LAMB, Patrick		19	M	Laborer	15Ju02Bf
Catherine		28	F	Spinster	15Ju02Bf
Bernard		36	M	Laborer	15Ju02Bf
John		34	M	Laborer	15Ju02Bf
Elizabeth		10	F	Spinster	15Ju02Bf
Bridget		08	F	Child	15Ju02Bf
CASEY, John		06	M	Child	15Ju02Bf
MCGEE, Margret		04	F	Child	15Ju02Bf
NENAN, Daniel		22	M	Laborer	15Ju02Bf
CURRY, Mary		26	F	Dressmaker	15Ju02Bf
DUFFY, Ann		24	F	Dressmaker	15Ju02Bf
DUNN, Mary		20	F	Spinster	15Ju02Bf
FLANAGAN, Thomas-K.		22	M	Clerk	15Ju02Bf
Rebecca		22	F	Spinster	15Ju02Bf
KERNAN, Mary-A.		21	F	Spinster	15Ju02Bf
MAURICE, Mary		36	F	Spinster	15Ju02Bf
BROPHY, Roddy		11	M	Spinster	15Ju02Bf
LAWLESS, Christopher		24	M	Laborer	15Ju02Bf
Elizabeth	(W)	22	F	Spinster	15Ju02Bf
POWER, William		23	M	Lawyer	15Ju02Bf
DUNN, Patrick		35	M	Laborer	15Ju02Bf

NAMES OF PASSENGERS		A G E	S E X	OCCUPATIONS	DATE PORT SHIP	NAMES OF PASSENGERS		A G E	S E X	OCCUPATIONS	DATE PORT SHIP
KENTING, John		20	M	Laborer	15Ju02Bf	DIVINE, Mary		19	F	Spinster	15Ju02Bf
FARREL, James		58	M	Laborer	15Ju02Bf	KENEDY, Margret		21	F	Dressmaker	15Ju02Bf
Mary	(W)	50	F	Spinster	15Ju02Bf	FAIN, Bridget		10	F	Spinster	15Ju02Bf
Mary	(D)	20	F	Spinster	15Ju02Bf	CAUGHLIN, James		16	M	Laborer	15Ju02Bf
Morris	(S)	18	M	Laborer	15Ju02Bf	LINCH, Catharine		24	F	Spinster	15Ju02Bf
James	(S)	16	M	Laborer	15Ju02Bf	CUNNINGHAM, Bridget		20	F	Spinster	15Ju02Bf
Madge	(D)	14	F	Laborer	15Ju02Bf	DONELLY, Michael		18	M	Laborer	15Ju02Bf
Jerry	(S)	12	M	Laborer	15Ju02Bf						
Daniel	(S)	10	M	Laborer	15Ju02Bf						
Ellen	(D)	08	F	Child	15Ju02Bf						
Patrick	(S)	06	M	Child	15Ju02Bf						
John	(S)	01	F	Child	15Ju02Bf						
Narry		36	M	Laborer	15Ju02Bf						
William		02		Child	15Ju02Bf			**GREAT-WESTERN 15 JUNE 1846**				
CORRINGHAM, Francis		20	M	Laborer	15Ju02Bf						
MOAN, Francis		12	M	Laborer	15Ju02Bf			From Liverpool				
HUSTON, John		24	M	Laborer	15Ju02Bf						
Frances	(W)	26	F	Spinster	15Ju02Bf						
John	(S)	01	M	Child	15Ju02Bf	CHICHESTER, Chas.		40	M	Ay-Ltcol	15Ju02Cy
CRAYON, Catharine		20	F	Spinster	15Ju02Bf	C.	(W)	36	F	Wife	15Ju02Cy
LAYLOR, Mary		20	F	Spinster	15Ju02Bf	Amy	(D)	06	F	Child	15Ju02Cy
SHANEN, Timothy		23	M	Laborer	15Ju02Bf	C.	(D)	05	F	Child	15Ju02Cy
ROGERS, Ann		52	F	Spinster	15Ju02Bf	HUGHES, S.		20	F	Servant	15Ju02Cy
John		15	M	Laborer	15Ju02Bf	GRADY, C.		25	F	Servant	15Ju02Cy
Eliza		09	F	Laborer	15Ju02Bf	FLEUSETT, J.		26	M	Servant	15Ju02Cy
LAWER, Mary		21	F	Spinster	15Ju02Bf	MORSON, L.		27	F	Lady	15Ju02Cy
BARRETT, Ellen		23	F	Spinster	15Ju02Bf	MILLS, Thos.		26	M	Gentleman	15Ju02Cy
CARLY, Ellen		20	F	Spinster	15Ju02Bf	E.	(W)	23	F	Wife	15Ju02Cy
COSGROVE, William		30	M	Laborer	15Ju02Bf	Wm.	(S)	02	M	Child	15Ju02Cy
EGMYTON, Wellimy		21	M	Laborer	15Ju02Bf	Clara	(D)	04	F	Child	15Ju02Cy
Ellen		18	F	Spinster	15Ju02Bf	WATTS, M.		26	F	Servant	15Ju02Cy
DAILY, James		26	M	Laborer	15Ju02Bf	WOODS, L.		36	F	Lady	15Ju02Cy
ROCKFORD, Edward		42	M	Laborer	15Ju02Bf	U	(S)	10	M	Unknown	15Ju02Cy
LEONARD, Mary		24	F	Spinster	15Ju02Bf	J.	(D)	04	F	Child	15Ju02Cy
RORKE, Catharine		20	F	Spinster	15Ju02Bf	Geo.	(S)	05	M	Child	15Ju02Cy
KILY, John		26	M	Laborer	15Ju02Bf	HALLEN, G.		52	M	Gentleman	15Ju02Cy
Mary		25	F	Spinster	15Ju02Bf	S.	(W)	50	F	Wife	15Ju02Cy
CLANAN, Ann		15	F	Carpenter	15Ju02Bf	GALT, M.		40	F	Lady	15Ju02Cy
MURPHY, Catharine		15	F	Unknown	15Ju02Bf	CRUISE, Anna		20	F	Lady	15Ju02Cy
MAIDE, James		26	M	Laborer	15Ju02Bf	HOWELL, E.		17	M	Ay-Lt	15Ju02Cy
Mary		23	F	Spinster	15Ju02Bf	PAULSON, G.		29	M	Merchant	15Ju02Cy
CROAK, James		27	M	Carpenter	15Ju02Bf	LENDAM, W.		25	M	Merchant	15Ju02Cy
Bridget	(W)	29	F	Spinster	15Ju02Bf	ROBINSON, T.		26	M	Gentleman	15Ju02Cy
John	(S)	.05	M	Infant	15Ju02Bf	BIRT, W.		50	M	Gentleman	15Ju02Cy
CAMPBELL, William		30	M	Laborer	15Ju02Bf	BRADLEY, J.N.		32	M	Gentleman	15Ju02Cy
MURRY, John		24	M	Laborer	15Ju02Bf	M.	(W)	21	F	Wife	15Ju02Cy
Ann		19	F	Spinster	15Ju02Bf	BRISTED, C.A.		22	M	Merchant	15Ju02Cy
LINCHAN, Anna		19	F	Spinster	15Ju02Bf	PUNNETT, Jno.		34	M	Gentleman	15Ju02Cy
PHURA, Catharine		19	F	Spinster	15Ju02Bf	J.	(W)	20	F	Wife	15Ju02Cy
CROAK, John		26	M	Laborer	15Ju02Bf	M.		21	F	Lady	15Ju02Cy
Margaret		26	F	Spinster	15Ju02Bf	M.E.		22	F	Lady	15Ju02Cy
HORE, James		22	M	Spinster	15Ju02Bf	PROCTOR, T.H.		30	M	Merchant	15Ju02Cy
Bridget		18	F	Spinster	15Ju02Bf	RICKETTS, H.		13	M	Gentleman	15Ju02Cy
COSTELLA, Honora		18	F	Spinster	15Ju02Bf	WILLETT, A.		23	M	Gentleman	15Ju02Cy
BIRNE, Hugh		22	M	Laborer	15Ju02Bf	BICKFORD, C.		36	M	Gentleman	15Ju02Cy
Michael		23	M	Laborer	15Ju02Bf	BROOKE, Jno.		27	M	Merchant	15Ju02Cy
ROPER, Nancy		15	F	Spinster	15Ju02Bf	FORMIN, Wm.		30	M	Gentleman	15Ju02Cy
DOUGHERTY, John		26	M	Blacksmith	15Ju02Bf	ROBINSON, Wm.		34	M	Gentleman	15Ju02Cy
MCINREW, Joseph		30	M	Blacksmith	15Ju02Bf	MAHARG, J.		20	F	Lady	15Ju02Cy
KEOGH, James		27	M	Blacksmith	15Ju02Bf	WILSON, M.		22	F	Servant	15Ju02Cy
Catharine	(W)	27	F	Spinster	15Ju02Bf	HAMPTON, Ann		22	F	Servant	15Ju02Cy
Margret	(D)	01	F	Child	15Ju02Bf						
MILLIN, Thomas		24	M	Laborer	15Ju02Bf						
Mary		00	F	Spinster	15Ju02Bf						
ODONELL, Jane		30	F	Spinster	15Ju02Bf						
SMITH, Conner		25	M	Unknown	15Ju02Bf			**REGULUS 16 JUNE 1846**				
ONEIL, Hugh		18	M	Butcher	15Ju02Bf						
SCANNELL, William		50	M	Laborer	15Ju02Bf			From Liverpool				
James	(S)	20	M	Laborer	15Ju02Bf						
Timothy	(S)	18	M	Laborer	15Ju02Bf						
FRAZER, Ann		20	F	Spinster	15Ju02Bf						
KEY, Hannah		17	F	Spinster	15Ju02Bf	ROWAN, Thomas		42	M	Servant	16Ju02Ep
FAY, Martin		20	M	Surveyor	15Ju02Bf	U		40	M	Servant	16Ju02Ep
CAURSIN, Mary		10	F	Spinster	15Ju02Bf	Kitty	(D)	08	F	Child	16Ju02Ep
Bridget		23	F	Spinster	15Ju02Bf						

NAMES OF PASSENGERS	A G E	S E X	OCCUPATIONS	DATE PORT SHIP	NAMES OF PASSENGERS	A G E	S E X	OCCUPATIONS	DATE PORT SHIP
ROWAN, Walty	(S)	06 M	Child	16Ju02Ep	STEPHENSON, Ann	23 F	Servant	16Ju02Ep
Anthony	(S)	04 M	Child	16Ju02Ep	DENN, William	30 M	Servant	16Ju02Ep
William	(S)	01 M	Child	16Ju02Ep	MCDERMISH, Terry	30 M	Servant	16Ju02Ep
RAGAN, John		26 M	Servant	16Ju02Ep	Bridget	30 F	Servant	16Ju02Ep
_atherine		05 F	Child	16Ju02Ep	Nenny	26 F	Servant	16Ju02Ep
ODONAL, John		46 M	Servant	16Ju02Ep	Mary	11 F	Servant	16Ju02Ep
Mary	(W)	44 F	Servant	16Ju02Ep	Patrick	09 M	Child	16Ju02Ep
James	(S)	03 M	Child	16Ju02Ep	Bridget	.00 F	Infant	16Ju02Ep
SHIELDS, U		30 M	Servant	16Ju02Ep	CLAGY, Abraham	18 M	Servant	16Ju02Ep
James		20 M	Tailor	16Ju02Ep	KERGON, Margret	22 F	Servant	16Ju02Ep
Silvaster		02 M	Child	16Ju02Ep	MARTIN, Mary	19 F	Servant	16Ju02Ep
ONEAL, Biddy		25 F	Servant	16Ju02Ep				
WELSH, William		27 M	Servant	16Ju02Ep				
Ellen		25 F	Servant	16Ju02Ep				
FURGISON, David		27 M	Servant	16Ju02Ep				
WENNCYSE, James		25 M	Servant	16Ju02Ep				
Mary		45 F	Servant	16Ju02Ep	JOHN-CAMPBELL 16 JUNE 1846			
REED, James		16 M	Servant	16Ju02Ep				
QUIHIN, James		25 M	Servant	16Ju02Ep	From Liverpool			
Mary		21 F	Servant	16Ju02Ep				
FITZPATRICK, Mick		23 M	Servant	16Ju02Ep				
Honora		24 F	Servant	16Ju02Ep	ATHERLEE, William	21 M	Laborer	16Ju02Eq
MURRAY, Mary		35 F	Servant	16Ju02Ep	REARDON, John	22 M	Laborer	16Ju02Eq
Biddy		13 F	Servant	16Ju02Ep	DUNN, William	24 M	Laborer	16Ju02Eq
Patrick		11 M	Servant	16Ju02Ep	ATHERLEE, Michael	22 M	Laborer	16Ju02Eq
John		09 M	Child	16Ju02Ep	HANLEY, Timothy	19 M	Laborer	16Ju02Eq
Michal		07 M	Child	16Ju02Ep	FERROLL, Edward	21 M	Laborer	16Ju02Eq
Mary		05 F	Child	16Ju02Ep	HENNESSY, Ellen	17 F	Laborer	16Ju02Eq
Thomas		02 M	Child	16Ju02Ep	John	21 M	Laborer	16Ju02Eq
HESHIN, Patrick		32 M	Farmer	16Ju02Ep	MCINTYRE, Susan	18 F	Laborer	16Ju02Eq
Michael		26 M	Farmer	16Ju02Ep	REILLY, Mary	18 F	Laborer	16Ju02Eq
MURRAY, John		23 M	Farmer	16Ju02Ep	KELLY, Margaret	21 F	Laborer	16Ju02Eq
MALLOY, Michal		48 M	Farmer	16Ju02Ep	Thomas	19 M	Laborer	16Ju02Eq
Bridget	(W)	48 F	Unknown	16Ju02Ep	SLATTERY, John	25 M	Laborer	16Ju02Eq
John	(S)	08 M	Child	16Ju02Ep	WOLF, Henry-Boyle	25 M	Clerk	16Ju02Eq
MARRIN, Bridget		13 F	Unknown	16Ju02Ep	MARSHALL, Bridget	26 F	Servant	16Ju02Eq
BUTLER, Catherine		22 F	Unknown	16Ju02Ep	Johanna	22 F	Servant	16Ju02Eq
GREALEY, Patrick		19 M	Farmer	16Ju02Ep	COTTES, Mary	19 F	Servant	16Ju02Eq
BILL, Benn		19 M	Farmer	16Ju02Ep	Ellen	17 F	Servant	16Ju02Eq
KENEDY, Robert		28 M	Farmer	16Ju02Ep	REALLY, Martin	25 M	Servant	16Ju02Eq
Ann		24 F	Unknown	16Ju02Ep	SWEENEY, Patrick	21 M	Servant	16Ju02Eq
WILSON, James		36 M	Farmer	16Ju02Ep	DORAN, Samuel	28 M	Servant	16Ju02Eq
ROSS, U		35 M	Farmer	16Ju02Ep	CORBETT, William	20 M	Servant	16Ju02Eq
Joseph		13 M	Servant	16Ju02Ep	MAHONEY, Dennis	27 M	Servant	16Ju02Eq
William		11 M	Servant	16Ju02Ep	Mary	23 F	Servant	16Ju02Eq
FERGUSON, Dwardy		45 M	Servant	16Ju02Ep	FENNELL, Bridget	21 F	Servant	16Ju02Eq
ALLAR, Mary		40 F	Servant	16Ju02Ep	MAHON, Catherine	27 F	Servant	16Ju02Eq
Joseph		22 M	Servant	16Ju02Ep	CALLAHAN, James	26 M	Servant	16Ju02Eq
James		19 M	Servant	16Ju02Ep	HAYS, Martin	22 M	Servant	16Ju02Eq
Eliza		20 F	Servant	16Ju02Ep	Bridget	20 F	Servant	16Ju02Eq
Ann		11 F	Servant	16Ju02Ep	Catherine	18 F	Servant	16Ju02Eq
Catherine		09 F	Child	16Ju02Ep	MCGARRITY, Biddy	19 F	Servant	16Ju02Eq
RAFFERTY, Edward		30 M	Servant	16Ju02Ep	MCLANE, Ellen	19 F	Servant	16Ju02Eq
Mary		03 F	Child	16Ju02Ep	HAGAN, Sarah	20 F	Servant	16Ju02Eq
Catherine		02 F	Child	16Ju02Ep	MCQUADE, Sarah	29 F	Servant	16Ju02Eq
GWAEY, Rose		26 F	Servant	16Ju02Ep	Owen	23 M	Servant	16Ju02Eq
BARR, James		24 M	Servant	16Ju02Ep	HOBBS, John	18 M	Servant	16Ju02Eq
MCCARDLE, Edward		40 M	Servant	16Ju02Ep	NORMAN, Margaret	20 F	Servant	16Ju02Eq
Elisabethe		35 F	Servant	16Ju02Ep	LITTLE, Mary	19 F	Servant	16Ju02Eq
Judth		22 F	Servant	16Ju02Ep	Simon	16 M	Farmer	16Ju02Eq
Rose	(D)	08 F	Child	16Ju02Ep	John	11 M	Farmer	16Ju02Eq
Mary	(D)	04 F	Child	16Ju02Ep	U, Martin	53 M	Farmer	16Ju02Eq
Ann	(D)	01 F	Child	16Ju02Ep	MCCABE, John	24 M	Farmer	16Ju02Eq
ROULAND, William		15 M	Servant	16Ju02Ep	QUIGLEY, Thomas	19 M	Farmer	16Ju02Eq
Elisabeth		17 F	Servant	16Ju02Ep	CAMERON, James	30 M	Farmer	16Ju02Eq
James		15 M	Servant	16Ju02Ep	GERSTON, Catherine	27 F	Servant	16Ju02Eq
GILY, Elledever		22 M	Servant	16Ju02Ep	COLEMAN, John	30 M	Servant	16Ju02Eq
MCGURR, John		23 M	Servant	16Ju02Ep	U	(W)	30 F	Servant	16Ju02Eq
MARIT, Margret		28 F	Servant	16Ju02Ep	U	.00 U	Infant	16Ju02Eq
MALAHY, Ellen		80 F	Servant	16Ju02Ep	Patrick	27 M	Servant	16Ju02Eq
Edward	(S)	36 M	Servant	16Ju02Ep	RADDY, Michael	20 M	Servant	16Ju02Eq
Mary	(L)	30 F	Servant	16Ju02Ep	U	.00 U	Infant	16Ju02Eq
Thomas	(S)	.00 M	Infant	16Ju02Ep	INWRIGH, Thos.	36 M	Servant	16Ju02Eq
FAREY, Biddy		60 F	Servant	16Ju02Ep	DAWSON, James	22 M	Servant	16Ju02Eq
STEPHENSON, David		28 M	Servant	16Ju02Ep				

NAMES OF PASSENGERS		AGE	SEX	OCCUPATIONS	DATE PORT SHIP	NAMES OF PASSENGERS	AGE	SEX	OCCUPATIONS	DATE PORT SHIP
DAWSON, U	(W)	21	F	Servant	16Ju02Eq	JONES, Elizabeth	22	F	Servant	16Ju02Eq
ENWRIGHT, Thomas		22	M	Servant	16Ju02Eq	U	.00	U	Infant	16Ju02Eq
U	(W)	20	F	Servant	16Ju02Eq	MCCLORKEY, Auther	18	M	Laborer	16Ju02Eq
DAWSON, Ellen		21	F	Servant	16Ju02Eq	GANNON, Dennis	06	M	Child	16Ju02Eq
MCDONNELL, Thomas		24	M	Servant	16Ju02Eq	MAHONE, Dennis	27	M	Laborer	16Ju02Eq
DEERMODY, James		27	M	Servant	16Ju02Eq	CAMPBELL, Edward	20	M	Laborer	16Ju02Eq
James		22	M	Servant	16Ju02Eq	GEUOLE, Edward	21	M	Laborer	16Ju02Eq
MURPHY, Jonas		20	M	Servant	16Ju02Eq	FEENEY, James	26	M	Laborer	16Ju02Eq
MCLANE, James		20	M	Servant	16Ju02Eq	RAY, James	28	M	Laborer	16Ju02Eq
DIMOND, Charles		24	M	Servant	16Ju02Eq	BANATT, John	23	M	Laborer	16Ju02Eq
FULTON, Margaret		21	F	Servant	16Ju02Eq	COLEMAN, James	30	M	Laborer	16Ju02Eq
John		19	M	Servant	16Ju02Eq	GORMLEY, Mark	30	M	Servant	16Ju02Eq
MURPHY, Johanna		34	F	Servant	16Ju02Eq	HEMMING, Michael	26	M	Servant	16Ju02Eq
U		.00	U	Infant	16Ju02Eq	BOHEN, Michael	22	M	Servant	16Ju02Eq
CONNOR, Patrick		33	M	Servant	16Ju02Eq	KEENEY, Patrick	27	M	Servant	16Ju02Eq
HIGGINS, John		21	M	Servant	16Ju02Eq	CONELLY, Patrick	31	M	Servant	16Ju02Eq
MULLIN, Mary		23	F	Servant	16Ju02Eq	DORAN, Samuel	28	M	Servant	16Ju02Eq
MARTIN, Mary		19	F	Servant	16Ju02Eq	SWEENEY, William	33	M	Laborer	16Ju02Eq
SHAW, William		23	M	Servant	16Ju02Eq	GILL, Ann	18	F	Laborer	16Ju02Eq
U	(W)	21	F	Servant	16Ju02Eq	HUGHES, Ann	23	F	Laborer	16Ju02Eq
Elizabeth		17	F	Servant	16Ju02Eq	U	.00	U	Infant	16Ju02Eq
MCCARTY, Charles		30	M	Servant	16Ju02Eq	MCCARRA, Bridget	19	F	Laborer	16Ju02Eq
DAVY, Mary		18	F	Servant	16Ju02Eq	CAVERY, Bridget	20	F	Laborer	16Ju02Eq
SHE, Michael		46	M	Servant	16Ju02Eq	U	.00	U	Infant	16Ju02Eq
Bridget		20	F	Servant	16Ju02Eq	GILL, Bridget	35	F	Laborer	16Ju02Eq
Mary		17	F	Servant	16Ju02Eq	MCDERMOT, Bridget	25	F	Laborer	16Ju02Eq
CAFFEE, Eliza.		20	F	Servant	16Ju02Eq	CAROLINE, Catherine	20	F	Laborer	16Ju02Eq
MCTAGGART, John		18	M	Servant	16Ju02Eq	MCGORMAN, Catherine	18	F	Servant	16Ju02Eq
Ellen		17	F	Servant	16Ju02Eq	CANNON, Bridget	19	F	Servant	16Ju02Eq
MCCOLLEN, Peter		17	M	Servant	16Ju02Eq	KEENEY, Elizabeth	26	F	Servant	16Ju02Eq
Elizabeth		18	F	Servant	16Ju02Eq	LIVERTY, Honora	19	F	Servant	16Ju02Eq
BRADY, Ellen		17	F	Servant	16Ju02Eq	POWER, Johanna	21	F	Servant	16Ju02Eq
Ellen		24	F	Servant	16Ju02Eq	BURNS, Margaret	22	F	Servant	16Ju02Eq
Hugh		24	M	Servant	16Ju02Eq	MURPHY, Mary-Ann	30	F	Servant	16Ju02Eq
REILLY, Mary		22	F	Servant	16Ju02Eq	CONNOR, Thomas	22	M	Servant	16Ju02Eq
MCCARTHY, Margt.		21	F	Servant	16Ju02Eq	MCDERMOT, Richard	22	M	Servant	16Ju02Eq
BRADY, Patrick		24	M	Servant	16Ju02Eq	MALONE, Mike	21	M	Servant	16Ju02Eq
Biddy		21	F	Servant	16Ju02Eq	OHARRA, Michael	22	M	Servant	16Ju02Eq
Margaret		30	F	Servant	16Ju02Eq	NAILER, John	19	M	Servant	16Ju02Eq
HINES, Morris		30	M	Servant	16Ju02Eq	CONNELL, John	22	M	Servant	16Ju02Eq
SMITH, Patrick		26	M	Servant	16Ju02Eq	CONDEN, John	25	M	Servant	16Ju02Eq
U	(W)	22	F	Servant	16Ju02Eq	SULLIVAN, Michael	24	M	Servant	16Ju02Eq
Bridget		20	F	Servant	16Ju02Eq	CAMPBELL, Patrick	21	M	Servant	16Ju02Eq
HUGHES, John		22	M	Laborer	16Ju02Eq	KELLY, Patrick	30	M	Servant	16Ju02Eq
MURRAY, Michael		21	M	Laborer	16Ju02Eq	Catherine	20	F	Servant	16Ju02Eq
Atley		18	M	Laborer	16Ju02Eq	MCCOUNT, Kenneth	20	M	Servant	16Ju02Eq
COLEMAN, Michael		20	M	Laborer	16Ju02Eq	CRAWLEY, Thomas	21	M	Servant	16Ju02Eq
MONAHAN, Elizabeth		16	F	Servant	16Ju02Eq	WARD, Patrick	29	M	Servant	16Ju02Eq
CASEY, Matthew		30	M	Servant	16Ju02Eq	KEAN, Morris	27	M	Servant	16Ju02Eq
BUCK, Mary		26	F	Servant	16Ju02Eq	NOON, Peter	25	M	Servant	16Ju02Eq
Catherine		22	F	Servant	16Ju02Eq	KEAN, Kitty	20	F	Servant	16Ju02Eq
CAFRADY, Phillp		22	M	Servant	16Ju02Eq	CALLAHAN, James	26	M	Servant	16Ju02Eq
Biddy		18	F	Servant	16Ju02Eq	HAGAN, James	24	M	Servant	16Ju02Eq
Catherine		18	F	Servant	16Ju02Eq	MAY, Larry	22	M	Servant	16Ju02Eq
FEGAN, John		16	M	Servant	16Ju02Eq	GELMOUR, Johanna	21	F	Servant	16Ju02Eq
DONAHUE, Thomas		40	M	Servant	16Ju02Eq	POWER, Mary-Anna	19	F	Servant	16Ju02Eq
MUNSTAR, Peter		19	M	Servant	16Ju02Eq	NOLFERMAN, Catherine	22	F	Servant	16Ju02Eq
SMITH, Michael		24	M	Servant	16Ju02Eq	DONNELLY, John	20	M	Servant	16Ju02Eq
NOLAN, Bridget		19	F	Servant	16Ju02Eq	BOGLER, Thomas	16	M	Servant	16Ju02Eq
HUGHES, Bridget		21	F	Servant	16Ju02Eq	DARLING, James	22	M	Servant	16Ju02Eq
FEE, Mary		13	F	Servant	16Ju02Eq	MCCARTHY, Donald	22	M	Servant	16Ju02Eq
Ellen		11	F	Servant	16Ju02Eq	LYONS, Ellen	19	F	Servant	16Ju02Eq
Alexander		09	M	Child	16Ju02Eq	CAMPBELL, John	22	M	Servant	16Ju02Eq
KENNEDY, Edward		31	M	Servant	16Ju02Eq	MCKELLAN, Ann	19	F	Servant	16Ju02Eq
KELLY, Patrick		31	M	Servant	16Ju02Eq	MCGUINESS, Bridget	20	F	Servant	16Ju02Eq
Catherine		30	F	Servant	16Ju02Eq	ONEAL, Bridget	16	F	Servant	16Ju02Eq
BUCK, Catherine		20	F	Servant	16Ju02Eq	BRADLEY, Margaret	22	F	Servant	16Ju02Eq
COURLEY, Thomas		18	M	Servant	16Ju02Eq	GOULDING, Ann	18	F	Servant	16Ju02Eq
QUIN, Hugh		22	M	Servant	16Ju02Eq	BURNS, Catherine	21	F	Servant	16Ju02Eq
Biddy		18	F	Servant	16Ju02Eq	CORMICK, John	29	M	Servant	16Ju02Eq
MURPHY, John		34	M	Servant	16Ju02Eq	MAHON, Michael	24	M	Servant	16Ju02Eq
BOREY, Patrick		21	M	Servant	16Ju02Eq	LYONS, Ellen	18	F	Servant	16Ju02Eq
EARLY, Catherine		22	F	Servant	16Ju02Eq	MCCARTHY, Mary	19	F	Seamstress	16Ju02Eq
U		.00	U	Infant	16Ju02Eq	QUINLAN, Johanna	30	F	Seamstress	16Ju02Eq
HIGGINBOTTOM, William		40	M	Servant	16Ju02Eq	Bridget	27	F	Seamstress	16Ju02Eq

NAMES OF PASSENGERS		A G E	S E X	OCCUPATIONS	DATE PORT SHIP
MAHON, Catherine		13	F	Seamstress	16Ju02Eq
REILLY, Mary		19	F	Seamstress	16Ju02Eq
ONEAL, Bridget		16	F	Seamstress	16Ju02Eq
SWEENEY, Morris		22	M	Laborer	16Ju02Eq
NOON, Peter		25	M	Laborer	16Ju02Eq

LAUREL 16 JUNE 1846

From Liverpool

NAMES OF PASSENGERS		A G E	S E X	OCCUPATIONS	DATE PORT SHIP
BURNE, Eliza		40	F	Wife	16Ju02Er
Eliza	(D)	20	F	Unknown	16Ju02Er
Isabella	(D)	18	F	Unknown	16Ju02Er
Wm.	(S)	18	M	Unknown	16Ju02Er
Ursulla	(D)	10	F	Unknown	16Ju02Er
Saml.	(S)	09	M	Child	16Ju02Er
Epheralme	(S)	07	M	Child	16Ju02Er
CASLULLY, Dennis		20	M	Laborer	16Ju02Er
Peggy		40	F	Unknown	16Ju02Er
Bridget		06	F	Child	16Ju02Er
Mebe		04	U	Child	16Ju02Er
Dennis		02	M	Child	16Ju02Er
Margt.		.00	F	Infant	16Ju02Er
TULLY, Cathe.		24	F	Spinster	16Ju02Er
CONLAN, Pat.		25	M	Laborer	16Ju02Er
QUIGLEY, Chas.		20	M	Laborer	16Ju02Er
CARTY, Mary		24	F	Spinster	16Ju02Er
CAMPBELL, Jas.		26	M	Laborer	16Ju02Er
Ann		28	F	Unknown	16Ju02Er
Mary		35	F	Unknown	16Ju02Er
LEVIN, Martha		22	F	Spinster	16Ju02Er
Francis		20	M	Unknown	16Ju02Er
CAVANAGH, Pat		28	M	Laborer	16Ju02Er
Mary		20	F	Unknown	16Ju02Er
Jane		10	F	Unknown	16Ju02Er
Athe.	(C)	07	F	Child	16Ju02Er
Wm.		05	M	Child	16Ju02Er
BROWN, Ally		40	F	Wife	16Ju02Er
Ann	(D)	04	F	Child	16Ju02Er
Thos.	(S)	04	M	Child	16Ju02Er
Jos.	(S)	02	M	Child	16Ju02Er
Jane	(M)	70	F	Unknown	16Ju02Er
Cathe.		50	F	Unknown	16Ju02Er
ADAMS, Mary		19	F	Spinster	16Ju02Er
FARRELL, Cathe.		20	F	Unknown	16Ju02Er
KENNEDY, Jno.		40	M	Laborer	16Ju02Er
Jno.	(S)	19	M	Unknown	16Ju02Er
Bridget	(D)	18	F	Unknown	16Ju02Er
FERNEY, Biddy		24	F	Spinster	16Ju02Er
KENNY, Thos.		12	M	Laborer	16Ju02Er
Pat.	(B)	10	M	Unknown	16Ju02Er
Margt.	(T)	16	F	Unknown	16Ju02Er
MULLIGAN, Cathe.		18	F	Spinster	16Ju02Er
MCKEAN, Martha		15	F	Spinster	16Ju02Er
Eliza		03	F	Child	16Ju02Er
Wm.		.00	M	Infant	16Ju02Er
REID, Chr.		21	M	Laborer	16Ju02Er
Bridget		18	F	Unknown	16Ju02Er
Francis		18	M	Unknown	16Ju02Er
Frances		21	F	Unknown	16Ju02Er
CARTY, Ann		21	F	Spinster	16Ju02Er
ANGES, Mary		21	F	Spinster	16Ju02Er
Cathe.		18	F	Unknown	16Ju02Er
WILLIAMS, Jos.		54	M	Laborer	16Ju02Er
Sarah	(W)	50	F	Unknown	16Ju02Er
Thos.	(S)	18	M	Unknown	16Ju02Er
Saml.	(S)	19	M	Unknown	16Ju02Er
Nora	(D)	12	F	Unknown	16Ju02Er
Reese	(S)	09	M	Child	16Ju02Er
WILLIAMS, Jerenan	(S)	07	M	Child	16Ju02Er
KERR, Robt.		35	M	Laborer	16Ju02Er
Jane	(W)	30	F	Unknown	16Ju02Er
Martha	(D)	10	F	Child	16Ju02Er
Jas.	(S)	06	M	Child	16Ju02Er
MCNEIL, Edw.		21	M	Laborer	16Ju02Er
Mary		20	F	Spinster	16Ju02Er
TIGHE, Michl.		21	M	Laborer	16Ju02Er
JOHNSON, Jno.		25	M	Laborer	16Ju02Er
Ann	(W)	21	F	Unknown	16Ju02Er
Danl.	(S)	04	M	Child	16Ju02Er
LARKIN, Ellen		25	F	Spinster	16Ju02Er
WALDEN, Jane		09	F	Child	16Ju02Er
WALSH, Eliza		21	F	Child	16Ju02Er
CAMPBELL, Jas.		25	M	Laborer	16Ju02Er
BURN, Marla		18	F	Spinster	16Ju02Er
FLYNN, Mary		18	F	Spinster	16Ju02Er
BROLATOR, Ann		12	F	Spinster	16Ju02Er
DOWNEY, Ann		18	F	Spinster	16Ju02Er
MADDON, Biddy		21	F	Spinster	16Ju02Er
FLANNIGAN, Jno.		30	M	Laborer	16Ju02Er
Judith		30	F	Unknown	16Ju02Er
Domonick		17	M	Unknown	16Ju02Er
Bridget		20	F	Unknown	16Ju02Er
CONNSHAW, Mary		13	F	Spinster	16Ju02Er
KENNEY, Ann		18	F	Spinster	16Ju02Er
Cathe.		07	F	Child	16Ju02Er
MACKAY, Mary		21	F	Spinster	16Ju02Er
BERRY, Eliza		18	F	Spinster	16Ju02Er
LEDWICH, Honora		18	F	Spinster	16Ju02Er
MURRAY, Mary		21	F	Spinster	16Ju02Er
JONES, Cathe.		18	F	Spinster	16Ju02Er
Ann		20	F	Spinster	16Ju02Er
FITZGERALD, Geo.		.00	M	Infant	16Ju02Er
SULLIVAN, Julia		18	F	Spinster	16Ju02Er
BERRY, Jno.		20	M	Laborer	16Ju02Er
MANGAN, Geo.		27	M	Laborer	16Ju02Er
CHURCHARD, Mary		20	F	Unknown	16Ju02Er
MCMULLEN, Pat		20	M	Farmer	16Ju02Er
GRAHAM, Jane		40	F	Unknown	16Ju02Er
HENDERSON, Jane		20	F	Unknown	16Ju02Er
BYRNES, Chas.		54	M	Laborer	16Ju02Er
Mary	(W)	54	F	Unknown	16Ju02Er
Jane	(D)	18	F	Unknown	16Ju02Er
Ann	(D)	16	F	Unknown	16Ju02Er
Jos.	(S)	12	M	Unknown	16Ju02Er
Chas.	(S)	11	M	Unknown	16Ju02Er
MCGOVERN, Julia		25	F	Unknown	16Ju02Er
Thos.		13	M	Unknown	16Ju02Er
ABRAHAM, Jno.		25	M	Laborer	16Ju02Er
Chas.		21	M	Laborer	16Ju02Er
MCMALEON, Susan		40	F	Unknown	16Ju02Er
Jas.	(S)	11	M	Unknown	16Ju02Er
Miller	(S)	09	M	Child	16Ju02Er
Mary	(D)	07	F	Child	16Ju02Er
DERMODY, Ann		21	F	Spinster	16Ju02Er
RYAN, Ann		21	F	Spinster	16Ju02Er
MURRAY, Cathe.		18	F	Spinster	16Ju02Er
CLEFFEY, Ellen		22	F	Spinster	16Ju02Er
WALSH, Henry		21	M	Laborer	16Ju02Er
Eliza		18	F	Unknown	16Ju02Er
NORRIS, Henry		26	M	Farmer	16Ju02Er
Chas.		.00	M	Infant	16Ju02Er
HEFFRON, Bridget		21	F	Spinster	16Ju02Er
BERRY, Rose		20	F	Spinster	16Ju02Er
DALEY, Rose		18	F	Spinster	16Ju02Er
KENNEY, Julia		18	F	Spinster	16Ju02Er
PRIOR, Mary		18	F	Spinster	16Ju02Er
GANNON, Jno.		18	M	Laborer	16Ju02Er
WARD, Mary		30	F	Unknown	16Ju02Er
Walker	(S)	08	M	Child	16Ju02Er
Jas.	(S)	06	M	Child	16Ju02Er
Alfred	(S)	04	M	Child	16Ju02Er
Lucy	(D)	02	F	Child	16Ju02Er
HENDERSON, Jas.		20	M	Laborer	16Ju02Er

NAMES OF PASSENGERS		AGE	SEX	OCCUPATIONS	DATE PORT SHIP
HENDERSON, Jno.		.00	M	Infant	16Ju02Er
GRAHAM, Thos.		25	M	Farmer	16Ju02Er
Saml.		23	M	Farmer	16Ju02Er
MCDOWELL, Edwd.		26	M	Farmer	16Ju02Er
HERRINGTON, Ellen		16	F	Spinster	16Ju02Er
KELLAHAN, Mary		40	F	Spinster	16Ju02Er
HIGGINS, Michl.		24	M	Laborer	16Ju02Er
BORMINGHAM, Margt.		40	F	Wi	16Ju02Er
Cathe.	(D)	13	F	Unknown	16Ju02Er
Bridget	(D)	11	F	Unknown	16Ju02Er
Edwd.	(S)	09	M	Child	16Ju02Er
Thos.	(S)	07	M	Child	16Ju02Er
Martin	(S)	05	M	Child	16Ju02Er
DEANE, Jane		18	F	Spinster	16Ju02Er
Eliza	(M)	42	F	Spinster	16Ju02Er
Wm.	(B)	22	M	Unknown	16Ju02Er
Rebecca	(T)	13	F	Unknown	16Ju02Er
Duke	(B)	23	M	Unknown	16Ju02Er
MORGAN, Cathe.		28	F	Spinster	16Ju02Er
NESBETT, Deny		25	M	Unknown	16Ju02Er
WHELAN, Rose		13	F	Spinster	16Ju02Er
GRAY, Ellen		13	F	Spinster	16Ju02Er
ROONEY, Biddy		18	F	Spinster	16Ju02Er
DILLON, Pat		22	M	Laborer	16Ju02Er
Margt.		21	F	Laborer	16Ju02Er
FARNEY, Nancy		20	F	Spinster	16Ju02Er
Jane		.00	F	Infant	16Ju02Er
HARTEY, Thos.		30	M	Laborer	16Ju02Er
Ellen		30	F	Unknown	16Ju02Er
Mary-Jane		18	F	Unknown	16Ju02Er
FARLEY, Pat		20	M	Unknown	16Ju02Er
SHERIDAN, Al.		20	M	Farmer	16Ju02Er
BLACK, Thos.		22	M	Farmer	16Ju02Er
MCFADDEN, Jno.		20	M	Farmer	16Ju02Er
Jno.		21	M	Farmer	16Ju02Er
Bessy		09	F	Child	16Ju02Er
FALEY, Pat		25	M	Farmer	16Ju02Er
LOO, Pat		21	M	Farmer	16Ju02Er
CORWELLY, Jas.		20	M	Farmer	16Ju02Er
DAVISON, Jno.		22	M	Farmer	16Ju02Er
STEELE, Sally		20	F	Spinster	16Ju02Er
LEEHAN, John		21	M	Farmer	16Ju02Er
HAGAN, John		30	M	Unknown	16Ju02Er
CALEHAN, Edwd.		27	M	Unknown	16Ju02Er
OBRIAN, Pat		21	M	Unknown	16Ju02Er
GARVEY, Mary		21	F	Unknown	16Ju02Er
STOODAUH, Wm.		30	M	Laborer	16Ju02Er
U	(W)	28	F	Unknown	16Ju02Er
ROWE, U-Mrs.		25	F	Unknown	16Ju02Er
Jno.		04	M	Child	16Ju02Er
MCCARTY, Jas.		35	M	Laborer	16Ju02Er
Mary		35	F	Unknown	16Ju02Er
SULLIVAN, Mary		18	F	Spinster	16Ju02Er
MCCONLEY, Jno.		11	M	Farmer	16Ju02Er
Dennis		.00	M	Infant	16Ju02Er
BAILEY, Michl.		30	M	Farmer	16Ju02Er
Cathe.	(W)	30	F	Unknown	16Ju02Er
Biddy	(D)	05	F	Child	16Ju02Er
Mary	(D)	04	F	Child	16Ju02Er
Pat	(S)	.00	M	Infant	16Ju02Er
BRENNAN, Jas.		19	M	Laborer	16Ju02Er
SULLIVAN, Tim		26	M	Laborer	16Ju02Er
DWYER, Mary		19	F	Spinster	16Ju02Er
ALCOCK, Thos.		25	M	Farmer	16Ju02Er
U	(W)	20	F	Unknown	16Ju02Er
Thos.	(S)	.00	M	Infant	16Ju02Er
FITZGERALD, Agnes		20	F	Spinster	16Ju02Er
MCDOWELL, Thos.		16	M	Laborer	16Ju02Er
FARRELL, Pat		11	M	Laborer	16Ju02Er
Jno.		09	M	Child	16Ju02Er
MCDONNOUGH, Bridget		18	F	Spinster	16Ju02Er
BRANAN, Margt.		40	F	Spinster	16Ju02Er
Rose	(D)	09	F	Child	16Ju02Er
Bridget	(D)	05	F	Child	16Ju02Er
Jno.	(S)	.00	M	Infant	16Ju02Er
BRANAN, Jno.	(S)	19	M	Unknown	16Ju02Er
MCAVOY, Thos.		19	M	Laborer	16Ju02Er
HULTON, Jane		18	F	Spinster	16Ju02Er
BRENNAN, U-Mrs.		21	F	Unknown	16Ju02Er
Cathe		18	F	Unknown	16Ju02Er
CARLISHE, Jas.		48	M	Laborer	16Ju02Er
Phebe	(W)	43	F	Unknown	16Ju02Er
David	(S)	19	M	Unknown	16Ju02Er
Jos.	(S)	18	M	Unknown	16Ju02Er
Eliza	(D)	13	F	Unknown	16Ju02Er
Jane	(D)	12	F	Unknown	16Ju02Er
Mary	(D)	11	F	Unknown	16Ju02Er
Ellen	(D)	07	F	Child	16Ju02Er
Jas.	(S)	04	M	Child	16Ju02Er
Thos.	(S)	.00	M	Infant	16Ju02Er
MCARDLE, Jas.		19	M	Farmer	16Ju02Er
DUNWAY, Cathe.		21	F	Spinster	16Ju02Er
DONOVAN, Abby		19	F	Spinster	16Ju02Er
ONEIL, U		21	F	Spinster	16Ju02Er
Florence		18	F	Spinster	16Ju02Er
MCVOY, Ann		18	F	Spinster	16Ju02Er
GIBSON, Jas.		35	M	Laborer	16Ju02Er
Jno.	(S)	11	M	Unknown	16Ju02Er
Abby	(D)	09	F	Child	16Ju02Er
Kelly	(D)	07	F	Child	16Ju02Er
Jas.	(S)	05	M	Child	16Ju02Er
REEL, Lucia		11	F	Unknown	16Ju02Er
MCHUGH, Jeremiah		16	M	Unknown	16Ju02Er
MORRISON, Jas.		25	M	Unknown	16Ju02Er
JORDAN, Jno.		28	M	Unknown	16Ju02Er
CROSS, Eliza		18	F	Unknown	16Ju02Er
GRELIAM, Jas.		70	M	Unknown	16Ju02Er
Jas.		18	M	Unknown	16Ju02Er
Jno.		18	M	Unknown	16Ju02Er
HOLEHAN, Johanna		20	F	Unknown	16Ju02Er
HIGGINS, Cathe.		15	F	Unknown	16Ju02Er
BRENNAN, Ellen		40	F	Unknown	16Ju02Er
Hannah		20	F	Unknown	16Ju02Er
COLMAN, Ellen		30	F	Unknown	16Ju02Er
Pat		05	M	Child	16Ju02Er
DUNORE, Michl.		22	M	Unknown	16Ju02Er
RALLAKER, Wm.		18	M	Unknown	16Ju02Er
WHITE, Sam.		30	M	Unknown	16Ju02Er
MCQUEENY, Dolly		21	F	Unknown	16Ju02Er
RERCORE, James		25	M	Unknown	16Ju02Er
EGAN, Margt.		05	F	Child	16Ju02Er
DEVINE, John		.00	M	Infant	16Ju02Er
DONOHUE, Mary		19	F	Spinster	16Ju02Er
DEVLIN, Jas.		12	M	Laborer	16Ju02Er
Hannah		09	F	Child	16Ju02Er
WALKER, Henry		20	M	Unknown	16Ju02Er
CALLAGHER, Timothy		29	M	Farmer	16Ju02Er
Mary	(W)	24	F	Unknown	16Ju02Er
James	(S)	06	M	Child	16Ju02Er
Wm.	(S)	08	M	Child	16Ju02Er
John	(S)	04	M	Child	16Ju02Er
Henry	(S)	.00	M	Infant	16Ju02Er
WHELAN, Mary		36	F	Spinster	16Ju02Er
Jerry		40	M	Laborer	16Ju02Er
CONNOLLY, James		18	M	Laborer	16Ju02Er
FUTE, Wm.		40	M	Laborer	16Ju02Er
HARRISON, U-Mrs.		30	F	Unknown	16Ju02Er
Mary		18	F	Unknown	16Ju02Er
HENRY, Mary		13	F	Spinster	16Ju02Er
MANGAN, Wm.		40	M	Laborer	16Ju02Er
SULLIVAN, Harriet		24	F	Unknown	16Ju02Er
CONROY, Jas.		18	M	Unknown	16Ju02Er
FEENEY, Wm.		13	M	Unknown	16Ju02Er
CAVANAGH, Jas.		19	M	Unknown	16Ju02Er
WEHLAN, Jno.		20	M	Unknown	16Ju02Er
STANTON, Jas.		40	M	Unknown	16Ju02Er
BRADLEY, Wm.		40	M	Unknown	16Ju02Er
MCIVEN, Henry		19	M	Unknown	16Ju02Er
FARRELL, Jas.		.00	M	Infant	16Ju02Er
RUDLOW, Jno.		10	M	Laborer	16Ju02Er

NAMES OF PASSENGERS		AGE	SEX	OCCUPATIONS	DATE PORT SHIP
RUDLOW, Maria		20	F	Unknown	16Ju02Er
James	(S)	04	M	Child	16Ju02Er
Henry	(S)	.00	M	Infant	16Ju02Er
Ann		06	F	Child	16Ju02Er
Jeremiah	(S)	02	M	Child	16Ju02Er
AGNES, Chas.		34	M	Farmer	16Ju02Er
Mary	(W)	54	F	Unknown	16Ju02Er
Jane	(D)	18	F	Unknown	16Ju02Er
Ann	(D)	16	F	Unknown	16Ju02Er
Josh.	(S)	12	M	Unknown	16Ju02Er
Chas.	(S)	11	M	Unknown	16Ju02Er
MCGOVERN, Julia		25	F	Spinster	16Ju02Er
Thos.		13	M	Unknown	16Ju02Er
ABRAHAM, Jno.		25	M	Laborer	16Ju02Er
Chas.		21	M	Unknown	16Ju02Er
MCMAHON, Susan		40	F	Unknown	16Ju02Er
Jas.	(S)	11	M	Unknown	16Ju02Er
Miller	(S)	09	M	Child	16Ju02Er
Mary	(D)	07	F	Child	16Ju02Er
DENODY, Ann		21	F	Spinster	16Ju02Er
RYAN, Ann		21	F	Spinster	16Ju02Er
MURRAY, Cathe.		18	F	Spinster	16Ju02Er
CLIFFEY, Ellen		22	F	Spinster	16Ju02Er
WALSH, Henry		21	M	Laborer	16Ju02Er
Eliza		18	F	Spinster	16Ju02Er
MORRIS, Henry		26	M	Laborer	16Ju02Er
Chas.		.00	M	Infant	16Ju02Er
HEFFRON, Bridget		21	F	Spinster	16Ju02Er
BERRY, Rose		21	F	Spinster	16Ju02Er
DALEY, Rose		18	F	Spinster	16Ju02Er
KENNEY, Julia		18	F	Spinster	16Ju02Er
PRIOR, Mary		18	F	Unknown	16Ju02Er
LUNNORE, Jno.		18	M	Laborer	16Ju02Er
WARD, Mary		30	F	Spinster	16Ju02Er
Walker	(S)	08	M	Child	16Ju02Er
ALFRED, Jas.		06	M	Child	16Ju02Er
Alfred		04	M	Child	16Ju02Er
Lucy		02	F	Child	16Ju02Er

LOUISA 16 JUNE 1846

From Waterford

NAMES OF PASSENGERS		AGE	SEX	OCCUPATIONS	DATE PORT SHIP
SEXTON, Mary		21	F	Servant	16Jul6Ev
PHELAN, James		25	M	Servant	16Jul6Ev
CASEY, James		25	M	Servant	16Jul6Ev
KENNEDY, Patrick		26	M	Servant	16Jul6Ev
HANNIGAN, Thomas		22	M	Servant	16Jul6Ev
EGARD, John		21	M	Servant	16Jul6Ev
MCCARTHY, Lawrence		20	M	Servant	16Jul6Ev
EGARD, Ellen		26	F	Servant	16Jul6Ev
KEANOR, John		24	M	Servant	16Jul6Ev
HASOR, Thomas		20	M	Servant	16Jul6Ev
CAIN, Thomas		22	M	Servant	16Jul6Ev
Patt		21	M	Servant	16Jul6Ev
MULLALLY, Mary		26	F	Servant	16Jul6Ev
WALSH, Alice		25	F	Servant	16Jul6Ev
HACKETT, Peggy		23	F	Servant	16Jul6Ev
KEHOL, Mary		20	F	Servant	16Jul6Ev
Catherine		22	F	Servant	16Jul6Ev
HAMILTON, Johanna		26	F	Servant	16Jul6Ev
George		03	M	Child	16Jul6Ev
STONAS, Ann		17	F	Servant	16Jul6Ev
LYONS, Martin		22	M	Servant	16Jul6Ev
DUNN, Richard		23	M	Servant	16Jul6Ev
POWER, Anthony		26	M	Servant	16Jul6Ev
COTTER, Patrick		30	M	Servant	16Jul6Ev
GRIFFIN, Andrew		20	M	Servant	16Jul6Ev
GREEN, Davis		21	M	Servant	16Jul6Ev

NAMES OF PASSENGERS		AGE	SEX	OCCUPATIONS	DATE PORT SHIP
KENSINGTON, Mary		21	F	Servant	16Jul6Ev
PHELAN, Patrick		23	M	Servant	16Jul6Ev
FORRESTAL, Thomas		21	M	Servant	16Jul6Ev
CLANCEY, Thomas		22	M	Servant	16Jul6Ev
John		17	M	Servant	16Jul6Ev
LYNCH, Vince		18	M	Servant	16Jul6Ev
FITZGERALD, William		20	M	Servant	16Jul6Ev
SWEENY, Johannah		21	F	Servant	16Jul6Ev
QULIAN, Thomas		22	M	Servant	16Jul6Ev
WALSH, Edmond		26	M	Servant	16Jul6Ev
MORRIS, Alice		22	F	Servant	16Jul6Ev
REDDY, Thomas		20	M	Servant	16Jul6Ev
NOALAN, Michael		25	M	Servant	16Jul6Ev
STAPLETON, Michael		26	M	Servant	16Jul6Ev
MULCAHEY, Patt		17	M	Servant	16Jul6Ev
Nancy		19	F	Servant	16Jul6Ev
QUINN, Mary		20	F	Servant	16Jul6Ev
HARRIS, Thomas		22	M	Servant	16Jul6Ev
WALSH, William		25	M	Servant	16Jul6Ev
DUNN, Thomas		24	M	Servant	16Jul6Ev
GOFF, Mary		21	F	Servant	16Jul6Ev
Johanna		21	F	Servant	16Jul6Ev
LYONS, James		22	M	Servant	16Jul6Ev
FITZGERALD, John		35	M	Servant	16Jul6Ev
TOBY, Daniel		40	M	Servant	16Jul6Ev
Margret	(W)	35	F	Servant	16Jul6Ev
Edmond	(S)	10	M	Child	16Jul6Ev
Betsy	(D)	08	F	Child	16Jul6Ev
Michael	(S)	05	M	Child	16Jul6Ev
SUTTON, Catherine		03	F	Child	16Jul6Ev
HANNEY, Patrick		46	M	Farmer	16Jul6Ev
Bridget	(W)	35	F	Farmer	16Jul6Ev
William	(S)	12	M	Farmer	16Jul6Ev
Edward	(S)	10	M	Farmer	16Jul6Ev
Patrick	(S)	08	M	Farmer	16Jul6Ev
John	(S)	06	M	Farmer	16Jul6Ev
Thomas	(S)	04	M	Farmer	16Jul6Ev
Daniel	(S)	03	M	Farmer	16Jul6Ev
Cath.	(D)	02	F	Farmer	16Jul6Ev
John	(B)	34	M	Farmer	16Jul6Ev
Mary	(W)	30	F	Farmer	16Jul6Ev
Catherine	(D)	10	F	Farmer	16Jul6Ev
William	(S)	08	M	Child	16Jul6Ev
Bridget	(D)	06	F	Child	16Jul6Ev
Judy	(D)	04	F	Child	16Jul6Ev
Mary	(D)	03	F	Child	16Jul6Ev
Thomas	(S)	02	M	Child	16Jul6Ev
John	(S)	01	M	Child	16Jul6Ev
MAHER, John		22	M	Servant	16Jul6Ev
HALLORAN, Patrick		20	M	Servant	16Jul6Ev
GRIFFITH, Judy		21	F	Servant	16Jul6Ev
RYAN, Cornelius		17	M	Servant	16Jul6Ev
CLEARY, Marie		19	F	Servant	16Jul6Ev
CAIN, Dennis		40	M	Servant	16Jul6Ev
Owen		27	M	Servant	16Jul6Ev
NOWLAN, Thomas		26	M	Servant	16Jul6Ev
Ellen	(W)	25	F	Servant	16Jul6Ev
James	(S)	04	M	Child	16Jul6Ev
Mary	(D)	04	F	Child	16Jul6Ev
RYAN, Pheoby		30	F	Servant	16Jul6Ev
HICKEY, Mary		25	F	Servant	16Jul6Ev
BRYAN, Richard		20	M	Servant	16Jul6Ev
CARY, John		21	M	Servant	16Jul6Ev
ENOHY, Margret		25	F	Servant	16Jul6Ev
QUIGLAN, Margret		20	F	Servant	16Jul6Ev
NOLAN, Ann		17	F	Servant	16Jul6Ev

EMPIRE 17 JUNE 1846

From Liverpool

NAMES OF PASSENGERS	A G E	S E X	OCCUPATIONS	DATE PORT SHIP
HILLON, Danl.	26	M	Mechanic	17Ju02Al
MCCALDEN, Wm.	26	M	Merchant	17Ju02Al
MURRAY, George	26	M	Engineer	17Ju02Al
Cath.	16	F	Engineer	17Ju02Al
CHAMPONY, Edwd.	30	M	Farmer	17Ju02Al
Eliza	24	F	Farmer	17Ju02Al
CALLOW, Stephn.	27	M	Farmer	17Ju02Al
Ann	25	F	Farmer	17Ju02Al
ZACHERLY, Geo.	29	M	Clerk	17Ju02Al
BUSH, Wm.	26	M	Miner	17Ju02Al
Hanna	46	F	Miner	17Ju02Al
WILSON, John	29	M	Joiner	17Ju02Al
Elizabeth	26	F	Joiner	17Ju02Al
RICHARDSON, Ellen	20	F	Spinster	17Ju02Al
MARRIOT, Wm.	30	M	Farmer	17Ju02Al
Hannah	26	F	Farmer	17Ju02Al
Eliza	05	F	Child	17Ju02Al
BRADLEY, Saml.	46	M	Farmer	17Ju02Al
Ann (W)	44	F	Farmer	17Ju02Al
Eliza (D)	16	F	Farmer	17Ju02Al
Ann (D)	15	F	Farmer	17Ju02Al
Thos. (S)	14	M	Farmer	17Ju02Al
John (S)	12	M	Farmer	17Ju02Al
Isaac (S)	10	M	Farmer	17Ju02Al
Jas. (S)	06	M	Child	17Ju02Al
David (S)	04	M	Child	17Ju02Al
George (S)	02	M	Child	17Ju02Al
HAGERTY, John	25	M	Farmer	17Ju02Al
BEGGIN, James	30	M	Farmer	17Ju02Al
MOORE, Jas.	23	M	Servant	17Ju02Al
SELLER, Abram	34	M	Blacksmith	17Ju02Al
Martha (W)	32	F	Unknown	17Ju02Al
George (S)	12	M	Unknown	17Ju02Al
Abram (S)	06	M	Child	17Ju02Al
Sarah (D)	06	F	Child	17Ju02Al
Ann (D)	03	F	Child	17Ju02Al
Mary (D)	01	F	Child	17Ju02Al
ROBERTS, Jas.	57	M	Currier	17Ju02Al
Ann (W)	60	F	Currier	17Ju02Al
Hanna (D)	27	F	Currier	17Ju02Al
Jacob (S)	23	M	Currier	17Ju02Al
Jas. (S)	13	M	Currier	17Ju02Al
George (S)	03	M	Child	17Ju02Al
Alice (D)	02	F	Child	17Ju02Al
MCGUINESS, Patt	30	M	Farmer	17Ju02Al
COSSETTY, Ellen	20	F	Spinster	17Ju02Al
CUNNINGHAM, Sarah	21	F	Spinster	17Ju02Al
MCAVOY, Neil	45	M	Saddler	17Ju02Al
Thos. (S)	20	M	Saddler	17Ju02Al
Jas. (S)	25	M	Saddler	17Ju02Al
George	18	M	Saddler	17Ju02Al
Ann	40	F	Saddler	17Ju02Al
Mary	14	F	Saddler	17Ju02Al
FEATHERTON, John	29	M	Laborer	17Ju02Al
HEANY, John	24	M	Carpenter	17Ju02Al
Eliza	21	F	Spinster	17Ju02Al
ELDER, Mary	20	F	Spinster	17Ju02Al
TORNES, Sam.	25	M	Merchant	17Ju02Al
PATTERSON, Robt.	20	M	Farmer	17Ju02Al
BOYLE, Jas.	21	M	Farmer	17Ju02Al
CLARKE, Saml.	50	M	Lnbl	17Ju02Al
Hannah (W)	40	F	Lnbl	17Ju02Al
David (S)	20	M	Lnbl	17Ju02Al
Mary (D)	18	F	Lnbl	17Ju02Al
Margt. (D)	16	F	Lnbl	17Ju02Al
CLARKE, Hannah (D)	12	F	Lnbl	17Ju02Al
Jas. (S)	08	M	Child	17Ju02Al
Agnes-Jane (D)	04	F	Child	17Ju02Al
CAMBLE, Wm.	21	M	Tailor	17Ju02Al
KELLY, Andrew	21	M	Wheelwright	17Ju02Al
CAMBLE, Henry	13	M	Wheelwright	17Ju02Al
COOPER, Saml.	20	M	Laborer	17Ju02Al
ROBERTS, Henry	24	M	Mnftr	17Ju02Al
BELL, Robt.	47	M	Farmer	17Ju02Al
Martha (W)	35	F	Farmer	17Ju02Al
Saml. (S)	10	M	Farmer	17Ju02Al
John (S)	08	M	Farmer	17Ju02Al
Eliza (D)	06	F	Farmer	17Ju02Al
Robt. (S)	04	M	Farmer	17Ju02Al
George (S)	02	M	Farmer	17Ju02Al
David (S)	.00	M	Infant	17Ju02Al
GAMBLE, Margt.	20	F	Spinster	17Ju02Al
GOLD, John	57	M	Miner	17Ju02Al
Margt.	49	F	Miner	17Ju02Al
John	24	M	Miner	17Ju02Al
George	20	M	Miner	17Ju02Al
SCEALLY, Thos.	46	M	Mason	17Ju02Al
Mary	40	F	Mason	17Ju02Al
Jas.	19	M	Mason	17Ju02Al
Joshua	16	M	Mason	17Ju02Al
Eliza	18	F	Mason	17Ju02Al
Virtu	10	F	Mason	17Ju02Al
Mary-Ann	07	F	Child	17Ju02Al
STRODE, Wm.	18	M	Mason	17Ju02Al
EDMONDS, Mary-Ann	.00	F	Infant	17Ju02Al
EDMOND, Caroline	30	F	Spinster	17Ju02Al
HENDOO, Aron	35	M	Farmer	17Ju02Al
Eliza (W)	30	F	Farmer	17Ju02Al
Aron (S)	.00	M	Infant	17Ju02Al
PEACH, Francis-B.	24	M	Farmer	17Ju02Al
ALSOM, Chas.	19	M	Farmer	17Ju02Al
KEAN, Peter	26	M	Laborer	17Ju02Al
Biddy	24	F	Laborer	17Ju02Al
MCCARROLL, Patt	40	M	Blacksmith	17Ju02Al
LEVY, Cath.	18	F	Servant	17Ju02Al
NALLY, Eliza	16	F	Servant	17Ju02Al
MORAN, Eliza	18	F	Servant	17Ju02Al
Mary	24	F	Servant	17Ju02Al
WHITE, Wm.	24	M	Blacksmith	17Ju02Al
TRISKET, Ellen	30	F	Servant	17Ju02Al
ROACH, Mary	20	F	Servant	17Ju02Al
ROWLAND, Julia	20	F	Servant	17Ju02Al
ROACH, Ellen	19	F	Servant	17Ju02Al
CORKIN, Mary	22	F	Servant	17Ju02Al
Colin	24	M	Servant	17Ju02Al
Mary	.00	F	Infant	17Ju02Al
MCCRELE, Ellen	20	F	Servant	17Ju02Al
PRITCHARD, Wm.	27	M	Miner	17Ju02Al
WILDEN, Mary	28	F	Miner	17Ju02Al
Eliza	08	F	Child	17Ju02Al
John	03	M	Child	17Ju02Al
EXLEY, Wm.	30	M	Clothier	17Ju02Al
DAVIS, John	43	M	Mechanic	17Ju02Al
Jane (W)	31	F	Mechanic	17Ju02Al
Eliza (D)	13	F	Mechanic	17Ju02Al
Jane (D)	09	F	Child	17Ju02Al
John (S)	10	M	Mechanic	17Ju02Al
Griffith (S)	08	M	Mechanic	17Ju02Al
THOMAS, John	35	M	Miner	17Ju02Al
Mary-Ann	30	F	Miner	17Ju02Al
Wm.	08	M	Child	17Ju02Al
Mary	06	F	Child	17Ju02Al
Eliza	03	F	Child	17Ju02Al
Martha	.00	F	Infant	17Ju02Al
GRIFFITH, Stepn.	32	M	Miner	17Ju02Al
Sarah	29	F	Miner	17Ju02Al
Thos.	.00	M	Infant	17Ju02Al
JONES, Henry	26	M	Carpenter	17Ju02Al
KENNEY, Hannah	29	F	None	17Ju02Al
Martha (D)	12	F	None	17Ju02Al

NAMES OF PASSENGERS		AGE	SEX	OCCUPATIONS	DATE PORT SHIP
KENNEY, Thos.	(S)	07	M	Child	17Ju02AI
George	(S)	04	M	Child	17Ju02AI
Saml.	(S)	.00	M	Infant	17Ju02AI
MONROE, David		28	M	Laborer	17Ju02AI
HOGAN, Patt		30	M	Laborer	17Ju02AI
LEWIS, Thos.		25	M	Laborer	17Ju02AI
WILLIAMS, Thos.		40	M	Miner	17Ju02AI
PROSSER, John		24	M	Miner	17Ju02AI
CLEARY, Dennis		25	M	Laborer	17Ju02AI
Patt		24	M	Laborer	17Ju02AI
Biddy		27	F	Laborer	17Ju02AI
HANNA, John		27	M	Laborer	17Ju02AI
Jas.		26	M	Laborer	17Ju02AI
SMITH, Eliza		20	F	Servant	17Ju02AI
IRVIN, Edwd.		40	M	Farmer	17Ju02AI
SHEWLIN, Jas.		38	M	Miner	17Ju02AI
Mary	(W)	30	F	Miner	17Ju02AI
Patt	(S)	07	M	Child	17Ju02AI
GALLAGHER, Nell		22	M	Laborer	17Ju02AI
WHITE, Archy		32	M	Carpenter	17Ju02AI
BLACK, Adam		30	M	Farmer	17Ju02AI
WHITE, Jane		24	F	Spinster	17Ju02AI
CASSIDY, Jas.		25	M	Laborer	17Ju02AI
MORAN, Peter		21	M	Laborer	17Ju02AI
WEST, Wm.		36	M	Weaver	17Ju02AI
Mary		30	F	Weaver	17Ju02AI
Mart.		11	F	Weaver	17Ju02AI
Robt.		09	M	Weaver	17Ju02AI
John		04	M	Weaver	17Ju02AI
Hannah		07	F	Weaver	17Ju02AI
Isabella		02	F	Weaver	17Ju02AI
DOYLE, Henry		23	M	Laborer	17Ju02AI
LEWIS, Eliza		18	F	Spinster	17Ju02AI
MAGHAN, Ann		30	F	Spinster	17Ju02AI
SWAN, Chas.		20	M	None	17Ju02AI
DUNN, Cath.		22	F	Servant	17Ju02AI
FINNEGAN, Mary		45	F	Servant	17Ju02AI
DUFFY, Francis		12	M	Servant	17Ju02AI
Patt.		10	M	Servant	17Ju02AI
Wm.		02	M	Servant	17Ju02AI
CONLY, Mary		40	F	Spinster	17Ju02AI
Biddy		10	F	Spinster	17Ju02AI
Mary		20	F	Spinster	17Ju02AI
Jas.		03	M	Child	17Ju02AI
SHERLOCK, John		24	M	Farmer	17Ju02AI
DREW, John		35	M	Laborer	17Ju02AI
BURK, Mary		21	F	Servant	17Ju02AI
DOLAN, Mary		20	F	Servant	17Ju02AI
DREW, Thos.		06	M	Child	17Ju02AI
KIDD, John		17	M	Draper	17Ju02AI
Robt.		18	M	Draper	17Ju02AI
MCINTYRE, Wm.		40	M	Mason	17Ju02AI
Rose		30	F	Mason	17Ju02AI
CRERON, Margt.		20	F	Mason	17Ju02AI
MCGUIRE, Susan		19	F	Mason	17Ju02AI
Patt		10	M	Mason	17Ju02AI
Margt.		08	F	Child	17Ju02AI
Cath.		06	F	Child	17Ju02AI
John		04	M	Child	17Ju02AI
Jos.		03	M	Child	17Ju02AI
Wm.		.00	M	Infant	17Ju02AI
CRABTREE, Johnathan		37	M	Farmer	17Ju02AI
Mary	(W)	36	F	Farmer	17Ju02AI
Ann	(D)	16	F	Farmer	17Ju02AI
Jas.	(S)	14	M	Farmer	17Ju02AI
George	(S)	12	M	Farmer	17Ju02AI
John	(S)	10	M	Farmer	17Ju02AI
Matthew	(S)	08	M	Farmer	17Ju02AI
Susan	(D)	06	F	Farmer	17Ju02AI
Sarah	(D)	04	F	Child	17Ju02AI
Margaret	(D)	02	F	Child	17Ju02AI
FOX, Maria		29	F	Servant	17Ju02AI
MCDONALD, Margt.		21	F	Servant	17Ju02AI
REID, Ann		21	F	Servant	17Ju02AI
SHAW, Wm.		26	M	Laborer	17Ju02AI
STEVENSON, John		30	M	Mechanic	17Ju02AI
MOSES, Sam.		20	M	Weaver	17Ju02AI
MANION, Thos.		22	M	Laborer	17Ju02AI
HOBBINS, Jas.		25	M	Laborer	17Ju02AI
TOWES, Mary		24	F	Spinster	17Ju02AI
DEVLIN, Rose		20	F	Spinster	17Ju02AI
HUGHES, Kate		20	F	Spinster	17Ju02AI
EWORT, Wm.		25	M	Laborer	17Ju02AI
IRVIN, Alex		24	M	Laborer	17Ju02AI
MCGUIRE, Michl.		25	M	Laborer	17Ju02AI
MORAN, John		20	M	Laborer	17Ju02AI
KELLY, Patt		24	M	Laborer	17Ju02AI
PRIOR, Anne		18	F	Spinster	17Ju02AI
Anne		18	F	Spinster	17Ju02AI
DEGNAN, Biddy		25	F	Spinster	17Ju02AI
DORLY, Mary		18	F	Spinster	17Ju02AI
Nancy		25	F	Spinster	17Ju02AI
KEENAN, Martin		.00	M	Infant	17Ju02AI
COCOREN, Cath.		18	F	Spinster	17Ju02AI
BOREN, Hannah		27	F	Spinster	17Ju02AI
TRACY, Mary		19	F	Spinster	17Ju02AI
CASINS, Mary		18	F	Spinster	17Ju02AI
DEVENY, Biddy		21	F	Servant	17Ju02AI
JOHNSON, Wm.		63	M	Farmer	17Ju02AI
Eliza		52	F	Farmer	17Ju02AI
Wm.	(S)	18	M	Farmer	17Ju02AI
Margt.	(D)	20	F	Farmer	17Ju02AI
Isabella	(D)	18	F	Farmer	17Ju02AI
Eliza	(D)	16	F	Farmer	17Ju02AI
Ann	(D)	12	F	Farmer	17Ju02AI
David	(S)	16	M	Farmer	17Ju02AI
Kennedy	(S)	06	M	Child	17Ju02AI
John	(S)	10	M	Farmer	17Ju02AI
MORRIS, Hugh		24	M	Foundryman	17Ju02AI
MCFAUL, Ann		16	F	None	17Ju02AI
MCCALLEY, Wm.John		20	M	Farmer	17Ju02AI
WENLOCK, Wm.		65	M	Farmer	17Ju02AI
David	(S)	26	M	Farmer	17Ju02AI
Richard	(S)	17	M	Farmer	17Ju02AI
Ellen	(D)	15	M	Farmer	17Ju02AI
Mary	(D)	20	M	Farmer	17Ju02AI
TENOR, Wm.		22	M	Farmer	17Ju02AI
Mary-Jane		19	F	Farmer	17Ju02AI
MILLER, John		24	M	Weaver	17Ju02AI
Eliza	(W)	25	F	Weaver	17Ju02AI
HARRISON, John		17	M	Weaver	17Ju02AI
GRIFFIN, Patt		24	M	Laborer	17Ju02AI
LOUGHLIN, Thos.		21	M	Laborer	17Ju02AI
SCALLON, John		28	M	Laborer	17Ju02AI
MURRIEN, Jos.		25	M	Carpenter	17Ju02AI
Mary		30	F	Carpenter	17Ju02AI
CURRIGEN, Jane		25	F	Spinster	17Ju02AI
MCGINN, Ann		38	F	Spinster	17Ju02AI
HENDRAY, John		25	M	Laborer	17Ju02AI
FOGGART, Jas.		25	M	Wool Comber	17Ju02AI
PADEN, Biddy		21	F	Servant	17Ju02AI
KELLY, Jane		20	F	Servant	17Ju02AI
Mary		20	F	Servant	17Ju02AI
MCCUE, Biddy		25	F	Servant	17Ju02AI
Margt.		30	F	Servant	17Ju02AI
CONLY, Thos.		40	M	Farmer	17Ju02AI
Mary	(W)	35	F	Farmer	17Ju02AI
Robt.		26	M	Farmer	17Ju02AI
Ann		23	F	Farmer	17Ju02AI
James		20	M	Farmer	17Ju02AI
Mary		18	F	Farmer	17Ju02AI
Ellen		13	F	Farmer	17Ju02AI
Eliza		13	F	Farmer	17Ju02AI
Margt.		10	F	Farmer	17Ju02AI
Susan		18	F	Farmer	17Ju02AI
DOHERTY, Cath.		23	F	Dressmaker	17Ju02AI
MCGUIRE, Mary		24	F	Servant	17Ju02AI
John		18	M	Servant	17Ju02AI
Patt		20	M	Laborer	17Ju02AI
Biddy		.00	F	Infant	17Ju02AI

NAMES OF PASSENGERS	A G E	S E X	OCCUPATIONS	DATE PORT SHIP	NAMES OF PASSENGERS	A G E	S E X	OCCUPATIONS	DATE PORT SHIP
QUIN, Isabella	20	F	Servant	17Ju02AI	MCCOOL, Jos.	46	M	Farmer	17Ju02AI
ANDERSON, Eliza-Jane	26	F	Servant	17Ju02AI	Jane	44	F	Farmer	17Ju02AI
Eliza	21	F	Dressmaker	17Ju02AI	Robt.	09	M	Child	17Ju02AI
REGNEY, John	24	M	Laborer	17Ju02AI	John	05	M	Child	17Ju02AI
DEGNAN, Tom	25	M	Laborer	17Ju02AI	Mary	04	F	Child	17Ju02AI
James	25	M	Laborer	17Ju02AI	Eliza	02	F	Child	17Ju02AI
KEANAN, Edwd.	40	M	Laborer	17Ju02AI	Adam	.00	M	Infant	17Ju02AI
Biddy	30	F	Laborer	17Ju02AI	WOODS, John	25	M	Farmer	17Ju02AI
LARKIN, Ellen	19	F	Unknown	17Ju02AI	DOOLIN, Jas.	19	M	Farmer	17Ju02AI
John	25	M	Laborer	17Ju02AI	MCDONALD, Rose	28	F	Spinster	17Ju02AI
MCBRIDE, Mary	43	F	Laborer	17Ju02AI	ENNIS, Margt.	26	F	Spinster	17Ju02AI
Wm.	12	M	Laborer	17Ju02AI	BURNS, Edwd.	16	M	Laborer	17Ju02AI
John	10	M	Laborer	17Ju02AI	CONOLY, Hugh	25	M	Laborer	17Ju02AI
Jane-Ann	07	F	Child	17Ju02AI	MCKENNA, Margt.	24	F	Laborer	17Ju02AI
Mary	05	F	Child	17Ju02AI	DONLY, Mary	28	F	Laborer	17Ju02AI
Isabella	02	F	Child	17Ju02AI	Patt	08	M	Child	17Ju02AI
PRITCHARD, Martha	29	F	Laborer	17Ju02AI	John	06	M	Child	17Ju02AI
Hugh	(S) .00	M	Infant	17Ju02AI	Ann	04	F	Child	17Ju02AI
CHERRY, Betsey	17	F	Servant	17Ju02AI	Frank	.00	M	Infant	17Ju02AI
MCANALLY, Cath.	28	F	Servant	17Ju02AI	MONAGHAN, Jas.	23	M	Laborer	17Ju02AI
MCGEE, Ellen	17	F	Servant	17Ju02AI	CONRAN, Mary	06	F	Child	17Ju02AI
DONLY, Sarah	20	F	Servant	17Ju02AI	Wm.	05	M	Child	17Ju02AI
GRAHAM, Patt	34	M	Laborer	17Ju02AI	KING, Michl.	18	M	Laborer	17Ju02AI
COYNE, Jas.	22	M	Laborer	17Ju02AI	Patt	11	M	Laborer	17Ju02AI
Ann	20	F	Laborer	17Ju02AI	MONOR, Patt	24	M	Laborer	17Ju02AI
GAHER, Madge	20	F	Servant	17Ju02AI	Robt.	21	M	Laborer	17Ju02AI
LAVING, Charlotte	17	F	Servant	17Ju02AI	Ann	21	F	Spinster	17Ju02AI
KELLY, Robt.	24	M	Tanner	17Ju02AI	GREEN, John	47	M	Laborer	17Ju02AI
MCDADE, Thos.	21	M	Farmer	17Ju02AI	Isabella	(W) 45	F	Laborer	17Ju02AI
MCGEE, Henry	24	M	Farmer	17Ju02AI	John	(S) 16	M	Laborer	17Ju02AI
REILLY, Wm.	25	M	Mason	17Ju02AI	Jas.	(S) 14	M	Laborer	17Ju02AI
PATTERSON, Jos.	18	M	Laborer	17Ju02AI	Bernrd	(S) 11	M	Laborer	17Ju02AI
MCLOUGHLIN, Danl.	18	M	Farmer	17Ju02AI	Patt	(S) 08	M	Laborer	17Ju02AI
FARRELL, Chas.	21	M	Teacher	17Ju02AI	Cath.	(D) 05	F	Laborer	17Ju02AI
ROADES, John	41	M	Laborer	17Ju02AI	MCTEAGUE, Jas.	20	M	Laborer	17Ju02AI
SMITH, Bessey	16	F	Servant	17Ju02AI	MCELLROY, Jas.	38	M	Laborer	17Ju02AI
Michael	12	M	Servant	17Ju02AI	Mary	(W) 38	F	Laborer	17Ju02AI
Mary	10	F	Servant	17Ju02AI	Barny	(S) 08	M	Child	17Ju02AI
MORAN, Sally	30	F	Servant	17Ju02AI	Thos.	(S) 06	M	Child	17Ju02AI
HANLY, Biddy	21	F	Servant	17Ju02AI	Jas.	(S) 04	M	Child	17Ju02AI
NORTAN, Honor	28	F	Servant	17Ju02AI	REHILL, Mich.	29	M	Laborer	17Ju02AI
MALANNY, Rody	09	F	Servant	17Ju02AI	MCGUIRE, Kierman	24	M	Laborer	17Ju02AI
John	04	M	Child	17Ju02AI	BOUGHAN, Ellen	21	F	Spinster	17Ju02AI
John	40	M	Child	17Ju02AI	Susan	24	F	Spinster	17Ju02AI
Honora	30	F	Child	17Ju02AI	GAINTY, John	24	M	Laborer	17Ju02AI
Ellen	.00	F	Infant	17Ju02AI	MAGNAN, Michl.	25	M	Laborer	17Ju02AI
GIBBIN, Patt	02	M	Child	17Ju02AI	MCKENNA, Thos.	28	M	Laborer	17Ju02AI
Sarah	22	F	Unknown	17Ju02AI	FAHY, Ann	19	F	Spinster	17Ju02AI
ORR, Alex	24	M	Laborer	17Ju02AI	DALY, Cath.	18	F	Spinster	17Ju02AI
BROLY, Wm.	17	M	Laborer	17Ju02AI	LEWIS, Thos.	69	M	None	17Ju02AI
MULLAN, Patt	25	M	Laborer	17Ju02AI	Died-At-Sea				
Jas.	08	M	Child	17Ju02AI					
John	04	M	Child	17Ju02AI					
NOHAN, Mary	16	F	Servant	17Ju02AI					
FLYN, Margt.	21	F	Servant	17Ju02AI					
MASON, Robt.	27	M	Spinner	17Ju02AI					
Wm.	25	M	Spinner	17Ju02AI	BALTIC 17 JUNE 1846				
Thos.	21	M	Spinner	17Ju02AI					
HANEY, Rose	17	F	Servant	17Ju02AI	From Trinidad De Cuba				
FARLY, Biddy	17	F	Servant	17Ju02AI					
GAFFNEY, Ann	16	F	Servant	17Ju02AI					
CASERLY, Mary	18	F	Servant	17Ju02AI					
PERCE, Wm.	21	M	Laborer	17Ju02AI	WOOLEY, E.	35	M	Unknown	17Ju74Fb
MCANNLTY, Jas.	30	M	Laborer	17Ju02AI	U	(W) 20	F	Unknown	17Ju74Fb
Mary	20	F	Laborer	17Ju02AI	U	05	U	Child	17Ju74Fb
HANLY, Michl.	30	M	Laborer	17Ju02AI	U	08	U	Child	17Ju74Fb
CORKIN, Susan	40	F	Laborer	17Ju02AI	SURTY, J.K.	35	M	None	17Ju74Fb
Hugh	35	M	Laborer	17Ju02AI					
John	30	M	Laborer	17Ju02AI					
Patt	27	M	Laborer	17Ju02AI					
Frank	13	M	Laborer	17Ju02AI					
Mick	10	M	Laborer	17Ju02AI					
Biddy	08	F	Laborer	17Ju02AI					
Thos.	06	M	Laborer	17Ju02AI					
Peter	04	M	Child	17Ju02AI					

NAMES OF PASSENGERS	AGE	SEX	OCCUPATIONS	DATE PORT SHIP
PLANTER 18 JUNE 1846				
From PICTOU,N.S.				
BUME, Anna	20	F	Servant	18Ju43Fc
LIVERPOOL 18 JUNE 1846				
From Liverpool				
WILLEN, Thomas	29	M	Laborer	18Ju02Bo
Mary (W)	27	F	Servant	18Ju02Bo
John (S)	03	M	Child	18Ju02Bo
Martin (S)	01	M	Child	18Ju02Bo
WALSH, John	22	M	Laborer	18Ju02Bo
CUNNINGHAM, Bridget	26	F	Servant	18Ju02Bo
WALL, Mary	25	F	Servant	18Ju02Bo
Catherine	23	F	Servant	18Ju02Bo
ISSON, James	18	M	Laborer	18Ju02Bo
Michael	22	M	Bricklayer	18Ju02Bo
MILLS, Joseph	21	M	Gdnr	18Ju02Bo
SHERIDAN, James	26	M	Farmer	18Ju02Bo
Bridget	22	F	Farmer	18Ju02Bo
MANNING, Michael	64	M	Ploughman	18Ju02Bo
KELLY, Patrick	24	M	Shepherd	18Ju02Bo
MOONY, Patrick	21	M	Courier	18Ju02Bo
MAHOR, Mary	20	F	Servant	18Ju02Bo
LOBBER, Mary	50	F	Servant	18Ju02Bo
CARROLE, Anne	20	F	Servant	18Ju02Bo
DOHEN, Daniel	45	M	Milkman	18Ju02Bo
KAY, Michael	22	M	Laborer	18Ju02Bo
---LLER, Jeremiah	30	M	Laborer	18Ju02Bo
BANNER, Margaret	25	F	Servant	18Ju02Bo
MCGLEED, Margaret	25	F	Servant	18Ju02Bo
MCGUIRE, Anne	18	F	Servant	18Ju02Bo
BURN, Michael	20	M	Laborer	18Ju02Bo
DAULEN, Thomas	25	M	Stone Mason	18Ju02Bo
Michael	20	M	Stone Mason	18Ju02Bo
KNOWLAN, Martin	28	M	Laborer	18Ju02Bo
Thomas	08	M	Child	18Ju02Bo
NORN, Winifred	16	F	Servant	18Ju02Bo
BRINNARD, Thomas	20	M	Ploughman	18Ju02Bo
BRANAND, Ann	20	F	Servant	18Ju02Bo
TEASSY, John	26	M	Ploughman	18Ju02Bo
Catherine	18	F	Servant	18Ju02Bo
HANNAH, Margret	20	F	Servant	18Ju02Bo
HILAND, Margret	18	F	Servant	18Ju02Bo
KILPATRICK, Francis	18	M	Coachman	18Ju02Bo
CARROLL, Michael	30	M	Stone Mason	18Ju02Bo
COOLLACHEN, Patrick	26	M	Tailor	18Ju02Bo
HORN, Michael	22	M	Ploughman	18Ju02Bo
DONEHON, Thomas	22	M	Shepherd	18Ju02Bo
SWOONY, Michael	20	M	Laborer	18Ju02Bo
HILLY, Patrick	22	M	Laborer	18Ju02Bo
Lawrence	12	M	Laborer	18Ju02Bo
SCULLY, Hebener	21	F	Servant	18Ju02Bo
BRIDDY, Francis	53	M	Laborer	18Ju02Bo
Clare	40	F	None	18Ju02Bo
Bridget	21	F	Servant	18Ju02Bo
James	20	M	Laborer	18Ju02Bo
Ann	13	F	None	18Ju02Bo
Terrence	12	M	None	18Ju02Bo
Mary	08	F	Child	18Ju02Bo

NAMES OF PASSENGERS	AGE	SEX	OCCUPATIONS	DATE PORT SHIP
BRIDDY, Patrick	03	M	Child	18Ju02Bo
SULLIVAN, Mary	19	F	Servant	18Ju02Bo
Ann	21	F	Servant	18Ju02Bo
SMITH, Mary	18	F	Servant	18Ju02Bo
HARNEY, John	24	M	Blacksmith	18Ju02Bo
Mary	22	F	None	18Ju02Bo
HUNTER, Patrick	31	M	Laborer	18Ju02Bo
Anne	30	F	None	18Ju02Bo
BRIMER, Bridget	22	F	Servant	18Ju02Bo
Ellen	20	F	Servant	18Ju02Bo
CLINCH, Patrick	26	M	Laborer	18Ju02Bo
Margaret	26	F	None	18Ju02Bo
DUNN, Patrick	20	M	Stone Mason	18Ju02Bo
MCQUE, Michael	20	M	Laborer	18Ju02Bo
HARNES, Thomas	20	M	Blacksmith	18Ju02Bo
KNOLLAN, Patrick	23	M	Laborer	18Ju02Bo
DONAGHUE, James	50	M	Weaver	18Ju02Bo
Susan (D)	19	F	Servant	18Ju02Bo
Peter (S)	17	M	Weaver	18Ju02Bo
Bridget (D)	13	F	None	18Ju02Bo
Margaret (D)	11	F	None	18Ju02Bo
CUNNINGHAM, James	30	M	Servant	18Ju02Bo
Merle	26	F	None	18Ju02Bo
FLYNN, Margaret	21	F	Servant	18Ju02Bo
CONNELL, Patrick	50	M	Laborer	18Ju02Bo
Anne	52	F	None	18Ju02Bo
LAWLESS, Mills	13	M	None	18Ju02Bo
ONEILL, James	26	M	Laborer	18Ju02Bo
CANADA, Sarah	28	F	Servant	18Ju02Bo
-LINTON, Lawrence	23	M	Butcher	18Ju02Bo
TOURELL, Thomas	19	M	Tailor	18Ju02Bo
MONOHAN, James	30	M	Laborer	18Ju02Bo
HEDEN, Matthew	23	M	Laborer	18Ju02Bo
CLEARY, Jeremiah	50	M	Plumber	18Ju02Bo
John	22	M	Plumber	18Ju02Bo
Eliza	18	F	None	18Ju02Bo
Margaret	16	F	None	18Ju02Bo
Jeremiah	14	M	None	18Ju02Bo
George	12	M	None	18Ju02Bo
Ellen	09	F	Child	18Ju02Bo
Anne	06	F	Child	18Ju02Bo
RYAN, John	26	M	Laborer	18Ju02Bo
KEEFF, Martin	20	M	Laborer	18Ju02Bo
CUMMINS, Alex	22	F	Servant	18Ju02Bo
SHINTIN, Bridger	23	F	Servant	18Ju02Bo
RYAN, Margaret	20	F	Servant	18Ju02Bo
MACHEL, James	52	M	Laborer	18Ju02Bo
ALLEN, Thomas	22	M	Carpenter	18Ju02Bo
HANRY, James	16	M	Laborer	18Ju02Bo
MORGAN, Mary	25	F	Servant	18Ju02Bo
MACKEN, Mary	17	F	Servant	18Ju02Bo
GANLEN, Bridget	24	F	Servant	18Ju02Bo
DENEHY, Mary	40	F	Servant	18Ju02Bo
Margaret	11	F	Servant	18Ju02Bo
Bernard	07	M	Child	18Ju02Bo
Catherine	04	F	Child	18Ju02Bo
CLARKE, Mary	25	F	Servant	18Ju02Bo
CORMAN, Sarah	30	F	Servant	18Ju02Bo
COUGHLEN, John	28	M	Laborer	18Ju02Bo
CORNMAR, Edward	28	M	Laborer	18Ju02Bo
TUCKER, James	27	M	Laborer	18Ju02Bo
Sarah	20	F	None	18Ju02Bo
MCGENNIS, Ellen	20	F	Servant	18Ju02Bo
FITZPATRICK, Bridget	21	F	Dressmaker	18Ju02Bo
STATON, Patrick	26	M	Laborer	18Ju02Bo
MORRIS, Anne	26	F	Servant	18Ju02Bo
CLAFFY, Michael	48	M	Farmer	18Ju02Bo
Bridget	30	F	None	18Ju02Bo
Patrick	14	M	None	18Ju02Bo
CONNOLLY, Bridget	20	F	Servant	18Ju02Bo
STANTON, Thomas	28	M	Laborer	18Ju02Bo
CUNNINGHAM, John	20	M	Laborer	18Ju02Bo
MCDERMONT, Daniel	20	M	Laborer	18Ju02Bo
MARTIN, Bridget	21	F	Servant	18Ju02Bo
MCELEVENCE, Helen	35	F	Servant	18Ju02Bo

NAMES OF PASSENGERS	AGE	SEX	OCCUPATIONS	DATE PORT SHIP
POWELL, James	20	M	Laborer	18Ju02Bo
MCMARRA, Patrick	27	M	Shoemaker	18Ju02Bo
MAGUIRE, Martin	25	M	Laborer	18Ju02Bo
CULLIN, Daniel	27	M	Blacksmith	18Ju02Bo
MANGAN, John	28	M	Laborer	18Ju02Bo
KENON, Suzanne	20	F	Servant	18Ju02Bo
MCCLEER, Bridget	16	F	Servant	18Ju02Bo
Susanah	72	F	Servant	18Ju02Bo
FLANAGAN, Suzannah	19	F	Servant	18Ju02Bo
MAYRAH, Michael	26	M	Laborer	18Ju02Bo
MCGRAH, Julia	27	F	Servant	18Ju02Bo
Anne	20	F	Servant	18Ju02Bo
Bridget	18	F	Servant	18Ju02Bo
SWEENEY, Dominick	20	M	Laborer	18Ju02Bo
KENCE, Michael	25	M	Laborer	18Ju02Bo
BUTLER, Richard	50	M	Laborer	18Ju02Bo
Bridget	70	F	None	18Ju02Bo
Judith	50	F	None	18Ju02Bo
Patrick	18	M	Laborer	18Ju02Bo
Thomas	16	M	Laborer	18Ju02Bo
Bridget	14	F	None	18Ju02Bo
Margaret	12	F	None	18Ju02Bo
Mathew	09	M	Child	18Ju02Bo
SADDLER, John	20	M	Laborer	18Ju02Bo
WHELTON, Thomas	34	M	Laborer	18Ju02Bo
HALLORAN, John	24	M	Laborer	18Ju02Bo
HOWARD, Patrick	26	M	Laborer	18Ju02Bo
HALLORAN, John	24	M	Laborer	18Ju02Bo
WILLETT, James	30	M	Laborer	18Ju02Bo
CONSADINE, Mary	25	F	Servant	18Ju02Bo
MCNAMARA, Bridget	18	F	Servant	18Ju02Bo
HALLARAN, Anne	20	F	Servant	18Ju02Bo
RUSSELL, Anne	20	F	None	18Ju02Bo
WHEELAN, Bridget	20	F	Servant	18Ju02Bo
FRAYNE, Michael	22	M	Laborer	18Ju02Bo
DUFFY, Richard	21	M	Laborer	18Ju02Bo
MOONY, Dennis	23	M	Laborer	18Ju02Bo
Bridget	20	F	Dressmaker	18Ju02Bo
MCDERMONT, Ellen	23	F	Servant	18Ju02Bo
CLINCH, Bridget	23	F	Servant	18Ju02Bo
CLARE, Rosett	17	F	Servant	18Ju02Bo
DWIRE, Patrick	18	M	Laborer	18Ju02Bo
Denis	13	M	Laborer	18Ju02Bo
DALY, James	18	M	Plumber	18Ju02Bo
Mary	21	F	Servant	18Ju02Bo
MORGAN, Mary	18	F	Servant	18Ju02Bo
MURRY, Michael	25	M	Laborer	18Ju02Bo
Anne	20	F	Servant	18Ju02Bo
MOLVILLY, Bridget	30	F	Servant	18Ju02Bo
MCMAUGLE, Mary	20	F	Servant	18Ju02Bo
MCQULEN, Rose	17	F	Servant	18Ju02Bo
HUGHES, Henry	25	M	Shoemaker	18Ju02Bo
MCLUHY, Henry	24	M	Laborer	18Ju02Bo
Eliza	22	F	None	18Ju02Bo
MCDONOUGH, Hugh	28	M	Laborer	18Ju02Bo
Mary (W)	28	F	None	18Ju02Bo
U (S)	.00	M	Infant	18Ju02Bo
Born-At-Sea				
CUNNINGHAM, Anne	16	F	Servant	18Ju02Bo
BRADY, Morgan	18	M	Servant	18Ju02Bo
DONEGAN, John	22	M	Laborer	18Ju02Bo
Mary	14	F	None	18Ju02Bo
COLEMAN, Lawrence	20	M	Shoemaker	18Ju02Bo
CROWLY, Timothy	22	M	Laborer	18Ju02Bo
MIHEGAN, Michael	21	M	Iron Monger	18Ju02Bo
Ellen	18	F	Servant	18Ju02Bo
RUSSELL, Johannah	22	F	Servant	18Ju02Bo
MCCARTHY, Ellen	48	F	Servant	18Ju02Bo
MCELBREY, Samuel	60	M	Farmer	18Ju02Bo
MCCAUGHRY, James	27	M	Unknown	18Ju02Bo

HARRIET-AND-JESSIE 19 JUNE 1846

From Liverpool

NAMES OF PASSENGERS	AGE	SEX	OCCUPATIONS	DATE PORT SHIP
SIGHE, Ellen	23	F	None	19Ju02FI
STAFFORD, Susan	18	F	None	19Ju02FI
LEE, John	19	M	Farmer	19Ju02FI
LORAN, Susanna	25	F	None	19Ju02FI
MURPHY, Phillip	22	M	Farmer	19Ju02FI
MARSH, William	49	M	Laborer	19Ju02FI
GREEN, Ann	21	F	None	19Ju02FI
LITTLE, Robert	13	M	None	19Ju02FI
SMITH, Rose	17	F	None	19Ju02FI
Andrew	22	M	Laborer	19Ju02FI
MULHOLLAND, Daniel	19	M	Farmer	19Ju02FI
Mary	17	F	None	19Ju02FI
ONEIL, Mary	21	F	None	19Ju02FI
MAKER, Timothy	35	M	Laborer	19Ju02FI
CASSIDY, Peter	19	M	Laborer	19Ju02FI
BAXTER, Charles	27	M	Laborer	19Ju02FI
MCGUIRE, Thomas	15	M	Laborer	19Ju02FI
Mary	17	F	None	19Ju02FI
GAVIN, Michael	24	M	Laborer	19Ju02FI
MOORE, Mary	20	F	None	19Ju02FI
Bridget	29	F	None	19Ju02FI
MEAN, William	17	M	None	19Ju02FI
Joseph	22	M	None	19Ju02FI
MCDREW, Cath.	17	F	None	19Ju02FI
MEEKHAM, James	22	M	Laborer	19Ju02FI
COCKRAN, John	22	M	Laborer	19Ju02FI
Mary	20	F	None	19Ju02FI
TIERNEY, William	22	M	Laborer	19Ju02FI
Thos.	20	M	Laborer	19Ju02FI
HARRASS, Geo.	17	M	Laborer	19Ju02FI
DUFFY, Judy	28	F	None	19Ju02FI
James	.00	M	Infant	19Ju02FI
MCKENNA, Hugh	19	M	Laborer	19Ju02FI
BRENNAN, Peter	22	M	Laborer	19Ju02FI
MAHON, Thomas	21	M	Laborer	19Ju02FI
BRENNAN, Mary	20	F	None	19Ju02FI
MEHAN, Honora	18	F	None	19Ju02FI
Mary	19	F	None	19Ju02FI
CORRORAN, Francis	22	M	Laborer	19Ju02FI
BAGD, Catherine	21	F	None	19Ju02FI
CORRORAN, William	28	M	Laborer	19Ju02FI
MCGUIRE, Phillip	19	M	Laborer	19Ju02FI
DAGHERTY, Margret	21	F	None	19Ju02FI
ODONNELL, Pat	20	M	Laborer	19Ju02FI
MCCANN, Cath.	20	F	None	19Ju02FI
SATTER, William	25	M	Laborer	19Ju02FI
HICKIE, Martin	24	M	Farmer	19Ju02FI
KENSHALA, John	25	M	Farmer	19Ju02FI
BURNE, James	26	M	Farmer	19Ju02FI
ALL, John	21	M	Farmer	19Ju02FI
GUTHRIE, John	19	M	Farmer	19Ju02FI
MCGAHAN, Richard	51	M	Farmer	19Ju02FI
Harriet	49	F	None	19Ju02FI
Catherine	24	F	None	19Ju02FI
Thomas	22	M	None	19Ju02FI
Richard	19	M	None	19Ju02FI
Peater	16	M	None	19Ju02FI
James	12	M	None	19Ju02FI
Margret	10	F	Child	19Ju02FI
George	08	M	Child	19Ju02FI
Rose	07	F	Child	19Ju02FI
Alice	06	F	Child	19Ju02FI
CARROLL, Eleanor	27	F	None	19Ju02FI
Patrick	12	M	None	19Ju02FI
CONNOR, John	35	M	Farmer	19Ju02FI

NAMES OF PASSENGERS		AGE	SEX	OCCUPATIONS	DATE PORT SHIP
CONNOR, Ann	(W)	31	F	None	19Ju02FI
Henrey	(S)	04	M	Child	19Ju02FI
John	(S)	02	M	Child	19Ju02FI
Eleanor	(D)	.00	F	Infant	19Ju02FI
HOGAN, Dennis		27	M	None	19Ju02FI
CALLAHAN, Betty		48	F	None	19Ju02FI
DUFFY, Michael		19	M	Laborer	19Ju02FI
BRADY, John		19	M	Laborer	19Ju02FI
Ann		19	F	None	19Ju02FI
RICHARDS, Benjamin		26	M	Laborer	19Ju02FI
Walter		23	M	Laborer	19Ju02FI
PETERS, Francis		27	M	Laborer	19Ju02FI
THOMAS, Stephen		30	M	Laborer	19Ju02FI
DRENNAN, Thos.		39	M	Laborer	19Ju02FI
POWERS, John		28	M	Laborer	19Ju02FI
WILLIAMS, Ann		20	F	Laborer	19Ju02FI
HAVEY, Cathn.		20	F	Laborer	19Ju02FI
MURRAY, John		17	M	Laborer	19Ju02FI
Simon		56	M	Farmer	19Ju02FI
Catherine		49	F	None	19Ju02FI
Eliza		13	F	None	19Ju02FI
Simon		11	M	None	19Ju02FI
Lucy		09	F	Child	19Ju02FI
Michael		07	M	Child	19Ju02FI
FLEMING, John		50	M	Farmer	19Ju02FI
BOYLE, James		20	M	Farmer	19Ju02FI
HOGAN, Mary		25	F	Farmer	19Ju02FI
RYAN, Thomas		21	M	Farmer	19Ju02FI
DELUREY, James		25	M	Farmer	19Ju02FI
WHITE, Richard		24	M	Laborer	19Ju02FI
MURRAY, James		20	M	Laborer	19Ju02FI
DELUREY, John		26	M	Laborer	19Ju02FI
CARDY, Margaret		20	F	None	19Ju02FI
WELSH, Margaret		23	F	None	19Ju02FI
MCGRATH, John		25	M	Laborer	19Ju02FI
Johanna		20	F	None	19Ju02FI
LACY, Bridget		24	F	None	19Ju02FI
ROYAL, Marg.		24	F	None	19Ju02FI
Mary	(D)	.00	F	Infant	19Ju02FI
EAGAN, John		45	M	None	19Ju02FI
Margt.		40	F	None	19Ju02FI
Elizabeth	(D)	08	F	Child	19Ju02FI
Michael	(S)	11	M	None	19Ju02FI
Mary	(D)	12	F	None	19Ju02FI
Bridget	(D)	16	F	None	19Ju02FI
CASS, Margt.		21	F	None	19Ju02FI
KELLY, Bridget		20	F	None	19Ju02FI
MULLOONEY, Mary		20	F	None	19Ju02FI
OLEARY, Elizabeth		24	F	None	19Ju02FI
MINCHEN, Michael		23	M	Laborer	19Ju02FI
Mary		22	F	None	19Ju02FI
Michael		.00	M	Infant	19Ju02FI
NUGENT, Ellen		16	F	Dressmaker	19Ju02FI
RICE, Roderick		37	M	Farmer	19Ju02FI
Mary	(W)	37	F	None	19Ju02FI
Thomas	(S)	13	M	None	19Ju02FI
George	(S)	11	M	None	19Ju02FI
James	(S)	08	M	Child	19Ju02FI
Hannah	(D)	05	F	Child	19Ju02FI
Griffeth	(S)	02	M	Child	19Ju02FI
GRIFFETH, Ann		24	F	None	19Ju02FI
EVANS, Richd.		37	M	Farmer	19Ju02FI
Margt.	(W)	29	F	None	19Ju02FI
John	(S)	08	M	Child	19Ju02FI
Richard	(S)	06	M	Child	19Ju02FI
Margt.	(D)	03	F	Child	19Ju02FI
MUSNEN, Jane		00	F	Unknown	19Ju02FI

ARABIAN 19 JUNE 1846

From Liverpool

NAMES OF PASSENGERS		AGE	SEX	OCCUPATIONS	DATE PORT SHIP
HOLMES, Thomas		22	M	Laborer	19Ju02FJ
FARRELLY, William		30	M	Laborer	19Ju02FJ
Ann		20	F	Laborer	19Ju02FJ
SMITH, Patrick		25	M	Laborer	19Ju02FJ
Jane		27	F	Laborer	19Ju02FJ
JONES, Lawrence		30	M	Laborer	19Ju02FJ
Margaret		30	F	Laborer	19Ju02FJ
LARKIN, Edward		25	M	Laborer	19Ju02FJ
FLOOD, Betty		16	F	Laborer	19Ju02FJ
GEARTY, Betty		20	F	Laborer	19Ju02FJ
FOX, Kitty		22	F	Laborer	19Ju02FJ
CARLIN, Mary		22	F	Laborer	19Ju02FJ
KELLY, Ann		22	F	Laborer	19Ju02FJ
WAKELY, Margt.		22	F	Laborer	19Ju02FJ
HALFPENNY, Pat		32	M	Laborer	19Ju02FJ
HOLLIGAN, James		32	M	Laborer	19Ju02FJ
MCQUADE, Henry		20	M	Laborer	19Ju02FJ
ODONELL, Michael		24	M	Laborer	19Ju02FJ
WALSH, John		30	M	Laborer	19Ju02FJ
GRUNDY, George		26	M	Laborer	19Ju02FJ
SMITH, Alfred		17	M	Laborer	19Ju02FJ
DAVIS, U-Mr.		36	M	Laborer	19Ju02FJ
NORRIS, Joseph		30	M	Laborer	19Ju02FJ
HAMILTON, U-Mr.		30	M	Laborer	19Ju02FJ
U	(W)	30	F	Laborer	19Ju02FJ
Elizabeth	(D)	10	F	Child	19Ju02FJ
James	(S)	07	M	Child	19Ju02FJ
John	(S)	06	M	Child	19Ju02FJ
George	(S)	02	M	Child	19Ju02FJ
William	(S)	.00	M	Infant	19Ju02FJ
MCKNIGHT, Edward		30	M	Laborer	19Ju02FJ
U	(W)	26	F	Laborer	19Ju02FJ
DAVIS, U-Mr.		20	M	Laborer	19Ju02FJ
MCKNIGHT, Elizabeth		05	F	Child	19Ju02FJ
HULL, Thomas		21	M	Laborer	19Ju02FJ
WALSH, U-Mrs.		30	F	Laborer	19Ju02FJ
Ann		16	F	Laborer	19Ju02FJ
Alicia		13	F	Laborer	19Ju02FJ
Eliza-Jane		09	F	Child	19Ju02FJ
MURPHY, Maria		20	F	Laborer	19Ju02FJ
FITZSIMMONS, Michael		28	M	Laborer	19Ju02FJ
Mary	(W)	25	F	Laborer	19Ju02FJ
Mary	(D)	02	F	Child	19Ju02FJ
Patrick	(S)	.00	M	Infant	19Ju02FJ
NORRIS, Joseph-G.		13	M	Laborer	19Ju02FJ
KELLER, Margt.		20	F	Laborer	19Ju02FJ
PROUDLY, Michael		20	M	Laborer	19Ju02FJ
CASSIDY, Ann		20	F	Laborer	19Ju02FJ
CARLON, Jas.		30	M	Laborer	19Ju02FJ
CARNEY, John		20	M	Laborer	19Ju02FJ
HANERTY, Lawrence		24	M	Laborer	19Ju02FJ
U	(W)	20	F	Laborer	19Ju02FJ
HEAH, Robert		35	M	Laborer	19Ju02FJ
TROPUN, Isiah		33	M	Laborer	19Ju02FJ
IRWEN, Jas.		22	M	Laborer	19Ju02FJ
HALL, Joseph		26	M	Laborer	19Ju02FJ
BURKE, Thomas		26	M	Laborer	19Ju02FJ
FLOOD, John		23	M	Laborer	19Ju02FJ
GILMORE, John		24	M	Laborer	19Ju02FJ
MCGANNEY, Patrick		20	M	Laborer	19Ju02FJ
HEART, William		23	M	Laborer	19Ju02FJ
DORRAN, Hugh		20	M	Laborer	19Ju02FJ
BRADY, Chris		20	M	Laborer	19Ju02FJ
CADY, Thomas		42	M	Laborer	19Ju02FJ
BURKE, Michael		27	M	Laborer	19Ju02FJ

NAMES OF PASSENGERS		AGE	SEX	OCCUPATIONS	DATE PORT SHIP
DONOGHUE, Mary		21	F	Laborer	19Ju02FJ
MARKY, Edward		22	M	Laborer	19Ju02FJ
Bridget		23	F	Laborer	19Ju02FJ
BURKE, John		21	M	Laborer	19Ju02FJ
BLAKE, George		36	M	Laborer	19Ju02FJ
JORDAN, Lawrence		21	M	Laborer	19Ju02FJ
GALLAGAN, Catharine		25	F	Laborer	19Ju02FJ
Mary		24	F	Laborer	19Ju02FJ
BELL, Hannah		21	F	Laborer	19Ju02FJ
LOFTUS, Michael		20	M	Laborer	19Ju02FJ
HARSWORD, Ann		34	F	Laborer	19Ju02FJ
Ellen		13	F	Laborer	19Ju02FJ
Wilson		07	M	Child	19Ju02FJ
KELLY, James		19	M	Child	19Ju02FJ
FLOSENN, Edward		23	M	Child	19Ju02FJ
U	(W)	23	F	Child	19Ju02FJ
KELLY, Teresa		18	F	Child	19Ju02FJ
BUTLER, Mary		20	F	Child	19Ju02FJ
Mary		.00	F	Infant	19Ju02FJ
NORTON, Andrew		26	M	Laborer	19Ju02FJ
U	(W)	25	F	Laborer	19Ju02FJ
Bridget	(D)	06	F	Child	19Ju02FJ
Thomas	(S)	02	M	Child	19Ju02FJ
James	(S)	01	M	Child	19Ju02FJ
Thomas		50	M	Laborer	19Ju02FJ
Michl.		24	M	Laborer	19Ju02FJ
FARLEY, James		25	M	Laborer	19Ju02FJ
U	(W)	25	F	Laborer	19Ju02FJ
Mary	(D)	07	F	Child	19Ju02FJ
Frances	(D)	03	F	Child	19Ju02FJ
John	(S)	01	M	Child	19Ju02FJ
MCDONNELL, Bridget		19	F	Laborer	19Ju02FJ
LAMB, Nicholas		26	M	Laborer	19Ju02FJ
LYNCH, Peter		22	M	Laborer	19Ju02FJ
CAROLAN, Pete		22	M	Laborer	19Ju02FJ
U	(W)	22	F	Laborer	19Ju02FJ
Mary	(D)	05	F	Child	19Ju02FJ
Thomas		19	M	Laborer	19Ju02FJ
John		20	M	Laborer	19Ju02FJ
CAFFRAY, Rose		20	F	Laborer	19Ju02FJ
CORGEN, Catharine		18	F	Laborer	19Ju02FJ
FINNEGAN, Catharine		18	F	Laborer	19Ju02FJ
SMITH, Mary		19	F	Laborer	19Ju02FJ
SMART, Michael		32	M	Laborer	19Ju02FJ
ROURKE, Thomas		35	M	Laborer	19Ju02FJ
RYAN, Patrick		22	M	Laborer	19Ju02FJ
POWELL, Joseph		20	M	Laborer	19Ju02FJ
LYNN, Timothy		35	M	Laborer	19Ju02FJ
CARROLL, Patrick		20	M	Laborer	19Ju02FJ
LYNCH, Thomas		20	M	Laborer	19Ju02FJ
U	(W)	25	F	Laborer	19Ju02FJ
CONNELL, Patt		24	M	Laborer	19Ju02FJ
DWYER, Ellen		22	F	Laborer	19Ju02FJ
CARROLL, Michl.		24	M	Laborer	19Ju02FJ
U	(W)	23	F	Laborer	19Ju02FJ
WEYMANS, John		26	M	Laborer	19Ju02FJ
HAPLETON, Philip		28	M	Laborer	19Ju02FJ
BLACK, John		24	M	Laborer	19Ju02FJ
U	(W)	22	F	Laborer	19Ju02FJ
Bridget	(D)	01	F	Child	19Ju02FJ
HARLEY, John		24	M	Laborer	19Ju02FJ
U	(W)	22	F	Laborer	19Ju02FJ
MCADAM, John		21	M	Laborer	19Ju02FJ
WALSH, Wm.		19	M	Laborer	19Ju02FJ
FARLEY, Mary		19	F	Laborer	19Ju02FJ
FESTON, Mary		20	F	Laborer	19Ju02FJ
Ellen		20	F	Laborer	19Ju02FJ
GARRETY, Michael		30	M	Laborer	19Ju02FJ
DALTON, James		26	M	Laborer	19Ju02FJ
U	(W)	24	F	Laborer	19Ju02FJ
U	(D)	01	F	Infant	19Ju02FJ
BERRY, Thomas		40	M	Laborer	19Ju02FJ
U	(W)	34	F	Laborer	19Ju02FJ
James	(S)	13	M	Laborer	19Ju02FJ
Patrick	(S)	13	M	Laborer	19Ju02FJ
BERRY, John	(S)	11	M	Laborer	19Ju02FJ
Thomas	(S)	09	M	Child	19Ju02FJ
Michael	(S)	08	M	Child	19Ju02FJ
Ann	(D)	06	F	Child	19Ju02FJ
U	(D)	.00	F	Infant	19Ju02FJ
MCCALL, Lawrence		24	M	Laborer	19Ju02FJ
Ann		20	F	Laborer	19Ju02FJ
SHERIDAN, U-Mrs.		40	F	Laborer	19Ju02FJ
Jane	(D)	20	F	Laborer	19Ju02FJ
MILLER, U-Mrs.		20	F	Laborer	19Ju02FJ
FORD, Mary-Ann		19	F	Laborer	19Ju02FJ
BRADY, David		12	M	Laborer	19Ju02FJ
JESSON, Robert		20	M	Laborer	19Ju02FJ
BUTLER, Robert		30	M	Laborer	19Ju02FJ
Mary		40	F	Laborer	19Ju02FJ
FOX, Thomas		20	M	Laborer	19Ju02FJ
DENBONEY, Catharine		20	F	Laborer	19Ju02FJ
BURKE, John		24	M	Laborer	19Ju02FJ
BRATTEN, Wm.		22	M	Laborer	19Ju02FJ
CURRAN, Daniel		30	M	Laborer	19Ju02FJ
Dennis		26	M	Laborer	19Ju02FJ
Mary		60	F	Laborer	19Ju02FJ
MARTIN, Catharine		20	F	Laborer	19Ju02FJ
FEANEY, Thomas		21	M	Laborer	19Ju02FJ
Muld---, John		22	M	Laborer	19Ju02FJ
QUIGLEY, Charles		35	M	Laborer	19Ju02FJ
MCGEOUGH, Ann		45	F	Laborer	19Ju02FJ
MCCANNA, Mary		25	F	Laborer	19Ju02FJ
QUIGLEY, Susan		23	F	Laborer	19Ju02FJ
SHEA, Mary		30	F	Laborer	19Ju02FJ
CURRAN, Mary		20	F	Laborer	19Ju02FJ
SHEA, Judy		25	F	Laborer	19Ju02FJ
SULLIVAN, John		25	M	Laborer	19Ju02FJ
DALLY, Johanna		17	F	Laborer	19Ju02FJ
CURRAN, Dennis		25	M	Laborer	19Ju02FJ
CLARK, Ann		20	F	Laborer	19Ju02FJ
HUSIAN, Catharine		20	F	Laborer	19Ju02FJ
RYAN, John		27	M	Laborer	19Ju02FJ
KELLY, Hugh		25	M	Laborer	19Ju02FJ
HEART, Michl.		25	M	Laborer	19Ju02FJ
BRAINER, Mary		23	F	Laborer	19Ju02FJ
CLARK, Honora		20	F	Laborer	19Ju02FJ
MURRAY, Owen		26	M	Laborer	19Ju02FJ
Bridget		24	F	Laborer	19Ju02FJ
FINERTY, Owen		28	M	Laborer	19Ju02FJ
Bridget		40	F	Laborer	19Ju02FJ
OHARA, Thomas		25	M	Laborer	19Ju02FJ
John		21	M	Laborer	19Ju02FJ
Martin		07	M	Child	19Ju02FJ
SAVAGE, Robert		21	M	Laborer	19Ju02FJ
CARROLL, Patrick		22	M	Laborer	19Ju02FJ
FINN, Lawrence		26	M	Laborer	19Ju02FJ
KELLY, John		16	M	Laborer	19Ju02FJ
FINN, Michael		02	M	Child	19Ju02FJ
COUGHLIN, John		11	M	Laborer	19Ju02FJ
CAWLEY, Loughlin		26	M	Laborer	19Ju02FJ
HENAN, Margt.		11	F	Laborer	19Ju02FJ
DOUGLAS, John		24	M	Laborer	19Ju02FJ
GOROUGHTY, Bridget		23	F	Laborer	19Ju02FJ
DAVIS, Catharine		24	F	Laborer	19Ju02FJ
MCHUGH, John		21	M	Laborer	19Ju02FJ
CARROLL, U-Mrs.		50	F	Laborer	19Ju02FJ
Ellen	(D)	20	F	Laborer	19Ju02FJ
Bridget	(D)	14	F	Laborer	19Ju02FJ
Eliza	(D)	18	F	Laborer	19Ju02FJ
Ann	(D)	17	F	Laborer	19Ju02FJ
CONROY, Biddy		20	F	Laborer	19Ju02FJ
CONDRON, Cathe		20	F	Laborer	19Ju02FJ
MOONEY, Cathe		20	F	Laborer	19Ju02FJ
FOX, Gabrial		20	M	Laborer	19Ju02FJ
FARREL, James		19	M	Laborer	19Ju02FJ
CONWAY, John		18	M	Laborer	19Ju02FJ
Thomas		20	M	Laborer	19Ju02FJ

NAMES OF PASSENGERS	A G E	S E X	OCCUPATIONS	DATE PORT SHIP

HANNAH-KERR 20 JUNE 1846

From Liverpool

NAMES OF PASSENGERS	A G E	S E X	OCCUPATIONS	DATE PORT SHIP	NAMES OF PASSENGERS	A G E	S E X	OCCUPATIONS	DATE PORT SHIP
					CALLAGHER, Peter	18	M	Servant	20Ju02Gq
					Ellen	20	F	Servant	20Ju02Gq
					SHERIDAN, Margat	13	F	Servant	20Ju02Gq
					MCGOWEN, John	25	M	Servant	20Ju02Gq
					MCGORLEY, Thomas	27	M	Servant	20Ju02Gq
					GONYAN, Cath.	16	F	Servant	20Ju02Gq
					FALKES, Mathew	25	M	Laborer	20Ju02Gq
					TALBOT, Thomas	24	M	Laborer	20Ju02Gq
					BRYON, Michael	18	M	Laborer	20Ju02Gq
DONAL, Joseph	31	M	Farmer	20Ju02Gq	Patt	17	M	Laborer	20Ju02Gq
MULLOR, Mary-Ann	20	F	Farmer	20Ju02Gq	Edmond	16	M	Laborer	20Ju02Gq
KNIGHTLY, Richard	22	M	Farmer	20Ju02Gq	James	35	M	Laborer	20Ju02Gq
GREEN, Thomas	36	M	Farmer	20Ju02Gq	RYAN, John	28	M	Laborer	20Ju02Gq
MCGAGHANAN, Peter	22	M	Farmer	20Ju02Gq	BYRON, Bridget	36	F	Laborer	20Ju02Gq
MCGAHNY, Thomas	26	M	Farmer	20Ju02Gq	Cath	13	F	Laborer	20Ju02Gq
LITTLE, James	17	M	Farmer	20Ju02Gq	Honora	12	F	Laborer	20Ju02Gq
BYRNES, John	18	M	Farmer	20Ju02Gq	Mary	10	F	Laborer	20Ju02Gq
SHERIDAN, Patrick	22	M	Farmer	20Ju02Gq	Ellen	08	F	Child	20Ju02Gq
REILLY, Ann	20	F	Farmer	20Ju02Gq	Margaret	06	F	Child	20Ju02Gq
CARR, Mary	18	F	Farmer	20Ju02Gq	Michael	20	M	Laborer	20Ju02Gq
MCCABE, Mary	35	F	Farmer	20Ju02Gq	WALSH, Margt.	20	M	Laborer	20Ju02Gq
HUGHES, James	26	M	Farmer	20Ju02Gq	GORMLEY, Edward	21	M	Laborer	20Ju02Gq
LYNSKEY, Walter	20	M	Farmer	20Ju02Gq	Mary	70	F	Laborer	20Ju02Gq
CAHILL, Bridget	30	F	Farmer	20Ju02Gq	SHAW, Phoebe	20	F	Laborer	20Ju02Gq
COUGHLON, Mary	20	F	Farmer	20Ju02Gq	DILLON, Neal	61	M	Laborer	20Ju02Gq
QUINN, Edward	30	M	Farmer	20Ju02Gq	ANTHONY, Cathy	21	F	WI	20Ju02Gq
Bridget	30	F	Servant	20Ju02Gq	HAMILTON, William	20	M	Laborer	20Ju02Gq
Rose	20	F	Servant	20Ju02Gq	GROWNEY, U	18	F	Laborer	20Ju02Gq
MANNEON, Mary	11	F	Servant	20Ju02Gq	FLINT, Kath	25	F	Laborer	20Ju02Gq
RUAN, Cath	20	F	Servant	20Ju02Gq	MADEGAN, Mary	17	F	Laborer	20Ju02Gq
CRAVEN, John	25	M	Servant	20Ju02Gq	Stephen	06	M	Child	20Ju02Gq
Margaret	18	F	Servant	20Ju02Gq	Thom	20	F	Laborer	20Ju02Gq
LEERY, Bridget	30	F	Servant	20Ju02Gq	DWYER, U-Mrs.	15	F	Laborer	20Ju02Gq
GIBBINS, Thomas	19	M	Servant	20Ju02Gq	SHANLEY, Tim	22	M	Laborer	20Ju02Gq
BARWOOD, Eliza	16	F	Servant	20Ju02Gq	BEGAN, Edward	20	M	Servant	20Ju02Gq
CRAVEN, Michael	20	M	Servant	20Ju02Gq	BLACKNLY, Mary-Ann	20	F	Servant	20Ju02Gq
GAFFNEY, Luke	24	M	Servant	20Ju02Gq	John	20	M	Servant	20Ju02Gq
SCULLY, Michael	26	M	Servant	20Ju02Gq	SULLIVAN, James	16	M	Servant	20Ju02Gq
BYRNE, Mary	32	F	Servant	20Ju02Gq	TELFORD, Fanny	24	F	Servant	20Ju02Gq
COOK, Patrick	26	M	Servant	20Ju02Gq	DAGG, Edward	35	M	Servant	20Ju02Gq
CLARKE, Catherine	15	F	Servant	20Ju02Gq	MCDONNELL, John	35	M	Servant	20Ju02Gq
Abby	17	F	Servant	20Ju02Gq	COLLIN, William	24	M	Servant	20Ju02Gq
SMITH, Mary	16	F	Servant	20Ju02Gq	CULLIN, John	20	M	Servant	20Ju02Gq
REILLY, Cath.	07	F	Child	20Ju02Gq	Ann	.00	F	Infant	20Ju02Gq
HANLEY, Mary	17	F	Laborer	20Ju02Gq	Jos.	36	M	Servant	20Ju02Gq
ROURKE, U	20	F	Laborer	20Ju02Gq	MURRAY, Margaret	24	F	Servant	20Ju02Gq
Ann	30	F	Laborer	20Ju02Gq	NEWGEN, Ellen	20	F	Servant	20Ju02Gq
Cath	11	F	Laborer	20Ju02Gq	DUNMARY, Honora	.00	F	Infant	20Ju02Gq
Mary	09	F	Child	20Ju02Gq	FINCENIA, Honora	24	F	Servant	20Ju02Gq
SMITH, Bernard	07	M	Child	20Ju02Gq	Ann	17	F	Servant	20Ju02Gq
James	30	M	Servant	20Ju02Gq	DRWER, John	13	M	Servant	20Ju02Gq
Ann	19	F	Servant	20Ju02Gq	MCCRACKEN, Jack	11	M	Servant	20Ju02Gq
MCCORMACK, Ellen	30	F	Servant	20Ju02Gq	Hugh	24	M	Servant	20Ju02Gq
FLOOD, Ann	20	F	Servant	20Ju02Gq	KENNEDY, Martin	25	M	Servant	20Ju02Gq
CON, Mary	21	F	Servant	20Ju02Gq	Cath.	23	F	Servant	20Ju02Gq
GANNOR, Margt.	20	F	Servant	20Ju02Gq	John	22	M	Servant	20Ju02Gq
BROWN, George	20	M	Servant	20Ju02Gq	U (W)	21	F	Servant	20Ju02Gq
REILLY, Ann	18	F	Servant	20Ju02Gq	Henry	13	M	Servant	20Ju02Gq
Mary	17	F	Servant	20Ju02Gq	Alex	40	F	Servant	20Ju02Gq
GREEN, Cath.	19	F	Servant	20Ju02Gq	NORTON, Martin	20	M	Laborer	20Ju02Gq
KEVANNY, John	59	M	Servant	20Ju02Gq	MCCANDY, John	25	M	Laborer	20Ju02Gq
Bridget	50	F	Servant	20Ju02Gq	MCCABE, Cath	18	F	Laborer	20Ju02Gq
Margaret	21	F	Servant	20Ju02Gq	MULLIGAN, Owen	20	M	Laborer	20Ju02Gq
Bridget	19	F	Servant	20Ju02Gq	MCGRAW, Sarah	20	F	Laborer	20Ju02Gq
Catherine	17	F	Servant	20Ju02Gq	MCCRACKEN, James	36	M	Laborer	20Ju02Gq
Winifred	12	F	Servant	20Ju02Gq	Patrick	06	M	Child	20Ju02Gq
MCGOWIN, Patrick	19	M	Servant	20Ju02Gq	KENNEDY, Patrick	25	M	Laborer	20Ju02Gq
CONIGAN, Cecella	18	F	Servant	20Ju02Gq	Thomas	20	M	Laborer	20Ju02Gq
MULDOON, Mary	19	F	Servant	20Ju02Gq	Nancy	26	F	Laborer	20Ju02Gq
QUINN, Nancy	17	F	Servant	20Ju02Gq	Bridget	11	F	Laborer	20Ju02Gq
WALLACE, Nancy	16	M	Servant	20Ju02Gq	MALEY, Julia	23	F	Laborer	20Ju02Gq
DWYER, John	22	M	Servant	20Ju02Gq	Thomas	20	M	Laborer	20Ju02Gq
Jeremiah	17	M	Servant	20Ju02Gq	CAMPION, Jeremiah	21	M	Laborer	20Ju02Gq
MCDERMOTT, Ann	32	F	Servant	20Ju02Gq	SIMMONS, Ellen	20	F	Laborer	20Ju02Gq
					KIERNAN, Margret	17	F	Laborer	20Ju02Gq

172

NAMES OF PASSENGERS	AGE	SEX	OCCUPATIONS	DATE PORT SHIP
MURPHY, Mathew	21	M	Laborer	20Ju02Gq
COYLE, Nicholas	30	M	Laborer	20Ju02Gq
KELLY, May	16	F	Laborer	20Ju02Gq
GANNON, Abby	20	F	Laborer	20Ju02Gq
NULTY, Patt	22	M	Laborer	20Ju02Gq
MCKEAN, Hugh	25	M	Laborer	20Ju02Gq
REILLY, Phillip	20	M	Laborer	20Ju02Gq
CAHILL, Margaret	19	F	Laborer	20Ju02Gq
MASTERSON, Ann	19	F	Laborer	20Ju02Gq
GAFFENEY, Mary	09	F	Child	20Ju02Gq
MCDONALD, Biddy	20	F	Laborer	20Ju02Gq
BRAHAN, Peter	20	M	Laborer	20Ju02Gq
CRINNER, Dennis	25	M	Laborer	20Ju02Gq
DENNISTON, Patt	50	M	Laborer	20Ju02Gq
May	13	F	Laborer	20Ju02Gq
Biddy	11	F	Laborer	20Ju02Gq
Cath	09	F	Child	20Ju02Gq
LAVRY, Alice	10	F	Laborer	20Ju02Gq
MCCORMICK, Biddy	19	F	Laborer	20Ju02Gq
MCEARLY, Biddy	50	F	Laborer	20Ju02Gq
James	18	M	Laborer	20Ju02Gq
Patt	16	M	Laborer	20Ju02Gq
Phillip	15	M	Laborer	20Ju02Gq
Biddy	20	F	Laborer	20Ju02Gq
GROVEY, Biddy	20	F	Laborer	20Ju02Gq
BRONEY, U-Mrs.	30	F	Laborer	20Ju02Gq
Ann (D)	.00	F	Infant	20Ju02Gq
MURRAY, Richard	23	M	Servant	20Ju02Gq
FRICAY, Mary	17	F	Servant	20Ju02Gq
FLANSBURY, William	50	M	Servant	20Ju02Gq
James	29	M	Servant	20Ju02Gq
REILLY, Edward	21	M	Servant	20Ju02Gq
LYNCH, Peter	21	M	Servant	20Ju02Gq
CUSHING, Thomas	19	M	Servant	20Ju02Gq
Cath	18	F	Servant	20Ju02Gq
GEORGE, Mary-Jane	18	F	Servant	20Ju02Gq
WRIGHT, Jane	19	F	Laborer	20Ju02Gq
KAUGHER, Mary	30	F	Laborer	20Ju02Gq
MORAN, Patrick	25	M	Laborer	20Ju02Gq
DONNELLY, Dennis	24	M	Laborer	20Ju02Gq
FLANNY, Hugh	25	M	Laborer	20Ju02Gq
KEARNS, Mary	40	F	Laborer	20Ju02Gq
BLAKE, Richard	27	M	Laborer	20Ju02Gq
Bridget	26	F	Laborer	20Ju02Gq
GOGHAN, Honora	21	F	Laborer	20Ju02Gq
Patrick	28	M	Laborer	20Ju02Gq
Peggy	25	F	Laborer	20Ju02Gq
Francis	23	M	Laborer	20Ju02Gq
DOGHERTY, John	14	M	Laborer	20Ju02Gq
BANNAN, Cath	25	F	Laborer	20Ju02Gq
Ellen	22	F	Laborer	20Ju02Gq
COUGHTON, John	24	M	Laborer	20Ju02Gq
KEARNY, John	40	M	Laborer	20Ju02Gq
U (W)	40	F	Laborer	20Ju02Gq
Mary (D)	18	F	Laborer	20Ju02Gq
Ellen (D)	10	F	Laborer	20Ju02Gq
CREER, Stephen	24	M	Laborer	20Ju02Gq
WALSH, John	18	M	Laborer	20Ju02Gq
KELROW, Thomas	18	M	Laborer	20Ju02Gq
MCGUINNIS, John	27	M	Laborer	20Ju02Gq
CUEL, Patrick	23	M	Laborer	20Ju02Gq
WRIGHT, Robt.	17	M	Laborer	20Ju02Gq
MCCONNELL, William	50	M	Laborer	20Ju02Gq
Elizabeth (W)	48	F	Laborer	20Ju02Gq
Margret (D)	18	F	Laborer	20Ju02Gq
Andrew (S)	16	M	Laborer	20Ju02Gq
Jane (D)	15	F	Laborer	20Ju02Gq
MCNIELE, Isabella	17	F	Laborer	20Ju02Gq
CULLEN, Mary	20	F	Laborer	20Ju02Gq
COLLINS, Sarah	20	F	Laborer	20Ju02Gq
ARMSTRONG, Isabella	21	F	Laborer	20Ju02Gq
BRADIE, Mary	21	F	WI	20Ju02Gq
DODD, Henry	24	M	Laborer	20Ju02Gq
Bridget	23	F	Laborer	20Ju02Gq
Mary	03	F	Child	20Ju02Gq

NAMES OF PASSENGERS	AGE	SEX	OCCUPATIONS	DATE PORT SHIP
DODD, Patt	02	M	Child	20Ju02Gq
Cath.	.00	F	Infant	20Ju02Gq
FANNY, John	23	M	Laborer	20Ju02Gq
Sarah	20	F	Laborer	20Ju02Gq
CAVANAH, Patt	20	M	Laborer	20Ju02Gq
WHITE, Cath	20	F	Laborer	20Ju02Gq
MCGARVEY, Bernard	18	M	Laborer	20Ju02Gq
Abbey	15	M	Laborer	20Ju02Gq
HENRY, Mary	36	F	Laborer	20Ju02Gq
ARMSTRONG, Jane	25	F	Laborer	20Ju02Gq
BRUCE, Jane	22	F	Laborer	20Ju02Gq
FARRELL, Patrick	19	M	Laborer	20Ju02Gq
BRADFIELD, Ann	19	F	Laborer	20Ju02Gq
BROWN, James	24	M	Servant	20Ju02Gq
U (W)	21	F	Wife	20Ju02Gq
HUTTERY, Cath	40	F	Cook	20Ju02Gq
Edmond	24	M	Laborer	20Ju02Gq
Cath	12	F	None	20Ju02Gq
Mary	10	F	None	20Ju02Gq
Edmond	07	M	Child	20Ju02Gq
Briodget	12	F	None	20Ju02Gq

HENDRIK-HUDSON 20 JUNE 1846

From London

NAMES OF PASSENGERS	AGE	SEX	OCCUPATIONS	DATE PORT SHIP
ALEXANDER, Esther	38	F	Lady	20Ju21Bh
LEWIS, Anne-E.	28	F	None	20Ju21Bh
David	24	M	Merchant	20Ju21Bh
BROWN, Peter	68	M	Captain	20Ju21Bh
MCDONALD, Alexander	24	M	Farmer	20Ju21Bh
MONTAGUE, Edward-P.	29	M	Doctor	20Ju21Bh
THOMAS, Henry	27	M	Draper	20Ju21Bh
HELMES, James	30	M	Iron Monger	20Ju21Bh
Mary (W)	29	F	Wife	20Ju21Bh
James (S)	04	M	Child	20Ju21Bh
Mary (D)	03	F	Child	20Ju21Bh
BROWN, Charley	17	M	Student	20Ju21Bh
WELLSDEN, Elizabeth	30	F	Student	20Ju21Bh
Anne (D)	13	F	Student	20Ju21Bh
Elizabeth (D)	11	F	Student	20Ju21Bh
Ellen (D)	09	F	Child	20Ju21Bh
Richard (S)	08	M	Child	20Ju21Bh
Simson (S)	.00	M	Infant	20Ju21Bh
Died-At-Sea				
PURRILL, Chaarles	40	M	Bookmaker	20Ju21Bh
Mary	56	F	Bookmaker	20Ju21Bh
Charles	06	M	Child	20Ju21Bh
Sarah	04	F	Child	20Ju21Bh
John	03	M	Child	20Ju21Bh
FREEMAN, William	38	M	Druggist	20Ju21Bh
Caroline (W)	38	F	Wife	20Ju21Bh
William (S)	10	M	None	20Ju21Bh
Catherine (D)	04	F	Child	20Ju21Bh
CLUMM, Augustus	50	M	Merchant	20Ju21Bh
Maria (W)	48	F	Wife	20Ju21Bh
Augustus (S)	13	M	None	20Ju21Bh
Phillip (S)	12	M	None	20Ju21Bh
Edwin (S)	09	M	Child	20Ju21Bh
CRAMP, Robert	47	M	Laborer	20Ju21Bh
GONDEY, Thomas	22	M	Printer	20Ju21Bh
MARTIN, William	38	M	Bootmaker	20Ju21Bh
KING, James	14	M	None	20Ju21Bh
LAVENDER, William	34	M	Currier	20Ju21Bh
PARK, George	41	M	Farmer	20Ju21Bh
HANDS, Robert	34	M	Farmer	20Ju21Bh
LAMBERT, Maria	46	F	Lady	20Ju21Bh
Sarah	16	F	Lady	20Ju21Bh
SCARR, Alfred-S.	35	M	Merchant	20Ju21Bh

NAMES OF PASSENGERS	AGE	SEX	OCCUPATIONS	DATE PORT SHIP
SHRICH, Charles	23	M	Merchant	20Ju21Bh
KISBY, William	23	M	Laborer	20Ju21Bh
DIVINE, John	39	M	Blacksmith	20Ju21Bh
FROST, Daniel	27	M	Farmer	20Ju21Bh
John	21	M	Farmer	20Ju21Bh
FULLOCK, Charles	25	M	Farmer	20Ju21Bh

ASHBURTON 22 JUNE 1846

From Liverpool

NAMES OF PASSENGERS	AGE	SEX	OCCUPATIONS	DATE PORT SHIP
MAHON, Michael	50	M	Farmer	22Ju02Bd
Bridget	40	F	Farmer	22Ju02Bd
John	22	M	Farmer	22Ju02Bd
William	13	M	Farmer	22Ju02Bd
Eleanor	06	F	Child	22Ju02Bd
RYAN, Pat	35	M	None	22Ju02Bd
MCLAUGHLIN, Thos.	23	M	Farmer	22Ju02Bd
Ellen	22	F	Farmer	22Ju02Bd
RACEY, Joseph	40	M	Shoemaker	22Ju02Bd
SPERRING, John	44	M	Farmer	22Ju02Bd
LEARY, John	50	M	Farmer	22Ju02Bd
Keady	25	M	Farmer	22Ju02Bd
Michael	24	M	Farmer	22Ju02Bd
David	23	M	Farmer	22Ju02Bd
RAFFERTY, James	40	M	None	22Ju02Bd
Mary	40	F	None	22Ju02Bd
Catherine	09	F	Child	22Ju02Bd
Michael	06	M	Child	22Ju02Bd
Dennis	02	M	Child	22Ju02Bd
Died-At-Sea				
CONNOR, James	33	M	None	22Ju02Bd
Mary	33	F	None	22Ju02Bd
Thomas	12	M	None	22Ju02Bd
Edmond	08	M	Child	22Ju02Bd
Mary	36	F	None	22Ju02Bd
Pat	02	M	Child	22Ju02Bd
GORMAN, Nelly	28	F	None	22Ju02Bd
CRANLY, Mary	02	F	Child	22Ju02Bd
AGNEW, Michael	36	M	Tailor	22Ju02Bd
Ellen	30	F	Tailor	22Ju02Bd
MADDEN, Thos.	23	M	Farmer	22Ju02Bd
Mary	25	M	Farmer	22Ju02Bd
NICHOLSON, Pat	18	M	Farmer	22Ju02Bd
MAYLEY, Mary	18	F	Farmer	22Ju02Bd
GAHAN, Eliza	19	F	Farmer	22Ju02Bd
SULLIVAN, Ann	27	F	Farmer	22Ju02Bd
BELL, John	28	M	Weaver	22Ju02Bd
MCLEAR, Hugh	22	M	Shoemaker	22Ju02Bd
Mary	19	F	Shoemaker	22Ju02Bd
Robert	18	M	Shoemaker	22Ju02Bd
MCCARTNEY, Pat	25	M	Shoemaker	22Ju02Bd
ODONNELL, Mike	30	M	Shoemaker	22Ju02Bd
MCSTAY, Mike	20	M	Sail Maker	22Ju02Bd
HORN, Martin	21	M	None	22Ju02Bd
KELLY, John	30	M	None	22Ju02Bd
Bridget	25	F	None	22Ju02Bd
CARTHON, Thomas	29	M	None	22Ju02Bd
Catherine	22	F	None	22Ju02Bd
ONEIL, John	37	M	None	22Ju02Bd
Margaret	24	F	None	22Ju02Bd
Mary-Ann	01	F	Child	22Ju02Bd
BIRMINGHAM, Catherine	18	F	None	22Ju02Bd
MAHAN, Margaret	18	F	None	22Ju02Bd
MULDON, Joseph	22	M	Weaver	22Ju02Bd
Nancy	22	F	Weaver	22Ju02Bd
MCNELLY, Felix	47	M	Sail Maker	22Ju02Bd
James	19	M	None	22Ju02Bd
MCCARTY, John	28	M	Weaver	22Ju02Bd
HUMBLE, Jane	21	F	None	22Ju02Bd
ANTHONY, Elisabeth	36	F	None	22Ju02Bd
DONLIN, Nelly	18	F	None	22Ju02Bd
GANETZ, Mary	20	F	None	22Ju02Bd
JOHNSON, Rebecca	25	F	None	22Ju02Bd
MCEVANS, Thos.	32	M	Farmer	22Ju02Bd
John	05	M	Child	22Ju02Bd
Rose	26	F	None	22Ju02Bd
Sarah-Ann	03	F	Child	22Ju02Bd
Lititia	01	F	Child	22Ju02Bd
CHANDLER, James	39	M	None	22Ju02Bd
Jane	38	F	None	22Ju02Bd
Joseph	09	M	None	22Ju02Bd
Emily	04	F	Child	22Ju02Bd
Fredk.	02	M	Child	22Ju02Bd
Elizabeth	01	F	Child	22Ju02Bd
SHANLEY, Tim	22	M	None	22Ju02Bd
BLEWIT, John	20	M	Butcher	22Ju02Bd
SARTON, James	19	M	None	22Ju02Bd
BUTLER, Pat	22	M	None	22Ju02Bd
SULLIVAN, James	16	M	None	22Ju02Bd
SMITH, Mary	20	F	None	22Ju02Bd
CREID, Michael	26	M	None	22Ju02Bd
OCONNELL, Thos.	18	M	None	22Ju02Bd
Ann	16	F	None	22Ju02Bd
ONEIL, Catherine	18	F	None	22Ju02Bd
MURRY, Judy	19	F	None	22Ju02Bd
DUNN, Mary	10	F	None	22Ju02Bd
Michael	12	M	None	22Ju02Bd
MAUGAN, Daniel	25	M	Farmer	22Ju02Bd
John	25	M	Farmer	22Ju02Bd
DANIEL, Pat	25	M	Bricklayer	22Ju02Bd
John	23	M	Bricklayer	22Ju02Bd
LOURNE, Mary	11	F	Bricklayer	22Ju02Bd
CASY, Pat	25	M	None	22Ju02Bd
MULLIGAN, David	23	M	Farmer	22Ju02Bd
WHITE, Thos.	26	M	Carpenter	22Ju02Bd
DYER, Thos.	45	M	None	22Ju02Bd
Mary	40	F	None	22Ju02Bd
Mike	70	M	None	22Ju02Bd
Mike	15	M	None	22Ju02Bd
Pat	07	M	Child	22Ju02Bd
Bridget	09	F	Child	22Ju02Bd
Margaret	18	F	None	22Ju02Bd
Judy	17	F	None	22Ju02Bd
Mary	03	F	Child	22Ju02Bd
Thos.	02	M	Child	22Ju02Bd
HETHERMONT, Dennis	50	M	None	22Ju02Bd
Ellen	50	F	None	22Ju02Bd
Pat	16	M	None	22Ju02Bd
Mary	14	F	None	22Ju02Bd
Ellen	12	F	None	22Ju02Bd
Mike	07	M	Child	22Ju02Bd
FARRELL, James	23	M	Child	22Ju02Bd
SHEALES, Pat	24	M	None	22Ju02Bd
LIVINGSTON, John	25	M	None	22Ju02Bd
Ann	55	F	None	22Ju02Bd
Mary	20	F	None	22Ju02Bd
DOCHERTY, John	23	M	None	22Ju02Bd
BURKE, Steven	27	M	None	22Ju02Bd
BURN, Mike	30	M	None	22Ju02Bd
Saul	25	M	None	22Ju02Bd
Martin	27	M	None	22Ju02Bd
Bridget	25	F	None	22Ju02Bd
Mary	02	F	Child	22Ju02Bd
WINTER, Pat	18	M	None	22Ju02Bd
DOWNES, Edmond	24	M	Farmer	22Ju02Bd
FITZPATRICK, Barney	37	M	Unknown	22Ju02Bd
MCHONNOGILL, Phil	30	M	None	22Ju02Bd
Thos.	22	M	None	22Ju02Bd
Margaret	18	F	None	22Ju02Bd
Rose	13	F	None	22Ju02Bd
Mary	12	F	None	22Ju02Bd
FLINER, Mike	20	M	None	22Ju02Bd

NAMES OF PASSENGERS	AGE	SEX	OCCUPATIONS	DATE PORT SHIP
HAVER, John	20	M	Unknown	22Ju02Bd
Ann	28	F	Unknown	22Ju02Bd
JENNEY, James	20	M	Unknown	22Ju02Bd
DENNY, Catherine	21	F	Unknown	22Ju02Bd
JENNY, Jane	17	F	Unknown	22Ju02Bd
FLANIGAN, John	20	M	Unknown	22Ju02Bd
Catherine	18	F	Unknown	22Ju02Bd
MORE, William	26	M	Unknown	22Ju02Bd
Bridget	23	F	Unknown	22Ju02Bd
Masy	02	F	Child	22Ju02Bd
Bridget	23	F	None	22Ju02Bd
WELSH, Thomas	24	M	None	22Ju02Bd
Pat	22	M	None	22Ju02Bd
GIBSON, Mary	18	F	None	22Ju02Bd
GLINN, Dianna	30	F	None	22Ju02Bd
HUGHES, Martha	20	F	None	22Ju02Bd
KENNISON, Joseph	23	M	None	22Ju02Bd
BLYTHE, James	20	M	None	22Ju02Bd
MORRE, Sally	29	F	None	22Ju02Bd
Thos.	07	M	Child	22Ju02Bd
Catherine	05	F	Child	22Ju02Bd
Margaret	03	F	Child	22Ju02Bd
William	01	M	Child	22Ju02Bd
GEHEN, Elizabeth	44	F	Unknown	22Ju02Bd
Margaret	19	F	Unknown	22Ju02Bd
Ellen	10	F	Unknown	22Ju02Bd
MORRE, John	18	M	Unknown	22Ju02Bd
MCGUINNES, Mary	10	F	Unknown	22Ju02Bd
BENNETT, John	19	M	Tailor	22Ju02Bd
William	16	M	Unknown	22Ju02Bd
DONOUGHUE, John	20	M	Unknown	22Ju02Bd
DOCHERTY, Thos.	45	M	Unknown	22Ju02Bd
Betty	45	F	Unknown	22Ju02Bd
Mary	16	F	Unknown	22Ju02Bd
Martha	13	F	Unknown	22Ju02Bd
Joseph	12	M	Unknown	22Ju02Bd
MCCARTY, William	04	M	Child	22Ju02Bd
Ellen	05	F	Child	22Ju02Bd
CANESTY, Patrick	20	M	Unknown	22Ju02Bd
MCDONNELL, Pat	27	M	Unknown	22Ju02Bd
FLINNEGAN, Margaret	28	F	Unknown	22Ju02Bd
SIMS, William	23	M	Unknown	22Ju02Bd
BRUNELL, Ellen	23	F	Unknown	22Ju02Bd
DOYLE, Joanna	23	F	Unknown	22Ju02Bd
CONDON, Mary	24	F	Unknown	22Ju02Bd
FAY, Susan	21	F	Unknown	22Ju02Bd
MCGAYNE, Mary	21	F	Unknown	22Ju02Bd
FITZSIMMONS, John	24	M	Lnknown	22Ju02Bd
MACINALLY, Pat	10	M	None	22Ju02Bd
Mary	06	F	Child	22Ju02Bd
Edd.	08	M	Child	22Ju02Bd
MCLAUGHLIN, Mary	22	F	None	22Ju02Bd
MACINALLY, Mary	20	F	None	22Ju02Bd
LAWLESS, Pat	30	M	None	22Ju02Bd
DAILY, Martha	20	F	None	22Ju02Bd
MACINTYRE, Mary	50	F	None	22Ju02Bd
Saml.	20	M	None	22Ju02Bd
Ann	18	M	None	22Ju02Bd
PAN, Margaret	20	F	None	22Ju02Bd
CALLAN, Mary	16	F	None	22Ju02Bd
Patt (S)	07	M	Child	22Ju02Bd
CLEARY, Dennis	23	M	Shipwright	22Ju02Bd
MITCHELL, James	23	M	Farmer	22Ju02Bd
MILLER, Alexn.	16	M	None	22Ju02Bd
Rose-Ann	18	F	None	22Ju02Bd
FORD, Mary	20	F	None	22Ju02Bd
MONAHAN, Honor	19	F	None	22Ju02Bd
SMITH, Catherine	20	F	None	22Ju02Bd
LEASY, John	21	M	None	22Ju02Bd
COLLINS, James	17	M	None	22Ju02Bd
Mike	16	M	Joiner	22Ju02Bd
CHRISTY, Martha	20	F	None	22Ju02Bd
DUNLOP, Peggy-Jane	19	F	None	22Ju02Bd
CLARK, Ellen	18	F	None	22Ju02Bd
STENCELL, Sarah	20	F	None	22Ju02Bd
QUEEN, Mike	30	M	None	22Ju02Bd
ROGAN, William	30	M	None	22Ju02Bd
Ellen	25	F	None	22Ju02Bd
BUTLER, Ellen	30	F	None	22Ju02Bd
CONNOL, Mary	20	F	None	22Ju02Bd
HELYAN, Ann	23	F	None	22Ju02Bd
MORN, Kitty	60	F	None	22Ju02Bd
FLYNE, Ellen	35	F	None	22Ju02Bd
Mary	13	F	None	22Ju02Bd
Catherine	10	F	None	22Ju02Bd
Mike	02	M	Child	22Ju02Bd
CAMPBELL, Pat	60	M	None	22Ju02Bd
Mary	50	F	None	22Ju02Bd
Francis	17	M	None	22Ju02Bd
Pat	15	M	None	22Ju02Bd
Moses	13	M	None	22Ju02Bd
John	12	M	None	22Ju02Bd
James	10	M	None	22Ju02Bd
FLOYD, John	26	M	Farmer	22Ju02Bd
PUSEY, Catherine	17	F	None	22Ju02Bd
FELLON, Catherine	15	F	None	22Ju02Bd
PLUNKET, Thomas	25	M	None	22Ju02Bd
BARRY, John	22	M	None	22Ju02Bd
MAXWELL, John	20	M	None	22Ju02Bd
LINCHAN, John	16	M	None	22Ju02Bd
HAMILTON, Charles	16	M	None	22Ju02Bd
John	22	M	None	22Ju02Bd
Mary-Ann	20	F	None	22Ju02Bd
Judy	14	F	None	22Ju02Bd
HARRIGAN, Kit	25	F	None	22Ju02Bd
BUST, Mike	22	M	None	22Ju02Bd
RYAN, Mike	18	M	None	22Ju02Bd
KIPP, Joanna	25	F	None	22Ju02Bd
Mary	02	F	Child	22Ju02Bd
William	05	M	Child	22Ju02Bd
MULLIGAN, Robert	18	M	None	22Ju02Bd
BURNS, John	24	M	None	22Ju02Bd
CARLIN, Mike	28	M	None	22Ju02Bd
BURGAN, John	26	M	None	22Ju02Bd
DALIN, James	24	M	None	22Ju02Bd
MCCARTY, Wm.	19	M	None	22Ju02Bd
MCDERMOT, Ann	20	F	None	22Ju02Bd
HARTFORD, Dorothy	22	F	None	22Ju02Bd
GRAHAM, Owen	26	M	Farmer	22Ju02Bd
MCDONNOLL, Mary	24	F	Farmer	22Ju02Bd
GOLDEN, Catherine	21	F	Farmer	22Ju02Bd
QUEEN, Mary	21	F	None	22Ju02Bd
DUFFY, Margaret	25	F	None	22Ju02Bd
GOLDEN, Margaret	23	F	None	22Ju02Bd
RIPLEY, Alexr.	22	M	None	22Ju02Bd
SEALY, John	21	M	Engraver	22Ju02Bd
ADAMSON, Susan	18	F	None	22Ju02Bd
KELLY, Mike	21	M	Gdnr	22Ju02Bd
COOK, William	22	M	None	22Ju02Bd
SMITH, Daniel	24	M	Shoemaker	22Ju02Bd
Margaret	19	F	None	22Ju02Bd
ODONNELL, Edward	31	M	Farmer	22Ju02Bd
BAJAN, Dawer	21	M	None	22Ju02Bd
Mary	17	F	None	22Ju02Bd
FLINN, John	21	M	None	22Ju02Bd
QUEEN, Pat	25	M	None	22Ju02Bd
FLINN, Perry	13	M	None	22Ju02Bd
FLEMMING, Saml.	24	M	None	22Ju02Bd
Eliza	24	F	None	22Ju02Bd
Rebeccah	01	F	Child	22Ju02Bd
SLIVEN, Sally	18	F	None	22Ju02Bd
Susan	16	F	None	22Ju02Bd
PATTEN, Mary	24	F	None	22Ju02Bd
MEDLY, Mary-Ann	17	F	None	22Ju02Bd
MURRAY, Edward	24	M	None	22Ju02Bd
Ellen	27	F	None	22Ju02Bd
PERRYMAN, Pat	20	M	None	22Ju02Bd
MURRAY, Nick	21	M	None	22Ju02Bd
MORN, James	26	M	Boatmaker	22Ju02Bd
WEBB, Catherine	22	M	None	22Ju02Bd

NAMES OF PASSENGERS		AGE	SEX	OCCUPATIONS	DATE PORT SHIP
BROGAN, Mary		15	F	None	22Ju02Bd
ODONNELL, Hugh		28	M	None	22Ju02Bd
SKELLY, Daniel		24	M	None	22Ju02Bd
COUGHAN, Bridget		18	F	None	22Ju02Bd
RAFFERTY, Mary		25	F	None	22Ju02Bd
Sally		24	F	None	22Ju02Bd
PEAK, George		30	M	Weaver	22Ju02Bd
CASEY, Bess		20	F	None	22Ju02Bd
Catherine		22	F	None	22Ju02Bd
GOODWIN, Edward		24	M	None	22Ju02Bd
LEAD, Fanny		43	F	None	22Ju02Bd
Mary		11	F	None	22Ju02Bd
Robert		13	M	None	22Ju02Bd
MILLS, Bridget		20	F	None	22Ju02Bd
CHADWICK, John		30	M	None	22Ju02Bd
RODGER, Mary		30	F	None	22Ju02Bd
Retu		05	U	Child	22Ju02Bd
Pat		02	M	Child	22Ju02Bd
John		01	M	Child	22Ju02Bd
ROONEY, Biddy		23	F	None	22Ju02Bd
LAMFIER, Andrew		61	M	None	22Ju02Bd
Mary		53	F	None	22Ju02Bd
Joseph		18	M	None	22Ju02Bd
Dennis		13	M	None	22Ju02Bd
Ambrose		15	M	None	22Ju02Bd
Judy		22	F	None	22Ju02Bd
DEARY, Dennis		20	M	None	22Ju02Bd
LEACH, Margan		18	U	None	22Ju02Bd
GARVEY, John		28	M	None	22Ju02Bd
Ann		20	F	None	22Ju02Bd
KELLY, John		20	M	None	22Ju02Bd
MCDERMOT, Mike		36	M	None	22Ju02Bd
HEGIN, Mike		27	M	Cooper	22Ju02Bd
BULKLEY, James		32	M	None	22Ju02Bd
MULLEN, Mike		30	M	None	22Ju02Bd
HAULIN, John		28	M	None	22Ju02Bd
GAVY, Martin		29	M	None	22Ju02Bd
EYRE, Thos.		22	M	None	22Ju02Bd
BERGEN, Massdew		23	U	None	22Ju02Bd
EASTWOOD, Benj.		40	M	Butcher	22Ju02Bd
Hannah		40	F	None	22Ju02Bd
FOX, Fanny		25	F	None	22Ju02Bd
ONEY, Peter		19	M	None	22Ju02Bd
WALLACE, Pat		22	M	None	22Ju02Bd
CASLY, James		23	M	None	22Ju02Bd
EARLY, Julia		20	F	None	22Ju02Bd
Mary		20	F	None	22Ju02Bd
LOONEY, Bridget		16	F	None	22Ju02Bd
MAHAN, Rebecca		18	F	None	22Ju02Bd
FITZGERALD, Ann		22	F	None	22Ju02Bd
DONAGHUE, Julia		20	F	None	22Ju02Bd
SHANLY, Margaret		19	F	None	22Ju02Bd
GASSIDE, Jonathan		27	M	None	22Ju02Bd
BARR, Thomas		25	M	None	22Ju02Bd
FARRAL, Dominic		20	M	None	22Ju02Bd

JOSEPH-CUNARD 23 JUNE 1846

From Liverpool

NAMES OF PASSENGERS		AGE	SEX	OCCUPATIONS	DATE PORT SHIP
MORRISON, Wm.		30	M	Laborer	23Ju02Hn
PATTON, Patt		26	M	Laborer	23Ju02Hn
RAFFERTY, John		24	M	Laborer	23Ju02Hn
Ann		30	F	Spinster	23Ju02Hn
BYRNE, John		25	M	Laborer	23Ju02Hn
SMITH, Cathrin		20	F	Spinster	23Ju02Hn
MILLER, Corey		22	M	Laborer	23Ju02Hn
RYAN, Patrick		24	M	Laborer	23Ju02Hn
Margaret		22	F	Spinster	23Ju02Hn
WALSH, Jno.		20	M	Laborer	23Ju02Hn
CARROLL, Patrick		22	M	Laborer	23Ju02Hn
HAYES, Judith		18	F	Spinster	23Ju02Hn
FAHAY, Cath.		20	F	Spinster	23Ju02Hn
CRAWFORD, William		25	M	Laborer	23Ju02Hn
CASHMAN, Danl.		30	M	Laborer	23Ju02Hn
LACKINGTON, James		28	M	Laborer	23Ju02Hn
RYAN, Ellen		20	F	Spinster	23Ju02Hn
RENOLDS, Mary		20	F	Spinster	23Ju02Hn
CARR, Peggy		50	F	Spinster	23Ju02Hn
Francis	(S)	18	M	Laborer	23Ju02Hn
Jno.	(S)	16	M	Laborer	23Ju02Hn
Catherine	(D)	14	F	Spinster	23Ju02Hn
Thomas	(S)	13	M	Laborer	23Ju02Hn
Mary	(D)	04	F	Child	23Ju02Hn
Rosey	(D)	09	F	Child	23Ju02Hn
Dennis	(S)	07	M	Child	23Ju02Hn
Francis	(S)	05	M	Child	23Ju02Hn
PENDER, Margrt.		40	F	Laborer	23Ju02Hn
Peter		40	M	Laborer	23Ju02Hn
DORAN, Jno.		30	M	Laborer	23Ju02Hn
BARTON, Jno.		25	M	Laborer	23Ju02Hn
U	(W)	24	F	Wife	23Ju02Hn
MCCALL, Jan.		40	F	Laborer	23Ju02Hn
WOODS, Jno.		39	M	Laborer	23Ju02Hn
Patt		28	M	Laborer	23Ju02Hn
Bridget		03	F	Child	23Ju02Hn
TRACY, Patrick		25	M	Laborer	23Ju02Hn
Rose		24	F	Laborer	23Ju02Hn
ONEAL, Cormick		40	M	Laborer	23Ju02Hn
Ann	(W)	38	F	Wife	23Ju02Hn
Chas.	(S)	16	M	Laborer	23Ju02Hn
Bessey	(D)	13	F	Laborer	23Ju02Hn
Joseph	(S)	09	M	Child	23Ju02Hn
DIERAN, Martin		40	M	Laborer	23Ju02Hn
Mary		20	F	Laborer	23Ju02Hn
TERRAN, Maria		20	F	Laborer	23Ju02Hn
RING, Betty		27	F	Laborer	23Ju02Hn
Cath.		20	F	Laborer	23Ju02Hn
WIELKS, Peter		18	M	Laborer	23Ju02Hn
TIRNEN, John		20	M	Laborer	23Ju02Hn
NEILL, John		25	M	Laborer	23Ju02Hn
BOWES, Thomas		36	M	Laborer	23Ju02Hn
RYAN, James		28	M	Laborer	23Ju02Hn
MAN, Mary		26	F	Laborer	23Ju02Hn
CAHILL, Thomas		27	M	Laborer	23Ju02Hn
MAGUIRE, Jno.		25	M	Laborer	23Ju02Hn
ONEAL, May		30	F	Laborer	23Ju02Hn
DUNEAN, James		18	M	Laborer	23Ju02Hn
HENNAGHAN, Martin		24	M	Laborer	23Ju02Hn
OBRIEN, Honora		25	F	Laborer	23Ju02Hn
Ellen		20	F	Laborer	23Ju02Hn
WALLACE, Geo.		30	M	Laborer	23Ju02Hn
PHILLIPS, Jas.		30	M	Laborer	23Ju02Hn
BRIEN, Jno.		26	M	Laborer	23Ju02Hn
OBRIEN, Winifred		24	F	Laborer	23Ju02Hn
Cathin.		12	F	Laborer	23Ju02Hn
Martin		10	M	Laborer	23Ju02Hn
Bessey		08	F	Laborer	23Ju02Hn
Lucy		04	F	Laborer	23Ju02Hn
GLESON, Mich.		32	M	Laborer	23Ju02Hn
Margret		34	F	Laborer	23Ju02Hn
Julia		30	F	Laborer	23Ju02Hn
James		14	M	Laborer	23Ju02Hn
Mary		.00	F	Infant	23Ju02Hn
DOYLE, Patt		28	M	Laborer	23Ju02Hn
Charles		24	M	Laborer	23Ju02Hn
Mary		20	F	Laborer	23Ju02Hn
NEWMAN, John		30	M	Laborer	23Ju02Hn
Cathrin		26	F	Laborer	23Ju02Hn
DUNN, Matthew		30	M	Laborer	23Ju02Hn
Mary	(W)	28	F	Wife	23Ju02Hn
Cath.	(D)	10	F	Child	23Ju02Hn
Sally	(D)	08	F	Child	23Ju02Hn
Martin	(S)	04	M	Child	23Ju02Hn

NAMES OF PASSENGERS		AGE	SEX	OCCUPATIONS	DATE PORT SHIP
MOORE, John		30	M	Laborer	23Ju02Hn
WHELAN, Patt		30	M	Laborer	23Ju02Hn
DUNN, Mary		25	F	Laborer	23Ju02Hn
Mary		10	F	Laborer	23Ju02Hn
DELANY, Michl.		40	M	Laborer	23Ju02Hn
BAXTER, Mary		40	F	Laborer	23Ju02Hn
REYNOLDS, Betty		35	F	Laborer	23Ju02Hn
FLYNN, Ellen		20	F	Laborer	23Ju02Hn
STEWART, John		18	M	Laborer	23Ju02Hn
LOCKET, James		25	M	Laborer	23Ju02Hn
CONIGHTY, Michl.		24	M	Laborer	23Ju02Hn
MALON, Michl.		28	M	Laborer	23Ju02Hn
Sicily		24	F	Laborer	23Ju02Hn
MURRAY, Margt.		20	F	Laborer	23Ju02Hn
CLUCAS, Chal.		25	M	Laborer	23Ju02Hn
U	(W)	23	F	Wife	23Ju02Hn
Margaret	(D)	.00	F	Infant	23Ju02Hn
GRIFFITHS, James		25	M	Laborer	23Ju02Hn
WALLACE, Wm.		24	M	Laborer	23Ju02Hn
MCCURDY, Saml.		20	M	Laborer	23Ju02Hn
PRIOR, Hugh		30	M	Laborer	23Ju02Hn
Alice	(W)	26	F	Wife	23Ju02Hn
John	(S)	09	M	Child	23Ju02Hn
Andrew	(S)	03	M	Child	23Ju02Hn
MCAUHILL, James		25	M	Laborer	23Ju02Hn
Sarah		22	F	Laborer	23Ju02Hn
BARTON, John		28	M	Laborer	23Ju02Hn
Susan		26	F	Laborer	23Ju02Hn
KENNEDY, Margt.		38	F	Laborer	23Ju02Hn
DORSEY, Elisa		30	F	Laborer	23Ju02Hn
JOHNSTON, Bridget		16	F	Laborer	23Ju02Hn
COURTNEY, Mary		38	F	Laborer	23Ju02Hn
Thomas	(H)	30	M	Laborer	23Ju02Hn
Thomas-Jr.	(S)	16	M	Laborer	23Ju02Hn
Bridget	(D)	14	F	Laborer	23Ju02Hn
VASEY, John		18	M	Laborer	23Ju02Hn
REILLY, Cath.		20	F	Laborer	23Ju02Hn
SMITH, Patt		30	M	Laborer	23Ju02Hn
Mary	(W)	28	F	Wife	23Ju02Hn
Bridget	(D)	06	F	Child	23Ju02Hn
MCGODRICK, Margt.		18	F	Laborer	23Ju02Hn
DWYER, Anthony		40	M	Laborer	23Ju02Hn
BROWN, Michl.		30	M	Laborer	23Ju02Hn
MAHER, Patt		18	M	Laborer	23Ju02Hn
BROWN, Phillip		16	M	Laborer	23Ju02Hn
CARROLL, Thomas		25	M	Laborer	23Ju02Hn
Bridget	(W)	23	F	Wife	23Ju02Hn
Nelly	(D)	06	F	Child	23Ju02Hn
WATERS, Thos.		28	M	Laborer	23Ju02Hn
CANTFIELD, Pat		30	M	Laborer	23Ju02Hn
Daniel		18	M	Laborer	23Ju02Hn
BRENAN, Jas.		20	M	Laborer	23Ju02Hn
WALKER, William		25	M	Laborer	23Ju02Hn
BREWSTER, Saml.		24	M	Laborer	23Ju02Hn
Mary		20	F	Laborer	23Ju02Hn
COFNE, John		18	M	Laborer	23Ju02Hn
BRADY, James		23	M	Laborer	23Ju02Hn
Mary		18	F	Laborer	23Ju02Hn
FITZPATRICK, James		40	M	Laborer	23Ju02Hn
REGNET, Jas.D.		30	M	Laborer	23Ju02Hn
MOORE, Helen		16	F	Laborer	23Ju02Hn
HANAGHAN, Michl.		28	M	Laborer	23Ju02Hn
Mary		26	F	Laborer	23Ju02Hn
CORCORAN, Peter		28	M	Laborer	23Ju02Hn
COLHELEN, Bridget		24	F	Laborer	23Ju02Hn
SHELAN, Eny		22	F	Laborer	23Ju02Hn
BURKE, Margt.		24	F	Laborer	23Ju02Hn
Wm.		18	M	Laborer	23Ju02Hn
OCONNELL, Danl.		18	M	Laborer	23Ju02Hn
CONNORS, Wm.		30	M	Laborer	23Ju02Hn
CULET, Mary		28	F	Laborer	23Ju02Hn
SHEHAN, Margt.		16	F	Laborer	23Ju02Hn
DREW, James		24	M	Laborer	23Ju02Hn
ODONNELL, Magt.		23	F	Laborer	23Ju02Hn
Cath.		20	F	Laborer	23Ju02Hn
DREW, Johnna		24	F	Laborer	23Ju02Hn
RYAN, Margt.		27	F	Laborer	23Ju02Hn
FOGARTY, Wm.		30	M	Laborer	23Ju02Hn
MOORE, Jno.		24	M	Laborer	23Ju02Hn
May	(W)	19	F	Wife	23Ju02Hn
Sarah	(D)	03	F	Child	23Ju02Hn
BOYLAN, Thos.		20	M	Laborer	23Ju02Hn
MOORE, Bridget		25	F	Laborer	23Ju02Hn
KEEFE, Timothy		24	M	Laborer	23Ju02Hn
WELLS, U		27	F	Laborer	23Ju02Hn
MURPHY, Tim		30	M	Laborer	23Ju02Hn
Catherine	(W)	26	F	Wife	23Ju02Hn
May	(D)	06	F	Child	23Ju02Hn
Barthew.	(S)	03	M	Child	23Ju02Hn
TOOHEY, Jas.		30	M	Laborer	23Ju02Hn
BRYAN, Mary		18	F	Laborer	23Ju02Hn
NOWLAN, Thos.		28	M	Laborer	23Ju02Hn
Bridget	(W)	24	F	Wife	23Ju02Hn
John	(S)	10	M	Laborer	23Ju02Hn
Bridget	(D)	08	F	Child	23Ju02Hn
FANNAN, Pat		40	M	Laborer	23Ju02Hn
Anne		32	F	Laborer	23Ju02Hn
DROUT, Thos.		18	M	Laborer	23Ju02Hn
MCNALLY, Wm.		27	M	Laborer	23Ju02Hn
LAWLER, John		24	M	Laborer	23Ju02Hn
Cath.		20	F	Laborer	23Ju02Hn
CALLAN, Bryan		30	M	Laborer	23Ju02Hn
HOGAN, Ellen		35	F	Laborer	23Ju02Hn
KILMARTIN, Thos.		27	M	Laborer	23Ju02Hn
HEALY, James		23	M	Laborer	23Ju02Hn
GURLEY, Patt		30	M	Laborer	23Ju02Hn
CARNAUGHT, Michl.		18	M	Laborer	23Ju02Hn
CALLAHAN, Arthur		19	M	Laborer	23Ju02Hn
MCLARKEY, Cath.		14	F	Laborer	23Ju02Hn
GARNIN, Pat		30	M	Laborer	23Ju02Hn
MARTIN, James		26	M	Laborer	23Ju02Hn
Mary	(W)	22	F	Wife	23Ju02Hn
Bridget	(D)	03	F	Child	23Ju02Hn
CARDLE, Bridget		18	F	Laborer	23Ju02Hn
FLEMING, Thomas		16	M	Laborer	23Ju02Hn
GLEESON, Jno.		30	M	Laborer	23Ju02Hn
LIGHERTY, Wm.		32	M	Laborer	23Ju02Hn
KEELY, Jno.		27	M	Laborer	23Ju02Hn
FLEMING, Jno.		24	M	Laborer	23Ju02Hn
JOHNSTON, James		29	M	Laborer	23Ju02Hn
Thos.		27	M	Laborer	23Ju02Hn
Sarah		08	F	Child	23Ju02Hn
James-Jr.	(S)	06	M	Child	23Ju02Hn
Bridget		04	F	Child	23Ju02Hn
HUGHES, Thos.		29	M	Laborer	23Ju02Hn
Rachel	(W)	25	F	Wife	23Ju02Hn
Francis	(S)	04	M	Child	23Ju02Hn
Susan	(D)	01	F	Child	23Ju02Hn
FLEMING, Thos.		38	M	Laborer	23Ju02Hn
FLINN, Saml.		35	M	Laborer	23Ju02Hn
Rachl.	(W)	36	F	Wife	23Ju02Hn
Margt.	(D)	10	F	Laborer	23Ju02Hn
Sarah	(D)	08	F	Child	23Ju02Hn
Thos.	(S)	05	M	Child	23Ju02Hn
HUGHES, Sal.		26	M	Laborer	23Ju02Hn
DENOIT, P.		24	M	Laborer	23Ju02Hn
JONES, S.		18	M	Laborer	23Ju02Hn
THOMPSON, P.		22	M	Laborer	23Ju02Hn
Ellen		18	F	Laborer	23Ju02Hn
ROBERTS, Richd.		38	M	Laborer	23Ju02Hn
Sarah	(W)	35	F	Wife	23Ju02Hn
Jane	(D)	06	F	Child	23Ju02Hn
Alex	(S)	03	M	Child	23Ju02Hn
KENNEY, Peter		29	M	Laborer	23Ju02Hn
Jane	(W)	25	F	Wife	23Ju02Hn
Sam.	(S)	09	M	Child	23Ju02Hn
Luke	(S)	07	M	Child	23Ju02Hn
Thos.	(S)	03	M	Child	23Ju02Hn
DEVITT, Saml.		30	M	Laborer	23Ju02Hn
FINCH, Hugh		27	M	Laborer	23Ju02Hn

NAMES OF PASSENGERS		AGE	SEX	OCCUPATIONS	DATE PORT SHIP
KELLY, Tom		40	M	Laborer	23Ju02Hn
Sams.		38	M	Laborer	23Ju02Hn
HICKSON, Andw.		28	M	Laborer	23Ju02Hn
May	(W)	26	F	Wife	23Ju02Hn
Ellen	(D)	05	F	Child	23Ju02Hn
MCGUIRE, James		30	M	Laborer	23Ju02Hn
THOMAS, Richd.		32	M	Laborer	23Ju02Hn
JONES, Saml.		27	M	Laborer	23Ju02Hn
LYNCH, Thos.		29	M	Laborer	23Ju02Hn
MULLIGAN, Robt.		34	M	Laborer	23Ju02Hn
JOHNTON, Thos.		28	M	Laborer	23Ju02Hn
STEWART, Isaac		35	M	Laborer	23Ju02Hn
May	(W)	30	F	Wife	23Ju02Hn
Eliza	(D)	10	F		23Ju02Hn
James	(S)	07	M	Laborer	23Ju02Hn
Ellen	(D)	04	F	Laborer	23Ju02Hn
SHAW, Jas.		24	M	Laborer	23Ju02Hn
Jane	(W)	20	F	Wife	23Ju02Hn
Jno.	(S)	03	M	Child	23Ju02Hn
Mary	(D)	01	F	Child	23Ju02Hn
JONES, Margt.		18	F	Laborer	23Ju02Hn
FLINN, Sam.		38	M	Laborer	23Ju02Hn
Ellen	(W)	36	F	Wife	23Ju02Hn
Mary	(D)	09	F	Child	23Ju02Hn
James	(S)	07	M	Child	23Ju02Hn
Nancy	(D)	03	F	Child	23Ju02Hn
MAGEUNIS, P.		29	M	Laborer	23Ju02Hn
Jno.		27	M	Laborer	23Ju02Hn
U		.00	U	Infant	23Ju02Hn
Born-At-Sea					
U		00	U	Unknown	23Ju02Hn
U		00	U	Unknown	23Ju02Hn
U		00	U	Unknown	23Ju02Hn
U		00	U	Unknown	23Ju02Hn
U		00	U	Unknown	23Ju02Hn
U		00	U	Unknown	23Ju02Hn
U		00	U	Unknown	23Ju02Hn
U		00	U	Unknown	23Ju02Hn
U		00	U	Unknown	23Ju02Hn
U		00	U	Unknown	23Ju02Hn
U		00	U	Unknown	23Ju02Hn
U		00	U	Unknown	23Ju02Hn
U		00	U	Unknown	23Ju02Hn

ADAM-CARR 23 JUNE 1846

From Glasgow

NAMES OF PASSENGERS		AGE	SEX	OCCUPATIONS	DATE PORT SHIP
GILL, E.		22	F	Spinster	23Ju04Aw
WEIR, Wm.		21	M	Weaver	23Ju04Aw
ARTHUR, Gordon		45	M	Farmer	23Ju04Aw
DALLY, Alexia		25	F	Spinster	23Ju04Aw
LATHWAITE, Grace		30	F	Spinster	23Ju04Aw
MCGAVIN, Bridget		30	F	Spinster	23Ju04Aw
DONNELLY, Francis		30	M	Laborer	23Ju04Aw
Sarah		18	F	Spinster	23Ju04Aw
MCCUTCHEON, Alexr.		20	M	Laborer	23Ju04Aw
Robt.		19	M	Laborer	23Ju04Aw
HAMILTON, James		55	M	Farmer	23Ju04Aw
Margaret		15	F	None	23Ju04Aw
Isabella		09	F	Child	23Ju04Aw
PHILLIPS, S.M.		31	M	Surgeon	23Ju04Aw
STEWART, Jas.		22	M	Farmer	23Ju04Aw
U	(W)	24	F	Wife	23Ju04Aw
SIMPSON, Henry		24	M	Laborer	23Ju04Aw
DURNEY, Hugh		26	M	Laborer	23Ju04Aw
DUFFY, James		30	M	Laborer	23Ju04Aw
MCCLEAN, Jas.		30	M	Laborer	23Ju04Aw

NAMES OF PASSENGERS		AGE	SEX	OCCUPATIONS	DATE PORT SHIP
MCCLEAN, Chas.	(S)	.09	M	Infant	23Ju04Aw
Seraw-Jane	(D)	14	F	None	23Ju04Aw
FERRY, Eleanor		20	F	Spinster	23Ju04Aw
HAMILTON, Ann		19	F	Spinster	23Ju04Aw
MCCLEAN, Catherine		30	F	Wife	23Ju04Aw
MCGREGOR, Edward		50	M	Laborer	23Ju04Aw

RAPPAHANOCK 24 JUNE 1846

From Liverpool

NAMES OF PASSENGERS		AGE	SEX	OCCUPATIONS	DATE PORT SHIP
HAYES, Wm.		57	M	Farmer	24Ju02Dm
Sarah	(W)	40	F	Wife	24Ju02Dm
Richard	(S)	26	M	Farmer	24Ju02Dm
John	(S)	23	M	Farmer	24Ju02Dm
Daniel	(S)	19	M	Farmer	24Ju02Dm
Albino	(S)	15	M	Farmer	24Ju02Dm
Ellen	(D)	12	F	Farmer	24Ju02Dm
Thomas	(S)	09	M	Child	24Ju02Dm
Sarah	(D)	05	F	Child	24Ju02Dm
LEMON, John		20	M	Farmer	24Ju02Dm
MADDEN, Michael		20	M	Farmer	24Ju02Dm
GRADY, Nancy		20	F	Farmer	24Ju02Dm
Biddy		15	F	Farmer	24Ju02Dm
WALSH, Alexander		25	M	Farmer	24Ju02Dm
MITCHEL, Thomas		21	M	Farmer	24Ju02Dm
MOONY, Peggy		.06	F	Infant	24Ju02Dm
DENT, Thomas		40	M	Farmer	24Ju02Dm
Dorothy	(W)	37	F	Wife	24Ju02Dm
William	(S)	13	M	Farmer	24Ju02Dm
Thomas	(S)	11	M	Farmer	24Ju02Dm
Elizabeth	(D)	09	F	Child	24Ju02Dm
Richard	(S)	07	M	Child	24Ju02Dm
Ansby	(S)	05	M	Child	24Ju02Dm
Dorothy	(D)	03	F	Child	24Ju02Dm
KINSELA, Margaret		23	F	Farmer	24Ju02Dm
JOHNSON, Robert		40	M	Farmer	24Ju02Dm
Mary	(W)	35	F	Wife	24Ju02Dm
Fanny		21	F	Farmer	24Ju02Dm
Mary		19	F	Farmer	24Ju02Dm
Eliz.		17	F	Farmer	24Ju02Dm
Anna		09	F	Child	24Ju02Dm
Jennina		05	F	Child	24Ju02Dm
NESBIT, Mary		25	F	Farmer	24Ju02Dm
MILES, James		36	M	Farmer	24Ju02Dm
Ann	(W)	34	F	Wife	24Ju02Dm
Robt.	(S)	13	M	Farmer	24Ju02Dm
SMITH, Mary-Ann		23	F	Servant	24Ju02Dm
BROWN, Mary		23	F	Servant	24Ju02Dm
BRAUMUSH, Ann		23	F	Servant	24Ju02Dm
CONNOR, Eliza		20	F	Servant	24Ju02Dm
PRESTON, Mary		22	F	Servant	24Ju02Dm
MILLS, Eliza		20	F	Servant	24Ju02Dm
ANNIS, Robert		25	M	Laborer	24Ju02Dm
Margaret	(W)	22	F	Wife	24Ju02Dm
WRIGHT, Thomas		13	M	None	24Ju02Dm
ANNIS, Margaret		.06	F	Infant	24Ju02Dm
CLENDENING, Andrew		30	M	Farmer	24Ju02Dm
Ann	(W)	35	F	Wife	24Ju02Dm
Ann	(D)	.06	F	Infant	24Ju02Dm
James		38	M	Farmer	24Ju02Dm
Janet	(W)	32	F	Wife	24Ju02Dm
Agnes	(D)	13	F	None	24Ju02Dm
William	(S)	07	M	Child	24Ju02Dm
Mary	(D)	06	F	Child	24Ju02Dm
James	(S)	03	M	Child	24Ju02Dm
Jannet	(D)	.03	F	Infant	24Ju02Dm
TURNER, Stephen		40	M	Farmer	24Ju02Dm
Mary	(W)	37	F	Wife	24Ju02Dm

NAMES OF PASSENGERS		AGE	SEX	OCCUPATIONS	DATE PORT SHIP
TURNER, Charles	(S)	13	M	Farmer	24Ju02Dm
William	(S)	11	M	Farmer	24Ju02Dm
STODARD, William		30	M	Farmer	24Ju02Dm
Mary	(W)	28	F	Wife	24Ju02Dm
ROWAN, William		25	M	Farmer	24Ju02Dm
John		43	M	Farmer	24Ju02Dm
GALAGER, Catherine		24	F	Servant	24Ju02Dm
Eliza		52	F	None	24Ju02Dm
CROTTON, Ann		18	F	Servant	24Ju02Dm
Joseph		20	M	Laborer	24Ju02Dm
BEST, Robt.		33	M	Laborer	24Ju02Dm
AGNES, Francis		45	M	Farmer	24Ju02Dm
Ann	(W)	30	F	Wife	24Ju02Dm
Charles	(S)	12	M	Farmer	24Ju02Dm
George	(S)	05	M	Child	24Ju02Dm
William	(S)	.02	M	Infant	24Ju02Dm
COBS, William		23	M	Laborer	24Ju02Dm
BANNON, Ann		23	F	Servant	24Ju02Dm
BARNETT, Charles		60	M	Farmer	24Ju02Dm
Betty	(W)	58	F	Wife	24Ju02Dm
Richard	(S)	20	M	Farmer	24Ju02Dm
DONELY, Rosey		60	F	Farmer	24Ju02Dm
KELLY, Catherine		21	F	Servant	24Ju02Dm
HAMLIN, Fanny		22	F	Servant	24Ju02Dm
OKEAN, Neal		25	M	Laborer	24Ju02Dm
WALLACE, Ally		60	F	Laborer	24Ju02Dm
Christian		50	M	Farmer	24Ju02Dm
William	(S)	22	M	Farmer	24Ju02Dm
Allan	(S)	20	M	Farmer	24Ju02Dm
John	(S)	16	M	Farmer	24Ju02Dm
Hellen	(D)	20	F	Farmer	24Ju02Dm
Agnes	(D)	13	F	Farmer	24Ju02Dm
Martha	(D)	07	F	Child	24Ju02Dm
Jennet	(D)	05	F	Child	24Ju02Dm
MUIR, Thomas		24	M	Farmer	24Ju02Dm
SHAW, Jay		06	M	Child	24Ju02Dm
MCCARTY, Margaret		.06	F	Infant	24Ju02Dm
BRADY, Bridget		20	F	Servant	24Ju02Dm
BUDDAN, Ehlly		20	F	Servant	24Ju02Dm
MATINAS, Emanuel		24	M	Farmer	24Ju02Dm
Jonena	(W)	23	F	Wife	24Ju02Dm
Matilda	(D)	.03	F	Infant	24Ju02Dm
MCCONNELL, Mary		22	F	Servant	24Ju02Dm
Jane		18	F	Servant	24Ju02Dm
Margaret		15	F	Servant	24Ju02Dm
GLEN, Thomas		24	M	Laborer	24Ju02Dm
BARNARD, William		21	M	Laborer	24Ju02Dm
Martha		23	F	Laborer	24Ju02Dm
Thomas		22	M	Laborer	24Ju02Dm
Ann		19	F	Laborer	24Ju02Dm
CONNER, Mary		22	F	Servant	24Ju02Dm
GILLESPIE, Martin		26	M	Laborer	24Ju02Dm
RICHARDSON, Wm.		14	M	Laborer	24Ju02Dm
PATTERSON, John		17	M	Laborer	24Ju02Dm
HUGS, Catherine		16	F	Servant	24Ju02Dm
BOYLE, Margaret		25	F	Servant	24Ju02Dm
DAOG, William		16	M	Servant	24Ju02Dm
MURPHY, Bridget		25	F	Servant	24Ju02Dm
DOAG, Catherine		18	F	Servant	24Ju02Dm
MURPHY, Mary		20	F	Servant	24Ju02Dm
MCGRALE, Ann		30	F	Servant	24Ju02Dm
James	(S)	10	M	Servant	24Ju02Dm
Rosanna	(D)	08	F	Child	24Ju02Dm
Jane	(D)	06	F	Child	24Ju02Dm
John	(S)	04	M	Child	24Ju02Dm
CROW, William		15	M	None	24Ju02Dm
MCLAUGHLIN, James		22	M	Farmer	24Ju02Dm
Mary		50	F	Farmer	24Ju02Dm
John		50	M	Farmer	24Ju02Dm
Ellen		20	F	None	24Ju02Dm
GRANGE, Edward		22	M	Laborer	24Ju02Dm
MAHER, James		27	M	Laborer	24Ju02Dm
Jane	(W)	24	F	Wife	24Ju02Dm
Margaret	(D)	03	F	Child	24Ju02Dm
James	(S)	02	M	Child	24Ju02Dm
DOWNY, Betty		11	F	None	24Ju02Dm
BOWDIN, Mary		20	F	Servant	24Ju02Dm
DOLAN, James		26	M	Laborer	24Ju02Dm
LOVE, Bill		26	M	Laborer	24Ju02Dm
GALAGHER, Jane		20	F	Servant	24Ju02Dm
GREEN, Mary		19	F	Servant	24Ju02Dm
OBRIEN, Mary		19	F	Servant	24Ju02Dm
CORNELL, Peggy		18	F	Servant	24Ju02Dm
MCCLUSKY, Anthony		21	M	Laborer	24Ju02Dm
Ann		14	F	None	24Ju02Dm
DORAN, Michael		18	M	None	24Ju02Dm
HUGHES, James		12	M	None	24Ju02Dm
JUTHINSON, John		29	M	Farmer	24Ju02Dm
NESBET, James		.06	M	Infant	24Ju02Dm
LOUIS, John		22	M	Laborer	24Ju02Dm
CHAPMAN, George		34	M	None	24Ju02Dm
Belinda	(W)	34	F	Wife	24Ju02Dm
Robert	(S)	02	M	Child	24Ju02Dm
Eliza	(D)	.04	F	Infant	24Ju02Dm
IRVIN, Mary-Ann		20	F	Servant	24Ju02Dm
Andrew		19	M	Laborer	24Ju02Dm
MCHUTTON, Jane		20	F	Servant	24Ju02Dm
GALVIN, William		27	M	Laborer	24Ju02Dm
KING, Mary		16	F	None	24Ju02Dm
QUEENEY, Ann		36	F	Servant	24Ju02Dm
TAYLOR, William		30	M	Farmer	24Ju02Dm
WOOLRICH, John		27	M	Farmer	24Ju02Dm
Mary	(W)	25	F	Wife	24Ju02Dm
Isaach	(S)	.06	M	Infant	24Ju02Dm
CORNITH, Francis		40	M	Farmer	24Ju02Dm
Mary	(W)	35	F	Wife	24Ju02Dm
Edwin	(S)	21	M	None	24Ju02Dm
Eliza	(D)	17	F	None	24Ju02Dm
Frances	(D)	13	F	None	24Ju02Dm
Sallos	(D)	11	F	None	24Ju02Dm
Arthur	(S)	09	M	Child	24Ju02Dm
MOFFET, William		27	M	Farmer	24Ju02Dm
PENNELL, Catherine		21	F	Servant	24Ju02Dm
FLINN, Margaret		18	F	Servant	24Ju02Dm
MCGRATH, John		16	M	None	24Ju02Dm
IRVIN, Thomas		40	M	Farmer	24Ju02Dm
Jane		23	F	None	24Ju02Dm
GOATE, Ellen		23	F	None	24Ju02Dm
DRONE, Edward		27	M	Laborer	24Ju02Dm
DRINN, Edward		28	M	Laborer	24Ju02Dm
DORAN, Margaret		26	F	Servant	24Ju02Dm
Allice		16	F	Servant	24Ju02Dm
GAFFY, Bridget		18	F	Servant	24Ju02Dm
MURRY, Mary		18	F	Servant	24Ju02Dm
SHIEL, John		19	M	Laborer	24Ju02Dm
DELANY, John		21	M	Laborer	24Ju02Dm
GURDARAH, Ally		28	F	Laborer	24Ju02Dm
KEAN, Pat		24	M	Laborer	24Ju02Dm
GANEGAR, John		21	M	Laborer	24Ju02Dm
SCANLIN, Lawrence		21	M	Laborer	24Ju02Dm
FRAIN, Roderic		50	M	Farmer	24Ju02Dm
Mary	(W)	40	F	Wife	24Ju02Dm
John	(S)	18	M	None	24Ju02Dm
Filex	(S)	15	M	None	24Ju02Dm
Pat	(S)	13	M	None	24Ju02Dm
Jim	(S)	11	M	None	24Ju02Dm
Honora	(D)	09	F	Child	24Ju02Dm
WALSH, Julia		19	F	Servant	24Ju02Dm
DOBSAN, Ellen		20	F	Servant	24Ju02Dm
EGAN, Jean		20	F	Servant	24Ju02Dm
MOLONE, Catherine		19	F	Servant	24Ju02Dm
HAMMAN, Pat		28	M	Farmer	24Ju02Dm
PHILIPS, John		28	M	Farmer	24Ju02Dm
MCKENNA, James		27	M	Farmer	24Ju02Dm
OWENS, Martin		20	M	Farmer	24Ju02Dm
COYLE, Peter		20	M	Farmer	24Ju02Dm
MCGENTY, Robert		20	M	Farmer	24Ju02Dm
MCGINTY, Mary		40	F	None	24Ju02Dm
Susan		19	F	None	24Ju02Dm
Catherine		20	F	None	24Ju02Dm

NAMES OF PASSENGERS	A G E	S E X	OCCUPATIONS	DATE PORT SHIP	NAMES OF PASSENGERS	A G E	S E X	OCCUPATIONS	DATE PORT SHIP
MCCARTY, Pat	20	M	Laborer	24Ju02Dm	PEARSON, Samuel	.04	M	Infant	24Ju02Dm
MCKEY, John	20	M	Laborer	24Ju02Dm	RYAN, Andrew	27	M	Farmer	24Ju02Dm
SULIVAN, Timothy	02	M	Child	24Ju02Dm	COMER, David	25	M	Farmer	24Ju02Dm
MCKEY, Catherine	19	F	Servant	24Ju02Dm	Bridget	20	F	Servant	24Ju02Dm
SULTY, James	30	M	Farmer	24Ju02Dm	SLATTERY, Margaret	20	F	Servant	24Ju02Dm
MATHIEU, Patt	40	M	Farmer	24Ju02Dm	COLLINS, Philip	40	M	Farmer	24Ju02Dm
Ellen (W)	40	F	Wife	24Ju02Dm	Mary	18	F	None	24Ju02Dm
Eliza	25	F	None	24Ju02Dm	Margaret	04	F	Child	24Ju02Dm
Thomas	11	M	None	24Ju02Dm	Allice	28	F	None	24Ju02Dm
Owen	02	M	Child	24Ju02Dm	Mary	02	F	Child	24Ju02Dm
Hugh	.06	M	Infant	24Ju02Dm	BANNAN, John	16	M	None	24Ju02Dm
GUNNELL, Mary	20	F	Servant	24Ju02Dm	FITZPATRICK, Patt	06	M	Child	24Ju02Dm
CUSHING, Michael	21	M	Laborer	24Ju02Dm	William	04	M	Child	24Ju02Dm
KEIF, David	46	M	Laborer	24Ju02Dm	ONEIL, James	18	M	None	24Ju02Dm
MARTIN, Samuel	25	M	Laborer	24Ju02Dm	DUNN, James	26	M	Farmer	24Ju02Dm
CALAGER, John	24	M	Laborer	24Ju02Dm	KEARNY, Bridget	21	F	Servant	24Ju02Dm
BIRMINGHAM, John	24	M	Laborer	24Ju02Dm	DONELLY, Susan	18	F	Servant	24Ju02Dm
DONOVAN, Mary	19	F	Servant	24Ju02Dm	MURRY, Bryan	40	M	Farmer	24Ju02Dm
BROWN, Peggy	19	F	Servant	24Ju02Dm	Mary (W)	35	F	Wife	24Ju02Dm
LYNCH, John	25	M	Farmer	24Ju02Dm	Frances (D)	08	F	Child	24Ju02Dm
Dennis	19	M	Farmer	24Ju02Dm	Mary (D)	.06	F	Infant	24Ju02Dm
Peggy	20	F	None	24Ju02Dm	Catherine (D)	.06	F	Infant	24Ju02Dm
Mary	18	F	None	24Ju02Dm	MULLEN, Mary	18	F	Servant	24Ju02Dm
HENNISY, Paddy	37	M	Farmer	24Ju02Dm	Margaret	10	F	None	24Ju02Dm
BOORMAN, Thomas	37	M	Farmer	24Ju02Dm	Bryant	06	M	Child	24Ju02Dm
OTTERMAN, Dennis	32	M	Farmer	24Ju02Dm	SMYTH, John	14	M	None	24Ju02Dm
SMYTH, Patt	40	M	Farmer	24Ju02Dm	Ann	16	F	None	24Ju02Dm
ANDERSON, James	18	M	Farmer	24Ju02Dm	CLIVIN, Darbes	25	F	Servant	24Ju02Dm
THORNTON, James	30	M	Farmer	24Ju02Dm	MCCABE, Patt	18	M	Laborer	24Ju02Dm
Hannah (W)	28	F	Wife	24Ju02Dm	KORKER, Allice	20	F	Servant	24Ju02Dm
James (S)	03	M	Child	24Ju02Dm	NESBIT, Adam	30	M	Farmer	24Ju02Dm
Catherine (D)	02	F	Child	24Ju02Dm	MCCABE, Nancy	18	F	Servant	24Ju02Dm
Elizabeth (D)	.06	F	Infant	24Ju02Dm	Mary	21	F	Servant	24Ju02Dm
DEEBLE, Allice	16	F	Servant	24Ju02Dm	FITZPATRICK, Philip	18	M	Laborer	24Ju02Dm
RILEY, Edward	28	M	Servant	24Ju02Dm	MULLIGAN, James	50	M	Farmer	24Ju02Dm
Robert	20	M	Laborer	24Ju02Dm	Thomas	18	M	Farmer	24Ju02Dm
Ann	17	F	Servant	24Ju02Dm	Ellen	13	F	None	24Ju02Dm
SALLY, Michael	25	M	Laborer	24Ju02Dm	MCAVOY, Margaret	18	F	Servant	24Ju02Dm
GLOSSITT, Cornelius	27	M	Laborer	24Ju02Dm	Thomas (S)	01	M	Child	24Ju02Dm
COGHLAN, Margaret	30	F	None	24Ju02Dm	FLANNIGAN, Ann	18	F	None	24Ju02Dm
MCCARTY, Michael	25	M	Farmer	24Ju02Dm	WELCH, Robert	30	M	Farmer	24Ju02Dm
Patt	20	M	Farmer	24Ju02Dm	MCCARTY, James	44	M	Farmer	24Ju02Dm
MULHORN, Timothy	50	M	Farmer	24Ju02Dm	Eliza (W)	36	F	Wife	24Ju02Dm
Mary (W)	50	F	Wife	24Ju02Dm	John (S)	12	M	None	24Ju02Dm
Ann (D)	16	F	None	24Ju02Dm	Michael (S)	10	M	None	24Ju02Dm
Elisa (D)	13	F	None	24Ju02Dm	Eliza (D)	06	F	Child	24Ju02Dm
Dennis (S)	16	M	None	24Ju02Dm	Joseph (S)	04	M	Child	24Ju02Dm
Winifred (D)	.06	F	Infant	24Ju02Dm	CUNNIFF, Honora	19	F	None	24Ju02Dm
CROMY, Mary	60	F	None	24Ju02Dm	CAREY, Michael	30	M	Farmer	24Ju02Dm
Robert	22	M	Farmer	24Ju02Dm	CAMPBELL, Mary	26	F	Servant	24Ju02Dm
Richard	19	M	Farmer	24Ju02Dm	BRENNAN, Michael	25	M	Laborer	24Ju02Dm
HILL, Henry	28	M	Farmer	24Ju02Dm	MARTIN, Owen	18	M	Carpenter	24Ju02Dm
Edward	23	M	Farmer	24Ju02Dm	GRADY, Catherine	18	F	Servant	24Ju02Dm
Frederick	21	M	Farmer	24Ju02Dm	NAULIN, John	20	M	Laborer	24Ju02Dm
MORE, Margareth-Jane	21	F	Servant	24Ju02Dm	BRENAN, Honora	18	F	Servant	24Ju02Dm
MCCANN, Samuel	21	M	Laborer	24Ju02Dm	ONEIL, Margaret	13	F	None	24Ju02Dm
Mary-Ann	20	F	Servant	24Ju02Dm	SHIELDS, Ellen	18	F	None	24Ju02Dm
HARGROVE, Isabela	22	F	Servant	24Ju02Dm	JARVEL, William	09	M	Child	24Ju02Dm
MORE, John	24	M	Laborer	24Ju02Dm	NEALY, Mary	18	F	None	24Ju02Dm
HUGHES, Patt	20	M	Laborer	24Ju02Dm	GALIGAN, Bridget	20	F	Servant	24Ju02Dm
BOYER, James	25	M	Laborer	24Ju02Dm	KENNADY, Jane	18	F	Servant	24Ju02Dm
COFFEY, Michael	23	M	Laborer	24Ju02Dm	FITZPATRICK, Mary	21	F	Servant	24Ju02Dm
Margaret	20	F	Servant	24Ju02Dm	COPELAND, Jny.	25	M	Laborer	24Ju02Dm
CHAPMAN, Edward	26	M	Farmer	24Ju02Dm	Emily (W)	24	F	Wife	24Ju02Dm
Mary	50	F	None	24Ju02Dm	Emily (D)	.06	F	Infant	24Ju02Dm
Lidia	22	F	None	24Ju02Dm	DUGGAN, Catherine	30	F	Servant	24Ju02Dm
Margaret-Ann	19	F	None	24Ju02Dm	Peggy (D)	09	F	Child	24Ju02Dm
GRAY, Andrew	45	M	Farmer	24Ju02Dm	Rose (D)	07	F	Child	24Ju02Dm
Samuel	48	M	Farmer	24Ju02Dm	MCIINTYRE, Ellen	16	F	Servant	24Ju02Dm
Jeramiah	21	M	Farmer	24Ju02Dm	GUDARAH, Mary	20	F	Servant	24Ju02Dm
Mary	24	F	None	24Ju02Dm	CUSHING, Richard	30	M	Laborer	24Ju02Dm
PEARSON, Thomas	25	M	Farmer	24Ju02Dm	DOLAN, Thomas	50	M	Farmer	24Ju02Dm
WHEELAN, Mary	19	F	None	24Ju02Dm	Ann (W)	50	F	Wife	24Ju02Dm
PEARSON, Rebecca	29	F	None	24Ju02Dm	Biddy (D)	12	F	None	24Ju02Dm
STORIG, Walter	30	M	Farmer	24Ju02Dm	Mary (D)	10	F	None	24Ju02Dm

NAMES OF PASSENGERS		AGE	SEX	OCCUPATIONS	DATE PORT SHIP
DOLAN, Kitty	(D)	08	F	Child	24Ju02Dm
MCAVOY, William		21	M	Laborer	24Ju02Dm
WHELAN, Sarah		18	F	None	24Ju02Dm
LAP, Bridget		18	F	Servant	24Ju02Dm
REDDING, Mary		21	F	Servant	24Ju02Dm
MCCARTY, Catherine		20	F	Servant	24Ju02Dm
GRACE, Catherine		50	F	None	24Ju02Dm
Edward		22	M	Farmer	24Ju02Dm
William		20	M	Farmer	24Ju02Dm
FULTON, Thomas		20	M	Farmer	24Ju02Dm
HATTON, John		21	M	Farmer	24Ju02Dm
WILSON, Jane		30	F	Servant	24Ju02Dm
Robert	(S)	08	M	Child	24Ju02Dm
Agnes	(D)	06	F	Child	24Ju02Dm
Eliza	(D)	03	F	Child	24Ju02Dm
MACK, Daniel		20	M	Laborer	24Ju02Dm
Bridget		12	F	Laborer	24Ju02Dm
Mary		09	F	Child	24Ju02Dm
Timothy		07	M	Child	24Ju02Dm
SULLIVAN, Mary		25	F	Servant	24Ju02Dm
Patt	(S)	05	M	Child	24Ju02Dm
Anne	(D)	03	F	Child	24Ju02Dm
HAGAN, James		20	M	Farmer	24Ju02Dm
Bernard		19	M	Farmer	24Ju02Dm
SULLIVAN, Michael		20	M	Farmer	24Ju02Dm
MORONEY, Ellen		21	F	Servant	24Ju02Dm
Sarah		13	F	None	24Ju02Dm
Morris		12	M	None	24Ju02Dm
MCGIVEN, Cathn.		20	F	None	24Ju02Dm
MCGILL, Bernard		20	M	Laborer	24Ju02Dm
BAILIE, Daniel		18	M	Laborer	24Ju02Dm
DAVEUGH, Daniel		28	M	Laborer	24Ju02Dm
Isabela		19	F	Servant	24Ju02Dm
James		20	M	Laborer	24Ju02Dm
CASEY, Catherine		20	F	Servant	24Ju02Dm
KENAN, James		34	M	Farmer	24Ju02Dm
CLINTON, Patt		34	M	Farmer	24Ju02Dm
LIDDY, Jerome		20	M	Farmer	24Ju02Dm
DOLAN, Anne		20	F	Servant	24Ju02Dm
FOLEY, Thomas		30	M	Farmer	24Ju02Dm
RILEY, Christopher		23	M	Farmer	24Ju02Dm
LEE, Wm.		21	M	Farmer	24Ju02Dm
RILEY, Anne		30	F	None	24Ju02Dm
BRANOCK, Michael		24	M	Farmer	24Ju02Dm
RYAN, Michael		20	M	Farmer	24Ju02Dm
Patt		21	M	Farmer	24Ju02Dm
DOYLE, Patt		27	M	Farmer	24Ju02Dm
Mary	(W)	26	F	Wife	24Ju02Dm
Anne	(D)	02	F	Child	24Ju02Dm
DOOLAN, James		24	M	Farmer	24Ju02Dm
HENRY, Jane		24	F	None	24Ju02Dm
SIMMONS, Eliza		16	F	None	24Ju02Dm
WATSON, Eliza		24	F	Servant	24Ju02Dm
Sarah		22	F	Servant	24Ju02Dm
MCGUNN, Alice		22	F	Servant	24Ju02Dm
Margaret		17	F	Servant	24Ju02Dm
HILL, Edward		27	M	Farmer	24Ju02Dm
Mary	(W)	26	F	Wife	24Ju02Dm
Mary	(D)	02	F	Child	24Ju02Dm
SHEDY, Patt		26	M	Laborer	24Ju02Dm
Jane	(W)	25	F	Wife	24Ju02Dm
Sarah	(D)	.06	F	Infant	24Ju02Dm
ANDERSON, Mary		40	F	None	24Ju02Dm
Isabella	(D)	12	F	None	24Ju02Dm
Richard	(S)	10	M	None	24Ju02Dm
Anne	(D)	08	F	Child	24Ju02Dm
John	(S)	05	M	Child	24Ju02Dm
George	(S)	.06	M	Infant	24Ju02Dm
FARREL, Barny		23	M	Farmer	24Ju02Dm
LAMB, Thomas		56	M	Farmer	24Ju02Dm
John		28	M	Farmer	24Ju02Dm
LOWRY, Thomas		32	M	Farmer	24Ju02Dm
SIMPSON, Robert		30	M	Farmer	24Ju02Dm
RILEY, John		28	M	Farmer	24Ju02Dm
SIMPSON, George		03	M	Child	24Ju02Dm

NAMES OF PASSENGERS		AGE	SEX	OCCUPATIONS	DATE PORT SHIP
LOWRY, Grace		32	F	None	24Ju02Dm
LAMB, Sarah		19	F	Servant	24Ju02Dm
SIMPSON, Jane		28	F	Servant	24Ju02Dm
LAMB, Grace		18	F	Servant	24Ju02Dm
FRIN, Eliza		06	F	Child	24Ju02Dm
Ann		03	F	Child	24Ju02Dm
NICHOL, Wm.		20	M	Carpenter	24Ju02Dm
HOLME, Jane		21	F	Servant	24Ju02Dm
VERSAIL, Frances		24	F	Servant	24Ju02Dm
Mary		18	F	Servant	24Ju02Dm
BLENDING, Eppenence		19	F	Servant	24Ju02Dm
JENKS, James		20	M	Unknown	24Ju02Dm
WENSKET, Joseph		30	M	Unknown	24Ju02Dm
TEREL, Joseph		24	M	Unknown	24Ju02Dm
Esther		20	F	None	24Ju02Dm
John		21	M	None	24Ju02Dm
LEITH, Haorad		22	M	Merchant	24Ju02Dm
LANSLY, Mary		40	F	None	24Ju02Dm
Catherine		10	F	None	24Ju02Dm
ABERTHNOT, John		40	M	None	24Ju02Dm

ANN-STILLE 24 JUNE 1846

From NASSAU,Eleuthera

NAMES OF PASSENGERS	AGE	SEX	OCCUPATIONS	DATE PORT SHIP
COOK, U-Mrs.	30	F	Lady	24Ju52Hw

PRINCE-ALBERT 25 JUNE 1846

From London

NAMES OF PASSENGERS		AGE	SEX	OCCUPATIONS	DATE PORT SHIP
NEWTON, William		25	M	Clerk	25Ju21Bn
MORTIMORE, John		53	M	Farmer	25Ju21Bn
John	(S)	22	M	Farmer	25Ju21Bn
William	(S)	15	M	Farmer	25Ju21Bn
Henry	(S)	12	M	Farmer	25Ju21Bn
Elizabeth	(W)	50	F	Wife	25Ju21Bn
Elizabeth	(D)	19	F	Farmer	25Ju21Bn
GRACE, Cornelius		23	M	Clerk	25Ju21Bn
RILEY, John		14	M	None	25Ju21Bn
Bridget		45	F	None	25Ju21Bn
TASKER, Fanny		23	F	Servant	25Ju21Bn
Mary		19	F	Servant	25Ju21Bn
POTTER, Ann		35	F	None	25Ju21Bn
James	(S)	06	M	Child	25Ju21Bn
Austin	(S)	03	M	Child	25Ju21Bn
Edwin	(S)	.07	M	Infant	25Ju21Bn
EASLEY, William		21	M	Carpenter	25Ju21Bn
BRIDSON, Elisabeth		60	F	None	25Ju21Bn
HEWITT, Ann		69	F	None	25Ju21Bn
SPERNEY, Peter		25	M	Saddler	25Ju21Bn
RUSSELL, Jacob		29	M	Baker	25Ju21Bn
ABEL, George		27	M	Laborer	25Ju21Bn
Mary		21	F	Laborer	25Ju21Bn
RANNEY, Alexander		21	M	Baker	25Ju21Bn
GRAFF, Thomas		39	M	Carpenter	25Ju21Bn
Harriet	(W)	30	F	Wife	25Ju21Bn
Rosina	(D)	06	F	Child	25Ju21Bn
Hellen	(D)	03	F	Child	25Ju21Bn
BENNET, Samuel		27	M	Carpenter	25Ju21Bn
WOODWARD, Paul		40	M	Tanner	25Ju21Bn
HACKER, John		31	M	Tailor	25Ju21Bn
BEST, Thomas		43	M	Farmer	25Ju21Bn

NAMES OF PASSENGERS		AGE	SEX	OCCUPATIONS	DATE PORT SHIP
STEPHENS, George		35	M	Engineer	25Ju21Bn
EARL, John		45	M	Paper Maker	25Ju21Bn
Mary	(W)	44	F	Wife	25Ju21Bn
James	(S)	13	M	None	25Ju21Bn
Joseph	(S)	06	M	Child	25Ju21Bn
William	(S)	03	M	Child	25Ju21Bn
BORNER, James		20	M	Tailor	25Ju21Bn
ONEAL, Patrick		44	M	Shopkeeper	25Ju21Bn
GREAVES, George		40	M	Painter	25Ju21Bn
Rebecca	(W)	35	F	Wife	25Ju21Bn
Charles	(S)	13	M	None	25Ju21Bn
James	(S)	11	M	None	25Ju21Bn
George	(S)	06	M	Child	25Ju21Bn
CAMPBELL, George		24	M	Carpenter	25Ju21Bn
DREW, Thomas		30	M	Tailor	25Ju21Bn
FREEMAN, John		25	M	Baker	25Ju21Bn
YALLOP, James		28	M	Surgeon	25Ju21Bn
Frances	(W)	26	F	Wife	25Ju21Bn
Callene	(D)	.06	F	Infant	25Ju21Bn
THOMAS, Elisabeth		22	F	None	25Ju21Bn
BURTON, Robert		42	M	Piano Maker	25Ju21Bn
Thomas	(S)	16	M	Piano Maker	25Ju21Bn
George	(S)	13	M	Piano Maker	25Ju21Bn
Sarah	(D)	12	F	None	25Ju21Bn
Elisa	(D)	09	F	Child	25Ju21Bn
LOWTER, Ann		49	F	None	25Ju21Bn
Catherine		19	F	None	25Ju21Bn
SINGLETON, William		45	M	Smith	25Ju21Bn
Mary	(W)	36	F	None	25Ju21Bn
KEMP, Samuel		20	M	Clerk	25Ju21Bn
GORDON, Isaac		44	M	Farmer	25Ju21Bn
PIERCE, Thomas		35	M	Laborer	25Ju21Bn

MAYFIELD 25 JUNE 1846

From Liverpool

NAMES OF PASSENGERS		AGE	SEX	OCCUPATIONS	DATE PORT SHIP
REYNOLDS, Wm.		30	M	Farmer	25Ju02lg
U	(W)	26	F	Wife	25Ju02lg
BATH, Jas.		15	M	Farmer	25Ju02lg
Benj.		24	M	Farmer	25Ju02lg
DESMOND, Henry		23	M	Laborer	25Ju02lg
Pat.		26	M	Laborer	25Ju02lg
Cath.		22	F	Spinster	25Ju02lg
Josh		20	M	None	25Ju02lg
Pat		25	M	Farmer	25Ju02lg
BOYLE, John		21	M	None	25Ju02lg
EARLY, Jno.		.31	M	None	25Ju02lg
Robt.	(S)	05	M	Child	25Ju02lg
DUNN, Pat		28	M	Laborer	25Ju02lg
HARVEY, Wm.		20	M	Laborer	25Ju02lg
MCCAFFERTY, Isabella		20	F	Spinster	25Ju02lg
WHOLEY, Dennis		20	M	None	25Ju02lg
BURKE, Wm.		25	M	Laborer	25Ju02lg
MCCORMICK, Wm.		55	M	Laborer	25Ju02lg
Alice	(W)	46	F	Wife	25Ju02lg
Hugh	(S)	15	M	None	25Ju02lg
Jane	(D)	13	F	None	25Ju02lg
MEHOR, Edw.		24	M	None	25Ju02lg
REYNOLDS, Ann		26	F	Spinster	25Ju02lg
Judy	(D)	.00	F	Infant	25Ju02lg
ARMSTRONG, U		19	F	Spinster	25Ju02lg
GAILEY, John		21	M	Laborer	25Ju02lg
Eadward		21	M	Laborer	25Ju02lg
AYRES, Denis		30	M	Laborer	25Ju02lg
MCGINN, Jane		20	F	Spinster	25Ju02lg
BRANNIGAN, Jno.		40	M	Laborer	25Ju02lg
MURRAY, Jno.		25	M	Laborer	25Ju02lg
DEVENALL, Edwd.		19	M	Laborer	25Ju02lg
MARCHONS, Job.		22	M	Laborer	25Ju02lg
ALLEN, Louisa		22	F	Laborer	25Ju02lg
BATTON, Ann		22	F	Spinster	25Ju02lg
DEVERAL, Jane		23	F	Spinster	25Ju02lg
Ann	(D)	02	F	Child	25Ju02lg
SINGER, John		23	M	None	25Ju02lg
KELLY, Michl.		22	M	Laborer	25Ju02lg
John		21	M	Laborer	25Ju02lg
Margt.		01	F	Child	25Ju02lg
Margt.		18	F	Spinster	25Ju02lg
GLEESON, Jas.		22	M	Laborer	25Ju02lg
Mary-Ann		20	F	None	25Ju02lg
HALVERT, Jas.		30	M	None	25Ju02lg
HENKINSON, Bridget		20	F	Spinster	25Ju02lg
KENNEDY, Judy		20	F	Spinster	25Ju02lg
MANGAN, Barney		20	M	Laborer	25Ju02lg
CARROLL, Peggy		20	F	Spinster	25Ju02lg
MCCANN, Sarah		21	F	Spinster	25Ju02lg
MATTHEW, John		25	M	Laborer	25Ju02lg
MOORE, Cath.		25	F	Spinster	25Ju02lg
Rose		19	F	Spinster	25Ju02lg
MCCARDLE, Mary		20	F	Spinster	25Ju02lg
BISHOP, Stephen		40	M	Laborer	25Ju02lg
GREEN, Ann		22	F	Spinster	25Ju02lg
MCCOMEN, Jane		23	F	Spinster	25Ju02lg
GAVIN, Margt.		20	F	Spinster	25Ju02lg
BUTLER, Thos.		29	M	Laborer	25Ju02lg
SULLIVAN, Pat		24	M	Laborer	25Ju02lg
Honora		24	F	None	25Ju02lg
Jas.		23	M	None	25Ju02lg
Honora		16	F	None	25Ju02lg
CHURCH, Pat		30	M	Laborer	25Ju02lg
MURPHY, Mary		25	F	Spinster	25Ju02lg
CHURCH, John		23	M	Laborer	25Ju02lg
MCCLEAN, Martin		34	M	Laborer	25Ju02lg
CODY, Mich.		21	M	Laborer	25Ju02lg
Johanna		.00	F	Infant	25Ju02lg
COLEMAN, Wm.		50	M	Laborer	25Ju02lg
INGMAN, Wm.		23	M	Laborer	25Ju02lg
FLYNN, Cathn.		21	F	None	25Ju02lg
POLLOCK, Mary-Ann		22	F	None	25Ju02lg
MCCOLLONGE, Sally		17	F	Spinster	25Ju02lg
Mary		16	F	None	25Ju02lg
DINNEMAN, Nancy		19	F	None	25Ju02lg
LUDDY, Michl.		15	M	None	25Ju02lg
FARRELLY, Owen		11	M	None	25Ju02lg
WALKER, Eliza		24	F	None	25Ju02lg
CAHER, Pat		23	M	Laborer	25Ju02lg
Ann		22	F	None	25Ju02lg
PAGE, John-A.		28	M	Laborer	25Ju02lg
SWEENEY, Michl.		20	M	Laborer	25Ju02lg
HORAN, Gerald		20	M	Laborer	25Ju02lg
ORAMUS, Edwd.		20	M	Laborer	25Ju02lg
HORAN, David		20	M	Laborer	25Ju02lg
MEGSON, Margt.		30	F	Laborer	25Ju02lg
KELLY, Sarah		19	F	Laborer	25Ju02lg
CREMIN, Dennis		19	M	Laborer	25Ju02lg
MCENTIRE, Jas.		20	M	Laborer	25Ju02lg
CORCORAN, Pat		20	M	Laborer	25Ju02lg
CLARKE, Luke		23	M	Laborer	25Ju02lg
Biddy		19	F	Laborer	25Ju02lg
CRUSE, Jas.		19	M	Laborer	25Ju02lg
THOMPSON, Owen		18	M	Laborer	25Ju02lg
SHERIDAN, Owen		24	M	Laborer	25Ju02lg
ROCHE, Maurice		20	M	Laborer	25Ju02lg
Elizth.		17	F	Laborer	25Ju02lg
Rich.		11	M	Laborer	25Ju02lg
MONTGOMERY, Sarah		40	F	Laborer	25Ju02lg
MULHOLLAND, Henry		13	M	Laborer	25Ju02lg
Ann		14	F	Laborer	25Ju02lg
WHITE, Mary		.00	F	Infant	25Ju02lg
HUGHES, Denis		20	M	Laborer	25Ju02lg
U	(W)	20	F	Wife	25Ju02lg
Cath.	(D)	06	F	Child	25Ju02lg
Eliza	(D)	04	F	Child	25Ju02lg

NAMES OF PASSENGERS		AGE	SEX	OCCUPATIONS	DATE PORT SHIP
HUGHES, Margt.	(D)	.00	F	Infant	25Ju02Ig
SMITH, Wm.		20	M	Laborer	25Ju02Ig
Cath.		21	F	Laborer	25Ju02Ig
KENNY, Mary		20	F	Laborer	25Ju02Ig
HAMILTON, Eleanor		40	F	Laborer	25Ju02Ig
Thos.		17	M	Laborer	25Ju02Ig
Ellen		.00	F	Infant	25Ju02Ig
KEIRNAN, Pat		35	M	Laborer	25Ju02Ig
Mary	(W)	35	F	Wife	25Ju02Ig
Rose	(D)	05	F	Child	25Ju02Ig
Julia	(D)	03	F	Child	25Ju02Ig
MANGLE, Mary		20	F	Laborer	25Ju02Ig
SULLIVAN, Mary		12	F	Laborer	25Ju02Ig
CONNOR, Sam		56	M	Laborer	25Ju02Ig
Margt.	(W)	40	F	Wife	25Ju02Ig
Biddy	(D)	17	F	Laborer	25Ju02Ig
Mary	(D)	15	F	Laborer	25Ju02Ig
John	(S)	08	M	Child	25Ju02Ig
KEAN, John		30	M	Laborer	25Ju02Ig
MCMAHON, John		21	M	Laborer	25Ju02Ig
KELLY, Danl.		22	M	Laborer	25Ju02Ig
BUCKLEY, Simson		22	M	Laborer	25Ju02Ig
LYNCH, Thos.		21	M	Laborer	25Ju02Ig
CONNOR, Thos.		16	M	Laborer	25Ju02Ig
MCNAMARA, Thos.		22	M	Laborer	25Ju02Ig
CONROY, Connor		27	M	Laborer	25Ju02Ig
U	(W)	27	F	Wife	25Ju02Ig
Thos.	(S)	09	M	Child	25Ju02Ig
Jas.	(S)	11	M	Laborer	25Ju02Ig
OBRIEN, Margt.		20	F	Laborer	25Ju02Ig
FLANNAGAN, Owen		25	M	Laborer	25Ju02Ig
Mary		28	F	Laborer	25Ju02Ig
BURKE, Eliza		25	F	Laborer	25Ju02Ig
MCGRATH, Patt.		70	M	Laborer	25Ju02Ig
Ellen		22	F	Laborer	25Ju02Ig
Nancy		24	F	Laborer	25Ju02Ig
MAHON, Nancy		18	F	Laborer	25Ju02Ig
MURPHY, Jas.		42	M	Laborer	25Ju02Ig
Ann	(W)	41	F	Wife	25Ju02Ig
Jane	(D)	12	F	Laborer	25Ju02Ig
Ann	(D)	10	F	Laborer	25Ju02Ig
Pat	(S)	07	M	Child	25Ju02Ig
John	(S)	05	M	Child	25Ju02Ig
Wm.	(S)	03	M	Child	25Ju02Ig
SEVERN, Jane		29	F	Laborer	25Ju02Ig
Susan	(D)	04	F	Child	25Ju02Ig
Marla	(D)	02	F	Child	25Ju02Ig
BUCKLEY, Mary		22	F	Laborer	25Ju02Ig
MULROONNEY, Cath.		30	F	Laborer	25Ju02Ig
CONNELL, Michl.		30	M	Laborer	25Ju02Ig
U	(W)	20	F	Wife	25Ju02Ig
DEVINE, Jas.		25	M	Laborer	25Ju02Ig
Ann		18	F	Laborer	25Ju02Ig
RUSSELL, Margt.		22	F	Laborer	25Ju02Ig
GALLAGHER, Margt.		26	F	Laborer	25Ju02Ig
U	(W)	24	F	Laborer	25Ju02Ig
MCARDIFF, Michl.		25	M	Laborer	25Ju02Ig
U	(W)	20	F	Wife	25Ju02Ig
MCGOVERN, Biddy		50	F	Laborer	25Ju02Ig
John	(H)	40	M	Laborer	25Ju02Ig
Mich	(S)	11	M	Laborer	25Ju02Ig
Biddy	(D)	09	F	Child	25Ju02Ig
FORSTER, John		20	M	Laborer	25Ju02Ig
PITCHER, Thos.		20	M	Laborer	25Ju02Ig
MELIN, Peter		25	M	Laborer	25Ju02Ig
DARCY, John		25	M	Laborer	25Ju02Ig
LEESON, Jas.		25	M	Laborer	25Ju02Ig
REILLY, Phil		30	M	Laborer	25Ju02Ig
MULLOY, John		20	M	Laborer	25Ju02Ig
Ann		25	F	Laborer	25Ju02Ig
Geo.		18	M	Laborer	25Ju02Ig
LANGAN, Jno.		22	M	Laborer	25Ju02Ig
DILLON, Mary		26	F	Laborer	25Ju02Ig
CONNOR, Frank		25	M	Laborer	25Ju02Ig
POWER, Jas.		26	M	Laborer	25Ju02Ig
POWER, Julia		22	F	Laborer	25Ju02Ig
REARDON, Jas.		40	M	Laborer	25Ju02Ig
Danl.	(S)	13	M	Laborer	25Ju02Ig
Mary	(D)	12	F	Laborer	25Ju02Ig
MANION, Bryan		20	M	Laborer	25Ju02Ig
FEENY, Mary		22	F	Laborer	25Ju02Ig
Judy		20	F	Laborer	25Ju02Ig
KELLY, Sarah		20	F	Laborer	25Ju02Ig
QUINLAN, Cella		20	F	Laborer	25Ju02Ig
FINEGAN, Honora		17	F	Laborer	25Ju02Ig
TOBIN, Jno.		30	M	Laborer	25Ju02Ig
COUGHLAN, Denis		40	M	Laborer	25Ju02Ig
Christy		20	M	Laborer	25Ju02Ig
REDFERN, Jas.		20	M	Laborer	25Ju02Ig
Marla		19	F	Laborer	25Ju02Ig
MANNE, U		21	M	Laborer	25Ju02Ig
DOLAN, Jas.		23	M	Laborer	25Ju02Ig
Honora		21	F	Laborer	25Ju02Ig
CONLEY, Thos.		20	M	Laborer	25Ju02Ig
REILLY, Margt.		20	F	Laborer	25Ju02Ig
QUINN, Patt		20	M	Laborer	25Ju02Ig
BANNEN, Michl.		18	M	Laborer	25Ju02Ig
CAMPBELL, Sarah		20	F	Laborer	25Ju02Ig
OHANLON, Denis		66	M	Laborer	25Ju02Ig
CULLEN, Biddy		20	F	Laborer	25Ju02Ig
DOLAN, Mary		26	F	Laborer	25Ju02Ig
ONEILL, Margt.		13	F	Laborer	25Ju02Ig
PHILLIPS, Ann		30	F	Laborer	25Ju02Ig
Matilda	(D)	10	F	Child	25Ju02Ig
REILLY, Mary		18	F	Laborer	25Ju02Ig
GLEESON, Thos.		24	M	Laborer	25Ju02Ig
DALEY, Cathn.		20	F	Laborer	25Ju02Ig
MANION, Jno.		26	M	Laborer	25Ju02Ig
FANION, Jas.		26	M	Laborer	25Ju02Ig
MANION, Mary		20	F	Laborer	25Ju02Ig
MCCANLEY, Margt.		17	F	Laborer	25Ju02Ig
MCCORMACK, Margt.		16	F	Laborer	25Ju02Ig
REILLY, Eliza		20	F	Laborer	25Ju02Ig
Peter		18	M	Laborer	25Ju02Ig
BURKE, Cathn.		05	F	Child	25Ju02Ig
EGAN, Margt.		16	F	Laborer	25Ju02Ig
Elizth.		14	F	Laborer	25Ju02Ig
DWYER, Peter		22	M	Laborer	25Ju02Ig
Ann		18	F	Laborer	25Ju02Ig
MCCORMICK, Francis		25	M	Laborer	25Ju02Ig
MORAN, Edwd.		18	M	Laborer	25Ju02Ig
DOLAN, Cathn.		18	F	Laborer	25Ju02Ig
PENDER, Mary		19	F	Laborer	25Ju02Ig
HANELY, Susan		15	F	Laborer	25Ju02Ig
SHERIDAN, Patk.		19	M	Laborer	25Ju02Ig
REILLY, Terence		57	M	Laborer	25Ju02Ig
PENDER, Peter		23	M	Laborer	25Ju02Ig
HALFPENNY, Patk.		27	M	Laborer	25Ju02Ig
MULLIN, Ellen		28	F	Laborer	25Ju02Ig
KAIN, Barbara		19	F	Laborer	25Ju02Ig
CASSIDY, Patk.		17	M	Laborer	25Ju02Ig
MCALLISTER, Rosey		24	F	Laborer	25Ju02Ig
SEAL, Michl.		35	M	Laborer	25Ju02Ig
John		20	M	Laborer	25Ju02Ig
CARROLL, Bridgt.		15	F	Laborer	25Ju02Ig
FLATTERY, Cathn.		17	F	Laborer	25Ju02Ig
BARREY, Bridgt.		20	F	Laborer	25Ju02Ig
KENT, Ann		48	F	Laborer	25Ju02Ig
Wm.	(S)	20	M	Laborer	25Ju02Ig
Emma	(D)	19	F	Laborer	25Ju02Ig
Geo.	(S)	10	M	Child	25Ju02Ig
Henry	(S)	08	M	Child	25Ju02Ig
ROSSENT, Ann		40	F	Laborer	25Ju02Ig
CONWAY, Barney		35	M	Laborer	25Ju02Ig
Barney	(S)	09	M	Child	25Ju02Ig
DALEY, Jas.		17	M	Laborer	25Ju02Ig
DOUGHERTY, Mary		17	F	Laborer	25Ju02Ig
BRENNARD, Mary		52	F	Laborer	25Ju02Ig
Cornl.	(S)	27	M	Laborer	25Ju02Ig
MCDONALD, R.		20	U	Laborer	25Ju02Ig

NAMES OF PASSENGERS		AGE	SEX	OCCUPATIONS	DATE PORT SHIP
CORRIGAN, Honor		22	F	Laborer	25Ju02Ig
SULLIVAN, Michl.		19	M	Laborer	25Ju02Ig
Richd.		23	M	Laborer	25Ju02Ig
MCCARTY, Chas.		25	M	Laborer	25Ju02Ig
Ellen		21	F	Laborer	25Ju02Ig
CARTY, Ellen		19	F	Laborer	25Ju02Ig
ANDREW, Francis		29	F	Laborer	25Ju02Ig
James		21	M	Laborer	25Ju02Ig
CALAHAN, Jno.		41	M	Laborer	25Ju02Ig
Mary	(W)	38	F	Wife	25Ju02Ig
Wm.	(S)	10	M	Child	25Ju02Ig
Jas.	(S)	08	M	Child	25Ju02Ig
Saml.	(S)	06	M	Child	25Ju02Ig
Ann	(D)	04	F	Child	25Ju02Ig
Julia	(D)	02	F	Child	25Ju02Ig
Biddy	(D)	.00	F	Infant	25Ju02Ig
Jane		21	F	Laborer	25Ju02Ig
JONES, Margt.		18	F	Laborer	25Ju02Ig
SHERIDAN, Jas.		21	M	Laborer	25Ju02Ig
Cathn.		17	F	Laborer	25Ju02Ig
DEVINE, Martin		21	M	Laborer	25Ju02Ig
U		23	F	Laborer	25Ju02Ig

BRILLIANT 29 JUNE 1846

From Liverpool

NAMES OF PASSENGERS		AGE	SEX	OCCUPATIONS	DATE PORT SHIP
MANSFIELD, Henry		56	M	Farmer	29Ju02Iy
Mary	(W)	48	F	Wife	29Ju02Iy
Ralph	(S)	22	M	Carpenter	29Ju02Iy
William	(S)	18	M	Laborer	29Ju02Iy
Mary	(D)	15	F	None	29Ju02Iy
Elizabeth	(D)	13	F	None	29Ju02Iy
Jane	(D)	10	F	None	29Ju02Iy
Susan	(D)	08	F	None	29Ju02Iy
Henry	(S)	03	M	None	29Ju02Iy
BOLE, Lary		21	M	Clerk	29Ju02Iy
NAPIER, John		24	M	Farmer	29Ju02Iy
KEANE, Pat		22	M	Clerk	29Ju02Iy
MAHONY, Michael		60	M	Carpenter	29Ju02Iy
Mary	(W)	55	F	Wife	29Ju02Iy
Catherine	(D)	26	F	None	29Ju02Iy
MOORE, John		60	M	Cooper	29Ju02Iy
Margaret	(W)	48	F	Wife	29Ju02Iy
Joseph	(S)	22	M	Farmer	29Ju02Iy
Francis	(S)	19	M	Farmer	29Ju02Iy
James	(S)	16	M	None	29Ju02Iy
Peter	(S)	12	M	None	29Ju02Iy
Mary	(D)	14	F	None	29Ju02Iy
MAGEE, Ann		12	F	None	29Ju02Iy
Thomas		25	M	Farmer	29Ju02Iy
MULDOON, Pat.		40	M	Laborer	29Ju02Iy
Ellen		30	F	None	29Ju02Iy
KEATON, Fanton		31	M	Farmer	29Ju02Iy
Julia		20	F	None	29Ju02Iy
PATRICK, Catherine		25	F	None	29Ju02Iy
SHERIDAN, Briene		25	M	Laborer	29Ju02Iy
NASON, Margaret		20	F	None	29Ju02Iy
SULLEVAN, Mary		60	F	None	29Ju02Iy
KING, Edward		20	M	Farmer	29Ju02Iy
CURRY, Michael		28	M	Laborer	29Ju02Iy
GRAY, Pat		26	M	Laborer	29Ju02Iy
Rose	(W)	25	F	Wife	29Ju02Iy
Michael	(S)	04	M	Child	29Ju02Iy
Catherine	(S)	01	F	Child	29Ju02Iy
STONE, John		30	M	Farmer	29Ju02Iy
MURRY, Pat		30	M	Farmer	29Ju02Iy
FILLEY, Thomas		32	M	Carpenter	29Ju02Iy
LAYNUM, Ann		50	F	None	29Ju02Iy
CRILLEY, Betsey		26	F	None	29Ju02Iy
LIAP, Beddy		20	F	None	29Ju02Iy
LAYNUM, Barney		17	M	Laborer	29Ju02Iy
Catherin		14	F	None	29Ju02Iy
Ellen		10	F	Child	29Ju02Iy
GRIMES, Mary		18	F	None	29Ju02Iy
MORRIS, Ann		18	F	None	29Ju02Iy
TRIER, Ann		20	F	None	29Ju02Iy
WORTE, Margaret		18	F	None	29Ju02Iy
ARMSTRONG, James		38	M	Painter	29Ju02Iy
Matilda	(W)	23	F	Wife	29Ju02Iy
Sarah-A.	(D)	.07	F	Infant	29Ju02Iy
GORMAN, John		26	M	Laborer	29Ju02Iy
Ann		25	F	None	29Ju02Iy
MARTIN, Patrick		35	M	Farmer	29Ju02Iy
Owwin		21	M	Laborer	29Ju02Iy
MCCABE, Pat		21	M	Laborer	29Ju02Iy
Catherine		26	F	None	29Ju02Iy
NORTON, John		30	M	Laborer	29Ju02Iy
Mary		30	F	None	29Ju02Iy
MULDOON, Hannah		20	F	None	29Ju02Iy
SCOTT, James		26	M	Laborer	29Ju02Iy
PENDERGARST, Michael		35	M	Laborer	29Ju02Iy
Mary	(W)	25	F	Wife	29Ju02Iy
Edward	(S)	03	M	Child	29Ju02Iy
James	(S)	02	M	Child	29Ju02Iy
THOMAS, Richard		28	M	Laborer	29Ju02Iy
DUNN, James		25	M	Laborer	29Ju02Iy
CONNER, Mathew		25	M	Laborer	29Ju02Iy
LAYSON, Mathew		27	M	Laborer	29Ju02Iy
MCKENNEY, Catherine		50	F	None	29Ju02Iy
GOVER, Margaret		22	F	None	29Ju02Iy
MCCABE, Margaret		17	F	None	29Ju02Iy
Rose		15	F	None	29Ju02Iy
Ellen		09	F	Child	29Ju02Iy
Pat		21	M	Laborer	29Ju02Iy
John		12	M	None	29Ju02Iy
John	(P)	50	M	Laborer	29Ju02Iy
Mary	(M)	52	F	None	29Ju02Iy
SMITH, Joseph		21	M	Mason	29Ju02Iy
CANNADA, Michael		19	M	Clerk	29Ju02Iy
DAVIDSON, Hamilton		18	M	Carpenter	29Ju02Iy
VARNEY, John		18	M	Laborer	29Ju02Iy
BELL, Margaret		24	F	None	29Ju02Iy
MCTAMNEY, John		23	M	Tailor	29Ju02Iy
WALLACE, Thomas		72	M	Farmer	29Ju02Iy
MCLELLAN, Betsey		18	F	None	29Ju02Iy
MONAGHAN, Mary		18	F	None	29Ju02Iy
MCCLUSKEY, Eliza		23	F	None	29Ju02Iy
Jane		18	F	None	29Ju02Iy
John		16	M	None	29Ju02Iy
Mary		13	F	None	29Ju02Iy
Eliza		07	F	Child	29Ju02Iy
Catherine		04	F	Child	29Ju02Iy
David		10	M	Child	29Ju02Iy
HOGAN, William		29	M	Laborer	29Ju02Iy
Julia	(W)	26	F	Wife	29Ju02Iy
Margaret	(D)	04	F	Child	29Ju02Iy
FALAHEE, John		21	M	Laborer	29Ju02Iy
TRIER, Michael		25	M	Laborer	29Ju02Iy
BIGGAN, Dinnes		21	M	Weaver	29Ju02Iy
MCCARTY, Dinnes		19	M	Weaver	29Ju02Iy
HAGAN, Malaca		26	M	Laborer	29Ju02Iy
FINNALE, John		20	M	Laborer	29Ju02Iy
GRIFFEN, Michael		50	M	Laborer	29Ju02Iy
Ellen	(W)	35	F	Wife	29Ju02Iy
Pat	(S)	14	M	None	29Ju02Iy
Thimety	(S)	11	M	None	29Ju02Iy
John	(S)	09	M	Child	29Ju02Iy
Ellen	(D)	05	F	Child	29Ju02Iy
Margaret		20	F	None	29Ju02Iy
GATELY, Marla		16	F	None	29Ju02Iy
HANNEN, Bridget		18	F	None	29Ju02Iy
GELLEGAN, Betty		17	F	None	29Ju02Iy

HARRIET 29 JUNE 1846

From Bermuda

NAMES OF PASSENGERS	AGE	SEX	EX	OCCUPATIONS	DATE PORT SHIP
GORRY, John	30	M		Gentleman	29Ju75Jb

JOHN-R.SKIDDY 01 JULY 1846

From Liverpool

NAMES OF PASSENGERS	AGE	SEX	EX	OCCUPATIONS	DATE PORT SHIP
CAMBELL, Bridget	50	F		Laborer	01J102Ac
MULLEN, Paul	28	M		Laborer	01J102Ac
MULVEY, James	21	M		Laborer	01J102Ac
HUGHES, Cathn.	30	F		Servant	01J102Ac
Margt.	21	F		Servant	01J102Ac
ONEIL, James	21	M		Laborer	01J102Ac
Arthur	18	M		Laborer	01J102Ac
GINTY, Mary	35	F		Servant	01J102Ac
Mary	22	F		Servant	01J102Ac
BROGAN, Peter	28	M		Laborer	01J102Ac
HIGGINS, Ann	16	F		Servant	01J102Ac
KILLROY, Ann	20	F		Servant	01J102Ac
Rose	16	F		Servant	01J102Ac
KEENAN, Nancy	20	F		Servant	01J102Ac
MULLEN, Bernard	22	M		Farmer	01J102Ac
WOODS, Bridget	17	F		Servant	01J102Ac
Mary	20	F		Servant	01J102Ac
AUSTIN, Thos.	40	M		Laborer	01J102Ac
Michl.	22	M		Laborer	01J102Ac
Margt.	20	F		Servant	01J102Ac
CASSADY, James	24	M		Farmer	01J102Ac
Ann	22	F		Servant	01J102Ac
Ellen	20	F		Servant	01J102Ac
Bridget	18	F		Servant	01J102Ac
Mary	19	F		Servant	01J102Ac
BOLAND, Patt	20	M		Laborer	01J102Ac
KELLY, Wm.	24	M		Laborer	01J102Ac
Margt.	20	F		Laborer	01J102Ac
Mary	.02	F		Infant	01J102Ac
ROBINSON, Jas.	35	M		Laborer	01J102Ac
Jane	28	F	(W)	Wife	01J102Ac
Jane	05	F	(D)	Child	01J102Ac
DIXON, James	32	M		Laborer	01J102Ac
Eliza	31	F	(W)	Wife	01J102Ac
Thos.	09	M	(S)	Child	01J102Ac
Margt.	12	F	(D)	Unknown	01J102Ac
Mary	07	F	(D)	Child	01J102Ac
Rich.	05	M	(S)	Child	01J102Ac
Andrew	03	M	(S)	Child	01J102Ac
Jno.	01	M	(S)	Child	01J102Ac
EDGAR, Mary	50	F		Laborer	01J102Ac
RICE, Margt.	40	F		Laborer	01J102Ac
Elizth.	19	F	(D)	Laborer	01J102Ac
Jno.	18	M	(S)	Laborer	01J102Ac
Ellen	16	F	(D)	Laborer	01J102Ac
Ann.	12	F	(D)	Laborer	01J102Ac
Margt.	09	F		Child	01J102Ac
Wm.	07	M	(S)	Child	01J102Ac
HUGHES, Michl.	18	M		Laborer	01J102Ac
DONNELLY, Hugh	30	M		Laborer	01J102Ac
MCBENNETT, Susan	16	F		Laborer	01J102Ac
HESLEM, Wm.	24	M		Laborer	01J102Ac
U	21	F	(W)	Laborer	01J102Ac
HESLEM, Martha	20	F		Laborer	01J102Ac
Sarah	18	F		Laborer	01J102Ac
Rich.	06	M		Child	01J102Ac
Elizth.	04	F		Child	01J102Ac
CUNNINGHAM, Margt.	19	F		Laborer	01J102Ac
Patt	35	M		Laborer	01J102Ac
Esther	17	F		Laborer	01J102Ac
BROWNE, Cathn.	19	F		Laborer	01J102Ac
CONNELL, Jane	20	F		Laborer	01J102Ac
MCTEAR, Jno.	21	M		Laborer	01J102Ac
WALLS, Roger	28	M		Laborer	01J102Ac
GREEN, Patt	24	M		Laborer	01J102Ac
REGAN, James	25	M		Laborer	01J102Ac
Jno.	24	M		Laborer	01J102Ac
KENNY, Thos.	23	M		Laborer	01J102Ac
CLARKE, Laurence	19	M		Laborer	01J102Ac
DONOHUE, Cathn.	20	F		Laborer	01J102Ac
MARRIN, Patt	40	M		Laborer	01J102Ac
Margt.	36	F		Laborer	01J102Ac
Michl.	22	M		Laborer	01J102Ac
Terisa	18	F		Laborer	01J102Ac
Mary	14	F		Servant	01J102Ac
Wm.	12	M		Laborer	01J102Ac
Ann	09	F		Child	01J102Ac
ENNIS, Margt.	21	F		Servant	01J102Ac
DONNOVAN, Bridget	21	F		Servant	01J102Ac
GAHAN, Cathn.	18	F		Servant	01J102Ac
BRENNAN, Margt.	21	F		Servant	01J102Ac
NOONAN, Mary	19	F		Servant	01J102Ac
MCCUSKER, Feilx	24	M		Farmer	01J102Ac
CAMPBELL, Jno.	23	M		Farmer	01J102Ac
GORMELY, Jno.	22	M		Farmer	01J102Ac
MCCUSKER, Peter	21	M		Farmer	01J102Ac
CONDRON, James	20	M		Farmer	01J102Ac
STANLEY, Morris	31	M		Comedian	01J102Ac
Mary-Ann	27	F		Dressmaker	01J102Ac
Wm.	10	M		Child	01J102Ac
Julia	06	F		Child	01J102Ac
Mary-Ann	.03	F		Infant	01J102Ac
FARRELL, Cathn.	20	F		Servant	01J102Ac
DEVAN, Margt.	24	F		Servant	01J102Ac
MCMULLEN, Jno.	25	M		Laborer	01J102Ac
KEENAN, Jos.	40	M		Laborer	01J102Ac
Rose	40	F	(W)	Wife	01J102Ac
Margt.	14	F	(D)	Unknown	01J102Ac
Frs.	12	M	(S)	Unknown	01J102Ac
Bryan	10	M	(S)	Child	01J102Ac
Ann	08	F	(D)	Child	01J102Ac
HOGAN, Ann	14	F		Laborer	01J102Ac
BAXTER, Jno.	20	M		Farmer	01J102Ac
RODY, Bridget	25	F		Servant	01J102Ac
Jas.	14	M		Joiner	01J102Ac
MCGINN, Rose	20	F		Servant	01J102Ac
HANNAHAN, Cathn.	19	F		Servant	01J102Ac
Ann	15	F		Servant	01J102Ac
BAXTER, Bridget	20	F		Servant	01J102Ac
BRUDY, Jas.	23	M		Laborer	01J102Ac
COONEY, Terence	25	M		Laborer	01J102Ac
COOKE, Patt	21	M		Laborer	01J102Ac
DREW, Michl.	30	M		Laborer	01J102Ac
Jas.	20	M		Laborer	01J102Ac
Mary	22	F		Laborer	01J102Ac
Jas.	.01	M		Infant	01J102Ac
KELLY, Peggy	20	F		Laborer	01J102Ac
Cathn.	18	F		Laborer	01J102Ac
CARROLL, Elsey	22	F		Laborer	01J102Ac
FINN, Bridget	18	F		Laborer	01J102Ac
GIBSON, Robt.	21	M		Weaver	01J102Ac
NULTY, Frank	22	M		Weaver	01J102Ac
GAYNOR, Michl.	24	M		Farmer	01J102Ac
MCCORMICK, Thos.	21	M		Farmer	01J102Ac
BLAKE, Thos.	23	M		Farmer	01J102Ac
GIBSON, Geo.	22	M		Farmer	01J102Ac
RICE, Ellen	19	F		Dressmaker	01J102Ac
MONNAHAGN, James	30	M		Laborer	01J102Ac

NAMES OF PASSENGERS	A G E	S E X	OCCUPATIONS	DATE PORT SHIP	NAMES OF PASSENGERS	A G E	S E X	OCCUPATIONS	DATE PORT SHIP
MONNAHAGN, Ellen		27	F	Laborer	01J102Ac	MAGARRY, Ellen		13	F	Servant	01J102Ac
FARRELL, Margt.		21	F	Laborer	01J102Ac	CULLEN, Eliza		24	F	Servant	01J102Ac
Rose		20	F	Laborer	01J102Ac	THOMSON, Margt.		21	F	Servant	01J102Ac
MADDEN, Edw.		25	M	Laborer	01J102Ac	CAMPBELL, Michl.		20	M	Laborer	01J102Ac
Jno.		22	M	Laborer	01J102Ac	FITZSIMONS, Michl.		26	M	Stctr	01J102Ac
GLEESON, Michl.		24	M	Laborer	01J102Ac	CAMPBELL, Jno.		60	M	Baker	01J102Ac
BOYDE, Jno.		20	M	Laborer	01J102Ac	Henry		14	M	Baker	01J102Ac
MCCABE, Michl.		29	M	Laborer	01J102Ac	Mary		48	F	Baker	01J102Ac
CURRAN, Bernard		29	M	Laborer	01J102Ac	Mary		12	F	Baker	01J102Ac
PARR, Jas.		18	M	Laborer	01J102Ac	Eliza		08	F	Child	01J102Ac
CAMPBELL, Owen		23	M	Laborer	01J102Ac	Arthur		06	M	Child	01J102Ac
MCCARROLL, Hugh		17	M	Laborer	01J102Ac	MURPHY, Johanna		24	F	Servant	01J102Ac
QUINN, Mary		24	F	Laborer	01J102Ac	Ellen		20	F	Servant	01J102Ac
MCGUIRE, Jas.		19	M	Laborer	01J102Ac	Patt		17	M	Servant	01J102Ac
MALONEY, Mary		26	F	Laborer	01J102Ac	Maria		16	F	Servant	01J102Ac
LAVEL, Patt		23	M	Laborer	01J102Ac	MULVADY, Jas.		50	M	Laborer	01J102Ac
MCNAMEE, Patt		13	M	Laborer	01J102Ac	Judy (W)		47	F	Wife	01J102Ac
LOGUE, Jno.		55	M	Merchant	01J102Ac	James (S)		24	M	Laborer	01J102Ac
Jno. (S)		18	M	Merchant	01J102Ac	Frs. (S)		16	M	Laborer	01J102Ac
Jas. (S)		16	M	Merchant	01J102Ac	Patt (S)		14	M	Laborer	01J102Ac
Thos. (S)		13	M	Merchant	01J102Ac	Michl. (S)		12	M	Laborer	01J102Ac
Ann (D)		10	F	Child	01J102Ac	Bridget (D)		10	F	Child	01J102Ac
Alex. (S)		20	M	None	01J102Ac	HAGNEY, Michl.		23	M	Laborer	01J102Ac
CASEY, Jas.		25	M	Farmer	01J102Ac	CLINE, Mary		24	F	Laborer	01J102Ac
NAGLE, Margt.		15	F	Servant	01J102Ac	LUDWITH, Bridget		22	F	Laborer	01J102Ac
COLLINS, Hy		22	M	Laborer	01J102Ac	FLOOD, Bessy		23	F	Laborer	01J102Ac
CONNELL, Jno.		24	M	Laborer	01J102Ac	MCANALLY, Bryan		25	M	Laborer	01J102Ac
GIBSON, Alex		24	M	Laborer	01J102Ac	BOULTON, Edw.		36	M	Laborer	01J102Ac
FITZGERALD, Jno.		20	M	Laborer	01J102Ac	SUTTON, Julia		55	F	Laborer	01J102Ac
HIGGINS, Dennis		24	M	Laborer	01J102Ac	Thos.		10	M	Child	01J102Ac
Wm.		22	M	Laborer	01J102Ac	Honora		08	F	Child	01J102Ac
Mary		22	F	Laborer	01J102Ac	SULLIVAN, Edw.		30	M	Laborer	01J102Ac
Thos.		20	M	Laborer	01J102Ac	DUFFY, Sarah		24	F	Laborer	01J102Ac
Bridget		17	F	Laborer	01J102Ac	Patt		22	M	Laborer	01J102Ac
Julie		12	F	Laborer	01J102Ac	HAMMELL, Mary		60	F	Laborer	01J102Ac
WHITE, Jno.		20	M	Weaver	01J102Ac	Owen		21	M	Laborer	01J102Ac
DEASEY, Michl.		45	M	Laborer	01J102Ac	Sylvester		19	M	Laborer	01J102Ac
Mary		21	F	Laborer	01J102Ac	SALSBURY, Sarah		19	F	Laborer	01J102Ac
TRIANOR, Geo.		26	M	Laborer	01J102Ac	COSGROVE, Patt		20	M	Laborer	01J102Ac
BRANNIN, Edw.		26	M	Laborer	01J102Ac	Jas.		17	M	Laborer	01J102Ac
Eliza		24	F	Laborer	01J102Ac	MCGEE, Jane		30	F	Laborer	01J102Ac
HOLAN, Timo.		25	M	Laborer	01J102Ac	CALVEY, Eliza		07	F	Child	01J102Ac
Mary		19	F	Laborer	01J102Ac	COSTELLO, Bern.		17	M	Unknown	01J102Ac
LEADER, Thos.		19	M	Farmer	01J102Ac	MCGEE, Danl.		12	M	Unknown	01J102Ac
MCMANUS, Jno.		20	M	Farmer	01J102Ac	CAHILL, Alice		34	F	Unknown	01J102Ac
DANIELS, Margt.		19	F	Servant	01J102Ac	Mary (D)		10	F	Child	01J102Ac
PEACOCK, Henry		25	M	Laborer	01J102Ac	Henry (S)		08	M	Child	01J102Ac
Jane		18	F	Laborer	01J102Ac	Ann (D)		06	F	Child	01J102Ac
HENSHAW, Jno.		25	M	Laborer	01J102Ac	Rose (D)		03	F	Child	01J102Ac
Dennis		17	M	Laborer	01J102Ac	MCILVOY, Jno.		20	M	Laborer	01J102Ac
Margt.		23	F	Laborer	01J102Ac	LEMON, Rose		30	F	Laborer	01J102Ac
Mary		21	F	Laborer	01J102Ac	MORAN, Patt		24	M	Laborer	01J102Ac
MEHAN, Biddy		50	F	Laborer	01J102Ac	CASEY, Jane		21	F	Laborer	01J102Ac
Mary (W)		45	F	Wife	01J102Ac	SLIVEN, Ann		22	F	Laborer	01J102Ac
Thos. (S)		12	M	Servant	01J102Ac	DOYLE, Cathn.		20	F	Laborer	01J102Ac
Ann (D)		13	F	Servant	01J102Ac	SCULLY, Mary		20	F	Laborer	01J102Ac
Jno. (S)		20	M	Servant	01J102Ac	NOLAN, Cathn.		21	F	Laborer	01J102Ac
HOPKINS, Jno.		23	M	Shoemaker	01J102Ac	COYLE, Susan		19	F	Laborer	01J102Ac
MALLADY, Patt		50	M	Laborer	01J102Ac	MCGRADY, Thos.		20	M	Laborer	01J102Ac
Patt (S)		13	M	Laborer	01J102Ac	BRENNAN, Jas.		27	M	Laborer	01J102Ac
Ann (W)		40	F	None	01J102Ac	MCCULLUM, Cathn.		21	F	Laborer	01J102Ac
Biddy (D)		13	F	None	01J102Ac	BYRNE, Jas.		18	M	Laborer	01J102Ac
Betty (D)		11	F	None	01J102Ac	CONAHAN, Jas.		23	M	Laborer	01J102Ac
PARKER, Geo.		23	M	Farmer	01J102Ac	DONNELLY, Cathn.		31	F	Laborer	01J102Ac
Mary		21	F	Farmer	01J102Ac	HALEY, Cathn.		18	F	Laborer	01J102Ac
HUGHES, Cathn.		19	F	Servant	01J102Ac	BYRNE, Mary		20	F	Laborer	01J102Ac
FARRIS, Mary		20	F	Servant	01J102Ac	DOUGHERTY, Ann		17	F	Servant	01J102Ac
LOOBY, Mary		20	F	Servant	01J102Ac	MOSS, Alice		25	F	Servant	01J102Ac
LYNAM, Mary		20	F	Servant	01J102Ac	MCMULKERIN, Michl.		30	M	Farmer	01J102Ac
MCKEY, Jno.		20	M	Clerk	01J102Ac	MCSORLEY, Cathn.		17	F	Servant	01J102Ac
TIERNAN, Patt		20	M	Laborer	01J102Ac	ALCORN, Mary		21	F	Servant	01J102Ac
MCDONNELL, Jane		21	F	Servant	01J102Ac	MCLAUGHLIN, Cathn.		22	F	Servant	01J102Ac
JONES, Charles		41	M	Farmer	01J102Ac	OBRIEN, Jno.		17	M	Servant	01J102Ac
VANCE, Chamber		16	M	Farmer	01J102Ac	Matilda		46	F	Servant	01J102Ac
CROW, Geo.		19	M	Laborer	01J102Ac	COLLINS, Margt.		38	F	Servant	01J102Ac

NAMES OF PASSENGERS		AGE	SEX	OCCUPATIONS	DATE PORT SHIP
COLLINS, Ellen	(D)	17	F	Servant	01J102Ac
Jno.	(S)	11	M	Servant	01J102Ac
Cathn.	(D)	10	F	Servant	01J102Ac
Charles	(S)	08	M	Child	01J102Ac
Margt.	(D)	06	F	Child	01J102Ac
James	(S)	04	M	Child	01J102Ac
Mary-Ann	(D)	01	F	Child	01J102Ac
OBRIEN, Jas.		17	M	Servant	01J102Ac
COX, Mary		21	F	Servant	01J102Ac
GLYNN, Winnefred		22	F	Servant	01J102Ac
FARRELLY, Mary		25	F	Servant	01J102Ac
MCGOVERN, Mary		25	F	Servant	01J102Ac
ROWE, Jane		34	F	Servant	01J102Ac
WARD, Ellzth.		11	F	Servant	01J102Ac
Peter		08	M	Servant	01J102Ac
BRADLY, Rosanna		22	F	Servant	01J102Ac
DORAN, Ellzth.		21	F	Servant	01J102Ac
CAMPBELL, Margt.		17	F	Servant	01J102Ac
Ellzth.		12	F	Servant	01J102Ac
CAMPION, Michl.		25	M	Tailor	01J102Ac
PRUNTY, Thos.		20	M	Laborer	01J102Ac
BARRETT, Thos.		33	M	Gdnr	01J102Ac
LYNCH, Patt		40	M	Laborer	01J102Ac
FOGARTY, Jno.		25	M	Laborer	01J102Ac
EGAN, Biddy		20	F	Laborer	01J102Ac
GINTY, Cathn.		20	F	Laborer	01J102Ac
WALKER, James		29	M	Bricklayer	01J102Ac
Mary	(W)	30	F	Wife	01J102Ac
Thos.	(S)	10	M	Bricklayer	01J102Ac
Wm.	(S)	08	M	Child	01J102Ac
Jno.	(S)	06	M	Child	01J102Ac
Patt	(S)	.09	M	Infant	01J102Ac
MURRAY, Jane		26	F	Servant	01J102Ac
WALSH, Christian		19	M	Servant	01J102Ac
DOWLEY, Patt		18	M	Servant	01J102Ac
Frs.		17	M	Servant	01J102Ac
James		15	M	Servant	01J102Ac
CONDRIN, Patt		21	M	Servant	01J102Ac
FITZGERALD, Cathn.		24	F	Servant	01J102Ac
COLVILL, James		35	M	Laborer	01J102Ac
CAMPION, Margt.		25	F	Servant	01J102Ac
DILLON, Bridget		20	F	Servant	01J102Ac
HACKETT, Bridget		19	F	Servant	01J102Ac
SMITH, Michl.		22	M	Weaver	01J102Ac
Bridget		20	F	Weaver	01J102Ac
MURPHY, Mary		25	F	Dressmaker	01J102Ac
DEGNAN, Thos.		20	M	Laborer	01J102Ac
Ann		18	F	Laborer	01J102Ac
BRADY, Jas.		28	M	Laborer	01J102Ac
Patt	(S)	07	M	Child	01J102Ac
GRAY, Andrew		30	M	Farmer	01J102Ac
Terrance		27	M	Farmer	01J102Ac
BRADY, Patt		21	M	Farmer	01J102Ac
Mary		20	F	Servant	01J102Ac
WALSH, Jno.		25	M	Laborer	01J102Ac
Thos.		12	M	Laborer	01J102Ac
LYNCH, Ann		19	F	Laborer	01J102Ac
Bridget		17	F	Laborer	01J102Ac
STANLEY, Margt.		34	F	Laborer	01J102Ac
DAVIS, Jane		20	F	Laborer	01J102Ac
STANLEY, Wm.		21	M	Laborer	01J102Ac
VANCE, Ellzth.		18	F	Servant	01J102Ac
ELVEY, Frs.		32	M	Cbtmkr	01J102Ac
KEENAN, Alice		32	F	Laborer	01J102Ac
MCCLUSKY, Bridget		33	F	Laborer	01J102Ac
MCBARREN, Jas.		06	M	Child	01J102Ac
MCILVOY, Ann		25	F	Laborer	01J102Ac
KIRBY, Nanny		17	F	Laborer	01J102Ac
HORMS, Frs.		18	M	Laborer	01J102Ac
CONNOR, Ann		24	F	Laborer	01J102Ac
Jas.	(S)	03	M	Child	01J102Ac
Ellzth.	(D)	.06	F	Infant	01J102Ac
MCNULTY, Patt		24	M	Laborer	01J102Ac
ADAMS, Jno.		17	M	Laborer	01J102Ac
MCKEE, Wm.		13	M	Laborer	01J102Ac

NAMES OF PASSENGERS		AGE	SEX	OCCUPATIONS	DATE PORT SHIP
MCKEE, George		10	M	Laborer	01J102Ac
GRANGIN, Ellzth.		29	F	Milliner	01J102Ac
DEEHAN, Roger		20	M	Servant	01J102Ac
ONEILL, James		08	M	Child	01J102Ac
Jno.		06	M	Child	01J102Ac
Cathn.		12	F	Child	01J102Ac
MEEHAN, Mary		60	F	Unknown	01J102Ac
CONNOR, Ellen		23	F	Servant	01J102Ac
COOGAN, Bridget		20	F	Servant	01J102Ac
GAFFNEY, Peter		37	M	Laborer	01J102Ac
U	(W)	50	F	Laborer	01J102Ac
CAVANAGH, James		14	M	Laborer	01J102Ac
MITCHELL, Ann		20	F	Laborer	01J102Ac
KEYS, Wm.		30	M	Laborer	01J102Ac
REILLEY, Chas.		30	M	Laborer	01J102Ac
LOOBY, Jno.		30	M	Laborer	01J102Ac
DONNELLY, Jno.		27	M	Laborer	01J102Ac
DOWNES, James		20	M	Laborer	01J102Ac
Margt.		04	F	Child	01J102Ac
DONAHUE, Oney		29	M	Laborer	01J102Ac
DELAHUNTY, Mary		16	F	Laborer	01J102Ac
GREENNAN, Patt		24	M	Laborer	01J102Ac
Cathn.		19	F	Laborer	01J102Ac
BROWN, Thos.		56	M	Merchant	01J102Ac
Ann	(W)	50	F	Merchant	01J102Ac
STERLING, George		60	M	Merchant	01J102Ac
Mary	(W)	60	F	Merchant	01J102Ac

EVANDER 01 JULY 1846

From Eleuthera

NAMES OF PASSENGERS	AGE	SEX	OCCUPATIONS	DATE PORT SHIP
FISHER, Elizabeth	50	F	Htlkpr	01J141Fo

LORD-ASHBURTON 02 JULY 1846

From Liverpool

NAMES OF PASSENGERS		AGE	SEX	OCCUPATIONS	DATE PORT SHIP
SCOTT, U		76	M	Servant	02J102Fp
U	(W)	72	F	Servant	02J102Fp
HITTER, U-Mrs		34	F	Servant	02J102Fp
WILSON, William		26	M	Servant	02J102Fp
Samuel		24	M	Servant	02J102Fp
James		22	M	Servant	02J102Fp
Robert		18	M	Servant	02J102Fp
COURTNEY, Andrew		22	M	Servant	02J102Fp
Margt.		21	F	Servant	02J102Fp
WHALEY, Geo.		22	M	Servant	02J102Fp
FLINN, John		40	M	Servant	02J102Fp
Mary	(W)	36	F	Wife	02J102Fp
Rosanna	(D)	17	F	None	02J102Fp
Mary-Ann	(D)	06	F	Child	02J102Fp
James	(S)	02	M	Child	02J102Fp
ANGLEY, Mary-Ann		20	F	Servant	02J102Fp
MORGAN, Ann		26	F	Servant	02J102Fp
CONNOR, Bernard		30	M	Servant	02J102Fp
Ellen	(W)	30	F	Servant	02J102Fp
Marla	(D)	01	F	Child	02J102Fp
FARLEY, Peter		21	M	Servant	02J102Fp
CHANCE, Thomas		25	M	Servant	02J102Fp
Mary		21	F	Servant	02J102Fp
BRIDGE, Sarah		25	F	Milliner	02J102Fp
Ephriam	(S)	06	M	Child	02J102Fp

NAMES OF PASSENGERS		AGE	SEX	OCCUPATIONS	DATE PORT SHIP
BRIDGE, Robert	(S)	04	M	Child	02J102Fp
REILLY, Michael		28	M	Servant	02J102Fp
Catherine		26	F	Servant	02J102Fp
SMITH, John		22	M	Servant	02J102Fp
STEEL, Nathl.		21	M	Servant	02J102Fp
WALMSLEY, James		27	M	Servant	02J102Fp
Betsey	(W)	24	F	Wife	02J102Fp
William	(S)	04	M	Child	02J102Fp
KINN, Marmgt.		35	F	Servant	02J102Fp
Bernard		17	M	Servant	02J102Fp
Joseph	(S)	06	M	Child	02J102Fp
John	(S)	04	M	Child	02J102Fp
Peter	(S)	02	M	Child	02J102Fp
MCBRYAN, Catherine		18	F	Servant	02J102Fp
Ann		16	F	Servant	02J102Fp
DUNN, Catherine		23	F	Servant	02J102Fp
CARR, Ellen		30	F	Servant	02J102Fp
MCGRATH, Mary		30	F	Servant	02J102Fp
SADUNN, Catherine		16	F	Servant	02J102Fp
CONNOLLY, Robt.		26	M	Servant	02J102Fp
Christopher		24	M	Servant	02J102Fp
Peter		20	M	Servant	02J102Fp
CUBBISON, James		22	M	Servant	02J102Fp
Mary		24	F	Servant	02J102Fp
SPRATT, Agnes		22	F	Servant	02J102Fp
CHAMBERS, Mary		22	F	Servant	02J102Fp
CARSON, John		24	M	Servant	02J102Fp
NEWELL, Robert		21	M	Servant	02J102Fp
Margaret	(W)	20	F	Servant	02J102Fp
Francis	(S)	01	M	Child	02J102Fp
GILLIES, Mary-Ann		23	F	Servant	02J102Fp
PURVIS, Alexd.		21	M	Servant	02J102Fp
Mary	(W)	20	F	Servant	02J102Fp
Martha	(D)	01	F	Child	02J102Fp
DOLAN, Ann		50	F	Servant	02J102Fp
BUTLER, Catherine		26	F	Servant	02J102Fp
CORIGAN, Dennis		25	M	Servant	02J102Fp
SMITH, Mary		26	F	Servant	02J102Fp
LAWLER, James		21	M	Servant	02J102Fp
CARROLL, Thos.		25	M	Servant	02J102Fp
FLOOD, Andrew		24	M	Servant	02J102Fp
BROGAN, Mary		19	F	Servant	02J102Fp
LYNCH, Mary		20	F	Servant	02J102Fp
MCCANN, James		23	M	Servant	02J102Fp
OCONNOR, Michl.		19	M	Servant	02J102Fp
DALEY, Maria		30	F	Servant	02J102Fp
Wm.	(S)	08	M	Child	02J102Fp
Jane	(D)	01	F	Child	02J102Fp
SMITH, Mary		25	F	Servant	02J102Fp
NULTY, Catherine		18	F	Servant	02J102Fp
GRAYSON, Michael		25	M	Laborer	02J102Fp
LAVEY, Chris		21	M	Laborer	02J102Fp
CAMPBELL, James		24	M	Laborer	02J102Fp
Mary		60	F	Cook	02J102Fp
Ann		20	F	Servant	02J102Fp
HART, Francis		11	M	Servant	02J102Fp
MASON, Mary		40	F	Servant	02J102Fp
MCGUIRE, Ann		19	F	Servant	02J102Fp
MURPHY, Peter		30	M	Servant	02J102Fp
GALLAGHER, Jas.		19	M	Servant	02J102Fp
HARRAHAN, Wm.		21	M	Servant	02J102Fp
IVAY, Jno.		44	M	Servant	02J102Fp
Phillip		44	M	Servant	02J102Fp
John		22	M	Servant	02J102Fp
Jane		19	F	Servant	02J102Fp
Henry		19	M	Servant	02J102Fp
Eliza.		14	F	Servant	02J102Fp
Isaac		12	M	Servant	02J102Fp
William		10	M	Servant	02J102Fp
Susan		08	F	Child	02J102Fp
Mary		06	F	Child	02J102Fp
Jane		04	F	Child	02J102Fp
Elizabeth		02	F	Child	02J102Fp
Jas.Henry		01	M	Child	02J102Fp
DAVIS, John		23	M	Servant	02J102Fp
EAVES, Wm.		21	M	Servant	02J102Fp
MCFARLANE, Wm.		25	M	Servant	02J102Fp
Jessie	(W)	25	F	Servant	02J102Fp
John	(S)	01	M	Child	02J102Fp
SMITH, Samuel		14	M	Servant	02J102Fp
PATTERSON, John		33	M	Servant	02J102Fp
Christina	(W)	29	F	Servant	02J102Fp
Jessie	(D)	06	F	Child	02J102Fp
Francis	(S)	05	M	Child	02J102Fp
Ellen	(D)	03	F	Child	02J102Fp
Christina	(D)	01	F	Child	02J102Fp
GAFFNEY, James		38	M	Servant	02J102Fp
Ann	(W)	33	F	Servant	02J102Fp
Michl.	(S)	04	M	Child	02J102Fp
Catherine	(D)	02	F	Child	02J102Fp
FARRELL, Thos.		26	M	Servant	02J102Fp
MCDONALD, Mary		28	F	Servant	02J102Fp
ROACH, Christopher		34	M	Servant	02J102Fp
Mary		25	F	Servant	02J102Fp
Peter		27	M	Servant	02J102Fp
CARROLL, James		35	M	Servant	02J102Fp
Bridget		33	F	Servant	02J102Fp
FEEHAN, Terence		30	M	Servant	02J102Fp
KELLY, Thomas		27	M	Servant	02J102Fp
EATON, Mary		19	F	Servant	02J102Fp
Martha		16	F	Servant	02J102Fp
HUTCHESON, John		18	M	Servant	02J102Fp
ROURKE, Thomas		14	M	Servant	02J102Fp
MCDERMOTT, Catherine		18	F	Servant	02J102Fp
LACEY, Jas.		22	M	Servant	02J102Fp
MILLIGAN, John		13	M	Servant	02J102Fp
LARKIN, Mary		24	F	Servant	02J102Fp
MULLIGAN, Ann		40	F	Servant	02J102Fp
Elizabeth	(D)	18	F	Servant	02J102Fp
Jas.	(S)	02	M	Child	02J102Fp
LARKIN, Honora		18	F	Servant	02J102Fp
HAGAN, Catherine		24	F	Servant	02J102Fp
FISHER, Catherine		60	F	Servant	02J102Fp
Joseph		20	M	Farmer	02J102Fp
Thos.		22	M	Farmer	02J102Fp
CONNOLLY, Peter		24	M	Farmer	02J102Fp
KEOGH, Michael		30	M	Farmer	02J102Fp
Judith		60	F	Cook	02J102Fp
Catherine		25	F	Servant	02J102Fp
BRENNAN, Catherine		17	F	Servant	02J102Fp
Patrick		30	M	Servant	02J102Fp
FOGERTY, Wm.		30	M	Servant	02J102Fp
GILROY, Wm.		25	M	Servant	02J102Fp
Margaret		25	F	Servant	02J102Fp
KELLY, Pat.		24	M	Servant	02J102Fp
Ann	(W)	24	F	Servant	02J102Fp
Joseph	(S)	02	M	Child	02J102Fp
Esther	(D)	01	F	Child	02J102Fp
FREEMAN, Pat		20	M	Servant	02J102Fp
FEELEY, Pat		27	M	Servant	02J102Fp
Cathne.	(W)	24	F	Servant	02J102Fp
James	(S)	01	M	Child	02J102Fp
Michael		20	M	Servant	02J102Fp
Bridget		19	F	Servant	02J102Fp
CONSIDINE, Corns.		22	M	Servant	02J102Fp
HOGAN, Corns.		22	M	Servant	02J102Fp
NEW, William		22	M	Servant	02J102Fp
JERDEN, Thos.		22	M	Servant	02J102Fp
BLAIR, Elizabeth		20	F	Servant	02J102Fp
SMITH, Margt-Jane		18	F	Servant	02J102Fp
HAYS, Cathne.		23	F	Servant	02J102Fp
MCGUINESS, Cathne.		40	F	Servant	02J102Fp
ROACH, John		22	M	Servant	02J102Fp
CLENNAN, Elizabeth		20	F	Servant	02J102Fp
BAHON, Ann		16	F	Servant	02J102Fp
FOX, James		25	M	Farmer	02J102Fp
MARCH, Henry		24	M	Farmer	02J102Fp
MALLERY, James		24	M	Farmer	02J102Fp
MORRIS, Martin		21	M	Farmer	02J102Fp
MURNAN, Wm.		34	M	Farmer	02J102Fp

NAMES OF PASSENGERS		AGE	SEX	OCCUPATIONS	DATE PORT SHIP
MURNAN, Sarah	(W)	30	F	Servant	02J102Fp
John	(S)	02	M	Child	02J102Fp
FILEY, Johanna		22	F	Servant	02J102Fp
POLAN, Pat		26	M	Servant	02J102Fp
BEERY, William		21	M	Tailor	02J102Fp
IRVINE, John		28	M	Tailor	02J102Fp
LEONARD, Bridget		22	F	Servant	02J102Fp
WRINKLE, Mary		24	F	Servant	02J102Fp
Rose		54	F	Servant	02J102Fp
MALEARY, Dominick		25	M	Servant	02J102Fp
OWENS, Wm.		21	M	Servant	02J102Fp
Joseph		24	M	Servant	02J102Fp
FLANNAGAN, James		21	M	Servant	02J102Fp
DEERING, Bridget		16	F	Servant	02J102Fp
QUINN, Ellen		25	F	Servant	02J102Fp
SMITH, John		28	M	Servant	02J102Fp
Margaret		20	F	Servant	02J102Fp
MORAN, Mary		30	F	Servant	02J102Fp
MCCORMICK, Bridget		11	F	Servant	02J102Fp
SHINNERS, Ann		20	F	Servant	02J102Fp
Richard		35	M	Servant	02J102Fp
CONNALLY, James		25	M	Servant	02J102Fp
Catharine	(W)	25	F	Servant	02J102Fp
Margaret	(D)	04	F	Child	02J102Fp
GRAHAM, James		50	M	Servant	02J102Fp
Alex	(S)	16	M	Servant	02J102Fp
Ann	(D)	20	F	Servant	02J102Fp
Mary	(D)	16	F	Servant	02J102Fp
MUSSEY, John		22	M	Servant	02J102Fp
MAHARA, Alex		23	M	Servant	02J102Fp
SHEA, Mary		20	F	Servant	02J102Fp
TOOEY, Johanna		30	F	Milliner	02J102Fp
FOLEY, Maurice		20	M	Servant	02J102Fp
James		15	M	Servant	02J102Fp
CREED, James		21	M	Servant	02J102Fp
Michl.		21	M	Servant	02J102Fp
SHIELL, James		23	M	Servant	02J102Fp
Mary		20	F	Servant	02J102Fp
DONOVAN, Margt.		19	F	Servant	02J102Fp
COTTER, Mary		50	F	Servant	02J102Fp
Hugh		20	M	Servant	02J102Fp
James		18	M	Servant	02J102Fp
John		13	M	Servant	02J102Fp
CLEARY, Patrick		20	M	Servant	02J102Fp
MCCRITT, Ellen		20	F	Servant	02J102Fp
MCGUALLY, Ellen		23	F	Servant	02J102Fp
Charlotte		25	F	Servant	02J102Fp
FARRELL, Pat		22	M	Servant	02J102Fp
GALVIN, Dennis		22	M	Servant	02J102Fp
DUFFY, Catherine		22	F	Servant	02J102Fp
MCNAMARA, Mary		20	F	Servant	02J102Fp
TEIRNEY, Catherine		30	F	Servant	02J102Fp
Ann	(D)	15	F	Servant	02J102Fp
Bridget	(D)	12	F	Servant	02J102Fp
Margaret	(D)	09	F	Child	02J102Fp
CONLON, Mary		20	F	Servant	02J102Fp
Christopher		21	M	Servant	02J102Fp
MCCULLOCK, George		22	M	Tailor	02J102Fp
James		19	M	Tailor	02J102Fp
CONNELLY, Ellen		20	F	Tailor	02J102Fp
KROGH, John		26	M	Tailor	02J102Fp
John		22	M	Tailor	02J102Fp
John		06	M	Child	02J102Fp
Timothy		01	M	Child	02J102Fp
Johanna		23	F	Servant	02J102Fp
WINNE, Catherine		30	F	Servant	02J102Fp
DUFFY, Ann		18	F	Servant	02J102Fp
RAGG, Fanny-Margt.		18	F	Servant	02J102Fp
RAY, John		17	M	Servant	02J102Fp
BRENNAN, John		20	M	Servant	02J102Fp
STURGEN, Thos.		20	M	Servant	02J102Fp
COGHLAN, Danl.		18	M	Servant	02J102Fp
WHITE, Laurence		20	M	Servant	02J102Fp
BUCKLEY, Mary		20	F	Servant	02J102Fp
WHITE, Joanna		18	F	Servant	02J102Fp
MALONEY, Anna		21	F	Servant	02J102Fp
BRYAN, Timothy		18	M	Tailor	02J102Fp
HOY, Pat		40	M	Farmer	02J102Fp
Mary	(W)	40	F	Farmer	02J102Fp
Thos.	(S)	14	M	Farmer	02J102Fp
Laurence	(S)	10	M	Farmer	02J102Fp
Mary	(D)	08	F	Child	02J102Fp
Margt.	(D)	05	F	Child	02J102Fp
COYLE, Margt.		17	F	None	02J102Fp
John		15	M	None	02J102Fp
PLUNKET, Mary		18	F	None	02J102Fp
WARD, Betsey		18	F	None	02J102Fp
CARBERRY, Michl.		18	M	None	02J102Fp
NASSEY, Michl.		20	M	None	02J102Fp
DONOCASE, Mary		50	F	None	02J102Fp
DONOVAN, Danl.		20	M	None	02J102Fp
Catherine		18	F	None	02J102Fp
Pat		16	M	None	02J102Fp
Mary		13	F	None	02J102Fp
HOG, John		20	M	Laborer	02J102Fp
Pat		22	M	Laborer	02J102Fp
KENNAN, Michl.		22	M	Laborer	02J102Fp
SULLIVAN, John		22	M	Laborer	02J102Fp
REARDON, Ellen		20	F	Servant	02J102Fp
CALLAHAN, Johanna		20	F	Servant	02J102Fp
MAHONEY, Jane		22	F	Servant	02J102Fp
REARDON, John		18	M	Servant	02J102Fp
ONEAL, Julia		22	F	Servant	02J102Fp
MCCALL, Ann		20	F	Servant	02J102Fp
TIERNEY, Rose		20	F	Servant	02J102Fp
TOBIN, Ellen		60	F	Servant	02J102Fp
Catherine		22	F	Servant	02J102Fp
MURRAY, Bernard		21	M	Servant	02J102Fp
Margt.	(W)	22	F	Servant	02J102Fp
Mary	(D)	01	F	Child	02J102Fp
HIGGINS, David		30	M	Servant	02J102Fp
Catherine		35	F	Servant	02J102Fp
BAILEY, Mathew		16	M	Servant	02J102Fp
MALONE, Michl.		28	M	Servant	02J102Fp
FOY, Peter		30	M	Servant	02J102Fp
COYLE, Michl.		20	M	Servant	02J102Fp
RICKET, Mary		25	F	Servant	02J102Fp
Rose		22	F	Servant	02J102Fp
CORMICK, Margt.		16	F	Dressmaker	02J102Fp
DUFFY, Catherine		20	F	Dressmaker	02J102Fp
TAMONY, Ann		17	F	Dressmaker	02J102Fp
HUGHES, Mary		19	F	Dressmaker	02J102Fp
MCELROY, Ann		24	F	Dressmaker	02J102Fp
BURNS, Rose		21	F	Servant	02J102Fp
GORMAN, John		58	M	Servant	02J102Fp
Keron	(S)	20	M	Servant	02J102Fp
Ellen	(D)	18	F	Servant	02J102Fp
KANALLY, Ann		72	F	Servant	02J102Fp
William		26	M	Servant	02J102Fp
Ann		28	F	Servant	.02J102Fp
HICKEY, James		19	M	Servant	02J102Fp
BRISBANE, Peter		28	M	Servant	02J102Fp
Bridget		28	F	Servant	02J102Fp
BIRMINGHAM, Pat		45	M	Servant	02J102Fp
FOX, Mary		21	F	Servant	02J102Fp
HANLON, Margt.		19	F	Servant	02J102Fp
EVANS, Martha		31	F	Servant	02J102Fp
NEVENS, Francis		25	M	Servant	02J102Fp
CAVANAUGH, Pat		30	M	Servant	02J102Fp
Mary	(W)	29	F	Servant	02J102Fp
Jane	(D)	10	F	Servant	02J102Fp
Patrick	(S)	07	M	Child	02J102Fp
Wm.	(S)	05	M	Child	02J102Fp
HICKEY, Mary		16	F	Servant	02J102Fp
CONNELL, Rose		17	F	Servant	02J102Fp
BODKIN, James		18	M	Tailor	02J102Fp
FOX, Edward		20	M	Laborer	02J102Fp

NAMES OF PASSENGERS	AGE	SEX	OCCUPATIONS	DATE PORT SHIP

BELFAST 02 JULY 1846

From St.Vincent

NAMES OF PASSENGERS		AGE	SEX	OCCUPATIONS	DATE PORT SHIP
REID, Elizabeth		32	F	Lady	02J140Du
BROWN, Thomas-A.		30	M	Minister	02J140Du
EDWARDS, Richard		28	M	Gentleman	02J140Du
CHECKLEY, Francis		16	M	Gentleman	02J140Du

POLAND 03 JULY 1846

From Havana

CURELL, Charles		27	M	Merchant	03J106Hs

CORNELIA 06 JULY 1846

From Liverpool

POTTS, John-Turperent		36	M	Gentleman	06J102Am
Jane-Francis	(W)	36	F	Wife	06J102Am
Elizabeth	(D)	08	F	Child	06J102Am
William	(S)	06	M	Child	06J102Am
Henry	(S)	05	M	Child	06J102Am
John	(S)	03	M	Child	06J102Am
James	(S)	01	M	Child	06J102Am
MCBOY, Ann		40	F	Servant	06J102Am

SIR-C.CAMPBELL 07 JULY 1846

From Liverpool

FITZGERALD, Daniel		28	M	Laborer	07J102Jg
CRAWFORD, Mary-Ann		35	F	WI	07J102Jg
Matilda	(D)	18	F	Unknown	07J102Jg
Betsey		13	F	Servant	07J102Jg
KELLS, Robert		25	M	Laborer	07J102Jg
CARR, Isabella		21	F	Servant	07J102Jg
CONNOR, Hugh		25	M	Weaver	07J102Jg
Mary		24	F	Servant	07J102Jg
John		17	M	Laborer	07J102Jg
Nancy		19	F	Servant	07J102Jg
Martha		01	F	Child	07J102Jg
Margaret		.05	F	Infant	07J102Jg
CHAMBERS, William		26	M	Weaver	07J102Jg
U, U		15	M	Weaver	07J102Jg
MONTGOMERY, James		26	M	Weaver	07J102Jg
AULD, Thomas		30	M	Farmer	07J102Jg
Jane	(W)	30	F	Servant	07J102Jg
Agnes	(D)	10	F	Unknown	07J102Jg
John	(S)	08	M	Child	07J102Jg
AULD, Josiah	(S)	04	M	Child	07J102Jg
Martha	(D)	02	F	Child	07J102Jg
MILFORD, Mary		40	F	Servant	07J102Jg
William	(S)	17	M	Servant	07J102Jg
Sarah	(D)	19	F	Servant	07J102Jg
Robert	(S)	16	M	Servant	07J102Jg
Agnes	(D)	12	F	Servant	07J102Jg
STEPHENSON, William		50	M	Farmer	07J102Jg
Sarah	(W)	50	F	Farmer	07J102Jg
John	(S)	20	M	Farmer	07J102Jg
Sarah	(D)	18	F	Servant	07J102Jg
William	(S)	13	M	Servant	07J102Jg
David	(S)	12	M	Unknown	07J102Jg
Samuel	(S)	10	M	Unknown	07J102Jg
HANLON, Biddy		38	F	Servant	07J102Jg
Catharine	(D)	13	F	Servant	07J102Jg
IRWIN, Elizabeth		18	F	Servant	07J102Jg
. John		16	M	Weaver	07J102Jg
SCOTT, John		35	M	Farmer	07J102Jg
Mary	(W)	30	F	Farmer	07J102Jg
Mary	(D)	12	F	Servant	07J102Jg
Samuel	(S)	10	M	Unknown	07J102Jg
Sarah	(D)	04	F	Child	07J102Jg
Mathew	(S)	06	M	Child	07J102Jg
David	(S)	01	M	Child	07J102Jg
FOX, William-J.		45	M	Surgeon	07J102Jg
Mary-Ann	(W)	30	F	Wife	07J102Jg
William-John		17	M	Surgeon	07J102Jg
Rachael	(D)	15	F	Spinster	07J102Jg
Mary-Ann	(D)	10	F	Unknown	07J102Jg
George	(S)	08	M	Child	07J102Jg
Christiana	(D)	06	F	Child	07J102Jg
Margaret	(D)	05	F	Child	07J102Jg
Ewing	(S)	03	M	Child	07J102Jg
Jas.Campbell	(S)	.00	M	Infant	07J102Jg
LEWIS, Thos.		28	M	Farmer	07J102Jg
SLOANE, Sarah		27	F	Servant	07J102Jg
Elizabeth		22	F	Servant	07J102Jg
MCULLOUGH, James		23	M	Weaver	07J102Jg
HARBISON, James		18	M	Laborer	07J102Jg
DUNN, John		25	M	Clerk	07J102Jg
MDONALD, Donald		32	M	Laborer	07J102Jg
MACDONALD, Elizabeth		24	F	Laborer	07J102Jg
GIRSIDE, Thomas		22	M	Laborer	07J102Jg
GIRDSIDE, John		20	M	Laborer	07J102Jg
SMYTH, Samuel		20	M	Clerk	07J102Jg
ONEILL, Catharine		21	F	Servant	07J102Jg
HAY, David-Lowry		17	M	Clerk	07J102Jg
BAILEY, Marg.		21	F	Servant	07J102Jg
FITZSIMMONS, Isabella		25	F	Servant	07J102Jg
MCANULLY, Jane		20	F	Servant	07J102Jg
PARKESHAM, James		25	M	Weaver	07J102Jg
Elizabeth		20	F	Weaver	07J102Jg
HOWELL, Robert		26	M	Weaver	07J102Jg
ANDERSON, William		25	M	Laborer	07J102Jg
MORRISON, Agnes		21	F	Servant	07J102Jg
OAKMAN, Clement		18	M	Weaver	07J102Jg
DENVIR, Margaret		18	F	Servant	07J102Jg
ORR, John		19	M	Weaver	07J102Jg
CORR, Mary		18	F	Servant	07J102Jg
JACKSON, John		35	M	Laborer	07J102Jg
Mary		21	F	Servant	07J102Jg
Eleanor		18	F	Servant	07J102Jg
MORGAN, William		18	M	Laborer	07J102Jg
HARKIN, David		25	M	Weaver	07J102Jg
ROBINSON, Betty		50	F	Servant	07J102Jg
Maria	(D)	16	F	Servant	07J102Jg
TODD, James		18	M	Laborer	07J102Jg
ROBINSON, Peter		30	M	Farmer	07J102Jg
Mary		25	F	Farmer	07J102Jg
LINDEN, Mary		18	F	Servant	07J102Jg
ADAMS, John		25	M	Shoemaker	07J102Jg
MCKEE, John		22	M	Carpenter	07J102Jg
Jane	(D)	02	F	Child	07J102Jg
MACKAY, John		20	M	Carpenter	07J102Jg

NAMES OF PASSENGERS		AGE	SEX	OCCUPATIONS	DATE PORT SHIP
LOUGHEY, Nancy		20	F	Servant	07J102Jg
MOORE, Elizabeth		20	F	Servant	07J102Jg
BLEAKLEY, Johnston		21	M	Clerk	07J102Jg
WATERS, Jas.M.		25	M	Carpenter	07J102Jg
HEPBURN, Sarah		23	F	Servant	07J102Jg
BRYSON, Robert		30	M	Weaver	07J102Jg
FLANAGAN, Mary		21	F	Weaver	07J102Jg
DONEGAN, Patt		25	M	Weaver	07J102Jg
Jane		23	F	Servant	07J102Jg
May		13	F	Servant	07J102Jg
MCMAHON, Liddy		19	F	Servant	07J102Jg
Margt.		14	F	Servant	07J102Jg
WETHERS, James		20	M	Carpenter	07J102Jg
BISHOP, David		23	M	Carpenter	07J102Jg
CONNERY, Mary		22	F	Servant	07J102Jg
MAHONNY, Alex.		28	M	Laborer	07J102Jg
MCFEINN, Alx.		20	M	Laborer	07J102Jg
STEPHENSON, James		25	M	Laborer	07J102Jg
TARNEY, Thos.		19	M	Laborer	07J102Jg
MACLINDOX, Thos.		25	M	Laborer	07J102Jg
CURRIER, James		18	M	Laborer	07J102Jg
KERN, Margaret		20	F	Spinster	07J102Jg
BLANY, Archy		28	M	Laborer	07J102Jg
BLANEY, Elizabeth		29	F	Servant	07J102Jg
MCCULLOUGH, Henry		13	M	Weaver	07J102Jg
Saml.		19	M	Weaver	07J102Jg
ARMSTRONG, Francis		27	M	Laborer	07J102Jg
Ellen		25	F	Servant	07J102Jg
John		13	M	Weaver	07J102Jg
Robt.		05	M	Child	07J102Jg
Mary-Anne		03	F	Child	07J102Jg
Eliza-Jane		03	F	Child	07J102Jg
David		.00	M	Infant	07J102Jg
MCCAN, John		21	M	Weaver	07J102Jg
SMITH, James		25	M	Weaver	07J102Jg
AICKEN, Jane		20	F	Servant	07J102Jg
BEATTY, Mary-Ann		18	F	Servant	07J102Jg
HUTCHINSON, Mary-Ann		20	F	Servant	07J102Jg
BOYLE, Mary-Ann		19	F	Servant	07J102Jg
MCIVOR, Mary-Ann		20	F	Servant	07J102Jg
LENOX, Henry		23	M	Weaver	07J102Jg
Andrew		21	M	Weaver	07J102Jg
SLOANE, James		25	M	Weaver	07J102Jg
MUNDELL, U-Miss		25	F	Servant	07J102Jg
CUDDY, Henry		22	M	Weaver	07J102Jg
HUGHES, James		25	M	Clerk	07J102Jg
Sarah	(W)	21	F	Wife	07J102Jg
MCGEE, Patrick		25	M	Weaver	07J102Jg
MOORE, Marg.		25	F	Servant	07J102Jg
HIGGINSON, Robert		24	M	Weaver	07J102Jg
LORIMER, Wm.		28	M	Weaver	07J102Jg
Fanny	(W)	25	F	Servant	07J102Jg
Mary-Ann	(D)	03	F	Child	07J102Jg
Marg.	(D)	.00	F	Infant	07J102Jg
Bridget		50	F	Servant	07J102Jg
BURNS, Eliza		25	F	Servant	07J102Jg
TODD, James		30	M	Weaver	07J102Jg
BYRNES, James		26	M	Weaver	07J102Jg
OSWALD, Hugh		24	M	Weaver	07J102Jg
PATTERSON, Rob.		50	M	Farmer	07J102Jg
Barbara	(W)	50	F	Farmer	07J102Jg
Jas.Henry	(S)	17	M	Farmer	07J102Jg
Sarah-Ann	(D)	15	F	Servant	07J102Jg
Jane	(D)	12	F	Servant	07J102Jg
Eliza	(D)	08	F	Child	07J102Jg
MCGINN, Arthur		20	M	Weaver	07J102Jg
BOYD, Archy		25	M	Weaver	07J102Jg
Robert		23	M	Weaver	07J102Jg
BIGHAM, Thos.		60	M	Farmer	07J102Jg
Agnes	(D)	20	F	Farmer	07J102Jg
Eliza		.00	F	Infant	07J102Jg
ALLEN, Jane		20	F	Servant	07J102Jg
MILLEN, Thos.		20	M	Weaver	07J102Jg
MARROW, James		27	M	Weaver	07J102Jg
FALKNER, Andw.		21	M	Weaver	07J102Jg
FALKNER, George		23	M	Weaver	07J102Jg
HARKNESS, Saml.		21	M	Weaver	07J102Jg
Cathn.		22	F	Weaver	07J102Jg
Hamilton		24	M	Weaver	07J102Jg
ROBINSON, Saml.		21	M	Weaver	07J102Jg
Anne		22	F	Weaver	07J102Jg
ONEILL, Hugh		25	M	Laborer	07J102Jg
CLARK, Elizabeth		23	F	Servant	07J102Jg
ANDERSON, Eliza		21	F	Servant	07J102Jg
STEPHENSON, Marg.		21	F	Servant	07J102Jg
DICKSON, Edwd.		18	M	Weaver	07J102Jg
Charlotte		21	F	Weaver	07J102Jg
JOHNSTON, Wm.		25	M	Laborer	07J102Jg
WILLIAMS, Jane		21	F	Servant	07J102Jg
MORAN, Nancy		22	F	Servant	07J102Jg
WHITE, John		25	M	Laborer	07J102Jg
JOHNSTON, Martha		23	F	Servant	07J102Jg
David		20	M	Weaver	07J102Jg
CARNEY, John		40	M	Farmer	07J102Jg
Henry	(S)	20	M	Farmer	07J102Jg
KEANE, Margt.		19	F	Servant	07J102Jg
DONELLY, Wm.		20	M	Laborer	07J102Jg
MCCAHOY, Mary		18	F	Servant	07J102Jg
MCBRIDE, Patrick		36	M	Laborer	07J102Jg
ARMSTRONG, George		18	M	Laborer	07J102Jg
JOHNSTON, Mary		18	F	Servant	07J102Jg
KEAN, Catherine		19	F	Servant	07J102Jg
SPIERS, Mary		20	F	Servant	07J102Jg
BROWN, John		22	M	Laborer	07J102Jg
MULLHOLLAND, Mary		40	F	Servant	07J102Jg
WILLIAMS, Fred		25	M	Laborer	07J102Jg
WARD, Allen		21	F	Laborer	07J102Jg
MINNIS, Andr.		26	M	Laborer	07J102Jg
CONWAY, Marg.		21	F	Servant	07J102Jg
Mary		17	F	Servant	07J102Jg
MACCRACKEN, Rob.		20	M	Laborer	07J102Jg
Anne		19	F	Weaver	07J102Jg
HUTCHINSON, Andrew		19	M	Weaver	07J102Jg
JOHNSTONE, Rob.		18	M	Weaver	07J102Jg
FENTON, Marg.		20	F	Servant	07J102Jg
MURPHY, U-Mrs.		30	F	Servant	07J102Jg
John	(S)	04	M	Child	07J102Jg
Mary-Ann	(D)	02	F	Child	07J102Jg
CORNETT, Wilm.		25	M	Laborer	07J102Jg
FLANNAGAN, B.		17	M	Laborer	07J102Jg

FOAM 07 JULY 1846

From Tampico

NAMES OF PASSENGERS	AGE	SEX	OCCUPATIONS	DATE PORT SHIP
MCDOWELL, Archibald	11	M	Student	07J176Jh
Stewart	13	M	Student	07J176Jh

ST.MARGARET 08 JULY 1846

From St.JOHN,Cape Nf.

NAMES OF PASSENGERS	AGE	SEX	OCCUPATIONS	DATE PORT SHIP
CONNORS, Edward	27	M	Blacksmith	08J177JI
KENNEDY, Wm.	21	M	None	08J177JI
CONNORS, Patrick	30	M	None	08J177JI
POWER, Alice	18	F	None	08J177JI

NAMES OF PASSENGERS		AGE	SEX	OCCUPATIONS	DATE PORT SHIP

CLAUSMAN 08 JULY 1846

From Glasgow

NAMES OF PASSENGERS		AGE	SEX	OCCUPATIONS	DATE PORT SHIP
MURROGH, Catherine		18	F	Servant	08J104JJ
DOCKERTY, Fanney		19	F	Servant	08J104JJ

WESTMINSTER 10 JULY 1846

From London

NAMES OF PASSENGERS		AGE	SEX	OCCUPATIONS	DATE PORT SHIP
TAYLER, Emma		26	F	None	10J121Br
HILL, Caroline		33	F	None	10J121Br
RENNBOLL, Emma		19	F	None	10J121Br
PETERS, William		65	M	Farmer	10J121Br
PRESTON, Mary		44	F	Farmer	10J121Br
HOPE, Edward		26	M	Draper	10J121Br
HEATHORN, Henry		26	M	None	10J121Br
OVINGTON, Isaac		46	M	Printer	10J121Br
GAY, William		60	M	Farmer	10J121Br
Sarah-Ann		55	F	Farmer	10J121Br
CRONY, Elizabeth		25	F	Servant	10J121Br
SMITH, William		34	M	None	10J121Br
Hanna	(W)	29	F	Hairdresser	10J121Br
Will-Henry	(S)	04	M	Child	10J121Br
KELLA, Patric		37	M	Laborer	10J121Br
CLARK, Joseph		25	M	Cnf	10J121Br
Mary-Ann		23	F	Cnf	10J121Br
WILKENSON, Arthur-N.		18	M	Bootmaker	10J121Br
BROOKS, Charles		18	M	Coachman	10J121Br
PURVIS, James		25	M	Surveyor	10J121Br
ASHLY, Fredc.		18	M	Tailor	10J121Br
BALL, John		35	M	Currier	10J121Br
CUTTING, Hervey		27	M	Bootmaker	10J121Br
Sarah		31	F	Bootmaker	10J121Br
MAIZE, George		11	M	Child	10J121Br
CUTTING, Henry		11	M	Child	10J121Br
CAVENER, Ann		52	F	None	10J121Br
Mary-Ann	(D)	14	F	None	10J121Br
FOULGER, Edward		25	M	Tailor	10J121Br
Harriet	(W)	25	F	Tailor	10J121Br
Elizabeth	(D)	09	F	Child	10J121Br
STEWARD, William		06	M	Child	10J121Br
FOULGER, John		02	M	Child	10J121Br
EVERENDEN, George		52	M	Bootmaker	10J121Br
Mary	(W)	48	F	Bootmaker	10J121Br
George	(S)	22	M	Bootmaker	10J121Br
William	(S)	16	M	Bootmaker	10J121Br
Sarah	(D)	13	F	Bootmaker	10J121Br
Eliza	(D)	10	F	Child	10J121Br
Lueazer	(D)	08	F	Child	10J121Br
WEBSTER, John		20	M	Laborer	10J121Br
FOSKETT, John		22	M	Goldbeater	10J121Br
Amelia		20	F	Goldbeater	10J121Br
MARA, John		30	M	Servant	10J121Br
Emma		21	F	Servant	10J121Br
HANSELL, Thomas		24	M	Tailor	10J121Br
FISHER, James		25	M	Laborer	10J121Br

NEW-YORK 13 JULY 1846

From Liverpool

NAMES OF PASSENGERS		AGE	SEX	OCCUPATIONS	DATE PORT SHIP
SEWELL, Henry-D.		39	M	Gentleman	13J102Bk
Charlotte		36	F	Lady	13J102Bk
PARTON, Ann		25	F	Lady	13J102Bk
FLOOD, Bridget		24	F	Lady	13J102Bk
LAVERICK, Mary		24	F	Lady	13J102Bk
CLEEFF, Edward		13	M	None	13J102Bk
DOLIER, George		17	M	Gentleman	13J102Bk
PUGH, James		31	M	Gentleman	13J102Bk
U	(W)	31	F	Lady	13J102Bk
DAWSON, Phebe		05	F	Child	13J102Bk
BILLINGTON, John		62	M	Laborer	13J102Bk
U	(W)	60	F	Laborer	13J102Bk
Mary-Ann	(D)	20	F	Laborer	13J102Bk
James	(S)	14	M	Laborer	13J102Bk
CONALY, Philip		32	M	Laborer	13J102Bk
KEAVLIN, John		35	M	Laborer	13J102Bk
GRAHAM, Terence		26	M	Laborer	13J102Bk
U	(W)	28	F	Laborer	13J102Bk
Julia	(D)	06	F	Child	13J102Bk
MCFARLAND, John		21	M	Laborer	13J102Bk
RAFFERTY, Edward		25	M	Laborer	13J102Bk
CONNLY, Bessey		38	F	Farmer	13J102Bk
EAMES, Bessey		20	F	Farmer	13J102Bk
SHERRY, Michel		38	M	Farmer	13J102Bk
John		40	M	Farmer	13J102Bk
MOSS, Ann		36	F	Farmer	13J102Bk
John	(S)	09	M	Child	13J102Bk
MULLEN, Michel		19	M	Farmer	13J102Bk
HAYES, Pat.		22	M	Shoemaker	13J102Bk
Catherine		20	F	Shoemaker	13J102Bk
GERAGHTY, Margort		21	F	Shoemaker	13J102Bk
MCCANN, Eliza		18	F	Shoemaker	13J102Bk
MCCARRAN, Margaret		20	F	Laborer	13J102Bk
MCDERMOTT, Edward		25	M	Laborer	13J102Bk
LANGANE, Margt.		24	F	Laborer	13J102Bk
BRASMAN, Mary		22	F	Laborer	13J102Bk
CONAGHTY, Bridget		20	F	Laborer	13J102Bk
BYRNES, Bridget		19	F	Laborer	13J102Bk
CONAGHTY, Pat		21	M	Laborer	13J102Bk
MENES, Mary		17	F	Laborer	13J102Bk
KILELINE, Mary		20	F	Laborer	13J102Bk
KELLY, Mary-Ann		22	F	Farmer	13J102Bk
CARRY, Margaret		30	F	Farmer	13J102Bk
HASKINS, Wm.		20	M	Farmer	13J102Bk
SNELL, John		02	M	Child	13J102Bk
BROW, Pat		29	M	Laborer	13J102Bk
WHITE, Ellin		20	F	Laborer	13J102Bk
TANCEY, James		28	M	Laborer	13J102Bk
CULLEN, U-Mrs.		40	F	Laborer	13J102Bk
GERAGHTY, Tully		20	M	Laborer	13J102Bk
NEILSON, Rose		23	F	Laborer	13J102Bk
FOX, Mary		22	F	Laborer	13J102Bk
DALEY, Mary		22	F	Laborer	13J102Bk
MALONE, Joseph		18	M	Laborer	13J102Bk
James		16	M	Laborer	13J102Bk
PERKINS, John		28	M	Laborer	13J102Bk
U	(W)	26	F	Laborer	13J102Bk
ECCLES, Edward		19	M	Laborer	13J102Bk
AUGUSTAS, Ann		20	F	Laborer	13J102Bk
CHELDRING, Wm.		27	M	Laborer	13J102Bk
BRYCE, U-Mrs.		45	F	Laborer	13J102Bk
Catherine	(D)	23	F	Laborer	13J102Bk
William	(S)	20	M	Laborer	13J102Bk
REILLY, Mary		18	F	Laborer	13J102Bk
SNELL, John		21	M	Laborer	13J102Bk

NAMES OF PASSENGERS		A G E	S E X	OCCUPATIONS	DATE PORT SHIP
HUGH, Phelim-M.		40	M	Laborer	13J102Bk
U	(W)	40	F	Laborer	13J102Bk
Mary	(D)	17	F	Laborer	13J102Bk
John	(S)	15	M	Laborer	13J102Bk
Thomas	(S)	13	M	Laborer	13J102Bk
James	(S)	12	M	Laborer	13J102Bk
Michel	(S)	20	M	Laborer	13J102Bk
EAGAN, Mathew		24	M	Laborer	13J102Bk
Margaret		19	F	Laborer	13J102Bk
KELLY, Pat		30	M	Laborer	13J102Bk
MCCABE, Esther		19	F	Laborer	13J102Bk
Susan		15	F	Laborer	13J102Bk
WALSH, James		35	M	Laborer	13J102Bk
U	(W)	23	F	Laborer	13J102Bk
Pat	(S)	.01	M	Infant	13J102Bk
Born-At-Sea					
Maria	(D)	01	F	Child	13J102Bk
MCNALLY, Mary		20	F	Laborer	13J102Bk
MURRY, Susan		17	F	Laborer	13J102Bk
MORAN, Danial		35	M	Laborer	13J102Bk
KELLY, Biddy		13	F	Laborer	13J102Bk
PENDERGRASS, Pat		14	M	Laborer	13J102Bk
DULY, Thos.		24	M	Laborer	13J102Bk
TYRLE, Thomas		24	M	Laborer	13J102Bk
GLASON, Michel		40	M	Laborer	13J102Bk
Catherine	(D)	19	F	Laborer	13J102Bk
DWYER, Ann		18	F	Laborer	13J102Bk
RYAN, Pat		21	M	Laborer	13J102Bk
DONOHUE, Pat		27	M	Laborer	13J102Bk
U	(W)	24	F	Laborer	13J102Bk
Jane	(D)	.01	F	Infant	13J102Bk
Born-At-Sea					
Thos.	(S)	15	M	Laborer	13J102Bk
Died-At-Sea					
James	(S)	13	M	Laborer	13J102Bk
William	(S)	03	M	Child	13J102Bk
DUGGAN, James		20	M	Laborer	13J102Bk
Edward		13	M	Laborer	13J102Bk
Biddy		20	F	Laborer	13J102Bk
Hannah		14	F	Laborer	13J102Bk
DELANCY, Wm.		35	M	Laborer	13J102Bk
DUNN, Grace		20	F	Laborer	13J102Bk
PHEBAM, Judeth		18	F	Laborer	13J102Bk
FOULKNER, Eliza		18	F	Laborer	13J102Bk
Magt.		20	F	Laborer	13J102Bk
MOFFAT, Jane		21	F	Laborer	13J102Bk
HOGSHEAD, Thos.		19	M	Laborer	13J102Bk
WARD, Michel		20	M	Laborer	13J102Bk
ROBERTS, David		56	M	Laborer	13J102Bk
U	(W)	53	F	Laborer	13J102Bk
Robert	(S)	20	M	Laborer	13J102Bk
William	(S)	28	M	Laborer	13J102Bk
Catherine	(D)	30	F	Laborer	13J102Bk
COLLEBY, Catherin		18	F	Laborer	13J102Bk
WILLIAMS, Eliza		20	F	Laborer	13J102Bk
William		21	M	Laborer	13J102Bk
Robert		30	M	Laborer	13J102Bk
U-Mrs.		29	F	Laborer	13J102Bk
Sydney		05	M	Child	13J102Bk
Catherine		03	F	Child	13J102Bk
Jane		.02	F	Infant	13J102Bk
GRIFFITHS, Elijah		21	M	Laborer	13J102Bk
COULD, Bell-M.		19	F	Laborer	13J102Bk
BUCKLEY, James		22	M	Laborer	13J102Bk
CORNISH, Pat		22	M	Laborer	13J102Bk
FINN, Rita		22	F	Laborer	13J102Bk
MALONE, Mary		20	F	Laborer	13J102Bk
KENNEY, Edward		24	M	Laborer	13J102Bk
HAYES, Thomas		04	M	Infant	13J102Bk
KELLY, Cathn.		26	F	Laborer	13J102Bk
HAYES, Hannah		03	F	Child	13J102Bk
Catherine		01	F	Child	13J102Bk
SUTTON, Wm.		28	M	Laborer	13J102Bk
NOLAN, Maria		18	F	Laborer	13J102Bk
WINTER, Pat.		25	M	Laborer	13J102Bk
COLFOR, Walter		22	M	Laborer	13J102Bk
CARRY, Ann		20	F	Laborer	13J102Bk
MURRY, Charles-M.		20	M	Laborer	13J102Bk
TYLER, Mathew		38	M	Laborer	13J102Bk
U	(W)	25	F	Laborer	13J102Bk
ONEIL, Chas.		34	M	Laborer	13J102Bk
MCNALLY, Barney		12	M	Laborer	13J102Bk
Ellin		05	F	Child	13J102Bk
MALOY, Tim		25	M	Child	13J102Bk
SCARROTT, Betty		22	F	Child	13J102Bk
NOWD, Winefred		20	M	Child	13J102Bk
HAINAHAN, Pat.		20	M	Laborer	13J102Bk
FLOOD, Wm.		25	M	Laborer	13J102Bk
WORDHILL, Sampson		25	M	Laborer	13J102Bk
DARBY, Eliza		20	F	Laborer	13J102Bk
GROVE, Wm.		24	M	Laborer	13J102Bk
DANIALS, John		23	M	Laborer	13J102Bk
FIELD, Mary		20	F	Laborer	13J102Bk
WHITE, Wm.		29	M	Laborer	13J102Bk
U	(W)	25	F	Laborer	13J102Bk
BELL, Agness		17	F	Laborer	13J102Bk
Essy		15	F	Laborer	13J102Bk
SOSAGHIN, Bessy		20	F	Laborer	13J102Bk
Mary-Ann	(D)	02	F	Child	13J102Bk
FARRILS, Biddy		16	F	Laborer	13J102Bk
CLUSKEY, James		20	M	Laborer	13J102Bk
COLLEBY, Margaret		20	F	Laborer	13J102Bk
CLARK, Owin		22	M	Laborer	13J102Bk
KELLHAN, Pat		20	M	Laborer	13J102Bk
WILSON, Michel		28	M	Laborer	13J102Bk
PARK, John		24	M	Laborer	13J102Bk
COLLEN, John		24	M	Laborer	13J102Bk
PARK, John		30	M	Laborer	13J102Bk
MIDDLETON, John		30	M	Laborer	13J102Bk
MAHON, Owen		50	M	Laborer	13J102Bk
U	(W)	40	F	Laborer	13J102Bk
Mary		30	F	Laborer	13J102Bk
Ann		20	F	Laborer	13J102Bk
LEARY, Danial		19	M	Laborer	13J102Bk
LANDEIS, John		40	M	Laborer	13J102Bk
U	(W)	34	F	Laborer	13J102Bk
William	(S)	09	M	Child	13J102Bk
Pat	(S)	07	M	Child	13J102Bk
Mary	(D)	04	F	Child	13J102Bk
Nicholas		01		Child	13J102Bk
WALSH, Mary		20	F	Laborer	13J102Bk
BARRY, John		21	M	Laborer	13J102Bk
KANE, John		24	M	Laborer	13J102Bk
SWANY, Timothy		06	M	Child	13J102Bk
SULLIVAN, Mary		13	F	Laborer	13J102Bk
CROWLY, Carus		22	M	Laborer	13J102Bk
FEE, Thomas		25	M	Laborer	13J102Bk
FLOOD, Barnard		20	M	Laborer	13J102Bk
CURRIN, Bridget		22	F	Laborer	13J102Bk
DUNN, Catherine		17	F	Laborer	13J102Bk
Ann		13	F	Laborer	13J102Bk
Suenrena		12	F	Laborer	13J102Bk
Eliza		09	F	Child	13J102Bk
OCONNER, Ellin		24	F	Laborer	13J102Bk
FINGAN, Ann		29	F	Laborer	13J102Bk
MCDERMET, Pat		07	M	Laborer	13J102Bk
MUNGAN, Michel		14	M	Laborer	13J102Bk
BYRNE, Margaret		30	F	Laborer	13J102Bk
James		17	M	Laborer	13J102Bk
Henry		15	M	Laborer	13J102Bk
Honora		12	F	Laborer	13J102Bk
Patt		10	M	Child	13J102Bk
Martin		08	M	Child	13J102Bk
John		06	M	Child	13J102Bk
MCGINN, Rose		40	F	Laborer	13J102Bk
Thomas	(S)	18	M	Laborer	13J102Bk
Owen	(S)	14	M	Laborer	13J102Bk
James	(S)	13	M	Laborer	13J102Bk
DUGGAN, John		60	M	Laborer	13J102Bk
John	(S)	22	M	Laborer	13J102Bk

NAMES OF PASSENGERS		AGE	SEX	OCCUPATIONS	DATE PORT SHIP
DUGGAN, Rose	(D)	20	F	Laborer	13J102Bk
Thomas	(S)	14	M	Laborer	13J102Bk
Biddy	(D)	04	F	Child	13J102Bk
FITZPATRICK, Michel		20	M	Laborer	13J102Bk
WOODS, Margaret		25	F	Laborer	13J102Bk
Jane		18	F	Laborer	13J102Bk
MCCREDEN, Danial		16	M	Laborer	13J102Bk
Mary		21	F	Laborer	13J102Bk
PATTEN, Michel		14	M	Laborer	13J102Bk
PALMER, Wm.		15	M	Laborer	13J102Bk
FLANAGAN, Pat.		30	M	Laborer	13J102Bk
Jully		35	F	Laborer	13J102Bk
DOLAN, Michel		22	M	Laborer	13J102Bk
FARRELL, Mary		22	F	Laborer	13J102Bk
GORMLY, Mary		12	F	Laborer	13J102Bk
Ann		10	F	Laborer	13J102Bk
HANLY, Honer		20	F	Laborer	13J102Bk
DONOHUE, Ann		21	F	Laborer	13J102Bk
MCCONGLY, Ann		12	F	Laborer	13J102Bk
James		08	M	Child	13J102Bk
Mary		06	F	Child	13J102Bk
MCKION, Peter		14	M	Laborer	13J102Bk
Margaret		13	F	Laborer	13J102Bk
MCGURCK, Ann		12	F	Laborer	13J102Bk
TULLY, James		30	M	Laborer	13J102Bk
MELODY, Pat.		22	M	Laborer	13J102Bk
CUNNINGHAM, Mary		20	F	Laborer	13J102Bk
STINSON, Thomas		18	M	Laborer	13J102Bk
SMITH, Cathn.		14	F	Laborer	13J102Bk
MCARNN, Ann		18	F	Laborer	13J102Bk
SMITH, Mary		18	F	Laborer	13J102Bk
BOGGSON, Gilbert		32	M	Laborer	13J102Bk
Ann		28	F	Laborer	13J102Bk
MANION, James		40	M	Laborer	13J102Bk
Ellen	(D)	08	F	Child	13J102Bk
SHIELDS, Cathn.		20	F	Laborer	13J102Bk
Cathn.		10	F	Laborer	13J102Bk
REAINS, Mary		17	F	Laborer	13J102Bk
CASEY, Barthm.		22	M	Laborer	13J102Bk
SCULLIN, John		30	M	Laborer	13J102Bk
CON, John		18	M	Laborer	13J102Bk
COHILL, Catherin		21	F	Laborer	13J102Bk
WHITE, Margaret		24	F	Laborer	13J102Bk
LAVENY, Robt.		16	M	Laborer	13J102Bk
Mary-Ann		10	F	Child	13J102Bk
Elitia		08	F	Child	13J102Bk
James		05	M	Child	13J102Bk
WALKER, Mary-A.		30	F	Laborer	13J102Bk
Anna	(D)	05	F	Child	13J102Bk
MCDONNELL, Danial		12	M	Laborer	13J102Bk
BERNE, Henry		20	M	Laborer	13J102Bk
Pat.		18	M	Laborer	13J102Bk
DONOHOE, Mary		21	F	Laborer	13J102Bk
Michel		14	M	Laborer	13J102Bk
Julia		12	F	Laborer	13J102Bk
MCNAMARA, Michl.		22	M	Laborer	13J102Bk
KENNY, Cathn.		20	F	Laborer	13J102Bk
JUDGE, John		18	M	Laborer	13J102Bk
KELLS, Margaret		26	F	Laborer	13J102Bk
Hannah		24	F	Laborer	13J102Bk
David		13	M	Laborer	13J102Bk
HAYS, John		24	M	Laborer	13J102Bk
Margaret		24	F	Laborer	13J102Bk
CONLON, Mary		18	F	Laborer	13J102Bk
LYONS, Mary		16	F	Laborer	13J102Bk
DENNEY, Mary		40	F	Laborer	13J102Bk
Pat	(S)	09	M	Child	13J102Bk
DELANY, Rose		40	F	Laborer	13J102Bk
DENNEY, Mary		09	F	Child	13J102Bk
Hugh		08	M	Child	13J102Bk
Peter		05	M	Child	13J102Bk
Cathn.		03	F	Child	13J102Bk
LYNCH, Rose		20	F	Laborer	13J102Bk
SNOW, Cathn.		20	F	Laborer	13J102Bk
MULRY, Hugh		22	M	Laborer	13J102Bk

NAMES OF PASSENGERS		AGE	SEX	OCCUPATIONS	DATE PORT SHIP
ROGERS, Mathews		40	M	Laborer	13J102Bk
CONNOLLY, Mary		15	F	Laborer	13J102Bk
EDWARDS, Emma		38	F	Laborer	13J102Bk
PHILIPS, Mary		28	F	Laborer	13J102Bk
Ann		12	F	Laborer	13J102Bk
MCEVANS, Ann		26	F	Laborer	13J102Bk
LOUGHLIN, Catherin-M.		29	F	Laborer	13J102Bk
Ann	(D)	09	F	Child	13J102Bk
BYRNE, Owin		30	M	Laborer	13J102Bk
MCGAVEY, Bridget		25	F	Laborer	13J102Bk
MCGINN, Bridget		22	F	Laborer	13J102Bk
GIXMAN, Jane		22	F	Laborer	13J102Bk
LYNCH, Bridget		22	F	Laborer	13J102Bk
DONLON, Peter		20	M	Laborer	13J102Bk
MULLIGAN, Pat.		16	M	Laborer	13J102Bk
Bridget		12	F	Laborer	13J102Bk
KANE, Rose-O.		18	F	Laborer	13J102Bk
FINDLEY, Jane		30	F	Laborer	13J102Bk
Jesse		25	F	Laborer	13J102Bk
CAMPBELL, John		20	M	Laborer	13J102Bk
MANGIN, Mary		20	F	Laborer	13J102Bk
RILEY, Ann		34	F	Laborer	13J102Bk
Edward	(S)	08	M	Child	13J102Bk
Peggy	(D)	06	F	Child	13J102Bk
Biddy	(D)	03	F	Child	13J102Bk
LAVINDER, Julia		24	F	Laborer	13J102Bk
Julia	(D)	08	F	Child	13J102Bk
NEWLAN, Cathn.		24	F	Laborer	13J102Bk
COFFIN, Mary		18	F	Laborer	13J102Bk
FINX, Hannah		16	F	Laborer	13J102Bk
NEWMAN, Ann		22	F	Laborer	13J102Bk
WILLIAMS, Griffetts		50	M	Laborer	13J102Bk
U	(W)	30	F	Laborer	13J102Bk
CLARK, Peter		22	M	Laborer	13J102Bk
John		21	M	Laborer	13J102Bk
HILL, Jane		20	F	Laborer	13J102Bk
MCGRINE, Magguy		30	F	Laborer	13J102Bk
FULLER, Cathn.		30	F	Laborer	13J102Bk
Ann		25	F	Laborer	13J102Bk
Margaret		13	F	Laborer	13J102Bk
Pat.		07	M	Child	13J102Bk
James		06	M	Child	13J102Bk
NEWLAN, Margaret		20	F	Laborer	13J102Bk
KENNY, Mary		20	F	Laborer	13J102Bk
GILLICK, Francis		20	F	Laborer	13J102Bk
PENDERGAST, John		25	M	Laborer	13J102Bk
Mary		30	F	Laborer	13J102Bk
KEHR, Ann		20	F	Laborer	13J102Bk
KELLY, Mary		20	F	Laborer	13J102Bk
ROLLY, Margaret		20	F	Laborer	13J102Bk
MURPHEY, Judith		20	F	Laborer	13J102Bk
CONNOR, James		20	M	Laborer	13J102Bk
FARRELLY, Rose		20	F	Laborer	13J102Bk
MCCLUSKEY, Cathn.		20	F	Laborer	13J102Bk

MILLICETE 13 JULY 1846

From Liverpool

NAMES OF PASSENGERS		AGE	SEX	OCCUPATIONS	DATE PORT SHIP
MCDONNELL, Thomas		25	M	None	13J102Jq
U	(W)	26	F	None	13J102Jq
James	(S)	06	M	Child	13J102Jq
MAHER, Pat		35	M	Farmer	13J102Jq
Julia		30	F	Farmer	13J102Jq
DEERLY, Julia		21	F	Laborer	13J102Jq
BROPHY, Margaret		21	F	Laborer	13J102Jq
MEEN, Patk.		26	M	Laborer	13J102Jq
MALERY, Pat		28	M	Laborer	13J102Jq
U	(W)	26	F	Laborer	13J102Jq

NAMES OF PASSENGERS	A G E	S E X	OCCUPATIONS	DATE PORT SHIP
MOFFET, Patk.	27	M	Laborer	13J102Jq
U	(W) 26	F	Laborer	13J102Jq
SLACK, George	24	M	Laborer	13J102Jq
HALL, Geo.	24	M	Laborer	13J102Jq
CUNNINGHAM, M.	24	M	Laborer	13J102Jq
COLLIN, Mary	19	F	Spinster	13J102Jq
DOOLEY, Michl.	25	M	Laborer	13J102Jq
Mary	55	F	Laborer	13J102Jq
Mary	28	F	Laborer	13J102Jq
WISE, Mary	09	F	Child	13J102Jq
SULLIVAN, Martin	27	M	Laborer	13J102Jq
U	(W) 22	F	Laborer	13J102Jq
William	19	M	Laborer	13J102Jq
STEPHENS, Wm.	26	M	Laborer	13J102Jq
DALZEL, George	21	M	Laborer	13J102Jq
MCDONNELL, Patt	28	M	Laborer	13J102Jq
U	(W) 26	F	Laborer	13J102Jq
Mary	(D) 02	F	Child	13J102Jq
WHELAN, Pat	28	M	Laborer	13J102Jq
HENNESSY, John	22	M	Laborer	13J102Jq
U	(W) 21	F	Laborer	13J102Jq
MCNULTY, Mary	40	F	Mechanic	13J102Jq
PULLY, Fredrick	36	M	Mechanic	13J102Jq
U	(W) 30	F	Mechanic	13J102Jq
Fredrick	(S) 11	M	Child	13J102Jq
Henry	(S) 02	M	Child	13J102Jq
Emily	(D) 01	F	Child	13J102Jq
MCCABE, Bridget	24	F	Spinster	13J102Jq
WATSON, James	20	M	Laborer	13J102Jq
MCCANN, Michl.	26	M	Laborer	13J102Jq
U	(W) 22	F	Laborer	13J102Jq
CONLEY, Ann	21	F	Spinster	13J102Jq
NEWMAN, Cathn.	21	F	Spinster	13J102Jq
MCPHILLIPS, James	24	M	Laborer	13J102Jq
James	22	M	Laborer	13J102Jq
Cath.	18	F	Laborer	13J102Jq
MCCANN, Ellas	25	M	Laborer	13J102Jq
U	(W) 23	F	Laborer	13J102Jq
DONEGAN, Ellen	21	F	Spinster	13J102Jq
HUNTER, Rosy	22	F	Spinster	13J102Jq
DUDDY, Richd.	24	M	Laborer	13J102Jq
U	(W) 22	F	Laborer	13J102Jq
MCCARTHY, Dana	18	M	Laborer	13J102Jq
CALDENCE, Wm.	20	M	Laborer	13J102Jq
Rebecca	19	F	Laborer	13J102Jq
CEARN, Benjamin	42	M	Laborer	13J102Jq
MCILROY, John	30	M	Laborer	13J102Jq
ARMSTRONG, Thos.	22	M	Laborer	13J102Jq
HURST, Mary	20	F	Spinster	13J102Jq
SUMMERVILLE, Eliza	30	F	Spinster	13J102Jq
Cathn.	20	F	Spinster	13J102Jq
MCLOUGHLIN, Wm.	03	M	Child	13J102Jq
KELLY, William	22	M	Laborer	13J102Jq
HORAN, Cennot	28	M	Laborer	13J102Jq
U	(W) 27	F	Laborer	13J102Jq
CHRISTY, Richd.	30	M	Laborer	13J102Jq
CALLIHAN, Lily	30	F	Laborer	13J102Jq
BRYAN, Pat	24	M	Laborer	13J102Jq
FITZPATRICK, John	25	M	Laborer	13J102Jq
MARTIN, John	21	M	Laborer	13J102Jq
CONNER, Hugh	20	M	Laborer	13J102Jq
CREGHTON, Mary	20	F	Spinster	13J102Jq
DALY, May	25	F	Spinster	13J102Jq
CROSGROVE, Cathn.	20	F	Spinster	13J102Jq
Sarah	16	F	Spinster	13J102Jq
DONOHUE, Mary-Ann	16	F	Spinster	13J102Jq
RESPINE, Mary	20	F	Spinster	13J102Jq
LITTLE, Bridget	20	F	Spinster	13J102Jq
GILMORE, Thos.	22	M	Laborer	13J102Jq
TERNEY, Bernard	26	M	Laborer	13J102Jq
LANLIN, Mary	21	F	Spinster	13J102Jq
Bridget	20	F	Spinster	13J102Jq
MCDERMOTT, James	26	M	Farmer	13J102Jq
U	(W) 22	F	None	13J102Jq
William	(S) .00	M	Infant	13J102Jq
BRYAN, Thomas	19	M	None	13J102Jq
MULHOLLAND, Danl.	28	M	None	13J102Jq
MCQUILLEN, Robert	21	M	None	13J102Jq
DRUMMOND, Peter	20	M	Laborer	13J102Jq
AIGNEN, Mary	22	F	None	13J102Jq
CREENEN, Mathew	23	M	None	13J102Jq
Maria	18	F	None	13J102Jq
DOUGHERTY, Margaret	02	F	Child	13J102Jq
MURTAGH, Mary	19	F	Spinster	13J102Jq
Mary	20	F	Spinster	13J102Jq
Agnes	11	F	Child	13J102Jq
HENNESSY, John	14	M	Laborer	13J102Jq
WARD, John	26	M	None	13J102Jq
MCGULLICK, Michl.	26	M	None	13J102Jq
FERGUSON, Richd.	24	M	None	13J102Jq
MCAUELY, John	21	M	None	13J102Jq
BRIAN, Pat	21	M	None	13J102Jq
MALLON, Margaret	22	F	None	13J102Jq
LYNCH, Margaret	22	F	Spinster	13J102Jq
KEARNEY, Cathn.	24	F	Spinster	13J102Jq
HARDFORD, Margaret	20	F	Spinster	13J102Jq
EDWARDS, James	21	M	Laborer	13J102Jq
MARTIN, Mathew	17	M	Laborer	13J102Jq
LYONS, Owen	24	M	Laborer	13J102Jq
WARD, Francis	24	M	Laborer	13J102Jq
CAVANAHA, Michl.	20	M	Laborer	13J102Jq
U-Mrs.	40	F	Laborer	13J102Jq
HANLON, Thos.	28	M	Laborer	13J102Jq
CAVANAHA, Bridget	16	F	Spinster	13J102Jq
Patt	11	M	Child	13J102Jq
MALLON, Bridget	17	F	Spinster	13J102Jq
QUIGLEY, Hugh	47	M	Laborer	13J102Jq
Cathn.	19	F	None	13J102Jq
Margaret	16	F	None	13J102Jq
William	13	M	None	13J102Jq
CRANFORD, Margaret	20	F	Spinster	13J102Jq
YOUNG, Ann	32	F	Spinster	13J102Jq
Pat	(S) 08	M	Child	13J102Jq
DONOHUE, Rose	64	F	WI	13J102Jq
James	(S) 13	M	None	13J102Jq
Henry	(S) 10	M	Child	13J102Jq
MCGOVERN, Mary	20	F	Spinster	13J102Jq
HARRIS, Wm.	28	M	Laborer	13J102Jq
U	(W) 24	F	None	13J102Jq
Mary-Ann	(D) 03	F	Child	13J102Jq
Martha	(D) 01	F	Child	13J102Jq
John	(H) 25	M	Laborer	13J102Jq
FERGUSON, Frances	52	F	Laborer	13J102Jq
Frances	(D) 20	F	Laborer	13J102Jq
Sampson	(S) 16	M	Laborer	13J102Jq
GARRAGHTY, Ann	21	F	Spinster	13J102Jq
MOORE, John	25	M	Laborer	13J102Jq
GARRAGHTY, Thos.	20	M	Laborer	13J102Jq
Ann	30	F	Laborer	13J102Jq
QUINN, John	28	M	Laborer	13J102Jq
SMITH, Pat	24	M	Laborer	13J102Jq
REYNOLDS, Cath.	20	F	Spinster	13J102Jq
MCGINNESS, U-Mrs.	40	F	WI	13J102Jq
Chas.	(S) 08	M	Child	13J102Jq
Geo.	(S) 10	M	Child	13J102Jq
Mary	(D) 06	F	Child	13J102Jq
CURTIS, Wm.	50	M	Farmer	13J102Jq
FITZPATRICK, Denis	15	M	None	13J102Jq
GORAN, Ellen	60	F	Wife	13J102Jq
Bridget	(D) 20	F	None	13J102Jq
John	(S) 18	M	None	13J102Jq
Ellen	(D) 16	F	None	13J102Jq
Thomas	(S) 08	M	Child	13J102Jq
Jane	(D) 09	F	Child	13J102Jq
SHARKEY, John	59	M	Laborer	13J102Jq
Cathn.	50	F	None	13J102Jq
BROWN, Thomas	26	M	None	13J102Jq
Mary	13	F	None	13J102Jq
MARSHEW, John	25	M	Laborer	13J102Jq
MILLS, Wm.	26	M	None	13J102Jq

NAMES OF PASSENGERS		A G E	S E X	OCCUPATIONS	DATE PORT SHIP
MARSHINE, Eduard		28	M	Laborer	13J102Jq
HERAN, Ann		28	F	None	13J102Jq
U-Mrs.		21	F	None	13J102Jq
HART, Henry		27	M	Spinner	13J102Jq
CORREGAN, Ellen		21	F	None	13J102Jq
Margaret		20	F	None	13J102Jq
LOUGHLAN, Mary-Ann		02	F	None	13J102Jq
MURPHY, Joseph		25	M	Laborer	13J102Jq
MCMULLEN, James		30	M	Laborer	13J102Jq
Janey		19	F	Laborer	13J102Jq
James		07	M	Child	13J102Jq
Ellen		05	F	Child	13J102Jq
GLEESTON, Mary		03	F	Child	13J102Jq
MCMULLEN, Thomas		.00	M	Infant	13J102Jq
Ellen	(M)	23	F	Spinster	13J102Jq
GREGG, John		20	M	Laborer	13J102Jq
U	(W)	21	F	Laborer	13J102Jq
LEIGHBRIDGE, Nell		64	M	Laborer	13J102Jq
Noelle	(D)	20	F	Laborer	13J102Jq
Pat	(S)	10	M	Child	13J102Jq
Mary	(D)	12	F	Laborer	13J102Jq
Ann	(D)	22	F	Laborer	13J102Jq
Mary	(W)	50	F	Laborer	13J102Jq
SCULLY, Thos.		30	M	Laborer	13J102Jq
John	(S)	02	M	Child	13J102Jq
Sarah	(D)	.00	F	Infant	13J102Jq
MULRANEY, Pat		21	M	Laborer	13J102Jq
GANNON, U-Mrs.		40	F	Laborer	13J102Jq
Ellen	(D)	18	F	Laborer	13J102Jq
James	(S)	13	M	Laborer	13J102Jq
Bridget	(D)	11	F	Laborer	13J102Jq
MCPEAKE, James		25	M	Laborer	13J102Jq
MCVEIGH, Henry		20	M	Laborer	13J102Jq
ONEILLE, John		20	M	Laborer	13J102Jq
MCCULLEN, Archy		40	M	Laborer	13J102Jq
Mary	(W)	33	F	Spinster	13J102Jq
Richd.	(D)	06	M	Child	13J102Jq
MCCALLA, Nancy		20	F	Laborer	13J102Jq
BOYLAN, Michl.		27	M	Laborer	13J102Jq
Rose		24	F	Laborer	13J102Jq
CONNOLY, Nancy		16	F	Laborer	13J102Jq
TRAINOR, Fanny		22	F	Laborer	13J102Jq
BOYLAN, Cath.		01	F	Child	13J102Jq
Ann		.00	F	Infant	13J102Jq
KELLY, Agnes		15	F	Spinster	13J102Jq
MCCARTNEY, Sarah		22	F	Spinster	13J102Jq
MCCULLOCH, Ann		33	F	Spinster	13J102Jq
Sarah		19	F	Spinster	13J102Jq
MCCANN, Mary		20	F	Spinster	13J102Jq
SCOTT, Wm.		25	M	Spinster	13J102Jq
SHERIDAN, John		20	M	Farmer	13J102Jq
FAY, Philip		26	M	Farmer	13J102Jq
HUGHES, John		21	M	Farmer	13J102Jq
Cathn.		19	F	Farmer	13J102Jq
CASEY, James		30	M	Farmer	13J102Jq
BERNICK, Bryan		22	M	Laborer	13J102Jq
Rose	(M)	50	F	Laborer	13J102Jq
Rose-Ann	(T)	13	F	Laborer	13J102Jq
LONG, John		00	M	Farmer	13J102Jq
Bridget		00	F	Farmer	13J102Jq
RILEY, Owen		21	M	Farmer	13J102Jq
MURPHY, Judith		22	F	Farmer	13J102Jq
MCGOVERN, Bridget		18	F	Farmer	13J102Jq
LAULER, Margaret		16	F	Farmer	13J102Jq
SPELMAN, Pat		41	M	Farmer	13J102Jq
MURRAY, John		22	M	Farmer	13J102Jq
MOODY, Eliza		26	F	Farmer	13J102Jq
COURTEN, Richd.		24	M	Farmer	13J102Jq
RILEY, John		.00	M	Infant	13J102Jq
Hugh		18	M	Farmer	13J102Jq
Michl.		21	M	Farmer	13J102Jq
Ann		22	F	Farmer	13J102Jq
Rose		28	F	Farmer	13J102Jq
SMITH, Henry		32	M	Farmer	13J102Jq
HOOPS, Mary		46	F	Farmer	13J102Jq

NAMES OF PASSENGERS		A G E	S E X	OCCUPATIONS	DATE PORT SHIP
HOOPS, Eliza	(D)	24	F	Farmer	13J102Jq
John	(S)	18	M	Farmer	13J102Jq
Eduard		32	M	Farmer	13J102Jq
Anty.	(S)	19	M	Farmer	13J102Jq
OKEEFE, Arthur		21	M	Farmer	13J102Jq
CAHILL, Michl.		27	M	Farmer	13J102Jq
MILLER, James		18	M	Farmer	13J102Jq
U-Mrs.		30	F	Farmer	13J102Jq
MCDONNELL, Bridget		40	F	Farmer	13J102Jq
John		21	M	Farmer	13J102Jq
ROSS, James		28	M	Farmer	13J102Jq
MARTIN, Mathew		22	M	Farmer	13J102Jq
MCDONNELL, Martha		10	F	Child	13J102Jq
James		06	M	Child	13J102Jq
Thomas		04	M	Child	13J102Jq
BATE, Geo.		26	M	None	13J102Jq
MCGLOWN, Hanna		22	F	None	13J102Jq
CURREN, Pat		22	M	None	13J102Jq
MCGLONE, Cathn.		22	F	Spinster	13J102Jq
CHRISTAL, Thos.		22	M	Laborer	13J102Jq
TRAINOR, John		38	M	Laborer	13J102Jq
TOOLE, Stephen		20	M	Laborer	13J102Jq
FARRE, Rose		25	F	Spinster	13J102Jq
MCGUIGAN, James		20	M	Laborer	13J102Jq
Mary	(M)	24	F	Laborer	13J102Jq
FENEGAN, Mary		18	F	Laborer	13J102Jq
BALL, Thos.		20	M	Laborer	13J102Jq
Wm.		25	M	Laborer	13J102Jq
James		25	M	Laborer	13J102Jq
DAVENPORT, Thos.		.00	M	Infant	13J102Jq
Mary	(M)	22	F	Laborer	13J102Jq
CORKURELLE, Saml.		18	M	Laborer	13J102Jq
Harriett		30	F	Laborer	13J102Jq
William		30	M	Laborer	13J102Jq
Eduard		09	M	Child	13J102Jq
Harriett		07	F	Child	13J102Jq
Richard		05	M	Child	13J102Jq

INDEPENDENCE 14 JULY 1846

From Liverpool

NAMES OF PASSENGERS		A G E	S E X	OCCUPATIONS	DATE PORT SHIP
PEARCE, Ephraim		21	M	Laborer	14J102Hf
U	(W)	20	F	Servant	14J102Hf
PENNY, Ann		60	F	Servant	14J102Hf
Mary	(D)	26	F	Servant	14J102Hf
Ellen	(D)	26	F	Servant	14J102Hf
Sarah	(D)	24	F	Servant	14J102Hf
Margaret	(D)	22	F	Servant	14J102Hf
Thomas	(S)	20	M	Servant	14J102Hf
Danl.	(S)	18	M	Servant	14J102Hf
William	(S)	17	M	Servant	14J102Hf
DOBIN, William		36	M	Servant	14J102Hf
MEALY, Thomas		26	M	Servant	14J102Hf
U	(W)	22	F	Servant	14J102Hf
HUGHES, Jane		22	F	Servant	14J102Hf
Bridget		19	F	Servant	14J102Hf
KEATING, Joanna		18	F	Servant	14J102Hf
Ellen	(M)	40	F	Servant	14J102Hf
SENNEL, David		18	M	Servant	14J102Hf
KEATING, Patrick		16	M	Servant	14J102Hf
NEENAN, Mary		20	F	Servant	14J102Hf
DOYLE, Mary		50	F	Servant	14J102Hf
Mary	(D)	20	F	Servant	14J102Hf
OBRIEN, Bryan		20	M	Servant	14J102Hf
James		16	M	Servant	14J102Hf
Mary		08	F	Child	14J102Hf
DOYLE, Patrick		23	M	Laborer	14J102Hf
HAYES, Patrick		36	M	Laborer	14J102Hf

NAMES OF PASSENGERS		AGE	SEX	OCCUPATIONS	DATE PORT SHIP
HAYES, Ellen	(W)	30	F	Laborer	14J102Hf
Patrick	(S)	06	M	Child	14J102Hf
CONNELL, Mary		19	F	Laborer	14J102Hf
TREACEY, William		27	M	Laborer	14J102Hf
Margret		25	F	Laborer	14J102Hf
CONNILLY, Thomas		25	M	Laborer	14J102Hf
BEAN, Angus		20	M	Laborer	14J102Hf
MCKENYN, Alexander		26	M	Laborer	14J102Hf
HOGAN, Daniel		20	M	Laborer	14J102Hf
BEATY, Mary		18	F	Servant	14J102Hf
MCQUADE, Ellen		17	F	Servant	14J102Hf
MCGLINN, Ann		19	F	Servant	14J102Hf
DUNLEAVY, Ann		20	F	Dressmaker	14J102Hf
DEVINE, Pat		21	M	Laborer	14J102Hf
Ann		20	F	Servant	14J102Hf
COOK, Archibald		54	M	Servant	14J102Hf
Betty	(W)	47	F	Servant	14J102Hf
Isabella	(D)	19	F	Servant	14J102Hf
Mary	(D)	17	F	Servant	14J102Hf
Robert	(S)	13	M	Servant	14J102Hf
Archibald	(S)	11	M	Child	14J102Hf
Eliza	(D)	08	F	Child	14J102Hf
Margret	(D)	05	F	Child	14J102Hf
KILLBRIDE, Mary		17	F	Servant	14J102Hf
CARTY, Mary		66	F	Servant	14J102Hf
YOUNG, Mary		21	F	Servant	14J102Hf
KELLY, Honora		20	F	Servant	14J102Hf
MICHAELS, Andrew		27	M	Servant	14J102Hf
BURNEY, Jane		18	F	Servant	14J102Hf
PATERSON, Isabella		18	F	Servant	14J102Hf
SCALLY, Margret		20	F	Servant	14J102Hf
GILHOLY, Patrick		23	M	Servant	14J102Hf
ELLIOTT, Robert		25	M	Servant	14J102Hf
COX, Bryan		25	M	Servant	14J102Hf
BOYDE, Ellen		20	F	Servant	14J102Hf
SCULLEN, Teady		26	M	Servant	14J102Hf
ONEIL, Rosey		19	F	Servant	14J102Hf
KEENAN, Mary-Ann		19	F	Servant	14J102Hf
MCARLANE, Thomas		16	M	Servant	14J102Hf
WALSH, Richard		26	M	Servant	14J102Hf
FARRELL, Honora		20	F	Servant	14J102Hf
BATCHELOR, Jacob		36	M	Servant	14J102Hf
FITZSIMMONS, Rosey		25	F	Servant	14J102Hf
GRIFFITH, Ellen		20	F	Servant	14J102Hf
FAHEY, Mary		30	F	Servant	14J102Hf
SHANLY, Thomas		20	M	Servant	14J102Hf
PARROT, William		20	M	Servant	14J102Hf
U	(W)	19	F	Servant	14J102Hf
KINGSTON, Samuel		20	M	Servant	14J102Hf
MCDERMOT, Francis		50	M	Servant	14J102Hf
U	(W)	50	F	Servant	14J102Hf
Bidy	(D)	15	F	Servant	14J102Hf
Rosey	(D)	11	F	Child	14J102Hf
Susanna	(D)	11	F	Child	14J102Hf
John	(S)	13	M	Servant	14J102Hf
Mary	(D)	09	F	Child	14J102Hf
Frank	(S)	06	M	Child	14J102Hf
MCGOVERN, James		25	M	Laborer	14J102Hf
Margaret		19	F	Laborer	14J102Hf
Judith		26	F	Laborer	14J102Hf
MCCULLOUGH, Helen		24	F	Laborer	14J102Hf
CLARKE, Michael		19	M	Laborer	14J102Hf
OBRIEN, William		30	M	Laborer	14J102Hf
MCLOUGHLEN, Thomas		50	M	Laborer	14J102Hf
U	(W)	45	F	Laborer	14J102Hf
Cath.	(D)	13	F	Laborer	14J102Hf
Mary	(D)	11	F	Child	14J102Hf
Rose	(D)	09	F	Child	14J102Hf
Thomas	(S)	04	M	Child	14J102Hf
BRANNAN, Peter		35	M	Laborer	14J102Hf
Bidy	(W)	27	F	Servant	14J102Hf
Helen	(D)	09	F	Child	14J102Hf
Sally	(D)	.00	F	Infant	14J102Hf
Mary	(D)	.00	F	Infant	14J102Hf
KEANEY, James		20	M	Servant	14J102Hf
LYNCH, Peter		20	M	Servant	14J102Hf
SMITH, Owen		20	M	Servant	14J102Hf
MCCLINCHEY, Michael		17	M	Servant	14J102Hf
WELLS, James		35	M	Servant	14J102Hf
BRADY, Bernard		23	M	Servant	14J102Hf
CALLAN, Phil.		25	M	Servant	14J102Hf
FOX, Cath.		50	F	Servant	14J102Hf
MAGRATH, Jane		12	F	Servant	14J102Hf
FOX, Carney		50	M	Servant	14J102Hf
CLARK, John		24	M	Servant	14J102Hf
Ann	(W)	22	F	Servant	14J102Hf
John	(S)	.00	M	Infant	14J102Hf
KANE, U-Mrs.		50	F	Servant	14J102Hf
U		13	U	Child	14J102Hf
U		11	U	Child	14J102Hf
U		09	U	Child	14J102Hf
U		08	U	Child	14J102Hf
U		07	U	Child	14J102Hf
U, U		19	U	Servant	14J102Hf
BURKE, Richard		22	M	Servant	14J102Hf
Pat		22	M	Servant	14J102Hf
OMEALEY, Bidy		19	F	Servant	14J102Hf
CONNELLY, Bidy		19	F	Servant	14J102Hf
MCNAMARA, Michael		34	M	Servant	14J102Hf
CULLEN, James		30	M	Servant	14J102Hf
Mary		28	F	Servant	14J102Hf
CALLAND, Pat		38	M	Servant	14J102Hf
James	(S)	13	M	Servant	14J102Hf
Mary	(D)	10	F	Child	14J102Hf
Jane	(D)	07	F	Child	14J102Hf
Pat	(D)	04	F	Child	14J102Hf
Bidy	(D)	.00	F	Infant	14J102Hf
MORRIS, James		20	M	Servant	14J102Hf
ONEIL, James		30	M	Servant	14J102Hf
QUINN, James		28	M	Servant	14J102Hf
MORRIS, Teresa		24	F	Servant	14J102Hf
BLANEY, Ellen		26	F	Servant	14J102Hf
KAY, Thomas		25	M	Servant	14J102Hf
BLUE, Pat		30	M	Servant	14J102Hf
Mary		30	F	Servant	14J102Hf
Rosey		25	F	Servant	14J102Hf
Arthur		01	M	Child	14J102Hf
MCGREGOR, Mary		19	F	Servant	14J102Hf
CORCORAN, Margret		20	F	Servant	14J102Hf
QUIN, Mary		21	F	Servant	14J102Hf
Eliza		18	F	Servant	14J102Hf
CURRAN, Bridget		21	F	Servant	14J102Hf
ONEIL, Cath.		18	F	Servant	14J102Hf
MULLIGAN, Patrick		20	M	Servant	14J102Hf
DONOHOE, John		35	M	Servant	14J102Hf
Bridget	(W)	30	F	Servant	14J102Hf
Cath.	(D)	15	F	Servant	14J102Hf
Ann	(D)	12	F	Servant	14J102Hf
Bridget	(D)	05	F	Child	14J102Hf
FARRELL, Cath.		30	F	Servant	14J102Hf
GIBSON, Alex.		21	M	Servant	14J102Hf
CARBERRY, Phillip		22	M	Servant	14J102Hf
Cath.		20	F	Servant	14J102Hf
Alexander		21	M	Servant	14J102Hf
LOCKART, Mary		21	F	Servant	14J102Hf
MORRISON, Mary		20	F	Servant	14J102Hf
MOORE, Margret		15	F	Servant	14J102Hf
MURTHA, Margret		24	F	Servant	14J102Hf
LEE, Thomas		10	M	Child	14J102Hf
MCMANUS, Pat		50	M	Servant	14J102Hf
MCCARTY, Mary		24	F	Servant	14J102Hf
DOWNEY, Ellen		07	F	Child	14J102Hf
Margt.		05	F	Child	14J102Hf
Mary		02	F	Child	14J102Hf
Cath.		01	F	Child	14J102Hf
CLEMENTS, Margret		27	F	Servant	14J102Hf
John	(S)	10	M	Child	14J102Hf
Elizabeth	(D)	07	F	Child	14J102Hf
William	(S)	04	M	Child	14J102Hf
Ann	(D)	02	F	Child	14J102Hf

NAMES OF PASSENGERS		AGE	SEX	OCCUPATIONS	DATE PORT SHIP
MCINROE, James		.00	M	Infant	14J102Hf
Mary		26	F	Servant	14J102Hf
Cath.		28	F	Servant	14J102Hf
LYNCH, Ann		24	F	Servant	14J102Hf
GALLIGAN, Ann		21	F	Servant	14J102Hf
HYLAND, Mary		25	F	Servant	14J102Hf
MORAN, Cath.		21	F	Servant	14J102Hf
STRICKLAND, Mary		20	F	Servant	14J102Hf
MURPHY, Thomas		20	M	Servant	14J102Hf
MAYERMAN, James		20	M	Servant	14J102Hf
KILLROY, Cath.		19	F	Servant	14J102Hf
RAY, Cath.		09	F	Child	14J102Hf
MCNICHOLE, James		24	M	Servant	14J102Hf
SCULLEN, Bridget		21	F	Servant	14J102Hf
WOODS, Francis		20	M	Servant	14J102Hf
GOODMAN, Michael		20	M	Servant	14J102Hf
John		19	M	Servant	14J102Hf
MCPHILLIPS, Betty		30	F	Servant	14J102Hf
GARVEY, Mary		03	F	Child	14J102Hf
DONAN, Ann		21	F	Servant	14J102Hf
REYNOLDS, Honora		24	F	Servant	14J102Hf
CONNOR, Bridget		50	F	Servant	14J102Hf
CALLAHAN, Dani.		20	M	Servant	14J102Hf
TRAYNOR, James		30	M	Servant	14J102Hf
QUINN, Ann		19	F	Servant	14J102Hf
BRADY, Bridget		26	F	Servant	14J102Hf
MCCARTY, Ellen		24	F	Servant	14J102Hf
LONGWARD, U		25	M	Servant	14J102Hf
BAIN, George		24	M	Servant	14J102Hf
LEE, Cath.		60	F	Servant	14J102Hf
ROONEY, Elizabeth		26	F	Servant	14J102Hf
MURRAY, Elizabeth		24	F	Servant	14J102Hf
TAYLOR, Thomas		13	M	Servant	14J102Hf
RIELY, Cath.		24	F	Servant	14J102Hf
Lelly		23	F	Servant	14J102Hf
CRENTON, Catherin		22	F	Servant	14J102Hf
MCGUIRE, Pat		21	M	Servant	14J102Hf
CARTER, Eliza		20	F	Servant	14J102Hf
BLANY, John		47	M	Servant	14J102Hf
William		28	M	Servant	14J102Hf
GALLAGHER, Margret		19	F	Servant	14J102Hf
3RADY, Francis		26	M	Servant	14J102Hf
BRANAGAN, Judy		21	F	Servant	14J102Hf
REIDER, Michael		31	M	Servant	14J102Hf
Ellen	(W)	25	F	Servant	14J102Hf
Margret	(D)	.00	F	Infant	14J102Hf
GALLARVAN, Margret		14	F	Servant	14J102Hf
LACY, Michael		24	M	Servant	14J102Hf
DUFFY, Ann		18	F	Servant	14J102Hf
CLARK, Hugh		21	M	Servant	14J102Hf
SPALLAN, Patrick		20	M	Servant	14J102Hf
DOYLE, Mary		18	F	Servant	14J102Hf
EVERS, Elizabeth		17	F	Servant	14J102Hf

UNITED-KINGDOM 14 JULY 1846

From Liverpool

NAMES OF PASSENGERS		AGE	SEX	OCCUPATIONS	DATE PORT SHIP
BIGGLE, Elizabeth		66	F	Servant	14J102Js
CASEY, Biddy		30	F	Servant	14J102Js
MULONY, Jane		50	F	Servant	14J102Js
James	(S)	19	M	Laborer	14J102Js
Maria	(D)	14	F	Servant	14J102Js
MACAFEE, Rose		23	F	Servant	14J102Js
DARAGH, Wm.John		28	M	Laborer	14J102Js
Margaret		22	F	Servant	14J102Js
Elizabeth		20	F	Servant	14J102Js
BLAIR, Jane		17	F	Servant	14J102Js
IRWIN, Samuel		19	M	Laborer	14J102Js

NAMES OF PASSENGERS		AGE	SEX	OCCUPATIONS	DATE PORT SHIP
IRWIN, Robert		17	M	Laborer	14J102Js
MACGARTH, Catharine		25	F	Servant	14J102Js
CASSADY, James		20	M	Laborer	14J102Js
Mary		18	F	Servant	14J102Js
KELLY, Ann		20	F	Servant	14J102Js
ROULSTON, Joseph		18	M	Laborer	14J102Js
BARRETT, John		17	M	Laborer	14J102Js
WALSH, John		19	M	Laborer	14J102Js
MACDONALD, John		20	M	Laborer	14J102Js
ALLSOP, John		21	M	Laborer	14J102Js
REILLY, Chas.		21	M	Laborer	14J102Js
DALEY, James		34	M	Laborer	14J102Js
LEE, John		26	M	Laborer	14J102Js
REYNOLDS, Andrew		20	M	Laborer	14J102Js
MATTHEWS, Richd.		53	M	Laborer	14J102Js
Mary	(W)	45	F	Servant	14J102Js
Joseph	(S)	28	M	Laborer	14J102Js
Marg.	(D)	14	F	Servant	14J102Js
Richd.	(S)	12	M	Laborer	14J102Js
Thos.	(S)	10	M	Child	14J102Js
Alice	(D)	08	F	Child	14J102Js
James	(S)	06	M	Child	14J102Js
GUOGON, Christopher		21	M	Laborer	14J102Js
Bryan		18	M	Laborer	14J102Js
Bridget	(M)	50	F	Servant	14J102Js
DRUM, Bridget		20	F	Servant	14J102Js
DORLAN, Patt		40	M	Laborer	14J102Js
Matt	(S)	16	M	Laborer	14J102Js
BURNS, James		30	M	Laborer	14J102Js
TALLON, Mary		16	F	Servant	14J102Js
HALFPENNY, Mary		16	F	Servant	14J102Js
MOYLES, Pat		26	M	Laborer	14J102Js
Mary	(W)	21	F	Servant	14J102Js
Mary	(D)	.00	F	Infant	14J102Js
WHITE, Garrett		23	M	Laborer	14J102Js
BURNS, Bridget		30	F	Servant	14J102Js
CRYNGON, Mary		25	F	Laborer	14J102Js
BURNS, Ann		04	F	Child	14J102Js
GOODWIN, James		28	M	Laborer	14J102Js
HASE, Andrew		35	M	Laborer	14J102Js
Mary		45	F	Servant	14J102Js
Andrew		45	M	Laborer	14J102Js
DIXON, Ellin		20	F	Servant	14J102Js
CAMPBELL, Mary		21	F	Servant	14J102Js
Ann		19	F	Servant	14J102Js
KELLY, John		30	M	Laborer	14J102Js
Eliza		28	F	Servant	14J102Js
MOORE, Thos.		22	M	Laborer	14J102Js
MCKENNA, Feilx		19	F	Servant	14J102Js
Mary		17	F	Servant	14J102Js
QUIN, Mary		26	F	Servant	14J102Js
JACKSON, Rebecca		30	F	Servant	14J102Js
Wm.Jas.	(S)	05	M	Child	14J102Js
HALL, Ricd.		28	M	Laborer	14J102Js
Jackson		26	M	Laborer	14J102Js
Joshua		19	M	Laborer	14J102Js
PALMER, Richd.		23	M	Laborer	14J102Js
KENNEDY, Michael		24	M	Laborer	14J102Js
Peter		22	M	Laborer	14J102Js
Ellen		19	F	Servant	14J102Js
Ellen		17	F	Servant	14J102Js
MCQUIRK, Thos.		24	M	Laborer	14J102Js
Andrew		22	M	Laborer	14J102Js
GOOLEY, Mary		40	F	Servant	14J102Js
MACKENNA, Francis		30	M	Laborer	14J102Js
James		21	M	Laborer	14J102Js
MULRAY, Chas.		27	M	Laborer	14J102Js
HIND, Hugh		21	M	Laborer	14J102Js
MATTHESON, James		23	M	Laborer	14J102Js
BASSETT, Jas.		19	M	Laborer	14J102Js
Eliza		28	F	Servant	14J102Js
DUEKIN, Patt		20	M	Laborer	14J102Js
GALLAGHER, John		23	M	Laborer	14J102Js
BATTER, Sarah		16	F	Servant	14J102Js
James		07	M	Child	14J102Js

NAMES OF PASSENGERS		A G E	S E X	OCCUPATIONS	DATE PORT SHIP
FLINN, Thos.		24	M	Laborer	14J102Js
ARTHUR, Mary		36	F	Servant	14J102Js
MACCRACKEN, Biddy		25	F	Servant	14J102Js
MCQUIRK, Ann		18	F	Servant	14J102Js
CONWAY, Rosey		20	F	Servant	14J102Js
DONNELLY, Peter		50	M	Laborer	14J102Js
MACILHATON, Pat		25	M	Servant	14J102Js
TIERNEY, James		04	M	Child	14J102Js
CAPPY, Chas.M.		22	M	Laborer	14J102Js
MCLAUGHLON, Sally		30	F	Servant	14J102Js
MCSUNLY, James		23	M	Laborer	14J102Js
NUGENT, John		16	M	Laborer	14J102Js
KERR, Mich.		30	M	Laborer	14J102Js
Mary	(W)	25	F	Servant	14J102Js
Essy	(D)	03	F	Child	14J102Js
Bridget	(D)	.00	F	Infant	14J102Js
DUNN, Robt.		30	M	Laborer	14J102Js
MCKEE, Marg.		19	F	Servant	14J102Js
MARPLE, Jane		24	F	Servant	14J102Js
Mary-Jane	(D)	.00	F	Infant	14J102Js
JACKSON, John		22	M	Laborer	14J102Js
Harriet		27	F	Servant	14J102Js
BRADY, Rose		18	F	Servant	14J102Js
COYLE, Ann		24	F	Servant	14J102Js
BERGIN, Marg.		21	F	Servant	14J102Js
FIGHE, John		35	M	Laborer	14J102Js
Jas.		32	M	Laborer	14J102Js
Marg.		29	F	Servant	14J102Js
Mary		40	F	Servant	14J102Js
NEVIN, Patt		20	M	Laborer	14J102Js
QUIN, Ann		23	F	Servant	14J102Js
Elizabeth		23	F	Servant	14J102Js
GOULDING, Jos.		16	M	Laborer	14J102Js
MACGARTH, John		18	M	Laborer	14J102Js
IRWIN, Thos.		23	M	Laborer	14J102Js
SHEANN, Timothy		29	M	Laborer	14J102Js
GORE, James		32	M	Laborer	14J102Js
John		30	M	Laborer	14J102Js
U-Mrs.		30	F	Servant	14J102Js
Bridget		10	F	Child	14J102Js
Ben		11	M	Child	14J102Js
Arthur		08	M	Child	14J102Js
CURTIS, Michl.		21	M	Laborer	14J102Js
MCCABE, Archy		22	M	Laborer	14J102Js
John		23	M	Laborer	14J102Js
RILEY, Bridget		18	F	Servant	14J102Js
MCDONALD, Mary		22	F	Servant	14J102Js
MCKEANEY, Michl.		18	M	Laborer	14J102Js
MCBRIDE, John		23	M	Laborer	14J102Js
MARTIN, Peggy		32	F	Servant	14J102Js
BERN, Gerrard		27	M	Laborer	14J102Js
Ann		14	F	Servant	14J102Js
Rose		20	F	Servant	14J102Js
Mary		19	F	Servant	14J102Js
LAWSON, Edward		24	M	Laborer	14J102Js
Jane		22	F	Servant	14J102Js
MACDERMOTT, Richd.		17	M	Laborer	14J102Js
LINDSEY, Martha		24	F	Servant	14J102Js
SCANLON, Francis		25	M	Servant	14J102Js
Isabel		21	F	Servant	14J102Js
COLLINS, James		22	M	Servant	14J102Js
FARLEY, Catharine		18	F	Servant	14J102Js
COYLE, Catharine		15	F	Servant	14J102Js
SMITH, Ann		20	F	Servant	14J102Js
BELL, Mary		18	F	Servant	14J102Js
DOYLE, Dennis		28	M	Laborer	14J102Js
Catharine	(W)	34	F	Servant	14J102Js
Patt	(S)	02	M	Child	14J102Js
KENNY, Rose		24	F	Servant	14J102Js
LUDEN, Mary		24	F	Servant	14J102Js
Bridget		22	F	Servant	14J102Js
LACEY, Honora		20	F	Servant	14J102Js
BURKE, Ann		28	F	Servant	14J102Js
LOCKE, Ann		27	F	Servant	14J102Js
STENSON, Jane		18	F	Servant	14J102Js
STENSON, Robert		25	M	Laborer	14J102Js
ELLIS, Thos.		21	M	Laborer	14J102Js
MILLS, John		19	M	Laborer	14J102Js
BRENAN, Henry		47	M	Laborer	14J102Js
KEARNEY, Cathn.		30	F	Servant	14J102Js
Bridget	(D)	11	F	Child	14J102Js
Elizabeth	(D)	09	F	Child	14J102Js
Eleanor	(D)	06	F	Child	14J102Js
Rosannah	(D)	.00	F	Infant	14J102Js
BRENAN, Marg.		08	F	Child	14J102Js
Thomas		05	M	Child	14J102Js
GUMPLE, Samuel		28	M	Laborer	14J102Js
DAWSON, Willm.		16	M	Laborer	14J102Js
Eliza		12	F	Servant	14J102Js
GARTLAND, John		26	M	Laborer	14J102Js
Mary	(W)	26	F	Servant	14J102Js
Peter	(S)	.00	M	Infant	14J102Js
Sarah		22	F	Servant	14J102Js
CAMPBELL, Eliza		22	F	Servant	14J102Js
BEATTIE, Robert		18	M	Laborer	14J102Js
GARTLAND, John		18	M	Laborer	14J102Js
CULBERT, John		24	M	Laborer	14J102Js
Ann	(W)	24	F	Servant	14J102Js
William	(S)	.00	M	Infant	14J102Js
MOORE, William		20	M	Laborer	14J102Js
LEVISON, David		24	M	Laborer	14J102Js
Elizabeth		35	F	Servant	14J102Js
George		.00	M	Infant	14J102Js
BOWEN, Marg.		20	F	Servant	14J102Js
BRYAN, Mary		19	F	Servant	14J102Js
MORRISON, Mary		19	F	Servant	14J102Js
FITZSIMMONS, Rosey		19	F	Servant	14J102Js
Marg.		18	F	Servant	14J102Js
COOK, Cath.		18	F	Servant	14J102Js
IRVING, Susan		20	F	Servant	14J102Js
DOONEY, Willm.		23	M	Laborer	14J102Js
Mary		25	F	Servant	14J102Js
FARRELL, Cath.		20	F	Servant	14J102Js
Eliza		07	F	Child	14J102Js
MCLOUGHLIN, Mary		25	F	Servant	14J102Js
ONEIL, Henry		26	M	Laborer	14J102Js
Susan		23	F	Servant	14J102Js
MCCLUREN, Jas.		35	M	Laborer	14J102Js
Mary	(W)	30	F	Servant	14J102Js
Ann	(D)	10	F	Child	14J102Js
Thomas	(S)	06	M	Child	14J102Js
Alexander	(S)	02	M	Child	14J102Js
FINNONS, Patrick		24	M	Laborer	14J102Js
DONOVAN, James		40	M	Laborer	14J102Js
Peter	(S)	14	M	Laborer	14J102Js
WAUGH, Robert		31	M	Laborer	14J102Js
MULVANY, Bridget		22	F	Servant	14J102Js
SHIEL, Thos.		30	M	Laborer	14J102Js
U	(W)	27	F	Wife	14J102Js
Patrick	(S)	08	M	Child	14J102Js
Jane	(D)	06	F	Child	14J102Js
Bessey	(D)	04	F	Child	14J102Js
William	(S)	02	M	Child	14J102Js
BROOMLEY, Hugh		30	M	Child	14J102Js
U	(W)	27	F	Servant	14J102Js
REILLY, John		22	M	Laborer	14J102Js
BOYLAN, Mary		15	F	Servant	14J102Js
Hugh		12	M	Laborer	14J102Js
CLARKING, Ann		18	F	Servant	14J102Js
TULLY, Cath.		20	F	Servant	14J102Js
Eliza		19	F	Servant	14J102Js
GRAHAM, Julia		30	F	Servant	14J102Js
Michl.	(S)	02	M	Child	14J102Js
CLARKIN, Hugh		19	M	Laborer	14J102Js
MCCABE, Wm.		19	M	Laborer	14J102Js
CLARKIN, Isaac		24	M	Laborer	14J102Js
Rosey		15	F	Servant	14J102Js
Catharine		12	F	Servant	14J102Js
FINNEGAN, John		20	M	Laborer	14J102Js
Ann		00	F	Unknown	14J102Js

NAMES OF PASSENGERS		AGE	SEX	OCCUPATIONS	DATE PORT SHIP
CLARK, Patt		34	M	Laborer	14J102Js
Ann		34	F	Servant	14J102Js
CONNELL, Bessey		19	F	Servant	14J102Js
CANNON, Cathr.		18	F	Servant	14J102Js
TERRIS, Kate		19	F	Servant	14J102Js
MORANS, Mary		14	F	Servant	14J102Js
COLLINS, Mich.		24	M	Laborer	14J102Js
CULLINS, Bridget		20	F	Servant	14J102Js
ONEIL, Jane		18	F	Servant	14J102Js
BROMLEY, Mary-Ann		13	F	Servant	14J102Js
James		11	M	None	14J102Js
Jane		08	F	Child	14J102Js
Elizabeth		.00	F	Infant	14J102Js
WALSH, Thos.		18	M	Laborer	14J102Js
Jas.		17	M	Laborer	14J102Js
TUCKNEY, Ann		18	F	Servant	14J102Js
PATTERSON, Mary		25	F	Servant	14J102Js
CLARKE, Mary		06	F	Child	14J102Js
John		03	M	Child	14J102Js
TOOLE, Patt		20	M	Laborer	14J102Js
MORRIS, Rose		17	F	Servant	14J102Js
DOYLE, Cath.		21	F	Servant	14J102Js
NEIL, Laurence		20	M	Laborer	14J102Js
BRADY, Francis		26	M	Laborer	14J102Js
BRANNIGAN, Judy		21	F	Servant	14J102Js
CARTY, Mich.		30	M	Laborer	14J102Js
Ann		28	F	Servant	14J102Js
MALEY, Mary		28	F	Servant	14J102Js
HUGHSON, U-Mrs.		50	F	Servant	14J102Js
MCGIVALY, Frances		41	F	Servant	14J102Js
MACCORMICK, Mary		19	F	Servant	14J102Js
TROWE, U		30	M	Laborer	14J102Js
FARLEY, John		25	M	Laborer	14J102Js
MCCABE, Catha.		18	F	Servant	14J102Js
CORR, Sarah		19	F	Servant	14J102Js
CATHCART, Mary		19	F	Servant	14J102Js
CAVANNAH, Jas.		15	M	Laborer	14J102Js
MCPHILLIPS, Jas.		22	M	Laborer	14J102Js
MACCARROLL, Wm.		22	M	Laborer	14J102Js
Ann		23	F	Servant	14J102Js
Catharine		18	F	Servant	14J102Js
HOOD, U-Mrs.		35	F	Servant	14J102Js
U	(D)	11	F	None	14J102Js
TURMAN, Patrick		23	M	Laborer	14J102Js
REILLY, Frances		23	M	Laborer	14J102Js
Marg.		21	F	Servant	14J102Js
ROURKE, Bernard		21	M	Laborer	14J102Js
MCKENNA, Hugh		21	M	Laborer	14J102Js
CORMING, Lary		20	F	Servant	14J102Js
REILLY, Terrence		22	M	Laborer	14J102Js
GARVIN, Jas.		24	M	Laborer	14J102Js
Mary		18	F	Servant	14J102Js
FLANAGAN, Mich.		24	M	Laborer	14J102Js
Marg.	(W)	20	F	Servant	14J102Js
Thomas	(S)	.00	M	Infant	14J102Js
KEENAN, Wm.		28	M	Laborer	14J102Js
GOUGH, Bridget		28	F	Servant	14J102Js
CASSYDE, Thos.		19	M	Laborer	14J102Js
HAIGH, Thos.		20	M	Laborer	14J102Js
DOWNES, Jas.		36	M	Laborer	14J102Js
Marg.	(D)	04	F	Child	14J102Js
DONALDY, John		24	M	Laborer	14J102Js
Judy		24	F	Servant	14J102Js
MCCORMACK, Catharine		18	F	Servant	14J102Js
Biddy		21	F	Servant	14J102Js
GARDEN, Michl.		35	M	Laborer	14J102Js
SWEENEY, Ann		21	F	Servant	14J102Js
DENNESON, Mary		21	F	Servant	14J102Js
DERWIN, Sally		22	F	Servant	14J102Js
MCCARROLL, Patt.		24	M	Laborer	14J102Js
MCCARTHY, Elliott		25	M	Laborer	14J102Js
DUGGAN, Stephen		20	M	Laborer	14J102Js
WHELAN, Ed.		24	M	Laborer	14J102Js
U-Mrs.		45	F	Servant	14J102Js
GREEN, Mich.		25	M	Laborer	14J102Js
CARMORE, Ellen		19	F	Servant	14J102Js
CONNOR, John		30	M	Laborer	14J102Js
KEADON, Patt		21	M	Laborer	14J102Js
TUEL, John		21	M	Laborer	14J102Js
ALKIN, Philp		22	M	Laborer	14J102Js
GILLICK, Laurenc		22	M	Laborer	14J102Js
FARRELL, Laurenc		22	M	Laborer	14J102Js
PLUNKETT, Mary		18	F	Servant	14J102Js
MASS, Thos.		21	M	Laborer	14J102Js
FAGAN, Marg.		21	F	Servant	14J102Js
MARTIN, Ellen		20	F	Servant	14J102Js
CUNNINGHAM, Ann		22	F	Servant	14J102Js
BYRNE, Bridget		20	F	Servant	14J102Js
Bridget		22	F	Servant	14J102Js
ROONEY, Cath.		19	F	Servant	14J102Js
BARREN, Pat.		17	M	Laborer	14J102Js
Marg.		16	F	Servant	14J102Js
MURRAY, Bridget		20	F	Servant	14J102Js
MURPHY, Phillp		08	M	Child	14J102Js
OBRIEN, Edmund		38	M	Laborer	14J102Js
Mary	(W)	30	F	Servant	14J102Js
Patrick	(S)	05	M	Child	14J102Js
Mary-Ann	(D)	04	F	Child	14J102Js
CONNOR, James		30	M	Laborer	14J102Js
Mary	(W)	28	F	Laborer	14J102Js
Laurence	(S)	10	M	Child	14J102Js
Jemima	(D)	05	F	Child	14J102Js
Bridget	(D)	.00	F	Infant	14J102Js
KELLWIN, John		19	M	Laborer	14J102Js
OBRIEN, Mary-Ann		.00	F	Infant	14J102Js
MACHOLLAND, Mary		22	F	Servant	14J102Js
BOFFY, Mich.		35	M	Laborer	14J102Js
HAIGH, Marg.		19	F	Servant	14J102Js
FIFE, Thos.		24	M	Laborer	14J102Js
RIDDELL, Ellen		20	F	Servant	14J102Js
Sarah		23	F	Servant	14J102Js
John		02	M	Child	14J102Js
FITZSIMMONS, Wm.		26	M	Laborer	14J102Js
CASSIDY, Henry		20	M	Laborer	14J102Js
MCPECK, Eliza		26	F	Servant	14J102Js
MCCOY, Mary		18	F	Servant	14J102Js
HOLLIDAY, Thos.		30	M	Laborer	14J102Js
CREELY, John		27	M	Laborer	14J102Js
SCALLON, John		16	M	Laborer	14J102Js
WALLACE, John		40	M	Laborer	14J102Js
FITZPATRICK, Dominick		17	M	Laborer	14J102Js
LEWIS, Catha.		15	F	Servant	14J102Js
FAMES, Mary		20	F	Servant	14J102Js
MARMION, Rody		28	M	Laborer	14J102Js
MCCORT, Marg.		24	F	Servant	14J102Js
MCKERNA, Ed.		20	M	Laborer	14J102Js
CORNELL, Cath.		18	F	Servant	14J102Js
BOYLAND, Felix		49	M	Laborer	14J102Js
U	(W)	40	F	Servant	14J102Js
KNEADON, Marg.		08	F	Child	14J102Js
CROSSON, Biddy		25	F	Servant	14J102Js
BOYLAN, Thos.		16	M	Laborer	14J102Js
BRYANS, Eliza		24	F	Servant	14J102Js
Ann		23	F	Servant	14J102Js
BOYLE, Biddy		25	F	Servant	14J102Js
MOULDEN, John		25	M	Laborer	14J102Js
RYAN, Owen		24	M	Laborer	14J102Js
BEGGS, Mary		24	F	Servant	14J102Js
DOUGHERTY, Mary		23	F	Servant	14J102Js
Mary	(D)	04	F	Child	14J102Js
LOUGHLIN, Cath.		21	F	Servant	14J102Js
DUFF, Luke		28	M	Laborer	14J102Js
NULTY, Christy		18	M	Laborer	14J102Js
EGAN, Step.		21	M	Laborer	14J102Js
Mary		20	F	Servant	14J102Js
RIGWAY, Biddy		20	F	Servant	14J102Js
RIGNEY, Patt		22	M	Laborer	14J102Js
CURLEY, Pat		24	M	Laborer	14J102Js
Eliza	(W)	21	F	Servant	14J102Js
Mary	(D)	.00	F	Infant	14J102Js

NAMES OF PASSENGERS		AGE	SEX	OCCUPATIONS	DATE PORT SHIP
CURLEY, Catharine		18	F	Servant	14J102Js
KELLY, Ellen		20	F	Servant	14J102Js
PENDER, Edwd.		24	M	Laborer	14J102Js
U	(W)	32	F	Servant	14J102Js
WHELAN, Jas.		25	M	Laborer	14J102Js
MAHON, Jas.		21	M	Laborer	14J102Js
WHELAN, Mary		19	F	Servant	14J102Js
BLACKMADDER, John		22	M	Laborer	14J102Js
EVERSON, Wm.		20	M	Laborer	14J102Js
TOOHEY, Dennis		20	M	Laborer	14J102Js
ODONNELL, John		15	M	Laborer	14J102Js
BERMINGHAM, Mary		30	F	Servant	14J102Js
BUTLER, Patt		30	M	Laborer	14J102Js
MCGARTH, Mich.		21	M	Laborer	14J102Js
TIVANEY, Michael		23	M	Laborer	14J102Js
U	(W)	20	F	Servant	14J102Js
STARKEY, John		23	M	Laborer	14J102Js
Michael		19	M	Laborer	14J102Js
DERWIN, Patt		18	M	Laborer	14J102Js
SHEA, Jas.		20	M	Laborer	14J102Js
MATHEWS, Willm.		22	M	Laborer	14J102Js
CONNELL, Phill.		19	M	Laborer	14J102Js
GALLIGAN, Patt		19	M	Laborer	14J102Js
TONER, Bryan		19	M	Laborer	14J102Js
Ann		18	F	Servant	14J102Js
Biddy		17	F	Servant	14J102Js
CONNOR, Ann		25	F	Servant	14J102Js
RYAN, Geo.		30	M	Laborer	14J102Js
KELLY, Jas.		19	M	Laborer	14J102Js
U	(W)	19	F	Servant	14J102Js
FLOOD, Mich.		17	M	Laborer	14J102Js
Cath.		17	F	Servant	14J102Js
DIXON, U		31	M	Laborer	14J102Js
Mary		30	F	Servant	14J102Js
GRAHAM, Jas.		21	M	Laborer	14J102Js
Eliza		30	F	Servant	14J102Js
MCQUILLAN, John		20	M	Laborer	14J102Js
Catharine		22	F	Servant	14J102Js
Mary-Jane		24	F	Servant	14J102Js
TEMBS, Ann		19	F	Servant	14J102Js
DOYLE, James		19	M	Laborer	14J102Js
Mary		20	F	Servant	14J102Js
GRAHAM, Ann		02	F	Child	14J102Js
John		.00	M	Infant	14J102Js
DIXON, Ann		04	F	Child	14J102Js
John		.00	M	Infant	14J102Js
MCGEE, Sarah		20	F	Servant	14J102Js
Betty		18	F	Servant	14J102Js
VANCE, John		20	M	Laborer	14J102Js
SMITH, John		20	M	Laborer	14J102Js
REILLY, Catha.		26	F	Servant	14J102Js
KENNEDY, Mark		22	M	Laborer	14J102Js
TULLY, Mary		19	F	Servant	14J102Js
CASSET, Juddy		19	F	Servant	14J102Js
SMITH, Mary		16	F	Servant	14J102Js
BRADY, Larry		41	M	Laborer	14J102Js
Barry	(S)	18	M	Laborer	14J102Js
Peter	(S)	16	M	Laborer	14J102Js
Teresa	(D)	13	F	Servant	14J102Js
Larry	(S)	12	M	Laborer	14J102Js
James	(S)	10	M	Child	14J102Js
Catharine	(D)	08	F	Child	14J102Js
Maria	(D)	06	F	Child	14J102Js
John	(S)	05	M	Child	14J102Js
Patt	(S)	03	M	Child	14J102Js
REILLY, Catharine		16	F	Servant	14J102Js
CASSIDY, Hugh		17	M	Laborer	14J102Js
KELLY, Willm.		32	M	Laborer	14J102Js
TOLING, Thos.		28	M	Laborer	14J102Js
FARLEY, Connor		20	M	Laborer	14J102Js
GLEESON, Patt		20	M	Laborer	14J102Js
KELLY, Catha.		20	F	Servant	14J102Js
BRANNAN, Emily		40	F	Servant	14J102Js
U		.00	F	Infant	14J102Js
MANLY, Matt		25	M	Laborer	14J102Js
MANLY, Rosey	(W)	22	F	Servant	14J102Js
Mary	(D)	04	F	Child	14J102Js
DOWNEY, Marg.		22	F	Servant	14J102Js
JONES, Ann		13	F	Servant	14J102Js
OBRIEN, John		22	M	Laborer	14J102Js
POWER, Ellen		21	F	Servant	14J102Js
FOUGHERTY, Martin		30	M	Laborer	14J102Js
Mary	(W)	27	F	Servant	14J102Js
Ellen	(D)	.00	F	Infant	14J102Js

OCEAN 14 JULY 1846

From Liverpool

NAMES OF PASSENGERS		AGE	SEX	OCCUPATIONS	DATE PORT SHIP
BROWN, Thomas		38	M	Unknown	14J102Jx
U	(W)	38	F	Unknown	14J102Jx
Martha	(D)	09	F	Child	14J102Jx
Joseph	(S)	07	M	Child	14J102Jx
George	(S)	05	M	Child	14J102Jx
Susannah	(D)	03	F	Child	14J102Jx
Jonathan	(S)	.00	M	Infant	14J102Jx
VILE, U-Mrs.		24	F	Unknown	14J102Jx
U	(H)	34	M	Unknown	14J102Jx
Benjamin	(S)	08	M	Child	14J102Jx
MCDERMOT, M.		28	U	Unknown	14J102Jx
OBRIEN, Ellen		29	F	Unknown	14J102Jx
NEIL, Joseph		49	M	Unknown	14J102Jx
U		18	F	Unknown	14J102Jx
William		14	M	Unknown	14J102Jx
John		12	M	Unknown	14J102Jx
James-Joseph		04	M	Child	14J102Jx
CURLY, Margt.		29	F	Unknown	14J102Jx
Letitia		19	F	Unknown	14J102Jx
GYLES, U		16	U	Unknown	14J102Jx
CARROLL, Thomas		41	M	Unknown	14J102Jx
U	(W)	42	F	Unknown	14J102Jx
Bridget	(D)	21	F	Unknown	14J102Jx
MOORE, Bridget		19	F	Unknown	14J102Jx
RICE, Jane		49	F	Unknown	14J102Jx
U-Mrs.		39	F	Unknown	14J102Jx
Patt-Curtis		45	M	Unknown	14J102Jx
U-Mrs.		42	F	Unknown	14J102Jx
Margaret		20	F	Unknown	14J102Jx
Bernerd		14	M	Unknown	14J102Jx
R---		14	U	Unknown	14J102Jx
Patt		11	M	None	14J102Jx
James		05	M	Child	14J102Jx
REILLY, Margt.		20	F	Unknown	14J102Jx
ROAKE, Cath.		20	F	Unknown	14J102Jx
PRIER, Mary		20	F	Unknown	14J102Jx
Biddy		17	F	Unknown	14J102Jx
Emma		.00	F	Infant	14J102Jx
Died-At-Sea					
MAHAN, Ann		22	F	Unknown	14J102Jx
BAXTER, Michl.		45	M	Unknown	14J102Jx
U	(W)	41	F	Unknown	14J102Jx
Patt	(S)	18	M	Unknown	14J102Jx
Cath.	(D)	15	F	Unknown	14J102Jx
Frances	(D)	13	F	Unknown	14J102Jx
Ann	(D)	09	F	Child	14J102Jx
Mary	(D)	07	F	Child	14J102Jx
Margt.	(D)	05	F	Child	14J102Jx
John	(S)	.00	M	Infant	14J102Jx
TUMALTY, Jane		19	F	Unknown	14J102Jx
CARRY, Bridget		19	F	Unknown	14J102Jx
MAHON, James		23	M	Unknown	14J102Jx
DOGHARTY, Patrick		12	M	Unknown	14J102Jx
Margt.		11	F	None	14J102Jx
REGAN, Mary		18	F	Unknown	14J102Jx

NAMES OF PASSENGERS		AGE	SEX	OCCUPATIONS	DATE PORT SHIP
MAHER, Mary		20	F	Unknown	14J102Jx
RUSSELL, Mary		16	F	Unknown	14J102Jx
CLEW, Cath.		20	F	Unknown	14J102Jx
FITZPATRICK, Bridget		20	F	Unknown	14J102Jx
RYAN, Teddy		28	M	Unknown	14J102Jx
COYLE, May		50	F	Unknown	14J102Jx
Ellen		40	F	Unknown	14J102Jx
OHARA, Arthur		20	M	Unknown	14J102Jx
MCCARTY, Danl.		20	M	Unknown	14J102Jx
FLANAGIN, Wm.		25	M	Unknown	14J102Jx
Alice		21	F	Unknown	14J102Jx
DONNAN, Danl.		07	M	Child	14J102Jx
SCOTT, Olive		24	F	Unknown	14J102Jx
STAUNTON, Julia		21	F	Unknown	14J102Jx
BRODERICK, Cath.		24	F	Unknown	14J102Jx
BRETHEN, James		26	M	Unknown	14J102Jx
Wm.		23	M	Unknown	14J102Jx
MONAGEN, Bridget		27	F	Unknown	14J102Jx
Bernard		.00	M	Infant	14J102Jx
Died-At-Sea					
DOLAN, Wm.		30	M	Unknown	14J102Jx
Harriett	(W)	30	F	Unknown	14J102Jx
James	(S)	03	M	Child	14J102Jx
Rose-Ann	(D)	.00	F	Infant	14J102Jx
MALQUARY, Dennis		26	M	Unknown	14J102Jx
Ann		22	F	Unknown	14J102Jx
DONAGHAN, Andrew		30	M	Unknown	14J102Jx
FEENY, Ellen		20	F	Unknown	14J102Jx
Dolly		25	F	Unknown	14J102Jx
Mary		03	F	Child	14J102Jx
Edward		.00	M	Infant	14J102Jx
PINKNEY, John		28	M	Unknown	14J102Jx
WALTERS, Robert		25	M	Unknown	14J102Jx
LEE, Joseph		20	M	Unknown	14J102Jx
WIGHTMAN, Ann		33	F	Unknown	14J102Jx
HICKEY, Nicholas		20	M	Unknown	14J102Jx
GUGAN, Mary		18	F	Unknown	14J102Jx
NIXON, Joseph		20	M	Unknown	14J102Jx
ROWE, James		40	M	Unknown	14J102Jx
U	(W)	35	F	Unknown	14J102Jx
An	(D)	16	F	Unknown	14J102Jx
George	(S)	15	M	Unknown	14J102Jx
Thomas	(S)	12	M	Unknown	14J102Jx
James	(S)	07	M	Child	14J102Jx
John	(S)	04	M	Child	14J102Jx
Mary-Ann	(D)	02	F	Child	14J102Jx
Emma	(D)	.00	F	Infant	14J102Jx
REIMAN, Thomas		22	M	Unknown	14J102Jx
U	(W)	22	F	Unknown	14J102Jx
COLLINS, Margt.		25	F	Unknown	14J102Jx
MCCALL, Michl.		20	M	Unknown	14J102Jx
Margt.		21	F	Unknown	14J102Jx
CLARKE, Rosey		19	F	Unknown	14J102Jx
MCCALL, Eduard		21	M	Unknown	14J102Jx
Ellen		20	F	Unknown	14J102Jx
DANIEL, Patt		20	M	Unknown	14J102Jx
EAKEN, James		18	M	Unknown	14J102Jx
DUFFY, Frances		20	F	Unknown	14J102Jx
James		20	M	Unknown	14J102Jx
Rose		19	F	Unknown	14J102Jx
MANEN, John		22	M	Unknown	14J102Jx
Judith		21	F	Unknown	14J102Jx
BEGAN, Patt		21	M	Unknown	14J102Jx
Agnes		20	F	Unknown	14J102Jx
DONAGHY, Nathl.		21	M	Unknown	14J102Jx
MONOGAN, Patt		40	M	Unknown	14J102Jx
Kitty	(W)	30	F	Unknown	14J102Jx
Michael		18	M	Unknown	14J102Jx
Susan	(D)	11	F	Unknown	14J102Jx
Daniel	(S)	09	M	Child	14J102Jx
Catherine	(D)	07	F	Child	14J102Jx
James	(S)	05	M	Child	14J102Jx
Bernard	(S)	.00	M	Infant	14J102Jx
SUTTEFFE, Wm.		21	M	Unknown	14J102Jx
MALLOY, Mary		49	F	Unknown	14J102Jx
MALLOY, Ann	(D)	29	F	Unknown	14J102Jx
John-Harry	(S)	29	M	Unknown	14J102Jx
LALLY, Mich.		30	M	Unknown	14J102Jx
MCCORMICK, Ellen		21	F	Unknown	14J102Jx
LACKIN, Wm.		28	M	Unknown	14J102Jx
SWIFT, Patt		18	M	Unknown	14J102Jx
MALONY, Eliza		11	F	None	14J102Jx
SLATER, Ann		18	F	Unknown	14J102Jx
Eliza		14	F	Unknown	14J102Jx
Thomlson		10	M	None	14J102Jx
RATTICAN, Betty		21	F	Unknown	14J102Jx
GONNAN, Patt		30	M	Unknown	14J102Jx
RYAN, John		05	M	Child	14J102Jx
Mary		07	F	Child	14J102Jx
MATHEWS, Mary		52	F	Unknown	14J102Jx
Danl.	(S)	12	M	Unknown	14J102Jx
BALFE, Francis		21	M	Unknown	14J102Jx
Rose		08	F	Child	14J102Jx
James		10	M	None	14J102Jx
HART, Bridget		30	F	Unknown	14J102Jx
Bridget	(D)	07	F	Child	14J102Jx
James	(S)	04	M	Child	14J102Jx
COLLINS, Patt		12	M	Unknown	14J102Jx
John		10	M	None	14J102Jx
CARROLL, James		15	M	Unknown	14J102Jx
DOUGHERTY, U-Mrs.		46	F	Unknown	14J102Jx
Betty	(D)	23	F	Unknown	14J102Jx
Thomas	(S)	18	M	Unknown	14J102Jx
Mary	(D)	13	F	Unknown	14J102Jx
CALLAHAN, Miles		30	M	Unknown	14J102Jx
HENNESSY, Morris		26	M	Unknown	14J102Jx
U	(W)	28	F	Unknown	14J102Jx
Betty		20	F	Unknown	14J102Jx
DECOURCY, U-Mrs.		30	F	Unknown	14J102Jx
William	(S)	11	M	None	14J102Jx
TOOLE, Patt		28	M	Unknown	14J102Jx
FRAZIER, Wm.		22	M	Unknown	14J102Jx
MCWEECKY, John		21	M	Unknown	14J102Jx
DWIER, Eduard		20	M	Unknown	14J102Jx
CORCORAN, Henry		23	M	Unknown	14J102Jx
GILLOONEY, Wm.		22	M	Unknown	14J102Jx
Cath.		20	F	Unknown	14J102Jx
DOOLAN, Fanny		19	F	Unknown	14J102Jx
STUFFERD, Judy		29	F	Unknown	14J102Jx
MCCANLY, Adam		27	M	Unknown	14J102Jx
SHAW, Martin		23	M	Unknown	14J102Jx
Mary		25	F	Unknown	14J102Jx
FARRALLY, Jno.		24	M	Unknown	14J102Jx
CANNING, Bridget		20	F	Unknown	14J102Jx
CORREGAN, Mary		20	F	Unknown	14J102Jx
REILLY, Margt.		20	F	Unknown	14J102Jx
REGAN, John		30	M	Unknown	14J102Jx
WINTER, Patt		50	M	Unknown	14J102Jx
John	(S)	22	M	Unknown	14J102Jx
Patt	(S)	18	M	Unknown	14J102Jx
Susan	(D)	16	F	Unknown	14J102Jx
HILL, Mary		21	F	Unknown	14J102Jx
Ann		19	F	Unknown	14J102Jx
BROTHERTEN, Robert		50	M	Unknown	14J102Jx
Ann	(W)	40	F	Unknown	14J102Jx
Hugh	(S)	18	M	Unknown	14J102Jx
Robert	(S)	11	M	None	14J102Jx
Wm.	(S)	12	M	Unknown	14J102Jx
Ann	(D)	07	F	Child	14J102Jx
Catherine	(D)	04	F	Child	14J102Jx
DONOVAN, Margt.		22	F	Unknown	14J102Jx
COLLINS, Cath.		17	F	Unknown	14J102Jx
HUGGERTY, Catherin		22	F	Unknown	14J102Jx
CARREL, Michael		55	M	Unknown	14J102Jx
U	(W)	55	F	Unknown	14J102Jx
Thomas	(S)	24	M	Unknown	14J102Jx
Eliza		51	F	Unknown	14J102Jx
Bridget	(D)	18	F	Unknown	14J102Jx
MCGEE, Isabella		16	F	Unknown	14J102Jx
William		13	M	Unknown	14J102Jx

NAMES OF PASSENGERS		AGE	SEX	OCCUPATIONS	DATE PORT SHIP
MCGEE, Rebecca		10	F	Child	14J102Jx
MORTON, Charles		28	M	Unknown	14J102Jx
SPRUTO, Thomas		29	M	Unknown	14J102Jx
MULLIN, Ann		21	F	Unknown	14J102Jx
Bridget		23	F	Unknown	14J102Jx
SKERRINGTON, Eduard		24	M	Unknown	14J102Jx
CONLAN, John		24	M	Unknown	14J102Jx
Peter		22	M	Unknown	14J102Jx
SOAMS, Ellen		35	F	Unknown	14J102Jx
SMITH, Ann		18	F	Unknown	14J102Jx
MILTON, James		24	M	Unknown	14J102Jx
BARRY, Wm.		22	M	Unknown	14J102Jx
MONAGEN, Thomas		21	M	Unknown	14J102Jx
DAVIDSON, George		40	M	Unknown	14J102Jx
BRASSNELL, Andrew		32	M	Unknown	14J102Jx
Martha	(W)	21	F	Unknown	14J102Jx
Sarah	(D)	04	F	Child	14J102Jx
Hannah	(D)	04	F	Child	14J102Jx
Thomas	(S)	02	M	Child	14J102Jx
Fanny	(D)	02	F	Child	14J102Jx
Died-At-Sea					
BRATTEN, Wm.		35	M	Unknown	14J102Jx
Mary	(W)	37	F	Unknown	14J102Jx
Jane	(D)	06	F	Child	14J102Jx
Sarah-Ann	(D)	05	F	Child	14J102Jx
Fanny	(D)	02	F	Child	14J102Jx
U, U		.00	U	Infant	14J102Jx
Born-At-Sea					

PRINCE-HENRY 14 JULY 1846

From YARMOUTH,N.S.

NAMES OF PASSENGERS	AGE	SEX	OCCUPATIONS	DATE PORT SHIP
WYMAN, Hannah	38	F	Lady	14J157Jy
DURKEE, Jane	28	F	Lady	14J157Jy

MIRACLE 14 JULY 1846

From Liverpool

NAMES OF PASSENGERS		AGE	SEX	OCCUPATIONS	DATE PORT SHIP
CRUMLEY, Mary		40	F	Wife	14J102Jz
Wm.	(S)	17	M	Laborer	14J102Jz
John	(S)	15	M	Laborer	14J102Jz
James	(S)	13	M	Laborer	14J102Jz
Geo.	(S)	11	M	Laborer	14J102Jz
Rebecca	(D)	09	F	Child	14J102Jz
Thos.	(S)	06	M	Child	14J102Jz
Andrew	(S)	04	M	Child	14J102Jz
DAGGON, Hugh		20	M	Weaver	14J102Jz
FLANIGAN, Mary		09	F	Child	14J102Jz
Edw.		06	M	Child	14J102Jz
TOBIN, Margt.		40	F	Unknown	14J102Jz
COKLAN, Anty.		07	M	Child	14J102Jz
Jas.		05	M	Child	14J102Jz
MULLARKEY, Mary		18	F	Spinster	14J102Jz
ALLEN, Wesley		18	M	Laborer	14J102Jz
BURKE, Honora		18	F	Spinster	14J102Jz
STENTON, Julia		21	F	Spinster	14J102Jz
BRODERICK, Cathere.		21	F	Spinster	14J102Jz
ODONNELL, Patk.		22	M	Laborer	14J102Jz
CONNOR, James		25	M	Wheelwright	14J102Jz
FRANKLIN, Wm.		20	M	Laborer	14J102Jz
NEWELL, Richard		30	M	Farmer	14J102Jz

NAMES OF PASSENGERS		AGE	SEX	OCCUPATIONS	DATE PORT SHIP
LANGAN, Jas.		50	M	Farmer	14J102Jz
CASEY, Alice		05	F	Child	14J102Jz
LANGAN, Jas.		20	M	Laborer	14J102Jz
Margt.	(M)	50	F	Unknown	14J102Jz
Thos.	(B)	19	M	Laborer	14J102Jz
PHILLIPS, Jas.		16	M	Laborer	14J102Jz
Peter		06	M	Child	14J102Jz
WOODS, Mary		21	F	Spinster	14J102Jz
Rose		12	F	Unknown	14J102Jz
Ann		09	F	Child	14J102Jz
KELLY, Bridget		21	F	Spinster	14J102Jz
MURPHY, Robt.		04	M	Child	14J102Jz
PHELAN, Bridget		21	F	Spinster	14J102Jz
DAY, Eliza		40	F	Unknown	14J102Jz
Ann	(D)	16	F	Spinster	14J102Jz
Jas.	(S)	04	M	Child	14J102Jz
Peter	(S)	02	M	Child	14J102Jz
TOBIN, Anthy.		21	M	Laborer	14J102Jz
Nath., Patk.		06	M	Child	14J102Jz
FOSTER, Geo.		24	M	Printer	14J102Jz
Ann	(W)	23	F	Unknown	14J102Jz
John	(S)	.00	M	Infant	14J102Jz
DAYRFIELD, Davd.		27	M	Farmer	14J102Jz
Sarah	(W)	28	F	Farmer	14J102Jz
Ann	(D)	03	F	Child	14J102Jz
Edw.	(S)	.00	M	Infant	14J102Jz
THOMPSON, Jos.		26	M	Laborer	14J102Jz
REEVES, John		28	M	Laborer	14J102Jz
Mathew		26	M	Laborer	14J102Jz
Saml.		03	M	Child	14J102Jz
Fanny		.00	F	Infant	14J102Jz
SPENCE, Wm.		21	M	Unknown	14J102Jz
Geo.		20	M	Unknown	14J102Jz
ALLEN, Arthur		25	M	Printer	14J102Jz
WRIGHT, Samuel		29	M	Baker	14J102Jz
Mary	(W)	25	F	Unknown	14J102Jz
Eliza	(D)	03	F	Child	14J102Jz
Margt.	(D)	.00	F	Infant	14J102Jz
TRACEY, Thos.		20	M	Laborer	14J102Jz
Rosana.	(W)	18	F	Unknown	14J102Jz
Cathe.	(D)	.00	F	Infant	14J102Jz
DUNN, Hiram		24	M	Laborer	14J102Jz
Steward		16	M	Unknown	14J102Jz
Eliza		24	F	Unknown	14J102Jz
Mary		04	F	Child	14J102Jz
Wm.		.00	M	Infant	14J102Jz
TOWNLY, Michl.		40	M	Farmer	14J102Jz
John		25	M	Farmer	14J102Jz
James		17	M	Farmer	14J102Jz
DONAGHUE, Hugh		20	M	Dyer	14J102Jz
WORSCOTT, John		30	M	Blacksmith	14J102Jz
Bridget	(W)	26	F	Unknown	14J102Jz
Edwd.	(S)	02	M	Child	14J102Jz
HANOLAN, Maria		20	F	Spinster	14J102Jz
FLANNERY, Martin		22	M	Laborer	14J102Jz
MANGER, Wm.		26	M	Laborer	14J102Jz
MEHA, John		23	M	Laborer	14J102Jz
SAUNDERS, Wm.		21	M	Laborer	14J102Jz
DUCKETT, Charles		25	M	Laborer	14J102Jz
HARTLEY, Josh		25	M	Laborer	14J102Jz
WARD, Mary		08	F	Child	14J102Jz
Elizabeth		30	F	Wife	14J102Jz
MCNIGHT, Jos.		22	M	Laborer	14J102Jz
FEATHERSON, Richd.		40	M	Farmer	14J102Jz
AIYRE, Wm.		19	M	Laborer	14J102Jz
ROBINSON, Mgt.		21	F	Spinster	14J102Jz
HALLORAN, Mgt.		20	F	Spinster	14J102Jz
BAIREY, Judith		24	F	Wife	14J102Jz
Mary	(D)	02	F	Child	14J102Jz
FITZPATRICK, John		20	M	Laborer	14J102Jz
Mary		21	F	Spinster	14J102Jz
Ann		24	F	Spinster	14J102Jz
QUINN, John		26	M	Farmer	14J102Jz
U	(W)	22	F	Farmer	14J102Jz
CORCORAN, Christr.		21	M	Laborer	14J102Jz

NAMES OF PASSENGERS		AGE	SEX	OCCUPATIONS	DATE PORT SHIP
CORCORAN, U	(W)	20	F	Unknown	14J102Jz
GIBNEY, Patk.		21	M	Wool Dyer	14J102Jz
FAYLE, John		21	M	Laborer	14J102Jz
Patk.		21	M	Laborer	14J102Jz
BARRETT, Eliza		21	F	Spinster	14J102Jz
MCDONOUGH, Andrew		34	M	Distiller	14J102Jz
BOWERS, David		36	M	Farmer	14J102Jz
U	(W)	33	F	Farmer	14J102Jz
Wm.		19	M	Unknown	14J102Jz
Jane		17	F	Unknown	14J102Jz
BONES, Thos.		16	M	Unknown	14J102Jz
THOMAS, James		28	M	Unknown	14J102Jz
BONES, Maria		11	F	Unknown	14J102Jz
Mary-Hannah		06	F	Child	14J102Jz
David		04	M	Child	14J102Jz
Charles		.00	M	Infant	14J102Jz
DAUSON, Chas.		19	M	Laborer	14J102Jz
BONES, Elizabeth		19	F	Wife	14J102Jz
LATIMORE, David		21	M	Composer	14J102Jz
MCDONNELL, Mary-Ann		20	F	Spinster	14J102Jz
MAGUIRE, Patk.		20	M	Laborer	14J102Jz
MOORE, Anastatia		30	F	Spinster	14J102Jz
Jinney		18	F	Spinster	14J102Jz
MANIES, John		22	M	Laborer	14J102Jz
MCMANUS, Mary		22	F	Spinster	14J102Jz
MAXWELL, Jas.		21	M	Laborer	14J102Jz
MOPHY, John		18	M	Laborer	14J102Jz
FITZSIMMER, Phil.		19	M	Laborer	14J102Jz
Ann		20	F	Spinster	14J102Jz
HALTON, Ann		21	F	Spinster	14J102Jz
BURNS, Robt.		40	M	Farmer	14J102Jz
U	(W)	36	F	Wife	14J102Jz
REILLY, Philip		20	M	Laborer	14J102Jz
MCBRIDE, Betty		21	F	Spinster	14J102Jz
SMALLS, Jas.		20	M	Laborer	14J102Jz
DOGHERTY, Cathr.		21	F	Spinster	14J102Jz
MCGLIVCHY, Mary		21	F	Spinster	14J102Jz
FRAME, Wm.		22	M	Laborer	14J102Jz
MCELLENY, Wm.		21	M	Turner	14J102Jz
DALEY, Jas.		30	M	Farmer	14J102Jz
MCMONAGLE, Wm.		20	M	Laborer	14J102Jz
DAILEY, Wm.		06	M	Child	14J102Jz
DEVINE, Michl.		25	M	Laborer	14J102Jz
BYRNE, Dani.		22	M	Laborer	14J102Jz
MCMANUS, John		25	M	Laborer	14J102Jz
MARTIN, Jas.		22	M	Laborer	14J102Jz
BELRINGTON, Thos.		20	M	Laborer	14J102Jz
Jas.		17	M	Laborer	14J102Jz
Ann		14	F	Unknown	14J102Jz
GLYNN, Cathr.		21	F	Spinster	14J102Jz
LYNCHAN, Dani.		20	M	Smith	14J102Jz
DENNIS, Hugh		21	M	Laborer	14J102Jz
MCKENNA, Cathr.		16	F	Spinster	14J102Jz
MCGIRR, Arthur		13	M	Unknown	14J102Jz
Ann		20	F	Spinster	14J102Jz
Margt.		15	F	Spinster	14J102Jz
SMITH, Henry		26	M	Laborer	14J102Jz
Cathe.		24	F	Wife	14J102Jz
Mary	(D)	03	F	Child	14J102Jz
Charles		22	M	Laborer	14J102Jz
PHELAN, Anthy.		24	M	Laborer	14J102Jz
DELANEY, John		30	M	Laborer	14J102Jz
COFFEY, James		20	M	Laborer	14J102Jz
FARRELL, John		18	M	Laborer	14J102Jz
ROSS, Mary		21	F	Unknown	14J102Jz
COFFEY, James		30	M	Laborer	14J102Jz
U	(W)	25	F	Unknown	14J102Jz
Mary	(D)	01	F	Child	14J102Jz
DUGAN, Michl.		20	M	Wood Carver	14J102Jz
NEARY, Patk.		27	M	Laborer	14J102Jz
GRUMBY, John		27	M	Locksmith	14J102Jz
MCGEE, Wm.Henry		22	M	Machinist	14J102Jz
U-Miss		20	F	Spinster	14J102Jz
Ann		19	F	Spinster	14J102Jz
CORLAHAN, Michl.		21	M	Laborer	14J102Jz

NAMES OF PASSENGERS		AGE	SEX	OCCUPATIONS	DATE PORT SHIP
BROTHER, Jas.		26	M	Laborer	14J102Jz
HENRY, Jas.		24	M	Laborer	14J102Jz
OSBORN, Ellen		22	F	Spinster	14J102Jz
Henry		20	M	Laborer	14J102Jz
WOODS, Michl.		28	M	Laborer	14J102Jz
U	(W)	27	F	Wife	14J102Jz
Jane	(D)	06	F	Child	14J102Jz
Robt.	(S)	04	M	Child	14J102Jz
John	(S)	.00	M	Infant	14J102Jz
GIBBS, Hugh		32	M	Carpenter	14J102Jz
U	(W)	30	F	Unknown	14J102Jz
John	(S)	10	M	Unknown	14J102Jz
Sally	(D)	08	F	Child	14J102Jz
Henry	(S)	06	M	Child	14J102Jz
Mary	(D)	03	F	Child	14J102Jz
Jane	(D)	.00	F	Infant	14J102Jz
MALONEY, Timothy		40	M	Carpenter	14J102Jz
U	(W)	38	F	Unknown	14J102Jz
Jane	(D)	13	F	Unknown	14J102Jz
Robt.	(S)	10	M	Unknown	14J102Jz
Timothy	(S)	06	M	Child	14J102Jz
Mary	(D)	03	F	Child	14J102Jz
Sally	(D)	.00	F	Infant	14J102Jz
OBRIEN, Thos.		26	M	Laborer	14J102Jz
U	(W)	24	F	Unknown	14J102Jz
Henry	(S)	04	M	Child	14J102Jz
David	(S)	02	M	Child	14J102Jz
Sally	(D)	.00	F	Infant	14J102Jz
TODD, George		32	M	Mechanic	14J102Jz
U	(W)	30	F	Wife	14J102Jz
Mary	(D)	13	F	Unknown	14J102Jz
John	(S)	10	M	Unknown	14J102Jz
Sally	(D)	04	F	Child	14J102Jz
George	(S)	03	M	Child	14J102Jz
Robt.	(S)	.00	M	Infant	14J102Jz
BOLAND, Mary		21	F	Spinster	14J102Jz
Judith		10	F	Unknown	14J102Jz
BURNS, Mary		13	F	Unknown	14J102Jz
Geo.		10	M	Unknown	14J102Jz
Bobt.		04	M	Child	14J102Jz
ONEIL, Hugh		30	M	Laborer	14J102Jz
U	(W)	30	F	Wife	14J102Jz
Michl.	(S)	10	M	Unknown	14J102Jz
Catherine	(D)	10	M	Unknown	14J102Jz
John	(S)	02	M	Child	14J102Jz
SMITH, Joseph		36	M	Farmer	14J102Jz
Judith	(W)	35	F	Wife	14J102Jz
Francis	(S)	13	M	Unknown	14J102Jz
Mary-Ann	(D)	11	F	Unknown	14J102Jz
Margt.	(D)	08	F	Child	14J102Jz
Patk.	(S)	03	M	Child	14J102Jz
Sally	(D)	.00	F	Infant	14J102Jz

LIVERPOOL 14 JULY 1846

From Liverpool

NAMES OF PASSENGERS		AGE	SEX	OCCUPATIONS	DATE PORT SHIP
HINDS, Philip		40	M	Victualler	14J102Bo
ODONNELL, James		34	M	Doctor	14J102Bo
Rebecca	(W)	26	F	Wife	14J102Bo
Allen	(S)	06	M	Child	14J102Bo
Rebecca	(D)	04	F	Child	14J102Bo
Fredrick	(S)	02	M	Child	14J102Bo
MCCARTY, Patt		50	M	Laborer	14J102Bo
Margt.	(W)	50	F	Laborer	14J102Bo
Pat	(S)	27	M	Laborer	14J102Bo
David	(S)	17	M	Laborer	14J102Bo
William	(S)	16	M	Laborer	14J102Bo
Richard	(S)	13	M	Laborer	14J102Bo

NAMES OF PASSENGERS		AGE	SEX	OCCUPATIONS	DATE PORT SHIP
CALLAGHAN, John		25	M	Tailor	14J102Bo
Margt.	(W)	20	F	Tailor	14J102Bo
Denis	(S)	05	M	Child	14J102Bo
Cathe.	(D)	04	F	Child	14J102Bo
Bridget	(D)	02	F	Child	14J102Bo
John	(S)	.00	M	Infant	14J102Bo
KENNEDY, Ellen		20	F	Servant	14J102Bo
COUFIELD, Thos.		27	M	Laborer	14J102Bo
ONEILL, James		28	M	Laborer	14J102Bo
QUINN, Thomas		30	M	Laborer	14J102Bo
Hannah		20	F	Servant	14J102Bo
MCCARTNEY, Barth		50	M	Laborer	14J102Bo
Mary	(W)	36	F	Laborer	14J102Bo
Cathe.	(D)	05	F	Child	14J102Bo
John	(S)	03	M	Child	14J102Bo
Mary	(D)	.00	F	Infant	14J102Bo
DOGHERTY, Julias		50	M	Farmer	14J102Bo
Mary	(W)	40	F	Wife	14J102Bo
Bridget	(D)	18	F	Servant	14J102Bo
ONEILL, John		19	M	Laborer	14J102Bo
BURKE, John		30	M	Laborer	14J102Bo
Mary	(W)	25	F	Wife	14J102Bo
MORGAN, Richd.		20	M	Cbtmkr	14J102Bo
BANETT, John		20	M	Laborer	14J102Bo
Mary		18	F	Laborer	14J102Bo
CLINTON, Pat		26	M	Laborer	14J102Bo
QUIGLEY, Pat		24	M	Laborer	14J102Bo
KENNEDY, Mary		19	F	Servant	14J102Bo
HALLARIN, John		27	M	Laborer	14J102Bo
Ann	(W)	25	F	Laborer	14J102Bo
John	(S)	07	M	Child	14J102Bo
Thomas	(S)	05	M	Child	14J102Bo
Patrick	(S)	03	M	Child	14J102Bo
John		18	M	Laborer	14J102Bo
HUGHES, Margt.		20	F	Servant	14J102Bo
RYAN, Andrew		25	M	Laborer	14J102Bo
Mary	(W)	20	F	Wife	14J102Bo
MADDEN, Peter		25	M	Laborer	14J102Bo
MCCLUSKEY, Pat		19	M	Laborer	14J102Bo
SKEFFINGTON, Betty		19	F	Wife	14J102Bo
Sarah		18	F	Wife	14J102Bo
John		26	M	Laborer	14J102Bo
CALLAGHAN, Cornelius		28	M	Laborer	14J102Bo
MCCUSKER, Pat		21	M	Laborer	14J102Bo
LEARY, Daniel		24	M	Laborer	14J102Bo
Catherine		10	F	Laborer	14J102Bo
CALLMAN, Cathe.		21	F	Laborer	14J102Bo
MCCARTNEY, Saml.		25	M	Shoemaker	14J102Bo
Mathew		25	M	Shoemaker	14J102Bo
MANAGH, Anthony		28	M	Weaver	14J102Bo
SULLIVAN, Giles		25	M	Laborer	14J102Bo
MCGOWAN, Biddy		30	F	Laborer	14J102Bo
James	(S)	09	M	Child	14J102Bo
Mary	(D)	06	F	Child	14J102Bo
Matilda	(D)	03	F	Child	14J102Bo
DOHERTY, Mary		80	F	Servant	14J102Bo
Died-At-Sea					
LEADY, John		21	M	Servant	14J102Bo
DUNNERY, Daniel		24	M	Servant	14J102Bo
HAMELL, Michl.		25	M	Servant	14J102Bo
WOODS, Ann		30	F	Servant	14J102Bo
Pat	(S)	10	M	Servant	14J102Bo
Ellen	(D)	08	F	Servant	14J102Bo
JOYCE, Denis		27	M	Laborer	14J102Bo
CUNNIFF, Bridget		17	F	Servant	14J102Bo
HARKIN, John		11	M	Servant	14J102Bo
Peter		07	M	Servant	14J102Bo
MCGARRY, Eliza		18	F	Servant	14J102Bo
COGHLAN, Mary		20	F	Servant	14J102Bo
MCCARDLE, Henry		21	M	Sailor	14J102Bo
MURRAY, Cathe.		24	F	Housewife	14J102Bo
Henry		15	M	Servant	14J102Bo
Pat		12	M	None	14J102Bo
Cathe.		09	F	Child	14J102Bo
Mary-Ann		05	F	Child	14J102Bo
MURRAY, Ellen		02	F	Child	14J102Bo
COULTER, Harry		21	M	Servant	14J102Bo
Mary	(W)	18	F	Wife	14J102Bo
FETHERSTON, John		13	M	Servant	14J102Bo
SMITH, Cathe.		21	F	Servant	14J102Bo
Susan		18	F	Servant	14J102Bo
DUNN, Eliza		21	F	Servant	14J102Bo
BURN, Eliza		20	F	Servant	14J102Bo
LAWLER, Margt.		20	F	Servant	14J102Bo
PHELAN, Margt.		21	F	Seamstress	14J102Bo
GRIFFIN, Michl.		35	M	Carpenter	14J102Bo
Sarah	(W)	25	F	Wife	14J102Bo
Mary	(D)	02	F	Child	14J102Bo
RILEY, Eliza		20	F	Servant	14J102Bo
MULDOON, Cathe.		20	F	Servant	14J102Bo
Ann		18	F	Servant	14J102Bo
LODDOCKE, Winifred		21	F	Servant	14J102Bo
LYNCH, Peter		21	M	Laborer	14J102Bo
FLOOD, Phillp		20	M	Laborer	14J102Bo
John		56	M	Farmer	14J102Bo
MARTIN, Mary-Ann		24	F	Servant	14J102Bo
Isabella		22	F	Servant	14J102Bo
CARAGY, Jane		20	F	Servant	14J102Bo
MCCABE, James		25	M	Laborer	14J102Bo
Rose		20	F	Servant	14J102Bo
GALLIGAN, Cathe.		20	F	Servant	14J102Bo
BEATTY, James		40	M	Mason	14J102Bo
Hannah	(W)	40	F	Wife	14J102Bo
James	(S)	23	M	Laborer	14J102Bo
Eliza	(D)	16	F	Laborer	14J102Bo
Mary	(D)	13	F	Laborer	14J102Bo
Jane	(D)	10	F	Laborer	14J102Bo
Biddy	(D)	08	F	Child	14J102Bo
Ann	(D)	06	F	Child	14J102Bo
Joseph	(S)	04	M	Child	14J102Bo
BARRY, Ann		23	F	Servant	14J102Bo
GERATY, Pat		18	M	Laborer	14J102Bo
WALSH, Thos.		60	M	Laborer	14J102Bo
HARPER, Alexr.		22	M	Weaver	14J102Bo
WARD, Mary		18	F	Servant	14J102Bo
Nancy		23	F	Servant	14J102Bo
ONEILL, Michl.		20	M	Laborer	14J102Bo
MCCAULEY, Richd.		23	M	Laborer	14J102Bo
Thomas		20	M	Laborer	14J102Bo
HIGINSON, Richd.		25	M	Farmer	14J102Bo
COFFEY, John		40	M	Cooper	14J102Bo
CONNER, Thomas		25	M	Cooper	14J102Bo
BARRETY, James		20	M	Cooper	14J102Bo
MCCABE, Felix		20	M	Baker	14J102Bo
LONEY, Michl.		20	M	Laborer	14J102Bo
SHIELDS, Robt.		22	M	Gdnr	14J102Bo
MATTHEWS, Wm.		22	M	Laborer	14J102Bo
MULLEN, Susan		18	F	Laborer	14J102Bo
RILEY, Thos.		20	M	Laborer	14J102Bo
CAHILL, Thos.		25	M	Servant	14J102Bo
MOONE, Eliza		20	F	Servant	14J102Bo
CLEAR, Wm.		22	M	Laborer	14J102Bo
MOORE, James		45	M	Blacksmith	14J102Bo
CAHILL, Margt.		45	F	Wife	14J102Bo
ROWAN, Ellany		20	F	Servant	14J102Bo
DOYLE, John		30	M	Laborer	14J102Bo
KENT, Brinda		58	F	Lady	14J102Bo
Theresa	(D)	23	F	Lady	14J102Bo
BROWN, Marke		25	M	Farmer	14J102Bo
Robert	(S)	.00	M	Infant	14J102Bo
Meolena		19	F	Wife	14J102Bo
NORTON, Barney		20	M	Laborer	14J102Bo
REYNOLDS, Kitty		24	F	Seamstress	14J102Bo
REGAN, Martin		28	M	Laborer	14J102Bo
Michl.		24	M	Laborer	14J102Bo
Cathe.		18	F	Servant	14J102Bo
Mary		14	F	Servant	14J102Bo
JOHNSTON, Edward		20	M	Farmer	14J102Bo
Harriet		18	F	Lady	14J102Bo
LYONS, Michl.		20	M	Laborer	14J102Bo

NAMES OF PASSENGERS		AGE	SEX	OCCUPATIONS	DATE PORT SHIP
LATMER, John		27	M	Blacksmith	14J102Bo
Eliza		18	F	Servant	14J102Bo
TAYLOR, Wm.		20	M	Groom	14J102Bo
Betty		18	F	Servant	14J102Bo
GILLESPIE, Henry		29	M	Carpenter	14J102Bo
HAMILL, Eliza		18	F	Seamstress	14J102Bo
RAFFERTY, Mary		28	F	Seamstress	14J102Bo
MARTLAN, James		27	M	Farmer	14J102Bo
WILSON, Sarah		27	F	Wife	14J102Bo
Eliza	(D)	.00	F	Infant	14J102Bo
ELLIOTT, John		27	M	Carpenter	14J102Bo
GRINDER, Eliza		45	F	Servant	14J102Bo
MCHURSTH, Mary-Ann		40	F	Wi	14J102Bo
Wm.James	(S)	08	M	Child	14J102Bo
FORREST, Ellen		20	F	Servant	14J102Bo
MOORE, Eliza		18	F	Servant	14J102Bo
Mary		15	F	Servant	14J102Bo
Cathe.		13	F	Servant	14J102Bo
CARROLL, Edward		17	M	Servant	14J102Bo
Luke		15	M	Servant	14J102Bo
THOMPSON, Robert		25	M	Clerk	14J102Bo
HAMILTON, John		20	M	Farmer	14J102Bo
Jane		20	F	Servant	14J102Bo
SPEER, Eliza		24	F	Servant	14J102Bo
DELANER, Mary-Ann		17	F	Servant	14J102Bo
REYNOLDS, Pat		20	M	Tailor	14J102Bo
BOYD, Isaac		40	M	Laborer	14J102Bo
Isaac	(S)	18	M	Laborer	14J102Bo
Mary		48	F	Spinster	14J102Bo
TIDDY, John		24	M	Laborer	14J102Bo
EVERAN, Susan		18	F	Seamstress	14J102Bo
LINTON, Cathe.		20	F	Servant	14J102Bo
Eliza		22	F	Servant	14J102Bo
OBRIEN, John		21	M	Saddler	14J102Bo
GAFNEY, Francis		20	M	Laborer	14J102Bo
RANKIN, Wm.		20	M	Laborer	14J102Bo
Susan		21	F	Servant	14J102Bo
MURPHY, Denis		25	M	Laborer	14J102Bo
POWER, Nicholas		30	M	Tailor	14J102Bo
WALSH, Thomas		20	M	Butcher	14J102Bo
MULHAM, John		23	M	Farmer	14J102Bo
QUINN, Isabella		40	F	Laborer	14J102Bo
TOBIN, John		19	M	Weaver	14J102Bo
WEBB, James		60	M	Farmer	14J102Bo
Mary-Ann		05	F	Child	14J102Bo
LYNCH, Mary-Ann		20	F	Servant	14J102Bo
DOOLEY, Martin		46	M	Laborer	14J102Bo
Mary	(W)	40	F	Wife	14J102Bo
Mary	(D)	15	F	Unknown	14J102Bo
John	(S)	12	M	Unknown	14J102Bo
Pat	(S)	09	M	Child	14J102Bo
Margt.	(D)	14	F	Unknown	14J102Bo
KENNY, Cathe.		20	F	Servant	14J102Bo
CURLEY, Marhta		20	F	Servant	14J102Bo
LARKIN, Ann		20	F	Servant	14J102Bo
KEASH, Billy		20	M	Laborer	14J102Bo
DALTON, John		20	M	Laborer	14J102Bo
WARD, John		20	M	Laborer	14J102Bo
KELLY, John		20	M	Laborer	14J102Bo
Mary		20	F	Laborer	14J102Bo
BEEGAN, Michl.		14	M	Laborer	14J102Bo
Maria		13	F	Laborer	14J102Bo
Catherine		09	F	Laborer	14J102Bo
Bridget		07	F	Laborer	14J102Bo
CROZIER, Robert		30	M	Millwright	14J102Bo
Jane	(W)	28	F	Wife	14J102Bo
MCFARLAN, Eliza		25	F	Servant	14J102Bo
MCCORMICK, Cathe.		21	F	Servant	14J102Bo
Ann		21	F	Servant	14J102Bo
RIEL, Ann		25	F	Servant	14J102Bo
MURPHY, John		22	M	Laborer	14J102Bo
COROVEN, Michl.		18	M	Laborer	14J102Bo
WARNACK, Richd.		21	M	Farmer	14J102Bo
Fanny	(W)	21	F	Wife	14J102Bo
BURN, Grace		18	F	Servant	14J102Bo
CHRISTIE, Thos.		20	M	Laborer	14J102Bo
TIERNEY, Edwd.		25	M	Farmer	14J102Bo
REARDON, Wm.		30	M	Laborer	14J102Bo
Ellen	(W)	30	F	Wife	14J102Bo
MURPHY, Ellen		25	F	Servant	14J102Bo
Danl.	(S)	.00	M	Infant	14J102Bo
WARD, Bernard		25	M	Laborer	14J102Bo
LINCHEN, Biddy		30	F	Wife	14J102Bo
Denis	(H)	30	M	Laborer	14J102Bo
John	(S)	05	M	Child	14J102Bo
Michl.	(S)	.00	M	Infant	14J102Bo
FLYNN, Michl.		30	M	Laborer	14J102Bo
LALLY, John		30	M	Clerk	14J102Bo
Martin		05	M	Child	14J102Bo
GATELY, Mary		11	F	Servant	14J102Bo
CROCKEWLL, Maria		09	F	Servant	14J102Bo
MCFARLAND, Eliza		21	F	Servant	14J102Bo
SKALLY, Cathe.		20	F	Servant	14J102Bo
HOLMES, Raphael		62	M	Laborer	14J102Bo
Eliza	(W)	62	F	Wife	14J102Bo
Mathw.	(S)	17	M	Laborer	14J102Bo
Raphael	(S)	12	M	Laborer	14J102Bo
Robert	(S)	10	M	Laborer	14J102Bo
Mary	(D)	05	F	Child	14J102Bo
MCJELLNEY, Edward		21	M	Laborer	14J102Bo
DONNELLY, Cathe.		12	F	Servant	14J102Bo
MCCORMICK, Cathe.		21	F	Servant	14J102Bo
MACKIN, Peter		25	M	Weaver	14J102Bo
Jane	(W)	25	F	Wife	14J102Bo
James	(S)	02	M	Child	14J102Bo
John	(S)	.00	M	Infant	14J102Bo
MCKENNA, Mary		21	F	Servant	14J102Bo
BLACK, John		30	M	Shoemaker	14J102Bo
James	(S)	07	M	Child	14J102Bo
CROOKS, Ellen		22	F	Servant	14J102Bo
SKIVINGTON, Mary		.09	F	Infant	14J102Bo

ELIZABETH-DENISON 20 JULY 1846

From Liverpool

NAMES OF PASSENGERS		AGE	SEX	OCCUPATIONS	DATE PORT SHIP
MCLLRAN, Isaac		00	M	Laborer	20J102Jn
SPENCE, George		28	M	Farmer	20J102Jn
William		20	M	Farmer	20J102Jn
LAWRENCE, William		42	M	Minister	20J102Jn
PRATT, Jane		20	F	Unknown	20J102Jn
Anne		18	F	Unknown	20J102Jn
KERR, Jane		30	F	Unknown	20J102Jn
RILEY, Catharine		27	F	Unknown	20J102Jn
MURPHY, Mary		18	F	Unknown	20J102Jn
HAMILTON, Samuel		17	M	Laborer	20J102Jn
KEEGAN, Mary		18	F	Unknown	20J102Jn
FARRELL, Peter		24	M	Laborer	20J102Jn
GAMGAN, Peter		24	M	Laborer	20J102Jn
GUINE, Bernard		50	M	Carpenter	20J102Jn
Margaret	(W)	49	F	Unknown	20J102Jn
Hannah	(D)	14	F	Unknown	20J102Jn
Robert	(S)	11	M	Unknown	20J102Jn
Isabella	(D)	18	F	Unknown	20J102Jn
BOYLE, Ellen		20	F	Unknown	20J102Jn
CLARK, Sally		16	F	Unknown	20J102Jn
MCCABE, Francis		23	M	Laborer	20J102Jn
SMITH, Patt		23	M	Carpenter	20J102Jn
DALY, Thomas		20	M	Laborer	20J102Jn
CONNOR, Larry		24	M	Shoemaker	20J102Jn
KRANE, David		29	M	Laborer	20J102Jn
MURPHY, Joseph		25	M	Laborer	20J102Jn
Mary	(W)	30	F	Unknown	20J102Jn
Mary	(D)	.00	F	Infant	20J102Jn

NAMES OF PASSENGERS		AGE	SEX	OCCUPATIONS	DATE PORT SHIP		NAMES OF PASSENGERS		AGE	SEX	OCCUPATIONS	DATE PORT SHIP
MCGARY, James		19	M	Laborer	20J102Jn		DAWSON, Agnes	(D)	04	F	Child	20J102Jn
PHILLIPS, Pat		21	M	Laborer	20J102Jn		William-J.	(S)	02	M	Child	20J102Jn
SHORT, William		12	M	Laborer	20J102Jn		DRISCOLL, Honora		21	F	Unknown	20J102Jn
MELLUM, John		50	M	Laborer	20J102Jn		Timothy		16	M	Unknown	20J102Jn
MCELLROY, Catharine		60	F	Unknown	20J102Jn		MCELLRAY, William		20	M	Laborer	20J102Jn
KELLY, Mary		18	F	Unknown	20J102Jn		DEALEY, Thomas		18	M	Laborer	20J102Jn
MCGINN, Mary		16	F	Unknown	20J102Jn		SHAW, Thomas		24	M	Laborer	20J102Jn
MCGUIGAN, Mary		19	F	Unknown	20J102Jn		CULLEN, Mary		26	F	Servant	20J102Jn
HUGHES, Bridget		24	F	Unknown	20J102Jn		MCATEE, Mary		20	F	Servant	20J102Jn
ASHCROFT, Robert		19	M	Laborer	20J102Jn		MCGUIN, Mary		19	F	Servant	20J102Jn
MICKLE, James		33	M	Laborer	20J102Jn		DIVER, Nancy		21	F	Servant	20J102Jn
THOMPSON, John		20	M	Weaver	20J102Jn		GORDON, John		40	M	Farmer	20J102Jn
SHAFFREY, Patrick		29	M	Laborer	20J102Jn		Sarah	(W)	39	F	Farmer	20J102Jn
COLLINS, James		25	M	Butcher	20J102Jn		DOUGHERTY, Catharine		18	F	Servant	20J102Jn
MONTGOMERY, Nathaniel		21	M	Clerk	20J102Jn		BOYLE, Catharine		29	F	Servant	20J102Jn
HAYNES, Edward		26	M	Cooper	20J102Jn		Francis	(S)	04	M	Child	20J102Jn
LAFFERTY, Ellen		24	F	Servant	20J102Jn		MCMANUS, Anne		18	F	Unknown	20J102Jn
MCANARTY, Eliza		24	F	Servant	20J102Jn		PHILLIPS, Francis		20	M	Unknown	20J102Jn
SLAVID, Eliza		20	F	Servant	20J102Jn		Thomas		17	M	Unknown	20J102Jn
MCNAUGHTEN, Moses		24	M	Laborer	20J102Jn		Mary		12	F	Unknown	20J102Jn
Eliza		18	F	Unknown	20J102Jn		GILL, Daniel		18	M	Laborer	20J102Jn
NUGAN, Jane		13	F	Servant	20J102Jn		DOWLING, Ann		30	F	Unknown	20J102Jn
MCBRIDE, John		16	M	Unknown	20J102Jn		COWEL, Wm.		28	M	Surgeon	20J102Jn
James		12	M	Unknown	20J102Jn							
Ann		24	F	Unknown	20J102Jn							
BOWSTAN, William		29	M	Laborer	20J102Jn							
CURRAN, Pat		24	M	Laborer	20J102Jn							
FINN, Ann		20	F	Servant	20J102Jn							
MALERY, John		24	M	Laborer	20J102Jn		**SIDDONS 20 JULY 1846**					
GARY, John		21	M	Laborer	20J102Jn							
CARY, Cely		24	F	Servant	20J102Jn		**From Liverpool**					
FARRELL, Mary		21	F	Servant	20J102Jn							
HOPKIN, Mary		24	F	Servant	20J102Jn							
CUNN, Catharine		20	F	Servant	20J102Jn							
MCGREAN, Daniel		45	M	Shoemaker	20J102Jn		NOLAN, Harriet		24	F	Unknown	20J102Bx
John		17	M	Shoemaker	20J102Jn		FEDIGAN, Patrick		28	M	Laborer	20J102Bx
MURPHY, Bryan		21	M	Laborer	20J102Jn		U	(W)	28	F	Laborer	20J102Bx
Nathan		20	M	Tailor	20J102Jn		Lawrence	(S)	10	M	Laborer	20J102Bx
Anne		21	F	Tailor	20J102Jn		Patrick	(S)	08	M	Laborer	20J102Bx
HOGAN, Anne		20	F	Servant	20J102Jn		Thomas	(S)	.00	M	Infant	20J102Bx
PRENDERGAST, George		29	M	Laborer	20J102Jn		GRIMES, Bridget		22	F	Laborer	20J102Bx
MCCANNA, Hugh		24	M	Laborer	20J102Jn		WHESTON, William		21	M	Laborer	20J102Bx
REILEY, Kelly		29	M	Laborer	20J102Jn		IRWIN, James		29	M	Laborer	20J102Bx
OBRIEN, John		26	M	Laborer	20J102Jn		SLOAN, Saml.		20	M	Laborer	20J102Bx
Luke		24	M	Laborer	20J102Jn		REID, James		20	M	Laborer	20J102Bx
Catharine		21	F	Servant	20J102Jn		MURPHY, Thomas		21	M	Laborer	20J102Bx
MAXWELL, Mary		20	F	Servant	20J102Jn		CASEY, Bridget		23	F	Laborer	20J102Bx
DIGUAN, Mary		39	F	Unknown	20J102Jn		FLEMING, James		23	M	Laborer	20J102Bx
Terence		10	F	Child	20J102Jn		HARRISON, Lark		30	M	Laborer	20J102Bx
REYNOLDS, Edward		24	M	Laborer	20J102Jn		U	(W)	30	F	Laborer	20J102Bx
OWENS, John		21	M	Laborer	20J102Jn		Lovell		11	U	Laborer	20J102Bx
MCNEAL, Bernard		20	M	Laborer	20J102Jn		Sarah	(D)	07	F	Child	20J102Bx
CLINE, Bridget		13	F	Servant	20J102Jn		Thomas	(S)	04	M	Child	20J102Bx
TRACY, Mary		20	F	Servant	20J102Jn		John	(S)	02	M	Child	20J102Bx
MCDONALD, Anne		20	F	Servant	20J102Jn		CURTIS, Sarah		30	F	Laborer	20J102Bx
BARNETT, William		16	M	Laborer	20J102Jn		WALL, Bridget		20	F	Laborer	20J102Bx
Catharine		18	F	Unknown	20J102Jn		BOYLE, Maria		20	F	Laborer	20J102Bx
Mary-J.		16	F	Unknown	20J102Jn		HANLEY, Michl.		30	M	Laborer	20J102Bx
SUGHLHAW, Sarah		25	F	Unknown	20J102Jn		DUFFY, Thomas		20	M	Laborer	20J102Bx
MOGHALY, Thomas		21	M	Laborer	20J102Jn		MOORE, John		21	M	Laborer	20J102Bx
HAYES, Mary		20	F	Servant	20J102Jn		SMITH, Terrence		20	M	Laborer	20J102Bx
MATHESON, Ellen		27	F	Servant	20J102Jn		BRADY, Anne		22	F	Laborer	20J102Bx
MURPHY, John		21	M	Laborer	20J102Jn		Mary		12	F	Laborer	20J102Bx
RAFFERTY, Patrick		50	M	Laborer	20J102Jn		MANGING, Ellen		20	F	Laborer	20J102Bx
Sally	(W)	49	F	Unknown	20J102Jn		DALTON, Maria		20	F	Laborer	20J102Bx
CAMPBELL, Eliza		40	F	Unknown	20J102Jn		Anne		11	F	Laborer	20J102Bx
MCCLEAN, Nancy		35	F	Unknown	20J102Jn		VINTON, Anne		35	F	Laborer	20J102Bx
Margaret	(D)	11	F	Unknown	20J102Jn		Anne	(D)	12	F	Laborer	20J102Bx
Wm. James	(S)	09	M	Child	20J102Jn		John	(S)	06	M	Child	20J102Bx
Eliza	(D)	06	F	Child	20J102Jn		Mary	(D)	03	F	Child	20J102Bx
WHITE, James		22	M	Weaver	20J102Jn		Louisa	(D)	01	F	Child	20J102Bx
DUFFY, Susan		17	F	Servant	20J102Jn		JENKINS, Mary		58	F	Laborer	20J102Bx
HARTIGAN, James		26	M	Laborer	20J102Jn		Lewis		54	M	Laborer	20J102Bx
DAWSON, John		29	M	Weaver	20J102Jn		Margt.	(D)	17	F	Laborer	20J102Bx
Mary	(W)	23	F	Unknown	20J102Jn		Lewis	(S)	12	M	Laborer	20J102Bx

207

NAMES OF PASSENGERS		A G E	S E X	OCCUPATIONS	DATE PORT SHIP	NAMES OF PASSENGERS		A G E	S E X	OCCUPATIONS	DATE PORT SHIP
JEFFREYS, James		22	M	Laborer	20J102Bx	MURPHY, John.		26	M	Laborer	20J102Bx
MCMULLEN, Wm.		44	M	Laborer	20J102Bx	HANLON, Christ.		40	M	Laborer	20J102Bx
U	(W)	35	F	Laborer	20J102Bx	U	(W)	30	F	Laborer	20J102Bx
Martha	(D)	15	F	Laborer	20J102Bx	Margt.	(D)	07	F	Child	20J102Bx
Mary	(D)	13	F	Laborer	20J102Bx					Died-At-Sea	
Jane	(D)	11	F	Laborer	20J102Bx	KANE, Daniel		30	M	Laborer	20J102Bx
Margt.	(D)	07	F	Child	20J102Bx	MCKEGNEY, Mary-A.		25	F	Laborer	20J102Bx
Anne	(D)	03	F	Child	20J102Bx	Elizabeth	(D)	05	F	Child	20J102Bx
Elizabeth	(D)	02	F	Child	20J102Bx	Felix	(S)	03	M	Child	20J102Bx
James	(S)	.09	M	Infant	20J102Bx	MCDONNELL, Anne		26	F	Laborer	20J102Bx
MURRAY, Peter		20	M	Laborer	20J102Bx	James	(S)	06	M	Child	20J102Bx
SHAMON, Saml.		21	M	Laborer	20J102Bx	GOLDING, Robt.		30	M	Laborer	20J102Bx
MCCOY, Wm.		21	M	Laborer	20J102Bx	KENEDY, Nancy		22	F	Laborer	20J102Bx
HAMILTON, Sarah		20	F	Laborer	20J102Bx	MANNION, Michl.		21	M	Laborer	20J102Bx
GOUGH, James		25	M	Laborer	20J102Bx	ROGERS, Michael		25	M	Laborer	20J102Bx
WYATT, Philip		27	M	Laborer	20J102Bx	Anne		22	F	Laborer	20J102Bx
DONOGHUE, Timothy		18	M	Laborer	20J102Bx	TIERNEY, Mary		21	F	Laborer	20J102Bx
REILLY, Bernard		31	M	Laborer	20J102Bx	ROGERS, Cathe.		05	F	Child	20J102Bx
MCMAHON, Stephen		36	M	Laborer	20J102Bx	LYNCH, Edward		20	M	Laborer	20J102Bx
MEAR, Martin		30	M	Laborer	20J102Bx	CRAWFORD, Thomas		22	M	Laborer	20J102Bx
FLAHERTY, Margaret		20	F	Laborer	20J102Bx	LYNCH, Ellen		18	F	Laborer	20J102Bx
LIDDY, Catherine		21	F	Laborer	20J102Bx	LYNCH, Margt.		18	F	Laborer	20J102Bx
WATERS, Sarah		36	F	Laborer	20J102Bx	NELSON, Margt.		21	F	Laborer	20J102Bx
NOLAN, Pat		23	M	Laborer	20J102Bx	PATTESON, Jane		21	F	Laborer	20J102Bx
FITZPATRICK, Mary		20	F	Laborer	20J102Bx	WHITTAKER, Geo.		26	M	Laborer	20J102Bx
SCULLY, Thomas		18	M	Laborer	20J102Bx	EATON, William		21	M	Laborer	20J102Bx
HYLAND, Martha		21	F	Laborer	20J102Bx	LIGHTHOLDER, Jos.		22	M	Laborer	20J102Bx
Mathew		20	M	Laborer	20J102Bx	JONES, James		32	M	Laborer	20J102Bx
WRIGHT, William		30	M	Laborer	20J102Bx	MOORHOUSE, John		29	M	Laborer	20J102Bx
Henry		31	M	Laborer	20J102Bx	CRAWLEY, Michl.		26	M	Laborer	20J102Bx
Sarah		29	F	Laborer	20J102Bx	HAND, Anne		30	F	Laborer	20J102Bx
Henry		06	M	Child	20J102Bx	Cathe.		15	F	Laborer	20J102Bx
CUMMINGS, Bernard		21	M	Laborer	20J102Bx	Owen		11	M	Laborer	20J102Bx
Richard		35	M	Laborer	20J102Bx	ROBINSON, Saml.		30	M	Laborer	20J102Bx
Mary		30	F	Laborer	20J102Bx	WALDRON, Teresa		19	F	Laborer	20J102Bx
William		12	M	Laborer	20J102Bx	MCGUIRK, John		21	M	Laborer	20J102Bx
Anne		10	F	Laborer	20J102Bx	WORDING, Hannah		33	F	Laborer	20J102Bx
John		06	M	Laborer	20J102Bx	Anne	(D)	12	F	Laborer	20J102Bx
Mary-Anne		06	F	Laborer	20J102Bx	John	(S)	10	M	Laborer	20J102Bx
Daniel		.05	M	Infant	20J102Bx	Thomas	(S)	08	M	Child	20J102Bx
GONGALY, Theodore		49	M	Laborer	20J102Bx	Mary	(D)	06	F	Child	20J102Bx
U	(W)	44	F	Laborer	20J102Bx	Jane	(D)	04	F	Child	20J102Bx
Rachel	(D)	15	F	Laborer	20J102Bx	Richd.	(S)	02	M	Child	20J102Bx
Charles	(S)	12	M	Laborer	20J102Bx	Henry	(S)	01	M	Child	20J102Bx
Anthony		20	M	Laborer	20J102Bx	MURPHY, Peter		21	M	Laborer	20J102Bx
U	(W)	20	F	Laborer	20J102Bx	GLEESON, Timothy		36	M	Laborer	20J102Bx
MCKEE, Michl.		33	M	Laborer	20J102Bx	Sally		13	F	Laborer	20J102Bx
Bridget	(W)	30	F	Laborer	20J102Bx	KENNAGH, John		13	M	Laborer	20J102Bx
Sarah	(D)	07	F	Child	20J102Bx	SHERIDAN, Pat		18	M	Laborer	20J102Bx
Margaret	(D)	01	F	Child	20J102Bx	GIBNEY, Richd.		28	M	Laborer	20J102Bx
CONLAN, James		22	M	Laborer	20J102Bx	SHERIDAN, Bridget		15	F	Laborer	20J102Bx
Mary	(W)	20	F	Laborer	20J102Bx	John		12	M	Laborer	20J102Bx
Sarah	(D)	.00	F	Infant	20J102Bx	CASEY, U-Mrs.		30	F	Laborer	20J102Bx
PICKETT, Lawrence		28	M	Laborer	20J102Bx	Kate	(D)	11	F	Laborer	20J102Bx
U	(W)	26	F	Laborer	20J102Bx	Mary-Anne	(D)	09	F	Laborer	20J102Bx
Mary	(D)	06	F	Child	20J102Bx	DONNELLY, Sarah		24	F	Laborer	20J102Bx
William	(S)	02	M	Child	20J102Bx	MCEVOY, Thomas		24	M	Laborer	20J102Bx
James	(S)	.00	M	Infant	20J102Bx	CARROLL, Mary		24	F	Laborer	20J102Bx
DALY, Honora		21	F	Laborer	20J102Bx	WRIGHT, Elizabeth		22	F	Laborer	20J102Bx
HENNESSY, John		26	M	Laborer	20J102Bx	GRAHAM, William		20	M	Laborer	20J102Bx
U	(W)	24	F	Laborer	20J102Bx	REILLY, Ellen		35	F	Laborer	20J102Bx
ODONNELL, Wm.		24	M	Laborer	20J102Bx	Elizabeth	(D)	15	F	Laborer	20J102Bx
Cathe.		21	F	Laborer	20J102Bx	James	(S)	12	M	Laborer	20J102Bx
Anne		20	F	Laborer	20J102Bx	MCDONNELL, Patk.		33	M	Laborer	20J102Bx
KAYES, John		24	M	Laborer	20J102Bx	DIVINE, Timothy		28	M	Laborer	20J102Bx
GARVEY, Owen		22	M	Laborer	20J102Bx	MURPHY, Eliza		23	F	Laborer	20J102Bx
STINTON, Mary-A.		20	F	Laborer	20J102Bx	BRENAN, Thomas		29	M	Laborer	20J102Bx
CASEY, Michl.		26	M	Laborer	20J102Bx	FALLON, Rose		18	F	Laborer	20J102Bx
HARRINGTON, James		20	M	Laborer	20J102Bx	MCLOUGHLIN, Edwd.		35	M	Laborer	20J102Bx
BENNETT, James		30	M	Laborer	20J102Bx	Cathe.	(W)	27	F	Laborer	20J102Bx
U	(W)	28	F	Laborer	20J102Bx	Michael	(S)	07	M	Child	20J102Bx
KEOUGH, John		24	M	Laborer	20J102Bx	DILLON, Sarah		26	F	Laborer	20J102Bx
READDEN, John		24	M	Laborer	20J102Bx	DONOSKY, Susan		20	F	Laborer	20J102Bx
CROMWAY, Ellen		20	F	Laborer	20J102Bx	CARSON, Anne		19	F	Laborer	20J102Bx
CARVILLE, Patrick		26	M	Laborer	20J102Bx	DYER, John		21	M	Laborer	20J102Bx
						DOYLE, Pat.		22	M	Laborer	20J102Bx

NAMES OF PASSENGERS		A G E	S E X	OCCUPATIONS	DATE PORT SHIP	NAMES OF PASSENGERS		A G E	S E X	OCCUPATIONS	DATE PORT SHIP
DOYLE, Mary		20	F	Laborer	20J102Bx	COYNE, John		20	M	Laborer	20J102Bx
Rose		19	F	Laborer	20J102Bx	MCGUINNESS, John		19	M	Laborer	20J102Bx
DUFFY, Rose		10	F	Laborer	20J102Bx	Margaret		17	F	Laborer	20J102Bx
GAFFREY, Alice		20	F	Laborer	20J102Bx	CRAWFORD, James		50	M	Laborer	20J102Bx
LARDNER, Susanna		29	F	Laborer	20J102Bx	Charlotte	(W)	45	F	Laborer	20J102Bx
Wm.	(S)	09	M	Laborer	20J102Bx	John-Henry	(S)	12	M	Laborer	20J102Bx
Anne	(D)	06	F	Laborer	20J102Bx	Robert	(S)	09	M	Laborer	20J102Bx
Mary	(D)	05	F	Laborer	20J102Bx	James	(S)	06	M	Laborer	20J102Bx
James	(S)	02	M	Laborer	20J102Bx	Charlotte	(D)	04	F	Laborer	20J102Bx
PENDER, Mary		20	F	Laborer	20J102Bx	Prudentia	(D)	02	F	Laborer	20J102Bx
Mary		19	F	Laborer	20J102Bx	Eleanor	(D)	01	F	Laborer	20J102Bx
HAMILL, Bridget		21	F	Laborer	20J102Bx	Saml.		44	M	Laborer	20J102Bx
INGHAM, Joseph		30	M	Laborer	20J102Bx	Jane	(W)	44	F	Laborer	20J102Bx
U	(W)	23	F	Laborer	20J102Bx	Jane	(D)	20	F	Laborer	20J102Bx
William	(S)	06	M	Child	20J102Bx	Robert	(S)	19	M	Laborer	20J102Bx
SLACK, Anne		21	F	Laborer	20J102Bx	Ellen	(D)	17	F	Laborer	20J102Bx
Francis		15	M	Laborer	20J102Bx	James	(S)	12	M	Unknown	20J102Bx
Nathaniel		12	M	Laborer	20J102Bx	Jane		30	F	Unknown	20J102Bx
WILDMAN, John		30	M	Laborer	20J102Bx	HENDERSON, James		32	M	Laborer	20J102Bx
SMITH, John		24	M	Laborer	20J102Bx	MCMURRAY, John		20	M	Laborer	20J102Bx
Peter		22	M	Laborer	20J102Bx	MCINTYRE, Sarah		20	F	Laborer	20J102Bx
GILLICK, Patrick		18	M	Laborer	20J102Bx	BLAKE, Thomas		20	M	Laborer	20J102Bx
FITZPATRICK, Pat.		22	M	Laborer	20J102Bx	REORDEN, James		29	M	Laborer	20J102Bx
Sally		20	F	Laborer	20J102Bx	JONES, Elizabeth		32	F	Laborer	20J102Bx
HENNESSY, Anne		19	F	Laborer	20J102Bx	Thomas	(S)	06	M	Child	20J102Bx
MORRIS, Edward		25	M	Laborer	20J102Bx	John	(S)	04	M	Child	20J102Bx
KAYE, James		20	M	Laborer	20J102Bx	Elizabeth	(D)	01	F	Child	20J102Bx
COMLAN, Nathan		20	M	Laborer	20J102Bx	Mary		25	F	Laborer	20J102Bx
LANSBOROUGH, Saml.		25	M	Laborer	20J102Bx	Mary	(D)	01	F	Child	20J102Bx
DEGNAN, James		21	M	Laborer	20J102Bx	CARROLL, Henry		22	M	Laborer	20J102Bx
PAUL, John		50	M	Laborer	20J102Bx	GREENWOOD, Wm.		30	M	Laborer	20J102Bx
U	(W)	50	F	Laborer	20J102Bx	Thomas	(S)	06	M	Child	20J102Bx
Elizabeth	(D)	12	F	Laborer	20J102Bx	JOHNSON, Oliver		04	M	Child	20J102Bx
BARTLEY, James		28	M	Laborer	20J102Bx	BARRY, Robert		22	M	Laborer	20J102Bx
U	(W)	28	F	Laborer	20J102Bx	STAPLETON, James		22	M	Laborer	20J102Bx
Jane	(D)	05	F	Child	20J102Bx	CORBITT, Pat		22	M	Laborer	20J102Bx
Andrew	(S)	03	M	Child	20J102Bx	NIBLOCK, Stewart		25	M	Laborer	20J102Bx
Margt.	(D)	.10	F	Infant	20J102Bx	Margt.		18	F	Laborer	20J102Bx
WALKER, John		26	M	Laborer	20J102Bx	PEACOCK, Geo.		24	M	Laborer	20J102Bx
U	(W)	24	F	Laborer	20J102Bx	Thomas		25	M	Laborer	20J102Bx
Mary	(D)	01	F	Child	20J102Bx	CORE, Margt.		18	F	Laborer	20J102Bx
HINTON, John		21	M	Laborer	20J102Bx	WOODS, William		27	M	Laborer	20J102Bx
CRAWFORD, Andrew		24	M	Laborer	20J102Bx	ROURKE, Bridget		18	F	Laborer	20J102Bx
MCDONNELL, Mary		18	F	Laborer	20J102Bx	GRAHAM, William		21	M	Laborer	20J102Bx
MORCHAM, Thomas		22	M	Laborer	20J102Bx	JONES, Mary		30	F	Laborer	20J102Bx
Mary		22	F	Laborer	20J102Bx	FAHY, Pierce		19	M	Laborer	20J102Bx
SEVILLE, William		21	M	Laborer	20J102Bx	BINGLEY, Thomas		22	M	Laborer	20J102Bx
CAMPBELL, Anne		20	F	Laborer	20J102Bx	SHEKLOG, Jos.		19	M	Laborer	20J102Bx
Cathe.		17	F	Laborer	20J102Bx	SLOAN, Belle		40	F	Laborer	20J102Bx
GREEN, Margt.		20	F	Laborer	20J102Bx	OBRIEN, James		22	M	Laborer	20J102Bx
Elizabeth		25	F	Laborer	20J102Bx	Dennis		26	M	Laborer	20J102Bx
HAMILTON, Cathe.		20	F	Laborer	20J102Bx	ASHMORE, John		23	M	Laborer	20J102Bx
CONNOR, Cathe.		19	F	Laborer	20J102Bx	Mary	(W)	23	F	Laborer	20J102Bx
DALY, Ellen		26	F	Laborer	20J102Bx	William	(S)	.05	M	Infant	20J102Bx
PICKETT, Catherine		18	F	Laborer	20J102Bx	COYNE, Lawrence		20	M	Laborer	20J102Bx
Mary		20	F	Laborer	20J102Bx	Cathe.		18	F	Laborer	20J102Bx
MCLOUGHLIN, Sarah		20	F	Laborer	20J102Bx	FITZPATRICK, Christ.		40	M	Laborer	20J102Bx
CURLEY, Bridget		20	F	Laborer	20J102Bx	EVANS, John		20	M	Laborer	20J102Bx
MURPHY, Patk.		26	M	Laborer	20J102Bx	MOONEY, John		20	M	Laborer	20J102Bx
CRANSIE, Catherine		20	F	Laborer	20J102Bx	WILSON, Robert		24	M	Laborer	20J102Bx
MCLEOD, Francis		26	M	Laborer	20J102Bx	DALY, Peter		21	M	Laborer	20J102Bx
MCLOUGHLIN, Jane		30	F	Laborer	20J102Bx	BARRY, U-Miss		15	F	Laborer	20J102Bx
WARK, Henry		40	M	Laborer	20J102Bx	KEEGAN, Eliza		16	F	Laborer	20J102Bx
SMITH, Moore		20	M	Laborer	20J102Bx	KANE, Ellen		18	F	Laborer	20J102Bx
MCCABE, Patk.		10	M	Laborer	20J102Bx	EGAN, John		20	M	Laborer	20J102Bx
RIGNEY, Patk.		27	M	Laborer	20J102Bx	James		18	M	Laborer	20J102Bx
Eliza	(W)	25	F	Laborer	20J102Bx	HALL, Eliza		16	F	Laborer	20J102Bx
Stephen	(S)	03	M	Child	20J102Bx	WILSON, John		22	M	Laborer	20J102Bx
Joseph	(S)	01	M	Child	20J102Bx	EVANS, William		23	M	Laborer	20J102Bx
HOOLAHAN, Mary		21	F	Laborer	20J102Bx	CURTIS, John		21	M	Laborer	20J102Bx
BRADY, Betsey		30	F	Laborer	20J102Bx	WHEELAN, Nichs.		12	M	Laborer	20J102Bx
HANLON, Anne		20	F	Laborer	20J102Bx	SHERIDAN, Pat		23	M	Laborer	20J102Bx
MCQUILLAN, Jane		25	F	Laborer	20J102Bx	CAVANAGH, Chas.		25	M	Laborer	20J102Bx
NELSON, Anne		25	F	Laborer	20J102Bx	BRANNAN, Andrew		30	M	Laborer	20J102Bx
COYNE, William		22	M	Laborer	20J102Bx	CARSON, Mary-A.		19	F	Laborer	20J102Bx

NAMES OF PASSENGERS		AGE	SEX	OCCUPATIONS	DATE PORT SHIP
TAYLOR, William		39	M	Laborer	20J102Bx
U	(W)	37	F	Laborer	20J102Bx
Fanny	(D)	15	F	Laborer	20J102Bx
Elizabeth	(D)	12	F	Laborer	20J102Bx
Gilder		10	U	Laborer	20J102Bx
FANNING, John		23	M	Laborer	20J102Bx
Richd.		42	M	Laborer	20J102Bx
REEVE, Alfred		31	M	Laborer	20J102Bx
Jeffrey		26	M	Laborer	20J102Bx
RYAN, Patk.		32	M	Laborer	20J102Bx
U	(W)	27	F	Laborer	20J102Bx
Cathe.	(D)	06	F	Child	20J102Bx

AFFGHAN 20 JULY 1846

From Marseilles

TIMMONS, Hugh		30	M	Labr-Mnr	20J178Ka
CARRONS, John		30	M	Labr-Mnr	20J178Ka
BRION, John		28	M	Laborer	20J178Ka
Ann		23	F	Wife	20J178Ka
Francis	(S)	01	M	Child	20J178Ka
Mary	(D)	.04	F	Infant	20J178Ka

MARGARET-EVANS 20 JULY 1846

From London

NEWELL, Wm.B.		21	M	Clerk	20J1211p
DONALDSON, John		23	M	Clerk	20J1211p
MOORE, Jeremiah		42	M	Weaver	20J1211p
DARTON, Mary		29	F	Unknown	20J1211p

GREAT-BRITAIN 21 JULY 1846

From Liverpool

LAMBERT, R.		36	M	Merchant	21J102Hp
MUNKITTRICK, A.		35	M	Merchant	21J102Hp
TIGHE, Salei		20	M	Army	21J102Hp
MOORE, S.R.		26	M	Gentleman	21J102Hp
U	(W)	22	F	Unknown	21J102Hp
KERR, S.		27	M	Merchant	21J102Hp

YUCATAN 22 JULY 1846

From Liverpool

MCKINLIN, John		30	M	Farmer	22J102Kf
Margt.		17	F	None	22J102Kf
GREEN, Thadeus		12	M	None	22J102Kf

NAMES OF PASSENGERS		AGE	SEX	OCCUPATIONS	DATE PORT SHIP
BROWN, Ricld.		30	M	Farmer	22J102Kf
STANTAN, Thomas		27	M	Farmer	22J102Kf
GRELY, Martin		21	M	Farmer	22J102Kf
LOVELL, Austin		21	M	Farmer	22J102Kf
TIERNEY, John		20	M	Farmer	22J102Kf
STANTAN, Sabina		28	F	Farmer	22J102Kf
CONNELL, Anthy.		24	M	Farmer	22J102Kf
BEIRNE, Ann		19	F	Servant	22J102Kf
Mary		17	F	Servant	22J102Kf
Catherin		13	F	None	22J102Kf
MOLLOY, Wm.		62	M	Farmer	22J102Kf
U	(W)	60	F	None	22J102Kf
Wm.	(S)	24	M	Farmer	22J102Kf
Margt.	(D)	11	F	Child	22J102Kf
REYNOLDS, Jno.		25	M	Mechanic	22J102Kf
MOLLOY, Cathe.		20	F	Servant	22J102Kf
CROHAM, Cathe.		18	F	Servant	22J102Kf
CADEY, Bridget		13	F	Servant	22J102Kf
MORGAN, Margt.		18	F	Servant	22J102Kf
GIBSON, David		20	M	Tailor	22J102Kf
MCCALL, Agnes		20	F	Laborer	22J102Kf
RHALL, Patk.		20	M	Laborer	22J102Kf
James		20	M	Laborer	22J102Kf
LYNCH, Bridget		20	F	Servant	22J102Kf
DONOHOE, Bessy		20	F	Servant	22J102Kf
QUINN, Wm.		24	M	Farmer	22J102Kf
CAIN, Denis		20	M	Farmer	22J102Kf
CLARY, Lawrence		20	M	Farmer	22J102Kf
CORMICK, James		35	M	Farmer	22J102Kf
CREIGHTON, John		60	M	Farmer	22J102Kf
Michl.		30	M	Farmer	22J102Kf
John		35	M	Farmer	22J102Kf
GRIFFITHS, Robt.		28	M	Farmer	22J102Kf
HAMILTON, James		50	M	Farmer	22J102Kf
CREIGHTON, Elizth.		26	F	None	22J102Kf
Grace		20	F	None	22J102Kf
FORREST, Margt.		06	F	Child	22J102Kf
CREIGHTON, Mary		26	F	Servant	22J102Kf
GRIFFITHS, James		04	M	Child	22J102Kf
Ann		.00	F	Infant	22J102Kf
HAGGERTY, Elizth.		50	F	None	22J102Kf
Joseph		36	M	Farmer	22J102Kf
Anne		23	F	None	22J102Kf
John		13	M	None	22J102Kf
Isabella		11	F	Child	22J102Kf
Anne		09	F	Child	22J102Kf
Edwd.		17	M	None	22J102Kf
Rosanna		05	F	Child	22J102Kf
Mary		03	F	Child	22J102Kf
Joseph		.00	M	Infant	22J102Kf
GINTEY, Owen		24	M	Farmer	22J102Kf
Bridget		28	F	Servant	22J102Kf
QUINN, Mary-Ann		13	F	Servant	22J102Kf
Joseph		12	M	Servant	22J102Kf
SMITH, John		20	M	Laborer	22J102Kf
BARTAN, James		20	M	Laborer	22J102Kf
IRVINE, James		36	M	Laborer	22J102Kf
HUMPHREYS, George		34	M	Farmer	22J102Kf
KENNEDY, Robt.		22	M	Farmer	22J102Kf
BARTAN, Archibd.		50	M	Farmer	22J102Kf
James	(S)	22	M	Farmer	22J102Kf
Rose	(D)	20	F	Farmer	22J102Kf
Cathe.	(D)	12	F	Farmer	22J102Kf
Mary	(W)	50	F	Farmer	22J102Kf
Catherin		28	F	None	22J102Kf
Mary-Jane	(D)	07	F	Child	22J102Kf
Margt.	(D)	03	F	Child	22J102Kf
Cathe.	(D)	.00	F	Infant	22J102Kf
COLMAN, Mary		20	F	Servant	22J102Kf
Honor		20	F	Servant	22J102Kf
CONLY, Lawe.		20	M	Laborer	22J102Kf
KEATING, John		20	M	Laborer	22J102Kf
MCCLUSKEY, Bridgt.		20	F	Servant	22J102Kf
MITCHELL, John		17	M	Laborer	22J102Kf
Mary		20	F	Servant	22J102Kf

NAMES OF PASSENGERS		AGE	SEX	OCCUPATIONS	DATE PORT SHIP
FARRELL, Danl.		25	M	Farmer	22J102Kf
MULLIN, Mary		13	F	Servant	22J102Kf
MEHIGAN, John		36	M	Laborer	22J102Kf
Timothy		30	M	Laborer	22J102Kf
POOLE, Cathe.		13	F	None	22J102Kf
DONOVAN, Mary		30	F	Servant	22J102Kf
Cathe.	(D)	13	F	Servant	22J102Kf
HEMPAN, Cathe.		19	F	Servant	22J102Kf
SULLIVAN, Julia		18	F	Servant	22J102Kf
HEMPAN, Patk.		12	M	None	22J102Kf
TURNER, Mary-Ann		20	F	Servant	22J102Kf
Mary-Ann		20	F	Servant	22J102Kf
Mary		.00	F	Infant	22J102Kf
NEAN, Cathe.		30	F	Servant	22J102Kf
Mary-Ann		20	F	Servant	22J102Kf
Susan	(D)	11	F	Child	22J102Kf
Cathe.	(D)	10	F	Child	22J102Kf
Owen	(S)	09	M	Child	22J102Kf
Michl.	(S)	08	M	Child	22J102Kf
Hugh	(S)	05	M	Child	22J102Kf
TOBIN, Robert		20	M	Mechanic	22J102Kf
CROLIN, James		20	M	Laborer	22J102Kf
SHEA, John		30	M	Mechanic	22J102Kf
DOWD, Michl.		30	M	Mechanic	22J102Kf
BEATY, U		20	F	Servant	22J102Kf
MCGOWAN, Mary		20	F	Servant	22J102Kf
QUAYLE, Charles		40	M	Farmer	22J102Kf
MCMASTER, Robt.		12	M	None	22J102Kf
SHAW, Ann		16	F	Servant	22J102Kf
Matilda		13	F	Servant	22J102Kf
FEEGAN, Edw.		21	M	Laborer	22J102Kf
OHARA, John		23	M	Laborer	22J102Kf
SHAW, Sam		30	M	Laborer	22J102Kf
MURRAY, Jas.		27	M	Laborer	22J102Kf
HART, Hy.		27	M	Laborer	22J102Kf
U	(W)	24	F	None	22J102Kf
DAVIS, U-Mrs.		45	F	None	22J102Kf
U	(H)	45	M	Farmer	22J102Kf
Ellz.	(D)	20	F	None	22J102Kf
David	(S)	17	M	None	22J102Kf
Ann	(D)	15	F	None	22J102Kf
John	(S)	13	M	None	22J102Kf
Jos.	(S)	11	M	Child	22J102Kf
Hannah	(D)	09	F	Child	22J102Kf
Thos.	(S)	06	M	Child	22J102Kf
Margt.	(D)	05	F	Child	22J102Kf
Evan	(S)	.00	M	Infant	22J102Kf
KEYS, Mich.		27	M	Laborer	22J102Kf
MCGRATH, Margt.		21	F	Servant	22J102Kf
CONELL, Mary		24	F	Servant	22J102Kf
MCCONNELL, Betty		19	F	Servant	22J102Kf
BAKER, Wm.		20	M	None	22J102Kf
DONOHUE, Thos.		40	M	None	22J102Kf
Bridget	(D)	19	F	None	22J102Kf
Ann	(D)	18	F	None	22J102Kf
Mary	(D)	09	F	Child	22J102Kf
HORAN, Mary		10	F	Child	22J102Kf
SHERIDAN, Mary		26	F	Servant	22J102Kf
MCDERMOTT, Ann		20	F	Servant	22J102Kf
CALLAHAN, Pat		20	M	None	22J102Kf
Peggy		18	F	None	22J102Kf
CULLOUGH, Michl.		24	M	Laborer	22J102Kf
DONOHUE, John		20	M	Laborer	22J102Kf
MALADY, Jas.		24	M	Laborer	22J102Kf
WALSH, Thos.		26	M	Laborer	22J102Kf
MCKIELY, Bl---		26	F	Servant	22J102Kf
GROGAN, Pat		26	M	None	22J102Kf
MCCLUSKEY, Jane		30	F	None	22J102Kf
CAVANAUGH, Cath.		28	F	None	22J102Kf
Margaret	(D)	04	F	Child	22J102Kf
ROARK, Ellz.		49	F	None	22J102Kf
COONEY, Mgt.		47	F	None	22J102Kf
Tina	(D)	19	F	None	22J102Kf
NORTHERN, Mich.		26	M	Laborer	22J102Kf
Ann		19	F	None	22J102Kf
MULLIN, Jas.		25	M	None	22J102Kf
BRADY, Mary		20	F	None	22J102Kf
Mich.		16	M	None	22J102Kf
Bridget		26	F	None	22J102Kf
QUINN, Cath.		25	F	None	22J102Kf
Cath.		18	F	None	22J102Kf
Bridget		04	F	Child	22J102Kf
DEVLIN, Ann		18	F	None	22J102Kf
FEELY, Maurice		24	M	Laborer	22J102Kf
Bidy		20	F	None	22J102Kf
MCNULTY, Terence		27	M	None	22J102Kf
FARRALL, Ann		20	F	None	22J102Kf
ROE, Bridget		20	F	None	22J102Kf
MCGOVERN, Pat		18	M	None	22J102Kf
TIERNAN, John		30	M	None	22J102Kf
U		25	F	None	22J102Kf
Thos.	(S)	03	M	Child	22J102Kf
Mary	(D)	.00	F	Infant	22J102Kf
Pat		28	M	None	22J102Kf
Ann		21	F	None	22J102Kf
MCGUINN, Cath.		20	F	Servant	22J102Kf
GANNON, Ellz.		25	F	Servant	22J102Kf
Donld.	(S)	04	M	Child	22J102Kf
Cath.	(D)	.00	F	Infant	22J102Kf
GEERY, Mary		25	F	None	22J102Kf
FEENEY, Ellen		25	F	None	22J102Kf
MACK, Danl.		34	M	Laborer	22J102Kf
SHOCKPENNY, U		20	F	None	22J102Kf
ENNESSY, Thos.		25	M	Farmer	22J102Kf
U-Mrs.		30	F	None	22J102Kf
Mary		45	F	None	22J102Kf
HIGGINS, John		30	M	Farmer	22J102Kf
Mary		20	F	None	22J102Kf
Susan		20	F	None	22J102Kf
Cath.		19	F	None	22J102Kf
MCKENNA, Mary		20	F	Servant	22J102Kf
KING, Owen		20	M	Laborer	22J102Kf
MORAN, Cath.		19	F	Servant	22J102Kf
DELANY, Cath.		20	F	Servant	22J102Kf
DUNN, Anthy.		26	M	Laborer	22J102Kf
COYLE, Hugh		21	M	Laborer	22J102Kf
CASSADY, Wm.		22	M	Laborer	22J102Kf
MARRNELL, Jas.		21	M	Laborer	22J102Kf
CAVANAUGH, Danl.		21	M	Laborer	22J102Kf
UNGER, Peter		20	M	Laborer	22J102Kf
MULLEN, Mary		25	M	Laborer	22J102Kf
Ann		.00	F	Infant	22J102Kf
CALLAHAN, Mary		20	F	None	22J102Kf
BUCKLY, Ellen		20	F	None	22J102Kf
HEADY, Danl.		24	M	Laborer	22J102Kf
Cath.	(W)	24	F	None	22J102Kf
Denis	(S)	.00	M	Infant	22J102Kf
LEONARD, Mary		18	F	Servant	22J102Kf
REILLY, Cath.		20	F	Servant	22J102Kf
Pat		20	M	Laborer	22J102Kf
FINN, Mich.		40	M	Laborer	22J102Kf
Ellen		40	F	None	22J102Kf
CLARKSON, Ellz.		20	F	None	22J102Kf
SHIELS, John		35	M	None	22J102Kf
HAMILTON, John		32	M	Farmer	22J102Kf
Ann	(W)	26	F	None	22J102Kf
Anna	(D)	05	F	Child	22J102Kf
KENNEDY, Mary		20	F	None	22J102Kf
Peter		23	M	None	22J102Kf
KAVANAUGH, Mich.		40	M	Farmer	22J102Kf
U	(W)	40	F	None	22J102Kf
Cath.	(D)	12	F	None	22J102Kf
Math.	(S)	10	M	Child	22J102Kf
Bridget	(D)	08	F	Child	22J102Kf
Rose	(D)	02	F	Child	22J102Kf
Mary	(D)	.00	F	Infant	22J102Kf
Thos.	(S)	.00	M	Infant	22J102Kf
COOK, Jas.		30	M	Laborer	22J102Kf
GIBBONS, Susan		30	F	Servant	22J102Kf
SCOTT, Jas.		34	M	Laborer	22J102Kf

NAMES OF PASSENGERS		AGE	SEX	OCCUPATIONS	DATE PORT SHIP
URISTON, Wm.		28	M	Laborer	22J102Kf
Betsey		28	F	Laborer	22J102Kf
MCCREA, Abh.		25	M	Laborer	22J102Kf
HICKS, Jane		20	F	Laborer	22J102Kf
HARRISON, Jas.		57	M	Laborer	22J102Kf
Sarah	(W)	50	F	Laborer	22J102Kf
John	(S)	18	M	Laborer	22J102Kf
Wm.	(S)	11	M	Child	22J102Kf
Rach.	(D)	04	F	Child	22J102Kf
STEPHENS, Hugh		23	M	Mechanic	22J102Kf
QUIGLEY, Owen		13	M	None	22J102Kf
KEARNAN, John		23	M	Laborer	22J102Kf
ROCKE, Eliza		16	F	Servant	22J102Kf
MOFFATT, Rose		17	F	Servant	22J102Kf
DUNN, Danl.		30	M	Laborer	22J102Kf
Rose-Ann		20	F	Servant	22J102Kf
Mary		29	F	Servant	22J102Kf
RIDDING, Patk.		43	M	Farmer	22J102Kf
U	(W)	29	F	None	22J102Kf
CONNELL, James		21	M	Laborer	22J102Kf

CHARLEMAGNE 23 JULY 1846

From Liverpool

NAMES OF PASSENGERS		AGE	SEX	OCCUPATIONS	DATE PORT SHIP
LOUGHERY, John		40	M	Laborer	23J102Kc
Abby		50	F	None	23J102Kc
DOWNY, Thomas		19	M	Stone Mason	23J102Kc
DONELLY, Michael		25	M	Laborer	23J102Kc
CUMMINS, John		30	M	Nail Maker	23J102Kc
MITCHELL, Rose		50	F	Nail Maker	23J102Kc
COLLINS, Mary-Jane		20	F	Nail Maker	23J102Kc
BUCKETT, William		22	M	Carpenter	23J102Kc
Isabela	(W)	22	F	None	23J102Kc
Robert	(S)	04	M	Child	23J102Kc
Eliza	(D)	.00	F	Infant	23J102Kc
MURPHY, James		40	M	Laborer	23J102Kc
Ann	(W)	30	F	None	23J102Kc
Margaret	(D)	06	F	Child	23J102Kc
Mary-Jane	(D)	03	F	Child	23J102Kc
James	(S)	.00	M	Infant	23J102Kc
COUCH, John		19	M	Farmer	23J102Kc
GINN, James		30	M	Farmer	23J102Kc
MILIGAN, Ann		20	F	Farmer	23J102Kc
CARROLL, Ann		20	F	Farmer	23J102Kc
John		24	M	Laborer	23J102Kc
REYNOLDS, Ellen		20	F	None	23J102Kc
CAMEL, Ann		20	F	None	23J102Kc
DONELLY, Bridget		18	F	None	23J102Kc
REYNOLDS, Oliver		21	M	Laborer	23J102Kc
GOODIN, Terence		27	M	Teacher	23J102Kc
Mary	(W)	24	F	None	23J102Kc
Ann	(D)	.00	F	Infant	23J102Kc
MCARDLE, John		17	M	Laborer	23J102Kc
Betsey	(M)	50	F	None	23J102Kc
NUGENT, Ann		21	F	None	23J102Kc
MCARDLE, Michael		11	M	Child	23J102Kc
KELLEY, Susan		24	F	None	23J102Kc
ANDERSON, John		21	F	Farmer	23J102Kc
Mathew		18	F	Farmer	23J102Kc
DOLLAN, James		30	F	Farmer	23J102Kc
MURPHY, Pat		23	M	Servant	23J102Kc
FAGAN, Anthony		25	M	Laborer	23J102Kc
MCGINIS, Ellen		18	F	None	23J102Kc
HOPKINS, John		12	M	None	23J102Kc
HIGGINS, Robert		30	M	None	23J102Kc
Mary		13	F	None	23J102Kc
TRAYNOR, James		20	M	Laborer	23J102Kc
Francis		15	M	None	23J102Kc

NAMES OF PASSENGERS		AGE	SEX	OCCUPATIONS	DATE PORT SHIP
MCKENNEY, Francis		23	M	Farmer	23J102Kc
Catherine		20	F	None	23J102Kc
MCCUSKER, Sally		18	F	None	23J102Kc
EDGAR, Francis		40	M	Clerk	23J102Kc
SAVAGE, Henry		24	M	Laborer	23J102Kc
COUGHLIN, Mary		20	F	None	23J102Kc
CARROLL, Ann		19	F	None	23J102Kc
MULHERN, James		37	M	Farmer	23J102Kc
FITZPATRICK, Bridget		17	F	None	23J102Kc
GALVOONY, Catherine		30	F	None	23J102Kc
CARTY, Mary		18	F	None	23J102Kc
Ann		17	F	None	23J102Kc
PIERCE, Michael		23	M	Laborer	23J102Kc
MCCABE, Mary-Ann		19	F	None	23J102Kc
CAREY, Mary-Ann		21	F	None	23J102Kc
REED, John		24	M	Laborer	23J102Kc
DONAGHO, Catherine		20	F	None	23J102Kc
MCIHENNEY, Mary		20	F	None	23J102Kc
LEDAY, Thomas		20	M	Laborer	23J102Kc
Mary		19	F	None	23J102Kc
WISE, Ann		20	F	None	23J102Kc
MCGRAGH, Pat		21	M	Laborer	23J102Kc
WHITE, George		30	M	Grocer	23J102Kc
PLUNKET, Thomas		21	M	Laborer	23J102Kc
NAUGHTON, Maria		18	F	None	23J102Kc
COYLE, Mary		20	F	None	23J102Kc
MAHAN, Thomas		25	M	Laborer	23J102Kc
CLANCY, William		20	M	Laborer	23J102Kc
BARY, Peter		21	M	Laborer	23J102Kc
TRACIE, Constantine		25	M	Laborer	23J102Kc
BARY, Betsey		12	F	None	23J102Kc
FEENEY, Ellen		18	F	None	23J102Kc
GUY, Thomas		20	M	Laborer	23J102Kc
DOWD, Pat		18	M	Laborer	23J102Kc
SIMPLE, Margaret		21	F	Unknown	23J102Kc
MCTHOWN, Henry		27	M	Laborer	23J102Kc
Mary		26	F	None	23J102Kc
ARCHES, Betsey		20	F	None	23J102Kc
NIGHT, William		20	M	Laborer	23J102Kc
HOEN, Alexander		24	M	Laborer	23J102Kc
Susannah		25	F	None	23J102Kc
BROOKS, Susan		50	F	None	23J102Kc
DONELY, Eliza		17	F	None	23J102Kc
TAYLOR, John		12	M	None	23J102Kc
BURNS, John		22	M	Laborer	23J102Kc
Ann		19	F	None	23J102Kc
COYLE, Pat		20	M	Laborer	23J102Kc
MORE, Margaret		21	F	None	23J102Kc
ROBERTS, James-J.		25	M	Merchant	23J102Kc
Cherubina		20	F	None	23J102Kc
Mary		18	F	None	23J102Kc
John		14	M	None	23J102Kc
NUGENT, Mary		22	F	None	23J102Kc
GILL, Thomas		21	M	Laborer	23J102Kc
LORD, Ann		18	F	None	23J102Kc
TWOLON, Michael		21	M	Laborer	23J102Kc
MCDONELL, Ann		18	F	None	23J102Kc
LOVETT, John		21	M	Architect	23J102Kc
Joseph		24	M	Laborer	23J102Kc
DIVINE, Michael		24	M	Laborer	23J102Kc
CAIN, Margaret		20	F	None	23J102Kc
BOURKE, Jane		28	F	None	23J102Kc
GORDEN, Mary		25	F	None	23J102Kc
MCBRIDE, Owen		30	M	Shoemaker	23J102Kc
BUCKLEY, Catherine		25	F	None	23J102Kc
CUSHIN, Ann		18	F	None	23J102Kc
PAYE, William		40	M	Lawyer	23J102Kc
Ann	(W)	40	F	None	23J102Kc
Mary	(D)	13	F	None	23J102Kc
Patter	(S)	12	M	None	23J102Kc
Katherine	(D)	10	F	Child	23J102Kc
Ann	(D)	06	F	Child	23J102Kc
Emily	(D)	05	F	Child	23J102Kc
William	(S)	02	M	Child	23J102Kc
SLATTERS, Mary		16	F	None	23J102Kc

NAMES OF PASSENGERS		AGE	SEX	OCCUPATIONS	DATE PORT SHIP
LOAN, Hannah		30	F	None	23J102Kc
Sarah		03	F	Child	23J102Kc
MCKEN, Sally		16	F	Laborer	23J102Kc
MCALLISTER, Catherine		20	F	None	23J102Kc
HYNDMAN, John		20	M	Laborer	23J102Kc
CAVANAGH, Mary		30	F	None	23J102Kc
MCKENNEY, Jane		23	F	None	23J102Kc
SPRATT, John		20	M	Weaver	23J102Kc
MCMAHON, Thomas		30	M	Nail Maker	23J102Kc
DUNN, Margaret		50	F	None	23J102Kc
Hugh	(S)	18	M	None	23J102Kc
Samuel	(S)	15	M	None	23J102Kc
Margaret	(D)	10	F	Child	23J102Kc
Mary	(D)	08	F	Child	23J102Kc
James	(S)	06	M	Child	23J102Kc
MILLET, Thomas		25	M	Laborer	23J102Kc
Jane		20	F	None	23J102Kc
MCCLAFERTY, Mary		18	F	None	23J102Kc
NOLAND, Margare		20	F	None	23J102Kc
CRYSTAL, Eliza		21	F	None	23J102Kc
WHITECRAFT, Judith		50	F	None	23J102Kc
Judith	(D)	12	F	None	23J102Kc
CAREY, Michael		25	M	None	23J102Kc
COYLE, Mary		11	F	Child	23J102Kc
MAHAN, Hugh		21	M	Joiner	23J102Kc
MCNAMARA, Mary		20	F	None	23J102Kc
HAMILTON, John		20	M	None	23J102Kc
DOUGHERTY, Hannah		21	F	None	23J102Kc
LAWLER, Catherine		13	F	None	23J102Kc
Mary		10	F	Child	23J102Kc
Michael		08	M	Child	23J102Kc
David		06	M	Child	23J102Kc
U		.00	U	Infant	23J102Kc
Born-At-Sea					
ROWNDTMEN, Elizabeth		17	F	None	23J102Kc
ALLEN, Mary		27	F	None	23J102Kc
Jane		15	F	None	23J102Kc
RILEY, Farel		20	M	Laborer	23J102Kc
TRAYNON, Rodger		39	M	Bootmaker	23J102Kc
DEMPSEY, Bernard		24	M	Laborer	23J102Kc
HENRY, Michael		27	M	None	23J102Kc
DOLAND, Bridget		21	F	None	23J102Kc
ROKE, John		28	M	Clerk	23J102Kc
OGARA, Domick		27	M	Collier	23J102Kc
FEELEY, Michael		27	M	Cbtmkr	23J102Kc
MCDONNELL, Daniel		26	M	Farmer	23J102Kc
Ann		24	F	None	23J102Kc
HILLER, John		28	M	Farmer	23J102Kc
COYNE, Mary		20	F	None	23J102Kc
MCDONNELLY, Mary		.00	F	Infant	23J102Kc
FINN, Marcella		21	F	None	23J102Kc
CONALLY, Marcella		50	F	None	23J102Kc
Teresa	(D)	13	F	None	23J102Kc
MCGOWEN, Margaret		21	F	None	23J102Kc
Rose		20	F	None	23J102Kc
RYAN, Mary		30	F	None	23J102Kc
John	(S)	13	M	None	23J102Kc
Patrick	(S)	10	M	Child	23J102Kc
REED, Michael		21	M	Laborer	23J102Kc
REYNOLDS, Catherine		20	F	None	23J102Kc
FALTON, Rose		18	F	None	23J102Kc
CONELLY, Pat		20	M	Laborer	23J102Kc
MORE, Grace-Ann		21	F	None	23J102Kc
TALE, Bridget		12	F	None	23J102Kc
SHAHANESSY, Joseph		21	M	Laborer	23J102Kc
DUNN, Mary		20	F	None	23J102Kc
COWLEY, Pat.		21	M	Laborer	23J102Kc
DUNN, Margaret		18	F	None	23J102Kc
FINIGAN, Pat		28	M	Carpenter	23J102Kc
LYONS, Ann		20	F	None	23J102Kc
PETERS, John		21	M	Farmer	23J102Kc
DILLON, Patrick		21	M	Laborer	23J102Kc
HICKEY, Ann		21	F	None	23J102Kc
ARTHUR, Thomas		10	M	Child	23J102Kc
Margaret		09	F	Child	23J102Kc
ARTHUR, Martin		05	M	Child	23J102Kc
FARRELL, John		20	M	Surveyor	23J102Kc
HICKEY, Margaret		21	F	None	23J102Kc
WHEELAN, Michael		25	M	Laborer	23J102Kc
WYSE, Mary		10	F	Child	23J102Kc
Eliza		08	F	Child	23J102Kc
JOHNSTON, Thomas		23	M	None	23J102Kc
Catherine		21	F	None	23J102Kc
Louisa		16	F	None	23J102Kc
Mary-Ann	(D)	03	F	Child	23J102Kc
Catharine	(D)	.00	F	Infant	23J102Kc
ELLIOT, Mary		25	F	None	23J102Kc
GRACE, Richard		25	M	Laborer	23J102Kc
ADAMS, George		25	M	Farmer	23J102Kc
BANON, Matilda		30	F	None	23J102Kc
Jane	(D)	08	F	Child	23J102Kc
Ellen	(D)	06	F	Child	23J102Kc

HOWARD 23 JULY 1846

From Liverpool

NAMES OF PASSENGERS		AGE	SEX	OCCUPATIONS	DATE PORT SHIP
BURKE, William		30	M	Laborer	23J102Kd
Judy	(W)	22	F	None	23J102Kd
Mary	(D)	.05	F	Infant	23J102Kd
Mary		22	F	None	23J102Kd
COMERFORD, Gerrold		30	M	Laborer	23J102Kd
PHELAN, John		28	M	Carpenter	23J102Kd
Margaret		27	F	None	23J102Kd
BURNS, James		28	M	Laborer	23J102Kd
COSTIGAN, Johanna		27	F	Servant	23J102Kd
KELLY, Hannah		18	F	Servant	23J102Kd
MAKON, Susan-Maria		16	F	Servant	23J102Kd
JOHNSON, Sarah		19	F	Servant	23J102Kd
ROWE, Thomas		18	M	Laborer	23J102Kd
Rebecca		22	F	Servant	23J102Kd
ATWELL, Eliza		20	F	Dressmaker	23J102Kd
GRIFFIN, Arthur		21	M	Laborer	23J102Kd
MALLEN, John		20	M	Laborer	23J102Kd
DUFFY, Thomas		27	M	Laborer	23J102Kd
Mary	(W)	20	F	None	23J102Kd
Owen	(S)	01	M	Child	23J102Kd
FINNIGAN, Michl.		45	M	Laborer	23J102Kd
Nancy		23	F	None	23J102Kd
MCGREGHAN, Susan		25	F	Servant	23J102Kd
SHIELD, Henry		20	M	Carpenter	23J102Kd
John		18	M	Carpenter	23J102Kd
BRACKEN, Robert		27	M	Mechanic	23J102Kd
MCFLINN, Arthur		22	M	Weaver	23J102Kd
DIAMOND, James		18	M	Weaver	23J102Kd
Ann		28	F	None	23J102Kd
PARK, Robt.		30	M	Weaver	23J102Kd
MCMULLIN, Ann		18	F	Servant	23J102Kd
BOW, Judy		22	F	Servant	23J102Kd
MCCABE, Ellen		22	F	Servant	23J102Kd
CONLON, John		21	M	Iron Turner	23J102Kd
WILSON, Wm.		21	M	Iron Turner	23J102Kd
CONNOR, Cathe.		18	F	Servant	23J102Kd
DOWNES, Eliza		18	F	Servant	23J102Kd
Michl.		18	M	Carpenter	23J102Kd
CUMMINGS, Michl.		15	M	Carpenter	23J102Kd
GREGSON, Mary		22	F	Servant	23J102Kd
RYAN, Mary		18	F	Servant	23J102Kd
EATON, Hugh		19	M	Farmer	23J102Kd
HALL, David		19	M	Carpenter	23J102Kd
MCKENNA, Edwd.		18	M	Carpenter	23J102Kd
Cathr.		19	F	Servant	23J102Kd
MCCOURT, Barnard		22	M	Laborer	23J102Kd
Cathr.		21	F	None	23J102Kd

NAMES OF PASSENGERS		AGE	SEX	OCCUPATIONS	DATE PORT SHIP
BREHANY, Pat		30	M	Laborer	23J102Kd
Ellen		25	F	Servant	23J102Kd
RYAN, Thos.		20	M	Servant	23J102Kd
WARD, Mary		22	F	Servant	23J102Kd
DONOHUE, John		20	M	Laborer	23J102Kd
James		12	M	Laborer	23J102Kd
MCCAVE, Francis		18	M	Laborer	23J102Kd
GREEN, Mary-Ann		12	F	Servant	23J102Kd
KELLY, James		18	M	Shoemaker	23J102Kd
DONOHUE, Ally		12	F	Servant	23J102Kd
GREEN, Ann		30	F	Servant	23J102Kd
CONROY, Fanny		17	F	Servant	23J102Kd
QUATE, Charles		23	M	Laborer	23J102Kd
BURKE, Eliza		17	F	Servant	23J102Kd
DONALD, Samuel		25	M	Shoemaker	23J102Kd
QUAYLE, Hugh		20	M	Laborer	23J102Kd
MCLOUGHLIN, Cathr.		12	F	Servant	23J102Kd
MCKIFF, Rose		17	F	Servant	23J102Kd
Fergus		11	M	Child	23J102Kd
KRAMAR, John		23	M	Laborer	23J102Kd
QUAYLE, Owen		13	M	Laborer	23J102Kd
RILEY, Ann		16	F	Servant	23J102Kd
WHEELER, Wm.		26	M	Bookkeeper	23J102Kd
CLARK, Pat		40	M	Laborer	23J102Kd
Mary	(W)	30	F	None	23J102Kd
Martin	(S)	12	M	None	23J102Kd
John	(S)	10	M	Child	23J102Kd
Hannah	(D)	10	F	Child	23J102Kd
SHERDAN, Mary		20	F	Child	23J102Kd
CONLEY, James		23	M	Laborer	23J102Kd
KILCATTY, Owen		24	M	Laborer	23J102Kd
MILIGAN, Barnard		25	M	Laborer	23J102Kd
Bridget		28	F	None	23J102Kd
SURLY, Michl.		20	M	Laborer	23J102Kd
MCPATE, Thos.		35	M	Laborer	23J102Kd
FRENEY, Cathr.		23	F	Servant	23J102Kd
BURKE, Pat		25	M	Servant	23J102Kd
Julia		25	F	None	23J102Kd
STEVENS, John		23	M	Servant	23J102Kd
WALSH, Thos.		26	M	Servant	23J102Kd
HEFFERN, Ewd.		22	M	Laborer	23J102Kd
DUGGAN, Michl.		22	M	Laborer	23J102Kd
COYNE, Thomas		20	M	Laborer	23J102Kd
KELLY, Mary		20	F	Servant	23J102Kd
HUME, John		20	M	Laborer	23J102Kd
GAFFY, Pat		18	M	Laborer	23J102Kd
CLARK, Peggy		30	F	Servant	23J102Kd
TIMOTHY, Cathr.		19	F	Servant	23J102Kd
CARDY, James		24	M	Porter	23J102Kd
ASBOURNE, Peggy		19	F	Servant	23J102Kd
DACY, Cornelius		70	M	Laborer	23J102Kd
TOBIN, John		50	M	Laborer	23J102Kd
Elln	(W)	30	F	None	23J102Kd
Bridget	(D)	03	F	Child	23J102Kd
GALLAGHER, Mary		11	F	Child	23J102Kd
DONOHUE, John		33	M	Laborer	23J102Kd
Dennis		31	M	Laborer	23J102Kd
SULLIVAN, H.		24	M	Laborer	23J102Kd
WHITE, Mary		20	F	Servant	23J102Kd
MANYAN, Mary		20	F	Servant	23J102Kd
FELEAN, Nabby		20	F	Servant	23J102Kd
EVAN, Maty		20	M	Laborer	23J102Kd
FITZMAURICE, Ewd.		19	M	Laborer	23J102Kd
KELLY, Peggy		16	F	Servant	23J102Kd
CARR, Cathr.		24	F	Servant	23J102Kd
KEATING, Jacob		30	M	Laborer	23J102Kd
TUTON, Hannah		23	F	Servant	23J102Kd
GIBSON, John		22	M	Laborer	23J102Kd
Robt.		20	M	Laborer	23J102Kd
OGRADY, Stephen		27	M	Laborer	23J102Kd
Cathr.	(M)	60	F	Servant	23J102Kd
WATKINS, William		20	M	Butcher	23J102Kd
FOX, Ellen		25	F	Dressmaker	23J102Kd
LANE, Andr.		18	M	Laborer	23J102Kd
CASEY, Wm.		26	M	Laborer	23J102Kd
KILROW, James		21	M	Laborer	23J102Kd
FLINN, Tom		74	M	Laborer	23J102Kd
Jane		40	F	None	23J102Kd
Cathr.		16	F	None	23J102Kd
Mary		12	F	None	23J102Kd
Michl.		14	M	None	23J102Kd
MCHERRY, Honora		24	F	Servant	23J102Kd
DALY, Bridget		22	F	Servant	23J102Kd
MAGNUS, Robt.		18	M	Laborer	23J102Kd
Dennis		12	M	Laborer	23J102Kd
Margaret	(M)	50	F	None	23J102Kd
BURNS, Nancy		24	F	Servant	23J102Kd
PURDY, Henry		25	M	Laborer	23J102Kd
Margaret	(W)	20	F	None	23J102Kd
Asa	(D)	.05	F	Infant	23J102Kd
DUGGAN, Mary		18	F	Servant	23J102Kd
FITZPATRICK, Bell		40	F	Servant	23J102Kd
MCGLOCHLIN, Bell		20	F	Servant	23J102Kd
DACY, Ellen		26	F	Servant	23J102Kd
Cathr.		23	F	Servant	23J102Kd
MADDIGAN, Hannah		22	F	Servant	23J102Kd
DEMPSEY, John		20	M	Carpenter	23J102Kd
Michl.		45	M	Carpenter	23J102Kd
Sarah		40	F	None	23J102Kd
James		20	M	Carpenter	23J102Kd
Ally		20	F	None	23J102Kd
Nancy		17	F	None	23J102Kd
Sally		15	F	None	23J102Kd
Rosanna		12	F	None	23J102Kd
Mary		12	F	None	23J102Kd
Michl.		08	M	Child	23J102Kd
William		04	M	Child	23J102Kd
Cathr.		01	F	Child	23J102Kd
DONALD, Ellen		19	F	None	23J102Kd
Margaret	(D)	.06	F	Infant	23J102Kd
CROYN, Kitty		23	F	Servant	23J102Kd

YORKSHIRE 31 JULY 1846

From Liverpool

NAMES OF PASSENGERS		AGE	SEX	OCCUPATIONS	DATE PORT SHIP
DELANY, Michael		40	M	Weaver	31J102Bz
Mary	(W)	38	F	None	31J102Bz
Mary	(D)	20	F	None	31J102Bz
Winefred	(D)	18	F	None	31J102Bz
Ann	(D)	12	F	None	31J102Bz
REDMAN, John		30	M	Weaver	31J102Bz
DUNN, John		20	M	Weaver	31J102Bz
GLENNING, John		26	M	Clfn	31J102Bz
CARROL, James		50	M	Plasterer	31J102Bz
Mary	(W)	40	F	Plasterer	31J102Bz
Helena	(D)	10	F	Child	31J102Bz
James	(S)	08	M	Child	31J102Bz
Pat	(S)	.00	M	Infant	31J102Bz
Eliza	(D)	07	F	Child	31J102Bz
BAKER, Samuel		23	M	Tailor	31J102Bz
EUSHEL, John		30	M	Potter	31J102Bz
Anna-Mrs.		30	F	Potter	31J102Bz
SAMONSON, John		50	M	Weaver	31J102Bz
PEERS, Thos.		26	M	Ctnsp	31J102Bz
TAYLOR, John		26	M	Wool Sorter	31J102Bz
PALEAU, James		34	M	Baker	31J102Bz
Ann	(W)	30	F	Baker	31J102Bz
James	(S)	06	M	Child	31J102Bz
Fredk.	(S)	04	M	Child	31J102Bz
Wllm.	(S)	02	M	Child	31J102Bz
DAVIS, John		28	M	Mechanic	31J102Bz
Mary	(M)	50	F	Mechanic	31J102Bz
Elizabeth	(T)	23	F	Mechanic	31J102Bz

NAMES OF PASSENGERS		AGE	SEX	OCCUPATIONS	DATE PORT SHIP
REYNELES, James		28	M	Wire Worker	31J102Bz
PITCHFORD, Wllm.		22	M	Mechanic	31J102Bz
Ann	(W)	23	F	Mechanic	31J102Bz
Martha	(D)	.00	F	Infant	31J102Bz
COLLEN, Mary		50	F	Blacksmith	31J102Bz
Wllm.	(H)	51	M	Blacksmith	31J102Bz
Robt.	(S)	18	M	Blacksmith	31J102Bz
George	(S)	16	M	Blacksmith	31J102Bz
Emma	(D)	21	F	Blacksmith	31J102Bz
BEVIN, Richd.		60	M	Farmer	31J102Bz
PHILLIPS, John		35	M	Weaver	31J102Bz
Elizabeth	(W)	32	F	Weaver	31J102Bz
Hugh	(S)	13	M	Weaver	31J102Bz
Ann	(D)	11	F	Child	31J102Bz
Jane	(D)	07	F	Child	31J102Bz
Elizabeth	(D)	05	F	Child	31J102Bz
John	(S)	.00	M	Infant	31J102Bz
OWENS, James		40	M	Farmer	31J102Bz
Ann	(W)	35	F	Farmer	31J102Bz
Barna	(D)	16	F	Farmer	31J102Bz
Peter	(S)	11	M	Child	31J102Bz
Phillp	(S)	09	M	Child	31J102Bz
James	(S)	07	M	Child	31J102Bz
John	(S)	04	M	Child	31J102Bz
Emily	(D)	.00	F	Infant	31J102Bz
Frances	(D)	.00	F	Infant	31J102Bz
GAINSON, Mary		20	F	Farmer	31J102Bz
BATEMAN, Thos.		35	M	Farmer	31J102Bz
RATLISH, Mary		24	F	Farmer	31J102Bz
KAIN, Peggy		25	F	Farmer	31J102Bz
MCGUIN, Thos.		26	M	Farmer	31J102Bz
KILLENNY, Thos.		26	M	Farmer	31J102Bz
STUART, Margaret		11	F	Child	31J102Bz
THOMPSON, Mary		16	F	Farmer	31J102Bz
MCCABE, John		26	M	Farmer	31J102Bz
HAMILTON, William		30	M	Mechanic	31J102Bz
TAYLOR, Andrew		24	M	Mechanic	31J102Bz
GORMLEY, Patrick		30	M	Farmer	31J102Bz
KIRK, Susan		20	F	Farmer	31J102Bz
PATERSON, David		40	M	Servant	31J102Bz
TACKNEY, James		20	M	Blacksmith	31J102Bz
HEERY, Mary		20	F	Blacksmith	31J102Bz
MCDONALD, Catharine		21	F	Blacksmith	31J102Bz
FAREAL, Mary		20	F	Blacksmith	31J102Bz
DOHERTY, Rachall		20	F	Blacksmith	31J102Bz
BONNER, Thos.		26	M	Farmer	31J102Bz
WALKER, Thos.		44	M	Farmer	31J102Bz
Alice	(W)	40	F	Farmer	31J102Bz
Richard	(S)	18	M	Farmer	31J102Bz
William	(S)	16	M	Farmer	31J102Bz
Elizabeth	(D)	13	M	Farmer	31J102Bz
Thos.Jepherson	(S)	08	M	Child	31J102Bz
Sarah-Jane	(D)	06	M	Child	31J102Bz
Alice	(D)	.00	F	Infant	31J102Bz
KENNEDY, Mary		12	F	None	31J102Bz
MEEHAN, Wllm.		25	M	Ploughman	31J102Bz
MULLIGAN, Edwd.		20	M	Farmer	31J102Bz
HALE, Robt.		16	M	Farmer	31J102Bz
PARKER, John		26	M	Farmer	31J102Bz
CORK, Samuel		40	M	Farmer	31J102Bz
Thos.		30	M	Farmer	31J102Bz
CLARKE, Mary		20	F	Farmer	31J102Bz
OBRIEN, Ann		20	F	Farmer	31J102Bz
MOORE, Ann		20	F	None	31J102Bz
LOOMIE, John		20	M	Bootmaker	31J102Bz
MCCABE, Ann		20	F	Dry Goods	31J102Bz
GIBBON, John-P.		25	M	Laborer	31J102Bz
WALDRON, Michael		11	M	Child	31J102Bz
Mary		09	F	Child	31J102Bz
CART, Wllm.		13	M	Laborer	31J102Bz
CLYNES, Ann		35	F	Laborer	31J102Bz
BUOVEY, John		20	M	Grocer	31J102Bz
JONES, Charles		20	M	Coppersmith	31J102Bz
PEKIN, James		25	M	Clergyman	31J102Bz
JOHNSON, Archbd.		20	M	Shopman	31J102Bz
MCKEE, Wllm.		20	M	Carpenter	31J102Bz
BOLE, Agnes		60	F	Carpenter	31J102Bz
HAYES, Patrick		.00	M	Infant	31J102Bz
WATERS, Helen		20	F	Carpenter	31J102Bz
WHELAN, Patrick		30	M	Baker	31J102Bz
Margaret		28	F	Baker	31J102Bz
ARMSTRONG, Margaret		25	F	Baker	31J102Bz
MOORE, Margaret		18	F	Baker	31J102Bz
SCALEY, John		23	M	Cooper	31J102Bz
KENNEDY, Mary		22	F	Cooper	31J102Bz
BELL, Mary		22	F	Cooper	31J102Bz
WILSON, James		20	M	Laborer	31J102Bz
HUNTER, Hugh		50	M	Laborer	31J102Bz
Esther	(W)	50	F	Laborer	31J102Bz
Wllm.	(S)	18	M	Laborer	31J102Bz
BOYD, Robt.		18	M	Laborer	31J102Bz
BROWN, Mary		20	F	Laborer	31J102Bz
OBRIEN, James		36	M	Hatter	31J102Bz
RESPIN, John		25	M	Brewer	31J102Bz
MATTHEWS, Patrick		23	M	Barber	31J102Bz
CARAHA, Dennis		26	M	Slater	31J102Bz
BYRNE, Ann		12	F	Slater	31J102Bz
MORRISON, John		20	M	Mechanic	31J102Bz
CRONAN, Ellzb.		25	F	Mechanic	31J102Bz
SHERIDON, Michael		24	M	Tailor	31J102Bz
Peter		22	M	Tailor	31J102Bz
Patk.		20	M	Barber	31J102Bz
Bridget		20	F	Barber	31J102Bz
BRADY, Biddy		20	F	Barber	31J102Bz
CAMPDEN, Robt.		49	M	Farmer	31J102Bz
MCCEATLY, Margt.		20	F	Farmer	31J102Bz
HERN, Hanh.		20	F	Farmer	31J102Bz
CONSATINE, Thos.		30	M	Laborer	31J102Bz
RILEY, Patck.		26	M	Laborer	31J102Bz
RYAN, Patck.		30	M	Laborer	31J102Bz
RYLEY, Edwd.		24	M	Laborer	31J102Bz
FERGUSON, Mary		21	F	Laborer	31J102Bz
RILEY, Patck.		20	M	Baker	31J102Bz
ALDINGTON, George		30	M	Baker	31J102Bz
Jane	(W)	29	F	Baker	31J102Bz
Helen	(D)	02	F	Child	31J102Bz
CREARY, Catharine		21	F	Baker	31J102Bz
SLACK, Elizabeth		36	F	Baker	31J102Bz
Esther	(D)	09	F	Child	31J102Bz
Marla	(D)	.00	F	Infant	31J102Bz
TRAINER, James		25	M	Groom	31J102Bz
MCELGROVE, John		20	M	Farmer	31J102Bz
COUGHLAN, Daniel		20	M	Farmer	31J102Bz
MALONE, Bridget		31	F	Farmer	31J102Bz
COMLEY, Wllm.		24	M	Fitter	31J102Bz
Harrete	(W)	22	F	Fitter	31J102Bz
Ellzb.	(D)	04	F	Child	31J102Bz
Ann	(D)	.00	F	Infant	31J102Bz
BLACKSTACK, James		20	M	Gameskeeper	31J102Bz
Margaret		20	F	Gameskeeper	31J102Bz
BARRY, James		40	M	Builder	31J102Bz
Margaret	(W)	40	F	Builder	31J102Bz
Jane	(D)	25	F	Builder	31J102Bz
Marla	(D)	12	F	Builder	31J102Bz
SIMPSON, Marmaduke		20	M	Farmer	31J102Bz
HAYES, John		09	M	Tailor	31J102Bz
Ellen		04	F	Tailor	31J102Bz
WALSH, Mary		30	F	Farmer	31J102Bz
BARNS, Catharine		20	F	Farmer	31J102Bz
OBRIEN, Margaret		24	F	Farmer	31J102Bz
CLARKE, Frances		30	M	Tailor	31J102Bz
Mary	(W)	30	F	Tailor	31J102Bz
Frances	(S)	04	M	Tailor	31J102Bz
SHERIDAN, Catharine		04	F	Child	31J102Bz
CLARKE, Catharine		.00	F	Infant	31J102Bz
REED, Wllliam		35	M	Musician	31J102Bz
Ellzabeth	(W)	30	F	Musician	31J102Bz
John	(S)	07	M	Child	31J102Bz
Agnes	(D)	05	F	Child	31J102Bz
James	(S)	04	M	Child	31J102Bz

NAMES OF PASSENGERS		AGE	SEX	OCCUPATIONS	DATE PORT SHIP
REED, William	(S)	02	M	Child	31J102Bz
Mary-Ann	(D)	.00	F	Infant	31J102Bz
FIELDING, Ann		40	F	Musician	31J102Bz
Mary	(D)	22	F	Musician	31J102Bz
Elizabeth	(D)	18	F	Musician	31J102Bz
Ann	(D)	13	F	Musician	31J102Bz
BURNS, Mona		23	F	Fisherman	31J102Bz
MALONE, Mary		20	F	Fisherman	31J102Bz
CASSADY, Catharine		27	F	Fisherman	31J102Bz
HART, Stephen		20	M	Tailor	31J102Bz
FINNIGIN, Michael		20	M	Pot Boy	31J102Bz
LYNCH, Patck.		30	M	Laborer	31J102Bz
LOOMIE, Bridget		19	F	Laborer	31J102Bz
SULLIVAN, Mary-Ann		16	F	Laborer	31J102Bz
HEFFERNAN, Margaret		30	F	Laborer	31J102Bz
Richard	(S)	12	M	Laborer	31J102Bz
Ellen	(D)	10	F	Child	31J102Bz
Mary	(D)	08	F	Child	31J102Bz
John	(S)	04	M	Child	31J102Bz
William	(S)	.00	M	Imfant	31J102Bz
BRADY, Richard		50	M	Laborer	31J102Bz
Catharine	(D)	13	F	Laborer	31J102Bz
Thos.	(S)	16	M	Laborer	31J102Bz
CALVERT, Thos.		58	M	Farmer	31J102Bz
Samuel	(S)	20	M	Farmer	31J102Bz
Nathl.	(S)	20	M	Farmer	31J102Bz
Elizabeth	(D)	09	F	Child	31J102Bz
Catharine	(W)	37	F	Farmer	31J102Bz
LAFFRAN, Margaret		25	F	Farmer	31J102Bz
BYRNES, James		18	M	Laborer	31J102Bz
Ann		13	F	Laborer	31J102Bz
Jane		07	F	Child	31J102Bz
BRENAN, Sasha		25	F	Laborer	31J102Bz
RYAN, Mary		24	F	Laborer	31J102Bz
BRENAN, Patck.		40	M	Laborer	31J102Bz
Margaret	(W)	40	F	Laborer	31J102Bz
Catatharine	(D)	20	F	Laborer	31J102Bz
GORMAN, Bridget		20	F	Laborer	31J102Bz
SMITH, Mary		12	F	Laborer	31J102Bz
MILLEDY, Christopher		35	M	Laborer	31J102Bz
KEARNY, Bridget		16	F	Laborer	31J102Bz
FARRINDY, Laurence		20	M	Laborer	31J102Bz
BARRY, Mary		60	F	Laborer	31J102Bz
Edmund	(S)	13	M	Laborer	31J102Bz
WILSON, Willm.		17	M	Laborer	31J102Bz
COOGAN, Thos.		40	M	Laborer	31J102Bz
Essy	(D)	13	F	Laborer	31J102Bz
Catharine	(D)	12	F	Laborer	31J102Bz
John	(S)	10	M	Child	31J102Bz
WATERS, John		50	M	Bt-Shmk	31J102Bz
Ann	(W)	50	F	Bt-Shmk	31J102Bz
Thomas	(S)	12	M	Bt-Shmk	31J102Bz
ENGLISH, Margaret		20	F	Bt-Shmk	31J102Bz
LYONS, Mary		16	F	Bt-Shmk	31J102Bz
HAYES, John		40	M	Tailor	31J102Bz
KELLY, Mary		29	F	Tailor	31J102Bz
CARTWRIGHT, Hannah		30	F	Tailor	31J102Bz
Joseph	(S)	04	M	Child	31J102Bz
Maray	(D)	.00	F	Infant	31J102Bz
KELNAN, Bridget		50	F	Tailor	31J102Bz
Margaret	(D)	08	F	Child	31J102Bz
Thomas	(S)	06	M	Child	31J102Bz
RILEY, Norah		25	F	Tailor	31J102Bz
TOOKER, Ann		37	F	Tailor	31J102Bz
Virginia-Piasscot	(D)	.00	F	Infant	31J102Bz
KENTON, Oliver		16	M	Tailor	31J102Bz
Frances		14	U	Tailor	31J102Bz
Helena		07	F	Child	31J102Bz
Fena		05	F	Child	31J102Bz
CARN, John		20	M	Laborer	31J102Bz
QUINLIONN, Thos.		13	M	Laborer	31J102Bz
LEAVY, Catharine		27	F	Laborer	31J102Bz
Catharine	(D)	.00	F	Infant	31J102Bz
MARTIN, James		25	M	Laborer	31J102Bz
GROGAN, Ann		40	F	Laborer	31J102Bz
GROGAN, Mary-Ann	(D)	02	F	Child	31J102Bz
Rose	(D)	.00	F	Infant	31J102Bz
CAIN, Bridget		23	F	Laborer	31J102Bz
Winifred		24	F	Laborer	31J102Bz
JONES, Elizabeth		28	F	Laborer	31J102Bz
LATTAMORE, Catharine		50	F	Laborer	31J102Bz
FLANAGAN, Dennis		28	M	Laborer	31J102Bz
FITZPATRICK, Elizth.		40	F	Laborer	31J102Bz
WHEELAAN, Laurence		26	M	Laborer	31J102Bz
RILEY, Charles		25	M	Laborer	31J102Bz
DONELLY, Thomas		29	M	Laborer	31J102Bz
MCGUIRE, Ann		35	F	Laborer	31J102Bz
LYNCH, Patrick		06	M	Child	31J102Bz
COPESTOCK, William		20	M	Lace Maker	31J102Bz
LEWIS, Henry		20	M	Potter	31J102Bz
STEPHENSON, Edward-Edw		13	M	Potter	31J102Bz
FEE, Mary		45	M	Potter	31J102Bz
James	(S)	12	M	Potter	31J102Bz
DRUM, Owen		06	M	Child	31J102Bz
Catharine		05	F	Child	31J102Bz
NELLY, Mary		55	F	Potter	31J102Bz
ONIEL, Edward		30	M	Weaver	31J102Bz
Margaret		23	F	Weaver	31J102Bz
GILLESPIE, William		41	M	Tailor	31J102Bz
Elizabeth	(W)	41	F	Tailor	31J102Bz
James	(S)	21	M	Tailor	31J102Bz
William	(S)	13	N	Tailor	31J102Bz
Mary	(D)	19	F	Tailor	31J102Bz
Thomas	(S)	10	M	Child	31J102Bz
John	(S)	08	M	Child	31J102Bz
Bernard	(S)	04	M	Child	31J102Bz
Margaret	(D)	02	F	Child	31J102Bz
Edward	(S)	.00	M	Infant	31J102Bz
FREEMAN, Alice		20	F	Laborer	31J102Bz
MCDONALD, Andrew		24	M	Laborer	31J102Bz
CARBERRY, James		12	M	Laborer	31J102Bz
DWYER, Catharine		20	F	Laborer	31J102Bz
DELANY, Bridget		20	F	Laborer	31J102Bz
SHEA, Mary		20	F	Laborer	31J102Bz
Margaret		17	F	Laborer	31J102Bz
CAHILLAN, Patck.		22	M	Laborer	31J102Bz
KEARNY, Thos.		38	M	Mason	31J102Bz
MURPHY, Thos.		18	M	Laborer	31J102Bz
Judy		20	F	Laborer	31J102Bz
MCINTYRE, Owen		20	M	Laborer	31J102Bz
Bridget		15	F	Laborer	31J102Bz
MCKENNER, John		13	M	Laborer	31J102Bz
MCINNELEY, Mary		66	F	Laborer	31J102Bz
MCMANING, Catharine		26	F	Laborer	31J102Bz
Thos.	(S)	06	M	Child	31J102Bz
John	(S)	01	M	Child	31J102Bz
LEE, Mary		25	F	Laborer	31J102Bz
MCENERY, Catharine		25	F	Laborer	31J102Bz
SIMS, William		22	M	Mason	31J102Bz
OBRIEN, Edward		26	M	Laborer	31J102Bz
John		16	M	Laborer	31J102Bz
EGAN, Margaret		20	F	Laborer	31J102Bz
JEFFE, Nancy		22	F	Laborer	31J102Bz
PINKERTON, Ann		20	F	Laborer	31J102Bz
DOOLEY, Edward		30	M	Laborer	31J102Bz
SCOTT, Mary		20	F	Laborer	31J102Bz
CAFFREY, Jane		60	F	Laborer	31J102Bz
DWYER, Frances		18	U	Laborer	31J102Bz
BRADY, Sasha		20	F	Laborer	31J102Bz
Bridget		16	F	Laborer	31J102Bz
SMITH, Rose		18	F	Laborer	31J102Bz
FINNAGIN, Catharine		14	F	Laborer	31J102Bz
RYAN, Margaret		14	F	Laborer	31J102Bz
HAGGARTY, William		17	M	Laborer	31J102Bz
HEFFERNAN, Margaret		37	F	Laborer	31J102Bz
Christopher	(S)	07	M	Child	31J102Bz
MCGAHAY, Ann		21	F	Laborer	31J102Bz
MAGEE, Margaret		20	F	Laborer	31J102Bz
JOHNSTON, Elizabeth		20	F	Laborer	31J102Bz
BRADY, Margaret		30	F	Laborer	31J102Bz

NAMES OF PASSENGERS		AGE	SEX	OCCUPATIONS	DATE PORT SHIP
COLEMAN, Mary		46	F	Laborer	31J102Bz
Mary	(D)	14	F	Laborer	31J102Bz
Nora	(D)	13	F	Laborer	31J102Bz
Patck.	(S)	10	M	Child	31J102Bz
Judy	(D)	04	F	Child	31J102Bz
FERRY, Margaret		12	F	Laborer	31J102Bz
CONLON, Mary		16	F	Laborer	31J102Bz
SULLIVAN, Ann		18	F	Laborer	31J102Bz
CANNIVAN, Barnard		40	M	Farmer	31J102Bz
Ellen	(W)	30	F	Farmer	31J102Bz
Catharine	(D)	11	F	Child	31J102Bz
Ann	(D)	08	F	Child	31J102Bz
Ellen	(D)	06	F	Child	31J102Bz
Barnard	(S)	02	M	Child	31J102Bz
Daniel	(S)	.00	M	Infant	31J102Bz
MCGAWLEY, Mary		35	F	Farmer	31J102Bz
DAVIS, Bridget		07	F	Child	31J102Bz
CULLEN, Margaret		28	F	Farmer	31J102Bz
Peter	(S)	02	M	Child	31J102Bz
Patck.	(S)	.00	M	Infant	31J102Bz
ROARKE, Catharine		25	F	Farmer	31J102Bz
NICHOLSON, Honey		18	F	Farmer	31J102Bz
Maria		16	F	Farmer	31J102Bz
MAHON, Ann		24	F	Farmer	31J102Bz
Margaret		16	F	Farmer	31J102Bz
MOLLOY, Daniel		23	M	Shoemaker	31J102Bz
FINNERTY, Ann		24	F	Shoemaker	31J102Bz
Thos.	(S)	04	M	Child	31J102Bz
John	(S)	03	M	Child	31J102Bz
KELLY, Mary		19	F	None	31J102Bz
RONAN, Ann		21	F	None	31J102Bz
WILLIAMS, William		28	M	Laborer	31J102Bz

COLUMBIA 31 JULY 1846

From Liverpool

NAMES OF PASSENGERS		AGE	SEX	OCCUPATIONS	DATE PORT SHIP
MALONE, James		37	M	Farmer	31J102Hx
Alice	(W)	40	F	None	31J102Hx
Richd.	(S)	12	M	None	31J102Hx
Bridget	(D)	09	F	None	31J102Hx
John	(S)	07	M	None	31J102Hx
James	(S)	05	M	None	31J102Hx
Bernard	(S)	02	M	None	31J102Hx
Mary	(D)	11	F	None	31J102Hx
BOYLAND, Mary		40	F	None	31J102Hx
MCNEALLY, William		18	M	Shop Boy	31J102Hx
ATKINS, Eliza		22	F	None	31J102Hx
CORBETT, Lawrence		25	M	Painter	31J102Hx
Catharine		17	F	None	31J102Hx
MEAGLE, James		32	M	Servant	31J102Hx
Catharine		34	F	Servant	31J102Hx
MURPHY, James		19	M	Servant	31J102Hx
HONEYFORD, John		25	M	Cbtmkr	31J102Hx
MCGRAME, Michael		20	M	Servant	31J102Hx
BURNS, Pat.		28	M	Laborer	31J102Hx
CLINCH, Pat		20	M	Laborer	31J102Hx
BROWN, David		23	M	Surgeon	31J102Hx
MARSHALL, Jno.		20	M	Clerk	31J102Hx
FAHAY, Pat.		18	M	Clerk	31J102Hx
CROWLEY, Matthew		17	M	Laborer	31J102Hx
REILL, Pat		30	M	Farmer	31J102Hx
Elizabeth	(W)	29	F	None	31J102Hx
Mary-Ann	(D)	06	F	Child	31J102Hx
JOHNSTON, Robt.		28	M	Laborer	31J102Hx
MALLENCY, Michael		23	M	Carpenter	31J102Hx
Abby		19	F	None	31J102Hx
MCGLON, Patr.		30	M	Weaver	31J102Hx
LEE, Wm.		19	M	Farmer	31J102Hx
LEE, Ann		21	F	None	31J102Hx
RILEY, Patr.		21	M	Laborer	31J102Hx
Richd.		18	M	Laborer	31J102Hx
BROWN, Michael		20	M	Laborer	31J102Hx
GAFFNY, Matthew		21	M	Laborer	31J102Hx
EDWARDS, Kate		23	F	None	31J102Hx
Bridget	(D)	03	F	Child	31J102Hx
Margaret	(D)	02	F	Child	31J102Hx
HENNESSY, Mary		19	F	None	31J102Hx
MORESSY, Bryan		29	M	Bootmaker	31J102Hx
Ellen	(W)	23	F	None	31J102Hx
Andrew	(S)	02	M	Child	31J102Hx
CONWAY, Mary		22	F	None	31J102Hx
DONOVAN, Danl.		23	M	Laborer	31J102Hx
CONWAY, Mary		06	F	Child	31J102Hx
BRADY, Hugh		18	M	Laborer	31J102Hx
COPPINGER, John		19	M	Laborer	31J102Hx
MALONEY, Thos.		21	M	Laborer	31J102Hx
SKERRY, Martin		27	M	Weaver	31J102Hx
Ann		23	F	None	31J102Hx
KEFF, John		15	M	None	31J102Hx
MARTIN, Thos.		13	M	None	31J102Hx
COCHRANE, George		13	M	None	31J102Hx
MULLANEY, Henry		28	M	Gdnr	31J102Hx
ADAMS, Jno.		17	M	Laborer	31J102Hx
ARMSTRONG, Wm.		20	M	Laborer	31J102Hx
ONEAL, Biddy		19	F	None	31J102Hx
Ellen		17	F	None	31J102Hx
MCCOY, Thos.		55	M	Laborer	31J102Hx
Jane		30	F	None	31J102Hx
Abraham		21	M	Laborer	31J102Hx
Thos.		17	M	Laborer	31J102Hx
Rose		13	F	Jone	31J102Hx
Mary		08	F	Child	31J102Hx
ROGERS, Catharine		17	F	None	31J102Hx
Patr.		08	M	Child	31J102Hx
ANLEY, Ellen		21	F	None	31J102Hx
ATCHISON, Margaret		20	F	None	31J102Hx
YOUNG, Martha		20	F	None	31J102Hx
MCLEAN, Mary		22	F	None	31J102Hx
HUNGERFORD, Mary		20	F	None	31J102Hx
RILEY, Patr.		33	M	Laborer	31J102Hx
DOOLEY, Catharine		17	F	None	31J102Hx
BRADY, Helen		13	F	None	31J102Hx
CASSOCK, Thomas		19	M	Laborer	31J102Hx
Pat		11	M	Child	31J102Hx
Jno.		10	M	Child	31J102Hx
REIDY, Ann		55	F	None	31J102Hx
PATTON, Thomas		25	M	Laborer	31J102Hx
WALKER, Thomas		19	M	Laborer	31J102Hx
HARRISON, Bridget		60	F	None	31J102Hx
FINLAND, Jno.		13	M	None	31J102Hx
DUNN, Bridget		29	F	None	31J102Hx
Thomas	(S)	03	M	Child	31J102Hx
Matilda	(D)	01	F	Child	31J102Hx
CANON, Mary		25	F	Servant	31J102Hx
RYAN, Sally		25	F	Servant	31J102Hx
James	(S)	04	M	Child	31J102Hx
Thos.	(S)	02	M	Child	31J102Hx
WARNOCK, Bridget		20	F	None	31J102Hx
QUINN, Mary		20	F	None	31J102Hx
Catharine		22	F	None	31J102Hx
HAYES, Mary		09	F	Child	31J102Hx
Thos.		06	M	Child	31J102Hx
FARRELL, Ann		21	F	None	31J102Hx
KENNEDY, Bridget		30	F	None	31J102Hx
GLASGOW, Honora		20	F	None	31J102Hx
HOGAN, Wm.		23	M	Laborer	31J102Hx
MONTGOMERY, John		17	M	Clerk	31J102Hx
HOGAN, Mary		20	F	None	31J102Hx
KENNEDY, Ann		16	F	None	31J102Hx
DOOLAN, Bernard		22	M	Laborer	31J102Hx
MCAFEE, Mary-Ann		07	F	Child	31J102Hx
SIMSKEY, Ann		20	F	None	31J102Hx
ALLEY, Bridget		18	F	None	31J102Hx

NAMES OF PASSENGERS		AGE	SEX	OCCUPATIONS	DATE PORT SHIP	NAMES OF PASSENGERS		AGE	SEX	OCCUPATIONS	DATE PORT SHIP
KING, Margaret		18	F	None	31J102Hx	GRISKELL, Nora		17	F	None	31J102Hx
ROONEY, Michael		26	M	Laborer	31J102Hx	COSTALLEZ, James		25	M	Weaver	31J102Hx
MULLEN, Susan		19	F	None	31J102Hx	MCGINNESS, James		25	M	Laborer	31J102Hx
MANAHAN, Eliza		14	F	None	31J102Hx	MARSHALL, William		13	M	Laborer	31J102Hx
FINN, Bridget		20	F	None	31J102Hx	BRADFORD, Jno.		21	M	Laborer	31J102Hx
MCGUIRE, Mary		25	F	None	31J102Hx	JORDAN, Miles		28	M	Laborer	31J102Hx
Susan		21	F	None	31J102Hx	FINN, Pat		19	M	Laborer	31J102Hx
FLINN, Catharine		20	F	None	31J102Hx	DONOVAN, John		20	M	Laborer	31J102Hx
Alley		28	F	None	31J102Hx	MCGUCKIN, Paul		24	M	Laborer	31J102Hx
ONEIL, Matthew		19	M	Laborer	31J102Hx	RILEY, Jane		18	F	Laborer	31J102Hx
KERRY, Margaret		20	F	None	31J102Hx	BRADY, Mary		21	F	Laborer	31J102Hx
MANNESS, Margaret		19	F	None	31J102Hx	MOORE, Martha		40	F	Laborer	31J102Hx
SAXON, Michael		32	M	Clerk	31J102Hx	Jemima	(D)	17	F	Laborer	31J102Hx
Margaret	(W)	32	F	None	31J102Hx	Mary-Jane	(D)	10	F	Child	31J102Hx
John	(S)	11	M	Child	31J102Hx	James	(S)	08	M	Child	31J102Hx
Catharine		70	F	None	31J102Hx	John	(S)	06	M	Child	31J102Hx
Nora		17	F	None	31J102Hx	BROCK, Mary		26	F	None	31J102Hx
JORDAN, Matthew		20	M	Laborer	31J102Hx	Ann		19	F	None	31J102Hx
LINSKY, Patr.		25	M	Laborer	31J102Hx	MCGOLAN, Ann		20	F	None	31J102Hx
BOYD, James		50	M	Laborer	31J102Hx	LEDDY, Margaret		18	F	None	31J102Hx
Margaret	(D)	19	F	None	31J102Hx	DELANEY, James		21	M	Laborer	31J102Hx
Sarah	(D)	17	F	None	31J102Hx	KING, Catharine		19	F	None	31J102Hx
CASSALY, Mary		28	F	None	31J102Hx	KERMAN, Ann		20	F	None	31J102Hx
OGGAN, Margaret		19	F	None	31J102Hx	HERLY, Ann		20	F	None	31J102Hx
BARRY, Eliza		16	F	None	31J102Hx	NUGEN, Ann		21	F	None	31J102Hx
WELCH, Edward		22	M	Shoemaker	31J102Hx	MCCOY, Eliza		21	F	None	31J102Hx
DOWDELL, Robert		28	M	Laborer	31J102Hx	GREEN, Mary		20	F	None	31J102Hx
BROCKER, Eliza		26	F	None	31J102Hx	MCCOY, Betsey		15	F	None	31J102Hx
DOWDELL, Walter		26	M	Laborer	31J102Hx	SEWELL, Mary		16	F	None	31J102Hx
TEGG, John		20	M	Laborer	31J102Hx	TAYLOR, Susan		16	F	None	31J102Hx
Jane		18	F	Laborer	31J102Hx	THOMPSON, John		17	M	Laborer	31J102Hx
KINNER, James		38	M	Mason	31J102Hx	CORBETT, Danl.		27	M	Laborer	31J102Hx
Margaret	(W)	28	F	None	31J102Hx	GALLAGHER, Biddy		19	M	Laborer	31J102Hx
Julia	(D)	05	F	Child	31J102Hx	SEWELL, John		24	M	Carpenter	31J102Hx
Edward	(S)	02	M	Child	31J102Hx	Margaret		17	F	None	31J102Hx
RUSSELL, Robt.		30	M	Laborer	31J102Hx	MCMONAGAN, Susan		17	F	None	31J102Hx
Ann		30	F	None	31J102Hx	RYAN, Pat		23	M	Laborer	31J102Hx
CLUSKY, John		17	M	None	31J102Hx	THOMPSON, Helen		16	F	None	31J102Hx
MOONEY, James		20	M	None	31J102Hx	RILEY, Rose		26	F	None	31J102Hx
HETHERINGTON, Michael		20	M	None	31J102Hx	Catharine		10	F	Child	31J102Hx
Maria		11	F	Child	31J102Hx	Bridget		03	F	Child	31J102Hx
BRADY, James		24	M	None	31J102Hx	James		01	M	Child	31J102Hx
Mary		18	F	None	31J102Hx	MULVANEY, Julia		24	F	None	31J102Hx
CURRISS, Ann		20	F	None	31J102Hx	Biddy		10	F	Child	31J102Hx
NOLAND, Michael		20	M	Blacksmith	31J102Hx	CALLAN, Timothy		26	M	Mason	31J102Hx
GUIRE, James		30	M	Laborer	31J102Hx	Mary		70	F	None	31J102Hx
Patrick		29	M	Laborer	31J102Hx	TERRAN, Eliza		13	F	None	31J102Hx
THORPE, Mary		40	F	None	31J102Hx	MURRAY, Mary		10	F	Child	31J102Hx
Biddy	(D)	15	F	None	31J102Hx	LILOR, Bridget		20	F	None	31J102Hx
Thomas	(S)	11	M	Child	31J102Hx	TERRENCE, Mary		16	F	None	31J102Hx
Catharine	(D)	10	F	Child	31J102Hx	SIMPSON, Essey		18	F	None	31J102Hx
Rodnie	(S)	07	M	Child	31J102Hx	MASON, Henry		03	M	Child	31J102Hx
William	(S)	05	M	Child	31J102Hx	OCONNELL, Mary		13	F	None	31J102Hx
Martin	(S)	03	M	Child	31J102Hx	DOUGHERTY, Michael		23	M	Laborer	31J102Hx
MALONE, John		30	M	Laborer	31J102Hx	MCCAN, Mary		19	F	None	31J102Hx
Mary	(W)	36	F	None	31J102Hx	GILLAN, Nora		18	F	None	31J102Hx
Mary	(D)	01	F	Child	31J102Hx	FITZPARKER, Betsey		17	F	None	31J102Hx
Helen	(D)	06	F	Child	31J102Hx	DOCKIN, Martin		60	M	Laborer	31J102Hx
Edward	(S)	04	M	Child	31J102Hx	Mary	(W)	60	F	None	31J102Hx
FARRELL, Michael		30	M	Tailor	31J102Hx	Patrick	(S)	12	M	None	31J102Hx
Bridget		22	F	None	31J102Hx	MCNEALLY, Mary		20	F	None	31J102Hx
PETTERY, Mary		17	F	None	31J102Hx	SHERIDAN, Margaret		19	F	None	31J102Hx
Margaret		12	F	None	31J102Hx	WARD, Mary		19	F	None	31J102Hx
REYNOLDS, Mary		17	F	None	31J102Hx	DOCKIN, Margaret		20	F	None	31J102Hx
COFFY, Nancy		30	F	None	31J102Hx	MAHON, Catharine		20	F	None	31J102Hx
John	(S)	08	M	Child	31J102Hx	WALL, Catharine		19	F	None	31J102Hx
SHANNON, Catharine		17	F	None	31J102Hx	REED, James		13	M	None	31J102Hx
ONEIL, Elizabeth		26	F	None	31J102Hx	MCDONALD, Mary		17	F	None	31J102Hx
OCONNELL, Daniel		15	M	None	31J102Hx	BROCKING, Mickey		23	M	Laborer	31J102Hx
Mary		12	F	None	31J102Hx	VAUGHAN, Susan		28	F	None	31J102Hx
Rose		10	F	Child	31J102Hx	BROCKING, Mary		21	F	None	31J102Hx
BRADY, Rose		30	F	None	31J102Hx	DOON, Mary		45	F	None	31J102Hx
REYNOLDS, Mary		13	F	None	31J102Hx	LOWELL, Thomas		16	M	Laborer	31J102Hx
Mary		13	F	None	31J102Hx	RILEY, Bridget		18	F	None	31J102Hx
GRISKELL, Johanna		19	F	None	31J102Hx	MURPHY, Betsy		25	F	None	31J102Hx

NAMES OF PASSENGERS		AGE SEX	OCCUPATIONS	DATE PORT SHIP
HANEY, Catharine		20 F	None	31J102Hx
MARTIN, Catharine		25 F	None	31J102Hx
MCKAY, Mary		23 F	None	31J102Hx
WARD, Patr.		20 M	Laborer	31J102Hx
HOWARD, Patr.		08 M	Child	31J102Hx
HUNTER, Jno.		30 M	Laborer	31J102Hx
DONOVAN, Margaret		21 F	None	31J102Hx
QUIGLY, Ann		23 F	None	31J102Hx
KEENAN, Helen		22 F	None	31J102Hx
ODONNELL, James		24 M	Laborer	31J102Hx
BROWN, Margaret		21 F	None	31J102Hx
MCINTYRE, Catharine		46 F	None	31J102Hx
William	(S)	16 M	None	31J102Hx
GONALLY, James		40 M	None	31J102Hx
Eliza	(D)	20 F	None	31J102Hx
Jane	(D)	12 F	None	31J102Hx
Ann	(D)	09 F	Child	31J102Hx
WARD, Biddy		30 F	None	31J102Hx
Mary	(D)	11 F	None	31J102Hx
Helen	(D)	09 F	Child	31J102Hx
Thomas	(S)	07 M	Child	31J102Hx
Jane	(D)	04 F	Child	31J102Hx
Catharine	(D)	02 F	Child	31J102Hx
MICKLENOY, Margaret		25 F	None	31J102Hx
KEENAN, Ann		16 F	None	31J102Hx
CASSEY, Helen		14 F	None	31J102Hx
MOONEY, Catharine		30 F	None	31J102Hx
DONNELLY, Ann		25 F	None	31J102Hx
FARRELL, Margaret		30 F	None	31J102Hx
RILEY, Alice		32 F	None	31J102Hx
FLANNAGAN, Jane		25 F	None	31J102Hx
LYONS, Ann		16 F	None	31J102Hx
GALLAHER, Mary		20 F	None	31J102Hx
JERVIS, Rose		20 F	None	31J102Hx
WHITE, Betsey		25 F	None	31J102Hx
BURNS, Margaret		18 F	None	31J102Hx
WHITE, Ann		15 F	None	31J102Hx
MCNELLY, Isabella		15 F	None	31J102Hx
FARRELL, Timothy		46 M	Laborer	31J102Hx
FLINN, Barnard		25 M	Laborer	31J102Hx
OHARA, Catharine		19 F	None	31J102Hx
MCDONALD, James		26 M	Laborer	31J102Hx
ONEIL, Nicholas		24 M	Laborer	31J102Hx
MCLAUGHLIN, Helen		40 F	Laborer	31J102Hx
Mary	(D)	12 F	Laborer	31J102Hx
Nell	(S)	07 M	Child	31J102Hx
James	(S)	21 M	None	31J102Hx
CREDDICK, Martin		45 M	Laborer	31J102Hx
FOX, Michael		21 M	Laborer	31J102Hx
CREDDICK, Patrick		02 M	Child	31J102Hx
RILEY, Margaret		18 F	None	31J102Hx
KING, Jane		31 F	None	31J102Hx
Edward	(S)	01 M	Child	31J102Hx
Mary	(D)	02 F	Child	31J102Hx
MURPHY, George		20 M	Clerk	31J102Hx
HODGE, James		40 M	Laborer	31J102Hx
Rose	(W)	30 F	None	31J102Hx
Mary-Jane	(D)	13 F	None	31J102Hx
Sally	(D)	11 F	None	31J102Hx
James	(S)	09 M	Child	31J102Hx
Thomas	(S)	08 M	Child	31J102Hx
Eliza	(D)	04 F	Child	31J102Hx
Saml.	(S)	01 M	Child	31J102Hx
HOW, Nancy		66 F	None	31J102Hx
MCKEENEY, Ann		19 F	None	31J102Hx
MCNELLY, Margaret		17 F	None	31J102Hx
FLINN, Patrick		18 M	Shoemaker	31J102Hx
COCHLIN, Michael		21 M	Laborer	31J102Hx
HUTCHINSON, Ann		19 F	None	31J102Hx
Barbary		17 F	None	31J102Hx
SEWELL, Ann		34 F	None	31J102Hx
Betsy	(D)	16 F	None	31J102Hx
Patrick	(S)	14 M	None	31J102Hx
James	(S)	12 M	None	31J102Hx
Ann	(D)	10 F	Child	31J102Hx

NAMES OF PASSENGERS		AGE SEX	OCCUPATIONS	DATE PORT SHIP
SEWELL, Francis	(S)	08 M	Child	31J102Hx
Mary	(D)	01 F	Child	31J102Hx
CONNELL, Ann		18 F	None	31J102Hx
GLESON, Mary		19 F	None	31J102Hx
MCKNIGHT, Elizabeth		20 F	None	31J102Hx
Mary		18 F	None	31J102Hx
MCCADE, Ann		20 F	None	31J102Hx
CAMP, Robt.		04 M	Child	31J102Hx
LITTLE, Jno.		25 M	Farmer	31J102Hx
Jane	(W)	24 F	None	31J102Hx
John	(S)	04 M	Child	31J102Hx
Isaac	(S)	02 M	Child	31J102Hx
MOGAN, Nancy		20 F	None	31J102Hx
MANILLA, Mary		17 F	None	31J102Hx
Nancy		15 F	None	31J102Hx
OHARE, Francis		23 M	Laborer	31J102Hx
ODONAHUE, Mary		21 F	None	31J102Hx
CARR, Alex		21 M	Laborer	31J102Hx
Mary		22 F	None	31J102Hx
BENSON, James		20 M	Seminarian	31J102Hx
BRADY, John		35 M	Farmer	31J102Hx
Abby	(W)	30 F	None	31J102Hx
Mary	(D)	09 F	Child	31J102Hx
George	(S)	07 M	Child	31J102Hx
MURPHY, Mary-Ann		23 F	None	31J102Hx
MALOY, Henry		18 M	Clerk	31J102Hx
Mary		19 F	None	31J102Hx
COURTNEY, Mary-Ann		25 F	None	31J102Hx
HALY, John		19 M	None	31J102Hx
LOVELOCK, Mary-Ann		17 F	None	31J102Hx
MONTGOMERY, Jane		19 F	None	31J102Hx
Elizabeth		25 F	None	31J102Hx
ROBINSON, Alex.		00 M	Merchant	31J102Hx
BYRNE, William		37 M	Teacher	31J102Hx
Bridget		30 F	None	31J102Hx

ST.GEORGE 03 AUGUST 1846

From Liverpool

NAMES OF PASSENGERS		AGE SEX	OCCUPATIONS	DATE PORT SHIP
MORIARTY, Edw.		36 M	Laborer	03Au02Av
Bridget	(W)	29 F	Wife	03Au02Av
Ellen	(D)	09 F	Child	03Au02Av
Cathe.	(D)	08 F	Child	03Au02Av
Henry	(S)	06 M	Child	03Au02Av
James	(S)	03 M	Child	03Au02Av
BROSNAN, Thos.		28 M	Nail Maker	03Au02Av
Mary	(W)	26 F	Unknown	03Au02Av
U	(D)	.00 F	Infant	03Au02Av
Mary		24 F	Unknown	03Au02Av
Margt.		26 F	Unknown	03Au02Av
Sarah		09 F	Child	03Au02Av
CURREN, Patk.		26 M	Laborer	03Au02Av
KELLY, Jno.		22 M	Laborer	03Au02Av
KING, Mary		24 F	Unknown	03Au02Av
Ann		17 F	Unknown	03Au02Av
MCDERMOTT, Jno.		22 M	Laborer	03Au02Av
HUGHES, Thomas		21 M	Laborer	03Au02Av
BANNIGAN, Michl.		17 M	Laborer	03Au02Av
MADDIN, Cathe.		26 F	Unknown	03Au02Av
U	(D)	.00 F	Infant	03Au02Av
Jno.	(S)	05 M	Child	03Au02Av
LAVELL, Patk.		24 M	Laborer	03Au02Av
GARRITY, James		28 M	Laborer	03Au02Av
Anne		26 F	Unknown	03Au02Av
ENNIS, Danl.		22 M	Blacksmith	03Au02Av
BELL, Mary		46 F	Unknown	03Au02Av
WHITE, Hugh		19 M	Saddler	03Au02Av
MCCULLEN, Bernd.		23 M	Laborer	03Au02Av

219

NAMES OF PASSENGERS		A G E	S E X	OCCUPATIONS	DATE PORT SHIP	NAMES OF PASSENGERS		A G E	S E X	OCCUPATIONS	DATE PORT SHIP
QUINN, Patt		18	M	Laborer	03Au02Av	FINLAY, Patt		21	M	Laborer	03Au02Av
CAIRNS, Racheal		20	F	Unknown	03Au02Av	USHER, Mary		17	F	Unknown	03Au02Av
MCKAGUE, Robert		50	M	Laborer	03Au02Av	KEENAN, Patk.		22	M	Laborer	03Au02Av
Margaret	(W)	35	F	Unknown	03Au02Av	MCGOWAN, Jno.		19	M	Laborer	03Au02Av
Jane	(D)	13	F	Unknown	03Au02Av	MCLOUGHLIN, Geo.		24	M	Servant	03Au02Av
Robt.	(S)	12	M	Unknown	03Au02Av	Margaret		23	F	Unknown	03Au02Av
Edw.	(S)	09	M	Child	03Au02Av	SHEEHAN, James		28	M	Laborer	03Au02Av
MOUNTFORD, Malcolm		13	M	Unknown	03Au02Av	BYRNES, Rose		18	F	Unknown	03Au02Av
OHARRA, James		40	M	Cord Maker	03Au02Av	MCCARTY, Kitty		36	F	Unknown	03Au02Av
MOUNTFORD, Cathe.		36	F	Unknown	03Au02Av	COREY, Judith		22	F	Unknown	03Au02Av
U	(D)	.00	F	Infant	03Au02Av	MULLEN, Ann		30	F	Unknown	03Au02Av
Mary	(D)	12	F	Child	03Au02Av	MIZEN, Sarah		22	F	Unknown	03Au02Av
Alex.	(S)	10	M	Child	03Au02Av	WALSH, Ellen		47	F	Unknown	03Au02Av
William	(S)	08	M	Child	03Au02Av	Johanna	(D)	16	F	Unknown	03Au02Av
Samuel	(S)	06	M	Child	03Au02Av	CAREY, Mary		22	F	Unknown	03Au02Av
Martha	(D)	04	F	Child	03Au02Av	BRADY, Richd.		08	M	Child	03Au02Av
Sarah	(D)	02	F	Child	03Au02Av	George		06	M	Child	03Au02Av
MCCLUSKEY, Cathe.		25	F	Unknown	03Au02Av	DUNNE, Ann		20	F	Unknown	03Au02Av
MCKEOWN, Patk.		26	M	Bricklayer	03Au02Av	Francis		22	M	Laborer	03Au02Av
Mary	(W)	24	F	Unknown	03Au02Av	Sarah		50	F	Unknown	03Au02Av
U	(D)	.00	F	Infant	03Au02Av	BOYLAN, Ann		10	F	Unknown	03Au02Av
CASSIDY, Bernd.		18	M	Carter	03Au02Av	Roseanne		08	F	Child	03Au02Av
RATTIGAN, Mary		18	F	Unknown	03Au02Av	HUNTER, Mary		17	F	Unknown	03Au02Av
WHITE, Mary		19	F	Unknown	03Au02Av	CONNOLLY, Patk.		16	M	Laborer	03Au02Av
MILLS, William		70	M	Weaver	03Au02Av	DUNNE, Jno.		32	M	Laborer	03Au02Av
KEEFE, Mary		21	F	Unknown	03Au02Av	CAMPBELL, Ellen		15	F	Unknown	03Au02Av
MCDONNELL, Daly		18	F	Unknown	03Au02Av	COYNE, Ann		16	F	Unknown	03Au02Av
CORCORAN, Bridget		18	F	Unknown	03Au02Av	FITZPATRICK, Cathe.		20	F	Unknown	03Au02Av
CONNIMS, Margt.		20	F	Unknown	03Au02Av	Mary		11	F	Child	03Au02Av
NEAD, Michl.		35	M	Laborer	03Au02Av	MCGOLRICK, Allice		20	F	Unknown	03Au02Av
HEFFERNAN, David		30	M	Carpenter	03Au02Av	HOLLINS, Jane		21	F	Unknown	03Au02Av
Julia		24	F	Unknown	03Au02Av	Mary-Ann		22	F	Unknown	03Au02Av
U	(D)	.00	F	Infant	03Au02Av	Sarah		19	F	Unknown	03Au02Av
Catherine		16	F	Unknown	03Au02Av	DALY, Bridget		40	F	Unknown	03Au02Av
FLANNIGIN, Jno.		25	M	Mason	03Au02Av	Michl.	(S)	19	M	Unknown	03Au02Av
WORKMAN, Jno.		27	M	Miller	03Au02Av	Danl.	(S)	17	M	Unknown	03Au02Av
COMMONS, James		21	M	Laborer	03Au02Av	Mary	(D)	09	F	Child	03Au02Av
ROONEY, Thomas		25	M	Weaver	03Au02Av	Nancy	(D)	09	F	Child	03Au02Av
Jno.		50	M	Weaver	03Au02Av	LINASEY, Jane		36	F	Unknown	03Au02Av
Sarah		50	F	Unknown	03Au02Av	Cathe.	(D)	11	F	Unknown	03Au02Av
REILEY, William		22	M	Laborer	03Au02Av	CONNELL, Timothy		20	M	Unknown	03Au02Av
KELLY, Issaba.		25	F	Unknown	03Au02Av	Catherine		11	F	Unknown	03Au02Av
BAIR, Mary		20	F	Unknown	03Au02Av	DOOLAN, Thomas		60	M	Laborer	03Au02Av
MCCORMICK, Mary		20	F	Unknown	03Au02Av	Nancy	(W)	60	F	Unknown	03Au02Av
MCCAHARY, Mary		20	F	Unknown	03Au02Av	James		20	M	Unknown	03Au02Av
MCGEEHAN, Bridget		20	F	Unknown	03Au02Av	Rose		16	F	Unknown	03Au02Av
Eliza		18	F	Unknown	03Au02Av	Ann		12	F	Unknown	03Au02Av
MCWILLIAMS, Patk.		18	M	Laborer	03Au02Av	Ellen		08	F	Unknown	03Au02Av
MCGEEHAN, Edw.		16	M	Laborer	03Au02Av	Maria		23	F	Unknown	03Au02Av
ACHESON, Andw.		24	M	Laborer	03Au02Av	U		.00	F	Infant	03Au02Av
KELLY, Gilbert		17	M	Tailor	03Au02Av	COOGAN, Bridget		18	F	Unknown	03Au02Av
RIFFAN, Jane		18	F	Unknown	03Au02Av	MCGILL, Patt		19	M	Laborer	03Au02Av
GERWIN, Joseph		60	M	Mason	03Au02Av	GILROY, Margt.		50	F	Unknown	03Au02Av
Elizth.	(W)	56	F	Unknown	03Au02Av	ANDERSON, Jno.		22	M	Laborer	03Au02Av
Sarah	(D)	25	F	Unknown	03Au02Av	BYRNES, Ellen		20	F	Unknown	03Au02Av
Issaba.	(D)	20	F	Unknown	03Au02Av	MCINTIRE, Thos.		70	M	Laborer	03Au02Av
KELLY, Anne		36	F	Unknown	03Au02Av	BARCLAY, Margt.		18	F	Unknown	03Au02Av
Jane	(D)	18	F	Unknown	03Au02Av	COSGROVE, Robt.		26	M	Shoemaker	03Au02Av
Dennis	(S)	16	M	Unknown	03Au02Av	Elisa		24	F	Unknown	03Au02Av
Mary	(D)	14	F	Unknown	03Au02Av	Patk.		15	M	Unknown	03Au02Av
James	(S)	11	M	Unknown	03Au02Av	GOUGH, Michl.		40	M	Laborer	03Au02Av
Michl.	(S)	05	M	Child	03Au02Av	Ann	(W)	36	F	Unknown	03Au02Av
Bridget	(D)	03	F	Child	03Au02Av	Judith	(D)	14	F	Unknown	03Au02Av
WALSH, Ellen		22	F	Unknown	03Au02Av	John	(S)	02	M	Child	03Au02Av
COWBER, Dorah		19	F	Unknown	03Au02Av	GREANY, Patt		21	M	Nail Maker	03Au02Av
FLYNN, Edw.		21	M	Laborer	03Au02Av	CULLENAN, Mary		17	F	Unknown	03Au02Av
Ellen		19	F	Unknown	03Au02Av	MCDONNELL, Wm.		25	M	Shoemaker	03Au02Av
MAHON, Patt		40	M	Laborer	03Au02Av	Catherine		23	F	Unknown	03Au02Av
Kitty		28	F	Unknown	03Au02Av	BERGEN, Mary		24	F	Unknown	03Au02Av
U	(D)	.00	F	Infant	03Au02Av	SMITH, Bessey		25	F	Unknown	03Au02Av
Thos.	(S)	05	M	Child	03Au02Av	GORDON, Ann		20	F	Unknown	03Au02Av
Jno.	(S)	03	M	Child	03Au02Av	BURKE, Mary		50	F	Unknown	03Au02Av
Martin	(S)	02	M	Child	03Au02Av	Edw.	(S)	20	M	Laborer	03Au02Av
Jno.	(S)	10	M	Child	03Au02Av	DEGNAN, Chas.		20	M	Laborer	03Au02Av
SCALLY, Julia		21	F	Dressmaker	03Au02Av	CALWELL, David		15	M	Laborer	03Au02Av

NAMES OF PASSENGERS	A G E	S E X	OCCUPATIONS	DATE PORT SHIP	NAMES OF PASSENGERS	A G E	S E X	OCCUPATIONS	DATE PORT SHIP
CALWELL, U	14	M	Laborer	03Au02Av	SHEA, John	25	M	Laborer	10Au02Cd
Mary	18	F	Unknown	03Au02Av	STEWART, James	20	M	Laborer	10Au02Cd
STRAW, Thos.	22	M	Unknown	03Au02Av	GRAY, Ellen	36	F	None	10Au02Cd
FIELD, Thomas	40	M	Painter	03Au02Av	William	11	M	Child	10Au02Cd
MCTIER, Ellen	32	F	Unknown	03Au02Av	GAULT, Robert	18	M	Laborer	10Au02Cd
					OSBURN, Deborah	50	F	None	10Au02Cd
					Thomas (S)	22	M	Weaver	10Au02Cd
					John (S)	20	M	Weaver	10Au02Cd
					William (S)	18	M	Weaver	10Au02Cd
					Hugh (S)	14	M	None	10Au02Cd
AVALANCHE 03 AUGUST 1846					Ezekial (S)	12	M	None	10Au02Cd
					Francis (S)	08	M	Child	10Au02Cd
From London					DEVEREUX, Anthony	25	M	Laborer	10Au02Cd
					SMITH, Ann	53	F	None	10Au02Cd
					Thomas (S)	13	M	None	10Au02Cd
DAILY, Thomas	47	M	Tailor	03Au21Eu	Mary (D)	11	F	Child	10Au02Cd
Mary (D)	16	F	Unknown	03Au21Eu	MCGLOUGHLAN, Patrick	23	M	Laborer	10Au02Cd
					ECCLES, Patrick	23	M	Laborer	10Au02Cd
					PURCELL, Bridget	28	F	None	10Au02Cd
					COUGHLAN, Mary	27	F	None	10Au02Cd
					Ann (D)	05	F	Child	10Au02Cd
					Maria (D)	02	F	Child	10Au02Cd
ANN-HARLEY 03 AUGUST 1846					RILEY, John	20	M	Laborer	10Au02Cd
					James	07	M	Child	10Au02Cd
From Glasgow					Felix	05	M	Child	10Au02Cd
					GLEESON, John	34	M	Blacksmith	10Au02Cd
					Ellen	32	F	None	10Au02Cd
KILDARE, Cathrine	35	F	Wife	03Au04Db	DUGAN, Mary	17	F	None	10Au02Cd
Agnes (D)	05	F	Child	03Au04Db	Catharine	17	F	None	10Au02Cd
William (S)	07	M	Child	03Au04Db	Mary	16	F	None	10Au02Cd
Cathrine (D)	03	F	Child	03Au04Db	Nancy	12	F	None	10Au02Cd
James (S)	.05	M	Infant	03Au04Db	MCNESBITT, Bridget	24	F	None	10Au02Cd
DONAHUE, Margaret	30	F	Spinster	03Au04Db	James	22	M	Laborer	10Au02Cd
					COMESGAN, Bridget	20	F	None	10Au02Cd
					CONOLY, Bridget	27	F	None	10Au02Cd
					BEARNE, James	28	M	Laborer	10Au02Cd
					Andrew	27	M	Laborer	10Au02Cd
					ONEILL, John	20	M	Servant	10Au02Cd
					COLLINS, William	23	M	Hrsm	10Au02Cd
STEPHEN-WHITNEY 10 AUGUST 1846					CONDON, Patrick	23	M	Laborer	10Au02Cd
					CONLEY, Margaret	30	F	None	10Au02Cd
From Liverpool					John (S)	07	M	Child	10Au02Cd
					Catharine (D)	04	F	Child	10Au02Cd
					RILEY, Margaret	09	F	Child	10Au02Cd
					MALLEY, Patrick	22	M	Laborer	10Au02Cd
PORTER, James-Andrew-G	18	M	None	10Au02Cd	DUNLOP, Samuel	16	M	Laborer	10Au02Cd
WILSON, Edward-B.Lieut	22	M	Army	10Au02Cd	WILTON, Marianne	26	F	None	10Au02Cd
HAYDEN, John	18	M	None	10Au02Cd	GALLAGHER, James	23	M	Laborer	10Au02Cd
U	20	F	None	10Au02Cd	GAVIN, Michael	20	M	Laborer	10Au02Cd
H.	15	F	None	10Au02Cd	KEARNEY, Patrick	23	M	Laborer	10Au02Cd
BENITT, Edward	18	M	Laborer	10Au02Cd	Martin	21	M	Tailor	10Au02Cd
SHARKEY, Francis	20	M	Laborer	10Au02Cd	TEARAN, Martin	24	M	Tailor	10Au02Cd
MARTIN, Patrick	23	M	Laborer	10Au02Cd	Catharine	21	F	None	10Au02Cd
Bridget	21	F	None	10Au02Cd	HAILEY, John	43	M	Laborer	10Au02Cd
MCDONALD, Michael	21	M	Laborer	10Au02Cd	MCGOVERN, James	21	M	Laborer	10Au02Cd
ONEILL, Michael	38	M	Laborer	10Au02Cd	Walter	14	M	None	10Au02Cd
HART, William	28	M	Carpenter	10Au02Cd	MORNE, Mary	18	F	None	10Au02Cd
FITZPATRICK, William	18	M	Laborer	10Au02Cd	SWEENY, Bridget	17	F	None	10Au02Cd
GOWIST, Mary	17	F	None	10Au02Cd	HIGGINS, Sarah	17	F	None	10Au02Cd
Rosey	28	F	None	10Au02Cd	DALY, Bridget	18	F	None	10Au02Cd
MURPHY, Martha	21	F	None	10Au02Cd	SHERDAN, Edward	24	M	Laborer	10Au02Cd
RILEY, Martin	22	M	Cooper	10Au02Cd	GLASTIRCK, Catharine	07	F	Child	10Au02Cd
Margaret	18	F	None	10Au02Cd	Thomas	14	M	None	10Au02Cd
KEENAH, Bridget	17	F	None	10Au02Cd	RAINEY, Eliza	18	F	None	10Au02Cd
BURKE, Mary	30	F	None	10Au02Cd	PARKER, Anne	32	F	None	10Au02Cd
Michael	12	M	Child	10Au02Cd	CASSIDY, Mary-Jane	15	F	None	10Au02Cd
Maria	05	F	Child	10Au02Cd	GRANGE, Ashanhinst	34	M	None	10Au02Cd
Catharine	00	F	None	10Au02Cd	Jane-Elizabeth	20	F	None	10Au02Cd
OLOUGHLAN, Bridget	20	F	None	10Au02Cd	Helena	26	F	None	10Au02Cd
MALONY, Catharine	20	F	None	10Au02Cd	Martha	24	F	None	10Au02Cd
GOUMONT, William	27	M	Laborer	10Au02Cd	NEILL, Julia	20	F	None	10Au02Cd
John	09	M	Child	10Au02Cd	MURPHY, Mary-Jane	35	F	None	10Au02Cd
Terrence	11	M	Child	10Au02Cd	GILDEA, John	62	M	Smith	10Au02Cd
Patrick	07	M	Child	10Au02Cd	OMEARA, Patrick	26	M	Shoemaker	10Au02Cd
					MCWHITE, Robert	22	M	Farmer	10Au02Cd

NAMES OF PASSENGERS		A G E	S E X	OCCUPATIONS	DATE PORT SHIP	NAMES OF PASSENGERS		A G E	S E X	OCCUPATIONS	DATE PORT SHIP
MCWHITE, Jane	(W)	20	F	None	10Au02Cd	MCPHILIPS, John		19	M	Mechanic	10Au02Cd
James	(S)	.03	M	Infant	10Au02Cd	CAROLL, Peter		24	M	Currier	10Au02Cd
HERNON, James		46	M	Farmer	10Au02Cd	MCGOWAN, James		60	M	None	10Au02Cd
Mary	(W)	40	F	None	10Au02Cd	DEVINE, Ellenor		60	F	None	10Au02Cd
Marianne	(D)	10	F	None	10Au02Cd	HAINEY, Robert		13	M	None	10Au02Cd
Elizabeth	(D)	08	F	Child	10Au02Cd	HAGAN, Edward		34	M	Laborer	10Au02Cd
Susannah	(D)	18	F	None	10Au02Cd	Eneas		08	M	Child	10Au02Cd
George	(S)	15	M	None	10Au02Cd	MAGHER, Margaret		16	F	None	10Au02Cd
James	(S)	12	M	None	10Au02Cd	MULLAN, Margaret		60	F	None	10Au02Cd
FLINN, William		32	M	Laborer	10Au02Cd	HARVEY, Mary		32	F	None	10Au02Cd
FLOOD, Peter		30	M	Laborer	10Au02Cd	MCGUIRE, John		12	M	None	10Au02Cd
Bridget	(W)	24	F	None	10Au02Cd	Patrick		11	M	None	10Au02Cd
Jane	(D)	06	F	Child	10Au02Cd	RUTLEDGE, Catharine		24	F	None	10Au02Cd
Michael	(S)	.05	M	Infant	10Au02Cd	DONLEY, Mary		20	F	None	10Au02Cd
Catharine		26	F	None	10Au02Cd	Bridget		14	F	None	10Au02Cd
MCMAHON, William		22	M	Laborer	10Au02Cd	HALL, Mary		15	F	None	10Au02Cd
John		24	M	Laborer	10Au02Cd	MORNE, Ann		16	F	None	10Au02Cd
PLUNKET, Mary		21	F	None	10Au02Cd	DERMOODIE, Ann		24	F	None	10Au02Cd
CAHILL, Catharine		22	F	None	10Au02Cd	Patrick	(S)	04	M	Child	10Au02Cd
CARLAN, Catharine		17	F	None	10Au02Cd	John	(S)	02	M	Child	10Au02Cd
MOGON, Julia		20	F	None	10Au02Cd	Maria	(D)	.08	F	Infant	10Au02Cd
BAGLEY, Eliza		16	F	None	10Au02Cd	CANARY, Mary		20	F	None	10Au02Cd
MCCANN, Judith		16	F	None	10Au02Cd	COTTER, Johannah		18	F	None	10Au02Cd
FLYNN, Mary		23	F	None	10Au02Cd	MCCLUCKER, Catharine		20	F	None	10Au02Cd
Margaret		18	F	None	10Au02Cd	MCRINN, Catharine		25	F	None	10Au02Cd
HAGAN, Edward		26	M	Laborer	10Au02Cd	Michael		23	M	Laborer	10Au02Cd
Ann		24	F	None	10Au02Cd	EAGAN, Mary		17	F	None	10Au02Cd
MCGUINN, Martin		22	M	Laborer	10Au02Cd	Julia		14	F	None	10Au02Cd
Martin	(S)	.07	M	Infant	10Au02Cd	DONALLAN, Mary		18	F	None	10Au02Cd
GALLAGHER, Winnifred		25	F	None	10Au02Cd	BYRNE, Catharine		18	F	None	10Au02Cd
CAREY, Winnifred		18	F	None	10Au02Cd	CULL, Roger		27	M	Saddler	10Au02Cd
BOYCE, Mary		18	F	None	10Au02Cd	BULMAN, Patrick		16	M	None	10Au02Cd
COX, Mary		20	F	None	10Au02Cd	FOSTER, Charles		21	M	Shoemaker	10Au02Cd
DEVINE, Ellen		20	F	None	10Au02Cd	PATTERSON, Alexander		30	M	Laborer	10Au02Cd
DOGHERTY, Bernard		45	M	None	10Au02Cd	Jane	(W)	28	F	None	10Au02Cd
MURRAY, Patrick		18	M	Laborer	10Au02Cd	James	(S)	11	M	None	10Au02Cd
Ann		17	F	None	10Au02Cd	John	(S)	08	M	Child	10Au02Cd
DOGHERTY, Elizabeth		30	F	None	10Au02Cd	Mary	(D)	06	F	Child	10Au02Cd
FEENY, Cecilia		16	F	None	10Au02Cd	Jane	(D)	03	F	Child	10Au02Cd
HAYES, Dennis		25	M	None	10Au02Cd	Libby	(D)	01	F	Child	10Au02Cd
DOLAN, Patrick		18	M	Laborer	10Au02Cd	Bessie		20	F	None	10Au02Cd
CASEY, Joseph		19	M	Laborer	10Au02Cd	RODGERS, Patrick		20	M	Groom	10Au02Cd
REID, Thomas		26	M	Flaxdr	10Au02Cd	DOCKRY, Bridget		23	F	None	10Au02Cd
CRUMLISH, John		22	M	Flaxdr	10Au02Cd	Michael		20	M	Groom	10Au02Cd
GARNER, Fanny		18	F	None	10Au02Cd	SMITH, Anthony		21	M	Laborer	10Au02Cd
ROBERTS, Jane		20	F	None	10Au02Cd	KENCANNON, Patrick		18	M	Laborer	10Au02Cd
MCKELVIE, Jane		24	F	None	10Au02Cd	Bridget		17	F	None	10Au02Cd
BRADY, Patrick		30	M	Farmer	10Au02Cd	LYONS, Madge		18	F	None	10Au02Cd
CROAK, Richard		23	M	Farmer	10Au02Cd	MARTIN, Edward		35	M	Farmer	10Au02Cd
FEE, Peter		16	M	None	10Au02Cd	Susan	(M)	70	F	None	10Au02Cd
BRADY, U-Mrs.		60	F	None	10Au02Cd	Martha	(D)	14	F	None	10Au02Cd
MALONY, Mary		19	F	None	10Au02Cd	Susan	(D)	04	F	Child	10Au02Cd
MURRAY, Margaret		16	F	None	10Au02Cd	CUFF, Maria		23	F	None	10Au02Cd
LANKINS, Bessie		20	F	None	10Au02Cd	SMITH, Louise		20	F	None	10Au02Cd
CONGENDON, Catharine		40	F	None	10Au02Cd	MCDERMOTT, Mary		12	F	None	10Au02Cd
MCGONIGLE, Mary		18	F	None	10Au02Cd	ANDERSON, William		21	M	Bookkeeper	10Au02Cd
WILLIAMS, James		19	M	None	10Au02Cd	Eliza		20	F	None	10Au02Cd
CASEY, Lawrence		26	M	Saddler	10Au02Cd	DUFFY, James		21	M	Laborer	10Au02Cd
FARLEY, James		16	M	None	10Au02Cd	MCCORMICK, James		18	M	Laborer	10Au02Cd
Peter		13	M	None	10Au02Cd	John		16	M	Laborer	10Au02Cd
Patrick		11	M	None	10Au02Cd	KURAN, Eliza		26	F	None	10Au02Cd
Ellen		09	F	Child	10Au02Cd	MACKIN, Ellen		16	F	None	10Au02Cd
Catharine	(M)	46	F	None	10Au02Cd	CALDERS, Mary		36	F	None	10Au02Cd
CALWELL, Mary		22	F	None	10Au02Cd	Ann	(D)	12	F	None	10Au02Cd
HAMILTON, Edward		19	M	Laborer	10Au02Cd	CAMPBELL, William		19	M	Laborer	10Au02Cd
James		16	M	Laborer	10Au02Cd	MCCABE, Michael		22	M	Laborer	10Au02Cd
Ellen		50	F	None	10Au02Cd	CARTY, Patrick		25	M	Laborer	10Au02Cd
Sarah		12	F	None	10Au02Cd	BRENNAN, Patrick		19	M	Laborer	10Au02Cd
Ellen		14	F	None	10Au02Cd	MONTIETH, Margaret		11	F	None	10Au02Cd
Anne		10	F	None	10Au02Cd	COIL, Ann		53	F	None	10Au02Cd
CONNELL, Alice		18	F	None	10Au02Cd	Ellen	(D)	18	F	None	10Au02Cd
SMITH, Michael		35	M	Shoemaker	10Au02Cd	SMITH, Margaret		14	F	None	10Au02Cd
MCGUIRE, Hugh		19	M	Laborer	10Au02Cd	YOUNG, Michael		20	M	Laborer	10Au02Cd
MAROONEY, Patrick		17	M	Laborer	10Au02Cd	ANDERSON, Edward		22	M	Laborer	10Au02Cd
FERRIS, Michael		26	M	Laborer	10Au02Cd	BRADY, Patrick		23	M	Laborer	10Au02Cd

NAMES OF PASSENGERS	A G E	S E X	OCCUPATIONS	DATE PORT SHIP	NAMES OF PASSENGERS	A G E	S E X	OCCUPATIONS	DATE PORT SHIP
LEDDY, Ann	60	F	None	10Au02Cd	BARNES, Roseann	17	F	None	10Au02Cd
Daniel (S)	15	M	None	10Au02Cd	Ellen	16	F	None	10Au02Cd
Thomas (S)	12	M	None	10Au02Cd	COFFER, Mary	19	F	None	10Au02Cd
MCKENNA, Sally	60	F	None	10Au02Cd	Catherine	17	F	None	10Au02Cd
Mary	11	F	Child	10Au02Cd	IRVIN, Mary	30	F	Servant	10Au02Cd
CULLY, Mary	18	F	None	10Au02Cd					

Illustrated London News, May 10, 1851.

EMIGRANTS ON THE QUAY AT CORK, 1851.

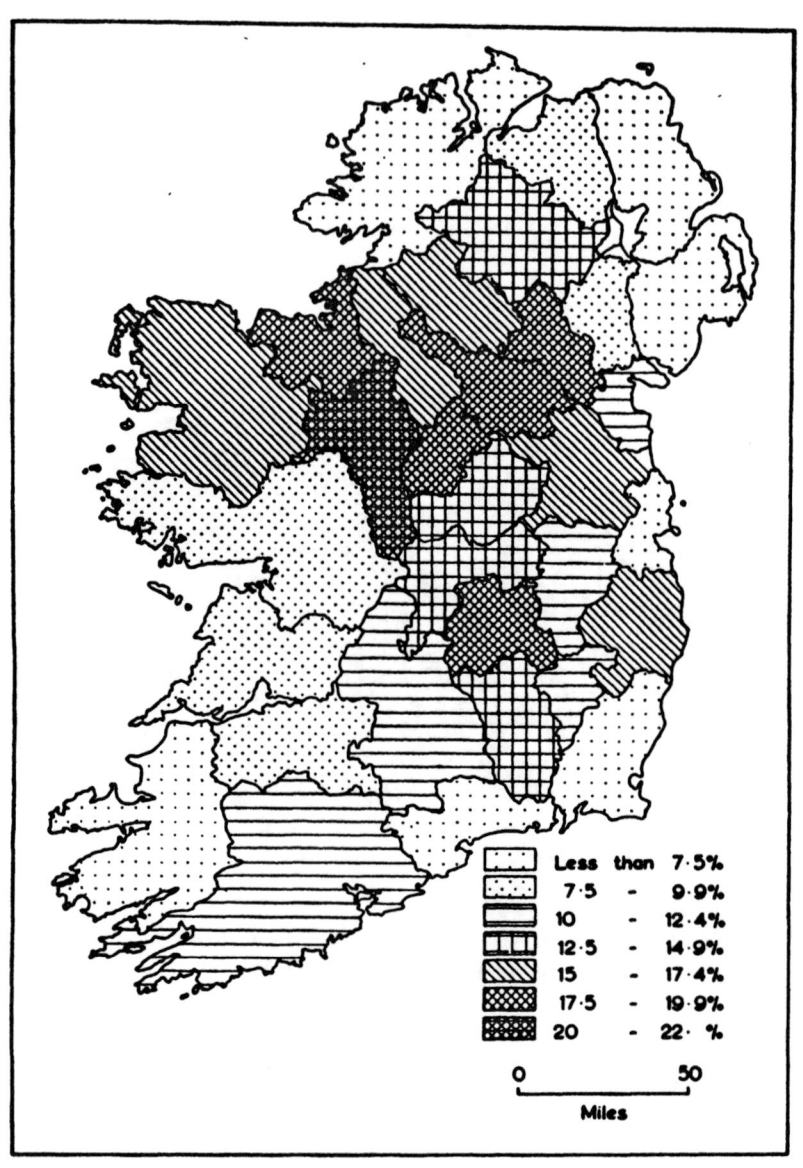

	Less than 7·5%
	7·5 – 9·9%
	10 – 12·4%
	12·5 – 14·9%
	15 – 17·4%
	17·5 – 19·9%
	20 – 22· %

0   50

Miles

**EMIGRATION DURING THE FAMINE, 1846-1851,
AS A PERCENTAGE OF THE POPULATION IN 1841**

From "The Regional Pattern of Emigration During the Great Irish Famine,
1846-1851," by S. H. Cousens, in *Transactions and Papers of the Institute of British
Geographers*, No. 28, 1960. Reprinted with permission.

					GIVIMY, Judy	19	F	Servant	10Au02Fm
					OGAN, Cath.	21	F	Servant	10Au02Fm
					MORRIS, Thomas	30	M	Servant	10Au02Fm
					Teresa	30	F	Servant	10Au02Fm
OCEAN-QUEEN 10 AUGUST 1846					WILLIAMS, Mary	26	F	Servant	10Au02Fm
					Margret (D)	04	F	Child	10Au02Fm
From Liverpool					MARMION, Ryan	24	M	Servant	10Au02Fm
					Daniel	20	M	Servant	10Au02Fm
					BRADY, Andrew	20	M	Servant	10Au02Fm
					Cath.	21	F	Servant	10Au02Fm
KENNY, Peter	27	M	Laborer	10Au02Fm	REILLY, Thomas	03	M	Child	10Au02Fm
Mary	20	F	Servant	10Au02Fm	FULLY, Patrick	21	M	Servant	10Au02Fm
QUINN, Elenor	19	F	Servant	10Au02Fm	KENNY, John	19	M	Servant	10Au02Fm
Eliza	20	F	Servant	10Au02Fm	MORROW, Jane	20	F	Servant	10Au02Fm
MCCARRON, Alice	20	F	Servant	10Au02Fm	MCWILLIAM, Alice	30	F	Servant	10Au02Fm
CANNON, Mary	20	F	Servant	10Au02Fm	MCMULLIN, Clarabell	19	F	Servant	10Au02Fm
DONNELLY, Ellen	20	F	Servant	10Au02Fm	BRADY, James	20	M	Servant	10Au02Fm
BAYLEY, Elizabeth	17	F	Servant	10Au02Fm	KENNEDDY, Thimothy	21	M	Servant	10Au02Fm
CAIRNES, Mary	18	F	Servant	10Au02Fm	Susanah	18	F	Servant	10Au02Fm
KEAN, Patrick	45	M	Servant	10Au02Fm	BRACKEN, Margret	21	F	Servant	10Au02Fm
U (W)	40	F	Servant	10Au02Fm	ROURKE, Mary	21	F	Servant	10Au02Fm
Mary (D)	22	F	Servant	10Au02Fm	Mary	36	F	Servant	10Au02Fm
Eliza (D)	20	F	Servant	10Au02Fm	MCCABE, James	21	M	Servant	10Au02Fm
Bridget (D)	13	F	Servant	10Au02Fm	HAMMILL, Peter	21	M	Servant	10Au02Fm
John (S)	12	M	Servant	10Au02Fm	MILES, James	20	M	Servant	10Au02Fm
Harriett (D)	03	F	Child	10Au02Fm	DOWN, Rosey	19	F	Servant	10Au02Fm
LENHAN, Ann	17	F	Servant	10Au02Fm	James	16	M	Servant	10Au02Fm
Mary	11	F	Servant	10Au02Fm	WHITE, James	22	M	Servant	10Au02Fm
WALSH, John	16	M	Servant	10Au02Fm	WILLIAMS, William	35	M	Servant	10Au02Fm
ROWLAN, Mary	26	F	Servant	10Au02Fm	HUTCHINS, Thomas	35	M	Servant	10Au02Fm
Biddy (D)	04	F	Child	10Au02Fm	EVANS, William	20	M	Servant	10Au02Fm
Mary (D)	03	F	Child	10Au02Fm	KENNY, Mary	28	F	Servant	10Au02Fm
LANFORD, Marcella	17	F	Servant	10Au02Fm	Cath. (D)	08	F	Child	10Au02Fm
CUSBY, Judy	16	F	Servant	10Au02Fm	Elizabeth (D)	03	F	Child	10Au02Fm
POWER, Margaret	17	F	Servant	10Au02Fm	James (S)	01	M	Child	10Au02Fm
CARROLL, Francis	50	M	Servant	10Au02Fm	Sarah	26	F	Servant	10Au02Fm
U (W)	45	F	Servant	10Au02Fm	MCLAUGHLIN, John	25	M	Servant	10Au02Fm
Ellen (D)	16	F	Servant	10Au02Fm	DUFFY, Michael	20	M	Servant	10Au02Fm
Cath. (D)	10	F	Servant	10Au02Fm	MURPHY, Margret	18	F	Servant	10Au02Fm
Patrick (S)	06	M	Child	10Au02Fm	PURCELL, Patt	20	M	Servant	10Au02Fm
GLEASON, Judy	20	F	Servant	10Au02Fm	Margret	19	F	Servant	10Au02Fm
CARROLL, Mary	25	F	Servant	10Au02Fm	TEIRNEY, Darby	19	M	Servant	10Au02Fm
Judy	20	F	Servant	10Au02Fm	TREACY, Patt	19	M	Servant	10Au02Fm
Margaret	18	F	Servant	10Au02Fm	HIGHLAND, Maria	18	F	Servant	10Au02Fm
TINDELL, Thomas	40	M	Servant	10Au02Fm	SULLIVAN, Jane	18	F	Servant	10Au02Fm
SHERRY, Robert	28	M	Servant	10Au02Fm	MCFALLAND, Robert	28	M	Servant	10Au02Fm
MCGOWAN, Ann	30	F	Servant	10Au02Fm	Martha (W)	23	F	Servant	10Au02Fm
BOND, Thomas	12	M	Servant	10Au02Fm	Jane (D)	.00	F	Infant	10Au02Fm
DALEY, Bridget	19	F	Servant	10Au02Fm	CASEY, Judith	19	F	Servant	10Au02Fm
Cath.	18	F	Servant	10Au02Fm	GRAY, James	21	M	Servant	10Au02Fm
CUNNINGHAM, Ellen	16	F	Servant	10Au02Fm	HICKEY, Biddy	30	F	Servant	10Au02Fm
Cath.	20	F	Servant	10Au02Fm	CASEY, Julia	15	F	Servant	10Au02Fm
Bridget	11	F	Unknown	10Au02Fm	MCALARNEY, Biddy	19	F	Servant	10Au02Fm
Mary-Ann	12	F	Unknown	10Au02Fm	TOLEY, Catherine	21	F	Servant	10Au02Fm
Daniel	09	M	Child	10Au02Fm	RYAN, Thomas	23	M	Servant	10Au02Fm
John	03	M	Child	10Au02Fm	KELLY, Eliza	19	F	Servant	10Au02Fm
DONALD, Ann	16	F	Servant	10Au02Fm	HAGGERTY, Ann	19	F	Servant	10Au02Fm
MCCABE, Mary	14	F	Servant	10Au02Fm	SPELLMAN, Michael	19	M	Servant	10Au02Fm
CRAWLEY, Thomas	30	M	Servant	10Au02Fm	RYAN, Biddy	14	F	Servant	10Au02Fm
Bridget (W)	30	F	Servant	10Au02Fm	FINNIGAN, Patt	25	M	Servant	10Au02Fm
James (S)	05	M	Child	10Au02Fm	Ann (W)	20	F	Servant	10Au02Fm
SMITH, Andrew	19	M	Servant	10Au02Fm	Biddy (D)	.00	F	Infant	10Au02Fm
MCKEE, Terence	19	M	Servant	10Au02Fm	QUIGLY, Paddy	20	M	Laborer	10Au02Fm
WOOD, Susan	17	F	Servant	10Au02Fm	KADDIGAN, James	19	M	Laborer	10Au02Fm
HODGES, Ann	18	F	Servant	10Au02Fm	CONNOLLY, Biddy	19	F	Servant	10Au02Fm
SULLY, U	36	M	Servant	10Au02Fm	CAIN, Mary	19	F	Servant	10Au02Fm
FLAHERTY, U-Mrs.	49	F	Servant	10Au02Fm	MALADY, Ann	36	F	Servant	10Au02Fm
U	17	F	Servant	10Au02Fm	DOUGHERTY, Mary	11	F	Unknown	10Au02Fm
KEARNEY, Maria	20	F	Servant	10Au02Fm	Peggy	04	F	Child	10Au02Fm
HODGERS, Mary	24	F	Servant	10Au02Fm	James	00	M	Unknown	10Au02Fm
MCINTOCH, Mary	20	F	Servant	10Au02Fm	Ann	00	F	Unknown	10Au02Fm
BRADLEY, Ann	36	F	Servant	10Au02Fm	CONROY, Miles	40	M	Unknown	10Au02Fm
CROSSLEY, U	20	F	Servant	10Au02Fm	FINNIGAN, Cath.	02	F	Child	10Au02Fm
RYAN, Michael	20	M	Servant	10Au02Fm	CONROY, Ann	40	F	Unknown	10Au02Fm
ROARK, John	17	M	Servant	10Au02Fm	CARNEY, Ann	18	F	Unknown	10Au02Fm

NAMES OF PASSENGERS	AGE	SEX	OCCUPATIONS	DATE PORT SHIP	NAMES OF PASSENGERS	AGE	SEX	OCCUPATIONS	DATE PORT SHIP
REYNOLDS, Bess	16	F	Servant	10Au02Fm	MADDEN, Thomas	50	M	Servant	10Au02Fm
FLEAMAN, Michael	30	M	Servant	10Au02Fm	William	18	M	Servant	10Au02Fm
RYAN, Honora	20	F	Servant	10Au02Fm	Honora	16	F	Servant	10Au02Fm
WATERS, William	22	M	Servant	10Au02Fm	Patrick	13	M	Servant	10Au02Fm
NEUMAN, J.	30	M	Servant	10Au02Fm	Mary	11	F	Unknown	10Au02Fm
Sophia	30	F	Servant	10Au02Fm	Daniel	06	M	Child	10Au02Fm
Abraham	50	M	Servant	10Au02Fm	CARLTON, Mary	32	F	Servant	10Au02Fm
GRENON, Helena	19	F	Servant	10Au02Fm	Ellen	30	F	Cook	10Au02Fm
HEPSTAM, Sophia	50	F	Servant	10Au02Fm	HENRIGHT, Daniel	35	M	Servant	10Au02Fm
COFFMAN, Levy	19	M	Servant	10Au02Fm	GROGAN, John	40	M	Servant	10Au02Fm
Alvin	50	M	Servant	10Au02Fm	HUNT, James	35	M	Servant	10Au02Fm
OCHTAUGN, Mena	18	F	Servant	10Au02Fm	CONNELL, Denny	30	M	Servant	10Au02Fm
DENAN, Mic	07	F	Child	10Au02Fm	BERWICK, Mathew	21	M	Servant	10Au02Fm
Mary	06	F	Child	10Au02Fm	MONALENY, Mary	18	F	Servant	10Au02Fm
Kissy	.00	F	Infant	10Au02Fm	COAKLEY, Dennis	58	M	Servant	10Au02Fm
DALY, Arthur	54	M	Servant	10Au02Fm	U (W)	50	F	Servant	10Au02Fm
Ellen	23	F	Servant	10Au02Fm	CAIN, Daniel	30	M	Servant	10Au02Fm
Mary	20	F	Servant	10Au02Fm	Mary	25	F	[ervant	10Au02Fm
Ellen	15	F	Servant	10Au02Fm	MCCARTHY, Alexander	20	M	Servant	10Au02Fm
DOONAN, Ann	05	F	Child	10Au02Fm	MCGUNNEY, James	20	M	Servant	10Au02Fm
FINNGAN, Peggy	35	F	Servant	10Au02Fm	WALSH, Bridget	40	F	Servant	10Au02Fm
CRAVEN, Ann	18	F	Servant	10Au02Fm	REARDON, Cath.	17	F	Servant	10Au02Fm
MCFEE, William	20	M	Servant	10Au02Fm	GLEASON, Teddy	17	M	Servant	10Au02Fm
KING, James	20	M	Servant	10Au02Fm	GAMBLE, Samuel	35	M	Servant	10Au02Fm
BLACK, Nell	20	M	Servant	10Au02Fm	SCOTT, James	34	M	Servant	10Au02Fm
Peggy-Jane	18	F	Servant	10Au02Fm	TRACEY, Pat	46	M	Servant	10Au02Fm
KING, Mary	17	F	Servant	10Au02Fm	KITCHEN, Danl.	30	M	Servant	10Au02Fm
Mary-Jane	21	F	Servant	10Au02Fm	REARDON, Peggy	20	F	Servant	10Au02Fm
HUNTER, James	20	M	Servant	10Au02Fm	SENA, Mary	65	F	Servant	10Au02Fm
MCKILLAY, Isabella	19	F	Servant	10Au02Fm	John	22	M	Servant	10Au02Fm
MCGREEGAN, Thomas	20	M	Servant	10Au02Fm	Catherine	26	F	Servant	10Au02Fm
Sally	19	F	Servant	10Au02Fm	ONEILL, John	40	M	Servant	10Au02Fm
Bridget	32	F	Servant	10Au02Fm	Ann	18	F	Servant	10Au02Fm
MCGUIRE, Ann	19	F	Servant	10Au02Fm	BRESLIN, Wm.	26	M	Servant	10Au02Fm
JOHNSTON, James	31	M	Servant	10Au02Fm	Ellen (W)	20	F	Servant	10Au02Fm
MCCREALAND, Michael	46	M	Servant	10Au02Fm	John (S)	.00	M	Infant	10Au02Fm
ROBERTS, Humphrey	50	M	Servant	10Au02Fm	RYAN, Tim	27	M	Servant	10Au02Fm
Henry	26	M	Farmer	10Au02Fm	Bridget	22	F	Servant	10Au02Fm
John	23	M	Farmer	10Au02Fm	Ann	22	F	Servant	10Au02Fm
Owen	11	M	Farmer	10Au02Fm	MALONEY, Austin	25	M	Servant	10Au02Fm
Humphrey	22	M	Servant	10Au02Fm	Margt.	23	F	Servant	10Au02Fm
GIDNISS, Francis	19	M	Servant	10Au02Fm	CLARKSON, Thos.	56	M	Servant	10Au02Fm
URYNHART, Robert	25	M	Servant	10Au02Fm	LEDDIE, Henry	22	M	Servant	10Au02Fm
WHILIE, Andrew	30	M	Servant	10Au02Fm	Mark	21	M	Servant	10Au02Fm
NELSON, William	30	M	Servant	10Au02Fm	HAGAN, Michl.	29	M	Servant	10Au02Fm
NICKEL, George	45	M	Servant	10Au02Fm	FITZPATRICK, Thomas	27	M	Servant	10Au02Fm
NELSON, Maria	20	F	Servant	10Au02Fm	WILLIAMSON, James	30	M	Laborer	10Au02Fm
TAYLOR, Joseph	28	M	Servant	10Au02Fm	ISANLONE, David	30	M	Laborer	10Au02Fm
PRICE, Ann	13	F	Servant	10Au02Fm	HARDING, Robert	60	M	Laborer	10Au02Fm
KEGHAN, Sally	20	F	Servant	10Au02Fm	Sarah	20	F	Wife	10Au02Fm
DOWLAN, Jane	24	F	Servant	10Au02Fm	U (W)	60	F	Wife	10Au02Fm
WHITES, Pat	24	M	Servant	10Au02Fm	BRYAN, Mary	20	F	Unknown	10Au02Fm
U (W)	25	F	Servant	10Au02Fm	U, U	.00	U	Infant	10Au02Fm
ARMSTRONG, Elizabeth	21	F	Servant	10Au02Fm	Born-At-Sea				
HUCKEDY, James	30	M	Servant	10Au02Fm					
MCCARTHY, Pat	40	M	Servant	10Au02Fm					
DUNN, Thomas	18	M	Servant	10Au02Fm					
COMERTY, Maria	20	F	Servant	10Au02Fm					
LENNAGON, Eliza	21	F	Servant	10Au02Fm					
HAYS, Eliza	21	F	Servant	10Au02Fm	GREAT-WESTERN 10 AUGUST 1846				
HARPER, Jane	20	F	Servant	10Au02Fm					
FLYNN, Mary	18	F	Servant	10Au02Fm	From Liverpool				
Sarah	45	F	Servant	10Au02Fm					
HOLIDAY, Cath.	28	F	Servant	10Au02Fm					
Eliza	12	F	Servant	10Au02Fm					
George	27	M	Servant	10Au02Fm	SMITH, Peter	45	M	Gentleman	10Au02Cy
BRYAN, Patt	30	M	Servant	10Au02Fm	Patrick	46	M	Gentleman	10Au02Cy
MACHAN, James	24	M	Servant	10Au02Fm	U	14	F	Lady	10Au02Cy
SHEANS, Corney	24	M	Servant	10Au02Fm					
Owen	30	M	Servant	10Au02Fm					
MCDUFF, Phillip	25	M	Servant	10Au02Fm					
Mary	13	F	Servant	10Au02Fm					
Eliza	05	F	Child	10Au02Fm					
Ellen	55	F	Servant	10Au02Fm					
Noray	03	F	Child	10Au02Fm					

NORTHUMBERLAND 12 AUGUST 1846

From London

NAMES OF PASSENGERS		AGE	SEX	OCCUPATIONS	DATE PORT SHIP
ALMA, Mary		19	F	Unknown	12Au21Cg
Emily-J.		17	F	Unknown	12Au21Cg
Edward-J.		13	M	Unknown	12Au21Cg
Catharine		07	F	Child	12Au21Cg
BRADSHAW, Thos.		38	M	Gentleman	12Au21Cg
Mary	(W)	26	F	Lady	12Au21Cg
Maria-A.	(D)	06	F	Child	12Au21Cg
SEABROOK, Mary-A.		48	F	Unknown	12Au21Cg
FLETCHER, Sarah		27	F	Unknown	12Au21Cg
CRAMPTON, Joseph		20	M	Engineer	12Au21Cg
SUMMERS, George-J.		15	M	Unknown	12Au21Cg
CHANDLER, James		45	M	Artist	12Au21Cg
Sarah	(W)	53	F	Unknown	12Au21Cg
Jane	(D)	13	F	Unknown	12Au21Cg
Elizabeth	(D)	11	F	Child	12Au21Cg
WILLIAMSON, Thomas		47	M	Laborer	12Au21Cg
MAITEN, John		29	M	Farmer	12Au21Cg
SULIVAN, John		36	M	Carpenter	12Au21Cg
SHEPHERD, Joseph		48	M	Brewer	12Au21Cg
Mary	(W)	48	F	Unknown	12Au21Cg
Joseph	(S)	18	M	Unknown	12Au21Cg
Saml.	(S)	13	M	Unknown	12Au21Cg
Mary	(D)	10	F	Unknown	12Au21Cg
PENTIN, Ann		18	F	Unknown	12Au21Cg
PAVES, Mary-A.		38	F	Unknown	12Au21Cg
Mary-A.	(D)	07	F	Child	12Au21Cg
SHEPHERD, Ann		28	F	Unknown	12Au21Cg
ADES, John		33	M	Butcher	12Au21Cg
DEGGS, George		27	M	Butcher	12Au21Cg
HOPKINS, Thos.		16	M	Butcher	12Au21Cg
ROBERTS, Emily		23	F	Unknown	12Au21Cg
PEASAT, Wm.		11	M	Child	12Au21Cg
MCKAY, Julia		57	F	Unknown	12Au21Cg
CONNER, Chas.		23	M	Laborer	12Au21Cg
PARSONS, Robt.		24	M	Clerk	12Au21Cg
NICHOLAS, Edward		38	M	Clerk	12Au21Cg
CEMALE, Geo.W.		17	M	Carpenter	12Au21Cg
VANCE, Cornelius		17	M	Joiner	12Au21Cg
ELIOTT, Mary		35	F	Unknown	12Au21Cg
James	(S)	15	M	Unknown	12Au21Cg
Mary	(D)	14	F	Unknown	12Au21Cg
Eliza	(D)	12	F	Unknown	12Au21Cg
Jerry	(S)	11	M	Unknown	12Au21Cg
George	(S)	07	M	Child	12Au21Cg
JACOB, Joseph		24	M	Brf	12Au21Cg
Mary-A.		20	F	Unknown	12Au21Cg
TOWNE, Thos.		33	M	Farrier	12Au21Cg
ELDRED, John		25	M	Farrier	12Au21Cg
Edward		22	M	Wheelwright	12Au21Cg
ELLIS, Matigen		25	M	Farmer	12Au21Cg
DUKES, John		38	M	Engineer	12Au21Cg
WELLES, Lucy		26	F	Unknown	12Au21Cg
Wm.	(S)	01	M	Child	12Au21Cg
CRAFT, Frank		24	M	Clerk	12Au21Cg
WATSON, George		25	M	Farmer	12Au21Cg
William		22	M	Farmer	12Au21Cg
SAUNTER, William		40	M	Saw Maker	12Au21Cg
Jane	(W)	35	F	Unknown	12Au21Cg
Jane	(D)	17	F	Unknown	12Au21Cg
Ann	(D)	12	F	Unknown	12Au21Cg
Ellen	(D)	13	F	Unknown	12Au21Cg
Selina	(D)	11	F	Unknown	12Au21Cg
William	(S)	06	M	Child	12Au21Cg
METCALF, Wm.		29	M	Blacksmith	12Au21Cg
Henry		26	M	Grocer	12Au21Cg
METCALF, John		24	M	Grocer	12Au21Cg
Frank		15	M	Grocer	12Au21Cg
Sarah		32	F	Unknown	12Au21Cg
Jane		30	F	Unknown	12Au21Cg
HAYWOOD, Sophia		40	F	Unknown	12Au21Cg
BOSTELO, Wm.		54	M	Painter	12Au21Cg
MESHEN, Reuben		25	M	Farrier	12Au21Cg
HENLEY, Edw.		05	M	Child	12Au21Cg
PILS, Sarah		41	F	Unknown	12Au21Cg
Eliza		12	F	Unknown	12Au21Cg
John		08	M	Child	12Au21Cg
Mary		06	F	Child	12Au21Cg
Sarah		04	F	Child	12Au21Cg

CHAOS 12 AUGUST 1846

From Liverpool

NAMES OF PASSENGERS		AGE	SEX	OCCUPATIONS	DATE PORT SHIP
FITZ, William-Thomas		25	M	Cbtmkr	12Au02Gg
Charlotte-Jane		22	F	None	12Au02Gg
MARA, Patt		23	M	Carpenter	12Au02Gg
Elizabeth		19	F	None	12Au02Gg
DOYLE, Martin		20	M	Laborer	12Au02Gg
KELLY, Catherine		20	F	Servant	12Au02Gg
MCSORLEY, Margaret		30	F	Shoemaker	12Au02Gg
Bridget		21	F	Shoemaker	12Au02Gg
Michael		10	M	Unknown	12Au02Gg
Mary		08	F	Child	12Au02Gg
Patrick		05	M	Child	12Au02Gg
John		02	M	Child	12Au02Gg
Died-At-Sea					
Maryann		.00	F	Infant	12Au02Gg
GAKINS, William		40	M	Laborer	12Au02Gg
Margaret	(W)	35	F	None	12Au02Gg
Sarah	(D)	05	F	Child	12Au02Gg
Letitia	(D)	02	F	Child	12Au02Gg
MAGUIRE, Peter		51	M	Butcher	12Au02Gg
Owen		15	M	Butcher	12Au02Gg
MCNAMARA, Owen		24	M	Laborer	12Au02Gg
MCMURREY, John		20	M	Laborer	12Au02Gg
CURLEY, Ann		16	F	Servant	12Au02Gg
PADDEN, Bridget		18	F	Servant	12Au02Gg
CORCORAN, Bridget		19	F	Servant	12Au02Gg
Patrick	(S)	10	M	Unknown	12Au02Gg
MCLAUGHLIN, Thomas		21	M	Laborer	12Au02Gg
MURPHY, John		20	M	Laborer	12Au02Gg
LEAN, Josiah		21	M	Laborer	12Au02Gg
KEEGAN, William		24	M	Laborer	12Au02Gg
FARRELL, Jane		23	F	Servant	12Au02Gg
KAVANAGH, John		28	M	Laborer	12Au02Gg
DOLAN, Sarah		22	F	Servant	12Au02Gg
Catherine		25	F	Servant	12Au02Gg
TEWBET, Catherine		20	F	Servant	12Au02Gg
ROACH, Celia		22	F	Servant	12Au02Gg
FARRALL, Mary		22	F	Servant	12Au02Gg
LAMB, Patt		21	M	Whitesmith	12Au02Gg
Mary		26	F	Servant	12Au02Gg
MOORE, William		24	M	Laborer	12Au02Gg
Mary		15	F	Servant	12Au02Gg
MCGOVERN, Patrick		20	M	Laborer	12Au02Gg
KEARNEY, Mark		20	M	Laborer	12Au02Gg
CAINS, Mary		18	F	Servant	12Au02Gg
NEVINS, Mary		19	F	Servant	12Au02Gg
CAFFREY, Mary		15	F	Servant	12Au02Gg
STANS, Michael		20	M	Laborer	12Au02Gg
LYNCH, Patrick		18	M	Laborer	12Au02Gg
MCKUCKIN, Mary		19	F	Servant	12Au02Gg
CASEY, Mary		28	F	Servant	12Au02Gg
John	(S)	.00	M	Infant	12Au02Gg

NAMES OF PASSENGERS		AGE	SEX	OCCUPATIONS	DATE PORT SHIP
MCKENNA, Hannah		18	F	Servant	12Au02Gg
CAMPBELL, Mary		10	F	Unknown	12Au02Gg
MOFFAT, George		22	M	Laborer	12Au02Gg
Mary-Ann		14	F	Servant	12Au02Gg
CAUGHLIN, Ann		14	F	Servant	12Au02Gg
MALLON, Catherine		18	F	Servant	12Au02Gg
MCELROY, Barney		22	M	Laborer	12Au02Gg
DORAN, Roberts		21	M	Laborer	12Au02Gg
MAGHAN, Patrick		18	M	Tailor	12Au02Gg
RYAN, Bridget		18	F	Servant	12Au02Gg
DOLAN, Bernard		29	M	Tailor	12Au02Gg
OBRIEN, Lawrence		21	M	Shoemaker	12Au02Gg
BOURKE, William		28	M	Laborer	12Au02Gg
Ann	(W)	30	F	None	12Au02Gg
Mary	(D)	.09	F	Infant	12Au02Gg
GALLIGAN, Matthew		21	M	Laborer	12Au02Gg
Ann		19	F	None	12Au02Gg
MCINTER, Catherine		20	F	Servant	12Au02Gg
MCKENNA, Hugh		21	M	Laborer	12Au02Gg
TEARNEY, John		22	M	Laborer	12Au02Gg
AIKEN, John		18	M	Clerk	12Au02Gg
BRADLEY, John		17	M	Servant	12Au02Gg
CLAREE, Catherine		38	F	Servant	12Au02Gg

QUEEN-OF-THE-WEST 12 AUGUST 1846

From Liverpool

NAMES OF PASSENGERS		AGE	SEX	OCCUPATIONS	DATE PORT SHIP
JACKSON, John		26	M	Tailor	12Au02Cn
Jane	(W)	26	F	Unknown	12Au02Cn
Catharine		23	F	Unknown	12Au02Cn
Sarah	(D)	04	F	Child	12Au02Cn
Mary	(D)	02	F	Child	12Au02Cn
John	(S)	.09	M	Infant	12Au02Cn
BEATTY, Mary		18	F	Unknown	12Au02Cn
HIGGINS, Ann		18	F	Unknown	12Au02Cn
Bridget		20	F	Unknown	12Au02Cn
MCBRERETY, Margt.		35	F	Unknown	12Au02Cn
FOY, Bridget		20	F	Unknown	12Au02Cn
BYRNE, Edward		48	M	Merchant	12Au02Cn
MARSHALL, Wm.		30	M	Carpenter	12Au02Cn
CROOKS, Mary-Ann		15	F	Unknown	12Au02Cn
MURRY, Pat		20	M	Shoemaker	12Au02Cn
EDWARDS, James		24	M	Butcher	12Au02Cn
Bridget	(W)	17	F	Unknown	12Au02Cn
Maria	(D)	.07	F	Infant	12Au02Cn
OBRIEN, Dennis		36	M	Cooper	12Au02Cn
HONAN, Edward		22	M	Butcher	12Au02Cn
MORGAN, John		35	M	Miner	12Au02Cn
Margaret	(W)	30	F	Unknown	12Au02Cn
Wm.	(S)	.05	M	Infant	12Au02Cn
BIRT, Ezekiel		28	M	Unknown	12Au02Cn
Hannah		25	F	Unknown	12Au02Cn
WALKER, Michael		20	M	Hatter	12Au02Cn
MONAHAN, Jane		18	F	Unknown	12Au02Cn
GILL, Ann		18	F	Unknown	12Au02Cn
MULLANEY, Thomas		30	M	Laborer	12Au02Cn
MOHER, Hugh		20	M	Farmer	12Au02Cn
Margaret		30	F	Unknown	12Au02Cn
Maria		28	F	Unknown	12Au02Cn
Eleanor		24	F	Unknown	12Au02Cn
Nancy		30	F	Unknown	12Au02Cn
MACKEY, Mary		25	F	Unknown	12Au02Cn
FITZGERALD, Eliza		30	F	Unknown	12Au02Cn
Hanna	(D)	.07	F	Infant	12Au02Cn
Catharine		30	F	Unknown	12Au02Cn
TUITE, Philip		20	M	Laborer	12Au02Cn
DOOLEY, John		40	M	Farmer	12Au02Cn
Mary	(W)	40	F	Unknown	12Au02Cn

NAMES OF PASSENGERS		AGE	SEX	OCCUPATIONS	DATE PORT SHIP
DOOLEY, Pat	(S)	15	M	Unknown	12Au02Cn
Peggy	(D)	12	F	Unknown	12Au02Cn
Catharine	(D)	09	F	Child	12Au02Cn
Ann	(D)	07	F	Child	12Au02Cn
Mary	(D)	09	F	Child	12Au02Cn
Mary		20	F	Ynknown	12Au02Cn
GORRY, Andrew		20	M	Bricklayer	12Au02Cn
FOX, Timothy		18	M	Laborer	12Au02Cn
HACHETT, Simon		48	M	Farmer	12Au02Cn
Mary	(W)	48	F	Unknown	12Au02Cn
Kitty	(D)	20	F	Unknown	12Au02Cn
Bridget	(D)	19	F	Unknown	12Au02Cn
Thomas	(S)	25	M	Tailor	12Au02Cn
CLARENDEN, Matthew		23	M	Farmer	12Au02Cn
Peter		23	M	Farmer	12Au02Cn
Thomas		20	M	Farmer	12Au02Cn
GOOSEY, Thomas		26	M	Laborer	12Au02Cn
JACKSON, George		17	M	Clerk	12Au02Cn
WALSH, Wm.		26	M	Clerk	12Au02Cn
VAUGHAN, Charlotte		16	F	Unknown	12Au02Cn
Arther		12	M	Unknown	12Au02Cn
BAILY, Margaret		17	F	Unknown	12Au02Cn
HANNON, John		55	M	Joiner	12Au02Cn
Ralph	(S)	19	M	Joiner	12Au02Cn
SUFFER, Saml.		20	M	Grocer	12Au02Cn
CAIRN, James		30	M	Grocer	12Au02Cn
BRADLEY, Catharine		18	F	Unknown	12Au02Cn
HENNESEY, Margaret		18	F	Unknown	12Au02Cn
MUSSY, Margaret		20	F	Unknown	12Au02Cn
DONOHUE, Wm.		20	M	Laborer	12Au02Cn
SAMPSON, John		33	M	Stctr	12Au02Cn
Ann		22	F	Unknown	12Au02Cn
Eliza		18	F	Unknown	12Au02Cn
CAMPBELL, Patt		40	M	Currier	12Au02Cn
CONNER, Ann		30	F	Unknown	12Au02Cn
John	(S)	03	M	Child	12Au02Cn
Dennis	(S)	.08	M	Infant	12Au02Cn
HARRINGTON, Peter		25	M	Laborer	12Au02Cn
BOYLIN, Catharine		20	F	Unknown	12Au02Cn
BRADY, James		03	M	Child	12Au02Cn
CROWLEY, Jeremiah		40	M	Laborer	12Au02Cn
Nelly	(W)	40	F	Unknown	12Au02Cn
Mary	(D)	15	F	Unknown	12Au02Cn
John	(S)	09	M	Child	12Au02Cn
THOMPSON, Ann		23	F	Unknown	12Au02Cn
ALLEN, Margaret		22	F	Unknown	12Au02Cn
MCCARTHY, Catharine		31	F	Unknown	12Au02Cn
Owen	(S)	12	M	Unknown	12Au02Cn
Catharine	(D)	09	F	Child	12Au02Cn
Eliza	(D)	07	F	Child	12Au02Cn
HARRINGTON, Dennis		36	M	Laborer	12Au02Cn
Honora	(W)	32	F	Unknown	12Au02Cn
Michael	(S)	09	M	Child	12Au02Cn
John	(S)	06	M	Child	12Au02Cn
Mary	(D)	02	F	Child	12Au02Cn
GREEN, Ellen		25	F	Unknown	12Au02Cn
HERBERT, Wm.		20	M	Servant	12Au02Cn
MULLHOLLAND, Henry		23	M	Farmer	12Au02Cn
DURHAM, Joseph		18	M	Unknown	12Au02Cn
SPALLON, Wm.		27	M	Tailor	12Au02Cn
Catharine		25	F	Unknown	12Au02Cn
MCDONALD, John		12	M	Unknown	12Au02Cn
Bridget		13	F	Unknown	12Au02Cn
DIVINE, Michael		23	M	Unknown	12Au02Cn
HENRY, Alice		18	F	Unknown	12Au02Cn
MAJOR, George		25	M	Farmer	12Au02Cn
BYRNE, Henry		20	M	Miner	12Au02Cn
GRAY, John		13	M	Unknown	12Au02Cn
MCCLUSKY, James		20	M	Grocer	12Au02Cn
WALSH, Ann		22	F	Unknown	12Au02Cn
FURLONG, Esther		13	F	Unknown	12Au02Cn
CARLIN, Patt		22	M	Laborer	12Au02Cn
DONNELL, John		19	M	Laborer	12Au02Cn
GOLDSBURG, Richard		25	M	Laborer	12Au02Cn
LANAGAN, Mary		18	F	Unknown	12Au02Cn

NAMES OF PASSENGERS		AGE	SEX	OCCUPATIONS	DATE PORT SHIP
SHERIDAN, Margaret		18	F	Unknown	12Au02Cn
DARCY, Michael		20	M	Laborer	12Au02Cn
MALOY, John		20	M	Grocer	12Au02Cn
STONEY, James		25	M	Storekeeper	12Au02Cn
DWYER, James		30	M	Laborer	12Au02Cn
BUTLER, Pat		26	M	Coachman	12Au02Cn
Catharine		24	F	Unknown	12Au02Cn
WALSH, John		25	M	Laborer	12Au02Cn
CORNWALL, James		25	M	Traveller	12Au02Cn
FORAN, Mary		18	F	Laborer	12Au02Cn
MCCARTY, Danl.		22	M	Laborer	12Au02Cn
MURPHY, Eliza		12	F	Unknown	12Au02Cn
WILSON, Sarah		25	F	Unknown	12Au02Cn
MAYLAND, Henry		11	M	Unknown	12Au02Cn
Joseph		09	M	Child	12Au02Cn
RUSSELL, Jane		26	F	Unknown	12Au02Cn
MEGINNISS, Mark		20	M	Laborer	12Au02Cn
MCKENNA, James		25	M	Tailor	12Au02Cn
Isabella	(W)	20	F	Unknown	12Au02Cn
Mary	(D)	.05	F	Infant	12Au02Cn
Died-At-Sea					
SULLIVAN, Mary		28	F	Unknown	12Au02Cn
HIGGINS, John		30	M	Laborer	12Au02Cn
SULLIVAN, Peter		03	M	Child	12Au02Cn
John		.07	M	Infant	12Au02Cn
BLACK, John		20	M	Servant	12Au02Cn
NEWLAN, Peter		07	M	Child	12Au02Cn
Bridget		11	F	Unknown	12Au02Cn
HOGAN, Pat		21	M	Carpenter	12Au02Cn
GOOD, Michael		07	M	Child	12Au02Cn
Bridget		04	F	Child	12Au02Cn
Susan		.05	F	Infant	12Au02Cn
HAVERTY, James		18	M	Carpenter	12Au02Cn
RIELEY, Bridget		21	F	Unknown	12Au02Cn
MCMANUS, Henry		21	M	Laborer	12Au02Cn
FLINN, Mary		21	F	Unknown	12Au02Cn
GANLEY, Mary		21	F	Unknown	12Au02Cn
GUNN, Catharine		20	F	Unknown	12Au02Cn
LUITE, Thomas		16	M	Clerk	12Au02Cn
GORDON, Jane		18	F	Unknown	12Au02Cn
Eliza		16	F	Unknown	12Au02Cn
LOBIN, Mary-Ann		18	F	Unknown	12Au02Cn
Edward		09	M	Child	12Au02Cn
LOMBARD, Mary		13	F	Unknown	12Au02Cn
GARRY, Danl.		50	M	Laborer	12Au02Cn
Ann	(W)	50	F	Unknown	12Au02Cn
Ellen	(D)	10	F	Unknown	12Au02Cn
Edmond	(S)	08	M	Child	12Au02Cn
David	(S)	06	M	Child	12Au02Cn
Catharine	(D)	04	F	Child	12Au02Cn
Ann	(D)	.09	F	Infant	12Au02Cn
MCDONALD, Mary		50	F	Unknown	12Au02Cn
Honora	(D)	18	F	Unknown	12Au02Cn
FITZSIMMONS, Mary		50	F	Unknown	12Au02Cn
John		25	M	Laborer	12Au02Cn

WARD-CHIPMAN 12 AUGUST 1846

From Liverpool

NAMES OF PASSENGERS		AGE	SEX	OCCUPATIONS	DATE PORT SHIP
SULLIVAN, Mary		43	F	Unknown	12Au02Gw
Cath.	(D)	17	F	Unknown	12Au02Gw
Edw.	(S)	11	M	Unknown	12Au02Gw
DAVIS, John		31	M	Unknown	12Au02Gw
DALY, Ann		34	F	Unknown	12Au02Gw
HAGAN, Barney		24	M	Laborer	12Au02Gw
KEAN, Nancy		19	F	Servant	12Au02Gw
Bell		18	F	Servant	12Au02Gw
GAFNY, Maria		20	F	Unknown	12Au02Gw

NAMES OF PASSENGERS		AGE	SEX	OCCUPATIONS	DATE PORT SHIP
BARRETT, John		25	M	Farmer	12Au02Gw
Michl.		20	M	Darmer	12Au02Gw
Tim.		20	M	Farmer	12Au02Gw
Mrgt.		18	F	Unknown	12Au02Gw
Lucy		19	F	Unknown	12Au02Gw
KELLY, Maria		20	F	Unknown	12Au02Gw
SITDRAFF, Byran		20	M	Servant	12Au02Gw
BARRETT, U		25	F	Unknown	12Au02Gw
SULLIVAN, Mary		45	F	None	12Au02Gw
Danl.	(S)	06	M	Child	12Au02Gw
KILCHEN, Elizabeth		50	F	None	12Au02Gw
SULLIVAN, John		18	M	Laborer	12Au02Gw
LYNCH, Anne		30	F	Servant	12Au02Gw
DELANY, John		50	M	Farmer	12Au02Gw
Cathe.		40	F	None	12Au02Gw
TIERNEY, Margt.		30	F	None	12Au02Gw
Michl.	(S)	05	M	Child	12Au02Gw
Mary	(D)	02	F	Child	12Au02Gw
Biddy	(D)	.00	F	Infant	12Au02Gw
BANNON, Ann		23	F	Servant	12Au02Gw
PICKENS, Edwd.		20	M	Mechanic	12Au02Gw
Mary		40	F	Unknown	12Au02Gw
FITZGERALD, Mary		25	F	Servant	12Au02Gw
COYNE, Bridget		20	F	Servant	12Au02Gw
MCCORMICK, Bridget		25	F	Servant	12Au02Gw
CONWAY, Honor		13	F	Servant	12Au02Gw
SPRING, Patk.		20	M	Laborer	12Au02Gw
OBRIEN, Thomas		20	M	Laborer	12Au02Gw
CAVAN, Patk.		20	M	Laborer	12Au02Gw
KELLY, Margt.		22	F	Servant	12Au02Gw
MCHUGH, Jane		45	F	None	12Au02Gw
Patk.	(S)	19	M	Laborer	12Au02Gw
Rose-Ann	(D)	12	F	Unknown	12Au02Gw
Bridget	(D)	08	F	Child	12Au02Gw
Ellen	(D)	05	F	Child	12Au02Gw
Mary	(D)	03	F	Child	12Au02Gw
HAGGARD, Frank		40	M	Mechanic	12Au02Gw
Alice	(W)	38	F	None	12Au02Gw
Jane	(D)	19	F	Unknown	12Au02Gw
Harriet	(D)	11	F	Child	12Au02Gw
Ann	(D)	09	F	Child	12Au02Gw
John	(S)	04	M	Child	12Au02Gw
James	(S)	.00	M	Infant	12Au02Gw
BOYD, Harriet		70	F	Unknown	12Au02Gw
COLBERT, John		25	M	Farmer	12Au02Gw
Thomas		40	M	Farmer	12Au02Gw
DELANY, Anne		40	F	None	12Au02Gw
James	(S)	07	M	Child	12Au02Gw
William	(S)	04	M	Child	12Au02Gw
BUCKLEY, Hannah		00	F	Unknown	12Au02Gw
MORTAL, John		00	M	Unknown	12Au02Gw
MCGANN, Patk.		00	M	Unknown	12Au02Gw
U	(W)	00	F	Unknown	12Au02Gw
ONEAL, Rose		00	F	Unknown	12Au02Gw
LITTLE, James		00	M	Unknown	12Au02Gw
U	(W)	00	F	Unknown	12Au02Gw
Christy		00	F	Unknown	12Au02Gw
Sarah		00	F	Unknown	12Au02Gw
Mary		00	F	Unknown	12Au02Gw
Elizabeth		00	F	Unknown	12Au02Gw
Rachel		00	F	Unknown	12Au02Gw
Jane		00	F	Unknown	12Au02Gw
Margaret		00	F	Unknown	12Au02Gw
LAWRENCE, John		00	M	Unknown	12Au02Gw
CARROLL, Nicholas		00	M	Unknown	12Au02Gw
GILES, George		20	M	Laborer	12Au02Gw
BURKE, Biddy		25	F	Unknown	12Au02Gw
LAWLER, Cathe.		20	F	Unknown	12Au02Gw
PHILLIPS, Martin		26	M	Unknown	12Au02Gw
FLANERY, Michl.		19	M	Unknown	12Au02Gw
MCMANUS, Ellen		22	F	Servant	12Au02Gw
PHILIPS, Mary		20	F	Servant	12Au02Gw
FITZPATRICK, Margt.		26	F	Servant	12Au02Gw
PHILIPS, Nancy		20	F	Servant	12Au02Gw
KELLY, Margt.		20	F	Servant	12Au02Gw

NAMES OF PASSENGERS		AGE	SEX	OCCUPATIONS	DATE PORT SHIP
CONNOR, Pat		50	M	Laborer	12Au02Gw
Rose	(W)	40	F	Unknown	12Au02Gw
Bridget	(D)	12	F	Unknown	12Au02Gw
KILLEN, Cathe.		20	F	Unknown	12Au02Gw
BLACKBURN, Wm.		22	M	Laborer	12Au02Gw
John		46	M	Laborer	12Au02Gw
Samuel		26	M	Laborer	12Au02Gw
CASEY, John		20	M	Laborer	12Au02Gw
COHEN, Biddy		23	F	Unknown	12Au02Gw
WARD, John		21	M	Laborer	12Au02Gw
CUE, Peggy		20	F	Unknown	12Au02Gw
CASEY, Mary		22	F	Unknown	12Au02Gw
BOYD, Berkley		26	M	Laborer	12Au02Gw
DELANY, Mary		20	F	Unknown	12Au02Gw
COYLE, Owen		60	M	Laborer	12Au02Gw
Denis	(S)	20	M	Laborer	12Au02Gw
Nancy	(W)	58	F	Unknown	12Au02Gw
Rose	(D)	13	F	Unknown	12Au02Gw
WALSH, Mary		20	F	Unknown	12Au02Gw
HORAN, James		22	M	Laborer	12Au02Gw
MORAN, Thomas		23	M	Laborer	12Au02Gw
MCKINNY, John		20	M	Laborer	12Au02Gw
FAGAN, Thomas		20	M	Laborer	12Au02Gw
U	(W)	20	F	Unknown	12Au02Gw
WALL, Michl.		22	M	Laborer	12Au02Gw
U	(W)	22	F	Unknown	12Au02Gw
BOYLE, Terence		21	M	Laborer	12Au02Gw
MOFFOTT, Ann		11	F	Child	12Au02Gw
MCGUIRE, Margaret		19	F	Servant	12Au02Gw
MCLAUGHLIN, James		28	M	Laborer	12Au02Gw
RYAN, Cathe.		20	F	Servant	12Au02Gw
Sarah		18	F	Servant	12Au02Gw
JENNINGS, Margt.		30	F	Servant	12Au02Gw
SHAW, Elisa		30	F	Servant	12Au02Gw
ENNIS, Martha		27	F	Servant	12Au02Gw
Mary		12	F	Servant	12Au02Gw
Agnes	(D)	.00	F	Infant	12Au02Gw
MULLIN, Rose		40	F	Servant	12Au02Gw
Patk.	(S)	11	M	Servant	12Au02Gw
Peter	(S)	09	M	Child	12Au02Gw
Mary	(D)	07	F	Child	12Au02Gw
Rose	(D)	03	F	Child	12Au02Gw
MCCABE, James		20	M	Laborer	12Au02Gw
GREEN, Bridget		18	F	Servant	12Au02Gw
BROGAN, Mary		20	F	Servant	12Au02Gw
EWING, Mary		18	F	Servant	12Au02Gw
REILY, John		17	M	Laborer	12Au02Gw
CULLEN, Bridget		16	F	Servant	12Au02Gw
DOLAN, Ann		30	F	Servant	12Au02Gw
FARRELL, Patk.		30	M	Farmer	12Au02Gw
Mary		27	F	Servant	12Au02Gw
DOLAN, Peter		12	M	None	12Au02Gw
Cathe.		08	F	Child	12Au02Gw
John		05	M	Child	12Au02Gw
Bridget		02	F	Child	12Au02Gw
FARRELL, Bridget		.00	F	Infant	12Au02Gw
MITCHELL, James		55	M	Farmer	12Au02Gw
U	(W)	50	F	None	12Au02Gw
Patk.	(S)	17	M	None	12Au02Gw
Margt.	(D)	13	F	None	12Au02Gw
Mary	(D)	17	F	None	12Au02Gw
James	(S)	12	M	None	12Au02Gw
Thomas	(S)	12	M	None	12Au02Gw
Michl.	(S)	04	M	Child	12Au02Gw
John	(S)	03	M	Child	12Au02Gw
Frances	(S)	.00	M	Infant	12Au02Gw
Anne	(D)	08	F	Child	12Au02Gw
Peter	(S)	11	M	Child	12Au02Gw
CULLIN, James		19	M	Laborer	12Au02Gw
COYLE, Cathe.		20	F	Servant	12Au02Gw
James		20	M	Servant	12Au02Gw
Peter		20	M	Laborer	12Au02Gw
Thomas		09	M	Child	12Au02Gw
CULLIN, Mary		20	F	Servant	12Au02Gw
MITCHELL, Hugh		23	M	Farmer	12Au02Gw
MITCHELL, Hugh		13	M	Unknown	12Au02Gw
Bridget		10	F	Unknown	12Au02Gw
Cathe.		09	F	Child	12Au02Gw
CUSACK, Patk.		30	M	Farmer	12Au02Gw
Kelly		25	F	Servant	12Au02Gw
Kelly		13	F	Servant	12Au02Gw
BENSON, Charles		40	M	Mechanic	12Au02Gw
Mary	(W)	37	F	None	12Au02Gw
Anne	(D)	20	F	Servant	12Au02Gw
Wm.	(S)	15	M	None	12Au02Gw
Robert	(S)	10	M	Unknown	12Au02Gw
Peter	(S)	08	M	Child	12Au02Gw
Bell	(D)	07	F	Child	12Au02Gw
Charles	(S)	05	M	Child	12Au02Gw
Christopher	(S)	03	M	Child	12Au02Gw
WILKIN, Margt.		17	F	Servant	12Au02Gw
KIERNAN, B.R.		20	M	Mechanic	12Au02Gw
NEU, John		50	M	Farmer	12Au02Gw
DARRON, John		45	M	Farmer	12Au02Gw
Alice	(W)	45	F	None	12Au02Gw
James	(S)	17	M	None	12Au02Gw
Charles	(S)	13	M	None	12Au02Gw
Anne	(D)	11	F	Child	12Au02Gw
Margaret	(D)	09	F	Child	12Au02Gw
Ellen	(D)	07	F	Child	12Au02Gw
Eliza	(D)	.00	F	Infant	12Au02Gw
BRANSFIELD, Mary		23	F	Servant	12Au02Gw
Bridget		21	F	Servant	12Au02Gw
RATIGAN, Patk.		20	M	Laborer	12Au02Gw
MOONEY, Theresa		16	F	Servant	12Au02Gw
MACK, Cathe.		16	F	Servant	12Au02Gw
Connor		10	M	Servant	12Au02Gw
Anne		12	F	Servant	12Au02Gw
WALPOLE, Mary		11	F	Child	12Au02Gw
HARRIS, Hyam		27	M	Laborer	12Au02Gw
FOX, Hyram		25	M	Laborer	12Au02Gw
FREDLIGH, Harris		22	M	Laborer	12Au02Gw
BURTON, Bethel		20	M	Laborer	12Au02Gw
BLANEY, James		30	M	Laborer	12Au02Gw
CARROLL, Thomas		25	M	Laborer	12Au02Gw
GRADY, Richd.		25	M	Laborer	12Au02Gw
Martha		25	F	Laborer	12Au02Gw
WALKER, Emily		16	F	Laborer	12Au02Gw
CARROLL, Martha		.00	F	Infant	12Au02Gw
KEY, Charles		29	M	Laborer	12Au02Gw
Jane	(W)	27	F	Laborer	12Au02Gw
Robert	(S)	04	M	Child	12Au02Gw
LYONS, Thomas		29	M	Laborer	12Au02Gw
RUSSELL, David		30	M	Laborer	12Au02Gw
Sabrina	(W)	30	F	Laborer	12Au02Gw
Thomas	(S)	04	M	Child	12Au02Gw
Wm.	(S)	04	M	Child	12Au02Gw
Mary	(D)	03	F	Child	12Au02Gw
CLUSKER, Christopher		40	M	Laborer	12Au02Gw
Judy	(W)	38	F	Laborer	12Au02Gw
Cathe.	(D)	05	F	Child	12Au02Gw
Mary	(D)	.00	F	Infant	12Au02Gw
CLARKE, Betsey		38	F	Laborer	12Au02Gw
CRAVEN, Anne		08	F	Child	12Au02Gw
MURRAY, Luke		20	M	Laborer	12Au02Gw
COHEN, Lewis		25	M	Laborer	12Au02Gw
LYNCH, Bernard		22	M	Laborer	12Au02Gw
HEANEY, Frank		37	M	Laborer	12Au02Gw
FAIRTY, Mary		21	F	Laborer	12Au02Gw
MONOHAN, Cathe.		55	F	Laborer	12Au02Gw
MCDERMOTT, James		27	M	Laborer	12Au02Gw
REYNOLDS, Biddy		20	F	Laborer	12Au02Gw
ANDERSON, Mary		20	F	Laborer	12Au02Gw
MURPHY, Mathew		24	M	Laborer	12Au02Gw
WARD, John		30	M	Laborer	12Au02Gw
Biddy		30	F	Laborer	12Au02Gw
FARRELL, Biddy		20	F	Servant	12Au02Gw
MULVEY, Bailley		28	M	Laborer	12Au02Gw
Bridget		28	F	Laborer	12Au02Gw
Michl.		20	M	Laborer	12Au02Gw

NAMES OF PASSENGERS		A G E	S E X	OCCUPATIONS	DATE PORT SHIP
BOYLE, Margt.		20	F	Laborer	12Au02Gw
CONLAN, Lawr.		25	M	Laborer	12Au02Gw
U	(W)	30	F	Laborer	12Au02Gw
Michl.	(S)	.00	M	Infant	12Au02Gw
Kitty	(D)	04	F	Child	12Au02Gw
LANDON, Hy		25	M	Laborer	12Au02Gw
Ay., Martha		39	F	Laborer	12Au02Gw
Cathe.		20	F	Laborer	12Au02Gw
COHEN, Mark		20	M	Laborer	12Au02Gw
MARTFORD, Wm.		27	M	Laborer	12Au02Gw
MCHEY, John		27	M	Laborer	12Au02Gw
Fanny		26	F	Laborer	12Au02Gw
Ann		20	F	Laborer	12Au02Gw
Hy.		.00	M	Infant	12Au02Gw
MCBRIDE, May		22	F	Laborer	12Au02Gw
BROTH, Jas.		17	M	Laborer	12Au02Gw
REYNOLDS, Mary		20	F	Laborer	12Au02Gw
MCKINNA, Jas.		29	M	Laborer	12Au02Gw
QUINN, Patt		24	M	Laborer	12Au02Gw
DALEY, Darby		25	M	Laborer	12Au02Gw
NOLAN, John		44	M	Laborer	12Au02Gw
Mary	(W)	34	F	Laborer	12Au02Gw
Alice	(D)	17	F	Laborer	12Au02Gw
Michl.	(S)	08	M	Child	12Au02Gw
Phillp	(S)	04	M	Child	12Au02Gw
Patk.	(S)	.00	M	Infant	12Au02Gw
MCCURRY, Hy.		21	M	Laborer	12Au02Gw
Mary		20	F	Laborer	12Au02Gw
FENTON, Margt.		20	F	Laborer	12Au02Gw
GRIFFITH, Ellz.		60	F	Laborer	12Au02Gw
Eliza	(D)	17	F	Laborer	12Au02Gw
HARRIS, Thos.		24	M	Laborer	12Au02Gw
MULLHOLLAND, Margt.		23	F	Laborer	12Au02Gw
Betty		20	F	Laborer	12Au02Gw
BYRAN, H.		19	F	Laborer	12Au02Gw
MCCABE, Eliza		21	F	Laborer	12Au02Gw
TORNEY, David		20	M	Laborer	12Au02Gw
John		06	M	Child	12Au02Gw
Ellen		06	F	Child	12Au02Gw

CONSTITUTION 13 AUGUST 1846

From Liverpool

NAMES OF PASSENGERS		A G E	S E X	OCCUPATIONS	DATE PORT SHIP
FOVLY, Pat		25	M	Unknown	13Au02HI
Ann		20	F	Unknown	13Au02HI
PENDERGAST, Julia		20	F	Unknown	13Au02HI
MORRAL, Honora		40	F	Servant	13Au02HI
Alice	(D)	15	F	Servant	13Au02HI
Patt	(S)	12	M	Child	13Au02HI
Mary	(D)	04	F	Child	13Au02HI
John	(S)	.00	M	Infant	13Au02HI
CONNOR, Thomas		30	M	Laborer	13Au02HI
Margt.		20	F	Servant	13Au02HI
DEMFRY, John		22	M	Laborer	13Au02HI
Eliza		25	F	Seamstress	13Au02HI
GAFNEY, Easther		13	F	Seamstress	13Au02HI
MCGUINESS, Ellen		23	F	Seamstress	13Au02HI
HAMILTON, Grace		19	F	Dressmaker	13Au02HI
PAN, Cath.		19	F	Unknown	13Au02HI
KEN, Will		30	M	Laborer	13Au02HI
U	(W)	20	F	Laborer	13Au02HI
WHELAN, Judy		30	F	Laborer	13Au02HI
Honora	(D)	03	F	Child	13Au02HI
MCLOUGHLIN, Edward		28	M	Laborer	13Au02HI
MCCLUSKEY, Margret		22	F	Laborer	13Au02HI
DALY, John		30	M	Laborer	13Au02HI
U	(W)	25	F	Laborer	13Au02HI
ODONNEL, John		22	M	Laborer	13Au02HI
ODONNEL, Cath.		13	F	Laborer	13Au02HI
BLAKE, Mick		20	M	Laborer	13Au02HI
MADILL, U		46	M	Laborer	13Au02HI
U-Jr.	(S)	20	M	Laborer	13Au02HI
LAWRENCE, U		22	M	Laborer	13Au02HI
COLLINS, Will		30	M	Laborer	13Au02HI
Wineferd	(W)	25	F	Laborer	13Au02HI
John	(S)	03	M	Child	13Au02HI
Cath.	(D)	.00	F	Infant	13Au02HI
MCGEE, Eliza		19	F	Laborer	13Au02HI
MCNIEL, Jane		20	F	Laborer	13Au02HI
CAPERLY, Margt.		25	F	Laborer	13Au02HI
CORMICK, Mary		17	F	Laborer	13Au02HI
RIGNACY, John		25	M	Laborer	13Au02HI
Ann		19	F	Servant	13Au02HI
Ann		19	F	Servant	13Au02HI
JESSOP, George		20	M	Servant	13Au02HI
OBRIEN, Will		20	M	Servant	13Au02HI
SMITH, Ann		17	F	Servant	13Au02HI
KEOUGH, John		32	M	Servant	13Au02HI
MARTIN, Rose		28	F	Servant	13Au02HI
Cath.	(D)	07	F	Child	13Au02HI
Mary	(D)	05	F	Child	13Au02HI
Will	(S)	.00	M	Infant	13Au02HI
SMITH, Mary		35	F	Servant	13Au02HI
Betty	(D)	11	F	Servant	13Au02HI
Jane	(D)	07	F	Child	13Au02HI
Anthony	(S)	02	M	Child	13Au02HI
MCGARTH, John		38	M	Servant	13Au02HI
FIELDS, Will		38	M	Servant	13Au02HI
FARLEY, Jas.		26	M	Servant	13Au02HI
Kitty	(W)	20	F	Servant	13Au02HI
John	(S)	.00	M	Infant	13Au02HI
DUNN, James		36	M	Mechanic	13Au02HI
WARD, Will		30	M	Mechanic	13Au02HI
LANN, Jos.		26	M	Mechanic	13Au02HI
Anthony		25	M	Mechanic	13Au02HI
Mary		06	F	Child	13Au02HI
Biddy		04	F	Child	13Au02HI
Ellen		02	F	Child	13Au02HI
Pat		.00	M	Infant	13Au02HI
MALACTRY, Biddy		17	F	Laborer	13Au02HI
Ellen		04	F	Child	13Au02HI
FINNECUN, Richard		24	M	Laborer	13Au02HI
Hanna		22	F	Laborer	13Au02HI
RING, Namy		19	F	Laborer	13Au02HI
Mary		17	F	Laborer	13Au02HI
MCCONAGHY, Jas.		45	M	Laborer	13Au02HI
Eliza	(D)	12	F	Laborer	13Au02HI
Colhoon	(S)	07	M	Child	13Au02HI
Mathew	(S)	01	M	Child	13Au02HI
LITTLE, Ann		20	F	Laborer	13Au02HI
DEPRY, Susan		20	F	Laborer	13Au02H
HUGHES, Mary		22	F	Laborer	13Au02H
MCQUADE, Nancy		20	F	Laborer	13Au02H
Mary		18	F	Laborer	13Au02H.
BRENNAN, Bridget		20	F	Laborer	13Au02H.
SEHENY, Michael		21	M	Laborer	13Au02H
LAMB, Pat		22	M	Laborer	13Au02H
SIMPLE, John		22	M	Laborer	13Au02H
JENKINS, Jas.		50	M	Laborer	13Au02H
STEWART, Robert		37	M	Laborer	13Au02H
U	(W)	40	F	Laborer	13Au02H
NEIL, Margret		23	F	Laborer	13Au02H
Mary		14	F	Laborer	13Au02H
BYRNE, Hugh		22	M	Laborer	13Au02H
HUTCHINSON, Bob		19	M	Laborer	13Au02H
HUTCHINGSON, Mary		21	F	Servant	13Au02H
QUINN, Margret		20	F	Servant	13Au02H
ROONEY, Mary		30	F	Servant	13Au02H
Cath.		18	F	Servant	13Au02H
BRENNAN, Patrick		35	M	Servant	13Au02H
CONNOR, Pat		19	M	Servant	13Au02H
FARRELL, John		17	M	Servant	13Au02H
MCENRU, Margret		24	F	Servant	13Au02H

229

NAMES OF PASSENGERS		AGE	SEX	OCCUPATIONS	DATE PORT SHIP
MCENRU, Ellen		07	F	Child	13Au02HI
CLARKIN, Ann		24	F	Servant	13Au02HI
BODLE, John		44	M	Servant	13Au02HI
Bridget	(W)	42	F	Servant	13Au02HI
Thos.	(S)	16	M	Servant	13Au02HI
Robt.	(S)	13	M	Servant	13Au02HI
Eliza	(D)	12	F	Servant	13Au02HI
Jane	(D)	10	F	Servant	13Au02HI
Dan	(S)	05	M	Child	13Au02HI
Susan	(D)	08	F	Child	13Au02HI
Francis	(S)	02	M	Child	13Au02HI
Charles	(S)	.00	M	Infant	13Au02HI
DALY, Cath.		20	F	Laborer	13Au02HI
FOLEY, Pat		13	M	Laborer	13Au02HI
Mary		36	F	Laborer	13Au02HI
MCBRIDE, Margt.		24	F	Laborer	13Au02HI
DONALDSON, Richard		42	M	Laborer	13Au02HI
Pat	(S)	18	M	Laborer	13Au02HI
Eliza	(D)	16	F	Laborer	13Au02HI
KERR, Will		21	M	Laborer	13Au02HI
MACNAMARA, Will		22	M	Laborer	13Au02HI
Mary		24	F	Laborer	13Au02HI
BRETT, Jas.		22	M	Laborer	13Au02HI
LEDWICH, Christy		50	F	Laborer	13Au02HI
Marrella		11	F	Laborer	13Au02HI
John		09	M	Child	13Au02HI
Mary		02	F	Child	13Au02HI
DARF, Mary		23	F	Laborer	13Au02HI
Ann	(D)	04	F	Child	13Au02HI
BRADY, Jane		20	F	Laborer	13Au02HI
GILLIGAN, Martin		22	M	Laborer	13Au02HI
BAIL, George		25	M	Laborer	13Au02HI
U	(W)	20	F	Laborer	13Au02HI
HERBRET, Jas.		20	M	Laborer	13Au02HI
PEPPER, Pat		30	M	Laborer	13Au02HI
Thos.	(S)	03	M	Child	13Au02HI
MCCORMICK, Will		30	M	Laborer	13Au02HI
Jane	(W)	32	F	Laborer	13Au02HI
Eliza	(D)	13	F	Laborer	13Au02HI
Kenny	(S)	11	M	Laborer	13Au02HI
Charles	(S)	07	M	Child	13Au02HI
Edwd.	(S)	02	M	Child	13Au02HI
Marla	(D)	05	F	Child	13Au02HI
Margret	(D)	.00	F	Infant	13Au02HI
WARD, Hugh		29	M	Laborer	13Au02HI
Sarah		26	F	Laborer	13Au02HI
COURTNEY, Jas.		20	M	Laborer	13Au02HI
SCUCKINDER, Moses		50	M	Laborer	13Au02HI
GANAGAN, Jas.		21	M	Laborer	13Au02HI
Mary		19	F	Laborer	13Au02HI
MULLEN, Jas.		11	M	Laborer	13Au02HI
Owen		06	M	Laborer	13Au02HI
SMITH, Ann		12	F	Laborer	13Au02HI
MCGOUGH, Alice		20	F	Laborer	13Au02HI
MCNULTY, Peter		21	M	Laborer	13Au02HI
DUFFY, Jas.		17	M	Laborer	13Au02HI
MAKLER, Mary		18	F	Laborer	13Au02HI
QUINN, Cath.		11	F	Laborer	13Au02HI
Thos.		08	M	Child	13Au02HI
MCGAR, Ann		18	F	Laborer	13Au02HI
DALEY, Barnard		24	M	Laborer	13Au02HI
HILLS, Robt.		25	M	Laborer	13Au02HI
WILLSON, George		22	M	Laborer	13Au02HI
GLUNBER, Phil.		23	M	Laborer	13Au02HI
ANDRICK, Robt.		25	M	Laborer	13Au02HI
JONES, Susan		20	F	Laborer	13Au02HI
CUMISKY, Mick		20	M	Laborer	13Au02HI
HUGHS, Julia		13	F	Laborer	13Au02HI
HENRY, Mary		20	F	Laborer	13Au02HI
ALLEN, Richd.		43	M	Laborer	13Au02HI
Jane	(D)	11	F	Laborer	13Au02HI
Isabella	(D)	16	F	Laborer	13Au02HI
John	(S)	12	M	Laborer	13Au02HI
James	(S)	08	M	Child	13Au02HI
Martha	(D)	05	F	Child	13Au02HI
ALLEN, Ann	(D)	07	F	Child	13Au02HI
Alex	(S)	.00	M	Infant	13Au02HI
Samuel	(S)	.00	M	Infant	13Au02HI
Richard	(S)	.00	M	Infant	13Au02HI
MCNOLBY, Ann		35	F	Laborer	13Au02HI
Cath.	(D)	18	F	Laborer	13Au02HI
THOMPSON, Isabella		13	F	Laborer	13Au02HI
Mary		12	F	Laborer	13Au02HI
GAFFERY, Jas.		20	M	Laborer	13Au02HI
CRAWFORD, Bridget		24	F	Laborer	13Au02HI
DONALDSON, Charles		06	M	Child	13Au02HI

GREENOCK 18 AUGUST 1846

From Liverpool

NAMES OF PASSENGERS		AGE	SEX	OCCUPATIONS	DATE PORT SHIP
GILMOUR, James		13	M	Grocer	18Au02Hm
LEMON, Peter		19	M	Baker	18Au02Hm
Catharine		16	F	Spinster	18Au02Hm
MCKENNA, Patrick		25	M	Laborer	18Au02Hm
OFLAHERTY, H.L.		25	M	Unknown	18Au02Hm
CUNNINGHAM, Margaret		22	F	Spinster	18Au02Hm
MCCUSHER, John		24	M	Laborer	18Au02Hm
COULAN, Mary		19	F	Servant	18Au02Hm
CAMMON, Thomas		16	M	Laborer	18Au02Hm
CARR, John		25	M	Laborer	18Au02Hm
CAULFIELD, James		31	M	Stone Mason	18Au02Hm
MULLIGAN, Ann		20	F	Dressmaker	18Au02Hm
CUNNINGHAM, Catharine		00	F	Spinster	18Au02Hm
DERLIN, Bridget		21	F	Unknown	18Au02Hm
LOVELY, Susan		30	F	Spinster	18Au02Hm
Maria	(D)	03	F	Child	18Au02Hm
Ann	(D)	02	F	Child	18Au02Hm
FITZPATRICK, Rose		20	F	Spinster	18Au02Hm
Mary		15	F	Spinster	18Au02Hm
CLINE, Bernard		23	M	Laborer	18Au02Hm
DOYLE, Bridget		17	F	Servant	18Au02Hm
MCGRANE, Rose		17	F	Spinster	18Au02Hm
Mary		19	F	Spinster	18Au02Hm
MULVEY, James		19	M	Laborer	18Au02Hm
CASSIDY, Michael		12	M	Servant	18Au02Hm
HOLTON, Rose		20	F	Servant	18Au02Hm
Judy		40	F	Servant	18Au02Hm
Michael		16	M	Servant	18Au02Hm
Patrick		12	M	Servant	18Au02Hm
John		10	M	None	18Au02Hm
James		08	M	None	18Au02Hm
FLANNIGAN, Mary		40	F	Servant	18Au02Hm
James	(S)	11	M	None	18Au02Hm
Mary	(D)	08	F	Child	18Au02Hm
Ellen	(D)	07	F	Child	18Au02Hm
Ann	(D)	06	F	Child	18Au02Hm
GALLAGHER, Mary		30	F	Servant	18Au02Hm
MCKERRON, Catharine		19	F	Servant	18Au02Hm
GILMORE, Margaret		11	F	Spinster	18Au02Hm
FARRELL, Catharine		20	F	Dressmaker	18Au02Hm
NAUGHTON, James		20	M	Laborer	18Au02Hm
MURTOGH, Elizabeth		19	F	Spinster	18Au02Hm
FARRELL, Ellen		21	F	Spinster	18Au02Hm
MAHON, Thomas		21	M	Wheelwright	18Au02Hm
MOLONEY, Ann		11	F	Child	18Au02Hm
BRENNEN, Edwd.		25	M	Laborer	18Au02Hm
ROONEY, Patrick		60	M	Laborer	18Au02Hm
OWENS, Mary		17	F	Servant	18Au02Hm
PADDEN, Charles		25	M	Grocer	18Au02Hm
Marla		22	F	Wife	18Au02Hm
Eliza	(D)	.00	F	Infant	18Au02Hm
DROYRE, John		25	M	Laborer	18Au02Hm
Bridget		28	F	Wife	18Au02Hm

NAMES OF PASSENGERS	AGE	SEX	OCCUPATIONS	DATE PORT SHIP
KILROY, Ann	17	F	Servant	18Au02Hm
BURK, Ann	17	F	Servant	18Au02Hm
OUYLE, Andrew	20	M	Butcher	18Au02Hm
OSBORNE, Ann	27	F	Spinster	18Au02Hm
DOYLE, Cath.	21	F	Spinster	18Au02Hm
FOSTER, Robt.	22	M	Carpenter	18Au02Hm
PHILIPS, John	65	M	Gentleman	18Au02Hm
U	60	F	Wife	18Au02Hm
Dorothy-Ann (D)	20	F	Spinster	18Au02Hm
HEGGINBOTTOM, Nathan	15	M	Surgeon	18Au02Hm
Ann-Jane	19	F	Spinster	18Au02Hm
Mary	17	F	Spinster	18Au02Hm
GAHAN, James	21	M	Laborer	18Au02Hm
FLYNER, William	24	M	Butcher	18Au02Hm
CONROY, Mary	20	F	Spinster	18Au02Hm
CUNNIFF, Catharine	24	F	Spinster	18Au02Hm
Ann	20	F	Spinster	18Au02Hm
NULTY, Margaret	18	F	Spinster	18Au02Hm
LANEY, Patrick	09	M	Child	18Au02Hm
CONNOR, Patrick	20	M	Laborer	18Au02Hm
BOYLE, Peter	19	M	Wool Comber	18Au02Hm
GREY, Thomas	09	M	Laborer	18Au02Hm
Terence	14	M	Laborer	18Au02Hm
John	10	M	Laborer	18Au02Hm
Ann	30	F	Laborer	18Au02Hm
Patrick	01	M	Child	18Au02Hm
DOWNEY, Patrick	12	M	None	18Au02Hm
Bernard	10	M	None	18Au02Hm
SMITH, Biddy	24	F	Spinster	18Au02Hm
KELLY, Sarah	19	F	Spinster	18Au02Hm
DONNELL, Rebecca	27	F	Spinster	18Au02Hm
GREY, Mary	31	F	Cook	18Au02Hm
PHILLIPS, Elizabeth	20	F	Wife	18Au02Hm
James	10	M	Child	18Au02Hm
William	02	M	Child	18Au02Hm
MITCHELL, Catharine	20	F	Spinster	18Au02Hm
HIGGINS, Nicholas	50	M	Miner	18Au02Hm
John (S)	24	M	Miner	18Au02Hm
GLANEY, Hugh	28	M	Laborer	18Au02Hm
U	26	F	Wife	18Au02Hm
John (S)	11	M	Child	18Au02Hm
Betsy (D)	08	F	Child	18Au02Hm
MCAVEMA, John	21	M	Pmbr-Gzr	18Au02Hm
BOWE, Michael	17	M	Laborer	18Au02Hm
MCLEAN, Bridget	17	F	Spinster	18Au02Hm
Mary	16	F	Spinster	18Au02Hm
DOYLE, William	22	M	Miner	18Au02Hm
LOUGHLIN, Catharine	19	F	Spinster	18Au02Hm
NEIGHAN, Catharine	19	F	Spinster	18Au02Hm
KERRIGAN, Isabella	16	F	Spinster	18Au02Hm
BRENNAN, Mary	16	F	Spinster	18Au02Hm
MCBRIEN, Mary	11	F	Spinster	18Au02Hm
OBRIEN, Rosey	16	F	Spinster	18Au02Hm
DEVINES, John	27	M	Laborer	18Au02Hm
DALY, Elias	26	M	Missionary	18Au02Hm
DORLING, Bernardine	34	F	Missionary	18Au02Hm
EDWARDS, Francis	38	M	Missionary	18Au02Hm
VERE, Lewis	15	M	Missionary	18Au02Hm
MARIA, Benedick	35	M	Missionary	18Au02Hm
GILLIGAN, John	30	M	Surveyor	18Au02Hm
BRADY, Peter	22	M	Laborer	18Au02Hm
ODO, Margaret	50	F	Spinster	18Au02Hm
Mary (D)	24	F	Spinster	18Au02Hm
FARRELL, William	24	M	Coppersmith	18Au02Hm
MANGIN, Catharine	22	F	Wife	18Au02Hm
WRIGHT, Alexander	25	M	Watchmaker	18Au02Hm
MCLOUGHLIN, Mary	23	F	Spinster	18Au02Hm
DELANEY, Patrick	21	M	Shoemaker	18Au02Hm
KELLY, Catharine	20	F	Spinster	18Au02Hm
SIMPSON, Alexander	40	M	Clerk	18Au02Hm
Mary-Ann	32	F	Wife	18Au02Hm
Ann-Maria	08	F	Child	18Au02Hm
William-Alexander	06	M	Child	18Au02Hm
Francis-Henry	03	M	Child	18Au02Hm
Robert-Gordon	.00	M	Infant	18Au02Hm
HARRISON, Robert	27	M	Laborer	18Au02Hm
QUIM, Mary	17	F	Spinster	18Au02Hm
KANE, Richard	30	M	Gdnr	18Au02Hm
U	20	F	Wife	18Au02Hm
BURNS, Margaret	17	F	Spinster	18Au02Hm
FITZSIMONS, Elizabeth	17	F	Spinster	18Au02Hm
GRENNAN, Bridget	19	F	Spinster	18Au02Hm
SMITH, Mary	19	F	Spinster	18Au02Hm
TURLEY, Cornelius	30	M	Weaver	18Au02Hm
NORTON, Ellen	19	F	Spinster	18Au02Hm
NOLAN, Catharine	20	F	Spinster	18Au02Hm
ROACH, Ann	17	F	Spinster	18Au02Hm
SOLOHAN, Patrick	30	M	Joiner	18Au02Hm
FLINON, Mary	19	F	Spinster	18Au02Hm
SMART, James	21	M	Joiner	18Au02Hm
LYNAN, Ann	30	F	Spinster	18Au02Hm
TRUGBY, Juila	23	F	Spinster	18Au02Hm
DUNNE, Frances	19	F	Spinster	18Au02Hm
SHACKLETON, John	19	M	Laborer	18Au02Hm
Elizabeth (S)	11	F	Spinster	18Au02Hm
KENNEDY, Thomas	21	M	Laborer	18Au02Hm
John	12	M	Child	18Au02Hm
Thomas	09	M	Child	18Au02Hm
EUSTANU, James	35	M	Laborer	18Au02Hm
REYNOLDS, John	23	M	Farmer	18Au02Hm
Thomas	20	M	Farmer	18Au02Hm
KIERNAN, Patrick	30	M	Farmer	18Au02Hm
MCGUINNESS, Patrick	20	M	Farmer	18Au02Hm
FARRADY, Silvester	33	M	Farmer	18Au02Hm
Sarah	25	F	Wife	18Au02Hm
MCTISMAN, Patrick	21	M	Stableman	18Au02Hm
MCAVENNY, John	24	M	Laborer	18Au02Hm
BROPHY, Ellen	19	F	Spinster	18Au02Hm
FINNIGAN, Mary	21	F	Spinster	18Au02Hm
MCCARTHY, U	66	F	Wi	18Au02Hm
MCAULIFF, Mary	12	F	Spinster	18Au02Hm
DAVIS, Ann	33	F	Wife	18Au02Hm
Jane (D)	09	F	Child	18Au02Hm
John (S)	07	M	Child	18Au02Hm
Robert (S)	04	M	Child	18Au02Hm
Ann (D)	02	F	Child	18Au02Hm
HOGAN, Joanna	40	F	Wife	18Au02Hm
Margaret	20	F	Wife	18Au02Hm
William	16	M	Unknown	18Au02Hm
David	70	M	Husband	18Au02Hm
BARRY, John	30	M	Fisherman	18Au02Hm
Honora	50	F	Wife	18Au02Hm
JOHNS, J.F.	29	F	Poet	18Au02Hm
WARD, Luke	20	M	Mason	18Au02Hm
CONNOR, Cornelius	34	M	Farmer	18Au02Hm
Catharine	34	F	Wife	18Au02Hm
Margaret (D)	04	F	Child	18Au02Hm
Ann (D)	03	F	Child	18Au02Hm
BROWN, Catharine	13	F	Spinster	18Au02Hm
Margaret (S)	10	F	Spinster	18Au02Hm
Joanna (S)	08	F	Spinster	18Au02Hm
DONOHOE, Catharine	23	F	Spinster	18Au02Hm
Nancy (S)	21	F	Spinster	18Au02Hm
SAMUEL, Biddy	22	F	Spinster	18Au02Hm
MUNRIN, Henry	20	M	Joiner	18Au02Hm
DUFFEY, Margaret	23	F	Spinster	18Au02Hm
FITZGERALD, George	23	M	Farmer	18Au02Hm
Catharine	30	F	Wife	18Au02Hm
NASH, John	13	M	Farmer	18Au02Hm
SAHIFF, Honora	16	F	Unknown	18Au02Hm
BURK, Thomas	27	M	Laborer	18Au02Hm
MURPHY, Michael	30	M	Mason	18Au02Hm
KENNEDY, John	45	M	Grocer	18Au02Hm
Thomas (S)	09	M	Child	18Au02Hm
MAGINNIS, Margaret	22	F	Spinster	18Au02Hm
WOODS, Elisabeth	22	F	Spinster	18Au02Hm
MCNUESS, Elisabeth-Ann	20	F	Dressmaker	18Au02Hm
MCGOVERN, Margaret	20	F	Spinster	18Au02Hm
GREY, Sarah	20	F	Spinster	18Au02Hm
MCGOWEN, Ellen	20	F	Spinster	18Au02Hm

NAMES OF PASSENGERS		A G E	S E X	OCCUPATIONS	DATE PORT SHIP	NAMES OF PASSENGERS		A G E	S E X	OCCUPATIONS	DATE PORT SHIP
SANLEY, William		21	M	Laborer	18Au02Hm	CARROLL, Ann	(D)	18	F	Spinster	18Au02Hm
LEDDY, Mary		24	F	Spinster	18Au02Hm	Catharine	(D)	16	F	Spinster	18Au02Hm
REILLY, Margaret		11	F	Spinster	18Au02Hm	MCGEE, Charles		30	M	Farmer	18Au02Hm
CATHING, James		27	M	Butcher	18Au02Hm	MULLIN, Henry		20	M	Laborer	18Au02Hm
KISSICK, James		22	M	Dealer	18Au02Hm	OBRIEN, Margaret		20	F	Spinster	18Au02Hm
HUGHES, Hercules		30	M	Butcher	18Au02Hm	Isabella		20	F	Spinster	18Au02Hm
DOWING, Catharine		15	F	Spinster	18Au02Hm	RYAN, James		21	M	Laborer	18Au02Hm
John		13	M	Barmer	18Au02Hm	BURNS, Peter		24	M	Joiner	18Au02Hm
MCALLISTER, William		30	M	Engd	18Au02Hm	CLARK, William		23	M	Laborer	18Au02Hm
U		22	F	Wife	18Au02Hm	HANLEY, John		22	M	Laborer	18Au02Hm
BLACK, Elisabeth		31	F	Servant	18Au02Hm						
CRAIG, Jane		61	F	Servant	18Au02Hm						
Margaret	(D)	17	F	Servant	18Au02Hm						
MCNEILLS, Donald		52	M	Unknown	18Au02Hm						
HARRISON, Grace		18	F	Spinster	18Au02Hm						
BLACKFIELD, John		25	M	Forester	18Au02Hm			SHERIDAN 20 AUGUST 1846			
RYAN, Ralph		19	M	Groom	18Au02Hm						
REYNOLDS, William		26	M	Miller	18Au02Hm			From Liverpool			
WALSH, John		20	M	Laborer	18Au02Hm						
MULLADY, Mary		20	F	Spinster	18Au02Hm						
HANLON, Biddy		30	F	Wife	18Au02Hm						
Biddy	(D)	03	F	Child	18Au02Hm	ADAMS, James		26	M	Laborer	20Au02Do
MARTIN, Patrick		25	M	Merchant	18Au02Hm	CROSSON, Patk.		20	M	Laborer	20Au02Do
DAVIS, William		27	M	Farmer	18Au02Hm	BLAKELY, Wm.		46	M	Laborer	20Au02Do
CONOLLY, William		25	M	Shoemaker	18Au02Hm	U	(W)	45	F	Unknown	20Au02Do
SHORT, Joseph		20	M	Laborer	18Au02Hm	Eliza	(D)	05	F	Child	20Au02Do
DONOHOE, Patrick		20	M	Laborer	18Au02Hm	Sarah-Ann	(D)	18	F	Unknown	20Au02Do
MULLINS, Andrew		34	M	Laborer	18Au02Hm	BATTY, Saml.		24	M	Unknown	20Au02Do
Michael		30	M	Laborer	18Au02Hm	U	(W)	24	F	Unknown	20Au02Do
MURRAY, Wm.		40	M	Laborer	18Au02Hm	U		.00	U	Infant	20Au02Do
U		40	F	Wife	18Au02Hm	FEASHY, John-B.		26	M	Carpenter	20Au02Do
Edward	(S)	19	M	Spinner	18Au02Hm	U	(W)	25	F	Wife	20Au02Do
LYNCH, James		24	M	Laborer	18Au02Hm	BURGES, John		15	M	Shoemaker	20Au02Do
MURRAY, Catharine		00	F	Unknown	18Au02Hm	Geo.		13	M	Laborer	20Au02Do
MCNEILL, Ann		16	F	Spinster	18Au02Hm	CARTER, James		25	M	Laborer	20Au02Do
OLEARY, Ann		17	F	Spinster	18Au02Hm	CHILLON, Saml.		25	M	Laborer	20Au02Do
KEEGAN, Betsy		16	F	Spinster	18Au02Hm	HANSON, Hans-C.		24	M	Laborer	20Au02Do
LEARY, Biddy		18	F	Spinster	18Au02Hm	DROOMGOOLE, Thos.		26	M	Laborer	20Au02Do
MCCARTHY, U		28	F	Wife	18Au02Hm	THORPE, Charles		30	M	Laborer	20Au02Do
James	(S)	09	M	Child	18Au02Hm	SWIFT, James		39	M	Laborer	20Au02Do
Michael	(S)	.00	M	Infant	18Au02Hm	SCHOFIELD, Thos.		24	M	Laborer	20Au02Do
MCGURE, Patrick		20	M	Laborer	18Au02Hm	U	(W)	23	F	Unknown	20Au02Do
CORR, Patrick		30	M	Mason	18Au02Hm	U		02	U	Child	20Au02Do
SWEENEY, Luke		25	M	Policeman	18Au02Hm	Lydie		67	F	Unknown	20Au02Do
U		20	F	Wife	18Au02Hm	MARKEY, James		25	M	Servant	20Au02Do
SLAVEN, Daniel		20	M	Laborer	18Au02Hm	CUMMINGS, Mary		21	F	Unknown	20Au02Do
Michael		10	M	Laborer	18Au02Hm	MCCORMICK, John		45	M	Laborer	20Au02Do
KELLY, Margaret		13	F	Spinster	18Au02Hm	Margt.		40	F	Laborer	20Au02Do
WYNN, Biddy		34	F	Spinster	18Au02Hm	Ewd.		13	M	Laborer	20Au02Do
HEAVEY, James		40	M	Laborer	18Au02Hm	Rosana		12	F	Unknown	20Au02Do
HIGGINS, Patrick		35	M	Laborer	18Au02Hm	John		08	M	Child	20Au02Do
MCAVENNY, Ann		16	F	Spinster	18Au02Hm	CANFIELD, Mary		20	F	Laborer	20Au02Do
BREESON, Charles		24	M	Laborer	18Au02Hm	DUNNE, John		07	M	Child	20Au02Do
MCNAMMARA, Michael		24	M	Tailor	18Au02Hm	Maria		05	F	Child	20Au02Do
BREESON, U-Miss		24	F	Spinster	18Au02Hm	BURKE, Thos.		20	M	Laborer	20Au02Do
CUSHIN, Mary		24	F	Spinster	18Au02Hm	COLLIER, Thos.		04	M	Child	20Au02Do
FRY, John		43	M	Farmer	18Au02Hm	QUINN, Margt.		20	F	Unknown	20Au02Do
Mary		40	F	Wife	18Au02Hm	GILISHINHAM, Mary		50	F	Unknown	20Au02Do
Eliza	(D)	16	F	None	18Au02Hm	BUTLER, Patt		33	M	Laborer	20Au02Do
Sarah	(D)	15	F	None	18Au02Hm	REILEY, Bridget		38	F	Unknown	20Au02Do
Margaret	(D)	13	F	None	18Au02Hm	Michael	(S)	12	M	Unknown	20Au02Do
Hannah	(D)	09	F	Child	18Au02Hm	Patrick	(S)	10	M	Child	20Au02Do
Alexander	(S)	11	M	None	18Au02Hm	Thos.	(S)	08	M	Child	20Au02Do
Rachel	(D)	07	F	Child	18Au02Hm	FARRELL, Mary		23	F	Unknown	20Au02Do
William	(S)	04	M	Child	18Au02Hm	Margt.		20	F	Unknown	20Au02Do
Edward	(S)	02	M	Child	18Au02Hm	FEALAY, William		26	M	Smith	20Au02Do
Elias	(S)	.00	M	Infant	18Au02Hm	U	(W)	24	F	Unknown	20Au02Do
DARLEY, Kitty		19	F	Spinster	18Au02Hm	MCCABE, James		21	M	Laborer	20Au02Do
MATTHEWS, Richard		20	M	Servant	18Au02Hm	U	(W)	20	F	Unknown	20Au02Do
HENNING, Laurence		35	M	Laborer	18Au02Hm	REYNOLDS, Margt.		20	F	Unknown	20Au02Do
Honora		22	F	Spinster	18Au02Hm	BLESTO, James		35	M	Laborer	20Au02Do
GEICHY, Margaret		19	F	Spinster	18Au02Hm	U	(W)	30	F	Unknown	20Au02Do
LEONARD, Mary		20	F	Spinster	18Au02Hm	U		.00	U	Infant	20Au02Do
KEAN, Ellen		18	F	Spinster	18Au02Hm	Anne	(D)	09	F	Child	20Au02Do
CARROLL, Margaret		45	F	Spinster	18Au02Hm	FERTH, Henry		22	M	Laborer	20Au02Do

NAMES OF PASSENGERS		AGE	SEX	OCCUPATIONS	DATE PORT SHIP
GOODHILL, Thos.		23	M	Laborer	20Au02Do
HAMPSHIRE, Robt.		25	M	Laborer	20Au02Do
U	(W)	25	F	Unknown	20Au02Do
U		.00	U	Infant	20Au02Do
BROCK, James		25	M	Laborer	20Au02Do
U	(W)	24	F	Unknown	20Au02Do
RYMES, U-Mrs.		32	F	Unknown	20Au02Do
Thos.		11	M	Child	20Au02Do
Geo.		25	M	Laborer	20Au02Do
U	(W)	20	F	Unknown	20Au02Do
Anne		18	F	Unknown	20Au02Do
Sarah		08	F	Child	20Au02Do
Benjamin		17	M	Unknown	20Au02Do
Joseph		09	M	Child	20Au02Do
BROWN, Mary		20	F	Unknown	20Au02Do
DECLAY, Mary		20	F	Unknown	20Au02Do
SMALLWOOD, James		22	M	Laborer	20Au02Do
Mary		20	F	Qnknown	20Au02Do
HARRISON, William		40	M	Laborer	20Au02Do
FITZSIMONS, Patt		25	M	Laborer	20Au02Do
MATHEWS, Fanny		25	F	Laborer	20Au02Do
BOURSEY, Anne		19	F	Unknown	20Au02Do
CANNER, Patk.		25	M	Laborer	20Au02Do
LEITH, John		26	M	Laborer	20Au02Do
HAWKINS, Elizabeth		21	F	Laborer	20Au02Do
BRADLEY, Thos.		21	M	Laborer	20Au02Do
U	(W)	20	F	Laborer	20Au02Do
U		.00	U	Infant	20Au02Do
FOX, Alice		21	F	Laborer	20Au02Do
GALAGAR, U-Mrs.		20	F	Laborer	20Au02Do
HANE, Cathe.		20	F	Laborer	20Au02Do
FASTER, U-Mrs.		23	F	Laborer	20Au02Do
Richd.	(S)	02	M	Child	20Au02Do
NUGENT, Bridget		21	F	Laborer	20Au02Do
U		.00	U	Infant	20Au02Do
DALEY, Cathe.		20	F	Laborer	20Au02Do
RICHARDSON, John		25	M	Laborer	20Au02Do
WHITE, Mathew		30	M	Laborer	20Au02Do
U		.00	U	Infant	20Au02Do
RICHARDSON, Sarah		09	F	Child	20Au02Do
John		12	M	Child	20Au02Do
Ebenezar		07	M	Child	20Au02Do
MCHERMAN, Anne		22	F	Servant	20Au02Do
CLANCY, Thos.		24	M	Laborer	20Au02Do
MCPARTLAN, Mary		21	F	Unknown	20Au02Do
MCGUIRE, Nabby		22	F	Unknown	20Au02Do
CLUSKEY, Owen		24	M	Laborer	20Au02Do
CRINNAN, Mary		21	F	Laborer	20Au02Do
TIFFLE, U		24	M	Laborer	20Au02Do
LOWRY, M.C.		21	U	Laborer	20Au02Do
WOODS, Eliza		22	F	Laborer	20Au02Do
NUGENT, Michl.		30	M	Laborer	20Au02Do
MUBRYAN, Biddy		16	F	Laborer	20Au02Do
MCLAUGHLIN, Cathe.		17	F	Laborer	20Au02Do
GORMON, Patt		18	M	Laborer	20Au02Do
MURPHY, Charles		20	M	Laborer	20Au02Do
ROGERS, Charles		20	M	Laborer	20Au02Do
RAFFERTY, Thos.		20	M	Laborer	20Au02Do
CAILLER, Wm.		53	M	Laborer	20Au02Do
Elizabeth	(W)	53	F	Unknown	20Au02Do
Mary	(D)	19	F	Unknown	20Au02Do
MOHAN, Charles		24	M	Laborer	20Au02Do
Anne		21	F	Laborer	20Au02Do
CARNEY, Patrick		20	M	Laborer	20Au02Do
DOWD, Cathe.		25	F	Laborer	20Au02Do
REYNOLDS, Mary		20	F	Laborer	20Au02Do
MCDERMOT, Anne		20	F	Laborer	20Au02Do
HANLEY, Catherine		20	F	Laborer	20Au02Do
WALKER, Ellen		30	F	Laborer	20Au02Do
John		12	M	Laborer	20Au02Do
MCDONNELL, Mary		21	F	Laborer	20Au02Do
MCKENNA, Mary		20	F	Laborer	20Au02Do
MCDONNELL, Biddy		18	F	Laborer	20Au02Do
DOYLE, Cathe.		22	F	Laborer	20Au02Do
COLLIER, Thos.		18	M	Laborer	20Au02Do

NAMES OF PASSENGERS		AGE	SEX	OCCUPATIONS	DATE PORT SHIP
MCGEE, Michl.		00	M	Laborer	20Au02Do
Michl.		00	M	Laborer	20Au02Do
Cathe.		00	F	Maborer	20Au02Do
CAVENCH, Wm.		14	M	Laborer	20Au02Do
Sabina		22	F	Unknown	20Au02Do

PANTHEA 20 AUGUST 1846

From Liverpool

NAMES OF PASSENGERS		AGE	SEX	OCCUPATIONS	DATE PORT SHIP
NAUGHTON, Michael		28	M	Laborer	20Au02Ds
LEE, Bridget		21	F	None	20Au02Ds
HAYDEN, Margaret		22	F	None	20Au02Ds
GORMAN, Mary		18	F	None	20Au02Ds
FLYNN, Patk.		21	M	Farmer	20Au02Ds
DALANNOR, Cath.		23	F	None	20Au02Ds
Owen		19	M	None	20Au02Ds
CAMREN, Patk.		35	M	Farmer	20Au02Ds
MCCORMACK, Cath.		18	F	None	20Au02Ds
MADDEN, Cath.		20	F	None	20Au02Ds
SINNOTT, Hannah		24	F	None	20Au02Ds
MCCABE, Cath.		40	F	None	20Au02Ds
HUGHES, Rose		30	F	None	20Au02Ds
Mary	(D)	05	F	Child	20Au02Ds
Frances	(D)	03	F	Child	20Au02Ds
LANE, Patk.		41	M	Farmer	20Au02Ds
QUIGGIN, John		21	M	Farmer	20Au02Ds
HUOY, Cath.		21	F	None	20Au02Ds
BOYLE, Alice		20	F	None	20Au02Ds
MCKENNA, Bridget		20	F	None	20Au02Ds
GERWIN, Mary		36	F	None	20Au02Ds
Patk.	(S)	10	M	Child	20Au02Ds
William	(S)	09	M	Child	20Au02Ds
DALEY, Michael		18	M	Farmer	20Au02Ds
COYLE, Cath.		41	F	None	20Au02Ds
DEGGEN, Mary		13	F	None	20Au02Ds

ROBERT-A.PARKE 21 AUGUST 1846

From Liverpool

NAMES OF PASSENGERS		AGE	SEX	OCCUPATIONS	DATE PORT SHIP
OLEARY, Patrick		13	M	Laborer	21Au02Ir
MCLEAN, John		26	M	Laborer	21Au02Ir
George		24	M	Laborer	21Au02Ir
Agnes		21	F	Laborer	21Au02Ir
GORLEY, Peter		22	M	Laborer	21Au02Ir
MCKELVEY, Wm.		50	M	Laborer	21Au02Ir
BRODDIE, James		46	M	Laborer	21Au02Ir
U	(W)	44	F	Laborer	21Au02Ir
Margret	(D)	19	F	Laborer	21Au02Ir
Hugh	(S)	13	M	Laborer	21Au02Ir
James	(S)	20	M	Laborer	21Au02Ir
David	(S)	11	M	Child	21Au02Ir
John	(S)	10	M	Child	21Au02Ir
William	(S)	05	M	Child	21Au02Ir
Alexander	(S)	03	M	Child	21Au02Ir
KANE, Walter		25	M	Servant	21Au02Ir
BRYEN, Patrick		25	M	Servant	21Au02Ir
MONAGHAN, Owen		26	M	Servant	21Au02Ir
FITZSIMONS, Rose		25	F	Servant	21Au02Ir
DONHOE, Ann		22	F	Servant	21Au02Ir
MARKS, Susan		20	F	Servant	21Au02Ir
DIXON, Stephen		40	M	Servant	21Au02Ir

NAMES OF PASSENGERS		AGE	SEX	OCCUPATIONS	DATE PORT SHIP
DIXON, U	(W)	40	F	Servant	21Au02Ir
HOLMES, Wm.		28	M	Unknown	21Au02Ir
U	(W)	24	F	Unknown	21Au02Ir
Ann	(D)	.00	F	Infant	21Au02Ir
MCCLEAN, Susan		40	F	Unknown	21Au02Ir
REED, Mary		27	F	Unknown	21Au02Ir
WOODRUN, Agnes		18	F	Unknown	21Au02Ir
CROSS, Rose-Ann		60	F	Unknown	21Au02Ir
TWEEDY, Wm.		23	M	Laborer	21Au02Ir
LARSILN, James		25	M	Laborer	21Au02Ir
Cath.	(W)	23	F	Laborer	21Au02Ir
Bridget	(D)	.00	F	Infant	21Au02Ir
HIGGINS, Andrew		30	M	Laborer	21Au02Ir
MATHEWS, Bernard		21	M	Laborer	21Au02Ir
Alley		20	F	Laborer	21Au02Ir
LITTLE, Mary-Ann		20	F	Laborer	21Au02Ir
FLENNING, Peter		28	M	Laborer	21Au02Ir
PATTON, Wm.		19	M	Laborer	21Au02Ir
FANNON, James		17	M	Laborer	21Au02Ir
CLARK, Robert		20	M	Laborer	21Au02Ir
THOMAS, John		30	M	Laborer	21Au02Ir
HENDS, Alley		20	F	Laborer	21Au02Ir
QUINN, Bridget		20	F	Laborer	21Au02Ir
BURK, Thomas		20	M	Laborer	21Au02Ir
QUINN, Thomas		27	M	Laborer	21Au02Ir
LYONS, John		20	M	Laborer	21Au02Ir
MORGAN, James		20	M	Laborer	21Au02Ir
Judy	(M)	50	F	Laborer	21Au02Ir
Thomas		09	M	Child	21Au02Ir
MURRAY, Mathew		30	M	Laborer	21Au02Ir
MOORE, Thomas		19	M	Laborer	21Au02Ir
CARR, Hugh		40	M	Laborer	21Au02Ir
Mary	(D)	10	F	Child	21Au02Ir
Biddy	(D)	08	F	Seamstress	21Au02Ir
James	(S)	05	M	Child	21Au02Ir
John	(S)	04	M	Child	21Au02Ir
Henry	(S)	.00	M	Infant	21Au02Ir
FINNIK, Betty		50	F	Laborer	21Au02Ir
Ann-Jane	(D)	21	F	Laborer	21Au02Ir
Margret	(D)	19	F	Laborer	21Au02Ir
Mary	(D)	16	F	Laborer	21Au02Ir
WEIGH, Mary-M.		20	F	Laborer	21Au02Ir
MULLEN, Mary		21	F	Laborer	21Au02Ir
KERNAN, James		30	M	Laborer	21Au02Ir
DONNELEY, Mary		27	F	Laborer	21Au02Ir
Thomas	(S)	03	M	Child	21Au02Ir
MCCORMAC, Barney		19	M	Laborer	21Au02Ir
Pat		19	M	Laborer	21Au02Ir
KEEMAN, Thomas		19	M	Laborer	21Au02Ir
HANLON, Eliza		23	F	Laborer	21Au02Ir
FAY, Mary		21	F	Laborer	21Au02Ir
HYNES, Michael		30	M	Laborer	21Au02Ir
BURKE, Peter		20	M	Laborer	21Au02Ir
THOLLANS, Jos.		30	M	Laborer	21Au02Ir
U	(W)	25	F	Laborer	21Au02Ir
GLANCEY, Fanny		19	F	Laborer	21Au02Ir
MCDOWALL, Mary		18	F	Laborer	21Au02Ir
CUSLIGAN, Judy		35	F	Laborer	21Au02Ir
GLEESON, Mary		09	F	Child	21Au02Ir
MAHER, Cathy		18	F	Laborer	21Au02Ir
LONGDON, Pat		37	M	Laborer	21Au02Ir
MCNEIL, Hugh		22	M	Laborer	21Au02Ir
CARR, Dennis		25	M	Laborer	21Au02Ir
BUER, James		30	M	Laborer	21Au02Ir
WALLACE, Margret		19	F	Laborer	21Au02Ir
KELLY, Margret		19	F	Laborer	21Au02Ir
Johanna		19	F	Laborer	21Au02Ir
WALSH, Alice		20	F	Laborer	21Au02Ir
MULLEN, Mary		21	F	Laborer	21Au02Ir
MORAN, Mary		20	F	Laborer	21Au02Ir
Wm.		21	M	Laborer	21Au02Ir
Mary		19	F	Laborer	21Au02Ir
Ann		11	F	Child	21Au02Ir
FORK, Martha-Jane		20	F	Laborer	21Au02Ir
Martha		18	F	Laborer	21Au02Ir

NAMES OF PASSENGERS		AGE	SEX	OCCUPATIONS	DATE PORT SHIP
SWEENY, Ann		26	F	Laborer	21Au02Ir
TANNER, David		19	M	Laborer	21Au02Ir
TOOMEY, Michael		35	M	Laborer	21Au02Ir
MURPHY, Martha		23	F	Laborer	21Au02Ir
BLANEY, Ann		24	F	Laborer	21Au02Ir
Thomas		08	M	Child	21Au02Ir
George		05	M	Ahild	21Au02Ir
ROONEY, Ellen		24	F	Unknown	21Au02Ir
MORGAN, Thomas		23	M	Unknown	21Au02Ir

MARMION 22 AUGUST 1846

From Liverpool

NAMES OF PASSENGERS		AGE	SEX	OCCUPATIONS	DATE PORT SHIP
FOSTER, Francis		26	M	Farmer	22Au02Hc
VAUGHAN, Samuel		33	M	Machinist	22Au02Hc
Elizabeth		10	F	None	22Au02Hc
Mary		07	F	Child	22Au02Hc
Emma		04	F	Child	22Au02Hc
DONOHOE, Ann		35	F	None	22Au02Hc
HART, William		35	M	Weaver	22Au02Hc
Rachel	(W)	29	F	None	22Au02Hc
James	(S)	09	M	Child	22Au02Hc
Elizabeth	(D)	07	F	Child	22Au02Hc
Samuel	(S)	04	M	Child	22Au02Hc
ADAMS, Mary-Jane		26	F	None	22Au02Hc
John		07	M	Child	22Au02Hc
Robert		04	M	Child	22Au02Hc
William-James		01	M	Child	22Au02Hc
CAMPBELL, John		20	M	Laborer	22Au02Hc
BEIGH, Mary		20	F	Servant	22Au02Hc
CONNOR, Christopher		26	M	Laborer	22Au02Hc
Bridget	(W)	25	F	Wife	22Au02Hc
Patrick	(S)	01	M	Child	22Au02Hc
MCGUALLAN, John		22	M	Laborer	22Au02Hc
MCMULLEN, James		25	M	Laborer	22Au02Hc
SIMPSON, John		26	M	Laborer	22Au02Hc
HOLARAN, Susan		28	F	Servant	22Au02Hc
Mary		22	F	Servant	22Au02Hc
MCNICHOLL, Isabella		19	F	Servant	22Au02Hc
HANAGAN, Bridgett		20	F	Servant	22Au02Hc
HIGGINS, Terence		62	M	Weaver	22Au02Hc
Ann		31	F	None	22Au02Hc
John		12	M	None	22Au02Hc
KING, Sarah		13	F	None	22Au02Hc
MCKENNA, John		20	M	Laborer	22Au02Hc
KIRNAN, Philip		30	M	Laborer	22Au02Hc
Ann	(M)	67	F	None	22Au02Hc
DUNPHY, Julia		24	F	Servant	22Au02Hc
MCTULLOGH, Thomas		30	M	Laborer	22Au02Hc
KENNAY, Michael		24	M	Tailor	22Au02Hc
Mary		05	F	Child	22Au02Hc
FLYNN, Mary		40	F	Servant	22Au02Hc
SMITH, Biddy		49	F	Servant	22Au02Hc
COLLINS, Biddy		20	F	Servant	22Au02Hc
COYLE, Patrick		27	M	Laborer	22Au02Hc
LALOR, Dennis		30	M	Builder	22Au02Hc
Sarah	(W)	24	F	None	22Au02Hc
Joanna	(D)	03	F	Child	22Au02Hc
Eliza	(D)	.03	F	Infant	22Au02Hc
CUNNINGHAM, James		28	M	Laborer	22Au02Hc
Eleanor	(W)	25	F	None	22Au02Hc
Francis	(S)	.07	M	Infant	22Au02Hc
Died-At-Sea					
Bridgett	(D)	05	F	Child	22Au02Hc

NAMES OF PASSENGERS	AGE	SEX	OCCUPATIONS	DATE PORT SHIP

OXFORD 22 AUGUST 1846

From Liverpool

NAMES OF PASSENGERS	AGE	SEX	OCCUPATIONS	DATE PORT SHIP
KIRKPATRICK, James	20	M	Weaver	22Au02AJ
Jane	20	F	Unknown	22Au02AJ
WHALEN, Judy	28	F	Servant	22Au02AJ
MCMANN, Mary	19	F	Unknown	22Au02AJ
BERGEN, Bridgett	16	F	Unknown	22Au02AJ
Mary	13	F	Unknown	22Au02AJ
KEHOE, James	13	M	Unknown	22Au02AJ
LYNCH, Thomas	26	M	Unknown	22Au02AJ
LINDSAY, Mike	20	M	Laborer	22Au02AJ
KELLEY, Mary	03	F	Child	22Au02AJ
TOWNER, James	22	M	Laborer	22Au02AJ
LINDSAY, Mary	29	F	Servant	22Au02AJ
Jane	22	F	Servant	22Au02AJ
TURNEY, Mary	20	F	Servant	22Au02AJ
DOCKERTY, Margrett	20	F	Servant	22Au02AJ
James	30	M	Laborer	22Au02AJ
HUNT, Pat	19	M	Laborer	22Au02AJ
HERN, John	20	M	Laborer	22Au02AJ
MCCURRIE, Mary	19	F	Servant	22Au02AJ
BURNS, Mag	16	F	Servant	22Au02AJ
BLESSING, Mary	30	F	Servant	22Au02AJ
MOORE, Winney	19	F	Servant	22Au02AJ
SHANLEY, Margrett	22	F	Servant	22Au02AJ
GILSHIN, James	38	M	Laborer	22Au02AJ
HUGHES, U	24	M	Weaver	22Au02AJ
Peter	14	M	Weaver	22Au02AJ
OHARARA, William	24	M	Laborer	22Au02AJ
CAMPBELL, Mary	21	F	Dressmaker	22Au02AJ
HUGHES, Ann	38	F	Servant	22Au02AJ
CARL, Mary	22	F	Servant	22Au02AJ
MCDANNIEL, Pat	23	M	Laborer	22Au02AJ
HAGAN, Pat	17	M	Laborer	22Au02AJ
HANLIN, Pat	30	M	Cooper	22Au02AJ
GRAHAM, James	23	M	Carpenter	22Au02AJ
MADDEN, Mary	20	F	Servant	22Au02AJ
Pat	18	M	Soap Maker	22Au02AJ
FITZGERALD, Amelia	11	F	Child	22Au02AJ
MCKENMER, Pat	22	M	Laborer	22Au02AJ
BOLDS, James	21	M	Weaver	22Au02AJ
STEVENSON, Margrett	25	F	Milliner	22Au02AJ
GORMAN, Harriett	20	F	Milliner	22Au02AJ
Ann	25	F	Servant	22Au02AJ
Kate	22	F	Servant	22Au02AJ
ODWINE, Mary	28	F	Dressmaker	22Au02AJ
SHELLEY, Mary	23	F	Dressmaker	22Au02AJ
KITON, Mary	22	F	Servant	22Au02AJ
ODWINE, Philip	03	M	Child	22Au02AJ
FALLAN, Mary	26	F	Servant	22Au02AJ
REYNOLDS, Margrett	12	F	Servant	22Au02AJ
MURPHY, Bridgett	17	F	Servant	22Au02AJ
Rose	26	F	Servant	22Au02AJ
BURKE, Frank	26	M	Laborer	22Au02AJ
BARNEY, James	40	M	Chandler	22Au02AJ
MULLER, Mary	26	F	Servant	22Au02AJ
DOYLE, Ellen	24	F	Servant	22Au02AJ
GEFFANEY, Elisha	25	M	Laborer	22Au02AJ
MURRY, Thomas	24	M	Tailor	22Au02AJ
JORDON, Biddy	17	F	Dressmaker	22Au02AJ
TONMAY, Biddy	25	F	Dressmaker	22Au02AJ
DONAHOE, Mathew	19	M	Laborer	22Au02AJ
LENNARD, Charles	18	M	Laborer	22Au02AJ
GOODWIN, Peter	20	M	Laborer	22Au02AJ
CONLEY, Pat	16	M	Unknown	22Au02AJ
Frank	11	M	Child	22Au02AJ
FOX, Mary	26	F	Unknown	22Au02AJ
FOX, Mike	04	M	Child	22Au02AJ
John	24	M	Unknown	22Au02AJ
AIKIN, Judy	24	F	Servant	22Au02AJ
MURPHY, Catharine	22	F	Unknown	22Au02AJ
LOCHERBY, Mary	38	F	Unknown	22Au02AJ
MCCABE, Mike	26	M	Clerk	22Au02AJ
MCDONOUGH, James	21	M	Clerk	22Au02AJ
COONEY, Brigett	34	F	Servant	22Au02AJ
FITZGERALD, Ann	29	F	Servant	22Au02AJ
FLINN, Maria	11	F	Child	22Au02AJ
FAGAN, Magrett	22	F	Unknown	22Au02AJ
MOONEY, Judy	36	F	Unknown	22Au02AJ
MCCAHAN, Pat	40	M	Laborer	22Au02AJ
Mary (W)	35	F	Servant	22Au02AJ
James (S)	13	M	Laborer	22Au02AJ
Bartley (S)	12	M	Laborer	22Au02AJ
Terrence (S)	11	M	Laborer	22Au02AJ
Margt. (D)	10	F	Servant	22Au02AJ
Pat (S)	08	M	Child	22Au02AJ
Brian (S)	06	M	Child	22Au02AJ
Thomas (S)	03	M	Child	22Au02AJ
STOST, Cornelius	40	M	Laborer	22Au02AJ
GRAHAM, Mary-Ann	22	F	Unknown	22Au02AJ
FARSLOW, Catharine	48	F	Servant	22Au02AJ
John	18	M	Laborer	22Au02AJ
BUTLER, Sarah	17	F	Unknown	22Au02AJ
TREER, Arthur	24	M	Farmer	22Au02AJ
FARSLOW, James	28	M	Laborer	22Au02AJ
ROCKWELL, Susan	53	F	Unknown	22Au02AJ
Mary (D)	19	F	Servant	22Au02AJ
Rubin (S)	14	M	Unknown	22Au02AJ
KEENER, Mike	60	M	Laborer	22Au02AJ
James (S)	24	M	Unknown	22Au02AJ
Frank (S)	22	M	Unknown	22Au02AJ
Rose (W)	54	F	Unknown	22Au02AJ
Pat (S)	18	M	Unknown	22Au02AJ
Ann (D)	24	F	Unknown	22Au02AJ
REARD, John	12	M	Unknown	22Au02AJ
YOUNG, John	44	M	Tailor	22Au02AJ
William	20	M	Laborer	22Au02AJ
ROGAN, John	20	M	Shoemaker	22Au02AJ
ADAMS, Martin	25	M	Tanner	22Au02AJ
MADDIGIN, John	39	M	Laborer	22Au02AJ
FLINT, William	17	M	Laborer	22Au02AJ
OBRIEN, Mary	19	F	Servant	22Au02AJ
ANDERSON, Margrett	18	F	Servant	22Au02AJ
DEMPSEY, Kate	15	F	Servant	22Au02AJ
OBRIEN, Ellen	19	F	Servant	22Au02AJ
SULLIVAN, Pat	23	M	Laborer	22Au02AJ
WELCH, Mary	13	F	Servant	22Au02AJ
MIDDLETON, John	50	M	Laborer	22Au02AJ
Mary	14	F	Servant	22Au02AJ
BRENNEN, Mary	23	F	Dressmaker	22Au02AJ
ONEIL, Kate	25	F	Servant	22Au02AJ
HAMILTON, Mary	41	F	Weaver	22Au02AJ
SENNETT, Bartlett	27	M	Laborer	22Au02AJ
COFFEE, John	24	M	Laborer	22Au02AJ

SOUTHERNER 25 AUGUST 1846

From Liverpool

NAMES OF PASSENGERS	AGE	SEX	OCCUPATIONS	DATE PORT SHIP
ARMSTRONG, Patrick	21	M	Mechanic	25Au02Dy
FURY, James	50	M	Mechanic	25Au02Dy
CORROAN, Cornelius	42	M	Mechanic	25Au02Dy
RODGERS, Patrick	19	M	Laborer	25Au02Dy
FENAN, Michael	25	M	Laborer	25Au02Dy
COSTOLE, Owen	32	M	Laborer	25Au02Dy
FOWLER, Charles	23	M	Laborer	25Au02Dy

NAMES OF PASSENGERS		AGE	SEX	OCCUPATIONS	DATE PORT SHIP
CARROLL, Margt.		25	F	Laborer	25Au02Dy
RYAN, Michael		24	M	Laborer	25Au02Dy
U	(W)	28	F	Laborer	25Au02Dy
BEATY, Bridget		30	F	Laborer	25Au02Dy
BRADY, Catherine		21	F	Laborer	25Au02Dy
SMITH, Mary		17	F	Laborer	25Au02Dy
Margt.		16	F	Naborer	25Au02Dy
MARA, Michael		20	M	Laborer	25Au02Dy
MCCAWLEY, Cornelius		30	M	Laborer	25Au02Dy
U	(W)	25	F	Laborer	25Au02Dy
CLONNAN, Thomas		19	M	Laborer	25Au02Dy
CANNON, Dorothy		19	F	Laborer	25Au02Dy
COYLE, Mary		20	F	Laborer	25Au02Dy
KERNAN, John		28	M	Laborer	25Au02Dy
U	(W)	23	F	Laborer	25Au02Dy
KITYDOWN, Bridget		21	F	Laborer	25Au02Dy
HANDWRIGHT, Bridget		26	F	Laborer	25Au02Dy
SMITH, William		40	M	Mechanic	25Au02Dy
FAYGIN, Michael		20	M	Mechanic	25Au02Dy
KEARNEY, Rodger		36	M	Mechanic	25Au02Dy
BYRNS, John		40	M	Mechanic	25Au02Dy
GRIFFIN, Patrick		33	M	Mechanic	25Au02Dy
John		13	M	Unknown	25Au02Dy
William		11	M	Child	25Au02Dy
Patrick		09	M	Child	25Au02Dy
Thomas		02	M	Child	25Au02Dy
WILSON, James		24	M	Mechanic	25Au02Dy
KEATING, Peter		22	M	Mechanic	25Au02Dy
NAUGHTON, Patrick		23	M	Mechanic	25Au02Dy
KING, Ellen		22	F	Unknown	25Au02Dy
KEATIN, Catherine		21	F	Wife	25Au02Dy
Mary-Ann	(D)	01	F	Child	25Au02Dy
KENAN, Jane		26	F	Unknown	25Au02Dy
DEKIN, Hannah		24	F	Unknown	25Au02Dy

NAMES OF PASSENGERS		AGE	SEX	OCCUPATIONS	DATE PORT SHIP
OBRIEN, James	(S)	35	M	Farmer	27Au02Is
Bridget	(D)	29	F	Unknown	27Au02Is
Bridget		01	F	Child	27Au02Is
MEADE, Patty		35	F	Servant	27Au02Is
ODONNELL, Mary		29	F	Unknown	27Au02Is
NEWMAN, Betsey		40	F	Unknown	27Au02Is
MCCORMICK, Ann		11	F	Child	27Au02Is
James	(B)	07	M	Child	27Au02Is
PHILAN, Johanna		35	F	Servant	27Au02Is
CAMPBELL, James		68	M	Laborer	27Au02Is
Ellen	(D)	14	F	Unknown	27Au02Is
Catherine	(D)	16	F	Unknown	27Au02Is
PHELAN, Bessy		18	F	Servant	27Au02Is
CAFFREY, Catherine		17	F	Servant	27Au02Is
CUSHMAN, Bridget		25	F	Servant	27Au02Is
CAREY, Michael		13	M	Unknown	27Au02Is
FALLON, Mary		34	F	Unknown	27Au02Is
MCKENNY, Andrew		20	M	Laborer	27Au02Is
Ellen		18	F	Servant	27Au02Is
KELLY, Catherine		20	F	Servant	27Au02Is
BROWN, George		21	M	Clerk	27Au02Is
MCDERMOT, John		24	M	Laborer	27Au02Is
ENNIS, Luke		21	M	Laborer	27Au02Is
MALONE, Catherine		18	F	Servant	27Au02Is
HUNT, Patrick		30	M	Laborer	27Au02Is
John		22	M	Laborer	27Au02Is
CURRAY, Margaret		50	F	Unknown	27Au02Is
William	(S)	15	M	Unknown	27Au02Is
FORD, Margaret		35	F	Unknown	27Au02Is
Margaret	(D)	05	F	Child	27Au02Is
Jane	(D)	03	F	Child	27Au02Is
OSULLIVAN, Patk.		32	M	Clergyman	27Au02Is

SEA-OF-NEW-YORK 27 AUGUST 1846

From Liverpool

NAMES OF PASSENGERS		AGE	SEX	OCCUPATIONS	DATE PORT SHIP
KEANE, Patrick		35	M	Peddler	27Au02Is
BOGAN, Robert		48	M	Sailor	27Au02Is
HAGGARTY, James		35	M	Laborer	27Au02Is
MCGINTY, Patrick		40	M	Peddler	27Au02Is
SHIELDS, Elinor		20	F	Servant	27Au02Is
Zachariah		19	M	Laborer	27Au02Is
William		12	M	Child	27Au02Is
SLAVIN, James		37	M	Laborer	27Au02Is
Mary		15	F	Servant	27Au02Is
CARNEY, Ann		50	F	Unknown	27Au02Is
Mary	(D)	20	F	Servant	27Au02Is
Bridget	(D)	14	F	Servant	27Au02Is
KIND, Catherine		30	F	Servant	27Au02Is
MULDRY, Mary		19	F	Servant	27Au02Is
HENRY, Dominick		24	M	Laborer	27Au02Is
KENNEDY, Philip		19	M	Laborer	27Au02Is
TERMAN, Martin		24	M	Laborer	27Au02Is
BURKE, Patrick		24	M	Blacksmith	27Au02Is
FITZPATRICK, Betsy		28	F	Servant	27Au02Is
SALMON, Catherine		18	F	Servant	27Au02Is
MCCAFFREY, Ellen		18	F	Servant	27Au02Is
MCCORMICK, Jane		17	F	Servant	27Au02Is
TURNAN, James		20	M	Laborer	27Au02Is
John		22	M	Laborer	27Au02Is
Mary		18	F	Servant	27Au02Is
GRIFFIN, William		30	M	Laborer	27Au02Is
Eliza		30	F	Unknown	27Au02Is
RYAN, James		53	M	Farmer	27Au02Is
CONNOR, Catherine		22	F	Servant	27Au02Is
OBRIEN, Terence		76	M	Farmer	27Au02Is

VIRGINIAN 27 AUGUST 1846

From Liverpool

NAMES OF PASSENGERS		AGE	SEX	OCCUPATIONS	DATE PORT SHIP
PERRIN, George		30	M	Tailor	27Au02Ap
Elizabeth		26	F	Wife	27Au02Ap
Jane	(D)	06	F	Child	27Au02Ap
Henry	(S)	01	M	Child	27Au02Ap
BROWN, John		35	M	Tailor	27Au02Ap
Marcella		30	F	Unknown	27Au02Ap
MCCORMICK, Pat		27	M	Carpenter	27Au02Ap
Mary		26	F	Wife	27Au02Ap
Betsey	(D)	06	F	Child	27Au02Ap
John	(S)	04	M	Child	27Au02Ap
Francis	(S)	02	M	Child	27Au02Ap
Catherine	(D)	.01	F	Infant	27Au02Ap
CAULEY, Mary		50	F	Domestic	27Au02Ap
Roger	(S)	18	M	Laborer	27Au02Ap
Mary	(D)	14	F	Unknown	27Au02Ap
Betsey	(D)	12	F	Unknown	27Au02Ap
Margret	(D)	09	F	Child	27Au02Ap
Patrick	(S)	06	M	Child	27Au02Ap
Michael		47	M	Weaver	27Au02Ap
ARGY, Sarah		45	F	Wife	27Au02Ap
Margret	(D)	14	F	Unknown	27Au02Ap
Jane	(D)	12	F	Unknown	27Au02Ap
John	(S)	10	M	Child	27Au02Ap
Charles		07	M	Child	27Au02Ap
Alexander	(S)	02	M	Child	27Au02Ap
FINERTY, Roger		25	M	Laborer	27Au02Ap
James		24	M	Laborer	27Au02Ap
Mary		01	F	Child	27Au02Ap
HEURTON, Sarah		37	F	Domestic	27Au02Ap
William		16	M	Laborer	27Au02Ap
Elizabeth		12	F	Unknown	27Au02Ap
CUSHAN, Richard		21	M	Tailor	27Au02Ap

NAMES OF PASSENGERS		AGE	SEX	OCCUPATIONS	DATE PORT SHIP
DURVAN, Ellen		29	F	Domestic	27Au02Ap
EFFERAN, Alex		17	M	Laborer	27Au02Ap
KILMARTIN, Patrick		21	M	Laborer	27Au02Ap
OBRIEN, Catherine		21	F	Unknown	27Au02Ap
HARLOW, John		18	M	Glove Maker	27Au02Ap
Sarah		20	F	Unknown	27Au02Ap
Mary-Jane		12	F	Unknown	27Au02Ap
Michael		14	M	Unknown	27Au02Ap
BELL, John		22	M	Tailor	27Au02Ap
Eliza		19	F	Domestic	27Au02Ap
Sarah		17	F	Unknown	27Au02Ap
STRANNEY, Margret		20	F	Unknown	27Au02Ap
CORMACKERN, Mary		16	F	Unknown	27Au02Ap
OBRIEN, Patrick		19	M	Laborer	27Au02Ap
Ellen		16	F	Domestic	27Au02Ap
SMITH, Mary		16	F	Unknown	27Au02Ap
BURKE, Michael		23	M	Laborer	27Au02Ap
DONLER, Bridget		20	F	Servant	27Au02Ap
VINGLEY, Peter		20	M	Laborer	27Au02Ap
CAHAO, Thomas		20	M	Unknown	27Au02Ap
OBRIEN, Jane		20	F	Domestic	27Au02Ap
CORMACKERN, Mary		20	F	Domestic	27Au02Ap
CARBRO, Bridget		14	F	Domestic	27Au02Ap
James		10	M	Child	27Au02Ap
HIGGINS, Biddy		46	F	Domestic	27Au02Ap
Thomas	(S)	13	M	Unknown	27Au02Ap
OWENS, Catherine		35	F	Domestic	27Au02Ap
Biddy	(D)	05	F	Child	27Au02Ap
Ann	(D)	03	F	Child	27Au02Ap
Mary	(D)	.11	F	Infant	27Au02Ap
SMITH, Andrew		20	M	Laborer	27Au02Ap
WORKE, Margret		20	F	Domestic	27Au02Ap
GILLENY, Ann		33	F	Domestic	27Au02Ap
SHANLEY, Edward		10	M	Child	27Au02Ap
MCGOVAN, Mary		20	F	Domestic	27Au02Ap
MONEY, Rose		16	F	Domestic	27Au02Ap
HOPPER, Catherine		18	F	Domestic	27Au02Ap
DONAGHAN, John		17	M	Laborer	27Au02Ap
Mary		12	F	Unknown	27Au02Ap
CORKMAN, Michael		12	M	Unknown	27Au02Ap
QUIN, Martin		22	M	Tailor	27Au02Ap
RYAN, Mathew		28	M	Laborer	27Au02Ap
MCINTIRE, Jane		18	F	Seamstress	27Au02Ap
LOWRY, Ellen		30	F	Domestic	27Au02Ap
MCGARTH, Mary		22	F	Domestic	27Au02Ap
FLANETY, Margret		22	F	Tailor	27Au02Ap
GAYNOR, Eliza		22	F	Tailor	27Au02Ap
GILWAY, Wm.		19	M	Laborer	27Au02Ap
LESLIE, Robert		35	M	Farmer	27Au02Ap
Nancy		24	F	Unknown	27Au02Ap
CRUSE, Daniel		18	M	Painter	27Au02Ap
COULY, Michael		23	M	Laborer	27Au02Ap
HAGIN, John		28	M	Turner	27Au02Ap
BALL, Francis		22	M	Shoemaker	27Au02Ap
Joshua		12	M	Unknown	27Au02Ap
John		06	M	Child	27Au02Ap
HONE, Ellen		23	F	Unknown	27Au02Ap
MCMANNUS, Jane		12	F	Unknown	27Au02Ap
STANN, James		24	M	Painter	27Au02Ap
Caroline		23	F	Unknown	27Au02Ap
COCKRAN, Mary		30	F	Domestic	27Au02Ap
Mariah	(D)	03	F	Child	27Au02Ap
Thomas	(S)	05	M	Child	27Au02Ap
Samuel	(S)	.06	M	Infant	27Au02Ap
CLINTON, Ann		30	F	Domestic	27Au02Ap
Rosannah	(D)	13	F	Unknown	27Au02Ap
James	(S)	09	M	Child	27Au02Ap
KELLY, Ann		22	F	Laborer	27Au02Ap
RUSSELL, Mary		45	F	Domestic	27Au02Ap
MONNEY, Mary		30	F	Domestic	27Au02Ap
LITTLE, Susannah		25	F	Domestic	27Au02Ap
Ellen		19	F	Domestic	27Au02Ap
Matilda		16	F	Domestic	27Au02Ap
HARRINGTON, Mary		23	F	Seamstress	27Au02Ap
MCCLOUR, Mary		15	F	Unknown	27Au02Ap
FONGY, Mary		20	F	Servant	27Au02Ap
MALONE, Mary		17	F	Servant	27Au02Ap
TROY, Mary		19	F	Servant	27Au02Ap
CARROL, John		36	M	Glass Maker	27Au02Ap
Sarah		36	F	Wife	27Au02Ap
Thomas	(S)	14	M	Unknown	27Au02Ap
MURPHY, Margret		35	F	Domestic	27Au02Ap
NOLAN, Catherine		16	F	Unknown	27Au02Ap
MEEKMAN, Ellen		43	F	Unknown	27Au02Ap
CURRY, Mary		03	F	Child	27Au02Ap
Catherine	(M)	23	F	Unknown	27Au02Ap
John		12	M	Unknown	27Au02Ap
MCCOSLEN, Ann		27	F	Unknown	27Au02Ap
CURRY, Patrick		06	M	Child	27Au02Ap
MCMAN, John		25	M	Laborer	27Au02Ap
GILOOLY, James		21	M	Unknown	27Au02Ap
OWEN, Bridget		19	F	Domestic	27Au02Ap
FORD, Bently		20	M	Laborer	27Au02Ap
DONLAN, Patrick		20	M	Laborer	27Au02Ap
HADLY, William		16	M	Laborer	27Au02Ap
MAKINAH, John		17	M	Laborer	27Au02Ap
CAIN, Thomas		13	M	Laborer	27Au02Ap
FITZPATRICK, James		14	M	Laborer	27Au02Ap
VIRTUE, Patrick		20	M	Laborer	27Au02Ap
MCGARTH, Mathew		32	M	Laborer	27Au02Ap
PHENY, Owen		26	M	Laborer	27Au02Ap
GAHON, John		28	M	Laborer	27Au02Ap
FLANETY, Martin		20	M	Laborer	27Au02Ap
GALLAGHER, Barney		20	M	Tinman	27Au02Ap
Thomas		18	M	Bell Hanger	27Au02Ap
GLEASON, Patrick		30	M	Laborer	27Au02Ap
HICKEY, Edward		24	M	Blacksmith	27Au02Ap
Mary		21	F	Domestic	27Au02Ap
FOWLY, John		22	M	Laborer	27Au02Ap
MAHONY, Sarah		17	F	Domestic	27Au02Ap
RAWEN, Margret		17	F	Domestic	27Au02Ap
TIVLAN, Patrick		50	M	Laborer	27Au02Ap
Mary		18	F	Domestic	27Au02Ap
HUSE, Biddy		20	F	Domestic	27Au02Ap
HAMAGEN, Cornelius		30	M	Farmer	27Au02Ap
TIGHE, Peter		23	M	Laborer	27Au02Ap
MAHON, Thomas		25	M	Laborer	27Au02Ap

ADIRONDACK 01 SEPTEMBER 1846

From Liverpool

NAMES OF PASSENGERS		AGE	SEX	OCCUPATIONS	DATE PORT SHIP
DUMINE, Ann		24	F	Unknown	01Se02Om
Ann		20	F	Unknown	01Se02Om
EADE, Ellnaleck		24	M	Carpenter	01Se02Om
U	(W)	24	F	Unknown	01Se02Om
Edwin	(S)	.06	M	Infant	01Se02Om
GARRETT, James		25	M	Blacksmith	01Se02Om
KELLY, Edw.		23	M	Laborer	01Se02Om
Mary		20	F	Unknown	01Se02Om
LYNCH, Mary		20	F	Unknown	01Se02Om
CONWAY, Martha		23	F	Unknown	01Se02Om
MCEVOY, Bridget		25	F	Unknown	01Se02Om
Catherine		20	F	Unknown	01Se02Om
Patrick		50	M	Unknown	01Se02Om
MADDEN, Michael		24	M	Laborer	01Se02Om
Mary		28	F	Unknown	01Se02Om
MCCORMICK, Rich.		22	M	Laborer	01Se02Om
MCCLUSKEY, James		24	M	Tailor	01Se02Om
FREEBORN, Jane		60	F	Unknown	01Se02Om
ELLIOTT, Isabella		21	F	Unknown	01Se02Om
BOWDEN, Margt.		20	F	Unknown	01Se02Om
MUNDY, Mark		25	M	Laborer	01Se02Om
U	(W)	37	F	Unknown	01Se02Om

NAMES OF PASSENGERS		AGE	SEX	OCCUPATIONS	DATE PORT SHIP
MALLOY, Jno.		25	M	Accountant	01Se02Cm
MALONE, Edwd.		23	M	Cooper	01Se02Cm
SAVILLE, Joseph		50	M	Weaver	01Se02Cm
Joseph		17	M	Unknown	01Se02Cm
George		10	M	Unknown	01Se02Cm
MORRIS, Margt.		24	F	Unknown	01Se02Cm
DUNN, Dolly		24	F	Unknown	01Se02Cm
WILLIAMS, Mary		25	F	Unknown	01Se02Cm
John		25	M	Miner	01Se02Cm
Thomas		20	M	Miner	01Se02Cm
Charles		20	M	Miner	01Se02Cm
JAY, Ann		20	F	Unknown	01Se02Cm
JAMES, Thos.		21	M	Carpenter	01Se02Cm
Catherine	(W)	21	F	Unknown	01Se02Cm
David	(S)	02	M	Child	01Se02Cm
COFFEE, Thos.		23	M	Carpenter	01Se02Cm
U	(W)	27	F	Unknown	01Se02Cm
John	(S)	03	M	Child	01Se02Cm
Thomas	(S)	.06	M	Infant	01Se02Cm
Died-At-Sea					
FARRELL, Timothy		32	M	Laborer	01Se02Cm
FISK, U		35	M	Weaver	01Se02Cm
PRICE, Francis		22	M	Weaver	01Se02Cm
LINDSAY, George		24	M	Tailor	01Se02Cm
BURKE, Michael		22	M	Laborer	01Se02Cm
FLYNN, Thos.		60	M	Laborer	01Se02Cm
WALSH, John		21	M	Laborer	01Se02Cm
Died-At-Sea					
LONIE, Thos.		25	M	Laborer	01Se02Cm
DONELLY, Pat		22	M	Laborer	01Se02Cm
BYRNE, Owen		26	M	Laborer	01Se02Cm
JAMISON, Wm.		20	M	Carpenter	01Se02Cm
COLLIGAN, Biddy		28	F	Unknown	01Se02Cm
MYLES, Ann		28	F	Unknown	01Se02Cm
Edw.	(S)	06	M	Child	01Se02Cm
CALLIGHAN, Biddy		28	F	Unknown	01Se02Cm
Hannah		12	F	Unknown	01Se02Cm
Mary		11	F	Unknown	01Se02Cm
Dennis		08	M	Child	01Se02Cm
TIERNEY, James		33	M	Blacksmith	01Se02Cm
Johanna	(W)	32	F	Unknown	01Se02Cm
James	(S)	12	M	Unknown	01Se02Cm
David	(S)	08	M	Child	01Se02Cm
Thomas	(S)	05	M	Child	01Se02Cm
John	(S)	01	M	Child	01Se02Cm
Edw.	(S)	.06	M	Infant	01Se02Cm
BENNETT, Pat		26	M	Laborer	01Se02Cm
CRONAN, Pat		20	M	Laborer	01Se02Cm
HEENAN, Mick		20	M	Laborer	01Se02Cm
Ony		20	M	Unknown	01Se02Cm
RYAN, Ann		18	F	Unknown	01Se02Cm
FIELDEN, Thos.		20	M	Blacksmith	01Se02Cm
SHANLEY, Pat		20	M	Laborer	01Se02Cm
ONEIL, U		22	M	Carpenter	01Se02Cm
U	(W)	20	F	Unknown	01Se02Cm
DRUMMOND, Mary		21	F	Unknown	01Se02Cm
HANBERY, Peter		20	M	Tailor	01Se02Cm
MCGUIRE, Edw.		21	M	Laborer	01Se02Cm
MURPHY, Edw.		11	M	Laborer	01Se02Cm
CONDRON, John		23	M	Laborer	01Se02Cm
Mary		22	F	Unknown	01Se02Cm
DILLON, Edw.		50	M	Laborer	01Se02Cm
Edw.		16	M	Laborer	01Se02Cm
CROUGHWELL, Jno.		22	M	Carpenter	01Se02Cm
HARRIGAN, Cath.		25	F	Unknown	01Se02Cm
Bridget	(D)	03	F	Child	01Se02Cm
Michael	(S)	.06	M	Infant	01Se02Cm
CARRACK, Mary		20	F	Unknown	01Se02Cm
BENSEN, Wm.		24	M	Weaver	01Se02Cm
PHILIPS, Jas.		23	M	Tailor	01Se02Cm
DUNNE, John		20	M	Laborer	01Se02Cm
BRIGAN, Pat		22	M	Laborer	01Se02Cm
KNOX, James		20	M	Carpenter	01Se02Cm
KENNEDY, Jno.		30	M	Carpenter	01Se02Cm
Eliza		30	F	Unknown	01Se02Cm
HAMILTON, Jas.		40	M	Tailor	01Se02Cm
SHIELDS, Jno.		25	M	Tailor	01Se02Cm
MOORE, Alex.		18	M	Laborer	01Se02Cm
CAUGHLAN, Jno.		30	M	Laborer	01Se02Cm
Martha	(W)	21	F	Unknown	01Se02Cm
Martha	(D)	.08	F	Infant	01Se02Cm
MCDOUGALL, Martha		18	F	Unknown	01Se02Cm
FONENG, Mary		24	F	Unknown	01Se02Cm
BLAIR, Jane		18	F	Unknown	01Se02Cm
FINLEY, Betsey		18	F	Unknown	01Se02Cm
MURPHEY, Wm.		23	M	Blacksmith	01Se02Cm
BRIAN, Bridget		40	F	Unknown	01Se02Cm
Patrick	(S)	06	M	Child	01Se02Cm
LONG, Wm.		30	M	Carpenter	01Se02Cm
Julia	(W)	27	F	Unknown	01Se02Cm
David		22	M	Unknown	01Se02Cm
Rebecca		20	F	Unknown	01Se02Cm
Eliza	(D)	06	F	Child	01Se02Cm
Henry	(S)	04	M	Child	01Se02Cm
Hannah	(D)	.06	F	Infant	01Se02Cm
EVANS, Reese		40	M	Miner	01Se02Cm
Elizabeth	(W)	40	F	Unknown	01Se02Cm
Thomas		16	M	Unknown	01Se02Cm
David		26	M	Unknown	01Se02Cm
Margt.		28	F	Unknown	01Se02Cm
Ann		.06	F	Infant	01Se02Cm
MORGAN, Abm.		33	M	Unknown	01Se02Cm
Elizabeth		36	F	Unknown	01Se02Cm
JENKINS, Mary		07	F	Child	01Se02Cm
JONES, Wm.		20	M	Miner	01Se02Cm
FREENY, Cath.		20	F	Unknown	01Se02Cm
PARRY, Thos.		23	M	Miner	01Se02Cm
Ann		26	F	Unknown	01Se02Cm
Margt.		18	F	Unknown	01Se02Cm
CARTY, Bridget		20	F	Unknown	01Se02Cm
HIGGINS, Mary		18	F	Unknown	01Se02Cm
HEALEY, Pat		20	M	Laborer	01Se02Cm
ATLEY, Ellen		40	F	Unknown	01Se02Cm
Nancy		24	F	Unknown	01Se02Cm
Julia		10	F	Unknown	01Se02Cm
William		08	M	Child	01Se02Cm
FOLE, Margt.		18	F	Unknown	01Se02Cm
MCKEENAN, Bryan		50	M	Laborer	01Se02Cm
Bridget		30	F	Unknown	01Se02Cm
Thomas		19	M	Unknown	01Se02Cm
Rose		08	F	Child	01Se02Cm
Bridget		04	F	Child	01Se02Cm
Ann		.06	F	Infant	01Se02Cm
MATTHEWS, Ann		20	F	Unknown	01Se02Cm
BYRNE, Rose		19	F	Unknown	01Se02Cm
CONROY, David		25	M	Laborer	01Se02Cm
MURPHEY, John		28	M	Laborer	01Se02Cm
MADDEN, Luke		25	M	Laborer	01Se02Cm
KENNEDY, Jno.		20	M	Accountant	01Se02Cm
CLARKE, Thos.		20	M	Tailor	01Se02Cm
KELLY, Margt.		23	F	Unknown	01Se02Cm
BRENNAN, Ellen		16	F	Unknown	01Se02Cm
MCDONNELL, Edw.		18	M	Laborer	01Se02Cm
MEEHAN, Julia		20	F	Unknown	01Se02Cm
CEARNES, Peter		20	M	Blacksmith	01Se02Cm
GLEASON, Kitty		20	F	Unknown	01Se02Cm
GORMAN, James		18	M	Laborer	01Se02Cm
FALLON, Timy.		21	M	Laborer	01Se02Cm
MALONY, Ann		18	F	Unknown	01Se02Cm
MORRISEY, Susan		18	F	Unknown	01Se02Cm
OBRIEN, Mary		13	F	Unknown	01Se02Cm
STEELE, Saml.		18	M	Laborer	01Se02Cm
CONAGHTON, Bryan		68	M	Laborer	01Se02Cm
Elizabeth	(W)	68	F	Unknown	01Se02Cm
Mary	(D)	36	F	Unknown	01Se02Cm
Bernard	(S)	27	M	Laborer	01Se02Cm
OFLAGHERTY, Thos.		18	M	Laborer	01Se02Cm
Eliza		17	F	Unknown	01Se02Cm
BRONNE, Mary		12	F	Unknown	01Se02Cm
OKEEFE, Bridget		18	F	Unknown	01Se02Cm

NAMES OF PASSENGERS		AGE	SEX	OCCUPATIONS	DATE PORT SHIP
MCCARTY, Mary		30	F	Unknown	01Se02Cm
JARVIS, Wm.		18	M	Laborer	01Se02Cm
ONEIL, Ann		22	F	Unknown	01Se02Cm
MCCRYSTAL, Jane		68	F	Unknown	01Se02Cm
Bridget		28	F	Unknown	01Se02Cm
Thomas		.06	M	Infant	01Se02Cm
MOORE, Robert		17	M	Laborer	01Se02Cm
WILSON, Jane		36	F	Unknown	01Se02Cm
REID, Eliza		18	F	Unknown	01Se02Cm
RATTICAN, Maria		30	F	Unknown	01Se02Cm
Ann	(D)	.08	F	Infant	01Se02Cm
BRENNAN, Winifred		20	F	Unknown	01Se02Cm
MCDONALD, Mary		18	F	Unknown	01Se02Cm
MCGLYAN, Honora		18	F	Unknown	01Se02Cm
BYRNE, Michael		25	M	Laborer	01Se02Cm
CASEY, Jos.		40	M	Laborer	01Se02Cm
GORMAN, Mary-Ann		40	F	Unknown	01Se02Cm
BEESON, Ann		13	F	Unknown	01Se02Cm
COWAN, Hugh		66	M	Laborer	01Se02Cm
Hugh		22	M	Laborer	01Se02Cm
Jane		21	F	Unknown	01Se02Cm
Betty		60	F	Unknown	01Se02Cm
Died-At-Sea					
Joseph		.05	M	Infant	01Se02Cm
STRONG, Mary		25	F	Unknown	01Se02Cm
BARRETT, Eliz.		20	F	Unknown	01Se02Cm
FEMAL, Margt.		20	F	Unknown	01Se02Cm
HUTCHISON, Eliza		19	F	Unknown	01Se02Cm
CONAUGTHY, Thos.		20	M	Laborer	01Se02Cm
COMER, Philip		21	M	Laborer	01Se02Cm
DOYLE, John		21	M	Laborer	01Se02Cm
MCMARNELL, Jno.		21	M	Laborer	01Se02Cm
MCCLAIN, Jno.		21	M	Laborer	01Se02Cm
MCNOE, John		53	M	Weaver	01Se02Cm
Agnes	(W)	50	F	Unknown	01Se02Cm
Jannett	(D)	22	F	Unknown	01Se02Cm
Evan	(S)	17	M	Unknown	01Se02Cm
William		.06	M	Infant	01Se02Cm
ANDERSON, Rich.		25	M	Miner	01Se02Cm
James		31	M	Miner	01Se02Cm
Joseph		18	M	Miner	01Se02Cm
Grace		23	F	Unknown	01Se02Cm
COCK, John		27	M	Mechanic	01Se02Cm
William	(S)	01	M	Child	01Se02Cm
ANDERSON, Mary-Ann		09	F	Child	01Se02Cm
BELL, Wm.		36	M	Blacksmith	01Se02Cm
HUGHES, Mary		20	F	Unknown	01Se02Cm
RYAN, Pat		21	M	Laborer	01Se02Cm
LENNON, Mary		16	F	Unknown	01Se02Cm
NEIL, Mary		16	F	Unknown	01Se02Cm
SUTLIFFE, Danl.		25	M	Laborer	01Se02Cm
Philip		20	M	Laborer	01Se02Cm
MITCHELL, Alfred		20	M	Laborer	01Se02Cm
STAUNTON, Mary		30	F	Unknown	01Se02Cm
PEARSON, David		40	M	Carpenter	01Se02Cm
GILLIGAN, Mary		18	F	Unknown	01Se02Cm
MOORE, Edw.		40	M	Blacksmith	01Se02Cm
FINTON, Eliza		11	F	Unknown	01Se02Cm
MCCORMICK, Thos.		18	M	Laborer	01Se02Cm
HARKIN, Jane		28	F	Unknown	01Se02Cm
Martha		22	F	Unknown	01Se02Cm
FENELLA, Hanna		21	F	Unknown	01Se02Cm
Margaret		20	F	Unknown	01Se02Cm
MCCORMICK, Cath.		30	F	Unknown	01Se02Cm
HEREN, Dennis		18	M	Laborer	01Se02Cm
Marry		18	F	Unknown	01Se02Cm
JOYCE, Edwd.		48	M	Laborer	01Se02Cm
Johanna	(W)	50	F	Unknown	01Se02Cm
Henry	(S)	16	M	Unknown	01Se02Cm
Keenan	(S)	13	M	Unknown	01Se02Cm
Thomas	(S)	11	M	Unknown	01Se02Cm
Mary-Ann	(D)	10	F	Unknown	01Se02Cm
Edward	(S)	08	M	Child	01Se02Cm
Henry	(S)	08	M	Child	01Se02Cm
Catherine	(D)	06	F	Child	01Se02Cm

NAMES OF PASSENGERS		AGE	SEX	OCCUPATIONS	DATE PORT SHIP
HAYES, Pat		30	M	Laborer	01Se02Cm
Catherine		26	F	Unknown	01Se02Cm
FLYNN, Pat		40	M	Laborer	01Se02Cm
Betsey	(D)	13	F	Unknown	01Se02Cm
Michael	(S)	10	M	Unknown	01Se02Cm
Ann	(D)	09	F	Child	01Se02Cm
FITZSIMMONS, Rose		20	F	Unknown	01Se02Cm
MILLER, Carroll		20	M	Laborer	01Se02Cm
GRANGER, David		24	M	Laborer	01Se02Cm
MULCAHY, Pat		20	M	Laborer	01Se02Cm
BRONNE, John		20	M	Weaver	01Se02Cm
DUFFY, Winifred		19	F	Unknown	01Se02Cm
CONLAN, Ann		19	F	Unknown	01Se02Cm
JAMES, Morgan		40	M	Tailor	01Se02Cm
PEET, U		38	M	Unknown	01Se02Cm
U	(W)	24	F	Unknown	01Se02Cm
WEST, U		38	M	Unknown	01Se02Cm
U	(W)	38	F	Unknown	01Se02Cm
OFLANNAGAN, U		25	M	Unknown	01Se02Cm
MURPHEY, U		24	M	Unknown	01Se02Cm

SWITZERLAND 04 SEPTEMBER 1846

From London

COCKMAN, Agnes		27	F	Servant	04Se21Al

SARACEN 04 SEPTEMBER 1846

From Glasgow

DENNY, E.		20	F	Unknown	04Se04Ah
CASH, Henry		30	M	Grocer	04Se04Ah
LEE, James		40	M	Spinner	04Se04Ah
Agnes	(D)	17	F	Unknown	04Se04Ah
Elizabeth	(D)	15	F	Unknown	04Se04Ah
Thomas	(S)	13	M	Unknown	04Se04Ah
James	(S)	11	M	Unknown	04Se04Ah
Mary	(D)	08	F	Child	04Se04Ah
Agnes	(W)	40	F	Unknown	04Se04Ah
MILONE, Charles		21	M	Weaver	04Se04Ah
Agnes		23	F	Servant	04Se04Ah
MCCHEYNE, Margaret		24	F	Servant	04Se04Ah
DENNY, Cathrine		22	F	Servant	04Se04Ah
MCGLOCKEN, Harriet		18	F	Spinner	04Se04Ah
COLWELL, Margaret		20	F	Bleacher	04Se04Ah
GUTHRIE, Benjamin		76	M	Farmer	04Se04Ah
Martha		64	F	Unknown	04Se04Ah
Mary		25	F	Milliner	04Se04Ah
Ann		23	F	Servant	04Se04Ah
Jane		21	F	Servant	04Se04Ah
Elizabeth		18	F	Servant	04Se04Ah
KANE, John		26	M	Laborer	04Se04Ah
MCPHAIL, Mary		23	F	Milliner	04Se04Ah

NAMES OF PASSENGERS	A G E	S E X	OCCUPATIONS	DATE PORT SHIP

SAMUEL-HICKS 04 SEPTEMBER 1846

From Liverpool

NAMES OF PASSENGERS	AGE	SEX	OCCUPATIONS	DATE PORT SHIP
HENRY, Micheal	23	M	Laborer	04Se02Bs
LAUGHTON, Rosanna	23	F	None	04Se02Bs
MALONE, Mary	70	F	None	04Se02Bs
KEENAN, James	19	M	Laborer	04Se02Bs
Isabella	17	F	None	04Se02Bs
MCLANGLEY, Margret	40	F	None	04Se02Bs
Rosey	30	F	None	04Se02Bs
Bridget	09	F	Child	04Se02Bs
Sarah	07	F	Child	04Se02Bs
CARANUGH, Mary	19	F	None	04Se02Bs
MURRY, Stephen	20	M	Laborer	04Se02Bs
Catherine	18	F	None	04Se02Bs
RYAN, John	22	M	Laborer	04Se02Bs

ST.PATRICK 05 SEPTEMBER 1846

From Liverpool

NAMES OF PASSENGERS	AGE	SEX	OCCUPATIONS	DATE PORT SHIP
MOORE, John	55	M	Farmer	05Se02Bw
Rose	00	F	Unknown	05Se02Bw
MURPHY, William-B.	23	M	Merchant	05Se02Bw

RELIANCE 07 SEPTEMBER 1846

From Kingston

NAMES OF PASSENGERS	AGE	SEX	OCCUPATIONS	DATE PORT SHIP
WEBSTER, Joseph		25	M	Merchant	07Se23Dw
Jane	(W)	25	F	Lady	07Se23Dw

SOUTH-CAROLINA 07 SEPTEMBER 1846

From Liverpool

NAMES OF PASSENGERS	AGE	SEX	OCCUPATIONS	DATE PORT SHIP
ELLIOTT, James	30	M	Miner	07Se02Fd
BLACK, Robert	20	M	Weaver	07Se02Fd
GALLAGAN, Rose	13	F	Servant	07Se02Fd
HOGG, John	25	M	Farmer	07Se02Fd
BRADY, Elizabeth	18	F	Servant	07Se02Fd
EDWARDS, William	22	M	Farmer	07Se02Fd
BROWN, Jane	40	F	Dressmaker	07Se02Fd
OCONNER, Ambrose	20	M	Mechanic	07Se02Fd
CLARKSON, Ann	20	F	Servant	07Se02Fd
SEXTON, Mary	20	F	Servant	07Se02Fd
KING, John	50	M	Farmer	07Se02Fd
MURPHY, Ann	25	F	Servant	07Se02Fd
SHAW, William	35	M	Farmer	07Se02Fd
MADDIN, Patrick	30	M	Farmer	07Se02Fd

NAMES OF PASSENGERS		AGE	SEX	OCCUPATIONS	DATE PORT SHIP
MADDIN, Ann	(W)	30	F	Unknown	07Se02Fd
Margaret	(D)	12	F	Unknown	07Se02Fd
James	(S)	11	M	Unknown	07Se02Fd
Peter	(S)	09	M	Child	07Se02Fd
Thomas	(S)	07	M	Child	07Se02Fd
Catherine	(D)	05	F	Child	07Se02Fd
Patrick	(S)	01	M	Child	07Se02Fd
ARNOLD, William		30	M	Weaver	07Se02Fd
HARTY, John		62	M	Merchant	07Se02Fd
John		30	M	Clerk	07Se02Fd
William		22	M	Baker	07Se02Fd
ATKINSON, Susan		40	F	Dressmaker	07Se02Fd
Helen	(D)	03	F	Child	07Se02Fd
MURPHEY, Helen		25	F	Servant	07Se02Fd
Margaret		23	F	Servant	07Se02Fd
DIGNON, John		22	M	Farmer	07Se02Fd
Mary		40	F	Wife	07Se02Fd
MARTIN, Sarah		40	F	Dressmaker	07Se02Fd
Hants		10	U	Unknown	07Se02Fd
ROCHE, Thomas		26	M	Mechanic	07Se02Fd
Nicholas		11	M	Mechanic	07Se02Fd
FINEGAN, Johanah-Mrs.		30	F	Servant	07Se02Fd
Margaret	(D)	13	F	Servant	07Se02Fd
Helen	(D)	07	F	Child	07Se02Fd
Jerry	(S)	03	M	Child	07Se02Fd
Mary-Ann	(D)	01	F	Child	07Se02Fd
CONAUGHTON, Michael		45	M	Laborer	07Se02Fd
Jane	(W)	45	F	Unknown	07Se02Fd
Jane	(T)	50	F	Unknown	07Se02Fd
Mary	(D)	20	F	Ctnsp	07Se02Fd
Catherine	(D)	18	F	Ctnsp	07Se02Fd
Michael	(S)	16	M	Ctnsp	07Se02Fd
John	(S)	12	M	Ctnsp	07Se02Fd
James	(S)	08	M	Child	07Se02Fd
CAWLY, Patrick		21	M	Clerk	07Se02Fd
Margret	(W)	20	F	Unknown	07Se02Fd
MAHAN, Margaret		48	F	Servant	07Se02Fd
Mary		20	F	Servant	07Se02Fd
LOFTUS, Nicholas		22	M	Ctnsp	07Se02Fd
Michael		23	M	Ctnsp	07Se02Fd
HEANEY, Bernard		24	M	Farmer	07Se02Fd
SHERNON, John		40	M	Ctnsp	07Se02Fd
Bridget	(W)	36	F	Ctnsp	07Se02Fd
Mary	(D)	20	F	Ctnsp	07Se02Fd
Helen	(D)	17	F	Ctnsp	07Se02Fd
John	(S)	13	M	Ctnsp	07Se02Fd
Michael	(S)	07	M	Child	07Se02Fd
ODOYLE, John		04	M	Child	07Se02Fd

MEDIATOR 10 SEPTEMBER 1846

From London

NAMES OF PASSENGERS	AGE	SEX	OCCUPATIONS	DATE PORT SHIP
LANDER, David	65	M	Gentleman	10Se21Dt
Elizabeth	60	F	Lady	10Se21Dt
Louisa	20	F	Lady	10Se21Dt
John	31	M	Gentleman	10Se21Dt
Fredrick	29	M	Gentleman	10Se21Dt
JAMES, James-F.	38	M	Gentleman	10Se21Dt
Jane	23	F	Lady	10Se21Dt
SPIRES, William	25	M	Gentleman	10Se21Dt
COLLIER, Thomas	31	M	Gentleman	10Se21Dt
LEEN, James	34	M	Gentleman	10Se21Dt
BRYAN, Matilda	68	F	Lady	10Se21Dt
BURNLEM, Mary-Ann	12	F	Lady	10Se21Dt
MEMFIEL, Henry	16	M	Merchant	10Se21Dt
GOURLEY, John	70	M	Farmer	10Se21Dt
PARR, John	55	M	Brewer	10Se21Dt
William	17	M	Unknown	10Se21Dt

NAMES OF PASSENGERS	A G E	S E X	OCCUPATIONS	DATE PORT SHIP
FLEMING, Jane	34	F	Unknown	10Se21Dt
George	14	M	Unknown	10Se21Dt
Daniel	08	M	Child	10Se21Dt
John	04	M	Child	10Se21Dt
William	02	M	Child	10Se21Dt
HEADING, John-P.	30	M	Brewer	10Se21Dt
BROWN, Thomas	33	M	Draper	10Se21Dt
WILKEY, Henry	20	M	Oilman	10Se21Dt
SHEPPERD, William	18	M	Draper	10Se21Dt
GARNER, Joseph	22	M	Tea Dealer	10Se21Dt
WATSON, Thomas	48	M	Bricklayer	10Se21Dt
FOSTER, George	21	M	Grocer	10Se21Dt
OTTS, John	18	M	Polisher	10Se21Dt
ISAACSON, Henry	18	M	Mariner	10Se21Dt
Terresa	23	F	Unknown	10Se21Dt
Katherine	02	F	Child	10Se21Dt
LOYNES, James	40	M	Carpenter	10Se21Dt
Sarah	34	F	Unknown	10Se21Dt
MCDONALD, Thomas	25	M	Carpenter	10Se21Dt

ISABELLA 11 SEPTEMBER 1846

From Liverpool

NAMES OF PASSENGERS	A G E	S E X	OCCUPATIONS	DATE PORT SHIP
SEYMORE, Samuel	25	M	Carpenter	11Se02Fe
U (W)	24	F	Unknown	11Se02Fe
Hannah	03	F	Child	11Se02Fe
Eliza	01	F	Child	11Se02Fe
WRIGHT, William	28	M	Laborer	11Se02Fe
U (W)	25	F	Labrw	11Se02Fe
TRACY, Mary	36	F	Unknown	11Se02Fe
Eliza	13	F	Unknown	11Se02Fe
Catherine	06	F	Child	11Se02Fe
LAWSON, Robert	42	M	Farmer	11Se02Fe
Ann	30	F	Unknown	11Se02Fe
Robert	01	M	Child	11Se02Fe
Thos.	17	M	Unknown	11Se02Fe
George	15	M	Unknown	11Se02Fe
Eliza	14	F	Unknown	11Se02Fe
Caroline	13	F	Unknown	11Se02Fe
Charles	12	M	Unknown	11Se02Fe
Abraham	10	M	Unknown	11Se02Fe
Mary-Ann	08	F	Child	11Se02Fe
Emma	06	F	Child	11Se02Fe
THORNTON, Eliza	20	F	Unknown	11Se02Fe
James	21	M	Laborer	11Se02Fe
Peter	22	M	Laborer	11Se02Fe
CORNER, Timothy	30	M	Laborer	11Se02Fe
HAYS, Bessy	30	F	Unknown	11Se02Fe
FANIX, Charles	17	M	Laborer	11Se02Fe
MASON, Charles	26	M	Gentleman	11Se02Fe
U (W)	22	F	Lady	11Se02Fe
MOON, Robert	26	M	Laborer	11Se02Fe
U (W)	24	F	Unknown	11Se02Fe
SMITH, John	25	M	Laborer	11Se02Fe
PRYZER, Thos.	31	M	Laborer	11Se02Fe
Sarah	40	F	Unknown	11Se02Fe
Mary-Ann	13	F	Unknown	11Se02Fe
Alfred	10	M	Child	11Se02Fe
Eliza	06	F	Child	11Se02Fe
Harriet	04	F	Child	11Se02Fe
CAVANAH, Thos.	24	M	Laborer	11Se02Fe
DUNN, John	21	M	Laborer	11Se02Fe
CARTY, Pat.	26	M	Laborer	11Se02Fe
U (W)	24	F	Unknown	11Se02Fe
James	07	M	Child	11Se02Fe
Bridget	03	F	Child	11Se02Fe
Julia	.06	F	Infant	11Se02Fe
WHITING, John	22	M	Laborer	11Se02Fe

NAMES OF PASSENGERS	A G E	S E X	OCCUPATIONS	DATE PORT SHIP
SMITH, Catherine	40	F	Unknown	11Se02Fe
Mary	18	F	Unknown	11Se02Fe
John	16	M	Unknown	11Se02Fe
KELLEY, Terrence	21	M	Laborer	11Se02Fe
Bridget	20	F	Unknown	11Se02Fe
MCGUIRE, Rose	20	F	Unknown	11Se02Fe
FLANEGEN, Ann	20	F	Unknown	11Se02Fe
LYNCH, Ellen	54	F	Unknown	11Se02Fe
Ann	15	F	Unknown	11Se02Fe
Timothy	09	M	Unknown	11Se02Fe
JACKSON, Thos.	30	M	Seaman	11Se02Fe
FAWSETT, William	24	M	Laborer	11Se02Fe
ROADS, Thos.	27	M	Laborer	11Se02Fe
BURGES, Felix	22	M	Laborer	11Se02Fe
BOLLARD, James	30	M	Laborer	11Se02Fe
U (W)	26	F	Unknown	11Se02Fe
QUEENLAND, Edward	22	M	Laborer	11Se02Fe
DOUGLAS, Michal	24	M	Laborer	11Se02Fe
MCKENNA, John	19	M	Laborer	11Se02Fe
LONLAN, Thos.	20	M	Laborer	11Se02Fe
ASH, Robt.	30	M	Laborer	11Se02Fe
U (W)	28	F	Unknown	11Se02Fe
Rebeca	09	F	Child	11Se02Fe
MATTEWS, Mary	20	F	Unknown	11Se02Fe
Mary	.06	F	Infant	11Se02Fe
THOMPSON, William	24	M	Laborer	11Se02Fe
Thos.	25	M	Laborer	11Se02Fe
NELSON, George	30	M	Laborer	11Se02Fe
RILEY, Andrew	21	M	Laborer	11Se02Fe
U (W)	24	F	Unknown	11Se02Fe
Bridget	05	F	Child	11Se02Fe
WILDERS, U-Mrs.	22	F	Unknown	11Se02Fe
MURPHY, Mary	39	F	Unknown	11Se02Fe
Thos.	17	M	Laborer	11Se02Fe
Michal	16	M	Laborer	11Se02Fe
POWER, William	22	M	Laborer	11Se02Fe
FLYNN, James	40	M	Laborer	11Se02Fe
BYNNES, William	24	M	Laborer	11Se02Fe
JOHNSON, Isabella	20	F	Unknown	11Se02Fe
Matilda	18	F	Unknown	11Se02Fe
KNOX, William	20	F	Laborer	11Se02Fe
TOOL, Henry	51	F	Laborer	11Se02Fe
U (W)	50	F	Unknown	11Se02Fe
Ellen	15	F	Unknown	11Se02Fe
Mary	12	F	Unknown	11Se02Fe
William	10	M	Unknown	11Se02Fe
Henry	08	M	Child	11Se02Fe
Daniel	06	M	Child	11Se02Fe
Robert	.06	M	Infant	11Se02Fe
VALERY, Hugh	22	M	Laborer	11Se02Fe
COSTELLO, Margaret	40	F	Unknown	11Se02Fe
BYRNES, Mary	20	F	Unknown	11Se02Fe
GRAY, James	24	M	Laborer	11Se02Fe
U (W)	18	F	Unknown	11Se02Fe
MAINS, Nancy	40	F	Unknown	11Se02Fe
STONES, Mary	36	F	Unknown	11Se02Fe
FINERGAN, Catherine	21	F	Laborer	11Se02Fe
SPANKEY, John	27	M	Laborer	11Se02Fe
TOMEY, Catherine	60	F	Unknown	11Se02Fe
Edward	16	M	Unknown	11Se02Fe
SHERMAN, John	44	M	Laborer	11Se02Fe
Ellen	42	F	Unknown	11Se02Fe
John	13	M	Unknown	11Se02Fe
Michal	11	M	Unknown	11Se02Fe
Catherine	09	F	Child	11Se02Fe
Ellen	06	F	Child	11Se02Fe
Robert	02	M	Child	11Se02Fe
RUSSELL, Francis	22	M	Laborer	11Se02Fe
PIGOTT, Morris	16	M	Laborer	11Se02Fe
WALLACE, Nancy	64	F	Unknown	11Se02Fe
Nancy	26	F	Unknown	11Se02Fe
DORAN, Mary	20	F	Unknown	11Se02Fe
FLANERY, Bridget	47	F	Unknown	11Se02Fe
FANAGAN, Peter	18	M	Laborer	11Se02Fe
HEPWORTH, Joseph	18	M	Unknown	11Se02Fe

NAMES OF PASSENGERS		AGE	SEX	OCCUPATIONS	DATE PORT SHIP
HARE, Mathew		20	M	Laborer	11Se02Fe
JAMES, Thos.		20	M	Laborer	11Se02Fe
HEALY, Thos.		20	M	Unknown	11Se02Fe
Bridget		20	F	Unknown	11Se02Fe
Eliza		.06	F	Infant	11Se02Fe
COALMAN, Mark		20	M	Laborer	11Se02Fe
JUDGE, Catherine		20	F	Unknown	11Se02Fe
CARR, Mary		25	F	Unknown	11Se02Fe
BYRNES, Mgt.		22	F	Unknown	11Se02Fe
DOYLE, Michal		40	M	Laborer	11Se02Fe
SAXON, Edward		18	M	Laborer	11Se02Fe
DUFFY, James		17	M	Laborer	11Se02Fe

HELEN 11 SEPTEMBER 1846

From Liverpool

NAMES OF PASSENGERS		AGE	SEX	OCCUPATIONS	DATE PORT SHIP
MORGAN, Patrick		20	M	Laborer	11Se02Fg
KANE, Henry		40	M	Laborer	11Se02Fg
MURPHY, Joseph		30	M	Laborer	11Se02Fg
HART, James		21	M	Laborer	11Se02Fg
U	(W)	20	F	Laborer	11Se02Fg
DANIEL, Patrick		25	M	Laborer	11Se02Fg
Helen		25	F	Servant	11Se02Fg
DUFFY, Ann		20	F	Servant	11Se02Fg
CASTROL, Ellen		22	F	Servant	11Se02Fg
CONNORY, Ron		21	M	Laborer	11Se02Fg
CORCRAN, Bridget		25	F	Servant	11Se02Fg
MALEN, Joseph		25	M	Laborer	11Se02Fg
U	(W)	24	F	Unknown	11Se02Fg
Clara	(D)	02	F	Child	11Se02Fg
Louisa	(D)	01	F	Child	11Se02Fg
Wm.		23	M	Laborer	11Se02Fg
U	(W)	20	F	Unknown	11Se02Fg
Reuben		21	M	Laborer	11Se02Fg
SIMMONS, John		47	M	Laborer	11Se02Fg
U	(W)	47	F	Unknown	11Se02Fg
Elizabeth	(D)	09	F	Child	11Se02Fg
Mary	(D)	07	F	Child	11Se02Fg
Palmyra	(D)	03	F	Child	11Se02Fg
Phebe	(D)	01	F	Child	11Se02Fg
MURRAY, John		36	M	Laborer	11Se02Fg
U	(W)	35	F	Unknown	11Se02Fg
Jessie	(D)	11	F	Unknown	11Se02Fg
Robert	(S)	09	M	Child	11Se02Fg
Elizabeth	(D)	06	F	Child	11Se02Fg
Jane	(D)	04	F	Child	11Se02Fg
TOMLINSON, Wm.		25	M	Laborer	11Se02Fg
U	(W)	24	F	Unknown	11Se02Fg
John	(S)	03	M	Child	11Se02Fg
George	(S)	01	M	Child	11Se02Fg
THOMAS, Edward-Mrs.		36	F	Servant	11Se02Fg
Mary	(D)	15	F	Unknown	11Se02Fg
Sarah	(D)	12	F	Unknown	11Se02Fg
KELLY, Mary		19	F	Servant	11Se02Fg
STEVENSON, Dorothy		22	F	Servant	11Se02Fg
DONACHY, Barnard		45	M	Laborer	11Se02Fg
MCRORIE, Hugh		25	M	Laborer	11Se02Fg
Mary		50	F	Unknown	11Se02Fg
Patrick		15	M	Unknown	11Se02Fg
Margaret		08	F	Child	11Se02Fg
Mary		11	F	Child	11Se02Fg
KELLY, Ellen		24	F	Servant	11Se02Fg
Anthony		30	M	Laborer	11Se02Fg
LATTY, Michael		36	M	Laborer	11Se02Fg
U	(W)	34	F	Unknown	11Se02Fg
Arthur		15	M	Unknown	11Se02Fg
MCCURTY, Michael		28	M	Laborer	11Se02Fg
U	(W)	25	F	Unknown	11Se02Fg
HIGHLY, U		32	F	Servant	11Se02Fg
CONWAY, Ann		21	F	Servant	11Se02Fg
MACHANAN, John		36	M	Laborer	11Se02Fg
CARNAMAN, Joseph		50	M	Laborer	11Se02Fg
PURSELE, Michael		34	M	Laborer	11Se02Fg
ROACH, Ann		20	F	Servant	11Se02Fg
May		16	F	Unknown	11Se02Fg
HAGG, Ellen		24	F	Servant	11Se02Fg
GARMER, Wm.		30	M	Laborer	11Se02Fg
U		27	M	Unknown	11Se02Fg
MALLIN, Ann		24	F	Servant	11Se02Fg
MCCALL, Wm.		31	M	Laborer	11Se02Fg
Wm.		31	M	Unknown	11Se02Fg
Thomas		08	M	Child	11Se02Fg
George		05	M	Child	11Se02Fg
James		02	M	Child	11Se02Fg
ROACH, Mary		17	F	Servant	11Se02Fg
JONES, William		45	M	Laborer	11Se02Fg
EVANS, William		26	M	Laborer	11Se02Fg
BRONSEN, Wm.		40	M	Unknown	11Se02Fg
LEARY, U		24	M	Laborer	11Se02Fg
U	(W)	22	F	Unknown	11Se02Fg
KENNEDY, Margaret		18	F	Servant	11Se02Fg
CHATTERLY, Sampson		26	M	Laborer	11Se02Fg
U	(W)	24	F	Unknown	11Se02Fg
James		06	M	Child	11Se02Fg
LEONARD, James		34	M	Laborer	11Se02Fg
U	(W)	23	F	Unknown	11Se02Fg
Henrietta	(D)	04	F	Child	11Se02Fg
George	(S)	02	M	Child	11Se02Fg
Arabella	(D)	04	F	Child	11Se02Fg
RILLY, Catherine		01	F	Child	11Se02Fg
CALLAGAN, Dennis		45	M	Laborer	11Se02Fg
U	(W)	26	F	Unknown	11Se02Fg
John	(S)	06	M	Child	11Se02Fg
William	(S)	04	M	Child	11Se02Fg
Patrick	(S)	02	M	Child	11Se02Fg
Joseph	(S)	01	M	Child	11Se02Fg
COGAN, Margaret		15	F	Servant	11Se02Fg
OATS, Ellen		20	F	Servant	11Se02Fg
NUGENT, Ann		15	F	Servant	11Se02Fg
FLYNN, Michael		30	M	Laborer	11Se02Fg
U	(W)	30	F	Servant	11Se02Fg
John	(S)	10	M	Child	11Se02Fg
Mary-Ann	(D)	05	F	Child	11Se02Fg
ODOWNS, Bridget		20	F	Unknown	11Se02Fg
Owen		18	F	Servant	11Se02Fg
LOAN, Ann		35	F	Servant	11Se02Fg
FACHIE, Bridget		22	F	Servant	11Se02Fg
Thomas		12	M	Child	11Se02Fg
QUINN, Patrick		30	M	Laborer	11Se02Fg
Mary		27	F	Unknown	11Se02Fg
CASTROL, Betsy		21	F	Servant	11Se02Fg
CURRIN, Timothy		45	M	Laborer	11Se02Fg
MURPHY, Jenny		27	F	Servant	11Se02Fg
CONNER, John		32	M	Laborer	11Se02Fg
PRUSH, Elizabeth		30	F	Unknown	11Se02Fg
Patrick		32	M	Laborer	11Se02Fg
HETHEN, Ann		24	F	Servant	11Se02Fg
HAAGEN, Bridget		20	F	Servant	11Se02Fg
KENNEDY, Mary		18	F	Servant	11Se02Fg
RIGHUN, Patrick		15	M	Unknown	11Se02Fg
MUNNY, Bridget		21	F	Servant	11Se02Fg
Gannet		24	F	Servant	11Se02Fg
HUGHES, John		27	M	Laborer	11Se02Fg
COLLARY, James		32	M	Laborer	11Se02Fg
Bridget		30	F	Servant	11Se02Fg
SCOTT, Thomas		50	M	Laborer	11Se02Fg
HAGAN, John		34	M	Laborer	11Se02Fg
MCLAUGHLIN, Thomas		50	M	Laborer	11Se02Fg
Patrick		28	M	Laborer	11Se02Fg
Michael		19	M	Laborer	11Se02Fg
Mary		19	F	Servant	11Se02Fg
Margaret		15	F	Servant	11Se02Fg
Sarah		13	F	Unknown	11Se02Fg

NAMES OF PASSENGERS		AGE	SEX	OCCUPATIONS	DATE PORT SHIP
GUE, Bridget		13	F	Servant	11Se02Fg
MCNAMARA, Patrick		47	M	Laborer	11Se02Fg
MCLEAR, Daniel		37	M	Laborer	11Se02Fg
MORAN, John		24	M	Laborer	11Se02Fg
FARREL, James		31	M	Laborer	11Se02Fg
COLLINS, John		40	M	Laborer	11Se02Fg
ONEIL, Wm.		21	M	Laborer	11Se02Fg
BARMICK, Wm.		40	M	Laborer	11Se02Fg
BROADLIN, Frances		27	F	Servant	11Se02Fg
ODONNELL, John		22	M	Laborer	11Se02Fg
JONES, Hugh		19	M	Laborer	11Se02Fg
Ellen		17	F	Unknown	11Se02Fg
HUGHES, John		24	M	Laborer	11Se02Fg
MCCUTCHIN, John		34	M	Laborer	11Se02Fg
U	(W)	30	F	Unknown	11Se02Fg
Mary		14	F	Unknown	11Se02Fg
James		12	M	Unknown	11Se02Fg
Ellen		10	F	Unknown	11Se02Fg
DOMECK, Michael		34	M	Laborer	11Se02Fg
Bridget	(W)	29	F	Unknown	11Se02Fg
Patrick		14	M	Unknown	11Se02Fg
Eliza		10	F	Unknown	11Se02Fg
RYAN, Michael		30	M	Laborer	11Se02Fg
U	(W)	28	F	Unknown	11Se02Fg
John	(S)	04	M	Child	11Se02Fg
Mary	(D)	04	F	Child	11Se02Fg
CANNING, Mark		24	M	Laborer	11Se02Fg
IVAN, U-Mrs.		21	F	Servant	11Se02Fg
GAGE, John		14	M	Unknown	11Se02Fg
SCANN, Patrick		27	M	Laborer	11Se02Fg
U	(W)	25	F	Unknown	11Se02Fg
U		.00	U	Infant	11Se02Fg
Born-At-Sea					
BREAKEN, Andrew		27	M	Laborer	11Se02Fg
U	(W)	21	F	Unknown	11Se02Fg
SWANN, John-George		42	M	Laborer	11Se02Fg
MILLER, Henry		21	M	Laborer	11Se02Fg
GILMANY, Andrew		27	M	Laborer	11Se02Fg
U	(W)	26	F	Unknown	11Se02Fg
LUCA, Thomas		27	M	Laborer	11Se02Fg
HEFFERON, John		24	M	Laborer	11Se02Fg
KENNEDY, Margaret		20	F	Servant	11Se02Fg
DUGAN, Mary		24	F	Servant	11Se02Fg
MCLAUGHLIN, U		21	M	Servant	11Se02Fg
GANETT, Thomas		15	M	Unknown	11Se02Fg
FAIRCHURCH, Matthew		27	M	Laborer	11Se02Fg
SAMSON, Samuel		42	M	Laborer	11Se02Fg
MULRICK, Thomas		24	M	Laborer	11Se02Fg
U	(W)	24	F	Unknown	11Se02Fg
WADE, Hugh		27	M	Laborer	11Se02Fg
U	(W)	25	F	Unknown	11Se02Fg
HAY, Patrick		24	M	Laborer	11Se02Fg
HAILY, Bernard		22	M	Laborer	11Se02Fg
MCJUNT, John		24	M	Laborer	11Se02Fg
ANCHOR, Thomas		14	M	Unknown	11Se02Fg
ROACH, Wm.		25	M	Laborer	11Se02Fg
U	(W)	23	F	Unknown	11Se02Fg
SWEENY, Philip		21	M	Laborer	11Se02Fg
OATS, John		20	M	Laborer	11Se02Fg
BREWNIT, Charles		15	M	Unknown	11Se02Fg
DUGHAN, James		40	M	Servant	11Se02Fg
Edward		02	M	Child	11Se02Fg
U	(W)	25	F	Servant	11Se02Fg
John	(S)	01	M	Infant	11Se02Fg
DOUGHERTY, Ann		18	F	Servant	11Se02Fg
ORONALD, Mary		30	F	Servant	11Se02Fg
WHEELAN, Patrick		30	M	Laborer	11Se02Fg
U	(W)	37	F	Servant	11Se02Fg
Catherine	(D)	09	F	Child	11Se02Fg
Mary-Ann	(D)	07	F	Child	11Se02Fg
John	(S)	05	M	Child	11Se02Fg
James	(S)	03	M	Child	11Se02Fg
Patrick	(S)	01	M	Child	11Se02Fg
HICKS, John		36	M	Laborer	11Se02Fg
U	(W)	34	F	Servant	11Se02Fg
HICKS, Jane	(D)	14	F	Unknown	11Se02Fg
Mary	(D)	12	F	Unknown	11Se02Fg
Ann	(D)	09	F	Child	11Se02Fg
Elizabeth	(D)	07	F	Child	11Se02Fg
Stephen	(S)	03	M	Child	11Se02Fg
John	(S)	01	M	Child	11Se02Fg
JENKINS, Joseph		25	M	Laborer	11Se02Fg
JONES, Thomas		24	M	Laborer	11Se02Fg
WILLIAMS, David		27	M	Laborer	11Se02Fg
GAND, Joseph		31	M	Laborer	11Se02Fg
U	(W)	30	F	Unknown	11Se02Fg
John	(S)	09	M	Child	11Se02Fg
Esther	(D)	07	F	Child	11Se02Fg
Joseph	(S)	01	M	Child	11Se02Fg
POWELL, Thomas		26	M	Laborer	11Se02Fg
U	(W)	24	F	Unknown	11Se02Fg
Ann	(D)	03	F	Child	11Se02Fg
JONES, Margaret		24	F	Servant	11Se02Fg
LOYD, Wm.		21	M	Laborer	11Se02Fg
JAMES, Edward		36	M	Laborer	11Se02Fg
U	(W)	32	F	Unknown	11Se02Fg
David	(S)	15	M	Unknown	11Se02Fg
Thomas	(S)	12	M	Unknown	11Se02Fg
BUNKER, John		27	M	Laborer	11Se02Fg
U	(W)	25	F	Unknown	11Se02Fg
Jemima	(D)	05	F	Child	11Se02Fg
MCGUIRE, Mary		35	F	Servant	11Se02Fg
Bridget		22	F	Servant	11Se02Fg
Owen		12	M	Unknown	11Se02Fg
WILLIAMS, U-Mrs.		00	F	Unknown	11Se02Fg
Died-At-Sea					
GAND, Frederick		00	M	Unknown	11Se02Fg
Died-At-Sea					
LARKEN, James		00	M	Unknown	11Se02Fg
Died-At-Sea					
MURRAY, Richard		00	M	Unknown	11Se02Fg
Died-At-Sea					
MCCALL, Jane		00	F	Unknown	11Se02Fg
Died-At-Sea					

ROCHESTER 11 SEPTEMBER 1846

From Liverpool

NAMES OF PASSENGERS		AGE	SEX	OCCUPATIONS	DATE PORT SHIP
WOODHEAD, Wm.		61	M	Farmer	11Se02Ak
Lydia		57	F	Unknown	11Se02Ak
Ann		20	F	Unknown	11Se02Ak
Lydia		18	F	Unknown	11Se02Ak
Elizabeth		14	F	Unknown	11Se02Ak
NOBLE, John		25	M	Farmer	11Se02Ak
U	(W)	20	F	Unknown	11Se02Ak
U		.00	U	Infant	11Se02Ak
TEMPEST, Joseph		70	M	Farmer	11Se02Ak
Elizabeth		67	F	Unknown	11Se02Ak
BROADBENT, Joseph		20	M	Carpenter	11Se02Ak
FORD, James		30	M	Carpenter	11Se02Ak
MALONE, Mary		29	F	Servant	11Se02Ak
Cath.		10	F	Servant	11Se02Ak
CASH, Ann		26	F	Servant	11Se02Ak
MCAVOY, Mgt.		20	F	Servant	11Se02Ak
LOOLAN, Betty		19	F	Servant	11Se02Ak
DENWORTH, Mary		09	F	Servant	11Se02Ak
DONOHUE, Bridget		12	F	Servant	11Se02Ak
BROWN, James		30	M	Laborer	11Se02Ak
Ann		20	F	Unknown	11Se02Ak
POWELL, Mary-Ann		24	F	Unknown	11Se02Ak
MATHEWS, Mathew		30	M	Laborer	11Se02Ak
U	(W)	36	F	Unknown	11Se02Ak
John	(S)	08	M	Child	11Se02Ak

NAMES OF PASSENGERS		A G E	S E X	OCCUPATIONS	DATE PORT SHIP	NAMES OF PASSENGERS		A G E	S E X	OCCUPATIONS	DATE PORT SHIP
MATHEWS, Ann	(D)	06	F	Child	11Se02Ak	OBRIEN, John		30	M	Laborer	11Se02Ak
Mgt.	(D)	.00	F	Infant	11Se02Ak	Mary		21	F	Unknown	11Se02Ak
CLIFFORD, Pat		20	M	Laborer	11Se02Ak	BYRNE, John		30	M	Laborer	11Se02Ak
MURPHY, Mgt.		20	F	Unknown	11Se02Ak	BREARLEY, John		40	M	Carpenter	11Se02Ak
DANAN, Wm.		22	M	Weaver	11Se02Ak	SNOWDEN, R.		30	M	Molder	11Se02Ak
Ann		26	F	Weaver	11Se02Ak	U		27	F	Unknown	11Se02Ak
Mary		26	F	Weaver	11Se02Ak	MCHUGH, Wm.		60	M	Laborer	11Se02Ak
EDWARDS, Eliza		20	F	Unknown	11Se02Ak	Mary		13	F	Unknown	11Se02Ak
BUCKLEY, Nick.		19	M	Laborer	11Se02Ak	Biddy		15	F	Unknown	11Se02Ak
DRAKE, Johanna		15	F	Unknown	11Se02Ak	Francis		20	M	Laborer	11Se02Ak
ROBINSON, Fred.		22	M	Weaver	11Se02Ak	CONLEY, Mick.		20	M	Unknown	11Se02Ak
John		20	M	Weaver	11Se02Ak	KEEFE, Ellen		24	F	Unknown	11Se02Ak
FARMER, John		34	M	Carpenter	11Se02Ak	U		.00	U	Infant	11Se02Ak
KELLY, Ann		20	F	Unknown	11Se02Ak	CONNOR, Ellen		20	F	Unknown	11Se02Ak
HOWARTH, John		24	M	Merchant	11Se02Ak	COOK, Joseph		27	M	Tailor	11Se02Ak
BUTLER, U		63	M	Farmer	11Se02Ak	DONOVAN, Ann		25	F	Unknown	11Se02Ak
U-Mrs.		33	F	Unknown	11Se02Ak	Ellen		02	F	Child	11Se02Ak
U		32	M	Unknown	11Se02Ak	HONNIGAN, James		25	M	Unknown	11Se02Ak
ABBOTT, Wm.		37	M	Unknown	11Se02Ak	MORAN, Mick.		25	M	Laborer	11Se02Ak
U	(W)	38	F	Unknown	11Se02Ak	BUTLER, Mgt.		20	F	Unknown	11Se02Ak
Edw.	(S)	11	M	Unknown	11Se02Ak	BRADWICK, Luke		13	M	Unknown	11Se02Ak
Mary	(D)	09	F	Child	11Se02Ak	HUGHY, Mary		25	F	Unknown	11Se02Ak
Martin	(S)	08	M	Child	11Se02Ak	RIDLEY, Edmond		28	M	Weaver	11Se02Ak
Alice	(D)	05	F	Child	11Se02Ak	FARRUT, Henderson		27	M	Weaver	11Se02Ak
Susan	(D)	04	F	Child	11Se02Ak	BEALE, Thos.		32	M	Laborer	11Se02Ak
Henry (	(S)	01	M	Child	11Se02Ak	HALL, Wm.		30	M	Farmer	11Se02Ak
Eliz.	(D)	.02	F	Infant	11Se02Ak	U	(W)	25	F	Unknown	11Se02Ak
LORD, John		60	M	Weaver	11Se02Ak	Jane	(D)	04	F	Unknown	11Se02Ak
Alice	(W)	55	F	Weaver	11Se02Ak	Thos.	(S)	10	M	Unknown	11Se02Ak
Saml.	(S)	28	M	Weaver	11Se02Ak	GRACY, Edw.		40	M	Unknown	11Se02Ak
Priscilla	(D)	18	F	Weaver	11Se02Ak	Hugh		12	M	Farmer	11Se02Ak
RAMSBOTTOM, Ellen		13	F	Unknown	11Se02Ak	REGAN, Pat.		23	M	Laborer	11Se02Ak
HASTERN, Thomas		36	M	Laborer	11Se02Ak	EAGAN, John		10	M	Laborer	11Se02Ak
WHITFIELD, Geo.		30	M	Machinist	11Se02Ak	Mgt.		08	F	Laborer	11Se02Ak
Sarah		30	F	Unknown	11Se02Ak	FLOWRE, Wm.		18	M	Unknown	11Se02Ak
Robt.		09	M	Child	11Se02Ak	MCGIVNY, Sarah		18	F	Unknown	11Se02Ak
Saml.		02	M	Child	11Se02Ak	EDGAR, George		25	M	Merchant	11Se02Ak
Sarah		05	F	Child	11Se02Ak	MARTIN, Howle		20	M	Merchant	11Se02Ak
NOBLE, Joseph		27	M	Farmer	11Se02Ak	CRAIG, Pat.		22	M	Laborer	11Se02Ak
U	(W)	30	F	Unknown	11Se02Ak	Fenton		30	M	Laborer	11Se02Ak
U		.00	U	Unknown	11Se02Ak	BENNETT, Anthony		23	M	Laborer	11Se02Ak
HUMPHREYS, Jeremiah		25	M	Tailor	11Se02Ak	NEBLOCK, Mary		20	F	Unknown	11Se02Ak
FARLEY, Thos.		29	M	Cbtmkr	11Se02Ak	HANLON, John		25	M	Shoemaker	11Se02Ak
U	(W)	25	F	Unknown	11Se02Ak	MCKEON, Martha		25	F	Unknown	11Se02Ak
Mary	(D)	04	F	Unknown	11Se02Ak	TORNBERRY, Eliza		23	F	Unknown	11Se02Ak
REDDING, Francis		23	M	Cbtmkr	11Se02Ak	MCGOVERN, Ann		23	F	Unknown	11Se02Ak
CLARKE, Bridget		23	F	Unknown	11Se02Ak	ALLAN, Eliz.		21	F	Unknown	11Se02Ak
SLOAVER, Mgt.		20	F	Unknown	11Se02Ak	HENRY, James		22	M	Carpenter	11Se02Ak
DOUGLAS, James		26	M	Unknown	11Se02Ak	GRAMWOOD, Rich.		53	M	Farmer	11Se02Ak
GORAN, Pat.		20	M	Unknown	11Se02Ak	PHELP, Anderson		23	M	Farmer	11Se02Ak
DOUGLAS, Mary-Ann		23	F	Unknown	11Se02Ak	U	(W)	30	F	Unknown	11Se02Ak
WYLER, John		43	M	Unknown	11Se02Ak	Eliz.		09	F	Child	11Se02Ak
FLOOD, Mathew		40	M	Laborer	11Se02Ak	Mary-Anne		05	F	Child	11Se02Ak
U	(W)	00	F	Unknown	11Se02Ak	Anderson		.00	M	Infant	11Se02Ak
John		.00	M	Infant	11Se02Ak	MELROY, John		45	M	Farmer	11Se02Ak
Mathew		04	M	Child	11Se02Ak	U	(W)	40	F	Unknown	11Se02Ak
Bridget		10	F	Child	11Se02Ak	Thos.	(S)	03	M	Child	11Se02Ak
MURPHY, Thos.		20	M	Laborer	11Se02Ak	MACKAY, John		30	M	Laborer	11Se02Ak
U	(W)	19	F	Unknown	11Se02Ak	U	(W)	30	F	Unknown	11Se02Ak
BYRNE, John		18	M	Unknown	11Se02Ak	COLGAN, Betty		18	F	Unknown	11Se02Ak
Mgt.		19	F	Unknown	11Se02Ak	TAYLOR, Robt.		20	M	Farmer	11Se02Ak
Thos.		26	M	Unknown	11Se02Ak	U	(W)	21	F	Unknown	11Se02Ak
CHADWICK, Elly		23	M	Tailor	11Se02Ak	WILSON, Wm.		24	M	Blacksmith	11Se02Ak
DUFFY, Saml.		23	M	Laborer	11Se02Ak	Wm.		56	M	Blacksmith	11Se02Ak
DANIEL, Rich		31	M	Laborer	11Se02Ak	THOMPSON, Ann		13	F	Unknown	11Se02Ak
BYRNY, Cath.		20	F	Unknown	11Se02Ak	LITTLE, Abm.		20	M	Unknown	11Se02Ak
Sarah		21	F	Unknown	11Se02Ak	DUNBALLY, Nick.		20	M	Unknown	11Se02Ak
COOPER, Chas.		20	M	Carpenter	11Se02Ak	Bridget		18	F	Unknown	11Se02Ak
DOWNEY, Cath.		40	F	Unknown	11Se02Ak	CLIFFORD, Mary		50	F	Unknown	11Se02Ak
GRIFFIN, Mary		11	F	Unknown	11Se02Ak	Julia		09	F	Child	11Se02Ak
CONNELL, Helen		18	F	Unknown	11Se02Ak	Jane		07	F	Child	11Se02Ak
LYNCH, Bridget		20	F	Unknown	11Se02Ak	Mary		05	F	Child	11Se02Ak
FIELDING, U		24	M	Farmer	11Se02Ak	Timothy		.00	M	Infant	11Se02Ak
John		05	M	Unknown	11Se02Ak	QUIGLEY, U		26	F	Unknown	11Se02Ak
OBRIEN, Wm.		70	M	Laborer	11Se02Ak	Mary-Ann		26	F	Unknown	11Se02Ak

NAMES OF PASSENGERS	AGE	SEX	OCCUPATIONS	DATE PORT SHIP
QUIGLEY, Mary	03	F	Child	11Se02Ak
Eliza	.00	F	Infant	11Se02Ak
Susanna	03	F	Unknown	11Se02Ak
CONLINN, Cornelius	20	M	Carpenter	11Se02Ak
Mary	06	F	Child	11Se02Ak
OCONNELL, Cath.	08	F	Child	11Se02Ak
Mary	05	F	Child	11Se02Ak
GALWAY, Julia	21	F	Unknown	11Se02Ak
ROLLFE, U	57	F	Unknown	11Se02Ak
MATHEWS, Mary	30	F	Unknown	11Se02Ak
MASTRISON, Pat.	25	M	Laborer	11Se02Ak
BOOTH, Saml.	36	M	Weaver	11Se02Ak
Eliza	32	F	Weaver	11Se02Ak
Ann	10	F	Child	11Se02Ak
Saml.	08	M	Child	11Se02Ak
Wm.	04	M	Child	11Se02Ak
Hy.	10	M	Child	11Se02Ak

LIBERTY 11 SEPTEMBER 1846

From Liverpool

NAMES OF PASSENGERS	AGE	SEX	OCCUPATIONS	DATE PORT SHIP
MCTEAGUE, Peter	17	M	Unknown	11Se02Fw
Ellen	20	F	Unknown	11Se02Fw
PADDEN, Bridget	22	F	Cook	11Se02Fw
RIGLEY, Michael	19	M	Laborer	11Se02Fw
MASTERSON, Mary	24	F	Servant	11Se02Fw
DEMPSEY, Geo.	65	M	Shopkeeper	11Se02Fw
WHITMORE, Mary	50	F	Unknown	11Se02Fw
DEMPSEY, Susan	15	F	Hatter	11Se02Fw
Mary-A.	18	F	Governess	11Se02Fw
DUNN, Margaret	24	F	Hatter	11Se02Fw
ORMSBY, Fanny	21	F	Dressmaker	11Se02Fw
CONLY, Pat.	22	M	Hrsm	11Se02Fw
SMITH, Geo.	26	M	Farmer	11Se02Fw
GLOVER, Wm.	21	M	Laborer	11Se02Fw
LENAGHAN, Maria	24	F	Servant	11Se02Fw
SMITH, Mary	25	F	Dressmaker	11Se02Fw
SHERRY, Sally	21	F	Servant	11Se02Fw
HENRY, Thomas	31	M	Farmer	11Se02Fw
MYHAN, Malachi	19	M	Tailor	11Se02Fw
OHARA, Bridget	35	F	Unknown	11Se02Fw
THINNESS, John	22	M	Carpenter	11Se02Fw
CONNER, Barney	20	M	Tailor	11Se02Fw
KELLAGHER, Hugh	20	M	Shoemaker	11Se02Fw
MCCOFFRY, William	21	M	Tailor	11Se02Fw
EAGAN, Thomas	35	M	Bootmaker	11Se02Fw
SMITH, Mary	05	F	Child	11Se02Fw
Fanny	08	F	Child	11Se02Fw
EAGAN, James	09	M	Child	11Se02Fw
OROHO, Thomas	38	M	Laborer	11Se02Fw
Francis	10	M	Unknown	11Se02Fw
John	08	M	Child	11Se02Fw
FLAHERTY, Margaret	48	F	Unknown	11Se02Fw
John	24	M	Laborer	11Se02Fw
DENNIGAN, Andrew	28	M	Laborer	11Se02Fw
BURNS, Maria	19	F	Unknown	11Se02Fw
CRAWFORD, Sarah	30	F	Unknown	11Se02Fw
Matilda	08	F	Child	11Se02Fw
Nancy	05	F	Child	11Se02Fw
Isabella	03	F	Child	11Se02Fw
MCDONALD, Mary	60	F	Unknown	11Se02Fw
CRATON, Ann	15	F	Unknown	11Se02Fw
SHERRY, Teressa	03	F	Child	11Se02Fw
DONNELLY, John	14	M	Unknown	11Se02Fw
Margt.	18	F	Unknown	11Se02Fw
BLAKE, John	24	M	Servant	11Se02Fw
MULLEN, James	26	M	Hatter	11Se02Fw
John	24	M	Mason	11Se02Fw

NAMES OF PASSENGERS	AGE	SEX	OCCUPATIONS	DATE PORT SHIP
MULLEN, Richard	12	M	Unknown	11Se02Fw
MCKINNEY, Bridget	40	F	Unknown	11Se02Fw
Margt.	16	F	Unknown	11Se02Fw
ROBB, Eliza	19	F	Servant	11Se02Fw
JOSEPH, Mary	18	F	Unknown	11Se02Fw
WARD, Pat.	32	M	Laborer	11Se02Fw
CLARKE, Michael	10	M	Unknown	11Se02Fw
RILEY, Ellen	16	F	Servant	11Se02Fw
KEARNEY, Catherin	20	F	Unknown	11Se02Fw
Margaret	14	F	Unknown	11Se02Fw
Edward	09	M	Unknown	11Se02Fw
Ann	08	F	Unknown	11Se02Fw
DONOHUE, Mary	20	F	Servant	11Se02Fw
Bridget	14	F	Servant	11Se02Fw
CONLY, Margt.	18	F	Servant	11Se02Fw
BOYLE, Charles	21	M	Laborer	11Se02Fw
HICKY, Dennis	36	M	Gdnr	11Se02Fw
John	12	M	Gdnr	11Se02Fw
James	13	M	Gdnr	11Se02Fw
MCGUIRE, Hugh	18	M	Unknown	11Se02Fw
KINNARD, James	25	M	Storekeeper	11Se02Fw
PATTERSON, Mary-J.	21	F	Dressmaker	11Se02Fw
BRADLEY, Mary	21	F	Dressmaker	11Se02Fw
PATTERSON, Henry	50	M	Farmer	11Se02Fw
MULHOLLAND, Eliza.	22	F	Servant	11Se02Fw
SCOTT, Margt.	21	F	Servant	11Se02Fw
SERRIER, Isabella	20	F	Hatter	11Se02Fw
MULLIKEN, Wm.	25	M	Unknown	11Se02Fw
WOODS, John	26	M	Printer	11Se02Fw
MOONEY, John	24	M	Printer	11Se02Fw
SMITH, Pat.	22	M	Printer	11Se02Fw
RITCHIE, Joseph	24	M	Bookkeeper	11Se02Fw
Eliza-Jane	22	F	Unknown	11Se02Fw
BARCLAY, Thomas	24	M	Farmer	11Se02Fw

TAROLINTA 11 SEPTEMBER 1846

From Glasgow

NAMES OF PASSENGERS	AGE	SEX	OCCUPATIONS	DATE PORT SHIP
TENNENT, H.L.	28	M	Advocate	11Se04Fx
COVENTRY, Janet	12	F	Laborer	11Se04Fx
U-Mrs.	33	F	Wife	11Se04Fx
MORE, James	15	M	Wife	11Se04Fx
ROSS, Cathr.	20	F	Dressmaker	11Se04Fx
SMITH, Charles	22	M	Shoemaker	11Se04Fx
WATTSON, James	13	M	Farmer	11Se04Fx
STRUTHERS, Thomas	24	M	Upholsterer	11Se04Fx
COVENTRY, John	10	M	Unknown	11Se04Fx

CAMBRIDGE 12 SEPTEMBER 1846

From Liverpool

NAMES OF PASSENGERS	AGE	SEX	OCCUPATIONS	DATE PORT SHIP
CREAMER, John	16	M	Laborer	12Se02Ea
Marshall	18	M	Laborer	12Se02Ea
SHEA, William	19	M	Laborer	12Se02Ea
MCCORMICK, Bernard	20	M	Laborer	12Se02Ea
MCCABE, Matthew	20	M	Laborer	12Se02Ea
Martin	16	M	Laborer	12Se02Ea
Matthew	60	M	Laborer	12Se02Ea
Ellen	30	F	Unknown	12Se02Ea
SHOCKNER, Hugh	50	M	Laborer	12Se02Ea
Ann	50	F	Unknown	12Se02Ea

NAMES OF PASSENGERS	A G E	S E X	OCCUPATIONS	DATE PORT SHIP	NAMES OF PASSENGERS	A G E	S E X	OCCUPATIONS	DATE PORT SHIP
MCCARTHY, Cath.	20	F	Unknown	12Se02Ea	HILL, Mary	20	F	Unknown	12Se02Ea
CULLAN, Ellen	50	F	Unknown	12Se02Ea	DOUGLASS, Sarah	20	F	Unknown	12Se02Ea
WARD, Catherine	40	F	Unknown	12Se02Ea	MCCLARE, George	20	M	Laborer	12Se02Ea
MURPHY, Mary	15	F	Unknown	12Se02Ea	MCGUIRE, Patt.	18	M	Clerk	12Se02Ea
John	13	M	Unknown	12Se02Ea	KILCARY, Thos.	27	M	Miner	12Se02Ea
Patrick	11	M	Unknown	12Se02Ea	Wm.	25	M	Laborer	12Se02Ea
Ann	09	F	Unknown	12Se02Ea	WALSH, John	19	M	Tailor	12Se02Ea
Cath.	.08	F	Infant	12Se02Ea	MCCRUE, Martha	38	F	Unknown	12Se02Ea
CORCORAN, Peter	17	M	Laborer	12Se02Ea	SLOAN, James	21	M	Laborer	12Se02Ea
BISHOP, Cath.	50	F	Unknown	12Se02Ea	ONEIL, Margt.	26	F	Unknown	12Se02Ea
Elizabeth	20	F	Unknown	12Se02Ea	DALEY, Mary	20	F	Unknown	12Se02Ea
LEAHY, Mary	11	F	Unknown	12Se02Ea	COSGROVE, Letitia	30	F	Unknown	12Se02Ea
Honora	10	F	Unknown	12Se02Ea	Mary	20	F	Unknown	12Se02Ea
GILCHRIST, Bridget	20	F	Unknown	12Se02Ea	Alice	06	F	Unknown	12Se02Ea
Ann	24	F	Unknown	12Se02Ea	Catherine	05	F	Unknown	12Se02Ea
DOURELLE, Bernard	23	M	Laborer	12Se02Ea	John	03	M	Unknown	12Se02Ea
Bridget	05	F	Unknown	12Se02Ea	Bridget	.06	F	Infant	12Se02Ea
OHARA, Margt.	20	F	Unknown	12Se02Ea	BORIE, Elizabeth	47	F	Unknown	12Se02Ea
Ellen	16	F	Unknown	12Se02Ea	MCGARVAN, Thos.	13	M	Unknown	12Se02Ea
COLEMAN, Mary	20	F	Unknown	12Se02Ea	COROAN, Elizabeth	20	F	Unknown	12Se02Ea
STANFORD, Ann	20	F	Unknown	12Se02Ea	DUFFY, Mary	23	F	Unknown	12Se02Ea
COP, Maria	16	F	Unknown	12Se02Ea	KELLY, Peggy	50	F	Unknown	12Se02Ea
KEVILL, Ann	20	F	Unknown	12Se02Ea	Mary	13	F	Unknown	12Se02Ea
CARROLL, Ann	20	F	Unknown	12Se02Ea	HOGG, Ann	18	F	Unknown	12Se02Ea
MORLICK, Edw.	18	M	Laborer	12Se02Ea	Honora	13	F	Unknown	12Se02Ea
MORAN, Mary	19	F	Unknown	12Se02Ea	HASSON, Isabella	24	F	Unknown	12Se02Ea
MCGRATH, Betsey	20	F	Unknown	12Se02Ea	MORAN, Rose	20	F	Unknown	12Se02Ea
KELLY, Peggy	50	F	Unknown	12Se02Ea	MURPHY, William	11	M	Unknown	12Se02Ea
Mary	13	F	Unknown	12Se02Ea	MCLURE, George	20	M	Laborer	12Se02Ea
CLARK, Alice	24	F	Unknown	12Se02Ea	CLEARLEY, Ann	19	F	Unknown	12Se02Ea
GALLIGAN, Wm.	20	M	Laborer	12Se02Ea	MCGUIRES, John	20	M	Laborer	12Se02Ea
CERLEY, Arthur	67	M	Mason	12Se02Ea	Thos.	05	M	Unknown	12Se02Ea
BYRNE, Ann	26	F	Unknown	12Se02Ea	Francis	07	M	Unknown	12Se02Ea
FLYNN, Cath.	20	F	Unknown	12Se02Ea	CARR, Bridget	40	F	Unknown	12Se02Ea
BIRN, Mary	26	F	Unknown	12Se02Ea	JOHNSTONE, John	37	M	Tailor	12Se02Ea
COOK, Michael	20	M	Laborer	12Se02Ea	LINDSEY, William	36	M	Tailor	12Se02Ea
FITZBECKETT, Patrick	50	M	Laborer	12Se02Ea	FOLHES, James	30	M	Tailor	12Se02Ea
Susan	14	F	Unknown	12Se02Ea	LEE, Ann	30	F	Unknown	12Se02Ea
Mark	12	M	Unknown	12Se02Ea	Sarah	20	F	Unknown	12Se02Ea
Ellen	10	F	Unknown	12Se02Ea	KERR, Margt.	40	F	Unknown	12Se02Ea
John	08	M	Unknown	12Se02Ea	Mary	20	F	Unknown	12Se02Ea
Patrick	06	M	Unknown	12Se02Ea	CAHILL, James	18	M	Laborer	12Se02Ea
James	05	M	Unknown	12Se02Ea	Eliza	16	F	Unknown	12Se02Ea
Died-At-Sea					GUIRE, Dominick	18	M	Unknown	12Se02Ea
LEES, John	28	M	Laborer	12Se02Ea	MCGOVERN, Bridget	11	F	Unknown	12Se02Ea
PATTERSON, Mary	20	F	Unknown	12Se02Ea	DELANY, John	25	M	Laborer	12Se02Ea
MCALLISTER, Ellen	20	F	Unknown	12Se02Ea	DODD, George	40	M	Shoemaker	12Se02Ea
HIGHLAND, Mary	20	F	Unknown	12Se02Ea	Jane	40	F	Unknown	12Se02Ea
Patrick	18	M	Unknown	12Se02Ea	Nancy	21	F	Unknown	12Se02Ea
Bridget	17	F	Unknown	12Se02Ea	Eliza	20	F	Unknown	12Se02Ea
Cath.	13	F	Unknown	12Se02Ea	GILL, Catherine	30	F	Unknown	12Se02Ea
Susan	12	F	Unknown	12Se02Ea	Mary	12	F	Unknown	12Se02Ea
Sarah	10	F	Unknown	12Se02Ea	John	08	M	Unknown	12Se02Ea
John	07	M	Unknown	12Se02Ea	Richard	05	M	Unknown	12Se02Ea
Ann	04	F	Unknown	12Se02Ea	Patrick	03	M	Unknown	12Se02Ea
WARD, Edward	21	M	Laborer	12Se02Ea	Edw.	.09	M	Infant	12Se02Ea
HIGGINS, Ann	24	F	Unknown	12Se02Ea	Died-At-Sea				
BRADY, Cormick	26	M	Laborer	12Se02Ea	STEVENSON, Moses	25	M	Laborer	12Se02Ea
John	40	M	Laborer	12Se02Ea	LOGAN, Robt.	20	M	Laborer	12Se02Ea
REILLEY, Ann	20	F	Unknown	12Se02Ea	OHARA, Cath.	26	F	Unknown	12Se02Ea
HANLON, Kelly	18	M	Unknown	12Se02Ea	CONNOLLY, Mary	14	F	Unknown	12Se02Ea
CURRIE, Cath.	15	F	Unknown	12Se02Ea	HILLARD, James	20	M	Laborer	12Se02Ea
BROWN, James	23	M	Laborer	12Se02Ea	TURLEY, Hugh	20	M	Laborer	12Se02Ea
QUIGLEY, Hugh	44	M	Laborer	12Se02Ea	LANGTON, Patrick	30	M	Laborer	12Se02Ea
HILLARD, Eliza	22	F	Unknown	12Se02Ea	Alice	20	F	Unknown	12Se02Ea
MITCHELL, Sarah	39	F	Unknown	12Se02Ea	HIGGINS, Mary	18	F	Unknown	12Se02Ea
Timothy	20	M	Laborer	12Se02Ea					
ROBERTS, Ellen	40	F	Unknown	12Se02Ea					
HENESSEY, Mary	24	F	Unknown	12Se02Ea					
BROWN, John	30	M	Farmer	12Se02Ea					
Margt.	10	F	Unknown	12Se02Ea					
Mary	08	F	Child	12Se02Ea					
Joanna	06	F	Child	12Se02Ea					
Elizabeth	04	F	Child	12Se02Ea					
Margt.	.09	F	Infant	12Se02Ea					

NAMES OF PASSENGERS	A G E	S E X	OCCUPATIONS	DATE PORT SHIP

ALVERTON 12 SEPTEMBER 1846

From Liverpool

NAMES OF PASSENGERS	AGE	SEX	OCCUPATIONS	DATE PORT SHIP
WIDERMORE, Narvy	30	M	Laborer	12Se02Gc
Cathie	08	F	Unknown	12Se02Gc
RYAN, Catlin	25	F	Unknown	12Se02Gc
MAHER, Margaret	25	F	Unknown	12Se02Gc
CROSSIN, Will.	40	M	Carpenter	12Se02Gc
Margt.	30	F	Unknown	12Se02Gc
MCCORMICK, Margt.	20	F	Unknown	12Se02Gc
EMMANUEL, Jos.	45	M	Laborer	12Se02Gc
GAFFENEY, Mary	11	F	Unknown	12Se02Gc
BUTLER, John	28	M	Unknown	12Se02Gc
SMITH, Ann	20	F	Unknown	12Se02Gc
MALOWNEY, Pat	13	M	Laborer	12Se02Gc
John	12	M	Laborer	12Se02Gc
Lo---, Samuel	43	M	Laborer	12Se02Gc
Norris	20	F	Unknown	12Se02Gc
ODONNEL, U	25	M	Carpenter	12Se02Gc
MALOWNEY, John	20	M	Unknown	12Se02Gc
MCCARTY, Dennis	13	M	Laborer	12Se02Gc
MAYNOR, Edw.	40	M	Laborer	12Se02Gc
THOMAS, Eliza	37	F	Unknown	12Se02Gc
John	12	M	Unknown	12Se02Gc
Robt.	10	M	Unknown	12Se02Gc
Mary	08	F	Child	12Se02Gc
Eliza	.00	F	Infant	12Se02Gc
JONES, Edw.	47	M	Laborer	12Se02Gc
Mary	46	F	Unknown	12Se02Gc
Jane	14	F	Unknown	12Se02Gc
CUSAER, Peter	21	M	Laborer	12Se02Gc
U (W)	20	F	Unknown	12Se02Gc
MATHEWS, Biddy	25	F	Unknown	12Se02Gc
Pat.	.00	M	Infant	12Se02Gc
REARSON, Alex.	37	M	Laborer	12Se02Gc
KINEY, Maria	47	F	Unknown	12Se02Gc
Isabella	14	F	Unknown	12Se02Gc
MCCORMICK, Catlin	40	F	Unknown	12Se02Gc
Pat.	11	M	Unknown	12Se02Gc
Biddy	09	F	Unknown	12Se02Gc
John	07	M	Unknown	12Se02Gc
Ellen	.00	F	Infant	12Se02Gc
Margt.	13	F	Unknown	12Se02Gc
MCCAW, James	50	M	Laborer	12Se02Gc
MULLIN, Mary-Ann	30	F	Unknown	12Se02Gc
ROCK, Ann	20	F	Unknown	12Se02Gc
CINTON, Ann	12	F	Unknown	12Se02Gc
CALAHAN, Ann	20	F	Unknown	12Se02Gc
Mary	18	F	Unknown	12Se02Gc
Thomas	20	M	Laborer	12Se02Gc
MURTAGH, Edw.	20	M	Laborer	12Se02Gc
DERMODY, Pat.	20	M	Laborer	12Se02Gc
MCGATH, Elizabeth	37	F	Unknown	12Se02Gc
Biddy	20	F	Unknown	12Se02Gc
CEARUS, Honora	32	F	Unknown	12Se02Gc
Catlin	10	F	Unknown	12Se02Gc
Nancy	08	F	Unknown	12Se02Gc
John	05	F	Unknown	12Se02Gc
Mary	.00	F	Infant	12Se02Gc
WALSH, James	26	M	Laborer	12Se02Gc
MCGEARNY, Pat.	45	M	Laborer	12Se02Gc
Mary	43	F	Unknown	12Se02Gc
James	12	M	Laborer	12Se02Gc
Pat.	10	M	Laborer	12Se02Gc
Michael	06	M	Laborer	12Se02Gc
James	.00	M	Infant	12Se02Gc
FURGERSON, Sarah	20	F	Unknown	12Se02Gc
CULLEN, Mary	30	F	Unknown	12Se02Gc

NAMES OF PASSENGERS	AGE	SEX	OCCUPATIONS	DATE PORT SHIP
GLURMOR, Pullen	20	M	Laborer	12Se02Gc
FLYNN, Sarah	18	F	Unknown	12Se02Gc
MCCAVIN, Bridget	20	F	Unknown	12Se02Gc
DONOVER, John	12	M	Unknown	12Se02Gc
Mary	10	F	Unknown	12Se02Gc
LANGLIN, John	12	M	Unknown	12Se02Gc
CALLAGHAN, Thos.	40	M	Unknown	12Se02Gc
MAGEER, Mary-Ann	13	F	Unknown	12Se02Gc
MORAN, Margt.	09	F	Unknown	12Se02Gc
Owen	12	M	Unknown	12Se02Gc
Cathrn.	10	F	Unknown	12Se02Gc
HYNES, Phil	10	M	Unknown	12Se02Gc
Thos.	09	M	Unknown	12Se02Gc
Ellen	04	F	Unknown	12Se02Gc
KEGLEY, Ann	13	F	Unknown	12Se02Gc
KEANLEY, Ann	28	F	Unknown	12Se02Gc
MCKNGLEY, Pat.	21	M	Unknown	12Se02Gc
CALLAGHAN, Cathrn.	12	F	Unknown	12Se02Gc
James	16	M	Unknown	12Se02Gc
MCGURRIE, Peter	20	M	Unknown	12Se02Gc
CONNER, Rose	18	F	Unknown	12Se02Gc
Hanna	13	F	Unknown	12Se02Gc
DOYLE, Mary	25	F	Unknown	12Se02Gc
TLOVE, Margt.	26	F	Unknown	12Se02Gc
COURTNEY, Ann	27	F	Unknown	12Se02Gc
LYNCH, James	11	M	Laborer	12Se02Gc
Thos.	09	M	Laborer	12Se02Gc
ODONNELL, John	30	M	Laborer	12Se02Gc
Ann	04	F	Child	12Se02Gc
KELLY, John	25	M	Laborer	12Se02Gc
HANNIE, W.	30	M	Laborer	12Se02Gc
Cohanne	25	M	Laborer	12Se02Gc
MCIVER, Hugh	20	M	Laborer	12Se02Gc
MCDONOUGH, Mary	18	F	Laborer	12Se02Gc
CULLEN, James	50	M	Laborer	12Se02Gc
BARRY, J.	28	M	Laborer	12Se02Gc
Cathrn.	27	F	Unknown	12Se02Gc
Mary	02	F	Child	12Se02Gc
Cathrn.	.00	F	Infant	12Se02Gc
THOMPSON, Carolin	43	F	Unknown	12Se02Gc
JONES, Emily	22	F	Unknown	12Se02Gc
HOPE, Erwin	60	M	Laborer	12Se02Gc
Edw.	40	M	Laborer	12Se02Gc
HAYES, Wm.	60	M	Unknown	12Se02Gc
Mary-Ann	60	F	Unknown	12Se02Gc
WALSH, Michael	28	M	Laborer	12Se02Gc
KING, James	36	M	Laborer	12Se02Gc
CLUTHAN, Samuel	20	M	Laborer	12Se02Gc
CALMON, Bridget	50	F	Unknown	12Se02Gc
Ellen	20	F	Unknown	12Se02Gc
Margt.	11	F	Unknown	12Se02Gc
Peter	15	M	Laborer	12Se02Gc

QUEBEC 14 SEPTEMBER 1846

From London

NAMES OF PASSENGERS	AGE	SEX	OCCUPATIONS	DATE PORT SHIP
BURK, Catharine	29	F	Unknown	14Se21Au
Winifred	25	F	Unknown	14Se21Au
RETINGER, Sarah	34	F	Unknown	14Se21Au
Christopher	10	M	Unknown	14Se21Au
Sarah	08	F	Unknown	14Se21Au
Joanna	02	F	Unknown	14Se21Au
KEMP, Mary	26	F	Unknown	14Se21Au
SHIPPEN, Eliza	36	F	Unknown	14Se21Au
CARTER, Geo.	19	M	Unknown	14Se21Au
Robt.	17	M	Unknown	14Se21Au
HORSNELL, Eliza	30	F	Unknown	14Se21Au
George	24	M	Farmer	14Se21Au

NAMES OF PASSENGERS	AGE	SEX	OCCUPATIONS	DATE PORT SHIP
HORSNELL, Wm.	14	M	Farmer	14Se21Au
DENNIS, Susan	31	F	Unknown	14Se21Au
Eliza	04	F	Unknown	14Se21Au
Susan	02	F	Unknown	14Se21Au
SHEPPARD, Alston	24	M	Bookbinder	14Se21Au
Ann	50	F	Unknown	14Se21Au
Amelia	17	F	Unknown	14Se21Au
Wm.	14	M	Unknown	14Se21Au
RICHARDSON, James	19	M	Stationer	14Se21Au
Thos.	17	M	Unknown	14Se21Au
WARDON, Wm.	40	M	Piano Maker	14Se21Au
WYATT, Edward	25	M	Unknown	14Se21Au
Ann	22	F	Unknown	14Se21Au
Edward	01	M	Unknown	14Se21Au
RETTINGER, Eliza	04	F	Unknown	14Se21Au
MCFARLAN, John	28	M	Artist	14Se21Au
Emona-Maria	25	F	Artist	14Se21Au
GUIETA, Chas.	33	M	Unknown	14Se21Au
WILLIAMS, Sally	19	F	Unknown	14Se21Au
HART, Thos.	36	M	Hairdresser	14Se21Au
Mary-Ann	25	F	Unknown	14Se21Au
WATKINS, Lucy	24	F	Laborer	14Se21Au
Thos.-A.	01	M	Unknown	14Se21Au
DEAKINS, Eliza-S.	25	F	Unknown	14Se21Au
DUNN, John	32	M	Comedian	14Se21Au
Louisa	28	F	Unknown	14Se21Au
Rose	06	F	Unknown	14Se21Au
John	04	M	Unknown	14Se21Au
Mary-Ann	01	F	Unknown	14Se21Au
MONTAGUE, Alexr.	24	M	Unknown	14Se21Au
Clara	24	F	Unknown	14Se21Au
Amy	06	F	Unknown	14Se21Au
Alfred	04	M	Unknown	14Se21Au
MELTON, John	22	M	Unknown	14Se21Au

SILAS-HOLMES 14 SEPTEMBER 1846

From Liverpool

NAMES OF PASSENGERS	AGE	SEX	OCCUPATIONS	DATE PORT SHIP
BURSTALL, Francis	47	M	Merchant	14Se02Gf
JOHNSON, Robert	34	M	Clergyman	14Se02Gf
WATSON, Jonathan	29	M	Merchant	14Se02Gf
WALTON, Thomas	41	M	Merchant	14Se02Gf
WILSON, David	28	M	Carpenter	14Se02Gf
Mary	20	F	Servant	14Se02Gf
MAINE, John	22	M	Carpenter	14Se02Gf
LATHRAM, Joseph	33	M	Butcher	14Se02Gf
LOYD, James	25	M	Wlmcht	14Se02Gf
BOWS, Jonathan	30	M	Chandler	14Se02Gf
Mary-Ann (W)	25	F	Unknown	14Se02Gf
Elizabeth-Jane (D)	.02	F	Infant	14Se02Gf
REINE, Jane	60	F	WI	14Se02Gf
Henry	16	M	Joiner	14Se02Gf
BYERS, Mary	58	F	Wife	14Se02Gf
Robert	34	M	Carpenter	14Se02Gf
SIMPSON, James	28	M	Farmer	14Se02Gf
STUART, Matilda	20	F	Servant	14Se02Gf
Margt.	18	F	Servant	14Se02Gf
CALDER, Margt.	17	F	Servant	14Se02Gf
TAYLOR, Saml.	21	M	Wlmcht	14Se02Gf
RICHARDS, Mathew	50	M	Miner	14Se02Gf
Mary (W)	45	F	Unknown	14Se02Gf
Hannah (D)	14	F	Unknown	14Se02Gf
Elizabeth (D)	12	F	Unknown	14Se02Gf
Matthew (S)	10	M	Unknown	14Se02Gf
Barth. (S)	08	M	Unknown	14Se02Gf
Eliza (D)	06	F	Unknown	14Se02Gf
Sarah (D)	04	F	Unknown	14Se02Gf
Avis (D)	02	F	Unknown	14Se02Gf

NAMES OF PASSENGERS	AGE	SEX	OCCUPATIONS	DATE PORT SHIP
BOYLE, Robert	22	M	Weaver	14Se02Gf
Agnes (W)	22	F	Wife	14Se02Gf
MORTON, Lucinda	20	F	Wife	14Se02Gf
BROWN, Robert	19	M	Shoemaker	14Se02Gf
MCCAULEY, James	21	M	Laborer	14Se02Gf
BROWN, George	12	M	Child	14Se02Gf
Margt.	18	F	Servant	14Se02Gf
MCKOWN, John	21	M	Laborer	14Se02Gf
Rachael (W)	21	F	Wife	14Se02Gf
SAMPSON, Sarah	22	F	Servant	14Se02Gf
Mary	20	F	Wife	14Se02Gf
BROWN, Mary	28	F	Servant	14Se02Gf
FENNOCK, Margt.	25	F	Wife	14Se02Gf
Alex.	36	M	Miner	14Se02Gf
Anna	01	F	Infant	14Se02Gf
DOYLE, John	20	M	Clerk	14Se02Gf
CAMPBELL, Tom	15	M	Brf	14Se02Gf
CONWAY, Pat.	27	M	Sawer	14Se02Gf
Margt. (W)	26	F	Wife	14Se02Gf
Cath. (D)	02	F	Child	14Se02Gf
Sarah (D)	04	F	Child	14Se02Gf
Margt. (D)	.06	F	Infant	14Se02Gf
BULMER, Henry	68	M	Weaver	14Se02Gf
Jane (W)	70	F	Wife	14Se02Gf
MURPHY, Margt.	22	F	Servant	14Se02Gf
CALLIGAN, Sarah	17	F	Servant	14Se02Gf
Margt.	10	F	Servant	14Se02Gf
FENWICK, William	03	M	Child	14Se02Gf
KNIEVOS, William	29	M	Miner	14Se02Gf
Elizabeth (W)	27	F	Wife	14Se02Gf
WEST, Mary	18	F	Servant	14Se02Gf
Mary-Jane (D)	01	F	Child	14Se02Gf
JACKSON, Robt.	19	M	Miner	14Se02Gf
DALE, John	20	M	Engd	14Se02Gf
BANKS, James	33	M	Miner	14Se02Gf
Mary (W)	29	F	Wife	14Se02Gf
James (S)	08	M	Child	14Se02Gf
Peter (S)	04	M	Child	14Se02Gf
RICHY, Biddy	18	F	Servant	14Se02Gf
BRADY, Mary	19	F	Servant	14Se02Gf
KEEGAN, Margt.	16	F	Servant	14Se02Gf
ELLET, Elizabeth	24	F	Servant	14Se02Gf
Cath.	22	F	Servant	14Se02Gf
LEENHEN, Pat.	19	M	Unknown	14Se02Gf
COSTELLO, Arch.	25	M	Farmer	14Se02Gf
Elizabeth (W)	23	F	Wife	14Se02Gf
James (S)	06	M	Child	14Se02Gf
William (S)	04	M	Child	14Se02Gf
Joseph (S)	02	M	Child	14Se02Gf
HILES, Hannah	50	F	Wife	14Se02Gf
Ann (D)	21	F	None	14Se02Gf
NICHOLSON, James	47	M	Collier	14Se02Gf
John	22	M	Miner	14Se02Gf
WAUGH, John	29	M	Miner	14Se02Gf
TATE, Jacob	37	M	Miner	14Se02Gf
MITCHELSON, David	29	M	Miner	14Se02Gf
MCDERMOTT, Pat.	24	M	Furrier	14Se02Gf
Isabella (W)	22	F	Wife	14Se02Gf
LAUGHLIN, Cath.	18	F	Servant	14Se02Gf
WILLIAMSON, Mary	20	F	Servant	14Se02Gf
PHILLIPS, Mary	20	F	Wife	14Se02Gf
WEBB, Richd.	30	M	Miner	14Se02Gf
WILLIAMS, Zach.	21	M	Miner	14Se02Gf
MANAND, Tom	31	M	Miner	14Se02Gf
EUDY, Joseph	22	M	Miner	14Se02Gf
SICCOMB, Henry	23	M	Miner	14Se02Gf
PRINGLE, Wm.	30	M	Blacksmith	14Se02Gf
Elizabeth (W)	29	F	Wife	14Se02Gf
UPPINGHAM, Henry	46	M	Merchant	14Se02Gf
HARRIS, Robert	35	M	Farmer	14Se02Gf
SMITH, William	24	M	Farmer	14Se02Gf
DUNCAN, George	48	M	Farmer	14Se02Gf
ROBERTS, Tom.	53	M	Miner	14Se02Gf
Ann (W)	51	F	None	14Se02Gf
Tom (S)	21	M	None	14Se02Gf

NAMES OF PASSENGERS		AGE	SEX	OCCUPATIONS	DATE PORT SHIP
ROBERTS, Henry	(S)	14	M	None	14Se02Gf
Ann	(D)	12	F	None	14Se02Gf
James	(S)	10	M	None	14Se02Gf
BENNETT, George		19	M	Miner	14Se02Gf
MCDONALD, John		17	M	Sawer	14Se02Gf
BYRNES, Peter		15	M	Unknown	14Se02Gf
FITZSIMMONS, Biddy		20	F	Servant	14Se02Gf
KELLEY, Jane		40	F	Wi	14Se02Gf
MADISON, Mary		20	F	Servant	14Se02Gf
MCMULLEN, Pat.		35	M	Flaxdr	14Se02Gf
Ellen	(W)	24	F	Wife	14Se02Gf
ONEAL, Sarah		36	F	Wife	14Se02Gf
RICHARDSON, James		11	M	None	14Se02Gf
Mary		03	F	Child	14Se02Gf
MCGINNIS, Mary		40	F	Wi	14Se02Gf
Philip	(S)	17	M	None	14Se02Gf
Kate		19	F	Servant	14Se02Gf
Betsey		13	F	Servant	14Se02Gf
Margt.		15	F	Servant	14Se02Gf
Tom	(S)	20	M	None	14Se02Gf
Bernard	(S)	11	M	None	14Se02Gf
OBRIEN, Tim		31	M	Weaver	14Se02Gf
Margt.	(W)	30	F	Wife	14Se02Gf
Henry	(S)	05	M	Child	14Se02Gf
HARRIGAN, Tom		60	M	Carpenter	14Se02Gf
Ann	(W)	50	F	Wife	14Se02Gf
Honorah	(D)	13	F	None	14Se02Gf
Hannah	(D)	04	F	Child	14Se02Gf
DOLZELL, Tom		67	M	Weaver	14Se02Gf
BUSTED, John		20	M	Flaxdr	14Se02Gf
MCCRUM, Sarah		17	F	Servant	14Se02Gf
LEECH, Ellen		24	F	Servant	14Se02Gf
BARY, Ellen		12	F	Servant	14Se02Gf
HAMILTON, William		19	M	Butcher	14Se02Gf
GILMARTIN, Tom		23	M	Baker	14Se02Gf
CAMPBELL, Dennis		37	M	Laborer	14Se02Gf
GARETY, Michael		19	M	Tailor	14Se02Gf
MORGAN, Tom		21	M	Laborer	14Se02Gf
Biddy	(W)	21	F	Wife	14Se02Gf
Biddy		19	F	Servant	14Se02Gf
CAMEDON, Francis		27	M	Tailor	14Se02Gf
Grace	(W)	25	F	Wife	14Se02Gf
CAZZON, William		30	M	Tailor	14Se02Gf
May	(W)	30	F	Wife	14Se02Gf
Eliza	(D)	09	F	Child	14Se02Gf
Harriet	(D)	01	F	Child	14Se02Gf
OFARRELL, Dominick		28	M	Merchant	14Se02Gf
Pat.		17	M	Clerk	14Se02Gf
Henry		13	M	Clerk	14Se02Gf
BRIERDY, Pat.		19	M	Laborer	14Se02Gf
Ann	(W)	18	F	Wife	14Se02Gf
Mary		40	F	Wi	14Se02Gf
OGORMAND, James		55	M	Blacksmith	14Se02Gf
MCCORMICK, Maria		32	F	Wi	14Se02Gf
RILEY, Mary		47	F	Wife	14Se02Gf
James	(S)	11	M	None	14Se02Gf
Mary-Ann	(D)	19	F	None	14Se02Gf
John	(S)	13	M	None	14Se02Gf
William	(S)	10	M	None	14Se02Gf
LINDSEY, Margt.		40	F	Wife	14Se02Gf
William	(S)	15	M	None	14Se02Gf
Mary	(D)	12	F	None	14Se02Gf
Frances	(D)	10	F	None	14Se02Gf
Jane	(D)	08	F	Child	14Se02Gf
Ruth	(D)	05	F	Child	14Se02Gf
KEERSON, Mary		18	F	Servant	14Se02Gf
BRADY, Cath.		16	F	Servant	14Se02Gf
CRONEN, Ellen		17	F	Servant	14Se02Gf
DURNEY, Mary		35	F	Wife	14Se02Gf
Mary-Ann	(D)	03	F	Child	14Se02Gf
Ellen	(D)	09	F	Child	14Se02Gf
James	(S)	12	M	None	14Se02Gf
James	(S)	01	M	Child	14Se02Gf
WERNON, Mary		33	F	Wi	14Se02Gf
John	(S)	13	M	None	14Se02Gf
WERNON, Tom	(S)	11	M	None	14Se02Gf
Biddy	(D)	07	F	Child	14Se02Gf
HARDIGAN, James		25	M	Carpenter	14Se02Gf
FOLEY, Edw.		21	M	Baker	14Se02Gf
STRAM, James		18	M	Weaver	14Se02Gf
Jane		20	F	Servant	14Se02Gf
RAFTER, Cath.		50	F	Wife	14Se02Gf
FITZPATRICK, Mary		25	F	Servant	14Se02Gf
DUCK, Edw.		16	M	Unknown	14Se02Gf
SMITH, Pat.		21	M	Farmer	14Se02Gf
ROURKE, Mary		16	F	Servant	14Se02Gf
Margt.		14	F	Servant	14Se02Gf
MCLEARY, Margt.		18	F	Servant	14Se02Gf
MCGIVNEY, Pat		40	M	Unknown	14Se02Gf
MCNAMEE, Pat.		25	M	Shoemaker	14Se02Gf

WILLIAM-CAULDWELL 16 SEPTEMBER 1846

From Halifax

NAMES OF PASSENGERS	AGE	SEX	OCCUPATIONS	DATE PORT SHIP
DIVINE, Wm.	18	M	Unknown	16Se22GJ

GARRICK 16 SEPTEMBER 1846

From Liverpool

NAMES OF PASSENGERS	AGE	SEX	OCCUPATIONS	DATE PORT SHIP
NALLY, Catharine	16	F	Spinster	16Se02Aa
AHERN, Patrick	30	M	Laborer	16Se02Aa
Margaret	20	F	Spinster	16Se02Aa
DUNLAN, Thomas	20	M	Farmer	16Se02Aa
DUNNE, Martin	13	M	Farmer	16Se02Aa
SMITH, Mary	17	F	Spinster	16Se02Aa
MARKEY, Anne	20	F	Spinster	16Se02Aa
Peter	17	M	Joiner	16Se02Aa
CONLAN, Mary	50	F	Unknown	16Se02Aa
Francis	13	M	Laborer	16Se02Aa
COOPER, R.	25	M	Laborer	16Se02Aa
CALLAGHAN, Bridget	32	F	Farmer	16Se02Aa
Edward	08	M	Farmer	16Se02Aa
Anne	.00	F	Infant	16Se02Aa
Mary	.00	F	Infant	16Se02Aa
SMALL, Mary	27	F	Spinster	16Se02Aa
LEDWITCH, John	20	M	Laborer	16Se02Aa
Mary	20	F	Laborer	16Se02Aa
BRODLE, Margaret	16	F	Laborer	16Se02Aa
ANNELLEY, Michael	20	M	Laborer	16Se02Aa
FLOOD, Mathew	18	M	Laborer	16Se02Aa
KEEFE, Anne	18	F	Laborer	16Se02Aa
CROWLEY, Humphrey	50	M	Laborer	16Se02Aa
RING, Bridget	20	F	Spinster	16Se02Aa
Mary	18	F	Spinster	16Se02Aa
JOHNSTONE, Henry	30	M	Farmer	16Se02Aa
DONAGHEY, John	60	M	Farmer	16Se02Aa
Rose	50	F	Farmer	16Se02Aa
Mary-Ann	20	F	Farmer	16Se02Aa
VALLERE, Rebecca	30	F	Spinster	16Se02Aa
MCMASTER, George	20	M	Mason	16Se02Aa
MCCORMICK, Arthur	24	M	Farmer	16Se02Aa
U-Mrs.	21	F	Farmer	16Se02Aa
MCKIVENGAN, James	25	M	Farmer	16Se02Aa
CUNNA, Anne	22	F	Spinster	16Se02Aa
HAMILL, Mary	20	F	Spinster	16Se02Aa
SCOTT, Steward	33	M	Clerk	16Se02Aa

NAMES OF PASSENGERS	AGE	SEX	OCCUPATIONS	DATE PORT SHIP
MCNULTY, James	40	M	Laborer	16Se02Aa
CLEARY, Ann	20	F	Servant	16Se02Aa
CARTY, Timothy	25	M	Laborer	16Se02Aa
CLOYNES, Thomas	30	M	Farmer	16Se02Aa
Eliza	32	F	Farmer	16Se02Aa
PAGE, Joseph	38	M	Farmer	16Se02Aa
Sarah (W)	25	F	Wife	16Se02Aa
Joseph-Henry	02	M	Child	16Se02Aa
Henry	.00	M	Infant	16Se02Aa
MAXWELL, Henry	30	M	Unknown	16Se02Aa
DEMPSEY, John	17	M	Unknown	16Se02Aa
SHAUGHNESSY, Peggy	50	F	Spinster	16Se02Aa
KELLY, Margaret	22	F	Spinster	16Se02Aa
LOUGHRAN, Eliza	30	F	Spinster	16Se02Aa
SARLEY, Sarah	18	F	Servant	16Se02Aa
ANDERSON, Sarah	17	F	Spinster	16Se02Aa
FLEMING, Michael	36	M	Farmer	16Se02Aa
Geo.	16	M	Farmer	16Se02Aa
Mary-Ann	13	F	Unknown	16Se02Aa
John	11	M	Unknown	16Se02Aa
Michael	09	M	Unknown	16Se02Aa
Thomas	07	M	Unknown	16Se02Aa
SMITH, George	26	M	Laborer	16Se02Aa
SINGLETON, Thomas	60	M	Laborer	16Se02Aa
Jane	60	F	Laborer	16Se02Aa
Thomas	27	M	Laborer	16Se02Aa
DAWSON, Wm.	50	M	Laborer	16Se02Aa
FAIRLEY, James	29	M	Laborer	16Se02Aa
SIMONS, John	36	M	Laborer	16Se02Aa
DAVIES, James	09	M	Laborer	16Se02Aa
MOORE, Julia	20	F	Spinster	16Se02Aa
NEIL, Eliza	18	F	Spinster	16Se02Aa
RYAN, Jane	18	F	Spinster	16Se02Aa
DONOHUE, James	25	M	Laborer	16Se02Aa
TRUMBLE, Margaret	30	F	Laborer	16Se02Aa
Margaret	08	F	Child	16Se02Aa
John	05	M	Child	16Se02Aa
Thomas	02	M	Child	16Se02Aa
Jane	.00	F	Infant	16Se02Aa
MARTIN, James	35	M	Laborer	16Se02Aa
Margaret	30	F	Laborer	16Se02Aa
BLACK, Rose	60	F	Farmer	16Se02Aa
MARTIN, Charles	16	M	Farmer	16Se02Aa
Mary-Rose-Ann	13	F	Farmer	16Se02Aa
John	08	M	Farmer	16Se02Aa
James	06	M	Farmer	16Se02Aa
Ellen	03	F	Farmer	16Se02Aa
Robt.	.00	M	Infant	16Se02Aa
CALLAGHAN, James	32	M	Farmer	16Se02Aa
CRANKSHAW, Emma	03	F	Unknown	16Se02Aa
WALKER, Mathew	30	M	Laborer	16Se02Aa
Charles	12	M	Laborer	16Se02Aa
SMITH, Catharine	18	F	Spinster	16Se02Aa
MCKINNEY, Sarah	30	F	Servant	16Se02Aa
James	07	M	Child	16Se02Aa
Francis	04	M	Child	16Se02Aa
Rosanna	.00	F	Infant	16Se02Aa
DOLAN, Ellen	19	F	Servant	16Se02Aa
Maria	16	F	Servant	16Se02Aa
Josh	03	M	Child	16Se02Aa
BRENAN, Michael	20	M	Tailor	16Se02Aa
STANLEY, Timothy	12	M	Servant	16Se02Aa
Bernard	09	M	Child	16Se02Aa
BENIGAN, Wm.	21	M	Farmer	16Se02Aa
John	35	M	Farmer	16Se02Aa
HANNA, Wm.	24	M	Farmer	16Se02Aa
Mary	19	F	Farmer	16Se02Aa
MACKLE, Hugh	18	M	Laborer	16Se02Aa
Henry	20	M	Laborer	16Se02Aa
BARKER, George	21	M	Farmer	16Se02Aa
BOYD, Mary	30	F	Farmer	16Se02Aa
ONEILL, Mary	19	F	Farmer	16Se02Aa
MCCULLOUGH, Salley	36	F	Farmer	16Se02Aa
KENT, Sarah	19	F	Farmer	16Se02Aa
HENRY, Hugh	21	M	Farmer	16Se02Aa
MICKELE, Henry	22	M	Farmer	16Se02Aa
Hugh	24	M	Farmer	16Se02Aa
CASEY, Bridget	.00	F	Infant	16Se02Aa
CLARK, Thomas	22	M	Laborer	16Se02Aa
OCOLVILL, Robt.	18	M	Laborer	16Se02Aa
BATES, Hugh	20	M	Joiner	16Se02Aa
MCGOUGH, Mary	22	F	Servant	16Se02Aa
MCMULLEN, Edward	30	M	Joiner	16Se02Aa
MOLLOY, John	21	M	Joiner	16Se02Aa
KIRKWOOD, Margaret	22	F	Servant	16Se02Aa
LOGAN, Mary	19	F	Servant	16Se02Aa
MCALLISTER, Patt.	40	M	Farmer	16Se02Aa
Mary	40	F	Unknown	16Se02Aa
James	04	M	Unknown	16Se02Aa
SHEEHAN, Nelly	21	F	Spinster	16Se02Aa
PROCTOR, Mary (W)	38	F	Wife	16Se02Aa
Mary (D)	03	F	Child	16Se02Aa
GARLAND, Margaret	24	F	Spinster	16Se02Aa
DOYLE, John	34	M	Farmer	16Se02Aa
U (W)	30	F	Wife	16Se02Aa
Charles (S)	09	M	Child	16Se02Aa
Amelia (D)	08	F	Child	16Se02Aa
John (S)	04	M	Child	16Se02Aa
Lucretia (D)	03	F	Child	16Se02Aa
Alfred (S)	.00	M	Infant	16Se02Aa
BAXTER, Charles	25	M	Laborer	16Se02Aa
DICK, Mat.	25	M	Laborer	16Se02Aa
BROWN, Gabriel	08	M	Child	16Se02Aa
U-Mrs.	30	F	Servant	16Se02Aa
GALLAGHER, James	20	M	Farmer	16Se02Aa
HIGGINS, Michael	30	M	Farmer	16Se02Aa
HARRISSTON, Susan	25	F	Servant	16Se02Aa
MCKIVERIGAN, Margaret	19	F	Servant	16Se02Aa
CARTIRE, Camelis	20	F	Spinster	16Se02Aa
Catharine	18	F	Spinster	16Se02Aa
Eliza	26	F	Spinster	16Se02Aa
SPILMAN, Michael	25	M	Farmer	16Se02Aa
U-Mrs.	20	F	Wife	16Se02Aa
HANLON, Wm.	25	M	Farmer	16Se02Aa
ROBINSON, Margaret	20	F	Spinster	16Se02Aa
Mary	18	F	Spinster	16Se02Aa
MALTIN, Anne	18	F	Spinster	16Se02Aa
QUINN, Mary	18	F	Spinster	16Se02Aa
MALTIN, Maria	18	F	Spinster	16Se02Aa
QUINN, Mary	18	F	Servant	16Se02Aa
MORGAN, Mary-Anne	21	F	Servant	16Se02Aa
MAMALE, Margaret	26	F	Servant	16Se02Aa
TOOMERY, Wm.	30	M	Farmer	16Se02Aa
OHARA, Stephen	30	M	Farmer	16Se02Aa
NEILL, Geo.	25	M	Farmer	16Se02Aa
DONOVAN, Daniel	24	M	Mason	16Se02Aa
MURPHY, Sarah	22	F	Servant	16Se02Aa
RILEY, Margaret	20	F	Servant	16Se02Aa
POWELL, Bridget	40	F	Servant	16Se02Aa
MARTIN, Ann	16	F	Servant	16Se02Aa
HIGGINS, Susan	18	F	Servant	16Se02Aa
CORLEY, Philip	32	M	Laborer	16Se02Aa
SMITH, Mary	20	F	Spinster	16Se02Aa
MAGUIRE, Patt.	20	M	Servant	16Se02Aa
Mary	18	F	Servant	16Se02Aa
CLARK, James	20	M	Servant	16Se02Aa
CARTY, Thos.	18	M	Farmer	16Se02Aa
HYDE, Wm.	20	M	Farmer	16Se02Aa
MCCUNE, Peter	20	M	Farmer	16Se02Aa
KELLEY, Thomas	20	M	Farmer	16Se02Aa
BRITTON, Anne	55	F	Farmer	16Se02Aa
Jane	20	F	Farmer	16Se02Aa
Wm.	19	M	Farmer	16Se02Aa
WALKER, James	60	M	Farmer	16Se02Aa
Died-At-Sea				
Ellen	55	F	Farmer	16Se02Aa
OHARA, Anne-Jane	22	F	Servant	16Se02Aa
MCCLEAN, Henry	28	M	Servant	16Se02Aa
Ann	26	F	Servant	16Se02Aa
John	32	M	Servant	16Se02Aa

NAMES OF PASSENGERS	AGE	SEX	OCCUPATIONS	DATE PORT SHIP		NAMES OF PASSENGERS	AGE	SEX	OCCUPATIONS	DATE PORT SHIP
GREEN, Margaret	20	F	Servant	16Se02Aa						
WOODS, Thomas	30	M	Joiner	16Se02Aa						
MCDERMOTT, James	34	M	Farmer	16Se02Aa						
BERIGAN, James	05	M	Child	16Se02Aa						
Wm.	.00	M	Infant	16Se02Aa		MONTEZUMA 17 SEPTEMBER 1846				
Margaret	08	F	Child	16Se02Aa						
Mary	04	F	Child	16Se02Aa		From Liverpool				
Mary	20	F	Unknown	16Se02Aa						
Margery	30	F	Unknown	16Se02Aa						
KAINE, Daniel	27	M	Carpenter	16Se02Aa						
CARSON, Dennis	30	M	Unknown	16Se02Aa		FRANCIS, Thos.	40	M	Gentleman	17Se02Ao
FARRELL, John	30	M	Blacksmith	16Se02Aa		SPAWFORTH, John	39	M	Merchant	17Se02Ao
HUNTER, Bessy	40	F	Unknown	16Se02Aa		SORBY, Walter	40	M	Merchant	17Se02Ao
Wm.	15	M	Unknown	16Se02Aa		LEWSON, Spurcheim	15	M	Merchant	17Se02Ao
Robt.	10	M	Unknown	16Se02Aa		FORESTER, William	27	M	Merchant	17Se02Ao
BLACK, Wm.	28	M	Farmer	16Se02Aa		William	05	M	Child	17Se02Ao
ROSS, Hannah	50	F	Servant	16Se02Aa		NICHOLSON, Sarah	40	F	Lady	17Se02Ao
Hannah	30	F	Servant	16Se02Aa		GREGG, U	29	M	Clergyman	17Se02Ao
Mary	07	F	Child	16Se02Aa		BLAKE, Lewis	19	M	Officer	17Se02Ao
Nancy	.00	F	Infant	16Se02Aa		HOGG, Ann	22	F	Lady	17Se02Ao
SCOTT, Patt.	30	M	Joiner	16Se02Aa		METZGER, John	22	M	Unknown	17Se02Ao
DELANEY, Martin	23	M	Tailor	16Se02Aa		KEY, Henry	22	M	Laborer	17Se02Ao
NEIL, John	26	M	Servant	16Se02Aa		PORTNEY, Sarah	54	F	Servant	17Se02Ao
MCDONALD, Pat.	20	M	Servant	16Se02Aa		DALEY, Mary	25	F	Servant	17Se02Ao
LARKIN, Thomas	18	M	Clerk	16Se02Aa		FITZPATRICK, Ann	20	F	Servant	17Se02Ao
WHELAN, Patt.	35	M	Unknown	16Se02Aa		DUFFY, Terrence	21	M	Servant	17Se02Ao
RILEY, Edward	30	M	Laborer	16Se02Aa		CORR, James	23	M	Servant	17Se02Ao
Mary	20	F	Unknown	16Se02Aa		MCNEVINE, Catherine	25	F	Servant	17Se02Ao
BROGAN, Margaret	20	F	Unknown	16Se02Aa		DUNN, Henry	30	M	Engineer	17Se02Ao
TAYLOR, John	.00	M	Infant	16Se02Aa		U (W)	31	F	Collier	17Se02Ao
REDMOND, John	32	M	Unknown	16Se02Aa		U	.00	U	Infant	17Se02Ao
Sally	28	F	Unknown	16Se02Aa		Julia-Ann	60	F	Unknown	17Se02Ao
Lawrence	.00	M	Infant	16Se02Aa		Mary-Sophia	45	F	Unknown	17Se02Ao
BURNS, Thomas	18	M	Unknown	16Se02Aa		JENKS, Mary	51	F	Servant	17Se02Ao
GRIER, James	18	M	Unknown	16Se02Aa		Julia-Ann	03	F	Child	17Se02Ao
CARROLL, Robert	16	M	Unknown	16Se02Aa		DAVEY, Wm.	36	M	Mechanic	17Se02Ao
Patrick	13	M	Unknown	16Se02Aa		Charles	13	M	Mechanic	17Se02Ao
CONNOR, James	17	M	Unknown	16Se02Aa		HALL, Thomas	30	M	Laborer	17Se02Ao
ONEELEY, John	17	M	Unknown	16Se02Aa		GILLON, Patrick	28	M	Laborer	17Se02Ao
HENRY, John	14	M	Unknown	16Se02Aa		WOOD, Francis	24	M	Carpenter	17Se02Ao
						HUNTER, James	24	M	Carpenter	17Se02Ao
						SULLIVAN, Dennis	31	M	Laborer	17Se02Ao
						Ellen	29	F	Laborer	17Se02Ao
						FLYNN, Mary	26	F	Servant	17Se02Ao
						ROBERTS, Michael	34	M	Tailor	17Se02Ao
ATLAS 16 SEPTEMBER 1846						LOT, John	27	M	Laborer	17Se02Ao
						BILLMAN, Mary	21	F	Servant	17Se02Ao
From Liverpool						GRADY, Mary	22	F	Servant	17Se02Ao
						DUDLEY, U-Mrs.	26	F	Servant	17Se02Ao
						MURPHY, William	25	M	Laborer	17Se02Ao
DUNN, Wm.	34	M	None	16Se02Ec		Margt.	24	F	Laborer	17Se02Ao
INGLEDIR, James	30	M	None	16Se02Ec		James	.00	M	Infant	17Se02Ao
Hanah (W)	30	F	Wife	16Se02Ec		BROOKS, Alice	20	F	Laborer	17Se02Ao
Junley (D)	09	F	Child	16Se02Ec		CHESTER, Thomas	24	M	Laborer	17Se02Ao
Hanah (D)	02	F	Child	16Se02Ec		GRAHAM, John	47	M	Laborer	17Se02Ao
ABBOTT, Francis	21	M	Farmer	16Se02Ec		LEE, Craven	21	M	Laborer	17Se02Ao
MORRISON, Benj.	44	M	Farmer	16Se02Ec		DAVIES, David	41	M	Laborer	17Se02Ao
Rose (W)	40	F	Wife	16Se02Ec		Elizabeth	21	F	Laborer	17Se02Ao
Elizabeth (D)	16	F	None	16Se02Ec		Elisa	18	F	Laborer	17Se02Ao
Hanah (D)	13	F	None	16Se02Ec		MCHAND, John	25	M	Laborer	17Se02Ao
Benjamin (S)	12	M	None	16Se02Ec		TAYLOR, Jane	20	F	Laborer	17Se02Ao
Hanah (D)	11	F	None	16Se02Ec		DALEY, Mary	26	F	Laborer	17Se02Ao
Solomon (S)	06	M	Child	16Se02Ec		MCKINNEY, Joseph	21	M	Laborer	17Se02Ao
Rebecc (D)	04	F	Child	16Se02Ec		MCCORMICK, Mary	18	F	Servant	17Se02Ao
Benj. (S)	.00	M	Infant	16Se02Ec		SMITH, John	31	M	Laborer	17Se02Ao
LYN, Morris	48	M	Farmer	16Se02Ec		WHITTERS, William	21	M	Laborer	17Se02Ao
JOYCE, James	40	M	Farmer	16Se02Ec		Grace	05	F	Child	17Se02Ao
						Francis	04	M	Child	17Se02Ao
						Lattimer	03	M	Child	17Se02Ao
						Caroline	02	F	Child	17Se02Ao
						GREALY, Patrick	29	M	Laborer	17Se02Ao
						DONNELLY, B.	40	M	Laborer	17Se02Ao
						CRAWFORD, Wm.	29	M	Merchant	17Se02Ao
						U (W)	25	F	Unknown	17Se02Ao
						KNOWLES, Jonas	30	M	Unknown	17Se02Ao

NAMES OF PASSENGERS	AGE	SEX	OCCUPATIONS	DATE PORT SHIP
GILLESPIE, Francis	22	M	Laborer	17Se02Ao
Rachael	20	F	Unknown	17Se02Ao
WATERTON, Margt.	20	F	Unknown	17Se02Ao
CONNER, Mary	20	F	Servant	17Se02Ao
CROGAN, Catherin	21	F	Servant	17Se02Ao
CONNER, Eliza	20	F	Servant	17Se02Ao
MCGUIN, Wm.	31	M	Laborer	17Se02Ao
Mr.	30	M	Laborer	17Se02Ao
HENESSEY, Norah	28	F	Servant	17Se02Ao
TATTERSALL, David	24	M	Tailor	17Se02Ao
MCGOVERN, Patrick	26	M	Laborer	17Se02Ao
TURY, Michael	36	M	Laborer	17Se02Ao
NOLAN, Ellen	22	F	Servant	17Se02Ao
Eliza	20	F	Servant	17Se02Ao
CAHAGAN, Thomas	28	M	Servant	17Se02Ao
John	06	M	Child	17Se02Ao
MULVEY, Thomas	26	M	Servant	17Se02Ao
ERNITZ, James	35	M	Servant	17Se02Ao
BATES, John	25	M	Laborer	17Se02Ao
MCCOOMB, Wm.	59	M	Laborer	17Se02Ao
Marietta	24	F	Unknown	17Se02Ao
MCGARRIF, Margt.	21	F	Unknown	17Se02Ao
BAMPTON, Wm.	40	M	Laborer	17Se02Ao
Martha	36	F	Unknown	17Se02Ao
Jane	07	M	Child	17Se02Ao
Martha	05	F	Child	17Se02Ao
John	.00	M	Infant	17Se02Ao
Robert	.00	M	Infant	17Se02Ao
NEWLADY, Julia	21	F	Unknown	17Se02Ao
DERMODY, Ellen	22	F	Unknown	17Se02Ao
FINN, Daniel	40	M	Laborer	17Se02Ao
Ann	34	F	Unknown	17Se02Ao
Sally	03	F	Child	17Se02Ao
Norris	02	M	Child	17Se02Ao
Died-At-Sea				
MCGEE, James	31	M	Peddler	17Se02Ao
Elizabeth	22	F	Unknown	17Se02Ao
Elizabeth	.00	F	Infant	17Se02Ao
CARROLL, Susan	22	F	Servant	17Se02Ao
HOBSON, Joseph	44	M	Mechanic	17Se02Ao
PORTER, U-Widow	45	F	Servant	17Se02Ao
Edding-BROOK, Henry	40	M	Laborer	17Se02Ao
U-Mrs. (W)	35	F	Wife	17Se02Ao
Harriet	02	F	Child	17Se02Ao
BREENAN, Edmund	24	M	Laborer	17Se02Ao
DUNSMITH, Sarah-Jane	28	F	Servant	17Se02Ao
Matilda	24	F	Servant	17Se02Ao
HEIGH, Martha-Jane	28	F	Servant	17Se02Ao
Rebecca	20	F	Servant	17Se02Ao
MCHEARD, Mary-Ann	27	F	Servant	17Se02Ao
MCCARLY, J.	26	M	Laborer	17Se02Ao
DOWLEY, Patrick	20	M	Laborer	17Se02Ao
HENESAY, Michael	25	M	Laborer	17Se02Ao
MULLINS, Michael	30	M	Laborer	17Se02Ao
QUINLON, Thomas	26	M	Laborer	17Se02Ao
PRITCHETT, Catherine	21	F	Servant	17Se02Ao
LYONS, Ann	28	F	Servant	17Se02Ao
MCELROY, Ann	24	F	Servant	17Se02Ao
HESLIN, Patrick	18	M	Servant	17Se02Ao
DAVIES, Mary	28	F	Servant	17Se02Ao
Margt.	22	F	Servant	17Se02Ao
LINDSLEY, Jane	18	F	Servant	17Se02Ao
MCCHESTER, U	40	F	Wi	17Se02Ao
MCTENNANT, Mary	30	F	Servant	17Se02Ao
Patt.	29	M	Servant	17Se02Ao
Marianne	10	F	Child	17Se02Ao
DOLAN, Fidella	13	F	Servant	17Se02Ao
MCCRAW, Bridget	20	M	Servant	17Se02Ao
KELLY, James	26	M	Laborer	17Se02Ao
MACHIE, Patt.	22	M	Laborer	17Se02Ao
MCQUIN, Bridget	22	F	Servant	17Se02Ao
CAMERON, Ellen	20	F	Servant	17Se02Ao
GRAY, Thomas	26	M	Servant	17Se02Ao
CAMERON, Mary	18	F	Servant	17Se02Ao
OLDHAM, Emma	25	F	Servant	17Se02Ao
BROOKE, Mary-Ann	22	F	Servant	17Se02Ao
HACKETT, Mary	40	F	Servant	17Se02Ao
Mary	20	F	Servant	17Se02Ao
Ellen	04	F	Child	17Se02Ao
PURCELL, Patrick	22	M	Laborer	17Se02Ao
SHANNON, Robert	24	M	Laborer	17Se02Ao
ARMSTRONG, James	26	M	Laborer	17Se02Ao
TAGGART, Kitty	17	F	Laborer	17Se02Ao
Leslie	19	M	Laborer	17Se02Ao
Sarah-Jane	..00	F	Infant	17Se02Ao
MCKNIGHT, Mary	22	F	Servant	17Se02Ao
Thomas	14	M	Servant	17Se02Ao
MCIVER, Sarah	18	F	Servant	17Se02Ao
BLANDON, Mary	19	F	Servant	17Se02Ao
MCCARTY, Ellen	20	F	Servant	17Se02Ao
BATTER, Catherine	21	F	Servant	17Se02Ao
WHITING, Daniel	27	M	Servant	17Se02Ao
MULLICK, Ellen	29	F	Servant	17Se02Ao
Mary	06	F	Child	17Se02Ao
Jane	03	F	Child	17Se02Ao
DAVEY, Isabella	26	F	Servant	17Se02Ao
Margt.	21	F	Servant	17Se02Ao
FOLLETT, Robert	23	M	Servant	17Se02Ao
FLANNAGAN, Betsey	21	F	Servant	17Se02Ao
REID, James	18	M	Servant	17Se02Ao
MURRY, Darly	19	M	Servant	17Se02Ao
MCKEON, Mary	20	F	Servant	17Se02Ao
FAGAN, Margt.	20	F	Servant	17Se02Ao
TRAINOR, Mary-Eliza	21	F	Servant	17Se02Ao
Eliza	18	F	Servant	17Se02Ao
RYDER, Margt.	17	F	Servant	17Se02Ao
Martin	16	M	Servant	17Se02Ao
WATSON, Mathias	20	M	Servant	17Se02Ao
Jane	18	F	Servant	17Se02Ao
KENNEDY, Jane	21	F	Servant	17Se02Ao
MORBRAY, Jane	50	F	Servant	17Se02Ao
Bridget	18	F	Servant	17Se02Ao
Henry	16	M	Servant	17Se02Ao
Peter	14	M	Servant	17Se02Ao
Mary	12	F	Servant	17Se02Ao
Bridget	10	F	Servant	17Se02Ao
MADDEN, John	22	M	Servant	17Se02Ao
MORBRAY, Ellen	10	F	Child	17Se02Ao
FITZGERALD, David	63	M	Weaver	17Se02Ao
Mary	50	F	Weaver	17Se02Ao
Julien	20	M	Weaver	17Se02Ao
James	15	M	Weaver	17Se02Ao
HANEY, Julia	21	F	Servant	17Se02Ao
LYRUS, Frances	20	M	Servant	17Se02Ao
REDBRAID, Catherine	20	F	Servant	17Se02Ao
REYNOLDS, Ann	21	F	Servant	17Se02Ao
POTER, Nancy	21	F	Servant	17Se02Ao
MCCRANN, Patt.	19	M	Laborer	17Se02Ao
CARTER, Wm.	21	M	Laborer	17Se02Ao
BROWN, John	24	M	Laborer	17Se02Ao
REYNOLDS, Edw.	34	M	Laborer	17Se02Ao
TIERNAN, Mary	21	F	Laborer	17Se02Ao
PHILIPS, Wm.	43	M	Laborer	17Se02Ao
Given	32	U	Laborer	17Se02Ao
Howell	07	M	Child	17Se02Ao
William	03	M	Child	17Se02Ao
David	.00	M	Infant	17Se02Ao
SHERGOLD, Richard	43	M	Peddler	17Se02Ao
Catherine	33	F	Unknown	17Se02Ao
William	08	M	Child	17Se02Ao
Rebecca	05	F	Child	17Se02Ao
Isaac	.00	M	Infant	17Se02Ao
PROPER, John	43	M	Laborer	17Se02Ao
GIMLETT, James	51	M	Laborer	17Se02Ao
JONES, James	40	M	Peddler	17Se02Ao
Ann	35	F	Unknown	17Se02Ao
John	13	M	Unknown	17Se02Ao
Sarah	11	F	Unknown	17Se02Ao
Mary	10	F	Child	17Se02Ao
Martha	08	F	Child	17Se02Ao

NAMES OF PASSENGERS	AGE	SEX	OCCUPATIONS	DATE PORT SHIP
JONES, Evan	07	M	Child	17Se02Ao
Ann	04	F	Child	17Se02Ao
William	.00	M	Infant	17Se02Ao
KELLY, Moses	30	M	Servant	17Se02Ao
JONES, Margt.	50	F	Servant	17Se02Ao
Jane	25	F	Servant	17Se02Ao
Humphrey	20	M	Servant	17Se02Ao
HEALEY, James	30	M	Servant	17Se02Ao
COOPER, Patt.	26	M	Servant	17Se02Ao
Minor	24	M	Servant	17Se02Ao
Hugh	03	M	Child	17Se02Ao
ONEILL, Martin	24	M	Clothier	17Se02Ao
DAVIES, Andrew	32	M	Laborer	17Se02Ao
HERON, Richard	22	M	Laborer	17Se02Ao
MURPHY, Martin	22	M	Laborer	17Se02Ao
STAPLETON, Edward	30	M	Carpenter	17Se02Ao
RYAN, Judith	35	F	Servant	17Se02Ao
PHELAN, Mary	35	F	Servant	17Se02Ao
Catherine	20	F	Servant	17Se02Ao
KEALTY, Honora	20	F	Servant	17Se02Ao
PURCELL, Catherine	03	F	Child	17Se02Ao
SMITH, T.	27	U	Unknown	17Se02Ao
U (W)	30	F	Unknown	17Se02Ao
Richard	24	M	Unknown	17Se02Ao
GRACE, William	24	M	Unknown	17Se02Ao
QUIRK, John	24	M	Unknown	17Se02Ao
MCCABE, James	24	M	Shoemaker	17Se02Ao
CALAGHAN, Peter	18	M	Laborer	17Se02Ao
LYKES, Thomas	30	M	Mechanic	17Se02Ao
TOGG, James	19	M	Mechanic	17Se02Ao
SAVAGE, Grace	18	F	Servant	17Se02Ao
MCMANUS, John	19	M	Servant	17Se02Ao
RYDER, Peter	44	M	Broker	17Se02Ao
Margt.	40	F	Unknown	17Se02Ao
LACKEY, Henry	15	M	Laborer	17Se02Ao
OBRIEN, Thomas	28	M	Laborer	17Se02Ao
TAYLOR, Henry	30	M	Laborer	17Se02Ao
Sarah	28	F	Unknown	17Se02Ao
James	.00	M	Infant	17Se02Ao
DUNN, Francis	25	M	Laborer	17Se02Ao
KNOWLES, Jno.	26	M	Hatter	17Se02Ao
Hannah	24	F	Unknown	17Se02Ao
Jane	10	F	Child	17Se02Ao
FITZPATRICK, William	22	M	Laborer	17Se02Ao
CURREN, James	20	M	Laborer	17Se02Ao
HANNAN, John	26	M	Servant	17Se02Ao
Ann	21	F	Servant	17Se02Ao
KENNEDY, Ann	23	F	Servant	17Se02Ao
COFFEE, John	25	M	Servant	17Se02Ao
Richard	27	M	Servant	17Se02Ao
CARROLL, Thos.	29	M	Servant	17Se02Ao
Mary	21	F	Servant	17Se02Ao
MORAN, Ann	20	F	Servant	17Se02Ao
John	14	M	Servant	17Se02Ao
OBRIEN, Bridget	24	F	Servant	17Se02Ao
NELSON, Rachael	26	F	Unknown	17Se02Ao
CALAGHAN, Mary	22	F	Unknown	17Se02Ao
BRYAN, John	26	M	Laborer	17Se02Ao
BOBSON, John	19	M	Laborer	17Se02Ao

CATHERINE 17 SEPTEMBER 1846

From Liverpool

NAMES OF PASSENGERS	AGE	SEX	OCCUPATIONS	DATE PORT SHIP
TURNER, James	22	M	Laborer	17Se02Gr
SHILDON, Denny	22	M	Laborer	17Se02Gr
HARTMAN, Wm.	28	M	Laborer	17Se02Gr
CURREN, Catherine	52	F	Laborer	17Se02Gr
CURAN, Betsey	18	F	Laborer	17Se02Gr

NAMES OF PASSENGERS	AGE	SEX	OCCUPATIONS	DATE PORT SHIP
CURAN, John	13	M	Mechanic	17Se02Gr
MALLADALE, Thos.	18	M	Mechanic	17Se02Gr
HEMPSTED, Henry	30	M	Mechanic	17Se02Gr
John	24	M	Mechanic	17Se02Gr
GREENFIELD, Amy	35	F	Housekeeper	17Se02Gr
Eliza	13	F	Housekeeper	17Se02Gr
LEASON, Ann	27	F	Mtmkr	17Se02Gr
KENNEDY, Eliza	13	F	Unknown	17Se02Gr
RUSSELL, William	28	M	Silk Weaver	17Se02Gr
Mary-Ann	28	F	Unknown	17Se02Gr
GOVERN, James	19	M	Laborer	17Se02Gr
DOLAN, Martin	19	M	Laborer	17Se02Gr
HANDY, Thomas	20	M	Laborer	17Se02Gr
HENEGAN, Biddy	19	F	Dressmaker	17Se02Gr
CURAN, Margaret	15	F	Servant	17Se02Gr
KELLY, Mary	19	F	Dressmaker	17Se02Gr
LYNCH, Margaret	20	F	Dressmaker	17Se02Gr
Mary	18	F	Servant	17Se02Gr
CAMPBELL, Rosey	20	F	Servant	17Se02Gr
KERRAN, Betsey	18	F	Servant	17Se02Gr
GOVERN, Mary	20	F	Dressmaker	17Se02Gr
MALLALY, Biddy	24	F	Servant	17Se02Gr
PUTSON, Mary	64	F	Servant	17Se02Gr
Ann	23	F	Milliner	17Se02Gr
John	20	M	Sailor	17Se02Gr
SMITH, Mick	31	M	Laborer	17Se02Gr

MACON 18 SEPTEMBER 1846

From Liverpool

NAMES OF PASSENGERS	AGE	SEX	OCCUPATIONS	DATE PORT SHIP
NICHOLSON, James	21	M	Farmer	18Se02Gs
PARKINSON, William	22	M	Farmer	18Se02Gs
TAYLOR, George	75	M	Farmer	18Se02Gs
Jane	45	F	Farmer	18Se02Gs
George	19	M	Farmer	18Se02Gs
Margret	13	F	Farmer	18Se02Gs
Letty	10	F	Farmer	18Se02Gs
Mary	08	F	Child	18Se02Gs
Betty	03	F	Child	18Se02Gs
DONELEY, Michael	30	M	Farmer	18Se02Gs
TAYLOR, Eliza	14	F	Farmer	18Se02Gs
MCMAHON, Mearyn	33	F	Farmer	18Se02Gs
MCCALL, Mary	18	F	Farmer	18Se02Gs
JOHNSON, Isabella	50	F	Farmer	18Se02Gs
Joseph	15	M	Farmer	18Se02Gs
MCFINK, Peter	30	M	Farmer	18Se02Gs
RUSSELL, John	22	M	Farmer	18Se02Gs
GAVAN, John	24	M	Laborer	18Se02Gs
Patrick	30	M	Laborer	18Se02Gs
Mary	25	F	Laborer	18Se02Gs
BROWN, James	30	M	Laborer	18Se02Gs
MCCANN, Michael	30	M	Laborer	18Se02Gs
JOHNSON, Robert	38	M	Laborer	18Se02Gs
Martha	23	F	Laborer	18Se02Gs
Robert	05	M	Child	18Se02Gs
John	03	M	Child	18Se02Gs
Rebecca	.00	F	Infant	18Se02Gs
HOPE, Bridget	20	F	Laborer	18Se02Gs
MCMURROW, Dennis	21	M	Laborer	18Se02Gs
FLEGHERTY, Mathew	23	M	Laborer	18Se02Gs
BOYLE, Peter	20	M	Laborer	18Se02Gs
YOUGHER, Pat.	26	M	Laborer	18Se02Gs
FOX, Ann	19	F	Laborer	18Se02Gs
ONEIL, James	25	M	Laborer	18Se02Gs
DIAMOND, Robert	40	M	Laborer	18Se02Gs
U (W)	36	F	Laborer	18Se02Gs
OBRYAN, Jane	20	F	Laborer	18Se02Gs
RAFFERTY, Francis	40	M	Laborer	18Se02Gs

253

NAMES OF PASSENGERS	A G E	S E X	OCCUPATIONS	DATE PORT SHIP	NAMES OF PASSENGERS	A G E	S E X	OCCUPATIONS	DATE PORT SHIP
RAFFERTY, Mary	40	F	Laborer	18Se02Gs	BRYAN, James	24	M	Laborer	18Se02Gs
MCCARROLL, Pat.	20	F	Laborer	18Se02Gs	OHARA, Martin	18	M	Laborer	18Se02Gs
FINNANS, Pat.	19	M	Laborer	18Se02Gs	MURPHY, Mary	19	F	Laborer	18Se02Gs
HUGHES, Ann	20	F	Laborer	18Se02Gs	HAGAN, Michael	19	M	Laborer	18Se02Gs
MULLIGAN, Judy	30	F	Laborer	18Se02Gs	Peter	24	M	Laborer	18Se02Gs
Ann	06	F	Child	18Se02Gs	DUFFY, Mary	20	F	Laborer	18Se02Gs
Margret	11	F	Unknown	18Se02Gs	ENGLAND, Joseph	45	M	Laborer	18Se02Gs
FARRELL, Pat.	17	M	Farmer	18Se02Gs	PARMOIL, Mary-Ann	50	F	Laborer	18Se02Gs
KELANER, James	07	M	Child	18Se02Gs	RODGERS, Ann	18	F	Laborer	18Se02Gs
TAMANY, Ellen	20	F	Farmer	18Se02Gs	GALLIGAN, David	30	M	Laborer	18Se02Gs
BYRNE, Thomas	30	M	Farmer	18Se02Gs	MAILER, John	17	M	Laborer	18Se02Gs
LYDEN, Luke	35	M	Farmer	18Se02Gs	MANNION, Biddy	30	F	Laborer	18Se02Gs
WALSH, Francis	25	M	Farmer	18Se02Gs	SULLIVAN, John	35	M	Laborer	18Se02Gs
SCULLY, Bernard	20	M	Farmer	18Se02Gs	Margret	30	F	Laborer	18Se02Gs
URE, William	20	M	Farmer	18Se02Gs	Maria	04	F	Child	18Se02Gs
MCDERMOTT, Ann	40	F	Farmer	18Se02Gs	RODGERS, Eliza	57	F	Laborer	18Se02Gs
Eliza	10	F	Child	18Se02Gs	Sarah	13	F	Laborer	18Se02Gs
Thomas	08	M	Child	18Se02Gs	John	12	M	Laborer	18Se02Gs
CARROLL, Mary	20	F	Farmer	18Se02Gs	William	10	M	Child	18Se02Gs
MCCARTIN, Mary	28	F	Farmer	18Se02Gs	CARLTON, Thomas	30	M	Laborer	18Se02Gs
DILLON, Biddy	20	F	Farmer	18Se02Gs	William	28	M	Laborer	18Se02Gs
FOX, John	25	M	Laborer	18Se02Gs	U	.00	M	Infant	18Se02Gs
Biddy	24	F	Laborer	18Se02Gs	U	.00	M	Infant	18Se02Gs
Ellen	.00	F	Infant	18Se02Gs	RODGERS, Priscilla	50	F	Laborer	18Se02Gs
MOORE, Thomas	20	M	Laborer	18Se02Gs	MCNAMEE, Eneas	39	F	Laborer	18Se02Gs
Fanny	18	F	Laborer	18Se02Gs	Mary	12	F	Laborer	18Se02Gs
Frank	10	M	Laborer	18Se02Gs	Ann	10	F	Laborer	18Se02Gs
CALLANAN, Thomas	30	M	Laborer	18Se02Gs	MCLAUGHLIN, William	24	M	Laborer	18Se02Gs
KANE, Susan	17	F	Laborer	18Se02Gs	CONNELL, M.C.	21	M	Laborer	18Se02Gs
Catherine	16	F	Laborer	18Se02Gs	MCIVER, John	19	M	Laborer	18Se02Gs
MCKENNA, Mary	40	F	Laborer	18Se02Gs	Jane	25	F	Laborer	18Se02Gs
Margaret	11	F	Laborer	18Se02Gs	MURRAY, Sally	28	F	Laborer	18Se02Gs
Part	07	M	Child	18Se02Gs	DAYLEY, John	21	M	Laborer	18Se02Gs
FOX, Ellen	50	F	Farmer	18Se02Gs	Bridget	24	F	Laborer	18Se02Gs
Pat.	05	M	Child	18Se02Gs	U	.00	F	Infant	18Se02Gs
OHARA, Ann	22	F	Farmer	18Se02Gs	Julia	06	F	Child	18Se02Gs
LYONS, Charles	28	M	Farmer	18Se02Gs	May	04	F	Child	18Se02Gs
WOLF, Ann	30	F	Farmer	18Se02Gs	U	.00	F	Infant	18Se02Gs
FOX, Ann	17	F	Farmer	18Se02Gs	LEHEY, Paul	64	M	Laborer	18Se02Gs
MOWLAN, John	22	M	Farmer	18Se02Gs	TURNLY, Honor	45	F	Laborer	18Se02Gs
Sarah	19	F	Farmer	18Se02Gs	CLARKIN, Mary	26	F	Laborer	18Se02Gs
FLYNN, James	21	M	Farmer	18Se02Gs	TIERNEY, John	23	M	Laborer	18Se02Gs
U (W)	24	F	Farmer	18Se02Gs	Sally	20	F	Laborer	18Se02Gs
Mary	.00	F	Infant	18Se02Gs	Michael	18	M	Laborer	18Se02Gs
CORCORAN, Ann	20	F	Laborer	18Se02Gs	FARRELEY, Ann	40	F	Laborer	18Se02Gs
KELLY, Patrick	26	M	Laborer	18Se02Gs	John	11	M	Laborer	18Se02Gs
NOON, Dennis	26	M	Laborer	18Se02Gs	Cath.	09	F	Child	18Se02Gs
DUFF, Eliza	26	F	Laborer	18Se02Gs	James	.00	M	Infant	18Se02Gs
DONAHU, Biddy	20	F	Laborer	18Se02Gs	JACKSON, Thomas	24	M	Laborer	18Se02Gs
CONDRON, Ann	19	F	Laborer	18Se02Gs	U (W)	21	F	Laborer	18Se02Gs
LUKES, William	28	M	Laborer	18Se02Gs	WARD, James	46	M	Laborer	18Se02Gs
Elizabeth	26	F	Laborer	18Se02Gs	U (W)	40	F	Laborer	18Se02Gs
Benjamin	08	M	Child	18Se02Gs	Pat.	18	M	Laborer	18Se02Gs
BYRNE, Thomas	21	M	Laborer	18Se02Gs	Ann	09	F	Laborer	18Se02Gs
LEHY, Jeremiah	36	M	Laborer	18Se02Gs	ONEIL, John	24	M	Laborer	18Se02Gs
MABSON, Thomas	25	M	Laborer	18Se02Gs	ROURKE, Mary	11	F	Laborer	18Se02Gs
MURPHY, Michael	35	M	Laborer	18Se02Gs	MCMAHON, Edward	17	M	Laborer	18Se02Gs
LOUGHLIN, Bridget	20	F	Laborer	18Se02Gs					
SMITH, Ann	20	F	Laborer	18Se02Gs					
MCLELLAND, U-Mrs.	50	F	Laborer	18Se02Gs					
MCCARTY, Eliza	03	F	Child	18Se02Gs					
SULLIVAN, John	28	M	Laborer	18Se02Gs					
U (W)	20	F	Laborer	18Se02Gs	PACIFIC 19 SEPTEMBER 1846				
Elizabeth	.00	F	Infant	18Se02Gs					
DUFFY, Mary	18	F	Laborer	18Se02Gs	From Liverpool				
MCLAUGHLIN, Cath.	15	F	Laborer	18Se02Gs					
MCFARLANE, Andrew	30	M	Laborer	18Se02Gs					
BOYLE, James	27	M	Laborer	18Se02Gs					
FINN, John	40	M	Laborer	18Se02Gs	MAHAN, U	46	F	None	19Se02BJ
U (W)	31	F	Laborer	18Se02Gs	BEATTY, Thomas	24	M	Farmer	19Se02BJ
Pat.	07	M	Child	18Se02Gs	Bridget	22	F	Servant	19Se02BJ
MCGREGOR, J.G.	30	M	Laborer	18Se02Gs	QUINN, Elizth.	30	F	Servant	19Se02BJ
SIMPSON, John	20	M	Laborer	18Se02Gs	PHELAN, Mary	27	F	Servant	19Se02BJ
ONEILL, James	24	M	Laborer	18Se02Gs	KEARNY, Ann	19	F	Servant	19Se02BJ
HOLTON, Henry	21	M	Laborer	18Se02Gs	HALY, Margt.	21	F	Servant	19Se02BJ

NAMES OF PASSENGERS		AGE	SEX	OCCUPATIONS	DATE PORT SHIP
TRAYNOR, Henry		25	M	Laborer	19Se02BJ
U	(W)	24	F	Wife	19Se02BJ
Henry	(S)	03	M	Child	19Se02BJ
LENAHAN, James		40	M	Farmer	19Se02BJ
CONAGHTY, Mary		45	F	None	19Se02BJ
GREEN, Henry		21	M	Laborer	19Se02BJ
ROGERS, Jane		40	F	Servant	19Se02BJ
FEENY, Ellen		18	F	Servant	19Se02BJ
MCLOUGHLIN, Wm.		20	M	Laborer	19Se02BJ
LANE, Mary		19	F	Servant	19Se02BJ
Thomas		19	M	Laborer	19Se02BJ
SEERY, Danl.		21	M	Laborer	19Se02BJ
REYNOLDS, Michl.		30	M	Laborer	19Se02BJ
U	(W)	30	F	Wife	19Se02BJ
Lawrence	(S)	.00	M	Infant	19Se02BJ
TRAYNOR, Michl.		40	M	Farmer	19Se02BJ
U	(W)	40	F	Wife	19Se02BJ
Margt.	(D)	12	F	None	19Se02BJ
James	(S)	06	M	None	19Se02BJ
Sarah	(D)	05	F	None	19Se02BJ
DORAS, Mary		17	F	Servant	19Se02BJ
MARLIN, Thomas		45	M	Miner	19Se02BJ
U	(W)	50	F	Wife	19Se02BJ
KELLY, Neal		45	M	Farmer	19Se02BJ
Sarah	(W)	40	F	Wife	19Se02BJ
Charles	(S)	13	M	None	19Se02BJ
Neal	(S)	09	M	Child	19Se02BJ
Lunty	(S)	07	M	Child	19Se02BJ
Bridget	(D)	04	F	Child	19Se02BJ
MORMAN, Bridget		19	F	Servant	19Se02BJ
KEARNY, Timothy		20	M	Laborer	19Se02BJ
LONG, Patt		16	M	Laborer	19Se02BJ
Mary		18	F	Servant	19Se02BJ
Denis		12	M	Servant	19Se02BJ
EVANS, Essy		25	F	Servant	19Se02BJ
Jane		18	F	Servant	19Se02BJ
MITCHELL, Essy		18	F	Servant	19Se02BJ
HANAWAY, Margt.		19	F	Servant	19Se02BJ
KENNEDY, Archd.		40	M	Mechanic	19Se02BJ
MCNAMARA, Mary		35	F	Servant	19Se02BJ
Michl.	(S)	09	M	Child	19Se02BJ
EGAN, Edward		24	M	Laborer	19Se02BJ
NOLAN, Eliza		16	F	Servant	19Se02BJ
ROWLEY, George		25	M	Laborer	19Se02BJ
MCGUIRE, John		29	M	Laborer	19Se02BJ
FITZPATRICK, Thos.		19	M	Laborer	19Se02BJ
DALEY, Cathe.		60	F	None	19Se02BJ
CLEMENTS, John		25	M	Laborer	19Se02BJ
KENNEDY, Patt		24	M	Laborer	19Se02BJ
MCGUIRE, Roger		64	M	Farmer	19Se02BJ
Mary	(W)	50	F	Wife	19Se02BJ
Mary	(D)	24	F	Servant	19Se02BJ
Cathe.	(D)	12	F	None	19Se02BJ
DOWLAN, Michl.		45	M	Farmer	19Se02BJ
Jane	(W)	30	F	Wife	19Se02BJ
Mary	(D)	10	F	Child	19Se02BJ
Cathe.	(D)	09	F	Child	19Se02BJ
Margt.	(D)	08	F	Child	19Se02BJ
Jane	(D)	07	F	Child	19Se02BJ
James	(S)	06	M	Child	19Se02BJ
Ellen	(D)	05	F	Child	19Se02BJ
Catherine	(D)	04	F	Child	19Se02BJ
SMITH, Ann		30	F	Servant	19Se02BJ
Mary	(D)	08	F	Child	19Se02BJ
Ann	(D)	06	F	Child	19Se02BJ
MCGOVERN, Rose		16	F	Servant	19Se02BJ
CONWAY, Michl.		25	M	Laborer	19Se02BJ
GRAY, Michl.		20	M	Laborer	19Se02BJ
BONE, Michl.		25	M	Laborer	19Se02BJ
U	(W)	30	F	Wife	19Se02BJ
BRAWNER, Wm.		25	M	Farmer	19Se02BJ
U	(W)	22	F	Wife	19Se02BJ
COPLE, Maria		25	F	Servant	19Se02BJ
KEARNEY, Mary		24	F	Servant	19Se02BJ
Ellen		18	F	Servant	19Se02BJ
KEARNEY, John		04	M	Child	19Se02BJ
Michl.		01	M	Child	19Se02BJ
CAMPBELL, Jane		25	F	Servant	19Se02BJ
HANLY, Michl.		28	M	Farmer	19Se02BJ
U	(W)	26	F	Wife	19Se02BJ
Mary-Ann	(D)	01	F	Child	19Se02BJ
DUNSTER, Wm.		19	M	Mechanic	19Se02BJ
EVAN, Thos.		22	M	Mechanic	19Se02BJ
CARROLL, Owen		20	M	Mechanic	19Se02BJ
CONNERTY, Ann		17	F	Servant	19Se02BJ
FLYNN, Mary		15	F	Servant	19Se02BJ
SMITH, U-Mrs.		17	F	None	19Se02BJ
SPRINTHROP, Bessy		31	F	Servant	19Se02BJ
MCNULTY, Thomas		24	M	Laborer	19Se02BJ
MCCURRY, Margt.		22	F	Servant	19Se02BJ
MCLOUGHLIN, John		13	M	None	19Se02BJ
James		12	M	None	19Se02BJ
Sally		09	F	Child	19Se02BJ
Michl.		07	M	Child	19Se02BJ
Mary		03	F	Child	19Se02BJ
TORPEY, Michl.		20	M	Laborer	19Se02BJ
Sarah		18	F	Servant	19Se02BJ
Wm.		06	M	Child	19Se02BJ
REYNOLDS, Cathe.		17	F	Servant	19Se02BJ
DOWLAN, Patt		20	M	Laborer	19Se02BJ
ARMSTRONG, U-Mrs.		58	F	None	19Se02BJ
U	(D)	24	F	Servant	19Se02BJ
MCNULTY, Patt		25	M	Laborer	19Se02BJ
MCGUIRE, Patt		27	M	Laborer	19Se02BJ
U	(W)	25	F	Wife	19Se02BJ
DUNCAN, Thomas		50	M	Miner	19Se02BJ
MCMAHAN, Ann		28	F	Servant	19Se02BJ
RIDDLE, Alexr.		35	M	Mechanic	19Se02BJ
MCKINNY, James		25	M	Mechanic	19Se02BJ
HOOPER, Thomas		34	M	Mechanic	19Se02BJ
BYRNE, Alice		22	F	Servant	19Se02BJ
GRIFFIN, Cathe.		35	F	Servant	19Se02BJ
GORMAN, Patt		30	M	Farmer	19Se02BJ
SHERRIDAN, Bernd.		20	M	Farmer	19Se02BJ
BRADY, Ann		20	F	Servant	19Se02BJ
KELLY, John		30	M	Farmer	19Se02BJ
Thomas	(S)	06	M	Child	19Se02BJ
RIDDLETON, Martin		28	M	Farmer	19Se02BJ
MCGINTY, Mary		20	F	Servant	19Se02BJ
ODONOVAN, Mary		24	F	Servant	19Se02BJ
MCCAUL, Richd.		18	M	Laborer	19Se02BJ
OHARA, Garret		20	M	Laborer	19Se02BJ
PETRIE, James		25	M	Laborer	19Se02BJ
Cathe.		23	F	Servant	19Se02BJ
KINSELLA, Ellen		17	F	Servant	19Se02BJ
KELLY, Cathe.		18	F	Servant	19Se02BJ
SCHLESENGER, Herman		19	M	Servant	19Se02BJ
GALAWAY, James		18	M	Carpenter	19Se02BJ
CARY, Richd.		22	M	Carpenter	19Se02BJ
FITZGERALD, Rose		22	F	Servant	19Se02BJ
Sally		17	F	Servant	19Se02BJ
Ellen		18	F	Servant	19Se02BJ
DALY, Elizabeth		30	F	Servant	19Se02BJ
MULLIGAN, Bridget		20	F	Servant	19Se02BJ
WILSON, Rose		17	F	Servant	19Se02BJ
CANNON, John		40	M	Farmer	19Se02BJ
HORAN, Margt.		30	F	Servant	19Se02BJ
KEENAN, Madgie		18	F	Servant	19Se02BJ
CURREN, William		41	M	Mechanic	19Se02BJ
TRACEY, Michael		22	M	Laborer	19Se02BJ
CLARKE, George		52	M	Farmer	19Se02BJ
KERR, Patrick		17	M	Farmer	19Se02BJ
DAVIS, William		27	M	Farmer	19Se02BJ
CARRET, John		21	M	Farmer	19Se02BJ
PRICE, John		27	M	Farmer	19Se02BJ
TALBOT, Thos.		21	M	Farmer	19Se02BJ
LEDDON, William		24	M	Farmer	19Se02BJ
LEECH, William		20	M	Farmer	19Se02BJ
Edward		21	M	Farmer	19Se02BJ
MAHER, Michl.		46	M	Mechanic	19Se02BJ

NAMES OF PASSENGERS		AGE	SEX	OCCUPATIONS	DATE PORT SHIP
MOONEY, Hugh		20	M	Mechanic	19Se02BJ
MAHER, Mary		10	F	None	19Se02BJ
HAFFSTEAD, Julia		23	F	Servant	19Se02BJ
CULLEN, Mary		25	F	Servant	19Se02BJ
CONNOR, Mary		20	F	Servant	19Se02BJ
HUSSY, Ellen		17	F	None	19Se02BJ
HARANCE, Larry		43	M	Mechanic	19Se02BJ
DESERD, Thomas		28	M	Mechanic	19Se02BJ
KERR, Ann		48	F	None	19Se02BJ
Martha	(D)	17	F	Servant	19Se02BJ
William	(S)	09	M	Child	19Se02BJ
Mary	(D)	08	F	Child	19Se02BJ
MCCABE, Mary		23	F	Servant	19Se02BJ
BRADY, Cathe.		18	F	Servant	19Se02BJ
Essy		21	F	Servant	19Se02BJ
MCCANNA, Ross		34	M	Servant	19Se02BJ
COOGAN, Mary		18	F	Servant	19Se02BJ
RUSSELL, Wm.		50	M	Farmer	19Se02BJ
KEAN, James		37	M	Farmer	19Se02BJ
RUSSELL, Patt		30	M	Farmer	19Se02BJ
Mary		25	F	None	19Se02BJ
MUNROE, Mary		17	F	Servant	19Se02BJ
RUSSELL, Peter		04	M	Child	19Se02BJ
MURPHY, Patt		35	M	Farmer	19Se02BJ
MINNIAN, James		40	M	Farmer	19Se02BJ
U	(W)	30	F	Wife	19Se02BJ
Biddy	(D)	13	F	None	19Se02BJ
BUTLER, My.		13	F	None	19Se02BJ
U		32	F	None	19Se02BJ
ABBOTT, Wm.		34	M	Miner	19Se02BJ
U	(W)	38	F	Wife	19Se02BJ
Edward	(S)	11	M	None	19Se02BJ
Mary	(D)	09	F	Child	19Se02BJ
Martin	(S)	08	M	Child	19Se02BJ
Allice	(D)	05	F	Child	19Se02BJ
Susan	(D)	04	F	Child	19Se02BJ
Henry	(S)	02	M	Child	19Se02BJ
Ely	(S)	.00	M	Infant	19Se02BJ
PAINTER, Wm.		32	M	Miner	19Se02BJ
COLLINS, Maria		19	F	Servant	19Se02BJ
MOORE, Wm.		60	M	None	19Se02BJ
WILSON, Thomas		23	M	Laborer	19Se02BJ
Eliza		20	F	None	19Se02BJ
DOAN, Cathe.		19	F	Servant	19Se02BJ
HUNTER, Saml.		21	M	Laborer	19Se02BJ
MCKENNY, Charles		23	M	Laborer	19Se02BJ
MCCARTHY, Mary		20	F	Servant	19Se02BJ
FOGG, Biddy		19	F	Servant	19Se02BJ
DOMMAS, Ann		13	F	Servant	19Se02BJ
Thomas		10	M	Child	19Se02BJ
SAVITT, Ann		15	F	Servant	19Se02BJ
KENNY, Ann		17	F	Servant	19Se02BJ
NOWLAN, Bridget		19	F	Servant	19Se02BJ
KANE, Ellen		24	F	Servant	19Se02BJ
BUTLER, U-Mrs.		64	F	Unknown	19Se02BJ
HUSSEY, U		26	F	Unknown	19Se02BJ

BROOKSBY 21 SEPTEMBER 1846

From Glasgow

NAMES OF PASSENGERS	AGE	SEX	OCCUPATIONS	DATE PORT SHIP
MCCASK, Jno.	21	M	Smith	21Se04Ex
BURNS, William	22	M	Smith	21Se04Ex
MILLER, Henry	20	M	Smith	21Se04Ex

INDEPENDENCE 22 SEPTEMBER 1846

From Liverpool

NAMES OF PASSENGERS		AGE	SEX	OCCUPATIONS	DATE PORT SHIP
BURNS, John		11	M	None	22Se02Hf
CALLERGHAN, Ann		20	F	None	22Se02Hf
HIGGINS, John		25	M	Laborer	22Se02Hf
WARD, Mary		42	F	Laborer	22Se02Hf
Mary-Ann	(D)	18	F	Laborer	22Se02Hf
Teresa	(D)	17	F	Laborer	22Se02Hf
John	(S)	12	M	Laborer	22Se02Hf
Eliza	(D)	11	F	Laborer	22Se02Hf
Julia	(D)	10	F	Laborer	22Se02Hf
CARROLL, John		24	M	Tailor	22Se02Hf
MCGRATH, Stephen		22	M	Laborer	22Se02Hf
BRADY, Rose		20	F	Laborer	22Se02Hf
Bessey		18	F	Laborer	22Se02Hf
DOLAN, Ann		25	F	Laborer	22Se02Hf
Ellen		12	F	Laborer	22Se02Hf
KILLEN, Bridget		21	F	Laborer	22Se02Hf
BOLAND, Thos.		23	M	Laborer	22Se02Hf
CANE, James		32	M	Laborer	22Se02Hf
FOX, Mary		17	F	Laborer	22Se02Hf
FLINN, Charles		30	M	Laborer	22Se02Hf
MULLIN, Eliza		14	F	Laborer	22Se02Hf
Rosannah		10	F	Laborer	22Se02Hf
MCFADDEN, Susan		50	F	Laborer	22Se02Hf
DOYLE, Patrick		21	M	Miner	22Se02Hf
MCCOMB, Mary-Ann		20	F	None	22Se02Hf
FOX, Julia		40	F	None	22Se02Hf
STANTON, John		25	M	Laborer	22Se02Hf
SHIFFLIN, Wm.		19	M	Tailor	22Se02Hf
SCOTT, Loughlin		36	M	Farmer	22Se02Hf
MONTAGUE, James		15	M	Butcher	22Se02Hf
MCANALLY, James		18	M	Laborer	22Se02Hf
DONOHOE, Bridget		36	F	None	22Se02Hf
Hugh	(S)	07	M	Child	22Se02Hf
GARRY, Patrick		17	M	Laborer	22Se02Hf
EARLY, Eliza		18	F	None	22Se02Hf
SHEA, Mary		18	F	None	22Se02Hf
HUGHS, Nicholas		20	M	Laborer	22Se02Hf
Mary		17	F	Laborer	22Se02Hf
CONNOR, Michel		22	M	Laborer	22Se02Hf
OLIVER, Jane		21	F	Laborer	22Se02Hf
MULLEN, Dennis		50	M	None	22Se02Hf
DAY, James		21	M	Laborer	22Se02Hf
BROWN, Margaret		20	F	None	22Se02Hf
OLIVER, Catherine-M.		43	F	None	22Se02Hf
WILLIAMS, Catherine		23	F	None	22Se02Hf
SCOTT, Elizabeth		22	F	None	22Se02Hf
ARMSTRONG, Catherine		30	F	None	22Se02Hf
LOUGHRAN, Thomas		24	M	Nailer	22Se02Hf
DRISCOLL, Ellen		25	F	None	22Se02Hf
WALSH, James		21	M	Laborer	22Se02Hf
DOWN, John		20	M	Shoemaker	22Se02Hf
DORAN, Cath.		15	F	None	22Se02Hf
MCSWEENEY, Edward		22	M	Laborer	22Se02Hf
FLINN, Mary		40	F	None	22Se02Hf
FINNIRAN, Mary		12	F	None	22Se02Hf
BRENNAN, James		50	M	Farmer	22Se02Hf
COCHRAN, John		19	M	Tailor	22Se02Hf
ROBB, James		23	M	Clerk	22Se02Hf
RAHIL, Mary		19	F	None	22Se02Hf
QUIGLAN, Catherine		21	F	None	22Se02Hf
FOSTER, Margaret		60	F	None	22Se02Hf
MONTGOMERY, Alex		21	M	Tailor	22Se02Hf
BRINNAN, Biddy		17	F	None	22Se02Hf
MCHALE, Patrick		40	M	Butcher	22Se02Hf
DOYLE, Ann		20	F	None	22Se02Hf

NAMES OF PASSENGERS	AGE EX	SEX	OCCUPATIONS	DATE PORT SHIP
DOYLE, Rose	18	F	None	22Se02Hf
Hugh	14	M	None	22Se02Hf
REILLY, James	22	M	Tinsmith	22Se02Hf
Margaret	(W) 19	F	Wife	22Se02Hf
Thomas	(S) .11	M	Infant	22Se02Hf
LARKIN, Patrick	22	M	Laborer	22Se02Hf
RILLEY, Michel	23	M	Tailor	22Se02Hf
FLINN, James	25	M	Farmer	22Se02Hf
CLUSKEY, Charles	26	M	Weaver	22Se02Hf
FREASY, John	22	M	Shoemaker	22Se02Hf
SMITH, Rose	20	F	None	22Se02Hf
DONOHOE, Mary	37	F	None	22Se02Hf
GREGORY, Sarah	22	F	None	22Se02Hf
NOTTUS, Joseph	48	M	Miner	22Se02Hf
John	27	M	Miner	22Se02Hf
Ellinor	26	F	Miner	22Se02Hf
Mary	22	F	Miner	22Se02Hf
Joseph	.03	M	Infant	22Se02Hf
MCVICKERS, Sarah	22	F	Miner	22Se02Hf
DOWNEY, Patick	28	M	Bricklayer	22Se02Hf
Allice	60	F	Bricklayer	22Se02Hf
WILLIAMSON, Allice	14	F	Bricklayer	22Se02Hf
PARKHILL, James	28	M	Weaver	22Se02Hf
HARPER, James	21	M	Weaver	22Se02Hf
GODSON, John	57	M	Chwkr	22Se02Hf
Susannah	(W) 63	F	Wife	22Se02Hf
Sybil	(D) 22	F	Chwkr	22Se02Hf
LAWTON, Daniel	30	M	Farmer	22Se02Hf
HARPER, Robert	23	M	Miner	22Se02Hf
Jane	(W) 21	F	Wife	22Se02Hf
John	(S) .04	M	Infant	22Se02Hf
MURRY, John	20	M	Laborer	22Se02Hf
James	26	M	Laborer	22Se02Hf
Margaret	22	F	Laborer	22Se02Hf
LYNN, Jane	26	F	Laborer	22Se02Hf
Margaret	19	F	Laborer	22Se02Hf
LEMON, Hugh	19	M	Weaver	22Se02Hf
MCCANN, Bernard	21	M	Seaman	22Se02Hf
FITZPATRICK, Ann	67	F	Laborer	22Se02Hf
ABBOTT, Eliza	18	F	Laborer	22Se02Hf
HANNIGAN, Mary	18	F	None	22Se02Hf
HEDWIN, Andr.	22	M	Carpenter	22Se02Hf
OBRIEN, Denis	20	M	Tailor	22Se02Hf
James	11	M	None	22Se02Hf
MCILARNY, Peter	35	M	Tailor	22Se02Hf
CASSEDY, James	25	M	Shoemaker	22Se02Hf
ROBINSON, John	28	M	Laborer	22Se02Hf
MARSHALL, Margaret	18	F	None	22Se02Hf
KELLY, Judith	30	F	None	22Se02Hf
COTTER, Catherine	22	F	None	22Se02Hf
Anne	(D) 01	F	Child	22Se02Hf
LEARY, William	30	M	Laborer	22Se02Hf
MCKEE, Patrick	32	M	Laborer	22Se02Hf
QUINN, Catherine	20	F	Laborer	22Se02Hf
BURNES, William	23	M	Laborer	22Se02Hf
COGHLAN, Margaret	24	F	Laborer	22Se02Hf
DEVINE, Martin	38	M	Shoemaker	22Se02Hf
Anne	(W) 30	F	Wife	22Se02Hf
James	(S) 12	M	None	22Se02Hf
Precilla	(D) 11	F	None	22Se02Hf
Elizabeth	(D) 05	F	Child	22Se02Hf
John	(S) 02	M	Child	22Se02Hf
MULLIGAN, Mary	27	F	None	22Se02Hf
Michael	(S) 02	M	Child	22Se02Hf
EGAN, Michl.	19	M	Tailor	22Se02Hf
CHAPMAN, Margaret	18	F	None	22Se02Hf
KILRAIN, Francis	36	M	Laborer	22Se02Hf
John	(S) 11	M	Laborer	22Se02Hf
Michael	(S) 09	M	Child	22Se02Hf
REYNOLDS, Ellen	40	F	None	22Se02Hf
Rose	(D) 10	F	None	22Se02Hf
Bridget	(D) 09	F	Child	22Se02Hf
CROFTON, Edward	21	M	Carpenter	22Se02Hf
SEXTON, Michl.	15	M	Laborer	22Se02Hf
SMITH, Elizabeth	18	F	Tailor	22Se02Hf
CALAN, Jane	50	F	Unknown	22Se02Hf
Alex	20	M	Laborer	22Se02Hf
TATE, John	21	M	Tailor	22Se02Hf
KELLEY, John	30	M	Laborer	22Se02Hf
Betty	(W) 26	F	Wife	22Se02Hf
Mary	(D) 05	F	Child	22Se02Hf
Patt	(S) 04	M	Child	22Se02Hf
Bessey	(D) .04	M	Infant	22Se02Hf
COONEY, John	18	M	Unknown	22Se02Hf
CORMACK, Cath.	17	F	Unknown	22Se02Hf
LEWIS, Mary	33	F	None	22Se02Hf
Mala	(D) 07	F	Child	22Se02Hf
Emerey	(S) 01	M	Child	22Se02Hf
MCCARTHY, Augustus	32	M	Seaman	22Se02Hf
SINGLETON, Joseph	25	M	Farmer	22Se02Hf
CASTELLEO, Bernard	18	M	Butcher	22Se02Hf
DOYLE, John	34	M	Miner	22Se02Hf
SINGLETON, John	18	M	Baker	22Se02Hf
BREAN, Patt	30	M	Miner	22Se02Hf
Elizabeth	(W) 28	F	Wife	22Se02Hf
James	(S) .10	M	Infant	22Se02Hf
FIELD, Richard	45	M	Farmer	22Se02Hf
REDDING, Patt	21	M	None	22Se02Hf
REULLEY, Martin	28	M	None	22Se02Hf
CONNELL, Catherine	35	F	Unknown	22Se02Hf
PIERCE, Michel	25	M	Clerk	22Se02Hf
MCDONNAL, Patt	36	M	Laborer	22Se02Hf
Jane	(W) 40	F	Wife	22Se02Hf
Tereca	(D) 03	F	Child	22Se02Hf
MURRAY, Gamane	18	M	Farmer	22Se02Hf
SHAW, Ann	18	F	Farmer	22Se02Hf
BOWIN, Ann	20	F	Farmer	22Se02Hf
HESLIN, Henry	18	M	None	22Se02Hf
MURRY, Ann-Mala	12	F	None	22Se02Hf
Mary-Jane	09	F	Child	22Se02Hf
NORMAN, Cath.	42	F	None	22Se02Hf
JEFFERS, Jane	20	F	None	22Se02Hf
Margaret	18	F	None	22Se02Hf
DOYLE, Cath.	17	F	None	22Se02Hf
MCEVERTT, James	37	M	Tailor	22Se02Hf
John	20	M	Tailor	22Se02Hf
MORAN, John	20	M	Tailor	22Se02Hf
KELLEY, Thos.	25	M	Draper	22Se02Hf
SMITH, Robert	45	M	Farmer	22Se02Hf
DOOLEY, Mary	20	F	Farmer	22Se02Hf

MANCHESTER 25 SEPTEMBER 1846

From Liverpool

NAMES OF PASSENGERS	AGE EX	SEX	OCCUPATIONS	DATE PORT SHIP
GILL, Bridget	21	F	Domestic	25Se02Hu
HEYDEN, Catharine	36	F	Domestic	25Se02Hu
Robert	(S) 10	M	Child	25Se02Hu
MACKDONOUGH, Martin	26	M	Farmer	25Se02Hu
Patrick	07	M	Child	25Se02Hu
WELTON, Mary-Anna	27	F	Farmer	25Se02Hu
Anna	(D) 09	F	Child	25Se02Hu
George	(S) 08	M	Child	25Se02Hu
Mary	(D) 06	F	Child	25Se02Hu
Charles	(S) 03	M	Child	25Se02Hu
KEEFE, James	40	M	Farmer	25Se02Hu
Ellen	(W) 30	F	Wife	25Se02Hu
U	.00	U	Infant	25Se02Hu
YOUER, John	20	M	Farmer	25Se02Hu
Jane	14	F	Farmer	25Se02Hu
Died-At-Sea				
HOPKINS, Anna	24	F	Laborer	25Se02Hu
CASEY, Ellen	24	F	Laborer	25Se02Hu
DOWNEY, Michl.	24	M	Laborer	25Se02Hu

NAMES OF PASSENGERS	AGE	SEX	OCCUPATIONS	DATE PORT SHIP	NAMES OF PASSENGERS	AGE	SEX	OCCUPATIONS	DATE PORT SHIP
DOWNEY, Bridget	22	F	Laborer	25Se02Hu	TAYLOR, Margt.	21	F	Servant	25Se02Hu
GOODWIN, John	29	M	Engraver	25Se02Hu	MOONEY, Sarah	20	F	Servant	25Se02Hu
MCEVOY, Michael	19	M	Laborer	25Se02Hu	LAUGHEY, James	35	M	Farmer	25Se02Hu
DOYLE, Patrick	25	M	Monk	25Se02Hu	DARAGH, Sarah	40	F	Servant	25Se02Hu
MURPHY, Augustine	26	M	Monk	25Se02Hu	Sarah (D)	13	F	Servant	25Se02Hu
DELENA, John	28	M	Monk	25Se02Hu	MURRAY, Bridget	40	F	Servant	25Se02Hu
WALSH, George	25	M	Millwright	25Se02Hu	Eliza (D)	20	F	None	25Se02Hu
Elise (W)	24	F	Wife	25Se02Hu	Thomas (S)	17	M	None	25Se02Hu
U	.00	U	Infant	25Se02Hu	Rose-Anna (D)	15	F	None	25Se02Hu
John	11	M	Millwright	25Se02Hu	Joseph (S)	12	M	None	25Se02Hu
Edmund	09	M	Child	25Se02Hu	Michael (S)	10	M	None	25Se02Hu
Theophilus	05	M	Child	25Se02Hu	MCDONNEL, Johanna	44	F	Milliner	25Se02Hu
Eliza	05	F	Child	25Se02Hu	Francis (D)	20	F	Milliner	25Se02Hu
MOLINEAUX, Sarah-A.	19	F	Servant	25Se02Hu	Johanna (D)	18	F	Milliner	25Se02Hu
MACMANNUS, Anna	19	F	Spinster	25Se02Hu	HARBISON, Andrew	20	M	Farmer	25Se02Hu
REILLY, James	20	M	Gdnr	25Se02Hu	KENEDY, Catharine	20	F	Farmer	25Se02Hu
THIRK, Gilmore	20	M	Laborer	25Se02Hu	MCCARTIN, Charles	20	M	Musician	25Se02Hu
Jane	18	F	Laborer	25Se02Hu	DEBOY, Margaret	17	F	Musician	25Se02Hu
BELL, Jane	20	F	Servant	25Se02Hu	ASH, John	25	M	Miner	25Se02Hu
BRADY, Judeth	15	F	Servant	25Se02Hu	GIBBONS, John	24	M	Laborer	25Se02Hu
CONNOLLY, Daniel	15	M	Clerk	25Se02Hu	DONAHY, John	24	M	Laborer	25Se02Hu
FINLIN, Patrick	25	M	Clerk	25Se02Hu	REILEY, Catharine	50	F	Laborer	25Se02Hu
GAROCY, Michael	21	M	Farmer	25Se02Hu	MARTIN, Sarah	50	F	Merchant	25Se02Hu
MCCORMICK, Catharine	21	F	Mtmkr	25Se02Hu	ALLEN, Elizebeth	30	F	Servant	25Se02Hu
TYRRELL, Thomas	26	M	Shoemaker	25Se02Hu	CROLLY, Mary-Ann	25	F	Servant	25Se02Hu
HIGGINSON, William	47	M	Farmer	25Se02Hu	MARTIN, Margt.	20	F	Servant	25Se02Hu
MCCABE, Bridget	35	F	Laborer	25Se02Hu	STEWART, Mary	08	F	Child	25Se02Hu
Mary	15	F	Laborer	25Se02Hu	ROCHE, Margaret	18	F	Servant	25Se02Hu
MCVEY, Anna	25	F	Laborer	25Se02Hu	CARROLL, Mary	18	F	Servant	25Se02Hu
MCDONNEL, Catharine	26	F	Laborer	25Se02Hu	HANLY, Biddy	20	F	Servant	25Se02Hu
U	.00	U	Infant	25Se02Hu	CONNOLY, Mary	12	F	Servant	25Se02Hu
MCNALLY, Hugh	32	M	Tailor	25Se02Hu	STAPLETON, Robert	19	M	Clerk	25Se02Hu
HANLEY, Catharine	21	F	Servant	25Se02Hu	FORTUNE, Moses	19	M	Clerk	25Se02Hu
REYNOLDS, Thomas	25	M	Farmer	25Se02Hu	REYNOLDS, Su-Jane	20	F	Clerk	25Se02Hu
Richard	23	M	Farmer	25Se02Hu	DORAN, John	20	M	Weaver	25Se02Hu
Ann	22	F	Farmer	25Se02Hu	HARRIS, Mary	19	F	Weaver	25Se02Hu
U	.00	U	Infant	25Se02Hu	HANLEY, Patt	22	M	Laborer	25Se02Hu
Margt.	32	F	Servant	25Se02Hu	FARRELL, Catharine	20	F	Servant	25Se02Hu
Charles	17	M	Servant	25Se02Hu	BIRCH, Margaret	20	F	Servant	25Se02Hu
Mary	11	F	Servant	25Se02Hu	MCMULLIN, Peter	18	M	Weaver	25Se02Hu
MCGUIRE, Anna	19	F	Servant	25Se02Hu	FERRIS, Mary	17	F	Weaver	25Se02Hu
MCDONNELL, Mary	28	F	Servant	25Se02Hu	U	.00	U	Infant	25Se02Hu
CARROLL, Mary	22	F	Servant	25Se02Hu	MCMULLIN, Rose-Anna	16	F	Weaver	25Se02Hu
CAVANAGH, Saml.	30	M	Laborer	25Se02Hu	MCIVER, Margt.	50	F	Farmer	25Se02Hu
Mary (W)	26	F	Wife	25Se02Hu	Dennis (S)	26	M	Clerk	25Se02Hu
U	.00	U	Infant	25Se02Hu	Margt. (D)	16	F	Servant	25Se02Hu
PEAT, George	29	M	Clerk	25Se02Hu	SPARKS, Richard	17	M	Clerk	25Se02Hu
FORD, James	16	M	Carpenter	25Se02Hu	Ann	24	F	Clerk	25Se02Hu
RODGER, Hugh	23	M	Bleacher	25Se02Hu	DOYLE, Mary	60	F	Weaver	25Se02Hu
Elizebeth (W)	25	F	Wife	25Se02Hu	MCMULLIN, Cathrine	02	F	Child	25Se02Hu
U	.00	U	Infant	25Se02Hu					
Esther	50	F	Mtmkr	25Se02Hu					
MULBEN, Anna	25	F	Servant	25Se02Hu					
COLLINS, Anna	25	F	Servant	25Se02Hu					
U	.00	U	Infant	25Se02Hu					
DOYLE, Betty	21	F	Servant	25Se02Hu					
DOGHERTY, Anty	28	F	Servant	25Se02Hu		WATERLOO 26 SEPTEMBER 1846				
DELLANEY, Anna	21	F	Servant	25Se02Hu					
Anna	19	F	Servant	25Se02Hu		From Liverpool				
STANTON, Patt	22	M	Laborer	25Se02Hu					
KELLY, David	20	M	Shoemaker	25Se02Hu					
Agnes	18	F	Shoemaker	25Se02Hu	PERRIN, W.Sedley	31	M	Merchant	26Se02As
Sarah	25	F	Shoemaker	25Se02Hu	SANDS, U (W)	29	F	Lady	26Se02As
MCDONALD, Mary	20	F	Servant	25Se02Hu	LOREE, Robt.	64	M	Gentleman	26Se02As
KERR, John	27	M	Coach Maker	25Se02Hu	GARLIN, Bridget	20	F	Servant	26Se02As
MCCORMICK, Willim.	40	M	Farmer	25Se02Hu	Nicholas	14	M	Servant	26Se02As
Anna (W)	29	F	Wife	25Se02Hu	CRAVEN, Thos.	24	M	Laborer	26Se02As
U	.00	U	Infant	25Se02Hu	FURGUSON, Catharine	22	F	None	26Se02As
Anne (D)	07	F	Child	25Se02Hu	Ellen (D)	02	F	Child	26Se02As
Ellen (D)	05	F	Child	25Se02Hu	COLLINS, Cath.	40	F	None	26Se02As
Marat.	29	F	Farmer	25Se02Hu	Michl.	28	M	None	26Se02As
MCGUIGGAN, John	21	M	Clerk	25Se02Hu	Joseph	12	M	None	26Se02As
Catharine (W)	20	F	Wife	25Se02Hu	KENNY, John	23	M	Unknown	26Se02As
U	.00	U	Infant	25Se02Hu	Michl.	22	M	Unknown	26Se02As
HILL, Mary	20	F	Servant	25Se02Hu	Anne	17	F	Unknown	26Se02As

NAMES OF PASSENGERS		AGE	SEX	OCCUPATIONS	DATE PORT SHIP
BRENNAN, Anne		20	F	Servant	26Se02As
DOHERTY, William		21	M	Laborer	26Se02As
MOFFAT, Irwin		20	M	Laborer	26Se02As
BURNS, Edward		24	M	Tailor	26Se02As
HENRY, Patrick		19	M	Laborer	26Se02As
CARR, George		40	M	Laborer	26Se02As
Robt.	(S)	17	M	Laborer	26Se02As
MCDONNELL, Margt.		19	F	Servant	26Se02As
MCLOUGHLIN, Timothy		26	M	Laborer	26Se02As
RABBIT, Mary		16	F	Laborer	26Se02As
TAGGART, John		19	M	Laborer	26Se02As
RELCHRIEST, James		26	M	Laborer	26Se02As
MCNAMARA, Thos.		26	M	Laborer	26Se02As
Margt.		21	F	None	26Se02As
HAYS, Mary		20	F	Servant	26Se02As
WATERS, Mary		27	F	Servant	26Se02As
Mary		20	F	Servant	26Se02As
DALY, Bridget		18	F	Servant	26Se02As
CLOHESY, Alley		21	F	Servant	26Se02As
TYRELL, Bridget		26	F	None	26Se02As
George	(S)	04	M	Child	26Se02As
John	(S)	03	M	Child	26Se02As
NAUGHTON, John		30	M	Laborer	26Se02As
Catharine		22	F	Laborer	26Se02As
REILY, Rose		19	F	Servant	26Se02As
DENNANY, Mary		40	F	Servant	26Se02As
Alice	(D)	10	F	Child	26Se02As
Owen	(S)	08	M	Child	26Se02As
NORTON, Thomas		24	M	Laborer	26Se02As
BROWNE, Thomas		20	M	Laborer	26Se02As
Bridget		11	F	Laborer	26Se02As
Elizabeth		09	F	Child	26Se02As
LOVE, Mary		20	F	Servant	26Se02As
MCMANUS, Bridget		19	F	Servant	26Se02As
MCQUINN, Margt.		16	F	Servant	26Se02As
COOKLEY, Michl.		19	M	Servant	26Se02As
KING, Mary		21	F	Servant	26Se02As
DUFFY, Rose		27	F	Servant	26Se02As
Thos.	(S)	08	M	Child	26Se02As
Rose	(D)	07	F	Child	26Se02As
CAMPBELL, Mary		50	F	None	26Se02As
William	(S)	21	M	None	26Se02As
MCNEIVE, Michl.		36	M	None	26Se02As
AYLWARD, John		24	M	None	26Se02As
CATTACAN, Patt		21	M	Bootmaker	26Se02As
U	(W)	22	F	Wife	26Se02As
CASTLE, Timothy		21	M	Bootmaker	26Se02As
Mary		20	F	None	26Se02As
WILLIAMS, Anne		18	F	Servant	26Se02As
LEIRANS, Mary		17	F	Servant	26Se02As
KENRY, Mary		20	F	Servant	26Se02As
DAVIS, Esther		16	F	Servant	26Se02As
FLEMING, Bridget		16	F	Servant	26Se02As
REILY, Garrett		30	M	Laborer	26Se02As
Judy	(W)	26	F	Wife	26Se02As
Kate	(D)	.00	F	Infant	26Se02As
James		38	M	Unknown	26Se02As
MCGENNISS, Bridget		24	F	Servant	26Se02As
GALWIN, Peter		29	M	None	26Se02As
U	(W)	21	F	Wife	26Se02As
Eliza		12	F	None	26Se02As
John		08	M	Child	26Se02As
Micheal		02	M	Child	26Se02As
Peter		02	M	Child	26Se02As
SIMPSON, Thomas		22	M	Laborer	26Se02As
ADIGAN, Stephen		21	M	Laborer	26Se02As
LARKIN, Thos.		21	M	Tailor	26Se02As
U	(W)	21	F	Wife	26Se02As
John	(S)	.00	M	Infant	26Se02As
DUNLEAVY, Micheal		34	M	None	26Se02As
Seragh	(W)	30	F	Wife	26Se02As
Martin	(S)	12	M	None	26Se02As
Micheal	(S)	10	M	Child	26Se02As
William	(S)	09	M	Child	26Se02As
Daniel	(S)	07	M	Child	26Se02As
DUNLEAVY, Mary	(D)	05	F	Child	26Se02As
John	(S)	02	M	Child	26Se02As
NOON, Peter		30	M	Farmer	26Se02As
U-Mrs.	(W)	26	F	Wife	26Se02As
Died-At-Sea					
Anne	(D)	11	F	None	26Se02As
John	(S)	09	M	Child	26Se02As
Peter	(S)	07	M	Child	26Se02As
Nicholas	(S)	04	M	Child	26Se02As
Mary	(D)	01	F	Child	26Se02As
MURPHY, Patt		27	M	None	26Se02As
Mary		24	F	None	26Se02As
Anne		29	F	None	26Se02As
Ellen		19	F	None	26Se02As
TIMLIN, Bridget		16	F	None	26Se02As
Thomas		13	M	None	26Se02As
MCNALTY, Martin		27	M	None	26Se02As
KANE, Martin		26	M	Laborer	26Se02As
U	(W)	30	F	Wife	26Se02As
BURKE, Bridget		20	F	Servant	26Se02As
HOLMES, Robt.		26	M	Laborer	26Se02As
U	(W)	21	F	Wife	26Se02As
WARD, Thomas		20	M	Laborer	26Se02As
KELLY, Cathn.		18	F	Servant	26Se02As
HARS, Micheal		19	F	Servant	26Se02As
OBRYAN, Patt		21	F	Laborer	26Se02As
BRYAN, U-Mrs.		40	F	Laborer	26Se02As
DAVIS, James		27	M	Laborer	26Se02As
TOOLE, John		25	M	Laborer	26Se02As
DOONAN, John		30	M	Laborer	26Se02As
Catharine	(W)	24	F	Wife	26Se02As
Henry	(S)	05	M	Child	26Se02As
Anne	(D)	03	F	Child	26Se02As
James	(S)	02	M	Child	26Se02As
Died-At-Sea					
FARRELL, Anne		20	F	None	26Se02As
MURPHY, Betty		19	F	Servant	26Se02As
POOL, Anne		19	F	Servant	26Se02As
MCDONNELL, Paul		20	M	None	26Se02As
Marla		17	F	Servant	26Se02As
MCFARLAN, Charles		18	M	Laborer	26Se02As
RORKE, James		31	M	Laborer	26Se02As
Mary		22	F	None	26Se02As
WALLACE, Robt.		18	M	Laborer	26Se02As
John		17	M	Laborer	26Se02As
Marla		40	F	None	26Se02As
MCKNIGHT, U-Mrs.		40	F	None	26Se02As
Margt.Ann	(D)	15	F	None	26Se02As
MURTAGH, Mat		00	M	None	26Se02As
KEARNY, Betty		18	F	None	26Se02As
DOONAN, James		01	M	Child	26Se02As
MORAN, Anne		25	F	Servant	26Se02As
Catharine		20	F	Servant	26Se02As
GALLAHER, Bridget		22	F	Servant	26Se02As
HARKER, Bridget		24	F	Servant	26Se02As
HALLORAN, Edward		26	M	None	26Se02As
KEARNEY, Margt.		20	F	Servant	26Se02As
MOLONEY, Honor		19	F	Servant	26Se02As
MCKEWN, Matilda		34	F	Servant	26Se02As
Catharine	(D)	13	F	Servant	26Se02As
Mary-Ann	(D)	06	F	Child	26Se02As
Ellen	(D)	04	F	Child	26Se02As
MCGURREN, Patt		21	M	None	26Se02As
FITZPATRICK, Patrick		40	M	Laborer	26Se02As
MCARDLE, Peter		26	M	Laborer	26Se02As
PARKEN, U-Mrs.		40	F	None	26Se02As
TYRELL, Henry		07	M	Child	26Se02As
TURNAN, Cath.		22	F	Servant	26Se02As
Anne		22	F	Servant	26Se02As
FLOHERTY, Bernard		26	M	Servant	26Se02As
LEE, Patt		20	M	Servant	26Se02As
MCKNIGHT, Barbara		22	F	None	26Se02As
Mary		16	F	None	26Se02As
CROFTON, Mary		16	F	None	26Se02As
Mary		13	F	None	26Se02As

NAMES OF PASSENGERS		A G E	S E X	OCCUPATIONS	DATE PORT SHIP
CROFTON, Margt.		09	F	Child	26Se02As
Anne		07	F	Child	26Se02As
MCTAGRUE, James		40	M	None	26Se02As
MULLIGAN, Hugh		19	M	None	26Se02As
Cath.		20	F	None	26Se02As
Anne		11	F	None	26Se02As
WHEELEN, Mary		20	F	Servant	26Se02As
DALTON, Anne		18	F	Servant	26Se02As
FEGAN, Mathew-H.		26	M	Unknown	26Se02As
JACKSON, Thos.		30	M	None	26Se02As
Margt.	(W)	30	F	Wife	26Se02As
James	(S)	09	M	Child	26Se02As
Eliza	(D)	06	F	Child	26Se02As
MURRAY, John		00	M	Child	26Se02As
ARMSTRONG, James		00	M	Laborer	26Se02As
FARRELL, Micheal		30	M	None	26Se02As
John		28	M	None	26Se02As
HARROHER, Patt		28	M	None	26Se02As
FINNIGAN, Margt.		22	F	None	26Se02As
Mary		18	F	None	26Se02As
HOGG, U		17	F	None	26Se02As
MCLOUGHLIN, Bridget		18	F	None	26Se02As
GALLAGHER, Anne		13	F	Servant	26Se02As
FOULEY, Patt		24	M	Laborer	26Se02As
SCULLY, Daniel		24	M	Miner	26Se02As
FITZGERALD, John		24	M	Miner	26Se02As
JONES, Mary		26	F	Servant	26Se02As
SWEENEY, Timothy		20	M	Shoemaker	26Se02As
WATERS, James		25	M	Laborer	26Se02As
GORMLY, Peter		20	M	Laborer	26Se02As
MCGOWRAN, Patt		21	M	Laborer	26Se02As
U	(W)	20	F	Wife	26Se02As
OCONNOR, Micheal		20	M	Clerk	26Se02As
OSULLIVAN, Micheal		20	M	Servant	26Se02As
GALLAGHER, Biddy		11	F	Servant	26Se02As
GRACE, Thomas		14	M	Servant	26Se02As
Ellen		18	F	Servant	26Se02As
Rose		20	F	Servant	26Se02As
HAYDEN, Eliza		22	F	Servant	26Se02As
CALLIN, Michl.		23	M	Laborer	26Se02As
Joseph		12	M	Laborer	26Se02As
MARSH, John		11	M	Laborer	26Se02As
KENT, Peter		17	M	Laborer	26Se02As

GREAT-WESTERN 30 SEPTEMBER 1846

From Liverpool

NAMES OF PASSENGERS		A G E	S E X	OCCUPATIONS	DATE PORT SHIP
HOUGHTON, J.R.		24	M	Gentleman	30Se02Cy
CARLETON, F.		26	M	Gentleman	30Se02Cy
FERRIER, James		46	M	Gentleman	30Se02Cy
G.D.	(S)	21	M	Gentleman	30Se02Cy
U	(W)	45	F	Lady	30Se02Cy
M.	(D)	18	F	Lady	30Se02Cy
Mary	(D)	16	F	Lady	30Se02Cy
PARSONS, W.		60	M	Merchant	30Se02Cy
B.		20	M	Gentleman	30Se02Cy
HARBIN, E.		17	M	Gentleman	30Se02Cy
HUMBERT, D.		40	M	Merchant	30Se02Cy
DAVIS, W.		35	M	Merchant	30Se02Cy
SELL, J.		29	M	Merchant	30Se02Cy
ORR, James-R.		39	M	Merchant	30Se02Cy
JOHNSON, Geo.		35	M	Gentleman	30Se02Cy
COPLAND, N.		25	F	Servant	30Se02Cy
GRIFFITHS, John		26	M	Gentleman	30Se02Cy
U	(W)	21	F	Lady	30Se02Cy
RAWLINGS, Thos.		38	M	Gentleman	30Se02Cy
FANALLY, W.		25	M	Gentleman	30Se02Cy

OHIO 01 OCTOBER 1846

From Liverpool

NAMES OF PASSENGERS		A G E	S E X	OCCUPATIONS	DATE PORT SHIP
HEARN, Patk.		50	M	Farmer	01Oc02Bm
Allice		35	F	None	01Oc02Bm
Catherine	(D)	11	F	None	01Oc02Bm
Mathew		08	M	Child	01Oc02Bm
Bridgett	(D)	06	F	Child	01Oc02Bm
John		04	M	Child	01Oc02Bm
Richard		03	M	Child	01Oc02Bm
Purse		01	M	Child	01Oc02Bm
METHUNE, Marth		00	F	None	01Oc02Bm
GAMBLE, Robert		34	M	Farmer	01Oc02Bm
Jane	(W)	34	F	Wife	01Oc02Bm
William	(S)	10	M	Child	01Oc02Bm
Margrett	(D)	08	F	Child	01Oc02Bm
James	(S)	06	M	Child	01Oc02Bm
Hugh	(S)	04	M	Child	01Oc02Bm
Isabell	(D)	02	F	Child	01Oc02Bm
FREEMAN, Alex.		42	M	Laborer	01Oc02Bm
Died-At-Sea					
BARRY, Mary		45	F	None	01Oc02Bm
DUNN, Ellen		03	F	Child	01Oc02Bm
MARR, Catherine		30	F	None	01Oc02Bm
SHERRARD, William		35	M	Farmer	01Oc02Bm
Maria		22	F	None	01Oc02Bm
MCCRACKEN, James		36	M	Farmer	01Oc02Bm
MARTIN, John		37	M	Farmer	01Oc02Bm
CONNELLY, Paul		21	M	Farmer	01Oc02Bm
BURK, Cathn.		17	F	Servant	01Oc02Bm
RUSSELL, Bartholemew		64	M	Mason	01Oc02Bm
Mathew		18	M	Mason	01Oc02Bm
Margrett		17	F	None	01Oc02Bm
CALLAHAN, Norra		18	F	None	01Oc02Bm
SLEET, Cathn.		50	F	None	01Oc02Bm
John	(S)	21	M	Laborer	01Oc02Bm
BRADY, Ann		49	F	None	01Oc02Bm
BURNS, Martin		40	M	Laborer	01Oc02Bm
INNIS, Mary		30	F	None	01Oc02Bm
SWORDS, Mary		12	F	None	01Oc02Bm
BOWSHER, John		19	M	Laborer	01Oc02Bm
FRENCH, Will		20	M	Laborer	01Oc02Bm
DUNN, Thos.		15	M	Laborer	01Oc02Bm
TEARNEY, Thos.		26	M	Farmer	01Oc02Bm
Margrett		60	F	None	01Oc02Bm
Margrett		17	F	Servant	01Oc02Bm
DUGGEN, James		23	M	Mason	01Oc02Bm
Catherine		50	F	None	01Oc02Bm
Daniell		19	M	Mason	01Oc02Bm
Bridgett		16	F	Servant	01Oc02Bm
MCMEHAN, Ann		23	F	Servant	01Oc02Bm
BALLENTINE, Hugh		50	M	Farmer	01Oc02Bm
Mary	(W)	45	F	Wife	01Oc02Bm
Ann	(D)	18	F	None	01Oc02Bm
Letitia	(D)	16	F	None	01Oc02Bm
Mary-Ellen	(D)	14	F	None	01Oc02Bm
Hugh	(S)	16	M	None	01Oc02Bm
James	(S)	07	M	Child	01Oc02Bm
COCHREN, Mary-Ann		17	F	None	01Oc02Bm
MURRY, Bridgett		17	F	Servant	01Oc02Bm
MCGORMLEY, Thos.		21	M	Carpenter	01Oc02Bm
BUTLER, John		18	M	Farmer	01Oc02Bm

NAMES OF PASSENGERS		AGE	SEX	OCCUPATIONS	DATE PORT SHIP

NIAGARA 01 OCTOBER 1846

From Liverpool

NAMES OF PASSENGERS		AGE	SEX	OCCUPATIONS	DATE PORT SHIP
HUMPHREYS, Robert		20	M	Weaver	010c02Ab
TRIMBLE, John		23	M	Laborer	010c02Ab
CORNIFF, Bernard		25	M	Laborer	010c02Ab
TARREEL, John		39	M	Weaver	010c02Ab
REID, Nancy		40	F	Domestic	010c02Ab
Ann	(D)	10	F	Child	010c02Ab
Margaret	(D)	08	F	Child	010c02Ab
MURPHY, Nancy		30	F	Domestic	010c02Ab
CRIMPAL, Margaret		18	F	Domestic	010c02Ab
Mery		10	F	Domestic	010c02Ab
Rosey		08	F	Child	010c02Ab
CONNEGAN, Esther		22	F	Domestic	010c02Ab
CANNEY, Catherine		20	F	Domestic	010c02Ab
MELIA, Eliza		13	F	Domestic	010c02Ab
CORMME, Barbara		22	F	Domestic	010c02Ab
Mary	(D)	.02	F	Infant	010c02Ab
Patrick	(S)	01	M	Child	010c02Ab
CHEANEY, Ann		22	F	Domestic	010c02Ab
IRWIN, Edmund		26	M	Weaver	010c02Ab
MCDOWELL, John		15	M	Tailor	010c02Ab
DRANEY, Thomas		21	M	Weaver	010c02Ab
DEWIT, Edward		20	M	Laborer	010c02Ab
CROFIT, Thomas		25	M	Weaver	010c02Ab
Margaret		58	F	Domestic	010c02Ab
Jane		27	F	Domestic	010c02Ab
Christina		15	F	Domestic	010c02Ab
SHAY, Henry		19	M	Laborer	010c02Ab
QUID, Thomas		19	M	Laborer	010c02Ab
FLOAGINS, Philip		22	M	Tailor	010c02Ab
SHEARS, Andrew		56	M	Farmer	010c02Ab
MOORE, Rosa		17	F	Domestic	010c02Ab
DAGNAL, Ann		17	F	Domestic	010c02Ab
DUFFEY, Mary		17	F	Domestic	010c02Ab
MADDON, Agnes		16	F	Domestic	010c02Ab
KEELY, Patrick		20	M	Blacksmith	010c02Ab
MACLEANY, Daniel		23	M	Weaver	010c02Ab
JAMESOON, Thomas		19	M	Weaver	010c02Ab
MCIINTIRE, Samuel		22	M	Laborer	010c02Ab
FERSIDE, Jane		30	F	Domestic	010c02Ab
CURLY, Mary		30	F	Domestic	010c02Ab
Ann		13	F	Domestic	010c02Ab
John		11	M	Domestic	010c02Ab
FAYLOR, George		21	M	Saddler	010c02Ab
MCINTIRE, Andrew		22	M	Laborer	010c02Ab
MACGOWAN, John		24	M	Groom	010c02Ab
LALARCH, Patrick		18	M	Laborer	010c02Ab
MCMARRA, John		43	M	Weaver	010c02Ab
James	(S)	18	M	Painter	010c02Ab
William	(S)	14	M	Painter	010c02Ab
CALLAGHAN, James		18	M	Tailor	010c02Ab
FAUL, Hugh		22	M	Fisherman	010c02Ab
Allen		25	M	Fisherman	010c02Ab
Mary		22	F	Domestic	010c02Ab
COCKERAN, Bryan		25	M	Laborer	010c02Ab
Mary	(W)	24	F	Wife	010c02Ab
Alice	(D)	.06	F	Infant	010c02Ab
REYLY, Owen		35	M	Laborer	010c02Ab
Terrence	(S)	10	M	Laborer	010c02Ab
Catherine	(D)	14	F	Laborer	010c02Ab
Ann	(D)	11	F	Laborer	010c02Ab
Owen	(S)	07	M	Child	010c02Ab
Charles	(S)	05	M	Child	010c02Ab
Patrick	(S)	03	M	Child	010c02Ab
John	(S)	02	M	Child	010c02Ab
Bridget	(W)	36	F	Wife	010c02Ab
SULLIVAN, Thomas		22	M	Shoemaker	010c02Ab
Rosa		22	F	Domestic	010c02Ab
SHARON, Margaret		25	F	Domestic	010c02Ab
MCDOWELL, Caroline		25	F	Domestic	010c02Ab
COFFER, Michael		39	M	Laborer	010c02Ab
Bridget	(W)	39	F	Wife	010c02Ab
Thomas	(S)	13	M	Laborer	010c02Ab
Edward	(S)	09	M	Child	010c02Ab
Mary	(D)	12	F	Laborer	010c02Ab
Catherine	(D)	07	F	Child	010c02Ab
Eliza	(D)	04	F	Child	010c02Ab
LARGEN, James		23	M	Laborer	010c02Ab
MCLUSKY, Michael		22	M	Shoemaker	010c02Ab
MCOLLUM, James		25	M	Carpenter	010c02Ab
PHELIM, William		26	M	Laborer	010c02Ab
LARGEN, Rosa		26	F	Servant	010c02Ab
Mary		19	F	Servant	010c02Ab
Jane		17	F	Servant	010c02Ab
COLLOTHN, Margaret		25	F	Servant	010c02Ab
REILLY, Rose		28	F	Servant	010c02Ab
FITZPATRICK, Mary		24	F	Servant	010c02Ab
BURN, Cecella		19	F	Servant	010c02Ab
Ann		17	F	Servant	010c02Ab
NUGENT, Peira		30	M	Painter	010c02Ab
Alice	(W)	26	F	Wife	010c02Ab
Edmund	(S)	08	M	Child	010c02Ab
Thomas	(S)	05	M	Child	010c02Ab
Margaret	(D)	03	F	Child	010c02Ab
HIGGISON, Robert		22	M	Laborer	010c02Ab
Allx		27	M	Laborer	010c02Ab
ONEIL, Margaret		28	F	Lady	010c02Ab
MCNELLY, Mary		20	F	Dressmaker	010c02Ab
DONLY, Ellen		35	F	Dressmaker	010c02Ab
LLOYD, Eliza		21	F	Seamstress	010c02Ab
MCANN, John		23	M	Printer	010c02Ab
TATE, Mary-Ann		31	F	Seamstress	010c02Ab
George	(S)	13	M	None	010c02Ab
Mary	(D)	10	F	Child	010c02Ab
Margaret	(D)	08	F	Child	010c02Ab
WHITE, Julia		26	F	Ctnsp	010c02Ab
COLLOGER, Biddy		20	F	Domestic	010c02Ab
RICHARD, Mary		20	F	Domestic	010c02Ab
WARD, Catherine		18	F	Domestic	010c02Ab
FITZGERALD, Beddy		18	F	Domestic	010c02Ab
Patrick	(F)	40	M	Laborer	010c02Ab
Margaret	(M)	40	F	Wife	010c02Ab
Catherine	(T)	14	F	None	010c02Ab
Ann	(T)	08	F	Child	010c02Ab
CLARK, Charles		21	M	Mason	010c02Ab
MCLUSKEY, Michael		17	M	Laborer	010c02Ab
MCDOWELL, John		25	M	Stnsp	010c02Ab
Agnes	(W)	26	F	Wife	010c02Ab
James	(S)	03	M	Child	010c02Ab
William-John	(S)	01	M	Child	010c02Ab
SERVICE, Agnes		20	F	Domestic	010c02Ab
Ann-Jane		17	F	Domestic	010c02Ab
KELLY, Charles		48	M	Farmer	010c02Ab
Catherine		33	F	Dressmaker	010c02Ab
ROGERS, Thomas		20	M	Laborer	010c02Ab
Mary		24	F	None	010c02Ab
FLINN, Mary		30	F	Domestic	010c02Ab
John	(S)	01	M	Child	010c02Ab
MCGUIRE, Mary		24	F	None	010c02Ab
Patrick	(S)	01	M	Child	010c02Ab
REYNOLDS, Joseph		26	M	Ppstr	010c02Ab
PORK, George		30	M	Laborer	010c02Ab
CRAYDON, Ann		14	F	Domestic	010c02Ab
GALLIGHAN, Jane		23	F	Domestic	010c02Ab
Betty		20	F	Domestic	010c02Ab
COX, James		35	M	Laborer	010c02Ab
Catherine		30	F	Laborer	010c02Ab
DOWEN, James		61	M	Laborer	010c02Ab
Elizabeth		64	F	None	010c02Ab
REED, Hugh		30	M	Loom Maker	010c02Ab
MCARRON, Patrick		24	M	Laborer	010c02Ab

NAMES OF PASSENGERS		A G E	S E X	OCCUPATIONS	DATE PORT SHIP	NAMES OF PASSENGERS		A G E	S E X	OCCUPATIONS	DATE PORT SHIP
DRURY, Owen		20	M	Laborer	010c02Ab	TURNER, William		46	M	Iron Worker	030c44lJ
SMITH, Patrick		30	M	Laborer	010c02Ab	Sarah	(W)	48	F	Wife	030c44lJ
MCGOWAN, James		25	M	Laborer	010c02Ab	Kedgwin	(S)	20	M	Iron Worker	030c44lJ
MURRY, Bridget		20	F	Domestic	010c02Ab	Sarah-Ann	(D)	16	F	None	030c44lJ
BURKE, Maria		18	F	Domestic	010c02Ab	Wm.Jr.	(D)	11	M	Iron Worker	030c44lJ
DONOVEN, Ann		20	F	Domestic	010c02Ab	Matilda	(D)	09	F	Child	030c44lJ
JAMES, William		24	M	Farmer	010c02Ab	Henrietta	(D)	07	F	Child	030c44lJ
John		21	M	Farmer	010c02Ab	John	(S)	05	M	Child	030c44lJ
Robert		16	M	Farmer	010c02Ab	Thomas	(S)	03	M	Child	030c44lJ
COGHLAN, Margaret		36	F	Domestic	010c02Ab	WILLIAMS, Mary-Mrs.		51	F	Tailor	030c44lJ
John	(S)	13	M	Domestic	010c02Ab	David	(S)	20	M	Iron Worker	030c44lJ
Margaret	(D)	06	F	Child	010c02Ab	William	(S)	12	M	Iron Worker	030c44lJ
MERGRADY, Mary		32	F	Child	010c02Ab	MATHEWS, Daniel		38	M	Carpenter	030c44lJ
Sarah	(D)	05	F	Child	010c02Ab	Esther	(W)	39	F	Wife	030c44lJ
CARLEY, John		36	M	Laborer	010c02Ab	Watkin	(S)	13	M	Carpenter	030c44lJ
MOONEY, Daniel		23	M	Laborer	010c02Ab	David	(S)	11	M	Carpenter	030c44lJ
CONNER, Patrick		20	M	Laborer	010c02Ab	William	(S)	09	M	Child	030c44lJ
HICKS, William		18	M	Laborer	010c02Ab	Ebenezer	(S)	09	M	Child	030c44lJ
BLACKBURN, Jane		20	F	Domestic	010c02Ab	MAGGS, Thirza		35	F	Wife	030c44lJ
WILSON, Ellen		15	F	Domestic	010c02Ab	Thirza	(D)	07	F	Child	030c44lJ
LYONS, Timothy		28	M	Tailor	010c02Ab	John	(S)	01	M	Child	030c44lJ
Mary	(W)	25	F	Wife	010c02Ab	STEADDER, Mary		24	F	Wife	030c44lJ
CLARK, Mary		15	F	Domestic	010c02Ab						
ROCK, Peggy		19	F	Domestic	010c02Ab						
MCCABE, Mickey		21	M	Laborer	010c02Ab						
MONNCE, Edward		35	M	Laborer	010c02Ab						
CORNWALL, Corney		35	M	Laborer	010c02Ab						
SHEEAN, William		35	M	Laborer	010c02Ab						
HIGGINS, Catherine		16	F	Domestic	010c02Ab		FIDELIA 05 OCTOBER 1846				
Mary		18	F	Domestic	010c02Ab						
CANOVER, Ann		19	F	Domestic	010c02Ab		From Liverpool				
MACALLY, Bessy		25	F	Domestic	010c02Ab						
COFF, John		20	M	Painter	010c02Ab						
KELLY, James		18	M	Clerk	010c02Ab	REYNOLDS, Mary		21	F	None	050c02Ax
LEECH, Nicholas		26	M	Cbtmkr	010c02Ab	BROWN, Wm.J.		30	M	Merchant	050c02Ax
JAMES, Lucy		20	F	Servant	010c02Ab	MACGHAN, Peter		25	M	Farmer	050c02Ax
JONES, Eliza		21	F	Servant	010c02Ab	HENNESEY, James		36	M	Farmer	050c02Ax
Mary		23	F	Servant	010c02Ab	Ellen	(W)	32	F	Wife	050c02Ax
WOOD, Joseph		30	M	Grocer	010c02Ab	Bridget	(D)	08	F	Child	050c02Ax
REILLY, Margaret		19	F	Domestic	010c02Ab	John	(S)	05	M	Child	050c02Ax
CONNER, Margaret		17	F	Domestic	010c02Ab	Nancy	(D)	03	F	Child	050c02Ax
Ann		16	F	Domestic	010c02Ab	Eliza	(D)	01	F	Child	050c02Ax
MCHESNRY, Eliza		23	F	Weaver	010c02Ab	WALSH, Bridget		20	F	Laborer	050c02Ax
Eliza		10	F	Weaver	010c02Ab	RYAN, Ellen		14	F	Laborer	050c02Ax
Jane		21	F	Weaver	010c02Ab	OCONNELL, Dan		21	M	Laborer	050c02Ax
Isabella		18	F	Weaver	010c02Ab	HORAN, Make		25	M	Gdnr	050c02Ax
Margaret		16	F	Weaver	010c02Ab	Gat---, Eliza		25	F	None	050c02Ax
Harriet		14	F	Weaver	010c02Ab	CHEATHAM, Margaret		25	F	None	050c02Ax
CARLEY, Constantine		60	M	Farmer	010c02Ab	John-L.	(S)	01	M	Child	050c02Ax
Patrick	(S)	26	M	Farmer	010c02Ab	MARSHALL, Mary		40	F	Laborer	050c02Ax
Constantine	(S)	17	M	Farmer	010c02Ab	MCNUT, Eliza		32	F	Laborer	050c02Ax
Bridges	(W)	56	F	Wife	010c02Ab	BOULES, Margt.		13	F	Laborer	050c02Ax
Mary	(D)	21	F	Domestic	010c02Ab	HERON, Margt.		38	F	Laborer	050c02Ax
EVENT, Eliza		18	F	Milliner	010c02Ab	Margt.	(D)	18	F	Laborer	050c02Ax
KENNAN, Patrick		40	M	Butcher	010c02Ab	John	(S)	11	M	Laborer	050c02Ax
Mary		24	F	Domestic	010c02Ab	SMITH, Sarah		20	F	Laborer	050c02Ax
BRANCY, Miles		22	M	Laborer	010c02Ab	WHELTOKE, U		32	M	Laborer	050c02Ax
MULLEN, Malach		29	M	Laborer	010c02Ab	Eliza	(W)	00	F	Wife	050c02Ax
HIGHLAND, Hannah		60	F	Domestic	010c02Ab	Ellen	(D)	07	F	Child	050c02Ax
WIGMORE, Arthur		17	M	Gentleman	010c02Ab	Henry	(S)	05	M	Child	050c02Ax
HOWELL, Henry		30	M	Gentleman	010c02Ab	Charles	(S)	02	M	Child	050c02Ax
CLARK, Alicia		17	F	Lady	010c02Ab	MALOW, A.		26	U	Laborer	050c02Ax
						CUNNINGHAM, F.		30	U	Laborer	050c02Ax
						Sarah		30	F	Laborer	050c02Ax
						CARTY, Ann		42	F	Laborer	050c02Ax
						CAMPBEL, E.		50	U	Laborer	050c02Ax
						MULHOLLAND, Henry		34	M	Laborer	050c02Ax
	CORSAIR 03 OCTOBER 1846					LAUREE, Hugh		18	M	Laborer	050c02Ax
						BOWMAN, U		20	U	Laborer	050c02Ax
	From NEWPORT, Wales					DEEN, Dennis		25	M	Laborer	050c02Ax
						MURTAGH, Mary		18	F	Laborer	050c02Ax
						Bu---, Cath.		30	F	Laborer	050c02Ax
						HARPER, Ann		17	F	Laborer	050c02Ax
JONES, Sarah-Mrs.		23	F	Lady	030c44lJ	NEIL, Henry		25	M	Laborer	050c02Ax
Henry	(S)	02	M	Child	030c44lJ	Susan		22	F	Laborer	050c02Ax

NAMES OF PASSENGERS		A G E	S E X	OCCUPATIONS	DATE PORT SHIP	NAMES OF PASSENGERS		A G E	S E X	OCCUPATIONS	DATE PORT SHIP
NEIL, Betsey		21	F	Laborer	050c02Ax	CORAGAN, Michl.		25	M	None	050c02Ax
MCLOOA, Susan		19	F	Laborer	050c02Ax	KENNEDY, Cathn.		21	F	None	050c02Ax
OKENSHY, Gushe		30	U	Laborer	050c02Ax	HIGGINS, B.		26	U	None	050c02Ax
Tuafh		25	U	Laborer	050c02Ax	RYAN, H.		16	U	None	050c02Ax
Michan		03	U	Child	050c02Ax	Mary		13	F	None	050c02Ax
Eliza		00	F	Child	050c02Ax	COMLEN, Chr.		13	F	None	050c02Ax
INGRAHAM, Alex		23	M	Laborer	050c02Ax	FLYNN, B.		20	U	None	050c02Ax
FALEY, Mary		17	F	Laborer	050c02Ax	May		23	F	None	050c02Ax
DUFFY, Eliza		30	F	Laborer	050c02Ax	MURPHY, Cathr.		18	F	None	050c02Ax
HALE, Jno.		18	M	Laborer	050c02Ax	MCCAFFRY, Jno.		21	M	None	050c02Ax
Elizabeth		24	F	Laborer	050c02Ax	MCINTIRE, B.		20	U	None	050c02Ax
ELLIOTT, Agnes		35	F	Laborer	050c02Ax	MCLAE, Nancy		19	F	None	050c02Ax
NESBET, Cath.		21	F	Laborer	050c02Ax	GORDEN, Anty-P.		30	M	None	050c02Ax
MALONE, Jno.		20	M	Laborer	050c02Ax	HARGAN, Denl.		21	M	None	050c02Ax
FERNEY, Eliza		20	F	Laborer	050c02Ax	FYE, Margt.		23	F	None	050c02Ax
MCKEA, Ann		19	F	Laborer	050c02Ax	LEDWICK, Ann		22	F	None	050c02Ax
WINTERBOTTUM, Sarah		26	F	Laborer	050c02Ax	DUFFEY, Ann		04	F	Child	050c02Ax
Mary-Ann	(D)	05	F	Child	050c02Ax	GREENAN, Margt.		20	F	None	050c02Ax
Charles	(S)	.03	M	Infant	050c02Ax	BECK, Alexr.		20	M	None	050c02Ax
HALEY, Rebecca		20	F	Laborer	050c02Ax	Jane		40	F	None	050c02Ax
OWEN, Wm.		25	M	Laborer	050c02Ax	Alexander		07	M	Child	050c02Ax
RUSSELL, C.T.		35	M	Laborer	050c02Ax	James		06	M	Child	050c02Ax
FOX, Ellen		18	F	Laborer	050c02Ax	Emily		03	F	Child	050c02Ax
SMITH, Bridget		19	F	Laborer	050c02Ax	HENRY, Edwd.		20	M	None	050c02Ax
FITZPATRICK, Alice		18	F	Laborer	050c02Ax	NICOLSON, Dera.		13	U	None	050c02Ax
MORUS, Patrick		25	M	Laborer	050c02Ax	ANDERSON, James		30	M	None	050c02Ax
OSULIVAN, Ellen		20	F	Laborer	050c02Ax	DUFFY, Ed.		13	M	None	050c02Ax
MCCARTY, Eliza		29	F	Laborer	050c02Ax	DALEY, James		19	M	None	050c02Ax
Timothy	(S)	10	M	Child	050c02Ax	CARR, Ann		23	F	None	050c02Ax
John	(S)	07	M	Child	050c02Ax	ANDON, Elizabeth		25	F	None	050c02Ax
SCOTT, Mary-Ann		27	F	Laborer	050c02Ax	JOYCE, M.		27	U	None	050c02Ax
William	(S)	05	M	Child	050c02Ax	CASY, James		28	U	None	050c02Ax
James	(S)	03	M	Child	050c02Ax	Patt		30	U	None	050c02Ax
Ann	(D)	01	F	Child	050c02Ax	HAYS, Alice		19	F	None	050c02Ax
FLEMING, Jane		25	F	Laborer	050c02Ax	TOBIN, Ellen		20	F	None	050c02Ax
MCMATH, Margaret		24	F	Laborer	050c02Ax	Honora		18	F	None	050c02Ax
DAYTON, Betsey		22	F	Laborer	050c02Ax	YORK, Pat		56	M	None	050c02Ax
CHAPMAN, Michl.		24	M	Laborer	050c02Ax	SHEA, Thos.		21	M	None	050c02Ax
QUIN, Bridget		26	F	Laborer	050c02Ax	Mary		23	F	None	050c02Ax
DOWNEY, Marla		30	F	Laborer	050c02Ax	MINAHE, Patt		24	M	None	050c02Ax
Ellen	(D)	10	F	Child	050c02Ax	SULLIVAN, Ann		19	F	None	050c02Ax
Maurice	(S)	07	M	Child	050c02Ax	Mary		19	F	None	050c02Ax
Owen	(S)	09	M	Child	050c02Ax	KELLY, Mary		20	F	None	050c02Ax
Margaret	(D)	04	F	Child	050c02Ax	PUNDER, Thos.		30	M	None	050c02Ax
John	(S)	.06	M	Infant	050c02Ax	Mary		21	F	None	050c02Ax
Died-At-Sea						CONNER, Michl.		23	M	None	050c02Ax
GRIFFITH, Margaret		30	F	Laborer	050c02Ax	HELDER, James		35	M	None	050c02Ax
Lauren		10	F	Child	050c02Ax	DOWLING, Andr.		32	M	None	050c02Ax
FERGUSON, Jno.		20	M	Laborer	050c02Ax	Maria		31	F	None	050c02Ax
Ann		16	F	Laborer	050c02Ax	MAHER, E.		29	U	None	050c02Ax
JOYCE, Ellen		52	F	Laborer	050c02Ax	Maria		10	F	None	050c02Ax
MARONEY, Jno.		45	M	Laborer	050c02Ax	CORLEFF, Michl.		32	M	Laborer	050c02Ax
BOWMAN, Mary		40	F	Laborer	050c02Ax	Elizabeth		26	F	None	050c02Ax
MCCARTER, Mary		22	F	Laborer	050c02Ax	CLAY, Michl.		27	M	Laborer	050c02Ax
GARRETY, Alice		20	F	Laborer	050c02Ax	Nora		20	F	None	050c02Ax
MCGUIRE, Jane		19	F	Laborer	050c02Ax	BRADLEY, Francis		60	M	None	050c02Ax
MAGGAN, Susan		18	F	Laborer	050c02Ax	HEENNAN, Thom.		16	M	None	050c02Ax
ZORMAL, Ann		25	F	Laborer	050c02Ax	Patt		20	M	None	050c02Ax
MURRY, Brigt.		22	F	Laborer	050c02Ax	MORGAN, Brgt.		20	F	None	050c02Ax
KELLY, Jno.		27	M	Laborer	050c02Ax	SWEENY, Correy		20	U	None	050c02Ax
OHARRA, B.		18	U	Laborer	050c02Ax	CRONITY, Charles		17	M	None	050c02Ax
FLYNN, Mary		50	F	Laborer	050c02Ax	MCCANRY, E.		27	U	None	050c02Ax
CARENY, M.		20	U	Laborer	050c02Ax	MOONY, Cath.		18	F	None	050c02Ax
GIDDEM, Josph.		20	M	Laborer	050c02Ax	TOKER, Elith.		63	F	None	050c02Ax
CORCORAN, Joseph		32	M	Laborer	050c02Ax	OSULLIVAN, Dan.		53	M	None	050c02Ax
Margt.	(D)	11	F	Laborer	050c02Ax	Mary	(W)	36	F	Wife	050c02Ax
Thoms.	(S)	07	M	Child	050c02Ax	Margaret	(D)	11	F	None	050c02Ax
DESSAY, Rose		32	F	Laborer	050c02Ax	Mehale		09	U	Child	050c02Ax
RONIN, Mary		22	F	Laborer	050c02Ax	Daniel	(S)	07	M	Child	050c02Ax
SHERIDEN, Jno.		18	M	Laborer	050c02Ax	James	(S)	04	M	Child	050c02Ax
REGAN, R.		26	U	Laborer	050c02Ax	Johanna	(D)	02	F	Child	050c02Ax
MACK, James		21	M	Laborer	050c02Ax	Died-At-Sea					
Elizabth.		25	F	None	050c02Ax	BRADLEY, Ed.		25	M	None	050c02Ax
FOX, Mary		24	F	None	050c02Ax	Mary	(W)	28	F	Wife	050c02Ax
KENNEDY, Jno.		30	M	None	050c02Ax	John	(S)	04	M	Child	050c02Ax

NAMES OF PASSENGERS		A S G E E X	OCCUPATIONS	DATE PORT SHIP	NAMES OF PASSENGERS		A S G E E X	OCCUPATIONS	DATE PORT SHIP
BRADLEY, Edward	(S)	02 M	Child	050c02Ax					
Mary	(D)	.06 F	Infant	050c02Ax					
MCDONALD, Cath.		50 F	None	050c02Ax					
MURPHY, Dan.		15 M	None	050c02Ax					
MCCARRAL, Geo.		42 M	Carpenter	050c02Ax		HENDRIK-HUDSON 05 OCTOBER 1846			
Elizabeth	(W)	42 F	Wife	050c02Ax					
Elizabeth	(D)	17 F	None	050c02Ax		From London			
Catherine	(D)	12 F	None	050c02Ax					
George	(S)	06 M	Child	050c02Ax					
WHELECK, Rose		40 F	None	050c02Ax					
CONNOR, Mary		48 F	None	050c02Ax	GLIDDON, George-R.		36 M	Lecturer	050c21Bh
Jane	(D)	17 F	None	050c02Ax	Henry-A.		17 M	None	050c21Bh
Patrick	(S)	12 M	None	050c02Ax	BASSETT, John-W.		29 M	Druggist	050c21Bh
MARUY, Winfred		20 M	None	050c02Ax	AUSTIN, Maria		42 F	None	050c21Bh
DUGGAN, Mary		20 F	None	050c02Ax	WALKER, John		55 M	Musdir	050c21Bh
WOODS, Bridget		19 F	None	050c02Ax	Amelia		30 F	None	050c21Bh
FITZGERALD, Ellen		26 F	None	050c02Ax	CLARK, Richard-E.		27 M	Gentleman	050c21Bh
Honora		23 F	None	050c02Ax	Jane-S.		23 F	None	050c21Bh
MORIARTY, Michl.		22 M	None	050c02Ax	HORE, Edward		33 M	Druggist	050c21Bh
Sarah		19 F	None	050c02Ax	Ann	(W)	22 F	Wife	050c21Bh
LAN, Timothy		25 M	None	050c02Ax	Charles-E.	(S)	01 M	Child	050c21Bh
CARCY, James-De		22 M	None	050c02Ax	Mary-A.	(D)	.05 F	Infant	050c21Bh
BOLDING, Jno.		28 M	Tailor	050c02Ax	BREWER, Fanny		17 F	None	050c21Bh
BRADLEY, Jno.		30 M	Miller	050c02Ax	RAPHAEL, George-C.		31 M	Merchant	050c21Bh
Francis		24 M	Painter	050c02Ax	Elizabeth	(W)	30 F	Wife	050c21Bh
William		20 M	Shoemaker	050c02Ax	George-C.	(S)	03 M	Child	050c21Bh
FRASEY, Mich.		24 M	Miner	050c02Ax	Gertrude	(D)	.10 F	Infant	050c21Bh
HARPER, Michl.		30 M	Laborer	050c02Ax	John-C.		29 M	Merchant	050c21Bh
ROBERTS, Willm.		60 M	Gdnr	050c02Ax	STOKES, Joseph-H.		31 M	Grocer	050c21Bh
Ann	(W)	60 F	Wife	050c02Ax	SIMEON, Godfrey		74 M	Iron Monger	050c21Bh
Willm.	(S)	21 M	Gdnr	050c02Ax	CHAPMAN, William		29 M	Coachman	050c21Bh
FORCE, Jno.		19 M	Laborer	050c02Ax	CROXON, Henry		31 M	Butcher	050c21Bh
HEYDEN, Patt		30 M	None	050c02Ax	Ann	(W)	25 F	Wife	050c21Bh
Ann		28 F	None	050c02Ax	Clara	(D)	01 F	Child	050c21Bh
CANOY, Elenor		26 F	None	050c02Ax	VERLIN, Rebecca		19 F	None	050c21Bh
DONALD, Susan		17 F	None	050c02Ax	Maria	(M)	50 F	None	050c21Bh
ELLWELL, Bridget		17 F	None	050c02Ax	LEVY, Elizabeth		54 F	None	050c21Bh
JOYCE, Jno.		46 M	None	050c02Ax	Catharine	(D)	15 F	None	050c21Bh
MURRY, Mary		16 F	None	050c02Ax	John	(S)	11 M	None	050c21Bh
TRACY, Sarah		19 F	None	050c02Ax	WALSH, Mary		20 F	None	050c21Bh
MCGARNEY, Jno.		39 M	None	050c02Ax	REED, John		26 M	Tailor	050c21Bh
JOHNSON, Rot.		45 M	None	050c02Ax	COX, William		40 M	Gdnr	050c21Bh
Mary	(W)	46 F	Wife	050c02Ax	Mary	(W)	40 F	Wife	050c21Bh
Jane	(D)	12 F	None	050c02Ax	Mary-A.	(D)	21 F	None	050c21Bh
James	(S)	10 M	None	050c02Ax	William	(S)	16 M	None	050c21Bh
Betsey	(D)	08 F	Child	050c02Ax	Ellen	(D)	09 F	Child	050c21Bh
DARCY, H.		17 U	None	050c02Ax	WILLIAMS, Robert-F.		29 M	Clerk	050c21Bh
CUMING, Jno.		24 M	None	050c02Ax	BRISCO, William		35 M	Schm	050c21Bh
Mary		24 F	None	050c02Ax	Jane		35 F	None	050c21Bh
LYNCH, Michl.		24 M	None	050c02Ax	PORTER, Thomas		22 M	Painter	050c21Bh
HUSTON, Charles		27 M	None	050c02Ax	THOMPSON, Joseph		31 M	Ppstr	050c21Bh
EAGAN, James		30 M	None	050c02Ax	Mary-A.	(W)	28 F	Wife	050c21Bh
PEATERY, U		30 M	None	050c02Ax	Joseph	(S)	09 M	Child	050c21Bh
BAILY, Rob.		30 M	None	050c02Ax	Mary-A.	(D)	07 F	Child	050c21Bh
DOYLE, B.		22 M	None	050c02Ax	John	(S)	06 M	Child	050c21Bh
Ann		20 F	None	050c02Ax	Elizabeth	(D)	03 F	Child	050c21Bh
GILL, Ann		22 F	None	050c02Ax	George	(S)	.02 M	Infant	050c21Bh
DONNALL, Ann		20 F	None	050c02Ax	SIM, Robert		21 M	Draper	050c21Bh
HIGGINS, Rse		21 F	None	050c02Ax	MCMILLAN, James		30 M	Ldpr	050c21Bh
BUTE, Rose		23 F	None	050c02Ax	Christina	(W)	30 F	Wife	050c21Bh
CONNEL, Patt		27 M	None	050c02Ax	Jesse	(D)	04 F	Child	050c21Bh
MCDONNELL, Thos.		27 M	None	050c02Ax	Elizabeth	(D)	03 F	Child	050c21Bh
MCGUINN, Patt		25 M	None	050c02Ax	Christina	(D)	01 F	Child	050c21Bh
SWENEY, Ellen		18 F	None	050c02Ax	MENZIES, Mary		35 F	None	050c21Bh
QUEN, Mary		20 F	None	050c02Ax	MACK, James		22 M	Baker	050c21Bh
LYNCH, Mary		18 F	None	050c02Ax	BAILEY, Joseph		28 M	Miller	050c21Bh
LANNIN, Cahte.		26 F	None	050c02Ax	DORMAN, William		28 M	Barber	050c21Bh
NOLAND, Margaret		25 F	None	050c02Ax	Louisa	(W)	33 F	Wife	050c21Bh
Died-At-Sea					STYLES, Charles		20 M	Grocer	050c21Bh
					FOSTER, Elizabeth		55 F	None	050c21Bh
					Mary-A.	(D)	23 F	None	050c21Bh
					Neville	(S)	22 M	None	050c21Bh
					Henry	(S)	19 M	None	050c21Bh
					Charlotte	(D)	17 F	None	050c21Bh
					George	(S)	13 M	None	050c21Bh

NAMES OF PASSENGERS		AGE	SEX	OCCUPATIONS	DATE PORT SHIP
BARRY, Thomas		56	M	Tailor	050c21Bh
SCHOFIELD, Robert		54	M	Tailor	050c21Bh
RANDALL, Henry		20	M	Shoemaker	050c21Bh
BUTCHER, William		33	M	Laborer	050c21Bh
Catharine	(W)	37	F	Wife	050c21Bh
Henry	(S)	13	M	None	050c21Bh
William	(S)	10	M	None	050c21Bh
James	(S)	06	M	Child	050c21Bh
CORKER, William		26	M	Bookkeeper	050c21Bh
SAVAGE, Henry		21	M	Blacksmith	050c21Bh
Frederick		18	M	Blacksmith	050c21Bh
EVANS, David		28	M	Tanner	050c21Bh
INGGRAM, Amelia		63	F	None	050c21Bh
HASLAM, Amelia		26	F	None	050c21Bh
HERSEE, Jane		62	F	None	050c21Bh
Fanny	(D)	20	F	None	050c21Bh
Edmund	(S)	18	M	Farmer	050c21Bh
PENTECOST, Refrain		58	F	None	050c21Bh
Edward	(S)	20	M	Tailor	050c21Bh
John	(S)	16	M	None	050c21Bh
WOOD, Thomas		31	M	Cbfmkr	050c21Bh
Eliza-E.	(W)	30	F	Wife	050c21Bh
Marla	(D)	07	F	Child	050c21Bh
Charlotte	(D)	05	F	Child	050c21Bh
MILLAN, Frances		42	F	None	050c21Bh
ROBERTSON, Daniel		38	M	Painter	050c21Bh
Sophia-E.	(W)	30	F	Wife	050c21Bh
Anna-S.	(D)	12	F	None	050c21Bh
Rosa-I.	(D)	10	F	None	050c21Bh
George-A.	(S)	09	M	Child	050c21Bh
Charles-T.	(S)	06	M	Child	050c21Bh
Jesse-S.	(D)	03	F	Child	050c21Bh
John	(S)	.10	M	Infant	050c21Bh
TRENCH, George		56	M	None	050c21Bh
Mary		54	F	None	050c21Bh
THOMPSON, Ann		15	F	None	050c21Bh
GAHAN, Elizabeth		27	F	None	050c21Bh
ARNOLD, William		31	M	Farmer	050c21Bh
MURRAY, William		39	M	Tailor	050c21Bh
Amelia	(W)	30	F	Wife	050c21Bh
Amelia	(D)	05	F	Child	050c21Bh
William	(S)	03	F	Child	050c21Bh

HUGUENOT 05 OCTOBER 1846

From Liverpool

NAMES OF PASSENGERS		AGE	SEX	OCCUPATIONS	DATE PORT SHIP
BOLES, James		26	M	Hatter	050c02Be
Marla		32	F	None	050c02Be
BUCHAN, Sarah		43	F	None	050c02Be
BOWLES, Sarah		16	F	None	050c02Be
Thomas		11	M	None	050c02Be
Eliza-Ann		10	F	None	050c02Be
Frances		07	M	Child	050c02Be
Marla		05	F	Child	050c02Be
MARTIN, James		22	M	Mechanic	050c02Be
Elizabeth		24	F	None	050c02Be
LENNON, Patric		24	M	Mechanic	050c02Be
REILLY, James		21	M	None	050c02Be
Hugh		30	M	Laborer	050c02Be
MULLIGAN, John		25	M	Laborer	050c02Be
MCDONAL, Mary		18	F	None	050c02Be
REILLY, Jane		20	F	None	050c02Be
MCGUIRE, Mary-Ann		18	F	None	050c02Be
BOWLES, Mary-Ann		18	F	None	050c02Be
EARLY, Mary		24	F	None	050c02Be
SHUNHAN, Margt.		40	F	None	050c02Be
Thaddy	(S)	02	M	Child	050c02Be
BIRNSFORD, Mary		48	F	None	050c02Be

NAMES OF PASSENGERS		AGE	SEX	OCCUPATIONS	DATE PORT SHIP
ELLIS, Sarah		38	F	None	050c02Be
Sarah	(D)	11	F	None	050c02Be
George	(S)	06	M	Child	050c02Be
CORCORAN, Mintagh		16	M	Laborer	050c02Be
GRIFFITH, James		15	M	Laborer	050c02Be
RUIMERY, U-Mrs.		41	F	None	050c02Be
Edward	(H)	39	M	Laborer	050c02Be
Thomas	(S)	08	M	Child	050c02Be
Mary	(D)	09	F	Child	050c02Be
Michael	(S)	10	M	Child	050c02Be
WOODBURN, Wm.		35	M	Druggist	050c02Be
DORNY, Hugh		41	M	Laborer	050c02Be
BURKE, Sarah		16	F	None	050c02Be
COUREY, Robert		24	M	Carpenter	050c02Be
MAHON, John		26	M	Laborer	050c02Be
Briget		26	F	None	050c02Be
CONNELL, Mich.G.		24	F	Clergyman	050c02Be
KINENY, Ann		35	F	None	050c02Be
Cath.	(D)	07	F	Child	050c02Be
Thomas	(S)	05	M	Child	050c02Be
SCOTT, James		30	M	Weaver	050c02Be
GAYLOR, Margt.		18	F	None	050c02Be
SHIELDS, Mary-Ann		17	F	None	050c02Be
GARRY, Mich.		24	M	Laborer	050c02Be
GANLEY, Thomas		21	M	Mnftr	050c02Be
BROWN, Robt.		19	M	Laborer	050c02Be
WILIAMSON, Henry		25	M	Laborer	050c02Be
HOSSEY, Terms		19	M	Laborer	050c02Be
HOMAN, Alex		20	M	Laborer	050c02Be
MOINS, Margt.		18	F	None	050c02Be
BURNS, Patrick		54	M	Gentleman	050c02Be
GALLON, James		18	M	None	050c02Be
FRANKE, John		16	M	None	050c02Be

ADAM-CARR 06 OCTOBER 1846

From Glasgow

NAMES OF PASSENGERS		AGE	SEX	OCCUPATIONS	DATE PORT SHIP
MALONE, Joseph		12	M	None	060c04Aw
Susan	(M)	40	F	Wife	060c04Aw

PRATENCOLE 07 OCTOBER 1846

From St.JOHN,Cape Nf.

NAMES OF PASSENGERS		AGE	SEX	OCCUPATIONS	DATE PORT SHIP
MCCORMICK, U		25	M	Clerk	070c77ll

VERONICA 08 OCTOBER 1846

From St.JOHN,Cape Nf.

NAMES OF PASSENGERS		AGE	SEX	OCCUPATIONS	DATE PORT SHIP
BURKE, John		28	M	Clerk	080c77lm

NAMES OF PASSENGERS	AGE	SEX	OCCUPATIONS	DATE PORT SHIP	NAMES OF PASSENGERS	AGE	SEX	OCCUPATIONS	DATE PORT SHIP

NEW-YORK-PACKET 12 OCTOBER 1846

From St.JOHN,Cape Nf.

NAMES OF PASSENGERS		AGE	SEX	OCCUPATIONS	DATE PORT SHIP
HURLEY, Michael		35	M	Trader	120c77An
MULROY, Thomas		20	M	Tailor	120c77An
BEALY, James		41	M	Laborer	120c77An
Margaret	(W)	43	F	Wife	120c77An
Mary	(D)	11	F	None	120c77An
Bridget	(D)	09	F	Child	120c77An
Catherine	(D)	07	F	Child	120c77An
Patrick	(S)	03	M	Child	120c77An
DUNN, Patrick		18	M	Tailor	120c77An
James	(B)	11	M	None	120c77An
Thos.	(B)	09	M	Child	120c77An
Cath.	(M)	40	F	None	120c77An
Mary	(T)	22	F	None	120c77An
SIMMONS, Mary		22	F	None	120c77An

PANAMA 12 OCTOBER 1846

From Liverpool

NAMES OF PASSENGERS		AGE	SEX	OCCUPATIONS	DATE PORT SHIP
CARROLL, Christopher		25	M	Laborer	120c02In
NAUGHTON, John		24	M	Laborer	120c02In
Catharine		22	F	None	120c02In
MCCAULEY, Bridget		11	F	None	120c02In
NOON, Mary		22	F	Servant	120c02In
NALLY, John		25	M	Shoemaker	120c02In
U	(W)	27	F	Wife	120c02In
Patk.	(S)	03	M	Child	120c02In
Mary-Ann	(D)	04	F	Child	120c02In
LANGAN, Mary		68	F	None	120c02In
SMITH, Mary		22	F	Servant	120c02In
MITCHELL, Jane		20	F	Servant	120c02In
KELLIN, Patk.		47	M	Musician	120c02In
Maria	(W)	40	F	Wife	120c02In
Margaret	(D)	19	F	None	120c02In
LYNCH, Jas.		30	M	Tailor	120c02In
MCNAMARA, Wm.		21	M	Tailor	120c02In
BURNS, Cath.		26	F	Servant	120c02In
GOLDING, Brien		26	M	Laborer	120c02In
BRIEN, Eliza		32	F	Servant	120c02In
Andrew	(S)	07	M	Child	120c02In
MCGARRY, Cormick		44	M	Laborer	120c02In
Ellen		40	F	None	120c02In
BRENNAN, Cath.		30	F	Servant	120c02In
RYAN, Dennis		24	M	Laborer	120c02In
LYNA, Margaret		25	F	Servant	120c02In
Mary		20	F	Servant	120c02In
DARBY, Betsy		22	F	Servant	120c02In
SMITH, Jas.		25	M	Laborer	120c02In
KILLROY, Bridget		20	F	Servant	120c02In

RAPID 12 OCTOBER 1846

From St.JOHN,Cape Nf.

NAMES OF PASSENGERS		AGE	SEX	OCCUPATIONS	DATE PORT SHIP
BURNS, U		40	M	Schm	120c77Io
U	(W)	30	F	Seamstress	120c77Io
Elizabeth	(D)	09	F	Child	120c77Io
Joseph	(S)	07	M	Child	120c77Io
Charles	(S)	04	M	Child	120c77Io

MARGARET-EVANS 12 OCTOBER 1846

From Liverpool

NAMES OF PASSENGERS		AGE	SEX	OCCUPATIONS	DATE PORT SHIP
WALDRON, Andr.		25	M	Gentleman	120c02Ip
Julia	(W)	25	F	Lady	120c02Ip
Alfred	(S)	03	M	Child	120c02Ip
Laura	(D)	01	F	Child	120c02Ip
MARTIN, Isabella		20	F	Lady	120c02Ip
John		18	M	Clerk	120c02Ip
BUCKLEY, Samuel		23	M	Shoemaker	120c02Ip
JACKSON, Thos.		24	M	Mechanic	120c02Ip
WILLIAMSON, Jno.		61	M	Mechanic	120c02Ip
Elizth.		67	F	None	120c02Ip
TURNER, Thos.		22	M	Mechanic	120c02Ip
Margt.		20	F	None	120c02Ip
POLLOCK, Wm.		19	M	Mechanic	120c02Ip
WALTON, Thos.		13	M	Mechanic	120c02Ip
NOTT, Geo.		25	M	Mechanic	120c02Ip
THOMSON, Letitia		18	F	Spinster	120c02Ip
DUFF, Violet		18	F	Spinster	120c02Ip
DAVIDSON, Thos.		21	M	Mechanic	120c02Ip
TAYLOR, Danl.		20	M	Mechanic	120c02Ip
CHESTNUT, Jno.		24	M	Mechanic	120c02Ip
Wilm.		23	M	Mechanic	120c02Ip
MCCORMICK, Patk.		18	M	Farmer	120c02Ip
MELLOR, Rose		60	F	None	120c02Ip
Jane		00	F	None	120c02Ip
HARPER, Jno.		20	M	Farmer	120c02Ip
IRWIN, Mary-J.		18	F	None	120c02Ip
MCDONNELL, Thos.		18	M	Farmer	120c02Ip
DOYLE, Mary		24	F	None	120c02Ip
MCALOON, Thos.		15	M	Farmer	120c02Ip
SHEELS, Luke		30	M	Farmer	120c02Ip
KELLY, Catherine		21	F	None	120c02Ip
SWEENY, Eliza		30	F	None	120c02Ip
MORRIS, Mary		30	F	None	120c02Ip
Michl.	(S)	.00	M	Infant	120c02Ip
FEELY, Brian		20	M	Farmer	120c02Ip
ROONY, Jas.		18	M	Farmer	120c02Ip
COWEN, Dennis		18	M	Farmer	120c02Ip
Peggy		20	F	None	120c02Ip
Honor		17	F	None	120c02Ip
WATERS, Jno.		22	M	Servant	120c02Ip
MCKENAN, Wm.		24	M	Farmer	120c02Ip
WILSON, Robt.		23	M	Farmer	120c02Ip
COWLEY, Hugh		20	M	Farmer	120c02Ip
KERR, Mary		18	F	None	120c02Ip
MCFADDEN, Ally		18	F	None	120c02Ip
MCKENNA, Ellen		18	F	Servant	120c02Ip
KEEVER, Mary		27	F	Servant	120c02Ip
Cathre.	(D)	06	F	Child	120c02Ip
Micl.	(S)	.00	M	Infant	120c02Ip

NAMES OF PASSENGERS		AGE	SEX	OCCUPATIONS	DATE PORT SHIP
KENNEDY, Hugh		32	M	Farmer	120c02lp
DUNCAN, Chas.		30	M	Farmer	120c02lp
KILROE, Jno.		26	M	Farmer	120c02lp
RYAN, Eliza		22	F	Servant	120c02lp
MURTON, Thos.		24	M	Servant	120c02lp
Jno.		22	M	Servant	120c02lp
TRAYNER, Margt.		31	F	Servant	120c02lp
DELLON, Chas.		31	M	Servant	120c02lp
Peter		17	M	Servant	120c02lp
Anna		21	F	Servant	120c02lp
Marsella		18	F	Servant	120c02lp
Elizabeth		30	F	Servant	120c02lp
KEARNEY, Peter		27	M	Servant	120c02lp
Mary	(W)	28	F	Wife	120c02lp
Edwd.	(S)	03	M	Child	120c02lp
Michl.	(S)	.00	M	Infant	120c02lp
HUGHS, Jas.		40	M	Servant	120c02lp
Jane		40	F	Servant	120c02lp
MCMANNEL, Anne		24	F	Servant	120c02lp
RYAN, Patk.		23	M	Servant	120c02lp
GALLIGER, Mary		20	F	Servant	120c02lp
Jas.		07	M	Child	120c02lp
Moony		09	M	Child	120c02lp
Mary		03	F	Child	120c02lp
Catherine		.00	F	Infant	120c02lp
MARTIN, Bridget		18	F	Servant	120c02lp
CALLEGHAN, Rose		25	F	Servant	120c02lp
SHERRIDAN, Ann		17	F	Servant	120c02lp
MAGRATH, Ann		20	F	Servant	120c02lp
BRADY, Thos.		40	M	Servant	120c02lp
Magt.	(W)	40	F	Wife	120c02lp
Alice	(D)	12	F	None	120c02lp
Catherine	(D)	12	F	None	120c02lp
Margt.	(D)	08	F	Child	120c02lp
Mary	(D)	06	F	Child	120c02lp
Ellen	(D)	04	F	Child	120c02lp
SMYTHE, Farrell		25	M	Servant	120c02lp
Rosanna		15	F	None	120c02lp
Margt.		18	F	None	120c02lp

HOTTINGUER 12 OCTOBER 1846

From Liverpool

NAMES OF PASSENGERS		AGE	SEX	OCCUPATIONS	DATE PORT SHIP
MCALLICE, Samuel		50	M	Laborer	120c02Bc
Martha	(D)	23	F	Servant	120c02Bc
Jane	(D)	21	F	Servant	120c02Bc
KILLEN, Lucinda		16	F	Servant	120c02Bc
DOLIN, Pat		24	M	Laborer	120c02Bc
Jane	(W)	24	F	Wife	120c02Bc
Mary	(D)	02	F	Child	120c02Bc
John	(S)	.00	M	Infant	120c02Bc
REDMOND, Canilar		33	F	None	120c02Bc
Catherine	(D)	07	F	Child	120c02Bc
William-E.	(S)	02	M	Child	120c02Bc
BEECHMAN, Elisa		18	F	Servant	120c02Bc
Mary		20	F	Servant	120c02Bc
Jane		15	F	Servant	120c02Bc
Fanny		17	F	Servant	120c02Bc
Mary-Ann		11	F	Servant	120c02Bc
Leavia		13	F	Servant	120c02Bc
BOWDAN, John-W.		25	M	Mctr	120c02Bc
WILD, Ebenezer		30	M	Laborer	120c02Bc
LAWTON, Charles		25	M	Laborer	120c02Bc
PARKER, Sarah		18	F	None	120c02Bc
SMITH, Sarah-G.		20	F	Servant	120c02Bc
Eliza		18	F	Servant	120c02Bc
HILTON, Robert		19	M	Wlmcht	120c02Bc
LOSIN, George		28	M	Shoemaker	120c02Bc
LOSIN, Mary		25	F	None	120c02Bc
MCQUEESTON, Joseph		21	M	Farmer	120c02Bc
Thomas		20	M	Farmer	120c02Bc
James		18	M	Farmer	120c02Bc
Margaret		08	F	Child	120c02Bc
Marla		10	F	Child	120c02Bc
Sarah-A.		22	F	None	120c02Bc
Catherine		16	F	None	120c02Bc
Thomas		50	M	Farmer	120c02Bc
Margaret		40	F	Wife	120c02Bc
GRAHAM, George		50	M	Farmer	120c02Bc
MCKAY, Daniel		21	M	Farmer	120c02Bc
MCCORMICK, Jeremiah		27	M	Clerk	120c02Bc
Eliza	(W)	20	F	Wife	120c02Bc
Marla	(D)	06	F	Child	120c02Bc
HATCHNAH, Marg.		25	F	Servant	120c02Bc
MITCHELL, Andrew		21	M	Laborer	120c02Bc
Thomas		21	M	Laborer	120c02Bc
MCCONNOLL, James		31	M	Laborer	120c02Bc
CHERRY, Samuel		22	M	Laborer	120c02Bc
COOPER, Mary-Ann		25	F	None	120c02Bc
Eliza-J.		.00	F	Infant	120c02Bc
Eliza		18	F	Servant	120c02Bc
GILBERT, Henry		15	M	Servant	120c02Bc
WHITE, John		20	M	Weaver	120c02Bc
SIMPSON, William		20	M	Weaver	120c02Bc
ARMSTRONG, Samuel		20	M	Weaver	120c02Bc
MAYERS, James		30	M	Carpenter	120c02Bc
Rachel	(W)	25	F	Wife	120c02Bc
John	(S)	.00	M	Infant	120c02Bc
MCCARRY, Richard		30	M	Weaver	120c02Bc
Eliza	(W)	30	F	Wife	120c02Bc
Sara	(D)	10	F	Child	120c02Bc
Habella	(D)	05	F	Child	120c02Bc
David	(S)	02	M	Child	120c02Bc
BLYGH, William		20	M	Servant	120c02Bc
Thomas		20	M	Servant	120c02Bc
HORSFALL, Charles		20	M	Servant	120c02Bc
ROBINSON, William		20	M	Dyer	120c02Bc
FOWLER, John		31	M	Tailor	120c02Bc
DEMSEY, John		48	M	Laborer	120c02Bc
Catherine		28	F	Servant	120c02Bc
Mary		24	F	Servant	120c02Bc
Hannah		22	F	Servant	120c02Bc
COHAL, Biddy		21	F	Servant	120c02Bc
TURNER, William		30	M	Trader	120c02Bc
MCLEANE, Alexander		18	M	Servant	120c02Bc
LONGHEAD, John		18	M	Laborer	120c02Bc
EWING, George		32	M	Laborer	120c02Bc
FERGUSON, John		36	M	Laborer	120c02Bc
BRASEL, Michael		25	M	Laborer	120c02Bc
TURNER, Charles		44	M	Laborer	120c02Bc
James		19	M	Laborer	120c02Bc
POLLOCK, William		36	M	Laborer	120c02Bc
Alexander		40	M	Laborer	120c02Bc
MCANANY, Sarah		21	F	Servant	120c02Bc
Mary		19	F	Servant	120c02Bc
MURTHAT, Ellen		19	F	Servant	120c02Bc
QUIRK, James		20	M	Laborer	120c02Bc
COLLINS, Pat		19	M	Laborer	120c02Bc
BAILEY, Sarah		32	F	None	120c02Bc
Francis	(S)	08	M	Child	120c02Bc
John	(S)	06	M	Child	120c02Bc
James	(S)	04	M	Child	120c02Bc
May-J.	(D)	.00	F	Infant	120c02Bc
Died-At-Sea					
TABB, Henry		22	M	Laborer	120c02Bc
WILLIAMS, Henry		36	M	Laborer	120c02Bc
IRWIN, Samuel		30	M	Laborer	120c02Bc
WILSON, Isabella		20	F	Servant	120c02Bc
SUTTON, Elizabeth		20	F	Servant	120c02Bc
HAMILTON, May-J.		18	F	Servant	120c02Bc
Died-At-Sea					
SMITH, Sarah		18	F	Servant	120c02Bc
EWING, Thomas		28	M	Laborer	120c02Bc

NAMES OF PASSENGERS		AGE	SEX	OCCUPATIONS	DATE PORT SHIP
EWING, Eliza		20	F	None	120c02Bc
CAVERTY, Paul		27	M	Laborer	120c02Bc
DIMSEY, Francis		35	M	Laborer	120c02Bc
CANNON, Ann		20	F	Servant	120c02Bc
ODONNELL, Catherine		21	F	Servant	120c02Bc
Ann		18	F	Servant	120c02Bc
MULHALLAN, Michael		30	M	Weaver	120c02Bc
Mary	(W)	30	F	Wife	120c02Bc
John	(S)	03	M	Child	120c02Bc
SMITH, Elizabeth		20	F	Servant	120c02Bc
LUNAN, Margaret		18	F	Servant	120c02Bc
MCCALLIN, Margaret		28	F	Servant	120c02Bc
Edward	(S)	05	M	Child	120c02Bc
CONOLY, Edmond		40	M	Laborer	120c02Bc
CONNELL, John		25	M	Laborer	120c02Bc
MEEHAN, Michael		30	M	Laborer	120c02Bc
KILLEEN, Martin		32	M	Tailor	120c02Bc
Bridget	(W)	25	F	Wife	120c02Bc
Pat	(S)	02	M	Child	120c02Bc
John	(S)	.00	M	Infant	120c02Bc
JONES, William		20	M	Tailor	120c02Bc
BLUNT, Thomas		20	M	Servant	120c02Bc
NAVITT, James		20	M	Servant	120c02Bc
Thomas		18	M	Servant	120c02Bc
ONEAL, Dennis		21	M	Weaver	120c02Bc
Jane		18	F	None	120c02Bc
BRANIN, Thomas		40	M	Laborer	120c02Bc
FOORA, Hanora		18	F	Servant	120c02Bc
BURNS, Robert		21	M	Shoemaker	120c02Bc
MCCANN, Fenix		22	M	Laborer	120c02Bc
MCCABE, James		25	M	Laborer	120c02Bc
FINLEY, Joseph		20	M	Laborer	120c02Bc
THOMPSON, Jane		.00	F	Infant	120c02Bc
William	(P)	25	M	Weaver	120c02Bc
Sarah		23	F	None	120c02Bc
Margaret		02	F	Child	120c02Bc

ROSCIUS 12 OCTOBER 1846

From Liverpool

NAMES OF PASSENGERS		AGE	SEX	OCCUPATIONS	DATE PORT SHIP
HAMILTON, Thos.		27	M	Unknown	120c02Bf
MOONY, John		17	M	Unknown	120c02Bf
PHILIPS, Wm.		26	M	Unknown	120c02Bf
WHISTLER, Ana		40	F	Unknown	120c02Bf
GOLD, Mary		70	F	Unknown	120c02Bf
MILES, Eliza		20	F	Unknown	120c02Bf
SHADLEY, Marie		20	F	Unknown	120c02Bf
STANTON, Mary		40	F	Unknown	120c02Bf
Wm.	(H)	40	M	Unknown	120c02Bf
U		00	U	Child	120c02Bf
U		00	U	Child	120c02Bf
U		00	U	Child	120c02Bf
U		00	U	Child	120c02Bf
U		00	U	Child	120c02Bf
LOUGHELTY, Mary		20	F	Unknown	120c02Bf
LOCHLIN, Mary		20	F	Unknown	120c02Bf
PARRY, Wm.		26	M	Unknown	120c02Bf
Owen		22	M	Unknown	120c02Bf
Laura		50	F	Unknown	120c02Bf
Laura		20	F	Unknown	120c02Bf
KENNEY, John		30	M	Unknown	120c02Bf
DOUGHERTY, Jas.		28	M	Unknown	120c02Bf
TOWNSEND, Wm.		30	M	Unknown	120c02Bf
ELLIOT, Fred		26	M	Unknown	120c02Bf
OTOOL, M.		22	U	Unknown	120c02Bf
RICE, Thos.		30	M	Unknown	120c02Bf
MCNIEL, H.		40	U	Unknown	120c02Bf
RADWAY, Ewd.		24	M	Unknown	120c02Bf
TOWNSEND, John		30	M	Unknown	120c02Bf
LOCHLIN, Mary		18	F	Unknown	120c02Bf
MASSY, Mary		30	F	Unknown	120c02Bf
GRAY, Pat		24	M	Unknown	120c02Bf
CAVEN, Michl.		24	M	Unknown	120c02Bf
WENTWORTH, Pat.		30	M	Unknown	120c02Bf
MULHOLAND, Owen		25	M	Unknown	120c02Bf
WENTWORTH, Cathr.		18	F	Unknown	120c02Bf
MCGOWAN, Frank		17	M	Unknown	120c02Bf
HIGINS, Henery		30	M	Unknown	120c02Bf
TOMPSON, Wm.		45	M	Unknown	120c02Bf
DUNK, Thos.		00	M	Unknown	120c02Bf
U		00	U	Child	120c02Bf
Sarah		00	F	Unknown	120c02Bf
PASCOE, Wm.		54	M	Unknown	120c02Bf
Ana	(W)	56	F	Wife	120c02Bf
Ann	(D)	16	F	Unknown	120c02Bf
ADAMS, John		56	M	Unknown	120c02Bf
GAMBLE, John		35	M	Unknown	120c02Bf
MOON, Ann		35	F	Unknown	120c02Bf
ARINA, Eliza		18	F	Unknown	120c02Bf
CONEGAN, Kate		19	F	Unknown	120c02Bf
SPELLAND, Ann		18	F	Unknown	120c02Bf
FITZPATRICK, Mary		22	F	Unknown	120c02Bf
DOYLE, Thos.		32	M	Unknown	120c02Bf
GALLAGHER, Thos.		35	M	Unknown	120c02Bf
BRENNER, John		22	M	Unknown	120c02Bf
GALLAGHER, Kate		40	F	Unknown	120c02Bf
Bridget		30	F	Unknown	120c02Bf
ALTON, Thos.		40	M	Unknown	120c02Bf
DONARTY, Nathan		30	M	Unknown	120c02Bf
CARTY, John		20	M	Unknown	120c02Bf
CARDEN, Thos.		30	M	Unknown	120c02Bf
KEOUGH, Peter		40	M	Unknown	120c02Bf
CONWAY, Edward		40	M	Unknown	120c02Bf
REMERY, Kate		20	F	Unknown	120c02Bf
MULLHOLLAN, Mary		19	F	Unknown	120c02Bf
DELANEY, Kate		20	F	Unknown	120c02Bf
MULLHOLLEND, Math.		40	M	Unknown	120c02Bf
DOYLE, Kate		21	F	Unknown	120c02Bf
DELANEY, Mat		43	M	Unknown	120c02Bf
ROONEY, Jas.		23	M	Unknown	120c02Bf
BLAIR, David		50	M	Unknown	120c02Bf
COCHERN, A.		23	U	Unknown	120c02Bf
LEWIS, Saml.		16	M	Unknown	120c02Bf
TONPSON, John		30	M	Unknown	120c02Bf
MCNAUGHTON, Anne.		31	F	Unknown	120c02Bf
MCKNIGHT, Eliza		23	F	Unknown	120c02Bf
PENROSE, Jas.		24	M	Unknown	120c02Bf
TREBLECOCK, Mike		21	M	Unknown	120c02Bf
MOORE, Kate		18	F	Unknown	120c02Bf
KNOWLAND, Ellen		17	F	Unknown	120c02Bf
KENNEY, Ann		15	F	Unknown	120c02Bf
DONLAN, Jullet		19	F	Unknown	120c02Bf
ROUKE, Pat		39	M	Unknown	120c02Bf
GALLATER, Pat		40	M	Unknown	120c02Bf
LANGAN, Pat		40	M	Unknown	120c02Bf
CARLIN, Grace		17	F	Laborer	120c02Bf
DEVENEY, Ann		35	F	Laborer	120c02Bf
MARINA, Mary		19	F	Laborer	120c02Bf
MCGUIRE, Pat		18	M	Laborer	120c02Bf
LILLEY, Jas.		15	M	Laborer	120c02Bf
COSGUFF, John		22	M	Laborer	120c02Bf
WARD, Jas.		23	M	Laborer	120c02Bf
GOLDEN, Thos.		40	M	Laborer	120c02Bf
May	(W)	40	F	Wife	120c02Bf
U		00	U	Child	120c02Bf
U		00	U	Child	120c02Bf
U		00	U	Child	120c02Bf
U		00	U	Child	120c02Bf
U		00	U	Child	120c02Bf
LOCHIN, Ann		18	F	Laborer	120c02Bf
POWER, Jullet		18	F	Laborer	120c02Bf
ROGERS, Chas.		30	M	Laborer	120c02Bf
NOCTON, Mike		35	M	Laborer	120c02Bf

NAMES OF PASSENGERS		AGE	SEX	OCCUPATIONS	DATE PORT SHIP
MARINA, Bridget		19	F	Laborer	120c02Bf
KENWORTHY, Thos.		59	M	Laborer	120c02Bf
Ann	(W)	59	F	Wife	120c02Bf
Mary	(D)	16	F	Laborer	120c02Bf
BENAN, Ann		31	F	Laborer	120c02Bf
DEREN, Wm.		52	M	Laborer	120c02Bf
WEBB, John		24	M	Laborer	120c02Bf
GRANGER, Bridget		15	F	Laborer	120c02Bf
Ellen		13	F	Laborer	120c02Bf
FOGER, Chas.		19	M	Laborer	120c02Bf
THOMAS, J.		50	U	Laborer	120c02Bf
NEWCOMB, Wm.		38	M	Laborer	120c02Bf
BROWN, Hugh		34	M	Laborer	120c02Bf
Francis		26	M	Laborer	120c02Bf
CAVANNAH, Jas.		27	M	Laborer	120c02Bf
SHIELS, John		30	M	Laborer	120c02Bf
Jas.		28	M	Laborer	120c02Bf
WILLKINSON, Wm.		27	M	Laborer	120c02Bf
ANDERSEN, Robt.		22	M	Laborer	120c02Bf
FAYLER, John		34	M	Laborer	120c02Bf
GASHIER, Wm.		25	M	Laborer	120c02Bf
NIEL, Thos.		40	M	Laborer	120c02Bf
HUGHES, Mary		28	F	Laborer	120c02Bf
WALLEY, Jane		24	F	Laborer	120c02Bf
HUGHES, Ellen		26	F	Laborer	120c02Bf
GREENWORTH, Wm.		31	M	Laborer	120c02Bf
Sara	(W)	32	F	Wife	120c02Bf
John	(S)	10	M	Child	120c02Bf
CALLAGAH, Kate		33	F	Unknown	120c02Bf
Francis		38	M	Unknown	120c02Bf
WEBB, Mary		26	F	Unknown	120c02Bf
WILLSON, Martha		27	F	Unknown	120c02Bf
Wm.		28	M	Unknown	120c02Bf
HOSKINS, Nathl.		23	M	Laborer	120c02Bf
GILCHRIST, John		24	M	Laborer	120c02Bf
HOWER, John		26	M	Laborer	120c02Bf
SPILLEN, Ellen		60	F	Laborer	120c02Bf
HECHEN, Ellen		13	F	Laborer	120c02Bf
LILLEY, Mag		20	F	Laborer	120c02Bf
Bridget		21	F	Laborer	120c02Bf
BENSTEET, Jas.		30	M	Laborer	120c02Bf
Rebecca		28	F	Laborer	120c02Bf
Ewd.		28	M	Laborer	120c02Bf
CEAMES, Anthy		45	M	Laborer	120c02Bf
Kate		25	F	Laborer	120c02Bf
Bryan		30	M	Laborer	120c02Bf
Pat		20	M	Laborer	120c02Bf
GLYNN, Kate		30	F	Laborer	120c02Bf
LAURENCE, Mary		32	F	Laborer	120c02Bf
BANKS, Jas.		32	M	Laborer	120c02Bf
Ellen		59	F	Laborer	120c02Bf
Eliza		22	F	Laborer	120c02Bf
Ellen		12	F	Laborer	120c02Bf
GUNN, Jas.		32	M	Laborer	120c02Bf
Frances		28	F	Laborer	120c02Bf
ORILEY, Kate		27	F	Laborer	120c02Bf
KENEDEY, Mag		15	F	Laborer	120c02Bf
SUGGARA, Susan		73	F	Laborer	120c02Bf
CALVERT, Mary		24	F	Laborer	120c02Bf
MCGUIRE, B.		18	U	Laborer	120c02Bf
Henery		35	M	Laborer	120c02Bf
Mary		30	F	Laborer	120c02Bf
MOON, Barney		25	M	Laborer	120c02Bf
MCDONOUGH, Bill		31	M	Laborer	120c02Bf
MOONEY, Thos.		26	M	Laborer	120c02Bf
RAFFERTY, Ewd.		29	M	Laborer	120c02Bf
PARRY, Seaney		29	M	Laborer	120c02Bf
Sara		28	F	Laborer	120c02Bf
Henery		17	M	Laborer	120c02Bf
Francis		13	M	Laborer	120c02Bf
John		06	M	Child	120c02Bf
CALLAHAN, Jas.		17	M	Unknown	120c02Bf
Robt.		10	M	Child	120c02Bf
Mary		06	F	Child	120c02Bf
Kate		02	F	Child	120c02Bf
CALLAHAN, Sarah		.00	F	Infant	120c02Bf
KELLY, Margt.		18	F	Unknown	120c02Bf
Wm.		25	M	Unknown	120c02Bf
Allen		50	M	Unknown	120c02Bf
DELANY, Mary		15	F	Unknown	120c02Bf
KELLY, Pat		18	M	Unknown	120c02Bf
GRANIS, Elizabeth		60	F	Unknown	120c02Bf
RICHARDSON, Ann		30	F	Unknown	120c02Bf
Jas.	(S)	06	M	Child	120c02Bf
GREENFISH, Jas.		19	M	Unknown	120c02Bf
CLARK, Mary		50	F	Unknown	120c02Bf
GREELY, Bridget		16	F	Unknown	120c02Bf
Ann		14	F	Unknown	120c02Bf
MURRY, Asa		18	M	Unknown	120c02Bf
CAROL, Thos.		25	M	Unknown	120c02Bf
CARROL, Cathrn.		23	F	Unknown	120c02Bf
Bridget		25	F	Unknown	120c02Bf
SWANSON, Robt.		26	M	Unknown	120c02Bf
Wm.		23	M	Unknown	120c02Bf
BOWTON, Bridget		20	F	Unknown	120c02Bf
SWEENY, Mary		24	F	Unknown	120c02Bf
BAKER, Mary		18	F	Unknown	120c02Bf
STEANEY, Mary		03	F	Child	120c02Bf
TOBIN, Wm.		32	M	Unknown	120c02Bf
Jane	(W)	27	F	Wife	120c02Bf
Joseph	(S)	06	M	Child	120c02Bf
Thos.	(S)	04	M	Child	120c02Bf
SCHAIN, Danl.		30	M	Unknown	120c02Bf
OCHASE, Jerry		40	M	Unknown	120c02Bf
MURPHY, Jas.		30	M	Unknown	120c02Bf
RILEY, Grace		23	F	Unknown	120c02Bf
Ann		21	F	Unknown	120c02Bf
RILROY, Mary		16	F	Unknown	120c02Bf
RILEY, Denis		30	M	Unknown	120c02Bf
Margt.	(W)	25	F	Wife	120c02Bf
Mary	(D)	06	F	Child	120c02Bf
Pat	(S)	04	M	Child	120c02Bf
Thos.	(S)	03	M	Child	120c02Bf
BARK, Jerry		37	M	Unknown	120c02Bf
Susan	(W)	27	F	Wife	120c02Bf
Mary	(D)	09	F	Child	120c02Bf
Susan	(D)	07	F	Child	120c02Bf
Doreathea	(D)	03	F	Child	120c02Bf
CONLY, Michl.		24	M	Unknown	120c02Bf
RILEY, Jas.		17	M	Unknown	120c02Bf
FLYNN, Henery		19	M	Unknown	120c02Bf
MCDONALD, Stephen		07	M	Child	120c02Bf
KELLY, Michael		26	M	Unknown	120c02Bf
Margt.	(D)	01	F	Child	120c02Bf
FINNAGAN, Ann		30	F	Unknown	120c02Bf
KELLY, Kate		18	F	Unknown	120c02Bf
CLARK, Ann		16	F	Unknown	120c02Bf
CAKINS, Ann		23	F	Unknown	120c02Bf
HARLEY, Cathn.		34	F	Unknown	120c02Bf
Mary	(D)	07	F	Child	120c02Bf
Jas.	(S)	04	M	Child	120c02Bf
LOGAN, Eliza		15	F	Unknown	120c02Bf
MISHELLY, Jas.		50	M	Unknown	120c02Bf
CREDEN, Pat		21	M	Unknown	120c02Bf
DONOVAN, Danl.		27	M	Unknown	120c02Bf
RAFFERTY, Wm.		22	M	Unknown	120c02Bf
Bridget		18	F	Unknown	120c02Bf
CAVING, Pat		19	M	Unknown	120c02Bf
DOWD, Pat		23	M	Unknown	120c02Bf
WELLS, Anthony		25	M	Unknown	120c02Bf
DONOHUGH, Mary		18	F	Unknown	120c02Bf
RAFFERTY, Sara		18	F	Unknown	120c02Bf
MCGOWAN, Ann		20	F	Unknown	120c02Bf
GAFFERY, Bridget		26	F	Unknown	120c02Bf
Ann	(D)	05	F	Child	120c02Bf
Martha	(D)	07	F	Child	120c02Bf
John	(S)	04	M	Child	120c02Bf
BRENAN, Bryan		44	M	Unknown	120c02Bf
Ann	(W)	36	F	Wife	120c02Bf
Mary	(D)	14	F	Unknown	120c02Bf

NAMES OF PASSENGERS		AGE	SEX	OCCUPATIONS	DATE PORT SHIP
BRENAN, Michael	(S)	12	M	Unknown	120c02Bf
John	(S)	10	M	Unknown	120c02Bf
Margaret	(D)	07	F	Child	120c02Bf
Ann	(D)	05	F	Child	120c02Bf
Bridget	(D)	03	F	Child	120c02Bf
Mary	(D)	01	F	Child	120c02Bf
LYNCH, Bridget		20	F	Unknown	120c02Bf
FUNE, Eliza		24	F	Unknown	120c02Bf
Margaret	(D)	04	F	Child	120c02Bf
Pat	(S)	02	M	Child	120c02Bf
VIRTUE, Mary		25	F	Unknown	120c02Bf
QUENTIN, Mary		54	F	Unknown	120c02Bf
MCGREECH, Michl.		23	M	Unknown	120c02Bf
DUNWORTH, John		13	M	Unknown	120c02Bf
KELLY, Cornelius		23	M	Unknown	120c02Bf
Nora		17	F	Unknown	120c02Bf
DEVINE, Michael		23	M	Unknown	120c02Bf
AUSTIN, A.		50	U	Unknown	120c02Bf
Mary		45	F	Unknown	120c02Bf
COSTEGAN, Ann		50	F	Unknown	120c02Bf
Pat		19	M	Unknown	120c02Bf
SPENCER, Bridget		14	F	Unknown	120c02Bf
MADDEN, Peter		50	M	Unknown	120c02Bf
HANAY, Cathrn.		60	F	Unknown	120c02Bf
Cathrn.		22	F	Unknown	120c02Bf
Thos.		07	M	Child	120c02Bf
DOYLE, Andrew		30	M	Unknown	120c02Bf
LEONARD, David		27	M	Unknown	120c02Bf
POWER, Jas.		25	M	Unknown	120c02Bf
FINCH, Elizabeth		23	F	Unknown	120c02Bf
Alice	(D)	03	F	Child	120c02Bf
Mary	(D)	01	F	Child	120c02Bf
CARDEGAN, Bridget		15	F	Laborer	120c02Bf
SMITH, Mary		18	F	Laborer	120c02Bf
COLLINS, Alice		20	F	Laborer	120c02Bf
WELKS, Jane		40	F	Laborer	120c02Bf
Susan	(D)	10	F	Child	120c02Bf
John	(S)	08	M	Child	120c02Bf
William	(S)	06	M	Child	120c02Bf
Cathrn.	(D)	04	F	Child	120c02Bf
NIXON, Jane		20	F	Laborer	120c02Bf
RENTE, Ann		22	F	Laborer	120c02Bf
Thos.		25	M	Laborer	120c02Bf
NIEL, Ellen		20	F	Laborer	120c02Bf
FLONE, Ann		21	F	Laborer	120c02Bf
CARNIE, Pat		30	M	Laborer	120c02Bf
Mary	(W)	28	F	Wife	120c02Bf
Walter	(S)	08	M	Child	120c02Bf
John	(S)	06	M	Child	120c02Bf
Pat	(S)	03	M	Child	120c02Bf
Tom	(S)	01	M	Child	120c02Bf
QUINN, Brian		24	M	Laborer	120c02Bf
John		18	M	Laborer	120c02Bf
HUGH, Francis		20	M	Laborer	120c02Bf
HART, Mary		22	F	Laborer	120c02Bf
Jane		20	F	Laborer	120c02Bf
CURRIN, Jas.		37	M	Laborer	120c02Bf
Thos.	(S)	13	M	Laborer	120c02Bf
Ann	(D)	11	F	Laborer	120c02Bf
Mary	(D)	07	F	Child	120c02Bf
James	(S)	03	M	Child	120c02Bf
John	(S)	01	M	Child	120c02Bf
GILMORE, Mary		20	F	Laborer	120c02Bf
BODKIN, Mag		25	F	Laborer	120c02Bf
BUSH, Mary		22	F	Laborer	120c02Bf
GILMORE, John		02	M	Child	120c02Bf
Mary		01	F	Child	120c02Bf
John		22	M	Laborer	120c02Bf
CAVANNA, Pat		24	M	Laborer	120c02Bf
DRUMOND, James		23	M	Laborer	120c02Bf
Margt.		24	F	Laborer	120c02Bf
MCGUIRE, Julia		19	F	Laborer	120c02Bf
CORNWALL, Jas.		26	M	Laborer	120c02Bf
Edw.		23	M	Laborer	120c02Bf
BOYLE, Pat		18	M	Laborer	120c02Bf
GIRAFTY, Owen		30	M	Laborer	120c02Bf
MANUN, Timothy		30	M	Laborer	120c02Bf
GLANNIN, Jas.		20	M	Laborer	120c02Bf
GALLAGHER, John		21	M	Laborer	120c02Bf
MCCLUE, Mary		28	F	Laborer	120c02Bf
MUTHALL, Jas.		40	M	Laborer	120c02Bf
BRENNAN, Ewd.		26	M	Laborer	120c02Bf
DOYLE, Bryan		25	M	Laborer	120c02Bf
HART, John		24	M	Laborer	120c02Bf
MURPHY, Mary		25	F	Laborer	120c02Bf
GORMER, Mary		19	F	Laborer	120c02Bf
KELLY, Winifred		28	F	Laborer	120c02Bf
DELANY, Ann		25	F	Laborer	120c02Bf
CONNER, Margt.		17	F	Laborer	120c02Bf
SHIELDS, Ellen		18	F	Laborer	120c02Bf
OHIEM, Mag		15	F	Laborer	120c02Bf
CONDIEL, Julia		17	F	Laborer	120c02Bf
BURN, Margaret		20	F	Laborer	120c02Bf
RYAN, Bridget		35	F	Laborer	120c02Bf
Cathr.		20	F	Laborer	120c02Bf
Sara		19	F	Laborer	120c02Bf
MCCONE, Pat		47	M	Laborer	120c02Bf
CONWAY, John		23	M	Laborer	120c02Bf
GREEN, Jas.		26	M	Laborer	120c02Bf
HAUGH, Jas.		18	M	Laborer	120c02Bf
GREEN, John		28	M	Laborer	120c02Bf
CONNER, Cathr.		40	F	Laborer	120c02Bf
LONG, Magt.		26	F	Laborer	120c02Bf
DOYLE, Cathr.		18	F	Laborer	120c02Bf
MANGAN, L.		08	U	Child	120c02Bf
Jas.		06	M	Child	120c02Bf
GLENMORE, Bridget		30	F	Laborer	120c02Bf
John		16	M	Laborer	120c02Bf
Michl.		04	M	Child	120c02Bf
John		01	M	Child	120c02Bf
SULIVAN, Mathew		27	M	Laborer	120c02Bf
Mary	(W)	23	F	Wife	120c02Bf
Margaret	(D)	03	F	Child	120c02Bf
DONATHY, Mary		23	F	Laborer	120c02Bf
BLACK, Thos.B.		00	M	Unknown	120c02Bf

LUCONIA 13 OCTOBER 1846

From Liverpool

NAMES OF PASSENGERS		AGE	SEX	OCCUPATIONS	DATE PORT SHIP
PATTIGAN, Harriet		18	F	Servant	130c02lt
SHERRED, Robert		23	M	Farmer	130c02lt
GALLAGHER, Alexr.		25	M	Laborer	130c02lt
Margaret	(W)	25	F	Wife	130c02lt
CLARK, Jane		42	F	Servant	130c02lt
JUDGE, Wm.		50	M	Servant	130c02lt
Matty	(D)	13	F	None	130c02lt
BRADY, Edward		40	M	Laborer	130c02lt
CARROLL, James		24	M	Carpenter	130c02lt
CARR, Catherine		50	F	Servant	130c02lt
Eliza	(D)	19	F	Servant	130c02lt
FOYLE, Margret		20	F	Servant	130c02lt
COLLAGHAN, Eliza		28	F	Servant	130c02lt
Catherine		30	F	Servant	130c02lt
GRAHAM, Pat		22	M	Shoemaker	130c02lt
DIVER, Wm.		24	M	Student	130c02lt
BLAKE, Geo.		22	M	Shoemaker	130c02lt
FEGAN, Dan		60	M	Laborer	130c02lt
Biddy	(W)	55	F	Wife	130c02lt
Allice	(D)	20	F	None	130c02lt
Anne	(D)	16	F	None	130c02lt
Agnus	(D)	13	F	None	130c02lt
DUFFY, Pat		09	M	Child	130c02lt

NAMES OF PASSENGERS	A G E	S E X	OCCUPATIONS	DATE PORT SHIP
DOLPHIN 13 OCTOBER 1846				
From St.JOHNS,N.B.				
RAMSAY, Jane	18	F	None	130c79Iz
Margaret	28	F	None	130c79Iz
Nancy	25	F	None	130c79Iz
BURLINGTON 14 OCTOBER 1846				
From Liverpool				
SIMPSON, Thomas	33	M	Laborer	140c02Ja
Sally (W)	30	F	Wife	140c02Ja
Thomas (S)	02	M	Child	140c02Ja
Margt. (D)	.00	F	Infant	140c02Ja
CONBORY, Anty.	20	M	Laborer	140c02Ja
Mary	20	F	None	140c02Ja
RYAN, William	28	M	Laborer	140c02Ja
DEVINE, Ned	25	M	Laborer	140c02Ja
CONROY, Dennis	20	M	Laborer	140c02Ja
KELLY, Judy	20	F	None	140c02Ja
FALLON, Ellen	20	F	None	140c02Ja
DONNELL, James	30	M	Laborer	140c02Ja
SPENCE, Ann	25	F	None	140c02Ja
Mary	40	F	None	140c02Ja
Jane	23	F	None	140c02Ja
DONNELLY, Mary	24	F	Unknown	140c02Ja
Ellen	12	F	None	140c02Ja
SPENCE, Margt.	04	F	Child	140c02Ja
Vernon	.00	M	Infant	140c02Ja
DONNELLY, Jas.	22	M	Laborer	140c02Ja
MCDONNELL, Jas.	20	M	Laborer	140c02Ja
REILLY, Mary	20	F	None	140c02Ja
CAVEY, Ann	25	F	None	140c02Ja
APPLEBY, U-Mrs.	40	F	None	140c02Ja
KEYS, Henry	20	M	Laborer	140c02Ja
BROOKS, Thos.	20	M	Laborer	140c02Ja
FLYN, Alice	20	F	None	140c02Ja
GLYN, P.	20	M	Laborer	140c02Ja
FADORS, Jas.	25	M	Laborer	140c02Ja
ANDREWS, Maria	30	F	None	140c02Ja
MCLEAN, Ann	60	F	None	140c02Ja
MCWEENEY, Ann	17	F	None	140c02Ja
FARRELL, Cath.	20	F	None	140c02Ja
GANNON, Mary	21	F	None	140c02Ja
INGLEBY, Bridg.	18	F	None	140c02Ja
MCGUIRE, Cathe.	17	F	None	140c02Ja
SPARROW, Michl.	23	M	Laborer	140c02Ja
BROWN, Eliza	30	F	None	140c02Ja
David (S)	08	M	Child	140c02Ja
Mary (D)	04	F	Child	140c02Ja
Eliza (D)	.00	F	Infant	140c02Ja
Sarah	21	F	None	140c02Ja
RILEY, Margt.	20	F	None	140c02Ja
Jane	18	F	None	140c02Ja
AIKEN, Jas.	45	M	Laborer	140c02Ja
Sarah (W)	42	F	Wife	140c02Ja
Jas. (S)	13	M	Laborer	140c02Ja
John (S)	11	M	Laborer	140c02Ja
Henry (S)	06	M	Child	140c02Ja
Saml. (S)	03	M	Child	140c02Ja
Margt. (D)	.00	F	Infant	140c02Ja
LARKIN, Ann	20	F	None	140c02Ja
LYNCH, Michael	16	M	None	140c02Ja
HALPIN, Ann	20	F	None	140c02Ja
DOHERTY, Patk.	21	M	Laborer	140c02Ja
NASH, Winifred	18	F	None	140c02Ja
Ann	11	F	None	140c02Ja
WATT, Mary	36	F	None	140c02Ja
Eliza	24	F	None	140c02Ja
MEITHLYN, Margt.	40	F	None	140c02Ja
HAMPSON, Sarah	35	F	None	140c02Ja
Eliza (D)	15	F	None	140c02Ja
Mary (D)	13	F	None	140c02Ja
Ann (D)	11	F	None	140c02Ja
Jane (D)	09	F	Child	140c02Ja
Sarah (D)	06	F	Child	140c02Ja
Charles (S)	.00	M	Infant	140c02Ja
HOLMES, Michl.	30	M	Laborer	140c02Ja
Jane (W)	30	F	Wife	140c02Ja
Edward (S)	03	M	Child	140c02Ja
Michael (S)	.00	M	Infant	140c02Ja
THOMPSON, Eliza	35	F	None	140c02Ja
James (S)	12	M	None	140c02Ja
Eliza (D)	09	F	Child	140c02Ja
William (S)	06	M	Child	140c02Ja
MCQUEENEY, Ellen	18	F	None	140c02Ja
BRANNON, Mary	22	F	None	140c02Ja
KEAN, Martin	25	M	Laborer	140c02Ja
HEWETT, Thomas	34	M	Laborer	140c02Ja
REYNOLDS, Robert	23	M	Laborer	140c02Ja
MCGANNERTY, Ellen	23	F	None	140c02Ja
KELLY, John	20	M	Laborer	140c02Ja
Nancy	19	F	None	140c02Ja
DEVLIN, Peter	23	M	Laborer	140c02Ja
Sally	18	F	None	140c02Ja
RAINEY, Mary	20	F	None	140c02Ja
Saml.	13	M	None	140c02Ja
MAHANY, Rose	30	F	None	140c02Ja
MCGILL, Wm.	19	M	None	140c02Ja
BROWN, Saml.	18	M	None	140c02Ja
WOODS, Robert	19	M	None	140c02Ja
KINEAR, Wm.	14	M	None	140c02Ja
JANNEY, Bernd.	13	M	None	140c02Ja
CROW, Wm.	30	M	None	140c02Ja
ONEILL, Maria	27	F	None	140c02Ja
Eliza (D)	03	F	Child	140c02Ja
GILLESPIE, Matilda	50	F	None	140c02Ja
DONNELLY, Jane	17	F	None	140c02Ja
Arthur	15	M	None	140c02Ja
WALKER, Chas.	28	M	Laborer	140c02Ja
MCILEAN, Ellen	18	F	None	140c02Ja
QUILLAN, Timothy	23	M	Laborer	140c02Ja
GILLESPIE, Nancy	30	F	None	140c02Ja
RUSSELL, Andr.	18	M	None	140c02Ja
SWEENEY, Dennis	20	M	Laborer	140c02Ja
QUILLAN, Mary	50	F	None	140c02Ja
HOFFMAN, Mary	09	F	Child	140c02Ja
DALTON, Michael	20	M	Laborer	140c02Ja
SHEPPARD, Richd.	22	M	Laborer	140c02Ja
ROBINSON, James	27	M	Laborer	140c02Ja
ELLIOTT, William	20	M	Laborer	140c02Ja
MEEAN, Judith	19	F	None	140c02Ja
GILLY, U	25	M	Laborer	140c02Ja
BUNTING, U-Mrs.	24	F	None	140c02Ja
MCHUGH, Mary	17	F	None	140c02Ja
SHINE, John	26	M	Laborer	140c02Ja
Ellen	22	F	None	140c02Ja
SAMPSON, Jas.	24	M	Laborer	140c02Ja
HARDING, U	45	M	Laborer	140c02Ja
U (W)	26	F	Wife	140c02Ja
KELLY, U-Mrs.	35	F	Wife	140c02Ja
ROBINSON, Isabela	25	F	None	140c02Ja
DIRKSON, Daniel	44	M	Laborer	140c02Ja
Joseph (S)	20	M	Laborer	140c02Ja
Bridget (D)	16	F	None	140c02Ja
Daniel (S)	13	M	None	140c02Ja

NAMES OF PASSENGERS		A G E	S E X	OCCUPATIONS	DATE PORT SHIP
DIRKSON, Ann	(D)	10	F	None	140c02Ja
STEVENSON, Jas.		24	M	Laborer	140c02Ja
U	(W)	22	F	Wife	140c02Ja
CROOKS, Geo.		24	M	Laborer	140c02Ja
CRAVEN, Wm.		29	M	Laborer	140c02Ja
JACKSON, John		22	M	Laborer	140c02Ja
DAGGAN, Margt.		21	F	None	140c02Ja
Abby		21	F	None	140c02Ja
John		20	M	Laborer	140c02Ja
Mick		19	M	Laborer	140c02Ja
Jas.		17	M	Laborer	140c02Ja
LYNCH, Peter		19	M	Laborer	140c02Ja
COWAN, Thos.		20	M	Laborer	140c02Ja
LYONS, Morris		20	M	Laborer	140c02Ja
BURRETT, John		31	M	Laborer	140c02Ja
MARRS, Bridget		28	F	None	140c02Ja
GRIFFIN, Jno.		25	M	Laborer	140c02Ja
MCGOVERN, Anthony		19	M	Laborer	140c02Ja
HANOLL, Jno.		19	M	Laborer	140c02Ja
REGAN, Mick		21	M	Laborer	140c02Ja
JORDAN, Bridget		20	F	None	140c02Ja
Cicely		22	F	None	140c02Ja
HUGHES, Thos.		21	M	Laborer	140c02Ja
BOYD, John		29	M	Laborer	140c02Ja
HARGROVE, David		23	M	Laborer	140c02Ja
Eliza		20	F	None	140c02Ja
Margt.		21	F	None	140c02Ja
KELLY, Rody		40	M	Laborer	140c02Ja
Hannah		70	F	None	140c02Ja
Mary		28	F	None	140c02Ja
NOLAN, John		15	M	None	140c02Ja
U-Mrs.		35	F	None	140c02Ja
STEVENSON, Jno.		40	M	Laborer	140c02Ja
Mary	(D)	14	F	None	140c02Ja
Margt.	(D)	11	F	None	140c02Ja
John	(S)	08	M	Child	140c02Ja
Brigt.	(D)	06	F	Child	140c02Ja
ROCHE, Ann		22	F	None	140c02Ja
MCGUN, Patrick		35	M	Laborer	140c02Ja
BYRNE, Patk.		15	M	None	140c02Ja
U-Mrs.		28	F	None	140c02Ja
RING, Eliza		35	F	None	140c02Ja
LAWLER, Ann		20	F	None	140c02Ja
COLLINS, Jas.		20	M	Laborer	140c02Ja
Mary	(W)	26	F	Wife	140c02Ja
Bessy	(D)	.00	F	Infant	140c02Ja
TOWRY, Thos.		36	M	Laborer	140c02Ja
WEREXEN, John		36	M	Laborer	140c02Ja
BURKE, Patt		65	M	Laborer	140c02Ja
DALY, Thos.		40	M	Laborer	140c02Ja
BOURKE, Wm.		23	M	Laborer	140c02Ja
Jas.		16	M	None	140c02Ja
John		12	M	None	140c02Ja
Wm.		09	M	Child	140c02Ja
Danl.		07	M	Child	140c02Ja
Mick		05	M	Child	140c02Ja
Thos.		.00	M	Infant	140c02Ja
BURKE, Ellen		60	F	None	140c02Ja
Ellen		35	F	None	140c02Ja
ROACH, Ellen		40	F	None	140c02Ja
Michl.	(S)	11	M	None	140c02Ja
Johanna	(D)	09	F	Child	140c02Ja
Mary	(D)	07	F	Child	140c02Ja
DUGGAN, Catharine		40	F	None	140c02Ja
Jeremiah	(S)	14	M	None	140c02Ja
GYLNN, Patrick		20	M	Laborer	140c02Ja
DUNN, Charles		24	M	Laborer	140c02Ja
RUSSELL, U		00	M	None	140c02Ja
U	(W)	00	F	Wife	140c02Ja
LAWSON, U		00	M	None	140c02Ja
BELL, U		00	M	None	140c02Ja

VERMONT 19 OCTOBER 1846

From Glasgow

NAMES OF PASSENGERS		A G E	S E X	OCCUPATIONS	DATE PORT SHIP
MORTON, Charles		20	M	Draper	190c04Jc
CONTS, Wm.		20	M	Farmer	190c04Jc
FULLERTON, Peter		26	M	Farmer	190c04Jc
Agnes		24	F	None	190c04Jc
CREE, Rober-T.		28	M	Clerk	190c04Jc
TYFE, David		30	M	Farmer	190c04Jc
MCKENZIE, Alex		17	M	Mechanic	190c04Jc
MINN, Ellen		30	F	Tailor	190c04Jc
FOSTER, Margt.		17	F	Servant	190c04Jc
WARDREP, John		27	M	Farmer	190c04Jc
Margret		18	F	Farmer	190c04Jc
MATN, James		40	M	Weaver	190c04Jc
Robert	(S)	12	M	Spinner	190c04Jc
Agnes	(D)	17	F	Spinner	190c04Jc
LAFFERTY, James		35	M	Weaver	190c04Jc
BURN, Margret		22	F	Isb	190c04Jc
MCKECHN, Mey		18	F	Bookbinder	190c04Jc
ROBB, Alex		16	M	Frngmr	190c04Jc
STEWAT, Wm.		25	M	Baker	190c04Jc
MENZIES, Mary		25	F	Tailor	190c04Jc
SIM, Hugh		27	M	Ptmkr	190c04Jc
BOAG, Peter		40	M	Servant	190c04Jc
Mary		20	F	Tenter	190c04Jc
LEATH, Thomas		21	M	Weaver	190c04Jc
FITZGERALD, John		30	M	Servant	190c04Jc
Ann		26	F	None	190c04Jc
HORN, Archibald		30	M	Baker	190c04Jc
RUSSEL, David		31	M	Tailor	190c04Jc
Rohn		23	M	Tailor	190c04Jc
Margret		02	F	Child	190c04Jc
MARTIN, Thomas		12	M	Saddler	190c04Jc
CROWN, Robert		24	M	None	190c04Jc
ROAY, Peter-Jr.		09	M	Child	190c04Jc

ELEUTHERIA 23 OCTOBER 1846

From Tralee

NAMES OF PASSENGERS		A G E	S E X	OCCUPATIONS	DATE PORT SHIP
MURPHY, John		22	M	Laborer	230c53Jd
U	(W)	20	F	Wife	230c53Jd
FLYNN, Patrick		30	M	Laborer	230c53Jd
U	(W)	26	F	Wife	230c53Jd

ASHBURTON 27 OCTOBER 1846

From Liverpool

NAMES OF PASSENGERS	A G E	S E X	OCCUPATIONS	DATE PORT SHIP
DASTON, William	27	M	Baker	270c02Bd
Ann-Jane	26	F	None	270c02Bd
DONNELLY, Jane	22	F	Servant	270c02Bd
HAMILTON, Matilda	19	F	Servant	270c02Bd
OCALLAGHAN, James	26	M	Laborer	270c02Bd
GRAVES, Owen	22	M	Doctor	270c02Bd

NAMES OF PASSENGERS		AGE	SEX	OCCUPATIONS	DATE PORT SHIP
GRAVES, Bridget		20	F	None	270c02Bd
Eliza		12	F	None	270c02Bd
Thomas		08	M	Child	270c02Bd
Francis		07	M	Child	270c02Bd
ODONOVAN, David		28	M	Clerk	270c02Bd
FLINN, James		09	M	Child	270c02Bd
MCCAULEY, James		36	M	Printer	270c02Bd
Cathe.	(W)	32	F	Wife	270c02Bd
Emily	(D)	13	F	None	270c02Bd
Julia	(D)	10	F	None	270c02Bd
William	(S)	08	M	Child	270c02Bd
Stephen	(S)	05	M	Child	270c02Bd
GILLIN, Ann		19	F	None	270c02Bd
HAILEY, Julia		22	F	None	270c02Bd
KELLAHAN, Hannah		14	F	None	270c02Bd
RYAN, Mary		30	F	None	270c02Bd
John	(S)	05	M	Child	270c02Bd
William	(S)	03	M	Child	270c02Bd
Died-At-Sea					
ROURKE, Judy		30	F	None	270c02Bd
FEGAN, Edward		24	M	Laborer	270c02Bd
PIERPOINT, James		19	M	Laborer	270c02Bd
MCCABE, John		16	M	Laborer	270c02Bd
CONNOLL, Edward		30	M	Laborer	270c02Bd
BUTLER, Peter		22	M	Laborer	270c02Bd
KINGSTON, Thomas		24	M	Farmer	270c02Bd
PRIOR, John		21	M	Cooper	270c02Bd
WARD, Thomas		21	M	Japanner	270c02Bd
DOLAN, Francis		22	M	Carpenter	270c02Bd
MURRAY, Thomas		20	M	Laborer	270c02Bd
LARKIN, Philip		26	M	Laborer	270c02Bd
MOORE, Alexr.		17	M	Laborer	270c02Bd
CLARKE, Patk.		30	M	Laborer	270c02Bd
Bridget		22	F	Laborer	270c02Bd
KINKAID, Geo.		35	M	Laborer	270c02Bd
MCINTYRE, Philip		20	M	Laborer	270c02Bd
DOYLE, Andrew		20	M	Shoemaker	270c02Bd
COOLEY, Thomas		38	M	Laborer	270c02Bd
RANDALS, William		22	M	Laborer	270c02Bd
FOX, Mathew		18	M	Laborer	270c02Bd
Rosey		20	F	None	270c02Bd
MCTAG, Patrick		20	M	Laborer	270c02Bd
MANNING, Patrick		21	M	Laborer	270c02Bd
MCCORMICK, Patrick		20	M	Laborer	270c02Bd
CARTER, James		20	M	Laborer	270c02Bd
MCGRATH, Michl.		20	M	Laborer	270c02Bd
FAULKNER, James		21	M	Laborer	270c02Bd
CONNOR, John		20	M	Tailor	270c02Bd
CARR, Peter		20	M	Saddler	270c02Bd
KINKAID, Alexr.		35	M	Farmer	270c02Bd
TIERNEY, Patrick		35	M	Tailor	270c02Bd
SMITH, Michl.		21	M	Laborer	270c02Bd
BLAKENY, John		20	M	Laborer	270c02Bd
MCGUINESS, Francis		21	M	Laborer	270c02Bd
FLOOD, Margt.		20	F	None	270c02Bd
CAMPBELL, Patrick		24	M	Laborer	270c02Bd
MURPHY, Michl.		21	M	Laborer	270c02Bd
MCQUINNEY, Wm.		20	M	Laborer	270c02Bd
Margt.		18	F	Laborer	270c02Bd
CONNOR, Bernard		24	M	Laborer	270c02Bd
JENNINGS, Patrick		19	M	Laborer	270c02Bd
STINGEN, Patrick		21	M	Laborer	270c02Bd
MURTOCH, John		24	M	Laborer	270c02Bd
HOGAN, Thomas		15	M	Laborer	270c02Bd
Mary		50	F	Laborer	270c02Bd
Donald		21	M	Laborer	270c02Bd
David		11	M	None	270c02Bd
MURPHY, Michl.		20	M	Laborer	270c02Bd
Ann	(W)	25	F	Wife	270c02Bd
Mary	(D)	01	F	Child	270c02Bd
BANNAN, Ann		20	F	None	270c02Bd
Hugh		23	M	Weaver	270c02Bd
BRADY, Ellen		18	F	Dressmaker	270c02Bd
CAREY, Eve		18	F	None	270c02Bd
Harriet		17	F	None	270c02Bd
HAYBURN, Archd.		27	M	Painter	270c02Bd
MCGUIRE, Thomas		22	M	Laborer	270c02Bd
Ann		20	F	None	270c02Bd
TRACEY, John		20	M	Laborer	270c02Bd
TURLEY, James		25	M	Laborer	270c02Bd
LEE, Michl.		15	M	Laborer	270c02Bd
Rose		12	F	None	270c02Bd
Margt.		15	F	None	270c02Bd
MALONE, Bridget		20	F	None	270c02Bd
BRADY, Mary		18	F	None	270c02Bd
BOHAN, Andrew		22	M	Physician	270c02Bd
KENNEY, Michl.		20	M	Physician	270c02Bd
RILEY, Philip		40	M	Laborer	270c02Bd
BEGLON, Bridget		16	F	None	270c02Bd
BURNS, Ann		18	F	None	270c02Bd
KENNON, Cornelius		20	M	Laborer	270c02Bd
Michl.		15	M	Laborer	270c02Bd
James		13	M	None	270c02Bd
MCCARTNEY, Mary		22	F	None	270c02Bd
CLARK, Alexr.		20	M	Weaver	270c02Bd
DRUM, Patrick		30	M	Laborer	270c02Bd
CAFFRAY, Lawrence		18	M	Hatter	270c02Bd
GAFFNEY, Ann		30	F	None	270c02Bd
RILEY, Bridget		16	F	None	270c02Bd
CULVIN, Rose		16	F	None	270c02Bd
RILEY, Bridget		15	F	None	270c02Bd
COUCHNEY, Ann		17	F	None	270c02Bd
RONNON, Mary		18	F	None	270c02Bd
CULREARY, Ann		18	F	Dressmaker	270c02Bd
DALEY, Mary		15	F	Dressmaker	270c02Bd
FITZPATRICK, Rose		19	F	Dressmaker	270c02Bd
DONOGHUE, Jane		19	F	Dressmaker	270c02Bd
DONNELLY, Ann		19	F	Dressmaker	270c02Bd
RILEY, Ellen		15	F	None	270c02Bd
MCGOVERN, Bessey		20	F	None	270c02Bd
MCCABE, Mary		20	F	None	270c02Bd
AIKENS, Francis		22	M	Laborer	270c02Bd
Mary		25	F	None	270c02Bd
CRAHAN, Peter		25	M	Laborer	270c02Bd
Kate		22	F	None	270c02Bd
DUNLUN, Thomas		30	M	Laborer	270c02Bd
Mary		26	F	None	270c02Bd
Elizh.		20	F	None	270c02Bd
HANLEY, Patrick		26	M	Laborer	270c02Bd
REARDON, Mathew		19	M	Laborer	270c02Bd
FOLEY, Bartw.		25	M	Laborer	270c02Bd
Julia		23	F	None	270c02Bd
MILEY, James		20	M	Tailor	270c02Bd
BARRETT, Thos.		30	M	Laborer	270c02Bd
Bridget		30	F	None	270c02Bd
DONNELLY, John		25	M	Laborer	270c02Bd
BARNETT, Geo.		20	M	Laborer	270c02Bd
Margt.		20	F	None	270c02Bd
FALLON, Richd.		28	M	Laborer	270c02Bd
Magt.	(W)	24	F	Wife	270c02Bd
Thomas	(S)	03	M	Child	270c02Bd
LOGAN, Frank		55	M	Laborer	270c02Bd
VICTORY, Michl.		20	M	Laborer	270c02Bd
BRENNON, Mary		20	F	None	270c02Bd
William		01	M	Child	270c02Bd
Murph		19	M	None	270c02Bd
Bridget		21	F	None	270c02Bd
John		05	M	Child	270c02Bd
Ellen		09	F	Child	270c02Bd
Catherine		04	F	Child	270c02Bd
LANGAN, Edwd.		16	M	Tailor	270c02Bd
Patrick		20	M	Laborer	270c02Bd
Betty		60	F	None	270c02Bd
MANHAN, Mary		40	F	None	270c02Bd
Cathe.		03	F	Child	270c02Bd
LEVAN, Margt.		24	F	None	270c02Bd
MAHON, Mary		14	F	None	270c02Bd
James		07	M	Child	270c02Bd
CRENNEN, Ellen		14	F	None	270c02Bd
CAMPBELL, Hugh		19	M	Laborer	270c02Bd

NAMES OF PASSENGERS		A G E	S E X	OCCUPATIONS	DATE PORT SHIP
CAMPBELL, Ann		12	F	None	270c02Bd
KELLY, Betty		16	F	None	270c02Bd
MCVEY, Sally		16	F	None	270c02Bd
MCALLY, Alice		30	F	Dressmaker	270c02Bd
HIGGINS, John		18	M	Laborer	270c02Bd
Patt		16	M	Shoemaker	270c02Bd
BRENNAN, Bridget		25	F	None	270c02Bd
BURKE, Michael		32	M	Laborer	270c02Bd
Ellen		20	F	None	270c02Bd
FLINN, Catherine		18	F	None	270c02Bd
KILLER, James		30	M	None	270c02Bd
Nabby	(W)	30	F	Wife	270c02Bd
Mary-Ann	(D)	03	F	Child	270c02Bd
John	(S)	02	M	Child	270c02Bd
FITZMORRIS, Thomas		30	M	Laborer	270c02Bd
Margt.	(W)	22	F	Wife	270c02Bd
Mary	(D)	04	F	Child	270c02Bd
KELLY, Peter		26	M	None	270c02Bd
DONNELLY, Winifred		17	F	None	270c02Bd
BURN, Patrick		21	M	None	270c02Bd
COUGHLIN, Ann		30	F	None	270c02Bd
Patrick	(S)	01	M	Child	270c02Bd
CADEN, Patrick		25	M	Laborer	270c02Bd
RILEY, Martin		22	M	Laborer	270c02Bd
MANNON, Patt		28	M	Gdnr	270c02Bd
CAHAN, Bridget		18	F	None	270c02Bd
CAHAL, Ann		18	F	None	270c02Bd
DUGGAN, Ann		18	F	None	270c02Bd
GOTTY, Ann		21	F	None	270c02Bd
HAGAN, Bridget		29	F	None	270c02Bd
Ann		19	F	None	270c02Bd
MCGUIRE, Thomas		18	M	Laborer	270c02Bd
POWER, Mary		25	F	None	270c02Bd
KEN, Margt.		12	F	None	270c02Bd
SHANLY, Maria		19	F	None	270c02Bd
OVERTON, Martha		22	F	None	270c02Bd
CASEY, Thomas		39	M	None	270c02Bd
SWEENEY, Hugh		35	M	Cooper	270c02Bd
Bridget		35	F	None	270c02Bd
Peggy		23	F	None	270c02Bd
CASEY, Mary		38	F	None	270c02Bd
Mary	(D)	18	F	None	270c02Bd
Ann	(D)	12	F	None	270c02Bd
Lawrence	(S)	09	M	Child	270c02Bd
GOUGH, Bridget		20	F	None	270c02Bd
CLINE, Mary		21	F	None	270c02Bd
BOLAN, Peggy		19	F	None	270c02Bd
DUNGAN, Cathe.		20	F	None	270c02Bd
MCKENNA, Mary		20	F	None	270c02Bd
COSTELLO, John		45	M	Laborer	270c02Bd
Mary		40	F	None	270c02Bd
MCQUIRK, Mary		20	F	None	270c02Bd
KING, Martin		35	M	Laborer	270c02Bd
Mary	(W)	30	F	Wife	270c02Bd
Mary	(D)	10	F	Child	270c02Bd
Oney	(D)	08	F	Child	270c02Bd
LUDDY, Ann		26	F	None	270c02Bd
MARCEY, Ellen		20	F	None	270c02Bd
READY, Ellen		20	F	None	270c02Bd
DUNNINGAN, Thos.		40	M	Laborer	270c02Bd
JOYCE, Ellen		24	F	None	270c02Bd
DOWD, Darby		40	M	Cooper	270c02Bd
CONDROY, Peter		40	M	Laborer	270c02Bd
MCBRIDE, Cathe.		30	F	None	270c02Bd
Patrick	(S)	01	M	Child	270c02Bd
SKELLY, Margt.		20	F	None	270c02Bd
HUGHES, Mary		30	F	None	270c02Bd
James	(S)	05	M	Child	270c02Bd
MCTEE, Bridget		23	F	None	270c02Bd
LYNCH, Mary-Ann		22	F	None	270c02Bd
Mary-Ann	(D)	01	F	Child	270c02Bd
MORGAN, Mathew		69	M	Carpenter	270c02Bd
CAMPBELL, John		26	M	Laborer	270c02Bd
CUMMINS, Patrick		25	M	Laborer	270c02Bd
KELLY, John		25	M	Laborer	270c02Bd
OTTERSON, Thomas		42	M	Laborer	270c02Bd
Cathe.	(W)	40	F	Wife	270c02Bd
Nancy	(D)	14	F	None	270c02Bd
Andrew	(S)	12	M	None	270c02Bd
Daniel	(S)	10	M	None	270c02Bd
Died-At-Sea					
Catherine	(D)	08	F	Child	270c02Bd
Thomas	(S)	06	M	Child	270c02Bd
Died-At-Sea					
Samuel	(S)	02	M	Child	270c02Bd
Died-At-Sea					
CRAWFORD, James		20	M	Laborer	270c02Bd
Ann		20	F	None	270c02Bd
MAHON, Ellen		30	F	None	270c02Bd
CUNNINGHAM, Mathew		14	M	None	270c02Bd
BOYLE, Lawrence		27	M	Carpenter	270c02Bd
Bridget		27	F	None	270c02Bd
MARTIN, Bridget		20	F	None	270c02Bd
NANN, Margt.		18	F	None	270c02Bd
BERRELL, Cathe.		35	F	None	270c02Bd
MCKEATON, Henry		22	M	Slater	270c02Bd
Patrick		20	M	Laborer	270c02Bd
Margt.		18	F	None	270c02Bd
ROBINSON, Catherine		14	F	None	270c02Bd
ROSNEY, Martin		24	M	Laborer	270c02Bd
Betty		22	F	None	270c02Bd
DOLAN, Cathe.		20	F	None	270c02Bd
DONNELLY, Fanny		22	F	None	270c02Bd
HURLEY, Arthur		40	M	Shoemaker	270c02Bd
CLARK, William		22	M	Clerk	270c02Bd
RILEY, Martin		25	M	Laborer	270c02Bd
COCHLIN, Joseph		26	M	Laborer	270c02Bd
FALLOUGHAN, Edwd.		08	M	Child	270c02Bd
Pat		07	M	Child	270c02Bd
Ann		05	F	Child	270c02Bd
RILEY, Winifred		22	F	None	270c02Bd
Cathe.		27	F	None	270c02Bd
James		18	M	None	270c02Bd
BALDWIN, H.		21	M	Mariner	270c02Bd
JOHNSON, James		24	M	Weaver	270c02Bd
LYNES, Patrick		26	M	Laborer	270c02Bd
CUSHAN, Robt.		34	M	Laborer	270c02Bd
Ellen	(W)	34	F	Wife	270c02Bd
Thomas	(S)	08	M	Child	270c02Bd
Mary	(D)	06	F	Child	270c02Bd
Margt.	(D)	04	F	Child	270c02Bd
John	(S)	03	M	Child	270c02Bd
OREILLY, Patrick		45	M	Farmer	270c02Bd
TRACEY, Peter		18	M	Laborer	270c02Bd
CARTER, Ann		18	F	None	270c02Bd
LOGRAN, Mary		26	F	None	270c02Bd
MCGUIRE, Cathe.		20	F	None	270c02Bd
MOLLOY, Cathe.		30	F	None	270c02Bd
KNIGHT, Jane		22	F	None	270c02Bd
MCGINNIS, Mary		14	F	None	270c02Bd
DOLAN, Cathe.		20	F	None	270c02Bd
MEHAN, Ellen		21	F	None	270c02Bd
KILLONLY, Bridget		25	F	None	270c02Bd
BOYLE, Ann		19	F	None	270c02Bd
BOYD, Amelia		16	F	Dressmaker	270c02Bd
CASEY, Thomas		30	M	Typesetter	270c02Bd
MCCARTNEY, Ann		19	F	None	270c02Bd
MURRAY, Ann		22	F	None	270c02Bd
FELLEY, Cathe.		19	F	None	270c02Bd
WHITELAW, Ann		21	F	None	270c02Bd
MANNAN, Owen		26	M	Laborer	270c02Bd
Peter		19	M	Laborer	270c02Bd
MARTIN, Martha		25	F	None	270c02Bd
MALONE, Garrett		20	M	Laborer	270c02Bd
BARLOW, Sarah		17	F	None	270c02Bd
LELAHAN, Bernard		22	M	Laborer	270c02Bd
MARTIN, Ellen		40	F	None	270c02Bd
MANAHAN, Mary		26	F	None	270c02Bd
RODGERSON, Cathe.		17	F	None	270c02Bd
HENNAN, Sally		17	F	None	270c02Bd

NAMES OF PASSENGERS		AGE	SEX	OCCUPATIONS	DATE PORT SHIP
ROCHSON, Biddy		18	F	None	27Oc02Bd
KEEFE, Ann		20	F	None	27Oc02Bd
BYRNE, Mary		19	F	None	27Oc02Bd
BURKE, Johanna		20	F	None	27Oc02Bd
KIERMAN, Thomas		28	M	Laborer	27Oc02Bd
COFFIN, Thomas		40	M	Laborer	27Oc02Bd
Mary		40	F	None	27Oc02Bd
SISK, John		25	M	Painter	27Oc02Bd
COFFIN, Mary		20	F	None	27Oc02Bd
Catherine		15	F	None	27Oc02Bd
FLOOD, John		00	M	None	27Oc02Bd
A.		00	F	None	27Oc02Bd
H.		00	F	None	27Oc02Bd
C.		00	F	None	27Oc02Bd

EUROPE 29 OCTOBER 1846

From Liverpool

NAMES OF PASSENGERS		AGE	SEX	OCCUPATIONS	DATE PORT SHIP
MCDONUGH, Ann		20	F	Laborer	29Oc02BI
IGOT, Michl.		18	M	Laborer	29Oc02BI
BONIK, Biddy		16	F	Laborer	29Oc02BI
LINREN, Margt.		18	F	Laborer	29Oc02BI
MCMANNUS, Thomas		16	M	Laborer	29Oc02BI
ROBINSON, Anges		12	F	Laborer	29Oc02BI
Joseph		14	M	Laborer	29Oc02BI
INFERLD, Charles		40	M	Laborer	29Oc02BI
John		14	M	Laborer	29Oc02BI
DENNERSON, Margt.		38	F	Laborer	29Oc02BI
Henery	(S)	12	M	Laborer	29Oc02BI
Thomas	(S)	08	M	Child	29Oc02BI
WILLIAMS, U-Mrs.		22	F	Laborer	29Oc02BI
FITZGERALD, U-Mrs.		38	F	Laborer	29Oc02BI
U		.00	U	Infant	29Oc02BI
John	(S)	02	M	Child	29Oc02BI
William	(S)	04	M	Child	29Oc02BI
BODOKIN, Bernard		28	M	Laborer	29Oc02BI
Charles		27	M	Laborer	29Oc02BI
DONOUGH, Patrick		22	M	Laborer	29Oc02BI
KELLY, Mary		24	F	Laborer	29Oc02BI
NEILE, Ann		24	F	Laborer	29Oc02BI
HEATH, Cath.		18	F	Laborer	29Oc02BI
MCCABE, Mary		34	F	Laborer	29Oc02BI
LINSEY, William		24	M	Laborer	29Oc02BI
COYLE, Rosey		18	F	Laborer	29Oc02BI
SULLIVAN, Michl.		28	M	Laborer	29Oc02BI
Margt.		49	F	Laborer	29Oc02BI
Mary		24	F	Laborer	29Oc02BI
KELLY, Bridget		20	F	Laborer	29Oc02BI
LINE, Mauric		30	M	Laborer	29Oc02BI
MURPHY, James		28	M	Laborer	29Oc02BI
Died-At-Sea					
MCCARTY, Patrick		30	M	Laborer	29Oc02BI
Cath.		26	F	Laborer	29Oc02BI
DONORS, John		20	M	Laborer	29Oc02BI
DOWNEY, William		09	M	Child	29Oc02BI
LESLIE, Frank		27	M	Laborer	29Oc02BI
MCCANLEY, Betsey		12	F	Laborer	29Oc02BI
FOWLER, Saml.		14	M	Laborer	29Oc02BI
BURKE, Mary		16	F	Laborer	29Oc02BI
MCLOUGHLIN, Mary		18	F	Laborer	29Oc02BI
MCCABER, Rosanna		10	F	Laborer	29Oc02BI
FOSTER, Geo.		24	M	Laborer	29Oc02BI
KEATING, Ellen		22	F	Laborer	29Oc02BI
CASSIDY, Ellinor		28	F	Laborer	29Oc02BI
DALEY, Edward		26	M	Laborer	29Oc02BI
SIMMONS, Michl.		10	M	Laborer	29Oc02BI
MURAY, Elizh.		14	F	Laborer	29Oc02BI
DUNN, Cath.		24	F	Laborer	29Oc02BI

NAMES OF PASSENGERS		AGE	SEX	OCCUPATIONS	DATE PORT SHIP
GANNON, John		18	M	Laborer	29Oc02BI
LINNREN, Patrick		14	M	Laborer	29Oc02BI
STONE, Sarah		49	F	Laborer	29Oc02BI
MULLEN, Bridget		10	F	Laborer	29Oc02BI
DUNN, Rose		25	F	Laborer	29Oc02BI
Ann		22	F	Laborer	29Oc02BI
Ann		03	F	Child	29Oc02BI
Mary		06	F	Child	29Oc02BI
Died-At-Sea					
SMITH, Hugh		10	M	Laborer	29Oc02BI
GORMLEY, Mary		20	F	Laborer	29Oc02BI
MCAVICKON, Susan		18	F	Laborer	29Oc02BI
LYDDY, Patrick		32	M	Laborer	29Oc02BI
ONEILE, James		14	M	Laborer	29Oc02BI
HART, Cath.		18	F	Laborer	29Oc02BI
KELLEY, Mary		20	F	Laborer	29Oc02BI
FISHER, Anthony		07	M	Child	29Oc02BI
CLARK, Eliza		38	F	Laborer	29Oc02BI
Sarah	(D)	14	F	Laborer	29Oc02BI
Grace	(D)	12	F	Laborer	29Oc02BI
Garrett	(S)	09	M	Child	29Oc02BI
Alexander	(S)	04	M	Child	29Oc02BI
QUINN, Margt.		26	F	Laborer	29Oc02BI
PIERRE, James		20	M	Laborer	29Oc02BI
Blewett		22	M	Laborer	29Oc02BI
RODDER, Michl.		12	M	Laborer	29Oc02BI
BRADY, Mary		22	F	Laborer	29Oc02BI
Magt.		06	F	Child	29Oc02BI
MONTGOMERY, Eliza		12	F	Laborer	29Oc02BI
BRADY, Patrick		10	M	Laborer	29Oc02BI
DOLAN, Michl.		18	M	Laborer	29Oc02BI
MCMANNUS, Thos.		22	M	Laborer	29Oc02BI
FERGUSON, Elizh.		23	F	Laborer	29Oc02BI
GINNIS, Richd.		18	M	Laborer	29Oc02BI
DALEY, Owen		40	M	Laborer	29Oc02BI
GIBNEY, Thos.		22	M	Laborer	29Oc02BI
Ellen		24	F	Laborer	29Oc02BI
KINAR, Ann		20	F	Laborer	29Oc02BI
FISHER, Mary		20	F	Laborer	29Oc02BI
SCOTT, John		22	M	Laborer	29Oc02BI
CARTEY, Margt.		18	F	Laborer	29Oc02BI
DOWD, Mary		38	F	Laborer	29Oc02BI
MULLADY, Peter		10	M	Laborer	29Oc02BI
HARPER, Wm.		22	M	Laborer	29Oc02BI
BRADY, Mary		04	F	Child	29Oc02BI
MCGIRON, Patrick		20	M	Laborer	29Oc02BI
MCMANNUS, John		22	M	Laborer	29Oc02BI
STINSON, Edward		22	M	Laborer	29Oc02BI
CARROLL, Ann		18	F	Laborer	29Oc02BI
WILLIS, Mary		20	F	Laborer	29Oc02BI
SMITH, Quen		22	M	Laborer	29Oc02BI
CONOR, Patrick		16	M	Laborer	29Oc02BI
MCDONALD, James		22	M	Laborer	29Oc02BI
KEARNS, Thomas		57	M	Laborer	29Oc02BI
U	(W)	50	F	Wife	29Oc02BI
Honor	(D)	16	F	Laborer	29Oc02BI
Patrick	(S)	10	M	Laborer	29Oc02BI
MCGRANE, Mary		48	F	Laborer	29Oc02BI
MURPHY, Bridget		16	F	Laborer	29Oc02BI
ROOK, Mary		12	F	Laborer	29Oc02BI
BEATY, Mary		18	F	Laborer	29Oc02BI
LEARY, Mary		20	F	Laborer	29Oc02BI
CONNOR, Owen		18	M	Laborer	29Oc02BI
ODOWELL, Chas.		20	M	Laborer	29Oc02BI
NEVAN, Thos.		18	M	Laborer	29Oc02BI
MULLAHAN, Ann		16	F	Laborer	29Oc02BI
FOLEY, Mary		14	F	Laborer	29Oc02BI
DELANY, John		28	M	Laborer	29Oc02BI
WILLIAMS, Stephen		32	M	Laborer	29Oc02BI
CHILL, Charles		24	M	Laborer	29Oc02BI
SEWELL, George		57	M	Laborer	29Oc02BI
DUNBAR, Michl.		16	M	Laborer	29Oc02BI
KEATING, Chris		49	M	Laborer	29Oc02BI
Ann	(D)	12	F	Laborer	29Oc02BI
John	(S)	12	M	Laborer	29Oc02BI

NAMES OF PASSENGERS		AGE	SEX	OCCUPATIONS	DATE PORT SHIP
KEATING, Cath.	(D)	10	F	Laborer	290c02BI
Eliza	(D)	10	F	Laborer	290c02BI
James	(S)	08	M	Child	290c02BI
Ellen	(D)	06	F	Child	290c02BI
GOOBY, Ellen		18	F	Laborer	290c02BI
DEVERIN, Mary		20	F	Laborer	290c02BI
HOOLEY, John		42	M	Laborer	290c02BI
ROSNAN, Marry		38	F	Laborer	290c02BI
Mary	(D)	07	F	Child	290c02BI
Julia	(D)	02	F	Child	290c02BI
DALEY, Bridgt.		46	F	Laborer	290c02BI
LEENALL, Magt.		24	F	Laborer	290c02BI
DUNAR, Magt.		18	F	Laborer	290c02BI
MCCORMICK, Ann		14	F	Laborer	290c02BI
Jane		12	F	Laborer	290c02BI
SHANLEY, Bridgt.		14	F	Laborer	290c02BI
BOWN, Wallen		18	M	Laborer	290c02BI
Ann		22	F	Laborer	290c02BI
FREVAR, Saml.		26	M	Laborer	290c02BI
HENDERSON, Mary		22	F	Laborer	290c02BI
HENSON, Ellen		24	F	Laborer	290c02BI
FREEMAN, Mary		25	F	Laborer	290c02BI
GANLEY, Mary		18	F	Laborer	290c02BI
WARD, Magt.		20	F	Laborer	290c02BI
DELANY, Ann		28	F	Laborer	290c02BI
William		26	M	Laborer	290c02BI
Henry		24	M	Laborer	290c02BI
Died-At-Sea					
Ellen		19	F	Laborer	290c02BI
Martain		16	M	Laborer	290c02BI
Julia		16	F	Laborer	290c02BI
Jerimiah		14	M	Laborer	290c02BI
Mary		12	F	Laborer	290c02BI
BENNETT, O.		28	M	Laborer	290c02BI
MCAVOY, Timothy		20	M	Laborer	290c02BI
MCCAFFREY, Patrick		30	M	Laborer	290c02BI
LAWBER, Patt		42	M	Laborer	290c02BI
GRADY, Patrick		22	M	Laborer	290c02BI
CARTIGAN, Dennis		45	M	Laborer	290c02BI
U	(W)	29	F	Wife	290c02BI
MCAVOY, Michl.		22	M	Laborer	290c02BI
Betsey		18	F	Laborer	290c02BI
HOOSMAN, Frank		35	M	Laborer	290c02BI
MENSEY, Martain		26	M	Laborer	290c02BI
GARMAN, Peter		20	M	Laborer	290c02BI
RENDER, Mary		12	F	Laborer	290c02BI
OCONNOR, John		18	M	Laborer	290c02BI
David		15	M	Laborer	290c02BI
Martain		12	M	Laborer	290c02BI
Arthur		10	M	Laborer	290c02BI
Robt.		08	M	Child	290c02BI
SCULLY, Patrick		38	M	Laborer	290c02BI
MCMAHON, Peter		40	M	Laborer	290c02BI
BRADY, Patrick		18	M	Laborer	290c02BI
James		22	M	Laborer	290c02BI
MCCUE, Cath.		18	F	Laborer	290c02BI
BRADY, Magt.		19	F	Laborer	290c02BI
HINSEY, Patrick		20	M	Laborer	290c02BI
Cath.		21	F	Laborer	290c02BI
DEVINE, Thos.		22	M	Laborer	290c02BI
Ann		16	F	Laborer	290c02BI
OAKES, Ann		18	F	Laborer	290c02BI
Michl.		12	M	Laborer	290c02BI
HACKETT, Mary		48	F	Laborer	290c02BI
Biddy	(D)	12	F	Laborer	290c02BI
Mary	(D)	06	F	Child	290c02BI
WOOLT, Mary		26	F	Laborer	290c02BI
Henry		30	M	Laborer	290c02BI
GALLIGAN, Lawrence		16	M	Laborer	290c02BI
HARTLEY, James		18	M	Laborer	290c02BI
LIVINGSTON, Richd.		22	M	Laborer	290c02BI
JENKINS, Frank		24	M	Laborer	290c02BI
REYONALDS, Maxwell		24	M	Laborer	290c02BI
LAWBER, Fanton		20	M	Laborer	290c02BI
GODDARD, Geo.		03	M	Child	290c02BI

NAMES OF PASSENGERS		AGE	SEX	OCCUPATIONS	DATE PORT SHIP
CONWAY, John		27	M	Laborer	290c02BI
BURKE, James		24	M	Laborer	290c02BI
WILDER, Cath.		20	F	Laborer	290c02BI
BYNES, Patt		20	M	Laborer	290c02BI
MCDOUGALL, John		12	M	Laborer	290c02BI
BRADY, Mary		20	F	Laborer	290c02BI
FALLON, Nelly		14	F	Laborer	290c02BI
HENDWIN, Edward		50	M	Laborer	290c02BI
Julia		33	F	Laborer	290c02BI
KEATING, Mary-A.		24	F	Laborer	290c02BI
Ann	(D)	.00	F	Infant	290c02BI
REILY, James		08	M	Child	290c02BI
MCCAVERY, Patrick		26	M	Laborer	290c02BI
KING, Phillip		58	M	Laborer	290c02BI
Jane	(W)	50	F	Wife	290c02BI
MCGRATH, Mary		58	F	Laborer	290c02BI
Mary-Jane		06	F	Child	290c02BI
ARMSTRONG, Wm.		12	M	Laborer	290c02BI
Cath.		10	F	Laborer	290c02BI
BLASDALE, Mathew		28	M	Laborer	290c02BI
KILROY, Daniel		24	M	Laborer	290c02BI
JORDEN, Anthony		18	M	Laborer	290c02BI
MILES, Rosey		18	F	Laborer	290c02BI
COLLINS, Sarah		24	F	Laborer	290c02BI
Jane	(D)	04	F	Child	290c02BI
Thomas	(S)	02	M	Child	290c02BI
Susanah	(D)	01	F	Child	290c02BI
ONEILE, Magt.		18	F	Laborer	290c02BI
CONNOR, Bridgt.		20	F	Laborer	290c02BI
RAFFERTY, Bridgt.		16	F	Laborer	290c02BI
JOHNSON, Wm.		26	M	Laborer	290c02BI
BRANNIGAN, Mary		28	F	Laborer	290c02BI
MORRIS, Ann		26	F	Laborer	290c02BI
BOWEN, Cath.		28	F	Laborer	290c02BI
WILLIAMS, U-Mrs.		32	F	Laborer	290c02BI
CALDWELL, Ellen		20	F	Laborer	290c02BI
KEENAN, Marsilla		18	F	Laborer	290c02BI
ARMSTRONG, Michl.		16	M	Laborer	290c02BI
BROGAN, Ellen		18	F	Laborer	290c02BI
FENEY, Cath.		20	F	Laborer	290c02BI
FETES, James		35	M	Unknown	290c02BI
U	(W)	25	F	Wife	290c02BI
THOMPSON, Cath.		28	F	Unknown	290c02BI
MYERS, Cath.		00	F	Unknown	290c02BI
Died-At-Sea					
REILY, Mary		00	F	Unknown	290c02BI
Died-At-Sea					
WILLIAMS, John		00	M	Unknown	290c02BI
Died-At-Sea					
DELANY, Cath.		00	F	Unknown	290c02BI
Died-At-Sea					
FITZGERALD, William		00	M	Unknown	290c02BI
Died-At-Sea					
COSTIGAN, Patrick		00	M	Unknown	290c02BI
Died-At-Sea					

CHRISTIANA 29 OCTOBER 1846

From London

NAMES OF PASSENGERS	AGE	SEX	OCCUPATIONS	DATE PORT SHIP
QUARRY, Narissa	30	F	Lady	290c21Jo
HUTTON, John	26	M	Gentleman	290c21Jo

NAMES OF PASSENGERS	A G E	S E X	OCCUPATIONS	DATE PORT SHIP	NAMES OF PASSENGERS	A G E	S E X	OCCUPATIONS	DATE PORT SHIP
					COWEN, Thos.	39	M	Carpenter	03No21Bn
					STEPHENS, Edwd.	27	M	Clerk	03No21Bn
					GROVES, Peter	22	M	Clerk	03No21Bn

PRINCE-ALBERT 03 NOVEMBER 1846

From London

FINLAND 03 NOVEMBER 1846

NAMES OF PASSENGERS	A G E	S E X	OCCUPATIONS	DATE PORT SHIP	NAMES OF PASSENGERS	A G E	S E X	OCCUPATIONS	DATE PORT SHIP
OLIN, Stephen	44	M	Clergyman	03No21Bn					
RYERSON, John	46	M	Clergyman	03No21Bn	From Liverpool				
GREEN, Anson	46	M	Clergyman	03No21Bn					
FREEMAN, Rowland	60	M	Surgeon	03No21Bn					
Martha	35	F	None	03No21Bn	DUNN, John	30	M	Farmer	03No02Cb
PERRY, Henry	54	M	None	03No21Bn	Alley	25	F	Farmer	03No02Cb
PROCTOR, Charles	15	M	None	03No21Bn	Biddy	02	F	Child	03No02Cb
LOWTHER, Mary	30	F	None	03No21Bn	Pat	.07	M	Infant	03No02Cb
Sarah	25	F	None	03No21Bn	BAMBRICK, Elizabeth	35	F	Laborer	03No02Cb
HARVEY, Elizabeth	30	F	None	03No21Bn	Lucinda	19	F	Laborer	03No02Cb
Ellen	04	F	Child	03No21Bn	Claressa	12	F	Laborer	03No02Cb
JAMES, Jane	30	F	None	03No21Bn	Henry-Alfred	17	M	Laborer	03No02Cb
Ellen	12	F	None	03No21Bn	MUBRYEN, Mary	40	F	Laborer	03No02Cb
Emily	09	F	None	03No21Bn	MAGUIRE, Michael	30	M	Laborer	03No02Cb
Frederick	07	M	Child	03No21Bn	Mary	24	F	Laborer	03No02Cb
PRESTON, Mary	23	F	None	03No21Bn	HENRY, Pat	20	M	Laborer	03No02Cb
William	04	M	Child	03No21Bn	MCDERMOTT, Michael	19	M	Laborer	03No02Cb
Nathaniel	.08	M	Infant	03No21Bn	CRAFTON, Margret	15	F	Laborer	03No02Cb
FRAY, Marry-Ann	30	F	Servant	03No21Bn	SHEERAN, Thomas	04	M	Child	03No02Cb
HEATHER, Mary	45	F	None	03No21Bn	Mary	30	F	Laborer	03No02Cb
LAMBERT, Chas.	18	M	Servant	03No21Bn	MCCALL, Anna	50	F	Laborer	03No02Cb
HILL, Edward	29	M	Clergyman	03No21Bn	MCKERNIEN, Edward	30	M	Laborer	03No02Cb
CURRY, Maria	35	F	Servant	03No21Bn	Edward	07	M	Child	03No02Cb
John	11	M	Servant	03No21Bn	John	03	M	Child	03No02Cb
HUBDELL, William	30	M	Servant	03No21Bn	Pat	05	M	Child	03No02Cb
MALVILL, John	21	M	Servant	03No21Bn	HOGAN, Ellen	19	F	Laborer	03No02Cb
GRIFFITHS, Mesach	22	M	Carpenter	03No21Bn	MAGUIRE, Ellen	40	F	Laborer	03No02Cb
LANGHAM, William	28	M	Farmer	03No21Bn	MURTOCH, James	20	M	Laborer	03No02Cb
SMITH, Joseph	16	M	Farmer	03No21Bn	ONEIL, Patt	19	M	Laborer	03No02Cb
ADY, George	32	M	Butcher	03No21Bn	MCVEY, James	18	M	Laborer	03No02Cb
Mary	40	F	None	03No21Bn	JORDAN, Charles	18	M	Laborer	03No02Cb
CLARK, Wm.	60	M	None	03No21Bn	DAY, Michael	19	M	Laborer	03No02Cb
BROWN, Wm.	28	M	Farmer	03No21Bn	MEENEY, James	12	M	Servant	03No02Cb
SELMIS, Matthew	32	M	Stctr	03No21Bn	MCGOEY, Mary	22	F	Laborer	03No02Cb
BRETT, John	24	M	Gdnr	03No21Bn	IGOE, Anne	26	F	Laborer	03No02Cb
Chas.	19	M	Cbtmkr	03No21Bn	CONWAY, Rose	20	F	Servant	03No02Cb
Geo.	14	M	None	03No21Bn	MCGUIRE, Catherine	23	F	Servant	03No02Cb
Wm.	48	M	Cbtmkr	03No21Bn	DONALLY, Matilda	22	F	Servant	03No02Cb
HICK, Daniel	30	M	Carpenter	03No21Bn	ALLEN, Mary	20	F	Servant	03No02Cb
Dorothy	26	F	None	03No21Bn	GALLAGHER, Elizabeth	20	F	Servant	03No02Cb
Ann	05	F	Child	03No21Bn	ARMSTRONG, Thomas	20	M	Blacksmith	03No02Cb
Henry	04	M	Child	03No21Bn	MURRY, Elizabeth	16	F	Servant	03No02Cb
Danl.	02	M	Child	03No21Bn	HOSEMAN, Mary-Anne	20	F	Servant	03No02Cb
WRIGHT, Geo.	32	M	Sawer	03No21Bn	DALEY, Maria	43	F	Servant	03No02Cb
Catherine	34	F	None	03No21Bn	James	23	M	Cloth Maker	03No02Cb
Geo.	10	M	None	03No21Bn	Joseph	13	M	Cloth Maker	03No02Cb
COPE, Mary	40	F	None	03No21Bn	Michael	07	M	Child	03No02Cb
ELLIS, Edmund	42	M	Dyer	03No21Bn	HILL, Elizabeth	24	F	Cloth Maker	03No02Cb
Lydia	39	F	None	03No21Bn	MCCABE, Anne	45	F	Laborer	03No02Cb
Mary	17	F	None	03No21Bn	James	14	M	Laborer	03No02Cb
LANE, Caroline	60	F	None	03No21Bn	MARAN, James	40	M	Paper Maker	03No02Cb
COOK, Thos.	20	M	Mariner	03No21Bn	MURRY, Margret	21	F	Laborer	03No02Cb
BATLEY, Sarah	30	F	None	03No21Bn	Thomas	12	M	Laborer	03No02Cb
WARD, Margaret	31	F	None	03No21Bn	John	10	M	Laborer	03No02Cb
JACKSON, Joseph	44	M	Engineer	03No21Bn	Hugh	08	M	Child	03No02Cb
Elizabeth	40	F	None	03No21Bn	MCVEY, Judy	47	F	Laborer	03No02Cb
FULCHER, John	30	M	Weaver	03No21Bn	ALEXANDER, Charles	30	M	Soldier	03No02Cb
Mary	28	F	None	03No21Bn	FREYNE, Lorenza	60	M	Farmer	03No02Cb
John	05	M	Child	03No21Bn	TRACEY, Mary	45	F	Farmer	03No02Cb
Thos.	03	M	Child	03No21Bn	Anna	14	F	Farmer	03No02Cb
CLAYDON, Thos.	24	M	Farmer	03No21Bn	Mary	08	F	Child	03No02Cb
Mary	20	F	None	03No21Bn	Honora	06	F	Child	03No02Cb
WRINCH, Thos.	23	M	Clerk	03No21Bn	KENNY, Catherine	22	F	Servant	03No02Cb
JONES, John	23	M	Merchant	03No21Bn	DONELLY, Abbey	22	F	Servant	03No02Cb
COLLINS, John	18	M	Cigar Maker	03No21Bn	DOMONDY, James	29	M	Laborer	03No02Cb

NAMES OF PASSENGERS	AGE	SEX	OCCUPATIONS	DATE PORT SHIP	NAMES OF PASSENGERS	AGE	SEX	OCCUPATIONS	DATE PORT SHIP
DOMONDY, Biddy	30	F	Laborer	03No02Cb	DOONER, Biddy	20	F	Servant	03No02Cb
William	05	M	Child	03No02Cb	MARAH, Patt	21	M	Laborer	03No02Cb
James	03	M	Child	03No02Cb	BYRN, Mary	21	F	Servant	03No02Cb
Patrick	01	M	Child	03No02Cb	ROARKE, Michael	20	M	Laborer	03No02Cb
DOMLEN, Eliza	20	F	Laborer	03No02Cb	DWYER, Mary	19	F	Servant	03No02Cb
CASSIDY, Jane	25	F	Servant	03No02Cb	BUCKLEY, Maria	14	F	Servant	03No02Cb
Anne	26	F	Servant	03No02Cb	Marcella	12	F	Servant	03No02Cb
BALDWIN, Mary	27	F	Servant	03No02Cb	QUINLAN, Margaret	23	F	Seamstress	03No02Cb
FOSTER, Francis	17	M	Laborer	03No02Cb	COGGINS, Patt	25	M	Laborer	03No02Cb
CLARK, Mary	19	F	Servant	03No02Cb	HIGGINS, Daniel	21	M	Laborer	03No02Cb
Ellen	15	F	Servant	03No02Cb	RICHARDSON, Eliza	30	F	Servant	03No02Cb
FOX, Catherine	22	F	Servant	03No02Cb	MCGUIGAN, Thos.	35	M	Salter	03No02Cb
SHAWNESEY, Biddy	20	F	Servant	03No02Cb	CHAIR, Marianne	21	F	Servant	03No02Cb
MAGUIRE, Anne	18	F	Servant	03No02Cb	RICHARDSON, Alfred	25	M	Iron Monger	03No02Cb
Margret	17	F	Servant	03No02Cb	Eliza.	21	F	Iron Monger	03No02Cb
Dennis	14	M	Servant	03No02Cb	MCCLENACHAN, James	38	M	Weaver	03No02Cb
Terence	13	M	Servant	03No02Cb	Mary	36	F	Weaver	03No02Cb
Jerard	12	M	Servant	03No02Cb	James	16	M	Weaver	03No02Cb
Cornelius	08	M	Child	03No02Cb	Robert	14	M	Weaver	03No02Cb
Bernard	07	M	Child	03No02Cb	Mathew	12	M	Weaver	03No02Cb
Rose	01	F	Child	03No02Cb	John	08	M	Child	03No02Cb
HAYES, Catherine	43	F	Servant	03No02Cb	Jane	05	F	Child	03No02Cb
Anne	17	F	Servant	03No02Cb	CAHILL, Rose	24	F	Laborer	03No02Cb
MCCOURT, Biddy	17	F	Servant	03No02Cb	DUNN, Anne	05	F	Child	03No02Cb
MURPHY, Nelly	30	F	Servant	03No02Cb	LONGWORTH, Jane	21	F	Servant	03No02Cb
OBREIN, Thos.	26	M	Laborer	03No02Cb	FLYNN, John	19	M	Laborer	03No02Cb
HAYES, James	12	M	Laborer	03No02Cb	JOHNSTON, James	23	M	Surveyor	03No02Cb
MCDERMOTT, James	20	M	Laborer	03No02Cb	Mary	21	F	Surveyor	03No02Cb
MCCAFREY, Mary	19	F	Servant	03No02Cb	David	25	M	Laborer	03No02Cb
MCCARTIN, John	20	M	Laborer	03No02Cb	HALL, Joseph	45	M	Weaver	03No02Cb
ROOKE, Catherine	20	F	Servant	03No02Cb	Anne	35	F	Weaver	03No02Cb
KANE, Sally	17	F	Servant	03No02Cb	Hanna	65	F	Weaver	03No02Cb
GREY, Alley	18	F	Servant	03No02Cb	James	26	M	Tailor	03No02Cb
DUNNE, Betty	32	F	Servant	03No02Cb	Eliza.	11	F	None	03No02Cb
KILREANEY, Mary	22	F	Servant	03No02Cb	MANNING, Timothy	35	M	Servant	03No02Cb
FARRELL, Catherine	16	F	Servant	03No02Cb					
KANE, Patt	25	M	Laborer	03No02Cb					
GLACKIN, Owen	31	M	Laborer	03No02Cb					
CLARK, Catherine	15	F	Servant	03No02Cb					
DUFFY, Mary	21	F	Servant	03No02Cb					
BRADY, Michael	22	M	Laborer	03No02Cb					
BRADLEY, Mary	17	F	Servant	03No02Cb			JOHN-R.SKIDDY 04 NOVEMBER 1846		
MURPHY, Catherine	17	F	Servant	03No02Cb					
CORRAGAN, Brien	16	M	Laborer	03No02Cb			From Liverpool		
MATHEWS, Hugh	25	M	Laborer	03No02Cb					
REILEY, William	21	M	Laborer	03No02Cb					
RIELEY, John	20	M	Laborer	03No02Cb	WALSH, Edward	26	M	Cooper	04No02Ac
SPALLIN, Michael	30	M	Laborer	03No02Cb	Mary	20	F	None	04No02Ac
HARBISON, Ellen	20	F	Servant	03No02Cb	Johannah	04	F	Child	04No02Ac
FLYNN, Owen	43	M	Turner	03No02Cb	Mary	02	F	Child	04No02Ac
Cecilia	22	F	Turner	03No02Cb	Eliza	01	F	Child	04No02Ac
ODONNELL, Sally	21	F	Servant	03No02Cb	BURNS, Julia	50	F	Housekeeper	04No02Ac
HEAVEY, James	50	M	Laborer	03No02Cb	GALLAGHER, John	40	M	Dealer	04No02Ac
MAGHAN, Marcy	17	F	Servant	03No02Cb	DAY, Henry	29	M	Teacher	04No02Ac
KIERNAN, Mary	30	F	Servant	03No02Cb	BREEN, Dennis	24	M	Farmer	04No02Ac
CLARK, Anne	16	F	Laborer	03No02Cb	MCCLELLAND, Martha	25	F	Servant	04No02Ac
DONELLY, Anne	20	F	Laborer	03No02Cb	CLARK, Ann	25	F	Milliner	04No02Ac
DUGGAN, John	16	M	Laborer	03No02Cb	CASSEDAY, Miche.	30	M	Servant	04No02Ac
DERMOODY, Walt	22	M	Laborer	03No02Cb	Cathe.	26	F	Servant	04No02Ac
LEONARD, Rich.	21	M	Tailor	03No02Cb	SHEA, Stephen	28	M	Clerk	04No02Ac
BRENNAN, Mary	30	F	Laborer	03No02Cb	REYNOLDS, Owen	20	M	Clerk	04No02Ac
MURRY, Susan	20	F	Servant	03No02Cb	Patt	23	M	Shoemaker	04No02Ac
SWEENY, Michael	26	M	Laborer	03No02Cb	Elizabeth	40	F	Housekeeper	04No02Ac
Anne	22	F	Laborer	03No02Cb	Rosannah	17	F	Housekeeper	04No02Ac
FLINN, Sarah	17	F	Laborer	03No02Cb	HANLON, Reuben	21	M	Butcher	04No02Ac
MCDERMOTT, Catherine	23	F	Servant	03No02Cb	Margt.	22	F	Milliner	04No02Ac
FINARTY, John	19	M	Laborer	03No02Cb	DARDIS, Bridget	17	F	Servant	04No02Ac
Maryanne	22	F	Laborer	03No02Cb	FLEMING, Jane	20	F	Milliner	04No02Ac
GOULDING, Patt	21	M	Tailor	03No02Cb	LOWDEN, Dennis	30	M	Butcher	04No02Ac
FRENCH, Peter	24	M	Farmer	03No02Cb	Patrick	16	M	Butcher	04No02Ac
WALLACE, Latetia	29	F	Servant	03No02Cb	MCCARROLL, Mary	22	F	Servant	04No02Ac
KENNEDY, Catherine	21	F	Servant	03No02Cb	CURRIN, Rosannah	20	F	Servant	04No02Ac
HUNT, Thomas	27	M	Laborer	03No02Cb	MOON, Mary	19	F	Servant	04No02Ac
Margaret	27	F	Laborer	03No02Cb	KEAN, Hannah	21	F	Servant	04No02Ac
TOOHE, William	23	M	Laborer	03No02Cb	DINNON, Mary	16	F	Servant	04No02Ac

278

NAMES OF PASSENGERS	AGE	SEX	OCCUPATIONS	DATE PORT SHIP
MARTIN, George	28	M	Laborer	04No02Ac
GWYNN, James	20	M	Merchant	04No02Ac
STEELE, Robert	19	M	Wlmcht	04No02Ac
MCMULLEN, James	25	M	Wlmcht	04No02Ac
ENRAGHT, Thomas	22	M	Servant	04No02Ac
ADAMS, John	36	M	Servant	04No02Ac
Susan	37	F	Servant	04No02Ac
Jane	10	F	Servant	04No02Ac
KELLY, John	23	M	Laborer	04No02Ac
LEONARD, Charlotte	18	F	Servant	04No02Ac
MCGUIGGAN, Mary-Ann	18	F	Servant	04No02Ac
MORRIS, John	15	M	Hatter	04No02Ac
CUNNINGHAM, Chris	24	M	Laborer	04No02Ac
Cathe.	20	F	None	04No02Ac
Mary	01	F	Child	04No02Ac
DARDIS, Rosannah	18	F	Servant	04No02Ac
MCQUILLAN, Cathe.	25	F	Servant	04No02Ac
CONNELL, James-L.	20	M	Grocer	04No02Ac
George	17	M	Grocer	04No02Ac
CLIFFORD, Thomas	26	M	Laborer	04No02Ac
CAFFREY, Patt	21	M	Tailor	04No02Ac
Mary	29	F	Housekeeper	04No02Ac
MOLLOY, Ann	20	F	Servant	04No02Ac
COX, Ann	16	F	Servant	04No02Ac
MCDERMOTT, John	24	M	Laborer	04No02Ac
CONROY, Miche.	23	M	Laborer	04No02Ac
GLANEY, Mary	19	F	Servant	04No02Ac
MATHEWS, James	40	M	Laborer	04No02Ac
Mary	35	F	None	04No02Ac
Wm.	12	M	None	04No02Ac
Edward	10	M	None	04No02Ac
Bridget	10	F	None	04No02Ac
James	08	M	Child	04No02Ac
Patrick	06	M	Child	04No02Ac
Margt.	04	F	Child	04No02Ac
MCKEON, Margt.	16	F	Servant	04No02Ac
Peter	14	M	Carpenter	04No02Ac
MCGUIRE, Cathe.	15	F	Servant	04No02Ac
GRAY, Ann	21	F	Servant	04No02Ac
Mary	19	F	Servant	04No02Ac
GUNNING, Cathe.	14	F	Servant	04No02Ac
HICKEY, Ann	25	F	Servant	04No02Ac
SHANLEY, Miche.	26	M	Servant	04No02Ac
Mary-Ann	20	F	Servant	04No02Ac
CONNOR, Maurice	20	M	Laborer	04No02Ac
Ellen	19	F	Servant	04No02Ac
DRISCOLL, Ellen	19	F	Servant	04No02Ac
MCGUIRE, Cathe.	18	F	Servant	04No02Ac
GUNSHINA, Honora	18	F	Servant	04No02Ac
BOHAN, Ann	17	F	Servant	04No02Ac
SEARLES, Thomas	21	M	Gdnr	04No02Ac
BUCKLEY, Wm.	22	M	Servant	04No02Ac
BRADY, Dominic	32	M	Shoemaker	04No02Ac
Ann	30	F	Unknown	04No02Ac
CASEY, Thomas	38	M	Groom	04No02Ac
William	30	M	Wheelwright	04No02Ac
LOUGHLIN, Thomas	18	M	Laborer	04No02Ac
MCGRAIN, Thomas	18	M	Laborer	04No02Ac
CAHILL, Chris	35	M	Weaver	04No02Ac
Ann	31	F	Unknown	04No02Ac
Caroline	70	F	Unknown	04No02Ac
Caroline	08	F	Child	04No02Ac
Mary	06	F	Child	04No02Ac
Henry	04	M	Child	04No02Ac
Hugh	01	M	Child	04No02Ac
HAFEY, Johannah	60	F	Housekeeper	04No02Ac
RING, Miche.	20	M	Laborer	04No02Ac
GORMAN, Mary	20	F	Servant	04No02Ac
FARRELL, Margt.	20	F	Servant	04No02Ac
STEVENSON, Robert	25	M	Farmer	04No02Ac
MCLOUGHLIN, Mary-Ann	20	F	Milliner	04No02Ac
STEWART, Jane	20	F	Milliner	04No02Ac
ROONEY, Mary	20	F	Servant	04No02Ac
HAZLETON, Sally	20	F	Servant	04No02Ac
DOON, Rosey	19	F	Servant	04No02Ac
SMITH, James	11	M	Unknown	04No02Ac
John	09	M	Child	04No02Ac
Biddy	08	F	Child	04No02Ac
Mary	06	F	Child	04No02Ac
Died-At-Sea				
Patrick	04	M	Child	04No02Ac
Bridget	40	F	Housekeeper	04No02Ac
BURKE, Richard	30	M	Laborer	04No02Ac
WALSH, Miche.	30	M	Laborer	04No02Ac
MEEKHAM, John	30	M	Laborer	04No02Ac
HORE, Cathe.	28	F	Housekeeper	04No02Ac
Margt.	09	F	Child	04No02Ac
Martin	07	M	Child	04No02Ac
Patt	05	M	Child	04No02Ac
GILIBINS, Ellen	17	F	Servant	04No02Ac
HAYES, Mary-Ann	36	F	Milliner	04No02Ac
LYNCH, Rosey	20	F	Servant	04No02Ac
REILLEY, Cathe.	20	F	Servant	04No02Ac
FLEMING, David	18	M	Servant	04No02Ac
DONNELLY, Francis	24	M	Weaver	04No02Ac
Betty	24	F	Unknown	04No02Ac
Mary	01	F	Child	04No02Ac
Died-At-Sea				
MCGUIRE, Hugh	30	M	Laborer	04No02Ac
MURPHY, Dennis	33	M	Laborer	04No02Ac
Sarah	30	F	Unknown	04No02Ac
Margt.	07	F	Child	04No02Ac
James	05	M	Child	04No02Ac
Mary	03	F	Child	04No02Ac
Bridget	01	F	Child	04No02Ac
DONNELLY, Ann	16	F	Laborer	04No02Ac
MCDERMOTT, John	17	M	Laborer	04No02Ac
SHERIDAN, Patt	30	M	Tailor	04No02Ac
MAHAGIN, Wm.	26	M	Laborer	04No02Ac
KENNY, John	24	M	Servant	04No02Ac
Mary	24	F	Servant	04No02Ac
MACKASAY, Wm.	42	M	Blacksmith	04No02Ac
Cathe.	34	F	Unknown	04No02Ac
Philip	13	M	Unknown	04No02Ac
Mary-Ann	09	F	Child	04No02Ac
Died-At-Sea				
Sarah	07	F	Child	04No02Ac
Died-At-Sea				
George	02	M	Child	04No02Ac
Died-At-Sea				
William	02	M	Child	04No02Ac
Died-At-Sea				
ONEIL, Jane	25	F	Servant	04No02Ac
KELLY, Ellen	19	F	Servant	04No02Ac
MCCORMACK, Mary	28	F	Servant	04No02Ac
HARVEY, Sally	20	F	Servant	04No02Ac
MEAKHAM, Sarah	20	F	Servant	04No02Ac
Cathe.	06	F	Child	04No02Ac
Mary	35	F	Servant	04No02Ac
Bridget	04	F	Child	04No02Ac
William	02	M	Child	04No02Ac
George	18	M	Laborer	04No02Ac
Edw.	11	M	Laborer	04No02Ac
Margt.	09	F	Laborer	04No02Ac
REILLY, Margt.	22	F	Housekeeper	04No02Ac
Mary	03	F	Child	04No02Ac
KEEGAN, Cathe.	17	F	Servant	04No02Ac
REILLY, Patt	02	M	Child	04No02Ac
Died-At-Sea				
BARRETT, Wm.	24	M	Tailor	04No02Ac
GREADY, Miche.	26	M	Laborer	04No02Ac
HARVEY, Patt	13	M	Servant	04No02Ac
BLAKE, Patt	21	M	Servant	04No02Ac
PENDERGRIST, James	20	M	Servant	04No02Ac
DUFFY, Bridget	20	F	Servant	04No02Ac
GALLAGHER, Betty	17	F	Servant	04No02Ac
Bridget	19	F	Servant	04No02Ac
FLOOD, Francis	50	M	Laborer	04No02Ac
Francis	22	M	Laborer	04No02Ac
HURLY, Timothy	22	M	Laborer	04No02Ac

NAMES OF PASSENGERS	AGE	SEX	OCCUPATIONS	DATE PORT SHIP	NAMES OF PASSENGERS	AGE	SEX	OCCUPATIONS	DATE PORT SHIP
HURLY, Honora	18	F	Servant	04No02Ac	MCCABE, Margt.	25	F	Servant	04No02Ac
Mary-Ann	20	F	Servant	04No02Ac	HAGERTY, Peter	25	M	Laborer	04No02Ac
Margt.	12	F	Servant	04No02Ac	POWELL, John	21	M	Laborer	04No02Ac
Honora	20	F	Servant	04No02Ac	ROUNDTREE, Winifred	20	F	Servant	04No02Ac
Julia	18	F	Milliner	04No02Ac	CLARKE, Margt.	22	F	Servant	04No02Ac
ANGLUM, John	20	M	Gdnr	04No02Ac	MORAN, Cathe.	18	F	Servant	04No02Ac
FOLEY, Miche.	22	M	Laborer	04No02Ac	ROGERS, Cathe.	17	F	Servant	04No02Ac
KELLY, Mary	20	F	Servant	04No02Ac	MORAN, Paul	27	M	Laborer	04No02Ac
MATHEWS, Eliza.	18	F	Servant	04No02Ac	ODONNELL, Hugh	26	M	Laborer	04No02Ac
MOROHAN, Hugh	30	M	Laborer	04No02Ac	BRADLEY, John	23	M	Laborer	04No02Ac
Bessy	26	F	Unknown	04No02Ac	CAMPBELL, John	19	M	Mason	04No02Ac
James	01	M	Child	04No02Ac	CONWAY, Chas.	20	M	Tailor	04No02Ac
DUFFY, Mathew	30	M	Laborer	04No02Ac	KELLY, Miche.	19	M	Tailor	04No02Ac
HAND, Patt	27	M	Laborer	04No02Ac	MCCORMACK, Rich.	35	M	Laborer	04No02Ac
MCGEE, Cathe.	30	F	Servant	04No02Ac	BARNETT, Thomas	19	M	Laborer	04No02Ac
CAMPBELL, Bridget	23	F	Servant	04No02Ac	SHANLEY, John	20	M	Laborer	04No02Ac
CARROLL, Ann	45	F	Housekeeper	04No02Ac	CARROLL, Patt	30	M	Laborer	04No02Ac
Margaret	16	F	Servant	04No02Ac	Bridget	30	F	Servant	04No02Ac
Mary-Ann	14	F	Servant	04No02Ac	KEAN, Ann	17	F	Servant	04No02Ac
Cathe.	13	F	Servant	04No02Ac	PRIOR, Thomas	40	M	Laborer	04No02Ac
Sarah	11	F	None	04No02Ac	CLINE, Miche.	35	M	Laborer	04No02Ac
Eliza.	09	F	Child	04No02Ac	CARROLL, Ann -	18	F	Servant	04No02Ac
BELL, Mary	26	F	Cnf	04No02Ac	FALLON, Miche.	21	M	Laborer	04No02Ac
Mary-Ann	02	F	Child	04No02Ac	MOROHAN, Mary	30	F	Housekeeper	04No02Ac
Died-At-Sea					Timothy	09	M	Child	04No02Ac
SMITH, Nancy	50	F	Housekeeper	04No02Ac	Bernard	07	M	Child	04No02Ac
BOTHWELL, Sarah	60	F	Housekeeper	04No02Ac	Thomas	05	M	Child	04No02Ac
MCKEON, Margt.	35	F	Servant	04No02Ac	DAVEY, Mathew	21	M	Laborer	04No02Ac
Sarah-Ann	12	F	None	04No02Ac	James	20	M	Laborer	04No02Ac
Honora	10	F	None	04No02Ac	Died-At-Sea				
BOTHWELL, David	26	M	Farmer	04No02Ac	REONOLDS, Abbey	30	F	Servant	04No02Ac
Sarah-Ann	24	F	Servant	04No02Ac	BOHAN, Cathe.	18	F	Servant	04No02Ac
Maria	21	F	Servant	04No02Ac	Betty	18	F	Servant	04No02Ac
Martha	18	F	Servant	04No02Ac	MURRAY, Biddy	19	F	Servant	04No02Ac
GALLAGHER, Miche.	50	M	Laborer	04No02Ac	MCKIERNAN, Bridget	17	F	Servant	04No02Ac
BRADY, John	23	M	Laborer	04No02Ac	RORKE, Cathe	23	F	Servant	04No02Ac
CARR, Peter	22	M	Tailor	04No02Ac	Hugh	24	M	Servant	04No02Ac
GALLAGHER, Bryan	23	M	Laborer	04No02Ac	IRWIN, Thomas	10	M	Servant	04No02Ac
KIERNAN, Andw.	20	M	Laborer	04No02Ac	Eliza	09	F	Child	04No02Ac
DONNELLY, Mathew	18	M	Laborer	04No02Ac	WILD, James	25	M	Servant	04No02Ac
FLINN, Bridget	18	F	Milliner	04No02Ac	Mary	45	F	Servant	04No02Ac
Died-At-Sea					MATHEWS, Sarah	20	F	None	04No02Ac
COX, Mary	13	F	Servant	04No02Ac	MOORE, Chas.	25	M	None	04No02Ac
Mary	60	F	Servant	04No02Ac	DICKISON, John	24	M	None	04No02Ac
MORAN, Thomas	20	M	Laborer	04No02Ac	MARTIN, Robt.	36	M	None	04No02Ac
CHEEVERS, Chris	22	M	Laborer	04No02Ac	OCONNOR, Andw.	40	M	None	04No02Ac
CULLEN, Mary	18	F	Servant	04No02Ac	DELTRY, Wm.	25	M	None	04No02Ac
KELLY, Mary	18	F	Servant	04No02Ac	HOLDSTOCK, Jane	46	F	None	04No02Ac
REILLY, Ellen	22	F	Servant	04No02Ac	VANSLYCK, Sarah	40	F	None	04No02Ac
TIERNEY, James	18	M	Laborer	04No02Ac	BRICE, Thos.	40	M	None	04No02Ac
Thomas	16	M	Laborer	04No02Ac	Mary	16	F	None	04No02Ac
BRADY, Ellen	19	F	Servant	04No02Ac	Louisa	14	F	None	04No02Ac
OLWELL, Cathl.	17	F	Servant	04No02Ac	Elizth	11	F	None	04No02Ac
FITZPATRICK, Mary	17	F	Servant	04No02Ac	John	09	M	Child	04No02Ac
CLARKE, Patt	32	M	Farmer	04No02Ac	Thos.	08	M	Child	04No02Ac
Maria	10	F	None	04No02Ac	Wm.	06	M	Child	04No02Ac
Francis	08	M	Child	04No02Ac	Jane	04	F	Child	04No02Ac
Joseph	06	M	Child	04No02Ac	Harriott	01	F	Child	04No02Ac
John	04	M	Child	04No02Ac	Jane	38	F	Servant	04No02Ac
JORDAN, James	20	M	Farmer	04No02Ac	DAVYDS, Mathew	21	M	Servant	04No02Ac
CONNER, Edwd.	30	M	Farmer	04No02Ac	James	20	M	Servant	04No02Ac
Thomas	02	M	Child	04No02Ac	MONAHAN, Mary	25	F	Servant	04No02Ac
BURKE, Ann	37	F	Housekeeper	04No02Ac	Thomas	17	M	Servant	04No02Ac
Mary	13	F	Servant	04No02Ac	Bernard	07	M	Child	04No02Ac
REEHILL, Mary	18	F	Servant	04No02Ac	Thos.	05	M	Child	04No02Ac
MCCABE, Chas.	10	M	None	04No02Ac					
Mary	08	F	Child	04No02Ac					
MCLOUGHLIN, Miche.	25	M	Laborer	04No02Ac					
ALLIOTT, John	35	M	Shoemaker	04No02Ac					
BURKE, Patt	09	M	Child	04No02Ac					
FOLEY, Cathe.	40	F	Servant	04No02Ac					
ROGAN, Bridget	18	F	Servant	04No02Ac					
HERRICK, Honora	18	F	Servant	04No02Ac					
FARRELL, Ellen	20	F	Servant	04No02Ac					
BARTLEY, Salina	30	F	Servant	04No02Ac					

FAIR-FIELD 05 NOVEMBER 1846

From Liverpool

NAMES OF PASSENGERS	AGE	SEX	OCCUPATIONS	DATE PORT SHIP
MCDERMONT, U	40	F	WI	05No02CJ
Mary	16	F	WI	05No02CJ
MCNIFF, John	40	M	Shoemaker	05No02CJ
Bridget	15	F	None	05No02CJ
James	13	M	None	05No02CJ
Mary	11	F	None	05No02CJ
Thomas	07	M	Child	05No02CJ
Martha	09	F	Child	05No02CJ
MCDONOUGH, U	20	M	Laborer	05No02CJ
ONEILL, John	24	M	Laborer	05No02CJ
MCCONNILLE, Alice	22	F	None	05No02CJ
LELJEHOLM, J.E.	23	M	Laborer	05No02CJ
GILBERT, Hanel	35	F	Laborer	05No02CJ
James	30	M	Laborer	05No02CJ
Thomas	30	M	Laborer	05No02CJ
GILROY, Bridget	22	F	None	05No02CJ
MCDONALD, Margt.	20	F	None	05No02CJ
GAYNN, Ellzth	16	F	None	05No02CJ
LANUTY, Edward	18	M	Laborer	05No02CJ
MCCONNUTY, James	20	M	Laborer	05No02CJ
MCGANN, James	20	M	Laborer	05No02CJ
John	17	M	None	05No02CJ
MCCANNOR, Rose	20	F	None	05No02CJ
CLAREY, Eliza	19	F	None	05No02CJ
HAGAN, Margt.	20	F	None	05No02CJ
CLUCK, Ann	19	F	None	05No02CJ
STANTON, Jane	20	F	None	05No02CJ
ODONNELL, Michael	22	M	Laborer	05No02CJ
PERRY, Thomas	29	M	Laborer	05No02CJ
Isabella	29	F	None	05No02CJ
Joseph	03	M	Child	05No02CJ
Margaret	17	F	None	05No02CJ
BEAR, Mary	26	F	None	05No02CJ
HAND, Owen	17	M	None	05No02CJ
MCGRATH, Thomas	20	M	Laborer	05No02CJ
Honora	25	F	None	05No02CJ
John	18	M	Laborer	05No02CJ
DUNLIAVY, Martin	20	M	Laborer	05No02CJ
GOWE, Robert	16	M	None	05No02CJ
WATSON, John-C.	20	M	Laborer	05No02CJ
GRAHAM, John	21	M	Laborer	05No02CJ
James	19	M	Laborer	05No02CJ
HUGHES, Eliza	20	F	None	05No02CJ
MCGUIRE, John	20	M	Laborer	05No02CJ
DOLAN, John	30	M	Laborer	05No02CJ
KELLERY, Pat	20	M	Laborer	05No02CJ
KENNY, Thomas	20	M	Laborer	05No02CJ
CLARKE, John	20	M	Laborer	05No02CJ
FARRELL, James	26	M	Farmer	05No02CJ
DUNN, Pat	24	M	Farmer	05No02CJ
Alice	26	F	None	05No02CJ
WHELAN, Thomas	20	M	Laborer	05No02CJ
COLLEN, Biddy	18	F	None	05No02CJ
LEE, Thomas	24	M	Laborer	05No02CJ
HELWOOD, George	26	M	Laborer	05No02CJ
CLANCEY, William	50	M	Laborer	05No02CJ
Ann	50	F	None	05No02CJ
James	20	M	Laborer	05No02CJ
CLARK, Terrance	20	M	Laborer	05No02CJ
BOLLIN, Ann	22	F	None	05No02CJ
GILLES, Bridget	17	F	None	05No02CJ
MCGAURN, Owen	09	M	None	05No02CJ
Michael	07	M	Child	05No2CJ
MARKER, Catherine	16	F	None	05No02CJ
Peter	20	M	None	05No02CJ
NESBITT, John	30	M	Laborer	05No02CJ
BODDY, Thomas	26	M	Laborer	05No02CJ
SHEERAN, Richd.	30	M	Laborer	05No02CJ
BOYLE, Ann	20	F	None	05No02CJ
Peter	13	M	None	05No02CJ
RILEY, John	28	M	Laborer	05No02CJ
CREGAN, Bridget	18	F	None	05No02CJ
FARLEY, Margaret	20	F	None	05No02CJ
WARD, Margaret	20	F	None	05No02CJ
SEAGRAVE, Alice	16	F	None	05No02CJ
HAMLY, John	34	M	Laborer	05No02CJ
JOHNSTON, Thomas	22	M	Laborer	05No02CJ
STEPHENSON, James	26	M	Laborer	05No02CJ
KELLY, Joseph	24	M	Laborer	05No02CJ
Cath.	20	F	None	05No02CJ
HEALY, Ellen	40	F	None	05No02CJ
Margaret	10	F	None	05No02CJ
Johanna	09	F	None	05No02CJ
Edmund	12	M	None	05No02CJ
HAND, Mary	30	F	None	05No02CJ
HOGAN, Cath.	11	F	None	05No02CJ
PARRY, Sarah	21	F	None	05No02CJ
MCGANE, Margaret	20	F	None	05No02CJ
GORDAN, James	30	M	Laborer	05No02CJ
GALLAGHAN, Edward	14	M	None	05No02CJ
Catherine	22	F	None	05No02CJ
NELSON, Roger	23	M	Laborer	05No02CJ
HENNEALY, Pat	20	M	Laborer	05No02CJ
TOBIN, John	45	M	Laborer	05No02CJ
CALL, Thos.	30	M	Laborer	05No02CJ
WALSH, John	21	M	Laborer	05No02CJ
MAHEN, Margaret	21	F	None	05No02CJ
Mary	20	F	None	05No02CJ
John	40	M	Laborer	05No02CJ
Thomas	13	M	None	05No02CJ
Ann	12	F	None	05No02CJ
LYNCH, Mary	10	F	None	05No02CJ
MCGOWAN, Phillip	08	M	Child	05No02CJ
Ellen	20	F	None	05No02CJ
ELLIOTT, Margt.	22	F	None	05No02CJ
MURRAY, Judith	20	F	None	05No02CJ
FARLEY, Cath.	13	F	None	05No02CJ
MAHON, Ann	13	F	None	05No02CJ
GANLEY, Ellen	12	F	None	05No02CJ
BARRETT, Richd.	18	M	Laborer	05No02CJ
Mary	20	F	None	05No02CJ
COLEMAN, David	40	M	Laborer	05No02CJ
John	30	M	Laborer	05No02CJ
Mary	21	F	None	05No02CJ
Pat	06	M	Child	05No02CJ
BARRETT, James	42	M	Laborer	05No02CJ
Ellen	40	F	None	05No02CJ
U	.00	U	Infant	05No02CJ
Bridget	42	F	None	05No02CJ
CONNER, Ann	40	F	None	05No02CJ
BARRETT, John	09	M	None	05No02CJ
Thos.	19	M	Laborer	05No02CJ
Pat	06	M	Child	05No02CJ
BROWN, Pat	45	M	Laborer	05No02CJ
Mary	40	F	Laborer	05No02CJ
U	.00	U	Infant	05No02CJ
Frederick	07	M	Child	05No02CJ
Henry	06	M	Child	05No02CJ
Thomas	04	M	Child	05No02CJ
HILL, Edwin	28	M	Laborer	05No02CJ
Eliza	30	F	None	05No02CJ
SWEENEY, Pat	27	M	Laborer	05No02CJ
U (W)	24	F	None	05No02CJ
COLLINS, William	26	M	Laborer	05No02CJ
Sarah	28	F	None	05No02CJ
MILES, William	30	M	Farmer	05No02CJ
MALOWNEY, Thomas	30	M	Laborer	05No02CJ
MITCHELL, Sarah	17	F	None	05No02CJ
HERDING, Elizabeth	20	F	None	05No02CJ
DOUGHERTY, Catherine	16	F	None	05No02CJ

NAMES OF PASSENGERS	A G E	S E X	OCCUPATIONS	DATE PORT SHIP	NAMES OF PASSENGERS	A G E	S E X	OCCUPATIONS	DATE PORT SHIP
BROWN, John	30	M	Laborer	05No02CJ	HIGGINS, Hony	20	M	None	05No02CJ
U (W)	26	F	None	05No02CJ	DUFFY, Martha	20	F	None	05No02CJ
Ellen	31	F	None	05No02CJ	MURRAY, Patt	26	M	None	05No02CJ
DOOLEY, Tim	26	M	Laborer	05No02CJ	COX, Cath.	19	F	None	05No02CJ
CALLAGHIA, U-Mrs.	26	F	None	05No02CJ	MAHAN, Michael	26	M	None	05No02CJ
MCBARROW, Mary	17	F	None	05No02CJ	MCKENNA, Francis	36	M	None	05No02CJ
Catherine	15	F	None	05No02CJ	SMITH, Cath.	21	F	None	05No02CJ
Bridget	17	F	None	05No02CJ	William	20	M	Laborer	05No02CJ
Felix	15	M	None	05No02CJ	U (W)	18	F	None	05No02CJ
Bartholomew	12	M	None	05No02CJ	MAGUIRE, John	20	M	Laborer	05No02CJ
Mary	10	F	None	05No02CJ	BURKE, John	28	M	Laborer	05No02CJ
Ann	08	F	Child	05No02CJ	MCDONOUGHT, Michael	20	M	Laborer	05No02CJ
SWAINE, U-Mrs.	34	F	None	05No02CJ	GANGHAN, Richd.	21	M	Laborer	05No02CJ
William	30	M	Laborer	05No02CJ	MURPHY, Michael	18	M	Laborer	05No02CJ
BRIDEN, Jane	10	F	None	05No02CJ	CONNOR, Pat	22	M	Laborer	05No02CJ
William	30	M	Laborer	05No02CJ	KNOTWELL, Francis	27	M	Laborer	05No02CJ
MURRAY, Mary	06	F	Child	05No02CJ	PINE, John	25	M	Laborer	05No02CJ
MORRISON, Ann	20	F	None	05No02CJ	MCCANNON, Rosy	20	F	Laborer	05No02CJ
Matilda	20	F	None	05No02CJ					
LYNCH, Mary	20	F	None	05No02CJ					
MCGINNY, Rose	16	F	None	05No02CJ					
DWYRE, Cath.	20	F	None	05No02CJ					
HAVAET, Eilth	21	F	None	05No02CJ					
Rose	19	F	None	05No02CJ	DEVONSHIRE 06 NOVEMBER 1846				
DUNN, John	20	M	Laborer	05No02CJ					
KING, Alice	20	F	Laborer	05No02CJ	From Liverpool				
MULVANY, Biddy	30	F	Laborer	05No02CJ					
Ann	20	F	Laborer	05No02CJ					
BROWN, Mary	12	F	None	05No02CJ					
Maria	20	F	None	05No02CJ	STEWART, Margaret	14	F	None	06No02CI
MCCALL, Mary-A.	18	F	None	05No02CJ	MAREY, Daniel	24	M	Laborer	06No02CI
CONNOR, John	30	M	Laborer	05No02CJ	Mary	50	F	Spinster	06No02CI
Francis	28	M	None	05No02CJ	Mayant	14	F	Spinster	06No02CI
REILLY, Chas.	20	M	None	05No02CJ	Susan	11	F	Spinster	06No02CI
Mary	15	F	None	05No02CJ	Mary-Ann	08	F	Child	06No02CI
GALLIGHAN, Bridget	19	F	None	05No02CJ	MCMILLAN, James	30	M	Farmer	06No02CI
SMITH, Mary	16	F	None	05No02CJ	MCCUSKEN, Alexander	25	M	Farmer	06No02CI
SPENDAN, Mary	13	F	None	05No02CJ	NASH, Bridget	45	F	Farmer	06No02CI
SMITH, Ellen	09	F	None	05No02CJ	FLOOD, Alice	20	F	Farmer	06No02CI
ENNIS, Esther	18	F	None	05No02CJ	SMITH, Catherine	20	F	Farmer	06No02CI
BAINES, John	25	M	Laborer	05No02CJ	FLOOD, Ellen	50	F	Farmer	06No02CI
Marg.	18	F	Laborer	05No02CJ	MCKENNY, Rose	15	F	Servant	06No02CI
U	.00	U	Infant	05No02CJ	Cath.	13	F	Servant	06No02CI
MCBRIEN, Mary	20	F	None	05No02CJ	Isabella	24	F	Servant	06No02CI
GRAHAM, Hannah	20	F	None	05No02CJ	GREEN, George	24	M	Mechanic	06No02CI
MARTIN, Rose	20	F	None	05No02CJ	Ann	21	F	Mechanic	06No02CI
MCCUSKEN, Cath.	20	F	None	05No02CJ	William	27	M	Mechanic	06No02CI
MURPHY, Dennis	50	M	Laborer	05No02CJ	Joseph	23	M	Mechanic	06No02CI
U (W)	46	F	None	05No02CJ	Sarah	21	F	Mechanic	06No02CI
Dennis	18	M	Laborer	05No02CJ	Jane	.00	F	Infant	06No02CI
GININE, Betsy	22	F	None	05No02CJ	GARDNER, Martha	15	F	Unknown	06No02CI
Daniel	20	M	Laborer	05No02CJ	KELLEN, Alexander	30	M	Unknown	06No02CI
HOPKINS, Christopher	22	M	Laborer	05No02CJ	Margaret	70	F	Unknown	06No02CI
Wm.	12	M	Laborer	05No02CJ	Died-At-Sea				
MORRIS, Jane	22	F	None	05No02CJ	COPELAND, George	47	M	Mechanic	06No02CI
GALBRATH, Martha	20	F	None	05No02CJ	CONLIN, Mary	20	F	Unknown	06No02CI
Jane	18	F	None	05No02CJ	MCGARREN, Mary	20	F	Unknown	06No02CI
MANERY, Edward	20	M	Laborer	05No02CJ	Eliza	18	F	Unknown	06No02CI
Betty	18	F	None	05No02CJ	Died-At-Sea				
FALKNER, Mary	08	F	Child	05No02CJ	MAXWELL, Jack	73	M	Servant	06No02CI
FLANGAN, Catherine	22	F	Child	05No02CJ	BIGS, Joseph	17	M	Laborer	06No02CI
Robert	22	M	Laborer	05No02CJ	DAYTON, Rose	18	F	Laborer	06No02CI
MCANERY, Margaret	17	F	None	05No02CJ	BYRNES, Mary	21	F	Laborer	06No02CI
GAY, Walter	26	M	Laborer	05No02CJ	HAND, Bridget	24	F	Laborer	06No02CI
Ellen	22	F	None	05No02CJ	Ellen	19	F	Servant	06No02CI
U	.00	U	Infant	05No02CJ	MCPHILIP, Edward	16	M	Servant	06No02CI
MCSHANE, Lawrence	20	M	Laborer	05No02CJ	Alice	29	F	Servant	06No02CI
WOODS, Mary	20	F	None	05No02CJ	MARTIN, Thomas	44	M	Servant	06No02CI
BIRDY, Thomas	20	M	Laborer	05No02CJ	MCKNIGHT, Jan	19	M	Servant	06No02CI
LLOYD, Wm.	55	M	Laborer	05No02CJ	MCCUTCHEAN, John	28	M	Servant	06No02CI
ONEILL, Margret	20	F	None	05No02CJ	MURPHY, Robert	26	M	Servant	06No02CI
LLOYDS, James	24	M	Laborer	05No02CJ	Mary-Ann	20	F	Servant	06No02CI
U (W)	36	F	None	05No02CJ	MCDONOGH, Elizabeth	16	F	Servant	06No02CI
U-Miss.	16	F	None	05No02CJ	Catherine	16	F	Servant	06No02CI
William	18	M	None	05No02CJ	MULLADAY, Cath.	18	F	Servant	06No02CI

NAMES OF PASSENGERS	AGE	SEX	OCCUPATIONS	DATE PORT SHIP	NAMES OF PASSENGERS	AGE	SEX	OCCUPATIONS	DATE PORT SHIP
KENNEDY, Bridget	21	F	Farmer	06No02Cl	RELEY, Belsey	18	M	Servant	06No02Cl
BROOKS, Edward	26	M	Farmer	06No02Cl	FARLEY, Judy	30	F	Servant	06No02Cl
Julia	26	F	Farmer	06No02Cl	Ann	12	F	Servant	06No02Cl
Charles	02	M	Child	06No02Cl	Bridget	02	F	Child	06No02Cl
Joseph	01	M	Child	06No02Cl	MARTIN, Catherine	13	F	None	06No02Cl
BREEMER, Ann	24	F	Servant	06No02Cl	TRACEY, James	28	M	None	06No02Cl
Thomas	02	M	Child	06No02Cl	TACEY, Catherine	25	F	None	06No02Cl
WINN, Alice	19	F	Servant	06No02Cl	SMITH, Margaret	10	F	None	06No02Cl
LEVIN, Henry	24	M	Servant	06No02Cl	RILEY, Maria	18	F	None	06No02Cl
Henry	24	M	Servant	06No02Cl	SMITH, Mary	14	F	None	06No02Cl
KEARNES, James	20	M	Laborer	06No02Cl	Charles	12	M	None	06No02Cl
MCFARLAND, Alexander	45	M	Merchant	06No02Cl	DURFEY, Bridget	11	F	None	06No02Cl
Margaret	38	F	Merchant	06No02Cl	DOHERTY, Cecelia	21	F	None	06No02Cl
Elizabeth	18	F	Merchant	06No02Cl	MCDADE, Catherine	30	F	None	06No02Cl
Duncan	13	M	Merchant	06No02Cl	Margaret	.00	F	Infant	06No02Cl
Agnes	11	F	Merchant	06No02Cl	Michael	60	M	Servant	06No02Cl
Malcom	09	M	Merchant	06No02Cl	John	25	M	Servant	06No02Cl
Mary	06	F	Child	06No02Cl	James	23	M	Servant	06No02Cl
Jessie	03	M	Child	06No02Cl	DONNELL, Michael	21	M	Servant	06No02Cl
HAMELTON, Mary	30	F	Servant	06No02Cl	GARRETTY, James	20	M	Servant	06No02Cl
CERMACAN, Jane	20	F	Servant	06No02Cl	GERDEN, James	22	M	Laborer	06No02Cl
BURNS, Ellen	20	F	Servant	06No02Cl	Catherine	25	F	Laborer	06No02Cl
HAMELTON, Dennis	24	M	Servant	06No02Cl	MCCULLY, Robert	35	M	Servant	06No02Cl
PINKNEY, John	36	M	Servant	06No02Cl	HUGHES, Michael	18	M	Servant	06No02Cl
LEWIS, Mark	38	M	Servant	06No02Cl	CLOSE, Margaret	27	F	Servant	06No02Cl
NEWMAN, Anthony	58	M	Servant	06No02Cl	BERGEN, Cathe.	00	F	Servant	06No02Cl
SULLIVAN, Dennis	45	M	Servant	06No02Cl	Winnifrid	20	F	Servant	06No02Cl
Margaret	40	F	Servant	06No02Cl	Cathe.	20	F	Servant	06No02Cl
Thomas	20	M	Servant	06No02Cl	BROWNE, May	18	F	Servant	06No02Cl
Michael	18	M	Servant	06No02Cl	DENESAN, Mary	11	F	Servant	06No02Cl
John	12	M	Servant	06No02Cl	RILEY, Andrew	22	M	Laborer	06No02Cl
Mary	09	F	Servant	06No02Cl	CAMRIE, Patrick	20	M	Laborer	06No02Cl
Ellen	08	F	Child	06No02Cl	Ellen	24	F	Laborer	06No02Cl
BEHIGH, John	30	M	Laborer	06No02Cl	THOMAS, Cella	22	F	Laborer	06No02Cl
CARROL, James	26	M	Laborer	06No02Cl	STEWART, Patrick	26	M	Servant	06No02Cl
WILLIAMS, John	22	M	Laborer	06No02Cl	LAMONT, Jane	27	F	Servant	06No02Cl
KANE, James	26	M	Laborer	06No02Cl	JONES, Martha	42	F	Servant	06No02Cl
Margaret	26	F	Servant	06No02Cl	CONARD, Peter	25	M	Servant	06No02Cl
RAFFERTY, Eace	25	F	Servant	06No02Cl	BALATONE, Robert	23	M	Servant	06No02Cl
KNEELAN, Ann	19	F	Servant	06No02Cl	BRANNAN, Belenda	18	F	Servant	06No02Cl
MARTIN, Bridget	60	F	Servant	06No02Cl	SMITH, Mary	13	F	Servant	06No02Cl
NERTON, Mary	22	F	Servant	06No02Cl	FINLAY, Thomas	47	M	Servant	06No02Cl
CLARK, Catherine	28	F	Servant	06No02Cl	CAEGAN, Thomas	24	M	Servant	06No02Cl
MCMANUS, James	08	M	Child	06No02Cl	PETTS, Sarah	18	F	Servant	06No02Cl
Ellen	05	F	Child	06No02Cl	Margaret	14	F	Servant	06No02Cl
MCCULLOCH, George	24	M	Servant	06No02Cl	COCHRANS, John	41	M	Laborer	06No02Cl
RUSSEL, Thomas	23	M	Servant	06No02Cl	John	11	M	Laborer	06No02Cl
ELDRIDP, Mark	22	M	Servant	06No02Cl	VISON, James	23	M	Servant	06No02Cl
SUTTON, Michael	25	M	Servant	06No02Cl	JOHNSTON, John	42	M	Laborer	06No02Cl
Mary	23	F	Servant	06No02Cl	PENNERYS, Thomas	26	M	Servant	06No02Cl
HANNEGAN, Wm.	18	M	Servant	06No02Cl	LAMONT, Edward	25	M	Servant	06No02Cl
GANKNEY, Thomas	18	M	Laborer	06No02Cl	CROMLY, William	44	M	Servant	06No02Cl
CARSON, Jane	17	F	Servant	06No02Cl	Jane	37	F	Servant	06No02Cl
LENSEY, Catherine	17	F	Servant	06No02Cl	Jane	08	F	Child	06No02Cl
KELLEN, Mary	17	F	Servant	06No02Cl	BENNELL, Bridget	17	F	None	06No02Cl
HALLCEAN, Patt	22	M	Servant	06No02Cl	BRESSLY, John	20	M	None	06No02Cl
QUECK, John	17	M	Servant	06No02Cl	MCAVOY, Patt	23	M	None	06No02Cl
HILL, Joseph	25	M	Servant	06No02Cl	MARTIN, Susan	28	F	None	06No02Cl
KERR, Daniel	40	M	Laborer	06No02Cl	Ann	.00	F	Infant	06No02Cl
Anderson	07	M	Child	06No02Cl	TURNER, Mary	22	F	None	06No02Cl
MARTIN, James	25	M	Laborer	06No02Cl	SWEENEY, Bridget	28	F	None	06No02Cl
FAREL, Bridget	18	F	Laborer	06No02Cl	CARTER, Bridget	20	F	None	06No02Cl
DELLON, Ann	18	F	Laborer	06No02Cl	CONNOLY, Alice	14	F	None	06No02Cl
HOPPARD, Bridget	18	F	Laborer	06No02Cl	James	12	M	None	06No02Cl
COSTELLO, James	22	M	Laborer	06No02Cl	John	10	M	None	06No02Cl
THANEGAN, Danue	30	M	Laborer	06No02Cl	MCMANUS, James	19	M	None	06No02Cl
FARNEN, Michael	18	M	Laborer	06No02Cl	MCKEE, Bridget	17	F	None	06No02Cl
ROBOTTOM, Wm.	18	M	Laborer	06No02Cl	MEHIN, May	18	F	None	06No02Cl
Maria	40	F	Laborer	06No02Cl	CALLIGHAN, Hugh	25	M	None	06No02Cl
Francis	36	F	Laborer	06No02Cl	CORNEY, Peter	25	M	None	06No02Cl
Elizabeth	11	F	Laborer	06No02Cl	DONOHUE, Mary	31	F	None	06No02Cl
William	08	M	Child	06No02Cl	CLANCY, Mary	20	F	None	06No02Cl
Maria	04	F	Child	06No02Cl	VANCE, Cath.	28	F	Servant	06No02Cl
George	.00	F	Infant	06No02Cl	Margaret	05	F	Child	06No02Cl
HAFFTEN, Bridget	12	F	None	06No02Cl	Margaret	05	F	Child	06No02Cl

283

NAMES OF PASSENGERS	A G E	S E X	OCCUPATIONS	DATE PORT SHIP	NAMES OF PASSENGERS	A G E	S E X	OCCUPATIONS	DATE PORT SHIP
VANCE, John	07	M	Child	06No02CI	MCINTERE, William	21	M	Laborer	06No02CI
DUGGAN, James	19	M	Laborer	06No02CI	COCHRAN, James	20	M	Laborer	06No02CI
CLANCY, Miles	24	M	Laborer	06No02CI	MCINTERE, Margaret	12	F	Servant	06No02CI
FARR, George	37	M	Laborer	06No02CI	NEILLE, Henry	32	M	Servant	06No02CI
HYGENS, Richard	26	M	Laborer	06No02CI	MURPHY, John	20	M	Servant	06No02CI
Mary	23	F	Servant	06No02CI	CARR, Dennis	18	M	Servant	06No02CI
Joseph	.00	M	Infant	06No02CI	BULLER, Julia	20	F	Servant	06No02CI
OWENS, John	43	M	Servant	06No02CI	Maria	18	F	Servant	06No02CI
Ann	39	F	Servant	06No02CI	FAILDEN, William	55	M	Servant	06No02CI
TROY, Ann	72	F	Servant	06No02CI	BLUE, James	31	M	Servant	06No02CI
MORRIS, Thomas	39	M	Servant	06No02CI	COFFEE, Ellen	14	F	Servant	06No02CI
Jane	36	F	Servant	06No02CI	Johanna	19	F	Servant	06No02CI
Ann	37	F	Servant	06No02CI	Mary	09	F	Servant	06No02CI
Charles	.00	M	Infant	06No02CI	Robert	08	M	Child	06No02CI
TROY, Martha	37	F	Servant	06No02CI	Phillp	07	M	Child	06No02CI
Wm.	06	M	Child	06No02CI	Catherine	15	F	Unknown	06No02CI
John	03	M	Child	06No02CI	MCDANIEL, Turney	50	M	Unknown	06No02CI
Sarah	02	F	Child	06No02CI	Patt	19	M	Unknown	06No02CI
CUMMINGS, Patrick	30	M	Child	06No02CI	John	15	M	Laborer	06No02CI
Bridget	25	F	Child	06No02CI	Mary	12	F	Servant	06No02CI
Elizabeth	03	F	Child	06No02CI	Michael	10	M	Servant	06No02CI
Patt	02	M	Child	06No02CI	MCDANEL, Betsy	30	F	Servant	06No02CI
Mary-Ann	.00	F	Infant	06No02CI	MCDADE, Pat	21	M	Servant	06No02CI
HOBBY, Eliza	23	F	Servant	06No02CI	RYAN, John	20	M	Servant	06No02CI
Ellen	20	F	Servant	06No02CI	GARDNER, John	45	M	Servant	06No02CI
LACKEN, Esther	18	F	Servant	06No02CI	Julia	36	F	Servant	06No02CI
Laure	20	F	Servant	06No02CI	MALLON, Fredrick	25	M	Servant	06No02CI
HERD, Margaret	20	F	Servant	06No02CI	BLERHASSET, Joseph	35	M	Servant	06No02CI
KERNEY, Margaret	18	F	Servant	06No02CI	WELLINGTON, James	30	M	Servant	06No02CI
GACKNEY, Mary	15	F	Servant	06No02CI	Elizabeth	35	F	Servant	06No02CI
KENNEDY, Timothy	40	M	Laborer	06No02CI	Luke	19	M	Servant	06No02CI
DONOHUE, Patrick	30	M	Laborer	06No02CI	Sophia	15	F	Servant	06No02CI
COCHRAN, Michael	20	M	Laborer	06No02CI	John-Rollitt	21	M	Servant	06No02CI
MOOREHEAD, Mary-A.	20	F	Laborer	06No02CI	LAUTHARD, David	27	M	Servant	06No02CI
YOUNG, Hannah	20	F	Laborer	06No02CI					
ALLEN, Nancy	50	F	Laborer	06No02CI					
KIMBALL, James	17	M	Laborer	06No02CI					
Anthony	16	M	Laborer	06No02CI					
MELLIN, Pat	15	M	Laborer	06No02CI					
LINSON, Eliza	35	F	Laborer	06No02CI	NEW-YORK 06 NOVEMBER 1846				
Elijah	11	M	Laborer	06No02CI					
Enoch	10	M	Laborer	06No02CI	From Liverpool				
Francis	08	M	Child	06No02CI					
WINSER, Caleb	06	M	Child	06No02CI					
Joel	03	M	Child	06No02CI	LOVELL, John	29	M	Gentleman	06No02Bk
Clement	.00	M	Infant	06No02CI	ROCHE, E.	28	M	Unknown	06No02Bk
DOHERTY, Hannah	20	F	Servant	06No02CI	U-Miss	16	F	Unknown	06No02Bk
Ann	09	F	Servant	06No02CI	HUTTON, James	30	M	Unknown	06No02Bk
Eliza	08	F	Child	06No02CI	TUCKER, R.	40	M	Unknown	06No02Bk
WILKINSON, Mariana	20	F	Child	06No02CI	A.H.	13	M	Unknown	06No02Bk
FLANIGAN, Richard	18	M	Laborer	06No02CI	TYLER, Wm.	30	M	Mason	06No02Bk
CLENKEY, John	28	M	Laborer	06No02CI	MCWILLIAMS, Rose	36	F	Unknown	06No02Bk
GAFNEY, Wm.	20	M	Laborer	06No02CI	Ally	12	F	Unknown	06No02Bk
HUTCHINSON, Saml.	30	M	Farmer	06No02CI	Biddy	08	F	Child	06No02Bk
Jane	24	F	Servant	06No02CI	Sally	06	F	Child	06No02Bk
Alice	05	F	Child	06No02CI	MCGOWAN, Biddy	17	F	Unknown	06No02Bk
Robert	02	M	Child	06No02CI	HESLIN, Ann	19	F	Unknown	06No02Bk
REGERS, Henry	20	M	Servant	06No02CI	MCDOWALL, Cath.	20	F	Unknown	06No02Bk
Peter	18	M	Servant	06No02CI	MAHAN, Owen	20	M	Laborer	06No02Bk
KANE, Henry	19	M	Servant	06No02CI	BROWN, David	26	M	Carpenter	06No02Bk
FENLAY, William	18	M	Servant	06No02CI	REYNOLDS, James	30	M	Carpenter	06No02Bk
AGIN, John	45	M	Servant	06No02CI	U (W)	30	F	Wife	06No02Bk
David	11	M	Servant	06No02CI	Michael	12	M	Unknown	06No02Bk
William	00	M	Servant	06No02CI	MCGOWAN, Peggy	19	F	Unknown	06No02Bk
John	09	M	Servant	06No02CI	REYNOLDS, Biddy	11	F	Unknown	06No02Bk
Samuel	08	M	Child	06No02CI	Wm.	09	M	Child	06No02Bk
KERN, Ellen	07	F	Child	06No02CI	James	.00	M	Infant	06No02Bk
DUGAN, Mary	21	F	Servant	06No02CI	CASSIDY, Michael	18	M	Laborer	06No02Bk
CROSBY, Mary	17	F	Servant	06No02CI	SMITH, Jane	18	F	Unknown	06No02Bk
HUBBARD, Alice	16	F	Servant	06No02CI	MCCORR, Peter	50	M	Blacksmith	06No02Bk
ARKERT, Cath.	18	F	Servant	06No02CI	REYNOLDS, James	21	M	Shoemaker	06No02Bk
WOOD, Margaret	17	F	Servant	06No02CI	CONNELL, U-Mrs.	40	F	Unknown	06No02Bk
CUNNINGHAM, Bridget	16	F	Servant	06No02CI	LESTER, Ann	28	F	Unknown	06No02Bk
MURDEN, Catherine	21	F	Servant	06No02CI	CONNELL, James	18	M	Unknown	06No02Bk
GARRIGAN, Rose	10	F	Servant	06No02CI					

NAMES OF PASSENGERS	EX	AGE	SEX	OCCUPATIONS	DATE PORT SHIP
CONNELL, Hugh		16	M	Unknown	06No02Bk
Maria		11	F	Unknown	06No02Bk
MCGLYNN, Michael		22	M	Laborer	06No02Bk
SPELLMAN, Elinor		20	F	Unknown	06No02Bk
BRANNAN, Michael		35	M	Miller	06No02Bk
U	(W)	35	F	Unknown	06No02Bk
Mary	(D)	09	F	Child	06No02Bk
Ellen	(D)	05	F	Child	06No02Bk
Cath.	(D)	07	F	Child	06No02Bk
MULAHEY, Owen		17	M	Child	06No02Bk
DALEY, Winney		25	F	Unknown	06No02Bk
GAVENTY, Mary		38	F	Unknown	06No02Bk
CONNOR, Ann		19	F	Unknown	06No02Bk
DONOHUE, Cath.		22	F	Unknown	06No02Bk
REILLY, Ann		20	F	Unknown	06No02Bk
MITCHELL, Cath.		26	F	Unknown	06No02Bk
Jane		37	F	Unknown	06No02Bk
James		49	M	Tailor	06No02Bk
Bridget		36	F	Unknown	06No02Bk
Owen		08	M	Child	06No02Bk
Ann		07	F	Child	06No02Bk
Mary		02	F	Child	06No02Bk
Thos.		03	M	Child	06No02Bk
GREEN, Mary-A.		17	F	Unknown	06No02Bk
GAFFNEY, Rose		08	F	Child	06No02Bk
EARLY, Patrick		35	M	Tailor	06No02Bk
BLESSING, Peter		18	M	Tailor	06No02Bk
GOUGHNEY, Thos.		22	M	Shoemaker	06No02Bk
CAVE, Margaret		17	F	Unknown	06No02Bk
OBRIEN, Margaret		25	F	Unknown	06No02Bk
MATTHEWS, Ellen		18	F	Unknown	06No02Bk
FARRELL, James		27	M	Sail Maker	06No02Bk
U	(W)	24	F	Wife	06No02Bk
Thos.	(S)	.00	M	Infant	06No02Bk
YORK, James		26	M	Laborer	06No02Bk
U	(W)	30	F	Wife	06No02Bk
U		.00	U	Infant	06No02Bk
MCGOWEN, James		24	M	Post	06No02Bk
CONOREY, Patrick		25	M	Upholsterer	06No02Bk
Eliza		24	F	Unknown	06No02Bk
MCCONNER, Eliza		20	F	Unknown	06No02Bk
MCKAY, Nancy		18	F	Unknown	06No02Bk
BRADLEY, Grace		18	F	Unknown	06No02Bk
CASSIDEY, Nancy		17	F	Unknown	06No02Bk
CAMPBELL, Fanny		19	F	Unknown	06No02Bk
MCGOUGHLIN, Henry		22	M	Laborer	06No02Bk
CASSIDEY, James		22	M	Carpenter	06No02Bk
U	(W)	20	F	Wife	06No02Bk
CAWLEY, Aaron		46	M	Laborer	06No02Bk
CHANN, John		32	M	Collier	06No02Bk
MCMENTENSHIP, U		20	U	Unknown	06No02Bk
MAUGHTEN, David		40	M	Laborer	06No02Bk
U	(W)	30	F	Wife	06No02Bk
Cath.	(D)	12	F	Unknown	06No02Bk
Mary	(D)	11	F	Unknown	06No02Bk
Pat	(S)	08	M	Child	06No02Bk
Biddy	(D)	06	F	Child	06No02Bk
Sally	(D)	.00	F	Infant	06No02Bk
DEHAN, Pat		29	M	Unknown	06No02Bk
CASSIGER, Mary		16	F	Unknown	06No02Bk
MCCARTEY, James		27	M	Laborer	06No02Bk
DONOHUE, John		20	M	Unknown	06No02Bk
MCCARTEY, Ann		20	F	Unknown	06No02Bk
BERGAN, Bessy		20	F	Unknown	06No02Bk
MCDONNELL, Dominick		45	M	Laborer	06No02Bk
Honora		40	F	Unknown	06No02Bk
Margaret		20	F	Unknown	06No02Bk
MCDONALD, James		22	M	Painter	06No02Bk
MCCARTHY, James		20	M	Unknown	06No02Bk
REILLY, Catherine		20	F	Unknown	06No02Bk
Philip		20	M	Unknown	06No02Bk
LAWRENCE, Fanny		30	F	Unknown	06No02Bk
MCGOVERN, Philip		20	M	Unknown	06No02Bk
KING, Hugh		20	M	Unknown	06No02Bk
BRADY, Mary		18	F	Unknown	06No02Bk
BRADY, Ann		13	F	Unknown	06No02Bk
MCCARTHY, Susan		18	F	Unknown	06No02Bk
DAWSON, Nally		18	F	Unknown	06No02Bk
GILEANY, Mary		20	F	Unknown	06No02Bk
FRAZIER, Cath.		30	F	Unknown	06No02Bk
Fanny		05	F	Child	06No02Bk
HALEY, Felicia		16	F	Unknown	06No02Bk
FITZGERALD, Patrick		18	M	Unknown	06No02Bk
Mary		18	F	Unknown	06No02Bk
MURRAY, James		24	M	Laborer	06No02Bk
MEYAN, Bridget		40	F	Laborer	06No02Bk
WALLERS, Cath.		18	F	Laborer	06No02Bk
MCGINTY, Mary		17	F	Laborer	06No02Bk
ODONNELL, Susan		22	F	Laborer	06No02Bk
BEGGS, Jane		00	F	Laborer	06No02Bk
Lavinia		16	F	Laborer	06No02Bk
LYNCH, Biddy		26	F	Laborer	06No02Bk
CLUFF, Robt.		54	M	Glazier	06No02Bk
Jane		21	F	Unknown	06No02Bk
Edward		17	M	Unknown	06No02Bk
QUILLAN, Bridget		17	F	Unknown	06No02Bk
MURPHY, James		20	M	Unknown	06No02Bk
MCKEAN, Pat		21	M	Laborer	06No02Bk
Ann		20	F	Unknown	06No02Bk
REILLY, Rose		16	F	Unknown	06No02Bk
Rose		15	F	Unknown	06No02Bk
GAYNOR, Ann		17	F	Unknown	06No02Bk
Patrick		18	M	Unknown	06No02Bk
Julia		16	F	Unknown	06No02Bk
MCGINNISS, Henry		40	M	Glazier	06No02Bk
MCCANNA, Francis		40	M	Digger	06No02Bk
CAFFREY, Owen		27	M	Digger	06No02Bk
SMITH, Ellen		17	F	Unknown	06No02Bk
FITZPATRICK, Cath.		18	F	Unknown	06No02Bk
CONOLLY, Ellen		20	F	Unknown	06No02Bk
MCCAFFREY, Isabell		20	F	Unknown	06No02Bk
Margaret		12	F	Unknown	06No02Bk
WARD, Mary		10	F	Unknown	06No02Bk
DUFFIE, Biddy		10	F	Unknown	06No02Bk
REILLY, John		25	M	Shoemaker	06No02Bk
Mary		25	F	Unknown	06No02Bk
LUCAS, U		40	M	Tailor	06No02Bk
STEVENSON, John		26	M	Laborer	06No02Bk
MCCOSTEN, John		22	M	Post	06No02Bk
CULLEN, Mary		24	F	Unknown	06No02Bk
IRVINE, Cath.		18	F	Unknown	06No02Bk
ROONEY, U		25	M	Painter	06No02Bk
CULLEN, Martin		27	M	Shoemaker	06No02Bk
CORTEY, William		19	M	Unknown	06No02Bk
PHELAN, Thos.		25	M	Wheelwright	06No02Bk
MASTERMANN, Pat		18	M	Unknown	06No02Bk
KEARNY, Timothy		32	M	Laborer	06No02Bk
MCAVORY, Michael		23	M	Laborer	06No02Bk
KEALING, Maria		20	F	Unknown	06No02Bk
LONGHERY, Bernard		35	M	Last Maker	06No02Bk
LAMB, James		23	M	Laborer	06No02Bk
MULVEHIL, Henry		29	M	Unknown	06No02Bk
MORAN, Thos.		26	M	Laborer	06No02Bk
U	(W)	22	F	Unknown	06No02Bk
HALWELL, James		19	M	Unknown	06No02Bk
KING, Malachi		20	M	Unknown	06No02Bk
MCGAVERY, John		33	M	Laborer	06No02Bk
MULOY, Pat		21	M	Laborer	06No02Bk
SWEENEY, Pat		20	M	Laborer	06No02Bk
GAVAHA, Susan		20	F	Laborer	06No02Bk
SWEENEY, Margaret		20	F	Laborer	06No02Bk
KENNEDY, Bridget		21	F	Laborer	06No02Bk
DOUGHERTY, Thos.		25	M	Laborer	06No02Bk
Bridget		22	F	Unknown	06No02Bk
CLOSKEN, Patrick		20	M	Unknown	06No02Bk
MURPHY, Ann		20	F	Unknown	06No02Bk
SHANNON, John		27	M	Laborer	06No02Bk
HOY, Rose		25	F	Unknown	06No02Bk
Cath.		23	F	Unknown	06No02Bk
GAFFNEY, Michael		19	M	Unknown	06No02Bk

NAMES OF PASSENGERS		AGE	SEX	OCCUPATIONS	DATE PORT SHIP
CONNELLY, U-Mrs.		35	F	Unknown	06No02Bk
Eliza		19	F	Unknown	06No02Bk
H.J.		16	U	Unknown	06No02Bk
MARTIN, Alice		20	F	Unknown	06No02Bk
HANCOCK, U-Mrs.		30	F	Unknown	06No02Bk
Sarah	(D)	04	F	Child	06No02Bk
Mary	(D)	.00	F	Infant	06No02Bk
HOGG, Wm.		11	M	Unknown	06No02Bk
MINEALRY, Wm.		23	M	Laborer	06No02Bk
MATTHEWS, Robt.		29	M	Unknown	06No02Bk
WOODS, James		20	M	Unknown	06No02Bk
GREEN, Thomas-M.		24	M	Shoemaker	06No02Bk
John		24	M	Shoemaker	06No02Bk
COATES, Wm.		30	M	Collier	06No02Bk
KEEFFE, David		21	M	Laborer	06No02Bk
KEEFFEE, Michael		25	M	Laborer	06No02Bk
KEEFE, Peggy		32	F	Unknown	06No02Bk
Johanna		32	F	Unknown	06No02Bk
CONNILL, John		35	M	Smith	06No02Bk
ROBINSON, James		30	M	Unknown	06No02Bk
DOYLE, Eliza		20	F	Unknown	06No02Bk
MCQUEENEY, Timothy		29	M	Laborer	06No02Bk
MCGUIRE, Ann		18	F	Unknown	06No02Bk
RICE, Bernard		13	M	Unknown	06No02Bk
GAFFNEY, P.		22	U	Unknown	06No02Bk
GORMAN, P.		24	M	Laborer	06No02Bk
NIXON, Edward		30	M	Laborer	06No02Bk
COSLIN, Mary		18	F	Unknown	06No02Bk
EGLAN, Thos.		20	M	Unknown	06No02Bk
MOONSEY, Bridget		18	F	Unknown	06No02Bk
Pat		16	M	Unknown	06No02Bk
David		12	M	Unknown	06No02Bk
Alice		14	F	Unknown	06No02Bk
MCGREAL, Winifred		13	F	Unknown	06No02Bk
FITZPATRICK, Bridget		14	F	Unknown	06No02Bk
MCGREAL, Maria		10	F	Unknown	06No02Bk
FISHER, Catharine		20	F	Unknown	06No02Bk
DOUGLAS, John		17	M	Unknown	06No02Bk
COSTELLO, Mary		29	F	Unknown	06No02Bk
FARRELL, Mary		15	F	Unknown	06No02Bk
BRUEN, Michael		40	M	Laborer	06No02Bk
MCCARTY, Jane		08	F	Child	06No02Bk
BRAGAN, Pat		14	M	Unknown	06No02Bk
Cath.		11	F	Unknown	06No02Bk
Ann		09	F	Child	06No02Bk
WARD, Mary		21	F	Unknown	06No02Bk
ARMSTRONG, Cath.		30	F	Unknown	06No02Bk
GRANSFIELD, Robt.		20	M	Unknown	06No02Bk
FEENEY, John		27	M	Laborer	06No02Bk
Cath.		08	F	Child	06No02Bk
COWAN, Mary		20	F	Laborer	06No02Bk
BUSCOWE, Elizabeth		30	F	Laborer	06No02Bk
RILEY, Thos.		19	M	Laborer	06No02Bk
ROACH, Bridget		40	F	Laborer	06No02Bk
MULLIGAN, Cath.		20	F	Laborer	06No02Bk
Elizabeth		18	F	Laborer	06No02Bk
WOODS, Chas.		16	M	Laborer	06No02Bk
KELLY, Mary		30	F	Laborer	06No02Bk
Maria	(D)	05	F	Child	06No02Bk
Margaret	(D)	03	F	Child	06No02Bk
Catherine	(D)	.00	F	Infant	06No02Bk
RANOKE, Anna		16	F	Unknown	06No02Bk
JOHNSON, Marg.		30	F	Unknown	06No02Bk
Ellen	(D)	08	F	Child	06No02Bk
John	(S)	03	M	Child	06No02Bk
James	(S)	01	M	Child	06No02Bk
REILLY, Margaret		18	F	Unknown	06No02Bk
WILLSON, Robt.		20	M	Unknown	06No02Bk
BUBAGE, Joseph		18	M	Unknown	06No02Bk
KELLY, Cath.		17	F	Unknown	06No02Bk
BRENNAN, Michael		40	M	Blacksmith	06No02Bk
BOYLAN, Bridget		20	F	Unknown	06No02Bk
CLARK, Mary		18	F	Unknown	06No02Bk
MOORE, Mary		85	F	Unknown	06No02Bk
MCLAUGHLIN, Mary		15	F	Unknown	06No02Bk

NAMES OF PASSENGERS		AGE	SEX	OCCUPATIONS	DATE PORT SHIP
MELADEY, Margaret		50	F	Unknown	06No02Bk
Ann		20	F	Unknown	06No02Bk
COHILL, Margaret		40	F	Unknown	06No02Bk
LALEY, Michael		19	M	Unknown	06No02Bk
MORAN, Ellen		21	F	Unknown	06No02Bk
MALONE, Jane		20	F	Unknown	06No02Bk
DOLAN, Thos.		40	M	Laborer	06No02Bk
GILL, Barney		40	M	Laborer	06No02Bk
THOMPSON, Ann		18	F	Unknown	06No02Bk
CORONE, Biddy		17	F	Unknown	06No02Bk
GILLIGAN, Matthew		40	M	Laborer	06No02Bk
BRENNAN, Michael		.00	M	Infant	06No02Bk
Born-At-Sea					

WAGRAM 06 NOVEMBER 1846

From London

NAMES OF PASSENGERS		AGE	SEX	OCCUPATIONS	DATE PORT SHIP
BURNS, John		28	M	Blacksmith	06No21Dk
FITZGERALD, William		30	M	Tailor	06No21Dk
HARRINGTON, Patrick		33	M	Tailor	06No21Dk
FITZGERALD, Margaret		20	F	Unknown	06No21Dk
HARRINGTON, Mary		29	F	Unknown	06No21Dk

RAPPAHANOCK 11 NOVEMBER 1846

From Liverpool

NAMES OF PASSENGERS		AGE	SEX	OCCUPATIONS	DATE PORT SHIP
BRADY, Nancy		16	F	None	11No02Dm
FOX, Pat		21	M	Laborer	11No02Dm
GALLAGHER, Pat		60	M	Laborer	11No02Dm
Maria		18	F	Servant	11No02Dm
WALSH, Anthony		19	M	Unknown	11No02Dm
MCAMITY, Patt		20	M	Unknown	11No02Dm
CALPHIN, John		20	M	Unknown	11No02Dm
DINNIRY, John		25	M	Unknown	11No02Dm
BRENNAN, Thomas		25	M	Unknown	11No02Dm
CHAMBERLAIN, Thomas		20	M	Laborer	11No02Dm
FLYN, Patt		20	M	Laborer	11No02Dm
OBRIAN, John		25	M	Laborer	11No02Dm
Peter		25	M	Laborer	11No02Dm
GOWAN, Tim		30	M	Laborer	11No02Dm
MURPHY, Patt		36	M	Laborer	11No02Dm
Mary		36	F	None	11No02Dm
Died-At-Sea					
Honora		15	F	None	11No02Dm
Elisa		13	F	None	11No02Dm
Margaret		06	F	None	11No02Dm
Ellen		10	F	None	11No02Dm
Margaret		04	F	None	11No02Dm
COSTELLO, Thos.		23	M	Laborer	11No02Dm
SIMPSON, George		13	M	None	11No02Dm
MOORE, Marcy		20	F	None	11No02Dm
ASSAM, Margaret		20	F	None	11No02Dm
SOLOMON, David		20	M	Tailor	11No02Dm
MCGIVEN, James		30	M	Farmer	11No02Dm
Mary	(W)	30	F	Wife	11No02Dm
Anna	(D)	10	F	None	11No02Dm
Kitty	(D)	08	F	None	11No02Dm
Mary	(D)	05	F	None	11No02Dm
MCQUIRE, Francis		30	M	Farmer	11No02Dm
Mary		30	F	Farmer	11No02Dm
Margaret		09	F	Farmer	11No02Dm

NAMES OF PASSENGERS	AGE	SEX	OCCUPATIONS	DATE PORT SHIP
PITY, Ellen	20	F	Servant	11No02Dm
OHARA, Catherine	30	F	Servant	11No02Dm
COLLISON, Maria	20	F	Servant	11No02Dm
DISON, James	20	M	Farmer	11No02Dm
Mary	20	F	Farmer	11No02Dm
Ann	02	F	Child	11No02Dm
Thos.	01	M	Child	11No02Dm
CUDDEN, Robert-J.	20	M	Laborer	11No02Dm
BRYAN, James-J.	40	M	Laborer	11No02Dm
BRADY, James	50	M	Laborer	11No02Dm
Mary	20	F	Wife	11No02Dm
Rose	24	F	None	11No02Dm
Catherine	15	F	None	11No02Dm
MARKY, Mary	18	F	None	11No02Dm
HUGHS, Elisabeth	18	F	None	11No02Dm
MCGIVEN, Catherine	20	F	None	11No02Dm
NANUN, Thos.	25	M	None	11No02Dm
TAYLOR, Thos.	20	M	None	11No02Dm
WALSH, Thos.	24	M	None	11No02Dm
Jane	24	F	Servant	11No02Dm
MCGUIRE, Edward	42	M	Mechanic	11No02Dm
IRVIS, James	24	M	Laborer	11No02Dm
KELLY, Ann	20	F	Servant	11No02Dm
MCGEE, Ann	20	F	Servant	11No02Dm
MURPHY, Betty	20	F	Servant	11No02Dm
LENNEN, Eliza	22	F	Servant	11No02Dm
MCCORMICK, Eliza	22	F	Servant	11No02Dm
TUNUY, Ann	22	F	Servant	11No02Dm
BRADY, James	17	M	None	11No02Dm
RILEY, Michael	26	M	None	11No02Dm
Mary	23	F	Servant	11No02Dm
SMITH, Mary	24	F	Servant	11No02Dm
WALSH, Mary	26	F	Servant	11No02Dm
SHORLNISSY, James	39	M	Farmer	11No02Dm
Catherine	39	F	Farmer	11No02Dm
Thos.	19	M	Farmer	11No02Dm
Mary	13	F	Farmer	11No02Dm
Tibby	11	F	Farmer	11No02Dm
Michael	09	M	Child	11No02Dm
HADDIN, Thos.	20	M	Laborer	11No02Dm
KINAN, Michael	45	M	Laborer	11No02Dm
Mary	45	F	Unknown	11No02Dm
Ann	21	F	Unknown	11No02Dm
Cornelia	18	F	Unknown	11No02Dm
Catherine	15	F	Unknown	11No02Dm
John	13	M	Unknown	11No02Dm
Mary	09	F	Child	11No02Dm
Sally	04	F	Child	11No02Dm
Jane	06	F	Child	11No02Dm
Michael	02	M	Child	11No02Dm
MONAGAN, James	24	M	Farmer	11No02Dm
Sally (W)	26	F	Wife	11No02Dm
GALLAHER, Patt	50	M	None	11No02Dm
DONNELL, Francis	21	M	None	11No02Dm
GALLAHER, Kitty	35	F	None	11No02Dm
ELLIOT, Will	12	M	None	11No02Dm
Mary	10	F	None	11No02Dm
Kitty	08	F	None	11No02Dm
Cornellus	07	M	None	11No02Dm
MCCAFFERTY, John	20	M	Laborer	11No02Dm
Ann (W)	18	F	Wife	11No02Dm
BOYLE, Hannah	20	F	Laborer	11No02Dm
DILITH, Fanny	20	F	Laborer	11No02Dm
CARBY, John	20	M	Laborer	11No02Dm
Mary	18	F	None	11No02Dm
CAMPBELL, Alexander	24	M	Farmer	11No02Dm
Mary-Ann	20	F	Unknown	11No02Dm
WILSON, Thos.	40	M	Farmer	11No02Dm
COSTELLO, Fanny	18	F	None	11No02Dm
KANE, Henry	20	M	None	11No02Dm
MCLAUGHIN, Margaret	17	F	None	11No02Dm
BLACK, Wm.	70	M	Farmer	11No02Dm
James	40	M	Farmer	11No02Dm
Robt.	40	M	Farmer	11No02Dm
Mary-Ann	22	F	None	11No02Dm
BLACK, Wm.	03	M	Child	11No02Dm
Mary	02	F	Child	11No02Dm
Jane	.06	F	Infant	11No02Dm
MCCAFFY, Terence	30	M	Laborer	11No02Dm
ATWELL, George	22	M	Laborer	11No02Dm
MCKINNY, Alexander	25	M	Laborer	11No02Dm
WILSON, Allice	30	F	None	11No02Dm
Anna	28	F	None	11No02Dm
HUGHS, Mary	20	F	None	11No02Dm
MONTGOMERY, John	20	M	None	11No02Dm
NEIL, Catherine	35	F	Farmer	11No02Dm
Died-At-Sea				
Mary	17	F	Farmer	11No02Dm
DOUGH, Daniel	22	M	Farmer	11No02Dm
GILMAN, Philip	21	M	Farmer	11No02Dm
GIBON, James	22	M	Laborer	11No02Dm
HAGARTY, John	23	M	Laborer	11No02Dm
Died-At-Sea				
Mary	18	F	None	11No02Dm
DONOGHUE, Mary	15	F	None	11No02Dm
BRADY, Rose	17	F	None	11No02Dm
FITZPATRICK, Patt	30	M	Farmer	11No02Dm
MCCONNER, James	22	F	Farmer	11No02Dm
Catherine	26	F	Wife	11No02Dm
HASLETT, George	30	M	Farmer	11No02Dm
QUIGLEY, Betty	20	F	None	11No02Dm
Dennis	40	M	Farmer	11No02Dm
Mary	40	F	Farmer	11No02Dm
Thos.	02	M	Unknown	11No02Dm
Mary	01	F	Unknown	11No02Dm
BENIGAN, John	25	M	Laborer	11No02Dm
Mary (W)	20	F	Wife	11No02Dm
FITZPATRICK, Catherine	20	F	None	11No02Dm
BROPHERY, Bridget	20	F	None	11No02Dm
DILLANY, Anna	20	F	Servant	11No02Dm
FOGERTY, George	20	M	Laborer	11No02Dm
WILSON, John	25	M	Laborer	11No02Dm
WARD, John	20	M	Laborer	11No02Dm
MACKEY, Bernard	20	M	Laborer	11No02Dm
HALFPENNY, Mary	15	F	None	11No02Dm
WARD, Mary	16	F	None	11No02Dm
DOHERTY, Bridget	20	F	None	11No02Dm
FLANAGAN, Maria	20	F	None	11No02Dm
LAHIFF, John	32	M	Farmer	11No02Dm
Laura	30	F	Farmer	11No02Dm
Bridget	30	F	Farmer	11No02Dm
Michael	07	M	Farmer	11No02Dm
John	05	M	None	11No02Dm
Mary	03	F	None	11No02Dm
Thos.	01	M	None	11No02Dm
BRADY, James	20	M	Laborer	11No02Dm
Margaret	20	F	Servant	11No02Dm
KEELEHER, Wm.	26	M	Laborer	11No02Dm
GULEN, Patt	26	M	Laborer	11No02Dm
DEGNAN, Alice	26	F	Servant	11No02Dm
BYRNE, Mary	23	F	Servant	11No02Dm
GANAGAN, Mary	22	F	Servant	11No02Dm
MCKENNY, Patt	19	M	None	11No02Dm
DEGNAN, Rose	17	F	None	11No02Dm
TUNNAY, Ann	37	F	None	11No02Dm
MCKENNITH, Catherine	13	F	None	11No02Dm
Eliza	10	F	None	11No02Dm
CULLEN, Wm.	21	M	Laborer	11No02Dm
CRENEN, Peter	21	M	Laborer	11No02Dm
Rose	30	F	None	11No02Dm
Henry	02	M	None	11No02Dm
Maurice	03	M	None	11No02Dm
BELL, Robert	36	M	Farmer	11No02Dm
Jane	36	F	Unknown	11No02Dm
Margaret	48	F	Unknown	11No02Dm
Mary	50	F	Unknown	11No02Dm
Sampson	12	M	Unknown	11No02Dm
Eliza	08	F	Unknown	11No02Dm
Margaret	09	F	Unknown	11No02Dm
Ellen	06	F	Unknown	11No02Dm

NAMES OF PASSENGERS		AGE	SEX	OCCUPATIONS	DATE PORT SHIP
BELL, Ann		02	F	Unknown	11No02Dm
James		34	M	Farmer	11No02Dm
Sally		30	F	Unknown	11No02Dm
William		01	M	None	11No02Dm
Mary		08	F	None	11No02Dm
Sally		05	F	None	11No02Dm
MCKEE, Betty		30	F	Servant	11No02Dm
CARTY, Wm.		20	M	Laborer	11No02Dm
ONIEL, Edward		20	M	Laborer	11No02Dm
MAHON, Mary		40	F	None	11No02Dm
Patt		20	M	None	11No02Dm
Martin		16	M	None	11No02Dm
Thomas		18	M	None	11No02Dm
Judy		12	F	None	11No02Dm
Margaret		11	F	None	11No02Dm
Francis		06	M	None	11No02Dm
BERGIN, Patt		25	M	Laborer	11No02Dm
Peggy	(W)	30	F	Wife	11No02Dm
Ann		03	F	None	11No02Dm
MOONEY, John		20	M	Laborer	11No02Dm
DONLY, James		20	M	Laborer	11No02Dm
REID, Graham		40	M	None	11No02Dm
Isabella		20	F	None	11No02Dm
LAWLESS, Mary		19	F	None	11No02Dm
HAWKINS, Bridget		20	F	None	11No02Dm
MURPHY, Eliza		07	F	None	11No02Dm
FOSTER, Thomas		49	M	Farmer	11No02Dm
Martha	(W)	50	F	Wife	11No02Dm
Mary	(D)	19	F	Daughter	11No02Dm
DAILY, Henry		21	M	Laborer	11No02Dm
REAGAN, Rose		30	F	Servant	11No02Dm
BRADY, Mary		20	F	Servant	11No02Dm
DAWSON, Thomas		20	M	Laborer	11No02Dm
CASEY, Michael		25	M	Laborer	11No02Dm
KELLY, Daniel		20	M	Laborer	11No02Dm
GORNILY, Bridget		30	F	None	11No02Dm
FARNEY, Tim		25	M	Farmer	11No02Dm
Jane	(W)	20	F	Wife	11No02Dm
MORE, Wm.		40	M	Farmer	11No02Dm
Robert		20	M	Farmer	11No02Dm
LEWIS, Rice		40	M	Farmer	11No02Dm
Died-At-Sea					
WILSON, Thomas		50	M	Farmer	11No02Dm
John		15	M	Farmer	11No02Dm
Richard		11	M	None	11No02Dm
RADENS, Ally		20	F	None	11No02Dm
OWENS, Edward		22	M	None	11No02Dm
WHALEN, Jane		20	F	Servant	11No02Dm
GAHAGAN, Ellen		18	F	Servant	11No02Dm
CONBUS, John		06	M	None	11No02Dm
Phillip		04	M	None	11No02Dm
BOURKE, John		20	M	Laborer	11No02Dm
CARROL, Mary		30	F	None	11No02Dm
Michael		01	M	None	11No02Dm
COYLE, Peter		25	M	Laborer	11No02Dm
GARNITT, Agness		28	F	None	11No02Dm
Jane		12	F	None	11No02Dm
Eliza		04	F	None	11No02Dm
MOORE, James		20	M	Laborer	11No02Dm
MCINTIRE, Alice		18	F	Unknown	11No02Dm
DOOLAN, Mylo		20	M	Laborer	11No02Dm
MARTHA, Wm.		25	M	Laborer	11No02Dm
SHERIDAN, Charles		20	M	Laborer	11No02Dm
Mary	(W)	20	F	Wife	11No02Dm
CONNELLY, Mary		20	F	None	11No02Dm
WHITE, Bart		40	M	Farmer	11No02Dm
CARTY, Tim		25	M	Farmer	11No02Dm
Mary	(W)	25	F	Wife	11No02Dm
MCINTIRE, Mary		20	F	None	11No02Dm
WARREN, Mary		40	F	None	11No02Dm
James		16	M	None	11No02Dm
George		13	M	None	11No02Dm
Mary-Ann		11	F	None	11No02Dm
Anna		09	F	None	11No02Dm
Harriet		07	F	None	11No02Dm
TILFORD, Andrew		25	M	Laborer	11No02Dm
GALWAY, James		30	M	Laborer	11No02Dm
BERGEN, Margaret		01	F	None	11No02Dm
CRUNILY, Joseph		40	M	Farmer	11No02Dm
CALL, Wm.		24	M	Farmer	11No02Dm
LYNN, Jane		20	F	Servant	11No02Dm
QUIN, Mary		20	F	Servant	11No02Dm
John		20	M	Laborer	11No02Dm
RICHARDS, Mary		30	F	Servant	11No02Dm
FLANNAGAN, Mary		30	F	Servant	11No02Dm
BAXTER, Mary		30	F	Servant	11No02Dm
TURRETT, Samuel		30	M	Laborer	11No02Dm
KEHOE, Patt		30	M	Farmer	11No02Dm
Mary	(W)	30	F	Wife	11No02Dm
Eliza		06	F	None	11No02Dm
Edward		01	M	None	11No02Dm
GASPIN, Patt		20	M	None	11No02Dm
BASNEN, Jeramia		20	M	None	11No02Dm
SPLARN, Margaret		20	F	None	11No02Dm
MATHEW, Wm.		26	M	Laborer	11No02Dm
FURRY, Edward		25	M	Laborer	11No02Dm
Mary	(W)	20	F	Wife	11No02Dm
HEALY, Margaret		20	F	None	11No02Dm
BRADY, Esther		26	F	None	11No02Dm
Sarah		22	F	None	11No02Dm
GAFFENY, Patt		16	M	None	11No02Dm
Ann		18	F	None	11No02Dm
RYAE, Andrew		20	M	Laborer	11No02Dm
Catherine	(W)	21	F	Wife	11No02Dm
BROOM, Mary		25	F	Servant	11No02Dm
SMITH, Mary		25	F	Servant	11No02Dm
GRACES, Sidney		18	M	Servant	11No02Dm
WAUNSLY, Joseph		25	M	Laborer	11No02Dm
GALIGAN, Catherine		50	F	None	11No02Dm
COMISTY, Thomas		07	M	None	11No02Dm
DOLAN, Bridget		18	F	Servant	11No02Dm
KELLY, Sarah		15	F	None	11No02Dm
John		13	M	None	11No02Dm
Michael		10	M	None	11No02Dm
CLARK, Margaret		40	F	None	11No02Dm
Thomas		07	M	None	11No02Dm
John		04	M	None	11No02Dm
Ann		01	F	None	11No02Dm
Died-At-Sea					
FRENCH, Patt		20	M	Laborer	11No02Dm
HUGHS, Patt		18	M	Laborer	11No02Dm
MOONY, Ann		40	F	None	11No02Dm
Mary		20	F	None	11No02Dm
KERNAN, John		20	M	Laborer	11No02Dm
Edward		18	M	Laborer	11No02Dm
LINTON, Benjamin		25	M	Laborer	11No02Dm
REILY, John		50	M	Laborer	11No02Dm
John		21	M	Laborer	11No02Dm
Bridget		50	F	Wife	11No02Dm
Bridget		16	F	None	11No02Dm
Catherine		12	F	None	11No02Dm
KENNADY, Mary		19	F	None	11No02Dm
LINTON, Margaret		22	F	Servant	11No02Dm
RYAN, James		27	M	Laborer	11No02Dm
WILSON, George		26	M	Laborer	11No02Dm
BRADY, Rose		20	F	Servant	11No02Dm
FALON, Felix		40	M	Farmer	11No02Dm
FOX, Owen		52	M	Farmer	11No02Dm
Eliza	(W)	40	F	Wife	11No02Dm
MULRAN, Mary		20	F	None	11No02Dm
Owen		08	M	None	11No02Dm
Catherine		06	F	None	11No02Dm
Wm.		02	M	None	11No02Dm
Jane		01	F	None	11No02Dm
Died-At-Sea					
FOX, Sulet		25	M	Laborer	11No02Dm
GALHAHER, Francis		18	M	Laborer	11No02Dm
KELHER, Michael		40	M	Farmer	11No02Dm
Ellen	(W)	40	F	Wife	11No02Dm
Julia	(D)	13	F	Child	11No02Dm

NAMES OF PASSENGERS		AGE	SEX	OCCUPATIONS	DATE PORT SHIP
KELHER, Catherine	(D)	08	F	Child	11No02Dm
Johana	(D)	03	F	Child	11No02Dm
Ellen	(D)	.06	F	Infant	11No02Dm
Died-At-Sea					
Conny		24	M	Laborer	11No02Dm
FLYN, Tim		22	M	Laborer	11No02Dm
Margaret	(W)	21	F	Wife	11No02Dm
HONAGAN, Margaret		21	F	Servant	11No02Dm
MCINTIRE, Rose		17	F	Servant	11No02Dm
Nancy		12	F	None	11No02Dm
GONNS, James		20	M	Laborer	11No02Dm
BELL, Robert		30	M	Laborer	11No02Dm
MELWARD, Ann		30	F	Servant	11No02Dm
WRIGHT, George		25	M	Laborer	11No02Dm
RACHFORD, William		25	M	Janitor	11No02Dm
CHIDLOW, George		30	M	Laborer	11No02Dm
ONEIL, Catherine		15	F	None	11No02Dm
Mary		12	F	None	11No02Dm
NEAL, Jane		30	F	Servant	11No02Dm
CONLIN, James		20	M	Laborer	11No02Dm
Molly	(W)	20	F	Wife	11No02Dm
Catherine		25	F	None	11No02Dm
KENNY, Patt		25	M	Laborer	11No02Dm
DELANY, Luke		25	M	Laborer	11No02Dm
COHALL, John		20	M	Laborer	11No02Dm
GRIFFIN, Sarah		20	F	Servant	11No02Dm
MALLICE, Robert		27	M	Laborer	11No02Dm
HICH, Wm.		27	M	Laborer	11No02Dm

NEW-HAMPSHIRE 12 NOVEMBER 1846

From Liverpool

NAMES OF PASSENGERS		AGE	SEX	OCCUPATIONS	DATE PORT SHIP
COLEMAN, Daniel		23	M	Ctlh	12No02EI
Mary	(W)	24	F	Wife	12No02EI
FLANAGAN, Maria		23	F	Wife	12No02EI
KELLY, Bridget		20	F	None	12No02EI
MASON, Anna		24	F	Wife	12No02EI
HALL, George		22	M	Laborer	12No02EI
John		50	M	Laborer	12No02EI
Died-At-Sea					
LEONARD, Edrd.		20	M	Polisher	12No02EI
MONAGHEN, Thos.		50	M	Laborer	12No02EI
DOLAN, John		20	M	Laborer	12No02EI
DOYLE, Thos.		40	M	Servant	12No02EI
MICHE, David		17	M	Laborer	12No02EI
SODA, Isack		19	M	Laborer	12No02EI
AGEN, Andrew		48	M	Laborer	12No02EI
Died-At-Sea					
Cathe.	(W)	42	F	Wife	12No02EI
John		17	M	Laborer	12No02EI
David		12	M	Child	12No02EI
Mary		14	F	Child	12No02EI
Betty		09	F	Child	12No02EI
Ellen		06	F	Child	12No02EI
PARMIS, Jams.		18	M	Laborer	12No02EI
GRADY, Margt.		17	F	None	12No02EI
BIBAGE, W.		19	M	Laborer	12No02EI
HURREN, Michl.		20	M	Laborer	12No02EI
DUN, James		20	M	Shoemaker	12No02EI
TOOL, James		26	M	Shoemaker	12No02EI
VAUGHAN, John		20	M	Nailer	12No02EI
HUGHES, Michl.		23	M	Laborer	12No02EI
HOLLAND, Thos.		20	M	Laborer	12No02EI
CUNNINGHAM, Pat.		20	M	Laborer	12No02EI
Mary	(T)	22	F	None	12No02EI
Francis		13	M	Child	12No02EI
WATERS, Wm.		23	M	Laborer	12No02EI
WEARE, Jn.		20	M	Farmer	12No02EI
THANCE, Thos.		20	M	Shoemaker	12No02EI
SHANE, Michl.		20	M	Laborer	12No02EI
FITZPATRICK, Chrisr.		42	M	Nailer	12No02EI
Maria	(D)	12	F	Unknown	12No02EI
CAVENOT, Margt.		16	F	Unknown	12No02EI
FINLAND, Laurence		16	M	Laborer	12No02EI
DONAHUE, Barny		00	M	Unknown	12No02EI
LEWIS, Jn.		19	M	Tailor	12No02EI
COLLINS, Edd.		20	M	Laborer	12No02EI
PINKINGTON, Jn.		22	M	Shoemaker	12No02EI
Alice	(W)	20	F	Wife	12No02EI
MASON, Edd.		21	M	Laborer	12No02EI
Mary	(T)	19	F	None	12No02EI
MCDONAGH, Patk.		36	M	Tailor	12No02EI
Mart.	(T)	20	F	None	12No02EI
CONEY, Jn.		26	M	Laborer	12No02EI
Bridget	(W)	20	F	Wife	12No02EI
BRENNON, Luke		20	M	Laborer	12No02EI
Mary	(W)	21	F	Wife	12No02EI
BARRY, W.		34	M	Victualler	12No02EI
LEDDY, J.		20	M	Farmer	12No02EI
SOLWAN, Jams.		30	M	Laborer	12No02EI
KIRBY, Thos.		42	M	Bootmaker	12No02EI
Margt.	(W)	44	F	Wife	12No02EI
Anne	(D)	10	F	Child	12No02EI
Alice	(D)	08	F	Child	12No02EI
MCROBBINS, Jn.		28	M	Farmer	12No02EI
Mary	(W)	24	F	Wife	12No02EI
MCGOWEN, Anne		26	F	Wife	12No02EI
DUNAGAN, Anne		20	F	Wife	12No02EI
CLEARY, Michl.		26	M	Miller	12No02EI
Catharine	(W)	24	F	Wife	12No02EI
JUDGE, Peter		28	M	Miner	12No02EI
Anne	(W)	20	F	Wife	12No02EI
SWARRY, Andrew		18	M	Weaver	12No02EI
MCGUIRE, Thos.		21	M	Carpenter	12No02EI
BOGA, Jas.		37	M	Tailor	12No02EI
WELCH, Jas.		20	M	Farmer	12No02EI
MOFFAT, Pat.		20	M	Laborer	12No02EI
Mart.		20	F	Servant	12No02EI
RIDYAN, Jn.		25	M	Laborer	12No02EI
MCHUGH, Jn.		25	M	Laborer	12No02EI
Mary		20	F	Servant	12No02EI
GROYAN, Laurence		46	M	Laborer	12No02EI
U	(W)	40	F	Wife	12No02EI
John	(S)	12	M	None	12No02EI
Richd.	(S)	09	M	Child	12No02EI
Pat.	(S)	06	M	Child	12No02EI
Cathl.	(D)	04	F	Child	12No02EI
Mary	(D)	02	F	Child	12No02EI
ADAMS, Mary		18	F	Servant	12No02EI
Sally		17	F	Servant	12No02EI
MASTESON, Ellen		21	F	Servant	12No02EI
KEENAN, Betsy		20	F	Wife	12No02EI
HAND, Bessy		16	F	Wife	12No02EI
KEENAN, Cath.		03	F	Child	12No02EI
HATCH, Francis		31	M	Hatter	12No02EI
GORDON, Barthw.		17	M	Hatter	12No02EI
SMITH, Cathl.		17	F	Servant	12No02EI
FERGUSON, Margt.		20	F	Wife	12No02EI
Mary		12	F	Child	12No02EI
REILLY, Biddy		40	F	Wife	12No02EI
WELSH, Jn.		60	M	Farmer	12No02EI
Mary	(W)	50	F	Wife	12No02EI
Margt.		14	F	Child	12No02EI
MCCABB, Mary		16	F	Servant	12No02EI
MAXWELL, Cathe.		30	F	Servant	12No02EI
Died-At-Sea					
LITTLE, Hugh		25	M	Farmer	12No02EI
Mary	(W)	20	F	Wife	12No02EI
Mary-Ann	(T)	18	F	None	12No02EI
LAMB, Mary		20	F	Wife	12No02EI
MCGUIRE, Thos.		23	M	Laborer	12No02EI
Biddy	(W)	20	F	Wife	12No02EI
Betsy	(T)	20	F	None	12No02EI

NAMES OF PASSENGERS		A G E	S E X	OCCUPATIONS	DATE PORT SHIP	NAMES OF PASSENGERS		A G E	S E X	OCCUPATIONS	DATE PORT SHIP
MCGUIRE, Ann	(T)	18	F	None	12No02EI						
GORDON, Michl.		20	M	Laborer	12No02EI						
KILDY, Pat.		20	M	Laborer	12No02EI						
Jams.		18	M	Laborer	12No02EI						
COPT, Peter		43	M	Laborer	12No02EI			LIVERPOOL 16 NOVEMBER 1846			
COON, U-Mrs.		40	F	Wife	12No02EI						
Barney		30	M	Laborer	12No02EI			From Liverpool			
Cathl.		25	F	Wife	12No02EI						
FLINN, Mary		25	F	Wife	12No02EI						
KILLDAY, Mary		18	F	Child	12No02EI						
GAIGINE, Anne		28	F	Dressmaker	12No02EI	POWELL, John		28	M	Merchant	16No02Bo
COON, John		15	M	None	12No02EI	LAWLESS, Robert		20	M	Laborer	16No02Bo
FARREN, Barney		19	M	Shoemaker	12No02EI	Patt		11	M	Child	16No02Bo
MCGUIRE, Jn.		26	M	Fisherman	12No02EI	BRADY, Julia		20	F	Seamstress	16No02Bo
FARREN, Mary		32	F	Wife	12No02EI	MCKEE, Jno.		40	M	Laborer	16No02Bo
BRIAN, Christy		30	M	Laborer	12No02EI	Auky		09	M	Child	16No02Bo
WILSON, Margt.		38	F	Wife	12No02EI	WINTER, Mathew		40	M	Laborer	16No02Bo
Robt.		38	M	Watchmaker	12No02EI	U	(W)	40	F	Laborer	16No02Bo
Mary		16	F	None	12No02EI	Mathew	(S)	20	M	Laborer	16No02Bo
Jane		14	F	None	12No02EI	Jno.	(S)	18	M	Laborer	16No02Bo
Margt.		13	F	None	12No02EI	James	(S)	13	M	Laborer	16No02Bo
Robt.		12	M	None	12No02EI	Anne	(D)	11	F	Child	16No02Bo
Charlotte		08	F	Child	12No02EI	Bernard	(S)	09	M	Child	16No02Bo
John		03	M	Child	12No02EI	WAITER, Henry		10	M	Child	16No02Bo
HUMPHREYS, Wm.		20	M	Laborer	12No02EI	MCNAMAN, Rose		20	F	Servant	16No02Bo
REITTY, Jams.		16	M	Laborer	12No02EI	MANAY, Mary-A.		20	F	Servant	16No02Bo
MCGUIRE, Francis		26	M	Laborer	12No02EI	MCGUNAN, Michl.		20	M	Laborer	16No02Bo
MANAGHAN, Chrisr.		27	M	Laborer	12No02EI	BUCKLEY, D.		30	M	Mechanic	16No02Bo
BOOTERS, Chars.		25	M	Laborer	12No02EI	U	(W)	20	F	Mechanic	16No02Bo
MAUNDERS, Willm.		25	M	Shoemaker	12No02EI	Jos.		25	M	Mechanic	16No02Bo
BEAR, Thos.		22	M	Laborer	12No02EI	MOORE, Eliza		21	F	Servant	16No02Bo
LURTY, Js.		19	M	Clerk	12No02EI	TRACY, Jane		30	F	Servant	16No02Bo
MILLER, Henry		20	M	Farmer	12No02EI	James	(S)	09	M	Child	16No02Bo
MARTEN, John		20	M	Farmer	12No02EI	Mary	(D)	05	F	Child	16No02Bo
CARDY, Peggy		20	F	Servant	12No02EI	MCGILLAN, Terence		25	M	Laborer	16No02Bo
COLERAN, Mary		30	F	Wife	12No02EI	CUNNINGHAM, Cthe.		21	F	Servant	16No02Bo
MCMULLEN, Cathl.		20	F	Servant	12No02EI	DEOLIN, Mary		13	F	Servant	16No02Bo
LEWIS, Jane		20	F	Servant	12No02EI	CARBURY, Sarah		15	F	Servant	16No02Bo
SAJO, Mickl.		36	M	Clcp	12No02EI	GILLAN, Darly		30	M	Laborer	16No02Bo
Bridgt.	(W)	20	F	Wife	12No02EI	Christe.		35	M	Laborer	16No02Bo
MARTIN, Margt.		20	F	Servant	12No02EI	Bridget		18	F	Laborer	16No02Bo
GRAHAM, Jane		20	F	Servant	12No02EI	BRADY, Michl.		25	M	Laborer	16No02Bo
Died-At-Sea						Mary		20	F	Laborer	16No02Bo
GLEGG, Edd.		46	M	Wis	12No02EI	MANION, Patt		25	M	Laborer	16No02Bo
Js.		20	M	Wis	12No02EI	KEALEY, Patt		25	M	Laborer	16No02Bo
Ellen	(W)	50	F	Wife	12No02EI	Bridget		20	F	Laborer	16No02Bo
Edd.		12	M	None	12No02EI	KEARY, Pat		20	M	Laborer	16No02Bo
Sarah		10	F	None	12No02EI	SMITH, Bridget		20	F	Laborer	16No02Bo
MURRAY, Thos.		35	M	Laborer	12No02EI	QUINN, Bridget		20	F	Laborer	16No02Bo
Cathl.	(W)	32	F	Wife	12No02EI	GLEAR, Andy		20	M	Laborer	16No02Bo
Cathl.		08	F	Child	12No02EI	LAYS, Robt.		36	M	Farmer	16No02Bo
John		07	M	Child	12No02EI	Jane	(W)	38	F	Farmer	16No02Bo
Died-At-Sea						Wm.		25	M	Farmer	16No02Bo
Pat.		03	M	Child	12No02EI	Mary		22	F	Farmer	16No02Bo
CUMINGS, Ann		31	F	Servant	12No02EI	Oliver		19	M	Farmer	16No02Bo
SOMERVILLE, Mary		19	F	Servant	12No02EI	Robert		16	M	Farmer	16No02Bo
GOONON, Betty		22	F	Servant	12No02EI	John		12	M	Farmer	16No02Bo
MULLEN, Eliza.		20	F	Servant	12No02EI	Jos.		10	M	Child	16No02Bo
Peggy		22	F	Servant	12No02EI	Jane		07	F	Child	16No02Bo
SAMPLE, Ann		16	F	Servant	12No02EI	Margt.		05	F	Child	16No02Bo
MORGAN, Sarah		18	F	Servant	12No02EI	Anne		02	F	Child	16No02Bo
LOGAN, Biddy		26	F	Servant	12No02EI	HALLARHAN, James		25	M	Laborer	16No02Bo
HUGHES, Biddy		20	F	Servant	12No02EI	FOX, Patt		27	M	Laborer	16No02Bo
FARRELL, Mary		26	F	Servant	12No02EI	Rosey		23	F	Servant	16No02Bo
DOYLE, Ann		20	F	Servant	12No02EI	HALLARHAN, Ellen		25	F	Servant	16No02Bo
STONE, C.P.		20	M	Cuof	12No02EI	MCGUINN, Besey		20	F	Servant	16No02Bo
A.M.	(T)	27	F	None	12No02EI	MCGEE, Ann		18	F	Servant	16No02Bo
						MOONEY, Ann		20	F	Servant	16No02Bo
						Mary		18	F	Servant	16No02Bo
						BURNS, Mary		17	F	Servant	16No02Bo
						MCGUIN, Judy		20	F	Servant	16No02Bo
						LEERY, James		13	M	Servant	16No02Bo
						HOGAN, Richard		32	M	Carpenter	16No02Bo
						NAVAN, Bernard		20	M	Laborer	16No02Bo
						MCDANIEL, Mary		30	F	Wife	16No02Bo

NAMES OF PASSENGERS		A G E	S E X	OCCUPATIONS	DATE PORT SHIP	NAMES OF PASSENGERS		A G E	S E X	OCCUPATIONS	DATE PORT SHIP
MCDANIEL, Margt.	(D)	04	F	Child	16No02Bo	MARTIN, Thos.	(S)	02	M	Child	16No02Bo
GRITY, Danl.		30	M	Farmer	16No02Bo	DOWN, John		28	M	Laborer	16No02Bo
Clara	(W)	28	F	Wife	16No02Bo	HANA, Barthey.		45	M	Laborer	16No02Bo
Mary		14	F	Unknown	16No02Bo	SMITH, James		54	M	Farmer	16No02Bo
Fanny		01	F	Child	16No02Bo	Eliza		50	F	Farmer	16No02Bo
ROONEY, Richd.		25	M	Laborer	16No02Bo	HANTON, Mary		30	F	Laborer	16No02Bo
CRAVEN, James		20	M	Laborer	16No02Bo	Michl.		15	M	Laborer	16No02Bo
ROONEY, Bridget		20	F	Servant	16No02Bo	James		14	M	Laborer	16No02Bo
DEGNAN, Cathe.		21	F	Servant	16No02Bo	John		05	M	Child	16No02Bo
John		18	M	Servant	16No02Bo	MCGOWAN, James		20	M	Laborer	16No02Bo
Bridget		14	F	Servant	16No02Bo	FOOTE, John		32	M	Stoker	16No02Bo
Mary		12	F	Servant	16No02Bo	HAMAN, James		21	M	Gdnr	16No02Bo
HAGGRY, John		25	M	Servant	16No02Bo	ONEIL, Hugh		50	M	Laborer	16No02Bo
NOLAN, John		20	M	Laborer	16No02Bo	HAMILL, Patt		24	M	Laborer	16No02Bo
Ann		18	F	Servant	16No02Bo	RILLY, John		21	M	Laborer	16No02Bo
COONEY, Ann		25	F	Servant	16No02Bo	FANNER, James		50	M	Laborer	16No02Bo
CALLAGHAN, James		30	M	Farmer	16No02Bo	Bridgt.	(W)	50	F	Laborer	16No02Bo
Mary	(W)	30	F	Wife	16No02Bo	Patt	(S)	17	M	Laborer	16No02Bo
Margt.	(D)	06	F	Child	16No02Bo	Timothy	(S)	04	M	Child	16No02Bo
Anna-Lilley	(D)	01	F	Child	16No02Bo	HOONAN, Ellen		14	F	Servant	16No02Bo
ROCHE, Burly		22	M	Farmer	16No02Bo	BENTLEY, Jno.		35	M	Mechanic	16No02Bo
MCDERMOTT, Emma		20	F	Servant	16No02Bo	Cathe.		30	F	Mechanic	16No02Bo
FLANIGAN, Sally		20	F	Servant	16No02Bo	MULHEIRN, Wm.		20	M	Laborer	16No02Bo
BANEY, Margt.		20	F	Servant	16No02Bo	BERRY, Anthony		22	M	Laborer	16No02Bo
OWENS, Peter		35	M	Laborer	16No02Bo	Margt.		20	F	Laborer	16No02Bo
Margt.	(W)	30	F	Laborer	16No02Bo	QUINN, Francis		20	F	Laborer	16No02Bo
Bridget	(D)	12	F	Laborer	16No02Bo	GALLAN, Rose		20	F	Laborer	16No02Bo
Margt.	(D)	08	F	Child	16No02Bo	Bridget		20	F	Laborer	16No02Bo
James	(S)	03	M	Child	16No02Bo	TUENAN, James		20	M	Laborer	16No02Bo
Patt	(S)	.06	M	Infant	16No02Bo	DUMER, John		20	M	Laborer	16No02Bo
Died-At-Sea						KALLAGHER, Thos.		20	M	Laborer	16No02Bo
WINFIELD, James		20	M	Laborer	16No02Bo	DUMER, U-Mrs.		20	F	Laborer	16No02Bo
John		13	M	Laborer	16No02Bo	GILLAN, Biddy		20	F	Laborer	16No02Bo
ANDERSON, Isab.		20	F	Servant	16No02Bo	GILLINAN, Ellen		20	F	Laborer	16No02Bo
MORAN, Danl.		00	M	Laborer	16No02Bo	MAHON, Wm.		22	M	Laborer	16No02Bo
COUROG, Cathe.		15	F	Servant	16No02Bo	RODGERS, Ceila		20	F	Servant	16No02Bo
John		12	M	None	16No02Bo	CASEY, Ellen		20	F	Servant	16No02Bo
Biddy		07	F	Child	16No02Bo	RUDEN, Patt		18	M	Laborer	16No02Bo
ROONEY, Terence		36	M	Mason	16No02Bo	FITZPATRICK, Margt.		18	F	Laborer	16No02Bo
Mary	(W)	30	F	Wife	16No02Bo	TUFTS, Robert		19	M	Laborer	16No02Bo
Died-At-Sea						COSHMAN, Michl.		24	M	Laborer	16No02Bo
James	(S)	10	M	Unknown	16No02Bo	STRONG, Ellen		18	F	Servant	16No02Bo
Mary	(D)	08	F	Child	16No02Bo	TURNEY, Michl.		20	M	Laborer	16No02Bo
Died-At-Sea						KILLEN, Ann		30	F	Servant	16No02Bo
Bridget	(D)	04	F	Child	16No02Bo	Died-At-Sea					
Margt.	(D)	03	F	Child	16No02Bo	KILLY, Margt.		20	F	Servant	16No02Bo
Ann	(D)	.08	F	Infant	16No02Bo	Judy		22	F	Servant	16No02Bo
Died-At-Sea						COFFEY, Peter		20	M	Mechanic	16No02Bo
MEKIN, Margt.		24	F	Servant	16No02Bo	MURTHA, Michl.		20	M	Mechanic	16No02Bo
OWANS, John		30	M	Laborer	16No02Bo	Ann		18	F	Mechanic	16No02Bo
Dennick		28	M	Laborer	16No02Bo	COSHAELEY, Michl.		20	M	Mechanic	16No02Bo
Cathe.		20	F	Servant	16No02Bo	OBRIEN, Mary		20	F	Mechanic	16No02Bo
BRENAN, James		30	M	Laborer	16No02Bo	HAGG, Luke		25	M	Mechanic	16No02Bo
CANON, John		15	M	Laborer	16No02Bo	Biddy		20	F	Mechanic	16No02Bo
DOWNEY, Henry		13	M	Laborer	16No02Bo	KILLY, Betty		20	F	Mechanic	16No02Bo
James		11	M	Child	16No02Bo	BRANNEN, Mary		20	F	Mechanic	16No02Bo
HANNIGAN, Thos.		40	M	Shoemaker	16No02Bo	BYRN, Michl.		25	M	Mechanic	16No02Bo
KELLY, Hugh		30	M	Laborer	16No02Bo	John		20	M	Mechanic	16No02Bo
MCLAUGHLIN, Mary		18	F	Servant	16No02Bo	PARSINS, John		25	M	Mechanic	16No02Bo
MCGINNIS, John		30	M	Gdnr	16No02Bo	Mary	(W)	20	F	Mechanic	16No02Bo
Mary		15	F	Servant	16No02Bo	Mary	(D)	01	F	Child	16No02Bo
CAVENAGH, Chas.		05	M	Laborer	16No02Bo	NOWLAND, John		17	M	Laborer	16No02Bo
HUESTON, James		25	M	Laborer	16No02Bo	FARMER, Ann		15	F	Laborer	16No02Bo
STEWART, Christ.		30	M	Laborer	16No02Bo	Margt.		13	F	Laborer	16No02Bo
U	(W)	30	F	Laborer	16No02Bo	Betty		07	F	Child	16No02Bo
A.L.		.10	U	Infant	16No02Bo	Rose		05	F	Child	16No02Bo
MARTIN, Michl.		50	M	Laborer	16No02Bo	Ellen		01	F	Child	16No02Bo
Mary	(W)	50	F	Laborer	16No02Bo	JAMESON, Margt.		19	F	Laborer	16No02Bo
Martin	(S)	11	M	Child	16No02Bo	COLERAN, Thos.		40	M	Laborer	16No02Bo
Jno.	(S)	07	M	Child	16No02Bo	Betty	(W)	40	F	Laborer	16No02Bo
Biddy	(D)	09	F	Child	16No02Bo	Maria	(D)	09	F	Child	16No02Bo
Jane	(D)	04	F	Child	16No02Bo	Jno.	(S)	06	M	Child	16No02Bo
Malachea	(S)	02	M	Child	16No02Bo	Biddy	(D)	04	F	Child	16No02Bo
Michl.	(S)	01	M	Child	16No02Bo	Judy	(D)	02	F	Child	16No02Bo
Died-At-Sea						ODONNELL, Jno.		35	M	Laborer	16No02Bo

NAMES OF PASSENGERS		AGE	SEX	OCCUPATIONS	DATE PORT SHIP
FELIN, Peter		50	M	Laborer	16No02Bo
Biddy	(W)	50	F	Laborer	16No02Bo
James	(S)	25	M	Laborer	16No02Bo
Biddy	(D)	20	F	Laborer	16No02Bo
SHIELDS, Hugh		48	M	Laborer	16No02Bo
Kitty	(W)	40	F	Laborer	16No02Bo
Hugh	(S)	20	M	Laborer	16No02Bo
Mary	(S)	18	F	Laborer	16No02Bo
John	(S)	15	M	Laborer	16No02Bo
Rosey	(D)	13	F	Laborer	16No02Bo
Peter	(S)	11	M	Child	16No02Bo
Sally	(D)	09	F	Child	16No02Bo
Cathe.	(D)	06	F	Child	16No02Bo
Patt	(S)	03	M	Child	16No02Bo
Danl.	(S)	03	M	Child	16No02Bo
MCTAGGY, James		30	M	Mechanic	16No02Bo
MCBUARTY, James		30	M	Mechanic	16No02Bo
MURPHY, Michl.		29	M	Laborer	16No02Bo
Bridget	(W)	31	F	Laborer	16No02Bo
Michl.	(S)	10	M	Laborer	16No02Bo
Mary	(D)	05	F	Child	16No02Bo
Died-At-Sea					
Thos.	(S)	03	M	Child	16No02Bo
Martin	(S)	01	M	Child	16No02Bo
CROZARE, Hugh		25	M	Clerk	16No02Bo
HILL, John		25	M	Clerk	16No02Bo
TONNEY, Mary		17	F	Servant	16No02Bo
KILLY, Biddy		16	F	Servant	16No02Bo
CURRAN, Cathe.		21	F	Servant	16No02Bo
Mary		19	F	Servant	16No02Bo
Jno.		06	M	Child	16No02Bo
CANE, Cathe.		20	F	Servant	16No02Bo
STANTON, Biddy		12	F	Servant	16No02Bo
BRANIGAN, Pat.		20	M	Laborer	16No02Bo
SHERIDAN, James		20	M	Laborer	16No02Bo
GILLAN, Biddy		20	F	Servant	16No02Bo
MCNULTY, Wm.		40	M	Carpenter	16No02Bo
QUIN, Ellen		23	F	Servant	16No02Bo
CONNELLY, Jno.		20	M	Laborer	16No02Bo
BASK, Cathe.		20	F	Servant	16No02Bo
MORAN, Mary		20	F	Servant	16No02Bo
FANELL, Margt.		20	F	Dressmaker	16No02Bo
MCCALN, Eliza		26	F	Servant	16No02Bo
James		16	M	Servant	16No02Bo
CALLAGHAN, Jno.		22	M	Coachman	16No02Bo
MAHIN, Mary		20	F	Servant	16No02Bo
MARCHATT, Bridget		30	F	Servant	16No02Bo
Edward	(S)	08	M	Child	16No02Bo
Rose	(D)	04	F	Child	16No02Bo
Bridget	(D)	02	F	Child	16No02Bo
HAGAN, Margt.		11	F	Child	16No02Bo
TIERNEY, Michl.		37	M	Laborer	16No02Bo
Lobinia	(W)	37	F	Laborer	16No02Bo
Edward	(S)	10	M	Child	16No02Bo
Sally	(D)	08	F	Child	16No02Bo
Stephen	(S)	06	M	Child	16No02Bo
Jno.	(S)	03	M	Child	16No02Bo
Died-At-Sea					
MCGUNY, Ellen		25	F	Servant	16No02Bo
MULLIN, Terrence		23	M	Laborer	16No02Bo
KILLY, Anne		18	F	Servant	16No02Bo
HUGH, Alice		18	F	Servant	16No02Bo
GRAHAM, Hannah		20	F	Servant	16No02Bo
ONEIL, Mary		17	F	Servant	16No02Bo
MCCALLIN, Bridget		18	F	Servant	16No02Bo
Jane		21	F	Servant	16No02Bo
CAVANAGH, Mary		20	F	Servant	16No02Bo
CATTER, Hannah		18	F	Servant	16No02Bo
DAGAN, Cathe.		20	F	Servant	16No02Bo
DANVERDY, John		40	M	Musician	16No02Bo
MCCAY, James		30	M	Distiller	16No02Bo
MARTIN, Danl.		18	M	Laborer	16No02Bo
BURNSIDE, Hugh		21	M	Laborer	16No02Bo
MALDOON, Darly		25	M	Laborer	16No02Bo
HAUGH, John		25	M	Laborer	16No02Bo

NAMES OF PASSENGERS		AGE	SEX	OCCUPATIONS	DATE PORT SHIP
KEELY, Thos.		20	M	Laborer	16No02Bo
GOMELEY, Philip		30	M	Laborer	16No02Bo
REILLY, Mary		50	F	Servant	16No02Bo
GORDON, Michl.		30	M	Farmer	16No02Bo
Jno.		25	M	Tailor	16No02Bo
CROSBY, Bridget		25	F	Servant	16No02Bo
HANLEY, Cathe.		26	F	Servant	16No02Bo
Biddy		20	F	Servant	16No02Bo
Jno.		21	M	Laborer	16No02Bo
CASSIDY, Mary		18	F	Servant	16No02Bo
MARTIN, Bridget		11	F	Child	16No02Bo
CARTY, John		48	M	Farmer	16No02Bo
GAFNEY, Pat		29	M	Farmer	16No02Bo
DENING, Thos.		24	M	Laborer	16No02Bo
MCGRATH, Wm.		26	M	Laborer	16No02Bo
WALSH, Thos.		20	M	Laborer	16No02Bo
RYAN, Thos.		27	M	Butcher	16No02Bo
DONNELLY, Michael		21	M	Laborer	16No02Bo

GREAT-WESTERN 17 NOVEMBER 1846

From Liverpool

NAMES OF PASSENGERS		AGE	SEX	OCCUPATIONS	DATE PORT SHIP
LETHUN, Jno.		22	M	Gentleman	17No02Cy
HAYNES, Wm.H.		30	M	Gentleman	17No02Cy
GILMOUR, Thos.		24	M	Merchant	17No02Cy
HAGERMAN, U-Mrs.		42	F	Lady	17No02Cy
U	(D)	20	F	Lady	17No02Cy
HAUGHTON, Marla		26	F	Servant	17No02Cy
STUART, Chas.		32	M	Lawyer	17No02Cy
TOBIAS, E.W.		24	M	Merchant	17No02Cy
DODSON, U		22	F	Lady	17No02Cy
G.		19	F	Lady	17No02Cy
WELFORD, Chas.		33	M	Merchant	17No02Cy
DEWRY, W.		37	M	Minister	17No02Cy
KLINGARSE, M.G.		24	M	Merchant	17No02Cy
LEECH, Robt.		34	M	Merchant	17No02Cy
ROSSIE, F.		64	M	Merchant	17No02Cy
JONES, Thos.		25	M	Gentleman	17No02Cy
NERSELEYS, U		50	F	Lady	17No02Cy
ALLAN, G.W.		24	M	Gentleman	17No02Cy
U	(W)	21	F	Lady	17No02Cy
SINCLAIR, J.B.		35	M	Merchant	17No02Cy
BREHANT, W.H.		30	M	Gentleman	17No02Cy
BRAWBEE, Charlotte		22	F	Lady	17No02Cy
HOLFORD, Wm.		50	M	Gentleman	17No02Cy
COSSIN, S.		43	M	Merchant	17No02Cy
PAUL, James		28	M	Servant	17No02Cy
PIMS, Saml.		48	M	Gentleman	17No02Cy
MEGGS, U		22	F	Lady	17No02Cy

SCOTIA 18 NOVEMBER 1846

From Prince-Edward-Island

NAMES OF PASSENGERS		AGE	SEX	OCCUPATIONS	DATE PORT SHIP
WHEELAN, U		60	M	Cooper	18No51Hv
U	(W)	50	F	Wife	18No51Hv
Wm.	(S)	30	M	Cooper	18No51Hv
Donald	(S)	28	M	Cooper	18No51Hv
John	(S)	26	M	Cooper	18No51Hv
Eliza	(D)	24	F	None	18No51Hv
Paul	(S)	22	M	None	18No51Hv
Ellen	(D)	12	F	None	18No51Hv

NAMES OF PASSENGERS		AGE	SEX	OCCUPATIONS	DATE PORT SHIP
MCMANUS, Barney		29	M	Laborer	19No02Bz
FORELEY, Sarah		20	F	Nurse	19No02Bz
CULLIN, Eliza		40	F	Seamstress	19No02Bz
Peter	(S)	09	M	Child	19No02Bz
OBRIEN, Alin		30	F	Servant	19No02Bz
CONLY, Eliz.		40	F	Servant	19No02Bz
Hugh-M.	(S)	09	M	Child	19No02Bz
Sella-E.	(D)	07	F	Child	19No02Bz
GARAHAN, Owen		30	M	Farmer	19No02Bz
U	(W)	30	F	None	19No02Bz
Peter	(S)	09	M	Child	19No02Bz
Josal	(S)	07	M	Child	19No02Bz
M.Owen	(S)	05	M	Child	19No02Bz
James		29	M	None	19No02Bz
LYNCH, Mary		18	F	Seamstress	19No02Bz
THOMPSON, Charles		21	M	Wood Cutter	19No02Bz
CROUTH, Joseph		21	M	Clerk	19No02Bz
WALSH, Michael		20	M	Farmer	19No02Bz
FEENEY, Mary		28	F	None	19No02Bz
Eliz.		20	F	Cnf	19No02Bz
ROONEY, Pat.		27	M	Laborer	19No02Bz
RUNSTON, Robt.		25	M	Laborer	19No02Bz
MCGOVERN, Pat.		20	M	Laborer	19No02Bz
DOLLAN, Pat.		19	M	Laborer	19No02Bz
MADDON, Jas.		20	M	Laborer	19No02Bz
CLARK, Daniel		20	M	Farmer	19No02Bz
GRAHAM, Robert		23	M	Miller	19No02Bz
MCBURN, Edward		24	M	Tailor	19No02Bz
BURKE, Chris.		24	M	Tailor	19No02Bz
EAGLE, John		60	M	Laborer	19No02Bz
U	(W)	56	F	None	19No02Bz
Aloe.	(S)	20	M	Laborer	19No02Bz
Mary	(D)	20	F	None	19No02Bz
MCSHAW, Jas.		20	M	Pugilist	19No02Bz
CONNELL, John		24	M	Farmer	19No02Bz
EAGLE, Jas.		20	M	Farmer	19No02Bz
HUARD, Ann		20	F	Servant	19No02Bz
MILLOCK, Mary-S.		12	F	None	19No02Bz
CLARK, Ann		25	F	Servant	19No02Bz
MULLAN, Ann		25	F	Servant	19No02Bz
TEMPLE, Robt.		28	M	Farmer	19No02Bz
Margt.		20	F	None	19No02Bz
DUNN, Mary		20	F	Milkmaid	19No02Bz
JONES, James		40	M	Laborer	19No02Bz
U	(W)	40	F	None	19No02Bz
Jas.	(S)	20	M	None	19No02Bz
Mary-Ann	(D)	12	F	None	19No02Bz
Patk.	(S)	11	M	Child	19No02Bz
O.Luke	(S)	09	M	Child	19No02Bz
DUNN, Susanna		19	F	Servant	19No02Bz
CONNOLLY, Thos.		25	M	Tailor	19No02Bz
KELLY, Margt.		40	F	None	19No02Bz
Mary		40	F	None	19No02Bz
Thos.		07	M	Child	19No02Bz
Bridget		.00	F	Infant	19No02Bz
JONES, Mary		20	F	None	19No02Bz
GATELY, Betty		18	F	Nurse	19No02Bz
LEACH, Mary		18	F	None	19No02Bz
Kitty		17	F	None	19No02Bz
FARELL, John	(S)	.00	M	Infant	19No02Bz
CALAHAN, John		35	M	Farmer	19No02Bz
U	(W)	30	F	None	19No02Bz
John-Luke	(S)	08	M	Child	19No02Bz
CARELL, Samuel		18	M	None	19No02Bz
LAULAR, Sally		17	F	Singer	19No02Bz
HARVEY, John		30	M	Baker	19No02Bz
MURRY, Pat.		18	M	Miller	19No02Bz
Cath.		20	F	None	19No02Bz
RICE, Bell		18	F	None	19No02Bz
CAUTHERS, And.		40	M	Laborer	19No02Bz
U	(W)	40	F	None	19No02Bz
John	(S)	22	M	Tailor	19No02Bz
And.	(S)	16	M	None	19No02Bz
H.A.		12	U	None	19No02Bz
KELLY, James		30	M	Laborer	19No02Bz
U	(W)	26	F	None	19No02Bz
James-A.	(S)	06	M	Child	19No02Bz
Hugh	(S)	04	M	Child	19No02Bz
Ellen	(D)	.00	F	Infant	19No02Bz
PATTON, Eliz.		26	F	Nurse	19No02Bz
Mary		10	F	Child	19No02Bz
Ellen-E.		08	F	Child	19No02Bz
GOLT, Robt.		26	M	Farmer	19No02Bz
U	(W)	24	F	None	19No02Bz
Mary-A.	(D)	.00	F	Infant	19No02Bz
FAULKNER, R.		20	M	Laborer	19No02Bz
FINLEY, May		20	F	None	19No02Bz
GOLT, Jas.		60	M	Laborer	19No02Bz
Elz.	(W)	38	F	None	19No02Bz
Mary	(D)	22	F	None	19No02Bz
Nancy	(D)	21	F	None	19No02Bz
Ellen	(D)	20	F	None	19No02Bz
Jane	(D)	13	F	None	19No02Bz
Wm.	(S)	12	M	None	19No02Bz
BYRNE, Peter		20	M	Stctr	19No02Bz
Patt.		22	M	Laborer	19No02Bz
Mary		24	F	Walter	19No02Bz
JALLY, Ann		18	F	Seamstress	19No02Bz
WATKINS, W.		25	M	Laborer	19No02Bz
FEENY, Brid.		18	F	None	19No02Bz
BYRNE, Cath.		20	F	None	19No02Bz
U		25	M	Hatter	19No02Bz
BRINON, Mary		22	F	None	19No02Bz
MCNIGHT, Rose		13	F	None	19No02Bz
ROONEY, Jas.		20	M	Carter	19No02Bz
DIRAH, Thos.		20	M	Bricklayer	19No02Bz
Timothy		21	M	Farrier	19No02Bz
HALIN, John		45	M	Laborer	19No02Bz
Sarah	(W)	44	F	None	19No02Bz
John	(S)	20	M	None	19No02Bz
Thomas	(S)	17	M	None	19No02Bz
Eliz.	(D)	14	F	None	19No02Bz
John	(S)	26	M	None	19No02Bz
MILES, Nancy		20	F	Servant	19No02Bz
CAMPBELL, Wm.		80	M	Farmer	19No02Bz
John	(S)	55	M	Farmer	19No02Bz
Fanny	(D)	45	F	None	19No02Bz
Eliz.	(D)	35	F	None	19No02Bz
Isabella	(D)	33	F	None	19No02Bz
William	(S)	20	M	None	19No02Bz
George		18	M	None	19No02Bz
Sarah-G.		08	F	Child	19No02Bz
John		.00	M	Infant	19No02Bz
CLARK, Henry		20	M	Laborer	19No02Bz
LUM, Rich.		40	M	Laborer	19No02Bz
LUCK, Geo.		17	M	None	19No02Bz
FINLEY, W.		30	M	Hatter	19No02Bz
RODIN, Chas.		50	M	Mason	19No02Bz
Ellen	(W)	50	F	None	19No02Bz
Chas.	(S)	13	M	None	19No02Bz
LOFTHOUSE, Wm.		25	M	Bootmaker	19No02Bz
Mary	(W)	24	F	None	19No02Bz
Thos.	(S)	.00	M	Infant	19No02Bz
NICHOLSON, Marg.		25	M	Nurse	19No02Bz
FRIAN, Thos.		19	M	Laborer	19No02Bz
OHARA, Jas.		25	M	Mason	19No02Bz
Bridget		19	F	None	19No02Bz
SCULLY, Barbara		23	F	Lad	19No02Bz
BUTLER, Barney		20	M	Farmer	19No02Bz
Bridget		40	F	None	19No02Bz

NAMES OF PASSENGERS		AGE	SEX	OCCUPATIONS	DATE PORT SHIP	NAMES OF PASSENGERS		AGE	SEX	OCCUPATIONS	DATE PORT SHIP
MCCANN, Neill		19	M	Mason	19No02Bz	LOBER, Mary	(W)	20	F	None	19No02Bz
Rose		19	F	None	19No02Bz	Ann	(D)	02	F	Child	19No02Bz
Ellen		17	F	None	19No02Bz	JOHNSTON, Brld.		22	F	None	19No02Bz
FOULEY, Cath.		18	F	None	19No02Bz	CLAYTON, George		20	M	Laborer	19No02Bz
DUNN, Cath.		40	F	Midwife	19No02Bz	NORN, James		24	M	Mason	19No02Bz
Jas.	(S)	08	M	Child	19No02Bz	HALFPENNY, Brian		20	M	Farmer	19No02Bz
Cath.	(D)	07	F	Child	19No02Bz	BURN, Mag.		20	F	None	19No02Bz
COGHLAN, Jas.		22	M	Farmer	19No02Bz	LINDSAY, Henry		26	M	Bartender	19No02Bz
ROI, John		52	M	Balllff	19No02Bz	U	(W)	25	F	None	19No02Bz
DOE, John		26	M	Lawyer	19No02Bz	Rebecca	(D)	03	F	Child	19No02Bz
VERITY, Edwd.		20	M	Tailor	19No02Bz	Wright	(S)	02	M	Child	19No02Bz
MCGLUENY, Chas.		20	M	Baker	19No02Bz	Emma	(D)	.00	F	Infant	19No02Bz
MCCLENAHEN, Mich.		30	M	Laborer	19No02Bz	DONOLY, Ann		30	F	None	19No02Bz
MCGACHAN, U		17	F	None	19No02Bz	John		26	M	Laborer	19No02Bz
Cath.		04	F	Child	19No02Bz	TRAYNOR, Ann		18	F	None	19No02Bz
MCNEILL, Jas.		25	M	Farmer	19No02Bz	DONOLY, Bridget		05	F	Child	19No02Bz
GREEN, Brld.		20	F	Mangler	19No02Bz	MEEHAN, M.		25	M	Clerk	19No02Bz
MCNEILL, Ellen		20	F	None	19No02Bz	CONNOR, U		20	M	Mason	19No02Bz
GERITY, John		25	M	Stone Mason	19No02Bz	FLARITY, Mary		20	F	None	19No02Bz
MCGUIN, Phil.		22	M	Laborer	19No02Bz	FONLEY, Ann		20	F	None	19No02Bz
OHARA, Barry		23	M	Cutter	19No02Bz	EGAN, Thos.		20	M	Laborer	19No02Bz
FEENEY, John		25	M	Bartender	19No02Bz	TRACEY, Cath.		18	F	None	19No02Bz
U	(W)	20	F	None	19No02Bz	OBRIEN, Pat.		18	M	None	19No02Bz
Danl.	(S)	.00	M	Infant	19No02Bz	BUCK, H.		27	U	Chest Maker	19No02Bz
Died-At-Sea						CLINTON, Mary		19	F	None	19No02Bz
FEENY, Rose		21	F	None	19No02Bz	BODIN, Christen		22	M	Laborer	19No02Bz
DILLON, Bessy		21	F	Servant	19No02Bz	MCCOLLOCK, Mich.		30	M	None	19No02Bz
ROARKE, Patt.		20	M	Stctr	19No02Bz	WALLIS, Patt.		30	M	Bootblack	19No02Bz
JOHNSTON, John		30	M	Merchant	19No02Bz	CLUSKEY, Brian		24	M	Laborer	19No02Bz
U		25	M	None	19No02Bz	MOORE, U		60	M	Farmer	19No02Bz
STURMAN, Rich.		24	M	Painter	19No02Bz	U	(W)	60	F	None	19No02Bz
Ann		22	F	None	19No02Bz	Rich.	(S)	17	M	None	19No02Bz
Ellen		18	F	None	19No02Bz	CALLAGHAN, Felix		50	M	Laborer	19No02Bz
SCHMEID, Wm.		30	M	Midwife	19No02Bz	MALLARY, Jas.		10	M	Unknown	19No02Bz
CALAN, H.		30	M	Clerk	19No02Bz	Mary		07	F	Child	19No02Bz
MAARLET, M.M.		28	M	Bfcr	19No02Bz	OBRIEN, Mary		15	F	None	19No02Bz
U	(W)	26	F	None	19No02Bz	KEVELIHAN, Mary		20	F	None	19No02Bz
MCGUIRE, Owen		20	M	Laborer	19No02Bz	Jas.		15	M	None	19No02Bz
SCOVA, Patt.		24	M	Farmer	19No02Bz	MCLOUGHAN, John		20	M	Mason	19No02Bz
FARMOUTH, Ron		25	M	Farmer	19No02Bz	RODGERS, Peter		40	M	Cutler	19No02Bz
BELL, Wm.		20	M	Laborer	19No02Bz	Mary	(W)	35	F	None	19No02Bz
Sarah		20	F	None	19No02Bz	John	(S)	12	M	None	19No02Bz
Martha		18	F	None	19No02Bz	Mary	(D)	10	F	Child	19No02Bz
GLYNN, Cath.		20	F	Dancer	19No02Bz	Thos.	(S)	06	M	Child	19No02Bz
KELLY, Patt.		20	M	Musician	19No02Bz	Peter	(S)	.00	M	Infant	19No02Bz
Cath.		51	F	None	19No02Bz	JONES, Mary		20	F	Servant	19No02Bz
CONN, Mich.		20	M	Laborer	19No02Bz	Mary		05	F	Child	19No02Bz
GALLYN, Ann		20	F	Servant	19No02Bz	Ann		.00	F	Infant	19No02Bz
KELLY, Jas.		22	M	None	19No02Bz	FARRELL, Mich.		74	M	None	19No02Bz
Rose		08	F	Child	19No02Bz	LENNARD, Mary		18	F	None	19No02Bz
MCMAHON, Jas.		25	M	Laborer	19No02Bz	Rose		45	F	None	19No02Bz
Mary		55	F	None	19No02Bz	WHALEN, Stan		40	M	Mason	19No02Bz
Ann		14	F	None	19No02Bz	Ally	(W)	40	F	Unknown	19No02Bz
Phllip		11	M	Child	19No02Bz	Mich.	(S)	19	M	Laborer	19No02Bz
Mag.		09	F	Child	19No02Bz	COYNE, Wm.		24	M	Laborer	19No02Bz
CONNAUGHT, Connor		50	M	Violinist	19No02Bz	PHELAN, Ellen		12	F	None	19No02Bz
Biddy	(W)	50	F	None	19No02Bz	Ann		12	F	None	19No02Bz
Thos.	(S)	13	M	None	19No02Bz	Pat.		08	M	Child	19No02Bz
Martha	(D)	11	F	Child	19No02Bz	Wm.		19	M	None	19No02Bz
Peter	(S)	10	M	Child	19No02Bz	John		06	M	Child	19No02Bz
Patt.	(S)	09	M	Child	19No02Bz	Thos.		04	M	Child	19No02Bz
John	(S)	.00	M	Infant	19No02Bz	GATELY, Brld.		17	F	Dyer	19No02Bz
Died-At-Sea						BERRY, Bernard		15	M	None	19No02Bz
MURPHY, U		20	M	Laborer	19No02Bz	CASTILE, Pat.		40	M	Stctr	19No02Bz
Patt		20	M	Servant	19No02Bz	Judy	(D)	13	F	None	19No02Bz
Jas.		15	M	None	19No02Bz	Robt.	(S)	13	M	None	19No02Bz
Brld.		13	F	None	19No02Bz	Jos.	(S)	10	M	Child	19No02Bz
CURT, Patt.		25	M	Mason	19No02Bz	Pat.	(S)	07	M	Child	19No02Bz
CARROLE, John		21	M	Unknown	19No02Bz	Mich.	(S)	04	M	Child	19No02Bz
HENRY, Peter		22	M	Clerk	19No02Bz						
GANNON, John		22	M	Mason	19No02Bz						
FEEGAN, Mary		20	F	Servant	19No02Bz						
GUBNEY, Brld.		22	F	None	19No02Bz						
COOK, Marg.		25	F	Cook	19No02Bz						
LOBER, John		24	M	Sweeper	19No02Bz						

NAMES OF PASSENGERS		A G E	S E X	OCCUPATIONS	DATE PORT SHIP

COLUMBIA 19 NOVEMBER 1846

From Liverpool

NAMES OF PASSENGERS		AGE	SEX	OCCUPATIONS	DATE PORT SHIP
WRIGHT, Edward-P.		22	M	Merchant	19No02Hx
LAYTON, Wm.		24	M	Merchant	19No02Hx
MACLAUGHLIN, U		32	M	Merchant	19No02Hx
PORCH, Thomas	(S)	25	M	Farmer	19No02Hx
Anna	(D)	20	F	Farmer	19No02Hx
Charlotte	(D)	18	F	Farmer	19No02Hx
Ellen	(D)	16	F	Farmer	19No02Hx
Sidney	(S)	13	M	Farmer	19No02Hx
CAVE, William		60	M	Farmer	19No02Hx
RENDELL, Phoebe		50	F	Farmer	19No02Hx
Maryann	(D)	25	F	Farmer	19No02Hx
Ellen	(D)	22	F	Farmer	19No02Hx
William	(S)	20	M	Farmer	19No02Hx
Amella	(D)	18	F	Farmer	19No02Hx
Eliza	(D)	16	F	Farmer	19No02Hx
Stephen	(S)	14	M	Farmer	19No02Hx
Elizabeth	(D)	12	F	Farmer	19No02Hx
Frances	(D)	09	F	Farmer	19No02Hx
Amella	(D)	20	F	Farmer	19No02Hx
READING, Richard		30	M	Farmer	19No02Hx
Maryann		26	F	Farmer	19No02Hx
MITCHELL, Mathew		45	M	Mechanic	19No02Hx
BURNS, John		32	M	Mason	19No02Hx
LYNCH, James		31	M	Laborer	19No02Hx
Matilda	(D)	16	F	Laborer	19No02Hx
M.M.	(D)	12	F	Laborer	19No02Hx
BLUMER, Moses		57	M	Carpenter	19No02Hx
STANFIELD, Thomas		40	M	Farmer	19No02Hx
BROWN, Isaac		23	M	Farmer	19No02Hx
Ann	(W)	23	F	Farmer	19No02Hx
Margaret	(D)	02	F	Child	19No02Hx
KELLY, Patrick		23	M	Laborer	19No02Hx
MACANDRA, James		22	M	Laborer	19No02Hx
GOLLAGHER, Phil		22	M	Laborer	19No02Hx
RYAN, Mary		40	F	Child	19No02Hx
Kate	(D)	08	F	Child	19No02Hx
MACVAY, Mary		30	F	Farmer	19No02Hx
BRESLAN, Thomas		34	M	Farmer	19No02Hx
HINDS, Phil		27	M	Cooper	19No02Hx
CASSIDEY, U		27	M	Laborer	19No02Hx
COMMON, Thomas		22	M	Laborer	19No02Hx
Kate	(W)	20	F	Laborer	19No02Hx
Mary	(D)	01	F	Child	19No02Hx
TINEY, Martin		18	M	Laborer	19No02Hx
MULAVY, Pat		25	M	Laborer	19No02Hx
GARRETY, James		18	M	Laborer	19No02Hx
LAWLER, Michael		20	M	Laborer	19No02Hx
HOLMES, Thomas		18	M	Laborer	19No02Hx
MACINTOSH, James		31	M	Laborer	19No02Hx
HIGGINS, Pat		42	M	Laborer	19No02Hx
CURTIN, Johanna		20	F	Laborer	19No02Hx
Honora		18	F	Laborer	19No02Hx
HIGGINS, Mary		50	F	Laborer	19No02Hx
MACKABE, James		42	M	Laborer	19No02Hx
Margaret	(W)	38	F	Laborer	19No02Hx
Pat	(S)	13	M	Laborer	19No02Hx
James	(S)	11	M	Laborer	19No02Hx
Mary	(D)	09	F	Child	19No02Hx
MEEHAN, Susan		23	F	Laborer	19No02Hx
FIELD, Hugh		42	M	Laborer	19No02Hx
ROSE, Michael		20	M	Laborer	19No02Hx
Mary		25	F	Laborer	19No02Hx
HOGAN, Wm.		25	M	Laborer	19No02Hx
MACCUE, Mary		22	F	Laborer	19No02Hx
PURDON, Ann		18	F	Laborer	19No02Hx
MAGUIRE, Biddy		28	F	Laborer	19No02Hx
Ann		17	F	Laborer	19No02Hx
BROWN, James		20	M	Laborer	19No02Hx
Ann		18	F	Laborer	19No02Hx
SHORTIS, Saml.		40	M	Laborer	19No02Hx
SULLIVAN, Biddy		17	F	Laborer	19No02Hx
HIGGINS, Catherine		28	F	Laborer	19No02Hx
Ann		15	F	Laborer	19No02Hx
Biddy		13	F	Laborer	19No02Hx
Bess		07	F	Child	19No02Hx
Amella		05	F	Child	19No02Hx
LAMB, Ann		13	F	Laborer	19No02Hx
HIGGINS, Ann		17	F	Laborer	19No02Hx
MURPHY, Edward		35	M	Laborer	19No02Hx
FARREL, Catherine		23	F	Laborer	19No02Hx
Bessy		17	F	Laborer	19No02Hx
MULDOON, Peter		23	M	Laborer	19No02Hx
Cathn.		22	F	Laborer	19No02Hx
MACGOLDRICK, Hugh		37	M	Laborer	19No02Hx
Mary	(W)	35	F	Laborer	19No02Hx
Edward	(S)	13	M	Laborer	19No02Hx
Wm.	(S)	12	M	Laborer	19No02Hx
Ann	(D)	11	F	Laborer	19No02Hx
James	(S)	08	M	Child	19No02Hx
Hugh	(S)	04	M	Child	19No02Hx
William	(S)	02	M	Child	19No02Hx
Thomas	(S)	01	M	Child	19No02Hx
BRACELIN, Mary		45	F	Laborer	19No02Hx
Eliza	(D)	20	F	Laborer	19No02Hx
ONEIL, John		27	M	Laborer	19No02Hx
Ellen		50	F	Laborer	19No02Hx
Susan		17	F	Laborer	19No02Hx
Catherine		15	F	Laborer	19No02Hx
Ellen		12	F	Laborer	19No02Hx
KENNEY, Maria		20	F	Laborer	19No02Hx
DUNN, Martin		20	M	Laborer	19No02Hx
NEIL, Josh		21	M	Laborer	19No02Hx
CANNON, John		27	M	Laborer	19No02Hx
MACLOUGHLIN, Thomas		13	M	Laborer	19No02Hx
FLOOD, Richard		22	M	Laborer	19No02Hx
FINNIGAN, Thomas		27	M	Laborer	19No02Hx
LYNCH, Hugh		50	M	Laborer	19No02Hx
Mary	(W)	40	F	Laborer	19No02Hx
James	(S)	12	M	Laborer	19No02Hx
Biddy	(D)	09	F	Child	19No02Hx
John	(S)	05	M	Child	19No02Hx
Hugh	(S)	18	M	Laborer	19No02Hx
Owen	(S)	19	M	Laborer	19No02Hx
Anna	(D)	16	F	Laborer	19No02Hx
Margaret	(D)	13	F	Laborer	19No02Hx
MACBAKE, Mary		20	F	Laborer	19No02Hx
MACCORMIC, Susan		20	F	Laborer	19No02Hx
LYNCH, Mary		10	F	Child	19No02Hx
MACGORMAN, Charles		40	M	Laborer	19No02Hx
Catherine	(D)	07	F	Child	19No02Hx
Ellen	(D)	07	F	Child	19No02Hx
Mary	(D)	09	F	Child	19No02Hx
Peter	(S)	12	M	Laborer	19No02Hx
Terence	(S)	14	M	Laborer	19No02Hx
MORROWS, Biddy		45	F	Laborer	19No02Hx
BANNAN, Michael		22	M	Laborer	19No02Hx
HENRY, Thomas		50	M	Laborer	19No02Hx
Mary	(W)	45	F	Laborer	19No02Hx
Ann	(D)	17	F	Laborer	19No02Hx
Mary	(D)	22	F	Laborer	19No02Hx
Ella	(S)	02	M	Child	19No02Hx
Biddy	(D)	05	F	Child	19No02Hx
James	(S)	11	M	Child	19No02Hx
Catherine	(D)	07	F	Child	19No02Hx
GANNEN, Thomas		21	M	Laborer	19No02Hx
COSTELLO, Patrick		30	M	Laborer	19No02Hx
BRENNAN, Margaret		28	F	Laborer	19No02Hx
Biddy		28	F	Laborer	19No02Hx
CONNOR, John		05	M	Child	19No02Hx
CLORAN, Owen		25	M	Laborer	19No02Hx

NAMES OF PASSENGERS		AGE SEX	OCCUPATIONS	DATE PORT SHIP
CLORAN, Hugh		22 M	Laborer	19No02Hx
Richard		21 M	Laborer	19No02Hx
KILDARE, Charles		18 M	Laborer	19No02Hx
MIDGE, Pat		36 M	Laborer	19No02Hx
DAVY, Frank		30 M	Laborer	19No02Hx
MALONE, Mary		21 F	Laborer	19No02Hx
LOMAN, Mary		21 F	Laborer	19No02Hx
KINNAIRD, James		25 M	Laborer	19No02Hx
Bess		22 F	Laborer	19No02Hx
Sally		15 F	Laborer	19No02Hx
CAVENAGH, Pat		20 M	Laborer	19No02Hx
Catherine		22 F	Laborer	19No02Hx
CARL, Margaret		18 F	Laborer	19No02Hx
Catherine		16 F	Laborer	19No02Hx
TOOLE, Joseph		22 M	Laborer	19No02Hx
DUNN, Margaret		18 F	Laborer	19No02Hx
MACNALLY, John		48 M	Laborer	19No02Hx
Ann	(W)	45 F	Laborer	19No02Hx
Catherine	(D)	12 F	Laborer	19No02Hx
Mary	(D)	10 F	Child	19No02Hx
Julia	(D)	06 F	Child	19No02Hx
Margaret	(D)	03 F	Child	19No02Hx
Ann	(D)	11 F	Unknown	19No02Hx
Alice	(D)	07 F	Child	19No02Hx
Thomas	(S)	04 M	Child	19No02Hx
Patrick		20 M	Laborer	19No02Hx
John		01 M	Child	19No02Hx
GAFFNEY, Pat		35 M	Laborer	19No02Hx
Jane	(W)	25 F	Laborer	19No02Hx
Mary	(D)	02 F	Child	19No02Hx
Mike	(S)	01 M	Child	19No02Hx
DIVINE, Thomas		54 M	Laborer	19No02Hx
Biddy	(W)	40 F	Laborer	19No02Hx
Biddy	(D)	11 F	Child	19No02Hx
Margaret	(D)	09 F	Child	19No02Hx
Ellen	(D)	07 F	Child	19No02Hx
Bessy	(D)	05 F	Child	19No02Hx
Ann	(D)	03 F	Child	19No02Hx
Pat	(S)	13 M	Laborer	19No02Hx
MORRIS, Bell		40 F	Laborer	19No02Hx
Mary	(D)	11 F	Child	19No02Hx
Michael	(S)	09 M	Child	19No02Hx
Joseph	(S)	07 M	Child	19No02Hx
Nancy	(D)	05 F	Child	19No02Hx
GARREY, Thomas		40 M	Laborer	19No02Hx
Mary	(W)	25 F	Laborer	19No02Hx
Margaret	(D)	02 F	Child	19No02Hx
TAAF, John		21 M	Laborer	19No02Hx
SMITH, Bessy		20 F	Laborer	19No02Hx
MACGALLAGHER, Sam		24 M	Laborer	19No02Hx
CAREY, James		23 M	Laborer	19No02Hx
CARROL, Richd.		18 M	Laborer	19No02Hx
LOCKITT, Ann		20 F	Laborer	19No02Hx
MOONEY, Catherine		49 F	Laborer	19No02Hx
Pat	(S)	12 M	Laborer	19No02Hx
Biddy	(D)	24 F	Laborer	19No02Hx
QUIN, Rose		20 F	Laborer	19No02Hx
GILLENDER, Mary		17 F	Laborer	19No02Hx
HILL, Mary		30 F	Laborer	19No02Hx
Margaret	(D)	12 F	Laborer	19No02Hx
Elizabeth	(D)	10 F	Child	19No02Hx
Sarah	(D)	07 F	Child	19No02Hx
Hill	(S)	04 M	Child	19No02Hx
Andy	(S)	02 M	Child	19No02Hx
Jane		24 F	Laborer	19No02Hx
MULONY, Richard		34 M	Laborer	19No02Hx
Catherine		26 F	Laborer	19No02Hx
Mary	(D)	13 F	Laborer	19No02Hx
James	(S)	10 M	Child	19No02Hx
Judy	(D)	07 F	Child	19No02Hx
TWELVE, Paddy		54 M	Laborer	19No02Hx
ROBINSON, Martin		18 M	Laborer	19No02Hx
FORSYTH, Margaret		18 F	Laborer	19No02Hx
Rebecca		18 F	Laborer	19No02Hx
BRADY, Mary		55 F	Laborer	19No02Hx
BRADY, Pat	(S)	21 M	Laborer	19No02Hx
FITZPATRICK, John		24 M	Laborer	19No02Hx
MACGRATH, Owen		55 M	Laborer	19No02Hx
Mary	(W)	55 F	Laborer	19No02Hx
Margaret	(D)	07 F	Child	19No02Hx
DELANY, John		24 M	Laborer	19No02Hx
MACDANIEL, Wm.		31 M	Laborer	19No02Hx
BRADY, Margaret		31 F	Laborer	19No02Hx
Ellen	(D)	07 F	Child	19No02Hx
MACGUIRE, Thomas		18 M	Laborer	19No02Hx
KING, Francis		25 M	Laborer	19No02Hx
MACGUIRE, Judy		18 F	Laborer	19No02Hx
FITZPATRICK, Kate		19 F	Laborer	19No02Hx
Margaret		18 F	Laborer	19No02Hx
MACDONNEL, Mary		17 F	Laborer	19No02Hx
SHEENAN, Barney		20 M	Laborer	19No02Hx
Owen		18 M	Laborer	19No02Hx
James		21 M	Laborer	19No02Hx
MACTIGHT, Rose		30 F	Laborer	19No02Hx
CUSICK, James		20 M	Laborer	19No02Hx
WILLOUGHBY, Mary		21 F	Laborer	19No02Hx
CLARK, Bridget		22 F	Laborer	19No02Hx
GILMARTIN, Ann		20 F	Laborer	19No02Hx
MUNROE, Ann		14 F	Laborer	19No02Hx
MACKEENAN, James		21 M	Laborer	19No02Hx
Mary	(W)	21 F	Laborer	19No02Hx
Rose	(D)	03 F	Child	19No02Hx
Felix	(S)	02 M	Child	19No02Hx
CANNON, Catherine		16 F	Laborer	19No02Hx
MACMANON, Patrick		21 M	Laborer	19No02Hx
KEENAN, Bridget		19 F	Laborer	19No02Hx
HORAN, John		28 M	Laborer	19No02Hx
MACMANUS, Ann		21 F	Laborer	19No02Hx
MACANDREW, Michael		25 M	Laborer	19No02Hx
BRENNAN, Bridget		21 F	Laborer	19No02Hx
CALLAHAN, Jack		22 M	Laborer	19No02Hx
Libby		18 F	Laborer	19No02Hx
BRENNAN, Mary		12 F	Laborer	19No02Hx
MURPHY, Ann		23 F	Laborer	19No02Hx
LYNCH, Mary		40 F	Laborer	19No02Hx
SHEENAN, Mary		16 F	Laborer	19No02Hx
MCABE, Martin		15 M	Laborer	19No02Hx
OWEN, Hugh		20 M	Laborer	19No02Hx
BRADY, James		18 M	Laborer	19No02Hx
THOMMANY, Dan		25 M	Laborer	19No02Hx
HENRY, Ellen		19 F	Laborer	19No02Hx
Mary		40 F	Laborer	19No02Hx
Robt.		06 M	Child	19No02Hx
Hugh		10 M	Child	19No02Hx
Rose		18 F	Laborer	19No02Hx
John		12 M	Laborer	19No02Hx
SCHOLLIC, Jane		19 F	Laborer	19No02Hx
ORMISTON, Wm.		54 M	Laborer	19No02Hx
COX, Margaret		20 F	Laborer	19No02Hx
GILMORE, Hugh		20 M	Laborer	19No02Hx
CAHAN, Thomas		19 M	Laborer	19No02Hx
CARNEY, Mary		19 F	Laborer	19No02Hx
DOUGHTY, Ann		18 F	Laborer	19No02Hx
MACCABE, Biddy		17 F	Laborer	19No02Hx
BURN, John		40 M	Laborer	19No02Hx
Maria		25 F	Laborer	19No02Hx
Patrick	(S)	05 M	Child	19No02Hx
Thomas	(S)	03 M	Child	19No02Hx
John	(S)	01 M	Child	19No02Hx
MURPHY, Jane		19 F	Laborer	19No02Hx
BRADY, James		19 M	Laborer	19No02Hx
KELLY, Margaret		18 F	Laborer	19No02Hx
MACGORMAN, Pat		55 M	Laborer	19No02Hx
MORRISON, Abraham		26 M	Laborer	19No02Hx
Eliza		26 F	Laborer	19No02Hx
FORSYTH, Francis		19 M	Laborer	19No02Hx
BURKE, Fanny		21 F	Laborer	19No02Hx
Matilda		19 F	Laborer	19No02Hx
Susan		16 F	Laborer	19No02Hx
MARKEY, Lawrence		20 M	Laborer	19No02Hx

NAMES OF PASSENGERS		AGE	SEX	OCCUPATIONS	DATE PORT SHIP
AIKIN, Robt.		22	M	Laborer	19No02Hx
HANNON, Bridget		23	F	Laborer	19No02Hx
Mary		07	F	Child	19No02Hx
MACGUIRE, Pat		20	M	Laborer	19No02Hx
GAMBLE, James		20	M	Laborer	19No02Hx
BELLFORD, Joseph		18	M	Laborer	19No02Hx
LEONARD, Mary		20	F	Laborer	19No02Hx
DUNN, Margaret		16	F	Laborer	19No02Hx
LAMBERT, Johanna		19	F	Laborer	19No02Hx
REYNOLDS, Catherine		54	F	Laborer	19No02Hx
Dolly	(D)	16	F	Laborer	19No02Hx
Catherine	(D)	17	F	Laborer	19No02Hx
KEVLIN, Margaret		20	F	Laborer	19No02Hx
MAID, Katherine		20	F	Laborer	19No02Hx
RYAN, John		20	M	Laborer	19No02Hx
CLARK, Arnold		37	M	Laborer	19No02Hx
MACILVOY, Barney		20	M	Laborer	19No02Hx
DUFFEY, Edward		20	M	Laborer	19No02Hx
MACSHANE, James		30	M	Laborer	19No02Hx
Mary		20	F	Laborer	19No02Hx
HUGHS, Catherine		20	F	Laborer	19No02Hx
DUFFEY, Rose		20	F	Laborer	19No02Hx
MACGRATH, Jane		20	F	Laborer	19No02Hx
MORAN, Wm.		56	M	Laborer	19No02Hx
Elizh.	(W)	45	F	Laborer	19No02Hx
Wm.	(S)	10	M	Child	19No02Hx
Susan	(D)	04	F	Child	19No02Hx
Eliza	(D)	16	F	Laborer	19No02Hx
Frances	(D)	13	F	Laborer	19No02Hx
IRWINE, Martha		20	F	Laborer	19No02Hx
ROBINSON, Ann		16	F	Laborer	19No02Hx
WELSH, Mary		18	F	Laborer	19No02Hx
FAULKNER, Mary		18	F	Laborer	19No02Hx
SMITH, Mary		14	F	Laborer	19No02Hx
OBYRNE, Catherine		20	F	Laborer	19No02Hx
KING, Catherine		14	F	Laborer	19No02Hx
FEE, Mary		17	F	Laborer	19No02Hx
Margaret		07	F	Child	19No02Hx
Frances		09	F	Child	19No02Hx
FARREL, Mary		20	F	Laborer	19No02Hx
DOLAN, Ann		24	F	Laborer	19No02Hx
Catherine		25	F	Laborer	19No02Hx
BYRNES, Bridget		16	F	Laborer	19No02Hx
LOWE, Margaret		26	F	Laborer	19No02Hx
WHITE, James		21	M	Laborer	19No02Hx
GORDON, James		25	M	Laborer	19No02Hx
SMITH, Martha		19	F	Laborer	19No02Hx
DENNISON, Rachel		21	F	Laborer	19No02Hx
FAGAN, Maria		20	F	Laborer	19No02Hx
KINNAIRD, Judy		24	F	Laborer	19No02Hx
BRADY, Foster		30	M	Laborer	19No02Hx
Margaret	(W)	28	F	Laborer	19No02Hx
Betsy	(D)	04	F	Child	19No02Hx
Jane	(D)	02	F	Child	19No02Hx
HENDRAN, Edward		23	M	Butcher	19No02Hx
COFFEE, Joseph		50	M	Laborer	19No02Hx
KALEY, Nancy		10	F	Child	19No02Hx
Jeffry		07	M	Child	19No02Hx
MEEKIN, Francis		35	M	Brf	19No02Hx
Joseph	(S)	08	M	Child	19No02Hx
Mary-Ann	(D)	07	F	Child	19No02Hx
HANLAN, Ellen		19	F	Dressmaker	19No02Hx
KALWIN, Edward		19	M	Laborer	19No02Hx
KALLIGAN, James		28	M	Laborer	19No02Hx
SMITH, James		21	M	Laborer	19No02Hx
HOGAN, Michael		20	M	Laborer	19No02Hx

HENRY 20 NOVEMBER 1846

From Liverpool

NAMES OF PASSENGERS		AGE	SEX	OCCUPATIONS	DATE PORT SHIP
CONNOR, Martin		21	M	Laborer	20No02Ic
CLARKE, John		24	M	Laborer	20No02Ic
Eleanor		20	F	None	20No02Ic
Hannah		50	F	None	20No02Ic
Ellen		12	F	None	20No02Ic
LAFFERTY, Jane		20	F	None	20No02Ic
COCHRANE, Margt.		20	F	None	20No02Ic
Molly		19	F	None	20No02Ic
MURPHY, Jas.		45	M	Laborer	20No02Ic
Rose		60	F	None	20No02Ic
George		19	M	Laborer	20No02Ic
Henry		14	M	Laborer	20No02Ic
James		12	M	Laborer	20No02Ic
CORCORAN, Catharine		28	F	None	20No02Ic
Alexander	(S)	03	M	Child	20No02Ic
MCSHERRY, Edward		21	M	Laborer	20No02Ic
MCINTYRE, George		30	M	Laborer	20No02Ic
HAMSAY, John		24	M	Laborer	20No02Ic
DOUGHERTY, Wm.		20	M	Laborer	20No02Ic
RANKIN, Jane		20	F	None	20No02Ic
SMITH, Bessie		20	F	None	20No02Ic
PARK, Elisa		20	F	None	20No02Ic
MCGEE, Mary		21	F	None	20No02Ic
MALLON, Mary		26	F	None	20No02Ic
GROGAN, John		40	M	Laborer	20No02Ic
U	(W)	40	F	None	20No02Ic
Fanny	(D)	18	F	None	20No02Ic
George	(S)	12	M	None	20No02Ic
Charles	(S)	10	M	Child	20No02Ic
Richard	(S)	05	M	Child	20No02Ic
John	(S)	07	M	Child	20No02Ic
KILROY, James		40	M	Laborer	20No02Ic
REYNOLDS, Edward		22	M	Laborer	20No02Ic
Catharine		20	F	None	20No02Ic
HARGADON, Bridget		20	F	None	20No02Ic
REYNOLDS, Ann		20	F	None	20No02Ic
KILROY, Fanny		16	F	None	20No02Ic
MORAN, Thomas		20	M	Laborer	20No02Ic
HEARN, Thomas		20	M	Laborer	20No02Ic
Mary		19	F	None	20No02Ic
TAYANT, William		17	M	Laborer	20No02Ic
HALPIN, Thomas		18	M	Laborer	20No02Ic
BRAMAN, Margh.		28	F	None	20No02Ic
CROHAN, Mich.		27	M	Laborer	20No02Ic
REYNOLDS, Patt		35	M	Laborer	20No02Ic
U	(W)	35	F	None	20No02Ic
James	(S)	11	M	Child	20No02Ic
Ann	(D)	09	F	Child	20No02Ic
SMITH, Mathew		36	M	Laborer	20No02Ic
U	(W)	32	F	None	20No02Ic
Elizabeth	(D)	03	F	Child	20No02Ic
Mary-Ann	(D)	.08	F	Infant	20No02Ic
DARLY, Mary		25	F	None	20No02Ic
MCMANUS, Mary		22	F	None	20No02Ic
LANE, Michael		26	M	Laborer	20No02Ic
KELLY, Fanny		40	F	None	20No02Ic
FOSTER, John		40	M	Laborer	20No02Ic
STEWART, John-C.		34	M	Laborer	20No02Ic
Helen		26	F	None	20No02Ic
BLAIR, Margt.		36	F	None	20No02Ic
GILLES, J.		35	M	Laborer	20No02Ic
Margh.	(D)	05	F	Child	20No02Ic
BARTEN, Jno.		26	M	Laborer	20No02Ic
HAGAN, Mary		18	F	None	20No02Ic
Ellen		20	F	None	20No02Ic

NAMES OF PASSENGERS		AGE	SEX	OCCUPATIONS	DATE PORT SHIP
COONEY, Wm.		22	M	Laborer	20No02Ic
U	(W)	25	F	None	20No02Ic
KEARNES, John		20	M	Laborer	20No02Ic
Elizabeth		20	F	None	20No02Ic
ELWOOD, Thos.		20	M	Laborer	20No02Ic
Mary		22	F	None	20No02Ic
Bridget		18	F	None	20No02Ic
OWENS, Michael		22	M	Laborer	20No02Ic
Thomas		20	M	Laborer	20No02Ic
MCDONNELL, Thos.		24	M	Laborer	20No02Ic
CONCANNON, Honora		25	F	None	20No02Ic
THOMPSON, Bridget		19	F	None	20No02Ic
OWENS, Patrick		09	M	Child	20No02Ic
LARKIN, U-Mrs.		35	F	None	20No02Ic
Mary		18	F	None	20No02Ic
DEEHAN, Michael		40	M	None	20No02Ic
DEVIN, Rose		16	F	None	20No02Ic
JEMISON, Sarah		50	F	None	20No02Ic
MULLHEARNE, Jane		30	F	None	20No02Ic
YOUNG, Mary-Ann		24	F	None	20No02Ic
CALLIGAN, Jane		20	F	None	20No02Ic
PARKER, Thos.		22	M	Laborer	20No02Ic
Catharine		30	F	None	20No02Ic
William		13	M	Laborer	20No02Ic
Richard		11	M	Child	20No02Ic
Eliza-Jane		01	F	Child	20No02Ic
WEIR, Henry		22	M	Laborer	20No02Ic
Elizabeth		20	F	None	20No02Ic
BOWES, Joseph		26	M	Laborer	20No02Ic
Elizabeth		25	F	None	20No02Ic
Elizabeth		23	F	None	20No02Ic
Mary		18	F	None	20No02Ic
SULLIVAN, Catharine		20	F	None	20No02Ic
KAIN, Margarett		22	F	None	20No02Ic
RESLEY, Patrick		24	M	Laborer	20No02Ic
BRADY, Hugh		30	M	Laborer	20No02Ic
GALLAGHER, Patrick		23	M	Laborer	20No02Ic
U	(W)	20	F	None	20No02Ic
Michael		06	M	Child	20No02Ic
KAIN, Peter		30	M	Laborer	20No02Ic
Died-At-Sea					
MCGUIRE, Mary		25	F	None	20No02Ic
DONNELLY, Eliza		05	F	Child	20No02Ic
MCLOUGHLIN, John		28	M	Laborer	20No02Ic
U	(W)	26	F	None	20No02Ic
CALLIGAN, John		11	M	Child	20No02Ic
CORMICK, Thos.		24	M	Laborer	20No02Ic
FARRELLY, Patt		22	M	Laborer	20No02Ic
ONEAL, Owen		18	M	Laborer	20No02Ic
LYNCH, Bernard		25	M	Laborer	20No02Ic
KELLY, James		22	M	Laborer	20No02Ic
CARROLL, James		22	M	Laborer	20No02Ic
IBBS, James		34	M	Laborer	20No02Ic
Isaac		26	M	Laborer	20No02Ic
DACRES, Michael		30	M	Laborer	20No02Ic
NAUGHTON, Wm.		20	M	Laborer	20No02Ic
DURKIN, Mary		20	F	None	20No02Ic
MCDERMOTT, John		20	M	Laborer	20No02Ic
Maria		26	F	None	20No02Ic
Fanny		45	F	None	20No02Ic
RICHERSON, Eliza		12	F	None	20No02Ic
BURKE, Patk.		28	M	Laborer	20No02Ic
CANTLAN, John		22	M	Laborer	20No02Ic
Ann		16	F	None	20No02Ic
MOONEY, Jas.		24	M	Laborer	20No02Ic
LAFFY, Thomas		60	M	Laborer	20No02Ic
Honora	(D)	23	F	None	20No02Ic
Catharine	(D)	19	F	None	20No02Ic
JOHNSTON, Anthony		17	M	Laborer	20No02Ic
DOWD, Thos.		25	M	Laborer	20No02Ic
FAIN, Ann		24	F	None	20No02Ic
CORRIGAN, Patt		30	M	Laborer	20No02Ic
U	(W)	28	F	None	20No02Ic
John	(S)	12	M	None	20No02Ic
James	(S)	10	M	Child	20No02Ic

NAMES OF PASSENGERS		AGE	SEX	OCCUPATIONS	DATE PORT SHIP
CORRIGAN, Joseph	(S)	04	M	Child	20No02Ic
Margh.	(D)	.08	F	Infant	20No02Ic
John		26	M	Carpenter	20No02Ic
U	(W)	22	F	None	20No02Ic
Patt	(S)	01	M	Child	20No02Ic
Died-At-Sea					
ARMSTRONG, Jane		21	F	None	20No02Ic
LEE, Mary-Ann		20	F	None	20No02Ic
CUNNING, Hugh		30	M	Tailor	20No02Ic
James		20	M	Laborer	20No02Ic
Joseph		21	M	Laborer	20No02Ic
Bernard		24	M	Laborer	20No02Ic
MCCEMENTS, Wm.		23	M	Laborer	20No02Ic
MCLOUGHLIN, Richard		19	M	Laborer	20No02Ic
MCENTIRE, Ellen		20	F	None	20No02Ic
DARENEY, Susan		21	F	None	20No02Ic
GRAY, Robt.		30	M	Laborer	20No02Ic
MCLOUGHLIN, Rachael		17	F	None	20No02Ic
Ann		18	F	None	20No02Ic
MCCLEAR, John		24	M	Grocer	20No02Ic
MCENTEE, Patrick		30	M	Laborer	20No02Ic
CLARK, Edward		21	M	Laborer	20No02Ic
CANNON, John		20	M	Laborer	20No02Ic
MCCABE, Thos.		21	M	Laborer	20No02Ic
NEILSON, Thos.		17	M	Laborer	20No02Ic
CLARKE, Margarett		19	F	None	20No02Ic
Alice		17	F	None	20No02Ic
KAYNOR, Catharine		17	F	None	20No02Ic
CONNOR, Catharine		16	F	None	20No02Ic
SMITH, Margh.		18	F	None	20No02Ic
DUFFY, Judith		22	F	None	20No02Ic
MCCONNAN, Bridget		26	F	None	20No02Ic
CLARK, Owen		37	M	Miller	20No02Ic
U	(W)	32	F	None	20No02Ic
Mary	(D)	12	F	None	20No02Ic
Ann	(D)	12	F	None	20No02Ic
Thomas	(S)	08	M	Child	20No02Ic
Philip	(S)	06	M	Child	20No02Ic
John	(S)	02	M	Child	20No02Ic
Patrick		20	M	Laborer	20No02Ic
MCLOUGHLIN, Hugh		20	M	Laborer	20No02Ic
MCKENNA, Terrence		19	M	Tailor	20No02Ic
COMERFORD, Felix		20	M	Laborer	20No02Ic
TOOLE, John		21	M	Brazier	20No02Ic
KEOUGH, Bridget		20	F	None	20No02Ic
CONNOLLY, Mary		20	F	None	20No02Ic
LYNCH, Mary		21	F	None	20No02Ic
MCEVOY, Ellen		24	F	None	20No02Ic
MORROW, Mary		20	F	None	20No02Ic
REILEY, Biddy		20	F	None	20No02Ic
MCGUIRE, Honora		12	F	None	20No02Ic
MCKENNA, Frank		19	M	Laborer	20No02Ic
Ellen		18	F	None	20No02Ic
Catharan		16	F	None	20No02Ic
Biddy		15	F	None	20No02Ic
NEILEY, Rosanna		26	F	None	20No02Ic
Wm.	(S)	05	M	Child	20No02Ic
MORAN, Catharin		21	F	None	20No02Ic
REILEY, Patrick		30	M	Laborer	20No02Ic
U	(W)	28	F	None	20No02Ic
Andrew	(S)	04	M	Child	20No02Ic
James	(S)	03	M	Child	20No02Ic
Edward		20	M	None	20No02Ic
MACKIN, Bridget		22	F	None	20No02Ic
KENNEDY, Arthur		40	M	Farmer	20No02Ic
Died-At-Sea					
Mary	(W)	30	F	None	20No02Ic
Rose	(D)	19	F	None	20No02Ic
John	(S)	15	M	None	20No02Ic
Hugh	(S)	13	M	None	20No02Ic
Margt.	(D)	11	F	Child	20No02Ic
Philip	(S)	09	M	Child	20No02Ic
Maria	(D)	07	F	Child	20No02Ic
Ann	(D)	05	F	Child	20No02Ic
Edward	(S)	03	M	Child	20No02Ic

NAMES OF PASSENGERS	A G E	S E X	OCCUPATIONS	DATE PORT SHIP	NAMES OF PASSENGERS	A G E	S E X	OCCUPATIONS	DATE PORT SHIP
KENNEDY, Catharin	(D)	02 F	Child	20No02Ic	OCONNELL, Patt		35 M	Laborer	20No02Ic
MCINTYRE, James		24 M	Laborer	20No02Ic	Margh.		22 F	None	20No02Ic
MCKEOWN, Mary		30 F	None	20No02Ic	NOWLAN, John		24 M	Laborer	20No02Ic
Francis	(S)	04 M	Child	20No02Ic	U	(W)	20 F	None	20No02Ic
REILEY, Ann		30 F	None	20No02Ic	BURKE, U-Mrs.		50 F	None	20No02Ic
TIGHE, Anthony		24 M	Laborer	20No02Ic	Jno.	(S)	20 M	Laborer	20No02Ic
MOORE, Hannah		23 F	None	20No02Ic	Alice	(D)	18 F	None	20No02Ic
DEVINE, Michl.		21 M	Laborer	20No02Ic	GUINAN, Mary		20 F	None	20No02Ic
MULLIGAN, Patt		23 M	Laborer	20No02Ic	SHAUGHNESSY, Mary		18 F	None	20No02Ic
CORCORAN, Patt		22 M	Laborer	20No02Ic	CONNOLY, Catharin		22 F	None	20No02Ic
WRIGHT, Francis		35 M	Laborer	20No02Ic	Elisabeth		40 F	None	20No02Ic
MIMMIER, John		24 M	Laborer	20No02Ic	Mary		20 F	None	20No02Ic
HACKET, Geo.		40 M	Laborer	20No02Ic	BURNS, Mary		22 F	None	20No02Ic
Josiah	(S)	20 M	Laborer	20No02Ic	CARROLL, Cathn.		24 F	None	20No02Ic
CONNOLLY, James		24 M	Laborer	20No02Ic	KEOUGH, Margh.		40 F	None	20No02Ic
Patt		40 M	Laborer	20No02Ic	BRANIGAN, Isabella		20 F	None	20No02Ic
WHITE, Samuel		25 M	Laborer	20No02Ic	ONEIL, Charles		24 M	Laborer	20No02Ic
MCCAFFREY, John		24 M	Laborer	20No02Ic	Maria		20 F	None	20No02Ic
John		20 M	Laborer	20No02Ic	REILLY, Margh.		17 F	None	20No02Ic
Jane		19 F	Laborer	20No02Ic	KIERNAN, Dominick		27 M	Laborer	20No02Ic
FARRELL, Garett		26 M	Laborer	20No02Ic	U	(W)	22 F	None	20No02Ic
U	(W)	24 F	Laborer	20No02Ic	KILMARTIN, Ann		22 F	None	20No02Ic
CONROY, Frank		21 M	Laborer	20No02Ic	TIERNAN, W.		20 M	Laborer	20No02Ic
Patrick		19 M	Laborer	20No02Ic	DEVIN, Bernard		45 M	Laborer	20No02Ic
SPRATT, William		21 M	Laborer	20No02Ic	Mary-Ann	(W)	37 F	None	20No02Ic
MELLONS, Richard		19 M	Laborer	20No02Ic	Mary-Ann	(D)	16 F	None	20No02Ic
MCGUIRE, Margh.		19 F	None	20No02Ic	Margh.	(D)	14 F	None	20No02Ic
Bridget		18 F	None	20No02Ic	Susan-Jane	(D)	12 F	None	20No02Ic
GILLOOLY, Ann		20 F	None	20No02Ic	John	(S)	06 M	Child	20No02Ic
GREEN, Catharin		20 F	None	20No02Ic	Charlotte	(D)	04 F	Child	20No02Ic
FITZGIBBON, Patt		25 M	None	20No02Ic	Henrietta	(D)	02 F	Child	20No02Ic
FITZPATRICK, John		24 M	None	20No02Ic	HENRY, Wm.		.00 M	Infant	20No02Ic
U	(W)	20 F	None	20No02Ic	CASEY, Michael		30 M	Laborer	20No02Ic
COADY, Patrick		21 M	Engineer	20No02Ic	TORRY, Jas.		26 M	Laborer	20No02Ic
MOSLEY, U-Mrs.		40 F	None	20No02Ic	FARRELLY, Rose		24 F	None	20No02Ic
Elizabeth	(D)	12 F	None	20No02Ic	POOLE, Samuel		30 M	Laborer	20No02Ic
Ann	(D)	10 F	Child	20No02Ic	HAMILTON, Thomas		21 M	Laborer	20No02Ic
RICE, F.		30 M	Laborer	20No02Ic	ONEIL, Robt.		50 M	Laborer	20No02Ic
LYNCH, Peter		35 M	Laborer	20No02Ic	GROGAN, Eliza		20 F	None	20No02Ic
LAMB, George		32 M	Laborer	20No02Ic					
HANLEY, Patt		45 M	Laborer	20No02Ic					
REILEY, Thomas		20 M	Laborer	20No02Ic					
Charles		10 M	Child	20No02Ic					
Nicholas		17 M	Laborer	20No02Ic	**COLLECTOR 20 NOVEMBER 1846**				
NIGHT, James		20 M	Laborer	20No02Ic					
COX, John		17 M	Laborer	20No02Ic	From Halifax				
MURTAGH, Phillip		26 M	Laborer	20No02Ic					
Elizabeth		24 F	None	20No02Ic					
RIDGE, Jas.		21 M	Laborer	20No02Ic					
CONNOR, John		21 M	Laborer	20No02Ic	MURPHY, Thomas		28 M	Merchant	20No22Ie
KELLY, John		19 M	Laborer	20No02Ic	MCNAUGHTON, Alex		25 M	Merchant	20No22Ie
CARMICHAEL, John		50 M	Laborer	20No02Ic					
Isabella	(W)	48 F	None	20No02Ic					
Joseph	(S)	12 M	Laborer	20No02Ic					
Isaac	(S)	10 M	Child	20No02Ic	**AURELIUS 21 NOVEMBER 1846**				
John	(S)	08 M	Child	20No02Ic					
Samuel	(S)	06 M	Child	20No02Ic	From Liverpool				
Susanna	(D)	04 F	Child	20No02Ic					
NEWMAN, John		60 M	Laborer	20No02Ic					
U	(W)	50 F	None	20No02Ic	OWENS, William		22 M	Bootmaker	21No02If
Edward	(S)	33 M	Laborer	20No02Ic	MOONEY, John		20 M	Merchant	21No02If
John	(S)	30 M	Laborer	20No02Ic	Joseph		18 M	Merchant	21No02If
Thomas	(S)	22 M	Laborer	20No02Ic	POWELL, Thomas-B.		16 M	Student	21No02If
Biddy	(D)	24 F	Laborer	20No02Ic	BROWN, Thomas		35 M	Weaver	21No02If
Catharin	(D)	18 F	Laborer	20No02Ic	Mary	(W)	32 F	Weaver	21No02If
Mary	(D)	19 F	Laborer	20No02Ic	Samuel	(S)	12 M	Weaver	21No02If
William	(S)	13 M	Laborer	20No02Ic	John	(S)	10 M	Child	21No02If
MAKER, John		19 M	Laborer	20No02Ic	Henry	(S)	08 M	Child	21No02If
Alley		12 F	None	20No02Ic	Ellenor	(D)	04 F	Child	21No02If
GRIFFIN, John		22 M	Laborer	20No02Ic	Mary-Ann	(D)	01 F	Child	21No02If
SHEA, William		24 M	Laborer	20No02Ic	MCMANANY, Pat		36 M	Laborer	21No02If
DWYER, Fany		18 F	None	20No02Ic					
SPILLMAN, Mary		22 F	None	20No02Ic					
RYAN, Mary		18 F	None	20No02Ic					
SCOTT, Elisa		19 F	None	20No02Ic					

NAMES OF PASSENGERS		AGE	SEX	OCCUPATIONS	DATE PORT SHIP
MCMANANY, Mary	(W)	34	F	Laborer	21No02If
Peter	(S)	02	M	Child	21No02If
Roger		32	M	Laborer	21No02If
Nancy		22	F	Laborer	21No02If
KRBY, Michal		30	M	Laborer	21No02If
Catherine		25	F	Laborer	21No02If
QUINLAN, William		27	M	Laborer	21No02If
Johanna		22	F	Laborer	21No02If
SHEEHY, Edmond		27	M	Butcher	21No02If
Eliza	(W)	25	F	Butcher	21No02If
John	(S)	02	M	Child	21No02If
LOUGHAN, James		20	M	Farmer	21No02If
ROCK, Andrew		28	M	Laborer	21No02If
Sarah	(W)	26	F	Laborer	21No02If
Pat	(S)	06	M	Child	21No02If
John	(S)	03	M	Child	21No02If
Andrew		60	M	Laborer	21No02If
Marten		35	M	Farmer	21No02If
Mary	(W)	34	F	Farmer	21No02If
Andrew	(S)	10	M	Child	21No02If
John	(S)	08	M	Child	21No02If
Thomas	(S)	01	M	Child	21No02If
MCGUIRE, John		18	M	Farmer	21No02If
MCMAN, Mary		18	F	Servant	21No02If
AUTHER, Esebella		18	F	Servant	21No02If
TULLY, Catherine		12	F	Servant	21No02If
MCGOVERN, Ann		18	F	Servant	21No02If
TULLY, Catherine		17	F	Servant	21No02If
MCCATHY, Sarah		17	F	Servant	21No02If
ROCK, John		30	M	Laborer	21No02If
Catherine		20	F	Laborer	21No02If

CORNELIA 23 NOVEMBER 1846

From Liverpool

NAMES OF PASSENGERS		AGE	SEX	OCCUPATIONS	DATE PORT SHIP
MOONEY, Arthur		40	M	Merchant	23No02Am
BRENNAN, Owen		26	M	Laborer	23No02Am
Mary		28	F	Servant	23No02Am
Catherine		24	F	Servant	23No02Am
U	(S)	.00	M	Infant	23No02Am
KENNEDY, Margaret		40	F	Servant	23No02Am
Sally	(D)	20	F	Servant	23No02Am
John	(S)	13	M	Servant	23No02Am
William	(S)	12	M	Servant	23No02Am
Andrew	(S)	10	M	Child	23No02Am
Patrick	(S)	08	M	Child	23No02Am
Bridget	(D)	06	F	Child	23No02Am
TRAYNON, Dora		27	F	Servant	23No02Am
MALLON, James		22	M	Laborer	23No02Am
Charles		20	M	Laborer	23No02Am
William		16	M	Laborer	23No02Am
Robert		13	M	Laborer	23No02Am
Mary		18	F	Laborer	23No02Am
Sarah		46	F	Laborer	23No02Am
Died-At-Sea					
FERGUSSON, Jane		20	F	Servant	23No02Am
QUIN, Jane		21	F	Servant	23No02Am
SMITH, Isabella		22	F	Servant	23No02Am
MCKENNA, Sarah		17	F	Servant	23No02Am
TAYLOR, Benjamin		65	M	Farmer	23No02Am
Died-At-Sea					
Mary		54	F	None	23No02Am
HUTCHINSON, George		20	M	Laborer	23No02Am
MARTIN, William		16	M	Laborer	23No02Am
MCCOLLOUGH, Jane		21	F	Servant	23No02Am
BROOKS, Nancy		21	F	Servant	23No02Am
DICKEY, Betsey		20	F	Servant	23No02Am
MCNEARY, Margt.		18	F	Servant	23No02Am
WIGLEY, William		31	M	Laborer	23No02Am
JUNK, John		18	M	Laborer	23No02Am
MINDS, James		35	M	Cooper	23No02Am
Cath.	(W)	35	F	None	23No02Am
Mary	(D)	.09	F	Infant	23No02Am
Died-At-Sea					
SHERLAN, Pat		22	M	Laborer	23No02Am
CALLAGHAN, John		16	M	Servant	23No02Am
MCELROY, Ann		19	F	Servant	23No02Am
OHARE, Ellen		30	F	Servant	23No02Am
MINDS, Felix		11	M	Child	23No02Am
Ann		08	F	Child	23No02Am
Bridget		06	F	Child	23No02Am
Jane		04	F	Child	23No02Am
Catherine		02	F	Child	23No02Am
CULLEN, Elizabeth		24	F	Servant	23No02Am
MULLEN, Mary		17	F	Servant	23No02Am
MULRANNEY, John		22	M	Servant	23No02Am
REILINGTON, Michael		25	M	Laborer	23No02Am
Cath.		30	F	Servant	23No02Am
REALLY, James		75	M	Laborer	23No02Am
Died-At-Sea					
KELLY, Matt		22	M	Laborer	23No02Am
SERVELL, Edward		22	M	Laborer	23No02Am
MATHER, Mary		21	F	Servant	23No02Am
DICKEY, Mary		20	F	Servant	23No02Am
Sophia-Ann		16	F	Servant	23No02Am
FALLOON, Thomas		20	M	Laborer	23No02Am
MCGORAN, Biddy		21	F	Servant	23No02Am
MCCLUSKEY, Biddy		21	F	Servant	23No02Am
MCCANN, Sally		20	F	Servant	23No02Am
MULLEN, Cath.		20	F	Servant	23No02Am
ROURKE, Peter		50	M	Laborer	23No02Am
GUMBLE, Daniel		40	M	Laborer	23No02Am
Ann-Jane	(D)	16	F	Servant	23No02Am
CUREY, Catherin		19	F	Servant	23No02Am
HASSEY, William		24	M	Servant	23No02Am
Bridget		21	F	Servant	23No02Am
KENNEDY, Samuel		42	M	Laborer	23No02Am
Ellen	(D)	15	F	Servant	23No02Am
Mary	(D)	14	F	Mtmkr	23No02Am
Charles	(S)	12	M	None	23No02Am
Biddy	(D)	10	F	Child	23No02Am
Catherin	(D)	08	F	Child	23No02Am
Margaret	(D)	06	F	Child	23No02Am
KANE, Mary		50	F	Servant	23No02Am
Michael	(S)	26	M	Laborer	23No02Am
SWEENEY, William		25	M	Laborer	23No02Am
CONNOR, Maria		19	F	Servant	23No02Am
BRADY, Patrick		22	M	Laborer	23No02Am
Bridget		20	F	Servant	23No02Am
MCCABE, Ann		18	F	Servant	23No02Am
CALLAGHAN, Betsey		20	F	Servant	23No02Am
Nancy		18	F	Servant	23No02Am
HAMILTON, Hugh		12	M	Laborer	23No02Am
DUFFY, James		21	M	Servant	23No02Am
MCGEOUGH, James		22	F	Laborer	23No02Am
BRYAN, Mary		20	F	Servant	23No02Am
GILLERAN, John		28	M	Laborer	23No02Am
SCOTT, Jane		21	F	Servant	23No02Am
BANGHEN, Maria		18	F	Servant	23No02Am
WIGLEY, Edward		20	M	Farmer	23No02Am
BRADY, James		20	M	Laborer	23No02Am
SHARKEY, Patt		30	M	Laborer	23No02Am
CURRAN, James		45	M	Farmer	23No02Am
Mary	(W)	45	F	None	23No02Am
Bridget	(D)	18	F	None	23No02Am
Ann	(D)	16	F	None	23No02Am
James	(S)	13	M	None	23No02Am
Jane	(D)	12	F	None	23No02Am
Thomas	(S)	10	M	Child	23No02Am
Mary	(D)	06	F	Child	23No02Am
DARLESS, Michael		20	M	Servant	23No02Am
RAILLY, Michael		22	M	Servant	23No02Am
KENNEDY, Catherine		20	F	Servant	23No02Am

NAMES OF PASSENGERS	AGE	SEX	OCCUPATIONS	DATE PORT SHIP
BRYAN, Ann	19	F	Servant	23No02Am
LENNAN, Mary	20	F	Servant	23No02Am
CONNOR, Bess	19	F	Servant	23No02Am
CLARK, Marella	21	F	Servant	23No02Am
MILAGHAN, Michael	21	M	Laborer	23No02Am
MCKENNA, John	20	M	Laborer	23No02Am
HALL, Jane	22	F	Servant	23No02Am
CASSIDY, Christoph.	30	M	Tailor	23No02Am
U (W)	28	F	None	23No02Am
MORGAN, Patt	23	M	Laborer	23No02Am
SWORDS, Mary	24	F	Servant	23No02Am
ONEIL, Thos.	14	M	Laborer	23No02Am
GLACKEN, Mich.	24	M	Laborer	23No02Am
LYNCH, Ann	21	F	Servant	23No02Am
DUFFY, Mary	17	F	Servant	23No02Am
MEANON, Daniel	30	M	Bricklayer	23No02Am
ORCHARD, George	20	M	Weaver	23No02Am
TOUCEY, John	20	M	Laborer	23No02Am
COLLEGAN, Ann	23	F	Servant	23No02Am
MCCANN, Mary	19	F	Servant	23No02Am
QUINN, Catherine	19	F	Servant	23No02Am
Mary	18	F	Servant	23No02Am
BRADY, Burran	19	M	Laborer	23No02Am
FAY, Cath.	19	F	Servant	23No02Am
CASSIDY, Mark	28	M	Laborer	23No02Am
LORETT, Edward	27	M	Laborer	23No02Am
KAIN, Dominick	20	M	Laborer	23No02Am
BRANDON, Owen	20	M	Laborer	23No02Am
CAIN, John	17	M	Laborer	23No02Am
FITZPATRICK, James	14	M	Laborer	23No02Am
MCCANN, John	40	M	Laborer	23No02Am
Margt. (D)	17	F	Servant	23No02Am
WILKINSON, Ann	17	F	Servant	23No02Am
MCKEE, Margt.	24	F	Servant	23No02Am
MCMAHON, Wm.	26	M	Laborer	23No02Am
HAYES, Michael	30	M	Laborer	23No02Am
HOLPEN, Michael	68	M	Laborer	23No02Am
U (W)	60	F	Laborer	23No02Am
MCCOFFY, Margt.	30	F	Servant	23No02Am
ARMSTRONG, Cath.	25	F	Servant	23No02Am
PEARSON, Benj.	20	M	Laborer	23No02Am
MCLARKEY, Patt	18	M	Laborer	23No02Am
MONAGHAN, John	17	M	Laborer	23No02Am
Brien	16	M	Servant	23No02Am
Julia	20	F	Servant	23No02Am
Catharine	14	F	Servant	23No02Am
Ellen	17	F	Servant	23No02Am
Mary	18	F	Servant	23No02Am
LEMON, Margt.	16	F	Servant	23No02Am
REILLY, Sally	20	F	Servant	23No02Am
TRACEY, Jane	20	F	Servant	23No02Am
MCCELLAN, Biddy	27	F	Servant	23No02Am
KELLY, Mary	18	F	Servant	23No02Am
GIBBINS, Margt.	20	F	Servant	23No02Am
BLAKE, Peggy	20	F	Servant	23No02Am
IVERS, Biddy	16	F	Servant	23No02Am
MCDERMOTT, Patrick	24	M	Laborer	23No02Am
BEGLEY, Eliza	22	F	Servant	23No02Am
MCDERMOTT, Rose	24	F	Servant	23No02Am
Rose	20	F	Servant	23No02Am
CONORAN, John	35	M	Laborer	23No02Am
U (W)	35	F	Servant	23No02Am
Peter (S)	12	M	None	23No02Am
Ann (D)	.06	F	Infant	23No02Am
MCGLOUGHLIN, Ann	22	F	Servant	23No02Am
MANGAN, Thos.	24	M	Servant	23No02Am
MCCANN, Mary	27	F	Servant	23No02Am
CARROLL, Ann	25	F	Servant	23No02Am
KANE, Kitty	25	F	Servant	23No02Am
FITZPATRICK, Patrick	25	M	Laborer	23No02Am
U (W)	20	F	Servant	23No02Am
CAFFREY, Mary	40	F	Servant	23No02Am
Ellen (D)	15	F	Servant	23No02Am
Henry (S)	14	M	Servant	23No02Am
Mary (D)	11	F	Child	23No02Am

NAMES OF PASSENGERS	AGE	SEX	OCCUPATIONS	DATE PORT SHIP
KELLY, Rose	20	F	Servant	23No02Am
MURPHY, Michael	17	M	Servant	23No02Am
DONNELLY, Peter	26	M	Servant	23No02Am
GRANT, Michael	27	M	Servant	23No02Am
KEANNON, Bridget	25	F	Servant	23No02Am
FIX, Mary	17	F	Servant	23No02Am
CARNAY, Sarah	50	F	Servant	23No02Am
Margt. (D)	18	F	Servant	23No02Am
Patrick (S)	12	M	Servant	23No02Am
James	71	M	Servant	23No02Am
Died-At-Sea				
ELDER, Ann	18	F	Servant	23No02Am
GILLESPIE, Michael	20	M	Servant	23No02Am
KROUGH, Martin	20	M	Laborer	23No02Am
Ann	10	F	Child	23No02Am
CROGHAN, Mary	21	F	Servant	23No02Am
BRENNAN, Nelly	18	F	Servant	23No02Am
REED, John	35	M	Servant	23No02Am
MARTIN, James	20	M	Laborer	23No02Am
FITZPATRICK, Hugh	19	M	Laborer	23No02Am
DAGNALL, James	27	M	Laborer	23No02Am
U (W)	24	F	Laborer	23No02Am
Barney (S)	03	M	Child	23No02Am
Patrick (S)	01	M	Child	23No02Am
Died-At-Sea				
ROARKE, Bridget	60	F	Housekeeper	23No02Am
FOLEY, Mary	18	F	Housekeeper	23No02Am
MCDONALD, Rose	20	F	Servant	23No02Am
CROAN, Patrick	22	M	Servant	23No02Am
MCCANN, Alice	50	F	Servant	23No02Am
CASEY, Biddy	40	F	Servant	23No02Am
James	30	M	Laborer	23No02Am
Alice	17	F	Servant	23No02Am
Judith	13	F	Servant	23No02Am
Margaret	12	F	Servant	23No02Am
Catherine	11	F	Child	23No02Am
GILLON, Biddy	30	F	Servant	23No02Am
GALLOUGHLY, Hugh	21	M	Laborer	23No02Am
Ann	25	F	Servant	23No02Am
ROBINSON, Sarah	30	F	Housekeeper	23No02Am
Sarah	25	F	Servant	23No02Am
Elizabeth	60	F	None	23No02Am
Died-At-Sea				
Mary	20	F	Servant	23No02Am
Irvine	18	M	Laborer	23No02Am
Christopher	60	M	Laborer	23No02Am
Christopher	28	M	Laborer	23No02Am
IRVINE, Mary	25	F	Servant	23No02Am
ROBINSON, Joseph	40	M	Laborer	23No02Am
Rebecca (W)	40	F	Servant	23No02Am
Margt. (D)	12	F	Servant	23No02Am
Eliza (D)	10	F	Child	23No02Am
Joseph (D)	06	F	Child	23No02Am
Christopher (S)	04	M	Child	23No02Am
John (S)	01	M	Child	23No02Am
NOBLE, Alexander	30	M	Laborer	23No02Am
Eliza (W)	28	F	Servant	23No02Am
James (S)	07	M	Servant	23No02Am
Ann (D)	05	F	Servant	23No02Am
Johnstone (S)	02	M	Servant	23No02Am
U	.04	M	Infant	23No02Am
BRENNAN, Thos.Kerr	.00	M	Infant	23No02Am
Died-At-Sea				
MULHOLLAND, Ellen	20	F	Laborer	23No02Am
Catherine	20	F	Servant	23No02Am
Biddy	18	F	Servant	23No02Am
ARNAUD, James	23	M	Laborer	23No02Am
Elizabeth	20	F	Servant	23No02Am
WRIGHT, John	22	M	Laborer	23No02Am
Rachael	22	F	Servant	23No02Am
ANDERSON, Wm.	32	M	Laborer	23No02Am
U (W)	32	F	Servant	23No02Am
Mary (D)	04	F	Child	23No02Am
KEARNEY, Mary	18	F	House Maid	23No02Am
Bridget	17	F	Servant	23No02Am

NAMES OF PASSENGERS		AGE	SEX	OCCUPATIONS	DATE PORT SHIP
LYNCH, U-Mrs.		26	F	Servant	23No02Am
BRADY, Sally		18	F	Servant	23No02Am
LAMB, Patrick		40	M	Servant	23No02Am
U	(W)	35	F	Servant	23No02Am
MULREAN, Robert		22	M	Servant	23No02Am
MCELROY, James		37	M	Servant	23No02Am
U	(W)	30	F	Servant	23No02Am
Mary-Ann	(D)	03	F	Child	23No02Am
Biddy	(D)	.00	F	Infant	23No02Am
MURRAY, Thomas		20	M	Servant	23No02Am
U	(W)	20	F	Servant	23No02Am
DALY, Honor		20	F	Servant	23No02Am
Ann		18	F	Servant	23No02Am
MCGHEE, James		20	M	Servant	23No02Am
BRADY, Sally		25	F	House Maid	23No02Am
MENON, Mary		50	F	Servant	23No02Am
Margt.	(D)	10	F	Child	23No02Am
DUNN, U		37	M	Servant	23No02Am
U	(W)	36	F	Servant	23No02Am
EGAN, Joseph		25	M	Laborer	23No02Am
KELLY, Mary		22	F	Servant	23No02Am
Ellen		20	F	Servant	23No02Am
CONNAY, John		30	M	Laborer	23No02Am
KELLY, Peter		25	M	Laborer	23No02Am
KENNEDY, Hugh		25	M	Laborer	23No02Am
MONAGHAN, Wm.		30	M	Laborer	23No02Am
NEWMAN, Mich.		30	M	Servant	23No02Am
U	(W)	26	F	Servant	23No02Am
HOG, James		30	M	Laborer	23No02Am
U	(W)	30	F	Laborer	23No02Am
Patrick	(S)	.00	M	Infant	23No02Am
MCGOIN, John		19	M	Laborer	23No02Am
SALMON, Mary		16	F	Servant	23No02Am
QUINN, Peter		35	M	Servant	23No02Am
Jane		28	F	Servant	23No02Am
CLARY, Biddy		24	F	Servant	23No02Am
Kitty		34	F	Servant	23No02Am
TODD, Biddy		23	F	Servant	23No02Am
DUNN, Martin		25	M	Servant	23No02Am
Martin		31	M	Laborer	23No02Am
KENAGHAN, William		26	M	Sawer	23No02Am
Peggy		24	F	Servant	23No02Am
GORMAN, Daniel		30	M	Laborer	23No02Am
BURNS, Thomas		23	M	Laborer	23No02Am
DOUGHTERY, Daniel		22	M	Servant	23No02Am
DUNN, William		21	M	Laborer	23No02Am
CASEY, Edward		22	M	Ploughwoman	23No02Am
Bridget		17	F	Servant	23No02Am
Ann		16	F	Servant	23No02Am
TERRENCE, George		27	M	Merchant	23No02Am
MONAGHAN, Catherine		27	F	Servant	23No02Am
Ann		30	F	Servant	23No02Am
TERRALL, Elizabeth		30	F	Servant	23No02Am
MCDONALD, Terrence		40	M	Laborer	23No02Am
My.		30	F	Servant	23No02Am
John	(S)	07	M	Child	23No02Am
Charles	(S)	05	M	Child	23No02Am
BROLIN, John		22	M	Laborer	23No02Am
DUGGAN, Mary		22	F	Servant	23No02Am
MARTIN, Patt		22	M	Servant	23No02Am
ALLEN, Wm.		23	M	Servant	23No02Am
FARRALL, John		20	M	Laborer	23No02Am
GILLIGAN, Matt		40	M	Laborer	23No02Am
MCMANNA, Ann		20	F	Servant	23No02Am
BRENNAN, Catherine		75	F	None	23No02Am
NEUMAN, Edward		.05	M	Infant	23No02Am
KELLY, James		19	M	Laborer	23No02Am

MARGARET-EVANS 27 NOVEMBER 1846

From London

NAMES OF PASSENGERS		AGE	SEX	OCCUPATIONS	DATE PORT SHIP
WHITE, Elizabeth		16	F	None	27No21lp
BROWN, Mary		19	F	None	27No21lp
DOLAND, Martin		49	M	Laborer	27No21lp
DONOVAN, Nora		26	F	None	27No21lp
John	(S)	01	M	Child	27No21lp

MARMION 28 NOVEMBER 1846

From Liverpool

NAMES OF PASSENGERS		AGE	SEX	OCCUPATIONS	DATE PORT SHIP
WHITAKER, John		28	M	Merchant	28No02Hc
FOSTER, Ann		38	F	None	28No02Hc
Henrietta	(D)	11	F	Child	28No02Hc
Richard	(S)	07	M	Child	28No02Hc
William-H.	(S)	04	M	Child	28No02Hc
DONE, Mary		18	F	Dressmaker	28No02Hc
MCCAFFERY, James		47	M	Laborer	28No02Hc
Ann	(W)	40	F	None	28No02Hc
James	(S)	16	M	Laborer	28No02Hc
Mary-Ann	(D)	13	F	None	28No02Hc
Susan	(D)	11	F	None	28No02Hc
Barney	(S)	09	M	Child	28No02Hc
Biddy	(D)	06	F	Child	28No02Hc
Antony	(S)	02	M	Child	28No02Hc
MCCANN, Wm.		47	M	Laborer	28No02Hc
Nancy	(W)	44	F	None	28No02Hc
Biddy	(D)	14	F	None	28No02Hc
Ann	(D)	12	F	None	28No02Hc
Hannah	(D)	10	F	Child	28No02Hc
James	(S)	08	M	Child	28No02Hc
DONLEY, Mary		18	F	Servant	28No02Hc
MCCABE, Francis		25	M	Laborer	28No02Hc
Catherin		24	F	None	28No02Hc
MCGUAIRE, Jas.		22	M	Tailor	28No02Hc
NIXON, Jas.		14	M	Laborer	28No02Hc
TOMIN, Cathrn.		18	F	Servant	28No02Hc
GOODIN, Cathrn.		18	F	Servant	28No02Hc
NAUGHTEN, Patt		40	M	Laborer	28No02Hc
Cicely	(W)	32	F	None	28No02Hc
John	(S)	13	M	None	28No02Hc
Frank	(S)	12	M	None	28No02Hc
James	(S)	11	M	None	28No02Hc
Patt	(S)	09	M	Child	28No02Hc
Thomas	(S)	09	M	Child	28No02Hc
Mary	(D)	02	F	Child	28No02Hc
KELLY, Mary		29	F	Servant	28No02Hc
DUFFY, Hugh		34	M	Laborer	28No02Hc
REILLY, John		18	M	Laborer	28No02Hc
KERR, Jane		40	F	Servant	28No02Hc
Mary		21	F	Servant	28No02Hc
REILLY, Robt.		13	M	Laborer	28No02Hc
STEWART, James		25	M	Laborer	28No02Hc
Bridget		23	F	None	28No02Hc
Patt		01	M	Child	28No02Hc
HEALEY, John		36	M	Laborer	28No02Hc
Mary	(W)	30	F	None	28No02Hc
Bridget	(D)	11	F	None	28No02Hc
Ann	(D)	08	F	Child	28No02Hc
Antony	(S)	05	M	Child	28No02Hc

NAMES OF PASSENGERS		AGE EX	SEX	OCCUPATIONS	DATE PORT SHIP
HEALEY, Michal	(S)	03	M	Child	28No02Hc
Martin	(S)	01	M	Child	28No02Hc
SALAN, Ann		13	F	Servant	28No02Hc
COSGROVE, Ann		30	F	None	28No02Hc
GALLAGHAN, John		26	M	Laborer	28No02Hc
MCGRATH, Michl.		30	M	None	28No02Hc
HENELLY, Wm.		35	M	Laborer	28No02Hc
Mary	(W)	30	F	None	28No02Hc
Neddy	(D)	11	F	None	28No02Hc
Owen	(S)	09	M	Child	28No02Hc
Michal	(S)	07	M	Child	28No02Hc
John	(S)	05	M	Child	28No02Hc
Patt	(S)	03	M	Child	28No02Hc
Edward	(S)	01	M	Child	28No02Hc
DUGAN, Patt		26	M	Laborer	28No02Hc
Bridget	(W)	26	F	None	28No02Hc
Mark	(S)	01	M	Child	28No02Hc
Michel	(S)	02	M	Child	28No02Hc
James		25	M	Laborer	28No02Hc
John		27	M	None	28No02Hc
Michel		23	M	None	28No02Hc
Ann		22	F	Servant	28No02Hc
Maria		18	F	None	28No02Hc
Margrt.		50	F	None	28No02Hc
ROONY, John		46	M	Laborer	28No02Hc
MANY, Peter		30	M	None	28No02Hc
John		36	M	None	28No02Hc
Patt		18	M	None	28No02Hc
DUGAN, Peggy		24	F	Servant	28No02Hc
Patt		30	M	Laborer	28No02Hc
Mary		30	F	None	28No02Hc
Ann		03	F	Child	28No02Hc
Patt		01	M	Child	28No02Hc
John		30	M	Laborer	28No02Hc
MCCEW, Patt		35	M	None	28No02Hc
Bridget	(W)	35	F	None	28No02Hc
Cicely	(D)	08	F	Child	28No02Hc
John	(S)	07	M	Child	28No02Hc
BRADY, James		18	M	Laborer	28No02Hc
BRADIN, Mary		32	F	Servant	28No02Hc
Catherin		19	F	None	28No02Hc
Biddy		15	F	None	28No02Hc
Mary		11	F	Child	28No02Hc
John		10	M	Child	28No02Hc
CASTILLON, Honer		17	F	None	28No02Hc
LOCKLHIN, Biddy		28	F	None	28No02Hc
LENNERD, John		23	M	Miner	28No02Hc
Margh.		22	F	None	28No02Hc
Mary		21	F	None	28No02Hc
KEATEN, John		22	M	Laborer	28No02Hc
SHARKE, Bryan		34	M	None	28No02Hc
MCELERY, Catherin		29	F	Servant	28No02Hc
DAILY, Laurance		25	M	Laborer	28No02Hc
Catherin		20	F	Servant	28No02Hc
Bridget		21	F	None	28No02Hc
BRADY, Sarah		20	F	None	28No02Hc
DUNCAN, John		60	M	Laborer	28No02Hc
Mary	(W)	45	F	None	28No02Hc
Eliza	(D)	20	F	Servant	28No02Hc
Charles	(S)	14	M	None	28No02Hc
Elliot	(S)	12	M	None	28No02Hc
Selina	(D)	10	F	Child	28No02Hc
CARR, John		26	M	Tailor	28No02Hc
Mary		26	F	Servant	28No02Hc
MCFARDIN, Peggy		29	F	None	28No02Hc
MCBREATY, Frank		26	M	Laborer	28No02Hc
BROWN, Patt		14	M	None	28No02Hc
BENNETT, Wm.		24	M	None	28No02Hc
FENNEY, Michl.		32	M	None	28No02Hc
John		28	M	None	28No02Hc
Mary		19	F	None	28No02Hc
CONLAN, Barney		25	M	None	28No02Hc
BREADY, Thomas		19	M	None	28No02Hc
Biddy		19	F	None	28No02Hc
MULDON, Daniel		33	M	None	28No02Hc
BRYAN, Jas.		23	M	None	28No02Hc
Ann		22	F	Servant	28No02Hc
CALLAGHAN, Patt		20	M	Laborer	28No02Hc
Wm.		13	M	Laborer	28No02Hc
Betsey		20	F	Servant	28No02Hc
Bridget		24	F	None	28No02Hc
CARRALL, Ann		18	F	None	28No02Hc
Eliza		16	F	None	28No02Hc
MULLER, Jamarea		16	M	None	28No02Hc
Thimety		13	M	None	28No02Hc
QUINN, Jas.		19	M	Laborer	28No02Hc
RYDER, Honer		20	F	Servant	28No02Hc
MCCASHEN, Mary		18	F	None	28No02Hc
RELIY, Ellen		30	F	Servant	28No02Hc
Thomas		17	M	Laborer	28No02Hc
CARR, Henry		17	M	None	28No02Hc
ONEIL, Ann		37	F	Servant	28No02Hc
Jane	(D)	08	F	Child	28No02Hc
MONAGHAN, Jonna		23	F	None	28No02Hc
Mary		25	F	None	28No02Hc
HARLEY, John		23	M	Laborer	28No02Hc
Ann	(W)	26	F	Servant	28No02Hc
Hannah	(D)	06	F	Child	28No02Hc
Margt.	(D)	03	F	Child	28No02Hc
Catherin	(D)	01	F	Child	28No02Hc
TERRELL, Honer		50	F	None	28No02Hc
Simon	(S)	22	M	None	28No02Hc
Ann	(D)	17	F	None	28No02Hc
Mary	(D)	17	F	None	28No02Hc
Wm.	(S)	09	M	Child	28No02Hc
Mary	(D)	11	F	Child	28No02Hc
COLLINS, Ellen		50	F	None	28No02Hc
HARLEY, Thomas		40	M	Laborer	28No02Hc
MCQUADE, Michal		30	M	Laborer	28No02Hc
CONNEL, Patt		25	M	None	28No02Hc
Margh.	(W)	23	F	None	28No02Hc
Michal	(S)	04	M	Child	28No02Hc
Mary	(D)	02	F	Child	28No02Hc
GIVERNY, Cathern		30	F	Servant	28No02Hc
Cathern	(D)	05	F	Child	28No02Hc
KILROY, John		25	M	Laborer	28No02Hc
MURPHY, Patt		22	M	Schm	28No02Hc
GARDINER, Arhd.		50	M	Laborer	28No02Hc
Mary	(W)	42	F	None	28No02Hc
Wm.	(S)	12	M	None	28No02Hc
Frank	(S)	10	M	Child	28No02Hc
Rebeca	(D)	08	F	Child	28No02Hc
Thomas	(S)	06	M	Child	28No02Hc
Catherine	(D)	02	F	Child	28No02Hc
LYONS, John		31	M	Tailor	28No02Hc
PENDER, Wm.		28	M	Butcher	28No02Hc
WRENN, Patt		56	M	Weaver	28No02Hc
Ambros		27	M	None	28No02Hc
TYE, Henry		25	M	Laborer	28No02Hc
John	(S)	03	M	Child	28No02Hc
James	(S)	02	M	Child	28No02Hc
U	(W)	23	F	None	28No02Hc
MCGUIRE, Owen		26	M	Laborer	28No02Hc
COALMAN, Biddy		18	F	Servant	28No02Hc
Ann		15	F	None	28No02Hc
Mary		14	F	None	28No02Hc
GRONEY, Barney		18	M	None	28No02Hc

EMPIRE 30 NOVEMBER 1846

From Liverpool

NAMES OF PASSENGERS	AGE EX	SEX	OCCUPATIONS	DATE PORT SHIP
OBRIEN, Rose	18	F	Servant	30No02Al
GARRA, Theddy	25	M	Farmer	30No02Al

303

NAMES OF PASSENGERS		AGE	SEX	OCCUPATIONS	DATE PORT SHIP
BRYAN, Michael		25	M	Laborer	30No02AI
MCLAUGHLIN, Ann		19	F	Servant	30No02AI
BRYAN, John		21	M	Laborer	30No02AI
KELLY, John		28	M	Laborer	30No02AI
MCCAFFREY, Dennis		24	M	Laborer	30No02AI
CONROY, Michl.		58	M	Laborer	30No02AI
Peggy	(W)	58	F	Wife	30No02AI
Margaret	(D)	16	F	Unknown	30No02AI
MORAN, Thos.		22	M	Tailor	30No02AI
FITZPATRICK, Eliza		30	F	Servant	30No02AI
Winefred	(D)	07	F	Child	30No02AI
Martin	(S)	05	M	Child	30No02AI
Biddy	(D)	03	F	Child	30No02AI
DONNELLY, Patt		41	M	Laborer	30No02AI
SHARKEY, Jane		27	F	Servant	30No02AI
COLREAVEY, Cath.		21	F	Servant	30No02AI
MCCABE, John		46	M	Laborer	30No02AI
Ann	(W)	38	F	Wife	30No02AI
Barney	(S)	12	M	Unknown	30No02AI
CONLON, Mary		18	F	Servant	30No02AI
REILLY, Cath.		16	F	Servant	30No02AI
CUNNINGHAM, Ann		20	F	Servant	30No02AI
FORSTER, James		25	M	Laborer	30No02AI
HANNERY, Thos.		40	M	Laborer	30No02AI
Cath.	(D)	19	F	Servant	30No02AI
John	(S)	20	M	Laborer	30No02AI
Bridget	(D)	21	F	Servant	30No02AI
COGGINS, Patrick		21	M	Laborer	30No02AI
LARKIN, Michael		23	M	Laborer	30No02AI
KELLY, Cormick		43	M	Laborer	30No02AI
MCELROY, Francis		23	M	Laborer	30No02AI
Mary		23	F	Unknown	30No02AI
CONROY, Peter		53	M	Laborer	30No02AI
Ann	(W)	50	F	Unknown	30No02AI
Patt	(S)	22	M	Unknown	30No02AI
Thos.	(S)	18	M	Unknown	30No02AI
Ann	(D)	20	F	Unknown	30No02AI
Mary	(D)	16	F	Unknown	30No02AI
Cath.	(D)	14	F	Unknown	30No02AI
Michael	(S)	12	M	Unknown	30No02AI
Peter	(S)	09	M	Child	30No02AI
MCDANIEL, Daniel		26	M	Laborer	30No02AI
Bridget	(W)	26	F	Wife	30No02AI
Andrew	(S)	03	M	Child	30No02AI
Peter	(S)	.00	M	Infant	30No02AI
Died-At-Sea					30No02AI
DAILY, Julia		60	F	Servant	30No02AI
WELSH, Ann		21	F	Servant	30No02AI
FARRELL, Betty		20	F	Servant	30No02AI
MCCART, Michl.		20	M	Laborer	30No02AI
MCCAIRN, Patt		21	M	Laborer	30No02AI
BUCKLEY, Johanna		19	F	Servant	30No02AI
ROACH, Mary		22	F	Servant	30No02AI
MARK, James		25	M	Laborer	30No02AI
BENNETT, George		23	M	Laborer	30No02AI
REYNOLDS, Patt		50	M	Laborer	30No02AI
Ann	(W)	49	F	Wife	30No02AI
Mary	(D)	14	F	Unknown	30No02AI
John	(S)	12	M	Unknown	30No02AI
Sarah	(D)	10	F	Child	30No02AI
Margaret	(D)	07	F	Child	30No02AI
Jas.	(S)	05	M	Child	30No02AI
EARLY, Mary		25	F	Spinster	30No02AI
James		21	M	Laborer	30No02AI
MCCOURT, Gerald		21	M	Laborer	30No02AI
MCMANUS, Elleanor		21	F	Spinster	30No02AI
MCCOURT, Elleanor		19	F	Spinster	30No02AI
MCCAFFREY, John		21	M	Laborer	30No02AI
CORREGAN, Margt.		19	F	Servant	30No02AI
ROURKE, Rose		17	F	Servant	30No02AI
MCMANUS, Cath.		31	F	Servant	30No02AI
COLLINS, Edwd.		21	M	Laborer	30No02AI
TOWERS, Patt		16	M	Laborer	30No02AI
KILLELEAGH, Michl.		40	M	Laborer	30No02AI
ENGLISH, Barney		21	M	Laborer	30No02AI
WELSH, Michael		18	M	Laborer	30No02AI
FINNERLY, Cath.		18	F	Servant	30No02AI
ROGERS, Susan		16	F	Servant	30No02AI
HIGGINS, Bernard		34	M	Laborer	30No02AI
GREEN, Cath.		11	F	Unknown	30No02AI
William		09	M	Child	30No02AI
GALLEGAR, Owen		28	M	Laborer	30No02AI
Mary		12	F	Unknown	30No02AI
IRVIN, John		42	M	Laborer	30No02AI
STEWART, George		23	M	Laborer	30No02AI
JORDAN, Ellen		18	F	Servant	30No02AI
NAUGHTON, Cath.		21	F	Servant	30No02AI
BURNE, Cath.		22	F	Servant	30No02AI
LYONS, Cath.		19	F	Servant	30No02AI
CAIN, Bridgt.		18	F	Servant	30No02AI
Margaret		20	F	Servant	30No02AI
BERRY, Cath.		18	F	Servant	30No02AI
SPELLMAN, Mary		22	F	Servant	30No02AI
MCNAMAMEA, James		34	M	Seaman	30No02AI
BYRNE, Michl.		30	M	Laborer	30No02AI
MCLAUGHLIN, Eliza		25	F	Servant	30No02AI
FARRELLY, Ann		28	F	Servant	30No02AI
BUTLER, Ann		30	F	Servant	30No02AI
REEVE, Mary		21	F	Servant	30No02AI
REDDEN, Mary		20	F	Servant	30No02AI
MARRA, Cath.		20	F	Servant	30No02AI
CONNOR, James		40	M	Laborer	30No02AI
Ellen	(W)	34	F	Wife	30No02AI
Ellen	(D)	06	F	Child	30No02AI
Thos.	(S)	03	M	Child	30No02AI
Henry	(S)	01	M	Child	30No02AI
DOWNES, Michael		29	M	Laborer	30No02AI
DILLON, Henry		26	M	Laborer	30No02AI
Mary		25	F	Unknown	30No02AI
GRAHAM, James		50	M	Mechanic	30No02AI
WHELAN, Patt		22	M	Laborer	30No02AI
MCPORTLAND, Mary		20	F	Servant	30No02AI
CLARK, Anty.		21	M	Laborer	30No02AI
John		20	M	Laborer	30No02AI
James		21	M	Laborer	30No02AI
MCDONNEL, John		28	M	Tailor	30No02AI
OREILLY, Ellen		30	F	Servant	30No02AI
Patt		08	M	Child	30No02AI
Mary		17	F	Servant	30No02AI
Bridget		16	F	Servant	30No02AI
WHELAN, Mary		15	F	Unknown	30No02AI
FINLEY, Patt		21	M	Laborer	30No02AI
Belle		20	F	Servant	30No02AI
OREILLY, Cath.		20	F	Servant	30No02AI
FAHY, Ann		19	F	Servant	30No02AI
BREEN, John		22	M	Laborer	30No02AI
Michael		20	M	Laborer	30No02AI
HANERY, Patt		21	M	Laborer	30No02AI
SPELLMAN, Elleanor		18	F	Servant	30No02AI
GORMAN, Michl.		21	M	Laborer	30No02AI
MCGRATH, John		20	M	Laborer	30No02AI
Honora		19	F	Servant	30No02AI
FEAIN, Bridgt		20	F	Servant	30No02AI
Died-At-Sea					
Sarah		18	F	Servant	30No02AI
COOK, Mary		17	F	Servant	30No02AI
KELLY, Ann		19	F	Servant	30No02AI
QUEENY, Laurence		18	M	Laborer	30No02AI
Ellen		16	F	Unknown	30No02AI
SUMMERS, Bernard		21	M	Mechanic	30No02AI
ADAMS, John		26	M	Laborer	30No02AI
Cath.		20	F	Unknown	30No02AI
FINNARGHTY, Owen		28	M	Laborer	30No02AI
Honora		20	F	Laborer	30No02AI
John		11	M	Unknown	30No02AI
Mary		09	F	Child	30No02AI
Patrick		07	M	Child	30No02AI
Owen		03	M	Child	30No02AI
Michael		.00	M	Infant	30No02AI
Died-At-Sea					

NAMES OF PASSENGERS	AGE	SEX	OCCUPATIONS	DATE PORT SHIP
MULLIGAN, Rose	14	F	Servant	30No02AI
REYNOLDS, Francis	19	M	Laborer	30No02AI
LAFFERTY, Bridget	26	F	Servant	30No02AI
CHARLEY, Patt	30	M	Laborer	30No02AI
Ann (W)	40	F	Wife	30No02AI
Patt (S)	12	M	Unknown	30No02AI
MCDERMOTT, Mary	20	F	Spinster	30No02AI
MCCARTY, Biddy	20	F	Spinster	30No02AI
COX, Michl.	40	M	Laborer	30No02AI
SHARKEY, John	20	M	Laborer	30No02AI
COCORAN, John	30	M	Laborer	30No02AI
Patt	18	M	Unknown	30No02AI
Mary	30	F	Unknown	30No02AI
Mary	13	F	Unknown	30No02AI
JENNINGS, Patt	20	M	Mechanic	30No02AI
Honora	20	F	Unknown	30No02AI
PATTEN, Robt.	40	M	Laborer	30No02AI
Died-At-Sea				
Ann (W)	40	F	Wife	30No02AI
Wm. (S)	20	M	Laborer	30No02AI
John (S)	18	M	Laborer	30No02AI
Robt. (S)	16	M	Laborer	30No02AI
Jane	25	F	Unknown	30No02AI
Margaret	23	F	Unknown	30No02AI
Ann (D)	19	F	Unknown	30No02AI
Sarah (D)	17	F	Unknown	30No02AI
REYNOLDS, Maria	23	F	Servant	30No02AI
Rebecca	20	F	Servant	30No02AI
TAYLOR, Sally	20	F	Servant	30No02AI
MCAVAINY, Elleanor	20	F	Servant	30No02AI
MURPHY, Cath.	20	F	Servant	30No02AI
SULLIVAN, Thos.	18	M	Butcher	30No02AI
DRISCOLL, Patt	19	M	Laborer	30No02AI
Mary	16	F	Unknown	30No02AI
STUFFY, Ellen	21	F	Servant	30No02AI
FERRIS, Jos.	30	M	Blacksmith	30No02AI
HALEY, John	24	M	Laborer	30No02AI
Isabella	26	F	Unknown	30No02AI
COLLER, Mary	19	F	Unknown	30No02AI
Ann	18	F	Unknown	30No02AI
MCQUIRE, Patt	20	M	Mechanic	30No02AI
QUIGLY, Hugh	70	M	Laborer	30No02AI
BOYLE, Dennis	30	M	Laborer	30No02AI
QUIGLY, Becky	28	F	Spinster	30No02AI
MERRIGLE, Betty	18	F	Spinster	30No02AI
BYRN, Patt	21	M	Laborer	30No02AI
Bryan	21	M	Laborer	30No02AI
John	25	M	Laborer	30No02AI
ODONNEL, Wm.	18	M	Laborer	30No02AI
CALLAGHER, Cath.	21	F	Servant	30No02AI
STEVENSON, Ann	20	F	Servant	30No02AI
FORSTER, Eliza	20	F	Servant	30No02AI
ROBINSON, Thos.	25	M	Laborer	30No02AI
Ann	20	F	Unknown	30No02AI
FARFEY, Wm.	50	M	Weaver	30No02AI
Eliza (W)	46	F	Wife	30No02AI
Died-At-Sea				
Isabella (D)	12	F	Unknown	30No02AI
Mary-A. (D)	10	F	Child	30No02AI
Patt (S)	08	M	Child	30No02AI
WHITE, Jas.	40	M	Laborer	30No02AI
Agnes (W)	36	F	Wife	30No02AI
Margt. (D)	12	F	Unknown	30No02AI
George (S)	10	M	Child	30No02AI
GOURLY, Jas.	30	M	Laborer	30No02AI
Agnes (W)	20	F	Wife	30No02AI
Mary-J. (D)	.00	F	Infant	30No02AI
Died-At-Sea				
GORDON, Maria	25	F	Spinster	30No02AI
Wm.	21	M	Laborer	30No02AI
Thos.	10	M	Child	30No02AI
STEVENSON, John	30	M	Weaver	30No02AI
Jane (W)	25	F	Wife	30No02AI
Robt. (S)	09	M	Child	30No02AI
Mary-J. (D)	05	F	Child	30No02AI
STEVENSON, James (S)	02	M	Child	30No02AI
Died-At-Sea				
James	30	M	Unknown	30No02AI
MARTIN, Thos.	27	M	Laborer	30No02AI
BACON, Patt	25	M	Laborer	30No02AI
Mary	24	F	Unknown	30No02AI
MCDONNA, John	21	M	Laborer	30No02AI
NOWLAN, Patt	18	M	Laborer	30No02AI
MULLIN, Martin	30	M	Laborer	30No02AI
RYAN, John	40	M	Laborer	30No02AI
Catherine (W)	40	F	Wife	30No02AI
Cath. (D)	14	F	Unknown	30No02AI
Ann (D)	12	F	Unknown	30No02AI
Wm. (S)	10	M	Child	30No02AI
Biddy (D)	08	F	Child	30No02AI
Teressa (D)	06	F	Child	30No02AI
Eliza (D)	04	F	Child	30No02AI
Jos. (S)	.00	M	Infant	30No02AI
CASEY, Jas.	35	M	Laborer	30No02AI
Ann (W)	30	F	Wife	30No02AI
Patt (S)	08	M	Child	30No02AI
Ann (D)	10	F	Child	30No02AI
Wm.	04	M	Child	30No02AI
Margt.	.00	F	Infant	30No02AI
MULHIRIN, Jas.	22	M	Laborer	30No02AI
MCCARTY, Peter	20	M	Laborer	30No02AI
MCPEAK, Hugh	20	M	Laborer	30No02AI
DIVINE, Michl.	20	M	Laborer	30No02AI
MARTIN, Francis	32	M	Laborer	30No02AI
QUAIL, Thos.	32	M	Laborer	30No02AI
Mary-A. (W)	22	F	Wife	30No02AI
Margt. (D)	.00	F	Infant	30No02AI
BOLAND, Tim	30	M	Cooper	30No02AI
Edward (S)	03	M	Child	30No02AI
Johana (W)	30	F	Wife	30No02AI
BOYLE, Sarah	50	F	Unknown	30No02AI
MCQILL, Andrew	29	M	Laborer	30No02AI
Eliza (W)	30	F	Wife	30No02AI
Geo. (S)	03	M	Child	30No02AI
ALEXANDER, Thos.	30	M	Weaver	30No02AI
Rebecca	27	F	Unknown	30No02AI
Margt.	21	F	Unknown	30No02AI
Jos.	04	M	Child	30No02AI
Margaret	02	F	Child	30No02AI
PEEBLES, Ann	21	F	Servant	30No02AI
PHILLIPS, Jane	20	F	Servant	30No02AI
TAYLOR, Margaret-J.	17	F	Servant	30No02AI
FERRIS, John	23	M	Laborer	30No02AI
MCQUIRE, Esther	30	F	Servant	30No02AI
Bridget (D)	03	F	Child	30No02AI
Eliza (D)	.00	F	Infant	30No02AI
SHANNON, Cath.	19	F	Servant	30No02AI
KEENEYE, Path.	21	M	Laborer	30No02AI
Bridgt.	18	F	Servant	30No02AI
WHITE, Bridgt.	21	F	Servant	30No02AI
MCQUIRE, Bridget	06	F	Child	30No02AI
CLASPEY, Bridgt.	19	F	Servant	30No02AI
BANFIELD, Dorothy	20	F	Servant	30No02AI
GONLANY, Thos.	20	M	Laborer	30No02AI
GANLY, Michl.	21	M	Laborer	30No02AI
REILLY, Patt	25	M	Laborer	30No02AI
Chas.	26	M	Laborer	30No02AI
FORD, Mary	20	F	Servant	30No02AI
BROWN, Mary-J.	22	F	Servant	30No02AI
MCALISTER, James	19	M	Laborer	30No02AI
MARTEN, Saml.	18	M	Laborer	30No02AI
ELLIOT, Wm.	23	M	Laborer	30No02AI
NOBLE, Maria	17	F	Servant	30No02AI
Ellen	22	F	Servant	30No02AI
LAVAN, Michl.	28	M	Laborer	30No02AI
MCQUIRE, Richd.	09	M	Child	30No02AI
HANNERY, Biddy	18	F	Servant	30No02AI
HATTON, Simon	28	M	Merchant	30No02AI
Della	28	F	Unknown	30No02AI

NAMES OF PASSENGERS		A G E	S E X	OCCUPATIONS	DATE PORT SHIP

STEPHEN-WHITNEY 30 NOVEMBER 1846

From Liverpool

NAMES OF PASSENGERS		A G E	S E X	OCCUPATIONS	DATE PORT SHIP
MAURICE, George-J.		24	M	Farmer	30No02Cd
DEVLIN, William		25	M	Draper	30No02Cd
MULHOLLAND, Thomas		46	M	Draper	30No02Cd
MOORE, David		21	M	Farmer	30No02Cd
WALKER, Henry		28	M	Printer	30No02Cd
KIRVAN, Mary		24	F	None	30No02Cd
MENAN, Mary		25	F	None	30No02Cd
MACCRORY, Mary		26	F	None	30No02Cd
GILLESPIE, Patrick		40	M	Laborer	30No02Cd
Mary		26	F	None	30No02Cd
Eliza		36	F	None	30No02Cd
Margaret		06	F	Child	30No02Cd
Nancy		07	F	Child	30No02Cd
James		21	M	Laborer	30No02Cd
Ellen		13	F	None	30No02Cd
Alice		14	F	None	30No02Cd
Michael		09	M	Child	30No02Cd
KEARNEY, Martha		20	F	None	30No02Cd
John		25	M	Laborer	30No02Cd
Mathew		26	M	Merchant	30No02Cd
Mary		12	F	None	30No02Cd
DONLEY, Catharine		12	F	None	30No02Cd
DARA, James		22	M	Laborer	30No02Cd
Ellen		19	F	None	30No02Cd
HAGGARTY, Eliza		20	F	None	30No02Cd
Bridget		21	F	None	30No02Cd
COIL, John		30	M	Laborer	30No02Cd
Mary		23	F	None	30No02Cd
MACCRORY, Charles		21	M	Laborer	30No02Cd
MCQUAID, Bernard		78	M	None	30No02Cd
HOSKING, Philip		26	M	Laborer	30No02Cd
DONOGHUE, Maurice		26	M	Laborer	30No02Cd
ROWER, Martin		30	M	Laborer	30No02Cd
DUGAN, John		20	M	Laborer	30No02Cd
ARMSTRONG, Edward		34	M	Laborer	30No02Cd
Eliza		60	F	None	30No02Cd
Isabella		20	F	None	30No02Cd
SEXON, Johannah		20	F	None	30No02Cd
ALLEN, Mary		21	F	None	30No02Cd
NAMES, Thomas		27	M	Laborer	30No02Cd
COOK, John		13	M	None	30No02Cd
KELLY, Laurence		25	M	Laborer	30No02Cd
Mary		18	F	None	30No02Cd
SKELLY, Anna		20	F	None	30No02Cd
NEWNEN, Patrick		22	M	Laborer	30No02Cd
John		26	M	Laborer	30No02Cd
READ, David		28	M	Laborer	30No02Cd
Rachel		30	F	None	30No02Cd
GRAHAM, Frank		30	M	Farmer	30No02Cd
Jane	(W)	30	F	None	30No02Cd
John	(S)	09	M	Child	30No02Cd
William	(S)	07	M	Child	30No02Cd
Francis	(S)	05	M	Child	30No02Cd
Margaret	(D)	04	F	Child	30No02Cd
Thomas	(S)	02	M	Child	30No02Cd
MONTGOMERY, Robert		25	M	Farmer	30No02Cd
William		23	M	Farmer	30No02Cd
CURRY, Robin		19	M	Farmer	30No02Cd
GORDON, John		19	M	Farmer	30No02Cd
Robert		16	M	None	30No02Cd
Andrew		14	M	None	30No02Cd
Jane		12	F	None	30No02Cd
Mary		09	F	Child	30No02Cd
Jane		40	F	None	30No02Cd
HARE, George		25	M	Farmer	30No02Cd
RENNOX, Gordon		08	M	Child	30No02Cd
Ellen		10	F	Child	30No02Cd
Margaret		20	F	None	30No02Cd
Andrew		28	M	Farmer	30No02Cd
Bessie		.06	F	Infant	30No02Cd
DUFFIE, Peter		21	M	Laborer	30No02Cd
Anne		19	F	None	30No02Cd
DEAM, Michael		27	M	Farmer	30No02Cd
Ann		24	F	None	30No02Cd
DUFFIE, Rose		50	F	None	30No02Cd
Rose	(D)	18	F	None	30No02Cd
John	(S)	26	M	Farmer	30No02Cd
HANNAN, Rose		20	F	None	30No02Cd
MCCABE, Mary		18	F	None	30No02Cd
BURNS, Mary		17	F	None	30No02Cd
VOGAN, James		19	M	Farmer	30No02Cd
GRUMMAGE, David		26	M	Farmer	30No02Cd
LISTER, Anne		18	F	None	30No02Cd
ROBINSON, Hugh		20	M	Laborer	30No02Cd
READ, John		24	M	Tailor	30No02Cd
LOUGHRIDGE, James		20	M	Schm	30No02Cd
John		24	M	Tailor	30No02Cd
Daniel		21	M	Shoemaker	30No02Cd
Esther		24	F	None	30No02Cd
Anna		01	F	Child	30No02Cd
CAMERON, Samuel		21	M	Crpm	30No02Cd
KING, James		22	M	Saddler	30No02Cd
Martha		18	F	None	30No02Cd
RUSH, Michael		40	M	Schm	30No02Cd
Catherine	(W)	40	F	None	30No02Cd
Catherine	(D)	18	F	None	30No02Cd
Helen	(D)	06	F	Child	30No02Cd
Mary	(D)	01	F	Child	30No02Cd
SKERRY, Mary		19	F	None	30No02Cd
KINNEY, Margaret		22	F	None	30No02Cd
BRIEN, Catherine		16	F	None	30No02Cd
FARLEY, Mary		23	F	None	30No02Cd
SAUL, Catherine		25	F	None	30No02Cd
MALADY, Mary		25	F	None	30No02Cd
KELLY, Betty		23	F	None	30No02Cd
Ellen		30	F	None	30No02Cd
GLINN, Mary		25	F	None	30No02Cd
Michael		26	M	Laborer	30No02Cd
MARK, Patrick		30	M	Laborer	30No02Cd
MURRAY, Brian		18	M	Laborer	30No02Cd
DOYLE, William		24	M	Laborer	30No02Cd
Dorothea		23	F	None	30No02Cd
MCGUIRE, Mary		22	F	None	30No02Cd
Thomas		25	M	Laborer	30No02Cd
James		22	M	Laborer	30No02Cd
VINCENT, Anne		20	F	None	30No02Cd
HICKEY, William		35	M	Laborer	30No02Cd
COLHN, John		21	M	Laborer	30No02Cd
Ellen		22	F	None	30No02Cd
CLASSIE, Bridget		28	F	None	30No02Cd
Mary		24	F	None	30No02Cd
GALLAGHER, Catherine		20	F	None	30No02Cd
KELLY, Thomas		22	M	Laborer	30No02Cd
MALONE, Thomas		40	M	Clerk	30No02Cd
GINN, John		44	M	Carpenter	30No02Cd
ANDREWS, William		26	M	Laborer	30No02Cd
LALLY, John		28	M	Bricklayer	30No02Cd
Bridget	(W)	26	F	None	30No02Cd
Catharine	(D)	07	F	Child	30No02Cd
Micheal	(D)	05	M	Child	30No02Cd
John	(S)	03	M	Child	30No02Cd
Mary	(D)	.02	F	Infant	30No02Cd
CORMICK, Barrett		19	M	Laborer	30No02Cd
Bridget		21	F	None	30No02Cd
CASSIDY, Laurence		20	M	Laborer	30No02Cd
HARRISON, Edward		20	M	Saddler	30No02Cd
SKERRY, John		21	M	Millwright	30No02Cd
KELLY, Thomas		36	M	Whitesmith	30No02Cd
CURLEY, Catharine		22	F	None	30No02Cd
Eliza		20	F	None	30No02Cd

NAMES OF PASSENGERS		AGE	SEX	OCCUPATIONS	DATE PORT SHIP
LAMEY, Hugh		30	M	Laborer	30No02Cd
Rose	(W)	28	F	None	30No02Cd
Mary	(D)	10	F	Child	30No02Cd
Margaret	(D)	06	F	Child	30No02Cd
Patrick	(S)	04	M	Child	30No02Cd
Fahill	(S)	01	M	Child	30No02Cd
Died-At-Sea					
Farell		20	M	Laborer	30No02Cd
Margaret		18	F	None	30No02Cd
Rose		20	F	None	30No02Cd
COMESQUE, John		41	M	Laborer	30No02Cd
James	(S)	12	M	None	30No02Cd
MCCABE, Francis		24	M	Shoemaker	30No02Cd
Catherine		22	F	None	30No02Cd
SMITH, Phillm		20	M	Laborer	30No02Cd
John		19	M	Laborer	30No02Cd
OWDEN, Owen		26	M	Laborer	30No02Cd
MURPHY, Owen		20	M	Laborer	30No02Cd
Catharine		19	F	None	30No02Cd
DOWNIE, Anne		30	F	None	30No02Cd
KELLY, Patrick		20	M	Tailor	30No02Cd
BERRY, Wilham		20	M	Shoemaker	30No02Cd
KANE, Peter		27	M	Laborer	30No02Cd
YOUNG, Robert		16	M	Laborer	30No02Cd
William		18	M	Laborer	30No02Cd
Martha		40	F	None	30No02Cd
Andrew		14	M	None	30No02Cd
Joseph		11	M	None	30No02Cd
Margaret		09	F	Child	30No02Cd
KIERAN, Jane		30	F	None	30No02Cd
HAND, Andrew		21	M	Weaver	30No02Cd
DEVLIN, Henry		45	M	Weaver	30No02Cd
James	(S)	18	M	Weaver	30No02Cd
Francis	(S)	16	M	Weaver	30No02Cd
OWENS, Ann		20	F	None	30No02Cd
HORAH, Micheal		19	M	Laborer	30No02Cd
Bridget		17	F	None	30No02Cd
John		08	M	Child	30No02Cd
Ann		11	F	None	30No02Cd
James		14	M	None	30No02Cd
MCMAHON, Patrick		24	M	Laborer	30No02Cd
MCBRIEN, Owen		16	M	Laborer	30No02Cd
HENDERSON, Catharine		18	F	None	30No02Cd
KING, John		26	M	Laborer	30No02Cd
WOODS, Thomas		24	M	Butcher	30No02Cd
DONLEY, Amelia		26	F	None	30No02Cd
GALBRAITH, Thomas		22	M	None	30No02Cd
BRIEN, Micheal		32	M	Farmer	30No02Cd
Bridget	(W)	22	F	None	30No02Cd
Mary	(D)	.03	F	Infant	30No02Cd
Died-At-Sea					
QUAIL, Bridget		20	F	None	30No02Cd
RYAN, Bridget		20	F	None	30No02Cd
MEADOW, Dora		26	F	None	30No02Cd
FIFE, James		23	M	Blacksmith	30No02Cd
Anne		20	F	None	30No02Cd
MCMULLAN, Hannah		20	F	None	30No02Cd
CLAFFERTY, Mary		16	F	None	30No02Cd
WHITNEY, Bridget		18	F	None	30No02Cd
FITZPATRICK, James		48	M	Farmer	30No02Cd
Bridget	(W)	46	F	None	30No02Cd
Thomas	(S)	24	M	Farmer	30No02Cd
Phillm	(S)	19	M	Farmer	30No02Cd
Francis	(S)	14	M	Farmer	30No02Cd
James	(S)	12	M	None	30No02Cd
Edward	(S)	08	M	Child	30No02Cd
Thomas	(S)	06	M	Child	30No02Cd
MURDOCK, James		50	M	Laborer	30No02Cd
Margaret	(W)	40	F	None	30No02Cd
James	(S)	23	M	Laborer	30No02Cd
Samuel	(S)	13	M	None	30No02Cd
Winnifred	(D)	18	F	None	30No02Cd
Anna	(D)	12	F	None	30No02Cd
Sarah	(D)	10	F	Child	30No02Cd
Stephen	(S)	07	M	Child	30No02Cd

NAMES OF PASSENGERS		AGE	SEX	OCCUPATIONS	DATE PORT SHIP
MURDOCK, Robert	(S)	05	M	Child	30No02Cd
Susan	(D)	02	F	Child	30No02Cd
GRAHAM, Andrew		26	M	Laborer	30No02Cd
Jane		25	F	None	30No02Cd
Sarah		20	F	None	30No02Cd
HARRINGTON, George		21	M	Laborer	30No02Cd
WHITE, Mary-Anne		40	F	None	30No02Cd
Henry	(S)	14	M	Weaver	30No02Cd
Robert	(S)	20	M	Weaver	30No02Cd
RILEY, Anne		20	F	None	30No02Cd
MCGARRETY, Joseph		23	M	Laborer	30No02Cd
SMITH, Thomas		20	M	Laborer	30No02Cd
Rosey		22	F	None	30No02Cd
HUGHES, James		20	M	Tailor	30No02Cd
LEDDY, Thomas		21	M	Laborer	30No02Cd
CLARK, Patrick		20	M	Laborer	30No02Cd
RILEY, Peter		14	M	None	30No02Cd
MCCOMBS, Hugh		40	M	Laborer	30No02Cd
FLYNN, Timothy		30	M	Laborer	30No02Cd
COIL, Brian		19	M	Laborer	30No02Cd
Patrick		68	M	None	30No02Cd
Bridget		50	F	None	30No02Cd
Micheal		15	M	None	30No02Cd
John		32	M	Laborer	30No02Cd
Bridget		28	F	None	30No02Cd
Patrick		04	M	Child	30No02Cd
John		.06	M	Infant	30No02Cd
MCWILLIAMS, Mary		22	F	None	30No02Cd
BURK, Mary		17	F	None	30No02Cd
GOURK, Mary		25	F	None	30No02Cd
COHEAVY, Mary		20	F	None	30No02Cd
SHEA, Mary		24	F	None	30No02Cd
John	(S)	01	M	Child	30No02Cd
GROGAN, Anne		08	F	Child	30No02Cd
John		21	M	Laborer	30No02Cd
POWELL, Bridget		18	F	None	30No02Cd
DOYLE, Ellen		26	F	None	30No02Cd
MCDERMOTT, Margaret		18	F	None	30No02Cd
HAINEY, Catharine		16	F	None	30No02Cd
LEDDY, Margaret		26	F	None	30No02Cd
COCHRANE, Micheal		27	M	Laborer	30No02Cd
SMITH, Thomas		21	M	Laborer	30No02Cd
MCCARTY, Patrick		25	M	Laborer	30No02Cd
KEERAN, Bridget		12	F	None	30No02Cd
John		24	M	Laborer	30No02Cd
MURPHY, Thomas		06	M	Child	30No02Cd
Betty		09	F	Child	30No02Cd
Thomas		50	M	Laborer	30No02Cd
Eliza		50	F	None	30No02Cd
Ellen		27	F	None	30No02Cd
Patrick		07	M	Child	30No02Cd
Ellen		03	F	Child	30No02Cd
DERMOODIE, Mary		20	F	None	30No02Cd
MADDEN, Mary		17	F	None	30No02Cd
KELLY, Ellen		23	F	None	30No02Cd
GRIFFIN, Anne		20	F	None	30No02Cd
DOOLEY, William		30	M	Grocer	30No02Cd
ONEILL, James		28	M	Laborer	30No02Cd
JOHNSTON, Charles		24	M	Traveller	30No02Cd
NEWNEN, Cornelius		35	M	Laborer	30No02Cd
Mary-C.		33	F	None	30No02Cd
DELANY, Mary		26	F	None	30No02Cd
NEWNEN, William		05	M	Child	30No02Cd
Margaret		02	F	Child	30No02Cd
SHIELDS, James		30	M	Laborer	30No02Cd
Anne	(W)	24	F	None	30No02Cd
Thomas	(S)	05	M	Child	30No02Cd
GRIMES, Darby		25	M	Carpenter	30No02Cd
MOONEY, Ellen		26	F	None	30No02Cd
CARRELL, Micheal		30	M	Laborer	30No02Cd
FIELDS, Micheal		20	M	Laborer	30No02Cd
LARKIN, James		36	M	Laborer	30No02Cd
GALLAGHER, Bessie		22	F	None	30No02Cd
Barney	(H)	30	M	Laborer	30No02Cd
Bessie	(D)	.09	F	Infant	30No02Cd

NAMES OF PASSENGERS		AGE	SEX	OCCUPATIONS	DATE PORT SHIP
MCCABE, John		36	M	Laborer	30No02Cd
Margaret	(W)	30	F	None	30No02Cd
Anne	(D)	10	F	Child	30No02Cd
James	(S)	04	M	Child	30No02Cd
Margaret	(D)	.02	F	Infant	30No02Cd
MARYMAN, Thomas		24	M	Laborer	30No02Cd
HENRY, Thomas		30	M	Laborer	30No02Cd
DAVIS, James		20	M	Laborer	30No02Cd
DONLEY, Catharine		30	F	None	30No02Cd
Mary	(D)	08	F	Child	30No02Cd
Bridget	(D)	03	F	Child	30No02Cd
Patrick	(S)	01	M	Child	30No02Cd
ROWLAND, James		50	M	Publican	30No02Cd
Judith		46	F	None	30No02Cd
RILEY, Thomas		27	M	Laborer	30No02Cd
Mary		22	F	None	30No02Cd
STRATT, Archibald		35	M	Laborer	30No02Cd
Margaret	(W)	25	F	None	30No02Cd
Mary-Jane	(D)	07	F	Child	30No02Cd
Anne	(D)	05	F	Child	30No02Cd
George	(S)	03	M	Child	30No02Cd
Eliza	(D)	01	F	Child	30No02Cd
Died-At-Sea					
TURNIE, John		35	M	Laborer	30No02Cd
ROOHAN, Edward		30	M	Laborer	30No02Cd
HAINEY, Martin		38	M	Farmer	30No02Cd
Micheal	(S)	10	M	Child	30No02Cd
STRONG, Alexander		27	M	Laborer	30No02Cd
Elisabeth	(W)	24	F	None	30No02Cd
Elisabeth	(D)	03	F	Child	30No02Cd
Mary	(D)	01	F	Child	30No02Cd
Died-At-Sea					
BRADY, Anthony		26	M	Laborer	30No02Cd
MCGINSTRY, Mary		24	F	None	30No02Cd
William	(S)	01	M	Child	30No02Cd
Died-At-Sea					

ST.GEORGE 02 DECEMBER 1846

From Liverpool

NAMES OF PASSENGERS		AGE	SEX	OCCUPATIONS	DATE PORT SHIP
JACKSON, John		23	M	Laborer	02De02Av
BANKS, George		23	M	Laborer	02De02Av
MCCOUSIN, Phillip		25	M	Laborer	02De02Av
Jane	(W)	24	F	Wife	02De02Av
Patrick	(S)	.00	M	Infant	02De02Av
KING, John		40	M	Laborer	02De02Av
Mary	(D)	17	F	None	02De02Av
Ann	(D)	16	F	None	02De02Av
Margaret	(D)	11	F	None	02De02Av
Eliza	(D)	06	F	Child	02De02Av
James	(S)	14	M	Laborer	02De02Av
John	(S)	09	M	Child	02De02Av
Joseph	(S)	02	M	Child	02De02Av
ROONEY, John		30	M	Laborer	02De02Av
Ann	(W)	28	F	Wife	02De02Av
Died-At-Sea					
David	(S)	04	M	Child	02De02Av
John	(S)	02	M	Child	02De02Av
James	(S)	01	M	Child	02De02Av
Died-At-Sea					
MCGEE, Catherine.		22	F	None	02De02Av
MOOHAN, Susan		22	F	None	02De02Av
ARMSTRONG, Mark		30	M	Farmer	02De02Av
Betsy		24	F	None	02De02Av
William		20	M	Farmer	02De02Av
THORNTON, Abrahm		40	M	Farmer	02De02Av
Rose	(W)	36	F	Servant	02De02Av
Mary-Ann	(D)	14	F	Servant	02De02Av
THORNTON, Belle	(D)	13	F	Servant	02De02Av
William	(S)	02	M	Child	02De02Av
JERTON, Margaret		28	F	None	02De02Av
BOWES, Francis		40	M	Laborer	02De02Av
Died-At-Sea					
LYONS, Mary		50	F	None	02De02Av
Jane	(D)	17	F	None	02De02Av
Eliza	(D)	12	F	None	02De02Av
TRAINOR, Bernard		66	M	Laborer	02De02Av
Owen		40	M	Laborer	02De02Av
John		11	M	Child	02De02Av
Margaret		07	F	Child	02De02Av
MCCOFFRY, Francis		28	M	Laborer	02De02Av
GOLDING, Edward		24	M	Smith	02De02Av
John		14	M	None	02De02Av
SLEVIN, Patrick		19	M	Laborer	02De02Av
STENSON, Michael		18	M	Laborer	02De02Av
MARRON, Bridget		18	F	Servant	02De02Av
KENEDY, Margaret		18	F	Servant	02De02Av
CONNERTY, Micheal		21	M	Laborer	02De02Av
MCCAULY, Margaret		23	F	None	02De02Av
RIELLY, Patrick		26	M	Laborer	02De02Av
Ellen	(W)	24	F	Wife	02De02Av
Died-At-Sea					
Michael	(S)	.00	M	Infant	02De02Av
EGAN, Ann		20	F	None	02De02Av
MCNULTY, Cathe.		20	F	None	02De02Av
MAY, Patrick		24	M	Laborer	02De02Av
BROWN, John		21	M	Farmer	02De02Av
BRENNAN, Patt		24	M	Laborer	02De02Av
WILLIAMS, William		19	M	Blacksmith	02De02Av
PRIOR, James		20	M	Clerk	02De02Av
DALY, Patrick		22	M	Laborer	02De02Av
MCGREGOR, George		26	M	Weaver	02De02Av
MCDONALD, James		21	M	Mason	02De02Av
DEVANEY, Thomas		21	M	Clerk	02De02Av
FLANEGAN, John		28	M	Laborer	02De02Av
FURY, James		32	M	Laborer	02De02Av
BENNAN, David		20	M	Shoemaker	02De02Av
SHARP, Rose		25	F	None	02De02Av
BRAELAND, Grace		18	F	None	02De02Av
MCCUE, Margaret		20	F	None	02De02Av
Susan		19	F	None	02De02Av
BELL, Francis		21	F	None	02De02Av
NALLY, Catherine		16	F	None	02De02Av
BURKE, Maria		18	F	None	02De02Av
CROOK, George		26	M	Carpenter	02De02Av
UPPER, William		22	M	Farmer	02De02Av
Mary-Ann	(W)	22	F	Wife	02De02Av
Mary-Ann	(D)	.00	F	Infant	02De02Av
DOWNES, Thomas		21	M	Farmer	02De02Av
Judy		20	F	Farmer	02De02Av
ODONELL, John		20	M	Laborer	02De02Av
MCALLISTER, Issac		50	M	Laborer	02De02Av
GARITY, Mary		20	F	None	02De02Av
DOWNS, Thomas		20	M	Farmer	02De02Av
SMITH, Margaret		55	F	None	02De02Av
Thomas	(S)	24	M	Laborer	02De02Av
Micheal	(S)	17	M	Laborer	02De02Av
Mary	(D)	26	F	None	02De02Av
Ann	(D)	20	F	None	02De02Av
Eliza	(D)	13	F	None	02De02Av
Ellen	(D)	10	F	Child	02De02Av
FOLEY, Margaret		20	F	None	02De02Av
BARRY, Ann		50	F	None	02De02Av
Rodger	(S)	23	M	Laborer	02De02Av
Ann	(D)	13	F	None	02De02Av
Margaret	(D)	13	F	None	02De02Av
HOPE, Ann		20	F	None	02De02Av
Margaret		18	F	None	02De02Av
WHITE, Micheal		22	M	None	02De02Av
WHELAN, Michael		24	M	Laborer	02De02Av
Kitty		22	F	None	02De02Av
WALSH, William		40	M	Mason	02De02Av
Judy		40	F	None	02De02Av

NAMES OF PASSENGERS		AGE	SEX	OCCUPATIONS	DATE PORT SHIP
HOGAN, Catherine		20	F	None	02De02Av
CULLEN, Charles		20	M	Laborer	02De02Av
Mary		18	F	None	02De02Av
MCMANUS, Ann		18	F	None	02De02Av
STEATHERS, James		22	M	Carpenter	02De02Av
OBRIEN, Thomas		25	M	Laborer	02De02Av
Ann	(W)	20	F	Wife	02De02Av
Patrick	(S)	03	M	Child	02De02Av
Edward	(S)	02	M	Child	02De02Av
CORCORAN, Henry		28	M	Laborer	02De02Av
KEENAN, William		30	M	Shoemaker	02De02Av
John		30	M	Shoemaker	02De02Av
MCGLUSK, Patt		28	M	Laborer	02De02Av
Susan		20	F	None	02De02Av
WEIRS, James		40	M	Laborer	02De02Av
Ellen		40	F	None	02De02Av
MCGEVIN, John		25	M	Laborer	02De02Av
Mary	(W)	24	F	Wife	02De02Av
Jane	(D)	.00	F	Infant	02De02Av
COKELY, Mary		25	F	None	02De02Av
DAVIDSON, Henderson		19	M	Gentleman	02De02Av
Sarah		15	F	Lady	02De02Av
Jane		10	F	Child	02De02Av
OBRIEN, Thomas		28	M	Laborer	02De02Av
John		28	M	Laborer	02De02Av
FEREL, Bridget		18	F	Spinster	02De02Av
BURK, Joseph		20	M	Farmer	02De02Av
CUNNIFF, Micheal		20	M	Farmer	02De02Av
CONDLEY, Micheal		48	M	Laborer	02De02Av
Mary	(W)	38	F	Wife	02De02Av
Ellen	(D)	13	F	None	02De02Av
Patrick	(S)	11	M	Child	02De02Av
Della	(D)	09	F	Child	02De02Av
William	(S)	04	M	Child	02De02Av
Micheal	(S)	.00	M	Infant	02De02Av
MCWHERTER, Andrew		40	M	Laborer	02De02Av
Maggy		30	F	None	02De02Av
SMITH, Biddy		18	F	None	02De02Av
Mary		17	F	None	02De02Av
MCWHERTER, James		18	M	Laborer	02De02Av
Sarah		09	F	Child	02De02Av
Mary		06	F	Child	02De02Av
Thomas		04	M	Child	02De02Av
John		.00	M	Infant	02De02Av
Died-At-Sea					
Andrew		16	M	None	02De02Av
KEENAN, Michael		19	M	Smith	02De02Av
John		21	M	Laborer	02De02Av
Betty		20	F	None	02De02Av
CAHILL, Biddy		20	F	None	02De02Av
MCFARLANE, Mary		20	F	None	02De02Av
Mary		18	F	None	02De02Av
FITZGERALD, M.		40	M	Mason	02De02Av
Margaret	(W)	35	F	Wife	02De02Av
Peggy	(D)	.00	F	Infant	02De02Av
SMITH, Ellen		50	F	None	02De02Av
Judy	(D)	19	F	None	02De02Av
Biddy	(D)	17	F	None	02De02Av
COLE, M.A.		40	M	Blacksmith	02De02Av
LYONS, A.		35	M	Weaver	02De02Av
FITZSIMMONS, Thos.		20	M	Tanner	02De02Av
Ann		19	F	None	02De02Av
GALLAGAN, Mary		20	F	None	02De02Av
HYDE, Joseph		29	M	Stctr	02De02Av
GORMAN, Ann		19	F	None	02De02Av
CLARK, Wm.		30	M	Merchant	02De02Av
BRENNAN, Mary		20	F	None	02De02Av
JOHNSON, Robert		52	M	Farmer	02De02Av
Jane	(W)	48	F	Wife	02De02Av
Sarah	(D)	17	F	None	02De02Av
Margaret	(D)	15	F	None	02De02Av
John	(S)	12	M	None	02De02Av
Samuel	(S)	10	M	Child	02De02Av
Andrew	(S)	07	M	Child	02De02Av
RICE, Bernard		45	M	Laborer	02De02Av
RICE, Rose	(W)	45	F	Wife	02De02Av
Thomas	(S)	19	M	None	02De02Av
Peter	(S)	13	M	None	02De02Av
Mary	(D)	12	F	None	02De02Av
Henry	(S)	06	M	Child	02De02Av
Patt	(S)	04	M	Child	02De02Av
Cathrine	(D)	.00	F	Infant	02De02Av
RILEY, Charles		50	M	Farmer	02De02Av
Michael	(S)	20	M	Farmer	02De02Av
Margaret	(D)	18	F	None	02De02Av
FURY, John		45	M	Laborer	02De02Av
Patrick	(S)	20	M	Laborer	02De02Av
Ellen	(D)	16	F	None	02De02Av
GALLAGHER, James		20	M	Laborer	02De02Av
MCGINLEY, James		30	M	Laborer	02De02Av
Ann		28	F	Laborer	02De02Av
MIHAN, Patrick		22	M	Laborer	02De02Av
DARCY, Margaret		21	F	Servant	02De02Av
BARTLEY, William		10	M	Child	02De02Av
Ann		08	F	Child	02De02Av
BROWN, Wm.		30	M	Carpenter	02De02Av
COFFIN, John		18	M	Laborer	02De02Av
William		15	M	None	02De02Av
U-Mrs.		60	F	None	02De02Av
HOBBS, Margaret		20	F	None	02De02Av
CASSADY, Frank		40	M	Laborer	02De02Av
Catharine		60	F	None	02De02Av
Ann		20	F	None	02De02Av
MCMAHAN, Mary		27	F	None	02De02Av
KELLY, Catherine		20	F	None	02De02Av
Mary		25	F	None	02De02Av
WHITE, Catherine		24	F	None	02De02Av
MCDONALD, Mary		22	F	None	02De02Av
CONLY, Mary		12	F	None	02De02Av
MCCATREY, Ann		.00	F	Infant	02De02Av
MCCABE, Bernard		22	M	Laborer	02De02Av
NEIL, Kitty		23	F	None	02De02Av
TRAINOR, Patt		30	M	Laborer	02De02Av
MCKENNA, Rosey		25	F	None	02De02Av
GRAY, Betty		22	F	None	02De02Av
MCWILLIAMS, Ann		25	F	None	02De02Av
MOAN, Mary		25	F	None	02De02Av
DUFFY, Bidy		27	F	None	02De02Av
RILEY, William		28	M	Mason	02De02Av
James		28	M	Laborer	02De02Av
Caterine		28	F	None	02De02Av
CURMAN, Mary		20	F	None	02De02Av
FERNAN, Mary		18	F	None	02De02Av
MCCOTTER, A.		24	F	Spinster	02De02Av

DORCAS 03 DECEMBER 1846

From Limerick

MCCREA, John		28	M	Engineer	03De33HJ
CORTESS, Rebbeca		35	F	None	03De33HJ

WESTMINSTER 04 DECEMBER 1846

From London

JERVOIS, Gordon		21	M	Lieutenant	04De21Br
SCOLTOCK, Elizabeth		45	F	Lady	04De21Br

309

NAMES OF PASSENGERS		AGE	SEX	OCCUPATIONS	DATE PORT SHIP
BARBER, Walter		26	M	Clerk	04De21Br
WYATT, Percival		14	M	None	04De21Br
GRAHAM, Edward		40	M	None	04De21Br
BACON, William		21	M	Surveyor	04De21Br
SCOTT, John-William		22	M	Clerk	04De21Br
CARTER, George		36	M	Hrsm	04De21Br
Elizabeth		26	F	None	04De21Br
HALL, Harriet-S.		24	F	None	04De21Br
PASCOE, Thomas		25	M	Shoemaker	04De21Br
SCANLAN, Johannah		39	F	None	04De21Br
Thomas	(S)	12	M	None	04De21Br
SCHEIN, Margaret		32	F	None	04De21Br
FITZGERALD, Mary		29	F	None	04De21Br
SNARE, James		23	M	None	04De21Br
CAVENER, Joseph		40	M	Shoemaker	04De21Br
NAPPIER, William		34	M	Shoemaker	04De21Br
TALLON, Mary-Ann		30	F	None	04De21Br
William	(S)	.06	M	Infant	04De21Br
RICKETTS, George		21	M	None	04De21Br
WERNERKER, Emma		22	F	None	04De21Br
CARTER, David		28	M	Carpenter	04De21Br

AMERICAS 04 DECEMBER 1846

From Liverpool

NAMES OF PASSENGERS		AGE	SEX	OCCUPATIONS	DATE PORT SHIP
WATERS, Mary		44	F	Unknown	04De02Hk
Patrick	(S)	08	M	Child	04De02Hk
HOLLYWOOD, Edward		32	M	Farmer	04De02Hk
CLARKE, Pat		21	M	Farmer	04De02Hk
OATES, Catherine		24	F	Servant	04De02Hk
GILLOHAN, Winford		20	F	Servant	04De02Hk
PUNTY, Ann		20	F	Servant	04De02Hk
TRACY, Bridget		19	F	Servant	04De02Hk
Alies		21	F	Servant	04De02Hk
MORRISS, Mary		18	F	Servant	04De02Hk
MCLEAR, Mary		16	F	Milliner	04De02Hk
QUINE, Ann		17	F	Servant	04De02Hk
CURLEY, Mary		26	F	Servant	04De02Hk
MADDON, Michael		23	M	Farmer	04De02Hk
DOULEN, Thos.		23	M	Farmer	04De02Hk
HOBAN, John		26	M	Farmer	04De02Hk
Ellen		22	M	Farmer	04De02Hk
QUALTER, Mary		21	F	Servant	04De02Hk
CORNELL, Mary		23	F	Servant	04De02Hk
FAHEE, Peggy		26	F	Servant	04De02Hk
CURLEY, John		03	M	Child	04De02Hk
QUINLON, Jude		40	M	Farmer	04De02Hk
Johannah	(W)	38	F	Wife	04De02Hk
Margarett	(D)	06	F	Child	04De02Hk
MURPHY, John		35	M	Tanner	04De02Hk
Julia		25	F	Servant	04De02Hk
CONDUN, Michael		26	M	Farmer	04De02Hk
GROGAN, Michael		26	M	Farmer	04De02Hk
GILES, Mary-A.		16	F	None	04De02Hk
GREY, Ann		50	F	None	04De02Hk

SEA 08 DECEMBER 1846

From Liverpool

NAMES OF PASSENGERS		AGE	SEX	OCCUPATIONS	DATE PORT SHIP
THOMPSON, John		50	M	Laborer	08De02Bg
Mary		30	F	None	08De02Bg

NAMES OF PASSENGERS		AGE	SEX	OCCUPATIONS	DATE PORT SHIP
THOMPSON, William		24	M	Laborer	08De02Bg
LUCAS, John		20	M	Laborer	08De02Bg
THOMPSON, Sarah		11	F	None	08De02Bg
John		09	M	Child	08De02Bg
Mary-Ann		07	F	Child	08De02Bg
Thomas		05	M	Child	08De02Bg
James		03	M	Child	08De02Bg
Eliza		01	F	Child	08De02Bg
LARKIN, Michael		25	M	Mason	08De02Bg
Margaret		21	F	None	08De02Bg
MALONEY, Ann		20	F	None	08De02Bg
MCGONIGAL, Pat		37	M	Laborer	08De02Bg
FITZGERALD, Peter		30	M	Laborer	08De02Bg
Mary	(W)	21	F	Wife	08De02Bg
Ann	(D)	04	F	Child	08De02Bg
CARROLL, Timothy		40	M	Laborer	08De02Bg
CONLON, Michael		30	M	Laborer	08De02Bg
Margaret	(W)	20	F	Wife	08De02Bg
Thomas	(S)	01	M	Child	08De02Bg
WALSH, John		16	M	Laborer	08De02Bg
NUGENT, James		15	M	Laborer	08De02Bg
Jane		16	F	None	08De02Bg
MEDE, Ann		20	F	None	08De02Bg
MCCARTY, John		30	M	Laborer	08De02Bg
SMITH, Ann		27	F	None	08De02Bg
DUMPHY, Mary		18	F	None	08De02Bg
LARVIN, Patrick		30	M	Laborer	08De02Bg
Mary	(W)	26	F	Wife	08De02Bg
Patrick	(S)	01	M	Child	08De02Bg
RIDDINGTON, Patrick		30	M	Laborer	08De02Bg
Ann		32	F	None	08De02Bg
DUMPHY, Julia		21	F	None	08De02Bg
HOOK, John		32	M	Laborer	08De02Bg
DWYER, Michael		60	M	Laborer	08De02Bg
Peggy	(W)	51	F	Wife	08De02Bg
Catherine		14	F	None	08De02Bg
Edward		12	M	None	08De02Bg
Mary		02	F	Child	08De02Bg
STANLEY, Michael		42	M	Laborer	08De02Bg
Eliza	(W)	30	F	Wife	08De02Bg
Dolly	(D)	12	F	None	08De02Bg
Mary	(D)	06	F	Child	08De02Bg
Catherine	(D)	04	F	Child	08De02Bg
Anne	(D)	02	F	Child	08De02Bg
Sarah		01	F	Child	08De02Bg
GARRY, Ann		30	F	None	08De02Bg
MCLOUGHLIN, Thomas		23	M	Laborer	08De02Bg
DOWD, Anthony		25	M	None	08De02Bg
MAHON, Pat		19	M	Laborer	08De02Bg
GILVANY, Michael		26	M	Laborer	08De02Bg
MCCABE, Margaret		20	F	None	08De02Bg
ODOWD, Bridget		20	F	None	08De02Bg
GILLESPIE, Anthony		28	M	Laborer	08De02Bg
Catherine		20	F	None	08De02Bg
Eleanor		25	F	None	08De02Bg
CALLY, John		45	M	Laborer	08De02Bg
Bridget		34	F	None	08De02Bg
John		25	M	Laborer	08De02Bg
Hannah		22	F	None	08De02Bg
WELSH, Michael		28	M	Laborer	08De02Bg
DOLIN, Mary		24	F	None	08De02Bg
Honor		23	F	None	08De02Bg
CALLY, Mary		03	F	Child	08De02Bg
Bridget		01	F	Child	08De02Bg
DOVER, Francis		12	M	Laborer	08De02Bg
OBRIAN, Phillip		35	M	Laborer	08De02Bg
MCKENZIE, John		23	M	Laborer	08De02Bg
LANGAN, John		28	M	Laborer	08De02Bg
ROONEY, Thomas		22	M	Laborer	08De02Bg
ROGERS, Hannah		20	F	None	08De02Bg
OBRIEN, John		11	M	None	08De02Bg
ROACH, John		25	M	Laborer	08De02Bg
Larry		18	M	Laborer	08De02Bg
Bridget		20	F	None	08De02Bg
QUIN, Nancy		20	F	None	08De02Bg

NAMES OF PASSENGERS		AGE	SEX	OCCUPATIONS	DATE PORT SHIP
WELLS, Henry		40	M	Laborer	08De02Bg
LOFTUS, Anthony		30	M	Laborer	08De02Bg
Catherine		21	F	None	08De02Bg
TUNLING, Robert		40	M	Laborer	08De02Bg
Mary		33	F	None	08De02Bg
MCMAHON, John		50	M	Laborer	08De02Bg
Mary	(W)	45	F	Wife	08De02Bg
Catherine	(D)	19	F	None	08De02Bg
Mary	(D)	11	F	Child	08De02Bg
Margaret	(D)	09	F	Child	08De02Bg
John	(S)	07	M	Child	08De02Bg
MCCOYNE, Pat		20	M	Laborer	08De02Bg
COLTIN, Betty		20	F	None	08De02Bg
QUILLIAMS, Thomas		40	M	Laborer	08De02Bg
HUNT, Edward		34	M	Diactr	08De02Bg
WALDRON, Martin		47	M	Laborer	08De02Bg
Mary	(W)	45	F	Wife	08De02Bg
Mary	(D)	13	F	None	08De02Bg
Biddy	(D)	12	F	None	08De02Bg
Kitty	(D)	10	F	Child	08De02Bg
Ann	(D)	08	F	Child	08De02Bg
Sally	(D)	02	F	Child	08De02Bg
John	(S)	05	M	Child	08De02Bg
James	(S)	03	M	Child	08De02Bg
MCMANNS, John		24	M	Laborer	08De02Bg
MILLADY, Thomas		22	M	Laborer	08De02Bg
Mary		26	F	None	08De02Bg
FLANNAGAN, Margaret		40	F	None	08De02Bg
RILELINE, Patrick		18	M	Laborer	08De02Bg
Andrew		11	M	Laborer	08De02Bg
CONNOR, Bessy		40	F	None	08De02Bg
Biddy		17	F	None	08De02Bg
QUIGLEY, John		19	M	Laborer	08De02Bg
LYNCH, Mary		23	F	None	08De02Bg
COLGAN, Mary		80	F	None	08De02Bg
Died-At-Sea					
ROBINSON, Pat		31	M	Laborer	08De02Bg
MCGEEVER, Andrew		30	M	Laborer	08De02Bg
Katherine	(W)	36	F	Wife	08De02Bg
Mary	(D)	02	F	Child	08De02Bg
Frederick	(S)	01	M	Child	08De02Bg
GOLDING, Anthony		22	M	Laborer	08De02Bg
BEGGAN, Peter		21	M	Laborer	08De02Bg
HERBERT, Bridget		19	F	None	08De02Bg
MARTIN, Jane		40	F	None	08De02Bg
RILEY, John		54	M	Gdnr	08De02Bg
Michael		22	M	Laborer	08De02Bg
Patrick		27	M	Laborer	08De02Bg
Margaret		25	F	None	08De02Bg
Mary		27	F	None	08De02Bg
DOWDALL, Edward		26	M	Laborer	08De02Bg
Susan	(W)	24	F	Wife	08De02Bg
Elizabeth	(D)	03	F	Child	08De02Bg
William	(S)	02	M	Child	08De02Bg
FLOWER, Elizabeth		26	F	None	08De02Bg
Eliza		13	F	None	08De02Bg
Margaret		09	F	Child	08De02Bg
LYNCH, Peter		30	M	Farmer	08De02Bg
Mary		26	F	None	08De02Bg
Katherine		50	F	None	08De02Bg
Jane		22	F	None	08De02Bg
Mary		18	F	None	08De02Bg
James		14	M	Laborer	08De02Bg
Ellen		12	F	None	08De02Bg
KERRIGAN, Thomas		58	M	Farmer	08De02Bg
Bridget	(W)	56	F	Wife	08De02Bg
Ann	(D)	24	F	None	08De02Bg
Margaret	(D)	22	F	None	08De02Bg
Bridget	(D)	20	F	None	08De02Bg
Martin	(S)	15	M	Laborer	08De02Bg
Thomas	(S)	23	M	Laborer	08De02Bg
Michael	(S)	12	M	Laborer	08De02Bg
Elizabeth	(D)	10	F	Child	08De02Bg
MCGORLICH, Charles		26	M	Laborer	08De02Bg
ROONEY, John		15	M	Laborer	08De02Bg
LYONS, Hannah		27	F	None	08De02Bg
John	(S)	07	M	Child	08De02Bg
DUNN, Ann		20	F	None	08De02Bg
KANE, Patrick		17	M	Laborer	08De02Bg
OWENS, Peter		30	M	Farmer	08De02Bg
Ellen		50	F	None	08De02Bg
Margaret		30	F	None	08De02Bg
Mary		09	F	Child	08De02Bg
Phillip		13	M	Laborer	08De02Bg
Phillip		02	M	Child	08De02Bg
Thomas		28	M	Laborer	08De02Bg
John		15	M	Laborer	08De02Bg
Mary		15	F	None	08De02Bg
LITTLE, Jane		14	F	None	08De02Bg
DALY, John		45	M	Laborer	08De02Bg
Bridget	(D)	15	F	None	08De02Bg
Ann	(D)	15	F	None	08De02Bg
CALDRICH, Matthew		22	M	Laborer	08De02Bg
SMITH, Mary		15	F	None	08De02Bg
Ann		17	F	None	08De02Bg
CLERKSON, Charles		23	M	Laborer	08De02Bg
FLOOD, Pat		21	M	Laborer	08De02Bg
OWENS, Eliza		25	F	None	08De02Bg
LEONARD, Daniel		25	M	Laborer	08De02Bg
James		22	M	Laborer	08De02Bg
GALLAGHER, Pat		35	M	Groom	08De02Bg
Margaret		30	F	None	08De02Bg
CONLAN, Bridget		19	F	None	08De02Bg
MCCLEANAN, Alexander		38	M	Laborer	08De02Bg
BYRN, Thomas		20	M	Laborer	08De02Bg
Jane		20	F	None	08De02Bg
MURTHA, Patrick		20	M	Laborer	08De02Bg
CONNOR, Dennis		19	M	Groom	08De02Bg
KANE, Mary		20	F	None	08De02Bg
ROGERS, William		21	M	Laborer	08De02Bg
James		31	M	Laborer	08De02Bg
ORR, Elizabeth		21	F	None	08De02Bg
CONNOR, Winefred		23	F	None	08De02Bg
HACKET, Margaret		19	F	None	08De02Bg
KENNEDY, Patrick		16	M	Laborer	08De02Bg
DONNELLY, Jane		19	F	None	08De02Bg
KELLY, Betsy		25	F	None	08De02Bg
SLOAN, Betsy		23	F	None	08De02Bg
Alice		21	F	None	08De02Bg
COVE, Alice		20	F	None	08De02Bg
Betsy		18	F	None	08De02Bg
CARMIELO, Mary		20	F	None	08De02Bg
KENNEDY, Andrew		35	M	Laborer	08De02Bg
KEARNS, Andrew		40	M	Laborer	08De02Bg
Mary	(W)	35	F	Wife	08De02Bg
Peter	(S)	12	M	None	08De02Bg
Margaret	(D)	10	F	Child	08De02Bg
John	(S)	08	M	Child	08De02Bg
Michael	(S)	06	M	Child	08De02Bg
Thomas	(S)	04	M	Child	08De02Bg
Andrew	(S)	02	M	Child	08De02Bg
CONNELL, Patrick		24	M	Laborer	08De02Bg
Kitty		24	F	None	08De02Bg
Mary		09	F	Child	08De02Bg
Katherine		01	F	Child	08De02Bg
Teddy		06	M	Child	08De02Bg
KEAJAN, Mary		24	F	None	08De02Bg
MAGEE, Edward		35	M	Laborer	08De02Bg
Sally	(W)	35	F	Wife	08De02Bg
Mary	(D)	12	F	Child	08De02Bg
John	(S)	10	M	Child	08De02Bg
Bridget	(D)	05	F	Child	08De02Bg
Patrick	(S)	02	M	Child	08De02Bg
MARTIN, Hugh		20	M	Laborer	08De02Bg
OBRIEN, Matthew		16	M	Laborer	08De02Bg
HAGAN, Peter		23	M	Laborer	08De02Bg
FITZIMMINS, Mary		28	F	None	08De02Bg
CLIRKIN, Phillip		30	M	Laborer	08De02Bg
Mary	(W)	24	F	Wife	08De02Bg
Ann	(D)	01	F	Child	08De02Bg

NAMES OF PASSENGERS	A G E	S E X	OCCUPATIONS	DATE PORT SHIP		NAMES OF PASSENGERS	A G E	S E X	OCCUPATIONS	DATE PORT SHIP
MCNALLY, Daniel	80	M	Laborer	08De02Bg		MEANY, Sarah	21	F	Servant	08De02Hz
Mary	65	F	None	08De02Bg		FARRELL, Julia	16	F	Servant	08De02Hz
Thomas	20	M	Laborer	08De02Bg		MULLIN, Peter	28	M	Laborer	08De02Hz
MCHENRY, Francis	18	M	Laborer	08De02Bg		MCGLOGHLIN, Ann	17	F	None	08De02Hz
WELSH, Daniel	15	M	Laborer	08De02Bg		HALY, Henry	20	M	Laborer	08De02Hz
RILEY, Katherine	30	F	None	08De02Bg		GREEN, Mary	20	F	Servant	08De02Hz
Biddy	20	F	None	08De02Bg		DELEAVEY, Bridget	13	F	Servant	08De02Hz
LYNCH, Mary	46	F	None	08De02Bg		JOYCE, Patt	20	M	Laborer	08De02Hz
Katherine	13	F	None	08De02Bg		DOLAN, Luke	19	M	Laborer	08De02Hz
SHERIDAN, Ann	13	F	None	08De02Bg		TOBIN, Mich.	36	M	Laborer	08De02Hz
JOYCE, Biddy	24	F	None	08De02Bg		THOMPSON, George	22	M	Merchant	08De02Hz
						COSTELLO, Darby	20	M	Laborer	08De02Hz
						Peggy	19	F	Servant	08De02Hz
						CAIN, Peggy	20	F	Servant	08De02Hz
HAMPDEN 08 DECEMBER 1846						BLY, Biddy	18	F	Servant	08De02Hz
						BURKE, Biddy	26	F	Servant	08De02Hz
From Liverpool						GADDOCK, John	19	M	Laborer	08De02Hz
						BRITTAN, Thos.	26	M	Laborer	08De02Hz
						MONTAGUE, Anderew	30	M	Laborer	08De02Hz
						LALLEY, Wm.	20	M	Laborer	08De02Hz
						U (W)	18	F	Wife	08De02Hz
KERR, Wm.	18	M	Laborer	08De02Hz		Bridget	30	F	Servant	08De02Hz
MORAN, Cath.	30	F	Servant	08De02Hz		Mary	11	F	Child	08De02Hz
Mary	27	F	Servant	08De02Hz		Paul	08	M	Child	08De02Hz
FLYN, Cath.	20	F	Servant	08De02Hz		CONDRY, Ned	25	M	Laborer	08De02Hz
CARTWRIGHT, Thos.	27	M	Servant	08De02Hz		Margaret (W)	22	F	Wife	08De02Hz
MONAGEN, Wm.	22	M	Farmer	08De02Hz		John (S)	.00	M	Infant	08De02Hz
John	30	M	Farmer	08De02Hz		PRUSON, Ben	20	M	Laborer	08De02Hz
Ann	28	F	None	08De02Hz		MARLEY, Jas.	20	M	Laborer	08De02Hz
Eliza	07	F	Child	08De02Hz		JOYCE, Peter	24	M	Laborer	08De02Hz
Wm.	05	M	Child	08De02Hz		U (W)	22	F	None	08De02Hz
Jas.	03	M	Child	08De02Hz		MCERVEN, John	24	M	Rope Maker	08De02Hz
Thos.	.00	M	Infant	08De02Hz		U (W)	20	F	None	08De02Hz
HADDON, Wm.	20	M	Servant	08De02Hz		MILLIGAN, Jas.	30	M	Carpenter	08De02Hz
RICHARDSON, James	21	M	Laborer	08De02Hz		RUSS, J.P.	15	M	None	08De02Hz
MINIHAN, Marge	26	F	Laborer	08De02Hz		MOGAVIN, Catherine	23	F	None	08De02Hz
Cath.	16	F	Laborer	08De02Hz		FLYN, Hy.	21	M	Laborer	08De02Hz
MCDIVET, Danl.	39	M	Laborer	08De02Hz		GULLOCK, Biddy	25	F	Servant	08De02Hz
ALLEN, Danl.	38	M	Butcher	08De02Hz		LYNCH, Bernard	21	M	Laborer	08De02Hz
CONROY, Eliza	26	F	Servant	08De02Hz		CARPENTER, Biddy	18	F	Servant	08De02Hz
MCCANDEN, Cath	20	F	Servant	08De02Hz		CULLEN, Mat.	25	M	Laborer	08De02Hz
GALLEGER, Mary	26	F	Servant	08De02Hz		GARRATY, Mary-Ann	13	F	Servant	08De02Hz
DENARRY, Bess	20	F	Servant	08De02Hz		HEGAN, Peggy	40	F	Servant	08De02Hz
CUDDY, Biddy	18	F	Servant	08De02Hz		FEGAN, Mary	19	F	Servant	08De02Hz
MULLIN, Mary	26	F	Servant	08De02Hz		Cath.	09	F	Servant	08De02Hz
Nancy	20	F	Servant	08De02Hz		John	03	M	Child	08De02Hz
MCKENNA, Cath.	18	F	Servant	08De02Hz		BRADY, Bernard	25	M	Laborer	08De02Hz
MOSSY, Mary	40	F	Servant	08De02Hz		FINERTY, Wm.	30	M	Laborer	08De02Hz
WHITE, Pat	40	M	Laborer	08De02Hz		CAMBELL, Mich.	35	M	Laborer	08De02Hz
Cath.	16	F	None	08De02Hz		Honor	30	F	Servant	08De02Hz
PICKETT, Thos.	28	M	Laborer	08De02Hz		FINERTY, Sally	18	F	Servant	08De02Hz
Pat	25	M	Laborer	08De02Hz		MCANANY, John	19	M	Laborer	08De02Hz
Bridget	13	F	None	08De02Hz		HEGAN, Dennis	25	M	Carpenter	08De02Hz
CARUTHER, Thos.	30	M	Laborer	08De02Hz		Winney	20	M	None	08De02Hz
COLLIAN, Pat	23	M	Farmer	08De02Hz		MCKENNEDY, John	20	M	Laborer	08De02Hz
MAGRAIL, Patt	50	M	Laborer	08De02Hz		WUN, Wm.	24	M	Laborer	08De02Hz
Cath	20	F	None	08De02Hz		Mary	16	F	None	08De02Hz
HAWLEY, Ann	20	F	None	08De02Hz		MCFAGNE, Peggy	20	F	Servant	08De02Hz
Died-At-Sea						MULLIN, Bridget	30	F	Servant	08De02Hz
DUMPSEY, Ed.	30	M	Laborer	08De02Hz		Pat (S)	07	M	Child	08De02Hz
Jas.	25	M	Laborer	08De02Hz		Jane (D)	05	F	Child	08De02Hz
Cath.	24	F	Servant	08De02Hz		MCKEW, Francis	26	M	Butcher	08De02Hz
Bernard	.00	M	Infant	08De02Hz		HALL, Ann	18	F	Servant	08De02Hz
JOHNSON, Hy.	21	M	Laborer	08De02Hz		NUGENT, Francis	15	M	None	08De02Hz
GORR, Ralph	30	M	Laborer	08De02Hz		Mary	22	F	Servant	08De02Hz
Mary (W)	30	F	Servant	08De02Hz		CASSADY, Jane	24	F	Servant	08De02Hz
John (S)	10	M	Child	08De02Hz		Elizabeth	21	F	Servant	08De02Hz
Mary (D)	08	F	Child	08De02Hz		MCQUEENY, Cath.	18	F	Servant	08De02Hz
Eliza (D)	06	F	Child	08De02Hz		REYNOLDS, Eliza	21	F	Servant	08De02Hz
BUSH, James	23	M	Laborer	08De02Hz		HUGHES, John	25	M	Laborer	08De02Hz
Mary (D)	.00	F	Infant	08De02Hz		MCCABE, Jos.	20	M	Laborer	08De02Hz
Margaret (W)	25	F	Wife	08De02Hz		Jane	24	F	None	08De02Hz
Bridget (D)	.00	F	Infant	08De02Hz		BARNACLE, Mary	18	F	Servant	08De02Hz
WARRIN, J.E.	21	M	Nvof	08De02Hz		BRATT, Edwin	27	M	Farmer	08De02Hz
						U (W)	26	F	Wife	08De02Hz

312

NAMES OF PASSENGERS		AGE	SEX	OCCUPATIONS	DATE PORT SHIP
BRATT, Jas.	(S)	03	M	Child	08De02Hz
Mary	(D)	.00	F	Infant	08De02Hz
MCGUIRE, Sarah		30	F	Servant	08De02Hz
REILLY, Ann		40	F	Servant	08De02Hz
Cath.		17	F	Servant	08De02Hz
PRATT, Mary		22	F	Servant	08De02Hz
Ellen		22	F	Servant	08De02Hz
Martha		17	F	Servant	08De02Hz
FERGUSON, Eliza		22	F	Servant	08De02Hz
MOORE, Cath.		19	F	Servant	08De02Hz
MANNING, Alex.		24	M	Engineer	08De02Hz
WALLER, Maria		19	F	Servant	08De02Hz
CAHILL, Patt		40	M	Laborer	08De02Hz
Ed.		19	M	Laborer	08De02Hz
Margt.		16	F	None	08De02Hz
Mich.		09	M	Child	08De02Hz
Thos.		07	M	Child	08De02Hz
Kitty		04	F	Child	08De02Hz
LALLY, Anthony		14	M	None	08De02Hz
Bridget		12	F	None	08De02Hz
BURYIN, Ann		20	F	None	08De02Hz
HIGGINS, U-Mrs.		30	F	None	08De02Hz
Michael		50	M	Laborer	08De02Hz
U	(W)	50	F	Farmer	08De02Hz
Ann		20	F	Farmer	08De02Hz
Peter		19	M	Farmer	08De02Hz
Mary-Ann		10	F	Farmer	08De02Hz
Henry		02	M	Child	08De02Hz
Mary		.00	F	Infant	08De02Hz
Betty		11	F	Unknown	08De02Hz
Thos.		09	M	Child	08De02Hz
Died-At-Sea					
CAIN, Henry		60	M	Farmer	08De02Hz
U	(W)	56	F	Wife	08De02Hz
Mary		14	F	Farmer	08De02Hz
PUNTY, Cath.		20	F	Farmer	08De02Hz
MURRAY, Jas.		30	M	Farmer	08De02Hz
BRUCE, Malcomb		51	M	Farmer	08De02Hz
NAHAND, Mark		19	M	Clerk	08De02Hz
Anthony		20	M	None	08De02Hz
FARRELL, Mary		20	F	Servant	08De02Hz
TAYLOR, John		30	M	Laborer	08De02Hz
MCALINDER, Sarah		19	F	Servant	08De02Hz
NOUGTON, Pat		23	M	Laborer	08De02Hz
Sarah		20	F	Servant	08De02Hz
MCDONOUGH, Mich.		22	M	Laborer	08De02Hz
GLENNAN, Ed.		20	M	Laborer	08De02Hz
DELANY, Pat		20	M	Laborer	08De02Hz
Mary		19	F	None	08De02Hz
MULLIN, Martin		20	M	Laborer	08De02Hz
Mary		16	F	None	08De02Hz
MORRIS, Jas.		20	M	Laborer	08De02Hz
REILLY, John		20	M	Laborer	08De02Hz
Biddy		11	F	None	08De02Hz
FASLEY, Bridget		19	F	None	08De02Hz
MCGRATH, Cath.		19	F	None	08De02Hz
WINKIN, David		26	M	Laborer	08De02Hz
HEILLY, Jas.		20	M	Laborer	08De02Hz
MINAHAN, Jas.		20	M	Laborer	08De02Hz
SRADDEN, U		20	M	Laborer	08De02Hz
BACON, John		18	M	Laborer	08De02Hz
MULDEN, Margaret		46	F	Servant	08De02Hz
HILLY, Margt.		23	F	Servant	08De02Hz
SCOOKES, Sarah		21	F	Servant	08De02Hz
BURN, Pat		45	M	Laborer	08De02Hz
Mary		20	F	None	08De02Hz
Biddy		18	F	None	08De02Hz
MCLOUGLIN, Margt.		22	F	Servant	08De02Hz
Mary		20	F	Servant	08De02Hz
MCCOOURT, Anne		20	F	Servant	08De02Hz
LEVELL, Cath.		18	F	Farmer	08De02Hz
SIDNEY, A.A.		24	M	Merchant	08De02Hz
HENDERSON, J.B.		32	M	Mariner	08De02Hz
THOMAS, Chas.		17	M	Laborer	08De02Hz
MCDERMOTT, Patt		24	M	Laborer	08De02Hz
DALEM, Bernard		21	M	Laborer	08De02Hz
EARLY, Julia		16	F	Servant	08De02Hz
OREILLY, Walter		22	M	Doctor	08De02Hz
Susan		18	F	None	08De02Hz
HALL, Michael		30	M	None	08De02Hz
RYAN, Patt		32	M	None	08De02Hz
QUINN, Wm.		21	M	Laborer	08De02Hz
BARNACLE, Wm.		21	M	None	08De02Hz
Biddy		20	F	None	08De02Hz
GRIFFITH, Peter		28	M	None	08De02Hz
HANLEY, Cath.		19	F	Servant	08De02Hz
DALY, Wm.		24	M	Laborer	08De02Hz
DRUMMOND, B.		24	M	Groom	08De02Hz
Mcl.		20	M	Groom	08De02Hz
MURRAY, Ed.		19	M	Laborer	08De02Hz
MCGLOGHLIN, Barthn.		22	M	Clerk	08De02Hz
KELLY, David		20	M	Clerk	08De02Hz
REILLEY, Austin		30	M	Clerk	08De02Hz
U	(W)	29	F	Laborer	08De02Hz
BOYLE, Elsy		17	F	None	08De02Hz
ONEIL, Eliza		35	F	None	08De02Hz
Ann		12	F	None	08De02Hz
Mary		09	F	Child	08De02Hz
WILLIAMS, Hy.		25	M	Laborer	08De02Hz
Peggy		25	F	None	08De02Hz
ROCK, Bridget		17	F	Servant	08De02Hz
Pat		20	M	Laborer	08De02Hz
DAVIS, Wm.		38	M	Farmer	08De02Hz
LALLOR, Cath.		26	F	Farmer	08De02Hz
PRUSSALL, Martin		22	M	Farmer	08De02Hz
DILLON, Thos.		30	M	Farmer	08De02Hz
Bridget	(W)	25	F	Wife	08De02Hz
Michael	(S)	.00	M	Infant	08De02Hz
HAGGERTY, William		25	M	Laborer	08De02Hz
MCKENNA, Cath.		22	F	Servant	08De02Hz
Margt.		18	F	Servant	08De02Hz
WALKER, Jas.		13	M	Saddler	08De02Hz
MCCONNELL, Robt.		23	M	Laborer	08De02Hz
ARKIN, Alex.		24	M	Laborer	08De02Hz
REILLY, U-Mrs.		50	F	Laborer	08De02Hz
Thos.	(H)	50	M	Laborer	08De02Hz
Margt.	(D)	23	F	None	08De02Hz
Bridget	(D)	18	F	None	08De02Hz
Rose	(D)	15	F	None	08De02Hz
NUGENT, Ellen		18	F	None	08De02Hz
MCGUIRE, Mary		20	F	None	08De02Hz
MOLOY, Saml.		21	M	Laborer	08De02Hz
RUSSELL, Wm.		27	M	Laborer	08De02Hz
U-Mrs.	(W)	26	F	Wife	08De02Hz
George	(S)	03	M	Child	08De02Hz
MCCONNELL, Patt		22	M	Laborer	08De02Hz
MULLEY, John		00	M	Unknown	08De02Hz
Died-At-Sea					
FEGAN, Ann		00	F	Unknown	08De02Hz
Died-At-Sea					
CAMPBELL, Mary		00	F	Unknown	08De02Hz
Died-At-Sea					
MULLER, Michael		00	M	Unknown	08De02Hz
Died-At-Sea					
BUSH, Brien		00	M	Unknown	08De02Hz
Died-At-Sea					
HIGGINS, Hugh		00	M	Unknown	08De02Hz
Died-At-Sea					
RILEY, Michael		00	M	Unknown	08De02Hz
Died-At-Sea					

NAMES OF PASSENGERS		AGE	SEX	OCCUPATIONS	DATE PORT SHIP
DAVIS, John	(S)	12	M	Shoemaker	09De18Ga
Issac	(S)	10	M	None	09De18Ga
Elizabeth	(D)	08	F	Child	09De18Ga
Eliza	(D)	01	F	Child	09De18Ga

NORTHUMBERLAND 08 DECEMBER 1846

From London

NAMES OF PASSENGERS		AGE	SEX	OCCUPATIONS	DATE PORT SHIP
STUART, W.Capt.		41	M	Army	08De21Cg
Anne	(W)	36	F	None	08De21Cg
BENSLEY, John		25	M	Farmer	08De21Cg
WILLIAMS, George		25	M	Surgeon	08De21Cg
OLLIPHANT, Henry-W.		26	M	Gentleman	08De21Cg
MOER, Mary		60	F	None	08De21Cg
Phillipp		28	M	Merchant	08De21Cg
MITCHEL, Joseph		17	M	Druggist	08De21Cg
BREM, Thos.		28	M	Weaver	08De21Cg
HERBERT, George		26	M	Gentleman	08De21Cg
JEFFERD, Margaret		26	F	Lady	08De21Cg
WHITE, John		52	M	Stctr	08De21Cg
DIBBEN, Cadella		16	F	None	08De21Cg
COLMAN, George		46	M	Farmer	08De21Cg
FITZGERALD, Ann		25	F	Farmer	08De21Cg
Mary	(D)	01	F	Child	08De21Cg
WOOD, James		38	M	Farmer	08De21Cg
JONES, Christiana		46	F	Farmer	08De21Cg
Christ.	(D)	09	F	Child	08De21Cg
Sarah	(D)	07	F	Child	08De21Cg
Laura	(D)	03	F	Child	08De21Cg

COSMO 09 DECEMBER 1846

From Bristol

NAMES OF PASSENGERS		AGE	SEX	OCCUPATIONS	DATE PORT SHIP
JANES, Ann		22	F	None	09De18Ga
Mary		28	F	None	09De18Ga
Alfred		17	M	None	09De18Ga
MIRTO, Samuel		63	M	Shoemaker	09De18Ga
Pricilla		49	F	None	09De18Ga
BIGBEE, Sarah		49	F	None	09De18Ga
Mary-A.		20	F	None	09De18Ga
TURNER, Samuel		37	M	Farmer	09De18Ga
Jane	(W)	41	F	Wife	09De18Ga
Martha	(D)	15	F	None	09De18Ga
Joseph	(S)	13	M	None	09De18Ga
Fanny	(D)	12	F	None	09De18Ga
Stephen	(S)	17	M	None	09De18Ga
BODY, Elizabeth		56	F	None	09De18Ga
Elizabeth	(D)	18	F	None	09De18Ga
HARLEY, Charlotte		35	F	None	09De18Ga
STEPHEINS, Henry		25	M	None	09De18Ga
Ann	(W)	20	F	Wife	09De18Ga
Frederick	(S)	01	M	Child	09De18Ga
BOWEN, Wm.		31	M	None	09De18Ga
Eliza	(W)	26	F	Wife	09De18Ga
Elizabeth	(D)	06	F	Child	09De18Ga
Eliza	(D)	04	F	Child	09De18Ga
Harriet	(D)	02	F	Child	09De18Ga
ELLIS, Thos.		24	M	Hrsm	09De18Ga
Elizth.	(W)	18	F	Wife	09De18Ga
Sarah	(D)	04	F	Child	09De18Ga
BIRMINGHAM, Patrick		24	M	Tailor	09De18Ga
Mary		24	F	Tailor	09De18Ga
DAY, Emily		28	F	Tailor	09De18Ga
Jane	(D)	06	F	Child	09De18Ga
Ann	(D)	02	F	Child	09De18Ga
DAVIS, Martha		42	F	None	09De18Ga

ANN-HARLEY 11 DECEMBER 1846

From Glasgow

NAMES OF PASSENGERS		AGE	SEX	OCCUPATIONS	DATE PORT SHIP
MCTOPNEY, Patrick		45	M	Weaver	11De04Db
Hannah	(W)	32	F	Wife	11De04Db
Edward	(S)	10	M	Child	11De04Db
Patrick	(S)	.10	M	Infant	11De04Db
KERROL, Edward		21	M	Iron Turner	11De04Db
MCDEVITT, Janet		03	F	None	11De04Db
MCKAY, Bridgett		19	F	Spinster	11De04Db
HARGON, Daniel		40	M	Slt-Plstr	11De04Db
HURD, Agnes-Mrs.		50	F	Unknown	11De04Db
SLEITH, U-Mrs.		24	F	None	11De04Db

QUEEN-OF-THE-WEST 11 DECEMBER 1846

From Liverpool

NAMES OF PASSENGERS		AGE	SEX	OCCUPATIONS	DATE PORT SHIP
MCQUAY, William		25	M	Joiner	11De02Cn
Catherine	(W)	23	F	Wife	11De02Cn
Thos.	(S)	06	M	Child	11De02Cn
GILBEY, Mary		50	F	None	11De02Cn
Jane	(D)	20	F	None	11De02Cn
Robert	(S)	23	M	Laborer	11De02Cn
James		26	M	Laborer	11De02Cn
WHIRRY, Biddy		20	F	None	11De02Cn
GILLESPIE, Laurence		39	M	Laborer	11De02Cn
Honore	(W)	30	F	Wife	11De02Cn
Patt	(S)	.00	M	Infant	11De02Cn
Anthony	(S)	09	M	Child	11De02Cn
HENIHER, Patt		35	M	Laborer	11De02Cn
Kitty	(W)	30	F	Wife	11De02Cn
Martin	(S)	09	M	Child	11De02Cn
Bridget	(D)	12	F	None	11De02Cn
Thos.	(S)	02	M	Child	11De02Cn
ROCHE, Leonard		20	M	Laborer	11De02Cn
DOOLAN, Peter		50	M	Laborer	11De02Cn
Martin	(S)	20	M	Laborer	11De02Cn
Mary	(D)	16	F	None	11De02Cn
WALSHE, Ellen		20	F	None	11De02Cn
DOOLAN, Bridget		13	F	None	11De02Cn
Honner		10	F	Child	11De02Cn
Ned		07	M	Child	11De02Cn
Michael		07	M	Child	11De02Cn
BARNETT, Patt		20	M	Laborer	11De02Cn
GALLAGHER, Michael		19	M	Laborer	11De02Cn
LOUGHENY, Hannah		50	F	None	11De02Cn
Bernard	(S)	19	F	Laborer	11De02Cn
Jeremiah	(S)	18	F	Laborer	11De02Cn
Ellen	(D)	17	F	Laborer	11De02Cn
Mary	(D)	16	F	Laborer	11De02Cn
Kitty	(D)	13	F	Laborer	11De02Cn
Sally	(D)	12	F	Laborer	11De02Cn
Daniel	(S)	11	M	Laborer	11De02Cn
QUINN, Thomas		50	M	Laborer	11De02Cn
Mary	(W)	50	F	Wife	11De02Cn
Florence	(D)	15	F	None	11De02Cn

NAMES OF PASSENGERS		AGE	SEX	OCCUPATIONS	DATE PORT SHIP
QUINN, John	(S)	14	M	Wife	11De02Cn
Kitty	(D)	12	F	Wife	11De02Cn
Patt	(S)	08	M	Child	11De02Cn
Michael	(S)	06	M	Child	11De02Cn
Mary	(D)	03	F	Child	11De02Cn
Thos.	(S)	.00	M	Infant	11De02Cn
Tedy		20	M	Laborer	11De02Cn
Betty		10	F	Child	11De02Cn
Bernard		40	M	Laborer	11De02Cn
Mary		50	F	Laborer	11De02Cn
Michael	(S)	09	M	Child	11De02Cn
Thos.	(S)	07	M	Child	11De02Cn
Patt	(S)	03	M	Child	11De02Cn
CLARK, Joseph		15	M	Tailor	11De02Cn
MCGUGGAN, Bernard		16	M	Laborer	11De02Cn
COLLINS, John		20	M	Laborer	11De02Cn
REILLY, Dennis		22	M	Laborer	11De02Cn
John		24	M	Laborer	11De02Cn
Frank		20	M	Laborer	11De02Cn
Bridget		18	F	Laborer	11De02Cn
SMYTH, Anne		18	F	Laborer	11De02Cn
KELLY, Anna		30	F	Laborer	11De02Cn
BRANNAN, Bridget		35	F	Laborer	11De02Cn
HODGE, Thos.		25	M	Laborer	11De02Cn
Margaret		20	F	Laborer	11De02Cn
Catherine		18	F	Laborer	11De02Cn
HIGGINS, Michael		40	M	Shoemaker	11De02Cn
U	(W)	30	F	Wife	11De02Cn
John	(S)	03	M	Child	11De02Cn
Mary	(D)	04	F	Child	11De02Cn
Catherine	(D)	02	F	Child	11De02Cn
BYRNES, Patt		46	M	Laborer	11De02Cn
U	(W)	30	F	Wife	11De02Cn
Bridget	(D)	02	F	Child	11De02Cn
HANN, Patt		30	M	Laborer	11De02Cn
U	(W)	30	F	Wife	11De02Cn
Denis	(S)	02	M	Child	11De02Cn
ALLAN, Thos.		25	M	Laborer	11De02Cn
MCENTER, James		13	M	Shoemaker	11De02Cn
MORAN, Thos.		21	M	Laborer	11De02Cn
Ellen		21	F	Laborer	11De02Cn
BAINS, Timothy		21	M	Laborer	11De02Cn
Naby		21	F	Laborer	11De02Cn
REILLY, Francis		21	M	Laborer	11De02Cn
Bridget		21	F	Laborer	11De02Cn
MCCONNER, Bridget		21	F	Laborer	11De02Cn
REYNOLDS, Catherine		21	F	Laborer	11De02Cn
NOON, Peter		25	M	Laborer	11De02Cn
EARLY, Catherine		23	F	Laborer	11De02Cn
MAYLES, James		47	M	Laborer	11De02Cn
Winney		13	F	Laborer	11De02Cn
HANLON, David		27	M	Laborer	11De02Cn
HASKIN, Anne		20	F	Laborer	11De02Cn
GUMAN, Thos.		10	M	Child	11De02Cn
MCGEVIN, Anna		19	F	Laborer	11De02Cn
RUTLIDGE, John		35	M	Laborer	11De02Cn
Nanny		21	F	Laborer	11De02Cn
SHARP, Cornelius		35	M	Laborer	11De02Cn
MCDERMOTT, Connell		16	M	Laborer	11De02Cn
GREEN, John		25	M	Laborer	11De02Cn
GALLAGHER, Barney		32	M	Laborer	11De02Cn
MCDERMOTT, John		20	M	Laborer	11De02Cn
GALLAGHER, Mary		30	F	Laborer	11De02Cn
MILLS, Robert-H.		21	M	Clerk	11De02Cn
OLIVER, Mich.		30	M	Clerk	11De02Cn
READY, Bridget		20	F	Clerk	11De02Cn
OLIVER, Margt.		26	F	Clerk	11De02Cn
Honner		20	F	Clerk	11De02Cn
MCDONAGH, Ellen		22	F	Clerk	11De02Cn
MCKALE, Bridget		18	F	Clerk	11De02Cn
CODY, John		25	M	Laborer	11De02Cn
Mary	(W)	37	F	Wife	11De02Cn
Margt.	(D)	13	F	Laborer	11De02Cn
Thos.	(S)	10	M	Laborer	11De02Cn
Chas.	(S)	09	M	Child	11De02Cn
CODY, Ellen	(D)	07	F	Child	11De02Cn
Fanny	(D)	06	F	Child	11De02Cn
Mary	(D)	05	F	Child	11De02Cn
John	(S)	04	M	Child	11De02Cn
Newcome	(S)	.00	M	Infant	11De02Cn
HARRICOCK, Alice		30	F	Laborer	11De02Cn
MALONE, Margt.		20	F	Laborer	11De02Cn
MILEY, Michl.		28	M	Laborer	11De02Cn
Catherine	(W)	28	F	Wife	11De02Cn
Margt.	(D)	.00	F	Infant	11De02Cn
COONEY, Edward		40	M	Laborer	11De02Cn
RYDER, Peter		40	M	Laborer	11De02Cn
John	(S)	13	M	Laborer	11De02Cn
Patt	(S)	11	M	Laborer	11De02Cn
MULLEN, Patt		28	M	Laborer	11De02Cn
KELLY, Bridget		24	F	Laborer	11De02Cn
WALSHE, Anthony		20	M	Laborer	11De02Cn
GLANON, Patt		21	M	Laborer	11De02Cn
ROCKE, Edward		30	M	Laborer	11De02Cn
Sarah	(W)	30	F	Wife	11De02Cn
Bridget	(D)	.00	F	Infant	11De02Cn
REDDEN, Samuel		25	M	Shoemaker	11De02Cn
Ellen		21	F	None	11De02Cn
MOONEY, Michl.		17	M	Laborer	11De02Cn
HART, Wm.		22	M	Gdnr	11De02Cn
TRACY, Jane		15	F	None	11De02Cn
MARTIN, James		27	M	Laborer	11De02Cn
HANNON, Margt.		40	F	None	11De02Cn
Margt.	(D)	17	F	None	11De02Cn
FAGAN, Thos.		22	M	Laborer	11De02Cn
CANRY, Margt.		19	F	Laborer	11De02Cn
KINLEY, Bessy		21	F	None	11De02Cn
DUFFY, John		47	M	Teacher	11De02Cn
Margt.	(W)	42	F	Wife	11De02Cn
Julia	(D)	22	F	None	11De02Cn
James	(S)	18	M	None	11De02Cn
Rose	(D)	16	F	None	11De02Cn
Mary		30	F	None	11De02Cn
Joseph		13	M	None	11De02Cn
Bryan		11	M	None	11De02Cn
Patt		08	M	Child	11De02Cn
Joshua		07	M	Child	11De02Cn
Jane		05	F	Child	11De02Cn
Mary		.00	F	Infant	11De02Cn
TYRELL, Bridget		30	F	None	11De02Cn
Catherine	(D)	.00	F	Infant	11De02Cn
DUNNEY, Peter		33	M	Laborer	11De02Cn
BROWN, Marcella		21	F	Laborer	11De02Cn
HART, Jane		19	F	Laborer	11De02Cn
BLUM, Wm.		18	M	Bricklayer	11De02Cn
HIGGINS, Catherine		21	F	None	11De02Cn
DONOHUE, Patt		25	M	Laborer	11De02Cn
Catherine	(W)	25	F	None	11De02Cn
COWEN, James		22	M	Laborer	11De02Cn
Matthew		20	M	Laborer	11De02Cn
CARRIGHE, Lettia		16	F	Laborer	11De02Cn
COWEN, Fanny		16	F	Laborer	11De02Cn
LEONAN, John		30	M	Laborer	11De02Cn
BRADY, John		20	M	Laborer	11De02Cn
MITCHELL, John		30	M	Laborer	11De02Cn
U	(W)	20	F	Wife	11De02Cn
JOHNSTONE, U		20	F	Wife	11De02Cn
MAGIN, John		40	M	Laborer	11De02Cn
KING, Mich.		28	M	Laborer	11De02Cn
Mary		28	F	Laborer	11De02Cn
MCMULLIN, Toal		30	M	Farmer	11De02Cn
Margt.	(W)	30	F	Wife	11De02Cn
Hugh	(S)	08	M	Child	11De02Cn
Francis	(S)	06	M	Child	11De02Cn
Rosan	(D)	04	F	Child	11De02Cn
James	(S)	.00	M	Infant	11De02Cn
HUGHES, Wm.		30	M	Bootmaker	11De02Cn
HUGBOD, Isaac		25	M	Merchant	11De02Cn
U	(W)	24	F	Wife	11De02Cn
DALE, George		30	M	Plumber	11De02Cn

NAMES OF PASSENGERS	A G E	S E X	OCCUPATIONS	DATE PORT SHIP
DALE, Mary	20	F	Plumber	11De02Cn
Ellen	10	F	Plumber	11De02Cn
HORN, Thos.	30	M	Laborer	11De02Cn
Rose	20	F	Laborer	11De02Cn
MCCULLIFF, Mary	25	F	Laborer	11De02Cn
FARRELL, Bridget	30	F	None	11De02Cn
Ellen (D)	06	F	Child	11De02Cn
Died-At-Sea				
MCCULLIFF, Bridget	.00	F	Infant	11De02Cn
MONAGHAN, Mary	40	F	None	11De02Cn
Ellen (D)	12	F	None	11De02Cn
Mary (D)	11	F	None	11De02Cn
James (S)	08	M	Child	11De02Cn
MCMAUS, Phillip	30	M	None	11De02Cn
MAHON, Mich.	35	M	Mason	11De02Cn
CLEGG, James	33	M	Printer	11De02Cn
MCGARRY, Anne	20	F	None	11De02Cn
BRIAN, Patt	34	M	None	11De02Cn
MORRISON, Robert	27	M	Laborer	11De02Cn
BLAIR, Rebecca	20	F	Laborer	11De02Cn
STEPHENSON, William	19	M	Weaver	11De02Cn
MCKARR, Henry	44	M	Weaver	11De02Cn
Anne (W)	46	F	Wife	11De02Cn
M.	16	U	None	11De02Cn
TAYLOR, Edward	23	M	Laborer	11De02Cn
Mary	17	F	Laborer	11De02Cn
HENRY, Saml.	44	M	None	11De02Cn
U (W)	22	F	Wife	11De02Cn
IRWIN, Joseph	35	M	Weaver	11De02Cn
Margt. (W)	30	F	Wife	11De02Cn
Mary (D)	09	F	Child	11De02Cn
Wm. (S)	07	M	Child	11De02Cn
Richard (S)	05	M	Child	11De02Cn
George (S)	02	M	Child	11De02Cn
Henry (S)	.00	M	Infant	11De02Cn
Died-At-Sea				
HENFY, Mich.	36	M	Laborer	11De02Cn
Saml.	24	M	Laborer	11De02Cn
Anne	09	F	Child	11De02Cn
Michael	07	M	Child	11De02Cn
Patt	05	M	Child	11De02Cn
HINLEY, Sarah	03	F	Child	11De02Cn
Catherine	13	F	None	11De02Cn
CHRISTY, Anne	50	F	None	11De02Cn
MCDONALD, Arthur	48	M	Weaver	11De02Cn
Mary (W)	50	F	Wife	11De02Cn
Isabella (D)	20	F	None	11De02Cn
Sarah (D)	17	F	None	11De02Cn
Allice (D)	14	F	None	11De02Cn
Margt. (D)	10	F	None	11De02Cn
MCNIELL, Stewart	22	M	Laborer	11De02Cn
HINLEY, Patt	51	M	Laborer	11De02Cn
Alice (W)	50	F	Wife	11De02Cn
Jane (D)	13	F	None	11De02Cn
Nell (S)	08	M	Child	11De02Cn
Allice (D)	03	F	Child	11De02Cn
Mary (D)	09	F	Child	11De02Cn
HENDERSON, Rebecca	60	F	None	11De02Cn
ARCHER, Eliza	21	F	None	11De02Cn
Jane	25	F	None	11De02Cn
CROTHEN, George	26	M	Farmer	11De02Cn
Ellen (W)	26	F	None	11De02Cn
BRADY, Wm.	22	M	Laborer	11De02Cn
MAMSNEY, Anne-Jane	15	F	None	11De02Cn
John	11	M	None	11De02Cn
SHEENY, John	20	M	Carpenter	11De02Cn
FALKNER, Wm.	46	M	Farmer	11De02Cn
Danl. (S)	18	M	Farmer	11De02Cn
HENDERSON, Catherine	21	F	Farmer	11De02Cn
MCKEOWN, Jas.	30	M	Clerk	11De02Cn
MCCOY, John	20	M	Clerk	11De02Cn
MASON, George	30	M	Miner	11De02Cn
KELLY, Neal	25	M	Laborer	11De02Cn
Biddy	22	F	Laborer	11De02Cn

PANTHEA 12 DECEMBER 1846

From Liverpool

NAMES OF PASSENGERS	A G E	S E X	OCCUPATIONS	DATE PORT SHIP
LAMBE, Catherine-A.	29	F	Lady	12De02Ds
D.W.Caheen (S)	10	M	None	12De02Ds
CRAWFORD, John	20	M	Laborer	12De02Ds
MCCRACKEN, John	19	M	Laborer	12De02Ds
KNOX, George	20	M	Laborer	12De02Ds
BENNETT, Jane	60	F	None	12De02Ds
Ann	33	F	None	12De02Ds
John	12	M	Laborer	12De02Ds
MCNAUGHTON, Bryan	29	M	Laborer	12De02Ds
Martin	26	M	Laborer	12De02Ds
Peter	24	M	Laborer	12De02Ds
MACKAY, Cornelius	30	M	Laborer	12De02Ds
REDBURN, Jane	35	F	None	12De02Ds
Betty (D)	08	F	Child	12De02Ds
Joseph (S)	.00	M	Infant	12De02Ds
MERRILL, Mary	24	F	None	12De02Ds
APPLEGARD, Isabella	22	F	None	12De02Ds
MCALEER, Nicholas	50	M	Laborer	12De02Ds
John	21	M	Laborer	12De02Ds
COPE, Edwin	23	M	Laborer	12De02Ds
BRADY, Owen	20	M	Laborer	12De02Ds
DUFFIELD, George	22	M	Laborer	12De02Ds
COATES, Richd.	21	M	Laborer	12De02Ds
FITSGERALD, Michl.	20	M	Laborer	12De02Ds
SHERAUGH, George	18	M	Laborer	12De02Ds
KETTLEY, Thomas	20	M	Laborer	12De02Ds
Fanny	24	F	None	12De02Ds
MALLONEY, Anslake	20	F	None	12De02Ds
MULHOLL, Judy	18	F	None	12De02Ds
RYAN, Cathne.	22	F	None	12De02Ds
HOWE, Mary	21	F	None	12De02Ds
GALLESPIE, Margaret	16	F	None	12De02Ds
MCCALL, Robert	24	M	Laborer	12De02Ds
LEACY, Cathne.	35	F	None	12De02Ds
BRADLEY, Peter	21	M	Laborer	12De02Ds
Bridget	40	F	None	12De02Ds
Honora	20	F	None	12De02Ds
Patt	17	M	None	12De02Ds
Ann	14	F	None	12De02Ds
KENNEY, Rosey	18	F	None	12De02Ds
DINOLLEN, Maragret	21	F	None	12De02Ds
WALSH, Mary	48	F	Wi	12De02Ds
REDDAN, Rosey	20	F	None	12De02Ds
MARSDEN, Nancy	30	F	None	12De02Ds
Jane (D)	02	F	Child	12De02Ds
HARSON, Mary	50	F	None	12De02Ds
JOHNSTON, James	26	M	Laborer	12De02Ds
FREANY, Mary	18	F	None	12De02Ds
CONLON, Biddy	25	F	None	12De02Ds
DUNOLLY, Patt	26	M	Laborer	12De02Ds
Mary (W)	24	F	Wife	12De02Ds
Patt (S)	03	M	Child	12De02Ds
Owen (S)	.00	M	Infant	12De02Ds
MULLEN, Rose	12	F	None	12De02Ds
MCCONNOR, John	22	M	None	12De02Ds
BOWAN, Michael	20	M	None	12De02Ds
DOLAN, Alice	15	F	None	12De02Ds
MCNAMARA, Daniel	20	M	None	12De02Ds
MCPARLAIN, Charles	40	M	Laborer	12De02Ds
Biddy (D)	20	M	None	12De02Ds
Patt (S)	13	M	None	12De02Ds
Anne (D)	12	F	None	12De02Ds
John (S)	10	M	None	12De02Ds
James (S)	08	M	Child	12De02Ds
BAXTER, Patt	20	M	Laborer	12De02Ds

NAMES OF PASSENGERS		AGE	SEX	OCCUPATIONS	DATE PORT SHIP
BAXTER, Mary		40	F	None	12De02Ds
Mary		21	F	None	12De02Ds
Rosanna		14	F	None	12De02Ds
Tersia		11	F	None	12De02Ds
Thomas		09	M	Child	12De02Ds
MCKERNAN, Ann		20	F	None	12De02Ds
MCCARTAN, Anne		20	F	None	12De02Ds
BAXTER, Bridget		20	F	None	12De02Ds
MCNAMARA, Jane		19	F	Laborer	12De02Ds
WHITE, John		40	M	Laborer	12De02Ds
Bridget		37	F	None	12De02Ds
Mary		36	F	None	12De02Ds
Thomas		30	M	Laborer	12De02Ds
Janet		27	F	None	12De02Ds
Michael		26	M	Laborer	12De02Ds
John		24	M	Laborer	12De02Ds
Bessy		21	F	None	12De02Ds
Margaret		19	F	None	12De02Ds
Mary		18	F	None	12De02Ds
FOLLIN, Thomas		20	M	Laborer	12De02Ds
KING, Thomas		26	M	Laborer	12De02Ds
NEWLAN, Anne		27	F	None	12De02Ds
KING, Bridget		03	F	Child	12De02Ds
Margaret		02	F	Child	12De02Ds
John		.00	M	Infant	12De02Ds
DONOHOE, Mary		25	F	None	12De02Ds
COLLOE, Rose		22	F	None	12De02Ds
MCFARLANE, Alice		32	F	None	12De02Ds
MCNELLS, Bridget		25	F	None	12De02Ds
LYNCH, Patt		22	M	Laborer	12De02Ds
LEA, Michael		24	M	Laborer	12De02Ds
Sarah		44	F	None	12De02Ds
CONNOR, John		24	M	Laborer	12De02Ds
Biddy		20	F	None	12De02Ds
Mary		19	F	None	12De02Ds
MCDERMOTT, Thomas		19	M	None	12De02Ds
MULROY, John		19	M	None	12De02Ds
GOULDING, Harriet		20	F	None	12De02Ds
CAWN, James		24	M	Laborer	12De02Ds
WALLON, David		19	M	Laborer	12De02Ds
HUGHES, Arthur		45	M	Laborer	12De02Ds
Bridget	(W)	40	F	Wife	12De02Ds
Bridget	(D)	17	F	None	12De02Ds
Peter	(S)	09	M	Child	12De02Ds
Arthur	(S)	08	M	Child	12De02Ds
Susan	(D)	06	F	Child	12De02Ds
William	(S)	03	M	Child	12De02Ds
BRYAN, Patt		21	M	None	12De02Ds
MALLY, Bridget		18	F	None	12De02Ds
IRELAND, Eliza		17	F	None	12De02Ds
BARNETT, Thomas		30	M	Laborer	12De02Ds
PHELAN, Patrick		23	M	Laborer	12De02Ds
DAVINE, Michael		24	M	Laborer	12De02Ds
MCCARWIN, Michael		36	M	Laborer	12De02Ds
DOUGHERTY, John		25	M	Laborer	12De02Ds
KING, Patt		32	M	Laborer	12De02Ds
Sarah		23	F	None	12De02Ds
Bridget		22	F	None	12De02Ds
HAY, Francis		40	M	Laborer	12De02Ds
U	(W)	40	F	Wife	12De02Ds
HURLEY, Margt.		29	F	None	12De02Ds
KEEFE, Maria		22	F	None	12De02Ds
Bridget		20	F	None	12De02Ds
CALLAGHAN, John		26	M	Laborer	12De02Ds
NUGENT, Mary		30	F	None	12De02Ds
Ann		20	F	None	12De02Ds
FITZIMMONS, Patt		25	M	Laborer	12De02Ds
NISBETT, Joseph		40	M	Laborer	12De02Ds
U	(W)	30	F	Wife	12De02Ds
Sarah		60	F	None	12De02Ds
John	(S)	03	M	Child	12De02Ds
Mary-Anne	(D)	02	F	Child	12De02Ds
Jane	(D)	.00	F	Infant	12De02Ds
LORD, John		36	M	Laborer	12De02Ds
RILEY, Terence		23	M	Laborer	12De02Ds
RILEY, U	(W)	24	F	Wife	12De02Ds
COYLE, Rosey		16	F	None	12De02Ds
Bernard		24	M	Laborer	12De02Ds
U	(W)	22	F	Wife	12De02Ds
James		08	M	Child	12De02Ds
Patrick		.00	M	Infant	12De02Ds
QUIN, Patt		30	M	Laborer	12De02Ds
MCARTHUR, Gilbert		31	M	Laborer	12De02Ds
RILEY, Dan		50	M	Laborer	12De02Ds
EWAN, William		22	M	Laborer	12De02Ds
RILEY, Rose		36	F	None	12De02Ds
MCNAMEE, William		22	M	None	12De02Ds
BACON, George		19	M	None	12De02Ds
William		45	M	Laborer	12De02Ds
Anne		40	F	None	12De02Ds
Mary		17	F	None	12De02Ds
James		06	M	Child	12De02Ds
Robert		11	M	None	12De02Ds
MCGLUCHY, James		24	M	Laborer	12De02Ds
BEAGON, John		35	M	Laborer	12De02Ds
REGAN, Mary		30	F	None	12De02Ds
Elizabeth	(D)	05	F	Child	12De02Ds
Dennis	(S)	03	M	Child	12De02Ds
LYDEN, Ann		19	F	None	12De02Ds
GREY, Bryan		30	M	Laborer	12De02Ds
U	(W)	26	F	Wife	12De02Ds
Michael	(S)	04	M	Child	12De02Ds
Peter	(S)	.00	M	Infant	12De02Ds
Margaret		17	F	None	12De02Ds
PEATON, John		26	M	Laborer	12De02Ds
U	(W)	24	F	Wife	12De02Ds
KERWIN, Richard		25	M	Laborer	12De02Ds
Fanny		22	F	None	12De02Ds
Joseph		10	M	None	12De02Ds
HICKEY, Bridget		16	F	None	12De02Ds
WELDEN, David		20	M	Laborer	12De02Ds
Isabella		20	F	None	12De02Ds
Esther		40	F	None	12De02Ds
		Died-At-Sea			
Charlotte		08	F	Child	12De02Ds
EAGEN, Michael		18	M	None	12De02Ds
Morris		18	M	None	12De02Ds
FOX, Hugh		22	M	Laborer	12De02Ds
GROWNEY, Owen		26	M	Laborer	12De02Ds
FOX, Ann		18	F	None	12De02Ds
William		10	M	None	12De02Ds
DOUGHERTY, Margaret		19	F	None	12De02Ds
DUNOVAN, Patt		30	M	Laborer	12De02Ds
CRAWFORD, Thomas		35	M	Laborer	12De02Ds
MAGUIRE, Patt		21	M	Laborer	12De02Ds
FURNEY, James		22	M	Laborer	12De02Ds
HAYDEN, Judith		20	F	None	12De02Ds
SHERIDAN, Patt		23	M	None	12De02Ds
Jane		17	F	None	12De02Ds
HEALY, John		32	M	Laborer	12De02Ds
Anne	(W)	30	F	Wife	12De02Ds
John	(S)	08	M	Child	12De02Ds
CARLY, Margaret		30	F	None	12De02Ds
KENNY, William		30	M	Laborer	12De02Ds
U	(W)	25	F	Wife	12De02Ds
Mary-Anne	(D)	.00	F	Infant	12De02Ds
MCGOWAN, Mary		11	F	None	12De02Ds
RILEY, Owen		30	M	Laborer	12De02Ds
SCOLLEY, Mary		20	F	None	12De02Ds
CREATON, Catherine		20	F	None	12De02Ds
NAUGHTON, Jane		22	F	None	12De02Ds
Anne		14	F	None	12De02Ds
Mary		20	F	None	12De02Ds
QUINN, Felix		30	M	Laborer	12De02Ds
POPE, Stephen		24	M	Laborer	12De02Ds
BRANKS, William		24	M	Laborer	12De02Ds
DOUGHERTY, Andrew		70	M	Laborer	12De02Ds
MCKENNA, Margaret		21	F	None	12De02Ds
Nancy		55	F	None	12De02Ds
Patt		26	M	Laborer	12De02Ds

NAMES OF PASSENGERS		A G E	S E X	OCCUPATIONS	DATE PORT SHIP
MCKENNA, Maggy	(T)	22	F	None	12De02Ds
CONNOR, Watt		19	M	None	12De02Ds
DOGHERTY, Judy		.00	F	Infant	12De02Ds
LAIRD, Mary		26	F	None	12De02Ds
WITHERTON, Mary		26	F	None	12De02Ds
CUNNINGHAM, Patt		40	M	Laborer	12De02Ds
Rosey	(W)	35	F	Wife	12De02Ds
Mary	(D)	10	F	Child	12De02Ds
Ann	(D)	08	F	Child	12De02Ds
Cella	(D)	06	F	Child	12De02Ds
Andrew	(S)	04	M	Child	12De02Ds
Patt	(S)	.00	M	Infant	12De02Ds
KERR, James		24	M	Laborer	12De02Ds
U	(W)	30	F	Wife	12De02Ds
MORGAN, John		27	M	Laborer	12De02Ds
RYAN, Michael		28	M	Laborer	12De02Ds
DONNEGHAN, John		56	M	Laborer	12De02Ds
U	(W)	56	F	Wife	12De02Ds
Mary	(D)	30	F	None	12De02Ds
Ann	(D)	21	F	None	12De02Ds
James	(S)	19	M	None	12De02Ds
William	(S)	13	M	None	12De02Ds
HIGGINS, U-Mrs.		40	F	None	12De02Ds
W.	(H)	40	M	Laborer	12De02Ds
Marla	(D)	18	F	None	12De02Ds
Eliza	(D)	16	F	None	12De02Ds
Bedella	(D)	06	F	Child	12De02Ds
Ann	(D)	04	F	Child	12De02Ds
Susan	(D)	03	F	Child	12De02Ds
Theresa	(D)	.00	F	Infant	12De02Ds
FAHEY, Pat		20	M	Laborer	12De02Ds
SCHOLLEY, Peter		30	M	Laborer	12De02Ds
Pat		20	M	Laborer	12De02Ds
SPENGEROSS, David		30	M	Laborer	12De02Ds
HEARSON, Pat		19	M	Laborer	12De02Ds
DOOGAN, Peter		19	M	Laborer	12De02Ds
James		40	M	Laborer	12De02Ds
GALLAGHER, Harry		35	M	Laborer	12De02Ds
WALKER, William		30	M	Laborer	12De02Ds
GILL, Peter		21	M	Laborer	12De02Ds
PATON, John		19	M	Laborer	12De02Ds
Mary		17	F	None	12De02Ds

FRANCONIA 14 DECEMBER 1846

From Liverpool

NAMES OF PASSENGERS		A G E	S E X	OCCUPATIONS	DATE PORT SHIP
GAFFNEY, Michl.		18	M	Laborer	14De02Jr
Bridget		16	F	Laborer	14De02Jr
Cathrine		13	F	Laborer	14De02Jr
Ellen		12	F	Laborer	14De02Jr
Betsey		06	F	Child	14De02Jr
Margaret		05	F	Child	14De02Jr
MCDONNELL, William		45	M	Laborer	14De02Jr
U	(W)	34	F	Wife	14De02Jr
Margaret	(D)	05	F	Child	14De02Jr
John	(S)	03	M	Child	14De02Jr
Cornellus	(S)	.00	M	Infant	14De02Jr
TAYLOR, William		25	M	Laborer	14De02Jr
Margaret	(M)	58	F	Laborer	14De02Jr
Margaret	(T)	25	F	Laborer	14De02Jr
Patrick	(B)	22	M	Laborer	14De02Jr
Dennis	(B)	17	M	Laborer	14De02Jr
FRASIER, Francis		20	M	Laborer	14De02Jr
Marla		20	F	Laborer	14De02Jr
GREEN, John		40	M	Shoemaker	14De02Jr
Mary	(D)	12	F	Shoemaker	14De02Jr
Patrick	(S)	10	M	Shoemaker	14De02Jr
Peter	(S)	08	M	Child	14De02Jr

NAMES OF PASSENGERS		A G E	S E X	OCCUPATIONS	DATE PORT SHIP
GREEN, Ann	(D)	06	F	Child	14De02Jr
John	(S)	04	M	Child	14De02Jr
BRUNE, Michl.		25	M	Laborer	14De02Jr
Biddy		18	F	Laborer	14De02Jr
MURPHY, Alex.		15	M	Laborer	14De02Jr
BYERS, Sarah		45	F	Servant	14De02Jr
John	(S)	16	M	Servant	14De02Jr
Ellen	(D)	13	F	Servant	14De02Jr
Margaret	(D)	11	F	Servant	14De02Jr
MCNICHOLL, Walter		20	M	Laborer	14De02Jr
Mary	(W)	20	F	Wife	14De02Jr
Patrick	(S)	.00	M	Infant	14De02Jr
				Died-At-Sea	
DONLAN, James		26	M	Laborer	14De02Jr
Patrick		24	M	Laborer	14De02Jr
COGIER, Cathrine		25	F	Servant	14De02Jr
DOWLAN, Bridget		24	F	Servant	14De02Jr
BRETT, Ellen		22	F	Dressmaker	14De02Jr
MCHUGH, Mary		20	F	Servant	14De02Jr
BOYLE, Ann		20	F	Servant	14De02Jr
NAUN, Eliza		46	F	Servant	14De02Jr
Jane	(D)	21	F	Servant	14De02Jr
Wm.	(S)	16	M	Servant	14De02Jr
Margaret	(D)	16	F	Servant	14De02Jr
Eliza	(D)	13	F	Servant	14De02Jr
SMITH, Jane		25	F	Servant	14De02Jr
NAWN, George		11	M	Servant	14De02Jr
SHARP, Robert		18	M	Servant	14De02Jr
Beny		22	F	Servant	14De02Jr
Edward		21	M	Servant	14De02Jr
DEVENEY, Cathrine		16	F	Servant	14De02Jr
CAMPBELL, John		28	M	Laborer	14De02Jr
Robt.		30	M	Laborer	14De02Jr
MCQUEENEY, Pat		29	M	Laborer	14De02Jr
MCDERMOTT, Patrick		30	M	Laborer	14De02Jr
KENNEDY, Alex		23	M	Laborer	14De02Jr
FITZPATRICK, Mary		18	F	Servant	14De02Jr
BREMER, Edward		20	M	Laborer	14De02Jr
GANNON, Patrick		20	M	Laborer	14De02Jr
DOWLAN, Eleanor		30	F	Servant	14De02Jr
MONTGOMERY, John		27	M	Laborer	14De02Jr
DOYLE, Mary		19	F	Servant	14De02Jr
SMITH, Phillipp		21	M	Laborer	14De02Jr
ROE, Patrick		20	M	Laborer	14De02Jr
SMITH, Alex		21	M	Laborer	14De02Jr
ROCK, Mary		20	F	Servant	14De02Jr
MADDEN, Patrick		55	M	Laborer	14De02Jr
James		20	M	Laborer	14De02Jr
Michl.		09	M	Child	14De02Jr
Bridget		16	F	Laborer	14De02Jr
Cathrine		15	F	Laborer	14De02Jr
Margaret		11	F	Laborer	14De02Jr
WELSCH, Michl.		20	M	Laborer	14De02Jr
COLNEY, Thomas		20	M	Laborer	14De02Jr
MALEY, John		20	M	Laborer	14De02Jr
DARGEN, John		30	M	Weaver	14De02Jr
REILLY, Ellen		18	F	Servant	14De02Jr
Cathrine		20	F	Servant	14De02Jr
DELANY, Charles		55	M	Laborer	14De02Jr
U	(W)	50	F	Servant	14De02Jr
Charles	(S)	25	M	Servant	14De02Jr
Ann	(D)	21	F	Servant	14De02Jr
Biddy	(D)	19	F	Servant	14De02Jr
John	(S)	17	M	Servant	14De02Jr
Marsen	(S)	13	M	Servant	14De02Jr
Joseph	(S)	12	M	Servant	14De02Jr
TRACY, Ellen		46	F	Servant	14De02Jr
Edward	(S)	22	M	Servant	14De02Jr
Ann	(D)	20	F	Servant	14De02Jr
Ellen	(D)	13	F	Servant	14De02Jr
James	(S)	17	M	Servant	14De02Jr
Mary	(D)	12	F	Servant	14De02Jr
SCULLY, Daniel		21	M	Laborer	14De02Jr
WOOD, John		22	M	Weaver	14De02Jr
Patrick		18	M	Weaver	14De02Jr

NAMES OF PASSENGERS		AGE	SEX	OCCUPATIONS	DATE PORT SHIP
WOOD, Mary		24	F	Weaver	14De02Jr
Died-At-Sea					
Margt.		20	F	Weaver	14De02Jr
SCRAIVS, Patrick		25	M	Laborer	14De02Jr
COWAN, Luke		50	M	Laborer	14De02Jr
U	(W)	50	F	Servant	14De02Jr
KNOEKTAN, Martin		50	M	Laborer	14De02Jr
HAFFORD, Michael		22	M	Laborer	14De02Jr
Mary		23	F	Laborer	14De02Jr
MCCULLOCK, Alexand.		26	M	Laborer	14De02Jr
David		00	M	Laborer	14De02Jr
Jane		23	F	Laborer	14De02Jr
John		.00	M	Infant	14De02Jr
KILROY, Hugh		30	M	Laborer	14De02Jr
MCELVER, Patrick		25	M	Laborer	14De02Jr
HEARY, John		19	M	Laborer	14De02Jr
Philipp		16	M	Laborer	14De02Jr
MCELGREEN, Jeremiah		20	M	Laborer	14De02Jr
Biddy		21	F	Servant	14De02Jr
MARROW, Sarah		18	F	Servant	14De02Jr
FORSEDE, Richard		13	M	Laborer	14De02Jr
MALEY, William		17	M	Laborer	14De02Jr
NALLY, Ann		20	F	Servant	14De02Jr
MURTAGH, John		22	M	Laborer	14De02Jr
FRAZE, Bernard		28	M	Laborer	14De02Jr
Ann	(W)	21	F	Wife	14De02Jr
Andrew	(S)	.00	M	Infant	14De02Jr
MURPHY, Robert		30	M	Laborer	14De02Jr
MARTEN, Thomas		20	M	Laborer	14De02Jr
Mary-Ann		19	F	Servant	14De02Jr
CORLIS, William		20	M	Mason	14De02Jr
VELCH, Mary		27	F	Servant	14De02Jr
Eliza		11	F	Servant	14De02Jr
William		09	M	Child	14De02Jr
GRAHAM, Cathrine		23	F	Servant	14De02Jr
MONAGHAM, James		22	M	Laborer	14De02Jr
STURGEON, Thomas		23	M	Laborer	14De02Jr
GREEHAN, Mary		21	F	Servant	14De02Jr
MCDONNELL, Mary		20	F	Servant	14De02Jr
WELSCH, Mary		22	F	Servant	14De02Jr
GALLAGHER, Edward		24	M	Laborer	14De02Jr
DOHERTY, Patrick		24	M	Laborer	14De02Jr
CAMOCK, Frank		21	M	Laborer	14De02Jr
DUNN, Mathew		19	M	Laborer	14De02Jr
Eleanor		17	F	Laborer	14De02Jr
GAVIN, Thomas		19	M	Laborer	14De02Jr
FLYNN, Patrick		22	M	Laborer	14De02Jr
CORCAN, Patrick		24	M	Laborer	14De02Jr
LOUTH, Pat		20	M	Laborer	14De02Jr
TYSON, Henry		40	M	Laborer	14De02Jr
GALLAGHER, Ann		30	F	Servant	14De02Jr
KING, John		22	M	Laborer	14De02Jr
Margaret		20	F	Laborer	14De02Jr
BRINNINGHAM, Margt.		20	F	Laborer	14De02Jr
HARRIS, Edward		22	M	Silversmith	14De02Jr
Eliza		20	F	Silversmith	14De02Jr
NEATSH, John		20	M	Shoemaker	14De02Jr
LOFTUS, Daniel		24	M	Laborer	14De02Jr
KELLY, Lawrence		24	M	Tailor	14De02Jr
PHALAN, Eliza		20	F	Servant	14De02Jr
BRACELAN, Pat		25	M	Laborer	14De02Jr
CARL, Bartly		18	M	Laborer	14De02Jr
William	(P)	36	M	Shoemaker	14De02Jr
Margery	(M)	30	F	Shoemaker	14De02Jr
Cathrine	(T)	16	F	Shoemaker	14De02Jr
Robert	(B)	14	M	Shoemaker	14De02Jr
Elizabeth	(T)	12	F	Shoemaker	14De02Jr
Sarah-Ann	(T)	09	F	Child	14De02Jr
William	(B)	07	M	Child	14De02Jr
Stephen	(B)	03	M	Child	14De02Jr
HALL, William		24	M	Laborer	14De02Jr
MILES, Thos.		20	M	Laborer	14De02Jr
U	(W)	20	F	Servant	14De02Jr
Maria	(D)	.00	F	Infant	14De02Jr
OGARD, James		30	M	Laborer	14De02Jr
OGARD, U	(W)	30	F	Wife	14De02Jr
Mary		20	F	Laborer	14De02Jr
James	(S)	04	M	Child	14De02Jr
MCGLOWER, Michael		27	M	Blacksmith	14De02Jr
MCDONNELL, Bridget		40	F	Servant	14De02Jr
ODOWD, Patrick		20	M	Carpenter	14De02Jr
MCGHENE, U-Mrs.		27	F	Servant	14De02Jr
OBRIEN, Pat		24	M	Laborer	14De02Jr
HEALEY, Pat		19	M	Laborer	14De02Jr
HAMDEN, John		34	M	Farmer	14De02Jr
U	(W)	00	F	Wife	14De02Jr

SHERIDAN 15 DECEMBER 1846

From Liverpool

NAMES OF PASSENGERS		AGE	SEX	OCCUPATIONS	DATE PORT SHIP
FLOOD, U-Mrs.		25	F	None	15De02Do
HAM, John		25	M	Laborer	15De02Do
REILY, John		30	M	Laborer	15De02Do
DONELSON, Martin		30	M	Laborer	15De02Do
DONNELLAN, Thos.		25	M	Laborer	15De02Do
FINIGAN, John		22	M	Laborer	15De02Do
MCGRANE, Christopher		28	M	Laborer	15De02Do
MCCULLOUGH, Jas.		30	M	Laborer	15De02Do
U		18	F	None	15De02Do
MCBRIDE, U-Mrs.		22	F	Laborer	15De02Do
U		25	M	Laborer	15De02Do
CONNELL, A.Mrs.		25	F	Laborer	15De02Do
SMITH, Bridget		20	F	Domestic	15De02Do
ROURKE, John		21	M	Laborer	15De02Do
MEIHAN, Patt		22	M	Laborer	15De02Do
MCCANN, Michl.		22	M	Laborer	15De02Do
KANE, Cathn.		18	F	Domestic	15De02Do
LYNCH, Margt.		16	F	Domestic	15De02Do
WHALAN, Danl.		25	M	Laborer	15De02Do
CROONAN, John		27	M	Laborer	15De02Do
SHEPPARD, U-Mrs.		38	F	Laborer	15De02Do
Peter	(H)	38	M	Laborer	15De02Do
Cathn.	(D)	20	F	Laborer	15De02Do
Harriet	(D)	18	F	Laborer	15De02Do
Elizabeth	(D)	16	F	Laborer	15De02Do
Jane	(D)	14	F	Laborer	15De02Do
Margt.	(D)	12	F	Laborer	15De02Do
Maria	(D)	02	F	Child	15De02Do
OBRIEN, U		20	F	Laborer	15De02Do
Michl.		25	M	Laborer	15De02Do
SCULLY, Peter		26	M	Laborer	15De02Do
Timothy		24	M	Laborer	15De02Do
MCDONNELL, Ellen		18	F	Laborer	15De02Do
MURRY, U	(W)	30	F	Wife	15De02Do
Peter	(S)	16	M	Laborer	15De02Do
Cathn.	(D)	12	F	Laborer	15De02Do
Wm.	(S)	04	M	Child	15De02Do
SLOANE, John		28	M	Unknown	15De02Do
THORP, Jane		25	F	Domestic	15De02Do
Mary		23	F	Domestic	15De02Do
GRADY, Terrance		25	M	Laborer	15De02Do
CONNORS, Mary		24	F	None	15De02Do
CLARK, Wm.		20	M	None	15De02Do
DUFFY, Patt.		25	M	None	15De02Do
CONROY, James		35	M	None	15De02Do
U	(W)	32	F	Wife	15De02Do
Ann	(D)	10	F	Child	15De02Do
Mary	(D)	09	F	Child	15De02Do
John	(S)	07	M	Child	15De02Do
Thos.	(S)	06	M	Child	15De02Do
PIERCE, Anne		16	F	None	15De02Do
Mary		16	F	None	15De02Do
AGNEW, Thos.		35	M	Driller	15De02Do

NAMES OF PASSENGERS		AGE	SEX	OCCUPATIONS	DATE PORT SHIP
AGNEW, Eleanor	(W)	32	F	Wife	15De02Do
Hugh	(S)	10	M	Child	15De02Do
Cathr.	(D)	08	F	Child	15De02Do
FOSTER, Wm.		35	M	Farmer	15De02Do
U	(W)	34	F	Wife	15De02Do
Jas.	(S)	15	M	Farmer	15De02Do
Thos.	(S)	12	M	Farmer	15De02Do
Elizabeth	(D)	10	F	Farmer	15De02Do
LEPPER, Wm.		30	M	None	15De02Do
LENNON, John		30	M	Laborer	15De02Do
MUNNIN, Jas.		25	M	None	15De02Do
BRUCE, David		28	M	None	15De02Do
GARDNER, Geo.		28	M	None	15De02Do
POWER, Patt		30	M	Farmer	15De02Do
U	(W)	28	F	Wife	15De02Do
Bridget	(D)	06	F	Child	15De02Do
Nicholas	(S)	04	M	Child	15De02Do
Jane	(D)	03	F	Child	15De02Do
FITZPATRICK, Patt		30	M	Blacksmith	15De02Do
MCCABE, Michl.		25	M	None	15De02Do
REILY, Thos.		21	M	None	15De02Do
LAVERY, Francis		25	M	Laborer	15De02Do
REILY, Patt		24	M	None	15De02Do
RUDDEN, John		25	M	None	15De02Do
MULLIGAN, Judith		18	F	Servant	15De02Do
LLYNCH, Judith		18	F	Servant	15De02Do
FITZOMONS, Ellen		18	F	Servant	15De02Do
MCGOVAN, Jas.		16	M	Servant	15De02Do
COYNE, Patt		30	M	Farmer	15De02Do
U	(W)	29	F	Wife	15De02Do
Mch.	(S)	08	M	Child	15De02Do
Bridget	(D)	07	F	Child	15De02Do
Patt	(S)	05	M	Child	15De02Do
KANE, Thos.		22	M	Laborer	15De02Do
U	(W)	20	F	Wife	15De02Do
Mary	(D)	02	F	Child	15De02Do
DOLAN, Mary-Ann		28	F	Domestic	15De02Do
MONAGAN, Mary		25	F	Domestic	15De02Do
FLYNN, Nabby		18	F	Domestic	15De02Do
CONROY, Patk.		24	M	None	15De02Do
U	(W)	20	F	Wife	15De02Do
Thos.	(S)	02	M	Child	15De02Do
John	(S)	.09	M	Infant	15De02Do
GROGAN, Michl.		30	M	Laborer	15De02Do
LALLY, Martin		28	M	Laborer	15De02Do
GOVAN, Jas.		25	M	Laborer	15De02Do
MCDERNOT, Cath.		18	F	Domestic	15De02Do
KENNY, Patt		20	M	Laborer	15De02Do
HICKEY, Elizabeth		18	F	Domestic	15De02Do
LYNCH, Philip		20	M	Laborer	15De02Do
PARTLAN, Mary		18	F	Domestic	15De02Do
COLMAN, David		30	M	Laborer	15De02Do
U	(W)	28	F	Wife	15De02Do
Mary	(D)	10	F	Child	15De02Do
Patk.	(S)	08	M	Child	15De02Do
John	(S)	06	M	Child	15De02Do
Cecily	(D)	04	F	Child	15De02Do
HOWLEY, Cathn.		18	F	Laborer	15De02Do
MCGINNIS, Bridget		18	F	Domestic	15De02Do
Charles		17	M	Laborer	15De02Do
GRIFFIN, John		20	M	Musician	15De02Do
KILBRIDE, Lawrence		30	M	Laborer	15De02Do
LYNCH, Wm.		30	M	Laborer	15De02Do
RYAN, Patt		25	M	Laborer	15De02Do
FAHY, Patt		25	M	Laborer	15De02Do
BRYAN, John		24	M	Laborer	15De02Do
LYNCH, Cathr.		18	F	Domestic	15De02Do
SMITH, Margt.		18	F	Domestic	15De02Do
CURLEY, Barth.		35	M	Farmer	15De02Do
U	(W)	34	F	Wife	15De02Do
Peter	(S)	16	M	Farmer	15De02Do
Bridget	(D)	15	F	Farmer	15De02Do
Honora	(D)	12	F	Farmer	15De02Do
Michl.	(S)	10	M	Child	15De02Do
Cathn.	(D)	08	F	Child	15De02Do
CURLEY, Patt	(S)	04	M	Child	15De02Do
CUNINGHAM, Ann		20	F	Domestic	15De02Do
MATHEWS, Susan		20	F	Domestic	15De02Do
ROURKE, Jas.		40	M	Farmer	15De02Do
FOX, Michl.		38	M	Farmer	15De02Do
U	(W)	34	F	Wife	15De02Do
Patk.	(S)	14	M	Farmer	15De02Do
Mary	(D)	12	F	Farmer	15De02Do
Anne	(D)	10	F	Child	15De02Do
Michl.	(S)	08	M	Child	15De02Do
Francis	(S)	06	M	Child	15De02Do
James	(S)	04	M	Child	15De02Do
Margt.	(D)	02	F	Child	15De02Do
John	(S)	01	M	Child	15De02Do
BREMNAN, Wm.		30	M	Laborer	15De02Do
HAM, U-Mrs.		20	F	Laborer	15De02Do
LEONARD, Jas.		25	M	Laborer	15De02Do
MCGLOUGHLIN, Sally		25	F	Laborer	15De02Do
Wm.		27	M	Laborer	15De02Do
GORMAN, Francis		28	M	Laborer	15De02Do
U	(W)	26	F	Wife	15De02Do

GAZELLE 17 DECEMBER 1846

From St.JOHN,Cape Nf.

NAMES OF PASSENGERS		AGE	SEX	OCCUPATIONS	DATE PORT SHIP
BYRNE, James		30	M	Mechanic	17De77Ju
Helen	(W)	27	F	Wife	17De77Ju
James	(S)	01	M	Child	17De77Ju
CONNOR, M.		30	F	None	17De77Ju

PONTIAC 21 DECEMBER 1846

From Liverpool

NAMES OF PASSENGERS		AGE	SEX	OCCUPATIONS	DATE PORT SHIP
WILSON, James		49	M	Farmer	21De02Jw
Elizabeth	(W)	50	F	Wife	21De02Jw
Mary	(D)	24	F	Farmer	21De02Jw
James	(S)	20	M	Farmer	21De02Jw
Susannah	(D)	18	F	Farmer	21De02Jw
Martha	(D)	12	F	Farmer	21De02Jw
William	(S)	13	M	Farmer	21De02Jw
Robert	(S)	10	M	Child	21De02Jw
Joseph	(S)	08	M	Child	21De02Jw
Jane	(D)	06	F	Child	21De02Jw
Frederick	(S)	04	M	Child	21De02Jw
Jeanette	(D)	01	F	Child	21De02Jw
Died-At-Sea					
GAHARRIAN, Patrick		23	M	Farmer	21De02Jw
DAVY, Teddy		30	M	Farmer	21De02Jw
Eleanor	(W)	30	F	Wife	21De02Jw
Anna	(D)	01	F	Child	21De02Jw
THOMPSON, John		24	M	Sthmkr	21De02Jw
Margaret		22	F	Sthmkr	21De02Jw
FITZSIMMONS, Michael		45	M	Farmer	21De02Jw
Died-At-Sea					
Rose	(W)	44	F	Wife	21De02Jw
Ann	(D)	17	F	Farmer	21De02Jw
Rose	(D)	16	F	Farmer	21De02Jw
Kathleen	(D)	08	F	Child	21De02Jw
John	(S)	13	M	Farmer	21De02Jw
HAGAN, Michael		38	M	Farmer	21De02Jw
Died-At-Sea					

NAMES OF PASSENGERS		AGE	SEX	OCCUPATIONS	DATE PORT SHIP
WHITE, John		27	M	Farmer	21De02Jw
FITZPATRICK, John		37	M	Farmer	21De02Jw
SMITH, James		32	M	Farmer	21De02Jw
DELANY, Judy		30	F	Dressmaker	21De02Jw
CRUIKSHANKS, Esther		17	F	Servant	21De02Jw
BRADY, Sarah		22	F	Servant	21De02Jw
COMASKEE, Mary		18	F	Servant	21De02Jw
WARD, Thomas		55	M	Farmer	21De02Jw
Betsy	(D)	18	F	Farmer	21De02Jw
Michael	(S)	11	M	Farmer	21De02Jw
DONNAHOO, Michael		24	M	Farmer	21De02Jw
FLANNIGAN, Charles-Jr.		21	M	Farmer	21De02Jw
Bridget		17	F	Servant	21De02Jw
WEST, Ann		18	F	Servant	21De02Jw
MCGUIRE, Patrick		19	M	Baker	21De02Jw
Rose		20	F	Baker	21De02Jw
FLANNIGAN, Charles-Sen		60	M	Farmer	21De02Jw
Ann		60	F	Farmer	21De02Jw
Died-At-Sea					
ONEILL, James		20	M	Laborer	21De02Jw
WINTER, Patrick		18	M	Laborer	21De02Jw
BYRNE, John		18	M	Laborer	21De02Jw
BROWN, John		25	M	Laborer	21De02Jw
EATON, Michael		30	M	Laborer	21De02Jw
RONAN, John		20	M	Laborer	21De02Jw
BRANNAN, John		24	M	Laborer	21De02Jw
MARTIN, Patrick		25	M	Laborer	21De02Jw
KENNEDY, Patrick		24	M	Laborer	21De02Jw
Thomas		20	M	Laborer	21De02Jw
TYRE, John		21	M	Laborer	21De02Jw
MONNAGAN, Michael		18	M	Laborer	21De02Jw
MCLAUGHLIN, William		42	M	Shoemaker	21De02Jw
Margery	(W)	36	F	Wife	21De02Jw
Nancy	(D)	16	F	Shoemaker	21De02Jw
Sarah	(D)	15	F	None	21De02Jw
Eleanor	(D)	14	F	None	21De02Jw
Jane	(D)	13	F	None	21De02Jw
Mary	(D)	12	F	None	21De02Jw
Died-At-Sea					
Katherine	(D)	10	F	Child	21De02Jw
Bernard	(S)	09	M	Child	21De02Jw
James	(S)	07	M	Child	21De02Jw
Margaret	(D)	06	F	Child	21De02Jw
Margery	(D)	04	F	Child	21De02Jw
Rosanna	(D)	02	F	Child	21De02Jw
James		40	M	Shoemaker	21De02Jw
CASILLAN, Patrick		30	M	Farmer	21De02Jw
Bridget		20	F	Farmer	21De02Jw
MOGANN, Catherine		30	F	Servant	21De02Jw
FLAHARTY, Sarah		15	F	Servant	21De02Jw
NATTEN, Bridget		26	F	Servant	21De02Jw
Bridget-Jr.		17	F	Servant	21De02Jw
Died-At-Sea					
MCDERMOT, Thomas		20	M	Laborer	21De02Jw
Bridget		50	F	Servant	21De02Jw
HAGAN, Owen		30	M	Laborer	21De02Jw
Mary		14	F	Servant	21De02Jw
MALONEY, Thomas		20	M	Laborer	21De02Jw
Died-At-Sea					
ROCK, Patrick		14	M	Laborer	21De02Jw
Daniel		12	M	Laborer	21De02Jw
MAHONEY, Morris		22	M	Laborer	21De02Jw
Katherine		30	F	Laborer	21De02Jw
Mary		08	F	Child	21De02Jw
John		04	M	Child	21De02Jw
Narry		01	F	Child	21De02Jw
CROGHAN, Biddy		19	F	Servant	21De02Jw
ODONNELL, Mary		19	F	Dressmaker	21De02Jw
BOYD, Ann		18	F	Servant	21De02Jw
TEALAN, Mary		26	F	Servant	21De02Jw
ROONEY, Mary		19	F	Servant	21De02Jw
Died-At-Sea					
MAHONEY, John		30	M	Laborer	21De02Jw
DOLAN, John		19	M	Laborer	21De02Jw
MCGUIRE, Michael		22	M	Laborer	21De02Jw
BRANNER, John		22	M	Shoemaker	21De02Jw
Eliza		20	F	Shoemaker	21De02Jw
MCCONNOR, Alexander		22	M	Laborer	21De02Jw
HAGAN, Ellen		18	F	Servant	21De02Jw
MCKINNEY, Judy		26	F	Dressmaker	21De02Jw
Died-At-Sea					
DROGHERTY, Ann		17	F	Servant	21De02Jw
QUIGLEY, Ann		20	F	Servant	21De02Jw
Died-At-Sea					
DIVINE, Owen		22	M	Laborer	21De02Jw
MCCONNOR, Mary-Ann		21	F	Servant	21De02Jw

ELSINORE 22 DECEMBER 1846

From Liverpool

NAMES OF PASSENGERS		AGE	SEX	OCCUPATIONS	DATE PORT SHIP
LALLY, Bernd.		27	M	Laborer	22De02Ke
U	(W)	22	F	Servant	22De02Ke
HAYDEN, Richd.		40	M	Weaver	22De02Ke
U	(W)	34	F	Wife	22De02Ke
BERGIN, Fenton		27	M	Laborer	22De02Ke
DOOLIN, Mary		20	F	Servant	22De02Ke
Bridget		18	F	Servant	22De02Ke
BAILY, Francis		28	M	Laborer	22De02Ke
U	(W)	20	F	Wife	22De02Ke
U		30	F	Dressmaker	22De02Ke
KELLY, Ann		20	F	Servant	22De02Ke
FITZPATRICK, Margt.		20	F	Servant	22De02Ke
MCBRIEN, Susan		24	F	Servant	22De02Ke
FITZPATRICK, Bebby		26	F	Servant	22De02Ke
ALGIER, Martha		22	F	Servant	22De02Ke
CUMMINS, Wm.		26	M	Laborer	22De02Ke
RODY, Mary		40	F	Servant	22De02Ke
Martha	(D)	18	F	Servant	22De02Ke
TULLY, Ann		22	F	Servant	22De02Ke
KEOWN, Mary		22	F	Servant	22De02Ke
ROGERS, Biddy		22	F	Servant	22De02Ke
LAMB, Nancy		26	F	Servant	22De02Ke
MALLAY, James		24	M	Farmer	22De02Ke
RAYNOLDS, Thos.		20	M	Farmer	22De02Ke
RIDGE, Ann		20	F	Laborer	22De02Ke
FALKNER, John		51	M	Laborer	22De02Ke
Elizabeth	(W)	53	F	Servant	22De02Ke
Saml.	(S)	13	M	Laborer	22De02Ke
Caraline	(D)	10	F	Child	22De02Ke
MORE, William		28	M	Farmer	22De02Ke
U	(W)	26	F	Wife	22De02Ke
Wm.Jr.	(S)	04	M	Child	22De02Ke
FAULKNER, Isabel		03	F	Child	22De02Ke
James		.00	M	Infant	22De02Ke
PATRICK, James		25	M	Laborer	22De02Ke
U	(W)	20	F	Wife	22De02Ke
KEOUGH, James		24	M	Laborer	22De02Ke
MARTIN, Ann		26	F	Servant	22De02Ke
John	(S)	07	M	Child	22De02Ke
Mary	(D)	05	F	Child	22De02Ke
FENEGAN, Mary		22	F	Servant	22De02Ke
MULLIN, Mary		19	F	Servant	22De02Ke
MCCORMICK, Michl.		58	M	Farmer	22De02Ke
Ann	(W)	52	F	Wife	22De02Ke
Rose	(D)	21	F	Servant	22De02Ke
Patt	(S)	19	M	Laborer	22De02Ke
John	(S)	17	M	Shoemaker	22De02Ke
Peter	(S)	13	M	None	22De02Ke
Mary-Ann	(D)	12	F	None	22De02Ke
Michl.	(S)	11	M	None	22De02Ke
Eliza	(D)	08	F	Child	22De02Ke
Dennis	(S)	06	M	Child	22De02Ke
GROGAN, Mchl.		23	M	Laborer	22De02Ke

NAMES OF PASSENGERS		AGE	SEX	OCCUPATIONS	DATE PORT SHIP
DIGNAN, John		25	M	Laborer	22De02Ke
Ellen		25	F	Laborer	22De02Ke
DOOLY, Cathn.		25	F	Servant	22De02Ke
DUNNE, Brigt.		25	F	Servant	22De02Ke
HOLLAND, John		20	M	Laborer	22De02Ke
John		23	M	Laborer	22De02Ke
CAMPBELL, John		19	M	Laborer	22De02Ke
CUNNINGHAM, Margt.		17	F	Servant	22De02Ke
MCHUGH, Thos.		16	M	Servant	22De02Ke
BULLNER, Simeon		24	M	Blacksmith	22De02Ke
HUDSON, Wm.		24	M	Tailor	22De02Ke
MAHAN, Pat		13	M	None	22De02Ke
WALSH, Edwd.		21	M	Mechanic	22De02Ke
Ellen		19	F	None	22De02Ke
CLEARY, Danl.		22	M	Laborer	22De02Ke
NOONAN, Mary		20	F	Servant	22De02Ke
NIELSON, James		56	M	Farmer	22De02Ke
NEILSON, Eleanor		52	F	Wife	22De02Ke
Dennis	(S)	15	M	Farmer	22De02Ke
Charlotte	(D)	14	F	Farmer	22De02Ke
Hugh		33	M	Laborer	22De02Ke
Agnes		31	F	Dressmaker	22De02Ke
ANDERSON, James		50	M	Farmer	22De02Ke
Sarah	(W)	50	F	Wife	22De02Ke
Magt.	(D)	18	F	Farmer	22De02Ke
James-Jr.	(S)	15	M	Farmer	22De02Ke
BRANEGAN, Mart.		18	F	Servant	22De02Ke
REED, Betty		18	F	Servant	22De02Ke
LEE, Mary-Ann		21	F	Servant	22De02Ke
TALBOT, Alfred		22	M	Laborer	22De02Ke
FARREL, Mary-Ann		21	F	Servant	22De02Ke
CALLEARY, James		30	M	Laborer	22De02Ke
MORAN, James		22	M	Laborer	22De02Ke
U	(W)	22	F	Wife	22De02Ke
CALLEARY, Cathn.		26	F	Servant	22De02Ke
DYER, Mary		28	F	Servant	22De02Ke
MORAN, Brigt.		22	F	Servant	22De02Ke
ALERICK, Mary		20	F	Servant	22De02Ke
BRETT, Thos.		21	M	Laborer	22De02Ke
RODY, John		20	M	Laborer	22De02Ke
HOEY, Patt		21	M	Laborer	22De02Ke
THOMPSON, John		25	M	Laborer	22De02Ke
U	(W)	24	F	Wife	22De02Ke
Richd.	(S)	02	M	Child	22De02Ke
Died-At-Sea					
Henry	(S)	.00	M	Infant	22De02Ke
SORDEN, Michl.		42	M	Farmer	22De02Ke
Cathn.	(W)	42	F	Wife	22De02Ke
Mary	(D)	18	F	Farmer	22De02Ke
Dennis	(S)	14	M	Farmer	22De02Ke
Michl.	(S)	12	M	Farmer	22De02Ke
Timy.	(S)	05	M	Child	22De02Ke
Norry	(D)	10	F	Child	22De02Ke
SULLIVAN, Ellen		20	F	Servant	22De02Ke
HARLEY, Kitty		22	F	Servant	22De02Ke
MCKERNAN, Birgt.		20	F	Servant	22De02Ke
LYNCH, Martin		18	M	Laborer	22De02Ke
HAWKINS, Mary		25	F	Servant	22De02Ke
ORR, Alx.		35	M	Farmer	22De02Ke
Agnes	(W)	30	F	Wife	22De02Ke
Wm.	(S)	10	M	Child	22De02Ke
Issabella	(D)	06	F	Child	22De02Ke
Agnes	(D)	03	F	Child	22De02Ke
Magt.	(D)	.00	F	Infant	22De02Ke
Elizabeth		20	F	Farmer	22De02Ke
CLEMENTS, Mary		20	F	Servant	22De02Ke
DUNLAP, Fanny		20	F	Servant	22De02Ke
VISSARD, Patt		20	M	Laborer	22De02Ke
U	(W)	20	F	Wife	22De02Ke
BOYLAN, Edwd.		30	M	Blacksmith	22De02Ke
Ann	(W)	30	F	Wife	22De02Ke
Margt.	(D)	05	F	Child	22De02Ke
James	(S)	01	M	Child	22De02Ke
FAY, Margt.		24	F	Servant	22De02Ke
Mary		20	F	Servant	22De02Ke
BOYLAN, Brigt.		18	F	Servant	22De02Ke
FAY, Sally		24	F	Servant	22De02Ke
Brigt.		20	F	Servant	22De02Ke
MCGOW, P.		20	M	Laborer	22De02Ke
BOYLAN, Owen		22	M	Laborer	22De02Ke
MCEVOY, U-Mrs.		50	F	Weaver	22De02Ke
Edwd.	(S)	24	M	Laborer	22De02Ke
Patt	(S)	22	M	Laborer	22De02Ke
Oney	(S)	20	M	Laborer	22De02Ke
Eliza	(D)	19	F	Servant	22De02Ke
Mary	(D)	17	F	Weaver	22De02Ke
Ann	(D)	15	F	Weaver	22De02Ke
DELANEY, Michl.		22	M	Laborer	22De02Ke
WHELAN, James		24	M	Laborer	22De02Ke
BOW, Phantom		22	M	Laborer	22De02Ke
DALENY, Phanton		20	M	Laborer	22De02Ke
FORAN, Danl.		26	M	Laborer	22De02Ke
BOW, Ann		20	F	Servant	22De02Ke
CORCORAN, Cathn.		22	F	Servant	22De02Ke
SHEIL, Martin		22	M	Laborer	22De02Ke
BRIAN, Rose		24	F	Servant	22De02Ke
BURNET, Ellen		24	F	Servant	22De02Ke
LAWLAR, James		20	M	Joiner	22De02Ke
SUMMERS, Cathn.		20	F	Servant	22De02Ke
MURPHY, Brigt.		22	F	Servant	22De02Ke
Margt.		19	F	Servant	22De02Ke
Ann		18	F	Servant	22De02Ke
REILEY, Ann		30	F	Servant	22De02Ke
KERNAN, Mary		40	F	Servant	22De02Ke
CAHILL, Mary-Ann		22	F	Servant	22De02Ke
Alice		18	F	Servant	22De02Ke
DOLAN, Thos.		13	M	Servant	22De02Ke
KILHEANY, Ann		20	F	Servant	22De02Ke
CANNON, Brigt.		34	F	Servant	22De02Ke
REYNOLDS, Ellen		20	F	Servant	22De02Ke
GRUNAN, Ann		20	F	Servant	22De02Ke
DOWNES, Margt.		18	F	Servant	22De02Ke
JONES, Ann		17	F	Servant	22De02Ke
REILEY, Mary		17	F	Servant	22De02Ke
MURPHY, Judith		18	F	None	22De02Ke
Died-At-Sea					
REILEY, Brigt.		16	F	Servant	22De02Ke
CURMESKY, Brigt.		17	F	None	22De02Ke
Died-At-Sea					
CROSS, James		50	M	Farmer	22De02Ke
Margt.	(W)	50	F	Wife	22De02Ke
John	(S)	24	M	Farmer	22De02Ke
Eliza	(D)	18	F	Farmer	22De02Ke
Teresa	(D)	17	F	Farmer	22De02Ke
William	(S)	15	M	Farmer	22De02Ke
MCCORMICK, Wm.		24	M	Farmer	22De02Ke
MADGLY, Ann		20	F	Servant	22De02Ke
FLANNARY, Davd.		20	M	Clergyman	22De02Ke
LAUGHTON, Patt		56	M	Carpenter	22De02Ke
Edwd.		07	M	Child	22De02Ke
Margt.		06	F	Child	22De02Ke
HOGAN, Mary		33	F	Servant	22De02Ke
Maria		16	F	Servant	22De02Ke
NOWLAN, Margt.		17	F	Servant	22De02Ke
CAULFIELD, Wm.		24	M	Carpenter	22De02Ke
Eleanor		20	F	Carpenter	22De02Ke
HENDERSON, Wm.		24	M	Shoemaker	22De02Ke
Cathn.		19	F	Shoemaker	22De02Ke
SCALLIEN, Hugh		29	M	Tailor	22De02Ke
CURRAN, Mary		22	F	Servant	22De02Ke
HENDERSON, Margt.		20	F	Servant	22De02Ke
MCARNE, John		28	M	Laborer	22De02Ke
DOUGHERTY, Patt		21	M	Laborer	22De02Ke
Cathn.		20	F	Servant	22De02Ke
JORDAN, Cathn.		21	F	Servant	22De02Ke
MCDONNELL, Patt		26	M	Laborer	22De02Ke
James		27	M	Stone Mason	22De02Ke
MONIELEY, Dennis		21	M	Stone Mason	22De02Ke
COMMONS, Patt		21	M	Stone Mason	22De02Ke
RONAN, Patt		20	M	Laborer	22De02Ke

NAMES OF PASSENGERS		AGE	SEX	OCCUPATIONS	DATE PORT SHIP
MCCAFFREY, Michl.		22	M	Laborer	22De02Ke
LALLY, Ann		54	F	Lad	22De02Ke
John		16	M	Lad	22De02Ke
MCCORMICK, James		22	M	Clerk	22De02Ke
DOYLE, Patt		25	M	Laborer	22De02Ke
KEARY, Michl.		23	M	Laborer	22De02Ke
LANE, Patt		18	M	Laborer	22De02Ke
Mary		54	F	Lad	22De02Ke
CASEY, Owen		22	M	Laborer	22De02Ke
SULLIVAN, James		21	M	Laborer	22De02Ke
DOYLE, Mary		25	F	Servant	22De02Ke
HANSON, Patt		25	M	Laborer	22De02Ke
MULLEN, Honora		25	F	Servant	22De02Ke
REARDON, Abby		24	F	Servant	22De02Ke
MURPHY, Mary		22	F	Servant	22De02Ke
CREEDEN, John		30	M	Joiner	22De02Ke
GREER, Margt.		45	F	Servant	22De02Ke
John	(S)	14	M	Tailor	22De02Ke
Sarah	(D)	10	F	Tailor	22De02Ke
FALLON, Brigt.		20	F	Servant	22De02Ke
MCGOW, Stephen		20	M	Laborer	22De02Ke
John		14	M	Laborer	22De02Ke
SMITH, Mary		19	F	Servant	22De02Ke
KILLIAN, Thos.		26	M	Laborer	22De02Ke
BRENNAN, James		27	M	Laborer	22De02Ke
DONNELLY, James		14	M	Laborer	22De02Ke
SHIPMAN, Ann		50	F	Lace Maker	22De02Ke
Ann	(D)	22	F	Lace Maker	22De02Ke
JACKSON, Wm.		24	M	Laborer	22De02Ke
GARREY, Bernd.		22	M	Laborer	22De02Ke
MCDANIEL, John		27	M	Tailor	22De02Ke
LEE, Edwd.		21	M	Tailor	22De02Ke
MCGILL, Margt.		50	F	Stock Maker	22De02Ke
LENNON, James		27	M	Laborer	22De02Ke
Mary		20	F	Servant	22De02Ke

SOUTHERNER 26 DECEMBER 1846

From Liverpool

NAMES OF PASSENGERS		AGE	SEX	OCCUPATIONS	DATE PORT SHIP
CRAIG, Francis		50	M	Laborer	26De02Dy
Mary	(W)	50	F	Wife	26De02Dy
John	(S)	21	M	Laborer	26De02Dy
Frances	(D)	19	F	Laborer	26De02Dy
Mary	(D)	18	F	Laborer	26De02Dy
Ellen	(D)	19	F	Laborer	26De02Dy
Wm.	(S)	10	M	Child	26De02Dy
Sally	(D)	09	F	Child	26De02Dy
Bridget	(D)	06	F	Child	26De02Dy
GOLNDEN, John		50	M	Laborer	26De02Dy
Sally	(W)	50	F	Wife	26De02Dy
Mary	(D)	20	F	Laborer	26De02Dy
Henry	(S)	17	M	Laborer	26De02Dy
John	(S)	13	M	Laborer	26De02Dy
Patrick	(S)	12	M	Laborer	26De02Dy
Jas.	(S)	18	M	Laborer	26De02Dy
Frances	(D)	06	F	Child	26De02Dy
Sarah	(D)	04	F	Child	26De02Dy
MCMANNUS, Chas.		24	M	Laborer	26De02Dy
Mary		20	F	Laborer	26De02Dy
HORTHINGTON, Julia		21	F	Laborer	26De02Dy
Eliza		20	F	Laborer	26De02Dy
CUNAN, Elizabeth		20	F	Laborer	26De02Dy
JONES, Thos.		27	M	Laborer	26De02Dy
U	(W)	24	F	Wife	26De02Dy
May	(D)	10	F	Child	26De02Dy
John	(S)	08	M	Child	26De02Dy
Bridget	(D)	06	F	Child	26De02Dy
Mathew	(S)	03	M	Child	26De02Dy
JONES, Sarah	(D)	.00	F	Infant	26De02Dy
SMITH, Felix		50	M	Laborer	26De02Dy
U	(W)	47	F	Wife	26De02Dy
Ann	(D)	19	F	Laborer	26De02Dy
Catherine	(D)	12	F	Laborer	26De02Dy
Jane	(D)	10	F	Child	26De02Dy
Mag.	(D)	07	F	Child	26De02Dy
Sarah	(D)	.00	F	Infant	26De02Dy
WILSON, Mary		25	F	Laborer	26De02Dy
Isabel		12	F	Laborer	26De02Dy
Jane		09	F	Child	26De02Dy
Sarah		05	F	Child	26De02Dy
John		25	M	Laborer	26De02Dy
IGO, Mary		24	F	Laborer	26De02Dy
Mary		10	F	Child	26De02Dy
Ann		09	F	Child	26De02Dy
Hannah		08	F	Child	26De02Dy
Jas.		05	M	Child	26De02Dy
Catherine		02	F	Child	26De02Dy
INLEY, Michel		26	M	Laborer	26De02Dy
REILEY, Chas.		17	M	Laborer	26De02Dy
COYNE, Anthony		50	M	Laborer	26De02Dy
U	(W)	40	F	Wife	26De02Dy
Mitchell	(S)	10	M	Child	26De02Dy
Ann	(D)	09	F	Child	26De02Dy
Mary	(D)	.00	F	Infant	26De02Dy
MCGLYNN, Pat		40	M	Laborer	26De02Dy
NALLY, Jas.		25	M	Laborer	26De02Dy
CONNELLY, Catherine		18	F	Laborer	26De02Dy
WHELAN, Martin		25	M	Laborer	26De02Dy
SUTTON, Ann		20	F	Laborer	26De02Dy
SULLIVAN, Eliza		21	F	Laborer	26De02Dy
Ann		19	F	Laborer	26De02Dy
Mary		11	F	Laborer	26De02Dy
TOBIN, Robt.		28	M	Laborer	26De02Dy
Danl.		36	M	Laborer	26De02Dy
INLY, Bridget		25	F	Laborer	26De02Dy
Norah		12	F	Laborer	26De02Dy
Dennis		09	M	Child	26De02Dy
Pat		05	M	Child	26De02Dy
CLARK, Peter		26	M	Laborer	26De02Dy
MCDONNELL, Randell		26	M	Laborer	26De02Dy
U	(W)	25	F	Wife	26De02Dy
John	(S)	.00	M	Infant	26De02Dy
HENNEGAN, John		54	M	Laborer	26De02Dy
U	(W)	50	F	Wife	26De02Dy
Anthony	(S)	23	M	Laborer	26De02Dy
Micheal	(S)	22	M	Laborer	26De02Dy
John	(S)	06	M	Child	26De02Dy
Martin	(S)	06	M	Child	26De02Dy
Catherine	(D)	04	F	Child	26De02Dy
MULLIGAN, Ellen		22	F	Laborer	26De02Dy
CONNOR, Ellen		20	F	Laborer	26De02Dy
OHARE, Frans		25	M	Laborer	26De02Dy
Mary		20	F	Laborer	26De02Dy
Catherine		20	F	Laborer	26De02Dy
MCCONEL, Luke		40	M	Laborer	26De02Dy
BROWN, Mary		18	F	Laborer	26De02Dy
KELLY, Anthony		28	M	Laborer	26De02Dy
MCDONNELL, Michlll		28	M	Laborer	26De02Dy
HUGHES, Anthony		25	M	Laborer	26De02Dy
CLARKE, Jas.		21	M	Laborer	26De02Dy
MCGOHRAN, Pat		21	M	Laborer	26De02Dy
LYNCH, Julia		35	F	Laborer	26De02Dy
WALLACE, David		20	M	Laborer	26De02Dy
GILLIOR, Elizabeth		21	F	Laborer	26De02Dy
MAHAN, Mary		40	F	Laborer	26De02Dy
George	(S)	10	M	Child	26De02Dy
CARROLL, Bridget		30	F	Laborer	26De02Dy
MCCARLIE, Michel		24	M	Laborer	26De02Dy
Bridget		17	F	Laborer	26De02Dy
KENNEDY, Bridget		50	F	Laborer	26De02Dy
Kathrine	(D)	12	F	Laborer	26De02Dy
LENDGEMS, John		30	M	Laborer	26De02Dy
U	(W)	23	F	Wife	26De02Dy

NAMES OF PASSENGERS		AGE	SEX	OCCUPATIONS	DATE PORT SHIP
LENDGEMS, Andrew	(S)	05	M	Child	26De02Dy
KELLY, Barbarra		30	F	Laborer	26De02Dy
CASSIDY, Jas.		19	M	Laborer	26De02Dy
LENDGEMS, Ellen		00	F	Laborer	26De02Dy
Died-At-Sea					
RIELLY, Thos.		24	M	Laborer	26De02Dy
Martin		26	M	Laborer	26De02Dy
KELLY, Barbara		30	F	Laborer	26De02Dy
Jas.	(S)	13	M	Laborer	26De02Dy
HANLY, Murtaugh		24	U	Laborer	26De02Dy
HAYS, Murtaugh		40	U	Laborer	26De02Dy
Pat		40	M	Laborer	26De02Dy
LEMSKEY, John		26	M	Laborer	26De02Dy
Sally		16	F	Laborer	26De02Dy
CRAIG, Peter		13	M	Laborer	26De02Dy
MULLY, Mary		25	F	Laborer	26De02Dy
CAMPBELL, Kate		35	F	Laborer	26De02Dy
MADDEN, Matthew		24	M	Laborer	26De02Dy
BRINDS, Brigt.		20	F	Laborer	26De02Dy
FAGAN, Mary		20	F	Laborer	26De02Dy
Jane	(D)	.00	F	Infant	26De02Dy
MORGAN, Jas.		17	M	Laborer	26De02Dy
MURPHY, Michl.		25	M	Laborer	26De02Dy
Mary		11	F	Laborer	26De02Dy
Ann		16	F	Laborer	26De02Dy
COTANY, Magt.		20	F	Laborer	26De02Dy
MURRAY, Sarah		40	F	Laborer	26De02Dy
LANEY, U-Mrs.		35	F	Laborer	26De02Dy
HALL, John		30	M	Laborer	26De02Dy
TEMERAN, John		25	M	Laborer	26De02Dy
BUTTLER, Edwd.		50	M	Laborer	26De02Dy
U	(W)	48	F	Wife	26De02Dy
Anthony	(S)	17	M	Laborer	26De02Dy
Bridgt.	(D)	14	F	Laborer	26De02Dy
Mary	(D)	12	F	Laborer	26De02Dy
Abby	(D)	10	F	Child	26De02Dy
Kate	(D)	06	F	Child	26De02Dy
Michl.	(S)	06	M	Child	26De02Dy
Judy	(D)	04	F	Child	26De02Dy
Peggy	(D)	02	F	Child	26De02Dy
PRESLAN, Jas.		20	M	Laborer	26De02Dy
MCDONALD, John		20	M	Laborer	26De02Dy
Betsey		18	F	Laborer	26De02Dy
HUGHES, John		40	M	Laborer	26De02Dy
Mary	(D)	20	F	Laborer	26De02Dy
Bridgt.	(D)	18	F	Laborer	26De02Dy
John	(S)	12	M	Laborer	26De02Dy
Michl.	(S)	11	M	Laborer	26De02Dy
LOFTUS, Pat		27	M	Laborer	26De02Dy
U	(W)	26	F	Wife	26De02Dy
John	(S)	.00	M	Infant	26De02Dy
BROWN, Pat		20	M	Laborer	26De02Dy
BARTON, Ann		06	F	Child	26De02Dy
BARTLY, U-Mrs.		30	F	Laborer	26De02Dy
John	(S)	04	M	Child	26De02Dy
Jane	(D)	.00	F	Infant	26De02Dy
CALLAKEN, Enis		20	M	Laborer	26De02Dy
MCCEARN, John		50	M	Laborer	26De02Dy
Mary	(W)	40	F	Wife	26De02Dy
Rose	(D)	15	F	Laborer	26De02Dy
BROOKE, John		19	M	Laborer	26De02Dy
LOUSMAN, Michl.		25	M	Laborer	26De02Dy
DOSNEL, Magt.		22	F	Laborer	26De02Dy
CONNAUGHTON, Owen		25	M	Laborer	26De02Dy
KENNEDY, Magt.		20	F	Laborer	26De02Dy
COSTELLO, Magt.		20	F	Laborer	26De02Dy
MASTERSON, Magt.		20	F	Laborer	26De02Dy
Rose		18	F	Laborer	26De02Dy
DONEL, Pat		26	M	Laborer	26De02Dy
U	(W)	25	F	Wife	26De02Dy
Michl.	(S)	03	M	Child	26De02Dy
Francis	(S)	.00	M	Infant	26De02Dy
HIGGINS, May		12	F	Laborer	26De02Dy
HESLIN, Brigt.		20	F	Laborer	26De02Dy
GUNMAN, Abby		20	F	Laborer	26De02Dy
CARR, Thos.		20	M	Laborer	26De02Dy
WHELAN, Bridgt.		20	F	Laborer	26De02Dy
CONIGAN, Peter		28	M	Laborer	26De02Dy
MURRAY, Thos.		26	M	Laborer	26De02Dy
KILHOM, Mchl.		40	M	Laborer	26De02Dy
Bridgt.	(W)	26	F	Wife	26De02Dy
John	(S)	.00	M	Infant	26De02Dy
LEE, Mary		30	F	Laborer	26De02Dy
PILEN, Thos.		18	M	Laborer	26De02Dy
Horace		20	M	Laborer	26De02Dy
Hellen		22	F	Laborer	26De02Dy
KENNAN, U-Mrs.		19	F	Laborer	26De02Dy
Thos.		16	M	Laborer	26De02Dy
ROAKE, Dennis		28	M	Laborer	26De02Dy
Hugh		16	M	Laborer	26De02Dy
CHRISTOL, Sally		45	F	Laborer	26De02Dy
Jas.	(S)	22	M	Laborer	26De02Dy
Patrick	(S)	21	M	Laborer	26De02Dy
May	(D)	17	F	Laborer	26De02Dy
Bridget	(D)	14	F	Laborer	26De02Dy
SMITH, John		20	M	Laborer	26De02Dy
Jas.		22	M	Laborer	26De02Dy
GILPIL, William		24	M	Laborer	26De02Dy
Jane		20	F	Laborer	26De02Dy
Jas.		12	M	Laborer	26De02Dy
Mary		08	F	Child	26De02Dy
MARTIN, Owen		21	M	Laborer	26De02Dy
Phillip		26	M	Laborer	26De02Dy
U	(W)	18	F	Wife	26De02Dy
JOHNSON, Catherine		40	F	Laborer	26De02Dy
Henry	(S)	21	M	Laborer	26De02Dy
Betsey	(D)	13	F	Laborer	26De02Dy
FAGEN, Richd.		20	M	Laborer	26De02Dy
KALAHAN, U		20	U	Laborer	26De02Dy
CEA, U		20	U	Laborer	26De02Dy
HODGINS, Bridget		35	F	Laborer	26De02Dy
BURKE, Michl.		50	M	Laborer	26De02Dy
Betsey		50	F	Laborer	26De02Dy
GILL, John		22	M	Laborer	26De02Dy
Bridget		20	F	Laborer	26De02Dy
KELLY, Jos.		18	M	Laborer	26De02Dy
KNOX, Frans.		25	M	Laborer	26De02Dy
DUNN, Wm.		26	M	Laborer	26De02Dy
Frans.		24	M	Laborer	26De02Dy
NICHOLSON, Martin		30	M	Laborer	26De02Dy
Nancy	(W)	26	F	Wife	26De02Dy
Michel	(S)	.00	M	Infant	26De02Dy
MCLAUGHLIN, Mary		22	F	Laborer	26De02Dy
DONOHUE, Jas.		26	M	Laborer	26De02Dy
CRAIGS, Jas.		40	M	Laborer	26De02Dy
U	(W)	35	F	Wife	26De02Dy
Edwd.	(S)	07	M	Child	26De02Dy
MCCONEL, Betsey		40	F	Laborer	26De02Dy
Ellen	(D)	08	F	Child	26De02Dy
SIMMONS, Jas.		25	M	Laborer	26De02Dy
MAHON, Catherne		20	F	Laborer	26De02Dy
MULLUGAN, Frans.		18	U	Laborer	26De02Dy
REILY, Richd.		26	M	Laborer	26De02Dy
Jas.	(S)	08	M	Child	26De02Dy
CUNNINGHAM, John		20	M	Laborer	26De02Dy
MORGAN, Barnard		20	M	Laborer	26De02Dy
Mary		21	F	Laborer	26De02Dy
MCCONEL, Davd.		31	M	Laborer	26De02Dy
JOHNSTON, John		40	M	Laborer	26De02Dy
Elizabeth	(W)	40	F	Wife	26De02Dy
Sally	(D)	16	F	Laborer	26De02Dy
Robt.	(S)	12	M	Laborer	26De02Dy
Ann	(D)	10	F	Child	26De02Dy
Henry	(S)	06	M	Child	26De02Dy
MAGINNIS, M.		39	M	Laborer	26De02Dy
Jane	(W)	35	F	Wife	26De02Dy
Mary	(D)	08	F	Child	26De02Dy
Jas.	(S)	.00	M	Infant	26De02Dy
INNIS, John		20	M	Laborer	26De02Dy
GANNAN, Thos.		20	M	Laborer	26De02Dy

NAMES OF PASSENGERS		AGE	SEX	OCCUPATIONS	DATE PORT SHIP
BRENNAN, Cath.		20	F	Laborer	26De02Dy
MOON, Pat		60	M	Laborer	26De02Dy
Mary	(W)	50	F	Wife	26De02Dy
John		09	M	Child	26De02Dy
Henry		06	M	Child	26De02Dy
Pat		.00	M	Infant	26De02Dy
LEMSKEY, Pat		24	M	Laborer	26De02Dy
Sally		15	F	Laborer	26De02Dy
BENTON, Bridget		22	F	Laborer	26De02Dy
Ann		30	F	Laborer	26De02Dy
Hugh		19	M	Laborer	26De02Dy
Mary		09	F	Child	26De02Dy
Pat		05	M	Child	26De02Dy
John		03	M	Child	26De02Dy

OXFORD 26 DECEMBER 1846

From Liverpool

NAMES OF PASSENGERS		AGE	SEX	OCCUPATIONS	DATE PORT SHIP
HOSTON, John		24	M	Laborer	26De02AJ
MURDOCH, John		20	M	Laborer	26De02AJ
BEGS, Thomas		20	M	Laborer	26De02AJ
MCGIVEN, Patrick		29	M	Laborer	26De02AJ
Elizabeth		34	F	Servant	26De02AJ
RYAN, Catharine		19	F	Servant	26De02AJ
Margaret		18	F	Servant	26De02AJ
MCDERMOTT, Thomas		24	M	Laborer	26De02AJ
GILROY, Bessy		01	F	Child	26De02AJ
BURKE, Hugh		17	M	Blacksmith	26De02AJ
FEENEY, Eliza		30	F	Servant	26De02AJ
GHALLAGHER, Ann		25	F	Servant	26De02AJ
BURKE, Ann		20	F	Servant	26De02AJ
FEENEY, Helen		21	F	Servant	26De02AJ
FLOOD, Mary		26	F	Mtmkr	26De02AJ
Bridget		62	F	Mtmkr	26De02AJ
COX, Mary		19	F	Servant	26De02AJ
CONOLLY, Ellen		19	F	Servant	26De02AJ
FITZMORRIS, John		40	M	Laborer	26De02AJ
DUNN, Michael		25	M	Laborer	26De02AJ
DIGNAN, John		22	M	Laborer	26De02AJ
Bridget	(D)	01	F	Child	26De02AJ
KEARNADY, Catharine		13	F	Servant	26De02AJ
Mary		24	F	Servant	26De02AJ
Rose		22	F	Servant	26De02AJ
MCGUIRE, Mary		24	F	Servant	26De02AJ
HOLLOHAN, Francis		40	M	Laborer	26De02AJ
Bridget	(W)	40	F	Wife	26De02AJ
Mary	(D)	10	F	Child	26De02AJ
Peter	(S)	07	M	Child	26De02AJ
GILROY, Patrick		35	M	Laborer	26De02AJ
Jane	(W)	35	F	Wife	26De02AJ
Alice	(D)	13	F	Servant	26De02AJ
Ann	(D)	12	F	Servant	26De02AJ
James	(S)	10	M	Servant	26De02AJ
Frank	(S)	08	M	Child	26De02AJ
Owen	(S)	07	M	Child	26De02AJ
Catharine	(D)	06	F	Child	26De02AJ
Mary	(D)	05	F	Child	26De02AJ
HOLLOHAN, John		20	M	Laborer	26De02AJ
Thomas		26	M	Laborer	26De02AJ
Margaret		50	F	Weaver	26De02AJ
Elizabeth		28	F	Weaver	26De02AJ
Esther		27	F	Weaver	26De02AJ
TOYNE, Nancy		22	F	Servant	26De02AJ
TIERRAN, Anna		22	F	Servant	26De02AJ
SHANNON, John		20	M	Laborer	26De02AJ
GILROY, Thomas		21	M	Laborer	26De02AJ
MCCAFFREY, James		18	M	Laborer	26De02AJ
OBRIEN, Terence		23	M	Laborer	26De02AJ
MCQUADE, Rose		17	F	Servant	26De02AJ
BURKE, Bridget		21	F	Servant	26De02AJ
GARRETTY, Margaret		27	F	Servant	26De02AJ
MCDONALD, Peter		30	M	Laborer	26De02AJ
Peggy		28	F	Servant	26De02AJ
Pat		14	M	Servant	26De02AJ
Ann		16	F	Servant	26De02AJ
Margaret		12	F	Servant	26De02AJ
Catharine		09	F	Child	26De02AJ
Thomas		10	M	Child	26De02AJ
Maria		08	F	Child	26De02AJ
John		07	M	Child	26De02AJ
MCGUIRE, Helen		50	F	None	26De02AJ
Thomas	(S)	15	M	Servant	26De02AJ
Barney	(S)	09	M	Child	26De02AJ
MCQUADE, Catharine		21	F	Servant	26De02AJ
OCONOLLY, James		18	M	Laborer	26De02AJ
BRODERICK, Patrick		25	M	Laborer	26De02AJ
YOUNG, Joseph		30	M	Carpenter	26De02AJ
Mary	(W)	32	F	Wife	26De02AJ
William	(S)	09	M	Child	26De02AJ
Joseph	(S)	08	M	Child	26De02AJ
Walter	(S)	05	M	Child	26De02AJ
James	(S)	02	M	Child	26De02AJ
CASTELLO, William		18	M	Shoemaker	26De02AJ
HANDY, James		28	M	Stone Mason	26De02AJ
Mary	(W)	28	F	Wife	26De02AJ
Margt.		55	F	None	26De02AJ
Michael	(S)	.08	M	Infant	26De02AJ
Thomas	(S)	04	M	Child	26De02AJ
Maria	(D)	10	F	Child	26De02AJ
CONROY, Maria		20	F	Servant	26De02AJ
IGO, Ann		20	F	Servant	26De02AJ
CAVILL, Martin		48	M	Shoemaker	26De02AJ
Michael	(S)	14	M	Shoemaker	26De02AJ
Francis	(S)	12	M	Shoemaker	26De02AJ
FLINN, Sarah		40	F	Servant	26De02AJ
MCDONELL, Barny		20	M	Laborer	26De02AJ
FEDERTON, James		35	M	Shoemaker	26De02AJ
JANIDAN, Richd.		25	M	Laborer	26De02AJ
DOLAN, James		40	M	Laborer	26De02AJ
NEVILL, Jacob		25	M	Laborer	26De02AJ
NOLAN, Mary		35	F	Servant	26De02AJ
Thomas	(S)	12	M	Servant	26De02AJ
Ann	(D)	06	F	Child	26De02AJ
Michael	(S)	04	M	Child	26De02AJ
OCONNOR, Patrick		29	M	Laborer	26De02AJ
FARLEY, Mary		08	F	Child	26De02AJ
Michael		10	M	Child	26De02AJ
MULLANEY, Catharine		23	F	Servant	26De02AJ
STERNLY, Helen		25	F	Servant	26De02AJ
PIGEON, John		38	M	Weaver	26De02AJ
GEMMILL, John		30	M	Bricklayer	26De02AJ
GAMBLE, Maria		18	F	Servant	26De02AJ
CASTELLO, Helen		14	F	Servant	26De02AJ
TUOMY, Catherine		23	F	Servant	26De02AJ
MURPHY, Anty		28	F	Servant	26De02AJ
FLICK, Ann-Jane		06	F	Child	26De02AJ
Robert		08	M	Child	26De02AJ
CARRIGAN, Patrick		23	M	Shoemaker	26De02AJ
TIERRAN, Terence		17	M	Laborer	26De02AJ
Helen		14	F	Servant	26De02AJ
DONOVAN, Dennis		38	M	Weaver	26De02AJ
FREENEY, Felix		26	M	Laborer	26De02AJ
CORRIGAN, Edward		50	M	Laborer	26De02AJ
GLEECE, Michael		30	M	Laborer	26De02AJ
EATHAN, Tebble		27	F	Servant	26De02AJ
Sarah	(D)	07	F	Child	26De02AJ
Bessy	(D)	05	F	Child	26De02AJ
Ann	(D)	01	F	Child	26De02AJ
MADDEN, Biddy		40	F	None	26De02AJ
EAGAN, Pat		10	M	None	26De02AJ
COX, Julia		23	F	Servant	26De02AJ
Catherine		13	F	Servant	26De02AJ
MAHON, Catherine		30	F	Servant	26De02AJ

NAMES OF PASSENGERS		AGE	SEX	OCCUPATIONS	DATE PORT SHIP
BRADY, James		22	M	Laborer	26De02AJ
RILEY, John		30	M	Laborer	26De02AJ
MARTIN, Barney		20	M	Laborer	26De02AJ
NOLAN, Patrick		36	M	Laborer	26De02AJ
Eliza	(W)	33	F	Wife	26De02AJ
John	(S)	09	M	Child	26De02AJ
Thomas	(S)	01	M	Child	26De02AJ
John		50	M	Laborer	26De02AJ
Catherine		50	F	None	26De02AJ
MATHESON, Mary		26	F	Servant	26De02AJ
LYNCH, Mary		26	F	Servant	26De02AJ
OCONNOR, Michael		58	M	Laborer	26De02AJ
Bridget		60	F	None	26De02AJ
MCJAMES, James		27	M	Laborer	26De02AJ
OCONNOR, Rose		02	F	Child	26De02AJ
Kitty		13	F	Servant	26De02AJ
MORRAN, James		22	M	Laborer	26De02AJ
Mary		15	F	Servant	26De02AJ
WHEELAN, Patrick		16	M	Butcher	26De02AJ
Thomas		13	M	Butcher	26De02AJ
Ann		11	F	None	26De02AJ
DEGNON, Lawrence		40	M	Laborer	26De02AJ
Thomas		24	M	Laborer	26De02AJ
Ann		15	F	Servant	26De02AJ
Ann		35	F	Servant	26De02AJ
ODONNELL, William		25	M	Farmer	26De02AJ
OBRIEN, Francis		30	M	Laborer	26De02AJ
MULLIGAN, Michael		20	M	Laborer	26De02AJ
MALANY, James		25	M	Laborer	26De02AJ
FLINN, Alice		21	F	Servant	26De02AJ
ODONNELL, Alice		23	F	Servant	26De02AJ
COCHLAN, Michael		50	M	Laborer	26De02AJ
NESBETT, William		36	M	Laborer	26De02AJ
BURNIE, William		36	M	Laborer	26De02AJ
OBRIEN, Roger		35	M	Laborer	26De02AJ
William	(S)	03	M	Child	26De02AJ
Patrick	(S)	03	M	Child	26De02AJ
NEAL, Mary		19	F	Servant	26De02AJ
LOUGHERNE, Patrick		50	M	Laborer	26De02AJ
WHITE, Catherine		21	F	Servant	26De02AJ
KEATON, Judith		21	F	Servant	26De02AJ
ODONALD, William		21	M	Laborer	26De02AJ
KILKENNY, John		26	M	Laborer	26De02AJ
MURRAY, John		50	M	Laborer	26De02AJ
MCDONAGH, John		45	M	Laborer	26De02AJ
John	(S)	18	M	Laborer	26De02AJ
Bridget	(W)	40	F	Servant	26De02AJ
Michael	(S)	16	M	Servant	26De02AJ
Catherine	(D)	18	F	Servant	26De02AJ
Mary	(D)	14	F	Servant	26De02AJ
Thomas	(S)	18	M	Laborer	26De02AJ
Peter		28	M	Laborer	26De02AJ
LANDRIGAN, Thomas		30	M	Laborer	26De02AJ
MCGRATH, John		20	M	Laborer	26De02AJ
DEMSIE, Margaret		26	F	Servant	26De02AJ
John		27	M	Carpenter	26De02AJ
KENNEDY, Catherine		25	F	Servant	26De02AJ
MURPHY, Helen		25	F	Servant	26De02AJ
RUDDY, Francis		40	M	Laborer	26De02AJ
Helen	(D)	14	F	Servant	26De02AJ
KELLY, Ann		22	F	Servant	26De02AJ
DUNN, Maria		18	F	Servant	26De02AJ
MCGINTRY, Biddy		19	F	Servant	26De02AJ
FLINN, Michael		22	M	Farmer	26De02AJ
CASEY, Brian		25	M	Laborer	26De02AJ
JUDY, Hally		20	F	Servant	26De02AJ
SHALLY, Alice		24	F	Servant	26De02AJ
HINDS, Catherine		23	F	Servant	26De02AJ
RARRAHAN, Owen		29	M	Laborer	26De02AJ
MURPHY, Margaret		25	F	Servant	26De02AJ
Jerry		30	M	Laborer	26De02AJ
RILY, Barney		25	M	Laborer	26De02AJ
WADE, Trennce		25	M	Tailor	26De02AJ
FLAHERTY, Thomas		25	M	Laborer	26De02AJ
KEATON, Thomas		40	M	Farmer	26De02AJ

NAMES OF PASSENGERS		AGE	SEX	OCCUPATIONS	DATE PORT SHIP
KEATON, Judith	(W)	35	F	Servant	26De02AJ
Mary	(D)	14	F	Servant	26De02AJ
Ellen	(D)	08	F	Child	26De02AJ
Maurice	(S)	07	M	Child	26De02AJ
Judith	(D)	05	F	Child	26De02AJ
John	(S)	01	M	Child	26De02AJ
Judy		60	F	None	26De02AJ
HOGAN, Edward		40	M	Farmer	26De02AJ
Ellen	(W)	36	F	Servant	26De02AJ
Thomas	(S)	08	M	Child	26De02AJ
Dennis	(S)	06	M	Child	26De02AJ
Alice	(D)	04	F	Child	26De02AJ
John	(S)	02	M	Child	26De02AJ
HOGHLAN, John		30	M	Laborer	26De02AJ
CARROLL, William		23	M	Laborer	26De02AJ
James		25	M	Laborer	26De02AJ
DOBINS, David		25	M	Laborer	26De02AJ
COSGRAVE, Michael		38	M	Stctr	26De02AJ
Michael		20	M	Laborer	26De02AJ
Thomas		16	M	Laborer	26De02AJ
Catherine		23	F	Servant	26De02AJ
Marcella		16	F	Servant	26De02AJ
MARRHANNEY, Robert		00	M	Farmer	26De02AJ
DULOP, John		00	M	Clerk	26De02AJ
HOLLOHAN, Mary		15	F	Servant	26De02AJ
MARTIN, Matilda		06	F	Child	26De02AJ
John		17	M	Laborer	26De02AJ
FLOOD, Daniel		35	M	Shoemaker	26De02AJ
MCCAFFREY, Rose		22	F	Dressmaker	26De02AJ
EAGAN, Mary		08	F	Child	26De02AJ
MCDONOGH, Anne		07	F	Child	26De02AJ
Bridget		06	F	Child	26De02AJ
Died-At-Sea					
GORGAN, Mary		15	F	Servant	26De02AJ
GAVIN, Julia		18	F	Servant	26De02AJ
ARTHUR, Susan		40	F	None	26De02AJ
Ellen	(D)	16	F	None	26De02AJ
BATRON, Augustus-Frede		24	M	Surgeon	26De02AJ
DIVINE, Ann		23	F	Dressmaker	26De02AJ
CARROLL, Owen		24	M	Clergyman	26De02AJ
SMITH, Ann		22	F	Servant	26De02AJ
CLECK, John		13	M	Servant	26De02AJ
MURPHY, Mary		28	F	Servant	26De02AJ
ODONAGH, Michael		30	M	Laborer	26De02AJ
OBRIEN, Margaret		25	F	Servant	26De02AJ

HENRY-CLAY 26 DECEMBER 1846

From Liverpool

NAMES OF PASSENGERS		AGE	SEX	OCCUPATIONS	DATE PORT SHIP
FOY, Jas.		60	M	Innkeeper	26De02Co
Margt.		26	F	None	26De02Co
GLYNN, Mary		18	F	None	26De02Co
QUINN, Thos.		23	M	None	26De02Co
DAVIS, Thos.		40	M	None	26De02Co
Ann	(W)	36	F	Wife	26De02Co
Richard	(S)	20	M	Blacksmith	26De02Co
Thos.	(S)	16	M	None	26De02Co
John	(S)	13	M	None	26De02Co
Mary-Ann	(D)	11	F	None	26De02Co
Elizabeth	(D)	04	F	Child	26De02Co
SCULLY, Peter		25	M	None	26De02Co
Mary	(W)	24	F	Wife	26De02Co
Mary	(D)	03	F	Child	26De02Co
MERRY, Bridget		18	F	None	26De02Co
Andrew		26	M	None	26De02Co
Mary		24	F	None	26De02Co
RATICAN, Bridget		24	F	None	26De02Co
FARRELL, Ellen		22	F	None	26De02Co

NAMES OF PASSENGERS		A G E	S E X	OCCUPATIONS	DATE PORT SHIP	NAMES OF PASSENGERS		A G E	S E X	OCCUPATIONS	DATE PORT SHIP
BURK, John		17	M	None	26De02Co	FIRRIS, Timothy		28	M	None	26De02Co
FITZSIMON, Jas.		26	M	None	26De02Co	FARRELL, Michl.		24	M	Laborer	26De02Co
FITZSOMONS, Ann		22	F	None	26De02Co	KELLEY, Michl.		25	M	Laborer	26De02Co
HAYS, Brenard		20	M	None	26De02Co	Francis		21	M	Laborer	26De02Co
Ruth		18	F	None	26De02Co	LAWLES, John		20	M	Laborer	26De02Co
SHEREY, Jas.		20	M	None	26De02Co	HINDS, John		21	M	Laborer	26De02Co
DOLAND, Bridget		18	F	None	26De02Co	MCGOWEN, John		36	M	Laborer	26De02Co
Catherine		17	F	None	26De02Co	Nelley	(W)	36	F	Wife	26De02Co
Ann		30	F	None	26De02Co	Mary	(D)	08	F	Child	26De02Co
DUNDRE, Cathe.		19	F	None	26De02Co	Ann	(D)	06	F	Child	26De02Co
CAFFREY, Biddy		16	F	None	26De02Co	Cathn.	(D)	03	F	Child	26De02Co
RILEY, Ann		17	F	None	26De02Co	Bernard	(S)	01	M	Child	26De02Co
LAWLER, Ann		16	F	None	26De02Co	MARRON, Mary		40	F	Laborer	26De02Co
SMITH, Mary		18	F	None	26De02Co	Miles	(S)	20	M	Laborer	26De02Co
HARMON, Rose		15	F	None	26De02Co	Betty	(D)	17	F	Laborer	26De02Co
NEILL, Jas.		30	M	None	26De02Co	Thos.	(S)	15	M	Laborer	26De02Co
Ann	(W)	02	F	Wife	26De02Co	Francis	(D)	13	F	Laborer	26De02Co
John	(S)	02	M	Child	26De02Co	MCFULLEN, Jas.		18	M	Laborer	26De02Co
Bridget	(D)	01	F	Child	26De02Co	Judith		16	F	Laborer	26De02Co
FARRELLY, Margt.		35	F	None	26De02Co	Cathn.		12	F	Laborer	26De02Co
Jas.	(S)	05	M	Child	26De02Co	Bridget		08	F	Child	26De02Co
DUNNY, John		46	M	None	26De02Co	SHORT, Mary		19	F	Laborer	26De02Co
Margt.	(W)	40	F	Wife	26De02Co	MAHON, Patrick		23	M	Laborer	26De02Co
Rose	(D)	19	F	None	26De02Co	SWENEY, John		25	M	Laborer	26De02Co
Mary	(D)	17	F	None	26De02Co	DURNY, John		40	M	Laborer	26De02Co
Margt.	(D)	16	F	None	26De02Co	CHAMBERS, John		25	M	Laborer	26De02Co
ROGERS, Edwd.		21	M	None	26De02Co	COYL, Phillip		18	M	Laborer	26De02Co
MILES, Edwd.		24	M	None	26De02Co	SULLEY, Cathn.		18	F	Laborer	26De02Co
DUFFY, John		21	M	None	26De02Co	MCGOWEN, Owen		40	M	Laborer	26De02Co
ROGERS, Michael		20	M	None	26De02Co	Ann	(W)	40	F	Wife	26De02Co
KILLIAN, Ann		20	F	None	26De02Co	Mary	(D)	12	F	Laborer	26De02Co
SMITH, Mary		22	F	None	26De02Co	Jas.	(S)	05	M	Child	26De02Co
BOOTH, George		35	M	None	26De02Co	Michl.	(S)	03	M	Child	26De02Co
HARIGAN, Winifred		22	F	None	26De02Co	Margt.	(D)	01	F	Child	26De02Co
DUFFY, Peter		20	M	None	26De02Co	GRAHAM, Robt.		30	M	Farmer	26De02Co
Mary		19	F	None	26De02Co	Jane		23	F	None	26De02Co
BRESLIN, Mary		24	F	None	26De02Co	LYNCH, John		33	M	None	26De02Co
Phil.	(H)	22	M	None	26De02Co	OBRIEN, Mary		19	F	None	26De02Co
Augst.	(S)	01	M	Child	26De02Co	KEATING, Geo.		22	M	None	26De02Co
JONES, Wm.		50	M	None	26De02Co	Ann		20	F	None	26De02Co
Mary	(W)	40	F	Wife	26De02Co	MENGRESS, Owen		21	M	Farmer	26De02Co
Hugh	(S)	22	M	None	26De02Co	GAVANICH, Thos.		25	M	None	26De02Co
Mary	(D)	17	F	None	26De02Co	POWER, Wm.		32	M	None	26De02Co
John	(S)	21	M	None	26De02Co	FORRELTT, Geo.		35	M	None	26De02Co
Jas.	(S)	13	M	None	26De02Co	Jamina		32	F	None	26De02Co
Judith	(D)	11	F	None	26De02Co	Alwes		30	M	None	26De02Co
Ellen	(D)	08	F	Child	26De02Co	MCGOWEN, Michl.		20	M	None	26De02Co
Alice	(D)	06	F	Child	26De02Co	Owen		18	M	None	26De02Co
FEALY, Joseph		17	M	None	26De02Co	MCDOWELL, John		30	M	None	26De02Co
Sally		21	F	None	26De02Co	Firah	(W)	28	F	Wife	26De02Co
Mary		19	F	None	26De02Co	John	(S)	01	M	Child	26De02Co
MCANTHAN, Mary		20	F	None	26De02Co	Patrick		40	M	None	26De02Co
Biddy		19	F	None	26De02Co	Mary	(W)	35	F	Wife	26De02Co
DUHAN, U-Mrs.		50	F	None	26De02Co	John	(S)	01	M	Child	26De02Co
Jane	(D)	25	F	None	26De02Co	DAVIDSON, Robt.		30	M	Butcher	26De02Co
Mgt.	(D)	22	F	None	26De02Co	Wm.		23	M	None	26De02Co
MCGARRY, Ann		21	F	None	26De02Co	Ellzbth		20	F	None	26De02Co
LAPPEN, Mary		23	F	None	26De02Co	Sarah		24	F	None	26De02Co
MANGAN, Wm.		21	M	None	26De02Co	KINELLY, Alex.		40	M	None	26De02Co
MULVEY, Francis		23	M	None	26De02Co	MCCANN, Biddy		24	F	None	26De02Co
BOWN, Wm.		22	M	Mechanic	26De02Co	MURRY, Patrick		22	M	None	26De02Co
Ann		20	F	None	26De02Co	SWEENY, Danl.		22	M	Tailor	26De02Co
CUNNY, Michl.		25	M	None	26De02Co	MAHER, Paul		24	M	None	26De02Co
MCDONNELL, John		16	M	None	26De02Co	Margt.	(W)	27	F	Wife	26De02Co
Cathn.		17	F	None	26De02Co	Ann	(D)	06	F	Child	26De02Co
GINTY, Cathn.		16	F	None	26De02Co	Rhoda	(D)	05	F	Child	26De02Co
COSGROVE, Niel		27	M	None	26De02Co	Patrick	(S)	04	M	Child	26De02Co
Bridget	(W)	25	F	Wife	26De02Co	John	(S)	01	M	Child	26De02Co
Patrick	(S)	03	M	Child	26De02Co	COSTIGAN, Lawrence		38	M	Farmer	26De02Co
Patrick	(S)	01	M	Child	26De02Co	Margt	(W)	38	F	Wife	26De02Co
COMISKY, Pat		22	M	Laborer	26De02Co	John	(S)	06	M	Child	26De02Co
KINSSEY, John		20	M	None	26De02Co	Michl.	(S)	03	M	Child	26De02Co
GAREN, John		22	M	Laborer	26De02Co	Ann	(D)	01	F	Child	26De02Co
Jas.		24	M	None	26De02Co	Died-At-Sea					
KELLEY, Jas.		27	M	None	26De02Co	SWEENY, Patt		40	M	Farmer	26De02Co

NAMES OF PASSENGERS		AGE	SEX	OCCUPATIONS	DATE PORT SHIP
SWEENY, Bridget	(D)	18	F	None	26De02Co
Michl.	(S)	22	M	None	26De02Co
BRANARIEF, Wm.		25	M	None	26De02Co
MCGIBBEN, Jas.		25	M	None	26De02Co
YOUNG, Alxr.		25	M	Baker	26De02Co
BROWNLEE, Jas.		20	M	None	26De02Co
YOUNG, Mary		19	F	None	26De02Co
John		04	M	Child	26De02Co
JEMSON, Elizbeth		18	F	None	26De02Co
MCNALLY, Cath.		21	F	None	26De02Co
Cath.		20	F	None	26De02Co
Mary		17	F	None	26De02Co
Rose		16	F	None	26De02Co
Ann		21	F	None	26De02Co
KELLEY, John		25	M	None	26De02Co
MAHER, John		20	M	None	26De02Co
FITZPATRICK, Thos.		24	M	Farmer	26De02Co
CONLAN, Francis		16	M	None	26De02Co
LINCH, Mary		25	F	None	26De02Co
GILROY, Danl.		31	M	Farmer	26De02Co
Mary	(W)	30	F	Wife	26De02Co
Patrick	(S)	07	M	Child	26De02Co
Bryan	(S)	04	M	Child	26De02Co
John	(S)	02	M	Child	26De02Co
Bridget		46	F	None	26De02Co
Bridget		01	F	Child	26De02Co
Hugh		26	M	None	26De02Co
MURPHY, Edward		20	M	None	26De02Co
CURRAN, Cathe.		50	F	None	26De02Co
Peter	(S)	23	M	Farmer	26De02Co
Owen	(S)	16	M	None	26De02Co
Bridget	(D)	14	F	None	26De02Co
Thos.	(S)	09	M	Child	26De02Co
Cathn.	(D)	07	F	Child	26De02Co
Ann	(D)	04	F	Child	26De02Co
Eliza	(D)	01	F	Child	26De02Co
FITZPATRICK, Mary		21	F	Dressmaker	26De02Co
Margt.		18	F	None	26De02Co
BRYAN, Sarah		22	F	None	26De02Co
GLINCHY, Michl.		21	M	None	26De02Co
MCGAFFEN, Jas.		20	M	None	26De02Co
WOODS, John		20	M	None	26De02Co
WALLARTREE, John		20	M	Farmer	26De02Co
Sarah		16	F	None	26De02Co
MCCOURT, Bridget		20	F	None	26De02Co
MCCONER, Rose-Ann		18	F	None	26De02Co
MCSHANE, John		20	M	None	26De02Co
DOLON, Biddy		10	F	None	26De02Co
HEGANND, Patrick		30	M	None	26De02Co
U	(D)	06	F	Child	26De02Co
MCGARTY, Michl.		21	M	None	26De02Co
Bridget		20	F	None	26De02Co
HERON, Mary		20	F	None	26De02Co
GAFFREN, Peter		20	M	None	26De02Co
BRESLEN, Pat		24	M	None	26De02Co
DARCEY, Edward		22	M	None	26De02Co
GALNY, Fanny		20	F	None	26De02Co
SHEA, Michl.		35	M	Farmer	26De02Co
Julia	(D)	08	F	Child	26De02Co
FEGAN, Peter		21	M	None	26De02Co
MULROY, Michl.		20	M	None	26De02Co
GILLEM, Anne		20	F	None	26De02Co
CONNER, Patt		24	M	None	26De02Co
BRISNAN, Frank		27	M	Farmer	26De02Co
Bridget		24	F	None	26De02Co
BRADLEY, Alice		19	F	None	26De02Co
Ann	(D)	01	F	Child	26De02Co
MCARDLE, Ann		19	F	None	26De02Co
MCCALL, Cathn.		19	F	None	26De02Co
WARD, Ann		20	F	None	26De02Co
MURPHY, Cathn.		21	F	None	26De02Co
HAYES, Denis		06	M	Child	26De02Co
BRADY, Rose		18	F	None	26De02Co
NURRY, Bridget		18	F	None	26De02Co
SMITH, Rose		18	F	None	26De02Co

NAMES OF PASSENGERS		AGE	SEX	OCCUPATIONS	DATE PORT SHIP
SMITH, Pat		19	M	None	26De02Co
Francis		11	M	None	26De02Co
CONLAN, Thos.		56	M	None	26De02Co
KEEGAN, John		26	M	None	26De02Co
MURRY, John		20	M	None	26De02Co
HAYS, Patrick		40	M	Farmer	26De02Co
Mary		35	F	None	26De02Co
LEARY, Margt.		20	F	None	26De02Co
Peggy		00	F	None	26De02Co
Died-At-Sea					
SHEA, John		12	M	None	26De02Co
David		12	M	None	26De02Co
MCNALLY, Selvester		24	M	Farmer	26De02Co
Margt.		18	F	None	26De02Co
Robt.		15	M	None	26De02Co
DRACY, Francis		16	M	None	26De02Co
CAFFREY, Rose		49	F	None	26De02Co
Edward		30	M	None	26De02Co
John		04	M	Child	26De02Co
CUSACK, Mary		22	F	None	26De02Co
GLYNNE, Sabina		40	F	None	26De02Co
BARRON, Jenna		01	F	Child	26De02Co
MCCAFFREY, Sally		16	F	None	26De02Co
HARRIGAN, Thos.		35	M	None	26De02Co
HAYS, John		14	M	None	26De02Co

KALAMAZOO 28 DECEMBER 1846

From Liverpool

NAMES OF PASSENGERS		AGE	SEX	OCCUPATIONS	DATE PORT SHIP
CANNAGHAN, John		25	M	Farmer	28De02Bt
SCONNON, Thos.		20	M	Farmer	28De02Bt
SMYTH, Thos.		23	M	Farmer	28De02Bt
Jno.		20	M	Farmer	28De02Bt
Rose		15	F	None	28De02Bt
Michl.		13	M	Farmer	28De02Bt
Ann		50	F	None	28De02Bt
TRUANS, Jno.		20	M	Farmer	28De02Bt
GRAHAM, Mary		15	F	None	28De02Bt
LEE, Jno.		40	M	Farmer	28De02Bt
HURAN, Mary		35	F	None	28De02Bt
MCMAHON, Mary		40	F	None	28De02Bt
CARLIN, Ann		20	F	None	28De02Bt
DOLAN, Mary		20	F	None	28De02Bt
BYRNE, Bridget		20	F	None	28De02Bt
GROWCOCK, Geo.		20	M	Farmer	28De02Bt
KEARNEY, Dominick		20	M	Farmer	28De02Bt
WALSH, Michl.		30	M	Farmer	28De02Bt
Nancy	(W)	30	F	Wife	28De02Bt
Jno.	(S)	.00	M	Infant	28De02Bt
MCDERMOTT, Bridget		50	F	None	28De02Bt
Cathe.	(D)	11	F	None	28De02Bt
Michl.	(S)	18	M	None	28De02Bt
Betty	(D)	06	F	Child	28De02Bt
MURRAY, Jno.		25	M	None	28De02Bt
Ann		24	F	None	28De02Bt
JUAN, Martin		18	M	None	28De02Bt
DEAN, Jas.		40	M	None	28De02Bt
Bridget	(W)	40	F	Wife	28De02Bt
Jim	(S)	03	M	Child	28De02Bt
FARRELL, Margt.		30	F	Farmer	28De02Bt
Margt.	(D)	.00	F	Infant	28De02Bt
MURRAY, Pat		30	M	Farmer	28De02Bt
Mary		20	F	None	28De02Bt
GAVAN, Anthony		36	M	Farmer	28De02Bt
MURRAY, Bridget		.00	F	Infant	28De02Bt
HEALY, Michl.		43	M	Farmer	28De02Bt
U, Martin		35	M	Farmer	28De02Bt
MCDONAGH, Pat		32	M	Farmer	28De02Bt

NAMES OF PASSENGERS		AGE	SEX	OCCUPATIONS	DATE PORT SHIP
HEALY, Mary		25	F	Farmer	28De02B†
Biddy		20	F	Farmer	28De02B†
Martin		.00	M	Infant	28De02B†
Jno.		.00	M	Infant	28De02B†
Jno.		.00	M	Infant	28De02B†
MCDONAGH, Sally		24	F	None	28De02B†
HEALY, Mary		60	F	Farmer	28De02B†
WALSH, Biddy		11	F	Farmer	28De02B†
MCDONAGH, Mary		.00	F	Infant	28De02B†
HURST, Jno.		30	M	Farmer	28De02B†
U	(W)	23	F	Wife	28De02B†
Anthony	(S)	.00	M	Infant	28De02B†
Patt		20	M	None	28De02B†
GALLAGHER, Thomas		20	M	Farmer	28De02B†
MCDERMOTT, Cormick		40	M	Farmer	28De02B†
Mary		30	F	None	28De02B†
CULLIN, Mary		15	F	None	28De02B†
Ann		08	F	Child	28De02B†
Laurel		05	F	Child	28De02B†
DERMOTT, Jas.		03	M	Child	28De02B†
PHILLIPS, Edwd.		30	M	None	28De02B†
MCMANUS, Steve		30	M	None	28De02B†
U	(W)	30	F	Wife	28De02B†
Thos.	(S)	13	M	None	28De02B†
James	(S)	11	M	None	28De02B†
Jno.	(S)	06	M	Child	28De02B†
OFARA, Michl.		20	M	None	28De02B†
GAFFREY, Phil		40	M	None	28De02B†
Pat		20	M	None	28De02B†
Thos.		18	M	None	28De02B†
DALTON, Andley		45	M	None	28De02B†
Mary	(W)	40	F	Wife	28De02B†
Thos.	(S)	20	M	None	28De02B†
Ann	(D)	22	F	None	28De02B†
Luke	(S)	17	M	None	28De02B†
Chas.	(S)	20	M	None	28De02B†
Rose	(D)	08	F	Child	28De02B†
BRADY, Margt.		20	F	None	28De02B†
LYNCH, Ellen		40	F	None	28De02B†
HAVARD, Jos.		19	M	None	28De02B†
MCHUGH, Thos.		50	M	None	28De02B†
Mary	(W)	40	F	Wife	28De02B†
Ellen	(D)	18	F	None	28De02B†
Kitty	(D)	16	F	None	28De02B†
Michl.	(S)	12	M	None	28De02B†
Mary	(D)	08	F	Child	28De02B†
Thos.	(S)	07	M	Child	28De02B†
Martin	(S)	04	M	Child	28De02B†
MUNAGHAN, Jno.		22	M	None	28De02B†
MCEWING, Jas.		50	M	None	28De02B†
BOYLE, Mich.		30	M	None	28De02B†
Pat		27	M	None	28De02B†
Ellen		30	F	None	28De02B†
MCEWING, Mary		26	F	None	28De02B†
BOYLE, Mary		20	F	None	28De02B†
GALLAGHER, Ellen		34	F	None	28De02B†
DELBIN, Wm.		20	M	None	28De02B†
MARSHALL, Jas.		20	M	None	28De02B†
Robt.		18	M	None	28De02B†
WILEY, Wm.		20	M	None	28De02B†
DULIN, Michl.		26	M	None	28De02B†
FARRAND, Pat		28	M	None	28De02B†
NICHSON, Peggy		19	F	None	28De02B†
Cathe.		21	F	None	28De02B†
MAHON, Peggy		40	F	None	28De02B†
POWER, Peggy		60	F	None	28De02B†
Jas.	(S)	20	M	None	28De02B†
Jno.	(S)	22	M	None	28De02B†
ONIEL, Brigt.		20	F	None	28De02B†
CONLIN, Chas.		20	M	None	28De02B†
DYER, Jas.		24	M	None	28De02B†
LANDY, Jno.		30	M	None	28De02B†
WALL, Jno.		20	M	None	28De02B†
CLAM, Wm.		27	M	None	28De02B†
CONER, Wm.		35	M	None	28De02B†

NAMES OF PASSENGERS		AGE	SEX	OCCUPATIONS	DATE PORT SHIP
CONER, Pat	(S)	10	M	Child	28De02B†
Jno.	(S)	08	M	Child	28De02B†
DRURY, Jno.		30	M	None	28De02B†
U	(W)	26	F	Wife	28De02B†
Thos.	(S)	03	M	Child	28De02B†
GALLAGER, Pat		50	M	None	28De02B†
HILLIARD, Jno.		30	M	None	28De02B†
KENNEDY, Ally		22	F	None	28De02B†
GRADY, Mary		20	F	None	28De02B†
Cathe.		21	F	None	28De02B†
KELLY, Cathe.		19	F	None	28De02B†
EGAN, Brigt.		22	F	None	28De02B†
MCCULLIN, Lawrence		35	M	None	28De02B†
Mary	(W)	35	F	Wife	28De02B†
Ann	(D)	11	F	None	28De02B†
Biddy	(D)	09	F	Child	28De02B†
Thos.	(S)	07	M	Child	28De02B†
Edwd.	(S)	05	M	Child	28De02B†
Lawrence	(S)	02	M	Child	28De02B†
ANDREWS, Pat		35	M	None	28De02B†
Mary	(W)	35	F	Wife	28De02B†
Cushen	(D)	12	F	None	28De02B†
Jane	(D)	10	F	None	28De02B†
Martin	(S)	08	M	Child	28De02B†
Mary	(D)	06	F	Child	28De02B†
Biddy	(D)	04	F	Child	28De02B†
Margt.	(D)	.00	F	Infant	28De02B†
MCCABE, Jno.		30	M	None	28De02B†
Biddy		20	F	None	28De02B†
Michl.		20	M	None	28De02B†
Nichs.		30	M	None	28De02B†
MARAVEE, Mary		16	F	None	28De02B†
ELLIOTT, Chas.		17	M	None	28De02B†
MCGRATH, Jno.		24	M	None	28De02B†
CROSSIN, Philip		28	M	None	28De02B†
Maria		18	F	None	28De02B†
Margt.		.00	F	Infant	28De02B†
SHERIDAN, Thos.		21	M	None	28De02B†
Mary		18	F	None	28De02B†
CROSSIN, Thos.		18	M	None	28De02B†
Michl.		16	M	None	28De02B†
LYONS, Tim		12	M	None	28De02B†
SHERAN, Frank		22	M	None	28De02B†
OFARRA, Judy		20	F	None	28De02B†
RYAN, Jas.		42	M	None	28De02B†
DOYLE, Jno.		30	M	None	28De02B†
Maria	(D)	.00	F	Infant	28De02B†
Mary	(W)	30	F	Wife	28De02B†
WHALON, David		19	M	None	28De02B†
CURRY, Ann		32	F	None	28De02B†
ROWAN, Eliza		32	F	None	28De02B†
Michl.		18	M	None	28De02B†
Mary		17	F	None	28De02B†
JONES, Evan		31	M	None	28De02B†
DIVINE, Cathe.		50	F	None	28De02B†
Chas.	(S)	19	M	None	28De02B†
Brigt.	(D)	18	F	None	28De02B†
Ann	(D)	16	F	None	28De02B†
Chst.	(S)	12	M	None	28De02B†
RILEY, Ellen		35	F	None	28De02B†
Biddy		30	F	None	28De02B†
Jno.	(S)	04	M	Child	28De02B†
Mary	(D)	12	F	None	28De02B†
Alice	(D)	10	F	Child	28De02B†
Biddy	(D)	07	F	Child	28De02B†
MCGOVERN, Michl.		29	M	None	28De02B†
COLWELL, Mary		21	F	None	28De02B†
BRODERICK, Peter		30	M	None	28De02B†
Biddy	(W)	25	F	Wife	28De02B†
Mary	(D)	06	F	Child	28De02B†
Biddy	(D)	02	F	Child	28De02B†
Nancy	(D)	.00	F	Infant	28De02B†
EGAN, Jno.		26	M	None	28De02B†
Mary	(W)	24	F	Wife	28De02B†
Jas.	(S)	.00	M	Infant	28De02B†

NAMES OF PASSENGERS		AGE	SEX	OCCUPATIONS	DATE PORT SHIP
BURKE, Wm.		24	M	None	28De02Bt
U	(W)	22	F	Wife	28De02Bt
OBRIEN, Arthur		25	M	None	28De02Bt
MCKERIGAN, Jno.		21	M	None	28De02Bt
OBRIEN, Margt.		20	F	None	28De02Bt
Cathe.		20	F	None	28De02Bt
GINTY, Jas.		20	M	None	28De02Bt
Rose		20	F	None	28De02Bt
CURRIN, Cathe.		26	F	None	28De02Bt
MCCOSKER, Ann		20	F	None	28De02Bt
KEENAN, Ellen		40	F	None	28De02Bt
Mary	(D)	09	F	Child	28De02Bt
Leith	(D)	06	F	Child	28De02Bt
Jno.	(S)	04	M	Child	28De02Bt
Rose	(D)	02	F	Child	28De02Bt
THOMPSON, Robt.		34	M	None	28De02Bt
CAFFREY, Judy		12	F	None	28De02Bt
CAMBELL, Henry		30	M	None	28De02Bt
RILEY, Bridget		30	F	None	28De02Bt
MCCANN, Thos.		50	M	None	28De02Bt
U	(W)	49	F	Wife	28De02Bt
Jas.	(S)	25	M	None	28De02Bt
Nancy	(D)	20	F	None	28De02Bt
Mary	(D)	18	F	None	28De02Bt
Jane	(D)	12	F	None	28De02Bt
Wm.	(S)	11	M	None	28De02Bt
Ann	(D)	09	F	Child	28De02Bt
Denis	(S)	07	M	Child	28De02Bt
Thos.	(S)	06	M	Child	28De02Bt
CALLAGHAN, Peter		29	M	None	28De02Bt
U	(W)	36	F	Wife	28De02Bt
Mary		20	F	None	28De02Bt
MOONEY, Thos.		30	M	None	28De02Bt
CALLAGHAN, Maria		03	F	Child	28De02Bt
Jane		.00	F	Infant	28De02Bt
BOYLE, Jas.		35	M	None	28De02Bt
Bernd.		25	M	None	28De02Bt
MASTERSON, Pat		30	M	None	28De02Bt
Ann	(W)	24	F	Wife	28De02Bt
Pat	(S)	02	M	Child	28De02Bt
Mary	(D)	.00	F	Infant	28De02Bt
MCDOWNES, Arthur		18	M	None	28De02Bt
U-Mrs.	(M)	50	F	None	28De02Bt
Bessy	(T)	21	F	None	28De02Bt
Ann	(T)	13	F	None	28De02Bt
Jno.	(B)	12	M	None	28De02Bt
COHIT, Ellen		46	F	None	28De02Bt
Cathe.	(D)	18	F	None	28De02Bt
DOYLE, Pat		21	M	None	28De02Bt
Peggy		18	F	None	28De02Bt
KEWON, Pat		20	M	None	28De02Bt
Jno.		18	M	None	28De02Bt
MULLHOLLAND, Ann		08	F	Child	28De02Bt
Mary		03	F	Child	28De02Bt
Susan		11	F	None	28De02Bt
Ann		09	F	Child	28De02Bt
Jno.		07	M	Child	28De02Bt
MCGINN, Pat		20	M	None	28De02Bt
LEACH, Jas.		45	M	None	28De02Bt
MCCOURTT, Jas.		40	M	None	28De02Bt
GALLAGHER, Jas.		21	M	None	28De02Bt
Peter		17	M	None	28De02Bt
CERNIGHN, Jno.		26	M	None	28De02Bt
MCCOME, Ellen		19	F	None	28De02Bt
MULLIN, Michl.		36	M	None	28De02Bt
DUFFY, U		27	M	None	28De02Bt
STEER, Sally		47	F	None	28De02Bt
RILEY, Jas.		36	M	None	28De02Bt
MCQUADE, Pat		23	M	None	28De02Bt
KELLY, Roger		20	M	None	28De02Bt
Bridget		17	F	None	28De02Bt
MCDENT, Margt.		23	F	None	28De02Bt
CANN, Mary		17	F	None	28De02Bt
CRISTIE, Jno.		34	M	None	28De02Bt
Joh.		19	F	None	28De02Bt

NAMES OF PASSENGERS		AGE	SEX	OCCUPATIONS	DATE PORT SHIP
MCCAFFER, U-Mrs.		29	F	None	28De02Bt
KANE, Mary		18	F	None	28De02Bt
BEEDE, U		29	M	None	28De02Bt
KANE, U-Mrs.		35	F	None	28De02Bt
MATTHEWS, Henry		42	M	None	28De02Bt
FARRA, Patrick		19	M	None	28De02Bt

VIRGINIAN 29 DECEMBER 1846

From Liverpool

NAMES OF PASSENGERS		AGE	SEX	OCCUPATIONS	DATE PORT SHIP
DONNELLY, James		24	M	Farmer	29De02Ap
CALLEHAN, Owen		55	M	Laborer	29De02Ap
Catherine	(W)	50	F	Wife	29De02Ap
Mary	(D)	22	F	Laborer	29De02Ap
Ellen	(D)	18	F	Laborer	29De02Ap
Ann	(D)	12	F	Laborer	29De02Ap
John	(S)	10	M	Child	29De02Ap
Michael	(S)	09	M	Child	29De02Ap
Patrick	(S)	07	M	Child	29De02Ap
REILLY, James		20	M	Laborer	29De02Ap
John		18	M	Laborer	29De02Ap
KELLY, Michael		40	M	Laborer	29De02Ap
U	(W)	40	F	Wife	29De02Ap
Bessy	(D)	22	F	Laborer	29De02Ap
Petre	(S)	15	M	Laborer	29De02Ap
Mary	(D)	13	F	Laborer	29De02Ap
Michael	(S)	11	M	Laborer	29De02Ap
Matilda	(D)	09	F	Child	29De02Ap
SMALL, Henry		17	M	Laborer	29De02Ap
DENNAN, Daniel		42	M	Laborer	29De02Ap
COLWELL, Petre		39	M	Laborer	29De02Ap
CULLEN, John		60	M	Laborer	29De02Ap
CARROLL, Catherine		24	F	Laborer	29De02Ap
GUNN, William		20	M	Laborer	29De02Ap
OWENS, John		21	M	Laborer	29De02Ap
U	(W)	19	F	Wife	29De02Ap
Rose		23	F	Laborer	29De02Ap
CONNELLY, Henry		20	M	Laborer	29De02Ap
Henry		18	M	Laborer	29De02Ap
FOLEY, John		25	M	Laborer	29De02Ap
DUFFY, John		23	M	Laborer	29De02Ap
MCDANIEL, James		60	M	Laborer	29De02Ap
U-Mrs.		27	F	Laborer	29De02Ap
Edward		04	M	Child	29De02Ap
Thomas		03	M	Child	29De02Ap
Biddy		.02	F	Infant	29De02Ap
FARLEY, Michael		20	M	Laborer	29De02Ap
GIBNEY, Owen		22	M	Laborer	29De02Ap
Nancy		20	F	Laborer	29De02Ap
BOHAMA, Nancy		13	F	Laborer	29De02Ap
BLAKE, Patrick		26	M	Laborer	29De02Ap
CARVANNAH, Patrl.		16	M	Laborer	29De02Ap
KEAN, Patrick		20	M	Laborer	29De02Ap
Martin		18	M	Laborer	29De02Ap
MULOENEY, Dominick		35	M	Laborer	29De02Ap
HIGGINS, Michael		30	M	Laborer	29De02Ap
Teddy		22	M	Laborer	29De02Ap
LYAN, Andrew		25	M	Laborer	29De02Ap
MCGOWAN, Patrick		26	M	Laborer	29De02Ap
John		27	M	Laborer	29De02Ap
WILKINS, George		21	M	Laborer	29De02Ap
LIVELY, Bridget		40	F	Laborer	29De02Ap
MCBRYAN, Bridget		22	F	Laborer	29De02Ap
HIGGINS, Peggy		30	F	Laborer	29De02Ap
OMEALEY, Petre		20	M	Laborer	29De02Ap
OBOYLE, Hugh		32	M	Laborer	29De02Ap
Maider	(W)	32	F	Wife	29De02Ap
Mary	(D)	01	F	Child	29De02Ap

NAMES OF PASSENGERS		AGE	SEX	OCCUPATIONS	DATE PORT SHIP
MURPHY, John		23	M	Laborer	29De02Ap
HALEY, John		30	M	Laborer	29De02Ap
U	(W)	22	F	Wife	29De02Ap
John	(S)	.06	M	Infant	29De02Ap
EARLEY, Mary		22	F	Laborer	29De02Ap
MCELROY, James		30	M	Laborer	29De02Ap
Matty		27	M	Laborer	29De02Ap
Sarah		12	F	Laborer	29De02Ap
Eliza		10	F	Laborer	29De02Ap
James		08	M	Child	29De02Ap
Margaret		05	F	Child	29De02Ap
Matty		03	M	Child	29De02Ap
Edward		01	M	Child	29De02Ap
CONORAN, Owen		40	M	Laborer	29De02Ap
Catherine	(D)	13	F	Laborer	29De02Ap
SHERIDAN, Patrick		20	M	Laborer	29De02Ap
WARD, Biddy		19	F	Laborer	29De02Ap
CONNOLLY, Rose		40	F	Laborer	29De02Ap
REILLY, Catherine		20	F	Laborer	29De02Ap
SHERRIDAN, Bryan		30	M	Laborer	29De02Ap
Mary	(W)	30	F	Wife	29De02Ap
Michael	(S)	05	M	Child	29De02Ap
John	(S)	03	M	Child	29De02Ap
Bryan	(S)	02	M	Child	29De02Ap
Patrick	(S)	.06	M	Infant	29De02Ap
CAMPBLL, Robert		21	M	Laborer	29De02Ap
William		26	M	Laborer	29De02Ap
Susan		30	F	Laborer	29De02Ap
Ann-Maria		03	F	Child	29De02Ap
Margaret		24	F	Laborer	29De02Ap
William		01	M	Child	29De02Ap
Robert		03	M	Child	29De02Ap
CANNING, Thomas		40	M	Laborer	29De02Ap
Ann	(W)	40	F	Wife	29De02Ap
Ann	(D)	13	F	Laborer	29De02Ap
Catherine	(D)	12	F	Laborer	29De02Ap
Thomas	(S)	10	M	Child	29De02Ap
Bridget	(D)	08	F	Child	29De02Ap
SHERRIDAN, Thomas		20	M	Laborer	29De02Ap
CONORAN, Patrick		19	M	Laborer	29De02Ap
MULREHEN, Thomas		24	M	Laborer	29De02Ap
MCCOMMICK, Bernard		32	M	Farmer	29De02Ap
GALLAGHEN, Michael		23	M	Farmer	29De02Ap
Mary		18	F	Farmer	29De02Ap
OHARA, Thomas		19	M	Farmer	29De02Ap
MARTIN, Ellen		27	F	Farmer	29De02Ap
CLARK, Thomas		28	M	Carpenter	29De02Ap
Ellen		23	F	Dressmaker	29De02Ap
REILLY, Ann		20	F	None	29De02Ap
SMITH, Biddy		19	F	None	29De02Ap
CONLAN, Martha		22	F	None	29De02Ap
LATTIMER, John		23	M	Tailor	29De02Ap
KELLY, John		21	M	Laborer	29De02Ap
DONOHUE, Petre		19	M	Tailor	29De02Ap
HOUGHTON, Mary		40	F	None	29De02Ap
John	(S)	20	M	Laborer	29De02Ap
Catherine	(D)	15	F	Laborer	29De02Ap
Dennis	(S)	13	M	Laborer	29De02Ap
Francis	(S)	11	M	Laborer	29De02Ap
Biddy	(D)	10	F	Laborer	29De02Ap
Michael	(S)	07	M	Child	29De02Ap
QUINN, Michael		20	M	Laborer	29De02Ap
DOLAN, Anthony		20	M	Laborer	29De02Ap
DURKIN, Tilby		20	M	Laborer	29De02Ap
GALDING, John		24	M	Laborer	29De02Ap
Betty		20	F	Laborer	29De02Ap
SCANLAN, John		20	M	Laborer	29De02Ap
MITCHELL, Wm.		26	M	Laborer	29De02Ap
Ann		24	F	Laborer	29De02Ap
SMITH, John		24	M	Laborer	29De02Ap
Biddy		20	F	Laborer	29De02Ap
MALORY, Wm.		35	M	Laborer	29De02Ap
GILCOOLEY, Owen		25	M	Laborer	29De02Ap
Jane		24	F	Laborer	29De02Ap
MCDONAGH, Thomas		20	M	Laborer	29De02Ap

NAMES OF PASSENGERS		AGE	SEX	OCCUPATIONS	DATE PORT SHIP
BLUNT, John		21	M	Laborer	29De02Ap
Biddy		23	F	Laborer	29De02Ap
TIMM, Daniel		20	M	Laborer	29De02Ap
CONNELL, Michl.		30	M	Laborer	29De02Ap
Mary	(W)	27	F	Wife	29De02Ap
Patrick	(S)	03	M	Child	29De02Ap
Michael	(S)	.10	M	Infant	29De02Ap
HOGG, Thom.		24	M	Laborer	29De02Ap
Mary	(W)	26	F	Wife	29De02Ap
Bridget	(D)	01	F	Child	29De02Ap
EARLEY, Bridget		25	F	Laborer	29De02Ap
CALE, Bridget		21	F	Laborer	29De02Ap
MULVEY, Mary		20	F	Laborer	29De02Ap
KILLOLY, Bridget		20	F	Laborer	29De02Ap
GUCHEON, Mary		20	F	Laborer	29De02Ap
GROHAGAN, Cathn.		20	F	Laborer	29De02Ap
Patrick		14	M	Laborer	29De02Ap
CULLEN, James		11	M	Laborer	29De02Ap
Ellen		19	F	Laborer	29De02Ap
FLANNAGHAN, John		26	M	Laborer	29De02Ap
Catherine	(W)	24	F	Wife	29De02Ap
Patrick	(S)	.06	M	Infant	29De02Ap
BURNS, John		19	M	Merchant	29De02Ap
WILLIAMS, John		23	M	Clerk	29De02Ap
MANGAN, Patrick		25	M	Laborer	29De02Ap
MCDONOUGH, Bridget		20	F	Laborer	29De02Ap
MCILROY, Thomas		21	M	Laborer	29De02Ap
CANAGHAN, Martin		25	M	Laborer	29De02Ap
MITCHELL, Michael		20	M	Laborer	29De02Ap
MCDONOUGH, James		20	M	Laborer	29De02Ap
SCANLAN, Michl.		24	M	Laborer	29De02Ap
SHERRY, Patrick		25	M	Laborer	29De02Ap
DEVENY, Patrick		14	M	Laborer	29De02Ap
Mary-Ann		09	F	Child	29De02Ap
MORAN, James		23	M	Laborer	29De02Ap
Ellen		11	F	Laborer	29De02Ap
KIERNAN, Thomas		24	M	Laborer	29De02Ap
CORCORAN, Ellen		26	F	Laborer	29De02Ap
SMYTH, James		16	M	Laborer	29De02Ap
CARROLL, James		00	M	Unknown	29De02Ap
SAUNDERS, U-Mrs.		00	F	Unknown	29De02Ap

ORPHAN 30 DECEMBER 1846

From Liverpool

NAMES OF PASSENGERS		AGE	SEX	OCCUPATIONS	DATE PORT SHIP
DOWNEY, Margret		16	F	Servant	30De02DJ
MALIRE, Hugh		30	M	Laborer	30De02DJ
Sally	(W)	30	F	Wife	30De02DJ
Joseph	(S)	10	M	Child	30De02DJ
LOUGHLIN, John		12	M	Laborer	30De02DJ
WILLIAMSON, John		24	M	Laborer	30De02DJ
HALLIMAN, Samuel		24	M	Laborer	30De02DJ
Mary	(W)	30	F	Wife	30De02DJ
Eliza-Jane	(D)	01	F	Child	30De02DJ
STAFFORD, John		21	M	Laborer	30De02DJ
Hannah		20	F	Laborer	30De02DJ
MASTERSON, Joseph		20	M	Laborer	30De02DJ
MCDONNEL, Phil		20	M	Laborer	30De02DJ
Catherine		19	F	Laborer	30De02DJ
LAMB, Patt		37	M	Laborer	30De02DJ
REARY, William		27	M	Laborer	30De02DJ
Catherine	(W)	27	F	Wife	30De02DJ
Thomas	(S)	03	M	Child	30De02DJ
William	(S)	01	M	Child	30De02DJ
LOUGHLIN, William		27	M	Laborer	30De02DJ
Bridget	(W)	26	F	Wife	30De02DJ
Maria	(D)	01	F	Child	30De02DJ
FOGERTY, Judy		23	F	Laborer	30De02DJ

NAMES OF PASSENGERS		AGE	SEX	OCCUPATIONS	DATE PORT SHIP
MURPHY, Mary		23	F	Laborer	30De02DJ
MCQUADE, Jacob		30	M	Laborer	30De02DJ
Mary	(W)	25	F	Wife	30De02DJ
Elluza	(D)	01	F	Child	30De02DJ
COLLINS, Mary		60	F	Laborer	30De02DJ
Patrick		12	M	Laborer	30De02DJ
MCFURLAND, William		12	M	Laborer	30De02DJ
John		08	M	Child	30De02DJ
MCDONNEL, Eliza		20	F	Servant	30De02DJ
GENSITY, Bridget		60	F	Servant	30De02DJ
Marallas		12	F	Servant	30De02DJ
James		20	M	Servant	30De02DJ
MCDONNEL, Anthony		18	M	Servant	30De02DJ
RUYE, Merlin		20	M	Servant	30De02DJ
Bridget		20	F	Servant	30De02DJ
TOLAN, Mathew		20	M	Servant	30De02DJ
PARK, Samuel		20	M	Servant	30De02DJ
MCNULTY, Thos.		27	M	Servant	30De02DJ
Bridget		24	F	Servant	30De02DJ
MCRIEL, Mary		24	F	Servant	30De02DJ
GROGAN, Anne		20	F	Servant	30De02DJ
MAHON, Margt.		18	F	Servant	30De02DJ
HUM, Catherine		20	F	Servant	30De02DJ
QUERREL, Dorothea		20	F	Servant	30De02DJ
BABYA, Peter		20	M	Servant	30De02DJ
MCQUE, Pat		27	M	Servant	30De02DJ
GAVIN, Marlin		21	M	Servant	30De02DJ
KING, Biddy		20	F	Servant	30De02DJ
MCCULLEN, Robt.		20	M	Servant	30De02DJ
MULDOON, Edward		22	M	Laborer	30De02DJ
Patt		19	M	Laborer	30De02DJ
PHILLIPS, Anne		26	F	Laborer	30De02DJ
MCLURLEY, Bridget		24	F	Laborer	30De02DJ
KEAVIN, Charles		22	M	Laborer	30De02DJ
Francis		16	M	Laborer	30De02DJ
MCGUIRE, Charles		24	M	Laborer	30De02DJ
Jane	(W)	24	F	Wife	30De02DJ
Francis	(S)	03	M	Child	30De02DJ
Frances	(D)	01	F	Child	30De02DJ
MULDOON, Henry		27	M	Laborer	30De02DJ
Bell		25	M	Laborer	30De02DJ
Bridget		01	F	Child	30De02DJ
MCGUNE, Patt		50	M	Laborer	30De02DJ
Margret	(W)	46	F	Wife	30De02DJ
John	(S)	22	M	Laborer	30De02DJ
Francis	(S)	20	M	Laborer	30De02DJ
Patrick	(S)	18	M	Laborer	30De02DJ
Eliza	(D)	16	F	Laborer	30De02DJ
Mary	(D)	13	F	Laborer	30De02DJ
Margret	(D)	11	F	Laborer	30De02DJ
Anne	(D)	09	F	Child	30De02DJ
Robt.	(S)	07	M	Child	30De02DJ
James	(S)	04	M	Child	30De02DJ
Thos.	(S)	01	M	Child	30De02DJ
MULDOON, John		58	M	Laborer	30De02DJ
Bridget	(W)	59	F	Wife	30De02DJ
Patrick	(S)	32	M	Laborer	30De02DJ
Patrick	(S)	27	M	Laborer	30De02DJ
Michael	(S)	22	M	Laborer	30De02DJ
Danel	(S)	17	M	Laborer	30De02DJ
GOURLY, James		26	M	Laborer	30De02DJ
James		20	M	Laborer	30De02DJ
Patrick		22	M	Laborer	30De02DJ
John		23	M	Laborer	30De02DJ
MCPARRY, Samuel		25	M	Laborer	30De02DJ
GOURLY, Sarah		13	F	Laborer	30De02DJ
GILL, Bidy		20	F	Laborer	30De02DJ
SEALLY, James		18	M	Laborer	30De02DJ
FARREL, Biddy		25	F	Laborer	30De02DJ
FENGELTON, Edward		30	M	Laborer	30De02DJ
MCCAFRY, Cahml.		42	M	Laborer	30De02DJ
Died-At-Sea					
Anne		35	F	Laborer	30De02DJ
LAUGLIN, Saml.		23	M	Laborer	30De02DJ
MCGLIMHIN, Anne		18	F	Laborer	30De02DJ
STEWART, William		18	M	Laborer	30De02DJ
MCDONNEL, Arthur		60	M	Laborer	30De02DJ
RILEY, Thos.		24	M	Laborer	30De02DJ
LYNCH, James		40	M	Laborer	30De02DJ
Mary	(W)	40	F	Wife	30De02DJ
Judy	(D)	18	F	Laborer	30De02DJ
Ellen	(D)	16	F	Laborer	30De02DJ
Patt	(S)	12	M	Laborer	30De02DJ
Farrel	(S)	10	M	Laborer	30De02DJ
Anne	(D)	08	F	Child	30De02DJ
Catherine	(D)	06	F	Child	30De02DJ
James	(S)	04	M	Child	30De02DJ
Peter	(S)	04	M	Child	30De02DJ
Mary	(D)	02	F	Child	30De02DJ
Margret	(D)	01	F	Child	30De02DJ
JOHNSTON, Thos.		40	M	Laborer	30De02DJ
Mary	(W)	40	F	Wife	30De02DJ
Martha	(D)	18	F	Laborer	30De02DJ
Anne	(D)	15	F	Laborer	30De02DJ
James	(S)	12	M	Laborer	30De02DJ
Thomas	(S)	10	M	Laborer	30De02DJ
Jane	(D)	04	F	Child	30De02DJ
HODLIN, Hanll-M.		25	M	Laborer	30De02DJ
BENISE, Archd.		35	M	Laborer	30De02DJ
SHIPPEN, Mary		26	F	Servant	30De02DJ
CAMBELL, James		21	M	Laborer	30De02DJ
Bridget		21	F	Laborer	30De02DJ
FAY, Mathew		21	M	Laborer	30De02DJ
DEVYN, Michl.		33	M	Laborer	30De02DJ
Bridget		29	F	Laborer	30De02DJ
HARDMAN, Mary		23	F	Laborer	30De02DJ
GOLOCHEN, Patt		30	M	Laborer	30De02DJ
Catherine		30	F	Laborer	30De02DJ
MCKENNA, Patt		30	M	Laborer	30De02DJ
JOHNSTON, Anthony		30	M	Laborer	30De02DJ
TIMLIN, Michel		20	M	Laborer	30De02DJ
TWEARY, Owen		20	M	Laborer	30De02DJ
DORAN, Patt		40	M	Laborer	30De02DJ
Mary	(W)	40	F	Wife	30De02DJ
Bidy	(D)	12	F	Laborer	30De02DJ
Peter	(S)	11	M	Laborer	30De02DJ
Michael	(S)	09	M	Child	30De02DJ
Nancy	(D)	07	F	Child	30De02DJ
Frank	(S)	05	M	Child	30De02DJ
Mary	(D)	02	F	Child	30De02DJ
TAYLOR, James		25	M	Laborer	30De02DJ
BLUET, Thos.		25	M	Laborer	30De02DJ
BOLDS, John		30	M	Laborer	30De02DJ
Mary	(W)	30	F	Wife	30De02DJ
Mary	(D)	15	F	Laborer	30De02DJ
Catherine	(D)	12	F	Laborer	30De02DJ
Anne	(D)	10	F	Laborer	30De02DJ
Ellen	(D)	08	F	Child	30De02DJ
James	(S)	06	M	Child	30De02DJ
Bernard	(S)	04	M	Child	30De02DJ
Bridget	(D)	02	F	Child	30De02DJ
HINDES, Mary		25	F	Laborer	30De02DJ
CROSBY, Bridget		30	F	Laborer	30De02DJ
Catherine	(D)	09	F	Child	30De02DJ
Mary	(D)	01	F	Child	30De02DJ
GOLOCHEN, Peter		40	M	Laborer	30De02DJ
Died-At-Sea					
Margret	(W)	40	F	Wife	30De02DJ
Patt	(S)	20	M	Laborer	30De02DJ
John	(S)	18	M	Laborer	30De02DJ
Margret	(D)	13	F	Laborer	30De02DJ
Bridget	(D)	11	F	Laborer	30De02DJ
Peter	(S)	10	M	Laborer	30De02DJ
Thomas	(S)	08	M	Child	30De02DJ
Onorra		30	F	Laborer	30De02DJ
Patt	(S)	13	M	Laborer	30De02DJ
Catherine	(D)	11	F	Laborer	30De02DJ
Michael	(S)	13	M	Laborer	30De02DJ
GOUGHEY, Anthony		30	M	Laborer	30De02DJ
Catherine		30	F	Laborer	30De02DJ

NAMES OF PASSENGERS		AGE	SEX	OCCUPATIONS	DATE PORT SHIP
MCLEAN, Patt		20	M	Laborer	30De02DJ
LYONS, Patt		21	M	Laborer	30De02DJ
LEVERY, Peter		20	M	Laborer	30De02DJ
Marlin		21	M	Laborer	30De02DJ
Bridget		20	F	Laborer	30De02DJ
Nancy		30	F	Laborer	30De02DJ
LOFTUS, Peter		25	M	Laborer	30De02DJ
Gibey		25	M	Laborer	30De02DJ
RILEY, Bridget		25	F	Laborer	30De02DJ
MCQUEDT, James		26	M	Laborer	30De02DJ
GUBLER, Casper		25	M	Laborer	30De02DJ
MORRIE, Bidy		04	F	Child	30De02DJ
MCGOVEN, Mary		20	F	Laborer	30De02DJ
KEAN, Bidy		20	F	Laborer	30De02DJ
HURLEY, Samuel		50	M	Laborer	30De02DJ
MCKEW, William		20	M	Laborer	30De02DJ
MCCONNEL, Margret		20	F	Laborer	30De02DJ
WELCH, Richard		22	M	Gentleman	30De02DJ
Anne		50	F	Lady	30De02DJ
Catherine		30	F	Lady	30De02DJ
Mary-Julia		21	F	Lady	30De02DJ
Elizabeth		20	F	Lady	30De02DJ
HINDES, Ralph		02	M	Child	30De02DJ

CHAOS 02 JANUARY 1847

From Liverpool

NAMES OF PASSENGERS		AGE	SEX	OCCUPATIONS	DATE PORT SHIP
PHILLIPS, H.		40	M	Laborer	02Ja02Gg
Robt.		20	M	Laborer	02Ja02Gg
Francis		18	M	Laborer	02Ja02Gg
Mary		16	F	Unknown	02Ja02Gg
Andrew		13	M	None	02Ja02Gg
Henry	(S)	10	M	None	02Ja02Gg
DOOKER, A.		30	M	Farmer	02Ja02Gg
Frances		24	F	Unknown	02Ja02Gg
WALSH, T.		30	M	Farmer	02Ja02Gg
Pat		18	M	Laborer	02Ja02Gg
Mary		22	F	Unknown	02Ja02Gg
MCANDREW, M.		23	M	Laborer	02Ja02Gg
Eleanor		50	F	Unknown	02Ja02Gg
Bgt.		21	F	Unknown	02Ja02Gg
Danl.		13	M	None	02Ja02Gg
LOFTUS, A.		35	M	Laborer	02Ja02Gg
Bgt.		26	F	Unknown	02Ja02Gg
Thos.		02	M	Child	02Ja02Gg
Bgt.		20	F	Unknown	02Ja02Gg
Patt		01	M	Child	02Ja02Gg
DICKSON, G.		22	M	Laborer	02Ja02Gg
Cath.		20	F	Unknown	02Ja02Gg
GIBBONS, M.		40	M	Laborer	02Ja02Gg
John		17	M	Laborer	02Ja02Gg
Patt		12	M	None	02Ja02Gg
Mary		13	F	Unknown	02Ja02Gg
FISHER, M.A.		40	M	Farmer	02Ja02Gg
Matd.		15	F	Unknown	02Ja02Gg
Caroline		02	F	Child	02Ja02Gg
Walter		01	M	Child	02Ja02Gg
EVANS, H.		26	M	Laborer	02Ja02Gg
U	(W)	25	F	Wife	02Ja02Gg
Henry	(S)	03	M	Child	02Ja02Gg
Thomas	(S)	01	M	Child	02Ja02Gg
GILLESPIE, P.		40	M	Farmer	02Ja02Gg
Mary	(W)	31	F	Wife	02Ja02Gg
Thomas	(S)	07	M	Child	02Ja02Gg
Mary	(D)	06	F	Child	02Ja02Gg
FURLIN, A.		25	M	Laborer	02Ja02Gg
Ann		18	F	Unknown	02Ja02Gg
MCELROY, O.		20	M	Farmer	02Ja02Gg

NAMES OF PASSENGERS		AGE	SEX	OCCUPATIONS	DATE PORT SHIP
SMITH, J.		19	M	Laborer	02Ja02Gg
RILEY, J.		20	M	Laborer	02Ja02Gg
Phillip		30	M	Laborer	02Ja02Gg
Mgt.		26	F	Unknown	02Ja02Gg
WAGNER, J.		20	M	Laborer	02Ja02Gg
KEEN, J.		21	M	Laborer	02Ja02Gg
GALLAGHER, J.		25	M	Laborer	02Ja02Gg
Hannah		30	F	Unknown	02Ja02Gg
DALY, J.		20	M	Laborer	02Ja02Gg
GREENSON, T.		19	M	Laborer	02Ja02Gg
KERIGAN, P.		34	M	Laborer	02Ja02Gg
CARROLL, T.		20	M	Laborer	02Ja02Gg
MULLIGAN, T.		20	M	Laborer	02Ja02Gg
GOOLAN, M.		18	M	Laborer	02Ja02Gg
RELORY, P.		20	M	Laborer	02Ja02Gg
FAGHY, A.		17	M	Laborer	02Ja02Gg
QUIGLEY, R.		23	M	Laborer	02Ja02Gg
STOCKER, J.		23	M	Laborer	02Ja02Gg
WHITE, J.		27	M	Laborer	02Ja02Gg
CLOMAN, T.		24	M	Laborer	02Ja02Gg
KERIGAN, C.		20	M	Laborer	02Ja02Gg
MAGUIRE, A.		34	M	Laborer	02Ja02Gg
GALLAGHER, M.		20	F	Unknown	02Ja02Gg
SCOTT, M.		50	M	Laborer	02Ja02Gg
KELLY, D.		49	M	Laborer	02Ja02Gg
Cath.		49	F	Unknown	02Ja02Gg
Patt		18	M	None	02Ja02Gg
Mary		16	F	Unknown	02Ja02Gg
Mich.		10	M	None	02Ja02Gg
Ann		06	F	Child	02Ja02Gg
John		04	M	Child	02Ja02Gg
Ann		01	F	Child	02Ja02Gg
MCCURLY, M.		28	M	Laborer	02Ja02Gg
Fany	(W)	28	F	Wife	02Ja02Gg
Mich.	(S)	09	M	Child	02Ja02Gg
Thos.	(S)	02	M	Child	02Ja02Gg
Patt	(S)	01	M	Child	02Ja02Gg
Thos.		25	M	Laborer	02Ja02Gg
Bgt.		23	F	Unknown	02Ja02Gg
MONGHAN, J.		23	M	Laborer	02Ja02Gg
MAGUIRE, J.		35	M	Laborer	02Ja02Gg
Bgt.	(W)	30	F	Wife	02Ja02Gg
Cornelia	(D)	04	F	Child	02Ja02Gg
John	(S)	03	M	Child	02Ja02Gg
MURPHY, J.		22	M	Laborer	02Ja02Gg
BROWN, M.		20	M	Laborer	02Ja02Gg
Biddy		20	F	Unknown	02Ja02Gg
WARE, Betty		23	F	Unknown	02Ja02Gg
DUFFY, Kitty		23	F	Unknown	02Ja02Gg
YOUNG, Betsy		20	F	Unknown	02Ja02Gg
MARTIN, P.		20	M	Laborer	02Ja02Gg
LARIGAN, M.		25	M	Laborer	02Ja02Gg
Kitty		19	F	Unknown	02Ja02Gg
Phelan		13	M	None	02Ja02Gg
Barb.		11	F	Unknown	02Ja02Gg
FRENIS, Mary		20	F	Unknown	02Ja02Gg
LARIGAN, J.		50	M	Laborer	02Ja02Gg
Bgt.	(W)	50	F	Wife	02Ja02Gg
Mich.	(S)	22	M	Laborer	02Ja02Gg
Thomas	(S)	20	M	Laborer	02Ja02Gg
John	(S)	16	M	Laborer	02Ja02Gg
Mary	(D)	14	F	Unknown	02Ja02Gg
Ann	(D)	12	F	Unknown	02Ja02Gg
Patt	(S)	10	M	None	02Ja02Gg
Biddy	(D)	07	F	Child	02Ja02Gg
Peggy	(D)	01	F	Child	02Ja02Gg
YARR, Ann		56	F	Unknown	02Ja02Gg
Wm.		19	M	Laborer	02Ja02Gg
Bgt.		17	F	Unknown	02Ja02Gg
Ann		08	F	Child	02Ja02Gg
MCCAULY, P.		26	M	Laborer	02Ja02Gg
Bgt.	(W)	26	F	Wife	02Ja02Gg
Biddy	(D)	02	F	Child	02Ja02Gg
Mary	(D)	01	F	Child	02Ja02Gg
LAYLIN, Ellen		18	F	Unknown	02Ja02Gg

NAMES OF PASSENGERS		A G E	S E X	OCCUPATIONS	DATE PORT SHIP
MCSHEARN, O.		61	M	Laborer	02Ja02Gg
Martha	(W)	61	F	Wife	02Ja02Gg
Ann	(D)	20	F	Unknown	02Ja02Gg
John	(S)	18	M	Laborer	02Ja02Gg
WELCH, J.		25	M	Laborer	02Ja02Gg
Ann		21	F	Unknown	02Ja02Gg
HALY, J.		50	M	Laborer	02Ja02Gg
Mary		18	F	Unknown	02Ja02Gg
Biddy		10	F	Unknown	02Ja02Gg
Thomas		18	M	Laborer	02Ja02Gg
Mich.		20	M	Laborer	02Ja02Gg
Betsy		24	F	Unknown	02Ja02Gg
BRYAN, P.		40	M	Laborer	02Ja02Gg
Mary	(W)	35	F	Wife	02Ja02Gg
Stephen	(S)	10	M	None	02Ja02Gg
Ann	(D)	06	F	Child	02Ja02Gg
Mary	(D)	04	F	Child	02Ja02Gg
Ellen	(D)	01	F	Child	02Ja02Gg
STAPELTON, Mary		21	F	Unknown	02Ja02Gg
TOOKER, Mary		24	F	Unknown	02Ja02Gg
SEALY, Ann		24	F	Unknown	02Ja02Gg
BRANCHY, A.		34	M	Laborer	02Ja02Gg
Elizbt.		30	F	Unknown	02Ja02Gg
HERRY, M.		21	M	Laborer	02Ja02Gg
MCREN, J.		18	M	Laborer	02Ja02Gg
MALY, Mary		20	F	Unknown	02Ja02Gg
MCGARRY, Ellen		23	F	Unknown	02Ja02Gg
BATTIGAN, P.		21	M	Laborer	02Ja02Gg
GOLDING, J.		24	M	Laborer	02Ja02Gg
Mary		18	F	Unknown	02Ja02Gg
Mary		14	F	Unknown	02Ja02Gg
DOLAN, P.		25	M	Laborer	02Ja02Gg
Ellen		25	F	Unknown	02Ja02Gg
STIMLE, J.		40	M	Laborer	02Ja02Gg
Mary		18	F	Unknown	02Ja02Gg
MEARN, D.		30	M	Laborer	02Ja02Gg
Mary		30	F	Unknown	02Ja02Gg
DEVERY, T.		22	M	Laborer	02Ja02Gg
Honora	(W)	22	F	Wife	02Ja02Gg
Michl.	(S)	01	M	Child	02Ja02Gg
DONNEGAN, T.		28	M	Laborer	02Ja02Gg
MCALLEN, D.		30	M	Laborer	02Ja02Gg
COCHRAN, P.		34	M	Laborer	02Ja02Gg
TONCHER, Peggy		18	F	Unknown	02Ja02Gg
CORIDON, Mn.		11	F	Unknown	02Ja02Gg
MCJUSHY, E.		40	M	Laborer	02Ja02Gg
DENKIS, O.		30	M	Laborer	02Ja02Gg
BUTLER, T.		19	M	Laborer	02Ja02Gg
RILEY, P.		29	M	Laborer	02Ja02Gg
MORRIS, Mary		19	F	Unknown	02Ja02Gg
MURPHY, T.		20	M	Laborer	02Ja02Gg

NAMES OF PASSENGERS		A G E	S E X	OCCUPATIONS	DATE PORT SHIP
FLYNN, O.		24	M	Laborer	04Ja02Ko
BURK, M.		17	M	Laborer	04Ja02Ko
GILLAME, J.		40	M	Laborer	04Ja02Ko
KELARY, Bgt.		25	F	Unknown	04Ja02Ko
RYAN, Cath.		17	F	Unknown	04Ja02Ko
BURK, Cath.		20	F	Unknown	04Ja02Ko
MCGUIRE, P.		66	M	Laborer	04Ja02Ko
Pat		30	M	Laborer	04Ja02Ko
Grace		64	F	Unknown	04Ja02Ko
Hugh		25	M	Laborer	04Ja02Ko
Bernd.		23	M	Laborer	04Ja02Ko
Dennis		24	M	Laborer	04Ja02Ko
Ellias		20	M	Laborer	04Ja02Ko
Hanah		19	F	Unknown	04Ja02Ko
Mary		18	F	Unknown	04Ja02Ko
Rose		23	F	Unknown	04Ja02Ko
Mary		03	F	Child	04Ja02Ko
Pat		02	M	Child	04Ja02Ko
John		28	M	Mechanic	04Ja02Ko
Mary		26	F	Unknown	04Ja02Ko
Patk.		04	M	Child	04Ja02Ko
Thos.		02	M	Child	04Ja02Ko
Dennis		01	M	Child	04Ja02Ko
Anthony		30	M	Laborer	04Ja02Ko
Elizbt.		20	F	Unknown	04Ja02Ko
MEHAN, S.		24	M	Laborer	04Ja02Ko
LAUGHLIN, H.		22	M	Mechanic	04Ja02Ko
Michl.		18	M	Mechanic	04Ja02Ko
DAILEY, T.		30	M	Laborer	04Ja02Ko
BRADY, T.		40	M	Laborer	04Ja02Ko
Cath.		50	F	Unknown	04Ja02Ko
PLANT, Cath.		18	F	Unknown	04Ja02Ko
GLIGAN, Bgdt.		18	F	Unknown	04Ja02Ko
DUFFY, Cath.		19	F	Unknown	04Ja02Ko
CONLIN, Susan		18	F	Unknown	04Ja02Ko
MULLIN, W.M.		29	M	Laborer	04Ja02Ko
MARTIN, P.		29	M	Laborer	04Ja02Ko
DUFFY, B.		25	M	Laborer	04Ja02Ko
ODONNELL, J.		40	M	Laborer	04Ja02Ko
MIGINT, Mary		18	F	Unknown	04Ja02Ko
MCGOWAN, P.		18	M	Mechanic	04Ja02Ko
NAUGHTON, M.		17	M	Mechanic	04Ja02Ko
BRADY, Mary		16	F	Unknown	04Ja02Ko
Susan		20	F	Unknown	04Ja02Ko
NANY, Cath.		50	F	Unknown	04Ja02Ko

SAMUEL-HICKS 04 JANUARY 1847

From Liverpool

INDIANA 04 JANUARY 1847

From Liverpool

NAMES OF PASSENGERS		A G E	S E X	OCCUPATIONS	DATE PORT SHIP
ORNISH, W.B.		27	M	Merchant	04Ja02Ko
FISHER, E.		40	M	Mechanic	04Ja02Ko
Ed.F.Jr.		13	M	None	04Ja02Ko
Selena		07	F	Child	04Ja02Ko
DAVIS, J.		34	M	Mechanic	04Ja02Ko
Elizbt.	(W)	40	F	Wife	04Ja02Ko
Walter	(S)	08	M	Child	04Ja02Ko
Jane	(D)	07	F	Child	04Ja02Ko
Elizbt.	(D)	05	F	Child	04Ja02Ko
Sarah	(D)	04	F	Child	04Ja02Ko
Mary	(D)	01	F	Child	04Ja02Ko
GILLIAN, M.		40	M	Mechanic	04Ja02Ko
CARNEY, J.		20	M	Laborer	04Ja02Ko

NAMES OF PASSENGERS		A G E	S E X	OCCUPATIONS	DATE PORT SHIP
BIRNEY, G.		22	M	Merchant	04Ja02Bs
Louise		17	F	Unknown	04Ja02Bs
BANCROFT, J.		21	M	Merchant	04Ja02Bs
FERRIS, D.		48	M	Merchant	04Ja02Bs
SAVAGE, H.		40	M	Laborer	04Ja02Bs
Cath.	(W)	25	F	Wife	04Ja02Bs
Bdgt.	(D)	06	F	Child	04Ja02Bs
Cath.	(D)	02	F	Child	04Ja02Bs
MCGOWAN, D.		16	M	Laborer	04Ja02Bs
BRADY, Mary		22	F	Unknown	04Ja02Bs
MCGOWAN, Betty		18	F	Unknown	04Ja02Bs
BRADY, Mary		18	F	Unknown	04Ja02Bs
DONELLY, B.		34	M	Laborer	04Ja02Bs
MORAN, M.		50	M	Laborer	04Ja02Bs
Cath.	(W)	48	F	Wife	04Ja02Bs
Albnt.	(D)	06	F	Child	04Ja02Bs
Louisa	(D)	08	F	Child	04Ja02Bs
DENNERY, T.		19	M	Laborer	04Ja02Bs
John		17	M	Laborer	04Ja02Bs

NAMES OF PASSENGERS		AGE	SEX	OCCUPATIONS	DATE PORT SHIP
GRAHAM, A.		17	M	Laborer	04Ja02Bs
HELLEY, T.		30	M	Laborer	04Ja02Bs
DONNELLY, T.		24	M	Laborer	04Ja02Bs
Mary		25	F	Unknown	04Ja02Bs
LYNN, R.		35	M	Laborer	04Ja02Bs
Cath.	(W)	37	F	Wife	04Ja02Bs
Ellen	(D)	09	F	Child	04Ja02Bs
Cath.	(D)	07	F	Child	04Ja02Bs
Jas.	(S)	05	M	Child	04Ja02Bs
Mary-J.	(D)	03	F	Child	04Ja02Bs
Sarah	(D)	01	F	Child	04Ja02Bs
MCLAUGHLIN, Mgt.		17	F	Unknown	04Ja02Bs
MURPHY, P.		25	M	Laborer	04Ja02Bs
Mary		23	F	Unknown	04Ja02Bs
John		23	M	Laborer	04Ja02Bs
BARRETT, J.		24	M	Laborer	04Ja02Bs
BENNETT, Cath.		22	F	Unknown	04Ja02Bs
MOLYNOUX, W.		20	M	Laborer	04Ja02Bs
Mary	(W)	25	F	Wife	04Ja02Bs
Patk.	(S)	01	M	Child	04Ja02Bs
JOHNS, J.		40	M	Laborer	04Ja02Bs
Chat.	(W)	42	F	Wife	04Ja02Bs
Geog.	(S)	15	M	Laborer	04Ja02Bs
Edwd.	(S)	13	M	None	04Ja02Bs
Elizbt.	(D)	10	F	Unknown	04Ja02Bs
Thos.	(S)	06	M	Child	04Ja02Bs
Henrietta	(D)	03	F	Child	04Ja02Bs
John-E.	(S)	02	M	Child	04Ja02Bs
Jas.	(S)	01	M	Child	04Ja02Bs
HANLON, P.		21	M	Laborer	04Ja02Bs
DAVIDSON, W.		30	M	Laborer	04Ja02Bs
CONLON, D.		22	M	Laborer	04Ja02Bs
REILLY, Mgt.		22	F	Unknown	04Ja02Bs
MCQUIN, Mary		20	F	Unknown	04Ja02Bs
HOGAN, Jane		12	F	Unknown	04Ja02Bs
DOON, Alea		17	F	Unknown	04Ja02Bs
KIRKPATRICK, W.		24	M	Laborer	04Ja02Bs
Bella		22	F	Unknown	04Ja02Bs
WILSON, W.H.		13	M	Laborer	04Ja02Bs
BALDWIN, J.		24	M	Laborer	04Ja02Bs
BRENNAN, E.		26	M	Laborer	04Ja02Bs
GANNON, J.		20	M	Laborer	04Ja02Bs
DOUGHERTY, H.		25	M	Laborer	04Ja02Bs
Rose		23	F	Unknown	04Ja02Bs
MCALTY, R.		26	M	Laborer	04Ja02Bs
DOUGHERTY, W.		48	M	Laborer	04Ja02Bs
Cath.	(W)	48	F	Wife	04Ja02Bs
Rose	(D)	14	F	Unknown	04Ja02Bs
Davd.	(S)	11	M	None	04Ja02Bs
Eliza	(D)	09	F	Child	04Ja02Bs
CARSON, J.		30	M	Laborer	04Ja02Bs
Mary	(W)	26	F	Wife	04Ja02Bs
John	(S)	01	M	Child	04Ja02Bs

CAMBRIDGE 04 JANUARY 1847

From Liverpool

NAMES OF PASSENGERS		AGE	SEX	OCCUPATIONS	DATE PORT SHIP
MELIN, P.		30	M	Laborer	04Ja02Ea
DOWD, J.		21	M	Laborer	04Ja02Ea
KELLY, H.		20	M	Laborer	04Ja02Ea
OAKLY, F.		20	M	Laborer	04Ja02Ea
HICKBURN, Mary		30	F	Wife	04Ja02Ea
John		30	M	Laborer	04Ja02Ea
Hy	(S)	04	M	Child	04Ja02Ea
Emily	(D)	08	F	Child	04Ja02Ea
DENNING, J.		20	M	Laborer	04Ja02Ea
RANKS, B.		29	M	Laborer	04Ja02Ea
JACOB, S.		59	M	Laborer	04Ja02Ea

NAMES OF PASSENGERS		AGE	SEX	OCCUPATIONS	DATE PORT SHIP
JACOB, Nath.		28	M	Laborer	04Ja02Ea
Sarah		55	F	Unknown	04Ja02Ea
Rebecca		50	F	Unknown	04Ja02Ea
DONAHUE, F.		20	M	Laborer	04Ja02Ea
MCCANN, Ellen		20	F	Unknown	04Ja02Ea
HARY, Ann		20	F	Unknown	04Ja02Ea
SHEAN, M.		25	M	Laborer	04Ja02Ea
COONY, Betsy		25	F	Unknown	04Ja02Ea
DONNEGAN, Biddy		25	F	Unknown	04Ja02Ea
GRADY, Mary		50	F	Unknown	04Ja02Ea
MURRY, S.		12	M	None	04Ja02Ea
MCNEE, Cath.		11	F	Unknown	04Ja02Ea
BYRNS, J.		20	M	Laborer	04Ja02Ea
EDMUNSON, W.		68	M	Laborer	04Ja02Ea
Isabell	(W)	55	F	Wife	04Ja02Ea
Maty.	(S)	22	M	Laborer	04Ja02Ea
Mary	(D)	20	F	Unknown	04Ja02Ea
Ellen	(D)	15	F	Unknown	04Ja02Ea
Willm.	(S)	11	M	None	04Ja02Ea
MONTGOMERY, C.		19	M	Laborer	04Ja02Ea
GALLAHER, P.		40	M	Laborer	04Ja02Ea
IREVIRY, A.		50	M	Laborer	04Ja02Ea
Mary		20	F	Unknown	04Ja02Ea
DAKIN, A.		40	M	Laborer	04Ja02Ea
DAHN, P.		50	M	Laborer	04Ja02Ea
RYAN, Sarah		20	F	Unknown	04Ja02Ea
TIERNEY, Mgt.		20	F	Unknown	04Ja02Ea
Mary		01	F	Child	04Ja02Ea
John		20	M	Laborer	04Ja02Ea
KEITH, P.		20	M	Laborer	04Ja02Ea
FARRELL, W.		20	M	Laborer	04Ja02Ea
Thos.		20	M	Laborer	04Ja02Ea
BOYLAN, A.		20	M	Laborer	04Ja02Ea
Fras.		20	M	Laborer	04Ja02Ea
Mary		15	F	Unknown	04Ja02Ea
MOLED, Biddy		09	F	Child	04Ja02Ea
DOFTUS, Mary		26	F	Unknown	04Ja02Ea
GRENING, M.		20	M	Laborer	04Ja02Ea
LANS, J.		20	M	Laborer	04Ja02Ea
HIGGITY, Mary		40	F	Unknown	04Ja02Ea
SUNDY, H.		69	M	Laborer	04Ja02Ea
Mary	(W)	54	F	Wife	04Ja02Ea
Danl.	(S)	12	M	None	04Ja02Ea
Mgrt.	(D)	10	F	Unknown	04Ja02Ea
John	(S)	06	M	Child	04Ja02Ea
Elizbt.	(D)	03	F	Child	04Ja02Ea
Cath.	(D)	01	F	Child	04Ja02Ea
ONEIL, P.		29	M	Mechanic	04Ja02Ea
DONOVAN, J.		27	M	Mechanic	04Ja02Ea
MCCAFFREY, Ann		19	F	Unknown	04Ja02Ea
WALTON, J.		22	M	Mechanic	04Ja02Ea
Jane		22	F	Unknown	04Ja02Ea
EDWARDS, T.		30	M	Mechanic	04Ja02Ea
DOLAN, A.		20	M	Mechanic	04Ja02Ea
Jane		20	F	Unknown	04Ja02Ea
Chas.		22	M	Laborer	04Ja02Ea
Cath.		03	F	Child	04Ja02Ea
Mary		16	F	Unknown	04Ja02Ea
Cath.		14	F	Unknown	04Ja02Ea
MCGOWAN, P.		20	M	Laborer	04Ja02Ea
OBRIEN, M.		30	M	Laborer	04Ja02Ea
Biddy	(W)	20	F	Wife	04Ja02Ea
Pegg	(D)	01	F	Child	04Ja02Ea
Bgt.	(D)	02	F	Child	04Ja02Ea
GALLAHER, B.		50	M	Laborer	04Ja02Ea
COOK, J.		20	M	Farmer	04Ja02Ea
MCCULLAH, F.		20	M	Farmer	04Ja02Ea
MOUNTTEITH, J.		20	M	Farmer	04Ja02Ea
PHILLIPS, J.		20	M	Farmer	04Ja02Ea
BROWN, E.A.		20	M	Farmer	04Ja02Ea
CONOLLY, J.		20	M	Laborer	04Ja02Ea
NEW, J.		40	M	Laborer	04Ja02Ea
MAXWELL, J.		20	M	Laborer	04Ja02Ea
JORDEN, T.		20	M	Laborer	04Ja02Ea
Rich.		20	M	Laborer	04Ja02Ea

NAMES OF PASSENGERS		A G E	S E X	OCCUPATIONS	DATE PORT SHIP	NAMES OF PASSENGERS		A G E	S E X	OCCUPATIONS	DATE PORT SHIP
JORDEN, Mary		20	F	Unknown	04Ja02Ea	MCGRATH, Biddy		20	F	Unknown	04Ja02Ea
Mgt.		20	F	Unknown	04Ja02Ea	HOGAN, M.		38	M	Laborer	04Ja02Ea
MORTHESER, Magt.		20	F	Unknown	04Ja02Ea	Mary		28	F	Unknown	04Ja02Ea
HART, P.		20	M	Laborer	04Ja02Ea	DONNOHUE, T.		36	M	Laborer	04Ja02Ea
HARTLEY, W.		20	M	Laborer	04Ja02Ea	Bgdt.	(W)	30	F	Wife	04Ja02Ea
MCSHERRY, J.		12	M	None	04Ja02Ea	Pat	(S)	13	M	None	04Ja02Ea
DUNCAN, P.		40	M	Laborer	04Ja02Ea	Thomas	(S)	11	M	None	04Ja02Ea
Susan	(W)	30	F	Wife	04Ja02Ea	Francis	(S)	07	M	Child	04Ja02Ea
Jibby	(D)	07	F	Child	04Ja02Ea	Bernard	(S)	05	M	Child	04Ja02Ea
Dennis	(S)	01	M	Child	04Ja02Ea	Cath.	(D)	01	F	Child	04Ja02Ea
Sally	(D)	01	F	Child	04Ja02Ea	CASE, M.		30	M	Laborer	04Ja02Ea
MURRAY, T.		35	M	Laborer	04Ja02Ea	WALSH, Honor		35	F	Unknown	04Ja02Ea
Julia		18	F	Unknown	04Ja02Ea	DOYLE, Ann		40	F	Unknown	04Ja02Ea
Mich.		16	M	Laborer	04Ja02Ea	MURPHY, P.		22	M	Laborer	04Ja02Ea
Mary		11	F	Unknown	04Ja02Ea	HANLY, M.		20	M	Laborer	04Ja02Ea
RILY, B.		26	M	Laborer	04Ja02Ea	MCLOUGHLIN, Sarah		30	F	Unknown	04Ja02Ea
Peggy		20	F	Unknown	04Ja02Ea	Jameson		09	M	Child	04Ja02Ea
KERAN, P.		21	M	Laborer	04Ja02Ea	KELLY, Roddy		20	F	Unknown	04Ja02Ea
BURKE, J.		20	M	Laborer	04Ja02Ea	Bessy		20	F	Unknown	04Ja02Ea
RILEY, T.		20	M	Laborer	04Ja02Ea	WATSON, Cath.		30	F	Unknown	04Ja02Ea
Danl.		18	M	Laborer	04Ja02Ea	Peter		15	M	None	04Ja02Ea
WILLIAMS, Mary-A.		13	F	Unknown	04Ja02Ea	LYONS, Cath.		30	F	Unknown	04Ja02Ea
Thomas		11	M	None	04Ja02Ea	Timothy		06	M	Child	04Ja02Ea
ANDERSON, W.		24	M	Laborer	04Ja02Ea	SPARIR, Mary		25	F	Unknown	04Ja02Ea
DUCAN, T.		18	M	Laborer	04Ja02Ea	Cornelius		11	M	Unknown	04Ja02Ea
Mary		16	F	Unknown	04Ja02Ea	Honor		09	F	Child	04Ja02Ea
Ellen		11	F	Unknown	04Ja02Ea	DONNAHUE, J.		25	M	Laborer	04Ja02Ea
LOFTUS, M.		20	M	Laborer	04Ja02Ea	HALPIN, Betty		25	F	Unknown	04Ja02Ea
Biddy		20	F	Unknown	04Ja02Ea	Cath.		20	F	Unknown	04Ja02Ea
OHARA, Mary		01	F	Child	04Ja02Ea	Mary		11	F	Unknown	04Ja02Ea
BLACK, M.		20	M	Laborer	04Ja02Ea	Ann		09	F	Child	04Ja02Ea
MCNANY, M.		20	M	Laborer	04Ja02Ea	Eliza		06	F	Child	04Ja02Ea
MCCAFFREY, J.		50	M	Laborer	04Ja02Ea	Maggy		01	F	Child	04Ja02Ea
IVARS, Cath.		30	F	Unknown	04Ja02Ea	SANDS, Ellen		10	F	Unknown	04Ja02Ea
CARTY, Biddy		13	F	Unknown	04Ja02Ea	Betsy		08	F	Child	04Ja02Ea
Mary		10	F	Unknown	04Ja02Ea	DONNELLY, J.		11	M	None	04Ja02Ea
U		01	F	Infant	04Ja02Ea	HAYES, Ja.		40	M	Laborer	04Ja02Ea
MURPHY, J.		20	M	Laborer	04Ja02Ea	MACGLE, Ellen		20	F	Unknown	04Ja02Ea
Bgt.		20	F	Unknown	04Ja02Ea	HAYES, T.		11	M	None	04Ja02Ea
SWEENY, John		20	M	Laborer	04Ja02Ea	HENNISSEY, P.		30	M	Laborer	04Ja02Ea
John		30	M	Laborer	04Ja02Ea	Bgdt.		13	F	Unknown	04Ja02Ea
MERRICK, T.		35	M	Laborer	04Ja02Ea	CONNOLLY, Mary		25	F	Unknown	04Ja02Ea
Biddy	(W)	25	F	Wife	04Ja02Ea	FOY, L.		16	M	Laborer	04Ja02Ea
Ann	(D)	02	F	Child	04Ja02Ea	MCNAB, Rose		40	F	Unknown	04Ja02Ea
LOGAN, Susan		30	F	Unknown	04Ja02Ea	Michl.		30	M	Laborer	04Ja02Ea
Wm.		28	M	Laborer	04Ja02Ea	Jane		15	F	Unknown	04Ja02Ea
John		26	M	Laborer	04Ja02Ea	MCFALL, Mgt.		24	F	Unknown	04Ja02Ea
Edwd.		20	M	Laborer	04Ja02Ea	Rose		11	F	Unknown	04Ja02Ea
Sarah		06	F	Child	04Ja02Ea	KING, Bgdt.		35	F	Unknown	04Ja02Ea
Peter		04	M	Child	04Ja02Ea	Pat		08	M	Child	04Ja02Ea
Jane		13	F	Unknown	04Ja02Ea	James		05	M	Child	04Ja02Ea
Jane		02	F	Child	04Ja02Ea	MEREDITH, Ann		22	F	Unknown	04Ja02Ea
DOYLE, P.		20	M	Laborer	04Ja02Ea	MCGOWAN, T.		30	M	Laborer	04Ja02Ea
Mary		20	F	Unknown	04Ja02Ea	FORD, J.		20	M	Laborer	04Ja02Ea
HERN, P.		40	M	Laborer	04Ja02Ea	RYAN, M.		24	M	Laborer	04Ja02Ea
Bgt.		13	F	Unknown	04Ja02Ea	MALONE, J.		20	M	Laborer	04Ja02Ea
Jane		10	F	Unknown	04Ja02Ea	Ann		20	F	Unknown	04Ja02Ea
CONNOR, W.		31	M	Laborer	04Ja02Ea	GARESTIN, W.		20	M	Laborer	04Ja02Ea
Peggy	(W)	21	F	Wife	04Ja02Ea	NOLAN, T.		40	M	Laborer	04Ja02Ea
Edwd.	(S)	01	M	Child	04Ja02Ea	Bdgt.	(W)	40	F	Wife	04Ja02Ea
REYNOLDS, L.		21	M	Laborer	04Ja02Ea	Cath.	(D)	14	F	Unknown	04Ja02Ea
FLYNN, Mgt.		20	F	Unknown	04Ja02Ea	Pat	(S)	12	M	None	04Ja02Ea
SMITH, J.		12	M	None	04Ja02Ea	Mary	(D)	10	F	Unknown	04Ja02Ea
HART, Bgt.		11	F	Unknown	04Ja02Ea	Thos.	(S)	08	M	Child	04Ja02Ea
SMITH, Wm.		13	M	None	04Ja02Ea	Peter	(S)	06	M	Child	04Ja02Ea
Mary		14	F	Unknown	04Ja02Ea	MCLOUGHLIN, F.		26	M	Laborer	04Ja02Ea
BYRNE, M.		38	M	Laborer	04Ja02Ea	CRANE, M.		21	M	Laborer	04Ja02Ea
HEARNY, M.		20	M	Laborer	04Ja02Ea	Susan		30	F	Unknown	04Ja02Ea
MAHLONY, W.		27	M	Laborer	04Ja02Ea	MURPHY, J.		30	M	Laborer	04Ja02Ea
HISTIN, M.		20	M	Laborer	04Ja02Ea	Pat		20	M	Laborer	04Ja02Ea
MCTURNE, P.		40	M	Laborer	04Ja02Ea	CLARKE, T.		18	M	Laborer	04Ja02Ea
Sally	(W)	38	F	Wife	04Ja02Ea	MCCABE, L.		40	M	Laborer	04Ja02Ea
John	(S)	09	M	Child	04Ja02Ea	Mary		30	F	Unknown	04Ja02Ea
Ann	(D)	03	F	Child	04Ja02Ea	CLARKE, T.		04	M	Child	04Ja02Ea
Pat	(S)	01	M	Child	04Ja02Ea	CONNELL, J.		40	M	Laborer	04Ja02Ea

NAMES OF PASSENGERS		AGE	SEX	OCCUPATIONS	DATE PORT SHIP
SMITH, Bgdt.		29	F	Unknown	04Ja02Ea
Mary		18	F	Unknown	04Ja02Ea
U		04	F	Child	04Ja02Ea
U		06	F	Child	04Ja02Ea
Bdgt.		16	F	Unknown	04Ja02Ea
CURRAN, Mary		16	F	Unknown	04Ja02Ea
MCCABE, J.		20	M	Laborer	04Ja02Ea
RILY, J.		20	M	Laborer	04Ja02Ea
MCMAHON, H.		40	M	Laborer	04Ja02Ea
Kate	(W)	40	F	Wife	04Ja02Ea
Kate	(D)	20	F	Unknown	04Ja02Ea
Susan	(D)	10	F	Unknown	04Ja02Ea
Mgt.	(D)	07	F	Child	04Ja02Ea
Hugh	(S)	07	M	Child	04Ja02Ea
John	(S)	08	M	Child	04Ja02Ea
Pat	(S)	02	M	Child	04Ja02Ea
DENBY, T.		46	M	Laborer	04Ja02Ea
MCINALLY, T.		20	M	Laborer	04Ja02Ea
INNIS, W.		24	M	Laborer	04Ja02Ea
CARR, J.		20	M	Laborer	04Ja02Ea
STEWART, W.		20	M	Mechanic	04Ja02Ea
SOMERS, W.		50	M	Mechanic	04Ja02Ea
CABONE, L.		20	M	Laborer	04Ja02Ea
WILLIAMSON, J.		66	M	Laborer	04Ja02Ea
W., John		24	M	Laborer	04Ja02Ea
LOUGHLIN, S.		27	M	Laborer	04Ja02Ea
CASY, M.		27	M	Laborer	04Ja02Ea
COXE, Con.		24	F	Unknown	04Ja02Ea
WINTERS, J.		18	M	Laborer	04Ja02Ea
WALSH, M.		20	M	Laborer	04Ja02Ea
LUDGE, J.		20	M	Laborer	04Ja02Ea
DALY, Rose		20	F	Unknown	04Ja02Ea
MURPHY, M.		20	M	Laborer	04Ja02Ea
LANDEN, W.		20	M	Laborer	04Ja02Ea
MYER, Erne		02	F	Child	04Ja02Ea

RICHARD-WATSON 05 JANUARY 1847

From Sligo

NAMES OF PASSENGERS		AGE	SEX	OCCUPATIONS	DATE PORT SHIP
TIGHE, M.		26	M	Laborer	05Ja28Lf
Ann	(W)	26	F	Wife	05Ja28Lf
John	(S)	01	M	Child	05Ja28Lf
BEGLY, A.		26	M	Farmer	05Ja28Lf
Anne		26	F	Unknown	05Ja28Lf
OBEIRNE, H.		20	M	Farmer	05Ja28Lf
Bdgt.		00	F	Unknown	05Ja28Lf
COLEMAN, Ann		19	F	Unknown	05Ja28Lf
SCANLAN, P.		50	M	Farmer	05Ja28Lf
Magt.	(W)	50	F	Wife	05Ja28Lf
Mary	(D)	22	F	Unknown	05Ja28Lf
Ann	(D)	20	F	Unknown	05Ja28Lf
Pat	(S)	18	M	Farmer	05Ja28Lf
Cath.	(D)	16	F	Unknown	05Ja28Lf
Mgt.	(D)	14	F	Unknown	05Ja28Lf
Biddy	(D)	12	F	Unknown	05Ja28Lf
Julia	(D)	10	F	Unknown	05Ja28Lf
Wm.	(S)	08	M	Child	05Ja28Lf
MCGOWAN, M.		45	M	Laborer	05Ja28Lf
Mary	(W)	35	F	Wife	05Ja28Lf
Ellen	(D)	12	F	Unknown	05Ja28Lf
Winnfred	(D)	03	F	Child	05Ja28Lf
Mary	(D)	02	F	Child	05Ja28Lf
GEEVER, P.		32	M	Laborer	05Ja28Lf
Cath.		26	F	Unknown	05Ja28Lf
Cath.		19	F	Unknown	05Ja28Lf
TORNY, Mary		20	F	Unknown	05Ja28Lf
CONNELL, M.		21	M	Laborer	05Ja28Lf
MCHUGH, T.		37	M	Laborer	05Ja28Lf

NAMES OF PASSENGERS		AGE	SEX	OCCUPATIONS	DATE PORT SHIP
MCHUGH, M.	(W)	36	F	Wife	05Ja28Lf
Wm.	(S)	09	M	Child	05Ja28Lf
Bgt.	(D)	07	F	Child	05Ja28Lf
M.	(D)	05	F	Child	05Ja28Lf
Thos.	(S)	03	M	Child	05Ja28Lf
SCANLAN, O.		30	M	Laborer	05Ja28Lf
Ann	(W)	30	F	Wife	05Ja28Lf
Madvia	(D)	10	F	Unknown	05Ja28Lf
Mary	(D)	06	F	Unknown	05Ja28Lf
Martin	(S)	02	M	Unknown	05Ja28Lf
LADEN, Bgt.		17	F	Unknown	05Ja28Lf
OWENS, P.		22	M	Laborer	05Ja28Lf
Mgt.	(W)	25	F	Wife	05Ja28Lf
Biddy	(D)	02	F	Child	05Ja28Lf
ROURKE, D.		18	M	Laborer	05Ja28Lf
DYER, Bdgt.		28	F	Unknown	05Ja28Lf
MULLERY, Bdgt.		18	F	Unknown	05Ja28Lf
HART, P.		21	M	Laborer	05Ja28Lf
PARSONS, J.		20	M	Laborer	05Ja28Lf
Mary		23	F	Unknown	05Ja28Lf
MCSUNNAS, Bdgt.		19	F	Unknown	05Ja28Lf
SHANNON, Honor		28	F	Unknown	05Ja28Lf
DRURY, P.		30	M	Laborer	05Ja28Lf
Allse	(W)	30	F	Wife	05Ja28Lf
Peter	(S)	01	M	Child	05Ja28Lf
GALLAGHER, P.		24	M	Farmer	05Ja28Lf
Cath.		29	F	Unknown	05Ja28Lf
Ian		20	M	Laborer	05Ja28Lf
NEILAN, Cath.		16	F	Unknown	05Ja28Lf
Mary		18	F	Unknown	05Ja28Lf
GAFFREY, Mich.		34	M	Laborer	05Ja28Lf
Ellen	(W)	25	F	Wife	05Ja28Lf
Mary	(D)	01	F	Child	05Ja28Lf
MIDDLEDEN, R.		25	M	Farmer	05Ja28Lf
Mary-A.		22	F	Unknown	05Ja28Lf
LOFTUS, D.		25	M	Farmer	05Ja28Lf
Jane		24	F	Unknown	05Ja28Lf
HARN, A.		22	M	Farmer	05Ja28Lf
LOFTUS, O.		30	M	Farmer	05Ja28Lf
Pat		25	M	Farmer	05Ja28Lf
Anthy.		27	M	Farmer	05Ja28Lf
CARNAN, P.		45	M	Farmer	05Ja28Lf
DAVEY, P.		44	M	Farmer	05Ja28Lf
Mary	(W)	50	F	Wife	05Ja28Lf
Jno.	(S)	26	M	Farmer	05Ja28Lf
Cath.	(D)	20	F	Unknown	05Ja28Lf
Andr.	(S)	19	M	None	05Ja28Lf
Bgt.	(D)	17	F	Unknown	05Ja28Lf
Mary	(D)	14	F	Unknown	05Ja28Lf
Michl.	(S)	12	M	None	05Ja28Lf
Sarah	(D)	10	F	Unknown	05Ja28Lf
Arthur	(S)	08	M	Child	05Ja28Lf
MCDONOUGH, F.		35	M	Farmer	05Ja28Lf
Mary		35	F	Unknown	05Ja28Lf
Thos.		35	M	Farmer	05Ja28Lf
Frank		13	M	None	05Ja28Lf
Martin		11	M	None	05Ja28Lf
Bdgt.		07	F	Child	05Ja28Lf
Jno.		05	M	Child	05Ja28Lf
Pat		03	M	Child	05Ja28Lf
Jno.		02	M	Child	05Ja28Lf
Cath.		01	F	Child	05Ja28Lf
BURROWS, A.		28	M	Laborer	05Ja28Lf
Ann	(W)	28	F	Wife	05Ja28Lf
Wm.	(S)	09	M	Child	05Ja28Lf
Thos.	(S)	07	M	Child	05Ja28Lf
Jas.	(S)	05	M	Child	05Ja28Lf
Danl.	(S)	03	M	Child	05Ja28Lf
Jno.	(S)	01	M	Child	05Ja28Lf
PARKER, T.		52	M	Farmer	05Ja28Lf
WARE, Bdgt.		20	F	Unknown	05Ja28Lf
MCHUGH, Mary		20	F	Unknown	05Ja28Lf
GLENN, Elizbt.		02	F	Child	05Ja28Lf
Fdck.		29	M	Laborer	05Ja28Lf
Louise		21	F	Unknown	05Ja28Lf

NAMES OF PASSENGERS		AGE	SEX	OCCUPATIONS	DATE PORT SHIP
GLENN, Fdck.		02	M	Child	05Ja28Lf
Frns.		03	M	Child	05Ja28Lf
Marla		22	F	Unknown	05Ja28Lf
LONDON, A.		32	M	None	05Ja28Lf
Chuty		43	F	Unknown	05Ja28Lf
RARIN, J.		38	M	Laborer	05Ja28Lf
KELSO, J.		24	M	Laborer	05Ja28Lf
VIEBIS, Fdrk.		25	M	Laborer	05Ja28Lf
ROBIN, J.		28	M	Laborer	05Ja28Lf

ADIRONDACK 07 JANUARY 1847

From Liverpool

NAMES OF PASSENGERS		AGE	SEX	OCCUPATIONS	DATE PORT SHIP
ROCK, R.		50	M	Farmer	07Ja02Cm
MCGLADE, Mgt.		20	F	Unknown	07Ja02Cm
CORRIGAN, W.		26	M	Laborer	07Ja02Cm
Mary		24	F	Unknown	07Ja02Cm
DUFFY, J.		39	M	Mechanic	07Ja02Cm
My.	(W)	38	F	Unknown	07Ja02Cm
Cath.	(D)	04	F	Child	07Ja02Cm
Bessy	(D)	02	F	Child	07Ja02Cm
Mary		20	F	Unknown	07Ja02Cm
Patk.		18	M	Laborer	07Ja02Cm
HART, Bgt.		22	F	Unknown	07Ja02Cm
GALLAGHER, J.		25	M	Laborer	07Ja02Cm
Cath.		21	F	Unknown	07Ja02Cm
MCKENTY, J.		21	M	Laborer	07Ja02Cm
BYRNE, J.		25	M	Laborer	07Ja02Cm
REGAN, P.		22	M	Laborer	07Ja02Cm
CHERRY, H.L.		18	M	Laborer	07Ja02Cm
GRAGY, U-Mrs.		27	F	Unknown	07Ja02Cm
DAVIS, T.		28	M	Unknown	07Ja02Cm
U	(W)	26	F	Wife	07Ja02Cm
LEA, M.		21	M	Mechanic	07Ja02Cm
ISAAC, S.		22	M	Mechanic	07Ja02Cm
HINE, J.		20	M	Mechanic	07Ja02Cm
KERRY, Bgt.		20	F	Unknown	07Ja02Cm
DIRKIN, M.		20	M	Mechanic	07Ja02Cm
COCKROFT, W.		28	M	Mechanic	07Ja02Cm
THOMPSON, A.		39	M	Mechanic	07Ja02Cm
STANFORD, M.		21	M	Mechanic	07Ja02Cm
HILL, L.		35	M	Mechanic	07Ja02Cm
U	(W)	30	F	Unknown	07Ja02Cm
Bernd.	(S)	04	M	Child	07Ja02Cm
Cath.	(D)	01	F	Child	07Ja02Cm
T.		22	M	Mechanic	07Ja02Cm
DOHERTY, J.		21	M	Mechanic	07Ja02Cm
Mary		19	F	Unknown	07Ja02Cm
Rose		17	F	Unknown	07Ja02Cm
KELLY, Anne		13	F	Unknown	07Ja02Cm
WESLY, E.		20	F	Farmer	07Ja02Cm
JACKSON, U-Mrs.		50	F	Unknown	07Ja02Cm
Thomas	(S)	21	M	Mechanic	07Ja02Cm
Judy	(D)	13	F	Unknown	07Ja02Cm
DEMING, J.		20	M	Laborer	07Ja02Cm
MCGARR, Bgt.		40	F	Unknown	07Ja02Cm
John	(S)	20	M	Mechanic	07Ja02Cm
Cath.	(D)	18	F	Unknown	07Ja02Cm
Mary	(D)	16	F	Unknown	07Ja02Cm
Rose	(D)	07	F	Child	07Ja02Cm
Ellen	(D)	05	F	Child	07Ja02Cm
HYNES, U-Miss		20	F	Unknown	07Ja02Cm
TONER, Rose		30	F	Unknown	07Ja02Cm
HEINE, Cath.		03	F	Child	07Ja02Cm
Bgt.		07	F	Child	07Ja02Cm
CAIN, J.		56	M	Mechanic	07Ja02Cm
SCANLON, M.		20	M	Mechanic	07Ja02Cm
CASSIDY, Mary		20	F	Unknown	07Ja02Cm
GILLMAN, R.		30	M	Laborer	07Ja02Cm
Bgt.		22	F	Unknown	07Ja02Cm
MCGOWEN, J.		20	M	Mechanic	07Ja02Cm
Bdgt.		50	F	Unknown	07Ja02Cm
BRADY, Mn.		18	F	Unknown	07Ja02Cm
PATTERSON, D.		24	M	Mechanic	07Ja02Cm
Edwd.		20	M	Mechanic	07Ja02Cm
DUNCAN, W.		20	M	Laborer	07Ja02Cm
MCGALE, P.		21	M	Laborer	07Ja02Cm
LEA, M.		21	M	Mechanic	07Ja02Cm
CAHILL, M.		30	M	Mechanic	07Ja02Cm
Betty	(W)	30	F	Unknown	07Ja02Cm
Patk.	(S)	02	M	Child	07Ja02Cm
Peggy	(D)	03	F	Child	07Ja02Cm
BYRNE, P.		20	M	Laborer	07Ja02Cm
MCGILL, L.		19	M	Laborer	07Ja02Cm
WALSH, M.		20	M	Laborer	07Ja02Cm
QUINN, P.		50	M	Laborer	07Ja02Cm
Mary	(W)	40	F	Unknown	07Ja02Cm
Mary	(D)	13	F	Unknown	07Ja02Cm
Bgt.	(D)	11	F	Unknown	07Ja02Cm
James	(D)	09	M	Child	07Ja02Cm
Cath.	(D)	08	F	Child	07Ja02Cm
Thos.	(S)	06	M	Child	07Ja02Cm
Patk.	(S)	03	M	Child	07Ja02Cm
MULDOON, Mary		18	F	Unknown	07Ja02Cm
MANNING, Mary		19	F	Unknown	07Ja02Cm
LYONS, Lily		19	F	Unknown	07Ja02Cm
ODONNELL, P.		32	M	Laborer	07Ja02Cm
MCCAFFERTY, J.		36	M	Laborer	07Ja02Cm
MEE, J.		29	M	Laborer	07Ja02Cm
HURLY, J.		20	M	Laborer	07Ja02Cm
CROGAN, P.		24	M	Laborer	07Ja02Cm
FREENY, S.		35	M	Laborer	07Ja02Cm
Bgt.	(W)	30	F	Unknown	07Ja02Cm
Cath.	(D)	05	F	Child	07Ja02Cm
Mary	(D)	01	F	Child	07Ja02Cm
MCCOLLUM, J.		34	M	Mechanic	07Ja02Cm
Mary		22	F	Unknown	07Ja02Cm
Arthur		20	M	Mechanic	07Ja02Cm
Eliza		16	F	Unknown	07Ja02Cm
NEWTON, R.		30	M	Mechanic	07Ja02Cm
DERVANY, Kity		20	F	Unknown	07Ja02Cm
EVANS, W.		50	M	Laborer	07Ja02Cm
KNOWLES, W.R.		20	M	Laborer	07Ja02Cm
ROONEY, M.		20	M	Laborer	07Ja02Cm
COTTIGAN, M.		20	M	Laborer	07Ja02Cm
SCOTT, P.		19	M	Laborer	07Ja02Cm
Mary		18	F	Unknown	07Ja02Cm
Sydney		18	M	None	07Ja02Cm
CORMACK, M.		20	M	Laborer	07Ja02Cm
U	(W)	20	F	Unknown	07Ja02Cm
SHEAHAN, D.		40	M	Mechanic	07Ja02Cm
Anna	(W)	35	F	Unknown	07Ja02Cm
Martha	(D)	09	F	Child	07Ja02Cm
James	(S)	07	M	Child	07Ja02Cm
Thom.	(S)	05	M	Child	07Ja02Cm
Marla	(D)	03	F	Child	07Ja02Cm
Pat	(S)	01	M	Child	07Ja02Cm
FRET, A.		34	M	Laborer	07Ja02Cm
MCKENNA, Sus.		14	F	Unknown	07Ja02Cm
Anne		18	F	Unknown	07Ja02Cm
Cath.		20	F	Unknown	07Ja02Cm
MCGUIRE, Cath.		19	F	Unknown	07Ja02Cm
SMITH, Mary		25	F	Unknown	07Ja02Cm
HAGGETT, Mary		24	F	Unknown	07Ja02Cm
MCKENNA, P.		20	M	Mechanic	07Ja02Cm
MCCAHEY, J.		40	M	Mechanic	07Ja02Cm
U	(W)	35	F	Unknown	07Ja02Cm
Mary	(D)	13	F	Unknown	07Ja02Cm
John	(S)	11	M	None	07Ja02Cm
Cath.	(D)	09	F	Child	07Ja02Cm
James	(S)	07	M	Child	07Ja02Cm
Sarah	(D)	05	F	Child	07Ja02Cm
Mgt.	(D)	03	F	Child	07Ja02Cm

NAMES OF PASSENGERS		AGE	SEX	OCCUPATIONS	DATE PORT SHIP
MCCAHEY, Barny	(S)	01	M	Child	07Ja02Cm
MCCONN, F.		36	M	Laborer	07Ja02Cm
U	(W)	35	F	Unknown	07Ja02Cm
Mary	(D)	05	F	Child	07Ja02Cm
Owen	(S)	03	M	Child	07Ja02Cm
Sarah	(D)	01	F	Child	07Ja02Cm
MCKENNA, Cath.		20	F	Unknown	07Ja02Cm
CLARKE, O.		30	M	Laborer	07Ja02Cm
Chas.		24	M	Laborer	07Ja02Cm
MANN, L.		26	M	Laborer	07Ja02Cm
Mgt.		22	F	Unknown	07Ja02Cm
CULLEN, S.		40	M	Farmer	07Ja02Cm
Ann	(W)	40	F	Unknown	07Ja02Cm
Mary	(D)	13	F	Unknown	07Ja02Cm
John	(S)	11	M	None	07Ja02Cm
Bgt.	(D)	09	F	Child	07Ja02Cm
Ann	(D)	07	F	Child	07Ja02Cm
Joseph	(S)	05	M	Child	07Ja02Cm
James	(S)	02	M	Child	07Ja02Cm
Cicely	(D)	01	F	Child	07Ja02Cm
DOLAN, O.		40	M	Laborer	07Ja02Cm
Betty		35	F	Unknown	07Ja02Cm
Mary		40	F	Unknown	07Ja02Cm
Pat.		13	M	Unknown	07Ja02Cm
Thos.		11	M	None	07Ja02Cm
Ann		09	F	Child	07Ja02Cm
Peter		07	M	Child	07Ja02Cm
Biddy		05	F	Child	07Ja02Cm
John		02	M	Child	07Ja02Cm
SHEENY, M.		40	M	Laborer	07Ja02Cm
Mary-T.	(W)	35	F	Unknown	07Ja02Cm
Timy.	(S)	13	M	None	07Ja02Cm
Mary	(D)	11	F	Unknown	07Ja02Cm
Bgt.	(D)	09	F	Child	07Ja02Cm
Nancy	(D)	07	F	Child	07Ja02Cm
Cath.	(D)	05	F	Child	07Ja02Cm
Patk.	(S)	04	M	Child	07Ja02Cm
Brian	(S)	03	M	Child	07Ja02Cm
Ellen	(D)	01	F	Child	07Ja02Cm
DOLAN, F.		22	M	Laborer	07Ja02Cm
U	(W)	22	F	Unknown	07Ja02Cm
Mich.	(S)	03	M	Child	07Ja02Cm
Ellen	(D)	01	F	Child	07Ja02Cm
MCGUIRE, Mgt.		21	F	Unknown	07Ja02Cm
Marion		20	F	Unknown	07Ja02Cm
Pat		19	M	Mechanic	07Ja02Cm
Cicely		20	F	Unknown	07Ja02Cm
PATTERSON, S.		50	M	Farmer	07Ja02Cm
Mgt.		60	F	Unknown	07Ja02Cm
Jane		20	F	Unknown	07Ja02Cm
HAMILTON, J.		70	M	Mechanic	07Ja02Cm
HUTCHINSON, A.		50	M	Mechanic	07Ja02Cm
Wm.		11	M	None	07Ja02Cm
MCCAULY, Mgt.		47	F	Unknown	07Ja02Cm
Patk.	(S)	16	M	Unknown	07Ja02Cm
Mgt.	(D)	13	F	Unknown	07Ja02Cm
Mary-A.	(D)	11	F	Unknown	07Ja02Cm
PETER, J.		35	M	Mechanic	07Ja02Cm
U	(W)	33	F	Unknown	07Ja02Cm
Mgt.	(D)	09	F	Child	07Ja02Cm
John	(S)	07	M	Child	07Ja02Cm
Bdgt.	(D)	01	F	Child	07Ja02Cm
MCKILLOP, N.		21	M	Mechanic	07Ja02Cm
SMILIE, Mgt.		40	F	Unknown	07Ja02Cm
Wm.	(S)	17	M	Mechanic	07Ja02Cm
Hugh	(S)	10	M	None	07Ja02Cm
James	(S)	09	M	Child	07Ja02Cm
KENNEDY, P.		22	M	Laborer	07Ja02Cm
MULLEN, Sarah		20	F	Unknown	07Ja02Cm
WIGGINS, H.		22	M	Laborer	07Ja02Cm
BROWN, R.		20	M	Laborer	07Ja02Cm
FULLERTON, W.		25	M	Laborer	07Ja02Cm
GURREY, J.		18	M	Laborer	07Ja02Cm
CARTER, Ellen		18	F	Unknown	07Ja02Cm
MURRY, J.		28	M	Mechanic	07Ja02Cm
COOK, F.		30	M	Laborer	07Ja02Cm
CONLON, P.		20	M	Laborer	07Ja02Cm
DURKIN, P.		19	M	Laborer	07Ja02Cm
Biddy		20	F	Unknown	07Ja02Cm
BREMER, M.		20	M	Laborer	07Ja02Cm
LANGAN, J.		20	M	Laborer	07Ja02Cm
Sally		19	F	Unknown	07Ja02Cm
Mary		20	F	Unknown	07Ja02Cm
FINNEGAN, P.		27	M	Laborer	07Ja02Cm
LEE, H.		30	M	Mechanic	07Ja02Cm
Ann		50	F	Unknown	07Ja02Cm
Biddy		13	F	Unknown	07Ja02Cm
Ann		10	F	Unknown	07Ja02Cm
James		12	M	None	07Ja02Cm
HANNTY, Biddy		40	F	Unknown	07Ja02Cm
MORLIN, Mary		20	F	Unknown	07Ja02Cm
MCCABE, J.		25	M	Mechanic	07Ja02Cm
CARRAN, H.		24	M	Mechanic	07Ja02Cm
U	(W)	20	F	Unknown	07Ja02Cm
MONAGAN, P.		45	M	Laborer	07Ja02Cm
Mary	(W)	40	F	Unknown	07Ja02Cm
Mary	(D)	13	F	Unknown	07Ja02Cm
John	(S)	11	M	None	07Ja02Cm
Biddy	(D)	09	F	Child	07Ja02Cm
Cath.	(D)	08	F	Child	07Ja02Cm
Pat	(S)	07	M	Child	07Ja02Cm
Rose	(D)	06	F	Child	07Ja02Cm
Thomas	(S)	01	M	Child	07Ja02Cm
LEE, Bgt.		19	F	Unknown	07Ja02Cm
PURCELL, J.		22	M	Laborer	07Ja02Cm
KING, E.		20	M	Laborer	07Ja02Cm
CLOCKLY, J.		21	M	Laborer	07Ja02Cm
BURLINGTON, W.		18	M	Laborer	07Ja02Cm
KELLY, Mch.		35	M	Laborer	07Ja02Cm
MORAN, E.		21	M	Laborer	07Ja02Cm
RYAN, P.		28	M	Laborer	07Ja02Cm
GOWEN, Isb.		18	F	Unknown	07Ja02Cm
ROWLAND, Jane		30	F	Unknown	07Ja02Cm
FOLY, Timothy		22	M	Laborer	07Ja02Cm
WEEKS, W.		23	M	Laborer	07Ja02Cm
COX, Mgt.		50	F	Unknown	07Ja02Cm
DUFFY, M.		47	M	Laborer	07Ja02Cm
Ann		23	F	Unknown	07Ja02Cm
Mgt.		20	F	Unknown	07Ja02Cm
Mary		13	F	Unknown	07Ja02Cm
HUGHES, T.		35	M	Laborer	07Ja02Cm
Hanah		29	F	Unknown	07Ja02Cm
Mary		18	F	Unknown	07Ja02Cm
Eliza		04	F	Child	07Ja02Cm
Ann		01	F	Child	07Ja02Cm
MARO, W.		23	M	Laborer	07Ja02Cm
BYRNE, Ellen		18	F	Unknown	07Ja02Cm
KEENAN, J.		30	M	Laborer	07Ja02Cm
SOMMERS, J.		20	M	Laborer	07Ja02Cm
MCCORMICK, M.		20	M	Laborer	07Ja02Cm
MARTIN, F.		24	M	Laborer	07Ja02Cm
BRADY, M.		19	M	Laborer	07Ja02Cm
TATE, T.		25	M	Laborer	07Ja02Cm
LANGAN, P.		21	M	Laborer	07Ja02Cm
GALLAGHER, W.		20	M	Laborer	07Ja02Cm
BRENNAN, J.		23	M	Laborer	07Ja02Cm
FOLY, C.		17	M	Laborer	07Ja02Cm
WALSH, J.		22	M	Mechanic	07Ja02Cm
U	(W)	20	F	Unknown	07Ja02Cm
John	(S)	03	M	Child	07Ja02Cm
Thos.	(S)	01	M	Child	07Ja02Cm
KANE, U-Mrs.		30	F	Unknown	07Ja02Cm
Thos.	(S)	07	M	Child	07Ja02Cm
Michael	(S)	05	M	Child	07Ja02Cm
Mary	(D)	03	F	Child	07Ja02Cm
DRURY, U-Mrs.		26	F	Unknown	07Ja02Cm
Thomas	(S)	03	M	Child	07Ja02Cm
TIMINS, T.J.		25	M	Mechanic	07Ja02Cm
Sarah		20	F	Unknown	07Ja02Cm

METOKA 07 JANUARY 1847

From Liverpool

NAMES OF PASSENGERS		AGE	SEX	OCCUPATIONS	DATE PORT SHIP
BUNTY, U-Mrs.		24	F	Unknown	07Ja02MI
MAGNER, T.		25	M	Farmer	07Ja02MI
Ellen		20	F	Unknown	07Ja02MI
STAPLETON, E.		22	M	Farmer	07Ja02MI
BRADETT, Sarah		22	F	Unknown	07Ja02MI
MAGEE, Isb.		30	F	Unknown	07Ja02MI
DOOLY, J.		30	M	Farmer	07Ja02MI
U	(W)	08	F	Unknown	07Ja02MI
Mgt.	(D)	10	F	Unknown	07Ja02MI
Thos.	(S)	07	M	Child	07Ja02MI
Mary-Jane	(D)	05	F	Child	07Ja02MI
MURRY, H.		20	M	Farmer	07Ja02MI
COSGRAVE, Sally		00	F	Unknown	07Ja02MI
HARLY, P.		30	M	Farmer	07Ja02MI
U	(W)	26	F	Unknown	07Ja02MI
Edwd.	(S)	05	M	Child	07Ja02MI
Mgt.	(D)	03	F	Child	07Ja02MI
LOFTUS, T.		22	M	Farmer	07Ja02MI
CARTY, P.		22	M	Farmer	07Ja02MI
DUFF, W.		26	M	Farmer	07Ja02MI
WILSON, R.		23	M	Farmer	07Ja02MI
JONNIGER, J.		30	M	Farmer	07Ja02MI
ONEIL, Mgt.		60	F	Unknown	07Ja02MI
J.		26	M	Unknown	07Ja02MI
KINNERY, B.		25	M	Farmer	07Ja02MI
Mary		18	F	Unknown	07Ja02MI
WALSH, Ann		24	F	Unknown	07Ja02MI
DILLON, W.		20	M	Farmer	07Ja02MI
ONEIL, U-Miss		17	F	Unknown	07Ja02MI
SEXTON, E.		24	M	Farmer	07Ja02MI
Ellen		20	F	Unknown	07Ja02MI
JERRANDS, A.		20	M	Farmer	07Ja02MI
SIMPSON, W.		25	M	Farmer	07Ja02MI
CROSBY, J.		20	M	Farmer	07Ja02MI
DUFFY, J.		20	M	Farmer	07Ja02MI
Cath.		15	F	Unknown	07Ja02MI
Hus---, J.		26	M	Farmer	07Ja02MI
LONG, Mary		48	F	Unknown	07Ja02MI
Eliza		26	F	Unknown	07Ja02MI
Ann		25	F	Unknown	07Ja02MI
Mgt.		22	F	Unknown	07Ja02MI
Wm.		06	M	Child	07Ja02MI
Mary		04	F	Child	07Ja02MI
GREEN, Cath.		20	F	Unknown	07Ja02MI
MURPHY, Mgt.		20	F	Unknown	07Ja02MI
KEENAN, Ann		20	F	Unknown	07Ja02MI
DOOLAN, Ellen		20	F	Unknown	07Ja02MI
NOOLAN, Ann		20	F	Unknown	07Ja02MI
FRENCH, Mary		34	F	Unknown	07Ja02MI
MANN, U-Mrs.		24	F	Unknown	07Ja02MI
Mary	(D)	13	F	Unknown	07Ja02MI
Patk.	(S)	10	M	None	07Ja02MI
CASKEN, Alice		30	F	Unknown	07Ja02MI
James		11	M	None	07Ja02MI
HAY, P.		22	M	Laborer	07Ja02MI
ROONY, Mary		20	F	Unknown	07Ja02MI
TURGIN, Mary		20	F	Unknown	07Ja02MI
Martha		16	F	None	07Ja02MI
DRYDAN, J.		36	M	Laborer	07Ja02MI
ISAACS, T.		25	M	Laborer	07Ja02MI
Mary-J.	(W)	25	F	Unknown	07Ja02MI
Mary	(D)	08	F	Child	07Ja02MI
Patk.	(S)	01	M	Child	07Ja02MI
WALDRON, T.		28	M	Laborer	07Ja02MI
Mary		20	F	Unknown	07Ja02MI
WOODS, T.		50	M	Laborer	07Ja02MI
HARRIS, R.		45	M	Laborer	07Ja02MI
Jane		20	F	Unknown	07Ja02MI
Robt.		18	M	Laborer	07Ja02MI
Thos.		19	M	Laborer	07Ja02MI
SHERRY, R.		17	M	Laborer	07Ja02MI
Jno.		16	M	Laborer	07Ja02MI
Cath.		12	F	Unknown	07Ja02MI
HARRIS, D.		10	M	None	07Ja02MI
Isaac		08	M	Child	07Ja02MI
James		06	M	Child	07Ja02MI
Mary-A.		01	F	Child	07Ja02MI
REIN, J.		34	M	Laborer	07Ja02MI
Mary	(W)	33	F	Unknown	07Ja02MI
Martha	(D)	06	F	Child	07Ja02MI
KELLY, S.		20	M	Laborer	07Ja02MI
CUNIFF, Mary		20	F	Unknown	07Ja02MI
Mgt.		18	F	Unknown	07Ja02MI
GIBBON, Biddy		17	F	Unknown	07Ja02MI
ROGAN, J.		28	M	Laborer	07Ja02MI
DEVIS, P.		21	M	Laborer	07Ja02MI
Jane		22	F	Unknown	07Ja02MI
MCGINY, Cath.		20	F	Unknown	07Ja02MI
DEERYNE, Bgt.		19	F	Unknown	07Ja02MI
FINY, Mary		20	F	Unknown	07Ja02MI
Martha		18	F	Unknown	07Ja02MI
CADUAH, Sarah		16	F	Unknown	07Ja02MI
TULLY, Fr.		18	F	Unknown	07Ja02MI
MCKEON, J.		37	M	Laborer	07Ja02MI
ROBINSON, W.		08	M	Child	07Ja02MI
Winnie		30	F	Unknown	07Ja02MI
Jno.		11	M	None	07Ja02MI
Ian		08	M	Child	07Ja02MI
CALLAGHER, J.		20	M	Laborer	07Ja02MI
ROONEY, P.		18	M	Laborer	07Ja02MI
KENNEDY, Biddy		50	F	Unknown	07Ja02MI
Jno.		18	M	Laborer	07Ja02MI
Peter		12	M	None	07Ja02MI
LANNIDER, Mary		18	F	Unknown	07Ja02MI
EARLY, Biddy		30	F	Unknown	07Ja02MI
MCDERVOTT, Mary		00	F	Unknown	07Ja02MI
DUFFY, Mgt.		20	F	Unknown	07Ja02MI
Marta		30	F	Unknown	07Ja02MI
MASON, Isaac		20	M	Laborer	07Ja02MI
MURRY, P.		23	M	Laborer	07Ja02MI
DELANY, W.		21	M	Laborer	07Ja02MI
PULIHARD, Mary		19	F	Unknown	07Ja02MI
BUSNER, Mary		29	F	Unknown	07Ja02MI
FITZPATRICK, Julia		30	F	Unknown	07Ja02MI
TIGER, F.		28	M	Laborer	07Ja02MI
Mary		26	F	Unknown	07Ja02MI
CONIGAN, P.		29	M	Laborer	07Ja02MI
PHELAN, C.		25	M	Laborer	07Ja02MI
MUROHYER, P.		40	M	Laborer	07Ja02MI
NAGLE, Cath.		20	M	Laborer	07Ja02MI
KEATY, Mary		25	F	Unknown	07Ja02MI
Mary		25	F	Unknown	07Ja02MI
KEAN, Mgt.		15	F	Unknown	07Ja02MI
Mary		13	F	Unknown	07Ja02MI
Cath.		13	F	Unknown	07Ja02MI
FALERY, M.		21	M	Laborer	07Ja02MI
DUNOVAN, Elizt.		30	F	Unknown	07Ja02MI
FLYNN, Nan		20	F	Unknown	07Ja02MI
Joanna		23	F	Unknown	07Ja02MI
DURRY, M.		18	M	Laborer	07Ja02MI
OBRIEN, D.		23	M	Laborer	07Ja02MI
HICKEY, J.		18	M	Laborer	07Ja02MI
Mary		15	F	Unknown	07Ja02MI
Cath.		48	F	Unknown	07Ja02MI
CHILDS, A.		40	F	Unknown	07Ja02MI
SULLIVAN, D.		10	M	None	07Ja02MI
KINGS, P.		21	M	Laborer	07Ja02MI
Mary		50	F	Unknown	07Ja02MI
Ellen		40	F	Unknown	07Ja02MI
T.		25	F	Unknown	07Ja02MI

NAMES OF PASSENGERS		AGE	SEX	OCCUPATIONS	DATE PORT SHIP
HARTWELL, Jno.		19	M	Laborer	07Ja02MI
HITCHCOCK, S.		35	M	Laborer	07Ja02MI
HICKY, Mgt.		16	F	Unknown	07Ja02MI
Mary		16	F	Unknown	07Ja02MI
SPILLMAN, T.		23	M	Laborer	07Ja02MI
RYAN, Mary		24	F	Unknown	07Ja02MI
KENEDY, W.		26	M	Laborer	07Ja02MI
Cath.		26	F	Unknown	07Ja02MI
GRIFFIN, Elen		21	F	Unknown	07Ja02MI
WALSH, Mgt.		23	F	Unknown	07Ja02MI
Cath.		07	F	Child	07Ja02MI
COSTIN, J.		40	M	Laborer	07Ja02MI
Mgt.		40	F	Unknown	07Ja02MI
Biddy		40	F	Unknown	07Ja02MI
Thad.		07	M	Child	07Ja02MI
Mary		03	F	Child	07Ja02MI

HECTOR 15 JANUARY 1847

From Liverpool

NAMES OF PASSENGERS		AGE	SEX	OCCUPATIONS	DATE PORT SHIP
DONAHUE, M.		40	M	Laborer	15Ja02Ms
Ann	(W)	40	F	Unknown	15Ja02Ms
Bertha	(D)	18	F	Unknown	15Ja02Ms
Biddy	(D)	16	F	Unknown	15Ja02Ms
John	(S)	12	M	None	15Ja02Ms
Mich.	(S)	10	M	None	15Ja02Ms
Nich.	(S)	08	M	Child	15Ja02Ms
Patt	(S)	04	M	Child	15Ja02Ms
Ann	(D)	02	F	Child	15Ja02Ms
Maria	(D)	01	F	Child	15Ja02Ms
DALTON, P.		26	M	Farmer	15Ja02Ms
BAIN, M.		27	M	Farmer	15Ja02Ms
FEENY, Mary		40	F	Unknown	15Ja02Ms
Bgdt.		16	F	Unknown	15Ja02Ms
Dolly		16	F	Unknown	15Ja02Ms
Hanah		13	F	Unknown	15Ja02Ms
Pegg		11	F	Unknown	15Ja02Ms
Mich.		07	M	Child	15Ja02Ms
Mary		07	F	Child	15Ja02Ms
John		05	M	Child	15Ja02Ms
Matilda		03	F	Child	15Ja02Ms
SHERIDAN, Mary		20	F	Unknown	15Ja02Ms
MCCOMBS, J.		21	M	Mechanic	15Ja02Ms
MILLER, W.M.		21	M	Mechanic	15Ja02Ms
DYSON, J.		24	M	Mechanic	15Ja02Ms
BATES, J.		38	M	Mechanic	15Ja02Ms
Mary	(W)	32	F	Unknown	15Ja02Ms
Hugh	(S)	11	M	None	15Ja02Ms
Thos.	(S)	07	M	Child	15Ja02Ms
Meg	(D)	05	F	Child	15Ja02Ms
Francis	(S)	01	M	Child	15Ja02Ms
MEIMON, E.		35	M	Laborer	15Ja02Ms
EARLY, M.		30	M	Laborer	15Ja02Ms
Mary		25	F	Unknown	15Ja02Ms
FLINN, Jas.		25	M	Laborer	15Ja02Ms
Mary		25	F	Unknown	15Ja02Ms
Ellen		25	F	Unknown	15Ja02Ms
Michl.		03	M	Child	15Ja02Ms
WALSH, J.		32	M	Laborer	15Ja02Ms
Mary	(W)	32	F	Unknown	15Ja02Ms
Mich.	(S)	04	M	Child	15Ja02Ms
MELINGERY, M.		65	M	Laborer	15Ja02Ms
James		20	M	Laborer	15Ja02Ms
Cath.		20	F	Unknown	15Ja02Ms
FURNS, T.		20	M	Laborer	15Ja02Ms
SULLIGHER, A.		30	M	Laborer	15Ja02Ms
CONNER, J.		30	M	Laborer	15Ja02Ms
Biddy		55	F	Unknown	15Ja02Ms

NAMES OF PASSENGERS		AGE	SEX	OCCUPATIONS	DATE PORT SHIP
CONNER, Meg		13	F	Unknown	15Ja02Ms
Biddy		11	F	Unknown	15Ja02Ms
Bessy		09	F	Child	15Ja02Ms
Peggy		05	F	Child	15Ja02Ms
Michl.		23	M	Laborer	15Ja02Ms
FOY, J.		24	M	Laborer	15Ja02Ms
FERGURSON, P.		21	M	Laborer	15Ja02Ms
Meg		20	F	Unknown	15Ja02Ms
CONLAN, P.		20	M	Laborer	15Ja02Ms
Meg		40	F	Unknown	15Ja02Ms
MORAN, M.		20	M	Laborer	15Ja02Ms
SANGAR, Judy		19	F	Unknown	15Ja02Ms
HOLMES, O.		28	M	Laborer	15Ja02Ms
Mary	(W)	24	F	Wife	15Ja02Ms
Ruth	(D)	02	F	Child	15Ja02Ms
HARD, P.		30	M	Laborer	15Ja02Ms
Mary	(W)	30	F	Unknown	15Ja02Ms
Patt	(S)	02	M	Child	15Ja02Ms
COVANNA, T.		40	M	Laborer	15Ja02Ms
Anne	(W)	40	F	Unknown	15Ja02Ms
Patk.	(S)	11	M	None	15Ja02Ms
Martin	(S)	10	M	None	15Ja02Ms
James	(S)	08	M	Child	15Ja02Ms
Cath.	(D)	05	F	Child	15Ja02Ms
Mary	(D)	04	F	Child	15Ja02Ms
John	(S)	01	M	Child	15Ja02Ms
GREGAN, J.		21	M	Laborer	15Ja02Ms
HARTT, H.		20	M	Laborer	15Ja02Ms
Antny.		21	M	Laborer	15Ja02Ms
SCOTT, Ann		18	F	Unknown	15Ja02Ms
Pat		25	M	Laborer	15Ja02Ms
Biddy		25	F	Unknown	15Ja02Ms
LYNN, Meg		18	F	Unknown	15Ja02Ms
MULHORAN, J.		40	M	Laborer	15Ja02Ms
Nanny	(W)	40	F	Wife	15Ja02Ms
Teddy	(S)	17	M	Laborer	15Ja02Ms
Meg	(D)	12	F	Unknown	15Ja02Ms
John	(S)	10	M	Laborer	15Ja02Ms
Danl.	(S)	07	M	Child	15Ja02Ms
Cath.	(D)	02	F	Child	15Ja02Ms
Peggy	(D)	01	F	Child	15Ja02Ms
MCDENNETT, J.		25	M	Laborer	15Ja02Ms
John		35	M	Laborer	15Ja02Ms
NAIR, Mary-A.		16	F	Unknown	15Ja02Ms
MCCARICK, Jane		18	F	Unknown	15Ja02Ms
ROGH, J.		25	M	Laborer	15Ja02Ms
PATT, L.		30	M	Laborer	15Ja02Ms
FLANAGAN, E.		30	M	Laborer	15Ja02Ms
Cath.	(W)	26	F	Unknown	15Ja02Ms
Mary	(D)	06	F	Child	15Ja02Ms
Mich.	(S)	04	M	Child	15Ja02Ms
Bernard	(S)	02	M	Child	15Ja02Ms
HUNTER, J.		25	M	Laborer	15Ja02Ms
Francis		20	M	Laborer	15Ja02Ms
SHERIDAN, J.		20	M	Laborer	15Ja02Ms
NARENY, T.		25	M	Laborer	15Ja02Ms
U	(W)	25	F	Wife	15Ja02Ms
Cath.		20	F	Unknown	15Ja02Ms
Edwd.		10	M	None	15Ja02Ms
Cath.		09	F	Child	15Ja02Ms
Mary		07	F	Child	15Ja02Ms
Patt		05	M	Child	15Ja02Ms
Biddy		01	F	Child	15Ja02Ms
MCKERR, M.		20	M	Laborer	15Ja02Ms
SHERIDAN, M.		40	M	Laborer	15Ja02Ms
U	(W)	40	F	Unknown	15Ja02Ms
Edward	(S)	13	M	None	15Ja02Ms
William	(S)	07	M	Child	15Ja02Ms
Mathl.	(S)	04	M	Child	15Ja02Ms
STEVENSON, J.		02	M	Child	15Ja02Ms
CROSSIN, T.		22	M	Mechanic	15Ja02Ms
FOHNANY, J.		30	M	Mechanic	15Ja02Ms
U	(W)	30	F	Unknown	15Ja02Ms
Patt	(S)	11	M	None	15Ja02Ms
Mary	(D)	09	F	Child	15Ja02Ms

NAMES OF PASSENGERS		AGE SEX	OCCUPATIONS	DATE PORT SHIP	NAMES OF PASSENGERS		AGE SEX	OCCUPATIONS	DATE PORT SHIP
FOHNANY, Owen	(S)	06 M	Child	15Ja02Ms	KELLY, Sarah		16 F	Unknown	15Ja02Ms
Michl.	(S)	04 M	Child	15Ja02Ms	DURKIN, Honora		26 F	Unknown	15Ja02Ms
Ellen	(D)	02 F	Child	15Ja02Ms	HIGGINS, F.		17 M	Laborer	15Ja02Ms
MCSOWEN, P.		24 M	Laborer	15Ja02Ms	Eliza		19 F	Unknown	15Ja02Ms
Ellen	(W)	29 F	Unknown	15Ja02Ms	Edwd.		20 M	Laborer	15Ja02Ms
Honora	(D)	06 F	Child	15Ja02Ms	MCCONLY, D.		32 M	Laborer	15Ja02Ms
James	(S)	01 M	Child	15Ja02Ms	U	(W)	29 F	Unknown	15Ja02Ms
FOOLEY, P.		30 M	Laborer	15Ja02Ms	Mary	(D)	09 F	Child	15Ja02Ms
John		21 M	Laborer	15Ja02Ms	Ann	(D)	07 F	Child	15Ja02Ms
DOUGHERTY, J.		24 M	Laborer	15Ja02Ms	Martin	(S)	03 M	Child	15Ja02Ms
Bdgt.		25 F	Unknown	15Ja02Ms	Magt.	(D)	01 F	Child	15Ja02Ms
Mary		40 F	Unknown	15Ja02Ms	REED, Mary		25 F	Unknown	15Ja02Ms
Thos.		12 M	None	15Ja02Ms	MCMORRIS, P.		22 M	Laborer	15Ja02Ms
Mary		17 F	Unknown	15Ja02Ms	CEENLIN, W.		22 M	Laborer	15Ja02Ms
MCMURRY, M.		35 M	Laborer	15Ja02Ms	UKBLREN, Nancy		17 F	Unknown	15Ja02Ms
Eliza	(W)	30 F	Unknown	15Ja02Ms	AMSBY, Sidy		22 F	Unknown	15Ja02Ms
Matilda	(D)	03 F	Child	15Ja02Ms	SEYNE, T.		20 M	Laborer	15Ja02Ms
Arthur	(S)	01 M	Child	15Ja02Ms	James		10 M	None	15Ja02Ms
HUGHES, T.		39 M	Laborer	15Ja02Ms	MAKERLY, T.		22 M	Laborer	15Ja02Ms
Sarah	(W)	35 F	Unknown	15Ja02Ms	NEILSON, J.		20 M	Laborer	15Ja02Ms
Margt.	(D)	11 F	Unknown	15Ja02Ms	SLAVIN, J.		28 M	Laborer	15Ja02Ms
Thos.	(S)	09 M	Child	15Ja02Ms	KEIGAN, Bdgt.		18 F	Unknown	15Ja02Ms
Patt	(S)	07 M	Child	15Ja02Ms	MCDEULL, Carolina		16 F	Unknown	15Ja02Ms
Ellen	(D)	05 F	Child	15Ja02Ms	SEYNE, J.		08 M	Child	15Ja02Ms
Sarah	(D)	02 F	Child	15Ja02Ms					
WOODY, Susan		20 F	Unknown	15Ja02Ms					
BOYLAN, J.		20 M	Laborer	15Ja02Ms					
MCDEVELIN, H.		52 M	Laborer	15Ja02Ms					
U	(W)	52 M	Unknown	15Ja02Ms					
J.	(S)	26 M	Laborer	15Ja02Ms			**ATLAS 15 JANUARY 1847**		
Joseph	(S)	25 M	Laborer	15Ja02Ms					
Cath.	(D)	20 F	Unknown	15Ja02Ms			**From Liverpool**		
Elizbt.	(D)	16 F	Unknown	15Ja02Ms					
Jacob	(S)	11 M	None	15Ja02Ms					
WOLF, M.		21 M	Laborer	15Ja02Ms					
HEESAL, G.		21 M	Laborer	15Ja02Ms	CRONEY, Mark		38 M	Mechanic	15Ja02Ec
HEEVINER, J.		36 E	Laborer	15Ja02Ms	Jane	(W)	36 F	Unknown	15Ja02Ec
SYKES, J.		56 M	Laborer	15Ja02Ms	Ann	(D)	08 F	Child	15Ja02Ec
Meg	(W)	45 F	Unknown	15Ja02Ms	Bridget	(D)	04 F	Child	15Ja02Ec
John	(S)	22 M	Laborer	15Ja02Ms	Mary	(D)	04 F	Child	15Ja02Ec
Peggy	(D)	18 F	Unknown	15Ja02Ms	Cath.	(D)	01 F	Child	15Ja02Ec
James	(S)	10 M	None	15Ja02Ms	MOHAN, Pat.		26 M	Laborer	15Ja02Ec
Mary	(D)	08 F	Child	15Ja02Ms	CLARK, Bernard		21 M	Laborer	15Ja02Ec
MULLIGAN, Eliza		18 F	Unknown	15Ja02Ms	BOURNE, Mary-A.		27 F	Unknown	15Ja02Ec
ROCH, Mary		22 F	Unknown	15Ja02Ms	WARD, James		22 M	Laborer	15Ja02Ec
MCDENNETT, P.		25 M	Laborer	15Ja02Ms	RICK, James		19 M	Laborer	15Ja02Ec
Honora		22 F	Unknown	15Ja02Ms	FARRELL, Danl.		18 M	Laborer	15Ja02Ec
MCCORMICK, J.		24 M	Laborer	15Ja02Ms	TULLY, Hugh		17 M	Laborer	15Ja02Ec
ARMSTRONG, J.		48 M	Laborer	15Ja02Ms	GALLAGHER, Dennis		16 M	Laborer	15Ja02Ec
Lyny		22 M	Laborer	15Ja02Ms	MCLAUGHLIN, John		35 M	Laborer	15Ja02Ec
Mary-J.		15 F	Unknown	15Ja02Ms	QUILKIN, Pat.		23 M	Laborer	15Ja02Ec
Eliza		13 F	Unknown	15Ja02Ms	David		11 M	Laborer	15Ja02Ec
Smal.		11 M	None	15Ja02Ms	KELLEY, Charles		23 M	Laborer	15Ja02Ec
BREADY, W.		24 M	Laborer	15Ja02Ms	CAYNE, Owen		23 M	Laborer	15Ja02Ec
Eady.		20 M	Laborer	15Ja02Ms	Jane		23 F	Unknown	15Ja02Ec
SMITH, W.		18 M	Laborer	15Ja02Ms	BARRETT, Cecilia		20 F	Unknown	15Ja02Ec
Francis		17 M	Laborer	15Ja02Ms	CONLON, James		25 M	Laborer	15Ja02Ec
MCFARLANE, Cath.		15 F	Unknown	15Ja02Ms	NOWLAN, Michael		30 M	Laborer	15Ja02Ec
SREY, T.		25 M	Merchant	15Ja02Ms	KELLY, Bridget		23 F	Unknown	15Ja02Ec
KELLY, T.		30 M	Laborer	15Ja02Ms	MCLAUGHLIN, Mary		21 F	Unknown	15Ja02Ec
Bdgt.	(W)	28 F	Wife	15Ja02Ms	KELLEY, James		23 M	Laborer	15Ja02Ec
Martin	(S)	06 M	Child	15Ja02Ms	SHERIDAN, Michael		52 M	Laborer	15Ja02Ec
Bdgt.	(D)	03 F	Child	15Ja02Ms	Mary		24 F	Unknown	15Ja02Ec
Edwd.	(S)	01 M	Child	15Ja02Ms	Michael		26 M	Laborer	15Ja02Ec
HAWKINS, M.		20 M	Laborer	15Ja02Ms	MADDEN, Pat		34 M	Laborer	15Ja02Ec
Mary		18 F	Unknown	15Ja02Ms	Jane		10 F	Unknown	15Ja02Ec
CORMICK, Biddy		18 F	Unknown	15Ja02Ms	Walter		05 M	Child	15Ja02Ec
FAY, Math.		26 M	Laborer	15Ja02Ms	MCGOWAN, Thos.		28 M	Laborer	15Ja02Ec
Rebecca	(W)	20 F	Wife	15Ja02Ms	Cath.		26 F	Unknown	15Ja02Ec
Bdgt.	(D)	03 F	Child	15Ja02Ms	Bridget		24 F	Unknown	15Ja02Ec
Alis	(S)	01 M	Child	15Ja02Ms	Mary		.00 F	Infant	15Ja02Ec
CHURCHILL, M.		02 M	Child	15Ja02Ms	LEONARD, Anthony		26 M	Laborer	15Ja02Ec
KELLY, Ann-M.		26 F	Unknown	15Ja02Ms	Bridget	(W)	26 F	Unknown	15Ja02Ec
Hannah		18 F	Unknown	15Ja02Ms	Cath.	(D)	01 F	Child	15Ja02Ec
Biddy		20 F	Unknown	15Ja02Ms	Mary	(D)	.00 F	Infant	15Ja02Ec

NAMES OF PASSENGERS		AGE	SEX	OCCUPATIONS	DATE PORT SHIP
LYNOTT, Nancy		27	F	Unknown	15Ja02Ec
Peter		21	M	Laborer	15Ja02Ec
Bridget		22	F	Unknown	15Ja02Ec
Michael		02	M	Child	15Ja02Ec
Patrick		.00	M	Infant	15Ja02Ec
CLARK, John		35	M	Mechanic	15Ja02Ec
CURREY, Pat		23	M	Mechanic	15Ja02Ec
MILLS, Eliz.		43	F	Unknown	15Ja02Ec
SWEENEY, Michael		26	M	Laborer	15Ja02Ec
MUTAGH, Thos.		27	M	Laborer	15Ja02Ec
Eliz.		20	F	Unknown	15Ja02Ec
OMALLEY, James		19	M	Laborer	15Ja02Ec
CONROY, Michael		35	M	Laborer	15Ja02Ec
TOY, Wm.		24	M	Laborer	15Ja02Ec
DEVENEY, Hugh		20	M	Laborer	15Ja02Ec
RUMS, Dennis		24	M	Laborer	15Ja02Ec
BARNARD, James		40	M	Laborer	15Ja02Ec
James		22	M	Laborer	15Ja02Ec
HANCROFT, Rolph		55	M	Laborer	15Ja02Ec
SCOTT, Chas.		19	M	Laborer	15Ja02Ec
WOOD, Barnard		20	M	Laborer	15Ja02Ec
Cath.		25	F	Unknown	15Ja02Ec
BINBLE, Mary		30	F	Unknown	15Ja02Ec
DUFFER, Edward		40	M	Laborer	15Ja02Ec
CASSIDAY, Pat		40	M	Laborer	15Ja02Ec
Peggy	(W)	40	F	Unknown	15Ja02Ec
Ann	(D)	10	F	Unknown	15Ja02Ec
James	(S)	06	M	Child	15Ja02Ec
Peter	(S)	04	M	Child	15Ja02Ec
DOLAN, James		21	M	Laborer	15Ja02Ec
FINIGAN, James		18	M	Laborer	15Ja02Ec
Cath.		16	F	Unknown	15Ja02Ec
WARD, William		20	M	Laborer	15Ja02Ec
DORAN, Michael		30	M	Mechanic	15Ja02Ec
MCNULTY, James		24	M	Mechanic	15Ja02Ec
Nancy		18	F	Unknown	15Ja02Ec
FRANY, James		24	F	Unknown	15Ja02Ec
Mary		20	F	Unknown	15Ja02Ec
MCCUIN, Cornelius		55	M	Laborer	15Ja02Ec
Jane	(W)	45	F	Unknown	15Ja02Ec
Margt.	(D)	19	F	Unknown	15Ja02Ec
Mary	(D)	15	F	Unknown	15Ja02Ec
William	(S)	12	M	None	15Ja02Ec
Patrick	(S)	07	M	Child	15Ja02Ec
Cath.	(D)	04	F	Child	15Ja02Ec
MCKEFFEY, Bridget		24	F	Unknown	15Ja02Ec
Peggy		20	F	Unknown	15Ja02Ec
MCGLINN, Mary		15	F	Unknown	15Ja02Ec
Fanny		45	F	Unknown	15Ja02Ec
Cath.		10	F	Unknown	15Ja02Ec
Hugh		08	M	Child	15Ja02Ec
Peggy		06	F	Child	15Ja02Ec
Fanny		04	F	Child	15Ja02Ec
MCBRIDE, Michael		20	M	Laborer	15Ja02Ec
LANE, William		23	M	Laborer	15Ja02Ec
Isabella	(W)	23	F	Unknown	15Ja02Ec
Jane	(D)	.00	F	Infant	15Ja02Ec
CULLEN, Richd.		25	M	Laborer	15Ja02Ec
Eliza		26	F	Unknown	15Ja02Ec
MCCABE, Jno.		21	M	Laborer	18Ja02Ak
MCWILLIAMS, H.		50	M	Laborer	18Ja02Ak
CORNELL, Eliza		44	F	Unknown	18Ja02Ak
Hugh		17	M	Laborer	18Ja02Ak
Mary		20	F	Unknown	18Ja02Ak
Eliza		18	F	Unknown	18Ja02Ak
Ann-J.		16	F	Unknown	18Ja02Ak
Sarah		11	F	Unknown	18Ja02Ak
Agnes		09	F	Child	18Ja02Ak
John		14	M	Laborer	18Ja02Ak
DINSMORE, Isabella		23	F	Unknown	18Ja02Ak
MCBRIDE, John		36	M	Laborer	18Ja02Ak
Mary		13	F	Unknown	18Ja02Ak
Biddy		11	F	Unknown	18Ja02Ak
JERDEN, Peter		40	M	Laborer	18Ja02Ak
Mary	(W)	22	F	Unknown	18Ja02Ak
John	(S)	.09	M	Infant	18Ja02Ak
Antony	(S)	13	M	None	18Ja02Ak
HOBAN, Michl.		40	M	Laborer	18Ja02Ak
LOMETTE, Ellen		24	F	Unknown	18Ja02Ak
Honora		26	F	Unknown	18Ja02Ak
LANE, Wm.		35	M	Mechanic	18Ja02Ak
LYON, Chas.		22	M	Mechanic	18Ja02Ak
DAVIS, Caroline		27	F	Unknown	18Ja02Ak
Martha	(D)	07	F	Child	18Ja02Ak
Mary	(D)	04	F	Child	18Ja02Ak
Joseph	(S)	02	M	Child	18Ja02Ak
MALIN, Matt		23	M	Laborer	18Ja02Ak
PADDON, Dom.		25	M	Laborer	18Ja02Ak
DOHERTY, Roger		27	M	Laborer	18Ja02Ak
MCDONOUGH, Thos.		40	M	Laborer	18Ja02Ak
Eliza	(W)	40	F	Wife	18Ja02Ak
Mary	(D)	15	F	Unknown	18Ja02Ak
Jane	(D)	12	F	Unknown	18Ja02Ak
Eliza	(D)	10	F	Unknown	18Ja02Ak
Sarah	(D)	08	F	Child	18Ja02Ak
Mgt.	(D)	06	F	Child	18Ja02Ak
James	(S)	04	M	Child	18Ja02Ak
Rebecca	(D)	01	F	Child	18Ja02Ak
DOLPHIN, Thos.		27	M	Laborer	18Ja02Ak
Mary	(W)	27	F	Unknown	18Ja02Ak
Cath.	(D)	.10	F	Infant	18Ja02Ak
LAYNE, Jas.		35	M	Laborer	18Ja02Ak
Bridget	(W)	30	F	Unknown	18Ja02Ak
Pat	(S)	07	M	Child	18Ja02Ak
HEALEY, Biddy		18	F	Unknown	18Ja02Ak
TAYNE, Ed.		30	M	Laborer	18Ja02Ak
SCANLAN, Dom.		21	M	Laborer	18Ja02Ak
Biddy		30	F	Unknown	18Ja02Ak
Honora		15	F	Unknown	18Ja02Ak
Mary		12	F	Unknown	18Ja02Ak
ROWAN, Michl.		24	M	Laborer	18Ja02Ak
Pat		25	M	Laborer	18Ja02Ak
LANGAN, Pat		25	M	Laborer	18Ja02Ak
DUNCAN, Thos.		50	M	Laborer	18Ja02Ak
Nancy	(W)	40	F	Unknown	18Ja02Ak
Mich.	(S)	18	M	Laborer	18Ja02Ak
Mary	(D)	16	F	Unknown	18Ja02Ak
John	(S)	14	M	Laborer	18Ja02Ak
Pat	(S)	12	M	Laborer	18Ja02Ak
Thos.	(S)	10	M	Laborer	18Ja02Ak
James	(S)	08	M	Child	18Ja02Ak
Owen	(S)	08	M	Child	18Ja02Ak
Mgt.	(D)	05	F	Child	18Ja02Ak
CRONER, Danl.		22	M	Mechanic	18Ja02Ak
BANKS, Danl.		24	M	Mechanic	18Ja02Ak
ROWEN, Pat		20	M	Mechanic	18Ja02Ak
Biddy		21	F	Unknown	18Ja02Ak
MALONEY, Michl.		28	M	Laborer	18Ja02Ak
Mgt.		20	F	Unknown	18Ja02Ak
HEALEY, Pat		20	M	Laborer	18Ja02Ak
MORIN, Eliza		20	F	Unknown	18Ja02Ak
MCDONALD, Mgt.		30	F	Unknown	18Ja02Ak
GALLAGHER, Isaac		26	M	Laborer	18Ja02Ak
Betty		26	F	Unknown	18Ja02Ak

ROCHESTER 18 JANUARY 1847

From Liverpool

NAMES OF PASSENGERS		AGE	SEX	OCCUPATIONS	DATE PORT SHIP
BAWER, Wm.		19	M	Laborer	18Ja02Ak
BIRMINGHAM, Bridget		16	F	Unknown	18Ja02Ak
Nappy		15	F	Unknown	18Ja02Ak
HIGGINS, Jno.		40	M	Laborer	18Ja02Ak
Biddy		50	F	Unknown	18Ja02Ak

NAMES OF PASSENGERS		A G E	S E X	OCCUPATIONS	DATE PORT SHIP	NAMES OF PASSENGERS		A G E	S E X	OCCUPATIONS	DATE PORT SHIP
ODONNELL, James		36	M	Laborer	18Ja02Ak	FITZPATRICK, Jas.		21	M	Laborer	18Ja02Ak
Biddy	(W)	32	F	Unknown	18Ja02Ak	Jno.		23	M	Laborer	18Ja02Ak
Mary	(D)	06	F	Child	18Ja02Ak	FALLON, Mich.		30	M	Laborer	18Ja02Ak
Antony	(S)	04	M	Child	18Ja02Ak	Nelly	(W)	25	F	Unknown	18Ja02Ak
MCDERMOT, Mary		40	F	Unknown	18Ja02Ak	Ann	(D)	02	F	Child	18Ja02Ak
Michl.	(H)	40	M	Laborer	18Ja02Ak	Pat	(S)	05	M	Child	18Ja02Ak
Cath.	(D)	07	F	Child	18Ja02Ak	Jas.		25	M	Laborer	18Ja02Ak
Jno.	(S)	06	M	Child	18Ja02Ak	MCGILL, John		50	M	Laborer	18Ja02Ak
HOLDEN, Pat		20	M	Laborer	18Ja02Ak	RICE, John		13	M	Laborer	18Ja02Ak
MALARKEY, Pat		21	M	Laborer	18Ja02Ak	MCCANN, Dennis		31	M	Laborer	18Ja02Ak
Jno.		23	M	Laborer	18Ja02Ak	Mary	(W)	32	F	Unknown	18Ja02Ak
CAFFREY, Jno.		26	M	Laborer	18Ja02Ak	Jno.	(S)	09	M	Child	18Ja02Ak
Cath.		42	F	Unknown	18Ja02Ak	Biddy	(D)	07	F	Child	18Ja02Ak
Cath.		22	F	Unknown	18Ja02Ak	Ann	(D)	03	F	Child	18Ja02Ak
READY, David		30	M	Laborer	18Ja02Ak	Wm.	(S)	05	M	Child	18Ja02Ak
PURCELL, Jas.		22	M	Laborer	18Ja02Ak	Lewis	(S)	.09	M	Infant	18Ja02Ak
Mary		20	F	Unknown	18Ja02Ak	Francis		24	M	Laborer	18Ja02Ak
BARK, Biddy		21	F	Unknown	18Ja02Ak	Biddy		22	F	Unknown	18Ja02Ak
MCDERMOTT, Jno.		33	M	Laborer	18Ja02Ak	Cathl.		19	F	Unknown	18Ja02Ak
MONTGOMERY, Jas.		22	M	Laborer	18Ja02Ak	LANG, Jno.		23	M	Laborer	18Ja02Ak
Cath.	(W)	24	F	Unknown	18Ja02Ak	MCMURRAY, Frank		50	M	Laborer	18Ja02Ak
Ann	(D)	09	F	Child	18Ja02Ak	Mgt.	(W)	45	F	Unknown	18Ja02Ak
BRADY, Peter		21	M	Laborer	18Ja02Ak	Rose	(D)	22	F	Unknown	18Ja02Ak
SLEIM, Pat		50	M	Laborer	18Ja02Ak	Ed.	(S)	20	M	Laborer	18Ja02Ak
Dan		18	M	Laborer	18Ja02Ak	Mgt.	(D)	18	F	Unknown	18Ja02Ak
Jno.		16	M	Laborer	18Ja02Ak	M.A.	(D)	16	F	Unknown	18Ja02Ak
CAMPBELL, Ann		17	F	Unknown	18Ja02Ak	Jno.	(S)	14	M	Laborer	18Ja02Ak
DOUGAN, Eliza		18	F	Unknown	18Ja02Ak	Rose-C.	(D)	19	F	Unknown	18Ja02Ak
MARKEY, Owen		21	M	Laborer	18Ja02Ak	STIMITT, Wm.		21	M	Laborer	18Ja02Ak
Christ.		30	M	Laborer	18Ja02Ak	Betty		20	F	Unknown	18Ja02Ak
MCCUTCHEON, Saml.		15	M	Laborer	18Ja02Ak	DIVINE, Cathl.		50	F	Unknown	18Ja02Ak
ROGERS, Jas.		25	M	Laborer	18Ja02Ak	MCDERMOT, Pat.		21	M	Laborer	18Ja02Ak
Jno.		30	M	Laborer	18Ja02Ak	FANAGAN, Pat.		18	M	Laborer	18Ja02Ak
Biddy		26	F	Unknown	18Ja02Ak	Esther		13	F	Unknown	18Ja02Ak
Mary		.09	F	Infant	18Ja02Ak	CONNOLLY, Mary		18	F	Unknown	18Ja02Ak
KELLEY, Dennis		21	M	Laborer	18Ja02Ak	MCELROY, B.		20	M	Laborer	18Ja02Ak
Dudley		18	M	Laborer	18Ja02Ak	BLUCKLIN, Danl.		31	M	Laborer	18Ja02Ak
CAREY, Wm.		22	M	Laborer	18Ja02Ak	Chas.		10	M	None	18Ja02Ak
GRAY, Richd.		24	M	Laborer	18Ja02Ak	KELLY, John		22	M	Laborer	18Ja02Ak
MCGEE, Mich.		30	M	Laborer	18Ja02Ak	MORGAN, Ann		17	F	Unknown	18Ja02Ak
MONAGAN, Mich.		20	M	Laborer	18Ja02Ak	DAILEY, Cathl.		19	F	Unknown	18Ja02Ak
SWEENEY, Michl.		24	M	Laborer	18Ja02Ak	DARDY, Biddy		22	F	Unknown	18Ja02Ak
Biddy		23	F	Unknown	18Ja02Ak	KELLEY, Ann		24	F	Unknown	18Ja02Ak
BURKE, Honora		24	F	Unknown	18Ja02Ak	Mary		20	F	Unknown	18Ja02Ak
MCQUILTY, Peter		30	M	Laborer	18Ja02Ak	MCNALLY, Biddy		22	F	Unknown	18Ja02Ak
Quis	(W)	25	F	Unknown	18Ja02Ak	ROWLAND, Hy.		26	M	Mechanic	18Ja02Ak
Pat.	(S)	02	M	Child	18Ja02Ak	Eliza-J.		18	F	Unknown	18Ja02Ak
SWEENEY, Thos.		27	M	Laborer	18Ja02Ak	MALONEY, Ann		23	F	Unknown	18Ja02Ak
Mgt.		24	F	Unknown	18Ja02Ak	OBRIEN, Mich.		22	M	Laborer	18Ja02Ak
MAYER, Sebastian		63	M	Laborer	18Ja02Ak	Mgt.		52	F	Unknown	18Ja02Ak
Jacob		40	M	Laborer	18Ja02Ak	HIGGINS, Mary		10	F	Unknown	18Ja02Ak
Magdalina		30	F	Unknown	18Ja02Ak	MCGUIRE, Biddy		30	F	Unknown	18Ja02Ak
Jacob		16	M	Laborer	18Ja02Ak	REILEY, Biddy		23	F	Unknown	18Ja02Ak
Johanna		02	F	Child	18Ja02Ak	REGAN, Arthur		10	M	None	18Ja02Ak
BRUTCHER, Eliza		48	F	Unknown	18Ja02Ak	GAFFREY, John		02	M	Child	18Ja02Ak
Attica		20	F	Unknown	18Ja02Ak	Mary		.00	F	Infant	18Ja02Ak
Cyprelan		15	M	Laborer	18Ja02Ak	COLBRUN, Danl.		20	M	Mechanic	18Ja02Ak
RI--, Agatha		58	F	Unknown	18Ja02Ak	SCOTT, Richd.		20	M	Mechanic	18Ja02Ak
EISTER, Frans.		28	M	Laborer	18Ja02Ak	CURTIS, Wm.		25	M	Mechanic	18Ja02Ak
MAYER, Casper		35	M	Laborer	18Ja02Ak	U	(W)	23	F	Unknown	18Ja02Ak
Anola		13	F	Unknown	18Ja02Ak	ISLAY, Amelia		18	F	Unknown	18Ja02Ak
Francis		11	M	None	18Ja02Ak	OBRIEN, Pat		35	M	Laborer	18Ja02Ak
Magd.		05	F	Child	18Ja02Ak	GALLAGHER, Hannah		.00	F	Infant	18Ja02Ak
MAYO, Joseph		48	M	Laborer	18Ja02Ak	MCGLANE, Cath.		20	F	Unknown	18Ja02Ak
Christ.		46	M	Laborer	18Ja02Ak	U, U		.00	U	Infant	18Ja02Ak
Marin		18	M	Laborer	18Ja02Ak	Born-At-Sea					
Janetta		17	F	Unknown	18Ja02Ak	U		.00	U	Infant	18Ja02Ak
Agnes		10	F	Unknown	18Ja02Ak	Born-At-Sea					
Hodges		08	M	Child	18Ja02Ak						
Withel		04	M	Child	18Ja02Ak						
HAYS, Pat.		24	M	Laborer	18Ja02Ak						
FIELD, Jas.		26	M	Laborer	18Ja02Ak						
Wm.		24	M	Laborer	18Ja02Ak						
CUPPAL, C.		50	M	Laborer	18Ja02Ak						
DOLAN, Biddy		20	F	Unknown	18Ja02Ak						

PACIFIC 20 JANUARY 1847

From Liverpool

NAMES OF PASSENGERS		AGE	SEX	OCCUPATIONS	DATE PORT SHIP
WILEY, John		20	M	Farmer	20Ja02BJ
BURKE, Jas.		39	M	Farmer	20Ja02BJ
Mary	(W)	37	F	Wife	20Ja02BJ
Mich.		17	M	None	20Ja02BJ
Pat.	(S)	16	M	None	20Ja02BJ
Cathl.	(D)	13	F	Unknown	20Ja02BJ
Thos.	(S)	14	M	None	20Ja02BJ
Cathl.	(D)	13	F	Unknown	20Ja02BJ
Pat.	(S)	12	M	None	20Ja02BJ
RITIG, Math.		30	M	Farmer	20Ja02BJ
GRIFFITHS, Anna		29	F	Unknown	20Ja02BJ
MCCANN, Anna		20	F	Unknown	20Ja02BJ
FARRALL, Mich.		30	M	Farmer	20Ja02BJ
John		20	M	Farmer	20Ja02BJ
Mathd.		18	M	Farmer	20Ja02BJ
Ann		15	F	Unknown	20Ja02BJ
HUGHES, Wm.		28	M	Farmer	20Ja02BJ
SWEENEY, John		25	M	Farmer	20Ja02BJ
BACKIN, U-Mrs.		28	F	Unknown	20Ja02BJ
HAGAN, Bridget		20	F	Unknown	20Ja02BJ
HANDY, Math.		20	M	Farmer	20Ja02BJ
Cath.		18	F	Unknown	20Ja02BJ
FAGAN, Pat.		20	M	Farmer	20Ja02BJ
U	(W)	20	F	Wife	20Ja02BJ
LUCKLEY, Thos.		20	M	Farmer	20Ja02BJ
FINCH, Pat		29	M	Farmer	20Ja02BJ
Bridget	(W)	28	F	Unknown	20Ja02BJ
Thos.	(S)	08	M	Child	20Ja02BJ
Ann	(D)	07	F	Child	20Ja02BJ
Matt.	(S)	05	M	Child	20Ja02BJ
Henor	(S)	03	M	Child	20Ja02BJ
CUNIFF, Ann		25	F	Unknown	20Ja02BJ
Peter	(H)	24	M	Farmer	20Ja02BJ
Mich.	(S)	06	M	Child	20Ja02BJ
Ann	(D)	05	F	Child	20Ja02BJ
Andy	(S)	04	M	Child	20Ja02BJ
Owen	(S)	03	M	Child	20Ja02BJ
Mich.	(S)	02	M	Child	20Ja02BJ
GORDON, Jas.		40	M	Farmer	20Ja02BJ
Jane		40	F	Unknown	20Ja02BJ
Magt.		28	F	Unknown	20Ja02BJ
Math.		16	M	None	20Ja02BJ
Patk.		15	M	None	20Ja02BJ
Jas.		14	M	None	20Ja02BJ
Eliza		13	F	Unknown	20Ja02BJ
Thos.		12	M	None	20Ja02BJ
John		20	M	Farmer	20Ja02BJ
Ann		18	F	Unknown	20Ja02BJ
Rachel		28	F	Unknown	20Ja02BJ
MCCABE, Wm.		29	M	Farmer	20Ja02BJ
Chas.		28	M	Farmer	20Ja02BJ
John		23	M	Farmer	20Ja02BJ
CLERK, John		25	M	Farmer	20Ja02BJ
MALONY, Mich.		24	M	Farmer	20Ja02BJ
SMITH, John		23	M	Farmer	20Ja02BJ
Susan		22	F	Unknown	20Ja02BJ
MCCABE, Pat		25	M	Laborer	20Ja02BJ
LEONARD, John		26	M	Laborer	20Ja02BJ
Jane		24	F	Unknown	20Ja02BJ
MYDRON, Matt.		30	M	Mechanic	20Ja02BJ
U	(W)	28	F	Unknown	20Ja02BJ
BODEN, Moses		34	M	Farmer	20Ja02BJ
Hugh		10	M	None	20Ja02BJ
Thos.		08	M	Child	20Ja02BJ
MALONEY, M.		30	M	Farmer	20Ja02BJ
MCSHANE, Wm.		28	M	Farmer	20Ja02BJ
Jane	(W)	27	F	Unknown	20Ja02BJ
James	(S)	06	M	Child	20Ja02BJ
David	(S)	04	M	Child	20Ja02BJ
KENNEY, John		28	M	Farmer	20Ja02BJ
Thos.	(S)	03	M	Child	20Ja02BJ
U	(W)	27	F	Wife	20Ja02BJ
Bessey	(D)	02	F	Child	20Ja02BJ
CUMMIFFS, John		20	M	Mechanic	20Ja02BJ
JAURDON, Matt		40	M	Mechanic	20Ja02BJ
U	(W)	39	F	Unknown	20Ja02BJ
Mary	(D)	17	F	Unknown	20Ja02BJ
Chas.	(S)	15	M	None	20Ja02BJ
Cathl.	(D)	13	F	Unknown	20Ja02BJ
Martin	(S)	11	M	None	20Ja02BJ
Bernard	(S)	08	M	Child	20Ja02BJ
Peggy	(D)	05	F	Child	20Ja02BJ
Maria	(D)	04	F	Child	20Ja02BJ
Anna	(D)	02	F	Child	20Ja02BJ
BURTON, Nibben		28	M	Mechanic	20Ja02BJ
David		26	M	Mechanic	20Ja02BJ
OHARA, Rose		20	F	Unknown	20Ja02BJ
DOYLE, Pat		20	M	Mechanic	20Ja02BJ
Cathl.		18	F	Unknown	20Ja02BJ
GILLESPIE, Jas.		20	M	Mechanic	20Ja02BJ
FORD, Wm.		21	M	Mechanic	20Ja02BJ
BENNETT, John		22	M	Mechanic	20Ja02BJ
MURPHY, Jas.		25	M	Mechanic	20Ja02BJ
TUDOR, David		24	M	Mechanic	20Ja02BJ
CANNON, Pat		24	M	Mechanic	20Ja02BJ
U	(W)	20	F	Unknown	20Ja02BJ
TRAYNOR, Cathl.		18	F	Unknown	20Ja02BJ
COHAN, M.		21	M	Mechanic	20Ja02BJ
MCKENNA, Margt.		20	F	Unknown	20Ja02BJ
Mary		18	F	Unknown	20Ja02BJ
WYKOFF, Thos.		25	M	Farmer	20Ja02BJ
HOGAN, John		25	M	Farmer	20Ja02BJ
Pat.		23	M	Farmer	20Ja02BJ
OBRIEN, Pat.		24	M	Farmer	20Ja02BJ
JAMES, Wm.		26	M	Farmer	20Ja02BJ
MADDEN, Saml.		26	M	Farmer	20Ja02BJ
MCCABE, Barney		28	M	Farmer	20Ja02BJ
U	(W)	27	F	Unknown	20Ja02BJ
WYNNE, Geo.		38	M	Farmer	20Ja02BJ
Mary	(W)	38	F	Unknown	20Ja02BJ
Anne	(D)	12	F	Unknown	20Ja02BJ
Patk.	(S)	10	M	None	20Ja02BJ
Cathl.	(D)	08	F	Child	20Ja02BJ
James	(S)	06	M	Child	20Ja02BJ
CEVERN, B.		18	M	None	20Ja02BJ
SULLIVAN, Jas.		26	M	Farmer	20Ja02BJ
Cathl.	(W)	24	F	Unknown	20Ja02BJ
Cathl.	(D)	04	F	Child	20Ja02BJ
RILEY, Hugh		20	M	Farmer	20Ja02BJ
Patk.		18	M	Farmer	20Ja02BJ
GRADY, Dennis		36	M	Farmer	20Ja02BJ
Betty	(W)	35	F	Wife	20Ja02BJ
Cathl.	(D)	14	F	Unknown	20Ja02BJ
Mary	(D)	12	F	Unknown	20Ja02BJ
Corns.	(S)	10	M	None	20Ja02BJ
Thos.	(S)	08	M	Child	20Ja02BJ
Dennis	(S)	06	M	Child	20Ja02BJ
SANDERS, Leo.		28	M	Farmer	20Ja02BJ
U	(W)	26	F	Unknown	20Ja02BJ
MADDEN, Bridget		18	F	Unknown	20Ja02BJ
NAUGHTON, Pat.		40	M	Farmer	20Ja02BJ
Honor	(W)	38	F	Unknown	20Ja02BJ
Mary	(D)	14	F	Unknown	20Ja02BJ
Mihl.	(S)	12	M	None	20Ja02BJ
James	(S)	10	M	None	20Ja02BJ
Ann	(D)	08	F	Child	20Ja02BJ
Wm.	(S)	05	M	Child	20Ja02BJ
MELEAR, Michl.		20	M	Mechanic	20Ja02BJ
HANN, Geo.		20	M	Mechanic	20Ja02BJ
MOHER, John		20	M	Mechanic	20Ja02BJ

NAMES OF PASSENGERS		AGE	SEX	OCCUPATIONS	DATE PORT SHIP
BAND, John		30	M	Mechanic	20Ja02BJ
Bridget	(W)	28	F	Unknown	20Ja02BJ
Myles	(S)	08	M	Child	20Ja02BJ
Patk.	(S)	06	M	Child	20Ja02BJ
Thos.	(S)	05	M	Child	20Ja02BJ
Owen	(S)	04	M	Child	20Ja02BJ
Essey	(D)	.00	F	Infant	20Ja02BJ
Anne	(D)	.00	F	Infant	20Ja02BJ
Michl.		28	M	Farmer	20Ja02BJ
John		26	M	Farmer	20Ja02BJ
James		24	M	Farmer	20Ja02BJ
Esther		24	F	Unknown	20Ja02BJ
Jeremiah		20	M	Farmer	20Ja02BJ
Margt.		18	F	Unknown	20Ja02BJ
Sarah		17	F	Unknown	20Ja02BJ
Anne		14	F	Unknown	20Ja02BJ
Patk.		09	M	Child	20Ja02BJ
BROWN, Andy		20	M	Farmer	20Ja02BJ
DACY, John		20	M	Farmer	20Ja02BJ
FOGERTY, Cathl.		18	F	Unknown	20Ja02BJ
BYRNE, Thos.		21	M	Farmer	20Ja02BJ
KELLEY, John		20	M	Farmer	20Ja02BJ
BROCK, James		20	M	Farmer	20Ja02BJ
BRADY, Ellen		18	F	Unknown	20Ja02BJ
RAMKE, Pat.		20	M	Farmer	20Ja02BJ
MEHAN, Pat.		20	M	Farmer	20Ja02BJ
HADEN, Arthur		20	M	Farmer	20Ja02BJ
GORDON, Owen		20	M	Farmer	20Ja02BJ
CRIP, Thos.		28	M	Farmer	20Ja02BJ
U	(W)	26	F	Unknown	20Ja02BJ
MEHAN, Peter		24	M	Farmer	20Ja02BJ
HARDY, Danl.		27	M	Farmer	20Ja02BJ
Anne	(W)	25	F	Unknown	20Ja02BJ
Robt.	(S)	02	M	Child	20Ja02BJ
WILLSON, Wm.		40	M	Farmer	20Ja02BJ
Julia	(W)	38	F	Unknown	20Ja02BJ
Decen	(S)	16	M	Farmer	20Ja02BJ
Francis	(S)	12	M	None	20Ja02BJ
Wm.	(S)	10	M	None	20Ja02BJ
Rachel	(D)	07	F	Child	20Ja02BJ
WATERS, Hugh		26	M	Mechanic	20Ja02BJ
Honor		24	M	Mechanic	20Ja02BJ
BOLAN, John		20	M	Mechanic	20Ja02BJ
BARRON, Wm.		20	M	Mechanic	20Ja02BJ
WINBERLAND, Wm.		21	M	Mechanic	20Ja02BJ
TRACY, Pat.		28	M	Mechanic	20Ja02BJ
U	(W)	25	F	Unknown	20Ja02BJ
Mike	(S)	03	M	Child	20Ja02BJ
HANDS, U-Mrs.		28	F	Unknown	20Ja02BJ
U	(W)	25	F	Unknown	20Ja02BJ
U	(W)	25	F	Unknown	20Ja02BJ
PATHER, M.R.		29	M	Farmer	20Ja02BJ
HAZE, Moll.		26	F	Unknown	20Ja02BJ
PELGAN, James		24	M	Farmer	20Ja02BJ
TEENEY, Lard.		23	M	Farmer	20Ja02BJ
HEMSON, D.		23	M	Farmer	20Ja02BJ
IRWIN, M.		27	M	Farmer	20Ja02BJ
U	(W)	25	F	Wife	20Ja02BJ
Thos.	(S)	03	M	Child	20Ja02BJ
Jane	(D)	.00	F	Infant	20Ja02BJ
BURKE, Thos.		20	M	None	20Ja02BJ
LINNEY, John		20	M	None	20Ja02BJ
MCMARIN, John		22	M	None	20Ja02BJ
DAYHAN, Ann		18	F	Unknown	20Ja02BJ
GURDE, Philip		18	M	None	20Ja02BJ
MORTINGEN, U-Mrs.		28	F	Unknown	20Ja02BJ
ALLEN, U		27	M	None	20Ja02BJ
HERN, U		26	M	None	20Ja02BJ
Alex		24	M	None	20Ja02BJ

GARRICK 30 JANUARY 1847

From Liverpool

NAMES OF PASSENGERS		AGE	SEX	OCCUPATIONS	DATE PORT SHIP
AUSTIN, S.		22	M	Mechanic	30Ja02Aa
FIELDER, J.		20	M	Laborer	30Ja02Aa
GORDON, P.		25	M	Laborer	30Ja02Aa
WYLEY, J.		35	M	Laborer	30Ja02Aa
TAM, Ann		20	F	None	30Ja02Aa
WILEY, Cath.		20	F	None	30Ja02Aa
TROWER, Ann		15	F	None	30Ja02Aa
STILL, T.		18	M	Laborer	30Ja02Aa
GORMAN, E.		18	M	Laborer	30Ja02Aa
MCGILL, P.		21	M	Laborer	30Ja02Aa
STEVENS, J.		20	M	Mechanic	30Ja02Aa
SITINGAM, G.F.		30	M	Mechanic	30Ja02Aa
WRIGHT, R.		25	M	Farmer	30Ja02Aa
VOSS, J.		33	M	Farmer	30Ja02Aa
FARB, B.		24	M	Farmer	30Ja02Aa
PARKMEN, E.		25	M	Farmer	30Ja02Aa
Ann		21	F	None	30Ja02Aa
Edward		04	M	Child	30Ja02Aa
Wm.		02	M	Child	30Ja02Aa
Geog.		13	M	None	30Ja02Aa
STALY, P.		16	M	Farmer	30Ja02Aa
Mary		26	F	None	30Ja02Aa
HARANY, R.		12	M	Mechanic	30Ja02Aa
HALEY, P.		50	M	Laborer	30Ja02Aa
Bridget		12	F	None	30Ja02Aa
Thos.		26	M	Laborer	30Ja02Aa
Cath.		28	F	None	30Ja02Aa
Mary		26	F	None	30Ja02Aa
GRADY, J.		33	M	Laborer	30Ja02Aa
Mary		26	F	None	30Ja02Aa
Tedd		21	M	Laborer	30Ja02Aa
OBRIEN, A.		30	M	Laborer	30Ja02Aa
Peggy		20	F	None	30Ja02Aa
MCBRADY, M.		32	M	Laborer	30Ja02Aa
MCMOLY, Cath.		22	F	None	30Ja02Aa
TIENNY, Ann		54	F	None	30Ja02Aa
DANLY, P.		02	M	Child	30Ja02Aa
FARY, J.		55	M	Laborer	30Ja02Aa
MCMURPHY, M.		50	F	None	30Ja02Aa
MCGREGYAR, P.		20	M	Laborer	30Ja02Aa
MCQUADE, T.		30	M	Laborer	30Ja02Aa
Sarah		30	F	None	30Ja02Aa
Patk.		07	M	Child	30Ja02Aa
Bany		03	F	Child	30Ja02Aa
Mary		01	F	Child	30Ja02Aa
SLAVEN, J.		30	M	Laborer	30Ja02Aa
Anthony		30	M	Laborer	30Ja02Aa
Mary		07	F	Child	30Ja02Aa
Isabella		05	F	Child	30Ja02Aa
Patt		03	M	Child	30Ja02Aa
Binn		01	F	Child	30Ja02Aa
DALY, T.		20	M	Laborer	30Ja02Aa
T.		19	M	Laborer	30Ja02Aa
MCCLENNON, N.		22	M	Laborer	30Ja02Aa
STANTON, P.		29	M	Laborer	30Ja02Aa
SLAVEN, D.		16	M	Laborer	30Ja02Aa
MORAN, W.		36	M	Laborer	30Ja02Aa
STANTON, My.		18	F	None	30Ja02Aa
LYNCH, My.		17	F	None	30Ja02Aa
CALAN, My.		23	F	None	30Ja02Aa
PARKINSON, J.		40	M	Mechanic	30Ja02Aa
Judy		23	F	None	30Ja02Aa
HART, R.		35	M	Mechanic	30Ja02Aa
COYCE, J.		28	M	Mechanic	30Ja02Aa
MARION, J.		22	M	Mechanic	30Ja02Aa

NAMES OF PASSENGERS	AGE	SEX	OCCUPATIONS	DATE PORT SHIP
MARION, Hnna	22	F	None	30Ja02Aa
LAWSON, Ester	19	F	None	30Ja02Aa
MCGUIRE, Mary	22	F	None	30Ja02Aa
HYDE, Jane	22	F	None	30Ja02Aa
BULTER, J.	18	M	Laborer	30Ja02Aa
KELLY, P.	21	M	Laborer	30Ja02Aa
MULTWELL, J.	25	M	Laborer	30Ja02Aa
MCGUILLAM, Mgt.	25	F	None	30Ja02Aa
MULHOLD, Cath.	22	F	None	30Ja02Aa
HOLLOHAN, Mgt.	21	F	None	30Ja02Aa
KELLY, Mich	24	M	Laborer	30Ja02Aa
MUYEDER, O.	24	M	Laborer	30Ja02Aa
DONOHUE, P.	21	M	Laborer	30Ja02Aa
EVAN, J.	22	M	Laborer	30Ja02Aa
JOHNSON, T.	23	M	Laborer	30Ja02Aa
MCKENNA, P.	21	M	Laborer	30Ja02Aa
MARTIN, M.	30	M	Laborer	30Ja02Aa
Cath.	31	F	None	30Ja02Aa
Ann	19	F	None	30Ja02Aa
LUCKEY, J.	01	M	Child	30Ja02Aa
John	14	M	Farmer	30Ja02Aa
Margt.	19	F	None	30Ja02Aa
Ellen	12	F	None	30Ja02Aa
Elizth.	10	F	None	30Ja02Aa
Martha	08	F	Child	30Ja02Aa
Thos.	06	M	Child	30Ja02Aa
Peter	05	M	Child	30Ja02Aa
Sam.	01	M	Child	30Ja02Aa
FITZSIMMONS, F.	17	M	Mechanic	30Ja02Aa
RYLY, Biddy	19	F	None	30Ja02Aa
HIGGINS, Biddy	40	F	None	30Ja02Aa
MOORE, Mary	27	F	None	30Ja02Aa
MATHER, Elizth.	27	F	None	30Ja02Aa
NOLAN, L.	37	M	Laborer	30Ja02Aa
TREMBLE, W.	24	M	Laborer	30Ja02Aa
DIRE, P.	25	M	Laborer	30Ja02Aa
Cath.	25	F	None	30Ja02Aa
Ythos.	02	M	Child	30Ja02Aa
DEVLIN, J.	46	M	Laborer	30Ja02Aa
Ellen	47	F	None	30Ja02Aa
Sarah	22	F	None	30Ja02Aa
Frances	20	F	None	30Ja02Aa
Peter	19	M	None	30Ja02Aa
Mich.	13	M	None	30Ja02Aa
James	04	M	Child	30Ja02Aa
Mary	08	F	Child	30Ja02Aa
Ellen	04	F	Child	30Ja02Aa
CROFTER, M.	23	M	Laborer	30Ja02Aa
OBRIEN, J.	50	M	Laborer	30Ja02Aa
DUFFY, J.	20	M	Laborer	30Ja02Aa
CAMEGAR, J.	30	M	Laborer	30Ja02Aa
Mary	32	F	None	30Ja02Aa
Michl.	08	M	Child	30Ja02Aa
Cath.	02	F	Child	30Ja02Aa
DUNBY, A.	35	M	Laborer	30Ja02Aa
Margt.	28	F	None	30Ja02Aa
Thos.	09	M	Child	30Ja02Aa
P.	05	M	Child	30Ja02Aa
Anthony	03	M	Child	30Ja02Aa
Ann	02	F	Child	30Ja02Aa
John	30	M	Laborer	30Ja02Aa
Cath.	28	F	None	30Ja02Aa
John	06	M	Child	30Ja02Aa
Richard	04	M	Child	30Ja02Aa
FLERRY, J.	22	M	Laborer	30Ja02Aa
Patch	17	M	Laborer	30Ja02Aa
John	14	M	Laborer	30Ja02Aa
Cath.	19	F	None	30Ja02Aa
Ann	24	F	None	30Ja02Aa
CRANE, J.	24	M	Mechanic	30Ja02Aa
GRENAN, M.	44	M	Laborer	30Ja02Aa
FLANNAGAN, D.	48	M	Laborer	30Ja02Aa
WAYLAN, J.	24	M	Mechanic	30Ja02Aa
MATTHEW, J.	38	M	Laborer	30Ja02Aa
Peggy	32	F	None	30Ja02Aa
MATTHEW, Cath.	13	F	None	30Ja02Aa
Patch	10	M	None	30Ja02Aa
James	07	M	Child	30Ja02Aa
Owen	05	M	Child	30Ja02Aa
Teddy	04	M	Child	30Ja02Aa
Mary	03	F	Child	30Ja02Aa
JORDAN, T.	35	M	Farmer	30Ja02Aa
REGAN, J.	32	M	Farmer	30Ja02Aa
THOMPSON, M.	28	M	Farmer	30Ja02Aa
Thos.	22	M	Farmer	30Ja02Aa
MCPOLY, J.	35	M	Farmer	30Ja02Aa
Mary	23	F	None	30Ja02Aa
THOMSON, Hy	28	M	Laborer	30Ja02Aa
Biddy	01	F	Child	30Ja02Aa
GUILYAN, J.	09	M	Child	30Ja02Aa
DUMAS, D.	30	M	Laborer	30Ja02Aa
LIDDE, N.	23	M	Laborer	30Ja02Aa
DENEPHY, P.	20	M	Laborer	30Ja02Aa
Mary	10	F	None	30Ja02Aa
Pat	20	M	Laborer	30Ja02Aa
MCKEOWN, J.	30	M	Laborer	30Ja02Aa
DORSEY, P.	28	M	Laborer	30Ja02Aa
Biddy	28	F	None	30Ja02Aa
J.	05	M	Child	30Ja02Aa
Jas.	01	M	Child	30Ja02Aa
Biddy	05	F	Child	30Ja02Aa
WOFBITY, P.	19	M	Farmer	30Ja02Aa
LARR, N.	35	M	Farmer	30Ja02Aa
COOPER, J.	35	M	Farmer	30Ja02Aa
Cath.	35	F	None	30Ja02Aa
Daley	23	F	None	30Ja02Aa
LEECH, F.	40	M	Farmer	30Ja02Aa
Letitia	37	F	None	30Ja02Aa
DALEN, Biddy	23	F	None	30Ja02Aa
Peggy	24	F	None	30Ja02Aa
NOLAN, P.	30	M	Farmer	30Ja02Aa
Mgt.	30	F	None	30Ja02Aa
Mgt.	01	F	Child	30Ja02Aa
MCGREER, Bdgt.	18	F	None	30Ja02Aa
NARY, Mary	18	F	None	30Ja02Aa
LEGAN, P.	28	M	Laborer	30Ja02Aa
ONEIL, J.	20	M	Laborer	30Ja02Aa
BROWN, A.	27	M	Laborer	30Ja02Aa
MORAN, J.	22	M	Laborer	30Ja02Aa
GILLESPIE, P.	40	M	Laborer	30Ja02Aa
Bdgt.	40	F	None	30Ja02Aa
John	19	M	Laborer	30Ja02Aa
Patt	09	M	Child	30Ja02Aa
Michael	01	M	Child	30Ja02Aa
Ellen	02	F	Child	30Ja02Aa
LOFTUS, A.	20	M	Laborer	30Ja02Aa
LEERY, J.	30	M	Laborer	30Ja02Aa
BURK, M.	50	M	Laborer	30Ja02Aa
Mary	40	F	None	30Ja02Aa
Michael	08	M	Child	30Ja02Aa
Mary	16	F	None	30Ja02Aa
Sarah	04	F	Child	30Ja02Aa
PATTERSON, J.	35	M	Laborer	30Ja02Aa
Mary	36	F	None	30Ja02Aa
Chas.	07	M	Child	30Ja02Aa
Jane	08	F	Child	30Ja02Aa
Daniel	02	M	Child	30Ja02Aa
Mgt.	11	F	None	30Ja02Aa
MCCONNELL, Bdgt.	50	F	None	30Ja02Aa
W.	45	M	Laborer	30Ja02Aa
BURK, W.	27	M	Laborer	30Ja02Aa
MCMAHON, M.	30	M	Laborer	30Ja02Aa
Biddy	25	F	None	30Ja02Aa
Jane	04	F	Child	30Ja02Aa
Michael	02	M	Child	30Ja02Aa
Patt	04	M	Child	30Ja02Aa
MANN, P.	22	M	Laborer	30Ja02Aa
POTTER, J.	25	M	Mechanic	30Ja02Aa
SINUN, Biddy	30	F	None	30Ja02Aa
MORAN, Mary	20	F	None	30Ja02Aa

NAMES OF PASSENGERS	AGE	SEX	OCCUPATIONS	DATE PORT SHIP	NAMES OF PASSENGERS	AGE	SEX	OCCUPATIONS	DATE PORT SHIP
MORAN, Mary	23	F	None	30Ja02Aa	NOLAN, Mgt.	01	F	Child	30Ja02Aa
BURNS, J.	30	M	Mechanic	30Ja02Aa	HOPKINS, Mgt.	16	F	None	30Ja02Aa
MCGRERY, Bld.	25	F	None	30Ja02Aa	MISKELL, J.	25	M	Laborer	30Ja02Aa
GOIRRY, T.	25	M	Laborer	30Ja02Aa	Cath.	25	F	None	30Ja02Aa
MURPHY, P.	26	M	Laborer	30Ja02Aa	CANONTEN, M.	23	M	Laborer	30Ja02Aa
FITZSIMONS, Mary	20	F	None	30Ja02Aa	CANNON, P.	24	M	Laborer	30Ja02Aa
MURDEN, Ruth	40	F	None	30Ja02Aa	SCALLY, Mary	38	F	None	30Ja02Aa
Robt.	13	M	None	30Ja02Aa	Ann	16	F	None	30Ja02Aa
Wm.	11	M	None	30Ja02Aa	Biddy	14	F	None	30Ja02Aa
Ann	09	F	Child	30Ja02Aa	Mich	11	M	None	30Ja02Aa
James	05	M	Child	30Ja02Aa	Cath.	09	F	Child	30Ja02Aa
Greg	03	M	Child	30Ja02Aa	MEEY, J.	40	M	Laborer	30Ja02Aa
Dawn	01	F	Child	30Ja02Aa	Margt.	40	F	None	30Ja02Aa
DOYLE, J.	23	M	Laborer	30Ja02Aa	John	22	M	Farmer	30Ja02Aa
MORAN, J.	20	M	Laborer	30Ja02Aa	Cath.	20	F	None	30Ja02Aa
COOKE, T.	22	M	Laborer	30Ja02Aa	Ann	18	F	None	30Ja02Aa
HALY, J.	25	M	Laborer	30Ja02Aa	Patt	16	M	None	30Ja02Aa
NEELY, J.	27	M	Laborer	30Ja02Aa	Bdgt.	15	F	None	30Ja02Aa
KELLER, D.	23	M	Laborer	30Ja02Aa	James	11	M	None	30Ja02Aa
BRINE, Mary	18	F	None	30Ja02Aa	MCGLYNN, P.	23	M	Farmer	30Ja02Aa
MARTIN, J.	20	M	Laborer	30Ja02Aa	TACTER, W.	32	M	Laborer	30Ja02Aa
MCCARR, M.	30	M	Laborer	30Ja02Aa	MCGLYNN, Isb.	15	F	None	30Ja02Aa
Biddy	30	F	None	30Ja02Aa	Gllb.	19	M	None	30Ja02Aa
Barnett	05	M	Child	30Ja02Aa	Hugh	15	M	None	30Ja02Aa
Biddy	01	F	Child	30Ja02Aa	KELLY, P.	28	M	Laborer	30Ja02Aa
HENNETY, Mary	14	F	None	30Ja02Aa	Mary	25	F	None	30Ja02Aa
Peggy	12	F	None	30Ja02Aa	Thos.	02	M	Child	30Ja02Aa
MOORE, Judy	30	F	None	30Ja02Aa	John	01	M	Child	30Ja02Aa
Biddy	28	F	None	30Ja02Aa	DOLEN, J.	30	M	Laborer	30Ja02Aa
Thos.	07	M	Child	30Ja02Aa	Cath.	25	F	None	30Ja02Aa
Betty	06	F	Child	30Ja02Aa	Patk.	09	M	Child	30Ja02Aa
Barnett	03	M	Child	30Ja02Aa	Ann	06	F	Child	30Ja02Aa
OMOORE, U	30	M	Laborer	30Ja02Aa	Biddy	02	F	Child	30Ja02Aa
Pat	20	M	Laborer	30Ja02Aa	MURPHY, P.	35	M	Laborer	30Ja02Aa
John	18	M	Laborer	30Ja02Aa	GILBERT, D.	32	M	Laborer	30Ja02Aa
Mary	16	F	None	30Ja02Aa	Wm.	22	M	Laborer	30Ja02Aa
MCMULLEN, J.	40	M	Laborer	30Ja02Aa	Hester	28	F	None	30Ja02Aa
George	16	M	Laborer	30Ja02Aa	Roger	08	M	Child	30Ja02Aa
Mary	12	F	None	30Ja02Aa	Daniel	03	M	Child	30Ja02Aa
Ann	10	F	None	30Ja02Aa	SMITH, W.	28	M	Laborer	30Ja02Aa
WILSON, Fanny	23	F	None	30Ja02Aa	George	21	M	Laborer	30Ja02Aa
MCGOLAN, Mary	17	F	None	30Ja02Aa	CROFFON, R.	28	M	Laborer	30Ja02Aa
Cv., Sally	50	F	None	30Ja02Aa	Abram	26	M	Laborer	30Ja02Aa
Banee	42	M	Laborer	30Ja02Aa	Wm.	02	M	Child	30Ja02Aa
John	18	M	Laborer	30Ja02Aa	HOPKINS, T.	17	M	Laborer	30Ja02Aa
Barnett	16	M	Laborer	30Ja02Aa	HANSON, Cath.	16	F	None	30Ja02Aa
Mary-A.	13	F	None	30Ja02Aa	MARTIN, A.	40	M	Laborer	30Ja02Aa
Patt	11	M	None	30Ja02Aa	Cath.	60	F	None	30Ja02Aa
Hugh	09	M	Child	30Ja02Aa	Michl.	18	M	Laborer	30Ja02Aa
Hannah	07	F	Child	30Ja02Aa	John	09	M	Child	30Ja02Aa
James	05	M	Child	30Ja02Aa	P.	09	M	Child	30Ja02Aa
Brian	03	M	Child	30Ja02Aa	Mary	05	F	Child	30Ja02Aa
MCGOOLY, H.	19	M	Laborer	30Ja02Aa	Cath.	03	F	Child	30Ja02Aa
DICKON, J.	30	M	Laborer	30Ja02Aa	CAROLIN, Mary	30	F	None	30Ja02Aa
CONNER, P.	40	M	Laborer	30Ja02Aa	James	32	M	Laborer	30Ja02Aa
CALLIGHER, J.	25	M	Laborer	30Ja02Aa	HUGHS, J.	25	M	Laborer	30Ja02Aa
BROWN, M.	16	M	Laborer	30Ja02Aa	MARTIN, T.	30	M	Laborer	30Ja02Aa
BURK, C.	19	M	Laborer	30Ja02Aa	Hannah	22	F	None	30Ja02Aa
MCGLEE, E.	40	M	Laborer	30Ja02Aa	HUGHES, M.	27	M	Laborer	30Ja02Aa
DOHERTY, M.	32	M	Laborer	30Ja02Aa	GAUHKER, B.	32	M	Laborer	30Ja02Aa
ROACH, T.	24	M	Laborer	30Ja02Aa	Nelly	30	F	None	30Ja02Aa
Ann	03	F	Child	30Ja02Aa	HALY, Mary	01	F	Child	30Ja02Aa
John	01	M	Child	30Ja02Aa	COYAN, T.	22	M	Laborer	30Ja02Aa
RILEY, P.	23	M	Laborer	30Ja02Aa	MANN, Mgt.	06	F	Child	30Ja02Aa
BRADY, M.	22	M	Laborer	30Ja02Aa	DOBBS, Biddy	23	F	None	30Ja02Aa
CANNON, M.	19	M	Laborer	30Ja02Aa	KELLY, J.	01	M	Child	30Ja02Aa
NOBLE, Mgt.	20	F	None	30Ja02Aa	HUGHS, Biddy	17	F	None	30Ja02Aa
Sarah	18	F	None	30Ja02Aa	Michael	02	M	Child	30Ja02Aa
MCINTIRE, Mgt.	16	F	None	30Ja02Aa					
BRADY, Judy	20	F	None	30Ja02Aa					
DONOHUE, D.	25	M	Mechanic	30Ja02Aa					
Biddy	23	F	None	30Ja02Aa					
Peggy	24	F	None	30Ja02Aa					
NOLAN, P.	30	M	Mechanic	30Ja02Aa					
Mgt.	30	F	None	30Ja02Aa					

NAMES OF PASSENGERS	AGE	SEX	OCCUPATIONS	DATE PORT SHIP

SARDINIA 06 FEBRUARY 1847

From Liverpool

NAMES OF PASSENGERS	AGE	SEX	OCCUPATIONS	DATE PORT SHIP
CONNOR, Ann	40	F	Servant	06Fe02Gt
Bridget (D)	10	F	Servant	06Fe02Gt
Peter (S)	07	M	Child	06Fe02Gt
Nellie (D)	03	F	Child	06Fe02Gt
Anne (D)	.00	F	Infant	06Fe02Gt
KUNOCK, Edward	23	M	Laborer	06Fe02Gt
SHEEHAN, Patrick	14	M	Laborer	06Fe02Gt
LYONS, John	50	M	Laborer	06Fe02Gt
Mary	48	F	Laborer	06Fe02Gt
Mary	20	F	Laborer	06Fe02Gt
Catherine	18	F	Laborer	06Fe02Gt
Andrew	08	M	Child	06Fe02Gt
Biddy	09	F	Child	06Fe02Gt
John	14	M	Laborer	06Fe02Gt
BROWN, William	29	M	Laborer	06Fe02Gt
Mary	29	F	Laborer	06Fe02Gt
Geolbon	10	M	Laborer	06Fe02Gt
Benjamin	08	M	Child	06Fe02Gt
Tom	06	M	Child	06Fe02Gt
DAVIS, A.	24	M	Laborer	06Fe02Gt
LUNDY, Michael	25	M	Laborer	06Fe02Gt
Margaret	19	F	Laborer	06Fe02Gt
John	.00	M	Infant	06Fe02Gt
MCNICHOLS, Thomas	33	M	Laborer	06Fe02Gt
Margaret	28	F	Laborer	06Fe02Gt
John	.00	M	Infant	06Fe02Gt
Died-At-Sea				
ODRAGHETY, Charles	18	M	Laborer	06Fe02Gt
FLYNN, John	45	M	Laborer	06Fe02Gt
Eliza	47	F	Laborer	06Fe02Gt
Eliza	13	F	Laborer	06Fe02Gt
Mary-Ann	12	F	Laborer	06Fe02Gt
John	10	M	Laborer	06Fe02Gt
Isabella	08	F	Child	06Fe02Gt
David	06	M	Child	06Fe02Gt
George	04	M	Child	06Fe02Gt
MARMAN, Henry	28	M	Laborer	06Fe02Gt
TRAGET, Charles	27	M	Laborer	06Fe02Gt
BIRMINGHAM, Hartley	25	M	Laborer	06Fe02Gt
PLUNKETT, Margt.	18	F	Laborer	06Fe02Gt
Julia	16	F	Laborer	06Fe02Gt
BRADY, Mary	25	F	Laborer	06Fe02Gt
MALLOY, Terrence	25	M	Laborer	06Fe02Gt
Cath.	28	F	Laborer	06Fe02Gt
MCBRIE, Maris	20	M	Laborer	06Fe02Gt
MORAN, Patt	18	M	Laborer	06Fe02Gt
KALAHER, Pat	18	M	Laborer	06Fe02Gt
MCGOAN, Mary	36	F	Laborer	06Fe02Gt
Frances	08	F	Child	06Fe02Gt
MALONEY, Ellen	18	F	Laborer	06Fe02Gt
MOON, Biddy	18	F	Laborer	06Fe02Gt
Catherine	16	F	Laborer	06Fe02Gt
GALLAN, Ann	20	F	Laborer	06Fe02Gt
COLLINS, Mary	19	F	Laborer	06Fe02Gt
KELLY, Mary	28	F	Laborer	06Fe02Gt
CONNELL, Timothy	33	M	Laborer	06Fe02Gt
James	03	M	Child	06Fe02Gt
Bridget	.00	F	Infant	06Fe02Gt
Died-At-Sea				
HARGON, Juda	20	F	Laborer	06Fe02Gt
MURPHY, Ann	20	F	Laborer	06Fe02Gt
BOYLE, John	20	M	Laborer	06Fe02Gt
MCBRIDE, John	20	M	Laborer	06Fe02Gt
SWENY, John	20	M	Laborer	06Fe02Gt
KELLY, Patt	24	F	Laborer	06Fe02Gt
MCCARTY, Charles	21	M	Laborer	06Fe02Gt
John	22	M	Laborer	06Fe02Gt
Mary	18	F	Laborer	06Fe02Gt
Ellen	15	F	Laborer	06Fe02Gt
Davis	15	M	Laborer	06Fe02Gt
DARGIN, John	47	M	Laborer	06Fe02Gt
Cath.	50	F	Laborer	06Fe02Gt
Thomas	20	M	Laborer	06Fe02Gt
Patt	20	M	Laborer	06Fe02Gt
Bridget	12	F	Laborer	06Fe02Gt
John	06	M	Child	06Fe02Gt
MCGUIRE, Pat	22	M	Laborer	06Fe02Gt
James	20	M	Laborer	06Fe02Gt
DOLAN, Philip	30	M	Laborer	06Fe02Gt
MORAN, Patrick	24	M	Laborer	06Fe02Gt
MCNALLY, Thomas	22	M	Laborer	06Fe02Gt
OWENS, John	24	M	Laborer	06Fe02Gt
GIBSON, Lawrence	20	M	Laborer	06Fe02Gt
COLLINS, Catharine	23	F	Laborer	06Fe02Gt
TANNER, Ann	21	F	Laborer	06Fe02Gt
DOWLING, Robert	32	M	Laborer	06Fe02Gt
Mary	30	F	Laborer	06Fe02Gt
MCKENNAN, Michael	21	M	Laborer	06Fe02Gt
KELLY, Moriah	21	F	Laborer	06Fe02Gt
COLLEGAN, John	21	M	Laborer	06Fe02Gt
Jane	50	F	Laborer	06Fe02Gt
KELLY, Winifred	20	F	Laborer	06Fe02Gt
Bridget	20	F	Laborer	06Fe02Gt
COCHRIN, U-Mrs.	34	F	Laborer	06Fe02Gt
John	13	M	Laborer	06Fe02Gt
WAILINS, William	37	M	Laborer	06Fe02Gt
Mary	33	F	Laborer	06Fe02Gt
Eliza	11	F	Laborer	06Fe02Gt
Clara	06	F	Child	06Fe02Gt
Elizabeth	04	F	Child	06Fe02Gt
Thomas	12	M	Laborer	06Fe02Gt
Hubert	02	M	Child	06Fe02Gt
DONLEY, Bridget	20	F	Laborer	06Fe02Gt
Donley	00	2	F	06Fe02Gt
Catharine	35	2	F	06Fe02Gt
Bridget	06	F	Child	06Fe02Gt
Patrick	12	M	Laborer	06Fe02Gt
Thomas	08	M	Child	06Fe02Gt
Hugh	04	M	Child	06Fe02Gt
DIGNAN, John	19	M	Laborer	06Fe02Gt
MURPHEY, Mary	40	F	Laborer	06Fe02Gt
Margaret	09	F	Child	06Fe02Gt
William	11	M	Laborer	06Fe02Gt
Thomas	05	M	Child	06Fe02Gt
Patrick	04	M	Child	06Fe02Gt
MARTIN, John	22	M	Laborer	06Fe02Gt
BOYLE, Mary	19	F	Laborer	06Fe02Gt
SOHSTON, P.C.	30	U	Unknown	06Fe02Gt
JACKSON, Wm.	44	M	Unknown	06Fe02Gt
BROWN, J.	22	M	Unknown	06Fe02Gt
Eliza	23	F	Unknown	06Fe02Gt

HYNDERFORD 08 FEBRUARY 1847

From Glasgow

NAMES OF PASSENGERS	AGE	SEX	OCCUPATIONS	DATE PORT SHIP
PATTERSON, John	27	M	Farmer	08Fe04Kl

NAMES OF PASSENGERS		AGE	SEX	OCCUPATIONS	DATE PORT SHIP

NICHOLAS-BIDDLE 09 FEBRUARY 1847

From Liverpool

NAMES OF PASSENGERS		AGE	SEX	OCCUPATIONS	DATE PORT SHIP
GALLAGHER, John		20	M	Laborer	09Fe02Iq
MULLERNY, Peter		20	M	Laborer	09Fe02Iq
Anthy.		23	M	Laborer	09Fe02Iq
Michl.		14	M	Laborer	09Fe02Iq
Mary		14	F	Spinster	09Fe02Iq
Mary		20	F	Spinster	09Fe02Iq
James		.00	M	Infant	09Fe02Iq
GRULINNER, Walter		20	M	Mechanic	09Fe02Iq
RILEY, Hugh		18	M	Farmer	09Fe02Iq
WALSH, Patk.		26	M	Farmer	09Fe02Iq
Mary		22	F	Farmer	09Fe02Iq
Bridget		18	F	Farmer	09Fe02Iq
Peggy		09	F	Child	09Fe02Iq
LOFTUS, Biddy		18	F	Unknown	09Fe02Iq
MAHONEY, Mary		25	F	Servant	09Fe02Iq
Ellen		21	F	Servant	09Fe02Iq
John		03	M	Child	09Fe02Iq
Wm.		02	M	Child	09Fe02Iq
BRADLEY, Patt.		30	M	Servant	09Fe02Iq
MCALLEN, James		30	M	Servant	09Fe02Iq
MCCURRY, Margt.		25	F	Servant	09Fe02Iq
LEONARD, John		60	M	Farmer	09Fe02Iq
John		30	M	Mechanic	09Fe02Iq
Henry		28	M	Mechanic	09Fe02Iq
Felix		23	M	Mechanic	09Fe02Iq
Cathn.		26	F	Servant	09Fe02Iq
Ann		22	F	Servant	09Fe02Iq
Susan		20	F	Servant	09Fe02Iq
Mary		16	F	Servant	09Fe02Iq
Phillip		17	M	Servant	09Fe02Iq
CLELLAND, Wm.		40	M	Laborer	09Fe02Iq
James	(S)	20	M	Laborer	09Fe02Iq
Wm.	(S)	18	M	Laborer	09Fe02Iq
Mary	(D)	16	F	Laborer	09Fe02Iq
MAGUIRE, Margret		20	F	Servant	09Fe02Iq
MCMABEN, Bessey		13	F	Servant	09Fe02Iq
MCHUGH, Owen		21	M	Servant	09Fe02Iq
SWEENEY, John		28	M	Servant	09Fe02Iq
MCPORREY, James		21	M	Laborer	09Fe02Iq
KEYS, George		20	M	Laborer	09Fe02Iq
James		20	M	Laborer	09Fe02Iq
LYNCH, Margt.		18	F	Servant	09Fe02Iq

GLENMORE 09 FEBRUARY 1847

From Belfast

NAMES OF PASSENGERS		AGE	SEX	OCCUPATIONS	DATE PORT SHIP
BROWN, Rosanna		26	F	Spinster	09Fe07Km
BOYD, Jane		18	F	Spinster	09Fe07Km
SOUTAR, Jane		60	F	Mother	09Fe07Km
Margaret	(D)	19	F	Unknown	09Fe07Km
Jane	(D)	17	F	Unknown	09Fe07Km
Wm.	(S)	15	M	Unknown	09Fe07Km
David	(S)	14	M	Unknown	09Fe07Km
CRAWFORD, John		35	M	Weaver	09Fe07Km
Margaret		33	F	Wife	09Fe07Km
David	(S)	08	M	Child	09Fe07Km
John	(S)	04	M	Child	09Fe07Km
MONAGHAN, Mary		26	F	Spinster	09Fe07Km

NAMES OF PASSENGERS		AGE	SEX	OCCUPATIONS	DATE PORT SHIP
HANNA, Archibald		28	M	Farmer	09Fe07Km
Mary		25	F	Wife	09Fe07Km
MCCAFFERY, Catherine		60	F	WI	09Fe07Km
ROONEY, Ann		25	F	Spinster	09Fe07Km
MOORE, Mary		30	F	Spinster	09Fe07Km
STEWART, Samuel		45	M	Farmer	09Fe07Km
Martha		43	F	Wife	09Fe07Km
James	(S)	20	M	Unknown	09Fe07Km
Mary	(D)	18	F	Unknown	09Fe07Km
John	(S)	16	M	Unknown	09Fe07Km
Robert	(S)	14	M	Unknown	09Fe07Km
Sally	(D)	12	F	Unknown	09Fe07Km
Eliza	(D)	10	F	Child	09Fe07Km
Duncan	(S)	08	M	Child	09Fe07Km
Margaret	(D)	06	F	Child	09Fe07Km
Samuel	(S)	04	M	Child	09Fe07Km
JAMISON, Joseph		46	M	Farmer	09Fe07Km
Catherine		44	F	Wife	09Fe07Km
Eliza	(D)	15	F	Unknown	09Fe07Km
Margaret	(D)	11	F	Child	09Fe07Km
Mary	(D)	10	F	Child	09Fe07Km
Alexander	(S)	09	M	Child	09Fe07Km
Catherine	(D)	07	F	Child	09Fe07Km
Lucinda	(D)	05	F	Child	09Fe07Km
Joseph	(S)	02	M	Child	09Fe07Km
STEWART, Henry		35	M	Weaver	09Fe07Km
Catherine		32	F	Wife	09Fe07Km
Ann	(D)	07	F	Child	09Fe07Km
Dennis	(S)	05	M	Child	09Fe07Km
James	(S)	03	M	Child	09Fe07Km
Mary	(D)	01	F	Child	09Fe07Km
WILSON, Adam		35	M	Weaver	09Fe07Km
HOUSTON, Ann		37	F	WI	09Fe07Km
Mary-Ann	(D)	11	F	Child	09Fe07Km
Matilda	(D)	10	F	Child	09Fe07Km
Thomas	(S)	08	M	Child	09Fe07Km
GERAGHTY, Catherine		24	F	Spinster	09Fe07Km
MCCUE, Bernard		20	M	Weaver	09Fe07Km
Bell		16	F	Wife	09Fe07Km
RODGERS, James		40	M	Farmer	09Fe07Km
Mary		40	F	Wife	09Fe07Km
John	(S)	17	M	Unknown	09Fe07Km
Phillp	(S)	13	M	Unknown	09Fe07Km
James	(S)	11	M	Child	09Fe07Km
Catherine	(D)	10	F	Child	09Fe07Km
Bernard	(S)	09	M	Child	09Fe07Km
William	(S)	07	M	Child	09Fe07Km
Christy	(S)	05	M	Child	09Fe07Km
SLEAVIN, John		25	M	Laborer	09Fe07Km
GOODWIN, Catherine		24	F	Unknown	09Fe07Km
MCLAUGHLIN, Elisa		45	F	WI	09Fe07Km
Catherine	(D)	11	F	Child	09Fe07Km
Sally	(D)	10	F	Child	09Fe07Km
Jane	(D)	08	F	Child	09Fe07Km
Ann	(D)	06	F	Child	09Fe07Km
John	(S)	04	M	Child	09Fe07Km
GOODWIN, Biddy		11	F	Child	09Fe07Km
Rose		09	F	Child	09Fe07Km
Michael		07	M	Child	09Fe07Km
Philip		19	M	Weaver	09Fe07Km
ARMSTRONG, Ann		40	F	WI	09Fe07Km
Hugh	(S)	15	M	Unknown	09Fe07Km
Edward	(S)	11	M	Child	09Fe07Km
John	(S)	03	M	Child	09Fe07Km
MCCAFFRY, Catherine		22	F	Spinster	09Fe07Km
PRENTICE, Ann		25	F	Spinster	09Fe07Km
MOYNAGH, John		18	M	Laborer	09Fe07Km
LITTLE, Jane		18	F	Spinster	09Fe07Km
FOSTER, Jane		40	F	WI	09Fe07Km
Maria	(D)	23	F	Unknown	09Fe07Km
Jane	(D)	22	F	Unknown	09Fe07Km
Lucinda	(D)	17	F	Unknown	09Fe07Km
Mary	(D)	11	F	Child	09Fe07Km
MCELLROY, Patrick		25	M	Farmer	09Fe07Km
JOHNSTON, Catherine		21	F	Spinster	09Fe07Km

NAMES OF PASSENGERS		AGE	SEX	OCCUPATIONS	DATE PORT SHIP	NAMES OF PASSENGERS		AGE	SEX	OCCUPATIONS	DATE PORT SHIP
FORSYTHE, John		18	M	Weaver	09Fe07Km	MCMURRAY, Wm.		23	M	Weaver	09Fe07Km
GORDON, William		33	M	Farmer	09Fe07Km	BIRT, Bridget		30	F	Spinster	09Fe07Km
Jane		26	F	Wife	09Fe07Km	CUSKER, Michael		21	M	Farmer	09Fe07Km
Sarah	(D)	07	F	Child	09Fe07Km	John		19	M	Farmer	09Fe07Km
James	(S)	05	M	Child	09Fe07Km	WILSON, Mary		30	F	Spinster	09Fe07Km
David	(S)	03	M	Child	09Fe07Km	CROTHERS, James		30	M	Smith	09Fe07Km
William	(S)	01	M	Child	09Fe07Km	DOHERTY, Rosy		32	F	Spinster	09Fe07Km
JOHNSTON, Alexander		19	M	Laborer	09Fe07Km	CAMPBELL, Sarah		28	F	Spinster	09Fe07Km
HENDERSON, Francis		24	M	Weaver	09Fe07Km	LENOX, Francis		24	M	Shoemaker	09Fe07Km
FITZSIMMONS, John		60	M	Farmer	09Fe07Km	CONNOUR, Michael		25	M	Weaver	09Fe07Km
Jane		60	F	Wife	09Fe07Km	MCWILLIAMS, Andrew		22	M	Weaver	09Fe07Km
John	(S)	25	M	Unknown	09Fe07Km	SERVIA, John		34	M	Writer	09Fe07Km
Catherine	(D)	23	F	Unknown	09Fe07Km	MCKINNEY, Alexander		26	M	Weaver	09Fe07Km
Alice	(D)	21	F	Unknown	09Fe07Km	Matty		21	F	Wife	09Fe07Km
Margaret	(D)	19	F	Unknown	09Fe07Km	Michael	(S)	03	M	Child	09Fe07Km
Ann	(D)	19	F	Unknown	09Fe07Km	Chas.	(S)	01	M	Child	09Fe07Km
Patrick	(S)	17	M	Unknown	09Fe07Km	AGNEW, James		21	M	Clerk	09Fe07Km
John	(S)	01	M	Child	09Fe07Km	COMEVEY, Michael		28	M	Car Man	09Fe07Km
John	(S)	15	M	Unknown	09Fe07Km	OWEN, Mary		16	F	Unknown	09Fe07Km
INGRAM, Eliza		25	F	Spinster	09Fe07Km						
ORR, Wm.		25	M	Weaver	09Fe07Km						
DUNCAN, Grace		21	F	Spinster	09Fe07Km						
CROTHUS, Elizabeth		19	F	Spinster	09Fe07Km						
SLOANE, Robert		25	M	Unknown	09Fe07Km	**SARAH-SANDS 11 FEBRUARY 1847**					
Mary		25	F	Wife	09Fe07Km						
JENKINSON, Robert		25	M	Weaver	09Fe07Km	From Liverpool					
MITCIFF, Thomas		11	M	Child	09Fe07Km						
Anthony		09	M	Child	09Fe07Km						
HAMILTON, James		45	M	Farmer	09Fe07Km						
Lucy	(D)	15	F	Unknown	09Fe07Km	SCHVONMAKER, Hans		35	M	Peddler	11Fe02Kp
LYLE, David		25	M	Weaver	09Fe07Km	IRVIN, James		25	M	Farmer	11Fe02Kp
MILLAR, David		32	M	Farmer	09Fe07Km	ALLIGAN, John		50	M	Laborer	11Fe02Kp
Rose		30	F	Wife	09Fe07Km	ATKINS, George		35	M	Farmer	11Fe02Kp
Ann	(D)	10	F	Child	09Fe07Km	TAYLOR, Thomas		40	M	Farmer	11Fe02Kp
Mary-Jane	(D)	04	F	Child	09Fe07Km	Jane		30	F	Unknown	11Fe02Kp
Robert	(S)	01	M	Child	09Fe07Km	Susan		25	F	Unknown	11Fe02Kp
DOBSON, Henry		14	M	Weaver	09Fe07Km	PERRIE, J.A.		24	M	Merchant	11Fe02Kp
HOLMES, Jane		19	F	Spinster	09Fe07Km	GRAY, J.		22	M	Merchant	11Fe02Kp
RULE, Thomas		25	M	Weaver	09Fe07Km	CULLODERR, J.		30	M	Merchant	11Fe02Kp
Isabella		20	F	Wife	09Fe07Km	GELLILARR, H.A.		24	M	Merchant	11Fe02Kp
Wm.John	(S)	.00	M	Infant	09Fe07Km	MACLORNE, J.P.		24	M	Merchant	11Fe02Kp
WILSON, Alexander		22	M	Smith	09Fe07Km	MACTREVIN, A.H.		23	M	Gentleman	11Fe02Kp
Mary-Ann		20	F	Wife	09Fe07Km	PEABODY, T.		25	M	Merchant	11Fe02Kp
CONNOR, John		27	M	Weaver	09Fe07Km	LINASAY, J.		25	M	Merchant	11Fe02Kp
Margaret		25	F	Wife	09Fe07Km						
MCGUINIS, Catherine		21	F	Spinster	09Fe07Km						
DURCELL, Netty		20	F	Spinster	09Fe07Km						
BRADLEY, Biddy		18	F	Spinster	09Fe07Km						
HENDERSON, Henry		19	M	Weaver	09Fe07Km						
Edward		21	M	Weaver	09Fe07Km	**ELIZA 15 FEBRUARY 1847**					
MCCANN, John		40	M	Laborer	09Fe07Km						
Betty		36	F	Wife	09Fe07Km	From Belize					
Mary	(D)	09	F	Child	09Fe07Km						
Elizabeth	(D)	05	F	Child	09Fe07Km						
John	(S)	04	M	Child	09Fe07Km						
Felix	(S)	03	M	Child	09Fe07Km	TEVY, Joseph		50	M	Merchant	15Fe50Kt
Catherine	(D)	01	F	Child	09Fe07Km						
PRITCHARD, Thomas		40	M	Farmer	09Fe07Km						
ADAMSON, James		40	M	Farmer	09Fe07Km						
Agnes		35	F	Wife	09Fe07Km						
Henry	(S)	11	M	Child	09Fe07Km	**WATERLOO 19 FEBRUARY 1847**					
William	(S)	10	M	Child	09Fe07Km						
Jane	(D)	06	F	Child	09Fe07Km	From Liverpool					
John	(S)	02	M	Child	09Fe07Km						
CHATWORTHY, Agnes		40	F	Mother	09Fe07Km						
Frederick	(S)	07	M	Child	09Fe07Km						
COUTLER, John		25	M	Weaver	09Fe07Km						
Agnes		22	F	Wife	09Fe07Km	MONAGHAN, Phillip		50	M	Laborer	19Fe02As
BLACK, Margaret		19	F	Spinster	09Fe07Km	U		49	F	Wife	19Fe02As
BYRNE, Margaret		40	F	Wi	09Fe07Km	Terence	(S)	18	M	Unknown	19Fe02As
Benjamin	(S)	16	M	Unknown	09Fe07Km	Nancy	(D)	17	F	Unknown	19Fe02As
Margaretta	(D)	11	F	Child	09Fe07Km	Mary	(D)	15	F	Unknown	19Fe02As
Jurnessa	(D)	09	F	Child	09Fe07Km	Bridget	(D)	14	F	Unknown	19Fe02As
Edward	(S)	07	M	Child	09Fe07Km	Catharine	(D)	13	F	Unknown	19Fe02As
Susan	(D)	04	F	Child	09Fe07Km						

NAMES OF PASSENGERS		AGE	SEX	OCCUPATIONS	DATE PORT SHIP
MONAGHAN, Patt	(S)	11	M	Child	19Fe02As
Rose	(D)	09	F	Child	19Fe02As
Michael	(S)	08	M	Child	19Fe02As
SMITH, Bart		24	M	Laborer	19Fe02As
COYLE, Patt		21	M	Laborer	19Fe02As
SMITH, Mary		16	F	Servant	19Fe02As
COSGROVE, Jno.		20	M	Hrsm	19Fe02As
SMITH, Jas.		18	M	Laborer	19Fe02As
HARRIS, F.		22	M	Jeweller	19Fe02As
DEVLIN, Jno.		28	M	Rope Maker	19Fe02As
Mary		28	F	Unknown	19Fe02As
ONEILL, Ann		60	F	Unknown	19Fe02As
Mary	(D)	26	F	Unknown	19Fe02As
HOWELL, Isaiah		23	M	Weaver	19Fe02As
DEVLIN, Mary-Ann		06	F	Child	19Fe02As
Bartholomew		05	M	Child	19Fe02As
Margaret		03	F	Child	19Fe02As
Betty		.00	F	Infant	19Fe02As
MURRAY, Thomas		26	M	Shoemaker	19Fe02As
MCCORMICK, Roger		26	M	Shoemaker	19Fe02As
U		26	F	Wife	19Fe02As
HENRY, Margt.		18	F	Unknown	19Fe02As
MCGUIRE, Andrew		30	M	Laborer	19Fe02As
SMITH, Catharine		24	F	Servant	19Fe02As
Alice		18	F	Servant	19Fe02As
Peter		26	M	Servant	19Fe02As
KING, James		24	M	Gdnr	19Fe02As
CALLAHAN, Nichl.		20	M	Carpenter	19Fe02As
MURROW, Jas.		22	M	Laborer	19Fe02As
Frank		21	M	Laborer	19Fe02As
MCLANE, Jno.		20	M	Laborer	19Fe02As
EGAN, Thos.		18	M	Laborer	19Fe02As
FLAHERTY, Bridget		20	F	Servant	19Fe02As
MCDONNELL, Biddy		20	F	Servant	19Fe02As
STEANSON, Pat		25	M	Laborer	19Fe02As
Bar.		23	M	Laborer	19Fe02As
CONROY, Jas.		22	M	Laborer	19Fe02As
FLANNIGAN, Margaret		20	F	Unknown	19Fe02As
Mary		16	F	Unknown	19Fe02As
CANE, Eliza		30	F	Unknown	19Fe02As
Nancy		19	F	Unknown	19Fe02As
John		10	M	Child	19Fe02As
William		06	M	Child	19Fe02As
Maria		04	F	Child	19Fe02As
Catharine		.00	F	Infant	19Fe02As
MORRELAN, Garrett		40	M	Laborer	19Fe02As
Margaret		35	F	Wife	19Fe02As
Julia	(D)	05	F	Child	19Fe02As
James	(S)	03	M	Child	19Fe02As
U		.00	M	Infant	19Fe02As
BYRNE, James		15	M	Laborer	19Fe02As
STANLEY, U-Mrs.		24	F	Mother	19Fe02As
William	(S)	.00	M	Infant	19Fe02As
MCGOVERAN, Philip		24	M	Cooper	19Fe02As
CUFF, John		21	M	Laborer	19Fe02As
CULLEN, Jas.		21	M	Laborer	19Fe02As
DOCKEY, Pat		33	M	Laborer	19Fe02As
FARLEY, Charles		41	M	Laborer	19Fe02As
Biddy		38	F	Wife	19Fe02As
Nancy	(D)	10	F	Child	19Fe02As
Mary	(D)	08	F	Child	19Fe02As
Catharine	(D)	06	F	Child	19Fe02As
Thos.	(S)	04	M	Child	19Fe02As
Kitty	(D)	.00	F	Infant	19Fe02As
MULLIN, John		56	M	Laborer	19Fe02As
STINSON, Michael		40	M	Laborer	19Fe02As
Mary		40	F	Wife	19Fe02As
Barthw.	(S)	21	M	Laborer	19Fe02As
Michael	(S)	17	M	Laborer	19Fe02As
James	(S)	14	M	Laborer	19Fe02As
Catharine	(D)	12	F	Unknown	19Fe02As
Alice	(D)	09	F	Child	19Fe02As
Mary	(D)	04	F	Child	19Fe02As
HARRINGTON, Thomas		42	M	Laborer	19Fe02As
FAGAN, Nicholas		30	M	Laborer	19Fe02As

NAMES OF PASSENGERS		AGE	SEX	OCCUPATIONS	DATE PORT SHIP
FORD, John		21	M	Laborer	19Fe02As
Michael		28	M	Laborer	19Fe02As
Bernard		26	M	Laborer	19Fe02As
Pat		11	M	Child	19Fe02As
HARRINGTON, Martha		11	F	Child	19Fe02As
RICHARDSON, James		28	M	Laborer	19Fe02As
GORMAN, James		21	M	Laborer	19Fe02As
CANE, John		45	M	Laborer	19Fe02As
STEANSON, Burt		23	M	Laborer	19Fe02As
U, U		.00	U	Infant	19Fe02As
	Died-At-Sea				
U		.00	U	Infant	19Fe02As
	Born-At-Sea		Died-At-Sea		

MONTEZUMA 20 FEBRUARY 1847

From Liverpool

NAMES OF PASSENGERS		AGE	SEX	OCCUPATIONS	DATE PORT SHIP
ROGERS, U		23	M	Gentleman	20Fe02Ao
U	(W)	37	F	Lady	20Fe02Ao
DEADMAN, U		27	M	Gentleman	20Fe02Ao
U	(W)	25	F	Lady	20Fe02Ao
GODFREY, U		38	M	Gentleman	20Fe02Ao
U	(W)	28	F	Lady	20Fe02Ao
DEARDON, U		28	M	Merchant	20Fe02Ao
SHAW, U		21	M	Merchant	20Fe02Ao
MORLEY, U		41	M	Merchant	20Fe02Ao
RAY, U		38	M	Merchant	20Fe02Ao
U		31	M	Merchant	20Fe02Ao
RANKIN, U		25	M	Distiller	20Fe02Ao
HAY, U		30	M	Unknown	20Fe02Ao
GARDNER, U		30	M	Htlkpr	20Fe02Ao
U	(W)	29	F	Htlkpr	20Fe02Ao
MCGOVERN, James		44	M	Laborer	20Fe02Ao
Catharine		13	F	Unknown	20Fe02Ao
WALSH, Michael		26	M	Laborer	20Fe02Ao
FAY, Bridget		20	F	Servant	20Fe02Ao
LYNCH, Patrick		46	M	Laborer	20Fe02Ao
Mary	(W)	46	F	Unknown	20Fe02Ao
James	(S)	10	M	Child	20Fe02Ao
Michael	(S)	04	M	Child	20Fe02Ao
Charles	(S)	02	M	Child	20Fe02Ao
FITZPATRICK, Owen		30	M	Laborer	20Fe02Ao
U	(W)	29	F	Unknown	20Fe02Ao
Elizabeth	(D)	05	F	Child	20Fe02Ao
Patt	(S)	03	M	Child	20Fe02Ao
	Died-At-Sea				
MCCAFFREY, Patt		28	M	Laborer	20Fe02Ao
MCGUIRE, Mary		32	F	Laborer	20Fe02Ao
Dennis	(S)	10	M	Child	20Fe02Ao
Ann	(D)	08	F	Child	20Fe02Ao
	Died-At-Sea				
Patt	(S)	06	M	Child	20Fe02Ao
James	(S)	04	M	Child	20Fe02Ao
SMITH, U-Mrs.		60	F	Milliner	20Fe02Ao
ROARTLE, Mary		20	F	Milliner	20Fe02Ao
RYAN, U		34	M	Innkeeper	20Fe02Ao
Thomas	(S)	12	M	Unknown	20Fe02Ao
Catherine	(D)	08	F	Child	20Fe02Ao
Mary	(D)	06	F	Child	20Fe02Ao
John	(S)	10	M	Child	20Fe02Ao
Patt	(S)	04	M	Child	20Fe02Ao
BOYLE, Jane		19	F	Servant	20Fe02Ao
KNEEL, Martha		19	F	Servant	20Fe02Ao
COURTNEY, Wm.		23	M	Servant	20Fe02Ao
GAFFERY, Ann		20	F	Servant	20Fe02Ao
ROONY, Hugh		46	M	Laborer	20Fe02Ao
Margt.		36	F	Unknown	20Fe02Ao

NAMES OF PASSENGERS	A G E	S E X	OCCUPATIONS	DATE PORT SHIP	NAMES OF PASSENGERS		A G E	S E X	OCCUPATIONS	DATE PORT SHIP
SIMPSON, James	18	M	Laborer	20Fe02Ao	FLYNN, James	(S)	02	M	Child	22Fe02Ku
Died-At-Sea					Bridget	(D)	.00	F	Infant	22Fe02Ku
CONROY, Michael	22	M	Laborer	20Fe02Ao	MCNICHOL, Barlley		30	M	Laborer	22Fe02Ku
FLANNAGAN, Edward	24	M	Laborer	20Fe02Ao	U	(W)	27	F	None	22Fe02Ku
FULLERTON, James	21	M	Laborer	20Fe02Ao	Mary		13	F	None	22Fe02Ku
MCNEILL, Andrew	39	M	Weaver	20Fe02Ao	Martin		10	M	Child	22Fe02Ku
MCGLENROY, Rose	20	F	Unknown	20Fe02Ao	John	(S)	08	M	Child	22Fe02Ku
Died-At-Sea					Julia	(D)	06	F	Child	22Fe02Ku
HUDSON, Wm.Gregory	25	M	Baker	20Fe02Ao	Thomas	(S)	02	M	Child	22Fe02Ku
U	(W)	24	F	Unknown	20Fe02Ao	Patrick	(S)	.00	M	Infant	22Fe02Ku
MASON, Charles	24	M	Coachman	20Fe02Ao	DUCKIN, Thomas		30	M	Laborer	22Fe02Ku
Ann	22	F	Unknown	20Fe02Ao	U	(W)	30	F	None	22Fe02Ku
WINDUS, Thomas	24	M	Farmer	20Fe02Ao	HAYES, U-Mrs.		25	F	Unknown	22Fe02Ku
NOLIN, Patt	28	M	Carter	20Fe02Ao	Robt.		21	M	None	22Fe02Ku
COPELAND, James	24	M	Laborer	20Fe02Ao	BYRNE, Elizabeth		20	F	None	22Fe02Ku
MCKAGEN, John	21	M	Farmer	20Fe02Ao	RUPELL, Mary		20	F	None	22Fe02Ku
WOODS, John	22	M	Carpenter	20Fe02Ao	BRABAZON, Thomas		30	M	Laborer	22Fe02Ku
SMITH, Wm.	60	M	Farmer	20Fe02Ao	BRIEN, Winfred		22	M	None	22Fe02Ku
Bridget	20	F	Unknown	20Fe02Ao	Anne		21	F	None	22Fe02Ku
NEVINS, Michael	20	M	Unknown	20Fe02Ao	FANNON, John		45	M	None	22Fe02Ku
Died-At-Sea					MALLOM, Wm.		20	M	None	22Fe02Ku
MARTIN, James	20	M	Unknown	20Fe02Ao	FANNON, Mary		40	F	Wife	22Fe02Ku
					Catharine	(D)	13	F	Wife	22Fe02Ku
					Maria	(D)	10	F	Child	22Fe02Ku
INDEPENDENCE 20 FEBRUARY 1847					Bernard	(S)	08	M	Child	22Fe02Ku
					Patrick	(S)	04	M	Child	22Fe02Ku
From London					Daniel	(S)	01	M	Child	22Fe02Ku
					CASGROOVE, Henry		21	M	Laborer	22Fe02Ku
					CASSEY, Sarah		24	F	Laborer	22Fe02Ku
					GROMLY, John		26	M	Farmer	22Fe02Ku
CHATFIELD, Joseph	40	M	Gentleman	20Fe21Hf	Eleanor	(W)	20	F	None	22Fe02Ku
MILLISS, J.P.	26	M	Gentleman	20Fe21Hf	Peter	(S)	01	M	Child	22Fe02Ku
LOUNDER, Thomas	22	M	Gentleman	20Fe21Hf	Darby	(S)	.00	M	Infant	22Fe02Ku
AMON, John	25	M	Gentleman	20Fe21Hf	MCSURLY, Ann		18	F	Unknown	22Fe02Ku
MANEH, John	34	M	Gentleman	20Fe21Hf	MCCORMICK, Peter		22	M	Laborer	22Fe02Ku
TIERNEY, Timothy	22	M	Stctr	20Fe21Hf	Anne	(W)	23	F	None	22Fe02Ku
James	21	M	Carpenter	20Fe21Hf	Bridget	(D)	.00	F	Infant	22Fe02Ku
GIVINY, Patrick	21	M	Draper	20Fe21Hf	MCCARTHY, Timothy		40	M	Farmer	22Fe02Ku
CAMUS, William	17	M	Carpenter	20Fe21Hf	Judith	(W)	36	F	None	22Fe02Ku
ALLEN, Richard	36	M	Draper	20Fe21Hf	Ellen	(D)	13	F	Unknown	22Fe02Ku
MCKAY, William	33	M	Laborer	20Fe21Hf	Patrick	(S)	11	M	Child	22Fe02Ku
GRANT, Robert	18	M	Laborer	20Fe21Hf	John	(S)	09	M	Child	22Fe02Ku
BROWN, Elam	33	M	Engineer	20Fe21Hf	Margaret	(D)	05	F	Child	22Fe02Ku
Caroline	21	F	Unknown	20Fe21Hf	Michael	(S)	.00	M	Infant	22Fe02Ku
FISHE, Richard	30	M	Laborer	20Fe21Hf	FLOOD, John		29	M	Laborer	22Fe02Ku
					Michael		18	M	None	22Fe02Ku
					DALEY, John		35	M	Farmer	22Fe02Ku
					U	(W)	30	F	Unknown	22Fe02Ku
NEW-WORLD 22 FEBRUARY 1847					Bridget	(D)	13	F	Unknown	22Fe02Ku
					Mary	(D)	11	F	Child	22Fe02Ku
From Liverpool					Jane	(D)	09	F	Child	22Fe02Ku
					Winifred	(S)	07	M	Child	22Fe02Ku
					Eliza	(D)	05	F	Child	22Fe02Ku
					Catharine	(D)	03	F	Child	22Fe02Ku
					Anne	(D)	.00	F	Infant	22Fe02Ku
HYLAND, Marget.	18	F	None	22Fe02Ku	Died-At-Sea					
BUTTER, Ellen	14	F	None	22Fe02Ku	WALLACE, Mary		18	F	Unknown	22Fe02Ku
JONES, Alice	18	F	None	22Fe02Ku	SWEENEY, Margaret		32	F	Unknown	22Fe02Ku
KEENY, John	40	M	Laborer	22Fe02Ku	RODRIGUES, Jos.		28	M	Unknown	22Fe02Ku
Bridget	18	F	None	22Fe02Ku	SWEENEY, Eliza		12	F	None	22Fe02Ku
FLYNN, Patrick	40	M	Farmer	22Fe02Ku	Ellen		10	F	Child	22Fe02Ku
U	(W)	36	F	None	22Fe02Ku	Margaret		08	F	Child	22Fe02Ku
Mapply	(D)	14	F	None	22Fe02Ku	KING, Edward		29	M	Farmer	22Fe02Ku
John	(S)	13	M	None	22Fe02Ku	MCMAHON, Philip		21	M	Farmer	22Fe02Ku
Martin	(S)	09	M	Child	22Fe02Ku	GARRIGAN, Anne		20	F	Farmer	22Fe02Ku
Michael	(S)	07	M	Child	22Fe02Ku	Anne		17	F	Farmer	22Fe02Ku
Mary	(D)	13	F	None	22Fe02Ku	WALLACE, John		20	M	Laborer	22Fe02Ku
Catharine	(D)	16	F	None	22Fe02Ku	U	(W)	18	F	None	22Fe02Ku
Peggy	(D)	08	F	Child	22Fe02Ku	REILLY, Michael		40	M	Farmer	22Fe02Ku
Thomas	(S)	06	M	Child	22Fe02Ku	Judith	(W)	30	F	None	22Fe02Ku
Patrick	(S)	04	M	Child	22Fe02Ku	Catharine		15	F	Unknown	22Fe02Ku
					Bridget	(D)	13	F	Unknown	22Fe02Ku
					James	(S)	11	M	Child	22Fe02Ku
					Mary	(D)	11	F	Child	22Fe02Ku
					Michael	(S)	09	M	Child	22Fe02Ku

NAMES OF PASSENGERS		AGE	SEX	OCCUPATIONS	DATE PORT SHIP
REILLY, Betty	(D)	07	F	Child	22Fe02Ku
Thomas	(S)	05	M	Child	22Fe02Ku
John	(S)	03	M	Child	22Fe02Ku
Ellen	(D)	.00	F	Infant	22Fe02Ku
MCKENNA, Ellen		17	F	Unknown	22Fe02Ku
BYRNE, John		30	M	Farmer	22Fe02Ku
Catharine	(W)	30	M	None	22Fe02Ku
John	(S)	04	M	Child	22Fe02Ku
CONNOLLY, James		28	M	Farmer	22Fe02Ku
Isabella	(W)	26	F	Unknown	22Fe02Ku
Anne	(D)	06	F	Child	22Fe02Ku
Patrick	(S)	04	M	Child	22Fe02Ku
MCGRIMBY, James		25	M	Laborer	22Fe02Ku
IRVING, James		24	M	Laborer	22Fe02Ku
U	(W)	21	F	None	22Fe02Ku
Grace-Agnes	(D)	03	F	Child	22Fe02Ku
William	(S)	01	M	Child	22Fe02Ku
CLARKSON, Charlotte		13	F	None	22Fe02Ku
Mary-Ann		20	F	Unknown	22Fe02Ku
MULLIGAN, Mary		18	F	Unknown	22Fe02Ku
GORDON, Wm.		22	M	Unknown	22Fe02Ku
DONALDSON, James		19	M	Unknown	22Fe02Ku
PACEY, Thos.		55	M	Laborer	22Fe02Ku
LAGER, Wm.		13	M	None	22Fe02Ku
MCDOWELL, John		25	M	None	22Fe02Ku
Patrick		24	M	Farmer	22Fe02Ku
HURST, John		37	M	Farmer	22Fe02Ku
Mary-Ann	(W)	30	F	Unknown	22Fe02Ku
Alexander	(S)	12	M	Unknown	22Fe02Ku
MCCARTHY, Susan		20	F	Unknown	22Fe02Ku
FAHY, Anne		23	F	Unknown	22Fe02Ku
APPLETON, Fredk.		22	M	Unknown	22Fe02Ku
KENNEDY, Danl.		24	M	Unknown	22Fe02Ku
CARROLL, Mary		25	F	Unknown	22Fe02Ku
Eliza		21	F	Unknown	22Fe02Ku
KANE, Martin		27	M	Unknown	22Fe02Ku
SEARY, Owen		20	M	Unknown	22Fe02Ku
REILLY, Edward		22	M	Unknown	22Fe02Ku
LINAHAN, Jos.		21	M	Unknown	22Fe02Ku
Ann		15	F	Unknown	22Fe02Ku
Timothy		13	M	Unknown	22Fe02Ku
MURPHY, Mary-Ann		20	F	Unknown	22Fe02Ku
MCDONALD, Jas.		26	M	Unknown	22Fe02Ku
Catharine	(W)	24	F	Unknown	22Fe02Ku
Mary	(D)	.00	F	Infant	22Fe02Ku
WARD, John		25	M	Unknown	22Fe02Ku
BURKE, Thos.		29	M	Unknown	22Fe02Ku
CAMPBELL, Bridget		16	F	Unknown	22Fe02Ku
Patrick		12	M	Unknown	22Fe02Ku
DUCKIN, Martin		10	M	Child	22Fe02Ku
Thomas		09	M	Child	22Fe02Ku
Mary		07	F	Child	22Fe02Ku
CAMERON, Michael		40	M	Farmer	22Fe02Ku
Lawrence		16	M	None	22Fe02Ku
MCKEON, Patrick		16	M	None	22Fe02Ku
Bridget		13	F	None	22Fe02Ku
WALSH, John		25	M	Farmer	22Fe02Ku
DOLAN, John		27	M	Farmer	22Fe02Ku
Died-At-Sea					
U	(W)	22	F	None	22Fe02Ku
Margaret		20	F	None	22Fe02Ku
MCGOOM, James		25	M	Laborer	22Fe02Ku
U	(W)	20	F	None	22Fe02Ku
John	(S)	02	M	Child	22Fe02Ku
Died-At-Sea					
Mary		20	F	None	22Fe02Ku
SHEARLEY, John		24	M	Farmer	22Fe02Ku
WALSH, Patrick		40	M	Farmer	22Fe02Ku
U	(W)	35	F	None	22Fe02Ku
Nelley	(D)	06	F	Child	22Fe02Ku
Peggy	(D)	.00	F	Infant	22Fe02Ku
MCGOOM, Cormick		40	M	Farmer	22Fe02Ku
FITZGERALD, Saml.		30	M	Unknown	22Fe02Ku
BLAKELY, U-Miss		22	F	Unknown	22Fe02Ku
CASSIDY, Thomas		35	M	Farmer	22Fe02Ku
CASSIDY, Michael		20	M	Farmer	22Fe02Ku
MCCORMICK, Philip		45	M	Laborer	22Fe02Ku
Hugh		10	M	Child	22Fe02Ku
MCSURLY, Hugh		19	M	None	22Fe02Ku
HOTTON, Patrick		40	M	Laborer	22Fe02Ku
CANNON, Michael		25	M	Laborer	22Fe02Ku
SCOTT, Thos.		32	M	Laborer	22Fe02Ku
U	(W)	26	F	Unknown	22Fe02Ku
SPROTT, Robt.		30	M	Farmer	22Fe02Ku
MCCORMICK, John		30	M	Farmer	22Fe02Ku
Edward		16	M	None	22Fe02Ku
MCLAUGHLIN, Jas.		30	M	Farmer	22Fe02Ku
SMITH, Michael		27	M	Farmer	22Fe02Ku
U	(W)	20	F	None	22Fe02Ku
Ann	(D)	01	F	Child	22Fe02Ku
CONAGHRY, Jas.		38	M	Farmer	22Fe02Ku
U	(W)	28	F	None	22Fe02Ku
U	(D)	.00	F	Infant	22Fe02Ku
Frances	(D)	09	F	Child	22Fe02Ku
Bernard	(S)	05	M	Child	22Fe02Ku
Mary-Ann	(D)	02	F	Child	22Fe02Ku
HOOKS, Owen		27	M	Farmer	22Fe02Ku
LYNCH, Thos.		25	M	Farmer	22Fe02Ku
SLOBERDGER, John		49	M	Farmer	22Fe02Ku
SMITH, Philip		20	M	Farmer	22Fe02Ku
KELLEY, Jas.		30	M	Farmer	22Fe02Ku
Julia		25	F	None	22Fe02Ku
SMITH, John		31	M	Laborer	22Fe02Ku
BAILISS, U		24	M	None	22Fe02Ku
U	(W)	21	F	None	22Fe02Ku
Elizabeth		18	F	None	22Fe02Ku
MCGARTH, John		23	M	Farmer	22Fe02Ku
DUFFY, John		30	M	Farmer	22Fe02Ku
Thomas		04	M	Child	22Fe02Ku
EGAR, Albert		24	M	Laborer	22Fe02Ku
SMITH, Chas.		24	M	Laborer	22Fe02Ku
SHOMER, Wm.		24	M	Laborer	22Fe02Ku
Mary		22	F	Unknown	22Fe02Ku
Daniel		28	M	Farmer	22Fe02Ku
Henry		02	M	Child	22Fe02Ku
Edward		01	M	Child	22Fe02Ku
PEASER, Wm.		22	M	Farmer	22Fe02Ku
BARRETT, Elizabeth		50	F	None	22Fe02Ku
DUGGAN, Catharine		20	F	None	22Fe02Ku
ELLIS, Ell		40	M	None	22Fe02Ku
COCHRAN, Betty		40	F	None	22Fe02Ku
Betty	(D)	02	F	Child	22Fe02Ku
Died-At-Sea					
RUDOY, John		25	M	Farmer	22Fe02Ku
BYRNES, Michael		45	M	Farmer	22Fe02Ku
Ann	(W)	40	F	None	22Fe02Ku
Bridget	(D)	16	F	None	22Fe02Ku
Mary	(D)	12	F	None	22Fe02Ku
Ann	(D)	10	F	Child	22Fe02Ku
Pat	(S)	08	M	Child	22Fe02Ku
Martin	(S)	06	M	Child	22Fe02Ku
John	(S)	03	M	Child	22Fe02Ku
GORMAN, Bess		21	F	None	22Fe02Ku
BRAMAN, Mary		21	F	None	22Fe02Ku
KEILLY, John		25	M	Laborer	22Fe02Ku
DUFFY, U		35	F	Wife	22Fe02Ku
U		30	F	Wife	22Fe02Ku
MOORE, Pat.		26	M	Laborer	22Fe02Ku
BAKER, Mary		30	F	None	22Fe02Ku
Fanny	(D)	.00	F	Infant	22Fe02Ku
CALLAGHAR, Martin		50	M	Laborer	22Fe02Ku
Mary		27	F	None	22Fe02Ku
Died-At-Sea					
Peggy		40	F	None	22Fe02Ku
Thomas		11	M	Child	22Fe02Ku
John		09	M	Child	22Fe02Ku
Miles		07	M	Child	22Fe02Ku
James		.00	M	Infant	22Fe02Ku
Biddy		20	F	None	22Fe02Ku
BAYLEN, James		40	M	Laborer	22Fe02Ku

354

NAMES OF PASSENGERS		AGE	SEX	OCCUPATIONS	DATE PORT SHIP
BAYLEN, Catharine	(W)	37	F	None	22Fe02Ku
Biddy	(D)	09	F	Child	22Fe02Ku
Thomas	(S)	07	M	Child	22Fe02Ku
John	(S)	06	M	Child	22Fe02Ku
Margaret	(D)	02	F	Child	22Fe02Ku
Miles	(S)	.00	M	Infant	22Fe02Ku
KEEGAN, James		21	M	Laborer	22Fe02Ku
William		20	M	Laborer	22Fe02Ku
Betty		17	F	None	22Fe02Ku
WATSON, Wm.		27	M	Laborer	22Fe02Ku
STEWART, Mary		25	F	None	22Fe02Ku
ODONNELL, Mary		25	F	None	22Fe02Ku
CAMPBELL, John		20	M	Laborer	22Fe02Ku
Samuel		20	M	Laborer	22Fe02Ku
GILL, Joseph		39	M	Laborer	22Fe02Ku
U	(W)	30	F	Unknown	22Fe02Ku
Joseph	(S)	10	M	Child	22Fe02Ku
William	(S)	08	M	Child	22Fe02Ku
Mary-Ann	(D)	06	F	Child	22Fe02Ku
George	(S)	04	M	Child	22Fe02Ku
Charles	(S)	.00	M	Infant	22Fe02Ku
BRANLEY, Wm.		35	M	Farmer	22Fe02Ku
GORMAN, Saml.		24	M	Farmer	22Fe02Ku
HICKEY, John		26	M	Laborer	22Fe02Ku
WALSH, John		24	M	Laborer	22Fe02Ku
COUGHLAN, Pat		22	M	Laborer	22Fe02Ku
KELLY, William		20	M	Laborer	22Fe02Ku
HAULTON, Bryan		30	M	Laborer	22Fe02Ku
SMITH, Mary		20	F	None	22Fe02Ku
LEESON, Terrence		19	M	Farmer	22Fe02Ku
HAYES, Wm.		26	M	Farmer	22Fe02Ku
JONES, James		27	M	Laborer	22Fe02Ku
REYNOLDS, Chas.		20	M	Laborer	22Fe02Ku
DOYLE, Patrick		30	M	Laborer	22Fe02Ku
Judy		30	F	None	22Fe02Ku
ROAKE, James		24	M	Farmer	22Fe02Ku
NUGENT, Peter		28	M	None	22Fe02Ku
MCCOUGHLAN, Mathew		30	M	None	22Fe02Ku
Margaret	(W)	28	F	None	22Fe02Ku
Samuel	(S)	.00	M	Infant	22Fe02Ku
CRAWLEY, Paul		48	M	Farmer	22Fe02Ku
Ellenor	(W)	48	F	None	22Fe02Ku
Mary	(D)	07	F	Child	22Fe02Ku
Sarah	(D)	05	F	Child	22Fe02Ku
MULLIGAN, Jas.		30	M	Laborer	22Fe02Ku
Jane	(W)	28	F	None	22Fe02Ku
Pat	(S)	05	M	Child	22Fe02Ku
Mary	(D)	03	F	Child	22Fe02Ku
Margaret	(D)	.00	F	Infant	22Fe02Ku
FITZHAUS, John		24	M	Laborer	22Fe02Ku
John		.00	M	Infant	22Fe02Ku
BROOKS, George		20	M	Laborer	22Fe02Ku
GILLRAY, Patrick		18	M	Laborer	22Fe02Ku
Catherine		00	F	None	22Fe02Ku
VICTORY, Mary		30	F	None	22Fe02Ku
Jas.	(S)	08	M	Child	22Fe02Ku
Bernard	(S)	09	M	Child	22Fe02Ku
CALLAGAR, Dennis		25	M	Laborer	22Fe02Ku
CRUDON, Dennis		46	M	Laborer	22Fe02Ku
Jos.		25	M	Laborer	22Fe02Ku
CLARK, Nellie		28	M	Farmer	22Fe02Ku
U	(W)	28	F	None	22Fe02Ku
James		20	M	Farmer	22Fe02Ku
Ann		22	F	None	22Fe02Ku
Pat.		08	M	Child	22Fe02Ku
James		10	M	Child	22Fe02Ku
Nellie		06	M	Child	22Fe02Ku
Hugh		07	M	Child	22Fe02Ku
GAMRON, Thomas		40	M	Laborer	22Fe02Ku
U	(W)	40	F	None	22Fe02Ku
Philip	(S)	18	M	Laborer	22Fe02Ku
James	(S)	16	M	Laborer	22Fe02Ku
John	(S)	10	M	Child	22Fe02Ku
Catharine	(D)	12	F	None	22Fe02Ku
Michael		26	M	Farmer	22Fe02Ku

ROSCIUS 23 FEBRUARY 1847

From Liverpool

NAMES OF PASSENGERS		AGE	SEX	OCCUPATIONS	DATE PORT SHIP
MCCOCKING, Daniel		26	M	Laborer	23Fe02Bf
SHORT, John		29	M	Laborer	23Fe02Bf
CONMET, Margaret		20	F	Unknown	23Fe02Bf
MCHILL, Patrick		40	M	Laborer	23Fe02Bf
John	(S)	19	M	Laborer	23Fe02Bf
Bridget	(D)	13	F	Unknown	23Fe02Bf
OCONNELL, Michael		32	M	Laborer	23Fe02Bf
Bridget	(W)	32	F	Unknown	23Fe02Bf
Daniel	(S)	12	M	Laborer	23Fe02Bf
Margaret	(M)	60	F	Unknown	23Fe02Bf
WHITE, Mary		45	F	Unknown	23Fe02Bf
James		22	M	Farmer	23Fe02Bf
ROYEN, James		25	M	Laborer	23Fe02Bf
ANDERSON, Margaret		19	F	Unknown	23Fe02Bf
ROYEN, Mary		25	F	Unknown	23Fe02Bf
TOBY, Mary		22	F	Unknown	23Fe02Bf
BRENNING, James		26	M	Joiner	23Fe02Bf
Anne		26	F	Unknown	23Fe02Bf
PIKE, Ellen		26	F	Unknown	23Fe02Bf
Ann		08	F	Child	23Fe02Bf
OCONNOR, Bridget		25	F	Unknown	23Fe02Bf
Winny		27	M	Unknown	23Fe02Bf
Margaret		30	F	Unknown	23Fe02Bf
Bridget		18	F	Unknown	23Fe02Bf
MATTEKIN, Mary		22	F	Unknown	23Fe02Bf
BOYLE, John		40	M	Laborer	23Fe02Bf
TREASEY, Margaret		25	F	Unknown	23Fe02Bf
WHITE, Margaret		25	F	Unknown	23Fe02Bf
DORSEY, Garret		36	M	Farmer	23Fe02Bf
Mary-A.		22	F	Unknown	23Fe02Bf
BRANNEGAN, John		21	M	Farmer	23Fe02Bf
MCFARNELL, U		25	M	Laborer	23Fe02Bf
FAY, Dennis		56	M	Laborer	23Fe02Bf
Edward		30	M	Laborer	23Fe02Bf
Elizabeth	(W)	55	F	Unknown	23Fe02Bf
Sarah	(D)	23	F	Unknown	23Fe02Bf
Margaret	(D)	21	F	Unknown	23Fe02Bf
Catharine	(D)	19	F	Unknown	23Fe02Bf
Patrick	(S)	17	M	Laborer	23Fe02Bf
Dennis	(S)	16	M	Laborer	23Fe02Bf
Ellen	(D)	25	F	Unknown	23Fe02Bf
ROTHER, Margaret		28	F	Unknown	23Fe02Bf
REYNOLDS, Patrick		21	M	Laborer	23Fe02Bf
MCCORRICK, U		28	M	Laborer	23Fe02Bf
CONNOR, Catharine		25	F	Unknown	23Fe02Bf
U		00	U	Child	23Fe02Bf
U		00	U	Child	23Fe02Bf
U		00	U	Child	23Fe02Bf
U		00	U	Child	23Fe02Bf
U		00	U	Child	23Fe02Bf
FOUGETY, John		54	M	Laborer	23Fe02Bf
Mary		53	F	Unknown	23Fe02Bf
CUNNINGHAM, Barney		21	M	Laborer	23Fe02Bf
MCCORMICK, Patrick		24	M	Laborer	23Fe02Bf
FAY, Patrick		25	M	Laborer	23Fe02Bf
MCCAFFREY, John		21	M	Mason	23Fe02Bf
FAY, Patrick		40	M	Laborer	23Fe02Bf
DOBSON, Michael		20	M	Laborer	23Fe02Bf
Margaret	(W)	23	F	Laborer	23Fe02Bf
U		00	U	Child	23Fe02Bf
LOFTHOUSE, Bridget		30	F	Unknown	23Fe02Bf
JINNETTE, Frances		30	F	Unknown	23Fe02Bf
FRINGE, Patrick		38	M	Laborer	23Fe02Bf
TWING, Margaret		30	F	Unknown	23Fe02Bf
U		00	U	Child	23Fe02Bf

NAMES OF PASSENGERS		AGE	SEX	OCCUPATIONS	DATE PORT SHIP
TWING, U		00	U	Child	23Fe02Bf
U		00	U	Child	23Fe02Bf
U		00	U	Child	23Fe02Bf
U		00	U	Child	23Fe02Bf
U		00	U	Child	23Fe02Bf
SMITH, Jane		18	F	Unknown	23Fe02Bf
Helen		20	F	Unknown	23Fe02Bf
FRAZER, Helen		17	F	Unknown	23Fe02Bf
Sarah		19	F	Unknown	23Fe02Bf
MAGUIRE, Betsy		21	F	Unknown	23Fe02Bf
THOMPSON, Elizabeth		20	F	Unknown	23Fe02Bf
Archd.		23	M	Tailor	23Fe02Bf
CUMMINGS, Patrick		38	M	Laborer	23Fe02Bf
Ellen	(W)	36	F	Unknown	23Fe02Bf
U		00	U	Child	23Fe02Bf
U		00	U	Child	23Fe02Bf
U		00	U	Child	23Fe02Bf
U		00	U	Child	23Fe02Bf
U		00	U	Child	23Fe02Bf
CONWAY, John		36	M	Laborer	23Fe02Bf
Martin		25	M	Laborer	23Fe02Bf
U		00	U	Child	23Fe02Bf
CRIDDY, Peter		30	M	Laborer	23Fe02Bf
CONWAY, Mary		30	F	Unknown	23Fe02Bf
CELEY, Barney		30	M	Shoemaker	23Fe02Bf
MCCORMICK, Daniel		30	M	Laborer	23Fe02Bf
DALTON, William		17	M	Laborer	23Fe02Bf
LASHLEY, John		20	M	Laborer	23Fe02Bf
MCCARLE, Bejam.		26	M	Laborer	23Fe02Bf
DUFFLE, James		15	M	Joiner	23Fe02Bf
MCGOYNE, John		20	M	Laborer	23Fe02Bf
BOYLE, James		21	M	Laborer	23Fe02Bf
TUFNEE, Thomas		22	M	Laborer	23Fe02Bf
Daniel		26	M	Laborer	23Fe02Bf
HAULEY, James		40	M	Laborer	23Fe02Bf
Sarah	(W)	46	F	Unknown	23Fe02Bf
Patrick	(S)	21	M	Laborer	23Fe02Bf
Edmund	(S)	19	M	Laborer	23Fe02Bf
William	(S)	17	M	Laborer	23Fe02Bf
Nearlew	(D)	15	F	Unknown	23Fe02Bf
Catharine	(D)	13	F	Unknown	23Fe02Bf
James	(S)	12	M	Laborer	23Fe02Bf
Robert	(S)	10	M	Laborer	23Fe02Bf
Charles	(S)	07	M	Child	23Fe02Bf
Isabella	(D)	05	F	Child	23Fe02Bf
ODEAL, Patrick		30	M	Laborer	23Fe02Bf
Daniel		35	M	Farmer	23Fe02Bf
MCCLUE, Thomas		42	M	Laborer	23Fe02Bf
Ann	(W)	40	F	Unknown	23Fe02Bf
Catharine	(D)	21	F	Unknown	23Fe02Bf
Catharine	(D)	15	F	Unknown	23Fe02Bf
Bridget	(D)	13	F	Unknown	23Fe02Bf
Ann	(D)	11	F	Child	23Fe02Bf
James	(S)	09	M	Child	23Fe02Bf
Maria	(D)	06	F	Child	23Fe02Bf
Jane	(D)	03	F	Child	23Fe02Bf
GELLUBY, Ann		21	F	Unknown	23Fe02Bf
Patrick		30	M	Laborer	23Fe02Bf
Matthew		28	M	Laborer	23Fe02Bf
CARLEY, John		22	M	Tailor	23Fe02Bf
MCGUIRE, Thomas		20	M	Laborer	23Fe02Bf
Catharine		18	F	Unknown	23Fe02Bf
WELSH, Patrick		22	M	Laborer	23Fe02Bf
Mary		25	F	Laborer	23Fe02Bf
DENNING, Bartholomew		22	M	Laborer	23Fe02Bf
ROAKE, Bryan		22	M	Laborer	23Fe02Bf
DENNING, John		23	M	Laborer	23Fe02Bf
CONLEY, Peter		30	M	Laborer	23Fe02Bf
Bridget	(W)	28	F	Unknown	23Fe02Bf
Edward	(S)	10	M	Child	23Fe02Bf
John	(S)	08	M	Child	23Fe02Bf
Ann	(D)	06	F	Child	23Fe02Bf
Susan	(D)	03	F	Child	23Fe02Bf
James	(S)	.03	M	Infant	23Fe02Bf
MCMARE, Lawrence		25	M	Laborer	23Fe02Bf
SHARON, Thomas		21	M	Butcher	23Fe02Bf
CHARLES, Philip		19	M	Shoemaker	23Fe02Bf
BRADLEY, Barnabas		17	M	Laborer	23Fe02Bf
Jane		21	F	Unknown	23Fe02Bf
James		12	M	Unknown	23Fe02Bf
Edward		08	M	Child	23Fe02Bf
TWINGS, James		19	M	Joiner	23Fe02Bf
MCCOAL, Barnabas		40	M	Laborer	23Fe02Bf
CHARNEY, John		21	M	Laborer	23Fe02Bf
MCDONALD, John		30	M	Laborer	23Fe02Bf
GANLEY, Thomas		40	M	Laborer	23Fe02Bf
Mary	(W)	32	F	Unknown	23Fe02Bf
Thomas	(S)	10	M	Child	23Fe02Bf
Rose	(D)	08	F	Child	23Fe02Bf
DENWILL, Patrick		30	M	Laborer	23Fe02Bf
James		.09	M	Infant	23Fe02Bf
James		27	M	Laborer	23Fe02Bf
HOPKINS, Michael		30	M	Farmer	23Fe02Bf
NICHOLSON, James		29	M	Tailor	23Fe02Bf
Sarah	(W)	27	F	Unknown	23Fe02Bf
Mary	(D)	.03	F	Infant	23Fe02Bf
HENDERSON, Helen		20	F	Unknown	23Fe02Bf
FORD, Catharine		22	F	Unknown	23Fe02Bf
CARFORD, Michael		30	M	Laborer	23Fe02Bf
COOLING, John		25	M	Laborer	23Fe02Bf
James		30	M	Laborer	23Fe02Bf
HART, Mary		30	F	Unknown	23Fe02Bf
HANDLEY, Patrick		27	M	Laborer	23Fe02Bf
CARTER, Ann		15	F	Unknown	23Fe02Bf
William		17	M	Laborer	23Fe02Bf
OBRYAN, Edward		18	M	Laborer	23Fe02Bf
CARVINGS, Ann		20	F	Unknown	23Fe02Bf
Mary		17	F	Unknown	23Fe02Bf
GALERGON, Ann		20	F	Unknown	23Fe02Bf
RADY, Philip		30	M	Farmer	23Fe02Bf
Helen		27	F	Unknown	23Fe02Bf
John		13	M	Unknown	23Fe02Bf
Thomas		10	M	Child	23Fe02Bf
Barnabas		08	M	Child	23Fe02Bf
Helen		05	F	Child	23Fe02Bf
SMITH, Thomas		45	M	Bricklayer	23Fe02Bf
Mary	(W)	44	F	Unknown	23Fe02Bf
Catharine	(D)	21	F	Unknown	23Fe02Bf
Philip	(S)	19	M	Bricklayer	23Fe02Bf
Matthew		17	M	Joiner	23Fe02Bf
Francis		15	M	Laborer	23Fe02Bf
Ann		14	F	Unknown	23Fe02Bf
Ruth		11	F	Child	23Fe02Bf
Barnet		10	M	Child	23Fe02Bf
Thomas		07	M	Child	23Fe02Bf
MULVENEY, Rose		17	F	Laborer	23Fe02Bf
GOLEN, Catharine		17	F	Unknown	23Fe02Bf
MIDDINGS, Henry		18	M	Laborer	23Fe02Bf
SMITH, John		16	M	Laborer	23Fe02Bf
MCGERRAND, Owen		18	M	Laborer	23Fe02Bf
Henry		17	M	Laborer	23Fe02Bf
CULLMOOR, Michael		28	M	Laborer	23Fe02Bf
GROVES, Henry		45	M	Joiner	23Fe02Bf
Jane	(W)	40	F	Unknown	23Fe02Bf
Elizabeth	(D)	19	F	Unknown	23Fe02Bf
Jane	(D)	17	F	Unknown	23Fe02Bf
Henry	(S)	15	M	Unknown	23Fe02Bf
Catharine	(D)	09	F	Child	23Fe02Bf
Maria	(D)	06	F	Child	23Fe02Bf
PEARSHALL, Edward		26	M	Laborer	23Fe02Bf
GRACE, Mary		24	F	Unknown	23Fe02Bf
QUEEN, Catherine		21	F	Unknown	23Fe02Bf
CRISTIE, Thomas		40	M	Laborer	23Fe02Bf
Mary	(W)	38	F	Unknown	23Fe02Bf
Robert	(S)	21	M	Laborer	23Fe02Bf
Nopel	(D)	20	F	Unknown	23Fe02Bf
Irwin	(S)	11	M	Child	23Fe02Bf
George	(S)	09	M	Child	23Fe02Bf
CLARK, Ann		40	F	Unknown	23Fe02Bf
James		13	M	Unknown	23Fe02Bf

NAMES OF PASSENGERS		A G E	S E X	OCCUPATIONS	DATE PORT SHIP
PRESTON, Ann		24	F	Unknown	23Fe02Bf
RAINWOOD, Norman		30	M	Laborer	23Fe02Bf
Ann		22	F	Unknown	23Fe02Bf
YORK, Mary		18	F	Unknown	23Fe02Bf
MORTON, Mary		45	F	Unknown	23Fe02Bf
RICKTON, Michael		30	M	Laborer	23Fe02Bf
Catharine		26	F	Unknown	23Fe02Bf
FIDGAREL, Mary		27	F	Unknown	23Fe02Bf
DALTON, James		18	M	Farmer	23Fe02Bf
Mary		22	F	Unknown	23Fe02Bf
Patrick		30	M	Laborer	23Fe02Bf
SHINTHING, Dennis		14	M	Tailor	23Fe02Bf
MORLEY, John		22	M	Shoemaker	23Fe02Bf
THOMPSON, Thomas		12	M	Mason	23Fe02Bf
James		22	M	Mason	23Fe02Bf
Catharine		18	F	Unknown	23Fe02Bf
CONTON, Ellen		40	F	Unknown	23Fe02Bf
FARLEY, Peter		20	M	Laborer	23Fe02Bf
KELLY, Patrick		21	M	Laborer	23Fe02Bf
MCGUIRE, Aicher		14	M	Laborer	23Fe02Bf
MCCONNOR, Owen		26	M	Laborer	23Fe02Bf
Bridget		20	F	Unknown	23Fe02Bf
Ann		18	F	Unknown	23Fe02Bf
Micher		15	M	Laborer	23Fe02Bf
FORSYTH, John		49	M	Farmer	23Fe02Bf
Margaret	(W)	48	F	Unknown	23Fe02Bf
Ellen	(D)	22	F	Unknown	23Fe02Bf
Joseph	(S)	13	M	Unknown	23Fe02Bf
Margaret	(D)	10	F	Child	23Fe02Bf
Thomas	(S)	08	M	Child	23Fe02Bf
Mary-Ann	(D)	04	F	Child	23Fe02Bf
FITZPATRICK, Barnabas		20	M	Laborer	23Fe02Bf
SLURRY, Michael		15	M	Laborer	23Fe02Bf
MALLON, James		40	M	Laborer	23Fe02Bf
LEE, Patrick		25	M	Laborer	23Fe02Bf
DENCHMAN, Mark		19	M	Laborer	23Fe02Bf
SHARDEN, James		36	M	Laborer	23Fe02Bf
Elizabeth	(W)	33	F	Unknown	23Fe02Bf
Ellen	(D)	12	F	Unknown	23Fe02Bf
Rose	(D)	10	F	Child	23Fe02Bf
Mary	(D)	08	F	Child	23Fe02Bf
James	(S)	01	M	Child	23Fe02Bf
BRAGEN, James		28	M	Farmer	23Fe02Bf
CLARK, James		27	M	Farmer	23Fe02Bf
DODWELL, Catharine		27	F	Unknown	23Fe02Bf
Died-At-Sea					
CLARK, Mary		20	F	Unknown	23Fe02Bf
FOOL, Anthony		28	M	Laborer	23Fe02Bf
CURLEY, Dennis		20	M	Laborer	23Fe02Bf
Ann		18	F	Unknown	23Fe02Bf
John		16	M	Laborer	23Fe02Bf
Thomas		13	M	Unknown	23Fe02Bf
Bernard		10	M	Child	23Fe02Bf
Ellen		08	F	Child	23Fe02Bf
HOPPY, Patrick		20	M	Bricklayer	23Fe02Bf
CLARK, Thomas		29	M	Joiner	23Fe02Bf
Barnabas		22	M	Farmer	23Fe02Bf
MCCABBING, Michael		23	M	Laborer	23Fe02Bf
TOOL, Thomas		20	M	Laborer	23Fe02Bf
BRENNING, William		24	M	Laborer	23Fe02Bf
Jeannette	(W)	30	F	Unknown	23Fe02Bf
Moart	(S)	06	M	Child	23Fe02Bf
Margaret	(D)	01	F	Child	23Fe02Bf
HAMILTON, James		26	M	Butcher	23Fe02Bf
Sarah		35	F	Unknown	23Fe02Bf
James		14	M	Unknown	23Fe02Bf
Martha		08	F	Child	23Fe02Bf
Mary-Ellen		03	F	Child	23Fe02Bf
Margaret		.02	F	Infant	23Fe02Bf
MONEHAN, James		26	M	Laborer	23Fe02Bf
Bridget	(W)	24	F	Laborer	23Fe02Bf
Mary	(D)	01	F	Child	23Fe02Bf
Barbara	(D)	.03	F	Infant	23Fe02Bf
FARLEY, Lawrence		26	M	Farmer	23Fe02Bf
James		00	M	Unknown	23Fe02Bf

NAMES OF PASSENGERS		A G E	S E X	OCCUPATIONS	DATE PORT SHIP
TREASEY, Hugh		40	M	Laborer	23Fe02Bf
Hannah	(W)	36	F	Unknown	23Fe02Bf
James	(S)	08	M	Child	23Fe02Bf
Mary-Ann	(D)	05	F	Child	23Fe02Bf
Margaret	(D)	03	F	Child	23Fe02Bf
Rose	(D)	.09	F	Infant	23Fe02Bf
TOOL, Aicher		20	M	Laborer	23Fe02Bf
MCDONOGH, John		17	M	Laborer	23Fe02Bf

FIDELIA 23 FEBRUARY 1847

From Liverpool

NAMES OF PASSENGERS		A G E	S E X	OCCUPATIONS	DATE PORT SHIP
KELLY, Patrick		40	M	Doctor	23Fe02Ax
Mary	(D)	17	F	Unknown	23Fe02Ax
Robt.	(S)	10	M	Child	23Fe02Ax
THOMAS, W.T.		50	M	Machinist	23Fe02Ax
Hester	(W)	50	F	Unknown	23Fe02Ax
W.T.	(S)	20	M	Unknown	23Fe02Ax
Louisa	(D)	21	F	Unknown	23Fe02Ax
Susan	(D)	20	F	Unknown	23Fe02Ax
Covington	(S)	14	M	Unknown	23Fe02Ax
John	(S)	22	M	Unknown	23Fe02Ax
Died-At-Sea					
Emma-Jane	(D)	00	F	Unknown	23Fe02Ax
WALLACE, Edward		27	M	Mason	23Fe02Ax
DOYLE, Bridget		44	F	Unknown	23Fe02Ax
Mary	(D)	14	F	Unknown	23Fe02Ax
Barney	(S)	10	M	Child	23Fe02Ax
Thomas	(S)	04	M	Child	23Fe02Ax
Nelly	(D)	06	F	Child	23Fe02Ax
NEREL, John		37	M	Herd	23Fe02Ax
Bridget	(W)	35	F	Unknown	23Fe02Ax
Mary	(D)	13	F	Unknown	23Fe02Ax
Catherine	(D)	11	F	Child	23Fe02Ax
Patt	(S)	06	M	Child	23Fe02Ax
MONK, John		48	M	Accountant	23Fe02Ax
HENDERSON, Geo.		32	M	Unknown	23Fe02Ax
WALSH, Ann		21	F	Unknown	23Fe02Ax
LAWLESS, Esther		25	F	Unknown	23Fe02Ax
COONEY, Catherine		18	F	Unknown	23Fe02Ax
SMITH, Patt		25	M	Unknown	23Fe02Ax
Catherine		29	F	Unknown	23Fe02Ax
FLOOR, Margaret		20	F	Unknown	23Fe02Ax
MCGUIRE, Martin		30	M	Laborer	23Fe02Ax
RODDY, John		22	M	Laborer	23Fe02Ax
MAJOR, Thomas		32	M	Laborer	23Fe02Ax
MOONEY, Peter		25	M	Laborer	23Fe02Ax
MAHON, Bernard		24	M	Laborer	23Fe02Ax
SWEENEY, James		26	M	Laborer	23Fe02Ax
WICKLORE, Geo.		25	M	Servant	23Fe02Ax
DANFREY, Margaret		26	F	Servant	23Fe02Ax
SHORT, Amelia		29	F	Servant	23Fe02Ax
CONNOR, Michael		25	M	Servant	23Fe02Ax
FITZGERALD, Edward		20	M	Servant	23Fe02Ax
Morris		24	M	Servant	23Fe02Ax
SULLIVAN, Morris		60	M	Laborer	23Fe02Ax
Patrick	(S)	25	M	Laborer	23Fe02Ax
John	(S)	12	M	Laborer	23Fe02Ax
Mary	(D)	20	F	Laborer	23Fe02Ax
Bridget	(D)	16	F	Laborer	23Fe02Ax
CARR, Margaret		07	F	Child	23Fe02Ax
MANARREY, Jane		26	F	Laborer	23Fe02Ax
GALAHA, Manac		25	U	Laborer	23Fe02Ax
MCCARL, Grace		19	F	Laborer	23Fe02Ax
MCGLOVE, Winey		20	F	Laborer	23Fe02Ax
MCGEE, Cath.		20	F	Laborer	23Fe02Ax
CONNEL, Jennuah		40	F	Laborer	23Fe02Ax
Catherine		20	F	Laborer	23Fe02Ax

NAMES OF PASSENGERS		AGE	SEX	OCCUPATIONS	DATE PORT SHIP
SULLIVAN, Richard		44	M	Laborer	23Fe02Ax
DORIN, Francis		26	M	Laborer	23Fe02Ax
MILMORE, Mark		20	M	Laborer	23Fe02Ax
SMITH, Ann		50	F	Unknown	23Fe02Ax
Rosanah		14	F	Unknown	23Fe02Ax
HAYES, Ann		45	F	Unknown	23Fe02Ax
Mary		14	F	Unknown	23Fe02Ax
GOLPEY, Isabella		21	F	Unknown	23Fe02Ax
RAMSEY, Geo.		21	M	Cooper	23Fe02Ax
TRACY, Peter		22	M	Laborer	23Fe02Ax
KNOX, Sarah		38	F	Unknown	23Fe02Ax
Margaret	(D)	16	F	Unknown	23Fe02Ax
James	(S)	13	M	Unknown	23Fe02Ax
MOUN, Patt		41	M	Laborer	23Fe02Ax
DARE, Jno.		29	M	Unknown	23Fe02Ax
Ann		22	F	Unknown	23Fe02Ax
FLEMING, Biddy		15	F	Unknown	23Fe02Ax
RAILLY, Michael		17	M	Unknown	23Fe02Ax
ODONALD, Bryan		19	M	Unknown	23Fe02Ax
MCGUINN, Biddy		19	F	Unknown	23Fe02Ax
JUDGE, J.		21	M	Unknown	23Fe02Ax
Bridget		21	F	Unknown	23Fe02Ax
ODONALD, Patt		20	M	Unknown	23Fe02Ax
MCGLENSHA, Francis		25	M	Unknown	23Fe02Ax
DURRY, Michael		47	M	Unknown	23Fe02Ax
Catherine	(W)	32	F	Unknown	23Fe02Ax
Thomas	(S)	13	M	Unknown	23Fe02Ax
Biddy	(D)	09	F	Child	23Fe02Ax
Catherine	(D)	06	F	Child	23Fe02Ax
Peggy	(D)	02	F	Child	23Fe02Ax
FLARATY, Edward		44	M	Laborer	23Fe02Ax
Mary	(W)	42	F	Unknown	23Fe02Ax
Mary	(D)	12	F	Unknown	23Fe02Ax
Catherine	(D)	11	F	Child	23Fe02Ax
Ann	(D)	10	F	Child	23Fe02Ax
SULLIVAN, Ann		15	F	Servant	23Fe02Ax
Bridget		25	F	Servant	23Fe02Ax
GUFFIN, Joseph		22	M	Laborer	23Fe02Ax
CARL, Sarah		20	F	Servant	23Fe02Ax
CONOLLY, Bridget		18	F	Cook	23Fe02Ax
ARH, Ann		18	F	Servant	23Fe02Ax
FLYNN, Mo		30	M	Blacksmith	23Fe02Ax
CONROY, James		25	M	Laborer	23Fe02Ax
MORAN, James		29	M	Laborer	23Fe02Ax
ARMITAGE, Martha		23	F	Weaver	23Fe02Ax
Sarah	(D)	02	F	Child	23Fe02Ax
HOLT, James		25	M	Wool Comber	23Fe02Ax
Ann		24	F	Unknown	23Fe02Ax
FOSTER, Margaret		25	F	Unknown	23Fe02Ax
William		12	M	Unknown	23Fe02Ax
Robt.		01	M	Child	23Fe02Ax
GREEN, Ralph		25	M	Butcher	23Fe02Ax
MORRIS, Isaac		26	M	Laborer	23Fe02Ax
DOWNEY, Thomas		50	M	Unknown	23Fe02Ax
Johanna	(W)	48	F	Unknown	23Fe02Ax
James	(S)	20	M	Unknown	23Fe02Ax
John	(S)	15	M	Unknown	23Fe02Ax
Eliza	(D)	13	F	Unknown	23Fe02Ax
GUST, Saml.		20	M	Flock Maker	23Fe02Ax
BURNES, Arthur		20	M	Weaver	23Fe02Ax
Eliza-Jane	(W)	22	F	Unknown	23Fe02Ax
Ellen	(D)	03	F	Child	23Fe02Ax
REYNOLDS, Mary		26	F	Unknown	23Fe02Ax
KIRKWOOK, John		20	M	Unknown	23Fe02Ax
MOORE, John		29	M	Tailor	23Fe02Ax
MELOY, Michael		20	M	Laborer	23Fe02Ax
DONOHO, James		25	M	Laborer	23Fe02Ax
FLYNN, John		26	M	Laborer	23Fe02Ax
Bridget	(W)	26	F	Unknown	23Fe02Ax
Michael	(S)	02	M	Child	23Fe02Ax
MAWLAHA, Peter		20	M	Laborer	23Fe02Ax
Mary	(W)	20	F	Unknown	23Fe02Ax
Peter	(S)	.03	M	Infant	23Fe02Ax
KILDARE, Ricd.		21	M	Laborer	23Fe02Ax
Mary		20	F	Unknown	23Fe02Ax
BRANNAN, Edwd.		30	M	Laborer	23Fe02Ax
Ann	(W)	30	F	Unknown	23Fe02Ax
John	(S)	06	M	Child	23Fe02Ax
Mary	(D)	05	F	Child	23Fe02Ax
Michael	(S)	.07	M	Infant	23Fe02Ax
DONALD, Anthony		28	M	Laborer	23Fe02Ax
MCCLUSKY, Thos.		25	M	Laborer	23Fe02Ax
BURNES, James		28	M	Laborer	23Fe02Ax
KENNY, Mary		50	F	Laborer	23Fe02Ax
Catherine		20	F	Laborer	23Fe02Ax
LOYINS, Mary		09	F	Child	23Fe02Ax
Pat		03	M	Child	23Fe02Ax
QUIRK, Mary		30	F	Laborer	23Fe02Ax
DONALD, Margaret		24	F	Laborer	23Fe02Ax
QUIE, Catherine		26	F	Laborer	23Fe02Ax
JOHNSON, James		30	M	Laborer	23Fe02Ax
QUIE, James		28	M	Laborer	23Fe02Ax
GALAHA, Owen		24	M	Unknown	23Fe02Ax
MCCAN, Tully		19	M	Laborer	23Fe02Ax
SOFTIER, Patt		21	M	Unknown	23Fe02Ax
MCGUIN, Cather.		19	F	Laborer	23Fe02Ax
Mary		18	F	Unknown	23Fe02Ax
MARKEY, Michael		65	M	Laborer	23Fe02Ax
Patt	(S)	34	M	Unknown	23Fe02Ax
John	(S)	21	M	Unknown	23Fe02Ax
Catherine	(D)	20	F	Unknown	23Fe02Ax
Bridget	(D)	14	F	Unknown	23Fe02Ax
Ann	(D)	12	F	Unknown	23Fe02Ax
SMITH, Bryan		21	M	Laborer	23Fe02Ax
NEVEN, John		37	M	Laborer	23Fe02Ax
MCCABE, Henry		19	M	Unknown	23Fe02Ax
HOGG, Ann		30	F	Laborer	23Fe02Ax
FTIZSIMMONS, Philip		40	M	Laborer	23Fe02Ax
FARRLY, Peter		26	M	Laborer	23Fe02Ax
QULLUM, Philip		30	M	Laborer	23Fe02Ax
SMITH, James		25	M	Laborer	23Fe02Ax
LYNCH, Patt		25	M	Unknown	23Fe02Ax
GRIFFIN, John		28	M	Carpenter	23Fe02Ax
MARTIN, James		22	M	Unknown	23Fe02Ax
DONAHUE, John		28	M	Unknown	23Fe02Ax
DERMILY, John		40	M	Unknown	23Fe02Ax
Biddy	(W)	32	F	Unknown	23Fe02Ax
Michael	(S)	09	M	Child	23Fe02Ax
Catherine	(D)	08	F	Child	23Fe02Ax
Bridget	(D)	06	F	Child	23Fe02Ax
Thomas	(S)	03	M	Child	23Fe02Ax
DONOHUE, W.		18	U	Unknown	23Fe02Ax
CONLIN, Ellen		20	F	Unknown	23Fe02Ax
Bridget		18	F	Unknown	23Fe02Ax
CARR, Margaret		40	F	Unknown	23Fe02Ax
Condy		15	U	Unknown	23Fe02Ax
Ann	(D)	12	F	Unknown	23Fe02Ax
Grace	(D)	10	F	Child	23Fe02Ax
FLARATY, John		07	M	Child	23Fe02Ax
Pat		03	M	Child	23Fe02Ax
Margaret		01	F	Child	23Fe02Ax
HAWTHORNE, Adam		36	M	Unknown	23Fe02Ax
GILBURKE, Philip		21	M	Unknown	23Fe02Ax
COLEN, Terence		25	M	Unknown	23Fe02Ax
CHARLES, M.		21	U	Unknown	23Fe02Ax
MCCORMICK, Catherine		33	F	Unknown	23Fe02Ax
Patt	(S)	12	M	Unknown	23Fe02Ax
Thomas	(S)	10	M	Child	23Fe02Ax
Barney	(S)	09	M	Child	23Fe02Ax
John	(S)	05	M	Child	23Fe02Ax
Rose	(D)	02	F	Child	23Fe02Ax
CONNOR, John		25	M	Unknown	23Fe02Ax
KEENAR, James		21	M	Unknown	23Fe02Ax
CLARK, Bridget		32	F	Unknown	23Fe02Ax
WATHUNE, W.		17	M	Shoemaker	23Fe02Ax
JADES, Thos.		13	M	Unknown	23Fe02Ax
MCCORMICK, Jno.		17	M	Unknown	23Fe02Ax
WOODS, Jno.		20	M	Laborer	23Fe02Ax
MULLEY, Peter		14	M	Unknown	23Fe02Ax
KELLY, Mo		21	M	Laborer	23Fe02Ax

NAMES OF PASSENGERS	REL	AGE	SEX	OCCUPATION	DATE PORT SHIP
MALLOY, James		20	M	Laborer	23Fe02Ax

EUROPE 24 FEBRUARY 1847

From Liverpool

NAMES OF PASSENGERS	REL	AGE	SEX	OCCUPATION	DATE PORT SHIP
MOON, John		39	M	Laborer	24Fe02BI
U	(W)	30	F	Laborer	24Fe02BI
PHELAM, Phelam		05	U	Child	24Fe02BI
BARLOW, William		24	M	Laborer	24Fe02BI
GADDIS, John		44	M	Laborer	24Fe02BI
U	(W)	40	F	Laborer	24Fe02BI
James	(S)	18	M	Laborer	24Fe02BI
William	(S)	12	M	Laborer	24Fe02BI
Martha	(D)	07	F	Child	24Fe02BI
Ellsabeth	(D)	10	F	Child	24Fe02BI
John	(S)	08	M	Child	24Fe02BI
Samuel	(S)	03	M	Child	24Fe02BI
Margaret	(D)	.00	F	Infant	24Fe02BI
RADCLIFF, Samuel		30	M	Laborer	24Fe02BI
STEWART, William		30	M	Laborer	24Fe02BI
WEIGHT, John		12	M	Laborer	24Fe02BI
Cuphuma		14	U	Laborer	24Fe02BI
HUNT, Thomas		26	M	Laborer	24Fe02BI
MOON, Thomas		20	M	Laborer	24Fe02BI
MCDARMINT, Kelley		19	M	Laborer	24Fe02BI
MOORE, Jane		18	F	Laborer	24Fe02BI
SNANY, Biddy		20	F	Laborer	24Fe02BI
MULLAN, Michael		19	M	Laborer	24Fe02BI
BURN, John		26	M	Laborer	24Fe02BI
U	(W)	19	F	Laborer	24Fe02BI
James	(S)	01	M	Child	24Fe02BI
MOONEY, John		34	M	Laborer	24Fe02BI
U	(W)	28	F	Laborer	24Fe02BI
Ann	(D)	02	F	Child	24Fe02BI
CARROLL, Arthur		30	M	Laborer	24Fe02BI
BURN, James		23	M	Laborer	24Fe02BI
SHEA, Ellen		23	F	Laborer	24Fe02BI
CORCUAN, Ely		18	M	Laborer	24Fe02BI
GILHODY, John		21	M	Laborer	24Fe02BI
MCHANASAN, Jane		21	F	Laborer	24Fe02BI
SMITH, Byron		20	M	Laborer	24Fe02BI
Bridget		20	F	Laborer	24Fe02BI
KINNEY, John		19	M	Laborer	24Fe02BI
KING, Michael		20	M	Laborer	24Fe02BI
Mary		10	F	Child	24Fe02BI
Nancy		24	F	Laborer	24Fe02BI
FOX, Bryan		22	M	Laborer	24Fe02BI
CARBONY, Michael		24	M	Laborer	24Fe02BI
VAUGHN, Ann		20	F	Laborer	24Fe02BI
GALEIN, Margret		20	F	Laborer	24Fe02BI
RIAD, William		24	M	Laborer	24Fe02BI
COLOHM, John		24	M	Laborer	24Fe02BI
GUNAN, John		24	M	Laborer	24Fe02BI
GILLIN, Jane		20	F	Laborer	24Fe02BI
SABMAN, John		36	M	Laborer	24Fe02BI
WHITE, Thomas		28	M	Laborer	24Fe02BI
U	(W)	20	F	Laborer	24Fe02BI
Stephen		18	M	Laborer	24Fe02BI
Mary	(D)	02	F	Child	24Fe02BI
MARSHALL, George		30	M	Laborer	24Fe02BI
U	(W)	27	F	Laborer	24Fe02BI
MCDERRMOT, Regin		30	U	Laborer	24Fe02BI
BURNLY, James		21	M	Laborer	24Fe02BI
KING, Catherine		40	F	Laborer	24Fe02BI
Catherine		25	F	Laborer	24Fe02BI
Luke		10	M	Child	24Fe02BI
Mary		24	F	Laborer	24Fe02BI
John		24	M	Laborer	24Fe02BI
U, Pat		24	M	Laborer	24Fe02BI
MCLAUGHIN, John		20	M	Laborer	24Fe02BI
Catherine		18	F	Laborer	24Fe02BI
BOYD, Andrew		19	M	Laborer	24Fe02BI
WEATHERTON, John		34	M	Laborer	24Fe02BI
U	(W)	30	F	Laborer	24Fe02BI
MOONLONT, Alexander		30	M	Laborer	24Fe02BI
SYNCH, Margret		20	F	Laborer	24Fe02BI
WHITTY, James		20	M	Laborer	24Fe02BI
GALVIN, Thomas		24	M	Laborer	24Fe02BI
Ells.		20	F	Laborer	24Fe02BI
DRONVY, Timothy		20	M	Laborer	24Fe02BI
U	(W)	20	F	Laborer	24Fe02BI
Michael		08	M	Child	24Fe02BI
James		04	M	Child	24Fe02BI
Thomas		.00	M	Infant	24Fe02BI
CARNEY, Ann		12	F	Laborer	24Fe02BI
BEABY, Bridget		20	F	Laborer	24Fe02BI
FLYNG, Dennis		20	M	Laborer	24Fe02BI
John		30	M	Laborer	24Fe02BI
Elyn		20	M	Laborer	24Fe02BI
RUFLIRY, Thomas		18	M	Laborer	24Fe02BI
MURREY, Michael		29	M	Laborer	24Fe02BI
GRIFFIN, Anthy.		18	M	Laborer	24Fe02BI
MURREY, John		21	M	Laborer	24Fe02BI
MUSKEY, John		26	M	Laborer	24Fe02BI
SEARN, Michael		20	M	Laborer	24Fe02BI
KILLIAM, James		50	M	Laborer	24Fe02BI
John		14	M	Laborer	24Fe02BI
Mary		22	F	Laborer	24Fe02BI
Catherine		20	F	Laborer	24Fe02BI
FLATTEY, Pat		24	M	Laborer	24Fe02BI
U	(W)	24	F	Laborer	24Fe02BI
SHERIDAN, Thomas		21	M	Laborer	24Fe02BI
Mary		17	F	Laborer	24Fe02BI
GARNAN, John		36	M	Laborer	24Fe02BI
U	(W)	26	F	Laborer	24Fe02BI
SMITH, Michael		13	M	Laborer	24Fe02BI
FITZPATRICK, James		38	M	Laborer	24Fe02BI
Thomas		40	M	Laborer	24Fe02BI
COMILLY, Pat		40	M	Laborer	24Fe02BI
QUIN, Fredrick		30	M	Laborer	24Fe02BI
Thomas		25	M	Laborer	24Fe02BI
MACON, Mathew		30	M	Laborer	24Fe02BI
QUIN, Mary		19	F	Laborer	24Fe02BI
WILSON, Nathan		40	M	Laborer	24Fe02BI
MAY, Biddy		26	F	Laborer	24Fe02BI
BOYD, John		19	M	Laborer	24Fe02BI
MCGARTH, Fredrick		20	M	Laborer	24Fe02BI
SHAILS, James		24	M	Laborer	24Fe02BI
WOODS, Jane		32	F	Laborer	24Fe02BI
Mary	(D)	08	F	Child	24Fe02BI
William	(S)	04	M	Child	24Fe02BI
PADLOW, Susan		40	F	Laborer	24Fe02BI
James	(S)	23	M	Laborer	24Fe02BI
Richard	(S)	20	M	Laborer	24Fe02BI
Joseph	(S)	18	M	Laborer	24Fe02BI
Thomas	(S)	13	M	Laborer	24Fe02BI
Edwin	(S)	11	M	Child	24Fe02BI
Sarah	(D)	09	F	Child	24Fe02BI
WILKINS, William		36	M	Laborer	24Fe02BI
Isabella	(W)	30	F	Laborer	24Fe02BI
Francis	(S)	10	M	Child	24Fe02BI
Samuel	(S)	08	M	Child	24Fe02BI
William	(S)	03	M	Child	24Fe02BI
Ellsabeth	(D)	02	F	Child	24Fe02BI
ODONNEL, Charles		25	M	Laborer	24Fe02BI
HAGERTY, Pat		40	M	Laborer	24Fe02BI
QUIN, James		17	M	Laborer	24Fe02BI
BURN, Michael		39	M	Laborer	24Fe02BI
HALL, Henry		09	M	Child	24Fe02BI
Thomas		21	M	Laborer	24Fe02BI
COYLE, Mary		35	F	Laborer	24Fe02BI
Mary	(D)	11	F	Child	24Fe02BI
HORTON, William		29	M	Laborer	24Fe02BI

NAMES OF PASSENGERS		A G E	S E X	OCCUPATIONS	DATE PORT SHIP	NAMES OF PASSENGERS		A G E	S E X	OCCUPATIONS	DATE PORT SHIP
HORTON, Alice		18	F	Laborer	24Fe02BI						
CALLONHORN, Michael		20	M	Laborer	24Fe02BI						
MCCANNA, James		22	M	Laborer	24Fe02BI						
MCWALLEN, James		20	M	Laborer	24Fe02BI						
Catherine		13	F	Laborer	24Fe02BI						
DARBY, Darby		30	U	Laborer	24Fe02BI		**HYNDERFORD 24 FEBRUARY 1847**				
KANE, Thomas-H.		25	M	Laborer	24Fe02BI						
Susan	(W)	24	F	Laborer	24Fe02BI		**From Liverpool**				
Thomas	(S)	.00	M	Infant	24Fe02BI						
CULLING, Pat		35	M	Laborer	24Fe02BI						
Catherine	(W)	30	F	Laborer	24Fe02BI	FYE, Michael		47	M	Laborer	24Fe02KI
John	(S)	12	M	Laborer	24Fe02BI	MICHELL, Patrick		47	M	Laborer	24Fe02KI
Michael	(S)	10	M	Child	24Fe02BI	DOLAN, Mary		30	F	Unknown	24Fe02KI
Michael	(S)	08	M	Child	24Fe02BI	Cathn.		02	F	Child	24Fe02KI
Biddy	(D)	.00	F	Infant	24Fe02BI	KEAN, Margaret		20	F	Unknown	24Fe02KI
HARRIGALL, John		37	M	Laborer	24Fe02BI	DINNAHU, Bridget		20	F	Unknown	24Fe02KI
MCCAFEY, Larry		18	M	Laborer	24Fe02BI	Catharine		18	F	Unknown	24Fe02KI
Eleanor		10	F	Child	24Fe02BI	HASSAN, Pat.		38	M	Laborer	24Fe02KI
SHERIDAN, Catherine		20	F	Laborer	24Fe02BI	HEMY, Bernard		20	M	Laborer	24Fe02KI
RILEY, Kitty		19	F	Laborer	24Fe02BI	KELLY, Francis		20	M	Laborer	24Fe02KI
MCCANNA, Mary		20	F	Laborer	24Fe02BI	BRADLY, Mary		20	F	Unknown	24Fe02KI
SMITH, Pat		25	M	Laborer	24Fe02BI	OAKS, John		40	M	Unknown	24Fe02KI
MCCANNA, Thomas		14	M	Laborer	24Fe02BI	Cathn.	(W)	40	F	Unknown	24Fe02KI
SHERIDAN, James		20	M	Laborer	24Fe02BI	Rose	(D)	20	F	Unknown	24Fe02KI
DOWD, Mary		10	F	Child	24Fe02BI	May	(D)	18	F	Unknown	24Fe02KI
JOHNSON, George		21	M	Laborer	24Fe02BI	Ann	(D)	13	F	Unknown	24Fe02KI
NORSE, Francis		17	M	Laborer	24Fe02BI	Cathn.	(D)	11	F	Child	24Fe02KI
HAMINGTON, Josepth		27	M	Laborer	24Fe02BI	Betty	(D)	09	F	Child	24Fe02KI
John		15	M	Laborer	24Fe02BI	James	(S)	13	M	Unknown	24Fe02KI
Mary		12	F	Laborer	24Fe02BI	WILLIAMS, David		18	M	Laborer	24Fe02KI
CHANRY, Lucinda		18	F	Laborer	24Fe02BI	John		20	M	Laborer	24Fe02KI
FINNEY, Bridget		20	F	Laborer	24Fe02BI	GILLIGAN, Peter		25	M	Laborer	24Fe02KI
MOSS, Pat		01	M	Child	24Fe02BI	Ann		24	F	Unknown	24Fe02KI
TULLY, Hugh		21	M	Laborer	24Fe02BI	MURRAY, Francis		36	M	Laborer	24Fe02KI
DONAHUE, Bridget		18	F	Laborer	24Fe02BI	MCGERUN, Thos.		28	M	Laborer	24Fe02KI
CALAGHAN, Sir		20	M	Laborer	24Fe02BI	MCLAUGHLIN, Mary		30	F	Unknown	24Fe02KI
NOUGHTOM, John		50	M	Laborer	24Fe02BI	WHITE, Cathn.		18	F	Unknown	24Fe02KI
BANSFIELD, Elisabeth		19	F	Laborer	24Fe02BI	MULLOUNY, Jams.		24	M	Unknown	24Fe02KI
SHERIDAN, Richard		14	M	Laborer	24Fe02BI	MULLOCINER, Mary		24	F	Unknown	24Fe02KI
Catherine		11	F	Child	24Fe02BI	SMITH, Thos.		18	M	Unknown	24Fe02KI
MCCORNISH, Margret		19	F	Laborer	24Fe02BI	COMY, Margaret		18	F	Unknown	24Fe02KI
EDWARDS, John		18	M	Laborer	24Fe02BI	CLARK, Bridget		18	F	Unknown	24Fe02KI
Pat		08	M	Child	24Fe02BI	MCGREHAN, Thos.		20	M	Laborer	24Fe02KI
Bridget		06	F	Child	24Fe02BI	SMITH, Wm.		43	M	Unknown	24Fe02KI
MCLAUGHLIN, Michael		22	M	Laborer	24Fe02BI	Mary	(W)	30	F	Unknown	24Fe02KI
Ellen		18	F	Laborer	24Fe02BI	John	(S)	08	M	Child	24Fe02KI
MCNARL, John		04	M	Child	24Fe02BI	Robert	(S)	04	M	Child	24Fe02KI
ONEIL, Michael		28	M	Laborer	24Fe02BI	Elizabeth	(D)	03	F	Child	24Fe02KI
Mary		10	F	Child	24Fe02BI	Wm.	(S)	.09	M	Infant	24Fe02KI
CURNAN, Margret		24	F	Laborer	24Fe02BI	DEVET, Arthur		27	M	Laborer	24Fe02KI
WHITTY, James		24	M	Laborer	24Fe02BI	TOBY, Owen		35	M	Laborer	24Fe02KI
U	(W)	24	F	Laborer	24Fe02BI	HOLUHAN, Prine		22	M	Unknown	24Fe02KI
John	(S)	05	M	Child	24Fe02BI	HALIN, John		30	M	Unknown	24Fe02KI
Mary	(D)	03	F	Child	24Fe02BI	LAMB, Wm.		27	M	Unknown	24Fe02KI
REYNOLDS, M.		24	M	Laborer	24Fe02BI	MCCANNA, Pat.		23	M	Unknown	24Fe02KI
U	(W)	30	F	Laborer	24Fe02BI	MCPHILLIPS, Thos.		30	M	Unknown	24Fe02KI
Ann	(D)	04	F	Child	24Fe02BI	PADDAN, Michael		50	M	Farmer	24Fe02KI
Pat		02	U	Child	24Fe02BI	Mary	(W)	30	F	Unknown	24Fe02KI
COMER, Mary		24	F	Laborer	24Fe02BI	Catherine	(D)	10	F	Child	24Fe02KI
FALK, Marsilia		19	F	Laborer	24Fe02BI	Pat.	(S)	06	M	Child	24Fe02KI
WELMER, Mary		18	F	Laborer	24Fe02BI	John	(S)	04	M	Child	24Fe02KI
Catherine	(D)	.00	F	Infant	24Fe02BI	Michael	(S)	.10	M	Infant	24Fe02KI
MARSHALL, Sunis		27	U	Laborer	24Fe02BI	Biddy		16	F	Unknown	24Fe02KI
SMITH, Ruben		38	M	Laborer	24Fe02BI	HART, Martin		28	M	Laborer	24Fe02KI
Elisa		08	F	Child	24Fe02BI	CARROLL, Wm.		20	M	Laborer	24Fe02KI
Margret		05	F	Child	24Fe02BI	MURRAY, Thos.		18	M	Laborer	24Fe02KI
Mary		02	F	Child	24Fe02BI	RYAN, Thady		18	M	Laborer	24Fe02KI
GALAGAN, Pat		24	U	Laborer	24Fe02BI	GIBBINS, Thos.		30	M	Laborer	24Fe02KI
SWEITNER, Sarny		30	U	Laborer	24Fe02BI	MCGLAUGHLIN, Michael		30	M	Laborer	24Fe02KI
BUCK, John		29	M	Laborer	24Fe02BI						
HUGHS, Michael		31	M	Laborer	24Fe02BI						
MANSFIELD, George		00	M	Unknown	24Fe02BI						
FULLER, John		00	M	Unknown	24Fe02BI						
WOOD, Israel		00	M	Unknown	24Fe02BI						
Silas		00	M	Unknown	24Fe02BI						

MARMION 24 FEBRUARY 1847

From Liverpool

NAMES OF PASSENGERS	AGE	SEX	OCCUPATIONS	DATE PORT SHIP
JUST, Louisa-Augusta	63	F	Unknown	24Fe02Hc
COUTSTON, George-R.J.	23	M	Gentleman	24Fe02Hc
TEMPLEMAN, Robert-R.	16	M	Gentleman	24Fe02Hc
BYRNE, John	54	M	Weaver	24Fe02Hc
Ann (W)	54	F	Unknown	24Fe02Hc
Bridget (D)	24	F	Dressmaker	24Fe02Hc
Mary (D)	21	F	Milliner	24Fe02Hc
Ann (D)	10	F	None	24Fe02Hc
WHITE, Catherine	18	F	Servant	24Fe02Hc
HARNEY, William	22	M	Laborer	24Fe02Hc
MCCORMICK, Danl.	42	M	Laborer	24Fe02Hc
Mary (W)	40	F	None	24Fe02Hc
Mary (D)	12	F	None	24Fe02Hc
Danl. (S)	08	M	Child	24Fe02Hc
Ann (D)	07	F	Child	24Fe02Hc
Pat (S)	01	M	Child	24Fe02Hc
Biddy (D)	04	F	Child	24Fe02Hc
KILLEAN, Francis	18	M	Laborer	24Fe02Hc
THORNTON, John	30	M	Shoemaker	24Fe02Hc
Pat.	18	M	Laborer	24Fe02Hc
FAHER, T.	28	M	Laborer	24Fe02Hc
KINNEY, Edward	33	M	Laborer	24Fe02Hc
NEEDHAM, John	18	M	Laborer	24Fe02Hc
RAILEY, Jane	18	F	Servant	24Fe02Hc
LARKIN, Mary	19	F	Servant	24Fe02Hc
FARRELL, John	25	M	Tailor	24Fe02Hc
MACK, Thomas	30	M	Laborer	24Fe02Hc
Judy	28	F	None	24Fe02Hc
CAUNAVAN, Pat.	22	M	Laborer	24Fe02Hc
HANLEY, Michael	20	M	Laborer	24Fe02Hc
NOLLAN, Thomas	20	M	Laborer	24Fe02Hc
CAMPBELL, William	19	M	Laborer	24Fe02Hc
CALLE, Anthony	24	M	Laborer	24Fe02Hc
ODONALD, Conn	20	M	Laborer	24Fe02Hc
Ann	13	F	Servant	24Fe02Hc
GALLAGHER, Michael	14	M	Sailor	24Fe02Hc
BRANNAN, John	22	M	Laborer	24Fe02Hc
HUSTEN, Michael	21	M	Laborer	24Fe02Hc
ODONALD, Dennis	20	M	Laborer	24Fe02Hc
FOSTER, Archd.	45	M	Laborer	24Fe02Hc
Ann	45	F	None	24Fe02Hc
Margaret	30	F	Dressmaker	24Fe02Hc
Margaret	13	F	Dressmaker	24Fe02Hc
John	11	M	None	24Fe02Hc
Mary-Ann	07	F	Child	24Fe02Hc
Jane	05	F	Child	24Fe02Hc
Susan	02	F	Child	24Fe02Hc
CHAPMAN, Francis	22	M	Laborer	24Fe02Hc
MACADAMS, Richd.	16	M	Laborer	24Fe02Hc
MACDONALD, Mary	30	F	Servant	24Fe02Hc
KING, Jane	30	F	Servant	24Fe02Hc
George	01	M	Child	24Fe02Hc
TRAVIS, Owen	47	M	Weaver	24Fe02Hc
Patk.	17	M	Laborer	24Fe02Hc
HARRISON, Anthony	60	M	Carpenter	24Fe02Hc
Anthony (S)	22	M	Carpenter	24Fe02Hc
John (S)	20	M	Carpenter	24Fe02Hc
Kitty (D)	18	F	Servant	24Fe02Hc
Bridget (W)	60	F	None	24Fe02Hc
MACQUIRE, John	23	M	Laborer	24Fe02Hc
Biddy	22	F	None	24Fe02Hc
FORD, Thomas	40	M	Laborer	24Fe02Hc
Bridget (W)	34	F	None	24Fe02Hc
James (S)	10	M	None	24Fe02Hc
Thomas (S)	07	M	Child	24Fe02Hc
FORD, Ann (D)	05	F	Child	24Fe02Hc
Helen (D)	02	F	Child	24Fe02Hc
MACCORMICK, Michael	25	M	Shoemaker	24Fe02Hc
DONELLY, James	24	M	Laborer	24Fe02Hc
DURRIN, John	24	M	Laborer	24Fe02Hc
Pat.	21	M	Clerk	24Fe02Hc
CAFFLEY, Bernard	18	M	Laborer	24Fe02Hc
Mary	24	F	Servant	24Fe02Hc
MACCORMICK, Bernard	30	M	Laborer	24Fe02Hc
Ann (W)	24	F	None	24Fe02Hc
Mary	16	F	Servant	24Fe02Hc
Thomas (S)	03	M	Child	24Fe02Hc
Betsy (D)	01	F	Child	24Fe02Hc
MOIR, John	21	M	Laborer	24Fe02Hc
Thomas	19	M	Laborer	24Fe02Hc
Jane	16	F	Servant	24Fe02Hc
SHARP, George	24	M	Farmer	24Fe02Hc
Cathn. (W)	22	F	None	24Fe02Hc
Mary-Ann (D)	04	F	Child	24Fe02Hc
William (S)	02	M	Child	24Fe02Hc
MORTON, Charlotte	23	F	Milliner	24Fe02Hc
ODONNELL, Catherine	50	F	None	24Fe02Hc
Mary	19	F	Servant	24Fe02Hc
Sarah	07	F	Child	24Fe02Hc
HALLEY, James	19	M	Farmer	24Fe02Hc
Elizabeth	22	F	Servant	24Fe02Hc
CORIGAN, Michael	31	M	Laborer	24Fe02Hc
Mary	23	F	None	24Fe02Hc
SCOLLEN, Ann	22	F	Servant	24Fe02Hc
MACKAIRNEY, Dennis	28	M	Servant	24Fe02Hc
Ann (W)	24	F	Unknown	24Fe02Hc
Mary (D)	05	F	Child	24Fe02Hc
Frank (S)	01	M	Child	24Fe02Hc
HADEN, Judith	18	F	Servant	24Fe02Hc
WILLIAMSON, William	21	M	Laborer	24Fe02Hc
MACNAMARA, James	26	M	Laborer	24Fe02Hc
WISE, Jane	18	F	Servant	24Fe02Hc
RATTIGAN, Thomas	45	M	Laborer	24Fe02Hc
Mary (W)	40	F	None	24Fe02Hc
Thomas (S)	17	M	Laborer	24Fe02Hc
GRADY, Jane	30	F	Servant	24Fe02Hc
RATTIGAN, Edward	12	M	None	24Fe02Hc
Pat. (B)	10	M	None	24Fe02Hc
John (B)	07	M	Child	24Fe02Hc
Helen (T)	02	F	Child	24Fe02Hc
FAGAN, John	27	M	Grocer	24Fe02Hc
BRANNEN, Peter	28	M	Laborer	24Fe02Hc
Michael	26	M	Laborer	24Fe02Hc
Marcella	30	F	None	24Fe02Hc
ALLEN, William	24	M	Laborer	24Fe02Hc
COMLY, William	22	M	Laborer	24Fe02Hc
STAKING, Mathew	21	M	Laborer	24Fe02Hc
Catherine	18	F	Servant	24Fe02Hc
Judy	18	F	Servant	24Fe02Hc
HEART, Mary	19	F	Servant	24Fe02Hc
DURAS, Bridget	18	F	Servant	24Fe02Hc
CALLEGHAN, John	20	M	Laborer	24Fe02Hc
RALLEY, John	40	M	Laborer	24Fe02Hc
Marcella (W)	35	F	None	24Fe02Hc
John (S)	04	M	Child	24Fe02Hc
Helen (D)	02	F	Child	24Fe02Hc
HEATH, John	30	M	Shoemaker	24Fe02Hc
WINN, Patrick	22	M	Laborer	24Fe02Hc
BYRNE, Thomas	17	M	Stableman	24Fe02Hc
BALFOUR, Moses	60	M	Farmer	24Fe02Hc
Dally	55	F	None	24Fe02Hc
MCBRIEN, William	28	M	Grocer	24Fe02Hc
Sarah (W)	24	F	None	24Fe02Hc
Moses (S)	04	M	Child	24Fe02Hc
Jane (D)	01	F	Child	24Fe02Hc
MCMINUS, James	32	M	Laborer	24Fe02Hc
MCGORRELL, John	32	M	Laborer	24Fe02Hc
MCMINUS, Mary	22	F	None	24Fe02Hc
CODEY, Michael	21	M	Laborer	24Fe02Hc
ROUKE, John	19	M	Laborer	24Fe02Hc

NAMES OF PASSENGERS		AGE	SEX	OCCUPATIONS	DATE PORT SHIP
DOYLE, Pat.		26	M	Laborer	24Fe02Hc
WELCH, Margaret		18	F	Servant	24Fe02Hc
LARKIN, Pat		32	M	Painter	24Fe02Hc
Bridget		13	F	None	24Fe02Hc
Helen		09	F	Child	24Fe02Hc
NOGHOE, Bridget		07	F	Child	24Fe02Hc
RYAN, Timothy		34	M	Laborer	24Fe02Hc
GLEASON, Michael		33	M	Laborer	24Fe02Hc
BLAIR, John		40	M	Mason	24Fe02Hc
Jane	(W)	39	F	None	24Fe02Hc
Mary	(D)	20	F	Servant	24Fe02Hc
Jane	(D)	18	F	Servant	24Fe02Hc
John	(S)	17	M	Mason	24Fe02Hc
Ann	(D)	11	F	None	24Fe02Hc
Isabella	(D)	09	F	Child	24Fe02Hc
Sarah	(D)	06	F	Child	24Fe02Hc
Martha	(D)	04	F	Child	24Fe02Hc
William	(S)	03	M	Child	24Fe02Hc
BLAKE, Philip		66	M	Laborer	24Fe02Hc
Thomas	(S)	23	M	Laborer	24Fe02Hc
William	(S)	25	M	Laborer	24Fe02Hc
Ann		25	F	None	24Fe02Hc
Mary		28	F	None	24Fe02Hc
Mary		03	F	Child	24Fe02Hc
Bridget		02	F	Child	24Fe02Hc
Ann		01	F	Child	24Fe02Hc
WELCH, Ann		08	F	Child	24Fe02Hc
ADAMS, Mary		54	F	None	24Fe02Hc
LORENS, Peget		29	F	Dressmaker	24Fe02Hc
Robert	(S)	08	M	Child	24Fe02Hc
Ann	(D)	06	F	Child	24Fe02Hc
Jane	(D)	04	F	Child	24Fe02Hc
Catherine	(D)	01	F	Child	24Fe02Hc
PATTON, William		21	M	Laborer	24Fe02Hc
HORENS, Edward		24	M	Laborer	24Fe02Hc
FURLONG, Pat.		40	M	Laborer	24Fe02Hc
Helen	(W)	40	F	None	24Fe02Hc
William	(S)	09	M	Child	24Fe02Hc
JOHNSTONE, Edward		30	M	Smith	24Fe02Hc
DONOHUGE, Pat.		31	M	Laborer	24Fe02Hc
WAUGH, James		28	M	Carpenter	24Fe02Hc
Rose		26	F	None	24Fe02Hc
BYRNE, John		26	M	Gdnr	24Fe02Hc
FARRELL, James		26	M	Laborer	24Fe02Hc
KENNEDY, Pat.		25	M	Laborer	24Fe02Hc
KAILING, Michael		24	M	Servant	24Fe02Hc
Catherine		21	F	Servant	24Fe02Hc
HEFFRON, Michael		21	M	Grocer	24Fe02Hc
Catherine		20	F	None	24Fe02Hc
TRACEY, Honor		28	F	Servant	24Fe02Hc
WRIGHT, James		30	M	Laborer	24Fe02Hc
MCCOY, Pat.		21	M	Barber	24Fe02Hc
WELCH, Edward		21	M	Laborer	24Fe02Hc
BALFE, George		24	M	Physician	24Fe02Hc
Joseph		18	M	Physician	24Fe02Hc
DELADY, Mary		20	F	Servant	24Fe02Hc
MOLLAGAN, William		26	M	Laborer	24Fe02Hc
FLOOD, Peter		30	M	Laborer	24Fe02Hc
KEARNEN, Peter		28	M	Laborer	24Fe02Hc
KILGRACE, Francis		22	M	Weaver	24Fe02Hc
FLOOD, John		24	M	Laborer	24Fe02Hc
Catherine		20	F	None	24Fe02Hc
BROWN, Mary		20	F	Laborer	24Fe02Hc
CAPLA, Helen		50	F	None	24Fe02Hc
Ian	(S)	24	M	Laborer	24Fe02Hc
James	(S)	22	M	Laborer	24Fe02Hc
Pat.	(S)	17	M	Laborer	24Fe02Hc
Mary	(D)	11	F	None	24Fe02Hc
DOWNS, Biddy		20	F	Servant	24Fe02Hc
Biddy	(D)	.00	F	Infant	24Fe02Hc
Born-At-Sea					
RIDDEN, Daniel		24	M	Slater	24Fe02Hc
Hannah		25	F	Dressmaker	24Fe02Hc
DOUNEN, Michael		20	M	Clerk	24Fe02Hc
BERRY, John		24	M	Laborer	24Fe02Hc

NAMES OF PASSENGERS		AGE	SEX	OCCUPATIONS	DATE PORT SHIP
GREEN, Helen		21	F	None	24Fe02Hc
Timothy		19	M	Laborer	24Fe02Hc
MOLLAGAN, Mary		14	F	Servant	24Fe02Hc
MAIFFOR, Edward		21	M	Shoemaker	24Fe02Hc
BEYLON, Edward		45	M	Laborer	24Fe02Hc
Ann	(W)	40	F	None	24Fe02Hc
Mary	(D)	17	F	None	24Fe02Hc
Peter	(S)	17	M	None	24Fe02Hc
James	(S)	13	M	None	24Fe02Hc
Pat	(S)	11	M	None	24Fe02Hc
Ann	(D)	06	F	Child	24Fe02Hc
Bridget	(D)	01	F	Child	24Fe02Hc
CONNEY, Danl.		33	M	Laborer	24Fe02Hc
Mary		09	F	Child	24Fe02Hc
Catherine		07	F	Child	24Fe02Hc
CURGHEN, Catherine		30	F	Dressmaker	24Fe02Hc
MANGAN, William		18	M	Laborer	24Fe02Hc
DEVILIN, Jane		20	F	Unknown	24Fe02Hc
CLUGHIN, Ann		20	F	Servant	24Fe02Hc
LUNNEY, Michael		21	M	Stableman	24Fe02Hc
CLORNAN, Nancy		26	F	Servant	24Fe02Hc
BRADDY, Thomas		25	M	Laborer	24Fe02Hc
COYLE, Mary		21	F	Laborer	24Fe02Hc
GREEN, Mary		28	F	Servant	24Fe02Hc
FINNEGAN, John		20	M	Laborer	24Fe02Hc
Ann		15	F	None	24Fe02Hc
Barny		10	M	None	24Fe02Hc
Pat.		09	M	Child	24Fe02Hc
Thomas		05	M	Child	24Fe02Hc
Ann		45	F	None	24Fe02Hc
SMITH, Henry		34	M	Carpenter	24Fe02Hc
Bridget		24	F	None	24Fe02Hc
MCINTRYE, Sally		22	F	Servant	24Fe02Hc
CRAWFORD, Charles		35	M	Cooper	24Fe02Hc

THETIS 25 FEBRUARY 1847

From Belfast

NAMES OF PASSENGERS		AGE	SEX	OCCUPATIONS	DATE PORT SHIP
GONEGALL, William		21	M	Cooper	25Fe07Ae
MCCORMICK, William		25	M	Cooper	25Fe07Ae
Catherine		23	F	Wife	25Fe07Ae
DUNCAN, Alexander		28	M	Cooper	25Fe07Ae
Margaret	(W)	25	F	Wife	25Fe07Ae
Elizabeth		23	F	None	25Fe07Ae
KELLY, John		21	M	Farmer	25Fe07Ae
MCGLADEN, Eliza		18	F	Spinster	25Fe07Ae
MULLIGAN, Anne		40	F	Spinster	25Fe07Ae
BOYLE, Ellen		20	F	Spinster	25Fe07Ae
GORMON, Michael		22	M	Cooper	25Fe07Ae
CHAPMAN, Margaret		40	F	Wife	25Fe07Ae
Thos.	(S)	21	M	None	25Fe07Ae
Catherine	(D)	17	F	None	25Fe07Ae
John	(S)	13	M	None	25Fe07Ae
Margaret	(D)	11	F	None	25Fe07Ae
William	(S)	15	M	None	25Fe07Ae
REILLY, James		19	M	Farmer	25Fe07Ae
Margaret		15	F	Spinster	25Fe07Ae
William		13	M	None	25Fe07Ae
MCALESHER, John		48	M	Laborer	25Fe07Ae
BELL, Charles		29	M	Clerk	25Fe07Ae
James		24	M	Clerk	25Fe07Ae
Archy		22	M	Clerk	25Fe07Ae
Esther		20	F	Wife	25Fe07Ae
Eliza		20	F	Spinster	25Fe07Ae
Robert		03	M	Child	25Fe07Ae
Margaret		02	F	Child	25Fe07Ae
TURSDELL, Thomas		24	M	Cooper	25Fe07Ae
GORDEN, David		22	M	Cooper	25Fe07Ae

NAMES OF PASSENGERS	AGE	SEX	OCCUPATIONS	DATE PORT SHIP	NAMES OF PASSENGERS	AGE	SEX	OCCUPATIONS	DATE PORT SHIP
DUNN, Andrew	24	M	Cooper	25Fe07Ae					
KINKEAD, John	21	M	Cooper	25Fe07Ae					
GILLEN, James	29	M	Cooper	25Fe07Ae					
MCDONNELL, James	27	M	Cooper	25Fe07Ae	**NIAGARA 26 FEBRUARY 1847**				
HARDON, Felix	30	M	Cooper	25Fe07Ae					
MILLS, William	22	M	Cooper	25Fe07Ae	From Liverpool				
MILLIKEN, John	40	M	Cooper	25Fe07Ae					
FURGUSON, Thos.	21	M	Cooper	25Fe07Ae					
DOYLE, Patt	20	M	Cooper	25Fe07Ae					
GLOVER, Letitia	21	F	Spinster	25Fe07Ae					
BEST, Robert	22	M	Farmer	25Fe07Ae	SIMLIN, Michael	49	M	Laborer	26Fe02Ab
DUGAN, John	45	M	Farmer	25Fe07Ae	DURKIN, Bartley	22	M	Laborer	26Fe02Ab
CARLIN, Thos.	50	M	Farmer	25Fe07Ae	John	22	M	Laborer	26Fe02Ab
John	25	M	Farmer	25Fe07Ae	TIMLIN, Mary	20	F	Servant	26Fe02Ab
QUIN, Arthur	30	M	Farmer	25Fe07Ae	KILDAY, Ellen	20	F	Servant	26Fe02Ab
Bridget (W)	25	F	Wife	25Fe07Ae	GRAY, Mary	19	F	Servant	26Fe02Ab
BOWEN, Hugh	13	M	Clerk	25Fe07Ae	MCDONOUGH, Wm.	20	M	Laborer	26Fe02Ab
MCCROSSEN, Francis	19	M	Clerk	25Fe07Ae	MCMERNON, Michael	38	M	Laborer	26Fe02Ab
GLASGOW, Jane	19	F	Spinster	25Fe07Ae	MCGLAICHE, John	19	M	Laborer	26Fe02Ab
Lenora	16	F	Spinster	25Fe07Ae	WOODS, Abby	17	F	Servant	26Fe02Ab
Margaret	14	F	Spinster	25Fe07Ae	MCGUIRE, Mary	36	F	Servant	26Fe02Ab
NEELY, Sarah	45	F	Wi	25Fe07Ae	MCELROY, Mary	15	F	Servant	26Fe02Ab
Anabella (D)	13	F	None	25Fe07Ae	GRAY, Samuel	45	M	Weaver	26Fe02Ab
Mary (D)	11	F	None	25Fe07Ae	Susanna	17	F	Servant	26Fe02Ab
James (S)	09	M	Child	25Fe07Ae	MCBRIDE, Edward	25	M	Laborer	26Fe02Ab
Robert (S)	07	M	Child	25Fe07Ae	FORREST, John	23	M	Laborer	26Fe02Ab
Alexander (S)	05	M	Child	25Fe07Ae	FLYNN, Patrick	30	M	Laborer	26Fe02Ab
John (S)	03	M	Child	25Fe07Ae	CASEY, Ann	35	F	Servant	26Fe02Ab
Sarah (D)	.00	F	Infant	25Fe07Ae	Richard	10	M	None	26Fe02Ab
MCWILLIAMS, James	23	M	Clerk	25Fe07Ae	John	08	M	Child	26Fe02Ab
HENDERSON, George	24	M	Clerk	25Fe07Ae	GILHOOLY, Briget	20	F	Servant	26Fe02Ab
MCWILLIAMS, Jno.	23	M	Clerk	25Fe07Ae	GORMAN, Michael	27	M	Laborer	26Fe02Ab
MURRAY, William	45	M	Farmer	25Fe07Ae	MCCUEN, Biddy	21	F	Laborer	26Fe02Ab
Susanah (D)	10	F	None	25Fe07Ae	ROANE, Michael	43	M	Laborer	26Fe02Ab
John (S)	08	M	Child	25Fe07Ae	Margaret	40	F	Servant	26Fe02Ab
Eliza (D)	16	F	None	25Fe07Ae	Nancy	20	F	Servant	26Fe02Ab
MCKENNA, Jas.	50	M	Farmer	25Fe07Ae	Catherine	18	F	Servant	26Fe02Ab
Margret (W)	45	F	Wife	25Fe07Ae	Ann	16	F	Servant	26Fe02Ab
James-Jr. (S)	28	M	None	25Fe07Ae	Mary	14	F	Servant	26Fe02Ab
Eliza (D)	10	F	None	25Fe07Ae	Briget	11	F	Servant	26Fe02Ab
Charlotte (D)	08	F	Child	25Fe07Ae	Michael-Jr.	08	M	Child	26Fe02Ab
Reachel (D)	07	F	Child	25Fe07Ae	Rosanna	06	F	Child	26Fe02Ab
Martha (D)	05	F	Child	25Fe07Ae	Ann	03	F	Child	26Fe02Ab
Joseph (S)	04	M	Child	25Fe07Ae	Ellen	.03	F	Infant	26Fe02Ab
Margery (D)	02	F	Child	25Fe07Ae	LANELLE, Briget	18	F	Servant	26Fe02Ab
MCCOLLUM, Thomas	20	M	Farmer	25Fe07Ae	CAIN, Thomas	24	M	Laborer	26Fe02Ab
PARK, John	39	M	Farmer	25Fe07Ae	Mathew	20	M	Laborer	26Fe02Ab
CUNNINGHAM, James	29	M	Farmer	25Fe07Ae	Ann	22	F	Servant	26Fe02Ab
MCMURRAY, Samuel	46	M	Farmer	25Fe07Ae	ODONALD, James	23	M	Laborer	26Fe02Ab
OHARE, Jane	50	F	Wi	25Fe07Ae	Briget	26	F	Servant	26Fe02Ab
SMITH, Thomas	21	M	Farmer	25Fe07Ae	Mary	08	F	Child	26Fe02Ab
Maria (W)	20	F	Wife	25Fe07Ae	Mary	60	F	Servant	26Fe02Ab
ROBINSON, Thomas	40	M	Farmer	25Fe07Ae	Ann	12	F	Servant	26Fe02Ab
MOOREHEAD, John	33	M	Farmer	25Fe07Ae	Catherine	01	F	Child	26Fe02Ab
Rose (W)	30	F	Wife	25Fe07Ae	Died-At-Sea				
Mary	14	F	Spinster	25Fe07Ae	KEARNEY, John	.06	M	Infant	26Fe02Ab
Rose	10	F	None	25Fe07Ae	John	30	M	Farmer	26Fe02Ab
John	08	M	Child	25Fe07Ae	DOHERTY, John	32	M	Farmer	26Fe02Ab
Thomas	04	M	Child	25Fe07Ae	KELLY, George	28	M	Laborer	26Fe02Ab
Robert	01	M	Child	25Fe07Ae	MCCAEN, Hugh	20	M	Laborer	26Fe02Ab
LITTLE, William	20	M	Farmer	25Fe07Ae	Francis	28	M	Laborer	26Fe02Ab
Hugh	18	M	Farmer	25Fe07Ae	HENNEGAN, John	40	M	Laborer	26Fe02Ab
Jane	16	F	None	25Fe07Ae	MCNULTY, Francis	36	M	Laborer	26Fe02Ab
James	13	M	None	25Fe07Ae	Nancy	26	F	Servant	26Fe02Ab
WAID, Joseph	21	M	Tailor	25Fe07Ae	Michael	07	M	Child	26Fe02Ab
STITT, Francis	00	M	Merchant	25Fe07Ae	Died-At-Sea				
					Bridget	03	F	Child	26Fe02Ab
					Maria	01	F	Child	26Fe02Ab
					MCKOWAN, John	67	M	Farmer	26Fe02Ab
					Mary (W)	67	F	Wife	26Fe02Ab
					Died-At-Sea				
					John	26	M	Farmer	26Fe02Ab
					Henry	22	M	Farmer	26Fe02Ab
					Betsy	20	F	Servant	26Fe02Ab
					Owen	11	M	None	26Fe02Ab

NAMES OF PASSENGERS		A G E	S E X	OCCUPATIONS	DATE PORT SHIP	NAMES OF PASSENGERS		A G E	S E X	OCCUPATIONS	DATE PORT SHIP
BUCKLEY, Timothy		33	M	Tailor	26Fe02Ab	KELLY, Mary		30	F	Servant	26Fe02Ab
Ellen	(W)	32	F	Wife	26Fe02Ab	Bridget		19	F	Servant	26Fe02Ab
Thomas	(S)	09	M	Child	26Fe02Ab	HARTY, Mary		30	F	Servant	26Fe02Ab
Johanna	(D)	07	F	Child	26Fe02Ab	BLIGLEY, P.L.		28	M	Watchmaker	26Fe02Ab
James	(S)	03	M	Child	26Fe02Ab	KEARNEY, Edward		30	M	Farmer	26Fe02Ab
Ellen	(D)	01	F	Child	26Fe02Ab	Fanny	(W)	30	F	Wife	26Fe02Ab
QUINN, Thomas		22	M	Laborer	26Fe02Ab	Sarah	(D)	10	F	None	26Fe02Ab
Isabella		20	F	Laborer	26Fe02Ab	Catherine	(D)	08	F	Child	26Fe02Ab
WOODS, Robert		38	M	Laborer	26Fe02Ab	Patrick	(S)	05	M	Child	26Fe02Ab
COLSTON, Charles		17	M	Laborer	26Fe02Ab	Dennis	(S)	03	M	Child	26Fe02Ab
GORMAN, James		40	M	Farmer	26Fe02Ab	GRIFFIN, Hewitt-A.B.		35	M	Gentleman	26Fe02Ab
KELLY, John		66	M	Farmer	26Fe02Ab	U	(W)	25	F	Lady	26Fe02Ab
William		16	M	Farmer	26Fe02Ab						

THE ROLL CALL

"A double purpose is answered by the Roll-call — the verification of the passenger-list, and the medical inspection of the emigrants, on behalf of the captain and owners." *Illustrated London News*, July 6, 1850.

Gleeson's Pictorial, May 17, 1851.

THE BLACK BALL LINE PACKET *ISAAC WEBB,*

A Large Ship on the Liverpool — New York Run, with
Accommodation for 800 Steerage Passengers.

NAMES OF PASSENGERS	A G E	S E X	OCCUPATIONS	DATE PORT SHIP

ASHBURTON 26 FEBRUARY 1847

From Liverpool

NAMES OF PASSENGERS		AGE	SEX	OCCUPATIONS	DATE PORT SHIP
BUCHANAN, Wm.		28	M	Laborer	26Fe02Bd
DILLON, Henry		28	M	Laborer	26Fe02Bd
John		24	M	Laborer	26Fe02Bd
NEIL, Francis		26	M	Laborer	26Fe02Bd
Biddy		21	F	None	26Fe02Bd
MELVILLE, John		16	M	Laborer	26Fe02Bd
GILL, Thomas		30	M	Laborer	26Fe02Bd
REYNOLDS, Charles		22	M	Laborer	26Fe02Bd
REILEY, David		31	M	Laborer	26Fe02Bd
Ann	(W)	35	F	None	26Fe02Bd
Mary	(D)	07	F	Child	26Fe02Bd
Rose	(D)	05	F	Child	26Fe02Bd
Ann	(D)	02	F	Child	26Fe02Bd
GERRARD, Terance		28	M	Laborer	26Fe02Bd
KENNON, Thomas		20	M	Laborer	26Fe02Bd
RATTIGAN, Pat		22	M	Laborer	26Fe02Bd
BRADY, Pat		20	M	Laborer	26Fe02Bd
SMITH, Peter		27	M	Laborer	26Fe02Bd
KINNALY, Mike		25	M	Laborer	26Fe02Bd
KELLY, John		19	M	Laborer	26Fe02Bd
MORRISEY, John		29	M	Stctr	26Fe02Bd
Mary	(W)	29	F	None	26Fe02Bd
Helen	(D)	08	F	Child	26Fe02Bd
Joseph	(S)	06	M	Child	26Fe02Bd
Mary	(D)	02	F	Child	26Fe02Bd
MCGEE, John		20	M	Laborer	26Fe02Bd
MCCUSKY, Pat		20	M	Laborer	26Fe02Bd
TYE, Francis		26	M	Laborer	26Fe02Bd
Hugh		30	M	Laborer	26Fe02Bd
ROBINSON, Rodger		25	M	Engineer	26Fe02Bd
Margaret	(W)	29	F	None	26Fe02Bd
Caroline	(D)	10	F	None	26Fe02Bd
George	(S)	08	M	Child	26Fe02Bd
John	(S)	02	M	Child	26Fe02Bd
MCKINSTRY, Hugh		21	M	Saddler	26Fe02Bd
SMITH, Pat		20	M	Saddler	26Fe02Bd
CAVEN, Joseph		22	M	Laborer	26Fe02Bd
JENKINSON, Francis		22	M	Laborer	26Fe02Bd
BRIDGE, Joseph		30	M	Laborer	26Fe02Bd
HASEY, John		30	M	Laborer	26Fe02Bd
Sarah		33	F	None	26Fe02Bd
Saml.		22	M	Laborer	26Fe02Bd
REYNOLDS, Pat		28	M	None	26Fe02Bd
MCCUSKER, Fergess		21	M	Laborer	26Fe02Bd
MCGUIGAN, Mary		50	F	None	26Fe02Bd
GONNAN, Wm.		30	M	Laborer	26Fe02Bd
MCLAUGHLIN, James		30	M	Laborer	26Fe02Bd
KELLY, Matt		30	M	Laborer	26Fe02Bd
Margaret		30	F	None	26Fe02Bd
Sarah		20	F	None	26Fe02Bd
MCGOOLAND, James		25	M	Laborer	26Fe02Bd
MORRISON, John		40	M	Blacksmith	26Fe02Bd
GREVES, Catherine		19	F	None	26Fe02Bd
KEAN, Jane		20	F	None	26Fe02Bd
LYNCH, James		21	M	Laborer	26Fe02Bd
TRACY, Henry		28	M	Laborer	26Fe02Bd
Mary		24	F	None	26Fe02Bd
DENNIS, Wm.		38	M	Cooper	26Fe02Bd
BANNON, Terrance		20	M	Laborer	26Fe02Bd
MURRAY, Maurice		25	M	Laborer	26Fe02Bd
SMITH, Kate		18	F	None	26Fe02Bd
CONNELLY, Pat		30	M	Laborer	26Fe02Bd
JUDGE, James		40	M	Laborer	26Fe02Bd
Thomas	(S)	17	M	Laborer	26Fe02Bd
Frank	(S)	12	M	Unknown	26Fe02Bd
JUDGE, Ann	(D)	09	F	Child	26Fe02Bd
Francis		30	M	Laborer	26Fe02Bd
CONNELLY, Thomas		22	M	Laborer	26Fe02Bd
TILLEY, Ann		20	F	None	26Fe02Bd
BURKE, Sally		16	F	None	26Fe02Bd
MCMANERS, Kate		20	F	None	26Fe02Bd
BURKE, Dennis		22	M	Laborer	26Fe02Bd
MILLS, George		28	M	Laborer	26Fe02Bd
LANE, Pat		40	M	Laborer	26Fe02Bd
Mary	(D)	12	F	None	26Fe02Bd
Ann	(D)	08	F	Child	26Fe02Bd
Pat	(S)	02	M	Child	26Fe02Bd
KELLY, John		18	M	Laborer	26Fe02Bd
Pat		28	M	Laborer	26Fe02Bd
SMITH, Pat		44	M	Laborer	26Fe02Bd
Kate	(W)	40	F	None	26Fe02Bd
Mike	(S)	18	M	None	26Fe02Bd
Kate	(D)	19	F	None	26Fe02Bd
Sally	(D)	14	F	None	26Fe02Bd
James	(S)	12	M	None	26Fe02Bd
Pat	(S)	09	M	Child	26Fe02Bd
Mary	(D)	07	F	Child	26Fe02Bd
MCCANN, Arthur		50	M	Laborer	26Fe02Bd
Ellen	(W)	48	F	None	26Fe02Bd
Edward	(S)	15	M	None	26Fe02Bd
Peggy	(D)	12	F	None	26Fe02Bd
Paddy	(S)	09	M	Child	26Fe02Bd
Mike	(S)	06	M	Child	26Fe02Bd
Mary	(D)	03	F	Child	26Fe02Bd
Ellen	(D)	01	F	Child	26Fe02Bd
SHEARDAY, John		60	M	Laborer	26Fe02Bd
Mary	(W)	58	F	None	26Fe02Bd
Wm.	(S)	26	M	Laborer	26Fe02Bd
Pat	(S)	22	M	Laborer	26Fe02Bd
Hugh	(S)	24	M	Laborer	26Fe02Bd
Mike	(S)	20	M	Laborer	26Fe02Bd
John	(S)	16	M	Laborer	26Fe02Bd
Fanny	(D)	19	F	Laborer	26Fe02Bd
SHENDAN, Thomas		10	M	None	26Fe02Bd
Peter		08	M	Child	26Fe02Bd
LEARY, Pat		50	M	Laborer	26Fe02Bd
Mary		30	F	None	26Fe02Bd
Thomas		18	M	None	26Fe02Bd
Margaret		16	F	None	26Fe02Bd
Juda		14	F	None	26Fe02Bd
Mary		08	F	Child	26Fe02Bd
Edmond		07	M	Child	26Fe02Bd
Ellen		02	F	Child	26Fe02Bd
CHARLES, Pat		40	M	Laborer	26Fe02Bd
WILLIAM, Ellen		50	F	None	26Fe02Bd
DONOHUE, James		23	M	Laborer	26Fe02Bd
Thomas		19	M	None	26Fe02Bd
Francis		13	M	None	26Fe02Bd
Ellen		09	F	Child	26Fe02Bd
Peter		05	M	Child	26Fe02Bd
GRADY, James		38	M	Laborer	26Fe02Bd
Nelly	(W)	30	F	None	26Fe02Bd
Ellen	(D)	01	F	Child	26Fe02Bd
MCCARTY, Johanna		19	F	Servant	26Fe02Bd
HANNON, Mike		28	M	Servant	26Fe02Bd
KELLAN, Lew		20	M	Servant	26Fe02Bd
GRAY, Thos.		20	M	Servant	26Fe02Bd
WILLAN, Mike		32	M	Servant	26Fe02Bd
Eliza	(W)	30	F	None	26Fe02Bd
Kate	(D)	08	F	Child	26Fe02Bd
John	(S)	04	M	Child	26Fe02Bd
Anthony	(S)	01	M	Child	26Fe02Bd
KELLY, Mike		22	M	Laborer	26Fe02Bd
DANNAKIN, Mike		22	M	Laborer	26Fe02Bd
KEFF, James		26	M	Laborer	26Fe02Bd
FITZSIMMONS, Wat		26	M	Laborer	26Fe02Bd
John		19	M	Laborer	26Fe02Bd
KELLY, Thomas		26	M	Laborer	26Fe02Bd
NIELL, Kate		20	F	None	26Fe02Bd
DOHO, Thos.		25	M	Blacksmith	26Fe02Bd

NAMES OF PASSENGERS		AGE	SEX	OCCUPATIONS	DATE PORT SHIP
BOLIN, Martin		28	M	Tailor	26Fe02Bd
SHERIDAN, Sylvester		46	M	Laborer	26Fe02Bd
Jane	(W)	42	F	None	26Fe02Bd
John	(S)	26	M	Shoemaker	26Fe02Bd
Bridget	(L)	23	F	None	26Fe02Bd
Kate		01	F	Child	26Fe02Bd
John	(S)	20	M	Laborer	26Fe02Bd
James	(S)	20	M	Laborer	26Fe02Bd
RILEY, Frank		20	M	Laborer	26Fe02Bd
FITZSIMMONS, Pat		30	M	Laborer	26Fe02Bd
GILSHALL, Ellen		18	F	None	26Fe02Bd
GAFNEY, Pat		18	M	Cooper	26Fe02Bd
HARES, Mary		28	F	None	26Fe02Bd
BRADY, Rope		20	M	Laborer	26Fe02Bd
Peter		18	M	Shoemaker	26Fe02Bd
GRAIN, James		24	M	Laborer	26Fe02Bd
HEILY, Pat		21	M	Laborer	26Fe02Bd
MCGURK, Biddy		22	F	None	26Fe02Bd
MASTERSON, Mary		20	F	None	26Fe02Bd
JOHNSON, James		30	M	Weaver	26Fe02Bd
Mary	(W)	30	F	None	26Fe02Bd
Mary-Ann	(D)	03	F	Child	26Fe02Bd
COIL, Mike		70	M	None	26Fe02Bd
CAVIN, Joseph		23	M	None	26Fe02Bd
MCCORMACK, Mary		25	F	None	26Fe02Bd
DENNIS, Wm.		30	M	Laborer	26Fe02Bd
FARREL, Thos.		20	M	Laborer	26Fe02Bd
SMITH, Bryan		30	M	Laborer	26Fe02Bd
MCCUSKAN, Pat		16	M	Laborer	26Fe02Bd
Ann		20	F	None	26Fe02Bd
RILEY, Barnard		32	M	Laborer	26Fe02Bd
Ann	(W)	27	F	None	26Fe02Bd
Kate	(D)	10	F	None	26Fe02Bd
Margaret	(D)	05	F	Child	26Fe02Bd
James	(S)	02	M	Child	26Fe02Bd
GILBRIDE, Bernard		20	M	Laborer	26Fe02Bd
TOY, John		20	M	Shoemaker	26Fe02Bd
BANETT, John		22	M	Laborer	26Fe02Bd
Pat	(P)	60	M	Laborer	26Fe02Bd
Biddy	(T)	21	F	None	26Fe02Bd
Honor		11	F	None	26Fe02Bd
Pat		09	M	Child	26Fe02Bd
SHERIDAN, Pat		19	M	Laborer	26Fe02Bd
James		17	M	Laborer	26Fe02Bd
ALLWELL, Philip		50	M	Laborer	26Fe02Bd
Sally	(W)	50	F	None	26Fe02Bd
Philip	(S)	19	M	None	26Fe02Bd
Biddy	(D)	14	F	None	26Fe02Bd
John	(S)	11	M	None	26Fe02Bd
Nancy	(D)	08	F	Child	26Fe02Bd
ALPIN, Pat		40	M	Laborer	26Fe02Bd
HOLDEN, Felix		18	M	Laborer	26Fe02Bd
MACINALLY, Bernard		40	M	Laborer	26Fe02Bd
Mary	(W)	35	F	None	26Fe02Bd
Alanta	(S)	15	M	None	26Fe02Bd
Cormick	(S)	11	M	None	26Fe02Bd
Charles	(S)	08	M	Child	26Fe02Bd
Bernard	(S)	02	M	Child	26Fe02Bd
DONOHUE, Edward		22	M	Laborer	26Fe02Bd
Pat		18	M	None	26Fe02Bd
Mark		16	M	None	26Fe02Bd
Martin		14	M	None	26Fe02Bd
Ann		20	F	None	26Fe02Bd
LAWLER, Jas.		30	M	Carpenter	26Fe02Bd
WALL, John		25	M	Laborer	26Fe02Bd
CASHALL, Wm.		25	M	Laborer	26Fe02Bd
BOXER, Henry		19	M	Laborer	26Fe02Bd
CAVEN, Pat		21	M	Laborer	26Fe02Bd
Bridget		18	F	None	26Fe02Bd
SHERIDAN, Bernard		24	M	Laborer	26Fe02Bd
Mary		18	F	None	26Fe02Bd
Ellen		15	F	None	26Fe02Bd
CAFFREY, Rose		19	F	None	26Fe02Bd
GOLDEN, Ellen		20	F	None	26Fe02Bd
BRADY, Anna		20	F	None	26Fe02Bd
MULLEN, James		25	M	Laborer	26Fe02Bd
MCCONNOR, Ann		16	F	None	26Fe02Bd
MCGREGOR, Mike		25	M	Laborer	26Fe02Bd
BRADY, Pat		20	M	Laborer	26Fe02Bd
FITZSIMMONS, Robert		20	M	Laborer	26Fe02Bd
Ellen		18	F	None	26Fe02Bd
Rose		18	F	None	26Fe02Bd
PENDEGRASS, Pat		50	M	Laborer	26Fe02Bd
Mary	(W)	50	F	None	26Fe02Bd
Thomas	(S)	26	M	Laborer	26Fe02Bd
William	(S)	24	M	Laborer	26Fe02Bd
Edward	(S)	22	M	Laborer	26Fe02Bd
Robert	(S)	20	M	Laborer	26Fe02Bd
Mike	(S)	12	M	None	26Fe02Bd
John	(S)	10	M	None	26Fe02Bd
Pat	(S)	08	M	Child	26Fe02Bd
Kate	(D)	06	F	Child	26Fe02Bd
James	(S)	04	M	Child	26Fe02Bd
DOULING, Pat		26	M	Laborer	26Fe02Bd
WHITE, Mike		31	M	Laborer	26Fe02Bd
FLOOD, James		28	M	Carpenter	26Fe02Bd
RILEY, Kate		22	F	None	26Fe02Bd
GOSMONLY, Sarah		19	F	None	26Fe02Bd
OSTON, Pat		23	M	Brick Maker	26Fe02Bd
Johanna		26	F	None	26Fe02Bd
MCGURBRICK, Mary		17	F	None	26Fe02Bd
CLARK, Biddy		15	F	None	26Fe02Bd
Susan		13	F	None	26Fe02Bd
FITZPATRICK, Ann		19	F	None	26Fe02Bd
Mary		17	F	None	26Fe02Bd
MARTIN, John		16	M	None	26Fe02Bd
DOWD, John		19	M	None	26Fe02Bd
SKILLEY, Dennis		23	M	None	26Fe02Bd
OREILLY, John		26	M	None	26Fe02Bd
MANN, John		46	M	None	26Fe02Bd
Peggy	(W)	43	F	None	26Fe02Bd
Luke	(S)	12	M	None	26Fe02Bd
Biddy	(D)	10	F	None	26Fe02Bd
Alley	(D)	08	F	Child	26Fe02Bd
Thomas	(S)	06	M	Child	26Fe02Bd
Margaret	(D)	02	F	Child	26Fe02Bd
LARGE, Thomas		27	M	Shoemaker	26Fe02Bd
Elizabeth	(W)	30	F	None	26Fe02Bd
William	(S)	08	M	Child	26Fe02Bd
Henry	(S)	04	M	Child	26Fe02Bd
Deborah	(D)	01	F	Child	26Fe02Bd
JACKSON, Maria		26	F	None	26Fe02Bd
COLLINS, Kate		26	F	None	26Fe02Bd
FARRELL, Jane		25	F	None	26Fe02Bd
BOW, Thos.		26	M	Laborer	26Fe02Bd
SALMON, Thos.		20	M	Laborer	26Fe02Bd
OBRIEN, Bridget		19	F	None	26Fe02Bd
KENAHAN, Ellen		22	F	None	26Fe02Bd
MELOY, Timothy		72	M	Laborer	26Fe02Bd
MCGUIRE, Terrance		16	M	Cooper	26Fe02Bd
MCCULLEN, Mary		20	F	None	26Fe02Bd
HARVEY, John		19	M	Laborer	26Fe02Bd
SHAREY, Edward		24	M	Laborer	26Fe02Bd
KING, Hugh		22	M	Laborer	26Fe02Bd
Cat		24	M	Laborer	26Fe02Bd
Mike		23	M	Laborer	26Fe02Bd
DAVIS, Evan		30	M	Painter	26Fe02Bd
MARTIN, James		30	M	Tanner	26Fe02Bd
CASSIDY, Owen		25	M	Laborer	26Fe02Bd
CONNOR, James		35	M	Laborer	26Fe02Bd
Thomas	(S)	13	M	None	26Fe02Bd
Bridget	(W)	35	F	None	26Fe02Bd
Pat	(S)	11	M	None	26Fe02Bd
Daniel	(S)	07	M	Child	26Fe02Bd
Kate	(D)	02	F	Child	26Fe02Bd
MARKES, John		16	M	None	26Fe02Bd
DELLAMAN, Pat		20	M	None	26Fe02Bd
CASSIDY, Bernard		22	M	Laborer	26Fe02Bd
GREENAN, Thos.		20	M	Shoemaker	26Fe02Bd
John		17	M	None	26Fe02Bd

NAMES OF PASSENGERS		AGE	SEX	OCCUPATIONS	DATE PORT SHIP
MITNEY, Danl.		27	M	Laborer	26Fe02Bd
KAIN, Mike		24	M	Laborer	26Fe02Bd
HIGGINS, Bridget		25	F	None	26Fe02Bd
MCQUILL, Mike		32	M	Laborer	26Fe02Bd
Ann	(W)	32	F	None	26Fe02Bd
Mike	(S)	01	M	Child	26Fe02Bd
CLINTON, Lawrence		55	M	Laborer	26Fe02Bd
Mary	(W)	40	F	None	26Fe02Bd
Lawrence	(S)	12	M	None	26Fe02Bd
Hugh	(S)	12	M	None	26Fe02Bd
William	(S)	09	M	Child	26Fe02Bd
Mary	(D)	07	F	Child	26Fe02Bd
Christian	(S)	04	M	Child	26Fe02Bd
BARCLAY, Ellen		20	F	None	26Fe02Bd
Ann		19	F	None	26Fe02Bd
MCWILLIAMS, Sarah		18	F	None	26Fe02Bd
DOULINS, Margaret		18	F	None	26Fe02Bd
CUNNINGHAM, Wm.		24	M	Laborer	26Fe02Bd
James		26	M	Laborer	26Fe02Bd
MCCABE, Mathew		25	M	Laborer	26Fe02Bd
CUNNINGHAM, Sarah		22	F	None	26Fe02Bd
DANLY, Margaret		23	F	None	26Fe02Bd
Susan		17	F	None	26Fe02Bd
HANLY, Della		21	F	None	26Fe02Bd
WILSON, Jacob		25	M	Farmer	26Fe02Bd
SLAVIN, Margaret		21	F	None	26Fe02Bd
MCQUIDE, Hugh		40	M	Laborer	26Fe02Bd
Biddy	(W)	40	F	None	26Fe02Bd
Thomas	(S)	15	M	None	26Fe02Bd
Sarah	(D)	12	F	None	26Fe02Bd
Rosanna	(D)	10	F	None	26Fe02Bd
Bridget	(D)	08	F	Child	26Fe02Bd
Maria	(D)	05	F	Child	26Fe02Bd
Terrance		22	M	Stone Mason	26Fe02Bd
Isabel		20	F	None	26Fe02Bd
ODONNELL, John		21	M	Laborer	26Fe02Bd
MCKENNA, Hugh		22	M	Laborer	26Fe02Bd
MCGUY, Ellen		23	F	None	26Fe02Bd
SHERIDAN, Pat		25	M	Laborer	26Fe02Bd
MACISESSONY, Rose		17	F	None	26Fe02Bd
MERSTON, Bridget		17	F	None	26Fe02Bd
ROADEN, Mary		18	F	None	26Fe02Bd
MCGUIN, Thomas		22	M	Laborer	26Fe02Bd
BLIGGEN, James		21	M	Laborer	26Fe02Bd
SMITH, John		29	M	Farmer	26Fe02Bd
BRADY, Eliza		19	F	None	26Fe02Bd
KELLY, Martin		36	M	Laborer	26Fe02Bd
HYDE, Ellen		18	F	None	26Fe02Bd
WATERS, Alway		34	M	None	26Fe02Bd
William		02	M	Child	26Fe02Bd
HIGGIN, Mike		30	M	Laborer	26Fe02Bd
Mary	(W)	28	F	None	26Fe02Bd
Lettitia	(D)	04	F	Child	26Fe02Bd
John	(S)	02	M	Child	26Fe02Bd
MURPHY, Mike		58	M	Laborer	26Fe02Bd
Johanna		16	F	None	26Fe02Bd
Kate		14	F	None	26Fe02Bd
MCGUIN, Kate		19	F	None	26Fe02Bd
Biddy		17	F	None	26Fe02Bd
COSTLAN, Thos.		29	M	None	26Fe02Bd
Bridget	(W)	28	F	None	26Fe02Bd
Ellen	(D)	06	F	Child	26Fe02Bd
Maria	(D)	05	F	Child	26Fe02Bd
Barbara	(D)	03	F	Child	26Fe02Bd
GORDON, James		30	M	Laborer	26Fe02Bd
MCCABE, Mary		24	F	None	26Fe02Bd
MCCRUNAN, Mary		19	F	None	26Fe02Bd
DENNISON, John		30	M	Laborer	26Fe02Bd
MCAWINRY, Ann		27	F	None	26Fe02Bd
GOGERTY, George		26	M	Laborer	26Fe02Bd
DAILY, Pat		30	M	Laborer	26Fe02Bd
DAWBY, Margaret		22	F	None	26Fe02Bd
Susan		16	F	None	26Fe02Bd
CUMMINS, Sarah		19	F	None	26Fe02Bd
FAIVER, Terrance		30	M	None	26Fe02Bd

NAMES OF PASSENGERS		AGE	SEX	OCCUPATIONS	DATE PORT SHIP
FAIVER, Betty	(W)	30	F	None	26Fe02Bd
Owen	(S)	06	M	Child	26Fe02Bd
Elizabeth	(D)	04	F	Child	26Fe02Bd
Mary	(D)	01	F	Child	26Fe02Bd
				Died-At-Sea	
MICKLEMAN, Mary		22	F	None	26Fe02Bd
MCCONNOCKY, Mary		12	F	None	26Fe02Bd
RENALDS, Pat		24	M	Laborer	26Fe02Bd
Mary		24	F	None	26Fe02Bd
KELLY, Jane		20	F	None	26Fe02Bd
MCQUADE, Antony		22	M	Laborer	26Fe02Bd
MCGIVERN, Rose		15	F	None	26Fe02Bd
WALSH, Thos.		30	M	Laborer	26Fe02Bd
Nancy		22	F	None	26Fe02Bd
DUFFIE, Margaret		20	F	None	26Fe02Bd
Nancy		18	F	None	26Fe02Bd
STEVENS, J.W.		27	M	Gentleman	26Fe02Bd

BROOKSBY 27 FEBRUARY 1847

From Glasgow

NAMES OF PASSENGERS		AGE	SEX	OCCUPATIONS	DATE PORT SHIP
SMART, James		28	M	Laborer	27Fe04Ex
Isabella		26	F	Unknown	27Fe04Ex
DERMOTT, George		13	M	Laborer	27Fe04Ex
STODDURD, James		40	M	Laborer	27Fe04Ex
HAY, Andrew		75	M	Laborer	27Fe04Ex
John		25	M	Laborer	27Fe04Ex
DOTT, R.H.		30	M	Laborer	27Fe04Ex
BAILY, U-Mrs.		66	F	Unknown	27Fe04Ex
Eliza		17	F	Unknown	27Fe04Ex
PINKERTON, Daniel		30	M	Laborer	27Fe04Ex
Robt.		40	M	Laborer	27Fe04Ex
ROMY, Rich.		36	M	Laborer	27Fe04Ex
Cath.	(W)	34	F	Unknown	27Fe04Ex
U	(D)	11	F	Unknown	27Fe04Ex
Cath.	(D)	05	F	Child	27Fe04Ex
Mary-Ann	(D)	03	F	Child	27Fe04Ex
Margaret	(D)	01	F	Child	27Fe04Ex
RANKIN, Janet		40	F	Unknown	27Fe04Ex

ADAM-CARR 27 FEBRUARY 1847

From Glasgow

NAMES OF PASSENGERS		AGE	SEX	OCCUPATIONS	DATE PORT SHIP
HUTCHINSON, John		40	M	Gentleman	27Fe04Aw
GAIR, R.C.		23	M	Gentleman	27Fe04Aw
COLLINS, Mary		40	F	Lady	27Fe04Aw
Catharine		17	F	Lady	27Fe04Aw
MCILHONE, Bernard		26	M	Laborer	27Fe04Aw
Alay		22	F	Unknown	27Fe04Aw
SYNN, Pat		18	M	Laborer	27Fe04Aw
MCLEOD, John		28	M	Laborer	27Fe04Aw
MCFARLANE, James		19	M	Laborer	27Fe04Aw
SPINK, William		34	M	Laborer	27Fe04Aw

NAMES OF PASSENGERS		AGE	SEX	OCCUPATIONS	DATE PORT SHIP

F.MATHEWS 27 FEBRUARY 1847

From Sligo

NAMES OF PASSENGERS		AGE	SEX	OCCUPATIONS	DATE PORT SHIP
PATTERSON, Samuel		25	M	Clerk	27Fe28Lm
BRIDE, Ann		20	F	Servant	27Fe28Lm
LEONARD, Mary		23	F	Servant	27Fe28Lm
HAILY, John		56	M	Farmer	27Fe28Lm
John-Jr.	(S)	25	M	Farmer	27Fe28Lm
Bridget	(D)	22	F	Unknown	27Fe28Lm
Susan	(W)	50	F	Unknown	27Fe28Lm
Susan	(D)	20	F	Unknown	27Fe28Lm
FINN, Patrick		32	M	Farmer	27Fe28Lm
Patrick-Jr.	(S)	02	M	Child	27Fe28Lm
Mary	(W)	28	F	Unknown	27Fe28Lm
Ann	(D)	04	F	Child	27Fe28Lm
FINLEY, Bart		65	M	Farmer	27Fe28Lm
Bart-Jr.	(S)	20	M	Farmer	27Fe28Lm
Honor	(W)	65	F	Unknown	27Fe28Lm
Honor	(D)	18	F	Unknown	27Fe28Lm
Thomas	(S)	10	M	Unknown	27Fe28Lm
BRODIN, John		19	M	Tailor	27Fe28Lm
MCDONALD, Thos.		22	M	Laborer	27Fe28Lm
KELLY, Hugh		22	M	Tailor	27Fe28Lm
FOX, Michael		25	M	Laborer	27Fe28Lm
MORRAN, Michael		20	M	Laborer	27Fe28Lm
Ann		22	F	Unknown	27Fe28Lm
CONWAY, Bart		38	M	Laborer	27Fe28Lm
Ann	(W)	22	F	Unknown	27Fe28Lm
Ann	(D)	01	F	Child	27Fe28Lm
Bart-Jr.	(S)	07	M	Child	27Fe28Lm
OGOREN, Bridget		18	F	Servant	27Fe28Lm
SITTLE, Charles		24	M	Cooper	27Fe28Lm
KELLY, James		35	M	Laborer	27Fe28Lm

FALCON 27 FEBRUARY 1847

From Bermuda

NAMES OF PASSENGERS		AGE	SEX	OCCUPATIONS	DATE PORT SHIP
JONES, U		40	M	Gentleman	27Fe75Lp

THARTUS 01 MARCH 1847

From Belfast

NAMES OF PASSENGERS		AGE	SEX	OCCUPATIONS	DATE PORT SHIP
CULLEN, Catherine		50	F	Unknown	01Mr07Lq
MARDIN, Isabella		20	F	Unknown	01Mr07Lq
JOHNSTON, Daniel		25	M	Unknown	01Mr07Lq
Mary		20	F	Unknown	01Mr07Lq
STOTHERS, Robert		20	M	Unknown	01Mr07Lq
MEGARVY, Benard		25	M	Unknown	01Mr07Lq
HALLIDAY, Thomas		30	M	Turner	01Mr07Lq
Jane	(W)	30	F	Unknown	01Mr07Lq
John	(S)	04	M	Child	01Mr07Lq
Anne	(D)	02	F	Child	01Mr07Lq
FADEN, Saml.T.		21	M	Unknown	01Mr07Lq
MCCARN, Rose		23	F	Unknown	01Mr07Lq

NAMES OF PASSENGERS		AGE	SEX	OCCUPATIONS	DATE PORT SHIP
MCKEOWN, Mary		27	F	Unknown	01Mr07Lq
ROBINSON, Gawn		36	M	Shoemaker	01Mr07Lq
Wm.		18	M	Cooper	01Mr07Lq
MCCLEMENT, Lowey		18	M	Unknown	01Mr07Lq
SEYMOUR, Westly		16	M	Unknown	01Mr07Lq
MULDOUN, Bridget		35	F	Unknown	01Mr07Lq
HUGHES, John		40	M	Weaver	01Mr07Lq
Hannah		31	F	Unknown	01Mr07Lq
Walker		16	M	Unknown	01Mr07Lq
Sarah		06	F	Child	01Mr07Lq
Albert		04	M	Child	01Mr07Lq
Charlotte		02	F	Child	01Mr07Lq
MALLON, Sarah		20	F	Unknown	01Mr07Lq
MCCARN, Margaret		20	F	Unknown	01Mr07Lq
MONTGOMERY, Arthur		21	M	Cooper	01Mr07Lq
CAUGHEY, F.W.		20	M	Unknown	01Mr07Lq
MORE, Mary		20	F	Unknown	01Mr07Lq
MCMANUS, Ellen		21	F	Unknown	01Mr07Lq
HAMILL, Jas.		20	M	Weaver	01Mr07Lq
KINSBRY, Henry-W.		21	M	Unknown	01Mr07Lq
MULDOON, Catherine		25	F	Unknown	01Mr07Lq
MILLS, Fanny		17	F	Unknown	01Mr07Lq
Mary		21	F	Unknown	01Mr07Lq
Jane		19	F	Unknown	01Mr07Lq
MCCORT, F.		25	M	Cooper	01Mr07Lq
MCDOWELL, John		35	M	Brf	01Mr07Lq
MILLS, Mary		13	F	Unknown	01Mr07Lq
DILWORTH, Jane		20	F	Unknown	01Mr07Lq
GILLEN, John		40	M	Unknown	01Mr07Lq
ODONNELL, Mary		20	F	Unknown	01Mr07Lq
MCCAUGHEY, James		45	M	Unknown	01Mr07Lq
Catherine	(W)	40	F	Unknown	01Mr07Lq
Sarah	(D)	13	F	Unknown	01Mr07Lq
John	(S)	11	M	Unknown	01Mr07Lq
Mary	(D)	09	F	Child	01Mr07Lq
James	(S)	07	M	Child	01Mr07Lq
Ellen	(D)	03	F	Child	01Mr07Lq
Margaret	(D)	.00	F	Infant	01Mr07Lq
EARLY, Francis		22	M	Unknown	01Mr07Lq
ELVIN, Wm.		40	M	Unknown	01Mr07Lq
James		18	M	Unknown	01Mr07Lq
MAGILL, Patrick		50	M	Unknown	01Mr07Lq
Rose	(W)	45	F	Unknown	01Mr07Lq
Daniel	(S)	21	M	Tailor	01Mr07Lq
Patrick	(S)	16	M	Unknown	01Mr07Lq
Alex	(S)	13	M	Unknown	01Mr07Lq
Charles	(S)	11	M	Unknown	01Mr07Lq
Michael	(S)	09	M	Child	01Mr07Lq
Alice	(D)	16	F	Unknown	01Mr07Lq
Eliza	(D)	21	F	Unknown	01Mr07Lq
BUSH, James		21	M	Unknown	01Mr07Lq

AGINA 03 MARCH 1847

From Savanilla

NAMES OF PASSENGERS		AGE	SEX	OCCUPATIONS	DATE PORT SHIP
JONES, Jno.		30	M	Smith	03Mr62Ls

NAMES OF PASSENGERS	A G E	S E X	OCCUPATIONS	DATE PORT SHIP

FLORA 08 MARCH 1847

From Cadiz

NAMES OF PASSENGERS	A G E	S E X	OCCUPATIONS	DATE PORT SHIP
CARROLL, M.	23	M	Shoemaker	08Mr80Lt

HUGUENOT 09 MARCH 1847

From Liverpool

NAMES OF PASSENGERS	AGE SEX EX	OCCUPATIONS	DATE PORT SHIP	NAMES OF PASSENGERS	AGE SEX EX	OCCUPATIONS	DATE PORT SHIP
				BURKE, Patsey	23 M	Laborer	09Mr02Be
				Mary	20 F	Servant	09Mr02Be
				KELLY, Lawrence	30 M	Laborer	09Mr02Be
				CANARY, Thomas	20 M	Laborer	09Mr02Be
				Kitt	20 F	Servant	09Mr02Be
				FLYNN, Owen	24 M	Laborer	09Mr02Be
				Catherine (W)	20 F	Wife	09Mr02Be
				Thomas (S)	.00 M	Infant	09Mr02Be
				Edward (S)	01 M	Child	09Mr02Be
				OHARA, Pat	30 M	Laborer	09Mr02Be
				Bridget	26 F	Unknown	09Mr02Be
				BRADY, James	21 M	Baker	09Mr02Be
				MCCARTNEY, Bernard	35 M	Weaver	09Mr02Be
				MONOUGH, Patt	20 M	Laborer	09Mr02Be
				BRENNAN, Francis	18 M	Laborer	09Mr02Be
				FREEN, Martin	26 M	Laborer	09Mr02Be
				Mary	20 F	Servant	09Mr02Be
				SMITH, Bartholomew	20 M	Laborer	09Mr02Be
				NASH, Lawrence	38 M	Laborer	09Mr02Be
				MULLONEY, Mary	19 F	Servant	09Mr02Be
				HAGAN, Joseph	28 M	Laborer	09Mr02Be
				Ann	32 F	Servant	09Mr02Be
STANKARD, Peter	27 M	Herd	09Mr02Be	WELSH, Mary	28 F	Servant	09Mr02Be
Margaret	21 F	Unknown	09Mr02Be	LEE, Isabella	16 F	Servant	09Mr02Be
Margaret	18 F	Servant	09Mr02Be	DELANY, Michael	27 M	Laborer	09Mr02Be
POLING, U-Mrs.	35 F	Servant	09Mr02Be	KELLY, Honor	19 F	Servant	09Mr02Be
Julia (D)	.00 F	Infant	09Mr02Be	ALEXANDER, Thomas	50 M	Laborer	09Mr02Be
BUTLER, John	20 M	Laborer	09Mr02Be	Ann (W)	45 F	Wife	09Mr02Be
Pat	25 M	Laborer	09Mr02Be	John (S)	19 M	Laborer	09Mr02Be
PAYTE, Michael	21 M	Laborer	09Mr02Be	Smyth (S)	10 M	Laborer	09Mr02Be
FRENCH, Bartholomew	25 M	Laborer	09Mr02Be	Robert (S)	08 M	Child	09Mr02Be
REGAN, Austin	22 M	Laborer	09Mr02Be	Thomas (S)	06 M	Child	09Mr02Be
DOLAN, Patrick	24 M	Laborer	09Mr02Be	Martha (D)	04 F	Child	09Mr02Be
WALSH, Martin	20 M	Butcher	09Mr02Be	DOOLAN, Pat	22 M	Laborer	09Mr02Be
WATERS, Roger	20 M	Laborer	09Mr02Be	Edward	30 M	Laborer	09Mr02Be
OATES, U-Mrs.	26 F	Unknown	09Mr02Be	U-Mrs. (L)	30 F	Wife	09Mr02Be
TIERNEY, Thomas	22 M	Laborer	09Mr02Be	Mary (N)	03 F	Child	09Mr02Be
U (W)	25 F	Wife	09Mr02Be	LYNHAM, Ann	20 F	Unknown	09Mr02Be
Martha (D)	.00 F	Infant	09Mr02Be	Ellen	22 F	Unknown	09Mr02Be
MCGRATH, John	25 M	Laborer	09Mr02Be	FARREL, Mary	26 F	Unknown	09Mr02Be
Pat	20 M	Laborer	09Mr02Be	LAWLER, Patt.	46 M	Laborer	09Mr02Be
MANSON, Luke	21 M	Laborer	09Mr02Be	GILLIGAN, Bridget	24 F	Servant	09Mr02Be
TIERNEY, John	18 M	Laborer	09Mr02Be	Margaret	20 F	Servant	09Mr02Be
BURNS, Honor	20 F	Servant	09Mr02Be	BRYAN, Ann	18 F	Servant	09Mr02Be
CAUGHLIN, Mary	30 F	Servant	09Mr02Be	KELLY, Catharine	17 F	Servant	09Mr02Be
REYNOLDS, Patrick	47 M	Laborer	09Mr02Be	OATES, Thomas	27 M	Butcher	09Mr02Be
CAREY, John	25 M	Laborer	09Mr02Be	FERRIS, Henry	50 M	Laborer	09Mr02Be
Biddy (D)	07 F	Child	09Mr02Be	Ellen (W)	48 F	Wife	09Mr02Be
MCGUIRE, James	26 M	Laborer	09Mr02Be	Hugh (S)	21 M	Laborer	09Mr02Be
U (W)	24 F	Wife	09Mr02Be	John (S)	18 M	Laborer	09Mr02Be
Ellen	20 F	Servant	09Mr02Be	Henry (S)	13 M	Laborer	09Mr02Be
Francis (D)	.00 F	Infant	09Mr02Be	MCGUIRE, Hugh	21 M	Laborer	09Mr02Be
PEORDER, Mary	20 F	Servant	09Mr02Be	KELLY, Edward	22 M	Cooper	09Mr02Be
COSGROVE, Ellen	50 F	Servant	09Mr02Be	Biddy	20 F	Servant	09Mr02Be
RICHARDSON, John	23 M	Laborer	09Mr02Be	MCGENNESS, Ann	22 F	Servant	09Mr02Be
MULLIN, Richard	22 M	Carpenter	09Mr02Be	Mary	20 F	Servant	09Mr02Be
TRACY, Francis	22 M	Tailor	09Mr02Be	WARD, Owen	34 M	Laborer	09Mr02Be
RICHARDSON, John	23 M	Laborer	09Mr02Be	Margaret (W)	29 F	Wife	09Mr02Be
TOWLE, Michael	25 M	Laborer	09Mr02Be	Michael (S)	10 M	Laborer	09Mr02Be
SCAHAN, Pat	30 M	Laborer	09Mr02Be	MCCONLEY, Arthur	25 M	Servant	09Mr02Be
MCCULLUM, John	14 M	Laborer	09Mr02Be	Ann	26 F	Servant	09Mr02Be
James	13 M	Laborer	09Mr02Be	TAGUE, Mary	26 F	Servant	09Mr02Be
Ann	11 F	Unknown	09Mr02Be	James (S)	02 M	Child	09Mr02Be
Nell	09 M	Child	09Mr02Be	MCCUSKER, Mary	19 F	Servant	09Mr02Be
Peggy	04 F	Child	09Mr02Be	MORTON, Bernard	25 M	Nailer	09Mr02Be
Catharine	02 F	Child	09Mr02Be	Jane	33 F	Unknown	09Mr02Be
Eliza	.00 F	Infant	09Mr02Be	Susan	.00 F	Infant	09Mr02Be
BROWN, James	25 M	Laborer	09Mr02Be	KELLY, William	24 M	Plumber	09Mr02Be
SHIELDS, James	18 M	Laborer	09Mr02Be	Bridget	21 F	Servant	09Mr02Be
Mary	20 F	Servant	09Mr02Be	FOWLER, Pat	20 M	Laborer	09Mr02Be
Peggy	13 F	Servant	09Mr02Be	MONAGHAN, Pat.	22 M	Laborer	09Mr02Be
ONEIL, Sarah	35 F	Servant	09Mr02Be	ODONNELL, Judith	19 F	Servant	09Mr02Be
MCGAHERN, Rose	32 F	Servant	09Mr02Be	KENT, Pat.	28 M	Laborer	09Mr02Be
MOFFAT, William	28 M	Laborer	09Mr02Be	U (W)	25 F	Wife	09Mr02Be
Celia	24 F	Unknown	09Mr02Be	Walter (S)	.00 M	Infant	09Mr02Be

NAMES OF PASSENGERS		AGE	SEX	OCCUPATIONS	DATE PORT SHIP
MARLEY, James		19	M	Laborer	09Mr02Be
Edward		17	M	Laborer	09Mr02Be
KELLY, Daniel		21	M	Laborer	09Mr02Be
WARD, Catharine		23	F	Servant	09Mr02Be
MANKIN, Sarah		20	F	Servant	09Mr02Be
LANY, Mary		19	F	Servant	09Mr02Be
STUDDARD, Thomas		20	M	Laborer	09Mr02Be
GLENNON, Robert		17	M	Laborer	09Mr02Be
BRANAGAN, Pat		26	M	Laborer	09Mr02Be
Catharine	(W)	25	F	Wife	09Mr02Be
Barney	(S)	.00	M	Infant	09Mr02Be
RODDY, Bridget		24	F	Servant	09Mr02Be
MCCULLUM, Pat.		32	M	Rope Maker	09Mr02Be
Margaret	(W)	27	F	Wife	09Mr02Be
Ann	(D)	07	F	Child	09Mr02Be
Mary	(D)	03	F	Child	09Mr02Be
Anty.	(S)	01	M	Child	09Mr02Be
Eliza		24	F	Servant	09Mr02Be
MCCORMACK, Sarah		21	F	Servant	09Mr02Be
MCCULLUM, James		25	M	Overseer	09Mr02Be
Peggy	(W)	24	F	Wife	09Mr02Be
John	(S)	01	M	Child	09Mr02Be
LEECH, Mary		24	F	Servant	09Mr02Be
MCCULLUM, John		35	M	Laborer	09Mr02Be
Catharine		20	F	Unknown	09Mr02Be
LENNAN, Patrick		20	M	Laborer	09Mr02Be
KIRK, Richard		18	M	Laborer	09Mr02Be
ODONNELL, Peter		18	M	Laborer	09Mr02Be
GILLAN, James		55	M	Laborer	09Mr02Be
Margaret	(W)	54	F	Wife	09Mr02Be
Michael	(S)	12	M	Laborer	09Mr02Be
Margaret	(D)	09	F	Child	09Mr02Be
KENNEDY, Esther		24	F	Servant	09Mr02Be
Eleanor		22	F	Servant	09Mr02Be
MALEY, Richard		38	M	Laborer	09Mr02Be
Julia		30	F	Unknown	09Mr02Be
MULDOON, Hugh		20	M	Laborer	09Mr02Be
DOWNEY, James		20	M	Laborer	09Mr02Be
ODONNELL, Pat.		23	M	Laborer	09Mr02Be
MURRAY, Michael		21	M	Laborer	09Mr02Be
HENRY, James		40	M	Laborer	09Mr02Be
Biddy	(D)	16	F	Servant	09Mr02Be
Nancy	(D)	13	F	Servant	09Mr02Be
John	(S)	09	M	Child	09Mr02Be
Sarah	(D)	04	F	Child	09Mr02Be
MCANNALLY, Henry		32	M	Gdnr	09Mr02Be
LARAN, James		22	M	Laborer	09Mr02Be

HENDRIK-HUDSON 09 MARCH 1847

From London

NAMES OF PASSENGERS		AGE	SEX	OCCUPATIONS	DATE PORT SHIP
BROWN, Thomas		45	M	Whitesmith	09Mr21Bh
Phoebe	(W)	51	F	Unknown	09Mr21Bh
Martha	(D)	08	F	Child	09Mr21Bh
STARR, Anne		38	F	Unknown	09Mr21Bh
Ellen-A.		14	F	Unknown	09Mr21Bh
CROSS, George		48	M	Sprntr	09Mr21Bh
Jane		19	F	Unknown	09Mr21Bh
George-A.		.06	M	Infant	09Mr21Bh
CORNER, John		28	M	Painter	09Mr21Bh
MURRO, James		23	M	Painter	09Mr21Bh
ROBERTS, James		26	M	Baker	09Mr21Bh
Caroline		26	F	Unknown	09Mr21Bh
WILTON, John		24	M	Schm	09Mr21Bh
CLARK, Mary		12	F	Unknown	09Mr21Bh
QUEPELL, Mary-A.		24	F	Unknown	09Mr21Bh
BREWER, John		55	M	Sawer	09Mr21Bh
Elizabeth	(W)	54	F	Unknown	09Mr21Bh

NAMES OF PASSENGERS		AGE	SEX	OCCUPATIONS	DATE PORT SHIP
BREWER, Frances	(D)	19	F	Unknown	09Mr21Bh
Mary-C.	(D)	14	F	Unknown	09Mr21Bh
James	(S)	11	M	Unknown	09Mr21Bh

ABERFOIL 11 MARCH 1847

From Liverpool

NAMES OF PASSENGERS		AGE	SEX	OCCUPATIONS	DATE PORT SHIP
GALLAGHER, Patt		20	M	Unknown	11Mr02Lv
Catherine		40	F	Unknown	11Mr02Lv
Bridget		17	F	Unknown	11Mr02Lv
MCBARRON, John		25	M	Unknown	11Mr02Lv
MCGUIRE, Terence		28	M	Unknown	11Mr02Lv
Catherine	(W)	25	F	Unknown	11Mr02Lv
U		.00	U	Infant	11Mr02Lv
James		20	M	Unknown	11Mr02Lv
MCKENNA, Patt		21	M	Unknown	11Mr02Lv
Biddy		20	F	Unknown	11Mr02Lv
CANTWELL, John		24	M	Unknown	11Mr02Lv
Anne	(W)	22	F	Unknown	11Mr02Lv
U		.00	U	Infant	11Mr02Lv
TREACY, Anne		70	F	Unknown	11Mr02Lv
FAHEY, James		25	M	Unknown	11Mr02Lv
INBY, Mary		20	F	Unknown	11Mr02Lv
DUNN, Peggy		19	F	Unknown	11Mr02Lv
SUILLY, Ann		11	F	Unknown	11Mr02Lv
CANTWELL, Patt		04	M	Child	11Mr02Lv
Jeremiah		02	M	Child	11Mr02Lv
HARRIS, Edward		30	M	Unknown	11Mr02Lv
DOWNEY, Catherine		23	F	Unknown	11Mr02Lv
MCCLAVEN, Dominick		45	M	Unknown	11Mr02Lv
John		18	M	Unknown	11Mr02Lv
MCDONALD, Peter		50	M	Unknown	11Mr02Lv
U	(W)	46	F	Unknown	11Mr02Lv
Martin	(S)	19	M	Unknown	11Mr02Lv
James	(S)	18	M	Unknown	11Mr02Lv
Anne	(D)	13	F	Unknown	11Mr02Lv
Biron	(S)	11	M	Unknown	11Mr02Lv
Alicia	(D)	09	F	Child	11Mr02Lv
Margaret	(D)	07	F	Child	11Mr02Lv
Catherine	(D)	03	F	Child	11Mr02Lv
Fanny	(D)	.00	F	Infant	11Mr02Lv
FLEMING, Mary		20	F	Unknown	11Mr02Lv
SHIRITGON, Isaih		39	M	Unknown	11Mr02Lv
JEASON, Morris		49	M	Unknown	11Mr02Lv
DENGAN, James		48	M	Unknown	11Mr02Lv
Catherine		18	F	Unknown	11Mr02Lv
Mary		12	F	Unknown	11Mr02Lv
MCGUIRE, Patt		20	M	Unknown	11Mr02Lv
Ellen	(W)	18	F	Unknown	11Mr02Lv
U		.00	U	Infant	11Mr02Lv
Anne		16	F	Unknown	11Mr02Lv
REILLY, John		20	M	Unknown	11Mr02Lv
JACOB, Moses		19	M	Unknown	11Mr02Lv
WARD, Daniel		19	M	Unknown	11Mr02Lv
MCMANUS, John		20	M	Unknown	11Mr02Lv
CAWLEY, Daniel		40	M	Unknown	11Mr02Lv
MULLEN, John		40	M	Unknown	11Mr02Lv
Mary	(W)	40	F	Unknown	11Mr02Lv
Sally	(D)	17	F	Unknown	11Mr02Lv
George	(S)	13	M	Unknown	11Mr02Lv
Catherine	(D)	11	F	Unknown	11Mr02Lv
James	(S)	09	M	Child	11Mr02Lv
Mary	(D)	07	F	Child	11Mr02Lv
Rosana	(D)	05	F	Child	11Mr02Lv
Winifred	(D)	03	F	Child	11Mr02Lv
Gracey	(D)	02	F	Child	11Mr02Lv
RUTLEDGE, Joseph		26	M	Unknown	11Mr02Lv
Hester	(W)	22	F	Unknown	11Mr02Lv

NAMES OF PASSENGERS		AGE	SEX	OCCUPATIONS	DATE PORT SHIP
RUTLEDGE, U		.00	U	Infant	11Mr02Lv
WILSON, Eliza		25	F	Unknown	11Mr02Lv
BROWN, James		35	M	Unknown	11Mr02Lv
Margaret		30	F	Unknown	11Mr02Lv
DOADS, Thomas		28	M	Unknown	11Mr02Lv
U	(W)	20	F	Unknown	11Mr02Lv
U		.00	U	Infant	11Mr02Lv
MCGOWAN, John		25	M	Unknown	11Mr02Lv
Mary		20	F	Unknown	11Mr02Lv
FINAN, John		20	M	Unknown	11Mr02Lv
DENELLY, Patrick		22	M	Unknown	11Mr02Lv
BATEMAN, Danl.		20	M	Unknown	11Mr02Lv
FITZSIMMONS, Patrick		40	M	Unknown	11Mr02Lv
Margaret	(W)	16	F	Unknown	11Mr02Lv
U		.00	U	Infant	11Mr02Lv
PAGE, John		30	M	Unknown	11Mr02Lv
WALSH, Mary		17	F	Unknown	11Mr02Lv
ROCHE, Philip		20	M	Unknown	11Mr02Lv
LINCH, Mary		17	F	Unknown	11Mr02Lv
Patt		44	M	Unknown	11Mr02Lv
CAFFRE, John		30	M	Unknown	11Mr02Lv
Died-At-Sea					
HYGHES, Mahl		31	M	Unknown	11Mr02Lv
MALONE, Patt		30	M	Unknown	11Mr02Lv
Died-At-Sea					
MCHUGH, Owen		21	M	Unknown	11Mr02Lv
BUPHAC, Micl.		20	M	Unknown	11Mr02Lv
U	(M)	40	F	Unknown	11Mr02Lv
Mary	(T)	20	F	Unknown	11Mr02Lv
Abby	(W)	21	F	Unknown	11Mr02Lv
U		.00	U	Infant	11Mr02Lv
HOAN, Mary		20	F	Unknown	11Mr02Lv
MCKIENNA, Mich.		50	M	Unknown	11Mr02Lv
U	(W)	45	F	Unknown	11Mr02Lv
Caty	(D)	22	F	Unknown	11Mr02Lv
Rosay	(D)	18	F	Unknown	11Mr02Lv
Patt	(S)	20	M	Unknown	11Mr02Lv
Mich.	(S)	08	M	Child	11Mr02Lv
Ellen	(D)	10	F	Unknown	11Mr02Lv
DALE, Peter		20	M	Unknown	11Mr02Lv
MULLIGAN, Jas.		30	M	Unknown	11Mr02Lv
Jane	(W)	28	F	Unknown	11Mr02Lv
Patt	(S)	05	M	Child	11Mr02Lv
Mary	(D)	03	F	Child	11Mr02Lv
Margt.	(D)	.00	F	Infant	11Mr02Lv
CLARKE, Antony		50	M	Unknown	11Mr02Lv
Martin		12	M	Unknown	11Mr02Lv
STEWART, Wm.		25	M	Unknown	11Mr02Lv
JARVIN, U-Mrs.		21	F	Unknown	11Mr02Lv
JONES, Thos.		35	M	Unknown	11Mr02Lv
FAIRHUST, Pack.		40	M	Unknown	11Mr02Lv
U	(W)	30	F	Unknown	11Mr02Lv
Mich.	(S)	08	M	Child	11Mr02Lv
Jno.	(S)	06	M	Child	11Mr02Lv
WILLS, Al		22	M	Unknown	11Mr02Lv
MONOGHAN, John		21	M	Unknown	11Mr02Lv
DAVID, John		25	M	Unknown	11Mr02Lv
CALLAGHAN, Phil		42	M	Unknown	11Mr02Lv
GAMMON, Mich.		22	M	Unknown	11Mr02Lv
DILLON, Martin		20	M	Unknown	11Mr02Lv
FLOOD, Mat		19	M	Unknown	11Mr02Lv
TRAINOR, Bernard		21	M	Unknown	11Mr02Lv
SOUTHROLD, Thos.		23	M	Unknown	11Mr02Lv
BRANNON, Jas.		30	M	Unknown	11Mr02Lv
U	(W)	30	F	Unknown	11Mr02Lv
Biddy	(D)	06	F	Child	11Mr02Lv
Maney	(D)	04	F	Child	11Mr02Lv
Mary	(D)	03	F	Child	11Mr02Lv
Francis	(S)	.00	M	Infant	11Mr02Lv
IRWIN, Robt.		45	M	Unknown	11Mr02Lv
MAHONY, Jas.		32	M	Unknown	11Mr02Lv
Mary	(W)	30	F	Unknown	11Mr02Lv
Matilda-Ann	(D)	11	F	Unknown	11Mr02Lv
John	(S)	09	M	Child	11Mr02Lv
James	(S)	07	M	Child	11Mr02Lv

NAMES OF PASSENGERS		AGE	SEX	OCCUPATIONS	DATE PORT SHIP
BAZLES, Abraham		35	M	Unknown	11Mr02Lv
ROSS, Danl.		30	M	Unknown	11Mr02Lv
Eliza	(W)	25	F	Unknown	11Mr02Lv
Daniel	(S)	06	M	Child	11Mr02Lv
Damon	(S)	03	M	Child	11Mr02Lv
Hannah	(D)	.00	F	Infant	11Mr02Lv
DIAS, Robas		21	M	Unknown	11Mr02Lv
SMYTH, John		19	M	Unknown	11Mr02Lv
DOLAN, Phill		54	M	Unknown	11Mr02Lv
Hugh	(S)	23	M	Unknown	11Mr02Lv
Biddy	(D)	20	F	Unknown	11Mr02Lv
Catherine	(D)	13	F	Unknown	11Mr02Lv
BURN, John		26	M	Unknown	11Mr02Lv
KINNAN, Edward		23	M	Unknown	11Mr02Lv
MANAY, Ann		20	F	Unknown	11Mr02Lv
JENTIMS, Danl.		18	M	Unknown	11Mr02Lv
ROONEY, Pat		23	M	Unknown	11Mr02Lv
CAMPBELL, John		22	M	Unknown	11Mr02Lv
THOMPSON, John		30	M	Unknown	11Mr02Lv
U	(W)	30	F	Unknown	11Mr02Lv
U		.00	U	Infant	11Mr02Lv
JULLY, Thomas		23	M	Unknown	11Mr02Lv
SMITH, Thos.		22	M	Unknown	11Mr02Lv
SWEENY, John		32	M	Unknown	11Mr02Lv
Hanna		27	F	Unknown	11Mr02Lv
TRIMAN, Owen		24	M	Unknown	11Mr02Lv
Mary	(W)	21	F	Unknown	11Mr02Lv
Ally	(D)	03	F	Child	11Mr02Lv
Ann	(D)	01	F	Child	11Mr02Lv
Died-At-Sea					
Ally		50	F	Unknown	11Mr02Lv
Pat		20	M	Unknown	11Mr02Lv
Mary		18	F	Unknown	11Mr02Lv
Marg.		16	F	Unknown	11Mr02Lv
John		13	M	Unknown	11Mr02Lv
Ann		10	F	Unknown	11Mr02Lv
Ally		08	F	Child	11Mr02Lv
John		22	M	Unknown	11Mr02Lv
Ally		20	F	Unknown	11Mr02Lv
MCMURREY, Barney		20	M	Unknown	11Mr02Lv
DORAN, Ann		19	F	Unknown	11Mr02Lv
REILLY, Edward		20	M	Unknown	11Mr02Lv
Ann		20	F	Unknown	11Mr02Lv
John		10	M	Unknown	11Mr02Lv
Edward		09	M	Child	11Mr02Lv
GRAY, Wm.		21	M	Unknown	11Mr02Lv
REILLY, Wm.		20	M	Unknown	11Mr02Lv
Sally	(W)	20	F	Unknown	11Mr02Lv
U		.00	U	Infant	11Mr02Lv
Died-At-Sea					
WILSON, John		24	M	Unknown	11Mr02Lv
COGHAN, Wm.		20	M	Unknown	11Mr02Lv
John		13	M	Unknown	11Mr02Lv
SMITH, Catherine		24	F	Unknown	11Mr02Lv
Alice		18	F	Unknown	11Mr02Lv
Peter		26	M	Unknown	11Mr02Lv
HARVEY, Mary		18	F	Unknown	11Mr02Lv
U		.00	U	Infant	11Mr02Lv
CLERK, Wm.		44	M	Unknown	11Mr02Lv
KELLY, Saml.		13	M	Unknown	11Mr02Lv

OHIO 12 MARCH 1847

From Liverpool

NAMES OF PASSENGERS		AGE	SEX	OCCUPATIONS	DATE PORT SHIP
MOONEY, Samuel		21	M	Blacksmith	12Mr02Bm
MCTAMNAY, John		25	M	Barber	12Mr02Bm
CONNER, Patrick		17	M	Shoemaker	12Mr02Bm
HACKET, Caran		25	M	Laborer	12Mr02Bm

NAMES OF PASSENGERS		AGE	SEX	OCCUPATIONS	DATE PORT SHIP
DOYLE, James		20	M	Laborer	12Mr02Bm
FLYNN, Edward		19	M	Laborer	12Mr02Bm
LYNCH, John		46	M	Laborer	12Mr02Bm
WELSH, William		22	M	Brush Maker	12Mr02Bm
FRIGGS, Thomas		22	M	Brush Maker	12Mr02Bm
MCCORMICK, John		15	M	Unknown	12Mr02Bm
Mary-Ann		21	F	Seamstress	12Mr02Bm
GARVIN, Dominic		37	M	Laborer	12Mr02Bm
Betty	(W)	27	F	Unknown	12Mr02Bm
Rosy	(D)	06	F	Child	12Mr02Bm
John	(S)	03	M	Child	12Mr02Bm
Pat	(S)	01	M	Child	12Mr02Bm
John		27	M	Laborer	12Mr02Bm
Ann		25	F	Laborer	12Mr02Bm
CONNER, Rosy		20	F	Unknown	12Mr02Bm
BURKE, Martin		15	M	Laborer	12Mr02Bm
John		13	M	Laborer	12Mr02Bm
GARVIN, Mary		60	F	Unknown	12Mr02Bm
MAHAN, Pat		16	M	Miller	12Mr02Bm
Isabella		15	F	Unknown	12Mr02Bm
CRAIG, William		73	M	Laborer	12Mr02Bm
Alexander		35	M	Laborer	12Mr02Bm
BYRNE, Ann		30	F	Domestic	12Mr02Bm
John		04	M	Child	12Mr02Bm
HENNESSEY, Dennis		23	M	Laborer	12Mr02Bm
OBRIEN, Patrick		23	M	Laborer	12Mr02Bm
RYAN, Martin		30	M	Laborer	12Mr02Bm
MCDANIEL, Thomas		33	M	Laborer	12Mr02Bm
Margt.	(W)	35	F	Unknown	12Mr02Bm
Pat	(S)	06	M	Child	12Mr02Bm
Ann	(D)	03	F	Child	12Mr02Bm
CARNEY, Terry		55	M	Tailor	12Mr02Bm
Mary		15	F	Unknown	12Mr02Bm
HESTER, Thomas		22	M	Laborer	12Mr02Bm
MURRAY, Martin		30	M	Laborer	12Mr02Bm
Mary		25	F	Unknown	12Mr02Bm
GUNN, John		22	M	Laborer	12Mr02Bm
FLYNN, Margt.		60	F	Laborer	12Mr02Bm
James		20	M	Laborer	12Mr02Bm
John		18	M	Laborer	12Mr02Bm
BOLIN, Pat		20	M	Laborer	12Mr02Bm
FLYNN, Biddy		15	F	Unknown	12Mr02Bm
Wm.		22	M	Laborer	12Mr02Bm
Margt.		19	F	Unknown	12Mr02Bm
POWERS, Pat		18	M	Laborer	12Mr02Bm
BYRNE, Edward		10	M	Unknown	12Mr02Bm
John		08	M	Child	12Mr02Bm
James		40	M	Laborer	12Mr02Bm
Johanna		20	F	Unknown	12Mr02Bm
Margt.		.09	F	Infant	12Mr02Bm
FITZGERALD, Ann		16	F	Unknown	12Mr02Bm
FORRESTON, Jas.		35	M	Laborer	12Mr02Bm
Michl.		30	M	Laborer	12Mr02Bm
BRANNNON, John		24	M	Laborer	12Mr02Bm
MCGLYNN, Bryan		35	M	Laborer	12Mr02Bm
Mary	(W)	28	F	Unknown	12Mr02Bm
Ann	(D)	07	F	Child	12Mr02Bm
Michl.	(S)	05	M	Child	12Mr02Bm
Danl.	(S)	03	M	Child	12Mr02Bm
Peter	(S)	.07	M	Infant	12Mr02Bm
CAHILL, Lawrence		49	M	Brewer	12Mr02Bm
Rose		60	F	Unknown	12Mr02Bm
SMITH, Phil		25	M	Laborer	12Mr02Bm
OWENS, James		40	M	Laborer	12Mr02Bm
Jas.Jr.	(S)	18	M	Laborer	12Mr02Bm
Michl.	(S)	16	M	Laborer	12Mr02Bm
Cath.	(W)	40	F	Unknown	12Mr02Bm
Mary-Ann	(D)	14	F	Spinster	12Mr02Bm
Margt.	(D)	12	F	Unknown	12Mr02Bm
Bettsy	(D)	10	F	Unknown	12Mr02Bm
Cath.	(D)	08	F	Child	12Mr02Bm
Bridget	(D)	06	F	Child	12Mr02Bm
Thomas	(S)	04	M	Child	12Mr02Bm
MULLIGAN, Owen		26	M	Laborer	12Mr02Bm
ROURKE, Pat		30	M	Laborer	12Mr02Bm
ROURKE, Jane	(W)	27	F	Unknown	12Mr02Bm
Ellen	(D)	.03	F	Infant	12Mr02Bm
DIVINE, Pat		20	M	Servant	12Mr02Bm
LIMNERS, Pat		34	M	Laborer	12Mr02Bm
Ellen		22	F	Unknown	12Mr02Bm
Mary	(D)	06	F	Child	12Mr02Bm
James	(S)	04	M	Child	12Mr02Bm
Rosy	(D)	02	F	Child	12Mr02Bm
Peggy		28	F	Unknown	12Mr02Bm
MAHON, Bridget		17	F	Weaver	12Mr02Bm
LYNES, John		23	M	Carpenter	12Mr02Bm
HOGAN, Michl.		22	M	Laborer	12Mr02Bm
BRYDON, Daniel		24	M	Laborer	12Mr02Bm
HOLLY, John		25	M	Laborer	12Mr02Bm
William		30	M	Laborer	12Mr02Bm
Thos.		25	M	Laborer	12Mr02Bm
Ellen		25	F	Unknown	12Mr02Bm
DOLAN, Cath.		27	F	Unknown	12Mr02Bm
Pat	(S)	06	M	Child	12Mr02Bm
SHIELD, William		18	M	Laborer	12Mr02Bm
Cath.		20	F	Weaver	12Mr02Bm
FLYNN, Frances		22	F	Domestic	12Mr02Bm
SAVAGE, Mary		24	F	Domestic	12Mr02Bm
MULVEIGH, Thomas		15	M	Unknown	12Mr02Bm
Cath.		19	F	Seamstress	12Mr02Bm
ELLIOT, Mary		23	F	Seamstress	12Mr02Bm
MCGUIRE, Pat		26	M	Laborer	12Mr02Bm
MCQUILLON, James		25	M	Laborer	12Mr02Bm
Bridget		22	F	Laborer	12Mr02Bm
MULRAIGNE, Barney		28	M	Laborer	12Mr02Bm
MARTIN, Henry		21	M	Laborer	12Mr02Bm
Ann		24	F	Unknown	12Mr02Bm
HUGHES, Daniel		60	M	Laborer	12Mr02Bm
Martin		25	M	Laborer	12Mr02Bm
John		22	M	Laborer	12Mr02Bm
GALLAGHER, Bartlett		35	M	Laborer	12Mr02Bm
HUGHES, Mary		18	F	Unknown	12Mr02Bm
Ann		12	F	Unknown	12Mr02Bm
James		16	M	Unknown	12Mr02Bm
Peter		11	M	Unknown	12Mr02Bm
MULLONEY, Daniel		24	M	Laborer	12Mr02Bm
KENNEDY, John		26	M	Laborer	12Mr02Bm
GALLAGHER, John		19	M	Laborer	12Mr02Bm
KELLY, John		36	M	Laborer	12Mr02Bm
COSTELLO, John		40	M	Laborer	12Mr02Bm
MACKLIN, Michl.		24	M	Laborer	12Mr02Bm
BIGGIN, Barney		24	M	Blacksmith	12Mr02Bm
MAHAN, Michl.		20	M	Laborer	12Mr02Bm
GUNN, Phil		20	M	Laborer	12Mr02Bm
DEVLIN, Peter		30	M	Laborer	12Mr02Bm
MCKENNIFF, Bridget		60	F	Unknown	12Mr02Bm
Farl		12	M	Unknown	12Mr02Bm
MCGUIN, Mary		16	F	Domestic	12Mr02Bm
STEVENSON, Simon		37	M	Shoemaker	12Mr02Bm
DICKSON, John		20	M	Laborer	12Mr02Bm
SMITH, Phil		30	M	Laborer	12Mr02Bm
KERRIGAN, John		23	M	Joiner	12Mr02Bm
Cath.		20	F	Unknown	12Mr02Bm
Bridget		22	F	Unknown	12Mr02Bm
Bridget		.06	F	Infant	12Mr02Bm
SHAVLIN, Pat		21	M	Laborer	12Mr02Bm
Mary		20	F	Unknown	12Mr02Bm
MICHAEL, Pat		30	M	Laborer	12Mr02Bm
Cath.	(W)	28	F	Unknown	12Mr02Bm
Thos.	(S)	02	M	Child	12Mr02Bm
HOPKINS, Thos.		27	M	Laborer	12Mr02Bm
WEAVER, John		19	M	Laborer	12Mr02Bm
SUCKLEY, Martin		19	M	Laborer	12Mr02Bm
ROACH, Pat		26	M	Laborer	12Mr02Bm
Mary	(W)	24	F	Unknown	12Mr02Bm
John	(S)	02	M	Child	12Mr02Bm
Mary	(D)	04	F	Child	12Mr02Bm
John		22	M	Laborer	12Mr02Bm
William		17	M	Laborer	12Mr02Bm
BURKE, Jas.		24	M	Laborer	12Mr02Bm

NAMES OF PASSENGERS		AGE	SEX	OCCUPATIONS	DATE PORT SHIP
MAHAN, Bridget		17	F	Seamstress	12Mr02Bm
TEAGUE, Cath.		20	F	Seamstress	12Mr02Bm
Ann		15	F	Seamstress	12Mr02Bm
ROACH, Mary		21	F	Seamstress	12Mr02Bm
Peggy		19	F	Seamstress	12Mr02Bm
CARNEY, Bridget		18	F	Unknown	12Mr02Bm
Cathleen		16	F	Unknown	12Mr02Bm
RILEY, Anthony		29	M	Laborer	12Mr02Bm
LARINS, Pat		30	M	Laborer	12Mr02Bm
TEAGUE, Hugh		18	M	Laborer	12Mr02Bm
DORAN, John		18	M	Laborer	12Mr02Bm
ONEIL, Pat		20	M	Laborer	12Mr02Bm
QUINN, Pat		19	M	Laborer	12Mr02Bm
CONNER, Mathew		25	M	Laborer	12Mr02Bm
MURRAY, Pat		35	M	Laborer	12Mr02Bm
TRAYNER, John		19	M	Laborer	12Mr02Bm
ROSS, William		23	M	Laborer	12Mr02Bm
CLINTON, John		17	M	Laborer	12Mr02Bm
LAMB, John		18	M	Laborer	12Mr02Bm
ALTERSLEY, Abraham		20	M	Laborer	12Mr02Bm

ROSE 18 MARCH 1847

From Belize

NAMES OF PASSENGERS		AGE	SEX	OCCUPATIONS	DATE PORT SHIP
STIRLING, M.L.		27	M	Merchant	18Mr50Ma
EVANS, Edward		29	M	Merchant	18Mr50Ma
SMITH, Henry		32	M	Merchant	18Mr50Ma

MARGARET-EVANS 23 MARCH 1847

From London

NAMES OF PASSENGERS		AGE	SEX	OCCUPATIONS	DATE PORT SHIP
DOLAN, Honora		45	F	Unknown	23Mr21lp
John	(S)	11	M	Unknown	23Mr21lp
Ellen	(D)	03	F	Child	23Mr21lp
BYRNN, John		32	M	Dealer	23Mr21lp
Ellen	(W)	25	F	Unknown	23Mr21lp
Mary	(D)	03	F	Child	23Mr21lp
Ellen	(D)	01	F	Child	23Mr21lp
ARNOLD, William		42	M	Carpenter	23Mr21lp
THOMPSON, John		29	M	Painter	23Mr21lp
Frances		29	F	Unknown	23Mr21lp

SEA-OF-NEW-YORK 23 MARCH 1847

From Liverpool

NAMES OF PASSENGERS		AGE	SEX	OCCUPATIONS	DATE PORT SHIP
CONAGHAN, Edward		36	M	Laborer	23Mr02ls
Susan	(W)	30	F	Unknown	23Mr02ls
Patrick	(S)	04	M	Child	23Mr02ls
John	(S)	02	M	Child	23Mr02ls
RILEY, Francis		25	M	Laborer	23Mr02ls
Mary		27	F	Laborer	23Mr02ls
MORGAN, Pat		17	M	Laborer	23Mr02ls
KENNEDY, Thomas		30	M	Laborer	23Mr02ls
Betsey	(W)	26	F	Unknown	23Mr02ls
KENNEDY, Pat	(S)	04	M	Child	23Mr02ls
Anne	(D)	02	F	Child	23Mr02ls
Died-At-Sea					
KILMURRAY, James		30	M	Laborer	23Mr02ls
Mary	(W)	30	F	Unknown	23Mr02ls
Rose	(D)	04	F	Child	23Mr02ls
Pat	(S)	02	M	Child	23Mr02ls
MALONE, Bridget		30	F	Unknown	23Mr02ls
CUNNINGHAM, James		34	M	Laborer	23Mr02ls
DOLAN, Michael		21	M	Laborer	23Mr02ls
BRADBUIN, John		17	M	Groom	23Mr02ls
GLENNON, Catherine		24	F	Unknown	23Mr02ls
KILMURRAY, Ellen		22	F	Unknown	23Mr02ls
HYDE, Michael		26	M	Laborer	23Mr02ls
KILLIAN, Ellen		19	F	Unknown	23Mr02ls
SHEEIAN, James		25	M	Laborer	23Mr02ls
KEHOE, Mary		24	F	Unknown	23Mr02ls
MCANULTY, Dennis		19	M	Laborer	23Mr02ls
HAIKIN, John		18	M	Shoemaker	23Mr02ls
MCNEILL, Pat		23	M	Laborer	23Mr02ls
DUFFY, Hugh		21	M	Laborer	23Mr02ls
JENNINGS, Jane		17	F	Unknown	23Mr02ls
Bridget		01	F	Child	23Mr02ls
DAILY, Owen		35	M	Laborer	23Mr02ls
Mary		30	F	Unknown	23Mr02ls
MCGOVERAN, John		21	M	Laborer	23Mr02ls
MCDONOUGH, Ann		20	F	Unknown	23Mr02ls
Biddy		14	F	Unknown	23Mr02ls
Jane		12	F	Unknown	23Mr02ls
DOUGHERTY, John		22	M	Laborer	23Mr02ls
DAILY, Mary		18	F	Unknown	23Mr02ls
GALVIN, Bridget		18	F	Unknown	23Mr02ls
CONNER, John		21	M	Laborer	23Mr02ls
KELLY, Patrick		40	M	Laborer	23Mr02ls
Ann		19	F	Unknown	23Mr02ls
DUTTON, Thomas		30	M	Laborer	23Mr02ls
COWHAY, Martin		23	M	Butcher	23Mr02ls
NEVIN, John		21	M	Laborer	23Mr02ls
MOLLOY, John		23	M	Laborer	23Mr02ls
Arthur		22	M	Laborer	23Mr02ls
LEE, Daniel		34	M	Carpenter	23Mr02ls
MULVIGD, James		25	M	Musician	23Mr02ls
NALLY, Pat		25	M	Laborer	23Mr02ls
Maria		22	F	Laborer	23Mr02ls
MURRAY, Thomas		25	M	Laborer	23Mr02ls
Bridget		21	F	Unknown	23Mr02ls
CAMPION, Michael		30	M	Laborer	23Mr02ls
William		16	M	Laborer	23Mr02ls
BRACKEN, Thomas		26	M	Laborer	23Mr02ls
MURPHY, Pat		26	M	Laborer	23Mr02ls
Catherine	(W)	24	F	Unknown	23Mr02ls
Patrick	(S)	.02	M	Infant	23Mr02ls
HUNCHEN, Hugh		20	M	Laborer	23Mr02ls
KENNY, William		54	M	Laborer	23Mr02ls
Peggy	(W)	44	F	Unknown	23Mr02ls
Died-At-Sea					
Mary	(D)	20	F	Unknown	23Mr02ls
Kitty	(D)	18	F	Unknown	23Mr02ls
Patt	(S)	15	M	Unknown	23Mr02ls
Martin	(S)	13	M	Unknown	23Mr02ls
Edward	(S)	10	M	Unknown	23Mr02ls
Thomas	(S)	07	M	Child	23Mr02ls
SPALIN, Martin		20	M	Laborer	23Mr02ls
HINCHSEN, Ann		22	F	Unknown	23Mr02ls
HAND, Patrick		25	M	Laborer	23Mr02ls
GAUGHAN, John		48	M	Laborer	23Mr02ls
Mary	(W)	42	F	Unknown	23Mr02ls
Patt	(S)	19	M	Laborer	23Mr02ls
Bridget	(D)	12	F	Unknown	23Mr02ls
Mary	(D)	09	F	Child	23Mr02ls
John	(S)	07	M	Child	23Mr02ls
James	(S)	03	M	Child	23Mr02ls
James		30	M		23Mr02ls
Mary	(W)	30	F	Unknown	23Mr02ls
Judy	(D)	15	F	Unknown	23Mr02ls

NAMES OF PASSENGERS		AGE	SEX	OCCUPATIONS	DATE PORT SHIP
GAUGHAN, Martin	(S)	12	M	Unknown	23Mr02Is
Thomas	(S)	03	M	Child	23Mr02Is
Michael	(S)	02	M	Child	23Mr02Is
Bridget	(D)	.03	F	Infant	23Mr02Is
Died-At-Sea					
John		57	M	Farmer	23Mr02Is
Mary	(W)	42	F	Unknown	23Mr02Is
Bridget	(D)	22	F	Unknown	23Mr02Is
John	(S)	20	M	Unknown	23Mr02Is
Michael	(S)	18	M	Unknown	23Mr02Is
Peggy	(D)	12	F	Unknown	23Mr02Is
James	(S)	10	M	Unknown	23Mr02Is
Mary	(D)	08	F	Child	23Mr02Is
Thomas	(S)	05	M	Child	23Mr02Is
Martin	(S)	03	M	Child	23Mr02Is
Anthony	(S)	.08	M	Infant	23Mr02Is
Bryan		25	M	Laborer	23Mr02Is
Died-At-Sea					
Thomas		19	M	Laborer	23Mr02Is
Died-At-Sea					
CAIN, Margaret		17	F	Unknown	23Mr02Is
CAULY, Peter		35	M	Laborer	23Mr02Is
Thos.		30	M	Laborer	23Mr02Is
DALFIN, Wm.		30	M	Laborer	23Mr02Is
Mary	(W)	30	F	Unknown	23Mr02Is
Bridget	(D)	05	F	Child	23Mr02Is
Mary	(D)	03	F	Child	23Mr02Is
James	(S)	.09	M	Infant	23Mr02Is
SWEENEY, John		39	M	Farmer	23Mr02Is
Bridget	(W)	38	F	Unknown	23Mr02Is
Owen	(S)	22	M	Unknown	23Mr02Is
Nancy	(D)	20	F	Unknown	23Mr02Is
Biddy	(D)	17	F	Unknown	23Mr02Is
BOLIN, James		22	M	Laborer	23Mr02Is
SWEENEY, James		14	M	Unknown	23Mr02Is
Ann	(T)	11	F	Unknown	23Mr02Is
John	(B)	08	M	Child	23Mr02Is
Michael	(B)	05	M	Child	23Mr02Is
Owen	(B)	02	M	Child	23Mr02Is
OBRIEN, Patrick		25	M	Laborer	23Mr02Is
MEYRICK, John		26	M	Laborer	23Mr02Is
Honor		20	F	Unknown	23Mr02Is
QUIN, Mary		21	F	Unknown	23Mr02Is
MEYRICK, James		26	M	Laborer	23Mr02Is
Peggy		22	F	Unknown	23Mr02Is
WELSH, Martin		26	M	Laborer	23Mr02Is
Ellen		25	F	Unknown	23Mr02Is
Catherine		20	F	Unknown	23Mr02Is
Bridget		01	F	Child	23Mr02Is
GOODWIN, John		35	M	Weaver	23Mr02Is
Rose		30	F	Unknown	23Mr02Is
ONEILL, May		25	F	Unknown	23Mr02Is
Eleanor		21	F	Unknown	23Mr02Is
Eliza		19	F	Unknown	23Mr02Is
GOODWIN, Peter		03	M	Child	23Mr02Is
Betty	(T)	01	F	Child	23Mr02Is
MCGUIRE, Thomas		50	M	Cooper	23Mr02Is
Biddy	(W)	40	F	Unknown	23Mr02Is
Patrick	(S)	25	M	Unknown	23Mr02Is
Thomas	(S)	20	M	Unknown	23Mr02Is
Alice	(D)	16	F	Unknown	23Mr02Is
WARD, Wm.		19	M	Laborer	23Mr02Is
MARTIN, John		19	M	Laborer	23Mr02Is
MCGUIRE, May		20	F	Unknown	23Mr02Is
MCLOON, Mary		19	F	Unknown	23Mr02Is
OBRIEN, Mary		24	F	Unknown	23Mr02Is
DRISCOLL, Mary		24	F	Unknown	23Mr02Is
COONEY, Bartholomew		30	M	Laborer	23Mr02Is
Owen		28	M	Laborer	23Mr02Is
DUGGAN, Matthew		30	M	Laborer	23Mr02Is
Margaret		21	F	Unknown	23Mr02Is
KILCOLLIN, Pat		28	M	Laborer	23Mr02Is
Kate		20	F	Unknown	23Mr02Is
CONNOR, Thomas		30	M	Laborer	23Mr02Is
CONNELL, Catherine		28	F	Unknown	23Mr02Is
CONNELL, Mary	(D)	11	F	Unknown	23Mr02Is
Catherine	(D)	07	F	Child	23Mr02Is
Ellen	(D)	03	F	Child	23Mr02Is
Died-At-Sea					
SWEENY, John		40	M	Laborer	23Mr02Is
Cecilia	(W)	35	F	Unknown	23Mr02Is
Coll	(S)	20	M	Laborer	23Mr02Is
Michael	(S)	14	M	Unknown	23Mr02Is
Biddy	(D)	06	F	Child	23Mr02Is
Nancy	(D)	04	F	Child	23Mr02Is
John	(S)	03	M	Child	23Mr02Is
HERRIN, Martin		27	M	Draper	23Mr02Is
SULLIVAN, Cornelius		21	M	Servant	23Mr02Is
CLARK, Pat		30	M	Laborer	23Mr02Is
Mary		27	F	Laborer	23Mr02Is
BURKE, Michael		25	M	Laborer	23Mr02Is
Thomas		28	M	Laborer	23Mr02Is
BYRNE, John		23	M	Laborer	23Mr02Is
WHITE, John		30	M	Laborer	23Mr02Is
FITZGERALD, Mike		23	M	Laborer	23Mr02Is
RYAN, Thomas		20	M	Laborer	23Mr02Is
FITZPATRICK, Catherine		18	F	Unknown	23Mr02Is
RYAN, Mary		16	F	Unknown	23Mr02Is
JUDGE, John		35	M	Laborer	23Mr02Is
Ann	(W)	30	F	Unknown	23Mr02Is
James	(S)	10	M	Unknown	23Mr02Is
Patt	(S)	09	M	Child	23Mr02Is
Bridget	(D)	07	F	Child	23Mr02Is
William	(S)	04	M	Child	23Mr02Is
John	(S)	02	M	Child	23Mr02Is
FEENEY, Cecilia		19	F	Unknown	23Mr02Is
MELIDAY, Anthony		55	M	Farmer	23Mr02Is
Mary	(W)	50	F	Unknown	23Mr02Is
James	(S)	30	M	Laborer	23Mr02Is
Mike	(S)	16	M	Unknown	23Mr02Is
Anthony	(S)	12	M	Unknown	23Mr02Is
Bridget	(D)	17	F	Unknown	23Mr02Is
HEGARTY, Sibey		20	F	Unknown	23Mr02Is
QUINN, Wm.		20	M	Laborer	23Mr02Is
Bridget		20	F	Unknown	23Mr02Is
NOON, Michael		36	M	Laborer	23Mr02Is
Margaret	(W)	30	F	Unknown	23Mr02Is
Thomas	(S)	01	M	Child	23Mr02Is
ROBINSON, Maria		22	F	Unknown	23Mr02Is
DOUGHERTY, John		24	M	Laborer	23Mr02Is
Sarah		18	F	Unknown	23Mr02Is
Nancy		20	F	Unknown	23Mr02Is
MCAULIFFE, John		50	M	Laborer	23Mr02Is
Died-At-Sea					
Elizabeth	(W)	46	F	Unknown	23Mr02Is
Daniel	(S)	23	M	Laborer	23Mr02Is
Joseph	(S)	21	M	Laborer	23Mr02Is
John	(S)	12	M	Unknown	23Mr02Is
Died-At-Sea					
Michael	(S)	08	M	Child	23Mr02Is
SHEEHAN, Catherine		24	F	Unknown	23Mr02Is
Michael		27	M	Laborer	23Mr02Is
JOHNSTON, May		21	F	Servant	23Mr02Is
Ann		17	F	Servant	23Mr02Is
RAFFERTY, Andreaw		40	M	Tinker	23Mr02Is
LYNCH, Pat		30	M	Farmer	23Mr02Is
Catherine	(W)	26	F	Unknown	23Mr02Is
OHIGGINS, Danl.		18	M	Laborer	23Mr02Is
LYNCH, Ann-J.		08	F	Child	23Mr02Is
Pat	(B)	.06	M	Infant	23Mr02Is
MURPHY, James		50	M	Laborer	23Mr02Is
Michl.		20	M	Laborer	23Mr02Is
Winnivy		22	F	Unknown	23Mr02Is
MCKEE, Robt.		20	M	Wimcht	23Mr02Is
MULROY, John		24	M	Laborer	23Mr02Is
WILSON, James		24	M	Laborer	23Mr02Is
Honor		22	F	Unknown	23Mr02Is
KILLAWELL, Pat		23	M	Laborer	23Mr02Is
KENNEY, Pat		28	M	Laborer	23Mr02Is
KILLAWELL, Anthony		20	M	Laborer	23Mr02Is

NAMES OF PASSENGERS		AGE	SEX	OCCUPATIONS	DATE PORT SHIP
KILGAMMON, Ellen		18	F	Laborer	23Mr02Is
WHITE, John		17	M	Laborer	23Mr02Is
TRAINER, Mary		17	F	Unknown	23Mr02Is
Ann		18	F	Unknown	23Mr02Is
GALLAGHER, Pat		26	M	Laborer	23Mr02Is
LEGGETT, James		30	M	Mariner	23Mr02Is
NOON, Matthew		29	M	Laborer	23Mr02Is
Peggy		26	F	Unknown	23Mr02Is
MURPHY, Patrick		26	M	Laborer	23Mr02Is
SCOTT, John		24	M	Laborer	23Mr02Is
HUTCHINSON, May		58	F	Unknown	23Mr02Is
RAFFERTY, John		25	M	Shepherd	23Mr02Is
HAD, John		26	M	Laborer	23Mr02Is
MCCANN, Michael		20	M	Laborer	23Mr02Is
Margaret		29	F	Unknown	23Mr02Is
MCANDREWS, Thos.		20	M	Laborer	23Mr02Is
Margaret		29	F	Unknown	23Mr02Is
Catherine		25	F	Unknown	23Mr02Is
MAIN, Michael		20	M	Laborer	23Mr02Is
John		22	M	Laborer	23Mr02Is
Bridget		21	F	Unknown	23Mr02Is
KILGAMMON, Wm.		36	M	Laborer	23Mr02Is
CAVANAGH, John		39	M	Laborer	23Mr02Is
CURRY, Michael		30	M	Laborer	23Mr02Is
BRENNAN, Pat		40	M	Laborer	23Mr02Is
Rosanna	(W)	34	F	Unknown	23Mr02Is
Andrew	(S)	13	M	Unknown	23Mr02Is
Ellen	(D)	11	F	Unknown	23Mr02Is
Judy	(D)	09	F	Child	23Mr02Is
Ann	(D)	07	F	Child	23Mr02Is
Died-At-Sea					
James	(S)	.10	M	Infant	23Mr02Is
REILLY, Miles		20	M	Laborer	23Mr02Is
Died-At-Sea					
SAUL, John		20	M	Laborer	23Mr02Is
Michael		21	M	Laborer	23Mr02Is
CONNOR, James		24	M	Laborer	23Mr02Is
KELLY, Bryan		24	M	Laborer	23Mr02Is
Julia		22	F	Unknown	23Mr02Is
CLARKE, James		20	M	Clerk	23Mr02Is
NEVIN, Matthew		26	M	Laborer	23Mr02Is
Catherine		25	F	Unknown	23Mr02Is
DUFFY, Michael		20	M	Laborer	23Mr02Is
ALLEN, Payton		32	M	Gdnr	23Mr02Is
BEGNEY, Bridget		24	F	Unknown	23Mr02Is
ANDERSON, Geo.		18	M	Laborer	23Mr02Is
CONN, James		17	M	Laborer	23Mr02Is
ROBINSON, Henry		40	M	Laborer	23Mr02Is
Martha	(W)	40	F	Unknown	23Mr02Is
Sally	(D)	21	F	Unknown	23Mr02Is
Sarah	(D)	15	F	Unknown	23Mr02Is
Isabella	(D)	13	F	Unknown	23Mr02Is
Margaret	(D)	11	F	Unknown	23Mr02Is
Wm.Henry	(S)	07	M	Child	23Mr02Is
DUNCAN, Michael		23	M	Sawer	23Mr02Is
Marg	(W)	20	F	Unknown	23Mr02Is
Michael	(S)	.08	M	Infant	23Mr02Is
James		20	M	Laborer	23Mr02Is
SMITH, Phillip		21	M	Laborer	23Mr02Is
Mary-Ann		20	F	Unknown	23Mr02Is
RAHILL, Ellen		20	F	Unknown	23Mr02Is
ROURKE, Owen		26	M	Sawer	23Mr02Is
FARRELL, William		24	M	Laborer	23Mr02Is
Mary	(M)	50	F	Unknown	23Mr02Is
Died-At-Sea					
Mary	(T)	19	F	Unknown	23Mr02Is
LEVY, Margaret		19	F	Unknown	23Mr02Is
MCCORMICK, John		00	M	Laborer	23Mr02Is
CAVANAGH, Pat		40	M	Laborer	23Mr02Is
Mary	(W)	40	F	Unknown	23Mr02Is
Thos.	(S)	22	M	Unknown	23Mr02Is
Patrick	(S)	13	M	Unknown	23Mr02Is
Patrclk	(S)	16	M	Unknown	23Mr02Is
Sarah	(D)	18	F	Unknown	23Mr02Is
Mary	(D)	22	F	Unknown	23Mr02Is

NAMES OF PASSENGERS		AGE	SEX	OCCUPATIONS	DATE PORT SHIP
CAVANAGH, Bridget	(D)	12	F	Unknown	23Mr02Is
ODOWD, Michael		22	M	Laborer	23Mr02Is
MULDOWNEY, Mary		21	F	Unknown	23Mr02Is
DOWDICAN, Thos.		24	M	Laborer	23Mr02Is
Edward		17	M	Laborer	23Mr02Is
FINNEGAN, Elizabeth		19	F	Unknown	23Mr02Is
GILLOOLY, Thos.		21	M	Laborer	23Mr02Is
CRONIN, John		21	M	Servant	23Mr02Is
HASSELL, Mich.		22	M	Servant	23Mr02Is
Ellen		20	F	Unknown	23Mr02Is
DALY, John		30	M	Laborer	23Mr02Is
MCGRATH, Ann		20	F	Unknown	23Mr02Is
SWEENEY, Patrick		.00	M	Infant	23Mr02Is
Born-At-Sea					
DAVIS, Alexander		32	M	Mariner	23Mr02Is

FINLAND 25 MARCH 1847

From Liverpool

NAMES OF PASSENGERS		AGE	SEX	OCCUPATIONS	DATE PORT SHIP
GIBBENS, M.		25	M	Mechanic	25Mr02Cb
MCGRATH, Mary		17	F	Unknown	25Mr02Cb
CONROY, F.		20	M	Mechanic	25Mr02Cb
POWELL, G.		24	M	Mechanic	25Mr02Cb
U	(W)	24	F	Unknown	25Mr02Cb
Thos.	(S)	06	M	Child	25Mr02Cb
Benj.	(S)	04	M	Child	25Mr02Cb
BENARD, J.		22	M	Mechanic	25Mr02Cb
Eliza	(W)	22	F	Unknown	25Mr02Cb
Teresa	(D)	01	F	Child	25Mr02Cb
CURREY, F.		28	M	Mechanic	25Mr02Cb
NEWELL, J.		28	M	Mechanic	25Mr02Cb
Mary	(W)	26	F	Unknown	25Mr02Cb
Margr.	(D)	01	F	Child	25Mr02Cb
GOWNOR, M.		22	M	Mechanic	25Mr02Cb
MURPHY, H.		20	M	Mechanic	25Mr02Cb
CALLAGHAN, J.		36	M	Mechanic	25Mr02Cb
LOVE, J.		26	M	Mechanic	25Mr02Cb
Isabella		21	F	Unknown	25Mr02Cb
DEACON, Mary		20	F	Unknown	25Mr02Cb
LOVE, Alex		18	M	Mechanic	25Mr02Cb
NEY, S.		26	M	Mechanic	25Mr02Cb
OAWEAS, M.		26	M	Mechanic	25Mr02Cb
MCCEHATHIS, J.		22	M	Mechanic	25Mr02Cb
GALLAGHER, J.		30	M	Mechanic	25Mr02Cb
U	(W)	26	F	Unknown	25Mr02Cb
S.	(S)	04	M	Child	25Mr02Cb
Wm.	(S)	01	M	Child	25Mr02Cb
MCMAHON, H.		20	M	Mechanic	25Mr02Cb
BUTLER, P.		30	M	Mechanic	25Mr02Cb
J.		16	M	Mechanic	25Mr02Cb
Thos.		12	M	Mechanic	25Mr02Cb
FLYNN, C.		30	M	Mechanic	25Mr02Cb
U	(W)	24	F	Unknown	25Mr02Cb
J.	(S)	07	M	Child	25Mr02Cb
FREENER, M.		25	M	Mechanic	25Mr02Cb
REYNOLDS, Jas.		26	M	Mechanic	25Mr02Cb
U	(W)	20	F	Unknown	25Mr02Cb
Rose		24	F	Unknown	25Mr02Cb
Ann		21	F	Unknown	25Mr02Cb
DENNIS, Thos.		27	M	Mechanic	25Mr02Cb
KELLY, Thos.		30	M	Mechanic	25Mr02Cb
DAWNING, J.		22	M	Mechanic	25Mr02Cb
DURA, Margt.		25	F	Unknown	25Mr02Cb
REYNOLDS, M.		40	M	Mechanic	25Mr02Cb
U	(W)	22	F	Unknown	25Mr02Cb
Mary	(D)	01	F	Child	25Mr02Cb
Bryan		36	M	Mechanic	25Mr02Cb
Hugh		30	M	Mechanic	25Mr02Cb

NAMES OF PASSENGERS		AGE	SEX	OCCUPATIONS	DATE PORT SHIP
GALLAGHER, M.		19	M	Mechanic	25Mr02Cb
BYNN, R.		25	M	Mechanic	25Mr02Cb
SCULLY, J.		21	M	Mechanic	25Mr02Cb
CULREAVY, J.		21	M	Mechanic	25Mr02Cb
FLANIGAN, P.		40	M	Mechanic	25Mr02Cb
U	(W)	35	F	Unknown	25Mr02Cb
CAMPBELL, J.		40	M	Mechanic	25Mr02Cb
Biddy		38	F	Unknown	25Mr02Cb
HERLIN, J.		38	M	Mechanic	25Mr02Cb
Mary	(W)	36	F	Unknown	25Mr02Cb
Margt.	(D)	05	F	Child	25Mr02Cb
Biddy	(D)	02	F	Child	25Mr02Cb
Jas.	(S)	01	M	Child	25Mr02Cb
CAMPBELL, Jas.		25	M	Mechanic	25Mr02Cb
CONNOR, Mary		20	F	Unknown	25Mr02Cb
NAUGHTON, P.		19	M	Mechanic	25Mr02Cb
CURLEY, M.		12	M	Mechanic	25Mr02Cb
NAUGHTON, J.		29	M	Mechanic	25Mr02Cb
HAGAN, P.		40	M	Mechanic	25Mr02Cb
RUMY, Teresa		07	F	Child	25Mr02Cb
SWEHAN, J.		17	M	Mechanic	25Mr02Cb
BROOKS, J.		12	M	Mechanic	25Mr02Cb
CULLEN, Thos.		14	M	Mechanic	25Mr02Cb
U-Mr.		20	M	Mechanic	25Mr02Cb
GREY, Jan.		30	M	Mechanic	25Mr02Cb
Mary-A.		31	F	Unknown	25Mr02Cb
BRYAN, N.		35	M	Mechanic	25Mr02Cb
CORCORAN, Thos.		19	M	Mechanic	25Mr02Cb
N.		16	M	Mechanic	25Mr02Cb
CAHILL, N.		24	M	Mechanic	25Mr02Cb
CORCORAN, M.		30	M	Mechanic	25Mr02Cb
REYNOLDS, Jos.		16	M	Mechanic	25Mr02Cb
SHARKEY, Ann		01	F	Child	25Mr02Cb
SWEENEY, Michael		40	M	Unknown	25Mr02Cb
Bridget	(W)	40	F	Unknown	25Mr02Cb
Alexr.	(S)	18	M	Unknown	25Mr02Cb
Mary	(D)	13	F	Unknown	25Mr02Cb
SANDLEWOOD, Daniel		22	M	Unknown	25Mr02Cb
U	(W)	24	F	Unknown	25Mr02Cb
John	(S)	04	M	Child	25Mr02Cb
Mary-Jane	(D)	01	F	Child	25Mr02Cb
RURMISS, Isabella		50	F	Unknown	25Mr02Cb
MCCLUSKY, Jane		20	F	Unknown	25Mr02Cb
MCBURELL, Stephen		50	M	Unknown	25Mr02Cb
Noble		50	M	Unknown	25Mr02Cb
John		20	M	Unknown	25Mr02Cb
Edwd.		16	M	Unknown	25Mr02Cb
Clements		12	M	Unknown	25Mr02Cb
Peggy		10	F	Unknown	25Mr02Cb
Stephen		07	M	Child	25Mr02Cb
Irwin		05	M	Child	25Mr02Cb
Mary		03	F	Child	25Mr02Cb
DAVIS, Owen		30	M	Unknown	25Mr02Cb
MARTIN, Michael		36	M	Unknown	25Mr02Cb
U	(W)	34	F	Unknown	25Mr02Cb
Mary	(D)	06	F	Child	25Mr02Cb
U	(S)	04	M	Child	25Mr02Cb
Patk.	(S)	01	M	Child	25Mr02Cb
CORMICK, Ann		26	F	Unknown	25Mr02Cb
KERNRY, Peggy		25	F	Unknown	25Mr02Cb
KINNEY, Michael		30	M	Unknown	25Mr02Cb
Bridget		26	F	Unknown	25Mr02Cb
KAVISTON, Thos.		50	M	Unknown	25Mr02Cb
Ellen		21	F	Unknown	25Mr02Cb
Thos.		18	M	Unknown	25Mr02Cb
Cathr.		30	F	Unknown	25Mr02Cb
QUINN, Patk.		21	M	Unknown	25Mr02Cb
KEARNEY, Mary		07	F	Child	25Mr02Cb
KELLEY, Luke		50	M	Unknown	25Mr02Cb
Mary	(W)	50	F	Unknown	25Mr02Cb
Thos.	(S)	25	M	Unknown	25Mr02Cb
James	(S)	21	M	Unknown	25Mr02Cb
DEVINE, John		22	M	Unknown	25Mr02Cb
KELLEY, Michael		25	M	Unknown	25Mr02Cb
FORR, Mack		40	M	Mechanic	25Mr02Cb
FORR, Patk.		30	M	Laborer	25Mr02Cb
Cathn.		30	F	Unknown	25Mr02Cb
Cathn.		20	F	Unknown	25Mr02Cb
Mary		22	F	Unknown	25Mr02Cb
Owen		07	M	Child	25Mr02Cb
Hanick		01	M	Child	25Mr02Cb
LOUGHLIN, Mary		17	F	Unknown	25Mr02Cb
MULONI, Martin		20	M	Unknown	25Mr02Cb
Libby		18	F	Unknown	25Mr02Cb
CASSIDY, Thos.		35	M	Unknown	25Mr02Cb
Biddy	(W)	35	F	Unknown	25Mr02Cb
Cathn.	(D)	11	F	Unknown	25Mr02Cb
Mary	(D)	09	F	Child	25Mr02Cb
Biddy	(D)	07	F	Child	25Mr02Cb
Mary	(D)	05	F	Child	25Mr02Cb
Hannah	(D)	01	F	Child	25Mr02Cb
PHELEN, Biddy		21	F	Unknown	25Mr02Cb
BINGMAN, Mary		20	F	Unknown	25Mr02Cb
QUINN, Biddy		17	F	Unknown	25Mr02Cb
Mary		17	F	Unknown	25Mr02Cb
EAGAN, Bryan		40	M	Unknown	25Mr02Cb
Bridget		30	F	Unknown	25Mr02Cb
Cathn.		20	F	Unknown	25Mr02Cb
SHARKEY, Jas.		30	M	Unknown	25Mr02Cb
Mary		24	F	Unknown	25Mr02Cb
Mary		25	F	Unknown	25Mr02Cb
GILHARTON, J.		24	M	Unknown	25Mr02Cb
MCGARTH, Hugh		24	M	Unknown	25Mr02Cb
DORAN, Thos.		22	M	Unknown	25Mr02Cb
CARROL, John		20	M	Unknown	25Mr02Cb
GARVAN, Thos.		17	M	Unknown	25Mr02Cb
HANLEY, Patk.		30	M	Unknown	25Mr02Cb
U	(W)	27	F	Unknown	25Mr02Cb
Mary	(D)	06	F	Child	25Mr02Cb
Martin	(S)	04	M	Child	25Mr02Cb
Thos.	(S)	01	M	Child	25Mr02Cb
BOYLAN, Martin		28	M	Unknown	25Mr02Cb
U	(W)	26	F	Unknown	25Mr02Cb
James	(S)	04	M	Child	25Mr02Cb
Ann	(D)	02	F	Child	25Mr02Cb
George	(S)	01	M	Child	25Mr02Cb
CAMPBELL, Bernard		18	M	Mechanic	25Mr02Cb
CARNEY, Peter		50	M	Mechanic	25Mr02Cb
DONNELLY, Jas.		45	M	Mechanic	25Mr02Cb
MCELHALLAN, J.		26	M	Laborer	25Mr02Cb
WATTERS, Mary		24	F	Unknown	25Mr02Cb
SWEENEY, Clark		20	M	Unknown	25Mr02Cb
DENNIGAN, Ellen		18	F	Unknown	25Mr02Cb
KELLEY, Bridget		25	F	Unknown	25Mr02Cb
HUTCHINSON, Saml.		40	M	Mechanic	25Mr02Cb
MIGHT, S.		25	M	Mechanic	25Mr02Cb
SMYTH, Michael		30	M	Laborer	25Mr02Cb
CONLEY, Mary		18	F	Unknown	25Mr02Cb
GARDINER, Thos.		20	M	Mechanic	25Mr02Cb
KELLEY, Mary		20	F	Unknown	25Mr02Cb
MCCABE, Patk.		50	M	Unknown	25Mr02Cb
Margt.	(W)	40	F	Unknown	25Mr02Cb
W.	(S)	25	M	Mechanic	25Mr02Cb
Michael	(S)	23	M	Laborer	25Mr02Cb
James	(S)	20	M	Laborer	25Mr02Cb
Patk.	(S)	18	M	Laborer	25Mr02Cb
Edwd.	(S)	08	M	Child	25Mr02Cb
John	(S)	07	M	Child	25Mr02Cb
Hannah	(D)	11	F	Unknown	25Mr02Cb
GETTON, Anthony		30	M	Mechanic	25Mr02Cb
MURRAY, James		30	M	Laborer	25Mr02Cb
CADDEN, Ann		24	F	Unknown	25Mr02Cb

SIDDONS 31 MARCH 1847

From Liverpool

NAMES OF PASSENGERS		AGE SEX	OCCUPATIONS	DATE PORT SHIP
FRAY, L.		26 M	Laborer	31Mr02Bx
Jane	(W)	22 F	Unknown	31Mr02Bx
Ellen	(D)	02 F	Child	31Mr02Bx
CONLAN, C.		30 M	Laborer	31Mr02Bx
U	(W)	22 F	Unknown	31Mr02Bx
Peter		22 M	Laborer	31Mr02Bx
FOLLER, Bridget		17 F	Unknown	31Mr02Bx
CANEY, U-Miss		18 F	Unknown	31Mr02Bx
REILLY, B.		24 M	Laborer	31Mr02Bx
CARROLL, J.		21 M	Laborer	31Mr02Bx
MOON, Cath.		56 F	Unknown	31Mr02Bx
Alice		24 F	Unknown	31Mr02Bx
CULLEN, P.		26 M	Laborer	31Mr02Bx
SHARKE, Mary		26 F	Unknown	31Mr02Bx
Rose		22 F	Unknown	31Mr02Bx
CULLEN, Mary		18 F	Unknown	31Mr02Bx
PIOIRY, W.		25 M	Laborer	31Mr02Bx
Jas.		21 M	Laborer	31Mr02Bx
Cath.		18 F	Unknown	31Mr02Bx
Ann		18 F	Unknown	31Mr02Bx
Rose		50 F	Unknown	31Mr02Bx
ROGAN, D.		18 M	Laborer	31Mr02Bx
SWEENEY, Betsy		08 F	Child	31Mr02Bx
Rose		11 F	Child	31Mr02Bx
FINIGAN, Ann		02 F	Child	31Mr02Bx
GAUGHAN, Bridget		20 F	Unknown	31Mr02Bx
MONGAY, Bridget		20 F	Unknown	31Mr02Bx
COLEMAN, Mgt.		21 F	Unknown	31Mr02Bx
LYNAUGH, J.		22 M	Laborer	31Mr02Bx
HALL, J.		36 M	Laborer	31Mr02Bx
LANNY, P.		26 M	Laborer	31Mr02Bx
Anne	(W)	22 F	Unknown	31Mr02Bx
John	(S)	.00 M	Infant	31Mr02Bx
NOBLE, J.		21 M	Laborer	31Mr02Bx
DUFFY, P.		24 M	Laborer	31Mr02Bx
MCENTILL, C.		24 M	Laborer	31Mr02Bx
SMITH, C.		22 M	Laborer	31Mr02Bx
MCGUIN, P.		23 M	Laborer	31Mr02Bx
TUNIR, P.		22 M	Laborer	31Mr02Bx
MILLIGAN, P.		20 M	Laborer	31Mr02Bx
John		18 M	Laborer	31Mr02Bx
BUCHANAN, M.		28 M	Laborer	31Mr02Bx
STEWART, R.		24 M	Laborer	31Mr02Bx
BURDEN, P.		20 M	Laborer	31Mr02Bx
ELLIS, M.		26 M	Laborer	31Mr02Bx
FALLON, B.		08 M	Child	31Mr02Bx
LYNCH, P.		40 M	Laborer	31Mr02Bx
U	(W)	36 F	Unknown	31Mr02Bx
Patk.	(S)	07 M	Child	31Mr02Bx
John	(S)	05 M	Child	31Mr02Bx
MCANNY, P.		30 M	Laborer	31Mr02Bx
U	(W)	30 F	Unknown	31Mr02Bx
REILLY, G.		28 M	Laborer	31Mr02Bx
Peter		35 M	Laborer	31Mr02Bx
James		08 M	Child	31Mr02Bx
SHERIDAN, M.		36 M	Laborer	31Mr02Bx
NEWTON, G.		30 M	Laborer	31Mr02Bx
BYRNE, W.		19 M	Laborer	31Mr02Bx
Luke		17 M	Laborer	31Mr02Bx
EASTON, M.		00 M	Laborer	31Mr02Bx
U	(W)	00 F	Unknown	31Mr02Bx
TANSLY, W.		00 M	Laborer	31Mr02Bx
WILY, J.		37 M	Laborer	31Mr02Bx
GROWNLY, J.		25 M	Laborer	31Mr02Bx
Madge		16 F	Unknown	31Mr02Bx

NAMES OF PASSENGERS		AGE SEX	OCCUPATIONS	DATE PORT SHIP
SMITH, Judy		20 F	Unknown	31Mr02
MURRY, E.		40 M	Laborer	31Mr02
MCNALLY, Cath.		18 F	Unknown	31Mr02
MURRAY, J.		10 M	Child	31Mr02
Bridget		08 F	Child	31Mr02
MCNALLY, M.		22 M	Laborer	31Mr02
MORRIS, J.		22 M	Laborer	31Mr02
MASSEY, H.		19 M	Laborer	31Mr02
MCCANN, P.		22 M	Laborer	31Mr02
DERLIN, J.		22 M	Laborer	31Mr02
FOX, E.		20 M	Laborer	31Mr02
MCNAMEE, P.		17 M	Laborer	31Mr02
John		11 M	Child	31Mr02
U-Mrs.		21 F	Unknown	31Mr02
DUFF, Biddy		20 F	Unknown	31Mr02
Mary		19 F	Unknown	31Mr02
MCFADDEN, U-Mrs.		40 F	Unknown	31Mr02
J.	(S)	20 M	Laborer	31Mr02
Wm.	(S)	18 M	Laborer	31Mr02
BRADDY, J.		26 M	Laborer	31Mr02
CARTNEY, W.		27 M	Laborer	31Mr02
CLARKE, J.		25 M	Laborer	31Mr02
REILY, M.		24 M	Laborer	31Mr02
KELLEEN, D.		24 M	Laborer	31Mr02
GREEN, Fanny		50 F	Unknown	31Mr02
Barth	(S)	21 M	Laborer	31Mr02
Ann	(D)	17 F	Unknown	31Mr02
John	(S)	15 M	None	31Mr02
KILDREEN, P.		26 M	Laborer	31Mr02
GLANCY, B.		25 M	Laborer	31Mr02
U	(W)	24 F	Unknown	31Mr02
Michael	(S)	02 M	Child	31Mr02
Chas.	(S)	01 M	Child	31Mr02
JORDAN, C.		20 M	Laborer	31Mr02
DOUGHTY, H.		40 M	Laborer	31Mr02
EGAN, P.		37 M	Laborer	31Mr02
Michl.		25 M	Laborer	31Mr02
DOUGLAS, W.		24 M	Laborer	31Mr02
Nancy		18 F	Unknown	31Mr02
HARLY, P.		25 M	Laborer	31Mr02
MORAN, Mary		20 F	Unknown	31Mr02
KANE, Mary		19 F	Unknown	31Mr02
NEELAN, Bridget		20 F	Unknown	31Mr02
SHEAKIN, M.		20 M	Laborer	31Mr02
GARRIGAN, D.		24 M	Laborer	31Mr02
Mgt.		20 F	Unknown	31Mr02
QUIN, M.		20 M	Laborer	31Mr02
Anne		11 F	Child	31Mr02
BRADY, O.		22 M	Laborer	31Mr02
LYNCH, M.		23 M	Laborer	31Mr02
SWEENY, P.		26 M	Laborer	31Mr02
LYNCH, M.		00 M	Laborer	31Mr02
Philip	(P)	60 M	Laborer	31Mr02
U-Mrs.		26 F	Unknown	31Mr02
Jas.		20 M	Laborer	31Mr02
Cath.		19 F	Unknown	31Mr02
Janet		10 F	Child	31Mr02
MAHER, J.		46 M	Laborer	31Mr02
U	(W)	40 F	Unknown	31Mr02
MCKEEVER, Mary		18 F	Unknown	31Mr02
KELLY, O.		19 M	Laborer	31Mr02
GATELY, Mary		21 F	Unknown	31Mr02
DEVINE, J.		24 M	Laborer	31Mr02
WAUGH, M.		26 M	Laborer	31Mr02
ODONNELL, J.		21 M	Laborer	31Mr02
WILSON, M.		21 M	Laborer	31Mr02
KEARNSTON, H.		20 M	Laborer	31Mr02
KEENAN, T.		21 M	Laborer	31Mr02
MORAN, Mary		26 F	Unknown	31Mr02
SMITH, J.		24 M	Laborer	31Mr02
MCMALLY, Mary		20 F	Unknown	31Mr02
GALLIGAN, O.		40 M	Laborer	31Mr02
U	(W)	30 F	Unknown	31Mr02
GAFFREY, B.		26 M	Laborer	31Mr02
FINNIGAN, M.		20 F	Unknown	31Mr02

NAMES OF PASSENGERS		AGE	SEX	OCCUPATIONS	DATE PORT SHIP
REILLY, C.		20	M	Laborer	31Mr02Bx
Pat		20	M	Unknown	31Mr02Bx
BARRETT, J.		23	F	Unknown	31Mr02Bx
Mgt.		23	F	Unknown	31Mr02Bx
MELEN, Bridget		20	F	Unknown	31Mr02Bx
BARRETT, Bridget		02	F	Child	31Mr02Bx
Mgt.		01	F	Child	31Mr02Bx
REIFE, P.		39	M	Laborer	31Mr02Bx
U	(W)	39	F	Unknown	31Mr02Bx
Owen	(S)	20	M	Laborer	31Mr02Bx
Mgt.	(D)	21	F	Unknown	31Mr02Bx
Mary	(D)	19	F	Unknown	31Mr02Bx
Mich.	(S)	14	M	Unknown	31Mr02Bx
R.	(S)	12	M	Unknown	31Mr02Bx
Thos.	(S)	10	M	Child	31Mr02Bx
Bridget	(D)	08	F	Child	31Mr02Bx
Ellen	(D)	06	F	Child	31Mr02Bx
DEADY, J.		26	M	Laborer	31Mr02Bx
U	(W)	24	F	Unknown	31Mr02Bx
John		14	M	Laborer	31Mr02Bx
TULLEN, D.		30	M	Laborer	31Mr02Bx
U	(W)	30	F	Unknown	31Mr02Bx
DALONY, C.		23	M	Laborer	31Mr02Bx
HERLOHY, Bridget		23	F	Unknown	31Mr02Bx
SULLIVAN, Bridget		21	F	Unknown	31Mr02Bx
REILLY, J.		30	M	Laborer	31Mr02Bx
HENGEN, J.		22	M	Laborer	31Mr02Bx
DONALY, E.		20	M	Laborer	31Mr02Bx
PILLION, J.		26	M	Laborer	31Mr02Bx
DEVIN, Mary		16	F	Unknown	31Mr02Bx
Bridget		17	F	Unknown	31Mr02Bx
CLARKE, Mary		15	F	Unknown	31Mr02Bx
MARTHA, S.		28	M	Laborer	31Mr02Bx
SMITH, O.		26	M	Laborer	31Mr02Bx
MURPHY, J.		26	M	Laborer	31Mr02Bx
U	(W)	25	F	Unknown	31Mr02Bx
Martin	(S)	03	M	Child	31Mr02Bx
MITCHELL, Honore		22	F	Unknown	31Mr02Bx
MASTERSON, P.		40	M	Laborer	31Mr02Bx
Mary		07	F	Child	31Mr02Bx
GAUGHAN, M.		20	M	Laborer	31Mr02Bx
LYNCH, J.		27	M	Laborer	31Mr02Bx
Ellen		30	F	Unknown	31Mr02Bx
MASTERSON, J.		21	M	Laborer	31Mr02Bx
BUTLER, P.		30	M	Laborer	31Mr02Bx
DORAN, P.		28	M	Laborer	31Mr02Bx
ORR, Mgt.		40	F	Unknown	31Mr02Bx
Anne-J.	(D)	14	F	Unknown	31Mr02Bx
Mary	(D)	12	F	Unknown	31Mr02Bx
Abram.	(S)	10	M	Child	31Mr02Bx
Mgt.	(D)	08	F	Child	31Mr02Bx
Elizbt.	(D)	06	F	Child	31Mr02Bx
Jas.	(S)	02	M	Child	31Mr02Bx
GILLY, Rose		25	F	Unknown	31Mr02Bx
BRADY, Alice		16	F	Unknown	31Mr02Bx
GRIFFEN, M.		24	M	Laborer	31Mr02Bx
MALONEY, D.		24	M	Laborer	31Mr02Bx
John		19	M	Laborer	31Mr02Bx
John		18	M	Laborer	31Mr02Bx
KENNEDY, J.		24	M	Laborer	31Mr02Bx
CONNOR, J.		22	M	Laborer	31Mr02Bx
STACK, M.		20	M	Laborer	31Mr02Bx
WALSH, J.		21	M	Laborer	31Mr02Bx
GRIFFEN, J.		25	M	Laborer	31Mr02Bx
CONNOR, E.		22	M	Laborer	31Mr02Bx
LAWLER, T.		30	M	Laborer	31Mr02Bx
Mary	(W)	26	F	Unknown	31Mr02Bx
Patrk.	(S)	01	M	Child	31Mr02Bx
SCOLLARD, M.		24	M	Laborer	31Mr02Bx
HAYES, J.		20	M	Laborer	31Mr02Bx
GRIFFIN, Mgt.		19	F	Unknown	31Mr02Bx
DOOLAN, Mary		18	F	Unknown	31Mr02Bx
BARNCLE, J.		20	M	Laborer	31Mr02Bx
THOMPSON, J.		22	M	Laborer	31Mr02Bx
LLOYD, T.E.		22	M	Laborer	31Mr02Bx
ROBERTS, J.		10	M	Child	31Mr02
COSTIGAN, W.		35	M	Laborer	31Mr02
LOUGHAN, W.		21	M	Laborer	31Mr02
MEEHAN, E.		24	M	Laborer	31Mr02
LAWLER, M.		21	M	Laborer	31Mr02
CONROY, J.		27	M	Laborer	31Mr02
COLLOPS, Ann		20	F	Unknown	31Mr02
Mary		11	F	Child	31Mr02
Ellen		09	F	Child	31Mr02
BRODERICK, P.		25	M	Laborer	31Mr02
KEEFE, O.		21	M	Laborer	31Mr02
BROPHY, J.		21	M	Laborer	31Mr02
BROWN, A.		21	M	Laborer	31Mr02
FAY, P.		22	M	Laborer	31Mr02
WATSON, M.		36	M	Laborer	31Mr02
FITZPATRICK, P.		24	M	Laborer	31Mr02
MCGOWAN, F.		22	M	Laborer	31Mr02
ROWE, T.		23	M	Laborer	31Mr02
LOUGHAN, J.		24	M	Laborer	31Mr02
KELLY, R.		22	M	Laborer	31Mr02
U	(W)	22	F	Unknown	31Mr02
REILLY, P.		20	M	Laborer	31Mr02
Bryan		22	M	Laborer	31Mr02
WALSH, T.		29	M	Laborer	31Mr02
TONNER, Ann		31	F	Unknown	31Mr02
John		15	M	None	31Mr02
Cath.		11	F	Child	31Mr02
MCSWENE, D.		50	M	Laborer	31Mr02
Cecily	(D)	25	F	Unknown	31Mr02
Mary	(D)	22	F	Unknown	31Mr02
Betty	(D)	21	F	Unknown	31Mr02
Jane	(D)	20	F	Unknown	31Mr02
Nancy	(D)	18	F	Unknown	31Mr02
Danl.		03	M	Child	31Mr02
Edwd.	(S)	18	M	Laborer	31Mr02
John	(S)	30	M	Laborer	31Mr02
QUINN, G.		28	M	Laborer	31Mr02
Cath.		24	F	Unknown	31Mr02
BUCHANAN, R.		21	M	Laborer	31Mr02
LAWSON, A.		22	M	Laborer	31Mr02
MURPHY, J.		30	M	Laborer	31Mr02
GRANAHAN, P.		50	M	Laborer	31Mr02
Patk.		30	M	Laborer	31Mr02
Martin		30	M	Laborer	31Mr02
MURPHY, Nancy		30	F	Unknown	31Mr02
GRANAHAN, Bridget		20	F	Unknown	31Mr02
MCKENNA, C.		30	M	Laborer	31Mr02
FLAHERTY, D.		21	M	Laborer	31Mr02
MAHON, H.		26	M	Laborer	31Mr02
COCKRAN, M.		45	M	Laborer	31Mr02
Jane	(W)	40	F	Unknown	31Mr02
Nancy	(D)	16	F	Unknown	31Mr02
Mary	(D)	14	F	Unknown	31Mr02
Anthony	(S)	06	M	Child	31Mr02
MCELROY, J.		26	M	Laborer	31Mr02
Cath.		20	F	Unknown	31Mr02
GAULT, Elizbt.		26	F	Unknown	31Mr02
John		18	M	Laborer	31Mr02
Robt.		10	M	Child	31Mr02
Joseph		09	M	Child	31Mr02
FUNY, J.		30	M	Laborer	31Mr02
BOGAN, T.		24	M	Laborer	31Mr02
WALSH, Ellen		20	F	Unknown	31Mr02
ERWEN, J.		03	M	Child	31Mr02
KENNERSH, J.		25	M	Child	31Mr02
FOX, Mgt.		20	F	Unknown	31Mr02
MCCABE, Ann		24	F	Unknown	31Mr02
REYLEY, E.		25	M	Laborer	31Mr02
DOLAN, P.		18	M	Laborer	31Mr02
FITZSIMONS, M.		45	M	Laborer	31Mr02
U	(W)	32	F	Unknown	31Mr02
CONROY, Eliza		21	F	Unknown	31Mr02
BAIN, Mich.		30	M	Laborer	31Mr02
U	(W)	24	F	Unknown	31Mr02
U-Miss		17	F	Unknown	31Mr02

NAMES OF PASSENGERS		AGE	SEX	OCCUPATIONS	DATE PORT SHIP
BYRNE, Cath.		20	F	Unknown	31Mr02
CONAHAN, J.		20	M	Laborer	31Mr02
ANDERSON, Mary		19	F	Unknown	31Mr02
MAHONY, D.		26	M	Laborer	31Mr02
HUSSEY, M.		26	M	Laborer	31Mr02
GOON, J.		28	M	Laborer	31Mr02
BURK, J.		22	M	Laborer	31Mr02
VAUGHN, M.		30	M	Laborer	31Mr02
Mgt.	(W)	28	F	Unknown	31Mr02
Bdgt.	(D)	07	F	Child	31Mr02
Ann	(D)	05	F	Child	31Mr02
Cath.	(D)	03	F	Child	31Mr02
Rose	(D)	01	F	Child	31Mr02
DONOHUE, J.		27	M	Laborer	31Mr02
Ann		22	F	Unknown	31Mr02
Biddy		17	F	Unknown	31Mr02
Patk.		15	M	None	31Mr02
FARRELL, D.		30	M	Laborer	31Mr02
VAUGHN, T.		26	M	Laborer	31Mr02
James		25	M	Laborer	31Mr02
CORCORAN, M.		24	M	Laborer	31Mr02
GEE, T.		20	M	Laborer	31Mr02
GURRY, P.		25	M	Laborer	31Mr02
FIELDS, T.		22	M	Laborer	31Mr02
Mary-Ann		20	F	Unknown	31Mr02
MCCONNOR, J.		25	M	Laborer	31Mr02
Terence		07	M	Child	31Mr02
Mgt.		05	F	Child	31Mr02
OHEARN, Eliza		16	F	Unknown	31Mr02
OCONNELL, M.		18	F	Unknown	31Mr02
DOYLE, J.		08	M	Child	31Mr02
MEATH, P.		30	M	Laborer	31Mr02
DOYLE, J.H.		30	M	Laborer	31Mr02
U	(W)	30	F	Unknown	31Mr02
Jane	(D)	06	F	Child	31Mr02
Marla	(D)	04	F	Child	31Mr02
Ella	(D)	01	F	Child	31Mr02
Norma	(D)	01	F	Child	31Mr02
GOFFREY, P.		25	M	Laborer	31Mr02
MCDONNELL, J.		20	M	Laborer	31Mr02
JOHNSON, W.		30	M	Laborer	31Mr02
RYDER, J.		25	M	Laborer	31Mr02
HOGAN, T.		20	M	Laborer	31Mr02
DUNIGAN, J.		20	M	Laborer	31Mr02
GAFFREY, Mary		20	F	Unknown	31Mr02
GUNNAN, M.		50	F	Unknown	31Mr02
Mary	(D)	13	F	Unknown	31Mr02
Sarah	(D)	12	F	Unknown	31Mr02
ROCK, M.		48	M	Laborer	31Mr02
MONARTY, M.		24	M	Laborer	31Mr02
Timothy		23	M	Laborer	31Mr02
DOWLING, J.		30	M	Laborer	31Mr02
YORE, G.		20	M	Laborer	31Mr02
REBBEN, Betty		32	F	Unknown	31Mr02
Mgt.	(D)	06	F	Child	31Mr02
Michl.	(S)	03	M	Child	31Mr02
Ellzbt.	(D)	01	F	Child	31Mr02
Cath.		40	F	Unknown	31Mr02
COSTELLO, P.		20	M	Laborer	31Mr02
Anne		12	F	Unknown	31Mr02
FAY, Mary		24	F	Unknown	31Mr02
Andrew		18	M	Laborer	31Mr02
Sarah		22	F	Unknown	31Mr02
SMALL, Ellen		24	F	Unknown	31Mr02
KETHEN, P.		22	M	Laborer	31Mr02

YORKSHIRE 01 APRIL 1847

From Liverpool

NAMES OF PASSENGERS		AGE	SEX	OCCUPATIONS	DATE PORT SHIP
BURN, Cormack		25	M	Laborer	01Ap02Bz
HAVEN, James		25	M	Laborer	01Ap02Bz
QUINN, Wm.		24	M	Laborer	01Ap02Bz
MULVEY, Bridget		26	F	Laborer	01Ap02Bz
Nancy		20	F	Laborer	01Ap02Bz
BROWN, Ellen		17	F	Unknown	01Ap02Bz
LOWRY, Judy		21	F	Unknown	01Ap02Bz
HAVEN, Pat		40	M	Laborer	01Ap02Bz
Nancy	(W)	35	F	Unknown	01Ap02Bz
Peter	(S)	11	M	Unknown	01Ap02Bz
Thos.	(S)	09	M	Child	01Ap02Bz
Chas.	(S)	13	M	None	01Ap02Bz
Patt		20	M	Laborer	01Ap02Bz
SHIRLS, James		30	M	Laborer	01Ap02Bz
HAND, Jas.		21	M	Laborer	01Ap02Bz
Cathe		20	F	Unknown	01Ap02Bz
BRIEN, Mary		30	F	Unknown	01Ap02Bz
Michael		23	M	Laborer	01Ap02Bz
GARRY, Tom		19	M	Laborer	01Ap02Bz
SHELLEY, Mary		23	F	Unknown	01Ap02Bz
John		25	M	Laborer	01Ap02Bz
Rhody		20	F	Unknown	01Ap02Bz
GREENE, Edwd.		63	M	Laborer	01Ap02Bz
Esther		60	F	Unknown	01Ap02Bz
William	(S)	20	M	Laborer	01Ap02Bz
Michael	(S)	14	M	Laborer	01Ap02Bz
Margt.	(D)	16	F	Unknown	01Ap02Bz
LAMB, Margt.		17	F	Unknown	01Ap02Bz
KELLEY, Pat		14	M	Laborer	01Ap02Bz
Rich.		12	M	Unknown	01Ap02Bz
MINTURN, Thos.		21	M	Laborer	01Ap02Bz
Cath		21	F	Unknown	01Ap02Bz
CARROLL, Ann		21	F	Unknown	01Ap02Bz
MCCANN, Cathe.		27	F	Unknown	01Ap02Bz
James	(S)	08	M	Unknown	01Ap02Bz
Wm.	(S)	06	M	Unknown	01Ap02Bz
Thos.	(S)	04	M	Unknown	01Ap02Bz
Jane	(D)	03	F	Unknown	01Ap02Bz
Marla	(D)	02	F	Unknown	01Ap02Bz
GORMOLY, Pat		23	M	Laborer	01Ap02Bz
ROGERS, James		23	M	Laborer	01Ap02Bz
ONEIL, John		20	M	Laborer	01Ap02Bz
HANNOLY, Dan		25	M	Laborer	01Ap02Bz
MALLY, Jas.		26	M	Laborer	01Ap02Bz
Winford		21	M	Laborer	01Ap02Bz
Jas.		20	M	Laborer	01Ap02Bz
MCNIEL, Owen		26	M	Laborer	01Ap02Bz
MALLY, James		22	M	Laborer	01Ap02Bz
CANE, Tom		24	M	Laborer	01Ap02Bz
GAVIN, Martin		20	M	Laborer	01Ap02Bz
HAM, Jas.		20	M	Laborer	01Ap02Bz
GLORNEY, Tim		16	M	Laborer	01Ap02Bz
Bridget		20	F	Unknown	01Ap02Bz
MCGRAVY, Margt.		25	F	Unknown	01Ap02Bz
MCKEE, John		29	M	Laborer	01Ap02Bz
DELANY, Thos.		25	M	Laborer	01Ap02Bz
CONNELL, Thos.		26	M	Laborer	01Ap02Bz
CANON, Pat		22	M	Laborer	01Ap02Bz
RUSSELL, John		30	M	Laborer	01Ap02Bz
GILMARTIN, G.		20	M	Laborer	01Ap02Bz
Jas.		25	M	Laborer	01Ap02Bz
Bessy		16	F	Unknown	01Ap02Bz
HERGUSON, Jas.		24	M	Laborer	01Ap02Bz
OWENS, Mary		20	F	Unknown	01Ap02Bz
MULLIN, Nancy		16	F	Unknown	01Ap02Bz

NAMES OF PASSENGERS		AGE	SEX	OCCUPATIONS	DATE PORT SHIP
BROWN, Jas.		25	M	Laborer	01Ap02Bz
RICE, John		18	M	Laborer	01Ap02Bz
MURPHY, Jas.		30	M	Laborer	01Ap02Bz
FINAL, Isaac		24	M	Laborer	01Ap02Bz
Ell		27	M	Laborer	01Ap02Bz
WILSON, Thos.		40	M	Laborer	01Ap02Bz
AYRES, Thos.		59	M	Laborer	01Ap02Bz
MCGINNIS, Robt.		22	M	Laborer	01Ap02Bz
FITZGERALD, Alex		25	M	Laborer	01Ap02Bz
CHEIR, Logen		20	M	Laborer	01Ap02Bz
MCSHAW, John		25	M	Laborer	01Ap02Bz
Jas.		22	M	Laborer	01Ap02Bz
TONER, Pat		20	M	Laborer	01Ap02Bz
Jas.		20	M	Laborer	01Ap02Bz
GALLAGHER, Jas.		25	M	Laborer	01Ap02Bz
DEVEREAUX, Ann		36	F	Unknown	01Ap02Bz
CHRISTON, Ellen		20	F	Unknown	01Ap02Bz
DOLAN, Mary		21	F	Unknown	01Ap02Bz
HARRIGAN, Eliza		58	F	Unknown	01Ap02Bz
SMITH, Mary		18	F	Unknown	01Ap02Bz
DEVEREAUX, Philip		20	M	Laborer	01Ap02Bz
MALOONEY, Michl.		25	M	Laborer	01Ap02Bz
LUDY, Thos.		30	M	Laborer	01Ap02Bz
MURRAY, Thos.		12	M	Laborer	01Ap02Bz
GORMLY, Thos.		50	M	Laborer	01Ap02Bz
Mary	(W)	50	F	Wife	01Ap02Bz
Alice		06	F	Child	01Ap02Bz
Wm.		04	M	Child	01Ap02Bz
CONNELL, Jas.		30	M	Laborer	01Ap02Bz
CUFF, Patt		35	M	Laborer	01Ap02Bz
Richard	(S)	12	M	Unknown	01Ap02Bz
Bridget	(D)	10	F	Unknown	01Ap02Bz
Martin	(S)	08	M	Child	01Ap02Bz
Tony	(S)	04	M	Child	01Ap02Bz
QUIN, Bard.		21	M	Laborer	01Ap02Bz
CONNOR, Ann		11	F	Unknown	01Ap02Bz
LENARD, Pat		21	F	Unknown	01Ap02Bz
Margaret	(W)	21	F	Wife	01Ap02Bz
Margt.		20	F	Unknown	01Ap02Bz
CARNEY, Jas.		20	M	Laborer	01Ap02Bz
DAVY, Jas.		16	M	Laborer	01Ap02Bz
BAILEY, Michael		26	M	Laborer	01Ap02Bz
MCCANN, John		26	M	Laborer	01Ap02Bz
RILEY, Mary		56	F	Unknown	01Ap02Bz
John		23	M	Laborer	01Ap02Bz
KERWOOD, Jas.		22	M	Laborer	01Ap02Bz
RILEY, Ann		18	F	Unknown	01Ap02Bz
DOYLE, Jas.		23	M	Laborer	01Ap02Bz
Bridget		26	F	Unknown	01Ap02Bz
CALEN, Judy		25	F	Unknown	01Ap02Bz
DOYLE, Patt.		04	M	Child	01Ap02Bz
Michael		01	M	Child	01Ap02Bz
KEITH, Thos.		20	M	Laborer	01Ap02Bz
GORMAN, Michl.		23	M	Laborer	01Ap02Bz
MCCANY, Patt		24	M	Laborer	01Ap02Bz
PATTISON, Jas.		25	M	Laborer	01Ap02Bz
SMITH, Rose		22	F	Unknown	01Ap02Bz
MCDONALD, Peggy		60	F	Unknown	01Ap02Bz
SMITH, John		22	M	Laborer	01Ap02Bz
DERMOTT, Patt		20	M	Laborer	01Ap02Bz
BEGAN, Barry		20	M	Laborer	01Ap02Bz
GOCUNS, Pat		24	M	Laborer	01Ap02Bz
FALCONER, Pat		20	M	Laborer	01Ap02Bz
MURPHY, Mich.		21	M	Laborer	01Ap02Bz
MCDONALD, John		28	M	Laborer	01Ap02Bz
ROGERS, Francis		25	M	Laborer	01Ap02Bz
BADY, John		19	M	Laborer	01Ap02Bz
RILEY, Luke		23	M	Laborer	01Ap02Bz
HOGAN, Cathe.		23	F	Unknown	01Ap02Bz
BRENNON, Mary		20	F	Unknown	01Ap02Bz
HOGAN, Mary		20	F	Unknown	01Ap02Bz
MACODY, Jas.		20	M	Laborer	01Ap02Bz
CAREY, John		20	M	Laborer	01Ap02Bz
FARLEY, Michael		15	M	Laborer	01Ap02Bz
MANN, Cathe.		24	F	Unknown	01Ap02Bz
DORAN, John		18	M	Laborer	01Ap02Bz
Mattie		20	F	Unknown	01Ap02Bz
Bridget		06	F	Child	01Ap02Bz
MCLAUGHLIN, Bridget		28	F	Unknown	01Ap02Bz
Mary		07	F	Unknown	01Ap02Bz
CLARK, Mary		24	F	Unknown	01Ap02Bz
Margt.		24	F	Unknown	01Ap02Bz
Rose		02	F	Child	01Ap02Bz
MCCULLER, Bridget		20	F	Unknown	01Ap02Bz
MABURY, Louisa		19	F	Unknown	01Ap02Bz
MCCONNELL, John		27	M	Laborer	01Ap02Bz
Luzard		27	M	Laborer	01Ap02Bz
Sally	(D)	06	F	Child	01Ap02Bz
Mich	(S)	03	M	Child	01Ap02Bz
Biddy	(D)	01	F	Child	01Ap02Bz
RANSFORD, John		40	M	Laborer	01Ap02Bz
Mary		40	F	Unknown	01Ap02Bz
ANDREWS, Ann		18	F	Unknown	01Ap02Bz
FARLEY, Ann		29	F	Unknown	01Ap02Bz
RANSFORD, Jno.		.04	M	Infant	01Ap02Bz
CASSY, Jas.		62	M	Mechanic	01Ap02Bz
Patt		21	M	Laborer	01Ap02Bz
HART, Patt		22	M	Laborer	01Ap02Bz
Mich.		19	M	Laborer	01Ap02Bz
KEIN, Ann		15	F	Unknown	01Ap02Bz
RODNICK, John		15	M	Laborer	01Ap02Bz
Rose		17	F	Unknown	01Ap02Bz
Ann		10	F	Unknown	01Ap02Bz
Bartay		15	M	Laborer	01Ap02Bz
KALSH, Thos.		21	M	Laborer	01Ap02Bz
NOLAND, Thos.		20	M	Laborer	01Ap02Bz
YEASLEY, Thos.		27	M	Laborer	01Ap02Bz
MCCANICK, Jas.		47	M	Laborer	01Ap02Bz
RILEY, Thos.		19	M	Laborer	01Ap02Bz
Cathe.		22	F	Unknown	01Ap02Bz
BACKLAND, Ann		19	F	Unknown	01Ap02Bz
RILEY, Mich.		25	M	Laborer	01Ap02Bz
Mary		.01	F	Infant	01Ap02Bz
MCDONALD, John		21	M	Laborer	01Ap02Bz
GALLAGHIN, Mich.		25	M	Laborer	01Ap02Bz
MCDONALD, Bridget		18	F	Unknown	01Ap02Bz
GALLAGHIN, Biddy		18	F	Unknown	01Ap02Bz
HUGHES, Rose		60	F	Unknown	01Ap02Bz
Mary		20	F	Unknown	01Ap02Bz
Rose		17	F	Unknown	01Ap02Bz
NOLAN, Mary		22	F	Unknown	01Ap02Bz
MCDONALD, Rose		18	F	Unknown	01Ap02Bz
KELLEY, Danl.		28	M	Laborer	01Ap02Bz
LOWRY, Michl.		28	M	Laborer	01Ap02Bz
HAMMKIN, Thos.		60	M	Laborer	01Ap02Bz
MACABOY, Thos.		22	M	Laborer	01Ap02Bz
LINOKIN, Jas.		16	M	Laborer	01Ap02Bz
Mary		22	F	Unknown	01Ap02Bz
TAUNTY, Dennis		22	M	Laborer	01Ap02Bz
CORKAN, Peggy		19	F	Unknown	01Ap02Bz
MACABOY, Susan		18	F	Unknown	01Ap02Bz
COYLE, John		20	M	Laborer	01Ap02Bz
CORKS, Owen		19	M	Laborer	01Ap02Bz
Edw.		37	M	Laborer	01Ap02Bz
OBRIEN, Hugh		25	M	Laborer	01Ap02Bz
DICKONY, Ellen		30	F	Unknown	01Ap02Bz
Bridget		04	F	Child	01Ap02Bz
Owen		02	M	Child	01Ap02Bz
Bessey		01	F	Infant	01Ap02Bz
OBRIEN, Kitty		21	F	Unknown	01Ap02Bz
Alby		19	F	Unknown	01Ap02Bz
WOODS, Rose		18	F	Unknown	01Ap02Bz
FLOOD, Ian		23	M	Laborer	01Ap02Bz
HOGAN, John		24	M	Laborer	01Ap02Bz
OBRIEN, John		26	M	Laborer	01Ap02Bz
BROWN, Thos.		22	M	Laborer	01Ap02Bz
DELANEY, Pat		26	M	Laborer	01Ap02Bz
Mary		20	F	Unknown	01Ap02Bz
BROWN, Rose		20	F	Unknown	01Ap02Bz
BRIEN, Mary		20	F	Unknown	01Ap02Bz

NAMES OF PASSENGERS		AGE	SEX	OCCUPATIONS	DATE PORT SHIP	NAMES OF PASSENGERS		AGE	SEX	OCCUPATIONS	DATE PORT SHIP
MCGRATH, John		25	M	Laborer	01Ap02Bz	DONNS, Jas.		26	M	Laborer	01Ap02Bz
Mary	(W)	20	F	Unknown	01Ap02Bz	MCLAND, Jas.		30	M	Laborer	01Ap02Bz
Patt	(S)	03	M	Child	01Ap02Bz	ANDERSON, G.		24	M	Laborer	01Ap02Bz
CONNER, Jas.		25	M	Laborer	01Ap02Bz	RILEY, John		30	M	Laborer	01Ap02Bz
RYAN, Chas.		35	M	Laborer	01Ap02Bz	GUN, Peter		19	M	Laborer	01Ap02Bz
Mary	(W)	30	F	Unknown	01Ap02Bz	BRIEN, Mich.		23	M	Laborer	01Ap02Bz
Phil	(S)	06	M	Child	01Ap02Bz	HARMEN, John		25	M	Laborer	01Ap02Bz
Patt	(S)	04	M	Child	01Ap02Bz	BYRNN, Pat		20	M	Laborer	01Ap02Bz
Judy	(D)	.06	F	Infant	01Ap02Bz	SCOTT, Wm.		40	M	Laborer	01Ap02Bz
FITZPATRICK, Thos.		18	M	Laborer	01Ap02Bz	BRIEN, Chas.		25	M	Laborer	01Ap02Bz
KENNEDY, Peter		27	M	Laborer	01Ap02Bz	SHIRLEY, H.		23	M	Laborer	01Ap02Bz
KESLIN, John		40	M	Laborer	01Ap02Bz	NORTON, Gregory		26	M	Laborer	01Ap02Bz
KELSON, Wm.		14	M	Laborer	01Ap02Bz	ANDERSON, Kate		19	F	Unknown	01Ap02Bz
RILEY, Wm.		18	M	Laborer	01Ap02Bz	CRONIMS, Kate		27	F	Unknown	01Ap02Bz
Thos.		18	M	Laborer	01Ap02Bz	MATHEWS, John		28	M	Laborer	01Ap02Bz
BRIER, John		18	M	Laborer	01Ap02Bz	WHITAKER, John		23	M	Laborer	01Ap02Bz
LYNCH, Chas.		16	M	Laborer	01Ap02Bz	KAMIN, Frank		40	M	Laborer	01Ap02Bz
RILEY, Jas.		28	M	Laborer	01Ap02Bz	MASTERSON, Simon		38	M	Laborer	01Ap02Bz
Ann	(W)	28	F	Unknown	01Ap02Bz	Cathe.	(W)	35	F	Wife	01Ap02Bz
Margt.	(D)	02	F	Child	01Ap02Bz	Bridget	(D)	05	F	Child	01Ap02Bz
LYNCH, Cathe.		60	F	Unknown	01Ap02Bz	John	(S)	03	M	Child	01Ap02Bz
Margt.		20	F	Unknown	01Ap02Bz	Judy	(D)	07	F	Child	01Ap02Bz
Rose		16	F	Unknown	01Ap02Bz	KELE, Judy		09	F	Child	01Ap02Bz
RILEY, Bridget		18	F	Unknown	01Ap02Bz	Bridget		38	F	Unknown	01Ap02Bz
MAKIN, Corm.		26	M	Laborer	01Ap02Bz	LLOYD, Bitty		16	F	Unknown	01Ap02Bz
RILEY, Cathe.		20	F	Unknown	01Ap02Bz	Bitty		16	F	Unknown	01Ap02Bz
AYRES, Cathe.		20	F	Unknown	01Ap02Bz	Charlot		55	F	Unknown	01Ap02Bz
CORMICK, Thos.		36	M	Laborer	01Ap02Bz	Mary		14	F	Unknown	01Ap02Bz
DUNFEE, Peter		25	M	Laborer	01Ap02Bz	Richard		07	M	Child	01Ap02Bz
CROSSE, Ed.		21	M	Laborer	01Ap02Bz	William		05	M	Child	01Ap02Bz
MALONE, Henry		20	M	Laborer	01Ap02Bz	BRADEN, Peter		25	M	Laborer	01Ap02Bz
LOYD, Peter		20	M	Laborer	01Ap02Bz	ROCH, Mich.		22	M	Laborer	01Ap02Bz
CASSIDAY, Jas.		22	M	Laborer	01Ap02Bz	CARNEY, Jas.		20	M	Laborer	01Ap02Bz
DINIKER, Mich.		34	M	Laborer	01Ap02Bz	BURROWS, Patt		27	M	Laborer	01Ap02Bz
CAVANAGH, John		30	M	Laborer	01Ap02Bz	HARLEM, Wm.		25	M	Laborer	01Ap02Bz
CONROY, Jas.		20	M	Laborer	01Ap02Bz	Mary		27	F	Unknown	01Ap02Bz
RILEY, Rich.		30	M	Laborer	01Ap02Bz	Mary		08	F	Child	01Ap02Bz
FURMAN, Ann		15	F	Unknown	01Ap02Bz	Bessey		06	F	Child	01Ap02Bz
COLAN, Lucy		20	F	Unknown	01Ap02Bz	Rich.		04	M	Child	01Ap02Bz
LYTT, Margt.		17	F	Unknown	01Ap02Bz	Jas.		01	M	Infant	01Ap02Bz
LEDENS, Wm.		24	M	Laborer	01Ap02Bz	MURPHY, Cathe.		62	F	Unknown	01Ap02Bz
Agnes		16	F	Unknown	01Ap02Bz	Mary		27	F	Unknown	01Ap02Bz
RILEY, Stephen		24	M	Laborer	01Ap02Bz	LATIMER, Ann		63	F	Unknown	01Ap02Bz
MOORE, Luke		20	M	Laborer	01Ap02Bz	TIVINCLIFFE, J.W.		63	M	Laborer	01Ap02Bz
CRAIG, Robt.		28	M	Laborer	01Ap02Bz	SHELTON, Wm.		26	M	Laborer	01Ap02Bz
HORNE, Cathe.		20	F	Unknown	01Ap02Bz	SHANON, Jas.		27	M	Laborer	01Ap02Bz
DUNN, Thos.		25	M	Laborer	01Ap02Bz	MURTHA, Bridget		08	F	Child	01Ap02Bz
HANAGAN, John		24	M	Laborer	01Ap02Bz	CARL, Peggy		18	F	Child	01Ap02Bz
Cathe.		20	F	Unknown	01Ap02Bz	MURPHY, Cathe.		29	F	Child	01Ap02Bz
MCCORMICK, U		18	M	Laborer	01Ap02Bz	SMITH, B.		25	M	Laborer	01Ap02Bz
Mary		20	F	Unknown	01Ap02Bz	RILEY, R.		22	M	Laborer	01Ap02Bz
COLLINS, Sarah		25	F	Unknown	01Ap02Bz	Brien		18	M	Laborer	01Ap02Bz
LOOMES, Mich.		22	M	Laborer	01Ap02Bz	YOND, Robt.		17	M	Laborer	01Ap02Bz
WELSH, Peter		24	M	Laborer	01Ap02Bz	HOGAN, John		20	M	Laborer	01Ap02Bz
BATY, Alex		60	M	Laborer	01Ap02Bz	BRADY, John		25	M	Laborer	01Ap02Bz
Nancy		70	F	Unknown	01Ap02Bz	SMITH, Teddy		25	M	Laborer	01Ap02Bz
James		22	M	Laborer	01Ap02Bz	GRATT, John		30	M	Laborer	01Ap02Bz
Liddy		20	F	Unknown	01Ap02Bz	LEADY, Thos.		27	M	Laborer	01Ap02Bz
Margt.		01	F	Child	01Ap02Bz	KELLY, Cor.		27	M	Laborer	01Ap02Bz
SMITH, Andrew		20	M	Laborer	01Ap02Bz	KELE, Pat		27	M	Laborer	01Ap02Bz
OCANNIN, Patt		21	M	Laborer	01Ap02Bz	DUNN, Ed.		22	M	Laborer	01Ap02Bz
Mary-Ann		19	F	Unknown	01Ap02Bz	Cathe.		22	F	Unknown	01Ap02Bz
MOON, Phillp		28	M	Laborer	01Ap02Bz	MANN, Hugh		30	M	Laborer	01Ap02Bz
Nancy		22	F	Unknown	01Ap02Bz	Patt		22	M	Laborer	01Ap02Bz
Eliza		.08	F	Infant	01Ap02Bz	ROKE, Brien		30	M	Laborer	01Ap02Bz
MONTAGUE, Chas.		21	M	Laborer	01Ap02Bz	CARLEY, John		30	M	Laborer	01Ap02Bz
Rose		20	F	Unknown	01Ap02Bz	CRAWLEY, Mich.		30	M	Laborer	01Ap02Bz
John		01	M	Child	01Ap02Bz	ROKE, Brien		20	M	Laborer	01Ap02Bz
Bridget		50	F	Unknown	01Ap02Bz	DERMODY, John		26	M	Laborer	01Ap02Bz
MOON, Eliza		56	F	Unknown	01Ap02Bz	Mary		25	F	Unknown	01Ap02Bz
BRONS, Paddy		30	M	Laborer	01Ap02Bz	Pat		14	M	Unknown	01Ap02Bz
CARO, John		21	M	Laborer	01Ap02Bz	Tom		16	M	Unknown	01Ap02Bz
Margt.		23	F	Unknown	01Ap02Bz	MCCABE, Cathe.		25	F	Unknown	01Ap02Bz
WHALON, Mich.		21	M	Laborer	01Ap02Bz	KELLEY, Mary		21	F	Unknown	01Ap02Bz
David		18	M	Laborer	01Ap02Bz	LYNCH, Mary		21	F	Unknown	01Ap02Bz

NAMES OF PASSENGERS	A G E	S E X	OCCUPATIONS	DATE PORT SHIP	NAMES OF PASSENGERS	A G E	S E X	OCCUPATIONS	DATE PORT SHIP
PAT, Garvin	24	M	Laborer	01Ap02Bz	MORAN, Michele	24	M	Unknown	03Ap02Kn
William	21	M	Laborer	01Ap02Bz	CANULTY, Thos.	21	M	Unknown	03Ap02Kn
SMITH, Pat	20	M	Laborer	01Ap02Bz	Bridget	20	F	Unknown	03Ap02Kn
RILEY, Tom	15	M	Laborer	01Ap02Bz	KELLY, Thos.	20	F	Unknown	03Ap02Kn
BRADY, Bridget	19	F	Unknown	01Ap02Bz	Bridget	25	F	Unknown	03Ap02Kn
BOG, Mary	19	F	Unknown	01Ap02Bz	Mary	03	F	Child	03Ap02Kn
LOOFT, Cathe	18	F	Unknown	01Ap02Bz	HANUHAN, Eugene-O.	25	M	Farmer	03Ap02Kn
BRADY, Mary	15	F	Unknown	01Ap02Bz	HONAN, John	28	M	Farmer	03Ap02Kn
PLUMB, Bridget	16	F	Unknown	01Ap02Bz	FENLIN, Martin	24	M	Farmer	03Ap02Kn
MONOHAN, John	20	M	Laborer	01Ap02Bz	KEATING, Barnaby	28	M	Farmer	03Ap02Kn
LYNCH, Math.	18	M	Laborer	01Ap02Bz	LYNCH, Michel	20	M	Farmer	03Ap02Kn
Edward	16	M	Laborer	01Ap02Bz	BLUMAN, Anastacius	30	M	Shoemaker	03Ap02Kn
RITT, Tos.	20	M	Laborer	01Ap02Bz	CORRY, Mary	27	F	Shoemaker	03Ap02Kn
NUGENT, Chris	33	M	Laborer	01Ap02Bz	HARRAGAN, Ellen	21	F	Shoemaker	03Ap02Kn
Eliza	22	F	Unknown	01Ap02Bz	MILLIGAN, Mary	18	F	Shoemaker	03Ap02Kn
Patt.	03	M	Child	01Ap02Bz	BRANNEN, Honora	19	F	Shoemaker	03Ap02Kn
CANNON, Wm.	22	M	Laborer	01Ap02Bz	OMALLEY, James	25	M	Shoemaker	03Ap02Kn
REARN, Jas.	30	M	Laborer	01Ap02Bz	BEGLEY, Patrick	22	M	Shoemaker	03Ap02Kn
WILLIAMSON, John	30	M	Laborer	01Ap02Bz	GOGERTY, Margret	20	F	Shoemaker	03Ap02Kn
WHALON, Pat	25	M	Laborer	01Ap02Bz	Ann	18	F	Shoemaker	03Ap02Kn
FLEMING, Peter	30	M	Laborer	01Ap02Bz	DICKSIN, Charles	21	M	Farmer	03Ap02Kn
ROBERTS, John	40	M	Unknown	01Ap02Bz	CAHILL, Owen	40	M	Farmer	03Ap02Kn
ROBERTSON, John	37	M	Mechanic	01Ap02Bz	Catherine (W)	40	F	Farmer	03Ap02Kn
PEACOCK, James	37	M	Mechanic	01Ap02Bz	Phillip (S)	16	M	Farmer	03Ap02Kn
NEALE, George	37	M	Mechanic	01Ap02Bz	Rose (D)	12	F	Farmer	03Ap02Kn
BINSWANGER, U	41	M	Mechanic	01Ap02Bz	James (S)	10	M	Farmer	03Ap02Kn
U	18	F	Unknown	01Ap02Bz	Owen (S)	08	M	Child	03Ap02Kn
					PHILLIPS, Bernard	32	M	Farmer	03Ap02Kn
					Mary (W)	30	F	Farmer	03Ap02Kn
					Mary	21	F	Farmer	03Ap02Kn
WESTMINSTER 02 APRIL 1847					Patrick	11	M	None	03Ap02Kn
					Edward	09	M	Child	03Ap02Kn
From London					James	09	M	Child	03Ap02Kn
					John	35	M	Farmer	03Ap02Kn
					Ann (W)	33	F	Farmer	03Ap02Kn
					Conner (S)	14	M	Farmer	03Ap02Kn
					James (S)	09	M	Child	03Ap02Kn
BERRETT, Francis	25	M	Farmer	02Ap21Br	Ellen (D)	07	F	Child	03Ap02Kn
COLBERT, Mary	45	F	Unknown	02Ap21Br	Edward	30	M	Farmer	03Ap02Kn
Maurice	23	M	Laborer	02Ap21Br	CLARK, Rose	20	F	Seamstress	03Ap02Kn
COREY, Abbey	25	F	Unknown	02Ap21Br	BURNS, Mary	20	F	Seamstress	03Ap02Kn
TUDER, Wm.	30	M	Laborer	02Ap21Br	BRADY, Mary	20	F	Seamstress	03Ap02Kn
KNIGHT, Sarah	74	F	Laborer	02Ap21Br	MCKISNEY, Mary	21	F	Seamstress	03Ap02Kn
GUIVER, James	00	M	Basketmaker	02Ap21Br	BRADY, Ann	19	F	Seamstress	03Ap02Kn
FOX, Simon	22	M	Tailor	02Ap21Br	ROGERS, Judy	17	F	Seamstress	03Ap02Kn
HARRISON, George	26	M	Brick Maker	02Ap21Br	STEWARD, Maxwell	17	M	Seamstress	03Ap02Kn
NORTH, James	27	M	Carpenter	02Ap21Br	GUNN, Sarah	22	F	Seamstress	03Ap02Kn
WARTERS, Frederick	26	M	Miller	02Ap21Br	Francis	20	M	Seamstress	03Ap02Kn
MERSE, Robert	32	M	Laborer	02Ap21Br	SMITH, Ann	19	F	Seamstress	03Ap02Kn
BARKNON, Theodore	28	M	Carpenter	02Ap21Br	TRACY, James	22	M	Servant	03Ap02Kn
CAMRON, George	17	M	Engineer	02Ap21Br	HARMAN, Lawrence	20	M	Servant	03Ap02Kn
CAMERON, John	37	M	Engineer	02Ap21Br	Pat	21	M	Servant	03Ap02Kn
MOORE, Elizabeth	62	F	None	02Ap21Br	GALLIGAN, Matthew	25	M	Servant	03Ap02Kn
					KELLY, Wm.	24	M	Servant	03Ap02Kn
					Mary (W)	22	F	Wife	03Ap02Kn
					Martin	.00	M	Infant	03Ap02Kn
					MULLOY, Peter	40	M	Stctr	03Ap02Kn
COLONIST 03 APRIL 1847					Ann	36	F	Servant	03Ap02Kn
					Mary	20	F	Servant	03Ap02Kn
From Liverpool					KELLY, Catherine	18	F	Servant	03Ap02Kn
					HOGAN, Mary	20	F	Servant	03Ap02Kn
					HAMILTON, George	22	M	Servant	03Ap02Kn
					Wm.	22	M	Servant	03Ap02Kn
HIGGINS, Thos.	28	M	Farmer	03Ap02Kn	DICKINSON, Samuel	32	M	Servant	03Ap02Kn
U (W)	27	F	Wife	03Ap02Kn	Lydia (W)	30	F	Wife	03Ap02Kn
Pat (S)	.00	M	Infant	03Ap02Kn	John	09	M	Child	03Ap02Kn
MCDERMITT, Patrick	23	M	Farmer	03Ap02Kn	Mary	07	F	Child	03Ap02Kn
KENNEY, Michel	22	M	Farmer	03Ap02Kn	Charles	02	M	Child	03Ap02Kn
CONNELLY, Bridget	18	F	Unknown	03Ap02Kn	Wm.	.00	M	Infant	03Ap02Kn
GRIFFIN, Catherine	18	F	Unknown	03Ap02Kn	Ann	04	F	Child	03Ap02Kn
COLLOELY, Catherine	19	F	Unknown	03Ap02Kn	DALTON, Ann	18	F	Servant	03Ap02Kn
ICHES, Catherine	20	F	Unknown	03Ap02Kn	TRACEY, Judy	17	F	Servant	03Ap02Kn
Pat	20	M	Unknown	03Ap02Kn	CAMPBELL, Anthony	24	M	Laborer	03Ap02Kn
					Judy	22	F	Laborer	03Ap02Kn
					GERMANY, Henry	21	M	Laborer	03Ap02Kn

NAMES OF PASSENGERS		AGE	SEX	OCCUPATIONS	DATE PORT SHIP	NAMES OF PASSENGERS		AGE	SEX	OCCUPATIONS	DATE PORT SHIP
POWER, Michel		50	M	Laborer	03Ap02Kn	MAHONEY, Wm.	(S)	04	M	Child	03Ap02Kn
Margt.		40	F	Laborer	03Ap02Kn	MADDEN, Morgan		26	M	Servant	03Ap02Kn
MCGAFFREY, Biddy		14	F	Laborer	03Ap02Kn	MINNOT, Thos.		30	M	Servant	03Ap02Kn
Catherine		17	F	Laborer	03Ap02Kn	CASSIDY, Jas.		40	M	Servant	03Ap02Kn
HAYNES, Bridget		18	F	Laborer	03Ap02Kn	MONTGOMERY, Robt.		24	M	Servant	03Ap02Kn
GILLEAN, Pat		25	M	Laborer	03Ap02Kn	Margt.		22	F	Servant	03Ap02Kn
TUNNEY, Pat		30	M	Laborer	03Ap02Kn	OWENS, Pat		21	M	Servant	03Ap02Kn
SHINEY, Mary		25	F	Laborer	03Ap02Kn	CLARK, Catherine		20	F	Servant	03Ap02Kn
John		04	M	Child	03Ap02Kn	TREANER, Mary		20	F	Servant	03Ap02Kn
TULLY, John		19	M	Laborer	03Ap02Kn	CUNNINGHAM, Michel		19	M	Shoemaker	03Ap02Kn
Mary-Ann		15	F	Laborer	03Ap02Kn	Ellen		16	F	Dressmaker	03Ap02Kn
Thomas		05	M	Child	03Ap02Kn	MALMADOR, Pat		20	M	Dressmaker	03Ap02Kn
KEYSER, Benjamin		24	M	Laborer	03Ap02Kn	BARTON, John		16	M	Dressmaker	03Ap02Kn
Jane	(W)	22	F	Wife	03Ap02Kn	FOGERTY, Jas.		21	M	Dressmaker	03Ap02Kn
Ellen	(D)	04	F	Child	03Ap02Kn	Pat		22	M	Dressmaker	03Ap02Kn
Mary	(D)	02	F	Child	03Ap02Kn	CORR, Michel		22	M	Cobbler	03Ap02Kn
Andrew	(S)	.00	M	Infant	03Ap02Kn	Catherine	(W)	20	F	Wife	03Ap02Kn
Andrew		30	M	Laborer	03Ap02Kn	Hugh	(S)	01	M	Child	03Ap02Kn
Catherine		18	F	Laborer	03Ap02Kn	RYAN, Pat		24	M	Cobbler	03Ap02Kn
LAUGHLIN, Edward		22	M	Laborer	03Ap02Kn	Elizabeth		20	F	Cobbler	03Ap02Kn
Margret		50	F	Unknown	03Ap02Kn	HARTIGAN, John		24	M	Cobbler	03Ap02Kn
JANE, Eliza		18	F	Laborer	03Ap02Kn	MURPHY, John		20	M	Mason	03Ap02Kn
MARK, Henry		30	M	Laborer	03Ap02Kn	CARROLL, Michel		30	M	Mason	03Ap02Kn
HEALY, Thos.		24	M	Farmer	03Ap02Kn	Mary		24	F	Mason	03Ap02Kn
Margt.		21	F	Farmer	03Ap02Kn	SELK, Mary		20	F	Mason	03Ap02Kn
DWYER, Pat		25	M	Farmer	03Ap02Kn	TRANNEY, Catherine		13	F	Mason	03Ap02Kn
Michel		22	M	Farmer	03Ap02Kn	NESTLE, Mary		20	F	Mason	03Ap02Kn
MULLOY, Ann		24	F	Farmer	03Ap02Kn	HEFFERMAN, Manuel		20	M	Mason	03Ap02Kn
SHANNON, Mary		24	F	Farmer	03Ap02Kn	ELLIS, Thos.		20	M	Mason	03Ap02Kn
MALLOY, Owen		45	M	Farmer	03Ap02Kn	Mary-Jane		23	F	Mason	03Ap02Kn
Mary		46	F	Farmer	03Ap02Kn	MATTHEWS, Wm.		26	M	Farmer	03Ap02Kn
Martin		20	M	Farmer	03Ap02Kn	Pat		24	M	Farmer	03Ap02Kn
Ann		22	F	Farmer	03Ap02Kn	COODY, Wm.		32	M	Farmer	03Ap02Kn
Ellen		19	F	Farmer	03Ap02Kn	Eliza	(W)	30	F	Wife	03Ap02Kn
Patrick		13	M	Farmer	03Ap02Kn	Margt.	(D)	03	F	Child	03Ap02Kn
Michel		12	M	Farmer	03Ap02Kn	Pat	(S)	02	M	Child	03Ap02Kn
SHEILDS, Ellen		21	F	Farmer	03Ap02Kn	Maria	(D)	.00	F	Infant	03Ap02Kn
GLREAY, Thos.		20	M	Farmer	03Ap02Kn	BUTLER, Margt.		20	F	Farmer	03Ap02Kn
WALD, Joseph		41	M	Farmer	03Ap02Kn	HARVEY, Chas.		21	M	Farmer	03Ap02Kn
FENTHEY, Thos.		33	M	Tailor	03Ap02Kn	NUGENT, Catherine		20	F	Servant	03Ap02Kn
DONOUGH, Edward		60	M	Tailor	03Ap02Kn	CLEMENTS, James		26	M	Servant	03Ap02Kn
Pat		23	M	Tailor	03Ap02Kn	Jane		24	F	Servant	03Ap02Kn
Mary		19	F	Tailor	03Ap02Kn	Margt.		20	F	Servant	03Ap02Kn
Ann		12	F	Tailor	03Ap02Kn	Mary		.00	F	Infant	03Ap02Kn
John		11	M	Tailor	03Ap02Kn	LATTIMER, Robert		20	M	Servant	03Ap02Kn
MCMANUS, Catherine		20	F	Tailor	03Ap02Kn	MCDONALD, James		25	M	Servant	03Ap02Kn
Jane		17	F	Tailor	03Ap02Kn	MORRISON, Richard		32	M	Servant	03Ap02Kn
DALEY, Mary		16	F	Tailor	03Ap02Kn	HARRISON, Chas.		20	M	Servant	03Ap02Kn
MURPHY, Jas.		22	M	Tailor	03Ap02Kn	WAITLEY, Ellen		52	F	Servant	03Ap02Kn
GARGAN, Jas.		22	M	Blacksmith	03Ap02Kn	James		26	M	Farmer	03Ap02Kn
FALLEN, Wm.		24	M	Blacksmith	03Ap02Kn	LAFFERY, Peter		27	M	Farmer	03Ap02Kn
CARROLL, Jas.		22	M	Blacksmith	03Ap02Kn	Mary	(W)	27	F	Farmer	03Ap02Kn
MORAN, John		24	M	Blacksmith	03Ap02Kn	John	(S)	.00	M	Infant	03Ap02Kn
GREUDY, Catherine		20	F	Blacksmith	03Ap02Kn	MCKEAN, Ellen		24	F	Farmer	03Ap02Kn
COLE, Matthew		22	M	Blacksmith	03Ap02Kn	HEGAN, Daniel		21	M	Farmer	03Ap02Kn
WARD, Edward		24	M	Blacksmith	03Ap02Kn	KEEN, Mary		17	F	Farmer	03Ap02Kn
MORAN, Thos.		20	M	Blacksmith	03Ap02Kn	KERWIN, Thos.		22	M	Farmer	03Ap02Kn
GRAHAM, Pat		22	M	Blacksmith	03Ap02Kn	CUMMINS, Eliza		21	F	Farmer	03Ap02Kn
COYLE, Mary		20	F	Blacksmith	03Ap02Kn	Maria		18	F	Farmer	03Ap02Kn
HYLAND, Eliza		20	F	Blacksmith	03Ap02Kn	Michel		10	M	Farmer	03Ap02Kn
GARLORY, Magt.		20	F	Blacksmith	03Ap02Kn	Michel		10	M	Child	03Ap02Kn
COLLIGAN, Michel		25	M	Blacksmith	03Ap02Kn	MURPHY, Catherine		20	F	Farmer	03Ap02Kn
HAYES, John		25	M	Blacksmith	03Ap02Kn	GYLET, Mary		20	F	Farmer	03Ap02Kn
ROGAN, Bridget		21	F	Servant	03Ap02Kn	GLEEN, George		26	M	Farmer	03Ap02Kn
BREGAN, John		24	M	Servant	03Ap02Kn	LONAGH, James		28	M	Farmer	03Ap02Kn
STANTON, Thos.		24	M	Servant	03Ap02Kn	Susan	(W)	24	F	Farmer	03Ap02Kn
Bridget		23	F	Servant	03Ap02Kn	Patrick	(S)	.00	M	Infant	03Ap02Kn
KELLY, Stephen		28	M	Servant	03Ap02Kn	PICKETT, Wm.		20	M	Servant	03Ap02Kn
CASSIDY, Owen		21	M	Servant	03Ap02Kn	Mary		18	F	Servant	03Ap02Kn
MATTHEWS, Pat		25	M	Servant	03Ap02Kn	DUFFEY, Patrick		22	M	Servant	03Ap02Kn
MURPHY, Michel		30	M	Servant	03Ap02Kn	MALLEN, Rose		27	F	Servant	03Ap02Kn
MCDONALD, Mary		20	F	Servant	03Ap02Kn	RILEY, Terrence		21	M	Servant	03Ap02Kn
LENNON, Bridget		19	F	Servant	03Ap02Kn	OGDEN, George-B.		24	M	Servant	03Ap02Kn
MAHONEY, Pat		35	M	Servant	03Ap02Kn	Carolina		22	F	Servant	03Ap02Kn
Catherine	(W)	30	F	Wife	03Ap02Kn	SPRING, Wm.		22	M	Servant	03Ap02Kn

NAMES OF PASSENGERS		AGE	SEX	OCCUPATIONS	DATE PORT SHIP
SPRING, Susan		24	F	Servant	03Ap02Kn
HOLLINGWORTH, Mary		25	F	Servant	03Ap02Kn
Eliza		01	F	Child	03Ap02Kn
OLIVER, Wm.		25	M	Gdnr	03Ap02Kn
Jane	(W)	24	F	Wife	03Ap02Kn
John	(S)	06	M	Child	03Ap02Kn
Sarah-Ann	(D)	04	F	Child	03Ap02Kn
Eliza-Ann	(D)	02	F	Child	03Ap02Kn
GARDINER, Jas.		24	M	Gdnr	03Ap02Kn
HARE, Thos.-O.		24	M	Gdnr	03Ap02Kn
Alice		20	F	Gdnr	03Ap02Kn
MURREY, Michel		23	M	Gdnr	03Ap02Kn
JENNINGS, John		24	M	Gdnr	03Ap02Kn
MORRISEY, Richard		22	M	Gdnr	03Ap02Kn
CAHILL, Patk.		20	M	Farmer	03Ap02Kn
COOGAN, Thos.		20	M	Farmer	03Ap02Kn
STANTON, Bridget		22	F	Farmer	03Ap02Kn
GREEN, Lester		50	M	Farmer	03Ap02Kn
STANTON, Wm.		21	M	Farmer	03Ap02Kn
BYRNE, Daniel		24	M	Farmer	03Ap02Kn
CARROLL, Thos.		20	M	Farmer	03Ap02Kn
ROURKE, Jas.		21	M	Farmer	03Ap02Kn
NOLEN, Chas.		28	M	Farmer	03Ap02Kn
GALLAGHER, George		21	M	Farmer	03Ap02Kn
BRUSE, James		22	M	Farmer	03Ap02Kn
JOYCE, Samuel		25	M	Farmer	03Ap02Kn
Catherine	(W)	20	F	Wife	03Ap02Kn
Eliza	(D)	.00	F	Infant	03Ap02Kn
NEESON, Catherine		21	F	Farmer	03Ap02Kn
MAINDOR, Bridget		20	F	Farmer	03Ap02Kn
MIDREY, Bridget		.00	F	Infant	03Ap02Kn
MONTGOMERY, Patrick		.00	M	Infant	03Ap02Kn

BURLINGTON 03 APRIL 1847

From Liverpool

NAMES OF PASSENGERS		AGE	SEX	OCCUPATIONS	DATE PORT SHIP
GESHIGAN, Geo.		28	M	Laborer	03Ap02Ja
PACS, Danl.		38	M	Laborer	03Ap02Ja
Bridget	(W)	34	F	Wife	03Ap02Ja
Bridget	(D)	12	F	Unknown	03Ap02Ja
Hugh	(S)	11	M	Unknown	03Ap02Ja
James	(S)	07	M	Child	03Ap02Ja
Danl.	(S)	.00	M	Infant	03Ap02Ja
Mary	(D)	.00	F	Infant	03Ap02Ja
REEVE, Hugh		30	M	Laborer	03Ap02Ja
Ellen	(W)	25	F	Wife	03Ap02Ja
Pat	(S)	06	M	Child	03Ap02Ja
Thomas	(S)	.00	M	Infant	03Ap02Ja
Michl.	(S)	04	M	Child	03Ap02Ja
Hugh	(S)	.00	M	Infant	03Ap02Ja
GREEN, Pat		25	M	Laborer	03Ap02Ja
BILLAY, Mary		25	F	Unknown	03Ap02Ja
CONNELLY, John		20	M	Laborer	03Ap02Ja
FLANIGAN, Thomas		20	M	Laborer	03Ap02Ja
CONROY, Bridget		20	F	Unknown	03Ap02Ja
WALSH, Pat		20	M	Laborer	03Ap02Ja
CARNY, John		21	M	Laborer	03Ap02Ja
WALDEN, Pat		25	M	Laborer	03Ap02Ja
Mich.		23	M	Laborer	03Ap02Ja
Mary		20	F	Unknown	03Ap02Ja
FETHERSTON, Jas.		22	M	Laborer	03Ap02Ja
KELLY, Mary		20	F	Unknown	03Ap02Ja
HART, Mary		20	F	Unknown	03Ap02Ja
CALLEY, Thos.		20	M	Laborer	03Ap02Ja
COAN, Margaret		60	F	Unknown	03Ap02Ja
Patrick		18	M	Laborer	03Ap02Ja
John		17	M	Laborer	03Ap02Ja
Mary		19	F	Unknown	03Ap02Ja

NAMES OF PASSENGERS		AGE	SEX	OCCUPATIONS	DATE PORT SHIP
WINTERS, Catherine		18	F	Unknown	03Ap02Ja
LIVERING, Mich		22	M	Laborer	03Ap02Ja
FELSTON, Edwin		28	M	Laborer	03Ap02Ja
CLEGG, Mary		21	F	Unknown	03Ap02Ja
SHARKEY, David		27	M	Laborer	03Ap02Ja
DUNLEAVY, Maria		30	F	Unknown	03Ap02Ja
CLARK, L		25	M	Laborer	03Ap02Ja
Phil		30	M	Laborer	03Ap02Ja
DOBSON, David		36	M	Laborer	03Ap02Ja
DOLAN, Bridget		30	F	Unknown	03Ap02Ja
Cathe.		10	F	Unknown	03Ap02Ja
Martin		07	M	Child	03Ap02Ja
OLAS, Ellen		17	F	Unknown	03Ap02Ja
MCKEOWN, Pat		20	M	Laborer	03Ap02Ja
PHELAN, Richd.		50	M	Laborer	03Ap02Ja
Judy	(W)	50	F	Wife	03Ap02Ja
Tommy		22	M	Laborer	03Ap02Ja
Arthur		11	M	Laborer	03Ap02Ja
Danl.		09	M	Child	03Ap02Ja
Richard		28	M	Laborer	03Ap02Ja
BRIZEN, Michael		28	M	Laborer	03Ap02Ja
Judy		23	F	Unknown	03Ap02Ja
HEALEY, Cathe.		25	F	Unknown	03Ap02Ja
SHERIDAN, John		48	M	Laborer	03Ap02Ja
John	(S)	20	M	Laborer	03Ap02Ja
Bryan	(S)	13	M	Laborer	03Ap02Ja
FORK, Margt.		50	F	Unknown	03Ap02Ja
GRAHAM, Charles		20	M	Laborer	03Ap02Ja
GODSALL, Thos.		25	M	Laborer	03Ap02Ja
U	(W)	20	F	Wife	03Ap02Ja
Cathe.	(D)	.00	F	Infant	03Ap02Ja
HANE, Pat		30	M	Laborer	03Ap02Ja
FORK, John		12	M	Laborer	03Ap02Ja
Michl.		07	M	Child	03Ap02Ja
MCGUINNESS, James		22	M	Laborer	03Ap02Ja
CONNOR, James		18	M	Laborer	03Ap02Ja
WILLSON, Andrew		30	M	Laborer	03Ap02Ja
HARMAN, Biddy		18	F	Unknown	03Ap02Ja
NEEDHAM, Austin		20	M	Laborer	03Ap02Ja
COULEY, Pat		20	M	Laborer	03Ap02Ja
MORAN, Julia		17	F	Unknown	03Ap02Ja
LEE, Mary		20	F	Unknown	03Ap02Ja
HAGARTY, Bernard		20	M	Laborer	03Ap02Ja
RICE, John		34	M	Laborer	03Ap02Ja
BRADY, John		30	M	Laborer	03Ap02Ja
DUNN, John		55	M	Laborer	03Ap02Ja
Lucy		20	F	Unknown	03Ap02Ja
CREENAN, Cathe.		20	F	Unknown	03Ap02Ja
FARRELL, James		30	M	Laborer	03Ap02Ja
Mary		26	F	Unknown	03Ap02Ja
DORAN, Pat		27	M	Laborer	03Ap02Ja
Jas.		22	M	Laborer	03Ap02Ja
Ellen		19	F	Unknown	03Ap02Ja
Mary-Ann		15	F	Unknown	03Ap02Ja
DOLON, Ellen		16	F	Unknown	03Ap02Ja
GLEASON, Richd.		20	M	Laborer	03Ap02Ja
LONNIGAN, Finn		25	M	Laborer	03Ap02Ja
NOLAN, James		20	M	Laborer	03Ap02Ja
MALONE, Pat		40	M	Laborer	03Ap02Ja
GILMORE, Richard		24	M	Laborer	03Ap02Ja
KILBY, Pat		20	M	Laborer	03Ap02Ja
FEENY, Mary		20	F	Unknown	03Ap02Ja
WHILEY, Robt.		20	M	Laborer	03Ap02Ja
Matilda		11	F	Unknown	03Ap02Ja
CARRILL, Ellen		40	F	Unknown	03Ap02Ja
John		20	M	Laborer	03Ap02Ja
Fanny		12	F	Unknown	03Ap02Ja
DREENAN, Wm.		40	M	Laborer	03Ap02Ja
Pat		30	M	Laborer	03Ap02Ja
Ann		44	F	Unknown	03Ap02Ja
Richard		17	M	Laborer	03Ap02Ja
BROWN, Wm.		30	M	Laborer	03Ap02Ja
Mary	(W)	30	F	Wife	03Ap02Ja
Biddy	(D)	.00	F	Infant	03Ap02Ja
Pat	(S)	.00	M	Infant	03Ap02Ja

NAMES OF PASSENGERS	A G E	S E X	OCCUPATIONS	DATE PORT SHIP	NAMES OF PASSENGERS	A G E	S E X	OCCUPATIONS	DATE PORT SHIP
CAINES, Michael		37 M	Laborer	03Ap02Ja	BRADLY, T.		26 M	Laborer	03Ap02Ja
Mary		13 F	Child	03Ap02Ja	BUSTAN, Michel		20 M	Laborer	03Ap02Ja
PLAYER, Thos.		21 M	Laborer	03Ap02Ja	James		25 M	Laborer	03Ap02Ja
KING, John		18 M	Laborer	03Ap02Ja	FARWELL, Pat		25 M	Laborer	03Ap02Ja
CLARK, Mary		18 F	Unknown	03Ap02Ja	COYLE, Mary		20 F	Unknown	03Ap02Ja
MURPHY, Mary		20 F	Unknown	03Ap02Ja	CASEY, James		50 M	Laborer	03Ap02Ja
DALEY, Cathe.		20 F	Unknown	03Ap02Ja	James		13 M	Child	03Ap02Ja
CAYNON, Maria		08 F	Child	03Ap02Ja	CAROLL, Thomas		20 M	Laborer	03Ap02Ja
Bridget		06 F	Child	03Ap02Ja	SMITH, Peter		40 M	Laborer	03Ap02Ja
Cathe.		26 F	Unknown	03Ap02Ja	Mary	(W)	40 F	Unknown	03Ap02Ja
GRAY, James		25 M	Laborer	03Ap02Ja	John	(S)	20 M	Laborer	03Ap02Ja
PROGAN, Mary		18 F	Unknown	03Ap02Ja	James	(S)	19 M	Laborer	03Ap02Ja
HEALY, Mary		40 F	Unknown	03Ap02Ja	Michel	(S)	18 M	Laborer	03Ap02Ja
MURPHY, John		21 M	Laborer	03Ap02Ja	Mathew	(S)	15 M	Laborer	03Ap02Ja
Mary		04 F	Child	03Ap02Ja	Peter	(S)	13 M	Laborer	03Ap02Ja
CONNER, Ann		10 F	Unknown	03Ap02Ja	Bridget	(D)	10 F	Child	03Ap02Ja
DOLIN, Francis		30 M	Laborer	03Ap02Ja	Andy	(S)	08 M	Child	03Ap02Ja
Margt.	(W)	30 F	Unknown	03Ap02Ja	MURPHY, John		21 M	Laborer	03Ap02Ja
Margt.	(D)	07 F	Child	03Ap02Ja	Mary		04 F	Child	03Ap02Ja
Chary	(D)	04 F	Child	03Ap02Ja	CONNOR, Ann		11 F	Child	03Ap02Ja
Pat	(S)	.00 M	Infant	03Ap02Ja	DOLIN, Francis		30 M	Laborer	03Ap02Ja
FULLAN, Nancy		30 F	Unknown	03Ap02Ja	Margaret		30 F	Unknown	03Ap02Ja
SMITH, Nichos.		30 M	Laborer	03Ap02Ja	Chary	(D)	04 F	Child	03Ap02Ja
Nichos.		21 M	Laborer	03Ap02Ja	Pat	(S)	.00 M	Infant	03Ap02Ja
Ellen		20 F	Unknown	03Ap02Ja	FALLAN, Mary		30 F	Unknown	03Ap02Ja
COONEY, Pat		20 M	Laborer	03Ap02Ja	SMITH, Nicholas		30 M	Laborer	03Ap02Ja
RILEY, Ann		20 F	Unknown	03Ap02Ja	Nicholas		21 M	Laborer	03Ap02Ja
CARR, John		25 M	Laborer	03Ap02Ja	Ellen		20 F	Unknown	03Ap02Ja
MITCHELL, Peter		40 M	Laborer	03Ap02Ja	COAREY, Pat		20 M	Laborer	03Ap02Ja
Peggy	(W)	40 F	Unknown	03Ap02Ja	RILEY, Ann		20 F	Unknown	03Ap02Ja
Francis	(S)	20 M	Laborer	03Ap02Ja	CARR, John		25 M	Laborer	03Ap02Ja
Michael	(S)	18 M	Laborer	03Ap02Ja	HALEY, Mary		20 F	Unknown	03Ap02Ja
HEHAY, John		20 M	Laborer	03Ap02Ja	MITCHELL, Peter		40 M	Laborer	03Ap02Ja
U	(W)	20 F	Wife	03Ap02Ja	Peggy	(W)	40 F	Wife	03Ap02Ja
DEVING, Anthony		20 M	Laborer	03Ap02Ja	Thomas	(S)	20 M	Laborer	03Ap02Ja
Hetty		20 F	Unknown	03Ap02Ja	Michel	(S)	18 M	Laborer	03Ap02Ja
MCSHERRY, Bagan		50 M	Laborer	03Ap02Ja	HELRAY, John		20 M	Laborer	03Ap02Ja
Pat		21 M	Laborer	03Ap02Ja	U	(W)	20 F	Unknown	03Ap02Ja
Cathe.		18 F	Unknown	03Ap02Ja	DARING, Anthony		20 M	Laborer	03Ap02Ja
Bridget		16 F	Unknown	03Ap02Ja	MCSHERY, Bryan		50 M	Laborer	03Ap02Ja
MCMANN, Chas.		35 M	Laborer	03Ap02Ja	MCTHERY, Bryan		50 M	Laborer	03Ap02Ja
Biddy	(W)	35 F	Unknown	03Ap02Ja	Pat		21 M	Laborer	03Ap02Ja
Biddy	(D)	05 F	Child	03Ap02Ja	Catherine		18 F	Unknown	03Ap02Ja
Mary	(D)	.00 F	Infant	03Ap02Ja	Bridget		16 F	Unknown	03Ap02Ja
Pat	(S)	07 M	Child	03Ap02Ja	MCMAN, Charles		35 M	Laborer	03Ap02Ja
GALLAHER, Ann		18 F	Unknown	03Ap02Ja	Biddy	(W)	35 F	Unknown	03Ap02Ja
GRAY, Hugh		35 M	Laborer	03Ap02Ja	Biddy	(D)	05 F	Child	03Ap02Ja
Susan		30 F	Unknown	03Ap02Ja	Mary	(D)	.00 F	Infant	03Ap02Ja
Carn		19 M	Laborer	03Ap02Ja	Patty	(D)	07 F	Child	03Ap02Ja
Mary-Jane		03 F	Child	03Ap02Ja	GALLAGHER, Ann		18 F	Unknown	03Ap02Ja
Ann		.00 F	Infant	03Ap02Ja	GRAY, Hugh		35 M	Laborer	03Ap02Ja
GALLAGHER, Ellen		13 F	Child	03Ap02Ja	Susan		30 F	Unknown	03Ap02Ja
MCGAHAY, Dennis		20 M	Laborer	03Ap02Ja	Cary		19 M	Laborer	03Ap02Ja
CLARKE, U-Mrs.		30 F	Wife	03Ap02Ja	Mary-Jane		03 F	Child	03Ap02Ja
Rosa	(D)	06 F	Child	03Ap02Ja	Ann		.00 F	Infant	03Ap02Ja
Phil	(S)	02 M	Child	03Ap02Ja	LAND, Mary		20 F	Unknown	03Ap02Ja
CARLIN, Mary		20 F	Unknown	03Ap02Ja	KEATING, Farrell		20 M	Laborer	03Ap02Ja
DERMITT, Mary		20 F	Unknown	03Ap02Ja	CANTNAY, Eliza		35 F	Unknown	03Ap02Ja
CARLIN, John		18 M	Laborer	03Ap02Ja	Mick	(S)	12 M	Child	03Ap02Ja
Catherine		18 F	Unknown	03Ap02Ja	Pat	(H)	40 M	Laborer	03Ap02Ja
Biddy		16 F	Unknown	03Ap02Ja	FLANIGAN, John		20 M	Laborer	03Ap02Ja
Anne		20 F	Unknown	03Ap02Ja	COONEY, John		17 M	Laborer	03Ap02Ja
CONOLLY, Ann		18 F	Unknown	03Ap02Ja	MCANN, Pat		18 M	Laborer	03Ap02Ja
DEVLIN, Honora		18 F	Unknown	03Ap02Ja	Ellen		16 F	Unknown	03Ap02Ja
HERAN, David		40 M	Laborer	03Ap02Ja					
Pat	(S)	20 M	Laborer	03Ap02Ja					
Peggy	(D)	18 F	Laborer	03Ap02Ja					
Kitty	(W)	40 F	Unknown	03Ap02Ja					
LAFTENS, John		30 M	Laborer	03Ap02Ja					
Henora	(W)	30 F	Wife	03Ap02Ja					
Arthur	(S)	12 M	None	03Ap02Ja					
Mary	(D)	10 F	None	03Ap02Ja					
Pat	(S)	06 M	Child	03Ap02Ja					
Thomas	(S)	08 M	Child	03Ap02Ja					
John	(S)	09 M	Child	03Ap02Ja					

NAMES OF PASSENGERS	A G E	S E X	OCCUPATIONS	DATE PORT SHIP

BROTHERS 05 APRIL 1847

From Newry

NAMES OF PASSENGERS	A G E	S E X	OCCUPATIONS	DATE PORT SHIP
MCILNY, Wm.	42	M	Farmer	05Ap19Cr
GORMAN, Alex.	38	M	Farmer	05Ap19Cr
Cathe.	37	F	Unknown	05Ap19Cr
Ann	32	F	Unknown	05Ap19Cr
Biddy	29	F	Unknown	05Ap19Cr
Mary	27	F	Unknown	05Ap19Cr
Michael	24	M	Farmer	05Ap19Cr
Cathe	18	F	Unknown	05Ap19Cr
Margt.	19	F	Unknown	05Ap19Cr
HALLIDAY, Robt.	36	M	Farmer	05Ap19Cr
David	32	M	Farmer	05Ap19Cr
COLGAN, Hugh	41	M	Farmer	05Ap19Cr
MCILROY, Wm.	44	M	Farmer	05Ap19Cr
Agnes	38	F	Unknown	05Ap19Cr
Ann-J.	32	F	Unknown	05Ap19Cr
John	27	M	Farmer	05Ap19Cr
William	23	M	Farmer	05Ap19Cr
Agnes	14	F	Unknown	05Ap19Cr
GELIA, Elizabeth	17	F	Unknown	05Ap19Cr
GRANT, Pat	25	M	Farmer	05Ap19Cr
Stephen	26	M	Farmer	05Ap19Cr
MCCARTNEY, John	32	M	Farmer	05Ap19Cr
MORGAN, Rose	27	F	Unknown	05Ap19Cr
MCKEE, Wm.	39	M	Farmer	05Ap19Cr
Elizabeth	37	F	Unknown	05Ap19Cr
Elizabeth	28	F	Unknown	05Ap19Cr
Essey	26	F	Unknown	05Ap19Cr
David	22	M	Farmer	05Ap19Cr
Margt.	18	F	Unknown	05Ap19Cr
William	10	M	None	05Ap19Cr
FITZPATRICK, Cathe.	28	F	Unknown	05Ap19Cr
Shebly	24	F	Unknown	05Ap19Cr
WATSON, Henry	32	M	Laborer	05Ap19Cr
Mary	29	F	Unknown	05Ap19Cr
MCCABE, Cathe.	26	F	Unknown	05Ap19Cr
JAMISON, Wm.	36	M	Laborer	05Ap19Cr
Ann	33	F	Unknown	05Ap19Cr
Mary	27	F	Unknown	05Ap19Cr
Wm.-S.	.09	M	Infant	05Ap19Cr
NEILL, Hugh	44	M	Laborer	05Ap19Cr
FITZPATRICK, Mich.	34	M	Farmer	05Ap19Cr
ONEILL, Biddy	28	F	Unknown	05Ap19Cr
Kitty	12	F	Unknown	05Ap19Cr
MORGAN, John	35	M	Farmer	05Ap19Cr
James	41	M	Farmer	05Ap19Cr
MCKENNA, Pat	26	M	Farmer	05Ap19Cr
Pat	34	M	Farmer	05Ap19Cr
JOHNSTON, Robt.	36	M	Farmer	05Ap19Cr
MCCANNON, John	28	M	Farmer	05Ap19Cr
HARRIGAN, Jas.	22	M	Farmer	05Ap19Cr
MEIDER, John	33	M	Farmer	05Ap19Cr
WARD, Bernard	38	M	Farmer	05Ap19Cr
SANDERSON, Margt.	27	F	Unknown	05Ap19Cr
REID, Eliza	24	F	Unknown	05Ap19Cr
HALL, Ann	19	F	Unknown	05Ap19Cr
WARSLOW, Agnes	21	F	Unknown	05Ap19Cr
FLANNIGAN, Ellen	22	F	Unknown	05Ap19Cr
MCCANNON, Ann	27	F	Unknown	05Ap19Cr
DONNELLY, Ann	31	F	Unknown	05Ap19Cr
MAGEE, Dennis	29	M	Farmer	05Ap19Cr
MCBALLAGH, Betty	32	F	Unknown	05Ap19Cr
FAGAN, John	41	M	Farmer	05Ap19Cr
HIGGINS, Hugh	38	M	Farmer	05Ap19Cr
Cathe.	06	F	Child	05Ap19Cr
Mary	06	F	Child	05Ap19Cr
JARDINS, Saml.	28	M	Farmer	05Ap19Cr
Christy	24	F	Unknown	05Ap19Cr
Sarah	29	F	Unknown	05Ap19Cr
Nancy	39	F	Unknown	05Ap19Cr
GRANT, Pat	40	M	Farmer	05Ap19Cr
DOYLE, John	38	M	Farmer	05Ap19Cr
Bridget	37	F	Unknown	05Ap19Cr
KING, Patrick	29	M	Farmer	05Ap19Cr
Mary	26	F	Unknown	05Ap19Cr
Biddy	22	F	Unknown	05Ap19Cr
Cathe.	20	F	Unknown	05Ap19Cr
Thos.	18	M	Farmer	05Ap19Cr
Betsey	18	F	Unknown	05Ap19Cr
Betsey	17	F	Unknown	05Ap19Cr
Nancy	12	F	Unknown	05Ap19Cr
TOOLE, Michael	42	M	Farmer	05Ap19Cr
Alice	38	F	Unknown	05Ap19Cr
Patrick	24	M	Farmer	05Ap19Cr
John	22	M	Farmer	05Ap19Cr
Michael	19	M	Farmer	05Ap19Cr
Rose	17	F	Unknown	05Ap19Cr
Mary-Ann	12	F	Unknown	05Ap19Cr
CAMPBELL, Patk.	36	M	Farmer	05Ap19Cr
Mary	34	F	Unknown	05Ap19Cr
CALLAGHAN, James	25	M	Farmer	05Ap19Cr
Mary-Ann	05	F	Child	05Ap19Cr
KINNAN, John	28	M	Farmer	05Ap19Cr
Mary	33	F	Unknown	05Ap19Cr
ANDERSON, James	38	M	Farmer	05Ap19Cr
Elizabeth	34	F	Unknown	05Ap19Cr
BRADLEY, Bernard	27	M	Farmer	05Ap19Cr
ONIEL, Ann	.10	F	Infant	05Ap19Cr
OHANLAN, John	33	M	Farmer	05Ap19Cr
QUIGGINESS, Ann	32	F	Unknown	05Ap19Cr
ELLIOTT, John	42	M	Farmer	05Ap19Cr
Mary	38	F	Unknown	05Ap19Cr
Wm.	24	M	Farmer	05Ap19Cr
Jane	18	F	Unknown	05Ap19Cr
Eliza	15	F	Unknown	05Ap19Cr
GIBSON, John	32	M	Farmer	05Ap19Cr
HUGHES, Francis	34	M	Farmer	05Ap19Cr
Nancy	29	F	Unknown	05Ap19Cr
ROGAN, James	37	M	Farmer	05Ap19Cr
Billey	35	F	Unknown	05Ap19Cr
HERRING, Saml.	41	M	Farmer	05Ap19Cr
Thos.	39	M	Farmer	05Ap19Cr
REYNOLDS, Pat	27	M	Farmer	05Ap19Cr
GOWAN, John	33	M	Farmer	05Ap19Cr
Margt.	29	F	Unknown	05Ap19Cr
Jane	18	F	Unknown	05Ap19Cr
Ann	16	F	Unknown	05Ap19Cr
Joseph	14	M	Farmer	05Ap19Cr
Robt.-Jas.	13	M	Farmer	05Ap19Cr
Joseph	10	M	None	05Ap19Cr
DODDS, Jas.	33	M	Laborer	05Ap19Cr
THOMPSON, Hamilton	28	M	Laborer	05Ap19Cr
DICKINSON, Matt.	24	M	Laborer	05Ap19Cr
FEARON, Pat	22	M	Laborer	05Ap19Cr
Cathe.	21	F	Unknown	05Ap19Cr
John	.10	M	Infant	05Ap19Cr
LAVARY, Margt.	36	F	Unknown	05Ap19Cr
JOHNSTON, Wm.	44	M	Farmer	05Ap19Cr
MCCANN, Wm.	32	M	Farmer	05Ap19Cr
Ann	34	F	Unknown	05Ap19Cr
SANDERSON, John	37	M	Farmer	05Ap19Cr
THORP, John	29	M	Farmer	05Ap19Cr
Ann	27	F	Unknown	05Ap19Cr
HARROWAY, Biddy	32	F	Unknown	05Ap19Cr
GEORGE, John	41	M	Farmer	05Ap19Cr
Mary	38	F	Unknown	05Ap19Cr
Elizabeth	22	F	Unknown	05Ap19Cr
John	18	M	Farmer	05Ap19Cr
Mary-J.	15	F	Unknown	05Ap19Cr
Helena	12	F	Unknown	05Ap19Cr
Neama	09	F	Child	05Ap19Cr

NAMES OF PASSENGERS	A G E	S E X	OCCUPATIONS	DATE PORT SHIP	NAMES OF PASSENGERS	A G E	S E X	OCCUPATIONS	DATE PORT SHIP
LAWSON, Mary	35	F	Unknown	05Ap19Cr	OCONNEL, John	25	M	Laborer	05Ap14Ld
KIRKLAND, Wm.	38	M	Farmer	05Ap19Cr	Margt.	20	F	Unknown	05Ap14Ld
HEARTY, Sally	32	F	Unknown	05Ap19Cr	David	27	M	Laborer	05Ap14Ld
MARTIN, Wm.	41	M	Farmer	05Ap19Cr	FOLIN, Bridget	20	F	Unknown	05Ap14Ld
TEARON, Jas.	39	M	Farmer	05Ap19Cr	RYAN, Margt.	20	F	Unknown	05Ap14Ld
BOLTON, William	36	M	Farmer	05Ap19Cr	Michael	19	M	Laborer	05Ap14Ld
DARBY, Rose	34	F	Unknown	05Ap19Cr	BYRNE, M.-A.	18	F	Unknown	05Ap14Ld
Rose	13	F	Unknown	05Ap19Cr	GRANT, Henry	24	M	Laborer	05Ap14Ld
WHITE, Margt.	11	F	Unknown	05Ap19Cr	SULLIVAN, Pat	35	M	Laborer	05Ap14Ld
James	09	M	Child	05Ap19Cr	ARTCHAR, Edward	30	M	Laborer	05Ap14Ld
CONWAY, Pat	35	M	Farmer	05Ap19Cr	BROOKE, Edward	25	M	Laborer	05Ap14Ld
MAGANTY, Margt.	28	F	Unknown	05Ap19Cr	Honora	20	F	Unknown	05Ap14Ld
MURPHY, Patk.	44	M	Farmer	05Ap19Cr	MAHONY, Mary	50	F	Unknown	05Ap14Ld
Jane	38	F	Unknown	05Ap19Cr	Michael	22	M	Laborer	05Ap14Ld
Margt.	24	F	Unknown	05Ap19Cr	Jeremiah	20	M	Laborer	05Ap14Ld
Cathe	22	F	Unknown	05Ap19Cr	DALEY, Cathe.	20	F	Unknown	05Ap14Ld
Biddy	18	F	Unknown	05Ap19Cr	QUINLAN, Mary	20	F	Unknown	05Ap14Ld
Mary	16	F	Unknown	05Ap19Cr	POMPHRET, U	26	F	Unknown	05Ap14Ld
Peter	13	M	Farmer	05Ap19Cr	KEARN, John	25	M	Laborer	05Ap14Ld
Jane	12	F	None	05Ap19Cr	COTTON, Thos.	22	M	Laborer	05Ap14Ld
John	11	M	None	05Ap19Cr	Ellen	22	F	Unknown	05Ap14Ld
Eliza	09	F	Child	05Ap19Cr	NEALE, Betty	20	F	Unknown	05Ap14Ld
Ann	04	F	Child	05Ap19Cr	DONAVAN, Michael	20	M	Laborer	05Ap14Ld
KEARNEY, Pat.	38	M	Laborer	05Ap19Cr	Patt	17	M	Laborer	05Ap14Ld
Ann	36	F	Unknown	05Ap19Cr	DOMIAN, Catherine	16	F	Unknown	05Ap14Ld
Sally	29	F	Unknown	05Ap19Cr	PARKER, Robt.	29	M	Laborer	05Ap14Ld
MOAN, John	33	M	Laborer	05Ap19Cr	FITZGERALD, Michl.	21	M	Laborer	05Ap14Ld
MCFARLAND, Rose	32	F	Unknown	05Ap19Cr	NOONAN, James	20	M	Laborer	05Ap14Ld
LAMB, John	39	M	Laborer	05Ap19Cr	DONNEY, Timothy	21	M	Laborer	05Ap14Ld
DONNELLY, James	32	M	Laborer	05Ap19Cr	Johanah	22	F	Unknown	05Ap14Ld
SAVAGE, Mark	28	M	Laborer	05Ap19Cr	Tim	22	M	Laborer	05Ap14Ld
SMITH, Robt.	31	M	Laborer	05Ap19Cr	KANEBY, Michael	25	M	Laborer	05Ap14Ld
BYRNES, Hugh	29	M	Laborer	05Ap19Cr	COLHART, John	20	M	Laborer	05Ap14Ld
Margaret	27	F	Unknown	05Ap19Cr	COHNAN, Ebben	16	M	Laborer	05Ap14Ld
CALLAGHAN, Bernard	33	M	Laborer	05Ap19Cr	BRIER, John	36	M	Laborer	05Ap14Ld
Deborah	31	F	Unknown	05Ap19Cr	REGAN, Dennis	22	M	Laborer	05Ap14Ld
MURPHY, Mary	29	F	Unknown	05Ap19Cr	Anna	21	F	Unknown	05Ap14Ld
BRADY, Francis	38	M	Laborer	05Ap19Cr	Con	25	M	Laborer	05Ap14Ld
MCKEON, Ann	41	F	Unknown	05Ap19Cr	ROCKFORD, Thos.	24	M	Laborer	05Ap14Ld
Michael	32	M	Laborer	05Ap19Cr	BATEMAN, Mary	39	F	Unknown	05Ap14Ld
John	28	M	Laborer	05Ap19Cr	REGAN, Cathe.	20	F	Unknown	05Ap14Ld
Mary	21	F	Unknown	05Ap19Cr	WALKER, Wm.	24	M	Laborer	05Ap14Ld
DONNELLY, Felix	37	M	Laborer	05Ap19Cr	WHIGMORE, Wm.	25	M	Laborer	05Ap14Ld
KEANNY, Michael	29	M	Laborer	05Ap19Cr	Thos.	25	M	Laborer	05Ap14Ld
MCKENNA, John	25	M	Laborer	05Ap19Cr	DOYLE, Mary	30	F	Unknown	05Ap14Ld
MAGER, Lawrence	33	M	Laborer	05Ap19Cr	BAVY, David	26	M	Laborer	05Ap14Ld
LESTER, Jas.	40	M	Laborer	05Ap19Cr	LEHAY, John	24	M	Laborer	05Ap14Ld
HARPER, Alex.	29	M	Laborer	05Ap19Cr	KENADY, Chas.	25	M	Laborer	05Ap14Ld
					OLDEN, Wm.	24	M	Laborer	05Ap14Ld
					KENEDEY, Mamia	30	M	Laborer	05Ap14Ld
					LEARY, Dal.	23	M	Laborer	05Ap14Ld
					Mary	22	F	Unknown	05Ap14Ld
					MURPHY, Benj.	25	M	Laborer	05Ap14Ld
MAY-T.RUNDLET 05 APRIL 1847					Johana	21	F	Unknown	05Ap14Ld
					Elben	27	M	Laborer	05Ap14Ld
From Cork					DUNAVAN, Pat	21	M	Laborer	05Ap14Ld
					DRISCOLL, Con.	22	M	Laborer	05Ap14Ld
					SHANAHAN, Andrew	25	M	Laborer	05Ap14Ld
					DRISCOLL, Peggy	24	F	Unknown	05Ap14Ld
MANLEY, Dan	21	M	Laborer	05Ap14Ld	BROTHER, Mary	22	F	Unknown	05Ap14Ld
Betsey	22	F	Unknown	05Ap14Ld	LANE, John	26	M	Laborer	05Ap14Ld
DUNAVEN, Hanah	28	F	Unknown	05Ap14Ld	Tom	22	M	Laborer	05Ap14Ld
MCCARTY, Florence	22	M	Laborer	05Ap14Ld	LINEHAN, Timy	25	M	Laborer	05Ap14Ld
MURPHY, John	26	M	Laborer	05Ap14Ld	QUIRK, David	19	M	Laborer	05Ap14Ld
Mary-Ann	20	F	Unknown	05Ap14Ld	MARTIN, David	24	M	Laborer	05Ap14Ld
Mary	23	F	Unknown	05Ap14Ld	HANKART, Margt.	25	F	Unknown	05Ap14Ld
SINGLETON, Dennis	18	M	Laborer	05Ap14Ld	CONNELL, Thos.	28	M	Laborer	05Ap14Ld
CROSSIN, Dan	20	M	Laborer	05Ap14Ld	DUNN, James	30	M	Laborer	05Ap14Ld
HILLIAM, John	23	M	Laborer	05Ap14Ld	Mary	22	F	Unknown	05Ap14Ld
Dennis	21	M	Laborer	05Ap14Ld	GALLIVAN, Thos.	22	M	Laborer	05Ap14Ld
Jobarah	19	M	Laborer	05Ap14Ld	DUNN, Matt.	50	M	Laborer	05Ap14Ld
DEASEY, John	22	M	Laborer	05Ap14Ld	Ellen	(W)	50	F	Unknown	05Ap14Ld
BARRY, James	30	M	Laborer	05Ap14Ld	Dennis	(S)	20	M	Laborer	05Ap14Ld
Cathe	22	F	Unknown	05Ap14Ld	Mary	(D)	25	F	Unknown	05Ap14Ld
CRONAN, Margt.	19	F	Unknown	05Ap14Ld	Elizabeth	(D)	13	F	Unknown	05Ap14Ld

NAMES OF PASSENGERS		AGE	SEX	OCCUPATIONS	DATE PORT SHIP
ENRIGHT, Thos.		22	M	Laborer	05Ap14Ld
CONDOR, Michael		22	M	Laborer	05Ap14Ld
GORMAN, John		30	M	Laborer	05Ap14Ld
SHANAHAN, Jas.		26	M	Laborer	05Ap14Ld
CONDON, Richd.		25	M	Laborer	05Ap14Ld
HOGAN, John		30	M	Laborer	05Ap14Ld
Mary		24	F	Unknown	05Ap14Ld
COLOGAN, John		44	M	Laborer	05Ap14Ld
HINBY, Dennis		40	M	Laborer	05Ap14Ld
FOX, Thos.		21	M	Laborer	05Ap14Ld
LEAK, Wm.		22	M	Laborer	05Ap14Ld
GOLDEN, Eliza		21	F	Unknown	05Ap14Ld
Patrick		23	M	Laborer	05Ap14Ld
Daniel		19	M	Laborer	05Ap14Ld
DUNN, Ellen		20	F	Unknown	05Ap14Ld
LANE, Mannie		25	M	Laborer	05Ap14Ld
Johana		20	F	Unknown	05Ap14Ld
Betsey		18	F	Unknown	05Ap14Ld
DEBEA, Margt.		25	F	Unknown	05Ap14Ld
James		20	M	Laborer	05Ap14Ld
LONG, Mary		20	F	Unknown	05Ap14Ld
DORGAN, Johana		20	F	Unknown	05Ap14Ld
FETHERSTONE, Jas.		13	M	Child	05Ap14Ld

PATRICK-HENRY 05 APRIL 1847

From Liverpool

NAMES OF PASSENGERS		AGE	SEX	OCCUPATIONS	DATE PORT SHIP
DUDLEY, Walter		34	M	Merchant	05Ap02Cw
Ann	(W)	25	F	Unknown	05Ap02Cw
Walter	(S)	.03	M	Infant	05Ap02Cw
SUMMERFIELD, Lucy		22	F	Unknown	05Ap02Cw
CUNNINGHAM, Wm.		22	M	Laborer	05Ap02Cw
KIGGIE, Thos.-C.		26	M	Laborer	05Ap02Cw
BATTERSBY, Francis		30	M	Farmer	05Ap02Cw
John		26	M	Farmer	05Ap02Cw
WELSH, James		30	M	Farmer	05Ap02Cw
U	(W)	30	F	None	05Ap02Cw
James		05	M	Child	05Ap02Cw
Ellen		.00	F	Infant	05Ap02Cw
HANNIRT, Molvis		22	M	Farmer	05Ap02Cw
BRYAN, James		22	M	Farmer	05Ap02Cw
LASEN, John		23	M	Farmer	05Ap02Cw
FANK, James		24	M	Farmer	05Ap02Cw
U	(W)	22	F	Unknown	05Ap02Cw
LASEN, U		22	F	Unknown	05Ap02Cw
PARODISH, Wm.		22	M	Farmer	05Ap02Cw
MCQUIRK, James		24	M	Farmer	05Ap02Cw
FITZSIMMONS, James		20	M	Farmer	05Ap02Cw
WHELAN, John		24	M	Farmer	05Ap02Cw
DALY, Phanton		20	M	Farmer	05Ap02Cw
SMITH, Thos.		21	M	Farmer	05Ap02Cw
HICKEY, Mary		20	F	Unknown	05Ap02Cw
MALLAN, John		24	M	Farmer	05Ap02Cw
CARROLL, Patt		24	M	Farmer	05Ap02Cw
KELLEY, Peter		24	M	Farmer	05Ap02Cw
John		24	M	Farmer	05Ap02Cw
DEAKIN, John		46	M	Farmer	05Ap02Cw
CASTER, Henry		24	M	Farmer	05Ap02Cw
TOLBY, Lawrence		25	M	Farmer	05Ap02Cw
Mary		25	F	Unknown	05Ap02Cw
SULLIVAN, Wm.		24	M	Farmer	05Ap02Cw
James		20	M	Farmer	05Ap02Cw
CORCORAN, John		20	M	Farmer	05Ap02Cw
GILLESSON, Bernard		27	M	Farmer	05Ap02Cw
BEGUINAN, And.		20	M	Farmer	05Ap02Cw
James		20	M	Farmer	05Ap02Cw
BUTTY, Pat		20	M	Farmer	05Ap02Cw
SMITH, Hnd.		24	M	Farmer	05Ap02Cw

NAMES OF PASSENGERS		AGE	SEX	OCCUPATIONS	DATE PORT SHIP
GALLAGAN, Ed.		27	M	Farmer	05Ap02Cw
SMITH, Ann		24	F	Farmer	05Ap02Cw
MCGLINN, James		40	M	Farmer	05Ap02Cw
BELL, Geo.		22	M	Farmer	05Ap02Cw
U	(W)	20	F	Unknown	05Ap02Cw
PIGEON, Owen		21	M	Farmer	05Ap02Cw
STEPHENSON, R.		21	M	Farmer	05Ap02Cw
WHINTY, Cathe		25	F	Unknown	05Ap02Cw
MCDONNEL, Michl.		60	M	Farmer	05Ap02Cw
Ann	(W)	60	F	Unknown	05Ap02Cw
Bridget	(D)	28	F	Unknown	05Ap02Cw
Phillip	(S)	26	M	Farmer	05Ap02Cw
Caroline	(D)	24	F	Unknown	05Ap02Cw
Thos.	(S)	22	M	Farmer	05Ap02Cw
Matthew	(S)	20	M	Farmer	05Ap02Cw
Charles	(S)	18	M	Farmer	05Ap02Cw
John	(S)	18	M	Farmer	05Ap02Cw
Myche.	(S)	12	M	Farmer	05Ap02Cw
Mary	(D)	08	F	Child	05Ap02Cw
FITZSIMMONS, Neilin		40	M	Farmer	05Ap02Cw
Mary	(W)	40	F	Unknown	05Ap02Cw
Hugh	(S)	18	M	Farmer	05Ap02Cw
Patrick	(S)	16	M	Farmer	05Ap02Cw
Ellen	(D)	19	F	Unknown	05Ap02Cw
Cathe	(D)	17	F	Unknown	05Ap02Cw
Matthew	(S)	13	M	Farmer	05Ap02Cw
Mary	(D)	10	F	None	05Ap02Cw
Philin	(S)	01	M	Child	05Ap02Cw
DUNN, Patrick		30	M	Laborer	05Ap02Cw
PLUNKET, Pat.		61	M	Laborer	05Ap02Cw
Rose	(W)	60	F	Unknown	05Ap02Cw
James	(S)	23	M	Laborer	05Ap02Cw
Ann	(D)	21	F	Unknown	05Ap02Cw
Bridget	(D)	17	F	Unknown	05Ap02Cw
Margt.	(D)	17	F	Unknown	05Ap02Cw
Ryan	(S)	15	M	Laborer	05Ap02Cw
BENNETT, Wm.		20	M	Laborer	05Ap02Cw
FAY, Peter		30	M	Laborer	05Ap02Cw
Ellen		30	F	Unknown	05Ap02Cw
Anne		30	F	Unknown	05Ap02Cw
Peggy		30	F	Unknown	05Ap02Cw
FRETT, Peter		.00	M	Infant	05Ap02Cw
STENSON, Wm.		50	M	Merchant	05Ap02Cw
U	(W)	40	F	Unknown	05Ap02Cw
Wm.	(S)	24	M	Merchant	05Ap02Cw
James	(S)	21	M	Merchant	05Ap02Cw
Cathe	(D)	16	F	Unknown	05Ap02Cw
Ellen	(D)	15	F	Unknown	05Ap02Cw
KELLEY, Luke		24	M	Merchant	05Ap02Cw
HYDE, Wm.		35	M	Merchant	05Ap02Cw
CARMODY, John		40	M	Merchant	05Ap02Cw
U	(W)	27	F	Unknown	05Ap02Cw
Robt.	(S)	07	M	Child	05Ap02Cw
Jane	(D)	03	F	Child	05Ap02Cw
Wm.	(S)	05	M	Child	05Ap02Cw
LOWENY, Mary		01	F	Child	05Ap02Cw
SULLIVAN, John		50	M	Farmer	05Ap02Cw
U	(W)	50	F	Unknown	05Ap02Cw
Patrick	(S)	23	M	Farmer	05Ap02Cw
John	(S)	20	M	Farmer	05Ap02Cw
Rose	(D)	18	F	Unknown	05Ap02Cw
Eliza	(D)	16	F	Unknown	05Ap02Cw
Redmand	(S)	14	M	Farmer	05Ap02Cw
Ellen	(D)	12	F	Unknown	05Ap02Cw
Thos.	(S)	09	M	Child	05Ap02Cw
Betsey	(D)	26	F	Unknown	05Ap02Cw
CORRIGAN, Francis		45	M	Laborer	05Ap02Cw
U	(W)	45	F	Unknown	05Ap02Cw
John	(S)	.00	M	Infant	05Ap02Cw
LIVERNAY, John		24	M	Laborer	05Ap02Cw
U	(W)	24	F	Unknown	05Ap02Cw
CLARKE, Peter		50	M	Laborer	05Ap02Cw
James		18	M	Laborer	05Ap02Cw
RIVERAHON, Cathe.		20	F	Unknown	05Ap02Cw
HUGHES, Bridget		20	F	Unknown	05Ap02Cw

NAMES OF PASSENGERS	AGE	SEX	OCCUPATIONS	DATE PORT SHIP
HUGHES, Alice	16	F	Unknown	05Ap02Cw
SHANY, Peter	20	M	Laborer	05Ap02Cw
BUTHWILL, Richd.	22	M	Laborer	05Ap02Cw
COX, George	21	M	Laborer	05Ap02Cw
GRAHAM, Eliza	18	F	Unknown	05Ap02Cw
SUMMERVILLE, John	30	M	Farmer	05Ap02Cw
MCANALLY, James	28	M	Farmer	05Ap02Cw
DUNCAN, Pat.	24	M	Farmer	05Ap02Cw
HAYDEN, Cathe.	20	F	Unknown	05Ap02Cw
DAVIDSON, U	36	F	Unknown	05Ap02Cw
John (S)	02	M	Child	05Ap02Cw
Mary (D)	09	F	Child	05Ap02Cw
KUCY, Eliza	18	F	Unknown	05Ap02Cw
JEHAN, Patrick	22	M	Laborer	05Ap02Cw
STEPHENSON, James	21	M	Laborer	05Ap02Cw
DEMPSEY, Michael	57	M	Laborer	05Ap02Cw
John	30	M	Laborer	05Ap02Cw
Patrick	25	M	Laborer	05Ap02Cw
Mike	15	M	Laborer	05Ap02Cw
James	25	M	Laborer	05Ap02Cw
Mary	16	F	Unknown	05Ap02Cw
Mary	50	F	Unknown	05Ap02Cw
Nelly	26	F	Unknown	05Ap02Cw
Kate	12	F	Unknown	05Ap02Cw
Judy	11	F	Unknown	05Ap02Cw
Margt.	02	F	Child	05Ap02Cw
REGAN, Pat	30	M	Laborer	05Ap02Cw
DENTHIN, Mary	33	F	Unknown	05Ap02Cw
Patrick	16	M	Laborer	05Ap02Cw
Sarah	08	F	Child	05Ap02Cw
Ward	05	M	Child	05Ap02Cw
John	03	M	Child	05Ap02Cw
BRASKER, John	22	M	Farmer	05Ap02Cw
FANELI, Mary	21	F	Unknown	05Ap02Cw
CALLIGHAN, Rose	20	F	Unknown	05Ap02Cw
MULHOLLAND, Danl.	30	M	Farmer	05Ap02Cw
MCCANNA, Thos.	17	M	Farmer	05Ap02Cw
MCKESNEILL, U	24	F	Unknown	05Ap02Cw
Susan	02	F	Child	05Ap02Cw
KEANEY, Mary	20	F	Unknown	05Ap02Cw
CASSIDY, Wm.	20	M	Farmer	05Ap02Cw
MURPHY, Conner	56	M	Farmer	05Ap02Cw
Ann	15	F	Unknown	05Ap02Cw
CONNERFORD, John	37	M	Farmer	05Ap02Cw
MURPHY, Michael	38	M	Farmer	05Ap02Cw
DOLAN, Noyes	28	M	Farmer	05Ap02Cw
MURPHY, Danl.	28	M	Farmer	05Ap02Cw
KING, James	36	M	Farmer	05Ap02Cw
DUNN, Michael	24	M	Farmer	05Ap02Cw
DANSHOE, Patt	18	M	Farmer	05Ap02Cw
HANAGAN, John	24	M	Farmer	05Ap02Cw
Margt.	20	F	Unknown	05Ap02Cw
DOWE, Bernard	30	M	Farmer	05Ap02Cw
Rose	25	F	Unknown	05Ap02Cw
BLAMS, Isaac	24	M	Farmer	05Ap02Cw
Richard	20	M	Farmer	05Ap02Cw
HEAD, Wm.	20	M	Farmer	05Ap02Cw
ALLEN, Danl.	12	M	Farmer	05Ap02Cw
DAVIS, James	25	M	Farmer	05Ap02Cw
MCDONNELL, Patt	24	M	Farmer	05Ap02Cw
PITT, Saml.	21	M	Farmer	05Ap02Cw
LAWNDS, Fredk.	18	M	Farmer	05Ap02Cw
John	13	M	Farmer	05Ap02Cw
KENNEDY, Pat	60	M	Farmer	05Ap02Cw
MCCORMICK, Sarah	50	F	Unknown	05Ap02Cw
Maria (D)	25	F	Unknown	05Ap02Cw
John (S)	23	M	Farmer	05Ap02Cw
LYONS, Bridget	40	F	Unknown	05Ap02Cw
Cathe.	20	F	Unknown	05Ap02Cw
James	18	M	Farmer	05Ap02Cw
MCMAHON, John	22	M	Farmer	05Ap02Cw
NUGENT, Edd.	22	M	Farmer	05Ap02Cw
BRAIN, John	22	M	Farmer	05Ap02Cw
FITZGERALD, David	23	M	Farmer	05Ap02Cw
Mary	18	F	Unknown	05Ap02Cw
CLIFFY, Ellen	20	F	Unknown	05Ap02Cw
KNOX, John	27	M	Farmer	05Ap02Cw
KELLY, John	22	M	Farmer	05Ap02Cw
MCCLEAN, Chas.	30	M	Farmer	05Ap02Cw
COOKER, Ino.-W.	27	M	Farmer	05Ap02Cw
MCNULTY, Henry	25	M	Farmer	05Ap02Cw
LOCKHARDT, Jas.	25	M	Farmer	05Ap02Cw
WARTON, George	25	M	Farmer	05Ap02Cw
NEIL, Mary-J.	20	F	Unknown	05Ap02Cw
ADO, Margt.	18	M	Laborer	05Ap02Cw
Eliza	15	F	Unknown	05Ap02Cw
ODONNELL, Danl.	15	M	Laborer	05Ap02Cw
GALLAGHER, Owen	39	M	Laborer	05Ap02Cw
BOYLE, Mary	50	F	Unknown	05Ap02Cw
Hannah	20	F	Unknown	05Ap02Cw
PHIRKEY, Sally	20	F	Unknown	05Ap02Cw
BOYLE, Nancy	12	F	Child	05Ap02Cw
CORCORAN, John	13	M	Unknown	05Ap02Cw
DOUGHERTY, Chas.	25	M	Laborer	05Ap02Cw
BRENNA, Pat	24	M	Laborer	05Ap02Cw
GAVENEY, Pat	22	M	Laborer	05Ap02Cw
John	19	M	Laborer	05Ap02Cw
DAILEY, James	20	M	Laborer	05Ap02Cw
CONNY, Pat	18	M	Laborer	05Ap02Cw
DOYLE, Cato	20	M	Laborer	05Ap02Cw
Ellen	18	F	Unknown	05Ap02Cw
COLMAN, Bridget	09	F	Child	05Ap02Cw
EARLY, Margt.	30	F	Unknown	05Ap02Cw
KERRNAN, Margt.	20	F	Unknown	05Ap02Cw
FANY, Walt	26	M	Laborer	05Ap02Cw
Mary	22	F	Unknown	05Ap02Cw
MALONE, Ann	18	F	Unknown	05Ap02Cw
Bridget	11	F	Unknown	05Ap02Cw
CONROY, Ann	12	F	Unknown	05Ap02Cw
FOLEY, Ellen	02	F	Child	05Ap02Cw
James	.00	M	Infant	05Ap02Cw
WHITE, Mike	30	M	Laborer	05Ap02Cw
Peter	20	M	Laborer	05Ap02Cw
Cathe	18	F	Unknown	05Ap02Cw
MOONEY, John	20	M	Laborer	05Ap02Cw
CLARK, Pat	30	M	Laborer	05Ap02Cw
MCANGLISH, Ed.	20	M	Laborer	05Ap02Cw
Ellen	22	F	Unknown	05Ap02Cw
Jane	25	F	Unknown	05Ap02Cw
John	30	M	Laborer	05Ap02Cw
MOORE, James	25	M	Laborer	05Ap02Cw
Oliver	23	M	Laborer	05Ap02Cw
Charlotte	19	F	Unknown	05Ap02Cw
Ann	10	F	Unknown	05Ap02Cw
MULHOLLAND, John	30	M	Laborer	05Ap02Cw
Cathe.	20	F	Unknown	05Ap02Cw
MCERLIN, James	22	M	Laborer	05Ap02Cw
Hughes	22	M	Laborer	05Ap02Cw
MCGAUGHEN, Thos.	21	M	Laborer	05Ap02Cw
BONNER, James	18	M	Laborer	05Ap02Cw
MCCANNA, Mary	20	F	Unknown	05Ap02Cw
HIGGINS, Mary	20	F	Unknown	05Ap02Cw
CARROL, Pat	18	M	Laborer	05Ap02Cw
MCCANNA, Peggy	18	F	Unknown	05Ap02Cw
DOYLE, Edwd.	36	M	Laborer	05Ap02Cw
HEVORAN, Bridget	18	F	Unknown	05Ap02Cw
LOUGHEY, Mickey	22	M	Farmer	05Ap02Cw
CONWAY, Daniel	21	M	Farmer	05Ap02Cw
BRADLEY, James	20	M	Farmer	05Ap02Cw
OAKES, Thos.	40	M	Farmer	05Ap02Cw
MCVEIGH, Pat	17	M	Farmer	05Ap02Cw
MCMAHON, James	30	M	Farmer	05Ap02Cw
MARI, H.	22	M	Laborer	05Ap02Cw
MARRIT, U	20	F	Unknown	05Ap02Cw
DOYLE, Cornelius	20	M	Farmer	05Ap02Cw
BYRNES, James	40	M	Farmer	05Ap02Cw
U	40	F	Unknown	05Ap02Cw
Phillip	19	M	Farmer	05Ap02Cw
Mary	17	F	Unknown	05Ap02Cw
John	15	M	Farmer	05Ap02Cw

NAMES OF PASSENGERS	AGE	SEX	OCCUPATIONS	DATE PORT SHIP	NAMES OF PASSENGERS	AGE	SEX	OCCUPATIONS	DATE PORT SHIP
BYRNES, James	12	M	Farmer	05Ap02Cw	DUNLAP, John	.00	M	Infant	05Ap02Cw
Peter	09	M	Child	05Ap02Cw	RYAN, Tim	25	M	Laborer	05Ap02Cw
Hannah	06	F	Child	05Ap02Cw	Cathe.	(W) 25	F	Unknown	05Ap02Cw
Ed.	02	M	Child	05Ap02Cw	Mary	(D) .00	F	Infant	05Ap02Cw
Amy	04	F	Child	05Ap02Cw	CARROLL, Patt	30	M	Laborer	05Ap02Cw
Felix	60	M	Laborer	05Ap02Cw	WILLSON, Wm.	20	M	Laborer	05Ap02Cw
ROBINSON, Thos.	21	M	Laborer	05Ap02Cw					
COOGAN, Dennis	26	M	Laborer	05Ap02Cw					
Ann	20	F	Unknown	05Ap02Cw					
Felix	19	M	Laborer	05Ap02Cw					
James	06	M	Child	05Ap02Cw	NEW-YORK 05 APRIL 1847				
DILWORTH, Robt.	60	M	Laborer	05Ap02Cw					
U	(W) 50	F	Unknown	05Ap02Cw	From Liverpool				
Margt.	(D) 25	F	Unknown	05Ap02Cw					
Charlotte	(D) 25	F	Unknown	05Ap02Cw					
Helena	(D) 28	F	Unknown	05Ap02Cw					
JOHNSON, Chas.	32	M	Laborer	05Ap02Cw					
HAYNES, Robt.	22	M	Laborer	05Ap02Cw	HAGSON, G.	28	M	Laborer	05Ap02Bk
MURPHY, Luke	30	M	Laborer	05Ap02Cw	U	(W) 25	F	Laborer	05Ap02Bk
U	(W) 24	F	Unknown	05Ap02Cw	DUFFY, M.M.	22	M	Laborer	05Ap02Bk
Mary	(D) 02	F	Child	05Ap02Cw	My.A.	16	F	Unknown	05Ap02Bk
CLARK, Cathe.	50	F	Unknown	05Ap02Cw	TURN, U	23	F	Unknown	05Ap02Bk
John	20	M	Laborer	05Ap02Cw	DAY, W.	45	M	Laborer	05Ap02Bk
Honora	17	F	Unknown	05Ap02Cw	WRIGHT, T.	22	M	Laborer	05Ap02Bk
Cathe	15	F	Unknown	05Ap02Cw	SMITH, C.	24	M	Laborer	05Ap02Bk
MURPHY, John	20	M	Laborer	05Ap02Cw	MONTAGH, P.	20	M	Laborer	05Ap02Bk
MCGUIRE, John	25	M	Laborer	05Ap02Cw	FRAMAN, T.	19	M	Laborer	05Ap02Bk
RIELLEY, Owen	30	M	Laborer	05Ap02Cw	DOWLAN, Betty	18	F	Unknown	05Ap02Bk
HANIE, Francis	24	M	Laborer	05Ap02Cw	Jane	19	F	Unknown	05Ap02Bk
MCGUIRE, James	23	M	Laborer	05Ap02Cw	FRENN, Molly	16	F	Unknown	05Ap02Bk
FARLEY, Jas.	31	M	Laborer	05Ap02Cw	DICKEY, M.	30	M	Laborer	05Ap02Bk
Phillip	20	M	Laborer	05Ap02Cw	FITZPATRICK, N.	24	M	Laborer	05Ap02Bk
REYNOLDS, Tim	26	M	Laborer	05Ap02Cw	Sally	24	F	Unknown	05Ap02Bk
DONOVAN, James	27	M	Laborer	05Ap02Cw	George	26	M	Laborer	05Ap02Bk
U	(W) 24	F	Unknown	05Ap02Cw	AGNEW, J.	24	M	Laborer	05Ap02Bk
Thos.	(S) 02	M	Child	05Ap02Cw	M.	(W) 24	F	Unknown	05Ap02Bk
FARLEY, Cathe.	19	F	Unknown	05Ap02Cw	Mary	(D) 01	F	Child	05Ap02Bk
Cathe.	16	F	Unknown	05Ap02Cw	Margt.	18	F	Unknown	05Ap02Bk
Mary	15	F	Unknown	05Ap02Cw	Henry-J.	16	M	Laborer	05Ap02Bk
DEMAIN, Michael	29	M	Laborer	05Ap02Cw	RICKUS, W.	22	M	Laborer	05Ap02Bk
James	27	M	Laborer	05Ap02Cw	GARNER, J.	22	M	Laborer	05Ap02Bk
MAHER, Ed.	28	M	Laborer	05Ap02Cw	ROURKE, Y.	16	M	Laborer	05Ap02Bk
Pat	30	M	Laborer	05Ap02Cw	M.	18	F	Unknown	05Ap02Bk
ENNIS, Lawrence	20	M	Laborer	05Ap02Cw	KILLY, Ellen	18	F	Unknown	05Ap02Bk
CLARK, Cathe.	35	F	Unknown	05Ap02Cw	CALARAN, C.	30	M	Laborer	05Ap02Bk
LYNCH, Bridget	25	F	Unknown	05Ap02Cw	CAIRNS, P.	28	M	Laborer	05Ap02Bk
FITZSIMMONS, Bryan	40	M	Laborer	05Ap02Cw	DUNN, J.	60	M	Laborer	05Ap02Bk
SMYTH, Margt.	30	F	Unknown	05Ap02Cw	Thos.	26	M	Laborer	05Ap02Bk
FARLEY, Bridget	30	F	Unknown	05Ap02Cw	Bdgt.	50	F	Unknown	05Ap02Bk
BRADY, Bridget	18	F	Unknown	05Ap02Cw	Bdgt.	28	F	Unknown	05Ap02Bk
DAY, Wm.	46	M	Laborer	05Ap02Cw	MCCABE, O.	18	M	Laborer	05Ap02Bk
WIND, John	20	M	Laborer	05Ap02Cw	CLARKE, L.	22	M	Laborer	05Ap02Bk
HASCY, Mick	21	M	Laborer	05Ap02Cw	MCCABE, P.	18	M	Laborer	05Ap02Bk
NEIL, Samuel	21	M	Laborer	05Ap02Cw	Frances	25	F	Unknown	05Ap02Bk
SHEILDS, Pat	37	M	Farmer	05Ap02Cw	FARRELL, Ann	20	F	Unknown	05Ap02Bk
MCLAUGHLIN, John	30	M	Farmer	05Ap02Cw	DOOLEN, Margt.	18	F	Unknown	05Ap02Bk
Morris	20	M	Farmer	05Ap02Cw	M.	18	F	Unknown	05Ap02Bk
HARPER, Chas.	20	M	Farmer	05Ap02Cw	MOLANY, P.	30	M	Laborer	05Ap02Bk
THORMACK, J.	20	M	Farmer	05Ap02Cw	YORK, T.	09	M	Child	05Ap02Bk
WATSON, Thos.	20	M	Farmer	05Ap02Cw	Jas.	06	M	Child	05Ap02Bk
PORTER, Joshua	20	M	Farmer	05Ap02Cw	MITCHELL, M.	26	M	Laborer	05Ap02Bk
MCKAY, Michael	20	M	Farmer	05Ap02Cw	U	(W) 22	F	Unknown	05Ap02Bk
Richard	20	M	Farmer	05Ap02Cw	U	(D) 01	F	Child	05Ap02Bk
MCQUINLAN, John	20	M	Farmer	05Ap02Cw	Margt.	27	F	Unknown	05Ap02Bk
BRENNAN, James	20	M	Farmer	05Ap02Cw	Thos.	13	M	Laborer	05Ap02Bk
BARRY, Chas.	20	M	Farmer	05Ap02Cw	Marella	12	F	None	05Ap02Bk
DOOLADY, Peter	18	M	Farmer	05Ap02Cw	Mich.	09	M	Child	05Ap02Bk
SMITH, Henry	22	M	Farmer	05Ap02Cw	Pat	07	M	Child	05Ap02Bk
U	(W) 21	F	Unknown	05Ap02Cw	Hugh	05	M	Child	05Ap02Bk
Andy	22	M	Farmer	05Ap02Cw	Ann	03	M	Child	05Ap02Bk
PRIZZEL, Saml.	22	M	Farmer	05Ap02Cw	YORK, Margt.	30	M	Unknown	05Ap02Bk
TODD, Mary	25	F	Unknown	05Ap02Cw	BRENNAN, Mary	17	M	Unknown	05Ap02Bk
DUNLAP, John	24	M	Farmer	05Ap02Cw	MEYER, P.M.	16	M	Laborer	05Ap02Bk
Ellen	12	F	None	05Ap02Cw	REE, W.	11	M	None	05Ap02Bk
Wm.	12	M	None	05Ap02Cw	CONLY, M.	20	M	Laborer	05Ap02Bk

NAMES OF PASSENGERS		AGE	SEX	OCCUPATIONS	DATE PORT SHIP
MCKEARN, Eliza		18	F	Unknown	05Ap02Bk
SHAW, P.		18	M	Laborer	05Ap02Bk
SHIRIDEN, B.		32	M	Laborer	05Ap02Bk
MURRY, Cathe.		26	F	Unknown	05Ap02Bk
LOGAN, M.		20	M	Laborer	05Ap02Bk
Mary		19	F	Unknown	05Ap02Bk
Bgt.		18	F	Unknown	05Ap02Bk
MCGRATH, B.		22	M	Laborer	05Ap02Bk
Pat		19	M	Laborer	05Ap02Bk
Ellen		12	F	None	05Ap02Bk
Cathe.		10	F	None	05Ap02Bk
MCGLOCKLIN, N.		22	M	Laborer	05Ap02Bk
BENNETT, M.		24	M	Laborer	05Ap02Bk
FLANIGAN, Rose		20	F	Unknown	05Ap02Bk
COUGHLIN, Ny.		20	M	Laborer	05Ap02Bk
SHAW, Mary		18	F	Unknown	05Ap02Bk
COLLINS, P.		18	M	Laborer	05Ap02Bk
FLANY, Mary		18	F	Unknown	05Ap02Bk
GYNNIS, Mary		19	F	Unknown	05Ap02Bk
DALY, Bdgt.		18	F	Unknown	05Ap02Bk
FITZSIMMONS, Cath.		36	F	Unknown	05Ap02Bk
Pat		14	M	None	05Ap02Bk
Rot.		10	M	None	05Ap02Bk
FEGAN, Mary		16	F	Unknown	05Ap02Bk
MCGREER, Ann		19	F	Unknown	05Ap02Bk
FEGAN, Ann		11	F	Child	05Ap02Bk
HIGGIN, P.		25	M	Laborer	05Ap02Bk
LEELER, Ellen-W.		18	F	Unknown	05Ap02Bk
MCGURY, Biddy		20	F	Unknown	05Ap02Bk
CONNER, Ny.		36	M	Laborer	05Ap02Bk
Mary		30	F	Unknown	05Ap02Bk
John		03	M	Child	05Ap02Bk
Cathe.		24	F	Unknown	05Ap02Bk
Ann		20	F	Unknown	05Ap02Bk
DIGIN, T.		24	M	Laborer	05Ap02Bk
LOUGHAN, F.		20	M	Laborer	05Ap02Bk
HUNT, P.		20	M	Laborer	05Ap02Bk
FENTON, J.		36	M	Laborer	05Ap02Bk
U	(W)	30	F	Unknown	05Ap02Bk
Jane	(D)	18	F	Unknown	05Ap02Bk
Eliza	(D)	16	F	Unknown	05Ap02Bk
POLLARD, T.		24	M	Laborer	05Ap02Bk
MCLOUGHLIN, J.		28	M	Laborer	05Ap02Bk
COGAN, Eliza		16	F	Unknown	05Ap02Bk
GOFREY, P.		18	M	Unknown	05Ap02Bk
BOLHIL, Bgt.		30	F	Unknown	05Ap02Bk
Ann	(D)	08	F	Child	05Ap02Bk
Biddy	(D)	05	F	Child	05Ap02Bk
James	(S)	01	M	Child	05Ap02Bk
MAYER, Ann		28	F	Unknown	05Ap02Bk
HANLAY, F.		20	M	Laborer	05Ap02Bk
DOYLE, M.		40	M	Laborer	05Ap02Bk
U	(W)	40	F	Unknown	05Ap02Bk
Rura	(S)	20	M	Laborer	05Ap02Bk
Mich.	(S)	11	M	Laborer	05Ap02Bk
DUNN, Rose		19	F	Unknown	05Ap02Bk
Pat		07	M	Child	05Ap02Bk
DOYLE, Mary		19	F	Unknown	05Ap02Bk
Honor		19	F	Unknown	05Ap02Bk
Bdgt.		19	F	Unknown	05Ap02Bk
MCGOUGHLIN, J.		18	M	Laborer	05Ap02Bk
Ann		36	F	Unknown	05Ap02Bk
Bdgt.		18	F	Unknown	05Ap02Bk
DOYLE, R.		20	M	Laborer	05Ap02Bk
Pegy		21	F	Unknown	05Ap02Bk
DEVONOUSH, Ellen		20	F	Unknown	05Ap02Bk
CAMP, G.		30	M	Laborer	05Ap02Bk
MOONY, T.		30	M	Laborer	05Ap02Bk
WHITE, P.		27	M	Laborer	05Ap02Bk
MURPHY, P.		25	M	Laborer	05Ap02Bk
SIMPSON, J.		21	M	Laborer	05Ap02Bk
HYLAN, Mary		18	F	Unknown	05Ap02Bk
Biddy		11	F	Unknown	05Ap02Bk
SCULLY, P.		14	M	Laborer	05Ap02Bk
Eliza		12	F	Child	05Ap02Bk
WALSH, J.		22	M	Laborer	05Ap02Bk
Francis		20	M	Laborer	05Ap02Bk
FINN, Margt.		20	F	Unknown	05Ap02Bk
CONLEY, Cathe.		20	F	Unknown	05Ap02Bk
MALONEY, Mat		22	M	Laborer	05Ap02Bk
GIBNEY, J.		18	M	Laborer	05Ap02Bk
ONEIL, C.		18	M	Laborer	05Ap02Bk
GIBEY, Cathe.		26	F	Unknown	05Ap02Bk
SHARTUS, Betty		21	F	Unknown	05Ap02Bk
MCCORMICK, J.		20	M	Laborer	05Ap02Bk
Mary		18	F	Unknown	05Ap02Bk
GRIFFIN, Hon.		20	F	Unknown	05Ap02Bk
GUNN, Betty		19	F	Unknown	05Ap02Bk
Bdgt.		18	F	Unknown	05Ap02Bk
LONG, S.		35	M	Laborer	05Ap02Bk
CLARKE, Ny.		22	M	Laborer	05Ap02Bk
GOLDING, P.		20	M	Laborer	05Ap02Bk
ROGAN, M.		22	M	Laborer	05Ap02Bk
CANNICK, M.		35	M	Laborer	05Ap02Bk
U	(W)	30	F	Unknown	05Ap02Bk
Mary	(D)	01	F	Child	05Ap02Bk
CORMACK, P.		06	M	Child	05Ap02Bk
Jules		04	M	Child	05Ap02Bk
NEWMAN, R.		40	M	Laborer	05Ap02Bk
Michl.		13	M	None	05Ap02Bk
Simon		12	M	None	05Ap02Bk
John		11	M	None	05Ap02Bk
Margt.		10	F	None	05Ap02Bk
Ann		09	F	Child	05Ap02Bk
WALSH, E.		20	M	Laborer	05Ap02Bk
Mary		20	F	Unknown	05Ap02Bk
Mary		20	F	Unknown	05Ap02Bk
Margt.		20	F	Unknown	05Ap02Bk
MCCABE, Mary		20	F	Unknown	05Ap02Bk
MURPHY, D.		25	M	Laborer	05Ap02Bk
MCGIVIN, P.		26	M	Laborer	05Ap02Bk
Ann		01	F	Child	05Ap02Bk
Peter		26	M	Laborer	05Ap02Bk
Ann		26	F	Unknown	05Ap02Bk
Ann		20	F	Unknown	05Ap02Bk
HANLY, T.		22	M	Laborer	05Ap02Bk
FEATHERSTONE, T.		19	M	Laborer	05Ap02Bk
LARKIN, J.		20	M	Laborer	05Ap02Bk
CLINE, M.		30	M	Laborer	05Ap02Bk
DONOLY, Ann		20	F	Unknown	05Ap02Bk
MCGUNN, Biddy		22	F	Unknown	05Ap02Bk
Ellen		15	F	Unknown	05Ap02Bk
MCANNAR, Rose		20	F	Unknown	05Ap02Bk
GIBBINS, J.		24	M	Laborer	05Ap02Bk
BOYLE, Ann		22	F	Unknown	05Ap02Bk
MCGORIN, J.		21	M	Laborer	05Ap02Bk
LINDOR, J.		20	M	Laborer	05Ap02Bk
Cathe.		21	F	Unknown	05Ap02Bk
CLARK, P.		20	M	Laborer	05Ap02Bk
Cathe.		26	F	Unknown	05Ap02Bk
SCALLY, Ann		19	F	Unknown	05Ap02Bk
SMITH, J.		24	M	Laborer	05Ap02Bk
FYE, Margt.		19	F	Unknown	05Ap02Bk
GALLAGHER, Rose		18	F	Unknown	05Ap02Bk
DUFFY, Mary		18	F	Unknown	05Ap02Bk
MCCAHILL, Cathe.		17	F	Unknown	05Ap02Bk
Bgt.		16	F	Unknown	05Ap02Bk
BOYLAN, Ann		19	F	Unknown	05Ap02Bk
TOOL, P.		18	M	Laborer	05Ap02Bk
KELLY, P.		40	M	Laborer	05Ap02Bk
YATES, J.		20	M	Laborer	05Ap02Bk
MCCADDEN, N.		30	M	Laborer	05Ap02Bk
PATERSON, M.		18	M	Laborer	05Ap02Bk
DOTY, M.		20	M	Laborer	05Ap02Bk
SHERIDAN, P.		22	M	Laborer	05Ap02Bk
Bessy		14	F	Unknown	05Ap02Bk
HOY, D.		25	M	Laborer	05Ap02Bk
MCDURMOT, P.		25	M	Laborer	05Ap02Bk
FUNY, J.		24	M	Laborer	05Ap02Bk
Ann		12	F	None	05Ap02Bk

NAMES OF PASSENGERS		AGE	SEX	OCCUPATIONS	DATE PORT SHIP
LIGAREN, Biddy		17	F	None	05Ap02Bk
FOX, J.		16	M	Laborer	05Ap02Bk
HAY, J.		47	M	Laborer	05Ap02Bk
FOX, Mary		17	F	Unknown	05Ap02Bk
FARRELL, P.		19	M	Laborer	05Ap02Bk
MCCUEN, W.		25	M	Laborer	05Ap02Bk
KYGAN, Margt.		18	F	Unknown	05Ap02Bk
BLANE, Jane		18	F	Unknown	05Ap02Bk
Ann		16	F	Unknown	05Ap02Bk
HYLAN, Mary		18	F	Unknown	05Ap02Bk
CORCORAN, Bdgt.		18	F	Unknown	05Ap02Bk
KEARNAN, P.		50	M	Laborer	05Ap02Bk
U	(W)	50	F	Unknown	05Ap02Bk
Mary	(D)	01	F	Child	05Ap02Bk
Mary	(D)	08	F	Child	05Ap02Bk
FARRELL, Ellen		18	F	Unknown	05Ap02Bk
KELLY, Cat.		22	F	Unknown	05Ap02Bk
CAFRY, M.		22	F	Unknown	05Ap02Bk
Pat		02	M	Child	05Ap02Bk
COFFEE, M.		23	M	Laborer	05Ap02Bk
KOUGH, J.		25	M	Laborer	05Ap02Bk
MEHONY, J.		24	M	Laborer	05Ap02Bk
NASH, F.P.		45	M	Laborer	05Ap02Bk
Mary		08	F	Child	05Ap02Bk
HACKET, M.		21	F	Unknown	05Ap02Bk
BRADY, T.		17	M	Laborer	05Ap02Bk
BILLY, J.		17	M	Laborer	05Ap02Bk
FLOOD, J.		20	M	Laborer	05Ap02Bk
BROUGHAN, P.		30	M	Laborer	05Ap02Bk
MULHOLLAND, P.		35	M	Laborer	05Ap02Bk
FAGAN, Ny.		40	M	Laborer	05Ap02Bk
M.		30	F	Unknown	05Ap02Bk
Pat		01	M	Child	05Ap02Bk
John		02	M	Child	05Ap02Bk
Bgn.		35	M	Laborer	05Ap02Bk
Cathe.		36	F	Unknown	05Ap02Bk
MCCORNAN, P.		25	M	Laborer	05Ap02Bk
Mich.		18	M	Laborer	05Ap02Bk
HASPEN, Biddy		20	F	Unknown	05Ap02Bk
DENNIS, M.		40	M	Laborer	05Ap02Bk
Pat		35	M	Laborer	05Ap02Bk
Peter		14	M	Laborer	05Ap02Bk
CARLON, J.		30	M	Laborer	05Ap02Bk
Wm.		30	M	Laborer	05Ap02Bk
Edwd.		01	M	Child	05Ap02Bk
LEE, P.		56	M	Laborer	05Ap02Bk
Cath.	(W)	52	F	Unknown	05Ap02Bk
Hugh	(S)	20	M	Laborer	05Ap02Bk
Eliza	(D)	18	F	Unknown	05Ap02Bk
Bridget	(D)	16	F	Unknown	05Ap02Bk
Jane	(D)	14	F	Unknown	05Ap02Bk
Susan	(D)	13	F	Unknown	05Ap02Bk
Mary	(D)	08	F	Child	05Ap02Bk
MAGOINS, P.		20	M	Laborer	05Ap02Bk
GRIFFITHS, P.		20	M	Laborer	05Ap02Bk
GARVY, Biddy		17	F	Unknown	05Ap02Bk
DIGNAN, P.		20	M	Laborer	05Ap02Bk
FLOOD, J.		20	M	Laborer	05Ap02Bk
KERGAN, P.		20	M	Laborer	05Ap02Bk
GALLAGHER, J.		19	M	Laborer	05Ap02Bk
NULLY, J.		20	M	Laborer	05Ap02Bk
MCGARNEY, J.		19	M	Laborer	05Ap02Bk
DOWD, P.		19	M	Laborer	05Ap02Bk
GALLIGAN, M.		15	F	Unknown	05Ap02Bk
GALLIBACH, D.		16	M	Laborer	05Ap02Bk
NEALLGAN, Ann		16	F	Unknown	05Ap02Bk
ROGERS, C.		35	M	Laborer	05Ap02Bk
MCGARRY, P.		20	M	Laborer	05Ap02Bk
M.		17	F	Unknown	05Ap02Bk
KENNEDY, Ellen		30	F	Unknown	05Ap02Bk
HUGHES, M.		17	F	Unknown	05Ap02Bk
WALTERS, M.		22	M	Laborer	05Ap02Bk
TOANER, W.		31	M	Laborer	05Ap02Bk
BEHAN, T.		24	M	Laborer	05Ap02Bk
WINTERS, C.		22	M	Laborer	05Ap02Bk
DUGAN, Ann		20	F	Unknown	05Ap02Bk
CULLY, Bdgt.		20	F	Unknown	05Ap02Bk
Mary		12	F	Unknown	05Ap02Bk
MCCARTHY, Margt.		18	F	Unknown	05Ap02Bk
DUNN, Mary		27	F	Unknown	05Ap02Bk
MCGRATH, Jane		20	F	Unknown	05Ap02Bk
SCULLY, Jas.		40	M	Laborer	05Ap02Bk
U	(W)	22	F	Unknown	05Ap02Bk
MULGHAN, Ny.		19	M	Laborer	05Ap02Bk
Bern.		27	M	Laborer	05Ap02Bk
MULAVY, Cath.		19	F	Unknown	05Ap02Bk
Mary		25	F	Unknown	05Ap02Bk
LINDSEY, J.		20	M	Laborer	05Ap02Bk
MCGRATH, Cathe.		20	F	Unknown	05Ap02Bk
HEANY, J.		20	M	Laborer	05Ap02Bk
WALSH, C.		18	M	Laborer	05Ap02Bk
Cathe.		22	F	Unknown	05Ap02Bk
BROWN, Sarah		25	F	Unknown	05Ap02Bk
HUSBAND, Nurrut		15	F	Unknown	05Ap02Bk
BROWNE, Anne		04	F	Unknown	05Ap02Bk
DOYLE, M.		11	M	Laborer	05Ap02Bk
BROWN, Sarah		25	F	Unknown	05Ap02Bk
QUINN, J.		28	M	Laborer	05Ap02Bk
DUNN, G.		20	M	Laborer	05Ap02Bk
GALGAN, Cath.		30	F	Unknown	05Ap02Bk
GRADY, Ann		20	F	Unknown	05Ap02Bk
HALPERN, H.		20	M	Laborer	05Ap02Bk
KELLY, P.		20	M	Laborer	05Ap02Bk
CARNY, J.		40	M	Laborer	05Ap02Bk
SHANLY, M.		22	M	Laborer	05Ap02Bk
CONNER, J.		20	M	Laborer	05Ap02Bk
HEFFERN, M.		32	M	Laborer	05Ap02Bk
Danl.		19	M	Laborer	05Ap02Bk
Kitty		26	F	Unknown	05Ap02Bk
CULLEN, Cathe.		05	F	Child	05Ap02Bk
Ellen		29	F	Unknown	05Ap02Bk
Ellen		05	F	Child	05Ap02Bk
Alfred		23	M	Laborer	05Ap02Bk
DONLY, Ann		25	F	Unknown	05Ap02Bk
DUFFY, Cathe.		15	F	Unknown	05Ap02Bk
MANN, T.		14	F	Unknown	05Ap02Bk
FURY, W.		14	M	Laborer	05Ap02Bk
DUFFY, Ellen		15	F	Unknown	05Ap02Bk
DERRY, Ny.		46	M	Laborer	05Ap02Bk
FERNAN, Mary		18	F	Unknown	05Ap02Bk
FERREN, Betty		18	F	Unknown	05Ap02Bk
GRIFFIN, R.		40	M	Laborer	05Ap02Bk
HAY, Mary		20	F	Unknown	05Ap02Bk
CASKER, P.		24	M	Laborer	05Ap02Bk
REYNOLDS, Ann		08	F	Child	05Ap02Bk
GIDNY, Bgt.		50	F	Unknown	05Ap02Bk
Ann		17	F	Unknown	05Ap02Bk
Brine		13	F	Unknown	05Ap02Bk
Mgt.		11	F	Unknown	05Ap02Bk
Pat		08	M	Child	05Ap02Bk
Norma		07	F	Child	05Ap02Bk
Eliza		03	F	Child	05Ap02Bk
Ellen		02	F	Child	05Ap02Bk
Cathe.		01	F	Child	05Ap02Bk
MEHAN, M.		30	M	Laborer	05Ap02Bk
CUNIFF, Ann		30	F	Unknown	05Ap02Bk

ZENOBIA 06 APRIL 1847

From Liverpool

NAMES OF PASSENGERS	AGE	SEX	OCCUPATIONS	DATE PORT SHIP
KESTEVEN, Francis	39	M	Mechanic	06Ap02Lg
MCVEY, Ellen	18	F	Unknown	06Ap02Lg
BURKE, Kathe.	30	F	Unknown	06Ap02Lg

NAMES OF PASSENGERS		AGE	SEX	OCCUPATIONS	DATE PORT SHIP	NAMES OF PASSENGERS	AGE	SEX	OCCUPATIONS	DATE PORT SHIP
TRAINOR, Mary		18	F	Unknown	06Ap02Lg	FLYNN, Jno.	20	M	Mechanic	06Ap02Lg
MCVAY, Thos.		23	M	Mechanic	06Ap02Lg	Mary	18	F	Unknown	06Ap02Lg
SMITH, Francis		24	M	Mechanic	06Ap02Lg	SULLIVAN, Hannah	20	F	Unknown	06Ap02Lg
BURKE, Mich.		18	M	Mechanic	06Ap02Lg	FORD, Biddy	20	F	Unknown	06Ap02Lg
CAFFRAY, Peter		28	M	Mechanic	06Ap02Lg	CLARK, John	25	M	Laborer	06Ap02Lg
CROSS, Jas.		24	M	Laborer	06Ap02Lg	CASSIDY, Mich.	20	M	Laborer	06Ap02Lg
LAWLER, Michl.		18	M	Laborer	06Ap02Lg	Bridget	25	F	Unknown	06Ap02Lg
JONES, Thos.		28	M	Laborer	06Ap02Lg	BRANIGAN, Arthur	24	M	Laborer	06Ap02Lg
JERVIS, Jas.		24	M	Laborer	06Ap02Lg	MCMAND, Adam	30	M	Laborer	06Ap02Lg
DAVIS, Mary		19	F	Unknown	06Ap02Lg	DUNLURY, Pat	23	M	Laborer	06Ap02Lg
BOHAN, Mary		15	F	Unknown	06Ap02Lg	DONOHUGH, Mick	29	M	Laborer	06Ap02Lg
GLEASON, Ellen		28	F	Unknown	06Ap02Lg	DUNLEVY, Jane	13	F	Unknown	06Ap02Lg
Dennis		07	M	Child	06Ap02Lg	HOLMES, James	26	M	Laborer	06Ap02Lg
HART, Kitty		24	F	Unknown	06Ap02Lg	LUISON, Jermina	50	F	Unknown	06Ap02Lg
BURKE, John		30	M	Laborer	06Ap02Lg	LEO, Ephy	20	F	Unknown	06Ap02Lg
HARVEY, Mich.		30	M	Laborer	06Ap02Lg	DUNCAN, John	24	M	Laborer	06Ap02Lg
MCDOYLE, Jas.		33	M	Laborer	06Ap02Lg	John	17	M	Laborer	06Ap02Lg
FITZPATRICK, Cathe.		16	F	Unknown	06Ap02Lg	COSTELLO, Thos.	17	M	Laborer	06Ap02Lg
CASEY, Rose		20	F	Unknown	06Ap02Lg	KELLEY, Pat	19	M	Laborer	06Ap02Lg
CAFFNEY, Susan		09	F	Child	06Ap02Lg	MCGUIRE, Phehin	18	M	Laborer	06Ap02Lg
DOWD, Pat		29	M	Laborer	06Ap02Lg	Connor	17	M	Laborer	06Ap02Lg
FARRELL, Pat		30	M	Laborer	06Ap02Lg	GAFFNEY, Jas.	23	M	Laborer	06Ap02Lg
MCGRATH, Hugh		30	M	Laborer	06Ap02Lg	SWEENY, Danl.	21	M	Laborer	06Ap02Lg
Mary	(W)	24	F	Unknown	06Ap02Lg	MOLLOY, Edwd.	34	M	Laborer	06Ap02Lg
Cathe.	(D)	05	F	Child	06Ap02Lg	MULLIN, Austin	33	M	Laborer	06Ap02Lg
PURCELL, Thos.		24	M	Laborer	06Ap02Lg	ROWAN, Pat	25	M	Laborer	06Ap02Lg
Andrew		26	M	Laborer	06Ap02Lg	Mich.	22	M	Laborer	06Ap02Lg
BURKE, Mick		30	M	Laborer	06Ap02Lg	Winny	20	M	Laborer	06Ap02Lg
MAHER, Pat		21	M	Laborer	06Ap02Lg	FLEMING, Pat	24	M	Laborer	06Ap02Lg
Mary		18	F	Unknown	06Ap02Lg	John	23	M	Laborer	06Ap02Lg
CORCORAN, Pat		36	M	Laborer	06Ap02Lg	BEATY, John	22	M	Laborer	06Ap02Lg
Mary		30	F	Unknown	06Ap02Lg	FLEMING, Mary	20	F	Unknown	06Ap02Lg
Mich.		56	M	Laborer	06Ap02Lg	GANING, Thos.	16	M	Laborer	06Ap02Lg
HOBSON, U		22	M	Laborer	06Ap02Lg	Eleanor	18	F	Unknown	06Ap02Lg
John		19	M	Laborer	06Ap02Lg	FORD, Thos.	20	M	Laborer	06Ap02Lg
CAFFNEY, Owen		25	M	Laborer	06Ap02Lg	FLEMING, Winny	18	M	Laborer	06Ap02Lg
HARVEY, John		30	M	Laborer	06Ap02Lg	GUNING, Mary	20	F	Unknown	06Ap02Lg
John-Jr.	(S)	07	M	Child	06Ap02Lg	KELLEY, Jas.	25	M	Laborer	06Ap02Lg
Mary	(D)	08	F	Child	06Ap02Lg	Mary	22	F	Unknown	06Ap02Lg
Ellen	(W)	30	F	Unknown	06Ap02Lg	Honor	16	M	Laborer	06Ap02Lg
Ellen	(D)	02	F	Child	06Ap02Lg	COSTER, Jas.	23	M	Laborer	06Ap02Lg
BOHLIG, Wm.		30	M	Mechanic	06Ap02Lg	Mary	19	F	Unknown	06Ap02Lg
COHEN, Jacob		23	M	Mechanic	06Ap02Lg	FLYNN, Betsey	15	F	Unknown	06Ap02Lg
DOONAY, Maurice		28	M	Mechanic	06Ap02Lg	Ellen	03	F	Child	06Ap02Lg
Mary		23	F	Unknown	06Ap02Lg	CASS, John	16	M	Laborer	06Ap02Lg
FARRELL, John		30	M	Mechanic	06Ap02Lg	RYAN, Mich.	20	M	Laborer	06Ap02Lg
Mary	(W)	23	F	Unknown	06Ap02Lg	CASS, Margt.	20	F	Unknown	06Ap02Lg
Martha	(D)	04	F	Child	06Ap02Lg	SCULLY, Phil.	25	M	Laborer	06Ap02Lg
LYONS, Thos.		18	M	Mechanic	06Ap02Lg	DORAN, Jerry	26	M	Laborer	06Ap02Lg
BANFIELD, John		18	M	Mechanic	06Ap02Lg	MCCABE, Danl.	30	M	Laborer	06Ap02Lg
MULLEN, John		20	M	Mechanic	06Ap02Lg	Jno.	25	M	Laborer	06Ap02Lg
NICKENAN, John		22	M	Mechanic	06Ap02Lg	Pat	28	M	Laborer	06Ap02Lg
Rose		50	F	Unknown	06Ap02Lg	Mary	20	F	Unknown	06Ap02Lg
MACKEN, Ann		20	F	Unknown	06Ap02Lg	Ellen	25	F	Unknown	06Ap02Lg
MACKEENAN, Ellen		20	F	Unknown	06Ap02Lg	Ann	23	F	Unknown	06Ap02Lg
MACKTIERRID, John		25	M	Mechanic	06Ap02Lg	THOMPSON, Ed.	17	M	Laborer	06Ap02Lg
FLYNN, Patt.		18	M	Mechanic	06Ap02Lg	Jas.	14	M	Laborer	06Ap02Lg
LAUGHLIN, Jno.		24	M	Mechanic	06Ap02Lg	CHEVOLIN, Jas.	19	M	Laborer	06Ap02Lg
MCGANTY, Jno.		20	M	Mechanic	06Ap02Lg	MALONE, Pat	24	M	Laborer	06Ap02Lg
MCNALLY, Cathe.		20	F	Unknown	06Ap02Lg	KELLY, Pat	29	M	Laborer	06Ap02Lg
DUFF, Thos.		20	M	Mechanic	06Ap02Lg	Chas.	26	M	Laborer	06Ap02Lg
DOLAN, Cathe.		18	F	Unknown	06Ap02Lg	MURPHY, Pat	40	M	Laborer	06Ap02Lg
MCNALLY, Agnes		18	F	Unknown	06Ap02Lg	KELLY, Ellen	19	F	Unknown	06Ap02Lg
POWDERLY, Wm.		18	M	Mechanic	06Ap02Lg	GOODWIN, Mary	26	F	Unknown	06Ap02Lg
CUFF, Jas.		45	M	Mechanic	06Ap02Lg	DONOVAN, Mary	30	F	Unknown	06Ap02Lg
Eleanor	(W)	45	F	Unknown	06Ap02Lg	SHORTEN, Jno.	33	M	Laborer	06Ap02Lg
Bridget	(D)	20	F	Unknown	06Ap02Lg	Fran.	26	M	Laborer	06Ap02Lg
Christy	(S)	26	M	Mechanic	06Ap02Lg	Tom	01	M	Child	06Ap02Lg
DUFF, Pat		24	M	Mechanic	06Ap02Lg	SMITH, Ann	36	F	Unknown	06Ap02Lg
RALPH, Christy		14	M	Mechanic	06Ap02Lg	Ellen	14	F	Child	06Ap02Lg
LINGERD, David		35	M	Mechanic	06Ap02Lg	Nancy	11	F	Child	06Ap02Lg
Nancy	(W)	30	F	Unknown	06Ap02Lg	Thos.	09	M	Child	06Ap02Lg
FLYNN, Pat		25	M	Mechanic	06Ap02Lg	COX, Jas.	26	M	Laborer	06Ap02Lg
FINIGAN, Tim		25	M	Mechanic	06Ap02Lg	CRIBBIN, Phil	24	M	Laborer	06Ap02Lg
BURNS, Dennis		25	M	Mechanic	06Ap02Lg	LORD, Mich.	24	M	Laborer	06Ap02Lg

NAMES OF PASSENGERS		AGE	SEX	OCCUPATIONS	DATE PORT SHIP
MORAN, Jas.		30	M	Laborer	06Ap02Lg
CASE, Andrew		23	M	Laborer	06Ap02Lg
JOICE, Mary		20	F	Unknown	06Ap02Lg
RILEY, Martin		30	M	Laborer	06Ap02Lg
Cathe.	(W)	24	F	Unknown	06Ap02Lg
Bridget	(D)	02	F	Child	06Ap02Lg
HUNT, Mary		23	F	Unknown	06Ap02Lg
DEGAN, Cath.		36	F	Unknown	06Ap02Lg
Wm.		12	M	Child	06Ap02Lg
Eliza		13	F	Child	06Ap02Lg
Susanna		10	F	Child	06Ap02Lg
Mary		06	F	Child	06Ap02Lg
Jas.		04	M	Child	06Ap02Lg
MCCORMICK, Pat		40	M	Laborer	06Ap02Lg
Mary	(W)	40	F	Unknown	06Ap02Lg
Jno.	(S)	14	M	Laborer	06Ap02Lg
Jas.	(S)	12	M	Child	06Ap02Lg
Pat	(S)	10	M	Child	06Ap02Lg
Mich.	(S)	08	M	Child	06Ap02Lg
Ed.	(S)	06	M	Child	06Ap02Lg
Martin	(S)	01	M	Child	06Ap02Lg
RYAN, Kitty		22	F	Unknown	06Ap02Lg
GLEASON, Hugh		52	M	Laborer	06Ap02Lg
Mary	(W)	40	F	Unknown	06Ap02Lg
Ed.	(S)	16	M	Laborer	06Ap02Lg
Margt.	(D)	14	F	None	06Ap02Lg
Kiernan	(S)	12	M	None	06Ap02Lg
John	(S)	10	M	Child	06Ap02Lg
Mary	(D)	08	F	Child	06Ap02Lg
Richd.	(S)	06	M	Child	06Ap02Lg
Pat	(S)	03	M	Child	06Ap02Lg
LORD, Jas.		30	M	Laborer	06Ap02Lg
Mary		30	F	Unknown	06Ap02Lg
MURPHY, Michael		27	M	Laborer	06Ap02Lg
Winifred		24	F	Unknown	06Ap02Lg
MAHER, Martin		20	M	Laborer	06Ap02Lg
KELLEY, Jay		25	M	Laborer	06Ap02Lg
FITZGERALD, Jas.		30	M	Laborer	06Ap02Lg
COGAN, John		21	M	Laborer	06Ap02Lg
HAYDEN, Chas.		21	M	Laborer	06Ap02Lg
PENDERGAST, Jas.		28	M	Laborer	06Ap02Lg
Kitty	(W)	29	F	Unknown	06Ap02Lg
Pat	(S)	07	M	Child	06Ap02Lg
TOOLE, Michael		20	M	Laborer	06Ap02Lg
MAHER, John		24	M	Laborer	06Ap02Lg
CARTY, John		33	M	Laborer	06Ap02Lg
FLAHERTY, Ed.		26	M	Laborer	06Ap02Lg
FAGIN, Christy		40	M	Laborer	06Ap02Lg
KELLEY, Christy		22	M	Laborer	06Ap02Lg
FAGIN, Ann		30	F	Unknown	06Ap02Lg
Rose		25	F	Unknown	06Ap02Lg
Bridget		65	F	Unknown	06Ap02Lg
Peter		10	M	Child	06Ap02Lg
GINTY, Pat		40	M	Laborer	06Ap02Lg
Mick		13	M	Laborer	06Ap02Lg
Thos.		09	M	Child	06Ap02Lg
Mary		11	F	Child	06Ap02Lg
YANSY, Jas.		15	M	Laborer	06Ap02Lg
MICHEL, Pat		42	M	Laborer	06Ap02Lg
Alice		35	F	Unknown	06Ap02Lg
Bridget		19	F	Unknown	06Ap02Lg
Mary		22	F	Unknown	06Ap02Lg
Cathe.		18	F	Unknown	06Ap02Lg
Maryann		13	F	Unknown	06Ap02Lg
Bridget		04	F	Child	06Ap02Lg
Wm.		14	M	Laborer	06Ap02Lg
Pat		11	M	Laborer	06Ap02Lg
John		09	M	Child	06Ap02Lg
Francis		07	M	Child	06Ap02Lg
COSTELLO, Ann		50	F	Unknown	06Ap02Lg
CANNORD, John		33	M	Laborer	06Ap02Lg
Honor		08	M	Laborer	06Ap02Lg
Pat		06	M	Child	06Ap02Lg
HARGORAN, Pat		26	M	Laborer	06Ap02Lg
Francis		22	M	Laborer	06Ap02Lg

NAMES OF PASSENGERS		AGE	SEX	OCCUPATIONS	DATE PORT SHIP
HARGORAN, Bridget		27	F	Unknown	06Ap02Lg
John		25	M	Laborer	06Ap02Lg
Mary		24	F	Unknown	06Ap02Lg
GREEN, John		27	M	Laborer	06Ap02Lg
Mary	(W)	24	F	Unknown	06Ap02Lg
Pat	(S)	02	M	Child	06Ap02Lg
BLAND, Michl.		22	M	Laborer	06Ap02Lg
BOHAN, Rose		23	F	Unknown	06Ap02Lg
MCGOWAN, Biddy		22	F	Unknown	06Ap02Lg
CASSON, Wm.		19	M	Laborer	06Ap02Lg
KENNEDY, Mich.		30	M	Laborer	06Ap02Lg
CAMPBELL, Thos.		30	M	Laborer	06Ap02Lg
MCCARTY, Jas.		34	M	Mechanic	06Ap02Lg
MCGARRELL, Hugh		25	M	Mechanic	06Ap02Lg
MCHUGH, Jas.		19	M	Mechanic	06Ap02Lg
MONAHAN, Thos.		24	M	Mechanic	06Ap02Lg
Pat		22	M	Mechanic	06Ap02Lg
BOWDEN, Jas.		28	M	Mechanic	06Ap02Lg
EMERSON, Ann		19	F	Unknown	06Ap02Lg

NORTHUMBERLAND 06 APRIL 1847

From London

NAMES OF PASSENGERS		AGE	SEX	OCCUPATIONS	DATE PORT SHIP
JOHNSTON, James-C.		35	M	Merchant	06Ap21Cg
Cathe.	(W)	35	F	Unknown	06Ap21Cg
Cathe.	(D)	04	F	Child	06Ap21Cg
Ann	(D)	03	F	Child	06Ap21Cg
Agnes		22	F	Unknown	06Ap21Cg
FARLEY, Sarah		55	F	Unknown	06Ap21Cg
Mary		45	F	Unknown	06Ap21Cg
Caroline		35	F	Unknown	06Ap21Cg
MARKS, Helena		32	F	Unknown	06Ap21Cg
BOUGH, Win-O.		24	M	Gentleman	06Ap21Cg
CANIN, Abraham		29	M	Farmer	06Ap21Cg
Louisa		29	F	Unknown	06Ap21Cg
DUCK, James		28	M	Tailor	06Ap21Cg
GAASELEN, John		25	M	Engineer	06Ap21Cg
GESLING, Wm.		44	M	Farmer	06Ap21Cg
FITZGERALD, John		26	M	Mechanic	06Ap21Cg
SAUTEL, Henry		47	M	Farmer	06Ap21Cg
Ann	(W)	48	F	Unknown	06Ap21Cg
PEREY, Chas.		32	M	Farmer	06Ap21Cg
RAMTON, Anthony		23	M	Farmer	06Ap21Cg
MORRIS, James		33	S	Farmer	06Ap21Cg
Margaret	(W)	33	F	Unknown	06Ap21Cg
Dennis	(S)	03	M	Child	06Ap21Cg
David	(S)	01	M	Child	06Ap21Cg
GALLAGER, James		25	M	Mechanic	06Ap21Cg
Maria		17	F	Unknown	06Ap21Cg
MANSEL, George		21	M	Mechanic	06Ap21Cg
Henrietta		22	F	Unknown	06Ap21Cg
ROSE, Frederick-W.		10	M	Child	06Ap21Cg
SMITH, Robt.		30	M	Baker	06Ap21Cg
REGIS, Dani.		30	M	Baker	06Ap21Cg
Mary	(W)	30	F	Unknown	06Ap21Cg
Dani.	(S)	03	M	Child	06Ap21Cg
Betsey	(D)	01	F	Child	06Ap21Cg
LUNG, Kriss		20	M	Tailor	06Ap21Cg
JAREBS, James		28	M	Tailor	06Ap21Cg
FALKLAND, Frederick		29	M	Tailor	06Ap21Cg
SOUTHERN, John		20	M	Unknown	06Ap21Cg
BIDLETOM, Alfred		24	M	Unknown	06Ap21Cg
SOUTHERN, Caleb		19	M	Laborer	06Ap21Cg
SCHOOL, Joseph		26	M	Laborer	06Ap21Cg
Maria		25	F	Jobber	06Ap21Cg
PRICE, Dan		26	M	Laborer	06Ap21Cg
DIXON, George		26	M	Cloth Maker	06Ap21Cg
John		22	M	Bookbinder	06Ap21Cg

393

NAMES OF PASSENGERS		AGE	SEX	OCCUPATIONS	DATE PORT SHIP
CARREL, Mary		19	F	Unknown	06Ap21Cg
Cath.		40	F	Unknown	06Ap21Cg
Patrick		06	M	Child	06Ap21Cg
David		05	M	Child	06Ap21Cg
Mary-A.		03	F	Child	06Ap21Cg
WATERHOUSE, James		44	M	Unknown	06Ap21Cg
Kim	(W)	44	M	Unknown	06Ap21Cg
Wm.	(S)	26	M	Unknown	06Ap21Cg
John	(S)	24	M	Unknown	06Ap21Cg
James	(S)	22	M	Unknown	06Ap21Cg
Saml.	(S)	19	M	Unknown	06Ap21Cg
Sarah	(D)	26	F	Unknown	06Ap21Cg
Mary	(D)	26	F	Unknown	06Ap21Cg
Elen	(D)	13	F	Unknown	06Ap21Cg
Joseph	(S)	11	M	Unknown	06Ap21Cg
Harper	(S)	09	M	Unknown	06Ap21Cg
Frank	(S)	07	M	Unknown	06Ap21Cg

EMPIRE 07 APRIL 1847

From Liverpool

NAMES OF PASSENGERS		AGE	SEX	OCCUPATIONS	DATE PORT SHIP
MCGREGOR, T.D.		27	M	None	07Ap02AI
DYHRENFORTH, J.		33	M	None	07Ap02AI
Caroline		25	F	None	07Ap02AI
BIRCH, J.Hy.		23	M	None	07Ap02AI
DYHRENFORTH, R.J.Hy.		02	M	Child	07Ap02AI
Hy.E.		01	M	Child	07Ap02AI
HYDE, O.		41	M	Unknown	07Ap02AI
KELLY, J.		52	M	Laborer	07Ap02AI
Anthony		20	M	Laborer	07Ap02AI
HOLMES, Hy.		30	M	Laborer	07Ap02AI
BRANNEN, J.		40	M	Laborer	07Ap02AI
Ellen		18	F	Unknown	07Ap02AI
Bridget		11	F	Unknown	07Ap02AI
Mary		12	F	Unknown	07Ap02AI
MOONLY, Ellen		20	F	Unknown	07Ap02AI
CONOLLY, Mgt.		20	F	Unknown	07Ap02AI
SMITH, J.		29	M	Laborer	07Ap02AI
WHITE, Cathe.		20	F	Unknown	07Ap02AI
STRET, R.		22	M	Laborer	07Ap02AI
LETHLAND, J.		20	M	Laborer	07Ap02AI
MOLLON, J.		25	M	Laborer	07Ap02AI
MCCANN, Mary		30	F	Unknown	07Ap02AI
CAMPBELL, J.		30	M	Laborer	07Ap02AI
Mary		26	F	Unknown	07Ap02AI
FULLEN, Peggy		19	F	Unknown	07Ap02AI
CAMPBELL, J.		12	M	Laborer	07Ap02AI
Sarah		10	F	Child	07Ap02AI
Andrew		08	M	Child	07Ap02AI
Michl.		06	M	Child	07Ap02AI
Mary		02	F	Child	07Ap02AI
MCGINLEY, H.		25	M	Laborer	07Ap02AI
DERINEY, P.		20	M	Laborer	07Ap02AI
ARNOLD, N.		18	M	Laborer	07Ap02AI
BONER, P.		30	M	Laborer	07Ap02AI
Ellen		20	F	Unknown	07Ap02AI
CORR, M.		18	F	Unknown	07Ap02AI
Peter		17	M	Laborer	07Ap02AI
Terence		15	M	Laborer	07Ap02AI
Ellen		12	F	Unknown	07Ap02AI
Mary		15	F	Unknown	07Ap02AI
Mgt.		18	F	Unknown	07Ap02AI
REILLY, Ellen		15	F	Unknown	07Ap02AI
CORR, P.		18	M	Laborer	07Ap02AI
FITZPATRICK, Mary		40	F	Unknown	07Ap02AI
SMITH, M.		20	M	Laborer	07Ap02AI
Ann		18	F	Unknown	07Ap02AI
Thos.		15	M	Laborer	07Ap02AI

NAMES OF PASSENGERS		AGE	SEX	OCCUPATIONS	DATE PORT SHIP
SMITH, Cathe.		13	F	Unknown	07Ap02AI
GREFNY, Cathe.		20	F	Unknown	07Ap02AI
Owen		13	M	Child	07Ap02AI
HASLETT, J.		20	M	Laborer	07Ap02AI
Sarah		20	F	Unknown	07Ap02AI
RACHELL, J.		22	M	Laborer	07Ap02AI
SMITH, A.		27	M	Laborer	07Ap02AI
Pat		18	M	Laborer	07Ap02AI
Ben		30	M	Laborer	07Ap02AI
KELLY, M.		19	M	Laborer	07Ap02AI
Ellen		18	F	Unknown	07Ap02AI
DILSON, Mary		42	F	Unknown	07Ap02AI
Mich.	(S)	20	M	Laborer	07Ap02AI
James	(S)	18	M	Laborer	07Ap02AI
Mark	(S)	11	M	Laborer	07Ap02AI
Mary	(D)	08	F	Child	07Ap02AI
Judy	(D)	06	F	Child	07Ap02AI
SMITH, Eliza		16	F	Unknown	07Ap02AI
HALL, H.		25	M	Laborer	07Ap02AI
IRVINE, R.		23	M	Laborer	07Ap02AI
HAMILL, R.		28	M	Laborer	07Ap02AI
Mary		26	F	Unknown	07Ap02AI
DONNELLY, M.		30	M	Laborer	07Ap02AI
James		18	M	Laborer	07Ap02AI
Eliza		28	F	Unknown	07Ap02AI
Mgt.		02	F	Child	07Ap02AI
JACKSON, Ellen		23	F	Unknown	07Ap02AI
Ann		25	F	Unknown	07Ap02AI
BOOLAN, Cath.		20	F	Unknown	07Ap02AI
SHENAN, Bgt.		18	F	Unknown	07Ap02AI
QUINN, J.		34	M	Laborer	07Ap02AI
Mgt.		40	F	Unknown	07Ap02AI
Rose		08	F	Child	07Ap02AI
BOYLE, J.		23	M	Laborer	07Ap02AI
CONNOR, P.		26	M	Laborer	07Ap02AI
CONLAN, J.		20	M	Laborer	07Ap02AI
Michl.		25	M	Laborer	07Ap02AI
CREATIN, J.		20	M	Laborer	07Ap02AI
RILEY, W.		18	M	Laborer	07Ap02AI
KEARNY, Hy.		20	M	Laborer	07Ap02AI
FLYNN, Jane		40	F	Unknown	07Ap02AI
LEADIN, Mary		30	F	Unknown	07Ap02AI
MCGUINESS, D.		20	M	Laborer	07Ap02AI
GALVIN, W.		25	M	Laborer	07Ap02AI
MARMION, Hy.		20	M	Laborer	07Ap02AI
WINKY, Mgt.		20	F	Unknown	07Ap02AI
MELADY, Bgt.		20	F	Unknown	07Ap02AI
MONAHAN, Ann		20	F	Unknown	07Ap02AI
Patk.		20	M	Laborer	07Ap02AI
GILHOOLY, Bgt.		20	F	Unknown	07Ap02AI
QUINN, J.		20	M	Laborer	07Ap02AI
MCGARRIGH, Hy.		20	M	Laborer	07Ap02AI
HARRISON, P.		20	M	Laborer	07Ap02AI
CLASY, Ngt.		20	F	Unknown	07Ap02AI
BRADLY, M.		20	M	Laborer	07Ap02AI
DOYLE, P.		20	M	Laborer	07Ap02AI
RILY, Ann		20	F	Unknown	07Ap02AI
KENEDY, J.		29	M	Laborer	07Ap02AI
Mary		30	F	Unknown	07Ap02AI
Mary		40	F	Unknown	07Ap02AI
Ann		22	F	Unknown	07Ap02AI
Sarah		36	F	Unknown	07Ap02AI
Eliza		35	F	Unknown	07Ap02AI
HAMPHILL, Mary		09	F	Child	07Ap02AI
GILLON, W.		40	M	Laborer	07Ap02AI
Cathe.	(W)	40	F	Unknown	07Ap02AI
Mich.	(S)	08	M	Child	07Ap02AI
Mary	(D)	07	F	Child	07Ap02AI
Bgt.	(D)	02	F	Child	07Ap02AI
GLYNN, J.		20	M	Laborer	07Ap02AI
Michl.		21	M	Laborer	07Ap02AI
Cathe.		18	F	Unknown	07Ap02AI
KELLY, M.		20	M	Laborer	07Ap02AI
MURPHY, Ellen		18	F	Unknown	07Ap02AI
CAHIL, Mary		20	F	Unknown	07Ap02AI

NAMES OF PASSENGERS		AGE	SEX	OCCUPATIONS	DATE/PORT/SHIP
MCCORMICK, Elle		20	F	Unknown	07Ap02AI
MAGUIRE, Martin		20	M	Laborer	07Ap02AI
Ellen		18	F	Unknown	07Ap02AI
DYER, Elle		20	F	Unknown	07Ap02AI
COWAN, M.		25	M	Laborer	07Ap02AI
MURPHY, P.		20	M	Laborer	07Ap02AI
GALAHER, J.		20	M	Laborer	07Ap02AI
MURPHY, J.		20	M	Laborer	07Ap02AI
Mary		18	F	Unknown	07Ap02AI
Ellen		40	F	Unknown	07Ap02AI
HARE, A.		25	M	Laborer	07Ap02AI
MCGARRITY, W.		20	M	Laborer	07Ap02AI
BRADY, J.		20	M	Laborer	07Ap02AI
HARRIGAN, J.		20	M	Laborer	07Ap02AI
Cathe.		18	F	Unknown	07Ap02AI
MONIGAN, P.		20	M	Laborer	07Ap02AI
CLANCY, M.		25	M	Laborer	07Ap02AI
Dora		20	F	Unknown	07Ap02AI
CARN, Mary		20	F	Unknown	07Ap02AI
LANE, Bgt.		20	F	Unknown	07Ap02AI
CAVANAUGH, Mary		20	F	Unknown	07Ap02AI
CLANNY, W.		20	M	Laborer	07Ap02AI
DONNELLY, J.		22	M	Laborer	07Ap02AI
CARROLL, Rose		30	F	Unknown	07Ap02AI
Thos.		13	M	Laborer	07Ap02AI
Bern.		08	M	Child	07Ap02AI
Pat		04	M	Child	07Ap02AI
Eliza		01	F	Child	07Ap02AI
John		20	M	Laborer	07Ap02AI
KANE, Biddy		21	F	Unknown	07Ap02AI
Ellen		20	F	Unknown	07Ap02AI
BRADE, F.		48	M	Laborer	07Ap02AI
REVELY, D.		19	M	Laborer	07Ap02AI
CASY, D.		24	M	Laborer	07Ap02AI
Honora		40	F	Unknown	07Ap02AI
CONNOR, Hy.		21	M	Laborer	07Ap02AI
HADDEN, O.		40	M	Laborer	07Ap02AI
Julia		18	F	Unknown	07Ap02AI
Pat		11	M	Child	07Ap02AI
Mgt.		09	F	Child	07Ap02AI
Cathe.		20	F	Unknown	07Ap02AI
CASY, Jane		18	F	Unknown	07Ap02AI
GAFFNEY, Ann		18	F	Unknown	07Ap02AI
GILCHRIS, P.		40	M	Laborer	07Ap02AI
Eliza	(W)	40	F	Unknown	07Ap02AI
Bgt.	(D)	12	F	Child	07Ap02AI
Dane	(S)	05	M	Child	07Ap02AI
Ann	(D)	07	F	Child	07Ap02AI
MACKAY, N.		30	M	Laborer	07Ap02AI
Mich.		20	M	Laborer	07Ap02AI
Cath.		18	F	Unknown	07Ap02AI
MATHEWS, B.		41	M	Laborer	07Ap02AI
MURPHY, P.		29	M	Laborer	07Ap02AI
DONNELLY, F.		20	M	Laborer	07Ap02AI
Thos.		18	M	Laborer	07Ap02AI
MCKAY, Mgt.		40	F	Unknown	07Ap02AI
LARKIN, Mary		20	F	Unknown	07Ap02AI
KILANY, P.		20	M	Laborer	07Ap02AI
DOWNLY, J.		25	M	Laborer	07Ap02AI
MARTIN, Ann		23	F	Unknown	07Ap02AI
Ellen		18	F	Unknown	07Ap02AI
LYNCH, Mary		17	F	Unknown	07Ap02AI
Ann		20	F	Unknown	07Ap02AI
MCKENNA, O.		18	M	Laborer	07Ap02AI
SHEA, D.		12	M	Laborer	07Ap02AI
Mary		16	F	Unknown	07Ap02AI
DERMOODY, Mgt.		20	F	Unknown	07Ap02AI
BOYLE, C.		20	M	Laborer	07Ap02AI
CONLIN, Cath.		20	F	Unknown	07Ap02AI
FARRELL, W.		20	M	Laborer	07Ap02AI
WALSH, P.		20	M	Laborer	07Ap02AI
John		20	M	Laborer	07Ap02AI
BOYLAN, Ann		20	F	Unknown	07Ap02AI
CARTY, Cathe.		20	F	Unknown	07Ap02AI
CONNELL, Biddy		20	F	Unknown	07Ap02AI
PIDGEON, P.		21	M	Laborer	07Ap02AI
REGAN, Mary		21	F	Unknown	07Ap02AI
LERNMAN, Mary		20	F	Unknown	07Ap02AI
MURPHY, J.		30	M	Laborer	07Ap02AI
ENGLISH, Hy.		30	M	Laborer	07Ap02AI
CONNER, Mary		25	F	Unknown	07Ap02AI
BOYER, O.		20	M	Laborer	07Ap02AI
DALY, R.		25	M	Laborer	07Ap02AI
B.		20	M	Laborer	07Ap02AI
BRADY, Mary		18	F	Unknown	07Ap02AI
SHERIDAN, J.		20	M	Laborer	07Ap02AI
TAFFE, J.		20	M	Laborer	07Ap02AI
MORAN, P.		29	M	Laborer	07Ap02AI
HASS, P.		30	M	Laborer	07Ap02AI
Judy		28	F	Unknown	07Ap02AI
MOSER, P.		31	M	Laborer	07Ap02AI
SAHAGN, R.		23	M	Laborer	07Ap02AI
CONOR, W.		28	M	Laborer	07Ap02AI
CLOOM, J.		19	M	Laborer	07Ap02AI
LENM, J.		30	M	Laborer	07Ap02AI
CROONER, J.		40	M	Laborer	07Ap02AI
SANIGN, M.		49	M	Laborer	07Ap02AI
CROONER, Mary		30	F	Unknown	07Ap02AI
MCCARCUS, Jull		20	F	Unknown	07Ap02AI
Mary		20	F	Unknown	07Ap02AI
KELLY, Mary		18	F	Unknown	07Ap02AI
PLUNKETT, Jull		18	F	Unknown	07Ap02AI
COFFE, Mary		18	F	Unknown	07Ap02AI
KELLY, Betsy		10	F	None	07Ap02AI
OBRIEN, Bgt.		12	F	None	07Ap02AI
CONLER, M.		22	M	Laborer	07Ap02AI
KERIGAN, Hy.		22	M	Laborer	07Ap02AI
SCOTT, W.		30	M	Laborer	07Ap02AI
Ellen		20	F	Unknown	07Ap02AI
MONTAGH, M.		20	M	Laborer	07Ap02AI
ROURKE, C.		24	M	Laborer	07Ap02AI
CONLY, P.		26	M	Laborer	07Ap02AI
MORAN, L.		30	M	Laborer	07Ap02AI
WYMES, J.		58	M	Laborer	07Ap02AI
Mary		40	F	Unknown	07Ap02AI
James	(S)	28	M	Laborer	07Ap02AI
Ellen	(D)	24	F	Unknown	07Ap02AI
Thos.	(S)	07	M	Child	07Ap02AI
Haris	(S)	05	M	Child	07Ap02AI
Mary	(D)	03	F	Child	07Ap02AI
Ellen	(D)	02	F	Child	07Ap02AI
Cathe.	(D)	01	F	Child	07Ap02AI
SAYNAR, J.		20	M	Laborer	07Ap02AI
MALLIN, J.		21	M	Laborer	07Ap02AI
HOGAN, Cath.		24	F	Unknown	07Ap02AI
QUIGGAN, P.		18	M	Laborer	07Ap02AI
HEANLY, M.		22	M	Laborer	07Ap02AI
WOOD, J.		24	M	Laborer	07Ap02AI
CONNOLLY, J.		27	M	Laborer	07Ap02AI
RANDALL, J.		44	M	Laborer	07Ap02AI
MAKIN, P.		36	M	Laborer	07Ap02AI
Cathe.		09	F	Child	07Ap02AI
Hanah		26	F	Unknown	07Ap02AI
S.		20	M	Laborer	07Ap02AI
JOHNSON, J.		17	M	Laborer	07Ap02AI
DAVIDSON, J.		16	M	Laborer	07Ap02AI
HANNOTH, Ann		23	F	Unknown	07Ap02AI
HIGGINS, H.		26	M	Laborer	07Ap02AI
MATTHEWS, W.G.		28	M	Laborer	07Ap02AI
HIGGINS, W.		26	M	Laborer	07Ap02AI
BURNS, R.		40	M	Laborer	07Ap02AI
Sarah	(W)	41	F	Unknown	07Ap02AI
Robt.	(S)	13	M	Child	07Ap02AI
Isabell	(D)	10	F	Child	07Ap02AI
Mgt.	(D)	07	F	Child	07Ap02AI
MCCAHEDY, Wm.		50	M	Laborer	07Ap02AI
Sally	(W)	50	F	Unknown	07Ap02AI
Cathe.	(D)	10	F	Child	07Ap02AI
Ann	(D)	08	F	Child	07Ap02AI
Wm.	(S)	05	M	Child	07Ap02AI

NAMES OF PASSENGERS	AGE	SEX	OCCUPATIONS	DATE PORT SHIP	NAMES OF PASSENGERS		AGE	SEX	OCCUPATIONS	DATE PORT SHIP
RYE, J.	33	M	Laborer	07Ap02AI	KEARNY, Mary		21	F	Unknown	07Ap02AI
FARRELL, J.	21	M	Laborer	07Ap02AI	FANNIE, Bgt.		18	F	Unknown	07Ap02AI
ROGIN, Eliza	21	F	Unknown	07Ap02AI	BATTIGAN, Nona		16	F	Unknown	07Ap02AI
CUMMINGS, Mgt.	18	F	Unknown	07Ap02AI	MORAN, Mary		24	F	Unknown	07Ap02AI
DUNLOP, Bgt.	18	F	Unknown	07Ap02AI	REGAN, Ann		18	F	Unknown	07Ap02AI
Alice	15	F	Unknown	07Ap02AI	EGAN, Hy.		22	M	Laborer	07Ap02AI
COGAN, H.	24	M	Laborer	07Ap02AI	KELLY, Cathe.		20	F	Unknown	07Ap02AI
DALY, J.	18	M	Laborer	07Ap02AI	Mgt.		18	F	Unknown	07Ap02AI
MCCABE, Bgt.	14	F	Unknown	07Ap02AI	FLYNN, M.		24	M	Laborer	07Ap02AI
DOWNALE, W.	28	U	Unknown	07Ap02AI	RATTIGAN, Mary		03	F	Child	07Ap02AI
Mary	10	F	Child	07Ap02AI	Martin		22	M	Laborer	07Ap02AI
BARTH, Mary	36	F	Unknown	07Ap02AI	HIERN, J.		25	M	Laborer	07Ap02AI
Patch	12	M	None	07Ap02AI	BONEY, P.		30	M	Laborer	07Ap02AI
Thos.	05	M	Child	07Ap02AI	Mary		33	F	Unknown	07Ap02AI
Mary	04	F	Child	07Ap02AI	Eliza		02	F	Child	07Ap02AI
J.	02	M	Child	07Ap02AI	SILLAR, J.		34	M	Laborer	07Ap02AI
MCCORMICK, J.	24	M	Laborer	07Ap02AI	Mary	(W)	26	F	Unknown	07Ap02AI
Dane	22	M	Laborer	07Ap02AI	Mary	(D)	06	F	Child	07Ap02AI
Danl.	20	M	Laborer	07Ap02AI	Ann	(D)	04	F	Child	07Ap02AI
MALONY, C.	20	M	Laborer	07Ap02AI	James	(S)	01	M	Child	07Ap02AI
FITZSIMMONS, M.	24	M	Laborer	07Ap02AI	MCGOW, John		26	M	Laborer	07Ap02AI
GILHOOLY, O.	20	M	Laborer	07Ap02AI	Alice	(W)	23	F	Unknown	07Ap02AI
Tim	24	M	Laborer	07Ap02AI	Pat	(S)	01	M	Child	07Ap02AI
Mary	40	F	Unknown	07Ap02AI	GALLAGHER, P.		20	M	Laborer	07Ap02AI
Bgt.	20	F	Unknown	07Ap02AI	John		20	M	Laborer	07Ap02AI
Hy.	18	M	Laborer	07Ap02AI	SULLIVAN, J.		30	M	Laborer	07Ap02AI
FAHELLY, Bgt.	20	F	Unknown	07Ap02AI	SHERIHAN, Mary		60	F	Unknown	07Ap02AI
REGAN, C.	43	M	Laborer	07Ap02AI	SULLIVAN, Nancy		25	F	Unknown	07Ap02AI
Mgt.	38	F	Unknown	07Ap02AI	Dolly		25	F	Unknown	07Ap02AI
John	24	M	Laborer	07Ap02AI	CONNER, Ellen		18	F	Unknown	07Ap02AI
Mary	25	F	Unknown	07Ap02AI	MARKY, F.		20	M	Laborer	07Ap02AI
Nay	14	F	Unknown	07Ap02AI	DOWD, J.		22	M	Laborer	07Ap02AI
KEENAN, C.	23	U	Unknown	07Ap02AI	Patk.		24	M	Laborer	07Ap02AI
CURKE, J.	26	U	Unknown	07Ap02AI	MORE, E.		30	M	Laborer	07Ap02AI
CARROLL, M.	25	U	Unknown	07Ap02AI	Peggy		30	F	Unknown	07Ap02AI
KINNTY, J.	24	U	Unknown	07Ap02AI	REID, P.		27	M	Laborer	07Ap02AI
NOLAN, P.	21	U	Unknown	07Ap02AI	Adam		24	M	Laborer	07Ap02AI
MCDERMOTT, J.	23	U	Unknown	07Ap02AI	Saml.		20	M	Laborer	07Ap02AI
BURKE, P.	21	U	Unknown	07Ap02AI	MAYER, J.		21	M	Laborer	07Ap02AI
DUNN, Hy.	25	M	Unknown	07Ap02AI	MCLOUGHLIN, Jane		25	F	Unknown	07Ap02AI
DIGNAN, M.	18	U	Unknown	07Ap02AI	MORRISON, J.		18	M	Laborer	07Ap02AI
Patk.	21	M	Laborer	07Ap02AI	TAGGART, J.		20	M	Laborer	07Ap02AI
CALLAGHAN, B.	20	U	Unknown	07Ap02AI	LAMB, Elle		19	F	Unknown	07Ap02AI
FENNY, M.	24	U	Unknown	07Ap02AI	LANAHAN, Mary		18	F	Unknown	07Ap02AI
MCCABE, M.	35	U	Unknown	07Ap02AI	MCCANN, J.		20	M	Laborer	07Ap02AI
Dolly	25	F	Unknown	07Ap02AI	MULLIN, J.		20	M	Laborer	07Ap02AI
Thos.	09	M	Child	07Ap02AI	Michl.		20	M	Laborer	07Ap02AI
BYRNE, B.	25	M	Laborer	07Ap02AI	COORY, M.		18	M	Laborer	07Ap02AI
KING, Bgt.	20	F	Unknown	07Ap02AI	HALSY, E.		19	M	Laborer	07Ap02AI
DILLON, M.	20	F	Unknown	07Ap02AI	MULLIN, P.		18	M	Laborer	07Ap02AI
CANNYMIRE, W.	25	M	Laborer	07Ap02AI	MULLIGAN, Ellen		18	F	Unknown	07Ap02AI
CURLY, W.	18	M	Laborer	07Ap02AI	MULLIN, Bgt.		18	F	Unknown	07Ap02AI
SILLAN, J.	20	M	Laborer	07Ap02AI	COOLY, M.		18	M	Laborer	07Ap02AI
CALB, Mary	16	F	Unknown	07Ap02AI	HALYS, M.		35	M	Laborer	07Ap02AI
STARKE, J.	35	M	Laborer	07Ap02AI	Cathe.	(W)	30	F	Unknown	07Ap02AI
Peter	28	M	Laborer	07Ap02AI	Mary	(D)	12	F	Child	07Ap02AI
Ellen	40	F	Unknown	07Ap02AI	Biddy	(D)	10	F	Child	07Ap02AI
BOYD, U	25	F	Unknown	07Ap02AI	Winifred	(D)	01	F	Child	07Ap02AI
Biddy	02	F	Child	07Ap02AI	MILLER, A.		29	M	Laborer	07Ap02AI
Pat	01	M	Child	07Ap02AI	SCOTT, R.		25	M	Laborer	07Ap02AI
MCCARR, J.	22	M	Laborer	07Ap02AI	CAHILL, J.		23	M	Laborer	07Ap02AI
Biddy	20	F	Unknown	07Ap02AI	HUGHES, D.		25	M	Laborer	07Ap02AI
Eunice	21	F	Unknown	07Ap02AI	Bridget		24	F	Unknown	07Ap02AI
GILLESPIE, P.	22	M	Laborer	07Ap02AI	GORDON, Hy.		26	M	Laborer	07Ap02AI
DOUGHERTY, P.	22	M	Laborer	07Ap02AI	RIEGN, H.		60	M	Laborer	07Ap02AI
WELSON, D.	30	M	Laborer	07Ap02AI	Mary		30	F	Unknown	07Ap02AI
SWEENY, Hy.	30	M	Laborer	07Ap02AI	FALLON, P.		22	M	Laborer	07Ap02AI
FARRELL, J.	24	M	Laborer	07Ap02AI	Biddy		23	F	Unknown	07Ap02AI
NEILL, P.	20	M	Laborer	07Ap02AI	KELLY, Mary		16	F	Unknown	07Ap02AI
FARRAN, P.	20	M	Laborer	07Ap02AI	TOMLINSON, Emmy		18	F	Unknown	07Ap02AI
SCANLON, P.	22	M	Laborer	07Ap02AI						
DONNEGUE, J.	24	M	Laborer	07Ap02AI						
SCOTT, J.	20	M	Laborer	07Ap02AI						
KELLY, J.	22	M	Laborer	07Ap02AI						
SCANLON, Cela	20	F	Unknown	07Ap02AI						

LIVERPOOL 07 APRIL 1847

From Liverpool

NAMES OF PASSENGERS		AGE	SEX	OCCUPATIONS	DATE PORT SHIP
WILSON, Mary		33	F	Unknown	07Ap02Bo
Sarah	(D)	05	F	Child	07Ap02Bo
George	(S)	07	M	Child	07Ap02Bo
CONNELLY, J.		40	M	Laborer	07Ap02Bo
James	(S)	13	M	Laborer	07Ap02Bo
Cathe.	(D)	11	F	Unknown	07Ap02Bo
Maria	(D)	08	F	Child	07Ap02Bo
Michl.	(S)	06	M	Child	07Ap02Bo
ROURKE, Cathe.		65	F	Unknown	07Ap02Bo
HART, J.		50	M	Laborer	07Ap02Bo
Cathe.	(W)	50	F	Unknown	07Ap02Bo
Pat	(S)	30	M	Laborer	07Ap02Bo
Mary	(D)	25	F	Unknown	07Ap02Bo
Judy	(D)	22	F	Unknown	07Ap02Bo
Bdgt.	(D)	20	F	Unknown	07Ap02Bo
May	(D)	10	F	Child	07Ap02Bo
CLARKE, W.R.		30	M	Laborer	07Ap02Bo
MORRISSON, P.		58	M	Laborer	07Ap02Bo
Jas.		22	M	Laborer	07Ap02Bo
John		13	M	Laborer	07Ap02Bo
MURRAY, R.		30	M	Laborer	07Ap02Bo
May		25	F	Unknown	07Ap02Bo
Robt.	(S)	02	M	Child	07Ap02Bo
Wm.	(S)	01	M	Child	07Ap02Bo
MARKLEM, H.		40	M	Laborer	07Ap02Bo
Cathe.		18	F	Unknown	07Ap02Bo
CURLEY, O.		40	M	Laborer	07Ap02Bo
MCLOUGHLIN, J.		43	M	Laborer	07Ap02Bo
HIFERTY, Jane		23	F	Unknown	07Ap02Bo
MCCREARY, O.		30	M	Laborer	07Ap02Bo
GILLESPIE, J.		27	M	Laborer	07Ap02Bo
Andrew		20	M	Laborer	07Ap02Bo
BROWN, Mary		20	F	Unknown	07Ap02Bo
MAHR, J.		22	M	Laborer	07Ap02Bo
LYNON, Cath.		21	F	Unknown	07Ap02Bo
TRACY, J.		20	M	Laborer	07Ap02Bo
KENNEDY, E.		22	M	Laborer	07Ap02Bo
MCGLYNN, E.		07	M	Child	07Ap02Bo
John		30	M	Laborer	07Ap02Bo
Peggy		13	F	Unknown	07Ap02Bo
BROWN, H.		22	M	Laborer	07Ap02Bo
BRENNAN, Hy.		40	M	Laborer	07Ap02Bo
Betsy	(W)	37	F	Unknown	07Ap02Bo
Mary	(D)	13	F	Unknown	07Ap02Bo
Jay	(S)	10	M	Child	07Ap02Bo
Mary	(D)	07	F	Child	07Ap02Bo
HALLORAN, R.		25	M	Laborer	07Ap02Bo
REDDINGTON, P.		20	M	Laborer	07Ap02Bo
EAGER, J.		20	M	Laborer	07Ap02Bo
DONAHUE, P.		20	M	Laborer	07Ap02Bo
REDDINGTON, J.		20	M	Laborer	07Ap02Bo
DUNN, P.		25	M	Laborer	07Ap02Bo
CUGGAN, W.		25	M	Laborer	07Ap02Bo
COIN, P.		20	M	Laborer	07Ap02Bo
ROURKE, S.		20	M	Laborer	07Ap02Bo
Michl.		21	M	Laborer	07Ap02Bo
HANNIGAN, L.		21	M	Laborer	07Ap02Bo
Mary		20	F	Unknown	07Ap02Bo
HANLY, M.		20	M	Laborer	07Ap02Bo
COALL, M.		23	M	Laborer	07Ap02Bo
STUDDERS, H.		30	M	Laborer	07Ap02Bo
U	(W)	30	F	Unknown	07Ap02Bo
HULTER, W.		20	M	Laborer	07Ap02Bo
KERNIG, W.		30	M	Laborer	07Ap02Bo
FUCKER, P.		27	M	Laborer	07Ap02Bo
FUCKER, Ann		20	F	Unknown	07Ap02Bo
Maria		18	F	Unknown	07Ap02Bo
GLANCY, J.		20	M	Laborer	07Ap02Bo
HAWLEY, Hy.		30	M	Laborer	07Ap02Bo
Michl.		11	M	Laborer	07Ap02Bo
FEENEY, O.		20	M	Laborer	07Ap02Bo
U	(W)	20	F	Unknown	07Ap02Bo
CALLAHAN, M.		20	M	Laborer	07Ap02Bo
MCMANUS, P.		20	M	Laborer	07Ap02Bo
MCFARLEY, D.		38	M	Laborer	07Ap02Bo
ROURKE, Hy.		20	M	Laborer	07Ap02Bo
Bernard		16	M	Laborer	07Ap02Bo
KEARNEY, M.		16	M	Laborer	07Ap02Bo
Judith		32	F	Unknown	07Ap02Bo
GALLAGHER, Mary		16	F	Unknown	07Ap02Bo
KEARNEY, Ann		12	F	Unknown	07Ap02Bo
Richd.		10	M	Child	07Ap02Bo
Mary		08	F	Child	07Ap02Bo
Henry		06	M	Child	07Ap02Bo
Michl.		04	M	Child	07Ap02Bo
Biddy		01	F	Child	07Ap02Bo
RILEY, J.		20	M	Laborer	07Ap02Bo
MCGAVIN, B.		21	M	Laborer	07Ap02Bo
MORGAN, P.		25	M	Laborer	07Ap02Bo
BRADY, Mary		19	F	Unknown	07Ap02Bo
ROBINSON, Eliza		18	F	Unknown	07Ap02Bo
KEARNEY, M.		50	M	Laborer	07Ap02Bo
Mgt.	(W)	40	F	Unknown	07Ap02Bo
Patt	(S)	17	M	Laborer	07Ap02Bo
Ann	(D)	18	F	Unknown	07Ap02Bo
Rose	(D)	05	F	Child	07Ap02Bo
Judy	(D)	09	F	Child	07Ap02Bo
Mary	(D)	12	F	Child	07Ap02Bo
Honora	(D)	20	F	Unknown	07Ap02Bo
PRENDERGRASS, P.		20	M	Laborer	07Ap02Bo
SWANE, B.		19	M	Laborer	07Ap02Bo
DOUGLAS, G.		28	M	Laborer	07Ap02Bo
Ellen		24	F	Unknown	07Ap02Bo
JORDAN, Cathe.		26	F	Unknown	07Ap02Bo
MURPHY, Ann		30	F	Unknown	07Ap02Bo
WELDIN, Jane		24	F	Unknown	07Ap02Bo
MOONY, Eliza		22	F	Unknown	07Ap02Bo
KINSLY, Ny		25	M	Laborer	07Ap02Bo
WARD, Ny		25	M	Laborer	07Ap02Bo
DILLON, E.		30	M	Laborer	07Ap02Bo
MCDERMOTT, W.		28	M	Laborer	07Ap02Bo
GANNY, Bgt.		18	F	Unknown	07Ap02Bo
SMITH, F.		40	F	Unknown	07Ap02Bo
Joe		05	M	Child	07Ap02Bo
SMILY, R.		30	M	Laborer	07Ap02Bo
U-Mrs.		20	F	Unknown	07Ap02Bo
Thos.	(S)	03	M	Child	07Ap02Bo
BURKE, P.		20	M	Laborer	07Ap02Bo
BYRNE, J.		20	M	Laborer	07Ap02Bo
LAWLESS, J.		20	M	Laborer	07Ap02Bo
KELLY, H.		20	M	Laborer	07Ap02Bo
BURNES, Judy		50	F	Unknown	07Ap02Bo
BURNS, B.		20	F	Unknown	07Ap02Bo
Jas.		12	M	Laborer	07Ap02Bo
Ann		05	F	Child	07Ap02Bo
KELLY, P.		18	M	Laborer	07Ap02Bo
WINNIFRED, Bgt.		18	F	Unknown	07Ap02Bo
SHANLY, F.		40	M	Laborer	07Ap02Bo
Mary	(W)	40	F	Unknown	07Ap02Bo
Bern.	(S)	06	M	Child	07Ap02Bo
Mary	(D)	04	F	Child	07Ap02Bo
Betsy	(D)	02	F	Child	07Ap02Bo
Thos.	(S)	04	M	Child	07Ap02Bo
DONNELLY, Ann		20	F	Unknown	07Ap02Bo
GALWAY, Agnes		18	F	Unknown	07Ap02Bo
MCKEE, W.		18	M	Laborer	07Ap02Bo
MCQUEENY, Betsy		18	F	Unknown	07Ap02Bo
MCCAFFREY, Ann		20	F	Unknown	07Ap02Bo
DOLAN, Ann		20	F	Unknown	07Ap02Bo
Pat		01	M	Child	07Ap02Bo

NAMES OF PASSENGERS		AGE	SEX	OCCUPATIONS	DATE PORT SHIP	NAMES OF PASSENGERS		AGE	SEX	OCCUPATIONS	DATE PORT SHIP
HOBAN, Bgt.		30	F	Unknown	07Ap02Bo	RAMSEY, J.		22	M	Laborer	07Ap02Bo
Michl.		02	M	Child	07Ap02Bo	KERWIN, Ann		20	F	Unknown	07Ap02Bo
CALLAHAN, M.		40	M	Laborer	07Ap02Bo	COWAN, J.		25	M	Laborer	07Ap02Bo
U	(W)	30	F	Unknown	07Ap02Bo	Agnes		18	F	Unknown	07Ap02Bo
Mary	(D)	02	F	Child	07Ap02Bo	WAIT, J.		30	M	Laborer	07Ap02Bo
MCLOUGHLIN, Mary		20	F	Unknown	07Ap02Bo	RICE, E.		30	M	Laborer	07Ap02Bo
MAHON, Ann		25	F	Unknown	07Ap02Bo	BIRNE, J.		30	M	Laborer	07Ap02Bo
KEEFE, Mgt.		20	F	Unknown	07Ap02Bo	Ann		30	F	Unknown	07Ap02Bo
TACKNEY, J.		18	M	Laborer	07Ap02Bo	BRENNAN, Mary		17	F	Unknown	07Ap02Bo
CONNELLY, P.		20	M	Laborer	07Ap02Bo	BRAN, Sally		20	F	Unknown	07Ap02Bo
CONNELL, R.		22	M	Laborer	07Ap02Bo	CARRY, Mary		20	F	Unknown	07Ap02Bo
PURCELL, M.		30	M	Laborer	07Ap02Bo	Cathe.		19	F	Unknown	07Ap02Bo
FLINN, D.		26	M	Laborer	07Ap02Bo	CONNER, Ann		20	F	Unknown	07Ap02Bo
MAHON, J.		26	M	Laborer	07Ap02Bo	Jas.		22	M	Laborer	07Ap02Bo
James		24	M	Laborer	07Ap02Bo	DOYLE, M.		30	M	Laborer	07Ap02Bo
Ann		17	F	Unknown	07Ap02Bo	MAHON, J.		28	M	Laborer	07Ap02Bo
LANNIGAN, J.		26	M	Laborer	07Ap02Bo	Thos.		26	M	Laborer	07Ap02Bo
BRASHAW, M.		20	M	Laborer	07Ap02Bo	JONES, J.		20	M	Laborer	07Ap02Bo
N.Mara		23	M	Laborer	07Ap02Bo	Mary		18	F	Unknown	07Ap02Bo
Mary		25	F	Unknown	07Ap02Bo	GILREY, P.		21	M	Laborer	07Ap02Bo
Kitty		22	F	Unknown	07Ap02Bo	KELLY, Ward		50	F	Unknown	07Ap02Bo
DEVIN, Cath.		20	F	Unknown	07Ap02Bo	Mgt.		20	F	Unknown	07Ap02Bo
FOLY, Hy.		30	M	Laborer	07Ap02Bo	MCGINNIS, H.		20	M	Laborer	07Ap02Bo
Ellen		28	F	Unknown	07Ap02Bo	WALSH, J.		20	M	Laborer	07Ap02Bo
CAMPBELL, R.		20	M	Laborer	07Ap02Bo	GARROTY, Bgt.		20	F	Unknown	07Ap02Bo
MOOREHEAD, J.		19	M	Laborer	07Ap02Bo	Mgt.		18	F	Unknown	07Ap02Bo
DERMOTT, J.		20	M	Laborer	07Ap02Bo	MCDERMOTT, Betsy		40	F	Unknown	07Ap02Bo
LAWLESS, Ny		20	M	Laborer	07Ap02Bo	James		07	M	Child	07Ap02Bo
MCCABE, J.		18	M	Laborer	07Ap02Bo	Thos.		04	M	Child	07Ap02Bo
GORMAN, D.		20	M	Laborer	07Ap02Bo	Mary		01	F	Child	07Ap02Bo
Michl.		20	M	Laborer	07Ap02Bo	MURRY, Hy.		13	M	Unknown	07Ap02Bo
Cathe.		18	F	Unknown	07Ap02Bo	HAYNE, D.		20	M	Laborer	07Ap02Bo
STANTON, J.		18	M	Laborer	07Ap02Bo	Thos.		19	M	Laborer	07Ap02Bo
CORCORAN, J.		17	M	Laborer	07Ap02Bo	SHILL, Mary		13	F	Unknown	07Ap02Bo
BRENNAN, M.		25	M	Laborer	07Ap02Bo	MCCORMICK, F.		50	M	Laborer	07Ap02Bo
FLOOD, Hy.		20	M	Laborer	07Ap02Bo	Wm.		12	M	Child	07Ap02Bo
Ann		19	F	Unknown	07Ap02Bo	Rose		08	F	Child	07Ap02Bo
GREEN, J.		16	M	Laborer	07Ap02Bo	Mary		08	F	Child	07Ap02Bo
KING, Farrell		20	M	Laborer	07Ap02Bo	MCLAUGHLIN, Cathe.		19	F	Unknown	07Ap02Bo
BURIS, Hy.		20	M	Laborer	07Ap02Bo	CASEY, May		18	F	Unknown	07Ap02Bo
John		18	M	Laborer	07Ap02Bo	JONES, G.		21	M	Laborer	07Ap02Bo
Jane		17	F	Unknown	07Ap02Bo	MCDERMOTT, Hy.		26	M	Laborer	07Ap02Bo
DORAN, Cathe.		18	F	Unknown	07Ap02Bo	Mich.		24	M	Laborer	07Ap02Bo
Thos.		20	M	Laborer	07Ap02Bo	Honora		18	F	Unknown	07Ap02Bo
Pat		13	M	Laborer	07Ap02Bo	FANNA, P.		28	M	Laborer	07Ap02Bo
CONROY, Mary		30	F	Unknown	07Ap02Bo	Michael		31	M	Laborer	07Ap02Bo
Richd.	(S)	06	M	Child	07Ap02Bo	CARLAS, J.		12	M	Child	07Ap02Bo
Michl.	(S)	04	M	Child	07Ap02Bo	MCKEE, Mary		25	F	Unknown	07Ap02Bo
FITZPATRICK, R.		22	M	Laborer	07Ap02Bo	Eliza		25	F	Unknown	07Ap02Bo
CALLEGEN, Mary		20	F	Unknown	07Ap02Bo	CAMPBELL, H.		30	M	Laborer	07Ap02Bo
CONLAN, Biddy		15	F	Unknown	07Ap02Bo	Mary		25	F	Unknown	07Ap02Bo
DOWAN, Hy.		28	M	Laborer	07Ap02Bo	KENNEDY, M.		50	M	Laborer	07Ap02Bo
SPUKE, J.		30	M	Laborer	07Ap02Bo	Mich.		21	M	Laborer	07Ap02Bo
DODDY, W.		25	M	Laborer	07Ap02Bo	Owen		18	M	Laborer	07Ap02Bo
MCDONNEL, Ellen		19	F	Unknown	07Ap02Bo	Biddy		11	F	Child	07Ap02Bo
THOMPSON, P.		18	M	Laborer	07Ap02Bo	John		09	M	Child	07Ap02Bo
LISTER, F.		15	M	Laborer	07Ap02Bo	WHEELAN, P.		23	M	Laborer	07Ap02Bo
Thos.		20	M	Laborer	07Ap02Bo	COLLINS, J.		22	M	Laborer	07Ap02Bo
DOHERTY, Ann		13	F	Unknown	07Ap02Bo	Thos.		24	M	Laborer	07Ap02Bo
Betsey		10	F	Unknown	07Ap02Bo	BROWN, J.		20	M	Laborer	07Ap02Bo
HART, J.		24	M	Laborer	07Ap02Bo	KEARNY, B.		30	M	Laborer	07Ap02Bo
AGNEW, J.		25	M	Laborer	07Ap02Bo	U	(W)	30	F	Unknown	07Ap02Bo
Mary		25	F	Unknown	07Ap02Bo	GAFFREY, J.		30	M	Laborer	07Ap02Bo
Sam	(S)	08	M	Child	07Ap02Bo	MCKENNA, Bgt.		16	F	Unknown	07Ap02Bo
Mary	(D)	06	F	Child	07Ap02Bo	Mary		12	F	Child	07Ap02Bo
HEMAN, J.		21	M	Laborer	07Ap02Bo	MAHER, Mary		25	F	Unknown	07Ap02Bo
KELLY, M.		22	M	Laborer	07Ap02Bo	Honora		02	F	Child	07Ap02Bo
HOLCROFT, W.		25	M	Laborer	07Ap02Bo	Pat		01	M	Child	07Ap02Bo
Alice		12	F	Child	07Ap02Bo	CONLAN, O.		50	M	Laborer	07Ap02Bo
Sarah		09	F	Child	07Ap02Bo	Peter		25	M	Laborer	07Ap02Bo
ROSENBERG, P.		24	M	Laborer	07Ap02Bo	Jas.		23	M	Laborer	07Ap02Bo
REATH, Hy.		23	M	Laborer	07Ap02Bo	Cathe.		23	F	Unknown	07Ap02Bo
COYLE, J.		22	M	Laborer	07Ap02Bo	Anne		11	F	Child	07Ap02Bo
Ann		21	F	Unknown	07Ap02Bo	HORNER, J.		30	M	Laborer	07Ap02Bo
MCGOWE, W.		26	M	Laborer	07Ap02Bo	BOHAR, P.		25	M	Laborer	07Ap02Bo

NAMES OF PASSENGERS		AGE	SEX	OCCUPATIONS	DATE PORT SHIP
KITTINY, Betsy		20	F	Unknown	07Ap02Bo
STAUNTON, Biddy		20	F	Unknown	07Ap02Bo
MARTIN, M.		20	M	Laborer	07Ap02Bo
BOHAR, Cath.		20	F	Unknown	07Ap02Bo
TRACY, W.		25	M	Laborer	07Ap02Bo
MADDEN, Biddy		20	F	Unknown	07Ap02Bo
Michl.		18	M	Laborer	07Ap02Bo
REDDIN, C.		25	M	Laborer	07Ap02Bo
BEVERLY, Anne		21	F	Unknown	07Ap02Bo
YATS, W.		17	M	Laborer	07Ap02Bo
OHEIE, W.		30	M	Laborer	07Ap02Bo
LORRY, A.		30	M	Laborer	07Ap02Bo
MCERLIM, H.		20	M	Laborer	07Ap02Bo
MILLER, H.		16	M	Laborer	07Ap02Bo
Mary-A.		40	F	Unknown	07Ap02Bo
John	(H)	40	M	Laborer	07Ap02Bo
Isbe.	(D)	18	F	Unknown	07Ap02Bo
Bgt.	(D)	13	F	Child	07Ap02Bo
Mary	(D)	12	F	Child	07Ap02Bo
Pat	(S)	12	M	Child	07Ap02Bo
Hr.	(S)	09	M	Child	07Ap02Bo
Nancy	(D)	08	F	Child	07Ap02Bo
Betsy	(D)	06	F	Child	07Ap02Bo
John	(S)	04	M	Child	07Ap02Bo
Felix	(S)	02	M	Child	07Ap02Bo
Thos.	(S)	02	M	Child	07Ap02Bo
BOYN, P.		20	M	Laborer	07Ap02Bo
Betsy		18	F	Unknown	07Ap02Bo
MCDANIEL, O.		27	M	Unknown	07Ap02Bo
FANNA, Cathe.		20	F	Unknown	07Ap02Bo
TEIRNEY, P.		25	M	Laborer	07Ap02Bo
UNILL, Cathe.		20	F	Unknown	07Ap02Bo
MCNIFF, M.		25	M	Laborer	07Ap02Bo
BOYLE, P.		30	M	Laborer	07Ap02Bo
Mary		35	F	Unknown	07Ap02Bo
Peggy		24	F	Unknown	07Ap02Bo
Mich.		10	M	Child	07Ap02Bo
Mary		05	F	Child	07Ap02Bo
Cathe.		03	F	Child	07Ap02Bo
DORAN, J.		41	M	Laborer	07Ap02Bo
Peggy	(W)	38	F	Unknown	07Ap02Bo
Mary	(D)	11	F	Child	07Ap02Bo
Thos.	(S)	06	M	Child	07Ap02Bo
Edwd.	(S)	01	M	Child	07Ap02Bo
LAWLESS, M.		13	M	Child	07Ap02Bo
CORMACK, E.		20	M	Laborer	07Ap02Bo
BROWN, E.		20	M	Laborer	07Ap02Bo
DELANY, J.		30	M	Laborer	07Ap02Bo
Mary	(W)	30	F	Unknown	07Ap02Bo
John	(S)	06	M	Child	07Ap02Bo
Mich.	(S)	03	M	Child	07Ap02Bo
Wm.	(S)	01	M	Child	07Ap02Bo
LAWLESS, Hy.		25	M	Laborer	07Ap02Bo
Honora	(W)	22	F	Unknown	07Ap02Bo
Mary	(D)	01	F	Child	07Ap02Bo
STAPLETON, Mary		25	F	Unknown	07Ap02Bo
OHARA, D.		25	M	Laborer	07Ap02Bo
Cath.	(W)	21	F	Unknown	07Ap02Bo
John	(S)	01	M	Child	07Ap02Bo
BAIRD, P.		43	M	Laborer	07Ap02Bo
ROWE, P.		24	M	Laborer	07Ap02Bo
FOX, P.		23	M	Laborer	07Ap02Bo
DONALY, Bgt.		40	F	Unknown	07Ap02Bo
Anne		13	F	Child	07Ap02Bo
KINCAIN, Ely		20	F	Unknown	07Ap02Bo
Cath.		26	F	Unknown	07Ap02Bo
KELLY, J.		30	M	Laborer	07Ap02Bo
EAGER, C.		19	M	Laborer	07Ap02Bo
Cath.		17	F	Unknown	07Ap02Bo
RODGERS, J.		20	M	Laborer	07Ap02Bo
LEISTER, D.		24	M	Laborer	07Ap02Bo
HEALY, P.		30	M	Laborer	07Ap02Bo
FARRELL, Hy.		20	M	Laborer	07Ap02Bo
MCMAHON, J.		23	M	Laborer	07Ap02Bo
GILLIAN, J.		25	M	Laborer	07Ap02Bo

NAMES OF PASSENGERS		AGE	SEX	OCCUPATIONS	DATE PORT SHIP
HAWLY, M.		22	M	Laborer	07Ap02Bo
POOLE, S.		30	M	Laborer	07Ap02Bo
Mary		28	F	Unknown	07Ap02Bo
W.		08	M	Child	07Ap02Bo
HIGGIN, Bgt.		20	F	Unknown	07Ap02Bo
FORLEY, Cath.		20	F	Unknown	07Ap02Bo
DOYLE, M.		25	M	Laborer	07Ap02Bo
Cath.		25	F	Unknown	07Ap02Bo
ANDERSON, N.		20	M	Laborer	07Ap02Bo
BYRNE, P.		20	M	Laborer	07Ap02Bo
MCGOEY, Cath.		28	F	Unknown	07Ap02Bo
John		26	M	Laborer	07Ap02Bo
REYNOLDS, C.		25	M	Laborer	07Ap02Bo
BOYLE, Mary		30	F	Unknown	07Ap02Bo
FORHAR, Jenny		40	F	Unknown	07Ap02Bo
Mary		12	F	Child	07Ap02Bo
Eliza		10	F	Child	07Ap02Bo
CARTY, Mary		20	F	Unknown	07Ap02Bo
HOGAN, M.		20	M	Laborer	07Ap02Bo
MANNON, Betsy		20	F	Unknown	07Ap02Bo
GRADY, J.		20	M	Laborer	07Ap02Bo
CARLAND, W.		30	M	Laborer	07Ap02Bo
Mary		60	F	Unknown	07Ap02Bo
MCDERMOTT, Ann		05	F	Child	07Ap02Bo
Patt		11	M	Child	07Ap02Bo
John		02	M	Child	07Ap02Bo
Phillip		01	M	Child	07Ap02Bo
CARLAND, P.		22	M	Laborer	07Ap02Bo
Phillip		24	M	Laborer	07Ap02Bo
CROOKER, G.		40	M	Laborer	07Ap02Bo
Jane	(W)	40	F	Unknown	07Ap02Bo
Oliver	(S)	15	M	Unknown	07Ap02Bo
W.B.	(S)	13	M	Child	07Ap02Bo
Mary	(D)	12	F	Child	07Ap02Bo
Fran	(D)	10	F	Child	07Ap02Bo
Sarah	(D)	08	F	Child	07Ap02Bo
Thos.	(S)	06	M	Child	07Ap02Bo
Geo.	(S)	04	M	Child	07Ap02Bo
ALEXANDER, M.		25	M	Laborer	07Ap02Bo
ROCKE, J.		18	M	Laborer	07Ap02Bo
SMITH, P.		30	M	Laborer	07Ap02Bo
TOONEY, G.		08	M	Child	07Ap02Bo
BUCKLEY, J.		28	M	Laborer	07Ap02Bo
LARKIN, P.		20	M	Laborer	07Ap02Bo
Rose		08	F	Child	07Ap02Bo
LYONS, M.		12	M	Laborer	07Ap02Bo
CRUDDICK, Eliza		50	F	Unknown	07Ap02Bo
HUMPHREY, R.		25	M	Laborer	07Ap02Bo
DEVLIN, S.		25	M	Laborer	07Ap02Bo
NELSON, Jane		25	F	Unknown	07Ap02Bo
CULLOGAN, C.		21	M	Laborer	07Ap02Bo
GRACE, B.		28	M	Laborer	07Ap02Bo
NELSON, G.		04	M	Child	07Ap02Bo
SMILY, P.		01	M	Child	07Ap02Bo

MONTEREY 07 APRIL 1847

From Belfast

NAMES OF PASSENGERS		AGE	SEX	OCCUPATIONS	DATE PORT SHIP
BOOMER, John		25	M	Farmer	07Ap07Mt
Margaret	(W)	25	F	Wife	07Ap07Mt
Jane	(D)	02	F	Child	07Ap07Mt
Eliza	(D)	.00	F	Infant	07Ap07Mt
BROWN, Francis		00	M	Farmer	07Ap07Mt
Susana	(W)	40	F	Wife	07Ap07Mt
John	(S)	12	M	Child	07Ap07Mt
Joshua	(S)	10	M	Child	07Ap07Mt
Mary	(D)	08	F	Child	07Ap07Mt
Francis	(S)	06	M	Child	07Ap07Mt

NAMES OF PASSENGERS		AGE	SEX	OCCUPATIONS	DATE PORT SHIP
BROWN, Susy	(D)	04	F	Child	07Ap07Mt
Edward	(S)	02	M	Child	07Ap07Mt
Joseph	(S)	01	M	Child	07Ap07Mt
MURPHY, Patrick		34	M	Laborer	07Ap07Mt
Sarah	(W)	30	F	Wife	07Ap07Mt
Margaret	(D)	12	F	Child	07Ap07Mt
Anne	(D)	10	F	Child	07Ap07Mt
Alice	(D)	07	F	Child	07Ap07Mt
Catherine	(D)	03	F	Child	07Ap07Mt
Sarah	(D)	00	F	Child	07Ap07Mt
KANE, William		50	M	Farmer	07Ap07Mt
Isabella	(W)	48	F	Wife	07Ap07Mt
Sarah	(D)	18	F	Unknown	07Ap07Mt
Robert	(S)	15	M	Unknown	07Ap07Mt
Eliza	(D)	12	F	Child	07Ap07Mt
Joseph	(S)	10	M	Child	07Ap07Mt
William	(S)	08	M	Child	07Ap07Mt
Margaret	(D)	06	F	Child	07Ap07Mt
Marshal	(S)	03	M	Child	07Ap07Mt
GEDDIS, David		40	M	Farmer	07Ap07Mt
Margaret	(W)	40	F	Wife	07Ap07Mt
Margaret	(D)	19	F	Unknown	07Ap07Mt
Mary	(D)	17	F	Unknown	07Ap07Mt
William	(S)	15	M	Unknown	07Ap07Mt
Matty	(S)	10	F	Unknown	07Ap07Mt
James	(S)	07	M	Unknown	07Ap07Mt
Catherine	(D)	04	F	Unknown	07Ap07Mt
James		40	M	Farmer	07Ap07Mt
Mary	(W)	40	F	Wife	07Ap07Mt
Ann	(D)	12	F	Child	07Ap07Mt
Mary	(D)	10	F	Child	07Ap07Mt
Rebecca	(D)	08	F	Child	07Ap07Mt
Ellen	(D)	06	F	Child	07Ap07Mt
Matilda	(D)	04	F	Child	07Ap07Mt
Eliza	(D)	02	F	Child	07Ap07Mt
Sharlott	(D)	00	F	Child	07Ap07Mt
MCMINNIS, Margaret		29	F	Spinster	07Ap07Mt
WORKMAN, William		25	M	Laborer	07Ap07Mt
ALLEN, John		22	M	Laborer	07Ap07Mt
BIGGER, Alex		25	M	Clerk	07Ap07Mt
BEGGS, Sam		17	M	Tailor	07Ap07Mt
CARSON, John		16	M	Clerk	07Ap07Mt
Easter		18	F	Spinster	07Ap07Mt
CORRISTON, James		25	M	Clerk	07Ap07Mt
WATERS, Samuel		25	M	Clerk	07Ap07Mt
TRIMBLE, William		44	M	Farmer	07Ap07Mt
Martha	(W)	40	F	Wife	07Ap07Mt
John	(S)	38	M	Unknown	07Ap07Mt
Margaret	(D)	17	F	Unknown	07Ap07Mt
Jane	(D)	14	F	Unknown	07Ap07Mt
Robert	(S)	12	M	Child	07Ap07Mt
Mary	(D)	09	F	Child	07Ap07Mt
Ellen	(D)	06	F	Child	07Ap07Mt
Catherine	(D)	03	F	Child	07Ap07Mt
William	(S)	00	M	Child	07Ap07Mt
MARTIN, Thomas		46	M	Laborer	07Ap07Mt
John		18	M	Laborer	07Ap07Mt
PAUL, Marshal		50	M	Laborer	07Ap07Mt
Mary	(W)	40	F	Wife	07Ap07Mt
John	(S)	17	M	Unknown	07Ap07Mt
William	(S)	13	M	Child	07Ap07Mt
JOHNSON, Catherine		40	F	Spinster	07Ap07Mt
MOORE, Margeret		20	F	Spinster	07Ap07Mt
JOHNSTON, John		24	M	Clerk	07Ap07Mt
CLARKE, Sarah		22	F	Wife	07Ap07Mt
Hugh	(S)	02	M	Child	07Ap07Mt
John	(S)	00	M	Child	07Ap07Mt
MCCLINTY, Hugh		35	M	Laborer	07Ap07Mt
Eloner	(W)	25	F	Wife	07Ap07Mt
Catherine	(D)	10	F	Child	07Ap07Mt
John	(S)	08	M	Child	07Ap07Mt
Hessy	(D)	05	F	Child	07Ap07Mt
Jane	(D)	02	F	Child	07Ap07Mt
DARRAH, John		25	M	Laborer	07Ap07Mt
Anne	(W)	23	F	Wife	07Ap07Mt
WAHALEY, John		40	M	Farmer	07Ap07Mt
Mary	(W)	38	F	Wife	07Ap07Mt
John	(S)	14	M	Child	07Ap07Mt
William	(S)	12	M	Child	07Ap07Mt
Eliza	(D)	10	F	Child	07Ap07Mt
George	(S)	08	M	Child	07Ap07Mt
Jane	(D)	06	F	Child	07Ap07Mt
James	(S)	03	M	Child	07Ap07Mt
MCKEOWN, Robert		23	M	Laborer	07Ap07Mt
MCALLISTER, Alex		25	M	Laborer	07Ap07Mt
MCAFEE, Arch.		40	M	Laborer	07Ap07Mt
Jane	(W)	36	F	Wife	07Ap07Mt
William	(S)	04	M	Child	07Ap07Mt
GRAHAM, Jane		40	F	Wi	07Ap07Mt
Margaret	(D)	15	F	Unknown	07Ap07Mt
Richard	(S)	13	M	Child	07Ap07Mt
John	(S)	11	M	Child	07Ap07Mt
Jane	(D)	07	F	Child	07Ap07Mt
HAMELE, Thomas		18	M	Laborer	07Ap07Mt
Fanny		20	F	Unknown	07Ap07Mt
LORRENS, William		24	M	Laborer	07Ap07Mt
TAYLOR, Andrew		40	M	Laborer	07Ap07Mt
SMYTH, Hugh		24	M	Laborer	07Ap07Mt
COCHRIN, Susan		23	F	Spinster	07Ap07Mt
THOMPSON, Ellen		29	F	Spinster	07Ap07Mt
CLARKE, Hannah		24	F	Spinster	07Ap07Mt
KERNS, Robert		28	M	Laborer	07Ap07Mt
Margaret	(W)	24	F	Wife	07Ap07Mt
Mary	(D)	04	F	Child	07Ap07Mt
James	(S)	00	M	Child	07Ap07Mt
WALSH, Henry		55	M	Laborer	07Ap07Mt
Bell	(W)	54	F	Wife	07Ap07Mt
Henry	(S)	18	M	Unknown	07Ap07Mt
Adam	(S)	16	M	Unknown	07Ap07Mt
Sarah	(D)	15	F	Unknown	07Ap07Mt
Bele	(D)	13	F	Unknown	07Ap07Mt
Mary	(D)	11	F	Child	07Ap07Mt
SCULLION, Daniel		24	M	Laborer	07Ap07Mt
MCPEASH, Thomas		24	M	Laborer	07Ap07Mt
Biddy	(W)	23	F	Wife	07Ap07Mt
Biddy	(D)	01	F	Child	07Ap07Mt
DRENNAN, Margaret		57	F	Wi	07Ap07Mt
Biddy	(D)	25	F	Unknown	07Ap07Mt
LOCHEL, James		45	M	Laborer	07Ap07Mt
James	(S)	11	M	Child	07Ap07Mt
MCAFEE, John		40	M	Laborer	07Ap07Mt
MILLER, John		30	M	Laborer	07Ap07Mt
Jane	(W)	28	F	Wife	07Ap07Mt
Robert	(S)	02	M	Child	07Ap07Mt
John	(S)	00	M	Child	07Ap07Mt
HAMILTON, Simpson		29	M	Laborer	07Ap07Mt
FERGUSON, Nathaniel		20	M	Clerk	07Ap07Mt
MOORE, Nathaniel		21	M	Clerk	07Ap07Mt
Elizabeth		17	F	Spinster	07Ap07Mt
Anne		16	F	Spinster	07Ap07Mt
Mary		14	F	Spinster	07Ap07Mt
MCCAUGHEN, Daniel		30	M	Laborer	07Ap07Mt
Nancy	(W)	28	F	Wife	07Ap07Mt
Susan	(D)	05	F	Child	07Ap07Mt
Robert	(S)	00	M	Child	07Ap07Mt
Jane		26	F	Spinster	07Ap07Mt
Susan		24	F	Spinster	07Ap07Mt
BOYLE, Patrick		19	M	Laborer	07Ap07Mt
WHALEY, Samuel		21	M	Laborer	07Ap07Mt
COUSIN, Robert		20	M	Laborer	07Ap07Mt
John		18	M	Laborer	07Ap07Mt
Margaret	(W)	20	F	Wife	07Ap07Mt
Ellen	(D)	02	F	Child	07Ap07Mt
Jane	(D)	02	F	Child	07Ap07Mt
MCALLISTER, John		40	M	Farmer	07Ap07Mt
Jane	(W)	38	F	Wife	07Ap07Mt
John	(S)	12	M	Child	07Ap07Mt
Daniel	(S)	10	M	Child	07Ap07Mt
Catherine	(D)	08	F	Child	07Ap07Mt
Henry	(S)	06	M	Child	07Ap07Mt

NAMES OF PASSENGERS		AGE	SEX	OCCUPATIONS	DATE PORT SHIP
MCALLISTER, Jane	(D)	03	F	Child	07Ap07Mt
Mary	(D)	00	F	Child	07Ap07Mt
MOREHEAD, Robt.		29	M	Cooper	07Ap07Mt
WILSON, James		50	M	Laborer	07Ap07Mt
WATTERSON, John-S.		50	M	Gentleman	07Ap07Mt
MCGEE, James		26	M	Clothier	07Ap07Mt
BIGGER, Hugh		25	M	Naturalist	07Ap07Mt
GIBSON, Robert		35	M	Merchant	07Ap07Mt
HENDERSON, Francis		30	M	Clerk	07Ap07Mt

LIBERTY 08 APRIL 1847

From Liverpool

NAMES OF PASSENGERS		AGE	SEX	OCCUPATIONS	DATE PORT SHIP
FENELLY, William		19	M	None	08Ap02Fw
MORTON, William		24	M	Merchant	08Ap02Fw
BARKER, Chas.		42	M	None	08Ap02Fw
Sarah	(W)	45	F	Wife	08Ap02Fw
Sarah	(D)	15	F	None	08Ap02Fw
CAROLON, James		24	M	Mechanic	08Ap02Fw
Heath		27	M	Mechanic	08Ap02Fw
CONANE, James		18	M	Mechanic	08Ap02Fw
GIVEN, Andy		24	M	Mechanic	08Ap02Fw
HENRY, Michael		27	M	Mechanic	08Ap02Fw
Honor		17	M	Mechanic	08Ap02Fw
NOTOLAN, Maria		20	F	Unknown	08Ap02Fw
KEAN, Margt.		18	F	Unknown	08Ap02Fw
EDWARD, David		24	M	Mechanic	08Ap02Fw
LEWIS, Henry		26	M	Mechanic	08Ap02Fw
DAVID, Jane		22	F	Unknown	08Ap02Fw
Sarah	(D)	01	F	Child	08Ap02Fw
HEYNE, Christian		32	M	Mechanic	08Ap02Fw
Wilhelmina		28	F	Unknown	08Ap02Fw
CULLIAND, James		28	M	Mechanic	08Ap02Fw
Mary	(W)	26	F	Wife	08Ap02Fw
Mary	(D)	.00	F	Infant	08Ap02Fw
KEEFE, Danny		24	M	Mechanic	08Ap02Fw
COLLING, Cathe.		20	F	Unknown	08Ap02Fw
FOLEY, Pat.		24	M	Mechanic	08Ap02Fw
Mary		20	F	Unknown	08Ap02Fw
QUINLAN, Michael		35	M	Mechanic	08Ap02Fw
HALL, Pat		21	M	Mechanic	08Ap02Fw
KELLEY, Michael		21	M	Mechanic	08Ap02Fw
Daffey		24	M	Mechanic	08Ap02Fw
CASSIDY, John		22	M	Mechanic	08Ap02Fw
DUFFY, Pat		23	M	Mechanic	08Ap02Fw
LIDDY, Hehasey		25	M	Mechanic	08Ap02Fw
GRIFFITHS, John		34	M	Mechanic	08Ap02Fw
John		29	M	Mechanic	08Ap02Fw
MILLIAM, Lawrence		28	M	Mechanic	08Ap02Fw
EVANS, Lewis		68	M	Mechanic	08Ap02Fw
Solomon		27	M	Mechanic	08Ap02Fw
Ann		27	F	Unknown	08Ap02Fw
Ann		.00	F	Infant	08Ap02Fw
HUMPHREY, William		24	M	Mechanic	08Ap02Fw
WELSH, Mary		18	F	Unknown	08Ap02Fw
FURY, Pat.		22	M	Mechanic	08Ap02Fw
OWENS, William		25	M	Mechanic	08Ap02Fw
JONES, Evan		23	M	Mechanic	08Ap02Fw
Evan		24	M	Mechanic	08Ap02Fw
OWENS, Jane		18	F	Unknown	08Ap02Fw
EVANS, Evan		30	M	Mechanic	08Ap02Fw
DUNLOP, Gavin		31	M	Mechanic	08Ap02Fw
HILLIER, John		54	M	Mechanic	08Ap02Fw
William		31	M	Mechanic	08Ap02Fw
Fredk.		17	M	Mechanic	08Ap02Fw
Ellen		54	F	Unknown	08Ap02Fw
Caroline		15	F	Unknown	08Ap02Fw
BROWN, Jonah		28	M	Mechanic	08Ap02Fw

NAMES OF PASSENGERS		AGE	SEX	OCCUPATIONS	DATE PORT SHIP
BROWN, Mary	(W)	25	F	Wife	08Ap02Fw
Charles	(S)	.00	M	Infant	08Ap02Fw
DAILEY, Joseph		20	M	Mechanic	08Ap02Fw
James		19	M	Mechanic	08Ap02Fw
Luther		24	M	Mechanic	08Ap02Fw
SEMION, John		20	M	Mechanic	08Ap02Fw
MCMANY, Michael		24	M	Mechanic	08Ap02Fw
Maria		18	F	Unknown	08Ap02Fw
KENNEDY, Cathe.		24	F	Unknown	08Ap02Fw
LOUGH, James		24	M	Mechanic	08Ap02Fw
GILLAN, James		29	M	Mechanic	08Ap02Fw
LOUGH, Mary		18	F	Unknown	08Ap02Fw
Ann		16	F	Unknown	08Ap02Fw
BLAKE, Julia		18	F	Unknown	08Ap02Fw
DOOGAN, Kearns		31	M	Mechanic	08Ap02Fw
COFFEE, James		20	M	Mechanic	08Ap02Fw
Peggy		21	F	Unknown	08Ap02Fw
GANNON, Thos.		28	M	Mechanic	08Ap02Fw
James		27	M	Mechanic	08Ap02Fw
BOERMAN, Hugh		20	M	Mechanic	08Ap02Fw
MULVEIGHER, Bridget		20	F	Unknown	08Ap02Fw
LINAGH, James		19	M	Mechanic	08Ap02Fw
GANNON, Pat		20	M	Mechanic	08Ap02Fw
LINAGH, Rose		21	F	Unknown	08Ap02Fw
FEIGHLIN, Michael		24	M	Laborer	08Ap02Fw
CLARKE, Bridget		20	F	Unknown	08Ap02Fw
Martin		24	M	Laborer	08Ap02Fw
CARNEY, Michael		22	M	Laborer	08Ap02Fw
MURPHY, Pat		20	M	Laborer	08Ap02Fw
BYRNES, Owen		14	M	Laborer	08Ap02Fw
HOPKINS, Judy		20	F	Unknown	08Ap02Fw
BYRNE, Bridget		24	F	Unknown	08Ap02Fw
TIGHER, Kitty		20	F	Unknown	08Ap02Fw
KEELEY, Betty		24	F	Unknown	08Ap02Fw
KILLHOOLEY, Ann		20	F	Unknown	08Ap02Fw
CONOLLY, Pat		21	M	Laborer	08Ap02Fw
Bridget		20	F	Unknown	08Ap02Fw
BANKS, Betty		19	F	Unknown	08Ap02Fw
GREAVY, Walter		21	M	Laborer	08Ap02Fw
DUFFY, Martin		28	M	Laborer	08Ap02Fw
SHYAN, Larry		23	M	Laborer	08Ap02Fw
TULLY, Pat		25	M	Laborer	08Ap02Fw
MOORE, John		40	M	Laborer	08Ap02Fw
DONNELLY, Michael		25	M	Laborer	08Ap02Fw
Mary		22	F	Unknown	08Ap02Fw
Norah		20	F	Unknown	08Ap02Fw
Bridget		19	F	Unknown	08Ap02Fw
John		17	M	Laborer	08Ap02Fw
Michael		10	M	Laborer	08Ap02Fw
Daniel		09	M	Child	08Ap02Fw
Jerry		14	M	None	08Ap02Fw
CANNON, John		30	M	Laborer	08Ap02Fw
NEALE, Pat		40	M	Laborer	08Ap02Fw
HIGGINS, Pat		30	M	Laborer	08Ap02Fw
ROLLINS, John		20	M	Laborer	08Ap02Fw
KENNY, John		22	M	Laborer	08Ap02Fw
HYMES, Mary		20	F	Unknown	08Ap02Fw
RAFFERTY, Pat		27	M	Laborer	08Ap02Fw
MOORE, Michael		35	M	Laborer	08Ap02Fw
FOOLEY, Matt		20	M	Laborer	08Ap02Fw
Ellen		16	F	Unknown	08Ap02Fw
LEECH, Thos.		20	M	Laborer	08Ap02Fw
CORCORAN, Thos.		30	M	Laborer	08Ap02Fw
MCAVICKER, John		23	M	Laborer	08Ap02Fw
GAFFNEY, Thos.		24	M	Laborer	08Ap02Fw
MCNEALE, Thos.		21	M	Laborer	08Ap02Fw
KENNY, Ann		20	F	Unknown	08Ap02Fw
Cathe.		19	F	Unknown	08Ap02Fw
Eliza		12	F	Unknown	08Ap02Fw
REILLY, Pat		25	M	Laborer	08Ap02Fw
DANNAN, John		17	M	Laborer	08Ap02Fw
William		12	M	Laborer	08Ap02Fw
GILL, Michael		18	M	Laborer	08Ap02Fw
Cathe.		12	F	Unknown	08Ap02Fw
CUNNINGHAM, Cathe.		18	F	Unknown	08Ap02Fw

NAMES OF PASSENGERS		AGE	SEX	OCCUPATIONS	DATE PORT SHIP
GOODWIN, Robt.		24	M	Laborer	08Ap02Fw
Phillip		22	M	Laborer	08Ap02Fw
Mary		19	F	Unknown	08Ap02Fw
ARMSTRONG, Sarah		19	F	Unknown	08Ap02Fw
MCGUIGAN, Hugh		20	M	Laborer	08Ap02Fw
Mary		16	F	Unknown	08Ap02Fw
GUNLEY, Arthur		18	M	Laborer	08Ap02Fw
LAROOLES, Ann		20	F	Unknown	08Ap02Fw
BROWN, Winn		25	M	Laborer	08Ap02Fw
SHERIDAN, John		30	M	Laborer	08Ap02Fw
TIERNEY, Pat		20	M	Laborer	08Ap02Fw
HIGGINS, Michael		21	M	Laborer	08Ap02Fw
DIVINE, Ann		20	F	Unknown	08Ap02Fw
GILLILAN, Cathe.		19	F	Unknown	08Ap02Fw
DAGNAN, Bridget		18	F	Unknown	08Ap02Fw
SMITH, James		24	M	Laborer	08Ap02Fw
KENT, Hannah		21	F	Unknown	08Ap02Fw
DONEGAN, Hannah		10	F	Child	08Ap02Fw
CRAWFIELD, Wm.		42	M	Laborer	08Ap02Fw
DARCY, John		28	M	Laborer	08Ap02Fw
DARSEY, Betsey		25	F	Unknown	08Ap02Fw
James		22	M	Laborer	08Ap02Fw
REGAN, James		26	M	Laborer	08Ap02Fw
LIBERTY, Wm.		24	M	Laborer	08Ap02Fw
WHITE, Pat		24	M	Laborer	08Ap02Fw
HOGAN, Margt.		26	F	Unknown	08Ap02Fw
DIVINE, Thos.		32	M	Laborer	08Ap02Fw
GOODRICH, Thos.		31	M	Laborer	08Ap02Fw
Mary		26	F	Unknown	08Ap02Fw
DIVINE, Thos.		20	M	Mechanic	08Ap02Fw
WELSCH, John		20	M	Mechanic	08Ap02Fw
MATTHEWS, Jane		25	F	Unknown	08Ap02Fw
MAY, Pat		25	M	Mechanic	08Ap02Fw
MCKAIG, Hugh		24	M	Mechanic	08Ap02Fw
BERNARD, Henry		28	M	Mechanic	08Ap02Fw
FELIX, Henry		27	M	Mechanic	08Ap02Fw
GALAGAN, Pat		24	M	Mechanic	08Ap02Fw
Mary		20	F	Unknown	08Ap02Fw
CORLESS, Matt		24	M	Mechanic	08Ap02Fw
Mary		20	F	Unknown	08Ap02Fw
Ann		24	F	Unknown	08Ap02Fw
MCGUIRE, Dan		25	M	Mechanic	08Ap02Fw
KEHOE, Michael		50	M	Mechanic	08Ap02Fw
Luke	(S)	16	M	Mechanic	08Ap02Fw
Michal	(S)	14	M	Mechanic	08Ap02Fw
Margaret	(D)	10	F	Unknown	08Ap02Fw
Bridget	(W)	50	F	Wife	08Ap02Fw
Cathe.	(D)	18	F	Unknown	08Ap02Fw
TIGHES, Bridget		18	F	Unknown	08Ap02Fw
Mary		14	F	Unknown	08Ap02Fw
KEHOE, Jollen		20	F	Unknown	08Ap02Fw
CORCORAN, Tom		12	M	Mechanic	08Ap02Fw
WATSON, Jane		30	F	Unknown	08Ap02Fw
Mary-Ann		28	F	Unknown	08Ap02Fw
Ann-E.		.00	F	Infant	08Ap02Fw
LOCKWOOD, W.A.		25	M	Mechanic	08Ap02Fw
GOVERN, William		23	M	Mechanic	08Ap02Fw
HOGAN, Andrew		30	M	Mechanic	08Ap02Fw
Pat		28	M	Mechanic	08Ap02Fw
CRORY, John		26	M	Mechanic	08Ap02Fw
HOGIN, Betsey		24	F	Unknown	08Ap02Fw
MCDERMOT, Martin		21	M	Mechanic	08Ap02Fw
FINICAN, Pat		19	M	Mechanic	08Ap02Fw
MCDERMOT, Bridget		24	F	Unknown	08Ap02Fw
Mary		19	F	Unknown	08Ap02Fw
SMITH, Barny		26	M	Mechanic	08Ap02Fw
LEONARD, Owen		22	M	Mechanic	08Ap02Fw
MCGOVERN, Pat		21	M	Mechanic	08Ap02Fw
CORICAN, Thos.		18	M	Mechanic	08Ap02Fw
DUNN, Peter		18	M	Mechanic	08Ap02Fw
CANLEY, Thos.		22	M	Mechanic	08Ap02Fw
HUMPHREY, Sarah		60	F	Unknown	08Ap02Fw
Mary		21	F	Unknown	08Ap02Fw
Mihan.		20	M	Mechanic	08Ap02Fw
Robbert		16	M	Mechanic	08Ap02Fw
HUMPHREY, Ellen		12	F	Unknown	08Ap02Fw
FINN, Pat		28	M	Mechanic	08Ap02Fw
FARLEY, Bryan		30	M	Mechanic	08Ap02Fw
Rose		27	F	Unknown	08Ap02Fw
Margt.		15	F	Unknown	08Ap02Fw
Bridget		12	F	Unknown	08Ap02Fw
Edward		08	M	Child	08Ap02Fw
Catherine		04	F	Child	08Ap02Fw
MANAGAN, Susan		14	F	Unknown	08Ap02Fw
SHAY, Richard		26	M	Laborer	08Ap02Fw
Margaret		22	F	Unknown	08Ap02Fw
CORRIGAN, John		35	M	Laborer	08Ap02Fw
Margaret		12	F	Unknown	08Ap02Fw
Denny		10	M	None	08Ap02Fw
PHILLIPS, David		42	M	Laborer	08Ap02Fw
LYONS, Isaac		30	M	Laborer	08Ap02Fw
GANNAN, John		29	M	Laborer	08Ap02Fw
BERGAN, William		25	M	Laborer	08Ap02Fw
LARKIN, Margt.		19	F	Unknown	08Ap02Fw
MONAGHAN, John		24	M	Laborer	08Ap02Fw
CONNACK, Christopher		23	M	Laborer	08Ap02Fw
DAGNAN, Peter		25	M	Laborer	08Ap02Fw
DUFFY, John		24	M	Laborer	08Ap02Fw
DAGNAN, Pat		29	M	Laborer	08Ap02Fw
Cathe.		22	F	Unknown	08Ap02Fw
MORRIS, Joseph		29	M	Laborer	08Ap02Fw
MCGUIRE, Connor		28	M	Laborer	08Ap02Fw
KANE, Patrick		40	M	Laborer	08Ap02Fw
ROLSTON, Saml.		30	M	Laborer	08Ap02Fw
MAKEN, John		25	M	Laborer	08Ap02Fw
BONNER, Wm.		24	M	Laborer	08Ap02Fw
QUINN, William		24	M	Laborer	08Ap02Fw
HANNIGAN, Hugh		21	M	Laborer	08Ap02Fw
MCELWEE, Hugh		21	M	Laborer	08Ap02Fw
Bridget		20	F	Unknown	08Ap02Fw
ODONNELL, Roger		21	M	Laborer	08Ap02Fw
MCELWEE, Owen		24	M	Laborer	08Ap02Fw
MCCANN, Pat		24	M	Laborer	08Ap02Fw
Elizabeth		50	F	Unknown	08Ap02Fw
MCGINTY, Pat		32	M	Laborer	08Ap02Fw
MCMAINER, James		24	M	Laborer	08Ap02Fw
GILLESPIE, Saml.		40	M	Laborer	08Ap02Fw
Susanna	(W)	40	F	Wife	08Ap02Fw
Saml.	(S)	21	M	Laborer	08Ap02Fw
Hannah	(D)	19	F	Unknown	08Ap02Fw
Eliza	(D)	17	F	Unknown	08Ap02Fw
LIVINGSTON, Eliza		18	F	Unknown	08Ap02Fw
DALEY, Pat		20	M	Laborer	08Ap02Fw
Thos.		21	M	Laborer	08Ap02Fw
LIVEYS, John		20	M	Laborer	08Ap02Fw
HAGAN, Colon		21	M	Laborer	08Ap02Fw
MCLAUGHLIN, Mary		17	F	Unknown	08Ap02Fw
BANKER, Ann		18	F	Unknown	08Ap02Fw
QUADE, William		22	M	Laborer	08Ap02Fw
BARKER, Michael		24	M	Laborer	08Ap02Fw
LANAN, Pat		26	M	Laborer	08Ap02Fw
CANEY, Peter		24	M	Laborer	08Ap02Fw
MCKEOWN, John		22	M	Laborer	08Ap02Fw
MCENTAGART, Mary		20	F	Unknown	08Ap02Fw
MURRAY, Thos.		22	M	Laborer	08Ap02Fw
KANE, Thos.		25	M	Laborer	08Ap02Fw
CUNNAGHER, Bernard		30	M	Laborer	08Ap02Fw
Mary		25	F	Unknown	08Ap02Fw
WALSH, James		30	M	Laborer	08Ap02Fw
Mary	(W)	28	F	Wife	08Ap02Fw
Margaret	(D)	08	F	Child	08Ap02Fw
MANGAN, Thos.		30	M	Laborer	08Ap02Fw
Ann		28	F	Unknown	08Ap02Fw
KIERNAN, Rose		21	F	Unknown	08Ap02Fw

402

SIR-ROBERT-PEEL 08 APRIL 1847

From London

NAMES OF PASSENGERS	AGE	SEX	OCCUPATIONS	DATE PORT SHIP
FITZGERALD, Frederick	28	M	Gentleman	08Ap21Mu

ST.GEORGE 08 APRIL 1847

From Liverpool

NAMES OF PASSENGERS	AGE	SEX	OCCUPATIONS	DATE PORT SHIP
GILDAY, Charles	39	M	Mason	08Ap02Av
Phillip	35	M	Mason	08Ap02Av
BISHOP, William	24	M	Tailor	08Ap02Av
LOUGHRAY, John	21	M	Laborer	08Ap02Av
LAHEAY, James	22	M	Laborer	08Ap02Av
HOGANS, David	23	M	Glazier	08Ap02Av
HOGAN, Ann	22	F	Unknown	08Ap02Av
WHITTEY, Morris	25	M	Butcher	08Ap02Av
Margaret	23	F	Unknown	08Ap02Av
QUINN, Mary	18	F	Unknown	08Ap02Av
MAYLAND, Michael	26	M	Laborer	08Ap02Av
CLARK, Michael	20	M	Tailor	08Ap02Av
DOOLAN, Mary	18	F	Unknown	08Ap02Av
RILEY, Miles	20	M	Laborer	08Ap02Av
OCONNER, James	20	M	Laborer	08Ap02Av
WALKER, Thos.	28	M	Laborer	08Ap02Av
Ann (W)	24	F	Wife	08Ap02Av
Elizabeth (D)	06	F	Child	08Ap02Av
KANE, Peter	34	M	Laborer	08Ap02Av
SLEVIN, Michael	27	M	Laborer	08Ap02Av
EVERARD, Chas.	23	M	Laborer	08Ap02Av
HOREY, Michael	20	M	Carpenter	08Ap02Av
NOWLAN, David	23	M	Carpenter	08Ap02Av
Thomas	28	M	Carpenter	08Ap02Av
FREGAN, Patk.	24	M	Laborer	08Ap02Av
BYRNE, Lawrence	26	M	Laborer	08Ap02Av
Edward	28	M	Laborer	08Ap02Av
MOORE, Thomas	26	M	Laborer	08Ap02Av
DEVLIN, Peter	22	M	Laborer	08Ap02Av
TIGHE, Micheal	30	M	Laborer	08Ap02Av
Ann	26	F	Unknown	08Ap02Av
MORAN, Cathrine	26	F	Unknown	08Ap02Av
DOYLE, Bridget	21	F	Unknown	08Ap02Av
DONALLY, Patt	22	M	Laborer	08Ap02Av
GILLROY, James	21	M	Laborer	08Ap02Av
LALLY, John	21	M	Laborer	08Ap02Av
BYRNE, Thomas	24	M	Shoemaker	08Ap02Av
DEVLIN, Ann	20	F	Shoemaker	08Ap02Av
HEARY, Patrick	25	M	Laborer	08Ap02Av
Ann	20	F	Unknown	08Ap02Av
LONGMAN, Michl.	24	M	Laborer	08Ap02Av
Thomas	21	M	Laborer	08Ap02Av
MCGOURTY, Chas.	24	M	Laborer	08Ap02Av
Owen	18	M	Laborer	08Ap02Av
LONGMAN, Bridget	22	F	Laborer	08Ap02Av
MCGRALE, Mary	18	F	Unknown	08Ap02Av
MCGOURTY, Cicely	16	F	Unknown	08Ap02Av
PHELAN, Micheal	26	M	Laborer	08Ap02Av
GLACKIN, Patt	26	M	Laborer	08Ap02Av
BRADLEY, Patt	20	M	Tailor	08Ap02Av
MCCAULY, Wm.	18	M	Gdnr	08Ap02Av
James	20	M	Gdnr	08Ap02Av
FLYNN, Peter	21	M	Laborer	08Ap02Av
FLYNN, Peter	20	M	Laborer	08Ap02Av
BONER, Charles	24	M	Laborer	08Ap02Av
SWENY, David	22	M	Laborer	08Ap02Av
MCNULTY, James	22	M	Laborer	08Ap02Av
MCGREARTY, Bryan	20	M	Laborer	08Ap02Av
GOLAGHER, John	17	M	Laborer	08Ap02Av
MALERKEY, John	21	M	Laborer	08Ap02Av
HAROLD, Edward	50	M	Laborer	08Ap02Av
Biddy (W)	46	F	Wife	08Ap02Av
Patrick (S)	18	M	Laborer	08Ap02Av
Mary (D)	16	F	Unknown	08Ap02Av
Cathrine (D)	12	F	Unknown	08Ap02Av
Biddy (D)	09	F	Child	08Ap02Av
Daniel (S)	10	M	Laborer	08Ap02Av
John (S)	06	M	Child	08Ap02Av
DOUGHERTY, Patt	20	M	Laborer	08Ap02Av
FITZPATRICK, John	23	M	Laborer	08Ap02Av
Ann	21	F	Unknown	08Ap02Av
DRAKE, John	23	M	Carpenter	08Ap02Av
FEGAN, Francis	21	M	Laborer	08Ap02Av
SCALLY, Cathe.	20	F	Unknown	08Ap02Av
MONAGHAN, Mathw.	25	M	Laborer	08Ap02Av
GARRAY, Patt	26	M	Laborer	08Ap02Av
U (W)	24	F	Wife	08Ap02Av
Cathrine (D)	07	F	Child	08Ap02Av
Elizabeth (D)	01	F	Child	08Ap02Av
MURRAY, James	21	M	Laborer	08Ap02Av
MALONE, Thomas	22	M	Laborer	08Ap02Av
RUSH, James	30	M	Laborer	08Ap02Av
Ann (W)	30	F	Dressmaker	08Ap02Av
Thomas (S)	.06	M	Infant	08Ap02Av
Died-At-Sea				
Patrick	25	M	Laborer	08Ap02Av
CONROY, Bridget	25	F	Unknown	08Ap02Av
SHEVLIN, Manus	22	M	Tailor	08Ap02Av
MCGEEHAN, Danl.	22	M	Laborer	08Ap02Av
Peter	24	M	Laborer	08Ap02Av
GOODWIN, Henry	24	M	Farmer	08Ap02Av
Maria (W)	25	F	Wife	08Ap02Av
U (D)	.06	F	Infant	08Ap02Av
Cathrine	20	F	Unknown	08Ap02Av
KEARNY, U	21	F	Unknown	08Ap02Av
TAITE, James	26	M	Laborer	08Ap02Av
BYRNE, Thomas	24	M	Laborer	08Ap02Av
LAVERY, Philip	20	M	Laborer	08Ap02Av
Judith	22	F	Unknown	08Ap02Av
MONAHAN, Margaret	19	F	Unknown	08Ap02Av
MOONEY, Margaret	27	F	Unknown	08Ap02Av
Sally	18	F	Unknown	08Ap02Av
MALARGA, Darby	30	M	Laborer	08Ap02Av
GLANCY, William	32	M	Laborer	08Ap02Av
MCGOVERN, Bridget	20	F	Unknown	08Ap02Av
NOON, Honora	20	F	Unknown	08Ap02Av
IRWIN, Martin	24	M	Laborer	08Ap02Av
Rodger	22	M	Laborer	08Ap02Av
BOALIN, John	22	M	Laborer	08Ap02Av
CASSADY, Henry	21	M	Laborer	08Ap02Av
Bridget	17	F	Unknown	08Ap02Av
Frances	19	F	Unknown	08Ap02Av
Allice	18	F	Unknown	08Ap02Av
KING, Bessy	21	F	Unknown	08Ap02Av
MARTIN, Mary	20	F	Unknown	08Ap02Av
LOUGHRAN, Nicholas	22	M	Laborer	08Ap02Av
Betsey	24	F	Unknown	08Ap02Av
HENLEY, Thomas	23	M	Laborer	08Ap02Av
CONALLY, Pattk.	60	M	Laborer	08Ap02Av
Margaret	18	F	Unknown	08Ap02Av
Patt	32	M	Laborer	08Ap02Av
HOWE, Thomas	23	M	Laborer	08Ap02Av
RIELY, James	24	M	Laborer	08Ap02Av
Joseph	23	M	Laborer	08Ap02Av
Margaret	20	F	Laborer	08Ap02Av
MCKEOWN, Simeon	22	M	Laborer	08Ap02Av
MCMANUS, Phelan	40	M	Laborer	08Ap02Av
Ann	10	F	Unknown	08Ap02Av

NAMES OF PASSENGERS		A G E	S E X	OCCUPATIONS	DATE PORT SHIP	NAMES OF PASSENGERS		A G E	S E X	OCCUPATIONS	DATE PORT SHIP
MCDONALD, Bessy		20	F	Unknown	08Ap02Av	MILEAGH, Winney	(D)	08	F	Child	08Ap02Av
Theressa		16	F	Unknown	08Ap02Av	Cathe.	(D)	.06	F	Infant	08Ap02Av
MCGAFNEY, Mary		19	F	Unknown	08Ap02Av	HIGGONS, James		20	M	Laborer	08Ap02Av
SURRAY, James		25	M	Laborer	08Ap02Av	Bridget	(D)	.04	F	Infant	08Ap02Av
CURREN, James		25	M	Laborer	08Ap02Av	Bridget	(W)	20	F	Wife	08Ap02Av
John		23	M	Laborer	08Ap02Av	CUMMINS, Bridget		60	F	Unknown	08Ap02Av
DREW, Honora		21	F	Unknown	08Ap02Av	EARLY, Pattk.		45	M	Laborer	08Ap02Av
DUNDON, Honora		18	F	Unknown	08Ap02Av	Bridget	(W)	40	F	Wife	08Ap02Av
WALL, Richard		21	M	Laborer	08Ap02Av	Mary	(D)	18	F	Unknown	08Ap02Av
Mary		26	F	Unknown	08Ap02Av	Bridget	(D)	08	F	Child	08Ap02Av
Abby		21	F	Unknown	08Ap02Av	Ellen	(D)	.04	F	Infant	08Ap02Av
Ellenor		24	F	Unknown	08Ap02Av	Abbey	(D)	20	F	Unknown	08Ap02Av
PARKER, Margaret		18	F	Unknown	08Ap02Av	Honara	(D)	20	F	Unknown	08Ap02Av
CASEY, Mary		18	F	Unknown	08Ap02Av	FLANERY, Thomas		23	M	Laborer	08Ap02Av
Lawrence		22	M	Laborer	08Ap02Av	Cathrine	(W)	21	F	Unknown	08Ap02Av
MCCARTHY, Owen		30	M	Laborer	08Ap02Av	John	(S)	.03	M	Infant	08Ap02Av
SMITH, Micheal		22	M	Shoemaker	08Ap02Av	KELLY, John		20	M	Laborer	08Ap02Av
CORRIGAN, Patt		20	M	Laborer	08Ap02Av	Micheal		19	M	Laborer	08Ap02Av
STAY, William		20	M	Laborer	08Ap02Av	HANLEY, Micheal		20	M	Laborer	08Ap02Av
Julia		22	F	Unknown	08Ap02Av	KING, Patt		21	M	Laborer	08Ap02Av
GILLISPIE, Peter		31	M	Flaxdr	08Ap02Av	NELAN, Micheal		20	M	Laborer	08Ap02Av
Ellen	(W)	24	F	Wife	08Ap02Av	FETHERSTON, Martin		20	M	Laborer	08Ap02Av
John	(S)	.04	M	Infant	08Ap02Av	SMITH, Bridget		20	F	Unknown	08Ap02Av
CUNNINGHAM, Edwd.		24	M	Mason	08Ap02Av	MILEAGH, Cathe.		20	F	Unknown	08Ap02Av
Henry		20	M	Mason	08Ap02Av	CORRIGAN, Letty		20	F	Unknown	08Ap02Av
MCSHEON, John		22	M	Laborer	08Ap02Av	CORMICK, Peter		22	M	Laborer	08Ap02Av
MURPHY, Peter		22	M	Laborer	08Ap02Av	CARROLL, John		20	M	Laborer	08Ap02Av
CARR, James		21	M	Laborer	08Ap02Av	Micheal		18	M	Laborer	08Ap02Av
TRAYNOR, Owen		21	M	Laborer	08Ap02Av	KING, Micheal		18	M	Laborer	08Ap02Av
MCMANUS, Mary		16	F	Unknown	08Ap02Av	RILEY, Thomas		18	M	Laborer	08Ap02Av
DELACY, Ann		20	F	Unknown	08Ap02Av	MONAGHAN, Bridget		18	F	Unknown	08Ap02Av
WALSH, Richd.		30	M	Laborer	08Ap02Av	MURRAY, Ann		18	F	Unknown	08Ap02Av
WHELAN, Edwd.		22	M	Laborer	08Ap02Av	CRANE, Martin		30	M	Laborer	08Ap02Av
HEGARTY, Cathe.		20	F	Unknown	08Ap02Av	COLLYER, Thos.		25	M	Laborer	08Ap02Av
COSS, Mary		20	F	Unknown	08Ap02Av	BRENNAN, Martin		20	M	Laborer	08Ap02Av
Ann		20	F	Unknown	08Ap02Av	BROWN, Patt		20	M	Laborer	08Ap02Av
MCNEVIN, Patt		18	M	Hatter	08Ap02Av	WALKER, John		23	M	Laborer	08Ap02Av
MCCORMICK, Jas.		35	M	Laborer	08Ap02Av	CURRINE, John		30	M	Laborer	08Ap02Av
Margaret	(W)	30	F	Wife	08Ap02Av	BYRNE, Edward		22	M	Laborer	08Ap02Av
Mary	(D)	08	F	Child	08Ap02Av	MCARVILLE, Thos.		22	M	Tailor	08Ap02Av
HIGGINS, Bryan		27	M	Laborer	08Ap02Av	Francis		20	F	Unknown	08Ap02Av
Thomas		23	M	Laborer	08Ap02Av	Ann		18	F	Unknown	08Ap02Av
Margaret		14	F	Unknown	08Ap02Av	Micheal		20	M	Tailor	08Ap02Av
CLARK, Cathe.		17	F	Unknown	08Ap02Av	HOLLAND, Hugh		40	M	Weaver	08Ap02Av
COLEMAN, John		25	M	Laborer	08Ap02Av	SHEVLIN, Dennis		24	M	Farmer	08Ap02Av
Bridget		14	F	Unknown	08Ap02Av	LONGMAN, James		18	M	Laborer	08Ap02Av
CUNNINGHAM, Ann		20	F	Unknown	08Ap02Av	FISHER, Cathe.		20	F	Unknown	08Ap02Av
MCCULLY, Jno.		20	M	Shoemaker	08Ap02Av	Bridget		21	F	Unknown	08Ap02Av
HART, Bernard		44	M	Laborer	08Ap02Av	BOYLE, John		22	M	Laborer	08Ap02Av
Mary	(W)	40	F	Wife	08Ap02Av	Margaret		21	F	Unknown	08Ap02Av
Thomas	(S)	15	M	Unknown	08Ap02Av	BRESLINE, Patt		24	M	Laborer	08Ap02Av
Bridget	(D)	17	F	Unknown	08Ap02Av	SHARP, Patt		37	M	Laborer	08Ap02Av
Margaret	(D)	19	F	Unknown	08Ap02Av	GALLAGHER, Nancy		22	F	Unknown	08Ap02Av
Martha	(D)	13	F	Unknown	08Ap02Av	LEE, Charles		24	M	Laborer	08Ap02Av
MCCULLY, Margaret		20	F	Unknown	08Ap02Av	MAHON, Edward		22	M	Laborer	08Ap02Av
MCCABE, John		20	M	Laborer	08Ap02Av	GRIFFIN, Larry		23	M	Laborer	08Ap02Av
MCGEE, John		20	M	Laborer	08Ap02Av	KAVENAGH, Thos.		27	M	Laborer	08Ap02Av
LEONARD, James		20	M	Laborer	08Ap02Av	BISHOP, Anthony		35	M	Laborer	08Ap02Av
FITZPATRICK, Jas.		20	M	Laborer	08Ap02Av	Cathrine	(W)	27	F	Wife	08Ap02Av
HALMAN, Micheal		26	M	Laborer	08Ap02Av	Cathrine	(D)	03	F	Child	08Ap02Av
Johanna		26	F	Unknown	08Ap02Av	Ellen	(D)	.03	F	Infant	08Ap02Av
ROGERS, Thomas		46	M	Laborer	08Ap02Av	OBRIEN, Thos.		22	M	Mason	08Ap02Av
John		25	M	Laborer	08Ap02Av	KELLY, Cathe.		23	F	Unknown	08Ap02Av
Bridget		20	F	Unknown	08Ap02Av	EARLY, Cathe.		50	F	Unknown	08Ap02Av
Mary		18	F	Unknown	08Ap02Av	Patrick		22	M	Laborer	08Ap02Av
Nancy		17	F	Unknown	08Ap02Av	Rose		13	F	Unknown	08Ap02Av
Ellen		13	F	Unknown	08Ap02Av	BRADY, Bridget		13	F	Unknown	08Ap02Av
GURREN, Patt		20	M	Laborer	08Ap02Av	DELANEY, Thos.		32	M	Laborer	08Ap02Av
FINNERTY, Patt		30	M	Laborer	08Ap02Av	FINEGAN, Bridgt.		20	F	Unknown	08Ap02Av
Mary		25	F	Unknown	08Ap02Av	GIBBON, Thomas		25	M	Laborer	08Ap02Av
Ellen		40	F	Unknown	08Ap02Av	BRADY, John		16	M	Laborer	08Ap02Av
Ann		17	F	Unknown	08Ap02Av	Maria		14	F	Unknown	08Ap02Av
MILEAGH, John		35	M	Laborer	08Ap02Av	GALVIN, Rose		24	F	Unknown	08Ap02Av
Mary	(W)	30	F	Wife	08Ap02Av	DOYLE, Patk.		18	M	Laborer	08Ap02Av
Patt	(S)	12	M	Unknown	08Ap02Av	CUMMINS, John		21	M	Laborer	08Ap02Av

NAMES OF PASSENGERS		AGE	SEX	OCCUPATIONS	DATE PORT SHIP	NAMES OF PASSENGERS		AGE	SEX	OCCUPATIONS	DATE PORT SHIP
CUMMINS, Margaret		18	F	Unknown	08Ap02Av	RIPPAM, Alfred	(S)	01	M	Child	09Ap02Bw
QUIGLEY, Lawrence		14	M	Unknown	08Ap02Av	LINDEN, J.		20	M	Laborer	09Ap02Bw
BURNS, Margaret		20	F	Unknown	08Ap02Av	KEENAN, P.		30	M	Laborer	09Ap02Bw
REYNOLDS, James		36	M	Laborer	08Ap02Av	Nancy	(W)	30	F	Wife	09Ap02Bw
Micheal		21	M	Laborer	08Ap02Av	Thos.	(S)	12	M	Unknown	09Ap02Bw
SHEILDS, Jack		21	M	Laborer	08Ap02Av	GOULDING, P.		30	M	Laborer	09Ap02Bw
FLOOD, Bernard		24	M	Laborer	08Ap02Av	Mich.		25	M	Laborer	09Ap02Bw
U	(W)	30	F	Wife	08Ap02Av	Bdlt.		30	F	Unknown	09Ap02Bw
Micheal	(S)	07	M	Child	08Ap02Av	Betsy		15	F	Unknown	09Ap02Bw
Thomas	(S)	04	M	Child	08Ap02Av	ROSS, H.		20	F	Unknown	09Ap02Bw
James	(S)	03	M	Child	08Ap02Av	MONE, My.		49	F	Unknown	09Ap02Bw
John	(S)	.05	M	Infant	08Ap02Av	Patk.		28	M	Laborer	09Ap02Bw
NOONAN, Patt		47	M	Laborer	08Ap02Av	Frank		20	M	Laborer	09Ap02Bw
Lawrence		18	M	Laborer	08Ap02Av	My.		17	F	Unknown	09Ap02Bw
Patrick		15	M	Laborer	08Ap02Av	Robt.		12	M	Unknown	09Ap02Bw
GANVIN, Patk.		20	M	Laborer	08Ap02Av	Anty.		10	M	Unknown	09Ap02Bw
MCPHARLANE, Jas.		25	M	Laborer	08Ap02Av	Wm.		08	M	Child	09Ap02Bw
MARTIN, Bryan		20	M	Laborer	08Ap02Av	Neil		06	F	Child	09Ap02Bw
Margaret		20	F	Unknown	08Ap02Av	FLINN, J.		45	M	Laborer	09Ap02Bw
QUINN, Cathrine		22	F	Unknown	08Ap02Av	Winifred	(W)	40	F	Wife	09Ap02Bw
EDGLEY, Abbey		20	F	Unknown	08Ap02Av	Cath.	(D)	12	F	Unknown	09Ap02Bw
DONAHUE, Rose		13	F	Unknown	08Ap02Av	Ellen	(D)	10	F	Unknown	09Ap02Bw
MORGAN, Ellen		24	F	Unknown	08Ap02Av	Mich	(S)	08	M	Child	09Ap02Bw
GRANT, Margaret		23	F	Unknown	08Ap02Av	Saml.	(S)	06	M	Child	09Ap02Bw
COGLAN, Patt		24	M	Laborer	08Ap02Av	Doly	(D)	01	F	Child	09Ap02Bw
Cathrine		14	F	Unknown	08Ap02Av	My.	(D)	01	F	Child	09Ap02Bw
Christian		17	F	Unknown	08Ap02Av	KERNIGAN, Mgt.		15	F	Unknown	09Ap02Bw
SHANLEY, Thomas		20	M	Laborer	08Ap02Av	CONOLLY, S.		22	M	Laborer	09Ap02Bw
GUAGAN, Andrew		20	M	Laborer	08Ap02Av	Ellen		20	F	Unknown	09Ap02Bw
HENRY, Micheal		20	M	Laborer	08Ap02Av	IRWIN, My.		45	F	Unknown	09Ap02Bw
Ann		18	F	Unknown	08Ap02Av	Chas.		24	M	Laborer	09Ap02Bw
HUGHS, James		26	M	Laborer	08Ap02Av	Jane		24	F	Unknown	09Ap02Bw
CAWLEY, Esther		28	F	Unknown	08Ap02Av	Robt.		19	M	Laborer	09Ap02Bw
CAYNE, Bess		17	F	Unknown	08Ap02Av	Wm.		16	M	Laborer	09Ap02Bw
WILLIAMSON, Jas.		20	M	Laborer	08Ap02Av	IRVINE, C.		13	M	Laborer	09Ap02Bw
GLASS, James		30	M	Laborer	08Ap02Av	Jas.		12	M	Laborer	09Ap02Bw
Maria	(W)	28	F	Wife	08Ap02Av	Archibald		11	M	Laborer	09Ap02Bw
Maria	(D)	06	F	Child	08Ap02Av	Alexder.		09	M	Child	09Ap02Bw
William	(S)	04	M	Child	08Ap02Av	CHELTICK, Ann		25	F	Unknown	09Ap02Bw
BYRNE, Thomas		35	M	Laborer	08Ap02Av	Wm.		30	M	Laborer	09Ap02Bw
Mary	(W)	30	F	Wife	08Ap02Av	HEAGHY, Ann		30	F	Unknown	09Ap02Bw
John	(S)	11	M	Unknown	08Ap02Av	CLARKE, My.		48	F	Unknown	09Ap02Bw
Ann	(D)	03	F	Child	08Ap02Av	Patk.		22	M	Laborer	09Ap02Bw
Elizabeth	(D)	.04	F	Infant	08Ap02Av	Mich.		18	M	Laborer	09Ap02Bw
KEIFFE, John		19	M	Laborer	08Ap02Av	My.		13	F	Unknown	09Ap02Bw
MURPHY, Matthew		18	M	Laborer	08Ap02Av	MCANDREW, P.		30	M	Laborer	09Ap02Bw
WARD, John		25	M	Laborer	08Ap02Av	My.		25	F	Unknown	09Ap02Bw
KEIFFE, Micheal		30	M	Laborer	08Ap02Av	Ellen		23	F	Unknown	09Ap02Bw
Hannah		23	F	Unknown	08Ap02Av	DOHERTY, Mgt.		34	F	Unknown	09Ap02Bw
Patt		25	M	Laborer	08Ap02Av	John	(S)	09	M	Child	09Ap02Bw
TIERNEY, Edwd.		26	M	Laborer	08Ap02Av	Wm.	(S)	06	M	Child	09Ap02Bw
LAWLESS, James		50	M	Laborer	08Ap02Av	Patck.	(S)	04	M	Child	09Ap02Bw
Mary		20	F	Unknown	08Ap02Av	Bgt.	(D)	07	F	Child	09Ap02Bw
Jane		18	F	Unknown	08Ap02Av	OHARA, M.		60	M	Laborer	09Ap02Bw
James		15	M	Unknown	08Ap02Av	Patck.		21	M	Laborer	09Ap02Bw
MOORE, James		20	M	Laborer	08Ap02Av	Anthy.		12	M	Unknown	09Ap02Bw
DEVLIN, Susan		20	F	Unknown	08Ap02Av	MEELY, P.		39	M	Laborer	09Ap02Bw
						MORAN, J.		30	M	Laborer	09Ap02Bw
						NOLAN, Mgt.		22	F	Unknown	09Ap02Bw
						John		54	M	Laborer	09Ap02Bw
						Cella		01	F	Child	09Ap02Bw
ST.PATRICK 09 APRIL 1847						Peter		11	M	Unknown	09Ap02Bw
						Cella		13	F	Unknown	09Ap02Bw
From Liverpool						RYAN, Bgt.		50	F	Unknown	09Ap02Bw
						DOBBS, J.		13	M	Laborer	09Ap02Bw
						KILLAN, J.		40	M	Laborer	09Ap02Bw
						Bgt.	(W)	40	F	Wife	09Ap02Bw
CARLISLE, W.		40	M	Laborer	09Ap02Bw	Thos.	(S)	22	M	Laborer	09Ap02Bw
Eliza		14	F	Unknown	09Ap02Bw	Michal	(S)	20	M	Laborer	09Ap02Bw
Stewart		13	M	Unknown	09Ap02Bw	Lawrence	(S)	17	M	Laborer	09Ap02Bw
Alexander		10	C	Unknown	09Ap02Bw	John	(S)	17	M	Laborer	09Ap02Bw
RIPPAM, J.		24	M	Laborer	09Ap02Bw	Ann	(D)	21	F	Unknown	09Ap02Bw
Cath.	(W)	23	F	Wife	09Ap02Bw	Bgt.	(D)	18	F	Unknown	09Ap02Bw
George	(S)	02	M	Child	09Ap02Bw	LEYNARD, M.		22	M	Laborer	09Ap02Bw
						HEALY, P.		45	M	Laborer	09Ap02Bw

NAMES OF PASSENGERS		A G E	S E X	OCCUPATIONS	DATE PORT SHIP	NAMES OF PASSENGERS		A G E	S E X	OCCUPATIONS	DATE PORT SHIP
COYLE, T.		30	M	Laborer	09Ap02Bw	SCOTT, O.		30	M	Laborer	09Ap02Bw
Bgt.	(W)	30	F	Wife	09Ap02Bw	MCCORMICK, J.		09	M	Child	09Ap02Bw
Barny	(S)	09	M	Child	09Ap02Bw	NOLAN, T.		30	M	Laborer	09Ap02Bw
Mara	(D)	04	F	Child	09Ap02Bw	Jas.		20	M	Laborer	09Ap02Bw
Bdgt.	(D)	01	F	Child	09Ap02Bw	Mgt.		18	F	Unknown	09Ap02Bw
RYAN, M.		47	M	Laborer	09Ap02Bw	MCGANN, Bdy.		20	F	Unknown	09Ap02Bw
Mgt.		17	F	Unknown	09Ap02Bw	GALLAGHER, Ann		30	F	Unknown	09Ap02Bw
Timothy		12	M	Unknown	09Ap02Bw	DOLAN, Mgt.		20	F	Unknown	09Ap02Bw
CUMMINS, M.		31	M	Laborer	09Ap02Bw	BERRY, T.		30	M	Laborer	09Ap02Bw
My.		49	F	Unknown	09Ap02Bw	James		19	M	Laborer	09Ap02Bw
Nancy		29	F	Unknown	09Ap02Bw	MCGAN, S.		22	M	Laborer	09Ap02Bw
Michl.		21	M	Laborer	09Ap02Bw	CAMPBELL, K.		25	M	Laborer	09Ap02Bw
Patk.		25	M	Laborer	09Ap02Bw	Jas.		21	M	Laborer	09Ap02Bw
Thos.		23	M	Laborer	09Ap02Bw	Isabella		22	F	Unknown	09Ap02Bw
Cath.		21	F	Unknown	09Ap02Bw	Mgt.		20	F	Unknown	09Ap02Bw
My.		19	F	Unknown	09Ap02Bw	QUINN, Jane		18	F	Unknown	09Ap02Bw
Bdgt.		18	F	Unknown	09Ap02Bw	MCALEERY, P.		32	M	Laborer	09Ap02Bw
Judith		25	F	Unknown	09Ap02Bw	BLAIR, R.		20	M	Laborer	09Ap02Bw
EAGEN, Ellen		18	F	Unknown	09Ap02Bw	MARTIN, Eliza		25	F	Unknown	09Ap02Bw
REILLY, Ellen		20	F	Unknown	09Ap02Bw	DONNELL, J.		22	M	Laborer	09Ap02Bw
My.		30	F	Unknown	09Ap02Bw	Fanny		21	F	Unknown	09Ap02Bw
Rose		08	F	Child	09Ap02Bw	Mgt.		18	F	Unknown	09Ap02Bw
FLOYD, Ann		12	F	Unknown	09Ap02Bw	MCVAUGH, J.		40	M	Laborer	09Ap02Bw
Mgt.		08	F	Child	09Ap02Bw	MADDEN, Ann		20	F	Unknown	09Ap02Bw
BURNS, E.		24	M	Laborer	09Ap02Bw	My.		18	F	Unknown	09Ap02Bw
Mgt.		25	F	Unknown	09Ap02Bw	MCGRANE, Rose		20	F	Unknown	09Ap02Bw
RILY, P.		20	M	Laborer	09Ap02Bw	LORMER, Ann		20	F	Unknown	09Ap02Bw
MCBIDE, Cath.		20	F	Unknown	09Ap02Bw	CARLIN, H.		31	M	Laborer	09Ap02Bw
GIBSEN, P.T.		60	M	Laborer	09Ap02Bw	MCGUINNISS, C.		30	M	Laborer	09Ap02Bw
Winlfred	(W)	50	F	Wife	09Ap02Bw	BEARD, J.		20	M	Laborer	09Ap02Bw
Mgt.	(D)	20	F	Unknown	09Ap02Bw	DUFFY, My.		20	F	Unknown	09Ap02Bw
Bdgt.	(D)	20	F	Unknown	09Ap02Bw	LOMRISH, J.		22	M	Laborer	09Ap02Bw
KEENAN, Cath.		18	F	Unknown	09Ap02Bw	Patck.		18	M	Laborer	09Ap02Bw
Mich.	(S)	01	M	Child	09Ap02Bw	Ann		19	F	Unknown	09Ap02Bw
Jas.	(S)	01	M	Child	09Ap02Bw	Susan		61	F	Unknown	09Ap02Bw
DWYER, J.		22	M	Laborer	09Ap02Bw	Eliza		13	F	Unknown	09Ap02Bw
John		20	M	Laborer	09Ap02Bw	Patck.		12	L	Unknown	09Ap02Bw
FERRALL, P.		23	M	Laborer	09Ap02Bw	WILSON, T.		20	L	Laborer	09Ap02Bw
My.		16	F	Unknown	09Ap02Bw	MORRISS, M.		20	L	Laborer	09Ap02Bw
HANAGHAN, T.		20	M	Laborer	09Ap02Bw	BRYAN, H.		30	L	Laborer	09Ap02Bw
Cath.		16	F	Unknown	09Ap02Bw	SILK, Mgt.		20	F	Unknown	09Ap02Bw
CONN, Cath.		16	F	Unknown	09Ap02Bw	CONNOLLY, E.		24	M	Laborer	09Ap02Bw
Honora		16	F	Unknown	09Ap02Bw	BRUSLAN, H.		18	M	Laborer	09Ap02Bw
MCGUIRE, P.		27	F	Unknown	09Ap02Bw	Patck.		18	M	Laborer	09Ap02Bw
MCCAFFERTY, H.		35	M	Laborer	09Ap02Bw	John		24	M	Laborer	09Ap02Bw
PETTITT, A.		49	M	Laborer	09Ap02Bw	SWEENY, N.		24	M	Laborer	09Ap02Bw
Cella	(W)	40	F	Wife	09Ap02Bw	MOLLOY, B.		24	M	Laborer	09Ap02Bw
Jeanette	(D)	19	F	Unknown	09Ap02Bw	CRANNOR, P.		40	M	Laborer	09Ap02Bw
Jas.	(S)	17	M	None	09Ap02Bw	Mry.	(W)	40	F	Wife	09Ap02Bw
Patick	(S)	15	M	None	09Ap02Bw	Patck.	(S)	10	M	None	09Ap02Bw
Joseph	(S)	13	M	None	09Ap02Bw	Bernard	(S)	08	M	Child	09Ap02Bw
My.	(D)	11	F	Unknown	09Ap02Bw	Cath.	(D)	01	F	Child	09Ap02Bw
Mgt.	(D)	07	F	Child	09Ap02Bw	HENRY, P.		20	M	Laborer	09Ap02Bw
Cella	(D)	03	F	Child	09Ap02Bw	CRENNAN, P.		20	M	Laborer	09Ap02Bw
Andrew	(S)	08	M	Child	09Ap02Bw	CRANOR, B.		25	M	Laborer	09Ap02Bw
Christoph.	(S)	01	M	Child	09Ap02Bw	MCCLEARY, Ellen		20	F	Unknown	09Ap02Bw
COSTELLO, Cath.		30	F	Unknown	09Ap02Bw	MAHER, T.		30	M	Laborer	09Ap02Bw
LERNUM, Ann		18	F	Unknown	09Ap02Bw	AMBROSE, M.		25	M	Laborer	09Ap02Bw
Honora		20	F	Unknown	09Ap02Bw	DOLAN, M.		25	M	Laborer	09Ap02Bw
ROCHE, Cath.		20	F	Unknown	09Ap02Bw	DORAN, T.		16	M	Laborer	09Ap02Bw
LERNUM, J.		28	M	Laborer	09Ap02Bw	GLANCEY, P.		18	M	Laborer	09Ap02Bw
OLIVER, S.		43	M	Laborer	09Ap02Bw	MOONDER, M.		25	M	Laborer	09Ap02Bw
Amella		13	F	Unknown	09Ap02Bw	CONNER, J.		20	M	Laborer	09Ap02Bw
Michl.		03	M	Child	09Ap02Bw	HAHER, M.		25	M	Laborer	09Ap02Bw
John		02	M	Child	09Ap02Bw	CASEY, P.		20	M	Laborer	09Ap02Bw
Ann		20	F	Unknown	09Ap02Bw	Wm.		21	M	Laborer	09Ap02Bw
Harrett		20	F	Unknown	09Ap02Bw	FUIN, Mgt.		40	F	Unknown	09Ap02Bw
MCGUIRE, Ann		20	F	Unknown	09Ap02Bw	Maria	(D)	10	F	Unknown	09Ap02Bw
OLIVER, P.		20	M	Laborer	09Ap02Bw	Mgt.	(D)	16	F	Unknown	09Ap02Bw
KELLY, J.		20	M	Laborer	09Ap02Bw	John	(S)	06	M	Child	09Ap02Bw
Thos.		20	M	Laborer	09Ap02Bw	FEE, M.		20	M	Laborer	09Ap02Bw
MCGANELL, My.		20	F	Unknown	09Ap02Bw	MCHUGH, J.		20	M	Laborer	09Ap02Bw
BYRAN, T.		20	M	Laborer	09Ap02Bw	ROBINSON, J.		24	M	Laborer	09Ap02Bw
MARAN, P.		24	M	Laborer	09Ap02Bw	MAXWELL, A.		19	M	Laborer	09Ap02Bw
DUFFY, P.		25	M	Laborer	09Ap02Bw	MCCEABE, M.		40	M	Laborer	09Ap02Bw

NAMES OF PASSENGERS	AGE	SEX	OCCUPATIONS	DATE PORT SHIP
MOFFATT, N.	45	M	Laborer	09Ap02Bw
CAMPBELL, P.	18	M	Laborer	09Ap02Bw
DEVLIN, J.	21	M	Laborer	09Ap02Bw
Ellen	28	F	Unknown	09Ap02Bw
BURNE, C.	18	M	Laborer	09Ap02Bw
My.	16	F	Unknown	09Ap02Bw
GALLAGHER, My.	20	F	Unknown	09Ap02Bw
Ann	16	F	Unknown	09Ap02Bw
BURNES, My.	16	F	Unknown	09Ap02Bw
MCCANE, C.	18	M	Laborer	09Ap02Bw
EVART, D.	84	M	Laborer	09Ap02Bw
Jane	08	F	Child	09Ap02Bw
David	25	M	Laborer	09Ap02Bw
George	30	M	Laborer	09Ap02Bw
Eliza	32	F	Unknown	09Ap02Bw
David	07	M	Child	09Ap02Bw
Joseph	05	M	Child	09Ap02Bw
Thos.	03	M	Child	09Ap02Bw
Susan	01	F	Child	09Ap02Bw
MARTIN, T.	20	M	Laborer	09Ap02Bw
STOKER, C.R.	24	M	Laborer	09Ap02Bw
BURN, T.	20	M	Laborer	09Ap02Bw
MCAVOY, P.	20	M	Laborer	09Ap02Bw
Judith	18	F	Unknown	09Ap02Bw
CONNOLLY, M.	20	M	Laborer	09Ap02Bw
HARRIGAN, P.	20	M	Laborer	09Ap02Bw
BURNS, Cath.	30	F	Unknown	09Ap02Bw
KELLY, T.	25	M	Laborer	09Ap02Bw
EAGAN, M.	20	M	Laborer	09Ap02Bw
DEVINE, P.	27	M	Laborer	09Ap02Bw
GERRARTY, Bgt.	22	F	Unknown	09Ap02Bw
ROCHE, P.	24	M	Laborer	09Ap02Bw
Cath.	50	F	Unknown	09Ap02Bw
MOONY, P.	18	M	Laborer	09Ap02Bw
WEBSTER, R.	20	M	Laborer	09Ap02Bw
MULLER, E.	25	M	Laborer	09Ap02Bw
LOFTUS, J.	12	M	None	09Ap02Bw
Patck.	16	M	Laborer	09Ap02Bw
GUSKEAR, T.	20	M	Laborer	09Ap02Bw
MORAN, J.	20	M	Laborer	09Ap02Bw
JOYCE, M.	20	M	Laborer	09Ap02Bw
KATRICK, A.	20	M	Laborer	09Ap02Bw
Rose	20	F	Unknown	09Ap02Bw
RYAN, M.	24	M	Laborer	09Ap02Bw
LYNCH, Ann	20	F	Unknown	09Ap02Bw
GILLAN, My.	20	F	Unknown	09Ap02Bw
FOLY, My.	20	F	Unknown	09Ap02Bw
DONOVAN, Mgt.	20	F	Unknown	09Ap02Bw
BECHAM, T.	30	M	Laborer	09Ap02Bw
Patck.	21	M	Laborer	09Ap02Bw
MEEHAN, Ann	22	F	Unknown	09Ap02Bw
LYNCH, D.	25	M	Laborer	09Ap02Bw
COLLINS, Honor	30	F	Unknown	09Ap02Bw
DAY, Mgt.	12	F	Unknown	09Ap02Bw
GILLAN, Ann	20	F	Unknown	09Ap02Bw
MCGANN, M.	20	M	Laborer	09Ap02Bw
Rose	16	F	Unknown	09Ap02Bw
REILLY, Ann	18	F	Unknown	09Ap02Bw
Winifred	12	F	Unknown	09Ap02Bw
Anne	10	F	Unknown	09Ap02Bw
LOVE, T.	25	M	Laborer	09Ap02Bw
FORN, P.	20	M	Laborer	09Ap02Bw
Edwd.	20	M	Laborer	09Ap02Bw
MING, P.	25	M	Laborer	09Ap02Bw
My.	20	F	Unknown	09Ap02Bw
FISHER, N.	20	M	Laborer	09Ap02Bw
MALAY, F.	20	M	Laborer	09Ap02Bw
CLANCY, F.	20	M	Laborer	09Ap02Bw
FARRELL, B.	44	M	Laborer	09Ap02Bw
My.	44	F	Unknown	09Ap02Bw
Cath.	50	F	Unknown	09Ap02Bw
Mich.	13	M	None	09Ap02Bw
John	11	M	None	09Ap02Bw
My.	10	F	Unknown	09Ap02Bw
Nancy	08	F	Child	09Ap02Bw

NAMES OF PASSENGERS	AGE	SEX		OCCUPATIONS	DATE PORT SHIP
FARRELL, Bdgt.	07	F		Child	09Ap02Bw
Betty	05	F		Child	09Ap02Bw
FLINN, F.	18	M		Laborer	09Ap02Bw
NOLT, Cath.	16	F		Unknown	09Ap02Bw
DUFFY, Mgt.	13	F		Unknown	09Ap02Bw
CURRIGAN, Esther	13	F		Unknown	09Ap02Bw
MCSHANE, J.	21	M		Laborer	09Ap02Bw
My.	23	F		Unknown	09Ap02Bw
DUFFY, P.	21	M		Laborer	09Ap02Bw
DELMORE, Ellen	40	F		Unknown	09Ap02Bw
John	20	M		Laborer	09Ap02Bw
Cath.	19	F		Unknown	09Ap02Bw
My.	18	F		Unknown	09Ap02Bw
Peter	12	M		Unknown	09Ap02Bw
Laurence	09	M		Child	09Ap02Bw
MCGINNIS, C.	24	M		Laborer	09Ap02Bw
KELLY, A.	70	M		Laborer	09Ap02Bw
Cath.	25	F		Unknown	09Ap02Bw
Patck.	20	M		Laborer	09Ap02Bw
HARLY, O.	21	M		Laborer	09Ap02Bw
LYNHAM, M.	30	M		Laborer	09Ap02Bw
My.	22	F	(W)	Wife	09Ap02Bw
Patck.	03	M	(S)	Child	09Ap02Bw
Bryan	01	M	(S)	Child	09Ap02Bw
CONNER, Eliza	18	F		Unknown	09Ap02Bw
KERT, J.	24	M		Laborer	09Ap02Bw
CURRAN, J.	25	M		Laborer	09Ap02Bw
My.	24	F		Unknown	09Ap02Bw
SMITH, G.	45	M		Laborer	09Ap02Bw
My.	13	F		Unknown	09Ap02Bw
MULLIN, M.	22	M		Laborer	09Ap02Bw
BYRNE, J.	28	M		Laborer	09Ap02Bw
BOLAN, J.	22	M		Laborer	09Ap02Bw
COFFEY, T.	25	M		Laborer	09Ap02Bw
MCGRATH, P.	50	M		Laborer	09Ap02Bw
WALTER, J.	20	M		Laborer	09Ap02Bw
SMITH, My.	18	F		Unknown	09Ap02Bw
MCNELLY, My.	22	F		Unknown	09Ap02Bw
Cal---, A.	35	M		Laborer	09Ap02Bw
My.	33	F	(W)	Wife	09Ap02Bw
Bernd.	09	M	(S)	Child	09Ap02Bw
Cath.	08	F	(D)	Child	09Ap02Bw
Wm.	06	M	(S)	Child	09Ap02Bw
Alens	04	M	(S)	Child	09Ap02Bw
Pat	01	M	(S)	Child	09Ap02Bw
Mat.	26	M		Laborer	09Ap02Bw
Ann	50	F		Unknown	09Ap02Bw
REILLY, C.	20	M		Laborer	09Ap02Bw
OLAHER, A.	24	M		Laborer	09Ap02Bw

LOUISIANA 09 APRIL 1847

From Liverpool

NAMES OF PASSENGERS	AGE	SEX		OCCUPATIONS	DATE PORT SHIP
TOOLE, Geo.	26	M		Laborer	09Ap02Nq
Bridget	22	F	(W)	Wife	09Ap02Nq
Mary	02	F	(D)	Child	09Ap02Nq
Cathe.	.03	F	(D)	Infant	09Ap02Nq
MORAN, Edwd.	28	M		Laborer	09Ap02Nq
Mary	25	F	(W)	Wife	09Ap02Nq
Cicily	05	F	(D)	Child	09Ap02Nq
James	02	M	(S)	Child	09Ap02Nq
PETIT, John	30	M		Laborer	09Ap02Nq
KELLEY, Pat	20	M		Laborer	09Ap02Nq
John	21	M		Laborer	09Ap02Nq
FARRY, John	20	M		Laborer	09Ap02Nq
RATICAN, Cathe.	20	F		Unknown	09Ap02Nq
CONNOR, Pat	20	M		Laborer	09Ap02Nq
Michl.	25	M		Laborer	09Ap02Nq

NAMES OF PASSENGERS		AGE	SEX	OCCUPATIONS	DATE PORT SHIP
HOPPER, John		12	M	Laborer	09Ap02Nq
Thos.		08	M	Child	09Ap02Nq
CONNOR, Michl.		07	M	Child	09Ap02Nq
Pat		05	M	Child	09Ap02Nq
Joseph		02	M	Child	09Ap02Nq
Rose		40	F	Unknown	09Ap02Nq
Ellen		26	F	Unknown	09Ap02Nq
Margt.		20	F	Unknown	09Ap02Nq
Mary		.03	F	Infant	09Ap02Nq
HOPPER, Peggy		10	F	Unknown	09Ap02Nq
CROW, John		30	M	Laborer	09Ap02Nq
Alley	(W)	30	F	Wife	09Ap02Nq
Mary	(D)	07	F	Child	09Ap02Nq
Joseph	(S)	05	M	Child	09Ap02Nq
Eliza	(D)	01	F	Child	09Ap02Nq
CARR, Pat.		30	M	Laborer	09Ap02Nq
Biddy	(W)	30	F	Wife	09Ap02Nq
Mary	(D)	13	F	Unknown	09Ap02Nq
Thos.	(S)	12	M	None	09Ap02Nq
Margt.	(D)	11	F	Unknown	09Ap02Nq
Andw.	(S)	10	M	Unknown	09Ap02Nq
John	(S)	07	M	Child	09Ap02Nq
Michl.	(S)	05	M	Child	09Ap02Nq
Christ.	(D)	.05	F	Infant	09Ap02Nq
GINNES, Matt		25	M	Laborer	09Ap02Nq
Ann	(W)	25	F	Wife	09Ap02Nq
Wm.	(S)	06	M	Child	09Ap02Nq
Ellen	(D)	04	F	Child	09Ap02Nq
Pat	(S)	.03	M	Infant	09Ap02Nq
KENAN, Margt.		20	F	Unknown	09Ap02Nq
MURTLEY, Ann		20	F	Unknown	09Ap02Nq
BOYLE, Michl.		24	M	Laborer	09Ap02Nq
Margt.		21	F	Unknown	09Ap02Nq
CULLY, Pat		20	M	Laborer	09Ap02Nq
SEWERS, Wm.		20	M	Laborer	09Ap02Nq
CORMACK, Pat		40	M	Laborer	09Ap02Nq
Bridget		40	F	Unknown	09Ap02Nq
Peggy		30	F	Unknown	09Ap02Nq
Mary		05	F	Child	09Ap02Nq
Margt.		03	F	Child	09Ap02Nq
GALLOWAY, Thos.		20	M	Laborer	09Ap02Nq
RICKEY, Joseph		13	M	Laborer	09Ap02Nq
MURPHY, Terence		30	M	Laborer	09Ap02Nq
Cathe.	(W)	30	F	Wife	09Ap02Nq
Atty.	(D)	03	F	Child	09Ap02Nq
James	(S)	02	M	Child	09Ap02Nq
HARVEY, Ed.		25	M	Laborer	09Ap02Nq
Mary		30	F	Unknown	09Ap02Nq
MCFINE, John		19	M	Laborer	09Ap02Nq
GRIDDON, Nelly		25	F	Unknown	09Ap02Nq
PRENTY, James		30	M	Laborer	09Ap02Nq
GANNAN, John		28	M	Laborer	09Ap02Nq
OAKES, Francis		30	M	Laborer	09Ap02Nq
MURPHY, Ellen		24	F	Unknown	09Ap02Nq
DIAMON, James		20	M	Laborer	09Ap02Nq
GUNN, Patk.		20	M	Laborer	09Ap02Nq
IRWIN, Ann		24	F	Unknown	09Ap02Nq
NEWSTEAD, John		22	M	Laborer	09Ap02Nq
Wm.N.		07	M	Child	09Ap02Nq
Alich		05	M	Child	09Ap02Nq
FARLEY, Ed.		40	M	Laborer	09Ap02Nq
MURRAY, Phillip		20	M	Laborer	09Ap02Nq
Chas.		19	M	Laborer	09Ap02Nq
CAVANAGH, Michl.		20	M	Laborer	09Ap02Nq
MCGUIRE, Ann		19	F	Unknown	09Ap02Nq
SMITH, Alley		19	M	Laborer	09Ap02Nq
NEALE, Thos.		30	M	Laborer	09Ap02Nq
FLYNN, Thos.		30	M	Laborer	09Ap02Nq
Rose		20	F	Unknown	09Ap02Nq
SMITH, M.J.		22	F	Unknown	09Ap02Nq
Margt.		20	F	Unknown	09Ap02Nq
Joseph		15	M	Laborer	09Ap02Nq
MCTAGUE, Cathe.		20	F	Unknown	09Ap02Nq
RAFFERTY, Ed.		20	M	Laborer	09Ap02Nq
Margt.		22	F	Unknown	09Ap02Nq
GOULDERS, Lawrence		20	M	Laborer	09Ap02Nq
DODSON, Thos.		35	M	Laborer	09Ap02Nq
BROWN, David		21	M	Laborer	09Ap02Nq
MCDONALD, Pat		21	M	Laborer	09Ap02Nq
Jane		20	F	Unknown	09Ap02Nq
CAIREY, John		22	M	Laborer	09Ap02Nq
Cathe.		30	F	Unknown	09Ap02Nq
Essey		25	F	Unknown	09Ap02Nq
WATSON, Cathe.		16	F	Unknown	09Ap02Nq
Ellen		08	F	Child	09Ap02Nq
CRAIG, Peter		04	M	Child	09Ap02Nq
TAFFEE, John		30	M	Laborer	09Ap02Nq
COFFEE, Michl.		28	M	Laborer	09Ap02Nq
ORMUN, Mich.		30	M	Laborer	09Ap02Nq
WARD, Betty		22	F	Unknown	09Ap02Nq
MARTIN, Cathe.		30	F	Unknown	09Ap02Nq
REYNOLDS, Mary		26	F	Unknown	09Ap02Nq
Peggy		20	F	Unknown	09Ap02Nq
JORDON, Ann		30	F	Unknown	09Ap02Nq
SLATTERY, Matt		22	M	Laborer	09Ap02Nq
CUMMINS, Wm.		20	M	Laborer	09Ap02Nq
Margt.		18	F	Unknown	09Ap02Nq
KELLEY, Patt		30	M	Laborer	09Ap02Nq
Mary		30	F	Unknown	09Ap02Nq
GALAVAN, Ann		20	F	Unknown	09Ap02Nq
FULLER, Michl.		22	M	Laborer	09Ap02Nq
GALLAGHER, Ann		40	F	Unknown	09Ap02Nq
Mary		13	F	Unknown	09Ap02Nq
COSBY, John		20	M	Laborer	09Ap02Nq
James		20	M	Laborer	09Ap02Nq
CAMPBELL, Pat.		30	M	Farmer	09Ap02Nq
Bernard		25	M	Farmer	09Ap02Nq
Michael		18	M	Farmer	09Ap02Nq
Bridget		20	F	Unknown	09Ap02Nq
Rose		50	F	Unknown	09Ap02Nq
Rose		12	F	Unknown	09Ap02Nq
Cathe.		10	F	Unknown	09Ap02Nq
Bernd.		03	M	Child	09Ap02Nq
John		01	M	Child	09Ap02Nq
MCCABE, Pat.		23	M	Laborer	09Ap02Nq
MCDANIEL, Pat.		32	M	Laborer	09Ap02Nq
WILKIE, Robt.		30	M	Laborer	09Ap02Nq
MCCUE, Corns.		30	M	Laborer	09Ap02Nq
BLACK, Hugh		13	M	Laborer	09Ap02Nq
GOUDIE, Thos.		30	M	Laborer	09Ap02Nq
SMITH, Owen		20	M	Laborer	09Ap02Nq
FAGAN, John		30	M	Laborer	09Ap02Nq
Julia		30	F	Unknown	09Ap02Nq
REGAN, Bridget		25	F	Unknown	09Ap02Nq
MCDONALD, Bridget		40	F	Unknown	09Ap02Nq
Pat		20	M	Laborer	09Ap02Nq
MCDONNELL, And.		16	M	Laborer	09Ap02Nq
Michl.		12	M	Laborer	09Ap02Nq
CURRENY, Michael		20	M	Laborer	09Ap02Nq
MCCABE, Eliza		15	F	Unknown	09Ap02Nq
GARNLEY, Pat		21	M	Laborer	09Ap02Nq
MCELWAIN, Bessey		18	F	Unknown	09Ap02Nq
Alice		20	F	Unknown	09Ap02Nq
GARNLEY, Bridget		18	F	Unknown	09Ap02Nq
CONNER, Julia		22	F	Unknown	09Ap02Nq
Cicely		20	F	Unknown	09Ap02Nq
BANCHER, John		20	M	Laborer	09Ap02Nq
KEARY, Pat.		20	M	Laborer	09Ap02Nq
Mary		18	F	Unknown	09Ap02Nq
CARLIN, Mary		20	F	Unknown	09Ap02Nq
HORAN, Ed.		20	M	Laborer	09Ap02Nq
GRADY, Ann		20	F	Unknown	09Ap02Nq
CRASSHALL, Thos.		20	M	Laborer	09Ap02Nq
GRADY, Michael		20	M	Laborer	09Ap02Nq
BURKE, John		20	M	Laborer	09Ap02Nq
FITZPATK, Cathe.		20	F	Unknown	09Ap02Nq
MCGUIRE, Thos.		16	M	Laborer	09Ap02Nq
CARROLL, Mary		20	F	Unknown	09Ap02Nq
MCGUIRE, Thos.		16	M	Laborer	09Ap02Nq
FITZPATRICK, Rose		16	F	Unknown	09Ap02Nq

NAMES OF PASSENGERS		AGE	SEX	OCCUPATIONS	DATE/PORT/SHIP
SMITH, Cathe.		03	F	Child	09Ap02Nq
Bridget		05	F	Child	09Ap02Nq
LAWRENCE, Thos.		23	M	Laborer	09Ap02Nq
GORMAN, Thos.		25	M	Laborer	09Ap02Nq
HEANEY, H----		25	M	Laborer	09Ap02Nq
SMITH, Mary		25	F	Laborer	09Ap02Nq
Debora		23	F	Unknown	09Ap02Nq
Cathe.		20	F	Unknown	09Ap02Nq
CAIN, Andy		21	M	Laborer	09Ap02Nq
DERWIN, John		20	M	Laborer	09Ap02Nq
HAGAN, Cathe.		20	F	Unknown	09Ap02Nq
FITZPATRICK, Ellen		20	F	Unknown	09Ap02Nq
JOHNSTON, Ed.		30	M	Laborer	09Ap02Nq
GUNSHAND, Philip		20	M	Laborer	09Ap02Nq
SMITH, James		20	M	Laborer	09Ap02Nq
CURAHAN, Terence		20	M	Laborer	09Ap02Nq
JOHNSTON, Thos.		20	M	Laborer	09Ap02Nq
SMITH, John		20	M	Laborer	09Ap02Nq
COX, Thos.		20	M	Laborer	09Ap02Nq
SMITH, Rose		20	F	Unknown	09Ap02Nq
CUDLAN, Cathe.		13	F	Unknown	09Ap02Nq
GULSHANAN, Cathe.		20	F	Unknown	09Ap02Nq
MCDONALD, Margt.		20	F	Unknown	09Ap02Nq
CUMMAFORD, Jas.		47	M	Laborer	09Ap02Nq
LAMB, Lawrence		20	M	Laborer	09Ap02Nq
Ellen		20	F	Unknown	09Ap02Nq
MEHAN, Michael		20	M	Laborer	09Ap02Nq
WELCH, Jas.		20	M	Laborer	09Ap02Nq
DORAN, John		20	M	Laborer	09Ap02Nq
QUIGLEY, Pat		20	M	Laborer	09Ap02Nq
Anthy.		18	M	Laborer	09Ap02Nq
MURPHY, Jas.		13	M	Laborer	09Ap02Nq
Mary		18	F	Unknown	09Ap02Nq
Bridget		16	F	Unknown	09Ap02Nq
CAMPBELL, Berd.		50	M	Laborer	09Ap02Nq
BRADY, Bernd.		13	M	Laborer	09Ap02Nq
MCGUIGAN, Owen		40	M	Laborer	09Ap02Nq
Ann	(W)	38	F	Wife	09Ap02Nq
Bridget	(D)	07	F	Child	09Ap02Nq
Bernd.	(S)	06	M	Child	09Ap02Nq
Mary	(D)	04	F	Child	09Ap02Nq
Rose	(D)	02	F	Child	09Ap02Nq
FERGUSON, Mary		18	F	Unknown	09Ap02Nq
FARADAY, John		26	M	Laborer	09Ap02Nq
Biddy		24	F	Unknown	09Ap02Nq
Jerry		20	M	Laborer	09Ap02Nq
DURINGHAM, Ann		21	F	Unknown	09Ap02Nq
KEENAN, Bernard		25	M	Laborer	09Ap02Nq
Ellen		15	F	Unknown	09Ap02Nq
MURPHY, Pat		20	M	Laborer	09Ap02Nq
KENNINS, Phillip		20	M	Laborer	09Ap02Nq
Bridget		20	F	Unknown	09Ap02Nq
CUNNINGHAM, Jas.		20	M	Laborer	09Ap02Nq
Rose		20	F	Unknown	09Ap02Nq
LYNCH, Judy		20	F	Unknown	09Ap02Nq
MCGOVERN, Ellen		20	F	Unknown	09Ap02Nq
MONAGHAN, Ellen		15	F	Unknown	09Ap02Nq
Mary		13	F	Unknown	09Ap02Nq
Ann		11	F	Unknown	09Ap02Nq
John		09	M	Child	09Ap02Nq
Ed.		05	M	Child	09Ap02Nq
Ellen		40	F	Unknown	09Ap02Nq
Michl.		18	M	Laborer	09Ap02Nq
Bridget		14	F	Unknown	09Ap02Nq
Michl.		09	M	Child	09Ap02Nq
SMITH, Philip		20	M	Laborer	09Ap02Nq
GAFFNEY, Rose		45	F	Unknown	09Ap02Nq
James		25	M	Laborer	09Ap02Nq
Pat		20	M	Laborer	09Ap02Nq
Michl.		17	M	Laborer	09Ap02Nq
Bernd.		13	M	Laborer	09Ap02Nq
Margt.		17	F	Unknown	09Ap02Nq
MCGOVERN, Bridget		17	F	Unknown	09Ap02Nq
SMITH, Jas.		16	M	Laborer	09Ap02Nq
TIERNEY, Ann		16	F	Unknown	09Ap02Nq
COSBY, Archd.		18	M	Laborer	09Ap02Nq
GLASSEY, John		24	M	Laborer	09Ap02Nq
Matilda	(W)	25	F	Wife	09Ap02Nq
Jas.	(S)	.06	M	Infant	09Ap02Nq
GRAHAM, Saml.		16	M	Laborer	09Ap02Nq
Thos.		13	M	Laborer	09Ap02Nq
SWEENY, Henry		20	M	Laborer	09Ap02Nq
CORCORAN, John		52	M	Laborer	09Ap02Nq
Ann	(W)	50	F	Wife	09Ap02Nq
John	(S)	20	M	Laborer	09Ap02Nq
Pat	(S)	20	M	Laborer	09Ap02Nq
SHEERAN, Daniel		20	M	Laborer	09Ap02Nq
GERRATY, Michl.		20	M	Laborer	09Ap02Nq
Teddy		32	M	Laborer	09Ap02Nq
Nancy		32	F	Unknown	09Ap02Nq
John		32	M	Laborer	09Ap02Nq
John		26	M	Laborer	09Ap02Nq
Cathe.		18	F	Unknown	09Ap02Nq
HUGHES, Michl.		20	M	Laborer	09Ap02Nq
MEHAN, Mary		20	F	Unknown	09Ap02Nq
HOLDEN, Susan		20	F	Unknown	09Ap02Nq
REYNOLDS, Biddy		30	F	Unknown	09Ap02Nq
KILMARTIN, Mary		20	F	Unknown	09Ap02Nq
FEANY, Michael		25	M	Laborer	09Ap02Nq
Mary		28	F	Unknown	09Ap02Nq
GARVAN, Pat		20	M	Laborer	09Ap02Nq
Bridget		20	F	Unknown	09Ap02Nq
Margt.		13	F	Unknown	09Ap02Nq
ELDER, Robt.		27	M	Laborer	09Ap02Nq
PATTERSON, Wm.		20	M	Laborer	09Ap02Nq
GUNN, Thos.		40	M	Laborer	09Ap02Nq
Ellen		20	F	Unknown	09Ap02Nq
CONNELL, Peter		20	M	Laborer	09Ap02Nq
CAVANNAGH, Cathe.		06	F	Child	09Ap02Nq
Pat		03	M	Child	09Ap02Nq
Margt.		10	F	Unknown	09Ap02Nq
Jas.		12	M	Laborer	09Ap02Nq
Margt.		19	F	Unknown	09Ap02Nq
Bridget		13	F	Unknown	09Ap02Nq
DOWD, Mary		25	F	Unknown	09Ap02Nq
CARLAN, Cathe.		20	F	Unknown	09Ap02Nq
Jane		18	F	Unknown	09Ap02Nq
DOUGHERTY, Ann		20	F	Unknown	09Ap02Nq
Rosann		18	F	Unknown	09Ap02Nq
REILEY, Honora		40	F	Unknown	09Ap02Nq
Margt.	(D)	10	F	Unknown	09Ap02Nq
Pat	(S)	08	M	Child	09Ap02Nq
Martin	(S)	06	M	Child	09Ap02Nq
Thos.	(S)	04	M	Child	09Ap02Nq
John	(S)	02	M	Child	09Ap02Nq
WATTS, Josiah		20	M	Mechanic	09Ap02Nq
MCGAHAN, Ed.		35	M	Mechanic	09Ap02Nq
Cathe.		20	F	Unknown	09Ap02Nq
SWEENEY, Geo.		27	M	Mechanic	09Ap02Nq
MATTHEWS, Cathe.		25	F	Unknown	09Ap02Nq

ANN-HARLEY 09 APRIL 1847

From Glasgow

NAMES OF PASSENGERS		AGE	SEX	OCCUPATIONS	DATE/PORT/SHIP
DEVELIN, Patt		32	M	Laborer	09Ap04Db
Cathrine	(W)	30	F	Wife	09Ap04Db
Isabella	(D)	11	F	Unknown	09Ap04Db
GALAGHER, Patt		25	M	Laborer	09Ap04Db
MOHEN, Hugh		23	M	Laborer	09Ap04Db
MELDRON, Owen		18	M	Laborer	09Ap04Db
VILLALY, Hugh		40	M	Laborer	09Ap04Db
Barney		20	M	Laborer	09Ap04Db
MCKAY, William		20	M	Laborer	09Ap04Db

NAMES OF PASSENGERS		AGE	SEX	OCCUPATIONS	DATE PORT SHIP
MCGARLICK, Charles		30	M	Laborer	09Ap04Db
Margaret	(W)	26	F	Wife	09Ap04Db
Mary	(D)	06	F	Child	09Ap04Db
Died-At-Sea					
Patt	(S)	04	M	Child	09Ap04Db
Rose	(D)	.09	F	Infant	09Ap04Db
Patt		69	M	Laborer	09Ap04Db
Mary	(W)	53	F	Wife	09Ap04Db
John	(S)	24	M	Unknown	09Ap04Db
Cathrine	(D)	22	F	Unknown	09Ap04Db
Patt	(S)	29	M	Unknown	09Ap04Db
Biddy	(D)	13	F	Unknown	09Ap04Db
Felix	(S)	11	M	Unknown	09Ap04Db
MCGLYNN, Patt		25	M	Laborer	09Ap04Db
WARD, Oliver		25	M	Laborer	09Ap04Db
HERON, Owen		26	M	Laborer	09Ap04Db
DOCHERTY, Rose		20	F	Spinster	09Ap04Db
Mary		21	F	Spinster	09Ap04Db
MONAGHAN, Isabella		25	F	Spinster	09Ap04Db
MCGARLICK, Mary		25	F	Spinster	09Ap04Db
Susana		18	F	Spinster	09Ap04Db
RODDY, Michael		40	M	Laborer	09Ap04Db
Cathrine	(W)	40	F	Wife	09Ap04Db
Madge	(D)	10	F	Unknown	09Ap04Db
Owen	(S)	07	M	Child	09Ap04Db
Hugh	(S)	05	M	Child	09Ap04Db
Margaret	(D)	01	F	Child	09Ap04Db
MCILMOYLE, John		38	M	Laborer	09Ap04Db
Matilda	(W)	36	F	Wife	09Ap04Db
Mary-Ann	(D)	09	F	Child	09Ap04Db
John	(S)	11	M	Unknown	09Ap04Db
Mary-Jane	(D)	00	F	Unknown	09Ap04Db
BRYAN, Michael		55	M	Laborer	09Ap04Db
Mary	(W)	50	F	Wife	09Ap04Db
Michael	(S)	14	M	Unknown	09Ap04Db
Martha	(D)	10	F	Unknown	09Ap04Db
Biddy	(D)	21	F	Unknown	09Ap04Db
BRYSON, Bernard		36	M	Farmer	09Ap04Db
Hugh	(S)	13	M	Unknown	09Ap04Db
Mary	(D)	11	F	Unknown	09Ap04Db
Rose	(W)	36	F	Wife	09Ap04Db
James	(S)	01	M	Child	09Ap04Db
CONWAY, Patt		30	M	Farmer	09Ap04Db
Bridget	(W)	25	F	Wife	09Ap04Db
Ann	(D)	07	F	Child	09Ap04Db
Mary	(D)	03	F	Child	09Ap04Db
Died-At-Sea					
John	(S)	03	M	Child	09Ap04Db
Bridget	(D)	06	F	Child	09Ap04Db
CAMPBELL, Hugh		50	M	Farmer	09Ap04Db
Rose	(W)	45	F	Wife	09Ap04Db
Daniel	(S)	20	M	Unknown	09Ap04Db
John	(S)	18	M	Unknown	09Ap04Db
Patt	(S)	11	M	Unknown	09Ap04Db
Mary	(D)	07	F	Child	09Ap04Db
Swee----, Edward		25	M	Laborer	09Ap04Db
Jane	(W)	20	F	Wife	09Ap04Db
MCNALTY, Mary		16	F	Spinster	09Ap04Db
Jane		18	F	Spinster	09Ap04Db
KEENAN, Ann		20	F	Spinster	09Ap04Db
DOBINTY, Peter		27	M	Laborer	09Ap04Db
MACQUIRE, Patrick		60	M	Laborer	09Ap04Db
Cathrine	(W)	42	F	Wife	09Ap04Db
BROGAN, Hugh		26	M	Laborer	09Ap04Db
MOORE, James		40	M	Farmer	09Ap04Db
Mary-Ann	(W)	37	F	Wife	09Ap04Db
Samuel	(S)	15	M	Unknown	09Ap04Db
Eleanor	(D)	12	F	Unknown	09Ap04Db
Maria	(D)	09	F	Child	09Ap04Db
Bess	(D)	07	F	Child	09Ap04Db
Margaret-Jane	(D)	03	F	Child	09Ap04Db
Stewart	(S)	01	M	Child	09Ap04Db
GATES, John		50	M	Farmer	09Ap04Db
Joseph		24	M	Farmer	09Ap04Db
William		21	M	Farmer	09Ap04Db

NAMES OF PASSENGERS		AGE	SEX	OCCUPATIONS	DATE PORT SHIP
GATES, James		20	M	Farmer	09Ap04Db
Josheph		17	M	Farmer	09Ap04Db
ALCORN, Mathew		52	M	Farmer	09Ap04Db
Sarah	(W)	55	F	Wife	09Ap04Db
Susan	(D)	20	F	Unknown	09Ap04Db
John	(S)	16	M	Unknown	09Ap04Db
Hugh	(S)	16	M	Unknown	09Ap04Db
Helen-Jane	(D)	09	F	Child	09Ap04Db
MCCAY, Daniel		48	M	Farmer	09Ap04Db
Helen	(W)	40	F	Wife	09Ap04Db
George	(S)	21	M	Unknown	09Ap04Db
William	(S)	18	M	Unknown	09Ap04Db
Daniel	(S)	17	M	Unknown	09Ap04Db
Died-At-Sea					
John	(S)	13	M	Unknown	09Ap04Db
Charles	(S)	11	M	Unknown	09Ap04Db
Robert	(S)	08	M	Child	09Ap04Db
Samuel	(S)	04	M	Child	09Ap04Db
SMITH, Jane		36	F	Spinster	09Ap04Db
Isabella		34	F	Spinster	09Ap04Db
MCEWAN, Thomas		28	M	Laborer	09Ap04Db
KELLY, Hugh		29	M	Laborer	09Ap04Db
Mary	(W)	29	F	Wife	09Ap04Db
John	(S)	02	M	Child	09Ap04Db
Died-At-Sea					
Mary	(D)	.01	F	Infant	09Ap04Db
MCKINNON, Barny		24	M	Laborer	09Ap04Db
DOCHARTY, Patrick		28	M	Laborer	09Ap04Db
John		25	M	Laborer	09Ap04Db
Cathrine		13	F	Unknown	09Ap04Db
Daniel		10	M	Unknown	09Ap04Db
MORE, U		.00	U	Infant	09Ap04Db
Born-At-Sea					
MCDONALD, Donald		00	M	Unknown	09Ap04Db
NAIRNE, Charles-M.		00	M	Unknown	09Ap04Db

SOUTHERNER 10 APRIL 1847

From Liverpool

NAMES OF PASSENGERS		AGE	SEX	OCCUPATIONS	DATE PORT SHIP
DOUGHERTY, Danl.		30	M	Laborer	10Ap02Dy
DOYLE, Pat		30	M	Laborer	10Ap02Dy
U	(W)	30	F	Wife	10Ap02Dy
LEES, Wm.		24	M	Laborer	10Ap02Dy
DELONY, Wm.		24	M	Laborer	10Ap02Dy
ROONY, Luke		20	M	Laborer	10Ap02Dy
ENNIS, Nichs.		25	M	Laborer	10Ap02Dy
LEYMEN, John		30	M	Laborer	10Ap02Dy
BRYAN, Margt.		22	F	None	10Ap02Dy
ROONY, John		30	M	Laborer	10Ap02Dy
David		25	M	Laborer	10Ap02Dy
FLEMING, John		20	M	Laborer	10Ap02Dy
WELSCH, Abby		22	F	None	10Ap02Dy
FLYNN, Mary		20	F	None	10Ap02Dy
MARNY, Darly		26	F	None	10Ap02Dy
CURNAS, John		36	M	Laborer	10Ap02Dy
U	(W)	30	F	None	10Ap02Dy
Christy	(S)	05	M	Child	10Ap02Dy
Ed.	(S)	02	M	Child	10Ap02Dy
MCGARVY, Ceron		20	M	Laborer	10Ap02Dy
U	(W)	30	F	Wife	10Ap02Dy
CAMPBELL, Pat		50	M	Laborer	10Ap02Dy
U	(W)	48	F	None	10Ap02Dy
Margt.	(D)	20	F	None	10Ap02Dy
Elizabeth	(D)	17	F	None	10Ap02Dy
James	(S)	22	M	Laborer	10Ap02Dy
Patrick	(S)	13	M	Laborer	10Ap02Dy
KEFF, Ed.		26	M	Laborer	10Ap02Dy
CAMPBELL, Martin		07	M	Child	10Ap02Dy

NAMES OF PASSENGERS		AGE	SEX	OCCUPATIONS	DATE PORT SHIP
POLEY, Phillip		30	M	Laborer	10Ap02Dy
FALLON, Mark		19	M	Laborer	10Ap02Dy
COSTELLO, Thady		22	M	Laborer	10Ap02Dy
FARLEY, Martin		24	M	Laborer	10Ap02Dy
MANGAN, James		22	M	Laborer	10Ap02Dy
RONKE, Pat		26	M	Laborer	10Ap02Dy
CALDWELL, Hugh		26	M	Laborer	10Ap02Dy
Peggy	(W)	30	F	None	10Ap02Dy
Pat	(S)	01	M	Child	10Ap02Dy
Margt.		09	F	Child	10Ap02Dy
FITSIMMONS, Bridget		20	F	None	10Ap02Dy
Stephen		22	M	Laborer	10Ap02Dy
TOBIN, Michael		25	M	Laborer	10Ap02Dy
GALLAGHER, Margt.		25	F	None	10Ap02Dy
KINAHAN, And.		30	M	Laborer	10Ap02Dy
U	(W)	29	F	None	10Ap02Dy
GREELY, Maria		24	F	None	10Ap02Dy
MIZON, Peter		21	M	Laborer	10Ap02Dy
LESLEY, Martin		16	M	Laborer	10Ap02Dy
RILEY, Thos.		19	M	Laborer	10Ap02Dy
DWYER, Mal.		18	M	Laborer	10Ap02Dy
Thos.		17	M	Laborer	10Ap02Dy
MCGEE, John		36	M	Laborer	10Ap02Dy
Mary		27	F	None	10Ap02Dy
Cathe.		57	F	None	10Ap02Dy
Archy		40	M	Laborer	10Ap02Dy
Ann		26	F	None	10Ap02Dy
BRADEN, Pat		23	M	Laborer	10Ap02Dy
GLEASON, Dennis		20	M	Laborer	10Ap02Dy
CASLYAN, John		18	M	Laborer	10Ap02Dy
ROACH, Pat		25	M	Laborer	10Ap02Dy
Chas.	(B)	20	M	Laborer	10Ap02Dy
Anna	(M)	45	F	None	10Ap02Dy
Bridget	(T)	18	F	None	10Ap02Dy
Ellen	(T)	16	F	None	10Ap02Dy
Johana	(T)	12	F	None	10Ap02Dy
Fitzpatk., Anna		12	F	None	10Ap02Dy
MANN, Michael		24	M	Laborer	10Ap02Dy
BYRNES, Richd.		40	M	Laborer	10Ap02Dy
Maria	(D)	16	F	None	10Ap02Dy
Sally	(D)	10	F	None	10Ap02Dy
JUMETT, Saml.		25	M	Laborer	10Ap02Dy
KEENE, Richd.		07	M	Child	10Ap02Dy
ROBINSON, James		35	M	Mechanic	10Ap02Dy
Thos.		25	M	Mechanic	10Ap02Dy
Margt.		28	F	None	10Ap02Dy
CLARKSON, Thos.		25	M	Mechanic	10Ap02Dy
FOX, Burnan		30	M	Mechanic	10Ap02Dy
SURRY, Wm.		30	M	Mechanic	10Ap02Dy
Anna		60	F	None	10Ap02Dy
MULLIGAN, Betty		20	F	None	10Ap02Dy
Frank	(S)	02	M	Child	10Ap02Dy
Thos.	(H)	24	M	Mechanic	10Ap02Dy
MULLEN, Wm.		16	M	Mechanic	10Ap02Dy
HIGGINS, Mary		18	F	None	10Ap02Dy
HARVEY, Pat		20	M	Mechanic	10Ap02Dy
KILLEARNY, Pat		21	M	Mechanic	10Ap02Dy
COLLINS, Mary		20	F	None	10Ap02Dy
MCNULTY, M.		20	M	Mechanic	10Ap02Dy
MORTON, Bernice		19	F	None	10Ap02Dy
MCKEAN, James		22	M	Mechanic	10Ap02Dy
LINNON, Thos.		30	M	Mechanic	10Ap02Dy
Michael		20	M	Mechanic	10Ap02Dy
Patrick		12	M	Mechanic	10Ap02Dy
Peter		10	M	Mechanic	10Ap02Dy
SHANLY, Pat		20	M	Mechanic	10Ap02Dy
DELANY, Margt.		23	F	None	10Ap02Dy
SHARKEY, Bridget		09	F	Child	10Ap02Dy
STANTON, Michael		35	M	Mechanic	10Ap02Dy
MELBURN, Michael		40	M	Mechanic	10Ap02Dy
Michael	(S)	09	M	Child	10Ap02Dy
DINTY, Pat		30	M	Mechanic	10Ap02Dy
REES, Archd.		25	M	Mechanic	10Ap02Dy
CUMISKY, Mchl.		30	M	Mechanic	10Ap02Dy
MOLEON, John		50	M	Mechanic	10Ap02Dy
MOLEON, Martha	(D)	29	F	None	10Ap02Dy
Bridget	(D)	27	F	None	10Ap02Dy
Mary	(D)	16	F	None	10Ap02Dy
Patrick	(S)	25	M	Mechanic	10Ap02Dy
DENON, James		40	M	Mechanic	10Ap02Dy
LABDON, Ann		18	F	None	10Ap02Dy
CASSACK, Anna		16	F	None	10Ap02Dy
FARLY, Pat		12	M	None	10Ap02Dy
Mary		13	F	None	10Ap02Dy
ROYLER, Pat		17	M	Laborer	10Ap02Dy
KINNON, John		20	M	Laborer	10Ap02Dy
MCKEON, Pat		20	M	Laborer	10Ap02Dy
GAFFNEY, Pat		30	M	Laborer	10Ap02Dy
PURDY, Michael		25	M	Laborer	10Ap02Dy
ROAK, Wm.		28	M	Laborer	10Ap02Dy
BROWN, Pat		27	M	Laborer	10Ap02Dy
BURKE, U-Mrs.		30	F	None	10Ap02Dy
Thos.	(H)	30	M	Laborer	10Ap02Dy
BYRNS, Ellen		60	F	None	10Ap02Dy
MULLONY, John		30	M	Laborer	10Ap02Dy
BYRNES, John		26	M	Laborer	10Ap02Dy
Wm.		17	M	Laborer	10Ap02Dy
Martha		13	F	None	10Ap02Dy
James		20	M	Laborer	10Ap02Dy
Judy		21	F	None	10Ap02Dy
GREY, Jane		09	F	Child	10Ap02Dy
Lucy	(M)	30	F	None	10Ap02Dy
GALLAGHER, Pat		30	M	Laborer	10Ap02Dy
Bridget		19	F	None	10Ap02Dy
Anna		40	F	None	10Ap02Dy
MULLIGAN, Cathe.		40	F	None	10Ap02Dy
GORNY, Dennis		21	M	Laborer	10Ap02Dy
ROURKE, Thos.		21	M	Laborer	10Ap02Dy
TAYLOR, Patt		20	M	Laborer	10Ap02Dy
Cathe.		20	F	None	10Ap02Dy
LEASLEY, James		35	M	Laborer	10Ap02Dy
WALSH, Thos.		23	M	Laborer	10Ap02Dy
HACKETT, Jas.		32	M	Laborer	10Ap02Dy
WALSH, U-Mrs.		34	F	None	10Ap02Dy
HAKING, Margt.		20	F	None	10Ap02Dy
WALSH, Mary		07	F	Child	10Ap02Dy
Phillip		02	M	Child	10Ap02Dy
RYAN, Pat		24	M	Laborer	10Ap02Dy
Michl.		36	M	Laborer	10Ap02Dy
Margt.		24	F	None	10Ap02Dy
Lyda		10	F	None	10Ap02Dy
DAY, Peter		20	M	Laborer	10Ap02Dy
John		20	M	Laborer	10Ap02Dy
Pat		07	M	Child	10Ap02Dy
Mary		05	F	Child	10Ap02Dy
SAMPSON, Pat		18	M	Laborer	10Ap02Dy
CUMMINGS, Michael		29	M	Laborer	10Ap02Dy
Pat		22	M	Laborer	10Ap02Dy
COLLINS, Michael		22	M	Laborer	10Ap02Dy
U	(W)	26	F	None	10Ap02Dy
M.	(T)	24	F	None	10Ap02Dy
Joanna	(T)	15	F	None	10Ap02Dy
Michael	(B)	12	M	Laborer	10Ap02Dy
Collins	(B)	08	M	Child	10Ap02Dy
Charlotte	(T)	06	F	Child	10Ap02Dy
Sarah	(T)	04	F	Child	10Ap02Dy
Wm.	(B)	10	M	Child	10Ap02Dy
WEST, John		24	M	Laborer	10Ap02Dy
U	(W)	20	F	None	10Ap02Dy
Rose	(D)	01	F	Child	10Ap02Dy
GLASCON, Thos.		40	M	Laborer	10Ap02Dy
U	(W)	30	F	None	10Ap02Dy
Nelly	(D)	01	F	Child	10Ap02Dy
CASS, John		50	M	Laborer	10Ap02Dy
U	(W)	48	F	None	10Ap02Dy
John	(S)	24	M	Laborer	10Ap02Dy
Ellen	(D)	26	F	None	10Ap02Dy
Anna	(D)	22	F	None	10Ap02Dy
James	(B)	40	M	Laborer	10Ap02Dy
Patk.	(S)	20	M	Laborer	10Ap02Dy

NAMES OF PASSENGERS		AGE	SEX	OCCUPATIONS	DATE PORT SHIP
CASS, Kenny	(S)	17	M	Laborer	10Ap02Dy
Many	(S)	14	M	Laborer	10Ap02Dy
Joseph	(S)	11	M	Laborer	10Ap02Dy
Michael	(S)	09	M	Child	10Ap02Dy
Cathe.	(D)	22	F	None	10Ap02Dy
James	(S)	20	M	Laborer	10Ap02Dy
DARLING, Ed.		26	M	Laborer	10Ap02Dy
BROWN, Wm.		20	M	Laborer	10Ap02Dy
DUFFY, Bridget		20	F	None	10Ap02Dy
FITZPATRICK, Dennis		24	M	Laborer	10Ap02Dy
Mary		20	F	None	10Ap02Dy
FLYNN, Pat.		20	M	Laborer	10Ap02Dy
Rose		19	F	None	10Ap02Dy
BARRETT, Richd.		20	M	Laborer	10Ap02Dy
MARTIN, Geo.		20	M	Laborer	10Ap02Dy
REYNOLDS, Mary		19	F	None	10Ap02Dy
SCARREY, Thos.		35	M	Laborer	10Ap02Dy
U	(W)	30	F	None	10Ap02Dy
Margt.	(D)	04	F	Child	10Ap02Dy
LEYDON, Pat		24	M	Laborer	10Ap02Dy
BURKE, Michael		30	M	Laborer	10Ap02Dy
MCGLOIN, Cathe.		20	F	None	10Ap02Dy
Anna		20	F	None	10Ap02Dy
MCKANA, John		21	M	Laborer	10Ap02Dy
Owen	(P)	40	M	Laborer	10Ap02Dy
Pat	(B)	17	M	Laborer	10Ap02Dy
Rose	(T)	20	F	None	10Ap02Dy
Cathe.	(T)	13	F	None	10Ap02Dy
Many	(B)	12	M	Laborer	10Ap02Dy
REYNOLDS, Bridget		30	F	None	10Ap02Dy
GILCHRIST, John		25	M	Laborer	10Ap02Dy
MCDONAUGH, Ed.		20	M	Laborer	10Ap02Dy
CASSIDY, Anna		23	F	None	10Ap02Dy
Eliza		19	F	None	10Ap02Dy
CARNEY, Dennis		24	M	Laborer	10Ap02Dy
Mary		21	F	None	10Ap02Dy
CLEW, John		25	M	Laborer	10Ap02Dy
SMITH, Lacy		25	M	Laborer	10Ap02Dy
LEARY, John		25	M	Laborer	10Ap02Dy
NERNY, Martha		25	F	None	10Ap02Dy
ARMSTRONG, U-Mrs.		30	F	None	10Ap02Dy
Mary	(D)	09	F	Child	10Ap02Dy
John	(S)	06	M	Child	10Ap02Dy
Rose	(D)	04	F	Child	10Ap02Dy
Marla	(D)	02	F	Child	10Ap02Dy
Wm.	(H)	32	M	Laborer	10Ap02Dy
SCALLY, John		24	M	Laborer	10Ap02Dy
U	(W)	24	F	None	10Ap02Dy
Cathe.	(D)	04	F	Child	10Ap02Dy
DUNN, Dennis		24	M	Laborer	10Ap02Dy
DENMAN, Peter		24	M	Laborer	10Ap02Dy
NERMODY, Saml.		40	M	Laborer	10Ap02Dy
U	(W)	34	F	None	10Ap02Dy
Elizabeth	(D)	11	F	None	10Ap02Dy
George	(S)	07	M	Child	10Ap02Dy
Sophia	(D)	05	F	Child	10Ap02Dy
Mary	(D)	03	F	Child	10Ap02Dy
Hannah	(D)	02	F	Child	10Ap02Dy
John-T.	(S)	01	M	Child	10Ap02Dy
WEARING, Wm.		48	M	Laborer	10Ap02Dy
U	(W)	45	F	None	10Ap02Dy
LEO, James		21	M	Laborer	10Ap02Dy
PARKER, Wm.		20	M	Laborer	10Ap02Dy
SCOTT, Pat		27	M	Laborer	10Ap02Dy
Francis		26	M	Laborer	10Ap02Dy
KERNAN, Anna		20	F	None	10Ap02Dy
KILROY, Bridget		26	F	None	10Ap02Dy
CASTELLAN, Mary		40	F	None	10Ap02Dy
John	(S)	11	M	None	10Ap02Dy
Pat	(S)	08	M	Child	10Ap02Dy
Mike	(S)	07	M	Child	10Ap02Dy
Mary	(D)	03	F	Child	10Ap02Dy
Cathe.	(T)	35	F	None	10Ap02Dy
LUKE, Caroline		30	F	None	10Ap02Dy
Eliza	(D)	08	F	Child	10Ap02Dy
LUKE, Caroline	(D)	06	F	Child	10Ap02Dy
Ed.	(S)	05	M	Child	10Ap02Dy
REILLY, Michael		20	M	Laborer	10Ap02Dy
FARRELL, Anna		20	F	None	10Ap02Dy
FREELY, Phillip		34	M	Laborer	10Ap02Dy

JANE-AND-BARBARA 10 APRIL 1847

From Liverpool

NAMES OF PASSENGERS		AGE	SEX	OCCUPATIONS	DATE PORT SHIP
MORGAN, Charles		26	M	Farmer	10Ap02Of
Richard		24	M	Farmer	10Ap02Of
Bridget		20	F	Farmer	10Ap02Of
Bridget		22	F	Farmer	10Ap02Of
SHERIDAN, John		47	M	Farmer	10Ap02Of
U	(W)	40	F	Wife	10Ap02Of
Patt	(S)	14	M	None	10Ap02Of
Edward	(S)	13	M	None	10Ap02Of
Judy	(D)	11	F	None	10Ap02Of
Bridget	(D)	05	F	Child	10Ap02Of
Margaret	(D)	03	F	Child	10Ap02Of
Thomas	(S)	.00	M	Infant	10Ap02Of
RODGERS, James		30	M	Farmer	10Ap02Of
LOWNY, James		24	M	Farmer	10Ap02Of
NOWLAN, Laurence		20	M	Farmer	10Ap02Of
MCNAMARA, Nell		30	M	Farmer	10Ap02Of
U	(W)	25	F	Wife	10Ap02Of
Bridget	(D)	05	F	Child	10Ap02Of
Dennis	(S)	02	M	Child	10Ap02Of
James	(S)	.00	M	Infant	10Ap02Of
KENNEDY, Joseph		30	M	Farmer	10Ap02Of
John		30	M	Farmer	10Ap02Of
GALLAHER, John		26	M	Farmer	10Ap02Of
U	(W)	26	F	Wife	10Ap02Of
Peter		22	M	None	10Ap02Of
Paddy		20	M	None	10Ap02Of
Francis		18	M	None	10Ap02Of
Niell		14	M	None	10Ap02Of
Nancy		12	F	None	10Ap02Of
Nancy		20	F	None	10Ap02Of
CLARK, James		40	M	None	10Ap02Of
U	(W)	40	F	Wife	10Ap02Of
Bridget	(D)	20	F	Farmer	10Ap02Of
Pat	(S)	14	F	Farmer	10Ap02Of
Michael	(S)	12	F	Farmer	10Ap02Of
Owen	(S)	10	F	Farmer	10Ap02Of
Phillip	(S)	03	M	Child	10Ap02Of
Bridget	(D)	.00	F	Infant	10Ap02Of
WALSH, Mary		24	F	Farmer	10Ap02Of
Oliver	(S)	04	M	Child	10Ap02Of
Margaret	(D)	06	F	Child	10Ap02Of
James	(S)	02	M	Child	10Ap02Of
LYNCH, John		40	M	Farmer	10Ap02Of
Cath.	(W)	40	F	Wife	10Ap02Of
Judith	(D)	17	F	Farmer	10Ap02Of
John	(S)	13	M	Farmer	10Ap02Of
Honora	(D)	11	F	Farmer	10Ap02Of
Biddy	(D)	09	F	Child	10Ap02Of
Jane	(D)	07	F	Child	10Ap02Of
Thomas	(S)	05	M	Child	10Ap02Of
John	(S)	03	M	Child	10Ap02Of
Sally	(D)	02	F	Child	10Ap02Of
MCGRATH, John		40	M	Farmer	10Ap02Of
Mary	(W)	45	F	Wife	10Ap02Of
Pat	(S)	16	M	Farmer	10Ap02Of
John	(S)	11	M	Farmer	10Ap02Of
James	(S)	09	M	Child	10Ap02Of
Anne	(D)	07	F	Child	10Ap02Of
Thomas	(S)	05	M	Child	10Ap02Of

NAMES OF PASSENGERS		AGE	SEX	OCCUPATIONS	DATE PORT SHIP
MOGRATH, Rose	(D)	.00	F	Infant	10Ap020f
ROWLAND, Mary		36	F	Farmer	10Ap020f
MCCLUSKY, James		17	M	Farmer	10Ap020f
Cecily		13	F	Farmer	10Ap020f
James		11	M	Farmer	10Ap020f
Edward		02	M	Child	10Ap020f
Mary		01	F	Child	10Ap020f
ROWLAND, Sarah		17	F	Unknown	10Ap020f
Terry		13	M	Unknown	10Ap020f
Henry		11	M	Unknown	10Ap020f
Elizabeth		09	F	Child	10Ap020f
Michael		07	M	Child	10Ap020f
Mary		05	F	Child	10Ap020f
John		04	M	Child	10Ap020f
Ally		02	F	Child	10Ap020f
Ann		.00	F	Infant	10Ap020f
FURY, Peter		11	M	Farmer	10Ap020f
MCCLUSKY, Jos.		09	M	Child	10Ap020f
Peter		07	M	Child	10Ap020f
Maria		05	F	Child	10Ap020f
Judith		03	F	Child	10Ap020f
U		.00	U	Infant	10Ap020f
Rose-Ann		35	F	Unknown	10Ap020f
Cath-Gore.		35	F	Unknown	10Ap020f
MEALY, Mary		17	F	Unknown	10Ap020f
Henry		15	M	Unknown	10Ap020f
William		13	M	Unknown	10Ap020f
Robert		11	M	Unknown	10Ap020f
John		09	M	Child	10Ap020f
Margaret		07	F	Child	10Ap020f
Joseph		04	M	Child	10Ap020f
Edward		02	M	Child	10Ap020f
BREABY, Francis		31	M	Unknown	10Ap020f
Maria	(D)	12	F	Unknown	10Ap020f
Judy	(D)	11	F	Unknown	10Ap020f
Ester	(D)	09	F	Child	10Ap020f
Frank	(S)	07	M	Child	10Ap020f
Peggy	(D)	05	F	Child	10Ap020f
Edward	(S)	03	M	Child	10Ap020f
John	(S)	.00	M	Infant	10Ap020f
MCCLUSKY, Ellen		14	F	Unknown	10Ap020f
James		09	M	Child	10Ap020f
Edward		05	M	Child	10Ap020f
CONNELLY, M.		30	M	Unknown	10Ap020f
Mary	(W)	30	F	Wife	10Ap020f
Martin	(S)	02	M	Child	10Ap020f
Margaret	(D)	.00	F	Infant	10Ap020f
GLALEY, Thomas-M.		40	M	Unknown	10Ap020f
U	(W)	30	F	Wife	10Ap020f
Pat		23	M	Unknown	10Ap020f
Cath.		20	F	Unknown	10Ap020f
Peter		19	M	Unknown	10Ap020f
Thomas		15	M	Unknown	10Ap020f
Rosey		12	F	Unknown	10Ap020f
Ann		15	F	Unknown	10Ap020f
MCGATRICK, Nancy		50	F	Unknown	10Ap020f
Dennis	(S)	25	M	Unknown	10Ap020f
Bridget	(D)	20	F	Unknown	10Ap020f
Peter	(S)	18	M	Unknown	10Ap020f
James	(S)	16	M	Unknown	10Ap020f
Rosey	(D)	12	F	Unknown	10Ap020f
MCGALIN, Patt		30	M	Unknown	10Ap020f
U	(W)	25	F	Wife	10Ap020f
Rosey	(D)	10	F	Unknown	10Ap020f
Thomas	(S)	08	M	Child	10Ap020f
Hugh	(S)	06	M	Child	10Ap020f
Mary	(D)	04	F	Child	10Ap020f
Michael	(S)	.00	M	Infant	10Ap020f
James		25	M	Unknown	10Ap020f
U	(W)	25	F	Wife	10Ap020f
Thomas	(P)	45	M	Unknown	10Ap020f
CUMING, John		40	M	Unknown	10Ap020f
Ann	(D)	12	F	Unknown	10Ap020f
James	(S)	10	M	Unknown	10Ap020f
John	(S)	08	M	Child	10Ap020f

NAMES OF PASSENGERS		AGE	SEX	OCCUPATIONS	DATE PORT SHIP
CUMING, Sam.	(S)	06	M	Child	10Ap020f
Archy	(S)	04	M	Child	10Ap020f
Susan	(D)	02	F	Child	10Ap020f
BRODY, Peter		25	M	Unknown	10Ap020f
James		23	M	Unknown	10Ap020f
MCELLON, James		20	M	Unknown	10Ap020f
Ann		25	F	Unknown	10Ap020f
RING, Margret		20	F	Unknown	10Ap020f
Michael		29	M	Unknown	10Ap020f
Hugh		12	M	Unknown	10Ap020f
CROSSON, John		07	M	Child	10Ap020f
CRUMM, John		26	M	Unknown	10Ap020f

HOTTINGUER 10 APRIL 1847

From Liverpool

NAMES OF PASSENGERS		AGE	SEX	OCCUPATIONS	DATE PORT SHIP
BRADY, Francis		20	M	Laborer	10Ap02Bc
RILEY, Michael		34	M	Laborer	10Ap02Bc
HINSON, Hugh		60	M	Laborer	10Ap02Bc
Died-At-Sea					
Bridget	(W)	50	F	Wife	10Ap02Bc
Michael	(S)	23	M	Laborer	10Ap02Bc
Thomas	(S)	22	M	Laborer	10Ap02Bc
Died-At-Sea					
Stephen	(S)	18	M	Laborer	10Ap02Bc
Died-At-Sea					
Mary	(D)	16	F	Servant	10Ap02Bc
Bridget	(D)	12	F	Servant	10Ap02Bc
Died-At-Sea					
Margaret	(D)	09	F	Child	10Ap02Bc
James	(S)	07	M	Child	10Ap02Bc
SARGENT, Michael		25	M	Laborer	10Ap02Bc
Bridget		23	F	Servant	10Ap02Bc
Died-At-Sea					
JOHNSON, James		22	M	Laborer	10Ap02Bc
Died-At-Sea					
DONLON, Michael		24	M	Laborer	10Ap02Bc
John		28	M	Laborer	10Ap02Bc
Biddy		24	F	Servant	10Ap02Bc
Mary		19	F	Servant	10Ap02Bc
BURNS, Biddy		19	F	Servant	10Ap02Bc
NOLAN, Mary		20	F	Servant	10Ap02Bc
LONG, John		30	M	Laborer	10Ap02Bc
Thomas		24	M	Laborer	10Ap02Bc
Thomas		23	M	Laborer	10Ap02Bc
Ellen		22	F	Laborer	10Ap02Bc
Mary		24	F	Laborer	10Ap02Bc
Patrick		01	M	Child	10Ap02Bc
Died-At-Sea					
MCKANNA, Patrick		22	M	Laborer	10Ap02Bc
Catharine		21	F	Servant	10Ap02Bc
KENNY, John		56	M	Laborer	10Ap02Bc
Died-At-Sea					
John	(S)	12	M	Laborer	10Ap02Bc
Michael	(S)	10	M	Laborer	10Ap02Bc
Nelly	(W)	40	F	Wife	10Ap02Bc
Biddy	(D)	17	F	Servant	10Ap02Bc
Ellen	(D)	20	F	Servant	10Ap02Bc
Rose	(D)	14	F	Servant	10Ap02Bc
Catharine	(D)	01	F	Child	10Ap02Bc
Died-At-Sea					
BURKE, George		54	M	Laborer	10Ap02Bc
BOLAND, James		24	M	Laborer	10Ap02Bc
HENLEY, Thomas		20	M	Laborer	10Ap02Bc
KENNY, Michael		23	M	Laborer	10Ap02Bc
LAWLESS, James		12	M	Laborer	10Ap02Bc
Died-At-Sea					

NAMES OF PASSENGERS		AGE	SEX	OCCUPATIONS	DATE PORT SHIP	NAMES OF PASSENGERS		AGE	SEX	OCCUPATIONS	DATE PORT SHIP
Mathias		09	M	Child	10Ap02Bc	MCALLISTER, Margare	(D)	05	F	Child	10Ap02Bc
Died-At-Sea						Ann	(D)	02	F	Child	10Ap02Bc
LAWLESS, Mary	(M)	40	F	Servant	10Ap02Bc	CORCORAN, Martin		50	M	Laborer	10Ap02Bc
Died-At-Sea						Patrick	(S)	26	M	Laborer	10Ap02Bc
ONEAL, Ann		20	F	Seamstress	10Ap02Bc	Luke	(S)	19	M	Laborer	10Ap02Bc
FLINN, Mary		23	F	Servant	10Ap02Bc	Biddy	(D)	20	F	Laborer	10Ap02Bc
KELLY, Mary		21	F	Servant	10Ap02Bc	EARLEY, Thomas		40	M	Laborer	10Ap02Bc
CUFFE, Ellen		22	F	Servant	10Ap02Bc	Peggy	(W)	40	F	Wife	10Ap02Bc
SHEARN, Bridget		22	F	Servant	10Ap02Bc	Patrick	(S)	10	M	Laborer	10Ap02Bc
GALLAHER, Bridget		19	F	Servant	10Ap02Bc	LAVEL, James		35	M	Laborer	10Ap02Bc
MEHAN, Ellen		23	F	Servant	10Ap02Bc	KILROY, John		25	M	Laborer	10Ap02Bc
Ann	(D)	01	F	Child	10Ap02Bc	JONES, William		30	M	Laborer	10Ap02Bc
Owen	(H)	25	M	Servant	10Ap02Bc	DIMOND, Patrick		26	M	Laborer	10Ap02Bc
CONNOLLY, Bryan		25	M	Servant	10Ap02Bc	CORCORAN, Michael		25	M	Laborer	10Ap02Bc
GOLLAHER, Bryan		28	M	Servant	10Ap02Bc	DOHERTY, Hugh		35	M	Laborer	10Ap02Bc
Died-At-Sea						Biddy	(W)	30	F	Wife	10Ap02Bc
DERMOT, James		24	M	Servant	10Ap02Bc	Michael	(S)	10	M	Laborer	10Ap02Bc
John		30	M	Servant	10Ap02Bc	Nancy	(D)	07	F	Child	10Ap02Bc
MULLEN, James		25	M	Laborer	10Ap02Bc	Mary	(D)	04	F	Child	10Ap02Bc
John	(S)	02	M	Child	10Ap02Bc	Kitty	(D)	.06	F	Infant	10Ap02Bc
Mary	(W)	25	F	Unknown	10Ap02Bc	Died-At-Sea					
MCNICOLL, Jane		26	F	Servant	10Ap02Bc	BROGAN, John		21	M	Laborer	10Ap02Bc
CARMODY, John		27	M	Laborer	10Ap02Bc	HOLLAND, John		18	M	Laborer	10Ap02Bc
KENNEDY, Daniel		27	M	Laborer	10Ap02Bc	Died-At-Sea					
FURGUSON, John		19	M	Laborer	10Ap02Bc	CRANE, Anthony		25	M	Laborer	10Ap02Bc
MEHAN, Thomas		20	M	Laborer	10Ap02Bc	Died-At-Sea					
BLAKELY, Charles		25	M	Laborer	10Ap02Bc	CAVANAGH, Peter		19	M	Laborer	10Ap02Bc
CAIRN, James		26	M	Laborer	10Ap02Bc	MCDONALD, Michael		35	M	Laborer	10Ap02Bc
MULLIGAN, Patrick		24	M	Laborer	10Ap02Bc	Died-At-Sea					
Mary		19	F	Servant	10Ap02Bc	Honora	(W)	34	F	Wife	10Ap02Bc
FERGUSON, Ann		14	F	Servant	10Ap02Bc	Antony	(S)	04	M	Child	10Ap02Bc
Margaret		18	F	Servant	10Ap02Bc	Died-At-Sea					
RILEY, John		36	M	Servant	10Ap02Bc	Anna	(D)	01	F	Child	10Ap02Bc
Biddy	(W)	35	F	Servant	10Ap02Bc	WELSH, Peggy		22	F	Laborer	10Ap02Bc
Mary	(D)	08	F	Child	10Ap02Bc	John		27	M	Laborer	10Ap02Bc
Biddy	(D)	06	F	Child	10Ap02Bc	BARRETT, Thomas		23	M	Laborer	10Ap02Bc
Died-At-Sea						Thomas		24	M	Laborer	10Ap02Bc
Hugh	(S)	03	M	Child	10Ap02Bc	KELLY, John		20	M	Laborer	10Ap02Bc
Died-At-Sea						KENNEDY, John		20	M	Laborer	10Ap02Bc
James	(S)	01	M	Child	10Ap02Bc	MCGOVREN, Thomas		20	M	Laborer	10Ap02Bc
FURLONG, Patrick		27	M	Laborer	10Ap02Bc	MCKANNA, Patrick		20	M	Laborer	10Ap02Bc
MANNON, Mathew		26	M	Laborer	10Ap02Bc	FANNAN, John		35	M	Laborer	10Ap02Bc
FITZPATRICK, Frank		26	M	Laborer	10Ap02Bc	MCCABE, John		22	M	Laborer	10Ap02Bc
MCCABE, Terence		28	M	Laborer	10Ap02Bc	SULLIVAN, Catharine		16	F	Servant	10Ap02Bc
DONNELLY, Owen		30	M	Laborer	10Ap02Bc	RILEY, Sally		17	F	Servant	10Ap02Bc
John		12	M	Laborer	10Ap02Bc	MCMAHON, Catharine		17	F	Servant	10Ap02Bc
HUGHES, John		21	M	Laborer	10Ap02Bc	FANNON, Ellen		09	F	Child	10Ap02Bc
MCKUE, John		32	M	Laborer	10Ap02Bc	MURPHY, Margaret		15	F	Servant	10Ap02Bc
MURRAY, Christy		31	M	Laborer	10Ap02Bc	GROGAN, Nelly		19	F	Servant	10Ap02Bc
SHAILES, John		19	M	Laborer	10Ap02Bc	James		21	M	Laborer	10Ap02Bc
MARRAH, Bartle		19	M	Laborer	10Ap02Bc	Owen		28	M	Laborer	10Ap02Bc
MARTIN, Patrick		20	M	Laborer	10Ap02Bc	Died-At-Sea					
HENDERSON, Boyle		23	M	Laborer	10Ap02Bc	GRADY, Patrick		22	M	Laborer	10Ap02Bc
Anna		22	F	Laborer	10Ap02Bc	WALLIS, Mary		18	F	Laborer	10Ap02Bc
DOOLEY, Mary		30	F	Laborer	10Ap02Bc	KEENAN, Narrah		18	F	Laborer	10Ap02Bc
James	(S)	10	M	Laborer	10Ap02Bc	SHEA, Mary		20	F	Laborer	10Ap02Bc
DUFFE, Martin		30	M	Laborer	10Ap02Bc	John		20	M	Laborer	10Ap02Bc
SPELMAN, Michael		25	M	Laborer	10Ap02Bc	James		18	M	Laborer	10Ap02Bc
ROACH, Thomas		23	M	Laborer	10Ap02Bc	Sarra		25	F	Laborer	10Ap02Bc
Bridget		20	F	Laborer	10Ap02Bc	MARTIN, John		58	M	Laborer	10Ap02Bc
OATES, Patrick		26	M	Walter	10Ap02Bc	Owen	(S)	13	M	Laborer	10Ap02Bc
Mary	(W)	24	F	Wife	10Ap02Bc	FLINN, Owen		22	M	Laborer	10Ap02Bc
Ellen	(D)	04	F	Child	10Ap02Bc	MURPHY, James		27	M	Laborer	10Ap02Bc
Kitty	(D)	01	F	Child	10Ap02Bc	OHARE, Arthur		33	M	Laborer	10Ap02Bc
MCALLISTER, Daniel		50	M	Laborer	10Ap02Bc	Mary	(W)	33	F	Laborer	10Ap02Bc
Mary	(W)	45	F	Wife	10Ap02Bc	Ann	(D)	08	F	Child	10Ap02Bc
John	(S)	23	M	None	10Ap02Bc	Mary	(D)	06	F	Child	10Ap02Bc
Patrick	(S)	20	M	None	10Ap02Bc	Patrick	(S)	04	M	Child	10Ap02Bc
James	(S)	13	M	None	10Ap02Bc	James	(S)	01	M	Child	10Ap02Bc
Daniel	(S)	11	M	None	10Ap02Bc	WOODS, John		23	M	Laborer	10Ap02Bc
Nancy	(D)	20	F	None	10Ap02Bc	Michael		30	M	Laborer	10Ap02Bc
Mary	(D)	18	F	None	10Ap02Bc	Mary		30	F	Laborer	10Ap02Bc
Bridget	(D)	16	F	None	10Ap02Bc	Johanna		15	F	Laborer	10Ap02Bc
Died-At-Sea						KEENAN, James		35	M	Laborer	10Ap02Bc
Catharine	(D)	08	F	Child	10Ap02Bc	Ellen	(W)	40	F	Wife	10Ap02Bc

NAMES OF PASSENGERS		AGE	SEX	OCCUPATIONS	DATE PORT SHIP
KEENAN, William	(S)	14	M	Laborer	10Ap02Bc
Patrick	(S)	12	M	Laborer	10Ap02Bc
Thomas	(S)	09	M	Child	10Ap02Bc
Edward	(S)	06	M	Child	10Ap02Bc
MCDONALD, Richard		40	M	Laborer	10Ap02Bc
Ellen	(W)	40	F	Wife	10Ap02Bc
Died-At-Sea					
Johanna	(D)	18	F	Laborer	10Ap02Bc
Catharine	(D)	22	F	Laborer	10Ap02Bc
Catharine	(D)	.06	F	Infant	10Ap02Bc
Died-At-Sea					
Mary	(D)	05	F	Child	10Ap02Bc
Patrick	(S)	03	M	Child	10Ap02Bc
Died-At-Sea					
John	(B)	30	M	Laborer	10Ap02Bc
Richard	(S)	13	M	Laborer	10Ap02Bc
BOUSE, William		24	M	Laborer	10Ap02Bc
DUFFEE, Michael		30	M	Laborer	10Ap02Bc
KELLY, Thomas		59	M	Laborer	10Ap02Bc
Died-At-Sea					
CULLAN, William		24	M	Laborer	10Ap02Bc
SUMMERS, Robert		23	M	Laborer	10Ap02Bc
DOYLE, Edward		23	M	Laborer	10Ap02Bc
KENNEDY, James		23	M	Laborer	10Ap02Bc
Sarah		20	F	Laborer	10Ap02Bc
SOMERS, Mary		18	F	Laborer	10Ap02Bc
CARLETON, Hugh		24	M	Laborer	10Ap02Bc
PHILLIPS, Sarah		25	F	Servant	10Ap02Bc
DUANE, Elizabeth		19	F	Servant	10Ap02Bc
WELSH, Henry		25	M	Servant	10Ap02Bc
Catharine	(W)	23	F	Servant	10Ap02Bc
Catharine	(D)	01	F	Child	10Ap02Bc
James	(B)	17	M	Laborer	10Ap02Bc
CLARK, John		24	M	Carpenter	10Ap02Bc
CORR, Henry		40	M	Laborer	10Ap02Bc
Died-At-Sea					
BRADY, Patrick		30	M	Laborer	10Ap02Bc
Ellen		21	F	Laborer	10Ap02Bc
MCGILL, Margaret		30	F	Servant	10Ap02Bc
LARKIN, Bridget		26	F	Servant	10Ap02Bc
CONLAN, Alice		24	F	Servant	10Ap02Bc
JOHNSON, Ann		24	F	Servant	10Ap02Bc
MCDONALD, James		25	M	Laborer	10Ap02Bc
Sally	(W)	20	F	Laborer	10Ap02Bc
James	(S)	03	M	Child	10Ap02Bc
Patrick	(B)	28	M	Laborer	10Ap02Bc
Margaret	(L)	21	F	Laborer	10Ap02Bc
Mary	(N)	01	F	Child	10Ap02Bc
Died-At-Sea					
DUFFE, James		25	M	Laborer	10Ap02Bc
FLAHERTY, John		25	M	Laborer	10Ap02Bc
CAFFREE, John		40	M	Painter	10Ap02Bc
CHAMBER, William		40	M	Farmer	10Ap02Bc
CASSIDY, Patrick		19	M	Laborer	10Ap02Bc
MCFARLAND, William		19	M	Walter	10Ap02Bc
FREEHAN, Patrick		20	M	Walter	10Ap02Bc
RILEY, Thomas		20	M	Walter	10Ap02Bc
OWENS, Mary		19	F	Walter	10Ap02Bc
GAFFNEY, Michael		23	M	Laborer	10Ap02Bc
Biddy	(W)	20	F	Wife	10Ap02Bc
Mary	(D)	01	F	Child	10Ap02Bc
Died-At-Sea					
CONNOLLY, Catharine		17	F	Laborer	10Ap02Bc
Charles		18	M	Laborer	10Ap02Bc

CORNELIA 10 APRIL 1847

From Liverpool

NAMES OF PASSENGERS		AGE	SEX	OCCUPATIONS	DATE PORT SHIP
GOLLAGHER, John		28	M	Laborer	10Ap02Am
Catherine		26	F	Unknown	10Ap02Am
CARIBONE, Ann		28	F	Servant	10Ap02Am
LYNCH, Michl.		28	M	Laborer	10Ap02Am
HARRAN, John		28	M	Laborer	10Ap02Am
MCGLONE, Patk.		25	M	Laborer	10Ap02Am
MURPHY, John		20	M	Laborer	10Ap02Am
SWEENEY, Peggy		24	F	Servant	10Ap02Am
John	(S)	.00	M	Infant	10Ap02Am
KILFATHER, Owen		23	M	Servant	10Ap02Am
KENNY, Dennis		25	M	Servant	10Ap02Am
MCGOVERN, John		20	M	Servant	10Ap02Am
ARTHER, Alexn.		28	M	Miner	10Ap02Am
JOHNSTONE, John		20	M	Miner	10Ap02Am
ARTHER, Ann		25	F	Servant	10Ap02Am
JOHNSTON, Sarah		18	F	Servant	10Ap02Am
ARTHER, Benjn.		16	M	Laborer	10Ap02Am
SMITH, Patt		45	M	Laborer	10Ap02Am
Bridget	(D)	18	F	Servant	10Ap02Am
Catherine	(D)	10	F	Servant	10Ap02Am
Pat	(S)	08	M	Child	10Ap02Am
GOLLAGHER, John		20	M	Laborer	10Ap02Am
Mary		20	F	Servant	10Ap02Am
Catherine		18	F	Servant	10Ap02Am
NANGLE, Pat		30	M	Servant	10Ap02Am
MCDONOUGH, Peter		20	M	Laborer	10Ap02Am
CAREY, Mary		30	F	Servant	10Ap02Am
Ellen		20	F	Servant	10Ap02Am
FITZGIBBON, Judy		30	F	Servant	10Ap02Am
KENNEDY, Peggy		21	F	Servant	10Ap02Am
MCGORTY, Bridget		20	F	Servant	10Ap02Am
BARRY, Michl.		35	M	Laborer	10Ap02Am
Ellen	(W)	31	F	Servant	10Ap02Am
William	(S)	04	M	Child	10Ap02Am
Bessy	(D)	02	F	Child	10Ap02Am
Edmund	(S)	22	M	Miner	10Ap02Am
Cornelius	(S)	21	M	Miner	10Ap02Am
HENESSEY, Pat		25	M	Farmer	10Ap02Am
STREEHAN, John		20	F	Farmer	10Ap02Am
BUTLER, Mary		20	F	Servant	10Ap02Am
MURPHY, Bess		20	F	Servant	10Ap02Am
MCCARTY, Peggy		25	F	Servant	10Ap02Am
DESMOND, Ellen		20	F	Servant	10Ap02Am
OSTEIN, Pat		28	M	Laborer	10Ap02Am
Margt.	(W)	26	F	Wife	10Ap02Am
BRIEN, Dennis		25	M	Laborer	10Ap02Am
MURPHY, Mary		23	F	Servant	10Ap02Am
WHITE, John		23	M	Shoemaker	10Ap02Am
CONNELL, Margt.		23	F	Servant	10Ap02Am
DRISCOLL, Betsy		20	F	Servant	10Ap02Am
PYNE, Thomas		22	M	Miner	10Ap02Am
DARGIN, Abby		17	F	Servant	10Ap02Am
Martin		25	M	Laborer	10Ap02Am
HENESSEY, Charles		30	M	Farmer	10Ap02Am
James		20	M	Laborer	10Ap02Am
Bridget		02	F	Child	10Ap02Am
Died-At-Sea					
Johanna		01	F	Child	10Ap02Am
Died-At-Sea					
REA, Pat		30	M	Laborer	10Ap02Am
CONDON, Edmund		25	M	Laborer	10Ap02Am
Catherine		20	F	Servant	10Ap02Am
HAYES, Danl.		30	M	Miner	10Ap02Am
LYNCH, Michl.		19	M	Miner	10Ap02Am
CONDON, Pat		20	M	Groom	10Ap02Am

NAMES OF PASSENGERS	A G E	S E X	OCCUPATIONS	DATE PORT SHIP	NAMES OF PASSENGERS	A G E	S E X	OCCUPATIONS	DATE PORT SHIP
CONDON, Thomas	19	M	Groom	10Ap02Am	BUTLER, Pat	26	M	Laborer	10Ap02Am
ALEXANDER, Stephen	34	M	Gentleman	10Ap02Am	CANDERON, Pierce	18	M	Laborer	10Ap02Am
TOGHER, Wm.	25	M	Laborer	10Ap02Am	MAHON, Francis	22	M	Laborer	10Ap02Am
Thomas	22	M	Laborer	10Ap02Am	KEARNEY, John	20	M	Laborer	10Ap02Am
Jane	21	F	Laborer	10Ap02Am	LACEY, John	34	M	Laborer	10Ap02Am
MCGEE, Catherine	15	F	Servant	10Ap02Am	RYAN, Pat	18	M	Laborer	10Ap02Am
CONNELL, John	27	M	Gdnr	10Ap02Am	HEWITT, Wm.	18	M	Laborer	10Ap02Am
MACKIE, James	19	M	Laborer	10Ap02Am	DOWNEY, Joseph	45	M	Farmer	10Ap02Am
IVORY, William	31	M	Farmer	10Ap02Am	Eliza (W)	30	F	Unknown	10Ap02Am
JOYCE, Michl.	38	M	Laborer	10Ap02Am	Joseph (S)	11	M	Unknown	10Ap02Am
GAFFNEY, Michl.	24	M	Laborer	10Ap02Am	Michl. (S)	09	M	Child	10Ap02Am
DURDEN, Pat	20	M	Laborer	10Ap02Am	Stephen (S)	08	M	Child	10Ap02Am
Joseph	20	M	Laborer	10Ap02Am	John (S)	08	M	Child	10Ap02Am
DONAGHUE, John	25	M	Laborer	10Ap02Am	Eliza (D)	03	F	Child	10Ap02Am
GALLAGHAR, Danl.	20	M	Miner	10Ap02Am	FLANAGAN, Alice	23	F	Servant	10Ap02Am
U (W)	20	F	Wife	10Ap02Am	CLARK, Dennis	08	M	Child	10Ap02Am
Mary	20	F	Servant	10Ap02Am	MCHENRY, John	27	M	Laborer	10Ap02Am
MASTERSON, Edward	22	M	Laborer	10Ap02Am	Biddy (W)	28	F	Servant	10Ap02Am
MCCARL, Phil	20	M	Laborer	10Ap02Am	John (S)	02	M	Child	10Ap02Am
DUNN, James	19	M	Laborer	10Ap02Am	CLAFFEY, Joseph	30	M	Laborer	10Ap02Am
ROGERS, Michl.	16	M	Farmer	10Ap02Am	MULLONY, James	24	M	Laborer	10Ap02Am
Mary	24	F	Unknown	10Ap02Am	Michl.	19	M	Laborer	10Ap02Am
Bridget	15	F	Unknown	10Ap02Am	GORMAN, James	19	M	Laborer	10Ap02Am
FARRELL, Bridget	18	F	Servant	10Ap02Am	Pat (P)	60	M	Laborer	10Ap02Am
SMITH, Pat	21	M	Laborer	10Ap02Am	Died-At-Sea				
DONAGHAN, John	18	M	Laborer	10Ap02Am	Sarah (M)	50	F	Wife	10Ap02Am
MULLOY, James	30	M	Laborer	10Ap02Am	Rose (D)	13	F	Servant	10Ap02Am
LARAN, James	31	M	Laborer	10Ap02Am	Catherine (D)	09	F	Child	10Ap02Am
BRANNAN, Andrew	25	M	Laborer	10Ap02Am	John (S)	07	M	Child	10Ap02Am
MURPHY, Martin	25	M	Miner	10Ap02Am	Francis (S)	05	M	Child	10Ap02Am
DORNER, Bridget	22	F	Servant	10Ap02Am	KENNY, James	22	M	Laborer	10Ap02Am
KIERNAN, Bernard	24	M	Laborer	10Ap02Am	Laurence	20	M	Laborer	10Ap02Am
James	21	M	Laborer	10Ap02Am	MURRAY, John	30	M	Miner	10Ap02Am
CULLENAN, John	24	M	Shoemaker	10Ap02Am	Mary (D)	10	F	Unknown	10Ap02Am
WOODHEAD, Richd.	33	M	Butler	10Ap02Am	Catherine (D)	02	F	Child	10Ap02Am
LEE, Mary	20	F	Servant	10Ap02Am	Died-At-Sea				
OGDEN, James	34	M	Farmer	10Ap02Am	GALLAGHER, John	25	M	Miner	10Ap02Am
U (W)	41	F	Wife	10Ap02Am	Bridget	16	F	Servant	10Ap02Am
DAILEY, Patrick	25	M	Farmer	10Ap02Am	HANLY, Mary	19	F	Servant	10Ap02Am
Sally (W)	24	F	Wife	10Ap02Am	GARVEY, Pat	20	M	Laborer	10Ap02Am
Mary (D)	03	F	Child	10Ap02Am	Bridget	20	F	Servant	10Ap02Am
CLANCY, Catherine	17	F	Servant	10Ap02Am	GALLAGHER, Thos.	20	M	Miner	10Ap02Am
SHEARON, Charles	26	M	Servant	10Ap02Am	RILEY, Michl.	21	M	Laborer	10Ap02Am
KILLARNEY, Danl.	18	M	Laborer	10Ap02Am	GERATY, Danl.	36	M	Laborer	10Ap02Am
CURLY, John	18	M	Laborer	10Ap02Am	U (W)	30	F	Wife	10Ap02Am
KILFOYLE, Bessy	12	F	Servant	10Ap02Am	U	.00	U	Infant	10Ap02Am
CARRIBONE, John	24	M	Laborer	10Ap02Am	Margt. (D)	10	F	Unknown	10Ap02Am
MCCERRAN, Sarah	20	F	Laborer	10Ap02Am	Andw. (S)	08	M	Child	10Ap02Am
Catherine	14	F	Laborer	10Ap02Am	Garrett (S)	06	M	Child	10Ap02Am
KNAVESEY, Thomas	31	M	Laborer	10Ap02Am	SHANNON, Thos.	24	M	Farmer	10Ap02Am
Biddy	30	F	Unknown	10Ap02Am	U-Mrs. (M)	40	F	Unknown	10Ap02Am
Mary	24	F	Servant	10Ap02Am	Ann	22	F	Servant	10Ap02Am
CLEARY, Michl.	30	M	Laborer	10Ap02Am	Cathn.	18	F	Servant	10Ap02Am
Margt. (W)	28	F	Wife	10Ap02Am	COWEN, Bridget	24	F	Seamstress	10Ap02Am
John (S)	08	M	Child	10Ap02Am	FOY, James	24	M	Laborer	10Ap02Am
Margt. (D)	04	F	Child	10Ap02Am	REYNOLDS, Michl.	30	M	Farmer	10Ap02Am
Michl. (S)	.00	M	Infant	10Ap02Am	U (W)	27	F	Wife	10Ap02Am
DOOMELY, Bridget	16	F	Unknown	10Ap02Am	Bridget (D)	07	F	Child	10Ap02Am
QUINLAN, Andrew	20	M	Laborer	10Ap02Am	Pat (S)	04	M	Child	10Ap02Am
KILFOYLE, Mary	20	F	Servant	10Ap02Am	FOLEY, John	16	M	Servant	10Ap02Am
GATEBY, Robt.	56	M	Laborer	10Ap02Am	SULLIVAN, Dennis	21	M	Laborer	10Ap02Am
Margt. (W)	40	F	Wife	10Ap02Am	Ellen	19	F	Servant	10Ap02Am
Pat (S)	23	M	Laborer	10Ap02Am	ALENN, Edwd.	22	M	Laborer	10Ap02Am
Margt. (D)	18	F	Servant	10Ap02Am	MCGRATH, James	20	M	Laborer	10Ap02Am
REILLY, Mary	13	F	Servant	10Ap02Am	MCCARROLL, Bryan	30	M	Miner	10Ap02Am
CONNOR, Thos.	24	M	Laborer	10Ap02Am	Michl.	25	M	Miner	10Ap02Am
Jane	20	F	Servant	10Ap02Am	Margt.	22	F	Servant	10Ap02Am
DUGGAN, Charles	17	M	Miner	10Ap02Am	DUFFY, Bryan	25	M	Shoemaker	10Ap02Am
GOLLAGHER, John	21	M	Miner	10Ap02Am	U (W)	24	F	Wife	10Ap02Am
ODONNEL, Isabella	18	F	Servant	10Ap02Am	Mary	21	F	Unknown	10Ap02Am
LOFTUS, Danl.	30	M	Laborer	10Ap02Am	Owen (S)	.00	M	Infant	10Ap02Am
Owen	21	M	Laborer	10Ap02Am	MCCARL, Mary	26	F	Unknown	10Ap02Am
KENNY, Marla	24	F	Servant	10Ap02Am	MCGILL, John	33	M	Laborer	10Ap02Am
Bridget	20	F	Servant	10Ap02Am	U (W)	26	F	Unknown	10Ap02Am
KERRIVAN, Pat	23	M	Laborer	10Ap02Am	Peter (S)	05	M	Child	10Ap02Am

NAMES OF PASSENGERS		AGE	SEX	OCCUPATIONS	DATE PORT SHIP
MCGILL, Ann	(D)	03	F	Child	10Ap02Am
Pat	(S)	.00	M	Infant	10Ap02Am
GOSGROVE, John		25	M	Laborer	10Ap02Am
MARTIN, Owen		25	M	Laborer	10Ap02Am
RATTESTRON, Danl.		24	M	Laborer	10Ap02Am
Julia		16	F	Servant	10Ap02Am
OBRIEN, Thos.		26	M	Shoemaker	10Ap02Am
QUINCE, Wm.		23	M	Laborer	10Ap02Am
CONWAY, Bernard		26	M	Laborer	10Ap02Am
U	(W)	26	F	Wife	10Ap02Am
MCGOHAN, John		21	M	Laborer	10Ap02Am
MCCARTNEY, Francis		21	M	Laborer	10Ap02Am
MORAN, Mary		26	F	Servant	10Ap02Am
NOONAN, Lucy		20	F	Servant	10Ap02Am
BRENNAN, Bridget		20	F	Servant	10Ap02Am
NORTON, John		25	M	Miner	10Ap02Am
COLMAN, Pat		25	M	Miner	10Ap02Am
GILLIGAN, Wm.		20	M	Laborer	10Ap02Am
ROGERS, John		20	M	Laborer	10Ap02Am
DONOGHUE, Pat		20	M	Laborer	10Ap02Am
Frank		20	M	Laborer	10Ap02Am
Catha.		30	F	Servant	10Ap02Am
FITZSIMONS, Honor		20	F	Servant	10Ap02Am
RILEY, Mary		40	F	Servant	10Ap02Am
HIGGINS, Peter		22	M	Miner	10Ap02Am
MCCARTY, John		28	M	Miner	10Ap02Am
U	(W)	26	F	Wife	10Ap02Am
U		.00	U	Infant	10Ap02Am
James	(S)	04	M	Child	10Ap02Am
MCAULIFF, Honor		21	F	Servant	10Ap02Am
KELLY, Michl.		23	M	Laborer	10Ap02Am
COWLEY, Ned		30	M	Tailor	10Ap02Am
DEANE, Peter		20	M	Laborer	10Ap02Am
BANNAN, Peter		21	M	Laborer	10Ap02Am
John		20	M	Laborer	10Ap02Am
MCGRADY, James		22	M	Laborer	10Ap02Am
DERHAM, Mart.		20	F	Servant	10Ap02Am
NOBLE, Mark		20	M	Servant	10Ap02Am
KELLY, Bryan		18	M	Laborer	10Ap02Am
LANG, Mary		18	F	Servant	10Ap02Am
Died-At-Sea					
John		30	M	Laborer	10Ap02Am
U-Mrs.		29	F	Wife	10Ap02Am
HALE, Margt.		20	F	Servant	10Ap02Am
CLINCH, Patrick		30	M	Laborer	10Ap02Am
MURPHY, John		24	M	Laborer	10Ap02Am
Edd.		20	M	Laborer	10Ap02Am
Eliza.		18	F	Servant	10Ap02Am
FARRELL, Mary		15	F	Servant	10Ap02Am
MURRY, Rose		13	F	Servant	10Ap02Am
MCGARRY, Cathe.		16	F	Servant	10Ap02Am
SCALLY, Jas.		30	M	Laborer	10Ap02Am
EASTON, Wm.		20	M	Locksmith	10Ap02Am
KENNY, Danl.		24	M	Farmer	10Ap02Am
U	(W)	20	F	Wife	10Ap02Am
DANBY, Cathe.		27	F	Servant	10Ap02Am
MERVIN, Wm.		28	M	Miner	10Ap02Am
MCBRIESTY, James		25	M	Miner	10Ap02Am
MEHAN, John		20	M	Laborer	10Ap02Am
BYRNE, Sally		20	F	Servant	10Ap02Am
CUNNINGHAM, Biddy		17	F	Servant	10Ap02Am
Cormick		18	M	Servant	10Ap02Am
GALLAGHER, Thos.		22	M	Miner	10Ap02Am
Charles		24	M	Miner	10Ap02Am
Died-At-Sea					
CARL, James		24	M	Miner	10Ap02Am
SHIRLAN, John		24	M	Laborer	10Ap02Am
CARR, Danl.		25	M	Laborer	10Ap02Am
FAUL, Arthur		25	M	Miner	10Ap02Am
Pat.		27	M	Miner	10Ap02Am
MALONEY, Wm.		26	M	Laborer	10Ap02Am
DUFFY, Richd.		25	M	Farmer	10Ap02Am
THOMAS, Pat		20	M	Fsvnt	10Ap02Am
COWAN, Richd.		24	M	Laborer	10Ap02Am
SHEEDY, Dennis		24	M	Laborer	10Ap02Am
SHEEDY, Margt.		24	F	Unknown	10Ap02Am
CARY, Cathe.		26	F	Servant	10Ap02Am
KENNARD, Thos.		27	M	Laborer	10Ap02Am
CASSY, John		24	M	Laborer	10Ap02Am
CUNNINGHAM, Jas.		24	M	Laborer	10Ap02Am
RYLEY, Math.		18	M	Laborer	10Ap02Am
CUNNINGHAM, Mary		18	F	Servant	10Ap02Am
BARRY, Cathe.		18	F	Servant	10Ap02Am
CANNA, Henry		24	M	Servant	10Ap02Am
CAVANAGH, Pat		20	M	Laborer	10Ap02Am
James		21	M	Laborer	10Ap02Am
TIERNEY, Biddy		18	F	Servant	10Ap02Am
GILMOUR, David		24	M	Fsvnt	10Ap02Am
Atty.		16	M	Fsvnt	10Ap02Am
DUFFY, Mary		16	F	Servant	10Ap02Am
MCIVOY, Biddy		18	F	Servant	10Ap02Am
MOONEY, Cathe.		19	M	Mtmkr	10Ap02Am
CAVANAGH, Mary		20	F	Servant	10Ap02Am
FLYNN, James		30	M	Shoemaker	10Ap02Am
HELEY, Peter		25	M	Hatter	10Ap02Am
DRISCOLL, Michl.		25	M	Laborer	10Ap02Am
U	(W)	21	F	Wife	10Ap02Am
MOONEY, Hugh		25	M	Servant	10Ap02Am
DONLAN, John		24	M	Tailor	10Ap02Am
STANTON, Pat		24	M	Laborer	10Ap02Am
GROGAN, James		29	M	Laborer	10Ap02Am
Pat		20	M	Laborer	10Ap02Am
COOGAN, Francis		49	M	Laborer	10Ap02Am
U	(W)	49	F	Wife	10Ap02Am
DUFFY, Francis		30	M	Farmer	10Ap02Am
Wm.	(S)	03	M	Child	10Ap02Am
JACKSON, Jas.		20	M	Laborer	10Ap02Am
RICH, Pat		20	M	Laborer	10Ap02Am
Eliza		20	F	Unknown	10Ap02Am
Conn.		12	F	Unknown	10Ap02Am
John		10	M	Unknown	10Ap02Am
DUFFY, Ann		20	F	Unknown	10Ap02Am
Bridget		16	F	Unknown	10Ap02Am
CONLEY, Jas.		18	M	Laborer	10Ap02Am
WALSH, Jas.		18	M	Laborer	10Ap02Am
HARTNIGHT, John		50	M	Fmr-Fshmn	10Ap02Am
U	(W)	50	F	Wife	10Ap02Am
Wm.	(S)	22	M	Fmr-Fshmn	10Ap02Am
Thos.	(S)	21	M	Fmr-Fshmn	10Ap02Am
Margt.	(D)	23	F	Fmr-Fshmn	10Ap02Am
Andy	(S)	24	M	Unknown	10Ap02Am
Bessy	(D)	19	F	Unknown	10Ap02Am
Eliza	(D)	05	F	Child	10Ap02Am
LAUGHERY, Mihl.		24	M	Laborer	10Ap02Am
FARRELL, Pat		20	M	Laborer	10Ap02Am
Mary		20	F	Servant	10Ap02Am
Biddy		17	F	Servant	10Ap02Am
GRIMES, Pat		18	M	Laborer	10Ap02Am
Eliza		10	F	Servant	10Ap02Am
Pat		36	M	Miner	10Ap02Am
John		30	M	Miner	10Ap02Am
MCQUADE, Pat		19	M	Laborer	10Ap02Am
Pat		19	M	Laborer	10Ap02Am
BOLAN, Pat		24	M	Laborer	10Ap02Am
FARRELL, Margt.		19	F	Servant	10Ap02Am
Bridget		20	F	Servant	10Ap02Am
DOLAN, Mary		17	F	Servant	10Ap02Am
SWEENEY, Ellick		30	M	Laborer	10Ap02Am
Ann		23	F	Unknown	10Ap02Am
Ellick	(P)	60	M	Laborer	10Ap02Am
Joseph		22	M	Laborer	10Ap02Am
Thos.		20	M	Laborer	10Ap02Am
Pat		19	M	Laborer	10Ap02Am
ROURKE, Pat		11	M	Laborer	10Ap02Am
Rose		30	F	Servant	10Ap02Am
MALANNY, Chrisph.		30	M	Laborer	10Ap02Am
BERRIE, Margt.		18	F	Servant	10Ap02Am
GOLDING, Cathe.		24	F	Servant	10Ap02Am
SANDERSON, John		22	M	Laborer	10Ap02Am
MAHON, Wm.		29	M	Cooper	10Ap02Am

NAMES OF PASSENGERS	AGE	SEX	OCCUPATIONS	DATE PORT SHIP	NAMES OF PASSENGERS	AGE	SEX	OCCUPATIONS	DATE PORT SHIP
MCCABE, John	24	M	Laborer	10Ap02Am	TERRY, William	30	M	Laborer	10ap020a
CAFFURY, Ann	20	F	Servant	10Ap02Am	SULLIVAN, Edmond	32	M	Carpenter	10ap020a
FINN, Michl.	24	M	Laborer	10Ap02Am	BRIDE, James	30	M	Laborer	10ap020a
BRENAN, Crist.	24	M	Laborer	10Ap02Am	KEEF, Pat	40	M	Laborer	10ap020a
LYONS, John	26	M	Laborer	10Ap02Am	U (W)	35	F	Wife	10ap020a
EMMIT, Jas.	20	M	Laborer	10Ap02Am	POWELL, Michael	12	M	Laborer	10ap020a
GORMLEY, Ann	20	F	Servant	10Ap02Am	KEEF, Bartholomew	30	M	Laborer	10ap020a
EMMIT, Mary	20	F	Servant	10Ap02Am	Edward	35	M	Laborer	10ap020a
MCAVOY, Alexn.	20	M	Fsvnt	10Ap02Am	BURK, Darley	40	M	Laborer	10ap020a
WARD, James	20	M	Miner	10Ap02Am	ARROW, H.	22	M	Unknown	10ap020a
COMESKY, Rose	19	F	Servant	10Ap02Am	HACKETT, L.	25	M	Unknown	10ap020a
WARD, Bridget	18	F	Servant	10Ap02Am	John	20	M	Unknown	10ap020a
MOORE, Ann	17	F	Servant	10Ap02Am	Pat	28	M	Unknown	10ap020a
MCAVOY, Alice	22	M	Milliner	10Ap02Am	CUMMINGS, Pearse	27	M	Unknown	10ap020a
GILL, Michl.	20	M	Laborer	10Ap02Am	BRYAN, Pat	24	M	Unknown	10ap020a
CARNEY, Bessy	21	F	Servant	10Ap02Am	CANE, Edward	21	M	Unknown	10ap020a
DOYLE, Bridget	21	F	Servant	10Ap02Am	COX, Joseph	50	M	Cbtmkr	10ap020a
KELLY, Pat	21	M	Miner	10Ap02Am	Elizabeth (W)	50	F	Wife	10ap020a
MURPHY, Francis	24	M	Miner	10Ap02Am	Susan (D)	22	F	None	10ap020a
U (W)	21	F	Wife	10Ap02Am	Margarett (D)	20	F	None	10ap020a
Francis (S)	.00	M	Infant	10Ap02Am	Joseph (S)	18	M	Laborer	10ap020a
Nancy	19	F	Servant	10Ap02Am	Cathrine (D)	12	F	None	10ap020a
Cathe.	19	F	Servant	10Ap02Am	Robert (S)	10	M	None	10ap020a
Sally	18	F	Servant	10Ap02Am	John (S)	07	M	Child	10ap020a
Pat	12	M	Unknown	10Ap02Am	Joseph (S)	05	M	Child	10ap020a
Edwd.	09	M	Child	10Ap02Am	James (S)	03	M	Child	10ap020a
DAY, Owen	05	M	Child	10Ap02Am	John (S)	02	M	Child	10ap020a
					HALL, Ann	30	F	None	10ap020a
					PHILAN, Dennis	21	M	Laborer	10ap020a
					HEANEY, William	21	M	Laborer	10ap020a
					FOILE, John	21	M	Smith	10ap020a
ELLERSLIE 10 APRIL 1847					BRAMLEY, Pat	20	M	Laborer	10ap020a
					Mary	12	F	None	10ap020a
From Liverpool					MCKEE, James	20	M	Laborer	10ap020a
					REDDY, Thomas	21	M	Laborer	10ap020a
					DOGERTY, William	22	M	Laborer	10ap020a
					DOYLE, Matthew	30	M	Laborer	10ap020a
MORAN, Peter	20	M	Laborer	10ap020a	Joanna (W)	27	F	Wife	10ap020a
CADY, William	24	M	Laborer	10ap020a	Jerry (S)	01	M	Child	10ap020a
MARRS, Cathrine	30	F	Grocer	10ap020a	WALSH, Martin	24	M	Laborer	10ap020a
CADY, Mary	25	F	Grocer	10ap020a	GALLAHER, Pat	24	M	Laborer	10ap020a
HODGE, James	30	M	Mnre	10ap020a	Martin	18	M	Laborer	10ap020a
MCLAUGHLIN, Michael	24	M	Butcher	10ap020a	GILLESPIE, Michael	20	M	Laborer	10ap020a
Ann	20	F	Butcher	10ap020a	Martin	22	M	Laborer	10ap020a
MCSHURY, James	20	M	Smith	10ap020a	WALSH, Mary	20	F	None	10ap020a
John	18	M	Shoemaker	10ap020a	CORNEY, James	35	M	Laborer	10ap020a
Died-At-Sea					James	21	M	Laborer	10ap020a
KELLY, Mary	22	F	Shoemaker	10ap020a	Pat	21	M	Laborer	10ap020a
CAVANAGH, Cathrine	24	F	Shoemaker	10ap020a	CORMAN, Thomas	26	M	Laborer	10ap020a
OATS, Luke	28	M	Laborer	10ap020a	ROWAN, Thomas	21	M	Laborer	10ap020a
Ellen (W)	24	F	Wife	10ap020a	Bridget (W)	21	F	None	10ap020a
Dennis (S)	02	M	Child	10ap020a	Cathrine (D)	.00	F	Infant	10ap020a
Pat (S)	.00	M	Infant	10ap020a	MCASHFORD, Barney	40	M	Laborer	10ap020a
Dennis	16	M	Laborer	10ap020a	Mary (W)	35	F	Wife	10ap020a
MCCABES, Owen	21	M	Shoemaker	10ap020a	Ann (D)	13	F	None	10ap020a
TOOLE, Conner	30	M	Laborer	10ap020a	Rose (D)	12	F	None	10ap020a
CORCORAN, J.	21	M	Unknown	10ap020a	Frank (S)	11	M	None	10ap020a
CULIN, Pat	18	M	Unknown	10ap020a	Barney (S)	08	M	Child	10ap020a
MALONE, Thomas	25	M	Unknown	10ap020a	Ferris (S)	08	M	Child	10ap020a
Ann	20	F	Unknown	10ap020a	Susan (D)	03	F	Child	10ap020a
SMITH, John	18	M	Printer	10ap020a	LANGAN, P.	50	M	Farmer	10ap020a
SCANLON, Daniel	20	M	Draper	10ap020a	Margarett	24	F	None	10ap020a
CANE, John	25	M	Butler	10ap020a	KELLY, Patt	50	M	Laborer	10ap020a
Bridget	20	F	Unknown	10ap020a	Cathrine	20	F	None	10ap020a
Cathrine (M)	50	F	Unknown	10ap020a	CARRIGAN, Nancy	08	F	Child	10ap020a
COX, Betty	25	F	Unknown	10ap020a	Alley	03	F	Child	10ap020a
MCLAUGHLIN, Mary	20	F	Unknown	10ap020a	DONNELLY, James	30	M	Stone Mason	10ap020a
CAIN, Thomas	02	M	Child	10ap020a	Mary (W)	27	F	Wife	10ap020a
Timothy (P)	20	M	Butler	10ap020a	Alley (D)	11	F	Unknown	10ap020a
Bridget (M)	21	F	Unknown	10ap020a	Mary (D)	09	F	Unknown	10ap020a
HAGAN, William	39	M	Baker	10ap020a	Luke (S)	09	M	Unknown	10ap020a
BURK, Thomas	40	M	Laborer	10ap020a	Biddy (D)	05	F	Unknown	10ap020a
CANFORD, Pat	40	M	Laborer	10ap020a	Pat (S)	04	M	Unknown	10ap020a
U (W)	02	F	Wife	10ap020a	James (D)	02	M	Unknown	10ap020a
					Luke (S)	01	M	Unknown	10ap020a

NAMES OF PASSENGERS		AGE	SEX	OCCUPATIONS	DATE PORT SHIP
TOURNEY, Timothy		20	M	Laborer	10ap020a
MURPHY, Mary		19	F	None	10ap020a
GAYNEY, James		24	M	Butcher	10ap020a
CONNEY, Jeremiah		24	M	Laborer	10ap020a
GUANEY, Thomas		17	M	Seminarian	10ap020a
BUCKLY, J.		25	M	Laborer	10ap020a
Died-At-Sea					
Pat		24	M	Laborer	10ap020a
Died-At-Sea					
FALRY, M.		16	M	Unknown	10ap020a
MALONY, P.		25	M	Unknown	10ap020a
KENEDY, Steven		25	M	Unknown	10ap020a
Thomas		25	M	Unknown	10ap020a
GAVAN, Michael		20	M	Unknown	10ap020a
MCKEOWN, Patk.		27	M	Scer	10ap020a
Bessy	(W)	20	F	Wife	10ap020a
Thomas	(S)	.02	M	Infant	10ap020a
PACKINGHAM, Patk.		27	M	Carpenter	10ap020a
Ann	(W)	24	F	Wife	10ap020a
Mary	(D)	06	F	Child	10ap020a
Bessy	(D)	04	F	Child	10ap020a
Ann	(D)	02	F	Child	10ap020a
Kitty	(D)	.00	F	Infant	10ap020a
GARRIGAN, William		26	M	Laborer	10ap020a
Rose		23	F	None	10ap020a
Susan		39	F	None	10ap020a
VILLAS, Margaret		30	F	None	10ap020a
REELS, Cathrine		21	F	None	10ap020a
DODD, Phoeby		20	F	None	10ap020a
MORRIS, Bessy		18	F	None	10ap020a
RONEY, John		20	M	Laborer	10ap020a
LEDWICK, James		25	M	Laborer	10ap020a
Mary	(W)	20	F	Wife	10ap020a
U	(D)	.00	F	Infant	10ap020a
DEVINE, Bessy		24	F	None	10ap020a
FOGERTY, William		45	M	Laborer	10ap020a
Cathrine	(D)	11	F	None	10ap020a
Thomas	(S)	09	M	Child	10ap020a
MALONE, Thomas		20	M	Coachman	10ap020a
LINCH, John		27	M	Laborer	10ap020a
COLLINS, Thomas		29	M	Slater	10ap020a
Michael		31	M	Laborer	10ap020a
FAUGHTY, John		30	M	Laborer	10ap020a
GRUMBLY, William		46	M	Coachman	10ap020a
MCCOUGH, Pat		26	M	Laborer	10ap020a
KERWIN, James		28	M	Fisherman	10ap020a
CULLIN, Rose		28	F	None	10ap020a
PHILLIPS, Ann		25	F	None	10ap020a
DESMOND, Jeremiah		21	M	Laborer	10ap020a
Mary		20	F	None	10ap020a
LIDDY, Bridget		21	F	None	10ap020a
MCKAN, Ann		20	F	None	10ap020a
KENAN, Elizabeth		19	F	None	10ap020a
MALRONY, Pat		19	M	Laborer	10ap020a
REELY, Michael		20	M	Laborer	10ap020a
Mary		19	F	None	10ap020a
HUGHES, James		20	M	Laborer	10ap020a
SMITH, James		21	M	Laborer	10ap020a
BOYLE, John		21	M	Laborer	10ap020a
TRACY, Matthew		20	M	Laborer	10ap020a
GRIFFIN, Michael		20	M	Laborer	10ap020a
HEANEY, Thomas		40	M	Shoemaker	10ap020a
U	(W)	40	F	Wife	10ap020a
John	(S)	08	M	Child	10ap020a
Bridget	(D)	04	F	Child	10ap020a
OBRIEN, Cathrine		35	F	None	10ap020a
MCGILLOCK, Pat		21	M	Clerk	10ap020a
Barney		19	M	Clerk	10ap020a
John		22	M	Musician	10ap020a
CAINS, Daniel		19	M	Laborer	10ap020a
DAILY, Michael		31	M	Laborer	10ap020a
Rose		19	F	None	10ap020a
DUFFY, Betty		20	F	None	10ap020a
MYERS, Margaret		21	F	None	10ap020a
DAILY, Allen		22	M	None	10ap020a
SMITH, John		34	M	Shoemaker	10ap020a
Died-At-Sea					
CAMPBELL, Rosea		28	F	Dressmaker	10ap020a
BATE, Margaret		10	F	None	10ap020a
James		08	M	Child	10ap020a
Susan		06	F	Child	10ap020a
CAMPBELL, William		04	M	Child	10ap020a
Robert		02	M	Child	10ap020a
HEGAN, Pat		30	M	Laborer	10ap020a
Ann	(W)	24	F	Wife	10ap020a
Winford	(D)	02	M	Child	10ap020a
John	(S)	.00	M	Infant	10ap020a
CASSON, Pat		24	M	Weaver	10ap020a
CONNER, John		30	M	Slater	10ap020a
MCCARRANE, Elizabeth		22	F	None	10ap020a
Cornelius		30	M	Laborer	10ap020a
MCMALION, Edward		26	M	Laborer	10ap020a
Ann		28	F	None	10ap020a
GUNNING, Pat		40	M	Laborer	10ap020a
Rose-Ann	(W)	35	F	Wife	10ap020a
Mary	(D)	11	F	None	10ap020a
John	(S)	09	M	Child	10ap020a
Rose-Ann	(D)	06	F	Child	10ap020a
BARRETT, William		28	M	Clerk	10ap020a
GAFNEY, John		35	M	Laborer	10ap020a
Bridget	(W)	30	F	None	10ap020a
Jeremiah	(S)	03	M	Child	10ap020a
Eliza	(D)	01	F	Child	10ap020a
MCPHILIPS, Pat		25	M	Heckler	10ap020a
CARRASK, Joanna		60	F	Heckler	10ap020a
Jeremiah	(S)	26	M	Laborer	10ap020a
Daniel	(S)	24	M	Laborer	10ap020a
Timothy	(S)	21	M	Laborer	10ap020a
James	(S)	16	M	Laborer	10ap020a
Cathrine	(D)	12	F	None	10ap020a
Margaret	(D)	11	F	None	10ap020a
Daniel	(S)	10	M	None	10ap020a
Michael	(S)	08	M	Child	10ap020a
KENNEDY, Daniel		24	M	Laborer	10ap020a
BRUSNING, Michael		23	M	Laborer	10ap020a
Peggy		16	F	None	10ap020a
HANOLINS, Pat		23	M	Laborer	10ap020a
Jeremiah		22	M	Laborer	10ap020a
Honora		20	F	None	10ap020a
MURPHY, Mary		19	F	None	10ap020a
COLLINS, Michael		31	M	Laborer	10ap020a
MCMANUS, John		42	M	Laborer	10ap020a
CONNER, James		24	M	Stb	10ap020a
Mary		28	F	None	10ap020a
MARE, Michael		22	M	Laborer	10ap020a
U	(W)	22	F	Wife	10ap020a
Ann	(D)	02	F	Child	10ap020a
DONLON, Martin		27	M	Laborer	10ap020a
HINES, Teddy		23	M	Laborer	10ap020a
COLLINS, John		50	M	Mason	10ap020a
U	(W)	50	F	Wife	10ap020a
MCDONOUGH, Rose		18	F	None	10ap020a
CULLIN, Michael		30	M	Laborer	10ap020a
Garrett	(S)	11	M	Unknown	10ap020a
Patrick	(S)	09	M	Child	10ap020a
Peter	(S)	07	M	Child	10ap020a
Thomas	(S)	05	M	Child	10ap020a
Francis	(S)	02	M	Child	10ap020a
SLEVIN, Daniel		25	M	Laborer	10ap020a
CARRIGAN, Allen		26	M	None	10ap020a
James	(P)	50	M	Laborer	10ap020a
Farral		20	M	Laborer	10ap020a
Michael		17	M	Laborer	10ap020a
REYNOLDS, James		30	M	Laborer	10ap020a
BURK, Ellen		20	F	None	10ap020a
CAHILL, Thomas		25	M	Laborer	10ap020a
MCGOUGH, James		18	M	Laborer	10ap020a

ENGLAND 12 APRIL 1847

From Liverpool

NAMES OF PASSENGERS		AGE	SEX	OCCUPATIONS	DATE PORT SHIP
LEEKEN, Robert		23	M	Laborer	12Ap02Hg
ACHE, James		23	M	Mechanic	12Ap02Hg
HAY, Thomas		32	M	Mechanic	12Ap02Hg
GERHNAS, John		16	M	Laborer	12Ap02Hg
Ellen	(M)	40	F	None	12Ap02Hg
Berton		14	M	Laborer	12Ap02Hg
James		03	M	Child	12Ap02Hg
QUIRK, Thomas		26	M	Laborer	12Ap02Hg
BOYLAN, James		27	M	Laborer	12Ap02Hg
FLINN, William		28	M	Laborer	12Ap02Hg
SOALAN, Eduard		25	M	Laborer	12Ap02Hg
HORNOR, James		32	M	Laborer	12Ap02Hg
Joha.		34	F	None	12Ap02Hg
Mary		30	F	None	12Ap02Hg
DOULTON, Pat		30	M	Laborer	12Ap02Hg
Bessey	(W)	31	F	None	12Ap02Hg
Mary	(D)	07	F	Child	12Ap02Hg
Bridget	(D)	04	F	Child	12Ap02Hg
Edward	(S)	01	M	Child	12Ap02Hg
GADDY, Patt		30	M	Laborer	12Ap02Hg
Catharine		30	F	None	12Ap02Hg
CUSHICK, Catharine		69	F	None	12Ap02Hg
GADDY, Mary		06	F	Child	12Ap02Hg
Bridget		04	F	Child	12Ap02Hg
Jane		.03	F	Infant	12Ap02Hg
HENDERSON, Robt.		20	M	Mechanic	12Ap02Hg
SCOTT, Thomas		20	M	Laborer	12Ap02Hg
David		21	M	Laborer	12Ap02Hg
MCGOURRY, James		24	M	Laborer	12Ap02Hg
Catharine		23	F	None	12Ap02Hg
GLINN, Bridget-M.		20	F	None	12Ap02Hg
MCGARRY, Mary-Ann		20	F	None	12Ap02Hg
GERITY, Rose		22	F	None	12Ap02Hg
GAFFY, Mary-M.		24	F	None	12Ap02Hg
BARROT, John		24	M	Laborer	12Ap02Hg
Ann	(W)	25	F	Wife	12Ap02Hg
Thomas	(S)	02	M	Child	12Ap02Hg
DUFFY, Charles		40	M	Laborer	12Ap02Hg
MCGUIRE, James		25	M	Laborer	12Ap02Hg
Ellen		25	F	None	12Ap02Hg
DEVELLAN, Robt.		22	M	Laborer	12Ap02Hg
MULDOUN, Patt		21	M	Laborer	12Ap02Hg
GUINN, Peter		20	M	Laborer	12Ap02Hg
STEENSON, Wm.		43	M	Farmer	12Ap02Hg
John	(S)	17	M	Laborer	12Ap02Hg
Wm.	(S)	07	M	Child	12Ap02Hg
Thomas	(S)	05	M	Child	12Ap02Hg
FARRELL, James		27	M	Laborer	12Ap02Hg
Mary		27	F	None	12Ap02Hg
Ann		19	F	None	12Ap02Hg
Mary		02	F	Child	12Ap02Hg
CORLAND, John		25	M	Laborer	12Ap02Hg
Solomon		21	M	Laborer	12Ap02Hg
MCRANDLER, Mary-Ann		20	F	None	12Ap02Hg
TURNER, Margaret		21	F	None	12Ap02Hg
CAMPBELL, Sarah		21	F	None	12Ap02Hg
CASLAN, Margaret		20	F	None	12Ap02Hg
GLASIAN, Kitty		27	F	None	12Ap02Hg
ROYAN, Mary		26	F	None	12Ap02Hg
ANLEY, Margaret		22	F	None	12Ap02Hg
COAGAN, Mary		27	F	None	12Ap02Hg
MURRAY, Hugh		46	M	Laborer	12Ap02Hg
May	(W)	30	F	None	12Ap02Hg
Ann	(D)	04	F	Child	12Ap02Hg
Patt	(S)	01	M	Child	12Ap02Hg
MUNLEY, Patt		24	M	Laborer	12Ap02Hg
Meck		18	M	Laborer	12Ap02Hg
Bridget		07	F	Child	12Ap02Hg
MURPHY, John		20	M	Laborer	12Ap02Hg
Mary		12	F	None	12Ap02Hg
BROWN, Mick		30	M	Laborer	12Ap02Hg
MCANDREWS, Thomas		45	M	Laborer	12Ap02Hg
Mary		35	F	None	12Ap02Hg
WALSH, Bridget		30	F	None	12Ap02Hg
MCLAUGHAN, Christian		36	M	Laborer	12Ap02Hg
KELLY, Christian		30	M	Laborer	12Ap02Hg
BROWN, Owen		60	M	Laborer	12Ap02Hg
Patrick	(S)	18	M	Laborer	12Ap02Hg
TURNEY, Walter		19	M	Laborer	12Ap02Hg
CONNAH, Janey		09	F	Child	12Ap02Hg
LAWLESS, Martin		20	M	Laborer	12Ap02Hg
SMITH, James		20	M	Laborer	12Ap02Hg
CAMPBELL, Mary		20	F	None	12Ap02Hg
RILEY, Mary		40	F	None	12Ap02Hg
Judy		38	F	None	12Ap02Hg
TORMAY, Mary		11	F	None	12Ap02Hg
Catharine		10	F	None	12Ap02Hg
FAGAN, Bryan		24	M	Laborer	12Ap02Hg
BURNS, Bryan		27	M	Laborer	12Ap02Hg
FAGAN, Biddy		26	F	None	12Ap02Hg
SKEVERTON, Meck		24	M	Laborer	12Ap02Hg
Mary		23	F	None	12Ap02Hg
BRYAN, Con		30	M	Laborer	12Ap02Hg
Mary	(W)	20	F	Wife	12Ap02Hg
John	(S)	02	M	Child	12Ap02Hg
LEAMEY, Thomas		19	M	Laborer	12Ap02Hg
ROYAN, Patt		19	M	Laborer	12Ap02Hg
GLICON, Patt		26	M	Laborer	12Ap02Hg
BRYAN, John		21	M	Laborer	12Ap02Hg
DWIRE, Thomas		24	M	Laborer	12Ap02Hg
BURKE, Michell		29	M	Laborer	12Ap02Hg
GLICON, Patt		26	M	Laborer	12Ap02Hg
ROYAN, John		21	M	Laborer	12Ap02Hg
DWIRE, Thomas		24	M	Laborer	12Ap02Hg
GLICON, Michell		29	M	Laborer	12Ap02Hg
BURKE, Michell		29	M	Laborer	12Ap02Hg
James		25	M	Laborer	12Ap02Hg
BREAD, Robert		23	M	Laborer	12Ap02Hg
DWIRE, John		27	M	Laborer	12Ap02Hg
FANAN, Thomas		16	M	Laborer	12Ap02Hg
John		21	M	Laborer	12Ap02Hg
John	(P)	48	M	Laborer	12Ap02Hg
Margaret	(M)	46	F	None	12Ap02Hg
Michel		26	M	Laborer	12Ap02Hg
RENDLES, Mary-Ann		27	F	None	12Ap02Hg
FANAN, Ellen		24	F	None	12Ap02Hg
John		02	M	Child	12Ap02Hg
Patt		01	M	Child	12Ap02Hg
KERNIGAN, Michel		20	M	Laborer	12Ap02Hg
Ambrose	(P)	49	M	Laborer	12Ap02Hg
Mary	(M)	44	F	None	12Ap02Hg
Margaret		18	F	None	12Ap02Hg
Ambrose		14	M	Laborer	12Ap02Hg
Patt		12	M	None	12Ap02Hg
Catharine		10	F	None	12Ap02Hg
Biddy		07	F	Child	12Ap02Hg
Ann		02	F	Child	12Ap02Hg
Eliza		.10	F	Infant	12Ap02Hg
MCCARTY, Patt		24	M	Laborer	12Ap02Hg
Michel		12	M	Laborer	12Ap02Hg
COUGHAN, John		23	M	Laborer	12Ap02Hg
WILLIAMS, Martin		24	M	Laborer	12Ap02Hg
FLARTY, James		26	M	Laborer	12Ap02Hg
Catharine		23	F	None	12Ap02Hg
Biddy		24	F	None	12Ap02Hg
TROY, Rose		24	F	None	12Ap02Hg
BOYNE, Bartley		25	M	Laborer	12Ap02Hg
MORAN, Thomas		24	M	Laborer	12Ap02Hg
Pritchard		23	M	Laborer	12Ap02Hg
FARRELL, Mary-Ann		19	F	None	12Ap02Hg

NAMES OF PASSENGERS		AGE	SEX	OCCUPATIONS	DATE PORT SHIP
MOLY, Mary		19	F	None	12Ap02Hg
KEENAN, Mary-Ann		19	F	None	12Ap02Hg
ONEALE, Margaret		22	F	None	12Ap02Hg
HINNSEY, Milhal		24	F	None	12Ap02Hg
Thomas		60	M	Laborer	12Ap02Hg
LANLY, Thomas		23	M	Laborer	12Ap02Hg
ENGLISH, Dennis		24	M	Laborer	12Ap02Hg
MANANY, Mary		22	F	None	12Ap02Hg
Mary		22	F	None	12Ap02Hg
ROGAN, Catharine		25	F	None	12Ap02Hg
FARRELL, Mathew		40	M	Laborer	12Ap02Hg
Sarah		30	F	None	12Ap02Hg
DOUGHERTY, Catharine		30	F	None	12Ap02Hg
FARRELL, Martin		12	M	Laborer	12Ap02Hg
CULYON, Henry		36	M	Laborer	12Ap02Hg
WALSH, Luke		36	M	Laborer	12Ap02Hg
CULYAN, John		18	M	Laborer	12Ap02Hg
WALSH, Jane		14	F	None	12Ap02Hg
CULYAN, Margaret		09	F	Child	12Ap02Hg
MCGOWAN, James		28	M	Laborer	12Ap02Hg
Catharine		24	F	None	12Ap02Hg
Catharine		18	F	None	12Ap02Hg
FINNEY, Ann		26	F	Unknown	12Ap02Hg
NUN, Michael		12	M	Unknown	12Ap02Hg
MURRAY, John		25	M	Laborer	12Ap02Hg
FINN, Catharine		20	F	None	12Ap02Hg
Ann		19	F	None	12Ap02Hg
Peggy		33	F	None	12Ap02Hg
JENNIGAN, Honora		26	F	None	12Ap02Hg
Margaret	(D)	02	F	Child	12Ap02Hg
Horner	(S)	.06	M	Infant	12Ap02Hg
CONNLEY, Bridget		40	F	None	12Ap02Hg
Mary	(D)	18	F	None	12Ap02Hg
William	(S)	16	M	Laborer	12Ap02Hg
Bridget	(D)	11	F	None	12Ap02Hg
Ellen	(D)	10	F	None	12Ap02Hg
Homer	(S)	06	M	Child	12Ap02Hg
Catharine	(D)	06	M	Child	12Ap02Hg
GORAN, Mary		42	F	None	12Ap02Hg
Catharine	(D)	11	F	None	12Ap02Hg
SANDS, Ann		15	F	None	12Ap02Hg
CONLEY, John		50	M	Laborer	12Ap02Hg
DONNELL, Thomas		24	M	Laborer	12Ap02Hg
DONAGHUE, Mary		20	F	None	12Ap02Hg
BURKE, Patt		24	M	Laborer	12Ap02Hg
FANDE, Martin		20	M	Laborer	12Ap02Hg
DONOUGHU, Francis		33	M	Mechanic	12Ap02Hg
Honor		33	F	None	12Ap02Hg
COGAN, Betty		20	F	None	12Ap02Hg
COYNE, Winny		20	F	None	12Ap02Hg
DOUGHAN, Mary		07	F	Child	12Ap02Hg
Bridget		05	F	Child	12Ap02Hg
Mathew		01	M	Child	12Ap02Hg
REYNEY, Patt		25	M	Laborer	12Ap02Hg
Catharine		25	F	None	12Ap02Hg
DONOUGHAN, Martin		20	M	Laborer	12Ap02Hg
Mary		20	F	None	12Ap02Hg
DOUGTHER, Antony		30	M	Laborer	12Ap02Hg
Mary		32	F	None	12Ap02Hg
James		26	M	Laborer	12Ap02Hg
Mary		03	F	Child	12Ap02Hg
FLYN, Daniel		26	M	Laborer	12Ap02Hg
SMITH, Wm.		30	M	Laborer	12Ap02Hg
HEBERAN, Patt		36	M	Laborer	12Ap02Hg
LOGAN, Michael		26	M	Laborer	12Ap02Hg
TEWART, James		20	M	Laborer	12Ap02Hg
MULLAN, Peter		34	M	Laborer	12Ap02Hg
WARDE, Peter		19	M	Laborer	12Ap02Hg
MULLAN, Catharine		23	F	None	12Ap02Hg
KINLAN, Mary		23	F	None	12Ap02Hg
MULLAN, Patt		02	M	Child	12Ap02Hg
GRAMMAGAN, William		20	M	Laborer	12Ap02Hg
KELLY, Michael		20	M	Laborer	12Ap02Hg
William		48	M	Laborer	12Ap02Hg
Biddy		07	F	Child	12Ap02Hg
KELLY, Mary		09	F	Child	12Ap02Hg
Michael		60	M	Laborer	12Ap02Hg
Peggy		60	F	None	12Ap02Hg
Michael		23	M	Laborer	12Ap02Hg
Mary		20	F	None	12Ap02Hg
Bridget		02	F	Child	12Ap02Hg
FANDE, Ellen		25	F	None	12Ap02Hg
COLLINS, Mary		20	F	None	12Ap02Hg
Catharine		17	F	None	12Ap02Hg
RUDDY, Patrick		20	M	Laborer	12Ap02Hg
PARRILL, Ciddy		40	F	None	12Ap02Hg
RUDDY, Mary		15	F	None	12Ap02Hg
Sarah		16	F	None	12Ap02Hg
Michael		12	M	Laborer	12Ap02Hg
Thomas		10	M	Laborer	12Ap02Hg
John		10	M	Laborer	12Ap02Hg
LEFTARS, Michael		50	M	Laborer	12Ap02Hg
Biddy	(W)	40	F	None	12Ap02Hg
Patt	(S)	10	M	None	12Ap02Hg
Mary	(D)	08	F	Child	12Ap02Hg
MUNDY, Michael		40	M	Laborer	12Ap02Hg
RUDDY, Catharine		40	F	None	12Ap02Hg
BURK, Thomas		30	M	Laborer	12Ap02Hg
MINTY, Biddy		18	F	None	12Ap02Hg
GANLARAN, Peter		31	M	Laborer	12Ap02Hg
Meck		33	M	Farmer	12Ap02Hg
Fanny		25	F	None	12Ap02Hg
WATERS, Michal		20	M	Laborer	12Ap02Hg
Patt		26	M	Laborer	12Ap02Hg
LANARD, John		26	M	Laborer	12Ap02Hg
Ann		26	F	None	12Ap02Hg
GARRADY, Michael		16	M	Laborer	12Ap02Hg
Catharine		18	F	None	12Ap02Hg
WATERS, Ann		27	F	None	12Ap02Hg
MACK, James		40	M	Laborer	12Ap02Hg
BROWN, Thomas		30	M	Laborer	12Ap02Hg
John		20	M	Laborer	12Ap02Hg
CALLINAN, Patt		30	M	Laborer	12Ap02Hg
BROWN, Mark		50	M	Laborer	12Ap02Hg
Andy	(S)	26	M	Laborer	12Ap02Hg
Biddy	(D)	12	F	None	12Ap02Hg
May	(D)	16	F	None	12Ap02Hg
Peggy	(W)	50	F	Wife	12Ap02Hg
REGAN, Biddy		16	F	None	12Ap02Hg
MCMYNER, Thomas		22	M	Laborer	12Ap02Hg
Joseph		24	M	Laborer	12Ap02Hg
MURRAY, Mich		19	M	Laborer	12Ap02Hg
Patt		22	M	Laborer	12Ap02Hg
HEDDY, Hugh		21	M	Laborer	12Ap02Hg
William		23	M	Laborer	12Ap02Hg
MALY, Richard		23	M	Laborer	12Ap02Hg
GAVAN, William		21	M	Laborer	12Ap02Hg
DONLAN, John		22	M	Laborer	12Ap02Hg
Teddy		23	M	Laborer	12Ap02Hg
WRIGHT, Thomas		23	M	Laborer	12Ap02Hg
MURRAY, John		20	M	Laborer	12Ap02Hg
MCLOUGHLIN, Michael		25	M	Laborer	12Ap02Hg
John		29	M	Laborer	12Ap02Hg
Thomas		22	M	Laborer	12Ap02Hg
Catharine		17	F	None	12Ap02Hg
MCDONALD, Michael		23	M	Laborer	12Ap02Hg
Henry	(P)	50	M	Laborer	12Ap02Hg
Martin	(S)	25	M	Laborer	12Ap02Hg
Nelly	(D)	20	F	None	12Ap02Hg
HAGGERTY, Martin		24	M	Laborer	12Ap02Hg
John		25	M	Laborer	12Ap02Hg
MCDONALD, Biddy		23	F	None	12Ap02Hg
ELLIS, George		23	M	Mechanic	12Ap02Hg
HICKS, Thomas		23	M	Mechanic	12Ap02Hg
SMITH, Stephen		45	M	Mechanic	12Ap02Hg
Herriot		35	F	None	12Ap02Hg
SLOANE, Robert		35	M	Laborer	12Ap02Hg
TAYLOR, Mary		32	F	None	12Ap02Hg
Emma		12	F	None	12Ap02Hg
MORAN, Thomas		21	M	Laborer	12Ap02Hg

NAMES OF PASSENGERS		A G E	S E X	OCCUPATIONS	DATE PORT SHIP
JOHNSON, Bark.		31	M	Schm	12Ap02Hg
TAYLOR, Wm.		52	M	Mechanic	12Ap02Hg
TODD, Richard		22	M	Mechanic	12Ap02Hg
HICK, Trusen		24	M	Mechanic	12Ap02Hg
ELLIS, John		25	M	Mechanic	12Ap02Hg
SEPT, James-Robert		25	M	Mechanic	12Ap02Hg
ROWLAND, Benj.		31	M	Mechanic	12Ap02Hg
PEARCHAM, George		22	M	Mechanic	12Ap02Hg
BEHATTON, Thomas		25	M	Farmer	12Ap02Hg
FOX, Edward		24	M	Mechanic	12Ap02Hg
HORNER, Edward		25	M	Mechanic	12Ap02Hg
HOSHMER, William		65	M	Mechanic	12Ap02Hg
BLUTE, Patt		35	M	Farmer	12Ap02Hg
Biddy	(W)	20	F	Wife	12Ap02Hg
May	(D)	01	F	Child	12Ap02Hg
Sally	(D)	.02	F	Infant	12Ap02Hg

QUEEN OF THE WEST 12 APRIL 1847

From Liverpool

NAMES OF PASSENGERS		A G E	S E X	OCCUPATIONS	DATE PORT SHIP
DOWNWARD, John		50	M	Mechanic	12Ap02Cn
Ann	(W)	50	F	None	12Ap02Cn
Eliza	(D)	11	F	None	12Ap02Cn
Mary	(D)	07	F	Child	12Ap02Cn
Ann	(D)	06	F	Child	12Ap02Cn
Jane	(D)	04	F	Child	12Ap02Cn
John	(S)	02	M	Child	12Ap02Cn
HIND, U		35	M	Laborer	12Ap02Cn
U	(W)	00	F	None	12Ap02Cn
Wm.		10	M	None	12Ap02Cn
Saml.		05	M	Child	12Ap02Cn
LEWIS, Harris		25	M	Laborer	12Ap02Cn
Mary		24	F	None	12Ap02Cn
Eliza		18	F	None	12Ap02Cn
STONER, Thos.		25	M	Laborer	12Ap02Cn
U	(W)	26	F	Wife	12Ap02Cn
SMITH, Jas.		24	M	Laborer	12Ap02Cn
CARTER, U		18	F	None	12Ap02Cn
BURN, Hugh		40	M	Laborer	12Ap02Cn
CONINGHAM, Margt.		25	F	None	12Ap02Cn
MULVANY, Edw.		21	M	Laborer	12Ap02Cn
WILLIAMS, Wm.		28	M	Laborer	12Ap02Cn
MANAGAN, Cathe.		20	F	None	12Ap02Cn
DEDDY, And.		30	M	Laborer	12Ap02Cn
Bridget		30	F	None	12Ap02Cn
SMITH, John		25	M	Laborer	12Ap02Cn
GALLAGHER, Matt.		20	M	Laborer	12Ap02Cn
DORAN, John		18	M	Laborer	12Ap02Cn
MALLAGH, Wm.		20	M	Laborer	12Ap02Cn
RILEY, Bernd.		35	M	Laborer	12Ap02Cn
Bessey		20	F	None	12Ap02Cn
SMITH, Chas.		25	M	Laborer	12Ap02Cn
WILDE, Jas.		40	M	Laborer	12Ap02Cn
LEES, Ed.		30	M	Laborer	12Ap02Cn
CRAWDER, Richd.		24	M	Laborer	12Ap02Cn
Betty	(W)	24	F	Wife	12Ap02Cn
Mary-Ann	(D)	01	F	Child	12Ap02Cn
TAYLOR, Sally		40	F	None	12Ap02Cn
John	(S)	09	M	Child	12Ap02Cn
LACKEY, John		22	M	Laborer	12Ap02Cn
RILEY, Pat		18	M	Laborer	12Ap02Cn
SMITH, Bridget		16	F	None	12Ap02Cn
Ann		16	F	None	12Ap02Cn
Peter		20	M	Laborer	12Ap02Cn
Phillip		20	M	Laborer	12Ap02Cn
Mary		20	F	None	12Ap02Cn
Thos.		20	M	Laborer	12Ap02Cn
DOYLE, Jas.		32	M	Laborer	12Ap02Cn

NAMES OF PASSENGERS		A G E	S E X	OCCUPATIONS	DATE PORT SHIP
DOYLE, Pat		30	M	Laborer	12Ap02Cn
Cathe.		20	F	None	12Ap02Cn
Luke		22	M	Laborer	12Ap02Cn
CANA, Michael		20	M	Laborer	12Ap02Cn
Francis		20	M	Laborer	12Ap02Cn
Martha		23	F	None	12Ap02Cn
GEGAN, James		13	M	Laborer	12Ap02Cn
Luke		11	M	Laborer	12Ap02Cn
RISLAGHAN, Bridget		28	F	None	12Ap02Cn
John		29	M	Laborer	12Ap02Cn
MCGIVAN, Phillip		40	M	Laborer	12Ap02Cn
HIGGARTY, Candy		46	M	Laborer	12Ap02Cn
ONIEL, Michael		41	M	Laborer	12Ap02Cn
Eliza	(W)	30	F	None	12Ap02Cn
Jas.	(S)	04	M	Child	12Ap02Cn
John	(S)	01	M	Child	12Ap02Cn
MCGINLEY, Pat		20	M	Laborer	12Ap02Cn
HARLEY, Ed.		26	M	Laborer	12Ap02Cn
Jas.		20	M	Laborer	12Ap02Cn
BERIN, Jas.		20	M	Laborer	12Ap02Cn
Hannibal		25	M	Laborer	12Ap02Cn
GARTAGHAN, John		25	M	Laborer	12Ap02Cn
GARAH, John		20	M	Laborer	12Ap02Cn
FISHER, John		20	M	Laborer	12Ap02Cn
RILEY, Michall		18	M	Laborer	12Ap02Cn
Jas.		20	M	Laborer	12Ap02Cn
Ellen		20	F	None	12Ap02Cn
NICHOLSON, John		20	M	Laborer	12Ap02Cn
GREGSTON, Ed.		20	M	Laborer	12Ap02Cn
ELLIOT, Rbt.		22	M	Laborer	12Ap02Cn
BERRY, Thos.		25	M	Laborer	12Ap02Cn
MURPHY, John		20	M	Laborer	12Ap02Cn
CONNORS, John		20	M	Laborer	12Ap02Cn
MCQUADE, Cathe.		20	F	None	12Ap02Cn
QUIN, Mary		20	F	None	12Ap02Cn
FEGAN, Pat		20	M	Laborer	12Ap02Cn
CADY, Mary		20	F	None	12Ap02Cn
Peggy		20	F	None	12Ap02Cn
FITZPATRICK, Honora		20	F	None	12Ap02Cn
Joe		20	M	Laborer	12Ap02Cn
GREGGY, Cathe.		20	F	None	12Ap02Cn
QUINLAN, Biddy		10	F	None	12Ap02Cn
DOOLEY, Judy		20	F	None	12Ap02Cn
WATSON, Honora		20	F	None	12Ap02Cn
KENEDY, Mick		18	M	Laborer	12Ap02Cn
DILLON, Peggy		20	F	None	12Ap02Cn
RYAN, Tom		20	M	Laborer	12Ap02Cn
NOLAN, Essey		20	F	None	12Ap02Cn
FITZSIMMONS, Charles		14	M	Laborer	12Ap02Cn
DOLAN, Alexn.		20	M	Laborer	12Ap02Cn
BURN, John		20	M	Laborer	12Ap02Cn
Margt.		20	F	None	12Ap02Cn
Michl.		08	M	Child	12Ap02Cn
John		06	M	Child	12Ap02Cn
Jas.		04	M	Child	12Ap02Cn
Ed.		02	M	Child	12Ap02Cn
Maria		.06	F	Infant	12Ap02Cn
HAUGHLAHAN, Wm.		20	M	Laborer	12Ap02Cn
CAVANAGH, Judy		20	F	None	12Ap02Cn
BROPHY, Thos.		20	M	Laborer	12Ap02Cn
MURTHY, Jas.		20	M	Laborer	12Ap02Cn
BRADDOCK, James		20	M	Laborer	12Ap02Cn
WHELAN, John		20	M	Laborer	12Ap02Cn
BUTLER, Cathe.		20	F	None	12Ap02Cn
Mary		20	F	None	12Ap02Cn
POWER, James		20	M	Laborer	12Ap02Cn
Maria	(W)	20	F	Wife	12Ap02Cn
John	(S)	04	M	Child	12Ap02Cn
Margt.	(D)	03	F	Child	12Ap02Cn
Kitty	(D)	01	F	Child	12Ap02Cn
TIERNAY, Jas.		25	M	Laborer	12Ap02Cn
POWER, Ellen		20	F	None	12Ap02Cn
HIGGINS, John		25	M	Mechanic	12Ap02Cn
PORTER, John		20	M	Mechanic	12Ap02Cn
RIGNEY, M.		40	M	Mechanic	12Ap02Cn

NAMES OF PASSENGERS		A G E	S E X	OCCUPATIONS	DATE PORT SHIP
MCBRINTY, Ann		18	F	None	12Ap02Cn
CUNNINGHAM, Hannah		50	F	None	12Ap02Cn
Mary	(D)	20	F	None	12Ap02Cn
DOWD, Alley		18	F	None	12Ap02Cn
CRAWFORD, John		18	M	Mechanic	12Ap02Cn
OHARA, Bernard		25	M	Mechanic	12Ap02Cn
EWING, Thos.		20	M	Mechanic	12Ap02Cn
PINKERTON, Matt		18	M	Mechanic	12Ap02Cn
PARKER, John		18	M	Mechanic	12Ap02Cn
BARRY, Charles		25	M	Mechanic	12Ap02Cn
SHELLY, Bridget		20	F	None	12Ap02Cn
FOLEY, Thos.		40	M	Mechanic	12Ap02Cn
John	(S)	06	M	Child	12Ap02Cn
Danl.	(S)	04	M	Child	12Ap02Cn
NANGLE, Honora		20	F	None	12Ap02Cn
LEAMY, Danl.		20	M	Laborer	12Ap02Cn
MOORE, Michael		25	M	Laborer	12Ap02Cn
POWER, John		40	M	Laborer	12Ap02Cn
Harriet	(W)	40	F	Wife	12Ap02Cn
Pat	(S)	09	M	Child	12Ap02Cn
Michael	(S)	07	M	Child	12Ap02Cn
Margt.	(D)	04	F	Child	12Ap02Cn
Ellen	(D)	01	F	Child	12Ap02Cn
CROTTY, Bridget		18	F	None	12Ap02Cn
FOGARTY, Mary		20	F	None	12Ap02Cn
BERGIN, Mary		18	F	None	12Ap02Cn
MCGANTY, John		30	M	Mechanic	12Ap02Cn
Ann	(D)	08	F	Child	12Ap02Cn
MCCARTY, Bridget		20	F	None	12Ap02Cn
KELLEY, Pat		25	M	Laborer	12Ap02Cn
Cathe.		20	F	None	12Ap02Cn
Ellen		21	F	None	12Ap02Cn
MCGOVERN, Thos.		20	M	Mechanic	12Ap02Cn
BOND, Hugh		20	M	Mechanic	12Ap02Cn
HONORY, Geo.		25	M	Mechanic	12Ap02Cn
GLEASON, Cathe.		18	F	None	12Ap02Cn
FENLEY, Cathe.		20	F	None	12Ap02Cn
MITCHELL, Mary		19	F	None	12Ap02Cn
KENIGAN, Jas.		20	M	Laborer	12Ap02Cn
Mary		20	F	None	12Ap02Cn
Roger		30	M	Laborer	12Ap02Cn
Mary		20	F	None	12Ap02Cn
KENNEDY, Wm.		40	M	Laborer	12Ap02Cn
Cathe.	(W)	40	F	Wife	12Ap02Cn
Pat	(S)	20	M	Laborer	12Ap02Cn
Cathe.	(D)	16	F	None	12Ap02Cn
Eliza	(D)	10	F	None	12Ap02Cn
Margt.	(D)	08	F	Child	12Ap02Cn
Ellen	(D)	06	F	Child	12Ap02Cn
POOHEY, James		21	M	Laborer	12Ap02Cn
LAUGHNAN, Ann		20	F	None	12Ap02Cn
WOOD, Timothy		30	M	Laborer	12Ap02Cn
MAHONY, Danl.		25	M	Laborer	12Ap02Cn
Pat		20	M	Laborer	12Ap02Cn
GOVERTY, Dennis		20	M	Laborer	12Ap02Cn
CAWLAN, Cathe.		18	F	None	12Ap02Cn
FREEMAN, John		30	M	Laborer	12Ap02Cn
Mary		40	F	None	12Ap02Cn
PADDINGTON, Mary-A.		23	F	None	12Ap02Cn
LEVING, Pat		20	M	Laborer	12Ap02Cn
John		23	M	Laborer	12Ap02Cn
GALLAGHER, Pat		23	M	Laborer	12Ap02Cn
SPEAK, Wm.		30	M	Laborer	12Ap02Cn
PANSAY, Pat		24	M	Laborer	12Ap02Cn
WARD, Lewis		22	M	Laborer	12Ap02Cn
WALSH, Wm.		29	M	Laborer	12Ap02Cn
GALLAGHER, Robt.		30	M	Laborer	12Ap02Cn
SWEENEY, Pat		20	M	Laborer	12Ap02Cn
John		23	M	Laborer	12Ap02Cn
NEENAN, David		18	M	Laborer	12Ap02Cn
SWEENY, Hugh		22	M	Laborer	12Ap02Cn
MCBRIDE, Mary		23	F	None	12Ap02Cn
SHIELDS, Ann		25	F	None	12Ap02Cn
HEVERTY, Mary		25	F	None	12Ap02Cn
FREELL, Hugh		20	M	Laborer	12Ap02Cn

NAMES OF PASSENGERS		A G E	S E X	OCCUPATIONS	DATE PORT SHIP
KERR, Francis		20	M	Laborer	12Ap02Cn
FREEL, Biddy		19	F	None	12Ap02Cn
Ann		20	F	None	12Ap02Cn
DWHIR, Jane		20	F	None	12Ap02Cn
HOUSTIN, John		25	M	Laborer	12Ap02Cn
COOPER, John		40	M	Laborer	12Ap02Cn
Eliza	(W)	35	F	None	12Ap02Cn
Wm.	(S)	10	M	None	12Ap02Cn
Ann	(D)	01	F	Child	12Ap02Cn
CARROLL, Michl.		14	M	Laborer	12Ap02Cn
Cathe.		09	F	Child	12Ap02Cn
CROMER, John		20	M	Laborer	12Ap02Cn
MCNULTY, Mark		25	M	Laborer	12Ap02Cn
PREIMER, Henry		30	M	Laborer	12Ap02Cn
Susan		20	F	None	12Ap02Cn
PORTER, John		11	M	None	12Ap02Cn
HARDING, Danl.		30	M	Farmer	12Ap02Cn
Winifred		25	F	None	12Ap02Cn
GANY, Jas.		25	M	Farmer	12Ap02Cn
Thos.		20	M	Farmer	12Ap02Cn
MEEHAN, Eliza		21	F	None	12Ap02Cn
LENEY, Bryan		22	M	Farmer	12Ap02Cn
ROBERTS, James		50	M	Farmer	12Ap02Cn
Mary		25	F	None	12Ap02Cn
Kitty		08	F	Child	12Ap02Cn
Margt.		04	F	Child	12Ap02Cn
Mary		01	F	Child	12Ap02Cn
KINGSTON, Jas.		25	M	Farmer	12Ap02Cn
MORTON, John		30	M	Farmer	12Ap02Cn
WILLSON, John		30	M	Farmer	12Ap02Cn
KELLEY, Peter		20	M	Farmer	12Ap02Cn
Bridget		17	F	None	12Ap02Cn
MCLENNON, Pat		20	M	Farmer	12Ap02Cn
James		17	M	Farmer	12Ap02Cn
MCWILLIAMS, Sally		30	F	None	12Ap02Cn
DICKEY, David		22	M	Farmer	12Ap02Cn
KISSACK, Wm.		19	M	Farmer	12Ap02Cn
Margt.		17	F	None	12Ap02Cn
MCATER, Wm.		50	M	Farmer	12Ap02Cn
Mary	(D)	12	F	None	12Ap02Cn
SPILLAN, J.W.		24	M	Farmer	12Ap02Cn
MITCHELL, Martin		24	M	Farmer	12Ap02Cn
BROWN, U-Mrs.		51	F	None	12Ap02Cn
ONEILL, Letitia		06	F	Child	12Ap02Cn
REYNOLDS, Cathe.		36	F	None	12Ap02Cn
Francis	(S)	16	M	Mechanic	12Ap02Cn
IDEA, Henry		25	M	Mechanic	12Ap02Cn
John		20	M	Mechanic	12Ap02Cn
Geo.		22	M	Mechanic	12Ap02Cn
GURKEN, Cathe.		19	F	None	12Ap02Cn
MALLIN, Jas.		25	M	Mechanic	12Ap02Cn
GREGG, Michael		24	M	Mechanic	12Ap02Cn
MCNAMARA, Danl.		20	M	Mechanic	12Ap02Cn
HENESY, Thos.		20	M	Mechanic	12Ap02Cn
HUGHES, Thos.		18	M	Mechanic	12Ap02Cn
Mary		16	F	None	12Ap02Cn
EAGER, Wm.		22	M	Mechanic	12Ap02Cn
HOY, Chas.		20	M	Mechanic	12Ap02Cn
MCCABE, Perry		20	M	Mechanic	12Ap02Cn
MCCONNELL, Murty		20	M	Mechanic	12Ap02Cn
Thos.		21	M	Mechanic	12Ap02Cn
FITZGERALD, Alley		30	F	None	12Ap02Cn
DALY, Ellen		18	F	None	12Ap02Cn
HAND, Ann		20	F	None	12Ap02Cn
LYNAS, Robt.		20	M	Mechanic	12Ap02Cn
SKELLY, Margt.		21	F	None	12Ap02Cn
BENNET, Richd.		23	M	Mechanic	12Ap02Cn
FLINN, Ann		06	F	Child	12Ap02Cn
GRUNDY, Thos.		20	M	Mechanic	12Ap02Cn
GILBERT, John		20	M	Mechanic	12Ap02Cn
MELDRING, Richd.		20	M	Mechanic	12Ap02Cn
MONAGAN, Mary		18	F	None	12Ap02Cn
SUTTON, Jas.		24	M	Mechanic	12Ap02Cn
Ellen		20	F	None	12Ap02Cn
ROWLEY, Rose		25	F	None	12Ap02Cn

NAMES OF PASSENGERS		AGE	SEX	OCCUPATIONS	DATE PORT SHIP
RUTHORN, Luke		14	M	Mechanic	12Ap02Cn
NYLAN, Fanny		20	F	None	12Ap02Cn
Cathe.		20	F	None	12Ap02Cn
GALBRAITH, John		25	M	Mechanic	12Ap02Cn
BERGIN, Ann		20	F	None	12Ap02Cn
CORCORAN, Stephen		25	M	Mechanic	12Ap02Cn
BRODRICK, J.		25	M	Mechanic	12Ap02Cn
STAPLETON, Cathe.		30	F	None	12Ap02Cn
Ed.	(S)	04	M	Child	12Ap02Cn
Michael	(S)	03	M	Child	12Ap02Cn
METARNE, Mary		20	F	None	12Ap02Cn
CARTY, Margt.		20	F	None	12Ap02Cn
DEANE, James		25	M	Laborer	12Ap02Cn
CLARKE, And.		30	M	Laborer	12Ap02Cn
CARROLL, Michael		23	M	Laborer	12Ap02Cn
KEHOE, Pat		20	M	Laborer	12Ap02Cn
FOGARTY, Chas.		20	M	Laborer	12Ap02Cn
SMITH, Jas.		20	M	Laborer	12Ap02Cn
DALTON, Michl.		18	M	Laborer	12Ap02Cn
Margt.		15	F	None	12Ap02Cn
LEASON, Chas.		20	M	Laborer	12Ap02Cn
HEWITT, Harriett		25	F	None	12Ap02Cn
MCGRATH, Pat		25	M	Laborer	12Ap02Cn
RYAN, Jas.		24	M	Laborer	12Ap02Cn
BERN, John		25	M	Laborer	12Ap02Cn
SHEA, John		20	M	Laborer	12Ap02Cn
MURPHY, John		15	M	Laborer	12Ap02Cn
BOURKE, Michael		22	M	Laborer	12Ap02Cn
MOORE, John		25	M	Laborer	12Ap02Cn
Kieran		25	M	Laborer	12Ap02Cn
Edmund		23	M	Laborer	12Ap02Cn
KENEDY, Michael		18	M	Laborer	12Ap02Cn
CARROLL, Anthy.		25	M	Laborer	12Ap02Cn
FITZPATRICK, Wm.		20	M	Laborer	12Ap02Cn
BRADFIELD, R.		25	M	Laborer	12Ap02Cn
MCLAUGHLIN, John		25	M	Laborer	12Ap02Cn
BROWN, Bridget		18	F	None	12Ap02Cn
Cathe.		20	F	None	12Ap02Cn
LAUGHAN, Peggy		20	F	None	12Ap02Cn
WIND, Frank		30	M	Laborer	12Ap02Cn
COLL, John		20	M	Laborer	12Ap02Cn
REYNOLDS, Chas.		40	M	Laborer	12Ap02Cn
LEAN, Thos.		45	M	Laborer	12Ap02Cn
Ann		17	F	None	12Ap02Cn
Eliza		35	F	Wife	12Ap02Cn
MCCANN, Peter		30	M	Laborer	12Ap02Cn
BROWN, Chas.		52	M	Laborer	12Ap02Cn
FLINN, Mary		20	F	None	12Ap02Cn
MARA, Mary		20	F	None	12Ap02Cn
HURLEY, Thos.		25	M	Farmer	12Ap02Cn
CULNANE, Charles		25	M	Farmer	12Ap02Cn
CARROLL, Bridget		25	F	None	12Ap02Cn
John		30	M	Farmer	12Ap02Cn
DARCY, Michael		25	M	Farmer	12Ap02Cn
Rose	(W)	25	F	None	12Ap02Cn
John	(S)	01	M	Child	12Ap02Cn
MCGRALE, Fanny		18	F	None	12Ap02Cn
OWENS, James		30	M	Laborer	12Ap02Cn
DONNELLEY, Jas.		30	M	Laborer	12Ap02Cn
EARLEY, Owen		30	M	Laborer	12Ap02Cn
OWENS, Mary		30	F	None	12Ap02Cn
DONNELLY, Cathe.		38	F	None	12Ap02Cn
OWENS, Jas.		02	M	Child	12Ap02Cn
Ed.		.06	M	Infant	12Ap02Cn
DONNELLY, Mary		.06	F	Infant	12Ap02Cn
KELLEY, John		40	M	Laborer	12Ap02Cn
RICHARDSON, Wm.		24	M	Laborer	12Ap02Cn
Michael		18	M	Laborer	12Ap02Cn
CANNON, Thos.		20	M	Laborer	12Ap02Cn
ODONNELL, Pat		25	M	Laborer	12Ap02Cn
Dennis		23	M	Laborer	12Ap02Cn
Jeremiah		20	M	Laborer	12Ap02Cn
FINLAY, And.		25	M	Laborer	12Ap02Cn
Margt.		25	F	None	12Ap02Cn
WOODS, Owen		25	M	Laborer	12Ap02Cn
WOODS, Eliza		21	F	None	12Ap02Cn
SHEA, John		30	M	Laborer	12Ap02Cn
SULLIVAN, Danl.		30	M	Laborer	12Ap02Cn
HARRINGTON, Danl.		26	M	Laborer	12Ap02Cn
BROGAN, Thos.		25	M	Laborer	12Ap02Cn
Cathe.		20	F	None	12Ap02Cn
MOORE, Jane		18	F	None	12Ap02Cn
KINSIL, John		45	M	Laborer	12Ap02Cn
Margt.	(W)	45	F	Wife	12Ap02Cn
John	(S)	20	M	Laborer	12Ap02Cn
STAPLETON, Danl.		35	M	Laborer	12Ap02Cn
SMITH, Brighton		25	M	Laborer	12Ap02Cn
PURCELL, Ann		18	F	None	12Ap02Cn
BRENNAN, Bridget		20	F	None	12Ap02Cn
WELSH, Felln		20	M	Laborer	12Ap02Cn
MULLONE, Bridget		20	F	None	12Ap02Cn
HUNT, Bridget		20	F	None	12Ap02Cn
FLANNIGAN, John		20	M	Laborer	12Ap02Cn
FLYNN, Jas.		25	M	Laborer	12Ap02Cn
Thos.		12	M	Laborer	12Ap02Cn
SHIRLEY, Stephen		25	M	Laborer	12Ap02Cn
KENNEDY, Michael		25	M	Laborer	12Ap02Cn
MACKIN, John		20	M	Laborer	12Ap02Cn
QUINN, Bernard		30	M	Laborer	12Ap02Cn
DILLON, Mary		12	F	None	12Ap02Cn
REILLY, Cathe.		20	F	None	12Ap02Cn
DELANY, Jeremiah		25	M	Laborer	12Ap02Cn
HOPE, Cathe.		20	F	None	12Ap02Cn
BARRY, Cathe.		08	F	Child	12Ap02Cn
John		18	M	Laborer	12Ap02Cn
HAMILTON, Matilda		18	F	None	12Ap02Cn
FOGARTY, Michael		28	M	Laborer	12Ap02Cn
Mary	(W)	30	F	Wife	12Ap02Cn
Cathe.	(D)	09	F	Child	12Ap02Cn
John	(S)	07	M	Child	12Ap02Cn
Michael	(S)	05	M	Child	12Ap02Cn
Mary	(D)	01	F	Child	12Ap02Cn
Rosamund		30	F	None	12Ap02Cn
Jas.	(S)	08	M	Child	12Ap02Cn
Wm.	(S)	04	M	Child	12Ap02Cn
DOYLE, John		20	M	Laborer	12Ap02Cn
DUFFY, Thos.		20	M	Laborer	12Ap02Cn
HAVITT, James		30	M	Laborer	12Ap02Cn
HORAN, Mary		20	F	None	12Ap02Cn
STONE, Wm.		25	M	Laborer	12Ap02Cn
DELANY, Michael		25	M	Laborer	12Ap02Cn
Bridget		14	F	None	12Ap02Cn
MCCALLA, Mary		18	F	None	12Ap02Cn
MCGRATH, Rony		25	M	Laborer	12Ap02Cn
MCANULTY, Sarah		18	F	None	12Ap02Cn
OREENE, Letitia		40	F	None	12Ap02Cn
OKANE, Walter		40	M	Laborer	12Ap02Cn
FIGHER, Owen		20	M	Laborer	12Ap02Cn
CARTER, Ed.		25	M	Laborer	12Ap02Cn
MCDERMOTT, Cathe.		20	F	None	12Ap02Cn
GREENE, Ann		20	F	None	12Ap02Cn
KENNA, Margt.		20	F	None	12Ap02Cn
SKILLY, Ann		13	F	None	12Ap02Cn
NEWLAN, Maggy		20	F	None	12Ap02Cn
HANREGAN, Danl.		29	M	Laborer	12Ap02Cn
Margt.		21	F	None	12Ap02Cn
CROMER, Cathe.		02	F	Child	12Ap02Cn
GILLAN, Ann		20	F	None	12Ap02Cn
STAPLETON, John		20	M	Laborer	12Ap02Cn
RYAN, Mary		50	F	None	12Ap02Cn
Michael	(S)	20	M	Laborer	12Ap02Cn
Eliza	(D)	01	F	Child	12Ap02Cn
James	(S)	07	M	Child	12Ap02Cn
MORRIS, Peter		45	M	Mechanic	12Ap02Cn
Eliza	(W)	45	F	Wife	12Ap02Cn
Terry	(S)	12	M	None	12Ap02Cn
Peter	(S)	10	M	None	12Ap02Cn
Eliza	(D)	09	F	Child	12Ap02Cn
MCCAFFRAY, Ann		18	F	None	12Ap02Cn
DOLAN, Cathe.		11	F	None	12Ap02Cn

NAMES OF PASSENGERS		AGE	SEX	OCCUPATIONS	DATE PORT SHIP
BAXTER, Eliza		20	F	None	12Ap02Cn
Margt.		18	F	None	12Ap02Cn
MCMANUS, R.		50	M	Laborer	12Ap02Cn
Margt.	(W)	50	F	None	12Ap02Cn
John	(S)	20	M	Laborer	12Ap02Cn
CRAWFORD, John		20	M	Laborer	12Ap02Cn
CORCORAN, Matt		18	M	Laborer	12Ap02Cn
HAGGAN, Wm.		18	M	Laborer	12Ap02Cn
FINEGAN, Bridget		18	F	None	12Ap02Cn
OCONNOR, Donnld.		50	M	Laborer	12Ap02Cn
Donnld.	(S)	12	M	None	12Ap02Cn
Timothy	(S)	10	M	None	12Ap02Cn
HANVEY, Jas.A.		50	M	Ay-Off	12Ap02Cn
MORELH, H.P.		45	M	Ay-Off	12Ap02Cn
JONES, Alfred		27	M	Ay-Off	12Ap02Cn
ANTHONY, Ad.		28	M	Ay-Off	12Ap02Cn
MELROY, Robt.		34	M	None	12Ap02Cn
HUMPHREYS, Archd.		25	M	None	12Ap02Cn
SOLOMON, Julius		30	M	Merchant	12Ap02Cn
MOODIE, Wm.		33	M	Merchant	12Ap02Cn
MEREDITH, Jas.S.		25	M	Merchant	12Ap02Cn
GILMER, Isaac-C.		31	M	Merchant	12Ap02Cn
Janet	(W)	25	F	Wife	12Ap02Cn
KERR, Geo.		13	M	None	12Ap02Cn
GILMORE, Gabella		02	F	Child	12Ap02Cn
Jas.R.		.06	M	Infant	12Ap02Cn

MARION 12 APRIL 1847

From Londonderry

NAMES OF PASSENGERS		AGE	SEX	OCCUPATIONS	DATE PORT SHIP
STEVENSON, John		33	M	Farmer	12Ap01Oh
Susannah	(W)	33	F	Unknown	12Ap01Oh
Martha	(D)	13	F	Unknown	12Ap01Oh
Robert	(S)	08	M	Child	12Ap01Oh
Sarah	(D)	03	F	Child	12Ap01Oh
Jacob	(S)	03	M	Child	12Ap01Oh
Eliza	(D)	10	F	Unknown	12Ap01Oh
WILEY, Matha		18	F	Unknown	12Ap01Oh
STEVENSON, Robert-A.		20	M	Unknown	12Ap01Oh
DIVER, Nancy		25	F	Unknown	12Ap01Oh
REED, John		21	M	Saddler	12Ap01Oh
KERR, Saml.		20	M	Student	12Ap01Oh
GAMBLE, Willm.		17	M	Farmer	12Ap01Oh
MCBREATY, Cath.		36	F	Unknown	12Ap01Oh
MCCORMICK, Mary		17	F	Unknown	12Ap01Oh
James		09	M	Child	12Ap01Oh
Patrick		06	M	Child	12Ap01Oh
John		.03	M	Infant	12Ap01Oh
ACHLES, Denis		26	M	Unknown	12Ap01Oh
MOODY, Robert		20	M	Unknown	12Ap01Oh
PORTER, Allexander		22	M	Unknown	12Ap01Oh
MCGINNESS, Edward		20	M	Unknown	12Ap01Oh
BEARDON, Andrew		22	M	Unknown	12Ap01Oh
COLLIN, Willm.		20	M	Shoemaker	12Ap01Oh
MCAND, Francis		20	M	Laborer	12Ap01Oh
BRADLEY, Patk.		28	M	Unknown	12Ap01Oh
Mary		25	F	Unknown	12Ap01Oh
MCCORKELL, Margaret		17	F	Unknown	12Ap01Oh
Biddy		08	F	Child	12Ap01Oh
DUFFY, Jeremiah		35	M	Lrfhm	12Ap01Oh
Mary	(W)	30	F	Wife	12Ap01Oh
Margeret	(M)	60	F	Spinster	12Ap01Oh
Margret	(D)	05	F	Child	12Ap01Oh
Mary-Amella	(D)	03	F	Child	12Ap01Oh
Bridget	(D)	02	F	Child	12Ap01Oh
GALLAGHER, Mary		51	F	Spinster	12Ap01Oh
MCMENOMIN, Susan		19	F	Spinster	12Ap01Oh
John	(H)	18	M	Laborer	12Ap01Oh

NAMES OF PASSENGERS		AGE	SEX	OCCUPATIONS	DATE PORT SHIP
MCMENOMIN, John	(S)	01	M	Child	12Ap01Oh
DUFFY, Michel		20	M	Laborer	12Ap01Oh
KELLY, James		26	M	Laborer	12Ap01Oh
MOODY, Hopkins		24	M	Laborer	12Ap01Oh
MCMERROMIN, Patrick		20	M	Laborer	12Ap01Oh
MCLOUGHLIN, Daniel		19	M	Laborer	12Ap01Oh
GREGORY, Saml.		17	M	Laborer	12Ap01Oh
Sarah		15	F	Spinster	12Ap01Oh
MAGER, Rose		20	F	Spinster	12Ap01Oh
MCCOOL, Reamond		24	M	Laborer	12Ap01Oh
ODONNELL, Neal		23	M	Cooper	12Ap01Oh
Hugh		20	M	Cooper	12Ap01Oh
MURPHY, Thomas		20	M	Cooper	12Ap01Oh
HART, Patrick		24	M	Laborer	12Ap01Oh
GALLAGA, Biddy		20	F	Spinster	12Ap01Oh
Anna		08	F	Child	12Ap01Oh
Anna		28	F	Spinster	12Ap01Oh
BONNELL, Ellen		20	F	Spinster	12Ap01Oh
Eliza		20	F	Spinster	12Ap01Oh
LAIRD, Mary		60	F	Spinster	12Ap01Oh
BRADLEY, Eliza		20	F	Spinster	12Ap01Oh
Jane		22	F	Spinster	12Ap01Oh
MCKINNY, Patrick		22	M	Unknown	12Ap01Oh
MCDOUGALL, Rebecca		23	F	Spinster	12Ap01Oh
Joseph		21	M	Unknown	12Ap01Oh
Rebecca	(M)	53	F	Spinster	12Ap01Oh
Anne		20	F	Spinster	12Ap01Oh
Mary		14	F	Spinster	12Ap01Oh
George		16	F	Spinster	12Ap01Oh
STEWART, Jane		20	F	Spinster	12Ap01Oh
Mary		20	F	Spinster	12Ap01Oh
MCKEAVER, Charles		30	M	Unknown	12Ap01Oh
Hannah	(W)	30	F	Wife	12Ap01Oh
Ellen	(D)	08	F	Child	12Ap01Oh
Anne	(D)	07	F	Child	12Ap01Oh
Mary	(D)	05	F	Child	12Ap01Oh
Patrick	(S)	03	M	Child	12Ap01Oh
Barny	(S)	01	M	Child	12Ap01Oh
LYNCH, John		36	M	Unknown	12Ap01Oh
MCINTYRE, Wm.		60	M	Unknown	12Ap01Oh
Sarah	(W)	60	F	Wife	12Ap01Oh
Anne	(D)	25	F	Spinster	12Ap01Oh
Claudius	(S)	24	M	Unknown	12Ap01Oh
Alexander	(S)	24	M	Unknown	12Ap01Oh
Rebecca	(D)	20	F	Spinster	12Ap01Oh
BEGLEY, Wm.		22	M	Saddler	12Ap01Oh
THOMPSON, Wm.		48	M	Laborer	12Ap01Oh
Biddy	(W)	54	F	Wife	12Ap01Oh
Wm.	(S)	19	M	Unknown	12Ap01Oh
Anne	(D)	17	F	Spinster	12Ap01Oh
Biddy	(D)	07	F	Child	12Ap01Oh
FREEL, Maurice		18	M	Unknown	12Ap01Oh
MULHOLLAND, Bernard		21	M	Unknown	12Ap01Oh
MCBRIDE, Charles		18	M	Unknown	12Ap01Oh
BROWN, John		22	M	Unknown	12Ap01Oh
DOHERTY, Daniel		20	M	Unknown	12Ap01Oh
MCFADDEN, Cornes.		25	M	Unknown	12Ap01Oh
HARROLD, Barny		18	M	Unknown	12Ap01Oh
MCCAFFERTY, John		20	M	Unknown	12Ap01Oh
CURRAN, Richard		70	M	Unknown	12Ap01Oh
Neal	(S)	18	M	Unknown	12Ap01Oh
Barny	(S)	20	M	Unknown	12Ap01Oh
Maggy	(W)	60	F	Wife	12Ap01Oh
BRISLAND, Eleanor		25	F	Spinster	12Ap01Oh
GALLAGHER, Catharine		20	F	Spinster	12Ap01Oh
BAIRD, Rebecca		57	F	Spinster	12Ap01Oh
Anne-Jane	(D)	21	F	Spinster	12Ap01Oh
Margt.Sarah	(D)	18	F	Spinster	12Ap01Oh
MCLOUGHLIN, Charles		21	M	Unknown	12Ap01Oh
HUTCHINSON, Robert		20	M	Unknown	12Ap01Oh
Cath.		22	F	Spinster	12Ap01Oh
WILEY, Matty		20	F	Spinster	12Ap01Oh
KIRKLAND, George		21	M	Unknown	12Ap01Oh
Jane		28	F	Spinster	12Ap01Oh
Mary-Anne		24	F	Spinster	12Ap01Oh

NAMES OF PASSENGERS		AGE	SEX	OCCUPATIONS	DATE PORT SHIP
COLHOUN, Alexander		20	M	Currier	12Ap010h
Matty		17	F	Spinster	12Ap010h
CONNER, Joseph		20	M	Shoemaker	12Ap010h
Matilda		19	F	Spinster	12Ap010h
STEEL, RACHEL-MOORE		25	F	SPINSTER	12AP010H
KERR, Robert		18	M	Laborer	12Ap010h
MCGLINCHY, Charles		28	M	Carpenter	12Ap010h
COYLE, Bridget		20	F	Spinster	12Ap010h
CALLIGHAN, Patrick		25	M	Laborer	12Ap010h
BROWN, Eleanor		19	F	Spinster	12Ap010h
CARLAND, Nancy		20	F	Spinster	12Ap010h
GALLONAGH, Patrick		20	M	Shoemaker	12Ap010h
MCGLINCHY, Nancy		19	F	Mtmkr	12Ap010h
Percy		19	M	Miller	12Ap010h
SMILEY, Cath.		19	F	Spinster	12Ap010h
MCCORMICK, Hugh		25	M	Laborer	12Ap010h
MCGLINN, Edward		20	M	Laborer	12Ap010h
MCGONAGLE, Wm.		26	M	Laborer	12Ap010h
LOUGHRY, John		30	M	Laborer	12Ap010h
MCCANN, Margery		20	F	Spinster	12Ap010h
MCKEEVER, Denis		25	M	Laborer	12Ap010h
KYLE, John		25	M	Laborer	12Ap010h
Arch.		20	M	Blacksmith	12Ap010h
Mary		16	F	Spinster	12Ap010h
BRANDON, Wm.		14	M	Laborer	12Ap010h
FAULKNER, John		72	M	Laborer	12Ap010h
Mary-Anne	(D)	22	F	Dressmaker	12Ap010h
BROWN, Wm.		24	M	Laborer	12Ap010h
Jane		18	F	Spinster	12Ap010h
Eliza		16	F	Spinster	12Ap010h
Andrew		22	M	Laborer	12Ap010h
LANGAN, John		34	M	Laborer	12Ap010h
MCELHINNY, John		30	M	Laborer	12Ap010h
MELOY, Frank		24	M	Laborer	12Ap010h
BONER, Paddy		40	M	Laborer	12Ap010h
Biddy		21	F	Spinster	12Ap010h
MAFEE, Peter		20	M	Laborer	12Ap010h
PATTERSON, James		17	M	Laborer	12Ap010h
James		19	M	Laborer	12Ap010h
MCCOOL, Alexn.		55	M	Laborer	12Ap010h
SWEENY, John		40	M	Cooper	12Ap010h
SMILEY, James		17	M	Saddler	12Ap010h
ODONNELL, Rosy		18	F	Spinster	12Ap010h
VANCE, John		25	M	Laborer	12Ap010h
MCMEANS, Cath.		16	F	Spinster	12Ap010h
Matilda		14	F	Spinster	12Ap010h
WARNICK, Robert		66	M	Laborer	12Ap010h
Eliza	(W)	45	F	Wife	12Ap010h
Eliza	(D)	17	F	Spinster	12Ap010h
Jane	(D)	19	F	Spinster	12Ap010h
Mary	(D)	12	F	Spinster	12Ap010h
James	(S)	10	M	Laborer	12Ap010h
SIMPSON, James		21	M	Laborer	12Ap010h
James		21	M	Laborer	12Ap010h
HARGAN, George		20	M	Teacher	12Ap010h
TRACEY, Edward		44	M	Laborer	12Ap010h
Rose		44	F	Spinster	12Ap010h
GREENWOOD, James		24	M	Laborer	12Ap010h
MCLOUGHLIN, James		27	M	Laborer	12Ap010h
DOHERTY, Richd.		28	M	Laborer	12Ap010h
Jane		25	F	Spinster	12Ap010h
THOMPSON, Wm.		26	M	Laborer	12Ap010h
MULLAN, Daniel		21	M	Laborer	12Ap010h
MCGINNESS, Peggy		19	F	Spinster	12Ap010h
MCCAULEY, Bridget		18	F	Spinster	12Ap010h
DYSART, Joseph		21	M	Laborer	12Ap010h
GWYNNE, O.B.		24	M	Laborer	12Ap010h

Ayshire 13 April 1847

From Newry

NAMES OF PASSENGERS		AGE	SEX	OCCUPATIONS	DATE PORT SHIP
MCGAHAN, J.		40	M	Laborer	13Ap1901
May	(W)	35	F	Wife	13Ap1901
Patch	(S)	09	M	Child	13Ap1901
Thos.	(S)	08	M	Child	13Ap1901
Jas.	(S)	05	M	Child	13Ap1901
Judy	(D)	02	F	Child	13Ap1901
MEAKS, P.		17	M	Unknown	13Ap1901
CARROLL, M.		28	M	Unknown	13Ap1901
Anne		26	F	None	13Ap1901
MONAGH, My.		25	F	None	13Ap1901
Bdgt.	(D)	03	F	Child	13Ap1901
Ann	(D)	02	F	Child	13Ap1901
LEE, J.		30	M	Unknown	13Ap1901
Ann	(W)	32	F	Wife	13Ap1901
Thos.	(S)	05	M	Child	13Ap1901
Joseph		20	M	Unknown	13Ap1901
MARKY, Ann		21	F	None	13Ap1901
MCCUNAN, Eliza		22	F	None	13Ap1901
Bdgt.		20	F	None	13Ap1901
DAVIDSON, Anne		19	F	None	13Ap1901
DUFF, Sarah		20	F	None	13Ap1901
FRELAN, Mary-M.		18	F	None	13Ap1901
FARELL, S.		45	M	Unknown	13Ap1901
My.	(W)	45	F	Wife	13Ap1901
Laurence	(S)	13	M	None	13Ap1901
Barn.	(S)	11	M	None	13Ap1901
Owen	(S)	09	M	Child	13Ap1901
REID, W.		25	M	Unknown	13Ap1901
RIELY, P.		28	M	Unknown	13Ap1901
DOWNY, D.		24	M	Unknown	13Ap1901
CENDER, M.		20	M	Unknown	13Ap1901
MCKEE, P.		21	M	Unknown	13Ap1901
Mary		21	F	None	13Ap1901
CREENAN, Ellen		40	F	None	13Ap1901
CURAN, G.		11	M	Unknown	13Ap1901
My.A.		08	F	Child	13Ap1901
Thos., Cth.		22	F	None	13Ap1901
LANGE, My.		22	F	None	13Ap1901
GROSS, M.		25	M	Unknown	13Ap1901
My.	(W)	20	F	Wife	13Ap1901
Edwd.	(S)	02	M	Child	13Ap1901
CALLESLY, J.		19	M	Laborer	13Ap1901
MCAULLEN, H.		30	M	Unknown	13Ap1901
MURPHY, H.		20	M	Unknown	13Ap1901
HAUGHY, J.		30	M	Unknown	13Ap1901
Ferris		20	M	Unknown	13Ap1901
MCCANNON, D.		35	M	Unknown	13Ap1901
Ellen	(D)	12	F	None	13Ap1901
John	(S)	10	M	None	13Ap1901
MCAULLY, My.		13	F	None	13Ap1901
Sally		09	F	Child	13Ap1901
MCGREAN, Rose		69	F	None	13Ap1901
Sally	(D)	24	F	None	13Ap1901
Owen	(S)	19	M	Unknown	13Ap1901
RISE, Mgt.		24	F	None	13Ap1901
SMALL, J.		26	M	Unknown	13Ap1901
Ann	(W)	24	F	None	13Ap1901
My.	(D)	03	F	Child	13Ap1901
PARKS, S.		10	M	Unknown	13Ap1901
TRENBLE, J.		21	M	Unknown	13Ap1901
CAMPBELL, J.		20	M	Unknown	13Ap1901
MCANALLY, A.		30	M	Unknown	13Ap1901
J.Goss.		32	M	Unknown	13Ap1901
Cath.		28	F	None	13Ap1901
Patch		35	M	Unknown	13Ap1901

NAMES OF PASSENGERS		AGE	SEX	OCCUPATIONS	DATE PORT SHIP
MCANALLY, Rose	(M)	60	F	None	13Ap1901
Patch		10	M	None	13Ap1901
Francis		07	M	Child	13Ap1901
Bgt.		05	F	Child	13Ap1901
Andrew		03	M	Child	13Ap1901
Mgt.		01	F	Child	13Ap1901
MCDONALD, J.		21	M	Unknown	13Ap1901
Ellen		20	F	None	13Ap1901
MCCARROLL, F.		21	M	Unknown	13Ap1901
HUGHES, M.		21	M	Unknown	13Ap1901
CARROLL, J.		20	M	Unknown	13Ap1901
MALONE, J.		20	M	Unknown	13Ap1901
RICE, M.		19	M	Unknown	13Ap1901
MURPHY, H.		20	M	Unknown	13Ap1901
PARKER, J.		22	M	Unknown	13Ap1901
MCCARR, A.		18	M	Unknown	13Ap1901
MASTERSON, P.		25	M	Unknown	13Ap1901
HANLON, Bgt.		35	F	None	13Ap1901
Patch	(H)	35	M	Laborer	13Ap1901
John		17	M	Laborer	13Ap1901
Michel		13	M	Laborer	13Ap1901
Patch		13	M	Laborer	13Ap1901
Mgt.		35	F	None	13Ap1901
Rose-A.		34	F	None	13Ap1901
Bdgt.	(D)	15	F	None	13Ap1901
Patch	(S)	13	M	None	13Ap1901
James	(S)	11	M	None	13Ap1901
My.	(D)	08	F	Child	13Ap1901
John	(S)	06	M	Child	13Ap1901
Francis	(S)	04	M	Child	13Ap1901
Michl.	(S)	02	M	Child	13Ap1901
HARRISSON, E.		35	M	Unknown	13Ap1901
Rachel		21	F	None	13Ap1901
Susan	(D)	09	F	Child	13Ap1901
Jas.	(S)	04	M	Child	13Ap1901
My.	(D)	02	F	Child	13Ap1901
Edwd.		28	M	Unknown	13Ap1901
SHAW, S.		28	M	Unknown	13Ap1901
Mgt.	(D)	07	F	Child	13Ap1901
Robt.	(S)	05	M	Child	13Ap1901
Merla	(D)	03	F	Child	13Ap1901
Jud.		20	F	None	13Ap1901
TEAGUE, J.		19	F	Unknown	13Ap1901
Eliza		20	F	None	13Ap1901
COCHRAN, R.		35	M	Unknown	13Ap1901
MCCAFFERE, C.		03	M	Child	13Ap1901
WHELAN, W.		02	M	Child	13Ap1901
CAFFEY, Rose		34	F	None	13Ap1901
MCCULLEN, D.		09	M	Child	13Ap1901
Ann		09	F	Child	13Ap1901
Bgt.		01	F	Child	13Ap1901
HEANY, P.		50	M	Unknown	13Ap1901
Sally	(D)	24	F	None	13Ap1901
Jas.	(S)	25	M	Unknown	13Ap1901
MCCLELLAN, G.		18	M	Unknown	13Ap1901
SMITH, J.		21	M	Unknown	13Ap1901
LENNON, T.		24	M	Unknown	13Ap1901
VALLERTY, J.		19	M	Unknown	13Ap1901
MCGREW, Julia		50	F	None	13Ap1901
Sally	(D)	18	F	None	13Ap1901
Sara-A.	(D)	17	F	None	13Ap1901
Eleanor	(D)	07	F	Child	13Ap1901
Bella	(D)	05	F	Child	13Ap1901
Cath.	(D)	04	F	Child	13Ap1901
DUFFY, B.		22	M	Laborer	13Ap1901
Eliza		20	F	None	13Ap1901
ROBESON, W.		29	M	Unknown	13Ap1901
Merla	(W)	19	F	Wife	13Ap1901
Eliza	(D)	02	F	Child	13Ap1901
MCELROY, L.		20	M	Unknown	13Ap1901
CAMPBELL, T.		25	M	Unknown	13Ap1901
HEBEHEN, F.		24	M	Unknown	13Ap1901
MCELHILL, J.		10	M	Unknown	13Ap1901
MCCULLEN, W.		55	M	Unknown	13Ap1901
Eliza	(D)	15	F	None	13Ap1901
MCCULLEN, Sarah	(D)	12	F	None	13Ap1901
SAUNERY, Eliza		26	F	None	13Ap1901
HILL, My.		17	F	None	13Ap1901
CONNER, R.		28	M	Unknown	13Ap1901
GLEESON, J.		27	M	Unknown	13Ap1901
Finroty		45	M	Unknown	13Ap1901
No-----		27	F	None	13Ap1901
Jane		07	F	Child	13Ap1901
Ann		05	F	Child	13Ap1901
Eliza		02	F	Child	13Ap1901
John		01	M	Child	13Ap1901
BAYS, W.		22	M	Unknown	13Ap1901
THOMPSON, T.		18	M	Unknown	13Ap1901
GRAHAM, Eliza		24	F	None	13Ap1901
CARD, Alice		17	F	None	13Ap1901
RAFFETY, My.		17	F	None	13Ap1901
GRACLY, R.		45	M	Unknown	13Ap1901
Marth.	(W)	35	F	Wife	13Ap1901
Marth.	(D)	20	F	Wife	13Ap1901
Jane	(D)	17	F	Wife	13Ap1901
Flora	(D)	10	F	Wife	13Ap1901
Wm.	(S)	05	M	Child	13Ap1901
Ann	(D)	03	F	Child	13Ap1901
John	(S)	01	M	Child	13Ap1901
REECE, O.		26	M	Laborer	13Ap1901
REID, T.		40	M	Unknown	13Ap1901
Mgt.	(W)	40	F	Wife	13Ap1901
Mary	(D)	14	F	Wife	13Ap1901
Rose-Ann	(D)	11	F	Wife	13Ap1901
Sarah	(D)	07	F	Child	13Ap1901
Jane	(D)	06	F	Child	13Ap1901
Thos.	(S)	04	M	Child	13Ap1901
Frances	(D)	02	F	Child	13Ap1901
MCCALLITON, D.		12	M	None	13Ap1901
KANNASHY, C.		20	M	Unknown	13Ap1901
MALLON, T.		25	M	Unknown	13Ap1901
WOODS, B.		18	M	Unknown	13Ap1901
GOUGH, P.		22	M	Unknown	13Ap1901
BISHOP, Cath.		20	F	None	13Ap1901
Mgt.		18	F	None	13Ap1901
MCCURRY, Susan		20	F	None	13Ap1901
POLLY, J.		20	M	Unknown	13Ap1901
Mgt.		29	F	None	13Ap1901
WALKER, J.		60	M	Unknown	13Ap1901
Eliza	(W)	60	F	Wife	13Ap1901
John	(S)	22	M	Unknown	13Ap1901
Isb.	(D)	20	F	None	13Ap1901
Jane	(D)	01	F	Child	13Ap1901
Mgt.	(D)	19	F	None	13Ap1901
Alex.	(S)	16	M	None	13Ap1901
CROTTY, J.		14	M	Unknown	13Ap1901
WILSON, My.A.		11	F	None	13Ap1901
Sarah-Jonn.		28	F	None	13Ap1901
MAHAFFY, Mgt.A.		30	F	None	13Ap1901
BROWN, S.		25	M	Unknown	13Ap1901
H.		24	F	None	13Ap1901
WHITESIDE, A.		28	M	Unknown	13Ap1901
My.A.	(W)	24	F	Wife	13Ap1901
Wm.	(S)	03	M	Child	13Ap1901
Jane	(D)	02	F	Child	13Ap1901
MCSHANE, B.		45	M	Unknown	13Ap1901
Cath.	(D)	18	F	None	13Ap1901
Mgt.	(D)	17	F	None	13Ap1901
MCGUIRE, C.		56	M	Unknown	13Ap1901
Julia		50	F	None	13Ap1901

REPUBLIC 13 APRIL 1847

From Liverpool

NAMES OF PASSENGERS	A G E	S E X	OCCUPATIONS	DATE PORT SHIP
CRAGG, J.		50 M	Laborer	13Ap02Nv
Mary	(W)	50 F	Wife	13Ap02Nv
John	(S)	30 M	Unknown	13Ap02Nv
Patch	(S)	28 M	Unknown	13Ap02Nv
Jas.	(S)	26 M	Unknown	13Ap02Nv
Ann	(D)	15 F	None	13Ap02Nv
My.	(D)	23 F	None	13Ap02Nv
BOYD, H.		52 M	Unknown	13Ap02Nv
Jane	(D)	09 F	Child	13Ap02Nv
Rose	(D)	06 F	Child	13Ap02Nv
My.	(D)	03 F	Child	13Ap02Nv
Agnes	(D)	01 F	Child	13Ap02Nv
CASEY, F.		05 M	Child	13Ap02Nv
BECK, J.		40 M	Unknown	13Ap02Nv
My.	(W)	40 F	Wife	13Ap02Nv
Bdgt.	(D)	15 F	None	13Ap02Nv
John	(S)	12 M	None	13Ap02Nv
Ann	(D)	08 F	Child	13Ap02Nv
Cath.	(D)	06 F	Child	13Ap02Nv
CARRELL, P.		25 M	Unknown	13Ap02Nv
Mich.		30 M	Unknown	13Ap02Nv
SMITH, P.		22 M	Unknown	13Ap02Nv
LYNCH, Bgt.		22 F	None	13Ap02Nv
HECTOR, J.		39 M	Unknown	13Ap02Nv
My.	(W)	40 F	Wife	13Ap02Nv
Peter	(S)	17 M	Unknown	13Ap02Nv
Isaac	(S)	15 M	None	13Ap02Nv
John	(S)	10 M	None	13Ap02Nv
Mgt.	(D)	06 F	Child	13Ap02Nv
John	(S)	01 M	Child	13Ap02Nv
PONS, J.		27 M	Unknown	13Ap02Nv
DAVIS, W.		22 M	Unknown	13Ap02Nv
MCGERTY, H.		25 M	Unknown	13Ap02Nv
My.		24 F	None	13Ap02Nv
TONER, H.		21 M	Unknown	13Ap02Nv
HUTTON, J.		39 M	Unknown	13Ap02Nv
Elizbt.	(W)	39 F	Wife	13Ap02Nv
Jane	(D)	12 F	None	13Ap02Nv
Ann	(D)	10 F	None	13Ap02Nv
Sarah	(D)	07 F	Child	13Ap02Nv
Ann	(D)	06 F	Child	13Ap02Nv
J.	(S)	05 M	Child	13Ap02Nv
Horace	(S)	03 M	Child	13Ap02Nv
Bgt.	(D)	01 F	Child	13Ap02Nv
MURPHY, Alice		20 F	None	13Ap02Nv
Jane		19 F	None	13Ap02Nv
DUFFY, My.		20 F	None	13Ap02Nv
RICE, My.		20 F	None	13Ap02Nv
Cath.		19 F	None	13Ap02Nv
BURNS, P.		21 M	Unknown	13Ap02Nv
DAILY, W.		20 M	Unknown	13Ap02Nv
HUSTON, J.		29 M	Unknown	13Ap02Nv
Elizabeth		38 F	None	13Ap02Nv
Julia		12 F	None	13Ap02Nv
Emily		10 F	None	13Ap02Nv
Maria		06 F	Child	13Ap02Nv
Henry		04 M	Child	13Ap02Nv
Susan		02 F	Child	13Ap02Nv
ABLOUGHRAN, P.		20 M	Unknown	13Ap02Nv
Ann		29 F	None	13Ap02Nv
GALLIGAN, Biddy		18 F	None	13Ap02Nv
HEADLY, Honor		18 F	None	13Ap02Nv
MCHUGH, T.		60 M	Unknown	13Ap02Nv
Biddy		12 F	None	13Ap02Nv
KINNY, T.		43 M	Unknown	13Ap02Nv
KINNY, Biddy	(W)	43 F	Wife	13Ap02Nv
Mgt.	(D)	22 F	None	13Ap02Nv
Martin	(S)	19 M	Unknown	13Ap02Nv
Andrew	(S)	12 M	Unknown	13Ap02Nv
MOLLOY, Bgt.		19 F	None	13Ap02Nv
LENNIN, M.		22 M	Unknown	13Ap02Nv
MCHUGH, My.		03 F	Child	13Ap02Nv
LANON, W.		46 M	Unknown	13Ap02Nv
U	(W)	40 F	Wife	13Ap02Nv
COATS, M.		22 M	Unknown	13Ap02Nv
BANNON, Biddy		13 F	None	13Ap02Nv
Jenney		10 F	None	13Ap02Nv
Susan		08 F	Child	13Ap02Nv
John		05 M	Child	13Ap02Nv
Henry		02 M	Child	13Ap02Nv
SALMAN, My.		30 F	None	13Ap02Nv
Nicholas		30 M	Unknown	13Ap02Nv
MCELLISTER, E.		40 M	Laborer	13Ap02Nv
U	(W)	29 F	Wife	13Ap02Nv
Eliza	(D)	10 F	None	13Ap02Nv
Hugh	(S)	07 M	Child	13Ap02Nv
John	(S)	05 M	Child	13Ap02Nv
Bessy	(D)	12 F	None	13Ap02Nv
Biddy	(D)	01 F	Child	13Ap02Nv
CONLY, Nancy		22 F	None	13Ap02Nv
HULL, Cath.		11 F	None	13Ap02Nv
CLARK, T.		30 M	Unknown	13Ap02Nv
FARRING, Jane		21 F	None	13Ap02Nv
REYNOLDS, T.		30 M	Unknown	13Ap02Nv
DOLAN, M.		24 M	Unknown	13Ap02Nv
QUIN, P.		20 M	Unknown	13Ap02Nv
SALLY, W.		27 M	Unknown	13Ap02Nv
M.		13 F	None	13Ap02Nv
Hy.		10 M	None	13Ap02Nv
Bessy		06 F	Child	13Ap02Nv
John		05 M	Child	13Ap02Nv
Sarah		01 F	Child	13Ap02Nv
Jane		02 F	Child	13Ap02Nv
ALLEN, P.		25 M	Unknown	13Ap02Nv
My.		24 F	None	13Ap02Nv
MORAN, E.		21 M	Unknown	13Ap02Nv
MCGREW, Jane		01 F	Child	13Ap02Nv
ABARNUM, Anna		21 F	None	13Ap02Nv
Ellen		18 F	None	13Ap02Nv
Cath.		66 F	None	13Ap02Nv
John		04 M	Child	13Ap02Nv
CULLENS, J.		24 M	Unknown	13Ap02Nv
Cath.		24 F	None	13Ap02Nv
Thos.		20 M	Unknown	13Ap02Nv
My.		02 M	Child	13Ap02Nv
Sally		01 F	None	13Ap02Nv
HESLIN, J.		24 M	Unknown	13Ap02Nv
U	(W)	24 F	Wife	13Ap02Nv
CURREY, J.		18 M	Unknown	13Ap02Nv
BURNS, M.		30 M	Unknown	13Ap02Nv
GUINY, C.		11 M	Unknown	13Ap02Nv
DERNIN, A.		24 M	Unknown	13Ap02Nv
A.		24 M	Unknown	13Ap02Nv
CASY, H.		29 M	Unknown	13Ap02Nv
BURNS, M.		30 M	Laborer	13Ap02Nv
GRIMES, C.		11 M	None	13Ap02Nv
DWIRE, A.		24 M	Unknown	13Ap02Nv
COURY, H.		27 M	Unknown	13Ap02Nv
U-Mrs.		38 F	None	13Ap02Nv
Cath.		10 F	None	13Ap02Nv
Rose		09 F	Child	13Ap02Nv
SULLIVAN, W.		30 M	Unknown	13Ap02Nv
Michal		30 M	Unknown	13Ap02Nv
MCELISTER, E.		40 M	Unknown	13Ap02Nv
Mry.	(W)	29 F	Wife	13Ap02Nv
Eliza	(D)	10 F	None	13Ap02Nv
Hugh	(S)	07 M	Child	13Ap02Nv
John	(S)	05 M	Child	13Ap02Nv
Bessy	(D)	13 F	None	13Ap02Nv
Lucy	(D)	01 F	Child	13Ap02Nv

NAMES OF PASSENGERS		AGE	SEX	OCCUPATIONS	DATE PORT SHIP	NAMES OF PASSENGERS		AGE	SEX	OCCUPATIONS	DATE PORT SHIP
CONLY, Nancy		22	F	None	13Ap02Nv	GILMAN, J.		20	M	Unknown	13Ap02Nv
Huc--, Cath.		11	F	None	13Ap02Nv	QUATLON, J.		18	M	Unknown	13Ap02Nv
CLARK, T.		30	M	Unknown	13Ap02Nv	GLOWN, Honora		50	F	None	13Ap02Nv
JENNINGS, Jane		21	F	None	13Ap02Nv	Jane		50	F	None	13Ap02Nv
REYNOLDS, T.		30	M	Unknown	13Ap02Nv	BRENNEN, D.		20	M	Unknown	13Ap02Nv
DELAN, M.		24	M	Unknown	13Ap02Nv	U	(W)	18	F	Wife	13Ap02Nv
QUINN, P.		20	M	Unknown	13Ap02Nv	Martin		15	M	None	13Ap02Nv
LALLEY, W.		39	M	Unknown	13Ap02Nv	Michael		22	M	Unknown	13Ap02Nv
U	(W)	39	F	Wife	13Ap02Nv	Pat		26	M	Unknown	13Ap02Nv
Hy.	(S)	13	M	None	13Ap02Nv	ORILEY, F.		21	M	Unknown	13Ap02Nv
Bessy	(D)	10	F	None	13Ap02Nv	HENNLEY, B.		24	M	Unknown	13Ap02Nv
Lucy	(D)	06	F	Child	13Ap02Nv	CASTER, R.		24	M	Unknown	13Ap02Nv
John	(S)	05	M	Child	13Ap02Nv	Jas.		25	M	Unknown	13Ap02Nv
Sarah	(D)	01	F	Child	13Ap02Nv	Cath.		24	F	None	13Ap02Nv
Jane	(D)	02	F	Child	13Ap02Nv	Ann		18	F	None	13Ap02Nv
ALLEN, P.		20	M	Unknown	13Ap02Nv	WATERN, D.		21	M	Unknown	13Ap02Nv
Ann-My.		20	F	None	13Ap02Nv	KELLY, E.		24	M	Unknown	13Ap02Nv
MORGAN, E.		26	M	Unknown	13Ap02Nv	CAZELL, Eliza		23	F	None	13Ap02Nv
MOORE, Ann		23	F	None	13Ap02Nv	LOREN, J.		22	M	Unknown	13Ap02Nv
Ellen		18	M	None	13Ap02Nv	Maria		20	F	None	13Ap02Nv
Cath.		06	F	Child	13Ap02Nv	SMITH, M.		28	M	Unknown	13Ap02Nv
John		04	M	Child	13Ap02Nv	DUFF, J.		22	M	Unknown	13Ap02Nv
CULLEN, J.		24	M	Unknown	13Ap02Nv	Andrew		18	M	Unknown	13Ap02Nv
DOLAN, My.		18	F	None	13Ap02Nv	LEENON, Ann		20	F	None	13Ap02Nv
MCMURRY, M.		23	M	Unknown	13Ap02Nv	MAGHAN, T.		45	M	Unknown	13Ap02Nv
Cath.		21	F	None	13Ap02Nv	Thos.	(S)	18	M	Unknown	13Ap02Nv
Mry.		16	F	None	13Ap02Nv	Edwd.	(S)	17	M	Unknown	13Ap02Nv
GERRENTY, J.M.		22	M	Unknown	13Ap02Nv	Peter	(S)	19	M	Unknown	13Ap02Nv
MULLIN, C.		30	M	Unknown	13Ap02Nv	U	(W)	40	F	Wife	13Ap02Nv
WELSH, J.		30	M	Unknown	13Ap02Nv	CUNEFF, T.		27	M	Unknown	13Ap02Nv
U-Mrs.		50	F	None	13Ap02Nv	LALLY, P.		20	M	Unknown	13Ap02Nv
Maria		13	F	None	13Ap02Nv	Sally		26	F	None	13Ap02Nv
Mry.		11	F	None	13Ap02Nv	Ellen		22	F	None	13Ap02Nv
John		07	M	Child	13Ap02Nv	Pat		21	M	Laborer	13Ap02Nv
Jas.		07	M	Child	13Ap02Nv	BROMWALT, W.		22	M	Laborer	13Ap02Nv
Lawrence		04	M	Child	13Ap02Nv	OLOUGHAN, Jane		22	F	None	13Ap02Nv
Henry		02	M	Child	13Ap02Nv	U-Mrs.		24	F	None	13Ap02Nv
Emily		01	F	Child	13Ap02Nv	Wm.		20	M	Unknown	13Ap02Nv
CUSACK, G.		21	M	Unknown	13Ap02Nv	CRANLY, O.		45	M	Unknown	13Ap02Nv
MULLIN, J.		15	M	Unknown	13Ap02Nv	My.	(W)	40	F	Wife	13Ap02Nv
Michl.		13	M	Unknown	13Ap02Nv	Jane	(D)	13	F	None	13Ap02Nv
Owen		10	M	Unknown	13Ap02Nv	Pat	(S)	11	M	None	13Ap02Nv
John		07	M	Child	13Ap02Nv	Cath.	(D)	08	F	Child	13Ap02Nv
Christopher		04	M	Child	13Ap02Nv	Jas.	(S)	06	M	Child	13Ap02Nv
Mry.		02	F	Child	13Ap02Nv	Edwd.	(S)	03	M	Child	13Ap02Nv
RAY, P.		35	M	Unknown	13Ap02Nv	FINIGAN, Ellen		15	F	None	13Ap02Nv
My.	(W)	35	F	Wife	13Ap02Nv	DIXSON, P.		24	M	Unknown	13Ap02Nv
Mgt.	(D)	05	F	Child	13Ap02Nv	COYLAN, P.		20	M	Unknown	13Ap02Nv
Cath.	(D)	03	F	Child	13Ap02Nv	KEENE, Susan		19	F	None	13Ap02Nv
Jane	(D)	01	F	Child	13Ap02Nv	MCDONNA, Jane		24	F	None	13Ap02Nv
DOYLE, Bgt.		20	F	None	13Ap02Nv	BRADY, C.		24	M	Unknown	13Ap02Nv
Bessy	(D)	01	F	Child	13Ap02Nv	CORCORAN, Wm.		24	M	Unknown	13Ap02Nv
DUNN, F.		30	M	Unknown	13Ap02Nv	My.		19	F	None	13Ap02Nv
Cathe.	(W)	24	F	Unknown	13Ap02Nv	STEVENSON, J.		22	M	Unknown	13Ap02Nv
Thos.	(S)	01	M	Child	13Ap02Nv	BENSIN, M.		25	M	Unknown	13Ap02Nv
KENNON, Ellen		20	F	None	13Ap02Nv	COMBNER, P.		28	M	Unknown	13Ap02Nv
WALSH, J.		40	M	Unknown	13Ap02Nv	MCCANNEN, A.		48	M	Unknown	13Ap02Nv
Mry.	(W)	40	F	Wife	13Ap02Nv	MCLARY, M.		35	M	Unknown	13Ap02Nv
Mgt.	(D)	16	F	None	13Ap02Nv	IHAN, Jane		21	F	None	13Ap02Nv
Richd.	(S)	14	M	None	13Ap02Nv	STUART, C.		22	M	Unknown	13Ap02Nv
My.		45	F	None	13Ap02Nv	CONNER, A.		26	M	Unknown	13Ap02Nv
Richd.	(S)	17	M	Unknown	13Ap02Nv	BRADY, A.		24	M	Unknown	13Ap02Nv
Bgt.	(D)	14	F	None	13Ap02Nv	GLASSEN, P.		22	M	Unknown	13Ap02Nv
BURNS, J.		24	M	Unknown	13Ap02Nv	FITZGERALD, M.		26	M	Unknown	13Ap02Nv
My.		33	F	None	13Ap02Nv	FOWLY, H.		24	M	Unknown	13Ap02Nv
MURPHY, Jane		21	F	None	13Ap02Nv	DRURY, My.		20	M	Unknown	13Ap02Nv
PHILLEN, J.		18	M	Laborer	13Ap02Nv	MEYLAND, Fr.		26	M	Unknown	13Ap02Nv
HAES, P.		20	M	Laborer	13Ap02Nv	DOANES, J.		26	M	Unknown	13Ap02Nv
KENNEDY, M.		20	M	Laborer	13Ap02Nv	BUTT, C.		26	M	Unknown	13Ap02Nv
CAMP, Cath.		21	F	None	13Ap02Nv	SMITH, W.		28	M	Unknown	13Ap02Nv
TRACY, Mgt.		20	F	None	13Ap02Nv	Cath.		26	F	None	13Ap02Nv
RIES, My.		13	F	None	13Ap02Nv	COFFEE, S.		25	M	Unknown	13Ap02Nv
FLOGERTY, M.		09	M	Child	13Ap02Nv	CAVENAUGH, J.		25	M	Unknown	13Ap02Nv
PHILLIPS, J.		19	M	Unknown	13Ap02Nv	U	(W)	25	F	Wife	13Ap02Nv
My.		22	F	None	13Ap02Nv	Pat	(S)	05	M	Child	13Ap02Nv

429

NAMES OF PASSENGERS		AGE	SEX	OCCUPATIONS	DATE PORT SHIP
CAVENAUGH, My.	(D)	02	F	Child	13Ap02Nv
CARLY, B.		21	M	Unknown	13Ap02Nv
CAVENAUGH, J.		20	M	Unknown	13Ap02Nv
CORLY, U-Mrs.		20	F	None	13Ap02Nv
GREYSON, Jane		20	F	None	13Ap02Nv
TRACY, P.		24	M	Unknown	13Ap02Nv
MORAN, W.		50	M	Unknown	13Ap02Nv
U	(W)	46	F	Wife	13Ap02Nv
Jas.		30	M	Unknown	13Ap02Nv
Patty	(D)	18	F	None	13Ap02Nv
My.	(D)	14	F	None	13Ap02Nv
LAUGHAN, J.		21	M	Unknown	13Ap02Nv
WELSH, J.		20	M	Unknown	13Ap02Nv
WHELLAN, My.		32	F	None	13Ap02Nv
John	(S)	16	M	Unknown	13Ap02Nv
CAVENAUGH, J.		25	M	Unknown	13Ap02Nv
MOONY, R.		48	M	Unknown	13Ap02Nv
Nancy	(D)	16	F	None	13Ap02Nv
Jane	(D)	13	F	None	13Ap02Nv
FITZGERALD, C.		24	M	Unknown	13Ap02Nv
CLERY, Bess		20	F	None	13Ap02Nv
DONNELAN, J.		33	M	Unknown	13Ap02Nv
MORRIS, J.		33	M	Unknown	13Ap02Nv
MULLEN, B.		24	M	Unknown	13Ap02Nv
DEMPY, M.		20	M	Unknown	13Ap02Nv
Bgt.		19	F	None	13Ap02Nv
CASHAN, J.		24	M	Unknown	13Ap02Nv
Cath.		21	F	None	13Ap02Nv
WARD, P.		17	M	Unknown	13Ap02Nv
BOHEN, Cath.		22	F	None	13Ap02Nv
MAHON, P.		22	M	Unknown	13Ap02Nv
JONES, Ha--T		01	F	Child	13Ap02Nv
MORAN, M.		26	M	Unknown	13Ap02Nv
Sonv--, T.		24	M	Unknown	13Ap02Nv
THOMAS, S.		24	M	Unknown	13Ap02Nv
KANY, P.		25	M	Unknown	13Ap02Nv
DEAYNTON, A.		26	M	Unknown	13Ap02Nv
Mich.		25	M	Unknown	13Ap02Nv
U-Mrs.	(M)	56	F	None	13Ap02Nv
REAUGHTON, Hona.		28	F	None	13Ap02Nv
Patch		28	M	Laborer	13Ap02Nv
Anty.		23	M	Laborer	13Ap02Nv
Thos.		21	M	Laborer	13Ap02Nv
Anthy.		01	M	Child	13Ap02Nv
CORMICK, Ann		20	F	None	13Ap02Nv
BUCK, M.		21	M	Unknown	13Ap02Nv
Nicholas		21	M	Unknown	13Ap02Nv
GARRICK, P.		24	M	Unknown	13Ap02Nv
U-Mrs.		34	F	None	13Ap02Nv
BURNS, M.		21	M	Unknown	13Ap02Nv
MCANEAW, J.		26	M	Unknown	13Ap02Nv
DOUGHERTY, B.		26	M	Unknown	13Ap02Nv
U	(W)	20	F	Wife	13Ap02Nv
Bdgt.		20	F	Wife	13Ap02Nv
MCCORMICK, Bdgt.		21	F	Wife	13Ap02Nv
My.		27	F	Wife	13Ap02Nv
GRAHAM, D.		22	M	Unknown	13Ap02Nv
George		30	M	Unknown	13Ap02Nv
Elenora		21	F	None	13Ap02Nv
CARRINGTON, M.		24	M	Unknown	13Ap02Nv
BRADY, Mgt.		24	F	None	13Ap02Nv
Cath.	(D)	01	F	Child	13Ap02Nv
MOONY, R.		48	M	Unknown	13Ap02Nv
Mary	(D)	16	F	None	13Ap02Nv
Jane	(D)	13	F	None	13Ap02Nv
STEVENSON, J.		22	M	Unknown	13Ap02Nv
SARAN, Ann		20	F	None	13Ap02Nv
MONOHAN, T.		45	M	Unknown	13Ap02Nv
Edwrd.	(S)	17	M	Unknown	13Ap02Nv
Peter	(S)	13	M	Unknown	13Ap02Nv
U	(W)	40	F	Wife	13Ap02Nv
KUNIFF, T.		27	M	Unknown	13Ap02Nv
FLURY, P.		20	M	Unknown	13Ap02Nv
Sally		24	F	None	13Ap02Nv
Ellen		22	F	None	13Ap02Nv
KURLY, P.		21	M	Unknown	13Ap02Nv
BRADACK, Wm.		12	M	Unknown	13Ap02Nv
MCLAUGHLIN, J.		22	M	Unknown	13Ap02Nv
U	(W)	24	F	Wife	13Ap02Nv
Wm.		20	M	None	13Ap02Nv
MCLINSKE, My.		24	F	None	13Ap02Nv
LAUGHIN, W.		20	M	Laborer	13Ap02Nv
CURLY, C.		45	M	Unknown	13Ap02Nv
U	(W)	40	F	Wife	13Ap02Nv
John	(S)	13	M	None	13Ap02Nv
Patch	(S)	11	M	None	13Ap02Nv
Cath.	(D)	18	F	None	13Ap02Nv
James	(S)	06	M	Child	13Ap02Nv
Edwd.	(S)	03	M	Child	13Ap02Nv
My.	(D)	01	F	Child	13Ap02Nv
WALKER, M.		14	M	Unknown	13Ap02Nv
BURNS, M.		25	M	Unknown	13Ap02Nv

IMPERIAL 14 APRIL 1847

From Sligo

NAMES OF PASSENGERS		AGE	SEX	OCCUPATIONS	DATE PORT SHIP
THOMPSON, William		41	M	Laborer	14Ap280k
Nancy	(W)	45	F	Unknown	14Ap280k
John	(S)	18	M	Laborer	14Ap280k
Bridget	(D)	19	F	Unknown	14Ap280k
Mary	(D)	14	F	Unknown	14Ap280k
James	(S)	22	M	Laborer	14Ap280k
GALLAGHER, James		28	M	Laborer	14Ap280k
GORMAN, John		21	M	Laborer	14Ap280k
KENNY, James		35	M	Laborer	14Ap280k
MCGETTRICK, John		20	M	Laborer	14Ap280k
DANAGHER, Michael		26	M	Laborer	14Ap280k
GORMAN, John		21	M	Laborer	14Ap280k
Fanny		18	F	Unknown	14Ap280k
MULHERN, Ellen		18	F	Unknown	14Ap280k
DUNN, Patrick		19	M	Laborer	14Ap280k
WARD, James		19	M	Laborer	14Ap280k
DEVANY, Nancy		19	F	Unknown	14Ap280k
GRIMES, James		36	M	Laborer	14Ap280k
CUNLISK, James		18	M	Laborer	14Ap280k
MURRAY, Dan		21	M	Laborer	14Ap280k
GILLEN, Domnick		21	M	Laborer	14Ap280k
FINNEGAN, John		20	M	Laborer	14Ap280k
WATERS, James		22	M	Laborer	14Ap280k
Michael		18	M	Laborer	14Ap280k
Patrick		16	M	Laborer	14Ap280k
Henry		14	M	Laborer	14Ap280k
Cath.		11	F	Unknown	14Ap280k
DILLON, Daniel		22	M	Laborer	14Ap280k
ROONEY, Francis		20	M	Laborer	14Ap280k
Mary	(W)	22	F	Wife	14Ap280k
Kate	(D)	01	F	Child	14Ap280k
DEVANY, Michael		34	M	Laborer	14Ap280k
Mary	(D)	15	F	Unknown	14Ap280k
Michael	(S)	14	M	Laborer	14Ap280k
Alice	(D)	10	F	Unknown	14Ap280k
LOFTUS, Michael		30	M	Laborer	14Ap280k
Mary		35	F	Unknown	14Ap280k
Mary		20	F	Unknown	14Ap280k
Kate	(D)	10	F	Unknown	14Ap280k
Frank	(S)	10	M	Laborer	14Ap280k
MALANY, Owen		50	M	Laborer	14Ap280k
James		18	M	Laborer	14Ap280k
BARRET, John		45	M	Laborer	14Ap280k
Walter	(S)	20	M	Laborer	14Ap280k
Catharine	(D)	15	F	Unknown	14Ap280k
James	(S)	13	M	Laborer	14Ap280k
LOCHLIN, John		22	M	Laborer	14Ap280k

NAMES OF PASSENGERS	AGE	SEX	OCCUPATIONS	DATE PORT SHIP
LOCHLIN, Matthew	20	M	Laborer	14Ap280k
John	20	M	Laborer	14Ap280k
HILLIS, Michael	25	M	Laborer	14Ap280k
Mary	20	F	Unknown	14Ap280k
FINNEGAN, James	22	M	Laborer	14Ap280k
HANLY, Bele	20	F	Unknown	14Ap280k
HATLEY, Andrew	16	M	Laborer	14Ap280k
Mary	09	F	Child	14Ap280k
John	14	M	Laborer	14Ap280k
Mary (M)	51	F	Unknown	14Ap280k
FINNEGAN, Thomas	21	M	Laborer	14Ap280k
Nancy	19	F	Unknown	14Ap280k
James	14	M	Laborer	14Ap280k
Michael	14	M	Laborer	14Ap280k
MOFFIT, John	10	M	Laborer	14Ap280k
Margt.	21	F	Unknown	14Ap280k
Kate	23	F	Unknown	14Ap280k
DUNN, Hugh	18	M	Laborer	14Ap280k
KEARNY, Stephen	22	M	Laborer	14Ap280k
May	23	F	Unknown	14Ap280k
CULLEN, Owen	48	M	Laborer	14Ap280k
Honor	13	F	Unknown	14Ap280k
Mary	26	F	Unknown	14Ap280k
Ellen	08	F	Child	14Ap280k
KELLY, Biddy	43	F	Unknown	14Ap280k
John (S)	03	M	Child	14Ap280k
Bartholemew (S)	08	M	Child	14Ap280k
SMITH, Kate	21	F	Unknown	14Ap280k
FINNEGAN, Henry	22	M	Laborer	14Ap280k
FEENY, Mary	23	F	Unknown	14Ap280k
MCCOUL, Ann	15	F	Unknown	14Ap280k
KELLY, Ann	18	F	Unknown	14Ap280k
MAGUIRK, Teresa	19	F	Unknown	14Ap280k
FINNEGAN, Matthew	.00	M	Infant	14Ap280k
Born-At-Sea				
COYNE, Bridget	24	F	Unknown	14Ap280k

JOHN-BRIGHT 14 APRIL 1847

From Liverpool

NAMES OF PASSENGERS	AGE	SEX	OCCUPATIONS	DATE PORT SHIP
LYNCH, J.	00	M	Laborer	14Ap020J
Bridget	00	F	Unknown	14Ap020J
NOAM, Thomas	00	M	Laborer	14Ap020J
John	00	M	Laborer	14Ap020J
Nersiney	00	F	Unknown	14Ap020J
Patrick	00	M	Unknown	14Ap020J
Biddy	00	F	Unknown	14Ap020J
NEEDHAM, John	00	M	Laborer	14Ap020J
MULLONEY, Michael	00	M	Laborer	14Ap020J
COSTELLA, Thos.	00	M	Laborer	14Ap020J
SCAMMILL, William	00	M	Laborer	14Ap020J
Johanna	00	F	Unknown	14Ap020J
Margaret	00	F	Unknown	14Ap020J
Johanna	00	F	Unknown	14Ap020J
Mary	00	F	Unknown	14Ap020J
KAIN, James	00	M	Farmer	14Ap020J
Robt.	00	M	Farmer	14Ap020J
Biddy	00	F	Unknown	14Ap020J
Sarah	00	F	Unknown	14Ap020J
Daniel	00	M	Laborer	14Ap020J
NOAM, Michl.	00	M	Laborer	14Ap020J
Ann	00	F	Unknown	14Ap020J
Mary	00	F	Unknown	14Ap020J
John	00	M	Unknown	14Ap020J
Margaret	00	F	Unknown	14Ap020J
MCGUIRE, Hugh	00	M	Laborer	14Ap020J
Mary	00	F	Unknown	14Ap020J
Ann	00	F	Unknown	14Ap020J

NAMES OF PASSENGERS	AGE	SEX	OCCUPATIONS	DATE PORT SHIP
MCGUIRE, Biddy	00	F	Unknown	14Ap020J
MCDONNEUGH, James	00	M	Laborer	14Ap020J
KAYLOUGHTON, Norton	00	M	Laborer	14Ap020J
GRANEY, Michl.	00	M	Laborer	14Ap020J
GOULAGHTER, Park.	00	M	Laborer	14Ap020J
GRANEY, Jas.	00	M	Laborer	14Ap020J
KELLY, Jas.	00	M	Laborer	14Ap020J
WALSH, Barth.	00	M	Laborer	14Ap020J
MCLOUGHLIN, J.	00	M	Laborer	14Ap020J
BURKE, J.	00	M	Laborer	14Ap020J
GIBBON, Ellen	00	F	Unknown	14Ap020J
DORAN, Ann	00	F	Unknown	14Ap020J
FLOYD, Rose	00	F	Unknown	14Ap020J
Biddy	00	F	Unknown	14Ap020J
GERGE, Biddy	00	F	Unknown	14Ap020J
Margaret	00	F	Unknown	14Ap020J
JENNINS, Bridget	00	F	Unknown	14Ap020J
GAWLING, Michl.	00	M	Laborer	14Ap020J
PENDERGRAST, Jas.	00	M	Laborer	14Ap020J
Thos.	00	M	Laborer	14Ap020J
GANNON, Thos.	00	M	Laborer	14Ap020J
WALSH, Biddy	00	F	Unknown	14Ap020J
Cath.	00	F	Unknown	14Ap020J
DONNOLLAN, Margt.	00	F	Unknown	14Ap020J
BRANNON, Owen	00	M	Laborer	14Ap020J
Margt.	00	F	Unknown	14Ap020J
Edward	00	M	Unknown	14Ap020J
Patrick	00	M	Unknown	14Ap020J
MULREY, Timothy	00	M	Unknown	14Ap020J
CARICHER, Patrick	00	M	Laborer	14Ap020J
Jas.	00	M	Laborer	14Ap020J
HOTHER, Patrick	00	M	Laborer	14Ap020J
Mary	00	F	Unknown	14Ap020J
NORTON, Biddy	00	F	Unknown	14Ap020J
KEYMAN, Peter	00	M	Unknown	14Ap020J
Honor	00	F	Unknown	14Ap020J
Ann	00	F	Unknown	14Ap020J
Rose	00	F	Unknown	14Ap020J
Peter	00	M	Unknown	14Ap020J
Hugh	00	M	Unknown	14Ap020J
Cathe.	00	F	Unknown	14Ap020J
BURNS, Daniel	00	M	Unknown	14Ap020J
Biddy	00	F	Unknown	14Ap020J
John	00	M	Laborer	14Ap020J
THEY, D.	00	M	Laborer	14Ap020J
MULAN, Cath.	00	F	Unknown	14Ap020J
Ellen	00	F	Unknown	14Ap020J
MOONY, Cath.	00	F	Unknown	14Ap020J
COLEMAN, My.	00	F	Unknown	14Ap020J
WATERMAN, J.	00	M	Unknown	14Ap020J
HOPE, J.	00	M	Unknown	14Ap020J
HURANT, J.	00	M	Unknown	14Ap020J
KERWIN, P.	00	M	Unknown	14Ap020J
PARSEN, R.	00	M	Unknown	14Ap020J
JORDAN, P.	00	M	Unknown	14Ap020J
Ellen	00	F	Unknown	14Ap020J
Bgt.	00	F	Unknown	14Ap020J
MCMULLIN, F.	00	M	Laborer	14Ap020J
Anat.	00	M	Laborer	14Ap020J
Frans.	00	M	Laborer	14Ap020J
Mgt.	00	F	Unknown	14Ap020J
John	00	M	Unknown	14Ap020J
My.Jane	00	F	Unknown	14Ap020J
James	00	M	Unknown	14Ap020J
Cath.	00	F	Unknown	14Ap020J
KENNEDY, J.	00	M	Unknown	14Ap020J
Thos.	00	M	Unknown	14Ap020J
CONNY, M.	00	M	Unknown	14Ap020J
CORMICK, T.	00	M	Unknown	14Ap020J
JORDAN, P.	00	M	Unknown	14Ap020J
KENNEDY, M.	00	M	Unknown	14Ap020J
Bgt.	00	F	Unknown	14Ap020J
My.	00	F	Unknown	14Ap020J
MCCAUGH, J.	00	M	Unknown	14Ap020J
Mary	00	F	Unknown	14Ap020J

NAMES OF PASSENGERS		AGE	SEX	OCCUPATIONS	DATE PORT SHIP
MCCAUGH, Bridget		00	F	Unknown	14Ap020J
James		00	M	Unknown	14Ap020J
John		00	M	Unknown	14Ap020J
James		00	M	Unknown	14Ap020J
Mary		00	F	Unknown	14Ap020J
Bridget		00	F	Unknown	14Ap020J
Ellen		00	F	Unknown	14Ap020J
KENNEDY, Patrick		00	M	Laborer	14Ap020J
Con		00	M	Laborer	14Ap020J
KING, Domenica		00	M	Laborer	14Ap020J
MCHALE, Sarah		00	F	Laborer	14Ap020J
NELLAN, Patrick		00	M	Laborer	14Ap020J
Bridget		00	F	Laborer	14Ap020J
Mary		00	F	Laborer	14Ap020J
BARRETT, Ellen		00	F	Laborer	14Ap020J
MCNEILL, John		00	M	Laborer	14Ap020J
FLOYD, John		00	M	Laborer	14Ap020J
Jane		00	F	Laborer	14Ap020J

MARY-MORRIS 15 APRIL 1847

From Glasgow

NAMES OF PASSENGERS		AGE	SEX	OCCUPATIONS	DATE PORT SHIP
MCHUGH, James		33	M	Mechanic	15Ap040I
MCLINN, Martin		26	M	Laborer	15Ap040I
CONDIN, John		20	M	Laborer	15Ap040I
MCHUGH, Bgdgt.		22	F	None	15Ap040I
MCGRAPH, James		27	M	Laborer	15Ap040I
Peggy		20	F	None	15Ap040I
FLAMBY, Biddy		15	F	None	15Ap040I
BUCK, Patk.		42	M	Laborer	15Ap040I
James	(S)	05	M	Child	15Ap040I
John	(S)	11	M	None	15Ap040I
Sally	(D)	10	F	None	15Ap040I
MCCOUGHLIN, Jas.		35	M	Laborer	15Ap040I
OMOULIN, Judy		22	F	None	15Ap040I
Brdgt.	(D)	02	F	Child	15Ap040I
LANGDON, Thos.		40	M	None	15Ap040I
WELSH, Nelly		30	F	None	15Ap040I
John		20	M	None	15Ap040I
Nancy		22	F	None	15Ap040I
GAGHANN, Jas.		40	M	Laborer	15Ap040I
Nancy		40	F	None	15Ap040I
CORRY, Pat		25	M	Laborer	15Ap040I
W.		20	M	Laborer	15Ap040I
Nancy		15	F	None	15Ap040I
GAGHANN, Helen		13	F	None	15Ap040I
Brdg.		01	F	Child	15Ap040I
LAVELL, Antony		35	M	Laborer	15Ap040I
CORRY, Patk.		30	M	Laborer	15Ap040I
Nancy		30	F	None	15Ap040I
MCHUGH, John		03	M	Child	15Ap040I
CROWE, John		52	M	Laborer	15Ap040I
Mary	(D)	13	F	None	15Ap040I
OBRIAN, Helen		24	F	None	15Ap040I
Helen	(D)	.01	F	Infant	15Ap040I
DOBSON, Susan		19	F	None	15Ap040I
GAUGHAN, Edwd.		19	M	Laborer	15Ap040I
ABERNTHY, John		22	M	Farmer	15Ap040I
WALKEN, Patk.		25	M	Laborer	15Ap040I
GUNNING, Anthony		25	M	Laborer	15Ap040I
GORNGAIN, Patk.		20	M	Laborer	15Ap040I
CRANY, Frank		52	M	Farmer	15Ap040I
HUNTER, Mary		23	F	None	15Ap040I
CORK, Jane		16	F	None	15Ap040I
Benjn.		18	M	Laborer	15Ap040I
Mary		18	F	None	15Ap040I
James		16	M	None	15Ap040I
BOYLE, Willm.		45	M	Farmer	15Ap040I

NAMES OF PASSENGERS		AGE	SEX	OCCUPATIONS	DATE PORT SHIP
BOYLE, Elizbth.	(W)	36	F	Wife	15Ap040I
Jean	(D)	14	F	Wife	15Ap040I
Margt.	(D)	10	F	Wife	15Ap040I
Chas.	(S)	08	M	Child	15Ap040I
Willm.	(S)	05	M	Child	15Ap040I
James	(S)	01	M	Child	15Ap040I
MCCORMICK, John		25	M	Laborer	15Ap040I
DOBIN, James		22	M	Farmer	15Ap040I
Jean	(W)	22	F	Wife	15Ap040I
Willm.	(S)	02	M	Child	15Ap040I
Margt.	(D)	.09	F	Infant	15Ap040I
MCCONOLLY, Robt.		20	M	Mechanic	15Ap040I
Margt.	(W)	20	F	None	15Ap040I
Danl.	(S)	.04	M	Infant	15Ap040I
GALLAGHER, David		21	M	Merchant	15Ap040I
Cath.		25	F	None	15Ap040I
HUME, Patk.		24	M	Laborer	15Ap040I
MCCASKY, Thos.		21	M	Laborer	15Ap040I
GILRAID, Pat		45	M	Laborer	15Ap040I
Hannah		40	F	None	15Ap040I
HUNSTER, Alexr.		19	M	None	15Ap040I
GILRAID, Cathe.		13	F	None	15Ap040I
John		04	M	Child	15Ap040I
Bernard		02	M	Child	15Ap040I
MCCORMICK, Mich.		19	M	Laborer	15Ap040I
Jean		19	F	None	15Ap040I
SCOTT, Jas.Esq.		38	M	Unknown	15Ap040I
MCGEE, J.F.Esq.		35	M	Unknown	15Ap040I
BROWN, John		23	M	Unknown	15Ap040I
FRAZER, Mary		20	F	None	15Ap040I
BURNET, Eliza		29	F	None	15Ap040I
MCKIM, Jane		03	F	Child	15Ap040I
KASSON, Saml.		25	M	Laborer	15Ap040I
Mary		21	F	None	15Ap040I
IRVIN, Peggy		45	F	None	15Ap040I
STERLING, Mgt.		40	F	None	15Ap040I
JAMEISON, Alex.		50	M	Laborer	15Ap040I
Willm.	(S)	23	M	Mechanic	15Ap040I
Alex.	(S)	21	M	Farmer	15Ap040I
Sally	(D)	19	F	None	15Ap040I
John	(S)	17	M	Farmer	15Ap040I
Ellen	(D)	13	F	None	15Ap040I
James	(S)	10	M	None	15Ap040I
Danl.	(S)	07	M	Child	15Ap040I
Jane	(W)	50	F	Wife	15Ap040I
MCCURLY, Sally		37	F	None	15Ap040I
STEWART, Jas.		23	M	Laborer	15Ap040I
Andw.		22	M	Laborer	15Ap040I
NEIL, John		40	M	Mechanic	15Ap040I
Mary		44	F	None	15Ap040I
ALLEN, Hannah-M.		17	F	None	15Ap040I
James		14	M	None	15Ap040I
Bernard		10	M	None	15Ap040I
MALONY, Mary		21	F	None	15Ap040I
PATTERSON, James		22	M	Mechanic	15Ap040I
MCLANY, Margt.		23	F	None	15Ap040I
Willm.		16	M	Farmer	15Ap040I
James		18	M	Farmer	15Ap040I
LANGREY, Willm.		23	M	Mechanic	15Ap040I
DOURGHY, Jno.		19	M	Mechanic	15Ap040I
MURPHY, Denis		35	M	Mechanic	15Ap040I
Mary		30	F	None	15Ap040I
MULLIGAN, Jas.		60	M	Laborer	15Ap040I
Ann	(W)	60	F	Wife	15Ap040I
Ann	(D)	26	F	None	15Ap040I
Ellen	(D)	20	F	None	15Ap040I
Frances	(D)	24	F	None	15Ap040I
James	(S)	13	M	None	15Ap040I
Ann	(D)	13	F	None	15Ap040I
Margt.	(D)	08	F	Child	15Ap040I
Cathrn.	(D)	10	F	None	15Ap040I
Mary	(D)	.07	F	Infant	15Ap040I
CRAIG, Ann		50	F	None	15Ap040I
Thos.	(S)	23	M	None	15Ap040I
Betsey	(D)	20	F	None	15Ap040I

NAMES OF PASSENGERS		AGE	SEX	OCCUPATIONS	DATE PORT SHIP
CRAIG, Michael	(S)	14	M	None	15Ap0401
James	(S)	12	M	None	15Ap0401
Andrew	(S)	08	M	Child	15Ap0401
William	(S)	05	M	Child	15Ap0401
MCCADDIN, Thos.		24	M	Farmer	15Ap0401
Elizabeth		16	F	None	15Ap0401
CLARK, Geo.		40	M	Farmer	15Ap0401
Mgt.	(W)	40	F	Wife	15Ap0401
Andrew	(S)	20	M	Farmer	15Ap0401
George	(S)	13	M	None	15Ap0401
David	(S)	11	M	None	15Ap0401
Mary	(D)	09	F	Child	15Ap0401
Rose	(D)	07	F	Child	15Ap0401
HENRY, Willm.		24	M	Laborer	15Ap0401
MCNEIL, Willm.		20	M	Clerk	15Ap0401
MCCADDIN, Rosanna		15	F	None	15Ap0401
MCNEIL, Mary-A.		16	F	None	15Ap0401
Elizabeth		10	F	None	15Ap0401
Cathe.		06	F	Child	15Ap0401
MARIS, John		20	M	Laborer	15Ap0401
Archd.		17	M	Laborer	15Ap0401
SHIELD, Tho.		18	M	Mechanic	15Ap0401
GALLAGHER, Elizth.		40	F	None	15Ap0401
Mary	(D)	19	F	None	15Ap0401
MCELIN, Martha		20	F	None	15Ap0401
MCKINNA, Mary		21	F	None	15Ap0401
KELLEY, Jas.		16	M	None	15Ap0401
MCHENNRY, Jas.		21	M	Sawer	15Ap0401
MCGINIS, John		23	M	Mechanic	15Ap0401
MAKIN, Mary-J.M.		18	F	None	15Ap0401
Elizabeth		14	F	None	15Ap0401
KENNEYDY, Jas.		24	M	Laborer	15Ap0401
CLYDE, John		30	M	Laborer	15Ap0401
FANEL, John		18	M	Laborer	15Ap0401
MCRINN, James		28	M	Laborer	15Ap0401
Jane	(W)	28	F	Wife	15Ap0401
Jas.	(S)	08	M	Child	15Ap0401

CUSHLAMACHREE 15 APRIL 1847

From Galway

NAMES OF PASSENGERS		AGE	SEX	OCCUPATIONS	DATE PORT SHIP
KIREN, James		25	M	Laborer	15Ap110m
MONAGAN, John		24	M	Laborer	15Ap110m
DOLAN, William		18	M	Laborer	15Ap110m
Kitty		19	F	Laborer	15Ap110m
NEE, Pat		29	M	Laborer	15Ap110m
KEARNS, Pat		23	M	Laborer	15Ap110m
GRADY, Coleman		22	M	Laborer	15Ap110m
Elizabeth	(W)	00	F	Wife	15Ap110m
HERNON, Martin		25	M	Laborer	15Ap110m
Honor	(W)	22	F	Wife	15Ap110m
CUDDIN, Mary		16	F	Spinster	15Ap110m
CONOLY, Dominic		26	M	Laborer	15Ap110m
Mary	(W)	20	F	Wife	15Ap110m
MOYLAN, Bryan		28	M	Laborer	15Ap110m
Wineford	(W)	26	F	Wife	15Ap110m
SHAUGHNESSY, John		24	M	Laborer	15Ap110m
MEEHAN, Honor		18	F	Spinster	15Ap110m
DUNPHEY, Richd.		20	M	Laborer	15Ap110m
Mary		17	F	Spinster	15Ap110m
HAVERLY, Thomas		24	M	Laborer	15Ap110m
FORD, Biddy		17	F	Spinster	15Ap110m
MCCARTHY, Edward		29	M	Farmer	15Ap110m
James		27	M	Farmer	15Ap110m
Pat		25	M	Farmer	15Ap110m
Darby		24	M	Farmer	15Ap110m
Daniel		25	M	Farmer	15Ap110m
John		26	M	Farmer	15Ap110m

NAMES OF PASSENGERS		AGE	SEX	OCCUPATIONS	DATE PORT SHIP
KELLY, Simon		25	M	Farmer	15Ap110m
LEONARD, John		22	M	Laborer	15Ap110m
HESSIAN, James		23	M	Laborer	15Ap110m
TUNNY, John		25	M	Laborer	15Ap110m
ROONY, Michael		24	M	Laborer	15Ap110m
CONNOLLY, William		24	M	Laborer	15Ap110m
MORRISSY, John		21	M	Laborer	15Ap110m
FAHEY, Pat		20	M	Laborer	15Ap110m
MORROSSY, Mgt.		19	F	Spinster	15Ap110m
MURPHY, Cath.		18	F	Spinster	15Ap110m
MURRAY, James		28	M	Laborer	15Ap110m
Biddy	(W)	23	F	Wife	15Ap110m
Kate	(D)	03	F	Child	15Ap110m
MCGUIN, Cath.		17	F	Spinster	15Ap110m
FAHEY, John		27	M	Laborer	15Ap110m
Nelly	(W)	25	F	Wife	15Ap110m
DONALLEN, Bridget		17	F	Spinster	15Ap110m
KAIN, Michael		22	M	Laborer	15Ap110m
KEALY, Thos.		20	M	Laborer	15Ap110m
Judy	(W)	20	F	Wife	15Ap110m
Wm.	(S)	01	M	Child	15Ap110m
SULLIVAN, Mare		18	F	Dressmaker	15Ap110m
ROSS, Mary-Ellen		10	F	None	15Ap110m
WARD, Patt		20	M	Laborer	15Ap110m
MELLY, Thos.		23	M	Shoemaker	15Ap110m
CANARVAN, Nicholas		21	M	Shoemaker	15Ap110m
CARTY, Ann		17	F	Spinster	15Ap110m
Maria		17	F	Spinster	15Ap110m
Jane		18	F	Spinster	15Ap110m
Cath.		15	F	Spinster	15Ap110m
COSTELLO, Anna		35	F	Matron	15Ap110m
John	(S)	18	M	Laborer	15Ap110m
Thos.	(S)	10	M	Laborer	15Ap110m
Ellen	(D)	19	F	None	15Ap110m
CHADOOCK, Martin		21	M	Laborer	15Ap110m
John		23	M	Laborer	15Ap110m
Michael		22	M	Laborer	15Ap110m
Mary		29	F	Matron	15Ap110m
MITCHELL, Wm.		25	M	Laborer	15Ap110m
Bridget	(W)	20	F	Wife	15Ap110m
Thos.		22	M	None	15Ap110m
RYAN, John		45	M	Laborer	15Ap110m
Cicily	(W)	39	F	Wife	15Ap110m
Darly	(S)	21	M	Laborer	15Ap110m
Nelly	(D)	19	F	Spinster	15Ap110m
Biddy	(D)	18	F	Spinster	15Ap110m
Kitty	(D)	16	F	Spinster	15Ap110m
Cicila	(D)	15	F	Spinster	15Ap110m
James	(S)	12	M	Spinster	15Ap110m
PAREGHER, John		24	M	Laborer	15Ap110m
RYAN, James		75	M	Laborer	15Ap110m
				Died-At-Sea	
Peggy	(W)	63	F	Wife	15Ap110m
Winford	(D)	35	F	None	15Ap110m
John	(S)	40	M	Laborer	15Ap110m
Jerry	(S)	19	M	Laborer	15Ap110m
James	(S)	17	M	Laborer	15Ap110m
GARVY, Wm.		23	M	Laborer	15Ap110m
James		25	M	Laborer	15Ap110m
Bridget		00	F	Wife	15Ap110m
LEE, Danl.		32	M	Laborer	15Ap110m
Winneford	(W)	30	F	Wife	15Ap110m
Biddy	(D)	15	F	None	15Ap110m
John	(S)	10	M	Laborer	15Ap110m
Peter	(S)	08	M	Child	15Ap110m
KELLY, John		19	M	Laborer	15Ap110m
Mgt.	(W)	24	F	Wife	15Ap110m
FLAHERTY, Martin		25	M	Laborer	15Ap110m
Wm.		23	M	Laborer	15Ap110m
CONNOLY, L.		04	M	Child	15Ap110m
FAHEY, John		02	M	Child	15Ap110m
CALLAGAN, John		22	M	Laborer	15Ap110m
JOYCE, Richd.		25	M	Laborer	15Ap110m
Sella		25	F	Laborer	15Ap110m
Mary		20	F	Laborer	15Ap110m

NAMES OF PASSENGERS		AGE	SEX	OCCUPATIONS	DATE PORT SHIP
CRONAN, Malchy		35	M	Laborer	15Apl10m
Honor	(W)	32	F	Wife	15Apl10m
Honor	(D)	12	F	None	15Apl10m
Mary	(D)	10	F	None	15Apl10m
Tim	(S)	08	M	Child	15Apl10m
Hubert	(S)	06	M	Child	15Apl10m
MALIO, Patt		22	M	Laborer	15Apl10m
Bridget		18	F	None	15Apl10m
MILLIDAY, Michael		23	M	Laborer	15Apl10m
Mary	(W)	19	F	Wife	15Apl10m
BURN, John		23	M	Laborer	15Apl10m
Mgt.	(W)	20	F	Wife	15Apl10m
Biddy		18	F	Spinster	15Apl10m
FAHEY, John		25	M	Laborer	15Apl10m
MURRAY, Wm.		25	M	Laborer	15Apl10m
Judy	(W)	20	F	Wife	15Apl10m
CRAWAN, Thomas		28	M	Farmer	15Apl10m
COLGAN, Thomas		26	M	Farmer	15Apl10m
Honor	(W)	24	F	Wife	15Apl10m
Ann		22	F	Spinster	15Apl10m
Mgt.		16	F	Spinster	15Apl10m
Mary	(M)	40	F	Matron	15Apl10m
CARTY, Patt		24	M	Laborer	15Apl10m
BURK, Michael		22	M	Laborer	15Apl10m

OXFORD 15 APRIL 1847

From Liverpool

NAMES OF PASSENGERS		AGE	SEX	OCCUPATIONS	DATE PORT SHIP
TUNNY, John		18	M	Servant	15Ap02AJ
Rose		16	F	Servant	15Ap02AJ
DUNCAN, Michael		25	M	Farmer	15Ap02AJ
REYNOLDS, James		20	M	Laborer	15Ap02AJ
MCCANN, Daniel		21	M	Farmer	15Ap02AJ
REYNOLDS, Mary		21	F	Dressmaker	15Ap02AJ
HALIKAN, Margerit		34	F	Servant	15Ap02AJ
PLUNKETT, Richd.		20	M	Laborer	15Ap02AJ
Catherine		23	F	Servant	15Ap02AJ
GOODWIN, Michl.		20	M	Farmer	15Ap02AJ
LENNON, John		20	M	Clerk	15Ap02AJ
MAGUIRE, James		20	M	Shoemaker	15Ap02AJ
CROTTY, Francis		27	M	Engineer	15Ap02AJ
MULLAN, Francis		15	M	Laborer	15Ap02AJ
Sarah		14	F	Servant	15Ap02AJ
MONAHAN, Bernard		21	M	Blacksmith	15Ap02AJ
Margeret		20	F	Servant	15Ap02AJ
MOLLOY, Mary		14	F	Servant	15Ap02AJ
Hugh		11	M	Servant	15Ap02AJ
MULVEY, Jane		17	F	Servant	15Ap02AJ
MURRAY, John		10	M	None	15Ap02AJ
Patrick		12	M	None	15Ap02AJ
Mary-Anne		15	F	None	15Ap02AJ
HALLIGAN, Richard		15	M	None	15Ap02AJ
RILEY, Mary		20	F	Servant	15Ap02AJ
SWEENY, John		20	M	Laborer	15Ap02AJ
CLIFFORD, Bridget		20	F	Servant	15Ap02AJ
MCLOUGHLIN, Patrick		22	M	Blacksmith	15Ap02AJ
HAGARTY, Eliza.		50	F	None	15Ap02AJ
HARRINGTON, Ellen		18	F	Seamstress	15Ap02AJ
William		22	M	Laborer	15Ap02AJ
Edward		20	M	Laborer	15Ap02AJ
Adam		13	M	Laborer	15Ap02AJ
Susan		09	F	Child	15Ap02AJ
Ellen		30	F	Servant	15Ap02AJ
Sarah		20	F	Servant	15Ap02AJ
MCGRIFFIN, Mary		07	F	Child	15Ap02AJ
FITZGERALD, Martin		20	M	Laborer	15Ap02AJ
KENNEDY, Catharin		26	F	Servant	15Ap02AJ
CARROLE, James		22	M	Tailor	15Ap02AJ

NAMES OF PASSENGERS		AGE	SEX	OCCUPATIONS	DATE PORT SHIP
SMITH, Mary		18	F	Servant	15Ap02AJ
HAMMON, Sarah		60	F	Servant	15Ap02AJ
George	(S)	20	M	Laborer	15Ap02AJ
Anne	(D)	20	F	Servant	15Ap02AJ
TULLY, Rose		13	F	Servant	15Ap02AJ
WOODS, George		20	M	Laborer	15Ap02AJ
FREE, Julia		18	F	Servant	15Ap02AJ
Bridget		18	F	Servant	15Ap02AJ
DUNNE, Mary		18	F	Servant	15Ap02AJ
KELLY, Mary		18	F	Servant	15Ap02AJ
COOKE, Thomas		20	M	Laborer	15Ap02AJ
REARDON, John		20	M	Baker	15Ap02AJ
RILEY, Francis		20	M	Laborer	15Ap02AJ
REARTY, Rose		20	F	Servant	15Ap02AJ
COX, James		16	M	Servant	15Ap02AJ
Margaret		18	F	Servant	15Ap02AJ
CAHILL, Honora		20	F	Servant	15Ap02AJ
DALTON, Honora		20	F	Servant	15Ap02AJ
FLYNN, Ann		13	F	Servant	15Ap02AJ
FARRELL, Anne		18	F	Servant	15Ap02AJ
WARD, Ann		20	F	Servant	15Ap02AJ
BANNON, John		20	M	Laborer	14Ap02AJ
HEFFINEN, Mary		18	F	Laborer	15Ap02AJ
MURPHY, Mary		37	F	Servant	15Ap02AJ
Died-At-Sea					
Mary	(D)	05	F	Child	15Ap02AJ
John	(S)	03	M	Child	15Ap02AJ
RENN, James		20	M	Laborer	15Ap02AJ
RILEY, Patrick		20	M	Laborer	15Ap02AJ
MOLLOY, John		20	M	Shoemaker	15Ap02AJ
CLARKE, Mary		20	F	Servant	15Ap02AJ
GARTY, Richard		16	M	Tailor	15Ap02AJ
MCCEGLEY, Mary		20	F	Tailor	15Ap02AJ
MUNDAY, Ellen		17	F	Servant	15Ap02AJ
Patrick		20	M	Laborer	15Ap02AJ
BYRNES, Mary		13	F	Servant	15Ap02AJ
GUINN, John		22	M	Laborer	15Ap02AJ
DUNN, Anne		40	F	Laborer	15Ap02AJ
MCQUELLAN, Fanny		20	F	Servant	15Ap02AJ
Ann		20	F	Servant	15Ap02AJ
CAMPBELL, John		26	M	Laborer	15Ap02AJ
Margerit	(M)	44	F	Servant	15Ap02AJ
LAHEE, Dennis		40	M	Shoemaker	15Ap02AJ
U	(W)	40	F	Wife	15Ap02AJ
Catharine	(D)	20	F	Shoemaker	15Ap02AJ
Bridget	(D)	20	F	Shoemaker	15Ap02AJ
Julia	(D)	18	F	Shoemaker	15Ap02AJ
Dora	(D)	15	F	None	15Ap02AJ
John	(S)	13	M	None	15Ap02AJ
Jerry	(S)	02	M	Child	15Ap02AJ
Died-At-Sea					
MCGRATH, James		24	M	Farmer	15Ap02AJ
DENNING, Catherine		20	F	Servant	15Ap02AJ
GAUST, U		24	M	Carpenter	15Ap02AJ
HERN, David		18	M	Laborer	15Ap02AJ
Patrick		19	M	Laborer	15Ap02AJ
John		17	M	Laborer	15Ap02AJ
BRIEN, Margerit		20	F	Servant	15Ap02AJ
DENNING, Margerit		20	F	Servant	15Ap02AJ
QUIRK, Margerit		20	F	Servant	15Ap02A,
John		20	M	Servant	15Ap02AJ
BARRETT, Richard		20	M	Servant	15Ap02AJ
REILLY, Mary		20	F	Servant	15Ap02AJ
HOY, Patrick		40	M	Farmer	15Ap02A,
SWEETMAN, Patrick		24	M	Farmer	15Ap02A,
U	(W)	20	F	Wife	15Ap02A,
MANGAN, Richard		40	M	Currier	15Ap02A,
CASEY, James		25	M	Laborer	15Ap02A,
MARSHALL, Oliver		18	M	Clerk	15Ap02A,
BURKE, Bartm.		22	M	Clerk	15Ap02A,
HASTINGS, William		15	M	Clerk	15Ap02A,
CONNELL, Patrick		20	M	Saddler	15Ap02A,
KELLY, Mary		20	F	Servant	15Ap02A,
CUNNIFF, Catherine		20	F	Servant	15Ap02A,
CUMMING, Mary		20	F	Servant	15Ap02A,

NAMES OF PASSENGERS	AGE	SEX	OCCUPATIONS	DATE PORT SHIP	NAMES OF PASSENGERS	AGE	SEX	OCCUPATIONS	DATE PORT SHIP
CUMMING, Luke	20	M	Laborer	15Ap02AJ	SMITH, Eliza	20	F	Servant	15Ap02AJ
Thomas	20	M	Laborer	15Ap02AJ	MEYERS, William	24	M	Farmer	15Ap02AJ
ROWLEY, Bernard	20	M	Laborer	15Ap02AJ	Colevide	29	M	Farmer	15Ap02AJ
MCDONNELL, John	29	M	Laborer	15Ap02AJ	Robert	25	M	Farmer	15Ap02AJ
WALSH, Daniel	26	M	Gentleman	15Ap02AJ	Mary-Ann	21	F	Servant	15Ap02AJ
MCCAFFREY, Mary	16	F	Servant	15Ap02AJ	Martha	12	F	Servant	15Ap02AJ
CORNELL, Eliza	19	F	Servant	15Ap02AJ	Anabella	10	F	Servant	15Ap02AJ
MALONE, Margerlt	19	F	Servant	15Ap02AJ	OWENS, John	25	M	Farmer	15Ap02AJ
KEALY, John	19	M	Servant	15Ap02AJ	CALHOUN, John	23	M	Laborer	15Ap02AJ
David	24	M	Servant	15Ap02AJ	BYRNE, Terance	16	M	Laborer	15Ap02AJ
BEGLIN, Margerlt	21	F	Servant	15Ap02AJ	BRENNAN, James	20	M	Laborer	15Ap02AJ
PLUNKETT, Joseph	20	M	Farmer	15Ap02AJ	NEWMAN, Mathew	26	M	Laborer	15Ap02AJ
Patrick	20	M	Farmer	15Ap02AJ	NUGENT, Anne	25	F	Servant	15Ap02AJ
Mary	20	F	Farmer	15Ap02AJ	FAY, Julia	18	F	Servant	15Ap02AJ
BYRNE, Rose	17	F	Farmer	15Ap02AJ	BEYER, Mary	21	F	Servant	15Ap02AJ
MCGRANE, Mary	20	F	Farmer	15Ap02AJ	DOHERTY, John	30	M	Weaver	15Ap02AJ
Thomas	20	M	Nailer	15Ap02AJ	Edward	20	M	Laborer	15Ap02AJ
ROARTY, Daniel	10	M	Servant	15Ap02AJ	BRIEN, Mathew	20	M	Laborer	15Ap02AJ
HANNAGH, David	27	M	Weaver	15Ap02AJ	Patrick	06	M	Child	15Ap02AJ
U	(W)	25	F	Wife	15Ap02AJ	James	26	M	Laborer	15Ap02AJ
Margerlt	12	F	Servant	15Ap02AJ	Mary	06	F	Child	15Ap02AJ
SEDLEY, James	26	M	Laborer	15Ap02AJ	Julia	20	F	Laborer	15Ap02AJ
WOODS, Andrew	24	M	Laborer	15Ap02AJ	CLEARY, Rose	18	F	Servant	15Ap02AJ
BOIRES, James	30	M	Farmer	15Ap02AJ	HIGGINS, Andrew	18	M	Servant	15Ap02AJ
KEAFE, Patrick	24	M	Laborer	15Ap02AJ	RYAN, John	20	M	Farmer	15Ap02AJ
COYNE, Mathew	38	M	Laborer	15Ap02AJ	GAHAGAN, Peter	20	M	Laborer	15Ap02AJ
TANNER, John	20	M	Farmer	15Ap02AJ	Patrick	22	M	Laborer	15Ap02AJ
FLYNN, Denis	24	M	Blacksmith	15Ap02AJ	Anne	20	F	Servant	15Ap02AJ
MOLLOY, Michl.	20	M	Laborer	15Ap02AJ	Catherine	20	F	Servant	15Ap02AJ
DOOLAN, Cathrine	20	F	Servant	15Ap02AJ	BROTHERTON, Eliza	20	F	Teacher	15Ap02AJ
MCSORLEY, William	20	M	Engineer	15Ap02AJ	Alice	13	F	None	15Ap02AJ
CONOLLEY, Edward	20	M	Painter	15Ap02AJ	DONOVAN, Mary	22	F	Servant	15Ap02AJ
GOODWIN, Alice	20	F	Servant	15Ap02AJ	GILLIGAN, Eliza	22	F	Servant	15Ap02AJ
LAMBERT, John	35	M	Stone Mason	15Ap02AJ	John	26	M	Engraver	15Ap02AJ
Mary	(W)	27	F	Servant	15Ap02AJ	THORN, Mary	18	F	Servant	15Ap02AJ
Mary	(D)	05	F	Child	15Ap02AJ	HUGHES, Michael	20	M	Laborer	15Ap02AJ
Ann	(D)	03	F	Child	15Ap02AJ	MULLANY, William	20	M	Farmer	15Ap02AJ
MAKER, Ellen	20	F	Servant	15Ap02AJ	Patrick	20	M	Farmer	15Ap02AJ
MCNAMEE, Ann	20	F	Servant	15Ap02AJ	GRACE, Patrick	20	M	Farmer	15Ap02AJ
MCKEOWN, Patrick	20	M	Laborer	15Ap02AJ	NEIL, Morton	38	M	Saddler	15Ap02AJ
MACKEY, Patrick	20	M	Laborer	15Ap02AJ	ROBERTSON, Dorothy	20	F	Servant	15Ap02AJ
TUNNY, Patrick	60	M	Farmer	15Ap02AJ	Charlotte	17	F	Servant	15Ap02AJ
Thomas	(S)	22	M	Farmer	15Ap02AJ	FAIRLEY, Michael	25	M	Laborer	15Ap02AJ
William	(S)	20	M	Farmer	15Ap02AJ	Bridget	17	F	Servant	15Ap02AJ
GOODTHOUGHT, John	45	M	Gentleman	15Ap02AJ	Mary	18	F	Servant	15Ap02AJ
GREEN, William	20	M	Farmer	15Ap02AJ	MOONEY, Michael	22	M	Laborer	15Ap02AJ
CLANCY, Thomas	20	M	Laborer	15Ap02AJ	RIDGEWAY, John	30	M	Laborer	15Ap02AJ
Hugh	25	M	Laborer	15Ap02AJ	Ellen	(W)	30	F	Servant	15Ap02AJ
MATHEWS, Margerlt	20	F	Servant	15Ap02AJ	William	(S)	03	M	Child	15Ap02AJ
PRESTON, William	30	M	Laborer	15Ap02AJ	HALLIGAN, James	24	M	Servant	15Ap02AJ
U	(W)	25	F	Wife	15Ap02AJ	ARMSTRONG, Thomas	23	M	Gdnr	15Ap02AJ
U	01	U	Child	15Ap02AJ	KENNY, John	25	M	Farmer	15Ap02AJ
AUSTIN, Susan	14	F	None	15Ap02AJ	SMITH, Ellen	24	F	Servant	15Ap02AJ
HEALY, Mary	16	F	Servant	15Ap02AJ	KELLY, Eliza	24	F	Servant	15Ap02AJ
KELLY, Joseph	20	M	Tailor	15Ap02AJ	DALY, Patrick	20	M	Farmer	15Ap02AJ
CARROLL, Thomas	40	M	Laborer	15Ap02AJ	HYLAND, Susan	20	F	Servant	15Ap02AJ
HAYES, William	44	M	Laborer	15Ap02AJ	GOODWIN, Thomas	24	M	Laborer	15Ap02AJ
DELANY, Mary	20	F	Servant	15Ap02AJ	CARTY, Patrick	20	M	Groom	15Ap02AJ
BRIEN, William	30	M	Farmer	15Ap02AJ	Catharin	16	F	Servant	15Ap02AJ
WALSH, Michl.	20	M	Laborer	15Ap02AJ	MCCAFFREY, James	18	M	Tailor	15Ap02AJ
RILEY, Richard	20	M	Farmer	15Ap02AJ	Mary	14	F	Servant	15Ap02AJ
WHELAN, Patrick	19	M	Farmer	15Ap02AJ	RILEY, Ellen	18	F	Servant	15Ap02AJ
BURKE, James	22	M	Laborer	15Ap02AJ	DOYLE, Margeret	18	F	Servant	15Ap02AJ
DWYER, Patrick	26	M	Laborer	15Ap02AJ	HANNAN, Thomas	20	M	Laborer	15Ap02AJ
HARMAN, Eliza	25	F	Servant	15Ap02AJ	HARRINGTON, Thomas	20	M	Laborer	15Ap02AJ
Margeret	18	F	Servant	15Ap02AJ	Margaret	20	F	Servant	15Ap02AJ
WHELAN, Laurence	20	M	Joiner	15Ap02AJ	MORGAN, John	20	M	Servant	15Ap02AJ
Margerlt	18	F	Servant	15Ap02AJ	REYNOLDS, Francis	20	M	Tailor	15Ap02AJ
ONEIL, Christopher	30	M	Laborer	15Ap02AJ	Eliza	20	F	Seamstress	15Ap02AJ
Amelia	30	F	Laborer	15Ap02AJ	MCCONNELL, Anne	20	F	Servant	15Ap02AJ
DAWSON, Abraham	40	M	Butcher	15Ap02AJ	REYNOLDS, Margeret	16	F	Servant	15Ap02AJ
Henry	(S)	20	M	Butcher	15Ap02AJ	TIMMONS, Mary	25	F	Dressmaker	15Ap02AJ
DUFFY, Brian	26	M	Laborer	15Ap02AJ	DONAGHOE, Margerlt	20	F	Servant	15Ap02AJ
Ann	20	F	Laborer	15Ap02AJ	DRURY, John	20	M	Laborer	15Ap02AJ
SARHEW, Ann	30	F	Servant	15Ap02AJ	Mary	20	F	Servant	15Ap02AJ

NAMES OF PASSENGERS	AGE	SEX	OCCUPATIONS	DATE PORT SHIP
AUBREY, Mary-Ann	25	F	Milliner	15Ap02AJ
FAGAN, Thomas	25	M	Laborer	15Ap02AJ
MONAGHAN, Margerit	20	F	Servant	15Ap02AJ
OCONNOR, John	20	M	Servant	15Ap02AJ
HUGHES, Andrew	20	M	Servant	15Ap02AJ
ENGLISH, James	30	M	Laborer	15Ap02AJ
Catharin (W)	30	F	Wife	15Ap02AJ
Mark (S)	11	M	None	15Ap02AJ
Margerit (D)	10	F	None	15Ap02AJ
James (S)	07	M	Child	15Ap02AJ
Catharin (D)	04	F	Child	15Ap02AJ
OHARA, Charles	20	M	Tailor	15Ap02AJ
PIKE, Thomas	18	M	Laborer	15Ap02AJ
MCKENNA, Catharin	50	F	Servant	15Ap02AJ
Mary (D)	26	F	Servant	15Ap02AJ
Thomas	01	M	Child	15Ap02AJ
COSGRAVE, James	30	M	Laborer	15Ap02AJ
FINEGAN, Rose	20	F	Servant	15Ap02AJ
BYRNES, Margerit	20	F	Servant	15Ap02AJ
CULLY, Anne	50	F	Servant	15Ap02AJ
Patrick	20	M	Carpenter	15Ap02AJ
CLINTON, Catharin	27	F	Servant	15Ap02AJ
MAGUIRE, John	20	M	Laborer	15Ap02AJ
LOUGHROY, Mary	20	F	Servant	15Ap02AJ
DELANY, Ann	20	F	Servant	15Ap02AJ

PONS 16 APRIL 1847

From Waterford

NAMES OF PASSENGERS	AGE	SEX	OCCUPATIONS	DATE PORT SHIP
DONOVAN, John	21	M	Boatman	16Ap160s
DELLY, John	20	M	Boatman	16Ap160s
CAVANAUGH, Andrew	22	M	Boatman	16Ap160s
WALSH, John	27	M	Laborer	16Ap160s
ENGLISH, John	28	M	Boatman	16Ap160s
RICKETT, William	26	M	Boatman	16Ap160s
MURPHY, James	28	M	Laborer	16Ap160s
RENSHALD, John	27	M	Laborer	16Ap160s
MCGRATH, James	26	M	Laborer	16Ap160s
MOORE, Thomas	29	M	Laborer	16Ap160s
REILLY, Richd.	29	M	Laborer	16Ap160s
DEZER, Patrick	27	M	Laborer	16Ap160s
POWER, Richard	28	M	Laborer	16Ap160s
LOWBER, Walter	21	M	Laborer	16Ap160s
HENSEY, Pierce	20	M	Laborer	16Ap160s
DALEY, John	21	M	Laborer	16Ap160s
MCDONALD, Patrick	22	M	Smith	16Ap160s
Mary (W)	21	F	Wife	16Ap160s
SMITH, Mary	19	F	Spinster	16Ap160s
LUTHER, John	27	M	Boatman	16Ap160s
CHEA, Margaret	22	F	Spinster	16Ap160s
RYAN, Eliza	22	F	Spinster	16Ap160s
MUNSEY, William	26	M	Laborer	16Ap160s
Thomas	27	M	Laborer	16Ap160s
QUALEY, John	20	M	Laborer	16Ap160s
KAHRE, Michael	20	M	Laborer	16Ap160s
FARRELL, Patrick	21	M	Cooper	16Ap160s
CARROLL, James	19	M	Laborer	16Ap160s
HOLAN, John	21	M	Laborer	16Ap160s
COEBER, George	21	M	Laborer	16Ap160s
CHANAHARD, Anastia	23	F	Spinster	16Ap160s
NEIVEN, Michael	21	M	Laborer	16Ap160s
CORDY, John	20	M	Laborer	16Ap160s
MAKER, Catherine	22	F	Spinster	16Ap160s
GALLINAN, Midgett	28	F	Spinster	16Ap160s
Michael	30	M	Laborer	16Ap160s
MCHINNEY, Pierce	24	M	Laborer	16Ap160s
MULLER, James	34	M	Laborer	16Ap160s
GALLAVAN, Mary	04	F	Child	16Ap160s

NAMES OF PASSENGERS	AGE	SEX	OCCUPATIONS	DATE PORT SHIP
CUNNINGHAM, Patt	24	M	Laborer	16Ap160s
KEATING, James	21	M	Laborer	16Ap160s
ARSHTON, John	17	M	Laborer	16Ap160s
ARTHAR, Martin	18	M	Laborer	16Ap160s
HACKETT, Michael	28	M	Laborer	16Ap160s
DRENEN, Martin	27	M	Laborer	16Ap160s
FITZGERALD, Michael	18	M	Laborer	16Ap160s
WALL, James	40	M	Laborer	16Ap160s
Ellen (W)	36	F	Wife	16Ap160s
John (S)	13	M	None	16Ap160s
Andrew (S)	12	M	None	16Ap160s
Bridget (D)	10	F	None	16Ap160s
Anastia (D)	08	F	Child	16Ap160s
Ellen (D)	06	F	Child	16Ap160s
William (S)	04	M	Child	16Ap160s
MURPHY, James	30	M	Laborer	16Ap160s
Eliza (W)	26	F	Wife	16Ap160s
DURNEY, Catherin	27	F	Spinster	16Ap160s
MURPHY, Patrick	29	M	Laborer	16Ap160s
CRANLEY, Johanna	22	F	Spinster	16Ap160s
DURLEY, Martin	23	M	Laborer	16Ap160s
NUGENT, Johanna	20	F	Spinster	16Ap160s
Margaret	18	F	Spinster	16Ap160s
DANIEL, John	25	M	Laborer	16Ap160s
Margaret (W)	25	F	Wife	16Ap160s
Margaret (M)	45	F	Wife	16Ap160s
Mary (D)	04	F	Child	16Ap160s
Margaret	40	F	Wife	16Ap160s
Died-At-Sea				
Eliza	26	F	Spinster	16Ap160s
Died-At-Sea				
John	24	M	Laborer	16Ap160s
Alice	22	F	Spinster	16Ap160s
Alice	23	F	Spinster	16Ap160s
Margaret	19	F	Spinster	16Ap160s
Henry	17	M	Laborer	16Ap160s
MULLONEY, Alice	17	F	Spinster	16Ap160s
MURPHY, Thomas	23	M	Laborer	16Ap160s
James	22	M	Laborer	16Ap160s
DOYLE, John	23	M	Laborer	16Ap160s
VAUGHAN, Margaret	24	F	Spinster	16Ap160s
LYNCH, John	20	M	Clerk	16Ap160s
NEILE, Henry	24	M	Salter	16Ap160s
MACKEN, Susan	20	F	Spinster	16Ap160s
Charles	10	M	Carpenter	16Ap160s
KELLY, John	38	M	Laborer	16Ap160s
CULLIN, Thomas	17	M	Laborer	16Ap160s
TOBIN, James	28	M	Laborer	16Ap160s
CORCORAN, Michael	25	M	Laborer	16Ap160s
CONNOR, Rtn.	22	M	Laborer	16Ap160s
POWERS, Richd.	26	M	Laborer	16Ap160s
MOORE, Michael	20	M	Unknown	16Ap160s
HEKETON, James	24	M	Laborer	16Ap160s
Ellen (W)	23	F	Wife	16Ap160s
ALNAYANT, Richd.	25	M	Laborer	16Ap160s
MCGRATH, Timothy	17	M	Shoemaker	16Ap160s
RYAN, John	26	M	Laborer	16Ap160s
FOGERTY, Richd.	18	M	Laborer	16Ap160s
MCCORMICK, Patrick	18	M	Laborer	16Ap160s
DAY, Thomas	34	M	Laborer	16Ap160s
CARTEY, William	08	M	Laborer	16Ap160s
MCGRATH, Michael	17	M	Laborer	16Ap160s
ONEILL, John	22	M	Laborer	16Ap160s
OCONNOR, John	00	M	Laborer	16Ap160s
CLEARY, John	28	M	Laborer	16Ap160s
BRIEN, Patrick	20	M	Laborer	16Ap160s
ROGERS, Ellen	20	F	Spinster	16Ap160s
FOLEY, Margaret	20	F	Spinster	16Ap160s
CROTTY, Margaret	22	F	Spinster	16Ap160s
MURPHY, Alice	.00	F	Infant	16Ap160s
DANIEL, Anastasia	.00	F	Infant	16Ap160s
PHELAN, Edwd.	25	M	Laborer	16Ap160s
WALSH, John	21	M	Shopkeeper	16Ap160s
MAKMAN, Nicholas	24	M	Carpenter	16Ap160s

436

GREAT-BRITAIN 16 APRIL 1847

From Belfast

NAMES OF PASSENGERS	Rel	AGE	SEX	OCCUPATIONS	DATE PORT SHIP
PRESTON, William		28	M	Farmer	16Ap07Hp
BLAIN, William		45	M	Farmer	16Ap07Hp
Robert		40	M	Farmer	16Ap07Hp
John		20	M	Farmer	16Ap07Hp
James		18	M	Farmer	16Ap07Hp
Jane		13	F	Farmer	16Ap07Hp
Margret		11	F	Farmer	16Ap07Hp
CAMMERON, William		40	M	Farmer	16Ap07Hp
Eliza	(W)	40	F	Wife	16Ap07Hp
Ann	(D)	16	F	Farmer	16Ap07Hp
Jane	(D)	14	F	Farmer	16Ap07Hp
James	(S)	12	M	Farmer	16Ap07Hp
CORR, Hugh		18	M	Farmer	16Ap07Hp
Sarah		12	F	Farmer	16Ap07Hp
John		16	M	Farmer	16Ap07Hp
Mary-Jane		20	F	Farmer	16Ap07Hp
Sarah		10	F	Farmer	16Ap07Hp
ELVIN, James		08	M	Child	16Ap07Hp
Elizabeth		50	F	Wife	16Ap07Hp
John		50	M	Farmer	16Ap07Hp
Sarah-Ann		24	F	Farmer	16Ap07Hp
Elizabeth		22	F	Farmer	16Ap07Hp
Jane		20	F	Farmer	16Ap07Hp
James		13	M	Farmer	16Ap07Hp
Edward		11	M	Farmer	16Ap07Hp
Charlott		09	F	Child	16Ap07Hp
Annabella		07	F	Child	16Ap07Hp
Mary		05	F	Child	16Ap07Hp
KIRKLAND, Isaac		03	M	Child	16Ap07Hp
Eliza		25	F	Farmer	16Ap07Hp
Margret		21	F	Farmer	16Ap07Hp
NEWBERRY, William		30	M	Farmer	16Ap07Hp
Thomas		28	M	Farmer	16Ap07Hp
MULLIGAN, David		19	M	Laborer	16Ap07Hp
DELINEE, John		18	M	Laborer	16Ap07Hp
HAGNEY, Catherine		30	F	Laborer	16Ap07Hp
DONNELLY, Margret		20	F	Laborer	16Ap07Hp
CUMMINS, John		40	M	Laborer	16Ap07Hp
Ann	(W)	40	F	Wife	16Ap07Hp
John	(S)	15	M	Laborer	16Ap07Hp
Sarah	(D)	13	F	Laborer	16Ap07Hp
George	(S)	11	M	Laborer	16Ap07Hp
Francis-Ann	(D)	09	F	Child	16Ap07Hp
Martha	(D)	07	F	Child	16Ap07Hp
Alex.	(S)	05	M	Child	16Ap07Hp
William	(S)	03	M	Child	16Ap07Hp
Joseph	(S)	01	M	Child	16Ap07Hp
GOODWIN, Peter		25	M	Laborer	16Ap07Hp
ONEIL, Hugh		26	M	Laborer	16Ap07Hp
Bella		22	F	Laborer	16Ap07Hp
SMITH, James		28	M	Laborer	16Ap07Hp
Bridget		26	F	Laborer	16Ap07Hp
HANNAH, Joseph		24	M	Laborer	16Ap07Hp
MCCANN, John		28	M	Laborer	16Ap07Hp
Mary		20	F	Laborer	16Ap07Hp
BOYLE, Mary		21	F	Laborer	16Ap07Hp
MCCANN, Catherine		.00	F	Infant	16Ap07Hp
MARTIN, William		30	M	Laborer	16Ap07Hp
DONNELLY, Felix		26	M	Laborer	16Ap07Hp
Rose		20	F	Laborer	16Ap07Hp
ONEILL, Clements		22	M	Laborer	16Ap07Hp
Mary-Ann		19	F	Laborer	16Ap07Hp
MACNAMARA, Arthur		21	M	Laborer	16Ap07Hp
RICHARDSON, James		27	M	Laborer	16Ap07Hp
FOSTER, William		28	M	Farmer	16Ap07Hp
FOSTER, Mary		20	F	Farmer	16Ap07Hp
Catherine		22	F	Farmer	16Ap07Hp
MCILYNN, Mary		40	F	Farmer	16Ap07Hp
MCKEOWN, Henry		36	M	Farmer	16Ap07Hp
Nancy	(W)	34	F	Wife	16Ap07Hp
John	(S)	15	M	Farmer	16Ap07Hp
Mary	(D)	13	F	Farmer	16Ap07Hp
Patrick	(S)	11	M	Farmer	16Ap07Hp
Isabella	(D)	09	F	Child	16Ap07Hp
Sarah-Ann	(D)	07	F	Child	16Ap07Hp
Thomas	(S)	03	M	Child	16Ap07Hp
DARRAGH, Michael		29	M	Farmer	16Ap07Hp
Bernard		27	M	Farmer	16Ap07Hp
MCCANN, James		30	M	Farmer	16Ap07Hp
MOYNAH, James		32	M	Farmer	16Ap07Hp
MCATEER, William		27	M	Farmer	16Ap07Hp
FEE, James		30	M	Farmer	16Ap07Hp
CLOSE, John		28	M	Farmer	16Ap07Hp
CAMPBELL, John		21	M	Farmer	16Ap07Hp
MCCARNEY, William		19	M	Farmer	16Ap07Hp
MCGUIRE, Ann		23	F	Farmer	16Ap07Hp
Mary		23	F	Farmer	16Ap07Hp
HAGAN, Bernard		27	M	Farmer	16Ap07Hp
LEWIS, John		30	M	Farmer	16Ap07Hp
FOLLY, Joseph		29	M	Farmer	16Ap07Hp
MCNALLY, James		29	M	Farmer	16Ap07Hp
Mary		19	F	Farmer	16Ap07Hp
MULLEN, George		21	M	Farmer	16Ap07Hp
FLANNERY, Charles		22	M	Farmer	16Ap07Hp
NAVAN, John		36	M	Laborer	16Ap07Hp
Mary	(W)	34	F	Wife	16Ap07Hp
Bridget	(D)	13	F	Laborer	16Ap07Hp
Ann	(D)	11	F	Laborer	16Ap07Hp
Margt.	(D)	09	F	Child	16Ap07Hp
Mary	(D)	07	F	Child	16Ap07Hp
Owen	(S)	05	M	Child	16Ap07Hp
Thos.	(S)	03	M	Child	16Ap07Hp
Catherine	(D)	01	F	Child	16Ap07Hp
MAGUIRE, Robert		29	M	Laborer	16Ap07Hp
FITZPATRICK, Patrick		23	M	Laborer	16Ap07Hp
DOONE, Patrick		38	M	Farmer	16Ap07Hp
Ann	(W)	34	F	Farmer	16Ap07Hp
John	(S)	08	M	Child	16Ap07Hp
Mary	(D)	06	F	Child	16Ap07Hp
Catharine	(D)	04	F	Child	16Ap07Hp
Ann-Jane	(D)	02	F	Child	16Ap07Hp
MCCLARNON, Hugh		21	M	Farmer	16Ap07Hp
MCMANUS, William		21	M	Farmer	16Ap07H
Mary		20	F	Farmer	16Ap07Hp
YOUNG, Robert		30	M	Farmer	16Ap07Hp
COLLINS, Robert		30	M	Farmer	16Ap07Hp
BLACK, David		26	M	Farmer	16Ap07Hp
Elizabeth	(W)	24	F	Wife	16Ap07Hp
Joseph	(S)	03	M	Child	16Ap07Hp
MCMANUS, John		27	M	Farmer	16Ap07Hp
NANN, Owen		30	M	Farmer	16Ap07Hp
Sarah	(W)	28	F	Wife	16Ap07Hp
Mary	(D)	04	F	Child	16Ap07Hp
Margt.	(D)	02	F	Child	16Ap07Hp
STANS, Bernard		23	M	Farmer	16Ap07Hp

OSCEOLA 16 APRIL 1847

From Glasgow

NAMES OF PASSENGERS	Rel	AGE	SEX	OCCUPATIONS	DATE PORT SHIP
CAMPBELL, James		48	M	Farmer	16Ap04Ot
Eliza	(W)	40	F	None	16Ap04Ot
George	(S)	06	M	Child	16Ap04Ot
James	(S)	04	M	Child	16Ap04Ot

NAMES OF PASSENGERS	A G E	S E X	OCCUPATIONS	DATE PORT SHIP	NAMES OF PASSENGERS	A G E	S E X	OCCUPATIONS	DATE PORT SHIP
FERRY, James		23	M	Farmer	16Ap040†	BROWN, Eliza	(D)	12	F	None	16Ap040†
Rose		38	F	None	16Ap040†	SIMPSON, Margt.		21	F	None	16Ap040†
MCLANY, Andrew		30	M	Farmer	16Ap040†	MCLAUGHLAN, Bridget		40	F	None	16Ap040†
MULLAN, Cathe.		14	F	None	16Ap040†	Mary	(D)	17	F	None	16Ap040†
Sally		12	F	None	16Ap040†	Rose	(D)	15	F	None	16Ap040†
John		09	M	Child	16Ap040†	Ann	(D)	13	F	None	16Ap040†
Eleanor		07	F	Child	16Ap040†	Wm.	(S)	11	M	None	16Ap040†
TERRY, Mary		03	F	Child	16Ap040†	MCGOWAN, Pat		54	M	Laborer	16Ap040†
Pat		.06	M	Infant	16Ap040†	Cathe.	(W)	54	F	None	16Ap040†
ADAMS, John		44	M	Laborer	16Ap040†	Patrick	(S)	24	M	Laborer	16Ap040†
Sarah	(W)	44	F	Wife	16Ap040†	Graw.	(S)	19	M	Laborer	16Ap040†
Jane	(D)	19	F	None	16Ap040†	ROGAN, James		60	M	Laborer	16Ap040†
James	(S)	10	M	None	16Ap040†	Bridget	(W)	60	F	Wife	16Ap040†
Andrew	(S)	11	M	None	16Ap040†	Winifred	(D)	25	F	None	16Ap040†
Jonas	(S)	03	M	Child	16Ap040†	Bridget	(D)	22	F	None	16Ap040†
KELLEY, Geo.		20	M	Laborer	16Ap040†	Elizabeth	(D)	14	F	None	16Ap040†
NIXON, And.		21	M	Laborer	16Ap040†	James	(S)	25	M	Laborer	16Ap040†
Isabella		15	F	None	16Ap040†	PEOPLES, John		46	M	Laborer	16Ap040†
DONAGHY, Richd.		60	M	Laborer	16Ap040†	Cathe.	(W)	36	F	Wife	16Ap040†
James	(S)	23	M	Laborer	16Ap040†	Ellen	(D)	14	F	None	16Ap040†
Ann	(D)	25	F	Laborer	16Ap040†	Jane	(D)	12	F	None	16Ap040†
Joseph	(S)	21	M	Laborer	16Ap040†	Hugh	(S)	06	M	Child	16Ap040†
Mary	(D)	27	F	None	16Ap040†	Cathe.	(D)	04	F	Child	16Ap040†
Peter	(S)	14	M	Laborer	16Ap040†	Charles	(S)	02	M	Child	16Ap040†
SWEENEY, Alexn.		22	M	Laborer	16Ap040†	BUCHANNON, John		45	M	Laborer	16Ap040†
ROSS, Constantin		20	M	Laborer	16Ap040†	Flora	(W)	45	F	Wife	16Ap040†
MCILHENNY, Wm.		50	M	Laborer	16Ap040†	John	(S)	18	M	Laborer	16Ap040†
Mary	(W)	56	F	Wife	16Ap040†	James	(S)	16	M	Laborer	16Ap040†
Elizabeth	(D)	12	F	None	16Ap040†	Mary-J.	(D)	13	F	None	16Ap040†
BENNETT, Robt.		30	M	Laborer	16Ap040†	Wm.G.	(S)	10	M	Laborer	16Ap040†
Margt.	(W)	22	F	Wife	16Ap040†	Moses	(S)	03	M	Child	16Ap040†
Mary	(D)	.06	F	Infant	16Ap040†	RUSSELL, Joseph		29	M	Laborer	16Ap040†
BRISLAND, Wm.		21	M	Laborer	16Ap040†	Margaret	(W)	29	F	Wife	16Ap040†
GRAY, Robt.		16	M	Laborer	16Ap040†	Nancy	(M)	50	F	None	16Ap040†
FLEMMING, Wm.		20	M	Laborer	16Ap040†	Ann	(D)	05	F	Child	16Ap040†
MANAN, Sarah		20	F	None	16Ap040†	James	(S)	03	M	Child	16Ap040†
BRUSTER, James		50	M	Farmer	16Ap040†	Adam	(S)	01	M	Child	16Ap040†
Mary	(W)	48	F	Wife	16Ap040†	CAMPBELL, Alex.		40	M	Farmer	16Ap040†
Jane	(D)	20	F	None	16Ap040†	Jane	(W)	38	F	Wife	16Ap040†
CURLMAN, Hugh		16	M	Farmer	16Ap040†	Martha	(D)	18	F	None	16Ap040†
Ann		14	F	None	16Ap040†	James	(S)	13	M	None	16Ap040†
M.J.		.06	M	Infant	16Ap040†	Catharine	(D)	09	F	Child	16Ap040†
MCGUITLAN, V.A.		17	F	None	16Ap040†	James	(S)	06	M	Child	16Ap040†
BARMATIN, M.J.		20	F	None	16Ap040†	Grace	(D)	04	F	Child	16Ap040†
CALDWELL, Saml.		25	M	Farmer	16Ap040†	Alexn.	(S)	.04	M	Infant	16Ap040†
Mary	(W)	21	F	Wife	16Ap040†	TAYLOR, Hugh		31	M	Laborer	16Ap040†
Isabella	(D)	.06	F	Infant	16Ap040†	Margt.		25	F	None	16Ap040†
MCNAMEE, Ed.		19	M	Farmer	16Ap040†	SWEENEY, Michael		30	M	Laborer	16Ap040†
ARMSTRONG, Margt.		45	F	None	16Ap040†	Ann		20	F	None	16Ap040†
Margt.	(D)	13	F	None	16Ap040†	Peter		13	M	None	16Ap040†
Charles	(S)	04	M	Child	16Ap040†	Thomas		11	M	None	16Ap040†
Jane	(D)	03	F	Child	16Ap040†	Daniel		22	M	Laborer	16Ap040†
MANN, Wm.		17	M	Laborer	16Ap040†	RULLER, Andrew		22	M	Laborer	16Ap040†
WHARMEL, John		22	M	Laborer	16Ap040†	Georgiann	(W)	22	F	None	16Ap040†
LANG, John		23	M	Laborer	16Ap040†	Thomas	(S)	.07	M	Infant	16Ap040†
Margt.		22	F	None	16Ap040†	PATTERSON, James		22	M	Laborer	16Ap040†
TAGGART, Hugh		26	M	Laborer	16Ap040†	EARSLEY, Charles		40	M	Laborer	16Ap040†
MANVAGNEWS, Ellen		19	F	None	16Ap040†	Jane	(W)	38	F	Wife	16Ap040†
CAMPBELL, John		50	M	Laborer	16Ap040†	Jane	(D)	13	F	Wife	16Ap040†
Ellen	(W)	45	F	Wife	16Ap040†	William	(S)	12	M	Laborer	16Ap040†
Patrick	(S)	19	M	Laborer	16Ap040†	Mary	(D)	10	F	None	16Ap040†
John	(S)	16	M	Laborer	16Ap040†	Ellen	(D)	08	F	Child	16Ap040†
James	(S)	13	M	Laborer	16Ap040†	Mary	(D)	06	F	Child	16Ap040†
Ann	(D)	11	F	Laborer	16Ap040†	Margt.	(D)	04	F	Child	16Ap040†
FORD, Thos.		19	M	Laborer	16Ap040†	Cath.	(D)	.06	F	Infant	16Ap040†
MCSEAN, Niel		24	M	Laborer	16Ap040†	ODONNELL, John		41	M	Farmer	16Ap040†
Robt.		24	M	Laborer	16Ap040†	MCMORNETH, R.		28	M	Farmer	16Ap040†
MCFALL, Cathe.		22	F	None	16Ap040†	STEWART, Wm.		30	M	Farmer	16Ap040†
KENNEDY, John		25	M	Laborer	16Ap040†	Ann	(W)	25	F	Wife	16Ap040†
MCDOUGAL, Isabella		26	F	None	16Ap040†	Charles	(S)	07	M	Child	16Ap040†
Marion		23	F	None	16Ap040†	Isabella	(D)	04	F	Child	16Ap040†
Agnes		21	F	None	16Ap040†	John	(S)	02	M	Child	16Ap040†
BROWN, James		38	M	Laborer	16Ap040†	Jane	(D)	02	F	Child	16Ap040†
Isabella	(W)	38	F	None	16Ap040†	Robt.		14	M	Laborer	16Ap040†
Mary	(D)	15	F	None	16Ap040†	Margaret		24	F	None	16Ap040†

NAMES OF PASSENGERS		AGE	SEX	OCCUPATIONS	DATE PORT SHIP	NAMES OF PASSENGERS		AGE	SEX	OCCUPATIONS	DATE PORT SHIP
STEWART, Jane		20	F	None	16Ap040†						
WILLSON, Joseph		20	M	Laborer	16Ap040†						
Sarah		18	F	None	16Ap040†						
SIMPSON, Henry		22	M	Laborer	16Ap040†						
Ellen		24	F	None	16Ap040†						
WOOD, Wm.		24	M	Laborer	16Ap040†	**HARMONY 16 APRIL 1847**					
CAMPBELL, Jane		11	F	None	16Ap040†						
Hannah		09	F	Child	16Ap040†	From Liverpool					
Alex.		07	M	Child	16Ap040†						
Ann		05	F	Child	16Ap040†						
KENNEDY, Martha		36	F	None	16Ap040†	MCCARDLE, Owen		25	M	Laborer	16Ap020y
LYNCH, Isabella		25	F	None	16Ap040†	Mick		24	M	Laborer	16Ap020y
CLARK, Wm.		25	M	Farmer	16Ap040†	Mary		20	F	None	16Ap020y
MCCLOY, Cathe.		20	F	None	16Ap040†	ARMSTRONG, Martin		24	M	Laborer	16Ap020y
FRIZIL, Wm.		25	M	Farmer	16Ap040†	Margt.		32	F	None	16Ap020y
MCCORMICK, Pat		26	M	Farmer	16Ap040†	MANNON, Mary		20	F	None	16Ap020y
HEALY, Thos.		18	M	Farmer	16Ap040†	CORREY, Brady		20	M	Laborer	16Ap020y
MCCLOY, Fanny		24	F	None	16Ap040†	BRADLEY, James		28	M	Laborer	16Ap020y
FERRY, Brian		36	M	Farmer	16Ap040†	CASSIDY, Pat		25	M	Laborer	16Ap020y
Elizabeth	(W)	35	F	Wife	16Ap040†	John		20	M	Laborer	16Ap020y
George	(S)	12	M	Laborer	16Ap040†	MCGUIRE, James		23	M	Laborer	16Ap020y
Cathe.	(D)	10	F	None	16Ap040†	CLARK, James		26	M	Laborer	16Ap020y
William	(S)	09	M	Child	16Ap040†	NOONEY, Elizabeth		17	F	None	16Ap020y
Mary	(D)	07	F	Child	16Ap040†	RILEY, Bryan		18	M	Laborer	16Ap020y
Brian	(S)	05	M	Child	16Ap040†	Margt.		17	F	None	16Ap020y
Jane	(D)	04	F	Child	16Ap040†	SMITH, Phillip		22	M	Laborer	16Ap020y
Nancy	(D)	02	F	Child	16Ap040†	KELLEY, John		23	M	Laborer	16Ap020y
Elizabeth	(D)	.03	F	Infant	16Ap040†	ONEILE, Francis		26	M	Laborer	16Ap020y
MCCARRON, Brian		25	M	Laborer	16Ap040†	DOWNEY, John		50	M	Laborer	16Ap020y
Jane		30	F	None	16Ap040†	Ann	(W)	50	F	Wife	16Ap020y
LYNCH, Michael		20	M	Laborer	16Ap040†	Thos.	(S)	16	M	Laborer	16Ap020y
Rose	(M)	50	F	None	16Ap040†	John	(S)	14	M	Laborer	16Ap020y
Mary		30	F	None	16Ap040†	Ann	(D)	11	F	None	16Ap020y
Isabella		28	F	None	16Ap040†	James	(S)	09	M	Child	16Ap020y
Wm.		16	M	None	16Ap040†	Wm.	(S)	07	M	Child	16Ap020y
Rose		13	F	None	16Ap040†	BRANNAGAN, Peter		22	M	Farmer	16Ap020y
Susan		06	F	Child	16Ap040†	TRAINER, Mary		20	F	None	16Ap020y
Charles		04	M	Child	16Ap040†	SMITH, Michael		25	M	Farmer	16Ap020y
James		02	M	Child	16Ap040†	KEENAN, Thomas		25	M	Farmer	16Ap020y
WATSON, Mary		18	F	None	16Ap040†	BRANNAGAN, Rose		20	F	None	16Ap020y
Sally		18	F	None	16Ap040†	MCOWEN, Mary		27	F	None	16Ap020y
BRUCE, James		68	M	Laborer	16Ap040†	Peter		37	M	Farmer	16Ap020y
Wm.		64	M	Laborer	16Ap040†	KERR, Pat		22	M	Farmer	16Ap020y
Elizabeth		46	F	None	16Ap040†	Mary		22	F	None	16Ap020y
Jane		19	F	None	16Ap040†	KENNEDY, James		40	M	Farmer	16Ap020y
Ann		17	F	None	16Ap040†	KENNELLY, Mike		10	M	Farmer	16Ap020y
Ellen		15	F	None	16Ap040†	Cathe.		02	F	Child	16Ap020y
Wm.		13	M	Laborer	16Ap040†	Mary		08	F	Child	16Ap020y
James		12	M	Laborer	16Ap040†	Cathe.		38	F	Unknown	16Ap020y
Mary		10	F	None	16Ap040†	CASS, James		26	M	Laborer	16Ap020y
Keny		07	M	Child	16Ap040†	MCFARLAN, Ann		16	F	None	16Ap020y
Martha		02	F	Child	16Ap040†	Margt.		13	F	None	16Ap020y
FARRENS, Robert		30	M	Farmer	16Ap040†	Julia		11	F	None	16Ap020y
Cathe.		30	F	None	16Ap040†	Chas.		09	M	Child	16Ap020y
John		18	M	None	16Ap040†	MCGOWAN, Daniel		25	M	Mechanic	16Ap020y
MCNAMARA, Sally		35	F	None	16Ap040†	ROURKE, James		23	M	Mechanic	16Ap020y
MCLAUGHLAN, Danl.		27	M	Farmer	16Ap040†	DONOUGH, Thomas		20	M	Mechanic	16Ap020y
Cathe.		26	F	None	16Ap040†	WEBB, Jane		19	F	None	16Ap020y
LOUGHBRIDGE, John		30	M	Farmer	16Ap040†	BANNON, Kitty		18	F	None	16Ap020y
Danl.		18	M	Laborer	16Ap040†	REILLY, Mary		20	F	None	16Ap020y
WOODSIDE, Saml.		21	M	Farmer	16Ap040†	LYNCH, Dominick		25	M	Mechanic	16Ap020y
LOUGHBRIDGE, Saml.		60	M	Farmer	16Ap040†	Cathe.		20	F	None	16Ap020y
Martha		60	F	None	16Ap040†	SPELMAN, John		40	M	Mechanic	16Ap020y
MCCUTCHEON, Eliza		47	F	None	16Ap040†	KENNEDY, John		30	M	Mechanic	16Ap020y
Jane	(D)	17	F	None	16Ap040†	U	(W)	25	F	Wife	16Ap020y
						Cathe.		25	F	None	16Ap020y
						Mary	(D)	.00	F	Infant	16Ap020y
						RILEY, Bernard		30	M	Mechanic	16Ap020y
						Mary		14	F	None	16Ap020y
						Margt.		20	F	None	16Ap020y
						John		07	M	Child	16Ap020y
						Pebby		04	M	Child	16Ap020y
						Mary		02	F	Child	16Ap020y
						COLLIGAN, Thos.		40	M	Laborer	16Ap020y
						Bernard		30	M	Laborer	16Ap020y

NAMES OF PASSENGERS		AGE	SEX	OCCUPATIONS	DATE PORT SHIP	NAMES OF PASSENGERS		AGE	SEX	OCCUPATIONS	DATE PORT SHIP
COLLIGAN, Bridget		14	F	None	16Ap020y	LAUGHLIN, Cathe.		20	F	None	16Ap020y
DEVINE, John		25	M	Laborer	16Ap020y	SPENCER, Mary		05	F	Child	16Ap020y
Cathe.	(W)	20	F	Wife	16Ap020y	Eleanor		08	F	Child	16Ap020y
Susan	(D)	.00	F	Infant	16Ap020y	ROTH, John		20	M	Laborer	16Ap020y
HANDLEY, Peter		25	M	Laborer	16Ap020y	Tobias		20	M	Laborer	16Ap020y
MCCORMICK, James		20	M	Laborer	16Ap020y	PAISEY, Joseph		20	M	Laborer	16Ap020y
FLANNIGAN, John		21	M	Laborer	16Ap020y	TREMBLE, James		30	M	Laborer	16Ap020y
HARLEY, Cella		19	F	None	16Ap020y	Margt.	(W)	30	F	Wife	16Ap020y
KILRAN, Daniel		21	M	Laborer	16Ap020y	Thos.	(S)	09	M	Child	16Ap020y
CARR, Bernard		20	M	Laborer	16Ap020y	John	(S)	07	M	Child	16Ap020y
MCDANIEL, Winny		19	F	None	16Ap020y	James	(S)	05	M	Child	16Ap020y
NETTAR, Joseph		30	M	Laborer	16Ap020y	Eliza	(D)	03	F	Child	16Ap020y
KERR, Bridget		17	F	None	16Ap020y	Robt.	(S)	.00	M	Infant	16Ap020y
FITZGERALD, Thos.		44	M	Laborer	16Ap020y	WILEY, Garret		20	M	Laborer	16Ap020y
HAGARTY, Mary		15	F	None	16Ap020y	HAGARTY, Wm.		40	M	Laborer	16Ap020y
Wm.		13	M	None	16Ap020y	Margt.	(W)	40	F	Wife	16Ap020y
Thomas		11	M	None	16Ap020y	Jane	(D)	21	F	None	16Ap020y
Sarah		09	F	Child	16Ap020y	Margt.	(D)	19	F	None	16Ap020y
ONALLY, Charles		20	M	Farmer	16Ap020y	James	(S)	17	M	Laborer	16Ap020y
James		26	M	Farmer	16Ap020y	CASS, John		30	M	Laborer	16Ap020y
Peter	(P)	57	M	Farmer	16Ap020y	Mike		30	M	Laborer	16Ap020y
Patrick		21	M	Farmer	16Ap020y	Andy		15	M	Laborer	16Ap020y
Mary		20	F	None	16Ap020y	DAWLAN, Ed.		30	M	Laborer	16Ap020y
MCDONOUGH, Mary		20	F	None	16Ap020y	Cathe.	(W)	40	F	Wife	16Ap020y
KEAUGH, Morris		20	M	Farmer	16Ap020y	Mary	(D)	10	F	None	16Ap020y
ELLIS, Rosey		20	F	None	16Ap020y	CASS, Margt.		12	F	None	16Ap020y
Mary		05	F	Child	16Ap020y	Biddy		21	F	None	16Ap020y
MORAN, Mary		23	F	None	16Ap020y	Biddy		50	F	None	16Ap020y
MCCABE, James		18	M	Farmer	16Ap020y	DUNNE, Sarah		29	F	None	16Ap020y
CARTY, Owen		25	M	Farmer	16Ap020y	KELLEY, Pat		20	M	Laborer	16Ap020y
ONEILE, Martin		20	M	Farmer	16Ap020y	TAMIN, Pat		21	M	Laborer	16Ap020y
Kitty		19	F	None	16Ap020y	KELLEY, Mick		20	M	Laborer	16Ap020y
GIBBONS, Pat		25	M	Farmer	16Ap020y	Cathe.		19	F	None	16Ap020y
Biddy	(W)	25	F	Wife	16Ap020y	SEXTON, Thos.		26	M	Laborer	16Ap020y
John	(S)	.00	M	Infant	16Ap020y	BURNS, Patrick		21	M	Laborer	16Ap020y
COYNE, Pat		25	M	Farmer	16Ap020y	RYAN, Patrick		30	M	Laborer	16Ap020y
Nancy		19	F	None	16Ap020y	BROWN, Saml.		21	M	Laborer	16Ap020y
KERRIGAN, James		32	M	Farmer	16Ap020y	U	(W)	20	F	Wife	16Ap020y
Margt.		32	F	None	16Ap020y	ROCHE, Wm.		23	M	Laborer	16Ap020y
DUFFY, Mike		30	M	Farmer	16Ap020y	GYNN, Peter		50	M	Laborer	16Ap020y
Cathe.		25	F	None	16Ap020y	U	(W)	48	F	Wife	16Ap020y
CONNOR, John		40	M	Farmer	16Ap020y	William	(S)	22	M	Laborer	16Ap020y
GILL, Wm.		25	M	Farmer	16Ap020y	Cathe.	(D)	15	F	None	16Ap020y
CONNORS, Thos.		25	M	Farmer	16Ap020y	Bessey	(D)	10	F	None	16Ap020y
FADDEN, Mick		20	M	Farmer	16Ap020y	Bridget	(D)	08	F	Child	16Ap020y
GILL, Margt.		18	F	None	16Ap020y	Peter	(S)	06	M	Child	16Ap020y
MORAN, Nancy		30	F	None	16Ap020y	FINN, Bridget		26	F	None	16Ap020y
DARDIS, Patrick		18	M	Farmer	16Ap020y	MCKEON, Thos.		25	M	Laborer	16Ap020y
GAFFNEY, James		20	M	Farmer	16Ap020y	BYRNE, Dennis		27	M	Laborer	16Ap020y
GREENE, Hugh		30	M	Farmer	16Ap020y	Martin		25	M	Laborer	16Ap020y
MCFARLAN, Hugh		60	M	Farmer	16Ap020y	SULLIVAN, Dennis		20	M	Laborer	16Ap020y
James	(S)	17	M	Farmer	16Ap020y	SCULLY, Dennis		20	M	Laborer	16Ap020y
Mary	(D)	19	F	None	16Ap020y	BOOTH, John		25	M	Laborer	16Ap020y
Eleanor	(D)	18	F	None	16Ap020y	TIERNEY, Bridget		50	F	None	16Ap020y
GREEN, William		52	M	Laborer	16Ap020y	CONNORS, Mary		21	F	None	16Ap020y
U	(W)	52	F	Wife	16Ap020y	Nelly		19	F	None	16Ap020y
William	(S)	26	M	Laborer	16Ap020y	FINERON, Mary		20	F	None	16Ap020y
Daniel	(S)	24	M	Laborer	16Ap020y	PETIT, Nelly		18	F	None	16Ap020y
John	(S)	16	M	Laborer	16Ap020y	Winfrid		17	F	None	16Ap020y
Patrick	(S)	12	M	Laborer	16Ap020y						
Floria	(D)	08	F	Child	16Ap020y						
Julia	(D)	11	F	None	16Ap020y						
MCLEAN, Mike		30	M	Laborer	16Ap020y						
BOHILE, James		20	M	Laborer	16Ap020y						
John		20	M	Laborer	16Ap020y	DEFENCE 17 APRIL 1847					
MCMANUS, Pat		20	M	Laborer	16Ap020y						
BRADY, Pat		30	M	Laborer	16Ap020y	From Liverpool					
SMITH, John		18	M	Laborer	16Ap020y						
MCCABE, Thos.		18	M	Laborer	16Ap020y						
HEAVY, Thos.		40	M	Laborer	16Ap020y						
KROUGH, Mike		20	M	Laborer	16Ap020y	BANNIGAN, Mary		21	F	Spinster	17Ap020d
LAFFY, Larry		21	M	Laborer	16Ap020y	BARADY, Mary		20	F	Spinster	17Ap020d
SPERLIN, Mary		45	F	None	16Ap020y	GEARY, Danl.		22	M	Laborer	17Ap020d
SPENCER, Ann		30	F	None	16Ap020y	HEARN, James-A.		28	M	Laborer	17Ap020d
Bernard		22	M	Laborer	16Ap020y	TRACEY, Terence		20	M	Laborer	17Ap020d

440

NAMES OF PASSENGERS	AGE	SEX	OCCUPATIONS	DATE PORT SHIP
WHELEHAN, Bridget	20	F	Spinster	17Ap020d
PLUNKETT, Rosanna	11	F	Spinster	17Ap020d
Cathn.	09	F	Child	17Ap020d
BYRNE, Jane	20	F	Unknown	17Ap020d
MENASHAN, Ann	18	F	Spinster	17Ap020d
NERILLE, Stephen	20	M	Laborer	17Ap020d
CARROL, Bridget	06	F	Child	17Ap020d
BELL, Mathew	40	M	Laborer	17Ap020d
ELLIOTT, Thomas	14	M	Laborer	17Ap020d
Mary-Ann	08	F	Child	17Ap020d
Hester	05	F	Child	17Ap020d
Eliza	.00	F	Infant	17Ap020d
COLLINS, Patk.	50	M	Laborer	17Ap020d
Peggy (W)	45	F	Unknown	17Ap020d
Margaret (D)	10	F	Unknown	17Ap020d
Patk. (S)	08	M	Child	17Ap020d
Peter (S)	06	M	Child	17Ap020d
Arthur (S)	03	M	Child	17Ap020d
Cathn. (D)	.00	F	Infant	17Ap020d
PENN, Andrew	20	M	Laborer	17Ap020d
Bridget	18	F	Unknown	17Ap020d
CONNELY, Cathn.	25	F	Laborer	17Ap020d
FLANIGAN, Elisa	29	F	Wife	17Ap020d
James (S)	07	M	Child	17Ap020d
Jane (D)	05	F	Child	17Ap020d
Michl. (S)	03	M	Child	17Ap020d
Christopher (S)	.00	M	Infant	17Ap020d
HANGHURY, Edwd.	25	M	Laborer	17Ap020d
DONLAN, Owen	50	M	Unknown	17Ap020d
Julia (W)	45	F	Spinster	17Ap020d
John (S)	18	M	Laborer	17Ap020d
KELLEN, Pat	21	M	Laborer	17Ap020d
DEVLIN, Owen	60	M	Laborer	17Ap020d
MCCABE, Brisent	25	M	Laborer	17Ap020d
SALMON, John	20	M	Laborer	17Ap020d
WELDON, Pat	25	M	Laborer	17Ap020d
BRADY, Ann	21	F	Spinster	17Ap020d
MALVEY, Pat	20	M	Laborer	17Ap020d
FENN, Ellen	22	F	Spinster	17Ap020d
HAYES, John	21	M	Laborer	17Ap020d
MCDERMOTT, Biddy	19	F	Spinster	17Ap020d
KANE, Pat	25	M	Laborer	17Ap020d
Mary	18	F	Spinster	17Ap020d
TLARREL, Jane	39	F	Wife	17Ap020d
Ellen	35	F	Wife	17Ap020d
Sarah	20	F	Wife	17Ap020d
TAGGERT, Wm.J.	28	M	Laborer	17Ap020d
MCGEE, James	50	M	Laborer	17Ap020d
Sarah	45	F	Wife	17Ap020d
Sarah (D)	08	F	Child	17Ap020d
Nelie (S)	03	M	Child	17Ap020d
David (S)	05	M	Child	17Ap020d
REHETY, Neil	20	M	Laborer	17Ap020d
Hugh	21	M	Unknown	17Ap020d
MONES, John	45	M	Laborer	17Ap020d
LEARY, Cathn.	19	F	Spinster	17Ap020d
CONNOLY, Mary	20	F	Spinster	17Ap020d
LEARY, James	21	M	Laborer	17Ap020d
COCHLAN, Michl.	21	M	Laborer	17Ap020d
Cathn.	20	F	Unknown	17Ap020d
TECHIE, Mary	20	F	Spinster	17Ap020d
NEILE, Pat	20	M	Laborer	17Ap020d
DONERSEN, John	22	M	Laborer	17Ap020d
DINNEN, Peter	21	M	Laborer	17Ap020d
BALMER, Hugh	34	M	Laborer	17Ap020d
CONLIN, John	30	M	Laborer	17Ap020d
Mary	24	F	Laborer	17Ap020d
Margaret	40	F	Spinster	17Ap020d
Margaret	21	F	Spinster	17Ap020d
Mary (D)	.00	F	Infant	17Ap020d
HAYES, Daniel	40	M	Laborer	17Ap020d
Ellen	30	F	Wife	17Ap020d
Cathn.	26	F	Spinster	17Ap020d
Dennis	50	M	Laborer	17Ap020d
RYAN, Dennis	30	M	Laborer	17Ap020d
RYAN, John	16	M	Unknown	17Ap020d
Pat	13	M	Unknown	17Ap020d
Andrew	11	M	Unknown	17Ap020d
Dennis	08	M	Child	17Ap020d
LANIER, Bridget	30	F	Spinster	17Ap020d
Mary	20	F	Spinster	17Ap020d
LEDWITH, Thos.	20	M	Laborer	17Ap020d
James	18	M	Laborer	17Ap020d
SHAW, Laurence	25	M	Laborer	17Ap020d
MACKIN, Mary	20	F	Spinster	17Ap020d
MCDERMOTT, Saml.	18	M	Laborer	17Ap020d
Patk.	17	M	Unknown	17Ap020d
Francis	12	M	Unknown	17Ap020d
MCCAFFERTY, John	20	M	Laborer	17Ap020d
LYNCH, Mathew	22	M	Laborer	17Ap020d
Margaret	18	F	Spinster	17Ap020d
CURRY, Jane	45	F	Spinster	17Ap020d
TAGGERT, Sarah	20	F	Wife	17Ap020d
Agnes	18	F	Spinster	17Ap020d
James	09	M	Child	17Ap020d
BRENTON, Julia	40	F	Wife	17Ap020d
Christopher (H)	55	M	Laborer	17Ap020d
Michl. (S)	18	M	Unknown	17Ap020d
John (S)	20	M	Unknown	17Ap020d
Ann (D)	10	F	Unknown	17Ap020d
WALCH, Cathn.	40	F	Unknown	17Ap020d
Robert (S)	10	M	Unknown	17Ap020d
Hannah (D)	08	F	Child	17Ap020d
Ellen (D)	06	F	Child	17Ap020d
Hugh (S)	04	M	Child	17Ap020d
Cathn. (D)	02	F	Child	17Ap020d
CURREY, John	18	M	Laborer	17Ap020d
SWEENEY, William	20	M	Laborer	17Ap020d
Michl.	20	M	Laborer	17Ap020d
CUMMINGS, Sarah	40	F	Wife	17Ap020d
Henry (S)	18	M	Laborer	17Ap020d
REACH, Johannah	40	F	Wife	17Ap020d
David (S)	09	M	Child	17Ap020d
Margaret (D)	06	F	Child	17Ap020d
CURLIS, Wm.	25	M	Laborer	17Ap020d
COLEMAN, Mary	18	F	Spinster	17Ap020d
SYNAS, John	40	M	Laborer	17Ap020d
Cat. (D)	08	F	Child	17Ap020d
Timothy (S)	06	M	Child	17Ap020d
Margaret (D)	03	F	Child	17Ap020d
John (S)	.00	M	Infant	17Ap020d
MULVEY, Pat	20	M	Laborer	17Ap020d
James	24	M	Unknown	17Ap020d
DONNAN, Pat	20	M	Laborer	17Ap020d
OBRIAN, Jeremiah	21	M	Unknown	17Ap020d
MAGUIRE, Thos.	20	M	Unknown	17Ap020d
Eliza	20	F	Unknown	17Ap020d
SULLIVAN, Danl.	50	M	Unknown	17Ap020d
John (S)	25	M	Unknown	17Ap020d
Margaret (D)	18	F	Unknown	17Ap020d
CARROL, Mary	20	F	Unknown	17Ap020d
GLEESON, Mary	40	F	Wife	17Ap020d
Harriette	25	F	Spinster	17Ap020d
Margaret (D)	18	F	Unknown	17Ap020d
Mary (D)	21	F	Unknown	17Ap020d
Jeremiah (S)	11	M	Unknown	17Ap020d
FLOOD, Mary	14	F	Spinster	17Ap020d
REYNOLDS, Bridget	10	F	Spinster	17Ap020d
BUTLER, Jno.	20	M	Laborer	17Ap020d
MURRAY, Thos.	20	M	Unknown	17Ap020d
MORAN, Margaret	35	F	Wife	17Ap020d
Mo.	10	U	Unknown	17Ap020d
Laurence (S)	09	M	Child	17Ap020d
William (S)	06	M	Child	17Ap020d
Thomas (S)	.00	M	Infant	17Ap020d
LYNCH, James	20	M	Laborer	17Ap020d
CONNOR, Margaret	30	F	Wife	17Ap020d
Michl. (S)	10	M	Unknown	17Ap020d
Elisa (D)	08	F	Child	17Ap020d
Edward (S)	06	M	Child	17Ap020d

NAMES OF PASSENGERS		AGE	SEX	OCCUPATIONS	DATE PORT SHIP
TULLY, Bridget		20	F	Spinster	17Ap020d
COURTLEY, Bridget		20	F	Spinster	17Ap020d
WALCH, Thomas		25	M	Laborer	17Ap020d
HOGAN, George		32	M	Laborer	17Ap020d
Elisa	(W)	32	F	Unknown	17Ap020d
James	(S)	12	M	Unknown	17Ap020d
John	(S)	08	M	Child	17Ap020d
George	(S)	05	M	Child	17Ap020d
Isaac	(S)	.00	M	Infant	17Ap020d
MCFALL, Robert		50	M	Unknown	17Ap020d
MCDERMOTT, James		30	M	Laborer	17Ap020d
SMITH, Robert		19	M	Laborer	17Ap020d
FINNIGAN, Michl.		25	M	Laborer	17Ap020d
Mary		26	F	Unknown	17Ap020d
PLUNKETT, James		50	M	Laborer	17Ap020d
Maria		12	F	Unknown	17Ap020d
Michael		11	M	Unknown	17Ap020d
Thomas		08	M	Child	17Ap020d
BRADY, Cathn.		13	F	Spinster	17Ap020d
DINNIGAN, Thos.		20	M	Laborer	17Ap020d
Jno.		20	M	Unknown	17Ap020d
KELLY, Cathn.		20	F	Spinster	17Ap020d
Margaret		20	F	Spinster	17Ap020d
WARD, Patt		25	M	Laborer	17Ap020d
DARLING, James		30	M	Laborer	17Ap020d
WARD, Elisa		13	F	Spinster	17Ap020d
HANLEY, Anne		05	F	Child	17Ap020d
BOYLE, Margaret		20	F	Spinster	17Ap020d
GELLAGHEY, Sally		30	F	Spinster	17Ap020d
KANE, Thos.		03	M	Child	17Ap020d
MCDONNEL, Mary		21	F	Wife	17Ap020d
Margaret		18	F	Unknown	17Ap020d
DOWNEY, Jno.		25	M	Laborer	17Ap020d
GLEERY, Robert		20	M	Laborer	17Ap020d
Cathn.		13	F	Spinster	17Ap020d
FARREL, Cathn.		20	F	Spinster	17Ap020d
GETTY, Bridget		20	F	Spinster	17Ap020d
DOYLE, Michl.		24	M	Laborer	17Ap020d
HERN, Michl.		22	M	Laborer	17Ap020d
MCGEE, Jno.		24	M	Laborer	17Ap020d
GARR, Margaret		20	F	Spinster	17Ap020d
ELLIOTT, Thos.		20	M	Laborer	17Ap020d
MURPHY, Jane		18	F	Laborer	17Ap020d
Bryan		20	M	Laborer	17Ap020d
STROKES, Richd.		20	M	Laborer	17Ap020d
WELSH, Martin		20	M	Unknown	17Ap020d
DEAS, Michl.		20	M	Unknown	17Ap020d

ROGER-STEWART 17 APRIL 1847

From Greenock

NAMES OF PASSENGERS		AGE	SEX	OCCUPATIONS	DATE PORT SHIP
GOURMLY, Patt		20	M	Farmer	17Ap680g
John		24	M	Farmer	17Ap680g
Edward		17	M	Farmer	17Ap680g
Patt		25	M	Farmer	17Ap680g
BURNS, John		24	M	Sexton	17Ap680g
Cathrine	(W)	26	F	Wife	17Ap680g
Archibald	(S)	.04	M	Infant	17Ap680g
MCMILLIN, Connell		40	M	Farmer	17Ap680g
DONNELLY, Hugh		30	M	Farmer	17Ap680g
MOLLOY, Dennis		20	M	Farmer	17Ap680g
GOULACHER, Catherine		19	F	Dressmaker	17Ap680g
QUIN, Mary		19	F	Dressmaker	17Ap680g
GOURMLY, Mary		18	F	Dressmaker	17Ap680g
MONAGHAN, Arthur		34	M	Farmer	17Ap680g
Ann	(W)	32	F	Wife	17Ap680g
Michael	(S)	16	M	Unknown	17Ap680g
Susan	(D)	15	F	Unknown	17Ap680g
MONAGHAN, Mary	(D)	13	F	Unknown	17Ap680g
Cathrine	(D)	11	F	Unknown	17Ap680g
Ann	(D)	09	F	Child	17Ap680g
John	(S)	02	M	Child	17Ap680g
BOYLE, John		58	M	Weaver	17Ap680g
Patt		17	M	Weaver	17Ap680g
GOODWIN, John		23	M	Unknown	17Ap680g
CAMELL, Denis		30	M	Unknown	17Ap680g
MCHANE, Hugh		22	M	Unknown	17Ap680g
BRADLY, Christy		48	M	Shoemaker	17Ap680g
Francy	(W)	48	F	Wife	17Ap680g
John	(S)	14	M	Unknown	17Ap680g
Michael	(S)	11	M	Unknown	17Ap680g
Peter	(S)	24	M	Unknown	.17Ap680g
CAMPBELL, John		48	M	Farmer	17Ap680g
COX, Mary		50	F	Spinster	17Ap680g
Ketty	(D)	20	F	Spinster	17Ap680g
Mary	(D)	16	F	Spinster	17Ap680g
Ellen	(D)	13	F	Spinster	17Ap680g
Biddy	(D)	08	F	Child	17Ap680g
Ann	(D)	05	F	Child	17Ap680g
MCSHERRY, Teddy		35	M	Weaver	17Ap680g
Mary	(W)	30	F	Wife	17Ap680g
Mary	(D)	12	F	Unknown	17Ap680g
John	(S)	10	M	Unknown	17Ap680g
Patt	(S)	07	M	Child	17Ap680g
Dan	(S)	05	M	Child	17Ap680g
Cathrine	(D)	.06	F	Infant	17Ap680g
HOUGHY, Richard		30	M	Farmer	17Ap680g
J------E, Jane		24	F	Spinster	17Ap680g
Ruth		22	F	Spinster	17Ap680g
Matty		28	F	Spinster	17Ap680g
MCKINLAY, Michael		19	M	Fisherman	17Ap680g
HIGGIN, William		30	M	Laborer	17Ap680g
COAL, William		21	M	Laborer	17Ap680g
CUNNINGHAM, John		20	M	Laborer	17Ap680g
MCKEELHANY, Connell		24	M	Tailor	17Ap680g
Bridget	(W)	24	F	Wife	17Ap680g
Peter	(S)	01	M	Child	17Ap680g
SHAW, Henry		24	M	Courier	17Ap680g
MCMALIGHAN, Robert		25	M	Tailor	17Ap680g
SMITH, Annabella		12	F	Dressmaker	17Ap680g
TIFFENY, Nell		35	M	Laborer	17Ap680g
MCGOWAN, Terris		50	M	Laborer	17Ap680g
Margt.	(W)	36	F	Wife	17Ap680g
Bryan	(S)	12	M	Unknown	17Ap680g
Betty	(D)	19	F	Unknown	17Ap680g
Terrace	(S)	10	M	Unknown	17Ap680g
Mary	(D)	08	F	Child	17Ap680g
Hugh	(S)	05	M	Child	17Ap680g
John	(S)	03	M	Child	17Ap680g
EARLY, Michael		35	M	Laborer	17Ap680g
Mary	(W)	26	F	Wife	17Ap680g
GOUGHAN, Teddy		23	M	Farmer	17Ap680g
MCGUIRE, Terrace		25	M	Farmer	17Ap680g
NAUGHTON, Francis		20	M	Tailor	17Ap680g
CHELAN, Pat		22	M	Farmer	17Ap680g
LYNCH, James		28	M	Farmer	17Ap680g
Betty	(W)	22	F	Wife	17Ap680g
Mary	(D)	.07	F	Infant	17Ap680g
Edmond	(S)	03	M	Child	17Ap680g
Edwaard		24	M	Farmer	17Ap680g
Margt.	(W)	20	F	Wife	17Ap680g
BURKE, Edward		50	M	Farmer	17Ap680g
Michael		20	M	Farmer	17Ap680g
RODGERS, John		18	M	Farmer	17Ap680g
KERGAN, Oner		13	F	Spinster	17Ap680g
CONRY, Martin		55	M	Farmer	17Ap680g
Margt.	(W)	50	F	Wife	17Ap680g
Margt.	(D)	13	F	Unknown	17Ap680g
Edward	(S)	09	M	Child	17Ap680g
Ketty	(D)	11	F	Unknown	17Ap680g
EARLY, Sibbey		20	F	Spinster	17Ap680g
DENRY, Antony		40	M	Farmer	17Ap680g
Mary	(W)	40	F	Wife	17Ap680g

NAMES OF PASSENGERS		AGE	SEX	OCCUPATIONS	DATE PORT SHIP
DENRY, Bridget	(D)	12	F	Unknown	17Ap680g
Nelly	(D)	10	F	Unknown	17Ap680g
Mary	(D)	08	F	Child	17Ap680g
James	(S)	06	M	Child	17Ap680g
John	(S)	04	M	Child	17Ap680g
TIVY, Bridget		60	F	Spinster	17Ap680g
John		45	M	Farmer	17Ap680g
BURN, Bridget		30	F	Spinster	17Ap680g
NEILL, Henry		40	M	Farmer	17Ap680g
Mary	(W)	40	F	Wife	17Ap680g
Henry	(S)	15	M	Unknown	17Ap680g
Franics	(S)	13	M	Unknown	17Ap680g
Ellen	(D)	09	F	Child	17Ap680g
ANDERSON, William		20	M	Farmer	17Ap680g
BLANEY, John		30	M	Weaver	17Ap680g
Kathrine	(W)	30	F	Wife	17Ap680g
John	(S)	10	M	Unknown	17Ap680g
Daniel	(S)	04	M	Child	17Ap680g
DOUGHERTY, Mary		20	F	Weaver	17Ap680g
COSGROVE, Ann		24	F	Seamstress	17Ap680g
ONEILL, Ellen		22	F	Seamstress	17Ap680g
MILHOLLAND, Sarah		30	F	Seamstress	17Ap680g
ANDERSON, John		30	M	Farmer	17Ap680g
Ellen	(W)	30	F	Wife	17Ap680g
James	(S)	12	M	Unknown	17Ap680g
JOHNSTONE, Mary		22	F	Spinster	17Ap680g
MCDERMOTT, Sarah		29	F	Wife	17Ap680g
MCGLOUGHLAN, Henry		12	M	Unknown	17Ap680g
Dan		10	M	Unknown	17Ap680g
Patrick		07	M	Child	17Ap680g
Ellen		06	F	Child	17Ap680g
Jane		04	F	Child	17Ap680g
HAUGHERTY, Patrick		44	M	Laborer	17Ap680g
SPENCE, Ann		56	F	Spinster	17Ap680g
Catherine		24	F	Wife	17Ap680g
John	(S)	20	M	Farmer	17Ap680g
Henry	(S)	16	M	Farmer	17Ap680g
William	(S)	14	M	Farmer	17Ap680g
James	(S)	10	M	Farmer	17Ap680g
MARTIN, Ann		02	F	Child	17Ap680g
George		.06	M	Infant	17Ap680g
DOUGHERTY, James		12	M	Unknown	17Ap680g
Patrick		00	M	Unknown	17Ap680g

NO RECORD OF SHIP

From Liverpool

NAMES OF PASSENGERS		AGE	SEX	OCCUPATIONS	DATE PORT SHIP
KELLEY, Joseph		30	M	Farmer	17Ap02
Mary		30	F	Farmer	17Ap02
Anne		11	F	Farmer	17Ap02
MCDONNALD, Sarah		19	F	Unknown	17Ap02
DERMAN, Ellen		19	F	Unknown	17Ap02
Died-At-Sea					
JUDGE, Mary		36	F	Unknown	17Ap02
Robert	(S)	.08	M	Infant	17Ap02
LEARY, William		40	M	Trade Man	17Ap02
Ellen	(W)	24	F	Trade Man	17Ap02
Catherine	(D)	01	F	Child	17Ap02
Bridget	(D)	09	F	Child	17Ap02
Patrick	(S)	06	M	Child	17Ap02
HYLAND, Catherine		21	F	Unknown	17Ap02
RAYNOLD, John		24	M	Farmer	17Ap02
Margaret-R.	(W)	28	F	Farmer	17Ap02
John	(S)	02	M	Child	17Ap02
CONNEL, Patrick		22	M	Farmer	17Ap02
HIGHLAND, Margaret		23	F	Unknown	17Ap02
SHORT, Margaret		20	F	Unknown	17Ap02
HANNAN, Rhody		22	M	Laborer	17Ap02

NAMES OF PASSENGERS		AGE	SEX	OCCUPATIONS	DATE PORT SHIP
HANNAN, Betsey		23	F	Laborer	17Ap02
KELLEY, Bridget		23	F	Laborer	17Ap02
MCDENNAH, Sarah		19	F	Laborer	17Ap02
Catherine		17	F	Laborer	17Ap02
CAMMEL, Margaret		24	F	Laborer	17Ap02
MCWITHER, Thomas		22	M	Mason	17Ap02
Edward		18	M	Laborer	17Ap02
MCCARDELE, Patrick		28	M	Farmer	17Ap02
Mary		28	F	Farmer	17Ap02
James		05	M	Child	17Ap02
Margaret		19	F	Unknown	17Ap02
Ellen		20	F	Unknown	17Ap02
TONER, Dennis		26	M	Farmer	17Ap02
ROACH, John		28	M	Farmer	17Ap02
James		26	M	Farmer	17Ap02
James		50	M	Laborer	17Ap02
Margaret		50	F	Laborer	17Ap02
Mary		24	F	Laborer	17Ap02
Patrick		20	M	Laborer	17Ap02
Edward		18	M	Laborer	17Ap02
Ellen		14	F	Laborer	17Ap02
Michael		13	M	Laborer	17Ap02
David		10	M	Laborer	17Ap02
KERNON, John		23	M	Laborer	17Ap02
MCVOY, James		23	M	Servant	17Ap02
GARRETTY, John		21	M	Smith	17Ap02
HARVEY, Samuel		32	M	Farmer	17Ap02
MALONE, Thomas		29	M	Carpenter	17Ap02
Christy	(W)	26	F	Carpenter	17Ap02
James	(S)	.06	M	Infant	17Ap02
Bridget		26	F	Laborer	17Ap02
REILY, Jane		19	F	Laborer	17Ap02
MEKOOHAN, Rose		18	F	Laborer	17Ap02
TAYLOR, Catherine		19	F	Laborer	17Ap02
MALONE, John		23	M	Laborer	17Ap02
NUGENT, Michael		54	M	Laborer	17Ap02
Francis	(S)	18	M	Laborer	17Ap02
James	(S)	14	M	Laborer	17Ap02
Rose	(D)	22	F	Laborer	17Ap02
Theresa	(D)	12	F	Laborer	17Ap02
KENNERY, Michael		24	M	Blacksmith	17Ap02
Kitty	(W)	22	F	Laborer	17Ap02
Ann	(D)	02	F	Child	17Ap02
LYNCH, John		40	M	Laborer	17Ap02
Catherine		25	F	Laborer	17Ap02
HYDE, Johanna		20	F	Laborer	17Ap02
MCDONNALD, Ann		28	F	Laborer	17Ap02
MOONEY, John		30	M	Laborer	17Ap02
FALL, Patrick		27	M	Laborer	17Ap02
FETHERSTON, Peter		30	M	Laborer	17Ap02
MCDONNALD, Catherine-B		24	F	Laborer	17Ap02
Michael		02	M	Child	17Ap02
CAIN, Patrick		26	M	Laborer	17Ap02
Mary		16	F	Laborer	17Ap02
HANLY, Michael		30	M	Laborer	17Ap02
CANE, James		30	M	Laborer	17Ap02
HANLY, Catherine		27	F	Laborer	17Ap02
MCDERMOTT, Ann		20	F	Laborer	17Ap02
CANE, Winefred		28	F	Laborer	17Ap02
MCDERMOTT, Michael		20	M	Laborer	17Ap02
GARVENTON, Martin		20	M	Laborer	17Ap02
BECKETT, Bea		20	F	Laborer	17Ap02
Ann		18	F	Laborer	17Ap02
EGAN, Margaret		23	F	Laborer	17Ap02
STEWART, Susan		18	F	Laborer	17Ap02
DULHINTY, Patrick		25	M	Trade Man	17Ap02
ENGLISH, John		24	M	Trade Man	17Ap02
LACY, Piercy		26	M	Laborer	17Ap02
SHEA, Lawrence		20	M	Laborer	17Ap02
ROACH, Mary		19	F	Laborer	17Ap02
KENNEY, Thomas		35	M	Trade Man	17Ap02
MCGARRY, Ann		20	F	Laborer	17Ap02
LOGAN, Lawrence		20	M	Laborer	17Ap02
MCGLOEKLIN, Luke		30	M	Laborer	17Ap02
MANNIN, Martin		25	M	Laborer	17Ap02

NAMES OF PASSENGERS		AGE	SEX	OCCUPATIONS	DATE PORT SHIP
KNOX, John		24	M	Trade Man	17Ap02
DALLY, Stephen		23	M	Blacksmith	17Ap02
RAFTER, William		20	M	Laborer	17Ap02
POWER, Joseph		20	M	Laborer	17Ap02
MULLY, John		24	M	Trade Man	17Ap02
Patrick		20	M	Trade Man	17Ap02
DURNEY, Lawrence		35	M	Laborer	17Ap02
James	(S)	12	M	Laborer	17Ap02
BOURK, James		19	M	Laborer	17Ap02
Ann		22	F	Laborer	17Ap02
Michael		27	M	Laborer	17Ap02
GARTLAND, Patrick		18	M	Laborer	17Ap02
CASSIDY, Catherine		18	F	Laborer	17Ap02
MCVICKER, Mary		21	F	Laborer	17Ap02
MCKINNER, Catherine		26	F	Laborer	17Ap02
SULLIVAN, Mary		60	F	Laborer	17Ap02
Owen	(S)	18	M	Farmer	17Ap02
William	(S)	15	M	Farmer	17Ap02
Margaret	(D)	22	F	Farmer	17Ap02
Catherine	(D)	20	F	Farmer	17Ap02
MACKIN, Patrick		23	M	Carpenter	17Ap02
SULLIVAN, Mary		21	F	Laborer	17Ap02
MICHIN, Ellen		24	F	Laborer	17Ap02
John	(S)	.08	M	Infant	17Ap02
MULINY, John		33	M	Laborer	17Ap02
FORD, Thomas		20	M	Laborer	17Ap02
TOOLAND, Patrick		25	M	Laborer	17Ap02
TEARIAN, Edward		27	M	Laborer	17Ap02
LYNCH, Martin		26	M	Mechanic	17Ap02
MEGAREY, Michael		27	M	Laborer	17Ap02
Catherine	(W)	24	F	Laborer	17Ap02
Michael	(S)	02	M	Child	17Ap02
Jane	(D)	03	F	Child	17Ap02
Paatrick	(S)	.09	M	Infant	17Ap02
CASEY, Thomas		22	M	Laborer	17Ap02
MEHANEY, Michael		23	M	Laborer	17Ap02
IRVING, Patrick		22	M	Laborer	17Ap02
QUIN, John		22	M	Laborer	17Ap02
NEAL, Thomas		34	M	Laborer	17Ap02
COLLIER, Julia		46	F	Unknown	17Ap02
Eliza		15	F	Unknown	17Ap02
BYRNS, Ann		26	F	Unknown	17Ap02
GALLOGHY, Michael		30	M	Farmer	17Ap02
KELLEY, Thomas		27	M	Farmer	17Ap02
CORRIN, Catherine		28	F	Unknown	17Ap02
MCNARY, John		28	M	Farmer	17Ap02
Mary		26	F	Farmer	17Ap02
CARROLL, Owen		30	M	Cooper	17Ap02
BUCKLEY, Dennis		21	M	Laborer	17Ap02
OBRIAN, Catherine		21	F	Laborer	17Ap02
LOGAN, Luke		28	M	Schm	17Ap02
MACNEAL, Patrick		11	M	Unknown	17Ap02
LOGAN, Catherine		68	F	Unknown	17Ap02
NOWLAND, John		30	M	Laborer	17Ap02
Mary		20	F	Laborer	17Ap02
HANEY, Richard		35	M	Clerk	17Ap02
ALEY, Margaret		19	F	Servant	17Ap02
WHAILLY, John		20	M	Laborer	17Ap02
BARRY, John		19	M	Laborer	17Ap02
JOHNSEN, James		23	M	Laborer	17Ap02
CATE, John		37	M	Laborer	17Ap02
CARMICHAEL, Patrick		25	M	Tailor	17Ap02
Ann		18	F	Tailor	17Ap02
OBRIAN, Bernerd		25	M	Laborer	17Ap02
GLANON, Michael		30	M	Laborer	17Ap02
CAHILL, Michael		30	M	Bootmaker	17Ap02
Susan	(W)	25	F	Laborer	17Ap02
William	(S)	06	M	Child	17Ap02
DONDLE, Jane		18	F	Laborer	17Ap02
Catherine		16	F	Laborer	17Ap02
ROACH, William		41	M	Laborer	17Ap02
Bridget		47	F	Laborer	17Ap02
Ellen		35	F	Laborer	17Ap02
NAUGHTON, Thomas		26	M	Laborer	17Ap02
Mary		50	F	Laborer	17Ap02
NAUGHTON, John		23	M	Laborer	17Ap02
Catherine		20	F	Laborer	17Ap02
Margaret		17	F	Laborer	17Ap02
Michael		15	M	Laborer	17Ap02
Neal		11	M	Laborer	17Ap02
MORGAN, James		26	M	Laborer	17Ap02
JACKSON, John		21	M	Laborer	17Ap02
OBRIEN, Timothy		28	M	Laborer	17Ap02
CASHEEN, Thomas		20	M	Laborer	17Ap02
ODONNELL, Mathew		25	M	Laborer	17Ap02
OBRIEN, Mary		22	F	Laborer	17Ap02
CASHEEN, Mary		22	F	Laborer	17Ap02
SHEA, Jeremiah		23	M	Laborer	17Ap02
Catherine		16	F	Laborer	17Ap02
REA, James		25	M	Laborer	17Ap02
Thomas		22	M	Laborer	17Ap02
IRWIN, Patrick		22	M	Laborer	17Ap02
SCULLY, Thomas		25	M	Shoemaker	17Ap02
Mary		19	F	Shoemaker	17Ap02
COLMAN, John		28	M	Laborer	17Ap02
CURTEN, Patrick		26	M	Laborer	17Ap02
PENI, Edward		25	M	Laborer	17Ap02
Michael		28	M	Laborer	17Ap02
CONNALLY, Ann		26	F	Laborer	17Ap02
MCCARTEY, Dennis		27	M	Farmer	17Ap02
SHEA, James		21	M	Tailor	17Ap02
HALEY, Margaret		20	F	Unknown	17Ap02

UNDINE 17 APRIL 1847

From Limerick

NAMES OF PASSENGERS		AGE	SEX	OCCUPATIONS	DATE PORT SHIP
FLYNN, Thos.		22	M	Farmer	17Ap33On
MURNAIN, James		22	M	Farmer	17Ap33On
John		24	M	Farmer	17Ap33On
DALEY, Michael		21	M	Farmer	;7Ap33On
BOSHAN, Patrick		21	M	Farmer	17Ap33On
IRWIN, Wm.		24	M	Carpenter	17Ap33On
BENSON, Johanna		17	F	Spinster	17Ap33On
Margaret		15	F	Spinster	17Ap33On
OMEALY, John		22	M	Laborer	17Ap33On
Michael		25	M	Laborer	17Ap33On
Bridget		50	F	Matron	17Ap33On
CLANCKY, John		23	M	Laborer	17Ap33On
HANLY, Francis		33	M	Farmer	17Ap33On
Jane	(W)	30	F	Unknown	17Ap33On
Patrick	(S)	12	M	Unknown	17Ap33On
Larry	(S)	08	M	Child	17Ap33On
John	(S)	06	M	Child	17Ap33On
Elisa	(D)	04	F	Child	17Ap33On
Margret	(D)	02	F	Child	17Ap33On
James	(S)	.00	M	Infant	17Ap33On
MURRY, Thos.		28	M	Laborer	17Ap33On
REAL, John		31	M	Laborer	17Ap33On
Patrick		29	M	Laborer	17Ap33On
Margret		21	F	Unknown	17Ap33On
RIORDAN, Mary		40	F	Matron	17Ap33On
Margret	(D)	13	F	Unknown	17Ap33On
Patrick	(S)	05	M	Child	17Ap33On
HART, John		13	M	Unknown	17Ap33On
MADEN, Thos.		32	M	Laborer	17Ap33On
LEE, Edward		29	M	Laborer	17Ap33On
PUNCH, Wm.		23	M	Laborer	17Ap33On
RYAN, John		32	M	Farmer	17Ap33On
Mary	(W)	30	F	Unknown	17Ap33On
Jeremiah	(S)	12	M	Unknown	17Ap33On
Bridget	(D)	10	F	Unknown	17Ap33On
John	(S)	05	M	Child	17Ap33On
Honora	(D)	.00	F	Infant	17Ap33On

NAMES OF PASSENGERS	AGE	SEX	OCCUPATIONS	DATE PORT SHIP
GLEASON, Denis	20	M	Laborer	17Ap33On
HANLY, Margret	19	F	Spinster	17Ap33On
MURPHY, Thos.	18	M	Laborer	17Ap33On
LYONS, Dan	24	M	Shoemaker	17Ap33On
SHUHY, John	23	M	Carpenter	17Ap33On
GAYNOR, Catherine	24	F	Spinster	17Ap33On
DOWNY, John	26	M	Plasterer	17Ap33On
ARCHER, Richard	21	M	Laborer	17Ap33On
MATIGAN, Bridget	24	F	Spinster	17Ap33On
GLEASON, Mary	20	F	Spinster	17Ap33On
MCNAMARA, Michael	28	M	Cooper	17Ap33On
COLLINS, Maurice	22	M	Cooper	17Ap33On
Michael	25	M	Cooper	17Ap33On
MENAHAN, John	28	M	Cooper	17Ap33On
BRIDGMEN, Joseph	26	M	Cooper	17Ap33On
NARRIS, Robert	36	M	Cooper	17Ap33On
DIRNDON, Francis	29	M	Cooper	17Ap33On
MCMAHON, Richard	30	M	Cooper	17Ap33On
MCMARA, Thos.	20	M	Cooper	17Ap33On
BOLAN, Bridget	45	F	Matron	17Ap33On
DOWNEY, Thos.	30	M	Cooper	17Ap33On
QUAID, Timothy	33	M	Cooper	17Ap33On
MANNING, John	29	M	Cooper	17Ap33On
KELLY, Michael	22	M	Laborer	17Ap33On

ROYAL-SOVEREIGN 19 APRIL 1847

From Liverpool

NAMES OF PASSENGERS	AGE	SEX	OCCUPATIONS	DATE PORT SHIP
MCBRIDE, Michael	28	M	Laborer	19Ap02Oo
MCCUE, Francis	20	M	Laborer	19Ap02Oo
CONIGAN, James	20	M	Laborer	19Ap02Oo
CAREY, Cristy	20	M	Laborer	19Ap02Oo
GALLAGHAN, Henry	21	M	Laborer	19Ap02Oo
DUFFY, Edwd.	21	M	Laborer	19Ap02Oo
Dennis	24	M	Laborer	19Ap02Oo
MOON, Jeremia	26	M	Laborer	19Ap02Oo
Rebecca	20	F	Laborer	19Ap02Oo
MCLAUGHLIN, Elisa	40	F	Laborer	19Ap02Oo
Anthony (S)	11	M	Laborer	19Ap02Oo
Catherine (D)	08	F	Child	19Ap02Oo
Francis (S)	06	M	Child	19Ap02Oo
Bernard (S)	.00	M	Infant	19Ap02Oo
MCDERMOT, Bernard	25	M	Laborer	19Ap02Oo
OWENS, Patrick	25	M	Laborer	19Ap02Oo
Michael	08	M	Child	19Ap02Oo
John	05	M	Child	19Ap02Oo
GRADY, Herra	20	M	Laborer	19Ap02Oo
BROGAN, Patrick	30	M	Laborer	19Ap02Oo
Margaret (W)	35	F	Laborer	19Ap02Oo
Thomas (S)	07	M	Child	19Ap02Oo
MAGUIRE, Catherine	11	F	Laborer	19Ap02Oo
SWEENY, John	30	M	Laborer	19Ap02Oo
U (W)	28	F	Laborer	19Ap02Oo
WRIGHT, John	50	M	Laborer	19Ap02Oo
Edward	17	M	Laborer	19Ap02Oo
James	30	M	Laborer	19Ap02Oo
GAFFREY, Catherine	19	F	Laborer	19Ap02Oo
SHERIDAN, Ann	20	F	Laborer	19Ap02Oo
ROCHE, Mary	19	F	Laborer	19Ap02Oo
GUNN, Felix	60	M	Laborer	19Ap02Oo
Died-At-Sea				
Pat	30	M	Laborer	19Ap02Oo
Andey	22	M	Laborer	19Ap02Oo
Ed.	20	M	Laborer	19Ap02Oo
Felix	03	M	Child	19Ap02Oo
MARTIN, Mary	22	F	Unknown	19Ap02Oo
GILROY, John	25	M	Farmer	19Ap02Oo
Mary	23	F	Unknown	19Ap02Oo

NAMES OF PASSENGERS	AGE	SEX	OCCUPATIONS	DATE PORT SHIP
GILROY, Margaret	20	F	Unknown	19Ap02Oo
Patrick	10	M	Farmer	19Ap02Oo
BRADY, William	34	M	Farmer	19Ap02Oo
MCMULLEN, Jane	22	F	Unknown	19Ap02Oo
HARRIS, Daniel	22	M	Farmer	19Ap02Oo
CONNES, John	30	M	Farmer	19Ap02Oo
U (W)	33	F	Unknown	19Ap02Oo
Dolly	24	F	Unknown	19Ap02Oo
Ann (D)	08	F	Child	19Ap02Oo
HERN, Michael	33	M	Farmer	19Ap02Oo
MCKIN, Pat	27	M	Farmer	19Ap02Oo
U (W)	23	F	Unknown	19Ap02Oo
MULDOON, Ellen	18	F	Unknown	19Ap02Oo
OHARA, Michael	25	M	Farmer	19Ap02Oo
U (W)	24	F	Unknown	19Ap02Oo
Henry (S)	08	M	Child	19Ap02Oo
Bessey (D)	06	F	Child	19Ap02Oo
MCLAUGHLIN, James	20	M	Laborer	19Ap02Oo
MCGAIRN, Bernard	20	M	Laborer	19Ap02Oo
CONLAN, Andrew	20	M	Laborer	19Ap02Oo
Cathe.	18	F	Unknown	19Ap02Oo
DONEGAN, Thomas	50	M	Laborer	19Ap02Oo
Margaret (W)	50	F	Unknown	19Ap02Oo
Ann (D)	30	F	Unknown	19Ap02Oo
John (S)	25	M	Laborer	19Ap02Oo
MULLIGAN, Bridget	20	F	Unknown	19Ap02Oo
ONEILE, Francis	40	M	Laborer	19Ap02Oo
Bernard	20	M	Laborer	19Ap02Oo
CASSIDAY, Edward	22	M	Laborer	19Ap02Oo
Mary	20	F	Unknown	19Ap02Oo
SULLIVAN, Mary	19	F	Unknown	19Ap02Oo
Eliz.	20	F	Unknown	19Ap02Oo
THOMPSON, John	19	M	Laborer	19Ap02Oo
HENNESSEY, Samuel	30	M	Laborer	19Ap02Oo
EAGAN, Michl.	21	M	Laborer	19Ap02Oo
MCGAVERN, Phillip	22	M	Laborer	19Ap02Oo
BURNS, Thomas	24	M	Laborer	19Ap02Oo
MCMANUS, James	20	M	Laborer	19Ap02Oo
MCLAUGHLIN, Bernard	26	M	Laborer	19Ap02Oo
MCNUTLY, John	20	M	Laborer	19Ap02Oo
SHANDLEY, John	25	M	Laborer	19Ap02Oo
Mary (W)	20	F	Unknown	19Ap02Oo
Mary (D)	05	F	Child	19Ap02Oo
Catherine (D)	.00	F	Infant	19Ap02Oo
CANNELLY, James	24	M	Farmer	19Ap02Oo
REILLY, John	27	M	Farmer	19Ap02Oo
REID, Ann	20	F	Unknown	19Ap02Oo
CANNELLY, Bridget	21	F	Unknown	19Ap02Oo
MCGUIN, John	20	M	Farmer	19Ap02Oo
Mary	13	F	Unknown	19Ap02Oo
BRYON, William	30	M	Farmer	19Ap02Oo
QUINN, Francis	19	M	Farmer	19Ap02Oo
BRADY, Hugh	26	M	Farmer	19Ap02Oo
Alice (W)	24	F	Unknown	19Ap02Oo
John (S)	.00	M	Infant	19Ap02Oo
CARBERRY, James	50	M	Farmer	19Ap02Oo
Cathe. (W)	45	F	Unknown	19Ap02Oo
Pat (S)	27	M	Farmer	19Ap02Oo
Bridget (D)	18	F	Unknown	19Ap02Oo
Mary (D)	13	F	Unknown	19Ap02Oo
Cathe. (D)	09	F	Child	19Ap02Oo
James (S)	.00	M	Infant	19Ap02Oo
SHARP, Margt.	24	F	Unknown	19Ap02Oo
Mary	02	F	Child	19Ap02Oo
MCLAUGHLIN, Ann	30	F	Unknown	19Ap02Oo
Mary (D)	10	F	Unknown	19Ap02Oo
Bryan (S)	07	M	Child	19Ap02Oo
John (S)	04	M	Child	19Ap02Oo
FEANAN, John	19	M	Farmer	19Ap02Oo
Margt.	17	F	Unknown	19Ap02Oo
HOGAN, Michael	21	M	Farmer	19Ap02Oo
HIGGINS, Patrick	25	M	Farmer	19Ap02Oo
Mary	03	F	Child	19Ap02Oo
Mary	09	F	Child	19Ap02Oo
Frank	07	M	Child	19Ap02Oo

NAMES OF PASSENGERS		AGE	SEX	OCCUPATIONS	DATE PORT SHIP
CASSIDY, Mary		21	F	Unknown	19Ap020o
Cathe.		22	F	Unknown	19Ap020o
CARNEY, John		21	M	Farmer	19Ap020o
MCCABE, Bridget		19	F	Unknown	19Ap020o
HANSKY, Richard		40	M	Farmer	19Ap020o
LYNCH, Michael		24	M	Farmer	19Ap020o
Margt.		24	F	Unknown	19Ap020o
CALLAGHAN, Bridget		18	F	Unknown	19Ap020o
HAMELL, Thomas		35	M	Farmer	19Ap020o
Ann		20	F	Unknown	19Ap020o
FOX, Bessey		20	F	Unknown	19Ap020o
ECCLES, Ann		20	F	Unknown	19Ap020o
CALLIGAN, Michael		22	M	Laborer	19Ap020o
MCGRAW, John		17	M	Laborer	19Ap020o
Patrick		18	M	Laborer	19Ap020o
MULLEN, James		35	M	Laborer	19Ap020o
CURREY, Maria		20	F	Unknown	19Ap020o
WRIGHT, Francis		20	M	Laborer	19Ap020o
KELLEY, James		35	M	Laborer	19Ap020o
Patt		30	M	Laborer	19Ap020o
MCGANN, Michael		31	M	Laborer	19Ap020o
SOMERS, Cathe.		17	F	Unknown	19Ap020o
WHALEN, James		30	M	Laborer	19Ap020o
Mary	(W)	27	F	Unknown	19Ap020o
Michael	(S)	.00	M	Infant	19Ap020o
DELIMERD, Bridget		20	F	Unknown	19Ap020o
DUNN, Thomas		27	M	Laborer	19Ap020o
REILLY, Elizabeth		28	F	Unknown	19Ap020o
DAWSON, Michael		27	M	Laborer	19Ap020o
KELLEY, Ann		50	F	Unknown	19Ap020o
Luke	(S)	24	M	Laborer	19Ap020o
Peggy	(D)	17	F	Unknown	19Ap020o
Edward	(S)	13	M	Laborer	19Ap020o
Biddy	(D)	11	F	Unknown	19Ap020o
CURRAN, Patrick		37	M	Laborer	19Ap020o
Jane	(W)	40	F	Unknown	19Ap020o
Ann	(D)	10	F	Unknown	19Ap020o
Thomas	(S)	08	M	Child	19Ap020o
Jane	(D)	07	F	Child	19Ap020o
Winifred	(S)	03	M	Child	19Ap020o
Margt.	(D)	.00	F	Infant	19Ap020o
ASHTON, John		19	M	Laborer	19Ap020o
LEONARD, Richard		27	M	Laborer	19Ap020o
BENNETT, Thomas		26	M	Laborer	19Ap020o
BROWN, Patrick		23	M	Laborer	19Ap020o
MULLIN, John		24	M	Laborer	19Ap020o
OHENRY, Mary		20	F	Unknown	19Ap020o
Mary		30	F	Unknown	19Ap020o
MANAGHAN, Ann		12	F	Unknown	19Ap020o
Bridget		10	F	Unknown	19Ap020o
U		04	F	Child	19Ap020o
SILLION, Allice		20	F	Unknown	19Ap020o
MCCUE, James		20	M	Laborer	19Ap020o
Mary		28	F	Unknown	19Ap020o
STEVENS, Margt.		21	F	Unknown	19Ap020o
ANDREWS, Joseph		29	M	Laborer	19Ap020o
KILROY, Patrick		22	M	Laborer	19Ap020o
Mary		44	F	Unknown	19Ap020o
Michael		17	M	Laborer	19Ap020o
WARBURTON, Thomas		40	M	Laborer	19Ap020o

LORD-DUFFERIN 19 APRIL 1847

From Liverpool

NAMES OF PASSENGERS		AGE	SEX	OCCUPATIONS	DATE PORT SHIP
MOONEY, Ellen		25	F	None	19Ap020p
MORRIS, Ben		21	M	Laborer	19Ap020p
REILLY, Margt.		15	F	None	19Ap020p
LANIGAN, Betty		20	F	None	19Ap020p
GROWERY, Peggy		16	F	None	19Ap020p
KEARNEY, Mary		25	F	None	19Ap020p
Thos.		17	M	None	19Ap020p
Eliza		16	F	None	19Ap020p
Kate		12	F	None	19Ap020p
Margt.		05	F	Child	19Ap020p
Mary		04	F	Child	19Ap020p
Pat		.00	M	Infant	19Ap020p
WHITELAW, Ellen		15	F	None	19Ap020p
CONOLLY, M.		20	F	None	19Ap020p
CAROLINE, Thos.		30	M	Laborer	19Ap020p
KING, Francis		45	M	Laborer	19Ap020p
HOLDAROFT, James		17	M	Laborer	19Ap020p
Rose		20	F	None	19Ap020p
MACKEY, Patk.		40	M	Laborer	19Ap020p
Judith	(W)	35	F	None	19Ap020p
Thomas	(S)	08	M	Child	19Ap020p
WHALON, John		19	M	Laborer	19Ap020p
James		21	M	Laborer	19Ap020p
MURRAY, W.		50	M	Laborer	19Ap020p
Roger	(S)	22	M	Laborer	19Ap020p
Cathe.	(D)	12	F	None	19Ap020p
Danl.	(S)	10	M	None	19Ap020p
James	(S)	09	M	Child	19Ap020p
Wm.	(S)	07	M	Child	19Ap020p
FEENEY, Thos.		21	M	Laborer	19Ap020p
ALLEN, Ellen		18	F	None	19Ap020p
GROGHAN, Ann		20	F	None	19Ap020p
YORK, Mary		40	F	None	19Ap020p
Frank		26	M	Laborer	19Ap020p
Bridget		24	F	None	19Ap020p
Mary		20	F	None	19Ap020p
Pat		17	M	Laborer	19Ap020p
Cathe.		16	F	None	19Ap020p
Ann		13	F	None	19Ap020p
Rose		11	F	None	19Ap020p
Eliza		09	F	Child	19Ap020p
Matt.		06	M	Child	19Ap020p
BROWN, Marcella		40	F	None	19Ap020p
LENAN, Mgt.		18	F	None	19Ap020p
KING, Rose		23	F	None	19Ap020p
BURNS, Kitty		20	F	None	19Ap020p
FAULKMAN, Patk.		30	M	Laborer	19Ap020p
WILSON, Ann		25	F	None	19Ap020p
FARRELL, Ann		21	F	None	19Ap020p
MAGINNIS, John		24	M	Laborer	19Ap020p
FARRELL, John		20	M	Laborer	19Ap020p
Ann		14	F	None	19Ap020p
NAUGHTON, Pat		20	M	Laborer	19Ap020p
Ellen		21	F	None	19Ap020p
KEENING, Ellen		24	F	None	19Ap020p
LYNCH, Peter		29	M	Laborer	19Ap020p
Francis		17	M	Laborer	19Ap020p
MORTIMER, Pat		17	M	Laborer	19Ap020p
MCCONNELL, Agnes		16	F	None	19Ap020p
MAHER, Martin		28	M	Laborer	19Ap020p
FARRELL, James		24	M	Laborer	19Ap020p
KANE, Pat		24	M	Laborer	19Ap020p
MATHEWS, Jas.		24	M	Laborer	19Ap020p
Pat		50	M	Laborer	19Ap020p
KELLY, John		21	M	Laborer	19Ap020p
Judy		19	F	None	19Ap020p
KING, John		23	M	Laborer	19Ap020p
Cathe.		18	F	None	19Ap020p
FAWKE, Jno.		20	M	Laborer	19Ap020p
CAHILL, Patrick		35	M	Laborer	19Ap020p
Patrick		26	M	Laborer	19Ap020p
Mary	(W)	25	F	None	19Ap020p
James	(S)	.00	M	Infant	19Ap020p
MCGRATH, Matthew		21	M	Laborer	19Ap020p
REILLY, Thomas		21	M	Laborer	19Ap020p
BAYLEY, John		21	M	Laborer	19Ap020p
REED, John		24	M	Laborer	19Ap020p
Cathe.		20	F	None	19Ap020p
MURRAY, Ellz.		20	F	None	19Ap020p

NAMES OF PASSENGERS	AGE SEX REL	AGE	SEX	OCCUPATIONS	DATE PORT SHIP
MURRAY, Mgt.		36	F	Laborer	19Ap020p
BRADY, Mt.		21	F	Laborer	19Ap020p
BROHANS, Thos.		30	M	Laborer	19Ap020p
BREESON, Cathe.		30	F	None	19Ap020p
Eliz.		40	F	None	19Ap020p
MCNICKLE, Danl.		26	M	Laborer	19Ap020p
George		26	M	Laborer	19Ap020p
MCCANN, Jas.		24	M	Laborer	19Ap020p
MCGUIRE, Hugh		24	M	Laborer	19Ap020p
Martin		21	M	Laborer	19Ap020p
BRENNAN, Rose		36	F	None	19Ap020p
CROPIER, Murtley		20	M	Laborer	19Ap020p
MCMAHON, Thos.		21	M	Laborer	19Ap020p
Mary		16	F	None	19Ap020p
KING, Mrgt.		26	F	None	19Ap020p
HARRIGAN, Thos.		26	M	Laborer	19Ap020p
SULLIVAN, Ellen		24	F	None	19Ap020p
HARRIGAN, Honora		26	F	None	19Ap020p
Patk.		20	M	Unknown	19Ap020p
MURRAY, Francis		21	M	Unknown	19Ap020p
FARRELL, John		22	M	Unknown	19Ap020p
KELAHEN, Madgey		20	F	None	19Ap020p
KENNY, Mrgt.		20	F	None	19Ap020p
GRUGLEY, Jas.		26	M	Laborer	19Ap020p
Mrgt.		20	F	None	19Ap020p
DUGAN, Cathe.		36	F	None	19Ap020p
FLOOD, Patk.		16	M	None	19Ap020p
OATES, Mary		26	F	None	19Ap020p
Terrence	(S)	02	M	Child	19Ap020p
MCBRIDE, Patk.		22	M	Laborer	19Ap020p
SMITH, Wm.		21	M	Laborer	19Ap020p
Cath.		20	F	None	19Ap020p
BRENNAN, Nancy		20	F	None	19Ap020p
Pat.		21	M	Laborer	19Ap020p
BRIEN, John		24	M	Laborer	19Ap020p
SWENEY, Martin		23	M	Laborer	19Ap020p
SHERIDAN, Patk.		50	M	Laborer	19Ap020p
Mrgt.	(W)	48	F	None	19Ap020p
James	(S)	24	M	Laborer	19Ap020p
John	(S)	20	M	Laborer	19Ap020p
Patk.	(S)	19	M	Laborer	19Ap020p
Edward	(S)	17	M	Laborer	19Ap020p
MCNALLY, Pat		34	M	Laborer	19Ap020p
BAYLAND, Cath.		16	F	None	19Ap020p
Mary		17	F	None	19Ap020p
MCDANIEL, Matthew		24	M	None	19Ap020p
CASSIDY, L.		04	M	Child	19Ap020p
Bryan		22	M	Unknown	19Ap020p
REYNOLDS, Charles		47	M	Laborer	19Ap020p
Ann	(W)	40	F	None	19Ap020p
Biddy	(D)	21	F	None	19Ap020p
Maurice	(S)	10	M	None	19Ap020p
Pat.	(S)	16	M	None	19Ap020p
Michael	(S)	12	M	None	19Ap020p
James	(S)	10	M	None	19Ap020p
BRADLEY, Mich.		32	M	Laborer	19Ap020p
Anne		24	F	None	19Ap020p
HOBBINS, Thos.		36	M	Laborer	19Ap020p
Mary	(W)	34	F	None	19Ap020p
Anne	(D)	10	F	None	19Ap020p
Wm.	(S)	07	M	Child	19Ap020p
Patk.	(S)	05	M	Child	19Ap020p
Cath.	(D)	.00	F	Infant	19Ap020p
Died-At-Sea					
FERRY, Widow		56	F	None	19Ap020p
Died-At-Sea					
Anne	(D)	24	F	None	19Ap020p
Peter	(S)	26	M	Laborer	19Ap020p
MCCOY, Abby		50	F	Laborer	19Ap020p
Mich.		19	M	Laborer	19Ap020p
FERRY, John		32	M	Laborer	19Ap020p
Jane	(W)	30	F	Laborer	19Ap020p
Jane	(D)	09	F	Child	19Ap020p
Maria	(D)	08	F	Child	19Ap020p
Anne	(D)	05	F	Child	19Ap020p
FERRY, Patt	(S)	.00	M	Infant	19Ap020p
SHANLEY, Widow		55	F	None	19Ap020p
Sarah	(D)	18	F	None	19Ap020p
Cathe.	(D)	16	F	None	19Ap020p
Biddy	(D)	15	F	None	19Ap020p
Edward	(S)	25	M	Laborer	19Ap020p
Cathe.	(D)	26	F	None	19Ap020p
EYRE, George		41	M	Laborer	19Ap020p
Mary	(W)	42	F	None	19Ap020p
Mary-Ann	(D)	19	F	None	19Ap020p
James	(S)	17	M	None	19Ap020p
Benjamin	(S)	13	M	None	19Ap020p
Jane	(D)	15	F	None	19Ap020p
Jackson	(S)	10	M	None	19Ap020p
George	(S)	07	M	Child	19Ap020p
Thomas	(S)	04	M	Child	19Ap020p
Mrgt.	(D)	02	F	Child	19Ap020p
DORAN, Maria		28	F	None	19Ap020p
SHERIDAN, Patk.		24	M	Laborer	19Ap020p
CULLEN, Michl.		23	M	None	19Ap020p
GORDON, John		20	M	None	19Ap020p
MCLANE, James		21	M	None	19Ap020p
MCGOVERN, Francis		22	M	Laborer	19Ap020p
CULLEN, Mary		18	F	None	19Ap020p
SHERIDAN, Bridget		20	F	None	19Ap020p
Peter		26	M	None	19Ap020p
DOLAN, James		22	M	Laborer	19Ap020p
Bridget	(W)	20	F	None	19Ap020p
Hugh	(S)	03	M	Child	19Ap020p
Mrgt.		25	F	None	19Ap020p
CULLEN, Patt		12	M	Laborer	19Ap020p
RYAN, James		24	M	Laborer	19Ap020p
CARTY, Mrgt.		23	F	None	19Ap020p
Cathe.		20	F	None	19Ap020p
Patrick		18	M	Laborer	19Ap020p
KIRKLAND, James		21	M	Laborer	19Ap020p
DOLAN, Patt		21	M	Laborer	19Ap020p
GALLAGHER, Farrell		22	M	Laborer	19Ap020p
EGAN, Michl.		31	M	Laborer	19Ap020p
FLANAGAN, Patt		55	M	Laborer	19Ap020p
Ann	(W)	50	F	None	19Ap020p
Eliza	(D)	20	F	None	19Ap020p
Susan	(D)	16	F	None	19Ap020p
James	(S)	17	M	None	19Ap020p
Mrgt.	(D)	11	F	None	19Ap020p
Pat.	(S)	09	M	Child	19Ap020p
HANNA, Sally		30	F	None	19Ap020p
DONOHOE, Bernard		33	M	Laborer	19Ap020p
Thos.		09	M	Child	19Ap020p
Anne		07	F	Child	19Ap020p
MURRAY, Thos.		44	M	Laborer	19Ap020p
U	(W)	44	F	None	19Ap020p
Mrgt.	(D)	07	F	Child	19Ap020p
Ann	(D)	04	F	Child	19Ap020p
COMEFORD, Mich.		26	M	Laborer	19Ap020p
MCDONALD, Thos.		21	M	Laborer	19Ap020p
U	(W)	19	F	None	19Ap020p
Anthony		18	M	Laborer	19Ap020p
Bridget	(D)	.00	F	Infant	19Ap020p
Died-At-Sea					
MCGRATH, Luke		22	M	Laborer	19Ap020p
U	(W)	22	F	None	19Ap020p
Honora	(D)	03	F	Child	19Ap020p
Mrgt.	(D)	.00	F	Infant	19Ap020p
DAVIS, Francis		50	M	Laborer	19Ap020p
HINES, Mich.		19	M	Laborer	19Ap020p
Judith		22	F	None	19Ap020p
Died-At-Sea					
WALSH, Thos.		46	M	Laborer	19Ap020p
Kitty	(W)	45	F	None	19Ap020p
Honora	(D)	20	F	None	19Ap020p
Biddy	(D)	16	F	None	19Ap020p
Mary	(D)	14	F	None	19Ap020p
Ellen	(D)	11	F	None	19Ap020p
John	(S)	09	M	Child	19Ap020p

NAMES OF PASSENGERS		A G E	S E X	OCCUPATIONS	DATE PORT SHIP	NAMES OF PASSENGERS		A G E	S E X	OCCUPATIONS	DATE PORT SHIP
WALSH, Lawrence	(P)	73	M	None	19Ap020p	KILROY, John		30	M	Laborer	20Ap020q
DOOLY, James		20	M	Laborer	19Ap020p	DUFFY, John		23	M	Laborer	20Ap020q
SHAKEY, Thos.		22	M	Laborer	19Ap020p	Rose		20	F	Laborer	20Ap020q
BOOTH, Thos.		28	M	Laborer	19Ap020p	ONEIL, Jane		20	F	Laborer	20Ap020q
Cath.	(W)	26	F	None	19Ap020p	John		.00	M	Infant	20Ap020q
Thos.	(S)	05	M	Child	19Ap020p	CULLEN, Edwd.		25	M	Laborer	20Ap020q
CULLEN, John		24	M	Laborer	19Ap020p	REASS, Anty.		62	M	Laborer	20Ap020q
GRACE, Thos.		22	M	Laborer	19Ap020p	Thos.		24	M	Laborer	20Ap020q
CONNER, Thos.		22	M	Laborer	19Ap020p	Edwd.		18	M	Laborer	20Ap020q
John		30	M	Laborer	19Ap020p	Martin		13	M	Laborer	20Ap020q
CASSIDY, Richd.		25	M	Laborer	19Ap020p	Bridget		12	F	Laborer	20Ap020q
MCGRATH, R.		25	M	Laborer	19Ap020p	W.Michael		20	M	Laborer	20Ap020q
CALLAN, Thos.		25	M	Laborer	19Ap020p	REDDINGTON, T.		20	U	Laborer	20Ap020q
WARD, Jno.		26	M	Laborer	19Ap020p	BURKE, Michl.		22	M	Laborer	20Ap020q
GRINDON, Jos.		20	M	Laborer	19Ap020p	RATTIGAN, Tim		25	M	Laborer	20Ap020q
CASSIDY, Emily		21	F	None	19Ap020p	GANNON, Michl.		24	M	Laborer	20Ap020q
PENTONY, Wm.		26	M	Laborer	19Ap020p	COLLINS, John		21	M	Laborer	20Ap020q
RUSSELL, Margt.		12	F	None	19Ap020p	FLAHERTY, W.		22	M	Laborer	20Ap020q
MCGARTY, Rosey		26	F	None	19Ap020p	Mary		26	F	Laborer	20Ap020q
MCGOVERN, Hugh		22	M	Laborer	19Ap020p	RUNROY, Bridget		20	F	Laborer	20Ap020q
HUNT, Wm.		35	M	Laborer	19Ap020p	HEVERAN, Tim		20	M	Laborer	20Ap020q
DALEY, Margt.		22	F	None	19Ap020p	Mary		20	F	Laborer	20Ap020q
GRIFFITH, Mich.		22	M	Laborer	19Ap020p	DONELAN, Cath.		22	F	Laborer	20Ap020q
CROWE, Patt.		19	M	Laborer	19Ap020p	GODFREY, Bridget		20	F	Laborer	20Ap020q
						NAUGHT, Edwd.		36	M	Laborer	20Ap020q
						CRONDEN, U-Mrs.		40	F	Laborer	20Ap020q
						Conner	(S)	13	M	Laborer	20Ap020q
						Ellen	(D)	11	F	Laborer	20Ap020q
						Jeremiah	(S)	06	M	Child	20Ap020q
BARLOW 20 APRIL 1847						DUFFIN, Patt		.00	M	Infant	20Ap020q
						CONDEN, John		22	M	Laborer	20Ap020q
From Liverpool						Nelly		20	F	Laborer	20Ap020q
						Susan		21	F	Laborer	20Ap020q
						MAHONY, John		23	M	Laborer	20Ap020q
						OBRIEN, George		20	M	Laborer	20Ap020q
HANLON, Ellen		25	F	Laborer	20Ap020q	DOUGHERTY, Barney		25	M	Laborer	20Ap020q
Catherine		15	F	Laborer	20Ap020q	MORTAGH, Mark		25	M	Laborer	20Ap020q
FLINN, Patt		25	M	Laborer	20Ap020q	Mary-Ann	(W)	22	F	Laborer	20Ap020q
MCGLIN, Mary		18	F	Laborer	20Ap020q	Alexander	(S)	.00	M	Infant	20Ap020q
John		13	M	Laborer	20Ap020q	James		18	M	Laborer	20Ap020q
CARNEY, Patt		09	M	Child	20Ap020q	Elizabeth		15	F	Laborer	20Ap020q
MCALARNEY, Jno.		21	M	Laborer	20Ap020q	MCDONNELL, Michl.		26	M	Laborer	20Ap020q
KERNGER, Patt		20	M	Laborer	20Ap020q	DOLAN, Edwd.		20	M	Laborer	20Ap020q
SULLIVAN, Patt		25	M	Laborer	20Ap020q	RALEY, Terence		20	M	Laborer	20Ap020q
MCDONNELD, Owen		25	M	Laborer	20Ap020q	Died-At-Sea					
CARNEY, Patt		25	M	Laborer	20Ap020q	JENNINGS, Thos.		56	M	Laborer	20Ap020q
Ann		20	F	Laborer	20Ap020q	Margt.		23	F	Laborer	20Ap020q
CONNELLY, Edwd.		45	M	Laborer	20Ap020q	Catherine		29	F	Laborer	20Ap020q
Alicia		25	F	Laborer	20Ap020q	Ellen		16	F	Laborer	20Ap020q
Cathe.		14	F	Laborer	20Ap020q	QUADE, William		22	M	Laborer	20Ap020q
Jane		12	F	Laborer	20Ap020q	BURKE, Michl.		22	M	Laborer	20Ap020q
Elizabeth		10	F	Laborer	20Ap020q	RUANE, Timothy		29	M	Laborer	20Ap020q
Edwd.		08	M	Child	20Ap020q	MULLLIN, Patt		22	M	Laborer	20Ap020q
Mary		02	F	Child	20Ap020q	GRIFFIN, Patt		22	M	Laborer	20Ap020q
Died-At-Sea						MCCARTNEY, Ellen		27	F	Laborer	20Ap020q
Felix		50	M	Laborer	20Ap020q	GRIFFIN, Frank		29	M	Laborer	20Ap020q
Alicia	(W)	50	F	Laborer	20Ap020q	FLEMING, Bridget		18	F	Laborer	20Ap020q
CURRY, Mary		17	F	Laborer	20Ap020q	FEAGAN, James		32	M	Laborer	20Ap020q
CONRY, Edwd.		21	M	Laborer	20Ap020q	Bessy	(W)	30	F	Laborer	20Ap020q
Cath.		18	F	Laborer	20Ap020q	Biddy	(D)	.00	F	Infant	20Ap020q
FEENY, Michl.		22	M	Laborer	20Ap020q	Mary		25	F	Laborer	20Ap020q
MAHER, Thos.		40	M	Laborer	20Ap020q	SULLIVAN, Bryan		22	M	Laborer	20Ap020q
Margt.	(W)	38	F	Laborer	20Ap020q	Mary		22	F	Laborer	20Ap020q
Bridget	(D)	18	F	Laborer	20Ap020q	Thomas		23	M	Laborer	20Ap020q
Rose	(D)	13	F	Laborer	20Ap020q	MANERON, Patt		21	M	Laborer	20Ap020q
Peter	(S)	12	M	Laborer	20Ap020q	MCDERMOTT, Michl.		23	M	Laborer	20Ap020q
Margt.	(D)	09	F	Child	20Ap020q	SULLIVAN, Owen		.00	M	Infant	20Ap020q
James	(S)	06	M	Child	20Ap020q	Thomas		23	M	Laborer	20Ap020q
Mary-Ann	(D)	03	F	Child	20Ap020q	MANION, Patt		21	M	Laborer	20Ap020q
Catherine	(D)	.00	F	Infant	20Ap020q	MCDERMOTT, Michl.		33	M	Laborer	20Ap020q
CONROY, Cath.		20	F	Laborer	20Ap020q	MANION, Margt.		33	F	Laborer	20Ap020q
DUFFY, Jas.		21	M	Laborer	20Ap020q	Michl.	(S)	10	M	Laborer	20Ap020q
Cath.		18	F	Laborer	20Ap020q	John	(S)	07	M	Child	20Ap020q
FEEHELY, Michael		22	M	Laborer	20Ap020q	Cathe.	(D)	05	F	Child	20Ap020q
BURKE, Danl.		20	M	Laborer	20Ap020q	Bridget	(D)	.00	F	Infant	20Ap020q

NAMES OF PASSENGERS		AGE	SEX	OCCUPATIONS	DATE PORT SHIP
MANION, Anne		20	F	Laborer	20Ap020q
CAFFREY, Terence		25	M	Laborer	20Ap020q
Anne	(W)	23	F	Laborer	20Ap020q
Richd.	(S)	.00	M	Infant	20Ap020q
Thos.		17	M	Laborer	20Ap020q
Patt		.00	M	Infant	20Ap020q
WEATHER, Laurence		20	M	Laborer	20Ap020q
VERNON, Jane		29	F	Laborer	20Ap020q
Jane		20	F	Laborer	20Ap020q
OHARA, James		56	M	Laborer	20Ap020q
Margt.	(W)	40	F	Laborer	20Ap020q
Mergt.	(D)	17	F	Laborer	20Ap020q
Michael	(S)	13	M	Laborer	20Ap020q
Terence	(S)	12	M	Laborer	20Ap020q
Charles	(S)	09	M	Child	20Ap020q
John	(S)	02	M	Child	20Ap020q
Belle	(D)	05	F	Child	20Ap020q
James	(S)	.00	M	Infant	20Ap020q
MCGINNITY, Patt		76	M	Laborer	20Ap020q
James		22	M	Laborer	20Ap020q
Jane		20	F	Laborer	20Ap020q
MCCARTY, Michl.		24	M	Laborer	20Ap020q
Danl.		24	M	Laborer	20Ap020q
CORBETT, Thos.		20	M	Laborer	20Ap020q
MCCARTY, Mary		28	F	Laborer	20Ap020q
Margt.		20	F	Laborer	20Ap020q
MURPHY, Patt		22	M	Laborer	20Ap020q
HERNE, Patt		30	M	Laborer	20Ap020q
John		47	M	Laborer	20Ap020q
John	(S)	12	M	Laborer	20Ap020q
CARROLL, Mary		26	F	Laborer	20Ap020q
Margt.		21	F	Laborer	20Ap020q
GAFFNEY, John		22	M	Laborer	20Ap020q
REED, Hamilton		10	M	Laborer	20Ap020q
Mary-Jane		08	F	Child	20Ap020q
John		04	M	Child	20Ap020q
WILSON, Hugh		36	M	Laborer	20Ap020q
Jane	(W)	35	F	Laborer	20Ap020q
George	(S)	10	M	Laborer	20Ap020q
Anne	(D)	08	F	Child	20Ap020q
Robert	(S)	03	M	Child	20Ap020q
Mary	(D)	.00	F	Infant	20Ap020q
MCKURLY, Edward		25	M	Laborer	20Ap020q
MCGATRY, Edward		25	M	Laborer	20Ap020q
TRAYNER, Bridget		20	F	Laborer	20Ap020q

JOHN-RAVENEL 20 APRIL 1847

From Liverpool

NAMES OF PASSENGERS	AGE	SEX	OCCUPATIONS	DATE PORT SHIP
MCMICHAEL, Francis	21	M	Laborer	20Ap020r
Patrick	17	M	Laborer	20Ap020r
Daniel	21	M	Laborer	20Ap020r
DOLAN, John	22	M	Miller	20Ap020r
MOAN, James	20	M	Shoemaker	20Ap020r
Thomas	13	M	Shoemaker	20Ap020r
MCKUGAN, Jas.	55	M	Weaver	20Ap020r
Jas.	19	M	Weaver	20Ap020r
MCCARTNEY, Edwd.	20	M	Wheelwright	20Ap020r
CALDWELL, Owen	21	M	Laborer	20Ap020r
GALLAGHER, Thos.	20	M	Laborer	20Ap020r
HUGHES, Patrick	25	M	Laborer	20Ap020r
Mary	20	F	Servant	20Ap020r
MALBORE, Anne	19	F	Servant	20Ap020r
MALLON, Mary	17	F	Servant	20Ap020r
WELSH, James	29	M	Laborer	20Ap020r
Anne	20	F	Servant	20Ap020r
DERMOTT, Peter	26	M	Laborer	20Ap020r
Mary	20	F	Servant	20Ap020r

NAMES OF PASSENGERS		AGE	SEX	OCCUPATIONS	DATE PORT SHIP
DERMOTT, Catherine		20	F	Servant	20Ap020r
Judy		50	F	Servant	20Ap020r
Patrick		11	M	Laborer	20Ap020r
Peter		.00	M	Infant	20Ap020r
Allice		26	F	Servant	20Ap020r
LYNCH, Owen		23	M	Shoemaker	20Ap020r
FOX, James		37	M	Laborer	20Ap020r
LYNCH, Anne		42	F	Servant	20Ap020r
SMITH, Bridget		32	F	Dressmaker	20Ap020r
COYLE, Dafrey		19	M	Laborer	20Ap020r
FITZPATRICK, Thomas		27	M	Shoemaker	20Ap020r
BRADY, Patrick		13	M	Laborer	20Ap020r
HIGHLAND, Mathew		27	M	Laborer	20Ap020r
BRADY, John		24	M	Laborer	20Ap020r
Jane		23	F	Servant	20Ap020r
MCGLOUGHLAN, Michael		27	M	Shoemaker	20Ap020r
FLEMING, James		24	M	Laborer	20Ap020r
MCGLOUGHLAN, Rose		40	F	None	20Ap020r
LUDY, Anne		18	F	Servant	20Ap020r
John		12	M	Servant	20Ap020r
George		10	M	Servant	20Ap020r
READY, Patrick		25	M	Clerk	20Ap020r
LENNAN, Terence		26	M	Laborer	20Ap020r
Thos.		29	M	Laborer	20Ap020r
DELANY, John		27	M	Laborer	20Ap020r
Timothy		23	M	Laborer	20Ap020r
HAGAN, Edward		28	M	Laborer	20Ap020r
MARTIN, Bridget		27	F	Servant	20Ap020r
DELANEY, Catherine		20	F	Servant	20Ap020r
FOGARTY, Nancy		23	F	Servant	20Ap020r
LENNAN, Bridget		22	F	Dressmaker	20Ap020r
COMERFORD, Bridget		21	F	Servant	20Ap020r
MOORE, Joseph		20	M	Carpenter	20Ap020r
Catherine		18	F	Dressmaker	20Ap020r
Catherine		27	F	Dressmaker	20Ap020r
Bridget		18	F	Dressmaker	20Ap020r
COYLE, Michael		26	M	Laborer	20Ap020r
DROMORE, Honor		22	F	Servant	20Ap020r
LAWLOR, Ellen		26	F	Servant	20Ap020r
HEELEY, James		54	M	Farmer	20Ap020r
BARRON, William		36	M	Laborer	20Ap020r
CORRIGAN, Danl.		30	M	Laborer	20Ap020r
MCINTEE, John		27	M	Shoemaker	20Ap020r
Mary	(W)	22	F	None	20Ap020r
John	(S)	02	M	Child	20Ap020r
ROGERS, Patrick		26	M	Laborer	20Ap020r
MCILROY, Henry		36	M	Laborer	20Ap020r
MCGARVEY, Bridget		18	F	Servant	20Ap020r
WARD, John		34	M	Laborer	20Ap020r
MCGRAIN, Charles		20	M	Laborer	20Ap020r
FARRELL, Elizabeth		27	F	Servant	20Ap020r
HEYAN, Eliza		19	F	Servant	20Ap020r
BELL, John		29	M	Servant	20Ap020r
Catherine		40	F	None	20Ap020r
GASH, William		27	M	Tanner	20Ap020r
HERINER, T.		40	M	Shoemaker	20Ap020r
NOWLAN, Jeremiah		24	M	Tailor	20Ap020r
POWERS, John		21	M	Laborer	20Ap020r
KELLEHER, Danl.		24	M	Laborer	20Ap020r
Ellen		26	F	None	20Ap020r
NOONAN, Edward		25	M	Laborer	20Ap020r
ROBERTS, Robert		30	M	Tanner	20Ap020r
MCGOVERN, John		50	M	Laborer	20Ap020r
Rosey		12	F	None	20Ap020r
MCGUIN, Catherine		17	F	Servant	20Ap020r
MCGOVERN, Mary		27	F	Servant	20Ap020r
KEERNAN, John		28	M	Laborer	20Ap020r
KILLAM, Edward		30	M	Laborer	20Ap020r
Anne		21	F	None	20Ap020r
CLERKE, Mathew		21	M	Servant	20Ap020r
Edward		08	M	Child	20Ap020r
HALDY, Robert		20	M	Laborer	20Ap020r
MCGUM, Peter		36	M	Laborer	20Ap020r
FORREST, Andrew		37	M	Laborer	20Ap020r

NAMES OF PASSENGERS		AGE	SEX	OCCUPATIONS	DATE PORT SHIP
KELLY, Michael		29	M	Laborer	20Ap020r
Died-At-Sea					
BUCKLEY, Denis		26	M	Laborer	20Ap020r
WELSH, Mary		30	F	Servant	20Ap020r
HUBBART, Mary		29	F	Servant	20Ap020r
WALSH, Edward		40	M	Laborer	20Ap020r
Ellen		27	F	None	20Ap020r
FORDE, Pate		37	M	Laborer	20Ap020r
Winefred		26	F	Servant	20Ap020r
Thomas		30	M	Laborer	20Ap020r
MAHON, Patrick		36	M	Laborer	20Ap020r
HICKEY, Denis		42	M	Laborer	20Ap020r
LEONARD, Mane		22	M	Laborer	20Ap020r
Julia		21	F	Servant	20Ap020r
BUCKLEY, Jeremiah		27	M	Shoemaker	20Ap020r
Ellen		40	F	Servant	20Ap020r
Michael	(S)	12	M	None	20Ap020r
Mary	(D)	09	F	Child	20Ap020r
HURBY, Teady		50	M	Laborer	20Ap020r
Died-At-Sea					
Mary	(W)	45	F	Servant	20Ap020r
William	(S)	24	M	Laborer	20Ap020r
Patrick	(S)	27	M	Laborer	20Ap020r
John	(S)	20	M	Laborer	20Ap020r
Teady	(S)	12	M	None	20Ap020r
Mary	(D)	10	F	None	20Ap020r
Bridget	(D)	08	F	Child	20Ap020r
FORDE, Michael		37	M	Laborer	20Ap020r
Mary	(W)	26	F	Servant	20Ap020r
Mary		13	F	None	20Ap020r
Terence	(S)	07	M	Child	20Ap020r
Patrick	(S)	06	M	Child	20Ap020r
DALEY, Michael		56	M	Laborer	20Ap020r
Died-At-Sea					
Mary	(W)	49	F	None	20Ap020r
Mary	(D)	20	F	Servant	20Ap020r
John	(S)	18	M	Laborer	20Ap020r
James	(S)	14	M	None	20Ap020r
Bridget	(D)	12	F	None	20Ap020r
Michael	(S)	11	M	None	20Ap020r
Patrick	(S)	04	M	Child	20Ap020r
Catherine	(D)	.00	F	Infant	20Ap020r
Pate		35	M	Laborer	20Ap020r
Pate		21	M	Laborer	20Ap020r
MURTHA, James		24	M	Laborer	20Ap020r
HEALY, John		36	M	Laborer	20Ap020r
MCKEON, Thomas		29	M	Tailor	20Ap020r
SHANLEY, Terence		37	M	Clerk	20Ap020r
Bridget	(W)	26	F	Servant	20Ap020r
Bernard	(S)	.00	M	Infant	20Ap020r
FEAGIN, Catherine		26	F	Servant	20Ap020r
KENNEDY, Emma		18	F	Laborer	20Ap020r
MAHER, Emma		19	F	Servant	20Ap020r
John		25	M	Laborer	20Ap020r
CORBET, Terry		25	M	Laborer	20Ap020r
CAUGHTON, Margret		20	F	Servant	20Ap020r
UGIN, James		27	M	Laborer	20Ap020r
Margret		26	F	Servant	20Ap020r
MURRAY, Richard		20	M	Laborer	20Ap020r
HEARY, Mary-Anne		17	F	Dressmaker	20Ap020r
CANTWELL, Patrick		23	M	Laborer	20Ap020r
Margret		24	F	Servant	20Ap020r
Died-At-Sea					
LUNDY, Anne		22	F	Servant	20Ap020r
TUSNY, Mary		28	F	Servant	20Ap020r
GUNNS, James		23	M	Laborer	20Ap020r
LYNCH, Peter		31	M	Laborer	20Ap020r
MADY, Patck.		27	M	Laborer	20Ap020r
RYAN, Edward		21	M	Laborer	20Ap020r
Johanah		27	F	Servant	20Ap020r
HUGHES, Edward		26	M	Laborer	20Ap020r
OBRIEN, Anne		19	F	Servant	20Ap020r
FITZPATRICK, James		31	M	Shoemaker	20Ap020r
HEYLAND, Philip		22	M	Laborer	20Ap020r
LYNCH, Thomas		27	M	Laborer	20Ap020r
GELESPIE, Sarah		27	F	Servant	20Ap020r
WALL, Patrick		31	M	Tailor	20Ap020r
MOODY, John		20	M	Laborer	20Ap020r
TOOMEY, George		28	M	Laborer	20Ap020r
KENEDY, Elisa		27	F	Servant	20Ap020r
CROGAN, James		37	M	Tanner	20Ap020r
Honora	(W)	25	F	Servant	20Ap020r
Patrick	(S)	.00	M	Infant	20Ap020r
GREAVEY, John		26	M	Laborer	20Ap020r
FITZGERALD, Giber		18	M	Laborer	20Ap020r
KILBODEN, Patrick		21	M	Laborer	20Ap020r
Mary		29	F	Servant	20Ap020r
RAN, Catherine		24	F	Servant	20Ap020r
MCANUF, Owen		21	M	Laborer	20Ap020r
DOGHERTY, Patrick		29	M	Laborer	20Ap020r
Margret	(W)	26	F	Servant	20Ap020r
Charles	(S)	.00	M	Infant	20Ap020r
Phil.		17	M	Laborer	20Ap020r
DELANY, William		27	M	Shoemaker	20Ap020r
Margret		21	F	Dressmaker	20Ap020r
Anne		20	F	Servant	20Ap020r
DERRAGAN, John		26	M	Laborer	20Ap020r
DORAN, James		20	M	Tanner	20Ap020r
BYRNE, John		21	M	Laborer	20Ap020r
LYNCH, Eugene		29	M	Laborer	20Ap020r
MULLHALL, William		28	M	Laborer	20Ap020r
TELLING, Kearney		20	M	Shoemaker	20Ap020r
WRIGHT, Michael		27	M	Blr	20Ap020r
HICKEY, James		28	M	Laborer	20Ap020r
MOORE, William		50	M	Laborer	20Ap020r
Mary	(W)	51	F	None	20Ap020r
Mary	(D)	17	F	Servant	20Ap020r
Margret	(D)	19	F	Servant	20Ap020r
Patrick	(S)	15	M	Laborer	20Ap020r
Bridget	(D)	13	F	None	20Ap020r
Ellen	(D)	11	F	None	20Ap020r
Catherine	(D)	09	F	Child	20Ap020r
Joseph	(S)	07	M	Child	20Ap020r
Judith	(D)	05	F	Child	20Ap020r
Thomas	(S)	03	M	Child	20Ap020r
Martha	(D)	.00	F	Infant	20Ap020r
MCKEON, John		29	M	Laborer	20Ap020r
DUNLANEY, James		21	M	Laborer	20Ap020r
Malichic		19	M	Laborer	20Ap020r
HUCHESON, Andrew		21	M	Laborer	20Ap020r
BOYLE, James		17	M	Laborer	20Ap020r
Susan		18	F	Servant	20Ap020r
EAGLE, Robert		26	M	Groom	20Ap020r
LAWLOR, Patrick		27	M	Laborer	20Ap020r
Mary	(W)	24	F	Servant	20Ap020r
Andy	(S)	04	M	Child	20Ap020r
Catherine	(D)	02	F	Child	20Ap020r
Timothy	(S)	.00	M	Infant	20Ap020r
MORRISON, John		28	M	Laborer	20Ap020r
Michael		27	M	Laborer	20Ap020r
MCDONALD, Loghlen		26	M	Laborer	20Ap020r
Mary	(W)	27	F	None	20Ap020r
Margret		17	F	Servant	20Ap020r
Catherine	(D)	02	F	Child	20Ap020r
LOWS, John		35	M	Clerk	20Ap020r
Esther		36	F	Dressmaker	20Ap020r
Elisa		25	F	Dressmaker	20Ap020r
Esther	(D)	.00	F	Infant	20Ap020r
POLLOCK, Andrew		27	M	Laborer	20Ap020r
Elisa		25	F	Servant	20Ap020r
PHILIPS, Sarah		18	F	Servant	20Ap020r
SCOTT, Anne		19	F	Servant	20Ap020r
STUART, Elisa		20	F	Servant	20Ap020r
TALBOT, Catherine		21	F	Dressmaker	20Ap020r
Martha		31	F	Dressmaker	20Ap020r
GUILLAN, Patrick		39	M	Laborer	20Ap020r
MCMINIGAL, Patrick		42	M	Laborer	20Ap020r
John		13	M	None	20Ap020r
KEARNEY, Mark		31	M	Laborer	20Ap020r
DARLEY, Thomas		26	M	Laborer	20Ap020r

NAMES OF PASSENGERS		AGE	SEX	OCCUPATIONS	DATE PORT SHIP
FOGARTY, Patrick		27	M	Laborer	20Ap02Or
MOODY, James		24	M	Tailor	20Ap02Or
MORRIS, John		27	M	Laborer	20Ap02Or
GUNIES, Arthur		24	M	Laborer	20Ap02Or
MURPHY, Anne		19	F	Servant	20Ap02Or
CLASSAN, James		26	M	Laborer	20Ap02Or
QUIGLY, James		24	M	Laborer	20Ap02Or
MULLANY, Catherine		18	F	Servant	20Ap02Or
LYONS, John		22	M	Laborer	20Ap02Or
Bridget		20	F	None	20Ap02Or
KILROY, Michael		22	M	Laborer	20Ap02Or
MANION, Catherine		26	F	Servant	20Ap02Or
MULDOON, Mary		21	F	Servant	20Ap02Or
MAHON, Malichl		29	M	Laborer	20Ap02Or
GLENNON, Hugh		26	M	Laborer	20Ap02Or
MALONE, Patrick		22	M	Laborer	20Ap02Or
SAVAGE, Thomas		21	M	Laborer	20Ap02Or
JOHNSTON, Henry		08	M	Child	20Ap02Or
John		31	M	Shoemaker	20Ap02Or
Jane		26	F	None	20Ap02Or
MCGOWAN, Margret		29	F	Servant	20Ap02Or
HUGHES, John		19	M	Laborer	20Ap02Or
Bridget		17	F	Servant	20Ap02Or
Patrick		16	M	Laborer	20Ap02Or
Catherine		18	F	Servant	20Ap02Or
COYLE, Sarah		27	F	None	20Ap02Or
GILMORE, James		28	M	Laborer	20Ap02Or
Catherine		21	F	Servant	20Ap02Or
SWEENEY, John		23	M	Laborer	20Ap02Or
Margret	(W)	21	F	Servant	20Ap02Or
U		.00	U	Infant	20Ap02Or

CEYLON 20 APRIL 1847

From Liverpool

NAMES OF PASSENGERS		AGE	SEX	OCCUPATIONS	DATE PORT SHIP
DOWED, Patt		35	M	Laborer	20Ap02Kw
DEAN, John		27	M	Laborer	20Ap02Kw
CURRIN, John		24	M	Laborer	20Ap02Kw
U	(W)	21	F	None	20Ap02Kw
DYLER, Thomas		20	M	Laborer	20Ap02Kw
MCGUIRE, Patt		20	M	Laborer	20Ap02Kw
Mary	(W)	18	F	None	20Ap02Kw
U		.00	U	Infant	20Ap02Kw
SOYAN, James		22	M	Laborer	20Ap02Kw
FLANNEY, Francis		20	M	Laborer	20Ap02Kw
HEANY, Patt		21	M	Laborer	20Ap02Kw
DELANEY, M.		17	M	None	20Ap02Kw
Mcc-----, U		19	U	None	20Ap02Kw
GILES, Charles		27	M	Laborer	20Ap02Kw
MCGUSS, Phillip		30	M	Laborer	20Ap02Kw
KEILY, Thomas		21	M	Laborer	20Ap02Kw
DARSEY, Hugh		27	M	Laborer	20Ap02Kw
John		20	M	Laborer	20Ap02Kw
MCMANS, Michael		20	M	Laborer	20Ap02Kw
KEELEHAN, Felix		28	M	Laborer	20Ap02Kw
Mary	(W)	23	F	None	20Ap02Kw
U		.00	U	Infant	20Ap02Kw
MCMANIS, Edward		27	M	Laborer	20Ap02Kw
GAFEERER, John		30	M	Laborer	20Ap02Kw
COOK, Mathew		25	M	None	20Ap02Kw
Olina	(W)	20	F	None	20Ap02Kw
John	(S)	03	M	Child	20Ap02Kw
Isabella	(D)	02	F	Child	20Ap02Kw
REILY, Pat		19	M	Laborer	20Ap02Kw
KEIDHIN, Mathew		40	M	Laborer	20Ap02Kw
U	(W)	20	F	None	20Ap02Kw
Frances		13	F	None	20Ap02Kw
Mary		11	F	None	20Ap02Kw
KEIDHIN, Ellen		09	F	Child	20Ap02Kw
Cathn.		06	F	Child	20Ap02Kw
Hugh		04	M	Child	20Ap02Kw
DOLAN, James		20	M	None	20Ap02Kw
REILEY, Pat		30	M	None	20Ap02Kw
Ellen		28	F	None	20Ap02Kw
G-------, Charles		25	M	Laborer	20Ap02Kw
Sally		15	F	None	20Ap02Kw
MALOY, John		24	M	Laborer	20Ap02Kw
EALY, Hugh		32	M	Laborer	20Ap02Kw
HUGHES, Mary		30	F	None	20Ap02Kw
MURPHEY, Wm.		21	M	Laborer	20Ap02Kw
LYNCH, Mary		40	F	None	20Ap02Kw
Pat	(S)	20	M	Laborer	20Ap02Kw
Peter	(S)	18	M	Laborer	20Ap02Kw
Catherine	(D)	11	F	None	20Ap02Kw
John	(S)	09	M	Child	20Ap02Kw
DAHEN, Pat		40	M	Laborer	20Ap02Kw
Mary	(D)	18	F	None	20Ap02Kw
Francis	(S)	20	M	Laborer	20Ap02Kw
FLYN, Michael		20	M	Laborer	20Ap02Kw
GALLEY, James		24	M	Laborer	20Ap02Kw
KEEGEN, Patt		27	M	Laborer	20Ap02Kw
Mary		17	F	None	20Ap02Kw
James		03	M	Child	20Ap02Kw
HUGHES, Mary		30	F	None	20Ap02Kw
MCCOURT, U		50	M	Laborer	20Ap02Kw
Mary	(W)	40	F	None	20Ap02Kw
James	(S)	12	M	None	20Ap02Kw
Owen	(S)	10	M	None	20Ap02Kw
Mary	(D)	08	F	Child	20Ap02Kw
Biddy	(D)	06	F	Child	20Ap02Kw
Rosey	(D)	04	F	Child	20Ap02Kw
U		.00	U	Infant	20Ap02Kw
DOUGHERTY, Andrew		20	M	Laborer	20Ap02Kw
Sally		23	F	None	20Ap02Kw
SMITH, James		22	M	Laborer	20Ap02Kw
FARRY, John		21	M	Laborer	20Ap02Kw
DOUGHERTY, Patt		23	M	Laborer	20Ap02Kw
MCNEWE, Owen		42	M	Laborer	20Ap02Kw
HARLEN, Michael		32	M	Laborer	20Ap02Kw
U	(W)	26	F	None	20Ap02Kw
John	(S)	06	M	Child	20Ap02Kw
Geo.	(S)	09	M	Child	20Ap02Kw
Michael	(S)	04	M	Child	20Ap02Kw
John		28	M	Laborer	20Ap02Kw
U	(W)	26	F	None	20Ap02Kw
Elizabeth	(D)	04	F	Child	20Ap02Kw
Tedy	(S)	02	M	Child	20Ap02Kw
John	(S)	.00	M	Infant	20Ap02Kw
James		25	M	Laborer	20Ap02Kw
FORNEN, Michael		22	M	Laborer	20Ap02Kw
FLANIGAN, Patt		18	M	Laborer	20Ap02Kw
HANKEN, Mary		27	F	None	20Ap02Kw
DONNELY, Thomas		25	M	Laborer	20Ap02Kw
CANE, U-Mrs.		21	F	None	20Ap02Kw
GRIMS, Nancy		19	F	None	20Ap02Kw
JOHNSON, James		45	M	Laborer	20Ap02Kw
Mary	(W)	43	F	None	20Ap02Kw
John	(S)	12	M	None	20Ap02Kw
James	(S)	10	M	None	20Ap02Kw
Mary	(D)	08	F	Child	20Ap02Kw
Anne	(D)	06	F	Child	20Ap02Kw
Hugh	(S)	05	M	Child	20Ap02Kw
Jacob	(S)	02	M	Child	20Ap02Kw
Sarah	(D)	.00	F	Infant	20Ap02Kw
MURPHEY, Ann		30	F	None	20Ap02Kw
Wm.	(S)	08	M	Child	20Ap02Kw
John	(S)	06	M	Child	20Ap02Kw
Sarah	(D)	04	F	Child	20Ap02Kw
Biddy	(D)	02	F	Child	20Ap02Kw
Patt	(S)	.00	M	Infant	20Ap02Kw
MCQUADE, John		20	M	Laborer	20Ap02Kw
GINEGAL, Jemey		25	M	None	20Ap02Kw
DENNEGEN, Denis		21	M	None	20Ap02Kw

NAMES OF PASSENGERS		AGE	SEX	OCCUPATIONS	DATE PORT SHIP	NAMES OF PASSENGERS		AGE	SEX	OCCUPATIONS	DATE PORT SHIP
DENNEGEN, U	(W)	20	F	None	20Ap02Kw	MCCRUM, James		31	M	Spinner	20Ap190u
U		.00	U	Infant	20Ap02Kw	WRIGHT, Andrew		19	M	Laborer	20Ap190u
KEEF, Patt		20	M	Laborer	20Ap02Kw	Alexander		18	M	Carpenter	20Ap190u
SENATE, Patt		60	M	Laborer	20Ap02Kw	MAGUIRE, Martha		20	F	Spinster	20Ap190u
BARLOW, Thomas		40	M	Laborer	20Ap02Kw	DONNELLY, Patrick		24	M	Laborer	20Ap190u
SEVALE, Patt		30	M	Laborer	20Ap02Kw	TRAINOR, Mary		27	F	Spinster	20Ap190u
BALLON, L.		26	M	Laborer	20Ap02Kw	ONEILL, James		24	M	Farmer	20Ap190u
Stephen		18	M	Laborer	20Ap02Kw	Mary		17	F	Spinster	20Ap190u
BARRET, Mary		20	F	None	20Ap02Kw	Sarah		15	F	Spinster	20Ap190u
LENALE, Bridget		24	F	None	20Ap02Kw	MCELROY, Jane		19	F	Spinster	20Ap190u
BALLON, Nancy		18	F	None	20Ap02Kw	RODGERS, Thomas		27	M	Farmer	20Ap190u
SEVALE, Mary		15	F	None	20Ap02Kw	ROLLERTON, Thomas		18	M	Carpenter	20Ap190u
CARRDIN, Mary		26	F	None	20Ap02Kw	Elizabeth		17	F	Spinster	20Ap190u
RELIN, John		40	M	Laborer	20Ap02Kw	CAMPBELL, James		44	M	Farmer	20Ap190u
John	(S)	19	M	None	20Ap02Kw	Agnes	(W)	37	F	Unknown	20Ap190u
Patt	(S)	12	M	None	20Ap02Kw	Died-At-Sea					
M.	(S)	07	M	Child	20Ap02Kw	Martha-Jane	(D)	22	F	Unknown	20Ap190u
Bridget	(D)	11	F	None	20Ap02Kw	James-Jr.	(S)	17	M	Unknown	20Ap190u
SENEHEN, Bryan		20	M	Laborer	20Ap02Kw	Saml.	(S)	15	M	Unknown	20Ap190u
SAMPSON, John		12	M	None	20Ap02Kw	Mary	(D)	09	F	Child	20Ap190u
Wm.		10	M	None	20Ap02Kw	Hannah	(D)	07	F	Child	20Ap190u
BIND, Thomas		26	M	Laborer	20Ap02Kw	Anne	(D)	05	F	Child	20Ap190u
ODONEL, John		26	M	Laborer	20Ap02Kw	Elizabeth	(D)	03	F	Child	20Ap190u
Mary		24	F	None	20Ap02Kw	Sarah	(D)	02	F	Child	20Ap190u
Honora		24	F	None	20Ap02Kw	Margaret		12	F	Unknown	20Ap190u
CURDER, Kit		24	F	None	20Ap02Kw	Susan	(D)	02	F	Child	20Ap190u
DOLAN, Patrick		24	M	Laborer	20Ap02Kw	BAIN, James		22	M	Painter	20Ap190u
FITZSIMONS, Mary		35	F	None	20Ap02Kw	CHARLETON, Henry		24	M	Farmer	20Ap190u
Mary	(D)	16	F	None	20Ap02Kw	Margaret		30	F	Spinster	20Ap190u
John	(S)	10	M	None	20Ap02Kw	DOWNEY, Margaret		30	F	Spinster	20Ap190u
James	(S)	07	M	Child	20Ap02Kw	MCCARTON, Elizabeth		19	F	Spinster	20Ap190u
Marg.	(D)	06	F	Child	20Ap02Kw	Ellen		18	F	Spinster	20Ap190u
U		.00	U	Infant	20Ap02Kw	LYNE, James		24	M	Farmer	20Ap190u
GILSON, Thomas		21	M	Laborer	20Ap02Kw	Margaret	(W)	23	F	Unknown	20Ap190u
FLANERTY, John		40	M	Laborer	20Ap02Kw	John		20	M	Laborer	20Ap190u
Cathn.		38	F	None	20Ap02Kw	Tristan		18	M	Laborer	20Ap190u
COOR, Sarah-Ann		27	F	None	20Ap02Kw	CHARLETON, Bernard		24	M	Farmer	20Ap190u
U		.00	U	Infant	20Ap02Kw	LYNE, Martha		12	F	Unknown	20Ap190u
FLANNERY, Thomas		30	M	Laborer	20Ap02Kw	Ellen-Jane		10	F	Unknown	20Ap190u
Margaret		20	F	None	20Ap02Kw	WALKER, George		28	M	Shoemaker	20Ap190u
LEE, Bridget		20	F	None	20Ap02Kw	MAGEE, Rose		19	F	Spinster	20Ap190u
TORMEY, Thomas		22	M	Laborer	20Ap02Kw	ROONEY, Bernard		28	M	Laborer	20Ap190u
KELLY, James		20	M	Laborer	20Ap02Kw	STEENSON, James		31	M	Farmer	20Ap190u
Coley		18	M	None	20Ap02Kw	John		28	M	Farmer	20Ap190u
TORMEY, John		20	M	Laborer	20Ap02Kw	Anne		12	F	Spinster	20Ap190u
EGAN, Ellen		18	F	None	20Ap02Kw	SMITH, William		21	M	Carpenter	20Ap190u
SMITH, John		26	M	Laborer	20Ap02Kw	Eliza-Jane		19	F	Spinster	20Ap190u
CAPE, Pat		19	M	Laborer	20Ap02Kw	BOYLE, Elizabeth		14	F	Spinster	20Ap190u
DEBLIN, Anne		19	F	None	20Ap02Kw	Martha		18	F	Spinster	20Ap190u
U, Eliza		00	F	None	20Ap02Kw	OBRIEN, Edwd.		40	M	Laborer	20Ap190u
POWERS, Honora		39	F	None	20Ap02Kw	Henry	(S)	19	M	Laborer	20Ap190u
BATTS, Mary		18	F	None	20Ap02Kw	Edwd.	(S)	21	M	Laborer	20Ap190u
MARSHALL, Geo.		24	M	Laborer	20Ap02Kw	Terence	(S)	24	M	Laborer	20Ap190u
Margret		22	F	None	20Ap02Kw	John	(S)	17	M	Laborer	20Ap190u
Elizabeth		19	F	None	20Ap02Kw	Catherine	(W)	50	F	Spinster	20Ap190u
Margret		16	F	None	20Ap02Kw	Rose	(D)	20	F	Spinster	20Ap190u
Isabella		.00	F	Infant	20Ap02Kw	John	(S)	18	M	Laborer	20Ap190u
HOLT, Allen		24	M	Laborer	20Ap02Kw	HENRY, Margaret		17	F	Spinster	20Ap190u
DOUGHERTY, James		30	M	Laborer	20Ap02Kw	FRASER, Isiah		18	M	Farmer	20Ap190u
Richd.		24	M	Laborer	20Ap02Kw	Isiah	(P)	57	M	Farmer	20Ap190u
						John		25	M	Unknown	20Ap190u
						Jane		23	F	Unknown	20Ap190u
						Margaret		16	F	Unknown	20Ap190u
						George		14	M	Unknown	20Ap190u
						Isaiah		12	M	Unknown	20Ap190u
MEG-LEE 20 APRIL 1847						Hannah		13	F	Unknown	20Ap190u
						MINAHAN, Joan		27	F	Spinster	20Ap190u
From Newry						MCKILSEY, Samuel		23	M	Laborer	20Ap190u
						MINOHAN, Thomas		25	M	Laborer	20Ap190u
						BREDIN, George		18	M	Laborer	20Ap190u
						HOWE, John		19	M	Farmer	20Ap190u
TINDALL, Anthony		30	M	Shoemaker	20Ap190u	Sarah		17	F	Spinster	20Ap190u
Eliza		27	F	Spinster	20Ap190u	William		.06	M	Infant	20Ap190u
SMITH, John		22	M	Laborer	20Ap190u	FLEMING, Catherine		32	F	WI	20Ap190u
MCCRUM, Alexander		35	M	Mechanic	20Ap190u	PATTERSON, William		23	M	Carpenter	20Ap190u

452

NAMES OF PASSENGERS		AGE	SEX	OCCUPATIONS	DATE PORT SHIP	NAMES OF PASSENGERS		AGE	SEX	OCCUPATIONS	DATE PORT SHIP
PATTERSON, Susan		21	F	Spinster	20Ap190u	COONEY, John	(S)	02	M	Child	20Ap110v
DONNELLY, Peter		25	M	Laborer	20Ap190u	KERIGAN, Michael		26	M	Laborer	20Ap110v
Rose	(W)	22	F	Unknown	20Ap190u	MORAN, Michael		24	M	Laborer	20Ap110v
JENNINGS, Samuel		18	M	Carpenter	20Ap190u	BUCHENY, Ann		22	F	Unknown	20Ap110v
						MCLAUGHLIN, Patrick		24	M	Laborer	20Ap110v
						QUINN, Martin		20	M	Laborer	20Ap110v
						SARPHY, James		16	M	Laborer	20Ap110v
						SULLY, Patt		14	M	Laborer	20Ap110v
						COONEY, Matt		28	M	Laborer	20Ap110v
ALBION 20 APRIL 1847						BARRY, Stephen		25	M	Laborer	20Ap110v
						Bridget		23	F	Unknown	20Ap110v
From Galway						BEATY, Patk.		23	M	Laborer	20Ap110v
						HOLWELL, James		16	M	Laborer	20Ap110v
						CREHAN, Pat		14	M	Laborer	20Ap110v
						Margt.		12	F	Unknown	20Ap110v
KAIN, John		30	M	Farmer	20Ap110v	COSTELLO, Kate		19	F	Unknown	20Ap110v
FALEY, Barth.		25	M	Farmer	20Ap110v	MCDONOUGH, Mary		17	F	Unknown	20Ap110v
Peter		20	M	Farmer	20Ap110v	KILKENNY, John		13	M	Laborer	20Ap110v
KAIN, Pat		20	M	Farmer	20Ap110v	PENDERGAST, John		20	M	Laborer	20Ap110v
EAGAN, Pat		19	M	Farmer	20Ap110v	Cathe.		19	F	Unknown	20Ap110v
RYAN, Thos.		20	M	Farmer	20Ap110v	CUNNIFFE, Margt.		26	F	Unknown	20Ap110v
Margt.		17	F	Unknown	20Ap110v	Honor		24	F	Laborer	20Ap110v
John		16	M	Farmer	20Ap110v	GILMAN, John		18	M	Laborer	20Ap110v
DONLY, Mary		19	F	Unknown	20Ap110v	Judy		16	F	Unknown	20Ap110v
RYNE, Pat		25	M	Farmer	20Ap110v	GREANY, Francis		20	M	Laborer	20Ap110v
GREANEY, Pat		23	M	Farmer	20Ap110v	BANE, Ellen		18	F	Unknown	20Ap110v
RYNE, Peter		21	M	Farmer	20Ap110v	BROGAN, Pat		19	M	Laborer	20Ap110v
Pat		29	M	Farmer	20Ap110v	DONELAN, Margt.		15	F	Unknown	20Ap110v
Michael		27	M	Farmer	20Ap110v	FORD, Michael		20	M	Laborer	20Ap110v
MCDERMOTT, Patt		29	M	Farmer	20Ap110v	BRADY, Patt		22	M	Laborer	20Ap110v
Kate	(W)	27	F	Unknown	20Ap110v	Biddy		20	F	Unknown	20Ap110v
Thomas	(S)	03	M	Child	20Ap110v	QUINN, Thos.		28	M	Laborer	20Ap110v
Michael	(S)	02	M	Child	20Ap110v	John		26	M	Laborer	20Ap110v
Patt	(S)	01	M	Child	20Ap110v	CREHAN, Ed.		25	M	Laborer	20Ap110v
KANE, Mary		30	F	Unknown	20Ap110v	Margt.		23	F	Unknown	20Ap110v
HANLEY, Thos.		25	M	Laborer	20Ap110v	BROWNE, Ed.		20	M	Laborer	20Ap110v
Martin		23	M	Laborer	20Ap110v	DILLON, James		30	M	Laborer	20Ap110v
KING, Horron		27	M	Laborer	20Ap110v	BAKER, Michael		28	M	Laborer	20Ap110v
John		25	M	Laborer	20Ap110v	CONNOR, Martin		26	M	Laborer	20Ap110v
Mark		23	M	Laborer	20Ap110v	Kate		24	F	Unknown	20Ap110v
CONNELLY, John		30	M	Laborer	20Ap110v	Thomas		22	M	Laborer	20Ap110v
CRADDOCK, Cathe.		28	F	Unknown	20Ap110v	SULLIVAN, Honora		30	F	Unknown	20Ap110v
DONOHOE, Pat		30	M	Laborer	20Ap110v	ROMEY, Michael		25	M	Laborer	20Ap110v
CRADDOCK, Richd.		36	M	Laborer	20Ap110v	Margt.		24	F	Unknown	20Ap110v
DONOHOE, Peter		35	M	Laborer	20Ap110v	TIERNEY, Thos.		27	M	Laborer	20Ap110v
Cathe.	(W)	38	F	Unknown	20Ap110v	MANION, Margt.		19	F	Unknown	20Ap110v
Sarah	(D)	08	F	Child	20Ap110v	MCDONOUGH, Michael		35	M	Laborer	20Ap110v
Monran	(D)	04	F	Child	20Ap110v	Phelim		33	M	Laborer	20Ap110v
BURKE, Matt		25	M	Laborer	20Ap110v	COOKE, Richd.		27	M	Laborer	20Ap110v
CREHAN, Pat		25	M	Laborer	20Ap110v	FLANIGAN, John		22	M	Laborer	20Ap110v
MANNON, Barth.		27	M	Laborer	20Ap110v	KAIN, Patrick		21	M	Laborer	20Ap110v
BRION, Thos.		24	M	Laborer	20Ap110v	WHEELAN, Morgan		26	M	Laborer	20Ap110v
Margt.		24	F	Unknown	20Ap110v	WALSH, John		35	M	Laborer	20Ap110v
Martin		30	M	Laborer	20Ap110v	FARRELL, Patrick		28	M	Laborer	20Ap110v
Patrick	(S)	01	M	Child	20Ap110v	DOWLON, Malechi		27	M	Laborer	20Ap110v
BRAWIN, Mary		18	F	Unknown	20Ap110v	HENNESSEY, Pat		25	M	Laborer	20Ap110v
ROACH, Pat		28	M	Farmer	20Ap110v	GULTERY, Martin		30	M	Laborer	20Ap110v
Ann		26	F	Unknown	20Ap110v	Margt.	(W)	26	F	Unknown	20Ap110v
Margt.		24	F	Unknown	20Ap110v	Theady	(S)	08	M	Child	20Ap110v
CONRY, Elizabeth		20	F	Unknown	20Ap110v	Mary	(D)	06	F	Child	20Ap110v
HALLORAN, Thos.		22	M	Farmer	20Ap110v	John	(S)	04	M	Child	20Ap110v
KYNE, Ellen		23	F	Unknown	20Ap110v	Bridget	(D)	02	F	Child	20Ap110v
WALSH, Ann		24	F	Unknown	20Ap110v	CAMBER, John		28	M	Laborer	20Ap110v
HYNES, Thomas		19	M	Farmer	20Ap110v	NAUGHATTY, John		26	M	Laborer	20Ap110v
Cathe.		16	F	Unknown	20Ap110v	MOONEY, Thos.		24	M	Laborer	20Ap110v
KAIN, Dennis		25	M	Farmer	20Ap110v	BRIHENY, Owen		20	M	Laborer	20Ap110v
CONNOR, Timothy		27	M	Farmer	20Ap110v	MULLOHAN, Anne		20	F	Unknown	20Ap110v
Michael		25	M	Farmer	20Ap110v	BRIHENY, Judy		21	F	Unknown	20Ap110v
Honor		23	M	Laborer	20Ap110v	Bridget		19	F	Unknown	20Ap110v
FINAGHTY, James		27	M	Farmer	20Ap110v	CARTHY, Barthw.		21	M	Laborer	20Ap110v
SUMMERLY, Thos.		35	M	Farmer	20Ap110v	HILAN, James		23	M	Laborer	20Ap110v
NELAND, Michl.		27	M	Farmer	20Ap110v	CURRIGAN, Danl.		26	M	Laborer	20Ap110v
CORCORAN, Patrick		25	M	Farmer	20Ap110v	Anne		19	F	Unknown	20Ap110v
COONEY, Michael		23	M	Farmer	20Ap110v	CANNON, Mary		17	F	Unknown	20Ap110v
Judy	(W)	21	F	Unknown	20Ap110v	CANNELL, Patrick		24	M	Laborer	20Ap110v

NAMES OF PASSENGERS		AGE	SEX	OCCUPATIONS	DATE PORT SHIP
CORMANE, Mary		22	F	Unknown	20Ap110v
Anne		20	F	Unknown	20Ap110v
MCGRATH, Ellen		21	F	Unknown	20Ap110v

ZANONI 20 APRIL 1847

From Liverpool

NAMES OF PASSENGERS		AGE	SEX	OCCUPATIONS	DATE PORT SHIP
MCALISTER, Sarah		04	F	Child	20Ap020w
Susan		03	F	Child	20Ap020w
DOWNING, Edward		30	M	Weaver	20Ap020w
MCPEAK, Bridget		20	F	Servant	20Ap020w
DOWNING, John		35	M	Laborer	20Ap020w
Bridget	(W)	22	F	Servant	20Ap020w
Ann	(D)	.09	F	Infant	20Ap020w
CASTELLO, Patrick		30	M	Carpenter	20Ap020w
BRIEN, Michael		20	M	Laborer	20Ap020w
TRAINER, Patrick		30	M	Laborer	20Ap020w
HUGES, Pat		20	M	Laborer	20Ap020w
DORISH, Ellen		35	F	None	20Ap020w
Neal	(S)	11	M	None	20Ap020w
James	(S)	09	M	Child	20Ap020w
Patrick	(S)	05	M	Child	20Ap020w
Ann	(D)	07	F	Child	20Ap020w
ary	(D)	13	F	None	20Ap020w
NELSON, Rebecca		20	F	None	20Ap020w
MCDONALD, James		28	M	Laborer	20Ap020w
REILLY, John		22	M	Laborer	20Ap020w
Barney		26	M	Laborer	20Ap020w
GOODWIN, Barnard		20	M	Laborer	20Ap020w
MCGINN, Owen		23	M	Laborer	20Ap020w
Catherine	(W)	20	F	None	20Ap020w
Rose	(D)	.03	F	Infant	20Ap020w
SMITH, Henry		30	M	Laborer	20Ap020w
Mary		25	F	None	20Ap020w
HAVANNAH, Pat		40	M	Weaver	20Ap020w
Bridget	(W)	44	F	None	20Ap020w
Died-At-Sea					
Peter	(S)	17	M	Laborer	20Ap020w
MCDONALD, James		17	M	Laborer	20Ap020w
ALWAY, Patrick		20	M	Grocer	20Ap020w
ROWAN, Robert		25	M	Laborer	20Ap020w
CORBET, John		20	M	Cooper	20Ap020w
STEWART, Henry		23	M	Laborer	20Ap020w
MCBURNEY, Robert		22	M	Weaver	20Ap020w
MCGINN, Terence		40	M	Laborer	20Ap020w
Ellen	(W)	35	F	None	20Ap020w
Rose	(D)	06	F	Child	20Ap020w
Edward	(S)	12	M	None	20Ap020w
Barney	(S)	15	M	None	20Ap020w
John		19	M	Laborer	20Ap020w
BIGLEY, John		45	M	Laborer	20Ap020w
CULLEN, David		28	M	Weaver	20Ap020w
CUSH, John		30	M	Weaver	20Ap020w
MCGREN, Terence		16	M	Tailor	20Ap020w
CAVANNAGH, John		30	M	Laborer	20Ap020w
SAGESON, James		20	M	Laborer	20Ap020w
MCDONALD, James		33	M	Laborer	20Ap020w
MCCOWELL, Patrick		21	M	Blacksmith	20Ap020w
MCGINNIS, Eliza		21	F	Servant	20Ap020w
MCCOWELL, Mary		22	F	Servant	20Ap020w
BIGLEY, Jane		14	F	Servant	20Ap020w
FANNY, Mary		19	F	Servant	20Ap020w
CORRIGAN, John		25	M	Laborer	20Ap020w
Sarah	(W)	26	F	None	20Ap020w
Margret	(D)	.05	F	Infant	20Ap020w
BRIEN, Winifer		25	F	Servant	20Ap020w
Mary		18	F	Servant	20Ap020w
FLOOD, John		25	M	Laborer	20Ap020w
KERRIGAN, Antony		37	M	Laborer	20Ap020w
COIN, Patrick		36	M	Carpenter	20Ap020w
BURNS, John		22	M	Laborer	20Ap020w
MARRA, Darby		54	M	Laborer	20Ap020w
Mary	(W)	38	F	None	20Ap020w
Patrick	(S)	09	M	Child	20Ap020w
FLOOD, George		18	M	Laborer	20Ap020w
DOYLE, Denis		30	M	Laborer	20Ap020w
TOOLE, James		32	M	Laborer	20Ap020w
DONNELY, Mary		19	F	Servant	20Ap020w
CAVANNAH, John		26	M	Laborer	20Ap020w
Bridget	(W)	20	F	Servant	20Ap020w
Margret	(D)	.00	F	Infant	20Ap020w
Born-At-Sea		Died-At-Sea			
FARRELL, Catherine		19	F	Servant	20Ap020w
MCHENERY, Luke		46	M	Laborer	20Ap020w
NEALE, Adam		32	M	Laborer	20Ap020w
Eliza	(W)	28	F	Servant	20Ap020w
Catherine	(D)	.09	F	Infant	20Ap020w
MOORE, Bridget		66	F	None	20Ap020w
MACANNALY, Mary		20	F	Servant	20Ap020w
DALY, Rose		35	F	Servant	20Ap020w
ONEALE, Ellen		20	F	Servant	20Ap020w
MILLER, Ann		13	F	Servant	20Ap020w
HAGAN, John		20	M	Laborer	20Ap020w
MAGLOTHLIN, Mary		20	F	Servant	20Ap020w
KEARNS, Thomas		31	M	Shopkeeper	20Ap020w
Rose		29	F	None	20Ap020w
NUGENT, Ann		24	F	Dressmaker	20Ap020w
Ann	(M)	55	F	None	20Ap020w
Mary-Ann	(D)	.06	F	Infant	20Ap020w
MONAGHAN, Arthur		22	M	Laborer	20Ap020w
MURRAY, James		19	M	Clerk	20Ap020w
WALKER, John		21	M	Weaver	20Ap020w
DEVLIN, John		30	M	Carpenter	20Ap020w
Bessy		28	F	Servant	20Ap020w
REILLY, Michael		36	M	Laborer	20Ap020w
Catherine	(W)	35	F	None	20Ap020w
Daniel	(S)	13	M	None	20Ap020w
Bridget	(D)	11	F	None	20Ap020w
Ann	(D)	09	F	Child	20Ap020w
Patrick	(S)	06	M	Child	20Ap020w
Owen	(S)	04	M	Child	20Ap020w
Catherine	(D)	02	F	Child	20Ap020w
BARRY, James		21	M	Laborer	20Ap020w
Patrick		24	M	Laborer	20Ap020w
MCAULIFFE, Denis		19	M	Laborer	20Ap020w
ATKINSON, William		32	M	Farmer	20Ap020w
Margret	(W)	28	F	None	20Ap020w
George	(S)	10	M	None	20Ap020w
Eliza	(D)	08	F	Child	20Ap020w
James	(S)	04	M	Child	20Ap020w
Sarah	(D)	.05	F	Infant	20Ap020w
COPELY, Hubert		27	M	Saddler	20Ap020w
HACKET, Mary		16	F	Servant	20Ap020w
MORAN, Ann		17	F	Servant	20Ap020w
HUNT, Catherine		15	F	Servant	20Ap020w
KYLAUGHER, Mary		16	F	Servant	20Ap020w
CONLON, Patrick		24	M	Laborer	20Ap020w
Roseann		22	F	Servant	20Ap020w
Sarah		16	F	Servant	20Ap020w
QUIN, Robert		30	M	Weaver	20Ap020w
TOOHIG, George-D.		31	M	Gentleman	20Ap020w
ROURKE, Biddy		26	F	Servant	20Ap020w
HIGGINS, Jane		24	F	Servant	20Ap020w
GILLESPY, Ann		25	F	Servant	20Ap020w
MCMANIS, Terence		26	M	Tailor	20Ap020w
MAHON, John		30	M	Laborer	20Ap020w
DOBSON, Stephen		42	M	Shopkeeper	20Ap020w
Catherine	(W)	35	F	None	20Ap020w
Mary-Jane	(D)	15	F	None	20Ap020w
Patrick	(S)	09	M	Child	20Ap020w
Ellen	(D)	07	F	Child	20Ap020w
John	(S)	02	M	Child	20Ap020w
CAVANNAH, Barney		26	M	Laborer	20Ap020w

NAMES OF PASSENGERS		AGE	SEX	OCCUPATIONS	DATE PORT SHIP
CAVANNAH, Michael	(B)	24	M	Laborer	20Ap020w
Michael	(P)	60	M	Laborer	20Ap020w
Denis	(B)	22	M	Laborer	20Ap020w
William	(B)	12	M	Laborer	20Ap020w
Bridget	(T)	13	F	Servant	20Ap020w
DELANY, Pat		24	M	Farmer	20Ap020w
COFFEY, James		23	M	Farmer	20Ap020w
Margret		22	F	Servant	20Ap020w
HUGHES, John		25	M	Carpenter	20Ap020w
Bridget		20	F	Servant	20Ap020w
BURNS, Thomas		25	M	Laborer	20Ap020w
Died-At-Sea					
KELLY, Bridget		25	F	Servant	20Ap020w
DEGAN, Bridget		24	F	Servant	20Ap020w
MONOGHAN, Patrick		20	M	Laborer	20Ap020w
Owen		18	M	Engineer	20Ap020w
GARVEY, Miles		20	M	Laborer	20Ap020w
Bridget		18	F	Servant	20Ap020w
MCCAEB, Mary		19	F	Servant	20Ap020w
NULTY, Catherine		20	F	Servant	20Ap020w
MCALISTER, James		30	M	Weaver	20Ap020w
Elizabeth		35	F	Servant	20Ap020w
MCGUIRE, James		23	M	Weaver	20Ap020w
FARRELL, Patrick		18	M	Shoemaker	20Ap020w
HAVANNAH, Mary-Ann		19	F	Servant	20Ap020w
Rose		24	F	Servant	20Ap020w
SULIVAN, Daniel		32	M	Laborer	20Ap020w
Catherine	(M)	60	F	None	20Ap020w
David	(B)	28	M	Laborer	20Ap020w
James	(B)	16	M	Shoemaker	20Ap020w
Mary	(T)	20	F	None	20Ap020w
BRIEN, Jerry		26	M	Laborer	20Ap020w
Mary		20	F	Servant	20Ap020w
GRIFFIN, Patrick		26	M	Laborer	20Ap020w
MILLIGAN, William		16	M	Laborer	20Ap020w
MILLER, Robert		30	M	Reed Maker	20Ap020w
DILLON, Andrew		36	M	Laborer	20Ap020w
Mary-Ann	(W)	31	F	None	20Ap020w
Mary	(D)	11	F	None	20Ap020w
Ellen	(D)	04	F	Child	20Ap020w
Died-At-Sea					
Thomas	(S)	07	M	Child	20Ap020w
Died-At-Sea					
SMOLLEN, Hugh		32	M	Laborer	20Ap020w
SNIPE, William		18	M	Shoemaker	20Ap020w
Robert		16	M	Laborer	20Ap020w
REID, John		22	M	Laborer	20Ap020w
BURNSIDE, William		24	M	Laborer	20Ap020w
MCADAM, Christopher		30	M	Weaver	20Ap020w
Mary	(W)	25	F	None	20Ap020w
Ann	(D)	02	F	Child	20Ap020w
Mary	(D)	.00	F	Infant	20Ap020w
Born-At-Sea	Died-At-Sea				
REILLY, Brien		20	M	Laborer	20Ap020w
GOULDEN, Peter		22	M	Laborer	20Ap020w
GROTTY, Rose		20	F	Dressmaker	20Ap020w
MCCLEAN, Bridget		17	F	Servant	20Ap020w
DONAR, Mary		35	F	None	20Ap020w
COIN, John		20	M	Laborer	20Ap020w
EVANS, Thomas		25	M	Laborer	20Ap020w
LYONS, Mathew		30	M	Laborer	20Ap020w
MCGINN, James		21	M	Laborer	20Ap020w
SHANLEY, Edward		50	M	Laborer	20Ap020w
Catherine	(W)	50	F	None	20Ap020w
Jane	(D)	13	F	None	20Ap020w
MCLAUGHLIN, Barney		23	M	Laborer	20Ap020w
Catherine	(W)	26	F	None	20Ap020w
James	(S)	.06	M	Infant	20Ap020w
SMITH, James		36	M	Laborer	20Ap020w
Mary	(W)	35	F	None	20Ap020w
Catherine	(D)	15	F	None	20Ap020w
Mary	(D)	04	F	Child	20Ap020w
Charles	(S)	07	M	Child	20Ap020w
CASTELLAN, Margret		19	F	Servant	20Ap020w
MCGARRY, Ann		17	F	Servant	20Ap020w

NAMES OF PASSENGERS		AGE	SEX	OCCUPATIONS	DATE PORT SHIP
SULLY, Ann		16	F	Servant	20Ap020w
CONNOR, Mary		22	F	Servant	20Ap020w
MARTIN, Connor		34	M	Laborer	20Ap020w
Philip		26	M	Laborer	20Ap020w
CONNOR, Charles		38	M	Weaver	20Ap020w
MCDERMOT, Michael		30	M	Laborer	20Ap020w
Mary	(W)	23	F	None	20Ap020w
James	(S)	04	M	Child	20Ap020w
Jane	(D)	06	F	Child	20Ap020w
Sarah	(D)	01	F	Child	20Ap020w
MILLETT, Patrick		20	M	Laborer	20Ap020w

COURTNEY 22 APRIL 1847

From Liverpool

NAMES OF PASSENGERS		AGE	SEX	OCCUPATIONS	DATE PORT SHIP
TIRRMAIM, James		19	M	Laborer	22Ap020x
Biddy		18	F	Laborer	22Ap020x
MONIGHAN, Patk.		18	M	Laborer	22Ap020x
BRODIGAN, Thomas		19	M	Laborer	22Ap020x
MCGUIN, Patk.		16	M	Laborer	22Ap020x
Susan		30	F	Laborer	22Ap020x
Mary		11	F	Laborer	22Ap020x
DOLAN, Hugh		25	M	Laborer	22Ap020x
MCGOOVIN, Andrew		26	M	Laborer	22Ap020x
Margt.	(W)	22	F	Laborer	22Ap020x
Cath.	(D)	05	F	Child	22Ap020x
John	(S)	03	M	Child	22Ap020x
Michael	(S)	.00	M	Infant	22Ap020x
KEENAN, Bernard		38	M	Laborer	22Ap020x
Winniford	(W)	28	F	Laborer	22Ap020x
Fanny	(D)	08	F	Child	22Ap020x
Peter	(S)	05	M	Child	22Ap020x
John	(S)	04	M	Child	22Ap020x
Bernard	(S)	.00	M	Infant	22Ap020x
Cath.W.		16	F	Laborer	22Ap020x
KURNAN, John		60	M	Laborer	22Ap020x
KULER, Mary-Ann		11	F	Laborer	22Ap020x
DOLAN, Thomas		18	M	Laborer	22Ap020x
DIVINE, James		21	M	Laborer	22Ap020x
Cath.		20	F	Laborer	22Ap020x
KEARY, John		25	M	Laborer	22Ap020x
Mgt.		20	F	Laborer	22Ap020x
MCCARTHY, James		25	M	Laborer	22Ap020x
Jaruk		22	M	Laborer	22Ap020x
HARLIN, John		19	M	Laborer	22Ap020x
Francis		00	M	Laborer	22Ap020x
Patrick		00	M	Laborer	22Ap020x
GOGIN, Cath.		19	F	Laborer	22Ap020x
BROWN, Arthur		21	M	Laborer	22Ap020x
MCEAGAN, Hugh		23	M	Laborer	22Ap020x
SHAWLAN, John		19	M	Laborer	22Ap020x
DUCKIN, Michl.		20	M	Laborer	22Ap020x
GREGORY, Mary		25	F	Laborer	22Ap020x
MCVAY, Wm.		20	M	Laborer	22Ap020x
EDGAR, Wm.		40	M	Laborer	22Ap020x
CARLTON, John		30	M	Laborer	22Ap020x
WALSH, Mat.		18	F	Laborer	22Ap020x
Honor		17	F	Laborer	22Ap020x
Cath.		15	F	Laborer	22Ap020x
LITTLE, James		18	M	Laborer	22Ap020x
MURPHY, Cath.		20	F	Laborer	22Ap020x
LITTLE, Sarah		18	F	Laborer	22Ap020x
MCNALLIN, Mary		18	F	Laborer	22Ap020x
BLACKBURN, Saml.		37	M	Laborer	22Ap020x
U	(W)	30	F	Laborer	22Ap020x
Wm.	(S)	10	M	Laborer	22Ap020x
Jane	(D)	08	F	Child	22Ap020x
Anna-Maria	(D)	06	F	Child	22Ap020x

NAMES OF PASSENGERS		AGE	SEX	OCCUPATIONS	DATE PORT SHIP
BLACKBURN, Saml.	(S)	11	M	Laborer	22Ap020x
Richd.	(P)	60	M	Laborer	22Ap020x
Ann	(T)	20	F	Laborer	22Ap020x
GORGON, Owen		47	M	Laborer	22Ap020x
CAVANNAH, Mary		40	F	Laborer	22Ap020x
Derby		29	F	Laborer	22Ap020x
SMITH, Bernard		40	M	Laborer	22Ap020x
U	(W)	30	F	Laborer	22Ap020x
Michl.	(S)	12	M	Laborer	22Ap020x
Pat	(S)	11	M	Laborer	22Ap020x
Edward	(S)	09	M	Child	22Ap020x
Peter	(S)	07	M	Child	22Ap020x
Bernard	(S)	05	M	Child	22Ap020x
Thos.	(S)	02	M	Child	22Ap020x
Cath.	(D)	03	F	Child	22Ap020x
CRANEER, Wm.		30	M	Laborer	22Ap020x
MCGIRR, A.Mrs.		26	F	Laborer	22Ap020x
Anne	(D)	07	F	Child	22Ap020x
DOYLE, Thos.		22	M	Laborer	22Ap020x
CARY, Patk.		20	M	Laborer	22Ap020x
David		18	M	Laborer	22Ap020x
FAGNARY, Thos.		26	M	Laborer	22Ap020x
KEALIN, Thos.		23	M	Laborer	22Ap020x
MCCORLY, Mary		22	F	Laborer	22Ap020x
GAMON, John		27	M	Laborer	22Ap020x
U	(W)	24	F	Laborer	22Ap020x
Ed.	(P)	65	M	Laborer	22Ap020x
SLOW, Wm.		30	M	Laborer	22Ap020x
DOWD, Wm.		03	M	Child	22Ap020x
DOLPHIN, Wm.		26	M	Laborer	22Ap020x
FLYN, Thos.		26	M	Laborer	22Ap020x
U	(W)	24	F	Laborer	22Ap020x
Thos.	(S)	02	M	Child	22Ap020x
MORAN, Ptk.		26	M	Laborer	22Ap020x
Bridget		24	F	Laborer	22Ap020x
Michl.		24	M	Laborer	22Ap020x
Farrell		22	M	Laborer	22Ap020x
RIN, Bernard		25	M	Laborer	22Ap020x
COSTIGAN, Lawrence		20	M	Laborer	22Ap020x
SMITH, George		24	M	Laborer	22Ap020x
Richd.		20	M	Laborer	22Ap020x
WELSH, Maurice		35	M	Laborer	22Ap020x
GORMANN, G.A.		27	M	Laborer	22Ap020x
CONNELL, Dennis		27	M	Laborer	22Ap020x
WHYLAN, Michl.		27	M	Laborer	22Ap020x
FOLRY, Simon		30	M	Laborer	22Ap020x
John		22	M	Laborer	22Ap020x
Cath.		20	F	Laborer	22Ap020x
DOWD, Michl.		30	M	Laborer	22Ap020x
HARNIS, Joseph		50	M	Laborer	22Ap020x
Mary	(W)	50	F	Laborer	22Ap020x
Joseph	(S)	23	M	Laborer	22Ap020x
Mary	(D)	18	F	Laborer	22Ap020x
HIGGINS, James		29	M	Laborer	22Ap020x
Bridget		36	F	Laborer	22Ap020x
MANGAN, Bridget		18	F	Laborer	22Ap020x
Mary		16	F	Laborer	22Ap020x
WALDRON, Thos.		17	M	Laborer	22Ap020x
Michl.		29	M	Laborer	22Ap020x
MAGNAN, Andrew		25	M	Laborer	22Ap020x
DYER, Domk.		25	M	Laborer	22Ap020x
WALDRON, Isaac		29	M	Laborer	22Ap020x
MCNURDY, Mgt.		18	F	Laborer	22Ap020x
HALLOVAN, John		28	M	Laborer	22Ap020x
Ann		30	F	Laborer	22Ap020x
LYNCH, Mary		11	F	Laborer	22Ap020x
LOUGHLIN, Michl.		35	M	Laborer	22Ap020x
U	(W)	30	F	Laborer	22Ap020x
Mary	(D)	.00	F	Infant	22Ap020x
Malachi	(S)	07	M	Child	22Ap020x
Francis	(S)	04	M	Child	22Ap020x
Bridget	(D)	03	F	Child	22Ap020x
John	(B)	30	M	Laborer	22Ap020x
U	(W)	30	F	Laborer	22Ap020x
Lehy	(D)	07	F	Child	22Ap020x

NAMES OF PASSENGERS		AGE	SEX	OCCUPATIONS	DATE PORT SHIP
LOUGHLIN, Patrick	(S)	05	M	Child	22Ap020x
Peter	(S)	03	M	Child	22Ap020x
John	(S)	01	M	Child	22Ap020x
Patrick	(B)	20	M	Laborer	22Ap020x
GRANT, John		25	M	Laborer	22Ap020x
U	(W)	25	F	Laborer	22Ap020x
HYLAND, Martin		25	M	Laborer	22Ap020x
CORLES, Duncan		25	M	Laborer	22Ap020x
KELLAGELLAN, Nancy		20	F	Laborer	22Ap020x
Mary		20	F	Laborer	22Ap020x
CORMANNON, John		40	M	Laborer	22Ap020x
U	(W)	44	F	Laborer	22Ap020x
John	(S)	19	M	Laborer	22Ap020x
Mgt.	(D)	17	F	Laborer	22Ap020x
Patk.	(S)	12	M	Laborer	22Ap020x
Eleanor	(D)	10	F	Laborer	22Ap020x
Thos.	(S)	08	M	Child	22Ap020x
Jas.	(S)	05	M	Child	22Ap020x
Michl.	(S)	.00	M	Infant	22Ap020x
DUFFY, James		24	M	Laborer	22Ap020x
CLOYNE, Lawrence		23	M	Laborer	22Ap020x
Mary		13	F	Laborer	22Ap020x
HUNT, Julia		23	F	Laborer	22Ap020x
FREEMAN, Mich.		19	M	Laborer	22Ap020x
DEY, Dennis		30	M	Laborer	22Ap020x
SHAW, Thos.		25	M	Laborer	22Ap020x
U	(W)	23	F	Laborer	22Ap020x
SHAUGHNESSY, Biddy		24	F	Laborer	22Ap020x
LAWLESS, Wm.		20	M	Laborer	22Ap020x
GARAGAN, Ann		17	F	Laborer	22Ap020x
MCLOUGHLIN, James		30	M	Laborer	22Ap020x
Patk.		28	M	Laborer	22Ap020x
R.		23	M	Laborer	22Ap020x
FIRKEY, Cathe.		18	F	Laborer	22Ap020x
Ellen		15	F	Laborer	22Ap020x
Thos.		12	M	Laborer	22Ap020x
Susan		10	F	Laborer	22Ap020x
KELLY, James		36	M	Laborer	22Ap020x
U	(W)	40	F	Laborer	22Ap020x
James	(S)	05	M	Child	22Ap020x
Michl.	(S)	03	M	Child	22Ap020x
Janey	(D)	01	F	Child	22Ap020x
Patrick	(B)	40	M	Laborer	22Ap020x
Terrence	(D)	01	F	Child	22Ap020x
Elizth.	(D)	09	F	Child	22Ap020x
John	(S)	05	M	Child	22Ap020x
Mary	(D)	03	F	Child	22Ap020x
MORVILLE, Patrick		24	M	Laborer	22Ap020x
MADDEN, Martin		30	M	Laborer	22Ap020x
MEEDLY, Michl.		30	M	Laborer	22Ap020x
MADDEN, John		25	M	Laborer	22Ap020x
Mgt.		23	F	Laborer	22Ap020x
TULLY, Benjamin		18	M	Laborer	22Ap020x
Mgt.		16	F	Laborer	22Ap020x
John		20	M	Laborer	22Ap020x
WARD, John		47	M	Laborer	22Ap020x
U	(W)	40	F	Laborer	22Ap020x
Rachel	(D)	17	F	Laborer	22Ap020x
Jas.	(S)	15	M	Laborer	22Ap020x
Mary	(D)	13	F	Laborer	22Ap020x
Jane	(D)	11	F	Laborer	22Ap020x
Nathl.	(S)	07	M	Child	22Ap020x
John	(S)	05	M	Child	22Ap020x
KELLY, Isabella		01	F	Child	22Ap020x
Kitty	(T)	03	F	Child	22Ap020x
DEAN, John		30	M	Laborer	22Ap020x
U	(W)	30	F	Laborer	22Ap020x
Edmund	(S)	.00	M	Infant	22Ap020x
LAWLESS, Wm.		20	M	Laborer	22Ap020x
GARRAGON, Ann		17	F	Laborer	22Ap020x
MCLOUGHLIN, James		30	M	Laborer	22Ap020x
Patk.		28	M	Laborer	22Ap020x
R.		23	M	Laborer	22Ap020x
KELLY, James		36	M	Laborer	22Ap020x
U	(W)	40	F	Laborer	22Ap020x

NAMES OF PASSENGERS		AGE	SEX	OCCUPATIONS	DATE PORT SHIP
KELLY, James	(S)	05	M	Child	22Ap020x
Michl.	(S)	03	M	Child	22Ap020x
Terry	(W)	40	F	Laborer	22Ap020x
Patk.	(B)	40	M	Laborer	22Ap020x
T.	(D)	11	F	Laborer	22Ap020x
Elizth.	(D)	09	F	Child	22Ap020x
Wm.	(S)	05	M	Child	22Ap020x
Mary	(D)	03	F	Child	22Ap020x
MANERELL, Patk.		24	M	Laborer	22Ap020x
MADDEN, Martin		20	M	Laborer	22Ap020x
MEDLY, Michl.		30	M	Laborer	22Ap020x
MADDEN, John		20	M	Laborer	22Ap020x
Mgt.		23	F	Laborer	22Ap020x
TULLY, Ben		18	M	Laborer	22Ap020x
Mgt.		16	F	Laborer	22Ap020x
John		20	M	Laborer	22Ap020x
WARD, Joseph		47	M	Laborer	22Ap020x
U	(W)	40	F	Laborer	22Ap020x
Rachel	(D)	17	F	Laborer	22Ap020x
Francis	(S)	15	M	Laborer	22Ap020x
Mary	(D)	13	F	Laborer	22Ap020x
Jane	(D)	11	F	Laborer	22Ap020x
Nathl.	(S)	07	M	Child	22Ap020x
John	(S)	05	M	Child	22Ap020x
Isabella	(D)	01	F	Child	22Ap020x
Kitty	(D)	03	F	Child	22Ap020x
GROGAN, John		26	M	Laborer	22Ap020x
U	(W)	26	F	Laborer	22Ap020x
Patk.	(S)	01	M	Child	22Ap020x
BOYLE, Michl.		30	M	Laborer	22Ap020x
U	(W)	25	F	Laborer	22Ap020x
John	(S)	05	M	Child	22Ap020x
MCLAUGHLIN, John		45	M	Laborer	22Ap020x
U	(W)	32	F	Laborer	22Ap020x
U	(S)	08	M	Child	22Ap020x
U	(S)	03	M	Child	22Ap020x
REILLY, John		30	M	Laborer	22Ap020x
DILLON, Patk.		30	M	Laborer	22Ap020x
COUSGRAVE, Peter		22	M	Laborer	22Ap020x
GREGG, Arthur		21	M	Laborer	22Ap020x
ARMSTRONG, Ellen		20	F	Laborer	22Ap020x

SEVEN-LASS 23 APRIL 1847

From Glasgow

NAMES OF PASSENGERS	AGE	SEX	OCCUPATIONS	DATE PORT SHIP
BRISLON, John	30	M	Shoemaker	23Ap04PJ
William	05	M	Child	23Ap04PJ

PETER-HATTRICK 23 APRIL 1847

From Liverpool

NAMES OF PASSENGERS	AGE	SEX	OCCUPATIONS	DATE PORT SHIP
GUNN, John	27	M	Carder	23Ap02Ck
FERRY, James	19	M	Laborer	23Ap02Ck
DUNN, James	40	M	Stctr	23Ap02Ck
PADDEN, John	21	M	Laborer	23Ap02Ck
SHANNON, Peter	27	M	Laborer	23Ap02Ck
KILLIAN, Darly	32	M	Laborer	23Ap02Ck
GALLIHER, Winfred	12	F	Servant	23Ap02Ck
BRANNAN, Jane	19	F	Servant	23Ap02Ck
SHACKLETON, Alexander	27	M	Clerk	23Ap02Ck
GOODWIN, Thomas	31	M	Laborer	23Ap02Ck

NAMES OF PASSENGERS		AGE	SEX	OCCUPATIONS	DATE PORT SHIP
SLOVEN, Frederick		25	M	Laborer	23Ap02Ck
MCMANUS, Catherine		18	F	Servant	23Ap02Ck
BLACK, Biddy		18	F	Servant	23Ap02Ck
MCGEA, Bridget		18	F	Servant	23Ap02Ck
MARTIN, John		20	M	Laborer	23Ap02Ck
Ellen	(W)	20	F	Wife	23Ap02Ck
Wm.	(S)	.06	M	Infant	23Ap02Ck
MCDONALD, Robert		25	M	Shoemaker	23Ap02Ck
MORAN, Barnard		25	M	Schm	23Ap02Ck
Biddy		25	F	Servant	23Ap02Ck
RILEY, Ann		20	F	Shopkeeper	23Ap02Ck
FITZPATRICK, James		27	M	Farmer	23Ap02Ck
Hugh		19	M	Shoemaker	23Ap02Ck
LYNCH, Catherine		20	F	Servant	23Ap02Ck
Francis		23	M	Shoemaker	23Ap02Ck
MCDONOUGH, Philip		22	M	Farmer	23Ap02Ck
DOUGLASS, Wallace-Smal		33	M	Farmer	23Ap02Ck
Hannah	(W)	24	F	Wife	23Ap02Ck
Mary-Ann	(D)	01	F	Infant	23Ap02Ck
PARKS, James		28	M	Brick Maker	23Ap02Ck
Elizabeth	(W)	30	F	Wife	23Ap02Ck
Ann	(D)	10	F	Child	23Ap02Ck
Arthur	(S)	05	M	Child	23Ap02Ck
GALLOWAY, Robert		27	M	Farmer	23Ap02Ck
Nancy	(W)	27	F	Wife	23Ap02Ck
Issabella	(D)	.06	F	Infant	23Ap02Ck
INGLISHY, Mary		17	F	Servant	23Ap02Ck
Bridget		17	F	Dressmaker	23Ap02Ck
GARVEY, Hannah		35	F	Housekeeper	23Ap02Ck
BRYAN, Oliver		26	M	Laborer	23Ap02Ck
MORAN, Thomas		55	M	Weaver	23Ap02Ck
LOVELL, Michael		22	M	Farmer	23Ap02Ck
Martin		20	M	Farmer	23Ap02Ck
BRADY, Thomas		30	M	Farmer	23Ap02Ck
FARLY, John		21	M	Laborer	23Ap02Ck
FIRNEY, James		19	M	Laborer	23Ap02Ck
FINEGAN, Ann		18	F	Servant	23Ap02Ck
SMITH, Rose		26	F	Servant	23Ap02Ck
Catharine		24	F	Servant	23Ap02Ck
WELSH, John		26	M	Laborer	23Ap02Ck
HOGARTY, Pat		27	M	Laborer	23Ap02Ck
SWEENEY, John		22	M	Laborer	23Ap02Ck
HANIGAN, Thomas		18	M	Laborer	23Ap02Ck
STORY, Geo.		35	M	Shopkeeper	23Ap02Ck
Mary-Ann	(W)	26	F	Wife	23Ap02Ck
RILEY, John		23	M	Laborer	23Ap02Ck
MCGEE, Bryan		42	M	Farmer	23Ap02Ck
Catherine	(W)	39	F	Wife	23Ap02Ck
Mary	(D)	20	F	Unknown	23Ap02Ck
Barny	(S)	16	M	Unknown	23Ap02Ck
Margaret	(D)	12	F	Unknown	23Ap02Ck
Fanny	(D)	10	F	Unknown	23Ap02Ck
Paddy	(S)	08	M	Child	23Ap02Ck
Kitty	(D)	05	F	Child	23Ap02Ck
Ellen	(D)	01	F	Child	23Ap02Ck
PEOPLES, Geo.		28	M	Blacksmith	23Ap02Ck
MCGEE, Manus		40	M	Tailor	23Ap02Ck
Barny		28	M	Tailor	23Ap02Ck
Michael		25	M	Blacksmith	23Ap02Ck
Peggy	(W)	25	F	Wife	23Ap02Ck
GALLIGHER, Pat		25	M	Carpenter	23Ap02Ck
MCGEIRLY, John		17	M	Laborer	23Ap02Ck
SWEENEY, Paddy		26	M	Tailor	23Ap02Ck
MCGENLEY, James		23	M	Laborer	23Ap02Ck
GALLIGHER, Patt		23	M	Laborer	23Ap02Ck
COLL, Thomas		20	M	Laborer	23Ap02Ck
James		20	M	Laborer	23Ap02Ck
GALLIGHER, William		28	M	Laborer	23Ap02Ck
Mary	(W)	30	F	Wife	23Ap02Ck
Kate	(D)	13	F	Unknown	23Ap02Ck
Jiley	(D)	10	F	Unknown	23Ap02Ck
Anthony	(S)	04	M	Child	23Ap02Ck
Hanibal	(D)	02	F	Child	23Ap02Ck
Nell		21	M	Laborer	23Ap02Ck
COYLE, John		30	M	Laborer	23Ap02Ck

457

NAMES OF PASSENGERS		A G E	S E X	OCCUPATIONS	DATE PORT SHIP	NAMES OF PASSENGERS		A G E	S E X	OCCUPATIONS	DATE PORT SHIP
FARRY, Tom		20	M	Laborer	23Ap02Ck	BRANNAN, Andrew		28	M	Brf	23Ap02Ck
MCGAREY, John		25	M	Laborer	23Ap02Ck	Catharine	(W)	32	F	Wife	23Ap02Ck
BOYLE, Conrad		20	M	Farmer	23Ap02Ck	ROURKE, Thomas		18	M	Laborer	23Ap02Ck
MCCAWLEY, John		20	M	Laborer	23Ap02Ck	Barnerd		19	M	Laborer	23Ap02Ck
BOYLE, Michael		24	M	Farmer	23Ap02Ck	KEENON, Eliza		15	F	Servant	23Ap02Ck
GALLIGHER, Nelly		18	F	Svnt-Nrs	23Ap02Ck	GRANY, James		24	M	Laborer	23Ap02Ck
MCFADDEN, Tague		18	M	Laborer	23Ap02Ck	COLIHAN, Mary		16	F	Servant	23Ap02Ck
COLL, Bryan		21	M	Laborer	23Ap02Ck	LYNCH, James		25	M	Laborer	23Ap02Ck
CARROLLAN, Michael		25	M	Laborer	23Ap02Ck	Eliza		23	F	Servant	23Ap02Ck
BRIDE, Michael		24	M	Laborer	23Ap02Ck	Ann		27	F	Servant	23Ap02Ck
BROGAN, Francis		19	M	Laborer	23Ap02Ck	BOHAN, Mary		50	F	Unknown	23Ap02Ck
FARRY, Maurice		22	M	Laborer	23Ap02Ck	Michael	(S)	13	M	Unknown	23Ap02Ck
BOYLE, Ned		18	M	Laborer	23Ap02Ck	CANSTON, Thomas		25	M	Laborer	23Ap02Ck
GALLIGHER, John		30	M	Laborer	23Ap02Ck	INGLISHY, Peter		28	M	Laborer	23Ap02Ck
COLL, James		22	M	Laborer	23Ap02Ck	SELLARD, Catharine		17	F	Servant	23Ap02Ck
BOYLE, James		22	M	Laborer	23Ap02Ck	AIKEN, Joseph		26	M	Weaver	23Ap02Ck
MCGEE, Owen		21	M	Weaver	23Ap02Ck	HAMILTON, Catharine-Ja		26	F	Servant	23Ap02Ck
MCFADDEN, Winny		20	F	Servant	23Ap02Ck	MCCONWAY, Hugh		19	M	Laborer	23Ap02Ck
FARRY, Mary		19	F	Servant	23Ap02Ck	MCCORMIC, Samuel		21	M	Blacksmith	23Ap02Ck
NALLOY, Neal		22	M	Laborer	23Ap02Ck	RILEY, Pat		26	M	Laborer	23Ap02Ck
BROWDEY, David		31	M	Farmer	23Ap02Ck	Margaret		20	F	Servant	23Ap02Ck
DOUGHERTY, Edward		25	M	Laborer	23Ap02Ck	HANTON, Mary		26	F	Servant	23Ap02Ck
Judy	(W)	23	F	Wife	23Ap02Ck	SEBRIEN, Michael		55	M	Laborer	23Ap02Ck
BRAWLY, Ann		22	F	Servant	23Ap02Ck	Catharine	(W)	54	F	Wife	23Ap02Ck
KEENAN, Betty		22	F	Servant	23Ap02Ck	Catharine	(D)	18	F	Dressmaker	23Ap02Ck
GALLIGHER, Pat		22	M	Laborer	23Ap02Ck	Biddy	(D)	16	F	Servant	23Ap02Ck
WARD, Owen		19	M	Carpenter	23Ap02Ck	John	(S)	14	M	Unknown	23Ap02Ck
GALLIGHER, John		28	M	Laborer	23Ap02Ck	Michael	(S)	13	M	Unknown	23Ap02Ck
Hannah	(W)	27	F	Wife	23Ap02Ck	AGAIN, Maggy		25	F	Servant	23Ap02Ck
Sophia	(D)	.02	F	Infant	23Ap02Ck	FINN, Betty		05	F	Child	23Ap02Ck
MCCALL, James		25	M	Laborer	23Ap02Ck	DAWSON, Thomas		30	M	Laborer	23Ap02Ck
Bridget	(W)	30	F	Wife	23Ap02Ck	MCCARROL, James		25	M	Laborer	23Ap02Ck
Oliver	(S)	.09	M	Infant	23Ap02Ck	MCELMEL, John		40	M	Clerk	23Ap02Ck
COLL, Charles		30	M	Laborer	23Ap02Ck	MCKEE, Pat		36	M	Farmer	23Ap02Ck
Hanible	(W)	30	F	Wife	23Ap02Ck	Mary		15	F	Unknown	23Ap02Ck
Michael	(S)	01	M	Child	23Ap02Ck	Margaret		12	F	Unknown	23Ap02Ck
GALLIGHER, Hugh		30	M	Laborer	23Ap02Ck	MULLIN, John		12	M	Unknown	23Ap02Ck
HORAN, John		36	M	Farmer	23Ap02Ck	Margaret		40	F	Dressmaker	23Ap02Ck
Jane	(W)	30	F	Wife	23Ap02Ck	Mary		45	F	Dressmaker	23Ap02Ck
Thomas	(S)	08	M	Child	23Ap02Ck	MCKINNA, James		60	M	Farmer	23Ap02Ck
Bridget	(D)	10	F	Unknown	23Ap02Ck	Bridget	(W)	50	F	Wife	23Ap02Ck
James	(B)	28	M	Laborer	23Ap02Ck	James	(S)	26	M	Farmer	23Ap02Ck
MCNAMARA, James		28	M	Laborer	23Ap02Ck	Ann	(W)	20	F	Wife	23Ap02Ck
Catharine	(W)	28	F	Wife	23Ap02Ck	WELSH, Pat		25	M	Farmer	23Ap02Ck
MAHON, Mary		19	F	Dressmaker	23Ap02Ck	LOMBARD, Michael		32	M	Laborer	23Ap02Ck
CARROLL, Michael		18	M	Laborer	23Ap02Ck	SCULLY, Ellen		34	F	Servant	23Ap02Ck
BROGAN, Biddy		15	F	Servant	23Ap02Ck	MCGUIRE, Cath.		30	F	Wife	23Ap02Ck
ASPINALL, John		28	M	Farmer	23Ap02Ck	Pat	(S)	06	M	Child	23Ap02Ck
Jane	(W)	28	F	Wife	23Ap02Ck	Margaret	(D)	03	F	Child	23Ap02Ck
BIDDLE, Catharine		23	F	Servant	23Ap02Ck	CONOLY, Ann		25	F	Servant	23Ap02Ck
HAGAN, Wm.		22	M	Servant	23Ap02Ck	GANNON, Margaret		19	F	Servant	23Ap02Ck
Marla	(W)	24	F	Wife	23Ap02Ck	GALLIGHER, Mary-Hattrl		.00	F	Infant	23Ap02Ck
NOLAN, John		34	M	Laborer	23Ap02Ck	Born-At-Sea					
Ellen		34	F	Servant	23Ap02Ck						
SHEE, Richard		21	M	Laborer	23Ap02Ck						
HAYBURN, Wm.		22	M	Laborer	23Ap02Ck						
BLESSING, Michael		25	M	Laborer	23Ap02Ck						
KELLY, Wm.		20	M	Blacksmith	23Ap02Ck						
Mary		22	F	Servant	23Ap02Ck	**YOUNG-QUEEN 24 APRIL 1847**					
HAGAN, Daniel		30	M	Stctr	23Ap02Ck						
WHITNEY, Biddy		16	F	Servant	23Ap02Ck	From Galway					
COFFEE, Bridget		25	F	Svnt-Nrs	23Ap02Ck						
MCGORRY, Pat		21	M	Servant	23Ap02Ck						
HICKEY, Edward		35	M	Laborer	23Ap02Ck						
GORMAN, Wm.		36	M	Laborer	23Ap02Ck	LAFFY, Joseph		27	M	Laborer	24Ap11Pk
MCKEE, Mary		16	F	Servant	23Ap02Ck	Bernard		25	M	Laborer	24Ap11Pk
OBRIEN, Mary		21	F	Servant	23Ap02Ck	Catherine		20	F	Spinster	24Ap11Pk
GORMAN, John		22	M	Laborer	23Ap02Ck	William		22	M	Laborer	24Ap11Pk
KENNY, Ellen		19	F	Domestic	23Ap02Ck	KEMPSEY, Barthl.		30	M	Laborer	24Ap11Pk
MCCARVINE, Cath.		17	F	Servant	23Ap02Ck	John		28	M	Laborer	24Ap11Pk
MCDONALD, John		38	M	Laborer	23Ap02Ck	Barth.		20	M	Laborer	24Ap11Pk
MAHON, Pat		38	M	Cabdriver	23Ap02Ck	LYONS, Michael		24	M	Laborer	24Ap11Pk
Mary	(W)	34	F	Wife	23Ap02Ck	Ellen		22	F	Spinster	24Ap11Pk
Miley	(S)	05	M	Child	23Ap02Ck	Judeth		18	F	Spinster	24Ap11Pk
John	(S)	02	M	Child	23Ap02Ck	Honora		15	F	Spinster	24Ap11Pk

NAMES OF PASSENGERS		AGE	SEX	OCCUPATIONS	DATE PORT SHIP
COLLINS, Peter		37	M	Watchmaker	24Ap11Pk
BOYLE, John		16	M	Carpenter	24Ap11Pk
LYONS, Margret		14	F	Spinster	24Ap11Pk
OCONNELL, William		66	M	Laborer	24Ap11Pk
Catherine	(W)	60	F	Spinster	24Ap11Pk
John	(S)	40	M	Laborer	24Ap11Pk
Patrick	(S)	38	M	Laborer	24Ap11Pk
Cath.	(D)	30	F	Spinster	24Ap11Pk
Margret	(D)	28	F	Spinster	24Ap11Pk
Honora	(D)	20	F	Spinster	24Ap11Pk
MALEY, Edward		36	M	Laborer	24Ap11Pk
Mary	(W)	35	F	Spinster	24Ap11Pk
Nancy		20	F	Spinster	24Ap11Pk
Kitty	(D)	18	F	Spinster	24Ap11Pk
Honora	(D)	16	F	Spinster	24Ap11Pk
James	(S)	14	M	Laborer	24Ap11Pk
Thomas	(S)	12	M	Laborer	24Ap11Pk
WALSH, John		18	M	Laborer	24Ap11Pk
Bridget		19	F	Spinster	24Ap11Pk
U		16	F	Spinster	24Ap11Pk
DOBBINS, George		36	M	Laborer	24Ap11Pk
Cath.	(W)	37	F	Wife	24Ap11Pk
William	(S)	20	M	Laborer	24Ap11Pk
George	(S)	18	M	Laborer	24Ap11Pk
Richard	(S)	16	M	Laborer	24Ap11Pk
MALEY, Owen		40	M	Laborer	24Ap11Pk
Mary	(W)	38	F	Spinster	24Ap11Pk
Cath.	(D)	18	F	Spinster	24Ap11Pk
James	(S)	16	M	Laborer	24Ap11Pk
Michael	(S)	13	M	None	24Ap11Pk
John	(S)	11	M	None	24Ap11Pk
KELLY, Biddy		08	F	Child	24Ap11Pk
MALEY, Ned		30	M	Laborer	24Ap11Pk
Winnefred	(B)	28	M	Carpenter	24Ap11Pk
Owen	(B)	20	M	Laborer	24Ap11Pk
John	(B)	18	M	Laborer	24Ap11Pk
Peter	(B)	15	M	Laborer	24Ap11Pk
Arthur	(B)	12	M	Laborer	24Ap11Pk
HEFRON, Dennis		28	M	Laborer	24Ap11Pk
BURKE, James		30	M	Laborer	24Ap11Pk
HESTON, Thomas		18	M	Laborer	24Ap11Pk
PHIBBIN, Mary		17	F	Spinster	24Ap11Pk
EDWARD, Mary		14	F	Spinster	24Ap11Pk
MALEY, John		12	M	Laborer	24Ap11Pk
CLOONAN, Bartley		18	M	Laborer	24Ap11Pk
MCDONOUGH, Biddy		30	F	Spinster	24Ap11Pk
HESSIAN, John		14	M	Laborer	24Ap11Pk
Honora		07	F	Child	24Ap11Pk
Daniel		06	M	Child	24Ap11Pk
WALSH, William		28	M	Laborer	24Ap11Pk
Patt		25	M	Laborer	24Ap11Pk
Acely		20	F	Unknown	24Ap11Pk
MELLETT, Martin		32	M	Unknown	24Ap11Pk
Bridget		12	F	Unknown	24Ap11Pk
Henry		08	M	Child	24Ap11Pk
JOYCE, Richard		40	M	Unknown	24Ap11Pk
Peggy	(W)	38	F	Unknown	24Ap11Pk
Michael	(S)	20	M	Unknown	24Ap11Pk
Catherine	(D)	18	F	Unknown	24Ap11Pk
Sally	(D)	16	F	Unknown	24Ap11Pk
Patt	(S)	13	M	Unknown	24Ap11Pk
BURKE, John		28	M	Unknown	24Ap11Pk
Cath.		20	F	Unknown	24Ap11Pk
Mary		15	F	Unknown	24Ap11Pk
JOYCE, Richard		46	M	Unknown	24Ap11Pk
Mary	(W)	44	F	Unknown	24Ap11Pk
Katty	(D)	22	F	Unknown	24Ap11Pk
Patt	(S)	20	M	Unknown	24Ap11Pk
Biddy	(D)	18	F	Unknown	24Ap11Pk
John	(S)	17	M	Unknown	24Ap11Pk
MOLLOY, William		50	M	Unknown	24Ap11Pk
Biddy	(W)	48	F	Unknown	24Ap11Pk
John	(S)	20	M	Unknown	24Ap11Pk
Biddy	(D)	18	F	Unknown	24Ap11Pk
Thomas	(S)	16	M	Unknown	24Ap11Pk

NAMES OF PASSENGERS		AGE	SEX	OCCUPATIONS	DATE PORT SHIP
MOLLOY, Mary	(D)	15	F	Unknown	24Ap11Pk
Catherine	(D)	13	F	Unknown	24Ap11Pk
Kate	(D)	11	F	Unknown	24Ap11Pk
Honor	(D)	07	F	Child	24Ap11Pk
William	(S)	04	M	Child	24Ap11Pk
BIGGINS, James		30	M	Unknown	24Ap11Pk
Biddy	(W)	28	F	Unknown	24Ap11Pk
Thomas	(S)	10	M	Unknown	24Ap11Pk
John	(S)	09	M	Child	24Ap11Pk
Mary	(D)	08	F	Child	24Ap11Pk
Patrick		30	M	Unknown	24Ap11Pk
Honora		25	F	Unknown	24Ap11Pk
Biddy		10	F	Unknown	24Ap11Pk
MCMANUS, James		28	M	Unknown	24Ap11Pk
COLLINS, Patt		45	M	Unknown	24Ap11Pk
Mary	(W)	43	F	Unknown	24Ap11Pk
Biddy	(D)	14	F	Unknown	24Ap11Pk
Honor	(D)	12	F	Unknown	24Ap11Pk
Nelly	(D)	08	F	Child	24Ap11Pk
LEE, Mary		20	F	Unknown	24Ap11Pk
Martin		16	M	Unknown	24Ap11Pk
LINNAM, Martin		38	M	Unknown	24Ap11Pk
ODONNELL, Thomas		40	M	Unknown	24Ap11Pk
RYDER, Mary		24	F	Unknown	24Ap11Pk
MCDONNELL, Mary		32	F	Unknown	24Ap11Pk

ACADIA 25 APRIL 1847

From Liverpool

NAMES OF PASSENGERS		AGE	SEX	OCCUPATIONS	DATE PORT SHIP
MCKENNA, John		22	M	Farmer	25Ap02Dq
WOODS, John		22	M	Farmer	25Ap02Dq
MCKENNA, John		20	M	Farmer	25Ap02Dq
Mary		21	F	Unknown	25Ap02Dq
Catherine		17	F	Unknown	25Ap02Dq
MORAN, John		45	M	Farmer	25Ap02Dq
Mary		30	F	Unknown	25Ap02Dq
MENOTAIN, Pat.		20	M	Farmer	25Ap02Dq
Eliza		05	F	Child	25Ap02Dq
MCDONALD, Jas.		42	M	Farmer	25Ap02Dq
U	(W)	40	F	Unknown	25Ap02Dq
John	(S)	13	M	Unknown	25Ap02Dq
Thos.	(S)	11	M	Unknown	25Ap02Dq
Catherine	(D)	09	F	Child	25Ap02Dq
Biddy	(D)	07	F	Child	25Ap02Dq
Mary-Ann	(D)	05	F	Child	25Ap02Dq
James	(S)	03	M	Child	25Ap02Dq
Margret	(D)	.00	F	Infant	25Ap02Dq
SMITH, Mary		20	F	Seamstress	25Ap02Dq
MCGUIRE, Mary		22	F	Seamstress	25Ap02Dq
SLOAN, Pat.		13	M	Unknown	25Ap02Dq
Elizabeth		20	F	Seamstress	25Ap02Dq
GANEY, Patrick		21	M	Unknown	25Ap02Dq
CALLEN, Wm.		13	M	Unknown	25Ap02Dq
MILLER, Jacob		26	M	Shoemaker	25Ap02Dq
U	(W)	25	F	Unknown	25Ap02Dq
Ellen	(D)	10	F	Unknown	25Ap02Dq
Matthew	(S)	09	M	Child	25Ap02Dq
John	(S)	07	M	Child	25Ap02Dq
Anne	(D)	05	F	Child	25Ap02Dq
Jane	(D)	02	F	Child	25Ap02Dq
George	(S)	.00	M	Infant	25Ap02Dq
GIBNEY, Michael		30	M	Shoemaker	25Ap02Dq
U	(W)	28	F	Unknown	25Ap02Dq
Mary	(D)	.00	F	Infant	25Ap02Dq
DARTY, Wm.		24	M	Shoemaker	25Ap02Dq
BLISLIN, Patrick		26	M	Shoemaker	25Ap02Dq
Michael		22	M	Shoemaker	25Ap02Dq
DUNCAN, Cornelius		19	M	Shoemaker	25Ap02Dq

NAMES OF PASSENGERS		AGE	SEX	OCCUPATIONS	DATE PORT SHIP
MCDERMOTT, Hugh		21	M	Shoemaker	25Ap02Dq
COOK, Patk.		18	M	Shoemaker	25Ap02Dq
REILLY, Hugh		20	M	Shoemaker	25Ap02Dq
MCMANUS, Patk.		24	M	Shoemaker	25Ap02Dq
Terrence		20	M	Shoemaker	25Ap02Dq
LYONS, Ellen		16	F	Unknown	25Ap02Dq
MCDERMOTT, Owen		24	M	Shoemaker	25Ap02Dq
U		22	M	Shoemaker	25Ap02Dq
WHITE, Rebeus		23	M	Shoemaker	25Ap02Dq
HANLOW, Rose		17	F	Unknown	25Ap02Dq
MCDERMOTT, Michael		30	M	Shoemaker	25Ap02Dq
Maria	(W)	26	F	Unknown	25Ap02Dq
Mary	(D)	06	F	Child	25Ap02Dq
John	(B)	22	M	Shoemaker	25Ap02Dq
Elizabeth	(M)	50	F	Unknown	25Ap02Dq
DAW, Michael		30	M	Shoemaker	25Ap02Dq
U	(W)	30	F	Unknown	25Ap02Dq
Michael	(S)	13	M	Unknown	25Ap02Dq
Owen	(S)	11	M	Unknown	25Ap02Dq
James	(S)	09	M	Child	25Ap02Dq
Jas.	(S)	06	M	Child	25Ap02Dq
John	(S)	02	M	Child	25Ap02Dq
Mary		20	M	Shoemaker	25Ap02Dq
MCCANN, Ann		20	F	Unknown	25Ap02Dq
CASEY, Mary		20	F	Unknown	25Ap02Dq
KELLETT, John		22	M	Shoemaker	25Ap02Dq
MENTOREY, Thos.		25	M	Shoemaker	25Ap02Dq
Simon		12	M	Shoemaker	25Ap02Dq
Bridget		21	F	Unknown	25Ap02Dq
DELAN, Patrick		25	M	Shoemaker	25Ap02Dq
HIGGINS, Patrick		12	M	Shoemaker	25Ap02Dq
HIGGENBOTTOM, John		22	M	Shoemaker	25Ap02Dq
WHEELAN, Pat.		20	M	Shoemaker	25Ap02Dq
MCGEE, Francis		24	M	Shoemaker	25Ap02Dq
U	(W)	22	F	Unknown	25Ap02Dq
John	(S)	.00	M	Infant	25Ap02Dq
MCVEY, John		26	M	Shoemaker	25Ap02Dq
FARRELL, Wm.		23	M	Farmer	25Ap02Dq
MCGUIRE, John		28	M	Farmer	25Ap02Dq
DOLOHAN, Margt.		20	F	Unknown	25Ap02Dq
BULL, Wm.		21	M	Farmer	25Ap02Dq
HARNEY, Patk.		22	M	Farmer	25Ap02Dq
LONGAN, Thos.		24	M	Farmer	25Ap02Dq
U	(W)	22	F	Unknown	25Ap02Dq
NOWLAN, Martin		25	M	Farmer	25Ap02Dq
HEUTH, George		26	M	Farmer	25Ap02Dq
John		04	M	Child	25Ap02Dq
MOOSE, Wm.		24	M	Blacksmith	25Ap02Dq
MOYHINNER, Arthur		25	M	Blacksmith	25Ap02Dq
FITZMOORES, Barry		22	M	Blacksmith	25Ap02Dq
U	(W)	20	F	Unknown	25Ap02Dq
MEE, U		33	M	Blacksmith	25Ap02Dq
BRENNER, Patk.		24	M	Blacksmith	25Ap02Dq
CARROLL, Thos.		24	M	Blacksmith	25Ap02Dq
FEEHILLY, Pat		27	M	Blacksmith	25Ap02Dq
U	(W)	20	F	Unknown	25Ap02Dq
CONWAY, Ellen		22	F	Unknown	25Ap02Dq
NAUGHTON, Mary		20	F	Unknown	25Ap02Dq
Bridget		18	F	Unknown	25Ap02Dq
Biddy		17	F	Unknown	25Ap02Dq
CUNNINGHAM, Wm.		41	M	Carpenter	25Ap02Dq
MCMORA, Martin		22	M	Carpenter	25Ap02Dq
MCDERMOTT, John		24	M	Carpenter	25Ap02Dq
MALONEY, Thos.		18	M	Weaver	25Ap02Dq
Betty		16	F	Unknown	25Ap02Dq
Rose		14	F	Unknown	25Ap02Dq
MCDONALD, Matthew		24	M	Weaver	25Ap02Dq
SHERRIDAN, Rose		25	F	Unknown	25Ap02Dq
WALSH, Edw.		28	M	Weaver	25Ap02Dq
MCILLE, Daniel		33	M	Weaver	25Ap02Dq
BRADY, Thos.		30	M	Weaver	25Ap02Dq
HINNEGER, George		23	M	Weaver	25Ap02Dq
Mary		18	F	Unknown	25Ap02Dq
George		19	M	Weaver	25Ap02Dq
HINESBURY, Henry		16	M	Spinner	25Ap02Dq

NAMES OF PASSENGERS		AGE	SEX	OCCUPATIONS	DATE PORT SHIP
CARN, Francis		14	M	Spinner	25Ap02Dq
CALLWELL, Stephen		15	M	Spinner	25Ap02Dq
MONKS, John		13	M	Spinner	25Ap02Dq
CANNIGHER, John		15	M	Spinner	25Ap02Dq
TURNIS, Thos.		12	M	Spinner	25Ap02Dq
U		11	F	Unknown	25Ap02Dq
BURRIS, Jas.		09	M	Child	25Ap02Dq
ROONEY, Daniel		07	M	Child	25Ap02Dq
U		05	F	Child	25Ap02Dq
Mary		03	F	Child	25Ap02Dq
Elizabeth		18	F	Unknown	25Ap02Dq
Wm.		16	M	Spinner	25Ap02Dq
James		14	M	Spinner	25Ap02Dq
Patk.		12	M	Spinner	25Ap02Dq
Peter		14	M	Spinner	25Ap02Dq
DUGGAN, Owen		16	M	Spinner	25Ap02Dq
RUNNER, O.		15	M	Spinner	25Ap02Dq
HERTY, Catherine		17	F	Unknown	25Ap02Dq
COLBERT, Johanna		19	F	Unknown	25Ap02Dq
HENRBAY, Catherine		21	F	Unknown	25Ap02Dq
MCCOFFIN, David		23	M	Spinner	25Ap02Dq
Mary		29	F	Unknown	25Ap02Dq
STEEL, Jane		25	F	Unknown	25Ap02Dq
MCCLURE, Agnes		23	F	Unknown	25Ap02Dq
KEENAN, John		22	M	Baker	25Ap02Dq
MCCONNE, Sarah		27	F	Unknown	25Ap02Dq
James		29	M	Baker	25Ap02Dq
Bridget		30	F	Unknown	25Ap02Dq
Mary		33	F	Unknown	25Ap02Dq
DONOUGHUE, Phillip		38	M	Baker	25Ap02Dq
Jas.		26	M	Baker	25Ap02Dq
MULLROY, Patk.		22	M	Tailor	25Ap02Dq
Thos.		18	M	Tailor	25Ap02Dq
Bridget		19	F	Unknown	25Ap02Dq
Mary		22	F	Unknown	25Ap02Dq
MCGINETY, Owen		18	M	Tailor	25Ap02Dq
SLIRNEY, Patk.		17	M	Tailor	25Ap02Dq
MULLROY, James		18	M	Tailor	25Ap02Dq
COYLE, Peter		16	M	Tailor	25Ap02Dq
CORR, Henry		36	M	Farmer	25Ap02Dq
Biddy	(W)	30	F	Unknown	25Ap02Dq
Mary	(D)	.00	F	Infant	25Ap02Dq
Albert	(S)	04	M	Child	25Ap02Dq
MCGUIRE, John		40	M	Farmer	25Ap02Dq
Mary		19	F	Unknown	25Ap02Dq
Rose		17	F	Unknown	25Ap02Dq
MCBRIDE, John		38	M	Farmer	25Ap02Dq
FOX, Chas.		27	M	Farmer	25Ap02Dq
Eleanor	(W)	25	F	Unknown	25Ap02Dq
Rosann	(D)	07	F	Child	25Ap02Dq
John	(S)	03	M	Child	25Ap02Dq
George	(S)	01	M	Child	25Ap02Dq
GLARY, Robert		23	M	Tailor	25Ap02Dq
U	(W)	21	F	Unknown	25Ap02Dq
Mary	(D)	.00	F	Infant	25Ap02Dq
LANEGAN, Peter		24	M	Tailor	25Ap02Dq
Catherine		18	F	Unknown	25Ap02Dq
SHELLY, Peter		12	M	Tailor	25Ap02Dq
FORMENY, Mary		18	M	Tailor	25Ap02Dq
HUGHES, Jas.		27	M	Tailor	25Ap02Dq
MCCARN, Wm.		27	M	Tailor	25Ap02Dq
ROWE, Edw.		24	M	Tailor	25Ap02Dq
CORCORAN, Francis		30	M	Blacksmith	25Ap02Dq
BINDER, Joseph		27	M	Blacksmith	25Ap02Dq
U, George		44	M	Blacksmith	25Ap02Dq
MCKEEGAN, John		22	M	Blacksmith	25Ap02Dq
MULDOON, John		20	M	Blacksmith	25Ap02Dq
Margt.		10	F	Unknown	25Ap02Dq
HALPIN, Richard		22	M	Blacksmith	25Ap02Dq
OREADIN, Jeremiah		23	M	Blacksmith	25Ap02Dq
Timothy		20	M	Blacksmith	25Ap02Dq
CLONY, Daniel		40	M	Blacksmith	25Ap02Dq
Catherine	(W)	40	F	Servant	25Ap02Dq
Mary	(D)	13	F	Servant	25Ap02Dq
Ann	(D)	11	F	Servant	25Ap02Dq

NAMES OF PASSENGERS		AGE	SEX	OCCUPATIONS	DATE PORT SHIP
CLONY, Jas.	(S)	06	M	Child	25Ap02Dq
MULMINE, Pas.		13	M	Servant	25Ap02Dq
Mary		13	F	Servant	25Ap02Dq
MURPHY, Richard		22	M	Servant	25Ap02Dq
WHITE, Jas.		40	M	Servant	25Ap02Dq
HEUTH, Wm.		25	M	Servant	25Ap02Dq
Biddy		22	F	Servant	25Ap02Dq
FOGARTY, Ann		21	F	Servant	25Ap02Dq
NEWMAN, Thos.		24	M	Servant	25Ap02Dq
SMITH, Wm.		24	M	Servant	25Ap02Dq
John		20	M	Servant	25Ap02Dq
KELLY, Bridget		24	F	Servant	25Ap02Dq
WARD, Thomas		23	M	Servant	25Ap02Dq
MATTHEWS, Thos.		34	M	Servant	25Ap02Dq
Biddy		25	F	Servant	25Ap02Dq
FOSWELL, Mary		18	F	Servant	25Ap02Dq
NEWMAN, Christ.		17	F	Servant	25Ap02Dq
Bridget		.00	F	Infant	25Ap02Dq
HUGHES, Jans.		14	M	Servant	25Ap02Dq
FOLLINON, Jas.		12	M	Servant	25Ap02Dq
GERRITY, Jno.		13	M	Servant	25Ap02Dq
Maria		11	F	Servant	25Ap02Dq
Michael		28	M	Servant	25Ap02Dq
Mary		26	F	Servant	25Ap02Dq
Patrick		23	M	Servant	25Ap02Dq
James		21	M	Servant	25Ap02Dq
WILSON, Thos.		14	M	Servant	25Ap02Dq
Wm.		15	M	Servant	25Ap02Dq
CHAMBERS, Jane		19	F	Servant	25Ap02Dq
WILSON, Catherine		17	F	Servant	25Ap02Dq
MOSS, George		28	M	Servant	25Ap02Dq
U	(W)	23	F	Servant	25Ap02Dq
WALLS, Edwin		17	M	Servant	25Ap02Dq
KEENAN, Jnos.		30	M	Servant	25Ap02Dq
John		28	M	Servant	25Ap02Dq
Isaac		26	M	Servant	25Ap02Dq
Eliza		24	F	Servant	25Ap02Dq
James		22	M	Servant	25Ap02Dq
George		20	M	Servant	25Ap02Dq
Isaac		18	M	Servant	25Ap02Dq
Jane		18	F	Servant	25Ap02Dq
COSGROVE, Bartley		17	M	Servant	25Ap02Dq
Honora		16	F	Servant	25Ap02Dq
Peggy		14	F	Servant	25Ap02Dq
Nancy		33	F	Servant	25Ap02Dq
Antony		26	M	Servant	25Ap02Dq
Margaret		27	F	Servant	25Ap02Dq
Catherine		34	F	Servant	25Ap02Dq
John		17	M	Servant	25Ap02Dq
Martin		15	M	Servant	25Ap02Dq
MCNALTY, Neal		42	M	Servant	25Ap02Dq
HEAN, Mary		36	F	Servant	25Ap02Dq
HAGGERTY, Nancy		29	F	Servant	25Ap02Dq
DUNKIN, Ann		46	F	Servant	25Ap02Dq
Mary		39	F	Servant	25Ap02Dq
John		62	M	Servant	25Ap02Dq
William		71	M	Servant	25Ap02Dq
WALSH, Paul		31	M	Servant	25Ap02Dq
Nancy		42	F	Servant	25Ap02Dq
Biddy		37	F	Servant	25Ap02Dq
MCNULTY, Teddy		35	M	Servant	25Ap02Dq
MCCORMACK, Jno.		26	M	Servant	25Ap02Dq
Owen		24	M	Servant	25Ap02Dq
Nelly		52	F	Servant	25Ap02Dq
Owen		39	M	Servant	25Ap02Dq
MCGREGOR, Nelly		17	F	Servant	25Ap02Dq
ALWICK, Dennis		16	M	Servant	25Ap02Dq
CROWLEY, Dennis		14	M	Servant	25Ap02Dq
ALCOCK, Dennis		31	M	Servant	25Ap02Dq
MAHONEY, Michael		27	M	Servant	25Ap02Dq
NEAL, Corns.		28	M	Servant	25Ap02Dq
CONNOR, Jno.		27	M	Servant	25Ap02Dq
COYLAN, James		30	M	Servant	25Ap02Dq
CAIN, Thomas		16	M	Servant	25Ap02Dq
Mary		24	F	Servant	25Ap02Dq

NAMES OF PASSENGERS		AGE	SEX	OCCUPATIONS	DATE PORT SHIP
CROWLEY, Jno.		23	M	Servant	25Ap02Dq
Thomas		27	M	Servant	25Ap02Dq
DOLAN, John		34	M	Servant	25Ap02Dq
BRADY, U		29	F	Servant	25Ap02Dq
Michael		36	M	Servant	25Ap02Dq
Patt		42	M	Servant	25Ap02Dq
Peter		61	M	Servant	25Ap02Dq
Catherine		37	F	Servant	25Ap02Dq
Ellen		29	F	Servant	25Ap02Dq
Cecilila		46	F	Servant	25Ap02Dq
Simon		26	M	Servant	25Ap02Dq
MCCONTOY, Edward		24	M	Servant	25Ap02Dq
Catherine		31	F	Servant	25Ap02Dq
Hugh		44	M	Servant	25Ap02Dq
Michaael		41	M	Servant	25Ap02Dq
Thomas		16	M	Servant	25Ap02Dq
Patt		23	M	Servant	25Ap02Dq
CARR, Jno.		17	M	Servant	25Ap02Dq
CONNOR, Jno.		46	M	Servant	25Ap02Dq
RUSKET, Catherine		32	F	Servant	25Ap02Dq
LEE, Michl.		17	M	Servant	25Ap02Dq
Anne		04	F	Child	25Ap02Dq
Thomas		10	M	Servant	25Ap02Dq
Anne		08	F	Child	25Ap02Dq

ROSE-STANDISH 26 APRIL 1847

From Havre

| NEUMAN, Petre | | 40 | M | Farmer | 26Ap05Pl |

ANNAMARIA 26 APRIL 1847

From Limerick

FARRELL, Dnnis-P.		38	M	Hatter	26Ap33Pm
Mary-O.	(W)	38	F	Wife	26Ap33Pm
CANNE, Francis-O.		24	M	Laborer	26Ap33Pm
Mary	(W)	24	F	Wife	26Ap33Pm
Margret	(D)	.06	F	Infant	26Ap33Pm
MAHERY, Julia		20	F	Servant	26Ap33Pm
LEONARD, M.		20	M	Laborer	26Ap33Pm
COFFEY, Michael		21	M	Farmer	26Ap33Pm
HAYES, John		22	M	Laborer	26Ap33Pm
Daniel		25	M	Laborer	26Ap33Pm
CONNORS, William		23	M	Laborer	26Ap33Pm
Catherine	(W)	21	F	Wife	26Ap33Pm
RUTTLE, Paul		22	M	Shoemaker	26Ap33Pm
Eliza		24	F	Spinster	26Ap33Pm
SCANLON, Michael		23	M	Farmer	26Ap33Pm
REODAN, John		20	M	Farmer	26Ap33Pm
HEALY, Catherine		22	F	Wife	26Ap33Pm
Michael	(S)	.09	M	Infant	26Ap33Pm
MCNAMARA, Frances		23	F	Servant	26Ap33Pm
COSTELLO, Ellen		23	F	Servant	26Ap33Pm
COLLIN, Dennis		44	M	Farmer	26Ap33Pm
Johanna	(W)	40	F	Wife	26Ap33Pm
Margaret	(D)	24	F	Spinster	26Ap33Pm
Jeremiah	(S)	13	M	Unknown	26Ap33Pm
Ellen	(D)	10	F	Unknown	26Ap33Pm
Edmund	(S)	08	M	Child	26Ap33Pm
Mary	(D)	.09	F	Infant	26Ap33Pm
Catherine	(D)	.09	F	Infant	26Ap33Pm

NAMES OF PASSENGERS		AGE	SEX	OCCUPATIONS	DATE PORT SHIP
CONNORS, David		30	M	Cooper	26Ap33Pm
MCMAN, Dennis		45	M	Cooper	26Ap33Pm
QUILLY, Michael		25	M	Cooper	26Ap33Pm
Simon		25	M	Cooper	26Ap33Pm
CONNORS, Ellen		40	F	Wife	26Ap33Pm
QUILLIGAN, Mary		13	F	Unknown	26Ap33Pm
MAHONEY, Mary		15	F	Servant	26Ap33Pm
FITZGERALD, Patt		25	M	Laborer	26Ap33Pm
BURN, Michael-O.		28	M	Laborer	26Ap33Pm
Bridget-O.	(W)	28	F	Wife	26Ap33Pm
SULLIVAN, Dennis		40	M	Gdnr	26Ap33Pm
FOX, Mary		25	F	Spinster	26Ap33Pm
KIRBY, Catherine		16	F	Dressmaker	26Ap33Pm
Jane		08	F	Child	26Ap33Pm
Bridget		06	F	Child	26Ap33Pm
KELOGG, David		36	M	Farmer	26Ap33Pm
CALLIGAN, Ann		35	F	Wife	26Ap33Pm
Mary	(D)	13	F	Unknown	26Ap33Pm
Michael	(S)	11	M	Unknown	26Ap33Pm
Alice	(D)	11	F	Unknown	26Ap33Pm
Richard	(S)	.09	M	Infant	26Ap33Pm
MARKSMAN, John		35	M	Laborer	26Ap33Pm
Dominick	(S)	10	M	Unknown	26Ap33Pm
Mary-Ann	(D)	08	F	Child	26Ap33Pm
Bridget	(D)	01	F	Child	26Ap33Pm
Died-At-Sea					
Mary	(W)	32	F	Wife	26Ap33Pm
NOUSTON, Michael		30	M	Nailer	26Ap33Pm
BROSDIN, Mary		22	F	Spinster	26Ap33Pm
Michael		12	M	Laborer	26Ap33Pm
Ellen		12	F	Unknown	26Ap33Pm
MOCHE, James		54	M	Farmer	26Ap33Pm
Catherine	(W)	48	F	Wife	26Ap33Pm
Annabella	(D)	27	F	Spinster	26Ap33Pm
CALLAGHAN, Patt		50	M	Farmer	26Ap33Pm
Died-At-Sea					
MARKE, Michael		23	M	Farmer	26Ap33Pm
Catherine	(T)	23	F	Spinster	26Ap33Pm
James	(B)	20	M	Farmer	26Ap33Pm
Bridget	(T)	15	F	Spinster	26Ap33Pm
Pat	(B)	13	M	Unknown	26Ap33Pm
Timothy	(B)	06	M	Child	26Ap33Pm
CONNORS, Margaret		01	F	Child	26Ap33Pm
OFARRELL, Esther		10	F	Unknown	26Ap33Pm

VIRGINIAN 26 APRIL 1847

From Liverpool

NAMES OF PASSENGERS		AGE	SEX	OCCUPATIONS	DATE PORT SHIP
MADDEN, Margaret		19	F	Lady	26Ap02Ap
COSLOLE, Edward		23	M	Butcher	26Ap02Ap
LYNN, Samuel		24	M	Laborer	26Ap02Ap
Sarah-Jane		22	F	Laborer	26Ap02Ap
PATEN, Margaret		30	F	Laborer	26Ap02Ap
Elizabeth		20	F	Laborer	26Ap02Ap
COOK, Mary		22	F	Laborer	26Ap02Ap
KELLY, Hugh		35	M	Laborer	26Ap02Ap
Ellen	(W)	32	F	Laborer	26Ap02Ap
Fanney	(D)	01	F	Child	26Ap02Ap
BONAR, Owen		44	M	Farmer	26Ap02Ap
Catherine		36	F	Unknown	26Ap02Ap
LYNCH, Bridget		20	F	Unknown	26Ap02Ap
MCLARCH, Sarah		20	F	Unknown	26Ap02Ap
SHAW, Isaac		31	M	Laborer	26Ap02Ap
Mun---, Patrick		30	M	Laborer	26Ap02Ap
Mary		30	F	Laborer	26Ap02Ap
FREEMAN, Mary		35	F	Laborer	26Ap02Ap
MASTERSON, Peter		25	M	Shoemaker	26Ap02Ap
Ann	(W)	22	F	Unknown	26Ap02Ap
MASTERSON, Joseph	(B)	22	M	Shoemaker	26Ap02Ap
Maary	(D)	.09	F	Infant	26Ap02Ap
FLANAGAN, Peter		24	M	Laborer	26Ap02Ap
WALSH, James		35	M	Unknown	26Ap02Ap
NOWLAN, Sally		18	F	Unknown	26Ap02Ap
SCHAN, Ellen		18	F	Unknown	26Ap02Ap
KANE, James		21	M	Unknown	26Ap02Ap
Patrick		26	M	Unknown	26Ap02Ap
KELLY, Patrick		20	M	Unknown	26Ap02Ap
CONNOR, Thomas		33	M	Unknown	26Ap02Ap
RUSSELLE, Patrick		26	M	Servant	26Ap02Ap
SMITH, William		35	M	Farmer	26Ap02Ap
PATTERSON, Alley		20	M	Unknown	26Ap02Ap
KELLEY, Charles		50	M	Unknown	26Ap02Ap
Edward	(S)	21	M	Unknown	26Ap02Ap
Ann	(D)	19	F	Unknown	26Ap02Ap
Charles	(S)	00	M	Unknown	26Ap02Ap
KEEFF, Patrick		00	M	Gdnr	26Ap02Ap
HEALEY, John		28	M	Gdnr	26Ap02Ap
Catherine	(M)	50	F	Unknown	26Ap02Ap
Patrick	(B)	15	M	Gdnr	26Ap02Ap
Catherine	(T)	18	F	Unknown	26Ap02Ap
Thomas	(B)	22	M	Gdnr	26Ap02Ap
Ann	(T)	17	F	Unknown	26Ap02Ap
MCDONNELL, Michael		34	M	Laborer	26Ap02Ap
Biddy		34	F	Laborer	26Ap02Ap
DANE, James		25	M	Farmer	26Ap02Ap
Bridget		20	F	Unknown	26Ap02Ap
Mary		17	F	Unknown	26Ap02Ap
BULLEN, James		18	M	Farmer	26Ap02Ap
BURKE, Patrick		21	M	Laborer	26Ap02Ap
Michael		24	M	Laborer	26Ap02Ap
FLINN, Peggy		22	F	Laborer	26Ap02Ap
Alley		18	F	Laborer	26Ap02Ap
MONGHAN, Peter		20	M	Laborer	26Ap02Ap
NAUGHTON, Thos.		20	M	Groom	26Ap02Ap
PICKETT, Patrick		28	M	Laborer	26Ap02Ap
John		24	M	Laborer	26Ap02Ap
RAFFE, Thomas		32	M	Laborer	26Ap02Ap
NOONAN, John		22	M	Laborer	26Ap02Ap
MOGRATH, Thomas		40	M	Laborer	26Ap02Ap
BRYAN, John		25	M	Shoemaker	26Ap02Ap
Margaret		23	F	Laborer	26Ap02Ap
FLINN, John		28	M	Laborer	26Ap02Ap
Bridget	(W)	28	F	Laborer	26Ap02Ap
Morriss	(S)	07	M	Child	26Ap02Ap
KEEFF, Jeramia		28	M	Laborer	26Ap02Ap
Johanna		25	F	Laborer	26Ap02Ap
CONNOR, Martin		22	M	Laborer	26Ap02Ap
KELLEY, Barnard		38	M	Blacksmith	26Ap02Ap
Elleanor		40	F	Unknown	26Ap02Ap
RYAN, Mathew		25	M	Carpenter	26Ap02Ap
FITZSIMMONS, U		20	F	Unknown	26Ap02Ap
Catherine		21	F	Unknown	26Ap02Ap
RYAN, Margaret		.05	F	Infant	26Ap02Ap
GRAY, Ann		40	F	Unknown	26Ap02Ap
MCDONNELL, Maria		05	F	Child	26Ap02Ap
FINLAN, Margaret		26	F	Laborer	26Ap02Ap
BELGER, Mary		22	F	Laborer	26Ap02Ap
CALLAHAN, Owen		22	M	Laborer	26Ap02Ap
FARRELL, James		33	M	Laborer	26Ap02Ap
GILPIN, Agel		49	M	Laborer	26Ap02Ap
Sally		18	F	Laborer	26Ap02Ap
FARRELL, James		14	M	Laborer	26Ap02Ap
Robert	(B)	03	M	Child	26Ap02Ap
Susan	(M)	33	F	Laborer	26Ap02Ap
KANE, John		60	M	Laborer	26Ap02Ap
Agness	(W)	55	F	Laborer	26Ap02Ap
Ellen	(D)	26	F	Laborer	26Ap02Ap
Ann	(D)	22	F	Laborer	26Ap02Ap
Peter	(S)	20	M	Laborer	26Ap02Ap
John	(S)	17	M	Laborer	26Ap02Ap
Mary-Ann	(D)	13	F	Laborer	26Ap02Ap
SIMPSON, James		20	M	Laborer	26Ap02Ap
Catherine		30	F	Laborer	26Ap02Ap

NAMES OF PASSENGERS		AGE	SEX	OCCUPATIONS	DATE PORT SHIP
SIMPSON, Ann	(D)	02	F	Child	26Ap02Ap
Margaret	(D)	01	F	Child	26Ap02Ap
DONNELY, Sarah		30	F	Laborer	26Ap02Ap
CASSIDY, Peter		47	M	Laborer	26Ap02Ap
LAWLER, Michael		18	M	Laborer	26Ap02Ap
Bridget		20	F	Laborer	26Ap02Ap
HASGRAVES, James		30	M	Laborer	26Ap02Ap
MULLOON, Thos.		19	M	Laborer	26Ap02Ap
CAUSGRIF, Catherine		24	F	Laborer	26Ap02Ap
MCCANNA, Pat		25	M	Laborer	26Ap02Ap
TAYLOR, M.		28	M	Laborer	26Ap02Ap
John	(B)	31	M	Laborer	26Ap02Ap
May	(W)	36	F	Laborer	26Ap02Ap
Prudence	(D)	13	F	Laborer	26Ap02Ap
John	(S)	04	M	Child	26Ap02Ap
Edward	(S)	08	M	Child	26Ap02Ap
LOUGHLON, James		18	M	Cooper	26Ap02Ap
DELANEY, Patrick		26	M	Laborer	26Ap02Ap
PIVINN, Stephen		21	M	Laborer	26Ap02Ap
KELEY, Nell		19	M	Laborer	26Ap02Ap
MCCONNELL, John		24	M	Laborer	26Ap02Ap
NELSON, James		27	M	Currier	26Ap02Ap
MCGRATH, Thomas		32	M	Farmer	26Ap02Ap
Mary	(W)	28	F	Unknown	26Ap02Ap
Mary	(D)	07	F	Child	26Ap02Ap
TOBIN, Catherine		24	F	Unknown	26Ap02Ap
ROCHE, John		39	M	Shoemaker	26Ap02Ap
COULTON, John		43	M	Farmer	26Ap02Ap
Susan	(W)	43	F	Unknown	26Ap02Ap
Mary	(D)	17	F	Unknown	26Ap02Ap
James	(S)	16	M	Farmer	26Ap02Ap
Jane	(D)	13	F	Unknown	26Ap02Ap
Thomas	(S)	11	M	Farmer	26Ap02Ap
Susannah	(D)	08	F	Child	26Ap02Ap
Sarah	(D)	06	F	Child	26Ap02Ap
Samuel	(S)	03	M	Child	26Ap02Ap
John	(S)	.06	M	Infant	26Ap02Ap
MCCRUDEN, Jane		18	F	Unknown	26Ap02Ap
OLIVER, Margaret		20	F	Unknown	26Ap02Ap
Eliza-Jane		17	F	Unknown	26Ap02Ap
CULLIN, Peter		26	M	Carpenter	26Ap02Ap
Luke		20	M	Blacksmith	26Ap02Ap
Mary		15	F	Unknown	26Ap02Ap
KELLEY, James		25	M	Laborer	26Ap02Ap
Rose	(M)	52	F	Unknown	26Ap02Ap
Mary		25	F	Unknown	26Ap02Ap
HIGGINS, Mathew		23	M	Farmer	26Ap02Ap
Biddy		21	F	Unknown	26Ap02Ap
Julia	(M)	50	F	Unknown	26Ap02Ap
LYNCH, John		25	M	Farmer	26Ap02Ap
TOUMAY, Bryan		22	M	Unknown	26Ap02Ap
HOPKINS, Samuel		38	M	Whitesmith	26Ap02Ap
REGAN, Mathew		30	M	Shoemaker	26Ap02Ap
GARRATTY, James		30	M	Distiller	26Ap02Ap
MCCANNA, James		21	M	Butcher	26Ap02Ap
DEER, William		25	M	Laborer	26Ap02Ap
Patrick	(B)	16	M	Laborer	26Ap02Ap
Bridget		22	F	Laborer	26Ap02Ap
DOLAN, Bridget		20	F	Laborer	26Ap02Ap
DUNNIGAN, John		30	M	Laborer	26Ap02Ap
Mary		30	F	Laborer	26Ap02Ap
CONNELL, William		34	M	Laborer	26Ap02Ap
James		13	M	Laborer	26Ap02Ap
CARLEY, John		46	M	Coachman	26Ap02Ap
CUNNINGHAM, John		23	M	Laborer	26Ap02Ap
LYE, Patrick		23	M	Laborer	26Ap02Ap
MORAN, Thomas		25	M	Laborer	26Ap02Ap
Edward		25	M	Laborer	26Ap02Ap
CUNNINGHAM, Rose		45	F	Laborer	26Ap02Ap
Mary	(D)	28	F	Laborer	26Ap02Ap
Margaret	(D)	24	F	Laborer	26Ap02Ap
Catherine	(D)	19	F	Laborer	26Ap02Ap
CONNOR, John		19	M	Laborer	26Ap02Ap
RYAN, Thomas		25	M	Laborer	26Ap02Ap
MCLOUGHTON, Bridget		30	F	Laborer	26Ap02Ap
IRVIN, George		37	M	Clerk	26Ap02Ap
RYAN, Michael		22	M	Laborer	26Ap02Ap
Andrew		20	M	Laborer	26Ap02Ap
Michael		20	M	Laborer	26Ap02Ap
CAVATTE, William		20	M	Laborer	26Ap02Ap
BURKE, Julia		25	F	Laborer	26Ap02Ap
RYAN, John		28	M	Shipper	26Ap02Ap
GLIMIN, John		30	M	Artist	26Ap02Ap
WALSH, Thomas		26	M	Laborer	26Ap02Ap
SPEARS, Ann		40	F	Laborer	26Ap02Ap
Eliza	(D)	18	F	Laborer	26Ap02Ap
MCMAHON, Edward		40	M	Farmer	26Ap02Ap
Honnora	(W)	36	F	Unknown	26Ap02Ap
John	(S)	19	M	Farmer	26Ap02Ap
Mary	(D)	17	F	Unknown	26Ap02Ap
Richard	(S)	10	M	Farmer	26Ap02Ap
Hannah	(D)	07	F	Child	26Ap02Ap
BODY, Michael		26	M	Laborer	26Ap02Ap
WOOLF, Patrick		20	M	Laborer	26Ap02Ap
GARVY, Daniel		26	M	Laborer	26Ap02Ap
Ellen		26	F	Unknown	26Ap02Ap
SULLIVAN, Patrick		25	M	Unknown	26Ap02Ap
MASTERSON, John		40	M	Carter	26Ap02Ap
SANDERS, John		24	M	Laborer	26Ap02Ap
Jenny	(W)	28	F	Laborer	26Ap02Ap
Richard	(S)	02	M	Child	26Ap02Ap
KENNE, Owen		23	M	Laborer	26Ap02Ap
Mary	(W)	22	F	Laborer	26Ap02Ap
Mary	(D)	.05	F	Infant	26Ap02Ap
CONNOR, Betty		18	F	Unknown	26Ap02Ap
WALL, James		20	M	Butcher	26Ap02Ap
MCCARTHY, Wm.		25	M	Shoemaker	26Ap02Ap
Mary		17	F	Unknown	26Ap02Ap
LYNCH, Patrick		25	M	Laborer	26Ap02Ap
LANE, Walter		54	M	Farmer	26Ap02Ap
Nancy	(W)	40	F	Unknown	26Ap02Ap
Sarah	(D)	19	F	Unknown	26Ap02Ap
MOORE, John		20	M	Farmer	26Ap02Ap
FITZGERALD, Mike		23	M	Farmer	26Ap02Ap
BOWLER, Ellen		38	F	Unknown	26Ap02Ap
Richard	(S)	02	M	Child	26Ap02Ap
SHEA, Thomas		24	M	Farmer	26Ap02Ap
Margaret		27	F	Unknown	26Ap02Ap
MORIN, Patrick		20	M	Farmer	26Ap02Ap
SHEAN, Manny		27	M	Farmer	26Ap02Ap
Catherine	(W)	20	F	Unknown	26Ap02Ap
Ellen	(D)	05	F	Child	26Ap02Ap
CONNORS, James		23	M	Farmer	26Ap02Ap
LYNCH, Patrick		24	M	Farmer	26Ap02Ap
Michael		23	M	Farmer	26Ap02Ap
CONNORS, Eliza		20	F	Unknown	26Ap02Ap
KALING, Laurence		20	M	Farmer	26Ap02Ap
OLOUGHTON, William		17	M	Farmer	26Ap02Ap
LEA, Margaret		16	F	Unknown	26Ap02Ap
Mary		18	F	Unknown	26Ap02Ap
BAYLAN, Michael		24	M	Farmer	26Ap02Ap
MURPHY, Peter		22	M	Farmer	26Ap02Ap
James		17	M	Farmer	26Ap02Ap
John		09	M	Child	26Ap02Ap
James		60	M	Farmer	26Ap02Ap
Ann	(W)	50	F	Unknown	26Ap02Ap
Ann		14	F	Unknown	26Ap02Ap
Margaret		20	F	Unknown	26Ap02Ap
Catherine		18	F	Unknown	26Ap02Ap
Elizabeth		10	F	Unknown	26Ap02Ap
DOOLAN, William		35	M	Farmer	26Ap02Ap
THORNTON, Francis		21	M	Farmer	26Ap02Ap
MULLIN, Thomas		21	M	Farmer	26Ap02Ap
BURN, Mary		28	F	Unknown	26Ap02Ap

NAMES OF PASSENGERS		A G E	S E X	OCCUPATIONS	DATE PORT SHIP

HENRY-CLAY 26 APRIL 1847

From Liverpool

NAMES OF PASSENGERS		A G E	S E X	OCCUPATIONS	DATE PORT SHIP
HOLLINS, George		40	M	Unknown	26Ap02Co
Lydia	(W)	32	F	Wife	26Ap02Co
Eleanor	(D)	10	F	None	26Ap02Co
Thos.	(S)	08	M	Child	26Ap02Co
Maria	(D)	06	F	Child	26Ap02Co
Eliza	(D)	04	F	Child	26Ap02Co
Anne	(D)	02	F	Child	26Ap02Co
Lydia	(D)	01	F	Child	26Ap02Co
KENNELLY, Mary		28	F	None	26Ap02Co
MORAN, Jas.M.		24	M	None	26Ap02Co
MONTGOMERY, Archibald		31	M	Unknown	26Ap02Co
PIM, Alfred		40	M	Packer	26Ap02Co
DUGGAN, Robt.		40	M	Unknown	26Ap02Co
Elizabeth		35	F	Unknown	26Ap02Co
RUSSELL, Jane		21	F	Unknown	26Ap02Co
Bessy		20	F	Unknown	26Ap02Co
SMITH, James		22	M	Laborer	26Ap02Co
GAUGHRAN, William		21	M	Laborer	26Ap02Co
CODD, Thomas		28	M	Weaver	26Ap02Co
John		26	M	Laborer	26Ap02Co
KELLY, John		24	M	Laborer	26Ap02Co
DUNNE, Mary		21	F	Laborer	26Ap02Co
Eliza		20	F	Laborer	26Ap02Co
WALSH, James		23	M	Laborer	26Ap02Co
Walter		23	M	Laborer	26Ap02Co
MAXWELL, John		28	M	Laborer	26Ap02Co
TRACEY, John		25	M	Laborer	26Ap02Co
GARGAN, Mary		28	F	Laborer	26Ap02Co
Martha	(D)	10	F	Laborer	26Ap02Co
Philip	(S)	08	M	Child	26Ap02Co
Anne	(D)	05	F	Child	26Ap02Co
Julia	(D)	01	F	Child	26Ap02Co
DEGNALL, Francis		21	M	Laborer	26Ap02Co
Maria		22	F	Laborer	26Ap02Co
GANNON, Mary		24	F	Laborer	26Ap02Co
Margaret		09	F	Child	26Ap02Co
Charles		23	M	Laborer	26Ap02Co
COLLINS, Margaret		24	F	Laborer	26Ap02Co
MARROW, Bridget		10	F	Laborer	26Ap02Co
MCFADDEN, Mary		24	F	Laborer	26Ap02Co
COYLE, John		24	M	Laborer	26Ap02Co
Michael		23	M	Laborer	26Ap02Co
DUFFY, Terance		21	M	Laborer	26Ap02Co
Michael		22	M	Laborer	26Ap02Co
Anne		24	F	Laborer	26Ap02Co
CAULFIELD, Betty		21	F	Laborer	26Ap02Co
NIXON, John		50	M	Unknown	26Ap02Co
Jane	(W)	50	F	Wife	26Ap02Co
John	(S)	22	M	Laborer	26Ap02Co
Robert	(S)	18	M	Laborer	26Ap02Co
Mary	(D)	20	F	Laborer	26Ap02Co
Francis	(B)	40	M	Laborer	26Ap02Co
BROWNE, Mary		56	F	Laborer	26Ap02Co
Southwell	(S)	05	M	Child	26Ap02Co
MOLLOY, James		20	M	Laborer	26Ap02Co
FITZSIMONS, Mary		18	F	Laborer	26Ap02Co
KELLY, William		20	M	Laborer	26Ap02Co
BLACK, Joseph		21	M	Laborer	26Ap02Co
MOORE, Elizabeth		19	F	Laborer	26Ap02Co
MCKEOWN, Martha-Jane		19	F	Laborer	26Ap02Co
STERLING, Robert		25	M	Laborer	26Ap02Co
Archibald		22	M	Laborer	26Ap02Co
Robert		24	M	Laborer	26Ap02Co
KELLY, Christopher		30	M	Laborer	26Ap02Co
FLOOD, Thomas		24	M	Laborer	26Ap02Co
FARRELLY, Thomas		24	M	Laborer	26Ap02Co
MCARDLE, Ellen		20	F	Unknown	26Ap02Co
FEEHAN, John		25	M	Tailor	26Ap02Co
MCEVOY, James		21	M	Laborer	26Ap02Co
WALSH, Mary		34	F	Laborer	26Ap02Co
Bridget	(D)	13	F	Laborer	26Ap02Co
Anthony	(S)	12	M	Laborer	26Ap02Co
Andrew	(S)	10	M	Laborer	26Ap02Co
James	(S)	08	M	Child	26Ap02Co
Catherine	(D)	03	F	Child	26Ap02Co
MARTIN, James		26	M	Laborer	26Ap02Co
REILLY, John		25	M	Laborer	26Ap02Co
CAFFREY, John		25	M	Laborer	26Ap02Co
DOOLAN, Luke		25	M	Laborer	26Ap02Co
TODD, Samuel		24	M	Laborer	26Ap02Co
Richard		25	M	Laborer	26Ap02Co
PATTERSON, Joseph		24	M	Laborer	26Ap02Co
Ann	(W)	22	F	Wife	26Ap02Co
Martha	(D)	.00	F	Infant	26Ap02Co
WHITE, James		22	M	Laborer	26Ap02Co
FINIGAN, Bridget		20	F	Laborer	26Ap02Co
KELLY, Mary		20	F	Laborer	26Ap02Co
LINEHAN, Kitty		20	F	Laborer	26Ap02Co
GILDEA, Patrick		25	M	Laborer	26Ap02Co
James		22	M	Laborer	26Ap02Co
BLACKBURN, John		20	M	Laborer	26Ap02Co
JOHNSON, Henry		26	M	Laborer	26Ap02Co
RIELLY, Peter		22	M	Laborer	26Ap02Co
SMITH, Ann		21	F	Laborer	26Ap02Co
Catherine		19	F	Laborer	26Ap02Co
CARROLL, Ellen		20	F	Laborer	26Ap02Co
LYNCH, Thomas		24	M	Laborer	26Ap02Co
MURPHY, Patrick		26	M	Laborer	26Ap02Co
Mary	(W)	24	F	Wife	26Ap02Co
Mary	(D)	.00	F	Infant	26Ap02Co
SHERIDAN, Ellen		20	F	Laborer	26Ap02Co
HOLLOWAY, Patt		21	M	Laborer	26Ap02Co
NEILL, Samuel		20	M	Laborer	26Ap02Co
Catherine		17	F	Laborer	26Ap02Co
NEWBERY, James		18	F	Laborer	26Ap02Co
MCHALE, Anne		50	F	Laborer	26Ap02Co
LYONS, Margaret		20	F	Laborer	26Ap02Co
MCGUIRE, Bridget		21	F	Laborer	26Ap02Co
RICHARDS, Richard		23	M	Merchant	26Ap02Co
BARWISE, William		23	M	Laborer	26Ap02Co
DERVIS, James		23	M	Laborer	26Ap02Co
PARR, William		39	M	Laborer	26Ap02Co
CUMMINS, John		18	M	Laborer	26Ap02Co
GRIFFIN, Joseph		24	M	Laborer	26Ap02Co
SEWELL, William		17	M	Laborer	26Ap02Co
KELLY, Martin		25	M	Laborer	26Ap02Co
Catherine		25	F	Laborer	26Ap02Co
MURRAY, Patt		20	M	Laborer	26Ap02Co
RUSH, Andrew		26	M	Laborer	26Ap02Co
GAGHAN, John		20	M	Laborer	26Ap02Co
Thomas		22	M	Laborer	26Ap02Co
Michael		22	M	Laborer	26Ap02Co
IRWIN, William		24	M	Laborer	26Ap02Co
MANLEY, John		30	M	Laborer	26Ap02Co
Mary		26	F	Laborer	26Ap02Co
CRAIG, Winifred		26	F	Laborer	26Ap02Co
MORAN, Bridget		18	F	Laborer	26Ap02Co
MILNAMS, Thomas		25	M	Laborer	26Ap02Co
FARRELL, James		22	M	Laborer	26Ap02Co
BYRNE, John		20	M	Laborer	26Ap02Co
MALONE, Michael		20	M	Laborer	26Ap02Co
FENAN, Michael		20	M	Laborer	26Ap02Co
DOONER, Anne		20	F	Laborer	26Ap02Co
Eliza		18	F	Laborer	26Ap02Co
IRELAND, Bridget		18	F	Laborer	26Ap02Co
FORD, Edward		26	M	Laborer	26Ap02Co
BLACKBURN, John		26	M	Merchant	26Ap02Co
Mary	(W)	23	F	Wife	26Ap02Co
James	(S)	08	M	Child	26Ap02Co
COURTNEY, Pat		40	M	Laborer	26Ap02Co

NAMES OF PASSENGERS		AGE	SEX	OCCUPATIONS	DATE PORT SHIP
COURTNEY, Mary		18	F	Laborer	26Ap02Co
LEWIS, William		22	M	Laborer	26Ap02Co
BROPHY, William		26	M	Laborer	26Ap02Co
Margaret		24	F	Laborer	26Ap02Co
FLOOD, Michael		26	M	Laborer	26Ap02Co
Mary	(W)	24	F	Wife	26Ap02Co
Alice	(D)	.00	F	Infant	26Ap02Co
CLARKE, Philip		21	M	Laborer	26Ap02Co
CROSTON, Mary-Anne		20	F	Laborer	26Ap02Co
MCGEE, Thomas		55	M	Laborer	26Ap02Co
Bridget	(D)	20	F	Laborer	26Ap02Co
Michael	(S)	19	M	Laborer	26Ap02Co
Mary	(D)	17	F	Laborer	26Ap02Co
Anne	(D)	15	F	Laborer	26Ap02Co
Catherine	(D)	13	F	Laborer	26Ap02Co
WARD, Jane		18	F	Laborer	26Ap02Co
KELLY, Mathew		24	M	Laborer	26Ap02Co
COLEMAN, Peggy		15	F	Laborer	26Ap02Co
Anne		19	F	Laborer	26Ap02Co
PLUNKET, Mary		21	F	Laborer	26Ap02Co
Bridget		17	F	Laborer	26Ap02Co
CLARKE, Catherine		18	F	Laborer	26Ap02Co
COFFY, Catherine		20	F	Laborer	26Ap02Co
HALFPENNY, Jane		16	F	Laborer	26Ap02Co
DOWN, Jane		28	F	Laborer	26Ap02Co
MONAGHAN, Biddy		20	F	Laborer	26Ap02Co
KELLY, Owen		19	M	Laborer	26Ap02Co
Bridget		20	F	Laborer	26Ap02Co
DUNNE, Bridget		24	F	Laborer	26Ap02Co
Anne		22	F	Laborer	26Ap02Co
WALSH, Betty		18	F	Laborer	26Ap02Co
MCANENY, Judy		24	F	Laborer	26Ap02Co
REYNOLDS, Thomas		35	M	Laborer	26Ap02Co
Mary	(W)	30	F	Wife	26Ap02Co
Catherine	(D)	02	F	Child	26Ap02Co
Patrick	(S)	.00	M	Infant	26Ap02Co
MCCONNIN, Biddy		14	F	Laborer	26Ap02Co
RAFFERTY, Thomas		18	M	Laborer	26Ap02Co
James		28	M	Laborer	26Ap02Co
LACY, Mary		20	F	Unknown	26Ap02Co
DWYER, Thomas		21	M	Tailor	26Ap02Co
MCGOUSK, James		28	M	Laborer	26Ap02Co
Margt.	(W)	24	F	Wife	26Ap02Co
Cath.	(D)	.00	F	Infant	26Ap02Co
CARROLL, James		26	M	Laborer	26Ap02Co
Mary		22	F	Laborer	26Ap02Co
CARNEY, Mary		50	F	Laborer	26Ap02Co
MCMAHON, John		50	M	Laborer	26Ap02Co
Mary	(W)	48	F	Wife	26Ap02Co
Patrick	(S)	24	M	Laborer	26Ap02Co
Oliver	(S)	22	M	Laborer	26Ap02Co
Edward	(S)	19	M	Laborer	26Ap02Co
Bryan	(S)	17	M	Laborer	26Ap02Co
MCMURTAGH, Andrew		60	M	Laborer	26Ap02Co
SMITH, Michael		22	M	Laborer	26Ap02Co
MCGOUGH, Betty		20	F	Laborer	26Ap02Co
CONLAN, Mary		18	F	Laborer	26Ap02Co
KAVANAGH, Mary		40	F	Laborer	26Ap02Co
Laurance	(S)	24	M	Laborer	26Ap02Co
Catherine	(D)	21	M	Laborer	26Ap02Co
Edward	(S)	19	M	Laborer	26Ap02Co
Honora	(D)	16	F	Laborer	26Ap02Co
Ellen	(D)	14	F	Laborer	26Ap02Co
Michael	(S)	12	M	Laborer	26Ap02Co
John	(S)	09	M	Child	26Ap02Co
Catherine		22	F	Laborer	26Ap02Co
Biddy	(D)	02	F	Child	26Ap02Co
MARTIN, George		26	M	Merchant	26Ap02Co
DEVERAUX, Mary		20	F	Unknown	26Ap02Co
KEHOE, Michael		14	M	Laborer	26Ap02Co
FENNAN, Charles		24	M	Laborer	26Ap02Co
Mary		22	F	Laborer	26Ap02Co
LYNCH, Bridget		21	F	Laborer	26Ap02Co
KAVANAGH, Patt		40	M	Laborer	26Ap02Co
Mary	(W)	35	F	Wife	26Ap02Co
KAVANAGH, Patrick	(S)	09	M	Child	26Ap02Co
Mary	(D)	04	F	Child	26Ap02Co
John	(S)	02	M	Child	26Ap02Co
MCCARTAN, Lawrance		21	M	Laborer	26Ap02Co
Phillip		19	M	Laborer	26Ap02Co
Amelia		20	F	Laborer	26Ap02Co
GRAHAM, James		30	M	Laborer	26Ap02Co
MCQUILLEN, Joseph		20	M	Laborer	26Ap02Co
Mary		18	F	Laborer	26Ap02Co
Anne		16	F	Laborer	26Ap02Co
DUNNE, Michael		22	M	Laborer	26Ap02Co
HEALY, Patt		22	M	Laborer	26Ap02Co
CAMPBELL, Michael		22	M	Laborer	26Ap02Co
BERRILL, Patrick		22	M	Laborer	26Ap02Co
CARPENTER, Margaret		16	F	Laborer	26Ap02Co
SANSEN, Anne		25	F	Laborer	26Ap02Co
MCKENNA, Hugh		22	M	Laborer	26Ap02Co
HARRICK, Patrick		24	M	Laborer	26Ap02Co
Michael		23	M	Laborer	26Ap02Co
MAXWELL, William		22	M	Laborer	26Ap02Co
HASLETT, William		35	M	Laborer	26Ap02Co
NIXON, Hugh		20	M	Laborer	26Ap02Co
Eliza		19	F	Laborer	26Ap02Co
Rebecca		25	F	Laborer	26Ap02Co
SMITH, William		21	M	Merchant	26Ap02Co
DOUGLAS, Samuel		26	M	Laborer	26Ap02Co
DEAN, Joseph		21	M	Laborer	26Ap02Co
THOMAS, Thomas		22	M	Laborer	26Ap02Co
MAHER, Mathew		25	M	Laborer	26Ap02Co
Maher		22	F	Laborer	26Ap02Co
RAHILL, Thomas		24	F	Laborer	26Ap02Co
BRAZELL, Thomas		24	F	Laborer	26Ap02Co
Maria		22	F	Laborer	26Ap02Co
GRIMES, Bridget		20	F	Laborer	26Ap02Co
QUIGLEY, John		30	M	Laborer	26Ap02Co
BLACKSTOCK, William		35	M	Laborer	26Ap02Co
PRITCHARD, Anne		25	F	Laborer	26Ap02Co
FARNAN, Joseph		21	M	Laborer	26Ap02Co
CONNOLLY, John		30	M	Laborer	26Ap02Co
MAHONY, James		30	M	Laborer	26Ap02Co
DONOHUE, Edward		21	M	Laborer	26Ap02Co
MALONEY, John		28	M	Laborer	26Ap02Co
NELSON, Mathew		24	M	Laborer	26Ap02Co
SULLIVAN, Daniel		40	M	Laborer	26Ap02Co
Ellen	(W)	40	F	Wife	26Ap02Co
James	(S)	20	M	Laborer	26Ap02Co
Patrick	(S)	17	M	Laborer	26Ap02Co
Elizabeth	(D)	15	F	Laborer	26Ap02Co
Catherine	(D)	13	F	Laborer	26Ap02Co
William	(S)	10	M	Laborer	26Ap02Co
OLEARY, Catherine		27	F	Laborer	26Ap02Co
SULLIVAN, Ellen		20	F	Laborer	26Ap02Co
COURTNEY, William		18	M	Laborer	26Ap02Co
NEALE, John		24	M	Laborer	26Ap02Co
KENEDY, Bridget		19	F	Laborer	26Ap02Co
Mary		16	F	Laborer	26Ap02Co
MURPHY, Anne		21	F	Laborer	26Ap02Co
OHARA, John		26	M	Laborer	26Ap02Co
Bridget		21	F	Laborer	26Ap02Co
TRACY, James		40	M	Laborer	26Ap02Co
BUCKLEY, Alice		21	F	Laborer	26Ap02Co
BURTON, Charles		30	M	Laborer	26Ap02Co
MAGEE, John		38	M	Laborer	26Ap02Co
DONEGAN, Patt		20	M	Laborer	26Ap02Co
HESTER, Patt		25	M	Laborer	26Ap02Co
WARD, Thomas		25	M	Laborer	26Ap02Co
Christopher		28	M	Laborer	26Ap02Co
Nicholas		26	M	Laborer	26Ap02Co
MCKENNA, Patt		35	M	Laborer	26Ap02Co
MINER, Adam		24	M	Laborer	26Ap02Co
CLARK, John		28	M	Laborer	26Ap02Co
KING, William		25	M	Laborer	26Ap02Co
BEAUMONT, John		27	M	Laborer	26Ap02Co
Hannah		28	F	Laborer	26Ap02Co
LESTER, Susan		50	F	Laborer	26Ap02Co

NAMES OF PASSENGERS		AGE	SEX	OCCUPATIONS	DATE PORT SHIP
LESTER, Eliza	(D)	25	F	Laborer	26Ap02Co
Rebecca	(D)	13	F	Laborer	26Ap02Co
Hester	(D)	10	F	Laborer	26Ap02Co
Thomas	(S)	09	M	Child	26Ap02Co
STODDARD, Bridget		70	F	Laborer	26Ap02Co
MIN, Thomas		26	M	Laborer	26Ap02Co
HANLEY, Edwd.		21	M	Laborer	26Ap02Co
LACEY, James		33	M	Laborer	26Ap02Co
EDWARDS, John		28	M	Laborer	26Ap02Co
MCARDLE, Henry		25	M	Laborer	26Ap02Co
JENKINS, William		24	M	Laborer	26Ap02Co
Alexander		23	M	Laborer	26Ap02Co
CONSTANTINE, Isaac		26	M	Laborer	26Ap02Co
GARDNER, John		30	M	Laborer	26Ap02Co
Rackes	(W)	28	F	Wife	26Ap02Co
Elizabeth	(D)	03	F	Child	26Ap02Co
John		.00	M	Infant	26Ap02Co
Andrew		13	M	Laborer	26Ap02Co
Anne		27	F	Laborer	26Ap02Co
HAYES, Anne		20	F	Laborer	26Ap02Co
YOUNG, John		18	M	Laborer	26Ap02Co
CLARKE, Elizabeth		42	F	Laborer	26Ap02Co
PLUNKETT, James		48	M	Merchant	26Ap02Co
John	(S)	16	M	Laborer	26Ap02Co
IRWINE, Robert		32	M	Laborer	26Ap02Co
WATSON, Mathew		26	M	Laborer	26Ap02Co
REID, Mary		23	F	Laborer	26Ap02Co
RANKIN, Nancy		20	F	Laborer	26Ap02Co
ONEILL, Eliza		20	F	Laborer	26Ap02Co
Sarah		18	F	Laborer	26Ap02Co
CUNNINGHAM, Mary		20	F	Laborer	26Ap02Co
COCHRANE, James		32	M	Laborer	26Ap02Co
Richard		32	M	Laborer	26Ap02Co
John		38	M	Merchant	26Ap02Co
Jane		34	F	None	26Ap02Co
Elizabeth		11	F	None	26Ap02Co
Andrew		09	M	Child	26Ap02Co
James		06	M	Child	26Ap02Co
Richard		05	M	Child	26Ap02Co
Benjamin		.00	M	Infant	26Ap02Co
MOON, Edward		25	M	Laborer	26Ap02Co
Mary	(W)	24	F	Wife	26Ap02Co
Letitia	(D)	01	F	Child	26Ap02Co
Died-At-Sea					
DOGHERTY, Michael		18	M	Laborer	26Ap02Co
ONEILL, James		21	M	Laborer	26Ap02Co
KEARNEY, Daniel		30	M	Laborer	26Ap02Co
TONER, Michael		25	M	Laborer	26Ap02Co
MCGUCKEN, Ellen		30	F	Laborer	26Ap02Co
Sarah	(D)	10	F	Laborer	26Ap02Co
Rose	(D)	07	F	Child	26Ap02Co
Catherine	(D)	06	F	Child	26Ap02Co
MCDONALD, James		21	M	Laborer	26Ap02Co
CLARK, John		21	M	Laborer	26Ap02Co
KERNEY, Michael		21	M	Laborer	26Ap02Co
MCPEAK, Mary		20	F	Laborer	26Ap02Co
KNIGHT, Alexander		36	M	Laborer	26Ap02Co
MOFFAT, Samuel		34	M	Laborer	26Ap02Co
ANDERSON, William		19	M	Laborer	26Ap02Co
KNIGHT, Alexander		18	M	Laborer	26Ap02Co
MAXWELL, Thomas		18	M	Laborer	26Ap02Co
MCCULLA, Charles		28	M	Laborer	26Ap02Co
MCNAMEE, John		25	M	Laborer	26Ap02Co
MCKENNA, Henry		30	M	Laborer	26Ap02Co
MCWILLIAMS, Michael		27	M	Laborer	26Ap02Co
MULLEN, Patt		26	M	Laborer	26Ap02Co
BRADLEY, Fran.		18	M	Laborer	26Ap02Co
Maria		17	F	Laborer	26Ap02Co
Margaret		16	F	Laborer	26Ap02Co
MORAN, Thomas		21	M	Laborer	26Ap02Co
MCKANE, David		30	M	Laborer	26Ap02Co
THOMPSON, William		25	M	Laborer	26Ap02Co
Betsey	(W)	24	F	Wife	26Ap02Co
William	(S)	02	M	Child	26Ap02Co
Charles	(B)	11	M	Laborer	26Ap02Co
DONOHUE, Bernard		45	M	Laborer	26Ap02Co
FARRELLY, Patrick		22	M	Laborer	26Ap02Co
MURPHY, Mary		27	F	Laborer	26Ap02Co
HENDERSON, James		20	M	Laborer	26Ap02Co
MCCULLA, John		20	M	Laborer	26Ap02Co
MCGARTY, Peter		34	M	Laborer	26Ap02Co
Alice	(W)	30	F	Wife	26Ap02Co
Michael	(S)	09	M	Child	26Ap02Co
Bridget	(D)	08	F	Child	26Ap02Co
Mary	(D)	06	F	Child	26Ap02Co
Catherine	(D)	04	F	Child	26Ap02Co
CANNON, James		27	M	Laborer	26Ap02Co
Mary		24	F	Laborer	26Ap02Co
ROURKE, Peter		56	M	Laborer	26Ap02Co
Stephen	(S)	18	M	Laborer	26Ap02Co
Cornelius	(S)	16	M	Laborer	26Ap02Co
CRAMER, Owen		50	M	Laborer	26Ap02Co
John	(S)	20	M	Laborer	26Ap02Co
KELLY, Kieran		24	M	Laborer	26Ap02Co
HAYES, Catherine		20	F	Laborer	26Ap02Co
KELLY, Michael		21	M	Laborer	26Ap02Co
HICKEY, Martin		20	M	Laborer	26Ap02Co
MCCARRON, Patt.		27	M	Laborer	26Ap02Co
Mary		26	F	Laborer	26Ap02Co
HUNT, Thomas		54	M	Laborer	26Ap02Co
Michael	(S)	09	M	Child	26Ap02Co
DOUGHERTY, Owen		21	M	Laborer	26Ap02Co
CONWAY, John		27	M	Laborer	26Ap02Co
MORRIS, Thomas-Stewart		30	M	Laborer	26Ap02Co
Mary		26	F	Laborer	26Ap02Co
MURROW, George		30	M	Laborer	26Ap02Co
SMITH, Michael		24	M	Laborer	26Ap02Co
MCGUIRE, James		21	M	Laborer	26Ap02Co
KENNY, Thomas		50	M	Laborer	26Ap02Co
Mary	(D)	18	F	Laborer	26Ap02Co
ABRAHAM, Stephen		45	M	Laborer	26Ap02Co
Margaret	(W)	40	F	Wife	26Ap02Co
Margaret	(D)	19	F	Laborer	26Ap02Co
Jane	(D)	20	F	Laborer	26Ap02Co
HUDSON, Mary		21	F	Laborer	26Ap02Co
WALLACE, Anne		20	F	Laborer	26Ap02Co
Mary		18	F	Laborer	26Ap02Co
MCLOUGHLIN, William		24	M	Laborer	26Ap02Co
FENNAN, James		20	M	Laborer	26Ap02Co
MCLOUGHLIN, Bryan		20	M	Laborer	26Ap02Co
Stephen		20	M	Laborer	26Ap02Co
Ellen		19	M	Laborer	26Ap02Co
LAVEY, Bridget		19	F	Laborer	26Ap02Co
BLANCHARD, Anne		22	M	Laborer	26Ap02Co
DAVID, Alice		15	M	Laborer	26Ap02Co
CUNNINGHAM, P.		17	M	Laborer	26Ap02Co
Anne		11	F	Laborer	26Ap02Co
SLAVIN, Mary		11	F	Laborer	26Ap02Co
EUSTACE, Bridget		20	F	Laborer	26Ap02Co
BRENNAN, Michael		27	F	Laborer	26Ap02Co
Bridget		20	F	Laborer	26Ap02Co
HOPKINS, Margaret		20	F	Laborer	26Ap02Co
KAIN, Michael		56	M	Laborer	26Ap02Co
Catherine	(W)	50	F	Wife	26Ap02Co
Anne	(D)	24	F	Unknown	26Ap02Co
Elizabeth	(D)	20	F	Unknown	26Ap02Co
Michael	(D)	14	F	Unknown	26Ap02Co
COFFY, Jane		19	F	Unknown	26Ap02Co
FLANAGAN, Peter		03	M	Child	26Ap02Co
MCDOOLE, Michael		30	M	Laborer	26Ap02Co
John		19	M	Laborer	26Ap02Co
BRADSHAW, Thomas		34	M	Laborer	26Ap02Co
Mary-Anne	(D)	07	F	Child	26Ap02Co
HUNT, Margaret		11	F	Laborer	26Ap02Co

SWITZERLAND 27 APRIL 1847

From London

ORPHAN 27 APRIL 1847

From Liverpool

NAMES OF PASSENGERS		AGE	SEX	OCCUPATIONS	DATE PORT SHIP	NAMES OF PASSENGERS		AGE	SEX	OCCUPATIONS	DATE PORT SHIP
GLASS, William		25	M	Unknown	27Ap21Al	STOCKHAM, G.H.		30	M	Gentleman	27Ap02DJ
CARTER, Leonard		33	M	Unknown	27Ap21Al	FINLAY, Joseph		22	M	Farmer	27Ap02DJ
Emma		24	F	Unknown	27Ap21Al	Bridget		18	F	Farmer	27Ap02DJ
Susannah	(M)	66	F	Unknown	27Ap21Al	MONAGLE, Pat.		45	M	Laborer	27Ap02DJ
KIMBER, Charles		13	M	Unknown	27Ap21Al	Betty	(W)	45	F	Wife	27Ap02DJ
KERG, Mathew		30	M	Farmer	27Ap21Al	Nancy	(D)	12	F	Laborer	27Ap02DJ
Katherine		22	F	Unknown	27Ap21Al	Biddy	(D)	10	F	Laborer	27Ap02DJ
HUME, William		27	M	Unknown	27Ap21Al	BOYLE, Mary		21	F	None	27Ap02DJ
FILMER, Johanne		37	F	Unknown	27Ap21Al	MEHAN, Frank		24	M	Mechanic	27Ap02DJ
SEAL, Peter		20	M	Unknown	27Ap21Al	BROWN, Thos.		24	M	Mechanic	27Ap02DJ
Richard		22	M	Unknown	27Ap21Al	VAUXES, Tom		52	M	Farmer	27Ap02DJ
BELL, Robert		37	M	Gdnr	27Ap21Al	John-P.	(S)	30	M	Farmer	27Ap02DJ
Ann		39	F	Unknown	27Ap21Al	Wm.	(S)	21	M	Farmer	27Ap02DJ
LEE, Catherine		25	F	Unknown	27Ap21Al	Susan	(W)	50	F	Wife	27Ap02DJ
STEEL, Charles		21	M	Laborer	27Ap21Al	Mary	(D)	18	F	None	27Ap02DJ
Eliza		21	F	Unknown	27Ap21Al	Susan	(D)	10	F	None	27Ap02DJ
KENNEDY, Dennis		30	M	Unknown	27Ap21Al	Ellen	(D)	06	F	Child	27Ap02DJ
RICE, Mary-Ann		22	F	Unknown	27Ap21Al	VILE, Saml.		25	M	Farmer	27Ap02DJ
SUNS, Avery		23	F	Unknown	27Ap21Al	Anne		27	F	None	27Ap02DJ
GOGGS, John		21	F	Unknown	27Ap21Al	GOLIGH, B.C.		22	M	Farmer	27Ap02DJ
CASTER, William		25	M	Painter	27Ap21Al	SMITH, Henry		26	M	Farmer	27Ap02DJ
ACKART, Charles		28	M	Unknown	27Ap21Al	Caroline		24	F	None	27Ap02DJ
HENNINGHAM, Richard		45	M	Unknown	27Ap21Al	KELLEY, Sally		40	F	None	27Ap02DJ
Ellen	(W)	43	F	Wife	27Ap21Al	NEALE, Francis		18	M	Farmer	27Ap02DJ
Eliza	(D)	21	F	Unknown	27Ap21Al	Cathe.		18	F	None	27Ap02DJ
Jemima	(D)	19	F	Unknown	27Ap21Al	HARRINGTON, John		20	M	Farmer	27Ap02DJ
Keziah	(D)	17	F	Unknown	27Ap21Al	BRADLEY, Matt.		15	M	Farmer	27Ap02DJ
Richard	(S)	12	M	Unknown	27Ap21Al	Mickl.		30	M	Farmer	27Ap02DJ
Harriet	(D)	08	F	Child	27Ap21Al	Mickl.		27	M	Farmer	27Ap02DJ
Josiah	(D)	06	M	Child	27Ap21Al	Ed.		20	M	Farmer	27Ap02DJ
Mary-Ann-Maria	(D)	03	F	Child	27Ap21Al	Ellen		25	F	None	27Ap02DJ
FULLER, Robert		63	M	Unknown	27Ap21Al	Ellen		20	F	None	27Ap02DJ
Phoebe		56	F	Unknown	27Ap21Al	DAILEY, Mathw.		20	M	Farmer	27Ap02DJ
MITCHELL, John-D.R.		34	M	Unknown	27Ap21Al	MCCALLEN, Rose		13	F	None	27Ap02DJ
Catherine	(W)	26	F	Wife	27Ap21Al	KANE, Mary		18	F	None	27Ap02DJ
John	(S)	03	M	Child	27Ap21Al	Sarah		23	F	None	27Ap02DJ
Catherine	(D)	.00	F	Infant	27Ap21Al	HARKIN, Dennis		30	M	Laborer	27Ap02DJ
STEWART, M.		24	M	Unknown	27Ap21Al	Bridget		21	F	None	27Ap02DJ
RAN, U-Mrs.		50	F	Unknown	27Ap21Al	DOGHERTY, Unity		16	F	None	27Ap02DJ
COLLINS, U-Mrs.		35	F	Unknown	27Ap21Al	MULGANY, John		45	M	Laborer	27Ap02DJ
U		04	U	Child	27Ap21Al	Thos.	(S)	20	M	Laborer	27Ap02DJ
FREEMAN, Otis-V.		25	M	Mariner	27Ap21Al	Maria	(W)	45	F	Wife	27Ap02DJ
TAYLOR, John		21	M	Prof-Lit	27Ap21Al	Ellen	(T)	30	F	None	27Ap02DJ
GADNEY, J.T.		19	M	Prof-Lit	27Ap21Al	HYLAND, Peter		06	M	Child	27Ap02DJ
MATHEWS, Oliver-H.		34	M	Unknown	27Ap21Al	GALLAGHER, John		21	M	Mechanic	27Ap02DJ
Hannah		28	F	Unknown	27Ap21Al	Daniel		16	M	Mechanic	27Ap02DJ
LEWIS, Geo.M.		30	M	Merchant	27Ap21Al	Biddy		19	F	None	27Ap02DJ
MAHONY, David		26	M	Physician	27Ap21Al	BYRNE, Hannah		30	F	None	27Ap02DJ
WEISMAN, Robert		22	M	Unknown	27Ap21Al	MILLER, John		30	F	None	27Ap02DJ
BARNASCO, Charles		21	M	Unknown	27Ap21Al	MCCALL, John		26	F	None	27Ap02DJ
Emil		19	M	Unknown	27Ap21Al	MILLER, Sarah		16	F	None	27Ap02DJ
BURES, Cornelias		46	M	Unknown	27Ap21Al	BYRNE, Margt.		17	F	None	27Ap02DJ
WEDLAKE, Henry-B.		22	M	Merchant	27Ap21Al	DEVLIN, John		31	M	Laborer	27Ap02DJ
EVANS, Robert-L.		21	M	Merchant	27Ap21Al	Mary		40	F	None	27Ap02DJ
NOVIS, Martin-W.		28	M	Bookbinder	27Ap21Al	Cathe.		16	F	None	27Ap02DJ
DWYER, James		23	M	Miller	27Ap21Al	Eise		19	F	None	27Ap02DJ
WRIGHT, Henry		22	M	Paper Maker	27Ap21Al	Nelly		12	F	None	27Ap02DJ
BURTON, Geo.		23	M	Farmer	27Ap21Al	Mary		10	F	None	27Ap02DJ
						Biddy		.06	F	Infant	27Ap02DJ
						KELLEY, John		18	M	Laborer	27Ap02DJ
						Andw.		22	M	Laborer	27Ap02DJ
						Andw.		30	M	Laborer	27Ap02DJ
						MCCULLUGH, Pat		35	M	Laborer	27Ap02DJ
						John		39	M	Laborer	27Ap02DJ
						MCCONWAY, Kitty		31	F	None	27Ap02DJ

NAMES OF PASSENGERS		AGE	SEX	OCCUPATIONS	DATE PORT SHIP
MCCULLOUGH, Mary		35	F	None	27Ap02DJ
BOYLE, James		25	M	Laborer	27Ap02DJ
SMITH, Patk.		40	M	Laborer	27Ap02DJ
Mary	(D)	19	F	None	27Ap02DJ
Cathe.	(D)	17	F	None	27Ap02DJ
CREEHAN, Phil.		20	M	Laborer	27Ap02DJ
Cathe.	(W)	20	F	Wife	27Ap02DJ
Patk.	(S)	.07	M	Infant	27Ap02DJ
KILMARTIN, Patk.		40	M	Laborer	27Ap02DJ
DOLAN, Michael		23	M	Laborer	27Ap02DJ
Philip		20	M	Laborer	27Ap02DJ
NOON, James		20	M	Laborer	27Ap02DJ
KERMEDY, Thos.		30	M	Mechanic	27Ap02DJ
MURPHY, Lawrence		21	M	Mechanic	27Ap02DJ
MULLEN, Martin		50	M	Laborer	27Ap02DJ
U	(W)	50	F	Wife	27Ap02DJ
Ellen	(D)	15	F	None	27Ap02DJ
Cathe.	(D)	13	F	None	27Ap02DJ
Bridget	(D)	07	F	Child	27Ap02DJ
Mathew	(S)	09	M	Child	27Ap02DJ
Patk.	(S)	05	M	Child	27Ap02DJ
John	(S)	02	M	Child	27Ap02DJ
MCGOWAN, Mary		26	F	None	27Ap02DJ
MCROWNEY, Owen		30	M	Laborer	27Ap02DJ
BRADLEY, Felix		13	M	Laborer	27Ap02DJ
KELLEY, Darby		30	M	Laborer	27Ap02DJ
COBB, Ed.		26	M	Laborer	27Ap02DJ
ARMSTRONG, Thos.		28	M	Laborer	27Ap02DJ
U	(W)	22	F	Wife	27Ap02DJ
Thos.	(S)	.09	M	Infant	27Ap02DJ
EGAN, Anne		20	F	None	27Ap02DJ
PICKETT, E.		25	M	Laborer	27Ap02DJ
HOLDEN, Wm.		30	M	Laborer	27Ap02DJ
MURRAY, Martin		23	M	Laborer	27Ap02DJ
BROWN, John		20	M	Laborer	27Ap02DJ
CLAVIN, Pat		26	M	Laborer	27Ap02DJ
Michl.		28	M	Laborer	27Ap02DJ
Bessey		28	F	None	27Ap02DJ
Cathe.		24	F	None	27Ap02DJ
Sarah		22	F	None	27Ap02DJ
John		03	M	Child	27Ap02DJ
Maria		.05	F	Infant	27Ap02DJ
MURPHY, Joseph		28	M	Laborer	27Ap02DJ
Cathe.		19	F	None	27Ap02DJ
AUGHAN, Ellen		22	F	None	27Ap02DJ
MURPHY, Patk.		.06	M	Infant	27Ap02DJ
MCCULLOGH, Pat.		20	M	Laborer	27Ap02DJ
Cathe.		20	F	None	27Ap02DJ
Roger		20	M	Laborer	27Ap02DJ
Alley		20	F	None	27Ap02DJ
CLARK, Owen		35	M	Laborer	27Ap02DJ
DUFFY, John		20	M	Laborer	27Ap02DJ
Cathe.		20	F	None	27Ap02DJ
Cathe.		20	F	None	27Ap02DJ
BARRETT, Cicily		20	F	None	27Ap02DJ
MCFAY, Hugh		25	M	Laborer	27Ap02DJ
Michael		20	M	Laborer	27Ap02DJ
John		.06	M	Infant	27Ap02DJ
HARVING, Mary		40	F	None	27Ap02DJ
MOORE, Thos.		11	M	None	27Ap02DJ
DUFFY, Cicily		20	F	None	27Ap02DJ
FITZPATRICK, Mary		48	F	None	27Ap02DJ
Michael	(S)	20	M	Mechanic	27Ap02DJ
John	(S)	13	M	None	27Ap02DJ
ONEILL, Biddy		20	F	None	27Ap02DJ
KEEFE, Thos.		29	M	Laborer	27Ap02DJ
KELLEY, Bridget		18	F	None	27Ap02DJ
MALONEY, Michl.		20	M	Laborer	27Ap02DJ
NORTH, John		40	M	Laborer	27Ap02DJ
Mary		30	F	None	27Ap02DJ
HANLON, Mary		20	F	None	27Ap02DJ
Thos.		20	M	None	27Ap02DJ
Patk.		15	M	None	27Ap02DJ
Mary		13	F	None	27Ap02DJ
WALSH, Wm.		30	M	Laborer	27Ap02DJ
OBRIEN, Hugh		20	M	Laborer	27Ap02DJ
FLYNN, Cathe.		20	F	None	27Ap02DJ
ARD, Thos.		30	M	Laborer	27Ap02DJ
SHAFFREY, Michael		25	M	Laborer	27Ap02DJ
Mary		20	F	None	27Ap02DJ
CAFFREY, Josh.		30	M	Laborer	27Ap02DJ
U	(W)	30	F	Wife	27Ap02DJ
Richd.	(S)	02	M	Child	27Ap02DJ
CONCANNON, Thos.		26	M	Laborer	27Ap02DJ
LINNON, Dennis		26	M	Laborer	27Ap02DJ
MULUCHALE, Thaddy		24	M	Laborer	27Ap02DJ
KENNEDY, Thos.		25	M	Laborer	27Ap02DJ
Bella		25	F	None	27Ap02DJ
Jane		18	F	None	27Ap02DJ
John		16	M	None	27Ap02DJ
THOMPSON, Jane		20	F	None	27Ap02DJ
MAYNARD, John		20	M	None	27Ap02DJ
CAMPBELL, George		20	M	None	27Ap02DJ
ARMSTRONG, Wm.		20	M	None	27Ap02DJ
SLOANE, Richd.		20	M	Mechanic	27Ap02DJ
MCFARRAND, Henry		25	M	Mechanic	27Ap02DJ
U	(W)	20	F	Wife	27Ap02DJ
WOOD, Matt.		20	M	Mechanic	27Ap02DJ
Susan		20	F	None	27Ap02DJ
MCCORMICK, Bernard		30	M	Mechanic	27Ap02DJ
U	(W)	30	F	Wife	27Ap02DJ
Sally	(D)	06	F	Child	27Ap02DJ
John	(S)	08	M	Child	27Ap02DJ
James	(S)	02	M	Child	27Ap02DJ
KEEGAN, Mary		25	F	None	27Ap02DJ
RIELY, John		26	M	Laborer	27Ap02DJ
Cathe.		15	F	None	27Ap02DJ
Eliza.		12	F	None	27Ap02DJ
Bridget		22	F	None	27Ap02DJ
LYNCH, Rose		18	F	None	27Ap02DJ
BRANNIGAN, Pat		21	M	Laborer	27Ap02DJ
CARROLL, Thos.		25	M	Laborer	27Ap02DJ
MCAREE, John		25	M	Laborer	27Ap02DJ
LOUGHEAD, Jas.		22	M	Laborer	27Ap02DJ
ARMSTRONG, Ann		20	F	None	27Ap02DJ
HICKEY, Patk.		22	M	Laborer	27Ap02DJ
REGAN, Michael		24	M	Laborer	27Ap02DJ
HURST, Thos.		25	M	Laborer	27Ap02DJ
U	(W)	20	F	Wife	27Ap02DJ
CAIN, John		20	M	Laborer	27Ap02DJ
Thos.		21	M	Laborer	27Ap02DJ
REGAN, Owen		20	M	Laborer	27Ap02DJ
BRENNAN, Jas.		20	M	Laborer	27Ap02DJ
DUFFY, Jerry		20	M	Laborer	27Ap02DJ
MCNULTY, Pat.		18	M	Laborer	27Ap02DJ
WALSH, Hannah		20	F	None	27Ap02DJ
MCDONNELL, John		20	M	Laborer	27Ap02DJ
U	(W)	20	F	Wife	27Ap02DJ
John	(S)	12	M	Laborer	27Ap02DJ
Jane	(D)	08	F	Child	27Ap02DJ
Anne	(D)	02	F	Child	27Ap02DJ
BYSON, Connor		25	M	Laborer	27Ap02DJ
OHINATY, John		21	M	Laborer	27Ap02DJ
DILLON, Ann		21	F	None	27Ap02DJ
Francis	(S)	02	M	Child	27Ap02DJ
MCGUIRE, Anne		20	F	None	27Ap02DJ
CARROLL, John		04	M	Child	27Ap02DJ
BOHEN, Bridget		21	F	None	27Ap02DJ
QUINN, Alice		21	F	None	27Ap02DJ
MARTIN, Peter		12	M	Laborer	27Ap02DJ
DAWDALL, Thos.		21	M	Laborer	27Ap02DJ
FLOODWOOD, Francis		25	M	Laborer	27Ap02DJ
WHALLEY, Cathe.		21	F	None	27Ap02DJ
DOLIN, Peter		40	M	Laborer	27Ap02DJ
Cathe.	(S)	16	F	None	27Ap02DJ
Mary	(D)	12	F	None	27Ap02DJ
Michael	(S)	10	M	None	27Ap02DJ
Peter	(S)	05	M	Child	27Ap02DJ
James	(D)	03	M	Child	27Ap02DJ
Cathe.	(D)	07	F	Child	27Ap02DJ

NAMES OF PASSENGERS		A G E	S E X	OCCUPATIONS	DATE PORT SHIP	NAMES OF PASSENGERS		A G E	S E X	OCCUPATIONS	DATE PORT SHIP
DOLIN, Peter		40	M	Laborer	27Ap02DJ	HACKETT, Darby		44	M	Farmer	28Ap02Pz
Cathe.	(W)	40	F	Wife	27Ap02DJ	Biddy	(W)	40	F	Wife	28Ap02Pz
Anne		25	F	None	27Ap02DJ	Catherine	(D)	09	F	Child	28Ap02Pz
Mary	(D)	13	F	None	27Ap02DJ	John	(S)	07	M	Child	28Ap02Pz
Cathe.	(D)	11	F	None	27Ap02DJ	Judy	(D)	05	F	Child	28Ap02Pz
Peter	(S)	07	M	Child	27Ap02DJ	Thomas	(S)	03	M	Child	28Ap02Pz
Michael	(S)	09	M	Child	27Ap02DJ	FLAERTY, Michael		24	M	Flaxdr	28Ap02Pz
CONLON, James		20	M	Laborer	27Ap02DJ	FEERY, John		20	M	Shoemaker	28Ap02Pz
MULLEN, Pat.		20	M	Laborer	27Ap02DJ	CAMPBELL, John		20	M	Laborer	28Ap02Pz
MILLER, John		20	M	Laborer	27Ap02DJ	SHANNON, Sarah		25	F	Spinster	28Ap02Pz
HEALEY, James		40	M	Laborer	27Ap02DJ	DOYLE, Henry		21	M	Weaver	28Ap02Pz
Mary	(W)	30	F	Wife	27Ap02DJ	Catherine	(W)	25	F	Wife	28Ap02Pz
Mary-O.	(D)	.07	F	Infant	27Ap02DJ	ROWATH, Catherine		25	F	Milliner	28Ap02Pz
SWEENEY, Michael		25	M	Laborer	27Ap02DJ	MCKANN, Thomas		22	M	Laborer	28Ap02Pz
KERINGHAN, Winefred		18	F	None	27Ap02DJ	CAMPBELL, John		27	M	Laborer	28Ap02Pz
Mary		18	F	None	27Ap02DJ	Margt.	(W)	24	F	Wife	28Ap02Pz
LAKE, Wm.		33	M	Laborer	27Ap02DJ	MCGOVERN, Phillip		21	M	Laborer	28Ap02Pz
JAKES, Wm.		30	M	Laborer	27Ap02DJ	OHARA, Charles		21	M	Unknown	28Ap02Pz
GAVIN, Ed.		30	M	Laborer	27Ap02DJ	MCBARTLAN, P.		21	M	Unknown	28Ap02Pz
Sarah		30	F	None	27Ap02DJ	DOLAN, P.		21	M	Unknown	28Ap02Pz
Sarah		20	F	None	27Ap02DJ	Bridget	(W)	19	F	Wife	28Ap02Pz
Peter		18	M	None	27Ap02DJ	Lydia	(T)	12	F	Unknown	28Ap02Pz
GRADY, Tim		20	M	None	27Ap02DJ	MCANELLY, Edward		50	M	Unknown	28Ap02Pz
MALLEY, Peggy		20	F	None	27Ap02DJ	U	(W)	40	F	Wife	28Ap02Pz
GAVIN, Patk.		16	M	None	27Ap02DJ	Mary	(D)	15	F	None	28Ap02Pz
John		13	M	None	27Ap02DJ	Eliz.	(D)	13	F	None	28Ap02Pz
Honora		12	F	None	27Ap02DJ	John	(S)	12	M	None	28Ap02Pz
Cathe.		10	F	None	27Ap02DJ	Catherine	(D)	10	F	None	28Ap02Pz
Thos.		08	M	Child	27Ap02DJ	Ellen	(D)	09	F	Child	28Ap02Pz
ROACH, Wm.		21	M	Laborer	27Ap02DJ	James	(D)	08	F	Child	28Ap02Pz
MORAN, And.		40	M	Laborer	27Ap02DJ	DAWN, Patk.		22	M	Laborer	28Ap02Pz
Mary		40	F	None	27Ap02DJ	KANE, Michael		24	M	Laborer	28Ap02Pz
CARRIGAN, Biddy		21	F	None	27Ap02DJ	Patk.		20	M	Laborer	28Ap02Pz
MORAN, Pat.		20	M	Laborer	27Ap02DJ	John		13	M	Laborer	28Ap02Pz
Michael		16	M	Laborer	27Ap02DJ	DELANY, Patk.		23	M	Laborer	28Ap02Pz
MCINTIRE, Thady		20	M	Laborer	27Ap02DJ	MCQUADE, Anthony		24	M	Laborer	28Ap02Pz
MORAN, Frank		30	M	Laborer	27Ap02DJ	GORMELY, Ann		20	F	Servant	28Ap02Pz
GROGAN, Thos.		16	M	Laborer	27Ap02DJ	KELLY, Mary		20	F	Servant	28Ap02Pz
BROGAN, Nancy		18	F	None	27Ap02DJ	COLGAN, Robert		24	M	Farmer	28Ap02Pz
GALLAGHER, Darnk.		30	M	Laborer	27Ap02DJ	Catherine	(W)	22	F	Wife	28Ap02Pz
U	(W)	30	F	Wife	27Ap02DJ	Bridgett	(T)	10	F	Spinster	28Ap02Pz
Patk.	(S)	02	M	Child	27Ap02DJ	CARR, Rosy		17	F	Spinster	28Ap02Pz
MONGHAN, Martin		40	M	Farmer	27Ap02DJ	BRICK, James		22	M	Carpenter	28Ap02Pz
Michael	(S)	20	M	Farmer	27Ap02DJ	John		12	M	Carpenter	28Ap02Pz
Patrick	(S)	18	M	Farmer	27Ap02DJ	EGAN, E.		60	M	Laborer	28Ap02Pz
FISCHER, Mary		40	F	None	27Ap02DJ	Cormick	(S)	24	M	Laborer	28Ap02Pz
Mary	(D)	20	F	None	27Ap02DJ	Ann	(L)	25	F	Wife	28Ap02Pz
John	(S)	20	M	Farmer	27Ap02DJ	Winfried	(D)	20	F	Spinster	28Ap02Pz
Jas.	(S)	25	M	Farmer	27Ap02DJ	MURPHY, Patk.		40	M	Laborer	28Ap02Pz
GALLAGHER, Jas.		.06	M	Infant	27Ap02DJ	CUMMINGS, Patk.		20	M	Laborer	28Ap02Pz
FADDEN, Biddy		30	F	None	27Ap02DJ	MCCORMICK, Martin		20	M	Laborer	28Ap02Pz
GALLAGHER, Jas.		30	M	Laborer	27Ap02DJ	GILLESPIE, Anthony		28	M	Glazier	28Ap02Pz
						MCCORMICK, Thomas		29	M	Laborer	28Ap02Pz
						GILROY, Mary		19	F	Servant	28Ap02Pz
						GILLESPIE, Winnie		19	F	Servant	28Ap02Pz
						MCGOWAN, Ann		20	F	Servant	28Ap02Pz
						WADE, Ellen		20	F	Servant	28Ap02Pz
ELLEN 28 APRIL 1847						DARBY, Catherine		16	F	Spinster	28Ap02Pz
						FLYNN, Thomas		24	M	Blacksmith	28Ap02Pz
From Liverpool						John		30	M	Tailor	28Ap02Pz
						TOPPIN, Robt.		40	M	Weaver	28Ap02Pz
						Esther	(W)	26	F	Wife	28Ap02Pz
						Margt.	(T)	22	F	Servant	28Ap02Pz
MCKENNA, Bridgett		20	F	Spinster	28Ap02Pz	Ellen		10	F	Seamstress	28Ap02Pz
ROONEY, Thomas		30	M	Laborer	28Ap02Pz	John		14	M	None	28Ap02Pz
Ann	(W)	30	F	Wife	28Ap02Pz	Hugh		12	M	None	28Ap02Pz
Thomas	(S)	03	M	Child	28Ap02Pz	Ann-Jane		10	F	None	28Ap02Pz
Patrick	(S)	04	M	Child	28Ap02Pz	Robert		08	M	Child	28Ap02Pz
John	(S)	01	M	Child	28Ap02Pz	Lucy		06	F	Child	28Ap02Pz
Owen	(B)	28	M	Bricklayer	28Ap02Pz	William		01	M	Child	28Ap02Pz
Patrick	(B)	28	M	Bricklayer	28Ap02Pz	WALSH, Patrick		15	M	Laborer	28Ap02Pz
Bridget	(L)	29	F	Wife	28Ap02Pz	Mary		13	F	None	28Ap02Pz
Patk.	(B)	24	M	Laborer	28Ap02Pz	MCSHOVE, Thomas		32	M	Laborer	28Ap02Pz
KELLEY, Michael		23	M	Laborer	28Ap02Pz	MANGAN, Eleanor		28	F	Servant	28Ap02Pz
Peter		20	M	Laborer	28Ap02Pz	Anthony		22	M	Laborer	28Ap02Pz

NAMES OF PASSENGERS		A G E	S E X	OCCUPATIONS	DATE PORT SHIP	NAMES OF PASSENGERS		A G E	S E X	OCCUPATIONS	DATE PORT SHIP
GALLAGHER, Wm.		24	M	Shoemaker	28Ap02Pz						
Bridgett	(W)	24	F	Wife	28Ap02Pz						
Mary	(D)	01	F	Child	28Ap02Pz						
DOLOLING, Patt.		21	M	Laborer	28Ap02Pz						
Nancy	(W)	21	F	Wife	28Ap02Pz				**DRYDEN 29 APRIL 1847**		
Wm.	(S)	01	M	Child	28Ap02Pz						
FEARON, Arthur		23	M	Watchmaker	28Ap02Pz					**From Unknown**	
Edward		26	M	Watchmaker	28Ap02Pz						
LYON, John		60	M	Flabr	28Ap02Pz						
Mary		40	F	Servant	28Ap02Pz						
John		24	M	Servant	28Ap02Pz	HALLINAN, David		35	M	Mechanic	29Ap00Qa
Daniel		20	M	Servant	28Ap02Pz	COLLIS, William		23	M	Mechanic	29Ap00Qa
Mary		20	F	Servant	28Ap02Pz	HALLINAN, Bernard		25	M	Laborer	29Ap00Qa
Patrick		12	M	None	28Ap02Pz	HENNESEY, Franses		23	M	Laborer	29Ap00Qa
John		10	M	None	28Ap02Pz	BRENNAN, James		26	M	Laborer	29Ap00Qa
Margt.		22	F	Servant	28Ap02Pz	Honora		20	F	Laborer	29Ap00Qa
SHEA, David		28	M	Brick Maker	28Ap02Pz	FOLLEY, John		30	M	Laborer	29Ap00Qa
FASTER, Miles		30	M	Laborer	28Ap02Pz	Julia		20	F	None	29Ap00Qa
Francis		28	M	Laborer	28Ap02Pz	Debora		24	F	None	29Ap00Qa
Mary		22	F	Wife	28Ap02Pz	CLIFFORD, Timothy		23	M	Laborer	29Ap00Qa
Richard		20	M	Laborer	28Ap02Pz	Honor		18	F	None	29Ap00Qa
KEARNS, Thomas		35	M	Laborer	28Ap02Pz	STACK, Daniel		22	M	Laborer	29Ap00Qa
BEGLEY, Dennis		30	M	Laborer	28Ap02Pz	CALLAGHAN, Patt.		25	M	Laborer	29Ap00Qa
MASSEY, Wm.		40	M	Farmer	28Ap02Pz	KISSANE, John		24	M	Laborer	29Ap00Qa
MCKINNA, Catherine		28	F	Servant	28Ap02Pz	CRANN, Thomas		27	M	Laborer	29Ap00Qa
MCEWAN, Hugh		20	M	Servant	28Ap02Pz	CAHILL, Thomas		22	M	Laborer	29Ap00Qa
MORGAN, John		27	M	Servant	28Ap02Pz	CAHLONE, Daniel		18	M	Laborer	29Ap00Qa
DALY, Catherine		18	F	Servant	28Ap02Pz	Thomas		20	M	Laborer	29Ap00Qa
MCAVOY, John		28	M	Laborer	28Ap02Pz	DUNLEY, Patk.		28	M	Laborer	29Ap00Qa
Catherine	(W)	28	F	Wife	28Ap02Pz	HOLLIHAN, Michael		27	M	Laborer	29Ap00Qa
Rosanna	(T)	23	F	Servant	28Ap02Pz	Mary		19	F	None	29Ap00Qa
Susan	(M)	64	F	Servant	28Ap02Pz	CANNING, James		20	M	Laborer	29Ap00Qa
Mary	(D)	02	F	Child	28Ap02Pz	THOMPSON, M.		24	M	Laborer	29Ap00Qa
Bartley	(S)	.06	M	Infant	28Ap02Pz	CURKIN, Daniel		27	M	Laborer	29Ap00Qa
MCADAM, Owen		33	M	Laborer	28Ap02Pz	Darby		25	M	Laborer	29Ap00Qa
GAGE, Wm.		45	M	Shoemaker	28Ap02Pz	RICE, Ellen		20	F	None	29Ap00Qa
Elizabeth	(W)	36	F	Wife	28Ap02Pz	HALLRAN, Jeremiah		30	M	Laborer	29Ap00Qa
BRENNAN, Patrick		40	M	Tailor	28Ap02Pz	ROURKE, John		18	M	Laborer	29Ap00Qa
Rosy	(W)	34	F	Wife	28Ap02Pz	SHEA, John		28	M	Laborer	29Ap00Qa
Andrew	(S)	13	M	None	28Ap02Pz	FITZGERALD, John		30	M	Laborer	29Ap00Qa
Ellen	(D)	11	F	None	28Ap02Pz						
Judy	(D)	09	F	Child	28Ap02Pz						
Ann	(D)	07	F	Child	28Ap02Pz						
James	(S)	.09	M	Infant	28Ap02Pz						
DOLAN, Bridgett		45	F	Wife	28Ap02Pz						
Mabey	(D)	17	F	None	28Ap02Pz				**OLINDER 29 APRIL 1847**		
Bridgett	(D)	12	F	None	28Ap02Pz						
Hannah	(D)	07	F	Child	28Ap02Pz					**From Liverpool**	
Mary	(D)	03	F	Child	28Ap02Pz						
FITZPATRICK, Terence		18	M	Laborer	28Ap02Pz						
MORAN, James		30	M	Laborer	28Ap02Pz						
MCDONALD, Thomas		30	M	Laborer	28Ap02Pz	MANION, Luke		24	M	Farmer	29Ap02Qb
DUFFY, Carmack		26	M	Laborer	28Ap02Pz	Laurance		22	M	Farmer	29Ap02Qb
KILMARTIN, George		36	M	Gdnr	28Ap02Pz	Mary		20	F	Farmer	29Ap02Qb
Mary	(W)	30	F	Wife	28Ap02Pz	GLEESON, Bridget		20	F	Farmer	29Ap02Qb
Mary	(D)	08	F	Child	28Ap02Pz	SULIVAN, Timothy		25	M	Farmer	29Ap02Qb
Andrew	(S)	03	M	Child	28Ap02Pz	Danl.		23	M	Farmer	29Ap02Qb
Bridgett	(D)	05	F	Child	28Ap02Pz	Mary		19	F	Farmer	29Ap02Qb
Betty	(T)	24	F	Unknown	28Ap02Pz	MULROONEY, Patk.		26	M	Farmer	29Ap02Qb
QUINN, Michael		35	M	Servant	28Ap02Pz	BYRNE, Jno.		25	M	Farmer	29Ap02Qb
Ann	(L)	30	F	Wife	28Ap02Pz	HINDLE, Ann		24	F	Farmer	29Ap02Qb
Patrick	(B)	32	M	Glazier	28Ap02Pz	Edwin	(S)	.00	M	Infant	29Ap02Qb
Ann	(T)	24	F	Servant	28Ap02Pz	SYNOT, James		24	M	Unknown	29Ap02Qb
GROGAN, Mary		24	F	Servant	28Ap02Pz	U	(W)	22	F	Wife	29Ap02Qb
RADY, Patk.		20	M	Laborer	28Ap02Pz	Thos.	(B)	25	M	Unknown	29Ap02Qb
COYNE, Andrew		30	M	Laborer	28Ap02Pz	James	(B)	21	M	Unknown	29Ap02Qb
Mary	(W)	30	F	Wife	28Ap02Pz	MCCORMACK, Thomas		25	M	Unknown	29Ap02Qb
Patrick	(S)	03	M	Child	28Ap02Pz	U	(W)	22	F	Wife	29Ap02Qb
Mary	(D)	02	F	Child	28Ap02Pz	TAYLOR, James		28	M	Unknown	29Ap02Qb
GORMLEY, Eliz.		16	F	Servant	28Ap02Pz	JONES, Len.		34	M	Unknown	29Ap02Qb
FEARON, Arthur		23	M	Laborer	28Ap02Pz	OHARA, James		24	M	Unknown	29Ap02Qb
Edward		26	M	Laborer	28Ap02Pz	Michl.	(B)	11	M	Unknown	29Ap02Qb
						Mary	(W)	25	F	Wife	29Ap02Qb
						Stephen	(S)	03	M	Child	29Ap02Qb
						Mary	(D)	.00	F	Infant	29Ap02Qb

NAMES OF PASSENGERS		AGE	SEX	OCCUPATIONS	DATE PORT SHIP
OHARA, Mary	(M)	50	F	Unknown	29Ap02Qb
GOODWIN, Pat.		26	M	Unknown	29Ap02Qb
U	(W)	24	F	Wife	29Ap02Qb
Thomas	(S)	03	M	Child	29Ap02Qb
Mary-Ann	(D)	.00	F	Infant	29Ap02Qb
MCDONNELL, Terrance		30	M	Unknown	29Ap02Qb
Mary		25	F	Unknown	29Ap02Qb
FALLON, Mary		18	F	Unknown	29Ap02Qb
RINNEYHAN, Betty		30	F	Unknown	29Ap02Qb
COSTELLY, Betty		18	F	Unknown	29Ap02Qb
KEANEYHAN, Betty		13	F	Unknown	29Ap02Qb
RINEHAN, Mary		09	F	Child	29Ap02Qb
CLEARY, James		21	M	Unknown	29Ap02Qb
HARRISON, John		24	M	Unknown	29Ap02Qb
Mary		20	F	Unknown	29Ap02Qb
Honora		20	F	Unknown	29Ap02Qb
BYRNE, Pat		40	M	Unknown	29Ap02Qb
Mary	(D)	16	F	Unknown	29Ap02Qb
Anne	(D)	12	F	Unknown	29Ap02Qb
Michael	(S)	10	M	Unknown	29Ap02Qb
JUDGE, James		40	M	Unknown	29Ap02Qb
U	(W)	40	F	Wife	29Ap02Qb
James	(S)	20	M	Unknown	29Ap02Qb
Bartley	(S)	16	M	Unknown	29Ap02Qb
John	(S)	14	M	Unknown	29Ap02Qb
Michael	(S)	11	M	Unknown	29Ap02Qb
Patrick	(S)	09	M	Child	29Ap02Qb
Darby	(S)	06	M	Child	29Ap02Qb
Thos.		23	M	Unknown	29Ap02Qb
U	(W)	22	F	Wife	29Ap02Qb
Bridget	(D)	01	F	Child	29Ap02Qb
COLE, William		35	M	Unknown	29Ap02Qb
KANE, James		04	M	Unknown	29Ap02Qb
John	(S)	20	M	Unknown	29Ap02Qb
Bridget		12	F	Unknown	29Ap02Qb
MULLIN, John		23	M	Unknown	29Ap02Qb
BYRNE, U-Mrs.		40	F	Unknown	29Ap02Qb
MULLEN, James		28	M	Unknown	29Ap02Qb
John		28	M	Unknown	29Ap02Qb
KENNEY, John		27	M	Unknown	29Ap02Qb
MULDIRE, Michl.		19	M	Unknown	29Ap02Qb
MCELDIN, Cella		24	F	Unknown	29Ap02Qb
Reddy	(S)	.00	M	Infant	29Ap02Qb
ENNIS, Phillip		21	M	Unknown	29Ap02Qb
CORMICK, Bernard-I.		19	M	Unknown	29Ap02Qb
HOWLEY, Mary		20	F	Unknown	29Ap02Qb
BRENNAN, Bridget		45	F	Unknown	29Ap02Qb
Catherine	(D)	13	F	Unknown	29Ap02Qb
OSULLIVAN, J.N.		26	M	Unknown	29Ap02Qb
RYAN, Jim-Y.		25	M	Unknown	29Ap02Qb
KAVANAGH, Jno.		50	M	Unknown	29Ap02Qb
Thomas	(S)	21	M	Unknown	29Ap02Qb
DEIGAN, Frank		24	M	Unknown	29Ap02Qb
REELEY, Martin		23	M	Unknown	29Ap02Qb
ASH, Margaret		40	F	Unknown	29Ap02Qb
Luke		30	M	Unknown	29Ap02Qb
HOWLEY, Mart.		24	M	Unknown	29Ap02Qb
RAKER, Thomas		24	M	Unknown	29Ap02Qb
ARMSTRONG, Wm.		54	M	Unknown	29Ap02Qb
Sophia	(W)	54	F	Wife	29Ap02Qb
Sarah	(D)	13	F	Unknown	29Ap02Qb
Ellzth.	(D)	18	F	Unknown	29Ap02Qb
Thos.	(S)	13	M	Unknown	29Ap02Qb
Noble	(S)	11	M	Unknown	29Ap02Qb
Mary-Anne	(D)	09	F	Child	29Ap02Qb
Andrew	(S)	07	M	Child	29Ap02Qb
CATHCART, Ann		26	F	Unknown	29Ap02Qb
BOYLE, James		52	M	Unknown	29Ap02Qb
Ellen	(W)	52	F	Wife	29Ap02Qb
Isabella	(D)	22	F	Unknown	29Ap02Qb
Margaret	(D)	15	F	Unknown	29Ap02Qb
William	(S)	12	M	Unknown	29Ap02Qb
Mary	(D)	10	F	Unknown	29Ap02Qb
BRADLEY, John		20	M	Unknown	29Ap02Qb
MCKEEN, Matilda		21	F	Unknown	29Ap02Qb
MAMM, Jno.		25	M	Unknown	29Ap02Qb
MCLOUGHLIN, Danl.		21	M	Unknown	29Ap02Qb
Michl.		20	M	Unknown	29Ap02Qb
Susan		18	F	Unknown	29Ap02Qb
Bridget		19	F	Unknown	29Ap02Qb
BRITLAND, Michael		22	M	Unknown	29Ap02Qb
Neal		20	M	Unknown	29Ap02Qb
MCGILLIS, James		20	M	Unknown	29Ap02Qb
MOLLOY, John		20	M	Unknown	29Ap02Qb
Susan		18	F	Unknown	29Ap02Qb
KILDIE, Teague		28	M	Unknown	29Ap02Qb
Mary	(W)	20	F	Wife	29Ap02Qb
Patrick	(S)	05	M	Child	29Ap02Qb
John	(S)	03	M	Child	29Ap02Qb
SWEENEY, Pat		23	M	Unknown	29Ap02Qb
CORCORAN, Jno.		20	M	Unknown	29Ap02Qb
PHELAN, Pat		25	M	Unknown	29Ap02Qb
MCHUGH, Barnard		21	M	Unknown	29Ap02Qb
MAGUIRE, Mgh.		20	F	Unknown	29Ap02Qb
NUGENT, Mary		17	F	Unknown	29Ap02Qb
ROGERS, Jno.		30	M	Unknown	29Ap02Qb
Anne	(D)	04	F	Child	29Ap02Qb
Patrick	(S)	03	M	Child	29Ap02Qb
HORE, Patrick		20	M	Unknown	29Ap02Qb
MAGUIRE, Patrick		20	M	Unknown	29Ap02Qb
Mary		22	F	Unknown	29Ap02Qb
MCCARTY, Jeremiah		24	M	Unknown	29Ap02Qb
NERVIN, Jno.		24	M	Unknown	29Ap02Qb
Cathe.		21	F	Unknown	29Ap02Qb
CASTLETON, Mary		21	F	Unknown	29Ap02Qb
HUGHES, Anne		30	F	Unknown	29Ap02Qb
Mary	(D)	11	F	Unknown	29Ap02Qb
Biddy	(D)	09	F	Child	29Ap02Qb
Nelly	(D)	07	F	Child	29Ap02Qb
DOYLE, Pat		40	M	Unknown	29Ap02Qb
John	(S)	13	M	Unknown	29Ap02Qb
Anne	(D)	10	F	Unknown	29Ap02Qb
CONNOR, Hugh		35	M	Unknown	29Ap02Qb
TRACEY, James		30	M	Unknown	29Ap02Qb
CAIN, James		36	M	Unknown	29Ap02Qb
U	(W)	30	F	Wife	29Ap02Qb
Biddy	(D)	09	F	Child	29Ap02Qb
Thomas	(S)	07	M	Child	29Ap02Qb
Honora	(D)	05	F	Child	29Ap02Qb
Margaret	(D)	03	F	Child	29Ap02Qb
James	(S)	.00	M	Infant	29Ap02Qb
NEVIN, William		19	M	Unknown	29Ap02Qb
OROURKE, Martin		21	M	Unknown	29Ap02Qb
MURPHY, Thos.		23	M	Unknown	29Ap02Qb
BURNS, Geo.		50	M	Unknown	29Ap02Qb
Jane	(W)	48	F	Wife	29Ap02Qb
Mary	(D)	10	F	Unknown	29Ap02Qb
Andy	(S)	07	M	Child	29Ap02Qb
William	(S)	05	M	Child	29Ap02Qb
Patk.		02	M	Child	29Ap02Qb
Ann	(D)	.00	F	Infant	29Ap02Qb
CALLEY, Margt.		20	F	Unknown	29Ap02Qb
PATTERSON, Robt.		20	M	Unknown	29Ap02Qb
HANNIGAN, Mary		19	F	Unknown	29Ap02Qb

JAVA 30 APRIL 1847

From Liverpool

NAMES OF PASSENGERS		AGE	SEX	OCCUPATIONS	DATE PORT SHIP
BOOTH, Hiram		21	M	Laborer	30Ap02Cx
GIBBONS, Michael		30	M	Laborer	30Ap02Cx
U	(W)	30	F	Wife	30Ap02Cx
WARD, Bryan		24	M	Laborer	30Ap02Cx
Catherine	(W)	24	F	Wife	30Ap02Cx

NAMES OF PASSENGERS	AGE	SEX	OCCUPATIONS	DATE PORT SHIP
WARD, James (S)	.00	M	Infant	30Ap02Cx
Sally (T)	20	F	Servant	30Ap02Cx
Kitty (T)	18	F	Servant	30Ap02Cx
Mary (T)	14	F	Servant	30Ap02Cx
ROWLAND, Robt.	24	M	Laborer	30Ap02Cx
DELANCY, Joshua	35	M	Laborer	30Ap02Cx
U (W)	30	F	Wife	30Ap02Cx
George (S)	12	M	Laborer	30Ap02Cx
Ann (D)	10	F	Laborer	30Ap02Cx
Sarah (D)	08	F	Child	30Ap02Cx
Susan (D)	06	F	Child	30Ap02Cx
Martha (D)	04	F	Child	30Ap02Cx
Ellen (D)	.00	F	Infant	30Ap02Cx
SIDY, Mathew	30	M	Laborer	30Ap02Cx
MULLINS, Mtta.	22	F	Laborer	30Ap02Cx
BRUNSINAN, John	24	M	Laborer	30Ap02Cx
GARVAN, John	27	M	Laborer	30Ap02Cx
U (W)	24	F	Wife	30Ap02Cx
MANAN, Mary	20	F	Laborer	30Ap02Cx
COLDSON, John	25	M	Laborer	30Ap02Cx
BROOKS, Thomas	27	M	Laborer	30Ap02Cx
TOMLINSON, Henry	21	M	Laborer	30Ap02Cx
CUMMINGS, Thomas	24	M	Laborer	30Ap02Cx
CAHILL, Corns.	40	M	Laborer	30Ap02Cx
Michael (S)	22	M	Laborer	30Ap02Cx
Julia (D)	20	F	Laborer	30Ap02Cx
Mary (D)	21	F	Laborer	30Ap02Cx
Thomas (S)	21	M	Laborer	30Ap02Cx
Martin (S)	09	M	Child	30Ap02Cx
Anthony (S)	03	M	Child	30Ap02Cx
ELSLONG, Thomas	26	M	Laborer	30Ap02Cx
BYRNE, James	22	M	Laborer	30Ap02Cx
DOUGGAN, James	24	M	Laborer	30Ap02Cx
John	20	M	Laborer	30Ap02Cx
MOLYNEUX, Mary	25	F	Laborer	30Ap02Cx
DOUGHERTY, Ann	26	F	Laborer	30Ap02Cx
HORTEN, John	34	M	Laborer	30Ap02Cx
GALLAGHER, John	30	M	Laborer	30Ap02Cx
LUCKEY, Thos.	30	M	Laborer	30Ap02Cx
GALLAGHER, Jane	15	F	Laborer	30Ap02Cx
DOBSON, Isabella	30	F	Laborer	30Ap02Cx
BUTLY, Mary	22	F	Laborer	30Ap02Cx
Margaret	18	F	Laborer	30Ap02Cx
MCEVOY, Bridget	18	F	Laborer	30Ap02Cx
MAGUIRE, John	25	M	Laborer	30Ap02Cx
U (W)	26	F	Wife	30Ap02Cx
MORAN, Edward	20	M	Unknown	30Ap02Cx
U (W)	22	F	Wife	30Ap02Cx
MCKEON, Michael	52	M	Laborer	30Ap02Cx
U (W)	40	F	Wife	30Ap02Cx
James (S)	18	M	Laborer	30Ap02Cx
Andrew (S)	16	M	Laborer	30Ap02Cx
Eliza (D)	14	F	Laborer	30Ap02Cx
Biddy (D)	11	F	Laborer	30Ap02Cx
Mary (D)	08	F	Child	30Ap02Cx
Pat (S)	06	M	Child	30Ap02Cx
John (S)	03	M	Child	30Ap02Cx
Peter (S)	.00	M	Infant	30Ap02Cx
MCGEE, Biddy	20	F	Laborer	30Ap02Cx
MONIGHAN, Ann	20	F	Laborer	30Ap02Cx
EGGLESTON, Margaret	18	F	Laborer	30Ap02Cx
TILLATSON, U	50	M	Laborer	30Ap02Cx
Eliza (D)	18	F	Laborer	30Ap02Cx
Isabella (D)	14	F	Laborer	30Ap02Cx
George (S)	17	M	Laborer	30Ap02Cx
EARLY, Mary	26	F	Laborer	30Ap02Cx
Laurence (S)	06	M	Child	30Ap02Cx
John (S)	04	M	Child	30Ap02Cx
Henry (S)	01	M	Child	30Ap02Cx
Ann (F)	.00	F	Infant	30Ap02Cx
FARRELL, James	29	M	Laborer	30Ap02Cx
MUNRIE, James	29	M	Laborer	30Ap02Cx
GUFFRIN, Thomas	21	M	Laborer	30Ap02Cx
DALY, Wm.	20	M	Laborer	30Ap02Cx
DOOLY, Bridget	20	F	Laborer	30Ap02Cx
WILSON, Edward	30	M	Laborer	30Ap02Cx
FITZPATRICK, Michael	30	M	Laborer	30Ap02Cx
U (W)	30	F	Wife	30Ap02Cx
Bridget (D)	05	F	Child	30Ap02Cx
WILD, Benj.	29	M	Laborer	30Ap02Cx
U (W)	24	F	Wife	30Ap02Cx
Martha (D)	06	F	Child	30Ap02Cx
John (S)	04	M	Child	30Ap02Cx
MCCORMICK, Arch.	60	M	Laborer	30Ap02Cx
U (W)	46	F	Wife	30Ap02Cx
James (S)	23	M	Laborer	30Ap02Cx
Mary (D)	20	F	Laborer	30Ap02Cx
Rose (D)	18	F	Laborer	30Ap02Cx
John (S)	13	F	Laborer	30Ap02Cx
M. (S)	10	F	Laborer	30Ap02Cx
Felix (S)	08	M	Child	30Ap02Cx
BRADY, Mary	40	F	Laborer	30Ap02Cx
Judith (D)	20	F	Laborer	30Ap02Cx
Mary (D)	18	F	Laborer	30Ap02Cx
Bryan (S)	16	M	Laborer	30Ap02Cx
John (S)	12	M	Laborer	30Ap02Cx
Thomas (S)	10	M	Laborer	30Ap02Cx
Biddy (D)	08	F	Child	30Ap02Cx
Sarah (D)	06	F	Child	30Ap02Cx
Catherine (D)	04	F	Child	30Ap02Cx
SMITH, Bridget	20	F	Laborer	30Ap02Cx
TOLHNE, Edward	45	M	Laborer	30Ap02Cx
Peggy (D)	16	F	Laborer	30Ap02Cx
Paddy (S)	22	M	Laborer	30Ap02Cx
BRADY, Andrew	40	M	Laborer	30Ap02Cx
HORAN, Joseph	25	M	Laborer	30Ap02Cx
MONGAN, Pat	26	M	Laborer	30Ap02Cx
FUREY, Arch.	26	M	Laborer	30Ap02Cx
KEAN, Mary	26	F	Laborer	30Ap02Cx
PARLON, Ann	20	F	Laborer	30Ap02Cx
MONGAN, Julia	20	F	Laborer	30Ap02Cx
Ellen	20	F	Laborer	30Ap02Cx
LOUGHRIN, Mary	18	F	Laborer	30Ap02Cx
MURPHY, James	19	M	Laborer	30Ap02Cx
GIBBS, Michl.	27	M	Laborer	30Ap02Cx
FAHONY, Dennis	26	M	Laborer	30Ap02Cx
CONWAY, Wm.	26	M	Laborer	30Ap02Cx
WELSH, Thomas	26	M	Laborer	30Ap02Cx
LUNDIGAN, Catharine	19	F	Laborer	30Ap02Cx
KENNIDY, Mary	20	F	Laborer	30Ap02Cx
DELANY, John	36	M	Laborer	30Ap02Cx
BLANFORD, Pat	30	M	Laborer	30Ap02Cx
MURRAY, Michl.	26	M	Laborer	30Ap02Cx
U (W)	23	F	Wife	30Ap02Cx
Catharine (T)	19	F	Laborer	30Ap02Cx
Maria (D)	05	F	Child	30Ap02Cx
HERN, Wm.	29	M	Laborer	30Ap02Cx
Bridget	26	F	Laborer	30Ap02Cx
HICKEY, Thos.	20	M	Laborer	30Ap02Cx
DUNFREY, Catharine	20	F	Laborer	30Ap02Cx
NEWLAND, John	20	M	Laborer	30Ap02Cx
HUGHES, Bernard	28	M	Laborer	30Ap02Cx
LYNCH, Tur.	25	M	Laborer	30Ap02Cx
Rose	22	F	Laborer	30Ap02Cx
FORD, Julia	25	F	Laborer	30Ap02Cx
KITCHER, Jer.	40	M	Laborer	30Ap02Cx
Catharine (W)	35	F	Wife	30Ap02Cx
Corns. (S)	20	M	Laborer	30Ap02Cx
Mary (D)	16	F	Laborer	30Ap02Cx
Catharine (D)	15	F	Laborer	30Ap02Cx
Nancy (D)	13	F	Laborer	30Ap02Cx
Mary (D)	12	F	Laborer	30Ap02Cx
Michl. (S)	15	M	Laborer	30Ap02Cx
John (S)	11	M	Laborer	30Ap02Cx
James (S)	09	M	Child	30Ap02Cx
DONGAN, Thomas	50	M	Laborer	30Ap02Cx
Mary (W)	50	F	Wife	30Ap02Cx
Thos. (S)	18	M	Laborer	30Ap02Cx
Matthew (S)	11	M	Laborer	30Ap02Cx
Ellen (D)	20	F	Laborer	30Ap02Cx

NAMES OF PASSENGERS		AGE	SEX	OCCUPATIONS	DATE PORT SHIP
DONGAN, Alice	(D)	16	F	Laborer	30Ap02Cx
Catharine	(D)	20	F	Laborer	30Ap02Cx
MCGOWAN, Bridget		16	F	Laborer	30Ap02Cx
John	(P)	40	M	Laborer	30Ap02Cx
Ellen		35	F	Laborer	30Ap02Cx
Martha		35	F	Laborer	30Ap02Cx
Martha	(T)	11	F	Laborer	30Ap02Cx
Thomas	(B)	09	M	Child	30Ap02Cx
James	(B)	07	M	Child	30Ap02Cx
Patrick	(B)	05	M	Child	30Ap02Cx
John	(B)	02	M	Child	30Ap02Cx
Mary-Ann	(T)	13	F	Laborer	30Ap02Cx
MALONEY, Robert		24	M	Laborer	30Ap02Cx
Sarah	(D)	21	F	Laborer	30Ap02Cx
GRIMES, John		27	M	Laborer	30Ap02Cx
WILSON, James		25	M	Laborer	30Ap02Cx
WHITE, Charly		25	M	Laborer	30Ap02Cx
FLYN, Alexander		30	M	Laborer	30Ap02Cx
Maggy		20	F	Laborer	30Ap02Cx
BLAIN, Mary-W.		11	F	Laborer	30Ap02Cx
BIRNE, John		13	M	Laborer	30Ap02Cx
John		18	M	Laborer	30Ap02Cx
MCANLEY, Daniel		19	M	Laborer	30Ap02Cx
Nancy		21	F	Laborer	30Ap02Cx
WELSH, May		23	F	Laborer	30Ap02Cx
RUSSEL, Edward		21	M	Laborer	30Ap02Cx
Catharin		20	F	Laborer	30Ap02Cx
SLAMON, Mike		24	M	Laborer	30Ap02Cx
Catharine		15	F	Laborer	30Ap02Cx
MCKINGNY, Larey		21	M	Laborer	30Ap02Cx
John		16	M	Laborer	30Ap02Cx
Sarah		12	F	Laborer	30Ap02Cx
HARFORD, Robert		52	M	Laborer	30Ap02Cx
MCIVORY, John		21	M	Laborer	30Ap02Cx
CURRY, Thomas		19	M	Laborer	30Ap02Cx
STEWART, Daniel		52	M	Laborer	30Ap02Cx
FITZGERALD, Daniel		50	M	Laborer	30Ap02Cx
Andrw.	(S)	15	M	Laborer	30Ap02Cx
Joseph	(S)	19	M	Laborer	30Ap02Cx
William	(S)	17	M	Laborer	30Ap02Cx
Ellen	(D)	20	F	Laborer	30Ap02Cx
MCILVEEN, John		18	M	Laborer	30Ap02Cx
HERNE, David		16	M	Laborer	30Ap02Cx
CASSIDY, Peter		20	M	Laborer	30Ap02Cx
ODONNELL, Dennis		35	M	Laborer	30Ap02Cx
Bridget	(W)	30	F	Wife	30Ap02Cx
Mary-Ann	(D)	07	F	Child	30Ap02Cx
Hugh	(S)	05	M	Child	30Ap02Cx
Thomas	(S)	03	M	Child	30Ap02Cx
BENNET, Mary		18	F	Laborer	30Ap02Cx
SHEAN, James		25	M	Laborer	30Ap02Cx
BROSSAN, Pat		28	M	Laborer	30Ap02Cx
Julia		24	F	Laborer	30Ap02Cx
Margaret		17	F	Laborer	30Ap02Cx
OCONNELL, Mary-F.		24	F	Laborer	30Ap02Cx
BOLAND, Pat		17	M	Laborer	30Ap02Cx
KISSAN, Pat		26	M	Laborer	30Ap02Cx
FAHY, Bridget		20	F	Laborer	30Ap02Cx
John		18	M	Laborer	30Ap02Cx
KEAN, Mary		24	F	Laborer	30Ap02Cx
HOLLOHAN, Honor		18	F	Laborer	30Ap02Cx

LUCONIA 30 APRIL 1847

From London

NAMES OF PASSENGERS		AGE	SEX	OCCUPATIONS	DATE PORT SHIP
MAKLEHAM, W.		45	M	Lawyer	30Ap21It
MILLER, J.		22	M	Farmer	30Ap21It
CONWAY, M.		25	M	Carpenter	30Ap21It

NAMES OF PASSENGERS		AGE	SEX	OCCUPATIONS	DATE PORT SHIP
CONWAY, Eliz.	(W)	25	F	Wife	30Ap21It
E.A.	(D)	02	F	Child	30Ap21It
U		.00	U	Infant	30Ap21It
PHILLIPS, Robert		36	M	Farmer	30Ap21It
MAXEN, Thomas		25	M	Baker	30Ap21It

ENTERPRISE 30 APRIL 1847

From Dublin

NAMES OF PASSENGERS		AGE	SEX	OCCUPATIONS	DATE PORT SHIP
GRESHAM, James		20	M	Laborer	30Ap20Hh
SHEA, Mary		20	F	Spinster	30Ap20Hh
Catherine		18	F	Spinster	30Ap20Hh
Jane		07	F	Child	30Ap20Hh
KEARY, Danl.		20	M	Laborer	30Ap20Hh
LOWREY, Ellen		24	F	Spinster	30Ap20Hh
MARTIN, Michael		21	M	Laborer	30Ap20Hh
U	(W)	19	F	Wife	30Ap20Hh
LEEMY, Laurence		24	M	Laborer	30Ap20Hh
FITZPATRICK, Thomas		22	M	Laborer	30Ap20Hh
DONOHOE, Patt		24	M	Laborer	30Ap20Hh
FEARY, Mary		40	F	Spinster	30Ap20Hh
Patt.	(S)	13	M	Laborer	30Ap20Hh
DONOHOE, Catherine		24	F	Spinster	30Ap20Hh
SHARKEY, Laurence		22	M	Watchmaker	30Ap20Hh
Mary		24	F	Spinster	30Ap20Hh
MCGYNNE, James		22	M	Mason	30Ap20Hh
RORKE, Michl.		20	M	Laborer	30Ap20Hh
BOLAND, Michl.		18	M	Laborer	30Ap20Hh
MCLYNNE, Mary		21	F	Spinster	30Ap20Hh
Catherine		30	F	Spinster	30Ap20Hh
WALSH, Patt		26	M	Laborer	30Ap20Hh
CALLAGHAN, John		21	M	Laborer	30Ap20Hh
U-Mrs.		30	F	Spinster	30Ap20Hh
Mary		26	F	Spinster	30Ap20Hh
FLANAGAN, M.		01	M	Child	30Ap20Hh
U		35	F	Wife	30Ap20Hh
John		30	M	Laborer	30Ap20Hh
Biddy		10	F	Spinster	30Ap20Hh
Eliza		08	F	Child	30Ap20Hh
Mary		06	F	Child	30Ap20Hh
Margt.		02	F	Child	30Ap20Hh
U		.00	U	Infant	30Ap20Hh
Died-At-Sea					
DONOHOE, Daniel		35	M	Weaver	30Ap20Hh
BUCKLEY, Thomas		36	M	Printer	30Ap20Hh
HART, U-Mrs.		53	F	Spinster	30Ap20Hh
QUEENE, Patt.		22	M	Carpenter	30Ap20Hh
QUINN, John		20	M	Laborer	30Ap20Hh
Ann		18	F	Spinster	30Ap20Hh
Rose		16	F	Spinster	30Ap20Hh
Patt.		22	M	Unknown	30Ap20Hh
Julia		00	U	Unknown	30Ap20Hh
MANGANNY, Thomas		30	M	Laborer	30Ap20Hh
U	(W)	26	F	Wife	30Ap20Hh
CURLEY, Barney		21	M	Farmer	30Ap20Hh
MURRAY, William		22	M	Farmer	30Ap20Hh
U	(W)	20	F	Wife	30Ap20Hh
DRUDY, James		45	M	Farmer	30Ap20Hh
U	(W)	40	F	Wife	30Ap20Hh
Ellen	(D)	21	F	Spinster	30Ap20Hh
Mary	(D)	19	F	Spinster	30Ap20Hh
Bridget	(D)	18	F	Spinster	30Ap20Hh
Michael	(S)	13	M	None	30Ap20Hh
Catherin	(D)	07	F	Child	30Ap20Hh
QUINN, Bridget		21	F	Glazier	30Ap20Hh
JOHNSON, Thomas		20	M	Glass Maker	30Ap20Hh
WILKENSON, Mary		36	F	Spinster	30Ap20Hh
Eliza	(W)	33	F	Wife	30Ap20Hh

NAMES OF PASSENGERS		A G E	S E X	OCCUPATIONS	DATE PORT SHIP	NAMES OF PASSENGERS		A G E	S E X	OCCUPATIONS	DATE PORT SHIP
WILKENSON, Ellen	(D)	.00	F	Infant	30Ap20Hh	CURLEY, Jane		24	F	Spinster	30Ap20Hh
MURPHY, Thomas		30	M	Astronomer	30Ap20Hh	QUINN, Michael		27	M	Farmer	30Ap20Hh
Ellen	(W)	33	F	Schms	30Ap20Hh	ENGLISH, Patt.		27	M	Farmer	30Ap20Hh
Catherine	(D)	00	F	Child	30Ap20Hh	DOWLING, Patt		33	M	Farmer	30Ap20Hh
COX, James		03	M	Child	30Ap20Hh	U	(W)	30	F	Wife	30Ap20Hh
BROWN, Essey		21	F	Spinster	30Ap20Hh	Michael	(S)	11	M	Unknown	30Ap20Hh
FYNN, Barth.		21	M	Laborer	30Ap20Hh	HARNAY, Thomas		35	M	Farmer	30Ap20Hh
MURTHA, John		27	M	Laborer	30Ap20Hh	MOORE, Martin		27	M	Farmer	30Ap20Hh
SAVAGE, U		20	F	Spinster	30Ap20Hh	U	(W)	26	F	Wife	30Ap20Hh
OBRIEN, Michael		30	M	Carpenter	30Ap20Hh	Bridget	(T)	26	F	Spinster	30Ap20Hh
U	(W)	28	F	Wife	30Ap20Hh	BARTLEY, Robt.		20	M	Weaver	30Ap20Hh
MCDERMOTT, Patt		47	M	Laborer	30Ap20Hh	U	(W)	26	F	Wife	30Ap20Hh
U	(W)	45	F	Wife	30Ap20Hh	CLARK, William		21	M	Laborer	30Ap20Hh
John	(S)	20	M	Laborer	30Ap20Hh	LENNON, U-Mrs.		20	F	Wife	30Ap20Hh
Bridget	(D)	18	F	Spinster	30Ap20Hh	William	(H)	26	M	Laborer	30Ap20Hh
Margret	(D)	16	F	Spinster	30Ap20Hh	SHARKALENY, Mark		20	M	Laborer	30Ap20Hh
Jane	(D)	13	F	None	30Ap20Hh	U	(W)	20	F	Wife	30Ap20Hh
Eliza	(D)	02	F	Child	30Ap20Hh	FISHBOURNE, Alex		24	F	Spinster	30Ap20Hh
Mary	(D)	09	F	Child	30Ap20Hh	U	(W)	24	F	Wife	30Ap20Hh
COONEY, Michael		24	M	Coppersmith	30Ap20Hh	DUDDLEY, John		30	M	Laborer	30Ap20Hh
FAHY, Edward		26	M	Tinker	30Ap20Hh	CURLEY, Patt.		35	M	Laborer	30Ap20Hh
U	(W)	35	F	Wife	30Ap20Hh	ALLEN, Charles		21	M	Laborer	30Ap20Hh
CASSIDY, Agustin		27	M	Cooper	30Ap20Hh	GORDEN, John		24	M	Laborer	30Ap20Hh
BRIEN, Tim		33	M	Cooper	30Ap20Hh	CARNEY, Patt.		20	M	Laborer	30Ap20Hh
U	(W)	28	F	Wife	30Ap20Hh	Biddy	(W)	20	F	Wife	30Ap20Hh
Ellen	(D)	01	F	Child	30Ap20Hh	Michael	(S)	01	M	Child	30Ap20Hh
Charles	(B)	28	M	Seaman	30Ap20Hh	Michael	(B)	20	M	Laborer	30Ap20Hh
U	(W)	25	F	Wife	30Ap20Hh	John	(B)	25	M	Laborer	30Ap20Hh
Thomas	(B)	30	M	Excavator	30Ap20Hh	KELLY, Asty.		20	M	Laborer	30Ap20Hh
BYRNE, Richard		24	M	Excavator	30Ap20Hh	GALLAGHER, Thomas		20	M	Laborer	30Ap20Hh
John		20	M	Laborer	30Ap20Hh	BUCKLEY, Francis		40	M	Laborer	30Ap20Hh
HEGAN, John		28	M	Laborer	30Ap20Hh	ROONEY, Mary		20	F	Servant	30Ap20Hh
DUNN, John		28	M	Laborer	30Ap20Hh	COOLEY, Thomas		20	M	Weaver	30Ap20Hh
DOOLEY, Michael		20	M	Laborer	30Ap20Hh	SALMON, Ann		20	F	Spinster	30Ap20Hh
HUSY, Thomas		30	M	Laborer	30Ap20Hh	Catherine		17	F	Spinster	30Ap20Hh
U	(W)	28	F	Wife	30Ap20Hh	MILLS, Ester		25	F	Spinster	30Ap20Hh
John	(P)	65	M	None	30Ap20Hh						
Jane	(D)	.00	F	Infant	30Ap20Hh						
LEATHAN, John		30	M	Laborer	30Ap20Hh						
U	(W)	28	F	Wife	30Ap20Hh	ELSINORE 01 MAY 1847					
George		15	M	Laborer	30Ap20Hh						
Bessey		13	F	None	30Ap20Hh	From Liverpool					
John	(S)	10	M	None	30Ap20Hh						
Edw.	(S)	07	M	Child	30Ap20Hh						
Mary	(D)	06	F	Child	30Ap20Hh						
Susanah	(D)	02	F	Child	30Ap20Hh	CASSIDY, Ann		60	F	Unknown	01Ma02Ke
EGAN, Andrew		26	M	Farmer	30Ap20Hh	Jas.		20	M	Laborer	01Ma02Ke
Martin		18	M	Farmer	30Ap20Hh	Margaret		17	F	Unknown	01Ma02Ke
U		55	F	Wi	30Ap20Hh	DOAGINS, Martin		20	M	Unknown	01Ma02Ke
Margaret		07	F	Child	30Ap20Hh	MCMANUS, Patrick		22	M	Unknown	01Ma02Ke
BERNE, Bessy		30	F	Spinster	30Ap20Hh	KERSEY, Thomas		20	M	Unknown	01Ma02Ke
DIXON, John		30	M	Farmer	30Ap20Hh	MURRAY, Patrick		20	M	Unknown	01Ma02Ke
Susan	(W)	26	F	Wife	30Ap20Hh	MCGRATH, Rose		30	F	Unknown	01Ma02Ke
Bridget		13	F	Spinster	30Ap20Hh	CUNNINGHAM, Cathe.		20	F	Unknown	01Ma02Ke
MCGRATH, John		20	M	Tailor	30Ap20Hh	COLE, Mary		20	F	Unknown	01Ma02Ke
MCDERMOTT, Michael		30	M	Tailor	30Ap20Hh	CLEARY, Thomas		22	M	Unknown	01Ma02Ke
U	(W)	24	F	Wife	30Ap20Hh	Margaret		20	F	Unknown	01Ma02Ke
Margt.	(D)	.00	F	Infant	30Ap20Hh	JENNINGS, Mary		20	F	Unknown	01Ma02Ke
CONNER, Ann		18	F	Spinster	30Ap20Hh	SHARP, Mary		19	F	Unknown	01Ma02Ke
KEEHER, Catherine		18	F	Spinster	30Ap20Hh	KEARNEY, Michl.		34	M	Unknown	01Ma02Ke
MCGLONNE, Ellen		21	F	Spinster	30Ap20Hh	Margaret	(W)	25	F	Unknown	01Ma02Ke
Danl.		24	M	Laborer	30Ap20Hh	Andrew	(S)	04	M	Child	01Ma02Ke
COSTELLO, Michael		22	M	Laborer	30Ap20Hh	Jas.	(S)	04	M	Child	01Ma02Ke
Maria		20	F	Spinster	30Ap20Hh	William	(S)	03	M	Child	01Ma02Ke
DELANEY, James		22	M	Carpenter	30Ap20Hh	Patrick	(S)	03	M	Child	01Ma02Ke
MORAN, Edward		20	M	Carpenter	30Ap20Hh	Michael	(S)	.04	M	Infant	01Ma02Ke
William		19	M	Mason	30Ap20Hh	CUNNINGHAM, John		24	M	Unknown	01Ma02Ke
CONROY, John		18	M	Mason	30Ap20Hh	Bessy		24	F	Unknown	01Ma02Ke
FAGAN, Catherine		20	F	Spinster	30Ap20Hh	MATHEWS, Margaret		20	F	Unknown	01Ma02Ke
U	(W)	22	F	Wife	30Ap20Hh	MEANY, May		20	F	Unknown	01Ma02Ke
John	(S)	02	M	Child	30Ap20Hh	OLIN, Darby		24	M	Unknown	01Ma02Ke
QUIGLEY, Thomas		21	M	Laborer	30Ap20Hh	Mary	(W)	23	F	Unknown	01Ma02Ke
Mary		18	F	Spinster	30Ap20Hh	Barny	(S)	03	M	Child	01Ma02Ke
GROGAN, Crist.		26	M	Laborer	30Ap20Hh						
CURLEY, Luke		26	M	Farmer	30Ap20Hh						

NAMES OF PASSENGERS		AGE	SEX	OCCUPATIONS	DATE PORT SHIP
OLIN, Raines	(S)	.08	M	Infant	01Ma02Ke
PHILLIPS, John		20	M	Unknown	01Ma02Ke
Mary		21	F	Unknown	01Ma02Ke
HUGHES, James		40	M	Unknown	01Ma02Ke
Margaret		25	F	Unknown	01Ma02Ke
William		18	M	Unknown	01Ma02Ke
REED, Mary-Ann		16	F	Unknown	01Ma02Ke
MCSHEE, Catherine		16	F	Unknown	01Ma02Ke
HEALY, Thomas		24	M	Unknown	01Ma02Ke
GERNEY, Bernard		24	M	Unknown	01Ma02Ke
Mary		21	F	Unknown	01Ma02Ke
SUDDEN, Thomas		24	M	Unknown	01Ma02Ke
GARRITY, Dominick		30	M	Laborer	01Ma02Ke
MORAN, Francis		28	M	Unknown	01Ma02Ke
GARRITY, John		30	M	Unknown	01Ma02Ke
MCGOWAN, Elizabeth		20	F	Unknown	01Ma02Ke
Farrell		12	M	Unknown	01Ma02Ke
MCGINN, Elizabeth		27	F	Unknown	01Ma02Ke
Catherine	(D)	08	F	Child	01Ma02Ke
Margaret	(D)	05	F	Child	01Ma02Ke
Alice	(D)	02	F	Child	01Ma02Ke
HUGHES, Patrick		20	M	Unknown	01Ma02Ke
MAHON, John		24	M	Unknown	01Ma02Ke
GILL, Catherine		20	F	Unknown	01Ma02Ke
BRADY, Mary		20	F	Unknown	01Ma02Ke
Ann		18	F	Unknown	01Ma02Ke
CASTELLO, Winnefred		20	M	Unknown	01Ma02Ke
POWERS, Ann		20	F	Unknown	01Ma02Ke
MCMAHON, Sarah		50	F	Unknown	01Ma02Ke
JOYCE, Mary		19	F	Unknown	01Ma02Ke
WALSH, Oliver		21	M	Unknown	01Ma02Ke
SAVAGE, Mary		20	F	Unknown	01Ma02Ke
LAWRENCE, Susan		20	F	Unknown	01Ma02Ke
MCCULLOUGH, Cathe.		30	F	Unknown	01Ma02Ke
LAWTON, James		20	M	Unknown	01Ma02Ke
MCCULLOUGH, Henry		07	M	Child	01Ma02Ke
HIGGIN, John		21	M	Unknown	01Ma02Ke
Ellen		20	F	Unknown	01Ma02Ke
Mary		19	F	Unknown	01Ma02Ke
OHARA, Catherine		03	F	Child	01Ma02Ke
MCGOWAN, Patrick		09	M	Child	01Ma02Ke
Mary		07	F	Child	01Ma02Ke
MCSHEE, Edw.		12	M	Unknown	01Ma02Ke
SINNEN, James		30	M	Unknown	01Ma02Ke
Elizabeth	(W)	27	F	Unknown	01Ma02Ke
Ann	(D)	02	F	Child	01Ma02Ke
Elizabeth	(D)	02	F	Child	01Ma02Ke
James	(S)	01	M	Child	01Ma02Ke
MURPHY, Edward		24	M	Unknown	01Ma02Ke
TIFFANY, Margaret		15	F	Unknown	01Ma02Ke
KENNEDY, William		20	M	Unknown	01Ma02Ke
HAMILTON, Jas.		20	M	Unknown	01Ma02Ke
DODDS, Thomas		24	M	Unknown	01Ma02Ke
DOOD, Mary		20	F	Unknown	01Ma02Ke
OHARA, Hugh		21	M	Unknown	01Ma02Ke
Lawrence		24	M	Unknown	01Ma02Ke
MURRY, Ellen		20	F	Unknown	01Ma02Ke
KEENAN, Jas.		22	M	Unknown	01Ma02Ke
OHARA, Hugh		24	M	Unknown	01Ma02Ke
BOWMAN, Thos.		19	M	Unknown	01Ma02Ke
WALKER, Thos.		30	M	Unknown	01Ma02Ke
MOULTEN, Ann		28	F	Unknown	01Ma02Ke
MAUNSELL, William		22	M	Unknown	01Ma02Ke
HAUGHY, Paul		30	M	Unknown	01Ma02Ke
John		32	M	Unknown	01Ma02Ke
DAVIS, Ernest		20	M	Unknown	01Ma02Ke
MCMAHON, John		18	M	Unknown	01Ma02Ke
KELLY, Patrick		24	M	Unknown	01Ma02Ke
Margaret		20	F	Unknown	01Ma02Ke
BRADLY, Bridget		20	F	Unknown	01Ma02Ke
HAGERTY, Susan		20	F	Unknown	01Ma02Ke
MADDEN, Isabella		22	F	Unknown	01Ma02Ke
KEARNEY, Mary		19	F	Unknown	01Ma02Ke
KENNEDY, Margaret		18	F	Unknown	01Ma02Ke
MCCAFFRY, Susan		20	F	Unknown	01Ma02Ke
MCCAFFRY, Mary		07	F	Child	01Ma02Ke
MCCANN, Rose-Ann		18	F	Unknown	01Ma02Ke
Mary		20	F	Unknown	01Ma02Ke
SARLIN, John		24	M	Unknown	01Ma02Ke
SAILLY, John		21	M	Unknown	01Ma02Ke
HIGGINS, Michael		18	M	Unknown	01Ma02Ke
JENNINGS, Ellen		21	F	Unknown	01Ma02Ke
WHITE, Edward		21	M	Unknown	01Ma02Ke
CEFF, Patrick		30	M	Unknown	01Ma02Ke
Sarah		27	F	Unknown	01Ma02Ke
Margaret		21	F	Unknown	01Ma02Ke
HAUGHY, Michael		40	M	Unknown	01Ma02Ke
OHARA, John		26	M	Unknown	01Ma02Ke
MCLEAN, Jas.		25	M	Unknown	01Ma02Ke
LOGAN, John		28	M	Unknown	01Ma02Ke
MCKEAGER, Rob.		20	M	Unknown	01Ma02Ke
BROWN, Thomas		21	M	Unknown	01Ma02Ke
MONTGOMERY, Smith		20	M	Unknown	01Ma02Ke
Saml.		19	M	Unknown	01Ma02Ke
MCIVOR, James		24	M	Laborer	01Ma02Ke
ADAMS, William		19	M	Unknown	01Ma02Ke
DUGGON, Ellen		20	F	Unknown	01Ma02Ke
MCCURDY, Danl.		24	M	Unknown	01Ma02Ke
Jas.		23	M	Unknown	01Ma02Ke
Mary		20	F	Unknown	01Ma02Ke
Elizabeth		03	F	Child	01Ma02Ke
Mathew		01	M	Child	01Ma02Ke
KEGAN, Catherine		.08	F	Infant	01Ma02Ke
HAMILTON, William		27	M	Unknown	01Ma02Ke
Matilda		22	F	Unknown	01Ma02Ke
MCSAFFERY, Dennis		20	M	Unknown	01Ma02Ke
CARNEY, Jas.		21	M	Unknown	01Ma02Ke
DORY, John		20	M	Unknown	01Ma02Ke
WIEL, William		25	M	Unknown	01Ma02Ke
MCGOWAN, Patrick		20	M	Unknown	01Ma02Ke
BROWN, Ally		20	F	Unknown	01Ma02Ke
Patrick		19	M	Unknown	01Ma02Ke
CARLIN, Ben.		20	M	Unknown	01Ma02Ke
ROLLAND, Francis		20	M	Farmer	01Ma02Ke
Mary		20	F	Unknown	01Ma02Ke
Catherine		18	F	Unknown	01Ma02Ke
WALSH, Cathe.		45	F	Unknown	01Ma02Ke
Mary		30	F	Unknown	01Ma02Ke
Honora		18	F	Unknown	01Ma02Ke
William		21	M	Unknown	01Ma02Ke
REYNOLDS, Catherine		27	F	Unknown	01Ma02Ke
QUIGBY, Thomas		26	M	Unknown	01Ma02Ke
MCGRINTIN, John		28	M	Unknown	01Ma02Ke
GILLIS, John		25	M	Unknown	01Ma02Ke
Betsey	(W)	23	F	Unknown	01Ma02Ke
Jane	(D)	02	F	Child	01Ma02Ke
Patrick	(S)	.08	M	Infant	01Ma02Ke
DONOHOE, Thos.		35	M	Unknown	01Ma02Ke
Mary	(W)	35	F	Unknown	01Ma02Ke
Margaret	(D)	03	F	Child	01Ma02Ke
Mary	(D)	.08	F	Infant	01Ma02Ke
NALLY, Judy		18	F	Unknown	01Ma02Ke
HUGHES, Michl.		18	M	Unknown	01Ma02Ke
Margaret		20	F	Unknown	01Ma02Ke
DREW, Catherine		24	F	Unknown	01Ma02Ke
MCFAILOR, Chas.		26	M	Laborer	01Ma02Ke
LINCH, Peter		33	M	Unknown	01Ma02Ke
MCFAILOR, Mary		24	F	Unknown	01Ma02Ke
LINCH, Mary		20	F	Unknown	01Ma02Ke
Catherine		18	F	Unknown	01Ma02Ke
RORKE, Bridget		21	F	Unknown	01Ma02Ke
Bridget		22	F	Unknown	01Ma02Ke
ALPIN, Michael		24	M	Unknown	01Ma02Ke
SHIELDS, Patrick		24	M	Unknown	01Ma02Ke
DELAN, John		22	M	Unknown	01Ma02Ke
HALPIN, Thos.		12	M	Unknown	01Ma02Ke
KEENAN, Thomas		40	M	Unknown	01Ma02Ke
PLUNKET, John		25	M	Unknown	01Ma02Ke
DUFFY, Felix		24	M	Unknown	01Ma02Ke
Lawrence		30	M	Unknown	01Ma02Ke

NAMES OF PASSENGERS		AGE	SEX	OCCUPATIONS	DATE PORT SHIP
DUFFY, Margaret		26	F	Unknown	01Ma02Ke
Biddy		20	F	Unknown	01Ma02Ke
Ann		15	F	Unknown	01Ma02Ke
BARREN, Jas.		20	M	Unknown	01Ma02Ke
GORLICK, Henry		29	M	Unknown	01Ma02Ke
LEAN, Henry		20	M	Unknown	01Ma02Ke
ELLERY, Michl.		18	M	Unknown	01Ma02Ke
MCKENNA, John		39	M	Unknown	01Ma02Ke
Mary	(W)	39	F	Unknown	01Ma02Ke
Bernard	(S)	10	M	Unknown	01Ma02Ke
Jonah	(S)	06	M	Child	01Ma02Ke
Margaret	(D)	04	F	Child	01Ma02Ke
Elizabeth	(D)	02	F	Child	01Ma02Ke
Margaret		60	F	Child	01Ma02Ke
DOLAN, Lawrence		30	M	Child	01Ma02Ke
Mary	(W)	30	F	Child	01Ma02Ke
Ann	(D)	07	F	Child	01Ma02Ke
Catherine	(D)	03	F	Child	01Ma02Ke
Patrick	(S)	.06	M	Infant	01Ma02Ke
MCSINN, Patrick		30	M	Unknown	01Ma02Ke
SCULLINS, Rose-Ann		20	F	Unknown	01Ma02Ke
DEVLIN, Ellen		30	F	Unknown	01Ma02Ke
Ann		20	F	Unknown	01Ma02Ke
FAIRLY, Mary		42	F	Unknown	01Ma02Ke
Thos.	(S)	22	M	Unknown	01Ma02Ke
Rebecca	(D)	17	F	Unknown	01Ma02Ke
FARLEY, Hugh		06	M	Child	01Ma02Ke
COYLE, Mary		22	F	Unknown	01Ma02Ke
MURPHY, Cornelius		40	M	Laborer	01Ma02Ke
Hannah	(W)	28	F	Unknown	01Ma02Ke
Jas.	(S)	03	M	Child	01Ma02Ke
Jas		26	M	Unknown	01Ma02Ke
Catherine		26	F	Unknown	01Ma02Ke
COLEMAN, Patrick		20	M	Unknown	01Ma02Ke
CALLIGHAN, Jas.		25	M	Unknown	01Ma02Ke
MCCANN, Jas.		22	M	Unknown	01Ma02Ke
DOLAN, Jas.		50	M	Unknown	01Ma02Ke
LEONARD, Hugh		22	M	Unknown	01Ma02Ke
MCGOVERN, Barry		21	M	Unknown	01Ma02Ke
MCCUE, John		20	M	Unknown	01Ma02Ke
DOLAN, Owen		19	M	Unknown	01Ma02Ke
Peggy		20	F	Unknown	01Ma02Ke
MCMANUS, Curdy		19	M	Unknown	01Ma02Ke
TORNEY, Michael		30	M	Unknown	01Ma02Ke
Biddy	(W)	30	F	Unknown	01Ma02Ke
Mary	(D)	10	F	Unknown	01Ma02Ke
Ellen	(D)	07	F	Child	01Ma02Ke
Michl.	(S)	04	M	Child	01Ma02Ke
NALLY, John		30	M	Unknown	01Ma02Ke
Biddy	(W)	30	F	Unknown	01Ma02Ke
Mary	(D)	.06	F	Infant	01Ma02Ke
Edward		25	M	Unknown	01Ma02Ke
CUNNINGHAM, Peggy		21	F	Unknown	01Ma02Ke
DUFFY, Michl.		19	M	Unknown	01Ma02Ke
MCGREA, Matilda		20	F	Unknown	01Ma02Ke
Ann		18	F	Unknown	01Ma02Ke
MULLAN, John		22	M	Unknown	01Ma02Ke
MCNEAL, Biddy		20	F	Unknown	01Ma02Ke
MCALLY, Danl.		20	M	Unknown	01Ma02Ke
Archy		13	M	Unknown	01Ma02Ke

ROBINSON 04 MAY 1847

From Newry

NAMES OF PASSENGERS		AGE	SEX	OCCUPATIONS	DATE PORT SHIP
HAUGHEY, Simon		50	M	Laborer	04Ma19Mr
Simon-Jr.	(S)	20	M	Laborer	04Ma19Mr
Catherine	(D)	23	F	Unknown	04Ma19Mr
HAMILTON, John		20	M	Laborer	04Ma19Mr

NAMES OF PASSENGERS		AGE	SEX	OCCUPATIONS	DATE PORT SHIP
DEANY, Felix		26	M	Laborer	04Ma19Mr
CALLAGHAN, Bernard		22	M	Laborer	04Ma19Mr
OHARA, Hugh		23	M	Laborer	04Ma19Mr
HAGGARD, Saml.		40	M	Mechanic	04Ma19Mr
FRASER, John		20	M	Mechanic	04Ma19Mr
Richard		18	M	Mechanic	04Ma19Mr
ELLIOTT, William		35	M	Farmer	04Ma19Mr
Letitia	(W)	35	F	Unknown	04Ma19Mr
Richard	(S)	10	M	Unknown	04Ma19Mr
Sarah	(D)	07	F	Child	04Ma19Mr
James	(S)	04	M	Child	04Ma19Mr
Jane	(D)	02	F	Child	04Ma19Mr
FORSYTHE, John		28	M	Merchant	04Ma19Mr
Mary		23	F	Unknown	04Ma19Mr
Martha		21	F	Unknown	04Ma19Mr
HAWTHORNE, Thos.		21	M	Mechanic	04Ma19Mr
FITZPATRICK, Margt.		40	F	Unknown	04Ma19Mr
Elizabeth		17	F	Unknown	04Ma19Mr
DALY, Patrick		17	M	Laborer	04Ma19Mr
AWA, Mary		16	F	Unknown	04Ma19Mr
RALSON, Ann		20	F	Unknown	04Ma19Mr
HANLON, Patrick		24	M	Mechanic	04Ma19Mr
CARBERRY, Jas.		25	M	Mechanic	04Ma19Mr
MCHENNA, Margt.		18	F	Unknown	04Ma19Mr
Francis		17	M	Mechanic	04Ma19Mr
MINTURN, John		30	M	Farmer	04Ma19Mr
Mary	(W)	22	F	Unknown	04Ma19Mr
Mary-Ann	(D)	01	F	Child	04Ma19Mr
MARTIN, William		23	M	Farmer	04Ma19Mr
MCGRAVY, Mary		40	F	Unknown	04Ma19Mr
Owen	(S)	20	M	Unknown	04Ma19Mr
Maria	(D)	17	F	Unknown	04Ma19Mr
Catherine	(D)	15	F	Unknown	04Ma19Mr
John	(S)	13	M	Unknown	04Ma19Mr
Bridget	(D)	10	F	Unknown	04Ma19Mr
MCCABE, Rose		40	F	Unknown	04Ma19Mr
John	(S)	14	M	Unknown	04Ma19Mr
James	(S)	12	M	Unknown	04Ma19Mr
Alice	(D)	10	F	Unknown	04Ma19Mr
Patrick	(S)	06	M	Child	04Ma19Mr
Mary		00	F	Unknown	04Ma19Mr
BRENNAN, Mary		19	F	Unknown	04Ma19Mr
COLGAN, Mary		40	F	Unknown	04Ma19Mr
Mary	(D)	18	F	Unknown	04Ma19Mr
MCKEFFEY, John		25	M	Mechanic	04Ma19Mr
James		17	M	Mechanic	04Ma19Mr
HUGHES, Daniel		32	M	Laborer	04Ma19Mr
Mary		28	F	Unknown	04Ma19Mr
BRENNAN, Wm.		19	M	Mechanic	04Ma19Mr
Rose		20	F	Unknown	04Ma19Mr
Cathl.		22	F	Unknown	04Ma19Mr
LARKIN, Bridget		21	F	Unknown	04Ma19Mr
JOHNSTON, Joseph		35	M	Farmer	04Ma19Mr
Elizabeth		30	F	Unknown	04Ma19Mr
Margaret		35	F	Unknown	04Ma19Mr
Robert		25	M	Laborer	04Ma19Mr
James		06	M	Child	04Ma19Mr
Eliza		04	F	Child	04Ma19Mr
Robert		01	M	Child	04Ma19Mr
SINE, Harriet		17	F	Unknown	04Ma19Mr
SINNS, Ann-Jane		20	F	Unknown	04Ma19Mr
MCGLONNE, Jas.		21	M	Mechanic	04Ma19Mr
MCCLEVEN, Wm.		40	M	Laborer	04Ma19Mr
MAHON, Terence		20	M	Unknown	04Ma19Mr
MCCULLOUGH, Mary		50	F	Unknown	04Ma19Mr
George	(H)	50	M	Laborer	04Ma19Mr
Samuel	(S)	23	M	Laborer	04Ma19Mr
William	(S)	20	M	Laborer	04Ma19Mr
Thomas	(S)	16	M	Laborer	04Ma19Mr
John	(S)	13	M	Laborer	04Ma19Mr
LOWE, James		20	M	Farmer	04Ma19Mr
MONTAGUE, John		20	M	Laborer	04Ma19Mr
MCGLINN, Hugh		20	M	Laborer	04Ma19Mr
MCCRATHALL, Cathl.		18	F	Unknown	04Ma19Mr
BRADLEY, James		30	M	Laborer	04Ma19Mr

NAMES OF PASSENGERS	AGE	SEX	OCCUPATIONS	DATE PORT SHIP
OWENS, Neal	30	M	Laborer	04Ma19Mr
MULLINS, James	32	M	Mechanic	04Ma19Mr
MCHENNA, Catherine	20	F	Unknown	04Ma19Mr
Pat.	01	M	Child	04Ma19Mr
CAMPBELL, John	50	M	Mechanic	04Ma19Mr
CULLEN, John	22	M	Laborer	04Ma19Mr
HANLON, John	22	M	Laborer	04Ma19Mr
Betty	20	F	Unknown	04Ma19Mr
REILLY, John	21	M	Laborer	04Ma19Mr
Mary (W)	20	F	Unknown	04Ma19Mr
Bridget (D)	01	F	Child	04Ma19Mr
WOODS, Lawrence	28	M	Laborer	04Ma19Mr
Ann (W)	21	F	Unknown	04Ma19Mr
Mary (D)	01	F	Child	04Ma19Mr
MCKEVILL, Owen	22	M	Laborer	04Ma19Mr
BOYLE, Thomas	25	M	Laborer	04Ma19Mr
Ann (W)	25	F	Unknown	04Ma19Mr
James (S)	03	M	Child	04Ma19Mr
OHARA, Ann	12	F	Unknown	04Ma19Mr
MCKENNA, Peter	38	M	Laborer	04Ma19Mr

FRANCIS-WATTS 04 MAY 1847

From Galway

NAMES OF PASSENGERS	AGE	SEX	OCCUPATIONS	DATE PORT SHIP
WHEELER, John	50	M	Mechanic	04Ma11Nc
John-Jr. (S)	20	M	Mechanic	04Ma11Nc
James (S)	15	M	Mechanic	04Ma11Nc
Richd. (S)	23	M	Mechanic	04Ma11Nc
Benj. (S)	13	M	Mechanic	04Ma11Nc
Mary	33	F	Unknown	04Ma11Nc
KENNEDY, Michl.	26	M	Mechanic	04Ma11Nc
Margt.	24	F	Unknown	04Ma11Nc
CUNNEFFE, John	28	M	Mechanic	04Ma11Nc
Biddy	23	F	Unknown	04Ma11Nc
Patt	26	M	Mechanic	04Ma11Nc
Michl.	20	M	Mechanic	04Ma11Nc
MORAN, John	19	M	Mechanic	04Ma11Nc
CONNILY, Thos.	18	M	Mechanic	04Ma11Nc
MORAN, Thos.	22	M	Mechanic	04Ma11Nc
Ann	18	F	Unknown	04Ma11Nc
CANICK, Richd.	23	M	Mechanic	04Ma11Nc
LYDEN, Bartley	23	M	Mechanic	04Ma11Nc
ATHEY, Ned	20	M	Mechanic	04Ma11Nc
Bridget	22	F	Unknown	04Ma11Nc
FLAHERTY, Rodger	28	M	Mechanic	04Ma11Nc
MANIN, Patt	21	M	Mechanic	04Ma11Nc
FOHEY, John	20	M	Mechanic	04Ma11Nc
QUINN, Michael	22	M	Mechanic	04Ma11Nc
Martin	25	M	Mechanic	04Ma11Nc
Peter	20	M	Mechanic	04Ma11Nc
Thos.	12	M	None	04Ma11Nc
John	02	M	Child	04Ma11Nc
Kitty	16	F	Unknown	04Ma11Nc
LEONARD, Cathr.	40	F	Unknown	04Ma11Nc
FURY, Martin	21	M	Farmer	04Ma11Nc
CURRAN, John	27	M	Farmer	04Ma11Nc
PENDEGRAST, Pat	21	M	Farmer	04Ma11Nc
John	18	M	Farmer	04Ma11Nc
SOLAN, Pat	37	M	Farmer	04Ma11Nc
Martin (S)	08	M	Child	04Ma11Nc
John (S)	06	M	Child	04Ma11Nc
Patt (S)	03	M	Child	04Ma11Nc
Peggy (W)	25	F	Unknown	04Ma11Nc
FITZPATRICK, Michael	26	M	Farmer	04Ma11Nc
Peter	19	M	Farmer	04Ma11Nc
MALEY, Michael	28	M	Farmer	04Ma11Nc
Nancy	18	F	Unknown	04Ma11Nc
John	.05	M	Infant	04Ma11Nc

NAMES OF PASSENGERS	AGE	SEX	OCCUPATIONS	DATE PORT SHIP
KYNE, Peter	25	M	Farmer	04Ma11Nc
NEWELL, Herbert	19	M	Farmer	04Ma11Nc
MURRAY, Thos.	25	M	Farmer	04Ma11Nc
GALLAGHER, Cathr.	14	F	Unknown	04Ma11Nc
CUNNOFFER, Kitty	18	F	Unknown	04Ma11Nc
QUINN, Honor	25	M	Unknown	04Ma11Nc
CUNNOFFER, Nancy	24	F	Unknown	04Ma11Nc

FEROZEPORE 04 MAY 1847

From Liverpool

NAMES OF PASSENGERS	AGE	SEX	OCCUPATIONS	DATE PORT SHIP
RONY, B.	60	M	Laborer	04Ma02Nd
Cath.	21	F	Unknown	04Ma02Nd
Mgt.	20	F	Unknown	04Ma02Nd
Saml.	15	M	None	04Ma02Nd
Alice	13	F	None	04Ma02Nd
Wm.	11	M	None	04Ma02Nd
Sarah	07	F	Child	04Ma02Nd
Mgt.	01	F	Child	04Ma02Nd
DOONY, J.	26	M	Unknown	04Ma02Nd
CORBITT, P.	26	M	Unknown	04Ma02Nd
Julie	28	F	Unknown	04Ma02Nd
MERY, Cath.	20	F	Unknown	04Ma02Nd
HOGAN, D.	16	M	None	04Ma02Nd
Cath.	14	F	Unknown	04Ma02Nd
FELAN, P.	20	M	Unknown	04Ma02Nd
Thos.	20	M	Unknown	04Ma02Nd
SMITH, Hale	18	F	Unknown	04Ma02Nd
SENOHE, C.	18	M	Unknown	04Ma02Nd
Cath.	20	F	Unknown	04Ma02Nd
Dan.	27	M	Unknown	04Ma02Nd
Cath.	27	F	Unknown	04Ma02Nd
MCCARTY, J.	39	M	Unknown	04Ma02Nd
Chart.	20	F	Unknown	04Ma02Nd
Andrew	28	M	Unknown	04Ma02Nd
Ann	27	F	Unknown	04Ma02Nd
J.	39	M	Unknown	04Ma02Nd
Charlott	20	F	Unknown	04Ma02Nd
Andrew	20	M	Unknown	04Ma02Nd
Ann	26	F	Unknown	04Ma02Nd
John	38	M	Unknown	04Ma02Nd
Ann	05	F	Child	04Ma02Nd
ROACH, Biddy	27	F	Unknown	04Ma02Nd
DOWN, Hannah	22	F	Unknown	04Ma02Nd
WHITE, Hannah	21	F	Unknown	04Ma02Nd
ROGGEN, J.	24	M	Unknown	04Ma02Nd
Hannah	25	F	Unknown	04Ma02Nd
HEARY, J.	29	M	Unknown	04Ma02Nd
Rich.	22	M	Unknown	04Ma02Nd
Bgt.	28	F	Unknown	04Ma02Nd
Cath.	03	F	Child	04Ma02Nd
THOMAS, M.	24	M	Unknown	04Ma02Nd
REILY, T.	24	M	Laborer	04Ma02Nd
CARY, J.	26	M	Unknown	04Ma02Nd
LENAH, J.	24	M	Unknown	04Ma02Nd
POAN, G.	18	M	Unknown	04Ma02Nd
W.	20	M	Unknown	04Ma02Nd
ENGLISH, Ally	20	F	Unknown	04Ma02Nd
BOYLE, T.	20	M	Unknown	04Ma02Nd
SULLIVAN, D.	30	M	Unknown	04Ma02Nd
U (W)	30	F	Unknown	04Ma02Nd
SWEENEY, P.	36	M	Unknown	04Ma02Nd
FREENEY, P.	30	M	Unknown	04Ma02Nd
JACKSON, G.	38	M	Unknown	04Ma02Nd
GUNN, M.	24	M	Unknown	04Ma02Nd
FRENEY, J.	22	M	Unknown	04Ma02Nd
LINCHEN, A.	25	M	Unknown	04Ma02Nd
Jane	19	F	Unknown	04Ma02Nd

NAMES OF PASSENGERS	(W/S/D/M)	AGE	SEX	OCCUPATIONS	DATE PORT SHIP
LINCHEN, Mich.		10	M	Child	04Ma02Nd
HIGGIN, P.		27	M	Unknown	04Ma02Nd
U		19	F	Unknown	04Ma02Nd
LANE, P.		21	M	Unknown	04Ma02Nd
DALY, T.		28	M	Unknown	04Ma02Nd
Cath.		20	F	Unknown	04Ma02Nd
Mary		30	F	Unknown	04Ma02Nd
LYNCH, Ann		29	F	Unknown	04Ma02Nd
MONDAY, D.		22	M	Unknown	04Ma02Nd
MCDONALD, B.		20	M	Unknown	04Ma02Nd
Mlore		18	F	Unknown	04Ma02Nd
SAMPSON, T.		31	F	Unknown	04Ma02Nd
Saml.		22	M	Unknown	04Ma02Nd
Jane		21	F	Unknown	04Ma02Nd
CLYDE, J.		24	M	Unknown	04Ma02Nd
RABB, A.		10	M	Child	04Ma02Nd
MCTOOKE, J.		25	M	Unknown	04Ma02Nd
MCGINLY, C.		24	M	Unknown	04Ma02Nd
BYRNE, M.		21	M	Unknown	04Ma02Nd
CUNNINGHAM, D.		24	M	Unknown	04Ma02Nd
DUNLEVY, F.		26	M	Unknown	04Ma02Nd
CUNGER, Sarah		18	F	Unknown	04Ma02Nd
CARR, C.		22	F	Unknown	04Ma02Nd
MCSHARK, C.		23	M	Unknown	04Ma02Nd
DUGGAN, P.		20	M	Unknown	04Ma02Nd
JOHNSTON, Ann		19	F	Unknown	04Ma02Nd
MALONE, Peggy		25	F	Unknown	04Ma02Nd
GARY, Mgt.		20	F	Unknown	04Ma02Nd
OATS, Biddy		21	F	Unknown	04Ma02Nd
CLUCKER, P.		20	M	Laborer	04Ma02Nd
ODONELL, Jane		20	F	Unknown	04Ma02Nd
COYE, Ellz.		20	F	Unknown	04Ma02Nd
SHORT, C.		20	M	Unknown	04Ma02Nd
MCHUGH, Ann		20	F	Unknown	04Ma02Nd
MCHESEY, Cath.		21	F	Unknown	04Ma02Nd
BELTON, Bld.		15	F	Unknown	04Ma02Nd
FAY, Cath.		21	F	Unknown	04Ma02Nd
MCDERMOTT, P.		08	M	Child	04Ma02Nd
CARROLL, A.		20	M	Unknown	04Ma02Nd
BRADY, J.		20	M	Unknown	04Ma02Nd
RENRY, E.		20	M	Unknown	04Ma02Nd
Bgt.		13	F	Unknown	04Ma02Nd
GURN, Ellen		20	F	Unknown	04Ma02Nd
MCCABE, J.		20	M	Unknown	04Ma02Nd
Ann		18	F	Unknown	04Ma02Nd
NORRIS, P.		20	M	Unknown	04Ma02Nd
Pat		15	M	None	04Ma02Nd
HANEY, D.		21	M	Unknown	04Ma02Nd
ODONNEL, A.		22	M	Unknown	04Ma02Nd
WARN, Mary		20	F	Unknown	04Ma02Nd
RODEN, M.		20	F	Unknown	04Ma02Nd
RED, T.		30	M	Unknown	04Ma02Nd
MEGHAN, N.		25	M	Unknown	04Ma02Nd
MALONEY, C.		27	M	Unknown	04Ma02Nd
CORLEY, J.		23	M	Unknown	04Ma02Nd
WARNTON, W.		35	M	Unknown	04Ma02Nd
Bgt.	(W)	34	F	Unknown	04Ma02Nd
Andrew	(S)	10	M	None	04Ma02Nd
Timothy	(S)	07	M	None	04Ma02Nd
Louisa	(D)	05	F	None	04Ma02Nd
Thos.	(S)	02	M	None	04Ma02Nd
KEALY, Bgt.		50	F	Unknown	04Ma02Nd
DOWNY, T.		30	M	Unknown	04Ma02Nd
TOURIS, P.		30	M	Unknown	04Ma02Nd
Peggy	(W)	30	F	Unknown	04Ma02Nd
Jas.	(S)	01	M	Child	04Ma02Nd
MCKEY, Mgt.		24	F	Unknown	04Ma02Nd
MURPHY, D.		24	M	Unknown	04Ma02Nd
TURNER, Nancy		33	F	Unknown	04Ma02Nd
Lawrence	(S)	13	M	None	04Ma02Nd
James	(S)	10	M	Child	04Ma02Nd
Patk.	(S)	07	M	Child	04Ma02Nd
BRYAN, J.		26	M	Unknown	04Ma02Nd
Owen		24	M	Unknown	04Ma02Nd
SEBEYER, Cath.		20	F	Unknown	04Ma02Nd
GLANCY, J.		20	M	Unknown	04Ma02Nd
Mgt.	(M)	50	F	Unknown	04Ma02Nd
Nora		19	F	Unknown	04Ma02Nd
Danl.		10	M	Child	04Ma02Nd
MCCARTHY, O.		21	M	Unknown	04Ma02Nd
GREGORY, H.		21	M	Unknown	04Ma02Nd
Rosey		24	F	Unknown	04Ma02Nd
MCANESPIE, Isa.		21	F	Unknown	04Ma02Nd
LYONS, R.		25	M	Unknown	04Ma02Nd
ROWE, P.		20	M	Unknown	04Ma02Nd
MCDONELL, S.		20	M	Unknown	04Ma02Nd
ROWE, M.		20	M	Unknown	04Ma02Nd
MCDOWD, Bridget		20	F	Unknown	04Ma02Nd
FARMER, Sally		20	F	Unknown	04Ma02Nd
Julia		20	F	Unknown	04Ma02Nd
EARLY, W.		20	M	Unknown	04Ma02Nd
Marc		18	M	Unknown	04Ma02Nd
DONNELLY, O.		25	M	Unknown	04Ma02Nd
MURPHY, J.		30	M	Unknown	04Ma02Nd
Biddy		11	F	Child	04Ma02Nd
MCSHEA, Mary		30	F	Unknown	04Ma02Nd
Pat		01	M	Child	04Ma02Nd
FANAGAN, Mgt.		60	F	Unknown	04Ma02Nd
Owen		25	M	Unknown	04Ma02Nd
Bdgt.		18	F	Unknown	04Ma02Nd
Cath.		16	F	Unknown	04Ma02Nd
MCGINN, P.		24	M	Unknown	04Ma02Nd
LOGAN, J.		30	M	Unknown	04Ma02Nd
RILEY, J.		30	M	Unknown	04Ma02Nd
LOGAN, J.		06	M	Child	04Ma02Nd
SHEELY, P.		27	M	Unknown	04Ma02Nd
MURPHY, P.		22	M	Unknown	04Ma02Nd
KELLY, Bgt.		20	F	Unknown	04Ma02Nd
HURNS, Mary		21	F	Unknown	04Ma02Nd
J.		22	M	Unknown	04Ma02Nd
CALLEN, D.		22	M	Laborer	04Ma02Nd
Pat		24	M	Unknown	04Ma02Nd
CARROLAN, F.		40	M	Unknown	04Ma02Nd
Ann		40	F	Unknown	04Ma02Nd
Mary		25	F	Unknown	04Ma02Nd
Henry		24	M	Unknown	04Ma02Nd
Rose		28	F	Unknown	04Ma02Nd
BRANNAN, Cath.		40	F	Unknown	04Ma02Nd
Mary	(D)	20	F	Unknown	04Ma02Nd
Biddy	(D)	13	F	Unknown	04Ma02Nd
Mary	(D)	10	F	Child	04Ma02Nd
KENFEUR, J.		30	M	Unknown	04Ma02Nd
MELLIN, M.		25	M	Unknown	04Ma02Nd
Thos.		21	M	Unknown	04Ma02Nd
Ellen		10	F	Child	04Ma02Nd
FITZSIMON, T.		25	M	Unknown	04Ma02Nd
Stephen		20	M	Unknown	04Ma02Nd
MAHON, J.		25	M	Unknown	04Ma02Nd
Mich.		24	M	Unknown	04Ma02Nd
DUNN, E.		23	M	Unknown	04Ma02Nd
DEVEAN, Cath.		21	F	Unknown	04Ma02Nd
FARRELLY, P.		50	M	Unknown	04Ma02Nd
Rose		19	F	Unknown	04Ma02Nd
ONEIL, G.		32	M	Unknown	04Ma02Nd
Jas.		15	M	None	04Ma02Nd
MCALAN, J.		20	M	Unknown	04Ma02Nd
Cath.		20	F	Unknown	04Ma02Nd
WHEELER, M.		26	M	Unknown	04Ma02Nd
WARD, J.		23	M	Unknown	04Ma02Nd
SPELLMAN, M.		26	M	Unknown	04Ma02Nd
Ann		23	F	Unknown	04Ma02Nd
DOCKSY, J.		26	M	Unknown	04Ma02Nd
BRESLIN, M.		23	M	Unknown	04Ma02Nd
MCGLINE, Cath.		22	F	Unknown	04Ma02Nd
MURPHY, U-Mrs.		24	F	Wife	04Ma02Nd
KELLY, P.		32	M	Unknown	04Ma02Nd
Mary	(W)	30	F	Unknown	04Ma02Nd
Pat	(S)	03	M	Child	04Ma02Nd
Thos.		24	M	Unknown	04Ma02Nd
Mary		21	F	Unknown	04Ma02Nd

NAMES OF PASSENGERS		AGE	SEX	OCCUPATIONS	DATE PORT SHIP	NAMES OF PASSENGERS		AGE	SEX	OCCUPATIONS	DATE PORT SHIP
BULEN, T.		20	M	Unknown	04Ma02Nd	WARD, T.		60	M	Unknown	04Ma02Nd
MCGREELY, Bdgt.		24	F	Unknown	04Ma02Nd	Mary	(W)	40	F	Unknown	04Ma02Nd
CALDEN, Ellen		08	F	Child	04Ma02Nd	Mich.	(S)	24	M	Unknown	04Ma02Nd
Pat		11	M	None	04Ma02Nd	Thos.	(S)	10	M	Child	04Ma02Nd
RILEY, Cath.		25	F	Unknown	04Ma02Nd	CANECHLIN, P.		20	M	Unknown	04Ma02Nd
Ann		15	F	Unknown	04Ma02Nd	CONRY, P.		23	M	Unknown	04Ma02Nd
Jas.		09	M	Child	04Ma02Nd	Sally		20	F	Unknown	04Ma02Nd
Mich.		13	M	None	04Ma02Nd	KENNA, P.		20	M	Unknown	04Ma02Nd
HICKEY, C.		25	M	Laborer	04Ma02Nd	Julia		20	F	Unknown	04Ma02Nd
MCGAUGHAN, J.		25	M	Unknown	04Ma02Nd	Martha		30	F	Unknown	04Ma02Nd
RAFFERTY, Sarah		18	F	Unknown	04Ma02Nd	Ann		18	F	Unknown	04Ma02Nd
Rob.		05	M	Child	04Ma02Nd	Ann		17	F	Unknown	04Ma02Nd
MCCANN, J.		25	M	Unknown	04Ma02Nd	MAHONY, J.		25	M	Laborer	04Ma02Nd
Mgt.		18	F	Unknown	04Ma02Nd	CONNELL, J.		25	M	Unknown	04Ma02Nd
CALLIN, Cath.		30	F	Unknown	04Ma02Nd	WARD, P.		40	M	Unknown	04Ma02Nd
Jno.		25	M	Unknown	04Ma02Nd	Jno.		17	M	Unknown	04Ma02Nd
Ann		18	F	Unknown	04Ma02Nd	Pat		19	M	Unknown	04Ma02Nd
Pat		20	M	Unknown	04Ma02Nd	Jno.		11	M	Child	04Ma02Nd
Thos.		21	M	Unknown	04Ma02Nd	Peter		04	M	Child	04Ma02Nd
Cath.		07	F	Child	04Ma02Nd	CODALHER, Biddy		20	F	Unknown	04Ma02Nd
FOYET, Bdgt.		20	F	Unknown	04Ma02Nd	NYELL, Ann		20	F	Unknown	04Ma02Nd
LILLY, Cath.		21	F	Unknown	04Ma02Nd	DUNCAN, M.		24	M	Unknown	04Ma02Nd
WALSH, M.		20	M	Unknown	04Ma02Nd	HANLY, Bdgt.		40	F	Unknown	04Ma02Nd
GERRATY, J.		20	M	Unknown	04Ma02Nd	Mich.		13	M	None	04Ma02Nd
COUR, J.		18	M	Unknown	04Ma02Nd	Mary		28	F	Unknown	04Ma02Nd
Mary		12	F	Unknown	04Ma02Nd	MCKELLY, M.		18	M	Unknown	04Ma02Nd
Mgt.		08	F	Child	04Ma02Nd	KERRY, J.		20	M	Unknown	04Ma02Nd
GALNER, Elisa		20	F	Unknown	04Ma02Nd	Sally		20	F	Unknown	04Ma02Nd
MURPHY, W.		20	M	Unknown	04Ma02Nd	MULLIN, Mgt.		17	F	Unknown	04Ma02Nd
Johanna		18	F	Unknown	04Ma02Nd	BURKE, J.		28	M	Unknown	04Ma02Nd
Mary		21	F	Unknown	04Ma02Nd	Walter		11	M	None	04Ma02Nd
KELLY, Rose		20	F	Unknown	04Ma02Nd	Jas.		22	M	Unknown	04Ma02Nd
HENRY, Cath.		21	F	Unknown	04Ma02Nd	DOHENY, J.		15	M	None	04Ma02Nd
BLACKY, Mary		20	F	Unknown	04Ma02Nd	HENNESSY, P.		25	M	Unknown	04Ma02Nd
DOOLY, J.		28	M	Unknown	04Ma02Nd	Thos.		23	M	Unknown	04Ma02Nd
FOX, Ann		20	F	Unknown	04Ma02Nd	Pat		20	M	Unknown	04Ma02Nd
DORNEY, Mgt.		20	F	Unknown	04Ma02Nd	Jas.		16	M	Unknown	04Ma02Nd
Patk.		10	M	Child	04Ma02Nd	Thos.		18	M	Unknown	04Ma02Nd
John		04	M	Child	04Ma02Nd	BYRNE, M.		22	M	Unknown	04Ma02Nd
MCGARY, J.		20	M	Unknown	04Ma02Nd	Bdgt.		18	F	Unknown	04Ma02Nd
Cath.		18	F	Unknown	04Ma02Nd	John		23	M	Unknown	04Ma02Nd
GARNER, Ann		18	F	Unknown	04Ma02Nd	SLATTY, Jane		25	F	Unknown	04Ma02Nd
DORAN, P.		20	M	Unknown	04Ma02Nd	MOORE, Cath.		21	F	Unknown	04Ma02Nd
ROGAN, U		20	F	Unknown	04Ma02Nd	Mary		18	F	Unknown	04Ma02Nd
GIBBONS, A.		25	M	Laborer	04Ma02Nd	HEALY, T.		25	M	Unknown	04Ma02Nd
Sarah		20	F	Unknown	04Ma02Nd	Mary		21	F	Unknown	04Ma02Nd
Bell		20	F	Unknown	04Ma02Nd	CARR, T.		18	M	Unknown	04Ma02Nd
MCNEIL, J.		24	M	Unknown	04Ma02Nd	FARLY, Ann		40	F	Unknown	04Ma02Nd
U	(W)	21	F	Unknown	04Ma02Nd	Thos.	(S)	20	M	Unknown	04Ma02Nd
Susan	(D)	01	F	Child	04Ma02Nd	Jas.	(S)	14	M	None	04Ma02Nd
Cath.		20	F	Unknown	04Ma02Nd	Frances	(D)	09	F	Child	04Ma02Nd
Biddy		14	F	Unknown	04Ma02Nd	CALDEN, Mary		16	F	Unknown	04Ma02Nd
Susan		11	F	Child	04Ma02Nd	Cath.		09	F	Child	04Ma02Nd
MARTIN, J.		25	M	Unknown	04Ma02Nd						
MCGAFFEY, J.		26	M	Unknown	04Ma02Nd						
MCCONALY, Mgt.		18	F	Unknown	04Ma02Nd						
Rose		15	F	Unknown	04Ma02Nd						
REILLY, E.		20	M	Unknown	04Ma02Nd						
FAY, J.		20	M	Unknown	04Ma02Nd	CHRISAN 05 MAY 1847					
BRADY, P.		20	M	Unknown	04Ma02Nd						
U	(W)	20	F	Unknown	04Ma02Nd	From Belfast					
BOYLE, Mary		15	F	Unknown	04Ma02Nd						
MURPHY, Ann		15	F	Unknown	04Ma02Nd						
DALY, J.		20	M	Unknown	04Ma02Nd						
NALLY, J.		20	M	Unknown	04Ma02Nd	LITTLE, Robt.		20	M	None	05Ma07Nk
REIFEN, J.		20	M	Unknown	04Ma02Nd	Elizabeth		18	F	Unknown	05Ma07Nk
BARKER, M.		20	M	Unknown	04Ma02Nd	Peggy		16	F	Unknown	05Ma07Nk
CARNEY, J.		30	M	Unknown	04Ma02Nd	HUTCHINSON, Adam		22	M	None	05Ma07Nk
Mary		35	F	Unknown	04Ma02Nd	TAYLOR, David		19	M	None	05Ma07Nk
RYAN, Jane		20	F	Unknown	04Ma02Nd	MCKINNEY, Alex.		30	M	None	05Ma07Nk
FITZGERALD, J.		20	M	Unknown	04Ma02Nd	MARTIN, Hugh		22	M	None	05Ma07Nk
GULIGHAN, T.		46	M	Unknown	04Ma02Nd	MCCRACKEN, Elise		27	F	Unknown	05Ma07Nk
Mary	(W)	35	F	Unknown	04Ma02Nd	MCCAMBRIDGE, Ellen		40	F	Unknown	05Ma07Nk
Dominick	(S)	16	M	Unknown	04Ma02Nd	Patrick	(S)	15	M	None	05Ma07Nk
Cath.	(D)	13	F	Unknown	04Ma02Nd	Cathe.	(D)	13	F	Unknown	05Ma07Nk

NAMES OF PASSENGERS	A G E	S E X	OCCUPATIONS	DATE PORT SHIP	NAMES OF PASSENGERS	A G E	S E X	OCCUPATIONS	DATE PORT SHIP
MCCAMBRIDGE, Robert	(S)	11 M	None	05Ma07Nk	MCCLEAN, James		30 M	Laborer	05Ma07Nk
Stewart	(S)	07 M	Child	05Ma07Nk	QUINN, Ann		50 F	Unknown	05Ma07Nk
Anne	(D)	03 F	Child	05Ma07Nk	Ellen	(D)	20 F	Unknown	05Ma07Nk
GALLAWAY, Margt.		25 F	Unknown	05Ma07Nk	Biddy	(D)	18 F	Unknown	05Ma07Nk
MCCLUNNY, John		23 M	None	05Ma07Nk	Mary	(D)	16 F	Unknown	05Ma07Nk
SHIELDS, Sarah		21 F	Unknown	05Ma07Nk	Thomas	(S)	14 M	Laborer	05Ma07Nk
WILLIAMSON, Mary		25 F	Unknown	05Ma07Nk	Ed.	(S)	12 M	None	05Ma07Nk
LOY, Neel		24 M	None	05Ma07Nk	John	(S)	10 M	Child	05Ma07Nk
JOHNSON, U-Mrs.		24 F	Unknown	05Ma07Nk	Patrick	(S)	08 M	Child	05Ma07Nk
James		22 M	None	05Ma07Nk	Joseph	(S)	07 M	Child	05Ma07Nk
Mage		20 F	Unknown	05Ma07Nk	WRIGHT, Wm.		65 M	Farmer	05Ma07Nk
Ellen		18 F	Unknown	05Ma07Nk	Ann		11 F	Child	05Ma07Nk
Andrew		25 M	None	05Ma07Nk	SHAW, Margt.		17 F	Unknown	05Ma07Nk
Thomas		12 M	None	05Ma07Nk	WILEY, Wm.		35 M	Farmer	05Ma07Nk
MILLIKEN, Alex.		25 M	None	05Ma07Nk	Mary	(W)	30 F	Unknown	05Ma07Nk
MCKENNA, Cathe.		20 F	Unknown	05Ma07Nk	Eliza	(D)	09 F	Child	05Ma07Nk
Mary		19 F	Unknown	05Ma07Nk	James	(S)	07 M	Child	05Ma07Nk
Margt.		24 F	Unknown	05Ma07Nk	Anne	(D)	06 F	Child	05Ma07Nk
LOGAN, Biddy		20 F	Unknown	05Ma07Nk	Richd.	(S)	02 M	Child	05Ma07Nk
MCKENNA, David		25 M	None	05Ma07Nk	Mary	(D)	.00 F	Infant	05Ma07Nk
GREENE, Mary		23 F	Unknown	05Ma07Nk	DODDS, Mary		55 F	Unknown	05Ma07Nk
Jane		25 F	Unknown	05Ma07Nk	Hannah		17 F	Unknown	05Ma07Nk
HOLBERT, Thos.		40 M	None	05Ma07Nk	KLEARNY, Cathe.		21 F	Unknown	05Ma07Nk
Margt.	(W)	38 F	Unknown	05Ma07Nk	Mary		20 F	Unknown	05Ma07Nk
Maria	(D)	16 F	Unknown	05Ma07Nk	BRADLEY, Polly		21 F	Unknown	05Ma07Nk
Patrick	(S)	13 M	None	05Ma07Nk	WHITFORD, Wm.		22 M	Laborer	05Ma07Nk
Anthony	(S)	11 M	Child	05Ma07Nk	Jane		18 F	Unknown	05Ma07Nk
MCHANLEY, Charles		34 M	Farmer	05Ma07Nk	KIRKER, Mary		18 F	Unknown	05Ma07Nk
Martha	(W)	32 F	Unknown	05Ma07Nk	RANN, Pat.		22 M	Laborer	05Ma07Nk
Daniel	(S)	08 M	Child	05Ma07Nk	SHARP, James		25 M	Laborer	05Ma07Nk
Sarah	(D)	05 F	Child	05Ma07Nk	SHAW, Jas.		50 M	Laborer	05Ma07Nk
Charles	(S)	02 M	Child	05Ma07Nk	Mabel	(W)	40 F	Unknown	05Ma07Nk
QUIGBY, Alexn.		40 M	Farmer	05Ma07Nk	Mary	(D)	10 F	Child	05Ma07Nk
Mary	(W)	30 F	Unknown	05Ma07Nk	Robt.	(S)	08 M	Child	05Ma07Nk
Hannah	(D)	01 F	Child	05Ma07Nk	James	(S)	05 M	Child	05Ma07Nk
Jane		37 F	Unknown	05Ma07Nk	Isabella	(D)	03 F	Child	05Ma07Nk
Ann		18 F	Unknown	05Ma07Nk	Agnes	(D)	02 F	Child	05Ma07Nk
SHAW, John		60 M	Farmer	05Ma07Nk	CUFT, Mgt.		00 F	Unknown	05Ma07Nk
Mary	(W)	50 F	Unknown	05Ma07Nk	COON, Pat.		22 M	Laborer	05Ma07Nk
John	(S)	25 M	Farmer	05Ma07Nk	SHARPE, James		25 M	Laborer	05Ma07Nk
Thomas	(S)	28 M	Farmer	05Ma07Nk	James		50 M	Laborer	05Ma07Nk
Peggy	(D)	17 F	Unknown	05Ma07Nk	Maid		40 M	Laborer	05Ma07Nk
MCCLEENE, Jane		50 F	Unknown	05Ma07Nk	Marg.		10 F	Child	05Ma07Nk
Thomas		20 M	Farmer	05Ma07Nk	Robt.		08 M	Child	05Ma07Nk
CULLY, Robt.		20 M	Farmer	05Ma07Nk	James		05 M	Child	05Ma07Nk
TWINER, Jas.		26 M	Farmer	05Ma07Nk	Isabella		03 F	Child	05Ma07Nk
Matilda		20 F	Unknown	05Ma07Nk	Agnes		02 F	Child	05Ma07Nk
DAVIDSON, John		67 M	Farmer	05Ma07Nk	Mgt.		.00 F	Infant	05Ma07Nk
Fanny	(W)	48 F	Unknown	05Ma07Nk	MCDERMOT, Laugh		25 M	Laborer	05Ma07Nk
James	(S)	18 M	Farmer	05Ma07Nk	ROBERTS, J.M.		29 M	Laborer	05Ma07Nk
George	(S)	14 M	Farmer	05Ma07Nk	Phoebe		25 F	Unknown	05Ma07Nk
John	(S)	06 M	Child	05Ma07Nk	BENNET, Chris.		10 F	Child	05Ma07Nk
James	(S)	28 M	Farmer	05Ma07Nk	BROWN, Wm.		35 M	Laborer	05Ma07Nk
Joseph	(S)	07 M	Child	05Ma07Nk	GORDON, John		36 M	Laborer	05Ma07Nk
TOWEEN, Eliza		26 F	Unknown	05Ma07Nk	QUINN, James		29 M	Laborer	05Ma07Nk
KENNAN, Ally		47 F	Unknown	05Ma07Nk	Eliza		27 F	Unknown	05Ma07Nk
Mary	(D)	20 F	Unknown	05Ma07Nk	PEDLOW, Robt.		21 M	Laborer	05Ma07Nk
James	(S)	18 M	Farmer	05Ma07Nk	Christiana		20 F	Unknown	05Ma07Nk
John	(S)	13 M	Farmer	05Ma07Nk	MCKEE, Mary		40 F	Unknown	05Ma07Nk
Atty	(S)	11 M	Child	05Ma07Nk	John		22 M	Laborer	05Ma07Nk
WOOD, Robert		45 M	Farmer	05Ma07Nk	Michael		20 M	Laborer	05Ma07Nk
Jane	(W)	45 F	Unknown	05Ma07Nk	BARLEY, James		30 M	Laborer	05Ma07Nk
Sarah	(D)	13 F	Unknown	05Ma07Nk	Eliza		56 F	Unknown	05Ma07Nk
Robert	(S)	10 M	Child	05Ma07Nk	DOYLE, Cathe.		30 F	Unknown	05Ma07Nk
John	(S)	08 M	Child	05Ma07Nk	Mgt.		10 F	Child	05Ma07Nk
William	(S)	06 M	Child	05Ma07Nk	ONEILL, Wm.		21 M	Laborer	05Ma07Nk
Agnes	(D)	.00 F	Infant	05Ma07Nk	QUINN, John		20 M	Laborer	05Ma07Nk
Mary	(D)	20 F	Unknown	05Ma07Nk	ONEIL, James		20 M	Laborer	05Ma07Nk
MARTIN, John		20 M	Farmer	05Ma07Nk	LOCKE, Francis		36 M	Laborer	05Ma07Nk
DAMEN, Thomas		21 M	Farmer	05Ma07Nk	Mary	(W)	36 F	Unknown	05Ma07Nk
CROCKETT, Eliza		20 F	Unknown	05Ma07Nk	Letitia	(D)	05 F	Child	05Ma07Nk
DOHERTY, Margt.		20 F	Unknown	05Ma07Nk	Wm.	(S)	03 M	Child	05Ma07Nk
ONEILL, John		24 M	Laborer	05Ma07Nk	Ruth	(D)	02 F	Child	05Ma07Nk
James		40 M	Laborer	05Ma07Nk	Thomas	(S)	.00 M	Infant	05Ma07Nk
THOMPSON, John		31 M	Laborer	05Ma07Nk	Elizabeth		20 F	Unknown	05Ma07Nk

NAMES OF PASSENGERS		A G E	S E X	OCCUPATIONS	DATE PORT SHIP	NAMES OF PASSENGERS		A G E	S E X	OCCUPATIONS	DATE PORT SHIP
HUNT, Letitia		06	F	Child	05Ma07Nk	DANNELLAN, Jas.		20	M	Unknown	05Ma20NI
						KEHER, Anne		20	F	Unknown	05Ma20NI
						BYRNE, Michael		21	M	Unknown	05Ma20NI
						MOORE, Thomas		36	M	Unknown	05Ma20NI
						U	(W)	36	F	Unknown	05Ma20NI
						Michael	(S)	17	M	Unknown	05Ma20NI
ATALANTA 05 MAY 1847						Mary	(D)	15	F	Unknown	05Ma20NI
						Jas.	(S)	13	M	Unknown	05Ma20NI
From Dublin						Patrick	(S)	11	M	Child	05Ma20NI
						Christy	(S)	09	M	Child	05Ma20NI
						Thomas	(S)	07	M	Child	05Ma20NI
						John	(S)	02	M	Child	05Ma20NI
HALE, William		26	M	Farmer	05Ma20NI	DOLAN, Patrick		28	M	Unknown	05Ma20NI
Margaret	(W)	26	F	Servant	05Ma20NI	Mary		20	F	Unknown	05Ma20NI
Johanna	(D)	02	F	Child	05Ma20NI	COLEMAN, Patrick		25	M	Unknown	05Ma20NI
John	(S)	.00	M	Infant	05Ma20NI	MURREY, Michael		25	M	Unknown	05Ma20NI
CASEY, Patrick		24	M	Servant	05Ma20NI	BYRNE, Michael		20	M	Unknown	05Ma20NI
Honora		17	F	Unknown	05Ma20NI	GRUGE, Patrick		24	M	Unknown	05Ma20NI
HAMMOND, Mary		20	F	Unknown	05Ma20NI	SANFORD, Martin		22	M	Unknown	05Ma20NI
AYLMER, U-Miss		20	F	Unknown	05Ma20NI	REDMOND, John		40	M	Unknown	05Ma20NI
BENNETT, Patrick		27	M	Servant	05Ma20NI	U	(W)	40	F	Unknown	05Ma20NI
SINES, Michael-F.		26	M	Unknown	05Ma20NI	William	(S)	20	M	Unknown	05Ma20NI
U	(W)	22	F	Unknown	05Ma20NI	Michl.	(S)	17	M	Unknown	05Ma20NI
John-F.	(S)	02	M	Child	05Ma20NI	Catherine	(D)	13	F	Unknown	05Ma20NI
CAULFIELD, Martin		26	M	Servant	05Ma20NI	John	(S)	11	M	Child	05Ma20NI
KELLY, John		21	M	Unknown	05Ma20NI	Andy	(S)	09	M	Child	05Ma20NI
MORRIS, William		21	M	Unknown	05Ma20NI	BEREDAN, Jas.		30	M	Unknown	05Ma20NI
MURPHY, Michael		18	M	Unknown	05Ma20NI	MCCONNELL, Cathe.		24	F	Unknown	05Ma20NI
BERGIN, Eliza		20	F	Servant	05Ma20NI	MULLANY, Mary		20	F	Unknown	05Ma20NI
KEENAN, Henry		30	M	Unknown	05Ma20NI	ONEIL, Martha		21	F	Unknown	05Ma20NI
Mary	(W)	32	F	Unknown	05Ma20NI	SHERLOCK, Martha		22	F	Unknown	05Ma20NI
Timothy	(S)	11	M	Child	05Ma20NI	CASSIDY, John		24	M	Unknown	05Ma20NI
Thomas	(S)	09	M	Child	05Ma20NI	Bridget		22	F	Unknown	05Ma20NI
Patrick	(S)	07	M	Child	05Ma20NI	CONNAGHTY, John		17	M	Unknown	05Ma20NI
William	(S)	.00	M	Infant	05Ma20NI	OHARA, Patrick		21	M	Unknown	05Ma20NI
DALEY, John		24	M	Unknown	05Ma20NI	HENNYBORN, Michl.		24	M	Unknown	05Ma20NI
EAGEN, Patrick		21	M	Unknown	05Ma20NI	MCCORMICK, John		34	M	Unknown	05Ma20NI
CARROLL, James		21	M	Servant	05Ma20NI	U	(W)	32	F	Unknown	05Ma20NI
MILLS, U-Mrs.		50	F	Unknown	05Ma20NI	Ellen	(D)	13	F	Unknown	05Ma20NI
Mary-Jane	(D)	20	F	Servant	05Ma20NI	John	(S)	11	M	Child	05Ma20NI
DAVIS, Peter		17	M	Unknown	05Ma20NI	Saml.	(S)	09	M	Child	05Ma20NI
MALONY, Peter		28	M	Unknown	05Ma20NI	William	(S)	07	M	Child	05Ma20NI
U	(W)	26	F	Servant	05Ma20NI	Gully	(S)	03	M	Child	05Ma20NI
WELSH, Martin		21	M	Unknown	05Ma20NI	Amity	(D)	.00	F	Infant	05Ma20NI
OAN, James		23	M	Servant	05Ma20NI	MOORE, Andrew		30	M	Unknown	05Ma20NI
U-Mrs.		40	F	Unknown	05Ma20NI	Sally	(W)	30	F	Unknown	05Ma20NI
Mary		25	F	Unknown	05Ma20NI	Jas.	(S)	07	M	Child	05Ma20NI
JAMISON, U-Mrs.		20	F	Unknown	05Ma20NI	Jane	(D)	.00	F	Infant	05Ma20NI
WILLIS, U-Mrs.		20	F	Unknown	05Ma20NI	BURKE, Ellen		31	F	Unknown	05Ma20NI
BRENNAN, John		22	M	Servant	05Ma20NI	MULLER, John		22	M	Unknown	05Ma20NI
MULLANEY, Mary		18	F	Servant	05Ma20NI	Sally		20	F	Unknown	05Ma20NI
Catherine		16	F	Unknown	05Ma20NI	BUTLER, John		20	M	Unknown	05Ma20NI
Ellen		15	F	Unknown	05Ma20NI	ENGLISH, William		26	M	Unknown	05Ma20NI
SHERIDAN, Mathew		39	M	Unknown	05Ma20NI	KELLY, John		24	M	Unknown	05Ma20NI
WALL, Jas.		40	M	Unknown	05Ma20NI	Sally		21	F	Unknown	05Ma20NI
GURGHEGNER, Mary		22	F	Unknown	05Ma20NI	James		11	M	Child	05Ma20NI
HANVEY, Thom.		27	M	Unknown	05Ma20NI	Ellen		09	F	Child	05Ma20NI
RUTHERFORD, John		33	M	Unknown	05Ma20NI	MOODY, William		24	M	Unknown	05Ma20NI
U	(W)	38	F	Unknown	05Ma20NI	BYRNE, John		34	M	Unknown	05Ma20NI
Maria	(D)	07	F	Child	05Ma20NI	ROONEY, Jas.		40	M	Unknown	05Ma20NI
Joseph	(S)	04	M	Child	05Ma20NI	SULLIVAN, Luke		37	M	Unknown	05Ma20NI
Isaac	(S)	01	M	Child	05Ma20NI	OHARE, Jas.		21	M	Unknown	05Ma20NI
Jas.		24	M	Unknown	05Ma20NI	OGORMAN, Richard		33	M	Unknown	05Ma20NI
BERJANE, Mary		25	F	Unknown	05Ma20NI						
DOLAN, Michael		21	M	Unknown	05Ma20NI						
KARNAGAN, Jas.F.		20	M	Unknown	05Ma20NI						
MULLANY, Sally		20	F	Unknown	05Ma20NI						
FLANIGAN, Bridget		20	F	Unknown	05Ma20NI						
GLANSEY, Eleanor		18	F	Unknown	05Ma20NI						
CONNOR, Henry		08	M	Child	05Ma20NI						
WOODSIDE, William		20	M	Unknown	05Ma20NI						
MCEVOY, Sarah		20	F	Unknown	05Ma20NI						
COLEMAN, Cathe.		20	F	Unknown	05Ma20NI						
SPAIN, Mary		20	F	Unknown	05Ma20NI						
BLYDE, Margt.		20	F	Unknown	05Ma20NI						

EMMANUEL 05 MAY 1847

From Liverpool

NAMES OF PASSENGERS	A G E	S E X	OCCUPATIONS	DATE PORT SHIP	NAMES OF PASSENGERS	A G E	S E X	OCCUPATIONS	DATE PORT SHIP
					STONE, Edwd.	(S)	09 M	Child	05Ma02Fq
					Richd.	(S)	01 M	Child	05Ma02Fq
					MCDONELL, P.		60 M	Unknown	05Ma02Fq
					James		40 M	Unknown	05Ma02Fq
					MCCAFFELY, P.		30 M	Unknown	05Ma02Fq
					Ellen		26 F	Unknown	05Ma02Fq
					Biddy		27 F	Unknown	05Ma02Fq
					RENAN, T.		35 M	Unknown	05Ma02Fq
					CALLIGHAN, T.		55 M	Unknown	05Ma02Fq
					Mary		40 F	Unknown	05Ma02Fq
CARTHY, T.		30 M	Laborer	05Ma02Fq	MANGAN, J.		24 M	Unknown	05Ma02Fq
Cath.	(W)	30 F	Unknown	05Ma02Fq	MCKELLY, A.		20 M	Unknown	05Ma02Fq
Timothy	(S)	05 M	Child	05Ma02Fq	SHEA, J.		30 M	Unknown	05Ma02Fq
Mary	(D)	03 F	Child	05Ma02Fq	ARCHER, J.		30 M	Unknown	05Ma02Fq
Mgt.	(D)	01 F	Child	05Ma02Fq	STANNEY, J.		30 M	Unknown	05Ma02Fq
ONEILL, D.		28 M	Unknown	05Ma02Fq	LANE, J.		60 M	Unknown	05Ma02Fq
John		22 M	Unknown	05Ma02Fq	Eliza		23 F	Unknown	05Ma02Fq
HICKEY, J.		19 M	Unknown	05Ma02Fq	Ellen		22 F	Unknown	05Ma02Fq
Joannah		20 F	Unknown	05Ma02Fq	GALLAGHAN, G.		21 M	Unknown	05Ma02Fq
Mgt.		25 F	Unknown	05Ma02Fq	Joanna		30 F	Unknown	05Ma02Fq
GOFF, T.		24 M	Unknown	05Ma02Fq	Charlotte		19 F	Unknown	05Ma02Fq
MARTIN, J.		24 M	Unknown	05Ma02Fq	Ellen		13 F	Unknown	05Ma02Fq
KENNEDY, P.		18 M	Unknown	05Ma02Fq	WHOLEY, T.		30 M	Laborer	05Ma02Fq
HORN, J.		24 M	Unknown	05Ma02Fq	Mary		27 F	Unknown	05Ma02Fq
Mich.		24 M	Unknown	05Ma02Fq	HARTIGAN, P.		35 M	Unknown	05Ma02Fq
MALONE, J.		24 M	Unknown	05Ma02Fq	Cath.		15 F	Unknown	05Ma02Fq
BRUEN, D.		23 M	Unknown	05Ma02Fq	SCULLION, M.		30 M	Unknown	05Ma02Fq
HANDFER, J.		22 M	Unknown	05Ma02Fq	Mary		25 F	Unknown	05Ma02Fq
Patk.		21 M	Unknown	05Ma02Fq	CONNER, T.		18 M	Unknown	05Ma02Fq
MCKENNA, Mary		21 F	Unknown	05Ma02Fq	MACK, P.		22 M	Unknown	05Ma02Fq
MURPHY, P.		22 M	Unknown	05Ma02Fq	COYLE, Biddy		18 F	Unknown	05Ma02Fq
ENNIS, M.		19 M	Unknown	05Ma02Fq	HUNT, M.		22 M	Unknown	05Ma02Fq
Cath.		22 F	Unknown	05Ma02Fq	John		21 M	Unknown	05Ma02Fq
MALONE, J.		24 M	Unknown	05Ma02Fq	MONEY, M.		25 M	Unknown	05Ma02Fq
FOLEY, J.		21 M	Unknown	05Ma02Fq	Biddy		22 F	Unknown	05Ma02Fq
Edwd.		19 M	Unknown	05Ma02Fq	FEIGHLY, T.		22 M	Unknown	05Ma02Fq
SHEA, J.		22 M	Unknown	05Ma02Fq	PATTEN, Ellen		21 F	Unknown	05Ma02Fq
DONOHOE, J.		27 M	Unknown	05Ma02Fq	OHARA, D.		31 M	Unknown	05Ma02Fq
MALONE, M.		20 M	Unknown	05Ma02Fq	MCCORMICK, M.		28 M	Unknown	05Ma02Fq
Cath.	(W)	20 F	Unknown	05Ma02Fq	Biddy		02 F	Child	05Ma02Fq
Mary	(D)	01 F	Child	05Ma02Fq	SMYTH, P.		22 M	Unknown	05Ma02Fq
MCLOUGHLIN, M.		20 M	Unknown	05Ma02Fq	FEEHERY, M.		16 M	Unknown	05Ma02Fq
MALONE, R.		20 M	Unknown	05Ma02Fq	MCKENNA, B.		30 M	Unknown	05Ma02Fq
ELLIS, J.		20 M	Unknown	05Ma02Fq	GUNDY, J.		25 M	Unknown	05Ma02Fq
Rosann		18 F	Unknown	05Ma02Fq	Mary		08 F	Child	05Ma02Fq
Richd.		15 M	Unknown	05Ma02Fq	DOOM, P.		30 M	Unknown	05Ma02Fq
Mgt.		12 F	Unknown	05Ma02Fq	John		25 M	Unknown	05Ma02Fq
Thos.		17 M	Unknown	05Ma02Fq	Mary		25 F	Unknown	05Ma02Fq
ARNOLD, J.		18 M	Unknown	05Ma02Fq	Ann		30 F	Unknown	05Ma02Fq
HANABY, Ann		37 F	Unknown	05Ma02Fq	Mary		01 F	Child	05Ma02Fq
ARMSTRONG, T.		30 M	Unknown	05Ma02Fq	MCCORMICK, Cath.		20 F	Unknown	05Ma02Fq
EVER, Bgt.		55 F	Unknown	05Ma02Fq	Ellen		19 F	Unknown	05Ma02Fq
CHRISTIAN, M.		19 M	Laborer	05Ma02Fq	BOYLE, C.		20 M	Unknown	05Ma02Fq
BUNTOR, M.		19 M	Unknown	05Ma02Fq	DUNN, W.		21 M	Unknown	05Ma02Fq
QUINN, Ellen		30 F	Unknown	05Ma02Fq	MURPHY, Biddy		20 F	Unknown	05Ma02Fq
MADDEN, Cath.		19 F	Unknown	05Ma02Fq	FITZSIMONS, C.		40 M	Unknown	05Ma02Fq
ARMSTRONG, Cath.		30 F	Unknown	05Ma02Fq	Ann	(W)	39 F	Unknown	05Ma02Fq
Ann		22 F	Unknown	05Ma02Fq	John	(S)	20 M	Unknown	05Ma02Fq
Mary		40 F	Unknown	05Ma02Fq	Mary	(D)	19 F	Unknown	05Ma02Fq
LUNN, M.		42 F	Unknown	05Ma02Fq	FARLY, P.		26 M	Unknown	05Ma02Fq
GUNN, J.		20 M	Laborer	05Ma02Fq	Martin		19 M	Unknown	05Ma02Fq
DOONA, M.		25 M	Unknown	05Ma02Fq	Cath.		20 F	Unknown	05Ma02Fq
John		20 M	Unknown	05Ma02Fq	BROWN, Biddy		40 F	Unknown	05Ma02Fq
BURKE, Mary		21 F	Unknown	05Ma02Fq	DAVIDSON, J.		22 M	Laborer	05Ma02Fq
Patt		01 M	Child	05Ma02Fq	STEALY, E.		28 M	Unknown	05Ma02Fq
GRAMES, J.		29 M	Unknown	05Ma02Fq	CLARK, Rose		40 F	Unknown	05Ma02Fq
Mary		30 F	Unknown	05Ma02Fq	LOUGH, Mary		40 F	Unknown	05Ma02Fq
SULLIVAN, J.		28 M	Unknown	05Ma02Fq	Thos.		20 M	Unknown	05Ma02Fq
Mary		28 F	Unknown	05Ma02Fq	LYNN, Mgt.		18 F	Unknown	05Ma02Fq
HUGHES, Mary		40 F	Unknown	05Ma02Fq	COMISKEY, T.		30 M	Unknown	05Ma02Fq
FOGARTY, P.		40 M	Unknown	05Ma02Fq	MURPHY, J.		30 M	Unknown	05Ma02Fq
Biddy		50 F	Unknown	05Ma02Fq	Eliza	(W)	28 F	Unknown	05Ma02Fq
STONE, Ellen		40 F	Unknown	05Ma02Fq	Patt	(S)	02 M	Child	05Ma02Fq
Ellen	(D)	15 F	Unknown	05Ma02Fq	John	(S)	01 M	Child	05Ma02Fq
James	(S)	12 M	Unknown	05Ma02Fq	DOYLE, Mary		18 F	Unknown	05Ma02Fq

NAMES OF PASSENGERS		AGE	SEX	OCCUPATIONS	DATE PORT SHIP
MCDONNELL, P.		27	M	Unknown	05Ma02Fq
Susan		26	F	Unknown	05Ma02Fq
James		20	M	Unknown	05Ma02Fq
Sarah		19	F	Unknown	05Ma02Fq
Eliza		18	F	Unknown	05Ma02Fq
Alice		10	F	Unknown	05Ma02Fq
Hugh		08	M	Child	05Ma02Fq
Mary		06	F	Child	05Ma02Fq
HEALY, Mary		25	F	Unknown	05Ma02Fq
FOX, J.		30	M	Unknown	05Ma02Fq
MCGAVIN, P.		40	M	Unknown	05Ma02Fq
EAGAN, W.		20	M	Unknown	05Ma02Fq
Anne		22	F	Unknown	05Ma02Fq
Mgt.		16	F	Unknown	05Ma02Fq
HEALY, Biddy		22	F	Unknown	05Ma02Fq
CAVANAGH, J.		25	M	Unknown	05Ma02Fq
FEHILLY, A.		60	M	Unknown	05Ma02Fq
Mgt.		19	F	Unknown	05Ma02Fq
DOCKEY, P.		21	M	Unknown	05Ma02Fq
CROGEN, Jane		20	F	Unknown	05Ma02Fq
MCGARTY, D.		24	M	Unknown	05Ma02Fq
Biddy		19	F	Unknown	05Ma02Fq
MCCOUR, Candy		20	F	Unknown	05Ma02Fq
MCCUE, D.		22	M	Unknown	05Ma02Fq
MINLY, B.		30	M	Unknown	05Ma02Fq
MCREILY, Carry		19	F	Unknown	05Ma02Fq
REILY, Bgt.		30	F	Unknown	05Ma02Fq
CRONER, E.		30	M	Unknown	05Ma02Fq
MURPHY, Ann		21	F	Unknown	05Ma02Fq

ELIZA-ANN 06 MAY 1847

From Liverpool

NAMES OF PASSENGERS		AGE	SEX	OCCUPATIONS	DATE PORT SHIP
BRADY, Philip		25	M	Laborer	06Ma02Nm
Cathe.	(W)	25	F	Unknown	06Ma02Nm
Mathew	(S)	07	M	Child	06Ma02Nm
Bridget	(D)	08	F	Child	06Ma02Nm
Ann	(D)	05	F	Child	06Ma02Nm
Cathe.	(D)	03	F	Child	06Ma02Nm
Margaret	(D)	.00	F	Infant	06Ma02Nm
MORTAGH, Brian		21	M	Unknown	06Ma02Nm
BOYLAN, Margaret		18	F	Unknown	06Ma02Nm
LYNCH, Jas.		30	M	Unknown	06Ma02Nm
Margaret	(W)	30	F	Unknown	06Ma02Nm
John	(S)	10	M	Unknown	06Ma02Nm
Thomas	(S)	08	M	Child	06Ma02Nm
Fanny	(D)	05	F	Child	06Ma02Nm
Bridget	(D)	03	F	Child	06Ma02Nm
Patrick	(S)	.00	M	Infant	06Ma02Nm
MONAGHAN, Tom		26	M	Farmer	06Ma02Nm
KELLY, John		29	M	Unknown	06Ma02Nm
Cathe.		29	F	Unknown	06Ma02Nm
DIXON, Peggy		30	F	Unknown	06Ma02Nm
PURDOCK, Martin		25	M	Laborer	06Ma02Nm
Rose		25	F	Unknown	06Ma02Nm
REILLY, Judy		28	F	Unknown	06Ma02Nm
TIGHE, Michael		20	M	Unknown	06Ma02Nm
Judy		16	F	Unknown	06Ma02Nm
FARRELL, John		30	M	Unknown	06Ma02Nm
BARRETT, John		30	M	Farmer	06Ma02Nm
Jane		35	F	Unknown	06Ma02Nm
Anthony		20	M	Unknown	06Ma02Nm
Patrick		17	M	Unknown	06Ma02Nm
Honora		12	F	Unknown	06Ma02Nm
Mary		09	F	Child	06Ma02Nm
Thos.		06	M	Child	06Ma02Nm
MULOONY, Alice		30	F	Unknown	06Ma02Nm
MURPHY, Cathe.		30	F	Unknown	06Ma02Nm
MURPHY, Michl.		06	M	Child	06Ma02Nm
CARTY, Thos.		55	M	Laborer	06Ma02Nm
PINKERTON, Henry		20	M	Unknown	06Ma02Nm
MILLIKEN, Geo.		25	M	Unknown	06Ma02Nm
Susan		20	F	Unknown	06Ma02Nm
WALSH, John		20	M	Laborer	06Ma02Nm
CLARK, Alex.		33	M	Unknown	06Ma02Nm
John		22	M	Unknown	06Ma02Nm
BARRETT, Jane		03	F	Child	06Ma02Nm
CUNNINGHAM, Michl.		20	M	Unknown	06Ma02Nm
HALLEN, Patrick		25	M	Unknown	06Ma02Nm
BRAY, Ann		20	F	Unknown	06Ma02Nm
Judy		20	F	Unknown	06Ma02Nm
BOHAN, Michl.		20	M	Laborer	06Ma02Nm
GRAVES, Camilla		28	F	Unknown	06Ma02Nm
Philip		30	M	Unknown	06Ma02Nm
MCLEAN, Elisa		20	F	Unknown	06Ma02Nm
GRAVES, John		07	M	Child	06Ma02Nm
Maria	(T)	03	F	Child	06Ma02Nm
Geo.	(B)	05	M	Child	06Ma02Nm
Patrick	(B)	.00	M	Infant	06Ma02Nm
KELLOWS, John		25	M	Unknown	06Ma02Nm
Geo.	(P)	50	M	Farmer	06Ma02Nm
HAMMOND, John		30	M	Laborer	06Ma02Nm
KELLOREN, Owen		30	M	Unknown	06Ma02Nm
MCDONAGH, Jas.		25	M	Unknown	06Ma02Nm
KILLEREN, Judy		25	F	Unknown	06Ma02Nm
HAMMOND, Bridget		25	F	Unknown	06Ma02Nm
KILLEREN, Margaret		25	F	Unknown	06Ma02Nm
KENNEDY, Jas.		20	M	Unknown	06Ma02Nm
Ellen		20	F	Unknown	06Ma02Nm
DOGAN, Jane		18	F	Unknown	06Ma02Nm
SAENY, Ellen		18	F	Unknown	06Ma02Nm
RAFFERTY, Sarah		18	F	Unknown	06Ma02Nm
CLARK, Edward		25	M	Unknown	06Ma02Nm
REILLY, Brien		28	M	Unknown	06Ma02Nm
CONLON, Thos.		21	M	Unknown	06Ma02Nm
FLATTERY, Catherine		20	F	Unknown	06Ma02Nm
NOON, Maria		20	F	Unknown	06Ma02Nm
CARROLL, Margt.		20	F	Unknown	06Ma02Nm
COLGAN, Mary		17	F	Unknown	06Ma02Nm
Andrew	(S)	03	M	Child	06Ma02Nm
Cathe.	(D)	.00	F	Infant	06Ma02Nm
TANNER, Ellen		40	F	Unknown	06Ma02Nm
Kieran		20	F	Unknown	06Ma02Nm
Betty		20	F	Unknown	06Ma02Nm
QUIN, Ann		70	F	Unknown	06Ma02Nm
Patrick		24	M	Laborer	06Ma02Nm
MURRAY, Bernard		25	M	Unknown	06Ma02Nm
Bridget		20	F	Unknown	06Ma02Nm
DONGAN, John		25	M	Unknown	06Ma02Nm
CLARK, Patrick		20	M	Unknown	06Ma02Nm
SHERY, Thos.		20	M	Unknown	06Ma02Nm
CUNNINGHAM, Betty		20	F	Unknown	06Ma02Nm
Reilly		20	F	Unknown	06Ma02Nm
MULHOLLAND, Peter		21	M	Unknown	06Ma02Nm
FARLEY, Mary		20	F	Unknown	06Ma02Nm
MCCABE, Michl.		20	M	Unknown	06Ma02Nm
Ann		13	F	Unknown	06Ma02Nm
MARTIN, Honora		20	F	Unknown	06Ma02Nm
HAND, Eliza		40	F	Unknown	06Ma02Nm
Thos.	(S)	20	M	Unknown	06Ma02Nm
Patrick	(S)	21	M	Unknown	06Ma02Nm
Catherine	(D)	11	F	Unknown	06Ma02Nm
HIGGINS, Cathe.		21	F	Unknown	06Ma02Nm
HEARY, Mary		21	F	Unknown	06Ma02Nm
MCCAFFAN, Geo.		25	M	Unknown	06Ma02Nm
EDAN, Margaret		40	F	Unknown	06Ma02Nm
RIGNEY, Michl.		25	M	Unknown	06Ma02Nm
Catherine	(W)	25	F	Unknown	06Ma02Nm
Patrick	(S)	03	M	Child	06Ma02Nm
John	(S)	.00	M	Infant	06Ma02Nm
ENWRIGHT, Mary		21	F	Unknown	06Ma02Nm
SCULLY, Patrick		21	M	Unknown	06Ma02Nm
HEGARTY, Chas.		21	M	Unknown	06Ma02Nm

NAMES OF PASSENGERS		AGE	SEX	OCCUPATIONS	DATE PORT SHIP
HAY, Margaret		18	F	Unknown	06Ma02Nm
FITZGERALD, John		25	M	Unknown	06Ma02Nm
WHEELALEAN, Ann		18	F	Unknown	06Ma02Nm
SMITH, Owen		21	M	Unknown	06Ma02Nm
MARTLY, John		25	M	Unknown	06Ma02Nm
Ellen		18	F	Unknown	06Ma02Nm
MURPHY, Bernard		25	M	Unknown	06Ma02Nm
FEENEY, Cameron		25	M	Unknown	06Ma02Nm
Rose		24	F	Unknown	06Ma02Nm
KEEN, James		25	M	Unknown	06Ma02Nm
Edward		25	M	Unknown	06Ma02Nm
SLINEY, John		25	M	Unknown	06Ma02Nm
BIRMINGHAM, James		30	M	Laborer	06Ma02Nm
Ann		25	F	Unknown	06Ma02Nm
Mary		20	F	Unknown	06Ma02Nm
Sarah		13	F	Unknown	06Ma02Nm
Eliza		.00	F	Infant	06Ma02Nm
CANN, Ann		20	F	Unknown	06Ma02Nm
MCKEEN, Patk.		30	M	Unknown	06Ma02Nm
Mary	(W)	30	F	Unknown	06Ma02Nm
Jas.	(S)	05	M	Child	06Ma02Nm
John	(S)	03	M	Child	06Ma02Nm
Patk.	(S)	.00	M	Infant	06Ma02Nm
HELORA, Susan		25	F	Unknown	06Ma02Nm
KEELY, John		20	M	Unknown	06Ma02Nm
Honora		20	F	Unknown	06Ma02Nm
ADAMS, Michl.		20	M	Unknown	06Ma02Nm
Fred		20	M	Unknown	06Ma02Nm
MCDONALD, Jas.		20	M	Unknown	06Ma02Nm
Marla		20	F	Unknown	06Ma02Nm
FLINN, James		20	M	Unknown	06Ma02Nm
KELLORN, Thomas		12	M	Unknown	06Ma02Nm
Sarah		10	F	Unknown	06Ma02Nm
HANNON, Margaret		.00	F	Infant	06Ma02Nm
Patrick		.00	M	Infant	06Ma02Nm
REDAHAN, Geo.		25	M	Unknown	06Ma02Nm
Catherine		25	F	Unknown	06Ma02Nm
Saml.		12	M	Unknown	06Ma02Nm
MURPHY, Martin		20	M	Unknown	06Ma02Nm
GIVAN, John		20	M	Unknown	06Ma02Nm
Margaret		10	F	Unknown	06Ma02Nm
Judy		08	F	Child	06Ma02Nm
COLGAN, John		25	M	Unknown	06Ma02Nm
RILEY, Martin		20	M	Unknown	06Ma02Nm
COLGAN, John		20	M	Unknown	06Ma02Nm
WHITE, William		20	M	Unknown	06Ma02Nm
RILEY, Ann		20	F	Unknown	06Ma02Nm
HOLGAN, Bridget		20	F	Unknown	06Ma02Nm
DONNELLY, Peter		30	M	Unknown	06Ma02Nm
MCNAMEE, Patrick		30	M	Unknown	06Ma02Nm
Mary	(M)	50	F	Unknown	06Ma02Nm
Francis	(B)	16	M	Unknown	06Ma02Nm
Patrick	(B)	13	M	Unknown	06Ma02Nm
BENNAN, Rose		21	F	Unknown	06Ma02Nm
CLARK, John		25	M	Laborer	06Ma02Nm
REILLY, Owen		20	M	Unknown	06Ma02Nm
GANNON, Patrick		22	M	Unknown	06Ma02Nm
Morris		20	M	Unknown	06Ma02Nm
Mary		18	F	Unknown	06Ma02Nm
SORAHAN, Mathew		60	M	Unknown	06Ma02Nm
H.		19	M	Unknown	06Ma02Nm
Abbey		18	F	Unknown	06Ma02Nm
Cathe.		16	F	Unknown	06Ma02Nm
KING, Bridget		17	F	Unknown	06Ma02Nm
SORAHAN, H.		12	M	Unknown	06Ma02Nm
RAYNE, Jas.		25	M	Unknown	06Ma02Nm
Betty		20	F	Unknown	06Ma02Nm
JERWEY, Patrick		20	M	Unknown	06Ma02Nm
CLARK, Jas.		21	M	Unknown	06Ma02Nm
MCCULLOUGH, Jas.		30	M	Unknown	06Ma02Nm
TELFORD, Margaret		19	F	Unknown	06Ma02Nm
KANE, Ellen		25	F	Unknown	06Ma02Nm
PERCIVAL, Jane		17	F	Unknown	06Ma02Nm
ROSE, Ellen		20	F	Unknown	06Ma02Nm
CAVENDER, John		25	M	Unknown	06Ma02Nm
SMITH, Mary		20	F	Unknown	06Ma02Nm
DARAGH, Mary		25	F	Unknown	06Ma02Nm
CARROLL, Bridget		28	F	Unknown	06Ma02Nm
MCCORMICK, Ann		20	F	Unknown	06Ma02Nm
PERCIVAL, Stephen		18	M	Unknown	06Ma02Nm
FARRELL, Margaret		24	F	Unknown	06Ma02Nm
SWESTON, Margaret		20	F	Unknown	06Ma02Nm
Ann		18	F	Unknown	06Ma02Nm
FREEMAN, Bridget		24	F	Unknown	06Ma02Nm
CRANSTON, Mary		20	F	Unknown	06Ma02Nm
LAW, Mary		18	F	Unknown	06Ma02Nm
CASERLY, Bridget		18	F	Unknown	06Ma02Nm
COMISKEY, Thos.		17	M	Unknown	06Ma02Nm
HEANIN, Lawrence		20	M	Unknown	06Ma02Nm
BALE, Thomas		20	M	Unknown	06Ma02Nm
DONOUGH, Patrick		23	M	Unknown	06Ma02Nm
Michl.		19	M	Unknown	06Ma02Nm
COOK, Hugh		25	M	Unknown	06Ma02Nm
CAIT, James		18	M	Laborer	06Ma02Nm
HANIAREL, Michl.		30	M	Unknown	06Ma02Nm
ROYBAN, Michl.		28	M	Unknown	06Ma02Nm
MOAN, James		25	M	Unknown	06Ma02Nm
HARE, Mary		06	F	Child	06Ma02Nm
BLACK, Thos.		27	M	Unknown	06Ma02Nm
HARE, Bridget		31	F	Unknown	06Ma02Nm
Alice		02	F	Child	06Ma02Nm
DUMMER, Ann		43	F	Unknown	06Ma02Nm
Ann		04	F	Child	06Ma02Nm
Ellen		02	F	Child	06Ma02Nm
KOOK, Thomas		21	M	Unknown	06Ma02Nm
Ann		21	F	Unknown	06Ma02Nm
DILLON, Caatherine		29	F	Unknown	06Ma02Nm
MORIARTY, Michl.		25	M	Unknown	06Ma02Nm
MOONE, Jas.		28	M	Unknown	06Ma02Nm
CULHIN, Mary		22	F	Unknown	06Ma02Nm
MOON, Jerry		28	M	Unknown	06Ma02Nm
MOHAN, Margaret		20	F	Unknown	06Ma02Nm
REILY, William		24	M	Unknown	06Ma02Nm
ROONEY, Michl.		28	M	Unknown	06Ma02Nm
Andrew		26	M	Unknown	06Ma02Nm
KIERNAN, Biddy		18	F	Unknown	06Ma02Nm
FITZGERALD, Saml.		32	M	Unknown	06Ma02Nm
Mary		31	F	Unknown	06Ma02Nm
COFFEE, Mary		28	F	Unknown	06Ma02Nm
HIGGEN, Ellen		25	F	Unknown	06Ma02Nm
HARRINGTON, Fanny		28	F	Unknown	06Ma02Nm
CARLIN, Thos.		24	M	Unknown	06Ma02Nm
HAWLEY, Michl.		18	M	Unknown	06Ma02Nm
HALLER, William		24	M	Unknown	06Ma02Nm
COOKS, Edward		18	M	Unknown	06Ma02Nm
MCGIFF, Rose		22	F	Unknown	06Ma02Nm
HEYEN, Ellen		18	F	Unknown	06Ma02Nm
CAVAUTH, Margaret		28	F	Unknown	06Ma02Nm
WHEELER, Henry		13	M	Unknown	06Ma02Nm
MCGOFFORD, Geo.		28	M	Unknown	06Ma02Nm
DILLON, Martin		27	M	Unknown	06Ma02Nm
HIGGINS, Mary		20	F	Unknown	06Ma02Nm
FAGAN, Ellen		18	F	Unknown	06Ma02Nm
CARROLL, Bridget		24	F	Unknown	06Ma02Nm
GLOVER, Bridget		22	F	Unknown	06Ma02Nm
CARLIN, Alice		20	F	Unknown	06Ma02Nm
FLATTERY, Maria		22	F	Unknown	06Ma02Nm
REILLY, Mary		22	F	Unknown	06Ma02Nm
HARRINGTON, Fanny		20	F	Unknown	06Ma02Nm
SMITH, Owen		28	M	Laborer	06Ma02Nm
MIKELL, Margaret		20	F	Unknown	06Ma02Nm
DUFFY, Bridget		20	F	Unknown	06Ma02Nm
OGDEN, Michael		27	M	Laborer	06Ma02Nm
Jane	(W)	26	F	Unknown	06Ma02Nm
Jane	(D)	06	F	Child	06Ma02Nm
Elizabeth	(D)	04	F	Child	06Ma02Nm
Mary	(D)	02	F	Child	06Ma02Nm

NAMES OF PASSENGERS		AGE	SEX	OCCUPATIONS	DATE PORT SHIP	NAMES OF PASSENGERS		AGE	SEX	OCCUPATIONS	DATE PORT SHIP
						DONOHOE, Susan		20	F	None	08Ma33Iz
						Biddy		17	F	None	08Ma33Iz
						HARTIGAN, Pat		19	M	Farmer	08Ma33Iz
						Cathe.		21	F	None	08Ma33Iz
DOLPHIN 08 MAY 1847						Biddy		12	F	None	08Ma33Iz
						LANG, Mary		22	F	None	08Ma33Iz
From Limerick						REILLY, Dennis		24	M	Farmer	08Ma33Iz
						KELLEY, Anne		22	F	None	08Ma33Iz
						CREWFORD, Owen		40	M	Farmer	08Ma33Iz
						SHAUGERY, M.A.		18	F	None	08Ma33Iz
MULGNER, Margt.		20	F	None	08Ma33Iz	CONNORS, Jno.		24	M	Farmer	08Ma33Iz
Hannah		15	F	None	08Ma33Iz	WHEALAN, Mary		14	F	None	08Ma33Iz
Mary		25	F	None	08Ma33Iz	QUINN, Martin		27	M	Farmer	08Ma33Iz
DAWNES, Pat		24	M	Farmer	08Ma33Iz	FITZGERALD, Ellen		00	F	Unknown	08Ma33Iz
Bridget		23	F	None	08Ma33Iz						
MURPHY, Pat		28	M	None	08Ma33Iz						
Margt.	(W)	28	F	Wife	08Ma33Iz						
John	(S)	03	M	Child	08Ma33Iz						
WHELAN, Eliza		20	F	None	08Ma33Iz						
WIXTED, Wm.		30	M	Farmer	08Ma33Iz	**ISABELLA 10 MAY 1847**					
COLEMAN, Ellen		21	F	None	08Ma33Iz						
ENRIGHT, Mary		20	F	None	08Ma33Iz	From Cork					
BREW, Michael		30	M	Farmer	08Ma33Iz						
Biddy	(W)	28	F	Wife	08Ma33Iz						
Mary-A.	(D)	03	F	Child	08Ma33Iz						
Kitty	(D)	01	F	Child	08Ma33Iz	HUNTY, Cornelius		50	M	Laborer	10Ma14Fe
KENEVAN, Thos.		24	M	Farmer	08Ma33Iz	Mary	(W)	50	F	Wife	10Ma14Fe
DUGAN, John		30	M	Farmer	08Ma33Iz	John	(S)	13	M	Laborer	10Ma14Fe
QUINN, Eliza		20	F	None	08Ma33Iz	Mary	(D)	11	F	None	10Ma14Fe
LAMASS, E.		20	F	None	08Ma33Iz	Cath.	(D)	10	F	None	10Ma14Fe
HAUGH, M.		20	F	None	08Ma33Iz	Thos.	(S)	08	M	Child	10Ma14Fe
Anne		13	F	None	08Ma33Iz	William	(S)	04	M	Child	10Ma14Fe
Mary		13	F	None	08Ma33Iz	Eliza	(D)	06	F	Child	10Ma14Fe
BLOOMFIELD, Thos.		50	M	Farmer	08Ma33Iz	Julia	(D)	02	F	Child	10Ma14Fe
Mary		50	F	None	08Ma33Iz	LAHY, Giles		45	M	Laborer	10Ma14Fe
PEDGAM, Thos.		52	M	Farmer	08Ma33Iz	CRORCORAN, John		30	M	Laborer	10Ma14Fe
Mary-A.	(D)	22	F	None	08Ma33Iz	Ellen		25	F	None	10Ma14Fe
Alicia	(D)	20	F	None	08Ma33Iz	DROZZ, Thos.		28	M	Laborer	10Ma14Fe
CLIFFORD, Thos.		38	M	Farmer	08Ma33Iz	BERRY, John		30	M	Laborer	10Ma14Fe
BURKE, John		26	M	Farmer	08Ma33Iz	BROWN, James		25	M	Laborer	10Ma14Fe
CASEY, Joseph		24	M	Farmer	08Ma33Iz	DANAGHAR, Thomas		20	M	Laborer	10Ma14Fe
DUHIG, Thomas		40	M	Farmer	08Ma33Iz	ROCHE, John		50	M	Laborer	10Ma14Fe
MORAN, Thos.		20	M	Farmer	08Ma33Iz	Mary	(W)	45	F	Wife	10Ma14Fe
HANELAN, John		27	M	Farmer	08Ma33Iz	John	(S)	16	M	Laborer	10Ma14Fe
Mary	(W)	26	F	Wife	08Ma33Iz	Michael	(S)	12	M	None	10Ma14Fe
Pat	(S)	06	M	Child	08Ma33Iz	Mary	(D)	10	F	None	10Ma14Fe
Johanna	(D)	03	F	Child	08Ma33Iz	FENTON, Timothy		20	M	Laborer	10Ma14Fe
M.	(S)	02	M	Child	08Ma33Iz	ROCHE, Mary		25	F	None	10Ma14Fe
Biddy	(D)	.10	F	Infant	08Ma33Iz	SHEEHAN, Jeremiah		25	M	Laborer	10Ma14Fe
MACKLER, Ellen		20	F	None	08Ma33Iz	Jane		23	F	None	10Ma14Fe
Richd.		30	M	Farmer	08Ma33Iz	FITZPATRICK, Ellen		19	F	None	10Ma14Fe
M.		20	M	Farmer	08Ma33Iz	SWEENY, Cons.		30	M	Laborer	10Ma14Fe
MOORE, Wm.		24	M	Farmer	08Ma33Iz	Eliza		17	F	None	10Ma14Fe
RYAN, Mary		22	F	None	08Ma33Iz	BROWN, Thos.		30	M	Laborer	10Ma14Fe
Judy		20	F	None	08Ma33Iz	DONOVAN, Ellen		35	F	None	10Ma14Fe
MCCOWAN, John		22	M	Farmer	08Ma33Iz	HOGAN, Michael		21	M	Laborer	10Ma14Fe
MADDAN, John		20	M	Farmer	08Ma33Iz	BAINS, James		18	M	Laborer	10Ma14Fe
Mary		24	F	None	08Ma33Iz	BARRATT, Michl.		29	M	Laborer	10Ma14Fe
LYNCH, Mi.		40	M	Farmer	08Ma33Iz	LEAKY, James		33	M	Laborer	10Ma14Fe
FOLEY, Jno.		20	M	Farmer	08Ma33Iz	DELANY, John		40	M	Laborer	10Ma14Fe
MEER, Thaddy		35	M	Farmer	08Ma33Iz	MULCAHY, Peggy		30	F	None	10Ma14Fe
Ellen	(W)	34	F	Wife	08Ma33Iz	NAGLE, Bridget		20	F	None	10Ma14Fe
Mary	(D)	15	F	None	08Ma33Iz	NIEL, John		23	M	Laborer	10Ma14Fe
CUSACK, James		35	M	Farmer	08Ma33Iz	DEE, Mary		18	F	None	10Ma14Fe
Margt.	(W)	34	F	Wife	08Ma33Iz	MILLMAN, Geo.		40	M	Laborer	10Ma14Fe
Pat	(S)	12	M	Farmer	08Ma33Iz	PARKER, M.D.		20	M	Laborer	10Ma14Fe
Thos.	(S)	10	M	None	08Ma33Iz	OWENS, Win.		25	M	Laborer	10Ma14Fe
Mary	(D)	08	F	Child	08Ma33Iz	HARRINGTON, U		40	M	Doctor	10Ma14Fe
Margt.	(D)	.09	F	Infant	08Ma33Iz	Owen		30	M	Laborer	10Ma14Fe
LEYDEN, P.		22	M	Farmer	08Ma33Iz	ANDY, Hy.		25	M	Laborer	10Ma14Fe
LUCKEY, Thos.		20	M	Farmer	08Ma33Iz	CALLAGHAN, Dennis		32	M	Laborer	10Ma14Fe
HEHER, Hull.		21	M	Farmer	08Ma33Iz	DEE, Owen		45	M	Laborer	10Ma14Fe
KERIN, Dennis		25	M	Farmer	08Ma33Iz	WARRINGTON, John		50	M	Laborer	10Ma14Fe
MCGINNPSEY, D.		40	M	Farmer	08Ma33Iz						
Margt.		26	F	None	08Ma33Iz						

NAMES OF PASSENGERS	A G E	S E X	OCCUPATIONS	DATE PORT SHIP	NAMES OF PASSENGERS		A G E	S E X	OCCUPATIONS	DATE PORT SHIP
					JILLE, Susan		30	F	Unknown	13Ma04No
					CHURCH, W.J.		22	M	Laborer	13Ma04No
					MCLEES, H.		23	M	Unknown	13Ma04No
					WALLES, D.		24	M	Unknown	13Ma04No
LORD-FITZGERALD 11 MAY 1847					BOYN, D.		47	M	Unknown	13Ma04No
					Jane	(W)	45	F	Unknown	13Ma04No
From Galway					Jane	(D)	13	F	Unknown	13Ma04No
					Moyen	(S)	11	M	Unknown	13Ma04No
					Alex.	(S)	09	M	Child	13Ma04No
					Andw.	(S)	07	M	Child	13Ma04No
MORAN, Jas.	20	M	Laborer	11Ma11Nn	Ruth	(D)	05	F	Child	13Ma04No
FITZGERALD, John	20	M	Laborer	11Ma11Nn	Danl.	(S)	02	M	Child	13Ma04No
GILDEN, Peter	25	M	Laborer	11Ma11Nn	MARTIN, Cath.		23	F	Unknown	13Ma04No
JOYCE, Thomas	25	M	Laborer	11Ma11Nn	TAYLOR, J.		25	M	Unknown	13Ma04No
CARTHY, John	34	M	Laborer	11Ma11Nn	ANDERSON, D.		30	M	Unknown	13Ma04No
LYDEN, Wm.	25	M	Laborer	11Ma11Nn	RANKIN, D.		30	M	Unknown	13Ma04No
DOHERTY, Pat	20	M	Laborer	11Ma11Nn	SMITH, S.		40	M	Unknown	13Ma04No
KENEDY, Margt.	23	F	Unknown	11Ma11Nn	Martha	(W)	34	F	Unknown	13Ma04No
FRENCH, James	19	M	Laborer	11Ma11Nn	Jane	(D)	09	F	Child	13Ma04No
Marla	18	F	Unknown	11Ma11Nn	Eliza	(D)	06	F	Child	13Ma04No
CANN, Bridget	22	F	Unknown	11Ma11Nn	Ruth-J.	(D)	02	F	Child	13Ma04No
CARNVAY, Pat	19	M	Laborer	11Ma11Nn	CAGHAN, Nancy		20	F	Unknown	13Ma04No
MACHARNAM, Bryan	26	M	Laborer	11Ma11Nn	Jane		23	F	Unknown	13Ma04No
Terence	22	M	Laborer	11Ma11Nn	Isa.		18	F	Unknown	13Ma04No
GORHAM, John	24	M	Laborer	11Ma11Nn	MCMEE, Mt.		21	M	Unknown	13Ma04No
GREEN, Jas.	36	M	Laborer	11Ma11Nn	SYNE, G.		23	M	Unknown	13Ma04No
FOLAN, Mary	28	F	Unknown	11Ma11Nn	MURNANE, J.		19	M	Unknown	13Ma04No
KEANE, Pat.	30	M	Laborer	11Ma11Nn	MILLER, R.		60	M	Unknown	13Ma04No
LYNOUGH, Pat	22	M	Laborer	11Ma11Nn	Jas.		29	M	Unknown	13Ma04No
MARKEN, Anthony	24	M	Laborer	11Ma11Nn	Richd.		21	M	Unknown	13Ma04No
HOWARD, Pat	23	M	Laborer	11Ma11Nn	Jane		23	F	Unknown	13Ma04No
MANNORI, John	21	M	Laborer	11Ma11Nn	Bdgt.		16	F	Unknown	13Ma04No
Homer	15	M	Laborer	11Ma11Nn	Wm.T.		13	M	Unknown	13Ma04No
OBRIEN, James	40	M	Laborer	11Ma11Nn	BURNS, Cath.		36	F	Unknown	13Ma04No
Margt.	20	F	Unknown	11Ma11Nn	MCGUNN, D.		21	M	Unknown	13Ma04No
MCMAHON, Thos.	25	M	Laborer	11Ma11Nn	MCBRIDE, P.		17	M	Unknown	13Ma04No
Margt.	20	F	Unknown	11Ma11Nn	Edw.		20	M	Unknown	13Ma04No
DONAHUE, Thos.	25	M	Laborer	11Ma11Nn	CARNAN, W.		26	M	Unknown	13Ma04No
Biddy	20	F	Unknown	11Ma11Nn	LONGBRAY, J.		21	M	Unknown	13Ma04No
KELLEY, Peter	20	M	Laborer	11Ma11Nn	M.		28	M	Laborer	13Ma04No
GALLERY, Bryan	25	M	Laborer	11Ma11Nn	MCKELVIN, H.		20	M	Unknown	13Ma04No
FAHERG, Michael	01	M	Child	11Ma11Nn	FINNEY, T.		25	M	Unknown	13Ma04No
MCGIRMELL, Michael	25	M	Laborer	11Ma11Nn	Cath.	(W)	25	F	Unknown	13Ma04No
HALLARAN, John	21	M	Laborer	11Ma11Nn	John	(S)	03	M	Child	13Ma04No
FAHEY, Pat	20	M	Laborer	11Ma11Nn	Ellzt.	(D)	01	F	Child	13Ma04No
CARTHARG, Pat	22	M	Laborer	11Ma11Nn	CRAIG, R.		17	M	Unknown	13Ma04No
HINES, Joseph	28	M	Laborer	11Ma11Nn	MINNOW, H.		20	M	Unknown	13Ma04No
Peter	23	M	Laborer	11Ma11Nn	MCNESTE, H.		29	M	Unknown	13Ma04No
MURPHY, Wm.	20	M	Laborer	11Ma11Nn	Cath.	(W)	27	F	Unknown	13Ma04No
Connor	31	M	Laborer	11Ma11Nn	Pat	(S)	02	M	Child	13Ma04No
Peggy	30	F	Unknown	11Ma11Nn	Cath.	(D)	03	F	Child	13Ma04No
FAHERG, John	25	M	Laborer	11Ma11Nn	CARLIN, R.		52	M	Unknown	13Ma04No
MURRAY, James	28	M	Laborer	11Ma11Nn	John	(S)	25	M	Unknown	13Ma04No
Nancy	28	F	Unknown	11Ma11Nn	Rosanne	(D)	20	F	Unknown	13Ma04No
KING, Martin	28	M	Laborer	11Ma11Nn	Mgt.	(D)	22	F	Unknown	13Ma04No
Bridget	28	F	Unknown	11Ma11Nn	Eleanor	(D)	13	F	Unknown	13Ma04No
NEALLY, Phillip	20	M	Laborer	11Ma11Nn	ENGLISH, J.		49	M	Unknown	13Ma04No
MURPHY, Thomas	26	M	Laborer	11Ma11Nn	Rose	(W)	50	F	Unknown	13Ma04No
HUME, Patt	26	M	Laborer	11Ma11Nn	Isabella	(D)	20	F	Unknown	13Ma04No
Phillip	21	M	Laborer	11Ma11Nn	Mary		01	F	Child	13Ma04No
Shady	18	M	Laborer	11Ma11Nn	James	(S)	23	M	Unknown	13Ma04No
FLAHERTY, Nancy	23	F	Unknown	11Ma11Nn	MCKEE, J.		50	M	Unknown	13Ma04No
					Sally	(W)	50	F	Unknown	13Ma04No
					Robt.	(S)	20	M	Unknown	13Ma04No
					Clark	(S)	18	M	Unknown	13Ma04No
					Alexr.	(S)	16	M	Unknown	13Ma04No
					John	(S)	13	M	None	13Ma04No
MONTICELLO 13 MAY 1847					George	(S)	13	M	None	13Ma04No
					Sally	(D)	07	F	Child	13Ma04No
From Glasgow					CLARKE, J.		21	M	Unknown	13Ma04No
					MCGUNGAN, J.		26	M	Unknown	13Ma04No
					RUDDER, E.		24	M	Unknown	13Ma04No
					MCKEERY, P.		20	M	Unknown	13Ma04No
KEE, M.	05	F	Child	13Ma04No	MORRISON, W.		14	M	None	13Ma04No
TRUER, Mgt.	18	F	Unknown	13Ma04No	BELL, S.		22	M	Unknown	13Ma04No

NAMES OF PASSENGERS		AGE	SEX	OCCUPATIONS	DATE PORT SHIP	NAMES OF PASSENGERS		AGE	SEX	OCCUPATIONS	DATE PORT SHIP
MILLER, D.		19	M	Unknown	13Ma04No						
MCLACHLIN, T.		20	M	Unknown	13Ma04No						
John		22	M	Unknown	13Ma04No						
MCSHEFERY, D.		35	M	Unknown	13Ma04No						
Mary		30	F	Unknown	13Ma04No			PELTONA 14 MAY 1847			
John		21	M	Unknown	13Ma04No						
Ann		06	F	Child	13Ma04No			From Liverpool			
Michl.		08	M	Child	13Ma04No						
Andrew		02	M	Child	13Ma04No						
GILLON, W.		20	M	Laborer	13Ma04No						
DOHERTY, J.		22	M	Unknown	13Ma04No	ARTHUR, Thomas		35	M	Laborer	14Ma02Np
James		16	M	Unknown	13Ma04No	Jane	(W)	25	F	Unknown	14Ma02Np
Sarah		40	F	Unknown	13Ma04No	Robert	(S)	02	M	Child	14Ma02Np
Mary		19	F	Unknown	13Ma04No	Anne	(D)	.00	F	Infant	14Ma02Np
Rose		30	F	Unknown	13Ma04No	NEILLY, Anne		25	F	Unknown	14Ma02Np
Sarah		30	F	Unknown	13Ma04No	James	(S)	.00	M	Infant	14Ma02Np
Mary		25	F	Unknown	13Ma04No	CLARKE, William		25	M	Laborer	14Ma02Np
Bdgt.		05	F	Child	13Ma04No	Mary-Jane		25	F	Unknown	14Ma02Np
Mgt.		03	F	Child	13Ma04No	Anne-Jane		40	F	Unknown	14Ma02Np
WILSON, W.		25	M	Unknown	13Ma04No	Samuel		20	M	Laborer	14Ma02Np
MCLACHLIN, P.		20	M	Unknown	13Ma04No	John		18	M	Mechanic	14Ma02Np
Mary		25	F	Unknown	13Ma04No	Jane		13	F	Unknown	14Ma02Np
LYNCH, P.		50	M	Unknown	13Ma04No	Bickly		11	M	Laborer	14Ma02Np
Mary	(W)	50	F	Unknown	13Ma04No	Esther		40	F	Unknown	14Ma02Np
James	(S)	20	M	Unknown	13Ma04No	Rachel		20	F	Unknown	14Ma02Np
Patk.	(S)	18	M	Unknown	13Ma04No	Sally		18	F	Unknown	14Ma02Np
Mary	(D)	15	F	Unknown	13Ma04No	George		11	M	Laborer	14Ma02Np
Mich.	(S)	13	M	None	13Ma04No	TOWNSEND, John		30	M	Laborer	14Ma02Np
Ellen	(D)	11	F	Unknown	13Ma04No	U	(W)	25	F	Unknown	14Ma02Np
Cath.	(D)	09	F	Child	13Ma04No	John	(S)	.00	M	Infant	14Ma02Np
HARKIN, D.		40	M	Unknown	13Ma04No	WHITE, Michael		24	M	Laborer	14Ma02Np
Mgt.	(W)	36	F	Unknown	13Ma04No	Ellen		24	F	Unknown	14Ma02Np
Dun.	(S)	09	M	Child	13Ma04No	CONNAY, Henry		21	M	Laborer	14Ma02Np
Danl.	(S)	06	M	Child	13Ma04No	Patt		23	M	Laborer	14Ma02Np
Mary	(D)	06	F	Child	13Ma04No	MCNEIL, Hugh		21	M	Laborer	14Ma02Np
Chas.	(S)	02	M	Child	13Ma04No	Jane		19	F	Unknown	14Ma02Np
Mgt.	(D)	01	F	Child	13Ma04No	MCMULLEN, Rose		22	F	Unknown	14Ma02Np
DOCKERY, W.		20	M	Unknown	13Ma04No	MURPHY, Isabella		25	F	Unknown	14Ma02Np
Ann		28	F	Unknown	13Ma04No	CUSACK, Jane		22	F	Unknown	14Ma02Np
Ann		26	F	Unknown	13Ma04No	BIRMINGHAM, W.		20	M	Laborer	14Ma02Np
Mgt.		03	F	Child	13Ma04No	Sarah		18	F	Unknown	14Ma02Np
Wm.		01	M	Child	13Ma04No	GARTLAND, Philip		30	M	Laborer	14Ma02Np
Isabella		26	F	Unknown	13Ma04No	Ellen		20	F	Unknown	14Ma02Np
Roseth		28	F	Unknown	13Ma04No	Anne		20	F	Unknown	14Ma02Np
MCAULT, Mary		20	F	Unknown	13Ma04No	DUFFY, James		20	M	Mechanic	14Ma02Np
GULL, J.		22	M	Unknown	13Ma04No	MCCABE, Michl.		20	M	Laborer	14Ma02Np
Mary		18	F	Unknown	13Ma04No	MCGARNE, Patt.		20	M	Laborer	14Ma02Np
Owen		30	M	Unknown	13Ma04No	Thomas		20	M	Laborer	14Ma02Np
GULLACHAN, Mgt.		28	F	Unknown	13Ma04No	COLLINS, Thomas		20	M	Mechanic	14Ma02Np
MCDERMOTT, J.		20	M	Laborer	13Ma04No	Margaret		20	F	Unknown	14Ma02Np
KILFEATHER, J.		22	M	Unknown	13Ma04No	HUGHES, James		13	M	Unknown	14Ma02Np
GOLDEN, J.		18	M	Unknown	13Ma04No	RYAN, Patt.		20	M	Farmer	14Ma02Np
MCAULY, Bdgt.		30	F	Unknown	13Ma04No	BEGLY, Joseph		24	M	Mechanic	14Ma02Np
Edwd.		33	M	Unknown	13Ma04No	U	(W)	24	F	Unknown	14Ma02Np
CARMSIN, J.		18	M	Unknown	13Ma04No	James		20	M	Unknown	14Ma02Np
DOCKERY, Harriet		25	F	Unknown	13Ma04No	DORAN, James		20	M	Unknown	14Ma02Np
Mary		23	F	Unknown	13Ma04No	HEALAN, William		22	M	Mechanic	14Ma02Np
TODD, J.		23	M	Unknown	13Ma04No	MURPHY, Isabella		20	F	Unknown	14Ma02Np
Danl.		49	M	Unknown	13Ma04No	WALSH, Christy		22	M	Mechanic	14Ma02Np
Mary		43	F	Unknown	13Ma04No	Sarah		19	F	Unknown	14Ma02Np
Nancy		13	F	Unknown	13Ma04No	Catherine		16	F	Unknown	14Ma02Np
John		11	M	Unknown	13Ma04No	Therese		17	F	Unknown	14Ma02Np
Alexan.		08	M	Child	13Ma04No	CARLY, John		20	M	Laborer	14Ma02Np
Mary-J.		06	F	Child	13Ma04No	Mary		18	F	Unknown	14Ma02Np
W.		03	M	Child	13Ma04No	CREAHNAN, Saml.		26	M	Laborer	14Ma02Np
LEITCH, D.		19	M	Unknown	13Ma04No	Margaret		37	F	Unknown	14Ma02Np
NEIL, Peggy		20	F	Unknown	13Ma04No	Charles		20	M	Laborer	14Ma02Np
CONNER, Rose		25	F	Unknown	13Ma04No	NOWLAN, Michl.		24	M	Farmer	14Ma02Np
WOODSIDE, R.		23	M	Unknown	13Ma04No	CASSIDY, John		24	M	Laborer	14Ma02Np
FRERIL, M.		30	M	Unknown	13Ma04No	DWYER, Margaret		20	F	Unknown	14Ma02Np
GILLESPIE, B.		21	M	Unknown	13Ma04No	Mary		11	F	Unknown	14Ma02Np
MCDOUGAN, T.		29	M	Unknown	13Ma04No	QUIN, Honor		20	F	Unknown	14Ma02Np
RUNAR, J.		22	M	Unknown	13Ma04No	Catherine		20	F	Unknown	14Ma02Np
FORBES, Eliza		29	F	Unknown	13Ma04No	RILEY, Bridget		20	F	Unknown	14Ma02Np
RUSS, W.		20	M	Unknown	13Ma04No	Catherine		20	F	Unknown	14Ma02Np

NAMES OF PASSENGERS	A G E	S E X	OCCUPATIONS	DATE PORT SHIP	NAMES OF PASSENGERS	A G E	S E X	OCCUPATIONS	DATE PORT SHIP
PRENDERGAST, Wm.	40	M	Farmer	14Ma02Np	HANEGAN, Margaret	20	F	Unknown	14Ma02Np
Mary (W)	36	F	Unknown	14Ma02Np	SCANLAN, Cath.	13	F	Unknown	14Ma02Np
John (S)	08	M	Child	14Ma02Np	REDMOND, Edward	23	M	Farmer	14Ma02Np
Patrick (S)	06	M	Child	14Ma02Np	Mary	21	F	Unknown	14Ma02Np
Kidith (S)	04	M	Child	14Ma02Np	SHIELDS, Hugh	24	M	Mechanic	14Ma02Np
WALSH, Anne	20	F	Unknown	14Ma02Np	Mary	20	F	Unknown	14Ma02Np
Kitty	20	F	Unknown	14Ma02Np	DALTON, Nicholas	20	M	Laborer	14Ma02Np
Margaret	20	F	Unknown	14Ma02Np	Cath.	19	F	Unknown	14Ma02Np
GALLAGHER, Michl.	28	M	Laborer	14Ma02Np	MCLERNEY, Jas.	20	M	Mechanic	14Ma02Np
Anne	22	F	Unknown	14Ma02Np	Cath.	20	F	Unknown	14Ma02Np
NEARY, Honor	20	F	Unknown	14Ma02Np	KELLY, Owen	20	M	Mechanic	14Ma02Np
HOPE, John	20	M	Laborer	14Ma02Np					
HARRINGTON, W.	20	M	Laborer	14Ma02Np					
LAWLIN, Eliza	20	F	Unknown	14Ma02Np					
Julia	20	F	Unknown	14Ma02Np					
WALSH, Thomas	20	M	Shepherd	14Ma02Np					
CAMPBELL, Henry	35	M	Walter	14Ma02Np		MONTEZUMA 14 MAY 1847			
MCMAHON, Bridget	20	F	Unknown	14Ma02Np					
FORSYTH, Anne	16	F	Unknown	14Ma02Np		From Liverpool			
MCKEE, Matilda	20	F	Unknown	14Ma02Np					
FIELDS, Richard	20	M	Laborer	14Ma02Np					
COGGINS, Anne	30	F	Unknown	14Ma02Np					
Mary	08	F	Child	14Ma02Np	COT, U-Mrs.	38	F	Unknown	14Ma02Ao
Anthony	05	M	Child	14Ma02Np	HEALIN, U-Mrs.	30	F	Unknown	14Ma02Ao
ALT, James	60	M	Laborer	14Ma02Np	EVANS, U-Mrs.	40	F	Unknown	14Ma02Ao
U (W)	50	F	Unknown	14Ma02Np	COMAN, A.	50	M	Physician	14Ma02Ao
Sally (D)	21	F	Unknown	14Ma02Np	WILEY, D.	40	M	Physician	14Ma02Ao
Jane (D)	19	F	Unknown	14Ma02Np	WEED, T.	38	M	None	14Ma02Ao
Nancy (D)	17	F	Unknown	14Ma02Np	TRIMAN, R.	22	M	None	14Ma02Ao
Anne (D)	15	F	Unknown	14Ma02Np	PRATT, T.	28	M	None	14Ma02Ao
Saml. (S)	13	M	Unknown	14Ma02Np	MEEDS, A.	23	M	Physician	14Ma02Ao
Andy (S)	11	M	Unknown	14Ma02Np	DANM, P.	28	M	Laborer	14Ma02Ao
James (S)	09	M	Child	14Ma02Np	CAUGHAN, Cath.	25	F	Unknown	14Ma02Ao
Matilda (D)	07	F	Child	14Ma02Np	HUGHES, J.	35	M	Unknown	14Ma02Ao
Liria (D)	05	F	Child	14Ma02Np	Elisabt.	25	F	Unknown	14Ma02Ao
Esther (D)	03	F	Child	14Ma02Np	MORGAN, W.	31	M	Unknown	14Ma02Ao
FARRELL, Edward	20	M	Laborer	14Ma02Np	Mary-N.	30	F	Unknown	14Ma02Ao
TIERNEY, Michael	20	M	Laborer	14Ma02Np	HALLAHAN, M.	30	M	Unknown	14Ma02Ao
MURRAY, Anne	20	F	Unknown	14Ma02Np	PRICE, J.	25	M	Unknown	14Ma02Ao
Lawrence	20	M	Laborer	14Ma02Np	JONES, T.	42	M	Unknown	14Ma02Ao
Margaret (W)	20	F	Unknown	14Ma02Np	Mary (W)	36	F	Unknown	14Ma02Ao
Edward (S)	.00	M	Infant	14Ma02Np	Mich. (S)	09	M	Child	14Ma02Ao
COMERTON, Michael	30	M	Laborer	14Ma02Np	BRADY, P.	20	M	Unknown	14Ma02Ao
U (W)	30	F	Unknown	14Ma02Np	TIERNY, P.	25	M	Unknown	14Ma02Ao
Catherine (D)	.00	F	Infant	14Ma02Np	REILY, Bgt.	20	F	Unknown	14Ma02Ao
MCGOWAN, Brian	40	M	Laborer	14Ma02Np	SMITH, Cath.	20	F	Unknown	14Ma02Ao
Bridget	40	F	Unknown	14Ma02Np	Bgt.	17	F	Unknown	14Ma02Ao
James	30	M	Laborer	14Ma02Np	LESTER, J.	26	M	Unknown	14Ma02Ao
Catherine	20	F	Unknown	14Ma02Np	SMITH, J.	25	M	Unknown	14Ma02Ao
Ann	20	F	Unknown	14Ma02Np	CONNERY, Mary	16	F	Unknown	14Ma02Ao
FAGAN, Patt.	24	M	Laborer	14Ma02Np	MONAGHAN, Mary	15	F	Unknown	14Ma02Ao
MURRAY, Martin	24	M	Miller	14Ma02Np	SMITH, M.	27	M	Unknown	14Ma02Ao
Margaret	20	F	Unknown	14Ma02Np	Cath.	20	F	Unknown	14Ma02Ao
KENNEY, Mary	20	F	Unknown	14Ma02Np	STARKPOOL, J.	42	M	Unknown	14Ma02Ao
FALLON, Ellen	20	F	Unknown	14Ma02Np	Mary (W)	40	F	Unknown	14Ma02Ao
MCDONALD, Martin	20	M	Laborer	14Ma02Np	Harriett (D)	17	F	Unknown	14Ma02Ao
Catherine	40	F	Unknown	14Ma02Np	Lucy (D)	14	F	Unknown	14Ma02Ao
HARRINGTON, Judy	20	F	Unknown	14Ma02Np	RUNEGER, Mgt.	42	F	Unknown	14Ma02Ao
GREENE, Pat.	30	M	Shepherd	14Ma02Np	Ellen	17	F	Unknown	14Ma02Ao
U (W)	20	F	Unknown	14Ma02Np	SULLIVAN, Biddy	46	F	Unknown	14Ma02Ao
Martin	20	M	Laborer	14Ma02Np	BOBINSON, T.	20	M	Unknown	14Ma02Ao
FALLON, Bernard	20	M	Laborer	14Ma02Np	WALKER, W.	20	M	Unknown	14Ma02Ao
EGAN, John	24	M	Laborer	14Ma02Np	MCCALLE, W.	22	M	Unknown	14Ma02Ao
DALY, Kan	24	M	Laborer	14Ma02Np	D.	18	M	Laborer	14Ma02Ao
MCGUIRE, Thos.	20	M	Laborer	14Ma02Np	GALLAGHER, C.	24	M	Unknown	14Ma02Ao
RILEY, Elisab.	20	F	Unknown	14Ma02Np	EATON, J.	34	M	Unknown	14Ma02Ao
DALY, Terence	20	M	Carpenter	14Ma02Np	U (W)	24	F	Unknown	14Ma02Ao
MCCAPPIN, Joe	20	M	Farmer	14Ma02Np	John-W. (S)	01	M	Child	14Ma02Ao
GILKINSON, John	20	M	Farmer	14Ma02Np	TENNARD, R.	22	M	Unknown	14Ma02Ao
FALES, John	20	M	Farmer	14Ma02Np	Ann	21	F	Unknown	14Ma02Ao
William	20	M	Farmer	14Ma02Np	John	23	M	Unknown	14Ma02Ao
DOWNES, Jane	20	F	Unknown	14Ma02Np	Elizbt.	64	F	Unknown	14Ma02Ao
Martha	20	F	Unknown	14Ma02Np	YORE, T.	23	M	Unknown	14Ma02Ao
Annie	20	F	Unknown	14Ma02Np	MCCAN, B.	25	M	Unknown	14Ma02Ao
HANEGAN, Hugh	20	M	Shepherd	14Ma02Np	CONUGH, T.	34	M	Unknown	14Ma02Ao

NAMES OF PASSENGERS		AGE	SEX	OCCUPATIONS	DATE PORT SHIP
CONUGH, Bgt.		21	F	Unknown	14Ma02Ao
FLYNN, M.		28	M	Unknown	14Ma02Ao
MORGAN, T.		24	M	Unknown	14Ma02Ao
BUSTLE, Cath.		19	F	Unknown	14Ma02Ao
ROBINSON, S.		28	M	Unknown	14Ma02Ao
KYS, J.		21	M	Unknown	14Ma02Ao
DUNN, A.		16	M	Unknown	14Ma02Ao
ROBINSON, M.		50	M	Unknown	14Ma02Ao
Mgt.		25	F	Unknown	14Ma02Ao
MCGORMAN, W.		20	M	Unknown	14Ma02Ao
HANLOTT, U.		16	M	Unknown	14Ma02Ao
KENNETH, Jane		17	F	Unknown	14Ma02Ao
GOHAN, Bgt.		18	F	Unknown	14Ma02Ao
MAKIN, D.		26	M	Unknown	14Ma02Ao
BOYLE, J.		20	M	Unknown	14Ma02Ao
MCTEAGUE, P.		20	M	Unknown	14Ma02Ao
REYNOLDS, J.		14	M	Unknown	14Ma02Ao
BRODEY, Mary		16	F	Unknown	14Ma02Ao
GADLY, M.		25	M	Unknown	14Ma02Ao
Mich.		20	M	Unknown	14Ma02Ao
BRUNBLE, T.		20	M	Unknown	14Ma02Ao
FAGAN, M.		20	M	Unknown	14Ma02Ao
CULLEN, Julia		22	F	Unknown	14Ma02Ao
Rose		19	F	Unknown	14Ma02Ao
MONAGHAN, T.		23	M	Unknown	14Ma02Ao
WELDEN, M.		22	M	Unknown	14Ma02Ao
FARLY, M.		28	M	Unknown	14Ma02Ao
MANATT, J.		30	M	Unknown	14Ma02Ao
Mary		60	F	Unknown	14Ma02Ao
Owen		19	M	Unknown	14Ma02Ao
KOWGAR, W.		30	M	Laborer	14Ma02Ao
Mos.		25	M	Unknown	14Ma02Ao
Ellen		20	F	Unknown	14Ma02Ao
Peggy		60	F	Unknown	14Ma02Ao
Anne		25	F	Unknown	14Ma02Ao
HEALY, Mary		15	F	Unknown	14Ma02Ao
Ellen		16	F	Unknown	14Ma02Ao
John		14	M	None	14Ma02Ao
CUSACK, J.		40	M	Unknown	14Ma02Ao
HANRATTY, Ann		19	F	Unknown	14Ma02Ao
NOON, J.		22	M	Unknown	14Ma02Ao
GILPIN, Denar		21	F	Unknown	14Ma02Ao
NONES, E.		24	M	Unknown	14Ma02Ao
BARNETT, J.		24	M	Unknown	14Ma02Ao
FLEMING, C.		34	M	Unknown	14Ma02Ao
U	(W)	23	F	Unknown	14Ma02Ao
Chris.	(S)	01	M	Child	14Ma02Ao
KELLY, J.		30	M	Unknown	14Ma02Ao
Jane		24	F	Unknown	14Ma02Ao
WARD, Eliza		22	F	Unknown	14Ma02Ao
BORAN, Jane		22	F	Unknown	14Ma02Ao
JOHNSON, Cath.		20	F	Unknown	14Ma02Ao
CAHILL, T.		20	M	Unknown	14Ma02Ao
MCGEE, J.		22	M	Unknown	14Ma02Ao
TURNER, T.		24	M	Unknown	14Ma02Ao
MCGERRY, N.		20	M	Unknown	14Ma02Ao
Cath.		18	F	Unknown	14Ma02Ao
MCGOWAN, P.		21	M	Unknown	14Ma02Ao
Cath.		23	F	Unknown	14Ma02Ao
JACKSON, T.		18	M	Unknown	14Ma02Ao
STEWART, G.		18	M	Unknown	14Ma02Ao
Thos.		14	M	None	14Ma02Ao
MCCRUTAT, P.		23	M	Unknown	14Ma02Ao
CARROLL, E.		27	M	Unknown	14Ma02Ao
Winifred		27	F	Unknown	14Ma02Ao
MCCABE, J.		20	M	Unknown	14Ma02Ao
COOK, Ann		14	F	Unknown	14Ma02Ao
Bgt.		16	F	Unknown	14Ma02Ao
DENNIS, J.		20	M	Unknown	14Ma02Ao
MCKEOWN, J.		20	M	Unknown	14Ma02Ao
Mary		20	F	Unknown	14Ma02Ao
SMITH, M.		18	M	Unknown	14Ma02Ao
CAFFRY, M.		20	M	Laborer	14Ma02Ao
CLIFFORD, F.		26	M	Unknown	14Ma02Ao
MCNULTY, J.		18	M	Unknown	14Ma02Ao
MCGAHAN, W.		30	M	Unknown	14Ma02Ao
MULLIGAN, Mary		22	F	Unknown	14Ma02Ao
MCCLAY, Ann		23	F	Unknown	14Ma02Ao
MCEVEY, Bgt.		30	F	Unknown	14Ma02Ao
SHANNON, T.		20	M	Unknown	14Ma02Ao
SHIELDS, N.		30	M	Unknown	14Ma02Ao
Ellen		30	F	Unknown	14Ma02Ao
GALLAGHAN, O.		21	M	Unknown	14Ma02Ao
COYLE, Susan		23	F	Unknown	14Ma02Ao
HORARTY, Jan		30	F	Unknown	14Ma02Ao
Hannah		20	F	Unknown	14Ma02Ao
Martha		19	F	Unknown	14Ma02Ao
James		23	M	Unknown	14Ma02Ao
Ann		21	F	Unknown	14Ma02Ao
STAR, S.		21	M	Unknown	14Ma02Ao
BRYAN, J.		25	M	Unknown	14Ma02Ao
PINDLE, M.		25	M	Unknown	14Ma02Ao
JORLENY, M.		24	M	Unknown	14Ma02Ao
COLLINS, J.		19	M	Unknown	14Ma02Ao
MOLLONE, W.		20	M	Unknown	14Ma02Ao
HOWARD, M.		35	M	Unknown	14Ma02Ao
Sarah		30	F	Unknown	14Ma02Ao
WILSON, J.		30	M	Unknown	14Ma02Ao
Rebecca	(W)	31	F	Unknown	14Ma02Ao
Elisbt.	(D)	01	F	Child	14Ma02Ao
SHEEHAN, Kitty		24	F	Unknown	14Ma02Ao
KELLY, Bgt.		21	F	Unknown	14Ma02Ao
LARAGHAN, M.		03	M	Child	14Ma02Ao
KELLY, J.		21	M	Unknown	14Ma02Ao
U	(W)	19	F	Unknown	14Ma02Ao
BANNACH, E.		26	M	Unknown	14Ma02Ao
RAINER, W.		43	M	Unknown	14Ma02Ao
U	(W)	43	F	Unknown	14Ma02Ao
Martha	(D)	13	F	Unknown	14Ma02Ao
U	(D)	12	F	Unknown	14Ma02Ao
Rachel	(D)	11	F	Unknown	14Ma02Ao
Sarh	(D)	10	F	Unknown	14Ma02Ao
Wm.	(S)	09	M	Child	14Ma02Ao
John	(S)	08	M	Child	14Ma02Ao
Alex.	(S)	01	M	Child	14Ma02Ao
MORTESEN, M.		24	M	Laborer	14Ma02Ao
Thos.		18	M	Laborer	14Ma02Ao
KELLY, Rose		20	M	Laborer	14Ma02Ao
COLYN, Mary		20	M	Laborer	14Ma02Ao
JAGHEN, Cath.		70	M	Laborer	14Ma02Ao
MCGUILL, Mary		15	M	Laborer	14Ma02Ao
ARMSTRONG, Mary		18	M	Laborer	14Ma02Ao
FAY, Mary		16	M	Laborer	14Ma02Ao
FARLY, Mgt.		21	M	Laborer	14Ma02Ao
MCGERAGE, M.		19	M	Laborer	14Ma02Ao
Mary		19	M	Laborer	14Ma02Ao
RICE, P.		20	M	Laborer	14Ma02Ao
MALLEN, P.		20	M	Laborer	14Ma02Ao
FITZPATRICK, Mgt.		20	F	Laborer	14Ma02Ao
COOLAHAN, Cath.		16	F	Laborer	14Ma02Ao
LORKIN, Elzt.		20	F	Laborer	14Ma02Ao
TUNY, Jane		20	F	Laborer	14Ma02Ao
GOLDIE, P.		14	M	Laborer	14Ma02Ao
TRIY, Mgt.		16	F	Laborer	14Ma02Ao
Michl.		18	M	Laborer	14Ma02Ao
NEARY, Rose		14	F	Laborer	14Ma02Ao
Bgt.		12	F	None	14Ma02Ao
COUGHLIN, D.		30	M	None	14Ma02Ao
GALLGHAR, Mary		20	F	None	14Ma02Ao
MURPHY, Mary		29	F	None	14Ma02Ao
OBRIEN, P.		16	M	None	14Ma02Ao
James		20	M	None	14Ma02Ao
MCHUGH, M.		20	F	None	14Ma02Ao
ARMSTRONG, J.		22	M	None	14Ma02Ao
BORKLEDGE, J.		28	M	None	14Ma02Ao
DALY, W.		23	F	None	14Ma02Ao
CARROLL, O.		24	M	None	14Ma02Ao
KENOK, J.		24	M	None	14Ma02Ao
MASSAEL, Mgt.		21	F	None	14Ma02Ao
WELSH, Jane		10	F	None	14Ma02Ao

NAMES OF PASSENGERS		AGE	SEX	OCCUPATIONS	DATE PORT SHIP
BARY, T.		26	M	None	14Ma02Ao
Patk.		20	M	None	14Ma02Ao
F.		17	M	None	14Ma02Ao
TEGAN, Rose		19	F	None	14Ma02Ao
CAVISH, Jane		18	F	None	14Ma02Ao
HAYGUS, W.		22	M	None	14Ma02Ao
HAGGERTY, J.		20	M	Laborer	14Ma02Ao
LEWIS, M.		28	M	Unknown	14Ma02Ao
Danl.		10	M	None	14Ma02Ao
Sarah		08	F	Child	14Ma02Ao
Mgt.		03	F	Child	14Ma02Ao
Wm.		01	M	Child	14Ma02Ao
BRADY, Mgt.		40	F	Unknown	14Ma02Ao
Joseph		16	M	Unknown	14Ma02Ao
Mary		09	F	Child	14Ma02Ao
DEMPSEY, O.		20	M	Unknown	14Ma02Ao
FARRELL, A.		20	M	Unknown	14Ma02Ao
MCCERY, Essy		10	F	Unknown	14Ma02Ao
Betsy		04	F	Child	14Ma02Ao
CLARK, Mary		70	F	Unknown	14Ma02Ao
DOLAN, J.		02	M	Child	14Ma02Ao
CONRY, John		24	M	Unknown	14Ma02Ao
SCANLON, E.		22	M	Unknown	14Ma02Ao
MALON, P.		24	M	Unknown	14Ma02Ao
STANLEY, T.		18	M	Unknown	14Ma02Ao
ROCHE, H.		24	M	Unknown	14Ma02Ao
HELGIN, P.		30	M	Unknown	14Ma02Ao
MORRATY, Mary		20	F	Unknown	14Ma02Ao
RUSH, Bgt.		22	F	Unknown	14Ma02Ao
DUFFY, Mary		20	F	Unknown	14Ma02Ao
SCALLY, Mary		26	F	Unknown	14Ma02Ao
Mary	(D)	01	F	Child	14Ma02Ao
CANLEN, P.		25	M	Unknown	14Ma02Ao
Eliza		12	F	Unknown	14Ma02Ao
Joseph		13	M	None	14Ma02Ao
Eliza		11	F	Unknown	14Ma02Ao
GRIFFIN, Cath.		13	F	Unknown	14Ma02Ao
Eliza		16	F	Unknown	14Ma02Ao
PYRE, T.		26	M	Unknown	14Ma02Ao
Bgt.		20	F	Unknown	14Ma02Ao
GURRY, P.		29	M	Unknown	14Ma02Ao
HEYN, D.		24	M	Unknown	14Ma02Ao
Cath.		30	F	Unknown	14Ma02Ao
John		12	M	None	14Ma02Ao
GILPIN, Susan		23	F	Unknown	14Ma02Ao
MCCORMICK, Mary		18	F	Unknown	14Ma02Ao
SORRY, T.		24	M	Unknown	14Ma02Ao
CAMPBELL, Abby		20	F	Unknown	14Ma02Ao
T.		19	M	Laborer	14Ma02Ao
OBRIEN, J.		30	M	Unknown	14Ma02Ao
CONNER, D.		11	M	None	14Ma02Ao
BRADY, Mgt.		70	F	Unknown	14Ma02Ao
James		27	M	Unknown	14Ma02Ao
Thos.		26	M	Unknown	14Ma02Ao
REILY, J.		30	M	Unknown	14Ma02Ao
Mary		20	F	Unknown	14Ma02Ao
MCCLINBERT, M.		40	M	Unknown	14Ma02Ao
MCCLEAR, M.		27	M	Unknown	14Ma02Ao
Louisa		18	F	Unknown	14Ma02Ao
NULLY, J.Mrs.		29	F	Unknown	14Ma02Ao
Ellen		28	F	Unknown	14Ma02Ao
SMITH, H.		30	M	Unknown	14Ma02Ao
MAHER, U-Mrs.		42	F	Unknown	14Ma02Ao
Mary	(D)	12	F	Unknown	14Ma02Ao
DELNAGH, B.		22	M	Unknown	14Ma02Ao
MCCORK, C.		16	M	Unknown	14Ma02Ao
PETER, Ann		18	F	Unknown	14Ma02Ao
BREY, Bgt.		18	F	Unknown	14Ma02Ao
REILY, Mgt.		20	F	Unknown	14Ma02Ao
PINHORN, E.		24	M	Unknown	14Ma02Ao
GULRYN, C.		16	M	Unknown	14Ma02Ao
DELEY, W.		22	M	Unknown	14Ma02Ao
DELHUS, Mgt.		18	F	Unknown	14Ma02Ao
MCLAUGHIN, M.		20	M	Unknown	14Ma02Ao
OHARE, P.		20	M	Unknown	14Ma02Ao

NAMES OF PASSENGERS		AGE	SEX	OCCUPATIONS	DATE PORT SHIP
SMITH, W.		60	M	Unknown	14Ma02Ao
Bgt.		19	F	Unknown	14Ma02Ao
MCEVEY, Ann		20	F	Unknown	14Ma02Ao
COOK, E.		61	M	Unknown	14Ma02Ao
Mgt.		20	F	Unknown	14Ma02Ao
Ann		19	F	Unknown	14Ma02Ao
KELLY, Cath.		19	F	Unknown	14Ma02Ao
WOODS, J.		28	M	Unknown	14Ma02Ao
SHANNAN, T.		22	M	Unknown	14Ma02Ao
KING, Cath.		20	F	Unknown	14Ma02Ao
FAGAN, Mgt.		18	F	Unknown	14Ma02Ao
REYBURN, P.		17	M	Unknown	14Ma02Ao
BEWES, J.		25	M	Unknown	14Ma02Ao
HALY, J.		24	M	Unknown	14Ma02Ao
MEEDY, Cath.		20	F	Unknown	14Ma02Ao
MCGEHAN, J.		20	M	Laborer	14Ma02Ao
PATTERSON, Cath.		20	F	Unknown	14Ma02Ao
HEYNES, D.		28	M	Unknown	14Ma02Ao
OHARA, Mary		46	F	Unknown	14Ma02Ao
CLEMEN, U-Mrs.		28	F	Unknown	14Ma02Ao
Ellen	(D)	05	F	Child	14Ma02Ao
John	(S)	03	M	Child	14Ma02Ao
DONOHUE, Mary		21	F	Unknown	14Ma02Ao
CAFFREY, Mary		15	F	Unknown	14Ma02Ao
SMITH, Bdgt.		16	F	Unknown	14Ma02Ao
HANARTY, Mary		12	F	Unknown	14Ma02Ao
COUNIER, M.		26	M	Unknown	14Ma02Ao
Wm.		21	M	Unknown	14Ma02Ao
CAHILL, Ann		40	F	Unknown	14Ma02Ao
GAVICAN, M.		04	M	Child	14Ma02Ao
CONOLLY, Betsy		19	F	Unknown	14Ma02Ao
Nancy		21	F	Unknown	14Ma02Ao
REDDY, R.		21	M	Unknown	14Ma02Ao
BAXTER, Jane		18	F	Unknown	14Ma02Ao
WOODS, Hannah		35	F	Unknown	14Ma02Ao
Ann	(D)	07	F	Child	14Ma02Ao
Mary	(D)	03	F	Child	14Ma02Ao
BRADY, H.		20	M	Unknown	14Ma02Ao
BOLTON, Judith		35	F	Unknown	14Ma02Ao
Mary	(D)	08	F	Child	14Ma02Ao
Ann	(D)	05	F	Child	14Ma02Ao
Edward	(S)	01	M	Child	14Ma02Ao
JENNINGS, Bgt.		60	F	Unknown	14Ma02Ao
Bdgt.		15	F	Unknown	14Ma02Ao
MALESON, Bdgt.		23	F	Unknown	14Ma02Ao
Bdgt.	(D)	02	F	Child	14Ma02Ao
ONEIL, Bgt.		16	F	Unknown	14Ma02Ao
GALLON, Mary		20	F	Unknown	14Ma02Ao
TAT, P.		27	M	Unknown	14Ma02Ao
CAFFRY, P.		21	M	Unknown	14Ma02Ao
Terence		18	M	Unknown	14Ma02Ao
Cath.		15	F	Unknown	14Ma02Ao
REILLY, Mary		30	F	Unknown	14Ma02Ao
James		20	M	Unknown	14Ma02Ao
DONOHOE, P.		18	M	Unknown	14Ma02Ao
FARRELL, G.		20	M	Unknown	14Ma02Ao
TREMBLE, J.		20	M	Unknown	14Ma02Ao
MCCORMICK, Mary		06	F	Child	14Ma02Ao
FITZGERALD, U		20	M	Laborer	14Ma02Ao
MURPHY, J.		27	M	Laborer	14Ma02Ao
COLSON, C.		24	M	Laborer	14Ma02Ao
QUIGLY, P.		22	M	Laborer	14Ma02Ao
REILLY, O.		20	M	Laborer	14Ma02Ao
RAMSEY, W.		25	M	Laborer	14Ma02Ao
LUNDAGNER, M.		26	M	Laborer	14Ma02Ao
MCDONNELL, J.		22	M	Laborer	14Ma02Ao
MCINTYRE, Mary		24	F	Laborer	14Ma02Ao
CROLY, Cath.		24	F	Laborer	14Ma02Ao
CAVANAGH, P.		36	M	Laborer	14Ma02Ao
Bgt.	(W)	36	F	Laborer	14Ma02Ao
Rich.	(S)	09	M	Child	14Ma02Ao
Cath.	(D)	06	F	Child	14Ma02Ao
John	(S)	03	M	Child	14Ma02Ao
Patt	(S)	02	M	Child	14Ma02Ao
OREEN, C.		20	M	Unknown	14Ma02Ao

NAMES OF PASSENGERS		A G E	S E X	OCCUPATIONS	DATE PORT SHIP	NAMES OF PASSENGERS		A G E	S E X	OCCUPATIONS	DATE PORT SHIP
MANTEN, M.		24	M	Unknown	14Ma02Ao	SHIRE, Elizbt.		19	F	Unknown	15Ma02Aa
Lawrence		20	M	Unknown	14Ma02Ao	STEWART, R.		26	M	Unknown	15Ma02Aa
WALSH, J.		16	M	Unknown	14Ma02Ao	DALY, P.		23	M	Unknown	15Ma02Aa
SORRY, C.		38	M	Unknown	14Ma02Ao	FINLY, W.		34	M	Unknown	15Ma02Aa
THONLEY, J.		16	M	Unknown	14Ma02Ao	CORTIE, A.J.		23	M	Unknown	15Ma02Aa
MARTIN, Mary-A.		18	F	Unknown	14Ma02Ao	CONSTATELA, W.		16	M	Unknown	15Ma02Aa
						PARR, B.		22	M	Unknown	15Ma02Aa
						RILEY, Mgt.		23	F	Unknown	15Ma02Aa
						SMITH, Mary		26	F	Unknown	15Ma02Aa
						COCHRAN, A.		23	M	Unknown	15Ma02Aa
GARRICK 15 MAY 1847						GALLAGHER, B.		21	M	Unknown	15Ma02Aa
						CORBETT, E.		23	M	Unknown	15Ma02Aa
From Liverpool						Mary-A.		21	F	Unknown	15Ma02Aa
						RALCLIFFE, J.		26	M	Unknown	15Ma02Aa
						MCCOSEN, J.		28	M	Unknown	15Ma02Aa
						Ann		22	F	Unknown	15Ma02Aa
						WATERFELL, J.		28	M	Unknown	15Ma02Aa
JACKSON, Alice		35	F	Unknown	15Ma02Aa	RYAN, J.		23	M	Unknown	15Ma02Aa
George-W.	(S)	14	M	None	15Ma02Aa	MULLEN, P.		23	M	Unknown	15Ma02Aa
Hugh	(S)	12	M	None	15Ma02Aa	KEARY, D.		20	M	Unknown	15Ma02Aa
COOPER, T.		26	M	Merchant	15Ma02Aa	EVANS, P.		25	M	Unknown	15Ma02Aa
BRADLY, T.		25	M	Merchant	15Ma02Aa	MARGEY, W.		20	M	Unknown	15Ma02Aa
BURNES, E.		19	M	Merchant	15Ma02Aa	GAHAGN, Mary		21	F	Unknown	15Ma02Aa
THORP, T.		39	M	Merchant	15Ma02Aa	MARTINS, Betty		20	F	Unknown	15Ma02Aa
Emily	(W)	28	F	Unknown	15Ma02Aa	MONE, Ann		37	F	Unknown	15Ma02Aa
Thos.	(S)	12	M	None	15Ma02Aa	RYAN, Mary		17	F	Unknown	15Ma02Aa
Chris.	(S)	10	M	None	15Ma02Aa	Bgt.		19	F	Unknown	15Ma02Aa
George	(S)	08	M	Child	15Ma02Aa	POLKE, Cath.		20	F	Unknown	15Ma02Aa
SKIDNER, U.		46	M	Merchant	15Ma02Aa	CAY, Bgt.		18	F	Unknown	15Ma02Aa
SAY, G.		40	M	Merchant	15Ma02Aa	KELLY, M.		20	M	Laborer	15Ma02Aa
Jane		17	F	Unknown	15Ma02Aa	Mich.		20	M	Laborer	15Ma02Aa
John		12	M	Unknown	15Ma02Aa	John		18	M	Laborer	15Ma02Aa
DAVIS, T.		32	M	Laborer	15Ma02Aa	RYAN, T.		23	M	Laborer	15Ma02Aa
Mgt.	(W)	31	F	Unknown	15Ma02Aa	KINNY, P.		20	M	Laborer	15Ma02Aa
Wm.	(S)	06	M	Child	15Ma02Aa	REILY, M.		23	M	Laborer	15Ma02Aa
Sarah-A.	(D)	04	F	Child	15Ma02Aa	ONEIL, Mary		16	F	Unknown	15Ma02Aa
COXWAN, J.		22	M	Unknown	15Ma02Aa	BURN, Cath.		18	F	Unknown	15Ma02Aa
BAMBUSH, Sarah-A.		10	F	Unknown	15Ma02Aa	GUNN, Ann		60	F	Unknown	15Ma02Aa
THEHUSH, W.		26	M	Unknown	15Ma02Aa	FLYN, Sarah		04	F	Child	15Ma02Aa
FLYN, W.		24	M	Unknown	15Ma02Aa	SHERIDAN, P.		40	M	Unknown	15Ma02Aa
Cath.		15	F	Unknown	15Ma02Aa	Mary	(W)	34	F	Unknown	15Ma02Aa
CONOUR, P.		25	M	Unknown	15Ma02Aa	Jane	(D)	15	F	Unknown	15Ma02Aa
LYNCH, J.		23	M	Unknown	15Ma02Aa	Mary	(D)	11	F	Unknown	15Ma02Aa
Thos.		30	M	Unknown	15Ma02Aa	Bgt.	(D)	07	F	Child	15Ma02Aa
CONDEN, M.		25	M	Unknown	15Ma02Aa	Mgt.	(D)	04	F	Child	15Ma02Aa
GOONAN, P.		21	M	Unknown	15Ma02Aa	Ann	(D)	01	F	Child	15Ma02Aa
RYAN, D.		27	M	Unknown	15Ma02Aa	BURNS, J.		20	M	Unknown	15Ma02Aa
DUNLAS, J.		26	M	Unknown	15Ma02Aa	BRADY, P.		21	M	Unknown	15Ma02Aa
Mary		30	F	Unknown	15Ma02Aa	GUNN, P.		30	M	Unknown	15Ma02Aa
BARRY, Ellen		16	F	Unknown	15Ma02Aa	SHEGN, J.		24	M	Unknown	15Ma02Aa
ROARKE, J.		21	M	Unknown	15Ma02Aa	CORNER, T.		22	M	Unknown	15Ma02Aa
KELLY, W.		20	M	Unknown	15Ma02Aa	TOORINY, P.		23	M	Unknown	15Ma02Aa
Jas.		21	M	Unknown	15Ma02Aa	CLONE, C.		26	M	Unknown	15Ma02Aa
BRADY, P.		30	M	Unknown	15Ma02Aa	M.		28	M	Unknown	15Ma02Aa
CLARKE, Susan		18	F	Unknown	15Ma02Aa	DENYSON, C.		28	M	Unknown	15Ma02Aa
RILEY, Mgt.		20	F	Unknown	15Ma02Aa	RILEY, T.		24	M	Unknown	15Ma02Aa
GASKIN, Mgt.		18	F	Unknown	15Ma02Aa	Edwd.		28	M	Unknown	15Ma02Aa
HARMON, T.		23	M	Unknown	15Ma02Aa	BELL, W.		19	M	Unknown	15Ma02Aa
BUNN, T.		23	M	Laborer	15Ma02Aa	FARRELL, P.		24	M	Unknown	15Ma02Aa
DONNELLY, J.		24	M	Unknown	15Ma02Aa	DONGAN, R.		25	M	Unknown	15Ma02Aa
FOX, T.		27	M	Unknown	15Ma02Aa	STEPHENS, W.J.		25	M	Unknown	15Ma02Aa
MCNAMARA, J.		23	M	Unknown	15Ma02Aa	TUNE, J.		25	M	Unknown	15Ma02Aa
BUTH, P.		40	M	Unknown	15Ma02Aa	BRANGHER, W.		26	M	Unknown	15Ma02Aa
Cath.	(W)	30	F	Unknown	15Ma02Aa	Ruth		22	F	Unknown	15Ma02Aa
Edwd.	(S)	02	M	Child	15Ma02Aa	Andrew		19	M	Unknown	15Ma02Aa
MCGUINN, J.		20	M	Unknown	15Ma02Aa	DUFFY, Elizth.		18	F	Unknown	15Ma02Aa
NARLEN, J.		20	M	Unknown	15Ma02Aa	KELLY, Jan		22	F	Unknown	15Ma02Aa
HENESSY, C.		24	M	Unknown	15Ma02Aa	PORTER, Agnes		20	F	Unknown	15Ma02Aa
MCDENIR, D.		18	M	Unknown	15Ma02Aa	HENRY, Sarah		40	F	Unknown	15Ma02Aa
GALLAGHER, P.		18	M	Unknown	15Ma02Aa	LORD, Sally		30	F	Unknown	15Ma02Aa
MCJAGEN, J.		20	M	Unknown	15Ma02Aa	Mary		20	F	Unknown	15Ma02Aa
Bgt.		25	F	Unknown	15Ma02Aa	BROWN, J.		24	M	Laborer	15Ma02Aa
MCDOWN, W.		20	M	Unknown	15Ma02Aa	Mgt.		17	F	Unknown	15Ma02Aa
Arthur		11	M	None	15Ma02Aa	LORD, R.		50	M	Unknown	15Ma02Aa
Eliza		37	F	Unknown	15Ma02Aa	John		40	M	Unknown	15Ma02Aa

NAMES OF PASSENGERS	A G E	S E X	OCCUPATIONS	DATE PORT SHIP	NAMES OF PASSENGERS	A G E	S E X	OCCUPATIONS	DATE PORT SHIP
DEAR, M.	25	M	Unknown	15Ma02Aa	WALSH, N.	23	M	Unknown	15Ma02Aa
HAY, J.	50	M	Unknown	15Ma02Aa	MCDONALD, E.	21	M	Laborer	15Ma02Aa
James	18	M	Unknown	15Ma02Aa	John	23	M	Unknown	15Ma02Aa
Johanna	06	F	Child	15Ma02Aa	Cath.	24	F	Unknown	15Ma02Aa
Mary	20	F	Unknown	15Ma02Aa	WAYLEN, Ann	21	F	Unknown	15Ma02Aa
BURY, M.	25	M	Unknown	15Ma02Aa	KILPATRICK, D.	30	M	Unknown	15Ma02Aa
GORDON, Bdgt.	20	F	Unknown	15Ma02Aa	Sarah-M. (W)	30	F	Unknown	15Ma02Aa
Jane	18	F	Unknown	15Ma02Aa	Sarah-M. (D)	05	F	Child	15Ma02Aa
HENY, J.	60	M	Unknown	15Ma02Aa	Ellsb.T. (D)	03	F	Child	15Ma02Aa
Mary (W)	55	F	Unknown	15Ma02Aa	BAKER, J.	35	M	Unknown	15Ma02Aa
Mgret. (D)	13	F	Unknown	15Ma02Aa	PENROSE, R.	24	M	Unknown	15Ma02Aa
Joseph (S)	22	M	Unknown	15Ma02Aa	WALMSBY, R.	21	M	Unknown	15Ma02Aa
SCANLON, W.	25	M	Unknown	15Ma02Aa	TELFER, Harriet	23	F	Unknown	15Ma02Aa
Rebecca	22	F	Unknown	15Ma02Aa	MILWEY, M.	25	M	Unknown	15Ma02Aa
CONNER, J.	22	M	Unknown	15Ma02Aa	Hy.	15	M	Unknown	15Ma02Aa
NERNE, T.	22	M	Unknown	15Ma02Aa	SLATT, R.	27	M	Unknown	15Ma02Aa
MCRANE, Esther	30	F	Unknown	15Ma02Aa	FAUN, Mary	45	F	Unknown	15Ma02Aa
SYMUS, B.	28	M	Unknown	15Ma02Aa	SWYN, Cath.	25	F	Unknown	15Ma02Aa
OWEN, S.	26	M	Unknown	15Ma02Aa	TUFF, Mgt.	20	F	Unknown	15Ma02Aa
RILEY, M.	30	M	Unknown	15Ma02Aa	MOORE, Jane	30	F	Unknown	15Ma02Aa
Cath.	30	F	Unknown	15Ma02Aa	MCARNLE, J.	35	M	Unknown	15Ma02Aa
GARAGH, Cath.	30	F	Unknown	15Ma02Aa	MOGN, P.	25	M	Unknown	15Ma02Aa
FANN, R.	23	M	Unknown	15Ma02Aa	CEUGHN, P.	35	M	Unknown	15Ma02Aa
MCREVY, M.	22	M	Unknown	15Ma02Aa	KELLY, Mgt.	19	F	Unknown	15Ma02Aa
ADAMS, T.	24	M	Unknown	15Ma02Aa	RILEY, Mgt.	28	F	Unknown	15Ma02Aa
MCARDLE, J.	23	M	Unknown	15Ma02Aa	JOYCE, R.	20	M	Unknown	15Ma02Aa
RODEN, J.	30	M	Unknown	15Ma02Aa	HEFFEN, T.	20	M	Unknown	15Ma02Aa
Owen	30	M	Unknown	15Ma02Aa	DONOHUE, P.	27	M	Unknown	15Ma02Aa
CONSTABLE, J.	26	M	Unknown	15Ma02Aa	NOON, F.	24	M	Unknown	15Ma02Aa
CLERY, P.	23	M	Unknown	15Ma02Aa	Mary	23	F	Unknown	15Ma02Aa
WALKER, C.	24	M	Unknown	15Ma02Aa	LORRGHAN, W.	25	M	Unknown	15Ma02Aa
WALEBARY, Sarah	06	F	Child	15Ma02Aa	FEN, T.	20	M	Unknown	15Ma02Aa
Emma	04	F	Child	15Ma02Aa	HANE, J.	27	M	Unknown	15Ma02Aa
RALSH, Eliza	19	F	Unknown	15Ma02Aa	LOSHNAGN, P.	34	M	Unknown	15Ma02Aa
STEWART, Alice-J.	22	F	Unknown	15Ma02Aa	LYNCH, P.	30	M	Unknown	15Ma02Aa
REILY, M.	30	M	Laborer	15Ma02Aa	WALKER, T.	22	M	Unknown	15Ma02Aa
Ruth (D)	01	F	Child	15Ma02Aa	FORN, M.	24	M	Unknown	15Ma02Aa
Mary (W)	23	F	Unknown	15Ma02Aa	TOBIN, Bgt.	20	F	Unknown	15Ma02Aa
DUFFY, N.	19	M	Unknown	15Ma02Aa	CROSBY, J.	23	M	Unknown	15Ma02Aa
BISHOP, J.	21	M	Unknown	15Ma02Aa	BIRNEY, R.	25	M	Unknown	15Ma02Aa
MCGUILL, D.	35	M	Unknown	15Ma02Aa	MCKELLAN, Ann	24	F	Unknown	15Ma02Aa
COLIN, B.	35	M	Unknown	15Ma02Aa	RYNNE, M.	20	M	Unknown	15Ma02Aa
Ann	08	F	Child	15Ma02Aa	KERNY, P.	26	M	Unknown	15Ma02Aa
Jane	18	F	Unknown	15Ma02Aa	KEARNY, M.	24	M	Laborer	15Ma02Aa
DWYER, R.	18	M	Unknown	15Ma02Aa	CLEAN, M.	24	M	Unknown	15Ma02Aa
BARRETT, R.	32	M	Unknown	15Ma02Aa	KENNY, Ellen	18	F	Unknown	15Ma02Aa
BENNET, Sarah	19	F	Unknown	15Ma02Aa	HASTINGS, Ann	23	F	Unknown	15Ma02Aa
WALKER, Sarah	30	F	Unknown	15Ma02Aa	CORBETT, Mgt.	20	F	Unknown	15Ma02Aa
MULRENY, P.	21	M	Unknown	15Ma02Aa	OCONN, Mgt.	20	F	Unknown	15Ma02Aa
FARREN, T.	17	M	Unknown	15Ma02Aa	FLAUGH, Ellen	23	F	Unknown	15Ma02Aa
HENRY, D.	60	M	Unknown	15Ma02Aa	MCNUNE, Mgt.	19	F	Unknown	15Ma02Aa
MCGEER, Susan	15	F	Unknown	15Ma02Aa	MCQUADE, Bessy	19	F	Unknown	15Ma02Aa
Eliza	17	F	Unknown	15Ma02Aa	Mary-N.	17	F	Unknown	15Ma02Aa
HURST, W.	19	M	Unknown	15Ma02Aa	CASSIDY, M.	31	F	Unknown	15Ma02Aa
SWAN, W.	23	M	Unknown	15Ma02Aa	Sarah	19	F	Unknown	15Ma02Aa
Jane	50	F	Unknown	15Ma02Aa	RILEY, P.	29	M	Unknown	15Ma02Aa
Mary-J.	18	F	Unknown	15Ma02Aa	John	22	M	Unknown	15Ma02Aa
Jane	11	F	Unknown	15Ma02Aa	KELLY, P.	26	M	Unknown	15Ma02Aa
BELL, A.	32	M	Unknown	15Ma02Aa	DONAHUE, Mary	19	F	Unknown	15Ma02Aa
Mary	30	F	Unknown	15Ma02Aa	ROARKE, P.	27	M	Unknown	15Ma02Aa
SHERN, H.	22	M	Unknown	15Ma02Aa	BRADY, E.	20	M	Unknown	15Ma02Aa
LAMB, Ann	21	F	Unknown	15Ma02Aa	CARRON, M.	30	M	Unknown	15Ma02Aa
CALLUM, Jane	15	F	Unknown	15Ma02Aa	REILLY, N.	30	M	Unknown	15Ma02Aa
CEVAGHN, M.	22	M	Unknown	15Ma02Aa	PRITCHARD, J.	21	M	Unknown	15Ma02Aa
MULLER, P.	20	M	Unknown	15Ma02Aa	CALAHAN, Sarah	25	F	Unknown	15Ma02Aa
BURY, D.	19	M	Unknown	15Ma02Aa	DONOHUE, Ann	17	F	Unknown	15Ma02Aa
B.	20	F	Unknown	15Ma02Aa	Mgt.	18	F	Unknown	15Ma02Aa
Cath.	15	F	Unknown	15Ma02Aa	Mgt.	20	F	Unknown	15Ma02Aa
LEONARD, R.	45	M	Unknown	15Ma02Aa	Ann	18	F	Unknown	15Ma02Aa
MCGUINN, M.	28	M	Unknown	15Ma02Aa	SKINNER, R.	21	M	Unknown	15Ma02Aa
MURRY, P.	22	M	Unknown	15Ma02Aa	WEMLY, S.	21	M	Unknown	15Ma02Aa
HARTIN, T.	20	M	Unknown	15Ma02Aa	WHILTON, W.	37	M	Unknown	15Ma02Aa
CONNER, E.	30	M	Unknown	15Ma02Aa	Emily	37	F	Unknown	15Ma02Aa
KERLY, M.	23	M	Unknown	15Ma02Aa	DOUGLAS, Mary	19	F	Unknown	15Ma02Aa
BURN, J.	28	M	Unknown	15Ma02Aa	TOHER, Julia	20	F	Unknown	15Ma02Aa

NAMES OF PASSENGERS	A G E X	S E	OCCUPATIONS	DATE PORT SHIP
FARRELY, Elizth.		47	F Unknown	15Ma02Aa
BEAMIS, R.		30	M Unknown	15Ma02Aa
Mary		18	F Unknown	15Ma02Aa
RUSH, Mary		17	F Unknown	15Ma02Aa
KIBIN, Mary		17	F Unknown	15Ma02Aa
RUSH, John		35	M Unknown	15Ma02Aa
Ann	(W)	33	F Unknown	15Ma02Aa
Mgt.	(D)	07	F Child	15Ma02Aa
Cath.	(D)	05	F Child	15Ma02Aa
Ann	(D)	03	F Child	15Ma02Aa
W.	(D)	01	F Child	15Ma02Aa
Mich.	(B)	40	M Laborer	15Ma02Aa
Mgt.	(L)	40	F Unknown	15Ma02Aa
M.	(N)	04	F Child	15Ma02Aa
W.	(M)	60	F Unknown	15Ma02Aa
BRYN, W.		22	M Unknown	15Ma02Aa
KELLY, M.		22	M Unknown	15Ma02Aa
NOON, J.		24	M Unknown	15Ma02Aa
GARAGHY, M.		24	M Unknown	15Ma02Aa
KELLY, J.		21	M Unknown	15Ma02Aa
DOLAN, P.		20	M Unknown	15Ma02Aa
Mgt.		23	F Unknown	15Ma02Aa
RYNE, F.		20	M Unknown	15Ma02Aa
NOBLY, E.		22	M Unknown	15Ma02Aa
Pat		24	M Unknown	15Ma02Aa
KELLY, P.		16	M Unknown	15Ma02Aa
GARAGHY, S.		23	M Unknown	15Ma02Aa
RYNE, M.		20	M Unknown	15Ma02Aa
GARAGHY, M.		20	M Unknown	15Ma02Aa
DONEGAN, J.		20	M Unknown	15Ma02Aa
GARAGHY, T.		20	M Unknown	15Ma02Aa
SWAN, S.		21	M Unknown	15Ma02Aa
GOW, J.		24	M Unknown	15Ma02Aa
Ann	(W)	20	F Unknown	15Ma02Aa
Thos.	(S)	01	M Child	15Ma02Aa
IRWIN, A.		25	M Unknown	15Ma02Aa
Elizb.		01	F Child	15Ma02Aa
ELROOD, Jane		04	F Child	15Ma02Aa
John		02	M Child	15Ma02Aa
GUN, Jane		45	F Unknown	15Ma02Aa
NOON, Ann		25	F Unknown	15Ma02Aa
CROOK, Rose		20	F Unknown	15Ma02Aa
FOLY, W.		28	M Unknown	15Ma02Aa
DONOHOE, P.		28	M Unknown	15Ma02Aa
Mgt.		28	F Unknown	15Ma02Aa
MARGETS, T.		36	M Unknown	15Ma02Aa
CHAPMAN, N.		23	M Unknown	15Ma02Aa
BUCES, S.		27	M Unknown	15Ma02Aa
FORD, S.		40	M Unknown	15Ma02Aa
COSEUFF, D.		21	M Unknown	15Ma02Aa
LIRRY, W.		27	M Unknown	15Ma02Aa
Elizabeth		29	F Unknown	15Ma02Aa
WALKER, J.		40	M Laborer	15Ma02Aa
VERTEGAN, E.		30	M Unknown	15Ma02Aa
M.	(W)	30	F Unknown	15Ma02Aa
Edwd.	(S)	08	M Child	15Ma02Aa
George	(S)	06	M Child	15Ma02Aa
SONLEN, Mary		23	F Unknown	15Ma02Aa
FARRELL, Mgt.		24	F Unknown	15Ma02Aa
GARAGTY, Mary		24	F Unknown	15Ma02Aa
TUNLY, Mgt.		17	F Unknown	15Ma02Aa
Mary		20	F Unknown	15Ma02Aa
MCQUE, Ann		18	F Unknown	15Ma02Aa
Mgt.		25	F Unknown	15Ma02Aa
Mgt.		20	F Unknown	15Ma02Aa
MURTEGH, M.		30	M Unknown	15Ma02Aa
Ann	(W)	30	F Unknown	15Ma02Aa
Pat	(S)	02	M Child	15Ma02Aa
Saml.	(S)	02	M Child	15Ma02Aa
CLERK, N.		20	M Unknown	15Ma02Aa

H.PATTERSON 15 MAY 1847

From Cork

NAMES OF PASSENGERS	A G E X	S E	OCCUPATIONS	DATE PORT SHIP
ODONNELL, Thos.		24	M Farmer	15Ma14Nr
Bridget		21	F Unknown	15Ma14Nr
WILLIAMS, Roger		46	M Farmer	15Ma14Nr
Mary	(W)	40	F Unknown	15Ma14Nr
Dennis	(S)	13	M None	15Ma14Nr
James	(S)	12	M None	15Ma14Nr
Ann	(D)	10	F Unknown	15Ma14Nr
Jesh	(S)	08	M Child	15Ma14Nr
Roger	(S)	06	M Child	15Ma14Nr
Thos.	(S)	03	M Child	15Ma14Nr
HORNE, John		30	M Farmer	15Ma14Nr
Baste		28	M Farmer	15Ma14Nr
FITZGERALD, Wm.		50	M Farmer	15Ma14Nr
Mgt.		28	F Unknown	15Ma14Nr
Nony		22	F Unknown	15Ma14Nr
POWER, Elizabeth		22	F Unknown	15Ma14Nr
HAWE, Wm.		06	M Child	15Ma14Nr
HORNE, Edwind		01	M Child	15Ma14Nr
REGAN, Ellen		19	F Unknown	15Ma14Nr
Margt.		17	F Unknown	15Ma14Nr
BARRY, Wm.		21	M Farmer	15Ma14Nr
Mgt.		18	F Unknown	15Ma14Nr
WESTON, Mary		20	F Unknown	15Ma14Nr
FITZGERALD, Wm.		26	M Farmer	15Ma14Nr
SULLIVAN, Timothy		50	M Farmer	15Ma14Nr
Julia		23	F Unknown	15Ma14Nr
MURPHY, Michael		35	M Farmer	15Ma14Nr
DOWNEY, John		20	M Farmer	15Ma14Nr
MCCARTHY, Michael		22	M Farmer	15Ma14Nr
MCRASEY, Pat		20	M Farmer	15Ma14Nr
SULLIVAN, John		23	M Farmer	15Ma14Nr
Bridget		21	F Unknown	15Ma14Nr
MOORE, John		27	M Farmer	15Ma14Nr
LEAHY, John		25	M Farmer	15Ma14Nr
MCDONALD, Michl.		22	M Farmer	15Ma14Nr
Mary		25	F Unknown	15Ma14Nr
SHEA, Richd.		21	M Farmer	15Ma14Nr
BRADDISH, Mary		27	F Unknown	15Ma14Nr
SHEA, Mary		06	F Child	15Ma14Nr
GARNER, Margt.		25	F Unknown	15Ma14Nr
NEUMAN, Mary		20	F Unknown	15Ma14Nr
SWEENY, Jeremiah		24	M Farmer	15Ma14Nr
MANNING, Daniel		24	M Farmer	15Ma14Nr
LYNCH, Timothy		45	M Farmer	15Ma14Nr
DONOVAN, John		23	M Farmer	15Ma14Nr
KENNEDY, Thos.		50	M Farmer	15Ma14Nr
Nony	(W)	50	F Unknown	15Ma14Nr
Ellen	(D)	21	F Unknown	15Ma14Nr
John		05	M Child	15Ma14Nr
CLIFFORD, Cathe.		20	F Unknown	15Ma14Nr
SULLIVAN, John		40	M Farmer	15Ma14Nr
Martin		24	M Farmer	15Ma14Nr

NICHOLAS-BIDDLE 15 MAY 1847

From Liverpool

NAMES OF PASSENGERS	A G E X	S E	OCCUPATIONS	DATE PORT SHIP
PORTER, T.		40	M Laborer	15Ma02Iq
Sarah	(W)	27	F Unknown	15Ma02Iq

NAMES OF PASSENGERS		AGE	SEX	OCCUPATIONS	DATE PORT SHIP	NAMES OF PASSENGERS		AGE	SEX	OCCUPATIONS	DATE PORT SHIP
PORTER, George	(S)	11	M	None	15Ma02lq	WELSH, Frances		26	F	Unknown	15Ma02lq
Ruth	(D)	05	F	Child	15Ma02lq	MCGACK, Ann		50	F	Unknown	15Ma02lq
Sidney	(S)	04	M	Child	15Ma02lq	John		30	M	Unknown	15Ma02lq
David	(S)	01	M	Child	15Ma02lq	Thos.		25	M	Unknown	15Ma02lq
GUMBLE, A.		20	M	Unknown	15Ma02lq	MURPHY, Cath.		12	F	Unknown	15Ma02lq
HOPKINS, T.		21	M	Unknown	15Ma02lq	Ann		10	F	Unknown	15Ma02lq
Betty		30	F	Unknown	15Ma02lq	JONES, J.		27	M	Laborer	15Ma02lq
Peggy		24	F	Unknown	15Ma02lq	DARCY, E.		25	M	Unknown	15Ma02lq
Nancy		30	F	Unknown	15Ma02lq	LOUGIN, P.		26	M	Unknown	15Ma02lq
CALLEVILLE, Betty		25	F	Unknown	15Ma02lq	CATOR, P.		39	M	Unknown	15Ma02lq
HENRY, P.		30	M	Unknown	15Ma02lq	DACEY, Doly		26	F	Unknown	15Ma02lq
Mary	(W)	30	F	Unknown	15Ma02lq	MURPHY, T.		26	M	Unknown	15Ma02lq
B.	(S)	09	M	Child	15Ma02lq	Esther		24	F	Unknown	15Ma02lq
John	(S)	07	M	Child	15Ma02lq	KENNY, J.		25	M	Unknown	15Ma02lq
Mary	(D)	05	F	Child	15Ma02lq	Nicholas		20	M	Unknown	15Ma02lq
Cath.	(D)	04	F	Child	15Ma02lq	Hannah		17	F	Unknown	15Ma02lq
CROFLEN, J.		50	M	Unknown	15Ma02lq	COLYN, B.		24	M	Unknown	15Ma02lq
Mary	(W)	50	F	Unknown	15Ma02lq	BOYEN, Ellen		21	F	Unknown	15Ma02lq
Mary	(D)	20	F	Unknown	15Ma02lq	KENNY, M.		30	M	Unknown	15Ma02lq
Andrew	(S)	20	M	Unknown	15Ma02lq	Peter		28	M	Unknown	15Ma02lq
SHENAN, P.		20	M	Unknown	15Ma02lq	CURTIS, A.		22	M	Unknown	15Ma02lq
Cath.		17	F	Unknown	15Ma02lq	AUSTIN, G.		20	M	Unknown	15Ma02lq
CULLIGAN, J.		22	M	Unknown	15Ma02lq	FAGAN, Ann		20	F	Unknown	15Ma02lq
KNOCKOLON, Ellen		20	F	Unknown	15Ma02lq	Mary		25	F	Unknown	15Ma02lq
DARBEY, R.		26	M	Unknown	15Ma02lq	LOGAN, P.		25	M	Unknown	15Ma02lq
John		24	M	Unknown	15Ma02lq	Collin	(W)	24	F	Unknown	15Ma02lq
GAFFREY, Bess		22	F	Unknown	15Ma02lq	Winny	(D)	01	F	Child	15Ma02lq
LARKIN, M.		26	M	Unknown	15Ma02lq	DILLON, P.		44	M	Unknown	15Ma02lq
Mary	(W)	20	F	Unknown	15Ma02lq	CAFF, T.		30	M	Unknown	15Ma02lq
Ann	(D)	04	F	Child	15Ma02lq	Bart		27	M	Unknown	15Ma02lq
KELLY, Mary		50	F	Unknown	15Ma02lq	FALLON, Ann		20	F	Unknown	15Ma02lq
FARNON, P.		25	M	Unknown	15Ma02lq	MCCREEN, J.		20	M	Unknown	15Ma02lq
BLACK, Mary		40	F	Unknown	15Ma02lq	WAKEFREE, J.		24	M	Unknown	15Ma02lq
Mary-Ann	(D)	15	F	Unknown	15Ma02lq	FERRY, D.		35	M	Unknown	15Ma02lq
Nancy	(D)	14	F	Unknown	15Ma02lq	CANHANSON, M.		20	M	Unknown	15Ma02lq
Ann	(D)	04	F	Child	15Ma02lq	FREENY, Honora		30	F	Unknown	15Ma02lq
Martha	(D)	12	F	Unknown	15Ma02lq	Pat	(S)	12	M	None	15Ma02lq
Wm.	(S)	02	M	Child	15Ma02lq	Honora	(D)	09	F	Child	15Ma02lq
WOOBEN, M.A.		19	M	Unknown	15Ma02lq	John	(S)	07	M	Child	15Ma02lq
Nancy		14	F	Unknown	15Ma02lq	Mary	(D)	04	F	Child	15Ma02lq
INGHAM, J.		57	M	Laborer	15Ma02lq	SELWRY, M.		30	M	Unknown	15Ma02lq
Sarah		55	F	Unknown	15Ma02lq	U-Mrs.		27	F	Unknown	15Ma02lq
JONES, D.		27	M	Unknown	15Ma02lq	MCDERMOT, B.		50	M	Unknown	15Ma02lq
Mary		27	F	Unknown	15Ma02lq	Unity	(W)	49	F	Unknown	15Ma02lq
Evan		27	M	None	15Ma02lq	Ann	(D)	20	F	Unknown	15Ma02lq
David		01	M	Child	15Ma02lq	Mary	(D)	15	F	Unknown	15Ma02lq
James		01	M	Child	15Ma02lq	John	(S)	19	M	Unknown	15Ma02lq
KENELY, T.		25	M	Unknown	15Ma02lq	BONNE, J.		19	M	Unknown	15Ma02lq
INGRALE, Elizt.		13	F	Unknown	15Ma02lq	MCMONAGH, D.		20	M	Laborer	15Ma02lq
Ann		09	F	Child	15Ma02lq	MOLLOY, D.		21	M	Unknown	15Ma02lq
GULLIAN, J.		25	M	Unknown	15Ma02lq	Nelly		20	F	Unknown	15Ma02lq
Mgt.		44	F	Unknown	15Ma02lq	MCCALLENS, N.		21	M	Unknown	15Ma02lq
Mgt.		01	F	Child	15Ma02lq	MORAN, J.		24	M	Unknown	15Ma02lq
Mgt.		01	F	Child	15Ma02lq	CAMPBELL, B.		24	M	Unknown	15Ma02lq
BOOMEN, Mary		76	F	Unknown	15Ma02lq	MOORE, J.		28	M	Unknown	15Ma02lq
MONTGUNY, M.		26	M	Unknown	15Ma02lq	BERNS, M.		24	M	Unknown	15Ma02lq
CAEN, J.		19	M	Unknown	15Ma02lq	HARKIN, J.		40	M	Unknown	15Ma02lq
HAMILL, J.		16	M	Unknown	15Ma02lq	BOYN, M.		21	M	Unknown	15Ma02lq
Eliza		32	F	Unknown	15Ma02lq	Dennis		20	M	Unknown	15Ma02lq
STINSON, J.		16	M	Unknown	15Ma02lq	FONY, Mary		19	F	Unknown	15Ma02lq
PAILENN, J.		20	M	Unknown	15Ma02lq	CANEYS, Sarah		21	F	Unknown	15Ma02lq
HAMILL, Eliza		02	F	Child	15Ma02lq	FARMER, B.		35	M	Unknown	15Ma02lq
James		05	M	Child	15Ma02lq	IGO, P.		24	M	Unknown	15Ma02lq
WALKER, N.		22	M	Unknown	15Ma02lq	MCDONELL, J.		40	M	Unknown	15Ma02lq
HALL, Nancy		29	F	Unknown	15Ma02lq	MCERLERRY, P.		35	M	Unknown	15Ma02lq
David		02	M	Child	15Ma02lq	Sally	(W)	40	F	Unknown	15Ma02lq
MCSURNIGH, M.		20	M	Unknown	15Ma02lq	John	(S)	14	M	None	15Ma02lq
GRAHAM, J.		22	M	Unknown	15Ma02lq	MENDY, F.		24	M	Unknown	15Ma02lq
HAMSON, C.		24	M	Unknown	15Ma02lq	Sally		20	F	Unknown	15Ma02lq
PAGE, J.		31	M	Unknown	15Ma02lq	Rebecca		18	F	Unknown	15Ma02lq
Ann		28	F	Unknown	15Ma02lq	Rebecca		52	F	Unknown	15Ma02lq
EARLY, D.		21	M	Unknown	15Ma02lq	Biddy		20	F	Unknown	15Ma02lq
U-Mrs.		38	F	Unknown	15Ma02lq	NOAH, J.		24	M	Unknown	15Ma02lq
JONES, T.		40	M	Unknown	15Ma02lq	MURLY, P.		22	M	Unknown	15Ma02lq
WELSH, J.		26	M	Unknown	15Ma02lq	Nell		07	M	Child	15Ma02lq

NAMES OF PASSENGERS	REL	AGE	SEX	OCCUPATIONS	DATE PORT SHIP
SPROLIN, F.		30	M	Unknown	15Ma02lq
BOYLE, Mary		21	F	Unknown	15Ma02lq
GORY, B.		30	M	Unknown	15Ma02lq
Rose	(W)	30	F	Unknown	15Ma02lq
Nancy	(D)	06	F	Child	15Ma02lq
Esther	(D)	03	F	Child	15Ma02lq
Wm.	(S)	01	M	Child	15Ma02lq
HUSSY, M.		39	M	Unknown	15Ma02lq
LARKEY, P.		28	M	Unknown	15Ma02lq
SLATNEY, J.		28	M	Unknown	15Ma02lq
FITZGERALD, R.		24	M	Unknown	15Ma02lq
MCGOWEN, J.		35	M	Unknown	15Ma02lq
Susannah	(W)	35	F	Unknown	15Ma02lq
Nancy	(D)	05	F	Child	15Ma02lq
MUIR, P.		28	M	Unknown	15Ma02lq
MCMINN, J.		26	M	Laborer	15Ma02lq
SCOTT, J.		24	M	Unknown	15Ma02lq
MCGUY, Peggy		40	F	Unknown	15Ma02lq
Mich.	(S)	14	M	Unknown	15Ma02lq
Fredck.	(S)	14	M	Unknown	15Ma02lq
Barny	(S)	16	M	Unknown	15Ma02lq
Cath.	(D)	20	F	Unknown	15Ma02lq
KERRY, M.		15	M	Unknown	15Ma02lq
VOGILLE, Cath.		15	F	Unknown	15Ma02lq
MCKEY, W.		20	M	Unknown	15Ma02lq
CAMPBELL, M.		28	M	Unknown	15Ma02lq
KELLY, Anne		18	F	Unknown	15Ma02lq
MCGUN, T.		26	M	Unknown	15Ma02lq
FELLER, Mgt.		20	F	Unknown	15Ma02lq
MARTIN, P.		24	M	Unknown	15Ma02lq
Eliza		28	F	Unknown	15Ma02lq
FOX, B.		24	M	Unknown	15Ma02lq
MCCORLAND, Jane		28	F	Unknown	15Ma02lq
Jane		60	F	Unknown	15Ma02lq
Thos.		25	M	Unknown	15Ma02lq
QUINER, Alice		20	F	Unknown	15Ma02lq
MCCALL, J.		20	M	Unknown	15Ma02lq
DONNER, Johanna		16	F	Unknown	15Ma02lq
HASKESS, M.		18	M	Unknown	15Ma02lq
CALLEGAN, J.		35	M	Unknown	15Ma02lq
Bdgt.	(W)	32	F	Unknown	15Ma02lq
James	(S)	11	M	None	15Ma02lq
John	(S)	09	M	Child	15Ma02lq
Mary	(D)	07	F	Child	15Ma02lq
Pat	(S)	03	M	Child	15Ma02lq
MCELLY, J.		20	M	Unknown	15Ma02lq
Cath.		12	F	Unknown	15Ma02lq
Sarah		11	F	Unknown	15Ma02lq
Bdgt.		08	F	Child	15Ma02lq
ROGERS, M.		15	M	Unknown	15Ma02lq
Mgt.		12	F	Unknown	15Ma02lq
Jas.		10	M	None	15Ma02lq
Cath.		05	F	Child	15Ma02lq
Bdgt.		09	F	Child	15Ma02lq
MCCAFLY, Ann		20	F	Unknown	15Ma02lq
BARBER, Cass		40	F	Unknown	15Ma02lq
Peter	(S)	14	M	None	15Ma02lq
Ellen	(M)	82	F	Unknown	15Ma02lq
LARKIN, T.		16	F	Unknown	15Ma02lq
FEGAN, W.		17	F	Unknown	15Ma02lq
James		17	M	Laborer	15Ma02lq
Ann		14	F	Unknown	15Ma02lq
Peter		11	M	Unknown	15Ma02lq
MANSFIELD, T.		50	M	Unknown	15Ma02lq
Lawrence	(S)	22	M	Unknown	15Ma02lq
Mich.	(S)	21	M	Unknown	15Ma02lq
Alice	(W)	50	F	Unknown	15Ma02lq
Thos.	(S)	12	M	Unknown	15Ma02lq
Margt.	(D)	10	F	Unknown	15Ma02lq
J.	(S)	08	M	Child	15Ma02lq
Cath.	(D)	06	F	Child	15Ma02lq
FLYNN, E.		20	M	Unknown	15Ma02lq
FERGUSON, J.		60	M	Unknown	15Ma02lq
Eliza.		15	F	Unknown	15Ma02lq
Saml.		18	M	Unknown	15Ma02lq

NAMES OF PASSENGERS	REL	AGE	SEX	OCCUPATIONS	DATE PORT SHIP
FLYNN, J.		23	M	Unknown	15Ma02lq
Pat		22	M	Unknown	15Ma02lq
ONEIL, Cath.		18	F	Unknown	15Ma02lq
WALL, P.		20	M	Unknown	15Ma02lq
Mary		06	F	Child	15Ma02lq
GREEN, D.		20	M	Unknown	15Ma02lq
HAWES, Cath.		18	F	Unknown	15Ma02lq
MCLADE, Ann		21	F	Unknown	15Ma02lq
REILY, J.		25	M	Unknown	15Ma02lq
MCCADE, Ann		18	F	Unknown	15Ma02lq
REILLY, J.		25	M	Unknown	15Ma02lq
MCCADE, A.		18	M	Unknown	15Ma02lq
Ann		16	F	Unknown	15Ma02lq
Bernd.		21	M	Unknown	15Ma02lq
Arthur		60	M	Unknown	15Ma02lq
TURNFEN, R.		22	M	Unknown	15Ma02lq
DEFELDY, J.		20	M	Unknown	15Ma02lq
Richd.		20	M	Unknown	15Ma02lq
DELAY, Ann		21	F	Unknown	15Ma02lq
DEGAN, Mary		21	F	Unknown	15Ma02lq
RODAN, Bdgt.		20	F	Unknown	15Ma02lq
HART, Mary		20	F	Unknown	15Ma02lq
MCSOOLY, Cath.		18	F	Unknown	15Ma02lq
HANRICK, J.		12	M	None	15Ma02lq
J.		11	M	None	15Ma02lq
SHENAN, O.		45	M	Laborer	15Ma02lq
Pat		20	M	Unknown	15Ma02lq
Mary		18	F	Unknown	15Ma02lq
HEERY, H.		40	M	Unknown	15Ma02lq
Ann	(D)	16	F	Unknown	15Ma02lq
James	(S)	14	M	None	15Ma02lq
Biddy	(D)	12	F	Unknown	15Ma02lq
Rose	(D)	08	F	Child	15Ma02lq
BENNETT, Julia		29	F	Unknown	15Ma02lq
John		08	M	Child	15Ma02lq
WHITE, Ann		36	F	Unknown	15Ma02lq
BARANLY, F.		30	M	Unknown	15Ma02lq
DALEY, P.		25	M	Unknown	15Ma02lq
SULLIVAN, F.		25	M	Unknown	15Ma02lq
BROOKS, N.		32	M	Unknown	15Ma02lq
Jacob		27	M	Unknown	15Ma02lq
Lawrence		35	M	Unknown	15Ma02lq
Emma		10	F	Unknown	15Ma02lq
BANISTER, J.		27	M	Unknown	15Ma02lq
Mary	(W)	27	F	Unknown	15Ma02lq
Hugh	(S)	01	M	Child	15Ma02lq
WOOLLEEN, J.		24	M	Unknown	15Ma02lq
TURNER, W.		26	M	Unknown	15Ma02lq
SMALL, W.		28	M	Unknown	15Ma02lq
MULLIN, Mgt.		28	F	Unknown	15Ma02lq
BUCKLY, D.		30	M	Unknown	15Ma02lq
SULLIVAN, M.		31	M	Unknown	15Ma02lq
WALL, J.		20	M	Unknown	15Ma02lq
Ellen		17	F	Unknown	15Ma02lq
EARLY, J.		20	M	Unknown	15Ma02lq
GOREN, W.		50	M	Unknown	15Ma02lq
Ann	(W)	42	F	Unknown	15Ma02lq
Pat	(S)	21	M	Unknown	15Ma02lq
Robt.	(S)	19	M	Unknown	15Ma02lq
Mary	(D)	17	F	Unknown	15Ma02lq
Cath.	(D)	15	F	Unknown	15Ma02lq
GAFFEY, E.		25	M	Unknown	15Ma02lq
Jane		24	F	Unknown	15Ma02lq
DUFFY, T.		18	M	Unknown	15Ma02lq
JONES, T.		40	M	Unknown	15Ma02lq
H.	(W)	30	F	Unknown	15Ma02lq
R.	(S)	04	M	Child	15Ma02lq
Mary	(D)	02	F	Child	15Ma02lq
FAGGAN, J.		22	M	Mechanic	15Ma02lq
ENNIS, J.		18	M	Unknown	15Ma02lq
REEF, M.		26	M	Unknown	15Ma02lq
SEIGEN, M.		24	M	Unknown	15Ma02lq
U	(W)	22	F	Unknown	15Ma02lq
RUSSELL, S.		29	M	Unknown	15Ma02lq
DANIELS, Eliza		37	F	Unknown	15Ma02lq

NAMES OF PASSENGERS	AGE	SEX	OCCUPATIONS	DATE PORT SHIP
WATER, Rose	18	F	Unknown	15Ma02Iq
HYLERN, P.	28	M	Unknown	15Ma02Iq
FEATHERSTON, J.	24	M	Unknown	15Ma02Iq
Mary	17	F	Unknown	15Ma02Iq
CONNY, P.	20	M	Unknown	15Ma02Iq
LEWS, R.	00	M	Unknown	15Ma02Iq

IOWA 15 MAY 1847

From Havre

NAMES OF PASSENGERS		AGE	SEX	OCCUPATIONS	DATE PORT SHIP
HACK, W.		42	M	Laborer	15Ma05Ns
Mary	(W)	42	F	Unknown	15Ma05Ns
Bgt.	(D)	15	F	Unknown	15Ma05Ns
John	(S)	12	M	Unknown	15Ma05Ns
Mich.	(S)	09	M	Child	15Ma05Ns
Wm.	(S)	07	M	Child	15Ma05Ns
James	(S)	04	M	Child	15Ma05Ns
MCCARTNEY, J.		22	M	Unknown	15Ma05Ns
Mary		16	F	Unknown	15Ma05Ns
Bronsh.		24	M	Unknown	15Ma05Ns
Patt.		14	M	Unknown	15Ma05Ns
Cath.		12	F	Unknown	15Ma05Ns
John		10	M	Unknown	15Ma05Ns
Barb.		08	F	Child	15Ma05Ns
Allen		08	M	Child	15Ma05Ns
JORDEN, Bgt.		28	F	Unknown	15Ma05Ns
DOLAN, Bgt.		19	F	Unknown	15Ma05Ns
HEYGEN, Bgt.		23	F	Unknown	15Ma05Ns
LYNN, J.		24	M	Unknown	15Ma05Ns
CORBLENY, Mgt.		20	F	Unknown	15Ma05Ns
CARLING, T.		26	M	Unknown	15Ma05Ns
MCCARTNEY, P.		36	M	Unknown	15Ma05Ns
Honora		55	F	Unknown	15Ma05Ns
LENNON, P.		27	M	Unknown	15Ma05Ns
GUSTON, S.		26	M	Unknown	15Ma05Ns
MCGELSE, Mary		24	F	Unknown	15Ma05Ns
Ellzth.		22	F	Unknown	15Ma05Ns
BIGLEY, D.		21	M	Unknown	15Ma05Ns
CASEY, A.		25	M	Unknown	15Ma05Ns
TARR, C.		24	M	Unknown	15Ma05Ns
MILL, J.		30	M	Unknown	15Ma05Ns
WHILLY, A.		22	M	Unknown	15Ma05Ns
BLEASSEN, A.		30	M	Unknown	15Ma05Ns
Mary		22	F	Unknown	15Ma05Ns
Ann		18	F	Unknown	15Ma05Ns
Sarah-A.		02	F	Child	15Ma05Ns
Ellzth.		01	F	Child	15Ma05Ns
MCCARTY, B.		24	M	Unknown	15Ma05Ns
Mary		22	F	Unknown	15Ma05Ns
HONPEEL, S.		23	M	Unknown	15Ma05Ns
BULMER, E.		33	M	Unknown	15Ma05Ns
MORN, F.		20	M	Unknown	15Ma05Ns
BALEY, P.		19	M	Laborer	15Ma05Ns
MURRAY, C.		25	M	Unknown	15Ma05Ns
MALON, T.		28	M	Unknown	15Ma05Ns
MONSEN, E.		20	M	Unknown	15Ma05Ns
GRIFFITH, E.		35	M	Unknown	15Ma05Ns
GREY, E.		27	M	Unknown	15Ma05Ns
MCMAN, P.		20	M	Unknown	15Ma05Ns
RILEY, Jane		15	F	Unknown	15Ma05Ns
MORROW, Rose		24	F	Unknown	15Ma05Ns
HOGAN, Helen		20	F	Unknown	15Ma05Ns
MCLENN, Ann		18	F	Unknown	15Ma05Ns
ANAN, J.		28	M	Unknown	15Ma05Ns
CONNER, T.		30	M	Unknown	15Ma05Ns
MURPHY, P.		24	M	Unknown	15Ma05Ns
HEESTER, M.		23	M	Unknown	15Ma05Ns
FATCHERN, J.		24	M	Unknown	15Ma05Ns
CONNER, Mary		24	F	Unknown	15Ma05Ns
GRALLY, M.		30	M	Unknown	15Ma05Ns
SMITH, P.		22	M	Unknown	15Ma05Ns
FLEMER, J.		20	M	Unknown	15Ma05Ns
GRALLY, Bgt.		50	F	Unknown	15Ma05Ns
MCQUADE, Betty		15	F	Unknown	15Ma05Ns
Arthur		22	M	Unknown	15Ma05Ns
GRODER, J.		18	M	Unknown	15Ma05Ns
MECHEGEN, J.		30	M	Unknown	15Ma05Ns
Bdgt.		20	F	Unknown	15Ma05Ns
Mary		15	F	Unknown	15Ma05Ns
Bdgt.		26	F	Unknown	15Ma05Ns
CULLEN, E.		29	M	Unknown	15Ma05Ns
DUNLEN, M.		29	M	Unknown	15Ma05Ns
DRENNAN, T.		36	M	Unknown	15Ma05Ns
FEALHISTE, P.		24	M	Unknown	15Ma05Ns
Cath.		22	F	Unknown	15Ma05Ns
MAY, Bdgt.		22	F	Unknown	15Ma05Ns
LAWDRY, J.		12	M	Unknown	15Ma05Ns
CALLEGAN, Cath.		26	F	Unknown	15Ma05Ns
CONDON, W.		23	M	Unknown	15Ma05Ns
M.		34	F	Unknown	15Ma05Ns
REILY, J.		18	M	Unknown	15Ma05Ns
BERTH, E.		34	M	Unknown	15Ma05Ns
DARLY, Pat		23	M	Unknown	15Ma05Ns
Helen		26	F	Unknown	15Ma05Ns
BRENNAN, J.		25	M	Laborer	15Ma05Ns
HUCKY, P.		25	M	Unknown	15Ma05Ns
REND, J.		23	M	Unknown	15Ma05Ns
BONRASH, J.		24	M	Unknown	15Ma05Ns
Man.		25	F	Unknown	15Ma05Ns
DELANY, J.		22	M	Unknown	15Ma05Ns
Dar.		19	M	Unknown	15Ma05Ns
DOWNEY, W.		27	M	Unknown	15Ma05Ns
JACKSON, A.		29	M	Unknown	15Ma05Ns
BURRIS, M.		23	M	Unknown	15Ma05Ns
MULLEN, B.		18	M	Unknown	15Ma05Ns
CARR, P.		23	M	Unknown	15Ma05Ns
FARREN, J.		23	M	Unknown	15Ma05Ns
MUIR, J.		23	M	Unknown	15Ma05Ns
BAILEY, J.		60	M	Unknown	15Ma05Ns
Cath.	(W)	45	F	Unknown	15Ma05Ns
James	(S)	00	M	None	15Ma05Ns
Cath.	(D)	08	F	Child	15Ma05Ns
FARRELL, T.		59	M	Unknown	15Ma05Ns
Cath.	(W)	30	F	Unknown	15Ma05Ns
Winifred	(D)	09	F	Child	15Ma05Ns
Edward	(S)	07	M	Child	15Ma05Ns
M.		20	M	Unknown	15Ma05Ns
Mark		18	M	Unknown	15Ma05Ns
CARROLL, Ann		20	F	Unknown	15Ma05Ns
Mary		17	F	Unknown	15Ma05Ns
THOMPSON, J.		21	M	Unknown	15Ma05Ns
BRACKEN, A.		20	M	Unknown	15Ma05Ns
Winford		29	F	Unknown	15Ma05Ns
Ann		22	F	Unknown	15Ma05Ns
MCGEE, Cath.		30	F	Unknown	15Ma05Ns
CARSON, T.		17	M	Unknown	15Ma05Ns
BRACKEN, P.		16	M	Unknown	15Ma05Ns
BROOKS, O.		30	M	Unknown	15Ma05Ns
CONLY, A.		20	M	Unknown	15Ma05Ns
Mary		13	F	Unknown	15Ma05Ns
Mark		17	M	Unknown	15Ma05Ns
MCCLERRY, P.		21	M	Unknown	15Ma05Ns
CAMPBELL, J.		39	M	Unknown	15Ma05Ns
M.	(W)	33	F	Unknown	15Ma05Ns
Brennan	(S)	15	M	Unknown	15Ma05Ns
Martha	(D)	13	F	Unknown	15Ma05Ns
Agnes	(D)	11	F	Unknown	15Ma05Ns
John	(S)	08	M	Child	15Ma05Ns
Edward	(S)	05	M	Child	15Ma05Ns
William	(S)	01	M	Child	15Ma05Ns
LAFORTY, D.		20	M	Laborer	15Ma05Ns
MUIR, Ellzth.		18	F	Unknown	15Ma05Ns
BYRNES, R.		30	M	Unknown	15Ma05Ns

NAMES OF PASSENGERS		AGE	SEX	OCCUPATIONS	DATE PORT SHIP	NAMES OF PASSENGERS		AGE	SEX	OCCUPATIONS	DATE PORT SHIP
LITTLE, F.		31	M	Unknown	15Ma05Ns	JERRY, Mgt.		13	F	Unknown	15Ma05Ns
KEYS, Eliza		23	F	Unknown	15Ma05Ns	Patt		09	M	Child	15Ma05Ns
ALEXANDER, J.		24	M	Unknown	15Ma05Ns	FEENY, Mary		05	F	Child	15Ma05Ns
Sarah	(W)	24	F	Unknown	15Ma05Ns	Cath.		14	F	Unknown	15Ma05Ns
Mgt.	(D)	01	F	Child	15Ma05Ns	SMITH, Mgt.		40	F	Unknown	15Ma05Ns
SWIFT, J.		30	M	Unknown	15Ma05Ns	M.		37	F	Unknown	15Ma05Ns
GANNON, J.		25	M	Unknown	15Ma05Ns	John		08	M	Child	15Ma05Ns
HOCKEY, P.		55	M	Unknown	15Ma05Ns	Peter		05	M	Child	15Ma05Ns
Ann	(W)	55	F	Unknown	15Ma05Ns	Mark		01	M	Child	15Ma05Ns
Ann	(D)	20	F	Unknown	15Ma05Ns	M.		56	M	Laborer	15Ma05Ns
Edward	(S)	14	M	None	15Ma05Ns	U	(W)	52	F	Unknown	15Ma05Ns
MICHAN, P.		24	M	None	15Ma05Ns	Bdgt.	(D)	18	F	Unknown	15Ma05Ns
Timothy		22	M	None	15Ma05Ns	Patt	(S)	15	M	Unknown	15Ma05Ns
HENRY, P.		20	M	None	15Ma05Ns	Mgt.	(D)	14	F	Unknown	15Ma05Ns
John		22	M	None	15Ma05Ns	MAHER, J.		22	M	Unknown	15Ma05Ns
ROURKE, J.		26	M	None	15Ma05Ns	John		20	M	Unknown	15Ma05Ns
KENNEDY, D.		36	M	None	15Ma05Ns	Mary		40	F	Unknown	15Ma05Ns
MCLARKEN, Cath.		16	F	None	15Ma05Ns	Nora		18	F	Unknown	15Ma05Ns
Mgt.		14	F	None	15Ma05Ns	NIGEL, M.		25	M	Unknown	15Ma05Ns
Mary		15	F	None	15Ma05Ns	Mary	(W)	24	F	Unknown	15Ma05Ns
Rosa		18	F	None	15Ma05Ns	M.	(D)	01	F	Child	15Ma05Ns
SULLIVAN, T.		22	M	None	15Ma05Ns	U		18	F	Unknown	15Ma05Ns
Mich.		23	M	None	15Ma05Ns	BERRY, P.		30	M	Unknown	15Ma05Ns
BENNETT, Mary		22	F	None	15Ma05Ns	Bdgt.		23	F	Unknown	15Ma05Ns
FITZGERALD, D.		23	M	None	15Ma05Ns						
MORIARTY, P.		22	M	None	15Ma05Ns						
GRIFFIN, J.		20	M	None	15Ma05Ns						
QUIGHAN, M.		30	M	None	15Ma05Ns						
Patt.		25	M	None	15Ma05Ns						
HIGGINS, Ma.		14	F	None	15Ma05Ns			QUEBEC 15 MAY 1847			
WHITE, Mgt.		20	F	None	15Ma05Ns						
HAMNIL, P.		70	M	None	15Ma05Ns			From London			
U	(W)	50	F	None	15Ma05Ns						
John	(S)	20	M	None	15Ma05Ns						
Martha	(D)	16	F	None	15Ma05Ns						
GILMER, Mary		18	F	None	15Ma05Ns	MEY, Mary-A.		50	F	Unknown	15Ma21Au
GORMAN, J.		20	M	Laborer	15Ma05Ns	THOMPSON, M.		23	M	None	15Ma21Au
William		45	M	Unknown	15Ma05Ns	WATCHOCH, T.		27	M	None	15Ma21Au
GORDON, R.		57	M	Unknown	15Ma05Ns	Julie		24	F	None	15Ma21Au
U	(W)	60	F	Unknown	15Ma05Ns	MANN, A.		30	M	Mechanic	15Ma21Au
Edwd.	(S)	29	M	Unknown	15Ma05Ns	ASHLY, W.		24	M	Unknown	15Ma21Au
Patt	(S)	27	M	Unknown	15Ma05Ns	DOBSON, G.		69	M	Unknown	15Ma21Au
Rich.	(S)	25	M	Unknown	15Ma05Ns	SHAW, C.		30	M	Unknown	15Ma21Au
Mary	(D)	25	F	Unknown	15Ma05Ns	JONES, S.		29	M	Unknown	15Ma21Au
Bgt.	(D)	22	F	Unknown	15Ma05Ns	COTT, T.		60	M	Unknown	15Ma21Au
John	(S)	18	M	Unknown	15Ma05Ns	Jemia	(W)	60	F	Unknown	15Ma21Au
LARRY, Jane		19	F	Unknown	15Ma05Ns	Wm.	(S)	18	M	Unknown	15Ma21Au
HANLEY, R.		26	M	Unknown	15Ma05Ns	George	(S)	16	M	Unknown	15Ma21Au
DONALD, J.		26	M	Unknown	15Ma05Ns	NOUKS, Mt.		27	F	Unknown	15Ma21Au
HIGGINS, H.		30	M	Unknown	15Ma05Ns	BALLAD, S.		20	M	Unknown	15Ma21Au
Mary		30	F	Unknown	15Ma05Ns	SNEEK, S.		30	M	Unknown	15Ma21Au
Ann		16	F	Unknown	15Ma05Ns	Ann		30	F	Unknown	15Ma21Au
Mary		08	F	Child	15Ma05Ns	SWEELLIN, J.		19	M	Unknown	15Ma21Au
James		04	M	Child	15Ma05Ns	ELNEGER, Eliza		34	F	Unknown	15Ma21Au
John		02	M	Child	15Ma05Ns	BIDEWER, E.		27	M	Unknown	15Ma21Au
LILLY, J.		28	M	Unknown	15Ma05Ns	JOHNSON, W.		21	M	Unknown	15Ma21Au
U	(W)	29	F	Unknown	15Ma05Ns	CHOLUND, Sophie		21	F	Unknown	15Ma21Au
Pat.		24	M	Unknown	15Ma05Ns	Elizth.		09	F	Child	15Ma21Au
MAKING, J.		28	M	Unknown	15Ma05Ns	STONE, J.		32	M	Unknown	15Ma21Au
CURRENS, M.		29	M	Unknown	15Ma05Ns	PENUGH, T.		58	M	Unknown	15Ma21Au
Mgt.		18	F	Unknown	15Ma05Ns	WHEAT, W.		23	M	Unknown	15Ma21Au
LYON, M.		24	M	Unknown	15Ma05Ns	TRENECH, W.		23	M	Unknown	15Ma21Au
John		22	M	Unknown	15Ma05Ns	CUFF, P.		37	M	Unknown	15Ma21Au
CORNER, J.		24	M	Unknown	15Ma05Ns	DEAN, G.		23	M	Laborer	15Ma21Au
KEET, Eliz.		20	F	Unknown	15Ma05Ns	ADAMS, A.		22	M	Unknown	15Ma21Au
SULLIVAN, P.		27	M	Unknown	15Ma05Ns	LEWIS, Ann		50	F	Unknown	15Ma21Au
Mary		21	F	Unknown	15Ma05Ns	Jas.		11	M	None	15Ma21Au
GLAHAN, B.		21	M	Unknown	15Ma05Ns	UPCRAFT, G.		46	M	Unknown	15Ma21Au
BERNEY, J.		28	M	Unknown	15Ma05Ns	Mary		36	F	Unknown	15Ma21Au
U	(W)	24	F	Unknown	15Ma05Ns	WARNER, W.		40	M	Unknown	15Ma21Au
John	(S)	01	M	Child	15Ma05Ns	M.		38	F	Unknown	15Ma21Au
FEENY, N.		20	M	Unknown	15Ma05Ns	SMITH, J.		25	M	Unknown	15Ma21Au
U-Mrs.		36	F	Unknown	15Ma05Ns	BALDWIN, J.		38	M	Unknown	15Ma21Au
JERRY, Cath.		14	F	Unknown	15Ma05Ns	Susan	(W)	34	F	Unknown	15Ma21Au
Bgt.		12	F	Unknown	15Ma05Ns	John	(S)	12	M	None	15Ma21Au

NAMES OF PASSENGERS		AGE	SEX	OCCUPATIONS	DATE PORT SHIP
BALDWIN, Mary	(D)	09	F	Child	15Ma21Au
Ann	(D)	06	F	Child	15Ma21Au
Robert	(S)	02	M	Child	15Ma21Au
DUNKLERY, T.		50	M	Unknown	15Ma21Au
Ann	(W)	42	F	Unknown	15Ma21Au
Elzbt.	(D)	19	F	Unknown	15Ma21Au
Ann	(D)	16	F	Unknown	15Ma21Au
Hen.	(S)	13	M	Unknown	15Ma21Au
Susan	(D)	12	F	Unknown	15Ma21Au
Mary	(D)	09	F	Child	15Ma21Au
Sarah	(D)	07	F	Child	15Ma21Au
MIGHT, Eliz.		70	F	Unknown	15Ma21Au
JELINGS, B.		18	M	Unknown	15Ma21Au
BANES, G.		24	M	Unknown	15Ma21Au
BENFIELD, R.		23	M	Unknown	15Ma21Au
MURRAY, M.L.		36	M	Unknown	15Ma21Au
Mary-A.		15	F	Unknown	15Ma21Au
Mgt.		13	F	Unknown	15Ma21Au
Matilda		07	F	Child	15Ma21Au
ROURKE, J.		17	M	Unknown	15Ma21Au
KENELL, E.J.		29	M	Unknown	15Ma21Au
Lucy		29	F	Unknown	15Ma21Au
Edwd.		11	M	Unknown	15Ma21Au
GREEN, E.D.		22	M	Unknown	15Ma21Au
Joseph		16	M	Unknown	15Ma21Au
FUR, P.D.		20	M	Unknown	15Ma21Au
RENELT, J.		20	M	Unknown	15Ma21Au
NULTY, N.		21	M	Unknown	15Ma21Au
RONEN, J.		20	M	Unknown	15Ma21Au
MCKERN, Eliza		01	F	Child	15Ma21Au
SOLOMAN, T.		27	M	Mechanic	15Ma21Au
Emma	(W)	23	F	Unknown	15Ma21Au
John	(S)	01	M	Child	15Ma21Au
MACKENZIE, Isa.		50	F	Unknown	15Ma21Au

CONSTITUTION 15 MAY 1847

From Liverpool

NAMES OF PASSENGERS	AGE	SEX	OCCUPATIONS	DATE PORT SHIP
RINGNEY, W.	55	M	Merchant	15Ma02HI
COLLINS, W.K.	50	M	Unknown	15Ma02HI
MCCLELLAN, D.G.	25	M	Unknown	15Ma02HI
KOUGH, T.	30	M	Unknown	15Ma02HI
MANNING, C.P.	28	M	Unknown	15Ma02HI
WILLIS, J.	30	M	Unknown	15Ma02HI
TREYNON, F.T.D.	24	M	Unknown	15Ma02HI
SIMSON, E.	45	M	Unknown	15Ma02HI
MCRUM, D.	48	M	Laborer	15Ma02HI
MURPHY, T.	25	M	Unknown	15Ma02HI
Teresa	24	F	Unknown	15Ma02HI
Cath.	18	F	Unknown	15Ma02HI
CONNER, J.	26	M	Unknown	15Ma02HI
FULLER, J.	25	M	Unknown	15Ma02HI
Cella	20	F	Unknown	15Ma02HI
ANSKIN, M.	20	M	Unknown	15Ma02HI
Ann	16	F	Unknown	15Ma02HI
Wilbur	13	M	None	15Ma02HI
MCCONKEY, W.	25	M	Unknown	15Ma02HI
LOWRY, R.	24	M	Unknown	15Ma02HI
ROSS, J.	50	M	Unknown	15Ma02HI
Wm.	20	M	Unknown	15Ma02HI
U	21	M	Unknown	15Ma02HI
Mgt.	19	F	Unknown	15Ma02HI
E.Jane	17	F	Unknown	15Ma02HI
Thos.	16	M	Unknown	15Ma02HI
Mary	23	F	Unknown	15Ma02HI
PINT, Jane	47	F	Unknown	15Ma02HI
BOWEN, J.	24	M	Unknown	15Ma02HI
BIRNY, T.	28	M	Unknown	15Ma02HI

NAMES OF PASSENGERS		AGE	SEX	OCCUPATIONS	DATE PORT SHIP
SHEIL, W.		25	M	Unknown	15Ma02HI
RYNEL, G.		20	M	Unknown	15Ma02HI
FEEHORN, D.		20	M	Unknown	15Ma02HI
BROGNEY, Ann		18	F	Unknown	15Ma02HI
LYNCH, B.		26	M	Unknown	15Ma02HI
Farrell		26	M	Unknown	15Ma02HI
CONNER, E.		25	M	Unknown	15Ma02HI
Ellen	(W)	24	F	Unknown	15Ma02HI
James	(S)	01	M	Child	15Ma02HI
NOLAN, P.		25	M	Unknown	15Ma02HI
Susan		25	F	Unknown	15Ma02HI
SEONAUGH, Mgt.		21	F	Unknown	15Ma02HI
ANDERSON, J.		20	M	Laborer	15Ma02HI
MCKEOWN, Eliza		20	F	Unknown	15Ma02HI
BURKE, J.		25	M	Unknown	15Ma02HI
HART, P.		25	M	Unknown	15Ma02HI
Ann		24	F	Unknown	15Ma02HI
James		20	M	Unknown	15Ma02HI
GURRY, W.		20	M	Unknown	15Ma02HI
BURKE, Su.		20	F	Unknown	15Ma02HI
Mgt.		18	F	Unknown	15Ma02HI
DAY, Mary		20	F	Unknown	15Ma02HI
DOLAN, Ann		20	F	Unknown	15Ma02HI
Cath.		50	F	Unknown	15Ma02HI
Thos.		25	M	Unknown	15Ma02HI
Peter		20	M	Unknown	15Ma02HI
MALY, Ann		20	F	Unknown	15Ma02HI
Fran.		12	M	None	15Ma02HI
FENNER, M.		25	M	Unknown	15Ma02HI
Cath.		21	F	Unknown	15Ma02HI
MALLY, Mary		18	F	Unknown	15Ma02HI
BURKE, J.		30	M	Unknown	15Ma02HI
Agnes	(W)	35	F	Unknown	15Ma02HI
George	(S)	02	M	Child	15Ma02HI
Jane	(D)	01	F	Child	15Ma02HI
COYLE, T.		25	M	Unknown	15Ma02HI
Ellen		18	F	Unknown	15Ma02HI
CUSH, M.		25	F	Unknown	15Ma02HI
BORPLY, Mgt.		20	F	Unknown	15Ma02HI
POLLOCK, Mary-A.		20	F	Unknown	15Ma02HI
ADAM, J.M.		40	M	Unknown	15Ma02HI
Ann	(W)	35	F	Unknown	15Ma02HI
John	(S)	04	M	Child	15Ma02HI
Ann	(D)	06	F	Child	15Ma02HI
SHERIDAN, J.		21	M	Unknown	15Ma02HI
CONNER, Cath.		21	F	Unknown	15Ma02HI
MCDONALD, J.		25	M	Unknown	15Ma02HI
SCANLAN, Mary		18	F	Unknown	15Ma02HI
CONROY, Mary		20	F	Unknown	15Ma02HI
HANLON, J.		20	M	Unknown	15Ma02HI
TAYLOR, T.		21	M	Unknown	15Ma02HI
MCKEON, M.		20	M	Unknown	15Ma02HI
FAGEN, J.		28	M	Unknown	15Ma02HI
Thos.		21	M	Unknown	15Ma02HI
CASEY, O.		25	M	Unknown	15Ma02HI
Mary		20	F	Unknown	15Ma02HI
HAHEY, T.		20	M	Unknown	15Ma02HI
SENGEND, Sarah		20	F	Unknown	15Ma02HI
MCCORMICK, Cath.		25	F	Unknown	15Ma02HI
Ann		20	F	Unknown	15Ma02HI
MACKLIN, Cath.		25	F	Unknown	15Ma02HI
Ellen		21	F	Unknown	15Ma02HI
DILLON, P.		20	M	Unknown	15Ma02HI
CONNELLY, Peggy		28	F	Unknown	15Ma02HI
John		09	M	Child	15Ma02HI
SULLIVAN, J.		25	M	Unknown	15Ma02HI
Timothy		11	M	Unknown	15Ma02HI
CASEY, J.		25	M	Unknown	15Ma02HI
James		20	M	Unknown	15Ma02HI
Ellen		12	F	Unknown	15Ma02HI
FITZGERALD, Eliza		40	F	Unknown	15Ma02HI
Isabella		20	F	Unknown	15Ma02HI
Ellen		21	F	Unknown	15Ma02HI
Bgt.		18	F	Unknown	15Ma02HI
MELEN, S.		28	M	Unknown	15Ma02HI

NAMES OF PASSENGERS	AGE	SEX	OCCUPATIONS	DATE PORT SHIP
MELEN, James	20	M	Unknown	15Ma02HI
Cath.	18	F	Unknown	15Ma02HI
MONE, Ann	20	F	Unknown	15Ma02HI
MAY, T.	25	M	Unknown	15Ma02HI
FOX, Eliza	50	F	Unknown	15Ma02HI
WARING, Dan.	23	M	Laborer	15Ma02HI
Wm.	20	M	Unknown	15Ma02HI
Jas.	13	M	None	15Ma02HI
Robt.	10	M	None	15Ma02HI
Mary	06	F	Child	15Ma02HI
Eliza	01	F	Child	15Ma02HI
DOUGLASS, J.	22	M	Unknown	15Ma02HI
MISS, J.	25	M	Unknown	15Ma02HI
ALEXANDER, Debra	20	F	Unknown	15Ma02HI
LITTLE, W.	30	M	Unknown	15Ma02HI
GILROY, J.	34	M	Unknown	15Ma02HI
Bgt.	21	F	Unknown	15Ma02HI
LISH, M.	24	M	Unknown	15Ma02HI
CUSHMAN, P.	25	M	Unknown	15Ma02HI
KURN, Honora	25	F	Unknown	15Ma02HI
John	21	M	Unknown	15Ma02HI
Wm.	18	M	Unknown	15Ma02HI
FINGER, T.	30	M	Unknown	15Ma02HI
Bgt.	06	F	Child	15Ma02HI
KEEP, Mgt.	20	F	Unknown	15Ma02HI
James	18	M	Unknown	15Ma02HI
DONNELY, T.	21	M	Unknown	15Ma02HI
MCGUSS, Alice	40	F	Unknown	15Ma02HI
Cath.	14	F	Unknown	15Ma02HI
GILCHRIST, Mary	21	F	Unknown	15Ma02HI
GORDAN, Eliza	50	F	Unknown	15Ma02HI
Peggy	25	F	Unknown	15Ma02HI
Richd.	23	M	Unknown	15Ma02HI
CORDON, J.	19	M	Unknown	15Ma02HI
Matilda	12	F	Unknown	15Ma02HI
John	10	M	None	15Ma02HI
CUNNINGHAM, C.	25	M	Unknown	15Ma02HI
Thos.	21	M	Unknown	15Ma02HI
Sarah	18	F	Unknown	15Ma02HI
BUCK, J.	30	M	Unknown	15Ma02HI
WALLIS, T.	25	M	Unknown	15Ma02HI
KERNAN, J.	20	M	Unknown	15Ma02HI
COLLINS, Bgt.	18	F	Unknown	15Ma02HI
MCGRATH, O.	28	M	Unknown	15Ma02HI
Mary	45	F	Unknown	15Ma02HI
Mary	20	F	Unknown	15Ma02HI
CONNER, Ann	20	F	Unknown	15Ma02HI
DAISY, M.	30	M	Laborer	15Ma02HI
Mich.	25	M	Unknown	15Ma02HI
Cath.	23	F	Unknown	15Ma02HI
MCCARTHY, J.	28	M	Unknown	15Ma02HI
WALSH, W.	24	M	Unknown	15Ma02HI
CONRY, J.	26	M	Unknown	15Ma02HI
ROACH, J.	28	M	Unknown	15Ma02HI
Cath.	20	F	Unknown	15Ma02HI
WELCH, Joanna	20	F	Unknown	15Ma02HI
DONOVAN, J.	20	M	Unknown	15Ma02HI
CALLAGHAN, J.	26	M	Unknown	15Ma02HI
John	19	M	Unknown	15Ma02HI
Daniel	17	M	Unknown	15Ma02HI
STEVENSON, J.	25	M	Unknown	15Ma02HI
KEATLY, S.	20	M	Unknown	15Ma02HI
DORAN, J.	26	M	Unknown	15Ma02HI
CONNER, P.	25	M	Unknown	15Ma02HI
Mary	25	F	Unknown	15Ma02HI
WRIGHT, W.	29	M	Unknown	15Ma02HI
FINNIGHAN, Judy	29	F	Unknown	15Ma02HI
Michl.	01	M	Child	15Ma02HI
KEATOR, J.	45	M	Unknown	15Ma02HI
Hannah	46	F	Unknown	15Ma02HI
KENT, J.	20	M	Unknown	15Ma02HI
LUDLOW, D.	20	M	Unknown	15Ma02HI
Joanna	30	F	Unknown	15Ma02HI
LISEO, W.	23	M	Unknown	15Ma02HI
MCKEAN, J.	17	M	Unknown	15Ma02HI
GORMAN, J.	35	M	Unknown	15Ma02HI
BUCKMAN, A.	32	M	Unknown	15Ma02HI
KENNEDY, J.	34	M	Unknown	15Ma02HI
MCLARNER, J.	35	M	Unknown	15Ma02HI
DOWN, F.	20	M	Unknown	15Ma02HI
NEWALL, J.	36	M	Unknown	15Ma02HI
Elizbt. (W)	23	F	Unknown	15Ma02HI
Frances (D)	03	F	Child	15Ma02HI
George (S)	01	M	Child	15Ma02HI
HAMILTON, Wm.	28	M	Unknown	15Ma02HI
GREEN, T.	25	M	Unknown	15Ma02HI
FITZGERALD, Ann	20	F	Unknown	15Ma02HI
WEARING, S.	60	M	Unknown	15Ma02HI
Dan.	25	M	Unknown	15Ma02HI
TABBOT, J.	36	M	Laborer	15Ma02HI
HARRIS, S.	30	M	Unknown	15Ma02HI
FORD, S.	25	M	Unknown	15Ma02HI
CANNON, S.	40	M	Unknown	15Ma02HI
Robt.	21	M	Unknown	15Ma02HI
John	25	M	Unknown	15Ma02HI
Saml.	18	M	Unknown	15Ma02HI
Mary	17	F	Unknown	15Ma02HI
DUGGAN, Honora	32	F	Unknown	15Ma02HI
CALLAGHAN, M.	30	M	Unknown	15Ma02HI
TOBIN, Bdgt.	20	F	Unknown	15Ma02HI
Bessy	18	F	Unknown	15Ma02HI
SPENSER, T.	26	M	Unknown	15Ma02HI
Cath.	26	F	Unknown	15Ma02HI
MCELROY, P.	25	M	Unknown	15Ma02HI
CLARK, P.	30	M	Unknown	15Ma02HI
MANLY, J.	42	M	Unknown	15Ma02HI
Mary (W)	45	F	Unknown	15Ma02HI
Chas. (S)	07	M	Child	15Ma02HI
DARCY, J.	20	M	Unknown	15Ma02HI
DAVY, C.	25	M	Unknown	15Ma02HI
SHENLAN, Ellen	25	F	Unknown	15Ma02HI
MALCONGAN, J.	20	M	Unknown	15Ma02HI
THOMPSON, G.	20	M	Unknown	15Ma02HI
LEE, W.	30	M	Unknown	15Ma02HI
Anne	26	F	Unknown	15Ma02HI
MADOCK, T.	29	M	Unknown	15Ma02HI
Honora (W)	24	F	Unknown	15Ma02HI
Wm. (S)	01	M	Child	15Ma02HI
KEARNY, P.	24	M	Unknown	15Ma02HI
Bdgt.	16	F	Unknown	15Ma02HI
BOYCE, Cath.	20	F	Unknown	15Ma02HI
Ann-Eliz.	16	F	Unknown	15Ma02HI
STEVENSON, R.	23	M	Unknown	15Ma02HI
MURRAY, J.	30	M	Unknown	15Ma02HI
Betty	28	F	Unknown	15Ma02HI
DISCOL, P.	14	M	Unknown	15Ma02HI
COGHLAN, D.	31	M	Unknown	15Ma02HI
Ellen	20	F	Unknown	15Ma02HI
HATTON, T.	30	M	Unknown	15Ma02HI
LAWLESS, D.	18	M	Unknown	15Ma02HI
DARSY, W.	36	M	Unknown	15Ma02HI
PERROTT, Cath.	28	F	Unknown	15Ma02HI
PHILLIP, J.	20	M	Laborer	15Ma02HI
FLEMING, T.	57	M	Unknown	15Ma02HI
Helen (W)	57	F	Unknown	15Ma02HI
Jno. (S)	34	M	Unknown	15Ma02HI
George (S)	30	M	Unknown	15Ma02HI
James (S)	21	M	Unknown	15Ma02HI
BETTY, C.	10	M	Unknown	15Ma02HI
KEANE, R.	50	M	Unknown	15Ma02HI
QUIGLEY, J.	25	M	Unknown	15Ma02HI
GALLUN, J.	20	M	Unknown	15Ma02HI
JOHNSON, R.	20	M	Unknown	15Ma02HI
BROWN, W.	26	M	Unknown	15Ma02HI
MCCLUSKY, Mary	25	F	Unknown	15Ma02HI
Cath.	25	F	Unknown	15Ma02HI
MCGUNN, P.	21	M	Unknown	15Ma02HI
MCAFEY, J.	24	M	Unknown	15Ma02HI
MCCALLOR, J.	25	M	Unknown	15Ma02HI
Eliza	20	F	Unknown	15Ma02HI

NAMES OF PASSENGERS		AGE	SEX	OCCUPATIONS	DATE PORT SHIP	NAMES OF PASSENGERS		AGE	SEX	OCCUPATIONS	DATE PORT SHIP
MCCALLOR, Sarah		18	F	Unknown	15Ma02HI	MONGAN, G.		30	M	Unknown	15Ma02HI
Pat		01	M	Child	15Ma02HI	MAY, J.		30	M	Unknown	15Ma02HI
MCQUA, Isb.		45	M	Unknown	15Ma02HI	Winifred		22	F	Unknown	15Ma02HI
Mich.		12	M	Unknown	15Ma02HI	CARLY, J.		23	M	Unknown	15Ma02HI
LINCH, T.		40	M	Unknown	15Ma02HI	NOLAN, N.		18	M	Unknown	15Ma02HI
MONAHAN, A.		31	M	Unknown	15Ma02HI	MCURN, Honora		18	F	Unknown	15Ma02HI
MCCARTNY, D.		31	M	Unknown	15Ma02HI	MULER, Barb.		17	F	Unknown	15Ma02HI
CLAXTON, D.		29	M	Unknown	15Ma02HI	HENRY, T.		30	M	Unknown	15Ma02HI
Hannah		23	F	Unknown	15Ma02HI	MCKEOWN, J.		40	M	Unknown	15Ma02HI
SMITH, T.		30	M	Unknown	15Ma02HI	FENIGAN, J.		20	M	Unknown	15Ma02HI
John		21	M	Unknown	15Ma02HI	MCDONALD, M.		20	M	Unknown	15Ma02HI
THOMPSON, W.		25	M	Unknown	15Ma02HI	MCKAIN, Sally		23	F	Unknown	15Ma02HI
U	(W)	25	F	Unknown	15Ma02HI	Bessy		19	F	Unknown	15Ma02HI
Eliza-J.	(D)	03	F	Child	15Ma02HI	MUCH, Ann		25	F	Unknown	15Ma02HI
Agnes		20	F	Unknown	15Ma02HI	KILEY, P.		30	M	Unknown	15Ma02HI
Sarah		01	F	Child	15Ma02HI	DOWLAN, M.		30	M	Unknown	15Ma02HI
NAAN, Mary		20	F	Unknown	15Ma02HI	STAPES, M.		40	M	Unknown	15Ma02HI
SALER, Sally		21	F	Unknown	15Ma02HI	KUGSNER, W.		28	M	Unknown	15Ma02HI
CATARALL, M.		20	M	Unknown	15Ma02HI	BROWN, J.		28	M	Unknown	15Ma02HI
PARKINS, J.		27	M	Unknown	15Ma02HI	WHITE, J.		40	M	Unknown	15Ma02HI
Mgt.	(W)	28	F	Unknown	15Ma02HI	Julie		20	F	Unknown	15Ma02HI
Elizbt.	(D)	09	F	Child	15Ma02HI	BOUKE, J.B.		56	M	Unknown	15Ma02HI
Thos.	(S)	01	M	Child	15Ma02HI	DONELLY, B.		56	M	Unknown	15Ma02HI
ROUGHAN, Bgt.		20	F	Unknown	15Ma02HI	Ann	(W)	56	F	Unknown	15Ma02HI
MORRISSEN, D.		21	M	Laborer	15Ma02HI	Bryan	(S)	17	M	Unknown	15Ma02HI
STEWART, S.		21	M	Unknown	15Ma02HI	Peggy	(D)	15	F	Unknown	15Ma02HI
WILLIAMS, T.		32	M	Unknown	15Ma02HI	Cath.	(D)	13	F	Unknown	15Ma02HI
Anna		28	F	Unknown	15Ma02HI	Ann	(D)	11	F	Unknown	15Ma02HI
FREEMAN, T.		23	M	Unknown	15Ma02HI	LAWLER, M.		30	M	Unknown	15Ma02HI
MULLIGAN, E.		18	M	Unknown	15Ma02HI	Jane		20	F	Unknown	15Ma02HI
SAMPSON, Mary		28	F	Unknown	15Ma02HI	LIVINGSTONE, H.		45	M	Laborer	15Ma02HI
MABLE, C.		22	M	Unknown	15Ma02HI	M.		20	M	Unknown	15Ma02HI
HORNER, T.		22	M	Unknown	15Ma02HI	Fan.		18	M	Unknown	15Ma02HI
KELLAN, P.		20	M	Unknown	15Ma02HI	ARGGEN, W.		16	M	Unknown	15Ma02HI
Mary		20	F	Unknown	15Ma02HI	LINGHEN, N.		20	M	Unknown	15Ma02HI
MCCONLY, C.		25	M	Unknown	15Ma02HI	KEHILL, W.		24	M	Unknown	15Ma02HI
Cath.		20	F	Unknown	15Ma02HI	Ann		18	F	Unknown	15Ma02HI
WELSH, J.		16	M	Unknown	15Ma02HI	Susan		18	F	Unknown	15Ma02HI
FUGLAN, J.		30	M	Unknown	15Ma02HI	LONGLIN, G.		18	M	Unknown	15Ma02HI
Ann		30	F	Unknown	15Ma02HI	CONLON, G.		20	M	Unknown	15Ma02HI
Deny		21	M	Unknown	15Ma02HI	MCKEE, A.		20	M	Unknown	15Ma02HI
Jane		18	F	Unknown	15Ma02HI	Joseph		35	M	Unknown	15Ma02HI
CORBANE, D.		20	M	Unknown	15Ma02HI	QUIN, H.		35	M	Unknown	15Ma02HI
Jos.		20	M	Unknown	15Ma02HI	Nancy	(W)	35	F	Unknown	15Ma02HI
SUNLER, Ann		20	F	Unknown	15Ma02HI	Mary	(D)	13	F	Unknown	15Ma02HI
GILLAN, T.		22	M	Unknown	15Ma02HI	Betty	(D)	12	F	Unknown	15Ma02HI
MCFARLEN, J.		20	M	Unknown	15Ma02HI	RUSSELL, J.		60	M	Unknown	15Ma02HI
NEWELL, J.		27	M	Unknown	15Ma02HI	U	(W)	69	F	Unknown	15Ma02HI
FOSTER, J.		27	M	Unknown	15Ma02HI	FERGUSON, B.		48	M	Unknown	15Ma02HI
Ellen		27	F	Unknown	15Ma02HI	Jane	(W)	40	F	Unknown	15Ma02HI
Elizbt.		25	F	Unknown	15Ma02HI	Jane	(D)	13	F	Unknown	15Ma02HI
Jas.		02	M	Child	15Ma02HI	Wm.	(S)	12	M	Unknown	15Ma02HI
Jos.		01	M	Child	15Ma02HI	Sarah	(D)	10	F	Unknown	15Ma02HI
SCOTT, J.		27	M	Unknown	15Ma02HI	Alex.	(S)	08	M	Child	15Ma02HI
Mary-J.		22	F	Unknown	15Ma02HI	Robt.	(S)	06	M	Child	15Ma02HI
ROBINSON, S.		26	M	Unknown	15Ma02HI	James	(S)	03	M	Child	15Ma02HI
Wm.		19	M	Unknown	15Ma02HI	Isabella	(D)	01	F	Child	15Ma02HI
LYONS, J.		20	M	Unknown	15Ma02HI	Isabella	(D)	17	F	Unknown	15Ma02HI
U, A.		25	M	Unknown	15Ma02HI	HAWAUTH, A.		20	M	Unknown	15Ma02HI
CLARK, Cath.		20	F	Unknown	15Ma02HI	John		21	M	Unknown	15Ma02HI
SEKEN, J.		28	M	Unknown	15Ma02HI	Bgt.		18	F	Unknown	15Ma02HI
GISSER, J.		35	M	Unknown	15Ma02HI	Mary		20	F	Unknown	15Ma02HI
Eliza		12	F	Unknown	15Ma02HI	KEOGH, D.		22	M	Unknown	15Ma02HI
CONNELLY, J.		35	M	Unknown	15Ma02HI	READ, J.		27	M	Unknown	15Ma02HI
Biddy		30	F	Unknown	15Ma02HI	Robt.		20	M	Unknown	15Ma02HI
HASBET, Robt.		02	M	Child	15Ma02HI	SAMPLER, W.		24	M	Unknown	15Ma02HI
LUCEY, P.		27	M	Laborer	15Ma02HI	HENSON, J.		35	M	Unknown	15Ma02HI
MCELROY, P.		21	M	Unknown	15Ma02HI	DUNN, D.		30	M	Unknown	15Ma02HI
Owen		19	M	Unknown	15Ma02HI	U	(W)	20	F	Unknown	15Ma02HI
Michl.		20	M	Unknown	15Ma02HI	HASBET, W.		26	M	Unknown	15Ma02HI
KEOGHANE, P.		24	M	Unknown	15Ma02HI	U	(W)	25	F	Unknown	15Ma02HI
MAHER, Mary		25	F	Unknown	15Ma02HI	Mgt.	(D)	03	F	Child	15Ma02HI
REYNOLDS, Ann		25	F	Unknown	15Ma02HI	ACLAND, J.		12	M	None	15Ma02HI
RANNEN, J.		30	M	Unknown	15Ma02HI	Joseph		10	M	None	15Ma02HI
FOGERTY, M.		30	M	Unknown	15Ma02HI	Roger		04	M	Child	15Ma02HI

NAMES OF PASSENGERS	A G E	S E X	OCCUPATIONS	DATE PORT SHIP
ACLAND, Jane	01	F	Child	15Ma02HI
BOWEN, J.	40	M	Laborer	15Ma02HI
KELLY, M.	35	M	Unknown	15Ma02HI
BOWEN, Bgt.	30	F	Unknown	15Ma02HI
JONES, Sarah	30	F	Unknown	15Ma02HI
Marie	01	F	Child	15Ma02HI
ABBOTT, R.	20	M	Unknown	15Ma02HI
George	25	M	Unknown	15Ma02HI
Mary	40	F	Unknown	15Ma02HI
CLARKE, J.	14	M	None	15Ma02HI
HAMILTON, W.	20	M	Unknown	15Ma02HI
HANNELL, A.	20	M	Unknown	15Ma02HI
Mary	20	F	Unknown	15Ma02HI
ROBINSON, J.	20	M	Unknown	15Ma02HI
MOORE, W.J.	20	M	Unknown	15Ma02HI
CONNEN, J.	24	M	Unknown	15Ma02HI
MCNALTY, P.	22	M	Unknown	15Ma02HI
GRUNTY, Mary	20	F	Unknown	15Ma02HI
MCNALTY, Cath.	20	F	Unknown	15Ma02HI
DONALD, J.	25	M	Unknown	15Ma02HI
Patk.	21	M	Unknown	15Ma02HI
MCFARLANE, J.	20	M	Unknown	15Ma02HI
HENRY, M.	20	M	Unknown	15Ma02HI
HUMPHREY, R.	50	M	Unknown	15Ma02HI
Rebecca (W)	55	F	Unknown	15Ma02HI
Mgt. (D)	20	F	Unknown	15Ma02HI
Susan (D)	17	F	Unknown	15Ma02HI
Thos. (S)	15	M	Unknown	15Ma02HI
Frans. (S)	14	M	Unknown	15Ma02HI
Wm. (S)	11	M	Unknown	15Ma02HI
BALLART, Mary	16	F	Unknown	15Ma02HI
HACKET, M.	30	M	Unknown	15Ma02HI
U (W)	30	F	Unknown	15Ma02HI
STEPHENS, J.	74	M	Unknown	15Ma02HI
MCNOLT, Betsy	02	F	Child	15Ma02HI
BROWN, P.	19	M	Unknown	15Ma02HI
Ann	25	F	Unknown	15Ma02HI
LIVINGSTONE, J.	43	M	Unknown	15Ma02HI
Isabella	43	F	Unknown	15Ma02HI
ONEIL, Cath.	20	F	Unknown	15Ma02HI
CANUGH, Mgt.	28	F	Unknown	15Ma02HI
Chas.	24	M	Unknown	15Ma02HI
PARKER, G.	50	M	Unknown	15Ma02HI
Ann (W)	30	F	Unknown	15Ma02HI
LAWSON, W.	11	M	Unknown	15Ma02HI
PARKER, Hannah	06	F	Child	15Ma02HI
Isabella (T)	04	F	Child	15Ma02HI
Mgt. (T)	02	F	Child	15Ma02HI
WATSON, T.	24	M	Unknown	15Ma02HI
William	22	M	Unknown	15Ma02HI
Esther	28	F	Unknown	15Ma02HI
Ann	02	F	Child	15Ma02HI
Mgt.	18	F	Unknown	15Ma02HI
MEHEY, A.	40	M	Unknown	15Ma02HI
DUNN, S.	24	M	Unknown	15Ma02HI
KENNEDY, T.	25	M	Unknown	15Ma02HI
William	24	M	Unknown	15Ma02HI
CASHELL, J.	30	M	Unknown	15Ma02HI
Ann	30	F	Unknown	15Ma02HI
QUOIN, J.	19	M	Unknown	15Ma02HI
Wm.	18	M	Unknown	15Ma02HI
CARROLL, J.	19	M	Unknown	15Ma02HI
ONEIL, W.N.	25	M	Unknown	15Ma02HI
BURN, A.M.	28	M	Unknown	15Ma02HI
Eliza	29	F	Unknown	15Ma02HI
PEPPER, T.	20	M	Unknown	15Ma02HI
MCBRIDE, Lucd.	21	F	Unknown	15Ma02HI
SPRATE, J.	22	M	Unknown	15Ma02HI
Ann	12	F	Unknown	15Ma02HI
Mgt.	11	F	Unknown	15Ma02HI
MATHER, J.	25	M	Unknown	15Ma02HI
MALONE, A.	28	M	Unknown	15Ma02HI
MCGILL, J.	20	M	Unknown	15Ma02HI
James	20	M	Unknown	15Ma02HI
MOORE, R.	27	M	Unknown	15Ma02HI

NAMES OF PASSENGERS	A G E	S E X	OCCUPATIONS	DATE PORT SHIP
ACLAND, R.	40	M	Unknown	15Ma02HI
Mary (W)	40	F	Unknown	15Ma02HI
Ann (D)	21	F	Unknown	15Ma02HI
Anthony	30	M	Unknown	15Ma02HI
Robt. (S)	19	M	Unknown	15Ma02HI
Wm. (S)	18	M	Unknown	15Ma02HI
CAROLINE, A.	25	M	Laborer	15Ma02HI
Francis	25	M	Unknown	15Ma02HI
Thos.	17	M	Unknown	15Ma02HI
Mary	40	F	Unknown	15Ma02HI
Mgt.	20	F	Unknown	15Ma02HI
Pat	11	M	None	15Ma02HI
MULLIGAN, T.	23	M	Unknown	15Ma02HI
CLARK, B.	21	M	Unknown	15Ma02HI
CASSELS, T.	30	M	Unknown	15Ma02HI
Ann	24	F	Unknown	15Ma02HI
SMITH, J.	20	M	Unknown	15Ma02HI
ROURKE, J.	25	M	Unknown	15Ma02HI
ROSS, T.	48	M	Unknown	15Ma02HI
Ann	42	F	Unknown	15Ma02HI
Ellen	31	F	Unknown	15Ma02HI
Ann	19	F	Unknown	15Ma02HI
Jane	17	F	Unknown	15Ma02HI
Thos.	15	M	None	15Ma02HI
Ruth	50	F	Unknown	15Ma02HI
LYNCH, J.	20	M	Unknown	15Ma02HI
Mary	50	F	Unknown	15Ma02HI
Bdgt.	18	F	Unknown	15Ma02HI
DONNELLY, P.	30	M	Unknown	15Ma02HI
U (W)	30	F	Unknown	15Ma02HI
CAVANAGH, Mary	35	F	Unknown	15Ma02HI
HORNE, Ann	22	F	Unknown	15Ma02HI
HALL, Eliza	20	F	Unknown	15Ma02HI
MCCANN, R.	30	M	Unknown	15Ma02HI
HALL, J.	30	M	Unknown	15Ma02HI
FITZPATRICK, M.	30	M	Unknown	15Ma02HI
Ann	25	F	Unknown	15Ma02HI
DORIN, Cath.	20	F	Unknown	15Ma02HI
COLMAN, J.	20	M	Unknown	15Ma02HI
NICOL, T.	19	M	Unknown	15Ma02HI
MCMAHON, C.	25	M	Unknown	15Ma02HI
HOGAN, P.	25	M	Unknown	15Ma02HI
RYAN, J.	20	M	Unknown	15Ma02HI
CRATOR, Mgt.	18	F	Unknown	15Ma02HI
LAWLESS, Ann	20	F	Unknown	15Ma02HI
MCELROY, J.	24	M	Unknown	15Ma02HI
JONES, T.	35	M	Unknown	15Ma02HI
Eliza	20	F	Unknown	15Ma02HI

DIANA 17 MAY 1847

From Liverpool

NAMES OF PASSENGERS	A G E	S E X	OCCUPATIONS	DATE PORT SHIP
SHORT, John	30	M	Farmer	17Ma02Nz
U (W)	30	F	Unknown	17Ma02Nz
Henry (S)	09	M	Child	17Ma02Nz
OKEEFE, Peter	25	M	Farmer	17Ma02Nz
CHENIARA, John	25	M	Farmer	17Ma02Nz
Sarah	20	F	Unknown	17Ma02Nz
Ann	18	F	Unknown	17Ma02Nz
QUIN, Darby	24	M	Farmer	17Ma02Nz
Eliza	22	F	Unknown	17Ma02Nz
MCGULLEY, Edward	25	M	Mechanic	17Ma02Nz
MCSLADE, Mary-Ann	14	F	Unknown	17Ma02Nz
MCCARTY, Chas.	45	M	Unknown	17Ma02Nz
SONTON, Mary	26	F	Unknown	17Ma02Nz
HOGAN, Pat.	21	M	Unknown	17Ma02Nz
MILLIGAN, William	24	M	Servant	17Ma02Nz
DECKERTON, Catherine	17	F	Unknown	17Ma02Nz

NAMES OF PASSENGERS		AGE	SEX	OCCUPATIONS	DATE PORT SHIP
MCDONNELL, Edw.		63	M	Servant	17Ma02Nz
NIXON, Lucinda		13	F	Servant	17Ma02Nz
Margaret		22	F	Servant	17Ma02Nz
John		24	M	Servant	17Ma02Nz
Julia		24	F	Servant	17Ma02Nz
COLLINS, Margaret		23	F	Servant	17Ma02Nz
SHEAHAN, John		26	M	Laborer	17Ma02Nz
CARROLL, Corns.		20	M	Laborer	17Ma02Nz
Ellen		18	F	Unknown	17Ma02Nz
Daniel		28	M	Laborer	17Ma02Nz
NAUGHAN, Michl.		24	M	Laborer	17Ma02Nz
SHEHAN, Patrick		25	M	Laborer	17Ma02Nz
SULLIVAN, Danl.		25	M	Mechanic	17Ma02Nz
MCCARTY, Danl.		27	M	Mechanic	17Ma02Nz
MCCARTHY, Robert		30	M	Mechanic	17Ma02Nz
MORRISON, Robert		26	M	Mechanic	17Ma02Nz
John		03	M	Child	17Ma02Nz
MCWHEENEY, John		41	M	Mechanic	17Ma02Nz
Cathe.	(W)	33	F	Mechanic	17Ma02Nz
Julia	(D)	13	F	Mechanic	17Ma02Nz
Ann	(D)	12	F	Mechanic	17Ma02Nz
Henry	(S)	09	M	Child	17Ma02Nz
Judy	(D)	07	F	Child	17Ma02Nz
MINIHAN, Bridget		10	F	Unknown	17Ma02Nz
MAHONY, Michl.		25	M	Mechanic	17Ma02Nz
Johanna		18	F	Unknown	17Ma02Nz
CANTY, Thomas		40	M	Mechanic	17Ma02Nz
Mary		30	F	Unknown	17Ma02Nz
Norah		23	F	Unknown	17Ma02Nz
ARTEUTHNEL, Margaret		25	F	Unknown	17Ma02Nz
WALSH, Robert		57	M	Mechanic	17Ma02Nz
Ellen	(W)	45	F	Unknown	17Ma02Nz
William	(S)	27	M	Farmer	17Ma02Nz
Michael	(S)	24	M	Farmer	17Ma02Nz
Cathe.	(D)	18	F	Unknown	17Ma02Nz
Mary	(D)	13	F	Unknown	17Ma02Nz
Ellen	(D)	04	F	Child	17Ma02Nz
KENT, John		24	M	Farmer	17Ma02Nz
MCCANNY, John		23	M	Farmer	17Ma02Nz
WALSH, Debby		20	F	Unknown	17Ma02Nz
DALY, Michael		17	M	Farmer	17Ma02Nz
SHEHAN, Dennis		19	M	Farmer	17Ma02Nz
MURPHY, U-Miss		24	F	Unknown	17Ma02Nz
DURAND, John		33	M	Farmer	17Ma02Nz
Elizabeth	(W)	28	F	Unknown	17Ma02Nz
Vincent	(S)	08	M	Child	17Ma02Nz
John	(S)	06	M	Child	17Ma02Nz
Jas.	(S)	05	M	Child	17Ma02Nz
BUTLER, Richard		24	M	Farmer	17Ma02Nz
Cathe.		23	F	Unknown	17Ma02Nz
MCEVOY, Hugh		26	M	Farmer	17Ma02Nz
U	(W)	24	F	Unknown	17Ma02Nz
Ann	(D)	04	F	Child	17Ma02Nz
DURAND, John		33	M	Farmer	17Ma02Nz
MAHONEY, Michael		25	M	Farmer	17Ma02Nz
Johanna		18	F	Unknown	17Ma02Nz
KENT, John		24	M	Farmer	17Ma02Nz
MCCANN, John		23	M	Farmer	17Ma02Nz
REGAN, Michael		27	M	Mechanic	17Ma02Nz
Elizabeth	(W)	17	F	Unknown	17Ma02Nz
Richard	(S)	01	M	Child	17Ma02Nz
DAGAN, Cahs.		31	M	Mechanic	17Ma02Nz
KENT, John		21	M	Mechanic	17Ma02Nz
Margaret		17	F	Unknown	17Ma02Nz
Ellen		15	F	Unknown	17Ma02Nz
MCCOURT, John		18	M	Mechanic	17Ma02Nz
MCBRIDE, Peter		18	M	Mechanic	17Ma02Nz
MCCOLLOUGH, Bernd.		17	M	Mechanic	17Ma02Nz
SULLY, James		22	M	Mechanic	17Ma02Nz
Mary		18	F	Unknown	17Ma02Nz
DEVLIN, Peter		24	M	Mechanic	17Ma02Nz
MCGIBBON, John		21	M	Mechanic	17Ma02Nz
MURRAY, Ellen		21	F	Unknown	17Ma02Nz
FENLON, Ellen		30	F	Unknown	17Ma02Nz
Ellen		30	F	Unknown	17Ma02Nz
FENLON, John		25	M	Mechanic	17Ma02Nz
REILY, Mary		21	F	Unknown	17Ma02Nz
KENNEDY, Mary		21	F	Unknown	17Ma02Nz
MCDONALD, Sarah		20	F	Unknown	17Ma02Nz
SHARKEY, John		33	M	Mechanic	17Ma02Nz
Anthy.		22	M	Mechanic	17Ma02Nz
Patrick		19	M	Mechanic	17Ma02Nz
ARBURTHER, M.		20	M	Mechanic	17Ma02Nz
Elizabeth	(M)	50	F	Unknown	17Ma02Nz
Geo.	(B)	20	M	Mechanic	17Ma02Nz
Sally-Ann	(T)	16	F	Unknown	17Ma02Nz
Margaret	(T)	13	F	Unknown	17Ma02Nz
Isabella	(T)	09	F	Child	17Ma02Nz
Chas.	(B)	29	M	Unknown	17Ma02Nz
Mary	(L)	25	F	Unknown	17Ma02Nz
Eliza	(N)	04	F	Child	17Ma02Nz
Margaret	(N)	03	F	Child	17Ma02Nz
William	(N)	01	M	Child	17Ma02Nz
MCCALLAN, Margt.Ann		23	F	Unknown	17Ma02Nz
THOMAS, John		22	M	Mechanic	17Ma02Nz
MINIHAN, Danl.		30	M	Mechanic	17Ma02Nz
Cathe.	(W)	25	F	Unknown	17Ma02Nz
Danl.	(S)	04	M	Child	17Ma02Nz
Cathe.	(D)	.00	F	Infant	17Ma02Nz
MURNAN, John		29	M	Laborer	17Ma02Nz
U	(W)	27	F	Unknown	17Ma02Nz
Judy	(D)	11	F	Unknown	17Ma02Nz
Jane	(D)	07	F	Child	17Ma02Nz
John	(S)	08	M	Child	17Ma02Nz
Michl.	(S)	05	M	Child	17Ma02Nz
Matilda	(D)	02	F	Child	17Ma02Nz
Henry	(S)	.00	M	Infant	17Ma02Nz
HEALY, Timothy		20	M	Mechanic	17Ma02Nz
Cathe.		21	F	Unknown	17Ma02Nz
Margaret		17	F	Unknown	17Ma02Nz
MCLAUGHLIN, Jas.		29	M	Mechanic	17Ma02Nz
LYNCH, Bridget		20	F	Unknown	17Ma02Nz
RAFERTY, Jas.		23	M	Mechanic	17Ma02Nz
Bridget		21	F	Unknown	17Ma02Nz
LYNN, John		20	M	Mechanic	17Ma02Nz
U-Mrs.		27	F	Unknown	17Ma02Nz
Margaret		04	F	Child	17Ma02Nz
MCMULLAN, John		47	M	Mechanic	17Ma02Nz
U	(W)	30	F	Unknown	17Ma02Nz
Danl.	(S)	07	M	Child	17Ma02Nz
Henry	(S)	04	M	Child	17Ma02Nz
Jane	(D)	03	F	Child	17Ma02Nz
MARLAND, Andrew		39	M	Mechanic	17Ma02Nz
Mary	(W)	32	F	Unknown	17Ma02Nz
Bridget	(D)	14	F	Unknown	17Ma02Nz
Thos.	(S)	11	M	Mechanic	17Ma02Nz
Jas.	(S)	09	M	Child	17Ma02Nz
John	(S)	07	M	Child	17Ma02Nz
Emily	(D)	02	F	Child	17Ma02Nz
MCCOURT, W.		25	M	Mechanic	17Ma02Nz
U	(W)	21	F	Unknown	17Ma02Nz
Margaret		15	F	Unknown	17Ma02Nz
LARLIN, Jas.		22	M	Mechanic	17Ma02Nz
John		19	M	Unknown	17Ma02Nz
LINDY, John		30	M	Mechanic	17Ma02Nz
U	(W)	27	F	Unknown	17Ma02Nz
U-Miss		20	F	Unknown	17Ma02Nz
Belle		19	F	Unknown	17Ma02Nz
Rose	(D)	04	F	Child	17Ma02Nz
REGAN, Catherine		20	F	Unknown	17Ma02Nz
MCWHEENEY, Emily		05	F	Child	17Ma02Nz
Bridget		03	F	Child	17Ma02Nz
Margaret		02	F	Child	17Ma02Nz
Biddy		.00	F	Infant	17Ma02Nz
MAGRATH, Hugh		27	M	Mechanic	17Ma02Nz
FARRELL, Henry		19	M	Mechanic	17Ma02Nz
WALSH, Isaac		17	M	Mechanic	17Ma02Nz
BOYLE, Jas.		21	M	Mechanic	17Ma02Nz
Ann	(W)	26	F	Unknown	17Ma02Nz
Honora	(D)	02	F	Child	17Ma02Nz

NAMES OF PASSENGERS		AGE	SEX	OCCUPATIONS	DATE PORT SHIP
BOYLE, James	(S)	.00	M	Infant	17Ma02Nz
Catherine		22	F	Unknown	17Ma02Nz
Jane		11	F	Unknown	17Ma02Nz
BRYAN, Peter		41	M	Mechanic	17Ma02Nz
U	(W)	37	F	Unknown	17Ma02Nz
Philip	(S)	13	M	Mechanic	17Ma02Nz
Johanna	(D)	11	F	Unknown	17Ma02Nz
Martha	(D)	07	F	Child	17Ma02Nz
Henry	(S)	05	M	Child	17Ma02Nz
Isabella	(D)	03	F	Child	17Ma02Nz
Michael	(S)	.00	M	Infant	17Ma02Nz
MCDONNELL, Patrick		22	M	Farmer	17Ma02Nz
Jane		27	F	Unknown	17Ma02Nz
Bridget		21	F	Unknown	17Ma02Nz
MORROW, Lawrence		31	M	Farmer	17Ma02Nz
U	(W)	27	F	Unknown	17Ma02Nz
John		19	M	Farmer	17Ma02Nz
DUFFY, Michael		29	M	Farmer	17Ma02Nz
Catherine		21	F	Unknown	17Ma02Nz
Catherine		19	F	Unknown	17Ma02Nz
MURRAY, Saml.		27	M	Farmer	17Ma02Nz
DEESON, Timy.		37	M	Farmer	17Ma02Nz
U	(W)	31	F	Unknown	17Ma02Nz
Julia	(D)	06	F	Child	17Ma02Nz
Felix	(S)	04	M	Child	17Ma02Nz
Jons.	(S)	11	M	Farmer	17Ma02Nz
GIBNEY, John		21	M	Laborer	17Ma02Nz
Henry		19	M	Laborer	17Ma02Nz
Ellen		17	F	Unknown	17Ma02Nz
James		21	M	Laborer	17Ma02Nz
HOPKINS, Michl.		27	M	Laborer	17Ma02Nz

PONTIAC 17 MAY 1847

From Belfast

NAMES OF PASSENGERS		AGE	SEX	OCCUPATIONS	DATE PORT SHIP
HARLETT, Grace		40	F	Unknown	17Ma07Jw
Jane		42	F	Unknown	17Ma07Jw
DEMPSTER, John		50	M	Farmer	17Ma07Jw
Mary	(W)	40	F	Unknown	17Ma07Jw
John	(S)	19	M	Farmer	17Ma07Jw
William	(S)	16	M	Unknown	17Ma07Jw
James	(S)	14	M	Unknown	17Ma07Jw
Elisabeth	(D)	12	F	Unknown	17Ma07Jw
Henry	(S)	10	M	Unknown	17Ma07Jw
Agnes	(D)	07	F	Child	17Ma07Jw
Andrew	(S)	03	M	Child	17Ma07Jw
Mary	(D)	03	F	Child	17Ma07Jw
KEE, James		28	M	Farmer	17Ma07Jw
KERR, James		22	M	Unknown	17Ma07Jw
Joseph		18	M	Unknown	17Ma07Jw
Eliza		20	F	Unknown	17Ma07Jw
Sarah		02	F	Child	17Ma07Jw
PAINE, Eliza		30	F	Unknown	17Ma07Jw
Eliza		12	F	Unknown	17Ma07Jw
MCCARY, Bernard		24	M	Unknown	17Ma07Jw
MCCARROLL, Jas.		24	M	Unknown	17Ma07Jw
HEBISON, Thos.		21	M	Unknown	17Ma07Jw
KERR, David		20	M	Unknown	17Ma07Jw
Mary	(W)	21	F	Unknown	17Ma07Jw
James	(S)	01	M	Child	17Ma07Jw
GORDON, George		30	M	Farmer	17Ma07Jw
Margt.	(W)	29	F	Unknown	17Ma07Jw
Elizabeth		16	F	Unknown	17Ma07Jw
John		18	M	Unknown	17Ma07Jw
Robert	(S)	04	M	Child	17Ma07Jw
FISHER, Jane		26	F	Unknown	17Ma07Jw
ALEIN, George		24	M	Mechanic	17Ma07Jw
GORDON, John-D.		11	M	Unknown	17Ma07Jw

NAMES OF PASSENGERS		AGE	SEX	OCCUPATIONS	DATE PORT SHIP
CUMMING, Jas.		24	M	Clerk	17Ma07Jw
Anne	(W)	24	F	Unknown	17Ma07Jw
William	(S)	.00	M	Infant	17Ma07Jw
FINLAY, William		20	M	Farmer	17Ma07Jw
MCKEE, Jas.		25	M	Farmer	17Ma07Jw
FREW, Margaret		17	F	Unknown	17Ma07Jw
MEIKIN, Alex.		05	M	Child	17Ma07Jw
SLOAN, James		25	M	Unknown	17Ma07Jw
MCBRIDE, Danl.		45	M	Farmer	17Ma07Jw
Mary	(W)	44	F	Unknown	17Ma07Jw
Eliza	(D)	17	F	Unknown	17Ma07Jw
William	(S)	09	M	Child	17Ma07Jw
Joseph	(S)	08	M	Child	17Ma07Jw
Martha	(D)	07	F	Child	17Ma07Jw
John	(S)	05	M	Child	17Ma07Jw
Thos.	(S)	00	M	Child	17Ma07Jw
CAIRNES, William		19	M	Laborer	17Ma07Jw
MCUSKER, Danl.		19	M	Laborer	17Ma07Jw
MOORE, Alex.		19	M	Laborer	17Ma07Jw
BUSBY, William		20	M	Mechanic	17Ma07Jw
Sarah		17	F	Unknown	17Ma07Jw
MORGAN, Cathe.		17	F	Unknown	17Ma07Jw
BRYNN, John		19	M	Clerk	17Ma07Jw
WILSON, Rob.B.M.		22	M	Surgeon	17Ma07Jw
IRWIN, William		21	M	Laborer	17Ma07Jw
Rebecca		20	F	Unknown	17Ma07Jw
SERGEANT, Ellen		30	F	Unknown	17Ma07Jw
Catherine		49	F	Unknown	17Ma07Jw
MORLAND, Eliza		25	F	Unknown	17Ma07Jw
REID, John		21	M	Laborer	17Ma07Jw
MURPHY, Hugh		30	M	Farmer	17Ma07Jw
Ellen	(W)	32	F	Unknown	17Ma07Jw
Ellen	(D)	07	F	Child	17Ma07Jw
Francis	(S)	04	M	Child	17Ma07Jw
John		25	M	Laborer	17Ma07Jw
Ann		30	F	Unknown	17Ma07Jw
MCCRAW, Biddy		32	F	Unknown	17Ma07Jw
Joseph		16	M	Laborer	17Ma07Jw
DUNAGHY, Terrence		21	M	Laborer	17Ma07Jw
KIRWOOD, Robert		35	M	Laborer	17Ma07Jw
BOYD, Jas.		20	M	Laborer	17Ma07Jw
SHANNON, Margt.		25	F	Unknown	17Ma07Jw
Mary		23	F	Unknown	17Ma07Jw
MOORE, David		25	M	Laborer	17Ma07Jw
WILSON, Saml.		31	M	Laborer	17Ma07Jw
CAMPBELL, Rob.		45	M	Mechanic	17Ma07Jw
Daniel		20	M	Mechanic	17Ma07Jw
JOHNSTON, Margt.		50	F	Unknown	17Ma07Jw
MCGRADY, Edw.		20	M	Mechanic	17Ma07Jw
BOYLE, Patrick		20	M	Mechanic	17Ma07Jw
GLASS, John		21	M	Mechanic	17Ma07Jw
CREEDY, Chas.		23	M	Mechanic	17Ma07Jw
MCMEIKIN, Jas.		57	M	Farmer	17Ma07Jw
Jane	(W)	50	F	Unknown	17Ma07Jw
Mary	(D)	18	F	Unknown	17Ma07Jw
Margaret	(D)	16	F	Unknown	17Ma07Jw
Rosanna	(D)	14	F	Unknown	17Ma07Jw
Isabella	(D)	12	F	Unknown	17Ma07Jw
John	(S)	09	M	Child	17Ma07Jw
William	(S)	07	M	Child	17Ma07Jw
MOORES, Haytt		28	M	Laborer -	17Ma07Jw
CARREN, Mary		25	F	Unknown	17Ma07Jw
BABE, William		44	M	Farmer	17Ma07Jw
Cathe.	(W)	42	F	Unknown	17Ma07Jw
Eliza	(D)	20	F	Unknown	17Ma07Jw
William	(S)	18	M	Unknown	17Ma07Jw
Jane	(D)	14	F	Unknown	17Ma07Jw
Mary	(D)	05	F	Child	17Ma07Jw
Isabella	(D)	03	F	Child	17Ma07Jw
MCHAFFER, Mary		25	F	Unknown	17Ma07Jw
Eliza		22	F	Unknown	17Ma07Jw
REA, Jane		20	F	Unknown	17Ma07Jw
MCDOWALL, Sarah		26	F	Unknown	17Ma07Jw
CALLIN, Ann		21	F	Unknown	17Ma07Jw
FRAMEN, Eliza		40	F	Unknown	17Ma07Jw

NAMES OF PASSENGERS	A G E	S E X	OCCUPATIONS	DATE PORT SHIP	NAMES OF PASSENGERS	A G E	S E X	OCCUPATIONS	DATE PORT SHIP
BROWNLOW, Rosella		09	F	Child	17Ma07Jw	ELLISON, Christophe(B)		11	M	Unknown	17Ma07Jw
MCKEOWEN, Henry		26	M	Laborer	17Ma07Jw	Henry	(B)	08	M	Child	17Ma07Jw
Jane		20	F	Unknown	17Ma07Jw	REID, Mary		24	F	Unknown	17Ma07Jw
GILLESPIE, Thos.		29	M	Laborer	17Ma07Jw	MALVANY, Sarah		21	F	Unknown	17Ma07Jw
Eliza	(W)	28	F	Unknown	17Ma07Jw	STEWART, Margt.		22	F	Unknown	17Ma07Jw
Saml.	(S)	12	M	Unknown	17Ma07Jw	FLEMING, Nancy		21	F	Unknown	17Ma07Jw
Agnes	(D)	10	F	Unknown	17Ma07Jw	SHAW, Thomas		20	M	Laborer	17Ma07Jw
MCCRACKAN, Saml.		30	M	Farmer	17Ma07Jw	KERR, John		20	M	Laborer	17Ma07Jw
DAWSON, Ellen		26	F	Unknown	17Ma07Jw	MCGEE, Wm.		60	M	Surgeon	17Ma07Jw
Thomas		15	M	Laborer	17Ma07Jw	Mary	(W)	58	F	Unknown	17Ma07Jw
Cathe.		13	F	Unknown	17Ma07Jw	John	(S)	24	M	Unknown	17Ma07Jw
William		04	M	Child	17Ma07Jw	Alicia	(D)	20	F	Unknown	17Ma07Jw
Martha		02	F	Child	17Ma07Jw	Margaret	(D)	17	F	Unknown	17Ma07Jw
WARWICK, James		21	M	Clerk	17Ma07Jw	William	(S)	14	M	Unknown	17Ma07Jw
HIRMANY, Robert		25	M	Mechanic	17Ma07Jw	GRUBB, William		24	M	Merchant	17Ma07Jw
Jas.		21	M	Mechanic	17Ma07Jw	Maria	(W)	24	F	Unknown	17Ma07Jw
QUIN, Joseph		22	M	Mechanic	17Ma07Jw	Alfred	(S)	07	M	Child	17Ma07Jw
Ann		21	F	Unknown	17Ma07Jw	Robert	(S)	03	M	Child	17Ma07Jw
Eliza		22	F	Unknown	17Ma07Jw	MCCONWAY, Mary		20	F	Unknown	17Ma07Jw
Mary		02	F	Child	17Ma07Jw	MCCONNELL, John		23	M	Farmer	17Ma07Jw
William		00	M	Child	17Ma07Jw	MCGRAW, John		22	M	Farmer	17Ma07Jw
DOUGLAS, John		35	M	Mechanic	17Ma07Jw	MARTIN, David		24	M	Farmer	17Ma07Jw
DANDEE, Chas.		18	M	Mechanic	17Ma07Jw	JOHNSTON, Andrew		20	M	Farmer	17Ma07Jw
MOORE, Hugh		17	M	Mechanic	17Ma07Jw	STENSON, John		17	M	Farmer	17Ma07Jw
LOGAN, Danl.		17	M	Mechanic	17Ma07Jw	MCGEE, John		28	M	Farmer	17Ma07Jw
MILLIGAN, Jas.		17	M	Mechanic	17Ma07Jw	WARWICK, William		23	M	Farmer	17Ma07Jw
HANNA, John		25	M	Clerk	17Ma07Jw	CUNNINGHAM, Jas.		21	M	Farmer	17Ma07Jw
MCCARTNEY, W.		39	M	Clerk	17Ma07Jw	REMEDY, Andrew		24	M	Clerk	17Ma07Jw
Nancy	(W)	38	F	Unknown	17Ma07Jw	Hugh		20	M	Clerk	17Ma07Jw
Archibald	(S)	19	M	Clerk	17Ma07Jw	MCLAINE, John		28	M	Clerk	17Ma07Jw
SNODGRASS, Alex.		22	M	Clerk	17Ma07Jw	ROSS, Jas.		25	M	Farmer	17Ma07Jw
Saml.		20	M	Clerk	17Ma07Jw	Jane	(W)	23	F	Unknown	17Ma07Jw
ROBINSON, Helen		19	F	Unknown	17Ma07Jw	Eliza	(D)	01	F	Child	17Ma07Jw
BROWNLOW, Archibald		14	M	Laborer	17Ma07Jw						
Anny		18	F	Unknown	17Ma07Jw						
MURPHY, Eleanor		02	F	Child	17Ma07Jw						
Cathe.		25	F	Unknown	17Ma07Jw						
COWAN, William		22	M	Laborer	17Ma07Jw						
Anne		19	F	Unknown	17Ma07Jw		BURNHOLM 17 MAY 1847				
MURPHY, Ellen		21	F	Unknown	17Ma07Jw						
ANDERSON, Mathew		23	M	Farmer	17Ma07Jw		From Liverpool				
Sarah		23	F	Unknown	17Ma07Jw						
David		20	M	Laborer	17Ma07Jw						
POLLACK, Saml.		26	M	Laborer	17Ma07Jw						
David		23	M	Unknown	17Ma07Jw	CONWAY, Catherine		22	F	Unknown	17Ma02Nt
CURRY, John		23	M	Laborer	17Ma07Jw	Anny		20	F	Unknown	17Ma02Nt
MOORE, William		18	M	Clerk	17Ma07Jw	BAYLEY, Francis		50	M	Farmer	17Ma02Nt
ADAIR, Robert		18	M	Clerk	17Ma07Jw	Mary	(W)	50	F	Unknown	17Ma02Nt
GRAHAM, William		16	M	Clerk	17Ma07Jw	Ann	(D)	16	F	Unknown	17Ma02Nt
HAWTHORN, David		18	M	Mechanic	17Ma07Jw	Jas.	(S)	19	M	Farmer	17Ma02Nt
BIGHAM, Robert		24	M	Mechanic	17Ma07Jw	BURNS, Ellen		20	F	Unknown	17Ma02Nt
William		18	M	Mechanic	17Ma07Jw	HIRNEY, Henry		20	M	Farmer	17Ma02Nt
HAMMOND, Benj.		20	M	Mechanic	17Ma07Jw	MCGANLIN, Patrick		29	M	Farmer	17Ma02Nt
MCHEVY, John		29	M	Mechanic	17Ma07Jw	HINSEY, Benjamin		26	M	Farmer	17Ma02Nt
Ellen		25	F	Unknown	17Ma07Jw	Mary	(W)	26	F	Unknown	17Ma02Nt
MCCLEERY, James		21	M	Mechanic	17Ma07Jw	James	(S)	07	M	Child	17Ma02Nt
BARRETT, George		24	M	Mechanic	17Ma07Jw	Mathias	(S)	05	M	Child	17Ma02Nt
GRAHAM, James		25	M	Mechanic	17Ma07Jw	David	(S)	02	M	Child	17Ma02Nt
BASID, Arthur		23	M	Mechanic	17Ma07Jw	MCCONNELL, Cathe.		20	F	Unknown	17Ma02Nt
MAGEE, William		23	M	Mechanic	17Ma07Jw	HUGHES, Bridget		21	F	Unknown	17Ma02Nt
BARRETT, Eliza		19	F	Unknown	17Ma07Jw	MCCANN, Elizabeth		20	F	Unknown	17Ma02Nt
AGNEW, Daniel		21	M	Mechanic	17Ma07Jw	HUGHES, Patrick		24	M	Unknown	17Ma02Nt
WARD, Kitty		20	F	Unknown	17Ma07Jw	MCCANN, Bradford		22	M	Unknown	17Ma02Nt
John		18	M	Laborer	17Ma07Jw	HANEY, Margaret		20	F	Unknown	17Ma02Nt
Mary		15	F	Unknown	17Ma07Jw	SMITH, Ellen		26	F	Unknown	17Ma02Nt
Rosey		11	F	Unknown	17Ma07Jw	George		04	M	Child	17Ma02Nt
Biddy		10	F	Unknown	17Ma07Jw	CONDON, Eliza		24	F	Unknown	17Ma02Nt
KIRK, Hugh		20	M	Laborer	17Ma07Jw	MCCARTHY, Horace		27	M	Unknown	17Ma02Nt
WILEY, Mary		25	F	Unknown	17Ma07Jw	SULLIVAN, John		21	M	Unknown	17Ma02Nt
Jane		23	F	Unknown	17Ma07Jw	John		12	M	Unknown	17Ma02Nt
MOFFAT, John		40	M	Mechanic	17Ma07Jw	ENGLISH, Jas.		50	M	Laborer	17Ma02Nt
ELLISON, John		26	M	Mechanic	17Ma07Jw	Saml.	(S)	15	M	Laborer	17Ma02Nt
Ellen	(M)	50	F	Unknown	17Ma07Jw	Mary	(D)	12	F	Unknown	17Ma02Nt
James	(B)	15	M	Unknown	17Ma07Jw	Jas.	(S)	10	M	Laborer	17Ma02Nt
Mathew	(B)	13	M	Unknown	17Ma07Jw	John	(S)	08	M	Child	17Ma02Nt

NAMES OF PASSENGERS		AGE	SEX	OCCUPATIONS	DATE PORT SHIP
ENGLISH, David	(S)	06	M	Child	17Ma02Nt
William	(S)	04	M	Child	17Ma02Nt
BOYLE, Jas.		35	M	Mechanic	17Ma02Nt
STORY, Mary-M.		20	F	Unknown	17Ma02Nt
PATTEN, Mary-Ann		02	F	Child	17Ma02Nt
ENGLISH, Thos.		48	M	Mechanic	17Ma02Nt
Augustus		42	M	Mechanic	17Ma02Nt
James		17	M	Mechanic	17Ma02Nt
Mary		16	F	Unknown	17Ma02Nt
MCDONNELL, Mary		09	F	Child	17Ma02Nt
Catherine	(T)	06	F	Child	17Ma02Nt
Molly	(T)	.00	F	Infant	17Ma02Nt
BRANIGAN, Jas.		19	M	Mechanic	17Ma02Nt
Catherine		19	F	Unknown	17Ma02Nt
FLEMING, Hugh		22	M	Farmer	17Ma02Nt
HOPKINS, John		30	M	Farmer	17Ma02Nt
DUNN, Patrick		24	M	Farmer	17Ma02Nt
Mary	(W)	22	F	Unknown	17Ma02Nt
Brian	(S)	.00	M	Infant	17Ma02Nt
BRAHALL, Jas.		22	M	Farmer	17Ma02Nt
DUNN, Michael		34	M	Farmer	17Ma02Nt
Jane		24	F	Unknown	17Ma02Nt
CROWELL, Jas.		24	M	Farmer	17Ma02Nt
Catherine		20	F	Unknown	17Ma02Nt
DOLAN, Ellen		24	F	Unknown	17Ma02Nt
HANANAH, Michl.		30	M	Farmer	17Ma02Nt
Jane		20	F	Unknown	17Ma02Nt
Margt.		25	F	Unknown	17Ma02Nt
Patrick		20	M	Farmer	17Ma02Nt
MCCOLE, Margt.		20	F	Unknown	17Ma02Nt
CROWLEY, Danl.		24	M	Farmer	17Ma02Nt
FITZPATRICK, Thos.		20	M	Farmer	17Ma02Nt
DOLAN, Ann		30	F	Unknown	17Ma02Nt
MCCOY, Saml.		35	M	Farmer	17Ma02Nt
MORTON, Clinot		23	M	Farmer	17Ma02Nt
John		30	M	Farmer	17Ma02Nt
FUTTON, Thomas		30	M	Farmer	17Ma02Nt
MCCOY, Ellen		28	F	Unknown	17Ma02Nt
KENNEDAN, Jas.		50	M	Farmer	17Ma02Nt
Mary	(W)	50	F	Unknown	17Ma02Nt
Mary	(D)	22	F	Unknown	17Ma02Nt
Patrick	(S)	24	M	Farmer	17Ma02Nt
HANNY, Patt		10	M	Farmer	17Ma02Nt
BYRNES, Edw.		25	M	Farmer	17Ma02Nt
Anna		21	F	Unknown	17Ma02Nt
HENGGAN, Patrick		22	M	Farmer	17Ma02Nt
Mary		14	F	Unknown	17Ma02Nt
MANN, John-M.		50	M	Farmer	17Ma02Nt
Jane	(W)	50	F	Unknown	17Ma02Nt
Robert	(S)	11	M	Unknown	17Ma02Nt
Joseph	(S)	07	M	Child	17Ma02Nt
Jas.	(S)	08	M	Child	17Ma02Nt
William	(S)	04	M	Child	17Ma02Nt
WHITE, Mary		56	F	Unknown	17Ma02Nt
John	(S)	20	M	Farmer	17Ma02Nt
Margaret	(D)	18	F	Unknown	17Ma02Nt
Eliza	(D)	15	F	Unknown	17Ma02Nt
Anna	(D)	12	F	Unknown	17Ma02Nt
Anna	(D)	09	F	Child	17Ma02Nt
HUTCHINSON, Bridget		50	F	Unknown	17Ma02Nt
John	(S)	24	M	Unknown	17Ma02Nt
Anna	(D)	22	F	Unknown	17Ma02Nt
Joseph	(S)	18	M	Farmer	17Ma02Nt
Anna	(D)	13	F	Unknown	17Ma02Nt
JOHNSON, Ellen		46	F	Unknown	17Ma02Nt
Mary-Ann	(D)	11	F	Unknown	17Ma02Nt
Ellen	(D)	13	F	Unknown	17Ma02Nt
ERWIN, Geo.		30	M	Farmer	17Ma02Nt
ROBINSON, Thos.		23	M	Farmer	17Ma02Nt
Martha	(W)	22	F	Unknown	17Ma02Nt
Martha	(D)	.00	F	Infant	17Ma02Nt
DONNELL, William		30	M	Farmer	17Ma02Nt
Ellen		25	F	Unknown	17Ma02Nt
Mary		23	F	Unknown	17Ma02Nt
KUGUS, Jane		25	F	Unknown	17Ma02Nt
MILLS, Marlad		18	F	Unknown	17Ma02Nt
DUNN, John		24	M	Farmer	17Ma02Nt
COAGAN, Timothy		22	M	Farmer	17Ma02Nt
MCDERMOTT, Henry		25	M	Farmer	17Ma02Nt
Ann		20	F	Unknown	17Ma02Nt
JOHNSON, Bridget		21	F	Unknown	17Ma02Nt
REGAN, Mary		20	F	Unknown	17Ma02Nt
MCDONNELL, John		40	M	Farmer	17Ma02Nt
Mary	(W)	40	F	Unknown	17Ma02Nt
Pat.	(S)	13	M	Farmer	17Ma02Nt
John	(S)	12	M	None	17Ma02Nt
ENGLISH, Henry		14	M	Mechanic	17Ma02Nt
Isabell	(T)	11	F	Unknown	17Ma02Nt
Chas.	(B)	09	M	Child	17Ma02Nt
Margaret	(T)	04	F	Child	17Ma02Nt
CRAIG, Margaret		25	F	Unknown	17Ma02Nt
MCCARTHY, Susan		24	F	Unknown	17Ma02Nt
Thomas	(B)	22	M	Mechanic	17Ma02Nt
Hugh	(B)	16	M	Mechanic	17Ma02Nt
Mary	(T)	05	F	Child	17Ma02Nt
STRANGER, William		21	M	Laborer	17Ma02Nt
GIBNER, John		17	M	Laborer	17Ma02Nt
HARVEY, Judith		17	F	Unknown	17Ma02Nt
BRADY, Patrick		40	M	Laborer	17Ma02Nt
Ann	(W)	36	F	Unknown	17Ma02Nt
Mary	(D)	14	F	Unknown	17Ma02Nt
Kirshed	(D)	11	F	Unknown	17Ma02Nt
MCGANLAN, Biddy		17	F	Unknown	17Ma02Nt
KENNEDY, Jas.		21	M	Laborer	17Ma02Nt
KIERN, Kate		20	F	Unknown	17Ma02Nt
HAUGH, Michael		26	M	Laborer	17Ma02Nt
HANLY, Mary		27	F	Unknown	17Ma02Nt
NAILOR, Mary		24	F	Unknown	17Ma02Nt
CRAIG, Mary-E.		34	F	Unknown	17Ma02Nt
Mary		17	F	Unknown	17Ma02Nt
CONLON, Michael		20	M	Laborer	17Ma02Nt
JONES, Paul		24	M	Laborer	17Ma02Nt
WILLIAMS, Jeremiah		50	M	Farmer	17Ma02Nt
Elizabeth	(W)	45	F	Unknown	17Ma02Nt
Jane	(D)	16	F	Unknown	17Ma02Nt
Hannah	(D)	11	F	Unknown	17Ma02Nt
David	(S)	08	M	Child	17Ma02Nt
FEATHER, Henry		27	M	Farmer	17Ma02Nt
MCGREELY, Dennis		24	M	Farmer	17Ma02Nt
GARIN, John		21	M	Farmer	17Ma02Nt
COYLE, M.		20	M	Farmer	17Ma02Nt
CALIGAN, Julia		21	F	Unknown	17Ma02Nt
Rose		19	F	Unknown	17Ma02Nt
RILEY, Jas.		23	M	Farmer	17Ma02Nt
MORRIS, Griffith		24	M	Farmer	17Ma02Nt
ROBERTS, Richard		24	M	Farmer	17Ma02Nt
HUMPHREYS, John		22	M	Farmer	17Ma02Nt

CAMBRIDGE 17 MAY 1847

From Liverpool

NAMES OF PASSENGERS		AGE	SEX	OCCUPATIONS	DATE PORT SHIP
HIGGINS, Martha		60	F	Unknown	17Ma02Ea
Owen	(S)	26	M	Laborer	17Ma02Ea
Martha	(D)	22	F	Unknown	17Ma02Ea
Mary	(D)	20	F	Unknown	17Ma02Ea
Alice	(D)	24	F	Unknown	17Ma02Ea
Rose	(D)	19	F	Unknown	17Ma02Ea
Judy	(D)	18	F	Unknown	17Ma02Ea
Bessy	(D)	15	F	Unknown	17Ma02Ea
MCGARREN, Judy		20	F	Unknown	17Ma02Ea
MCPALLIS, Susan		20	F	Unknown	17Ma02Ea
CONEY, Mary		24	F	Unknown	17Ma02Ea
BRIEN, D.		24	M	Unknown	17Ma02Ea

NAMES OF PASSENGERS		A G E	S E X	OCCUPATIONS	DATE PORT SHIP	NAMES OF PASSENGERS		A G E	S E X	OCCUPATIONS	DATE PORT SHIP
WARD, D.		20	M	Unknown	17Ma02Ea	CARY, O.		30	M	Laborer	17Ma02Ea
ROOSE, M.		20	M	Unknown	17Ma02Ea	U	(W)	30	F	Unknown	17Ma02Ea
ROLLINS, J.		22	M	Unknown	17Ma02Ea	John	(S)	12	M	None	17Ma02Ea
Eliza		16	F	Unknown	17Ma02Ea	Ann	(D)	09	F	Child	17Ma02Ea
SMITH, P.		25	M	Unknown	17Ma02Ea	Bdgt.	(D)	07	F	Child	17Ma02Ea
SHANLEY, P.		20	M	Unknown	17Ma02Ea	FITZPATRICK, P.		20	M	Unknown	17Ma02Ea
MORAN, B.		20	M	Unknown	17Ma02Ea	John		20	M	Unknown	17Ma02Ea
FARRELL, Mgt.		20	F	Unknown	17Ma02Ea	MURPHY, W.		20	M	Unknown	17Ma02Ea
Mary		20	F	Unknown	17Ma02Ea	MULLANY, J.		20	M	Unknown	17Ma02Ea
MCCONELL, Bgt.		20	F	Unknown	17Ma02Ea	CORR, J.		25	M	Unknown	17Ma02Ea
HUGHS, Mgt.		20	F	Unknown	17Ma02Ea	SHIELLS, Ann		20	F	Unknown	17Ma02Ea
MCGEE, Ellen		60	F	Unknown	17Ma02Ea	LEMON, Mary		20	F	Unknown	17Ma02Ea
Mgt.	(D)	30	F	Unknown	17Ma02Ea	QUIN, M.		20	M	Unknown	17Ma02Ea
Ellen	(D)	24	F	Unknown	17Ma02Ea	BYRNS, Mary		20	F	Unknown	17Ma02Ea
Maria	(D)	16	F	Unknown	17Ma02Ea	Bdgt.		20	F	Unknown	17Ma02Ea
Ann	(D)	12	F	Unknown	17Ma02Ea	WALSH, J.		20	M	Unknown	17Ma02Ea
CAFLER, Ema		03	F	Child	17Ma02Ea	MORN, Cath.		20	F	Unknown	17Ma02Ea
JACKSON, J.		20	M	Unknown	17Ma02Ea	GUNTY, Nancy		20	F	Unknown	17Ma02Ea
Mary		20	F	Unknown	17Ma02Ea	LOUGHAN, M.		20	M	Unknown	17Ma02Ea
Ann		20	F	Unknown	17Ma02Ea	MURRY, M.		24	M	Unknown	17Ma02Ea
Harry		20	M	Unknown	17Ma02Ea	GLASER, Mary		20	F	Unknown	17Ma02Ea
REILY, Ann		20	F	Unknown	17Ma02Ea	SPANE, Elizt.		18	F	Unknown	17Ma02Ea
MCGRACE, Letty		20	F	Unknown	17Ma02Ea	WILEY, M.		20	M	Unknown	17Ma02Ea
WARD, W.		20	M	Unknown	17Ma02Ea	Margt.		20	F	Unknown	17Ma02Ea
ENNISS, O.		30	M	Unknown	17Ma02Ea	CORBET, P.		20	M	Unknown	17Ma02Ea
Pat.		20	M	Unknown	17Ma02Ea	CANTLON, P.		20	M	Unknown	17Ma02Ea
LITTLE, R.		50	M	Unknown	17Ma02Ea	RYAN, J.		20	M	Unknown	17Ma02Ea
Edw.	(S)	18	M	Unknown	17Ma02Ea	Jeny		20	F	Unknown	17Ma02Ea
Jane	(D)	20	F	Unknown	17Ma02Ea	Mgt.		20	F	Unknown	17Ma02Ea
GRACE, Mgt.		20	F	Unknown	17Ma02Ea	William		20	M	Unknown	17Ma02Ea
THOMPSON, Chris.		20	F	Unknown	17Ma02Ea	GILLIRON, M.		30	M	Unknown	17Ma02Ea
ANSEY, Mary-A.		30	F	Unknown	17Ma02Ea	BETZ, U-Mrs.		20	F	Unknown	17Ma02Ea
SUIS, J.		25	M	Laborer	17Ma02Ea	MCDONALD, Rose		20	F	Unknown	17Ma02Ea
NOWLAN, P.		20	M	Unknown	17Ma02Ea	Bessy		20	F	Unknown	17Ma02Ea
MURPHY, J.		20	M	Unknown	17Ma02Ea	GREEN, J.		20	M	Unknown	17Ma02Ea
NOLAN, J.		20	M	Unknown	17Ma02Ea	MACTEAGUE, J.		20	M	Unknown	17Ma02Ea
Mary		20	F	Unknown	17Ma02Ea	WARD, P.		20	M	Unknown	17Ma02Ea
GAVAN, T.		30	M	Unknown	17Ma02Ea	Martha		20	F	Unknown	17Ma02Ea
Wm.		30	M	Unknown	17Ma02Ea	LYNCH, Mgt.		20	F	Unknown	17Ma02Ea
FANKEN, E.		20	M	Unknown	17Ma02Ea	EAGAN, W.		20	M	Laborer	17Ma02Ea
Marie		20	F	Unknown	17Ma02Ea	Cath.		20	F	Unknown	17Ma02Ea
REILLY, T.		20	M	Unknown	17Ma02Ea	Ellen		24	F	Unknown	17Ma02Ea
U	(W)	20	F	Unknown	17Ma02Ea	SEESON, S.		30	M	Unknown	17Ma02Ea
PASK, P.		30	M	Unknown	17Ma02Ea	BUCKLY, C.		30	M	Unknown	17Ma02Ea
MURRY, Jane		20	F	Unknown	17Ma02Ea	Mary		24	F	Unknown	17Ma02Ea
HALSON, Rose		20	F	Unknown	17Ma02Ea	Johana		20	F	Unknown	17Ma02Ea
KELLY, P.		20	M	Unknown	17Ma02Ea	MCCARTY, John		20	M	Unknown	17Ma02Ea
Mgt.		20	F	Unknown	17Ma02Ea	MERTHET, Mary		20	F	Unknown	17Ma02Ea
WHEATON, T.		29	M	Unknown	17Ma02Ea	PALY, Mary		20	F	Unknown	17Ma02Ea
RYAN, T.		24	M	Unknown	17Ma02Ea	PURCELL, Cath.		20	F	Unknown	17Ma02Ea
BRIEN, Mary		23	M	Unknown	17Ma02Ea	HALEEN, P.		30	M	Unknown	17Ma02Ea
MCGRATH, J.		26	M	Unknown	17Ma02Ea	CAMPAN, J.		30	M	Unknown	17Ma02Ea
SONNERY, E.		30	M	Unknown	17Ma02Ea	WHITE, M.		24	M	Unknown	17Ma02Ea
Honora	(W)	30	F	Unknown	17Ma02Ea	MASKIN, T.		19	M	Unknown	17Ma02Ea
Mgt.	(D)	12	F	Unknown	17Ma02Ea	DOWD, G.		20	M	Unknown	17Ma02Ea
Susanna	(D)	10	F	Unknown	17Ma02Ea	MASKIN, J.		17	M	Unknown	17Ma02Ea
David	(S)	08	M	Child	17Ma02Ea	Rose		04	F	Child	17Ma02Ea
Mary	(D)	06	F	Child	17Ma02Ea	BEGLIN, W.		20	M	Unknown	17Ma02Ea
John	(S)	02	M	Child	17Ma02Ea	LANNON, Mary		40	F	Unknown	17Ma02Ea
Leddy	(D)	01	F	Child	17Ma02Ea	Bart.	(S)	19	M	Unknown	17Ma02Ea
EAGAN, J.		25	M	Unknown	17Ma02Ea	Dennis	(S)	13	M	Unknown	17Ma02Ea
MALONE, M.		24	F	Unknown	17Ma02Ea	TRACY, Mary		20	F	Unknown	17Ma02Ea
EAGAN, J.		20	M	Unknown	17Ma02Ea	DOCKERY, J.		20	M	Unknown	17Ma02Ea
KENNY, P.		09	M	Child	17Ma02Ea	KERNAN, M.		45	M	Unknown	17Ma02Ea
MEYER, P.		38	M	Unknown	17Ma02Ea	FITZPATRICK, J.		20	M	Unknown	17Ma02Ea
Anna		30	F	Unknown	17Ma02Ea	REYNOLDS, T.		20	M	Unknown	17Ma02Ea
CUMMINS, R.		25	M	Unknown	17Ma02Ea	QUINTON, T.		20	M	Unknown	17Ma02Ea
Cath.		25	F	Unknown	17Ma02Ea	Sarah		18	F	Unknown	17Ma02Ea
SULLY, Honora		21	F	Unknown	17Ma02Ea	KERNO, Bdgt.		18	F	Unknown	17Ma02Ea
COLLINS, J.G.		41	M	Unknown	17Ma02Ea	John		09	M	Child	17Ma02Ea
U	(W)	41	F	Unknown	17Ma02Ea	FARRALL, Cath.		20	F	Unknown	17Ma02Ea
LEWIS, Ma.		26	F	Unknown	17Ma02Ea	DWYER, W.		28	M	Unknown	17Ma02Ea
BURKE, Nancy		18	F	Unknown	17Ma02Ea	WALSH, Eliza		20	F	Unknown	17Ma02Ea
COLLIS, Sarah		01	F	Child	17Ma02Ea	SMALLEN, S.		20	M	Unknown	17Ma02Ea
FARRISY, P.		20	M	Laborer	17Ma02Ea	DALTON, J.		20	M	Unknown	17Ma02Ea

NAMES OF PASSENGERS		AGE	SEX	OCCUPATIONS	DATE PORT SHIP
CURRY, Bdgt.		20	F	Unknown	17Ma02Ea
REILY, Mary		21	F	Unknown	17Ma02Ea
DAILY, Ma.		20	F	Unknown	17Ma02Ea
MADDEN, T.		40	M	Unknown	17Ma02Ea
Jane	(W)	40	F	Unknown	17Ma02Ea
James	(S)	20	M	Laborer	17Ma02Ea
Ellen	(D)	16	F	Unknown	17Ma02Ea
Mary	(D)	13	F	Unknown	17Ma02Ea
Danl.	(S)	11	M	None	17Ma02Ea
Christoph	(S)	09	M	Child	17Ma02Ea
FLOOD, Mary		20	F	Unknown	17Ma02Ea
ONEILL, N.		20	M	Laborer	17Ma02Ea
FLOOD, Elzt.		20	F	Unknown	17Ma02Ea
FOSTER, J.		20	M	Unknown	17Ma02Ea
RYNNE, M.		30	M	Unknown	17Ma02Ea
U	(W)	30	F	Unknown	17Ma02Ea
Thos.	(S)	13	M	None	17Ma02Ea
John	(S)	13	M	None	17Ma02Ea
Ann	(D)	11	F	Unknown	17Ma02Ea
Julia	(D)	09	F	Child	17Ma02Ea
Mgt.	(D)	07	F	Child	17Ma02Ea
MCGUIRE, W.		21	M	Unknown	17Ma02Ea
Ann		19	F	Unknown	17Ma02Ea
Rose		17	F	Unknown	17Ma02Ea
GILLIAN, M.		30	M	Unknown	17Ma02Ea
U	(W)	20	F	Unknown	17Ma02Ea
MCDONALD, Rose		20	F	Unknown	17Ma02Ea
Bessy		20	F	Unknown	17Ma02Ea
KILY, J.		20	M	Unknown	17Ma02Ea
FLOOD, Ann		15	F	Unknown	17Ma02Ea
KILY, Mary		10	F	Unknown	17Ma02Ea
Michl.		07	M	Child	17Ma02Ea
MCCORMICK, Cath.		20	F	Unknown	17Ma02Ea
MECHIN, Ellen		24	F	Unknown	17Ma02Ea
REYNOLDS, Honora		20	F	Unknown	17Ma02Ea
LOYD, G.		20	M	Unknown	17Ma02Ea
TIERNY, Eliza		20	F	Unknown	17Ma02Ea
KELLER, P.		12	M	Unknown	17Ma02Ea
MCNAUGHTON, Bgt.		20	F	Unknown	17Ma02Ea
FARRELL, D.		20	M	Unknown	17Ma02Ea
FREYNE, Mgt.		20	F	Unknown	17Ma02Ea
EGAN, T.		20	M	Unknown	17Ma02Ea
KELLY, T.		20	M	Unknown	17Ma02Ea
ROLLIN, Mgt.		16	F	Unknown	17Ma02Ea
GILLIGAN, Ann		18	F	Unknown	17Ma02Ea
RAHAL, Mary		20	F	Unknown	17Ma02Ea
DONOHUE, P.		24	M	Laborer	17Ma02Ea
Bernd.		26	M	Unknown	17Ma02Ea
SULLIVAN, Ellen		18	F	Unknown	17Ma02Ea
MCCOY, Mary		20	F	Unknown	17Ma02Ea
HAYES, U-Mrs.		50	F	Unknown	17Ma02Ea
Mary	(D)	26	F	Unknown	17Ma02Ea
Martha	(D)	24	F	Unknown	17Ma02Ea
John	(S)	20	M	Unknown	17Ma02Ea
Michael	(S)	20	M	Unknown	17Ma02Ea
Bdgt.	(D)	18	F	Unknown	17Ma02Ea
CALENDER, J.		20	M	Unknown	17Ma02Ea
GREY, Mary		09	F	Child	17Ma02Ea
BRADY, Cath.		30	F	Unknown	17Ma02Ea
BEATTY, J.		26	M	Unknown	17Ma02Ea
WREN, J.		20	M	Unknown	17Ma02Ea
SULLIVAN, J.		26	M	Unknown	17Ma02Ea
CLAY, E.		29	M	Unknown	17Ma02Ea
MCQUADE, W.		16	M	Unknown	17Ma02Ea
BROWN, M.		15	F	Unknown	17Ma02Ea
Ellen		12	F	Unknown	17Ma02Ea
Cornelius		10	M	None	17Ma02Ea
FANRY, Bgt.		20	F	Unknown	17Ma02Ea
HUGH, Judy		20	F	Unknown	17Ma02Ea
U		04	F	Child	17Ma02Ea
Mary		11	F	Unknown	17Ma02Ea
SULLIVAN, P.		24	M	Unknown	17Ma02Ea
TONE, J.		47	M	Unknown	17Ma02Ea
Mgt.		10	F	Unknown	17Ma02Ea
DUNN, P.		24	M	Unknown	17Ma02Ea
DUNN, Thos.		13	M	None	17Ma02Ea
RYNNE, Mary		20	F	Unknown	17Ma02Ea
KEANY, Cath.		20	F	Unknown	17Ma02Ea
Michl.		20	M	Unknown	17Ma02Ea
MCGINLEY, W.		20	M	Unknown	17Ma02Ea
KEANY, Mgt.		05	F	Child	17Ma02Ea
GIBBS, Samuel		20	M	Unknown	17Ma02Ea
MARTIN, Mary		20	M	Unknown	17Ma02Ea
KEEHAN, D.		13	M	None	17Ma02Ea
Dennis		08	M	Child	17Ma02Ea
CROWLY, J.		50	M	Unknown	17Ma02Ea
• GURDY, Judy		50	F	Unknown	17Ma02Ea
BRADY, L.		40	M	Unknown	17Ma02Ea
Cath.	(W)	30	F	Unknown	17Ma02Ea
James	(S)	11	M	None	17Ma02Ea
Mgt.	(D)	09	F	Child	17Ma02Ea
Alice	(D)	06	F	Child	17Ma02Ea
Hugh	(S)	06	M	Child	17Ma02Ea
Ellen	(D)	04	F	Child	17Ma02Ea
DODS, Mary		20	F	Unknown	17Ma02Ea
Pat		20	M	Laborer	17Ma02Ea
Mich.		20	M	Unknown	17Ma02Ea
Mgt.		09	F	Child	17Ma02Ea
Bdgt.		06	F	Child	17Ma02Ea
Cella		11	F	Unknown	17Ma02Ea
GUNHER, W.P.		50	M	Unknown	17Ma02Ea
U	(W)	50	F	Unknown	17Ma02Ea
Cath.		05	F	Child	17Ma02Ea
Biddy		05	F	Child	17Ma02Ea
NEILL, Mary		20	F	Unknown	17Ma02Ea
MCCAHILL, Mary		30	F	Unknown	17Ma02Ea
GAFREY, C.		20	M	Unknown	17Ma02Ea
LANNON, F.		30	M	Unknown	17Ma02Ea
LANG, Elzt.		20	F	Unknown	17Ma02Ea
GANTY, Ellen		20	F	Unknown	17Ma02Ea
CARY, J.		20	M	Unknown	17Ma02Ea
WHITE, Cath.		30	F	Unknown	17Ma02Ea
Wm.	(S)	05	M	Child	17Ma02Ea
James	(S)	03	M	Child	17Ma02Ea
Thos.	(S)	01	M	Child	17Ma02Ea
GAHAGN, Mary		12	F	Unknown	17Ma02Ea
MALONE, P.		20	M	Unknown	17Ma02Ea
Mary		12	F	Unknown	17Ma02Ea
NULLY, Ann		20	F	Unknown	17Ma02Ea
CONLY, P.		20	M	Unknown	17Ma02Ea
John		18	M	Unknown	17Ma02Ea
DALEY, J.		20	M	Unknown	17Ma02Ea
COMER, Bgt.		18	F	Unknown	17Ma02Ea
MCCABE, A.		02	M	Child	17Ma02Ea
LEY, Alice		20	F	Unknown	17Ma02Ea
DAWSON, Saml.		45	M	Unknown	17Ma02Ea
Wm.	(S)	09	M	Child	17Ma02Ea
Biddy	(D)	09	F	Child	17Ma02Ea
Mary	(D)	04	F	Child	17Ma02Ea
GALLEN, Ann		60	F	Unknown	17Ma02Ea
Mary		09	F	Child	17Ma02Ea
Agnes		07	F	Child	17Ma02Ea
Kitty		05	F	Child	17Ma02Ea
Pat		03	M	Child	17Ma02Ea
BRADY, Nora		18	F	Unknown	17Ma02Ea
MCCABE, P.		29	M	Unknown	17Ma02Ea
Mary		20	F	Unknown	17Ma02Ea
Bgt.		30	F	Unknown	17Ma02Ea
TOOLY, L.		10	M	None	17Ma02Ea
MONGER, Mary		40	F	Unknown	17Ma02Ea
ONEILL, D.		30	M	Unknown	17Ma02Ea
Mary	(W)	30	F	Unknown	17Ma02Ea
Mary	(D)	07	F	Child	17Ma02Ea
Wm.	(S)	06	M	Child	17Ma02Ea
George	(S)	05	M	Child	17Ma02Ea
MCGUIN, Ellen		20	F	Unknown	17Ma02Ea
U, W.		16	M	Unknown	17Ma02Ea
Mary		14	F	Unknown	17Ma02Ea
John		12	M	None	17Ma02Ea
Richd.		10	M	None	17Ma02Ea

NAMES OF PASSENGERS		AGE	SEX	OCCUPATIONS	DATE PORT SHIP
COOK, J.		41	M	Unknown	17Ma02Ea
Isabella	(W)	28	F	Unknown	17Ma02Ea
Hannah	(D)	05	F	Child	17Ma02Ea
Mary	(D)	03	F	Child	17Ma02Ea

ARCHIMEDES 17 MAY 1847

From Belfast .

MONROE, P.		48	M	Laborer	17Ma07Nu
Anne	(W)	46	F	Unknown	17Ma07Nu
James	(S)	20	M	Unknown	17Ma07Nu
Patrk.	(S)	20	M	Unknown	17Ma07Nu
John	(S)	18	M	Unknown	17Ma07Nu
Mary	(D)	16	F	Unknown	17Ma07Nu
Mgt.	(D)	14	F	Unknown	17Ma07Nu
Selena	(D)	12	F	Unknown	17Ma07Nu
Cath.	(D)	09	F	Child	17Ma07Nu
Richd.	(S)	03	M	Child	17Ma07Nu
Jane	(D)	01	F	Child	17Ma07Nu
TAGGAT, Isb.		22	F	Unknown	17Ma07Nu
MUNGETY, Mary		25	F	Unknown	17Ma07Nu
Elzbt.		21	F	Unknown	17Ma07Nu
CONSHER, N.		22	M	Unknown	17Ma07Nu
QUN, D.		19	M	Unknown	17Ma07Nu
Mary		22	F	Unknown	17Ma07Nu
VALENTER, R.		21	M	Unknown	17Ma07Nu
W.		22	M	Unknown	17Ma07Nu
WASON, D.		22	M	Unknown	17Ma07Nu
NIEL, W.		20	M	Unknown	17Ma07Nu
KELLY, T.		45	M	Unknown	17Ma07Nu
Patrk.	(S)	25	M	Unknown	17Ma07Nu
John	(S)	22	M	Unknown	17Ma07Nu
Wm.	(S)	15	M	Unknown	17Ma07Nu
Mary	(D)	11	F	Unknown	17Ma07Nu
James	(S)	08	M	Child	17Ma07Nu
CARRY, W.		32	M	Unknown	17Ma07Nu
HORNE, J.		23	M	Unknown	17Ma07Nu
BOYD, J.		25	M	Unknown	17Ma07Nu
CURRY, T.		25	M	Unknown	17Ma07Nu
HILL, R.		19	M	Unknown	17Ma07Nu
MCANULLY, H.		56	M	Unknown	17Ma07Nu
Cath.	(W)	50	F	Unknown	17Ma07Nu
Danl.	(S)	21	M	Unknown	17Ma07Nu
Henry	(S)	19	M	Unknown	17Ma07Nu
Saml.	(S)	17	M	Unknown	17Ma07Nu
Jane	(D)	16	F	Unknown	17Ma07Nu
Francis	(S)	14	M	None	17Ma07Nu
John	(S)	12	M	None	17Ma07Nu
Mary	(D)	10	F	Unknown	17Ma07Nu
P.	(S)	08	M	Child	17Ma07Nu
PANE, J.		30	M	Laborer	17Ma07Nu
Mary		29	F	Unknown	17Ma07Nu
Nancy		28	F	Unknown	17Ma07Nu
SIMPSON, W.		27	M	Unknown	17Ma07Nu
CALDERWOOD, J.		26	M	Unknown	17Ma07Nu
Henry		27	M	Unknown	17Ma07Nu
MCGLEECED, Eliza		20	F	Unknown	17Ma07Nu
Wm.		12	M	None	17Ma07Nu
Joseph		16	M	Unknown	17Ma07Nu
John		23	M	Unknown	17Ma07Nu
MCKEKLY, W.		20	M	Unknown	17Ma07Nu
Mary		20	F	Unknown	17Ma07Nu
MCCONN, J.		22	M	Unknown	17Ma07Nu
ENNICE, J.		20	M	Unknown	17Ma07Nu
WILSON, J.		20	M	Unknown	17Ma07Nu
Thos.		18	M	Unknown	17Ma07Nu
MCKUNLY, J.		35	M	Unknown	17Ma07Nu
Eliza	(W)	35	F	Unknown	17Ma07Nu

NAMES OF PASSENGERS		AGE	SEX	OCCUPATIONS	DATE PORT SHIP
MCKUNLY, Isabella	(D)	08	F	Child	17Ma07Nu
Joseph	(S)	05	M	Child	17Ma07Nu
Saml.	(S)	01	M	Child	17Ma07Nu
MCKITTRICK, J.		56	M	Unknown	17Ma07Nu
Mary	(W)	50	F	Unknown	17Ma07Nu
John	(S)	21	M	Unknown	17Ma07Nu
Eliza	(D)	20	F	Unknown	17Ma07Nu
WHITE, W.		25	M	Unknown	17Ma07Nu
Sarah		18	F	Unknown	17Ma07Nu
CROWE, Sarah		20	F	Unknown	17Ma07Nu
MCCORMICK, J.		30	M	Unknown	17Ma07Nu
GRIFFITH, S.		29	M	Unknown	17Ma07Nu
MORE, W.		25	M	Unknown	17Ma07Nu
Byron		22	M	Unknown	17Ma07Nu
CRAWFORD, N.		28	M	Unknown	17Ma07Nu
Sarah		25	F	Unknown	17Ma07Nu
Jane		20	F	Unknown	17Ma07Nu
DICKSON, R.		18	M	Unknown	17Ma07Nu
MCCLEARY, R.		18	M	Unknown	17Ma07Nu
MCANELLY, M.		19	M	Unknown	17Ma07Nu
Peter		18	M	Unknown	17Ma07Nu
MCDONELL, J.		41	M	Unknown	17Ma07Nu
Anne	(W)	38	F	Unknown	17Ma07Nu
J.	(S)	19	M	Laborer	17Ma07Nu
Anne	(D)	19	F	Unknown	17Ma07Nu
TAGGAT, Jane		17	F	Unknown	17Ma07Nu
BAIRLENT, J.		50	M	Unknown	17Ma07Nu
Bell		40	F	Unknown	17Ma07Nu
MCCUNGHEY, J.		30	M	Unknown	17Ma07Nu
Mary	(W)	28	F	Unknown	17Ma07Nu
George	(S)	08	M	Child	17Ma07Nu
Mgt.	(D)	03	F	Child	17Ma07Nu
Thonster	(S)	01	M	Child	17Ma07Nu
MCCUNE, G.		18	M	Unknown	17Ma07Nu
John		20	M	Unknown	17Ma07Nu
Sally		21	F	Unknown	17Ma07Nu
Betty		21	F	Unknown	17Ma07Nu
James		28	M	Unknown	17Ma07Nu
Mgt.		18	F	Unknown	17Ma07Nu
MCKING, G.		20	M	Unknown	17Ma07Nu
BLAIR, A.		26	M	Unknown	17Ma07Nu
MCNANN, M.		29	M	Unknown	17Ma07Nu
CRAWFORD, A.		29	M	Unknown	17Ma07Nu
MCANALLY, Ann		40	F	Unknown	17Ma07Nu
Saml.		39	M	Unknown	17Ma07Nu
MCILRATH, J.		20	M	Unknown	17Ma07Nu
BARR, J.		19	M	Unknown	17Ma07Nu
MCBRIDE, J.		17	M	Unknown	17Ma07Nu
GRILLIGER, J.		40	M	Unknown	17Ma07Nu
MONY, J.		45	M	Unknown	17Ma07Nu
Mary		39	F	Unknown	17Ma07Nu
MCGULLAN, Mary		29	F	Unknown	17Ma07Nu
JACKSON, J.		21	M	Unknown	17Ma07Nu
GAMBLE, D.		32	M	Unknown	17Ma07Nu
HILLAH, W.		23	M	Unknown	17Ma07Nu

CLIFTON 17 MAY 1847

From Liverpool

KELLY, Hugh		26	M	Laborer	17Ma02Nw
KEEMAN, Jas.		25	M	Laborer	17Ma02Nw
FLYNN, John		22	M	Laborer	17Ma02Nw
DUNN, Larry		28	M	Laborer	17Ma02Nw
MARAN, Anny		26	F	Unknown	17Ma02Nw
DOOLIN, Richd.		20	M	Laborer	17Ma02Nw
KELLY, Betty		19	F	Unknown	17Ma02Nw
WILLIAMS, John		40	M	Farmer	17Ma02Nw
U	(W)	38	F	Unknown	17Ma02Nw

NAMES OF PASSENGERS		AGE	SEX	OCCUPATIONS	DATE PORT SHIP
WILLIAMS, John	(S)	20	M	Unknown	17Ma02Nw
Margt.	(D)	16	F	Unknown	17Ma02Nw
Cathe.	(D)	10	F	Unknown	17Ma02Nw
Mary	(D)	08	F	Child	17Ma02Nw
David	(S)	05	M	Child	17Ma02Nw
KILLAN, Margt.		16	F	Unknown	17Ma02Nw
SCOTTY, Michl.		18	M	Farmer	17Ma02Nw
Michael		16	M	Unknown	17Ma02Nw
Pat		18	M	Unknown	17Ma02Nw
John		13	M	Unknown	17Ma02Nw
Michl.		11	M	Unknown	17Ma02Nw
Mary		10	F	Unknown	17Ma02Nw
Alice		08	F	Child	17Ma02Nw
Sarah		06	F	Child	17Ma02Nw
Catherine		04	F	Child	17Ma02Nw
COY, Edmond		32	M	Farmer	17Ma02Nw
KELLY, Martin		16	M	Laborer	17Ma02Nw
ROCHE, Edmond		32	M	Laborer	17Ma02Nw
KEAN, Patk.		26	M	Laborer	17Ma02Nw
MINNEY, John		20	M	Laborer	17Ma02Nw
CUNNINGHAM, E.		25	M	Laborer	17Ma02Nw
CALLAHAN, Michl.		50	M	Farmer	17Ma02Nw
U	(W)	27	F	Unknown	17Ma02Nw
Mary	(D)	28	F	Unknown	17Ma02Nw
Frances	(D)	27	F	Unknown	17Ma02Nw
John	(S)	17	M	Farmer	17Ma02Nw
John	(S)	20	M	Farmer	17Ma02Nw
Henry	(S)	15	M	Unknown	17Ma02Nw
Dennis	(S)	13	M	Unknown	17Ma02Nw
Corn.	(S)	10	M	Unknown	17Ma02Nw
Callahan	(S)	08	M	Child	17Ma02Nw
MORAN, Ellen		08	F	Child	17Ma02Nw
MURPHY, James		20	M	Unknown	17Ma02Nw
FOLLIN, Margt.		25	F	Unknown	17Ma02Nw
Biddy		20	F	Unknown	17Ma02Nw
MCCARTHY, Patt.		18	M	Unknown	17Ma02Nw
Ann		16	F	Unknown	17Ma02Nw
Hope		04	F	Child	17Ma02Nw
Ann		01	F	Child	17Ma02Nw
HOWARD, Jas.		20	M	Unknown	17Ma02Nw
SPAN, Michl.		30	M	Unknown	17Ma02Nw
Mary		28	F	Unknown	17Ma02Nw
FITZGERALD, Bessy		11	F	Unknown	17Ma02Nw
BLACKWELL, Wm.		20	M	Unknown	17Ma02Nw
HIGINBOTTOM, Susan		21	F	Unknown	17Ma02Nw
Eliza		18	F	Unknown	17Ma02Nw
RODGER, Saml.		20	M	Unknown	17Ma02Nw
Margt.		11	F	Unknown	17Ma02Nw
GORMON, James		20	M	Unknown	17Ma02Nw
Ann	(W)	19	F	Unknown	17Ma02Nw
U		01	U	Child	17Ma02Nw
LAWBER, William		20	M	Unknown	17Ma02Nw
KOHEN, Miles		25	M	Unknown	17Ma02Nw
HEISLER, Ann		19	F	Unknown	17Ma02Nw
CREDER, Michl.		24	M	Unknown	17Ma02Nw
KENNY, Ellen		18	F	Unknown	17Ma02Nw
MCCULLO, Patt		27	M	Unknown	17Ma02Nw
Ann		26	F	Unknown	17Ma02Nw
Bridget		22	F	Unknown	17Ma02Nw
Bridget		11	F	Laborer	17Ma02Nw
MCINTIRE, Margt.		20	F	Unknown	17Ma02Nw
MATHA, Susan		18	F	Unknown	17Ma02Nw
CLARK, Bryan		30	M	Unknown	17Ma02Nw
Maria		26	F	Unknown	17Ma02Nw
MURPHY, U-Mrs.		24	F	Unknown	17Ma02Nw
BUCKLEY, Mary		25	F	Unknown	17Ma02Nw
HACKETT, Mary		20	F	Unknown	17Ma02Nw
DOOLEN, John		28	M	Unknown	17Ma02Nw
Dean		17	M	Unknown	17Ma02Nw
Garrick		08	M	Child	17Ma02Nw
SARRY, John		24	M	Unknown	17Ma02Nw
FERNS, Ellen		25	F	Unknown	17Ma02Nw
Ann		24	F	Unknown	17Ma02Nw
CONWAY, Thomas		25	M	Unknown	17Ma02Nw
LEARD, James		20	M	Unknown	17Ma02Nw
CONIM, U-Mrs.		35	F	Unknown	17Ma02Nw
STARK, Edmond		28	M	Unknown	17Ma02Nw
BROWN, Jas.		22	M	Unknown	17Ma02Nw
BLAKE, John		25	M	Unknown	17Ma02Nw
MCCARTHY, Patt.		80	M	Unknown	17Ma02Nw
Michael		20	M	Unknown	17Ma02Nw
Mic.		12	M	Unknown	17Ma02Nw
BRYAN, Daniel		25	M	Unknown	17Ma02Nw
DRYER, Edmd.		47	M	Unknown	17Ma02Nw
Margt.	(W)	46	F	Unknown	17Ma02Nw
Margt.	(D)	21	F	Unknown	17Ma02Nw
Horace	(S)	19	M	Unknown	17Ma02Nw
Edmd.	(S)	13	M	Unknown	17Ma02Nw
Cathe.	(D)	08	F	Child	17Ma02Nw
Mary	(D)	06	F	Child	17Ma02Nw
John	(S)	01	M	Child	17Ma02Nw
CONNELLY, Patt.		25	M	Unknown	17Ma02Nw
LACY, John		20	M	Unknown	17Ma02Nw
ALLEN, Peggy		40	F	Unknown	17Ma02Nw
Mary	(D)	18	F	Unknown	17Ma02Nw
Nancy	(D)	13	F	Unknown	17Ma02Nw
Charles	(S)	11	M	Unknown	17Ma02Nw
George	(S)	08	M	Child	17Ma02Nw
Patt	(S)	07	M	Child	17Ma02Nw
DUGAN, Pat.		25	M	Unknown	17Ma02Nw
NEAL, Michael		20	M	Unknown	17Ma02Nw
SHANE, Lunira		29	F	Unknown	17Ma02Nw
MORAN, Jas.		30	M	Unknown	17Ma02Nw
Eliza	(W)	28	F	Unknown	17Ma02Nw
U		.00	U	Infant	17Ma02Nw
U		.00	U	Infant	17Ma02Nw
CLEWS, Joseph		13	M	Unknown	17Ma02Nw
John		08	M	Child	17Ma02Nw
Isabella		06	F	Child	17Ma02Nw
HOPKINS, James		40	M	Laborer	17Ma02Nw
U	(W)	39	F	Unknown	17Ma02Nw
U		.00	U	Infant	17Ma02Nw
Isaac	(S)	13	M	Unknown	17Ma02Nw
Mary	(D)	10	F	Unknown	17Ma02Nw
Richard	(S)	07	M	Child	17Ma02Nw
Hanna	(D)	05	F	Child	17Ma02Nw
SKINNER, William		24	M	Farmer	17Ma02Nw
WHITMORE, Richard		20	M	Unknown	17Ma02Nw
CHITTERLY, Wm.		64	M	Unknown	17Ma02Nw
HAMMOND, Geo.		24	M	Unknown	17Ma02Nw
WHITFIELD, Jas.		13	M	Unknown	17Ma02Nw
MALPEM, Danl.		27	M	Unknown	17Ma02Nw
U	(W)	26	F	Unknown	17Ma02Nw
Danl.	(S)	07	M	Child	17Ma02Nw
Robert	(S)	01	M	Child	17Ma02Nw
U		.00	U	Infant	17Ma02Nw
BEARDMORE, Wm.		28	M	Farmer	17Ma02Nw
MADDOCK, Thos.		26	M	Unknown	17Ma02Nw
KELLY, Michl.		40	M	Unknown	17Ma02Nw
Ellen	(W)	35	F	Unknown	17Ma02Nw
John-P.	(S)	19	M	Unknown	17Ma02Nw
Pierre	(S)	18	M	Unknown	17Ma02Nw
Cathe.		48	F	Unknown	17Ma02Nw
Pierre-P.		18	M	Unknown	17Ma02Nw
GIBRON, Ann		24	F	Unknown	17Ma02Nw
Cathe.		19	F	Unknown	17Ma02Nw
LOGAN, Michl.		24	M	Laborer	17Ma02Nw
SHINDON, John		20	M	Laborer	17Ma02Nw
MARET, Michl.		24	M	Unknown	17Ma02Nw
BUCKIN, Richard		27	M	Unknown	17Ma02Nw
U	(W)	24	F	Unknown	17Ma02Nw
U		.00	U	Infant	17Ma02Nw
MASTERSON, Jas.		24	M	Unknown	17Ma02Nw
U	(W)	24	F	Unknown	17Ma02Nw
MURTOGH, Ed.		27	M	Unknown	17Ma02Nw
MURPHY, John		24	M	Unknown	17Ma02Nw
HANCOCK, U-Mrs.		50	F	Unknown	17Ma02Nw
ROBERSON, Geo.		30	M	Laborer	17Ma02Nw
U	(W)	29	F	Unknown	17Ma02Nw
U		.00	U	Infant	17Ma02Nw

NAMES OF PASSENGERS		AGE	SEX	OCCUPATIONS	DATE PORT SHIP
ROBERSON, John	(S)	07	M	Child	17Ma02Nw
Sarah	(D)	02	F	Child	17Ma02Nw
SOMERFIELD, Geo.		45	M	Unknown	17Ma02Nw
U	(W)	24	F	Unknown	17Ma02Nw
Emma	(D)	13	F	Unknown	17Ma02Nw
BRADSHAW, William		45	M	Unknown	17Ma02Nw
U	(W)	45	F	Unknown	17Ma02Nw
Thos.	(S)	17	M	Unknown	17Ma02Nw
William	(S)	11	M	Unknown	17Ma02Nw
Henry	(S)	09	M	Child	17Ma02Nw
John	(S)	08	M	Child	17Ma02Nw
Isabella	(D)	07	F	Child	17Ma02Nw
PICKERING, Michl.		48	M	Unknown	17Ma02Nw
U	(W)	41	F	Unknown	17Ma02Nw
U		.00	U	Infant	17Ma02Nw
Eliza	(D)	17	F	Unknown	17Ma02Nw
Chas.	(S)	13	M	Unknown	17Ma02Nw
John	(S)	08	M	Child	17Ma02Nw
Joseph	(S)	12	M	Unknown	17Ma02Nw
Emma	(D)	07	F	Child	17Ma02Nw
Ellen	(D)	06	F	Child	17Ma02Nw
SMITH, Isaiah		35	M	Unknown	17Ma02Nw
U	(W)	35	F	Unknown	17Ma02Nw
U		.00	U	Infant	17Ma02Nw
Eliza	(D)	12	F	Unknown	17Ma02Nw
Emma	(D)	10	F	Unknown	17Ma02Nw
John	(S)	03	M	Child	17Ma02Nw
Sarah	(D)	06	F	Child	17Ma02Nw
Jas.	(S)	04	M	Child	17Ma02Nw
EVANS, Alex.		34	M	Unknown	17Ma02Nw
U	(W)	37	F	Unknown	17Ma02Nw
U		.00	U	Infant	17Ma02Nw
SMITH, Jim		09	M	Child	17Ma02Nw
Nic.		06	M	Child	17Ma02Nw
Fanny		04	F	Child	17Ma02Nw
CLEWS, Joseph		44	M	Unknown	17Ma02Nw
U	(W)	45	F	Unknown	17Ma02Nw
CALLAHAN, Abby		06	F	Child	17Ma02Nw
Julia		06	F	Child	17Ma02Nw
Margaret		18	F	Unknown	17Ma02Nw
MURPHY, John		20	M	Farmer	17Ma02Nw
SULLIVAN, John		40	M	Farmer	17Ma02Nw
Phil.		40	M	Farmer	17Ma02Nw
Stephen		16	M	Unknown	17Ma02Nw
Kitty		20	F	Unknown	17Ma02Nw
Bessy		16	F	Unknown	17Ma02Nw
STACK, Ellen		16	F	Unknown	17Ma02Nw
HAGGERTY, Margt.		20	F	Unknown	17Ma02Nw
SULLIVAN, Cathe.		22	F	Unknown	17Ma02Nw
CARNEY, Laurence		35	M	Unknown	17Ma02Nw
Johanna	(W)	30	F	Unknown	17Ma02Nw
Cathe.	(D)	10	F	Unknown	17Ma02Nw
Mary	(D)	08	F	Child	17Ma02Nw
Margt.	(D)	11	F	Unknown	17Ma02Nw
Julia	(D)	04	F	Child	17Ma02Nw
Bob	(S)	01	M	Child	17Ma02Nw
COFFIN, Danl.		40	M	Unknown	17Ma02Nw
Pat.		30	M	Unknown	17Ma02Nw
Gibby		25	M	Unknown	17Ma02Nw
John		18	M	Unknown	17Ma02Nw
James		10	M	Unknown	17Ma02Nw
Peggy		13	F	Unknown	17Ma02Nw
BUCKINHAM, Abram.		39	M	Miner	17Ma02Nw
U	(W)	36	F	Unknown	17Ma02Nw
Thomas	(S)	18	M	Unknown	17Ma02Nw
Abrm.	(S)	13	M	Unknown	17Ma02Nw
William	(S)	12	M	Unknown	17Ma02Nw
James	(S)	09	M	Child	17Ma02Nw
Richd.	(S)	07	M	Child	17Ma02Nw
Eliza	(D)	07	F	Child	17Ma02Nw
Martha	(D)	05	F	Child	17Ma02Nw
John	(S)	04	M	Child	17Ma02Nw
James	(S)	04	M	Child	17Ma02Nw
DARBY, Henry		30	M	Laborer	17Ma02Nw
U	(W)	28	F	Unknown	17Ma02Nw

NAMES OF PASSENGERS		AGE	SEX	OCCUPATIONS	DATE PORT SHIP
DARBY, Harlet	(D)	09	F	Child	17Ma02Nw
Eliza	(D)	07	F	Child	17Ma02Nw
FEND, Saml.		28	M	Unknown	17Ma02Nw

ATLAS 17 MAY 1847

From Liverpool

NAMES OF PASSENGERS		AGE	SEX	OCCUPATIONS	DATE PORT SHIP
TRACY, Michael		26	M	Laborer	17Ma02Ec
GILFOYLE, Cornelius		24	M	Mechanic	17Ma02Ec
COYLE, Patrick		30	M	Laborer	17Ma02Ec
Rose		24	F	Unknown	17Ma02Ec
GLENNON, Patrick		26	M	Laborer	17Ma02Ec
DOYLE, John		21	M	Mechanic	17Ma02Ec
COFFE, Michael		25	M	Laborer	17Ma02Ec
FITZMORRIS, Cathe.		11	F	Unknown	17Ma02Ec
HAVILAN, Michael		24	M	Laborer	17Ma02Ec
DEVELIN, Peter		30	M	Laborer	17Ma02Ec
Sarah		27	F	Unknown	17Ma02Ec
KIRWAN, Thomas		30	M	Laborer	17Ma02Ec
DEVELIN, Mary-Ann		02	F	Child	17Ma02Ec
John		.06	M	Infant	17Ma02Ec
Mary		28	F	Unknown	17Ma02Ec
Sarah		25	F	Unknown	17Ma02Ec
FLANAGAN, Peter		34	M	Farmer	17Ma02Ec
Patrick		24	M	Farmer	17Ma02Ec
MALADY, John		66	M	Laborer	17Ma02Ec
Ann	(W)	60	F	Unknown	17Ma02Ec
John	(S)	22	M	Farmer	17Ma02Ec
Thos.	(S)	19	M	Farmer	17Ma02Ec
Bridget	(D)	24	F	Unknown	17Ma02Ec
HOPKINS, Bridget		20	F	Unknown	17Ma02Ec
KENNEDY, Ann		19	F	Unknown	17Ma02Ec
TINLON, Thomas		32	M	Farmer	17Ma02Ec
Mary	(W)	30	F	Unknown	17Ma02Ec
Fanny	(D)	07	F	Child	17Ma02Ec
Mary	(D)	05	F	Child	17Ma02Ec
Thomas	(S)	03	M	Child	17Ma02Ec
Rebecca	(D)	01	F	Child	17Ma02Ec
FALKNER, Thos.		21	M	Laborer	17Ma02Ec
George		16	M	Laborer	17Ma02Ec
PATTERSON, Richd.		35	M	Laborer	17Ma02Ec
SHANNON, Patrick		16	M	Laborer	17Ma02Ec
Patrick		14	M	Laborer	17Ma02Ec
LACHRAN, Cathe.		20	F	Unknown	17Ma02Ec
FITZGIBBON, Thos.		26	M	Laborer	17Ma02Ec
Mary		28	F	Unknown	17Ma02Ec
Bridget		16	F	Unknown	17Ma02Ec
MICHEL, Bridget		18	F	Unknown	17Ma02Ec
James		16	M	Laborer	17Ma02Ec
RYAN, Patrick		22	M	Laborer	17Ma02Ec
MCCORMICK, John		22	M	Miller	17Ma02Ec
Michl.		16	M	Laborer	17Ma02Ec
Rose-Ann		18	F	Unknown	17Ma02Ec
SAULA, Ann		18	F	Unknown	17Ma02Ec
CROMLEY, Jas.		20	M	Laborer	17Ma02Ec
Cathe.		14	F	Unknown	17Ma02Ec
Ann		11	F	Unknown	17Ma02Ec
Christopher		17	M	Laborer	17Ma02Ec
NEWMAN, Jas.		18	M	Mechanic	17Ma02Ec
GARRICK, Jas.		20	M	Mechanic	17Ma02Ec
KELLY, Ellen		21	F	Unknown	17Ma02Ec
DOYLE, Thomas		23	M	Farmer	17Ma02Ec
Jas.		25	M	Farmer	17Ma02Ec
Cathe.		18	F	Unknown	17Ma02Ec
MULLINS, John		18	M	Laborer	17Ma02Ec
Patrick		15	M	Laborer	17Ma02Ec
John		12	M	Laborer	17Ma02Ec
MILET, Alice		18	F	Unknown	17Ma02Ec

NAMES OF PASSENGERS		AGE	SEX	OCCUPATIONS	DATE PORT SHIP	NAMES OF PASSENGERS		AGE	SEX	OCCUPATIONS	DATE PORT SHIP
MILET, Michael		15	M	Laborer	17Ma02Ec	DAVIS, John	(S)	04	M	Child	17Ma02Ec
Mary		12	F	Unknown	17Ma02Ec	Bridget	(D)	02	F	Child	17Ma02Ec
GARLAND, Elizabeth		40	F	Unknown	17Ma02Ec	Mary	(D)	01	F	Child	17Ma02Ec
Jas.		44	M	Laborer	17Ma02Ec	BURN, Maria		33	F	Unknown	17Ma02Ec
WILLIAMS, Sarah		17	F	Unknown	17Ma02Ec	Elizabeth	(D)	12	F	Unknown	17Ma02Ec
NOWLAN, Eliza		20	F	Unknown	17Ma02Ec	Bridget	(D)	09	F	Child	17Ma02Ec
LEE, Mary		24	F	Unknown	17Ma02Ec	Michael	(S)	07	M	Child	17Ma02Ec
SUSH, Robert		63	M	Merchant	17Ma02Ec	John	(S)	05	M	Child	17Ma02Ec
POND, William		36	M	Merchant	17Ma02Ec	Christopher	(S)	03	M	Child	17Ma02Ec
FORD, Hannah		30	F	Unknown	17Ma02Ec	SWEENY, Edward		22	M	Farmer	17Ma02Ec
DUFF, Peter		16	M	Laborer	17Ma02Ec	Bridget		50	F	Unknown	17Ma02Ec
MCINNALLY, Mary		64	F	Unknown	17Ma02Ec	John		20	M	Butcher	17Ma02Ec
Margaret		23	F	Unknown	17Ma02Ec	Jas.		17	M	Laborer	17Ma02Ec
Ellen		01	F	Child	17Ma02Ec	Cathe.		18	F	Unknown	17Ma02Ec
TURNER, Catherine		27	F	Unknown	17Ma02Ec	TUFFS, Jas.		21	M	Mechanic	17Ma02Ec
PARDEN, Simon		40	M	Servant	17Ma02Ec	LAWTON, Sarah		48	F	Unknown	17Ma02Ec
Ann		25	F	Unknown	17Ma02Ec	TURNER, Cathe.		26	F	Unknown	17Ma02Ec
MURPHY, Jas.		28	M	Mechanic	17Ma02Ec	FLINN, Eliza		21	F	Unknown	17Ma02Ec
Mary		28	F	Unknown	17Ma02Ec	CARROLL, John		30	M	Laborer	17Ma02Ec
MCCALL, Mary		28	F	Governess	17Ma02Ec	WILSON, Michael		32	M	Laborer	17Ma02Ec
Patrick		04	M	Child	17Ma02Ec	Jas.		26	M	Laborer	17Ma02Ec
SMITH, Philip		23	M	Laborer	17Ma02Ec	HOWARD, Timothy		25	M	Laborer	17Ma02Ec
Ann		20	F	Unknown	17Ma02Ec	ERVIN, Michs.		20	M	Laborer	17Ma02Ec
FITZPATRICK, Edw.		20	M	Laborer	17Ma02Ec	NORRIS, Philip		45	M	Laborer	17Ma02Ec
MAHAN, John		20	M	Laborer	17Ma02Ec	Nancy		32	F	Unknown	17Ma02Ec
Bridget		17	F	Unknown	17Ma02Ec	John		21	M	Laborer	17Ma02Ec
GILES, John		25	M	Mechanic	17Ma02Ec	Thomas		19	M	Laborer	17Ma02Ec
Ellen		30	F	Unknown	17Ma02Ec	Mary		17	F	Unknown	17Ma02Ec
DIGMAN, Michl.		20	M	Laborer	17Ma02Ec	Johanna		15	F	Unknown	17Ma02Ec
Jane		15	F	Unknown	17Ma02Ec	Catherine		13	F	Unknown	17Ma02Ec
GALLGAN, Anna		25	F	Unknown	17Ma02Ec	Michl.		11	M	Laborer	17Ma02Ec
FLYN, Michael		33	M	Laborer	17Ma02Ec	Philip		07	M	Child	17Ma02Ec
GALLIGAN, Patrick		18	M	Laborer	17Ma02Ec	LANIGAN, Jas.		24	M	Laborer	17Ma02Ec
QUILLIN, Patrick		40	M	Laborer	17Ma02Ec	MAHONY, Corns.		23	M	Farmer	17Ma02Ec
CONESKY, Chas.		40	M	Mechanic	17Ma02Ec	CONKLIN, William		26	M	Laborer	17Ma02Ec
Susan		15	F	Unknown	17Ma02Ec	NOOLAN, William		34	M	Farmer	17Ma02Ec
Cathe.		13	F	Unknown	17Ma02Ec	Cathe.	(W)	27	F	Unknown	17Ma02Ec
Ann		10	F	Unknown	17Ma02Ec	John	(S)	07	M	Child	17Ma02Ec
HIGGINS, Patrick		30	M	Laborer	17Ma02Ec	Jas.	(S)	04	M	Child	17Ma02Ec
FLYN, Mary		60	F	Unknown	17Ma02Ec	SEAHILL, Patrick		26	M	Mechanic	17Ma02Ec
Lawrence		11	M	Laborer	17Ma02Ec	Honorah		24	F	Unknown	17Ma02Ec
Andrew		08	M	Laborer	17Ma02Ec	MCCARTY, Danl.		24	M	Farmer	17Ma02Ec
John		06	M	Child	17Ma02Ec	SMITH, Owen		25	M	Laborer	17Ma02Ec
COLLINS, Michl.		39	M	Laborer	17Ma02Ec	Rose		20	F	Unknown	17Ma02Ec
Mary	(W)	32	F	Unknown	17Ma02Ec	MURRY, John		24	M	Laborer	17Ma02Ec
Bridget	(D)	08	F	Child	17Ma02Ec	BRANNAN, Edward		30	M	Farmer	17Ma02Ec
Michl.	(S)	05	M	Child	17Ma02Ec	GARLAND, John		24	M	Laborer	17Ma02Ec
Joseph	(S)	01	M	Child	17Ma02Ec	HARDY, Nichs.		30	M	Mechanic	17Ma02Ec
MICHEL, Dennis		60	M	Laborer	17Ma02Ec	BURNS, Jas.		21	M	Farmer	17Ma02Ec
Mary	(W)	60	F	Unknown	17Ma02Ec	LEE, Mathew		20	M	Mechanic	17Ma02Ec
Ann	(D)	20	F	Unknown	17Ma02Ec	HART, Ann-M.		22	F	Unknown	17Ma02Ec
GAFFY, John		12	M	Laborer	17Ma02Ec	Bridget		23	F	Unknown	17Ma02Ec
Patrick		02	M	Child	17Ma02Ec	Mary		19	F	Unknown	17Ma02Ec
MCCABE, Barnard		25	M	Laborer	17Ma02Ec	NOWLAND, David		30	M	Laborer	17Ma02Ec
Bridget		22	F	Unknown	17Ma02Ec	GAFFY, John		30	M	Laborer	17Ma02Ec
BRINE, John		25	M	Laborer	17Ma02Ec	Catherine		30	F	Unknown	17Ma02Ec
Catherine		22	F	Unknown	17Ma02Ec	Bridget		16	F	Unknown	17Ma02Ec
FOLEY, Patrick		25	M	Laborer	17Ma02Ec	Mary		14	F	Unknown	17Ma02Ec
LYNCH, Christopher		23	M	Laborer	17Ma02Ec	BAKER, Mary		23	F	Unknown	17Ma02Ec
Rose	(W)	24	F	Unknown	17Ma02Ec	CRAWIN, Johanna		23	F	Unknown	17Ma02Ec
Michael	(S)	03	M	Child	17Ma02Ec	AHERN, Edmund		22	M	Laborer	17Ma02Ec
FENEY, Patrick		32	M	Laborer	17Ma02Ec	MULLINS, John		25	M	Laborer	17Ma02Ec
MILLET, Margaret		19	F	Unknown	17Ma02Ec	Thos.		21	M	Laborer	17Ma02Ec
MCDOBRALD, Ann		19	F	Unknown	17Ma02Ec	Betsey		22	F	Unknown	17Ma02Ec
BUCKLY, John		27	M	Mechanic	17Ma02Ec	Johanna		18	F	Unknown	17Ma02Ec
William		22	M	Laborer	17Ma02Ec	CARAM, Michael		35	M	Laborer	17Ma02Ec
MCGLENMIN, John		16	M	Farmer	17Ma02Ec	MOORE, Michl.		31	M	Farmer	17Ma02Ec
MEGLENIN, Mary-Ann		14	F	Unknown	17Ma02Ec	WELSH, Morris		28	M	Laborer	17Ma02Ec
QUIN, Ann		30	F	Unknown	17Ma02Ec	FENNELE, Danl.		25	M	Laborer	17Ma02Ec
MEGLENIN, Francis		18	M	Laborer	17Ma02Ec	DOLAN, Cathe.		30	F	Unknown	17Ma02Ec
CARTY, John		26	M	Mechanic	17Ma02Ec	KING, Patrick		23	M	Mechanic	17Ma02Ec
Margaret		20	F	Unknown	17Ma02Ec	Johanna		18	F	Unknown	17Ma02Ec
Ann		18	F	Unknown	17Ma02Ec	SULLIVAN, John		20	M	Laborer	17Ma02Ec
DAVIS, Francis		30	M	Miner	17Ma02Ec	CANE, Jeremiah		24	M	Laborer	17Ma02Ec
Betsy	(W)	27	F	Unknown	17Ma02Ec	KANE, Ellen		19	F	Unknown	17Ma02Ec

NAMES OF PASSENGERS		A G E	S E X	OCCUPATIONS	DATE PORT SHIP	NAMES OF PASSENGERS		A G E	S E X	OCCUPATIONS	DATE PORT SHIP
BERNARD, Francis		45	M	Farmer	17Ma02Ec	NOLAND, Mathew		15	M	Farmer	17Ma02Ec
Thomas		42	M	Farmer	17Ma02Ec	Thos.		11	M	Farmer	17Ma02Ec
BRICK, Daniel		40	M	Farmer	17Ma02Ec	MCNAMARA, Patk.		34	M	Laborer	17Ma02Ec
Ann	(W)	30	F	Unknown	17Ma02Ec	MORAN, Michl.		20	M	Laborer	17Ma02Ec
Nancy	(D)	06	F	Child	17Ma02Ec	BURN, Patrick		20	M	Laborer	17Ma02Ec
KEEFE, Thomas		32	M	Laborer	17Ma02Ec	MORAN, Patrick		25	M	Laborer	17Ma02Ec
Margt.	(W)	25	F	Unknown	17Ma02Ec	NOONE, Mary		25	F	Unknown	17Ma02Ec
David	(S)	08	M	Child	17Ma02Ec	Michael		30	M	Laborer	17Ma02Ec
Ellen	(D)	01	F	Child	17Ma02Ec	Patrick	(S)	06	M	Child	17Ma02Ec
WILLIAMS, William		24	M	Laborer	17Ma02Ec	Ellen	(D)	04	F	Child	17Ma02Ec
CONNOR, John		27	M	Laborer	17Ma02Ec	CONWAY, Patrick		22	M	Laborer	17Ma02Ec
WOOD, Margaret		25	F	Unknown	17Ma02Ec	HIGHLAND, Mathew		27	M	Mechanic	17Ma02Ec
WILLIAMS, John		20	M	Laborer	17Ma02Ec	HART, Patrick		25	M	Farmer	17Ma02Ec
NOONAN, Eugene		33	M	Laborer	17Ma02Ec	ERDIGH, Maria		20	F	Unknown	17Ma02Ec
MULLINS, John		43	M	Laborer	17Ma02Ec	WALSH, Francis		46	M	Laborer	17Ma02Ec
CONKLIN, John		45	M	Laborer	17Ma02Ec	Maria	(W)	48	F	Unknown	17Ma02Ec
SHEA, Timothy		51	M	Laborer	17Ma02Ec	John	(S)	13	M	Laborer	17Ma02Ec
Biddy		13	F	Unknown	17Ma02Ec	Ann		40	F	Unknown	17Ma02Ec
John		15	M	Laborer	17Ma02Ec	Ann	(D)	12	F	Unknown	17Ma02Ec
WHITE, Timothy		25	M	Mechanic	17Ma02Ec	Francis	(S)	04	M	Child	17Ma02Ec
Bridget		20	F	Unknown	17Ma02Ec	James	(S)	07	M	Child	17Ma02Ec
SULLIVAN, Danl.		23	M	Laborer	17Ma02Ec	Thomas	(S)	.06	M	Infant	17Ma02Ec
LANE, Dennis		24	M	Laborer	17Ma02Ec	Bridget	(D)	06	F	Child	17Ma02Ec
Ann		23	F	Unknown	17Ma02Ec	CONNOR, Owen		23	M	Laborer	17Ma02Ec
WILLIS, Margaret		25	F	Unknown	17Ma02Ec	LEWIN, Patrick		19	M	Laborer	17Ma02Ec
Joseph		13	M	Laborer	17Ma02Ec	SMITH, Peter		30	M	Laborer	17Ma02Ec
MORRASEY, Michl.		30	M	Laborer	17Ma02Ec	Mary		28	F	Unknown	17Ma02Ec
John		26	M	Laborer	17Ma02Ec	Patrick		17	M	Laborer	17Ma02Ec
Patrick		23	M	Laborer	17Ma02Ec	HALEY, Catherine		25	F	Unknown	17Ma02Ec
Jas.		19	M	Laborer	17Ma02Ec	Ann		27	F	Unknown	17Ma02Ec
Ellen		28	F	Unknown	17Ma02Ec	WILLIS, Catherine		20	F	Unknown	17Ma02Ec
Alice		27	F	Unknown	17Ma02Ec						
Nancy		14	F	Unknown	17Ma02Ec						
TOBIN, James		20	M	Draper	17Ma02Ec						
Jas.		21	M	Laborer	17Ma02Ec						
FOLEY, Thomas		40	M	Laborer	17Ma02Ec	FAGAN-BEALAC 17 MAY 1847					
MORRASEY, James		24	M	Pawn Broker	17Ma02Ec						
FORD, Mathew		28	M	Farmer	17Ma02Ec	From Dublin					
FITZSIMMONS, Nichs.		30	M	Laborer	17Ma02Ec						
Cathe.	(W)	25	F	Unknown	17Ma02Ec						
Rose	(D)	04	F	Child	17Ma02Ec						
Christopher	(S)	01	M	Child	17Ma02Ec	DONOHUE, Jas.		35	M	Shepherd	17Ma20Nx
DONOHUE, James		26	M	Laborer	17Ma02Ec	Anne	(W)	30	F	Unknown	17Ma20Nx
Mary	(W)	28	F	Unknown	17Ma02Ec	John	(S)	09	M	Child	17Ma20Nx
Patrick	(S)	.06	M	Infant	17Ma02Ec	HANLEY, John		25	M	Shepherd	17Ma20Nx
ESPAN, Thomas		30	M	Mechanic	17Ma02Ec	Catherine		20	F	Unknown	17Ma20Nx
Rose		12	F	Unknown	17Ma02Ec	REDDY, Ann		20	F	Unknown	17Ma20Nx
John		10	M	Mechanic	17Ma02Ec	Catherine		18	F	Unknown	17Ma20Nx
KING, John		26	M	Laborer	17Ma02Ec	DEVOY, Bridget		30	F	Unknown	17Ma20Nx
COLLINS, Jame		20	F	Unknown	17Ma02Ec	Edward		40	M	Shepherd	17Ma20Nx
WOODS, Cathe.		20	F	Unknown	17Ma02Ec	CASSIDY, Peter		50	M	Farmer	17Ma20Nx
SHEHAN, Timothy		40	M	Servant	17Ma02Ec	Mary	(W)	46	F	Unknown	17Ma20Nx
Mary	(W)	33	F	Unknown	17Ma02Ec	Anne	(D)	20	F	Unknown	17Ma20Nx
Morris	(S)	14	M	Servant	17Ma02Ec	Mary	(D)	18	F	Unknown	17Ma20Nx
Mary	(D)	12	F	Unknown	17Ma02Ec	Jane	(D)	14	F	Unknown	17Ma20Nx
Isabella	(D)	05	F	Child	17Ma02Ec	Kate	(D)	12	F	Unknown	17Ma20Nx
John	(S)	03	M	Child	17Ma02Ec	Ellen	(D)	10	F	Unknown	17Ma20Nx
Margaret	(D)	02	F	Child	17Ma02Ec	Teresa	(D)	06	F	Child	17Ma20Nx
CONDIN, David		55	M	Farmer	17Ma02Ec	Pat.	(S)	23	M	Farmer	17Ma20Nx
Mary	(W)	50	F	Unknown	17Ma02Ec	POOLE, John		53	M	Pawn Broker	17Ma20Nx
Patsey	(D)	20	F	Unknown	17Ma02Ec	Eliza	(D)	21	F	Unknown	17Ma20Nx
Cathe.	(D)	21	F	Unknown	17Ma02Ec	Teresa	(D)	16	F	Unknown	17Ma20Nx
Mary	(D)	12	F	Unknown	17Ma02Ec	Joseph	(S)	14	M	Unknown	17Ma20Nx
Peggy	(D)	10	F	Unknown	17Ma02Ec	John	(S)	12	M	Unknown	17Ma20Nx
Jas.	(S)	08	M	Child	17Ma02Ec	Mary	(D)	18	F	Unknown	17Ma20Nx
DAVIN, Thomas		26	M	Laborer	17Ma02Ec	CONNOLLY, Patt		40	M	Farmer	17Ma20Nx
Bridget		28	F	Unknown	17Ma02Ec	U	(W)	39	F	Unknown	17Ma20Nx
SCANLON, Hannah		30	F	Unknown	17Ma02Ec	Mary	(D)	14	F	Unknown	17Ma20Nx
DALY, Martin		26	M	Laborer	17Ma02Ec	Ned	(S)	12	M	Unknown	17Ma20Nx
BURNS, John		40	M	Butcher	17Ma02Ec	Catherine	(D)	09	F	Child	17Ma20Nx
BRANNAN, John		20	M	Laborer	17Ma02Ec	Pat.	(S)	07	M	Child	17Ma20Nx
TAYLOR, William		23	M	Laborer	17Ma02Ec	Ann	(D)	.00	F	Infant	17Ma20Nx
FRASER, William		28	M	Farmer	17Ma02Ec	Nelly	(D)	03	F	Child	17Ma20Nx
DONALD, Michael		22	M	Farmer	17Ma02Ec	MALLOY, Benjamin		30	M	Laborer	17Ma20Nx
NOLAND, Daniel		35	M	Farmer	17Ma02Ec						

NAMES OF PASSENGERS		AGE	SEX	OCCUPATIONS	DATE PORT SHIP
KELLY, Francis		30	M	Farmer	17Ma20Nx
Catherine	(W)	28	F	Unknown	17Ma20Nx
Richard	(S)	02	M	Child	17Ma20Nx
Thos.	(S)	.00	M	Infant	17Ma20Nx
BURKE, Bessy		20	F	Unknown	17Ma20Nx
DARBY, Etty		26	F	Unknown	17Ma20Nx
BEHAN, Daniel		26	M	Servant	17Ma20Nx
HURLY, Daniel		20	M	Farmer	17Ma20Nx
Patt.		06	M	Child	17Ma20Nx
Mary		07	F	Child	17Ma20Nx
LENNE, Ann		20	F	Unknown	17Ma20Nx
ROGERS, Margaret		22	F	Unknown	17Ma20Nx
MURRAY, Margaret		22	F	Unknown	17Ma20Nx
SMYTH, Catherine		25	F	Unknown	17Ma20Nx
John	(S)	.00	M	Infant	17Ma20Nx
BUNE, John		35	M	Farmer	17Ma20Nx
Winny	(W)	30	F	Unknown	17Ma20Nx
Patt.	(S)	10	M	Unknown	17Ma20Nx
Bridget	(D)	04	F	Child	17Ma20Nx
BURNE, Mary		.00	F	Infant	17Ma20Nx
BURN, John		30	M	Mechanic	17Ma20Nx
FARRELL, Jane		20	F	Unknown	17Ma20Nx
CASSIDY, U-Mrs.		20	F	Unknown	17Ma20Nx
JOHNSON, Ann		20	F	Unknown	17Ma20Nx
COLMAN, Stephen		25	M	Laborer	17Ma20Nx
CARNEY, Elizab.		35	F	Unknown	17Ma20Nx
PERRIN, Richard		20	M	Laborer	17Ma20Nx
RUFFE, Jas.		25	M	Laborer	17Ma20Nx
Christopher		26	M	Laborer	17Ma20Nx
NOWLAND, Mary		23	F	Unknown	17Ma20Nx
Margaret		16	F	Unknown	17Ma20Nx
SMITH, Ellen		20	F	Unknown	17Ma20Nx
Mary		20	F	Unknown	17Ma20Nx
NUTLY, Andrew		25	M	Farmer	17Ma20Nx
WALSH, Michael		50	M	Trader	17Ma20Nx
John		14	M	Trader	17Ma20Nx
FOGARTY, Kate		23	F	Unknown	17Ma20Nx
REYNOLDS, Mary		17	F	Unknown	17Ma20Nx
MCEVOY, John		26	M	Mechanic	17Ma20Nx
ROGERS, Biddy		25	F	Unknown	17Ma20Nx
LAWLER, U		30	M	Laborer	17Ma20Nx
ROHAN, U		20	M	Laborer	17Ma20Nx
DUNPHY, Mary		25	F	Unknown	17Ma20Nx
BURKE, Nancy		25	F	Unknown	17Ma20Nx
DWYER, Mary		25	F	Unknown	17Ma20Nx
FANNIN, Mary		40	F	Unknown	17Ma20Nx
Peggy	(D)	20	F	Unknown	17Ma20Nx
Betsy	(D)	18	F	Unknown	17Ma20Nx
Biddy	(D)	08	F	Child	17Ma20Nx
Honor	(D)	.00	F	Infant	17Ma20Nx
FLYN, Judid		20	F	Unknown	17Ma20Nx
MAYERS, Mathew		20	M	Mechanic	17Ma20Nx
REGAN, Ann		16	F	Unknown	17Ma20Nx
FILAN, Betty		20	F	Unknown	17Ma20Nx
CONRAN, John		25	M	Laborer	17Ma20Nx
MCCORMICK, Richd.		20	M	Mechanic	17Ma20Nx
HOGARTY, Martin		25	M	Laborer	17Ma20Nx
DOWDALE, Henry		20	M	Farmer	17Ma20Nx
WALSH, Thomas		50	M	Laborer	17Ma20Nx
Mary	(W)	40	F	Unknown	17Ma20Nx
Patt.	(S)	22	M	Laborer	17Ma20Nx
Mary	(D)	06	F	Child	17Ma20Nx
ASPELL, William		20	M	Mechanic	17Ma20Nx
HEALY, Patt.		30	M	Butcher	17Ma20Nx
U	(W)	28	F	Unknown	17Ma20Nx
GILLIGAN, Thos.		22	M	Trader	17Ma20Nx
Patt.		18	M	Trader	17Ma20Nx
BERNEY, Thos.		18	M	Laborer	17Ma20Nx
Mary		19	F	Unknown	17Ma20Nx
MCKINSEY, Annie		19	F	Unknown	17Ma20Nx
HEALY, Patt.Jr.		06	M	Child	17Ma20Nx
CLARKTON, Thomas		20	M	Farmer	17Ma20Nx
HUGHES, Patrick		30	M	Shepherd	17Ma20Nx
JOHNSON, Geo.		30	M	Mechanic	17Ma20Nx
SHERIDAN, Bernard		18	M	Laborer	17Ma20Nx
SHERIDAN, Thomas		13	M	Laborer	17Ma20Nx
LAWRENCE, John		20	M	Organist	17Ma20Nx
MULICK, Michl.		22	M	Laborer	17Ma20Nx
MORA, John		26	M	Laborer	17Ma20Nx
HURLY, Cornelius		40	M	Farmer	17Ma20Nx
Ellen	(W)	38	F	Unknown	17Ma20Nx
John	(S)	09	M	Child	17Ma20Nx
Peggy	(D)	07	F	Child	17Ma20Nx
HYNES, John		20	M	Farmer	17Ma20Nx
DOOLY, John		20	M	Mechanic	17Ma20Nx
MATHEWS, Jas.		25	M	Mechanic	17Ma20Nx
HENRY, Jas.		30	M	Laborer	17Ma20Nx
John		20	M	Laborer	17Ma20Nx
Bessy		17	F	Unknown	17Ma20Nx
TOOMEY, Patt.		40	M	Shepherd	17Ma20Nx
Chas.		25	M	Shepherd	17Ma20Nx
Cathe.	(D)	17	F	Unknown	17Ma20Nx
Mary	(D)	19	F	Unknown	17Ma20Nx
CASSIDY, John		31	M	Laborer	17Ma20Nx
FLANAGAN, John		18	M	Laborer	17Ma20Nx
TWITE, Francis		22	M	Laborer	17Ma20Nx
HAYES, Patrick		20	M	Mechanic	17Ma20Nx
SULLIVAN, Mary		20	F	Unknown	17Ma20Nx
ALPINE, Christopher		25	M	Farmer	17Ma20Nx
DALY, John		20	M	Laborer	17Ma20Nx
BARNWELL, Thos.		30	M	Laborer	17Ma20Nx
HUBARD, Johana		30	M	Mechanic	17Ma20Nx
Keran		08	M	Child	17Ma20Nx
Edward		07	M	Child	17Ma20Nx
Mary		.00	F	Infant	17Ma20Nx
KANEY, Martin		25	M	Mechanic	17Ma20Nx
Mary	(W)	20	F	Unknown	17Ma20Nx
Thomas	(S)	.00	M	Infant	17Ma20Nx
Mary		18	F	Unknown	17Ma20Nx
NOONE, Thomas		40	M	Laborer	17Ma20Nx
Winney	(D)	15	F	Unknown	17Ma20Nx
Martin	(S)	15	M	Laborer	17Ma20Nx
Magnis	(D)	10	F	Unknown	17Ma20Nx
Owen	(S)	06	M	Child	17Ma20Nx
Martin-Jr.	(S)	08	M	Child	17Ma20Nx
Lawrence	(S)	04	M	Child	17Ma20Nx
Bridget	(D)	.00	F	Infant	17Ma20Nx
MACY, John		25	M	Musician	17Ma20Nx
RYAN, Thos.		23	M	Laborer	17Ma20Nx
CANTWELL, Danl.		20	M	Laborer	17Ma20Nx
MOONY, Michael		24	M	Laborer	17Ma20Nx
RYAN, William		30	M	Laborer	17Ma20Nx
QUINN, Neddy		25	M	Laborer	17Ma20Nx
Mary		25	F	Unknown	17Ma20Nx
HENDERSON, Bridget		21	F	Unknown	17Ma20Nx
Mary		18	F	Unknown	17Ma20Nx
LYNAN, Mary		20	F	Unknown	17Ma20Nx
CARRICK, Patrick		25	M	Butcher	17Ma20Nx
LURREY, John		20	M	Servant	17Ma20Nx
FANNIN, Jas.		21	M	Laborer	17Ma20Nx
Terence		20	M	Laborer	17Ma20Nx
SWEENEY, Edward		25	M	Laborer	17Ma20Nx
Margaret		22	F	Unknown	17Ma20Nx
Eliza		20	F	Unknown	17Ma20Nx
KEEGAN, Mary		.00	F	Infant	17Ma20Nx
Jas.		25	M	Mechanic	17Ma20Nx
DONOHUE, Patt.		20	M	Clerk	17Ma20Nx
Christopher		18	M	Laborer	17Ma20Nx
DONOVAN, Ellen		22	F	Unknown	17Ma20Nx
CAHILL, Jas.		25	M	Laborer	17Ma20Nx
Julia		20	F	Unknown	17Ma20Nx
CARLIERY, Margaret		17	F	Unknown	17Ma20Nx
CAHILL, Margaret		.00	F	Infant	17Ma20Nx
KEATING, John		25	M	Servant	17Ma20Nx
PARSTON, Elizabeth		21	F	Unknown	17Ma20Nx
ELLIS, Thomas		20	M	Mechanic	17Ma20Nx
LOVILL, Jas.		28	M	Laborer	17Ma20Nx
FINEGAN, Danl.		31	M	Laborer	17Ma20Nx
Judy		30	F	Unknown	17Ma20Nx
BOYLE, Michael		28	M	Laborer	17Ma20Nx

NAMES OF PASSENGERS	S X	AGE SEX OCCUPATIONS	DATE PORT SHIP
JOHNSON, Richard		25 M Farmer	17Ma20Nx
HYNES, John		27 M Baker	17Ma20Nx
William		21 M Baker	17Ma20Nx
Nicholas		18 M Baker	17Ma20Nx
MCDERMOTT, Barney		25 M Laborer	17Ma20Nx
Mary	(W)	20 F Unknown	17Ma20Nx
Jas.	(S)	.00 M Infant	17Ma20Nx
BRENNAN, James		25 M Laborer	17Ma20Nx
Mary		20 F Unknown	17Ma20Nx
BERRY, Thomas		25 M Laborer	17Ma20Nx
BERNE, Frank		28 M Mechanic	17Ma20Nx
BONNY, Winey		20 F Unknown	17Ma20Nx
DORAN, Patrick		25 M Farmer	17Ma20Nx
CONNOR, Mary		26 F Unknown	17Ma20Nx
KELLY, John		20 M Laborer	17Ma20Nx

MARMION 18 MAY 1847

From Liverpool

NAMES OF PASSENGERS	S X	AGE SEX OCCUPATIONS	DATE PORT SHIP
CARTY, Isaac		30 M Mechanic	18Ma02Hc
CAFFRY, Pat.		20 M Laborer	18Ma02Hc
WALSH, Edward		25 M Laborer	18Ma02Hc
Margaret		22 F Servant	18Ma02Hc
Catherine		20 F Servant	18Ma02Hc
BRIEN, Margaret		21 F Servant	18Ma02Hc
SCULLY, Martin		24 M Laborer	18Ma02Hc
MCCARLY, Maurice		30 M Mechanic	18Ma02Hc
MCLONIGI, Dennis		40 M Mechanic	18Ma02Hc
Nancy	(W)	40 F Unknown	18Ma02Hc
James		27 M Mechanic	18Ma02Hc
John		22 M Mechanic	18Ma02Hc
Pat.	(S)	17 M Mechanic	18Ma02Hc
James	(S)	14 M Mechanic	18Ma02Hc
Marlane	(D)	13 F Unknown	18Ma02Hc
DONELLY, Mary		24 F Unknown	18Ma02Hc
DALY, Rose		27 F Unknown	18Ma02Hc
RYAN, Mary		20 F Unknown	18Ma02Hc
BUTLER, Ellen		18 F Unknown	18Ma02Hc
KENNEDY, Thomas		30 M Servant	18Ma02Hc
Bridget		40 F Unknown	18Ma02Hc
DIGNAN, Thomas		35 M Laborer	18Ma02Hc
Margt.	(W)	34 F Unknown	18Ma02Hc
John	(S)	03 M Child	18Ma02Hc
CONDAN, Pat.		18 M Laborer	18Ma02Hc
WRIGHT, James		30 M Mechanic	18Ma02Hc
MURPHY, Gabriel		28 M Laborer	18Ma02Hc
BRENNAN, Mary		26 F Unknown	18Ma02Hc
MURPHY, Mathew		28 M Laborer	18Ma02Hc
CORCORAN, Betsy		20 F Unknown	18Ma02Hc
LARGY, Mary		20 F Unknown	18Ma02Hc
CORNANRON, W.		28 M Mechanic	18Ma02Hc
JOHNSON, Jas.		24 M Laborer	18Ma02Hc
WRIGHT, Jas.		24 M Laborer	18Ma02Hc
Betsy		25 F Unknown	18Ma02Hc
JOHNSTON, Martha		24 F Unknown	18Ma02Hc
Ellen		18 F Unknown	18Ma02Hc
WRIGHT, Nancy		21 F Unknown	18Ma02Hc
ROBINSON, John		22 M Butcher	18Ma02Hc
JOHNSTON, Wm.		38 M Mechanic	18Ma02Hc
BAILEY, George		22 M Mechanic	18Ma02Hc
JOHNSTON, William		22 M Mechanic	18Ma02Hc
OWENS, Rosanna		24 F Unknown	18Ma02Hc
FLANIGAN, Peter		24 M Laborer	18Ma02Hc
Mathew		24 M Laborer	18Ma02Hc
KIERNAN, John		63 M Laborer	18Ma02Hc
Rose	(W)	55 F Unknown	18Ma02Hc
Margt.	(D)	20 F Unknown	18Ma02Hc
Rose	(D)	16 F Unknown	18Ma02Hc
KIERNAN, James	(S)	15 M Unknown	18Ma02Hc
John	(S)	14 M Unknown	18Ma02Hc
BENSON, Maria		24 F Unknown	18Ma02Hc
Sarah		22 F Unknown	18Ma02Hc
KELLY, Henry		26 M Laborer	18Ma02Hc
John		33 M Laborer	18Ma02Hc
DUNN, Martin		33 M Laborer	18Ma02Hc
GRADY, Jas.		65 M Mechanic	18Ma02Hc
Bridget		60 F Unknown	18Ma02Hc
Daniel	(S)	28 M Laborer	18Ma02Hc
Patrick	(S)	24 M Mechanic	18Ma02Hc
Bridget	(D)	20 F Unknown	18Ma02Hc
James	(S)	25 M Laborer	18Ma02Hc
John	(S)	35 M Laborer	18Ma02Hc
Mary	(D)	30 F Unknown	18Ma02Hc
James	(S)	05 M Child	18Ma02Hc
Mary	(D)	07 F Child	18Ma02Hc
Michael	(S)	01 M Child	18Ma02Hc
CRUMMY, Sarah		70 F Unknown	18Ma02Hc
John		22 M Laborer	18Ma02Hc
James		30 M Laborer	18Ma02Hc
KELLY, Andrew		33 M Laborer	18Ma02Hc
CROGAN, Brian		30 M Laborer	18Ma02Hc
SHERIDAN, Mary		55 F Unknown	18Ma02Hc
KELLY, Mary		02 F Child	18Ma02Hc
James		01 M Child	18Ma02Hc
DEWEY, John		16 M Mechanic	18Ma02Hc
Elizabeth		12 F Unknown	18Ma02Hc
KELLY, John		05 M Child	18Ma02Hc
NOLAN, Michael		34 M Mechanic	18Ma02Hc
Letitia	(W)	32 F Unknown	18Ma02Hc
James	(S)	09 M Child	18Ma02Hc
Letitia	(D)	08 F Child	18Ma02Hc
William	(S)	07 M Child	18Ma02Hc
Michael	(S)	02 M Child	18Ma02Hc
REYNOLDS, Patrick		21 M Laborer	18Ma02Hc
Honora		50 F Unknown	18Ma02Hc
Thomas		22 M Laborer	18Ma02Hc
Bridget		19 F Unknown	18Ma02Hc
Edward		09 M Child	18Ma02Hc
KELSO, Henry		19 M Mechanic	18Ma02Hc
Sarah		50 F Unknown	18Ma02Hc
QUIGLY, Patrick		48 M Laborer	18Ma02Hc
Margaret	(W)	48 F Unknown	18Ma02Hc
Thomas	(S)	26 M Laborer	18Ma02Hc
John	(S)	22 M Laborer	18Ma02Hc
Elizabeth	(D)	20 F Unknown	18Ma02Hc
William	(S)	16 M Mechanic	18Ma02Hc
Rosanna	(D)	17 F Unknown	18Ma02Hc
Margaret	(D)	12 F Unknown	18Ma02Hc
Patrick	(S)	08 M Child	18Ma02Hc
Mary	(D)	30 F Unknown	18Ma02Hc
NELSON, Hannah		43 F Unknown	18Ma02Hc
HEALY, Jas.		20 M Laborer	18Ma02Hc
Anthy.		18 M Laborer	18Ma02Hc
KIERNAN, Michael		20 M Laborer	18Ma02Hc
Mary		20 F Unknown	18Ma02Hc
DUNN, Daniel		22 M Laborer	18Ma02Hc
George		24 M Laborer	18Ma02Hc
BRADY, Mary		18 F Unknown	18Ma02Hc
Fanny		12 F Unknown	18Ma02Hc
DONOGHUE, John		35 M Laborer	18Ma02Hc
MCDONALD, Paul		21 M Laborer	18Ma02Hc
QUIN, Rose		20 F Unknown	18Ma02Hc
MCKENNA, Hugh		17 M Laborer	18Ma02Hc
MOIER, Jas.		19 M Laborer	18Ma02Hc
Margt.		20 F Unknown	18Ma02Hc
Edward		13 M Unknown	18Ma02Hc
Mary		11 F Unknown	18Ma02Hc
KEENAN, Mary		20 F Unknown	18Ma02Hc
SHORT, Alice-M.		40 F Unknown	18Ma02Hc
HOGAN, Mary		32 F Unknown	18Ma02Hc
James	(S)	04 M Child	18Ma02Hc
WELSH, Patrick		24 M Servant	18Ma02Hc
BURKE, Judy		20 F Servant	18Ma02Hc

NAMES OF PASSENGERS		AGE	SEX	OCCUPATIONS	DATE PORT SHIP	NAMES OF PASSENGERS		AGE	SEX	OCCUPATIONS	DATE PORT SHIP
MCCUSKER, Patrick		24	M	Laborer	18Ma02Hc	MCGRATH, Mary-Ann		16	F	Unknown	18Ma02Hc
CARNS, John		27	M	Laborer	18Ma02Hc	TURNEY, Lucey		27	F	Unknown	18Ma02Hc
HIGGINS, Patrick		21	M	Laborer	18Ma02Hc	DAVVOY, Dennis		36	M	Mechanic	18Ma02Hc
KILLION, Bernard		25	M	Laborer	18Ma02Hc	GALLIGAN, Mary		52	F	Unknown	18Ma02Hc
Michael		20	M	Laborer	18Ma02Hc	MAGU, Barnard		30	M	Mechanic	18Ma02Hc
SPELLMAN, Mary		12	F	Unknown	18Ma02Hc	Rose	(W)	25	F	Unknown	18Ma02Hc
SHEPHARD, William		23	M	Mechanic	18Ma02Hc	Rosanna	(D)	03	F	Child	18Ma02Hc
FITZGERALD, Catherine		21	F	Unknown	18Ma02Hc	ELIFF, Alicia		50	F	Unknown	18Ma02Hc
MANSFIELD, Eliza		29	F	Unknown	18Ma02Hc	Richard		07	M	Child	18Ma02Hc
BURNS, Mary		20	F	Unknown	18Ma02Hc	REDWOOD, James		40	M	Laborer	18Ma02Hc
Ellen		21	F	Unknown	18Ma02Hc	Thomas		35	M	Laborer	18Ma02Hc
SMITH, Robert		30	M	Farmer	18Ma02Hc	Judith	(W)	22	F	Unknown	18Ma02Hc
Elizabeth	(W)	28	F	Unknown	18Ma02Hc	Thomas	(S)	01	M	Child	18Ma02Hc
Wm.John	(S)	01	M	Child	18Ma02Hc	KAY, John		32	M	Mechanic	18Ma02Hc
NAUST, Elizabeth		30	F	Unknown	18Ma02Hc	CARRIGAN, Bernard		25	M	Laborer	18Ma02Hc
GALLAGHAN, Patrick		18	M	Laborer	18Ma02Hc	LEARY, William		35	M	Laborer	18Ma02Hc
MCSORLEY, Arthur		20	M	Laborer	18Ma02Hc	KELLY, John		28	M	Laborer	18Ma02Hc
DOUGHERTY, Jas.		23	M	Laborer	18Ma02Hc	LEARY, Mary		26	F	Unknown	18Ma02Hc
Giley		54	F	Unknown	18Ma02Hc	Eliza		20	F	Unknown	18Ma02Hc
Michl.		20	M	Laborer	18Ma02Hc	GROHAM, Mary		30	F	Unknown	18Ma02Hc
Rosey		14	F	Unknown	18Ma02Hc	Ellen	(D)	10	F	Unknown	18Ma02Hc
MOORE, James		18	M	Laborer	18Ma02Hc	Thomas	(S)	08	M	Child	18Ma02Hc
MCCABE, Patrick		21	M	Laborer	18Ma02Hc	Mary	(D)	06	F	Child	18Ma02Hc
CROVELT, John		50	M	Laborer	18Ma02Hc	REILLY, Margaret		14	F	Unknown	18Ma02Hc
Catherine	(W)	48	F	Unknown	18Ma02Hc	MCGUERE, John		09	M	Child	18Ma02Hc
Andrew	(S)	20	M	Laborer	18Ma02Hc	SORAHGAN, Rose		21	F	Unknown	18Ma02Hc
Anne	(D)	18	F	Unknown	18Ma02Hc	SWEET, Nancy		17	F	Unknown	18Ma02Hc
John	(S)	10	M	Unknown	18Ma02Hc	CARROLL, Bridget		18	F	Unknown	18Ma02Hc
Patrick	(S)	04	M	Child	18Ma02Hc	BRADY, Mary		20	F	Unknown	18Ma02Hc
BELL, James		19	M	Laborer	18Ma02Hc	GULOITCH, Fanny		07	F	Child	18Ma02Hc
ONEIL, John		30	M	Laborer	18Ma02Hc	Mary		04	F	Child	18Ma02Hc
MCCLACKAN, Nancy		21	F	Unknown	18Ma02Hc	MCLASKEY, John		30	M	Mechanic	18Ma02Hc
Jane		19	F	Unknown	18Ma02Hc	LONER, Ann		28	F	Unknown	18Ma02Hc
VANDIN, Betsy		20	F	Unknown	18Ma02Hc	MITCHELL, Alex.		19	M	Mechanic	18Ma02Hc
KNOT, Ellen		21	F	Unknown	18Ma02Hc	Jane		20	F	Unknown	18Ma02Hc
MAYNIGHT, Mary		18	F	Unknown	18Ma02Hc	DAVIDSON, Robt.		18	M	Laborer	18Ma02Hc
TIERNNY, Patrick		24	M	Mechanic	18Ma02Hc	MCILVAIN, John		18	M	Laborer	18Ma02Hc
STANTON, Miles		27	M	Laborer	18Ma02Hc	FINN, Mathew		65	M	Laborer	18Ma02Hc
MORRISSY, Michl.		21	M	Laborer	18Ma02Hc	John		10	M	Laborer	18Ma02Hc
Mary		20	F	Unknown	18Ma02Hc	CASHIA, Patrick		18	M	Laborer	18Ma02Hc
DOYLE, James		35	M	Mechanic	18Ma02Hc	MCCLEAN, Margt.		16	F	Unknown	18Ma02Hc
Mary		30	F	Unknown	18Ma02Hc	James		14	M	Laborer	18Ma02Hc
HANIGAN, Anne		18	F	Unknown	18Ma02Hc	GREEN, Richard		48	M	Mechanic	18Ma02Hc
TOFFE, Bridget		24	F	Unknown	18Ma02Hc	JORDAN, Garret		60	M	Lawyer	18Ma02Hc
KENNEDY, Daniel		24	M	Laborer	18Ma02Hc	John		14	M	Laborer	18Ma02Hc
MCCORMAK, Bridgt.		25	F	Unknown	18Ma02Hc	MCLAUGHLIN, Michl.		24	M	Laborer	18Ma02Hc
COONEY, Rose		20	F	Unknown	18Ma02Hc	BIRNINGHAM, Michl.		20	M	Laborer	18Ma02Hc
MATTAN, Patrick		22	M	Laborer	18Ma02Hc	James		14	M	Laborer	18Ma02Hc
CARTTE, Thos.		35	M	Mechanic	18Ma02Hc	Thomas		08	M	Child	18Ma02Hc
FUREY, Michl.		10	M	Unknown	18Ma02Hc	Bridget		11	F	Unknown	18Ma02Hc
FARIGHAN, Peggy		50	F	Unknown	18Ma02Hc	OHARA, Ann		20	F	Unknown	18Ma02Hc
Patrick	(S)	25	M	Laborer	18Ma02Hc	GALLAGHER, Ann		20	F	Unknown	18Ma02Hc
Rose	(D)	20	F	Unknown	18Ma02Hc	MCGINNIS, Margt.		12	F	Unknown	18Ma02Hc
SMITH, William		50	M	Mechanic	18Ma02Hc	DONOHOE, Anne		12	F	Unknown	18Ma02Hc
GILL, Ellen		19	F	Unknown	18Ma02Hc	CONLEY, John		18	M	Mechanic	18Ma02Hc
COSGROVE, Cathe.		22	F	Unknown	18Ma02Hc	SHANNON, Honor		17	F	Unknown	18Ma02Hc
FARLEY, James		21	M	Laborer	18Ma02Hc	ROURKE, Bernard		22	M	Mechanic	18Ma02Hc
MAURAY, Hugh		26	M	Farmer	18Ma02Hc	NOWLAY, Martin		26	M	Laborer	18Ma02Hc
Catherine		23	F	Unknown	18Ma02Hc	Michael		16	M	Laborer	18Ma02Hc
Betty		20	F	Unknown	18Ma02Hc	Peter		09	M	Child	18Ma02Hc
BROWN, Pat.		24	M	Laborer	18Ma02Hc	Margt.		07	F	Child	18Ma02Hc
DOOLIN, John		21	M	Laborer	18Ma02Hc	Bridget		04	F	Child	18Ma02Hc
SEDWIGE, Jas.		28	M	Laborer	18Ma02Hc	JACKSON, Marry		57	F	Unknown	18Ma02Hc
SMITH, Laughlin		22	M	Mechanic	18Ma02Hc	Robert		50	M	Mechanic	18Ma02Hc
BRADY, Lawrence		19	M	Laborer	18Ma02Hc	John-Robert	(S)	20	M	Mechanic	18Ma02Hc
MILLIGAN, Lawrence		20	M	Laborer	18Ma02Hc	Catherine	(D)	18	F	Unknown	18Ma02Hc
DERMODY, Cathe.		21	F	Unknown	18Ma02Hc	Margaret	(D)	17	F	Unknown	18Ma02Hc
FAGAN, Eliza		25	F	Unknown	18Ma02Hc	Sarah	(D)	16	F	Unknown	18Ma02Hc
RILEY, Ann		20	F	Unknown	18Ma02Hc	DOWD, Nabby		24	F	Unknown	18Ma02Hc
DILLON, Mary		16	F	Unknown	18Ma02Hc	DOLAN, James		20	M	Laborer	18Ma02Hc
Ann		18	F	Unknown	18Ma02Hc	WILKINSON, Henry		25	M	Laborer	18Ma02Hc
FLANIGAN, Luke		20	M	Mechanic	18Ma02Hc	LOWE, James		21	M	Laborer	18Ma02Hc
Mary		06	F	Child	18Ma02Hc	WARD, Bridget		20	F	Unknown	18Ma02Hc
DIMOND, Hugh		21	M	Mechanic	18Ma02Hc	Nancy		18	F	Unknown	18Ma02Hc
MCGRATH, Cathe.		18	F	Unknown	18Ma02Hc	OWEN, Mary		28	F	Unknown	18Ma02Hc

NAMES OF PASSENGERS		AGE	SEX	OCCUPATIONS	DATE PORT SHIP
OWEN, Patrick	(S)	05	M	Child	18Ma02Hc
Biddy	(D)	02	F	Child	18Ma02Hc
IRWIN, William		26	M	Clerk	18Ma02Hc
Rebecca		65	F	Unknown	18Ma02Hc
STEVENS, William		20	M	Mechanic	18Ma02Hc
Euphemia		22	F	Unknown	18Ma02Hc
MCMANN, Peter		30	M	Merchant	18Ma02Hc
John		18	M	Unknown	18Ma02Hc
Ann		20	F	Unknown	18Ma02Hc
REILLY, Farrell		27	M	Farmer	18Ma02Hc
Margt.		26	F	Unknown	18Ma02Hc
KIPPEL, Michael		28	M	Laborer	18Ma02Hc
KEANNY, Cathe.		50	F	Unknown	18Ma02Hc
PHILLIPS, Honor		47	F	Unknown	18Ma02Hc
FALTY, Eliza		12	F	Unknown	18Ma02Hc
Patrick		07	M	Child	18Ma02Hc
BUCKINGHAM, Esther		21	F	Unknown	18Ma02Hc
Mary		19	F	Unknown	18Ma02Hc
FENKLEY, Cathe.		07	F	Child	18Ma02Hc
RIELLY, Thomas		48	M	Gdnr	18Ma02Hc

JANE-E.WILLIAMS 18 MAY 1847

From Londonderry

NAMES OF PASSENGERS		AGE	SEX	OCCUPATIONS	DATE PORT SHIP
MCCHONNY, A.		30	M	Laborer	18Ma01Qc
James		18	M	Laborer	18Ma01Qc
Isb.		60	F	Unknown	18Ma01Qc
Mich.		12	M	Unknown	18Ma01Qc
MCGULLIGAN, Biddy		45	F	Unknown	18Ma01Qc
Danl.		19	M	Unknown	18Ma01Qc
Mary		17	F	Unknown	18Ma01Qc
Park.		16	M	Unknown	18Ma01Qc
Fanny-A.		15	F	Unknown	18Ma01Qc
John		12	M	Unknown	18Ma01Qc
James		09	M	Child	18Ma01Qc
Thomas		07	M	Child	18Ma01Qc
GULLEN, J.		17	M	Unknown	18Ma01Qc
MCCAFFRY, J.		17	M	Unknown	18Ma01Qc
Arabelle		19	F	Unknown	18Ma01Qc
ALLEN, Mary		17	F	Unknown	18Ma01Qc
Turner		46	M	Unknown	18Ma01Qc
Nancy	(W)	45	F	Unknown	18Ma01Qc
Jane	(D)	12	F	Unknown	18Ma01Qc
MCNELLY, S.		21	M	Unknown	18Ma01Qc
GOWN, Mary		17	F	Unknown	18Ma01Qc
TURY, J.		21	M	Unknown	18Ma01Qc
Eliz.		22	F	Unknown	18Ma01Qc
QUIGBY, Susan		17	F	Unknown	18Ma01Qc
DONN, W.		17	M	Unknown	18Ma01Qc
Anne		21	F	Unknown	18Ma01Qc
MULLEN, M.		24	M	Unknown	18Ma01Qc
Cath.		23	F	Unknown	18Ma01Qc
OHEE, Jane		20	F	Unknown	18Ma01Qc
Mgt.		18	F	Unknown	18Ma01Qc
Bdgt.		50	F	Unknown	18Ma01Qc
MCNULTY, J.		45	M	Unknown	18Ma01Qc
Sally	(W)	48	F	Unknown	18Ma01Qc
U		16	M	Unknown	18Ma01Qc
Mary	(D)	06	F	Child	18Ma01Qc
Peggy		43	F	Unknown	18Ma01Qc
MCGORLY, G.		22	F	Unknown	18Ma01Qc
MCAR, Nelly		30	F	Unknown	18Ma01Qc
MCCENAND, M.		24	M	Unknown	18Ma01Qc
Mary		32	F	Unknown	18Ma01Qc
U		05	M	Child	18Ma01Qc
MCCAUL, Mary		05	F	Child	18Ma01Qc
Paddy		01	M	Child	18Ma01Qc
GULLOUGH, J.		45	M	Unknown	18Ma01Qc
GULLOUGH, Mary	(W)	45	F	Unknown	18Ma01Qc
Laghlin	(S)	21	M	Unknown	18Ma01Qc
Mary	(D)	19	F	Unknown	18Ma01Qc
Francis	(S)	12	M	None	18Ma01Qc
REILLY, Ann		25	F	Unknown	18Ma01Qc
MCCAUL, Pady		22	M	Unknown	18Ma01Qc
James		20	M	Unknown	18Ma01Qc
John		12	M	None	18Ma01Qc
Nelly		19	F	Unknown	18Ma01Qc
Nelly		45	F	Unknown	18Ma01Qc
Mary		20	F	Unknown	18Ma01Qc
MCGEE, D.		45	M	Unknown	18Ma01Qc
Mary	(W)	47	F	Unknown	18Ma01Qc
Mrgt.	(D)	15	F	Unknown	18Ma01Qc
MCELRY, P.		50	M	Unknown	18Ma01Qc
Grace	(W)	30	F	Unknown	18Ma01Qc
Mary	(D)	01	F	Child	18Ma01Qc
HERUGH, Cath.		19	F	Unknown	18Ma01Qc
FRYES, J.		22	M	Unknown	18Ma01Qc
BROGUES, J.		22	M	Unknown	18Ma01Qc
MCCLAFFORD, D.		20	M	Unknown	18Ma01Qc
PEOPLES, P.		23	M	Unknown	18Ma01Qc
MAYNE, P.		22	M	Unknown	18Ma01Qc
MOYNA, Mgt.		22	F	Unknown	18Ma01Qc
MORROW, T.		25	M	Unknown	18Ma01Qc
DOHEB, J.		45	M	Unknown	18Ma01Qc
Ellen		25	F	Unknown	18Ma01Qc
Mary		30	F	Unknown	18Ma01Qc
Nancy		10	F	Unknown	18Ma01Qc
GULLOGH, J.		54	M	Unknown	18Ma01Qc
KOLE, P.		28	M	Unknown	18Ma01Qc
MCNIVEER, P.		21	M	Unknown	18Ma01Qc
Bdgt.		30	F	Unknown	18Ma01Qc
COLE, Rosann		50	F	Unknown	18Ma01Qc
Alice	(D)	20	F	Unknown	18Ma01Qc
John	(S)	23	M	Unknown	18Ma01Qc
Jane	(D)	19	F	Unknown	18Ma01Qc
Chas.	(S)	15	M	Unknown	18Ma01Qc
HERRY, J.		48	F	Unknown	18Ma01Qc
MULLEN, Biddy		24	F	Unknown	18Ma01Qc
KOR, Jas.		28	M	Laborer	18Ma01Qc
LYNCH, D.		23	M	Unknown	18Ma01Qc
KORR, Letitia		01	F	Child	18Ma01Qc
Pat.		28	M	Unknown	18Ma01Qc
Michl.		24	M	Unknown	18Ma01Qc
MCLAUGHLIN, M.		48	M	Unknown	18Ma01Qc
KERNAN, J.		48	M	Unknown	18Ma01Qc
Martha	(W)	48	F	Unknown	18Ma01Qc
Mgt.	(D)	18	F	Unknown	18Ma01Qc
Susan	(D)	19	F	Unknown	18Ma01Qc
Jane	(D)	13	F	Unknown	18Ma01Qc
John	(S)	12	M	None	18Ma01Qc
DOHERTY, J.		15	M	None	18Ma01Qc
ODONNELL, C.		23	M	Unknown	18Ma01Qc
DOHERTY, G.		19	M	Unknown	18Ma01Qc
ALLEN, S.		16	M	Unknown	18Ma01Qc
John		08	M	Child	18Ma01Qc
Jos.		05	M	Child	18Ma01Qc
MCTAYNE, Sally		22	F	Unknown	18Ma01Qc
MULLEN, J.		13	M	Unknown	18Ma01Qc
HOPKINS, J.		17	M	Unknown	18Ma01Qc
KENY, M.		18	M	Unknown	18Ma01Qc
Mary		19	F	Unknown	18Ma01Qc
DOHERTY, T.		18	M	Unknown	18Ma01Qc
JACKSON, J.		58	M	Unknown	18Ma01Qc
Jane		60	F	Unknown	18Ma01Qc
KER, C.		24	M	Unknown	18Ma01Qc
Nancy	(W)	22	F	Unknown	18Ma01Qc
John	(S)	04	M	Child	18Ma01Qc
Mary-T.	(D)	01	F	Child	18Ma01Qc
LOUREN, J.		19	M	Unknown	18Ma01Qc
Jane		15	F	Unknown	18Ma01Qc
GEORGES, Fanny		24	F	Unknown	18Ma01Qc
Amelia		21	F	Unknown	18Ma01Qc
WOODS, A.		17	M	Unknown	18Ma01Qc

NAMES OF PASSENGERS		AGE	SEX	OCCUPATIONS	DATE PORT SHIP
KELLY, J.		20	M	Unknown	18Ma01Qc
MCLAUGHLIN, J.		30	M	Unknown	18Ma01Qc
MACGORTY, Elza.		52	F	Unknown	18Ma01Qc
Sarah	(D)	15	F	Unknown	18Ma01Qc
CAMPBELL, G.		16	M	Unknown	18Ma01Qc
WOODS, J.		46	M	Unknown	18Ma01Qc
W.	(S)	09	M	Laborer	18Ma01Qc
Andrew	(S)	17	M	Unknown	18Ma01Qc
Mgt.	(D)	16	F	Unknown	18Ma01Qc
Alexr.	(S)	15	M	Unknown	18Ma01Qc
Jane	(W)	48	F	Unknown	18Ma01Qc
Saml.	(S)	11	M	None	18Ma01Qc
James	(S)	13	M	None	18Ma01Qc
Cath.	(D)	05	F	Child	18Ma01Qc
Eliza	(D)	02	F	Child	18Ma01Qc
CLAY, T.W.		20	M	Unknown	18Ma01Qc
MILL, Fay		22	F	Unknown	18Ma01Qc
MCDORR, Mary		17	F	Unknown	18Ma01Qc
MCGRADY, Mgt.		20	F	Unknown	18Ma01Qc
RINDY, Bgt.		20	F	Unknown	18Ma01Qc
DOHERTY, P.		18	M	Unknown	18Ma01Qc
HENRY, E.		22	M	Unknown	18Ma01Qc
Danl.		24	M	Unknown	18Ma01Qc
Saml.		18	M	Unknown	18Ma01Qc
James		16	M	Unknown	18Ma01Qc
Martha		15	F	Unknown	18Ma01Qc
Robt.		14	M	None	18Ma01Qc
Dan.		11	M	None	18Ma01Qc
Jane		40	F	Unknown	18Ma01Qc
THOMAS, H.		24	F	Unknown	18Ma01Qc
MOREY, A.		22	M	Unknown	18Ma01Qc
DONALY, R.		24	M	Unknown	18Ma01Qc
Cath.		24	F	Unknown	18Ma01Qc
COOPER, W.		39	M	Unknown	18Ma01Qc
DOLY, Cath.		16	F	Unknown	18Ma01Qc
DENLER, Lucy		17	F	Unknown	18Ma01Qc
MCAUTYL, J.		21	M	Unknown	18Ma01Qc
MCMATEUR, U		20	F	Unknown	18Ma01Qc
MCCOUCH, M.		25	M	Unknown	18Ma01Qc
STAFFORD, J.		30	M	Unknown	18Ma01Qc
MCNALLY, T.		21	M	Unknown	18Ma01Qc

HOWARD 18 MAY 1847

From Liverpool

NAMES OF PASSENGERS		AGE	SEX	OCCUPATIONS	DATE PORT SHIP
DEGAN, James		35	M	Laborer	18Ma02Kd
James		22	M	Laborer	18Ma02Kd
HAYES, John		25	M	Laborer	18Ma02Kd
MONGAN, Patrick		30	M	Laborer	18Ma02Kd
Mary	(W)	23	F	Unknown	18Ma02Kd
John	(S)	02	M	Child	18Ma02Kd
Bridget	(D)	04	F	Child	18Ma02Kd
MARTIN, James		25	M	Laborer	18Ma02Kd
GOURLEY, James		18	M	Laborer	18Ma02Kd
HARD, Patrick		16	M	Laborer	18Ma02Kd
Margt.		18	F	Unknown	18Ma02Kd
MORTON, Ellen		20	F	Unknown	18Ma02Kd
KIRKPATRICK, James		25	M	Laborer	18Ma02Kd
CLARK, James		22	M	Laborer	18Ma02Kd
MCCLONACHAN, John		22	M	Laborer	18Ma02Kd
GIFF, David		19	M	Laborer	18Ma02Kd
BYRON, Michael		45	M	Laborer	18Ma02Kd
Margt.	(W)	40	F	Unknown	18Ma02Kd
Martin	(S)	18	M	Laborer	18Ma02Kd
Elisa	(D)	16	F	Unknown	18Ma02Kd
Patrick	(S)	14	M	Laborer	18Ma02Kd
Thomas	(S)	12	M	Laborer	18Ma02Kd
Mary	(D)	10	F	Unknown	18Ma02Kd
BYRON, Michael	(S)	07	M	Child	18Ma02Kd
Bridget	(D)	05	F	Child	18Ma02Kd
CONNER, Martin		30	M	Laborer	18Ma02Kd
Lawrence		17	M	Laborer	18Ma02Kd
Mary		25	F	Unknown	18Ma02Kd
MALONEY, Thos.		36	M	Laborer	18Ma02Kd
SCOTT, Richd.		27	M	Laborer	18Ma02Kd
Mary	(W)	26	F	Unknown	18Ma02Kd
Ann	(D)	06	F	Child	18Ma02Kd
Francis	(S)	03	M	Child	18Ma02Kd
Patrick	(S)	01	M	Child	18Ma02Kd
AGNEW, Francis		45	M	Laborer	18Ma02Kd
KENEY, John		20	M	Laborer	18Ma02Kd
BOGAN, Patrick		25	M	Laborer	18Ma02Kd
COHLAN, John		22	M	Laborer	18Ma02Kd
HUNT, Ann		22	F	Unknown	18Ma02Kd
Ellen		20	F	Unknown	18Ma02Kd
KELL, Mary		16	F	Unknown	18Ma02Kd
MURRAY, Michael		20	M	Laborer	18Ma02Kd
WELSH, Michael		18	M	Laborer	18Ma02Kd
DONOHUE, Nelly		35	F	Unknown	18Ma02Kd
BRADY, Thomas		16	M	Laborer	18Ma02Kd
HUNT, John		20	M	Laborer	18Ma02Kd
Mary		20	F	Unknown	18Ma02Kd
CORCORAN, James		20	M	Laborer	18Ma02Kd
KINEY, Winny		19	M	Laborer	18Ma02Kd
MAURAY, Bridget		20	F	Unknown	18Ma02Kd
FALLON, Ellen		20	F	Unknown	18Ma02Kd
HANLEY, Cathe.		18	F	Unknown	18Ma02Kd
WALLACE, Maria		18	F	Unknown	18Ma02Kd
SHANNON, Mary		30	F	Unknown	18Ma02Kd
MURRAY, James		26	M	Laborer	18Ma02Kd
Margt.	(W)	26	F	Unknown	18Ma02Kd
Michael	(S)	03	M	Child	18Ma02Kd
Cathe.		24	F	Unknown	18Ma02Kd
KING, Margt.		24	F	Unknown	18Ma02Kd
BURN, Ed.		20	M	Laborer	18Ma02Kd
Mary		18	F	Unknown	18Ma02Kd
WHILE, David		20	M	Laborer	18Ma02Kd
HAMILTON, Alexr.		18	M	Laborer	18Ma02Kd
MCDONALD, Michael		31	M	Laborer	18Ma02Kd
ROGERS, John		21	M	Laborer	18Ma02Kd
MUIR, James		52	M	Laborer	18Ma02Kd
Isabella		07	F	Child	18Ma02Kd
MURPHY, John		24	M	Laborer	18Ma02Kd
Cornelius		20	M	Laborer	18Ma02Kd
RENARD, Patrick		20	M	Laborer	18Ma02Kd
ORR, James		20	M	Laborer	18Ma02Kd
SHEA, Michaeal		31	M	Laborer	18Ma02Kd
Cathe.		25	F	Unknown	18Ma02Kd
EDGAR, Lawrence		30	M	Laborer	18Ma02Kd
Agnes		25	F	Unknown	18Ma02Kd
CARTY, Owen		50	M	Laborer	18Ma02Kd
Pat.	(S)	24	M	Laborer	18Ma02Kd
Dennis	(S)	18	M	Laborer	18Ma02Kd
Joseph	(S)	16	M	Laborer	18Ma02Kd
Rose	(D)	14	F	Unknown	18Ma02Kd
Mary	(D)	12	F	Unknown	18Ma02Kd
James	(S)	09	M	Child	18Ma02Kd
Cathe.	(D)	19	F	Unknown	18Ma02Kd
KELLEY, Margt.		30	F	Unknown	18Ma02Kd
Fanny	(D)	03	F	Child	18Ma02Kd
KATH, William		23	M	Laborer	18Ma02Kd
MURPHY, Dennis		21	M	Laborer	18Ma02Kd
DIGGAN, Terry		30	M	Laborer	18Ma02Kd
KING, Patk.		23	M	Laborer	18Ma02Kd
Ellen	(W)	23	F	Unknown	18Ma02Kd
Thomas	(S)	02	M	Child	18Ma02Kd
FINNEGAN, James		20	M	Laborer	18Ma02Kd
FENCE, Ann		15	F	Unknown	18Ma02Kd
COLEN, Michael		12	M	None	18Ma02Kd
Bridget		05	F	Child	18Ma02Kd
FINNEGAN, Mary		45	F	Unknown	18Ma02Kd
Patrick		14	M	None	18Ma02Kd
DONOHUE, Patrick		32	M	Laborer	18Ma02Kd

NAMES OF PASSENGERS		A G E	S E X	OCCUPATIONS	DATE PORT SHIP	NAMES OF PASSENGERS		A G E	S E X	OCCUPATIONS	DATE PORT SHIP
DONOHUE, Mary		23	F	Unknown	18Ma02Kd	FARRELL, James		16	M	Mechanic	18Ma02Kd
CALACHAN, Ellen		20	F	Unknown	18Ma02Kd	Michael		09	M	Child	18Ma02Kd
FISCHONEL, John		20	M	Laborer	18Ma02Kd	HUGHES, Thomas		20	M	Laborer	18Ma02Kd
SISE, James		45	M	Laborer	18Ma02Kd	DOCHARTY, Ellen		18	F	Unknown	18Ma02Kd
Agnes	(W)	30	F	Unknown	18Ma02Kd	FARRELL, Daniel		50	M	Laborer	18Ma02Kd
John	(S)	14	M	Laborer	18Ma02Kd	Bridget	(D)	12	F	Unknown	18Ma02Kd
Miles	(S)	09	M	Child	18Ma02Kd	Ellen	(D)	05	F	Child	18Ma02Kd
Hugh	(S)	05	M	Child	18Ma02Kd	Margt.	(D)	03	F	Child	18Ma02Kd
Mary	(D)	04	F	Child	18Ma02Kd	Rose	(D)	01	F	Child	18Ma02Kd
James	(S)	01	M	Child	18Ma02Kd	GOLDEN, Patrick		23	M	Laborer	18Ma02Kd
MITCHELL, Ed.		47	M	Farmer	18Ma02Kd	MCCARRY, John		20	M	Laborer	18Ma02Kd
Ed.	(S)	14	M	Farmer	18Ma02Kd	MUFFET, Joseph		18	M	Laborer	18Ma02Kd
Andrew	(S)	12	M	None	18Ma02Kd	DICKSON, Geo.		16	M	Laborer	18Ma02Kd
DEMSEY, Muty		26	M	Laborer	18Ma02Kd	MCGOWAN, Michael		30	M	Laborer	18Ma02Kd
Mary	(W)	24	F	Unknown	18Ma02Kd	Betsey	(W)	30	F	Unknown	18Ma02Kd
John	(S)	02	M	Child	18Ma02Kd	Mary	(D)	04	F	Child	18Ma02Kd
James	(S)	.06	M	Infant	18Ma02Kd	Eliza	(D)	03	F	Child	18Ma02Kd
CARRY, Michael		25	M	Laborer	18Ma02Kd	Betsey	(D)	01	F	Child	18Ma02Kd
Mary	(W)	23	F	Unknown	18Ma02Kd	POWELL, Ann		19	F	Unknown	18Ma02Kd
Cathe.	(D)	01	F	Child	18Ma02Kd	KANN, Sarah		50	F	Unknown	18Ma02Kd
NOWLAND, John		24	M	Laborer	18Ma02Kd	MCRAIN, John		24	M	Mechanic	18Ma02Kd
HAYS, Matt.		23	M	Laborer	18Ma02Kd	DENNIS, Andrew		28	M	Mechanic	18Ma02Kd
COCKLEY, Mary		20	F	Unknown	18Ma02Kd	Arthur		22	M	Mechanic	18Ma02Kd
COCHAN, Julia		22	F	Unknown	18Ma02Kd	SCOTT, Samuel		19	M	Mechanic	18Ma02Kd
MULHALL, Margt.		18	F	Unknown	18Ma02Kd	John		17	M	Mechanic	18Ma02Kd
MURRAY, Michael		20	M	Laborer	18Ma02Kd	CLARK, Eliza		17	F	Unknown	18Ma02Kd
CARLOW, David		20	M	Laborer	18Ma02Kd	GREAN, Margt.		21	F	Unknown	18Ma02Kd
WALLS, Eliza		18	F	Unknown	18Ma02Kd	BROWN, Margt.		17	F	Unknown	18Ma02Kd
FOY, Peter		25	M	Mechanic	18Ma02Kd	MCBRIDE, Eliza		18	F	Unknown	18Ma02Kd
HART, Robt.		21	M	Mechanic	18Ma02Kd	Sally		20	F	Unknown	18Ma02Kd
James		19	M	Mechanic	18Ma02Kd	WHITE, John		28	M	Mechanic	18Ma02Kd
FOLEY, John		40	M	Mechanic	18Ma02Kd	BAILEN, Robt.		22	M	Mechanic	18Ma02Kd
FOY, Cella		22	F	Unknown	18Ma02Kd	WALKER, William		22	M	Mechanic	18Ma02Kd
Cathe.		20	F	Unknown	18Ma02Kd	HAYWOOD, Thos.		22	M	Mechanic	18Ma02Kd
Mary-Ann		18	F	Unknown	18Ma02Kd	RAY, James		23	M	Mechanic	18Ma02Kd
MCNELLY, Honora		20	F	Unknown	18Ma02Kd	Agnes		20	F	Unknown	18Ma02Kd
Ellen		19	F	Unknown	18Ma02Kd	FARRELL, Cathe.		30	F	Unknown	18Ma02Kd
Mary		21	F	Unknown	18Ma02Kd	MALANEY, Margt.		30	F	Unknown	18Ma02Kd
MURRAY, Mary		23	F	Unknown	18Ma02Kd	COTIN, Perry		45	M	Laborer	18Ma02Kd
MCALLEN, Henry		29	M	Mechanic	18Ma02Kd	Margt.	(W)	40	F	Unknown	18Ma02Kd
MCALEN, Ritchell		27	F	Unknown	18Ma02Kd	Margt.	(D)	08	F	Child	18Ma02Kd
MUIR, Barbary		42	F	Unknown	18Ma02Kd	Patrick	(S)	05	M	Child	18Ma02Kd
Barbay	(D)	11	F	Unknown	18Ma02Kd	William	(S)	03	M	Child	18Ma02Kd
Fanny	(D)	02	F	Child	18Ma02Kd	MCGOWAN, Bryan		40	M	Laborer	18Ma02Kd
HAMILTON, John		23	M	Mechanic	18Ma02Kd	Fanny	(W)	35	F	Unknown	18Ma02Kd
MALONEY, Michael		26	M	Farmer	18Ma02Kd	Agnes	(D)	12	F	Unknown	18Ma02Kd
KENNEDY, John		24	M	Farmer	18Ma02Kd	Dunagan	(S)	03	M	Child	18Ma02Kd
DAY, Patrick		27	M	Farmer	18Ma02Kd	Hugh	(S)	02	M	Child	18Ma02Kd
Daniel		18	M	Farmer	18Ma02Kd	CARAGAN, Ed.		33	M	Laborer	18Ma02Kd
Bridget		50	F	Unknown	18Ma02Kd	LAWREGAN, John		23	M	Laborer	18Ma02Kd
Mary		26	F	Unknown	18Ma02Kd	CADY, John		24	M	Laborer	18Ma02Kd
LYNCH, Mary		17	F	Unknown	18Ma02Kd	LANDREGAN, Thos.		25	M	Laborer	18Ma02Kd
MALONEY, Margt.		17	F	Unknown	18Ma02Kd	MORGAN, William		27	M	Laborer	18Ma02Kd
KENNEDY, Cathe.		17	F	Unknown	18Ma02Kd	WELSH, Michael		35	M	Laborer	18Ma02Kd
OBRIAN, Ed.		30	M	Farmer	18Ma02Kd	LAVAN, Cormick		23	M	Laborer	18Ma02Kd
Carmon		27	M	Farmer	18Ma02Kd	CONNER, Patrick		21	M	Laborer	18Ma02Kd
CONLEY, Barth.		26	M	Farmer	18Ma02Kd	HOPKINS, William		25	M	Laborer	18Ma02Kd
MCCORMICK, James		21	M	Farmer	18Ma02Kd	NAUGHTON, James		36	M	Laborer	18Ma02Kd
LINEY, Bridget		26	F	Unknown	18Ma02Kd	Patrick		14	M	Laborer	18Ma02Kd
CROINCHEN, Cathe.		24	F	Unknown	18Ma02Kd	MOGRA, Margt.		18	F	Unknown	18Ma02Kd
CONDON, Cathe.		23	F	Unknown	18Ma02Kd	MCMARRET, Margt.		20	F	Unknown	18Ma02Kd
DORAN, Cathe.		21	F	Unknown	18Ma02Kd	SLOTTERY, Nelley		20	F	Unknown	18Ma02Kd
HURLEY, Mary		20	F	Unknown	18Ma02Kd	Margt.		18	F	Unknown	18Ma02Kd
LAWRY, William		25	M	Farmer	18Ma02Kd	MANEEL, Judy		20	F	Unknown	18Ma02Kd
William		24	M	Farmer	18Ma02Kd	COATES, Mary		14	F	Unknown	18Ma02Kd
HURLEY, Daniel		18	M	Farmer	18Ma02Kd	ROCHE, Patrick		27	M	Laborer	18Ma02Kd
Fr.		22	M	Farmer	18Ma02Kd	Thos.		23	M	Laborer	18Ma02Kd
LAWREY, Ellen		13	F	Unknown	18Ma02Kd	Bridget		50	F	Unknown	18Ma02Kd
KELLEY, Thomas		30	M	Mechanic	18Ma02Kd	Homer		24	M	Laborer	18Ma02Kd
FAREN, Betty		18	F	Unknown	18Ma02Kd	John		.03	M	Infant	18Ma02Kd
FARRELL, Mary		18	F	Unknown	18Ma02Kd	FINEGAN, James		60	M	Laborer	18Ma02Kd
BELAY, Mary		18	F	Unknown	18Ma02Kd	Patrick		21	M	Laborer	18Ma02Kd
WALLACE, Beaty		16	F	Unknown	18Ma02Kd	CHALL, Thomas		23	M	Laborer	18Ma02Kd
NOWLON, Bridget		18	F	Unknown	18Ma02Kd	MISCAL, Patrick		18	M	Laborer	18Ma02Kd
FARRELL, Patrick		22	M	Mechanic	18Ma02Kd	QUIGLEY, Patrick		23	M	Laborer	18Ma02Kd

NAMES OF PASSENGERS		AGE	SEX	OCCUPATIONS	DATE PORT SHIP
QUIGLEY, Ellen		25	F	Unknown	18Ma02Kd
DAILY, Patrick		20	M	Laborer	18Ma02Kd
FARRELL, Matthew		22	M	Laborer	18Ma02Kd
WOOD, John		21	M	Laborer	18Ma02Kd
Bridget		21	F	Unknown	18Ma02Kd
James		24	M	Laborer	18Ma02Kd
KELLIN, Cathe.		33	F	Unknown	18Ma02Kd
MCDONALD, Margt.		20	F	Unknown	18Ma02Kd
MCGUIRE, Margt.		22	F	Unknown	18Ma02Kd
DUNN, Eliza		20	F	Unknown	18Ma02Kd
BRISTOW, Margt.		20	F	Unknown	18Ma02Kd
BARN, Ann		20	F	Unknown	18Ma02Kd
MORGAN, Phillip		22	M	Laborer	18Ma02Kd
FAY, Chris.		19	M	Laborer	18Ma02Kd
DEARY, Jean		36	M	Laborer	18Ma02Kd
MILLIGAN, Eliza		20	F	Unknown	18Ma02Kd
Margt.		18	F	Unknown	18Ma02Kd
BAYLEY, Mary		20	F	Unknown	18Ma02Kd
DIVAN, Margt.		28	F	Unknown	18Ma02Kd
Bridget	(D)	07	F	Child	18Ma02Kd
Patrick	(S)	07	M	Child	18Ma02Kd
Thomas		31	M	Laborer	18Ma02Kd
FLINN, Patrick		26	M	Laborer	18Ma02Kd
DUGAN, Michael		28	M	Laborer	18Ma02Kd
MILLS, James		20	M	Laborer	18Ma02Kd
Lawrence		15	M	Laborer	18Ma02Kd
MILES, John		28	M	Laborer	18Ma02Kd
Christopher		25	M	Laborer	18Ma02Kd
CONLEY, Patrick		32	M	Laborer	18Ma02Kd
KINNA, William		25	M	Laborer	18Ma02Kd
James		23	M	Laborer	18Ma02Kd
Julia		20	F	Unknown	18Ma02Kd
NEVEN, Peter		25	M	Laborer	18Ma02Kd
DREW, Patrick		30	M	Laborer	18Ma02Kd
MCKAIL, Peter		25	M	Laborer	18Ma02Kd
MCMANAMAN, John		24	M	Laborer	18Ma02Kd
COMMON, John		34	M	Laborer	18Ma02Kd
MOORE, James		16	M	Laborer	18Ma02Kd
Hugh		18	M	Laborer	18Ma02Kd

AGILE 18 MAY 1847

From Cork

WALSH, Philip		30	M	Farmer	18Ma140b
DAGGAN, Thomas		25	M	Farmer	18Ma140b
CARROW, Wm.		18	M	Farmer	18Ma140b
MEARY, John		16	M	Farmer	18Ma140b
Andrew		30	M	Farmer	18Ma140b
LYAN, Margt.		20	F	Unknown	18Ma140b
COUGHLAN, Peggy		17	F	Unknown	18Ma140b
SHAW, Dennis		18	M	Farmer	18Ma140b
FLYNN, Cathe.		35	F	Unknown	18Ma140b
RYAN, Timy		49	M	Farmer	18Ma140b
Michael	(S)	24	M	Farmer	18Ma140b
John	(S)	19	M	Farmer	18Ma140b
James	(S)	07	M	Child	18Ma140b
Norry	(W)	47	F	Unknown	18Ma140b
Elizabeth	(D)	18	F	Unknown	18Ma140b
Peggy	(D)	12	F	Unknown	18Ma140b
Norry	(D)	09	F	Child	18Ma140b
MCCARTHY, Michael		30	M	Farmer	18Ma140b
Margt.		28	F	Unknown	18Ma140b
SAUNDERS, John		30	M	Farmer	18Ma140b
HEFFEMAN, Patt		20	M	Farmer	18Ma140b
RYAN, Margt.		18	F	Unknown	18Ma140b
MURPHY, James		16	M	Farmer	18Ma140b
CORNWALL, Geol		40	M	Farmer	18Ma140b
FARRALL, Patt		40	M	Farmer	18Ma140b

NAMES OF PASSENGERS		AGE	SEX	OCCUPATIONS	DATE PORT SHIP
FARRALL, Norry		24	F	Unknown	18Ma140b
FLYNN, Thos.		30	M	Farmer	18Ma140b
WALSH, William		40	M	Farmer	18Ma140b
DONNELLY, John		20	M	Farmer	18Ma140b
MANNING, Ellen		20	F	Unknown	18Ma140b
Cathe.		18	F	Unknown	18Ma140b
SULLIVAN, Pat.		30	M	Farmer	18Ma140b
Mary		27	F	Unknown	18Ma140b
DUNOHO, Cam.		30	M	Farmer	18Ma140b
Michael		30	M	Farmer	18Ma140b
DORGAN, Mary		25	F	Unknown	18Ma140b
DILLON, Ellen		27	F	Unknown	18Ma140b
FIELD, Ellen		27	F	Unknown	18Ma140b
BRIAN, Dennis		30	M	Farmer	18Ma140b
SHENY, David		16	M	Farmer	18Ma140b
WOODS, U		18	F	Unknown	18Ma140b
WALSH, Robt.		16	M	Farmer	18Ma140b
REARDON, Mary		30	F	Unknown	18Ma140b
FITZ, Cath.		30	F	Unknown	18Ma140b
KIPPEL, James		40	M	Farmer	18Ma140b
Honora		40	F	Unknown	18Ma140b
LAUGHLAN, Jno.		26	M	Farmer	18Ma140b
Timothy		13	M	Farmer	18Ma140b
Patrick		12	M	None	18Ma140b
MORONY, Margt.		18	F	Unknown	18Ma140b
FAKERRERY, Eliza		20	F	Unknown	18Ma140b
SHAHAN, Jas.		20	M	Farmer	18Ma140b
MALLIN, Wm.		25	M	Farmer	18Ma140b
GIRMY, Michael		20	M	Farmer	18Ma140b
HOLMES, Richd.		18	M	Farmer	18Ma140b
KILMARTIN, Sim.		40	M	Farmer	18Ma140b
MOWNY, Jno.		40	M	Farmer	18Ma140b
MINARD, Tim.		20	M	Farmer	18Ma140b
LINCHAN, Dennis		40	M	Farmer	18Ma140b
Margt.		20	F	Unknown	18Ma140b
CROWE, Michael		30	M	Farmer	18Ma140b
Margt.		20	F	Unknown	18Ma140b
BARRY, Jno.		40	M	Farmer	18Ma140b
WALSH, Wm.		20	M	Farmer	18Ma140b
ENGLISH, Wm.		50	M	Farmer	18Ma140b
FLYNN, Arthur		30	M	Farmer	18Ma140b
ENGLISH, Jno.		16	M	Farmer	18Ma140b
Mgt.		50	F	Unknown	18Ma140b
HICKS, Bridget		20	F	Unknown	18Ma140b
KUFFER, Mary		25	F	Unknown	18Ma140b
Jno.		14	M	Farmer	18Ma140b
BURKE, Ann		30	F	Unknown	18Ma140b
CORKERAN, Mary		30	F	Unknown	18Ma140b
LAUGHLAN, Ellen		17	F	Unknown	18Ma140b

SYMMETRY 18 MAY 1847

From Liverpool

LYNCH, J.		24	M	Farmer	18Ma020c
FALLON, D.		24	M	Unknown	18Ma020c
CONNELL, J.		40	M	Unknown	18Ma020c
U	(W)	40	F	Unknown	18Ma020c
Mary	(D)	17	F	Unknown	18Ma020c
Jno.	(S)	11	M	None	18Ma020c
Hannah	(D)	09	F	Child	18Ma020c
Corn.	(S)	03	M	Child	18Ma020c
WELSH, P.		34	M	Unknown	18Ma020c
Hannah	(W)	34	F	Unknown	18Ma020c
Hannah	(D)	08	F	Child	18Ma020c
Edwd.	(S)	05	M	Child	18Ma020c
James	(S)	03	M	Child	18Ma020c
Ellen	(D)	01	F	Child	18Ma020c
COLEMAN, D.		24	M	Laborer	18Ma020c

NAMES OF PASSENGERS		AGE	SEX	OCCUPATIONS	DATE PORT SHIP
LOGH, Bgt.		17	F	Unknown	18Ma020c
CONNERY, J.		25	M	Unknown	18Ma020c
MULLIGAN, Ann		20	F	Unknown	18Ma020c
DEVELIN, J.		40	M	Unknown	18Ma020c
MULLIGAN, J.		03	M	Child	18Ma020c
DEVIN, Honora		21	F	Unknown	18Ma020c
CASY, Cathn.		20	F	Unknown	18Ma020c
DOYLE, Biddy		20	F	Unknown	18Ma020c
Cath.		21	F	Unknown	18Ma020c
POWER, P.		35	M	Unknown	18Ma020c
Nancy		30	F	Unknown	18Ma020c
Lawrence		30	M	Unknown	18Ma020c
MATTHEWS, J.		35	M	Unknown	18Ma020c
Mary	(W)	30	F	Unknown	18Ma020c
Jas.	(S)	01	M	Child	18Ma020c
MORRISEY, T.		20	M	Unknown	18Ma020c
COOPER, J.		50	M	Unknown	18Ma020c
Mary	(W)	40	F	Unknown	18Ma020c
Pat	(S)	13	M	None	18Ma020c
Jno.	(S)	11	M	None	18Ma020c
Mich.	(S)	09	M	Child	18Ma020c
J.	(S)	07	M	Child	18Ma020c
Maria	(D)	05	F	Child	18Ma020c
LEWIS, G.		36	M	Unknown	18Ma020c
Ann		22	F	Unknown	18Ma020c
Tim		20	M	Unknown	18Ma020c
T.		21	M	Laborer	18Ma020c
Mary		25	F	Unknown	18Ma020c
James	(S)	01	M	Child	18Ma020c
ODONNELL, Cath.		40	F	Unknown	18Ma020c
Sally		40	F	Unknown	18Ma020c
Jno.		20	M	Unknown	18Ma020c
CONNELLY, Mary		20	F	Unknown	18Ma020c
WARD, J.		22	M	Unknown	18Ma020c
Mary		23	F	Unknown	18Ma020c
BRADLY, M.		20	M	Unknown	18Ma020c
Hugh		23	M	Unknown	18Ma020c
Rose	(W)	22	F	Unknown	18Ma020c
Dominick	(S)	01	M	Child	18Ma020c
FEERY, A.		26	M	Unknown	18Ma020c
CANN, M.		35	M	Unknown	18Ma020c
MCCAFFRY, O.		26	M	Unknown	18Ma020c
ROGERS, P.		30	M	Unknown	18Ma020c
Sarah		30	F	Unknown	18Ma020c
MCWILBURNS, M.		40	M	Unknown	18Ma020c
Cath.		30	F	Unknown	18Ma020c
KEELY, J.		78	M	Unknown	18Ma020c
Elsie		20	F	Unknown	18Ma020c
DUFFY, Mary		19	F	Unknown	18Ma020c
KELLY, M.		20	M	Unknown	18Ma020c
CONNELY, Mary		34	F	Unknown	18Ma020c
MCGALLY, J.		25	M	Unknown	18Ma020c
Biddy		46	F	Unknown	18Ma020c
Anne	(D)	06	F	Child	18Ma020c
TROWER, P.		40	M	Unknown	18Ma020c
Mary	(W)	30	F	Unknown	18Ma020c
Cath.	(D)	01	F	Child	18Ma020c
DOREON, D.		18	M	Unknown	18Ma020c
MCCALAGH, P.		18	M	Unknown	18Ma020c
MCCONNER, Peggy		16	F	Unknown	18Ma020c
HERST, F.		16	M	Unknown	18Ma020c
MILARY, Bgt.		20	F	Unknown	18Ma020c
KELLY, Mary		30	F	Unknown	18Ma020c
Cath.		14	F	Unknown	18Ma020c
BOYD, J.		24	M	Unknown	18Ma020c
GALLEN, J.		40	M	Unknown	18Ma020c
Mary	(W)	35	F	Unknown	18Ma020c
Ellen	(D)	02	F	Child	18Ma020c

DOWNS 19 MAY 1847

From Waterford

NAMES OF PASSENGERS		AGE	SEX	OCCUPATIONS	DATE PORT SHIP
FITZGERALD, Jas.		30	M	Farmer	19Ma16Pn
ROE, David		32	M	Farmer	19Ma16Pn
MORAN, Richard		24	M	Farmer	19Ma16Pn
GALVANN, John		26	M	Farmer	19Ma16Pn
Mary		19	F	Unknown	19Ma16Pn
John		18	M	Farmer	19Ma16Pn
LAURENCE, John		20	M	Farmer	19Ma16Pn
HENRY, William		22	M	Farmer	19Ma16Pn
MCGRATH, John		25	M	Farmer	19Ma16Pn
DUGGAN, Patrick		20	M	Farmer	19Ma16Pn
CONWAY, Patrick		20	M	Farmer	19Ma16Pn
POWER, John		31	M	Farmer	19Ma16Pn
Michael		20	M	Farmer	19Ma16Pn
Mary		15	F	Unknown	19Ma16Pn
MCDONALD, Alex.		00	M	Farmer	19Ma16Pn
MORAN, John		21	M	Farmer	19Ma16Pn
TORCHAM, John		21	M	Farmer	19Ma16Pn
READY, John		20	M	Farmer	19Ma16Pn
HEARNAN, Thomas		19	M	Farmer	19Ma16Pn
DORDY, Alice		18	F	Unknown	19Ma16Pn
FALEN, Patrick		21	M	Farmer	19Ma16Pn
CROTHEY, Danl.		22	M	Farmer	19Ma16Pn
HART, Laurence		28	M	Farmer	19Ma16Pn
SHEA, Walt.		24	M	Farmer	19Ma16Pn
SANCHER, Michael		23	M	Farmer	19Ma16Pn
LEARY, Mary		20	F	Unknown	19Ma16Pn
HARRINGTON, Mchl.		19	M	Farmer	19Ma16Pn
MURPHY, James		21	M	Farmer	19Ma16Pn
RYAN, Bridget		20	F	Unknown	19Ma16Pn
CASHIN, John		23	M	Farmer	19Ma16Pn
WALSH, Edmond		24	M	Farmer	19Ma16Pn
MENGUNN, William		29	M	Farmer	19Ma16Pn
BRYAN, Patrick		20	M	Farmer	19Ma16Pn
POWERS, Thomas		28	M	Farmer	19Ma16Pn
CAUGHLIN, Jas.		30	M	Farmer	19Ma16Pn
Mary	(W)	28	F	Wife	19Ma16Pn
Judith	(D)	07	F	Child	19Ma16Pn
Catherine	(D)	08	F	Child	19Ma16Pn
BERRY, Mary		20	F	Unknown	19Ma16Pn
John		20	M	Farmer	19Ma16Pn
Michael		20	M	Farmer	19Ma16Pn
Judith		21	F	Unknown	19Ma16Pn
Bridget		26	F	Unknown	19Ma16Pn
DOUGHERTY, Cathe.		29	F	Unknown	19Ma16Pn
LENNALY, Catherine		30	F	Unknown	19Ma16Pn
PENDERGAST, Edw.		21	M	Farmer	19Ma16Pn
BINGHAM, Michl.		19	M	Farmer	19Ma16Pn
BROWN, James		20	M	Farmer	19Ma16Pn
MORISSY, Patt.		19	M	Farmer	19Ma16Pn
WALSH, Anty.		19	M	Farmer	19Ma16Pn
Richd.		18	M	Farmer	19Ma16Pn
Alice		20	F	Unknown	19Ma16Pn
Ellen		26	F	Unknown	19Ma16Pn
MONAGHAN, Biddy		24	F	Unknown	19Ma16Pn
POWER, Patt.		25	M	Farmer	19Ma16Pn
OSHEA, John		30	M	Farmer	19Ma16Pn
DUMPHY, Patt.		28	M	Farmer	19Ma16Pn
OBRIEN, John		20	M	Farmer	19Ma16Pn
BUTLER, John		20	M	Farmer	19Ma16Pn
RYAN, Richard		20	M	Farmer	19Ma16Pn
CORBETT, Mary		22	F	Unknown	19Ma16Pn
WHITE, Thomas		21	M	Farmer	19Ma16Pn
CONNELL, Edward		20	M	Farmer	19Ma16Pn
John		19	M	Farmer	19Ma16Pn
Danl.		20	M	Farmer	19Ma16Pn

NAMES OF PASSENGERS	A G E / E X	A G E	S E X	OCCUPATIONS	DATE PORT SHIP
CONNELL, James		20	M	Farmer	19Ma16Pn
Rose		20	F	Unknown	19Ma16Pn
WHITE, John		20	M	Farmer	19Ma16Pn
Mary		19	F	Unknown	19Ma16Pn
Cathe.		19	F	Unknown	19Ma16Pn
Patt.		12	M	None	19Ma16Pn
FOUNTY, Patt		21	M	Farmer	19Ma16Pn
GREEN, Nancy		22	F	Unknown	19Ma16Pn
BRYAN, James		20	M	Farmer	19Ma16Pn
FLINN, Patt.		20	M	Farmer	19Ma16Pn
POWER, Thomas		20	M	Farmer	19Ma16Pn

COSMO 20 MAY 1847

From Bristol

NAMES OF PASSENGERS	A G E / E X	A G E	S E X	OCCUPATIONS	DATE PORT SHIP
COLE, W.		41	M	Mechanic	20Ma18Ga
Frances	(W)	40	F	Wife	20Ma18Ga
My.	(D)	19	F	None	20Ma18Ga
Ann	(D)	15	F	None	20Ma18Ga
Hellen	(D)	10	F	None	20Ma18Ga
Emily	(D)	09	F	Child	20Ma18Ga
Mgt.	(D)	05	F	Child	20Ma18Ga
GIBBS, J.		29	M	Unknown	20Ma18Ga
Elzt.	(W)	30	F	Wife	20Ma18Ga
Wm.	(S)	09	M	Child	20Ma18Ga
Elzt.	(D)	05	F	Child	20Ma18Ga
John	(S)	03	M	Child	20Ma18Ga
Susan	(D)	01	F	Child	20Ma18Ga
TALLYRAN, T.		27	M	Unknown	20Ma18Ga
Elzbt.		22	F	None	20Ma18Ga
FRY, Htt.		30	F	None	20Ma18Ga
HENNIT, J.		39	M	Unknown	20Ma18Ga
My.	(W)	37	F	Wife	20Ma18Ga
Louise	(D)	07	F	Child	20Ma18Ga
Elzbt.	(T)	28	F	None	20Ma18Ga
TAYLOR, T.		19	M	Unknown	20Ma18Ga
REES, T.		30	M	Unknown	20Ma18Ga
HAMPHION, J.		31	M	Unknown	20Ma18Ga
NIEL, W.		21	M	Unknown	20Ma18Ga
DACHERT, G.		20	M	Unknown	20Ma18Ga
BROWNING, R.		22	M	Unknown	20Ma18Ga
MARSH, R.		28	M	Unknown	20Ma18Ga
CROCKFORD, T.		24	M	Unknown	20Ma18Ga
Jane		06	F	Child	20Ma18Ga
CORCORAN, Mark		21	F	None	20Ma18Ga
MANN, S.		20	M	Unknown	20Ma18Ga
Ann		33	F	None	20Ma18Ga
BARTLETT, J.		34	M	Unknown	20Ma18Ga
Elzt.	(D)	08	F	Child	20Ma18Ga
FORD, Ann		01	F	Child	20Ma18Ga
RICKAN, G.		27	M	Unknown	20Ma18Ga
KITE, C.		18	M	Unknown	20Ma18Ga
BURNETT, G.		21	M	Unknown	20Ma18Ga
WEARITT, D.		35	M	Unknown	20Ma18Ga
Elza.	(W)	36	F	Wife	20Ma18Ga
My.	(D)	13	F	None	20Ma18Ga
WARD, Selina		35	F	None	20Ma18Ga
Wm.	(S)	09	M	Child	20Ma18Ga
HOOP, Ellst.		22	F	None	20Ma18Ga
ALLEN, A.		26	M	Unknown	20Ma18Ga
Fany.	(W)	21	F	Wife	20Ma18Ga
Ann	(D)	04	F	Child	20Ma18Ga
WEECKS, T.		21	M	Laborer	20Ma18Ga
HUDSON, J.		25	M	Unknown	20Ma18Ga
DRINAN, G.		43	M	Unknown	20Ma18Ga
Agnes	(W)	45	F	Wife	20Ma18Ga
Alfred	(S)	21	M	Unknown	20Ma18Ga
George	(S)	17	M	Unknown	20Ma18Ga
DRINAN, Edw.	(S)	11	M	None	20Ma18Ga
RICKAN, E.		17	M	Unknown	20Ma18Ga
Edw.		15	M	Unknown	20Ma18Ga
HUDSON, B.		50	M	Unknown	20Ma18Ga
Hana		40	F	None	20Ma18Ga
BURNS, W.		27	M	Unknown	20Ma18Ga
Harriet	(W)	23	F	Wife	20Ma18Ga
Thos.	(S)	03	M	Child	20Ma18Ga
GRANT, J.		26	M	Unknown	20Ma18Ga
Jas.	(P)	45	M	Unknown	20Ma18Ga
Fany	(M)	46	F	None	20Ma18Ga
MARTIN, W.		26	M	Unknown	20Ma18Ga
Marla		23	F	None	20Ma18Ga
SAGE, G.		31	M	Unknown	20Ma18Ga
My.	(W)	32	F	Wife	20Ma18Ga
Charlotte	(D)	06	F	Child	20Ma18Ga
Henry	(S)	04	M	Child	20Ma18Ga
GOFFY, H.		20	M	Unknown	20Ma18Ga
CLEMENTS, W.		35	M	Unknown	20Ma18Ga
Harriet	(W)	29	F	Wife	20Ma18Ga
Margt.	(D)	08	F	Child	20Ma18Ga
Helen	(D)	05	F	Child	20Ma18Ga
Sarah	(D)	04	F	Child	20Ma18Ga
SHIPTER, C.		26	M	Unknown	20Ma18Ga
Fanny	(W)	30	F	Wife	20Ma18Ga
My.	(D)	01	F	Child	20Ma18Ga
ALEXANDER, J.		23	M	Unknown	20Ma18Ga
Sybell		23	F	None	20Ma18Ga
Walter		20	M	Unknown	20Ma18Ga
Thos.		29	M	Unknown	20Ma18Ga
Barnett		23	M	None	20Ma18Ga
Walter		20	M	Mechanic	20Ma18Ga
Thos.		29	M	Unknown	20Ma18Ga
Harriet		29	F	None	20Ma18Ga
Emma		07	F	Child	20Ma18Ga
Oliver		05	M	Child	20Ma18Ga
Ruth		06	F	Child	20Ma18Ga
LEWIS, W.		36	M	Unknown	20Ma18Ga
My.	(W)	31	F	Wife	20Ma18Ga
Thos.	(S)	08	M	Child	20Ma18Ga
Geog.	(S)	06	M	Child	20Ma18Ga
Jane	(D)	04	F	Child	20Ma18Ga
Edw.	(S)	01	M	Child	20Ma18Ga
FORD, T.		24	M	Unknown	20Ma18Ga
Jane	(W)	24	F	Wife	20Ma18Ga
Arthur	(S)	03	M	Child	20Ma18Ga
Frank	(S)	01	M	Child	20Ma18Ga
BARTON, R.		20	M	Unknown	20Ma18Ga
HUMPHRIES, H.		22	M	Unknown	20Ma18Ga
WOODWARD, J.		25	M	Unknown	20Ma18Ga
Sarah	(W)	28	F	Wife	20Ma18Ga
Leleb	(D)	01	F	Child	20Ma18Ga
COLES, J.		40	M	Unknown	20Ma18Ga
Hannah	(W)	40	F	Wife	20Ma18Ga
Wm.	(S)	15	M	None	20Ma18Ga
Thos.	(S)	07	M	Child	20Ma18Ga
John	(S)	04	M	Child	20Ma18Ga
Caroline	(D)	08	F	Child	20Ma18Ga
ERVAN, N.		36	M	Unknown	20Ma18Ga
Eleanor	(W)	35	F	Wife	20Ma18Ga
Jeremiah	(S)	16	M	Unknown	20Ma18Ga
TURNER, G.		58	M	Unknown	20Ma18Ga
John	(S)	11	M	None	20Ma18Ga
ALLAN, C.		33	M	Unknown	20Ma18Ga
Susana	(W)	39	F	Wife	20Ma18Ga
Alfred	(B)	20	M	Unknown	20Ma18Ga
Stephen	(S)	09	M	Child	20Ma18Ga
Jane	(D)	01	F	Child	20Ma18Ga
BROOKS, Elzt.		20	F	None	20Ma18Ga
HATCH, G.		22	M	Unknown	20Ma18Ga
Richd.		19	M	Unknown	20Ma18Ga
DOWDEN, G.		42	M	Unknown	20Ma18Ga
Elizt.	(W)	42	F	Wife	20Ma18Ga
Selena	(D)	16	F	None	20Ma18Ga
Alfred	(S)	14	M	None	20Ma18Ga

NAMES OF PASSENGERS		AGE	SEX	OCCUPATIONS	DATE PORT SHIP
DOWDEN, Edmn.	(S)	11	M	None	20Ma18Ga
James	(S)	09	M	Child	20Ma18Ga
Geog.	(S)	08	M	Child	20Ma18Ga
Carolan	(D)	05	F	Child	20Ma18Ga
Frans.	(S)	04	M	Child	20Ma18Ga
Fredk.	(S)	02	M	Child	20Ma18Ga
Sarah-A.	(D)	01	F	Child	20Ma18Ga
ALEDONN, E.		38	M	Mechanic	20Ma18Ga
Agnes	(W)	39	F	Wife	20Ma18Ga
Mgt.	(D)	00	N	Wife	20Ma18Ga
Louisa	(D)	07	F	Child	20Ma18Ga
Jas.	(S)	02	M	Child	20Ma18Ga
Jane	(T)	29	F	None	20Ma18Ga
HAGAND, R.		16	M	Unknown	20Ma18Ga
WEEKS, W.		19	M	Unknown	20Ma18Ga
Chas.		17	M	Unknown	20Ma18Ga
John		48	M	Unknown	20Ma18Ga
Ann		30	F	None	20Ma18Ga
Geog.		09	M	Child	20Ma18Ga
Sarah		06	F	Child	20Ma18Ga
TOWNSEND, Elza.		38	F	None	20Ma18Ga
SMITH, S.		24	M	Unknown	20Ma18Ga
SIMMONS, T.		30	M	Unknown	20Ma18Ga
EVANS, J.		19	M	Unknown	20Ma18Ga
GOODHALE, J.		19	M	Unknown	20Ma18Ga
WEEKS, Jane		25	F	None	20Ma18Ga
ANDREWS, R.		45	M	Unknown	20Ma18Ga
Ann	(W)	45	F	Wife	20Ma18Ga
My.A.	(D)	16	F	None	20Ma18Ga
Ema	(D)	15	F	None	20Ma18Ga
Ephea	(D)	14	F	None	20Ma18Ga
Elzbt.	(D)	11	F	None	20Ma18Ga
Emily	(D)	10	F	None	20Ma18Ga
Edm.	(S)	08	M	Child	20Ma18Ga
Erynd.	(S)	06	M	Child	20Ma18Ga
Alex.	(S)	02	M	Child	20Ma18Ga

COMMERCE 20 MAY 1847

From Liverpool

NAMES OF PASSENGERS		AGE	SEX	OCCUPATIONS	DATE PORT SHIP
MAXWELL, Thomas		22	M	Laborer	20Ma02Po
Margt.		20	F	Unknown	20Ma02Po
FINN, James		19	M	Laborer	20Ma02Po
CARROLL, William		17	M	Laborer	20Ma02Po
Philip	(P)	53	M	Laborer	20Ma02Po
FLANAGAN, Michael		17	M	Laborer	20Ma02Po
CONAGAN, Christopher		21	M	Laborer	20Ma02Po
MAGINTRY, Peter		24	M	Laborer	20Ma02Po
JONES, Margaret		18	F	Unknown	20Ma02Po
MCGRA, Patrick		29	M	Laborer	20Ma02Po
LUDLOW, Mary		19	F	Unknown	20Ma02Po
MCMORRNICK, Margt.		17	F	Unknown	20Ma02Po
DONELY, Jas.		21	M	Laborer	20Ma02Po
ROGERS, Hugh		45	M	Laborer	20Ma02Po
Bess	(W)	43	F	Wife	20Ma02Po
Hugh-Jr.	(S)	16	M	Laborer	20Ma02Po
Sarah	(D)	11	F	Unknown	20Ma02Po
James	(S)	09	M	Child	20Ma02Po
LINSKY, John		50	M	Laborer	20Ma02Po
Mary	(W)	45	F	Wife	20Ma02Po
Michl.	(S)	20	M	Laborer	20Ma02Po
Thomas	(S)	16	M	Laborer	20Ma02Po
Peggy	(D)	12	F	Unknown	20Ma02Po
Mary	(D)	10	F	Unknown	20Ma02Po
MURPHY, John		40	M	Laborer	20Ma02Po
Cathe.	(W)	39	F	Wife	20Ma02Po
Patrick	(S)	13	M	Laborer	20Ma02Po
John-Jr.	(S)	11	M	Laborer	20Ma02Po

NAMES OF PASSENGERS		AGE	SEX	OCCUPATIONS	DATE PORT SHIP
MURPHY, Mary	(D)	09	F	Child	20Ma02Po
James	(S)	06	M	Child	20Ma02Po
Hugh	(S)	04	M	Child	20Ma02Po
Thomas	(S)	02	M	Child	20Ma02Po
Mary	(M)	86	F	Unknown	20Ma02Po
SULLIVAN, Jeremiah		20	M	Mechanic	20Ma02Po
James		18	M	Laborer	20Ma02Po
Jeremiah		35	M	Laborer	20Ma02Po
Mary		20	F	Unknown	20Ma02Po
CONNOR, Johanna		17	F	Unknown	20Ma02Po
BRENAN, Catherine		10	F	Unknown	20Ma02Po
MCGUINNIS, Ellen		21	F	Unknown	20Ma02Po
MCGRINNITY, William		17	M	Laborer	20Ma02Po
LEIVY, James		12	M	Laborer	20Ma02Po
FLINN, Mary		20	F	Unknown	20Ma02Po
JOHNSTON, Thos.		18	M	Engineer	20Ma02Po
CASHIN, Daniel		21	M	Laborer	20Ma02Po
HENDON, William		25	M	Laborer	20Ma02Po
CARROLL, Catherine		18	F	Unknown	20Ma02Po

COOLOCK 20 MAY 1847

From London

NAMES OF PASSENGERS		AGE	SEX	OCCUPATIONS	DATE PORT SHIP
MCLEOD, J.		24	M	Farmer	20Ma21Pp
U	(W)	22	F	Wife	20Ma21Pp
SCALY, J.		45	M	Unknown	20Ma21Pp
Cath.	(W)	45	F	Wife	20Ma21Pp
Laurence	(S)	29	M	Unknown	20Ma21Pp
Ann	(D)	19	F	None	20Ma21Pp
KELLY, U		24	F	None	20Ma21Pp
Monika		22	F	None	20Ma21Pp
Mgt.		20	F	None	20Ma21Pp
Eliza		18	F	None	20Ma21Pp
KEARNS, M.		27	M	Unknown	20Ma21Pp
U	(W)	27	F	Wife	20Ma21Pp
Pat	(S)	09	M	Child	20Ma21Pp
Elza.	(D)	04	F	Child	20Ma21Pp
Wm.	(S)	01	M	Child	20Ma21Pp
WRIGHT, Mgt.		15	F	None	20Ma21Pp
BOYD, T.		22	M	Unknown	20Ma21Pp
WARD, U-Mrs.		40	F	None	20Ma21Pp
Anabela	(D)	20	F	None	20Ma21Pp
REILLY, J.		45	M	Unknown	20Ma21Pp
U	(W)	40	F	Wife	20Ma21Pp
Martin	(S)	20	M	Unknown	20Ma21Pp
Michl.	(S)	17	M	Unknown	20Ma21Pp
Winnfd.	(D)	13	F	None	20Ma21Pp
DUFFY, My.		21	F	None	20Ma21Pp
LYNCH, My.		22	F	None	20Ma21Pp
DALY, L.		50	M	Unknown	20Ma21Pp
Garret	(S)	20	M	Unknown	20Ma21Pp
Bgt.	(D)	19	F	None	20Ma21Pp
My.	(D)	14	F	None	20Ma21Pp
Cath.	(D)	13	F	None	20Ma21Pp
Ann	(D)	11	F	None	20Ma21Pp
Mgt.	(D)	09	F	Child	20Ma21Pp
CARTY, Alice		20	F	None	20Ma21Pp
Ann		18	F	None	20Ma21Pp
COONY, R.		24	M	Unknown	20Ma21Pp
SMITH, M.		21	M	Unknown	20Ma21Pp
U	(W)	18	F	Wife	20Ma21Pp
COSTELLO, U-Mrs.		28	F	None	20Ma21Pp
Francis	(D)	11	F	None	20Ma21Pp
HANNLAN, P.		24	F	None	20Ma21Pp
HAMILTON, Hona.		22	F	None	20Ma21Pp
James		20	M	Laborer	20Ma21Pp
FARLY, Honora		24	F	None	20Ma21Pp
REILLY, J.		21	M	Unknown	20Ma21Pp

NAMES OF PASSENGERS		AGE	SEX	OCCUPATIONS	DATE PORT SHIP	NAMES OF PASSENGERS		AGE	SEX	OCCUPATIONS	DATE PORT SHIP
REILLY, Ann		22	F	None	20Ma21Pp	NUGENT, P.		30	M	Farmer	20Ma04Pq
CLARKE, M.		22	M	Unknown	20Ma21Pp	BURNET, F.C.		22	M	Farmer	20Ma04Pq
GILDAY, T.		20	M	Unknown	20Ma21Pp	COOK, T.		38	M	Farmer	20Ma04Pq
BRYAN, P.		46	M	Unknown	20Ma21Pp	Archibald		35	M	Farmer	20Ma04Pq
Ellen	(D)	10	F	None	20Ma21Pp	PORTER, W.		36	M	Farmer	20Ma04Pq
LAME, U-Mrs.		30	F	None	20Ma21Pp	MCINTYRE, N.		60	M	Farmer	20Ma04Pq
HERBERT, Bgt.		22	F	None	20Ma21Pp	Jane	(W)	40	F	Wife	20Ma04Pq
Ann		20	F	None	20Ma21Pp	James	(S)	21	M	Unknown	20Ma04Pq
DELANY, E.		20	M	Unknown	20Ma21Pp	My.J.	(D)	19	F	None	20Ma04Pq
READY, A.P.		25	M	Unknown	20Ma21Pp	Jane	(D)	16	F	None	20Ma04Pq
TANSY, O.		24	M	Unknown	20Ma21Pp	Nathan	(S)	13	M	None	20Ma04Pq
Thos.	(B)	22	M	Unknown	20Ma21Pp	Peggy-A.	(D)	09	F	Child	20Ma04Pq
My.	(M)	60	F	None	20Ma21Pp	Wm.	(S)	05	M	Child	20Ma04Pq
Owen	(B)	16	M	None	20Ma21Pp	MONTGOMERY, C.W.		20	M	Unknown	20Ma04Pq
HIGGINS, Cath.		20	F	None	20Ma21Pp	J.Thos.	(B)	18	M	Unknown	20Ma04Pq
REDDY, M.		20	M	Unknown	20Ma21Pp	Marla	(M)	59	F	None	20Ma04Pq
MCCABE, T.		30	M	Unknown	20Ma21Pp	Jane	(T)	21	F	None	20Ma04Pq
U	(W)	30	F	Wife	20Ma21Pp	MCLAUGHLIN, A.		21	M	Unknown	20Ma04Pq
Mich.	(S)	07	M	Child	20Ma21Pp	Peggy		23	F	None	20Ma04Pq
Ann	(D)	05	F	Child	20Ma21Pp	Martha		34	M	Unknown	20Ma04Pq
James	(S)	03	M	Child	20Ma21Pp	COCHRAN, A.		24	M	Unknown	20Ma04Pq
My.	(D)	01	F	Child	20Ma21Pp	MCCRACKEN, J.		18	M	Unknown	20Ma04Pq
Sally	(D)	13	F	None	20Ma21Pp	ROSS, M.		10	M	None	20Ma04Pq
SOUTHERN, J.		24	M	Unknown	20Ma21Pp	FOSTER, A.		58	M	Unknown	20Ma04Pq
WHELAN, M.		24	M	Unknown	20Ma21Pp	My.	(W)	48	F	Wife	20Ma04Pq
Judy		20	F	None	20Ma21Pp	Arthur	(S)	29	M	Unknown	20Ma04Pq
CLEMENT, C.		20	M	Unknown	20Ma21Pp	My.J.	(D)	30	F	None	20Ma04Pq
GRAHAM, W.		27	M	Unknown	20Ma21Pp	Thos.	(S)	15	M	None	20Ma04Pq
FITZPATRICK, J.		27	M	Unknown	20Ma21Pp	Andrew	(S)	10	M	None	20Ma04Pq
U	(W)	24	F	Wife	20Ma21Pp	Alexn.	(S)	21	M	None	20Ma04Pq
Ellen	(D)	01	F	Child	20Ma21Pp	Elza.	(D)	32	F	None	20Ma04Pq
RYAN, J.		21	M	Unknown	20Ma21Pp	GALVIN, P.		39	M	Unknown	20Ma04Pq
U	(W)	21	F	Wife	20Ma21Pp	FORSYTH, A.		35	M	Unknown	20Ma04Pq
FEE, T.		30	M	None	20Ma21Pp	Isabelle	(D)	09	F	Child	20Ma04Pq
Jane		33	F	None	20Ma21Pp	Elzbt.	(D)	08	F	Child	20Ma04Pq
Alice		20	F	None	20Ma21Pp	Wm.	(S)	06	M	Child	20Ma04Pq
Jane		20	F	None	20Ma21Pp	Mgt.	(D)	04	F	Child	20Ma04Pq
Alice		22	F	None	20Ma21Pp	Isabelle	(D)	01	F	Child	20Ma04Pq
Berl.		06	F	Child	20Ma21Pp	Jessica	(D)	01	F	Child	20Ma04Pq
Eliza		30	F	None	20Ma21Pp	MCALISTER, Jane		60	F	None	20Ma04Pq
Mgt.		25	F	None	20Ma21Pp	John	(S)	22	M	Mechanic	20Ma04Pq
Phelim		26	M	Laborer	20Ma21Pp	James	(S)	19	M	Unknown	20Ma04Pq
Mgt.		28	F	None	20Ma21Pp	Wm.	(S)	17	M	Unknown	20Ma04Pq
James		30	M	Unknown	20Ma21Pp	Jane	(D)	20	F	None	20Ma04Pq
HUNGERFORD, J.		30	M	Unknown	20Ma21Pp	MCLAUGHLIN, J.		17	M	Unknown	20Ma04Pq
M.	(D)	07	F	Child	20Ma21Pp	MURRAY, W.		36	M	Unknown	20Ma04Pq
Ryd.	(S)	06	M	Child	20Ma21Pp	HENRY, Mgt.		35	F	None	20Ma04Pq
Cecilia	(D)	01	F	Child	20Ma21Pp	Wm.	(S)	12	M	None	20Ma04Pq
Jonathan		25	M	Unknown	20Ma21Pp	Theresa	(D)	04	F	Child	20Ma04Pq
Richd.	(S)	09	M	Child	20Ma21Pp	Mgt.	(D)	01	F	Child	20Ma04Pq
James		20	M	Unknown	20Ma21Pp	CHARLES, J.		30	M	Unknown	20Ma04Pq
Jane	(W)	35	F	Wife	20Ma21Pp	Sara		30	F	None	20Ma04Pq
PEARSON, A.		32	M	Unknown	20Ma21Pp	GREG, J.		28	M	Unknown	20Ma04Pq
Jane		35	F	None	20Ma21Pp	FAIRBANKS, G.		20	M	Unknown	20Ma04Pq
Ann		20	F	None	20Ma21Pp	KANE, J.		35	M	Unknown	20Ma04Pq
John		13	M	None	20Ma21Pp	REYNOLDS, W.		60	M	Unknown	20Ma04Pq
Marth.		10	F	None	20Ma21Pp	DERMOTT, M.		42	M	Unknown	20Ma04Pq
Thos.		09	M	Child	20Ma21Pp	HARKIN, M.		19	M	Unknown	20Ma04Pq
My.		05	F	Child	20Ma21Pp	BURNSIDE, J.		26	M	Unknown	20Ma04Pq
Alexn.		01	M	Child	20Ma21Pp	MCQUAY, B.		26	M	Unknown	20Ma04Pq
JACKSON, R.		46	M	Unknown	20Ma21Pp	Sally	(W)	26	F	Wife	20Ma04Pq
Jane		40	F	None	20Ma21Pp	Mgt.	(D)	01	F	Child	20Ma04Pq
						MCMULLEN, C.		54	M	Unknown	20Ma04Pq
						Ann	(W)	44	F	Wife	20Ma04Pq
EMBLEM 20 MAY 1847						Mgt.	(D)	22	F	None	20Ma04Pq
						Ann	(D)	20	F	None	20Ma04Pq
From Glasgow						Susan	(D)	11	F	None	20Ma04Pq
						John	(S)	09	M	Child	20Ma04Pq
						Patrick	(S)	02	M	Child	20Ma04Pq
						LAVERTY, F.		50	M	Unknown	20Ma04Pq
						Jane	(D)	17	F	None	20Ma04Pq
						Susan	(D)	14	F	None	20Ma04Pq
						Ellen	(D)	12	F	None	20Ma04Pq
EDWARDS, J.		35	M	Farmer	20Ma04Pq	John	(S)	04	M	Child	20Ma04Pq
HOOD, R.		25	M	Farmer	20Ma04Pq	Sarah	(D)	01	F	Child	20Ma04Pq

523

NAMES OF PASSENGERS		AGE	SEX	OCCUPATIONS	DATE PORT SHIP
MCGEE, A.		20	M	Unknown	20Ma04Pq
Mgt.	(W)	50	F	None	20Ma04Pq
GALLOCHER, J.		25	M	Unknown	20Ma04Pq
ODONNELL, J.		20	M	Unknown	20Ma04Pq
WATT, J.		30	M	Unknown	20Ma04Pq
Eliza		26	F	None	20Ma04Pq
Thos.	(S)	06	M	Child	20Ma04Pq
John	(S)	03	M	Child	20Ma04Pq
MCINTYRE, D.		20	M	Laborer	20Ma04Pq
GRADY, Jane		22	F	None	20Ma04Pq
MCFADGEN, J.		40	M	Unknown	20Ma04Pq
Cath.	(W)	33	F	Wife	20Ma04Pq
Jas.	(S)	06	M	Child	20Ma04Pq
Wm.	(S)	02	M	Child	20Ma04Pq
Rose	(T)	22	F	None	20Ma04Pq
MONTGOMERY, Grace		18	F	None	20Ma04Pq
QUIN, J.		26	M	Unknown	20Ma04Pq
MCCAY, J.		23	M	Unknown	20Ma04Pq
Ellz.		15	F	None	20Ma04Pq
LAVERTY, J.		20	M	Mechanic	20Ma04Pq
BOYER, D.		28	M	Unknown	20Ma04Pq
ROSS, H.		25	M	Unknown	20Ma04Pq
HENNESSY, J.		30	M	Unknown	20Ma04Pq
GALLACHER, M.		33	M	Unknown	20Ma04Pq
Nelly	(W)	30	F	Wife	20Ma04Pq
Patch	(S)	01	M	Child	20Ma04Pq
MCLANY, Pegg.		20	F	None	20Ma04Pq
MCMURRY, D.		50	M	Unknown	20Ma04Pq
BOYD, J.		34	M	Unknown	20Ma04Pq
Rachel	(W)	30	F	Wife	20Ma04Pq
Elzt.	(D)	07	F	Child	20Ma04Pq
Wm.	(S)	05	M	Child	20Ma04Pq
Jane	(D)	03	F	Child	20Ma04Pq
James	(S)	01	M	Child	20Ma04Pq
CHESNUT, W.		21	M	Unknown	20Ma04Pq
STEVENSON, J.		24	M	Unknown	20Ma04Pq
PATERSON, T.		22	M	Unknown	20Ma04Pq
MCQUINN, J.		21	M	Unknown	20Ma04Pq
MCILLENN, W.		50	M	Unknown	20Ma04Pq
Rodger	(S)	30	M	Unknown	20Ma04Pq
Mgt.	(D)	28	F	None	20Ma04Pq
Nell	(S)	26	M	Unknown	20Ma04Pq
Hannah	(D)	24	F	None	20Ma04Pq
Wm.	(S)	22	M	Unknown	20Ma04Pq
Saml.	(S)	20	M	Unknown	20Ma04Pq
My.	(D)	18	F	None	20Ma04Pq
John	(S)	16	M	Unknown	20Ma04Pq
MCBRIDE, P.		25	M	Unknown	20Ma04Pq
Wm.	(S)	01	M	Child	20Ma04Pq
COLGARHAN, J.		19	M	Unknown	20Ma04Pq
Elzt.		10	F	None	20Ma04Pq
Sarah-J.		13	M	None	20Ma04Pq
MCFALLEN, W.		21	M	Unknown	20Ma04Pq
Janet		22	F	None	20Ma04Pq
SMITH, J.		42	M	Unknown	20Ma04Pq
Ellen		49	F	None	20Ma04Pq
YOUNGER, G.		19	M	Unknown	20Ma04Pq
MCGUNTY, H.		30	M	Unknown	20Ma04Pq
Nan.	(W)	25	F	Wife	20Ma04Pq
Jane	(D)	03	F	Child	20Ma04Pq
Fay	(D)	02	F	Child	20Ma04Pq
BOYLE, Nancy		20	F	None	20Ma04Pq
HAGERTY, Eliza		16	F	None	20Ma04Pq
YOUNG, A.		24	M	Laborer	20Ma04Pq
MCNEIL, S.		24	M	Laborer	20Ma04Pq
THOMSON, J.		20	M	Laborer	20Ma04Pq
LITTLE, T.		23	M	Laborer	20Ma04Pq
Ellen	(W)	27	F	Wife	20Ma04Pq
Rebecca	(D)	01	F	Child	20Ma04Pq
DOCKERTY, M.		30	M	Unknown	20Ma04Pq
MCCONNEL, W.		20	M	Unknown	20Ma04Pq
BRONNLLY, My.		18	F	None	20Ma04Pq
MCKINLY, J.		25	M	Unknown	20Ma04Pq
MCGREADY, H.		50	M	Unknown	20Ma04Pq
Fany	(W)	56	F	Wife	20Ma04Pq
MCGREADY, John	(S)	24	M	None	20Ma04Pq
Thos.	(S)	22	M	None	20Ma04Pq
Saml.	(S)	20	M	None	20Ma04Pq
Robt.	(S)	18	M	None	20Ma04Pq
Francis	(S)	17	M	None	20Ma04Pq
MACDERMOT, J.		17	M	None	20Ma04Pq
Eleanor		30	F	None	20Ma04Pq
Fany		26	F	None	20Ma04Pq
Alexn.		02	M	Child	20Ma04Pq
John		05	M	Child	20Ma04Pq
KILPATRICK, J.		19	M	Unknown	20Ma04Pq
John	(P)	63	M	Unknown	20Ma04Pq
Jane	(M)	60	F	None	20Ma04Pq
Gear.	(B)	31	M	Unknown	20Ma04Pq
Sarah	(T)	28	F	None	20Ma04Pq
John	(N)	10	M	None	20Ma04Pq
Gery.	(N)	06	M	Child	20Ma04Pq
James	(N)	06	M	Child	20Ma04Pq
My.J.	(N)	03	F	Child	20Ma04Pq
STUART, A.		35	M	Unknown	20Ma04Pq
Amelia	(W)	34	F	Wife	20Ma04Pq
Ezekiel	(S)	12	M	Wife	20Ma04Pq
Mgt.J.	(D)	10	F	None	20Ma04Pq
Amea.	(D)	07	F	Child	20Ma04Pq
Saml.	(S)	05	M	Child	20Ma04Pq
Addn.	(S)	03	M	Child	20Ma04Pq
Rebeca	(D)	01	F	Child	20Ma04Pq
MCKINLY, B.		21	M	Unknown	20Ma04Pq
BLAIR, A.		30	M	Farmer	20Ma04Pq
Mgt.	(W)	30	F	Wife	20Ma04Pq
Robt.	(S)	09	M	Child	20Ma04Pq
Je.	(S)	07	M	Child	20Ma04Pq
My.	(D)	04	F	Child	20Ma04Pq
MCALLISTER, C.		60	M	Unknown	20Ma04Pq
My.	(W)	58	F	Wife	20Ma04Pq
John	(S)	20	M	Unknown	20Ma04Pq
Nelly	(D)	17	F	None	20Ma04Pq
John	(S)	25	M	Unknown	20Ma04Pq
MCLAUGHLIN, A.		22	M	Unknown	20Ma04Pq
Neal		18	M	Unknown	20Ma04Pq
HAZELTON, J.		60	M	Unknown	20Ma04Pq
Bertha	(W)	50	F	Wife	20:Ma04Pq
Thos.	(S)	29	M	Unknown	20Ma04Pq
Alice	(D)	22	F	None	20Ma04Pq
Eliza	(D)	15	F	None	20Ma04Pq
PETERKIN, A.		29	M	Unknown	20Ma04Pq
TAIT, Sarah		30	F	None	20Ma04Pq
James	(S)	07	M	Child	20Ma04Pq
Martha	(D)	07	F	Child	20Ma04Pq
Martha	(D)	05	F	Child	20Ma04Pq
Stuart	(S)	03	M	Child	20Ma04Pq
WILKIN, Sara		31	F	None	20Ma04Pq
Saml.A.	(S)	09	M	Child	20Ma04Pq
Johnston	(S)	06	M	Child	20Ma04Pq
David	(S)	04	M	Child	20Ma04Pq
My.J.	(D)	03	F	Child	20Ma04Pq
Robt.	(S)	01	M	Child	20Ma04Pq
MCGEEHAN, W.		52	M	Unknown	20Ma04Pq
Cath.	(W)	50	F	Wife	20Ma04Pq
Biddy	(D)	15	F	None	20Ma04Pq
Mary	(D)	12	F	None	20Ma04Pq
My.	(D)	10	F	None	20Ma04Pq
Wm.	(S)	08	M	Child	20Ma04Pq
DITTON, J.		25	M	Unknown	20Ma04Pq
MCCAY, H.		30	M	Unknown	20Ma04Pq
GILLAM, H.		18	M	Unknown	20Ma04Pq
My.		19	F	None	20Ma04Pq
ADAMS, J.		32	M	Unknown	20Ma04Pq
My.		30	F	None	20Ma04Pq
CANNON, J.		28	M	Unknown	20Ma04Pq

LONDON 21 MAY 1847

From London

NAMES OF PASSENGERS		AGE	SEX	OCCUPATIONS	DATE PORT SHIP
WHELAN, Mgt.		25	F	None	21Ma21Pr
BOYLE, My.		25	F	None	21Ma21Pr
John		24	M	Laborer	21Ma21Pr
HOGAN, Julia		24	F	None	21Ma21Pr
DAVIDSON, S.		30	M	Unknown	21Ma21Pr
Elizabeth	(W)	25	F	Wife	21Ma21Pr
John	(S)	04	M	Child	21Ma21Pr
Eliza	(D)	03	F	Child	21Ma21Pr
Essy	(D)	01	F	Child	21Ma21Pr
MCCAULY, J.		56	M	Unknown	21Ma21Pr
Eliza	(W)	56	F	Wife	21Ma21Pr
My.A.	(D)	25	F	None	21Ma21Pr
Mgt.	(D)	23	F	None	21Ma21Pr
George	(S)	19	M	Unknown	21Ma21Pr
John	(S)	17	M	Unknown	21Ma21Pr
Wm.	(S)	13	M	None	21Ma21Pr
WILSON, J.		40	M	Unknown	21Ma21Pr
James	(S)	14	M	None	21Ma21Pr
Jane	(W)	35	F	Wife	21Ma21Pr
My.J.	(D)	12	F	None	21Ma21Pr
Sarah	(D)	10	F	None	21Ma21Pr
John	(S)	08	M	Child	21Ma21Pr
Martin	(S)	06	M	Child	21Ma21Pr
Robt.	(S)	04	M	Child	21Ma21Pr
CORBIT, J.		36	M	Unknown	21Ma21Pr
Sarah-A.		36	F	None	21Ma21Pr
MCGAZZAHER, G.		20	M	Unknown	21Ma21Pr
Jane		21	F	None	21Ma21Pr
BEAHAN, J.		17	M	Unknown	21Ma21Pr
BOLEYD, J.		27	M	Unknown	21Ma21Pr
Jane	(W)	25	F	Wife	21Ma21Pr
Moses	(S)	07	M	Child	21Ma21Pr
My.	(D)	05	F	Child	21Ma21Pr
Mgt.	(D)	02	F	Child	21Ma21Pr
MCCONELL, D.		25	M	Unknown	21Ma21Pr
Agnes	(W)	25	F	Wife	21Ma21Pr
Robt.	(S)	01	M	Child	21Ma21Pr
GALWIN, J.		30	M	Unknown	21Ma21Pr
STEVENSON, Bgt.		20	F	None	21Ma21Pr
CASEY, E.		21	M	Unknown	21Ma21Pr
Sarah		20	F	None	21Ma21Pr
WALSH, Bgt.		10	F	None	21Ma21Pr
ROGERSON, H.		19	M	Laborer	21Ma21Pr
MORROW, F.		25	M	Unknown	21Ma21Pr
ADAMS, J.		58	M	Unknown	21Ma21Pr
My.		40	F	None	21Ma21Pr
HOGAN, M.		35	M	Unknown	21Ma21Pr
Daniel		24	M	Unknown	21Ma21Pr
NOWLAND, J.		55	M	Unknown	21Ma21Pr
DEMPSEY, M.		23	M	Unknown	21Ma21Pr
MANN, Sarah		20	F	None	21Ma21Pr
ROXBURY, Sarah		11	F	None	21Ma21Pr
EGAN, M.		55	M	Unknown	21Ma21Pr
Nelly	(W)	50	F	Wife	21Ma21Pr
Mich.	(S)	20	M	Unknown	21Ma21Pr
Cath.	(D)	21	F	None	21Ma21Pr
Edward	(B)	60	M	Unknown	21Ma21Pr
Bgt.	(D)	22	F	None	21Ma21Pr
HOURGAN, J.		20	F	None	21Ma21Pr
WALSH, A.		50	M	Unknown	21Ma21Pr
My.	(W)	48	F	Wife	21Ma21Pr
My.	(D)	16	F	None	21Ma21Pr
QUIN, P.		24	M	Unknown	21Ma21Pr
MCLANE, Cath.		21	F	None	21Ma21Pr
OHARA, My.		09	F	Child	21Ma21Pr
OHARA, John		07	M	Child	21Ma21Pr
GREEN, Anastasia		20	F	None	21Ma21Pr
HURLY, Maria		21	F	None	21Ma21Pr
Anne		19	F	None	21Ma21Pr
HAGAN, P.		26	M	Unknown	21Ma21Pr
Martin	(S)	01	M	Child	21Ma21Pr
WALSH, M.		06	M	Child	21Ma21Pr
Sarah		04	F	Child	21Ma21Pr
Ellen		02	F	Child	21Ma21Pr
DOWDAL, J.		22	M	Unknown	21Ma21Pr
NEWALL, My.		20	F	None	21Ma21Pr
FITZPATRICK, Eliza		20	F	None	21Ma21Pr
CRAYTON, J.		36	M	Unknown	21Ma21Pr
MURPHY, Alice		19	F	None	21Ma21Pr
LYNCH, M.		25	M	Unknown	21Ma21Pr
Owen		21	M	Unknown	21Ma21Pr
MCKITTRICK, J.		22	M	Unknown	21Ma21Pr
GORNLY, Ann		24	F	None	21Ma21Pr
MORAN, J.		21	M	Laborer	21Ma21Pr
HANILY, C.		20	F	None	21Ma21Pr
Ellen		20	F	None	21Ma21Pr
Ellen		05	F	Child	21Ma21Pr
Ellen		03	F	Child	21Ma21Pr
MANN, Alice		20	F	None	21Ma21Pr
SULLIVAN, T.		22	M	Unknown	21Ma21Pr
Judith	(W)	20	F	Wife	21Ma21Pr
Cath.	(D)	07	F	Child	21Ma21Pr
GLYNN, P.		30	M	Unknown	21Ma21Pr
Mich.		29	M	Unknown	21Ma21Pr
Rosey		07	M	Child	21Ma21Pr
QUIN, J.		20	M	Unknown	21Ma21Pr
LYON, B.		22	M	Unknown	21Ma21Pr
SPELMAN, E.		19	M	Unknown	21Ma21Pr
CUNIFF, M.		20	M	Unknown	21Ma21Pr
LYONS, T.		19	M	Unknown	21Ma21Pr
FLYNN, M.		26	M	Unknown	21Ma21Pr
HAUGH, J.		24	M	Unknown	21Ma21Pr
CONWADDY, J.		25	M	Unknown	21Ma21Pr
CROWE, M.		27	M	Unknown	21Ma21Pr
QUINLAN, J.		24	M	Unknown	21Ma21Pr
COSTELLO, M.		22	M	Unknown	21Ma21Pr
TILLIS, P.		24	M	Unknown	21Ma21Pr
MCMAHON, My.		17	F	None	21Ma21Pr
Peggy		19	F	None	21Ma21Pr
HURLY, D.		50	M	Unknown	21Ma21Pr
Patch	(S)	09	M	Child	21Ma21Pr
My.	(D)	06	F	Child	21Ma21Pr
LACEY, J.		47	M	Unknown	21Ma21Pr
My.	(M)	62	F	None	21Ma21Pr
Saml.	(S)	12	M	None	21Ma21Pr
John	(S)	10	M	None	21Ma21Pr
Hugh	(S)	08	M	Child	21Ma21Pr
Ann	(D)	06	F	Child	21Ma21Pr
My.	(D)	04	F	Child	21Ma21Pr
James	(S)	02	M	Child	21Ma21Pr
Mich.	(S)	01	M	Child	21Ma21Pr
SCOTT, S.		00	M	None	21Ma21Pr
MATTHEWS, J.		13	M	None	21Ma21Pr
Isabella		11	F	None	21Ma21Pr
MCCORMICK, T.		26	M	None	21Ma21Pr
MCCONNEL, U-Mrs.		23	F	None	21Ma21Pr
Ann	(D)	01	F	Child	21Ma21Pr
MATTESON, J.		24	M	Laborer	21Ma21Pr
GALLAGHER, Cath.		30	F	None	21Ma21Pr
My.		20	F	None	21Ma21Pr
Hugh		20	M	Unknown	21Ma21Pr
Chas.		18	M	Unknown	21Ma21Pr
HALPEN, T.		22	M	Unknown	21Ma21Pr
FLANAGAN, T.		18	M	Unknown	21Ma21Pr
DUNOVAN, J.		10	M	None	21Ma21Pr

SEA-KING 21 MAY 1847

From Belfast

NAMES OF PASSENGERS		AGE	SEX	OCCUPATIONS	DATE PORT SHIP
MCAVERY, P.		24	M	Laborer	21Ma07Df
CASEY, O.		25	M	Laborer	21Ma07Df
Ann	(W)	20	F	Wife	21Ma07Df
U	(D)	01	F	Child	21Ma07Df
SHOULAN, My.		20	F	None	21Ma07Df
MCCARRY, M.		23	M	Unknown	21Ma07Df
MURPHY, D.		30	M	Unknown	21Ma07Df
CONNOR, G.		25	M	Unknown	21Ma07Df
BYRNES, O.		50	M	Unknown	21Ma07Df
FELY, D.		27	M	Unknown	21Ma07Df
Mgt.	(W)	23	F	Wife	21Ma07Df
U	(S)	01	M	Child	21Ma07Df
BYRNS, My.		18	F	None	21Ma07Df
Patt.		12	M	None	21Ma07Df
Bart.		10	F	None	21Ma07Df
Rose		08	F	Child	21Ma07Df
Cath.		06	F	Child	21Ma07Df
My.		01	F	Child	21Ma07Df
FEHELY, J.		18	M	Unknown	21Ma07Df
HANLY, M.		20	M	Unknown	21Ma07Df
DONNELL, J.		23	M	Unknown	21Ma07Df
WATSON, T.		27	M	Unknown	21Ma07Df
QUIN, W.		26	M	Unknown	21Ma07Df
Eliza		24	F	None	21Ma07Df
GRIFFIN, Cath.		40	F	None	21Ma07Df
MILDON, P.		35	M	Unknown	21Ma07Df
CASSEDY, J.		07	M	Child	21Ma07Df
MULDON, T.		21	M	Unknown	21Ma07Df
DOLAN, T.		21	M	Unknown	21Ma07Df
Mgt.	(D)	01	F	Child	21Ma07Df
MCGRATH, R.		24	M	Unknown	21Ma07Df
Ann		20	F	None	21Ma07Df
Cath.	(M)	50	F	None	21Ma07Df
DOLAN, T.		25	M	Unknown	21Ma07Df
MCGOVERN, O.		21	M	Unknown	21Ma07Df
SCOTT, J.		26	M	Unknown	21Ma07Df
MCCORMICK, T.		26	M	Unknown	21Ma07Df
U	(W)	23	F	Wife	21Ma07Df
Ann	(D)	01	F	Child	21Ma07Df
KEOWN, T.		28	M	Unknown	21Ma07Df
Eliza	(W)	28	F	Wife	21Ma07Df
H.	(S)	04	M	Child	21Ma07Df
Edmn.	(S)	02	M	Child	21Ma07Df
Francis	(S)	01	M	Child	21Ma07Df
Susan	(T)	26	F	None	21Ma07Df
POLLOCK, Hester		26	F	None	21Ma07Df
Jane		26	F	None	21Ma07Df
SILCOX, Carla		26	F	None	21Ma07Df
Francis	(H)	27	M	Laborer	21Ma07Df
My.J.	(D)	06	F	Child	21Ma07Df
Henry	(S)	04	M	Child	21Ma07Df
Thos.	(S)	02	M	Child	21Ma07Df
DURNAN, W.		30	M	Unknown	21Ma07Df
Cath.		30	F	None	21Ma07Df
Mgt.		30	F	None	21Ma07Df
My.		20	F	None	21Ma07Df
DOWD, W.		21	M	Unknown	21Ma07Df
Mgt.		18	F	None	21Ma07Df
Magt.		04	F	Child	21Ma07Df
ROLLAND, E.M.		26	M	Unknown	21Ma07Df
Bdgt.	(W)	26	F	Wife	21Ma07Df
Bdgt.	(D)	12	F	Wife	21Ma07Df
My.	(D)	07	F	Child	21Ma07Df
Patt.	(S)	04	M	Child	21Ma07Df
Ann	(D)	02	F	Child	21Ma07Df

NAMES OF PASSENGERS		AGE	SEX	OCCUPATIONS	DATE PORT SHIP
DOWNY, P.		02	M	Unknown	21Ma07Df
MCCANN, J.		23	M	Unknown	21Ma07Df
Jane		30	F	None	21Ma07Df
KAFFERTY, A.		25	M	Unknown	21Ma07Df
U	(W)	24	F	Wife	21Ma07Df
Patt.	(S)	01	M	Child	21Ma07Df
KAFFEKY, A.		20	M	Unknown	21Ma07Df
BRYAN, K.		20	M	Unknown	21Ma07Df
Lu-T.		20	M	Unknown	21Ma07Df
Bgt.		20	F	None	21Ma07Df
Judy		20	F	None	21Ma07Df
PHELAN, T.		20	M	Unknown	21Ma07Df
CASEY, J.		20	M	Unknown	21Ma07Df
CASHILL, J.		20	M	Unknown	21Ma07Df
HEANS, Cath.		22	M	Unknown	21Ma07Df
KENNEDY, J.		32	M	Unknown	21Ma07Df
LYNCH, M.		28	M	Unknown	21Ma07Df
DENPY, Bgt.		20	F	None	21Ma07Df
GILMERS, J.		18	M	Laborer	21Ma07Df
SLATE, A.		35	M	Unknown	21Ma07Df
U	(W)	30	F	Wife	21Ma07Df
James	(S)	04	M	Child	21Ma07Df
MOKINS, Ellen		20	F	None	21Ma07Df
MCFADDEN, Ellen		18	F	None	21Ma07Df
BIOTY, S.		16	M	Unknown	21Ma07Df
KEANNEN, P.		26	M	Unknown	21Ma07Df
Rose		15	F	None	21Ma07Df
Bgt.		13	F	None	21Ma07Df
MURPHY, J.		39	M	Unknown	21Ma07Df
Biddy	(W)	38	F	Wife	21Ma07Df
Ann	(D)	12	F	None	21Ma07Df
Jane	(D)	10	F	None	21Ma07Df
Jno.	(S)	08	M	Child	21Ma07Df
Sam	(S)	06	M	Child	21Ma07Df
Alice	(D)	04	F	Child	21Ma07Df
Emily	(D)	02	F	Child	21Ma07Df
Judy	(D)	01	F	Child	21Ma07Df
SHOGRUES, Julia		32	F	None	21Ma07Df
Saml.	(S)	09	M	Child	21Ma07Df
James	(S)	07	M	Child	21Ma07Df
Ann	(D)	05	F	Child	21Ma07Df
Jno.	(S)	03	M	Child	21Ma07Df
MURPHY, Ellen		25	F	None	21Ma07Df
Mgt.	(D)	02	F	Child	21Ma07Df
Thos.	(S)	01	M	Child	21Ma07Df
LEONCROFT, J.		25	M	Unknown	21Ma07Df
ALLEN, R.		30	M	Unknown	21Ma07Df
Danl.		23	M	Unknown	21Ma07Df
RYAN, W.		46	M	Unknown	21Ma07Df
Thos.	(S)	23	M	Unknown	21Ma07Df
Mgt.	(D)	21	F	None	21Ma07Df
Ellen	(D)	15	F	None	21Ma07Df
FITZGERALD, M.		32	M	Unknown	21Ma07Df
Mary	(W)	32	F	Wife	21Ma07Df
Jno.	(B)	27	M	Unknown	21Ma07Df
Thos.	(S)	03	M	Child	21Ma07Df
CONNOR, M.		30	M	Unknown	21Ma07Df
Ally		30	F	None	21Ma07Df
LOWRY, R.		24	M	Unknown	21Ma07Df
HUGHES, J.		27	M	Laborer	21Ma07Df
Cath.		22	F	None	21Ma07Df
GARGARTY, T.		30	M	Unknown	21Ma07Df
KILBRIDE, H.		32	M	Unknown	21Ma07Df
Cath.	(W)	27	F	Wife	21Ma07Df
Patt	(S)	08	M	Child	21Ma07Df
Bgt.	(D)	06	F	Child	21Ma07Df
Cath.	(D)	04	F	Child	21Ma07Df
Ann	(D)	02	F	Child	21Ma07Df
KILCRANE, P.		08	M	Child	21Ma07Df
Bessy	(B)	25	F	None	21Ma07Df
LADEN, J.		21	M	Unknown	21Ma07Df
KILKENNY, Ann		05	F	Child	21Ma07Df
Biddy		03	F	Child	21Ma07Df
Daniel		02	M	Child	21Ma07Df

NAMES OF PASSENGERS		AGE	SEX	OCCUPATIONS	DATE PORT SHIP
KILKENNY, Chas.		01	M	Child	21Ma07Df
CORSON, W.		35	M	Unknown	21Ma07Df
DEVINE, D.		30	M	Unknown	21Ma07Df
FITZGERALD, M.		19	M	Unknown	21Ma07Df
Richd.		17	M	Unknown	21Ma07Df
Mgt.		17	F	None	21Ma07Df
BOWER, A.		19	M	Unknown	21Ma07Df
CANTON, B.		24	M	Unknown	21Ma07Df
Jane		22	F	None	21Ma07Df
My.		21	F	None	21Ma07Df
BURK, Cath.		24	F	None	21Ma07Df
CLARK, A.		30	M	Unknown	21Ma07Df
MULLEN, My.		20	F	None	21Ma07Df
TIERNAN, O.M.		21	M	Unknown	21Ma07Df
Mgt.		01	F	None	21Ma07Df
BUSSEL, Cath.		20	F	None	21Ma07Df
ROWE, T.		25	M	Unknown	21Ma07Df
Biddy		20	F	None	21Ma07Df
Maria		35	F	None	21Ma07Df
BENNETT, W.		22	F	None	21Ma07Df
Jane		17	F	None	21Ma07Df
James		20	M	Unknown	21Ma07Df
RYAN, Bgt.		36	F	None	21Ma07Df
Cath.	(D)	28	F	None	21Ma07Df
My.	(D)	21	F	None	21Ma07Df
Mgt.	(D)	15	F	None	21Ma07Df
MATTHEWS, Mgt.		19	F	None	21Ma07Df
BURKE, T.		22	M	Laborer	21Ma07Df
HANLON, B.		18	M	Unknown	21Ma07Df
CONNOR, Ellen		19	F	None	21Ma07Df
Path.		17	M	Unknown	21Ma07Df
DANIEL, J.		19	M	Unknown	21Ma07Df
BYRNE, P.		30	M	Unknown	21Ma07Df
Bridget	(W)	25	F	Wife	21Ma07Df
My.A.	(D)	03	F	Child	21Ma07Df
ROACH, P.		20	M	Unknown	21Ma07Df
HEATHRIGHT, C.		20	M	Unknown	21Ma07Df
MITCHELL, Ann		24	F	None	21Ma07Df
Thos.	(B)	35	M	Unknown	21Ma07Df
U	(L)	30	F	Wife	21Ma07Df
BYRNES, M.		12	M	None	21Ma07Df
Michl.		03	M	Child	21Ma07Df
PARKER, T.		26	M	Unknown	21Ma07Df
Jessy	(W)	24	F	Wife	21Ma07Df
My.	(D)	03	F	Child	21Ma07Df
Eliza	(D)	01	F	Child	21Ma07Df
GRANT, J.		40	M	Unknown	21Ma07Df
Elizbt.	(W)	40	F	Wife	21Ma07Df
James	(S)	09	M	Child	21Ma07Df
Wm.	(B)	29	M	Unknown	21Ma07Df
Laurence	(S)	19	M	Unknown	21Ma07Df
Ann	(D)	19	F	None	21Ma07Df
CASSIDY, Ann		22	F	None	21Ma07Df
MORAN, J.		35	M	Unknown	21Ma07Df
Eliza		30	F	None	21Ma07Df
EAGAN, Mgt.		20	F	None	21Ma07Df
MCMURRY, B.		30	M	Unknown	21Ma07Df
Mary	(W)	28	F	Wife	21Ma07Df
My.	(D)	03	F	Child	21Ma07Df
Cath.	(D)	01	F	Child	21Ma07Df
MURPHY, E.		27	M	Unknown	21Ma07Df
EAGAN, M.		18	M	Unknown	21Ma07Df
MITCHELL, D.		08	M	Child	21Ma07Df
Thos.	(P)	35	M	Unknown	21Ma07Df
U	(M)	30	F	Wife	21Ma07Df
TENAN, Bgt.M.		17	F	None	21Ma07Df
Mar		16	F	None	21Ma07Df
SLOWEY, H.		17	M	Unknown	21Ma07Df
GUN, E.		30	M	Unknown	21Ma07Df
KEYS, Martha		17	F	None	21Ma07Df
MOONY, T.		25	M	Laborer	21Ma07Df
KING, M.		50	M	Unknown	21Ma07Df
James	(S)	17	M	Unknown	21Ma07Df
My.	(D)	16	F	None	21Ma07Df
GREEN, A.		20	M	Unknown	21Ma07Df

NAMES OF PASSENGERS		AGE	SEX	OCCUPATIONS	DATE PORT SHIP
RUFF, J.		20	M	Unknown	21Ma07Df
ROBINSON, J.		20	M	Unknown	21Ma07Df
Richd.		21	M	Unknown	21Ma07Df
Saml.		27	M	Unknown	21Ma07Df
Joseph		30	M	Unknown	21Ma07Df
MYERS, M.		27	M	Unknown	21Ma07Df
Mgt.		19	F	None	21Ma07Df
Jane		16	F	None	21Ma07Df
LYNCH, My.		15	F	None	21Ma07Df

VICTORY 21 MAY 1847

From Dublin

NAMES OF PASSENGERS		AGE	SEX	OCCUPATIONS	DATE PORT SHIP
MURRAY, Thomas		20	M	Farmer	21Ma20Ps
MARTIN, Briget		20	F	Unknown	21Ma20Ps
ORME, L.Mrs.		30	F	Unknown	21Ma20Ps
BARRETT, Anthony		18	M	Unknown	21Ma20Ps
PIERSON, U		20	F	Unknown	21Ma20Ps
U		18	F	Unknown	21Ma20Ps

VICTORY 21 MAY 1847

From Dublin

NAMES OF PASSENGERS		AGE	SEX	OCCUPATIONS	DATE PORT SHIP
MANN, Alex.		19	M	Farmer	21Ma20Ps
U-Mrs.	(M)	45	F	Unknown	21Ma20Ps
Sarah	(T)	20	F	Unknown	21Ma20Ps
Francis	(B)	18	M	Farmer	21Ma20Ps
Henry	(B)	18	M	Farmer	21Ma20Ps
Jane	(T)	07	F	Child	21Ma20Ps
Elizabeth	(T)	06	F	Child	21Ma20Ps
Joseph	(B)	12	M	Farmer	21Ma20Ps
HURLEY, Patt.		18	M	Unknown	21Ma20Ps
ACTON, William		20	M	Unknown	21Ma20Ps
THORP, Mathew		50	M	Unknown	21Ma20Ps
Robert	(S)	04	M	Child	21Ma20Ps
CONNOR, Mary		20	F	Unknown	21Ma20Ps
MCKANE, Rachel		19	F	Unknown	21Ma20Ps
KANE, Catherine		20	F	Unknown	21Ma20Ps
Patt.		23	M	Farmer	21Ma20Ps
LOUGHLIN, Martin		40	M	Unknown	21Ma20Ps
Mary		35	F	Unknown	21Ma20Ps
CROOK, Catherine		16	F	Unknown	21Ma20Ps
MORAN, Margt.		17	F	Unknown	21Ma20Ps
Eliza		15	F	Unknown	21Ma20Ps
FAHEY, Richard		20	M	Unknown	21Ma20Ps
MANN, James		20	M	Unknown	21Ma20Ps
U-Mrs.		33	F	Unknown	21Ma20Ps
DEMPSEY, John		20	M	Unknown	21Ma20Ps
DOOLEY, Chas.		21	M	Unknown	21Ma20Ps
CASH, Michael		34	M	Unknown	21Ma20Ps
U	(W)	30	F	Wife	21Ma20Ps
GARLAND, Pheling		16	M	Farmer	21Ma20Ps
MANN, Bernard		01	M	Child	21Ma20Ps
GALLIGAN, John		24	M	Unknown	21Ma20Ps
BOULGER, U		20	M	Unknown	21Ma20Ps
Thos.		24	M	Unknown	21Ma20Ps
MCKAY, U		20	F	Unknown	21Ma20Ps
MOORE, Sophia		11	F	Unknown	21Ma20Ps
Jas.		08	M	Child	21Ma20Ps
Edward		07	M	Child	21Ma20Ps
Saml.		04	M	Child	21Ma20Ps

527

NAMES OF PASSENGERS		A G E	S E X	OCCUPATIONS	DATE PORT SHIP
MCMANUS, Patk.		24	M	Unknown	21Ma20Ps
MADDEN, Valentine		20	M	Unknown	21Ma20Ps
MARTIN, Michl.		24	M	Unknown	21Ma20Ps
CONNELLY, Martin		13	M	Unknown	21Ma20Ps
Daniel		14	M	Unknown	21Ma20Ps
MULROY, Michl.		30	M	Unknown	21Ma20Ps
Nabby		20	F	Unknown	21Ma20Ps
Cathe.		12	F	Unknown	21Ma20Ps
OBRIEN, Mar		20	F	Unknown	21Ma20Ps
FLINN, George		21	M	Farmer	21Ma20Ps
MULLIGAN, Edwd.		35	M	Unknown	21Ma20Ps
Margt.		20	F	Unknown	21Ma20Ps
DUNNE, Mary		50	F	Unknown	21Ma20Ps
Thomas	(S)	20	M	Unknown	21Ma20Ps
Mary	(D)	14	F	Unknown	21Ma20Ps
POWER, Robert		20	M	Unknown	21Ma20Ps
MURRAY, My.		12	F	Unknown	21Ma20Ps
MCCORMACK, Jas.		20	M	Unknown	21Ma20Ps
DORMOR, Michl.		24	M	Unknown	21Ma20Ps
MCLAINE, Hugh		20	M	Unknown	21Ma20Ps
KANE, William		23	M	Unknown	21Ma20Ps
SARMAN, Patt.		21	M	Unknown	21Ma20Ps
U	(W)	21	F	Wife	21Ma20Ps
MORAN, Mary		20	F	Unknown	21Ma20Ps
DALY, Augustus		18	M	Unknown	21Ma20Ps
SMITH, Thomas		40	M	Unknown	21Ma20Ps
U	(W)	40	F	Wife	21Ma20Ps
Patrick	(S)	05	M	Child	21Ma20Ps
Eliza	(T)	27	F	Unknown	21Ma20Ps
Mary	(D)	12	F	Unknown	21Ma20Ps
Patrick	(S)	08	M	Child	21Ma20Ps
BRYAN, Jane		20	F	Unknown	21Ma20Ps
Cathe.		19	F	Unknown	21Ma20Ps
CARREN, Eliza		20	F	Unknown	21Ma20Ps
SMITH, Jas.		21	M	Unknown	21Ma20Ps
BEAGHAM, Cathe.		20	F	Unknown	21Ma20Ps
JONES, James		30	M	Farmer	21Ma20Ps
KIRWAN, U-Mrs.		34	F	Unknown	21Ma20Ps
Andrew	(S)	13	M	Farmer	21Ma20Ps
George	(S)	12	M	Farmer	21Ma20Ps
John	(S)	05	M	Child	21Ma20Ps
GILLERON, Loughlin		26	M	Unknown	21Ma20Ps
ELLIOT, Ab.		25	M	Unknown	21Ma20Ps
SHORT, Jas.		20	M	Unknown	21Ma20Ps
CALLAGHAN, William		18	M	Unknown	21Ma20Ps
FRANCIS, M.		20	F	Unknown	21Ma20Ps
ROACH, Margaret		20	F	Unknown	21Ma20Ps
Bridget		20	F	Unknown	21Ma20Ps
CARROLL, Mary		18	F	Unknown	21Ma20Ps
KENNEDY, John		25	M	Unknown	21Ma20Ps
WRIGHT, Patrick		30	M	Unknown	21Ma20Ps
Bernard		40	M	Unknown	21Ma20Ps
Jas.		02	M	Child	21Ma20Ps
TREACY, Michael		20	M	Unknown	21Ma20Ps
COFFEE, Adam		30	M	Unknown	21Ma20Ps
MCCLEAN, Mary		40	F	Unknown	21Ma20Ps
FAY, Ellen		50	F	Unknown	21Ma20Ps
Margaret		30	F	Unknown	21Ma20Ps
WRIGHT, Ann		17	F	Unknown	21Ma20Ps
CAMPBELL, Bridget		20	F	Unknown	21Ma20Ps
FARRELLY, Jas.		20	M	Unknown	21Ma20Ps
DOOLIN, Bridget		16	F	Unknown	21Ma20Ps
Jas.		13	M	Unknown	21Ma20Ps
DOUGHERTY, Jas.		21	M	Unknown	21Ma20Ps
MCGARRY, Anthy.		31	M	Unknown	21Ma20Ps
CALLIGAN, John		20	M	Unknown	21Ma20Ps
MCCLEAN, John		20	M	Unknown	21Ma20Ps
MCNABB, Edward		30	M	Unknown	21Ma20Ps
Ellen		40	F	Unknown	21Ma20Ps
Cath.		29	F	Unknown	21Ma20Ps
Patk.		20	M	Unknown	21Ma20Ps
Thomas		10	M	Unknown	21Ma20Ps
Ellen		09	F	Child	21Ma20Ps
Sophia		29	F	Unknown	21Ma20Ps
MOORE, Jas.		40	M	Unknown	21Ma20Ps
MOORE, Eliza	(W)	39	F	Wife	21Ma20Ps
Jemima	(D)	14	F	Unknown	21Ma20Ps
Ann	(D)	13	F	Unknown	21Ma20Ps
MCDERMOTT, Dominick		50	M	Farmer	21Ma20Ps
Rose	(W)	49	F	Unknown	21Ma20Ps
Cath.	(D)	20	F	Unknown	21Ma20Ps
Eliza	(D)	19	F	Unknown	21Ma20Ps
Nancy	(D)	12	F	Unknown	21Ma20Ps
Michl.	(S)	10	M	Unknown	21Ma20Ps
Biddy	(D)	08	F	Child	21Ma20Ps
TREACY, Ellen		19	F	Unknown	21Ma20Ps
DEERY, Edmond		23	M	Farmer	21Ma20Ps
RYAN, John		20	M	Unknown	21Ma20Ps
MCDONALD, Anthony		29	M	Unknown	21Ma20Ps
CONCANNON, Patrick		35	M	Unknown	21Ma20Ps
Dick		30	M	Unknown	21Ma20Ps
Michl.		29	M	Unknown	21Ma20Ps
Donald		27	M	Unknown	21Ma20Ps
Johanna		25	F	Unknown	21Ma20Ps
GOODFELLOW, Felix		35	M	Unknown	21Ma20Ps
John	(S)	12	M	Unknown	21Ma20Ps
BURNS, Patrick		17	M	Unknown	21Ma20Ps
MURRAY, Philip		35	M	Unknown	21Ma20Ps
Julia		34	F	Unknown	21Ma20Ps
GALLAGHER, Mary		18	F	Unknown	21Ma20Ps
Bridget		18	F	Unknown	21Ma20Ps
MURRAY, Margaret		07	F	Child	21Ma20Ps
Mary		06	F	Child	21Ma20Ps
DUFFY, Mary		20	F	Unknown	21Ma20Ps
BRADY, Bernard		50	M	Farmer	21Ma20Ps
Catherine	(W)	45	F	Wife	21Ma20Ps
John	(S)	18	M	Unknown	21Ma20Ps
Mary	(D)	16	F	Unknown	21Ma20Ps
Mathew	(S)	14	M	Unknown	21Ma20Ps
Simon	(S)	09	M	Child	21Ma20Ps
Alice	(D)	06	F	Child	21Ma20Ps
KANE, Eliza		24	F	Unknown	21Ma20Ps
John	(S)	01	M	Child	21Ma20Ps
MANAGHAN, Cath.		25	F	Unknown	21Ma20Ps
Mary	(D)	05	F	Child	21Ma20Ps
WILLIAMS, Richd.		22	M	Unknown	21Ma20Ps
CUMMINS, Thomas		26	M	Unknown	21Ma20Ps
KIRWAN, M.		24	M	Unknown	21Ma20Ps
John		34	M	Unknown	21Ma20Ps
MORAN, U		20	F	Unknown	21Ma20Ps
GANION, U		26	F	Unknown	21Ma20Ps
CARROLL, Rose		35	F	Unknown	21Ma20Ps
Thomas	(S)	11	M	Unknown	21Ma20Ps
HOLDEN, John		29	M	Farmer	21Ma20Ps
HANLY, Michael		24	M	Farmer	21Ma20Ps
KANE, Thomas		24	M	Farmer	21Ma20Ps
PLACK, Richard		24	M	Farmer	21Ma20Ps
HARMON, John		29	M	Farmer	21Ma20Ps
HOGAN, Michl.		24	M	Farmer	21Ma20Ps
HARMON, U-Mrs.		20	F	Farmer	21Ma20Ps
James	(S)	02	M	Child	21Ma20Ps
BARBER, Eliza		63	F	Unknown	21Ma20Ps
Patt.	(S)	26	M	Unknown	21Ma20Ps
Robert	(S)	28	M	Unknown	21Ma20Ps
Johanna	(D)	27	F	Unknown	21Ma20Ps
CARROLL, John		40	M	Unknown	21Ma20Ps
U	(W)	38	F	Wife	21Ma20Ps
Laurence	(S)	15	M	Unknown	21Ma20Ps
Jas.	(S)	12	M	Unknown	21Ma20Ps
Thomas	(S)	01	M	Child	21Ma20Ps
FITZPATRICK, Cath.		22	F	Unknown	21Ma20Ps
HEANY, Michl.		27	M	Unknown	21Ma20Ps
FLANAGAN, John		23	M	Unknown	21Ma20Ps
BURNS, William		21	M	Unknown	21Ma20Ps
Ann		16	F	Unknown	21Ma20Ps
MORRISS, Peter		14	M	Unknown	21Ma20Ps
BAHILL, Thos.		25	M	Unknown	21Ma20Ps
Bridget	(W)	25	F	Unknown	21Ma20Ps
Jas.	(S)	03	M	Child	21Ma20Ps
MCCANN, Patk.		16	M	Unknown	21Ma20Ps

NAMES OF PASSENGERS		AGE	SEX	OCCUPATIONS	DATE PORT SHIP
MCCANN, John		15	M	Unknown	21Ma20Ps
HAMILL, John		24	M	Unknown	21Ma20Ps
Michl.		23	M	Unknown	21Ma20Ps
DOOLEY, Dolly		21	F	Unknown	21Ma20Ps
CLARK, Patrick		30	M	Unknown	21Ma20Ps
Mary	(W)	20	F	Wife	21Ma20Ps
Michael	(S)	.00	M	Infant	21Ma20Ps
FOX, Mary		18	F	Unknown	21Ma20Ps
MCBRIDE, Mary		40	F	Unknown	21Ma20Ps
MCCULLOUGH, Patrick		30	M	Unknown	21Ma20Ps
NORWOOD, Benj.		21	M	Farmer	21Ma20Ps
ROBINSON, Fred.		22	M	Farmer	21Ma20Ps
Emily		24	F	Unknown	21Ma20Ps

SARDINIA 21 MAY 1847

From Liverpool

NAMES OF PASSENGERS		AGE	SEX	OCCUPATIONS	DATE PORT SHIP
CADDY, Anna		21	F	None	21Ma02Gt
Wm.		20	M	Laborer	21Ma02Gt
CANNON, P.		24	M	Unknown	21Ma02Gt
Martin		25	M	Unknown	21Ma02Gt
BIRCH, Mary		24	F	None	21Ma02Gt
CONNER, My.		24	F	None	21Ma02Gt
LANGAN, P.		24	M	Unknown	21Ma02Gt
My.	(W)	24	F	Wife	21Ma02Gt
My.	(D)	01	F	Child	21Ma02Gt
My.	(T)	20	F	None	21Ma02Gt
LAWLESS, P.		28	M	Unknown	21Ma02Gt
MAHONY, M.		30	M	Unknown	21Ma02Gt
CONLEN, J.		40	M	Unknown	21Ma02Gt
Bgt.		35	F	None	21Ma02Gt
ARCHER, Chat.		30	F	None	21Ma02Gt
Wm.	(S)	06	M	Child	21Ma02Gt
Richd.	(S)	04	M	Child	21Ma02Gt
Jane		20	F	None	21Ma02Gt
DANIGAN, My.		20	F	None	21Ma02Gt
GARNER, My.		21	F	None	21Ma02Gt
HANNON, A.		25	M	Unknown	21Ma02Gt
Barn.		24	F	Unknown	21Ma02Gt
CARRIGAN, Bgt.		24	F	None	21Ma02Gt
OWEN, J.		26	M	Unknown	21Ma02Gt
Q------, J.		16	M	Unknown	21Ma02Gt
OWENS, L.		21	M	Unknown	21Ma02Gt
PARKER, P.		25	M	Unknown	21Ma02Gt
HARLEN, P.		20	M	Unknown	21Ma02Gt
CANNON, M.		24	M	Unknown	21Ma02Gt
BRADY, M.		20	M	Unknown	21Ma02Gt
OWENS, L.		40	M	Unknown	21Ma02Gt
My.	(D)	18	F	None	21Ma02Gt
Thos.	(S)	17	M	Unknown	21Ma02Gt
Bgt.	(D)	15	F	None	21Ma02Gt
Danl.	(S)	12	M	None	21Ma02Gt
Luke	(S)	08	M	Child	21Ma02Gt
Mgt.	(D)	07	F	Child	21Ma02Gt
Ebna.	(S)	06	M	Child	21Ma02Gt
John	(S)	05	M	Child	21Ma02Gt
Jane	(W)	40	F	Wife	21Ma02Gt
Cath.	(D)	01	F	Child	21Ma02Gt
MCELROY, Eliza		19	F	None	21Ma02Gt
BASTOK, T.		32	M	Laborer	21Ma02Gt
CONNERY, J.		25	M	Unknown	21Ma02Gt
CALAGAN, M.		24	M	Unknown	21Ma02Gt
KELLY, J.		21	M	Unknown	21Ma02Gt
KEY, Maria		20	F	None	21Ma02Gt
SMITH, W.		31	M	Unknown	21Ma02Gt
GARNER, G.		24	M	Unknown	21Ma02Gt
BROWN, O.		24	M	Unknown	21Ma02Gt
Bgt.		28	F	None	21Ma02Gt

NAMES OF PASSENGERS		AGE	SEX	OCCUPATIONS	DATE PORT SHIP
GLYN, D.		20	M	Unknown	21Ma02Gt
Mich.		15	M	None	21Ma02Gt
SPELLMAN, E.		22	M	None	21Ma02Gt
Ellen		14	F	None	21Ma02Gt
KANE, M.		20	M	Unknown	21Ma02Gt
WALSH, Mgt.		16	F	None	21Ma02Gt
RAFFERTY, J.		44	M	Unknown	21Ma02Gt
DUNN, Peggy		22	F	None	21Ma02Gt
STEWART, W.		30	M	Unknown	21Ma02Gt
Chas.		40	M	Unknown	21Ma02Gt
Robt.		34	M	Unknown	21Ma02Gt
Susanah		28	F	None	21Ma02Gt
Jane		18	F	None	21Ma02Gt
My.		20	F	None	21Ma02Gt
Wm.		35	M	Unknown	21Ma02Gt
My.		20	F	None	21Ma02Gt
My.J.		01	F	Child	21Ma02Gt
LARKIN, F.		18	M	Unknown	21Ma02Gt
LISHTON, My.Eliza		16	F	None	21Ma02Gt
WILSON, Jane		18	F	None	21Ma02Gt
BROWN, A.		18	M	Unknown	21Ma02Gt
MARNIN, P.		22	M	Unknown	21Ma02Gt
Hana		16	F	None	21Ma02Gt
WILLIS, M.		46	M	Unknown	21Ma02Gt
George		26	M	Unknown	21Ma02Gt
Wm.		23	M	Unknown	21Ma02Gt
Henry		45	M	Unknown	21Ma02Gt
Mgt.		18	F	None	21Ma02Gt
MCKENY, Mgt.		28	F	None	21Ma02Gt
GRESHAM, W.		58	M	Unknown	21Ma02Gt
Jas.	(S)	23	M	Unknown	21Ma02Gt
My.	(D)	21	F	None	21Ma02Gt
SMITH, C.		40	M	Laborer	21Ma02Gt
CURRAN, J.		28	M	Unknown	21Ma02Gt
BRENNAN, W.		24	M	Unknown	21Ma02Gt
KENNY, J.		24	M	Unknown	21Ma02Gt
CLEERY, J.		20	M	Unknown	21Ma02Gt
BROCK, P.		21	M	Unknown	21Ma02Gt
KELLY, My.		30	F	None	21Ma02Gt
CLERY, Biddy		14	F	None	21Ma02Gt
GUFFIN, Cath.		18	F	None	21Ma02Gt
QUINN, W.		26	M	Unknown	21Ma02Gt
GALLHAN, P.		24	M	Unknown	21Ma02Gt
MCGANN, O.		38	M	Unknown	21Ma02Gt
PAGE, W.		45	M	Unknown	21Ma02Gt
My.	(W)	43	F	Wife	21Ma02Gt
Maria	(D)	21	F	None	21Ma02Gt
Betty	(D)	18	F	None	21Ma02Gt
My.	(D)	16	F	None	21Ma02Gt
Thos.	(S)	14	M	None	21Ma02Gt
STROUD, W.		40	M	None	21Ma02Gt
Hny.		38	M	None	21Ma02Gt
Thos.		12	M	None	21Ma02Gt
John		10	M	None	21Ma02Gt
Cath.		13	F	None	21Ma02Gt
Chatt.		08	M	Child	21Ma02Gt
My.		01	F	Child	21Ma02Gt
SMOLSON, C.		32	M	Unknown	21Ma02Gt
Hy.		21	M	Unknown	21Ma02Gt
Hanah		18	F	None	21Ma02Gt
Wm.		09	M	Child	21Ma02Gt
Elzbt.		03	F	Child	21Ma02Gt
HARTLY, E.		21	M	Unknown	21Ma02Gt
CLICKEY, R.		18	M	Unknown	21Ma02Gt
STEVENS, T.		23	M	Unknown	21Ma02Gt
CLICKEY, R.		29	M	Unknown	21Ma02Gt
My.	(W)	28	F	Wife	21Ma02Gt
My.	(D)	03	F	Child	21Ma02Gt
John	(S)	01	M	Child	21Ma02Gt
GANT, R.		25	M	Unknown	21Ma02Gt
Amelia		23	F	None	21Ma02Gt
Maria		20	F	None	21Ma02Gt
John	(S)	03	M	Child	21Ma02Gt
MAHON, J.		20	M	Unknown	21Ma02Gt
BARSTAN, E.		27	M	Laborer	21Ma02Gt

NAMES OF PASSENGERS		AGE	SEX	OCCUPATIONS	DATE PORT SHIP
BARSTAN, Henry		25	M	Laborer	21Ma02G†
WEST, J.		45	M	Laborer	21Ma02G†
My.		43	F	None	21Ma02G†
John		42	M	Unknown	21Ma02G†
John		17	M	Unknown	21Ma02G†
Thos.		21	M	Unknown	21Ma02G†
Harriet		12	F	None	21Ma02G†
CARTHE, T.		50	M	Unknown	21Ma02G†
My.	(W)	43	F	Wife	21Ma02G†
Wm.	(S)	20	M	Unknown	21Ma02G†
John	(S)	21	M	Unknown	21Ma02G†
Thos.	(S)	17	M	Unknown	21Ma02G†
Geg.	(S)	07	M	Child	21Ma02G†
Elizbt.	(D)	12	F	None	21Ma02G†
RANOLY, J.		48	M	Unknown	21Ma02G†
Cath.	(D)	16	F	None	21Ma02G†
Hanah	(D)	13	F	None	21Ma02G†
DOYLE, J.		33	M	Unknown	21Ma02G†
My.	(M)	50	F	None	21Ma02G†
Jane		28	F	None	21Ma02G†
Elzbt.		24	F	None	21Ma02G†
Hy.	(D)	03	F	Child	21Ma02G†
Mathew	(S)	02	M	Child	21Ma02G†
Wm.	(S)	01	M	Child	21Ma02G†
WATSON, J.		30	M	Unknown	21Ma02G†
CHANCE, T.		40	M	Unknown	21Ma02G†
Michl.	(S)	29	M	Unknown	21Ma02G†
GLENNON, Bgt.		17	F	None	21Ma02G†
SPEAKER, P.		19	M	Unknown	21Ma02G†
Mich.		20	M	Unknown	21Ma02G†
MURPHY, T.		21	M	Unknown	21Ma02G†
CARTY, J.		25	M	Unknown	21Ma02G†
COGHLAN, J.		19	M	Unknown	21Ma02G†
DALLAGER, M.		32	M	Unknown	21Ma02G†
SMITH, J.		24	M	Unknown	21Ma02G†
BRAYNARD, J.		40	M	Unknown	21Ma02G†
Saml.		30	M	Unknown	21Ma02G†
CARTY, J.		21	M	Unknown	21Ma02G†
BYRNE, Rose		09	F	Child	21Ma02G†
My.	(T)	01	F	Child	21Ma02G†
Hanah	(M)	40	F	None	21Ma02G†
BAGNALL, My.		30	F	None	21Ma02G†
HEANEY, P.		24	M	Laborer	21Ma02G†
Ann		21	F	None	21Ma02G†
GUNN, Julia		60	F	None	21Ma02G†
MCELLROY, Mgt.		20	F	None	21Ma02G†
MULREAN, Cath.		60	F	None	21Ma02G†
BRADY, Sarah		24	F	None	21Ma02G†
Danl.	(H)	25	M	Unknown	21Ma02G†
Mich.	(S)	01	M	Child	21Ma02G†
CANNON, John		20	M	Unknown	21Ma02G†
MCGLYN, Cath.		60	F	None	21Ma02G†
KENEDY, Cath.		16	F	None	21Ma02G†
REID, Mgt.		20	F	None	21Ma02G†
ONEIL, J.		40	M	Unknown	21Ma02G†
Patt.	(S)	04	M	Child	21Ma02G†
Cath.	(W)	40	F	Wife	21Ma02G†
Eliza	(D)	20	F	None	21Ma02G†
Alexn.	(S)	11	M	None	21Ma02G†
Bgt.	(D)	11	F	None	21Ma02G†
Cath.	(D)	07	F	Child	21Ma02G†
Owen	(S)	02	M	Child	21Ma02G†
FITZPATRICK, Mgt.		16	F	None	21Ma02G†
My.		13	F	None	21Ma02G†
STOTT, J.		40	M	Unknown	21Ma02G†
MCDEVIT, P.		20	M	Unknown	21Ma02G†
SWEENY, W.		18	M	Unknown	21Ma02G†
Rebeca		14	F	None	21Ma02G†
CROSSON, T.		28	M	Unknown	21Ma02G†
Cath.		40	F	None	21Ma02G†
Rose		08	F	Child	21Ma02G†
Thos.		06	M	Child	21Ma02G†
Andrew		04	M	Child	21Ma02G†
DWIRE, J.		46	M	Unknown	21Ma02G†
STEET, Ellen		26	F	None	21Ma02G†

NAMES OF PASSENGERS		AGE	SEX	OCCUPATIONS	DATE PORT SHIP
STEET, Cath.		16	F	None	21Ma02G†
DEVELIN, P.		20	M	Unknown	21Ma02G†
BRADY, J.		20	M	Unknown	21Ma02G†
GIBONS, L.		20	M	Unknown	21Ma02G†
WADE, L.		27	M	Unknown	21Ma02G†
KNOWLAN, M.		26	M	Unknown	21Ma02G†
Mich.		16	M	Unknown	21Ma02G†
Peter		09	M	Child	21Ma02G†
My.		07	F	Child	21Ma02G†
Bdgt.		04	F	Child	21Ma02G†
GRENNAN, J.		22	M	Laborer	21Ma02G†
DUNN, Bgt.		13	F	None	21Ma02G†
John		18	M	Unknown	21Ma02G†
MORGAN, T.		39	M	Unknown	21Ma02G†
Cath.		25	F	None	21Ma02G†
HASLETT, W.		20	M	Unknown	21Ma02G†
Ann	(M)	50	F	None	21Ma02G†
Mgt.	(T)	21	F	None	21Ma02G†
Jacob	(B)	18	M	Unknown	21Ma02G†
James	(B)	16	M	Unknown	21Ma02G†
Ann	(T)	17	M	Unknown	21Ma02G†
CHICKLY, G.		03	M	Child	21Ma02G†
ELLIS, T.		20	M	Unknown	21Ma02G†
DANCY, B.		21	M	Unknown	21Ma02G†
MCDONALD, T.		25	M	Unknown	21Ma02G†
STEWART, Ellen		23	F	None	21Ma02G†
BANON, T.		25	M	Unknown	21Ma02G†
DILLON, P.		29	M	Unknown	21Ma02G†
MCGEE, M.		18	M	Unknown	21Ma02G†
Cath.		24	F	None	21Ma02G†
Ann		16	F	None	21Ma02G†
DAVIS, F.		29	M	Unknown	21Ma02G†
SCULLY, T.		40	M	Unknown	21Ma02G†
Frank		30	M	Unknown	21Ma02G†
CONNOLLY, J.		35	M	Unknown	21Ma02G†
HANLY, Ann		20	F	None	21Ma02G†
RIVERS, J.		28	M	Unknown	21Ma02G†
MANGHAN, Sarah		20	F	None	21Ma02G†
BIRGHAN, Biddy		45	F	None	21Ma02G†
KELLY, T.		28	M	Unknown	21Ma02G†
GANAN, My.		18	F	None	21Ma02G†
KELLY, M.		20	M	Unknown	21Ma02G†
Ma.		22	M	Unknown	21Ma02G†
Patt		19	M	Unknown	21Ma02G†
MAGHER, My.		40	F	None	21Ma02G†
BRENNAN, T.		40	M	Unknown	21Ma02G†
KELLY, Mgt.		40	F	None	21Ma02G†
BRENNAN, P.		12	M	Unknown	21Ma02G†
KELLY, M.		10	M	None	21Ma02G†
My.		01	F	Child	21Ma02G†
KING, Eliza		27	F	None	21Ma02G†
MCGREEVY, Ann		26	F	None	21Ma02G†
Ann		26	F	None	21Ma02G†
GAHEY, My.		25	F	None	21Ma02G†
GLYNN, P.		37	M	Unknown	21Ma02G†
Ann		30	F	None	21Ma02G†
HUGHES, J.		19	M	Unknown	21Ma02G†
Cath.		35	F	None	21Ma02G†
Ellen		22	F	None	21Ma02G†
Wm.		02	M	Child	21Ma02G†
BRYAN, J.		04	M	Child	21Ma02G†
DEEGAN, J.		28	M	Unknown	21Ma02G†
MALONY, E.		30	M	Unknown	21Ma02G†
BRADY, W.		28	M	Unknown	21Ma02G†
My.		24	F	None	21Ma02G†
MCGLICHESTER, Mc.		20	M	Unknown	21Ma02G†
SPELLMAN, E.		34	M	Unknown	21Ma02G†
Elleanor		22	F	None	21Ma02G†
---ANE, M.		14	M	Unknown	21Ma02G†
WALCH, M.		20	M	Unknown	21Ma02G†
RAFFERTY, J.		16	M	Unknown	21Ma02G†
DUNN, Peggy		44	F	None	21Ma02G†
STEWART, W.		30	M	Unknown	21Ma02G†
Chas.		40	M	Unknown	21Ma02G†
HACKETT, M.		18	M	Unknown	21Ma02G†

NAMES OF PASSENGERS		AGE	SEX	OCCUPATIONS	DATE PORT SHIP
REILY, M.		65	M	Unknown	21Ma02Gt
Cath.		67	F	None	21Ma02Gt
BUCHANAN, B.		34	M	Unknown	21Ma02Gt
Mgt.	(W)	25	F	Wife	21Ma02Gt
Francis	(S)	02	M	Child	21Ma02Gt
John	(S)	01	M	Child	21Ma02Gt
KANE, Bgt.		21	F	None	21Ma02Gt
CONLY, M.		24	M	Unknown	21Ma02Gt
Cath.		16	F	None	21Ma02Gt
GAHAN, Mgt.		06	F	Child	21Ma02Gt
GROGHAN, Bgt.		28	F	None	21Ma02Gt
Jas.		20	F	None	21Ma02Gt
CONWAY, J.		09	M	Child	21Ma02Gt
MCAVERY, C.		25	M	Unknown	21Ma02Gt
MOFFIT, E.		17	M	Unknown	21Ma02Gt
GLENNON, Rose-A.		03	F	Child	21Ma02Gt
FLYNN, Ha.		18	F	None	21Ma02Gt
Mgt.		12	F	None	21Ma02Gt
MCDONELL, J.		27	M	Unknown	21Ma02Gt
HEFERNAN, J.		27	M	Unknown	21Ma02Gt
DAVIS, My.		29	F	None	21Ma02Gt
Amelia	(D)	04	F	Child	21Ma02Gt
Adolphus	(S)	01	M	Child	21Ma02Gt

NACOOCHEE 22 MAY 1847

From Dublin

NAMES OF PASSENGERS		AGE	SEX	OCCUPATIONS	DATE PORT SHIP
FARMLEY, U-Mrs.		30	F	None	22Ma20Pt
Margt.	(D)	07	F	Child	22Ma20Pt
Matilda	(D)	06	F	Child	22Ma20Pt
John	(S)	03	M	Child	22Ma20Pt
William	(S)	01	M	Child	22Ma20Pt
COLEGAN, Ann		24	F	None	22Ma20Pt
CONLAN, John		50	M	Mechanic	22Ma20Pt
U	(W)	46	F	Wife	22Ma20Pt
LUCKEN, Henry		24	M	Mechanic	22Ma20Pt
PINTLAND, Jas.		48	M	Mechanic	22Ma20Pt
Edward	(S)	22	M	Mechanic	22Ma20Pt
Eliza	(W)	48	F	None	22Ma20Pt
CALLEY, Michael		45	M	Mechanic	22Ma20Pt
U	(W)	40	F	Wife	22Ma20Pt
Bridget	(D)	10	F	None	22Ma20Pt
CONLAN, Judy		20	F	None	22Ma20Pt
Pat		27	M	Laborer	22Ma20Pt
Brian		30	M	Laborer	22Ma20Pt
U-Mrs.		25	F	None	22Ma20Pt
MCGEE, Rose		44	F	None	22Ma20Pt
FOX, Edmond		56	M	Laborer	22Ma20Pt
Mary	(W)	56	F	Wife	22Ma20Pt
Marla	(D)	28	F	None	22Ma20Pt
John	(S)	28	M	Laborer	22Ma20Pt
MCCABE, Catherine		12	F	None	22Ma20Pt
REYNOLDS, Ellen		18	F	None	22Ma20Pt
James		18	M	None	22Ma20Pt
COLLEY, Jullann		20	M	Laborer	22Ma20Pt
MACK, John		24	M	Laborer	22Ma20Pt
Eliza		22	F	None	22Ma20Pt
Mary		20	F	None	22Ma20Pt
COYLE, Peter		33	M	Laborer	22Ma20Pt
KAVANAGH, Bridget		24	F	None	22Ma20Pt
BURKE, James		31	M	Laborer	22Ma20Pt
CONALL, William		24	M	Laborer	22Ma20Pt
DAKENS, Ann		22	F	None	22Ma20Pt
CALAHAN, John		33	M	Laborer	22Ma20Pt
MACGRATH, Mary		34	F	None	22Ma20Pt
Bernard		34	M	Unknown	22Ma20Pt
Mathew		34	M	Laborer	22Ma20Pt
LAWLER, William		40	M	Laborer	22Ma20Pt

NAMES OF PASSENGERS		AGE	SEX	OCCUPATIONS	DATE PORT SHIP
LAWLER, My.	(W)	40	F	Wife	22Ma20Pt
Mary	(D)	12	F	None	22Ma20Pt
Patt	(S)	11	M	None	22Ma20Pt
NOBLE, U		40	F	None	22Ma20Pt
BRYAN, James		40	M	Laborer	22Ma20Pt
U	(W)	40	F	Wife	22Ma20Pt
Margt.	(D)	24	F	None	22Ma20Pt
Catherine	(D)	22	F	None	22Ma20Pt
Mary	(D)	20	F	None	22Ma20Pt
Bridget	(D)	18	F	None	22Ma20Pt
Sarah	(D)	15	F	None	22Ma20Pt
Ann	(D)	05	F	Child	22Ma20Pt
Peter	(S)	13	M	None	22Ma20Pt
James	(S)	11	M	None	22Ma20Pt
MCGRATH, James		38	F	None	22Ma20Pt
Margaret		39	F	None	22Ma20Pt
STAR, John		40	M	Laborer	22Ma20Pt
MCGRATH, Michl.		41	M	Laborer	22Ma20Pt
Francis		42	M	Laborer	22Ma20Pt
Thomas		43	M	Laborer	22Ma20Pt
Sarah		44	F	None	22Ma20Pt
Anne		46	F	None	22Ma20Pt
Mary		46	F	None	22Ma20Pt
Bridget		49	F	None	22Ma20Pt
Susan		48	F	None	22Ma20Pt
Patrick		45	M	Laborer	22Ma20Pt
MCALARNEY, Rose		56	F	None	22Ma20Pt
CRAWFORD, William		51	M	Laborer	22Ma20Pt
DOYLE, George		52	M	Laborer	22Ma20Pt
CARROLL, Patrick		53	M	Laborer	22Ma20Pt
KINSLEY, Thomas		55	M	Laborer	22Ma20Pt
Patrick		54	M	Laborer	22Ma20Pt
MURRAY, Patrick		54	M	Laborer	22Ma20Pt
WILLEY, James		59	M	Laborer	22Ma20Pt
REID, George		58	M	Laborer	22Ma20Pt
James		59	M	Laborer	22Ma20Pt
KEYLEY, Mary		60	F	None	22Ma20Pt
NUGENT, Eliza		20	F	None	22Ma20Pt
BARRY, James		24	M	Laborer	22Ma20Pt
CALLAHAN, Bridget		20	F	None	22Ma20Pt
MCDONNELL, Thomas		30	M	Laborer	22Ma20Pt
CASEY, Martin		30	M	Laborer	22Ma20Pt
CUNNINGHAM, Bridget		29	F	None	22Ma20Pt
HOGAN, Ellen		30	F	None	22Ma20Pt
FARRELL, James		29	M	Laborer	22Ma20Pt
REILLY, Owen		28	M	Laborer	22Ma20Pt
SMITH, Owen		29	M	Laborer	22Ma20Pt
DELANY, James		35	M	Laborer	22Ma20Pt
COGRAN, Andrew		40	M	Laborer	22Ma20Pt
CAMPLE, John		42	M	Laborer	22Ma20Pt
MCGRATH, Henry		44	M	Laborer	22Ma20Pt
MASON, James		43	M	Laborer	22Ma20Pt
SHERIDAN, Charles		46	M	Laborer	22Ma20Pt
GREEN, John		44	M	Laborer	22Ma20Pt
REDMOND, Pat		21	M	Laborer	22Ma20Pt
LEDDY, Rose		22	F	None	22Ma20Pt
FARLEY, Mary		20	F	None	22Ma20Pt
DALTRY, Kitty		22	F	None	22Ma20Pt
RILAND, Morris		30	M	Laborer	22Ma20Pt

EMIGRANT 22 MAY 1847

From Liverpool

NAMES OF PASSENGERS		AGE	SEX	OCCUPATIONS	DATE PORT SHIP
LARKIN, Luke		65	M	Farmer	22Ma02Pu
Ann	(D)	18	F	None	22Ma02Pu
BLACK, James		25	M	Farmer	22Ma02Pu
BOYD, John		25	M	Farmer	22Ma02Pu
ENGLISH, Dennis		25	M	Farmer	22Ma02Pu

NAMES OF PASSENGERS		AGE	SEX	OCCUPATIONS	DATE PORT SHIP		NAMES OF PASSENGERS		AGE	SEX	OCCUPATIONS	DATE PORT SHIP
BARRETT, Mich.		20	M	Farmer	22Ma02Pu		GALLAGHER, John		19	M	Laborer	22Ma02Pu
DAUGHERTY, James		20	M	Farmer	22Ma02Pu		FLOOD, Pat		20	M	Laborer	22Ma02Pu
MURPHY, Mary		20	F	None	22Ma02Pu		DONOHOE, Mary		22	F	None	22Ma02Pu
MALONEY, Biddy		30	F	None	22Ma02Pu		Johana		20	F	None	22Ma02Pu
PETERS, John		28	M	Farmer	22Ma02Pu		COGHLAN, Mary		11	F	None	22Ma02Pu
Peter		22	M	Farmer	22Ma02Pu		MALAWING, Mary		21	F	None	22Ma02Pu
U-Mrs.		28	F	None	22Ma02Pu		Ellen		22	F	None	22Ma02Pu
ONEIL, Pat		26	M	Farmer	22Ma02Pu		MCGINNIS, Cathe.		22	F	None	22Ma02Pu
U	(W)	24	F	Wife	22Ma02Pu		HENDRY, Ellen		19	F	None	22Ma02Pu
ALLEN, Cath.		14	F	None	22Ma02Pu		JANE, Sarah		22	F	None	22Ma02Pu
BEST, John		56	M	Farmer	22Ma02Pu		CAINE, John		26	M	Laborer	22Ma02Pu
U	(W)	56	F	Wife	22Ma02Pu		FICKLE, James		21	M	Laborer	22Ma02Pu
John	(S)	21	M	Farmer	22Ma02Pu		GLENN, Daniel		18	M	Laborer	22Ma02Pu
Thomas	(S)	18	M	Farmer	22Ma02Pu		THOMPSON, James		19	M	Laborer	22Ma02Pu
Nancy	(D)	16	F	None	22Ma02Pu		SMITH, Pat		36	M	Laborer	22Ma02Pu
Margt.	(D)	13	F	None	22Ma02Pu		SHEIL, Wm.		21	M	Laborer	22Ma02Pu
James	(S)	08	M	Child	22Ma02Pu		HOGAN, Rosey		50	F	None	22Ma02Pu
Susan	(D)	05	F	Child	22Ma02Pu		GARNER, Cathe.		40	F	None	22Ma02Pu
GRIBBIN, James		36	M	Laborer	22Ma02Pu		Bernard	(S)	20	M	Laborer	22Ma02Pu
U	(W)	25	F	Wife	22Ma02Pu		Rosamond	(D)	14	F	None	22Ma02Pu
Hugh	(S)	03	M	Child	22Ma02Pu		Margt.	(D)	10	F	None	22Ma02Pu
James	(S)	.00	M	Infant	22Ma02Pu		John	(S)	09	M	Child	22Ma02Pu
HAMILTON, Andrew		24	M	Laborer	22Ma02Pu		Terrence	(S)	04	M	Child	22Ma02Pu
GEORGE, Mary		18	F	None	22Ma02Pu		GLOVER, Cathe.		18	F	None	22Ma02Pu
BRADLEY, Arthur		30	M	Laborer	22Ma02Pu		MAHON, Thos.		30	M	Laborer	22Ma02Pu
James		17	M	Laborer	22Ma02Pu		LEHAN, John		24	M	Laborer	22Ma02Pu
Mary		19	F	None	22Ma02Pu		Wm.		22	M	Laborer	22Ma02Pu
COYLE, Barth.		40	M	Laborer	22Ma02Pu		WELSH, John		26	M	Laborer	22Ma02Pu
Margt.	(D)	26	F	None	22Ma02Pu		HOGAN, Timothy		21	M	Laborer	22Ma02Pu
DARBY, Patrick		30	M	Laborer	22Ma02Pu		QUINN, Pat		35	M	Laborer	22Ma02Pu
LAWNEY, John		30	M	Laborer	22Ma02Pu		GRADY, Allen		26	F	None	22Ma02Pu
MCGUIRE, Thomas		26	M	Laborer	22Ma02Pu		POLLOCK, James		25	M	Laborer	22Ma02Pu
SHANLEY, Pat		26	M	Laborer	22Ma02Pu		David		20	M	Laborer	22Ma02Pu
Mary		24	F	None	22Ma02Pu		Sarah		22	F	None	22Ma02Pu
KILDUFF, Susan		20	F	None	22Ma02Pu		Sarah		24	F	None	22Ma02Pu
LAUGHRY, Ann		20	F	None	22Ma02Pu		Peggy		02	F	Child	22Ma02Pu
Bridget		24	F	None	22Ma02Pu		MCINTYRE, Eliza		20	F	None	22Ma02Pu
MAXWELL, Michael		40	M	Laborer	22Ma02Pu		Ann		25	F	None	22Ma02Pu
Ann	(W)	30	F	Wife	22Ma02Pu		CAMPBELL, Sarah		20	F	None	22Ma02Pu
Ed.	(S)	12	M	None	22Ma02Pu		MURRAY, Nancy		50	F	None	22Ma02Pu
Thos.	(S)	10	M	None	22Ma02Pu		Rebecca	(D)	18	F	None	22Ma02Pu
READY, John		46	M	Laborer	22Ma02Pu		Gagahan		40	F	None	22Ma02Pu
U	(W)	36	F	Wife	22Ma02Pu		Ann	(D)	13	F	None	22Ma02Pu
Phillip	(S)	12	M	None	22Ma02Pu		Mgt.	(D)	12	F	None	22Ma02Pu
Richard	(S)	10	M	None	22Ma02Pu		Biddy	(D)	09	F	Child	22Ma02Pu
Bridget	(D)	09	F	Child	22Ma02Pu		MCCLEAN, Mich.		20	M	Farmer	22Ma02Pu
Margt.	(D)	08	F	Child	22Ma02Pu		FITZGERALD, James		22	M	Farmer	22Ma02Pu
Cath.	(D)	06	F	Child	22Ma02Pu		Hannah		18	F	None	22Ma02Pu
Farrell	(S)	04	M	Child	22Ma02Pu		YOHONY, John		25	M	Farmer	22Ma02Pu
DERMOODY, Andrew		26	M	Laborer	22Ma02Pu		MCGAWAN, John		20	M	Farmer	22Ma02Pu
HOGAN, Terrence		40	M	Laborer	22Ma02Pu		Bridget		22	F	None	22Ma02Pu
U	(W)	30	F	Wife	22Ma02Pu		MCDERMOT, Michael		25	M	Farmer	22Ma02Pu
Rosey	(D)	09	F	Child	22Ma02Pu		MCSHAW, Francis		20	M	Farmer	22Ma02Pu
John	(S)	10	M	None	22Ma02Pu		GLANEN, Hugh		18	M	Farmer	22Ma02Pu
Patt.	(S)	08	M	Child	22Ma02Pu		ONEIL, Bernard		19	M	Farmer	22Ma02Pu
Michael	(S)	06	M	Child	22Ma02Pu		MCSHAW, Sarah		16	F	None	22Ma02Pu
Bernard	(S)	04	M	Child	22Ma02Pu		MCGAVENY, Jacob		17	M	Farmer	22Ma02Pu
Terrence	(S)	.00	M	Infant	22Ma02Pu		MCGAW, Rose		15	F	None	22Ma02Pu
WALSH, James		41	M	Laborer	22Ma02Pu		FERGUSON, Wm.		30	M	Farmer	22Ma02Pu
Ann	(W)	37	F	Wife	22Ma02Pu		Sarah		25	F	None	22Ma02Pu
Ellen	(D)	14	F	None	22Ma02Pu		MORAY, Ann		13	F	None	22Ma02Pu
John	(S)	10	M	None	22Ma02Pu		DUNN, Stephen		21	M	Farmer	22Ma02Pu
James	(S)	09	M	Child	22Ma02Pu		MCCANN, Michael		21	M	Farmer	22Ma02Pu
Timothy	(S)	08	M	Child	22Ma02Pu		Pat		32	M	Farmer	22Ma02Pu
Ann	(D)	04	F	Child	22Ma02Pu		U-Mrs.		30	F	None	22Ma02Pu
Lawrence	(S)	03	M	Child	22Ma02Pu		John		25	M	Farmer	22Ma02Pu
Cath.	(D)	.00	F	Infant	22Ma02Pu		Bernard		05	M	Child	22Ma02Pu
CANNWELL, Eliza		38	F	None	22Ma02Pu		Mary		.00	F	Infant	22Ma02Pu
Ed.	(S)	07	M	Child	22Ma02Pu		Thomas		05	M	Child	22Ma02Pu
MADDEN, Wm.		22	M	Laborer	22Ma02Pu		CLYMORE, Wm.		20	M	Laborer	22Ma02Pu
U	(W)	22	F	Wife	22Ma02Pu		MCCABE, U-Mrs.		20	F	None	22Ma02Pu
LANNON, Thos.		22	M	Laborer	22Ma02Pu		SMITH, Ann		19	F	None	22Ma02Pu
CAIT, Cath.		20	F	None	22Ma02Pu		Cathe.		25	F	None	22Ma02Pu
GALLAGHER, Thos.		26	M	Laborer	22Ma02Pu		BLESSING, Terrence		30	M	Laborer	22Ma02Pu
Teddy		32	M	Laborer	22Ma02Pu		Bridget	(W)	23	F	Wife	22Ma02Pu

NAMES OF PASSENGERS		AGE	SEX	OCCUPATIONS	DATE PORT SHIP
BLESSING, Thomas	(S)	05	M	Child	22Ma02Pu
James	(S)	03	M	Child	22Ma02Pu
OBRYAN, James		26	M	Laborer	22Ma02Pu
CROHAN, Pat		22	M	Laborer	22Ma02Pu
SHARDIN, Wm.		26	M	Laborer	22Ma02Pu
HART, Bridget		26	F	None	22Ma02Pu
DELANEY, Wm.		20	M	Laborer	22Ma02Pu
Ellen		18	F	None	22Ma02Pu
MATTHEWS, John		22	M	Laborer	22Ma02Pu
Owin		22	M	Laborer	22Ma02Pu
Margt.		04	F	Child	22Ma02Pu
Francis		02	M	Child	22Ma02Pu
Mary		.00	F	Infant	22Ma02Pu
WHITFIELD, Cathe.		20	F	None	22Ma02Pu
CASEY, Pat		40	M	Laborer	22Ma02Pu
Mary	(W)	35	F	Wife	22Ma02Pu
Honora	(D)	09	F	Child	22Ma02Pu
COGHLAN, James		20	M	Laborer	22Ma02Pu
Margt.	(W)	20	F	Wife	22Ma02Pu
Thos.	(S)	.00	M	Infant	22Ma02Pu
MULLEN, Thos.		19	M	Laborer	22Ma02Pu
JOHNSON, Henry		21	M	Laborer	22Ma02Pu
Eliza	(W)	18	F	Wife	22Ma02Pu
Henry	(S)	.00	M	Infant	22Ma02Pu
Robt.	(B)	25	M	Farmer	22Ma02Pu
Jane	(L)	20	F	Wife	22Ma02Pu
Wm.	(N)	02	M	Child	22Ma02Pu
Eliza	(N)	.00	F	Infant	22Ma02Pu
ALLEN, Ed.		30	M	Farmer	22Ma02Pu
FLYNN, John		30	M	Farmer	22Ma02Pu
Mary	(W)	27	F	Wife	22Ma02Pu
Joseph	(S)	02	M	Child	22Ma02Pu
DONOUGH, James		27	M	Farmer	22Ma02Pu
Mary		20	F	None	22Ma02Pu
Ann		19	F	None	22Ma02Pu
Cathe.		17	F	None	22Ma02Pu
FLYNN, Cathe.		20	F	None	22Ma02Pu
Mary		21	F	None	22Ma02Pu
BOYLE, Pat		21	M	Farmer	22Ma02Pu
SWEENEY, James		22	M	Farmer	22Ma02Pu
Mary		22	F	None	22Ma02Pu
KINNEY, John		22	M	Farmer	22Ma02Pu
GALLAGHER, Pat		22	M	Farmer	22Ma02Pu
MCGINLEY, James		30	M	Farmer	22Ma02Pu
CANIFFE, Mich.		20	M	Farmer	22Ma02Pu
WELSH, Pat		24	M	Farmer	22Ma02Pu
REILLEY, Francis		24	M	Farmer	22Ma02Pu
HAND, Bridget		28	F	None	22Ma02Pu
TRACY, John		27	M	Farmer	22Ma02Pu
RAFFERTY, Martin		27	M	Farmer	22Ma02Pu
MURRAY, John		25	M	Farmer	22Ma02Pu
GARRETTY, John		22	M	Farmer	22Ma02Pu
Ann	(W)	22	F	Wife	22Ma02Pu
Michael	(S)	.00	M	Infant	22Ma02Pu
COSTELLO, Cath.		20	F	None	22Ma02Pu
MULLIGAN, Bridget		29	F	None	22Ma02Pu
FEENEY, Peter		25	M	Farmer	22Ma02Pu
CURRAN, John		25	M	Farmer	22Ma02Pu
GAWAN, John		25	M	Farmer	22Ma02Pu
COHAN, Martin		34	M	Farmer	22Ma02Pu
Michael		30	M	Farmer	22Ma02Pu
WYNN, Michael		22	M	Farmer	22Ma02Pu
KILLOLY, Thos.		20	M	Farmer	22Ma02Pu
James		22	M	Farmer	22Ma02Pu
Cath.		20	F	None	22Ma02Pu
HENNESSY, Ed.		20	M	Farmer	22Ma02Pu
Ellen		18	F	None	22Ma02Pu
MURRAY, Chs.		29	M	Farmer	22Ma02Pu
DUNN, Patt		24	M	Farmer	22Ma02Pu
WALKER, James		19	M	Farmer	22Ma02Pu
ROWE, Thos.		56	M	Farmer	22Ma02Pu
Cathe.	(W)	51	F	Wife	22Ma02Pu
James	(S)	18	M	Farmer	22Ma02Pu
John	(S)	17	M	Farmer	22Ma02Pu
FINNIGAN, Phil.		27	M	Farmer	22Ma02Pu
FLEMING, John		18	M	Farmer	22Ma02Pu
MARTIN, John		35	M	Farmer	22Ma02Pu
Mary	(W)	30	F	Wife	22Ma02Pu
Bernard		16	M	Farmer	22Ma02Pu
Eliza	(D)	08	F	Child	22Ma02Pu
Ann	(D)	06	F	Child	22Ma02Pu
Robt.	(S)	01	M	Child	22Ma02Pu
JORDAN, Mary		20	F	None	22Ma02Pu
MANAGHAN, Eliza		22	F	None	22Ma02Pu
COONAHAN, Thos.		25	M	Laborer	22Ma02Pu
Mary	(M)	45	F	None	22Ma02Pu
Margt.	(T)	13	F	None	22Ma02Pu
Lawrence	(B)	09	M	Child	22Ma02Pu
John	(B)	07	M	Child	22Ma02Pu
MCCABE, James		26	M	Laborer	22Ma02Pu
Cathe.	(M)	45	F	None	22Ma02Pu
Mary	(T)	20	F	None	22Ma02Pu
Alice	(T)	18	F	None	22Ma02Pu
Biddy	(T)	15	F	None	22Ma02Pu
MURPHY, Betty		19	F	None	22Ma02Pu
NULTY, Mary		28	F	None	22Ma02Pu
MCGEE, Peter		30	M	Laborer	22Ma02Pu
U	(W)	20	F	Wife	22Ma02Pu
GONE, Mgt.		20	F	None	22Ma02Pu
ALLEN, Brigan		30	M	Laborer	22Ma02Pu
CONNELL, Thos.		23	M	Laborer	22Ma02Pu
CASSIDY, Thos.		30	M	Laborer	22Ma02Pu
U	(W)	30	F	Wife	22Ma02Pu
Ann	(D)	03	F	Child	22Ma02Pu

ADAM-WRIGHT 22 MAY 1847

From Glasgow

NAMES OF PASSENGERS		AGE	SEX	OCCUPATIONS	DATE PORT SHIP
MCIVER, Michael		40	M	Farmer	22Ma04Pv
Mary	(W)	35	F	Wife	22Ma04Pv
Michael	(S)	16	M	None	22Ma04Pv
Ann	(D)	07	F	Child	22Ma04Pv
Patrick	(S)	05	M	Child	22Ma04Pv
MCDADE, Hannah		20	F	None	22Ma04Pv
Corns.	(P)	50	M	Farmer	22Ma04Pv
Corns.	(B)	24	M	Farmer	22Ma04Pv
Bridget	(T)	18	F	None	22Ma04Pv
Elizabeth	(T)	05	F	Child	22Ma04Pv
CULLINS, James		30	M	Laborer	22Ma04Pv
Daniel		28	M	Laborer	22Ma04Pv
MCCONALONG, Dani.		26	M	Laborer	22Ma04Pv
Mary		00	F	None	22Ma04Pv
TAGGART, Patrick		21	M	Laborer	22Ma04Pv
Nancy		20	F	None	22Ma04Pv
PORTER, Ann		18	F	Unknown	22Ma04Pv
DICK, John		38	M	Farmer	22Ma04Pv
Sarah	(W)	35	F	Wife	22Ma04Pv
James	(S)	15	M	None	22Ma04Pv
Mary-Ann	(D)	13	F	None	22Ma04Pv
William	(S)	11	M	None	22Ma04Pv
John	(S)	09	M	Child	22Ma04Pv
Alexander	(S)	06	M	Child	22Ma04Pv
Joseph	(S)	03	M	Child	22Ma04Pv
Jesse		21	F	None	22Ma04Pv
NELSON, Bridget		20	F	None	22Ma04Pv
MCSHEFREY, Dani.		22	M	Laborer	22Ma04Pv
LARKIN, Richard		26	M	Laborer	22Ma04Pv
NEILSON, George		18	M	Laborer	22Ma04Pv
CREELMAN, Robert		32	M	Farmer	22Ma04Pv
Eliza	(W)	32	F	Wife	22Ma04Pv
Thomas	(S)	09	M	Child	22Ma04Pv
Betty-Ann	(D)	06	F	Child	22Ma04Pv
Sarah-Jane	(D)	02	F	Child	22Ma04Pv

NAMES OF PASSENGERS		A G E	S E X	OCCUPATIONS	DATE PORT SHIP	NAMES OF PASSENGERS		A G E	S E X	OCCUPATIONS	DATE PORT SHIP
ALLAN, Charles		21	M	Laborer	22Ma04Pv	MCDONALD, Catherine	(D)	02	F	Child	22Ma04Pv
MCLAUGHLIN, Margaret		20	F	None	22Ma04Pv	DICK, Helen		26	F	None	22Ma04Pv
SMITH, William		18	M	Laborer	22Ma04Pv	KENNEDY, Robt.		37	M	Farmer	22Ma04Pv
MCCARRON, John		30	M	Laborer	22Ma04Pv	Letitia	(W)	37	F	Wife	22Ma04Pv
TORMY, Honoria		18	F	None	22Ma04Pv	Mary-Jane	(D)	13	F	None	22Ma04Pv
MICHAN, James		31	M	Laborer	22Ma04Pv	Letitia	(D)	05	F	Child	22Ma04Pv
MCGOWAN, Cath.		30	F	None	22Ma04Pv	Peggy-Ann	(D)	.01	F	Infant	22Ma04Pv
Giles	(S)	15	M	None	22Ma04Pv	DOHERTY, Patrick		22	M	Farmer	22Ma04Pv
DOCHERTY, John		30	M	Laborer	22Ma04Pv	RUDDY, James		00	M	Unknown	22Ma04Pv
William		20	M	Laborer	22Ma04Pv	BRIELAND, Patrick		25	M	None	22Ma04Pv
Bridget		20	F	None	22Ma04Pv	BARNES, James		00	M	Physician	22Ma04Pv
CALLAHAN, Bell		24	F	None	22Ma04Pv	WRIGHT, U-Mrs.		00	F	None	22Ma04Pv
CALHOUN, Sarah		24	F	None	22Ma04Pv						
STEVENSON, Robert		23	M	Laborer	22Ma04Pv						
BROWN, Ellen		20	F	None	22Ma04Pv						
MCDADE, Bridget		20	F	None	22Ma04Pv						
DOCHERTY, Owen		40	M	Farmer	22Ma04Pv						
Mary	(W)	40	F	Wife	22Ma04Pv						
Hugh	(S)	17	M	Farmer	22Ma04Pv						
Michael	(S)	15	M	Farmer	22Ma04Pv	**WATERLOO 22 MAY 1847**					
John	(S)	12	M	Farmer	22Ma04Pv						
James	(S)	10	M	Farmer	22Ma04Pv	From Liverpool					
Nancy	(D)	06	F	Child	22Ma04Pv						
Mary	(D)	.03	F	Infant	22Ma04Pv						
HASLET, James		40	M	Farmer	22Ma04Pv	COOK, Kath.		34	F	None	22Ma02As
Jane	(W)	32	F	Wife	22Ma04Pv	Wm.	(S)	06	M	Child	22Ma02As
Elizabeth	(D)	03	F	Child	22Ma04Pv	Frans.	(S)	04	M	Child	22Ma02As
Bridget	(M)	60	F	None	22Ma04Pv	HOUGHTON, Jane		40	F	None	22Ma02As
DONNELLY, James		29	M	Laborer	22Ma04Pv	BOGIN, A.		30	M	Unknown	22Ma02As
MCKEENY, Ann		40	F	None	22Ma04Pv	LIVINGSTON, J.		25	M	Unknown	22Ma02As
Patrick	(S)	20	M	Laborer	22Ma04Pv	COFFEE, Ann		47	F	None	22Ma02As
Michael	(S)	18	M	Laborer	22Ma04Pv	MCCARTHY, D.		40	M	Unknown	22Ma02As
Owen	(S)	10	M	Laborer	22Ma04Pv	Zina	(W)	34	F	Wife	22Ma02As
CULLEN, John		18	M	Laborer	22Ma04Pv	Rocknall	(S)	12	M	None	22Ma02As
MCCRACKEN, W.		50	M	Laborer	22Ma04Pv	Dalton	(S)	10	M	None	22Ma02As
AUSTIN, Archib.		22	M	Laborer	22Ma04Pv	Malden	(S)	08	M	Child	22Ma02As
Elizabeth	(W)	20	F	Wife	22Ma04Pv	John	(S)	03	M	Child	22Ma02As
Catherine	(D)	.02	F	Infant	22Ma04Pv	Ann	(D)	13	F	None	22Ma02As
CLYDE, John		60	M	Laborer	22Ma04Pv	MYLES, My.A.		42	F	None	22Ma02As
Jane	(D)	25	F	None	22Ma04Pv	Clara	(D)	04	F	Child	22Ma02As
BRADLY, Patrick		26	M	Farmer	22Ma04Pv	Magt.	(D)	01	F	Child	22Ma02As
Ann	(W)	26	F	Wife	22Ma04Pv	NORMAND, J.		19	M	Unknown	22Ma02As
Bridget	(D)	.03	F	Infant	22Ma04Pv	Woodgg--, T.		28	M	Unknown	22Ma02As
QUIG, Bridget		28	F	None	22Ma04Pv	ARSINACH, E.		21	M	Unknown	22Ma02As
Catherine	(D)	02	F	Child	22Ma04Pv	GREENSHAW, John		32	M	Unknown	22Ma02As
DOHERTY, Mary		30	F	None	22Ma04Pv	Eh.		19	M	Unknown	22Ma02As
MCCONALONG, Mary		30	F	None	22Ma04Pv	BLACK, W.K.		09	M	Child	22Ma02As
MCCASKEY, William		27	M	Laborer	22Ma04Pv	SHELLY, J.		25	M	Unknown	22Ma02As
Jane		20	F	None	22Ma04Pv	John		20	M	Unknown	22Ma02As
BARTON, Thomas		30	M	Laborer	22Ma04Pv	Mgt.		20	F	None	22Ma02As
KIRKPATRICK, Elizabeth		70	F	None	22Ma04Pv	GRAY, J.		20	M	Unknown	22Ma02As
Nelly		24	F	None	22Ma04Pv	MCGOVERN, W.		19	M	Unknown	22Ma02As
Harriet		.01	F	Infant	22Ma04Pv	Jane		19	F	None	22Ma02As
HOGG, Jane		18	F	None	22Ma04Pv	NEALAN, D.		51	M	Unknown	22Ma02As
BOLTON, Saml.		20	M	Laborer	22Ma04Pv	John	(S)	22	M	Unknown	22Ma02As
William		30	M	Laborer	22Ma04Pv	Denis	(S)	20	M	Unknown	22Ma02As
Ann		18	F	None	22Ma04Pv	James	(S)	18	M	Unknown	22Ma02As
MOORE, Maria		18	F	None	22Ma04Pv	GALAGHER, W.		27	M	Unknown	22Ma02As
BOLTON, Joseph		18	M	Laborer	22Ma04Pv	CONNELL, J.		22	M	Unknown	22Ma02As
SMITH, Neal		36	M	Laborer	22Ma04Pv	BRADLY, J.		26	M	Unknown	22Ma02As
John	(S)	13	M	Laborer	22Ma04Pv	T.		15	M	Unknown	22Ma02As
CAMPBELL, Charity		20	F	None	22Ma04Pv	CAMPBELL, Elzt.		20	F	None	22Ma02As
REID, George		36	M	Laborer	22Ma04Pv	BRADY, Bgt.		20	F	None	22Ma02As
CATHERWOOD, Jas.		25	M	Farmer	22Ma04Pv	MOIRS, Cath.		24	F	None	22Ma02As
William		21	M	Farmer	22Ma04Pv	HOONAN, Rosanne		24	F	None	22Ma02As
Jane		28	F	None	22Ma04Pv	MCGRATH, Cath.		16	F	None	22Ma02As
DUNCAN, James		19	M	Farmer	22Ma04Pv	GERGEN, M.M.		41	M	Unknown	22Ma02As
COOK, Edward		22	M	Farmer	22Ma04Pv	RINCH, T.		24	M	Unknown	22Ma02As
Ann		22	F	None	22Ma04Pv	BURKE, Mgt.		24	F	None	22Ma02As
RUDDEN, Ann		16	F	None	22Ma04Pv	GIBNEY, J.		27	M	Unknown	22Ma02As
MCDONALD, Betsy		38	F	None	22Ma04Pv	MANDER, J.		26	M	Unknown	22Ma02As
Mary	(D)	13	F	None	22Ma04Pv	U	(W)	24	F	Wife	22Ma02As
Ann	(D)	10	F	None	22Ma04Pv	GORMAN, Wlfrd.		19	F	None	22Ma02As
Margaret	(D)	08	F	Child	22Ma04Pv	BERINGHAM, My.		24	F	None	22Ma02As
Thomas	(S)	06	M	Child	22Ma04Pv	KIVNEY, P.		24	M	Unknown	22Ma02As
						MAHONY, My.		20	F	None	22Ma02As

534

NAMES OF PASSENGERS		AGE	SEX	OCCUPATIONS	DATE PORT SHIP
North-AT, J.		26	M	Unknown	22Ma02As
Judy		24	F	None	22Ma02As
DILLON, M.		24	M	Unknown	22Ma02As
ORMESBY, Mgt.		21	F	None	22Ma02As
FINLY, Bgt.		20	F	None	22Ma02As
CONNELL, O.		22	M	Unknown	22Ma02As
SMITH, P.		38	M	Unknown	22Ma02As
LYNCH, W.		34	M	Unknown	22Ma02As
Eleanor		30	F	None	22Ma02As
CARRIGAN, P.		34	M	Unknown	22Ma02As
GLERY, M.		34	M	Unknown	22Ma02As
Jas.		24	M	Unknown	22Ma02As
Ellen		28	F	None	22Ma02As
Ann		24	F	None	22Ma02As
Betty		20	F	None	22Ma02As
RILY, My.		24	M	Unknown	22Ma02As
GRAY, Ann		26	F	None	22Ma02As
RILY, Mgt.		25	F	None	22Ma02As
Pat		24	M	Unknown	22Ma02As
MASTERS, P.		18	M	Unknown	22Ma02As
MCCABE, Ann		54	F	None	22Ma02As
Eliza	(D)	21	F	None	22Ma02As
Ann	(D)	19	F	None	22Ma02As
Mgt.	(D)	17	F	None	22Ma02As
Cath.	(D)	10	F	None	22Ma02As
Susan	(D)	07	F	Child	22Ma02As
J.	(S)	05	M	Child	22Ma02As
LEAMY, M.		19	M	Unknown	22Ma02As
SMITH, T.		21	M	Unknown	22Ma02As
GALLAGHER, J.		27	M	Unknown	22Ma02As
KELLY, J.		28	M	Unknown	22Ma02As
MCCLOSKY, P.		26	M	Unknown	22Ma02As
CLARY, J.		27	M	Unknown	22Ma02As
SANDERS, M.		20	M	Unknown	22Ma02As
OBRIEN, W.		24	M	Unknown	22Ma02As
KEARNS, J.		27	M	Unknown	22Ma02As
Ann		20	F	None	22Ma02As
RYAN, T.		23	M	Unknown	22Ma02As
RIDDLE, H.		25	M	Unknown	22Ma02As
MCLELLAND, J.		19	M	Unknown	22Ma02As
BOWMAN, Jane		19	F	None	22Ma02As
GALLAGHER, J.		29	M	Unknown	22Ma02As
Edwd.		20	M	Unknown	22Ma02As
Hanah		24	F	None	22Ma02As
Hanah		18	F	None	22Ma02As
Sally		14	F	None	22Ma02As
Bdgt.		13	F	None	22Ma02As
Owen		08	M	Child	22Ma02As
Fanny		07	F	Child	22Ma02As
DOOGAN, E.		30	M	Unknown	22Ma02As
CHAPMAN, J.		20	M	Unknown	22Ma02As
U	(W)	26	F	Wife	22Ma02As
My.J.	(D)	03	F	Child	22Ma02As
Mgt.	(D)	01	F	Child	22Ma02As
MILLS, My.		20	F	None	22Ma02As
GALLGHER, M.		28	M	Unknown	22Ma02As
John		17	M	Unknown	22Ma02As
Peter		15	M	None	22Ma02As
Cath.		20	F	None	22Ma02As
BOYLE, D.		20	M	Unknown	22Ma02As
GALLAGHER, My.		16	F	None	22Ma02As
MURPHY, M.		20	M	Unknown	22Ma02As
HOLLINS, Cath.		20	F	None	22Ma02As
MINAHAN, A.		20	M	Unknown	22Ma02As
SHEEHY, D.		25	M	Unknown	22Ma02As
WHITE, T.		25	M	Unknown	22Ma02As
BARNTON, J.		20	M	Unknown	22Ma02As
CASTER, J.		24	M	Unknown	22Ma02As
Kate		20	F	None	22Ma02As
MCBAIN, J.		25	M	Laborer	22Ma02As
FINLY, R.		50	M	Unknown	22Ma02As
U	(W)	40	F	Wife	22Ma02As
Wm.	(S)	18	M	Unknown	22Ma02As
Alice	(D)	19	F	None	22Ma02As
Thos.	(S)	15	M	None	22Ma02As
FINLY, John	(S)	13	M	None	22Ma02As
G.N.	(D)	11	F	None	22Ma02As
Sarah	(D)	09	F	Child	22Ma02As
R.	(S)	07	M	Child	22Ma02As
Edwd.	(S)	05	M	Child	22Ma02As
Rosey	(S)	03	F	Child	22Ma02As
PRICE, N.		30	M	Unknown	22Ma02As
FITZSIMMONS, Cath.		26	F	None	22Ma02As
CAMPBELL, Mgt.		28	F	None	22Ma02As
CONNELL, C.		26	M	Unknown	22Ma02As
RING, P.		24	M	Unknown	22Ma02As
HAWKINS, G.		24	M	Unknown	22Ma02As
DUNN, J.		25	M	Unknown	22Ma02As
FOGARTY, Cath.		20	F	None	22Ma02As
DOYLE, Mgt.		20	F	None	22Ma02As
QUIN, J.		30	M	Unknown	22Ma02As
U	(W)	29	F	Wife	22Ma02As
HELLIGAN, T.		18	M	Unknown	22Ma02As
JEESON, J.		25	M	Unknown	22Ma02As
Thos.		25	M	Unknown	22Ma02As
ILIFT, H.		25	M	Unknown	22Ma02As
CASEY, T.		30	M	Unknown	22Ma02As
SMITH, J.		22	M	Unknown	22Ma02As
Cath.		24	F	None	22Ma02As
DENIS, J.		40	M	Unknown	22Ma02As
Bgt.		30	F	None	22Ma02As
GILL, My.		20	F	None	22Ma02As
WALSH, M.		24	M	Unknown	22Ma02As
CERINGHAM, J.		16	M	Unknown	22Ma02As
D.		22	F	None	22Ma02As
CUNNINGHAM, P.		30	M	Unknown	22Ma02As
MURPHY, M.		18	M	Unknown	22Ma02As
CAHER, Biddy		23	F	None	22Ma02As
NEARY, Biddy		21	F	None	22Ma02As
My.		21	F	None	22Ma02As
MAY, Biddy		21	F	None	22Ma02As
CAHER, My.		21	F	None	22Ma02As
NEARY, Biddy		21	F	None	22Ma02As
Cath.	(D)	01	F	Child	22Ma02As
KEY, J.		46	M	Laborer	22Ma02As
Marie	(D)	10	F	None	22Ma02As
John	(S)	09	M	Child	22Ma02As
Mich.	(S)	07	M	Child	22Ma02As
Mgt.	(D)	06	F	Child	22Ma02As
Pat	(S)	04	M	Child	22Ma02As
My.	(W)	35	F	Wife	22Ma02As
Joe	(S)	02	M	Child	22Ma02As
SMITH, Bgt.		20	F	None	22Ma02As
HOPKINS, J.		38	M	Unknown	22Ma02As
SMITH, C.		30	M	Unknown	22Ma02As
CORKERN, T.		38	M	Unknown	22Ma02As
GROUNY, P.		30	M	Unknown	22Ma02As
U	(W)	27	F	Wife	22Ma02As
Bgt.	(D)	09	F	Child	22Ma02As
Ann	(D)	07	F	Child	22Ma02As
Ellen	(D)	02	F	Child	22Ma02As
Ann	(D)	01	F	Child	22Ma02As
DUFFY, J.		27	M	Unknown	22Ma02As
My.		25	F	None	22Ma02As
John		19	M	Unknown	22Ma02As
CARMODY, M.		50	M	Unknown	22Ma02As
U	(W)	50	F	Wife	22Ma02As
Pat	(S)	30	M	Unknown	22Ma02As
Owen	(S)	28	M	Unknown	22Ma02As
Bryan	(S)	22	M	Unknown	22Ma02As
Peter	(S)	20	M	Unknown	22Ma02As
Ann	(D)	16	F	None	22Ma02As
Mich.	(S)	15	M	None	22Ma02As
Jas.	(S)	14	M	Unknown	22Ma02As
Cath.	(D)	13	F	None	22Ma02As
Biddy	(D)	05	F	Child	22Ma02As
LYNCH, Rose		20	F	None	22Ma02As
ROURKE, P.		21	M	Unknown	22Ma02As
QUIN, My.		24	F	None	22Ma02As
MCGUIRE, J.		22	M	Unknown	22Ma02As

NAMES OF PASSENGERS		A G E	S E X	OCCUPATIONS	DATE PORT SHIP
DALY, L.		21	M	Unknown	22Ma02As
SHANNON, S.		30	M	Unknown	22Ma02As
ROBINSON, J.		24	M	Unknown	22Ma02As
OWENS, F.		25	M	Laborer	22Ma02As
JUDGE, J.		49	M	Unknown	22Ma02As
Denis	(S)	19	M	Unknown	22Ma02As
James	(S)	16	M	Unknown	22Ma02As
BRADY, T.		24	M	Unknown	22Ma02As
RILY, Mgt.		30	F	None	22Ma02As
HICKY, W.		28	M	Unknown	22Ma02As
GUISEN, M.		25	F	None	22Ma02As
LEVY, P.		24	M	Unknown	22Ma02As
DUFFY, C.		23	M	Unknown	22Ma02As
FINY, H.		22	M	Unknown	22Ma02As
JESLYN, Ann		20	F	None	22Ma02As
CALLAGHAN, P.		23	M	Unknown	22Ma02As
My.		18	F	None	22Ma02As
Susan		18	F	None	22Ma02As
SMITH, B.		30	M	Unknown	22Ma02As
U	(W)	28	F	Wife	22Ma02As
KELLY, D.		28	M	Unknown	22Ma02As
Betsy	(W)	24	F	Wife	22Ma02As
John	(S)	04	M	Child	22Ma02As
Chas.	(B)	25	M	Unknown	22Ma02As
REARDEN, M.		28	M	Unknown	22Ma02As
KELLY, J.		28	M	Unknown	22Ma02As
MURPHY, Bessy		22	F	None	22Ma02As
CALLANAN, Mgt.		22	F	None	22Ma02As
BRANAGAN, P.		25	M	Unknown	22Ma02As
BARTLETT, H.		26	M	Unknown	22Ma02As
HILLARD, P.		25	M	Unknown	22Ma02As
CAPENTER, P.		30	M	Unknown	22Ma02As
Bgt.		25	F	None	22Ma02As
WALKER, C.		23	M	Unknown	22Ma02As
DALY, M.		24	M	Unknown	22Ma02As
BICK, J.		24	M	Unknown	22Ma02As
DELANY, D.		40	M	Unknown	22Ma02As
JONES, J.		44	M	Unknown	22Ma02As
My.	(W)	42	F	Wife	22Ma02As
Eliza	(D)	21	F	None	22Ma02As
Hebt.	(S)	16	M	Unknown	22Ma02As
Alice	(D)	13	F	None	22Ma02As
COLLINS, Cath.		22	F	None	22Ma02As
JONES, Ely.		09	M	Child	22Ma02As
Ann		11	F	None	22Ma02As
Chas.		06	M	Child	22Ma02As
John		04	M	Child	22Ma02As
CAVANAGH, B.		33	M	Laborer	22Ma02As
Cath.		30	F	None	22Ma02As
DELANY, Eliza		11	F	None	22Ma02As
Peter		09	M	Child	22Ma02As
Chas.		08	M	Child	22Ma02As
CARNAHAN, J.		02	M	Child	22Ma02As
HOGAN, J.		30	M	Unknown	22Ma02As
DART, G.		32	M	Unknown	22Ma02As
TURNER, P.		29	M	Unknown	22Ma02As
BIRNY, J.		24	M	Unknown	22Ma02As
OBRIEN, J.		50	M	Unknown	22Ma02As
Wifd.		40	F	None	22Ma02As
HAGAN, S.		66	M	Unknown	22Ma02As
REDFORD, T.		38	M	Unknown	22Ma02As
U	(W)	39	F	Wife	22Ma02As
W.	(S)	14	M	None	22Ma02As
Thos.	(S)	11	M	None	22Ma02As
George	(S)	05	M	Child	22Ma02As
WASHBURN, J.		25	M	Unknown	22Ma02As
GRAYSON, N.		42	M	Unknown	22Ma02As
ELEGREW, Hanah		22	F	None	22Ma02As
BRADY, Edwd.		21	M	Unknown	22Ma02As
NOONE, J.		34	M	Unknown	22Ma02As
My.	(W)	23	F	Wife	22Ma02As
Julia	(D)	02	F	Child	22Ma02As
Eliza	(D)	02	F	Child	22Ma02As
CORBETT, J.		20	M	Unknown	22Ma02As
CONNLY, M.		20	M	Unknown	22Ma02As

NAMES OF PASSENGERS		A G E	S E X	OCCUPATIONS	DATE PORT SHIP
HANSON, M.		20	M	Unknown	22Ma02As
Mich.		20	M	Unknown	22Ma02As
MCCORMICK, J.		40	M	Unknown	22Ma02As
Mgt.		24	F	None	22Ma02As
GRIFFEN, My.		27	F	None	22Ma02As
LYONS, P.		20	M	Unknown	22Ma02As
GRIFFEN, M.		24	F	None	22Ma02As
MCCORMICK, P.		16	M	Unknown	22Ma02As
NEWTON, My.		18	F	None	22Ma02As
CONNOR, My.		19	F	None	22Ma02As
NEWTON, My.A.		19	F	None	22Ma02As
FARMER, J.		17	F	None	22Ma02As
FAULKNER, D.		27	F	None	22Ma02As
Eliza		14	F	None	22Ma02As
ROACH, J.		21	M	Laborer	22Ma02As
U	(W)	21	F	Wife	22Ma02As
John	(S)	02	M	Child	22Ma02As
Richd.	(S)	01	M	Child	22Ma02As
GOODMAN, G.		26	M	Unknown	22Ma02As
MCNULTY, P.		27	M	Unknown	22Ma02As
LAHEEN, My.		20	F	None	22Ma02As
MCDERMOTT, J.		34	M	Unknown	22Ma02As
Jas.	(S)	03	M	Child	22Ma02As
Edwd.	(S)	01	M	Child	22Ma02As
Sarah	(W)	34	F	Wife	22Ma02As
Biddy	(M)	68	F	None	22Ma02As
LAFFERTY, Rose		22	F	None	22Ma02As
DOUGHERTY, N.		20	M	Unknown	22Ma02As
MCCALLINAN, O.		24	M	Unknown	22Ma02As
MURPHY, T.		50	M	Unknown	22Ma02As
John	(S)	24	M	Unknown	22Ma02As
Johanna	(W)	45	F	Wife	22Ma02As
SULLIVAN, E.		27	M	Unknown	22Ma02As
MCCAULY, F.		25	M	Unknown	22Ma02As
CURTIN, J.		40	M	Unknown	22Ma02As
Biddy		36	F	None	22Ma02As
Simon		35	M	Unknown	22Ma02As
John		38	M	Unknown	22Ma02As
JOHNSON, J.		45	M	Unknown	22Ma02As
POTTS, P.		25	M	Unknown	22Ma02As
HEARNE, M.		27	M	Unknown	22Ma02As
Marlb---, F.		22	M	Unknown	22Ma02As
Ja.		22	M	Unknown	22Ma02As
My.		18	F	None	22Ma02As
Bt.		17	F	None	22Ma02As
PUGH, R.		38	M	Unknown	22Ma02As
M.		15	F	None	22Ma02As
My.		23	F	None	22Ma02As
BLAKY, H.		16	M	Unknown	22Ma02As
JONSTON, J.		28	M	Unknown	22Ma02As
BARRETT, R.		47	M	Unknown	22Ma02As
TURNER, W.		37	M	Unknown	22Ma02As
M.		15	F	None	22Ma02As
M.		15	M	None	22Ma02As
FERGUSON, T.		45	M	Laborer	22Ma02As
WOODS, E.		30	M	Unknown	22Ma02As
REEVES, N.		12	M	Unknown	22Ma02As
BROWN, S.		34	M	Unknown	22Ma02As
CULLEN, F.		40	M	Unknown	22Ma02As
My.		16	F	None	22Ma02As
HERN, Mgt.		20	F	None	22Ma02As

GLENMORE 24 MAY 1847

From Belfast

NAMES OF PASSENGERS		A G E	S E X	OCCUPATIONS	DATE PORT SHIP
SMITH, Wm.		18	M	None	24Ma07Km
Alex.		16	M	None	24Ma07Km
MURRAY, Geo.		30	M	Farmer	24Ma07Km

NAMES OF PASSENGERS		AGE	SEX	OCCUPATIONS	DATE PORT SHIP
MURRAY, Susan	(W)	30	F	Wife	24Ma07Km
Mary	(D)	05	F	Child	24Ma07Km
George	(S)	07	M	Child	24Ma07Km
Jerrimla	(S)	03	M	Child	24Ma07Km
HUTCHISON, John		25	M	Farmer	24Ma07Km
MCMURRAY, Joseph		19	M	Farmer	24Ma07Km
SMITH, Anna		31	F	None	24Ma07Km
FIELD, Dennis		25	M	Farmer	24Ma07Km
MCALLISTER, Eliza		20	F	None	24Ma07Km
GALLAGHER, John		25	M	Farmer	24Ma07Km
BROWN, Robt.		20	M	Farmer	24Ma07Km
GALLAGHER, Sarah		20	F	None	24Ma07Km
MELLON, Betty		20	F	None	24Ma07Km
WOODS, William		25	M	Farmer	24Ma07Km
MARTIN, Saml.		21	M	Farmer	24Ma07Km
CORGIN, Henry		25	M	Farmer	24Ma07Km
Alley	(W)	23	F	Wife	24Ma07Km
Mary	(D)	03	F	Child	24Ma07Km
James	(S)	01	M	Child	24Ma07Km
LANE, Jas.		20	M	Laborer	24Ma07Km
Eliza	(W)	20	F	Wife	24Ma07Km
Robert	(S)	.10	M	Infant	24Ma07Km
TIMMANY, Peter		18	M	Laborer	24Ma07Km
MCGAWAN, James		35	M	Laborer	24Ma07Km
Jane	(D)	04	F	Child	24Ma07Km
Mary	(D)	03	F	Child	24Ma07Km
BOYD, Susan		20	F	None	24Ma07Km
BRITTON, James		19	M	Laborer	24Ma07Km
MCKEEVER, Biddy		49	F	None	24Ma07Km
George	(S)	19	M	Laborer	24Ma07Km
SMITH, Anne		25	F	None	24Ma07Km
MCCRACKEN, David		40	M	Laborer	24Ma07Km
Peggy		34	F	None	24Ma07Km
DALLAS, John		15	M	Laborer	24Ma07Km
GRAHAM, Peggy		24	F	None	24Ma07Km
MCCOOK, Mary		30	F	None	24Ma07Km
GARDNER, Alexn.		50	M	Laborer	24Ma07Km
James	(S)	21	M	Laborer	24Ma07Km
MULVENAN, Felice		25	F	None	24Ma07Km
MCCAFFREY, William		20	M	Laborer	24Ma07Km
CASSIDY, Jane		25	F	None	24Ma07Km
ONEILL, James		25	M	Laborer	24Ma07Km
Francis		16	M	Laborer	24Ma07Km
Michael		20	M	Laborer	24Ma07Km
Mary		18	F	None	24Ma07Km
MADDEN, Lawrence		20	M	Laborer	24Ma07Km
MULVENAN, Anna		22	F	None	24Ma07Km
CONWAY, Sarah		23	F	None	24Ma07Km
MELVAN, Lawrence		30	M	Laborer	24Ma07Km
MCMANUS, James		35	M	Laborer	24Ma07Km
MCCRAGSTAL, Anna		28	F	None	24Ma07Km
MCGUKEN, Daniel		42	M	Laborer	24Ma07Km
Mary	(W)	40	F	Wife	24Ma07Km
Daniel	(S)	18	M	Laborer	24Ma07Km
James	(S)	15	M	Laborer	24Ma07Km
Michael	(S)	13	M	Laborer	24Ma07Km
Patrick	(S)	11	M	Laborer	24Ma07Km
Anna	(D)	09	F	Child	24Ma07Km
Sarah	(D)	07	F	Child	24Ma07Km
Rosey	(D)	.08	F	Infant	24Ma07Km
CAWDEN, Mary		27	F	None	24Ma07Km
Rosey	(D)	.06	F	Infant	24Ma07Km
WARD, Owen		30	M	Laborer	24Ma07Km
PHILLIPS, John		28	M	Laborer	24Ma07Km
WRIGHT, John		28	M	Laborer	24Ma07Km
James		18	M	Laborer	24Ma07Km
WOODS, Mary		18	F	None	24Ma07Km
MCCULLOUGH, William		30	M	Laborer	24Ma07Km
Mary	(W)	28	F	Wife	24Ma07Km
Robert	(S)	11	M	None	24Ma07Km
John	(S)	02	M	Child	24Ma07Km
SWAN, Hugh		20	M	Laborer	24Ma07Km
GORDON, Allen		18	M	Laborer	24Ma07Km
Hugh		14	M	Laborer	24Ma07Km
DORAN, James		40	M	Laborer	24Ma07Km
DORAN, Sarah	(W)	40	F	Wife	24Ma07Km
John	(S)	20	M	Laborer	24Ma07Km
Anna	(D)	19	F	None	24Ma07Km
Jane	(D)	13	F	None	24Ma07Km
Thomas	(S)	11	M	Laborer	24Ma07Km
MULLINGTON, Wm.		21	M	Laborer	24Ma07Km
DILLON, Pat		25	M	Laborer	24Ma07Km
Sarah		12	F	None	24Ma07Km
MENAY, Neal		14	M	Laborer	24Ma07Km
MCQUADE, Pat		35	M	Laborer	24Ma07Km
CONNOR, Peter		11	M	Laborer	24Ma07Km
MCQUADE, Michael		40	M	Laborer	24Ma07Km
JACK, James		21	M	Laborer	24Ma07Km
Eliza		18	F	None	24Ma07Km
MCVEIGH, Seras		20	M	Laborer	24Ma07Km
EVANS, Hannah		20	F	None	24Ma07Km
Mary		18	F	None	24Ma07Km
STUART, Ed.		22	M	Laborer	24Ma07Km
Anna		20	F	None	24Ma07Km
MCGINNIS, Thos.		20	M	Laborer	24Ma07Km
WHITE, William		21	M	Laborer	24Ma07Km
GARRET, Robt.		22	M	Laborer	24Ma07Km
DRUMMOND, Michal		20	M	Laborer	24Ma07Km
William		18	M	Laborer	24Ma07Km
MCCRYSTAL, Pat		27	M	Laborer	24Ma07Km
MCNULTY, Bernard		16	M	Laborer	24Ma07Km
CROOKS, Saml.		35	M	Laborer	24Ma07Km
John		19	M	Laborer	24Ma07Km
MANON, Hugh		55	M	Laborer	24Ma07Km
Sarah		55	F	None	24Ma07Km
HAMPTON, Francis		30	M	Laborer	24Ma07Km
Sarah		30	F	None	24Ma07Km
LIVINGSTON, Eliza		30	F	None	24Ma07Km
HAMPTON, Matt		04	M	Child	24Ma07Km
John		02	M	Child	24Ma07Km
James		02	M	Child	24Ma07Km
DONAGHY, Mary		30	F	None	24Ma07Km
POTTS, John		40	M	Laborer	24Ma07Km
RAMSAY, Robt.		50	M	Laborer	24Ma07Km
MCCRAY, Francis		20	M	Laborer	24Ma07Km
MCGINNIS, John		25	M	Laborer	24Ma07Km
Margt.		22	F	None	24Ma07Km
BRENNAN, Michael		20	M	Laborer	24Ma07Km
CAIN, Henry		24	M	Laborer	24Ma07Km
DARAGLE, Anna		21	F	None	24Ma07Km
MCPELAN, Sarah		28	F	None	24Ma07Km
Argt.	(M)	24	F	None	24Ma07Km
GARDNER, Ellen		19	F	None	24Ma07Km
Saml.		14	M	Laborer	24Ma07Km
Mary		13	F	None	24Ma07Km
MCGOWAN, Neill		30	M	Laborer	24Ma07Km
George	(S)	05	M	Child	24Ma07Km
MCDERMOTT, Jas.		25	M	Laborer	24Ma07Km
OIR, John		50	M	Laborer	24Ma07Km
Margt.	(W)	50	F	Wife	24Ma07Km
Eliza	(D)	20	F	None	24Ma07Km
Susan	(D)	18	F	None	24Ma07Km
James	(S)	16	F	None	24Ma07Km
John	(S)	13	M	None	24Ma07Km
Margt.	(D)	12	F	None	24Ma07Km
REYNOLDS, Mary		18	F	None	24Ma07Km
DAVISON, Jane		18	F	None	24Ma07Km
MCKEOWN, John		28	M	Laborer	24Ma07Km
HUTCHISON, William		20	M	Laborer	24Ma07Km
MCKEOWN, Hannah		20	F	None	24Ma07Km
KRILLY, Patrick		40	M	Laborer	24Ma07Km
Susan		25	F	None	24Ma07Km
MCBRIDE, Michael		20	M	Laborer	24Ma07Km
MCCRYSTAL, John		18	M	Laborer	24Ma07Km
MCILWEE, Susan		18	F	None	24Ma07Km
SMITH, Robt.		30	M	Laborer	24Ma07Km
Eliza		20	F	None	24Ma07Km
James		18	F	None	24Ma07Km
MCILWANE, Pat		20	F	None	24Ma07Km
Charles		18	F	None	24Ma07Km

NAMES OF PASSENGERS		A G E	S E X	OCCUPATIONS	DATE PORT SHIP
MANEN, John		21	F	None	24Ma07Km
MCGINNIS, Patrick		30	F	None	24Ma07Km
MULVENEY, Patrick		30	F	None	24Ma07Km
Rose		28	F	None	24Ma07Km
MCANLEY, Sarah		25	F	None	24Ma07Km
MCCASH, Rose		20	F	None	24Ma07Km
MCILVENY, John		23	M	Laborer	24Ma07Km
Anna		20	F	None	24Ma07Km
LAMONNT, Robt.		25	M	Laborer	24Ma07Km
Mary		20	F	None	24Ma07Km
AUSTINN, Frank		16	M	Laborer	24Ma07Km
PALMER, Thomas		18	M	Laborer	24Ma07Km
DONAGHUE, James		30	M	Laborer	24Ma07Km
Mary		30	F	None	24Ma07Km

CLARENCE 24 MAY 1847

From Galway

NAMES OF PASSENGERS		A G E	S E X	OCCUPATIONS	DATE PORT SHIP
CALLIGHAN, John		25	M	Farmer	24Ma11Gp
Nancy	(W)	30	F	Wife	24Ma11Gp
John	(S)	07	M	Child	24Ma11Gp
Pat	(S)	06	M	Child	24Ma11Gp
Peter	(S)	03	M	Child	24Ma11Gp
MORRIS, Michael		17	M	Laborer	24Ma11Gp
HYNES, Ed.		34	M	Laborer	24Ma11Gp
Mary	(W)	32	F	Wife	24Ma11Gp
John	(S)	07	M	Child	24Ma11Gp
Mary	(D)	04	F	Child	24Ma11Gp
NAUGHTON, John		24	M	Laborer	24Ma11Gp
CONOLON, Pat		28	M	Laborer	24Ma11Gp
Bdgt.		24	F	None	24Ma11Gp
MCNAMARA, Matt		26	M	Laborer	24Ma11Gp
Hannah	(W)	34	F	Wife	24Ma11Gp
Anthy.	(D)	02	F	Child	24Ma11Gp
FATAY, James		27	M	Laborer	24Ma11Gp
Patt		29	M	Laborer	24Ma11Gp
Mary		28	F	None	24Ma11Gp
Mary		18	F	None	24Ma11Gp
Mary		05	F	Child	24Ma11Gp
MURPHY, Frank		32	M	Laborer	24Ma11Gp
Honor	(W)	35	F	Wife	24Ma11Gp
Mary		42	F	None	24Ma11Gp
Martin	(S)	09	M	Child	24Ma11Gp
Mary	(D)	07	F	Child	24Ma11Gp
Biddy	(D)	05	F	Child	24Ma11Gp
Frank	(S)	02	M	Child	24Ma11Gp
CONNOLLY, James		22	M	Farmer	24Ma11Gp
Martin	(B)	21	M	Farmer	24Ma11Gp
Patt	(B)	19	M	Farmer	24Ma11Gp
Cathe.	(M)	40	F	None	24Ma11Gp
WALSH, Michael		28	M	Farmer	24Ma11Gp
HALLORAN, Honor		28	F	None	24Ma11Gp
WALSHE, Mary		18	F	None	24Ma11Gp
Patt		12	M	None	24Ma11Gp
Thaddy		30	M	Farmer	24Ma11Gp
Honor		30	F	None	24Ma11Gp
Biddy		29	F	None	24Ma11Gp
Mary		05	F	Child	24Ma11Gp
Michael		03	M	Child	24Ma11Gp
DOWNES, Michael		24	M	Laborer	24Ma11Gp
WARD, David		21	M	Laborer	24Ma11Gp
FLANNERY, Wm.		38	M	Laborer	24Ma11Gp
HYNES, James		26	M	Laborer	24Ma11Gp
FAHAY, John		19	M	Laborer	24Ma11Gp
Patt		38	M	Laborer	24Ma11Gp
Bridget		34	F	None	24Ma11Gp
Bridget		28	F	None	24Ma11Gp
Mary		18	F	None	24Ma11Gp

NAMES OF PASSENGERS		A G E	S E X	OCCUPATIONS	DATE PORT SHIP
FAHAY, Bdgt.		09	F	Child	24Ma11Gp
Michael		07	M	Child	24Ma11Gp
MURPHY, Michael		18	M	Farmer	24Ma11Gp
FAHEY, Mary		27	F	None	24Ma11Gp
ROONY, Martin		21	M	Farmer	24Ma11Gp
MURPHY, James		28	M	Farmer	24Ma11Gp
Mary	(W)	21	F	Wife	24Ma11Gp
Peggy	(D)	07	F	Child	24Ma11Gp
Cathe.	(D)	05	F	Child	24Ma11Gp
CURRAN, Michael		32	M	Farmer	24Ma11Gp
Peggy	(W)	34	F	Wife	24Ma11Gp
John	(S)	07	M	Child	24Ma11Gp
HARE, Thos.		32	M	Laborer	24Ma11Gp
Biddy		38	F	None	24Ma11Gp
MANLEY, Martin		21	M	Laborer	24Ma11Gp
FOLAN, Patt		21	M	Laborer	24Ma11Gp
Mary		25	F	None	24Ma11Gp
HECKETT, Patt		21	M	Laborer	24Ma11Gp
JOYCE, Honor		32	F	None	24Ma11Gp
Patt	(S)	14	M	Laborer	24Ma11Gp
Maria	(D)	15	F	None	24Ma11Gp
LARKIN, John		16	M	Laborer	24Ma11Gp
NOLAN, Michael		21	M	Laborer	24Ma11Gp
HEGANS, Bdget.		22	F	None	24Ma11Gp
BURKE, Pat		27	M	Laborer	24Ma11Gp
FLANIGAN, Wm.		17	M	Laborer	24Ma11Gp
Mary		17	F	None	24Ma11Gp
DOOLAY, James		27	M	Laborer	24Ma11Gp
MALAY, Cathe.		28	F	None	24Ma11Gp
John	(H)	34	M	Laborer	24Ma11Gp
Mary	(D)	05	F	Child	24Ma11Gp
Chas.	(S)	04	M	Child	24Ma11Gp
Honora	(D)	03	F	Child	24Ma11Gp
GIBBON, Cathe.		22	F	None	24Ma11Gp
Rose		24	F	None	24Ma11Gp
Patk.		20	M	Laborer	24Ma11Gp
SEAHILL, Austin		17	M	Laborer	24Ma11Gp
DOHERTY, John		19	M	Laborer	24Ma11Gp
WALSHE, Mary		28	F	None	24Ma11Gp
MALEY, James		32	M	Laborer	24Ma11Gp
KINNEY, Michael		44	M	Laborer	24Ma11Gp
Darby		28	M	Laborer	24Ma11Gp
John		18	M	Laborer	24Ma11Gp
Julia		27	F	None	24Ma11Gp
Patt		.00	M	Infant	24Ma11Gp
Mgt.		05	F	Child	24Ma11Gp
WALSHE, James		05	F	Child	24Ma11Gp
ROONEY, Della		32	F	None	24Ma11Gp
Mgt.		27	F	None	24Ma11Gp
SWEENEY, Ann		18	F	None	24Ma11Gp
GOWAN, Maria		18	F	None	24Ma11Gp
Peter		32	M	Laborer	24Ma11Gp

WILLIAM-CARSON 24 MAY 1847

From Liverpool

NAMES OF PASSENGERS		A G E	S E X	OCCUPATIONS	DATE PORT SHIP
MAHER, Mary		26	F	Unknown	24Ma02Pv
Ellen		21	F	Unknown	24Ma02Pv
KELLY, Daniel		20	M	Farmer	24Ma02Pv
John		27	M	Unknown	24Ma02Pv
Judy		21	F	Unknown	24Ma02Pv
Ellen		04	F	Child	24Ma02Pv
Patt		02	M	Child	24Ma02Pv
James		.00	M	Infant	24Ma02Pv
MALONEY, Patt		20	M	Unknown	24Ma02Pv
MAGINISS, John		21	M	Unknown	24Ma02Pv
DEEHAN, John		40	M	Unknown	24Ma02Pv
James	(S)	20	M	Unknown	24Ma02Pv

NAMES OF PASSENGERS		AGE	SEX	OCCUPATIONS	DATE/PORT/SHIP
DEEHAN, Hannah	(D)	24	F	Unknown	24Ma02Pw
GALLAGHER, John		30	M	Unknown	24Ma02Pw
LAWLER, Betty		40	F	Unknown	24Ma02Pw
Mary	(D)	12	F	Unknown	24Ma02Pw
Thomas	(S)	10	M	Unknown	24Ma02Pw
Bess	(D)	06	F	Child	24Ma02Pw
Patt	(S)	03	M	Child	24Ma02Pw
Ann	(D)	02	F	Child	24Ma02Pw
KELLY, Patt		25	M	Unknown	24Ma02Pw
JEFFERS, John		25	M	Unknown	24Ma02Pw
WADE, John		25	M	Unknown	24Ma02Pw
COYLE, Patt		50	M	Unknown	24Ma02Pw
Michael	(S)	19	M	Unknown	24Ma02Pw
Margt.	(D)	12	F	Unknown	24Ma02Pw
Owen	(S)	10	M	Unknown	24Ma02Pw
Mary	(D)	08	F	Child	24Ma02Pw
Margt.	(D)	18	F	Unknown	24Ma02Pw
Patt	(S)	20	M	Unknown	24Ma02Pw
Michael	(S)	21	M	Unknown	24Ma02Pw
Abby	(D)	20	F	Unknown	24Ma02Pw
John	(S)	21	M	Unknown	24Ma02Pw
John	(S)	18	M	Unknown	24Ma02Pw
REILLY, Bridget		25	F	Unknown	24Ma02Pw
Margt.	(T)	22	F	Unknown	24Ma02Pw
Thomas	(P)	50	M	Unknown	24Ma02Pw
Math.	(B)	25	M	Unknown	24Ma02Pw
BURKE, Matt.		30	M	Unknown	24Ma02Pw
MULLIGAN, Edw.		30	M	Unknown	24Ma02Pw
Mary		25	F	Unknown	24Ma02Pw
CARSON, George		20	M	Farmer	24Ma02Pw
MAHER, Edmund		25	M	Unknown	24Ma02Pw
BESTION, Michael		23	M	Unknown	24Ma02Pw
Ellen		23	F	Unknown	24Ma02Pw
RIELLY, Con.		30	M	Unknown	24Ma02Pw
Patt.	(S)	10	M	Unknown	24Ma02Pw
MCADOO, John		35	M	Unknown	24Ma02Pw
FONDON, James		27	M	Unknown	24Ma02Pw
MCDERMOTT, W.		18	M	Unknown	24Ma02Pw
Peter		22	M	Unknown	24Ma02Pw
GREEN, George		25	M	Unknown	24Ma02Pw
CONNELL, Mary		20	F	Unknown	24Ma02Pw
JEFFREY, Mary		27	F	Unknown	24Ma02Pw
ELLIOTT, Eliza		25	M	Unknown	24Ma02Pw
Eliza	(D)	02	F	Child	24Ma02Pw
Georgiana	(D)	.00	F	Infant	24Ma02Pw
FALLON, John		26	M	Unknown	24Ma02Pw
DUFFY, John		36	M	Unknown	24Ma02Pw
CARLAN, Thos.		17	M	Unknown	24Ma02Pw
MCCHREA, Matt.		24	M	Unknown	24Ma02Pw
MCGLOGHERN, Matt.		19	M	Unknown	24Ma02Pw
John		22	M	Unknown	24Ma02Pw
CONLY, Sandy		25	M	Unknown	24Ma02Pw
MCINTEE, Danl.		21	M	Unknown	24Ma02Pw
Ellen		19	F	Unknown	24Ma02Pw
Ann		20	F	Unknown	24Ma02Pw
DULLARD, Jas.		37	M	Unknown	24Ma02Pw
Catherine		22	F	Unknown	24Ma02Pw
BRETT, James		28	M	Unknown	24Ma02Pw
RASWICK, Jas.		27	M	Unknown	24Ma02Pw
DELANY, Sally		21	F	Unknown	24Ma02Pw
REILLY, Bryan		22	M	Unknown	24Ma02Pw
James		11	M	Unknown	24Ma02Pw
MCNAMEE, Patt		12	M	Unknown	24Ma02Pw
MCGUIRE, Patt		40	M	Unknown	24Ma02Pw
Bridgt	(W)	35	F	Wife	24Ma02Pw
Margt.	(M)	60	F	Unknown	24Ma02Pw
Rose	(D)	05	F	Child	24Ma02Pw
Martin	(S)	04	M	Child	24Ma02Pw
Catherine	(D)	03	F	Child	24Ma02Pw
Peter	(S)	.00	M	Infant	24Ma02Pw
MARTINAN, Henry		12	M	Laborer	24Ma02Pw
FITZSIMONS, Cath.		15	F	Unknown	24Ma02Pw
Margt.		14	F	Unknown	24Ma02Pw
MCDERMOTT, Bessy		20	F	Unknown	24Ma02Pw
REILLY, Bridget		18	F	Unknown	24Ma02Pw

NAMES OF PASSENGERS		AGE	SEX	OCCUPATIONS	DATE/PORT/SHIP
SMITH, Patt.		20	M	Unknown	24Ma02Pw
Bridget		19	F	Unknown	24Ma02Pw
REILLY, Hugh		20	M	Laborer	24Ma02Pw
GAFNY, Patt.		20	M	Unknown	24Ma02Pw
REILLY, Rose		18	F	Unknown	24Ma02Pw
MCCARTHY, Dennis		29	M	Laborer	24Ma02Pw
Mary	(W)	29	F	Wife	24Ma02Pw
Margt.	(D)	02	F	Child	24Ma02Pw
BURNS, Eugene		24	M	Farmer	24Ma02Pw
MAHONY, Danl.		28	M	Farmer	24Ma02Pw
MCCARTHY, Jerem.		55	M	Farmer	24Ma02Pw
Mary		13	F	Unknown	24Ma02Pw
Michael	(S)	11	M	Unknown	24Ma02Pw
John	(S)	09	M	Child	24Ma02Pw
DONOVAN, John		19	U	Farmer	24Ma02Pw
HERSFELDT, Michl.		23	U	Farmer	24Ma02Pw
MACOOK, Ann		21	F	Unknown	24Ma02Pw
FLEMING, John		35	M	Unknown	24Ma02Pw
NELSON, John		20	M	Unknown	24Ma02Pw
Margaret	(M)	60	F	Unknown	24Ma02Pw
MCCOLOUGH, John		20	M	Unknown	24Ma02Pw
WILSON, Eliza		20	F	Unknown	24Ma02Pw
HEMMING, Grace		20	F	Unknown	24Ma02Pw
MCCOLOUGH, Fanny		60	F	Unknown	24Ma02Pw
Rebecca	(D)	17	F	Unknown	24Ma02Pw
Fanny	(D)	11	F	Unknown	24Ma02Pw
Eliza	(D)	16	F	Unknown	24Ma02Pw
DUFFY, Catherine		60	F	Unknown	24Ma02Pw
Dennis	(S)	30	M	Farmer	24Ma02Pw
Bridget	(L)	24	F	Wife	24Ma02Pw
John		.00	M	Infant	24Ma02Pw
HUDSON, Michl.		25	M	Unknown	24Ma02Pw
HOPKINS, Thomas		22	M	Unknown	24Ma02Pw
Margaret		20	F	Unknown	24Ma02Pw
Maria		20	F	Unknown	24Ma02Pw
SEALLY, Mary		20	F	Unknown	24Ma02Pw
LYON, Mary		22	F	Unknown	24Ma02Pw
MONAGHAN, Rosanna		12	F	Unknown	24Ma02Pw
MCMAHON, Cathe.		18	F	Unknown	24Ma02Pw
LEE, Eliza		23	F	Unknown	24Ma02Pw
MCGRATH, Bridgt.		24	F	Unknown	24Ma02Pw
Chas.	(H)	27	M	Laborer	24Ma02Pw
Patrick	(S)	06	M	Child	24Ma02Pw
Catherine	(D)	.00	F	Infant	24Ma02Pw
HAZARD, Richard		25	M	Unknown	24Ma02Pw
DALTON, Catherine		21	F	Unknown	24Ma02Pw
Thomas		19	M	Unknown	24Ma02Pw
DUFFY, Phillip		01	M	Child	24Ma02Pw

D.B. 24 MAY 1847

From Cork

NAMES OF PASSENGERS		AGE	SEX	OCCUPATIONS	DATE/PORT/SHIP
ONEIL, Thomas		35	M	Laborer	24Ma14Px
William		40	M	Laborer	24Ma14Px
HANON, Pat.O.		30	M	Laborer	24Ma14Px
DONOVAN, Danl.		28	M	Laborer	24Ma14Px
CHRISTOPHER, Mary		26	F	None	24Ma14Px
CONNERS, Daniel		60	M	Laborer	24Ma14Px
Catherine	(W)	60	F	Wife	24Ma14Px
Maria	(D)	28	F	None	24Ma14Px
Dennis	(S)	26	M	Laborer	24Ma14Px
Catherine	(D)	24	F	None	24Ma14Px
Ellen	(D)	22	F	None	24Ma14Px
John	(S)	20	M	Laborer	24Ma14Px
COLLINS, Pat.		45	M	Farmer	24Ma14Px
KELLEHER, Pat.		40	M	Farmer	24Ma14Px
FENNERY, John		25	M	Farmer	24Ma14Px
GRIELY, Martin		25	M	Farmer	24Ma14Px

NAMES OF PASSENGERS		A G E	S E X	OCCUPATIONS	DATE PORT SHIP	NAMES OF PASSENGERS		A G E	S E X	OCCUPATIONS	DATE PORT SHIP
GRIELY, Nancy		24	F	None	24Ma14Px	MURRAY, Bdgt.		20	F	None	24Ma71Py
HANNIGAN, John		30	M	Farmer	24Ma14Px	PATHERSON, John		18	M	Laborer	24Ma71Py
Catherine		28	F	None	24Ma14Px	SLOAN, Cathe.		20	F	None	24Ma71Py
FLEMING, Michael		26	M	Farmer	24Ma14Px	DEE, James		33	M	Laborer	24Ma71Py
CARROLL, John		23	M	Farmer	24Ma14Px	Johana		30	F	None	24Ma71Py
BERRY, John		20	M	Farmer	24Ma14Px	FITZGERALD, Hy.		35	M	Laborer	24Ma71Py
CURTIS, Jeremiah		23	M	Farmer	24Ma14Px	Mary		26	F	None	24Ma71Py
PHELAN, James		34	F	None	24Ma14Px	OBRIEN, Johana		20	F	None	24Ma71Py
RIGON, John		50	M	Farmer	24Ma14Px	BURKE, John		20	M	Laborer	24Ma71Py
COLEMAN, Ellen		60	F	None	24Ma14Px	KING, Ed.		33	M	Laborer	24Ma71Py
Mary	(D)	28	F	None	24Ma14Px	Mary	(W)	26	F	Wife	24Ma71Py
DOOLY, John		20	M	Farmer	24Ma14Px	John	(S)	06	M	Child	24Ma71Py
BROWN, Johanna		19	F	None	24Ma14Px	Patk.	(S)	04	M	Child	24Ma71Py
HYNES, Johanna		22	F	None	24Ma14Px	OBRIEN, Wm.		36	M	Laborer	24Ma71Py
FOLEY, John		23	M	Farmer	24Ma14Px	Ellen	(W)	30	F	Wife	24Ma71Py
HEA, Patrick		25	M	Farmer	24Ma14Px	Patk.	(S)	02	M	Child	24Ma71Py
MURPHY, Rachel		40	F	None	24Ma14Px	HYND, Ed.		20	M	Laborer	24Ma71Py
BARRY, Ellen		40	F	None	24Ma14Px	LYNCH, Cathe.		20	F	None	24Ma71Py
FOLEY, John		33	M	Farmer	24Ma14Px	BAURAL, Johanna		22	F	None	24Ma71Py
MORKIE, Jeremiah		41	M	Farmer	24Ma14Px	OBRIEN, Jane		20	F	None	24Ma71Py
WALSH, Corns.		24	M	Farmer	24Ma14Px	CROVAN, Matt.		26	M	Farmer	24Ma71Py
FENNERTY, Thos.		23	M	Farmer	24Ma14Px	DANE, John		30	M	Farmer	24Ma71Py
Elizabeth		19	F	None	24Ma14Px	BARRY, Mary		31	F	None	24Ma71Py
GURNY, John		20	M	Laborer	24Ma14Px	ONEILL, Mgt.		22	F	None	24Ma71Py
RICHARDS, Jas.		20	M	Laborer	24Ma14Px	RYAN, Ellen		24	F	None	24Ma71Py
GURLY, Marie		30	F	Laborer	24Ma14Px	HENNESSY, Michl.		32	M	Farmer	24Ma71Py
Norry		21	F	None	24Ma14Px	MURPHY, Johana		24	F	None	24Ma71Py
HARTSHAM, Jenny		31	F	None	24Ma14Px	HICKEY, Ellen		20	F	None	24Ma71Py
MORIARTY, Michael		41	M	Laborer	24Ma14Px	Nano		18	M	Farmer	24Ma71Py
BREARTY, Johanna		19	F	None	24Ma14Px	Peter		16	M	Farmer	24Ma71Py
MORIARTY, Bessy		21	F	None	24Ma14Px	CUSHION, John		38	M	Farmer	24Ma71Py
MARTIN, Jeremiah		50	M	Farmer	24Ma14Px	Ann	(W)	30	F	Wife	24Ma71Py
Mary		45	F	None	24Ma14Px	Wm.	(S)	04	M	Child	24Ma71Py
John		30	M	Farmer	24Ma14Px	Honorah	(D)	02	F	Child	24Ma71Py
James		25	M	Farmer	24Ma14Px	RYAN, Cathe.		25	F	None	24Ma71Py
HIGARTTY, John		30	M	Farmer	24Ma14Px	KEARN, John		30	M	Farmer	24Ma71Py
CROWELL, Hannah		20	F	None	24Ma14Px	Mary		33	F	None	24Ma71Py
Mary		18	F	None	24Ma14Px	KISSY, Mary		18	F	None	24Ma71Py
BAXTER, John		40	M	Farmer	24Ma14Px	COLEMAN, Mary		26	F	None	24Ma71Py
Mary		45	F	None	24Ma14Px	BUCKLEY, Cathe.		24	F	None	24Ma71Py
MCCARTHY, Dennis		30	M	Farmer	24Ma14Px	DONOVAN, Johana		33	F	None	24Ma71Py
MURPHY, Johanna		20	F	None	24Ma14Px	DENCHY, Anna		20	F	None	24Ma71Py
Timothy		19	M	Farmer	24Ma14Px	MOORE, John		26	M	Farmer	24Ma71Py
BUCKLY, Laurence		23	M	Farmer	24Ma14Px	CUNNINGHAM, Pat		28	M	Farmer	24Ma71Py
Norry		18	F	None	24Ma14Px	BUCKLEY, Cathe.		22	F	None	24Ma71Py
MCCARTHY, Timothy		21	M	Farmer	24Ma14Px	DARLEY, Mary		25	F	None	24Ma71Py
Mary		22	F	None	24Ma14Px	WALSHE, Ed.		44	M	Farmer	24Ma71Py
MAHONY, Bat.		23	M	Farmer	24Ma14Px	MANGAN, Thos.		22	M	Farmer	24Ma71Py
FITZGERALD, W.		26	M	Farmer	24Ma14Px	LINNANE, Jas.		36	M	Farmer	24Ma71Py
Judy		19	F	None	24Ma14Px	MALEATRY, Thos.		44	M	Farmer	24Ma71Py
Paddy		23	M	Farmer	24Ma14Px	MEALY, Jeremiah		16	M	Farmer	24Ma71Py
Catherine		19	F	None	24Ma14Px	MULLANY, Ellen		24	F	None	24Ma71Py
Ellen		.00	F	Infant	24Ma14Px	MCDONALD, Michael		22	M	Farmer	24Ma71Py
DALY, Dan		23	M	Farmer	24Ma14Px	CASHELL, And.		36	M	Farmer	24Ma71Py
FALLON, Eliza		17	F	None	24Ma14Px	Mary		31	F	None	24Ma71Py
Ralph	(S)	01	M	Child	24Ma14Px	Cathe.		24	F	None	24Ma71Py
ROCHE, Jas.		21	M	Farmer	24Ma14Px	John		22	M	Farmer	24Ma71Py
Mary		20	F	None	24Ma14Px	LYONS, Mgt.		14	F	None	24Ma71Py
						OBRIEN, Pat		28	M	Farmer	24Ma71Py
						BARRY, Alice		22	F	None	24Ma71Py
						CUNNINGHAM, Dennis		20	M	Farmer	24Ma71Py
						BROWN, Martin		22	M	Farmer	24Ma71Py
						John		28	M	Farmer	24Ma71Py
						LEE, Mary		22	F	None	24Ma71Py

CHARLES 24 MAY 1847

From Youghall

DARLING, Pat		32	M	Farmer	24Ma71Py
Mary	(W)	32	F	Wife	24Ma71Py
Mary	(D)	05	F	Child	24Ma71Py
Eliza	(D)	03	F	Child	24Ma71Py
PENDERNANT, Eliza		20	F	None	24Ma71Py
MURRAY, John		25	M	Laborer	24Ma71Py

FLORIDIAN 24 MAY 1847

From Londonderry

NAMES OF PASSENGERS		AGE	SEX	OCCUPATIONS	DATE PORT SHIP
GORMAN, Henry		36	M	Laborer	24Ma01Pf
Margt.		20	F	Unknown	24Ma01Pf
FOY, John		29	M	Weaver	24Ma01Pf
Mary		17	F	Unknown	24Ma01Pf
FOX, Margt.		23	F	Unknown	24Ma01Pf
MCDERMOTT, John		20	M	Miller	24Ma01Pf
KELLY, James		15	M	Mechanic	24Ma01Pf
William		20	M	Mechanic	24Ma01Pf
James		18	M	Mechanic	24Ma01Pf
MCBRIDE, Jas.		26	M	Mechanic	24Ma01Pf
FIRNY, Hugh		27	M	Mechanic	24Ma01Pf
WATERS, Peggy		22	F	Unknown	24Ma01Pf
John		31	M	Farmer	24Ma01Pf
COYLE, Michl.		.02	M	Infant	24Ma01Pf
Mabl.	(P)	19	M	Laborer	24Ma01Pf
MCGONAUGH, Sheeley		21	F	Unknown	24Ma01Pf
COYLE, Hannah		19	F	Unknown	24Ma01Pf
CARR, Dalty		20	M	Farmer	24Ma01Pf
John		22	M	Farmer	24Ma01Pf
An.		20	F	Unknown	24Ma01Pf
MALREAD, John		18	M	Laborer	24Ma01Pf
SHERIDAN, Grace		21	F	Unknown	24Ma01Pf
Biddy		28	F	Unknown	24Ma01Pf
LESLI, Alex.		19	M	Farmer	24Ma01Pf
Margt.		20	F	Unknown	24Ma01Pf
FOX, Mary-Ann		23	F	Unknown	24Ma01Pf
ALLISON, Sarah-J.		22	F	Unknown	24Ma01Pf
Cathe.		32	F	Unknown	24Ma01Pf
HUNTER, William		17	M	Laborer	24Ma01Pf
KEARNES, Owen-W.		23	M	Mechanic	24Ma01Pf
MCCRAY, Danl.		23	M	Mechanic	24Ma01Pf
MCGACK, Michl.		16	M	Farmer	24Ma01Pf
ROADLY, Frances		28	F	Unknown	24Ma01Pf
FLEMING, My.		46	F	Unknown	24Ma01Pf
James	(S)	21	M	Mechanic	24Ma01Pf
Archibald	(S)	06	M	Child	24Ma01Pf
DOAK, James		49	M	Mechanic	24Ma01Pf
George	(S)	20	M	Mechanic	24Ma01Pf
Jane	(D)	23	F	Unknown	24Ma01Pf
James	(S)	10	M	Unknown	24Ma01Pf
John	(S)	18	M	Unknown	24Ma01Pf
Mary	(D)	15	F	Unknown	24Ma01Pf
Elizabeth	(D)	12	F	Unknown	24Ma01Pf
James	(S)	01	M	Child	24Ma01Pf
Samuel	(S)	07	M	Child	24Ma01Pf
Rebecca	(D)	05	F	Child	24Ma01Pf
MILLER, Jane		46	F	Unknown	24Ma01Pf
MCFARLEN, Ann		19	F	Unknown	24Ma01Pf
Hugh		26	M	Laborer	24Ma01Pf
MALOY, James		17	M	Laborer	24Ma01Pf
DONALY, John		36	M	Laborer	24Ma01Pf
BARBER; John		20	M	Farmer	24Ma01Pf
KENNEDY, Alex.		30	M	Shopkeeper	24Ma01Pf
PORTER, Edward		18	M	Farmer	24Ma01Pf
MCMACKIN, Jane		32	M	Farmer	24Ma01Pf
MONAGHAN, Betsey		28	F	Unknown	24Ma01Pf
Mary		26	F	Unknown	24Ma01Pf
FEANIN, Ned		28	M	Farmer	24Ma01Pf
MCFETRIDGE, Wm.		49	M	Farmer	24Ma01Pf
Wm.		24	M	Farmer	24Ma01Pf
Mary-Jane		22	F	Unknown	24Ma01Pf
ELLIOTT, Margt.		19	F	Unknown	24Ma01Pf
RAMSAY, William		19	M	Farmer	24Ma01Pf
Ellen		21	F	Unknown	24Ma01Pf
AMMON, John		14	M	Laborer	24Ma01Pf
AMMON, Ellen	(M)	39	F	Unknown	24Ma01Pf
Jane	(T)	16	F	Unknown	24Ma01Pf
Andrew	(B)	12	M	Laborer	24Ma01Pf
HOOD, Wm.		55	M	Farmer	24Ma01Pf
Fanny	(W)	45	F	Wife	24Ma01Pf
John	(S)	16	M	Unknown	24Ma01Pf
Ann-Jane	(D)	14	F	Unknown	24Ma01Pf
Fanny	(D)	12	F	Unknown	24Ma01Pf
James	(S)	09	M	Child	24Ma01Pf
William	(S)	08	M	Child	24Ma01Pf
James	(S)	05	M	Child	24Ma01Pf
Sarah	(D)	04	F	Child	24Ma01Pf
Mary	(D)	03	F	Child	24Ma01Pf
Dennis	(S)	.02	M	Infant	24Ma01Pf
BROWN, Edwd.		24	M	Farmer	24Ma01Pf
BOYLE, Catherine		33	F	Unknown	24Ma01Pf
KENNEDY, Margt.		18	F	Unknown	24Ma01Pf
KELLY, John		16	M	Unknown	24Ma01Pf
MCCRISLATE, Mary		20	F	Unknown	24Ma01Pf
KEEFE, Peter		20	M	Farmer	24Ma01Pf
STEWART, Andrew		13	M	Farmer	24Ma01Pf
Catherine		16	F	Unknown	24Ma01Pf
FLINN, Isabella		60	F	Unknown	24Ma01Pf
DOMINSTON, Jas.		19	M	Farmer	24Ma01Pf
DOHARTY, John		15	M	Farmer	24Ma01Pf
Elizabeth		18	F	Unknown	24Ma01Pf
MULLIN, John		25	M	Farmer	24Ma01Pf
Catherine		20	F	Unknown	24Ma01Pf
MCLAUGHLIN, Mary		18	F	Unknown	24Ma01Pf
James		23	M	Farmer	24Ma01Pf
LOUGHENY, Edw.		23	M	Farmer	24Ma01Pf
MCLAUGHLIN, M.		24	M	Mechanic	24Ma01Pf
HARKIN, Michl.		19	M	Mechanic	24Ma01Pf
DOHERTY, Michl.		19	M	Mechanic	24Ma01Pf
SWEENY, John		19	M	Mechanic	24Ma01Pf
COON, William		49	M	Mechanic	24Ma01Pf
EWING, John		45	M	Mechanic	24Ma01Pf
My.		55	F	Unknown	24Ma01Pf
COON, U-Mrs.		58	F	Unknown	24Ma01Pf
CROW, William		20	M	Merchant	24Ma01Pf
Mary		21	F	Unknown	24Ma01Pf
Ann-Jane		19	F	Unknown	24Ma01Pf
Charly		18	M	Farmer	24Ma01Pf
James		14	M	Farmer	24Ma01Pf
John		12	M	Farmer	24Ma01Pf
Ann		10	F	Farmer	24Ma01Pf
David		08	M	Child	24Ma01Pf
George		03	M	Child	24Ma01Pf
Elizb.		01	F	Child	24Ma01Pf
RUTLIDGE, Mary		23	F	Unknown	24Ma01Pf
FLANNERLY, Danl.		20	M	Farmer	24Ma01Pf
GALLAGHER, John		28	M	Farmer	24Ma01Pf
DOHERTY, Fanny		20	F	Unknown	24Ma01Pf
MCLOUGHLIN, John		26	M	Farmer	24Ma01Pf
Nancy	(W)	25	F	Wife	24Ma01Pf
Jane	(M)	66	F	Unknown	24Ma01Pf
Henry	(S)	02	M	Child	24Ma01Pf
John	(S)	01	M	Child	24Ma01Pf
COX, William		44	M	Farmer	24Ma01Pf
MCCLUSKY, Ann		27	F	Unknown	24Ma01Pf
Mary		24	F	Unknown	24Ma01Pf
Elizabeth		18	F	Unknown	24Ma01Pf
Se----		13	F	Unknown	24Ma01Pf
Michael		07	M	Child	24Ma01Pf
MULLINS, Mary		15	F	Unknown	24Ma01Pf
Thomas		34	M	Farmer	24Ma01Pf
KENNEDY, Ann		20	F	Unknown	24Ma01Pf
Sarah		15	F	Unknown	24Ma01Pf
MCKOOG, John		14	M	Farmer	24Ma01Pf
Martha		10	F	Unknown	24Ma01Pf
POLLOCK, Jas.		20	M	Farmer	24Ma01Pf
WILLIAMSON, Jas.		24	M	Farmer	24Ma01Pf
LINDSAY, William		22	M	Farmer	24Ma01Pf
EVOY, Isaac		30	M	Farmer	24Ma01Pf
MCKEEG, Margt.		06	F	Child	24Ma01Pf

NAMES OF PASSENGERS		A G E	S E X	OCCUPATIONS	DATE PORT SHIP	NAMES OF PASSENGERS		A G E	S E X	OCCUPATIONS	DATE PORT SHIP
HAMILTON, W.		68	M	Farmer	24Ma01Pf	MANSPEN, Med.		02	F	Unknown	24Ma02Pg
Jane	(W)	49	F	Unknown	24Ma01Pf	CARROLL, P.		30	F	Unknown	24Ma02Pg
James	(S)	18	M	Unknown	24Ma01Pf	BARRETT, J.		30	F	Unknown	24Ma02Pg
John	(S)	16	M	Unknown	24Ma01Pf	SHEA, Judy		22	F	None	24Ma02Pg
MATHEWSON, Jas.		15	M	Unknown	24Ma01Pf	MEANY, M.		19	M	Unknown	24Ma02Pg
ANDERSON, Davl		58	M	Unknown	24Ma01Pf	WALSH, T.		22	M	Unknown	24Ma02Pg
Barbara	(W)	55	F	Unknown	24Ma01Pf	CROTTY, R.		22	M	Unknown	24Ma02Pg
James	(S)	19	M	Farmer	24Ma01Pf	BROGAN, Bgt.		20	F	None	24Ma02Pg
ROONEY, Thomas		25	M	Laborer	24Ma01Pf	JOHNSTON, E.		22	M	Unknown	24Ma02Pg
MILLEN, Gamble		27	M	Laborer	24Ma01Pf	Jane		16	F	None	24Ma02Pg
CALHOUN, David		19	M	Laborer	24Ma01Pf	Bart.		21	M	None	24Ma02Pg
MORROW, Mary-Jane		16	F	Unknown	24Ma01Pf	John		19	M	Unknown	24Ma02Pg
KELLY, Brady		18	M	Unknown	24Ma01Pf	MCALISH, D.		23	M	Unknown	24Ma02Pg
MCGANNON, Margt.		18	F	Unknown	24Ma01Pf	Michl.		19	M	Unknown	24Ma02Pg
ODONNELL, Grace		35	F	Unknown	24Ma01Pf	Sarall		20	F	None	24Ma02Pg
Mary	(D)	01	F	Child	24Ma01Pf	CAMPBELL, Ann		24	F	None	24Ma02Pg
RAMKIN, U-Mrs.		54	F	Unknown	24Ma01Pf	LOCRY, W.		24	M	Unknown	24Ma02Pg
WILSEN, Nancy		24	F	Unknown	24Ma01Pf	Mgt.		20	F	None	24Ma02Pg
						PENELL, Bgt.		20	F	None	24Ma02Pg
						FURNY, M		28	M	Unknown	24Ma02Pg
						REGAN, M.		25	M	Unknown	24Ma02Pg
						MCKOWN, J.		19	M	Unknown	24Ma02Pg
FRIENDSHIP 24 MAY 1847						Cath.	(M)	40	F	None	24Ma02Pg
						Cath.		22	F	None	24Ma02Pg
From Liverpool						FAY, B.		25	M	Unknown	24Ma02Pg
						CANAHAN, J.		20	M	Unknown	24Ma02Pg
						DRISCOL, T.		25	M	Unknown	24Ma02Pg
						DALY, D.		40	M	Unknown	24Ma02Pg
						GALAGHER, J.		55	M	Unknown	24Ma02Pg
WHELAN, W.		21	M	Laborer	24Ma02Pg	My.	(D)	21	F	None	24Ma02Pg
HIGGINS, B.		27	M	Unknown	24Ma02Pg	Ann	(D)	19	F	None	24Ma02Pg
HANSEN, M.		19	M	Unknown	24Ma02Pg	Elza.	(D)	16	F	None	24Ma02Pg
RODGERS, J.		26	M	Unknown	24Ma02Pg	Winlfd.	(D)	06	F	Child	24Ma02Pg
HENDERSON, J.		23	M	Unknown	24Ma02Pg	T.	(S)	22	M	Unknown	24Ma02Pg
FORD, T.		20	M	Unknown	24Ma02Pg	Patt.	(S)	22	M	Unknown	24Ma02Pg
FREUGH, Cath.		18	F	None	24Ma02Pg	Thos.	(S)	19	M	Unknown	24Ma02Pg
GREALY, T.		24	M	Unknown	24Ma02Pg	M.	(S)	10	M	None	24Ma02Pg
SCANLAN, P.		22	M	Unknown	24Ma02Pg	MCGEERY, P.		21	M	Laborer	24Ma02Pg
KIRNAN, T.		40	M	Unknown	24Ma02Pg	Cath.		19	F	None	24Ma02Pg
My.		35	F	None	24Ma02Pg	BROPHY, W.		54	M	Unknown	24Ma02Pg
DORNAN, O.		20	M	Unknown	24Ma02Pg	Ellza		54	F	None	24Ma02Pg
PRENDERGAST, J.		22	M	Unknown	24Ma02Pg	LACY, M.		24	M	Unknown	24Ma02Pg
DELAY, W.		23	M	Unknown	24Ma02Pg	BROPHY, W.		20	M	Unknown	24Ma02Pg
MAGRATH, E.		24	M	Unknown	24Ma02Pg	My.		18	F	None	24Ma02Pg
LEAY, W.		30	M	Unknown	24Ma02Pg	Patt.		09	M	Child	24Ma02Pg
CONOLY, J.		20	M	Unknown	24Ma02Pg	Judy		12	F	None	24Ma02Pg
HAND, J.		21	M	Unknown	24Ma02Pg	LAIY, W.		22	M	Unknown	24Ma02Pg
MCGONEHAN, O.		20	M	Unknown	24Ma02Pg	BARNES, D.		40	M	Unknown	24Ma02Pg
MCCONEN, T.		22	M	Unknown	24Ma02Pg	Martha		30	F	None	24Ma02Pg
Mgt.		21	F	None	24Ma02Pg	KELLY, D.		20	M	Unknown	24Ma02Pg
Patt.		20	M	Unknown	24Ma02Pg	BURNS, My.		24	F	None	24Ma02Pg
TRAYNOR, J.		21	M	Unknown	24Ma02Pg	HUGES, J.		25	M	Unknown	24Ma02Pg
CULLY, J.		24	M	Unknown	24Ma02Pg	MANLY, W.		25	M	Unknown	24Ma02Pg
STOKES, T.		22	M	Unknown	24Ma02Pg	Bldy		25	F	None	24Ma02Pg
STEER, Cath.		19	F	None	24Ma02Pg	LOCHEN, J.		25	M	Unknown	24Ma02Pg
MCGINN, J.		24	M	Unknown	24Ma02Pg	Johanna	(W)	24	F	Wife	24Ma02Pg
Thos.		20	M	Unknown	24Ma02Pg	Mgt.	(D)	01	F	Child	24Ma02Pg
Bgt.		19	F	None	24Ma02Pg	MANAHAN, Mgt.		24	F	None	24Ma02Pg
BROPHY, T.		20	M	Unknown	24Ma02Pg	My.		24	F	None	24Ma02Pg
M.		20	F	None	24Ma02Pg	MCMANUS, Bgt.		20	F	None	24Ma02Pg
BORGIN, J.		20	M	Unknown	24Ma02Pg	Mgt.		20	F	None	24Ma02Pg
Terence		20	M	Unknown	24Ma02Pg	MITCHELL, J.		14	M	None	24Ma02Pg
CROTTY, Betty		20	F	None	24Ma02Pg	Thos.		12	M	None	24Ma02Pg
RYAN, J.		20	M	Unknown	24Ma02Pg	DONOLY, J.		14	M	None	24Ma02Pg
Cath.		19	F	None	24Ma02Pg	Jane		16	F	None	24Ma02Pg
RIELLY, Mgt.		22	F	None	24Ma02Pg	LALY, Mgt.		20	F	None	24Ma02Pg
BROPHY, P.		02	M	Unknown	24Ma02Pg	DOYLE, Bgt.		20	F	None	24Ma02Pg
HUGH, My.		02	M	Unknown	24Ma02Pg	SMITH, W.		25	M	Unknown	24Ma02Pg
PHELAN, P.		24	M	Unknown	24Ma02Pg	U	(W)	22	F	Wife	24Ma02Pg
Ann		22	F	None	24Ma02Pg	BAGENS, J.		18	M	Unknown	24Ma02Pg
OCONNELL, M.		25	M	Laborer	24Ma02Pg	RYAN, J.		24	M	Unknown	24Ma02Pg
Johanna	(W)	24	F	Wife	24Ma02Pg						
Edwd.	(S)	01	M	Child	24Ma02Pg						
DONOHUE, P.		25	M	Unknown	24Ma02Pg						
MANSPEN, T.		24	M	Unknown	24Ma02Pg						

NAMES OF PASSENGERS	AGE	SEX	OCCUPATIONS	DATE PORT SHIP

WALKELLA 24 MAY 1847

From Galway

NAMES OF PASSENGERS	A G E	S E X	OCCUPATIONS	DATE PORT SHIP
SILK, Edward	24	M	Laborer	24Ma11Ph
GILLIAN, Michael	30	M	Laborer	24Ma11Ph
SILK, Sally	26	F	Unknown	24Ma11Ph
KELLY, John	54	M	Laborer	24Ma11Ph
FOY, John	22	M	Mechanic	24Ma11Ph
DUFFY, William	19	M	Laborer	24Ma11Ph
Margaret	23	F	Unknown	24Ma11Ph
LEAHY, Pat.	24	M	Laborer	24Ma11Ph
DUFFY, Kitty	24	F	Unknown	24Ma11Ph
F--G, Briget	23	F	Unknown	24Ma11Ph
KIMBALL, Robert	24	M	Laborer	24Ma11Ph
MUPHY, Michael	27	M	Laborer	24Ma11Ph
CURRAN, Patrick	27	M	Laborer	24Ma11Ph
Mary	20	F	Unknown	24Ma11Ph
CUNAN, Brydilla	02	F	Child	24Ma11Ph
Margaret	18	F	Unknown	24Ma11Ph
HYNES, John	22	M	Laborer	24Ma11Ph
MARTINE, Pat.	22	M	Laborer	24Ma11Ph
KENNEY, Thomas	24	M	Laborer	24Ma11Ph
LUFFIN, Thomas	23	M	Laborer	
DONOHUE, Redmond	26	M	Laborer	24Ma11Ph
MOON, Pat.	33	M	Laborer	24Ma11Ph
NEAL, Michael	21	M	Laborer	24Ma11Ph
KILKENNY, Danl.	20	M	Laborer	24Ma11Ph
MOON, Biddy	30	F	Unknown	24Ma11Ph
HARD, Thomas	29	M	Laborer	24Ma11Ph
WARD, Pat.	22	M	Laborer	24Ma11Ph
MANINAN, Pat.	21	M	Laborer	24Ma11Ph
CARR, Thomas	28	M	Laborer	24Ma11Ph
Cella	28	F	Unknown	24Ma11Ph
CUMMINGS, Nathe.	26	M	Laborer	24Ma11Ph
MANRY, John	30	M	Laborer	24Ma11Ph
RAFFERTY, Thos.	24	M	Mechanic	24Ma11Ph
FALLON, David	30	M	Laborer	24Ma11Ph
CARR, Nathl.	26	M	Laborer	24Ma11Ph
CALLINAN, Patrick	35	M	Laborer	24Ma11Ph
KELLY, Hugh	29	M	Laborer	24Ma11Ph
MCGRAFT, Bryan	22	M	Laborer	24Ma11Ph
MANRY, Nancey	20	F	Unknown	24Ma11Ph
MURRY, John	29	M	Laborer	24Ma11Ph
SHEKIT, Pat.	37	M	Laborer	24Ma11Ph
EARLY, Michael	20	M	Laborer	24Ma11Ph
CONNOR, Martin	20	M	Laborer	24Ma11Ph
Stephen	19	M	Laborer	24Ma11Ph
NAUGHTON, John	20	M	Mechanic	24Ma11Ph
ONEIL, Thomas	26	M	Laborer	24Ma11Ph
RYAN, Pat.	27	M	Laborer	24Ma11Ph
Mary	24	F	Unknown	24Ma11Ph
Thomas	26	M	Laborer	24Ma11Ph
CONNELLE, Simon	24	M	Laborer	24Ma11Ph
CAMPBELL, Ally	21	F	Unknown	24Ma11Ph
MCGRAFT, Thos.	22	M	Laborer	24Ma11Ph
CASSIDI, Howard	20	M	Laborer	24Ma11Ph
RINAN, Mary	19	F	Unknown	24Ma11Ph
MCGRAFT, Nappy	19	F	Unknown	24Ma11Ph
MAHON, John	27	M	Mechanic	24Ma11Ph
DEVLIN, Winey	58	F	Unknown	24Ma11Ph
FOLAN, John	29	M	Laborer	24Ma11Ph
KELLY, William	22	M	Laborer	24Ma11Ph
John	22	M	Laborer	24Ma11Ph
Michael	24	M	Mechanic	24Ma11Ph
Kate	30	F	Unknown	24Ma11Ph
FOLAN, Thomas	23	M	Laborer	24Ma11Ph
James	19	M	Laborer	24Ma11Ph
FOY, Ann	34	F	Unknown	24Ma11Ph

NAMES OF PASSENGERS		A G E	S E X	OCCUPATIONS	DATE PORT SHIP
FOY, Path.	(S)	16	M	Laborer	24Ma11Ph
TUNNY, Michael		21	M	Laborer	24Ma11Ph
LIDON, Judy		19	F	Unknown	24Ma11Ph
IRNITY, Marla		20	F	Unknown	24Ma11Ph
NEAL, Thomas		22	M	Laborer	24Ma11Ph
RULING, Pat.		21	M	Laborer	24Ma11Ph
GRATLY, Michael		22	M	Laborer	24Ma11Ph
MADDEN, Patrick		25	M	Laborer	24Ma11Ph
KILLALA, Thomas		28	M	Laborer	24Ma11Ph
Anne	(W)	28	F	Wife	24Ma11Ph
Mary	(D)	03	F	Child	24Ma11Ph
LYDON, James		17	M	Laborer	24Ma11Ph
LYNCHY, Dennis		31	M	Laborer	24Ma11Ph
SULLIVAN, Mary		22	F	Unknown	24Ma11Ph
Daniel		24	M	Mechanic	24Ma11Ph
MCDOUGH, Thomas		26	M	Mechanic	24Ma11Ph
Mary		19	F	Unknown	24Ma11Ph
John	(B)	23	M	Laborer	24Ma11Ph
Anna	(M)	40	F	Unknown	24Ma11Ph
CONNLY, Bridget		20	F	Unknown	24Ma11Ph
BARRET, Pat.		30	M	Mechanic	24Ma11Ph
KAIN, John		19	M	Laborer	24Ma11Ph
JKKCKSON, Michael		28	M	Laborer	24Ma11Ph
WALSH, Ellen		22	F	Unknown	24Ma11Ph
Biddy		20	F	Unknown	24Ma11Ph

HEATHER-BELL 24 MAY 1847

From Limerick

NAMES OF PASSENGERS		A G E	S E X	OCCUPATIONS	DATE PORT SHIP
NOONAN, T.		50	M	Farmer	24Ma33PI
Biddy	(W)	50	F	None	24Ma33PI
Pat	(S)	24	M	Unknown	24Ma33PI
My.	(D)	15	F	None	24Ma33PI
Jno.	(S)	06	M	Child	24Ma33PI
CARROLL, P.		23	M	Unknown	24Ma33PI
HALLERAN, M.		42	M	Unknown	24Ma33PI
My.	(W)	40	F	Wife	24Ma33PI
James	(S)	17	M	Unknown	24Ma33PI
My.	(D)	15	F	None	24Ma33PI
Mary	(D)	10	F	None	24Ma33PI
Pat	(S)	02	M	Child	24Ma33PI
DALY, P.		20	M	Unknown	24Ma33PI
BUNS, W.		50	M	Unknown	24Ma33PI
Mich.	(S)	22	M	Unknown	24Ma33PI
My.	(W)	50	F	Wife	24Ma33PI
Bdgt.	(D)	20	F	None	24Ma33PI
My.	(D)	17	F	None	24Ma33PI
Cath.	(D)	13	F	None	24Ma33PI
NOONAN, Mgt.		15	F	None	24Ma33PI
BYRNES, P.		20	M	Unknown	24Ma33PI
SCOTT, P.		20	M	Unknown	24Ma33PI
LYNCH, J.		20	M	Unknown	24Ma33PI
HANNON, M.		24	M	Unknown	24Ma33PI
My.		21	F	None	24Ma33PI
CUSACK, J.		22	M	Unknown	24Ma33PI
PURNELL, M.		24	M	Unknown	24Ma33PI
BOUCH, Jane		23	F	None	24Ma33PI
BOYLE, J.		26	M	Unknown	24Ma33PI
Johanna		30	F	None	24Ma33PI
My.		22	F	None	24Ma33PI
COSTELLO, My.		26	F	None	24Ma33PI
KENY, T.		40	M	Unknown	24Ma33PI
RING, Ellen		30	F	None	24Ma33PI
CONNOLY, My.		21	F	None	24Ma33PI
MCNAMEE, P.		21	M	Unknown	24Ma33PI
CARRELL, M.		22	M	Unknown	24Ma33PI
GLEESON, J.		24	M	Unknown	24Ma33PI
CROWE, C.		20	M	Unknown	24Ma33PI

NAMES OF PASSENGERS		AGE	SEX	OCCUPATIONS	DATE PORT SHIP
SMITH, J.		26	M	Unknown	24Ma33PI
BOYLE, Bgt.		34	F	None	24Ma33PI
CONNOR, J.		40	M	Farmer	24Ma33PI
LYNCH, D.		24	M	Unknown	24Ma33PI
NORRIS, My.		16	F	None	24Ma33PI
BRICE, T.		30	M	Unknown	24Ma33PI
MORRISON, W.		21	M	Unknown	24Ma33PI
CONNELL, R.		30	M	Unknown	24Ma33PI
Mgt.	(W)	20	F	Wife	24Ma33PI
My.	(D)	03	F	Child	24Ma33PI
MURRY, P.		40	M	Unknown	24Ma33PI
Sally	(W)	37	F	Wife	24Ma33PI
My.	(D)	13	F	Wife	24Ma33PI
Mary	(D)	09	F	Child	24Ma33PI
Jam.	(S)	04	M	Child	24Ma33PI
Denis	(S)	20	M	Unknown	24Ma33PI
Bgt.	(D)	01	F	Child	24Ma33PI
CROWE, Mgt.		26	F	None	24Ma33PI
MURRY, H.		24	M	Unknown	24Ma33PI
HALLORAN, M.		42	M	Unknown	24Ma33PI
My.	(W)	40	F	Wife	24Ma33PI
James	(S)	17	M	Unknown	24Ma33PI
My.	(D)	15	F	None	24Ma33PI
Mary	(D)	10	F	None	24Ma33PI
Pat	(S)	02	M	Child	24Ma33PI
HICKE, J.		20	M	Unknown	24Ma33PI
My.	(W)	20	F	Wife	24Ma33PI
Mich.	(S)	01	M	Child	24Ma33PI
MCMAHON, M.		15	M	Unknown	24Ma33PI
KENNY, My.		24	F	None	24Ma33PI
SULLIVAN, T.		28	M	Unknown	24Ma33PI
HOGAN, M.		34	M	Unknown	24Ma33PI
Ellen		30	F	None	24Ma33PI
CONNELL, J.		25	M	Unknown	24Ma33PI
MCMAHON, My.		23	F	None	24Ma33PI
HAUGH, J.		27	M	Unknown	24Ma33PI
COLLINS, Cath.		24	F	None	24Ma33PI
Pat	(H)	24	M	Unknown	24Ma33PI
Cath.	(D)	01	F	Child	24Ma33PI
HARE, T.		21	M	Unknown	24Ma33PI
DOWNS, Mgt.		23	F	None	24Ma33PI
KELLY, Sally		17	F	None	24Ma33PI
MILLS, J.		24	M	Unknown	24Ma33PI
ONEILL, W.		19	U	Unknown	24Ma33PI
CULLEN, G.		24	U	Unknown	24Ma33PI
CARNEY, D.		24	U	Unknown	24Ma33PI
CONNELLY, M.		30	U	Unknown	24Ma33PI
COUGHER, Mary		23	F	Unknown	24Ma33PI
CALLAN, Bdgt.		23	F	Unknown	24Ma33PI
PHELPS, P.		23	U	Unknown	24Ma33PI
DOWNES, Bgt.		20	F	Unknown	24Ma33PI
GARANEN, J.		28	U	Unknown	24Ma33PI
MALACHY, J.		21	U	Unknown	24Ma33PI
DONEL, My.		30	F	Unknown	24Ma33PI
DONOVAN, J.		23	U	Unknown	24Ma33PI
CARROLE, M.		25	U	Unknown	24Ma33PI
My.		14	F	Unknown	24Ma33PI
KEELY, My.		22	F	Unknown	24Ma33PI
HAGEN, W.		25	U	Unknown	24Ma33PI
GRIFFEN, J.		20	U	Unknown	24Ma33PI
DONOHAN, E.		18	U	Unknown	24Ma33PI
Patch		13	U	Unknown	24Ma33PI
TRADY, T.		27	U	Unknown	24Ma33PI
Mara		25	F	Unknown	24Ma33PI
Mgt.		16	F	Unknown	24Ma33PI
Be.		03	U	Child	24Ma33PI
HADEN, Wry.		01	U	Child	24Ma33PI
Peggy		01	F	Child	24Ma33PI
NEAL, J.		27	U	Unknown	24Ma33PI
Bgt.		28	F	Unknown	24Ma33PI
DONEVAN, P.		24	U	Unknown	24Ma33PI
DUNN, Mgt.		23	F	Unknown	24Ma33PI
BAY, Bgt.		25	F	Unknown	24Ma33PI
PROUD, Cath.		25	F	Unknown	24Ma33PI
MURPHY, P.		20	U	Unknown	24Ma33PI

NAMES OF PASSENGERS		AGE	SEX	OCCUPATIONS	DATE PORT SHIP
BARRETT, M.		40	U	Unknown	24Ma33PI
MACH, M.		28	U	Unknown	24Ma33PI
Bumgst., Ellen		30	F	Unknown	24Ma33PI
MARSH, P.		28	U	Unknown	24Ma33PI

DROMAHAIR 25 MAY 1847

From Sligo

NAMES OF PASSENGERS		AGE	SEX	OCCUPATIONS	DATE PORT SHIP
NESSON, Honor		21	F	Laborer	25Ma28Pa
CAULY, Thomas		21	M	Unknown	25Ma28Pa
NICHOLSON, Patt.		24	M	Unknown	25Ma28Pa
CLARK, Jane		56	F	Unknown	25Ma28Pa
GILDEA, Thos.		36	M	Unknown	25Ma28Pa
GANNON, Patt.		25	M	Unknown	25Ma28Pa
Rose	(W)	30	F	Wife	25Ma28Pa
Mary	(D)	03	F	Child	25Ma28Pa
MAY, Francis		23	M	Unknown	25Ma28Pa
Patt.	(B)	18	M	Unknown	25Ma28Pa
Mary	(M)	56	F	Unknown	25Ma28Pa
MCNULTY, Honor		20	F	Unknown	25Ma28Pa
JOHNSON, Bridget		21	F	Unknown	25Ma28Pa
Patt.		22	M	Unknown	25Ma28Pa
Ann		22	F	Unknown	25Ma28Pa
Bessey		.00	F	Infant	25Ma28Pa
William		23	M	Unknown	25Ma28Pa
Bryan		24	M	Unknown	25Ma28Pa
BRIEN, Patt.		21	M	Unknown	25Ma28Pa
WATERS, Stephen		25	M	Unknown	25Ma28Pa
FALLON, Anne		25	F	Unknown	25Ma28Pa
WALTERS, Roger		24	M	Unknown	25Ma28Pa
John		22	M	Unknown	25Ma28Pa
BYRNES, John		24	M	Unknown	25Ma28Pa
Eleanor	(W)	22	F	Unknown	25Ma28Pa
Thomas		15	M	None	25Ma28Pa
Bridget	(D)	.03	F	Infant	25Ma28Pa
Thomas	(S)	.02	M	Infant	25Ma28Pa
GILMARTIN, Thos.		29	M	Unknown	25Ma28Pa
James	(P)	62	M	Unknown	25Ma28Pa
Bridget	(T)	20	F	Unknown	25Ma28Pa
Mary	(M)	50	F	Unknown	25Ma28Pa
Sibly	(T)	16	F	Unknown	25Ma28Pa
Sally	(T)	14	F	Unknown	25Ma28Pa
Kitty	(T)	12	F	Unknown	25Ma28Pa
Winney	(T)	10	F	Unknown	25Ma28Pa
Mary	(T)	18	F	Unknown	25Ma28Pa
Nancy	(T)	11	F	Servant	25Ma28Pa
FEENEY, John		48	M	Servant	25Ma28Pa
GILDEA, Michl.		25	M	Servant	25Ma28Pa
JORDAN, Maria		20	F	Servant	25Ma28Pa
Catherine		18	F	Servant	25Ma28Pa
PRESTON, Thomas		30	M	Laborer	25Ma28Pa
Mary		20	F	Unknown	25Ma28Pa
PADDON, Sarah		56	F	Unknown	25Ma28Pa
MCTERNAN, Danl.		30	M	Unknown	25Ma28Pa
HART, Catherine		24	F	Unknown	25Ma28Pa
SCANLAN, Ann		20	F	Unknown	25Ma28Pa
Peter		23	M	Unknown	25Ma28Pa
WARD, Mary		22	F	Unknown	25Ma28Pa
SMYTH, Owen		26	M	Unknown	25Ma28Pa
MARTIN, Francis		25	M	Unknown	25Ma28Pa
Eleanor		25	F	Unknown	25Ma28Pa
COGAN, Mary		16	F	Unknown	25Ma28Pa
DOWD, Michael		44	M	Unknown	25Ma28Pa
Mary	(W)	30	F	Unknown	25Ma28Pa
Anne-Jane	(D)	11	F	Servant	25Ma28Pa
Matilda	(D)	09	F	Child	25Ma28Pa
John	(S)	07	M	Child	25Ma28Pa
Thomas	(S)	05	M	Child	25Ma28Pa

NAMES OF PASSENGERS		AGE	SEX	OCCUPATIONS	DATE PORT SHIP	NAMES OF PASSENGERS		AGE	SEX	OCCUPATIONS	DATE PORT SHIP
LAING, Michael		22	M	Unknown	25Ma28Pa	DUFFY, Margt.	(D)	08	F	Child	25Ma28Pa
Mary		19	F	Unknown	25Ma28Pa	Honor	(D)	06	F	Child	25Ma28Pa
Winnifred	(M)	48	F	Unknown	25Ma28Pa	Cathe.	(D)	04	F	Child	25Ma28Pa
THOMAS, Philip		24	M	Unknown	25Ma28Pa	Bridget	(D)	01	F	Child	25Ma28Pa
KILVLAGANN, James		25	M	Unknown	25Ma28Pa	Michael	(B)	35	M	Farmer	25Ma28Pa
Mary	(W)	20	F	Wife	25Ma28Pa	Rose	(L)	26	F	Unknown	25Ma28Pa
Catherine	(D)	03	F	Child	25Ma28Pa	Owen	(N)	11	M	Unknown	25Ma28Pa
Patt.	(S)	01	M	Child	25Ma28Pa	Peter	(N)	09	M	Child	25Ma28Pa
MCGETRICK, Bridget		30	F	Unknown	25Ma28Pa	Michl.	(N)	04	M	Child	25Ma28Pa
REGAN, Timothy		20	M	Farmer	25Ma28Pa	Thos.	(N)	06	M	Child	25Ma28Pa
LOFTUS, Peter		30	M	Unknown	25Ma28Pa	Rose	(N)	01	F	Child	25Ma28Pa
COGAN, Seamus		35	M	Unknown	25Ma28Pa	KILVIHAN, Peter		22	M	Unknown	25Ma28Pa
Margaret	(W)	22	F	Unknown	25Ma28Pa	Nancy		21	F	Unknown	25Ma28Pa
John	(S)	03	M	Child	25Ma28Pa	MCGLOIN, Martin		50	M	Unknown	25Ma28Pa
CLANCEY, James		30	M	Unknown	25Ma28Pa	Michl.		20	M	Unknown	25Ma28Pa
GOLDEN, William		60	M	Unknown	25Ma28Pa						
Mary	(W)	55	F	Unknown	25Ma28Pa						
Martin	(S)	26	M	Unknown	25Ma28Pa						
Mary	(D)	24	F	Unknown	25Ma28Pa						
Patt.	(S)	25	M	Unknown	25Ma28Pa						
Martin	(S)	22	M	Unknown	25Ma28Pa						
Peter	(S)	27	M	Unknown	25Ma28Pa	**HIBERNIA 27 MAY 1847**					
Margt.	(D)	18	F	Unknown	25Ma28Pa						
James	(S)	15	M	Unknown	25Ma28Pa	From New-Rush					
Eleanor	(D)	13	F	Unknown	25Ma28Pa						
Anne	(D)	12	F	Unknown	25Ma28Pa						
Bridget	(D)	24	F	Unknown	25Ma28Pa	READ, Pat		27	M	Laborer	27Ma61Pb
GALLAGHER, Jas.		22	M	Unknown	25Ma28Pa	M.A.		26	F	None	27Ma61Pb
MCTERNAN, John		28	M	Unknown	25Ma28Pa	WEAFER, John		28	M	Laborer	27Ma61Pb
NICHOLSON, Wm.		26	M	Unknown	25Ma28Pa	CHAPMAN, John		39	M	Laborer	27Ma61Pb
MCHUGH, Danl.		25	M	Unknown	25Ma28Pa	James		29	M	Laborer	27Ma61Pb
Mary		24	F	Unknown	25Ma28Pa	Bridget		28	F	None	27Ma61Pb
HART, Peter		24	M	Unknown	25Ma28Pa	ARCHBALD, Arch.		34	M	Laborer	27Ma61Pb
COGAN, Daniel		25	M	Unknown	25Ma28Pa	ROCHA, Micha.		32	M	Laborer	27Ma61Pb
Maria		19	F	Unknown	25Ma28Pa	POWER, E.O.		33	M	Laborer	27Ma61Pb
WATERS, Patrick		19	M	Unknown	25Ma28Pa	RILEY, Jas.		36	M	Laborer	27Ma61Pb
MULLONY, James		28	M	Unknown	25Ma28Pa	MURPHY, Danl.		21	M	Laborer	27Ma61Pb
Libby		25	F	Unknown	25Ma28Pa	LINN, Patt.		22	M	Laborer	27Ma61Pb
GERAGHTY, Corns.		24	M	Unknown	25Ma28Pa	Cathe.	(W)	22	F	Unknown	27Ma61Pb
Margt.		26	F	Unknown	25Ma28Pa	Martin	(S)	.00	M	Infant	27Ma61Pb
GILLEN, Francis		28	M	Unknown	25Ma28Pa	John	(S)	.00	M	Infant	27Ma61Pb
KIVLAGHEN, Thady		60	M	Unknown	25Ma28Pa	DOWNES, Fk.		22	M	Farmer	27Ma61Pb
Mary	(D)	22	F	Unknown	25Ma28Pa	MURPHY, Ch.		25	M	Farmer	27Ma61Pb
Cathe.	(D)	16	F	Unknown	25Ma28Pa	Patt.		26	M	Farmer	27Ma61Pb
John	(S)	24	M	Unknown	25Ma28Pa	QUIN, John		24	M	Farmer	27Ma61Pb
JORDAN, John		56	M	Unknown	25Ma28Pa	DUNN, John		31	M	Farmer	27Ma61Pb
Edward	(S)	22	M	Unknown	25Ma28Pa	MURPHY, W.		28	M	Farmer	27Ma61Pb
James	(S)	19	M	Laborer	25Ma28Pa	REACH, J.		31	M	Farmer	27Ma61Pb
Thomas	(S)	15	M	Unknown	25Ma28Pa	HOBIN, L.		22	M	Farmer	27Ma61Pb
FEENY, Honor		48	F	Unknown	25Ma28Pa	CARIN, W.		17	M	Farmer	27Ma61Pb
Patt.	(S)	18	M	Unknown	25Ma28Pa	Mary		19	F	Unknown	27Ma61Pb
John	(S)	16	M	Unknown	25Ma28Pa	FARRELL, H.		18	M	Farmer	27Ma61Pb
Cathe.	(D)	14	F	Unknown	25Ma28Pa	STILWELL, Mary		22	F	Farmer	27Ma61Pb
Mary	(D)	12	F	Unknown	25Ma28Pa	SHEA, Thos.		23	M	Farmer	27Ma61Pb
Bryan	(S)	09	M	Child	25Ma28Pa	Judith		19	M	Farmer	27Ma61Pb
Cecilia	(D)	08	F	Child	25Ma28Pa	Mary		18	F	Unknown	27Ma61Pb
Biddy	(D)	05	F	Child	25Ma28Pa	Cathe.		21	F	Unknown	27Ma61Pb
HATLEY, Patt.		26	M	Unknown	25Ma28Pa	Patt.		23	M	Laborer	27Ma61Pb
Rose	(W)	24	F	Unknown	25Ma28Pa	Martin		24	M	Laborer	27Ma61Pb
Cathe.	(D)	01	F	Child	25Ma28Pa	John		14	M	None	27Ma61Pb
Winney	(D)	01	F	Child	25Ma28Pa	Mary		16	F	Unknown	27Ma61Pb
BOYLE, Margaret		26	F	Unknown	25Ma28Pa	MURPHY, Martin		28	M	Laborer	27Ma61Pb
Nancey		24	F	Unknown	25Ma28Pa	DOYLE, Cathe.		25	F	Unknown	27Ma61Pb
CONLON, Anne		24	F	Unknown	25Ma28Pa	MCGRATH, Richd.		26	M	Laborer	27Ma61Pb
BRENNAN, Walter		24	M	Unknown	25Ma28Pa	LENNON, John		71	M	Farmer	27Ma61Pb
GILDEA, Betty		22	F	Unknown	25Ma28Pa	DUNNE, Patr.		18	M	Farmer	27Ma61Pb
Sarah	(D)	03	F	Child	25Ma28Pa	BURGESS, Pat		27	M	Farmer	27Ma61Pb
KELLY, Owen		30	M	Unknown	25Ma28Pa	SHEAL, John		28	M	Farmer	27Ma61Pb
Honor	(W)	21	F	Unknown	25Ma28Pa	COLLIN, Michael		25	M	Farmer	27Ma61Pb
Patrick	(S)	02	M	Child	25Ma28Pa	NEVILLE, Uanal		27	F	Unknown	27Ma61Pb
Mary-Ann	(D)	01	F	Child	25Ma28Pa	JOYCE, Mary		17	F	Unknown	27Ma61Pb
GILMER, Hugh		26	M	Unknown	25Ma28Pa	FOLLY, John		49	M	Farmer	27Ma61Pb
DUFFY, Danl.		40	M	Unknown	25Ma28Pa	BORDEN, Pat		20	M	Farmer	27Ma61Pb
Margt.	(W)	30	F	Unknown	25Ma28Pa	Mary		29	F	Unknown	27Ma61Pb
Mary	(D)	10	F	Child	25Ma28Pa	Bridget		25	F	Unknown	27Ma61Pb

NAMES OF PASSENGERS	EX	AGE	SEX	OCCUPATIONS	DATE PORT SHIP
SANS, Ellen		26	F	Unknown	27Ma61Pb
RIN, Cathe.E.		28	F	Unknown	27Ma61Pb
GORDON, Patt.		33	M	Farmer	27Ma61Pb
SIMMONS, Mary		34	F	Unknown	27Ma61Pb
DIXON, H.		36	F	Unknown	27Ma61Pb
CULLIN, Wm.		27	M	Farmer	27Ma61Pb
REDMOND, Cathe.		28	F	Unknown	27Ma61Pb
BUTLER, James		29	M	Farmer	27Ma61Pb
Mary		27	F	Unknown	27Ma61Pb
MURPHY, Anthony		28	M	Farmer	27Ma61Pb
Cathe.		14	F	Unknown	27Ma61Pb
U	(D)	.00	F	Infant	27Ma61Pb
ROACH, Moses		28	M	Farmer	27Ma61Pb
Ann		14	F	Unknown	27Ma61Pb
Mary		17	F	Unknown	27Ma61Pb
DOYLE, Michel		19	M	Farmer	27Ma61Pb
WALSH, James		21	M	Farmer	27Ma61Pb
Bridget	(W)	16	F	Unknown	27Ma61Pb
Bridget	(D)	.00	F	Infant	27Ma61Pb
NEVILLE, Mary		17	F	Unknown	27Ma61Pb
FINNLING, N.		18	M	Farmer	27Ma61Pb
BOYLE, P.		16	M	Farmer	27Ma61Pb
WHITTY, M.		21	M	Farmer	27Ma61Pb
SENOTT, James		13	M	Farmer	27Ma61Pb
ROSSITER, Patt.		17	M	Farmer	27Ma61Pb
MURPHY, John		19	M	Farmer	27Ma61Pb
Hannah	(M)	41	F	None	27Ma61Pb
DOYLE, Michl.		38	M	Farmer	27Ma61Pb
FLOOD, John		45	M	Farmer	27Ma61Pb
Magt.	(W)	40	F	Unknown	27Ma61Pb
Ely.		28	F	Unknown	27Ma61Pb
Hannah		26	F	Unknown	27Ma61Pb
M.		22	F	Unknown	27Ma61Pb
Mgt.		20	F	Unknown	27Ma61Pb
Geo.		18	M	Farmer	27Ma61Pb
John		16	M	Farmer	27Ma61Pb
NEVILLE, John		14	M	Farmer	27Ma61Pb

FIDELIA 27 MAY 1847

From Liverpool

NAMES OF PASSENGERS	EX	AGE	SEX	OCCUPATIONS	DATE PORT SHIP
QUIN, Ann		18	F	Unknown	27Ma02Ax
OREGAN, P.		27	M	Unknown	27Ma02Ax
Timety		20	M	Unknown	27Ma02Ax
Mich.		18	M	Unknown	27Ma02Ax
John		22	M	Unknown	27Ma02Ax
KELLY, C.		25	M	Unknown	27Ma02Ax
FLYNN, Elzbt.		20	F	Unknown	27Ma02Ax
My.		25	F	Unknown	27Ma02Ax
DALY, C.		25	M	Unknown	27Ma02Ax
GUTTEN, P.		64	M	Unknown	27Ma02Ax
Ann	(D)	18	F	None	27Ma02Ax
Ann	(W)	60	F	Unknown	27Ma02Ax
KELY, M.A.		16	F	Unknown	27Ma02Ax
IRWIN, Cath.		24	F	Unknown	27Ma02Ax
DALY, J.		18	M	Unknown	27Ma02Ax
SOUTHERAN, H.		25	M	Unknown	27Ma02Ax
OBRIEN, M.		18	F	Unknown	27Ma02Ax
PHAD, J.		20	M	Unknown	27Ma02Ax
HAY, J.		20	M	Unknown	27Ma02Ax
THOMPSON, P.		40	M	Unknown	27Ma02Ax
COLUDY, J.		28	M	Unknown	27Ma02Ax
HEYES, M.		20	M	Unknown	27Ma02Ax
DOYLE, J.		25	M	Unknown	27Ma02Ax
BYRN, Ellen		20	F	Unknown	27Ma02Ax
DENNIS, E.		21	M	Unknown	27Ma02Ax
SHEA, P.T.		40	M	Unknown	27Ma02Ax
M.	(W)	26	F	Unknown	27Ma02Ax
SHEA, My.	(D)	10	F	Unknown	27Ma02Ax
M.	(D)	07	F	Child	27Ma02Ax
WHITE, Cath.		04	F	Child	27Ma02Ax
Alice		01	F	Child	27Ma02Ax
KELY, T.		20	M	Laborer	27Ma02Ax
CARTY, H.		25	M	Unknown	27Ma02Ax
WILKINSON, J.		60	M	Unknown	27Ma02Ax
U-Mrs.		25	F	Unknown	27Ma02Ax
BANLON, W.		35	M	Unknown	27Ma02Ax
U	(W)	30	F	Unknown	27Ma02Ax
WILLIAMS, My.		23	F	Unknown	27Ma02Ax
MALY, Ma.		25	F	Unknown	27Ma02Ax
DALY, Cath.		18	F	Unknown	27Ma02Ax
KING, W.		28	M	Unknown	27Ma02Ax
KELLY, H.		36	M	Unknown	27Ma02Ax
GUNN, Ma.		22	M	Unknown	27Ma02Ax
GALING, Bgt.		36	F	Unknown	27Ma02Ax
GUNN, Elza.		28	F	Unknown	27Ma02Ax
REYNOLDS, C.		14	M	Unknown	27Ma02Ax
GARGAN, O.		03	M	Child	27Ma02Ax
MCNALLY, T.		20	M	Unknown	27Ma02Ax
BURN, M.		40	M	Unknown	27Ma02Ax
WHITE, M.		21	M	Unknown	27Ma02Ax
MCGRATH, Betsy		18	F	Unknown	27Ma02Ax
CREADY, R.		30	M	Unknown	27Ma02Ax
RIORDAN, R.		23	M	Unknown	27Ma02Ax
FITZGIBBON, Brt.		18	F	None	27Ma02Ax
MARTIN, J.		50	M	Unknown	27Ma02Ax
CORNAN, G.		45	M	Unknown	27Ma02Ax
HALLERN, My.		23	M	Unknown	27Ma02Ax
HAZELDEN, A.		45	M	Unknown	27Ma02Ax
DUNN, J.		25	M	Unknown	27Ma02Ax
BIRK, M.		23	M	Unknown	27Ma02Ax
My.J.		25	F	Unknown	27Ma02Ax
Ambrose		19	M	Unknown	27Ma02Ax
ORAWE, My.		40	F	Unknown	27Ma02Ax
SMITH, W.		25	M	Unknown	27Ma02Ax
CLARK, Ann		20	F	Unknown	27Ma02Ax
HOOLY, E.		25	M	Unknown	27Ma02Ax
SMITH, J.		30	M	Unknown	27Ma02Ax
My.		20	F	Unknown	27Ma02Ax
HART, Judith		09	F	Child	27Ma02Ax
Cath.		09	F	Child	27Ma02Ax
Jno.		09	M	Child	27Ma02Ax
J.		01	F	Child	27Ma02Ax
CLANCY, Cath.		20	F	Unknown	27Ma02Ax
SWEENEY, C.		25	M	Laborer	27Ma02Ax
WALSH, My.		18	F	Unknown	27Ma02Ax
KELLY, M.		20	M	Unknown	27Ma02Ax
FARR, Elza.		20	F	Unknown	27Ma02Ax
Honor		13	F	Unknown	27Ma02Ax
MACKEN, Elzbt.		28	F	Unknown	27Ma02Ax
OBRIEN, W.		20	M	Unknown	27Ma02Ax
GIFFEN, Alice		18	F	Unknown	27Ma02Ax
MCCURTIN, E.		20	M	Unknown	27Ma02Ax
DUFFY, Alice		18	F	Unknown	27Ma02Ax
ODONNEL, D.		27	M	Unknown	27Ma02Ax
Elza.	(W)	24	F	Unknown	27Ma02Ax
John	(S)	05	M	Child	27Ma02Ax
Myrt.	(D)	03	F	Child	27Ma02Ax
COWEN, M.		48	M	Unknown	27Ma02Ax
John	(S)	14	M	Unknown	27Ma02Ax
MCALLEN, Saml.		18	M	Unknown	27Ma02Ax
MCDERMOTT, J.		25	M	Unknown	27Ma02Ax
CASH, J.		25	M	Unknown	27Ma02Ax
MARSHAL, M.A.		21	F	Unknown	27Ma02Ax
HOUSTON, J.		20	M	Unknown	27Ma02Ax
BOYLE, Rose		16	F	Unknown	27Ma02Ax
MCCARROLL, An.		19	F	Unknown	27Ma02Ax
HART, M.		20	M	Unknown	27Ma02Ax
CON, Ann		24	F	Unknown	27Ma02Ax
BURNS, My.		23	F	Unknown	27Ma02Ax
KEEN, Cath.		20	F	Unknown	27Ma02Ax
BURNS, M.		17	M	Unknown	27Ma02Ax
KILLAN, Alice		16	F	Unknown	27Ma02Ax

NAMES OF PASSENGERS		AGE	SEX	OCCUPATIONS	DATE PORT SHIP
GRAYSON, N.		60	M	Unknown	27Ma02Ax
Ann	(W)	60	F	Unknown	27Ma02Ax
Joseph	(S)	20	M	Unknown	27Ma02Ax
Roz.	(D)	20	F	Unknown	27Ma02Ax
RYAN, Ma.		16	M	Unknown	27Ma02Ax
RYNOLDS, Brt.		25	M	Unknown	27Ma02Ax
LYNCH, E.		15	M	Unknown	27Ma02Ax
DEMPSEY, L.		35	M	Unknown	27Ma02Ax
My		35	F	Unknown	27Ma02Ax
MARA, Bgt.		17	F	Unknown	27Ma02Ax
My.		06	F	Child	27Ma02Ax
BUCK, Bety.		50	F	Unknown	27Ma02Ax
YOUNG, Ann		15	F	Unknown	27Ma02Ax
CARNEY, A.		28	M	Laborer	27Ma02Ax
Math.	(W)	28	F	Wife	27Ma02Ax
Sarah	(D)	09	F	Child	27Ma02Ax
Gah---, T.		15	M	Unknown	27Ma02Ax
CORY, M.		15	M	Unknown	27Ma02Ax
MCKUCHEON, My.		18	F	Unknown	27Ma02Ax
REID, Ma.		30	F	Unknown	27Ma02Ax
FANN, Ron		44	F	Unknown	27Ma02Ax
Sam.	(S)	21	M	Unknown	27Ma02Ax
James	(S)	19	M	Unknown	27Ma02Ax
John	(S)	15	M	Unknown	27Ma02Ax
Mgt.	(D)	12	F	Unknown	27Ma02Ax
MCCABE, Cath.		19	F	Unknown	27Ma02Ax
BENTON, My.A.		16	F	Unknown	27Ma02Ax
FURY, Cath.		58	F	Unknown	27Ma02Ax
KENY, P.		38	M	Unknown	27Ma02Ax
Patch	(S)	17	M	Unknown	27Ma02Ax
My.Ann		29	F	Unknown	27Ma02Ax
GUNN, Cath.		18	F	Unknown	27Ma02Ax
John		20	M	Unknown	27Ma02Ax
HUGHES, M.		20	F	Unknown	27Ma02Ax
MCCABE, J.		21	F	Unknown	27Ma02Ax
SMITH, Mrt.		17	F	None	27Ma02Ax
LEE, J.		33	M	Unknown	27Ma02Ax
RILY, L.		14	M	Unknown	27Ma02Ax
BRACKEN, D.		19	M	Unknown	27Ma02Ax
SHANAHAN, My.		20	F	Unknown	27Ma02Ax
LEARY, M.		40	M	Unknown	27Ma02Ax
NASON, Elen		35	F	Unknown	27Ma02Ax
LERY, Brt.		15	F	Unknown	27Ma02Ax
RYAN, D.		36	M	Unknown	27Ma02Ax
LYNCH, Cath.		14	F	Unknown	27Ma02Ax
John		15	M	Unknown	27Ma02Ax
Elen		12	F	Unknown	27Ma02Ax
Mgt.		20	F	Unknown	27Ma02Ax
CARR, My.		20	F	Unknown	27Ma02Ax
CRENY, Mgt.		10	F	Unknown	27Ma02Ax
John		23	M	Unknown	27Ma02Ax
ACHESON, J.		28	M	Unknown	27Ma02Ax
M.J.		24	F	Unknown	27Ma02Ax
BLAKE, M.		25	M	Laborer	27Ma02Ax
John		40	M	Laborer	27Ma02Ax
CAFREE, N.		30	M	Laborer	27Ma02Ax
MCGINN, C.		22	M	Unknown	27Ma02Ax
RILY, J.		22	M	Unknown	27Ma02Ax
BUTLER, M.		28	M	Unknown	27Ma02Ax
KELLY, J.		80	M	Unknown	27Ma02Ax
READY, Bgt.		16	F	Unknown	27Ma02Ax
PRENDERGAST, My.		16	F	Unknown	27Ma02Ax
SKELMAN, My.		16	F	Unknown	27Ma02Ax
SCOLLAN, My.		20	F	Unknown	27Ma02Ax
CUNNINGHAM, M.		20	M	Unknown	27Ma02Ax
DELANY, J.		18	M	Unknown	27Ma02Ax
Ellzbt.		18	F	Unknown	27Ma02Ax
FITZPATRICK, J.		18	M	Unknown	27Ma02Ax
PRENOUGH, P.		18	M	Unknown	27Ma02Ax
KENY, Ann		16	F	Unknown	27Ma02Ax
RABBIT, Bgt.		10	F	Unknown	27Ma02Ax
RAFFERTY, Ellen		22	F	Unknown	27Ma02Ax
DOUGLAS, G.		17	M	Unknown	27Ma02Ax
SHEEHAN, Bgt.		18	F	Unknown	27Ma02Ax
ARMSTRONG, J.		35	M	Unknown	27Ma02Ax
ARMSTRONG, My.		25	F	Unknown	27Ma02Ax
JAMES, U-Mrs.		30	F	Unknown	27Ma02Ax
My.Anne	(D)	06	F	Child	27Ma02Ax
ARMSTRONG, Jane		02	F	Child	27Ma02Ax
QUIN, Bgt.		14	F	Unknown	27Ma02Ax
EGAN, B.		18	M	Unknown	27Ma02Ax
COLLRIG, Mgt.		20	F	Unknown	27Ma02Ax
CALLAHAN, M.		20	M	Unknown	27Ma02Ax
MCNAMEE, Joanna		22	F	Unknown	27Ma02Ax
CONNOR, T.		20	M	Unknown	27Ma02Ax
KILDUFF, J.		20	M	Unknown	27Ma02Ax
Bgt.		18	F	Unknown	27Ma02Ax
HEAD, Mgt.		15	F	Unknown	27Ma02Ax
CLARKIN, P.		23	M	Unknown	27Ma02Ax
Bgt.		27	F	Unknown	27Ma02Ax
DONEVAN, T.		20	M	Unknown	27Ma02Ax
KINEELY, Bgt.		16	F	Unknown	27Ma02Ax
Gaurl-, Cath.		19	F	Unknown	27Ma02Ax
CARROL, Ellen		14	F	Unknown	27Ma02Ax
MCGLINN, P.		18	M	Unknown	27Ma02Ax
MASTERSON, My.		18	F	Unknown	27Ma02Ax
BRENNAN, P.		39	M	Laborer	27Ma02Ax
Bgt.	(W)	30	F	Unknown	27Ma02Ax
Betsey	(D)	11	F	Unknown	27Ma02Ax
Phillip	(S)	07	M	Child	27Ma02Ax
Rose	(D)	09	F	Child	27Ma02Ax
CROLLY, Judith		18	F	Unknown	27Ma02Ax
MCMAHON, J.		26	M	Unknown	27Ma02Ax
KELLY, Ann		18	F	Unknown	27Ma02Ax
Rose		15	F	Unknown	27Ma02Ax
ROARKE, Ann		18	F	Unknown	27Ma02Ax
My.A.		14	F	Unknown	27Ma02Ax
FRANE, Ellen		16	F	Unknown	27Ma02Ax
FORREST, Mgt.		19	F	Unknown	27Ma02Ax
MCGOWAN, Ann		11	F	Unknown	27Ma02Ax
FITZPATRICK, Ann		18	F	Unknown	27Ma02Ax
REILLY, Ann		29	F	Unknown	27Ma02Ax
Michl.	(S)	05	M	Child	27Ma02Ax
SHANAHAN, D.		19	M	Unknown	27Ma02Ax
CROWLY, Julia		40	F	Unknown	27Ma02Ax
KEENAN, E.		70	M	Unknown	27Ma02Ax
Jane	(W)	55	F	Unknown	27Ma02Ax
Cla.	(S)	13	M	Unknown	27Ma02Ax
Francis	(S)	12	M	Unknown	27Ma02Ax
Betty	(D)	11	F	None	27Ma02Ax
WALTERS, J.		21	M	Unknown	27Ma02Ax
Archibald		28	M	Unknown	27Ma02Ax
MCGEE, Sarah		28	F	Unknown	27Ma02Ax
BLASSY, P.		21	M	Unknown	27Ma02Ax
RADDLE, P.		19	M	Unknown	27Ma02Ax
BRADY, Bgt.		46	F	Unknown	27Ma02Ax
HOLLORAN, My.		23	F	Unknown	27Ma02Ax
Patch		30	M	Unknown	27Ma02Ax
MAHON, Mgt.		19	F	Unknown	27Ma02Ax
Peter		15	M	Unknown	27Ma02Ax
BROUGH, My.		24	F	None	27Ma02Ax
John	(S)	04	M	Child	27Ma02Ax
George	(S)	04	M	Child	27Ma02Ax
OTEMAN, W.		18	M	Unknown	27Ma02Ax
DORAN, W.		20	M	Unknown	27Ma02Ax
COFFE, G.		14	M	Unknown	27Ma02Ax
BRADY, B.		18	M	Unknown	27Ma02Ax
EARLY, C.B.		18	M	Laborer	27Ma02Ax
Michl.		16	M	Laborer	27Ma02Ax
DONNELY, E.		20	M	Laborer	27Ma02Ax
COFFELD, M.		40	M	Laborer	27Ma02Ax
SMITH, Cath.		13	F	Unknown	27Ma02Ax
LARKIN, My.		16	F	Unknown	27Ma02Ax
Julia		13	F	Unknown	27Ma02Ax
MCGEE, Bgt.		19	F	Unknown	27Ma02Ax
RIELLY, Ann		18	F	Unknown	27Ma02Ax
MCMORAN, Cath.		18	F	Unknown	27Ma02Ax
MCDARRA, My.		17	F	Unknown	27Ma02Ax
MCDANE, P.		05	M	Child	27Ma02Ax

FIDELIA 27 MAY 1847

From Liverpool

Name	Rel	Age	Sex	Occupation	Date/Port/Ship
MCDONNELL, My.		20	F	Unknown	27Ma02Ax
GUINY, Bgt.		20	F	Unknown	27Ma02Ax
Jane		19	F	Unknown	27Ma02Ax
DEANE, J.		25	M	Unknown	27Ma02Ax
CEARNY, D.		22	M	Unknown	27Ma02Ax
Michl.		20	M	Unknown	27Ma02Ax
GALLAGHER, H.		24	M	Unknown	27Ma02Ax
CAHILL, M.		24	M	Unknown	27Ma02Ax
REDDING, S.		22	M	Unknown	27Ma02Ax
MULLEN, My.		40	F	Unknown	27Ma02Ax
Arthur	(S)	20	M	Unknown	27Ma02Ax
John	(S)	16	M	Unknown	27Ma02Ax
Mgt.	(D)	14	F	Unknown	27Ma02Ax
My.	(D)	14	F	Unknown	27Ma02Ax
Cath.	(D)	09	F	Child	27Ma02Ax
CONNORS, My.		15	F	Unknown	27Ma02Ax
SEATON, Cath.		15	F	Unknown	27Ma02Ax
CURLY, My.		16	F	Unknown	27Ma02Ax
MCGUIRE, J.		21	M	Unknown	27Ma02Ax
Christopher		23	M	Unknown	27Ma02Ax
My.		02	F	Child	27Ma02Ax
CLARK, Rosann		15	2 F		27Ma02Ax
DUKE, Elzt.		22	2 F		27Ma02Ax
Elzt.	(M)	50	2 F		27Ma02Ax
CONNELL, Sally		18	2 F		27Ma02Ax
MOONY, Mgt.		11	2 F		27Ma02Ax
Bgt.		09	F	Child	27Ma02Ax
RYAN, Mgt.		35	F	Unknown	27Ma02Ax
CROWLY, J.		20	M	Unknown	27Ma02Ax
HENNEGAN, My.		50	F	Unknown	27Ma02Ax
J.	(H)	52	M	Laborer	27Ma02Ax
My.	(D)	18	F	Unknown	27Ma02Ax
Michl.	(S)	20	M	Unknown	27Ma02Ax
HYNES, M.		25	M	Unknown	27Ma02Ax
My.		20	F	Unknown	27Ma02Ax
FERGESSIN, Cath.		19	F	Unknown	27Ma02Ax
DOYLE, My.		20	F	Unknown	27Ma02Ax
GRATTAN, J.		30	M	Unknown	27Ma02Ax
SOUTHERLAND, W.		07	M	Child	27Ma02Ax
Hannah		05	F	Child	27Ma02Ax
Hellen		03	F	Child	27Ma02Ax
Thos.		09	M	Child	27Ma02Ax
Hugh		11	M	Unknown	27Ma02Ax
HERNAN, My.A.		30	F	None	27Ma02Ax
WHITE, My.		18	F	None	27Ma02Ax
CREALY, T.		16	M	Unknown	27Ma02Ax
CANN, M.		46	M	Unknown	27Ma02Ax
John	(S)	14	M	Unknown	27Ma02Ax
HANLAN, Isb.		44	F	Unknown	27Ma02Ax
Hanah	(D)	16	F	Unknown	27Ma02Ax
Robt.	(S)	11	M	Unknown	27Ma02Ax
Benjamin	(S)	09	M	Child	27Ma02Ax
Andrew	(S)	06	M	Child	27Ma02Ax
BRENNAN, H.		30	M	Unknown	27Ma02Ax
Mgt.	(W)	23	F	Wife	27Ma02Ax
Jas.P.	(S)	06	M	Child	27Ma02Ax

W.WARD 27 MAY 1847

From Liverpool

Name	Rel	Age	Sex	Occupation	Date/Port/Ship
HUNT, Ann		40	F	Unknown	27Ma02Pc
CORCORAN, D.		22	M	Laborer	27Ma02Pc
Maria		18	F	Unknown	27Ma02Pc
Mgt.		14	F	Unknown	27Ma02Pc
Michl.		11	M	Unknown	27Ma02Pc
Martin		07	M	Child	27Ma02Pc
MOONY, My.		20	F	Unknown	27Ma02Pc
WOODS, H.		25	M	Unknown	27Ma02Pc
CONAHER, J.		20	M	Unknown	27Ma02Pc
Bgt.	(W)	29	F	Wife	27Ma02Pc
My.	(D)	05	F	Child	27Ma02Pc
John	(S)	04	M	Child	27Ma02Pc
RINN, Cath.		24	F	None	27Ma02Pc
CARR, P.		25	M	Unknown	27Ma02Pc
My.		23	F	None	27Ma02Pc
DOLAN, J.		38	M	Unknown	27Ma02Pc
MURRY, U-Mrs.		18	F	Unknown	27Ma02Pc
CALDY, Elza.		17	F	Unknown	27Ma02Pc
DONLEN, Mary		20	F	Unknown	27Ma02Pc
GAHAGON, J.		20	F	Unknown	27Ma02Pc
Bryan		17	M	Unknown	27Ma02Pc
Han.		45	F	Unknown	27Ma02Pc
My.	(T)	26	F	None	27Ma02Pc
COCHRAN, Ann		03	F	Child	27Ma02Pc
HYNES, M.		46	M	Unknown	27Ma02Pc
Cath.	(D)	22	F	Unknown	27Ma02Pc
James	(S)	20	M	Unknown	27Ma02Pc
DOUGHTY, Rose		25	F	Unknown	27Ma02Pc
MCVEY, O.		50	M	Unknown	27Ma02Pc
Francis	(S)	18	M	Unknown	27Ma02Pc
Ellen	(D)	16	F	Unknown	27Ma02Pc
H.	(D)	12	F	Unknown	27Ma02Pc
Frances	(D)	05	F	Child	27Ma02Pc
CAHILL, M.		22	M	Unknown	27Ma02Pc
John		23	M	Unknown	27Ma02Pc
MAGHER, M.		23	M	Unknown	27Ma02Pc
KELLY, W.		20	M	Unknown	27Ma02Pc
DUNN, P.		26	M	Unknown	27Ma02Pc
DAWD, Bety		24	F	Unknown	27Ma02Pc
GRADY, Bgt.		20	F	Unknown	27Ma02Pc
DELAY, J.		23	M	Unknown	27Ma02Pc
FOLY, R.		24	M	Laborer	27Ma02Pc
RYAN, P.		23	M	Unknown	27Ma02Pc
FAHY, Ellen		22	F	Unknown	27Ma02Pc
WALSH, Ann		22	F	Unknown	27Ma02Pc
CROGAN, J.		22	M	Unknown	27Ma02Pc
HAUGHAST, T.		23	M	Unknown	27Ma02Pc
GEHAN, M.		28	M	Unknown	27Ma02Pc
My.		21	F	Unknown	27Ma02Pc
FANGLY, J.		20	M	Unknown	27Ma02Pc
Bgt.		24	F	Unknown	27Ma02Pc
James		22	M	Unknown	27Ma02Pc
Mgt.		26	F	Unknown	27Ma02Pc
STAPLETON, J.		21	M	Unknown	27Ma02Pc
Ellen	(M)	50	F	Unknown	27Ma02Pc
Pat	(P)	50	M	Unknown	27Ma02Pc
Mgt.	(T)	20	F	Unknown	27Ma02Pc
Emily	(T)	17	F	Unknown	27Ma02Pc
John	(B)	15	M	Unknown	27Ma02Pc
Edwrd.	(B)	14	M	Unknown	27Ma02Pc
Edmond	(B)	10	M	Unknown	27Ma02Pc
Judith		46	F	None	27Ma02Pc
John		32	M	Unknown	27Ma02Pc
LALLY, P.		01	M	Child	27Ma02Pc
Judy		34	F	Unknown	27Ma02Pc

NAMES OF PASSENGERS		AGE	SEX	OCCUPATIONS	DATE PORT SHIP
LALLY, Hannah		27	F	Unknown	27Ma02Pc
Honn., U		20	M	Unknown	27Ma02Pc
WHELAN, A.		20	M	Unknown	27Ma02Pc
OCONNELL, D.		22	M	Unknown	27Ma02Pc
CURLY, M.		20	F	Unknown	27Ma02Pc
Patt		19	M	Unknown	27Ma02Pc
DOWNY, B.		26	M	Unknown	27Ma02Pc
Jane	(W)	33	F	Wife	27Ma02Pc
Bgt.	(D)	02	F	Child	27Ma02Pc
Ann	(D)	01	F	Child	27Ma02Pc
KEOUGH, L.		24	M	Unknown	27Ma02Pc
BRADY, A.		30	M	Unknown	27Ma02Pc
My.		30	F	Unknown	27Ma02Pc
CASH, T.		21	M	Unknown	27Ma02Pc
KEEFE, B.		25	M	Unknown	27Ma02Pc
CONNELL, E.		21	M	Unknown	27Ma02Pc
John		24	M	Unknown	27Ma02Pc
MCCARTY, D.		22	M	Unknown	27Ma02Pc
D.		21	M	Laborer	27Ma02Pc
QUINN, P.		50	M	Laborer	27Ma02Pc
Mgt.	(W)	47	F	Wife	27Ma02Pc
Mich.	(S)	18	M	Unknown	27Ma02Pc
Marcella	(D)	16	F	Unknown	27Ma02Pc
Bdgt.	(D)	13	F	Unknown	27Ma02Pc
Mary	(D)	11	F	Unknown	27Ma02Pc
KENNY, J.		18	M	Unknown	27Ma02Pc
Thos.		13	M	Unknown	27Ma02Pc
Mich.		10	M	Unknown	27Ma02Pc
Peter		15	M	Unknown	27Ma02Pc
KELLY, Mgt.		28	F	Unknown	27Ma02Pc
MCILROY, M.		27	M	Unknown	27Ma02Pc
GEDDES, T.		22	M	Unknown	27Ma02Pc
MCGINLY, E.		24	M	Unknown	27Ma02Pc
EAGELY, J.		22	M	Unknown	27Ma02Pc
HORAN, H.		24	M	Unknown	27Ma02Pc
GARESIN, F.		21	M	Unknown	27Ma02Pc
FEGAN, M.		29	M	Unknown	27Ma02Pc
Rose	(W)	28	F	Unknown	27Ma02Pc
Anne	(D)	01	F	Child	27Ma02Pc
DALEY, M.		22	M	Unknown	27Ma02Pc
MENTON, L.		22	M	Unknown	27Ma02Pc
FEELING, B.		25	M	Unknown	27Ma02Pc
DUFFY, P.		24	M	Unknown	27Ma02Pc
BOTTOM, W.		16	M	Unknown	27Ma02Pc
Laurence		13	M	Unknown	27Ma02Pc
CARR, P.		16	M	Unknown	27Ma02Pc
FITZPATRICK, A.		24	M	Unknown	27Ma02Pc
DAFFEY, P.		40	M	Unknown	27Ma02Pc
Ann	(W)	40	F	Unknown	27Ma02Pc
Pat	(S)	21	M	Unknown	27Ma02Pc
My.	(D)	19	F	Unknown	27Ma02Pc
Mich.	(S)	17	M	Unknown	27Ma02Pc
Peter	(B)	45	M	Unknown	27Ma02Pc
James	(N)	14	M	Unknown	27Ma02Pc
Ann	(N)	12	F	Unknown	27Ma02Pc
John	(N)	10	M	Unknown	27Ma02Pc
Chas.	(N)	08	M	Child	27Ma02Pc
Eliza.	(N)	06	F	Child	27Ma02Pc
MURPHY, P.		30	M	Unknown	27Ma02Pc
BRYAN, J.		30	M	Unknown	27Ma02Pc
MONARN, R.		28	M	Laborer	27Ma02Pc
Mich.		24	M	Laborer	27Ma02Pc
SHINE, Jane		24	F	Unknown	27Ma02Pc
MURPHY, J.		20	U	Unknown	27Ma02Pc
Judy		25	F	Unknown	27Ma02Pc
John		34	M	Unknown	27Ma02Pc
John		22	M	Unknown	27Ma02Pc
Ellen		18	F	Unknown	27Ma02Pc
Ally		19	F	Unknown	27Ma02Pc
Mgt.		20	F	Unknown	27Ma02Pc
Cath.		19	F	Unknown	27Ma02Pc
GLYNN, W.		24	U	Unknown	27Ma02Pc
MUNSON, J.		21	U	Unknown	27Ma02Pc
OHARA, J.		21	U	Unknown	27Ma02Pc
U-Mrs.		20	F	Unknown	27Ma02Pc
OHARA, Patt		26	M	Unknown	27Ma02Pc
QUIN, E.		23	U	Unknown	27Ma02Pc
Cath.		20	F	Unknown	27Ma02Pc
EAGAN, J.		18	U	Unknown	27Ma02Pc
CULLOGH, Ch.		18	M	Unknown	27Ma02Pc
CROSSLAND, My.		20	F	Unknown	27Ma02Pc
HERRAN, B.		20	F	Unknown	27Ma02Pc
My.		18	F	Unknown	27Ma02Pc
BANNON, A.		20	F	Unknown	27Ma02Pc
HIND, Bidy		20	F	Unknown	27Ma02Pc
BARROW, Anne		21	F	Unknown	27Ma02Pc
QUIN, P----		30	U	Unknown	27Ma02Pc
HART, J.		05	U	Child	27Ma02Pc
ODONNEL, J.		24	U	Unknown	27Ma02Pc
CARR, B.		32	U	Unknown	27Ma02Pc
Thos.	(S)	06	M	Child	27Ma02Pc
Robt.	(S)	04	M	Child	27Ma02Pc
John	(S)	01	M	Child	27Ma02Pc
Ellen	(W)	30	F	Unknown	27Ma02Pc
Pat	(B)	34	M	Unknown	27Ma02Pc
KERRIGAN, Judy		20	F	Unknown	27Ma02Pc
JOHNSTON, Ann		24	F	Unknown	27Ma02Pc
HOGAN, P.		30	F	Unknown	27Ma02Pc
GREENWOOD, W.		20	F	Unknown	27Ma02Pc
CADWELL, J.		22	F	Unknown	27Ma02Pc
COCHRAN, J.		21	F	Unknown	27Ma02Pc
SMITH, W.		50	F	Unknown	27Ma02Pc
Cath.		40	F	Unknown	27Ma02Pc
JONES, J.		26	M	Laborer	27Ma02Pc
James		20	M	Unknown	27Ma02Pc
HUMPHY, J.		55	M	Unknown	27Ma02Pc
Hanna	(W)	50	F	Unknown	27Ma02Pc
James	(S)	18	M	Unknown	27Ma02Pc
Mgt.	(D)	20	F	Unknown	27Ma02Pc
Joshua	(S)	19	M	Unknown	27Ma02Pc
Thos.	(S)	11	M	None	27Ma02Pc
Cath.	(D)	09	F	Child	27Ma02Pc
OBRIEN, J.		07	M	Child	27Ma02Pc
CARTY, J.		40	M	Unknown	27Ma02Pc
Rose		35	F	Unknown	27Ma02Pc
Mich.		36	M	Unknown	27Ma02Pc
John		07	M	Child	27Ma02Pc
KELLY, J.		06	M	Child	27Ma02Pc
Laurence	(P)	30	M	Unknown	27Ma02Pc
My.		60	F	Unknown	27Ma02Pc
Phillip		20	M	Unknown	27Ma02Pc
DONEGAN, D.		20	M	Unknown	27Ma02Pc
MADDEN, J.		20	M	Unknown	27Ma02Pc
JAMES, T.		20	M	Unknown	27Ma02Pc
Marth.	(M)	50	F	Unknown	27Ma02Pc
WILLIAMS, A.		30	M	Unknown	27Ma02Pc
THOMAS, A.		19	M	Unknown	27Ma02Pc
Jack		13	M	None	27Ma02Pc
Agnes		05	F	Child	27Ma02Pc
Nat.		11	M	None	27Ma02Pc
John		07	M	Child	27Ma02Pc
Mgt.		04	F	Child	27Ma02Pc
Peter		02	M	Child	27Ma02Pc
Mgt.		19	F	Unknown	27Ma02Pc
Ire----, T.		25	M	Unknown	27Ma02Pc
My.		17	F	Unknown	27Ma02Pc
MCGLONE, My.		19	M	Unknown	27Ma02Pc
My.		18	F	Unknown	27Ma02Pc
War---, Cath.		30	F	Unknown	27Ma02Pc
Bgt.	(D)	09	F	Child	27Ma02Pc
M.		22	M	Unknown	27Ma02Pc
LENNEN, P.		09	M	Child	27Ma02Pc
Thos.		07	M	Child	27Ma02Pc
Honor		20	F	Unknown	27Ma02Pc
BRIEN, Ann-M.		14	F	None	27Ma02Pc
My.		30	F	None	27Ma02Pc
HURGAN, Cath.		08	F	Child	27Ma02Pc
Dani.		04	M	Child	27Ma02Pc
My.		16	F	Unknown	27Ma02Pc
HUNTER, M.		22	M	Laborer	27Ma02Pc

NAMES OF PASSENGERS		AGE	SEX	OCCUPATIONS	DATE PORT SHIP
LENNON, P.		29	M	Unknown	27Ma02Pc
Honora		25	F	Unknown	27Ma02Pc
MCGRATH, M.		23	M	Unknown	27Ma02Pc
MCGOLERICK, J.		18	M	Unknown	27Ma02Pc
Bgt.		18	F	Unknown	27Ma02Pc
FREE, R.		21	M	Unknown	27Ma02Pc
MCBANE, Cath.		16	F	Unknown	27Ma02Pc
MCMANUS, J.		28	M	Unknown	27Ma02Pc
LODGE, P.		50	M	Unknown	27Ma02Pc
BRENNAN, J.		22	M	Unknown	27Ma02Pc
Wm.		18	M	Unknown	27Ma02Pc
KEEFE, M.		16	M	Unknown	27Ma02Pc
FITZGERALD, T.		20	M	Unknown	27Ma02Pc
Cath.		18	F	Unknown	27Ma02Pc
Ed--Y, R.		16	M	Unknown	27Ma02Pc
JORDAN, E.		20	M	Unknown	27Ma02Pc
Cath.		14	F	Unknown	27Ma02Pc
My.		12	F	Unknown	27Ma02Pc
Walter		40	M	Unknown	27Ma02Pc
JORDEN, D.		18	M	Unknown	27Ma02Pc
Cath.		12	F	Unknown	27Ma02Pc
Edwd.		16	M	Unknown	27Ma02Pc
CARROLL, J.		12	M	Unknown	27Ma02Pc
B.		26	M	Unknown	27Ma02Pc
COLLINS, W.		24	M	Unknown	27Ma02Pc
DOWNY, M.		18	M	Unknown	27Ma02Pc
Mgt.		16	F	Unknown	27Ma02Pc
CARROLL, Betty		24	F	Unknown	27Ma02Pc
ONEIL, Cath.		16	F	Unknown	27Ma02Pc
QUINN, M.		18	M	Unknown	27Ma02Pc
DOWNY, Cath.		16	F	Unknown	27Ma02Pc
MENLAND, Bgt.		26	F	Unknown	27Ma02Pc
BELEW, Ann		16	F	Unknown	27Ma02Pc
My.		02	F	Child	27Ma02Pc
ONEILL, J.		26	M	Unknown	27Ma02Pc
DAVIS, My.		18	F	Unknown	27Ma02Pc
WATSON, My.		16	F	Unknown	27Ma02Pc
MAUGHTON, Cath.		12	F	Unknown	27Ma02Pc
NOLAN, J.		26	M	Laborer	27Ma02Pc
HOGAN, J.		12	M	Unknown	27Ma02Pc
KEENY, P.		10	M	Unknown	27Ma02Pc
MOLLOY, M.		26	M	Unknown	27Ma02Pc
Ann		20	F	Unknown	27Ma02Pc
MCDOWD, Bgt.		16	F	Unknown	27Ma02Pc
CURRAN, Bgt.		18	F	Unknown	27Ma02Pc
Cath.		14	F	Unknown	27Ma02Pc
CLERY, J.		12	M	Unknown	27Ma02Pc
My.		08	F	Child	27Ma02Pc
Mgt.		10	F	Unknown	27Ma02Pc
MCINTEE, J.		28	M	Unknown	27Ma02Pc
Cath.		20	F	None	27Ma02Pc

SPEED 28 MAY 1847

From Liverpool

NAMES OF PASSENGERS		AGE	SEX	OCCUPATIONS	DATE PORT SHIP
WHELAN, P.		40	M	Laborer	28Ma02Pd
U	(W)	35	F	Wife	28Ma02Pd
John	(S)	15	M	Unknown	28Ma02Pd
Thos.	(S)	11	M	Unknown	28Ma02Pd
Pat	(B)	39	M	Unknown	28Ma02Pd
MORTON, J.		29	M	Unknown	28Ma02Pd
Pat		27	M	Unknown	28Ma02Pd
Mary		30	F	Unknown	28Ma02Pd
Pat		30	M	Unknown	28Ma02Pd
MADDEN, My.		04	F	Child	28Ma02Pd
Pat	(B)	04	M	Child	28Ma02Pd
U-Mrs.	(M)	27	F	Unknown	28Ma02Pd
MCDOROY, P.		20	M	Unknown	28Ma02Pd
MOORE, W.		27	M	Unknown	28Ma02Pd
Jas.	(B)	24	M	Unknown	28Ma02Pd
U-Mrs.	(M)	50	F	Unknown	28Ma02Pd
John		11	M	None	28Ma02Pd
Ellen		07	F	Child	28Ma02Pd
LOVE, My.		24	F	Unknown	28Ma02Pd
ENWIGHT, Bgt.		24	F	Unknown	28Ma02Pd
HOWER, Joanne		25	F	None	28Ma02Pd
Cautl--, J.		24	M	Unknown	28Ma02Pd
STEDBURY, J.		30	M	Unknown	28Ma02Pd
APRIL, J.		30	M	Unknown	28Ma02Pd
STEDBURY, J.		28	M	Unknown	28Ma02Pd
Betty		40	F	Unknown	28Ma02Pd
Reuben		12	M	Unknown	28Ma02Pd
Ephraim		12	M	Unknown	28Ma02Pd
Sarah-A.		13	F	None	28Ma02Pd
Cora		06	F	Child	28Ma02Pd
Joseph		24	M	Unknown	28Ma02Pd
CAMPBELL, T.		25	M	Unknown	28Ma02Pd
WARD, J.		30	M	Unknown	28Ma02Pd
FLOYD, O.		22	M	Unknown	28Ma02Pd
Eliza		21	F	Unknown	28Ma02Pd
NEILSON, S.		25	M	Unknown	28Ma02Pd
BUCKLY, J.		23	M	Unknown	28Ma02Pd
STANLY, M.		27	M	Unknown	28Ma02Pd
My.		21	F	Unknown	28Ma02Pd
ROARKE, My.		21	F	Unknown	28Ma02Pd
LORD, F.L.		22	M	Unknown	28Ma02Pd
NALY, A.		60	M	Laborer	28Ma02Pd
KELLY, J.		50	M	Unknown	28Ma02Pd
EDWARDS, R.		27	M	Unknown	28Ma02Pd
STONE, J.		27	M	Unknown	28Ma02Pd
Eliza		13	F	Unknown	28Ma02Pd
P.		13	M	Unknown	28Ma02Pd
Mary		11	F	Unknown	28Ma02Pd
Thos.		17	M	Unknown	28Ma02Pd
Marla		16	F	Unknown	28Ma02Pd
Jane		16	F	Unknown	28Ma02Pd
Ellen		18	F	Unknown	28Ma02Pd
Cath.		09	F	Child	28Ma02Pd
Eliza.		06	F	Child	28Ma02Pd
My.		01	F	Child	28Ma02Pd
Bgt.		30	F	Unknown	28Ma02Pd
Mich.		24	M	Unknown	28Ma02Pd
John		01	M	Child	28Ma02Pd
CONNER, P.		30	M	Unknown	28Ma02Pd
Mary	(W)	24	F	Unknown	28Ma02Pd
Bgt.	(D)	01	F	Child	28Ma02Pd
MCEANY, T.		23	M	Unknown	28Ma02Pd
SWEENY, Cath.		34	F	Unknown	28Ma02Pd
CONNELL, J.		38	M	Unknown	28Ma02Pd
Tim		25	M	Unknown	28Ma02Pd
Jeffry		22	M	Unknown	28Ma02Pd
CARTY, T.		28	M	Unknown	28Ma02Pd
Danl.		21	M	Unknown	28Ma02Pd
Julia		22	F	Unknown	28Ma02Pd
REGAN, My.		10	F	Unknown	28Ma02Pd
CARY, T.		29	M	Unknown	28Ma02Pd
KILIAN, J.		26	M	Unknown	28Ma02Pd
DRISCOLL, P.		24	M	Unknown	28Ma02Pd
SULLIVAN, Joanne		24	F	Unknown	28Ma02Pd
Bess		26	F	Unknown	28Ma02Pd
Ellen		02	F	Child	28Ma02Pd
WHORTON, Ann		25	F	Unknown	28Ma02Pd
MURPHY, M.		25	M	Unknown	28Ma02Pd
SHATON, J.		25	M	Unknown	28Ma02Pd
FITZGERALD, E.		18	M	Unknown	28Ma02Pd
BUCKLY, T.		28	M	Unknown	28Ma02Pd
BARRETT, M.		27	M	Unknown	28Ma02Pd
OSBORNE, Ellen		20	F	Unknown	28Ma02Pd
LITTLE, M.		24	M	Farmer	28Ma02Pd
MANAHAN, M.		30	M	Unknown	28Ma02Pd
FENTON, T.		32	M	Unknown	28Ma02Pd
ELLIOTT, T.M.		20	M	Unknown	28Ma02Pd
LOOST, R.		23	M	Unknown	28Ma02Pd

NAMES OF PASSENGERS		AGE	SEX	OCCUPATIONS	DATE PORT SHIP
LOOST, Mary		18	F	Unknown	28Ma02Pd
DONOHOE, J.		40	M	Unknown	28Ma02Pd
Do--	(D)	19	F	Unknown	28Ma02Pd
John	(S)	17	M	Unknown	28Ma02Pd
Mich.	(S)	15	M	Unknown	28Ma02Pd
Cora	(D)	12	F	Unknown	28Ma02Pd
Redmond	(S)	09	M	Child	28Ma02Pd
Bess	(D)	07	F	Child	28Ma02Pd
CONNOR, J.		30	M	Unknown	28Ma02Pd
HENING, E.		45	M	Unknown	28Ma02Pd
Ellen		35	F	Unknown	28Ma02Pd
KENNEDY, T.		23	M	Unknown	28Ma02Pd
Peggy		27	F	Unknown	28Ma02Pd
Julia		01	F	Child	28Ma02Pd
Mostl--, J.		01	M	Child	28Ma02Pd
Pat		04	M	Child	28Ma02Pd
Mary		02	F	Child	28Ma02Pd
ELLIS, T.		27	M	Unknown	28Ma02Pd
U	(W)	28	F	Unknown	28Ma02Pd
THOMAS, Ellen		65	F	Unknown	28Ma02Pd
OSBORN, T.		25	M	Unknown	28Ma02Pd
Mich.		23	M	Unknown	28Ma02Pd
OBRIEN, P.		13	M	Unknown	28Ma02Pd
KETCHIN, O.		30	M	Unknown	28Ma02Pd
DOYLE, Mrgt.		25	F	Unknown	28Ma02Pd
OSBURN, Bgt.		25	F	Unknown	28Ma02Pd
DEVENNY, M.		15	M	Unknown	28Ma02Pd
DEVER, Cath.		04	F	Child	28Ma02Pd
John		18	M	Unknown	28Ma02Pd
Ann		17	F	Unknown	28Ma02Pd
Hugh		05	M	Child	28Ma02Pd
My.J.		11	F	Unknown	28Ma02Pd
Wm.		10	M	Unknown	28Ma02Pd
Mich.		09	M	Child	28Ma02Pd
Jane		06	F	Child	28Ma02Pd
Thy.		09	M	Child	28Ma02Pd
Kat.		05	F	Child	28Ma02Pd
DEVEREAUX, Soph.		03	F	Child	28Ma02Pd
MCCARTY, Ellen		21	F	Unknown	28Ma02Pd
GLORNY, Jane		20	F	Unknown	28Ma02Pd
BYRNES, D.		28	M	Unknown	28Ma02Pd
Mich.		25	F	Unknown	28Ma02Pd
My.		22	F	Unknown	28Ma02Pd
REGAN, D.		26	M	Unknown	28Ma02Pd
My.		38	F	Unknown	28Ma02Pd
MURPHY, My.		15	F	Unknown	28Ma02Pd
LEARY, C.		26	M	Unknown	28Ma02Pd
Ellen		24	F	Unknown	28Ma02Pd
LOHAN, H.		40	M	Unknown	28Ma02Pd
Bgt.	(W)	38	F	Wife	28Ma02Pd
Ann	(D)	13	F	Wife	28Ma02Pd
Hugh	(S)	11	M	Wife	28Ma02Pd
Thos.	(S)	08	M	Child	28Ma02Pd
Rose	(D)	06	F	Child	28Ma02Pd
Frances	(D)	03	F	Child	28Ma02Pd
John	(S)	01	M	Child	28Ma02Pd
MAHONY, D.		25	M	Unknown	28Ma02Pd
LEARY, T.		30	M	Unknown	28Ma02Pd
SULLIVAN, M.		20	M	Unknown	28Ma02Pd
Joanne		22	F	Unknown	28Ma02Pd
MURPHY, J.		50	M	Unknown	28Ma02Pd
My.	(D)	21	F	Unknown	28Ma02Pd
WALSH, My.		19	F	Unknown	28Ma02Pd
HALLERY, M.		21	M	Unknown	28Ma02Pd
John		09	M	Child	28Ma02Pd
Ellen		19	F	Unknown	28Ma02Pd
DONOVAN, D.		25	M	Unknown	28Ma02Pd
MAHONY, J.		22	M	Unknown	28Ma02Pd
CURACT, P.		27	M	Unknown	28Ma02Pd
SHAY, M.		45	M	Unknown	28Ma02Pd
Ann	(D)	13	F	Unknown	28Ma02Pd
CALLELY, F.		27	M	Unknown	28Ma02Pd
MANON, C.		30	M	Unknown	28Ma02Pd
Blow--, M.		30	M	Unknown	28Ma02Pd
VILLIER, P.		20	M	Unknown	28Ma02Pd

NAMES OF PASSENGERS		AGE	SEX	OCCUPATIONS	DATE PORT SHIP
GOWEN, J.		20	M	Unknown	28Ma02Pd
CANE, J.		22	M	Unknown	28Ma02Pd
Ellen		20	F	Unknown	28Ma02Pd
High----, J.		17	M	Unknown	28Ma02Pd
HIGHUNT, D.		42	M	Laborer	28Ma02Pd
Cat.	(D)	10	F	None	28Ma02Pd
Pat	(S)	08	M	Child	28Ma02Pd
Mgt.	(D)	06	F	Child	28Ma02Pd
Honor	(D)	03	F	Child	28Ma02Pd
Dani.	(S)	01	M	Child	28Ma02Pd
Honora	(W)	40	F	Wife	28Ma02Pd
SWEENY, Bgt.		18	F	Wife	28Ma02Pd
CALLEN, J.		30	M	Unknown	28Ma02Pd
SHEAHY, C.		28	M	Unknown	28Ma02Pd
SWEENY, N.H.		23	M	Unknown	28Ma02Pd
HERSTON, Cath.		20	F	None	28Ma02Pd
Joanna		18	F	None	28Ma02Pd
CONN, P.		23	M	Unknown	28Ma02Pd
MALLEY, Cath.		28	F	None	28Ma02Pd
OHARA, P.		25	M	Unknown	28Ma02Pd
RICH, O.J		23	M	Unknown	28Ma02Pd
My.		18	F	None	28Ma02Pd
BUCKLY, D.		25	M	Unknown	28Ma02Pd
MONAHAN, Elza.		23	N	Unknown	28Ma02Pd
CORY, P.		24	M	Unknown	28Ma02Pd
CULLEN, My.		22	F	None	28Ma02Pd
Hart.		20	F	None	28Ma02Pd
CONNOR, B.		20	M	Unknown	28Ma02Pd
COLLEY, C.		23	M	Unknown	28Ma02Pd
MCELY, P.		40	M	Unknown	28Ma02Pd
N.	(W)	32	F	Wife	28Ma02Pd
My.	(D)	04	F	Child	28Ma02Pd
Jas.	(S)	03	M	Child	28Ma02Pd
HAY, P.		40	M	Unknown	28Ma02Pd
MCGIVERN, Ann.		16	F	None	28Ma02Pd
My.		02	F	Child	28Ma02Pd
ROALY, J.		20	M	Unknown	28Ma02Pd
MCCAY, My.		16	F	None	28Ma02Pd
SHEA, Joanne		20	F	None	28Ma02Pd
RUMSTON, J.		30	M	Unknown	28Ma02Pd
MADDEN, Ja.		10	M	None	28Ma02Pd
MANAHAN, C.		30	M	None	28Ma02Pd
CURLY, P.		40	M	Unknown	28Ma02Pd
U	(W)	40	F	Wife	28Ma02Pd

PACIFIC 28 MAY 1847

From Liverpool

NAMES OF PASSENGERS		AGE	SEX	OCCUPATIONS	DATE PORT SHIP
CLINTON, Jas.C.		50	M	Farmer	28Ma02BJ
U	(W)	50	F	Wife	28Ma02BJ
Michael	(S)	25	M	Farmer	28Ma02BJ
James	(S)	25	M	Farmer	28Ma02BJ
Mary	(D)	20	F	None	28Ma02BJ
Catherine	(D)	15	F	None	28Ma02BJ
HARNALLY, Ann		20	F	Servant	28Ma02BJ
CUNNINGHAM, Alice		20	F	Servant	28Ma02BJ
MARTIN, Laurence		20	M	Laborer	28Ma02BJ
Catherine		18	F	Servant	28Ma02BJ
HALFPENNY, Paul		20	M	Laborer	28Ma02BJ
MAGANNON, John		20	M	Farmer	28Ma02BJ
CARROLL, Francis		20	M	Farmer	28Ma02BJ
WATERS, James		25	M	Farmer	28Ma02BJ
GOATLAND, Thos.		30	M	Farmer	28Ma02BJ
RODGERS, John		28	M	Farmer	28Ma02BJ
DONELLY, Bridget		20	F	Servant	28Ma02BJ
FERGUSON, Bridget		20	F	Servant	28Ma02BJ
Susan		22	F	Servant	28Ma02BJ
SMITH, Michael		40	M	Mechanic	28Ma02BJ

NAMES OF PASSENGERS		AGE	SEX	OCCUPATIONS	DATE PORT SHIP
WARD, Michael		50	M	Mechanic	28Ma02BJ
U	(W)	48	F	Wife	28Ma02BJ
John	(S)	20	M	Laborer	28Ma02BJ
Thomas	(S)	18	M	Laborer	28Ma02BJ
Bernard	(S)	16	M	Laborer	28Ma02BJ
Eleanor	(D)	12	F	None	28Ma02BJ
Mary	(D)	10	F	None	28Ma02BJ
Margaret	(D)	08	F	Child	28Ma02BJ
Peter	(S)	02	M	Child	28Ma02BJ
OHARE, John		20	M	Laborer	28Ma02BJ
DOHERTY, John		20	M	Laborer	28Ma02BJ
CUMMINGS, Michael		56	M	Mechanic	28Ma02BJ
U	(W)	43	F	Wife	28Ma02BJ
James	(S)	18	M	Laborer	28Ma02BJ
Christine	(D)	12	F	None	28Ma02BJ
Catherine	(D)	08	F	Child	28Ma02BJ
Betty	(D)	04	F	Child	28Ma02BJ
TIRRELL, Matt.		20	M	Mechanic	28Ma02BJ
Michael		20	M	Farmer	28Ma02BJ
VERNA, William		47	M	Farmer	28Ma02BJ
Samuel		40	M	Farmer	28Ma02BJ
James		20	M	Farmer	28Ma02BJ
Nancey		18	F	Servant	28Ma02BJ
Olivia		15	F	Servant	28Ma02BJ
Mary		08	F	Child	28Ma02BJ
Nancey		02	F	Child	28Ma02BJ
MANLEY, Saml.		30	M	Laborer	28Ma02BJ
Mary		25	F	Servant	28Ma02BJ
DUNLAP, Jane		25	F	Servant	28Ma02BJ
GIBSON, Mary-Ann		20	F	Servant	28Ma02BJ
CAMPBELL, Matilda		20	F	Servant	28Ma02BJ
RICHIE, Nancy		20	F	Servant	28Ma02BJ
STUART, John		58	M	Laborer	28Ma02BJ
Thomas		50	M	Laborer	28Ma02BJ
John		23	M	Laborer	28Ma02BJ
Oliver		20	M	Laborer	28Ma02BJ
Sarah		10	F	None	28Ma02BJ
Rachel		18	F	None	28Ma02BJ
Anne		06	F	Child	28Ma02BJ
Libbey		03	F	Child	28Ma02BJ
RICHARDSON, Vance		20	M	Laborer	28Ma02BJ
KAIRNES, Eliza		20	F	None	28Ma02BJ
RICHARDSON, Margt.		30	F	None	28Ma02BJ
Isabella		30	F	None	28Ma02BJ
MCHEA, John		40	M	Mechanic	28Ma02BJ
SMITH, James		35	M	Laborer	28Ma02BJ
WAINE, Joseph		20	M	Laborer	28Ma02BJ
NULLOCK, Henry		50	M	Laborer	28Ma02BJ
Thomas		48	M	Laborer	28Ma02BJ
John		10	M	Laborer	28Ma02BJ
Daniel		08	M	Child	28Ma02BJ
Elizabeth		06	F	Child	28Ma02BJ
Loucy		04	F	Child	28Ma02BJ
Joseph		03	M	Child	28Ma02BJ
Daniel		.00	M	Infant	28Ma02BJ
CONNOR, William		35	M	Laborer	28Ma02BJ
Jim		20	M	Laborer	28Ma02BJ
Mary		06	F	Child	28Ma02BJ
Peggy		03	F	Child	28Ma02BJ
GIBSON, U-Mrs.		20	F	Servant	28Ma02BJ
FINOCKER, Martha		20	F	Servant	28Ma02BJ
LYONS, Mary		20	F	Servant	28Ma02BJ
MURRY, Bridget		20	F	Servant	28Ma02BJ
James		20	M	Laborer	28Ma02BJ
GLEESON, Judy		35	F	Tailor	28Ma02BJ
Michael		20	M	Mechanic	28Ma02BJ
Julia		02	F	Child	28Ma02BJ
William		.00	M	Infant	28Ma02BJ
Jerry		.00	M	Infant	28Ma02BJ
Cornelius		.00	M	Infant	28Ma02BJ
QUIRK, Mary		20	F	Servant	28Ma02BJ
MCDONALD, Mary		30	F	Servant	28Ma02BJ
GOOHY, Mary		20	F	Servant	28Ma02BJ
SHANAHAN, James		35	M	Laborer	28Ma02BJ
GLEESON, Honor		40	F	None	28Ma02BJ
GLEESON, Bridget	(D)	20	F	None	28Ma02BJ
BIRMINGHAM, Pat.		35	M	Laborer	28Ma02BJ
DONOHUE, Catherine		20	F	Servant	28Ma02BJ
HAGAN, John		20	M	Laborer	28Ma02BJ
BELL, James		20	M	Laborer	28Ma02BJ
POWELL, Jos.		55	M	Laborer	28Ma02BJ
My.	(W)	50	F	Wife	28Ma02BJ
William	(S)	02	M	Child	28Ma02BJ
BANNON, Paul		36	M	Farmer	28Ma02BJ
NOON, George		25	M	Farmer	28Ma02BJ
Eleanor		20	F	Servant	28Ma02BJ
ONEIL, Elen		30	F	Servant	28Ma02BJ
HUGHES, Mary		30	F	Servant	28Ma02BJ
MCGIL, Thomas		40	M	Laborer	28Ma02BJ
U	(W)	35	F	Wife	28Ma02BJ
Michael	(S)	12	M	Laborer	28Ma02BJ
Winfrid	(S)	10	M	Laborer	28Ma02BJ
Catherine	(D)	08	F	Child	28Ma02BJ
Rose	(D)	04	F	Child	28Ma02BJ
JUDGE, Darby		50	M	Farmer	28Ma02BJ
James	(S)	20	M	Farmer	28Ma02BJ
Mary	(D)	18	F	Servant	28Ma02BJ
Margaret	(D)	14	F	Servant	28Ma02BJ
John	(S)	08	M	Child	28Ma02BJ
Mary	(D)	03	F	Child	28Ma02BJ
MCCORMICK, Bridgt.		20	F	Servant	28Ma02BJ
SHEHEY, Ann		20	F	Servant	28Ma02BJ
JUDGE, Catherine		20	F	Servant	28Ma02BJ
CONORTY, Margaret		35	F	Servant	28Ma02BJ
Edward	(H)	38	M	Laborer	28Ma02BJ
Thomas	(S)	03	M	Child	28Ma02BJ
DOHERTY, John		35	M	Laborer	28Ma02BJ
Ann	(W)	30	F	Servant	28Ma02BJ
Judy	(D)	05	F	Child	28Ma02BJ
Eliza	(D)	03	F	Child	28Ma02BJ
WHELAN, John		20	M	Laborer	28Ma02BJ
BURKE, Ned		20	M	Laborer	28Ma02BJ
CRAMPE, James		28	M	Laborer	28Ma02BJ
COFFEE, Paddy		28	M	Laborer	28Ma02BJ
Peggy		20	F	Servant	28Ma02BJ
RUSSELL, Barth.		28	M	Laborer	28Ma02BJ
SMITH, John		40	M	Laborer	28Ma02BJ
GIBSON, Alick		20	M	Laborer	28Ma02BJ
VANCE, James		20	M	Laborer	28Ma02BJ
MCCRONY, Susan		20	F	Servant	28Ma02BJ
RYAN, Mary		25	F	Servant	28Ma02BJ
MULLEN, Jerice-M.		30	F	Servant	28Ma02BJ
RUDDY, Fanny		28	F	Servant	28Ma02BJ
DARBY, Mary		20	F	Servant	28Ma02BJ
DOYLE, Catherine		35	F	Servant	28Ma02BJ
GREEN, James		26	M	Laborer	28Ma02BJ
DONALD, Michael		48	M	Laborer	28Ma02BJ
REID, M.		20	M	Laborer	28Ma02BJ
U	(W)	20	F	Wife	28Ma02BJ
Henry	(S)	03	M	Child	28Ma02BJ
BRENANN, Christe		20	F	Servant	28Ma02BJ
Eliza		20	F	Servant	28Ma02BJ
ONEIL, Mary-Ann		18	F	Servant	28Ma02BJ
HOPKINS, Julia		18	F	Servant	28Ma02BJ
LEADER, Patrick		23	M	Mechanic	28Ma02BJ
BATTER, Patrick		40	M	Servant	28Ma02BJ
LAHY, Ande.		60	M	Laborer	28Ma02BJ
KANE, John		25	M	Laborer	28Ma02BJ
MORAN, Ellen		30	F	Servant	28Ma02BJ
Margaret		20	F	None	28Ma02BJ
Catherine		10	F	None	28Ma02BJ
SMITH, Thomas		20	M	Laborer	28Ma02BJ
James		18	M	Laborer	28Ma02BJ
BIRNE, Cr--.		30	M	Laborer	28Ma02BJ
MCLAUGHLIN, Mathew		40	M	Laborer	28Ma02BJ
HANAUGHTY, Honor		20	F	None	28Ma02BJ
Patrick	(S)	.00	M	Infant	28Ma02BJ
DOHERTY, Corns.		.00	M	Infant	28Ma02BJ
BRADY, John		20	M	Laborer	28Ma02BJ
CARR, William		18	M	Laborer	28Ma02BJ

NAMES OF PASSENGERS	AGE	SEX	OCCUPATIONS	DATE PORT SHIP
SMITHWICK, U-Mrs.	35	F	Servant	28Ma02Bj
GRAHAM, Thomas	36	M	Laborer	28Ma02Bj
MANLY, Thomas	25	M	Laborer	28Ma02Bj
MCNELLY, Thomas	30	M	Laborer	28Ma02Bj
Mary	25	F	Servant	28Ma02Bj
GRIMES, Joseph	20	M	Laborer	28Ma02Bj
DRISKELL, James	20	M	Laborer	28Ma02Bj
MCDONALD, John	50	M	Laborer	28Ma02Bj
Brien	45	M	Laborer	28Ma02Bj
Bridget	20	F	None	28Ma02Bj
Paul	16	M	None	28Ma02Bj
Catherine	14	F	None	28Ma02Bj
John	12	M	None	28Ma02Bj
Ellen	08	F	Child	28Ma02Bj
Ann	06	F	Child	28Ma02Bj
FITZPATRICK, Ann	35	F	None	28Ma02Bj
John	20	M	Laborer	28Ma02Bj
Rose	03	F	Child	28Ma02Bj
DORSAY, Michael	25	M	Mechanic	28Ma02Bj
RIELLY, Mary	20	F	None	28Ma02Bj
BYRNE, Peter	20	M	Farmer	28Ma02Bj
MANN, Peter	20	M	Farmer	28Ma02Bj
KELLY, Catherine	20	F	Servant	28Ma02Bj
CHAMBERS, Williams	35	M	Farmer	28Ma02Bj
Robert	20	M	Farmer	28Ma02Bj
Mary	08	F	Child	28Ma02Bj
ROSS, William	20	M	Laborer	28Ma02Bj
Nancy	20	F	Servant	28Ma02Bj
JORDAN, James	25	M	Laborer	28Ma02Bj
LORNFORD, Isabella	30	F	Servant	28Ma02Bj
CHAMBERS, Elizabeth	20	F	Servant	28Ma02Bj
BURKE, Mary	25	F	Servant	28Ma02Bj
Annie	20	F	Servant	28Ma02Bj
HALIGAN, Thos.	30	M	Laborer	28Ma02Bj
MOORE, Richard	30	M	Laborer	28Ma02Bj
SMITH, Robert	32	M	Laborer	28Ma02Bj

ASHLAND 31 MAY 1847

From Liverpool

NAMES OF PASSENGERS		AGE	SEX	OCCUPATIONS	DATE PORT SHIP
MORAN, Patrick		23	M	Laborer	31Ma02Ny
Ann		21	F	None	31Ma02Ny
Thomas		60	M	Laborer	31Ma02Ny
Patrick		55	M	Laborer	31Ma02Ny
James		21	M	Laborer	31Ma02Ny
Michael		23	M	Laborer	31Ma02Ny
John		12	M	Laborer	31Ma02Ny
Bridget		18	F	None	31Ma02Ny
BERRY, Richard		24	M	Laborer	31Ma02Ny
BRYAN, Richard		21	M	Laborer	31Ma02Ny
Catherine		24	F	None	31Ma02Ny
Robert		26	M	Laborer	31Ma02Ny
CALLAHAN, James		25	M	Laborer	31Ma02Ny
HEALY, Timothy		35	M	Laborer	31Ma02Ny
SMITH, Michael		27	M	Laborer	31Ma02Ny
U	(W)	28	F	Wife	31Ma02Ny
Mary		17	F	None	31Ma02Ny
Andrew		27	M	Laborer	31Ma02Ny
Andrew		23	M	Laborer	31Ma02Ny
Marlana		26	F	None	31Ma02Ny
STANTON, Miles		36	M	Laborer	31Ma02Ny
Mary		28	F	None	31Ma02Ny
GIBBONS, Bridget		18	F	None	31Ma02Ny
MANNING, Patrick		26	M	Laborer	31Ma02Ny
BARCLAY, Samuel		25	M	Laborer	31Ma02Ny
CONNER, James		26	M	Laborer	31Ma02Ny
MAHONY, James		55	M	Laborer	31Ma02Ny
TOOMY, Dennis		26	M	Laborer	31Ma02Ny

NAMES OF PASSENGERS		AGE	SEX	OCCUPATIONS	DATE PORT SHIP
CONNELL, James		30	M	Laborer	31Ma02Ny
HARRINGTON, Mary		21	F	None	31Ma02Ny
Johanna		17	F	None	31Ma02Ny
Nelly		13	F	None	31Ma02Ny
HALLEHANT, Daniel		26	M	Laborer	31Ma02Ny
Gablells		22	M	Laborer	31Ma02Ny
CROWLEY, Tourmah		30	M	Laborer	31Ma02Ny
Julia		24	F	None	31Ma02Ny
DEASY, Patrick		26	M	Laborer	31Ma02Ny
DRULIN, Dennis		48	M	Laborer	31Ma02Ny
Michael	(S)	18	M	Laborer	31Ma02Ny
Catherine	(W)	48	F	Wife	31Ma02Ny
DONOVAN, Robert		24	M	Laborer	31Ma02Ny
BURKE, William		24	M	Laborer	31Ma02Ny
LEAHY, Daniel		23	M	Laborer	31Ma02Ny
William	(B)	25	M	Laborer	31Ma02Ny
Catherine	(M)	60	F	None	31Ma02Ny
Catherine		.00	F	Infant	31Ma02Ny
WALSH, Mich.		26	M	Laborer	31Ma02Ny
HAGGERTY, Patrick		25	M	Laborer	31Ma02Ny
STANTON, Michael		24	M	Laborer	31Ma02Ny
SPELLAN, Margaret		25	F	None	31Ma02Ny
ROACHE, Thomas		28	M	Laborer	31Ma02Ny
PIGOTT, Ellen		.00	F	Infant	31Ma02Ny
Mary	(M)	23	F	None	31Ma02Ny
DALEY, Catherine		25	F	None	31Ma02Ny
COCHRANE, Michael		26	M	Laborer	31Ma02Ny
DUHANY, James		22	M	Laborer	31Ma02Ny
SHOLAR, Ann		20	F	None	31Ma02Ny
HEALEY, Ally		21	F	None	31Ma02Ny
WELSH, Michael		26	M	Laborer	31Ma02Ny
Ann	(W)	25	F	Wife	31Ma02Ny
Ann	(D)	04	F	Child	31Ma02Ny
Martin	(S)	06	M	Laborer	31Ma02Ny
Michael	(S)	08	M	Laborer	31Ma02Ny
MOONY, Thomas		21	M	Laborer	31Ma02Ny
Sally		18	F	None	31Ma02Ny
WALSH, John		21	M	Laborer	31Ma02Ny
Martin		20	M	Laborer	31Ma02Ny
MOONEY, Margaret		19	F	None	31Ma02Ny
CONNER, Martin		22	M	Laborer	31Ma02Ny
BRININGAN, James		30	M	Laborer	31Ma02Ny
Catherine		29	F	None	31Ma02Ny
GRADY, Margaret		26	F	None	31Ma02Ny
GOODMAN, John		20	M	Laborer	31Ma02Ny
Patrick	(S)	.00	M	Infant	31Ma02Ny
Bridget	(W)	21	F	Wife	31Ma02Ny
Winfred	(T)	12	F	Laborer	31Ma02Ny
IGOR, Ann		14	F	None	31Ma02Ny
TANSAY, Bryan		22	M	Laborer	31Ma02Ny
SPELLMAN, Mary		16	F	None	31Ma02Ny
CONNELL, Ebron		30	M	Laborer	31Ma02Ny
MCDANNELLE, Joseph		21	M	Laborer	31Ma02Ny
DRUMMOND, Terence		45	M	Laborer	31Ma02Ny
U	(W)	45	F	Wife	31Ma02Ny
Sarah	(D)	24	F	None	31Ma02Ny
Mary	(D)	12	F	None	31Ma02Ny
CUMMING, Patrick		23	M	Laborer	31Ma02Ny
DRUMMOND, Terence		10	M	Laborer	31Ma02Ny
DAVIS, Mathew		23	M	Laborer	31Ma02Ny
COUGHLEY, John		46	M	Laborer	31Ma02Ny
DEMNICK, Dennis		24	M	Laborer	31Ma02Ny
David		24	M	Laborer	31Ma02Ny
Catherine		20	F	None	31Ma02Ny
CONNER, John		29	M	Laborer	31Ma02Ny
U	(W)	32	F	Wife	31Ma02Ny
Mary	(T)	21	F	None	31Ma02Ny
TYRELL, Edward		30	M	Laborer	31Ma02Ny
James		20	M	Laborer	31Ma02Ny
Kitty		23	F	None	31Ma02Ny
NAYLOR, Patrick		22	M	Laborer	31Ma02Ny
SANTTS, Erich		21	M	Laborer	31Ma02Ny
KELLY, Mich.		26	M	Laborer	31Ma02Ny
Ellen	(W)	25	F	Wife	31Ma02Ny
Biddy	(D)	01	F	Child	31Ma02Ny

NAMES OF PASSENGERS		A G E	S E X	OCCUPATIONS	DATE PORT SHIP	NAMES OF PASSENGERS		A G E	S E X	OCCUPATIONS	DATE PORT SHIP
TARRNA, Catherine		28	F	None	31Ma02Ny	EGAN, An.		50	F	None	31Ma02Pe
LINDELL, Peter		26	M	Laborer	31Ma02Ny	CLARK, Pat		20	M	None	31Ma02Pe
BURKE, Mostarn		35	M	Laborer	31Ma02Ny	Ma.		16	M	None	31Ma02Pe
WHITTEY, Samuel		40	M	Laborer	31Ma02Ny	CROGHAN, Ma.		15	M	None	31Ma02Pe
MCLEAN, Robert		27	M	Laborer	31Ma02Ny	MCGANN, J.		30	M	Unknown	31Ma02Pe
HAMILTON, William		20	M	Laborer	31Ma02Ny	Ann		20	F	None	31Ma02Pe
Mary	(W)	26	F	Wife	31Ma02Ny	DOCKERY, T.		26	M	Unknown	31Ma02Pe
Robert	(S)	01	M	Child	31Ma02Ny	Mgt.		26	F	None	31Ma02Pe
WHITE, Mather		22	M	Laborer	31Ma02Ny	KENNY, P.		23	M	Unknown	31Ma02Pe
Elizabeth	(D)	03	F	Child	31Ma02Ny	KELLY, M.		22	M	Unknown	31Ma02Pe
James	(H)	28	M	Laborer	31Ma02Ny	My.		22	F	None	31Ma02Pe
KELLY, Daniel		22	M	Laborer	31Ma02Ny	CARROL, E.		25	M	Unknown	31Ma02Pe
Catherine		18	F	None	31Ma02Ny	WHITE, W.		39	M	Unknown	31Ma02Pe
Mary		24	F	None	31Ma02Ny	Mgt.	(W)	36	F	Wife	31Ma02Pe
Felicia		20	F	None	31Ma02Ny	Ellen	(D)	14	F	None	31Ma02Pe
REYNOLDS, Mary		24	F	None	31Ma02Ny	Meas.	(D)	13	F	None	31Ma02Pe
FARLANE, Francis		18	M	Laborer	31Ma02Ny	Al.	(S)	11	M	None	31Ma02Pe
GALLGHER, Ellen		20	F	None	31Ma02Ny	Essy	(D)	10	F	None	31Ma02Pe
DUNN, Patrick		18	M	Laborer	31Ma02Ny	John	(S)	06	M	Child	31Ma02Pe
MYRICK, Mich.		30	M	Laborer	31Ma02Ny	Ricd.	(S)	08	M	Child	31Ma02Pe
WILSON, Thomas		20	M	Laborer	31Ma02Ny	Pat	(S)	04	M	Child	31Ma02Pe
HANLEY, Peter		19	M	Laborer	31Ma02Ny	HANDON, W.		25	M	Unknown	31Ma02Pe
CURNEN, Henry		24	M	Laborer	31Ma02Ny	Mat.		33	F	None	31Ma02Pe
Luke		19	M	Laborer	31Ma02Ny	My.		18	F	None	31Ma02Pe
MARAN, Peter		25	M	Laborer	31Ma02Ny	Michl.		14	M	None	31Ma02Pe
GAREY, Dennis		35	M	Laborer	31Ma02Ny	Bessy		20	F	None	31Ma02Pe
ROANE, Martin		20	M	Laborer	31Ma02Ny	DENNIS, C.		24	M	Unknown	31Ma02Pe
FAGE, Patrick		20	M	Laborer	31Ma02Ny	FITZSIMMONS, Mgt.		19	F	None	31Ma02Pe
Catherine		20	F	None	31Ma02Ny	CRAY, W.		22	M	Unknown	31Ma02Pe
CALLEY, Jane		20	F	None	31Ma02Ny	FITZSIMMONS, Rose		55	F	None	31Ma02Pe
FLANAGAN, Mary		36	F	None	31Ma02Ny	WILLIAMS, J.		24	M	Laborer	31Ma02Pe
Bridget	(D)	09	F	Child	31Ma02Ny	SHANAAN, J.		26	M	Laborer	31Ma02Pe
Mary	(D)	08	F	Child	31Ma02Ny	Judy		09	F	Child	31Ma02Pe
Ann	(D)	06	F	Child	31Ma02Ny	SLEVIN, Ann		06	F	Child	31Ma02Pe
Thomas	(S)	04	M	Child	31Ma02Ny	Cath.	(T)	02	F	Child	31Ma02Pe
John	(S)	02	M	Child	31Ma02Ny	Bess	(M)	40	F	None	31Ma02Pe
GAWAN, James		20	M	Laborer	31Ma02Ny	Henry		20	M	Unknown	31Ma02Pe
MCNULTY, William		20	M	Laborer	31Ma02Ny	DWYER, My.		24	F	None	31Ma02Pe
MCINTIRE, Barney		20	M	Laborer	31Ma02Ny	FITZGERALD, P.		10	M	None	31Ma02Pe
MCEWAN, James		20	M	Laborer	31Ma02Ny	MEHAN, J.		60	M	Unknown	31Ma02Pe
LYONS, John		20	M	Laborer	31Ma02Ny	Mgt.	(D)	08	F	Child	31Ma02Pe
CLEARY, James		20	M	Laborer	31Ma02Ny	MARTIN, J.		25	M	Unknown	31Ma02Pe
STEVENS, James		18	M	Laborer	31Ma02Ny	Nancy		29	F	None	31Ma02Pe
U	(W)	17	F	Wife	31Ma02Ny	MCCLUSKY, Nancy		19	F	None	31Ma02Pe
Ann	(T)	19	F	None	31Ma02Ny	CONNELL, J.		20	M	Unknown	31Ma02Pe
MORAN, Patt		18	M	Laborer	31Ma02Ny	MCKEE, J.		22	M	Unknown	31Ma02Pe
GIFFNEY, James		20	M	Laborer	31Ma02Ny	GREEN, C.		25	M	Unknown	31Ma02Pe
Mary		18	F	None	31Ma02Ny	KANE, T.		26	M	Unknown	31Ma02Pe
QUIGLEY, John		20	M	Laborer	31Ma02Ny	My.		21	F	None	31Ma02Pe
MORAN, Patt		24	M	Laborer	31Ma02Ny	GILKANNON, R.		40	M	Unknown	31Ma02Pe
Mary		24	F	None	31Ma02Ny	Ann-J.	(D)	24	F	None	31Ma02Pe
Margaret		10	F	None	31Ma02Ny	My.	(D)	22	F	None	31Ma02Pe
MCCAR, Patt		00	U	Unknown	31Ma02Ny	Thos.	(S)	20	M	Unknown	31Ma02Pe
						Eliza	(D)	16	F	None	31Ma02Pe
						DENHAM, J.		45	M	Unknown	31Ma02Pe
						Susan	(W)	43	F	Wife	31Ma02Pe
HINDOO 31 MAY 1847						Robt.	(B)	30	M	Unknown	31Ma02Pe
						Agnes	(D)	20	F	None	31Ma02Pe
From Liverpool						James	(S)	15	M	None	31Ma02Pe
						Sarah	(D)	10	F	None	31Ma02Pe
						Joseph	(S)	06	M	Child	31Ma02Pe
						SMART, R.		25	M	Unknown	31Ma02Pe
						MCDERMOTT, M.		17	M	Unknown	31Ma02Pe
						Mara		15	F	None	31Ma02Pe
JENNINGS, S.		20	M	Laborer	31Ma02Pe	CONDRAN, J.		25	M	Unknown	31Ma02Pe
DUNN, M.		26	F	None	31Ma02Pe	NOONAN, D.		23	M	Unknown	31Ma02Pe
EGAN, T.		18	M	Unknown	31Ma02Pe	My.An.		20	F	None	31Ma02Pe
MULLIGAN, My.		09	F	Child	31Ma02Pe	Pion---, R.		21	M	Unknown	31Ma02Pe
LAWLES, Honor		20	F	None	31Ma02Pe						
CUNNINGHAM, P.		41	M	Unknown	31Ma02Pe						
Ann	(W)	32	F	Wife	31Ma02Pe						
Danl.	(S)	11	M	Wife	31Ma02Pe						
Matthew	(S)	08	M	Child	31Ma02Pe						
Pat	(S)	03	M	Child	31Ma02Pe						
Maria	(D)	01	F	Child	31Ma02Pe						

NAMES OF PASSENGERS		AGE	SEX	OCCUPATIONS	DATE PORT SHIP

JOSEPHINE 01 JUNE 1847

From Galway

NAMES OF PASSENGERS		AGE	SEX	OCCUPATIONS	DATE PORT SHIP
CASEY, William		26	M	Laborer	01Ju11Kq
Catharine	(W)	26	F	None	01Ju11Kq
Joseph	(S)	.02	M	Infant	01Ju11Kq
GALLERY, Patrick		25	M	Laborer	01Ju11Kq
CAVENAUGH, Michael		20	M	Laborer	01Ju11Kq
FREEMAN, Morris		24	M	Laborer	01Ju11Kq
Mary	(W)	20	F	None	01Ju11Kq
KIRWAN, Eliza		30	F	None	01Ju11Kq
Margaret	(D)	07	F	Child	01Ju11Kq
George	(S)	04	M	Child	01Ju11Kq
SHANKS, John		21	M	Laborer	01Ju11Kq
MADAGAN, Michael		20	M	Laborer	01Ju11Kq
GURVEY, Patrick		29	M	Laborer	01Ju11Kq
HANLAN, James		25	M	Laborer	01Ju11Kq
REILY, Ann		35	F	None	01Ju11Kq
FLYNN, Catharine		26	F	None	01Ju11Kq
REILY, Luke		19	M	Laborer	01Ju11Kq
Catharine		12	F	None	01Ju11Kq
William		17	M	Laborer	01Ju11Kq
James		10	M	Laborer	01Ju11Kq
Thomas		09	M	Child	01Ju11Kq
John		08	M	Child	01Ju11Kq
Michael		06	M	Child	01Ju11Kq
Austin		05	M	Child	01Ju11Kq
Richard		04	M	Child	01Ju11Kq
MCHUGH, Patrick		24	M	Laborer	01Ju11Kq
SPILLMAN, Thomas		25	M	Laborer	01Ju11Kq
RAFERTY, Lawrence		19	M	Laborer	01Ju11Kq
Edward		11	M	Laborer	01Ju11Kq
Sylvester		08	M	Child	01Ju11Kq
Bridget		21	F	None	01Ju11Kq
CANNIN, Michael		25	M	Laborer	01Ju11Kq
RYAN, John		22	M	Laborer	01Ju11Kq
Bridget		19	F	None	01Ju11Kq
LEONARD, Martin		34	M	Laborer	01Ju11Kq
DALY, Thomas		35	M	Laborer	01Ju11Kq
Margaret	(W)	30	F	None	01Ju11Kq
Mary	(D)	02	F	Child	01Ju11Kq
Catharine	(D)	05	F	Child	01Ju11Kq
FLAHERTY, Bridget		20	F	None	01Ju11Kq
NIELAND, U-Mrs.		36	F	None	01Ju11Kq
NEILAND, Dennis		48	M	Laborer	01Ju11Kq
BANE, Murty		22	M	Laborer	01Ju11Kq
FLYNN, John		26	M	Laborer	01Ju11Kq
CROWLEY, Joseph		22	M	Laborer	01Ju11Kq

WRENHAM 01 JUNE 1847

From Belfast

NAMES OF PASSENGERS		AGE	SEX	OCCUPATIONS	DATE PORT SHIP
MORROW, J.		17	M	Laborer	01Ju07Kr
Betty		20	F	None	01Ju07Kr
Mgt.		18	F	None	01Ju07Kr
Rebecca	(M)	40	F	None	01Ju07Kr
HALL, W.		22	M	Unknown	01Ju07Kr
Mgt.		18	M	None	01Ju07Kr
MANKING, A.		27	M	Unknown	01Ju07Kr
HOLMES, S.		20	M	Unknown	01Ju07Kr
MORROW, R.		23	M	Unknown	01Ju07Kr

NAMES OF PASSENGERS		AGE	SEX	OCCUPATIONS	DATE PORT SHIP
BRADFORD, Ma.		20	F	None	01Ju07Kr
My.		22	F	None	01Ju07Kr
DAWSON, Mgt.		30	F	None	01Ju07Kr
Esther	(D)	13	F	None	01Ju07Kr
Joseph	(S)	01	M	Child	01Ju07Kr
MUSSIN, Cath.		25	F	None	01Ju07Kr
Mgt.		16	F	None	01Ju07Kr
BURLEIGH, W.		25	M	Unknown	01Ju07Kr
Elizbt.	(W)	23	F	None	01Ju07Kr
Geog.	(S)	03	M	Child	01Ju07Kr
My.	(D)	01	F	Child	01Ju07Kr
WOODS, M.		16	F	None	01Ju07Kr
HENSON, W.		18	M	Unknown	01Ju07Kr
My.	(M)	40	F	None	01Ju07Kr
MCNEIL, Rachel		40	F	None	01Ju07Kr
Jas.	(S)	22	M	Laborer	01Ju07Kr
Mgt.	(D)	13	F	None	01Ju07Kr
Chas.	(S)	10	M	None	01Ju07Kr
Archy	(S)	12	M	None	01Ju07Kr
FENNAN, N.		25	M	Unknown	01Ju07Kr
TAGGART, F.		24	M	Unknown	01Ju07Kr
HINES, Cath.		24	F	None	01Ju07Kr
ATKINS, G.		27	M	Unknown	01Ju07Kr
LIPEM, J.		20	M	Unknown	01Ju07Kr
BYRNE, A.		20	M	Unknown	01Ju07Kr
GIBBS, Ann		20	F	None	01Ju07Kr
My.		18	F	None	01Ju07Kr
GLOPHIS, Meg		25	F	None	01Ju07Kr
MINER, W.		21	M	Unknown	01Ju07Kr
BELL, A.		25	M	Unknown	01Ju07Kr
THOMPSON, Jane		60	M	Unknown	01Ju07Kr
DYNES, H.		20	M	Laborer	01Ju07Kr
H.		20	M	Laborer	01Ju07Kr
EGAN, A.		50	M	Unknown	01Ju07Kr
Mgt.	(D)	10	F	None	01Ju07Kr
Betty	(D)	09	F	Child	01Ju07Kr
Mary	(D)	07	F	Child	01Ju07Kr
John	(S)	05	M	Child	01Ju07Kr
Arthur	(S)	03	M	Child	01Ju07Kr
STEWART, Ann		40	F	None	01Ju07Kr
Jane		20	F	None	01Ju07Kr
BULLOCK, Robt.		20	M	Laborer	01Ju07Kr
BENSON, W.		40	M	Laborer	01Ju07Kr
Jane	(W)	40	F	Wife	01Ju07Kr
My.	(D)	16	F	None	01Ju07Kr
James	(S)	14	M	None	01Ju07Kr
Mgt.	(D)	13	F	None	01Ju07Kr
Eliza	(D)	11	F	None	01Ju07Kr
Saml.	(S)	09	M	Child	01Ju07Kr
Hannah	(D)	08	F	Child	01Ju07Kr
Rachel	(D)	04	F	Child	01Ju07Kr
PRESTON, J.		40	M	Laborer	01Ju07Kr
Mgt.	(W)	30	F	None	01Ju07Kr
William	(S)	01	M	Child	01Ju07Kr
JOHNSON, J.		22	M	Unknown	01Ju07Kr
MCMURTY, J.		25	M	Unknown	01Ju07Kr
TAYLOR, T.		21	M	Unknown	01Ju07Kr
MURDOCH, J.		20	M	Unknown	01Ju07Kr
MCBURY, H.		23	M	Unknown	01Ju07Kr
HENDERSON, H.		25	M	Unknown	01Ju07Kr
Jane		22	F	None	01Ju07Kr
FRICKLER, Eliza		40	F	None	01Ju07Kr
Eliza	(D)	15	F	None	01Ju07Kr
BOYD, W.		20	M	Unknown	01Ju07Kr
Hugh		18	M	Unknown	01Ju07Kr
SAULTERS, D.		20	M	Unknown	01Ju07Kr
YOUNG, A.		20	M	Unknown	01Ju07Kr
MCCULLOUGH, G.		25	M	Unknown	01Ju07Kr
KELLY, J.		29	M	Unknown	01Ju07Kr
FIRTHEY, R.		45	M	Unknown	01Ju07Kr
Jane	(W)	45	F	Wife	01Ju07Kr
Jane	(D)	18	F	None	01Ju07Kr
John	(S)	12	M	Unknown	01Ju07Kr
Robt.	(S)	15	M	Unknown	01Ju07Kr
H.	(S)	09	M	Child	01Ju07Kr

NAMES OF PASSENGERS		A G E	S E X	OCCUPATIONS	DATE PORT SHIP
FIRTHEY, Ann	(D)	11	F	None	01Ju07Kr
THOMPSON, S.		20	M	Laborer	01Ju07Kr
MCQUADE, J.		20	M	Unknown	01Ju07Kr
Peter		19	M	Unknown	01Ju07Kr
My.	(M)	49	F	None	01Ju07Kr
BECKLY, My.		18	F	None	01Ju07Kr
BLACK, Mgt.		18	F	None	01Ju07Kr
ROBINSON, E.		20	M	Laborer	01Ju07Kr
MCILMANN, R.		25	M	Laborer	01Ju07Kr
My.	(W)	22	F	Wife	01Ju07Kr
My.	(D)	03	F	Child	01Ju07Kr
John	(S)	01	M	Child	01Ju07Kr
BENNETT, W.		20	M	Child	01Ju07Kr
FECKLETON, My.		30	F	None	01Ju07Kr
PACK, Sarah		50	F	None	01Ju07Kr
Eliza	(D)	21	F	None	01Ju07Kr
TAGGART, R.		40	M	Unknown	01Ju07Kr
MERRICK, S.		27	M	Unknown	01Ju07Kr
QUIGLY, Ellen		40	F	None	01Ju07Kr
Jane	(D)	16	F	None	01Ju07Kr
My.	(D)	14	F	None	01Ju07Kr
MORRISON, T.		24	M	Unknown	01Ju07Kr
THOMPSON, J.		25	M	Unknown	01Ju07Kr
MCGOWN, J.		35	M	Unknown	01Ju07Kr
Ann		29	F	None	01Ju07Kr
BOYD, S.		30	M	Unknown	01Ju07Kr
Eliza	(W)	28	F	None	01Ju07Kr
Ann	(D)	05	F	Child	01Ju07Kr
My.	(D)	03	F	Child	01Ju07Kr
Wm.	(S)	01	M	Child	01Ju07Kr
HANON, G.		50	M	Laborer	01Ju07Kr
FRETON, J.		30	M	Laborer	01Ju07Kr
YOUNG, J.		17	M	Laborer	01Ju07Kr
Eliza		19	F	Laborer	01Ju07Kr
MCKEE, R.		50	M	Unknown	01Ju07Kr
Betty		49	F	None	01Ju07Kr
RACINE, J.		25	M	Unknown	01Ju07Kr
MAHER, Ann		20	F	None	01Ju07Kr
BEA, Mgt.		18	F	None	01Ju07Kr
Eliza	(D)	01	F	Child	01Ju07Kr
WADE, J.		50	M	Unknown	01Ju07Kr
Ellen	(W)	45	F	Wife	01Ju07Kr
Rachel	(D)	20	F	None	01Ju07Kr
ANDREWS, D.		40	M	Laborer	01Ju07Kr
Jane	(W)	41	F	Wife	01Ju07Kr
Martha	(D)	08	F	Child	01Ju07Kr
Wm.	(S)	06	M	Child	01Ju07Kr
Robt.	(S)	03	M	Child	01Ju07Kr
Eliza	(D)	01	F	Child	01Ju07Kr
CORI, P.		21	M	Unknown	01Ju07Kr
Thos.		20	M	Unknown	01Ju07Kr
WOODS, S.		25	M	Unknown	01Ju07Kr
SLOAN, Ellen		20	F	None	01Ju07Kr
SULLIVAN, G.		30	M	Unknown	01Ju07Kr
My.	(W)	28	F	None	01Ju07Kr
Isbl.	(D)	01	F	Child	01Ju07Kr
DELANY, A.		29	M	Unknown	01Ju07Kr
My.	(W)	27	F	None	01Ju07Kr
CARAN, Ann		26	F	None	01Ju07Kr
CURTIN, J.		29	M	Unknown	01Ju07Kr
Hy.		22	M	Unknown	01Ju07Kr
My.		21	F	None	01Ju07Kr
FINNIGAN, P.		21	M	Unknown	01Ju07Kr
Isb.		21	F	None	01Ju07Kr
LYLE, J.		21	M	Unknown	01Ju07Kr
WOODS, Ann		16	F	None	01Ju07Kr
TWEED, J.		25	M	Unknown	01Ju07Kr
MCCANDLS, J.		30	M	Unknown	01Ju07Kr
MCCAUGHY, M.		30	M	Unknown	01Ju07Kr
HANNON, Nelly		28	F	None	01Ju07Kr
STEWART, Rose		25	F	None	01Ju07Kr
WHITE, F.		25	M	Unknown	01Ju07Kr
Eliza		20	F	None	01Ju07Kr
SHIME, J.		50	M	Unknown	01Ju07Kr
ROBINSON, Jane		14	F	None	01Ju07Kr

NAMES OF PASSENGERS		A G E	S E X	OCCUPATIONS	DATE PORT SHIP
CRAY, D.		30	M	Unknown	01Ju07Kr
Mcs--Y, J.		20	M	Unknown	01Ju07Kr
Jane		18	F	None	01Ju07Kr
MASON, J.		40	M	Unknown	01Ju07Kr
My.		35	F	None	01Ju07Kr
Susan		20	F	None	01Ju07Kr
My.		15	F	None	01Ju07Kr
Mgt.		25	F	None	01Ju07Kr
CLEELLAND, W.		35	M	Laborer	01Ju07Kr
Wm.		30	M	Laborer	01Ju07Kr
Arthur		28	M	Laborer	01Ju07Kr
Robt.		26	M	Laborer	01Ju07Kr
Jane		24	F	None	01Ju07Kr
MUNSON, J.		22	M	Unknown	01Ju07Kr
LOWRY, Susan		20	F	None	01Ju07Kr
FLICKER, My.		18	F	None	01Ju07Kr
WARD, R.		20	M	Unknown	01Ju07Kr
SMITH, J.		20	M	Unknown	01Ju07Kr
MCKEE, W.		21	M	Unknown	01Ju07Kr
BARNES, My.		20	F	None	01Ju07Kr
SLOAN, Eliza		21	F	None	01Ju07Kr
My.		18	F	None	01Ju07Kr
BROWN, T.		59	M	Unknown	01Ju07Kr
Helen	(D)	23	F	None	01Ju07Kr
Martha	(D)	19	F	None	01Ju07Kr
Rose	(D)	16	F	None	01Ju07Kr
Jane	(D)	21	F	None	01Ju07Kr
HARPER, J.		30	M	Unknown	01Ju07Kr
Eliza	(W)	28	F	None	01Ju07Kr
Robt.	(S)	04	M	Child	01Ju07Kr
RUSSELL, Ellen		25	F	None	01Ju07Kr
ELHERTON, J.		25	M	Unknown	01Ju07Kr
Bernd.		20	M	Unknown	01Ju07Kr
GLASS, Isb.		20	F	None	01Ju07Kr
Saul		18	M	Laborer	01Ju07Kr
STOKS, N.		40	M	Laborer	01Ju07Kr
Mgt.		02	F	Child	01Ju07Kr
ROWAN, J.		02	M	Laborer	01Ju07Kr
SKEEN, J.		02	M	Laborer	01Ju07Kr
RACINE, Sarah		22	F	None	01Ju07Kr
MYERS, W.		25	M	Laborer	01Ju07Kr
MURRY, W.		24	M	Laborer	01Ju07Kr
MCGIFEN, W.		21	M	Laborer	01Ju07Kr
MAGEE, J.		18	M	Laborer	01Ju07Kr
HENASSIE, J.		17	M	Laborer	01Ju07Kr
MCKILTY, Cath.		21	F	None	01Ju07Kr
Jane	(D)	01	F	Child	01Ju07Kr
MEANY, J.		21	M	Laborer	01Ju07Kr
CARRYES, A.		15	M	Laborer	01Ju07Kr
WHITE, Jane		01	F	Child	01Ju07Kr

TALLERAND 01 JUNE 1847

From Glasgow

NAMES OF PASSENGERS		A G E	S E X	OCCUPATIONS	DATE PORT SHIP
MILLER, William		34	M	Laborer	01Ju04Ks
James		25	M	Laborer	01Ju04Ks
MCNEILL, John		24	M	Laborer	01Ju04Ks
SEWART, James		40	M	Laborer	01Ju04Ks
MCINTIRE, James		60	M	Laborer	01Ju04Ks
MCQUALE, Peter		30	M	Laborer	01Ju04Ks
Thomas		20	M	Laborer	01Ju04Ks
SHIELDS, Mary		25	F	None	01Ju04Ks
MCGINLAY, Peter		30	M	Laborer	01Ju04Ks
KENNEDY, John		22	M	Laborer	01Ju04Ks
Dennis	(P)	57	M	Laborer	01Ju04Ks
BURK, Edward		32	M	Laborer	01Ju04Ks
WEIR, James		28	M	Laborer	01Ju04Ks
Eliza		28	F	None	01Ju04Ks

NAMES OF PASSENGERS		AGE	SEX	OCCUPATIONS	DATE PORT SHIP
MCGILL, Daniel		35	M	Laborer	01Ju04Ks
SWEENY, Hugh		33	M	Laborer	01Ju04Ks
LOAG, James		48	M	Laborer	01Ju04Ks
Mary	(W)	35	F	None	01Ju04Ks
John	(S)	10	M	Child	01Ju04Ks
William	(S)	08	M	Child	01Ju04Ks
Mary	(D)	05	F	Child	01Ju04Ks
Peter	(S)	03	M	Child	01Ju04Ks
James	(S)	02	M	Child	01Ju04Ks
HARKIN, James		33	M	Laborer	01Ju04Ks
James		40	M	Laborer	01Ju04Ks
Catharine		40	F	None	01Ju04Ks
Mary		08	F	Child	01Ju04Ks
Catharine		05	F	Child	01Ju04Ks
Eliza		01	F	Child	01Ju04Ks
CARROLL, William		22	M	Laborer	01Ju04Ks
FOLKINER, George		20	M	Laborer	01Ju04Ks
MCGAROCK, Alexander		50	M	Laborer	01Ju04Ks
Sarah	(W)	40	F	None	01Ju04Ks
Hugh	(S)	18	M	Laborer	01Ju04Ks
Charlotte	(D)	12	F	None	01Ju04Ks
Patrick	(S)	10	M	Child	01Ju04Ks
Sarah	(D)	08	F	Child	01Ju04Ks
Alexander	(S)	06	M	Child	01Ju04Ks
John	(S)	03	M	Child	01Ju04Ks
CAMERON, Isabella		21	F	None	01Ju04Ks
BOYLE, Feilx		23	M	Laborer	01Ju04Ks
Margaret		20	F	None	01Ju04Ks
KEY, Henry		20	M	Laborer	01Ju04Ks
MCMULLEN, John		35	M	Laborer	01Ju04Ks
BRAWLEY, William		35	M	Laborer	01Ju04Ks
MCGEE, James		38	M	Laborer	01Ju04Ks
ALAMANY, Patrick		33	M	Laborer	01Ju04Ks
MCKERREN, Barny		40	M	Laborer	01Ju04Ks
Jane	(W)	33	F	None	01Ju04Ks
Eliza	(D)	12	F	None	01Ju04Ks
Mary	(D)	09	F	Child	01Ju04Ks
Patrick	(S)	06	M	Child	01Ju04Ks
MCHERMIT, Jane		35	F	None	01Ju04Ks
Ann	(D)	06	F	Child	01Ju04Ks
William	(S)	02	M	Child	01Ju04Ks
Alexander	(S)	02	M	Child	01Ju04Ks
HOLL, Samuel		22	M	Laborer	01Ju04Ks
MCCUGHAN, Robert		32	M	Laborer	01Ju04Ks
Andy		27	M	Laborer	01Ju04Ks
MAXWELL, John		21	M	Laborer	01Ju04Ks
FERGUSON, Wilson		20	M	Laborer	01Ju04Ks
MCGILL, Hugh		20	M	Laborer	01Ju04Ks
James		18	M	Laborer	01Ju04Ks
Margaret		16	F	None	01Ju04Ks
Ellen		14	F	None	01Ju04Ks
MCCORMACK, William		30	M	Laborer	01Ju04Ks
BROOKS, Jane		15	F	None	01Ju04Ks
MATHEWS, Jane		19	F	None	01Ju04Ks
MCKEY, Mary		17	F	None	01Ju04Ks
MILLER, Patrick		11	M	Child	01Ju04Ks
MCDOLL, John		40	M	Laborer	01Ju04Ks
Mary		20	F	None	01Ju04Ks
Daniel		20	M	Laborer	01Ju04Ks
Routh		07	F	Child	01Ju04Ks
Mary		20	F	None	01Ju04Ks
BURNSIDE, James		27	M	None	01Ju04Ks

MARY-H.KENDALL 01 JUNE 1847

From Unknown

NAMES OF PASSENGERS		AGE	SEX	OCCUPATIONS	DATE PORT SHIP
CHERRY, H.		18	M	Laborer	01Ju00Kv
MICHELL, Robt.		22	M	Laborer	01Ju00Kv

NAMES OF PASSENGERS		AGE	SEX	OCCUPATIONS	DATE PORT SHIP
CUNNINGHAM, Jos.		22	M	Laborer	01Ju00Kv
HIGGINS, Pat.		16	M	Laborer	01Ju00Kv
POWER, Wm.		40	M	Mechanic	01Ju00Kv
NESBIT, Wm.		24	M	Mechanic	01Ju00Kv
Elizabeth		24	F	None	01Ju00Kv
FRENN, John		40	M	Lawyer	01Ju00Kv
Bridget	(W)	28	F	None	01Ju00Kv
James	(S)	11	M	Child	01Ju00Kv
Maria	(D)	09	F	Child	01Ju00Kv
John	(S)	07	M	Child	01Ju00Kv
Thomas	(S)	03	M	Child	01Ju00Kv
Eliza		19	F	None	01Ju00Kv
MCGRITT, Peter		36	M	Laborer	01Ju00Kv
James	(S)	11	M	Child	01Ju00Kv
Sarah	(D)	04	F	Child	01Ju00Kv
MANGAN, Betty		19	F	None	01Ju00Kv
James		28	M	Laborer	01Ju00Kv
Catharine	(M)	50	F	None	01Ju00Kv
Alice		22	F	None	01Ju00Kv
QUINN, Jas.		24	M	Laborer	01Ju00Kv
Margaret		22	F	None	01Ju00Kv
John		35	M	Laborer	01Ju00Kv
Mary	(W)	32	F	None	01Ju00Kv
Rose	(D)	08	F	Child	01Ju00Kv
James	(S)	06	M	Child	01Ju00Kv
Michael	(S)	04	M	Child	01Ju00Kv
Sarah	(D)	02	F	Child	01Ju00Kv

CEYLON 01 JUNE 1847

From Liverpool

NAMES OF PASSENGERS		AGE	SEX	OCCUPATIONS	DATE PORT SHIP
CURMAN, John		21	M	Laborer	01Ju02Kw
Mary	(W)	21	F	None	01Ju02Kw
Mary	(D)	.00	F	Infant	01Ju02Kw
MASTERSON, Patt		35	M	Laborer	01Ju02Kw
Honora		30	F	None	01Ju02Kw
FARLY, Mathew		20	M	Laborer	01Ju02Kw
ROSH, Bryan		30	M	Laborer	01Ju02Kw
BRADLY, John		28	M	Laborer	01Ju02Kw
U	(W)	26	F	Wife	01Ju02Kw
MASTERSON, Pat		21	M	Laborer	01Ju02Kw
RILEY, Bryan		24	M	Laborer	01Ju02Kw
MCGOWEN, John		20	M	Laborer	01Ju02Kw
CULLEN, James		23	M	Laborer	01Ju02Kw
MITCHELL, Henry		24	M	Laborer	01Ju02Kw
Mary	(W)	24	F	None	01Ju02Kw
Anne		13	F	None	01Ju02Kw
Margaret	(D)	01	F	Child	01Ju02Kw
John	(S)	.00	M	Infant	01Ju02Kw
CURARS, John		25	M	Laborer	01Ju02Kw
DUFFY, William		48	M	Laborer	01Ju02Kw
MCGEE, Michael		22	M	Laborer	01Ju02Kw
CURRAN, John		22	M	Laborer	01Ju02Kw
MORAN, John		40	M	Laborer	01Ju02Kw
U	(W)	24	F	Wife	01Ju02Kw
Catharine	(D)	03	F	Child	01Ju02Kw
Mary	(D)	.00	F	Infant	01Ju02Kw
MCNAUGHTEN, Margaret		26	F	None	01Ju02Kw
MURRAY, Thomas		23	M	Laborer	01Ju02Kw
U-Mrs.		30	F	None	01Ju02Kw
Charles		22	M	Laborer	01Ju02Kw
Julia		.00	F	Infant	01Ju02Kw
MORRIS, Hugh		25	M	Laborer	01Ju02Kw
U	(W)	25	F	Wife	01Ju02Kw
Pat	(S)	.00	M	Infant	01Ju02Kw
BIRCHEVELL, Pat		25	M	Laborer	01Ju02Kw
Ann		24	F	None	01Ju02Kw
COUTH, William		30	M	Laborer	01Ju02Kw

NAMES OF PASSENGERS		A G E	S E X	OCCUPATIONS	DATE PORT SHIP	NAMES OF PASSENGERS		A G E	S E X	OCCUPATIONS	DATE PORT SHIP
TUNELLY, Ben		20	F	None	01Ju02Kw	PAINER, Rose	(D)	08	F	Child	01Ju02Kw
BREMAN, George		24	M	Laborer	01Ju02Kw	Terease	(D)	06	F	Child	01Ju02Kw
CASH, Michael		22	M	Laborer	01Ju02Kw	NUTT, James		20	M	Laborer	01Ju02Kw
Catharine		20	F	None	01Ju02Kw	SMITH, Ann		20	F	None	01Ju02Kw
MCDERMOTT, Philip		40	M	Laborer	01Ju02Kw	MAHER, Margaret		20	F	None	01Ju02Kw
Eliza	(D)	15	F	None	01Ju02Kw	SAVAGE, Mary		21	F	None	01Ju02Kw
PATTEN, Jane		20	F	None	01Ju02Kw	ORDANAH, John		25	M	Laborer	01Ju02Kw
BYRNE, George		21	M	Laborer	01Ju02Kw	REILLEY, Bernard		25	M	Laborer	01Ju02Kw
COLYEN, Thomas		49	M	Laborer	01Ju02Kw	MCGUINESS, Mich.		30	M	Laborer	01Ju02Kw
Mary	(W)	47	F	None	01Ju02Kw	DALTON, James		20	M	Laborer	01Ju02Kw
Patt	(S)	19	M	Laborer	01Ju02Kw	Kitty		20	F	None	01Ju02Kw
John	(S)	11	M	Child	01Ju02Kw	KRONEY, John		20	M	Laborer	01Ju02Kw
Biddy	(D)	09	F	Child	01Ju02Kw	MCCAN, James		28	M	Laborer	01Ju02Kw
Renan	(S)	06	M	Child	01Ju02Kw	MARROW, Pat		27	M	Laborer	01Ju02Kw
CLANSY, Andrew		32	M	Laborer	01Ju02Kw	CRAWFORD, Thomas		50	M	Laborer	01Ju02Kw
Bridget		48	F	None	01Ju02Kw	MURPHY, John		33	M	Laborer	01Ju02Kw
Rose		15	F	None	01Ju02Kw	Jane	(W)	33	F	Wife	01Ju02Kw
Pat		12	M	Laborer	01Ju02Kw	Mary	(D)	10	F	Child	01Ju02Kw
Mary		10	F	Child	01Ju02Kw	Sarah	(D)	04	F	Child	01Ju02Kw
John		10	M	Child	01Ju02Kw	Jane	(D)	02	F	Child	01Ju02Kw
Ann		07	F	Child	01Ju02Kw	John	(S)	.00	F	Infant	01Ju02Kw
MCQUADE, Catharine		20	F	None	01Ju02Kw	Sarah	(M)	60	F	None	01Ju02Kw
Isabella		27	F	None	01Ju02Kw	Mathew	(S)	.00	M	Infant	01Ju02Kw
SMITH, Jeremiah		18	M	Laborer	01Ju02Kw	GOULDING, Adam		50	M	Laborer	01Ju02Kw
Mary		15	F	None	01Ju02Kw	U	(W)	46	F	Wife	01Ju02Kw
HARVEY, William		24	M	Laborer	01Ju02Kw	Eliza	(D)	19	F	None	01Ju02Kw
MCDOOD, Patrick		25	M	Laborer	01Ju02Kw	Maria	(D)	17	F	None	01Ju02Kw
COAL, Pat		25	M	Laborer	01Ju02Kw	John	(S)	14	M	Laborer	01Ju02Kw
GRENAN, Cornelly		20	M	Laborer	01Ju02Kw	WINN, James		42	M	Laborer	01Ju02Kw
MCDOOD, Eleaner		24	F	None	01Ju02Kw	KINS, James		18	M	Laborer	01Ju02Kw
CARLES, Corinch		40	M	Laborer	01Ju02Kw	CATTEN, Charles		31	M	Laborer	01Ju02Kw
ROGERS, Edward		27	M	Laborer	01Ju02Kw	MURRAY, Hervey		24	M	Laborer	01Ju02Kw
ROSH, Edward		32	M	Laborer	01Ju02Kw	U	(W)	28	F	Wife	01Ju02Kw
Sarah		29	F	None	01Ju02Kw	LYNCH, Bernard		24	M	Laborer	01Ju02Kw
MCGOWAN, Margaret		27	F	None	01Ju02Kw	MCCALE, James		24	M	Laborer	01Ju02Kw
DONNELLY, Pat		19	M	Laborer	01Ju02Kw	CUNNINGHAM, John		55	M	Laborer	01Ju02Kw
Thomas		19	M	Laborer	01Ju02Kw	DOBSEN, Martha		70	F	None	01Ju02Kw
COFFERTY, Dennis		32	M	Laborer	01Ju02Kw	U-Mrs.	(D)	57	F	None	01Ju02Kw
LOUGHAN, Neal		19	M	Laborer	01Ju02Kw	Thomas		26	M	Laborer	01Ju02Kw
MOSS, Francis		56	M	Laborer	01Ju02Kw	Barbara		23	F	None	01Ju02Kw
Margaret	(W)	50	F	None	01Ju02Kw	Jane		18	F	None	01Ju02Kw
Mary	(D)	13	F	None	01Ju02Kw	GRAHAM, William		21	M	Laborer	01Ju02Kw
SMITH, Andrew		26	M	Laborer	01Ju02Kw	Eliza	(W)	19	F	None	01Ju02Kw
John		19	M	Laborer	01Ju02Kw	Johnston	(S)	.00	M	Infant	01Ju02Kw
MILES, John		33	M	Laborer	01Ju02Kw	SMITH, Thomas		30	M	Laborer	01Ju02Kw
SHELDEN, James		40	M	Laborer	01Ju02Kw	HINLEY, Alexander		25	M	Laborer	01Ju02Kw
Pat		35	M	Laborer	01Ju02Kw	NELSON, John		25	M	Laborer	01Ju02Kw
Arthur		27	M	Laborer	01Ju02Kw	Ann		20	F	None	01Ju02Kw
U-Mrs.		27	F	None	01Ju02Kw	CUNNINGHAM, Margaret		25	F	None	01Ju02Kw
James		01	M	Child	01Ju02Kw	Robert		20	M	Laborer	01Ju02Kw
Pat		.00	M	Infant	01Ju02Kw	COYLE, James		20	M	Laborer	01Ju02Kw
FARRELL, Francis		18	M	Laborer	01Ju02Kw	GRENNEN, James		20	M	Laborer	01Ju02Kw
CAMPBELL, John		30	M	Laborer	01Ju02Kw	KEARNEY, Thomas		30	M	Laborer	01Ju02Kw
Walter	(S)	12	M	Laborer	01Ju02Kw	MEHAN, John		26	M	Laborer	01Ju02Kw
VARAN, William		53	M	Laborer	01Ju02Kw	U	(W)	20	F	Wife	01Ju02Kw
MCGLAVE, Francis		30	M	Laborer	01Ju02Kw	GRAHAM, Robert		22	M	Laborer	01Ju02Kw
MAIDEN, Bryan		24	M	Laborer	01Ju02Kw	I-GNE, Mathew		20	M	Laborer	01Ju02Kw
MCANULTY, Mich.		19	M	Laborer	01Ju02Kw	WALKER, Isaac		60	M	Laborer	01Ju02Kw
Catharine		28	F	None	01Ju02Kw	CONNOR, Robert		30	M	Laborer	01Ju02Kw
Bridget		25	F	None	01Ju02Kw	Sarah		20	F	None	01Ju02Kw
MEAKEN, John		36	M	Laborer	01Ju02Kw	MCCARTY, Michael		24	M	Laborer	01Ju02Kw
CROPER, Ann		27	F	None	01Ju02Kw	RICHARDSON, William		37	M	Laborer	01Ju02Kw
MICKEN, J.		25	M	Laborer	01Ju02Kw	BUCKLY, Dennis		37	M	Laborer	01Ju02Kw
CAUL, John		32	M	Laborer	01Ju02Kw	HENIFICK, Pat		17	M	Laborer	01Ju02Kw
Hannah		32	F	None	01Ju02Kw	WILSON, James		20	M	Laborer	01Ju02Kw
HUNT, Sophia		30	F	None	01Ju02Kw	FRANKLIN, James		29	M	Laborer	01Ju02Kw
QUINN, Michael		30	M	Laborer	01Ju02Kw	GALLAGHER, Pat		20	M	Laborer	01Ju02Kw
GEORGE, Thomas		24	M	Laborer	01Ju02Kw	HACKETT, Thomas		27	M	Laborer	01Ju02Kw
Sarah	(W)	22	F	None	01Ju02Kw	ROURKE, Francis		22	M	Laborer	01Ju02Kw
Jane	(D)	.00	F	Infant	01Ju02Kw	Mary		40	F	None	01Ju02Kw
CARROLL, Jane		17	F	None	01Ju02Kw	Ann		16	F	None	01Ju02Kw
MULRAY, John		20	M	Laborer	01Ju02Kw	GOULDING, Dennis		19	M	Laborer	01Ju02Kw
PAINER, Bernard		35	M	Laborer	01Ju02Kw	MCCONNER, Eliza		27	F	None	01Ju02Kw
U	(W)	30	F	Wife	01Ju02Kw	CONNER, Cornelius		21	M	Laborer	01Ju02Kw
Mary	(D)	13	F	None	01Ju02Kw	SKERINGTON, John		17	M	Laborer	01Ju02Kw

NAMES OF PASSENGERS		AGE	SEX	OCCUPATIONS	DATE PORT SHIP
MCANNULLEN, Alice		23	F	None	01Ju02Kw
MCCOY, James		21	M	Laborer	01Ju02Kw
MCWILLIAMS, Joseph		15	M	Laborer	01Ju02Kw
Rose		24	F	None	01Ju02Kw
DOUGLASS, U		53	F	WI	01Ju02Kw
STUTT, Jane		26	F	None	01Ju02Kw
Pegga		23	F	None	01Ju02Kw
LEE, Bridget		40	F	None	01Ju02Kw
John	(S)	22	M	Laborer	01Ju02Kw
Catharine	(D)	22	F	None	01Ju02Kw
Pat	(S)	21	M	Laborer	01Ju02Kw
Mary	(D)	11	F	None	01Ju02Kw
Dennis	(S)	09	M	Child	01Ju02Kw
Cella	(D)	07	F	Child	01Ju02Kw
Pat	(S)	04	M	Child	01Ju02Kw
William	(S)	11	M	Child	01Ju02Kw
MCCORMICK, Bryen		19	M	Laborer	01Ju02Kw
Mary		40	F	None	01Ju02Kw
Mary		11	F	None	01Ju02Kw
Margaret		07	F	Child	01Ju02Kw
DRISCAL, Julien		50	M	Laborer	01Ju02Kw
Honora	(D)	10	F	Child	01Ju02Kw
Mary	(D)	07	F	Child	01Ju02Kw
COR, Samuel		24	M	Laborer	01Ju02Kw
John		10	M	Child	01Ju02Kw
ONEILE, Mary		40	F	None	01Ju02Kw
Mary	(D)	10	F	Child	01Ju02Kw
Patt	(S)	08	M	Child	01Ju02Kw
Bridget	(D)	06	F	Child	01Ju02Kw
CURLIN, Mary		20	F	None	01Ju02Kw
TRACY, Mary		18	F	None	01Ju02Kw
GERMAN, David		30	M	Laborer	01Ju02Kw
BRAKELEY, Pat		28	M	Laborer	01Ju02Kw
THOMAS, Thomas		21	M	Laborer	01Ju02Kw
Sarah		19	F	None	01Ju02Kw
RAINE, Pat		30	M	Laborer	01Ju02Kw
U	(W)	30	F	Wife	01Ju02Kw
John	(S)	05	M	Child	01Ju02Kw
Pat	(S)	.00	M	Infant	01Ju02Kw
HARLEY, David		20	M	Laborer	01Ju02Kw
DORRAN, Bernard		20	M	Laborer	01Ju02Kw
OWENS, James		24	M	Laborer	01Ju02Kw
Bridget		24	F	None	01Ju02Kw
MCCOY, Ann		20	F	None	01Ju02Kw
OWENS, Cath.		20	F	None	01Ju02Kw
SULLIVAN, John		35	M	Laborer	01Ju02Kw
Mary	(W)	35	F	None	01Ju02Kw
Thomas	(S)	09	M	Child	01Ju02Kw
William	(S)	07	M	Child	01Ju02Kw
Ann	(D)	05	F	Child	01Ju02Kw
John	(S)	03	M	Child	01Ju02Kw
Iris	(D)	.00	F	Infant	01Ju02Kw
BUTTY, Mary		18	F	None	01Ju02Kw
RATIGAN, Pat		24	M	Laborer	01Ju02Kw
CONORAD, George		21	M	Laborer	01Ju02Kw
MCSPOUND, Garin		21	M	Laborer	01Ju02Kw
C--L--, Dennis		17	M	Laborer	01Ju02Kw
WARD, James		25	M	Laborer	01Ju02Kw
Mary		09	F	Child	01Ju02Kw
BELL, Eliza		20	F	None	01Ju02Kw
George		22	M	Laborer	01Ju02Kw
SHETTLES, George		40	M	Laborer	01Ju02Kw
GIBSON, George		23	M	Laborer	01Ju02Kw
CURLIN, John		20	M	Laborer	01Ju02Kw
SALES, Edward		20	M	Laborer	01Ju02Kw
Mary		22	F	None	01Ju02Kw
DRAKNEY, Charles		30	M	Laborer	01Ju02Kw
Pat		20	M	Laborer	01Ju02Kw
COUGHAN, Michal		24	M	Laborer	01Ju02Kw
HATTERY, Pat		30	M	Laborer	01Ju02Kw
Susan	(W)	30	F	None	01Ju02Kw
U	(D)	09	F	Child	01Ju02Kw
Mathew	(S)	07	M	Child	01Ju02Kw
Mary	(D)	05	F	Child	01Ju02Kw
Susan	(D)	03	F	Child	01Ju02Kw

NAMES OF PASSENGERS		AGE	SEX	OCCUPATIONS	DATE PORT SHIP
HATTERY, Thomas	(S)	.00	M	Infant	01Ju02Kw
KNOWLES, Ann		25	F	None	01Ju02Kw
RATTIGEN, Pat		30	M	Laborer	01Ju02Kw
SKINNINGTON, Wm.		24	M	Laborer	01Ju02Kw
MCLOUGHLAN, Michal		28	M	Laborer	01Ju02Kw
Ann	(W)	20	F	None	01Ju02Kw
William	(S)	.00	M	Infant	01Ju02Kw
CONNOR, Margaret		22	F	None	01Ju02Kw
TALLAN, Eliza		30	F	None	01Ju02Kw
TANNING, Unider		25	F	None	01Ju02Kw
NIGHTOL, Frederick		25	M	Laborer	01Ju02Kw
TANNING, Mary		30	F	None	01Ju02Kw
YEATS, Jacob		36	M	Laborer	01Ju02Kw
CONN, U		38	M	Laborer	01Ju02Kw
HITCHPATRICK, Pat		27	M	Laborer	01Ju02Kw
WALLACE, James		30	M	Laborer	01Ju02Kw
ONEIL, William		24	M	Laborer	01Ju02Kw
John		17	M	Laborer	01Ju02Kw
GIBBONS, Mary		35	F	None	01Ju02Kw
Elvira		20	F	None	01Ju02Kw
HURSY, Ann		24	F	None	01Ju02Kw
CURIN, Lawrence		24	M	Laborer	01Ju02Kw
CARROLL, James		21	M	Laborer	01Ju02Kw
CLARK, Judith		22	F	None	01Ju02Kw
HAGGERTY, John		23	M	Laborer	01Ju02Kw
BYRNE, Bernard		19	M	Laborer	01Ju02Kw
DONNELL, Pat		25	M	Laborer	01Ju02Kw
DUGAN, Dan		22	M	Laborer	01Ju02Kw
BURNS, Charles		25	M	Laborer	01Ju02Kw
TURNER, John		24	M	Laborer	01Ju02Kw
OTIS, Samuel		20	M	Laborer	01Ju02Kw
GALLIGHER, Sally		20	F	None	01Ju02Kw
HAINY, Bridget		23	F	None	01Ju02Kw
FLAHERTY, Margaret		24	F	None	01Ju02Kw

LORD-ASHBURTON 01 JUNE 1847

From Liverpool

NAMES OF PASSENGERS		AGE	SEX	OCCUPATIONS	DATE PORT SHIP
MURPHY, M.		30	M	Farmer	01Ju02Fp
BOHAN, Robt.		30	M	Farmer	01Ju02Fp
U	(W)	25	F	None	01Ju02Fp
Mich.	(S)	06	M	Child	01Ju02Fp
Pat	(S)	04	M	Child	01Ju02Fp
My.	(D)	03	F	Child	01Ju02Fp
Thos.	(S)	01	M	Child	01Ju02Fp
SUTTON, Bdgt.		20	F	None	01Ju02Fp
Ann		30	F	None	01Ju02Fp
DERWARD, W.		26	M	Farmer	01Ju02Fp
KNOX, P.		22	M	Farmer	01Ju02Fp
CONDON, My.		45	F	None	01Ju02Fp
BURKE, G.		36	M	Farmer	01Ju02Fp
MAHAN, P.		24	M	Farmer	01Ju02Fp
CIOEN, Ann		20	F	None	01Ju02Fp
MCIVER, J.		40	M	Farmer	01Ju02Fp
U	(W)	42	F	None	01Ju02Fp
My.	(D)	18	F	None	01Ju02Fp
Patck.	(S)	15	M	Farmer	01Ju02Fp
James	(S)	13	M	Farmer	01Ju02Fp
Mgt.	(D)	12	F	None	01Ju02Fp
Eliza	(D)	08	F	Child	01Ju02Fp
Wm.	(S)	06	M	Child	01Ju02Fp
Robt.	(S)	04	M	Child	01Ju02Fp
H.	(D)	22	F	None	01Ju02Fp
MCQUADE, E.		29	M	Farmer	01Ju02Fp
HUGHES, Jane		21	F	None	01Ju02Fp
MULLAN, My.		19	F	None	01Ju02Fp
FOX, Rose		04	F	Child	01Ju02Fp
WALSH, M.		45	M	Farmer	01Ju02Fp

NAMES OF PASSENGERS	AGE	SEX	OCCUPATIONS	DATE PORT SHIP	NAMES OF PASSENGERS	AGE	SEX	OCCUPATIONS	DATE PORT SHIP
WALSH, Bgt. (W)	35	F	None	01Ju02Fp	PARKER, Chat.	20	F	None	01Ju02Fp
Mich. (S)	08	M	Child	01Ju02Fp	OBRIEN, Eliza	21	F	None	01Ju02Fp
Ann (D)	03	F	Child	01Ju02Fp	STRONG, My.	26	F	None	01Ju02Fp
Mara (D)	01	F	Child	01Ju02Fp	FLYNN, My.	30	F	None	01Ju02Fp
WANN, J.	36	M	Farmer	01Ju02Fp	Pat (S)	08	M	Child	01Ju02Fp
BOWES, S.	32	M	Farmer	01Ju02Fp	Wm. (S)	08	M	Child	01Ju02Fp
ABRAHAM, H.	49	M	Farmer	01Ju02Fp	Chas. (S)	02	M	Child	01Ju02Fp
BOREN, Cath.	30	F	None	01Ju02Fp	Thos. (H)	36	M	Farmer	01Ju02Fp
CREMIN, L.	26	M	Farmer	01Ju02Fp	EAGAN, E.	20	M	Farmer	01Ju02Fp
CAUFIELD, H.	24	M	Farmer	01Ju02Fp	James	26	M	Farmer	01Ju02Fp
LYNCH, W.	24	M	Farmer	01Ju02Fp	LUTTEREL, Ann	19	F	None	01Ju02Fp
DOWDALL, Bgt.	21	F	None	01Ju02Fp	DOYLE, M.	29	M	Farmer	01Ju02Fp
SUMMERS, P.	24	M	Farmer	01Ju02Fp	BROUGHTER, C.	29	M	Farmer	01Ju02Fp
Frances	23	F	None	01Ju02Fp	U (W)	21	F	None	01Ju02Fp
HUSTON, A.	52	M	Farmer	01Ju02Fp	KEEGAN, J.	26	M	Farmer	01Ju02Fp
CARSON, R.	27	M	Farmer	01Ju02Fp	Wllen (W)	25	F	None	01Ju02Fp
HEELAN, Cath.	21	F	None	01Ju02Fp	Ann (D)	01	F	Child	01Ju02Fp
CCONLAN, U	21	M	Farmer	01Ju02Fp	ROACH, Cath.	49	F	None	01Ju02Fp
CADY, W.	24	M	Farmer	01Ju02Fp	John (S)	20	M	Farmer	01Ju02Fp
CROSS, C.	24	M	Farmer	01Ju02Fp	Danl. (S)	10	M	Child	01Ju02Fp
WHALEN, My.	21	F	None	01Ju02Fp	MAHER, D.	09	M	Child	01Ju02Fp
CALLAGHAN, A.	19	M	Farmer	01Ju02Fp	Cath.	03	F	Child	01Ju02Fp
MCBRIDE, P.	22	M	Farmer	01Ju02Fp	BRENNAN, T.	20	M	Laborer	01Ju02Fp
MORAN, Bgt.	18	F	None	01Ju02Fp	SLACK, My.	25	F	None	01Ju02Fp
LANE, A.	27	M	Farmer	01Ju02Fp	Ellen	28	F	None	01Ju02Fp
KENNEY, J.	27	M	Farmer	01Ju02Fp	Peter	17	M	Laborer	01Ju02Fp
Wm.	18	M	Farmer	01Ju02Fp	CALLAN, Eliza	20	F	None	01Ju02Fp
Jno.	16	M	Farmer	01Ju02Fp	FANEY, J.	50	M	Laborer	01Ju02Fp
Miche.	14	M	Farmer	01Ju02Fp	My. (W)	50	F	None	01Ju02Fp
James	12	M	Farmer	01Ju02Fp	Pat (S)	24	M	Laborer	01Ju02Fp
Richd.	10	M	Child	01Ju02Fp	Eliza (D)	22	F	None	01Ju02Fp
Kate	08	F	Child	01Ju02Fp	Cath. (D)	20	F	None	01Ju02Fp
Julia	24	F	None	01Ju02Fp	Michl. (S)	18	M	Laborer	01Ju02Fp
Lucy	36	F	None	01Ju02Fp	My. (D)	16	F	None	01Ju02Fp
WALSH, M.	24	M	Farmer	01Ju02Fp	Jno. (S)	14	M	Laborer	01Ju02Fp
MANGAN, My.	36	F	None	01Ju02Fp	Brgt. (D)	16	F	None	01Ju02Fp
Patck.	35	M	Farmer	01Ju02Fp	Judith (D)	08	F	Child	01Ju02Fp
SCANLAN, M.	26	M	Farmer	01Ju02Fp	James (S)	07	M	Child	01Ju02Fp
OCALLAGHAN, E.	18	M	Farmer	01Ju02Fp	BURNS, B.	24	M	Laborer	01Ju02Fp
MAHANY, J.	24	M	Farmer	01Ju02Fp	WHELAN, U	24	M	Laborer	01Ju02Fp
My.	17	M	None	01Ju02Fp	Ann (W)	21	F	None	01Ju02Fp
SHEEHY, Cath.	28	F	None	01Ju02Fp	My. (D)	03	F	Child	01Ju02Fp
Jno.	26	M	Farmer	01Ju02Fp	KENNEDY, My.	21	F	None	01Ju02Fp
Thos.	20	M	Farmer	01Ju02Fp	MARA, Ann	25	F	None	01Ju02Fp
Bdgt.	20	F	None	01Ju02Fp	Pat	20	M	Laborer	01Ju02Fp
My.	22	F	None	01Ju02Fp	SMITH, Cath.	25	F	None	01Ju02Fp
WALLAGE, U	45	M	Farmer	01Ju02Fp	RIELY, T.	28	M	Laborer	01Ju02Fp
CARROLL, My.A.	60	F	None	01Ju02Fp	Thos.	18	M	Laborer	01Ju02Fp
Ann (D)	17	F	None	01Ju02Fp	Ellen	10	F	Child	01Ju02Fp
CASSIDY, M.	24	M	Farmer	01Ju02Fp	PATON, C.	30	M	Laborer	01Ju02Fp
HUGHES, P.	24	M	Farmer	01Ju02Fp	LENEHAN, J.	40	M	Laborer	01Ju02Fp
MCCABE, Hanah	24	F	None	01Ju02Fp	DUNN, J.	20	M	Laborer	01Ju02Fp
CARROLL, W.	20	M	Farmer	01Ju02Fp	FERGUSON, U	28	M	Laborer	01Ju02Fp
DAVIS, J.	27	M	Farmer	01Ju02Fp	COGHER, E.I.	45	M	Laborer	01Ju02Fp
Maria	25	F	None	01Ju02Fp	NEWMAN, J.	25	M	Laborer	01Ju02Fp
MAHON, J.	20	M	Farmer	01Ju02Fp	HIGGINS, J.	28	M	Laborer	01Ju02Fp
CONNER, Mrgt.	19	F	None	01Ju02Fp	Thos.	24	M	Laborer	01Ju02Fp
DAVIS, P.	26	M	Farmer	01Ju02Fp	James	19	M	Laborer	01Ju02Fp
James	25	M	Farmer	01Ju02Fp	DUNN, P.	25	M	Laborer	01Ju02Fp
Jno.	24	M	Farmer	01Ju02Fp	MANALLY, T.	23	M	Laborer	01Ju02Fp
MCEVER, E.	34	M	Farmer	01Ju02Fp	Mich.	16	M	Laborer	01Ju02Fp
SWAN, T.	35	M	Farmer	01Ju02Fp	CONDEN, Hanah	20	F	None	01Ju02Fp
RUNN, P.	08	M	Child	01Ju02Fp	PATRICK, W.	28	M	Farmer	01Ju02Fp
DONOUGH, T.	20	M	Farmer	01Ju02Fp	RAGGAN, B.	20	M	Farmer	01Ju02Fp
BLESSING, My.	20	F	None	01Ju02Fp	FARRELL, Betty	16	F	None	01Ju02Fp
My.	25	F	None	01Ju02Fp	Jno.	20	M	Farmer	01Ju02Fp
ROACH, Cath.	19	F	None	01Ju02Fp	MORRIS, B.	35	M	Farmer	01Ju02Fp
DUGGAN, H.	29	M	Farmer	01Ju02Fp	U (W)	35	F	None	01Ju02Fp
HALLARAN, Eliza.	18	F	None	01Ju02Fp	Jno.	21	M	Farmer	01Ju02Fp
BALTERS, My.	26	F	None	01Ju02Fp	Jas.	20	M	Farmer	01Ju02Fp
PENTEFACT, T.	19	M	Farmer	01Ju02Fp	Eliza	19	F	None	01Ju02Fp
GATES, B.	26	M	Farmer	01Ju02Fp	CONNOLLY, J.	25	M	Farmer	01Ju02Fp
SLATTERY, U	30	M	Farmer	01Ju02Fp	Danl.	25	M	Farmer	01Ju02Fp
MCHUGH, P.	25	M	Farmer	01Ju02Fp	ROSS, D.	40	M	Farmer	01Ju02Fp
MALONEY, J.	26	M	Farmer	01Ju02Fp	U (W)	36	F	None	01Ju02Fp

NAMES OF PASSENGERS		AGE	SEX	OCCUPATIONS	DATE PORT SHIP
ROSS, Eliza		36	F	None	01Ju02Fp
James		16	F	None	01Ju02Fp
MCDONALD, J.		35	M	Farmer	01Ju02Fp
Nancy		35	F	None	01Ju02Fp
MALAFEE, P.		34	M	Farmer	01Ju02Fp
WATERS, My.		20	F	None	01Ju02Fp
RIELY, Cath.		20	F	None	01Ju02Fp
GUFFEN, Cath.		25	F	None	01Ju02Fp
BOLAN, J.		26	M	Farmer	01Ju02Fp
Jenny		25	F	None	01Ju02Fp
Bldy		16	F	None	01Ju02Fp
U		28	M	Farmer	01Ju02Fp
My.		27	F	None	01Ju02Fp
Wm.		24	M	Farmer	01Ju02Fp
FREENY, J.		28	M	Farmer	01Ju02Fp
Martin		29	M	Farmer	01Ju02Fp
RYAN, M.		28	M	Farmer	01Ju02Fp
MASON, M.		12	M	Farmer	01Ju02Fp
MCCARTNEY, D.		25	M	Farmer	01Ju02Fp
SEXTON, Ann		26	F	None	01Ju02Fp
MCCARTNEY, D.		30	M	Farmer	01Ju02Fp
OFEAN, Brg.		20	F	None	01Ju02Fp
CONNER, Ellen		18	F	None	01Ju02Fp
CARROLL, T.		20	M	Farmer	01Ju02Fp
MCCUSKER, A.		40	M	Farmer	01Ju02Fp
MCCONNELL, W.		31	M	Farmer	01Ju02Fp
DELAN, Brgt.		20	F	None	01Ju02Fp
My.		21	F	None	01Ju02Fp
TATE, M.		28	M	Farmer	01Ju02Fp
P.		20	M	Laborer	01Ju02Fp
MITCHELL, C.H.		25	M	Laborer	01Ju02Fp
U	(W)	22	F	None	01Ju02Fp
My.		22	F	None	01Ju02Fp
ADAMS, T.		22	M	Laborer	01Ju02Fp
CROGAN, J.		35	M	Laborer	01Ju02Fp
Judith		22	F	None	01Ju02Fp
WHITE, J.		30	M	Laborer	01Ju02Fp
My.		25	F	None	01Ju02Fp
GANNON, M.		28	M	Laborer	01Ju02Fp
Eliza		26	F	None	01Ju02Fp
BARRETT, T.		30	M	Laborer	01Ju02Fp
DILLON, P.		40	M	Laborer	01Ju02Fp
DAVIS, W.		26	M	Laborer	01Ju02Fp
DONOLLY, M.		22	M	Laborer	01Ju02Fp
MARA, M.		25	M	Laborer	01Ju02Fp
MURPHY, J.		40	M	Laborer	01Ju02Fp
James	(S)	19	M	Laborer	01Ju02Fp
Steph.	(S)	19	M	Laborer	01Ju02Fp
Nicholas	(S)	09	M	Child	01Ju02Fp
POWER, J.		24	M	Laborer	01Ju02Fp
SHEA, J.		22	M	Laborer	01Ju02Fp
SULLIVAN, D.		30	M	Laborer	01Ju02Fp
BRENNAN, A.		27	M	Laborer	01Ju02Fp
MURPHY, D.		30	M	Laborer	01Ju02Fp
HALLERAN, R.		40	M	Laborer	01Ju02Fp
Mich.	(S)	22	M	Laborer	01Ju02Fp
Ellen	(D)	20	F	None	01Ju02Fp
Pat	(S)	12	M	Laborer	01Ju02Fp
Rich.	(S)	09	M	Child	01Ju02Fp
Fracs.	(S)	08	M	Child	01Ju02Fp
Honora	(D)	03	F	Child	01Ju02Fp
CASEY, Ellen		20	F	None	01Ju02Fp
DALEY, U		20	F	None	01Ju02Fp
RYAN, Cath.		21	F	None	01Ju02Fp
BERGEN, M.		20	M	Laborer	01Ju02Fp
HALLARAN, Ann		20	F	None	01Ju02Fp
STAPLETON, W.		55	M	Laborer	01Ju02Fp
W.	(W)	45	F	None	01Ju02Fp
Martin	(S)	21	M	Laborer	01Ju02Fp
Ann	(D)	18	F	None	01Ju02Fp
Bgt.	(D)	15	F	None	01Ju02Fp
J.	(S)	14	M	Farmer	01Ju02Fp
Eliza	(D)	12	F	None	01Ju02Fp
My.	(D)	09	F	Child	01Ju02Fp
MCANALLY, P.		09	M	Child	01Ju02Fp

NAMES OF PASSENGERS		AGE	SEX	OCCUPATIONS	DATE PORT SHIP
HUGGINS, O.		29	M	Farmer	01Ju02Fp
KENNY, P.		40	M	Farmer	01Ju02Fp
Ann	(D)	11	F	Child	01Ju02Fp
My.	(D)	07	F	Child	01Ju02Fp
GAVIN, T.		27	M	Farmer	01Ju02Fp
My.		24	F	None	01Ju02Fp
KILLOP, J.		29	M	Farmer	01Ju02Fp
Ma-.		22	F	None	01Ju02Fp
U-Mrs.		50	F	None	01Ju02Fp
Bgt.		18	F	None	01Ju02Fp
KEMP, U.		16	M	Farmer	01Ju02Fp
Chas.		25	M	Farmer	01Ju02Fp
BOWDEN, J.		21	M	Farmer	01Ju02Fp
WILSON, J.		25	M	Farmer	01Ju02Fp
Han---, F.		24	M	Farmer	01Ju02Fp
MURPHY, Bgt.		72	F	None	01Ju02Fp
MACK, Bgt.		20	F	None	01Ju02Fp
EMARY, J.		30	M	Farmer	01Ju02Fp
Mich.		21	M	Farmer	01Ju02Fp
WHITE, P.		21	M	Farmer	01Ju02Fp
Fany		19	F	None	01Ju02Fp
Mgt.		20	F	None	01Ju02Fp
CLUSKY, M.		32	M	Farmer	01Ju02Fp

ADAM-LODGE 02 JUNE 1847

From Liverpool

NAMES OF PASSENGERS	AGE	SEX	OCCUPATIONS	DATE PORT SHIP
HANNIGAN, P.	21	M	Laborer	02Ju02Kx
WILLIAMS, W.	30	M	Laborer	02Ju02Kx
John	23	M	Laborer	02Ju02Kx
MCKENDRIDGE, J.	20	M	Laborer	02Ju02Kx
LAW, P.	20	M	Laborer	02Ju02Kx
DONNELLY, F.	18	M	Laborer	02Ju02Kx
MCLOUGHLIN, D.	18	M	Laborer	02Ju02Kx
MCCANN, D.	20	M	Laborer	02Ju02Kx
MCKEEDGE, J.	27	M	Laborer	02Ju02Kx
CULLEN, R.	20	M	Laborer	02Ju02Kx
John	20	M	Laborer	02Ju02Kx
JOYCE, J.	21	M	Laborer	02Ju02Kx
DOYLE, J.	30	M	Laborer	02Ju02Kx
PENDER, P.	25	M	Laborer	02Ju02Kx
CUNNINS, J.	22	M	Laborer	02Ju02Kx
MCCAGHER, M.	22	M	Laborer	02Ju02Kx
GRACE, J.	40	M	Laborer	02Ju02Kx
CLARKE, P.	19	M	Laborer	02Ju02Kx
REDMOND, J.	25	M	Laborer	02Ju02Kx
KIELAN, J.	27	M	Laborer	02Ju02Kx
DAVIS, D.	05	M	Child	02Ju02Kx
Thos.	05	M	Child	02Ju02Kx
WALTERS, D.	24	M	Laborer	02Ju02Kx
BAKER, J.	23	M	Laborer	02Ju02Kx
THOMAS, Evan	32	M	Laborer	02Ju02Kx
MORGAN, D.	09	M	Child	02Ju02Kx
G.	06	M	Child	02Ju02Kx
EVANS, G.	01	M	Child	02Ju02Kx
WILLIAMS, D.	32	M	Laborer	02Ju02Kx
William	35	M	Laborer	02Ju02Kx
BRAZIL, E.	17	M	Laborer	02Ju02Kx
RICHARDS, W.	35	M	Laborer	02Ju02Kx
EVANS, D.	21	M	Laborer	02Ju02Kx
RICHARDS, J.	09	M	Child	02Ju02Kx
DWYER, J.	26	M	Laborer	02Ju02Kx
LUNTY, M.	21	M	Laborer	02Ju02Kx
KENNEALTY, H.	35	M	Laborer	02Ju02Kx
Chas.	25	M	Laborer	02Ju02Kx
RADCLIFFE, J.	30	M	Laborer	02Ju02Kx
KELLY, T.	22	M	Laborer	02Ju02Kx
GALLAGHER, M.	25	M	Laborer	02Ju02Kx

NAMES OF PASSENGERS	AGE	SEX	OCCUPATIONS	DATE PORT SHIP
CONLAN, Ann	18	F	None	02Ju02Kx
KEELTY, B.	16	F	None	02Ju02Kx
FITZGERALD, My.	23	F	None	02Ju02Kx
ELLIOTT, My.	25	F	None	02Ju02Kx
Betty	23	F	None	02Ju02Kx
WALSH, Ellen	21	F	None	02Ju02Kx
BOLAND, C.	19	F	None	02Ju02Kx
GLENN, My.	17	F	None	02Ju02Kx
HUGH, M.	26	F	None	02Ju02Kx
THOMPSON, M.	01	F	Child	02Ju02Kx
HILEDY, M.	20	F	None	02Ju02Kx
THERENTY, Ann	20	F	None	02Ju02Kx
FEEN, M.	18	F	None	02Ju02Kx
GRAY, A.	11	F	Child	02Ju02Kx
DEFIELD, M.	03	F	Child	02Ju02Kx
SODAN, M.	20	M	Laborer	02Ju02Kx
FARRELLY, O.	20	M	Laborer	02Ju02Kx
FITZSIMMONS, T.	24	M	Laborer	02Ju02Kx
MCEVOY, A.	18	M	Laborer	02Ju02Kx
MULLIGAN, C.	26	M	Laborer	02Ju02Kx
FAYLAN, T.	50	M	Laborer	02Ju02Kx
T.	39	M	Laborer	02Ju02Kx
Thos.	02	M	Child	02Ju02Kx
Joseph	23	M	Laborer	02Ju02Kx
MANCHESTER, J.	60	M	Laborer	02Ju02Kx
GREEN, J.	50	M	Laborer	02Ju02Kx
Wm. (S)	17	M	Laborer	02Ju02Kx
Joseph (S)	19	M	Laborer	02Ju02Kx
George (S)	13	M	Laborer	02Ju02Kx
CUSHION, J.	30	M	Laborer	02Ju02Kx
HEORTH, J.	23	M	Laborer	02Ju02Kx
RIPPON, S.	12	M	Laborer	02Ju02Kx
MCKENNA, T.	40	M	Laborer	02Ju02Kx
ROONY, P.	18	M	Laborer	02Ju02Kx
John	19	M	Laborer	02Ju02Kx
MEHAN, J.	22	M	Laborer	02Ju02Kx
SHEEHAN, M.	30	M	Laborer	02Ju02Kx
MILLIKEN, P.	21	M	Laborer	02Ju02Kx
RYAN, P.	26	M	Laborer	02Ju02Kx
HARNY, M.	25	M	Laborer	02Ju02Kx
COLLINS, J.	30	M	Laborer	02Ju02Kx
HEELY, P.	20	M	Laborer	02Ju02Kx
DOWNY, J.	25	M	Laborer	02Ju02Kx
FOLEY, J.	18	M	Laborer	02Ju02Kx
NEAL, E.	26	M	Laborer	02Ju02Kx
FOGARTY, M.	23	M	Laborer	02Ju02Kx
KELLY, E.	30	M	Laborer	02Ju02Kx
JENNINGS, E.	20	M	Laborer	02Ju02Kx
Mich.	18	M	Laborer	02Ju02Kx
GAFNEY, P.	23	M	Laborer	02Ju02Kx
WHITE, P.	36	M	Laborer	02Ju02Kx
GARGAN, J.	34	M	Laborer	02Ju02Kx
KELLY, M.	26	M	Laborer	02Ju02Kx
Mich.	24	M	Laborer	02Ju02Kx
BARRATT, P.	26	M	Laborer	02Ju02Kx
SAPEN, L.	30	M	Laborer	02Ju02Kx
NAUGHTON, T.	20	M	Laborer	02Ju02Kx
SOHEN, L.	30	M	Laborer	02Ju02Kx
ODONELL, T.	20	M	Laborer	02Ju02Kx
KELLY, D.	26	M	Laborer	02Ju02Kx
LYNCH, T.	24	M	Laborer	02Ju02Kx
LAWLESS, P.	18	M	Laborer	02Ju02Kx
MALONE, J.	27	M	Laborer	02Ju02Kx
CARLINGHAM, E.	27	M	Laborer	02Ju02Kx
HEPPIN, M.	56	M	Laborer	02Ju02Kx
KEYES, T.	20	M	Laborer	02Ju02Kx
KELLY, P.	21	M	Laborer	02Ju02Kx
GALLAGHER, O.	26	M	Laborer	02Ju02Kx
John	20	M	Laborer	02Ju02Kx
MCGINN, J.	19	M	Laborer	02Ju02Kx
MCGUIRK, P.	26	M	Laborer	02Ju02Kx
LYNCH, D.	01	M	Child	02Ju02Kx
Mich.	46	M	Laborer	02Ju02Kx
Thos.	17	M	Laborer	02Ju02Kx
REES, P.	30	M	Laborer	02Ju02Kx
MORGAN, T.	26	M	Laborer	02Ju02Kx
MORAN, P.	26	M	Laborer	02Ju02Kx
Mich.	22	M	Laborer	02Ju02Kx
John	20	M	Laborer	02Ju02Kx
SHALLY, P.	26	M	Laborer	02Ju02Kx
CONLIN, J.	24	M	Laborer	02Ju02Kx
MCCANN, O.	20	M	Laborer	02Ju02Kx
Path.	18	M	Laborer	02Ju02Kx
MURRY, D.	18	M	Laborer	02Ju02Kx
GALLAGHER, L.	24	M	Laborer	02Ju02Kx
Edwd.	25	M	Laborer	02Ju02Kx
CULLY, D.	22	M	Laborer	02Ju02Kx
GALLAGHER, H.	34	M	Laborer	02Ju02Kx
MAY, J.	16	M	Laborer	02Ju02Kx
FOLY, J.	25	M	Laborer	02Ju02Kx
MONAGHAN, G.	20	M	Laborer	02Ju02Kx
KEATING, M.	20	M	Laborer	02Ju02Kx
KINSHELLA, O.	25	M	Laborer	02Ju02Kx
MCCORMICK, P.	20	M	Laborer	02Ju02Kx
STUDAY, W.	22	M	Laborer	02Ju02Kx
THOMPSON, J.	30	M	Laborer	02Ju02Kx
H.	01	M	Child	02Ju02Kx
BUTHERFIELD, P.	29	M	Laborer	02Ju02Kx
WALSH, P.	25	M	Laborer	02Ju02Kx
HODGES, P.	50	M	Laborer	02Ju02Kx
KEVLIN, J.	26	M	Laborer	02Ju02Kx
DANGERD, D.	25	M	Laborer	02Ju02Kx
NAM, M.	22	M	Laborer	02Ju02Kx
GRACY, W.	13	M	Laborer	02Ju02Kx
WOODS, J.	20	M	Laborer	02Ju02Kx
SMITH, S.	26	M	Laborer	02Ju02Kx
WILKINSON, J.	21	M	Laborer	02Ju02Kx
LUCEY, M.	24	M	Laborer	02Ju02Kx
GREEN, N.	05	M	Child	02Ju02Kx
BLOCK, L.	24	M	Laborer	02Ju02Kx
GAFNEY, T.	01	M	Child	02Ju02Kx
LUCAS, Mgt.	18	F	None	02Ju02Kx
Ann	16	F	None	02Ju02Kx
MCCOURT, Ruth	20	F	None	02Ju02Kx
DONNELLY, Rose	17	F	None	02Ju02Kx
DUNAM, My.	18	F	None	02Ju02Kx
DONLON, Eliza	18	F	None	02Ju02Kx
CULLIN, My.	20	F	None	02Ju02Kx
JOYCE, My.	50	F	None	02Ju02Kx
Bdgt.	30	F	None	02Ju02Kx
DALTON, My.	17	F	None	02Ju02Kx
DAVIS, Elzbt.	25	F	None	02Ju02Kx
Rachel	60	F	None	02Ju02Kx
Prisilla	01	F	Child	02Ju02Kx
WALTERS, Elzt.	24	F	None	02Ju02Kx
Matilda (D)	01	F	Child	02Ju02Kx
BAKER, Matilda	26	F	None	02Ju02Kx
THOMAS, Ann	30	F	None	02Ju02Kx
MOYERS, Elzt.	55	F	None	02Ju02Kx
Elzt.	24	F	None	02Ju02Kx
RICHARDS, Janet	01	F	Child	02Ju02Kx
EVANS, Rach.	20	F	None	02Ju02Kx
DWYER, S.	22	F	None	02Ju02Kx
KENWALTY, A.	40	F	None	02Ju02Kx
FARRELLY, J.	16	F	None	02Ju02Kx
BACKER, Mgt.	24	F	None	02Ju02Kx
MAHER, Mgt.	25	F	None	02Ju02Kx
MCEVOY, Cath.	14	F	None	02Ju02Kx
SMITH, Bgt.	16	F	None	02Ju02Kx
LEEDWORD, S.	18	F	None	02Ju02Kx
HARINGTON, My.	20	F	None	02Ju02Kx
Jane	16	F	None	02Ju02Kx
TAYLER, Sarah	20	F	None	02Ju02Kx
Elzbt.	26	F	None	02Ju02Kx
Sarah	01	F	Child	02Ju02Kx
GREEN, Jane	46	F	None	02Ju02Kx
My. (D)	09	F	Child	02Ju02Kx
CASHMAN, Ann	28	F	None	02Ju02Kx
My.	09	F	Child	02Ju02Kx
SHEALT, Hat.	22	F	None	02Ju02Kx

NAMES OF PASSENGERS		AGE	SEX	OCCUPATIONS	DATE PORT SHIP	NAMES OF PASSENGERS		AGE	SEX	OCCUPATIONS	DATE PORT SHIP
RIPPON, S.		45	F	None	02Ju02Kx	MALEY, My.		21	F	None	02Ju02Ky
Ann	(D)	13	F	None	02Ju02Kx	OBRIEN, Cath.		22	F	None	02Ju02Ky
MCKEE, Cath.		30	F	None	02Ju02Kx	CANN, G.		25	M	Laborer	02Ju02Ky
ROSYN, R.		24	F	None	02Ju02Kx	BARTLY, T.		30	M	Laborer	02Ju02Ky
SHEHAN, N.		01	F	Child	02Ju02Kx	STEWART, B.		17	M	Laborer	02Ju02Ky
Cath.		01	F	Child	02Ju02Kx	JOHNSON, Eliza.		19	F	None	02Ju02Ky
GAFNEY, Ellen		25	F	None	02Ju02Kx	JEFFERS, J.		24	M	Laborer	02Ju02Ky
Bgt.		16	F	None	02Ju02Kx	DOYLE, Elzt.		20	F	None	02Ju02Ky
Ann		16	F	None	02Ju02Kx	MCMULLAN, J.		18	M	Laborer	02Ju02Ky
DALY, C.		23	F	None	02Ju02Kx	RAFTER, P.		20	M	Laborer	02Ju02Ky
CONNER, My.		22	F	None	02Ju02Kx	READY, P.		26	M	Laborer	02Ju02Ky
KELLY, B.		13	F	None	02Ju02Kx	KYTE, J.		24	M	Laborer	02Ju02Ky
FLYNN, H.		19	F	None	02Ju02Kx	HUMPHRIES, Ann		26	F	None	02Ju02Ky
KELLY, S.		16	F	None	02Ju02Kx	John	(S)	08	M	Child	02Ju02Ky
FENIRT, B.		13	F	None	02Ju02Kx	KYTE, Mgt.		19	F	None	02Ju02Ky
LEONARD, B.		24	F	None	02Ju02Kx	BROWN, J.		20	M	Laborer	02Ju02Ky
MURPHY, C.		24	F	None	02Ju02Kx	GARTY, P.		20	M	Laborer	02Ju02Ky
ROPPON, H.		10	F	Child	02Ju02Kx	Edwd.		21	M	Laborer	02Ju02Ky
KELLY, My.		20	F	Child	02Ju02Kx	FURY, B.		23	M	Laborer	02Ju02Ky
LYNCH, M.		21	F	None	02Ju02Kx	LYRD, P.		47	M	Laborer	02Ju02Ky
CULLEN, My.		22	F	None	02Ju02Kx	Cath.	(W)	35	F	None	02Ju02Ky
NOLAN, E.		24	F	None	02Ju02Kx	My.	(D)	13	F	None	02Ju02Ky
Bgt.		20	F	None	02Ju02Kx	Pat	(S)	10	M	Child	02Ju02Ky
BYRNE, A.		20	F	None	02Ju02Kx	Thos.	(S)	06	M	Child	02Ju02Ky
MACK, J.		20	F	None	02Ju02Kx	Cath.	(D)	02	F	Child	02Ju02Ky
GALLAGHER, A.		25	F	None	02Ju02Kx	CORNEL, Jula		20	F	None	02Ju02Ky
SOULY, E.M.		12	F	None	02Ju02Kx	RIELY, My.		30	F	None	02Ju02Ky
MCLOUGHLIN, J.		11	F	Child	02Ju02Kx	MCELROY, P.		18	M	Laborer	02Ju02Ky
REILY, B.		18	F	None	02Ju02Kx	Roger		17	M	Laborer	02Ju02Ky
BARTON, M.		23	F	None	02Ju02Kx	Edwd.		20	M	Laborer	02Ju02Ky
SHALLY, C.		23	F	None	02Ju02Kx	Ellen		17	F	None	02Ju02Ky
						Peter		03	M	Child	02Ju02Ky
						Isb.		50	F	None	02Ju02Ky
						Mgt.		01	F	Child	02Ju02Ky
						RAFFET, Mgt.		27	F	None	02Ju02Ky
BIRKINHEAD 02 JUNE 1847						MCELROY, Sam.		25	M	Laborer	02Ju02Ky
						CAMPBELL, O.		34	M	Laborer	02Ju02Ky
From Liverpool						GALVIN, M.		24	M	Laborer	02Ju02Ky
						STIFFORTE, M.		21	M	Laborer	02Ju02Ky
						MAHER, P.		20	M	Laborer	02Ju02Ky
						MCGOVERN, P.		20	M	Laborer	02Ju02Ky
						Mgt.		21	F	None	02Ju02Ky
MURRY, B.		26	M	Laborer	02Ju02Ky	Andrew		22	M	Laborer	02Ju02Ky
Fany	(W)	28	F	None	02Ju02Ky	CARTY, W.		40	M	Laborer	02Ju02Ky
Ma.	(D)	01	F	Child	02Ju02Ky	W--Y.		40	M	Laborer	02Ju02Ky
OMEARA, Ellb.		22	F	None	02Ju02Ky	NAUGHTON, A.		36	M	Laborer	02Ju02Ky
Mich.		23	M	Laborer	02Ju02Ky	HIGGINS, T.		36	F	None	02Ju02Ky
Jala.		21	M	Laborer	02Ju02Ky	Rose		36	F	None	02Ju02Ky
BRADY, P.		36	M	Laborer	02Ju02Ky	John		03	M	Child	02Ju02Ky
MCCABE, R.		17	M	Laborer	02Ju02Ky	NEE, P.		40	M	Laborer	02Ju02Ky
GARRY, M.		23	M	Laborer	02Ju02Ky	Ann	(W)	30	F	None	02Ju02Ky
MAHER, R.M.		25	M	Laborer	02Ju02Ky	Rose	(D)	04	F	Child	02Ju02Ky
Ann		20	F	None	02Ju02Ky	Jane	(D)	01	F	Child	02Ju02Ky
George		24	M	Laborer	02Ju02Ky	Cath.	(D)	01	F	Child	02Ju02Ky
MCCANN, M.		20	F	None	02Ju02Ky	Saml.		14	M	Laborer	02Ju02Ky
WILSON, G.		50	M	Laborer	02Ju02Ky	CARROLE, B.		25	M	Laborer	02Ju02Ky
Alexa.		45	M	Laborer	02Ju02Ky	CARTY, J.		40	M	Laborer	02Ju02Ky
Mgt.		26	F	None	02Ju02Ky	WARD, J.		60	M	Laborer	02Ju02Ky
PLACE, Ann		19	F	None	02Ju02Ky	Saml.		40	M	Laborer	02Ju02Ky
Edw.		12	M	Laborer	02Ju02Ky	My.		20	F	None	02Ju02Ky
WILSON, R.		12	M	Laborer	02Ju02Ky	Martha		14	F	None	02Ju02Ky
Alice		24	F	None	02Ju02Ky	Jacob		12	M	Laborer	02Ju02Ky
WALLER, R.		24	M	Laborer	02Ju02Ky	Harriet		10	F	Child	02Ju02Ky
SULLIVAN, D.		27	M	Laborer	02Ju02Ky	John		07	M	Child	02Ju02Ky
MCGINN, M.		21	M	Laborer	02Ju02Ky	George		05	M	Child	02Ju02Ky
RODGERS, Ann		19	F	None	02Ju02Ky	Betty		03	F	Child	02Ju02Ky
Thos.		28	M	Laborer	02Ju02Ky	Wm.		01	M	Child	02Ju02Ky
MCGINN, Ann		24	F	None	02Ju02Ky	MCMAHON, B.		23	M	Laborer	02Ju02Ky
U, Ele.		19	F	None	02Ju02Ky	Bgt.		20	F	None	02Ju02Ky
LEYAN, B.		23	F	None	02Ju02Ky	Bess		59	F	None	02Ju02Ky
FLYNN, Mgt.		19	F	None	02Ju02Ky	Mgt.		19	F	None	02Ju02Ky
LYNCH, P.		14	M	Laborer	02Ju02Ky	REILLY, J.		23	M	Laborer	02Ju02Ky
MALEY, J.		25	M	Laborer	02Ju02Ky	Cath.		18	F	None	02Ju02Ky
CONERY, J.		26	M	Laborer	02Ju02Ky	MULLIGAN, J.		20	M	Laborer	02Ju02Ky
MADDEN, P.		23	M	Laborer	02Ju02Ky	MURPHY, J.		32	M	Laborer	02Ju02Ky

NAMES OF PASSENGERS		AGE	SEX	OCCUPATIONS	DATE PORT SHIP	NAMES OF PASSENGERS		AGE	SEX	OCCUPATIONS	DATE PORT SHIP
MCGRATH, P.		30	M	Laborer	02Ju02Ky	GRAHAM, F.		24	M	Laborer	02Ju02Ky
COKEY, J.		22	M	Laborer	02Ju02Ky	LOWE, W.		26	M	Laborer	02Ju02Ky
PARKS, S.		23	M	Laborer	02Ju02Ky	GRAHAM, Jane		26	F	None	02Ju02Ky
SOLAN, M.		24	M	Laborer	02Ju02Ky	JOHNSTON, Eliza		23	F	None	02Ju02Ky
BRENNAN, T.		23	M	Laborer	02Ju02Ky	HEARNS, J.		24	M	Laborer	02Ju02Ky
SOLAN, M.		24	M	Laborer	02Ju02Ky	FINNEGAN, P.		30	M	Laborer	02Ju02Ky
BRENNAN, T.		23	M	Laborer	02Ju02Ky	BARNWWELL, J.		18	M	Laborer	02Ju02Ky
MADDEN, T.		18	M	Laborer	02Ju02Ky	FEELAN, P.		20	M	Laborer	02Ju02Ky
M.		24	F	None	02Ju02Ky	CARTY, P.		20	M	Laborer	02Ju02Ky
HALLARAN, S.		25	M	Laborer	02Ju02Ky	DANIEL, M.		23	M	Laborer	02Ju02Ky
FLANNAGAN, W.		20	M	Laborer	02Ju02Ky	MCCORMICK, C.		23	M	Laborer	02Ju02Ky
KELLY, W.		24	M	Laborer	02Ju02Ky	BENNETT, J.		22	M	Laborer	02Ju02Ky
PRICE, A.		24	M	Laborer	02Ju02Ky	CLARY, T.		30	M	Laborer	02Ju02Ky
MED, M.		22	M	Laborer	02Ju02Ky	BROOKARD, J.		28	M	Laborer	02Ju02Ky
Lyns.		25	F	None	02Ju02Ky	COOKE, J.		25	M	Laborer	02Ju02Ky
RIELLY, P.		68	M	Laborer	02Ju02Ky	HAM, J.		32	M	Laborer	02Ju02Ky
James	(S)	20	M	Laborer	02Ju02Ky	Cath.		28	F	None	02Ju02Ky
Ellen	(W)	60	F	None	02Ju02Ky	MCQUIN, J.		25	M	Laborer	02Ju02Ky
Thos.		02	M	Child	02Ju02Ky	Hester		22	F	None	02Ju02Ky
LOWPER, L.		24	M	Laborer	02Ju02Ky	REILLY, T.		26	M	Laborer	02Ju02Ky
Reyt.		18	F	None	02Ju02Ky	LAUGHLIN, T.		28	M	Laborer	02Ju02Ky
KENNY, Bgt.		22	F	None	02Ju02Ky	SULLIVAN, D.		23	M	Laborer	02Ju02Ky
ANTHONY, J.		20	M	Laborer	02Ju02Ky	Sally		19	F	None	02Ju02Ky
POOLE, J.		32	M	Laborer	02Ju02Ky	MURPHY, D.		23	F	None	02Ju02Ky
OHEARN, M.		30	M	Laborer	02Ju02Ky	CONNER, M.		34	F	None	02Ju02Ky
Cath.	(W)	25	F	None	02Ju02Ky	PHILLIPS, J.		73	F	None	02Ju02Ky
Eliza.	(D)	01	F	Child	02Ju02Ky	T.		28	M	Laborer	02Ju02Ky
HASSETT, W.		24	M	Laborer	02Ju02Ky	Biddy		20	F	None	02Ju02Ky
DREW, J.		31	M	Laborer	02Ju02Ky	WELSH, C.		18	M	Laborer	02Ju02Ky
DONOGHUE, R.		30	M	Laborer	02Ju02Ky	MCDONALD, C.		20	M	Laborer	02Ju02Ky
MEECHIN, My.		20	F	None	02Ju02Ky	RUTH, Bgt.		30	F	None	02Ju02Ky
REILLY, Cath.		18	F	None	02Ju02Ky	LOUGHAN, M.		28	F	None	02Ju02Ky
MURPHY, Ellen		17	F	None	02Ju02Ky	HEARNS, M.		26	M	Laborer	02Ju02Ky
MCCREW, J.		24	M	Laborer	02Ju02Ky	GOULDING, N.		24	M	Laborer	02Ju02Ky
BERRY, M.		18	M	Laborer	02Ju02Ky	HERN, Ann		19	F	None	02Ju02Ky
Br---EN, M.		22	M	Laborer	02Ju02Ky	BLYTH, Saml.		19	M	Laborer	02Ju02Ky
HILL, P.		24	M	Laborer	02Ju02Ky	MORGAN, P.		50	M	Laborer	02Ju02Ky
HAYS, J.		24	M	Laborer	02Ju02Ky	Martin		20	M	Laborer	02Ju02Ky
FOLEY, M.		25	M	Laborer	02Ju02Ky	SHEA, T.		20	M	Laborer	02Ju02Ky
WALSH, M.		20	M	Laborer	02Ju02Ky	HOLLAND, R.		40	M	Laborer	02Ju02Ky
FURY, W.		24	M	Laborer	02Ju02Ky	My.	(W)	41	F	None	02Ju02Ky
Joanna		28	F	None	02Ju02Ky	Robt.	(S)	10	M	Child	02Ju02Ky
Betty		05	F	Child	02Ju02Ky	Sarah	(D)	12	F	None	02Ju02Ky
WALSH, Kate		42	F	None	02Ju02Ky	BROUGH, G.		26	M	Laborer	02Ju02Ky
BYRNE, J.		24	M	Laborer	02Ju02Ky	CLEMENTS, T.		25	M	Laborer	02Ju02Ky
Marta		21	F	None	02Ju02Ky	Martha	(W)	25	F	None	02Ju02Ky
Denis		18	M	Laborer	02Ju02Ky	Mgt.	(D)	01	F	Child	02Ju02Ky
Pdck.		16	M	Laborer	02Ju02Ky	Th.	(S)	03	M	Child	02Ju02Ky
Judy		52	F	None	02Ju02Ky	Rebecca		27	F	None	02Ju02Ky
FREIN, J.		26	M	Laborer	02Ju02Ky	HAYES, J.		26	M	Laborer	02Ju02Ky
John		22	M	Laborer	02Ju02Ky	MARSHMAN, W.		56	M	Laborer	02Ju02Ky
Cath.		17	F	None	02Ju02Ky	Ann	(W)	56	F	None	02Ju02Ky
MALRAY, D.		31	M	Laborer	02Ju02Ky	Wm.	(S)	16	M	Laborer	02Ju02Ky
WASH, My.		22	F	None	02Ju02Ky	REILLY, Cath.		20	F	None	02Ju02Ky
HERTY, M.		24	M	Laborer	02Ju02Ky	My.		18	F	None	02Ju02Ky
John		20	M	Laborer	02Ju02Ky	SHEPARD, J.		19	M	Laborer	02Ju02Ky
My.		18	F	None	02Ju02Ky	Mry.		17	F	None	02Ju02Ky
James		15	M	Laborer	02Ju02Ky	HENSEY, M.		32	M	Laborer	02Ju02Ky
DOUGHERTY, Ann		18	F	None	02Ju02Ky	Cath.	(W)	28	F	None	02Ju02Ky
LOUGHLIN, D.		27	M	Laborer	02Ju02Ky	My.	(D)	02	F	Child	02Ju02Ky
Begt.		17	F	None	02Ju02Ky	Cath.	(D)	01	F	Child	02Ju02Ky
MADDEN, M.		29	M	Laborer	02Ju02Ky	KEARNY, L.		25	M	Laborer	02Ju02Ky
QUIRK, J.		20	M	Laborer	02Ju02Ky	DOWD, M.		20	M	Laborer	02Ju02Ky
Patch.		19	M	Laborer	02Ju02Ky	CAIN, T.		25	M	Laborer	02Ju02Ky
WRIGHT, R.		25	M	Laborer	02Ju02Ky	DOWD, M.		30	M	Laborer	02Ju02Ky
Rose		21	F	None	02Ju02Ky	MCORKAN, T.		35	M	Laborer	02Ju02Ky
COGHLAN, P.		25	M	Laborer	02Ju02Ky	FLENY, P.		28	M	Laborer	02Ju02Ky
Marta		27	F	None	02Ju02Ky	GALLAGHER, J.		30	M	Laborer	02Ju02Ky
DOYLE, B.		20	M	Laborer	02Ju02Ky	GILLIN, Elspet		30	F	None	02Ju02Ky
FLOOD, My.		36	F	None	02Ju02Ky	Elzbt.		50	F	None	02Ju02Ky
Simon		18	M	Laborer	02Ju02Ky	Elzbt.		05	F	Child	02Ju02Ky
CURRY, T.		21	M	Laborer	02Ju02Ky	Jas.		01	M	Child	02Ju02Ky
CONNOLLY, P.		21	M	Laborer	02Ju02Ky	Geog.		24	M	Laborer	02Ju02Ky
Mgt.		21	F	None	02Ju02Ky	Mgt.		27	F	None	02Ju02Ky
FLOOD, J.		22	M	Laborer	02Ju02Ky	A.		21	F	None	02Ju02Ky

NAMES OF PASSENGERS	AGE	SEX	OCCUPATIONS	DATE PORT SHIP	NAMES OF PASSENGERS	AGE	SEX	OCCUPATIONS	DATE PORT SHIP
GILLIN, Ann	26	F	None	02Ju02Ky	KILKENNY, Jane	26	F	None	03Ju01Kz
SWEENY, J.	50	M	Laborer	02Ju02Ky	MCLAUGHLIN, Margery	45	F	None	03Ju01Kz
My. (W)	50	F	None	02Ju02Ky	James (S)	29	M	Laborer	03Ju01Kz
Denis (S)	22	M	Laborer	02Ju02Ky	William (S)	28	M	Laborer	03Ju01Kz
Jery. (S)	20	M	Laborer	02Ju02Ky	Michael (S)	23	M	Laborer	03Ju01Kz
FARRELL, W.	24	M	Laborer	02Ju02Ky	Edward (S)	19	M	Laborer	03Ju01Kz
MCMAHON, T.	20	M	Laborer	02Ju02Ky	James (S)	17	M	Laborer	03Ju01Kz
MORRNOGH, G.	21	M	Laborer	02Ju02Ky	Mary (D)	12	F	None	03Ju01Kz
KEAN, Lucy	18	F	None	02Ju02Ky	Margery (D)	10	F	Child	03Ju01Kz
MCMAHON, Mgt.	22	F	None	02Ju02Ky	Ellen (D)	08	F	Child	03Ju01Kz
SPILSY, Hono.	18	F	None	02Ju02Ky	HISKEY, P.	26	M	Laborer	03Ju01Kz
B----N, P.	24	M	Laborer	02Ju02Ky	KENIGAN, G.	30	M	Laborer	03Ju01Kz
MACK, E.	24	M	Laborer	02Ju02Ky	MCGARRIGLE, P.	29	M	Laborer	03Ju01Kz
Cath.	24	F	None	02Ju02Ky	SUTTON, Rebecca	21	F	None	03Ju01Kz
FARRELL, Cath.	20	F	None	02Ju02Ky	CRAWFORD, Mary	19	F	None	03Ju01Kz
Bidy	20	F	None	02Ju02Ky	Mary	18	F	None	03Ju01Kz
FULLAN, Bidy	20	F	None	02Ju02Ky	Robert	12	M	None	03Ju01Kz
MCMEAN, J.	26	M	Laborer	02Ju02Ky	LUCAS, Isabella	26	F	None	03Ju01Kz
Cath. (W)	20	F	None	02Ju02Ky	CARSON, Margaret	20	F	None	03Ju01Kz
Ann (D)	02	F	Child	02Ju02Ky	CUNNINGHAM, J.	29	M	Laborer	03Ju01Kz
OHARA, J.	20	M	Laborer	02Ju02Ky	FERNSTON, Jane	22	F	None	03Ju01Kz
NOLAN, Ma.	20	F	None	02Ju02Ky	Farrtry	20	M	Laborer	03Ju01Kz
FINIGAN, Cath.	21	F	None	02Ju02Ky	MCCAB, Jas.	23	M	Laborer	03Ju01Kz
DOLAN, P.	26	M	Laborer	02Ju02Ky	Margaret	21	F	None	03Ju01Kz
Bgt. (W)	22	F	None	02Ju02Ky	Hugh	19	M	Laborer	03Ju01Kz
My. (D)	01	F	Child	02Ju02Ky	Andrew	17	M	Laborer	03Ju01Kz
LYONS, J.	22	M	Laborer	02Ju02Ky	Hannah	02	F	Child	03Ju01Kz
My.	22	F	None	02Ju02Ky	KELLY, Patrick	26	M	Laborer	03Ju01Kz
SMITH, J.	25	M	Laborer	02Ju02Ky	WINNEMAN, R.N.	44	M	Laborer	03Ju01Kz
MANNON, Mgt.	16	F	None	02Ju02Ky	Ann	34	F	None	03Ju01Kz
BOYLE, M.	25	M	Laborer	02Ju02Ky	JAMISON, J.	41	M	Laborer	03Ju01Kz
MEYER, T.	20	M	Laborer	02Ju02Ky	CLARKE, J.	39	M	Laborer	03Ju01Kz
					Wm.	29	M	Laborer	03Ju01Kz
					Isabella	19	F	None	03Ju01Kz
					Thomas	13	M	None	03Ju01Kz
					DAVIS, Rose	22	F	None	03Ju01Kz
					MCLAUGHLIN, J.	38	M	Laborer	03Ju01Kz

AILSA 03 JUNE 1847

From Londonderry

					MCNAMEE, B.	25	M	Laborer	03Ju01Kz
					Niel (P)	56	M	Laborer	03Ju01Kz
					Charles (B)	32	M	Laborer	03Ju01Kz
					Kiddy	11	F	Child	03Ju01Kz
					Rose	06	F	Child	03Ju01Kz
					SCANLAN, Mary	23	F	None	03Ju01Kz
JOHNSON, Arthur	40	M	Laborer	03Ju01Kz	HARRISON, Catharine	10	F	Child	03Ju01Kz
Sarah	30	F	None	03Ju01Kz	Charles	40	M	Laborer	03Ju01Kz
John	20	M	Laborer	03Ju01Kz	SCANLAN, D.	46	M	Laborer	03Ju01Kz
George	18	M	Laborer	03Ju01Kz	BOWEN, P.	35	M	Laborer	03Ju01Kz
James	13	M	Laborer	03Ju01Kz	RAMSAY, Fanny-A.	31	F	None	03Ju01Kz
William	11	M	Child	03Ju01Kz	David (S)	09	M	Child	03Ju01Kz
Mary	09	F	Child	03Ju01Kz	Martha	19	F	None	03Ju01Kz
Arthur	07	M	Child	03Ju01Kz	RASLEY, John	43	M	Laborer	03Ju01Kz
Isabella	05	F	Child	03Ju01Kz	RUE, Lateta	33	F	None	03Ju01Kz
Bessy	02	F	Child	03Ju01Kz	MCCONNELL, Eliza	24	F	None	03Ju01Kz
WILSON, Mary	28	F	None	03Ju01Kz	MCNAMEE, U-Mrs.	56	F	Wi	03Ju01Kz
WILLIAMS, Margaret	30	F	None	03Ju01Kz					
Thomas-D.	12	M	Laborer	03Ju01Kz					
MCFARLAND, Geo.	27	M	Laborer	03Ju01Kz					
DOHERTY, P.	25	M	Laborer	03Ju01Kz					
MCCLAY, D.	28	M	Laborer	03Ju01Kz					
MCKEEVER, D.	12	M	Laborer	03Ju01Kz					
FINEY, Fanny	09	F	Child	03Ju01Kz					
MCGEE, J.	45	M	Laborer	03Ju01Kz					
James	26	M	Laborer	03Ju01Kz	ABBY-PRATT 03 JUNE 1847				
FERRY, B.	28	M	Laborer	03Ju01Kz					
WALLACE, R.	35	M	Laborer	03Ju01Kz	From Liverpool				
Thomas	29	M	Laborer	03Ju01Kz					
Ellen	13	F	None	03Ju01Kz					
MCGLANKY, P.	26	M	Laborer	03Ju01Kz	JAYNT, Laurs.	28	M	None	03Ju02La
PATTERSON, J.	23	M	Laborer	03Ju01Kz	ASTON, Thos.	27	M	None	03Ju02La
Eliza	22	F	None	03Ju01Kz	WORKMAN, Thos.	19	M	None	03Ju02La
Maria	11	F	Child	03Ju01Kz	PORTER, Peter	21	M	None	03Ju02La
James	09	M	Child	03Ju01Kz	MORRIS, Maurice	37	M	None	03Ju02La
Jervis	10	M	Child	03Ju01Kz	Wm. (S)	13	M	None	03Ju02La
FINHEALLY, O.	31	M	Laborer	03Ju01Kz	Ed. (S)	09	M	Child	03Ju02La
KEGAN, M.	42	M	Laborer	03Ju01Kz	John (S)	08	M	Child	03Ju02La
					BIBBY, Maurice	17	M	Child	03Ju02La
					WILSON, Aug.H.	40	M	Captain	03Ju02La

NAMES OF PASSENGERS		A G E	S E X	OCCUPATIONS	DATE PORT SHIP
WARD, Madge		30	F	None	03Ju02La
James	(S)	07	M	Child	03Ju02La
Pat	(S)	.00	M	Infant	03Ju02La
LANEY, Thos.		30	M	Laborer	03Ju02La
MCKAY, John-G.		20	M	Laborer	03Ju02La
MARSHALL, Thos.		20	M	Laborer	03Ju02La
DAGLE, John		20	M	Laborer	03Ju02La
Pat		26	M	Laborer	03Ju02La
DEMPSEY, Margt.		25	F	None	03Ju02La
GORMAN, Owen		30	M	Laborer	03Ju02La
GILLISPIE, Pat		20	M	Laborer	03Ju02La
BARRY, Red.		20	M	Laborer	03Ju02La
MCDERMOT, James		30	M	Laborer	03Ju02La
BARNES, Joseph		40	M	Laborer	03Ju02La
HUGHIE, Jane		23	F	None	03Ju02La
RAWE, Robt.		50	M	Laborer	03Ju02La
MURRAY, Mary		60	F	None	03Ju02La
Mary		20	F	None	03Ju02La
WALSH, John		23	M	Laborer	03Ju02La
Margt.		20	F	None	03Ju02La
DUNN, Thos.		25	M	Laborer	03Ju02La
Maria		20	F	None	03Ju02La
MCCOMBE, John		20	M	Laborer	03Ju02La
Ellen		19	F	None	03Ju02La
LOYD, Cath.		19	F	None	03Ju02La
BARRY, Maria		18	F	None	03Ju02La
BURNS, Maria		21	F	None	03Ju02La
ASTERNE, James		48	M	Laborer	03Ju02La
U	(W)	38	F	Wife	03Ju02La
Margaret	(D)	19	F	None	03Ju02La
RAINY, Cathe.		19	F	None	03Ju02La
KEEFE, James		24	M	Farmer	03Ju02La
Eliza		17	F	None	03Ju02La
BARRY, John		40	M	Farmer	03Ju02La
U	(W)	38	F	None	03Ju02La
John	(S)	09	M	Child	03Ju02La
James	(S)	07	M	Child	03Ju02La
Mary	(D)	05	F	Child	03Ju02La
MCCARTHY, Jane		25	F	None	03Ju02La
OCALLAGHAN, Dennis		48	M	Laborer	03Ju02La
U	(W)	44	F	Wife	03Ju02La
Honora	(D)	20	F	None	03Ju02La
William	(S)	00	M	Child	03Ju02La
SULLIVAN, U-Mrs.		54	F	None	03Ju02La
Julia	(D)	11	F	Child	03Ju02La
DESMOND, James		30	M	Laborer	03Ju02La
U	(W)	25	F	Wife	03Ju02La
Ellen		24	F	None	03Ju02La
HALLORAN, Ellen		24	F	None	03Ju02La
CALLAGHAN, William		24	M	Laborer	03Ju02La
HARKNELL, Ellen		24	F	None	03Ju02La
JUSTICE, Bolton		26	M	Laborer	03Ju02La
KELLY, Pat.		23	M	Laborer	03Ju02La
KANDERSON, Pat		28	M	Laborer	03Ju02La
SMITH, Mary-N.		24	F	None	03Ju02La
ENNIS, Dennis		30	M	Laborer	03Ju02La
CALLAGHAN, James		37	M	Laborer	03Ju02La
U	(W)	30	F	Wife	03Ju02La
U	(D)	01	F	Child	03Ju02La
Mary	(D)	10	F	Child	03Ju02La
Kate	(D)	08	F	Child	03Ju02La
Joseph	(S)	06	M	Child	03Ju02La
Hanna	(D)	04	F	Child	03Ju02La
MITCHELL, Martin		25	M	Farmer	03Ju02La
U	(W)	29	F	None	03Ju02La
Mary		25	F	None	03Ju02La
LANNON, Ann		26	F	None	03Ju02La
KILLEN, Honora		24	F	None	03Ju02La
FORD, Peter		24	M	Laborer	03Ju02La
CLARK, Pat.		20	M	Laborer	03Ju02La
HUGHES, Danl.		18	M	Laborer	03Ju02La
CAFFREY, Bryan		25	M	Laborer	03Ju02La
HACKS, Robt.		25	M	Laborer	03Ju02La
U	(W)	21	F	None	03Ju02La
HOOKS, John		17	M	Laborer	03Ju02La
GILLIGAN, John		22	M	Laborer	03Ju02La
U	(W)	21	F	Wife	03Ju02La
GANLEY, Martin		21	M	Laborer	03Ju02La
Bridget		17	F	None	03Ju02La
SHAKEY, Barth.		28	M	Laborer	03Ju02La
GRIMES, John		36	M	Laborer	03Ju02La
Joseph		40	M	Laborer	03Ju02La
MCSHEA, James		61	M	Laborer	03Ju02La
U	(W)	56	F	Wife	03Ju02La
Cate	(D)	17	F	None	03Ju02La
Michel	(S)	18	M	Laborer	03Ju02La
BRASSIN, Michl.		22	M	Laborer	03Ju02La
Anna		20	F	None	03Ju02La
Margt.		56	F	None	03Ju02La
HANAFY, Betsey		19	F	None	03Ju02La
FLYNN, Betsey		18	F	None	03Ju02La
MOLONY, Mary		18	F	None	03Ju02La
WALSH, Charlath		22	F	None	03Ju02La
KELLY, Mary		16	F	None	03Ju02La
Eliz.		19	F	None	03Ju02La
LOYD, Rees		27	M	Laborer	03Ju02La
JONES, John		24	M	Laborer	03Ju02La
Hewsly		30	M	Laborer	03Ju02La
Mary		65	F	None	03Ju02La
Ed.		10	M	Child	03Ju02La
WILLIAMSON, Wm.		24	M	Farmer	03Ju02La
BURLINGTON, Wm.		27	M	Farmer	03Ju02La
Thomas		23	M	Farmer	03Ju02La
HUNTLIP, Wm.		21	M	Farmer	03Ju02La
MCCORMICK, Martin		30	M	Farmer	03Ju02La
Bryan		25	M	Farmer	03Ju02La
COOPER, Chas.		25	M	Farmer	03Ju02La
Corns.		40	M	Farmer	03Ju02La
MORRIS, Hugh		40	M	Farmer	03Ju02La
Wm.		40	M	Farmer	03Ju02La
Kate		25	F	None	03Ju02La
Ann		15	F	None	03Ju02La
CONNORS, John		35	M	Laborer	03Ju02La
KIRWIN, John		25	M	Laborer	03Ju02La
SMYTH, Isaac		37	M	Laborer	03Ju02La
Sarah		30	F	None	03Ju02La
Sarah		16	F	None	03Ju02La
CHARLWOOD, John		75	M	Laborer	03Ju02La
MOSS, Wm.		20	M	Laborer	03Ju02La
ADAMS, Wm.		27	M	Laborer	03Ju02La
NEWMAN, Pat.		49	M	Laborer	03Ju02La
Edwd.	(S)	25	M	Laborer	03Ju02La
Ed.	(S)	23	M	Laborer	03Ju02La
Kate	(D)	18	F	None	03Ju02La
Thomas	(S)	16	M	Laborer	03Ju02La
SHERLOCK, Richd.		22	M	Laborer	03Ju02La
U	(W)	28	F	Wife	03Ju02La
James		24	M	Laborer	03Ju02La
Michl.		22	M	Laborer	03Ju02La
CONDON, Pat.		26	M	Laborer	03Ju02La
U	(W)	23	F	Wife	03Ju02La
CRAVEL, Mary		30	F	None	03Ju02La
Margaret	(D)	14	F	None	03Ju02La
Cath.	(D)	11	F	Child	03Ju02La
KENWAN, Jane		24	F	None	03Ju02La
WALSH, John		28	M	Laborer	03Ju02La
BOWIE, Anne		30	F	None	03Ju02La
Mary	(D)	05	F	Child	03Ju02La
ROGARE, James		03	M	Child	03Ju02La
Margt.		.01	F	Infant	03Ju02La
HUTCHINSON, John		26	M	Laborer	03Ju02La
GRADY, Barth.		25	M	Laborer	03Ju02La
DARBY, Michl.		33	M	Laborer	03Ju02La
U	(W)	22	F	Wife	03Ju02La
John	(S)	02	M	Child	03Ju02La
WALSH, Ed.		70	M	Farmer	03Ju02La
William	(S)	25	M	Farmer	03Ju02La
Patrick	(S)	22	M	Farmer	03Ju02La
Richd.	(S)	13	M	Farmer	03Ju02La
Robt.	(S)	12	M	Farmer	03Ju02La

NAMES OF PASSENGERS		AGE	SEX	OCCUPATIONS	DATE PORT SHIP
WALSH, Michael	(S)	09	M	Child	03Ju02La
Mary	(D)	21	F	None	03Ju02La
Johanna	(D)	20	F	None	03Ju02La
HICKEY, Eliz.		25	F	None	03Ju02La
ONEILL, Mary		23	F	None	03Ju02La
HEFFERNAN, Arthur		18	M	Farmer	03Ju02La
Mary		22	F	None	03Ju02La
HAWE, Pat		23	M	Farmer	03Ju02La
Mary		25	F	None	03Ju02La
HICKY, Mary		25	F	None	03Ju02La
HAGERTY, James		60	M	Farmer	03Ju02La
James	(S)	17	M	Farmer	03Ju02La
Anne	(D)	17	F	None	03Ju02La
Napier	(S)	15	M	Farmer	03Ju02La
GALLAGHER, Jas.		05	M	Child	03Ju02La
FAHANY, Jas.		20	M	Laborer	03Ju02La
Cath.		19	F	None	03Ju02La
STEVENSON, David		22	M	Laborer	03Ju02La
William		19	M	Laborer	03Ju02La
DENNISON, Ed.		18	M	Laborer	03Ju02La
BIRMINGHAM, Rd.		16	M	Laborer	03Ju02La
LITTLOR, John		44	M	Laborer	03Ju02La
FRYER, Robt.		32	M	Laborer	03Ju02La
BIRCH, Richd.		23	M	Laborer	03Ju02La
KEANE, Michael		30	M	Laborer	03Ju02La
BARRETT, Simon		35	M	Laborer	03Ju02La
CROWLY, Pat.		29	M	Laborer	03Ju02La
FURLONG, John		19	M	Laborer	03Ju02La
GANNON, Pat.		18	M	Laborer	03Ju02La
MINNAHAN, Michael		20	M	Laborer	03Ju02La
Johanna		18	F	None	03Ju02La
DUNLANG, Rose		13	F	None	03Ju02La
Ann		11	F	Child	03Ju02La
REILLY, Thos.		45	M	Laborer	03Ju02La
U	(W)	40	F	Wife	03Ju02La
Thos.	(S)	21	M	Laborer	03Ju02La
Peter	(S)	18	M	Laborer	03Ju02La
FARRELL, Michael		25	M	Laborer	03Ju02La
Mary	(W)	22	F	None	03Ju02La
U	(D)	.01	F	Infant	03Ju02La
MURRAY, Pat.		28	M	Laborer	03Ju02La
Bridget		23	F	None	03Ju02La
U	(W)	23	F	Wife	03Ju02La
U	(S)	.01	M	Infant	03Ju02La
CAFFRY, Hugh		24	M	Laborer	03Ju02La

JUNO 03 JUNE 1847

From Liverpool

NAMES OF PASSENGERS		AGE	SEX	OCCUPATIONS	DATE PORT SHIP
MIDDLETON, J.		10	M	Child	03Ju02Lb
OCALLAGAN, D.		30	M	Laborer	03Ju02Lb
MURPHY, My.		24	F	None	03Ju02Lb
BANKS, My.		21	F	None	03Ju02Lb
GURNY, My.		60	F	None	03Ju02Lb
Edwd.	(S)	23	M	Laborer	03Ju02Lb
May	(D)	21	F	None	03Ju02Lb
CAHILL, U		26	M	Laborer	03Ju02Lb
GRIFFEN, Ellen		17	F	None	03Ju02Lb
CROMER, J.		33	M	Laborer	03Ju02Lb
BUCKLEY, J.		27	M	Laborer	03Ju02Lb
Ellen		18	F	None	03Ju02Lb
Hanna		16	F	None	03Ju02Lb
MURPHY, Mrgt.		19	F	None	03Ju02Lb
LEAHY, U		30	M	Laborer	03Ju02Lb
MURPHY, U		11	M	Child	03Ju02Lb
John		09	M	Child	03Ju02Lb
MCCARTY, D.		36	M	Laborer	03Ju02Lb
Slly.		25	U	Laborer	03Ju02Lb
MCCARTY, Mich.	(S)	04	M	Child	03Ju02Lb
James	(S)	02	M	Child	03Ju02Lb
G.		24	M	Child	03Ju02Lb
U	(W)	25	F	None	03Ju02Lb
SHAN, E.		23	M	Laborer	03Ju02Lb
FLYNN, My.		24	F	None	03Ju02Lb
WALL, R.		27	M	Laborer	03Ju02Lb
WALSH, P.		52	M	Laborer	03Ju02Lb
Edwd.	(S)	21	M	Laborer	03Ju02Lb
Rachel	(D)	19	F	None	03Ju02Lb
Ellen	(D)	22	F	None	03Ju02Lb
My.	(D)	16	F	None	03Ju02Lb
Cath.	(D)	13	F	None	03Ju02Lb
Hana	(D)	22	F	None	03Ju02Lb
Bgt.	(D)	15	F	None	03Ju02Lb
Mgt.	(D)	12	F	None	03Ju02Lb
Pat.	(S)	04	M	Child	03Ju02Lb
My.	(W)	50	F	None	03Ju02Lb
DOWNES, T.		22	M	Laborer	03Ju02Lb
GLEESON, P.		27	M	Laborer	03Ju02Lb
CALLAGHAN, J.		29	M	Laborer	03Ju02Lb
LANE, T.		23	M	Laborer	03Ju02Lb
T.		25	M	Laborer	03Ju02Lb
James		20	M	Laborer	03Ju02Lb
Mgt.		30	F	None	03Ju02Lb
John		10	M	Child	03Ju02Lb
Mich.		06	M	Child	03Ju02Lb
Ellen		03	F	Child	03Ju02Lb
TOWNES, T.		24	M	Laborer	03Ju02Lb
FINEGAN, M.		21	M	Laborer	03Ju02Lb
SULLIVAN, J.		24	M	Laborer	03Ju02Lb
FINEGAN, T.		40	M	Laborer	03Ju02Lb
DESMOND, P.		24	M	Laborer	03Ju02Lb
RUSETER, U		20	M	Laborer	03Ju02Lb
Joanna		18	F	None	03Ju02Lb
MUNSTER, J.		30	M	Laborer	03Ju02Lb
DALY, A.		34	M	Laborer	03Ju02Lb
Bgt.		23	F	None	03Ju02Lb
COFFIN, M.		26	M	Laborer	03Ju02Lb
HOLLAND, M.		21	M	Laborer	03Ju02Lb
John		09	M	Child	03Ju02Lb
Ellen		19	F	None	03Ju02Lb
MCCARTY, Eugene		21	U	None	03Ju02Lb
FURLONG, C.		20	M	Laborer	03Ju02Lb
HILL, J.		23	M	Laborer	03Ju02Lb
LOOIST, J.		20	M	Laborer	03Ju02Lb
CONNERS, My.		18	F	None	03Ju02Lb
BRYAN, M.		24	M	Laborer	03Ju02Lb
LYNCH, J.		20	M	Laborer	03Ju02Lb
SWEENEY, D.		30	M	Laborer	03Ju02Lb
CLERY, P.		40	M	Laborer	03Ju02Lb
My.	(W)	40	F	None	03Ju02Lb
James	(S)	05	M	Child	03Ju02Lb
DONOHUE, J.		26	M	Laborer	03Ju02Lb
Mich.		23	M	Laborer	03Ju02Lb
SCANILL, T.		31	M	Laborer	03Ju02Lb
CANAY, J.		28	M	Laborer	03Ju02Lb
Bess		19	F	None	03Ju02Lb
Pat		12	M	Laborer	03Ju02Lb
John		08	M	Child	03Ju02Lb
Jeremiah		20	M	Laborer	03Ju02Lb
DONOHUE, D.		23	M	Laborer	03Ju02Lb
LISLER, D.		35	M	Laborer	03Ju02Lb
COLLINS, My.		20	F	None	03Ju02Lb
SHEA, My.		19	F	None	03Ju02Lb
LISH, D.		18	M	Laborer	03Ju02Lb
HOWARD, T.		21	M	Laborer	03Ju02Lb
LANEYM, My.		30	F	None	03Ju02Lb
HANLY, Mgt.		30	F	None	03Ju02Lb
REGON, J.		26	M	Laborer	03Ju02Lb
HEALY, J.		26	M	Laborer	03Ju02Lb
My.		28	F	None	03Ju02Lb
COLLINS, M.		30	M	Laborer	03Ju02Lb
KILLY, T.		29	M	Laborer	03Ju02Lb
ROCK, J.		40	M	Laborer	03Ju02Lb

NAMES OF PASSENGERS		AGE	SEX	OCCUPATIONS	DATE PORT SHIP	NAMES OF PASSENGERS		AGE	SEX	OCCUPATIONS	DATE PORT SHIP
CALLAGHAN, J.		22	M	Laborer	03Ju02Lb	BROWN, W.		23	M	Laborer	03Ju02Lb
PALMER, Mary		13	F	None	03Ju02Lb	KENNEDY, T.		24	M	Laborer	03Ju02Lb
SULLIVAN, C.		28	M	Laborer	03Ju02Lb	DERDY, P.		22	M	Laborer	03Ju02Lb
Ellen		19	F	None	03Ju02Lb	DONOVAN, Mary		24	F	None	03Ju02Lb
Julia		19	F	None	03Ju02Lb	WALSH, T.		50	M	Laborer	03Ju02Lb
C.	(D)	04	F	Child	03Ju02Lb	My.	(W)	50	F	None	03Ju02Lb
D.		28	M	Laborer	03Ju02Lb	My.	(D)	25	F	None	03Ju02Lb
FARRY, Elzt.		50	F	None	03Ju02Lb	Betty	(D)	25	F	None	03Ju02Lb
Pat		40	M	Laborer	03Ju02Lb	Cath.	(D)	20	F	None	03Ju02Lb
SULLIVAN, M.		69	M	Laborer	03Ju02Lb	Path.	(S)	16	M	Laborer	03Ju02Lb
Denis	(S)	20	M	Laborer	03Ju02Lb	Thos.	(S)	14	M	Laborer	03Ju02Lb
John	(S)	20	M	Laborer	03Ju02Lb	R.		30	M	Laborer	03Ju02Lb
WALSH, J.		24	M	Laborer	03Ju02Lb	MEANY, D.		27	M	Laborer	03Ju02Lb
HAMILTON, J.		30	M	Laborer	03Ju02Lb	KITCHEN, J.		30	M	Laborer	03Ju02Lb
John		30	M	Laborer	03Ju02Lb	MADDEN, Ellen		21	F	None	03Ju02Lb
Ellen		01	F	Child	03Ju02Lb	TOOY, A.		23	M	Laborer	03Ju02Lb
CUSHMAN, J.		30	M	Laborer	03Ju02Lb	CLOUN, J.		23	M	Laborer	03Ju02Lb
CROWLY, J.		20	M	Laborer	03Ju02Lb	CONNELL, W.		20	M	Laborer	03Ju02Lb
BARRY, W.		24	M	Laborer	03Ju02Lb	TOHY, J.		46	M	Laborer	03Ju02Lb
Thos.		20	M	Laborer	03Ju02Lb	May	(W)	40	F	None	03Ju02Lb
Bess		20	F	None	03Ju02Lb	James	(S)	20	M	Laborer	03Ju02Lb
HENNSEY, O.		24	M	Laborer	03Ju02Lb	My.	(D)	12	F	None	03Ju02Lb
MURPHY, T.		22	M	Laborer	03Ju02Lb	Peggy	(D)	07	F	Child	03Ju02Lb
WALSH, J.		23	M	Laborer	03Ju02Lb	My.	(D)	05	F	Child	03Ju02Lb
COLLINS, J.		21	M	Laborer	03Ju02Lb	Mat.	(S)	02	M	Child	03Ju02Lb
CONDEN, J.		36	M	Laborer	03Ju02Lb	DUNN, A.		40	M	Laborer	03Ju02Lb
OLEARY, D.		24	M	Laborer	03Ju02Lb	Ellen	(W)	35	F	None	03Ju02Lb
MOANS, Ellen		26	F	None	03Ju02Lb	Pat	(S)	05	M	Child	03Ju02Lb
SHEEHAN, Ja.		27	M	Laborer	03Ju02Lb	Thos.	(S)	01	M	Child	03Ju02Lb
ROCHE, F.		35	M	Laborer	03Ju02Lb	MCCARTY, My.		29	F	None	03Ju02Lb
Ellen		26	F	None	03Ju02Lb	HOLLAND, D.		28	M	Laborer	03Ju02Lb
NAGLE, R.		29	M	Laborer	03Ju02Lb	MCGRATH, J.		44	M	Laborer	03Ju02Lb
OLARRY, D.		29	M	Laborer	03Ju02Lb	COONEY, J.		40	M	Laborer	03Ju02Lb
DERRY, W.		27	M	Laborer	03Ju02Lb	DESNAN, My.		18	F	None	03Ju02Lb
WHITE, E.		30	M	Laborer	03Ju02Lb	MURPHY, D.		26	M	Laborer	03Ju02Lb
MCDONELL, D.		34	M	Laborer	03Ju02Lb	Cath.		22	F	None	03Ju02Lb
REEDY, J.		24	M	Laborer	03Ju02Lb	SHEA, Hana		21	F	None	03Ju02Lb
CROWLY, T.		28	M	Laborer	03Ju02Lb	CROWE, J.		23	M	Laborer	03Ju02Lb
WHITE, Cath.		20	F	None	03Ju02Lb	MURPHY, P.		50	M	Laborer	03Ju02Lb
CANIFF, Ellen		22	F	None	03Ju02Lb	Ellen	(W)	48	F	None	03Ju02Lb
CONAN, J.		17	M	None	03Ju02Lb	MCGUIN, T.		17	M	Laborer	03Ju02Lb
Hana		26	F	None	03Ju02Lb	Danl.		08	M	Child	03Ju02Lb
Henry		14	M	Laborer	03Ju02Lb	Connor		04	M	Child	03Ju02Lb
DOWNY, B.		22	M	Laborer	03Ju02Lb	Kelly		02	M	Child	03Ju02Lb
RISNY, B.		56	M	Laborer	03Ju02Lb	Denis		48	M	Laborer	03Ju02Lb
Edwd.	(S)	17	M	Laborer	03Ju02Lb	GOWEN, P.		35	M	Laborer	03Ju02Lb
Mgt.	(D)	19	F	None	03Ju02Lb	U	(W)	27	F	None	03Ju02Lb
FORDE, J.		50	M	Laborer	03Ju02Lb	James	(S)	13	M	Laborer	03Ju02Lb
CROWLY, J.		20	M	Laborer	03Ju02Lb	Mich.	(S)	11	M	Child	03Ju02Lb
Julia	(W)	28	F	None	03Ju02Lb	My.	(D)	09	F	Child	03Ju02Lb
John	(S)	01	M	Child	03Ju02Lb	Cath.	(D)	07	F	Child	03Ju02Lb
CRANE, W.		29	M	Laborer	03Ju02Lb	D.	(D)	05	F	Child	03Ju02Lb
HARRINGTON, J.		29	M	Laborer	03Ju02Lb	John	(S)	02	M	Child	03Ju02Lb
SHEA, D.		29	M	Laborer	03Ju02Lb	WALSH, My.		18	F	None	03Ju02Lb
My.		25	F	None	03Ju02Lb	DOHERTY, B.		15	M	Laborer	03Ju02Lb
DELY, C.		39	M	Laborer	03Ju02Lb	Robt.		12	F	None	03Ju02Lb
Ann	(D)	13	F	None	03Ju02Lb	BAKER, My.		22	F	None	03Ju02Lb
Ann	(D)	11	F	Child	03Ju02Lb	John		18	M	Laborer	03Ju02Lb
My.	(D)	09	F	Child	03Ju02Lb	OBRIEN, D.		19	M	Laborer	03Ju02Lb
Joan	(W)	36	F	None	03Ju02Lb	BRADY, Ja.		26	M	Laborer	03Ju02Lb
Chas.	(S)	01	M	Child	03Ju02Lb	MIDDLETON, J.		70	M	Laborer	03Ju02Lb
DISCOLL, B.		29	M	Laborer	03Ju02Lb	My.	(W)	60	F	None	03Ju02Lb
HALLERY, M.		57	M	Laborer	03Ju02Lb	Richd.	(S)	20	M	Laborer	03Ju02Lb
John	(S)	30	M	Laborer	03Ju02Lb	LEAHY, R.		26	M	Laborer	03Ju02Lb
Thos.	(S)	28	M	Laborer	03Ju02Lb	GRIFFIN, M.		28	M	Laborer	03Ju02Lb
G.	(S)	24	M	Laborer	03Ju02Lb	KANE, Bgt.		20	F	None	03Ju02Lb
Mich.	(S)	16	M	Laborer	03Ju02Lb	LUTON, Elzt.		40	F	None	03Ju02Lb
Jane	(D)	14	F	None	03Ju02Lb	John	(S)	14	M	None	03Ju02Lb
Ellen	(D)	18	F	None	03Ju02Lb	LEAHY, Ellen		18	F	None	03Ju02Lb
LANE, Elyn.		22	F	None	03Ju02Lb	MAHY, Ellen		16	F	None	03Ju02Lb
SULLIVAN, T.		45	M	Laborer	03Ju02Lb	SHEHAN, T.		20	M	Laborer	03Ju02Lb
Mgt.	(W)	45	F	None	03Ju02Lb	MCKOWN, W.		20	M	Laborer	03Ju02Lb
Thos.	(S)	16	M	None	03Ju02Lb	DOWNE, Ellen		21	F	None	03Ju02Lb
My.	(D)	11	F	None	03Ju02Lb	MURPHY, J.		35	M	Laborer	03Ju02Lb
Joanna	(D)	09	F	Child	03Ju02Lb	DONELY, T.		23	M	Laborer	03Ju02Lb

NAMES OF PASSENGERS		AGE	SEX	OCCUPATIONS	DATE PORT SHIP
HEYES, B.		34	M	Laborer	03Ju02Lb
Mgt.	(D)	09	F	Child	03Ju02Lb
KING, J.		20	M	Laborer	03Ju02Lb
Mich.		18	M	Laborer	03Ju02Lb
WOODS, T.		28	M	Laborer	03Ju02Lb
U	(D)	05	F	Child	03Ju02Lb

HYNDERFORD 04 JUNE 1847

From Glasgow

NAMES OF PASSENGERS		AGE	SEX	OCCUPATIONS	DATE PORT SHIP
ABERCROMBIE, David		31	M	Farmer	04Ju04KI
Christine	(W)	30	F	None	04Ju04KI
David	(S)	06	M	Child	04Ju04KI
John	(S)	04	M	Child	04Ju04KI
William	(S)	03	M	Child	04Ju04KI
SCOTT, Jas.		26	M	Farmer	04Ju04KI
Margaret	(W)	24	F	None	04Ju04KI
Rebecca	(D)	03	F	Child	04Ju04KI
Martha	(D)	.10	F	Infant	04Ju04KI
ROAM, Hugh		19	M	Laborer	04Ju04KI
GALLOHAN, J.		19	M	Laborer	04Ju04KI
FANEN, C.		25	M	Laborer	04Ju04KI
QUIGLY, W.		20	M	Laborer	04Ju04KI
Grace		18	F	None	04Ju04KI
SMITH, J.		16	M	Laborer	04Ju04KI
BEATIE, Wm.		31	M	Farmer	04Ju04KI
Cath.	(W)	25	F	None	04Ju04KI
Daniel	(S)	06	M	Child	04Ju04KI
Elizabeth	(D)	01	F	Child	04Ju04KI
Alexander	(S)	04	M	Child	04Ju04KI
MORRISON, Wm.		16	M	Laborer	04Ju04KI
MULLVY, Ann		20	F	None	04Ju04KI
DOUGHERTY, O.		24	M	Laborer	04Ju04KI
Andrew		30	M	Laborer	04Ju04KI
MCGONAGLE, P.		30	M	Laborer	04Ju04KI
DOUGHERTY, Mary		26	F	None	04Ju04KI
GALLAGHER, Chas.		56	M	Farmer	04Ju04KI
Mary	(W)	50	F	None	04Ju04KI
Biddy	(D)	20	F	None	04Ju04KI
Betty	(D)	17	F	None	04Ju04KI
Mary	(D)	12	F	None	04Ju04KI
DONERTY, Peggy		20	F	None	04Ju04KI
Mary		24	F	None	04Ju04KI
Mary		08	F	Child	04Ju04KI
Hannah		03	F	Child	04Ju04KI
DOUGHERTY, Phil.		20	M	Laborer	04Ju04KI
MCCARTY, Jane		16	F	None	04Ju04KI
Betty		20	F	None	04Ju04KI
James		13	M	None	04Ju04KI
Elizabeth		11	F	Child	04Ju04KI
Rosie		05	F	Child	04Ju04KI
Nancy		02	F	Child	04Ju04KI
MCMICHEL, C.		25	M	Laborer	04Ju04KI
Rose-Ann		24	F	None	04Ju04KI
FITZPATRICK, P.		64	M	Farmer	04Ju04KI
Biddy	(D)	18	F	None	04Ju04KI
Theresa	(D)	15	F	None	04Ju04KI
MCGARDY, John		57	M	Farmer	04Ju04KI
Letty	(W)	55	F	None	04Ju04KI
Thos.	(S)	19	M	Farmer	04Ju04KI
Sally	(D)	20	F	None	04Ju04KI
Mary	(D)	18	F	None	04Ju04KI
Betty	(D)	12	F	None	04Ju04KI
Letty	(D)	08	F	Child	04Ju04KI
Esther	(D)	03	F	Child	04Ju04KI
GARDNER, Jane		28	F	None	04Ju04KI
MCMILLEN, Mary		20	F	None	04Ju04KI
Ann		18	F	None	04Ju04KI
MCIVER, Simon		53	M	Farmer	04Ju04KI
Mary	(W)	52	F	None	04Ju04KI
Simon	(S)	23	M	Farmer	04Ju04KI
Peggy	(D)	24	F	None	04Ju04KI
Oliver	(S)	21	M	Farmer	04Ju04KI
Eleanor	(D)	17	F	None	04Ju04KI
John	(S)	13	M	None	04Ju04KI
CHRISTIE, E.		26	M	Laborer	04Ju04KI
MITCHELL, J.		20	M	Laborer	04Ju04KI
MORRISON, W.		30	M	Laborer	04Ju04KI
Catharine	(W)	25	F	None	04Ju04KI
John	(S)	05	M	Child	04Ju04KI
GERMAN, M.		25	M	Farmer	04Ju04KI
BARNETT, N.		40	M	Farmer	04Ju04KI
Libby	(W)	30	F	None	04Ju04KI
Eliza	(D)	11	F	Child	04Ju04KI
Matilda	(D)	09	F	Child	04Ju04KI
William	(S)	07	M	Child	04Ju04KI
Robert	(S)	07	M	Child	04Ju04KI
Catharine	(D)	04	F	Child	04Ju04KI
Onaly	(D)	02	F	Child	04Ju04KI
Margaret	(D)	15	F	None	04Ju04KI
WILSON, John		38	M	Farmer	04Ju04KI
Mary	(W)	30	F	None	04Ju04KI
Joseph	(S)	06	M	Child	04Ju04KI
Matilda	(D)	.06	F	Infant	04Ju04KI
DURY, Thos.		60	M	Farmer	04Ju04KI
Sally	(D)	30	F	None	04Ju04KI
Rebecca	(D)	20	F	None	04Ju04KI
Nelly	(D)	14	F	None	04Ju04KI
KELLY, Owen		20	M	Laborer	04Ju04KI
DOUGHERTY, B.		35	M	Laborer	04Ju04KI
MCLOUGHLIN, Margt.		20	F	None	04Ju04KI
DOUGHERTY, Peggy		20	F	None	04Ju04KI
GILFELLEN, Ann		24	F	None	04Ju04KI
REMOGAN, F.		24	M	Laborer	04Ju04KI
Patk.		20	M	Laborer	04Ju04KI
FULLER, A.		34	M	Laborer	04Ju04KI
MCDONALD, A.		55	M	Farmer	04Ju04KI
Cath.	(W)	40	F	None	04Ju04KI
Archibald	(S)	17	M	Farmer	04Ju04KI
Duncan	(S)	13	M	None	04Ju04KI
Donald	(S)	11	M	Child	04Ju04KI
Catharine	(D)	09	F	Child	04Ju04KI
Alexander	(S)	07	M	Child	04Ju04KI
Nancy	(D)	05	F	Child	04Ju04KI
John	(S)	03	M	Child	04Ju04KI
Niel	(S)	.09	M	Infant	04Ju04KI
GAILHAIRTS, Peggy		24	F	None	04Ju04KI
WRIGHT, Jas.		45	M	Mechanic	04Ju04KI
Elizabeth	(W)	46	F	None	04Ju04KI
James	(S)	20	M	Mechanic	04Ju04KI
PLATT, Mary		37	F	None	04Ju04KI
MILLER, Cath.M.		16	F	None	04Ju04KI
MCDEVITT, J.		38	M	Laborer	04Ju04KI
YONNIE, Geo.		20	M	Farmer	04Ju04KI
Jas.		29	M	Farmer	04Ju04KI
BRANDESS, A.		24	M	Farmer	04Ju04KI
CARTHY, Ellen		60	F	None	04Ju04KI
MAVERS, A.		36	M	Farmer	04Ju04KI
BAILIE, Jno.		13	M	None	04Ju04KI
MILNE, Jno.		31	M	Farmer	04Ju04KI
Christiana		25	F	None	04Ju04KI
Janet		24	F	None	04Ju04KI
HUGH, Wm.		50	M	Farmer	04Ju04KI
Wm.	(S)	26	M	Farmer	04Ju04KI
PENDER, Thos.		26	M	Farmer	04Ju04KI
SMITH, D.		24	M	Farmer	04Ju04KI
PATERSON, Jos.		46	M	Farmer	04Ju04KI
Elizabeth	(W)	37	F	None	04Ju04KI
Christiana	(D)	06	F	Child	04Ju04KI
Elizabeth	(D)	12	F	None	04Ju04KI
John	(S)	04	M	Child	04Ju04KI
William	(S)	02	M	Child	04Ju04KI
DUNN, Jas.		30	M	Laborer	04Ju04KI

569

NAMES OF PASSENGERS		AGE	SEX	OCCUPATIONS	DATE PORT SHIP	NAMES OF PASSENGERS		AGE	SEX	OCCUPATIONS	DATE PORT SHIP
HUTCHINSON, Margaret		25	F	None	04Ju04KI	MULLOINE, John	(S)	13	M	None	04Ju02Qd
SMITH, Janet		30	F	None	04Ju04KI	Michael	(S)	12	M	None	04Ju02Qd
Isabella		34	F	None	04Ju04KI	Connor	(S)	07	M	Child	04Ju02Qd
GEMMELL, Jno.		20	M	Laborer	04Ju04KI	Biddy	(D)	09	F	Child	04Ju02Qd
BRUCE, Wm.		50	M	Farmer	04Ju04KI	Julia	(D)	20	F	None	04Ju02Qd
Elizabeth	(W)	30	F	None	04Ju04KI	EDWARDS, Biddy		21	F	None	04Ju02Qd
Ann	(D)	16	F	None	04Ju04KI	Ed.		19	M	Laborer	04Ju02Qd
John	(S)	14	M	None	04Ju04KI	MCGARN, William		20	M	Laborer	04Ju02Qd
Mary	(D)	14	F	None	04Ju04KI	Michael		21	M	Laborer	04Ju02Qd
Jane	(D)	07	F	Child	04Ju04KI	DONGAN, Anna		20	F	None	04Ju02Qd
Thomas	(S)	04	M	Child	04Ju04KI	MCCABE, Margt.		18	F	None	04Ju02Qd
Agnes	(D)	04	F	Child	04Ju04KI	SMITH, Bridget		20	F	None	04Ju02Qd
CAMPBELL, Thos.		26	M	Farmer	04Ju04KI	HAYES, Michael		40	M	Laborer	04Ju02Qd
ANDERSON, Ann		20	F	None	04Ju04KI	COLE, James		24	M	Laborer	04Ju02Qd
WATSON, A.		30	M	Farmer	04Ju04KI	BEATY, Hugh		35	M	Laborer	04Ju02Qd
Elizabeth	(W)	55	F	None	04Ju04KI	DOWD, Francis		21	M	Laborer	04Ju02Qd
Isabella	(T)	27	F	None	04Ju04KI	Hannah		20	F	None	04Ju02Qd
Matilda	(T)	27	F	None	04Ju04KI	MCCAVANAH, Eliza		45	F	None	04Ju02Qd
HENDERSON, Matilda		24	F	None	04Ju04KI	MCDERMOT, Ann		17	F	None	04Ju02Qd
MIDLETON, Jos.		24	M	Laborer	04Ju04KI	RORK, Roger		20	M	Laborer	04Ju02Qd
DAVIS, Jas.		24	M	Laborer	04Ju04KI	KELLEY, Julia		20	F	None	04Ju02Qd
MCCARTEY, Robt.		50	M	Farmer	04Ju04KI	ROGERS, Henry		12	M	None	04Ju02Qd
Rose	(W)	45	F	None	04Ju04KI	MULLAR, Peter		25	M	Laborer	04Ju02Qd
Robert	(S)	25	M	Farmer	04Ju04KI	U	(W)	20	F	None	04Ju02Qd
Mary	(D)	23	F	None	04Ju04KI	John	(S)	.00	M	Infant	04Ju02Qd
MORTON, Elizabeth		03	F	Child	04Ju04KI	DELANY, Bridget		25	F	None	04Ju02Qd
George		02	M	Child	04Ju04KI	HINCHE, Rose		33	F	None	04Ju02Qd
James		01	M	Child	04Ju04KI	Kitty	(D)	11	F	None	04Ju02Qd
JENKINS, Elizabeth		16	F	None	04Ju04KI	Eliza	(D)	09	F	Child	04Ju02Qd
MCALLISTER, John		30	M	Laborer	04Ju04KI	Sarah	(D)	07	F	Child	04Ju02Qd
DARCY, Wm.		21	M	Farmer	04Ju04KI	Ellen	(D)	04	F	Child	04Ju02Qd
						DEMPSEY, Julia		30	F	None	04Ju02Qd
						CURNES, Danl.		17	M	Laborer	04Ju02Qd
						SANDS, Sarah		25	F	None	04Ju02Qd
						HANDY, Cathe.		17	F	None	04Ju02Qd
						KENNEDY, John		19	M	Laborer	04Ju02Qd
HELENA 04 JUNE 1847						NEALE, Bryan		50	M	Laborer	04Ju02Qd
						OATES, Cathe.		40	F	None	04Ju02Qd
From Liverpool						Cathe.	(D)	07	F	Child	04Ju02Qd
						Michael	(S)	.00	M	Infant	04Ju02Qd
						HENIGAN, William		20	M	Laborer	04Ju02Qd
						CLYNES, Pat		20	M	Laborer	04Ju02Qd
DAISY, Patrick		30	M	Laborer	04Ju02Qd	LYNAN, Pat		38	M	Laborer	04Ju02Qd
U	(W)	30	F	None	04Ju02Qd	U	(W)	24	F	None	04Ju02Qd
Emma	(D)	.00	F	Infant	04Ju02Qd	Thos.	(S)	04	M	Child	04Ju02Qd
DAWD, James		24	M	Laborer	04Ju02Qd	Mary	(D)	02	F	Child	04Ju02Qd
BIGLANDS, Owen		28	M	Laborer	04Ju02Qd	DONOHUE, Margt.		20	F	None	04Ju02Qd
DAWD, Sarah		50	F	None	04Ju02Qd	LYNAN, Margt.		50	F	None	04Ju02Qd
Teddy	(S)	17	M	Laborer	04Ju02Qd	MCCARTHY, Pat		30	M	Laborer	04Ju02Qd
QUINN, U-Mrs.		30	F	None	04Ju02Qd	DAVIS, Stephen		20	M	Laborer	04Ju02Qd
Terence	(S)	09	M	Child	04Ju02Qd	BRIGHT, Patrick		24	M	Laborer	04Ju02Qd
KEEFE, Patrick		20	M	Laborer	04Ju02Qd	MCLAUGHLIN, John		27	M	Laborer	04Ju02Qd
KNAWLAND, Biddy		19	F	None	04Ju02Qd	Thos.		24	M	Laborer	04Ju02Qd
KENNEDY, Mary		19	F	None	04Ju02Qd	MCNICHOLS, James		19	M	Laborer	04Ju02Qd
RICE, James		22	M	Laborer	04Ju02Qd	JORDAN, John		12	M	None	04Ju02Qd
GILL, Thos.		50	M	Laborer	04Ju02Qd	James		11	M	None	04Ju02Qd
Margt.	(D)	17	F	None	04Ju02Qd	MCNICHOLS, Bridget		10	F	None	04Ju02Qd
Mary	(D)	19	F	None	04Ju02Qd	LOLLY, Michael		48	M	Laborer	04Ju02Qd
Honor	(D)	19	F	None	04Ju02Qd	Mary	(D)	22	F	None	04Ju02Qd
CURRY, Mary		18	F	None	04Ju02Qd	Patrick	(S)	13	M	None	04Ju02Qd
BRENNAN, Cathe.		40	F	None	04Ju02Qd	Maria	(D)	12	F	None	04Ju02Qd
Ann	(D)	13	F	None	04Ju02Qd	John	(S)	06	M	Child	04Ju02Qd
TURNER, Henry		30	M	Laborer	04Ju02Qd	Michael	(S)	09	M	Child	04Ju02Qd
MCDANIEL, Thos.		30	M	Laborer	04Ju02Qd	Jane	(D)	02	F	Child	04Ju02Qd
Mary		21	F	None	04Ju02Qd	Stephen	(S)	.00	M	Infant	04Ju02Qd
LOFTUS, Bridget		15	F	None	04Ju02Qd	CONNOLLY, Mary		60	F	None	04Ju02Qd
James		12	M	None	04Ju02Qd	NEALE, James		30	M	Laborer	04Ju02Qd
DUFFY, John		24	M	Laborer	04Ju02Qd	Julia		25	F	None	04Ju02Qd
PATTERSON, David		25	M	Laborer	04Ju02Qd	Cathe.		24	F	None	04Ju02Qd
Mary		20	F	None	04Ju02Qd	Patrick		02	M	Child	04Ju02Qd
MULLOINE, James		50	M	Laborer	04Ju02Qd	James		.00	M	Infant	04Ju02Qd
Mary	(W)	45	F	None	04Ju02Qd	MCQUADE, Roger		50	M	Laborer	04Ju02Qd
James	(S)	20	M	Laborer	04Ju02Qd	Wm.	(S)	15	M	Laborer	04Ju02Qd
Jamsey		32	M	Laborer	04Ju02Qd	John	(S)	11	M	None	04Ju02Qd
Timathy	(S)	18	M	Laborer	04Ju02Qd	Rose	(D)	10	F	None	04Ju02Qd

NAMES OF PASSENGERS		AGE	SEX	OCCUPATIONS	DATE PORT SHIP
WALSH, John		29	M	Laborer	04Ju02Qd
U	(W)	24	F	None	04Ju02Qd
Michael	(S)	.00	M	Infant	04Ju02Qd
AHIRON, Mich.		25	M	Laborer	04Ju02Qd
MCGUIRCK, John		30	M	Laborer	04Ju02Qd
U	(W)	30	F	None	04Ju02Qd
Wm.	(S)	06	M	Child	04Ju02Qd
Patrick	(S)	.00	M	Infant	04Ju02Qd
CONNOLLY, Ed.		20	M	Laborer	04Ju02Qd
DOYLE, James		20	M	Laborer	04Ju02Qd
SCOLLY, Peter	O	27	M	Laborer	04Ju02Qd
U	(W)	24	F	None	04Ju02Qd
Thos.	(S)	03	M	Child	04Ju02Qd
MCCARTHY, James		30	M	Laborer	04Ju02Qd
John		25	M	Laborer	04Ju02Qd
ROWLAND, Thos.		21	M	Laborer	04Ju02Qd
SCANLAN, John		30	M	Laborer	04Ju02Qd
KILLY, Martin		35	M	Laborer	04Ju02Qd

AERIEL 04 JUNE 1847

From Kilrush

NAMES OF PASSENGERS		AGE	SEX	OCCUPATIONS	DATE PORT SHIP
KEAN, Francis		25	M	Farmer	04Ju60Lc
MUDIGAN, Patrick		23	M	Farmer	04Ju60Lc
DOWNES, John		25	M	Farmer	04Ju60Lc
Mary		20	F	None	04Ju60Lc
BANCK, Michael		16	M	Farmer	04Ju60Lc
DOWNES, Joseph		.00	M	Infant	04Ju60Lc
ODEA, John		20	M	Laborer	04Ju60Lc
LILLIS, John		45	M	Laborer	04Ju60Lc
Mary		40	F	None	04Ju60Lc
NEWGENT, Ellen		27	F	None	04Ju60Lc
Patt		25	M	Laborer	04Ju60Lc
LILLIS, Ann		18	F	None	04Ju60Lc
Patrick		20	M	Laborer	04Ju60Lc
Margt.		17	F	None	04Ju60Lc
Mary		15	F	None	04Ju60Lc
Bridget		19	F	None	04Ju60Lc
NEWGENT, John		02	M	Child	04Ju60Lc
SPLICY, James		40	M	Farmer	04Ju60Lc
Cathe.	(W)	37	F	None	04Ju60Lc
Simon	(S)	02	M	Child	04Ju60Lc
Bridget	(D)	.00	F	Infant	04Ju60Lc
SHIOLEY, John		50	M	Farmer	04Ju60Lc
Mary	(W)	50	F	None	04Ju60Lc
Bridget	(D)	30	F	None	04Ju60Lc
Martin	(S)	22	M	Farmer	04Ju60Lc
Ellen	(D)	23	F	None	04Ju60Lc
SHEALEY, Michael		14	M	Farmer	04Ju60Lc
NOONAN, Johana		23	F	None	04Ju60Lc
MICHAN, James		28	M	Farmer	04Ju60Lc
MAHANEY, Mary		25	F	None	04Ju60Lc
MANGAN, Cathe.		25	F	None	04Ju60Lc
CARIGAY, Martin		26	M	Farmer	04Ju60Lc
James		25	M	Farmer	04Ju60Lc
KEATING, Michael		30	M	Farmer	04Ju60Lc
Johanna		28	F	None	04Ju60Lc
HICKEY, Jim		24	M	Farmer	04Ju60Lc
KEANY, Michael		25	M	Farmer	04Ju60Lc
GANILY, Terence		19	M	Farmer	04Ju60Lc
Patt	(P)	48	M	Farmer	04Ju60Lc
Nancy	(T)	16	F	None	04Ju60Lc
KEAN, Pat		25	M	Farmer	04Ju60Lc
DEALY, Michael		30	M	Laborer	04Ju60Lc
KEAN, Martin		28	M	Laborer	04Ju60Lc
BROWN, John		27	M	Laborer	04Ju60Lc
Ed.		28	M	Laborer	04Ju60Lc
REILEY, Hannah		28	F	None	04Ju60Lc

NAMES OF PASSENGERS		AGE	SEX	OCCUPATIONS	DATE PORT SHIP
SHAUGHNESSEY, James		27	M	Laborer	04Ju60Lc
CULLIGAN, Mary		23	F	None	04Ju60Lc
HASERTT, Hanaur		27	M	Laborer	04Ju60Lc
HOBIHAN, Darby		25	M	Laborer	04Ju60Lc
Anna		22	F	None	04Ju60Lc
CONNORS, Thready		24	M	Laborer	04Ju60Lc
MANGAN, John		25	M	Laborer	04Ju60Lc
GALVIN, Anne		22	F	None	04Ju60Lc
HAUGH, Dennis		23	M	Laborer	04Ju60Lc
Martin		24	M	Laborer	04Ju60Lc
HASSETT, Ellen		28	F	None	04Ju60Lc

JANE 04 JUNE 1847

From Liverpool

NAMES OF PASSENGERS		AGE	SEX	OCCUPATIONS	DATE PORT SHIP
NUGENT, Thomas		21	M	Laborer	04Ju02Dv
KILLEAVY, John		25	M	Laborer	04Ju02Dv
FITZGERALD, John		28	M	Laborer	04Ju02Dv
WALSH, John		25	M	Laborer	04Ju02Dv
FITZGERALD, Catherine		24	F	None	04Ju02Dv
Richard		28	M	Laborer	04Ju02Dv
FOLEY, Thomas		24	M	Laborer	04Ju02Dv
Michael		26	M	Laborer	04Ju02Dv
MANSFIELD, Thomas		28	M	Laborer	04Ju02Dv
COFFEE, Brian		39	M	Laborer	04Ju02Dv
John	(S)	19	M	Laborer	04Ju02Dv
Ellen	(D)	18	F	None	04Ju02Dv
Catharine	(D)	22	F	None	04Ju02Dv
Eliza	(D)	07	F	Child	04Ju02Dv
RILEY, Michael		20	M	Laborer	04Ju02Dv
DORMODY, James		24	M	Laborer	04Ju02Dv
CARNEY, Catharine		20	F	None	04Ju02Dv
GERARTY, Patk.		25	M	Laborer	04Ju02Dv
Catherine		25	F	None	04Ju02Dv
GALVIN, Mara		19	F	None	04Ju02Dv
GERARTY, William		26	M	Laborer	04Ju02Dv
Catharine		22	F	None	04Ju02Dv
SPROOL, Bridget		20	F	None	04Ju02Dv
DALTON, John		19	M	Laborer	04Ju02Dv
Richard		30	M	Laborer	04Ju02Dv
CORCORON, Thomas		21	M	Laborer	04Ju02Dv
HOGAN, Joseph		26	M	Laborer	04Ju02Dv
MAHER, Joseph		25	M	Laborer	04Ju02Dv
LANGAN, Biddy		17	F	None	04Ju02Dv
SHERAN, Mary		18	F	None	04Ju02Dv
Biddy	(M)	46	F	None	04Ju02Dv
Kitty	(T)	18	F	None	04Ju02Dv
COSGROVE, Mary		16	F	None	04Ju02Dv
DOLAN, Peter		20	M	Laborer	04Ju02Dv
LANGAN, Richard		30	M	Laborer	04Ju02Dv
Judith		20	F	None	04Ju02Dv
GERARTY, John		52	M	Laborer	04Ju02Dv
Ann	(W)	40	F	None	04Ju02Dv
Mary	(D)	20	F	None	04Ju02Dv
Johanna	(D)	16	F	None	04Ju02Dv
David	(S)	15	M	Laborer	04Ju02Dv
Susan	(D)	14	F	None	04Ju02Dv
Robert	(S)	11	M	None	04Ju02Dv
John	(S)	11	M	None	04Ju02Dv
KENNEDY, John		05	M	None	04Ju02Dv
HENNESSEY, Robert		05	M	None	04Ju02Dv
KEATING, James		24	M	Laborer	04Ju02Dv
Michael		25	M	Laborer	04Ju02Dv
CERMILL, Michael		22	M	Laborer	04Ju02Dv
HAMILL, Mary		21	F	None	04Ju02Dv
DOYLE, John		25	M	Laborer	04Ju02Dv
HARSGRAVE, Path.		27	M	Laborer	04Ju02Dv
Lawrence		24	M	Laborer	04Ju02Dv

571

NAMES OF PASSENGERS	AGE	SEX	OCCUPATIONS	DATE PORT SHIP
MCDONALD, Michael	21	M	Laborer	04Ju02Dv
RYAN, James	27	M	Laborer	04Ju02Dv
William	24	M	Laborer	04Ju02Dv
LOSEY, Catharine	21	F	None	04Ju02Dv
Gardiner	30	M	Laborer	04Ju02Dv
Catharine	27	F	None	04Ju02Dv
WALSH, James	22	M	Laborer	04Ju02Dv
CONNER, Mary	30	F	None	04Ju02Dv
BUTLER, U-Mrs.	30	F	None	04Ju02Dv
BASSETT, Cath.	20	F	None	04Ju02Dv
RYAN, Ellen	25	F	None	04Ju02Dv
BUTLER, Ellen	22	F	None	04Ju02Dv
CROSBY, Pat	25	M	Laborer	04Ju02Dv
STANLEY, James	24	M	Laborer	04Ju02Dv
Ann	21	F	None	04Ju02Dv
HALLIGAN, Andrew	20	M	Laborer	04Ju02Dv
John	21	M	Laborer	04Ju02Dv
MOORE, Charles	21	M	Laborer	04Ju02Dv
PIERCE, Chester	18	M	Laborer	04Ju02Dv
James	19	M	Laborer	04Ju02Dv
MURPHY, Arthur	28	M	Laborer	04Ju02Dv
John	25	M	Laborer	04Ju02Dv
FRAWLEY, John	20	M	Laborer	04Ju02Dv
Martin	20	M	Laborer	04Ju02Dv
FLYNN, James	65	M	Laborer	04Ju02Dv
MULONY, Mary	20	F	None	04Ju02Dv
MURRAY, Ann	18	F	None	04Ju02Dv
MAHON, Michael	23	M	Laborer	04Ju02Dv
BRYAN, Daniel	29	M	Laborer	04Ju02Dv
FLOOD, James	17	M	Laborer	04Ju02Dv
THOMPSON, Michael	20	M	Laborer	04Ju02Dv
KERNON, Michael	20	M	Laborer	04Ju02Dv
MCDERMOTT, Pat	21	M	Laborer	04Ju02Dv
Cath.	19	F	None	04Ju02Dv
YOUNG, Edward	20	M	Laborer	04Ju02Dv
BOYLE, James	30	M	Laborer	04Ju02Dv
Peggy (W)	30	F	None	04Ju02Dv
Mary (D)	.00	F	Infant	04Ju02Dv
REED, John	40	M	Laborer	04Ju02Dv
Susan	20	F	None	04Ju02Dv
BOYLE, Sam	03	M	Child	04Ju02Dv
GLENNON, James	21	M	Laborer	04Ju02Dv
Betty	20	F	None	04Ju02Dv
KELLY, Mary	21	F	None	04Ju02Dv
COYLE, Biddy	19	F	None	04Ju02Dv
GRIFFIN, Thomas	18	M	Laborer	04Ju02Dv
MINTHA, John	20	M	Laborer	04Ju02Dv
GARRAGHER, Hugh	28	M	Laborer	04Ju02Dv
U (W)	25	F	None	04Ju02Dv
Mary (D)	.00	F	Infant	04Ju02Dv
SHANNON, Peter	20	M	Laborer	04Ju02Dv
Andrew	21	M	Laborer	04Ju02Dv
CARLEY, Mary	18	F	None	04Ju02Dv
BINK, Catharine	23	F	None	04Ju02Dv
MALLALY, John	28	M	Laborer	04Ju02Dv
Catharine	28	F	None	04Ju02Dv
CLAFFEY, William	40	M	Laborer	04Ju02Dv
FLYNN, Mary	24	F	None	04Ju02Dv
SEERY, William	46	M	Laborer	04Ju02Dv
Ann (W)	44	F	None	04Ju02Dv
Maurice (S)	21	M	Laborer	04Ju02Dv
James (S)	20	M	Laborer	04Ju02Dv
Mary (D)	19	F	None	04Ju02Dv
Ann (D)	15	F	None	04Ju02Dv
Patrick (S)	13	M	Laborer	04Ju02Dv
William (S)	10	M	Child	04Ju02Dv
Luke (S)	07	M	Child	04Ju02Dv
Rose (D)	04	F	Child	04Ju02Dv
KENFOOT, Ellen	20	F	None	04Ju02Dv
BRADY, Patrick	21	M	Laborer	04Ju02Dv
WALSH, Cella	21	F	None	04Ju02Dv
METCALF, Isaac	20	M	Laborer	04Ju02Dv
Thomas	26	M	Laborer	04Ju02Dv
Mary	22	F	None	04Ju02Dv
STEPHENSON, John	26	M	Laborer	04Ju02Dv

NAMES OF PASSENGERS	AGE	SEX	OCCUPATIONS	DATE PORT SHIP
STEPHENSON, Elizabeth	24	F	None	04Ju02Dv

NEW-WORLD 07 JUNE 1847

From Liverpool

NAMES OF PASSENGERS	AGE	SEX	OCCUPATIONS	DATE PORT SHIP
WARD, J.A.	32	M	None	07Ju02Ku
FULLER, J.B.	21	M	None	07Ju02Ku
ANDERSON, J.	32	M	Mechanic	07Ju02Ku
PICKLES, R.	45	M	Unknown	07Ju02Ku
SCHOFFIELD, W.	22	M	Unknown	07Ju02Ku
Betty	20	F	None	07Ju02Ku
DIGGS, W.	55	M	Unknown	07Ju02Ku
HILL, W.	45	M	Unknown	07Ju02Ku
ADAMS, W.	40	M	Unknown	07Ju02Ku
MEASE, My.J.	23	F	None	07Ju02Ku
DAY, My.	19	F	None	07Ju02Ku
ROBURN, H.J.	21	M	None	07Ju02Ku
Wm.	26	M	None	07Ju02Ku
TAYLOR, G.	22	M	None	07Ju02Ku
WATSON, T.	28	M	None	07Ju02Ku
OWENS, J.	22	M	None	07Ju02Ku
SMITH, J.	24	M	None	07Ju02Ku
HANES, W.	24	M	None	07Ju02Ku
CREA, G.	26	M	None	07Ju02Ku
U (W)	24	F	None	07Ju02Ku
Ann	04	F	Child	07Ju02Ku
Mara	03	F	Child	07Ju02Ku
Cath.	01	F	Child	07Ju02Ku
CALLEY, Eliza	23	F	None	07Ju02Ku
MCBRIDE, My.	17	F	None	07Ju02Ku
MALENY, J.	35	M	Unknown	07Ju02Ku
John	13	M	None	07Ju02Ku
Thos.	15	M	None	07Ju02Ku
TOOLE, J.	16	M	None	07Ju02Ku
LEEMY, Pat	25	M	Unknown	07Ju02Ku
Cath.	24	F	None	07Ju02Ku
ODONNELL, E.	28	M	Unknown	07Ju02Ku
DUNN, J.	22	M	Unknown	07Ju02Ku
BUCKLY, E.	24	M	Unknown	07Ju02Ku
MACKEY, S.	23	M	Unknown	07Ju02Ku
My.	22	F	None	07Ju02Ku
KENNEDY, Susan	31	F	None	07Ju02Ku
Mich.	33	M	Unknown	07Ju02Ku
BLACK, P.	22	M	Unknown	07Ju02Ku
FITZPATRICK, J.	23	M	Unknown	07Ju02Ku
YOUNG, P.	24	M	Unknown	07Ju02Ku
DELANY, E.	25	M	Laborer	07Ju02Ku
MCGUIRE, Ann	20	F	None	07Ju02Ku
WALSH, Cath.	21	F	None	07Ju02Ku
DUNBY, Ann	26	F	None	07Ju02Ku
CORCORAN, J.	24	M	Laborer	07Ju02Ku
MURPHY, T.	25	M	Laborer	07Ju02Ku
PERKINSON, E.	26	M	Laborer	07Ju02Ku
ROGERS, P.	21	M	Laborer	07Ju02Ku
MCBREEN, P.	20	M	Laborer	07Ju02Ku
Pat.	21	M	Laborer	07Ju02Ku
Chas.	19	M	Laborer	07Ju02Ku
MONAHAN, P.	22	M	Laborer	07Ju02Ku
DUANE, W.	26	M	Laborer	07Ju02Ku
Pat	24	M	Laborer	07Ju02Ku
DYKES, Sarah	32	F	None	07Ju02Ku
NOSEDEN, Ann	22	F	None	07Ju02Ku
Frances	24	F	None	07Ju02Ku
WATSON, J.	15	M	Laborer	07Ju02Ku
CONROY, J.	20	M	Laborer	07Ju02Ku
LITTLE, My.	19	F	None	07Ju02Ku
HOUSTON, Jeanette	23	F	None	07Ju02Ku
MCKNABB, My.	24	F	None	07Ju02Ku

NAMES OF PASSENGERS	AGE	SEX	OCCUPATIONS	DATE PORT SHIP	NAMES OF PASSENGERS	AGE	SEX	OCCUPATIONS	DATE PORT SHIP
CAMPBELL, Eliza	22	F	None	07Ju02Ku	HANEY, P.	33	M	Laborer	07Ju02Ku
MCDADE, Bgt.	19	F	None	07Ju02Ku	SMITH, P.	24	M	Laborer	07Ju02Ku
James	36	M	Laborer	07Ju02Ku	MURPHY, M.	26	M	Laborer	07Ju02Ku
KENEDY, J.	45	M	Laborer	07Ju02Ku	SMITH, A.	24	M	Laborer	07Ju02Ku
John	22	M	Laborer	07Ju02Ku	MCLAUGHLIN, W.	45	M	Laborer	07Ju02Ku
Danl.	25	M	Laborer	07Ju02Ku	Robt.	26	M	Laborer	07Ju02Ku
Mgt. (W)	40	F	None	07Ju02Ku	Wm.	18	M	Laborer	07Ju02Ku
Bgt.	21	F	None	07Ju02Ku	Ellen	28	F	None	07Ju02Ku
Ann	20	F	None	07Ju02Ku	Hanah	26	F	None	07Ju02Ku
My.	23	F	None	07Ju02Ku	PURCELL, J.	24	M	Laborer	07Ju02Ku
Mgt.	01	F	Child	07Ju02Ku	Minne---, J.	20	M	Laborer	07Ju02Ku
HAYES, P.	22	M	Laborer	07Ju02Ku	GALAHER, J.	24	M	Laborer	07Ju02Ku
Cath.	25	F	None	07Ju02Ku	BROPHY, P.	50	M	Laborer	07Ju02Ku
BURKE, J.	24	M	Laborer	07Ju02Ku	Pat	21	M	Laborer	07Ju02Ku
Pat	20	M	Laborer	07Ju02Ku	Peter	26	M	Laborer	07Ju02Ku
BERKLY, B.	21	M	Laborer	07Ju02Ku	James	11	M	Child	07Ju02Ku
OBRIEN, H.	22	M	Laborer	07Ju02Ku	John	09	M	Child	07Ju02Ku
SHEA, Ann	24	F	None	07Ju02Ku	Bgt. (W)	50	F	None	07Ju02Ku
DREW, My.	02	F	Child	07Ju02Ku	Honora	19	F	None	07Ju02Ku
Thos.	03	M	Child	07Ju02Ku	Cath.	17	F	None	07Ju02Ku
HOGAN, T.	26	M	Laborer	07Ju02Ku	My.	14	F	None	07Ju02Ku
DWYER, J.	40	M	Laborer	07Ju02Ku	STEELE, T.	24	M	Laborer	07Ju02Ku
SMITH, Jane	30	F	None	07Ju02Ku	REILY, J.	22	M	Laborer	07Ju02Ku
OBRIEN, P.	07	M	Child	07Ju02Ku	DUFF, M.	24	M	Laborer	07Ju02Ku
DWYER, Mgt.	36	F	None	07Ju02Ku	NORTON, J.	25	M	Laborer	07Ju02Ku
COX, P.	27	M	Laborer	07Ju02Ku	Cath. (W)	24	F	None	07Ju02Ku
ALLEN, T.	20	M	Laborer	07Ju02Ku	Ann	02	F	Child	07Ju02Ku
KIERNAN, E.	40	M	Laborer	07Ju02Ku	MCGEE, Cath.	20	F	None	07Ju02Ku
Patck.	15	M	Laborer	07Ju02Ku	HALPIN, Brt.	21	F	None	07Ju02Ku
Edwd.	06	M	Child	07Ju02Ku	MCGEE, T.	23	M	Laborer	07Ju02Ku
Ellen	40	F	None	07Ju02Ku	LOYD, W.	25	M	Laborer	07Ju02Ku
Judith	19	F	None	07Ju02Ku	G.	24	M	Laborer	07Ju02Ku
Mgt.	08	F	Child	07Ju02Ku	CHARES, R.	22	M	Laborer	07Ju02Ku
My.	40	F	None	07Ju02Ku	LOYD, Th.	24	M	Laborer	07Ju02Ku
POWER, M.	20	M	Laborer	07Ju02Ku	FLAHEY, Ann	32	F	None	07Ju02Ku
GIBBONS, M.	20	M	Laborer	07Ju02Ku	Bgt.	26	F	None	07Ju02Ku
RYAN, P.	24	M	Laborer	07Ju02Ku	Bgt.	04	F	Child	07Ju02Ku
CRONAN, T.	24	M	Laborer	07Ju02Ku	Mgt.	18	F	None	07Ju02Ku
BRYNN, P.	26	M	Laborer	07Ju02Ku	Owen	32	M	Laborer	07Ju02Ku
WITHERTON, W.	20	M	Laborer	07Ju02Ku	Phillip.	55	M	Laborer	07Ju02Ku
CAFFY, C.	22	M	Laborer	07Ju02Ku	Bernd.	23	M	Laborer	07Ju02Ku
Bgt.	20	F	None	07Ju02Ku	GUCKEN, Mgt.	32	F	None	07Ju02Ku
BROWN, Ann	24	F	None	07Ju02Ku	JONES, D.	21	M	Laborer	07Ju02Ku
John	27	M	Laborer	07Ju02Ku	John	30	M	Laborer	07Ju02Ku
Jane	20	F	None	07Ju02Ku	ROBERTS, H.	23	M	Laborer	07Ju02Ku
NUGENT, M.	21	M	Laborer	07Ju02Ku	EVANS, D.	36	M	Laborer	07Ju02Ku
JORDAN, R.	35	M	Laborer	07Ju02Ku	Evan	32	M	Laborer	07Ju02Ku
Thos.	08	M	Child	07Ju02Ku	Eliza	36	F	None	07Ju02Ku
Bryan	07	M	Child	07Ju02Ku	Eliza	03	F	Child	07Ju02Ku
Peter	06	M	Child	07Ju02Ku	Sarah	24	F	None	07Ju02Ku
Ann	01	F	Child	07Ju02Ku	MARS, Ann	20	F	None	07Ju02Ku
Bgt. (W)	31	F	None	07Ju02Ku	MARRS, J.	40	M	Laborer	07Ju02Ku
KILBEY, Hana	18	F	None	07Ju02Ku	Hugh	24	M	Laborer	07Ju02Ku
SMITH, Ann	23	F	None	07Ju02Ku	Janet	01	F	Child	07Ju02Ku
MCKEW, Mgt.	22	F	None	07Ju02Ku	Ann	26	F	None	07Ju02Ku
Bryan	24	M	Laborer	07Ju02Ku	JONES, Mgt.	59	F	None	07Ju02Ku
CAROL, Jane	20	F	None	07Ju02Ku	ELLIS, Ellen	18	F	None	07Ju02Ku
HAND, Jane	30	F	None	07Ju02Ku	Elzbt.	72	F	None	07Ju02Ku
LYNCH, Jane	16	F	None	07Ju02Ku	Wm.	22	M	Laborer	07Ju02Ku
Bgt.	17	F	None	07Ju02Ku	SLIVERTON, S.	23	M	Laborer	07Ju02Ku
Mgt.	04	F	Child	07Ju02Ku	SHENELT, S.	24	M	Laborer	07Ju02Ku
MACKY, My.	20	F	None	07Ju02Ku	NERICK, M.	21	M	Laborer	07Ju02Ku
DALY, My.	21	F	None	07Ju02Ku	MCCABE, P.	18	M	Laborer	07Ju02Ku
CARNEY, Ann	40	F	None	07Ju02Ku	BOYLEN, L.	19	M	Laborer	07Ju02Ku
Bgt.	20	F	None	07Ju02Ku	QUIN, O.	21	M	Laborer	07Ju02Ku
Mgt.	17	F	None	07Ju02Ku	RILEY, R.	33	M	Laborer	07Ju02Ku
LYNCH, U	18	F	None	07Ju02Ku	ARMSTRONG, H.	24	M	Laborer	07Ju02Ku
DWYER, My.	19	F	None	07Ju02Ku	FARRELLY, J.	30	M	Laborer	07Ju02Ku
HARNE, J.	03	M	Child	07Ju02Ku	BOYLE, P.	24	M	Laborer	07Ju02Ku
WORTHINGTON, T.	26	M	Laborer	07Ju02Ku	FITZSIMMONS, P.	20	M	Laborer	07Ju02Ku
MULEHIER, P.	27	M	Laborer	07Ju02Ku	MCKEVER, Rose	21	F	None	07Ju02Ku
DONOHUE, M.	25	M	Laborer	07Ju02Ku	BOYLE, Ann	18	F	None	07Ju02Ku
HOGAN, J.	20	M	Laborer	07Ju02Ku	GRAHAM, J.	12	M	None	07Ju02Ku
BENSON, T.	24	M	Laborer	07Ju02Ku	Robert	10	M	Child	07Ju02Ku
MULEYAR, P.	25	M	Laborer	07Ju02Ku	John	05	M	Child	07Ju02Ku

NAMES OF PASSENGERS	AGE	SEX	OCCUPATIONS	DATE PORT SHIP	NAMES OF PASSENGERS	AGE	SEX	OCCUPATIONS	DATE PORT SHIP
MARTIN, R.	15	M	None	07Ju02Ku	DURNANE, Isb.	20	F	None	07Ju02Ku
GRAHAM, Fany	40	F	None	07Ju02Ku	OWENS, M.	21	F	None	07Ju02Ku
Fany	02	F	Child	07Ju02Ku	MCRORY, T.	30	M	Laborer	07Ju02Ku
COBB, Mgt.	21	F	None	07Ju02Ku	DALTON, J.	28	M	Laborer	07Ju02Ku
Mara	20	F	None	07Ju02Ku	CLENCHY, T.	28	M	Laborer	07Ju02Ku
CHRISTEN, Cella	25	F	None	07Ju02Ku	Jane	24	F	None	07Ju02Ku
John	25	M	Laborer	07Ju02Ku	MCCHEEVERS, Sarah	35	F	None	07Ju02Ku
Robt.	21	M	Laborer	07Ju02Ku	MCCARTNY, M.	25	M	Laborer	07Ju02Ku
HARRISON, R.	26	M	Laborer	07Ju02Ku	MCCHEEVERS, P.	40	M	Laborer	07Ju02Ku
COWLEY, W.	18	M	Laborer	07Ju02Ku	WARD, D.	23	M	Laborer	07Ju02Ku
FEARON, Mgt.	20	F	None	07Ju02Ku	CROSETT, T.	21	M	Laborer	07Ju02Ku
KISSIDY, Mgt.	17	F	None	07Ju02Ku	BARTLETT, W.	52	M	Laborer	07Ju02Ku
MULCRANE, T.	21	M	Laborer	07Ju02Ku	HOBIN, W.	20	M	Laborer	07Ju02Ku
BROPHY, C.	26	M	Laborer	07Ju02Ku	John	23	M	Laborer	07Ju02Ku
Peter	32	M	Laborer	07Ju02Ku	DUNN, R.	24	M	Laborer	07Ju02Ku
COSTIGAN, J.	25	M	Laborer	07Ju02Ku	MILLER, W.	25	M	Laborer	07Ju02Ku
Sarah	24	F	None	07Ju02Ku	HOBBS, A.	23	M	Laborer	07Ju02Ku
Ann	22	F	None	07Ju02Ku	BARTLETT, Ann	42	F	None	07Ju02Ku
SMITH, Betty	45	F	None	07Ju02Ku	MCGLEADY, Ellen	20	F	None	07Ju02Ku
Cath.	11	F	None	07Ju02Ku	TAYLOR, W.	25	M	Laborer	07Ju02Ku
Patt.	14	M	Laborer	07Ju02Ku	BRYAN, P.	26	M	Laborer	07Ju02Ku
EDWARDS, T.	40	M	Laborer	07Ju02Ku	KENNY, P.	24	M	Laborer	07Ju02Ku
GILPIN, R.	20	M	Laborer	07Ju02Ku	HOBIN, T.	22	M	Laborer	07Ju02Ku
SMITH, Betty	50	F	None	07Ju02Ku	COGGAN, W.	20	M	Laborer	07Ju02Ku
MURRY, P.	50	M	Laborer	07Ju02Ku	GRAHAM, J.	45	M	Laborer	07Ju02Ku
Mich.	25	M	Laborer	07Ju02Ku	CAMPBELL, J.	23	M	Laborer	07Ju02Ku
Pat	20	M	Laborer	07Ju02Ku	REID, P.	25	M	Laborer	07Ju02Ku
MONAHAN, J.	30	M	Laborer	07Ju02Ku	REILY, J.	22	M	Laborer	07Ju02Ku
RABBS, M.	24	M	Laborer	07Ju02Ku	Brnd.	14	M	None	07Ju02Ku
DUFFY, T.	45	M	Laborer	07Ju02Ku	DOWD, J.	30	M	Laborer	07Ju02Ku
Alice (W)	40	F	None	07Ju02Ku	BISSETT, J.	21	M	Laborer	07Ju02Ku
Cath.	19	F	None	07Ju02Ku	KELLY, P.	30	M	Laborer	07Ju02Ku
Alice	17	F	None	07Ju02Ku	LACY, J.	22	M	Laborer	07Ju02Ku
Judh.	15	F	None	07Ju02Ku	SANDS, P.	30	M	Laborer	07Ju02Ku
EANNES, J.	21	M	Laborer	07Ju02Ku	RYAN, J.	27	M	Laborer	07Ju02Ku
Trdch.	22	M	Laborer	07Ju02Ku	Pat	02	M	Child	07Ju02Ku
MINTEN, J.	21	M	Laborer	07Ju02Ku	Thos.	21	M	Laborer	07Ju02Ku
PETERS, M.	28	M	Laborer	07Ju02Ku	BUHAN, M.	27	M	Laborer	07Ju02Ku
FARELLY, T.	20	M	Laborer	07Ju02Ku	WALSH, J.	20	M	Laborer	07Ju02Ku
MCEVOY, P.	24	M	Laborer	07Ju02Ku	CURRAN, J.	26	M	Laborer	07Ju02Ku
CAVANAUGH, J.	25	M	Laborer	07Ju02Ku	HAYNES, J.	27	M	Laborer	07Ju02Ku
ONEALE, J.	25	M	Laborer	07Ju02Ku	REGAN, T.	25	M	Laborer	07Ju02Ku
CALLAN, My.	21	F	None	07Ju02Ku	JONES, James	34	M	Laborer	07Ju02Ku
COOGAN, Aly.	20	F	None	07Ju02Ku	Wm.	33	M	Laborer	07Ju02Ku
Ellen	21	F	None	07Ju02Ku	DUNN, N.	30	M	Laborer	07Ju02Ku
HEALY, Cath.	21	F	None	07Ju02Ku	REAS, J.	22	M	Laborer	07Ju02Ku
LACY, My.	20	F	None	07Ju02Ku	GALGER, L.	30	M	Laborer	07Ju02Ku
SMITH, P.	23	M	Laborer	07Ju02Ku	FITZSIMMONS, J.	25	M	Laborer	07Ju02Ku
OREILLY, P.	45	M	Laborer	07Ju02Ku	QUINN, F.	21	M	Laborer	07Ju02Ku
John	16	M	Laborer	07Ju02Ku	John	13	M	None	07Ju02Ku
LYNCH, P.	16	M	Laborer	07Ju02Ku	DEVAY, W.	21	M	Laborer	07Ju02Ku
DALTON, R.	26	M	Laborer	07Ju02Ku	MCKENNA, T.	20	M	Laborer	07Ju02Ku
Denis	18	M	Laborer	07Ju02Ku	Terence	18	M	Laborer	07Ju02Ku
REILLY, J.	22	M	Laborer	07Ju02Ku	TIGH, L.	50	M	Laborer	07Ju02Ku
KILPATRICK, W.	18	M	Laborer	07Ju02Ku	Wm.	33	M	Laborer	07Ju02Ku
Isabelle	30	F	None	07Ju02Ku	WALSH, My.	22	F	None	07Ju02Ku
KANE, My.	25	F	None	07Ju02Ku	OHEARN, Ann	21	F	None	07Ju02Ku
HOGG, Jane	30	F	None	07Ju02Ku	Ellen	22	F	None	07Ju02Ku
Elza.	06	F	Child	07Ju02Ku	MEADE, Elza.	21	F	None	07Ju02Ku
MCKENAN, T.	19	M	Laborer	07Ju02Ku	GANNON, Mgt.	20	F	None	07Ju02Ku
KENEDY, P.	24	M	Laborer	07Ju02Ku	GARGAN, Elza.	20	F	None	07Ju02Ku
MANGIN, T.	23	M	Laborer	07Ju02Ku	CURRAN, My.	26	F	None	07Ju02Ku
KENEDY, H.	25	M	Laborer	07Ju02Ku	DUNN, Bgt.	18	F	None	07Ju02Ku
HOUGH. W.	24	M	Laborer	07Ju02Ku	REGAN, Alice	22	F	None	07Ju02Ku
HENRY, J.	32	M	Laborer	07Ju02Ku	JONSON, Mgt.	29	F	None	07Ju02Ku
NUGENT, H.	24	M	Laborer	07Ju02Ku	Jane	10	F	Child	07Ju02Ku
GALAHER, J.	22	M	Laborer	07Ju02Ku	Isabelle	05	F	Child	07Ju02Ku
Patck.	24	M	Laborer	07Ju02Ku	Mary	02	F	Child	07Ju02Ku
TURNER, J.	23	M	Laborer	07Ju02Ku	MURPHY, Mgt.	19	F	None	07Ju02Ku
HEALY, W.	22	M	Laborer	07Ju02Ku	FITZSIMMONS, My.	20	F	None	07Ju02Ku
LYOD, J.	21	M	Laborer	07Ju02Ku	Betty	35	F	None	07Ju02Ku
DONALY, M.	19	F	None	07Ju02Ku	Fany	08	F	Child	07Ju02Ku
MORAN, Bgt.	17	F	None	07Ju02Ku	My.	21	F	None	07Ju02Ku
RILY, Cath.	40	F	None	07Ju02Ku	MCKEEN, Elen	20	F	None	07Ju02Ku
Bgt.	21	F	None	07Ju02Ku	HALL, Hanah	25	F	None	07Ju02Ku

NAMES OF PASSENGERS		AGE	SEX	OCCUPATIONS	DATE PORT SHIP
FRYNE, Mgt.		50	F	None	07Ju02Ku
Julia		30	F	None	07Ju02Ku
MURPHY, My.		18	F	None	07Ju02Ku
Ann		17	F	None	07Ju02Ku
Betty		10	F	Child	07Ju02Ku
Cath.		07	F	Child	07Ju02Ku
FLINN, My.		18	F	None	07Ju02Ku
GORDEN, Rose		26	F	None	07Ju02Ku
BANGHER, Ma.		14	F	None	07Ju02Ku
SHENAN, Mgt.		19	F	None	07Ju02Ku
OREILY, Elza.		15	F	None	07Ju02Ku

NEW-WORLD 07 JUNE 1847

From Liverpool

NAMES OF PASSENGERS		AGE	SEX	OCCUPATIONS	DATE PORT SHIP
BRADY, Ellen		28	F	None	07Ju02Ku
HOAMS, Ma.		18	F	None	07Ju02Ku
MUNSON, Ann		24	F	None	07Ju02Ku
MORRISON, C.		60	M	Laborer	07Ju02Ku
Jas.		26	M	Laborer	07Ju02Ku
Chas.		02	M	Child	07Ju02Ku
HOPKINS, T.		26	M	Laborer	07Ju02Ku
BAILEY, J.		22	M	Laborer	07Ju02Ku
JOHNSON, P.		22	M	Laborer	07Ju02Ku
Thos.	(P)	40	M	Laborer	07Ju02Ku
Pat		70	M	Laborer	07Ju02Ku
Chet.	(B)	30	M	Laborer	07Ju02Ku
TOOHAN, T.		27	M	Laborer	07Ju02Ku
BENNET, T.		24	M	Laborer	07Ju02Ku
Ja-.		25	M	Laborer	07Ju02Ku
MOORE, L.		25	M	Laborer	07Ju02Ku
Jas.		19	M	Laborer	07Ju02Ku
FINNEGAN, J.		24	M	Laborer	07Ju02Ku
JOHNSON, Ann		60	F	None	07Ju02Ku
BENNET, Ann		22	F	None	07Ju02Ku
NIEL, Ann		50	F	None	07Ju02Ku
My.	(D)	18	F	None	07Ju02Ku
COYNE, Elza.		22	F	None	07Ju02Ku
MCDONELL, N.		30	M	Laborer	07Ju02Ku
DWIRE, J.		22	M	Laborer	07Ju02Ku
KENEFICK, M.		28	M	Laborer	07Ju02Ku
COGAN, N.		24	M	Laborer	07Ju02Ku
NEIL, A.		10	M	Child	07Ju02Ku
FARELLY, J.		20	M	Laborer	07Ju02Ku
SAVAGE, R.		30	M	Laborer	07Ju02Ku
DELANY, J.		24	M	Laborer	07Ju02Ku
BERGEN, J.		25	M	Laborer	07Ju02Ku
CROWLY, J.		35	M	Laborer	07Ju02Ku
KENAN, W.		22	M	Laborer	07Ju02Ku
DAY, J.		22	M	Laborer	07Ju02Ku
FITZSIMMONS, Rose		18	F	None	07Ju02Ku
SAWYER, Honer		24	F	None	07Ju02Ku
DELENY, Mgt.		20	F	None	07Ju02Ku
DEWY, Ann		22	F	None	07Ju02Ku
MCCARTHY, Cath.		23	F	None	07Ju02Ku
OBRIEN, My.A.		22	F	None	07Ju02Ku
LAGRICK, Jane		20	F	None	07Ju02Ku
CAHY, My.		20	F	None	07Ju02Ku
ROCHESTER, Sarah		19	F	None	07Ju02Ku
Mgt.	(M)	45	F	None	07Ju02Ku
ROBERTS, Han.		15	F	None	07Ju02Ku
WILLIAMS, Elzbt.		17	F	None	07Ju02Ku
J.		20	M	Laborer	07Ju02Ku
HOAGEN, Jane		24	F	None	07Ju02Ku
LEE, Ann		27	F	None	07Ju02Ku
WELAN, Ma.		25	F	None	07Ju02Ku
RYAN, Mgt.		27	F	None	07Ju02Ku
My.	(D)	03	F	Child	07Ju02Ku
TOBIN, Bgt.		14	F	None	07Ju02Ku
RYAN, Mgt.		25	F	None	07Ju02Ku
BOYLE, Ann		18	F	None	07Ju02Ku
My.		15	F	None	07Ju02Ku
FITZSIMMONS, My.		19	F	None	07Ju02Ku
BUCKLER, Elza.		30	F	None	07Ju02Ku
James		20	M	Laborer	07Ju02Ku
Wm.		17	M	Laborer	07Ju02Ku
Thos.		11	M	Child	07Ju02Ku
WHITE, W.		22	M	Laborer	07Ju02Ku
HAND, B.		50	M	Laborer	07Ju02Ku
HINES, E--		20	F	None	07Ju02Ku
RYAN, E-		22	F	None	07Ju02Ku
MCDONELL, Chat.		25	F	None	07Ju02Ku
RILY, M.		19	M	Laborer	07Ju02Ku
SMITH, J.		21	M	Laborer	07Ju02Ku
ROCHE, M.		22	M	Laborer	07Ju02Ku
HOLLAND, J.		15	M	Laborer	07Ju02Ku
STACKPOLE, T.		12	M	Laborer	07Ju02Ku
John		10	M	Child	07Ju02Ku
My.		15	F	None	07Ju02Ku
FOLEY, My.		16	F	None	07Ju02Ku
Honora		15	F	None	07Ju02Ku
GIBBONS, Ellen		14	F	None	07Ju02Ku
DALY, Mgt.		18	F	None	07Ju02Ku
WHELAN, My.		14	F	None	07Ju02Ku
WAGNER, My.		10	F	Child	07Ju02Ku
BURRY, Johanna		15	F	None	07Ju02Ku
DONOHUE, P.		30	M	Laborer	07Ju02Ku
Owen		32	M	Laborer	07Ju02Ku
THOMPSON, O.		24	M	Laborer	07Ju02Ku
GILHOOLY, M.		60	M	Laborer	07Ju02Ku
Patck.	(S)	19	M	Laborer	07Ju02Ku
Cath.	(D)	15	F	None	07Ju02Ku
Mgt.	(D)	11	F	None	07Ju02Ku
BEATY, Bgt.		20	F	None	07Ju02Ku
DUNN, Sarah		17	F	None	07Ju02Ku
Mar.		20	M	Laborer	07Ju02Ku
HEIR, Ann-J.		30	F	None	07Ju02Ku
DRUM, John		21	M	Laborer	07Ju02Ku
LYONS, P.		26	M	Laborer	07Ju02Ku
LENNON, J.		24	M	Laborer	07Ju02Ku
HAMILL, A.		19	M	Laborer	07Ju02Ku
MENNON, W.		20	M	Laborer	07Ju02Ku
REDE, C.		19	M	Laborer	07Ju02Ku
DELANY, C.		30	M	Laborer	07Ju02Ku
DOOLAN, T.		30	M	Laborer	07Ju02Ku
FLANIGAN, R.		22	M	Laborer	07Ju02Ku
DEERY, J.		20	M	Laborer	07Ju02Ku
MURPHY, Alice		21	F	None	07Ju02Ku
DRENAN, Agnes		48	F	None	07Ju02Ku
Sarah	(D)	24	F	None	07Ju02Ku
Hanah	(D)	20	F	None	07Ju02Ku
Edward		50	M	Laborer	07Ju02Ku
Chas.		48	M	Laborer	07Ju02Ku
MYERS, J.		24	M	Laborer	07Ju02Ku
GRIFFITHS, W.		20	M	Laborer	07Ju02Ku
THOMPSON, E-		50	F	None	07Ju02Ku
BYRNES, P.		18	M	Laborer	07Ju02Ku
FOGARTY, P.		20	M	Laborer	07Ju02Ku
QURILISH, J.		22	M	Laborer	07Ju02Ku
CONNER, P.		40	M	Laborer	07Ju02Ku
Elza.	(D)	22	F	None	07Ju02Ku
GUINAN, Bgt.		23	F	None	07Ju02Ku
ROONY, Ann		20	F	None	07Ju02Ku
MULHERN, My.		21	F	None	07Ju02Ku
FREGAN, My.		19	F	None	07Ju02Ku
Jas.		18	M	Laborer	07Ju02Ku
GANNAN, J.		20	M	Laborer	07Ju02Ku
REILLY, P.		18	M	Laborer	07Ju02Ku
Edwd		35	M	Laborer	07Ju02Ku
John		36	M	Laborer	07Ju02Ku
Bernd.		10	M	Child	07Ju02Ku
Thos.		40	M	Laborer	07Ju02Ku
Matt		22	M	Laborer	07Ju02Ku

NAMES OF PASSENGERS		AGE	SEX	OCCUPATIONS	DATE PORT SHIP
REILLY, John		32	M	Laborer	07Ju02Ku
My.		30	F	None	07Ju02Ku
Mgt.		01	F	Child	07Ju02Ku
FARRELL, Jane		30	F	None	07Ju02Ku
MCNULTY, Betty		18	F	None	07Ju02Ku
THOMPSON, My.		17	F	None	07Ju02Ku
Ellen		21	F	None	07Ju02Ku
Honor		20	F	None	07Ju02Ku
MORAN, Ann		21	F	None	07Ju02Ku
MONAHAN, Elza.		17	F	None	07Ju02Ku
KENEDY, M.		50	F	None	07Ju02Ku
THOMPSON, P.		25	M	Laborer	07Ju02Ku
Mich.		20	M	Laborer	07Ju02Ku
HUGHES, J.		21	M	Laborer	07Ju02Ku
REID, J.		19	M	Laborer	07Ju02Ku
WALSH, J.		23	M	Laborer	07Ju02Ku
HARNE, J.		24	M	Laborer	07Ju02Ku
CARROLL, O.		26	M	Laborer	07Ju02Ku
MURPHY, J.		50	M	Laborer	07Ju02Ku
Pat	(S)	12	M	Laborer	07Ju02Ku
GUINAN, J.		26	M	Laborer	07Ju02Ku
SCOTT, F.		13	M	None	07Ju02Ku
FARRELL, J.		20	M	Laborer	07Ju02Ku
SCANLON, P.		40	M	Laborer	07Ju02Ku
N----	(D)	12	F	None	07Ju02Ku
M---	(D)	10	F	Child	07Ju02Ku
Pat	(S)	06	M	Child	07Ju02Ku
Ellen	(W)	39	F	None	07Ju02Ku
Bidy	(D)	14	F	None	07Ju02Ku
Cath.	(D)	03	F	Child	07Ju02Ku
MAYERS, Bgt.		22	F	None	07Ju02Ku
TIGH, Mgt.		14	F	None	07Ju02Ku
HART, Sarah		22	F	None	07Ju02Ku
MCDONNEL, J.		29	M	Laborer	07Ju02Ku
BAILY, P.		09	M	Child	07Ju02Ku
TIGH, N.		08	M	Child	07Ju02Ku
Phipp.		10	M	Child	07Ju02Ku

LEVERETT 07 JUNE 1847

From Kilrush

NAMES OF PASSENGERS		AGE	SEX	OCCUPATIONS	DATE PORT SHIP
KING, P.		45	M	Laborer	07Ju60Lh
Hugh		33	M	Laborer	07Ju60Lh
Cath.		10	F	Child	07Ju60Lh
Miles		08	M	Child	07Ju60Lh
Edwd.		06	M	Child	07Ju60Lh
Pat		01	M	Child	07Ju60Lh
DOYLE, J.		26	M	Laborer	07Ju60Lh
Cath.		22	F	None	07Ju60Lh
James	(P)	60	M	Laborer	07Ju60Lh
Thos.		21	M	Laborer	07Ju60Lh
Robt.		42	M	Laborer	07Ju60Lh
Jane		43	F	None	07Ju60Lh
Mich.		20	M	Laborer	07Ju60Lh
Bgt.		18	F	None	07Ju60Lh
My.		15	F	None	07Ju60Lh
Jas.		12	M	None	07Ju60Lh
Cath.		10	F	Child	07Ju60Lh
Louise		08	F	Child	07Ju60Lh
DOLLAN, P.		36	M	Laborer	07Ju60Lh
Bgt.	(W)	35	F	None	07Ju60Lh
Ken	(S)	01	M	Child	07Ju60Lh
Ellen	(D)	01	F	Child	07Ju60Lh
SHANAHAN, J.		50	M	Laborer	07Ju60Lh
CONNERY, J.		22	M	Laborer	07Ju60Lh
Anita		20	F	None	07Ju60Lh
SHEHORN, J.		20	M	Laborer	07Ju60Lh
LAWSON, W.		28	M	Laborer	07Ju60Lh

NAMES OF PASSENGERS		AGE	SEX	OCCUPATIONS	DATE PORT SHIP
LAWSON, My.		26	F	None	07Ju60Lh
TOBIN, M.		23	M	Laborer	07Ju60Lh
BURN, P.		24	M	Laborer	07Ju60Lh
DARCY, M.		36	M	Laborer	07Ju60Lh
FINNEGAN, M.		29	M	Laborer	07Ju60Lh
REID, Ellen		26	F	None	07Ju60Lh
COCHRAN, Mich.		21	M	Laborer	07Ju60Lh
MURPHY, Mils.		36	M	Laborer	07Ju60Lh
Mgt.	(W)	26	F	None	07Ju60Lh
Ann	(D)	03	F	Child	07Ju60Lh

GASPER 08 JUNE 1847

From Cork

NAMES OF PASSENGERS		AGE	SEX	OCCUPATIONS	DATE PORT SHIP
WARNER, Jas.		19	M	Farmer	08Ju14Le
DRISCOLL, Denis		21	M	Farmer	08Ju14Le
WALSH, Jas.		20	M	Farmer	08Ju14Le
SWEENY, Jno.		20	M	Farmer	08Ju14Le
TURCETT, Wm.		22	M	Farmer	08Ju14Le
NEVILLE, Marla		23	F	None	08Ju14Le
HARDING, Ann		17	F	None	08Ju14Le
BUCKLY, U-Mrs.		22	F	None	08Ju14Le
NEVILLE, Johannah		18	F	None	08Ju14Le
Margth.		18	F	None	08Ju14Le
DRISCOLL, Betty		18	F	None	08Ju14Le
BURK, Cath.		17	F	None	08Ju14Le
BRENNAN, Mary		18	F	None	08Ju14Le
KILLIHED, M.		22	M	Farmer	08Ju14Le
SPILLAN, Mary		18	F	None	08Ju14Le
CROW, Ellen		16	F	None	08Ju14Le
DONOUGHUE, Edwd.		18	M	Farmer	08Ju14Le
KIFFEE, Pat		20	M	Farmer	08Ju14Le
DESMONE, A.		22	M	Farmer	08Ju14Le
DWYER, R.		23	M	Farmer	08Ju14Le
BUCKLY, Ellen		20	F	None	08Ju14Le
GARVIN, M.		25	M	Farmer	08Ju14Le
REILY, M.		24	M	Farmer	08Ju14Le
NEWMAN, Jas.		24	M	Farmer	08Ju14Le
NIEL, Jos.		24	M	Farmer	08Ju14Le
DONOVAN, Cath.		17	F	None	08Ju14Le
KIELY, Brigt.		26	F	None	08Ju14Le
RYAN, Mary		18	F	None	08Ju14Le
POWER, Ellen		17	F	None	08Ju14Le
NIEL, Cath.		17	F	None	08Ju14Le
NOOLAN, Joh.		20	F	None	08Ju14Le
MAHONY, Mary		22	F	None	08Ju14Le
CONWAY, Pat		22	M	Farmer	08Ju14Le
SHEA, Pat		21	M	Farmer	08Ju14Le
Mich.		02	M	Child	08Ju14Le
FLANAGAN, Mich.		22	M	Farmer	08Ju14Le
ROACHE, L.		23	M	Farmer	08Ju14Le
SHEA, Jos.		06	M	Child	08Ju14Le
Thos.		04	M	Child	08Ju14Le
CONWAY, Mary		.00	F	Infant	08Ju14Le
SHEA, Mary		03	F	Child	08Ju14Le
CASHMAN, John		29	M	Farmer	08Ju14Le
HALLORAN, J.		23	M	Farmer	08Ju14Le
QUISHAN, J.		24	M	Farmer	08Ju14Le
GLAIEN, M.		25	M	Farmer	08Ju14Le
Ellen		21	F	Farmer	08Ju14Le
DEALY, Pat		22	M	Farmer	08Ju14Le
SPILLANE, Mich.		36	M	Farmer	08Ju14Le

NAMES OF PASSENGERS		AGE	SEX	OCCUPATIONS	DATE PORT SHIP

TASSIE 08 JUNE 1847

From Galway

NAMES OF PASSENGERS		AGE	SEX	OCCUPATIONS	DATE PORT SHIP
KELLY, Mary		22	F	None	08Ju11LI
KAIN, Ann		20	F	None	08Ju11LI
James		22	M	Laborer	08Ju11LI
BURK, Redmond		20	M	Laborer	08Ju11LI
Bridget		25	F	None	08Ju11LI
DEVINE, Patrick		44	M	Laborer	08Ju11LI
Michel	(S)	17	M	Laborer	08Ju11LI
Jno.	(S)	12	M	None	08Ju11LI
Martin	(S)	08	M	Child	08Ju11LI
Thos.	(S)	05	M	Child	08Ju11LI
Mary	(D)	15	F	None	08Ju11LI
Judy	(D)	01	F	Child	08Ju11LI
Mary	(W)	40	F	None	08Ju11LI
COSTELLO, Ed.		19	M	Laborer	08Ju11LI
Maria		13	F	None	08Ju11LI
BIRMINGHAM, Thos.		11	M	None	08Ju11LI
BURKE, Martin		26	M	Laborer	08Ju11LI
Cath.		20	F	None	08Ju11LI
KILLILIN, Martin		20	M	Laborer	08Ju11LI
CURLEY, Nic.		24	M	Laborer	08Ju11LI
KAIN, Joseph		26	M	Laborer	08Ju11LI
CORLASS, Cathe.		22	F	None	08Ju11LI
FLYNN, Richd.		19	M	Laborer	08Ju11LI
Cella		20	F	None	08Ju11LI
LEONARD, B.		21	F	None	08Ju11LI
Sabina		19	F	None	08Ju11LI
DONALLY, Margt.		26	F	None	08Ju11LI
CORNAKAN, Wm.		24	M	Laborer	08Ju11LI
GILL, Cathe.		55	F	None	08Ju11LI
Mary	(D)	20	F	None	08Ju11LI
John	(S)	27	M	Laborer	08Ju11LI
Rodger	(S)	18	M	Laborer	08Ju11LI
DURKAN, Bridget		20	F	None	08Ju11LI
CLOHERTY, Maria		24	F	None	08Ju11LI
MCGRATH, Cathe.		24	F	None	08Ju11LI
Mary		22	F	None	08Ju11LI
WALSH, Cathe.		24	F	None	08Ju11LI
BURK, Patk.		20	M	Laborer	08Ju11LI
SHAUGNESSY, Mary		25	F	None	08Ju11LI
DONOUGH, Mary-W.		22	F	None	08Ju11LI
Margt.		20	F	None	08Ju11LI
Patrick		21	M	Laborer	08Ju11LI
ROONEY, Pat		22	M	Laborer	08Ju11LI
William		25	M	Laborer	08Ju11LI
FLANAGAN, Jno.		25	M	Laborer	08Ju11LI
GANLAN, Pat		35	M	Laborer	08Ju11LI
Mary	(W)	27	F	None	08Ju11LI
Mary	(D)	07	F	Child	08Ju11LI
Jno.	(S)	04	M	Child	08Ju11LI
Bridget	(D)	02	F	Child	08Ju11LI
BURKE, Ed.		35	M	Laborer	08Ju11LI
MCHUGH, Austin		23	M	Laborer	08Ju11LI
FERN, Michl.		26	M	Laborer	08Ju11LI
Saml.	(B)	30	M	Laborer	08Ju11LI
John	(B)	24	M	Laborer	08Ju11LI
James		03	M	Child	08Ju11LI
Peggy	(M)	60	F	None	08Ju11LI
FONLAND, Peter		26	M	Laborer	08Ju11LI
CARR, Thos.		29	M	Laborer	08Ju11LI
HARLY, Matt		24	M	Laborer	08Ju11LI
FRANCIS, Thos.		25	M	Laborer	08Ju11LI
CLARK, Peter		21	M	Laborer	08Ju11LI
MORAN, James		25	M	Laborer	08Ju11LI
TANLEY, Hugh		33	M	Laborer	08Ju11LI
Cathe.		22	F	None	08Ju11LI

NAMES OF PASSENGERS	AGE	SEX	OCCUPATIONS	DATE PORT SHIP
DONNELLON, W.	23	M	Laborer	08Ju11LI
KEARNY, Michael	19	M	Laborer	08Ju11LI
LEDDY, Denis	22	M	Laborer	08Ju11LI
RUDY, Pat	25	M	Laborer	08Ju11LI
Peggy	22	F	None	08Ju11LI
KEARNS, Timy.	21	M	Laborer	08Ju11LI
Honor	21	F	None	08Ju11LI
WALSH, Michl.	25	M	Laborer	08Ju11LI
Edward	23	M	Laborer	08Ju11LI
Bridget	23	F	None	08Ju11LI
CLONAN, Ned	22	M	Laborer	08Ju11LI
Bently	30	M	Laborer	08Ju11LI
BUCK, Mary	25	F	None	08Ju11LI
FRANY, Peter	23	M	Laborer	08Ju11LI
GIBBONS, Thos.	28	M	Laborer	08Ju11LI
RICH, Nancy	20	F	None	08Ju11LI
FLAHERTY, Mary	20	F	None	08Ju11LI
GIBBONS, Biddy	20	F	None	08Ju11LI
KEARNS, Redmond	18	M	Laborer	08Ju11LI
OBRIEN, Dennis	27	M	Laborer	08Ju11LI
BARRETT, Pat	22	M	Laborer	08Ju11LI
Wm.	35	M	Laborer	08Ju11LI
BERKE, John	20	M	Laborer	08Ju11LI
JORDAN, Judy	28	F	None	08Ju11LI
Honor	30	F	None	08Ju11LI
LOFTUS, Pat	20	M	Laborer	08Ju11LI
Kate	20	F	None	08Ju11LI
SCULLY, John	35	M	Laborer	08Ju11LI
Cathe.	30	F	None	08Ju11LI
FLAHERTY, Thos.	30	M	Laborer	08Ju11LI
Bridget	20	F	None	08Ju11LI
BURNS, Martin	30	M	Laborer	08Ju11LI
Biddy	20	F	None	08Ju11LI
MORRISY, Pat	32	M	Laborer	08Ju11LI
LONG, John	25	M	Laborer	08Ju11LI
DUFFEY, Pat	31	M	Laborer	08Ju11LI
Mary	29	F	None	08Ju11LI

COXON 08 JUNE 1847

From Cork

NAMES OF PASSENGERS	AGE	SEX	OCCUPATIONS	DATE PORT SHIP
MCCARTHY, John	27	M	Farmer	08Ju14LJ
NEAL, M.	25	M	Farmer	08Ju14LJ
Cath.	22	F	None	08Ju14LJ
Mary	21	F	None	08Ju14LJ
GRIFFIN, D.	28	M	Laborer	08Ju14LJ
PEGOTT, J.	24	M	Laborer	08Ju14LJ
CARROLL, D.	24	M	Laborer	08Ju14LJ
Cath.	26	F	None	08Ju14LJ
MCCARTHY, Jos.	30	M	Servant	08Ju14LJ
CONNOLLY, N.	21	M	Servant	08Ju14LJ
Mary	22	F	None	08Ju14LJ
MCCARTHY, Jno.	30	M	Servant	08Ju14LJ
HAILEY, D.	36	M	Servant	08Ju14LJ
SHEHAN, J.	22	M	Servant	08Ju14LJ
MURPHY, P.	22	M	Servant	08Ju14LJ
EAGAN, J.	26	M	Servant	08Ju14LJ
Jno.	17	M	Servant	08Ju14LJ
Mary	30	F	None	08Ju14LJ
FITZGERALD, P.	30	M	Laborer	08Ju14LJ
Ellen	30	F	None	08Ju14LJ
NEAL, M.	02	M	Child	08Ju14LJ
MURPHY, W.	27	M	Farmer	08Ju14LJ
HOLLAND, D.	35	M	Farmer	08Ju14LJ
Mary	28	F	None	08Ju14LJ
WADE, Pat	30	M	Farmer	08Ju14LJ
BEAN, M.	28	M	Farmer	08Ju14LJ
COFFEE, Ed.	22	M	Farmer	08Ju14LJ

NAMES OF PASSENGERS	AGE	SEX	OCCUPATIONS	DATE PORT SHIP	NAMES OF PASSENGERS	AGE	SEX	OCCUPATIONS	DATE PORT SHIP
COFFEE, Cath.	30	F	None	08Ju14LJ	BEST, Ed.	27	M	Farmer	08Ju14LJ
Julia	27	F	None	08Ju14LJ	CLAN, Mich.H.	26	M	Farmer	08Ju14LJ
Ned	22	M	Laborer	08Ju14LJ	Mary-Ann	22	F	None	08Ju14LJ
Tade	50	M	Laborer	08Ju14LJ	ROCHE, Mary	20	F	None	08Ju14LJ
HAILY, Jos.	04	M	Child	08Ju14LJ	James	30	M	Farmer	08Ju14LJ
RAY, W.	02	M	Child	08Ju14LJ	SEAWELL, David	25	M	Farmer	08Ju14LJ
Cath. (M)	25	F	None	08Ju14LJ					
COLEMAN, Danl.	26	M	Laborer	08Ju14LJ					
Mary	26	F	None	08Ju14LJ					
Cath.	22	F	None	08Ju14LJ	CARTHAGE 09 JUNE 1847				
SPENCER, Rich.	30	M	Laborer	08Ju14LJ					
Wm.	20	M	Laborer	08Ju14LJ	From Liverpool				
Ann	25	F	None	08Ju14LJ					
WALSH, Nancy	20	F	None	08Ju14LJ					
FOLEY, Denis	24	M	Laborer	08Ju14LJ					
TERNEY, P.	30	M	Laborer	08Ju14LJ	BLAZE, Ann-J.	18	F	None	09Ju02Ln
MURPHY, C.	30	M	Laborer	08Ju14LJ	FALCONER, A.	56	M	Merchant	09Ju02Ln
Johannah	25	F	None	08Ju14LJ	MILLER, R.	46	M	Spinner	09Ju02Ln
Ellen	23	F	None	08Ju14LJ	ROBB, J.	21	M	Grocer	09Ju02Ln
Tim	25	M	Laborer	08Ju14LJ	REID, P.	16	M	Clerk	09Ju02Ln
Dan	30	M	Laborer	08Ju14LJ	HAYS, Jane	18	F	None	09Ju02Ln
Judy	30	F	None	08Ju14LJ	Walter	17	M	Tailor	09Ju02Ln
Judy	03	F	Child	08Ju14LJ	DONOGHUE, P.	22	M	Laborer	09Ju02Ln
LONY, Thos.	35	M	Farmer	08Ju14LJ	Mary	17	F	None	09Ju02Ln
Jeremiah	30	M	Farmer	08Ju14LJ	ROGERS, A.	28	M	Laborer	09Ju02Ln
Tim	25	M	Farmer	08Ju14LJ	NASH, Jas.	26	M	Laborer	09Ju02Ln
NEILL, M.	30	M	Farmer	08Ju14LJ	GILROY, Ph.	44	M	Laborer	09Ju02Ln
LOCK, Wm.	26	M	Farmer	08Ju14LJ	GREENAN, Th.	18	M	Laborer	09Ju02Ln
Sarah	22	F	None	08Ju14LJ	SHANLY, Ellen	18	F	None	09Ju02Ln
Robt.	20	M	Laborer	08Ju14LJ	OBRIEN, D.	20	M	Laborer	09Ju02Ln
Thos.	.00	M	Infant	08Ju14LJ	NORTON, Jas.	20	M	Laborer	09Ju02Ln
LYNCH, Tim	24	M	Laborer	08Ju14LJ	SOLAN, Mich.	30	M	Laborer	09Ju02Ln
Eliza	20	F	None	08Ju14LJ	CRAIN, H.	25	M	Laborer	09Ju02Ln
REILLY, Tim	35	M	Laborer	08Ju14LJ	NORTON, Mich.	24	M	Laborer	09Ju02Ln
MURPHY, D.	28	M	Laborer	08Ju14LJ	GILROY, Mary	18	F	None	09Ju02Ln
DAGER, W.	25	M	Laborer	08Ju14LJ	SULIVAN, Ellen	17	F	None	09Ju02Ln
John	33	M	Laborer	08Ju14LJ	NAIKER, Pat	24	M	Laborer	09Ju02Ln
SHAHAN, Pat	35	M	Laborer	08Ju14LJ	Bridget	24	F	None	09Ju02Ln
SHEA, Mich.	27	M	Laborer	08Ju14LJ	MOLLOY, Jno.	20	M	Laborer	09Ju02Ln
BARRY, Wm.	30	M	Laborer	08Ju14LJ	GRADY, T.	30	M	Laborer	09Ju02Ln
HIGGINS, D.	20	M	Laborer	08Ju14LJ	FARNEL, Pat	20	M	Laborer	09Ju02Ln
HUGS, P.	23	M	Laborer	08Ju14LJ	Margt.	14	F	None	09Ju02Ln
Jno.	20	M	Laborer	08Ju14LJ	DUFFY, Ann	20	F	None	09Ju02Ln
J.	16	M	Laborer	08Ju14LJ	ROGERS, John	29	M	Laborer	09Ju02Ln
Johannah	12	F	None	08Ju14LJ	KEENAN, Th.	20	M	Laborer	09Ju02Ln
Nancy	10	F	Child	08Ju14LJ	MURPHY, T.	30	M	Laborer	09Ju02Ln
Jno.	40	M	Laborer	08Ju14LJ	HOALHAM, T.	20	M	Laborer	09Ju02Ln
SEVENING, R.	27	M	Laborer	08Ju14LJ	DWIRE, M.	22	M	Laborer	09Ju02Ln
CASEY, Jas.	30	M	Laborer	08Ju14LJ	MCCAUNE, Pat	24	M	Laborer	09Ju02Ln
Cath. (W)	30	F	None	08Ju14LJ	CONNELLY, Pat	24	M	Laborer	09Ju02Ln
Jno. (S)	08	M	Child	08Ju14LJ	MCCANE, Mary	26	F	None	09Ju02Ln
Hannah (D)	07	F	Child	08Ju14LJ	FARRIL, Cath.	18	F	None	09Ju02Ln
James (S)	03	M	Child	08Ju14LJ	KENNY, J.	34	M	Laborer	09Ju02Ln
CRONIN, Bess	30	F	None	08Ju14LJ	Mich. (P)	70	M	Laborer	09Ju02Ln
FALRAY, Jno.	47	M	Laborer	08Ju14LJ	Mich.Jr. (S)	04	M	Child	09Ju02Ln
Jno. (S)	18	M	Laborer	08Ju14LJ	MCDALLION, Thos.	30	M	Laborer	09Ju02Ln
Patrick (S)	20	M	Laborer	08Ju14LJ	FARILY, Susan	20	F	None	09Ju02Ln
FUROLING, Julia	18	F	None	08Ju14LJ	Susan	15	F	None	09Ju02Ln
WOLF, Jas.	25	M	Laborer	08Ju14LJ	BRADY, Cath.	18	F	None	09Ju02Ln
FUROLING, Job	18	M	Laborer	08Ju14LJ	TAILOR, Jas.	18	M	Laborer	09Ju02Ln
Patrick	17	M	Laborer	08Ju14LJ	TRUMBEL, Cath.	25	F	None	09Ju02Ln
Jno.	15	M	Laborer	08Ju14LJ	DOYLE, Wm.	35	M	Laborer	09Ju02Ln
WALSH, Bat	22	M	Laborer	08Ju14LJ	JACKSON, Jno.	22	M	Spinner	09Ju02Ln
RYAN, Ally	36	F	None	08Ju14LJ	A.	25	M	Spinner	09Ju02Ln
DAVIS, L.	40	M	Farmer	08Ju14LJ	SHIELS, Jno.	22	M	Spinner	09Ju02Ln
HAILEY, J.	28	M	Farmer	08Ju14LJ	Margt.	21	F	None	09Ju02Ln
DOWNING, Jno.	40	M	Farmer	08Ju14LJ	Robt.	.00	M	Infant	09Ju02Ln
Jno. (S)	18	M	Farmer	08Ju14LJ	HUME, Jno.	25	M	Weaver	09Ju02Ln
Rebecca (D)	16	F	None	08Ju14LJ	JOHNSON, Jas.	26	M	Weaver	09Ju02Ln
Eliza (W)	40	F	None	08Ju14LJ	CREELMANN, Jno.	22	M	Weaver	09Ju02Ln
Mary (D)	18	F	None	08Ju14LJ	THOMAS, Elsa	40	F	None	09Ju02Ln
Ellen (D)	16	F	None	08Ju14LJ	Wm. (S)	13	M	None	09Ju02Ln
DALEY, Jer.	23	M	Farmer	08Ju14LJ	Hannah (D)	09	F	Child	09Ju02Ln
WALSH, Ann	28	F	None	08Ju14LJ					
MURRAY, M.	28	M	Farmer	08Ju14LJ					

NAMES OF PASSENGERS		AGE	SEX	OCCUPATIONS	DATE PORT SHIP
THOMAS, Thos.	(S)	05	M	Child	09Ju02Ln
CARR, Henry		39	M	Mechanic	09Ju02Ln
Elizth.	(W)	34	F	None	09Ju02Ln
Wm.	(S)	13	M	Mechanic	09Ju02Ln
DUFFY, Thos.		31	M	Mechanic	09Ju02Ln
CARR, Jno.		26	M	Mariner	09Ju02Ln
LEWIS, W.		35	M	Mechanic	09Ju02Ln
WALSH, Jno.		25	M	Mechanic	09Ju02Ln
Mary-A.		17	F	None	09Ju02Ln
ROCHFORD, Mary		30	F	None	09Ju02Ln
Cath.		23	F	None	09Ju02Ln
SCANLIN, Mich.		23	M	Mechanic	09Ju02Ln
Cath.		20	F	None	09Ju02Ln
MCARWY, Dennis		26	M	Laborer	09Ju02Ln
Mary	(W)	26	F	None	09Ju02Ln
Loghlin	(S)	07	M	Child	09Ju02Ln
Edward	(S)	04	M	Child	09Ju02Ln
Andrew	(S)	02	M	Child	09Ju02Ln
DONNELY, Jno.		25	M	Laborer	09Ju02Ln
Aben		28	M	Laborer	09Ju02Ln
Bridget		27	F	None	09Ju02Ln
FANTY, Rose		20	F	None	09Ju02Ln
GARRIGAN, Brian		29	M	Laborer	09Ju02Ln
Ann	(W)	19	F	None	09Ju02Ln
Ph.	(S)	03	M	Child	09Ju02Ln
HANA, Ann		18	F	None	09Ju02Ln
Judy		17	F	None	09Ju02Ln
STAPLETON, Wm.		22	M	Laborer	09Ju02Ln
SMYTH, Ann		30	F	None	09Ju02Ln
CARRIGAN, Ann		20	F	None	09Ju02Ln
MCMAHAN, Mary		17	F	None	09Ju02Ln
BOYLAN, Pat		20	M	Laborer	09Ju02Ln
MCRODE, N.		30	M	Laborer	09Ju02Ln
BAGNALL, Cath.		22	F	None	09Ju02Ln
Margt.		20	F	None	09Ju02Ln
TRAINOR, Mary		22	F	None	09Ju02Ln
LOGUE, Wm.		26	M	Laborer	09Ju02Ln
CULLIN, Jno.		20	M	Laborer	09Ju02Ln
REILY, Pat		44	M	Laborer	09Ju02Ln
Mary	(W)	50	F	None	09Ju02Ln
Joseph	(S)	13	M	None	09Ju02Ln
John	(S)	11	M	None	09Ju02Ln
George	(S)	09	M	Child	09Ju02Ln
Mary	(D)	07	F	Child	09Ju02Ln
GIBNEY, Mich.		40	M	Laborer	09Ju02Ln
KAVAUGH, Ph.		27	M	Laborer	09Ju02Ln
COTHINGTON, Mary		18	F	None	09Ju02Ln
MCSORLEY, Elizth.		26	F	None	09Ju02Ln
ROGAN, Jno.		20	M	Laborer	09Ju02Ln
RYAN, Mich.		23	M	Laborer	09Ju02Ln
HIGGINS, Cath.		22	F	None	09Ju02Ln
THOMPSON, Ann		19	F	None	09Ju02Ln
GERRITY, Mary		17	F	None	09Ju02Ln
DIGNAISS, Hannah		17	F	None	09Ju02Ln
GERITY, Law.		30	M	Laborer	09Ju02Ln
HURAL, Law.		26	M	Laborer	09Ju02Ln
ROBERTSON, Wm.		21	M	Laborer	09Ju02Ln
CONNOLY, Jno.		16	M	Laborer	09Ju02Ln
MCMULLEN, Jno.		25	M	Laborer	09Ju02Ln
GRADY, Jas.		21	M	Laborer	09Ju02Ln
MADDEN, Mary		19	F	None	09Ju02Ln
MORRISON, Thos.		25	M	Laborer	09Ju02Ln
BURNS, Ed.		25	M	Laborer	09Ju02Ln
Ellen		23	F	None	09Ju02Ln
HAMILTON, Alex.		20	M	Laborer	09Ju02Ln
MORPETH, Elizth.		30	F	None	09Ju02Ln
CARROL, Briget		22	F	None	09Ju02Ln
NOWLAN, Winford		28	F	None	09Ju02Ln
CHANY, J.		52	M	Mechanic	09Ju02Ln
J.Jr.	(S)	13	M	Mechanic	09Ju02Ln
HOGAN, Magt.		22	F	None	09Ju02Ln
KENNY, Mick		40	M	Laborer	09Ju02Ln
NORTON, Pat		19	M	Laborer	09Ju02Ln
FITZGERALD, M.		25	M	Laborer	09Ju02Ln
BRODRICK, D.		25	M	Mechanic	09Ju02Ln

NAMES OF PASSENGERS		AGE	SEX	OCCUPATIONS	DATE PORT SHIP
DILLON, Jno.		27	M	Mechanic	09Ju02Ln
BRODRICK, Briget		25	F	None	09Ju02Ln
CRAIN, Martin		22	M	Mechanic	09Ju02Ln
GANSEY, Jas.		60	M	Mechanic	09Ju02Ln
Jno.	(S)	30	M	Mechanic	09Ju02Ln
MCCANE, Jno.		28	M	Farmer	09Ju02Ln
BURKE, Thos.		37	M	Farmer	09Ju02Ln
Mary	(W)	28	F	None	09Ju02Ln
Thos.Jr.	(S)	07	M	Child	09Ju02Ln
John	(S)	05	M	Child	09Ju02Ln
Mary-A.	(D)	04	F	Child	09Ju02Ln
Sarah	(D)	02	F	Child	09Ju02Ln
John		24	M	Mechanic	09Ju02Ln
Michael		22	M	Mechanic	09Ju02Ln
Patrick		12	M	Mechanic	09Ju02Ln
LANNING, Pat.		21	M	Laborer	09Ju02Ln
HENEKIN, Ed.		27	M	Laborer	09Ju02Ln
FLYNN, Pat-Jr.		21	M	Laborer	09Ju02Ln
HUGHES, Jno.		27	M	Laborer	09Ju02Ln
FLYNN, Pat		56	M	Laborer	09Ju02Ln
COCKLY, B.		24	M	Laborer	09Ju02Ln
KENIVAN, Jas.		24	M	Laborer	09Ju02Ln
NEVIN, W.		33	M	Laborer	09Ju02Ln
CRAIN, Owen		25	M	Laborer	09Ju02Ln
Mary	(W)	20	F	None	09Ju02Ln
Ann	(D)	.00	F	Infant	09Ju02Ln
Thos.		20	M	Laborer	09Ju02Ln
CAMPION, Ed.		28	M	Laborer	09Ju02Ln
MOONY, Mich.		25	M	Laborer	09Ju02Ln
CAMPION, Mary		23	F	None	09Ju02Ln
GALAGER, Corns.		27	M	Laborer	09Ju02Ln
CORDY, Thos.		27	M	Laborer	09Ju02Ln
NEWGENT, Thos.		26	M	Laborer	09Ju02Ln

JAMES-REDDON 09 JUNE 1847

From Liverpool

NAMES OF PASSENGERS		AGE	SEX	OCCUPATIONS	DATE PORT SHIP
LEATHAM, Michael		20	M	Laborer	09Ju02Lo
CONNELLY, Thos.		21	M	Laborer	09Ju02Lo
KANE, Thos.		20	M	Laborer	09Ju02Lo
REILY, M.		20	M	Laborer	09Ju02Lo
ELLIS, Wm.		40	M	Farmer	09Ju02Lo
Cath.	(W)	40	F	None	09Ju02Lo
Mary	(D)	20	F	None	09Ju02Lo
Charles	(S)	20	M	Farmer	09Ju02Lo
Sally	(D)	20	F	None	09Ju02Lo
DOOLING, P.		20	M	Laborer	09Ju02Lo
MEALY, J.		20	M	Laborer	09Ju02Lo
GLEESON, D.		20	M	Laborer	09Ju02Lo
KILROE, Ed.		22	M	Laborer	09Ju02Lo
GALLATIN, G.		22	M	Laborer	09Ju02Lo
GRADY, J.		30	M	Laborer	09Ju02Lo
Aho.		21	F	None	09Ju02Lo
SHEAN, J.		30	M	Laborer	09Ju02Lo
U	(W)	21	F	None	09Ju02Lo
NORTON, Jno.		25	M	Laborer	09Ju02Lo
U	(W)	23	F	None	09Ju02Lo
TRACY, Mary		20	F	None	09Ju02Lo
Cath.		12	F	None	09Ju02Lo
NAUGHTEN, L.		49	M	Farmer	09Ju02Lo
Law.	(S)	20	M	Farmer	09Ju02Lo
Peggy	(D)	19	F	None	09Ju02Lo
Bridget	(D)	17	F	None	09Ju02Lo
MCDERMOTT, M.		20	M	Laborer	09Ju02Lo
CAMPBELL, P.		40	M	Laborer	09Ju02Lo
HEALY, M.		17	M	Laborer	09Ju02Lo
RIGBY, J.		20	M	Laborer	09Ju02Lo
GOOLEY, Ann		20	F	None	09Ju02Lo

NAMES OF PASSENGERS		AGE	SEX	OCCUPATIONS	DATE PORT SHIP
HITCHCOCK, J.		25	M	Laborer	09Ju02Lo
U	(W)	25	F	None	09Ju02Lo
Emma	(D)	11	F	None	09Ju02Lo
Eliza	(D)	05	F	Child	09Ju02Lo
HERMATAGE, W.		20	M	Mechanic	09Ju02Lo
BAINFENTS, Sarah		20	F	None	09Ju02Lo
JONES, Wm.		30	M	Laborer	09Ju02Lo
U	(W)	26	F	None	09Ju02Lo
MCDONALD, Thos.		26	M	Laborer	09Ju02Lo
COPELAND, Jas.		21	M	Laborer	09Ju02Lo
U	(W)	21	F	None	09Ju02Lo
GRANT, Daniel		30	M	Laborer	09Ju02Lo
U	(W)	26	F	None	09Ju02Lo
MAKIN, Chs.		22	M	Laborer	09Ju02Lo
Patk.		20	M	Laborer	09Ju02Lo
Susan		18	F	None	09Ju02Lo
Ann-G.		50	F	None	09Ju02Lo
MURRAY, Joe		20	M	Laborer	09Ju02Lo
NEVIN, Fanny		20	F	None	09Ju02Lo
Rose		20	F	None	09Ju02Lo
MCCONELL, M.		20	M	Laborer	09Ju02Lo
CONLAN, Jas.		20	M	Laborer	09Ju02Lo
Thomas		20	M	Laborer	09Ju02Lo
GLYNNE, Mary		20	F	None	09Ju02Lo
Cath.		20	F	None	09Ju02Lo
MACNAMARA, B.		20	M	Laborer	09Ju02Lo
COYNE, Jno.		20	M	Laborer	09Ju02Lo
GAHAGAN, Jno.		20	M	Laborer	09Ju02Lo
HUNT, Maria		20	F	None	09Ju02Lo
COYNE, Magt.		20	F	None	09Ju02Lo
GERAGHT, Ann		20	F	None	09Ju02Lo
CONRAY, Pat		32	M	Laborer	09Ju02Lo
VERNON, Richd.		28	M	Laborer	09Ju02Lo
Ann		20	F	None	09Ju02Lo
MALONEY, U		26	F	Wi	09Ju02Lo
GREENE, Ann		20	F	None	09Ju02Lo
MONKS, Elizabeth		20	F	None	09Ju02Lo
FAGAN, Cath.		20	F	None	09Ju02Lo
Mary		20	F	None	09Ju02Lo
DOYLE, Pat.		20	M	Laborer	09Ju02Lo
ROSNEY, Peter		20	M	Laborer	09Ju02Lo
OBRIEN, Danl.		40	M	Laborer	09Ju02Lo
U	(W)	40	F	None	09Ju02Lo
Rose	(D)	00	F	None	09Ju02Lo
HEWEN, S.		19	M	Laborer	09Ju02Lo
GALAHER, M.		22	M	Laborer	09Ju02Lo
CAMPBELL, A.		50	M	Laborer	09Ju02Lo
GILLESPIE, Jno.		19	M	Laborer	09Ju02Lo
GALAHER, Patt		20	M	Laborer	09Ju02Lo
KENNY, Mich.		22	M	Laborer	09Ju02Lo
MCMULLIGAN, Jas.		20	M	Laborer	09Ju02Lo
BULCKLEY, Denis		20	M	Laborer	09Ju02Lo
KEEFE, Pat		20	M	Laborer	09Ju02Lo
CAHAREN, Pat-F.		20	M	Laborer	09Ju02Lo

WINDSOR-CASTLE 09 JUNE 1847

From Liverpool

NAMES OF PASSENGERS		AGE	SEX	OCCUPATIONS	DATE PORT SHIP
DENNEY, Bridget		24	F	Servant	09Ju02Lw
Margaret		26	F	Servant	09Ju02Lw
HAUGH, Mary		21	F	Servant	09Ju02Lw
RYAN, Judy		30	F	Servant	09Ju02Lw
KELLEY, Wm.		31	M	Laborer	09Ju02Lw
DONOHUE, Nicholas		19	M	Laborer	09Ju02Lw
WHEELER, Stephen		16	M	Laborer	09Ju02Lw
Ann		17	F	Servant	09Ju02Lw
DONOHUE, John		19	M	Laborer	09Ju02Lw
KELLY, Mary		19	F	Servant	09Ju02Lw

NAMES OF PASSENGERS		AGE	SEX	OCCUPATIONS	DATE PORT SHIP
BATTY, Mary		19	F	Servant	09Ju02Lw
LINDSEY, Ellen		20	F	Servant	09Ju02Lw
GALLAGHER, Petrus		22	M	Laborer	09Ju02Lw
FALLER, Cora		30	F	Servant	09Ju02Lw
EUGEN, O.		31	M	Laborer	09Ju02Lw
WALSH, Pat		34	M	Laborer	09Ju02Lw
MCDONALD, D.		33	M	Laborer	09Ju02Lw
DALY, H.		29	M	Laborer	09Ju02Lw
FOWLER, Anne		19	F	Servant	09Ju02Lw
MAHONEY, Ellen		20	F	Servant	09Ju02Lw
CAMPBELL, John		21	M	Laborer	09Ju02Lw
QUIGLEY, Henry		19	M	Laborer	09Ju02Lw
Nell		18	M	Laborer	09Ju02Lw
LYNCH, James		17	M	Laborer	09Ju02Lw
DOUGHERTY, Ellen		20	F	Servant	09Ju02Lw
RIES, Mary-Ann		19	F	Servant	09Ju02Lw
DABY, Catharine		60	F	Servant	09Ju02Lw
HOGAN, Bridget		30	F	Servant	09Ju02Lw
LEON, Pat		31	M	Laborer	09Ju02Lw
MCNAUGHT, Pat		29	M	Laborer	09Ju02Lw
Bony		22	M	Laborer	09Ju02Lw
James		24	M	Laborer	09Ju02Lw
LINSBURY, Edward		19	M	Laborer	09Ju02Lw
Mary		18	F	None	09Ju02Lw
Moyent		16	M	Laborer	09Ju02Lw
RILEY, Michael		00	M	Laborer	09Ju02Lw
SMITH, P.		14	M	Laborer	09Ju02Lw
J.		15	M	Laborer	09Ju02Lw
SAXON, Rose		19	F	Servant	09Ju02Lw
RICE, Money		35	F	Servant	09Ju02Lw
Edward	(S)	13	M	None	09Ju02Lw
Daniel	(S)	12	M	None	09Ju02Lw
James	(S)	11	M	Child	09Ju02Lw
Mary	(D)	02	F	Child	09Ju02Lw
S.Jane	(D)	03	F	Child	09Ju02Lw
MATHEWS, Pat		36	M	Laborer	09Ju02Lw
James		30	M	Laborer	09Ju02Lw
Mary-J.		29	F	None	09Ju02Lw
Robert		14	M	None	09Ju02Lw
Laurence		13	M	None	09Ju02Lw
NOWLAND, Peter		31	M	Laborer	09Ju02Lw
Thomas		31	M	Laborer	09Ju02Lw
Mary-Ann		20	F	Servant	09Ju02Lw
Eliza		19	F	Servant	09Ju02Lw
MCGUNTER, Phil		32	M	Laborer	09Ju02Lw
Nabby	(W)	32	F	None	09Ju02Lw
Honora		50	F	None	09Ju02Lw
Barny	(S)	05	M	Child	09Ju02Lw
Thos.	(S)	03	M	Child	09Ju02Lw
Michl.	(S)	02	M	Child	09Ju02Lw
Died-At-Sea					
Catharine	(D)	.00	F	Infant	09Ju02Lw
Died-At-Sea					
RONETH, Dan		31	M	Laborer	09Ju02Lw
Cath.		29	F	None	09Ju02Lw
Charles		16	M	Laborer	09Ju02Lw
Thomas		18	M	Laborer	09Ju02Lw
Ellen		21	F	Servant	09Ju02Lw
WHITON, Mary		28	F	Servant	09Ju02Lw
MCDERMOTT, Mary		30	F	Servant	09Ju02Lw
RILEY, Ann		21	F	Servant	09Ju02Lw
Silas		22	M	Laborer	09Ju02Lw
MCRONE, Bony		35	M	Laborer	09Ju02Lw
WENZON, Thomas		29	M	Laborer	09Ju02Lw
MCRONE, Edmund		40	M	Laborer	09Ju02Lw
MULLEN, Mary		20	F	Servant	09Ju02Lw
BURNS, Wm.		29	M	Laborer	09Ju02Lw
DUFF, John		34	M	Laborer	09Ju02Lw
BORN, Daniel		38	M	Laborer	09Ju02Lw
DONBAR, James		39	M	Laborer	09Ju02Lw
HUGHES, Catharine		50	F	None	09Ju02Lw
WALLS, Bridget		23	F	Servant	09Ju02Lw
MALONE, Rose		28	F	Servant	09Ju02Lw
RANBY, Ann		29	F	Servant	09Ju02Lw
LALLY, Kate		30	F	Servant	09Ju02Lw

NAMES OF PASSENGERS		AGE	SEX	OCCUPATIONS	DATE PORT SHIP
LALLY, Ann		19	F	Servant	09Ju02Lw
COTHERN, H.		14	F	Servant	09Ju02Lw
BROWN, Isabella		30	F	Servant	09Ju02Lw
FOGHERTY, Miles		18	M	Laborer	09Ju02Lw
Bridget	(M)	50	F	None	09Ju02Lw
MCGOFF, James		16	M	None	09Ju02Lw
OASGOULD, Nay		29	M	None	09Ju02Lw
MCQUINN, Bryant		49	M	None	09Ju02Lw
Ellen	(W)	39	F	None	09Ju02Lw
Catharine	(D)	18	F	Servant	09Ju02Lw
LONEY, Bridget		19	F	Servant	09Ju02Lw
MCQUINN, Bridget		22	F	Servant	09Ju02Lw
BOTHEN, Napoleon		26	M	Laborer	09Ju02Lw
REY, Catharine		21	F	Servant	09Ju02Lw
Victoria		10	F	Child	09Ju02Lw
NOTTON, Peter		20	M	Laborer	09Ju02Lw
FLYNN, Mary		21	F	Servant	09Ju02Lw
MIGHT, Eliza		19	F	Servant	09Ju02Lw
THOMSON, Bridget		18	F	Servant	09Ju02Lw
HOYEN, Ann		20	F	Servant	09Ju02Lw
CORRALL, Honora		18	F	Servant	09Ju02Lw
John		17	M	None	09Ju02Lw
FULLER, Mary		16	F	Servant	09Ju02Lw
Thos.		17	M	None	09Ju02Lw
John		16	M	None	09Ju02Lw
Hugh		15	M	None	09Ju02Lw
Mary-Ann		19	F	Servant	09Ju02Lw
SULLIVAN, John		30	M	Laborer	09Ju02Lw
Kate		27	F	None	09Ju02Lw
RINGDON, Ellen		25	F	Servant	09Ju02Lw
COURTNEY, Ellen		16	F	Servant	09Ju02Lw
Mary		08	F	Child	09Ju02Lw
Bridget		04	F	Child	09Ju02Lw
Betty		02	F	Child	09Ju02Lw
SULLIVAN, Mary		16	F	Servant	09Ju02Lw
Mary		15	F	Servant	09Ju02Lw
Elizabeth		22	F	Servant	09Ju02Lw
Cora		15	F	Servant	09Ju02Lw
GAFFY, Jane		16	F	Servant	09Ju02Lw
KENEDER, Michael		25	M	Laborer	09Ju02Lw
WYNN, John		27	M	Laborer	09Ju02Lw
RONODER, Ellen		26	F	Servant	09Ju02Lw
Joshua		23	M	Laborer	09Ju02Lw
SCOMIE, Ellen		26	F	Servant	09Ju02Lw
EASTON, Betsey		21	F	Servant	09Ju02Lw
Died-At-Sea					
FLYNN, Michael		19	M	Laborer	09Ju02Lw
FITZGERALD, Charles		21	M	Laborer	09Ju02Lw
BANK, Michael		27	M	Laborer	09Ju02Lw
HAHER, Michael		40	M	Laborer	09Ju02Lw
Ellen	(W)	35	F	None	09Ju02Lw
Pat	(S)	16	M	None	09Ju02Lw
Michael	(S)	06	M	Child	09Ju02Lw
FALLON, James		19	M	Laborer	09Ju02Lw
Mary		19	F	Servant	09Ju02Lw
Margaret		20	F	Servant	09Ju02Lw
Biddy		16	F	Servant	09Ju02Lw
MCKENZE, Ann		17	F	Servant	09Ju02Lw
MULLHOLLAND, Thomas		16	M	None	09Ju02Lw
MCLYE, P.		24	M	Laborer	09Ju02Lw
Jas.		23	M	Laborer	09Ju02Lw
RILY, Pat		30	M	Laborer	09Ju02Lw
HAMER, Edward		35	M	Laborer	09Ju02Lw
James		30	M	Laborer	09Ju02Lw
REGAN, James		40	M	Laborer	09Ju02Lw
Tim		35	M	Laborer	09Ju02Lw
Bridget		65	F	None	09Ju02Lw
Bridget		20	F	None	09Ju02Lw
Ann		28	F	Servant	09Ju02Lw
Julia		06	F	Child	09Ju02Lw
COSGROVE, Richard		35	M	Laborer	09Ju02Lw
Wm.		30	M	Laborer	09Ju02Lw
Mary		20	F	None	09Ju02Lw
DOYLE, Cath.		25	F	Servant	09Ju02Lw
MILLS, Pat		26	M	Laborer	09Ju02Lw
MILLS, Ellen		23	F	Servant	09Ju02Lw
Edward		13	M	None	09Ju02Lw
James		07	M	Child	09Ju02Lw
MORTON, Robert		30	M	Laborer	09Ju02Lw
HALEY, Wm.		27	M	Laborer	09Ju02Lw
RONY, James		30	M	Laborer	09Ju02Lw
EGAN, Wm.		30	M	Laborer	09Ju02Lw
LOOMER, Thomas		25	M	Laborer	09Ju02Lw
Bridget		20	F	None	09Ju02Lw
Bridget		12	F	None	09Ju02Lw
Thomas		.00	M	Infant	09Ju02Lw
REILLY, Ellen		20	F	Servant	09Ju02Lw
REYNOLDS, Pat		25	M	Druggist	09Ju02Lw
Ann		20	F	Servant	09Ju02Lw
Ellen		19	F	Servant	09Ju02Lw
DONNELLY, Margaret		21	F	Servant	09Ju02Lw
HAMILTON, Bridget		22	F	Servant	09Ju02Lw
HERN, Biddy		30	F	Servant	09Ju02Lw
Mary		26	F	Servant	09Ju02Lw
FORESTER, Ellen		22	F	Servant	09Ju02Lw
BLACK, Mary		30	F	Servant	09Ju02Lw
Pat.		16	M	None	09Ju02Lw
Bridget	(D)	09	F	Child	09Ju02Lw
Peter	(S)	08	M	Child	09Ju02Lw
John	(S)	04	M	Child	09Ju02Lw
Mary	(D)	.00	F	Infant	09Ju02Lw
COLLINS, Francis		50	M	Laborer	09Ju02Lw
Bridget	(W)	50	F	None	09Ju02Lw
John	(S)	.00	M	Infant	09Ju02Lw
FERDON, Cecilly		20	F	Servant	09Ju02Lw
FINNEGAN, Chas.		24	M	Laborer	09Ju02Lw
PORTEREN, James		19	M	Laborer	09Ju02Lw
HAHERN, Danl.		18	M	Laborer	09Ju02Lw
Michl.		17	M	Laborer	09Ju02Lw
CRANEY, James		50	M	Laborer	09Ju02Lw
Rose	(W)	50	F	None	09Ju02Lw
James	(S)	20	M	Laborer	09Ju02Lw
John	(S)	19	M	Laborer	09Ju02Lw
Bridget	(D)	13	F	None	09Ju02Lw
Mary	(D)	12	F	None	09Ju02Lw
WADE, Edward		20	M	Laborer	09Ju02Lw
WRIGHT, John		20	M	Laborer	09Ju02Lw
REGAN, Mary		19	F	Servant	09Ju02Lw
Anne		18	F	Servant	09Ju02Lw
Mary		20	F	Servant	09Ju02Lw
KIRBY, Peggy		35	F	Servant	09Ju02Lw
James		30	M	Laborer	09Ju02Lw
Pat		18	M	Laborer	09Ju02Lw
James		19	M	Laborer	09Ju02Lw
Richard		16	M	Laborer	09Ju02Lw
DUNN, Olin		19	M	Laborer	09Ju02Lw
HOGAN, John		20	M	Laborer	09Ju02Lw
Sally		21	F	None	09Ju02Lw
HANISTRY, Peter		19	M	Laborer	09Ju02Lw
MAHON, G.		20	M	Laborer	09Ju02Lw
SMITH, Mat.		25	M	Laborer	09Ju02Lw
CRYSELAN, Mat.		29	M	Laborer	09Ju02Lw
STOUBRY, Antolny		30	M	Laborer	09Ju02Lw
ELLENBAUGH, Frdk.		21	M	Laborer	09Ju02Lw
Jacob		22	M	Laborer	09Ju02Lw
GREEN, John		27	M	Laborer	09Ju02Lw
GOLDEN, Mary		35	F	None	09Ju02Lw
James	(S)	13	M	None	09Ju02Lw
Ann	(D)	12	F	None	09Ju02Lw
Cath.	(D)	08	F	Child	09Ju02Lw
Martha	(D)	12	F	None	09Ju02Lw
CORMER, Pat		27	M	Laborer	09Ju02Lw
Bridget		25	F	None	09Ju02Lw
James		14	M	None	09Ju02Lw
Wm.		10	M	Child	09Ju02Lw
Eliza		09	F	Child	09Ju02Lw
DYAN, Barny		35	M	Laborer	09Ju02Lw
Jonas	(S)	14	M	Laborer	09Ju02Lw
MCLAUGHLIN, Barny		16	M	None	09Ju02Lw
BATES, Thomas		22	M	None	09Ju02Lw

NAMES OF PASSENGERS		AGE	SEX	OCCUPATIONS	DATE PORT SHIP
MCMAHON, John		26	M	None	09Ju02Lw
BARTLEY, Richd.		30	M	None	09Ju02Lw
MCQUIN, Ellen		21	F	Servant	09Ju02Lw
DORON, Charles		29	M	Laborer	09Ju02Lw
MCLEARY, Margaret		36	F	None	09Ju02Lw
James		30	M	Laborer	09Ju02Lw
MCMAHON, Rose		19	F	Servant	09Ju02Lw
DUFFY, Michael		21	M	Laborer	09Ju02Lw
MCLAUGHLIN, James		27	M	Laborer	09Ju02Lw
MURPHY, Pat		16	M	Laborer	09Ju02Lw
Mary		21	F	None	09Ju02Lw
MOONEY, Peter		20	M	Laborer	09Ju02Lw
HUGHES, James		18	M	Laborer	09Ju02Lw
EAGON, Wm.		22	M	Laborer	09Ju02Lw
FARMER, Pat		21	M	Laborer	09Ju02Lw
GIFFIN, James		19	M	Laborer	09Ju02Lw
DOYLE, Wm.		23	M	Laborer	09Ju02Lw
MULLEN, Pat		20	M	Laborer	09Ju02Lw

JAMES 09 JUNE 1847

From Dublin

NAMES OF PASSENGERS		AGE	SEX	OCCUPATIONS	DATE PORT SHIP
DAWSON, William		30	M	Laborer	09Ju20Lx
MACKEY, Peter		38	M	Laborer	09Ju20Lx
Roase	(W)	36	F	None	09Ju20Lx
Eliza	(D)	16	F	None	09Ju20Lx
Sarah	(D)	13	F	None	09Ju20Lx
John	(S)	11	M	None	09Ju20Lx
James	(S)	09	M	Child	09Ju20Lx
Eliza	(D)	07	F	Child	09Ju20Lx
Mary	(D)	05	F	Child	09Ju20Lx
Peter	(S)	.00	M	Infant	09Ju20Lx
CAVANAH, Patt		20	M	Laborer	09Ju20Lx
COYLE, Peter		33	M	Laborer	09Ju20Lx
BURKE, Thos.		36	M	Laborer	09Ju20Lx
U	(W)	30	F	None	09Ju20Lx
Thos.	(S)	08	M	Child	09Ju20Lx
John	(S)	06	M	Child	09Ju20Lx
Mary	(D)	04	F	Child	09Ju20Lx
Sarah	(D)	01	F	Child	09Ju20Lx
John		26	M	Laborer	09Ju20Lx
Michael		22	M	Laborer	09Ju20Lx
Patt		11	M	Laborer	09Ju20Lx
Laurence		09	M	Child	09Ju20Lx
MURPHY, Michael		24	M	Laborer	09Ju20Lx
MARTIN, Patt		40	M	Laborer	09Ju20Lx
GALLAGHER, James		40	M	Laborer	09Ju20Lx
BYRNE, Eliza		20	F	None	09Ju20Lx
DALY, John		27	M	Laborer	09Ju20Lx
BENHAM, Thos.		35	M	Laborer	09Ju20Lx
U	(W)	30	F	None	09Ju20Lx
Eliza	(D)	15	F	None	09Ju20Lx
Thos.	(S)	13	M	Laborer	09Ju20Lx
CARRICK, John		60	M	Laborer	09Ju20Lx
Mary	(W)	50	F	None	09Ju20Lx
Eliza	(D)	20	F	None	09Ju20Lx
William	(S)	18	M	Laborer	09Ju20Lx
Charles	(S)	16	M	Laborer	09Ju20Lx
Lucy	(D)	13	F	None	09Ju20Lx
Thos.	(S)	12	M	Laborer	09Ju20Lx
LEWIS, Joseph		24	M	Laborer	09Ju20Lx
MAHER, James		20	M	Laborer	09Ju20Lx
MORAN, Patt		30	M	Laborer	09Ju20Lx
Judy		27	F	None	09Ju20Lx
WALSH, Mary		20	F	None	09Ju20Lx
ENNIS, John		40	M	Laborer	09Ju20Lx
U-Mrs.		60	F	None	09Ju20Lx
Ann		25	F	None	09Ju20Lx

NAMES OF PASSENGERS		AGE	SEX	OCCUPATIONS	DATE PORT SHIP
ENNIS, John		03	M	Child	09Ju20Lx
MAGUIRE, James		40	M	Laborer	09Ju20Lx
Patk.	(S)	20	M	Laborer	09Ju20Lx
Mary	(D)	18	F	None	09Ju20Lx
Eliza	(D)	16	F	None	09Ju20Lx
John	(S)	10	M	Laborer	09Ju20Lx
KEOGH, William		24	M	Laborer	09Ju20Lx
U	(W)	20	F	None	09Ju20Lx
MAHER, Georgia		20	F	None	09Ju20Lx
MURPHY, Ann		20	F	None	09Ju20Lx
BYRNE, Matt		30	M	Laborer	09Ju20Lx
Eliza		25	F	None	09Ju20Lx
DOUGHERTY, Michl.		20	M	Laborer	09Ju20Lx
BIT, Thos.		40	M	Laborer	09Ju20Lx
BOYLE, Thos.		26	M	Laborer	09Ju20Lx
John		24	M	Laborer	09Ju20Lx
JENNETT, William		21	M	Laborer	09Ju20Lx
MURPHY, Jane		18	F	None	09Ju20Lx
MCTURTE, Mary		18	F	None	09Ju20Lx
REED, Eliza		17	F	None	09Ju20Lx
Ellen		16	F	None	09Ju20Lx
FEDIKEN, Mary		25	F	None	09Ju20Lx
Margaret		21	F	None	09Ju20Lx
MCCULLAGH, Ellen		24	F	None	09Ju20Lx
BALL, Catharine		21	F	None	09Ju20Lx
QUINN, Eliza		17	F	None	09Ju20Lx
MAHON, Bridget		20	F	None	09Ju20Lx
KELLY, Micheal		24	M	Laborer	09Ju20Lx
Eliza		22	F	None	09Ju20Lx
NOWLAND, Patt		26	M	Laborer	09Ju20Lx
KENNY, Edward		23	M	Laborer	09Ju20Lx
U	(W)	20	F	None	09Ju20Lx
WARD, John		34	M	Laborer	09Ju20Lx
HATTON, James		21	M	Laborer	09Ju20Lx
CONNAGHTY, Patt		35	M	Laborer	09Ju20Lx
Bridget		30	F	None	09Ju20Lx
DALEY, James		20	M	Laborer	09Ju20Lx
MARCE, Patt		27	M	Laborer	09Ju20Lx
MCLAUGHLAN, Catharine		20	F	Laborer	09Ju20Lx
TOOL, John		26	M	Laborer	09Ju20Lx
Michael		24	M	Laborer	09Ju20Lx
CARRIDY, Mary		40	F	None	09Ju20Lx
Mary		20	F	None	09Ju20Lx
MALONE, Essey		20	F	None	09Ju20Lx
FINTON, Patrick		25	M	Laborer	09Ju20Lx
Eliza	(W)	24	F	None	09Ju20Lx
Rodger	(S)	.00	M	Infant	09Ju20Lx
Mary		26	F	None	09Ju20Lx
HOGAN, Patt		25	M	Laborer	09Ju20Lx
CUNNINGHAM, Matt		16	M	Laborer	09Ju20Lx
NOLAN, Patrick		16	M	Laborer	09Ju20Lx
MANGIN, James		20	M	Laborer	09Ju20Lx
FARRELL, John		30	M	Laborer	09Ju20Lx
Catharine		25	F	None	09Ju20Lx
Mary		18	F	None	09Ju20Lx
Ellen		16	F	None	09Ju20Lx
MAHER, Michael		40	M	Laborer	09Ju20Lx
Judy		35	F	None	09Ju20Lx
BEGGS, Tutty		28	F	None	09Ju20Lx
Mary		26	F	None	09Ju20Lx

ORIZABA 10 JUNE 1847

From Liverpool

NAMES OF PASSENGERS		AGE	SEX	OCCUPATIONS	DATE PORT SHIP
DOOLAN, P.		21	M	Farmer	10Ju02Mb
Thos.		19	M	Farmer	10Ju02Mb
KEEGAN, P.		22	M	Farmer	10Ju02Mb
FITZGERALD, J.		23	M	Farmer	10Ju02Mb

NAMES OF PASSENGERS		AGE	SEX	OCCUPATIONS	DATE PORT SHIP	NAMES OF PASSENGERS		AGE	SEX	OCCUPATIONS	DATE PORT SHIP
BLAKE, Cath.		19	F	None	10Ju02Mb	MCNAMEE, John		15	M	None	10Ju02Mb
My.		30	F	None	10Ju02Mb	Mich.		12	M	None	10Ju02Mb
CARROLL, My.		03	F	Child	10Ju02Mb	Matthew		11	M	None	10Ju02Mb
KEEGAN, My.		16	F	None	10Ju02Mb	MURRY, Ann		23	F	None	10Ju02Mb
BROOK, My.		17	F	None	10Ju02Mb	GALLAGHER, J.		19	M	Farmer	10Ju02Mb
MCDERMOTT, P.		27	M	Farmer	10Ju02Mb	Cath.		18	F	None	10Ju02Mb
MALLAY, J.		21	M	Farmer	10Ju02Mb	MCDONALD, Ellen		17	F	None	10Ju02Mb
DANIEL, Ellen		18	F	None	10Ju02Mb	COYLE, John		33	M	Farmer	10Ju02Mb
Mgt.		18	F	None	10Ju02Mb	My.	(W)	26	F	None	10Ju02Mb
Johann		40	F	None	10Ju02Mb	Jane	(D)	01	F	Child	10Ju02Mb
BROWN, W.		40	M	Farmer	10Ju02Mb	SEMPLE, W.		22	M	Farmer	10Ju02Mb
My.	(W)	32	F	None	10Ju02Mb	MCSORLY, Cath.		40	F	None	10Ju02Mb
Elza.	(D)	09	F	Child	10Ju02Mb	Raye	(S)	18	M	Farmer	10Ju02Mb
LEDIG, B.		40	M	Farmer	10Ju02Mb	Sarah	(D)	14	F	None	10Ju02Mb
MURPHY, J.		22	M	Farmer	10Ju02Mb	John	(S)	12	M	None	10Ju02Mb
ONEIL, C.		28	M	Farmer	10Ju02Mb	MULLEN, Cath.		10	F	None	10Ju02Mb
MCDERMOTT, P.		24	M	Farmer	10Ju02Mb	My.		12	F	None	10Ju02Mb
BRADY, Bgt.		23	F	None	10Ju02Mb	MANKY, P.		60	M	Farmer	10Ju02Mb
CONNOR, J.		20	M	Farmer	10Ju02Mb	MCGINN, E.		50	M	Farmer	10Ju02Mb
Jas.		18	M	Farmer	10Ju02Mb	John	(S)	22	M	Farmer	10Ju02Mb
OCALLAGH, D.		30	M	Farmer	10Ju02Mb	Le---	(D)	20	F	None	10Ju02Mb
MANN, B.		22	M	Farmer	10Ju02Mb	Elyn.	(D)	18	F	None	10Ju02Mb
BENTLY, J.		21	M	Farmer	10Ju02Mb	COPELAND, R.		35	M	Farmer	10Ju02Mb
HOY, S.		28	M	Farmer	10Ju02Mb	My.	(W)	40	F	None	10Ju02Mb
Elza.	(W)	27	F	None	10Ju02Mb	Mgt.	(D)	20	F	None	10Ju02Mb
Stepn.	(S)	02	M	Child	10Ju02Mb	Ellen	(D)	10	F	None	10Ju02Mb
Bans.	(S)	06	M	Child	10Ju02Mb	John	(S)	09	M	Child	10Ju02Mb
RHOA, R.		40	M	Farmer	10Ju02Mb	Robt.	(S)	11	M	Child	10Ju02Mb
My.	(W)	40	F	None	10Ju02Mb	James		22	M	Farmer	10Ju02Mb
Wm.	(S)	13	M	None	10Ju02Mb	FLINN, J.		24	M	Farmer	10Ju02Mb
Mack	(S)	10	M	None	10Ju02Mb	FEELY, P.		22	M	Farmer	10Ju02Mb
Jas.	(S)	09	M	Child	10Ju02Mb	Jas.		20	M	Farmer	10Ju02Mb
Bryan	(S)	07	M	Child	10Ju02Mb	RILEY, My.		20	F	None	10Ju02Mb
Janette	(D)	01	F	Child	10Ju02Mb	GLENN, Ann		20	F	None	10Ju02Mb
Matthew	(P)	60	M	None	10Ju02Mb	DUNN, Bgt.		16	F	None	10Ju02Mb
HURST, Sarah		28	F	None	10Ju02Mb	KELLY, Elza.		17	F	None	10Ju02Mb
My.	(D)	03	F	Child	10Ju02Mb	MULLEN, Rose		30	F	None	10Ju02Mb
Ellen	(D)	01	F	Child	10Ju02Mb	MCKIRY, Cath.		48	F	None	10Ju02Mb
Joseph	(S)	07	M	Child	10Ju02Mb	NUGENT, Mgt.		23	F	None	10Ju02Mb
ROWAN, F.A.		30	M	Farmer	10Ju02Mb	HAMILTON, Ann		23	F	None	10Ju02Mb
My.	(W)	27	F	None	10Ju02Mb	DOWNY, P.		22	M	Farmer	10Ju02Mb
Fent.	(D)	04	F	Child	10Ju02Mb	Sarah		30	F	None	10Ju02Mb
Thos.	(S)	07	M	Child	10Ju02Mb	DEVIN, Alice		22	F	None	10Ju02Mb
Emily	(D)	02	F	Child	10Ju02Mb	KELLY, Jane		24	F	None	10Ju02Mb
Wm.	(S)	06	M	Child	10Ju02Mb	MURPHY, John		50	M	Farmer	10Ju02Mb
CHALWICK, Ruth		21	F	None	10Ju02Mb	Ann		52	F	None	10Ju02Mb
Richd.		22	M	Farmer	10Ju02Mb	Ann	(D)	20	F	None	10Ju02Mb
Wilson		20	M	Farmer	10Ju02Mb	Mgt.	(D)	17	F	None	10Ju02Mb
Wm.		24	M	Farmer	10Ju02Mb	Mgt.		40	F	None	10Ju02Mb
Geo.		25	M	Farmer	10Ju02Mb	Jas.	(S)	15	M	None	10Ju02Mb
DAVIS, Elzt.		68	F	None	10Ju02Mb	Patck.	(S)	13	M	None	10Ju02Mb
MCNAMA, M.		43	M	Farmer	10Ju02Mb	John	(S)	12	M	None	10Ju02Mb
Dermot		20	M	Farmer	10Ju02Mb	Sarah	(D)	07	F	Child	10Ju02Mb
FINGAN, P.		24	M	Farmer	10Ju02Mb	READ, My.		60	F	None	10Ju02Mb
MCEWEN, J.		25	M	Farmer	10Ju02Mb	Maria		30	F	None	10Ju02Mb
WAKEFIELD, E.		68	M	Farmer	10Ju02Mb	ARNSTEY, T.		11	M	None	10Ju02Mb
BOWER, W.		43	M	Farmer	10Ju02Mb	J.		13	F	None	10Ju02Mb
Anna	(D)	20	F	None	10Ju02Mb	MURPHY, J.		25	M	None	10Ju02Mb
Joseph	(S)	15	M	None	10Ju02Mb	RAFFERTY, J.		22	M	None	10Ju02Mb
ALEPIN, P.		35	M	Farmer	10Ju02Mb	Susan		21	F	None	10Ju02Mb
Ann	(D)	19	F	None	10Ju02Mb	Cath.		20	F	None	10Ju02Mb
Judith	(D)	15	F	None	10Ju02Mb	My.		03	F	Child	10Ju02Mb
BRADY, Ann		16	F	None	10Ju02Mb	Fances		01	F	Child	10Ju02Mb
LEVINE, Mgt.		30	F	None	10Ju02Mb	MCGANN, Ann		21	F	None	10Ju02Mb
Richd.	(S)	13	M	None	10Ju02Mb	GUY, Morriss		19	M	Farmer	10Ju02Mb
MILTY, J.		19	M	Farmer	10Ju02Mb	GEARY, D.		12	M	Laborer	10Ju02Mb
ANNON, Cath.		20	F	None	10Ju02Mb	Owen		09	M	Child	10Ju02Mb
LEONARD, Ellen		21	F	None	10Ju02Mb	My.		08	F	Child	10Ju02Mb
BRADY, My.		20	F	None	10Ju02Mb	OWENS, J.		34	M	Laborer	10Ju02Mb
COLTON, C.		28	M	Farmer	10Ju02Mb	RILY, P.		30	M	Laborer	10Ju02Mb
Alice	(W)	30	F	None	10Ju02Mb	OWENS, M.		20	M	Laborer	10Ju02Mb
John	(S)	11	M	None	10Ju02Mb	DWYER, P.		16	M	Laborer	10Ju02Mb
MCNAMEE, Cath.		50	F	None	10Ju02Mb	FERIGAN, M.		20	M	Laborer	10Ju02Mb
Michl.		70	M	Farmer	10Ju02Mb	MEAD, P.		20	M	Laborer	10Ju02Mb
My.		17	F	None	10Ju02Mb	MORAN, J.		25	M	Laborer	10Ju02Mb

NAMES OF PASSENGERS		A G E	S E X	OCCUPATIONS	DATE PORT SHIP
MCCLERY, Ellen		21	F	None	10Ju02Mb
MORGAN, Cath.		20	F	None	10Ju02Mb
FALLON, Bgt.		18	F	None	10Ju02Mb
POWER, P.		40	M	Laborer	10Ju02Mb
Bgt.	(W)	35	F	None	10Ju02Mb
Jas.		25	M	None	10Ju02Mb
Mich.	(S)	14	M	None	10Ju02Mb
My.	(D)	11	F	None	10Ju02Mb
Cath.	(D)	09	F	Child	10Ju02Mb
Robt.	(S)	07	M	Child	10Ju02Mb
Dan.	(S)	05	M	Child	10Ju02Mb
John	(S)	03	M	Child	10Ju02Mb
MCMULLEN, Cath.		21	F	None	10Ju02Mb
Jane		18	F	None	10Ju02Mb
COLLINS, Jane		20	F	None	10Ju02Mb
MCGEE, My.		30	F	None	10Ju02Mb
HENRY, Mar.		24	F	None	10Ju02Mb
WHELAN, Cath.		19	F	None	10Ju02Mb
NICHOLSON, Cath.		19	F	None	10Ju02Mb
BARKER, Ann		21	F	None	10Ju02Mb
FINEGAN, My.		18	F	None	10Ju02Mb
DOOLAN, My.		26	F	None	10Ju02Mb
MCGOWAN, M.		44	F	None	10Ju02Mb
My.		47	F	None	10Ju02Mb
DAY, Ann		26	F	None	10Ju02Mb
SNODY, Jane		19	F	None	10Ju02Mb
WARD, J.		24	M	Laborer	10Ju02Mb
U	(W)	20	F	None	10Ju02Mb
Ellen		18	F	None	10Ju02Mb
RIERDON, T.		23	M	Laborer	10Ju02Mb
MAHER, T.		30	M	Laborer	10Ju02Mb
RIERDON, J.		22	M	Laborer	10Ju02Mb
SMITH, J.		20	M	Laborer	10Ju02Mb
HOLDEN, M.		19	M	Laborer	10Ju02Mb
GAFFNEY, P.		18	M	Laborer	10Ju02Mb
BINNY, My.		19	F	None	10Ju02Mb
HIGGINS, W.		28	M	Laborer	10Ju02Mb
Elzbt.		20	F	None	10Ju02Mb
CONNELL, P.		40	M	Laborer	10Ju02Mb
RIELY, T.		19	M	Laborer	10Ju02Mb
DOLIN, E.		23	M	Laborer	10Ju02Mb
RILY, My.		19	F	None	10Ju02Mb
MCCABE, Mgt.		19	F	None	10Ju02Mb
Cath.		16	F	None	10Ju02Mb
MIGHT, Cath.		16	F	None	10Ju02Mb
MCNAGHEN, W.		48	M	Laborer	10Ju02Mb
Janet	(W)	48	F	None	10Ju02Mb
John	(S)	20	M	Laborer	10Ju02Mb
Jane	(D)	18	F	None	10Ju02Mb
Janet	(D)	16	F	None	10Ju02Mb
Elebt.	(D)	10	F	None	10Ju02Mb
BLACK, Mgt.		28	F	None	10Ju02Mb
Rose		18	F	None	10Ju02Mb
MCMAGAN, J.		22	M	Laborer	10Ju02Mb
LAGAN, W.		22	M	Laborer	10Ju02Mb
MCMAGAN, Jas.		18	M	Laborer	10Ju02Mb
DEVIN, J.		20	M	Laborer	10Ju02Mb
TRACY, M.		24	M	Laborer	10Ju02Mb
DORAN, P.		47	M	Laborer	10Ju02Mb
Bgt.	(W)	35	F	None	10Ju02Mb
Sarah	(D)	04	F	Child	10Ju02Mb
John	(S)	01	M	Child	10Ju02Mb
Cath.	(D)	03	F	Child	10Ju02Mb
DOLLARD, J.		30	M	Laborer	10Ju02Mb
Jas.		12	M	None	10Ju02Mb
DUNNE, Letitia		10	F	None	10Ju02Mb
MCMAGAN, Mary		22	F	None	10Ju02Mb
CHISTEN, J.		20	F	None	10Ju02Mb
TRACY, Bgt.		18	F	None	10Ju02Mb
Cath.		14	F	None	10Ju02Mb
KELLY, M.		25	M	Laborer	10Ju02Mb
RILY, B.		13	M	None	10Ju02Mb
Gratten	(B)	11	M	None	10Ju02Mb
My.	(M)	32	F	None	10Ju02Mb
Mgt.	(T)	09	F	Child	10Ju02Mb

NAMES OF PASSENGERS		A G E	S E X	OCCUPATIONS	DATE PORT SHIP
RILY, Jas.	(B)	07	M	Child	10Ju02Mb
Philip	(B)	05	M	Child	10Ju02Mb
Cath.	(T)	04	F	Child	10Ju02Mb
My.	(T)	02	F	Child	10Ju02Mb
FLINN, Mgt.		20	F	None	10Ju02Mb
ORGAN, J.		35	M	Laborer	10Ju02Mb
Canelus		23	M	Laborer	10Ju02Mb
Ellen		20	F	None	10Ju02Mb
GARGAN, Cath.		25	F	None	10Ju02Mb
DUNN, W.		28	M	Laborer	10Ju02Mb
COSLAN, P.		28	M	Laborer	10Ju02Mb
MADDEN, My.		18	F	None	10Ju02Mb
Elza.		16	F	None	10Ju02Mb
Joseph		13	M	None	10Ju02Mb
GANON, P.		30	M	Laborer	10Ju02Mb
GILMORE, J.		18	M	Laborer	10Ju02Mb
KELLY, J.		17	M	Laborer	10Ju02Mb
DORAN, Ann		20	F	None	10Ju02Mb
MURPHY, Bgt.		21	F	None	10Ju02Mb
RILEY, Ellen		20	F	None	10Ju02Mb
CRANE, C.		20	M	Laborer	10Ju02Mb
OCARELL, M.		28	M	Laborer	10Ju02Mb
MULLEN, M.		37	M	Laborer	10Ju02Mb
My.		57	F	None	10Ju02Mb
John		14	M	Laborer	10Ju02Mb
Patck.		12	M	None	10Ju02Mb
Christopher		10	M	None	10Ju02Mb
Mra.		05	F	Child	10Ju02Mb
Wm.		01	M	Child	10Ju02Mb
SCULLY, My.		20	F	None	10Ju02Mb
Sam.	(S)	02	M	Child	10Ju02Mb
Pady.		12	M	None	10Ju02Mb
Mgt.		18	F	None	10Ju02Mb
WESTON, J.		42	M	Laborer	10Ju02Mb
Elzt.	(W)	38	F	None	10Ju02Mb
Sarah	(D)	22	F	None	10Ju02Mb
Alnd.	(S)	19	M	Laborer	10Ju02Mb
Joseph	(S)	19	M	Laborer	10Ju02Mb
BABE, J.		40	M	Laborer	10Ju02Mb
Elzt.		42	F	None	10Ju02Mb
Robt.		64	M	Laborer	10Ju02Mb

CEYLON 10 JUNE 1847

From Liverpool

NAMES OF PASSENGERS		A G E	S E X	OCCUPATIONS	DATE PORT SHIP
POWER, John		23	M	Laborer	10Ju02Kw
Ellen		22	F	None	10Ju02Kw
Michel		19	M	Laborer	10Ju02Kw
DALTON, John		35	M	Laborer	10Ju02Kw
VAUGHAN, Joseph		25	M	Laborer	10Ju02Kw
Honora		24	F	None	10Ju02Kw
CAWHIG, Corn.		14	M	Laborer	10Ju02Kw
Johanna		.00	F	Infant	10Ju02Kw
MORRISON, James		19	M	Laborer	10Ju02Kw
Lanton		24	M	Laborer	10Ju02Kw
Ellen		14	F	None	10Ju02Kw
ALOHISSY, Corns.		22	M	Laborer	10Ju02Kw
Mary	(M)	50	F	None	10Ju02Kw
Cath.		20	F	None	10Ju02Kw
MCSWEENEY, Thos.		36	M	Laborer	10Ju02Kw
FLEMING, John		30	M	Laborer	10Ju02Kw
Thos.		40	M	Laborer	10Ju02Kw
MORRISON, Jno.		30	M	Laborer	10Ju02Kw
COLBERT, Jno.		35	M	Laborer	10Ju02Kw
Mary	(W)	35	F	None	10Ju02Kw
Johanna	(D)	11	F	None	10Ju02Kw
James	(S)	09	M	Child	10Ju02Kw
Pat	(S)	07	M	Child	10Ju02Kw

584

NAMES OF PASSENGERS	A G E	S E X	OCCUPATIONS	DATE PORT SHIP	NAMES OF PASSENGERS	A G E	S E X	OCCUPATIONS	DATE PORT SHIP
COLBERT, Jno.	(S)	.00 M	Infant	10Ju02Kw	MCHALE, Ann	(D)	20 F	None	10Ju02Kw
WHELAN, Richd.		30 M	Farmer	10Ju02Kw	Cathe.	(D)	14 F	None	10Ju02Kw
BARRY, Andw.		28 M	Farmer	10Ju02Kw	Jno.	(S)	18 M	Laborer	10Ju02Kw
COLEMAN, Ellen		13 F	None	10Ju02Kw	Alexn.	(S)	16 M	Laborer	10Ju02Kw
JONES, Owen		50 M	Farmer	10Ju02Kw	MCCUE, John		20 M	Laborer	10Ju02Kw
Cathe.	(D)	20 F	None	10Ju02Kw	HYNN, Tim		25 M	Laborer	10Ju02Kw
Owen	(S)	13 M	None	10Ju02Kw	SULLIVAN, Dan.		35 M	Laborer	10Ju02Kw
Ed.	(S)	08 M	Child	10Ju02Kw	COFFEE, Dennis		24 M	Laborer	10Ju02Kw
Robt.	(S)	06 M	Child	10Ju02Kw	MCLANE, Thos.		26 M	Laborer	10Ju02Kw
Patrick	(S)	04 M	Child	10Ju02Kw	TWOLES, Robt.		21 M	Laborer	10Ju02Kw
CONLAN, Frank		45 M	Farmer	10Ju02Kw	GALLAGAN, Susan		13 F	None	10Ju02Kw
James	(S)	18 M	Farmer	10Ju02Kw	Ann		12 F	None	10Ju02Kw
MALEADY, John		12 M	None	10Ju02Kw	Wiiham		13 M	Laborer	10Ju02Kw
BOWEN, John		30 M	Farmer	10Ju02Kw	Susan		12 F	None	10Ju02Kw
Bridgt.	(D)	.00 F	Infant	10Ju02Kw	BRADY, Margt.		14 F	None	10Ju02Kw
KELLY, James		30 M	Farmer	10Ju02Kw	KELLY, John		40 M	Laborer	10Ju02Kw
Bridget	(W)	30 F	None	10Ju02Kw	Pat	(S)	12 M	None	10Ju02Kw
Ann	(D)	04 F	Child	10Ju02Kw	Bridget	(D)	14 F	None	10Ju02Kw
DALEY, Ann		20 F	None	10Ju02Kw	CUSACK, Pat		29 M	Laborer	10Ju02Kw
CONNOR, Wm.		23 M	Laborer	10Ju02Kw	WALSH, Pat		20 M	Laborer	10Ju02Kw
Mcht.		23 M	Laborer	10Ju02Kw	LEE, Bridget		19 F	None	10Ju02Kw
MCCANN, Wm.		27 M	Laborer	10Ju02Kw	MCCALL, Barry		26 M	Laborer	10Ju02Kw
WARD, Jno.		22 M	Laborer	10Ju02Kw	HURST, Samul.		22 M	Laborer	10Ju02Kw
MCLANE, John		31 M	Laborer	10Ju02Kw	DAVIS, Mary		24 F	None	10Ju02Kw
MORISSAY, James		26 M	Laborer	10Ju02Kw	Jane		20 F	None	10Ju02Kw
GAFFNEY, Michl.		25 M	Laborer	10Ju02Kw	DUFFY, Thos.		20 M	Laborer	10Ju02Kw
Mary		24 F	None	10Ju02Kw	MULGRAW, Jane		20 F	None	10Ju02Kw
CULLEN, Wm.		22 M	Laborer	10Ju02Kw	DEVINE, Danl.		40 M	Laborer	10Ju02Kw
Ellen		20 F	None	10Ju02Kw	MCDONALD, Jno.		20 M	Laborer	10Ju02Kw
MCDONALD, James		14 M	Laborer	10Ju02Kw	DUNN, Mary		14 F	None	10Ju02Kw
CRAWFORD, Andw.		26 M	Laborer	10Ju02Kw	SPELLMAN, Jno.		32 M	Laborer	10Ju02Kw
LYNCH, Michl.		22 M	Laborer	10Ju02Kw	Honora		22 F	None	10Ju02Kw
GILLESPIE, Mary		20 F	None	10Ju02Kw	TIDLEY, James		40 M	Laborer	10Ju02Kw
Margt.		24 F	None	10Ju02Kw	REILLY, Peter		20 M	Laborer	10Ju02Kw
GENTY, Pat		31 M	Laborer	10Ju02Kw	CULLIN, Mich.		25 M	Laborer	10Ju02Kw
Marcella	(W)	30 F	None	10Ju02Kw	DELANY, Peggy		18 F	None	10Ju02Kw
Thos.	(S)	07 M	Child	10Ju02Kw	GAFFNEY, Peggy		20 F	None	10Ju02Kw
LEE, Pat		40 M	Laborer	10Ju02Kw	TERRY, Mary		13 F	None	10Ju02Kw
Ellen	(W)	40 F	None	10Ju02Kw	HERBERT, Ann		21 F	None	10Ju02Kw
Ann	(D)	13 F	None	10Ju02Kw	CONOLLY, Jno.		60 M	Laborer	10Ju02Kw
Patt	(S)	14 M	Laborer	10Ju02Kw	DOOHAN, Humphrey		20 M	Laborer	10Ju02Kw
Robt.	(S)	12 M	Laborer	10Ju02Kw	MCBRIDE, Pat		20 M	Laborer	10Ju02Kw
GALLNER, Michel		14 M	Laborer	10Ju02Kw	HUGGINS, Thos.		24 M	Laborer	10Ju02Kw
MORENS, Martin		25 M	Laborer	10Ju02Kw	NASH, Richd.		45 M	Laborer	10Ju02Kw
Margt.		12 F	None	10Ju02Kw	Thos.	(S)	24 M	Laborer	10Ju02Kw
Agnes		10 F	None	10Ju02Kw	Jno.	(S)	13 M	None	10Ju02Kw
David		08 M	None	10Ju02Kw	Ellen	(D)	20 F	None	10Ju02Kw
Alexn.		.00 M	Infant	10Ju02Kw	Johanna	(D)	11 F	None	10Ju02Kw
LEAVY, Danl.		26 M	Laborer	10Ju02Kw	Bridget	(D)	14 F	None	10Ju02Kw
DALEY, John		45 M	Laborer	10Ju02Kw	FITZGERALD, John		27 M	Laborer	10Ju02Kw
Mary	(W)	40 F	None	10Ju02Kw	SULLIVAN, James		14 M	Laborer	10Ju02Kw
Johannah	(D)	13 F	None	10Ju02Kw	GALLEGAN, Ann		50 F	None	10Ju02Kw
Margt.	(D)	11 F	None	10Ju02Kw	SULLIVAN, Pat		28 M	Laborer	10Ju02Kw
Mary	(D)	04 F	Child	10Ju02Kw	Peggy		13 F	None	10Ju02Kw
Ellen	(D)	.00 F	Infant	10Ju02Kw	CONNORS, Thos.		30 M	Laborer	10Ju02Kw
SLACK, Owen		37 M	Laborer	10Ju02Kw	Mary		21 F	None	10Ju02Kw
CORNELL, Ed.		25 M	Laborer	10Ju02Kw	LEEVY, Con.		25 M	Laborer	10Ju02Kw
MCCARTHY, Pat		25 M	Laborer	10Ju02Kw	Mary	(W)	40 F	None	10Ju02Kw
CONNORS, Dennis		19 M	Laborer	10Ju02Kw	Ann	(D)	14 F	None	10Ju02Kw
Cornl.		30 M	Laborer	10Ju02Kw	OFTIN, Jno.		22 M	Laborer	10Ju02Kw
Margt.	(W)	30 F	None	10Ju02Kw	Cathe.		21 F	None	10Ju02Kw
Mary	(D)	.00 F	Infant	10Ju02Kw	MADDEN, Jno.		41 M	Laborer	10Ju02Kw
BARRETT, Honora		22 F	None	10Ju02Kw	MCANTHY, Timy		34 M	Laborer	10Ju02Kw
NAGLE, Margt.		30 F	None	10Ju02Kw	DENEEN, Dennis		32 M	Laborer	10Ju02Kw
MCAULIFFE, Thos.		25 M	Laborer	10Ju02Kw	RYAN, Jno.		32 M	Laborer	10Ju02Kw
CULLIN, Johana		19 F	None	10Ju02Kw	MAHONY, Thos.		40 M	Laborer	10Ju02Kw
Margt.		14 F	None	10Ju02Kw	GOGGIN, David		21 M	Laborer	10Ju02Kw
MARNEN, Jno.		20 M	Laborer	10Ju02Kw	CAROLIN, Margt.		13 F	None	10Ju02Kw
MCGINTLY, And.		18 M	Laborer	10Ju02Kw	RINDAN, Dan		26 M	Laborer	10Ju02Kw
Michel.		23 M	Laborer	10Ju02Kw	Mgt.		24 F	None	10Ju02Kw
Cathe.		20 F	None	10Ju02Kw	Dan		24 M	Laborer	10Ju02Kw
SHAUGNESSY, Pat		13 M	Laborer	10Ju02Kw	SHEEHAN, Wm.		24 M	Laborer	10Ju02Kw
MCCORMICK, Ann		14 F	None	10Ju02Kw	Ellen		24 F	None	10Ju02Kw
TURNER, Cathe.		14 F	None	10Ju02Kw	DALY, Ann		23 F	None	10Ju02Kw
MCHALE, Jno.		43 M	Laborer	10Ju02Kw	James		23 M	Laborer	10Ju02Kw

NAMES OF PASSENGERS		A G E	S E X	OCCUPATIONS	DATE PORT SHIP	NAMES OF PASSENGERS		A G E	S E X	OCCUPATIONS	DATE PORT SHIP
BURKE, Jno.		50	M	Laborer	10Ju02Kw	TAYL, Ed.		07	M	Child	10Ju02Kw
Jno.	(S)	12	M	None	10Ju02Kw	Ann		06	F	Child	10Ju02Kw
REYNOLDS, Pat		28	M	Laborer	10Ju02Kw	MCCAINBOYD, Rose		19	F	None	10Ju02Kw
HAMMOND, Frank		28	M	Laborer	10Ju02Kw	REILLY, Wm.		21	M	Laborer	10Ju02Kw
WRIGHT, Fanny		20	F	None	10Ju02Kw	CHAMBERS, Joseph		18	M	Laborer	10Ju02Kw
OBRIEN, M.A.		18	F	None	10Ju02Kw						
Cathe.		16	F	None	10Ju02Kw						
ARNETT, Cath.		36	F	None	10Ju02Kw						
KING, Cath.		20	F	None	10Ju02Kw						
Mary-Ann		14	F	None	10Ju02Kw						
KELLEY, Christopher		30	M	Laborer	10Ju02Kw						
Margt.	(D)	05	F	Child	10Ju02Kw				SARAH-BOYDE 10 JUNE 1847			
Mary	(D)	.00	F	Infant	10Ju02Kw						
JOHNSTON, Mary		20	F	None	10Ju02Kw				From Sligo			
DALTON, Eliza		35	F	None	10Ju02Kw						
Pate	(S)	10	M	None	10Ju02Kw						
Jno.	(S)	06	M	Child	10Ju02Kw	GOLDEN, Pat		20	M	Farmer	10Ju28Mc
Martin	(S)	04	M	Child	10Ju02Kw	MCMURRAY, Pat		40	M	Farmer	10Ju28Mc
Biddy	(D)	13	F	None	10Ju02Kw	Pat	(S)	19	M	Farmer	10Ju28Mc
Mary	(D)	05	F	Child	10Ju02Kw	HIGGINS, John		23	M	Farmer	10Ju28Mc
Patrick		10	M	None	10Ju02Kw	Barthy.		22	M	Farmer	10Ju28Mc
Saml.		06	M	Child	10Ju02Kw	Michael		60	M	Farmer	10Ju28Mc
DOBLING, Ann		04	F	Child	10Ju02Kw	Mary		60	F	None	10Ju28Mc
LAWLAR, Ann		13	F	None	10Ju02Kw	Cathe.		28	F	None	10Ju28Mc
FOGERTY, Ann		05	F	Child	10Ju02Kw	Mary		25	F	None	10Ju28Mc
BROWN, Francis		30	M	Laborer	10Ju02Kw	Margt.		20	F	None	10Ju28Mc
MARTIN, Barry		22	M	Laborer	10Ju02Kw	CLABBY, Mary		22	F	None	10Ju28Mc
SULLIVAN, James		20	M	Laborer	10Ju02Kw	Ann		20	F	None	10Ju28Mc
Johannah		20	F	None	10Ju02Kw	Eleanor		10	F	None	10Ju28Mc
LEATHEN, Wm.		14	M	Laborer	10Ju02Kw	DUNN, Michael		30	M	Farmer	10Ju28Mc
Mary-A.	(W)	30	F	None	10Ju02Kw	Bridget	(W)	30	F	None	10Ju28Mc
MURRAY, Margt.		09	F	Child	10Ju02Kw	Pat	(S)	05	M	Child	10Ju28Mc
WRIGHT, Alice		30	F	None	10Ju02Kw	Barthy.	(S)	03	M	Child	10Ju28Mc
SWEENY, Sarah		30	F	None	10Ju02Kw	Bridget	(D)	02	F	Child	10Ju28Mc
Ned		33	M	Laborer	10Ju02Kw	Mary	(D)	.09	F	Infant	10Ju28Mc
Dennis		34	M	Laborer	10Ju02Kw	HIGGINS, Honor		15	F	None	10Ju28Mc
Rachael		30	F	None	10Ju02Kw	Ann		13	F	None	10Ju28Mc
Timy.		09	M	Child	10Ju02Kw	MCINTYRE, Thos.		20	M	Laborer	10Ju28Mc
CONNELL, Thos.		24	M	Laborer	10Ju02Kw	John		25	M	Laborer	10Ju28Mc
EDWARDS, Geo.		06	M	Child	10Ju02Kw	Kate		15	F	None	10Ju28Mc
ROGERS, Patt		.00	M	Infant	10Ju02Kw	DERRY, Mary		25	F	None	10Ju28Mc
KEEGAN, James		04	M	Child	10Ju02Kw	HISTER, Pat		45	M	Laborer	10Ju28Mc
CULLEN, Jno.		24	M	Farmer	10Ju02Kw	Pat	(S)	20	M	Laborer	10Ju28Mc
Biddy		24	F	None	10Ju02Kw	Thos.	(S)	18	M	Laborer	10Ju28Mc
SLAGON, Mary		28	F	None	10Ju02Kw	Mary	(W)	40	F	None	10Ju28Mc
Pat	(S)	.00	M	Infant	10Ju02Kw	Bridget	(D)	10	F	None	10Ju28Mc
Kate	(D)	.00	F	Infant	10Ju02Kw	CARL, Pat		30	M	Laborer	10Ju28Mc
RONAN, Pat		20	M	Farmer	10Ju02Kw	HEVERON, Owen		60	M	Laborer	10Ju28Mc
James		20	M	Farmer	10Ju02Kw	Pat	(S)	30	M	Laborer	10Ju28Mc
COFFEE, Michl.		50	M	Farmer	10Ju02Kw	John	(S)	28	M	Laborer	10Ju28Mc
Kate	(W)	50	F	None	10Ju02Kw	Winne.	(S)	20	M	Laborer	10Ju28Mc
James		45	M	Farmer	10Ju02Kw	Bridget	(W)	60	F	None	10Ju28Mc
Patt	(S)	14	M	Farmer	10Ju02Kw	Mary	(D)	20	F	None	10Ju28Mc
Mchl.	(S)	10	M	None	10Ju02Kw	Bridget	(D)	25	F	None	10Ju28Mc
FLYNN, Peter		04	M	Child	10Ju02Kw	BROWN, Mary		23	F	None	10Ju28Mc
Mary		06	F	Child	10Ju02Kw	FINEGAN, Michael		53	M	Laborer	10Ju28Mc
Mary-Ann		04	F	Child	10Ju02Kw	FINERON, Pat		20	M	Laborer	10Ju28Mc
REILLEY, Wm.		01	M	Child	10Ju02Kw	CONWAY, Anthony		35	M	Laborer	10Ju28Mc
Bridget		07	F	Child	10Ju02Kw	Celia	(W)	30	F	None	10Ju28Mc
Walter		04	M	Child	10Ju02Kw	Pat	(S)	01	M	Child	10Ju28Mc
MCLEER, Chas.		25	M	Laborer	10Ju02Kw	OCONNOR, Mary		47	F	None	10Ju28Mc
MACKEY, Peter		20	M	Laborer	10Ju02Kw	Bridget	(D)	22	F	None	10Ju28Mc
ASKIN, James		19	M	Laborer	10Ju02Kw	Ellen	(D)	16	F	None	10Ju28Mc
MCKENNON, Rose		20	F	None	10Ju02Kw	Hugh	(D)	12	M	Laborer	10Ju28Mc
Cathe.	(D)	06	F	Child	10Ju02Kw	FINNEGAN, Thos.		20	M	Laborer	10Ju28Mc
MCINTY, Michl.		16	M	Laborer	10Ju02Kw	FLATLEY, Andw.		40	M	Laborer	10Ju28Mc
MCKENNON, Mary		14	F	None	10Ju02Kw	MARTIN, Owen		35	M	Laborer	10Ju28Mc
MCCORMACK, Jno.		19	M	Laborer	10Ju02Kw	DONDICON, Bridget		50	F	None	10Ju28Mc
Jno.		15	M	Laborer	10Ju02Kw	MARTIN, Ann		20	F	None	10Ju28Mc
Patrick		12	M	Laborer	10Ju02Kw	BURNS, Honor		18	F	None	10Ju28Mc
Hugh		09	M	Child	10Ju02Kw	MCDERMOT, John		30	M	Laborer	10Ju28Mc
Margt.		07	F	Child	10Ju02Kw	Bridget		30	F	None	10Ju28Mc
Alice		06	F	Child	10Ju02Kw	KELLY, Pat		30	M	Laborer	10Ju28Mc
TAYL, Lawrence		05	M	Child	10Ju02Kw	JORDAN, Pat		32	M	Laborer	10Ju28Mc
Michael		02	M	Child	10Ju02Kw	Nancy		35	F	None	10Ju28Mc

NAMES OF PASSENGERS		A G E	S E X	OCCUPATIONS	DATE PORT SHIP
ELLIS, Cathe.		22	F	None	10Ju28Mc
JORDAN, Pat		.06	M	Infant	10Ju28Mc
OBRYAN, Betsey		18	F	None	10Ju28Mc
HART, Martin		32	M	Laborer	10Ju28Mc
DYER, Pat		35	M	Laborer	10Ju28Mc
CARLSON, John		25	M	Laborer	10Ju28Mc
FENEY, Pat		25	M	Laborer	10Ju28Mc
JORDAN, Andw.		25	M	Laborer	10Ju28Mc
Mary	(M)	57	F	None	10Ju28Mc
Bridget		22	F	None	10Ju28Mc
GILLEN, John		25	M	Laborer	10Ju28Mc
ROONEY, Neal		25	M	Laborer	10Ju28Mc
WATERS, Michael		25	M	Laborer	10Ju28Mc
WOOD, Henry		25	M	Laborer	10Ju28Mc
WATERS, Michael		25	M	Laborer	10Ju28Mc
HIGH, Mary		22	F	None	10Ju28Mc
BAGLEY, Mary		22	F	None	10Ju28Mc
GANNON, Cathe.		20	F	None	10Ju28Mc
John		22	M	Laborer	10Ju28Mc
Ann		18	F	None	10Ju28Mc
LARVIN, Danl.		22	M	Laborer	10Ju28Mc
FLINN, Ninies.		20	M	Laborer	10Ju28Mc
MATAMO, Mary		17	F	None	10Ju28Mc
FLINN, Bridget		21	F	None	10Ju28Mc
CARLEY, Michael		21	M	Mechanic	10Ju28Mc
DAVY, Pat		21	M	Mechanic	10Ju28Mc
MCGARIGHLAN, Darly		20	M	Mechanic	10Ju28Mc
MCLAUGHLIN, Pat		20	M	Mechanic	10Ju28Mc
CORREY, Pat		45	M	Mechanic	10Ju28Mc
Cella	(D)	17	F	None	10Ju28Mc
JONES, Luke		28	M	Mechanic	10Ju28Mc
FORD, Thos.		20	M	Mechanic	10Ju28Mc
MCLAUGHLIN, John		21	M	Mechanic	10Ju28Mc
Ann		23	F	None	10Ju28Mc
MCPARTHIN, Owen		21	M	Mechanic	10Ju28Mc
MCGOLDRICK, Pat		24	M	Mechanic	10Ju28Mc
MCDERMOT, Pat		26	M	Mechanic	10Ju28Mc
GILMARTIN, Ed.		25	M	Mechanic	10Ju28Mc
Mary		20	F	None	10Ju28Mc
COMER, Michael		57	M	Mechanic	10Ju28Mc
SARVILLE, Michael		23	M	Mechanic	10Ju28Mc
KELLEY, Anthy.		20	M	Mechanic	10Ju28Mc
SARVILLE, Bridget		18	F	None	10Ju28Mc
HOINE, Anthy.		28	M	Mechanic	10Ju28Mc
Michl.		25	M	Mechanic	10Ju28Mc
Bridget		29	F	None	10Ju28Mc
Margt.		29	F	None	10Ju28Mc
Mary		25	F	None	10Ju28Mc
PRESTON, Michael		50	M	Mechanic	10Ju28Mc
Thos.	(S)	20	M	Mechanic	10Ju28Mc
Mary	(W)	50	F	None	10Ju28Mc
Bridget	(D)	18	F	None	10Ju28Mc
Mary	(D)	17	F	None	10Ju28Mc
Sarah	(D)	16	F	None	10Ju28Mc
Margt.	(D)	14	F	None	10Ju28Mc
CONWAY, John		25	M	Mechanic	10Ju28Mc
Wm.		20	M	Mechanic	10Ju28Mc
Jas.		35	M	Mechanic	10Ju28Mc
Mary		60	F	None	10Ju28Mc
Nancy		23	F	None	10Ju28Mc
CORMICK, Thos.		25	M	Mechanic	10Ju28Mc
May		22	F	None	10Ju28Mc
MAY, James		30	M	Mechanic	10Ju28Mc
Nancy	(W)	24	F	None	10Ju28Mc
James	(S)	07	M	Child	10Ju28Mc
MORRICAN, Pat		60	M	Laborer	10Ju28Mc
John	(S)	20	M	Laborer	10Ju28Mc
James	(S)	15	M	Laborer	10Ju28Mc
Bridget	(D)	20	F	None	10Ju28Mc
Mary	(D)	18	F	None	10Ju28Mc
DUFFY, John		40	M	Laborer	10Ju28Mc
Pat		17	M	Laborer	10Ju28Mc
Bridget		50	F	None	10Ju28Mc
Ann		20	F	None	10Ju28Mc
Ellen		15	F	None	10Ju28Mc

BAVARIA 10 JUNE 1847

From Liverpool

NAMES OF PASSENGERS		A G E	S E X	OCCUPATIONS	DATE PORT SHIP
BULLON, J.		45	M	Laborer	10Ju02Md
Ann	(W)	46	F	None	10Ju02Md
Thos.	(S)	25	M	Laborer	10Ju02Md
Emily	(D)	16	F	None	10Ju02Md
Mara	(D)	13	F	None	10Ju02Md
Elzbt.	(D)	11	F	None	10Ju02Md
George	(S)	09	M	Child	10Ju02Md
Eleanor	(D)	06	F	Child	10Ju02Md
Wm.		45	M	Laborer	10Ju02Md
Ann		40	F	None	10Ju02Md
Ellen	(N)	07	F	Child	10Ju02Md
MORRELL, J.		41	M	Laborer	10Ju02Md
Martha	(W)	35	F	None	10Ju02Md
My.	(D)	09	F	Child	10Ju02Md
Hey.	(S)	01	M	Child	10Ju02Md
QUALE, L.		20	M	Laborer	10Ju02Md
U	(W)	20	F	None	10Ju02Md
JONES, J.		45	M	Laborer	10Ju02Md
FRANKLIN, T.		20	M	Laborer	10Ju02Md
Sopl.	(M)	66	F	None	10Ju02Md
CARROLL, Mgt.		36	F	None	10Ju02Md
James		10	M	None	10Ju02Md
Laurence		22	M	Laborer	10Ju02Md
James		19	M	Laborer	10Ju02Md
John		22	M	Laborer	10Ju02Md
Thos.		11	M	None	10Ju02Md
Wm.		14	M	None	10Ju02Md
Pat		09	M	Child	10Ju02Md
My.		23	F	None	10Ju02Md
Elza.		07	F	Child	10Ju02Md
Ellen		05	F	Child	10Ju02Md
Jane		01	F	Child	10Ju02Md
Robt.		50	M	Laborer	10Ju02Md
Ann		50	F	None	10Ju02Md
CAMPBELL, Robt.		20	M	Laborer	10Ju02Md
J.		20	M	Laborer	10Ju02Md
Jane		20	F	None	10Ju02Md
CONNOLLY, Jane		20	F	None	10Ju02Md
ARMSTRONG, J.		21	M	Laborer	10Ju02Md
MULLIN, J.		24	M	Laborer	10Ju02Md
Ann		20	F	None	10Ju02Md
HARNY, Mgt.		18	F	None	10Ju02Md
CRAWFORD, S.		10	M	None	10Ju02Md
WHITNEY, T.		19	M	Laborer	10Ju02Md
ELWOOD, J.		44	M	Laborer	10Ju02Md
Isb.		36	F	None	10Ju02Md
HART, C.		26	M	Laborer	10Ju02Md
SMITH, E.		21	M	Laborer	10Ju02Md
Peter		23	M	Laborer	10Ju02Md
COSGROVE, M.		29	M	Laborer	10Ju02Md
Peter		24	M	Laborer	10Ju02Md
Patck.		20	M	Laborer	10Ju02Md
SMITH, Ann		20	F	None	10Ju02Md
MULLGAN, Mgt.		12	F	None	10Ju02Md
LYNCH, P.		20	M	Laborer	10Ju02Md
Berd.		19	M	Laborer	10Ju02Md
FEGAN, M.		20	M	Laborer	10Ju02Md
James		23	M	Laborer	10Ju02Md
CLOCKER, J.		22	M	Laborer	10Ju02Md
My.		17	F	None	10Ju02Md
REILLY, My.		20	F	None	10Ju02Md
MCCORMACK, My.		19	F	None	10Ju02Md
HART, Cath.		20	F	None	10Ju02Md
HURSTLY, B.		30	M	Laborer	10Ju02Md
BURNS, J.		32	M	Laborer	10Ju02Md

NAMES OF PASSENGERS		A G E	S E X	OCCUPATIONS	DATE PORT SHIP
BURNS, John		30	M	Laborer	10Ju02Md
Mgt.		22	F	None	10Ju02Md
HOWARD, P.		30	M	Laborer	10Ju02Md
KNOWLES, J.		20	M	Laborer	10Ju02Md
DROPHIN, J.		28	M	Laborer	10Ju02Md
James	(S)	08	M	Child	10Ju02Md
John	(S)	01	M	Child	10Ju02Md
GUSTON, G.		43	M	Child	10Ju02Md
Charlotte		46	F	None	10Ju02Md
FINDLY, T.		33	M	Laborer	10Ju02Md
Sarah		28	F	None	10Ju02Md
KEENAN, Jane		19	F	None	10Ju02Md
SHEA, R.		26	M	Laborer	10Ju02Md
Bgt.		20	F	None	10Ju02Md
MARTINS, J.		25	M	Laborer	10Ju02Md
OPENSHAW, M.		26	F	None	10Ju02Md
HAWARTH, U-Mrs.		36	F	None	10Ju02Md
OPENSHAW, E.		06	M	Child	10Ju02Md
J.		06	M	Child	10Ju02Md
Lucy	(D)	01	F	None	10Ju02Md
ROURKE, P.		20	M	Laborer	10Ju02Md
Terence		20	M	Laborer	10Ju02Md
Bdgt.		45	F	None	10Ju02Md
KILKENY, Cath.		25	F	None	10Ju02Md
BODEY, W.		20	M	Laborer	10Ju02Md
HARTLY, A.		22	M	Laborer	10Ju02Md
LAHY, Elza.		20	F	None	10Ju02Md
ACKROYD, J.		24	M	Laborer	10Ju02Md
LAWLER, P.		26	M	Laborer	10Ju02Md
WALKENS, J.		23	M	Laborer	10Ju02Md
KELLY, J.		30	M	Laborer	10Ju02Md
Bldy		18	F	None	10Ju02Md
CLARK, P.		30	M	Laborer	10Ju02Md
GRILS, J.		20	M	Laborer	10Ju02Md
BROWN, M.		40	M	Laborer	10Ju02Md
Jane	(W)	40	F	None	10Ju02Md
Wm.	(S)	18	M	Laborer	10Ju02Md
IRVIN, T.		18	M	Laborer	10Ju02Md
DOYLE, Mgt.		20	F	None	10Ju02Md
Cath.		18	F	None	10Ju02Md
BROWN, E.		40	M	Laborer	10Ju02Md
Jas.	(S)	16	M	None	10Ju02Md
NELLEGAN, A.		25	M	None	10Ju02Md
My.		20	F	None	10Ju02Md
COOKE, G.		46	M	Laborer	10Ju02Md
INMAN, J.		26	M	Laborer	10Ju02Md
U	(W)	25	F	None	10Ju02Md
Josp.	(S)	01	M	Child	10Ju02Md
Mgt.	(D)	01	F	Child	10Ju02Md
LOWRY, W.		50	M	Laborer	10Ju02Md
Wm.	(S)	27	M	Laborer	10Ju02Md
Elzbt.	(D)	20	F	None	10Ju02Md
CAMPBELL, R.		26	M	Laborer	10Ju02Md
HUMPH, W.		25	M	Laborer	10Ju02Md
DALAYMPLE, W.		24	M	Laborer	10Ju02Md
SMITHS, J.		24	M	Laborer	10Ju02Md
U	(W)	21	F	None	10Ju02Md
MELORT, J.		21	M	Laborer	10Ju02Md
Mara		21	F	None	10Ju02Md
BRADY, Mgt.		40	F	None	10Ju02Md
My.	(D)	16	F	None	10Ju02Md
CADDAN, J.		16	M	Laborer	10Ju02Md
COOKE, W.		20	M	Laborer	10Ju02Md
MACKAY, T.		22	M	Laborer	10Ju02Md
CONNOR, G.		18	M	Laborer	10Ju02Md
MIKEALS, Ellen		20	F	None	10Ju02Md
FLANGAN, Cath.		20	F	None	10Ju02Md
STEWART, R.		18	M	Laborer	10Ju02Md
MCCALLEN, H.		24	M	Laborer	10Ju02Md
MCLOUGHLIN, P.		18	M	Laborer	10Ju02Md
HICKEY, J.		30	M	Laborer	10Ju02Md
WATSON, Elzt.		30	F	None	10Ju02Md
Alice-J.	(D)	12	F	None	10Ju02Md
Ellen	(D)	08	F	Child	10Ju02Md
Elzbt.	(D)	01	F	Child	10Ju02Md
KENNY, G.		30	M	Laborer	10Ju02Md
U	(W)	30	F	None	10Ju02Md
Mara	(D)	04	F	Child	10Ju02Md
Hry.	(S)	01	M	Child	10Ju02Md
FALT, An.		40	M	Mechanic	10Ju02Md
Matt	(S)	15	M	Mechanic	10Ju02Md
RILY, Sara		25	F	None	10Ju02Md
My.		20	F	None	10Ju02Md
GREENBOUGH, R.		20	M	Mechanic	10Ju02Md
Robert	(S)	07	M	Child	10Ju02Md
BERGEN, Elza.		20	F	None	10Ju02Md
Mich.		16	M	Mechanic	10Ju02Md
Thos.		15	M	Mechanic	10Ju02Md
BRESLIN, J.		21	M	Mechanic	10Ju02Md
QUIRK, My.		20	F	None	10Ju02Md
BRADY, B.		25	M	Mechanic	10Ju02Md
Cath.		24	F	None	10Ju02Md
Ellen	(D)	01	F	Child	10Ju02Md
Thos.	(S)	01	M	Child	10Ju02Md
FRISSLY, W.		40	M	Mechanic	10Ju02Md
Georg	(S)	20	M	Mechanic	10Ju02Md
FALLON, Ann		18	F	None	10Ju02Md
BYRNE, My.		20	F	None	10Ju02Md
MORRISS, E.		25	M	Mechanic	10Ju02Md
HELAN, J.B.		30	M	Mechanic	10Ju02Md
SMITH, S.		20	M	Mechanic	10Ju02Md
LYNCH, J.		25	M	Mechanic	10Ju02Md
Ann		20	F	None	10Ju02Md
DEGAN, M.		30	M	Mechanic	10Ju02Md
LYHAN, C.		19	M	Mechanic	10Ju02Md
WALL, J.		20	M	Mechanic	10Ju02Md
RILY, J.		24	M	Mechanic	10Ju02Md
GANGAN, M.		24	M	Mechanic	10Ju02Md
GRADY, J.		24	M	Mechanic	10Ju02Md
CALLOHAN, M.		25	M	Mechanic	10Ju02Md
MCCANN, My.		20	F	None	10Ju02Md
SLATTERY, J.		25	M	Mechanic	10Ju02Md
CROSS, P.		20	M	Mechanic	10Ju02Md
CONNOR, T.		20	M	Mechanic	10Ju02Md
MAN, J.		20	M	Mechanic	10Ju02Md
HILL, W.		30	M	Mechanic	10Ju02Md
BRANIGAN, C.		22	M	Mechanic	10Ju02Md
BAGLANN, B.		25	M	Mechanic	10Ju02Md
GALLAGHER, Ann		20	F	None	10Ju02Md
MASTERSON, Bgt.		30	F	None	10Ju02Md
James	(S)	05	M	Child	10Ju02Md
C.	(S)	01	M	Child	10Ju02Md
HALLEGAN, M.		25	M	Farmer	10Ju02Md
MAHON, C.		25	M	Farmer	10Ju02Md
DOHERTY, Rosann		14	F	None	10Ju02Md
Cath.		11	F	None	10Ju02Md
CORLESS, An		20	F	None	10Ju02Md
HAFFERN, W.		16	M	Farmer	10Ju02Md
MCDURN, J.		20	M	Farmer	10Ju02Md
Alan		11	M	None	10Ju02Md
Farh.		10	M	None	10Ju02Md
Mich.		08	M	Child	10Ju02Md
BRADY, J.		21	M	Farmer	10Ju02Md
U	(W)	24	F	None	10Ju02Md
MEYERS, M.		24	M	Farmer	10Ju02Md
LOCHAN, J.		24	M	Farmer	10Ju02Md
LAUGHLIN, Bt.		24	F	None	10Ju02Md
MARTIN, F.		24	M	Farmer	10Ju02Md
KELLY, P.		50	M	Farmer	10Ju02Md
Bgt.	(D)	25	F	None	10Ju02Md
Fran.	(S)	20	M	Farmer	10Ju02Md
Cath.	(D)	30	F	None	10Ju02Md
Ann	(D)	25	F	None	10Ju02Md
Jane	(W)	52	F	None	10Ju02Md
Thos.	(S)	22	M	Farmer	10Ju02Md
HENRY, W.R.		22	M	Farmer	10Ju02Md
REILY, J.N.		30	M	Farmer	10Ju02Md
NEVIN, R.N.		22	M	Farmer	10Ju02Md
LESTRURGE, C.		20	M	Farmer	10Ju02Md

FRANKLIN 11 JUNE 1847

From Unknown

NAMES OF PASSENGERS		AGE	SEX	OCCUPATIONS	DATE PORT SHIP
CAMPBELL, Margt.		22	F	None	11Ju00Me
LEVY, Pat		33	M	Farmer	11Ju00Me
U	(W)	36	F	None	11Ju00Me
Bridget		20	F	None	11Ju00Me
Mary		01	F	Child	11Ju00Me
CAVANAGH, Danl.		21	M	Laborer	11Ju00Me
SHERIDAN, C.		22	M	Laborer	11Ju00Me
COADY, Jno.		22	M	Laborer	11Ju00Me
KELLY, Peter		20	M	Laborer	11Ju00Me
PENDEGAST, M.		27	M	Laborer	11Ju00Me
FITZSIMMONS, Thos.		30	M	Laborer	11Ju00Me
PENDEGAST, Jno.		13	M	Laborer	11Ju00Me
Jane		15	F	None	11Ju00Me
CARTAY, Ann		45	F	None	11Ju00Me
GUSTED, Cath.		20	F	None	11Ju00Me
LENYENE, M.		35	M	Merchant	11Ju00Me
U	(W)	32	F	None	11Ju00Me
Magt.		22	F	None	11Ju00Me
REILY, Cath.		20	F	None	11Ju00Me
MURPHY, Jas.		20	M	Laborer	11Ju00Me
NOLAN, Jno.		35	M	Chandler	11Ju00Me
Mary	(W)	34	F	None	11Ju00Me
Sarah	(D)	13	F	None	11Ju00Me
Ellen	(D)	10	F	None	11Ju00Me
Mary-Ann	(D)	08	F	Child	11Ju00Me
Thos.	(S)	06	M	Child	11Ju00Me
Hannah	(D)	.00	F	Infant	11Ju00Me
LAPIER, Lewis-P.		24	M	Apothecary	11Ju00Me
U	(W)	22	F	None	11Ju00Me
ISAAC, Abm.		20	M	Tbcmcht	11Ju00Me
SHEARER, Jno.		26	M	Clothier	11Ju00Me
LAYAN, Jno.		19	M	Merchant	11Ju00Me
Wm.		09	M	Child	11Ju00Me
DEVENT, Jno.		30	M	Laborer	11Ju00Me
REID, Jno.		31	M	Laborer	11Ju00Me
DAVIS, Pat		31	M	Laborer	11Ju00Me
FEPENDEN, J.		20	M	Laborer	11Ju00Me
FARNUM, M.		20	M	Laborer	11Ju00Me
FETHERSTON, Thos.		20	M	Laborer	11Ju00Me
MORAND, Cath.		20	F	None	11Ju00Me
MURPHY, Thos.		24	M	Laborer	11Ju00Me
Jas.		21	M	Laborer	11Ju00Me
HOYLE, Jno.		33	M	Tailor	11Ju00Me
WHELAN, Jno.		19	M	Tailor	11Ju00Me
BROWN, Jno.		17	M	Tailor	11Ju00Me
CONELEY, Edw.		20	M	Tailor	11Ju00Me
HICKEY, U-Mrs.		40	F	None	11Ju00Me
Mary	(D)	23	F	None	11Ju00Me
James	(S)	20	M	Tailor	11Ju00Me
Denis	(S)	17	M	Tailor	11Ju00Me
Pat	(S)	15	M	None	11Ju00Me
Michel	(S)	12	M	None	11Ju00Me
Peter	(S)	10	M	None	11Ju00Me
MCLANE, W.		21	M	Laborer	11Ju00Me
H.		19	M	Laborer	11Ju00Me
RUPELL, Rich.		25	M	Laborer	11Ju00Me
Mary		24	F	None	11Ju00Me
FEGAN, B.		20	M	Laborer	11Ju00Me
RUPEL, M.		02	M	Child	11Ju00Me
Cath.	(T)	.03	F	Infant	11Ju00Me
MCDANIEL, Pat		30	M	Laborer	11Ju00Me
DUFFY, Pat		27	M	Laborer	11Ju00Me
U	(W)	25	F	None	11Ju00Me
Pat	(S)	03	M	Child	11Ju00Me
DWYER, John		24	M	Victualler	11Ju00Me
HEALY, T.		24	M	Baker	11Ju00Me
BYRNE, Jas.		24	M	Laborer	11Ju00Me
Bridget		20	F	None	11Ju00Me
MOORE, Step.		20	M	Laborer	11Ju00Me
Bridget		22	F	None	11Ju00Me
Margaret		24	F	None	11Ju00Me
DOWLING, Thos.		24	M	Laborer	11Ju00Me
REILY, B.		22	M	Laborer	11Ju00Me

TENNESSEE 11 JUNE 1847

From Belfast

NAMES OF PASSENGERS		AGE	SEX	OCCUPATIONS	DATE PORT SHIP
MURPHY, J.		20	M	Farmer	11Ju07Mf
Sarah		22	F	None	11Ju07Mf
Ann		20	F	None	11Ju07Mf
Bgt.		16	F	None	11Ju07Mf
MULLEN, Isb.		24	F	None	11Ju07Mf
MCCLUSKY, Ann		26	F	None	11Ju07Mf
RANKIN, Ann		14	F	None	11Ju07Mf
MCCAFFERTY, D.		43	M	Farmer	11Ju07Mf
Jane	(W)	43	F	None	11Ju07Mf
Wm.	(S)	23	M	Farmer	11Ju07Mf
John	(S)	22	M	Farmer	11Ju07Mf
Jane	(D)	20	F	None	11Ju07Mf
Robt.	(S)	18	M	Farmer	11Ju07Mf
Chas.	(S)	16	M	Farmer	11Ju07Mf
Ellen	(D)	14	F	None	11Ju07Mf
Dens.	(S)	12	M	None	11Ju07Mf
James	(S)	10	M	None	11Ju07Mf
Sophia	(D)	08	F	Child	11Ju07Mf
MCMULLEN, H.		46	M	Mechanic	11Ju07Mf
BAILER, J.		23	M	Mechanic	11Ju07Mf
Ann		22	F	None	11Ju07Mf
My.		29	F	None	11Ju07Mf
Eliza		21	F	None	11Ju07Mf
Hanah		14	F	None	11Ju07Mf
MILLS, Mgt.		21	F	None	11Ju07Mf
BONNER, A.		47	M	Mechanic	11Ju07Mf
Andrew	(S)	18	M	Mechanic	11Ju07Mf
Elza.J.	(D)	16	F	None	11Ju07Mf
John	(S)	13	M	None	11Ju07Mf
My.	(D)	12	F	None	11Ju07Mf
Sarah	(D)	04	F	Child	11Ju07Mf
MORRISON, Elza.		50	F	None	11Ju07Mf
Rachel	(D)	20	F	None	11Ju07Mf
Elza.	(D)	18	F	None	11Ju07Mf
Ellen	(D)	15	F	None	11Ju07Mf
Martha-J.	(D)	12	F	None	11Ju07Mf
Elzbt.	(D)	09	F	Child	11Ju07Mf
MUSCAMPBELL, J.		21	M	Mechanic	11Ju07Mf
John		18	M	Mechanic	11Ju07Mf
WHITE, G.		19	M	Mechanic	11Ju07Mf
CAGEN, O.		29	M	Mechanic	11Ju07Mf
Mrgt.		14	F	None	11Ju07Mf
MCGIBBON, J.		21	M	Mechanic	11Ju07Mf
Henry	(B)	15	M	Mechanic	11Ju07Mf
Racheal	(T)	13	F	None	11Ju07Mf
Sophia	(M)	40	F	None	11Ju07Mf
SHAW, S.		22	M	Mechanic	11Ju07Mf
Mgt.		22	F	None	11Ju07Mf
MCWILLIAM, J.		19	M	Mechanic	11Ju07Mf
LINN, W.		25	M	Mechanic	11Ju07Mf
Eliza		21	F	None	11Ju07Mf
CONNELLY, Jane		25	F	None	11Ju07Mf
WILLIAMS, R.		18	M	Mechanic	11Ju07Mf
Henrietta		17	F	None	11Ju07Mf
Elzabt.-A.		16	F	None	11Ju07Mf
WALLS, D.		38	M	Mechanic	11Ju07Mf

NAMES OF PASSENGERS		A G E	S E X	OCCUPATIONS	DATE PORT SHIP	NAMES OF PASSENGERS		A G E	S E X	OCCUPATIONS	DATE PORT SHIP
WALLS, Rose		36	F	None	11Ju07Mf	MCMAHON, Cath.A.		15	F	None	11Ju07Mf
MURPHY, My.		39	F	None	11Ju07Mf	BAFFET, Mgt.		16	F	None	11Ju07Mf
My.	(D)	10	F	Child	11Ju07Mf	WHIGHAM, T.		50	M	Farmer	11Ju07Mf
Archibald	(S)	19	M	Mechanic	11Ju07Mf	Mgt.	(W)	45	F	None	11Ju07Mf
Sarah		25	F	None	11Ju07Mf	Mgt.	(D)	19	F	None	11Ju07Mf
MANDILL, D.		20	M	Mechanic	11Ju07Mf	Sarah	(D)	19	F	None	11Ju07Mf
GILMORE, Cath.		25	F	None	11Ju07Mf	My.	(D)	15	F	None	11Ju07Mf
Rose-A.		30	F	None	11Ju07Mf	Isabella	(D)	13	F	None	11Ju07Mf
QUIN, J.		60	M	Mechanic	11Ju07Mf	John	(S)	11	M	None	11Ju07Mf
My.	(D)	32	F	None	11Ju07Mf	Thos.	(S)	09	M	Child	11Ju07Mf
MALONE, G.		20	M	Mechanic	11Ju07Mf	Elzbt.	(D)	07	F	Child	11Ju07Mf
WILSON, J.		25	M	Mechanic	11Ju07Mf	James	(S)	05	M	Child	11Ju07Mf
MARTIN, J.R.		25	M	Mechanic	11Ju07Mf	HAMMOND, J.		28	M	Farmer	11Ju07Mf
MCINTYRE, T.		30	M	Mechanic	11Ju07Mf	B.		24	M	Farmer	11Ju07Mf
Sarah		28	F	None	11Ju07Mf	MCELRATT, A.		50	M	Farmer	11Ju07Mf
GIVEN, My.		28	F	None	11Ju07Mf	MOONEY, P.		21	M	Farmer	11Ju07Mf
COMAB, R.		24	M	Mechanic	11Ju07Mf	MCDONALD, A.		20	M	Farmer	11Ju07Mf
My.A.		34	F	None	11Ju07Mf	WHITE, J.		20	M	Farmer	11Ju07Mf
BECK, J.		30	M	Mechanic	11Ju07Mf	ROACH, P.		25	M	Farmer	11Ju07Mf
Grace	(W)	24	F	None	11Ju07Mf	RAFFERTY, J.		18	M	Farmer	11Ju07Mf
John	(S)	05	M	Child	11Ju07Mf	ROACH, F.		50	M	Farmer	11Ju07Mf
James	(S)	03	M	Child	11Ju07Mf	CASSIDY, Jane		60	F	None	11Ju07Mf
Eliza		01	F	Child	11Ju07Mf	METCALF, Isb.		36	F	None	11Ju07Mf
STEWART, J.		36	M	Mechanic	11Ju07Mf	Jane	(D)	05	F	Child	11Ju07Mf
WRIGHT, A.		63	M	Mechanic	11Ju07Mf	Winnfd.	(D)	01	F	Child	11Ju07Mf
My.	(W)	61	F	None	11Ju07Mf	CAMPBELL, J.		66	M	Farmer	11Ju07Mf
James	(S)	28	M	Mechanic	11Ju07Mf	Thomas	(S)	21	M	Farmer	11Ju07Mf
Alexnd.	(S)	26	M	Mechanic	11Ju07Mf	Saml.	(S)	25	M	Farmer	11Ju07Mf
John	(S)	15	M	None	11Ju07Mf	Eliza.	(D)	22	F	None	11Ju07Mf
Agnes	(D)	25	F	None	11Ju07Mf	Cath.A.	(D)	18	F	None	11Ju07Mf
Abby	(D)	19	F	None	11Ju07Mf	WALLACE, Cath.		28	F	None	11Ju07Mf
Joseph		02	M	Child	11Ju07Mf	HENNESSY, W.		24	M	Farmer	11Ju07Mf
DONNELLY, Ellen		22	F	None	11Ju07Mf	Cath.	(W)	22	F	None	11Ju07Mf
THOMAS, Saml.		21	M	Mechanic	11Ju07Mf	James	(S)	01	M	Child	11Ju07Mf
KENDELL, Mgt.		19	F	None	11Ju07Mf	SLANE, My.A.		24	F	None	11Ju07Mf
MCGREAN, P.		22	M	Mechanic	11Ju07Mf	Grace		20	F	None	11Ju07Mf
CALVERT, J.		19	M	Mechanic	11Ju07Mf	SMITH, Mrgt.		22	F	None	11Ju07Mf
MCLAUGHLIN, H.		30	M	Mechanic	11Ju07Mf	SHIPPARD, S.		40	M	Farmer	11Ju07Mf
SAVANE, J.		25	M	Mechanic	11Ju07Mf	James	(S)	18	M	Farmer	11Ju07Mf
Cath.	(W)	23	F	None	11Ju07Mf	Benjamin	(S)	14	M	Farmer	11Ju07Mf
John	(S)	01	M	Child	11Ju07Mf	James	(S)	16	M	Farmer	11Ju07Mf
HEANIS, J.		40	M	Mechanic	11Ju07Mf	CAMPBELL, J.		27	M	Farmer	11Ju07Mf
Mgt.		35	F	None	11Ju07Mf	MCFARLAND, J.		26	M	Farmer	11Ju07Mf
James		26	M	Mechanic	11Ju07Mf	MCGIBBON, J.		24	M	Farmer	11Ju07Mf
John		14	M	Mechanic	11Ju07Mf	DONNELLY, P.		49	M	Farmer	11Ju07Mf
Isabelle		16	F	None	11Ju07Mf	STEWART, Elzt.		35	M	Farmer	11Ju07Mf
HALL, J.		24	M	Farmer	11Ju07Mf	MCQULLAN, Sarah		28	F	None	11Ju07Mf
FIELDS, Susan		56	F	None	11Ju07Mf	MCILVEEN, Mrgt.		14	F	None	11Ju07Mf
Susanah	(D)	20	F	None	11Ju07Mf	FOY, J.		21	M	Farmer	11Ju07Mf
Eliza	(D)	18	F	None	11Ju07Mf	BASSETT, W.		22	M	Farmer	11Ju07Mf
KELLY, J.		20	M	Farmer	11Ju07Mf	Ellen		26	F	None	11Ju07Mf
A---		18	F	None	11Ju07Mf						
Alexander		19	M	Farmer	11Ju07Mf						
MORRISON, Ann		40	F	None	11Ju07Mf						
My.A.	(D)	18	F	None	11Ju07Mf						
MITCHELL, Saml.J.		20	F	None	11Ju07Mf						
MCALTEN, R.		22	M	Farmer	11Ju07Mf		HINDOSTAN 11 JUNE 1847				
DIAMOND, F.		18	M	Farmer	11Ju07Mf						
PATTERSON, W.		20	M	Farmer	11Ju07Mf		From Liverpool				
MCALEER, Cth.		25	F	None	11Ju07Mf						
CHAMBERS, Matt.		18	M	Farmer	11Ju07Mf						
MOORE, Sarah		18	F	None	11Ju07Mf						
MITCHELL, My.A.		18	F	None	11Ju07Mf	LOCKE, W.		45	M	Farmer	11Ju02Mg
My.		66	F	None	11Ju07Mf	Harriet	(W)	35	F	None	11Ju02Mg
John		70	M	Farmer	11Ju07Mf	Wm.	(S)	18	M	Farmer	11Ju02Mg
BAILY, D.		37	M	Farmer	11Ju07Mf	Susan	(D)	16	F	None	11Ju02Mg
Mgt.	(W)	39	F	None	11Ju07Mf	Thos.	(S)	12	M	None	11Ju02Mg
James	(S)	12	M	None	11Ju07Mf	Eliza	(D)	13	F	None	11Ju02Mg
George	(S)	11	M	None	11Ju07Mf	Johana	(D)	10	F	None	11Ju02Mg
James		22	M	Farmer	11Ju07Mf	Bgt.	(D)	15	F	None	11Ju02Mg
MCKENNA, L.		21	M	Farmer	11Ju07Mf	Johanah	(D)	03	F	Child	11Ju02Mg
BAILEY, J.		13	M	None	11Ju07Mf	Danl.	(S)	01	M	Child	11Ju02Mg
MARTIN, J.		30	M	Farmer	11Ju07Mf	Francis	(S)	01	M	Child	11Ju02Mg
Ann		32	F	None	11Ju07Mf	My.		30	F	None	11Ju02Mg
MCMAHON, Mrgt.		19	F	None	11Ju07Mf	Jane		20	F	None	11Ju02Mg

NAMES OF PASSENGERS		A G E	S E X	OCCUPATIONS	DATE PORT SHIP	NAMES OF PASSENGERS		A G E	S E X	OCCUPATIONS	DATE PORT SHIP
HARKIN, J.		33	M	Farmer	11Ju02Mg	MULLIGAN, Hy.		21	M	Farmer	11Ju02Mg
Elza.		35	F	None	11Ju02Mg	John		20	M	Farmer	11Ju02Mg
BROWEN, W.		22	M	Farmer	11Ju02Mg	GIBBONS, My.		35	F	None	11Ju02Mg
Georgia		20	F	None	11Ju02Mg	Ellen		19	F	None	11Ju02Mg
LACKY, W.		17	F	None	11Ju02Mg	HANEY, Ann		22	F	None	11Ju02Mg
RUSSELL, J.		50	M	Farmer	11Ju02Mg	MCFENY, J.		24	F	None	11Ju02Mg
Jane	(W)	50	F	None	11Ju02Mg	GERY, J.		25	F	None	11Ju02Mg
My.	(D)	26	F	None	11Ju02Mg	MARTINS, E.		25	F	None	11Ju02Mg
John	(S)	28	M	Farmer	11Ju02Mg	Mgt.		24	F	None	11Ju02Mg
Susan	(D)	24	F	None	11Ju02Mg	FYE, My.		24	M	Farmer	11Ju02Mg
Amella	(D)	20	F	None	11Ju02Mg	SEXTON, J.		24	M	Farmer	11Ju02Mg
Charl.	(D)	19	F	None	11Ju02Mg	MCLOUGHLIN, R.		50	M	Farmer	11Ju02Mg
Sophia	(D)	17	F	None	11Ju02Mg	Sarah	(W)	50	F	None	11Ju02Mg
Saml.	(S)	14	M	None	11Ju02Mg	Bridey	(D)	18	F	None	11Ju02Mg
DONAHUE, T.		20	M	Farmer	11Ju02Mg	MCGUINNESS, M.		18	M	Farmer	11Ju02Mg
SANDESON, M.		27	M	Farmer	11Ju02Mg	SANDERSON, D.		30	M	Farmer	11Ju02Mg
GERAHETY, P.		20	M	Farmer	11Ju02Mg	MECHAN, J.		25	M	Farmer	11Ju02Mg
GERNSY, J.		20	M	Farmer	11Ju02Mg	BRYAN, P.		40	M	Farmer	11Ju02Mg
Johana		20	F	None	11Ju02Mg	HUSON, J.		30	M	Farmer	11Ju02Mg
TOUGHLAN, W.		20	M	Farmer	11Ju02Mg	MCFARLE, J.		20	M	Farmer	11Ju02Mg
MCANLEY, P.		45	M	Farmer	11Ju02Mg	My.		20	F	None	11Ju02Mg
Rosy	(W)	42	F	None	11Ju02Mg	FLANAGAN, Ann		13	F	None	11Ju02Mg
My.	(D)	17	F	None	11Ju02Mg	CONNER, C.		30	M	Farmer	11Ju02Mg
James	(S)	08	M	Child	11Ju02Mg	RYAN, Cath.		19	F	None	11Ju02Mg
Pat	(S)	05	M	Child	11Ju02Mg	Wm.		20	M	Farmer	11Ju02Mg
Ann	(D)	03	F	Child	11Ju02Mg	STARK, J.		22	M	Farmer	11Ju02Mg
Rosy	(D)	01	F	Child	11Ju02Mg	BANGHER, Jane		21	F	None	11Ju02Mg
GARBUSH, P.		45	M	Farmer	11Ju02Mg	SHANNON, Bgt.		40	F	None	11Ju02Mg
Bgt.	(W)	40	F	None	11Ju02Mg	Thos.	(S)	13	M	None	11Ju02Mg
Jas.	(S)	18	M	None	11Ju02Mg	Pat	(S)	12	M	None	11Ju02Mg
My.	(D)	16	F	None	11Ju02Mg	Cath.	(D)	10	F	None	11Ju02Mg
John	(S)	09	M	Child	11Ju02Mg	CARSON, L.		20	M	Farmer	11Ju02Mg
Peter	(S)	06	M	Child	11Ju02Mg	M.		21	M	Farmer	11Ju02Mg
Ann	(D)	03	F	Child	11Ju02Mg	HALL, J.		18	M	Farmer	11Ju02Mg
Hugh	(D)	01	F	Child	11Ju02Mg	GASSON, M.		30	M	Farmer	11Ju02Mg
MCGINN, T.		19	M	Farmer	11Ju02Mg	FEENY, T.		28	M	Farmer	11Ju02Mg
Cah.		17	F	None	11Ju02Mg	BANNON, J.		20	M	Farmer	11Ju02Mg
DONAHUE, Bgt.		20	F	None	11Ju02Mg	NUNN, J.		20	M	Farmer	11Ju02Mg
DOOLY, T.		40	M	Farmer	11Ju02Mg	RIBBON, W.		45	M	Farmer	11Ju02Mg
U	(W)	30	F	None	11Ju02Mg	Ann	(W)	40	F	None	11Ju02Mg
MELALY, M.		22	M	Farmer	11Ju02Mg	Elzbt.	(D)	24	F	None	11Ju02Mg
U	(W)	20	F	None	11Ju02Mg	Sarah	(D)	20	F	None	11Ju02Mg
DARSY, C.		35	M	Farmer	11Ju02Mg	Mgt.	(D)	14	F	None	11Ju02Mg
MCANLEY, Mgt.		36	F	None	11Ju02Mg	Robt.	(S)	12	M	None	11Ju02Mg
Peter	(S)	15	M	None	11Ju02Mg	Mera	(D)	10	F	None	11Ju02Mg
Bernd.	(S)	08	M	Child	11Ju02Mg	Isbell	(D)	08	F	Child	11Ju02Mg
Danl.	(S)	08	M	Child	11Ju02Mg	John	(S)	04	M	Child	11Ju02Mg
MCKENNON, B.		27	M	Farmer	11Ju02Mg	Mathilda	(D)	02	F	Child	11Ju02Mg
C.Stew.		40	M	Farmer	11Ju02Mg	SCOTT, Betty		18	F	None	11Ju02Mg
Robt.		11	M	Child	11Ju02Mg	EAGAN, T.		45	M	Farmer	11Ju02Mg
Stewrt.		09	M	Child	11Ju02Mg	Eliza	(W)	40	F	None	11Ju02Mg
MEAD, T.		24	M	Farmer	11Ju02Mg	Robt.	(S)	24	M	Farmer	11Ju02Mg
MURPHY, J.		23	M	Farmer	11Ju02Mg	Sarah	(D)	20	F	None	11Ju02Mg
Jane	(W)	33	F	None	11Ju02Mg	Isabella	(D)	16	F	None	11Ju02Mg
My.	(D)	08	F	Child	11Ju02Mg	Tho.	(D)	12	F	None	11Ju02Mg
Sarah	(D)	08	F	Child	11Ju02Mg	Margh.	(D)	10	F	None	11Ju02Mg
Jane	(D)	04	F	Child	11Ju02Mg	Mgt.	(D)	07	F	Child	11Ju02Mg
Ann	(D)	02	F	Child	11Ju02Mg	CARROLL, G.		40	M	Farmer	11Ju02Mg
Martha	(D)	01	F	Child	11Ju02Mg	Eliza	(W)	30	F	None	11Ju02Mg
Saml.		60	M	None	11Ju02Mg	Jane	(D)	12	F	None	11Ju02Mg
BALLY, E.		40	M	Farmer	11Ju02Mg	John	(S)	10	M	None	11Ju02Mg
U	(W)	40	F	None	11Ju02Mg	Mar.	(D)	08	F	Child	11Ju02Mg
Frns.	(S)	21	M	Farmer	11Ju02Mg	John	(S)	06	M	Child	11Ju02Mg
Ellen	(D)	18	F	None	11Ju02Mg	Dan	(S)	06	M	Child	11Ju02Mg
Bgt.	(D)	13	F	None	11Ju02Mg	HESLON, Cath.		20	F	None	11Ju02Mg
Ann	(D)	11	F	None	11Ju02Mg	TULLY, Ann		26	F	None	11Ju02Mg
Phillip	(S)	09	M	Child	11Ju02Mg	CALLAN, Elza.		27	F	None	11Ju02Mg
HESON, P.		30	M	Farmer	11Ju02Mg	DWYER, P.		20	M	Farmer	11Ju02Mg
U	(W)	25	F	None	11Ju02Mg	MYLES, Ewd.		19	M	Farmer	11Ju02Mg
Michl.	(S)	06	M	Child	11Ju02Mg	FOSTER, D.		20	M	Farmer	11Ju02Mg
Pat	(S)	04	M	Child	11Ju02Mg	Johana		12	F	None	11Ju02Mg
Mar.	(D)	03	F	Child	11Ju02Mg						
Theresa	(D)	01	F	Child	11Ju02Mg						
SUTTON, Bgt.		20	F	None	11Ju02Mg						
Ann		30	F	None	11Ju02Mg						

NAMES OF PASSENGERS	A G E	S E X	OCCUPATIONS	DATE PORT SHIP

GOLCONDA 12 JUNE 1847

From Bristol

NAMES OF PASSENGERS	A G E	S E X	OCCUPATIONS	DATE PORT SHIP
DEBEAUPREY, Ew.		25 M	Artist	12Jul8Mh
MORGAN, A.		21 M	Artist	12Jul8Mh
H.		24 F	None	12Jul8Mh
HUNT, J.		22 M	Artist	12Jul8Mh
U	(W)	26 F	None	12Jul8Mh
TAYLOR, U-Mrs.		45 F	None	12Jul8Mh
Kesia	(D)	13 F	None	12Jul8Mh
Maria	(D)	13 F	None	12Jul8Mh
Penelope	(D)	22 F	None	12Jul8Mh
HILES, U-Mrs.		50 F	None	12Jul8Mh
Emma	(D)	23 F	None	12Jul8Mh
U	(D)	21 F	None	12Jul8Mh
EVANS, Jno.		17 M	Farmer	12Jul8Mh
TAYLOR, Job		50 M	Farmer	12Jul8Mh
Wm.	(S)	21 M	Farmer	12Jul8Mh
Cornelius	(S)	18 M	Farmer	12Jul8Mh
Charles	(S)	17 M	Farmer	12Jul8Mh
FARNHAM, Maria		37 F	None	12Jul8Mh
SHEPPARD, Geo.		30 M	Farmer	12Jul8Mh
Anna	(W)	25 F	None	12Jul8Mh
Henry	(S)	07 M	Child	12Jul8Mh
Alfred	(S)	06 M	Child	12Jul8Mh
Anna	(D)	03 F	Child	12Jul8Mh
ALWCEY, James		32 M	Laborer	12Jul8Mh
Beppy	(W)	37 F	None	12Jul8Mh
Anna	(D)	17 F	None	12Jul8Mh
Sophia	(D)	11 F	None	12Jul8Mh
Amelia	(D)	08 F	Child	12Jul8Mh
John	(S)	02 M	Child	12Jul8Mh
VERRY, Jas.		55 M	Miner	12Jul8Mh
Wm.		60 M	Miner	12Jul8Mh
Wm.Jr.		25 M	Miner	12Jul8Mh
Elizabeth		33 F	None	12Jul8Mh
Mary		17 F	None	12Jul8Mh
WICKHAM, J.H.		18 M	Mechanic	12Jul8Mh
BOUTLING, A.		63 M	Laborer	12Jul8Mh
Ann	(W)	60 F	None	12Jul8Mh
Joseph	(S)	24 M	Laborer	12Jul8Mh
William	(S)	30 M	Laborer	12Jul8Mh
Sarah	(D)	25 F	None	12Jul8Mh
Jane	(D)	22 F	None	12Jul8Mh
Ruth	(D)	12 F	None	12Jul8Mh
Sidney	(S)	04 M	Child	12Jul8Mh
SAIRS, Sarah		40 F	None	12Jul8Mh
Martha	(D)	14 F	None	12Jul8Mh
Samuel	(S)	13 M	Laborer	12Jul8Mh
Ruth	(D)	11 F	None	12Jul8Mh
Henry	(S)	09 M	Child	12Jul8Mh
Sarah	(D)	07 F	Child	12Jul8Mh
Charles	(S)	03 M	Child	12Jul8Mh
MORE, Wm.		26 M	Farmer	12Jul8Mh
NAPPER, A.		23 M	Farmer	12Jul8Mh
WICKES, Ed.		25 M	Farmer	12Jul8Mh
Sarah		21 F	None	12Jul8Mh
LEWIS, Jno.		45 M	Farmer	12Jul8Mh
Mary-A.	(W)	43 F	None	12Jul8Mh
Wm.	(S)	22 M	Farmer	12Jul8Mh
Elizth.	(D)	17 F	None	12Jul8Mh
Edwd.	(S)	14 M	None	12Jul8Mh
Eliza	(D)	13 F	None	12Jul8Mh
George	(S)	05 M	Child	12Jul8Mh
Albert	(S)	03 M	Child	12Jul8Mh
QUIN, Henry		42 M	Laborer	12Jul8Mh
Johanna	(W)	42 F	None	12Jul8Mh
Henry	(S)	14 M	None	12Jul8Mh
QUIN, Mary	(D)	12 F	None	12Jul8Mh
Samuel	(S)	08 M	Child	12Jul8Mh
John	(S)	13 M	None	12Jul8Mh
Richard	(S)	10 M	None	12Jul8Mh
ROWE, Ed.		27 M	Laborer	12Jul8Mh
STAR, Thos.		55 M	Laborer	12Jul8Mh
JONES, John		30 M	Miner	12Jul8Mh
Jane	(D)	03 F	Child	12Jul8Mh
Mary	(D)	02 F	Child	12Jul8Mh
HALL, John		30 M	Mason	12Jul8Mh
Sarah	(W)	30 F	None	12Jul8Mh
Joseph	(S)	07 M	Child	12Jul8Mh
Robert	(S)	05 M	Child	12Jul8Mh
WENSLEY, Richd.		30 M	Laborer	12Jul8Mh
GLEECE, Wm.		22 M	Laborer	12Jul8Mh
Mary		26 F	None	12Jul8Mh
MCINTYRE, Hannah		32 F	None	12Jul8Mh
LANGLEY, Jane		16 F	None	12Jul8Mh
Elizabeth		11 F	None	12Jul8Mh
Ann		13 F	None	12Jul8Mh
TRAVIS, Thos.		43 M	Laborer	12Jul8Mh
JEFFRIES, S.		25 M	Laborer	12Jul8Mh

CALYPSO 15 JUNE 1847

From Cork

NAMES OF PASSENGERS	A G E	S E X	OCCUPATIONS	DATE PORT SHIP
HAYES, Eliza		23 F	None	15Jul14Ml
Ann		18 F	None	15Jul14Ml
MCNAMARA, Thos.		22 M	Laborer	15Jul14Ml
Sarah	(W)	26 F	None	15Jul14Ml
Jno.	(S)	01 M	Child	15Jul14Ml
HONEGAN, Pat		30 M	Laborer	15Jul14Ml
LEARY, P.		26 M	Laborer	15Jul14Ml
HONEGAN, A.		16 M	Laborer	15Jul14Ml
Mary		29 F	None	15Jul14Ml
DONOVAN, J.		20 M	Laborer	15Jul14Ml
SCREVIN, J.		27 M	Laborer	15Jul14Ml
DALEY, J.		20 M	Laborer	15Jul14Ml
RYAN, D.		25 M	Laborer	15Jul14Ml
MOORE, J.		30 M	Laborer	15Jul14Ml
Cath.		40 F	None	15Jul14Ml
GERALD, E.F.		40 M	Laborer	15Jul14Ml
Jno.H.	(S)	20 M	Laborer	15Jul14Ml
GAVEY, Jos.		18 M	Laborer	15Jul14Ml
Mich.		20 M	Laborer	15Jul14Ml
LENEHAN, Jno.		50 M	Laborer	15Jul14Ml
AHERN, Cath.		40 F	None	15Jul14Ml
LENHAN, Julia		13 F	None	15Jul14Ml
Will	(S)	10 M	None	15Jul14Ml
Kitty	(D)	08 F	None	15Jul14Ml
James	(S)	03 M	None	15Jul14Ml
MEENY, Jno.		28 M	Farmer	15Jul14Ml
DONLY, Mg.		30 F	None	15Jul14Ml
DOWLING, Joha.		32 F	None	15Jul14Ml
Jno	(S)	02 M	Child	15Jul14Ml
Mary	(D)	16 F	None	15Jul14Ml
Mich.	(S)	06 M	Child	15Jul14Ml
Neary	(S)	05 M	Child	15Jul14Ml
GOULD, Geo.		32 M	Laborer	15Jul14Ml
Robt.		30 M	Laborer	15Jul14Ml
COTTER, Cath.		24 F	None	15Jul14Ml
HAYES, Pat		24 M	Laborer	15Jul14Ml
GIMES, Ed.		24 M	Laborer	15Jul14Ml
MCAUFFEE, Thos.		50 M	Laborer	15Jul14Ml
Ivan	(W)	46 F	None	15Jul14Ml
Mich.	(S)	15 M	Laborer	15Jul14Ml
Mary	(D)	13 F	None	15Jul14Ml
Nancy	(D)	12 F	None	15Jul14Ml

NAMES OF PASSENGERS		AGE	SEX	OCCUPATIONS	DATE PORT SHIP	NAMES OF PASSENGERS		AGE	SEX	OCCUPATIONS	DATE PORT SHIP
MCAUFFEE, Ellen	(D)	10	F	None	15Jul4MI	DOWAL, Mary		46	F	None	15Jul4MI
Jeremiah	(S)	08	M	Child	15Jul4MI	SHEM, Margt.		20	F	None	15Jul4MI
Thomas	(S)	04	M	Child	15Jul4MI	HANIGAN, Lima.		30	F	None	15Jul4MI
GORDAN, Pat		25	M	Farmer	15Jul4MI	Johana.		30	F	None	15Jul4MI
HENLY, Jno.		23	M	Farmer	15Jul4MI	CAVERY, Julia		63	F	None	15Jul4MI
Cath.		24	F	None	15Jul4MI	SULLIVAN, J.		22	M	Laborer	15Jul4MI
LONG, Mich.		25	M	Farmer	15Jul4MI	WILLIAMS, Thos.		30	M	Laborer	15Jul4MI
Mary		36	F	None	15Jul4MI	SWANSON, Wm.		22	M	Laborer	15Jul4MI
Patience		07	F	Child	15Jul4MI	Charlotte		20	F	None	15Jul4MI
Richd.		05	M	Child	15Jul4MI	CERMER, Ed.		40	M	Laborer	15Jul4MI
Michl.		01	M	Child	15Jul4MI	GEERY, Cath.		20	F	None	15Jul4MI
BROWN, Mich.		35	M	Laborer	15Jul4MI	KELLY, Johana		20	F	None	15Jul4MI
MURPHY, T.		21	M	Laborer	15Jul4MI	LYNAKE, Thos.		25	M	Mechanic	15Jul4MI
D.		26	M	Laborer	15Jul4MI	SULLIVAN, Thos.		25	M	Laborer	15Jul4MI
CALLOGAN, Mary		26	F	None	15Jul4MI	Mary	(W)	20	F	None	15Jul4MI
Cath.		22	F	None	15Jul4MI	Mary	(D)	01	F	Child	15Jul4MI
Ann		17	F	None	15Jul4MI	KEIRTHY, Cath.		18	F	None	15Jul4MI
Thos.		24	M	Laborer	15Jul4MI	MAULEY, Tim		20	M	Laborer	15Jul4MI
MANNING, Jas.		30	M	Farmer	15Jul4MI	PARKER, Margt.		17	F	None	15Jul4MI
Danl.		22	M	Farmer	15Jul4MI	Jas.		16	M	Laborer	15Jul4MI
WARD, Jas.		25	M	Farmer	15Jul4MI	DALY, Mary		22	F	None	15Jul4MI
CARWELL, M.		26	M	Farmer	15Jul4MI	AUFFE, M.		20	M	Laborer	15Jul4MI
Jno.		22	M	Farmer	15Jul4MI	HEALLEN, P.		24	M	Laborer	15Jul4MI
Eliza		25	F	None	15Jul4MI	SMITH, M.		40	M	None	15Jul4MI
Mary		17	F	None	15Jul4MI	U	(W)	35	F	None	15Jul4MI
HARRIS, Richd.		40	M	Farmer	15Jul4MI	DUFF, U-Mrs.		38	F	None	15Jul4MI
Honorah	(W)	40	F	None	15Jul4MI	U	(D)	24	F	None	15Jul4MI
Timothy	(S)	27	M	Farmer	15Jul4MI	U	(D)	19	F	None	15Jul4MI
Mary-T.	(D)	24	F	None	15Jul4MI	U	(D)	16	F	None	15Jul4MI
BARRY, D.		28	M	Laborer	15Jul4MI	CYLE, U		28	M	None	15Jul4MI
HOWE, Ed.		22	M	Laborer	15Jul4MI	WARREN, U		21	M	None	15Jul4MI
Ellen		34	F	None	15Jul4MI	GRAGG, U		20	M	None	15Jul4MI
John		08	M	Child	15Jul4MI	U		19	F	None	15Jul4MI
Mary		06	F	Child	15Jul4MI	U		16	M	None	15Jul4MI
Cath.		03	F	Child	15Jul4MI	U		14	F	None	15Jul4MI
DISMOND, T.		34	M	Farmer	15Jul4MI						
COLLIGAN, Ellen		40	F	None	15Jul4MI						
Margt.	(W)	18	F	None	15Jul4MI						
Danl.		10	M	None	15Jul4MI						
Mary	(D)	07	F	Child	15Jul4MI						
LINEHAN, Hannah		18	F	None	15Jul4MI	MORGIANA 15 JUNE 1847					
MURPHY, Betty		35	F	None	15Jul4MI						
Paddy	(S)	17	M	Laborer	15Jul4MI	From Cork					
Johanna	(D)	15	F	None	15Jul4MI						
GRADY, Jno.		17	M	Laborer	15Jul4MI						
GOLLEY, Ellen		58	F	None	15Jul4MI						
Cath.	(D)	12	F	None	15Jul4MI	DALY, Denis		40	M	Laborer	15Jul4MJ
DAY, J.		30	M	Laborer	15Jul4MI	MURPHY, J.		33	M	Laborer	15Jul4MJ
Danl.		25	M	Laborer	15Jul4MI	JURTWUD, J.		17	M	Laborer	15Jul4MJ
Pat		27	M	Laborer	15Jul4MI	MURPHY, P.		16	M	Laborer	15Jul4MJ
Mich.		23	M	Laborer	15Jul4MI	BARRY, M.		30	M	Laborer	15Jul4MJ
Hannah		.00	F	Infant	15Jul4MI	Henry		25	M	Laborer	15Jul4MJ
Mary		06	F	Child	15Jul4MI	Cath.		08	F	Child	15Jul4MJ
Hannah		04	F	Child	15Jul4MI	Francis		12	F	None	15Jul4MJ
CARTHEY, Chr.		35	M	Farmer	15Jul4MI	Mary		22	F	None	15Jul4MJ
HEAFFY, J.		25	M	Farmer	15Jul4MI	DUSCOLE, D.		25	M	Laborer	15Jul4MJ
Thos.		14	M	Farmer	15Jul4MI	GALLARVAN, D.		24	M	Laborer	15Jul4MJ
HALPINE, Pat		20	M	Farmer	15Jul4MI	MURPHY, M.		50	M	Laborer	15Jul4MJ
MCCARPHY, Jno.		30	M	Farmer	15Jul4MI	M.	(S)	20	M	Laborer	15Jul4MJ
Johana	(W)	27	F	None	15Jul4MI	HALLORAN, D.		25	M	Laborer	15Jul4MJ
Johana	(D)	01	F	Child	15Jul4MI	Ellen		20	F	None	15Jul4MJ
MURRAY, Pat		20	M	Farmer	15Jul4MI	DILLON, Pat		24	M	Laborer	15Jul4MJ
Margaret	(M)	50	F	None	15Jul4MI	MEAULIFF, R.		25	M	Laborer	15Jul4MJ
James		10	M	None	15Jul4MI	GALLSEVOM, D.		30	M	Laborer	15Jul4MJ
Magt.		13	F	None	15Jul4MI	Mary	(W)	30	F	None	15Jul4MJ
GRIFFIN, Jos.		40	M	Farmer	15Jul4MI	Timothy	(S)	.01	M	Infant	15Jul4MJ
Cath.	(W)	40	F	None	15Jul4MI	SULLIVAN, Biddy		18	F	None	15Jul4MJ
Ann		30	F	None	15Jul4MI	BRADY, Margaret		17	F	None	15Jul4MJ
Patrick	(S)	22	M	Farmer	15Jul4MI	HUSBAND, G.		15	M	Laborer	15Jul4MJ
Mary	(D)	17	F	None	15Jul4MI	Margaret		17	F	None	15Jul4MJ
Joseph	(S)	13	M	None	15Jul4MI	SULLIVAN, Jerry		25	M	Laborer	15Jul4MJ
SULLIVAN, Jer.		30	M	Farmer	15Jul4MI	HEGAUTRY, Mary		18	F	None	15Jul4MJ
Ann	(W)	30	F	None	15Jul4MI	BROON, Cath.		04	F	Child	15Jul4MJ
Jona.	(D)	10	F	None	15Jul4MI	Alice		20	F	None	15Jul4MJ
John	(S)	07	M	Child	15Jul4MI	MCELIGOTTE, Thos.		20	M	Laborer	15Jul4MJ

NAMES OF PASSENGERS		AGE	SEX	OCCUPATIONS	DATE PORT SHIP
LEVITT, R.		25	M	Laborer	15Ju14MJ
Mary		22	F	None	15Ju14MJ
WALSOMY, D.		35	M	Laborer	15Ju14MJ
DONOMAGN, T.		35	M	Laborer	15Ju14MJ
TUNN, Jno.		30	M	Laborer	15Ju14MJ
CUNNINGHAM, W.		28	M	Laborer	15Ju14MJ
HARRINGTON, D.		35	M	Laborer	15Ju14MJ
HAROGAN, Mich.		30	M	Laborer	15Ju14MJ
DALY, M.		25	M	Laborer	15Ju14MJ
Mary		24	F	None	15Ju14MJ
DREW, Mich.		25	M	Laborer	15Ju14MJ
HUGAN, C.		25	M	Laborer	15Ju14MJ
RIORDAN, M.		30	M	Laborer	15Ju14MJ
MAHONEY, Eliza		20	F	None	15Ju14MJ
LUNY, Margaret		25	F	None	15Ju14MJ
HINEGAN, John		35	M	Laborer	15Ju14MJ
Johana		30	F	None	15Ju14MJ
MARTIN, Cath.		30	F	None	15Ju14MJ
MURPHY, Jno.		25	M	Laborer	15Ju14MJ
SULLIVAN, Mary		20	F	None	15Ju14MJ
James		20	M	Laborer	15Ju14MJ
DISCOLE, Pat		30	M	Laborer	15Ju14MJ
MCCARTHY, T.		30	M	Laborer	15Ju14MJ
WARD, Thos.		25	M	Laborer	15Ju14Fj
FITZGERALD, J.		50	M	Laborer	15Ju14MJ
John	(S)	25	M	Laborer	15Ju14MJ
CALLIGER, Jno.		35	M	Laborer	15Ju14MJ
THEABORER, Pat		25	M	Laborer	15Ju14MJ
STANTON, Ellen		30	F	None	15Ju14MJ
Mary		20	F	None	15Ju14MJ
Peggy		18	F	None	15Ju14MJ
Bridget		16	F	None	15Ju14MJ
SHINE, Don		35	M	Laborer	15Ju14MJ
COGGEN, J.		30	M	Laborer	15Ju14MJ
ROGAN, Mary		20	F	None	15Ju14MJ
HANNOGAN, J.		30	M	Laborer	15Ju14MJ
BARRETT, Wm.		25	M	Laborer	15Ju14MJ
BROZ, Mary		20	F	None	15Ju14MJ
HESHNEN, Margt.		20	F	None	15Ju14MJ
HANNEEN, Ed.		30	M	Laborer	15Ju14MJ
HUNT, Tim		25	M	Laborer	15Ju14MJ
SCANTON, M.		20	M	Laborer	15Ju14MJ
HUSTIAN, Magt.		35	F	None	15Ju14MJ
JAUNCE, Berry		25	M	Laborer	15Ju14MJ
JOHNSON, David		30	M	Laborer	15Ju14MJ
DUGAN, Cornelius		25	M	Laborer	15Ju14MJ
WILLIAMS, Julia		20	F	None	15Ju14MJ

SHAMROCK 16 JUNE 1847

From Limerick

NAMES OF PASSENGERS		AGE	SEX	OCCUPATIONS	DATE PORT SHIP
BAKER, Thos.		28	M	Farmer	16Ju33Mk
Mary		32	F	None	16Ju33Mk
Margt.		24	F	None	16Ju33Mk
Wm.	(S)	05	M	Child	16Ju33Mk
Thos.	(S)	01	M	Child	16Ju33Mk
Hanna	(D)	03	F	Child	16Ju33Mk
ANEY, M.		21	M	Laborer	16Ju33Mk
LYONS, W.		33	M	Laborer	16Ju33Mk
Ann		32	F	None	16Ju33Mk
Margt.		35	F	None	16Ju33Mk
Denis	(S)	02	M	Child	16Ju33Mk
Jas.	(S)	.11	M	Infant	16Ju33Mk
MCMAHON, J.		25	M	Farmer	16Ju33Mk
MCINNESSEY, J.		28	M	Mechanic	16Ju33Mk
AHERN, D.		20	M	Mechanic	16Ju33Mk
STRATTON, V.		21	M	Mechanic	16Ju33Mk
OHALLERON, Mary		28	F	None	16Ju33Mk

NAMES OF PASSENGERS		AGE	SEX	OCCUPATIONS	DATE PORT SHIP
OBRIEN, Mch.		24	M	Mechanic	16Ju33Mk
Margt.		20	F	None	16Ju33Mk
HOULIHAN, Jno.		25	M	Farmer	16Ju33Mk
HOURIGAN, Pat		22	M	Farmer	16Ju33Mk
SLATTERY, Thos.		24	M	Farmer	16Ju33Mk
CANTEY, Pat		26	M	Farmer	16Ju33Mk
HAYES, John		26	M	Farmer	16Ju33Mk
HANIGAN, Ellen		20	F	None	16Ju33Mk
SLATTERY, Bridget		45	F	None	16Ju33Mk
NEALIN, Mich.		21	M	Mechanic	16Ju33Mk
SULLIVAN, Jno.		14	M	Mechanic	16Ju33Mk
MARNANN, Mich.		36	M	Laborer	16Ju33Mk
BUCKLY, Jno.		22	M	Laborer	16Ju33Mk
MCMAHON, M.		25	M	Laborer	16Ju33Mk
Cath.		24	F	None	16Ju33Mk
CONNAY, Jas.		42	M	Laborer	16Ju33Mk
Mary	(W)	38	F	None	16Ju33Mk
Wm.	(S)	14	M	None	16Ju33Mk
Jas.	(S)	12	M	None	16Ju33Mk
Mary	(D)	10	F	Child	16Ju33Mk
Ellen	(D)	08	F	Child	16Ju33Mk
Edwd.	(S)	05	M	Child	16Ju33Mk
Thos.	(S)	04	M	Child	16Ju33Mk
John	(S)	02	M	Child	16Ju33Mk
FREEMAN, Margt.		18	F	None	16Ju33Mk
MCNAMARA, Sarah		21	F	None	16Ju33Mk
ONEIL, Mich.		23	M	Laborer	16Ju33Mk
Phoebe	(W)	24	F	None	16Ju33Mk
John	(S)	.00	M	Infant	16Ju33Mk
SANDEN, D.		27	M	Laborer	16Ju33Mk
MCNAMARA, D.		27	M	Laborer	16Ju33Mk
KENNEDY, D.		20	M	Laborer	16Ju33Mk
SHERING, Margt.		27	F	None	16Ju33Mk
DUNN, J.		27	M	Laborer	16Ju33Mk
CASEY, D.		20	M	Laborer	16Ju33Mk
DAILEY, Jno.		25	M	Laborer	16Ju33Mk
Mich.		23	M	Laborer	16Ju33Mk
MCCARTHY, Justin		21	M	Laborer	16Ju33Mk
ODONNELL, Margt.		32	F	None	16Ju33Mk
CORNNESS, Margt.		23	F	None	16Ju33Mk
Mary		23	F	None	16Ju33Mk
FAHY, Mary		30	F	None	16Ju33Mk
Jas.	(S)	17	M	Laborer	16Ju33Mk
HASSETT, Mary		28	F	None	16Ju33Mk
KEATING, Mat.		25	M	Laborer	16Ju33Mk
HALLORAN, Lucy		23	F	None	16Ju33Mk
MCNAMARA, D.		27	M	Laborer	16Ju33Mk
HASTINGS, P.		25	M	Laborer	16Ju33Mk
GLEASON, Mich.		22	M	Laborer	16Ju33Mk
John		19	M	Laborer	16Ju33Mk
Mary		24	F	None	16Ju33Mk
MALONEY, Pat		22	M	Laborer	16Ju33Mk
Martin		20	M	Laborer	16Ju33Mk
CONNOR, M.		27	M	Laborer	16Ju33Mk
Mary		25	F	None	16Ju33Mk
SCALAN, Pat		21	M	Laborer	16Ju33Mk
HALLORAN, Jim		32	M	Laborer	16Ju33Mk
Jas.		20	M	Laborer	16Ju33Mk
MCINERNY, Pat.		20	M	Laborer	16Ju33Mk
HERBERT, Peter		23	M	Laborer	16Ju33Mk
OBRIEN, Mich.		23	M	Laborer	16Ju33Mk
GREEN, Mich.		27	M	Laborer	16Ju33Mk
CASBIT, Mary		19	F	None	16Ju33Mk
GREEN, Jas.		24	M	Laborer	16Ju33Mk
CASBETT, Mich.		20	M	Laborer	16Ju33Mk
CARMODY, Jno.		24	M	Laborer	16Ju33Mk
MORRISSY, Thos.		24	M	Laborer	16Ju33Mk
CONWAY, Mary-A.		27	F	None	16Ju33Mk
KENNEY, Jno.		16	M	Laborer	16Ju33Mk
Mary		20	F	None	16Ju33Mk
FITZGERALD, G.		23	M	Laborer	16Ju33Mk
HALLORAN, Bridget		19	F	None	16Ju33Mk
MORRISSY, Jno.		34	M	Laborer	16Ju33Mk
HALLORAN, Mich.		32	M	Laborer	16Ju33Mk
MCMAHON, Pat		30	M	Laborer	16Ju33Mk

NAMES OF PASSENGERS		AGE	SEX	OCCUPATIONS	DATE PORT SHIP	NAMES OF PASSENGERS		AGE	SEX	OCCUPATIONS	DATE PORT SHIP
TRACY, Jas.		20	M	Laborer	16Ju33Mk	BOURKE, William		20	M	Farmer	18Ju02Jd
BANKS, Geo.		20	M	Laborer	16Ju33Mk	RYAN, Michl.		24	M	Farmer	18Ju02Jd
OCONNER, Mich.		23	M	Laborer	16Ju33Mk	ENGLISH, Patrick		40	M	Farmer	18Ju02Jd
MCINERNY, W.		24	M	Laborer	16Ju33Mk	Ellen		21	F	None	18Ju02Jd
RIORDAN, Robt.		27	M	Laborer	16Ju33Mk	BOURKE, Daniel		32	M	Farmer	18Ju02Jd
FITZGERALD, Margt.		23	F	None	16Ju33Mk	ENGLISH, Betty		18	F	None	18Ju02Jd
RYAN, Mary		25	F	None	16Ju33Mk	Jno.	(B)	06	M	Child	18Ju02Jd
LYNCH, Bridget		23	F	None	16Ju33Mk	Mary	(T)	01	F	Child	18Ju02Jd
Mich.		24	M	Laborer	16Ju33Mk	Julia	(M)	30	F	None	18Ju02Jd
MCMAHON, Susan		28	F	None	16Ju33Mk	RYAN, William		30	M	Carpenter	18Ju02Jd
SLATTERLY, Wm.		18	M	Laborer	16Ju33Mk	NEILL, Thomas		21	M	Carpenter	18Ju02Jd
Patrick	(P)	50	M	Laborer	16Ju33Mk	SHEEHAN, Thomas		23	M	Carpenter	18Ju02Jd
Cath.	(M)	48	F	None	16Ju33Mk	LYONS, James		30	M	Carpenter	18Ju02Jd
James	(B)	17	M	Laborer	16Ju33Mk	HICKIR, Jno.		26	M	Carpenter	18Ju02Jd
William	(B)	14	M	None	16Ju33Mk	Mary	(W)	27	F	None	18Ju02Jd
Maria	(T)	10	F	Child	16Ju33Mk	Patrick	(S)	01	M	Child	18Ju02Jd
Patrick	(B)	09	M	Child	16Ju33Mk	DILLON, Thomas		25	M	Carpenter	18Ju02Jd
John	(B)	07	M	Child	16Ju33Mk	Bridget		22	F	None	18Ju02Jd
FITZGERALD, Honora		23	F	None	16Ju33Mk	BROWN, Patrick		30	M	Carpenter	18Ju02Jd
FRANKLIN, Geo.		25	M	Laborer	16Ju33Mk	MAHONY, Michl.		28	M	Carpenter	18Ju02Jd
Ann	(W)	19	F	None	16Ju33Mk	LILLIS, Jno.		30	M	Carpenter	18Ju02Jd
Josha.	(S)	.07	M	Infant	16Ju33Mk	Mary	(W)	30	F	None	18Ju02Jd
WOODS, John		28	M	Laborer	16Ju33Mk	Owen		18	M	Carpenter	18Ju02Jd
DILLON, Jno.		25	M	Laborer	16Ju33Mk	Bridget	(D)	12	F	None	18Ju02Jd
FITZGILLON, Ellen		22	F	None	16Ju33Mk	Cath.	(D)	05	F	Child	18Ju02Jd
DWYER, Mary		23	F	None	16Ju33Mk	CASEY, William		30	M	Carpenter	18Ju02Jd
Ellen		18	F	None	16Ju33Mk	Maurice	(S)	02	M	Child	18Ju02Jd
MERRIT, Eliza		18	F	None	16Ju33Mk	Jane	(D)	01	F	Child	18Ju02Jd
PRESCOTT, Jnn.		19	M	Laborer	16Ju33Mk	Died-At-Sea					
MARA, Rodger		45	M	Laborer	16Ju33Mk	EAGAN, Peter		23	M	Carpenter	18Ju02Jd
Bridget	(W)	40	F	None	16Ju33Mk	Johanna	(W)	21	F	None	18Ju02Jd
Bridget	(D)	08	F	Child	16Ju33Mk	Michl.	(S)	07	M	Child	18Ju02Jd
John	(S)	06	M	Child	16Ju33Mk	James	(S)	04	M	Child	18Ju02Jd
Ellen	(D)	04	F	Child	16Ju33Mk	KEANE, Jno.		03	M	Child	18Ju02Jd
Thomas	(S)	01	M	Child	16Ju33Mk	MCAULIFFE, Jno.		40	M	Carpenter	18Ju02Jd
PUNCH, Mich.		28	M	Farmer	16Ju33Mk	Mary	(W)	36	F	None	18Ju02Jd
KEASY, Pat		26	M	Farmer	16Ju33Mk	Thos.	(S)	17	M	Carpenter	18Ju02Jd
Ellen		26	F	None	16Ju33Mk	Jno.	(S)	14	M	Carpenter	18Ju02Jd
Hanna		17	F	None	16Ju33Mk	Mary	(D)	09	F	Child	18Ju02Jd
SILLES, Richd.		20	M	Laborer	16Ju33Mk	Ellen	(D)	06	F	Child	18Ju02Jd
CASEY, Jas.		26	M	Laborer	16Ju33Mk	Michl.	(S)	04	M	Child	18Ju02Jd
OCONNER, Mch.		20	M	Laborer	16Ju33Mk	KILLY, Jno.		35	M	Carpenter	18Ju02Jd
DILLON, D.		30	M	Laborer	16Ju33Mk	Mary		22	F	None	18Ju02Jd
Bridget	(W)	25	F	None	16Ju33Mk	Morty		17	M	Carpenter	18Ju02Jd
Ellen	(D)	09	F	Child	16Ju33Mk	Biddy		15	F	None	18Ju02Jd
GRIFFEN, Mich.		30	M	Laborer	16Ju33Mk	BARRETT, James		30	M	Carpenter	18Ju02Jd
MCNAMARA, T.		24	M	Laborer	16Ju33Mk	Eliza		28	F	None	18Ju02Jd
GRADY, Jas.		23	M	Laborer	16Ju33Mk	Jno.		13	M	Carpenter	18Ju02Jd
Jane		22	F	None	16Ju33Mk	FITZGERALD, Patrick		35	M	Carpenter	18Ju02Jd
BRENNAN, Mary		22	F	None	16Ju33Mk	Michl.	(S)	06	M	Child	18Ju02Jd
MCINERNEY, Margt.		22	F	None	16Ju33Mk	ROCHE, Patrick		04	M	Child	18Ju02Jd
MENGAVIN, Jno.		30	M	Farmer	16Ju33Mk	Nany	(M)	35	F	None	18Ju02Jd
ODEA, Dennis		21	M	Farmer	16Ju33Mk	Patrick		20	M	Carpenter	18Ju02Jd
LYONS, U		.00	M	Infant	16Ju33Mk	KELLY, Edward		50	M	Cooper	18Ju02Jd
						Michl.	(S)	09	M	Child	18Ju02Jd
						HOGAN, Ellen		21	F	None	18Ju02Jd
						FRANKLYN, Danl.		40	M	Cooper	18Ju02Jd
						Cath.	(W)	36	F	None	18Ju02Jd
						Margt.	(D)	18	F	None	18Ju02Jd
ELEUTHERIA 18 JUNE 1847						Biddy	(D)	16	F	None	18Ju02Jd
						Thos.	(S)	12	M	Cooper	18Ju02Jd
From Liverpool						Kitty	(D)	09	F	Child	18Ju02Jd
						Jane	(D)	06	F	Child	18Ju02Jd
						Winney	(D)	04	F	Child	18Ju02Jd
						Margt.	(D)	03	F	Child	18Ju02Jd
CONNELL, Daniel		28	M	Farmer	18Ju02Jd	QUINLAN, Michl.		30	M	Carpenter	18Ju02Jd
Michael		25	M	Farmer	18Ju02Jd	Mary	(W)	28	F	None	18Ju02Jd
HAYS, Jno.		26	M	Farmer	18Ju02Jd	Kitty		16	F	None	18Ju02Jd
Bridget	(W)	26	F	None	18Ju02Jd	Danl.	(S)	09	M	Child	18Ju02Jd
Bridget	(D)	04	F	Child	18Ju02Jd	Mary	(D)	07	F	Child	18Ju02Jd
Jane	(M)	50	F	None	18Ju02Jd	Biddy	(D)	05	F	Child	18Ju02Jd
Patrick	(S)	03	M	Child	18Ju02Jd	Sally	(D)	01	F	Child	18Ju02Jd
Jane	(D)	01	F	Child	18Ju02Jd	MOORE, Thos.		40	M	Carpenter	18Ju02Jd
RUSSELL, John		20	M	Farmer	18Ju02Jd	Mary		20	F	None	18Ju02Jd
MYERS, Jno.		50	M	Farmer	18Ju02Jd	Michl.	(S)	20	M	Carpenter	18Ju02Jd

NAMES OF PASSENGERS		AGE	SEX	OCCUPATIONS	DATE PORT SHIP
MOORE, Mary		01	F	Child	18Ju02Jd
Kate		01	F	Child	18Ju02Jd
NANAN, Cornelius		23	M	Carpenter	18Ju02Jd
Jno.		18	M	Carpenter	18Ju02Jd
Michl.		12	M	Carpenter	18Ju02Jd
Nancy		08	F	Child	18Ju02Jd
Maurice		02	M	Child	18Ju02Jd
RYAN, Patrick		32	M	Carpenter	18Ju02Jd
Cath.	(W)	28	F	None	18Ju02Jd
Michl.	(S)	05	M	Child	18Ju02Jd
Jno.	(S)	03	M	Child	18Ju02Jd
Ellen		21	F	None	18Ju02Jd
Mary		18	F	None	18Ju02Jd
DWYER, Phil		30	M	Carpenter	18Ju02Jd
Mary	(W)	28	F	None	18Ju02Jd
Jno.	(S)	08	M	Child	18Ju02Jd
Michl.	(S)	04	M	Child	18Ju02Jd
Brdgt.	(D)	01	F	Child	18Ju02Jd
RYAN, Patrick		01	M	Child	18Ju02Jd
BARRETT, Mary		10	F	Child	18Ju02Jd
EGAN, Mary		01	F	Child	18Ju02Jd
MCAULIFFE, Biddy		01	F	Child	18Ju02Jd
RYAN, Ellen		00	F	Unknown	18Ju02Jd
James		00	M	Unknown	18Ju02Jd
HEALY, Cath.		00	F	Unknown	18Ju02Jd
HICKEY, Jno.		00	M	Unknown	18Ju02Jd
HALLINAN, William		00	M	Unknown	18Ju02Jd
HEALY, Cath.		00	F	Unknown	18Ju02Jd
CONDON, Cath.		22	F	None	18Ju02Jd
YEAN, Cath.		22	F	None	18Ju02Jd
VAUGHAN, Stephen		25	M	Carpenter	18Ju02Jd
RILIHAN, Timy.		45	M	Carpenter	18Ju02Jd
Jno.		26	M	Carpenter	18Ju02Jd
MCCORMACK, Margt.		18	F	None	18Ju02Jd
DWYER, Jno.		21	M	Gdnr	18Ju02Jd
Mary		21	F	None	18Ju02Jd
MCMAHON, Jno.		25	M	Gdnr	18Ju02Jd
SULLIVAN, Timy.		24	M	Gdnr	18Ju02Jd
Died-At-Sea					
Timy.		20	M	Gdnr	18Ju02Jd
Ellen		20	F	None	18Ju02Jd
KENNEDY, Jno.		40	M	Gdnr	18Ju02Jd
Bridgt.	(W)	40	F	None	18Ju02Jd
James	(S)	08	M	Child	18Ju02Jd
Jno.	(S)	05	M	Child	18Ju02Jd
LYNCH, Jno.		30	M	Gdnr	18Ju02Jd
Mary	(W)	30	F	None	18Ju02Jd
James		13	M	Gdnr	18Ju02Jd
Bridget	(D)	01	F	Child	18Ju02Jd
SULLIVAN, Lawrence		18	M	Gdnr	18Ju02Jd
BARRETT, Dani.		35	M	Gdnr	18Ju02Jd
Mary	(W)	30	F	None	18Ju02Jd
Cornelius		27	M	Gdnr	18Ju02Jd
Thomas	(S)	06	M	Child	18Ju02Jd
Jno.	(S)	03	M	Child	18Ju02Jd
KEANE, Thomas		40	M	Gdnr	18Ju02Jd
Ann		28	F	None	18Ju02Jd
NICHOLSON, Michl.		25	M	Gdnr	18Ju02Jd
HANLEY, Jno.		22	M	Gdnr	18Ju02Jd
James		21	M	Gdnr	18Ju02Jd
Mary		24	F	None	18Ju02Jd
Cath.		17	F	None	18Ju02Jd
Anastasia		12	F	None	18Ju02Jd
BLAKE, Henry		25	M	Gdnr	18Ju02Jd
Mary		25	F	None	18Ju02Jd
MANAGHAN, Patrick		28	M	Gdnr	18Ju02Jd
DONOGHOE, Mary		23	F	None	18Ju02Jd
Margt.		25	F	None	18Ju02Jd
COLLINS, Patrick		30	M	Gdnr	18Ju02Jd
PURTELL, William		25	M	Gdnr	18Ju02Jd
NUNAN, May		25	F	None	18Ju02Jd
CONNOR, Patrick		26	M	Gdnr	18Ju02Jd
HEALY, William		46	M	Gdnr	18Ju02Jd
Jno.	(S)	21	M	Gdnr	18Ju02Jd
Wm.	(S)	19	M	Gdnr	18Ju02Jd
HEALY, Denis	(S)	16	M	Gdnr	18Ju02Jd
Oliver	(S)	12	M	Gdnr	18Ju02Jd
CONNERS, Peggy		27	F	None	18Ju02Jd
HAYES, Cath.		28	F	None	18Ju02Jd
COFFEE, Richard		29	M	Gdnr	18Ju02Jd
HANLEY, Thomas		25	M	Gdnr	18Ju02Jd
MOLONY, James		27	M	Gdnr	18Ju02Jd
ODEA, Jno.		27	M	Gdnr	18Ju02Jd
CLANELRY, Patrick		25	M	Gdnr	18Ju02Jd
SPELLANY, Jno.		36	M	Victualler	18Ju02Jd
Ann	(W)	31	F	None	18Ju02Jd
Michl.	(S)	12	M	Victualler	18Ju02Jd
Catharine	(D)	09	F	Child	18Ju02Jd
Margt.	(D)	06	F	Child	18Ju02Jd
Ann	(D)	04	F	Child	18Ju02Jd
RYAN, Michael		30	M	Victualler	18Ju02Jd
Patrick		24	M	Victualler	18Ju02Jd
THOMEY, Margt.		21	F	None	18Ju02Jd
Died-At-Sea					
BARRETT, Mary		.00	F	Infant	18Ju02Jd
Born-At-Sea	Died-At-Sea				
DWYER, U		.00	U	Infant	18Ju02Jd

FANNY 18 JUNE 1847

From Glasgow

NAMES OF PASSENGERS		AGE	SEX	OCCUPATIONS	DATE PORT SHIP
KEAN, Thos.		35	M	Laborer	18Ju04Mn
BEATMAN, Jno.		32	M	Farmer	18Ju04Mn
Ellen		32	F	None	18Ju04Mn
WIER, Thos.		23	M	Farmer	18Ju04Mn
STEWARD, G.		30	M	Farmer	18Ju04Mn
U	(W)	30	F	None	18Ju04Mn
Jno.	(S)	.02	M	Infant	18Ju04Mn
BEARD, Jane		30	F	None	18Ju04Mn
CREMIE, Jas.		18	M	Farmer	18Ju04Mn
CAMPBELL, C.		21	M	Farmer	18Ju04Mn
Buchn.		13	M	None	18Ju04Mn
BROWN, Jno.		26	M	Clerk	18Ju04Mn
PATERSON, Silbias		25	F	None	18Ju04Mn
MCKENZIE, Geo.		25	M	Farmer	18Ju04Mn
U	(W)	25	F	None	18Ju04Mn
Alex	(S)	03	M	Child	18Ju04Mn
Ann	(D)	.09	F	Infant	18Ju04Mn
SMITH, Jas.		32	M	Farmer	18Ju04Mn
U	(W)	32	F	None	18Ju04Mn
James	(S)	04	M	Child	18Ju04Mn
Jean	(D)	02	F	Child	18Ju04Mn
Ann	(D)	.09	F	Infant	18Ju04Mn
Robert		24	M	Farmer	18Ju04Mn
U	(W)	26	F	None	18Ju04Mn
Jas.	(S)	.09	M	Infant	18Ju04Mn
Alexr.		23	M	Farmer	18Ju04Mn
MUSTARD, Wm.		35	M	Farmer	18Ju04Mn
Margt.		25	F	None	18Ju04Mn
NIMLEH, David		28	M	Farmer	18Ju04Mn
PATERSON, David		25	M	Farmer	18Ju04Mn
CAMPBELL, Jean		26	F	None	18Ju04Mn
David	(S)	.03	M	Infant	18Ju04Mn
Andrew	(S)	06	M	Child	18Ju04Mn
James	(S)	02	M	Child	18Ju04Mn
MILL, Ellen-W.		24	F	None	18Ju04Mn
PATERSON, Wm.		02	M	Child	18Ju04Mn
Jno.		02	M	Child	18Ju04Mn
GUY, Jas.		26	M	Mechanic	18Ju04Mn
MCALLISTER, Wm.		28	M	Mechanic	18Ju04Mn
GIBNY, James		30	M	Farmer	18Ju04Mn
MARSHALL, John		40	M	Farmer	18Ju04Mn
U	(W)	36	F	None	18Ju04Mn

NAMES OF PASSENGERS		AGE	SEX	OCCUPATIONS	DATE PORT SHIP
MARSHALL, Margt.	(D)	14	F	None	18Ju04Mn
Isabella	(D)	07	F	Child	18Ju04Mn
Cath.	(D)	05	F	Child	18Ju04Mn
Marjery	(D)	04	F	Child	18Ju04Mn
David	(S)	02	M	Child	18Ju04Mn
DAVIS, Jas.		29	M	Farmer	18Ju04Mn
Jean		21	F	None	18Ju04Mn
LOCKHART, H.		33	M	Farmer	18Ju04Mn
DAVIS, Martha		02	F	Child	18Ju04Mn
Rebecca	(T)	.11	F	Infant	18Ju04Mn
Thos.	(P)	34	M	Farmer	18Ju04Mn
Jean	(W)	28	F	None	18Ju04Mn
Joseph		18	M	Farmer	18Ju04Mn
Martha	(D)	04	F	Child	18Ju04Mn
Rachael	(D)	02	F	Child	18Ju04Mn
Isabella	(D)	.11	F	Infant	18Ju04Mn
CREIGHTON, Jas.		35	M	Farmer	18Ju04Mn
PATERSON, John		38	M	Mechanic	18Ju04Mn
BROWN, Geo.		19	M	Merchant	18Ju04Mn
MOORE, Thos.		30	M	Farmer	18Ju04Mn
LAURIE, Geo.		20	M	Farmer	18Ju04Mn
MCANDREWS, Robt.		29	M	Farmer	18Ju04Mn
LOCHREE, Peter		49	M	Farmer	18Ju04Mn
James		18	M	Farmer	18Ju04Mn
SWAVNEY, Danean		18	M	Farmer	18Ju04Mn
ROGERS, Robt.		40	M	Merchant	18Ju04Mn
Mary	(D)	16	F	None	18Ju04Mn
Margt.	(D)	12	F	None	18Ju04Mn
BIGLEY, Peter		30	M	Mechanic	18Ju04Mn
MOREN, John		33	M	Mechanic	18Ju04Mn
Mary		25	F	None	18Ju04Mn
Mary		13	F	None	18Ju04Mn
Patrick		11	M	Child	18Ju04Mn
Thos.		06	M	Child	18Ju04Mn
Michl.		.04	M	Infant	18Ju04Mn
MCROBERTS, Jno.		28	M	Farmer	18Ju04Mn
Elspeth	(W)	23	F	None	18Ju04Mn
MILLER, Mary		25	F	None	18Ju04Mn
MCROBERTS, Elspeth		01	F	Child	18Ju04Mn
Mary	(T)	.02	F	Infant	18Ju04Mn
BETHUNE, Peter		35	M	Farmer	18Ju04Mn
LAMB, Jas.		40	M	Farmer	18Ju04Mn
Jane		25	F	None	18Ju04Mn
MCALORN, Jas.		25	M	Farmer	18Ju04Mn
Dennis		22	M	Farmer	18Ju04Mn
John		20	M	Farmer	18Ju04Mn
MCNAMARA, Jas.		35	M	Farmer	18Ju04Mn
CLELAND, Wm.		32	M	Farmer	18Ju04Mn
Margt.	(W)	30	F	None	18Ju04Mn
George	(S)	11	M	Child	18Ju04Mn
John	(S)	09	M	Child	18Ju04Mn
Morris	(S)	06	M	Child	18Ju04Mn
Wm.	(S)	03	M	Child	18Ju04Mn
SMITH, Jas.		25	M	Farmer	18Ju04Mn
MILLER, Robt.		25	M	Farmer	18Ju04Mn
TAYLOR, Ebz.		23	M	Farmer	18Ju04Mn
MILLER, Robt.-Mrs.		25	F	None	18Ju04Mn
Janet	(D)	04	F	Child	18Ju04Mn
Jane	(D)	02	F	Child	18Ju04Mn
Nieve	(S)	01	M	Child	18Ju04Mn
Janet		67	F	None	18Ju04Mn
Helen		23	F	None	18Ju04Mn
Margt.	(D)	08	F	Child	18Ju04Mn
Wm.	(S)	02	M	Child	18Ju04Mn
ROBERTSON, Christina		12	F	None	18Ju04Mn
MCLAREN, Ed.		37	M	Mechanic	18Ju04Mn
LAURIE, Elizth.		18	F	None	18Ju04Mn
WRIGHT, Peter		27	M	Mechanic	18Ju04Mn
GOW, D.		25	M	Mechanic	18Ju04Mn
GORMAN, D.		16	M	Mechanic	18Ju04Mn
Mary		18	F	None	18Ju04Mn
MCGOURLICK, Ed.		24	M	Mechanic	18Ju04Mn
LONG, Sam		27	M	Mechanic	18Ju04Mn
SHIELS, Wm.		26	M	Mechanic	18Ju04Mn
MORRISON, And.		22	M	Mechanic	18Ju04Mn

NAMES OF PASSENGERS		AGE	SEX	OCCUPATIONS	DATE PORT SHIP
LONG, Magt.		21	F	None	18Ju04Mn
CONNER, Matt		50	M	Farmer	18Ju04Mn
Margt.	(W)	50	F	None	18Ju04Mn
Pat	(S)	30	M	Farmer	18Ju04Mn
Grace	(D)	25	F	None	18Ju04Mn
Thos.	(S)	20	M	Farmer	18Ju04Mn
Mary-Ann	(D)	16	F	None	18Ju04Mn
KNOX, Saml.		24	M	Farmer	18Ju04Mn
Mary	(W)	21	F	None	18Ju04Mn
Martin	(S)	01	M	Child	18Ju04Mn
Robert		20	M	Farmer	18Ju04Mn
BRYSON, Jno.		18	M	Farmer	18Ju04Mn
DUNLOP, Alex		50	M	Farmer	18Ju04Mn
Margt.	(W)	50	F	None	18Ju04Mn
Jas.	(S)	14	M	None	18Ju04Mn
Chas.	(S)	11	M	Child	18Ju04Mn
MCKENNA, Bridget		20	F	None	18Ju04Mn
GAGER, Alice		22	F	None	18Ju04Mn
DUNLOP, Matilda		50	F	None	18Ju04Mn
GALAGAR, Elsie		12	F	None	18Ju04Mn
Hannah		15	F	None	18Ju04Mn
GRAY, Miles		59	M	Farmer	18Ju04Mn
Cath.	(W)	49	F	None	18Ju04Mn
Isabella	(D)	11	F	Child	18Ju04Mn
Ellen	(D)	09	F	Child	18Ju04Mn
Andrew	(S)	07	M	Child	18Ju04Mn
ORR, Isabella		30	F	None	18Ju04Mn
REYNERS, Jno.		30	M	Farmer	18Ju04Mn
OBRIEN, Ann		20	F	None	18Ju04Mn
BRYSON, Mary		21	F	None	18Ju04Mn
WRAY, Henry-G.		22	M	Farmer	18Ju04Mn
Cath.		21	F	None	18Ju04Mn
COLLINS, Pat		29	M	Farmer	18Ju04Mn
Bridget		28	F	None	18Ju04Mn
Susan		20	F	None	18Ju04Mn
MCELVARY, Jno.		18	M	Farmer	18Ju04Mn
STERLING, Peter		24	M	Mechanic	18Ju04Mn
Isabella		26	F	None	18Ju04Mn
MCGREGOR, Peter		34	M	Mechanic	18Ju04Mn
FRAZER, Jane		35	F	None	18Ju04Mn
MCCARTY, R.		35	M	Mechanic	18Ju04Mn
RAMSAY, A.		20	M	Farmer	18Ju04Mn
FINDLAY, J.		27	M	Farmer	18Ju04Mn
RUSSEL, Joseph		40	M	Farmer	18Ju04Mn
TEMPLETON, Robt.		20	M	Farmer	18Ju04Mn
MCCARSON, Edwd.		17	M	Farmer	18Ju04Mn
CORR, Cath.		21	F	None	18Ju04Mn
KNOX, Mary		01	F	Child	18Ju04Mn
MCDEVITT, Jno.		46	M	Farmer	18Ju04Mn
HERRIT, William		46	M	Farmer	18Ju04Mn
SMITH, Jos.		30	M	Farmer	18Ju04Mn
Margt.	(W)	30	F	None	18Ju04Mn
Ann-Jane	(D)	.02	F	Infant	18Ju04Mn
HAGERTY, M.		39	M	Farmer	18Ju04Mn
GALAGER, Ellen		15	F	None	18Ju04Mn
ROBERTSON, R.		30	M	Farmer	18Ju04Mn
ROVIN, Mich.		22	M	Farmer	18Ju04Mn
HICK, Henry		32	M	Farmer	18Ju04Mn
David		30	M	Farmer	18Ju04Mn
FLEMING, And.		29	M	Farmer	18Ju04Mn
WILSON, Jno.		19	M	Farmer	18Ju04Mn
MITCHEL, Hugh		49	M	Farmer	18Ju04Mn
John	(S)	23	M	Farmer	18Ju04Mn
Janet	(D)	26	F	None	18Ju04Mn
Emily	(W)	40	F	None	18Ju04Mn
Margt.		30	F	None	18Ju04Mn
GRANT, D.		35	M	Farmer	18Ju04Mn
Isabella		40	F	None	18Ju04Mn
MCCRAE, R.		21	M	Farmer	18Ju04Mn
Margt.		18	F	None	18Ju04Mn
Cath.		16	F	None	18Ju04Mn
HUME, Wm.		27	M	Farmer	18Ju04Mn
Elizth.	(W)	28	F	None	18Ju04Mn
Elizth.	(D)	02	F	Child	18Ju04Mn
DUFFY, Abby		27	F	None	18Ju04Mn

NAMES OF PASSENGERS		AGE	SEX	OCCUPATIONS	DATE PORT SHIP
LANDON, Robt.		31	M	Farmer	18Ju04Mn
WATSON, Jno.		41	M	Farmer	18Ju04Mn

VICTOR 18 JUNE 1847

From Dublin

NAMES OF PASSENGERS		AGE	SEX	OCCUPATIONS	DATE PORT SHIP
WHITE, Wm.F.		25	M	Clerk	18Ju20Mo
Maria		20	F	None	18Ju20Mo
MEADE, B.		25	M	Laborer	18Ju20Mo
BURKE, John		28	M	Mechanic	18Ju20Mo
Eliza		25	F	None	18Ju20Mo
RAFFERTY, Mary-A.		18	F	None	18Ju20Mo
HAMILTON, Peter		30	M	Mechanic	18Ju20Mo
RAIT, Mary		25	F	None	18Ju20Mo
EVANS, Mary		25	F	None	18Ju20Mo
LAURENCE, Charles		21	M	Clerk	18Ju20Mo
GRIERSON, Joseph		25	M	Farmer	18Ju20Mo
HIGGINSON, Jane		30	F	None	18Ju20Mo
Thos.	(S)	13	M	None	18Ju20Mo
Mich.	(S)	11	M	Child	18Ju20Mo
MCDANIEL, Nich.		30	M	Laborer	18Ju20Mo
BREEN, Mich.		40	M	Laborer	18Ju20Mo
U	(W)	40	F	None	18Ju20Mo
DUMPHY, Frank		35	M	Laborer	18Ju20Mo
BYRNE, Cho.		25	M	Laborer	18Ju20Mo
GREEN, Danl.		25	M	Laborer	18Ju20Mo
BRODRICK, Jno.		25	M	Laborer	18Ju20Mo
BICKNELL, U-Mrs.		35	F	None	18Ju20Mo
Mellan	(D)	10	F	Child	18Ju20Mo
Eliza	(D)	09	F	Child	18Ju20Mo
George	(S)	07	M	Child	18Ju20Mo
Christopher	(S)	.00	M	Infant	18Ju20Mo
CASEY, Cath.		22	F	None	18Ju20Mo
MCGRATH, Pat		25	M	Mechanic	18Ju20Mo
KEATINGE, Mich.		30	M	Mechanic	18Ju20Mo
Eliza	(W)	25	F	None	18Ju20Mo
Michl.	(S)	03	M	Child	18Ju20Mo
Eliza	(D)	.00	F	Infant	18Ju20Mo
BURKE, Clara		22	F	None	18Ju20Mo
Elizth.		21	F	None	18Ju20Mo
Mary		18	F	None	18Ju20Mo
Harriet		17	F	None	18Ju20Mo
NUGENT, Fanny		25	F	None	18Ju20Mo
MELONY, Margt.		20	F	None	18Ju20Mo
LYNCH, John		26	M	Farmer	18Ju20Mo
JORING, Geo.		25	M	Farmer	18Ju20Mo
BUTTERLY, Jno.		30	M	Farmer	18Ju20Mo
KAYNN, Bernard		28	M	Laborer	18Ju20Mo
MOLYNEAUX, Wm.		24	M	Clerk	18Ju20Mo
Delice		20	F	None	18Ju20Mo
DUFFY, Wm.		21	M	Laborer	18Ju20Mo
Bessy		17	F	None	18Ju20Mo
DONEGAN, P.		30	M	Laborer	18Ju20Mo
HALPIN, Wm.		20	M	Laborer	18Ju20Mo
DUNNE, Jas.		30	M	Laborer	18Ju20Mo
Anne		25	F	None	18Ju20Mo
Ellen		23	F	None	18Ju20Mo
Mossy	(S)	.00	M	Infant	18Ju20Mo
DALY, Mary-Ann		38	F	None	18Ju20Mo
BYRNE, M.		48	M	Laborer	18Ju20Mo
J.	(S)	18	M	Laborer	18Ju20Mo
Wm.	(S)	17	M	Laborer	18Ju20Mo
MARKEY, Pat		25	M	Laborer	18Ju20Mo
TURNER, Jno.		30	M	Laborer	18Ju20Mo
Ann	(W)	24	F	None	18Ju20Mo
Joseph	(S)	.00	M	Infant	18Ju20Mo
RYAN, John		40	M	Farmer	18Ju20Mo
Cath.	(W)	35	F	None	18Ju20Mo
RYAN, Wm.	(S)	16	M	None	18Ju20Mo
Ed.	(S)	13	M	None	18Ju20Mo
Margt.	(D)	12	F	None	18Ju20Mo
Elizth.	(D)	04	F	Child	18Ju20Mo
Mich.	(S)	.00	M	Infant	18Ju20Mo
LAULER, Joseph		22	M	Mechanic	18Ju20Mo
KILLEN, Jno.		28	M	Mechanic	18Ju20Mo
HANBURY, Ed.		25	M	Mechanic	18Ju20Mo
DUMPHY, U-Mrs.		30	F	None	18Ju20Mo
FARRELL, R.		28	M	Farmer	18Ju20Mo
P.		30	M	Farmer	18Ju20Mo
U		22	F	None	18Ju20Mo
PLUNKETT, U		15	F	None	18Ju20Mo
CORRIGAN, Jas.		16	M	Farmer	18Ju20Mo
EGAN, Eliza		12	F	None	18Ju20Mo
QUINN, Mich.		28	M	Farmer	18Ju20Mo
Margt.		25	F	None	18Ju20Mo
GAFFNEY, Edwd.		25	M	Farmer	18Ju20Mo
ROCHE, Nich.		25	M	Farmer	18Ju20Mo
KELLY, J.		21	M	Clerk	18Ju20Mo
PARKER, Wm.		28	M	Clerk	18Ju20Mo
DOYLE, James		25	M	Mechanic	18Ju20Mo
CARROLL, J.		24	M	Mechanic	18Ju20Mo
M.		24	M	Mechanic	18Ju20Mo
KING, Pat		24	M	Laborer	18Ju20Mo
WHELAN, Thos.		22	M	Laborer	18Ju20Mo
DALY, Denis		30	M	Laborer	18Ju20Mo
ONEIL, Richd.		25	M	Laborer	18Ju20Mo
Jesse		20	F	None	18Ju20Mo
BRADY, Pat		30	M	Laborer	18Ju20Mo
Ann		27	F	None	18Ju20Mo
CODY, Ann		20	F	None	18Ju20Mo
REDMOND, Thos.		26	M	Laborer	18Ju20Mo
MAXWELL, H.B.		21	M	Laborer	18Ju20Mo
FEARER, U-Mrs.		30	F	None	18Ju20Mo
CONNOR, Hester		30	F	None	18Ju20Mo
EVANS, Thos.		20	M	Mechanic	18Ju20Mo
GOUGH, Jas.		25	M	Mechanic	18Ju20Mo
ELLIS, Thos.		30	M	Mechanic	18Ju20Mo
U	(W)	27	F	None	18Ju20Mo
Ed.	(S)	.00	M	Infant	18Ju20Mo
BULGER, Ed.		20	M	Laborer	18Ju20Mo
BEATTY, Pat		20	M	Laborer	18Ju20Mo
NICHOLSON, Mich.		22	M	Laborer	18Ju20Mo
REGAN, Eliza		22	F	None	18Ju20Mo
Mary	(M)	40	F	None	18Ju20Mo
Wm.	(B)	18	M	Laborer	18Ju20Mo
MCFEE, Pat		23	M	Laborer	18Ju20Mo

ASHBURTON 21 JUNE 1847

From Liverpool

NAMES OF PASSENGERS		AGE	SEX	OCCUPATIONS	DATE PORT SHIP
HIMSON, Francis		28	M	Merchant	21Ju02Bd
And.		28	M	Merchant	21Ju02Bd
St.JOHN, Thos.		50	M	Farmer	21Ju02Bd
Frances	(M)	70	F	None	21Ju02Bd
Ellen		25	F	None	21Ju02Bd
DAILY, Thos.		18	M	Farmer	21Ju02Bd
Jas.	(P)	48	M	Farmer	21Ju02Bd
Ann	(M)	42	F	None	21Ju02Bd
John	(B)	22	M	Farmer	21Ju02Bd
Wm.	(B)	20	M	Farmer	21Ju02Bd
Mary-A.	(T)	16	F	None	21Ju02Bd
Marcella	(T)	14	F	None	21Ju02Bd
Bridget	(T)	12	F	None	21Ju02Bd
Margt.	(T)	10	F	Child	21Ju02Bd
Cath.	(T)	08	F	Child	21Ju02Bd
James	(B)	06	M	Child	21Ju02Bd

NAMES OF PASSENGERS		A G E	S E X	OCCUPATIONS	DATE PORT SHIP	NAMES OF PASSENGERS		A G E	S E X	OCCUPATIONS	DATE PORT SHIP
DAILY, Alice	(T)	04	F	Child	21Ju02Bd	GARRICK, Bridget		23	F	None	21Ju02Bd
BARRY, Ann		18	F	None	21Ju02Bd	LEVY, Jno.		22	M	Farmer	21Ju02Bd
CHEEVERS, Mary		55	F	None	21Ju02Bd	TUMBLETON, Jas.		26	M	Farmer	21Ju02Bd
Jas.	(S)	30	M	Mechanic	21Ju02Bd	Margt.	(M)	52	F	None	21Ju02Bd
Richd.	(S)	29	M	Mechanic	21Ju02Bd	Frances	(T)	17	F	None	21Ju02Bd
Pat	(S)	27	M	Mechanic	21Ju02Bd	Ann	(T)	20	F	None	21Ju02Bd
George	(S)	23	M	Mechanic	21Ju02Bd	KINNALLY, Mich.		20	M	Farmer	21Ju02Bd
John	(S)	20	M	Mechanic	21Ju02Bd	JUDALE, Jas.		57	M	Farmer	21Ju02Bd
Mary	(D)	17	F	None	21Ju02Bd	Elizth.	(W)	50	F	None	21Ju02Bd
WARD, Laurence		50	M	Laborer	21Ju02Bd	Joshua	(S)	23	M	Farmer	21Ju02Bd
Ellen		30	F	None	21Ju02Bd	Sarah-A.	(D)	25	F	None	21Ju02Bd
James	(S)	16	M	Laborer	21Ju02Bd	Harriet	(D)	20	F	None	21Ju02Bd
FLOOD, Pat		28	M	Laborer	21Ju02Bd	William	(S)	13	M	None	21Ju02Bd
Ellen	(M)	42	F	None	21Ju02Bd	Grace	(D)	11	F	Child	21Ju02Bd
Thomas	(B)	14	M	Laborer	21Ju02Bd	Elizth.A.	(D)	09	F	Child	21Ju02Bd
Margt.	(T)	09	F	Child	21Ju02Bd	BRIAN, Pat		30	M	Laborer	21Ju02Bd
DIGNAN, Pat		31	M	Laborer	21Ju02Bd	Bridget		17	F	None	21Ju02Bd
Margt.		25	F	None	21Ju02Bd	CONNOR, John		30	M	Laborer	21Ju02Bd
NEWCOMBE, Martin		24	M	Laborer	21Ju02Bd	Cath.		25	F	None	21Ju02Bd
MURPHY, Thos.		20	M	Laborer	21Ju02Bd	Thos.		20	M	Laborer	21Ju02Bd
PEASELY, Thos.		25	M	Laborer	21Ju02Bd	QUIN, Ann		20	F	None	21Ju02Bd
Mary		27	F	None	21Ju02Bd	MCCARNAN, Geo.		16	M	Laborer	21Ju02Bd
DORIN, Cath.		62	F	None	21Ju02Bd	FITZPATRICK, B.		54	M	Laborer	21Ju02Bd
Pat	(S)	22	M	Laborer	21Ju02Bd	James	(S)	20	M	Laborer	21Ju02Bd
Martin	(S)	15	M	Laborer	21Ju02Bd	Thos.	(S)	14	M	Laborer	21Ju02Bd
Maria		13	F	None	21Ju02Bd	Margh.	(D)	19	F	None	21Ju02Bd
ROACH, Jno.		14	M	None	21Ju02Bd	FOLEY, Thos.		20	M	Laborer	21Ju02Bd
TOOLE, Pat		26	M	Laborer	21Ju02Bd	WOODS, Jno.		30	M	Laborer	21Ju02Bd
Mary	(W)	28	F	None	21Ju02Bd	FOSTER, Jno.		22	M	Laborer	21Ju02Bd
Bridget	(D)	03	F	Child	21Ju02Bd	CRONLEY, C.		27	M	Laborer	21Ju02Bd
Brian	(D)	01	M	Child	21Ju02Bd	MOORE, Pat.		20	M	Laborer	21Ju02Bd
JASH, Thos.		22	M	Laborer	21Ju02Bd	ROHAN, J.		30	M	Laborer	21Ju02Bd
ALPEN, Thos.		23	M	Laborer	21Ju02Bd	BURNS, D.		22	M	Laborer	21Ju02Bd
KELLY, Thos.		24	M	Laborer	21Ju02Bd	Ann	(W)	24	F	None	21Ju02Bd
HARPER, Eliza		20	F	None	21Ju02Bd	Cath.	(D)	.00	F	Infant	21Ju02Bd
TORMEY, Margt.		18	F	None	21Ju02Bd	CONWAY, Jas.		25	M	Laborer	21Ju02Bd
CARROLL, Mary		30	F	None	21Ju02Bd	Pat		23	M	Laborer	21Ju02Bd
DERMODY, Magt.		32	F	None	21Ju02Bd	Mary		21	F	None	21Ju02Bd
CARROLL, Cecilia		16	F	None	21Ju02Bd	GARRITY, O.		20	M	Laborer	21Ju02Bd
MEILAND, Deny		21	M	Laborer	21Ju02Bd	Bridget		17	F	None	21Ju02Bd
NOONAN, Jus.		25	M	Laborer	21Ju02Bd	HEARZ, Jane		20	F	None	21Ju02Bd
MCDONALD, Jno.		38	M	Laborer	21Ju02Bd	CARLAN, Richd.		05	M	Child	21Ju02Bd
Timothy	(S)	16	M	Laborer	21Ju02Bd	Cath.		07	F	Child	21Ju02Bd
MAR, Mich.		40	M	Laborer	21Ju02Bd	REE, Margt.		30	F	Child	21Ju02Bd
Bridget		38	F	None	21Ju02Bd	HAZELWOOD, Maria		27	F	Child	21Ju02Bd
FARLEY, Pat		24	M	Laborer	21Ju02Bd	MCCANISTER, Cath.		17	F	Child	21Ju02Bd
Ann		16	F	None	21Ju02Bd	Elizth.		21	F	Child	21Ju02Bd
BURKE, Thos.		26	M	Laborer	21Ju02Bd	MALDEN, Mary		23	F	Child	21Ju02Bd
FALLEN, Thos.		30	M	Farmer	21Ju02Bd	MOORE, Ellen		17	F	Child	21Ju02Bd
Eliza	(W)	30	F	None	21Ju02Bd	ROSSITER, Pat		25	M	Laborer	21Ju02Bd
Wm.	(S)	05	M	Child	21Ju02Bd	DEVON, Cath.		30	F	None	21Ju02Bd
John	(S)	04	M	Child	21Ju02Bd	GANLEY, Saml.		21	M	Mechanic	21Ju02Bd
Mary	(D)	01	F	Child	21Ju02Bd	Hannah		21	F	None	21Ju02Bd
HARMAN, Jno.		20	M	Laborer	21Ju02Bd	ATKIN, Geo.		27	M	Mechanic	21Ju02Bd
DOW, Margt.		14	F	None	21Ju02Bd	Sophy	(W)	28	F	None	21Ju02Bd
FARLEY, Mich.		25	M	Farmer	21Ju02Bd	Joseph	(S)	01	M	Child	21Ju02Bd
DERIVAN, Jno.		22	M	Laborer	21Ju02Bd	HAYDEN, Jas.		18	M	Mechanic	21Ju02Bd
OWENS, Elizth.		28	F	None	21Ju02Bd	RAINER, Thos.		30	M	Mechanic	21Ju02Bd
REGAN, Pat		23	M	Laborer	21Ju02Bd	SUTTON, Jas.		18	M	Mechanic	21Ju02Bd
HARRISON, Benj.		28	M	Laborer	21Ju02Bd	CARRINGTON, Pat		25	M	Mechanic	21Ju02Bd
HAGGERTY, Mich.		40	M	Laborer	21Ju02Bd	MURPHY, T.		27	M	Mechanic	21Ju02Bd
KELLY, Edwd.		22	M	Laborer	21Ju02Bd	GRAHAM, Thos.		22	M	Mechanic	21Ju02Bd
SHEE, Danl.		22	M	Laborer	21Ju02Bd	HARRIGAN, Jno.		30	M	Laborer	21Ju02Bd
MURPHY, Danl.		23	M	Laborer	21Ju02Bd	CLARK, Jno.		19	M	Laborer	21Ju02Bd
LYONS, Danl.		22	M	Laborer	21Ju02Bd	CARRIGAN, Jno.		49	M	Laborer	21Ju02Bd
RUTE, Thos.		23	M	Laborer	21Ju02Bd	Mary	(W)	47	F	None	21Ju02Bd
Bridget		21	F	None	21Ju02Bd	Ann	(D)	18	F	None	21Ju02Bd
GRIERSON, Adam		22	M	Farmer	21Ju02Bd	Chas.	(S)	14	M	None	21Ju02Bd
QUILL, Dennis		25	M	Farmer	21Ju02Bd	Wm.	(S)	12	M	None	21Ju02Bd
Mary		25	F	None	21Ju02Bd	Maria	(D)	10	F	Child	21Ju02Bd
Morris		24	M	Farmer	21Ju02Bd	DONOHOE, Ann		50	F	None	21Ju02Bd
RUDDLE, Jno.		26	M	Farmer	21Ju02Bd	Edwd.	(S)	20	M	Laborer	21Ju02Bd
HICKIE, Ann		21	F	None	21Ju02Bd	Margh.	(D)	22	F	None	21Ju02Bd
MCGRATH, Wm.		30	M	Farmer	21Ju02Bd	Cath.	(D)	15	F	None	21Ju02Bd
GARRICK, Thos.		28	M	Farmer	21Ju02Bd	Isabella	(D)	12	F	None	21Ju02Bd

NAMES OF PASSENGERS		AGE	SEX	OCCUPATIONS	DATE PORT SHIP
MCCARIN, Ann		20	F	None	21Ju02Bd
Rose		10	F	Child	21Ju02Bd
FINER, Jno.		18	M	Laborer	21Ju02Bd
DILLON, Jno.		34	M	Farmer	21Ju02Bd
Ellen	(W)	30	F	None	21Ju02Bd
John	(P)	60	M	Farmer	21Ju02Bd
Margt.	(M)	56	F	None	21Ju02Bd
Pat	(S)	14	M	None	21Ju02Bd
James	(S)	12	M	None	21Ju02Bd
Mich.	(S)	10	M	Child	21Ju02Bd
LAWLER, D.		35	M	Mechanic	21Ju02Bd
Margt.		26	F	None	21Ju02Bd
MCKENNON, Pat		28	M	Laborer	21Ju02Bd
Hannah		20	F	None	21Ju02Bd
GOGARTY, Chris.		30	M	Laborer	21Ju02Bd
PEG, Jno.		35	M	Laborer	21Ju02Bd
MARIN, Pat		23	M	Laborer	21Ju02Bd
Cath.		24	F	None	21Ju02Bd
QUINN, Sally		23	F	None	21Ju02Bd
HOGAN, Winne		18	F	None	21Ju02Bd
DUFF, Chrisa.		20	F	None	21Ju02Bd
CARNS, Cath.		24	F	None	21Ju02Bd
BREMMER, Henry		28	M	Laborer	21Ju02Bd
Sarah		29	F	None	21Ju02Bd
MURPHY, Jno.		18	M	Laborer	21Ju02Bd
Mary		19	F	None	21Ju02Bd
DAVIS, Cath.		22	F	None	21Ju02Bd
PHIAN, Jno.		30	M	Laborer	21Ju02Bd
GULLY, Margt.		25	F	None	21Ju02Bd
OHARRAN, Pat		27	M	Laborer	21Ju02Bd
HALFPENNY, Jno.		22	M	Laborer	21Ju02Bd
KERIST, Jno.A.		24	M	Laborer	21Ju02Bd
Louisiana		20	F	None	21Ju02Bd
HAGGERTY, Jas.		19	M	Mechanic	21Ju02Bd
Ann	(W)	.20	F	None	21Ju02Bd
Mary	(D)	01	F	Child	21Ju02Bd
HARZ, Ann		32	F	None	21Ju02Bd
SCULLY, Geo.		35	M	Mechanic	21Ju02Bd
Mary	(W)	35	F	None	21Ju02Bd
Ellen	(D)	07	F	Child	21Ju02Bd
Margt.	(D)	01	F	Child	21Ju02Bd
QUITTER, Edmd.		25	M	Mechanic	21Ju02Bd
DOYLE, John		24	M	Laborer	21Ju02Bd
RICHARDSON, Esther		50	F	None	21Ju02Bd
Thos.	(S)	23	M	Laborer	21Ju02Bd
Jno.	(S)	21	M	Laborer	21Ju02Bd
Sarah	(D)	19	F	None	21Ju02Bd
Ann	(D)	17	F	None	21Ju02Bd
Wm.	(S)	15	M	None	21Ju02Bd
Chris	(S)	12	M	None	21Ju02Bd
Esther	(D)	08	F	Child	21Ju02Bd
JORDAN, Pat		23	M	Laborer	21Ju02Bd
LOCKE, Richd.		25	M	Laborer	21Ju02Bd
MURPHY, Wm.		25	M	Laborer	21Ju02Bd
Nora		20	F	None	21Ju02Bd
Ellen		12	F	None	21Ju02Bd
Jno.		10	M	Child	21Ju02Bd
Julia		08	F	Child	21Ju02Bd
William		05	M	Child	21Ju02Bd
Bridget		03	F	Child	21Ju02Bd
TULLY, Jno.		23	M	Mechanic	21Ju02Bd
JEFFREY, Wm.		24	M	Mechanic	21Ju02Bd
HEBERTSON, A.		30	M	Mechanic	21Ju02Bd
ABRAHAMS, A.		20	M	Mechanic	21Ju02Bd
HAMERSLY, Jno.		27	M	Mechanic	21Ju02Bd
CROGAN, Mary		30	F	None	21Ju02Bd
PHILIPS, Edward		30	M	Mechanic	21Ju02Bd
Mary	(W)	30	F	None	21Ju02Bd
Mary-A.	(D)	09	F	Child	21Ju02Bd
Edward	(S)	07	F	Child	21Ju02Bd
Elizth.	(D)	05	F	None	21Ju02Bd
Eliza	(D)	03	F	None	21Ju02Bd
Samuel	(S)	02	M	None	21Ju02Bd
MILROY, Jno.		34	M	Farmer	21Ju02Bd
Jesse		24	F	None	21Ju02Bd
GRAHAM, Hugh		23	M	Farmer	21Ju02Bd
MCGRUNITY, Francis		20	M	Farmer	21Ju02Bd
GLIOKILL, Thos.		24	M	Mechanic	21Ju02Bd
HARRIS, Wm.		40	M	Mechanic	21Ju02Bd
BERNAN, Jas.		35	M	Mechanic	21Ju02Bd
Anna		28	F	None	21Ju02Bd
Mary		24	F	None	21Ju02Bd
Louisa	(D)	02	F	Child	21Ju02Bd
SPEED, Thos.		28	M	Mechanic	21Ju02Bd
Betsey		25	F	None	21Ju02Bd
KELLY, Owen		21	M	Mechanic	21Ju02Bd
Rose		17	F	None	21Ju02Bd
WHITTEY, Mich.		29	M	Mechanic	21Ju02Bd
KENNY, Margt.		23	F	None	21Ju02Bd
HENICKS, Judy		19	F	None	21Ju02Bd
STORER, Chas.D.		21	M	Mechanic	21Ju02Bd
HOBBS, Theo.		21	M	Mechanic	21Ju02Bd
CLARK, Jas.		33	M	Mechanic	21Ju02Bd
Jno.		18	M	Mechanic	21Ju02Bd
MILLS, Mary		36	F	None	21Ju02Bd
ROBERTS, Mary-J.		07	F	Child	21Ju02Bd
PEACOCK, Jona.		27	M	Mechanic	21Ju02Bd
GIBBIN, Pat		30	M	Laborer	21Ju02Bd
HILTON, Anna		34	F	None	21Ju02Bd
HINLEY, Pat		34	M	Laborer	21Ju02Bd
CLARK, Jno.		25	M	Laborer	21Ju02Bd
CONWAY, Pat		20	M	Laborer	21Ju02Bd
Jas.		25	M	Laborer	21Ju02Bd
Mary		18	F	None	21Ju02Bd
RAGAN, Mich.		40	M	Laborer	21Ju02Bd
Jas.	(B)	35	M	Laborer	21Ju02Bd
Pat	(B)	33	M	Laborer	21Ju02Bd
Thos.	(B)	34	M	Laborer	21Ju02Bd
Margt.	(M)	60	F	None	21Ju02Bd
Betty	(T)	25	F	None	21Ju02Bd
Kitty	(T)	24	F	None	21Ju02Bd
LAWLESS, Mich.		34	M	Mechanic	21Ju02Bd
Ann		31	F	None	21Ju02Bd
COCHRANE, Ann		23	F	None	21Ju02Bd
GANITZ, Ann		17	F	None	21Ju02Bd
Jas.		13	M	Mechanic	21Ju02Bd
FITZSIMMONS, Jerry		60	M	Farmer	21Ju02Bd
Nancy	(W)	40	F	None	21Ju02Bd
Ellen		35	F	None	21Ju02Bd
Mary	(D)	14	F	None	21Ju02Bd
Ann	(D)	12	F	None	21Ju02Bd
Thomas	(S)	08	M	Child	21Ju02Bd
John	(S)	03	M	Child	21Ju02Bd
MARTIN, Chris.		30	M	Mechanic	21Ju02Bd
MCGRATH, Jno.		24	M	Mechanic	21Ju02Bd
HIGGINS, John		28	M	Laborer	21Ju02Bd
BREEMER, Jas.		25	M	Laborer	21Ju02Bd
MEYER, A.		29	M	Laborer	21Ju02Bd
JONES, Mat		43	M	Laborer	21Ju02Bd
Helena	(W)	43	F	None	21Ju02Bd
Anna-M.	(D)	11	F	Child	21Ju02Bd
Elizth.	(D)	07	F	Child	21Ju02Bd
Agnes	(D)	.11	F	Infant	21Ju02Bd
ROSSELER, Nle		37	M	Mechanic	21Ju02Bd
Barbara	(W)	37	F	None	21Ju02Bd
Matthias	(S)	03	M	Child	21Ju02Bd
Gertrude	(D)	.10	F	Infant	21Ju02Bd
JONES, A.		35	M	Mechanic	21Ju02Bd
HAREN, Ed.		20	M	Farmer	21Ju02Bd
WHITE, Jno.		20	M	Farmer	21Ju02Bd
DANA, Ed.		20	M	Farmer	21Ju02Bd
COLEMAN, Wm.		11	M	Child	21Ju02Bd
GIBBIN, Thos.		12	M	Farmer	21Ju02Bd
WILSON, Henry		15	M	Farmer	21Ju02Bd
SMITH, Pat		16	M	Farmer	21Ju02Bd
FOX, Chas.		16	M	Farmer	21Ju02Bd
TAYLOR, Henry		22	M	Farmer	21Ju02Bd
HOLGATE, A.S.		00	M	Unknown	21Ju02Bd
DUNCAN, T.E.		00	M	Unknown	21Ju02Bd
FOWLER, Sam-L.		00	M	Unknown	21Ju02Bd

NAMES OF PASSENGERS		AGE	SEX	OCCUPATIONS	DATE PORT SHIP
LEVY, Levy		00	M	Unknown	21Ju02Bd
BRICKLEY, U-Mrs.		00	F	Unknown	21Ju02Bd
Jane		00	F	Unknown	21Ju02Bd
Mary		00	F	Unknown	21Ju02Bd
SHARPLESS, Geo.		00	M	Unknown	21Ju02Bd
U	(W)	00	F	Unknown	21Ju02Bd
ROBERTS, Wm.		00	M	Unknown	21Ju02Bd
Elizth.		00	F	Unknown	21Ju02Bd
JOHNSTON, Mary		00	F	Unknown	21Ju02Bd
LAMOURESON, M.H.		00	M	Unknown	21Ju02Bd
LOSE, Jrled.		00	M	Unknown	21Ju02Bd
GOTTTSBURGER, J.G.		00	M	Unknown	21Ju02Bd
REA, U		00	M	Physician	21Ju02Bd
DOUGLASS, James		00	M	Unknown	21Ju02Bd

ROSCINE 21 JUNE 1847

From Liverpool

NAMES OF PASSENGERS		AGE	SEX	OCCUPATIONS	DATE PORT SHIP
DOYLE, James		39	M	Laborer	21Ju02Mp
U	(W)	24	F	None	21Ju02Mp
CARROLL, James		24	M	Laborer	21Ju02Mp
Harriet		22	F	None	21Ju02Mp
BRADY, Patk.		35	M	Laborer	21Ju02Mp
BURNS, Mathew		30	M	Laborer	21Ju02Mp
Thos.	(P)	60	M	Laborer	21Ju02Mp
Peter	(B)	25	M	Laborer	21Ju02Mp
Bridget	(T)	20	F	None	21Ju02Mp
Ann	(T)	14	F	None	21Ju02Mp
DORLEY, Jane		20	F	None	21Ju02Mp
Mary		18	F	None	21Ju02Mp
DANBY, Michael		23	M	Laborer	21Ju02Mp
Cathe.		26	F	None	21Ju02Mp
BRAHANY, Edward		27	M	Laborer	21Ju02Mp
COYNE, Peter		18	M	Laborer	21Ju02Mp
Christopher		16	M	Laborer	21Ju02Mp
BRADLEY, Patk.		25	M	Laborer	21Ju02Mp
John		28	M	Laborer	21Ju02Mp
DORLAN, John		10	M	Child	21Ju02Mp
CALLAGHAN, Edward		25	M	Laborer	21Ju02Mp
Patrick		17	M	Laborer	21Ju02Mp
CARR, Miles		20	M	Laborer	21Ju02Mp
CHARLTON, Francis		18	M	Laborer	21Ju02Mp
Wm.		17	M	Laborer	21Ju02Mp
CLARK, Mary		40	F	None	21Ju02Mp
James	(S)	20	M	Laborer	21Ju02Mp
OKIEFE, John		34	M	Laborer	21Ju02Mp
MCCLURE, Eliza		17	F	None	21Ju02Mp
MURPHY, Michael		60	M	Laborer	21Ju02Mp
Charles	(S)	13	M	Laborer	21Ju02Mp
CONNOR, Margt.		18	F	None	21Ju02Mp
Mary		26	F	None	21Ju02Mp
ONIGHT, Wm.		55	M	Laborer	21Ju02Mp
Sarah	(W)	50	F	None	21Ju02Mp
Eliza	(D)	14	F	None	21Ju02Mp
DOLAN, Thos.		20	M	Laborer	21Ju02Mp
DORAUGHTY, Peter		22	M	Laborer	21Ju02Mp
MCGORNY, Peter		25	M	Laborer	21Ju02Mp
HUGHES, Peter		18	M	Laborer	21Ju02Mp
Wm.		15	M	Laborer	21Ju02Mp
RILEY, James		12	M	Laborer	21Ju02Mp
LALLAHLY, Patk.		32	M	Laborer	21Ju02Mp
BERYMAN, Robert		47	M	Laborer	21Ju02Mp
Catharine		57	F	None	21Ju02Mp
CARROLL, Patk.		30	M	Laborer	21Ju02Mp
HIGGINS, Patk.		20	M	Laborer	21Ju02Mp
BRUNCE, Ellen		18	F	None	21Ju02Mp
FRASER, Wm.		24	M	Laborer	21Ju02Mp
CLOWES, John		21	M	Laborer	21Ju02Mp
HARNEY, Flandrey		22	M	Laborer	21Ju02Mp
FURNS, Wm.		35	M	Laborer	21Ju02Mp
Mary		26	F	None	21Ju02Mp
THORNTON, Henry		30	M	Laborer	21Ju02Mp
WEST, Wm.		29	M	Laborer	21Ju02Mp
Eliza		26	F	None	21Ju02Mp
DOWLEY, John		40	M	Laborer	21Ju02Mp
Thos.	(S)	13	M	Laborer	21Ju02Mp
Tom.	(S)	09	M	Child	21Ju02Mp
Eliza	(D)	11	F	Child	21Ju02Mp
Mary	(W)	36	F	None	21Ju02Mp
Richard	(S)	06	M	Child	21Ju02Mp
Mary	(D)	04	F	Child	21Ju02Mp
DOROTY, Michael		30	M	Laborer	21Ju02Mp
BALL, James		18	M	Laborer	21Ju02Mp
U	(M)	49	F	None	21Ju02Mp
Happy	(T)	19	F	None	21Ju02Mp
Wm.	(B)	12	M	Laborer	21Ju02Mp
RACKHAM, John		37	M	Laborer	21Ju02Mp
Hannah		42	F	None	21Ju02Mp
ULTON, Wm.		25	M	Laborer	21Ju02Mp
John		24	M	Laborer	21Ju02Mp
EVORED, John		35	M	Laborer	21Ju02Mp
Alice		31	F	None	21Ju02Mp
Wm.		32	M	Laborer	21Ju02Mp
BRANNON, Peter		30	M	Laborer	21Ju02Mp
Bridget	(W)	26	F	None	21Ju02Mp
Peter	(S)	03	M	Child	21Ju02Mp
CADEY, Thos.		24	M	Laborer	21Ju02Mp
John		20	M	Laborer	21Ju02Mp
MULLIBAN, Thos.		18	M	Laborer	21Ju02Mp
DROGAN, Wm.		05	M	Child	21Ju02Mp
Edwd.		01	M	Child	21Ju02Mp
HASKIN, James		09	M	Child	21Ju02Mp
Thomas	(B)	12	M	Laborer	21Ju02Mp
James	(P)	34	M	Laborer	21Ju02Mp
JONES, James		35	M	Laborer	21Ju02Mp
RYAN, Timothy		22	M	Laborer	21Ju02Mp
Mary		23	F	None	21Ju02Mp
KELLY, Mary		19	F	None	21Ju02Mp
BODON, Conhol		33	M	Laborer	21Ju02Mp
Betsey		32	F	None	21Ju02Mp
MCDONNELL, John		22	M	Laborer	21Ju02Mp
MORAY, John		25	M	Laborer	21Ju02Mp
WILSON, Mary		18	F	None	21Ju02Mp
RICE, Mathew		25	M	Laborer	21Ju02Mp
CHAMSON, Jane		18	F	None	21Ju02Mp
SCULLION, Martha		18	F	None	21Ju02Mp
DONEY, Michael		18	M	Laborer	21Ju02Mp
LAMB, John		32	M	Laborer	21Ju02Mp
Cathe.		32	F	None	21Ju02Mp
BRIEN, Daniel		30	M	Laborer	21Ju02Mp
Cathe.		18	F	None	21Ju02Mp
REYNOLDS, Bernard		29	M	Laborer	21Ju02Mp
MCSHERRY, Matthew		25	M	Laborer	21Ju02Mp
COLLIER, Thomas		19	M	Laborer	21Ju02Mp
Rose		14	F	None	21Ju02Mp
OWENS, James		20	M	Laborer	21Ju02Mp
COLLIER, Charles		17	M	Laborer	21Ju02Mp
MORAN, Brigget		20	F	None	21Ju02Mp
CONROY, Owen		18	M	Laborer	21Ju02Mp
MORAN, Brigget		24	F	None	21Ju02Mp
STRANGE, Margt.		18	F	None	21Ju02Mp
CARNEY, Ellen		20	F	None	21Ju02Mp
WONNALL, James		19	M	Laborer	21Ju02Mp
ONEAL, John		18	M	Laborer	21Ju02Mp
HUGHES, Francis		20	M	Laborer	21Ju02Mp
MCCORMICK, Francis		21	M	Laborer	21Ju02Mp
DOROTY, Patk.		25	M	Laborer	21Ju02Mp
ONEAL, Sarah		16	F	None	21Ju02Mp
Cathe.		17	F	None	21Ju02Mp
CALLAGHAN, Peter		20	M	Laborer	21Ju02Mp
RILEY, Patk.		20	M	Laborer	21Ju02Mp
DAFFY, Bridget		60	F	None	21Ju02Mp

NAMES OF PASSENGERS		A G E	S E X	OCCUPATIONS	DATE PORT SHIP	NAMES OF PASSENGERS		A G E	S E X	OCCUPATIONS	DATE PORT SHIP
FURGISON, William		22	M	Laborer	21Ju02Mp	BURTINS, Martha	(W)	31	F	None	21Ju02Mp
DOHERTY, John		23	M	Laborer	21Ju02Mp	Mary	(D)	08	F	Child	21Ju02Mp
Owen		24	M	Laborer	21Ju02Mp	Thomas	(S)	06	M	Child	21Ju02Mp
Ann		22	F	None	21Ju02Mp	Sarah	(D)	03	F	Child	21Ju02Mp
CONNEY, Owen		45	M	Laborer	21Ju02Mp	Isabella	(D)	.03	F	Infant	21Ju02Mp
Honary	(D)	20	F	None	21Ju02Mp	SULLIVAN, Mary		25	F	None	21Ju02Mp
Michael	(S)	18	M	Laborer	21Ju02Mp	MCCONVILLE, Peter		55	M	Laborer	21Ju02Mp
Mary	(D)	16	F	None	21Ju02Mp	Mary	(W)	45	F	None	21Ju02Mp
Ann	(D)	14	F	None	21Ju02Mp	Patk.	(S)	22	M	Laborer	21Ju02Mp
KELLY, John		22	M	Laborer	21Ju02Mp	Rose	(D)	17	F	None	21Ju02Mp
Daniel		26	M	Laborer	21Ju02Mp	Mary	(D)	15	F	None	21Ju02Mp
Ellnear		24	F	None	21Ju02Mp	Alice	(D)	14	F	None	21Ju02Mp
Edward		.03	M	Infant	21Ju02Mp	Michael	(S)	11	M	Laborer	21Ju02Mp
Catharine		23	F	None	21Ju02Mp	DALEY, John		41	M	Laborer	21Ju02Mp
Mary		21	F	None	21Ju02Mp	Catharine		40	F	None	21Ju02Mp
Margaret		19	F	None	21Ju02Mp	CONNOR, John		40	M	Laborer	21Ju02Mp
COYLE, Daniel		40	M	Laborer	21Ju02Mp	Julia	(W)	30	F	None	21Ju02Mp
Rose		32	F	None	21Ju02Mp	Patrick	(S)	07	M	Child	21Ju02Mp
MURPHY, Patrick		36	M	Laborer	21Ju02Mp	Maria	(D)	04	F	Child	21Ju02Mp
Thos.		22	M	Laborer	21Ju02Mp	Julia	(D)	03	F	Child	21Ju02Mp
Ann		26	F	None	21Ju02Mp	KERNAN, Michael		11	M	Laborer	21Ju02Mp
Ellin		21	F	None	21Ju02Mp	BUTLER, Thos.		04	M	Child	21Ju02Mp
MARSHALL, Mary		25	F	None	21Ju02Mp	MCGAAH, Peter		25	M	Laborer	21Ju02Mp
SHORDAN, Mary		26	F	None	21Ju02Mp	BURKES, Thos.		25	M	Laborer	21Ju02Mp
Catharine		23	F	None	21Ju02Mp	Kitty		26	F	None	21Ju02Mp
PARLIN, John		65	M	Laborer	21Ju02Mp	Peter		25	F	None	21Ju02Mp
CONWAY, Timothy		20	M	Laborer	21Ju02Mp	Mary		24	F	None	21Ju02Mp
BRIEN, Thomas		25	M	Laborer	21Ju02Mp	TOWNEY, Mary		23	F	None	21Ju02Mp
CARDIN, Phillip		30	M	Laborer	21Ju02Mp	James		18	M	Laborer	21Ju02Mp
Mary		30	F	None	21Ju02Mp	KELLY, Brigget		20	F	None	21Ju02Mp
CONWAY, Michael		23	M	Laborer	21Ju02Mp	Patrick		24	M	Laborer	21Ju02Mp
LARY, Florence		24	F	None	21Ju02Mp	LARKIN, Mary		21	F	None	21Ju02Mp
MCCLEAN, Giles		17	M	Laborer	21Ju02Mp	MCCAB, Maria		18	F	None	21Ju02Mp
BOYLE, Mary		17	F	None	21Ju02Mp	BUCHSTEAD, Jacob		19	M	Laborer	21Ju02Mp
PUPLES, Rose		16	F	None	21Ju02Mp	Margaret		21	F	None	21Ju02Mp
CROSSLEY, James		25	M	Laborer	21Ju02Mp	Mary		20	F	None	21Ju02Mp
Mary		23	F	None	21Ju02Mp	LENT, Patk.		21	M	Laborer	21Ju02Mp
Patrick		21	M	Laborer	21Ju02Mp	RAGAN, James		20	M	Laborer	21Ju02Mp
HAGAR, Daniel		40	M	Mechanic	21Ju02Mp	LYNCH, Matthew		45	M	Laborer	21Ju02Mp
MCKEAGH, John		17	M	Laborer	21Ju02Mp	Brigget	(W)	45	F	None	21Ju02Mp
Mary		19	F	None	21Ju02Mp	Patk.	(S)	28	M	Laborer	21Ju02Mp
Kitty		19	F	None	21Ju02Mp	Rose	(D)	22	F	None	21Ju02Mp
Hannah		19	F	None	21Ju02Mp	Margaret	(D)	18	F	None	21Ju02Mp
MOHAN, Catharine		23	F	None	21Ju02Mp	Catharine	(D)	16	F	None	21Ju02Mp
CONNEL, Mathew		25	M	Laborer	21Ju02Mp	Daniel	(S)	13	M	Laborer	21Ju02Mp
Julia		26	F	None	21Ju02Mp	GARRAY, Hugh		40	M	Laborer	21Ju02Mp
DUGAN, Patrick		40	M	Laborer	21Ju02Mp	Cathe.		48	F	None	21Ju02Mp
Mary	(D)	14	F	None	21Ju02Mp	John		35	M	Laborer	21Ju02Mp
HAYNE, Daniel		40	M	Laborer	21Ju02Mp	Cathe.		18	F	None	21Ju02Mp
GILL, John		25	M	Laborer	21Ju02Mp	AMADY, Joseph		18	M	Laborer	21Ju02Mp
MADDEN, Patrick		30	M	Laborer	21Ju02Mp	Rose		16	F	None	21Ju02Mp
BYRNES, Michael		20	M	Laborer	21Ju02Mp	ONEAL, Arthur		20	M	Mechanic	21Ju02Mp
SHEARAN, Bridget		22	F	None	21Ju02Mp	Ann	(W)	20	F	None	21Ju02Mp
Nicholas		30	M	Laborer	21Ju02Mp	Margt.	(D)	.03	F	Infant	21Ju02Mp
GHASBAN, Richard		18	M	Laborer	21Ju02Mp	MORAN, Mary		16	F	None	21Ju02Mp
FLANNAGAN, Catharine		15	F	None	21Ju02Mp	HOLLAND, Arthur		20	M	Mechanic	21Ju02Mp
Margaret		16	F	None	21Ju02Mp	Mary		24	F	None	21Ju02Mp
LARKIN, John		27	M	Laborer	21Ju02Mp	KEICHLEY, Richd.		24	M	Laborer	21Ju02Mp
DOWEL, Bridget		30	F	None	21Ju02Mp	Mary		26	F	None	21Ju02Mp
William	(S)	06	M	Child	21Ju02Mp	CROOKE, Wm.		23	M	Laborer	21Ju02Mp
MONEY, Catharine		16	F	None	21Ju02Mp	MULLOHNY, Martin		27	M	Laborer	21Ju02Mp
HOCHEY, Richd.		30	M	Laborer	21Ju02Mp	RAWTON, Mary		19	F	None	21Ju02Mp
PANDAR, Patrick		22	M	Laborer	21Ju02Mp	CAIN, John		50	M	Mechanic	21Ju02Mp
MURPHY, Patrick		20	M	Laborer	21Ju02Mp	Elizabeth	(W)	48	F	None	21Ju02Mp
BYRNE, Alice		17	F	None	21Ju02Mp	Peter	(S)	21	M	Laborer	21Ju02Mp
MCKALANY, Patrick		30	M	Laborer	21Ju02Mp	John	(S)	18	M	Laborer	21Ju02Mp
NELSON, Patrick		30	M	Laborer	21Ju02Mp	Sarah	(D)	16	F	None	21Ju02Mp
DOYLE, John		20	M	Laborer	21Ju02Mp	Mary	(D)	13	F	None	21Ju02Mp
Martha		25	F	None	21Ju02Mp	Jeremiah	(S)	10	M	Laborer	21Ju02Mp
WALLACE, Thomas		19	M	Laborer	21Ju02Mp	Daniel	(S)	05	M	Child	21Ju02Mp
MCCONNYCH, James		28	M	Laborer	21Ju02Mp	SMALL, Thomas		40	M	Laborer	21Ju02Mp
COOPER, Charles		25	M	Laborer	21Ju02Mp	MCWILLIAM, Ellen		18	F	None	21Ju02Mp
OWENS, Thomas		50	M	Laborer	21Ju02Mp	John		20	M	Laborer	21Ju02Mp
FIELDEN, Philip		26	M	Laborer	21Ju02Mp	Brigget		05	F	Child	21Ju02Mp
BURTINS, Edmund		30	M	Mechanic	21Ju02Mp	Cathe.		08	F	Child	21Ju02Mp

NAMES OF PASSENGERS	A G E	S E X	OCCUPATIONS	DATE PORT SHIP	NAMES OF PASSENGERS	A G E	S E X	OCCUPATIONS	DATE PORT SHIP
MULLAGAN, Owen		30	M	Laborer	21Ju02Mp	KILLIAN, Thomas	(S)	25	M	Laborer	22Ju02Mv
MCKINNY, Patk.		35	M	Laborer	21Ju02Mp	Lawrence	(S)	28	M	Laborer	22Ju02Mv
REANAN, Patk.		20	M	Laborer	21Ju02Mp	Ellen	(W)	50	F	None	22Ju02Mv
Margt.		25	F	None	21Ju02Mp	Mary	(D)	21	F	None	22Ju02Mv
Owen		20	M	Laborer	21Ju02Mp	Bridget	(D)	18	F	None	22Ju02Mv
DOROTY, James		22	M	Laborer	21Ju02Mp	Catherine	(D)	08	F	Child	22Ju02Mv
John		30	M	Laborer	21Ju02Mp	Ellen	(D)	01	F	Child	22Ju02Mv
CONALY, Owen		25	M	Laborer	21Ju02Mp	Patrick	(S)	10	M	Laborer	22Ju02Mv
SHERIDAN, Wm.		25	M	Laborer	21Ju02Mp	STEWART, John		25	M	Laborer	22Ju02Mv
Ann		24	F	None	21Ju02Mp	FINNEGAN, John		20	M	Laborer	22Ju02Mv
DUGAN, Edmond		37	M	Laborer	21Ju02Mp	Mary		23	F	None	22Ju02Mv
Nancy		36	F	None	21Ju02Mp	MURPHY, Barney		35	M	Laborer	22Ju02Mv
Thos.	(S)	07	M	Child	21Ju02Mp	Ellen		22	F	None	22Ju02Mv
						James		55	M	Laborer	22Ju02Mv
						Daniel		16	M	Laborer	22Ju02Mv
						SHIELDS, John		16	M	Laborer	22Ju02Mv
VERONA 21 JUNE 1847						WADE, Richd.		30	M	Laborer	22Ju02Mv
						CATON, Eliza		30	F	None	22Ju02Mv
From Glasgow						FARRELL, Ann		17	F	None	22Ju02Mv
						KATING, Thos.		25	M	Laborer	22Ju02Mv
						Alice		24	F	None	22Ju02Mv
						GETTON, Michl.		30	M	Laborer	22Ju02Mv
						MILREA, John		16	M	Laborer	22Ju02Mv
CAMPBELL, John		27	M	Mechanic	21Ju04Mq	AIKEN, Robert		28	M	Laborer	22Ju02Mv
Rob.		25	M	Mechanic	21Ju04Mq	DILLON, Pat		19	M	Laborer	22Ju02Mv
BOYLE, Wm.		28	M	Mechanic	21Ju04Mq	DALEY, Pat		21	M	Mechanic	22Ju02Mv
MCQUILEM, D.		25	M	Mechanic	21Ju04Mq	Martin		21	M	Laborer	22Ju02Mv
OFERREL, H.		22	M	Merchant	21Ju04Mq	BRODERIC, Ann		18	F	None	22Ju02Mv
MCGARLIN, J.		20	M	Mechanic	21Ju04Mq	DONOHUE, Pat		26	M	Laborer	22Ju02Mv
MCCOURT, J.		09	M	Child	21Ju04Mq	CONWAY, John		40	M	Laborer	22Ju02Mv
MULLEN, Bridget		50	F	None	21Ju04Mq	Pat	(S)	20	M	Laborer	22Ju02Mv
MCCOURT, Magt.		14	F	None	21Ju04Mq	NOWLAN, Wm.		15	M	Laborer	22Ju02Mv
BAIN, John		57	M	Farmer	21Ju04Mq	GOODE, Edd.		56	M	Mechanic	22Ju02Mv
Ann	(W)	50	F	None	21Ju04Mq	CONWAY, Thos.		15	M	Mechanic	22Ju02Mv
James	(S)	23	M	Farmer	21Ju04Mq	KELLEY, Pat		19	M	Laborer	22Ju02Mv
Angus	(S)	22	M	Farmer	21Ju04Mq	MAGUIRE, Charles		24	M	Laborer	22Ju02Mv
John	(S)	13	M	None	21Ju04Mq	MCCONNELL, Adam		24	M	Laborer	22Ju02Mv
Robert	(S)	07	M	Child	21Ju04Mq	Anna		26	F	None	22Ju02Mv
Helen	(D)	18	F	None	21Ju04Mq	DOUN, Mary		17	F	None	22Ju02Mv
Magt.	(D)	09	F	Child	21Ju04Mq	John		14	M	Laborer	22Ju02Mv
Ellen-Mrs.		24	F	None	21Ju04Mq	GILHOOLY, Wm.		19	M	Laborer	22Ju02Mv
John	(S)	02	M	Child	21Ju04Mq	DONOHUE, Margt.		22	F	None	22Ju02Mv
Robb	(S)	05	M	Child	21Ju04Mq	CAREY, Hugh		28	M	Laborer	22Ju02Mv
MCBEATH, Helen		25	F	None	21Ju04Mq	RYAN, Timothy		40	M	Laborer	22Ju02Mv
MCRAY, D.F.		40	M	Farmer	21Ju04Mq	MCKENDRAN, Charles		16	M	Laborer	22Ju02Mv
WALSH, Thos.		40	M	Farmer	21Ju04Mq	OBRIEN, Pat		20	M	Laborer	22Ju02Mv
William		27	M	Farmer	21Ju04Mq	HOAR, Matt		26	M	Laborer	22Ju02Mv
ORR, Danl.		36	M	Mechanic	21Ju04Mq	DALEY, Catherine		20	F	None	22Ju02Mv
MULHALLER, A.		34	M	Laborer	21Ju04Mq	ROURKE, Cathe.		22	F	None	22Ju02Mv
Jane	(W)	31	F	None	21Ju04Mq	NOWLAN, William		20	M	Laborer	22Ju02Mv
John	(S)	10	M	None	21Ju04Mq	RILEY, Lawrence		19	M	Laborer	22Ju02Mv
Mary	(D)	07	F	Child	21Ju04Mq	GOUGH, Mary		20	F	None	22Ju02Mv
Andrew	(S)	04	M	Child	21Ju04Mq	Ann		16	F	None	22Ju02Mv
Barney	(S)	02	M	Child	21Ju04Mq	Bridget	(D)	01	F	Child	22Ju02Mv
						GILL, Pat		24	M	Laborer	22Ju02Mv
						Chrisr.		22	M	Laborer	22Ju02Mv
						James		20	M	Laborer	22Ju02Mv
SPARTAN 22 JUNE 1847						MCTEAGUE, Michl.		20	M	Laborer	22Ju02Mv
						MORGAN, James		24	M	Laborer	22Ju02Mv
From Liverpool						Jane		22	F	None	22Ju02Mv
						Ann		20	F	None	22Ju02Mv
						ALLEN, Pat		50	M	Laborer	22Ju02Mv
RELSH, Mary		16	F	None	22Ju02Mv	Thos.	(S)	22	M	Laborer	22Ju02Mv
BRADLEY, Mabrose		22	M	Farmer	22Ju02Mv	Mary	(D)	20	F	Laborer	22Ju02Mv
HOGAN, Mary		22	F	None	22Ju02Mv	HARMAN, Mary		20	F	Laborer	22Ju02Mv
Johanna		19	F	None	22Ju02Mv	MCWEEVEY, Charles		28	M	Farmer	22Ju02Mv
DOUN, Mary		24	F	None	22Ju02Mv	MCGARTY, Thos.		46	M	Farmer	22Ju02Mv
WALKER, Thos.		28	M	Farmer	22Ju02Mv	Ann	(D)	25	F	None	22Ju02Mv
KILLIAN, Patrick		50	M	Laborer	22Ju02Mv	MCGRAIL, John		20	M	Farmer	22Ju02Mv
John	(S)	22	M	Laborer	22Ju02Mv	GALLOGEHY, Cathe.		20	F	None	22Ju02Mv
James	(S)	14	M	Laborer	22Ju02Mv	CONBOY, Maria		46	F	None	22Ju02Mv
						FEARING, Ann		46	F	None	22Ju02Mv
						Bridget	(D)	20	F	None	22Ju02Mv
						Jane	(D)	16	F	None	22Ju02Mv
						Dennis	(S)	07	M	Child	22Ju02Mv

NAMES OF PASSENGERS		AGE	SEX	OCCUPATIONS	DATE PORT SHIP
FEARING, Mary	(D)	06	F	Child	22Ju02Mv
GRADY, Wm.		27	M	Laborer	22Ju02Mv
DUFFY, Pat		30	M	Laborer	22Ju02Mv
CLARK, James		27	M	Laborer	22Ju02Mv
NOWLAN, John		21	M	Laborer	22Ju02Mv
SHERWIN, Pat		24	M	Laborer	22Ju02Mv
CLINTON, James		25	M	Laborer	22Ju02Mv
Judea		36	M	Laborer	22Ju02Mv
BARGAN, Peter		40	M	Laborer	22Ju02Mv
MCNULTY, Pat.		18	M	Laborer	22Ju02Mv
MCKENNA, John		28	M	Laborer	22Ju02Mv
Eliza		25	F	None	22Ju02Mv
MCMULLAN, James		30	M	Laborer	22Ju02Mv
CARTY, Mary		20	F	None	22Ju02Mv
MULLONEY, Ellen		14	F	None	22Ju02Mv
CATON, John		30	M	Laborer	22Ju02Mv
BATEY, Luke		31	M	Laborer	22Ju02Mv
Pat	(P)	60	M	Laborer	22Ju02Mv
Bryan	(B)	31	M	Laborer	22Ju02Mv
Ann	(T)	20	F	None	22Ju02Mv
Mattw.		08	M	Child	22Ju02Mv
Michl.		05	M	Child	22Ju02Mv
Ellen		04	F	Child	22Ju02Mv
Mary		02	F	Child	22Ju02Mv
MURPHY, James		00	M	Laborer	22Ju02Mv
KILBRIDE, Michl.		00	M	Laborer	22Ju02Mv
TOMLINSON, Saml.		54	M	None	22Ju02Mv
ARGUE, Thos.		18	M	None	22Ju02Mv
KEARNAN, Mary		17	F	None	22Ju02Mv
Miles		06	M	Child	22Ju02Mv
TOMLINSON, Mary		36	F	None	22Ju02Mv
Danl.	(S)	15	M	Laborer	22Ju02Mv
John	(S)	13	M	Laborer	22Ju02Mv
Thomas	(S)	09	M	Child	22Ju02Mv
James	(S)	07	M	Child	22Ju02Mv
KERNAN, James		19	M	Laborer	22Ju02Mv
Mary		21	F	None	22Ju02Mv
KIERNAN, Edwd.		30	M	Laborer	22Ju02Mv
James		25	M	Laborer	22Ju02Mv
Alexander		27	M	Laborer	22Ju02Mv
Pat.		09	M	Child	22Ju02Mv
Thomas		02	M	Child	22Ju02Mv
GOUGH, Pat		49	M	Laborer	22Ju02Mv
U	(W)	36	F	Wife	22Ju02Mv
KELLY, Peter		30	M	Laborer	22Ju02Mv
U	(W)	30	F	Wife	22Ju02Mv
Pat		20	M	Laborer	22Ju02Mv
James	(S)	05	M	Child	22Ju02Mv
Mary	(D)	02	F	Child	22Ju02Mv
MCGOWAN, Thos.		28	M	Laborer	22Ju02Mv
Mary	(W)	26	F	None	22Ju02Mv
Jane	(D)	12	F	None	22Ju02Mv
Thomas	(S)	02	M	Child	22Ju02Mv
BATEY, Martin		22	M	Laborer	22Ju02Mv
Mathe.		08	M	Child	22Ju02Mv
Ellen		20	F	None	22Ju02Mv
Elizth.		17	F	None	22Ju02Mv
COSGROVE, Neal		70	M	Laborer	22Ju02Mv
Biddy	(W)	66	F	None	22Ju02Mv
Philip	(S)	27	M	Laborer	22Ju02Mv

FRANCONIA 22 JUNE 1847

From Liverpool

NAMES OF PASSENGERS		AGE	SEX	OCCUPATIONS	DATE PORT SHIP
LIMPSON, Thos.		30	M	Mechanic	22Ju02Jr
SMOLLEN, Owen		21	M	Mechanic	22Ju02Jr
BOWEN, Richd.		43	M	Mechanic	22Ju02Jr
John		24	M	Laborer	22Ju02Jr

NAMES OF PASSENGERS		AGE	SEX	OCCUPATIONS	DATE PORT SHIP
LYME, John		21	M	Laborer	22Ju02Jr
LANE, Dennis		30	M	Laborer	22Ju02Jr
Mary		25	F	None	22Ju02Jr
CRAHAN, Daniel		40	F	None	22Ju02Jr
BARRETT, Lawrence		20	F	None	22Ju02Jr
CASSIDY, Richd.		37	M	Mechanic	22Ju02Jr
Thos.		27	M	Mechanic	22Ju02Jr
NEVIN, Ann		27	F	None	22Ju02Jr
NAUGHTON, Margt.		20	F	None	22Ju02Jr
John		18	M	Mechanic	22Ju02Jr
MEATH, Darby		21	M	Laborer	22Ju02Jr
Thos.		24	M	Laborer	22Ju02Jr
MORLEY, Pat		18	M	Laborer	22Ju02Jr
HUGHES, Thos.		30	M	Laborer	22Ju02Jr
GREGORY, Pat		24	M	Laborer	22Ju02Jr
Sarah		45	F	None	22Ju02Jr
Sally		02	F	Child	22Ju02Jr
KELLY, Margt.		24	F	None	22Ju02Jr
SMITH, Bridget		20	F	None	22Ju02Jr
BREMAN, Pat		24	M	Laborer	22Ju02Jr
Mary		18	F	None	22Ju02Jr
FITZSIMMONS, Owen		18	M	Laborer	22Ju02Jr
WELDON, Edwd.		28	M	Laborer	22Ju02Jr
Lawrence		31	M	Laborer	22Ju02Jr
MASTERSON, John		20	M	Laborer	22Ju02Jr
WILSON, Mark		26	M	Laborer	22Ju02Jr
NICHOL, Henry		15	M	Laborer	22Ju02Jr
SOMERS, Thos.		20	M	Laborer	22Ju02Jr
HEIR, Thos.		20	M	Mechanic	22Ju02Jr
FAY, Owen		25	M	Laborer	22Ju02Jr
MAHON, Mary		20	F	None	22Ju02Jr
GARRATY, Pat		18	M	Laborer	22Ju02Jr
GOUGH, John		47	M	Laborer	22Ju02Jr
SHEA, Pat		30	M	Laborer	22Ju02Jr
James		19	M	Laborer	22Ju02Jr
DALTON, Thos.		18	M	Laborer	22Ju02Jr
CAULFIELD, Ann		20	F	None	22Ju02Jr
SCOLBY, Mary		20	F	None	22Ju02Jr
KELLY, Mattw.		26	M	Laborer	22Ju02Jr
DICKSON, John		62	M	Laborer	22Ju02Jr
U	(W)	52	F	Wife	22Ju02Jr
Hugh	(S)	20	M	Laborer	22Ju02Jr
John	(S)	17	M	Laborer	22Ju02Jr
Sarah	(D)	13	F	None	22Ju02Jr
NICHOLS, Joseph		04	M	Child	22Ju02Jr
DILLON, James		40	M	Laborer	22Ju02Jr
GREENE, Chester		17	M	Laborer	22Ju02Jr
MCDONNELL, Richd.		26	M	Laborer	22Ju02Jr
Miche.		22	M	Laborer	22Ju02Jr
Mary	(W)	23	F	None	22Ju02Jr
Mary	(D)	.00	F	Infant	22Ju02Jr
DUFFY, Michl.		56	M	Laborer	22Ju02Jr
Thos.	(S)	21	M	Laborer	22Ju02Jr
Ann	(D)	23	F	None	22Ju02Jr
Mary	(W)	56	F	None	22Ju02Jr
CLERKIN, Patk.		23	M	Laborer	22Ju02Jr
Peggy		20	F	None	22Ju02Jr
Mary		15	F	None	22Ju02Jr
CONNELL, Richd.		23	M	Laborer	22Ju02Jr
MCKEON, Michl.		21	M	Laborer	22Ju02Jr
WEIR, James		36	M	Laborer	22Ju02Jr
Margt.	(W)	34	F	None	22Ju02Jr
Eliza	(D)	17	F	None	22Ju02Jr
John	(S)	15	M	Laborer	22Ju02Jr
Ellen	(D)	14	F	None	22Ju02Jr
Margt.	(D)	10	F	None	22Ju02Jr
Steward	(S)	08	M	Child	22Ju02Jr
James	(S)	04	M	Child	22Ju02Jr
Crawford	(S)	.00	M	Infant	22Ju02Jr
DUNN, Cathe.		24	F	None	22Ju02Jr
NICHOLS, Mary		70	F	None	22Ju02Jr
SHOWELL, John		19	M	Laborer	22Ju02Jr
CREMINS, Deborah		45	F	None	22Ju02Jr
Ellen	(D)	10	F	None	22Ju02Jr
ELLIOTT, Elizabeth		38	F	None	22Ju02Jr

NAMES OF PASSENGERS		AGE SEX	OCCUPATIONS	DATE PORT SHIP
ELLIOTT, Olivia		28 F	None	22Ju02Jr
CALLAHAN, Bridget		50 F	None	22Ju02Jr
James	(S)	13 M	Laborer	22Ju02Jr
Catharine	(D)	11 F	None	22Ju02Jr
Philip	(S)	09 M	Child	22Ju02Jr
NELLY, Thos.		18 M	Laborer	22Ju02Jr
KENNEDY, John		55 M	Laborer	22Ju02Jr
U	(W)	55 F	Wife	22Ju02Jr
Dolly	(D)	20 F	None	22Ju02Jr
John	(S)	18 M	Laborer	22Ju02Jr
Ann	(D)	07 F	Child	22Ju02Jr
SPAIN, John		18 M	Laborer	22Ju02Jr
Mary		20 F	None	22Ju02Jr
ENGLISH, Jane		21 F	None	22Ju02Jr
MCCULLUM, Richd.		19 M	Laborer	22Ju02Jr
Thos.		21 M	Laborer	22Ju02Jr
Mary		26 F	None	22Ju02Jr
Nabby		25 F	None	22Ju02Jr
Michl.		.00 M	Infant	22Ju02Jr
GARDNER, John		30 M	Laborer	22Ju02Jr
U	(W)	25 F	Wife	22Ju02Jr
Patk.	(S)	03 M	Child	22Ju02Jr
Bridget	(D)	.00 F	Infant	22Ju02Jr
FLYNN, Michl.		24 M	Laborer	22Ju02Jr
Mary	(W)	23 F	None	22Ju02Jr
John	(S)	.00 M	Infant	22Ju02Jr
KANE, Patrick		30 M	Laborer	22Ju02Jr
Mary	(W)	26 F	None	22Ju02Jr
Thos.	(S)	04 M	Child	22Ju02Jr
Cathe.	(D)	.00 F	Infant	22Ju02Jr
WALSH, John		34 M	Laborer	22Ju02Jr
NULTY, James		26 M	Laborer	22Ju02Jr
SMITH, Billy		37 M	Laborer	22Ju02Jr
CARROLL, Edwd.		27 M	Laborer	22Ju02Jr
Thos.	(B)	23 M	Laborer	22Ju02Jr
Elizabeth	(M)	60 F	None	22Ju02Jr
Jane	(T)	21 F	None	22Ju02Jr
KENNEY, John		30 M	Laborer	22Ju02Jr
SMULLIN, Ann		16 F	None	22Ju02Jr
KENNEY, Ellen		20 F	None	22Ju02Jr
CARR, John		18 M	Laborer	22Ju02Jr
DOWNER, John		30 M	Laborer	22Ju02Jr
Harriet		30 F	None	22Ju02Jr
MAYFIELD, Joseph		30 M	Laborer	22Ju02Jr
DAWSON, John		25 M	Laborer	22Ju02Jr
ERSKINE, John		30 M	Laborer	22Ju02Jr
MCDERMOT, Richd.		22 M	Laborer	22Ju02Jr
John		25 M	Laborer	22Ju02Jr
MONAGHAN, Ann		18 F	None	22Ju02Jr

BARRINGTON 22 JUNE 1847

From Glasgow

NAMES OF PASSENGERS		AGE SEX	OCCUPATIONS	DATE PORT SHIP
HEALY, James		21 M	Mechanic	22Ju04Mw
Mary		18 F	None	22Ju04Mw
WARD, Danl.		25 M	Mechanic	22Ju04Mw
Pat		24 M	Mechanic	22Ju04Mw
Mary		27 F	None	22Ju04Mw
MCCALLIAN, B.		23 M	Farmer	22Ju04Mw
John		19 M	Farmer	22Ju04Mw
James		11 M	Farmer	22Ju04Mw
Daniel		09 M	Child	22Ju04Mw
Betty		20 F	None	22Ju04Mw
Margt.		13 F	None	22Ju04Mw
Bridget		21 F	None	22Ju04Mw
ANDREWS, Jane		20 F	None	22Ju04Mw
MCGEE, Jas.		25 M	Farmer	22Ju04Mw
MCKINDY, Jas.		58 M	Farmer	22Ju04Mw

NAMES OF PASSENGERS		AGE SEX	OCCUPATIONS	DATE PORT SHIP
MCKINDY, Chas.	(S)	18 M	Farmer	22Ju04Mw
Ann-Jane	(D)	16 F	None	22Ju04Mw
Saml.	(S)	11 M	Farmer	22Ju04Mw
MCVRAY, Thos.		30 M	Farmer	22Ju04Mw
SHEETS, M.Ann		29 F	None	22Ju04Mw
LINCH, Mich.		48 M	Farmer	22Ju04Mw
William	(S)	16 M	Farmer	22Ju04Mw
BOYLE, Cecilia		30 F	None	22Ju04Mw
MCCOLGAN, D.		26 M	Farmer	22Ju04Mw
KILPATRICK, Wm.		40 M	Farmer	22Ju04Mw
Bridget	(W)	50 F	None	22Ju04Mw
Hugh	(S)	19 M	Farmer	22Ju04Mw
Mary	(D)	16 F	None	22Ju04Mw
MCGONALS, Mary		16 F	None	22Ju04Mw
PETERSON, U-Mrs.		30 F	None	22Ju04Mw

SEA 23 JUNE 1847

From Liverpool

NAMES OF PASSENGERS		AGE SEX	OCCUPATIONS	DATE PORT SHIP
CRANE, Thos.		52 M	Mechanic	23Ju02Bg
LACE, D.		23 M	Mechanic	23Ju02Bg
CAIN, Robt.		18 M	Mechanic	23Ju02Bg
COILESS, Wm.		24 M	Mechanic	23Ju02Bg
LEWELLYN, Wm.		25 M	Mechanic	23Ju02Bg
Jane		17 F	None	23Ju02Bg
Margt.	(M)	58 F	None	23Ju02Bg
RICHARDS, Margt.		28 F	None	23Ju02Bg
Mary		06 F	Child	23Ju02Bg
Margt.		14 F	None	23Ju02Bg
HARRIS, Owen		29 M	Mechanic	23Ju02Bg
WHELAN, Thos.		25 M	Mechanic	23Ju02Bg
GRACE, Julia		22 F	None	23Ju02Bg
LITTLE, Thos.		21 M	Mechanic	23Ju02Bg
LINNER, Geo.		23 M	Mechanic	23Ju02Bg
Francis		31 M	Mechanic	23Ju02Bg
Sarah		31 F	None	23Ju02Bg
MOONEY, N.		20 M	Mechanic	23Ju02Bg
WILKINSON, D.		48 M	Mechanic	23Ju02Bg
D.	(S)	22 M	Mechanic	23Ju02Bg
Rebecca	(W)	50 F	None	23Ju02Bg
Mary-Ann	(D)	27 F	None	23Ju02Bg
Rebecca	(D)	17 F	None	23Ju02Bg
HAMERLY, R.		28 M	Mechanic	23Ju02Bg
RICHARDSON, Jno.		44 M	Mechanic	23Ju02Bg
WARD, James		34 M	Mechanic	23Ju02Bg
MCDONALD, Rose		22 F	None	23Ju02Bg
TIDER, Richd.		38 M	Mechanic	23Ju02Bg
FOSTER, Isaac		24 M	Mechanic	23Ju02Bg
Malg		25 F	None	23Ju02Bg
WILES, Richd.		59 M	Mechanic	23Ju02Bg
Grace	(W)	56 F	None	23Ju02Bg
David	(S)	18 M	Mechanic	23Ju02Bg
Ellen	(D)	16 F	None	23Ju02Bg
HOLLIDY, Elizth.		58 F	None	23Ju02Bg
Mag.		17 F	None	23Ju02Bg
WILKINSON, Geo.		20 M	Mechanic	23Ju02Bg
WARD, Wm.		24 M	Mechanic	23Ju02Bg
Elizth.		20 F	None	23Ju02Bg
DODSWORTH, Wm.		45 M	Mechanic	23Ju02Bg
Maria	(W)	44 F	None	23Ju02Bg
John	(S)	17 M	Farmer	23Ju02Bg
Wm.	(S)	14 M	Farmer	23Ju02Bg
Malg.	(D)	12 F	None	23Ju02Bg
Thos.	(S)	10 M	Farmer	23Ju02Bg
Peter	(S)	07 M	Child	23Ju02Bg
Elizth.	(D)	07 F	Child	23Ju02Bg
MCANALY, Thos.		16 M	Mechanic	23Ju02Bg
MCGUKEN, Malg.		22 F	None	23Ju02Bg

NAMES OF PASSENGERS		AGE	SEX	OCCUPATIONS	DATE PORT SHIP
MCGUKEN, Margt.		21	F	None	23Ju02Bg
SULLIVAN, Mary		16	F	None	23Ju02Bg
COLLINS, Cath.		17	F	None	23Ju02Bg
GOIMLY, W.		21	M	Mechanic	23Ju02Bg
BOOTH, Jas.		26	M	Mechanic	23Ju02Bg
MOORE, Ed.		20	M	Mechanic	23Ju02Bg
Jno.		22	M	Mechanic	23Ju02Bg
STEWARD, Jas.		25	M	Mechanic	23Ju02Bg
LEEY, Peter		27	M	Laborer	23Ju02Bg
James		30	M	Laborer	23Ju02Bg
CAMPBELL, Sarah		18	F	None	23Ju02Bg
KREIL, Barbara		17	F	None	23Ju02Bg
KENNY, Pat		35	M	Laborer	23Ju02Bg
MANIEL, M.		10	M	None	23Ju02Bg
Thos.		07	M	Child	23Ju02Bg
BIRMINGHAM, Wm.		12	M	None	23Ju02Bg
MCMICHAEL, J.		19	M	Laborer	23Ju02Bg
LEENY, Thos.		18	M	Laborer	23Ju02Bg
CASEY, D.		21	M	Laborer	23Ju02Bg
CAVAN, Peter		22	M	Laborer	23Ju02Bg
MCGRATH, J.		22	M	Laborer	23Ju02Bg
REYNOLDS, P.		30	M	Laborer	23Ju02Bg
SHERNIN, Mag.		64	F	None	23Ju02Bg
Pat	(S)	20	M	Laborer	23Ju02Bg
Ellen	(D)	18	F	None	23Ju02Bg
Alice	(D)	10	F	None	23Ju02Bg
DALTER, Thos.		20	M	Laborer	23Ju02Bg
WHITE, Thos.		44	M	Mechanic	23Ju02Bg
Eliza	(W)	44	F	None	23Ju02Bg
Jane	(D)	20	F	None	23Ju02Bg
Robert	(D)	16	F	None	23Ju02Bg
Fanny	(D)	13	F	None	23Ju02Bg
Eliza	(D)	11	F	None	23Ju02Bg
Letitia	(D)	08	F	Child	23Ju02Bg
TEMPLETON, Mary		31	F	None	23Ju02Bg
HENDERSON, Jane		08	F	Child	23Ju02Bg
Saml.		06	M	Child	23Ju02Bg
DEVON, Robert		40	M	Laborer	23Ju02Bg
Winifred		25	F	None	23Ju02Bg
Platt		22	M	Laborer	23Ju02Bg
Hubert		18	M	Laborer	23Ju02Bg
Cath.		17	F	None	23Ju02Bg
Margared		16	F	None	23Ju02Bg
REILY, Betty		12	F	None	23Ju02Bg
PONION, Jn.		28	M	Laborer	23Ju02Bg
HAGAN, Jas.		31	M	Laborer	23Ju02Bg
GIBBONS, David		60	M	Laborer	23Ju02Bg
Mary	(W)	55	F	None	23Ju02Bg
Letitia	(D)	27	F	None	23Ju02Bg
KELLY, Johanna		20	F	None	23Ju02Bg
LONITTS, B.		40	M	Laborer	23Ju02Bg
CLARKE, Pat		08	M	Child	23Ju02Bg
Jno.		07	M	Child	23Ju02Bg
TRACY, Malg.		14	F	None	23Ju02Bg
QUIN, Ann		18	F	None	23Ju02Bg
MCGOIAN, Thos.		45	M	Laborer	23Ju02Bg
KELLY, John		28	M	Laborer	23Ju02Bg
MCGEE, Ann		20	F	None	23Ju02Bg
WILKINSON, Rosanna		16	F	None	23Ju02Bg
DAVIS, K.		31	M	Laborer	23Ju02Bg
SARROCK, E.		26	M	Laborer	23Ju02Bg
KEENAN, Hugh		45	M	None	23Ju02Bg
Thos.	(S)	23	M	None	23Ju02Bg
POINTON, Wm.		28	M	None	23Ju02Bg
Saml.		21	M	None	23Ju02Bg
STIRLING, K.		45	M	None	23Ju02Bg

GIPSEY 23 JUNE 1847

From Dublin

NAMES OF PASSENGERS		AGE	SEX	OCCUPATIONS	DATE PORT SHIP
MORGAN, Richd.		25	M	Farmer	23Ju20Mx
WAFFRY, Cath.		25	F	None	23Ju20Mx
HENNAN, Peter		30	M	Laborer	23Ju20Mx
GANTLEY, Sarah		26	F	None	23Ju20Mx
MOORE, Ellen		20	F	None	23Ju20Mx
ROCH, Pat		25	M	Laborer	23Ju20Mx
LETITE, Pat		35	M	Laborer	23Ju20Mx
CACEY, Edmd.		26	M	Laborer	23Ju20Mx
Marcella		26	F	None	23Ju20Mx
Eliza		18	F	None	23Ju20Mx
RYAN, Marg.A.		27	F	None	23Ju20Mx
RICHARDSON, R.		40	M	Laborer	23Ju20Mx
MURPHY, R.		20	M	Laborer	23Ju20Mx
BRENNAN, Margt.		28	F	None	23Ju20Mx
CASSIDY, Gwen		20	F	None	23Ju20Mx
GREY, Rich.		24	M	Laborer	23Ju20Mx
Margt.		20	F	None	23Ju20Mx
MCDONALD, A.		24	M	Laborer	23Ju20Mx
DARAR, W.		24	M	Laborer	23Ju20Mx
DONOHOE, Thos.		20	M	Laborer	23Ju20Mx
BULLOCK, W.		62	M	Farmer	23Ju20Mx
Roden		50	F	None	23Ju20Mx
GAFFNEY, Ann		19	F	None	23Ju20Mx
BULLOCK, Mary.A.		26	F	None	23Ju20Mx
WELLS, Olin		24	M	Farmer	23Ju20Mx
MCKEE, Hugh		28	M	Farmer	23Ju20Mx
Ann		26	F	None	23Ju20Mx
JOHNSTON, Jno.		30	M	Farmer	23Ju20Mx
TOMKINS, W.		19	M	Mechanic	23Ju20Mx
BYRNE, Garret		28	M	Mechanic	23Ju20Mx
WHALEN, John		23	M	Mechanic	23Ju20Mx
OCONNELL, E.Mrs.		22	F	None	23Ju20Mx

SWAN 23 JUNE 1847

From Liverpool

NAMES OF PASSENGERS		AGE	SEX	OCCUPATIONS	DATE PORT SHIP
CONNER, William		23	M	Laborer	23Ju02Ix
John		16	M	Laborer	23Ju02Ix
BUCKLEY, Dan		23	M	Laborer	23Ju02Ix
DALEY, Joseph		23	M	Laborer	23Ju02Ix
WHEELAN, John		28	M	Laborer	23Ju02Ix
ROCHE, David		32	M	Laborer	23Ju02Ix
Ellen		28	F	None	23Ju02Ix
Mick		28	M	Laborer	23Ju02Ix
John		26	M	Laborer	23Ju02Ix
Margaret		07	F	Child	23Ju02Ix
Mary-Ann		02	F	Child	23Ju02Ix
OBRIEN, Mary		28	F	None	23Ju02Ix
FARRELL, Ellen		28	F	None	23Ju02Ix
SULLIVAN, Pat		30	M	Laborer	23Ju02Ix
DALTON, Dan		28	M	Laborer	23Ju02Ix
FARRINGTON, John		28	M	Laborer	23Ju02Ix
Bridget	(W)	28	F	None	23Ju02Ix
Bridget	(D)	.00	F	Infant	23Ju02Ix
SWEENEY, Danl.		25	M	Laborer	23Ju02Ix
John		23	M	Laborer	23Ju02Ix
LYNCH, John		23	M	Laborer	23Ju02Ix
Ellen		23	F	None	23Ju02Ix

NAMES OF PASSENGERS		AGE	SEX	OCCUPATIONS	DATE PORT SHIP
LYNCH, Mary		21	F	None	23Ju02lx
GRAYMER, Edward		28	M	Laborer	23Ju02lx
MURPHY, Ann		09	F	Child	23Ju02lx
COLWAY, James		25	M	Laborer	23Ju02lx
SULLIVAN, John		17	M	Laborer	23Ju02lx
MURRAY, David		40	M	Laborer	23Ju02lx
MCNAMARA, Bridget		30	F	None	23Ju02lx
MAURY, Mick		07	M	Child	23Ju02lx
CONNELL, Dennis		13	M	Laborer	23Ju02lx
Mary		11	F	None	23Ju02lx
CARROLL, Pat		26	M	Laborer	23Ju02lx
GROVE, Tom		20	M	Laborer	23Ju02lx
Robert		28	M	Laborer	23Ju02lx
BUCKLEY, Mary		40	F	None	23Ju02lx
CONNER, Bridget		26	F	None	23Ju02lx
COSGROVE, Cathe.		26	F	None	23Ju02lx
DELANY, John		16	M	Laborer	23Ju02lx
FARRELL, John		40	M	Laborer	23Ju02lx
U	(W)	40	F	Wife	23Ju02lx
Christe	(D)	23	F	None	23Ju02lx
James	(S)	19	M	Laborer	23Ju02lx
Mick	(S)	17	M	Laborer	23Ju02lx
Anne	(D)	16	F	None	23Ju02lx
Betsey	(D)	08	F	Child	23Ju02lx
FALLON, Mick		50	M	Laborer	23Ju02lx
CORCORAN, James		26	M	Laborer	23Ju02lx
GREENE, Thos.		26	M	Laborer	23Ju02lx
BRENNAN, George		19	M	Laborer	23Ju02lx
CORCORAN, Bridget		18	F	None	23Ju02lx
PLUNKETT, Francis		37	M	Laborer	23Ju02lx
U	(W)	30	F	Wife	23Ju02lx
HAYES, John		24	M	Laborer	23Ju02lx
U	(W)	23	F	Wife	23Ju02lx
CONNER, Mary		30	F	Wife	23Ju02lx
LARRIGAN, Judy		20	F	Wife	23Ju02lx
REYNOLDS, Charles		24	M	Laborer	23Ju02lx
MITCHELL, John		20	M	Laborer	23Ju02lx
MCELROY, Malachi		29	M	Laborer	23Ju02lx
MULREAD, John		27	M	Laborer	23Ju02lx
BOYLAN, Edwd.		22	M	Laborer	23Ju02lx
Ellen		18	F	None	23Ju02lx
KENNEDY, Mick		26	M	Laborer	23Ju02lx
Mary		22	F	None	23Ju02lx
FITZGERALD, Robert		35	M	Laborer	23Ju02lx
FEERY, Richard		30	M	Laborer	23Ju02lx
Mick		24	M	Laborer	23Ju02lx
Nelus		22	M	Laborer	23Ju02lx
Mary		07	F	Child	23Ju02lx
Charles		.00	M	Infant	23Ju02lx
CONNER, Pat		23	M	Infant	23Ju02lx
Mary	(W)	20	F	None	23Ju02lx
Biddy	(D)	.00	F	Infant	23Ju02lx
KENNEDY, James		22	M	Laborer	23Ju02lx
Biddy	(W)	20	F	None	23Ju02lx
James	(S)	.00	M	Infant	23Ju02lx
FITZGERALD, Mick		30	M	Laborer	23Ju02lx
BARBER, Ezekiel		26	M	Laborer	23Ju02lx
U	(W)	30	F	None	23Ju02lx
Charles	(S)	.00	M	Infant	23Ju02lx
Mary-Ann	(D)	03	F	Child	23Ju02lx
MCCABE, Pat		25	M	Laborer	23Ju02lx
WALTON, Mary		35	F	None	23Ju02lx
Thomas	(S)	13	M	Laborer	23Ju02lx
Jane	(D)	10	F	None	23Ju02lx
Fanny	(D)	03	F	Child	23Ju02lx
Robert	(S)	.00	M	Infant	23Ju02lx
DAVIES, Fredk.		35	M	Laborer	23Ju02lx
MORAN, Thos.		27	M	Laborer	23Ju02lx
U	(W)	24	F	None	23Ju02lx
REYNOLDS, Cathe.		18	F	None	23Ju02lx
BUTLER, Mary		19	F	None	23Ju02lx
COLLINS, James		60	M	Laborer	23Ju02lx
Mary	(W)	50	F	None	23Ju02lx
M.	(S)	19	M	Laborer	23Ju02lx
John	(S)	17	M	Laborer	23Ju02lx

NAMES OF PASSENGERS		AGE	SEX	OCCUPATIONS	DATE PORT SHIP
COLLINS, Pat	(S)	14	M	Laborer	23Ju02lx
Kate	(D)	13	F	None	23Ju02lx
Mick	(S)	11	M	Laborer	23Ju02lx
Bridget	(D)	09	F	Child	23Ju02lx
Martin	(S)	07	M	Laborer	23Ju02lx
Nancy	(D)	05	F	Child	23Ju02lx
James	(S)	03	M	Child	23Ju02lx
Mary	(D)	.00	F	Infant	23Ju02lx
MALACHI, Kewls		25	M	Laborer	23Ju02lx
MURPHY, Pat		25	M	Laborer	23Ju02lx
GRIFFIN, Danl.		26	M	Laborer	23Ju02lx
CONNER, Eugene		25	M	Laborer	23Ju02lx
MCSULLEY, Arthur		23	M	Laborer	23Ju02lx
MCLOON, Biddy		45	F	None	23Ju02lx
Pat	(S)	25	M	Laborer	23Ju02lx
Mary	(D)	16	F	None	23Ju02lx
BIRD, Pat		21	M	Laborer	23Ju02lx
MCLOON, Thos.		12	M	Laborer	23Ju02lx
Joanna		10	F	None	23Ju02lx
SMITH, Joseph		29	M	Laborer	23Ju02lx
LANE, Kate		30	F	None	23Ju02lx
GELORA, Acky-Du		40	M	Laborer	23Ju02lx
HANNER, B.		27	M	Laborer	23Ju02lx
CABULL, Joanna		.00	F	Infant	23Ju02lx
CROES, George		.00	M	Infant	23Ju02lx
REED, Robert		29	M	Laborer	23Ju02lx
LEBOEB, Gotlieb		29	M	Laborer	23Ju02lx
COVETT, Saml.		13	M	Laborer	23Ju02lx
St.JOHN, Richard		27	M	Laborer	23Ju02lx
U	(W)	24	F	Wife	23Ju02lx
Ellen	(D)	05	F	Child	23Ju02lx
James	(S)	02	M	Child	23Ju02lx
KITCHER, Mick		29	M	Laborer	23Ju02lx
FITZPATRICK, Ann		20	F	None	23Ju02lx
KELLEY, John		40	M	Laborer	23Ju02lx
CAMPLIN, Ellen		20	F	None	23Ju02lx
BRIGGS, Luke-M.		45	M	Laborer	23Ju02lx
MCCOLOHOY, James		30	M	Laborer	23Ju02lx
U	(W)	25	F	Wife	23Ju02lx
BROPHY, Wm.		18	M	Laborer	23Ju02lx
John		16	M	Laborer	23Ju02lx
LAWLER, Pat		18	M	Laborer	23Ju02lx
GROUM, J.		46	F	None	23Ju02lx
LYNCH, Pat		40	M	Laborer	23Ju02lx
Cathe.	(D)	11	F	None	23Ju02lx
KERNAN, Edwd.		07	M	Child	23Ju02lx
GARSEY, Christopher		30	M	Laborer	23Ju02lx
BYRNE, Bridget		20	F	None	23Ju02lx
SHEEHAN, Mick		31	M	Laborer	23Ju02lx
GARAHER, Stephen		30	M	Laborer	23Ju02lx
LYNCH, Edward		28	M	Laborer	23Ju02lx
U	(W)	22	F	Wife	23Ju02lx
Joseph	(S)	07	M	Child	23Ju02lx
Mary	(D)	08	F	Child	23Ju02lx
CONWAY, Pat		24	M	Laborer	23Ju02lx
OLEARY, Dennis		25	M	Laborer	23Ju02lx
MAHONEY, Ellen		25	F	None	23Ju02lx
FERRY, Richard		14	M	Laborer	23Ju02lx
THORP, Mary		22	F	None	23Ju02lx
Joseph		13	M	Laborer	23Ju02lx
WALKER, Sarah		25	F	None	23Ju02lx
DOYLE, Christopher		26	M	Laborer	23Ju02lx
Mary		26	F	None	23Ju02lx
Catharine		20	F	None	23Ju02lx
Essy		13	F	None	23Ju02lx
MCALLAN, Ella		22	F	None	23Ju02lx
CARR, Joseph		13	M	Laborer	23Ju02lx
SHANE, John		17	M	Laborer	23Ju02lx
BARBER, Ezekiel		26	M	Laborer	23Ju02lx
U	(W)	30	F	Wife	23Ju02lx
U	(D)	.00	F	Infant	23Ju02lx
Mary=Ann	(D)	03	F	Child	23Ju02lx
BOYLE, Ellen		19	F	None	23Ju02lx
HANNORAM, Mary		40	F	None	23Ju02lx
William	(S)	16	M	None	23Ju02lx

NAMES OF PASSENGERS		A G E	S E X	OCCUPATIONS	DATE PORT SHIP
HANNORAM, Jane	(D)	12	F	None	23Ju02Ix
Ducker	(S)	08	M	Child	23Ju02Ix
Thos.	(S)	06	M	Child	23Ju02Ix
George	(S)	04	M	Child	23Ju02Ix
CONNOR, Bryan		30	M	Laborer	23Ju02Ix
Cthe.	(D)	11	F	None	23Ju02Ix
Mary	(D)	03	F	Child	23Ju02Ix
Dennis	(S)	11	M	Laborer	23Ju02Ix
RYAN, J.G.		24	M	Laborer	23Ju02Ix
Pat		11	M	Laborer	23Ju02Ix
Edward		04	M	Child	23Ju02Ix
BRYAN, Bernard		29	M	Laborer	23Ju02Ix
U	(W)	30	F	Wife	23Ju02Ix
U		.00	U	Infant	23Ju02Ix
Mary	(D)	06	F	Child	23Ju02Ix
James		25	M	Laborer	23Ju02Ix
MCCARTY, Edward		27	M	Laborer	23Ju02Ix
EDMONDS, James		28	M	Laborer	23Ju02Ix
WHALING, Mark		26	M	Laborer	23Ju02Ix

CHRISTIANA 24 JUNE 1847

From Liverpool

NAMES OF PASSENGERS		A G E	S E X	OCCUPATIONS	DATE PORT SHIP
MCELGRUN, Ann		38	F	None	24Ju02Jo
Wm.	(S)	11	M	Laborer	24Ju02Jo
Steward	(S)	07	M	Child	24Ju02Jo
DOLE, Bridget		68	F	None	24Ju02Jo
CASEY, Bridget		15	F	None	24Ju02Jo
CONNOR, Joseph		20	M	Laborer	24Ju02Jo
CONNOLLEY, John		45	M	Laborer	24Ju02Jo
Mary	(W)	50	F	None	24Ju02Jo
Bridget	(D)	15	F	None	24Ju02Jo
KEARNS, Bernard		40	M	Laborer	24Ju02Jo
MURRAY, Margaret		25	F	None	24Ju02Jo
DRISCOLL, Mary		20	F	None	24Ju02Jo
RYAN, Nabbey		20	F	None	24Ju02Jo
EAGON, Margaret		15	F	None	24Ju02Jo
BREMAN, Mary		18	F	None	24Ju02Jo
MCLOUGHTON, Patrick		21	M	Laborer	24Ju02Jo
FAGAN, Michael		27	M	Laborer	24Ju02Jo
SAVAGE, Elizabeth		50	F	None	24Ju02Jo
James	(S)	21	M	Laborer	24Ju02Jo
RICE, Charles		21	M	Laborer	24Ju02Jo
James		18	M	Laborer	24Ju02Jo
John		17	M	Laborer	24Ju02Jo
KELLY, Michael		30	M	Laborer	24Ju02Jo
MCCARTEY, Bernard		70	M	Laborer	24Ju02Jo
Ann	(W)	60	F	None	24Ju02Jo
Ann-Jr.	(D)	28	F	None	24Ju02Jo
MULVEY, David		21	M	Laborer	24Ju02Jo
TOOKER, Edward		20	M	Laborer	24Ju02Jo
MEEHAN, Catharine		25	F	None	24Ju02Jo
MULVEY, Eliza		06	F	Child	24Ju02Jo
MANGAN, Catharine		40	F	None	24Ju02Jo
Eliza	(D)	13	F	None	24Ju02Jo
KEYLAN, John		33	M	Laborer	24Ju02Jo
TILSON, James		45	M	Laborer	24Ju02Jo
Mary	(D)	28	F	None	24Ju02Jo
MURFEY, Mary		31	F	None	24Ju02Jo
QUIN, Catharine		18	F	None	24Ju02Jo
HART, Catharine		20	F	None	24Ju02Jo
DONOHOE, James		17	M	Laborer	24Ju02Jo
Edwd.		13	M	Laborer	24Ju02Jo
Catharine		10	F	None	24Ju02Jo
DONOVAN, Patt		35	M	Laborer	24Ju02Jo
U		06	F	Child	24Ju02Jo
GRIMES, M.		00	U	Unknown	24Ju02Jo
GOOD, Bridget		00	F	Unknown	24Ju02Jo

NAMES OF PASSENGERS		A G E	S E X	OCCUPATIONS	DATE PORT SHIP
KENT, John		21	M	Laborer	24Ju02Jo
				Died-At-Sea	
RAY, John		21	M	Laborer	24Ju02Jo
DONOVAN, James		40	M	Laborer	24Ju02Jo
Ann		20	F	None	24Ju02Jo
Mary		25	F	None	24Ju02Jo
Patt		00	M	Laborer	24Ju02Jo
KEATING, Thos.		20	M	Laborer	24Ju02Jo
DELEPANT, Alice		21	F	None	24Ju02Jo
Mary		18	F	None	24Ju02Jo
DOLAN, Honor		18	F	None	24Ju02Jo
CONNOR, Judith		46	F	None	24Ju02Jo
Wm.	(S)	18	M	Laborer	24Ju02Jo
Anne	(D)	16	F	None	24Ju02Jo
WAKES, Julia		63	F	None	24Ju02Jo
KELLEY, Catharine		25	F	None	24Ju02Jo
CAIN, Mary		50	F	None	24Ju02Jo
Thos.	(S)	19	M	Laborer	24Ju02Jo
REILEY, John		16	M	Laborer	24Ju02Jo
FOREL, Daniel		19	M	Laborer	24Ju02Jo
MURRAY, Mary		19	F	None	24Ju02Jo
SMITH, Julia		20	F	None	24Ju02Jo
BRADY, Anne		10	F	None	24Ju02Jo
GRANES, Anne		26	F	None	24Ju02Jo
GOFREY, Andrew		18	M	Laborer	24Ju02Jo
An---		16	M	Laborer	24Ju02Jo
BRATEY, Rosa		12	F	None	24Ju02Jo
ATKINSON, Edward		36	M	Laborer	24Ju02Jo
Alice	(W)	30	F	None	24Ju02Jo
John	(S)	07	M	Child	24Ju02Jo
Sarah	(D)	09	F	Child	24Ju02Jo
Eliza	(D)	11	F	Child	24Ju02Jo
WARD, John		24	M	Laborer	24Ju02Jo
LENNETT, James		27	M	Laborer	24Ju02Jo
ONEAL, Bridget		60	F	None	24Ju02Jo
Wm.	(S)	17	M	Laborer	24Ju02Jo
COSTELLO, John		28	M	Laborer	24Ju02Jo
FLANIGAN, Martin		23	M	Laborer	24Ju02Jo
FARRAN, Bernard		50	M	Laborer	24Ju02Jo
Margaret	(W)	50	F	None	24Ju02Jo
Thomas	(S)	30	M	Laborer	24Ju02Jo
James	(S)	19	M	Laborer	24Ju02Jo
Ann	(D)	15	F	None	24Ju02Jo
Catharine	(D)	12	F	None	24Ju02Jo
HOLMES, Ellen		21	F	None	24Ju02Jo
MCDERMOTT, James		35	M	Laborer	24Ju02Jo
DUFFEY, Mary		00	F	None	24Ju02Jo
LANDERSON, Eliza		23	F	None	24Ju02Jo
RONEY, Pak.		30	M	Laborer	24Ju02Jo
HOWARD, Ann		10	F	None	24Ju02Jo
CONNOR, Pat		21	M	Laborer	24Ju02Jo
Thomas		19	M	Laborer	24Ju02Jo
BERRYMAN, James		22	M	Laborer	24Ju02Jo
Mary		13	F	None	24Ju02Jo
REYLEY, Hugh		23	M	Laborer	24Ju02Jo
Ellen		05	F	Child	24Ju02Jo
TILSON, Mary		05	F	Child	24Ju02Jo
James		03	M	Child	24Ju02Jo
Ellen		01	M	Child	24Ju02Jo
KING, Betsey		18	F	None	24Ju02Jo
Margaret		14	F	None	24Ju02Jo
DONOHOE, Thos.		19	M	Laborer	24Ju02Jo
KEARNAN, Margaret		18	F	None	24Ju02Jo
NOWLAN, James		22	M	Laborer	24Ju02Jo
MCNAMEE, James		20	M	Laborer	24Ju02Jo
MCCULLION, Daniel		22	M	Laborer	24Ju02Jo
SUMMERVILLE, Wm.		45	M	Laborer	24Ju02Jo
				Died-At-Sea	
Henrietta		32	F	None	24Ju02Jo
MCDONALD, Michael		27	M	Laborer	24Ju02Jo
LENNET, Peter		26	M	Laborer	24Ju02Jo
HUDDEN, Mary		20	F	None	24Ju02Jo
SKELTON, Sarah		16	F	None	24Ju02Jo
DOWLING, Patrick		29	M	Laborer	24Ju02Jo
Ellen	(W)	29	F	None	24Ju02Jo

NAMES OF PASSENGERS		AGE	SEX	OCCUPATIONS	DATE PORT SHIP
DOWLING, Maria	(D)	02	F	Child	24Ju02Jo
Patrick		26	M	Laborer	24Ju02Jo
MCANDRAN, John		22	M	Laborer	24Ju02Jo
DELLY, Michael		32	M	Laborer	24Ju02Jo
Isabella		35	F	None	24Ju02Jo
MCGUNOGAN, Honor		17	F	None	24Ju02Jo
KENEDY, Margaret		14	F	None	24Ju02Jo
Ellen		10	F	None	24Ju02Jo
James		08	M	Child	24Ju02Jo
David		04	M	Child	24Ju02Jo
COFFEY, Bridget		60	F	None	24Ju02Jo
CONNOUGHAM, Francis		16	M	Laborer	24Ju02Jo
MCGUICK, Bess		19	F	None	24Ju02Jo
HACKETT, Maria		27	F	None	24Ju02Jo
Margaret		25	F	None	24Ju02Jo
Bridget		23	F	None	24Ju02Jo
HEFFERIN, Catharine		18	F	None	24Ju02Jo
TOOHY, Ellen		24	F	None	24Ju02Jo
FRIEL, James		26	M	Laborer	24Ju02Jo
MCBRIDE, Patk.		26	M	Laborer	24Ju02Jo
HARKIN, Betsey		50	F	None	24Ju02Jo
Francis	(S)	15	M	Laborer	24Ju02Jo
Bidity	(D)	11	F	None	24Ju02Jo
Margaret	(D)	08	F	Child	24Ju02Jo
CONBOY, James		28	M	Laborer	24Ju02Jo
KELLEY, James		30	M	Laborer	24Ju02Jo
James		00	M	Laborer	24Ju02Jo
RESMAN, Christn.		35	M	Laborer	24Ju02Jo
BANIN, Owen		19	M	Laborer	24Ju02Jo
MCMERROW, Mary		21	F	None	24Ju02Jo
DOLSON, John		20	M	Laborer	24Ju02Jo
LARKIN, Catharine		50	F	None	24Ju02Jo
Michael	(S)	18	M	Laborer	24Ju02Jo
QUIN, Rachel		21	F	None	24Ju02Jo
LOCKHART, Thomas		18	M	Laborer	24Ju02Jo
MCCASHEN, James		20	M	Laborer	24Ju02Jo
Michael		22	M	Laborer	24Ju02Jo
SCALLY, Mary		23	F	None	24Ju02Jo
SHANNON, Ann		23	F	None	24Ju02Jo
SCALLY, Daniel		24	M	Laborer	24Ju02Jo
MORRAN, Catharine		17	F	None	24Ju02Jo
John		09	M	Child	24Ju02Jo
Ellen		07	F	Child	24Ju02Jo
RAHILL, Pat.		27	M	Laborer	24Ju02Jo

ATLANTIC 24 JUNE 1847

From Liverpool

NAMES OF PASSENGERS		AGE	SEX	OCCUPATIONS	DATE PORT SHIP
SMITH, Marg.		21	F	None	24Ju02My
CUNNINGHAM, Bessy		17	F	None	24Ju02My
Bessy		13	F	None	24Ju02My
FALLON, Mich.		20	M	Laborer	24Ju02My
MCCLURE, Mary		18	F	None	24Ju02My
REILY, Mary		26	F	None	24Ju02My
John		18	M	Laborer	24Ju02My
Margt.		16	F	None	24Ju02My
KEARY, Mich.		30	M	Farmer	24Ju02My
Mary	(W)	30	F	None	24Ju02My
John	(S)	05	M	Child	24Ju02My
WHEALIN, John		20	M	Farmer	24Ju02My
DOGHERTY, Hugh		19	M	Farmer	24Ju02My
Julia		15	F	None	24Ju02My
Wenny		13	M	None	24Ju02My
Thomas		11	M	None	24Ju02My
DOWLING, Pat		21	M	Mechanic	24Ju02My
KENEDY, Francis		21	M	Mechanic	24Ju02My
SMITH, James		20	M	Mechanic	24Ju02My
Ann		20	F	None	24Ju02My
MCMANUS, Jno.		20	M	Mechanic	24Ju02My
SMITH, Agnes		24	F	None	24Ju02My
FURNNES, Mary		30	F	None	24Ju02My
Cath.	(W)	25	F	None	24Ju02My
Pat.	(S)	10	M	None	24Ju02My
Harriet	(D)	09	F	Child	24Ju02My
Thos.	(S)	07	M	Child	24Ju02My
GREENE, Cath.		20	F	None	24Ju02My
BAILY, Mich.		20	M	Laborer	24Ju02My
EVANS, Bath.L.		40	M	Laborer	24Ju02My
Mary	(W)	35	F	None	24Ju02My
John	(S)	04	M	Child	24Ju02My
MCLURE, Martin		25	M	Laborer	24Ju02My
BANES, Jos.		40	M	Laborer	24Ju02My
Eliza	(W)	40	F	None	24Ju02My
Thomas	(S)	11	M	None	24Ju02My
Wm.	(S)	09	M	Child	24Ju02My
Joseph	(S)	07	M	Child	24Ju02My
John	(S)	05	M	Child	24Ju02My
Jane	(D)	03	F	Child	24Ju02My
MARANE, Cath.		20	F	None	24Ju02My
CASEY, Cath.		20	F	None	24Ju02My
REYNOLDS, Jas.		40	M	Laborer	24Ju02My
Ann	(W)	40	F	None	24Ju02My
Mary	(D)	06	F	Child	24Ju02My
Cath.	(D)	05	F	Child	24Ju02My
Wineford	(S)	03	M	Child	24Ju02My
Cormack	(S)	.00	M	Infant	24Ju02My
DOWN, H.		28	M	Laborer	24Ju02My
MCGUIRE, Owen		30	M	Laborer	24Ju02My
Ann		25	F	None	24Ju02My
BREMEN, Thos.		20	M	Laborer	24Ju02My
GAFFNEY, Thos.		20	M	Laborer	24Ju02My
HACKETT, Bridget		20	F	None	24Ju02My
WHITLOW, Pat.		20	M	Laborer	24Ju02My
COHILL, Law.		25	M	Laborer	24Ju02My
HAMIL, Ann		20	F	None	24Ju02My
Cath.		18	F	None	24Ju02My
LAUGHLIN, Jno.		25	M	Laborer	24Ju02My
CAREY, Jno.		20	M	Laborer	24Ju02My
MAHER, Cath.		18	F	None	24Ju02My
BROGAN, Mary		18	F	None	24Ju02My
REAGH, Cath.		20	F	None	24Ju02My
Bridget		12	F	None	24Ju02My
KADEN, Thos.		23	M	Laborer	24Ju02My
ANDERSON, Jos.		25	M	Laborer	24Ju02My
Jno.		24	M	Laborer	24Ju02My
RIGNEY, Ann		40	F	None	24Ju02My
KELLY, Thos.		30	M	Laborer	24Ju02My
HALLIGAN, Ed.		24	M	Laborer	24Ju02My
MCDONNELL, Eliza.		18	F	None	24Ju02My
BEATY, Thos.		32	M	Laborer	24Ju02My
LEE, Mich.		20	M	Laborer	24Ju02My
GILROY, Peter		20	M	Laborer	24Ju02My
BREARD, Richd.		34	M	Laborer	24Ju02My
Ann	(W)	34	F	None	24Ju02My
Eliza	(D)	.00	F	Infant	24Ju02My
NICHOLSON, Robt.		25	M	Laborer	24Ju02My
Mary		40	F	None	24Ju02My
Harriet		08	F	Child	24Ju02My
LUTE, Bridget		28	F	None	24Ju02My
MONGAN, Jno.		25	M	Mechanic	24Ju02My
Margt.		23	F	None	24Ju02My
WILDE, Rose		50	F	None	24Ju02My
POWER, Hannah		30	F	None	24Ju02My
Ems.		20	F	None	24Ju02My
Mich.	(S)	06	M	Child	24Ju02My
James	(S)	03	M	Child	24Ju02My
Jno.	(S)	.00	M	Infant	24Ju02My
Mary	(D)	.00	F	Infant	24Ju02My
COULTER, Jas.		24	M	Laborer	24Ju02My
MCINTOSH, Elizth.		20	F	None	24Ju02My
REILY, Pat		21	M	Laborer	24Ju02My
LAUTHER, A.		50	M	Laborer	24Ju02My
Janet	(W)	50	F	None	24Ju02My

NAMES OF PASSENGERS	AGE/EX	AGE	SEX	OCCUPATIONS	DATE PORT SHIP
LAUTHER, Adam	(S)	25	M	Laborer	24Ju02My
Garrett	(S)	24	M	Laborer	24Ju02My
Agnes	(D)	18	F	None	24Ju02My
INGLASS, Janet		24	F	None	24Ju02My
LAWTHER, Watty		12	F	None	24Ju02My
INGLASS, A.		03	M	Child	24Ju02My
KELLY, Agnes		23	F	None	24Ju02My
BRADY, J.		40	M	Farmer	24Ju02My
Bridget	(W)	40	F	None	24Ju02My
Dennis	(S)	20	M	Farmer	24Ju02My
John	(S)	11	M	None	24Ju02My
Mary	(D)	09	F	Child	24Ju02My
Owen	(S)	07	M	Child	24Ju02My
Cath.	(D)	04	F	Child	24Ju02My
James	(S)	02	M	Child	24Ju02My
RYON, Mary		18	F	None	24Ju02My
PRIDLE, Nat		54	M	Mechanic	24Ju02My
Sarah	(W)	40	F	None	24Ju02My
James	(S)	10	M	None	24Ju02My
Wm.	(S)	12	M	None	24Ju02My
SMITH, Jas.		20	M	Farmer	24Ju02My
MCKABE, Thos.		21	M	Farmer	24Ju02My
GALAGAN, B.		18	M	Laborer	24Ju02My
GAFFNEY, Ann		20	F	None	24Ju02My
Magt.		21	F	None	24Ju02My
GALLIGAN, Cath.		20	F	None	24Ju02My
COYLE, Alice		20	F	None	24Ju02My
SMITH, Ellen		20	F	None	24Ju02My
REILEY, Mary		20	F	None	24Ju02My
DOWNEY, Honora		41	F	None	24Ju02My
Eliza	(D)	13	F	None	24Ju02My
Hanora	(D)	10	F	None	24Ju02My
Mary	(D)	08	F	Child	24Ju02My
MCGUILY, Peggy		21	F	None	24Ju02My
BRIDE, Margt.		20	F	None	24Ju02My
SMITH, B.		20	M	Farmer	24Ju02My
WHITE, W.		20	M	Farmer	24Ju02My
Mary		18	F	None	24Ju02My
MALONEY, Ann		40	F	None	24Ju02My
John	(S)	28	M	Farmer	24Ju02My
E.	(S)	26	M	Farmer	24Ju02My
Dennis	(S)	30	M	Farmer	24Ju02My
NOLAN, Ann		18	F	None	24Ju02My
BAILY, Ed.		30	M	Farmer	24Ju02My
Bridget		30	F	None	24Ju02My
CONNELLY, M.		20	M	Laborer	24Ju02My
REILY, Mary		18	F	None	24Ju02My
Cth.		10	F	None	24Ju02My
HUNT, Pat.		25	M	Laborer	24Ju02My
GAHERTY, John		40	M	Laborer	24Ju02My
Cath.	(W)	40	F	None	24Ju02My
Francis	(S)	10	M	None	24Ju02My
Mary	(D)	12	F	None	24Ju02My
BAKER, Maria		40	F	None	24Ju02My
Jno.	(S)	10	M	None	24Ju02My
Margt.	(D)	08	F	Child	24Ju02My
Pat.	(S)	06	M	Child	24Ju02My
Charles	(S)	03	M	Child	24Ju02My
CONWAY, Wm.		25	M	Mechanic	24Ju02My
ACKRIDGE, Mary		36	F	None	24Ju02My
Ann	(D)	05	F	Child	24Ju02My
GRADY, James		30	M	Tanner	24Ju02My
Margt.		18	F	None	24Ju02My
Cath.		17	F	None	24Ju02My
ENNIS, Thos.		28	M	Tanner	24Ju02My
Mary		30	F	None	24Ju02My
SMITH, Matt		30	M	Farmer	24Ju02My
Rose		25	F	None	24Ju02My
Margt.		20	F	None	24Ju02My
HANA, Jno.		25	M	Farmer	24Ju02My
CORR, James		40	M	Mechanic	24Ju02My
Mary	(W)	40	F	None	24Ju02My
Mary-A.	(D)	15	F	None	24Ju02My
Margt.	(D)	15	F	None	24Ju02My
Joseph	(S)	13	M	None	24Ju02My
CORR, Julia	(D)	11	F	None	24Ju02My
Thomas	(S)	09	M	Child	24Ju02My
Ellen	(D)	08	F	Child	24Ju02My
John	(S)	06	M	Child	24Ju02My
BLACK, John		25	M	Laborer	24Ju02My
Ann	(W)	25	F	None	24Ju02My
Nich.	(S)	.00	M	Infant	24Ju02My
Bridget	(D)	.00	F	Infant	24Ju02My
FOLEY, Pat.		20	M	Laborer	24Ju02My
LAUGHERN, M.		40	M	Laborer	24Ju02My
CONNER, M.		18	M	Laborer	24Ju02My
NAHAL, Mary		18	F	None	24Ju02My
LAGARGON, P.		50	M	Laborer	24Ju02My
BLAKE, Ann		48	F	None	24Ju02My
HAYES, John		40	M	Farmer	24Ju02My
Pat.	(S)	07	M	Child	24Ju02My
Mary	(D)	05	F	Child	24Ju02My
Michl.	(S)	.00	M	Infant	24Ju02My
DECKER, Is.		45	M	Mechanic	24Ju02My
Paulina	(W)	40	F	None	24Ju02My
Eph.	(S)	10	M	None	24Ju02My
Dorotha	(D)	11	F	None	24Ju02My
Laman	(S)	.00	M	Infant	24Ju02My
SKIFF, David		42	M	Mechanic	24Ju02My
BRADY, M.		30	M	Mechanic	24Ju02My
P.		25	M	Mechanic	24Ju02My
Pat		21	M	Mechanic	24Ju02My
Margt.		20	F	None	24Ju02My
MCNAMEE, Biddy		19	F	None	24Ju02My
BUCK, Wm.		27	M	Mechanic	24Ju02My
Bridget	(W)	23	F	None	24Ju02My
Cella	(D)	08	F	Child	24Ju02My
Wm.	(S)	06	M	Child	24Ju02My
Ann	(D)	04	F	Child	24Ju02My
Cath.	(D)	09	F	Child	24Ju02My
Margt.		24	F	None	24Ju02My
Mary	(D)	.00	F	Infant	24Ju02My
BURNS, Pat		30	M	Farmer	24Ju02My
Law.		17	M	Farmer	24Ju02My
Edwd.		15	M	Farmer	24Ju02My
Jno.		13	M	None	24Ju02My
Martin		11	M	None	24Ju02My
James		08	M	Child	24Ju02My
Patk.		05	M	Child	24Ju02My
Magt.		40	F	None	24Ju02My
Mary		18	F	None	24Ju02My
Elizth.		15	F	None	24Ju02My
Cath.		13	F	None	24Ju02My
Ann		12	F	None	24Ju02My
James		05	M	Child	24Ju02My
GENNERSON, Jos.		45	M	Farmer	24Ju02My
Elizth.	(W)	49	F	None	24Ju02My
Robt.	(S)	21	M	Farmer	24Ju02My
Margt.	(D)	19	F	None	24Ju02My
Jane	(D)	16	F	None	24Ju02My
Jos.	(S)	12	M	None	24Ju02My
Alexn.	(S)	10	M	None	24Ju02My
Thomas	(S)	07	M	Child	24Ju02My
Hugh	(S)	09	M	Child	24Ju02My
Mary	(D)	23	F	None	24Ju02My
Ann	(D)	20	F	None	24Ju02My
Hannah	(D)	22	F	None	24Ju02My
LINDZEY, Sarah		40	F	None	24Ju02My
James	(S)	23	M	Farmer	24Ju02My
Margt.	(D)	21	F	None	24Ju02My
Sarah	(D)	16	F	None	24Ju02My
Elizth.	(D)	12	F	None	24Ju02My
Robert	(S)	09	M	Child	24Ju02My
BYRNS, Jas.		25	M	Farmer	24Ju02My
DENNISON, Bridget		21	F	None	24Ju02My
TWIGGS, Mary		50	F	None	24Ju02My
BROWNING, H.		45	M	Farmer	24Ju02My
Elizth.	(D)	20	F	None	24Ju02My
Emily	(D)	21	F	None	24Ju02My
Charlotte	(D)	18	F	None	24Ju02My

NAMES OF PASSENGERS		AGE	SEX	OCCUPATIONS	DATE PORT SHIP
BROWNING, Francis	(D)	13	F	None	24Ju02My
MCCLUSKIN, J.		23	M	Farmer	24Ju02My
Elisha		23	M	Farmer	24Ju02My
RUSSEL, Maria		20	F	None	24Ju02My
M.Ann	(D)	.00	F	Infant	24Ju02My
LYNOTT, Nath.		25	M	Farmer	24Ju02My
MULLINS, Wm.		20	M	Farmer	24Ju02My
KAVANAGH, Mary		20	F	None	24Ju02My
MONKS, A.		19	M	Laborer	24Ju02My
NOLAN, J.		20	M	Laborer	24Ju02My
CALNOR, Bridget		20	F	None	24Ju02My
LATTETS, P.		20	M	Laborer	24Ju02My
REILY, Ann		30	F	None	24Ju02My
RATING, Pat		35	M	Laborer	24Ju02My
GEGALAN, Ann		29	F	None	24Ju02My
CRAIG, Mary		20	F	None	24Ju02My
FITZGERALD, Mary		22	F	None	24Ju02My
CALLIAHN, P.		60	M	Farmer	24Ju02My
Sarah	(W)	55	F	None	24Ju02My
Patk.	(S)	29	M	Farmer	24Ju02My
Mary	(D)	25	F	None	24Ju02My
Fanny	(D)	20	F	None	24Ju02My
Dennis	(S)	16	M	Farmer	24Ju02My
Phil.	(S)	14	M	Farmer	24Ju02My
DONLY, Jno.		30	M	Farmer	24Ju02My
LAHOON, Bridget		22	F	None	24Ju02My
LIVLIS, Wm.		30	M	Farmer	24Ju02My
DONLY, Mary		23	F	None	24Ju02My
REILY, James		37	M	Farmer	24Ju02My
Ann		20	F	None	24Ju02My
MCNICKLEN, Margt.		14	F	None	24Ju02My
MULHAIN, Quig.		12	M	None	24Ju02My
HANEIR, Pat		18	M	Laborer	24Ju02My
MCNAFF, John		14	M	Laborer	24Ju02My

EUROPE 24 JUNE 1847

From Liverpool

NAMES OF PASSENGERS		AGE	SEX	OCCUPATIONS	DATE PORT SHIP
MCCANN, Jas.		25	M	Laborer	24Ju02BI
Bridget		60	F	None	24Ju02BI
Ellen		40	F	None	24Ju02BI
PATKINS, Ann		20	F	None	24Ju02BI
Margt.		18	F	None	24Ju02BI
LAUGHLIN, John		34	M	Laborer	24Ju02BI
U	(W)	24	F	Wife	24Ju02BI
Cath.	(D)	03	F	Child	24Ju02BI
Judith	(D)	02	F	Child	24Ju02BI
REILY, Hugh		18	M	Laborer	24Ju02BI
Margt.		12	F	None	24Ju02BI
SHERIDAN, Pat		45	M	Laborer	24Ju02BI
John	(S)	18	M	Laborer	24Ju02BI
Ellen	(D)	16	F	None	24Ju02BI
RENICK, Jno.		20	M	Laborer	24Ju02BI
SPROUL, Geo.		50	M	Laborer	24Ju02BI
Agnes	(W)	40	F	None	24Ju02BI
Fanny		30	F	None	24Ju02BI
Agnes	(D)	13	F	None	24Ju02BI
David	(S)	11	M	None	24Ju02BI
Alexander	(S)	06	M	Child	24Ju02BI
James	(S)	05	M	Child	24Ju02BI
MCGROTH, Jno.		31	F	None	24Ju02BI
Agnes		29	F	None	24Ju02BI
Mary		27	F	None	24Ju02BI
HAY, Janet		30	F	None	24Ju02BI
SPROUL, John		24	M	Mechanic	24Ju02BI
CUMMINGS, Jno.		35	M	Farmer	24Ju02BI
Mary	(W)	30	F	None	24Ju02BI
James	(S)	06	M	Child	24Ju02BI

NAMES OF PASSENGERS		AGE	SEX	OCCUPATIONS	DATE PORT SHIP
CUMMINGS, Grace	(D)	02	F	None	24Ju02BI
QUIGLEY, Richd.		14	M	Laborer	24Ju02BI
James		12	M	Laborer	24Ju02BI
RUTLEDGE, W.		20	M	Laborer	24Ju02BI
PATIGUE, James		18	M	Laborer	24Ju02BI
FAGAN, Wm.		50	M	Laborer	24Ju02BI
John	(S)	30	M	Laborer	24Ju02BI
James	(S)	28	M	Laborer	24Ju02BI
Patrick	(S)	26	M	Laborer	24Ju02BI
Michael	(S)	18	M	Laborer	24Ju02BI
DAGNON, Wm.		31	M	Laborer	24Ju02BI
MCCLUSKEY, Pat		19	M	Laborer	24Ju02BI
MACKEY, Mary		18	F	None	24Ju02BI
SMITH, Hugh		21	M	Laborer	24Ju02BI
GILL, Jas.		25	M	Laborer	24Ju02BI
Bridget		21	F	None	24Ju02BI
MATTEN, Jas.		24	M	Mechanic	24Ju02BI
MCDONALD, Pat		27	M	Laborer	24Ju02BI
MCDERMOTT, Pat		20	M	Laborer	24Ju02BI
Ellen		18	F	None	24Ju02BI
STALES, Hannah		12	F	None	24Ju02BI
BRYAN, Judy		18	F	None	24Ju02BI
Margt.		22	F	None	24Ju02BI
CUSSICK, Emma		15	F	None	24Ju02BI
MCMAHON, Mich.		60	M	Laborer	24Ju02BI
Pat	(S)	16	M	Laborer	24Ju02BI
MORAN, John		28	M	Laborer	24Ju02BI
Judith	(M)	55	F	None	24Ju02BI
Judy	(T)	18	F	None	24Ju02BI
Ellen	(T)	21	F	None	24Ju02BI
BLACK, John		40	M	Laborer	24Ju02BI
U	(W)	30	F	Wife	24Ju02BI
Pat	(S)	10	M	None	24Ju02BI
Thomas	(S)	08	M	Child	24Ju02BI
Bridget	(D)	06	F	Child	24Ju02BI
Mary	(D)	04	F	Child	24Ju02BI
SCOTT, James		37	M	Mechanic	24Ju02BI
Eliza	(W)	29	F	None	24Ju02BI
Ellen	(D)	02	F	Child	24Ju02BI
Robert	(S)	04	M	Child	24Ju02BI
Betsey	(D)	08	F	Child	24Ju02BI
Martin	(S)	02	M	Child	24Ju02BI
EAKEN, Saml.		71	M	Laborer	24Ju02BI
MCCABE, Jas.		16	M	Laborer	24Ju02BI
Hanna		13	F	None	24Ju02BI
BALDWIN, Jas.		29	M	Laborer	24Ju02BI
U	(W)	24	F	Wife	24Ju02BI
MCGLORE, Bridget		20	F	None	24Ju02BI
JONES, John		30	M	Laborer	24Ju02BI
Eliza		30	F	None	24Ju02BI
HOLMES, Pat		20	M	Laborer	24Ju02BI
WELSH, John		34	M	Laborer	24Ju02BI
Ellen	(W)	30	F	None	24Ju02BI
Bernard	(S)	04	M	Child	24Ju02BI
Edwd.	(S)	02	M	Child	24Ju02BI
GRANT, Ellen		26	F	None	24Ju02BI
MURPHY, Pat		18	M	Laborer	24Ju02BI
PARSONS, Jac.		57	M	Laborer	24Ju02BI
QUINN, Jas.		28	M	Laborer	24Ju02BI
Mary		24	F	None	24Ju02BI
FAY, Cath.		14	F	None	24Ju02BI
LANNAN, Jas.		30	M	Farmer	24Ju02BI
Ann		30	F	None	24Ju02BI
Margt.		18	F	None	24Ju02BI
Mary		16	F	None	24Ju02BI
Peter		14	M	Farmer	24Ju02BI
SMITH, Bridget		18	F	None	24Ju02BI
REDDING, John		21	M	None	24Ju02BI
COHILL, Cath.		20	F	None	24Ju02BI
VERDON, Margt.		20	F	None	24Ju02BI
CAVANAGH, Mary		22	F	None	24Ju02BI
CAMPBELL, Jno.		40	M	Mechanic	24Ju02BI
LYONS, Rose		18	F	None	24Ju02BI
WILSON, Cath.		30	F	None	24Ju02BI
CAINS, Rose		18	F	None	24Ju02BI

NAMES OF PASSENGERS		AGE	SEX	OCCUPATIONS	DATE PORT SHIP
CONNELL, Judith		50	F	None	24Ju02BI
Rose	(D)	18	F	None	24Ju02BI
OLNAN, Margt.		11	F	None	24Ju02BI
OBRIAN, Rose		12	F	None	24Ju02BI
CONCANNON, Mary		60	F	None	24Ju02BI
REILY, Jas.		24	M	Laborer	24Ju02BI
MCDONOHEGH, Magt.		22	F	None	24Ju02BI
SMITH, Jas.		23	M	Laborer	24Ju02BI
Mary		20	F	None	24Ju02BI
NANTLY, Ann		32	M	Laborer	24Ju02BI
SMITH, Betsey		13	F	None	24Ju02BI
Pat		14	M	Laborer	24Ju02BI
NANTLEY, Mich.		27	M	Laborer	24Ju02BI
MCCUE, Ann		17	F	None	24Ju02BI
John		16	M	Laborer	24Ju02BI
MCGUIL, Bridget		18	F	None	24Ju02BI
QUINLINE, Mary		21	F	None	24Ju02BI
FITZGIBBONS, Mary		25	F	None	24Ju02BI
HANLEY, Peter		30	M	Mechanic	24Ju02BI
Cath.	(W)	27	F	None	24Ju02BI
Martin	(S)	05	M	Child	24Ju02BI
Edward	(S)	03	M	Child	24Ju02BI
MULVANEY, Pat		40	M	Laborer	24Ju02BI
Judith		35	F	None	24Ju02BI
BARTLEY, Pat		30	M	Laborer	24Ju02BI
Rose		28	F	None	24Ju02BI
WHITE, Pat		20	M	Laborer	24Ju02BI
MCKNIGHT, Thos.		20	M	Laborer	24Ju02BI
MARTIN, Dom.		21	M	Farmer	24Ju02BI
FORESTER, Cath.		16	F	None	24Ju02BI
MCBRIDE, Cath.		14	F	None	24Ju02BI
FITZSIMMONS, Judy		15	F	None	24Ju02BI
HOGAN, Pat		18	M	Farmer	24Ju02BI
BRADY, Cath.		23	F	None	24Ju02BI
REILY, Rose		16	F	None	24Ju02BI
HOOD, Thos.		12	M	Laborer	24Ju02BI
GALLAHAN, Pat		18	M	Laborer	24Ju02BI
Owen		15	M	Laborer	24Ju02BI
ATKINSON, M.		20	M	Laborer	24Ju02BI
REILY, Pat		30	M	Laborer	24Ju02BI
COFFIELD, Jas.		40	M	Laborer	24Ju02BI
Rose		20	F	None	24Ju02BI
CARROL, Barny		25	M	Laborer	24Ju02BI
Mary		17	F	None	24Ju02BI
MURPHY, Bridget		18	F	None	24Ju02BI
KERINS, Rose-Ann		20	F	None	24Ju02BI
HORSEFALL, M.		40	M	Mechanic	24Ju02BI
WHITEHEAD, Chas.		30	M	Mechanic	24Ju02BI
Henry		20	M	Mechanic	24Ju02BI
TINKER, Jas.		20	M	Mechanic	24Ju02BI
MADDEN, Peter		30	M	Mechanic	24Ju02BI
MCGANLEY, Mich.		31	M	Laborer	24Ju02BI
MULROY, Bridget		43	F	None	24Ju02BI
BEATTY, Thos.		30	M	Laborer	24Ju02BI
SMITH, Bridget		20	F	None	24Ju02BI
CONNER, Cath.		55	F	None	24Ju02BI
Ellen	(D)	18	F	None	24Ju02BI
CANEN, Peter		30	M	Mechanic	24Ju02BI
Rose		28	F	None	24Ju02BI
Magt.		22	F	None	24Ju02BI
MULLEN, Mary		30	F	None	24Ju02BI
MCCLEERTY, Magt.		24	F	None	24Ju02BI
RIGHT, Bridget-E.		20	F	None	24Ju02BI
CONNER, Bridget-E.		22	F	None	24Ju02BI
MURPHY, Ellen		21	F	None	24Ju02BI
Ellen		10	F	None	24Ju02BI
MYERS, Cath.		30	F	None	24Ju02BI
John		20	M	None	24Ju02BI
COWEN, Cath.		28	F	None	24Ju02BI
MURPHY, Pat		70	M	Laborer	24Ju02BI
COHAN, Ann		26	F	None	24Ju02BI
MURPHY, Mary		25	F	None	24Ju02BI
DONALLY, Elizth.		27	F	None	24Ju02BI
HAMILTON, Ann		27	F	None	24Ju02BI
FAGAN, Ann		17	F	None	24Ju02BI

NAMES OF PASSENGERS		AGE	SEX	OCCUPATIONS	DATE PORT SHIP
GRAHAM, Jno.		18	M	Laborer	24Ju02BI
FARLEY, Cath.		18	F	None	24Ju02BI
GAINER, Rose		19	F	None	24Ju02BI
COCKLYNE, Jno.		47	M	Laborer	24Ju02BI
CARNEY, Bridget		20	F	None	24Ju02BI
LEARY, Jas.		26	M	Laborer	24Ju02BI
CONROY, Thos.		22	M	Laborer	24Ju02BI
DOCKERTY, Peter		28	M	Laborer	24Ju02BI

LEILA 24 JUNE 1847

From Galway

NAMES OF PASSENGERS		AGE	SEX	OCCUPATIONS	DATE PORT SHIP
BURKE, Miles		30	M	Laborer	24Jul1Mz
Bridget	(W)	27	F	None	24Jul1Mz
Mary-A.	(D)	07	F	Child	24Jul1Mz
Eliza	(D)	06	F	Child	24Jul1Mz
TOLAN, And.		25	M	Laborer	24Jul1Mz
Mary		20	F	None	24Jul1Mz
CONNOR, Sally		20	F	None	24Jul1Mz
TOLAN, Thos.		21	M	Laborer	24Jul1Mz
Bridget	(M)	40	F	None	24Jul1Mz
Pat	(B)	08	M	Child	24Jul1Mz
CORCANAN, Cath.		23	F	None	24Jul1Mz
CAIN, Bridget		25	F	None	24Jul1Mz
FLAHERTY, Sally		22	F	None	24Jul1Mz
Mary		20	F	None	24Jul1Mz
LOOKY, M.		22	M	Laborer	24Jul1Mz
MILAN, Pat		21	M	Laborer	24Jul1Mz
MCDONOUGH, Sam		20	M	Laborer	24Jul1Mz
WALSH, Peter		25	M	Laborer	24Jul1Mz
CONCANNON, Pat		23	M	Laborer	24Jul1Mz
MCKEON, C.		24	M	Laborer	24Jul1Mz
Celia		20	F	None	24Jul1Mz
Ann		18	F	None	24Jul1Mz
Sally		10	F	None	24Jul1Mz
Judy		18	F	None	24Jul1Mz
MCDONOUGH, Peter		18	M	Laborer	24Jul1Mz

HENRY-HOBBS 25 JUNE 1847

From Cork

NAMES OF PASSENGERS		AGE	SEX	OCCUPATIONS	DATE PORT SHIP
BASS, Thomas		48	M	Laborer	25Jul14Na
Margt.	(W)	47	F	None	25Jul14Na
Jane	(D)	26	F	None	25Jul14Na
Thomas	(S)	22	M	Laborer	25Jul14Na
Isaac	(S)	20	M	Laborer	25Jul14Na
Anne	(D)	16	F	None	25Jul14Na
William	(S)	26	M	Laborer	25Jul14Na
BIGLEY, Mary		20	F	None	25Jul14Na
Ellen		17	F	None	25Jul14Na
Julia		32	F	None	25Jul14Na
SULLIVAN, Cathe.		24	F	None	25Jul14Na
John		25	M	None	25Jul14Na
ROCHE, Michael		30	M	None	25Jul14Na
Ellen		23	F	None	25Jul14Na
FOLEY, Johanna		23	F	None	25Jul14Na
MUNDAY, John		18	M	Laborer	25Jul14Na
REARDY, Thos.		22	M	Laborer	25Jul14Na
MAFOONEY, Mary		23	F	None	25Jul14Na
REELY, Bridget		25	F	None	25Jul14Na
SWEENEY, Danl.		28	M	Laborer	25Jul14Na

NAMES OF PASSENGERS		AGE	SEX	OCCUPATIONS	DATE PORT SHIP	NAMES OF PASSENGERS		AGE	SEX	OCCUPATIONS	DATE PORT SHIP
BRIAN, John		25	M	Laborer	25Jul14Na	POPE, Catharine	(D)	28	F	None	25Jul14Na
Mary		20	F	None	25Jul14Na	Frances	(D)	26	F	None	25Jul14Na
Margt.		26	F	None	25Jul14Na	Mary	(D)	25	F	None	25Jul14Na
MCGUIRE, Arthur		24	M	Laborer	25Jul14Na	Ellen	(D)	25	F	None	25Jul14Na
Mary		28	F	None	25Jul14Na	Harriet	(D)	23	F	None	25Jul14Na
WALSH, William		50	M	Laborer	25Jul14Na	Frances	(D)	20	F	None	25Jul14Na
MCGRATH, Margaret		50	F	None	25Jul14Na	BURLEY, John		28	M	Laborer	25Jul14Na
John	(S)	09	M	Child	25Jul14Na	CROWLEY, Pat		25	M	Laborer	25Jul14Na
Jeremiah	(S)	07	M	Child	25Jul14Na	Jerry		50	M	Laborer	25Jul14Na
Pat	(H)	50	M	Laborer	25Jul14Na	GRIFFIN, Daniel		40	M	Laborer	25Jul14Na
FENTIN, James		13	M	Laborer	25Jul14Na	Wm.		30	M	Laborer	25Jul14Na
Dennis		15	M	Laborer	25Jul14Na	Daniel		18	M	Laborer	25Jul14Na
MAHONEY, John		26	M	Laborer	25Jul14Na	Hanora		60	F	None	25Jul14Na
Julia		22	F	None	25Jul14Na	CRUGAN, Mary		25	F	None	25Jul14Na
HARRIS, Hernora		20	F	None	25Jul14Na	MURRAY, Pat		24	M	Laborer	25Jul14Na
FENTIN, Johanna		28	F	None	25Jul14Na	Margt.		20	F	None	25Jul14Na
Timothy		15	M	Laborer	25Jul14Na	Bridget		18	F	None	25Jul14Na
Richard		16	M	Laborer	25Jul14Na	COBBENT, Matthew		28	M	Mechanic	25Jul14Na
John	(S)	01	M	Child	25Jul14Na	Thos.		24	M	Laborer	25Jul14Na
Michael	(S)	.09	M	Infant	25Jul14Na	DENNISON, Thos.		28	M	Laborer	25Jul14Na
Mary	(D)	01	F	Child	25Jul14Na	DRISCOLL, Timothy		36	M	Mechanic	25Jul14Na
DORGAN, Daniel		25	M	Laborer	25Jul14Na	JORDAN, Dennis		25	M	Laborer	25Jul14Na
James	(B)	22	M	Laborer	25Jul14Na	DONIVAN, Michael		22	M	Laborer	25Jul14Na
Ellen	(M)	55	F	None	25Jul14Na	FINN, Pat		30	M	Mechanic	25Jul14Na
Catharine	(T)	20	F	None	25Jul14Na	SULLIVAN, Betty		25	F	None	25Jul14Na
Ellen	(T)	15	F	None	25Jul14Na	GAYER, John		22	M	Laborer	25Jul14Na
Mary		01	F	Child	25Jul14Na	FITZGERALD, Pat		24	M	Laborer	25Jul14Na
BRIEN, Daniel		29	M	Laborer	25Jul14Na	Hanora		24	F	None	25Jul14Na
Judy		25	F	None	25Jul14Na	HERLIHY, Wm.		21	M	Laborer	25Jul14Na
SHICKEEN, Patrick		20	M	Laborer	25Jul14Na	QUINN, David		19	M	Laborer	25Jul14Na
MURPHY, Timothy		39	M	Laborer	25Jul14Na	Ellen		24	F	None	25Jul14Na
Johanna	(W)	34	F	None	25Jul14Na	FITZGERALD, Ann		24	F	None	25Jul14Na
Mary	(D)	09	F	Child	25Jul14Na	HAIGHT, Michael		21	M	Laborer	25Jul14Na
Margaret	(D)	06	F	Child	25Jul14Na	Catharine		19	F	None	25Jul14Na
Julia	(D)	06	F	Child	25Jul14Na	Mary		17	F	None	25Jul14Na
Catharine	(D)	03	F	Child	25Jul14Na	TIERNEY, Emanuel		24	M	Laborer	25Jul14Na
Daniel		34	M	Laborer	25Jul14Na	COLLINS, Timothy		22	M	Laborer	25Jul14Na
SWEENEY, Jeremiah		23	M	Laborer	25Jul14Na	LANONERGONS, Thos.		30	M	Laborer	25Jul14Na
Johanna		30	F	None	25Jul14Na	BOURK, Francis		25	M	Laborer	25Jul14Na
CONNELL, Hannah		24	F	None	25Jul14Na	BRIEN, Ellen		28	F	None	25Jul14Na
GOOD, Thos.		26	M	Laborer	25Jul14Na	HAILEY, Humphey		20	M	Laborer	25Jul14Na
William	(P)	50	M	Laborer	25Jul14Na	THOLAN, Mary		29	F	None	25Jul14Na
James	(B)	16	M	Laborer	25Jul14Na	GOWER, Hannah		20	F	None	25Jul14Na
Susan	(T)	20	F	None	25Jul14Na	MORRELL, Wm.		30	M	Laborer	25Jul14Na
Mary	(T)	18	F	None	25Jul14Na	Hannah		20	F	None	25Jul14Na
Tamson	(T)	30	F	None	25Jul14Na						
Mary	(M)	50	F	None	25Jul14Na						
CONNER, Daniel		29	M	Laborer	25Jul14Na						
MAHONEY, James		25	M	Laborer	25Jul14Na						
GOOD, Joseph		24	M	Laborer	25Jul14Na						
DEANE, Wm.		24	M	Laborer	25Jul14Na	LA-GRANGE 25 JUNE 1847					
CANIGAN, Jeremiah		37	M	Laborer	25Jul14Na						
Morry		30	F	None	25Jul14Na	From Newry					
DESMOND, Mary		25	M	Laborer	25Jul14Na						
MURPHY, John		30	M	Laborer	25Jul14Na						
Johanna	(W)	26	F	None	25Jul14Na						
Edmund	(S)	03	M	Child	25Jul14Na	HANRATTY, T.		35	M	Farmer	25Jul19Nb
John	(S)	.09	M	Infant	25Jul14Na	Anne		35	F	None	25Jul19Nb
CALLAGHAN, Dennis		22	M	Laborer	25Jul14Na	Nancy		30	F	None	25Jul19Nb
TOWNLEY, Maria		23	F	None	25Jul14Na	LONER, Anne		23	F	None	25Jul19Nb
ONIAL, Mary		26	F	None	25Jul14Na	DONLY, Anne		18	F	None	25Jul19Nb
FLYNN, Wm.		26	M	Laborer	25Jul14Na	ONEAL, Cath.		18	F	None	25Jul19Nb
HEGARTY, David		26	M	Laborer	25Jul14Na	TODD, J.		50	F	None	25Jul19Nb
CONNER, Wm.		26	M	Laborer	25Jul14Na	Ellen	(W)	50	F	None	25Jul19Nb
James		24	M	Laborer	25Jul14Na	Jane	(D)	09	F	Child	25Jul19Nb
KIEFFER, Mary		28	F	None	25Jul14Na	Jonathan	(S)	12	M	None	25Jul19Nb
BRIEN, John		30	M	Laborer	25Jul14Na	James	(S)	13	M	None	25Jul19Nb
LANGLEY, John		38	M	Laborer	25Jul14Na	Robt.R.	(S)	05	M	Child	25Jul19Nb
MCKENEDY, Michael		30	M	Laborer	25Jul14Na	WELSH, J.		19	M	Laborer	25Jul19Nb
SCANNELL, Bridget		27	F	None	25Jul14Na	DERLIS, Susannah		07	F	Child	25Jul19Nb
Ellen		25	F	None	25Jul14Na	MCMAHON, Ell.		30	F	None	25Jul19Nb
HEARLY, Wm.		45	M	Laborer	25Jul14Na	Sarah	(D)	06	F	Child	25Jul19Nb
Margt.	(D)	25	F	None	25Jul14Na	FITZGERALD, Betty		30	F	None	25Jul19Nb
John	(S)	22	M	Laborer	25Jul14Na	MCKIBBIN, J.		20	M	Laborer	25Jul19Nb
POPE, George		60	M	Laborer	25Jul14Na	SALT, Mgt.		23	F	None	25Jul19Nb

NAMES OF PASSENGERS		AGE	SEX	OCCUPATIONS	DATE PORT SHIP
SALT, Joseph		19	M	Laborer	25Ju19Nb
Elena		17	M	None	25Ju19Nb
Grm.		15	M	None	25Ju19Nb
Jane-E.		13	F	None	25Ju19Nb
Saml.		11	M	None	25Ju19Nb
Mgt.		07	F	Child	25Ju19Nb
Robt.		04	M	Child	25Ju19Nb
MCCAY, Esh.		25	F	None	25Ju19Nb
My.		27	F	None	25Ju19Nb
MCGIVEN, Mrgt.		14	F	None	25Ju19Nb
MARTIN, Jane-E.		18	F	None	25Ju19Nb
LITTLE, D.		50	M	Farmer	25Ju19Nb
Lucy	(W)	45	F	None	25Ju19Nb
James	(S)	21	M	Farmer	25Ju19Nb
Eliza	(D)	18	F	None	25Ju19Nb
John	(S)	16	M	None	25Ju19Nb
Joseph	(S)	15	M	None	25Ju19Nb
Thos.	(S)	14	M	None	25Ju19Nb
Wm.	(S)	12	M	None	25Ju19Nb
David	(S)	10	M	None	25Ju19Nb
Angus	(S)	08	M	None	25Ju19Nb
Isaac	(S)	06	M	None	25Ju19Nb
Robt.	(S)	03	M	None	25Ju19Nb
MORGAN, Cath.		50	F	None	25Ju19Nb
ROBINSON, W.		20	M	Farmer	25Ju19Nb
DOWNEY, P.		22	M	Unknown	25Ju19Nb
THOMPSON, My.J.		21	F	None	25Ju19Nb
Mgt.		19	F	None	25Ju19Nb
MCGUEHEGSON, J.		40	M	Unknown	25Ju19Nb
PATTERSON, Agnes		50	F	None	25Ju19Nb
Agnes	(D)	28	F	None	25Ju19Nb
MCCABE, J.		20	M	Unknown	25Ju19Nb
CUNNINGHAM, J.		23	M	Unknown	25Ju19Nb
SANDS, M.		23	M	Unknown	25Ju19Nb
Mary	(D)	01	F	Child	25Ju19Nb
Elsbt.	(D)	01	F	Child	25Ju19Nb
CAMPBELL, F.		21	M	Unknown	25Ju19Nb
Madol—, D.		44	M	Unknown	25Ju19Nb
Eliza	(W)	38	F	None	25Ju19Nb
Andw.	(S)	12	M	None	25Ju19Nb
Elza.J.	(D)	19	F	None	25Ju19Nb
John	(S)	09	M	Child	25Ju19Nb
Agnes	(D)	09	F	None	25Ju19Nb
Sam	(S)	05	M	None	25Ju19Nb
Robt.	(S)	03	M	None	25Ju19Nb
Mrgt.	(D)	02	M	None	25Ju19Nb
DONALY, P.		21	M	Unknown	25Ju19Nb
BRANTLY, Elzb.		38	F	None	25Ju19Nb
James	(S)	06	M	Child	25Ju19Nb
KELLY, T.		40	M	Unknown	25Ju19Nb
WARD, J.		41	M	Unknown	25Ju19Nb
DOWNY, P.		50	M	Unknown	25Ju19Nb
Biddy	(W)	43	F	None	25Ju19Nb
John	(S)	14	M	None	25Ju19Nb
MCCOURT, Ann		23	F	None	25Ju19Nb
Cath.		21	F	None	25Ju19Nb
OHARA, P.		41	M	Unknown	25Ju19Nb
REILLY, T.		40	M	Unknown	25Ju19Nb
GRAHAM, Ann		19	F	None	25Ju19Nb
MASTERSON, Joseph		46	M	Unknown	25Ju19Nb
Betty	(W)	40	F	None	25Ju19Nb
My.	(D)	18	F	None	25Ju19Nb
Sarah	(D)	14	F	None	25Ju19Nb
Ellen	(D)	15	F	None	25Ju19Nb
Eliza	(D)	09	F	None	25Ju19Nb
Ann-J.	(D)	06	F	Child	25Ju19Nb
LOONY, W.		18	M	Farmer	25Ju19Nb
LONGIN, E.		20	M	Unknown	25Ju19Nb
MAGILL, J.		30	M	Unknown	25Ju19Nb
Esther	(W)	30	F	None	25Ju19Nb
My.J.	(D)	02	F	Child	25Ju19Nb
Saml.	(S)	01	M	Child	25Ju19Nb
MITCHELL, W.		45	M	Unknown	25Ju19Nb
My.	(W)	40	F	None	25Ju19Nb
James	(S)	16	M	None	25Ju19Nb

NAMES OF PASSENGERS		AGE	SEX	OCCUPATIONS	DATE PORT SHIP
MITCHELL, David	(S)	12	M	None	25Ju19Nb
John	(S)	08	M	Child	25Ju19Nb
MCBONY, Sally		18	F	None	25Ju19Nb
My.J.		16	F	None	25Ju19Nb
BUCKY, Mgt.		18	F	None	25Ju19Nb
Sally		16	F	None	25Ju19Nb
My.		14	F	None	25Ju19Nb
Eliza		12	F	None	25Ju19Nb
DEVALIN, P.		44	M	Unknown	25Ju19Nb
Nancy	(W)	42	F	None	25Ju19Nb
John	(S)	17	M	Unknown	25Ju19Nb
Mgt.	(D)	15	F	None	25Ju19Nb
Saul	(S)	13	M	None	25Ju19Nb
My.	(D)	11	F	None	25Ju19Nb
Nancy	(D)	09	F	Child	25Ju19Nb
SALTS, A.		62	M	Unknown	25Ju19Nb
Ann		45	F	None	25Ju19Nb
MADIGAN, Cath.		20	F	None	25Ju19Nb
BELL, J.		50	M	Unknown	25Ju19Nb
Joseph	(S)	28	M	Unknown	25Ju19Nb
My.J.	(D)	24	F	None	25Ju19Nb
David	(S)	20	M	Unknown	25Ju19Nb
Eliza	(D)	18	F	None	25Ju19Nb
MCHANEY, M.		60	M	Unknown	25Ju19Nb
Michl.	(S)	24	M	Unknown	25Ju19Nb
Patch	(S)	28	M	Unknown	25Ju19Nb
Elza.	(S)	25	F	None	25Ju19Nb
MCCASWELL, Alice		35	F	None	25Ju19Nb
James		25	M	Unknown	25Ju19Nb
Patch		20	M	Unknown	25Ju19Nb
HAUGHEY, J.		48	M	Unknown	25Ju19Nb
Cath.	(W)	42	F	None	25Ju19Nb
Michl.	(S)	14	M	Farmer	25Ju19Nb
John	(S)	18	M	Farmer	25Ju19Nb
Anne	(D)	12	F	None	25Ju19Nb
Mgt.	(D)	10	F	None	25Ju19Nb
Eliza	(D)	05	F	Child	25Ju19Nb
Teresa	(D)	03	F	Child	25Ju19Nb
My.	(D)	08	F	Child	25Ju19Nb
MCARAB, M.		20	M	Unknown	25Ju19Nb
My.		23	F	None	25Ju19Nb
DORLY, M.		26	M	Unknown	25Ju19Nb
KERR, Alice		24	F	None	25Ju19Nb
Mgt.		22	F	None	25Ju19Nb
PARK, T.		20	M	Unknown	25Ju19Nb
MCGARRY, J.		26	M	Unknown	25Ju19Nb
Biddy		19	F	None	25Ju19Nb
TONER, P.		21	M	Unknown	25Ju19Nb
HAGAN, J.		19	M	Unknown	25Ju19Nb
My.		21	F	None	25Ju19Nb
MUCKER, T.		20	M	Unknown	25Ju19Nb
MURTAGH, P.		20	M	Unknown	25Ju19Nb
Magt.		21	F	None	25Ju19Nb
MCGUINY, H.		22	M	Unknown	25Ju19Nb
LITTLE, W.		55	M	Unknown	25Ju19Nb

ARCOLE 25 JUNE 1847

From Liverpool

NAMES OF PASSENGERS		AGE	SEX	OCCUPATIONS	DATE PORT SHIP
FARLEY, Edward		30	M	Laborer	25Ju02Ne
MONAHEN, Pat		36	M	Laborer	25Ju02Ne
COONEY, John		23	M	Laborer	25Ju02Ne
SHAD, Pat		27	M	Laborer	25Ju02Ne
HYNES, James		23	M	Laborer	25Ju02Ne
BRADY, James		21	M	Laborer	25Ju02Ne
GRADY, Andrew		21	M	Laborer	25Ju02Ne
PLUMKETE, James		27	M	Laborer	25Ju02Ne
CULLY, Hugh		22	M	Laborer	25Ju02Ne

NAMES OF PASSENGERS		A G E	S E X	OCCUPATIONS	DATE PORT SHIP	NAMES OF PASSENGERS		A G E	S E X	OCCUPATIONS	DATE PORT SHIP
CULLY, Bridget		19	F	None	25Ju02Ne	WARD, James		32	M	Laborer	25Ju02Ne
GERRY, Biddy		17	F	None	25Ju02Ne	Ann		21	F	None	25Ju02Ne
FITZGERALD, Mary		20	F	None	25Ju02Ne	COSTELLO, Catharine		36	F	None	25Ju02Ne
DARKIN, James		30	M	Laborer	25Ju02Ne	MURRAY, Mary		20	F	None	25Ju02Ne
Michael	(S)	03	M	Child	25Ju02Ne	SHERADON, Ann		20	F	None	25Ju02Ne
Biddy	(W)	29	F	Wife	25Ju02Ne	SMITH, Bridget		22	F	None	25Ju02Ne
John	(S)	.07	M	Infant	25Ju02Ne	Rose		14	F	None	25Ju02Ne
KEATING, Pat		25	M	Laborer	25Ju02Ne	Michael		18	M	Laborer	25Ju02Ne
OSBORNE, Michael		20	M	Laborer	25Ju02Ne	BOYLAN, Mary		22	F	None	25Ju02Ne
KILBY, Michael		30	M	Laborer	25Ju02Ne	BRADLEY, James		20	M	Laborer	25Ju02Ne
CHANCE, John		20	M	Laborer	25Ju02Ne	FARRELY, Pat		20	M	Laborer	25Ju02Ne
KELLY, Timothy		30	M	Laborer	25Ju02Ne	Margaret		20	F	None	25Ju02Ne
Catharine		25	F	None	25Ju02Ne	ARMSTRONG, Anthony		36	M	Laborer	25Ju02Ne
Mary		21	F	None	25Ju02Ne	BRADLEY, William		30	M	Laborer	25Ju02Ne
Johanna		19	F	None	25Ju02Ne	CATHIR, Margaret		25	F	None	25Ju02Ne
Johanna		.10	F	Infant	25Ju02Ne	Rosina		23	F	None	25Ju02Ne
MCANDREWS, Edward		30	M	Laborer	25Ju02Ne	Dorcas		24	F	None	25Ju02Ne
Pat	(B)	25	M	Laborer	25Ju02Ne	David		01	M	Child	25Ju02Ne
John	(B)	20	M	Laborer	25Ju02Ne	MCGATRICK, Pat		35	M	Laborer	25Ju02Ne
Thomas	(B)	17	M	Laborer	25Ju02Ne	Edward		16	M	Laborer	25Ju02Ne
Mary	(M)	50	F	None	25Ju02Ne	DOYLE, Eliza		19	F	None	25Ju02Ne
Mary	(T)	15	F	None	25Ju02Ne	CARTER, Charles		21	M	Laborer	25Ju02Ne
Bridget	(T)	22	F	None	25Ju02Ne	KILDUFF, Bridget		20	F	None	25Ju02Ne
MARTIN, Thomas		50	M	Laborer	25Ju02Ne	LAIRDEN, Ann		20	F	None	25Ju02Ne
Pat	(S)	20	M	Laborer	25Ju02Ne	LYNCH, James		35	M	Laborer	25Ju02Ne
Catharine	(D)	25	F	None	25Ju02Ne	Pat		24	M	Laborer	25Ju02Ne
Sarah	(D)	15	F	None	25Ju02Ne	Michael		20	M	Laborer	25Ju02Ne
Catharine	(D)	.11	F	Infant	25Ju02Ne	DALY, Pat		21	M	Laborer	25Ju02Ne
GAINY, Peter		33	M	Laborer	25Ju02Ne	Rose		25	F	None	25Ju02Ne
FINGLEY, William		30	M	Laborer	25Ju02Ne	MCCARRON, Hugh		22	M	Laborer	25Ju02Ne
Catharine		22	F	None	25Ju02Ne	THORNTON, Owen		58	M	Laborer	25Ju02Ne
Thomas		24	F	None	25Ju02Ne	Thomas	(S)	10	M	Laborer	25Ju02Ne
KELLY, Michael		26	F	None	25Ju02Ne	SADLER, Mary		31	F	None	25Ju02Ne
DALY, Catharine		20	F	None	25Ju02Ne	THORNTON, Margaret		17	F	None	25Ju02Ne
INFANT, Mary		16	F	None	25Ju02Ne	HARE, Andrew		70	M	Laborer	25Ju02Ne
MAXWELL, Ann		30	F	None	25Ju02Ne	HARRIS, Robert		28	M	Laborer	25Ju02Ne
CARTY, John		20	M	Laborer	25Ju02Ne	HARE, Sarah		60	F	None	25Ju02Ne
CORRIS, John		14	M	Laborer	25Ju02Ne	POLLARD, Mary		24	F	None	25Ju02Ne
NAUGHTON, Andrew		28	M	Laborer	25Ju02Ne	GROGAN, Bryan		34	M	Laborer	25Ju02Ne
Mary		20	F	None	25Ju02Ne	DORAN, Robert		19	M	Laborer	25Ju02Ne
HORAN, James		40	M	Laborer	25Ju02Ne	COOPER, H.		21	M	Laborer	25Ju02Ne
Edr.	(S)	24	M	Laborer	25Ju02Ne	FORREST, Wm.		37	M	Laborer	25Ju02Ne
Pat	(S)	20	M	Laborer	25Ju02Ne	Wm.	(S)	13	M	Laborer	25Ju02Ne
DONNELL, Morris		29	M	Laborer	25Ju02Ne	MONTGOMERY, James		28	M	Laborer	25Ju02Ne
BRADY, Margaret		18	F	None	25Ju02Ne	COSBY, Robert		26	M	Laborer	25Ju02Ne
Ann		16	F	None	25Ju02Ne	MOREHEAD, William		21	M	Laborer	25Ju02Ne
MORRAN, Mathew		30	M	Laborer	25Ju02Ne	MCCONNELL, Francis		26	M	Laborer	25Ju02Ne
SMITH, Catharine		17	F	None	25Ju02Ne	LONERY, Dan.		23	M	Laborer	25Ju02Ne
GAFFNEY, Thomas		20	M	Laborer	25Ju02Ne	MANAGH, Robert		22	M	Laborer	25Ju02Ne
MCCOLD, Eliza		20	F	None	25Ju02Ne	GREEN, Robert		22	M	Laborer	25Ju02Ne
HARTY, Michael		45	M	Laborer	25Ju02Ne	RICHMONDS, A.		24	M	Laborer	25Ju02Ne
Phil	(S)	17	M	Laborer	25Ju02Ne	Thomas	(S)	.11	M	Infant	25Ju02Ne
Harriet	(W)	34	F	Wife	25Ju02Ne	Rose		23	F	None	25Ju02Ne
Maria	(D)	16	F	Wife	25Ju02Ne	Maria		20	F	None	25Ju02Ne
Fanny	(D)	13	F	Wife	25Ju02Ne	LYONS, Bridget		20	F	None	25Ju02Ne
James	(S)	11	M	Laborer	25Ju02Ne	Mary		17	F	None	25Ju02Ne
Michael	(S)	09	M	Child	25Ju02Ne	Michael		20	M	Laborer	25Ju02Ne
Pat	(S)	06	M	Child	25Ju02Ne	KANE, Michael		45	M	Laborer	25Ju02Ne
Margaret	(D)	05	F	Child	25Ju02Ne	COONEY, Pat		20	M	Laborer	25Ju02Ne
Betty	(D)	02	F	Child	25Ju02Ne	GANNON, Mary		20	F	None	25Ju02Ne
Catharine	(D)	.03	F	Infant	25Ju02Ne	WHITESITS, Benjamin		28	M	Laborer	25Ju02Ne
BENNETT, John		19	M	Laborer	25Ju02Ne	Joseph		21	M	Laborer	25Ju02Ne
BALL, Thomas		13	M	Laborer	25Ju02Ne	BUTLER, Margaret		45	F	None	25Ju02Ne
FEGAN, John		26	M	Laborer	25Ju02Ne	Thomas	(S)	25	M	Laborer	25Ju02Ne
BRADY, John		26	M	Laborer	25Ju02Ne	William	(S)	11	M	Laborer	25Ju02Ne
GRAHAM, Margaret		20	F	None	25Ju02Ne	George	(S)	07	M	Child	25Ju02Ne
LYNCH, Catharine		20	F	None	25Ju02Ne	Mary	(D)	20	F	None	25Ju02Ne
BRADY, Am.		20	M	Laborer	25Ju02Ne	Ann	(D)	18	F	None	25Ju02Ne
HANDY, Pat		40	M	Laborer	25Ju02Ne	Margaret	(D)	15	F	None	25Ju02Ne
Catharine	(D)	16	F	None	25Ju02Ne	Jane	(D)	10	F	None	25Ju02Ne
MCBRIEN, Thomas		50	M	Laborer	25Ju02Ne	FARRELL, Jane		20	F	None	25Ju02Ne
Eliza		20	F	None	25Ju02Ne	KEEFE, Pat		20	M	Laborer	25Ju02Ne
LAMORE, Thomas		27	M	Laborer	25Ju02Ne	Mary		27	F	None	25Ju02Ne
LEE, Mary		20	F	None	25Ju02Ne	CROSBY, John		19	M	Laborer	25Ju02Ne
BRANNIM, James		40	M	Laborer	25Ju02Ne	FARRELL, Catharine		18	F	None	25Ju02Ne

NAMES OF PASSENGERS	AGE	SEX	EX	OCCUPATIONS	DATE PORT SHIP
OWENS, Rose	20	F		None	25Ju02Ne
MCCABE, Pat	25	M		Laborer	25Ju02Ne
KELLY, Mary	21	F		None	25Ju02Ne
GIBNEY, Charles	20	M		Laborer	25Ju02Ne
RANNON, James	60	M		Laborer	25Ju02Ne
James	16	M		Laborer	25Ju02Ne
Mary	30	F		None	25Ju02Ne
MAGUIRE, Mary	20	F		None	25Ju02Ne
BANNON, John	25	M		Laborer	25Ju02Ne
Michael	09	M		Child	25Ju02Ne
Joseph	13	M		Laborer	25Ju02Ne
Bridget	19	F		None	25Ju02Ne
MURPHY, Pat	20	M		Laborer	25Ju02Ne
CONNELL, Pat	27	M		Laborer	25Ju02Ne
Mary	65	F	(M)	None	25Ju02Ne
GEMERY, Honora	07	F		Child	25Ju02Ne
FINEGAN, Mathew	28	M		Laborer	25Ju02Ne
Pat	.11	M	(S)	Infant	25Ju02Ne
Eliza	25	F	(W)	None	25Ju02Ne
SHAW, Eliza	20	F		None	25Ju02Ne
WALSH, Mary	20	F		None	25Ju02Ne
COMEGHTY, Ellen	40	F		None	25Ju02Ne
Pat	03	M	(S)	Child	25Ju02Ne
Hugh	11	M	(S)	Laborer	25Ju02Ne
Catharine	.07	F	(D)	Infant	25Ju02Ne
KEEFE, James	23	M		Laborer	25Ju02Ne
SHERDON, Catharine	25	F		None	25Ju02Ne
Pat	09	M	(S)	Child	25Ju02Ne
James	30	M	(H)	Laborer	25Ju02Ne
MAGUIRE, Owen	56	M		Laborer	25Ju02Ne
BROBERN, Mary	20	F		None	25Ju02Ne
WALSH, Mary	20	F		None	25Ju02Ne
Mary	27	F		None	25Ju02Ne
MCCORMICK, Ann	20	F		None	25Ju02Ne
James	.10	M	(S)	Infant	25Ju02Ne
HOGAN, Catharine	20	F		None	25Ju02Ne
DOYLE, Mary	36	F		None	25Ju02Ne
James	02	M	(S)	Child	25Ju02Ne
GREEN, Mary	20	F		None	25Ju02Ne
DUNNING, Alice	21	F		None	25Ju02Ne
Mary	19	F		None	25Ju02Ne
COLES, Ellen	26	F		None	25Ju02Ne
MCDAID, Andrew	20	M		Laborer	25Ju02Ne
OBRIEN, Phil.	20	M		Laborer	25Ju02Ne
Bridget	15	F		None	25Ju02Ne
MCPHILLIPS, James	27	M		Laborer	25Ju02Ne
HALPHER, James	33	M		Laborer	25Ju02Ne
BERGAN, Berd.	21	M		Laborer	25Ju02Ne
SAUNDERS, Martin	40	M		Laborer	25Ju02Ne
CONROY, Catharine	15	F		None	25Ju02Ne
HOLLIDAY, Wm.	40	M		Laborer	25Ju02Ne
FARRELL, Pat	10	M		Laborer	25Ju02Ne
HORAN, Ed.	18	M		Laborer	25Ju02Ne
WOODS, Mary	20	F		None	25Ju02Ne
HAGABOTTEN, Mary	20	F		None	25Ju02Ne
MCELROY, Alice	33	F		None	25Ju02Ne
GREY, Wm.	16	M		Laborer	25Ju02Ne
Wm.	16	M		Laborer	25Ju02Ne
DALEY, Thomas	24	M		Laborer	25Ju02Ne
WALKER, James	20	M		Laborer	25Ju02Ne
John	18	M		Laborer	25Ju02Ne
FLANERY, Pat	40	M		Laborer	25Ju02Ne
Unifield	35	F	(W)	None	25Ju02Ne
Harriet	20	F	(D)	None	25Ju02Ne
John	08	M	(S)	Child	25Ju02Ne
ALARD, Anna	16	F		None	25Ju02Ne

SIBERIA 26 JUNE 1847

From Liverpool

NAMES OF PASSENGERS	AGE	SEX	EX	OCCUPATIONS	DATE PORT SHIP
CONNERY, Thos.	40	M		Farmer	26Ju02Nf
M.	30	F	(W)	None	26Ju02Nf
R.	12	M	(S)	None	26Ju02Nf
J.	05	M	(S)	Child	26Ju02Nf
J.	04	F	(D)	Child	26Ju02Nf
M.	02	M	(S)	Child	26Ju02Nf
E.	16	F	(D)	None	26Ju02Nf
A.	10	F	(D)	None	26Ju02Nf
STONE, M.	17	F		None	26Ju02Nf
CORCORAN, M.	30	M		Farmer	26Ju02Nf
MURPHY, P.	32	M		Farmer	26Ju02Nf
CRANE, O.	80	M		Farmer	26Ju02Nf
CLARK, M.	20	F		None	26Ju02Nf
OBRIEN, L.	21	F		None	26Ju02Nf
SULLIVAN, C.	22	F		None	26Ju02Nf
T.	02	M	(S)	Child	26Ju02Nf
CLARK, S.	21	F		None	26Ju02Nf
M.	17	F		None	26Ju02Nf
CONNELY, S.	21	F		None	26Ju02Nf
FINRIEN, M.	18	F		None	26Ju02Nf
LAVLEY, M.A.	27	F		None	26Ju02Nf
BYRNE, T.	20	M		Farmer	26Ju02Nf
MCGARTEE, R.	21	M		Farmer	26Ju02Nf
MAYONE, J.	34	M		Farmer	26Ju02Nf
WINNE, M.	18	F		None	26Ju02Nf
HANNAN, J.	26	M		Farmer	26Ju02Nf
HALL, T.	18	M		Farmer	26Ju02Nf
SULLIVAN, M.	50	M		Farmer	26Ju02Nf
KENIGAN, P.	10	M		None	26Ju02Nf
A.	55	F	(M)	None	26Ju02Nf
A.	24	M	(B)	Farmer	26Ju02Nf
C.	22	F	(T)	None	26Ju02Nf
P.	24	M	(B)	Farmer	26Ju02Nf
SMITH, A.	10	F		None	26Ju02Nf
REED, T.	25	M		Farmer	26Ju02Nf
MASON, J.	17	M		Farmer	26Ju02Nf
KINIGAN, M.	19	M		Farmer	26Ju02Nf
B.	60	F	(M)	None	26Ju02Nf
SULLIVAN, T.	22	M		Farmer	26Ju02Nf

JOHN-R.SKIDDY 26 JUNE 1847

From Liverpool

NAMES OF PASSENGERS	AGE	SEX	EX	OCCUPATIONS	DATE PORT SHIP
DOWLAN, Michl.	25	M		Trader	26Ju02Ac
Bridget	26	F	(W)	None	26Ju02Ac
James	.08	M	(S)	Infant	26Ju02Ac
LONG, Ann	26	F		None	26Ju02Ac
CARHAN, Pat	24	M		Laborer	26Ju02Ac
John	26	M		Laborer	26Ju02Ac
HATHAM, J.	26	M		Mechanic	26Ju02Ac
MCKENNA, M.	27	M		Mechanic	26Ju02Ac
KIRKE, Sarah	17	F		None	26Ju02Ac
Jas.	21	M		Laborer	26Ju02Ac
Catharine	18	F		None	26Ju02Ac
MOYSTON, J.	25	M		Laborer	26Ju02Ac
MCCRAMLISK, Ann	20	F		None	26Ju02Ac
NEWMAN, Cath.	18	F		None	26Ju02Ac
MCCULLOGH, Rose	20	F		None	26Ju02Ac

NAMES OF PASSENGERS		AGE	SEX	OCCUPATIONS	DATE PORT SHIP
MCCULLOGH, Cath.		18	F	None	26Ju02Ac
Michael		25	M	Laborer	26Ju02Ac
MILLER, W.G.		24	M	Carpenter	26Ju02Ac
BUCKLEY, John		30	M	Mechanic	26Ju02Ac
LOONEY, Edith		40	F	None	26Ju02Ac
Edith	(D)	20	F	None	26Ju02Ac
Jno.	(S)	19	M	Mechanic	26Ju02Ac
Mary-Ann	(D)	16	F	None	26Ju02Ac
Philip	(S)	12	M	Mechanic	26Ju02Ac
BARRET, Elizth.		21	F	None	26Ju02Ac
SMITH, Jno.		20	M	Mechanic	26Ju02Ac
Wm.		17	M	Mechanic	26Ju02Ac
BAYSON, Ph.		24	M	Mechanic	26Ju02Ac
CLARKE, P.		26	M	Mechanic	26Ju02Ac
MCCABE, P.		21	M	Mechanic	26Ju02Ac
JONES, J.		21	M	Mechanic	26Ju02Ac
CONNELL, Thos.		40	M	Laborer	26Ju02Ac
SMITH, Mich.		26	M	Laborer	26Ju02Ac
PRUNSEND, Wm.		22	M	Tailor	26Ju02Ac
CLARKE, Jno.		23	M	Mechanic	26Ju02Ac
CARTER, Mich.		22	M	Laborer	26Ju02Ac
BALL, Biddy		18	F	None	26Ju02Ac
CARTY, Ann		17	F	None	26Ju02Ac
STATWOOD, J.B.		40	M	Laborer	26Ju02Ac
U	(W)	30	F	Wife	26Ju02Ac
DONNELL, N.		25	M	Laborer	26Ju02Ac
JONES, Susan		19	F	None	26Ju02Ac
LEARY, Thos.		20	M	Mechanic	26Ju02Ac
CONNELLY, J.		40	M	Mechanic	26Ju02Ac
HILL, Hannah		20	F	None	26Ju02Ac
SPENCER, Jno.		40	M	Mechanic	26Ju02Ac
BARKER, P.		26	M	Laborer	26Ju02Ac
WHALEY, P.		24	M	Laborer	26Ju02Ac
WILSON, Jno.		25	M	Laborer	26Ju02Ac
CROWTHERS, Elizth.		21	F	None	26Ju02Ac
James		20	M	Laborer	26Ju02Ac
FOX, Pat		30	M	Laborer	26Ju02Ac
Ann	(W)	25	F	None	26Ju02Ac
Jno.	(S)	09	M	Child	26Ju02Ac
Ann	(D)	06	F	Child	26Ju02Ac
Cath.	(D)	05	F	Child	26Ju02Ac
SHEA, Elizth.		20	F	None	26Ju02Ac
MALONEY, Jno.		35	M	Laborer	26Ju02Ac
FERHAN, Jno.		35	M	Laborer	26Ju02Ac
BOYLE, Mary		25	F	None	26Ju02Ac
CARAN, Jas.		26	M	Mechanic	26Ju02Ac
Michl.		29	M	Mechanic	26Ju02Ac
Mary-Ann		23	F	None	26Ju02Ac
RAFFERTY, Mary-Ann		13	F	None	26Ju02Ac
KANE, Ann		30	F	None	26Ju02Ac
Essy		27	F	None	26Ju02Ac
OBRIEN, D.		23	M	Laborer	26Ju02Ac
CAMPION, Pat		30	M	Farmer	26Ju02Ac
KANE, Mich.		40	M	Farmer	26Ju02Ac
MCGOONAN, T.		17	F	Servant	26Ju02Ac
MCCARTIN, Jno.		35	M	Laborer	26Ju02Ac
Michl.		22	M	Laborer	26Ju02Ac
Bridget		18	F	None	26Ju02Ac
CORCORAN, Thos.		19	M	Laborer	26Ju02Ac
HAMMELL, O.		30	M	Mechanic	26Ju02Ac
GALSHAND, J.		24	M	Laborer	26Ju02Ac
HICKEES, P.		24	M	Laborer	26Ju02Ac
GALSHAND, Bridget		19	F	None	26Ju02Ac
NOWLAN, P.		27	M	Laborer	26Ju02Ac
BRYAN, S.		20	M	Laborer	26Ju02Ac
BRADY, Susan		28	F	None	26Ju02Ac
GAUGHRAN, Bridget		18	F	None	26Ju02Ac
FINNEGAN, Jas.		.10	M	Infant	26Ju02Ac
WARD, Jno.		25	M	Laborer	26Ju02Ac
GARTLAND, P.		44	M	Laborer	26Ju02Ac
KERLIM, Mary		20	F	None	26Ju02Ac
FARRELLY, Pat		36	M	Laborer	26Ju02Ac
Mary		35	F	None	26Ju02Ac
Wm.		20	M	Laborer	26Ju02Ac
Magt.		18	F	None	26Ju02Ac

NAMES OF PASSENGERS		AGE	SEX	OCCUPATIONS	DATE PORT SHIP
FITZSIMMONS, Wm.		22	M	Laborer	26Ju02Ac
Thos.		25	M	Laborer	26Ju02Ac
Ann		24	F	None	26Ju02Ac
FOX, James		25	M	Laborer	26Ju02Ac
BRADY, Ann		20	F	None	26Ju02Ac
DANPHY, Hy.		26	M	Laborer	26Ju02Ac
Edwd.		23	M	Laborer	26Ju02Ac
Judy		25	F	None	26Ju02Ac
Pat		13	M	Unknown	26Ju02Ac
Jno.		02	M	Child	26Ju02Ac
Mary		.04	F	Infant	26Ju02Ac
MASS, A.		28	M	Mechanic	26Ju02Ac
BUDROITT, Sarah		24	F	None	26Ju02Ac
BANNAR, F.		23	M	Farmer	26Ju02Ac
HATCHLINE, F.		23	M	Tailor	26Ju02Ac
Marianna		22	F	None	26Ju02Ac
CURLY, Jno.		27	M	Laborer	26Ju02Ac
CABY, Thos.		45	M	Laborer	26Ju02Ac
FLANNAGAN, F.		16	M	Laborer	26Ju02Ac
Mary		14	F	None	26Ju02Ac
FOSTER, Caroline		32	F	None	26Ju02Ac
Anna	(D)	08	F	Child	26Ju02Ac
Emma	(D)	05	F	Child	26Ju02Ac
Betty	(D)	03	F	Child	26Ju02Ac
FOX, James		40	M	Laborer	26Ju02Ac
Betty	(W)	30	F	None	26Ju02Ac
Ellen	(D)	13	F	None	26Ju02Ac
Ann	(D)	11	F	None	26Ju02Ac
James	(S)	09	M	Child	26Ju02Ac
John	(S)	05	M	Child	26Ju02Ac
KELLY, Mary		02	F	Child	26Ju02Ac
CORMICK, Pat		25	M	Laborer	26Ju02Ac
Jas.		20	M	Laborer	26Ju02Ac
Michl.		26	M	Laborer	26Ju02Ac
FOX, Thos.		16	M	Laborer	26Ju02Ac
REARDEN, Jno.		25	M	Mechanic	26Ju02Ac
MAHEN, Danl.		30	M	Laborer	26Ju02Ac
FREEMAN, Elizth.		19	F	None	26Ju02Ac
CAHAL, Mgrt.		50	F	None	26Ju02Ac
Ann	(D)	20	F	None	26Ju02Ac
Mary	(D)	22	F	None	26Ju02Ac
John	(S)	25	M	Laborer	26Ju02Ac
Thomas	(S)	17	M	Laborer	26Ju02Ac
Phil	(S)	16	M	Laborer	26Ju02Ac
Richd.	(S)	08	M	Child	26Ju02Ac
ORMAND, Pat		28	M	Laborer	26Ju02Ac
Bridget		24	F	None	26Ju02Ac
TUVAN, Fred		25	M	Laborer	26Ju02Ac
KENNEY, Mary		30	F	None	26Ju02Ac
Bridget	(D)	12	F	None	26Ju02Ac
KELLY, Mary		20	F	None	26Ju02Ac
KEELAN, P.		22	M	Laborer	26Ju02Ac
Michl.	(B)	18	M	Laborer	26Ju02Ac
Michl.	(P)	40	M	Laborer	26Ju02Ac
Mary	(T)	17	F	None	26Ju02Ac
Bernard	(B)	12	M	Unknown	26Ju02Ac
CONNER, Jas.		22	M	Laborer	26Ju02Ac
U-Mrs.	(M)	40	F	None	26Ju02Ac
CARROL, Peter		20	M	Laborer	26Ju02Ac
MCBRIDE, Ellen		20	F	None	26Ju02Ac
SMITH, Sarah		25	F	None	26Ju02Ac
RUTHERFORD, Eliza		22	F	None	26Ju02Ac
CONNELL, N.		18	M	Laborer	26Ju02Ac
MCNULTY, Jno.		47	M	Laborer	26Ju02Ac
BURNS, Hannah		21	F	None	26Ju02Ac
GITTINGS, Conor		41	M	Laborer	26Ju02Ac
MCGRATH, Margt.		20	F	None	26Ju02Ac
FOX, Mrgt.		21	F	None	26Ju02Ac
HERNY, Robt.		60	M	Laborer	26Ju02Ac
SIMPSON, Jno.		31	M	Mechanic	26Ju02Ac
Harriet	(W)	30	F	None	26Ju02Ac
Sophia	(D)	12	F	None	26Ju02Ac
WALSH, Pat		18	M	Laborer	26Ju02Ac
LEERY, Esther		18	F	None	26Ju02Ac
KELLY, Jno.		20	M	Laborer	26Ju02Ac

NAMES OF PASSENGERS		AGE	SEX	OCCUPATIONS	DATE PORT SHIP
CORCORAN, Pat		20	M	Laborer	26Ju02Ac
KIEFE, Jno.		28	M	Laborer	26Ju02Ac
WELSH, Allc		30	M	Laborer	26Ju02Ac
LATHRAND, Jermiah		23	M	Laborer	26Ju02Ac
KELLY, Anna		20	F	None	26Ju02Ac
LINDSEY, Ann		18	F	None	26Ju02Ac
Jas.		18	M	Laborer	26Ju02Ac
HART, B.		36	M	Laborer	26Ju02Ac
SHEA, Jno.		26	M	Laborer	26Ju02Ac
DEVINE, Julia		20	F	None	26Ju02Ac
MCQUILLAN, Jas.		20	M	Laborer	26Ju02Ac
OCONNER, Chas.		16	M	Laborer	26Ju02Ac
OBRIEN, Ellen		18	F	None	26Ju02Ac
Mary		15	F	None	26Ju02Ac
RYAN, Cath.		20	F	None	26Ju02Ac
BRADLEY, D.		60	M	Laborer	26Ju02Ac
Mary	(D)	21	F	None	26Ju02Ac
DIXON, Wm.		30	M	Laborer	26Ju02Ac
U	(W)	30	F	Wife	26Ju02Ac
Jno.	(S)	11	M	Unknown	26Ju02Ac
Mary	(D)	09	F	Child	26Ju02Ac
Sarah	(D)	06	F	Child	26Ju02Ac
E.Jane	(D)	03	F	Child	26Ju02Ac
SCULLY, James		21	M	Laborer	26Ju02Ac
DUNN, Jno.		23	M	Laborer	26Ju02Ac
CAREY, Jno.		10	M	Unknown	26Ju02Ac
COURY, Cath.		18	F	None	26Ju02Ac
KANE, Michl.		18	M	Laborer	26Ju02Ac
GANON, Thos.		17	M	Laborer	26Ju02Ac
NEAGLE, Ann		20	F	None	26Ju02Ac
Jno.		07	M	Child	26Ju02Ac
Laurence		04	M	Child	26Ju02Ac
HOPKINS, Thos.		29	M	Laborer	26Ju02Ac
MCDONOUGH, Mary		22	F	None	26Ju02Ac
DERRSIGAN, U		27	M	Laborer	26Ju02Ac
HUGHES, Jno.		35	M	Laborer	26Ju02Ac
MALLOW, Mary		19	F	None	26Ju02Ac
CARROLL, Michl.		38	M	Farmer	26Ju02Ac
BROPHY, Wm.		40	M	Farmer	26Ju02Ac
BALLEY, Jno.		22	M	Farmer	26Ju02Ac
JANDON, Jas.		20	M	Farmer	26Ju02Ac
LYNCH, Susan		20	F	None	26Ju02Ac
MCGAL, Bridget		20	F	None	26Ju02Ac
REILY, Ellen		03	F	Child	26Ju02Ac
RUDDY, Edwd.		25	M	Mechanic	26Ju02Ac
OHARA, Jno.		20	M	Mechanic	26Ju02Ac
Oliva		11	F	None	26Ju02Ac
GRADY, Magt.		23	F	None	26Ju02Ac
DONELLY, Ann		27	F	None	26Ju02Ac
CARNY, Barbara		50	F	None	26Ju02Ac
MCGRATH, Mgt.		25	F	None	26Ju02Ac
CORRIGAN, Eliza		20	F	None	26Ju02Ac
LAWLER, Thos.		19	M	Laborer	26Ju02Ac
FINNIGAN, Step.		30	M	Laborer	26Ju02Ac
Bridget		28	F	None	26Ju02Ac
MURPHY, Wm.		20	M	Laborer	26Ju02Ac
MCDOWELL, Ann		17	F	None	26Ju02Ac
MCGOWAN, Ellen		17	F	None	26Ju02Ac
NOONAN, Ellen		30	F	None	26Ju02Ac
MCGEE, Bryan		28	M	Laborer	26Ju02Ac
MCALLANY, Mary		20	F	None	26Ju02Ac
MCCABE, E.		20	F	None	26Ju02Ac
READY, Michl.		22	M	Laborer	26Ju02Ac
Rose		18	F	None	26Ju02Ac
MCGARRTY, Jno.		26	M	Laborer	26Ju02Ac
Bridget		20	F	None	26Ju02Ac
KERNEY, Michl.		45	M	Mechanic	26Ju02Ac
Mary	(W)	40	F	None	26Ju02Ac
Wm.	(S)	12	M	None	26Ju02Ac
Pat	(S)	10	M	None	26Ju02Ac
Michl.	(S)	06	M	Child	26Ju02Ac
Jno.	(S)	02	M	Child	26Ju02Ac
OCONNER, Wm.		60	M	Farmer	26Ju02Ac
LOUGHLAN, Ch.		28	M	Farmer	26Ju02Ac
Mary		20	F	None	26Ju02Ac

UNCAS 28 JUNE 1847

From Liverpool

.

NAMES OF PASSENGERS		AGE	SEX	OCCUPATIONS	DATE PORT SHIP
ROBINSON, E.		32	M	Farmer	28Ju02Ng
J.	(D)	15	F	None	28Ju02Ng
U	(D)	11	F	None	28Ju02Ng
HARRISON, A.		36	F	None	28Ju02Ng
A.	(D)	04	F	Child	28Ju02Ng
G.		00	M	Unknown	28Ju02Ng
JARROT, J.		20	M	Unknown	28Ju02Ng
SHALER, S.		22	M	Unknown	28Ju02Ng
MILLER, J.		22	M	Unknown	28Ju02Ng
RILLER, G.		27	M	Unknown	28Ju02Ng
B.		30	F	None	28Ju02Ng
PAINE, F.		30	F	None	28Ju02Ng
NARISS, J.		45	M	Farmer	28Ju02Ng
E.	(W)	42	F	None	28Ju02Ng
W.	(S)	08	M	Child	28Ju02Ng
M.	(D)	06	F	Child	28Ju02Ng
J.	(S)	03	M	Child	28Ju02Ng

PAOLI 28 JUNE 1847

From Liverpool

NAMES OF PASSENGERS		AGE	SEX	OCCUPATIONS	DATE PORT SHIP
WINCHESTER, James		44	M	Laborer	28Ju02Nh
Mary	(D)	23	F	None	28Ju02Nh
Sarah	(D)	20	F	None	28Ju02Nh
GOOGAN, Mary		16	F	None	28Ju02Nh
OWEN, Eleanor		30	F	None	28Ju02Nh
William	(S)	10	M	Laborer	28Ju02Nh
John	(S)	07	M	Child	28Ju02Nh
Owen	(S)	05	M	Child	28Ju02Nh
David	(S)	03	M	Child	28Ju02Nh
WARD, James		.00	M	Infant	28Ju02Nh
MOSHAM, Joseph		45	M	Laborer	28Ju02Nh
Zachariah	(S)	11	M	Laborer	28Ju02Nh
George	(S)	10	M	Laborer	28Ju02Nh
NEWPORT, Eliza		30	F	None	28Ju02Nh
WILLIAMS, Charles		12	M	Laborer	28Ju02Nh
Elizabeth		05	F	Child	28Ju02Nh
FOOLE, Jacob		21	M	Laborer	28Ju02Nh
SMITH, Henry		24	M	Laborer	28Ju02Nh
MEYER, Hugh		50	M	Laborer	28Ju02Nh
Margaret	(D)	09	F	Child	28Ju02Nh
JEVIN, William		60	M	Laborer	28Ju02Nh
Jane	(D)	20	F	None	28Ju02Nh
SULLIVAN, James		26	M	Laborer	28Ju02Nh
BOURNE, John		22	M	Laborer	28Ju02Nh
RALPH, William		24	M	Laborer	28Ju02Nh
U	(W)	22	F	Wife	28Ju02Nh
Thomas		21	M	Laborer	28Ju02Nh
James		25	M	Laborer	28Ju02Nh
BLANEY, George		40	M	Laborer	28Ju02Nh
TIERNEY, Michael		24	M	Laborer	28Ju02Nh
Mary		16	F	None	28Ju02Nh
CALAHAN, Platt		21	M	Laborer	28Ju02Nh
Sarah		18	F	None	28Ju02Nh
RYEN, Nath.		21	M	Laborer	28Ju02Nh
BELL, John		36	M	Laborer	28Ju02Nh
GUWA, Sally		17	F	None	28Ju02Nh
NICHOLS, Joseph		22	M	Laborer	28Ju02Nh

NAMES OF PASSENGERS		AGE	SEX	OCCUPATIONS	DATE PORT SHIP
NICHOLS, Nath.		19	M	Laborer	28Ju02Nh
RICHARDSON, William		24	M	Laborer	28Ju02Nh
SCHWEREN, Wm.		25	M	Laborer	28Ju02Nh
WALSH, Betty		16	F	None	28Ju02Nh
MCCORMICK, Johnson		21	M	Laborer	28Ju02Nh
HALEY, James		21	M	Laborer	28Ju02Nh
TRAVIS, James		50	M	Laborer	28Ju02Nh
Joseph	(S)	18	M	Laborer	28Ju02Nh
John	(S)	20	M	Laborer	28Ju02Nh
George	(S)	17	M	Laborer	28Ju02Nh
DALIPPE, Thomas		28	M	Laborer	28Ju02Nh
Thu.		26	M	Laborer	28Ju02Nh
Leven		22	M	Laborer	28Ju02Nh
GUSTLAR, J.		24	M	Laborer	28Ju02Nh
COTTNELL, Peter		23	M	Laborer	28Ju02Nh
MCNAMEE, John		22	M	Laborer	28Ju02Nh
SMITH, Margaret		45	F	None	28Ju02Nh
DURNIN, Thomas		60	M	Laborer	28Ju02Nh
John	(S)	30	M	Laborer	28Ju02Nh
James	(S)	22	M	Laborer	28Ju02Nh
Daniel	(S)	17	M	Laborer	28Ju02Nh
James	(S)	19	M	Laborer	28Ju02Nh
Mary	(D)	20	F	None	28Ju02Nh
KERLAN, Thomas		60	M	Laborer	28Ju02Nh
Margaret	(W)	60	F	None	28Ju02Nh
Benjamin	(S)	26	M	Laborer	28Ju02Nh
Merhlen	(S)	17	M	Laborer	28Ju02Nh
MURPHY, Patt		20	M	Laborer	28Ju02Nh
MURRAY, Ann		60	F	None	28Ju02Nh
DUNNE, John		04	M	Child	28Ju02Nh
HANATTY, Peter		19	M	Laborer	28Ju02Nh
MINIHAN, Bridget		26	F	None	28Ju02Nh
SMITH, Ann		16	F	None	28Ju02Nh
AVORY, Michael		18	M	Laborer	28Ju02Nh
Jane		20	F	None	28Ju02Nh
Margaret		18	F	None	28Ju02Nh
LANGTHORN, Francis		22	M	Laborer	28Ju02Nh
MCAVORY, U-Mrs.		23	F	None	28Ju02Nh
TWOHEY, Here.		50	M	Laborer	28Ju02Nh
John	(S)	23	M	Laborer	28Ju02Nh
Ann	(D)	24	F	None	28Ju02Nh
MCDERMOTT, Ann		28	F	None	28Ju02Nh
FIX, Sarah		45	F	None	28Ju02Nh
Eliza	(D)	18	F	None	28Ju02Nh
Sarah	(D)	16	F	None	28Ju02Nh
WILKINSON, W.		21	M	Laborer	28Ju02Nh
KENNY, Jacob		24	M	Laborer	28Ju02Nh
Maria	(W)	22	F	None	28Ju02Nh
U	(D)	06	F	Child	28Ju02Nh
John	(S)	01	M	Child	28Ju02Nh
FINLEY, Johanna		22	F	None	28Ju02Nh
Michael		24	M	Laborer	28Ju02Nh
HUGHES, James		21	M	Laborer	28Ju02Nh
MADHEES, Ann		40	F	None	28Ju02Nh
Ann	(D)	16	F	None	28Ju02Nh
WRIGHT, Robert		22	M	Laborer	28Ju02Nh
John		24	M	Laborer	28Ju02Nh
Ann		26	F	None	28Ju02Nh
REYNOLDS, John		15	M	Laborer	28Ju02Nh
BROWN, James		30	M	Laborer	28Ju02Nh
MULLIN, Edward		20	M	Laborer	28Ju02Nh
DIXON, James		20	M	Laborer	28Ju02Nh
Jane		20	F	None	28Ju02Nh
BURKE, Mary		.00	F	Infant	28Ju02Nh
MACKIN, Bridget		20	F	None	28Ju02Nh
BROWN, George		16	M	Laborer	28Ju02Nh
OWEN, Eleanor		30	F	None	28Ju02Nh
Wm.	(S)	10	M	Laborer	28Ju02Nh
John	(S)	07	M	Child	28Ju02Nh
Owen	(S)	05	M	Child	28Ju02Nh
David	(S)	03	M	Child	28Ju02Nh

PRINCE-DE-JOINVILLE 28 JUNE 1847

From Belfast

NAMES OF PASSENGERS		AGE	SEX	OCCUPATIONS	DATE PORT SHIP
MARRS, John		26	M	Mechanic	28Ju07NI
C.	(W)	25	F	None	28Ju07NI
B.	(S)	03	M	Child	28Ju07NI
M.	(D)	01	F	Child	28Ju07NI
BROWN, F.		18	F	None	28Ju07NI
MCTURK, J.		56	M	Farmer	28Ju07NI
S.	(S)	19	M	Farmer	28Ju07NI
J.	(D)	16	F	None	28Ju07NI
DENSMORE, H.		22	F	None	28Ju07NI
MOFFAT, J.		30	M	Farmer	28Ju07NI
M.	(W)	29	F	None	28Ju07NI
P.J.	(D)	06	F	Child	28Ju07NI
S.	(S)	.10	M	Infant	28Ju07NI
WHILLA, E.		22	F	None	28Ju07NI
RUMSEY, N.		70	F	None	28Ju07NI
W.		26	M	Mechanic	28Ju07NI
N.	(D)	40	F	None	28Ju07NI
H.		19	M	Mechanic	28Ju07NI
E.		14	F	None	28Ju07NI
N.M.		04	F	Child	28Ju07NI
R.		29	M	Mechanic	28Ju07NI
DARRAGH, S.		25	M	Mechanic	28Ju07NI
E.	(S)	07	M	Child	28Ju07NI
S.	(S)	02	M	Child	28Ju07NI
E.	(D)	05	F	Child	28Ju07NI
ABRAHAM, W.		22	M	Mechanic	28Ju07NI
F.		19	F	None	28Ju07NI
MCKENNA, E.		40	M	Mechanic	28Ju07NI
MCBRIDE, M.		50	F	None	28Ju07NI
M.	(D)	25	F	None	28Ju07NI
MURPHY, J.		17	M	Clerk	28Ju07NI
KIRK, J.		30	M	Mechanic	28Ju07NI
M.	(W)	29	F	None	28Ju07NI
J.	(D)	12	F	None	28Ju07NI
R.	(D)	.10	F	Infant	28Ju07NI
M.	(D)	09	F	Child	28Ju07NI
J.	(S)	06	M	Child	28Ju07NI
R.	(S)	02	M	Child	28Ju07NI
MURPHY, J.		54	M	Farmer	28Ju07NI
B.	(S)	17	M	Farmer	28Ju07NI
E.	(D)	19	F	Farmer	28Ju07NI
John	(S)	13	F	Farmer	28Ju07NI
W.	(S)	15	F	Farmer	28Ju07NI
CONELLY, T.		18	F	Farmer	28Ju07NI
BURNSS, J.		50	F	Farmer	28Ju07NI
C.	(W)	45	F	None	28Ju07NI
P.	(S)	18	M	Farmer	28Ju07NI
J.	(S)	13	M	Farmer	28Ju07NI
R.	(S)	11	M	Farmer	28Ju07NI
C.	(D)	06	F	Child	28Ju07NI
C.	(D)	.10	F	Infant	28Ju07NI
DONAN, J.		42	M	Mechanic	28Ju07NI
BROWN, P.		23	M	Mechanic	28Ju07NI
BRANIFF, W.		22	M	Mechanic	28Ju07NI
ALLEN, T.		75	M	Farmer	28Ju07NI
M.	(W)	63	F	None	28Ju07NI
T.	(S)	37	M	Farmer	28Ju07NI
M.	(L)	39	F	None	28Ju07NI
S.		06	M	Child	28Ju07NI
M.	(D)	04	F	Child	28Ju07NI
N.	(D)	.10	F	Infant	28Ju07NI
GILMORE, E.		40	M	Farmer	28Ju07NI
M.	(W)	46	F	None	28Ju07NI
J.	(D)	12	F	None	28Ju07NI
C.	(D)	10	F	None	28Ju07NI

NAMES OF PASSENGERS		AGE	SEX	OCCUPATIONS	DATE PORT SHIP	NAMES OF PASSENGERS		AGE	SEX	OCCUPATIONS	DATE PORT SHIP
GILMORE, B.	(D)	06	F	Child	28Ju07NI	WILSON, R.		21	M	Farmer	28Ju07NI
HAMILTON, D.		27	M	Farmer	28Ju07NI	MARON, W.		44	M	Farmer	28Ju07NI
MARION, J.		64	M	Farmer	28Ju07NI	GRIBBEN, J.		40	M	Farmer	28Ju07NI
AULD, W.		26	M	Farmer	28Ju07NI	C.	(W)	45	F	None	28Ju07NI
DIXON, J.		25	M	Farmer	28Ju07NI	T.	(S)	28	M	Farmer	28Ju07NI
JONES, M.		35	F	None	28Ju07NI	SMITH, R.		48	M	Mechanic	28Ju07NI
MCNIEL, E.		21	F	None	28Ju07NI	MCDONALD, F.		45	M	Mechanic	28Ju07NI
COWAN, J.		54	M	Farmer	28Ju07NI	BELL, W.		28	M	Mechanic	28Ju07NI
M.	(W)	55	F	None	28Ju07NI	A.		25	M	Mechanic	28Ju07NI
J.A.	(S)	20	M	Farmer	28Ju07NI	J.		19	F	None	28Ju07NI
J.	(D)	13	F	None	28Ju07NI	WILSON, J.		21	M	Mechanic	28Ju07NI
MCILROY, W.		30	M	Mechanic	28Ju07NI	BRADLEY, P.		20	M	Farmer	28Ju07NI
S.		36	F	None	28Ju07NI	ADAMS, J.		50	M	Farmer	28Ju07NI
CAMPBELL, R.		23	M	Farmer	28Ju07NI	J.	(W)	50	F	None	28Ju07NI
E.		24	F	None	28Ju07NI	M.J.	(D)	20	F	None	28Ju07NI
J.		16	F	None	28Ju07NI	C.	(D)	17	F	None	28Ju07NI
GAINTLE, Moses		50	M	Mechanic	28Ju07NI	J.	(S)	16	M	Farmer	28Ju07NI
J.	(W)	40	F	None	28Ju07NI	J.	(S)	13	M	None	28Ju07NI
L.	(D)	12	F	None	28Ju07NI	A.	(S)	12	M	None	28Ju07NI
E.	(D)	13	F	None	28Ju07NI	W.	(S)	10	M	None	28Ju07NI
BOYD, G.		40	M	Mechanic	28Ju07NI	WALKER, M.		22	F	None	28Ju07NI
E.	(W)	40	F	None	28Ju07NI	SIMPSON, J.		20	M	Mechanic	28Ju07NI
J.	(S)	20	M	Mechanic	28Ju07NI	BURNS, B.		20	M	Clerk	28Ju07NI
J.	(D)	17	F	None	28Ju07NI	HARVEY, A.		21	M	Farmer	28Ju07NI
MCIVOR, E.		24	M	Mechanic	28Ju07NI	WELSH, J.		22	M	Farmer	28Ju07NI
L.		29	F	None	28Ju07NI	HENRY, Edw.		22	M	Farmer	28Ju07NI
RONEY, J.		20	M	Mechanic	28Ju07NI	TRAINOR, M.		18	M	Farmer	28Ju07NI
MCILMEAL, D.		34	M	Farmer	28Ju07NI	MCGOWAN, J.		22	M	Laborer	28Ju07NI
M.	(W)	36	F	None	28Ju07NI	HALLIDAY, T.		23	M	Laborer	28Ju07NI
D.	(S)	04	M	Child	28Ju07NI	M.J.		16	F	None	28Ju07NI
E.		32	F	None	28Ju07NI	R.		14	F	None	28Ju07NI
M.		01	F	Child	28Ju07NI	A.		11	F	None	28Ju07NI
HILL, R.		60	M	Farmer	28Ju07NI	B.		09	F	Child	28Ju07NI
J.	(W)	57	F	None	28Ju07NI	GORDEN, C.		19	F	None	28Ju07NI
R.	(S)	21	M	Farmer	28Ju07NI	MCGEE, M.		18	F	None	28Ju07NI
J.	(D)	19	F	None	28Ju07NI	MEEHAN, J.		22	M	Farmer	28Ju07NI
E.	(D)	17	F	None	28Ju07NI	M.M.		25	F	None	28Ju07NI
S.	(D)	13	F	None	28Ju07NI	PITTS, D.		20	M	Farmer	28Ju07NI
J.	(S)	12	M	None	28Ju07NI	MUNHOLLAND, P.		14	M	Farmer	28Ju07NI
A.	(D)	09	F	Child	28Ju07NI	ARMSTRONG, W.		46	M	Mechanic	28Ju07NI
F.	(D)	06	F	Child	28Ju07NI	E.	(D)	19	F	None	28Ju07NI
COULTER, E.		22	F	None	28Ju07NI	M.E.	(D)	16	F	None	28Ju07NI
E.		24	F	None	28Ju07NI	J.	(D)	13	F	None	28Ju07NI
CURSON, J.		25	M	Laborer	28Ju07NI	ROGERS, A.		18	F	None	28Ju07NI
STOWELL, E.		22	F	None	28Ju07NI	GIBSON, F.		23	M	Farmer	28Ju07NI
HILL, J.		32	M	Mechanic	28Ju07NI	CARRIGAN, E.		33	M	Farmer	28Ju07NI
M.	(W)	26	F	None	28Ju07NI	GANLEY, E.		32	F	None	28Ju07NI
R.	(S)	06	M	Child	28Ju07NI	E.	(D)	03	F	Child	28Ju07NI
M.J.	(D)	02	F	Child	28Ju07NI	NIEL, J.C.		18	M	Farmer	28Ju07NI
J.	(S)	.06	M	Infant	28Ju07NI	GROGAN, P.		22	M	Farmer	28Ju07NI
HANNA, M.		28	F	None	28Ju07NI	MCCAN, J.		22	F	None	28Ju07NI
E.		26	F	None	28Ju07NI	MCCULLOUGH, J.		30	M	Farmer	28Ju07NI
A.		20	F	None	28Ju07NI	MOORE, J.		30	M	Farmer	28Ju07NI
MAXWELL, J.		27	M	Farmer	28Ju07NI	MCGERKIN, H.		37	M	Farmer	28Ju07NI
E.	(W)	22	F	None	28Ju07NI	M.	(W)	35	F	None	28Ju07NI
E.	(D)	03	F	Child	28Ju07NI	J.H.	(S)	15	M	Farmer	28Ju07NI
J.		13	M	Farmer	28Ju07NI	REID, M.		17	F	None	28Ju07NI
S.	(D)	01	F	Child	28Ju07NI	CUNNINGHAM, W.		19	M	Farmer	28Ju07NI
WINCHESTER, J.		48	M	Farmer	28Ju07NI	LYNAS, J.		18	M	Clerk	28Ju07NI
M.	(W)	48	F	None	28Ju07NI	TENER, W.		22	M	Clerk	28Ju07NI
J.	(D)	24	F	None	28Ju07NI	MATTHERS, J.		29	M	Farmer	28Ju07NI
J.	(D)	21	F	None	28Ju07NI						
W.	(S)	16	M	Farmer	28Ju07NI						
S.	(D)	13	M	None	28Ju07NI						
R.	(S)	12	M	None	28Ju07NI						
WILSON, S.		25	M	Mechanic	28Ju07NI						
SOUTEE, D.		34	M	Mechanic	28Ju07NI	EARL-DUNHAM 30 JUNE 1847					
MCCARRA, E.B.		20	F	None	28Ju07NI						
M.J.		18	F	None	28Ju07NI	From Liverpool					
VERNOY, A.		18	F	None	28Ju07NI						
MCHENNEY, M.		18	F	None	28Ju07NI						
SMITH, A.		28	F	None	28Ju07NI						
HUGHES, B.		26	F	None	28Ju07NI	BANK, Ed.		25	M	Farmer	30Ju02NJ
SHERLOCK, J.		28	M	Mechanic	28Ju07NI	Cath.		20	F	None	30Ju02NJ
MILLER, A.		24	M	Mechanic	28Ju07NI	Honora		20	F	None	30Ju02NJ

NAMES OF PASSENGERS		AGE	SEX	OCCUPATIONS	DATE PORT SHIP
MCDONNELL, C.		21	M	Farmer	30Ju02NJ
Cath.		16	F	None	30Ju02NJ
WELSH, Pat.		25	M	Farmer	30Ju02NJ
TOBIAS, John		28	M	Farmer	30Ju02NJ
REDMOND, John		25	M	Farmer	30Ju02NJ
DOUGHERTY, Pat		18	M	Farmer	30Ju02NJ
MCPHERNY, John		27	M	Farmer	30Ju02NJ
MCCALLEY, Mary		.00	F	Infant	30Ju02NJ
M.J.	(M)	25	F	None	30Ju02NJ
CALLAHAN, Hannah		20	F	None	30Ju02NJ
DOOLINS, Mary		25	F	None	30Ju02NJ
Jane		30	F	None	30Ju02NJ
Patk.		12	M	None	30Ju02NJ
RASSAN, James		24	M	Farmer	30Ju02NJ
Mary		22	F	None	30Ju02NJ
MARTIN, Jane		20	F	None	30Ju02NJ
MCCORNEBY, Mary		17	F	None	30Ju02NJ
WILDAN, Wm.		25	M	Farmer	30Ju02NJ
GRUZE, T.W.		25	M	Farmer	30Ju02NJ
U	(W)	25	F	Wife	30Ju02NJ
BRUMLEY, Wm.		30	M	Farmer	30Ju02NJ
HONEY, Winney		20	M	Farmer	30Ju02NJ
HALLEHAN, Dan		24	M	Farmer	30Ju02NJ
MOHLES, Pat		35	M	Farmer	30Ju02NJ
KENBEHAN, Jas.		30	M	Farmer	30Ju02NJ
COSNELL, Jas.		20	M	Farmer	30Ju02NJ
KILMARTIN, John		20	M	Farmer	30Ju02NJ
FLAHILLY, Bryan		36	M	Farmer	30Ju02NJ
FARNEY, Dan		30	M	Farmer	30Ju02NJ
U	(W)	25	F	Wife	30Ju02NJ
Baillie	(S)	.00	M	Infant	30Ju02NJ
Mary	(D)	02	F	Child	30Ju02NJ
HYNES, Timothy		28	M	Farmer	30Ju02NJ
Mary		26	F	None	30Ju02NJ
Margaret		24	F	None	30Ju02NJ
COLEMAN, Johana		25	F	None	30Ju02NJ
BARNES, John		28	M	Farmer	30Ju02NJ
Dorah	(W)	30	F	None	30Ju02NJ
Patrick	(S)	06	M	Child	30Ju02NJ
MCCALLEY, Bessey		25	F	None	30Ju02NJ
John	(S)	03	M	Child	30Ju02NJ
Pat	(H)	21	M	Farmer	30Ju02NJ
BAILE, Mary		15	F	None	30Ju02NJ
BYRNE, Arthur		20	M	Farmer	30Ju02NJ
CORMAN, Cathe.		50	F	None	30Ju02NJ
Allice	(D)	19	F	None	30Ju02NJ
Thos.	(S)	18	M	Farmer	30Ju02NJ
Ellen	(D)	12	F	None	30Ju02NJ
MAKES, John		48	M	Farmer	30Ju02NJ
Mary	(W)	50	F	None	30Ju02NJ
Judith	(D)	12	F	None	30Ju02NJ
BURKE, Wm.		27	M	Farmer	30Ju02NJ
Margt.		25	F	None	30Ju02NJ
John		24	M	Farmer	30Ju02NJ
Cathe.		21	F	None	30Ju02NJ
Michl.		.00	M	Infant	30Ju02NJ
MITCHEL, James		30	M	Farmer	30Ju02NJ
Margt.	(W)	24	F	None	30Ju02NJ
John	(S)	05	M	Child	30Ju02NJ
Eliza	(D)	.00	F	Infant	30Ju02NJ
SENEGLETS, Mary		26	F	None	30Ju02NJ
Bessey		25	F	None	30Ju02NJ
HARNEY, Joseph		28	M	Farmer	30Ju02NJ
Margt.		28	F	None	30Ju02NJ
BURLEY, Richd.		32	M	Farmer	30Ju02NJ
BROWN, Mary		40	F	None	30Ju02NJ
RYAN, James		28	M	Farmer	30Ju02NJ
DEVENISE, Johana		23	F	None	30Ju02NJ
FELLAN, Michael		25	M	Farmer	30Ju02NJ
Ambry.		20	M	Farmer	30Ju02NJ
MALONE, John		36	M	Farmer	30Ju02NJ
Eliza	(W)	30	F	None	30Ju02NJ
Mary	(D)	03	F	Child	30Ju02NJ
John	(S)	.00	M	Infant	30Ju02NJ
James	(S)	.00	M	Infant	30Ju02NJ
MALONE, Thos.		27	M	Farmer	30Ju02NJ
Ann		20	F	None	30Ju02NJ
DAWELL, Thos.		37	M	Farmer	30Ju02NJ
Janie		31	F	None	30Ju02NJ
BULLIONS, Evan		22	F	None	30Ju02NJ
Sally	(M)	50	F	None	30Ju02NJ
John	(B)	11	M	None	30Ju02NJ
FLYNN, Margt.		24	F	None	30Ju02NJ
ROBINSON, Mary		20	F	None	30Ju02NJ
GUNNANS, Thos.		20	M	Farmer	30Ju02NJ
HILLS, James		50	M	Farmer	30Ju02NJ
CAMONS, James		21	M	Farmer	30Ju02NJ
GRAFFNEY, John		20	M	Farmer	30Ju02NJ
Bridget		19	F	None	30Ju02NJ
FREEMAN, Tobias		40	M	Farmer	30Ju02NJ
Eliza	(D)	13	F	None	30Ju02NJ
Rachel	(D)	16	F	None	30Ju02NJ
Ralf	(S)	07	M	Child	30Ju02NJ
DAILEY, James		26	M	Farmer	30Ju02NJ
REILLY, John		42	M	Farmer	30Ju02NJ
Mary	(W)	35	F	None	30Ju02NJ
Pat	(S)	07	M	Child	30Ju02NJ
Biddy		35	F	None	30Ju02NJ
Mary		07	F	Child	30Ju02NJ
HIST, Geo.		25	M	Farmer	30Ju02NJ
Mary		30	F	None	30Ju02NJ
GRAHAM, Mary		50	F	None	30Ju02NJ
Michl.	(S)	21	M	Farmer	30Ju02NJ
James	(S)	11	M	None	30Ju02NJ
Margt.	(D)	08	F	Child	30Ju02NJ
DRISCOLL, John		60	M	Farmer	30Ju02NJ
Mag.	(W)	50	F	None	30Ju02NJ
Wm.	(S)	17	M	Farmer	30Ju02NJ
Mary	(D)	12	F	None	30Ju02NJ
Julia	(D)	11	F	None	30Ju02NJ
MCCORMICK, John		13	M	Farmer	30Ju02NJ
James		18	M	Farmer	30Ju02NJ
Ann		20	F	None	30Ju02NJ
MARIA, Bridget		16	F	None	30Ju02NJ
CANHY, Ann		17	F	None	30Ju02NJ
JONES, Cathe.		23	F	None	30Ju02NJ
Susan		20	F	None	30Ju02NJ
DORAN, James		20	M	Farmer	30Ju02NJ
CONDON, James		23	M	Farmer	30Ju02NJ
KEYSON, Mgt.		21	F	None	30Ju02NJ
FITZGERALD, John		25	M	Farmer	30Ju02NJ
Bridget		22	F	None	30Ju02NJ
DUFFEY, Pat		22	M	Farmer	30Ju02NJ
Cathe.		20	F	None	30Ju02NJ
POWER, Mich.		21	M	Farmer	30Ju02NJ
SHREES, Chas.		20	M	Farmer	30Ju02NJ
AYESTON, Robt.		24	M	Farmer	30Ju02NJ
EVANS, Magt.		23	F	None	30Ju02NJ
Ann	(D)	04	F	Child	30Ju02NJ
Elizb.	(D)	03	F	Child	30Ju02NJ
Mary	(D)	.00	F	Infant	30Ju02NJ
BANIMS, B.		25	M	Farmer	30Ju02NJ
Eliza		18	F	None	30Ju02NJ
Nancy		29	F	None	30Ju02NJ
CULLEN, James		30	M	Farmer	30Ju02NJ
DEVENALL, Wm.		30	M	Farmer	30Ju02NJ
WARBENSBURY, Nathan		22	M	Farmer	30Ju02NJ
Mary	(D)	04	F	Child	30Ju02NJ
John	(S)	02	M	Child	30Ju02NJ

INDEX

  James 480 , 515
  Jas. 178
  John 250 , 528
  Margaret 207
  Margt. 515
  Martin 182
  Mary 528
  Mich. 532
  Nancy 207
  Sarah-Jane 178
  Susan 234
  Wm.James 207
Mccleanan, Alexander
  311
Mcclear, John 298
  Louisa 490
  M. 490
Mccleary, Ellen 406
  R. 508
Mccleene, Jane 480
  Thomas 480
Mccleer, Bridget 169
  Susanah 169
Mccleerty, Magt. 612
Mccleary, James 504
Mccleland, Jane 96
  Mary 96
  Robert 96
  U-Mrs. 96
Mcclellan, D.G. 498
  G. 427
Mcclelland, James 112
  John 112
  Martha 278
  William 112
Mcclement, Lowey 367
Mcclenachan, James
  278
  Jane 278
  John 278
  Mary 278
  Mathew 278
  Robert 278
Mcclenahen, Mich. 294
Mcclennon, N. 346
Mcclerry, P. 496
Mcclery, Ellen 584
Mccleven, Wm. 476
Mcclinbert, M. 490
Mcclinchey, Michael
  197
Mcclintock, Alexander
  134
  Danl. 134
  James 134
  Jane 134
  Martha 134
  Mary 134
  William 33
Mcclinty, Catherine
  400
  Eloner 400
  Hessy 400
  Hugh 400
  Jane 400
  John 400
Mccloghey, Thos. 60
Mcclolan, Jane 153
Mcclonachan, John 517
Mcclorkey, Auther 161
Mcclorty, Mary 17
  Rose 17
Mccloskey, Cath. 134
  Edwd. 134
  Grace 134
  Hannah 134
  Mary , 134

Mccloskey, Robert 134
Mcclosky, Ann 134
  Nancy 134
  P. 535
Mccloud, Thos. 39
  William 110
Mcclour, Mary 237
Mccloy, Cathe. 439
  Fanny 439
Mcclucker, Catharine
  222
Mcclue, Ann 356
  Bridget 356
  Catharine 356
  James 356
  Jane 356
  Maria 356
  Mary 270
  Thomas 356
Mcclunny, John 480
Mcclure, Agnes 460
  Eliza 601
  Jas. 148
  John 6
  Joseph 148
  Mary 609
Mccluren, Alexander
  199
  Ann 199
  Jas. 199
  Mary 199
  Thomas 199
Mcclury, Robert 43
  Wm. 43
Mccluskey, Biddy 300
  Bridget 62
  Bridgt. 210
  Cathe. 220
  Catherine 184
  Cathn. 194
  Dan 96
  David 184
  Eliza 184
  James 237
  Jane 184 , 211
  Jas. 63
  John 50 , 184
  Margret 229
  Mary 3 , 184
  Pat 205 , 611
  Rosanna 3
Mccluskin, Elisha 611
  J. 611
Mcclusky, Ann 179 ,
  541 , 589
  Anthony 179
  Bridget 187
  Cath. 499
  Cath-Gore. 413
  Cecily 413
  Edward 413
  Elizabeth 541
  Ellen 413
  James 75 , 226 ,
  413
  Jane 375
  John 75
  Jos. 413
  Judith 413
  Maria 413
  Mary 75 , 413 , 499
  541
  Michael 541
  Nancy 75 , 554
  Peter 413
  Rose-Ann 413
  Se---- 541
  Thos. , 358

Mcclusky, U 413
Mccoal, Barnabas 356
Mccoanen, Chas. 125
  Mary 125
Mccocking, Daniel 355
Mccoffin, David 460
  Mary 460
Mccoffry, Francis 308
  William 245
Mccoffy, Margt. 301
Mccolagh, Andrew 29
Mccold, Eliza 615
Mccole, Margt. 505
Mccolgan, Cathe. 143
  D. 605
  Michl. 143
Mccollen, Elizabeth
  161
  Peter 161
Mccollim, Cath. 134
  Chas. 134
Mccollock, Mich. 294
Mccollom, Bridget 54
Mccollonge, Mary 182
  Sally 182
Mccollough, Bernd.
  502
  Jane 300
Mccollum, Arthur 338
  Eliza 338
  J. 338
  Mary 338
  Thomas 363
Mccolchoy, James 607
  U 607
Mccolough, Eliza 539
  Fanny 539
  Irvine 29
  Jane 29
  John 539
  Rebecca 539
Mccomb, Mary-Ann 256
Mccombe, Ellen 566
  John 566
Mccomble, Jno. 129
Mccombs, Hugh 307
  J. 341
Mccome, Ellen 330
Mccommick, Bernard
  331
  John 13
  Margreat 13
Mcconaghey, Isabella
  138
  Wm. 138
Mcconaghy, Anne 134
  Colhoon 229
  Eliza 229
  Jas. 229
  Mathew 229
Mcconahee, Margaret
  62
Mcconaid, John 117
  William 117
Mcconalong, Danl. 533
  Mary 533 , 534
Mcconaly, Mgt. 479
  Rose 479
Mccone, Eliza 23
  Matthew 23
  Pat 270
Mcconel, Betsey 324
  Davd. 324
  Ellen 324
  Luke 323
Mcconell, Agnes 525
  Bgt. 506
  D. , 525

Mcconell, M. 580
  Oliver 120
  Robt. 525
Mcconen, Mgt. 542
  Patt. 542
  T. 542
Mcconer, Rose-Ann 328
Mcconghan, Thos. 127
Mccongly, Ann 194
  James 194
  Mary 194
Mcconkey, W. 498
Mcconley, Ann 368
  Arthur 368
  Dennis 163
  Jno. 163
Mcconly, Ann 342
  C. 500
  Cath. 500
  D. 342
  Magt. 342
  Margt. 103
  Martin 342
  Mary 342
  U 342
Mcconn, F. 339
  J. 508
  Mary 339
  Owen 339
  Sarah 339
  U 339
Mcconnan, Bridget 298
Mcconne, Bridge
  James 460
  Mary 460
  Sarah 460
Mcconnel, Ann 525
  Margret 333
  U-Mrs. 525
  W. 524
Mcconnell, Adam 603
  Agnes 446
  Andrew 173
  Anna 603
  Anne 435
  Bdgt. 347
  Betty 211
  Biddy 379
  Bridget 19 , 61
  Catharine 48
  Cathe. 481 , 504
  Dennis 19
  Eliza 565
  Elizabeth 173
  Francis 615
  Jane 173 , 179
  Jas. 58
  John 58 , 379 , 463
  504
  Luzard 379
  Margaret 19
  Margret 173
  Mary 19 , 179
  Mich 379
  Murty 423
  Patk. 61
  Patt 313
  Randell 138
  Robt. 313
  Sally 379
  Sarah 58
  Susan 61
  Thos. 423
  U 58
  W. 347 , 561
  William 173
  Wm. 61
Mcconner, Bridget

INDEX

Simpson, Jane 181
Jno. 129 , 617
John 234 , 254
Margaret 463
Margt. 271 , 438
Marmaduke 215
Mary 43
Mary-Ann 231
Robert 181
Robert-Gordon 231
Robt. 43
Sally 271
Sophia 617
Thomas 259 , 271
W. 340 , 508
William 267
William-Alexander
231
Sims, Thos. 16
William 175 , 216
Simskey, Ann 217
Simson, E. 498
Sinclair, Henry 147
J.B. 292
Jno. 129
John 153
Mary 147
Sinconey, Dani. 145
Sine, Harriet 476
Sinehen, Dani. 137
Sines, John-F. 481
Michael-F. 481
U 481
Singer, John 182
Singleton, Dennis 386
Jane 250
John 257
Joseph 257
Mary 182
Thomas 250
William 182
Sinnen, Ann 475
Elizabeth 475
James 475
Sinnott, Eliza 61
Hannah 233
Sinns, Ann-Jane 476
Sinun, Biddy 347
Sise, Agnes 518
Hugh 518
James 518
John 518
Mary 518
Miles 518
Sisk, John 275
Sitdraff, Byran 227
Sitingam, G.F. 346
Sittle, Charles 367
Skally, Cathe. 206
Skeen, J. 556
Skeffington, Betty
205
John 205
Sarah 205
Skelley, Catherin 87
William 87
Skelly, Anna 306
Daniel 176
John 147
Margt. 274 , 423
Skelman, My. 547
Skelton, Sarah 608
Skerington, John 558
Skerrington, Eduard
203
Skerry, Ann 217
John 306
Martin , 217

Skerry, Mary 306
Skeverton, Mary 420
Meck 420
Skiddy, Michl. 127
Skidner, U. 491
Skiff, David 610
Skiffington, Mary 138
138
Skihan, Wm. 51
Skilley, Dennis 365
Skilly, Ann 424
Skinner, Mary 81
R. 492
William 509
Skinnington, Wm. 559
Skivington, Mary 206
Slack, Anne 209
Elizabeth 215
Ellen 560
Esther 215
Francis 209
George 195
Maria 215
My. 560
Nathaniel 209
Owen 585
Peter 560
Thomas 127
Slagon, Kate 586
Mary 586
Pat 586
Slamon, Catharine 473
Mike 473
Slan, Patrick 34
Slane, Grace 590
Mary 88
My.A. 590
Nancy 88
Slate, A. 526
James 526
U 526
Slater, Ann 202
Eliza 202
Margt. 144
Thomlson 202
Slatery, Bridget 116
Dolly 116
Jane 81
John 116
Mary 81
Patt 116
Slatney, J. 495
Slatt, R. 492
Slatterdy, Patk. 25
Slatterly, Cath. 595
James 595
John 595
Maria 595
Patrick 595
William 595
Wm. 595
Slatters, Mary 212
Slattery, Bridget 594
Denis 99
J. 588
John 160
Margaret 180
Matt. 408
Simon 104
Thos. 594
U 560
Wm. 6
Slatty, Jane 479
Patrick 137
Slaven, Anthony 346
Binn 346
D. 346
Daniel , 232

Slaven, Isabella 346
J. 346
Mary 346
Michael 232
Patk. 115
Patt 346
Slaver, Catherine 104
Francis 104
Slavid, Eliza 207
Slavin, Bridget 149
Ellen 121
Felix 133
J. 342
James 236
Margaret 366
Mary 236 , 466
Slayman, Elizabeth
156
John 156
Sleavin, John 350
Sleera, Michl. 100
Nancy 100
Sleet, Cathn. 260
John 260
Sleeter, Ellen 145
Sleight, Ann 48
Elizabeth 48
John 48
Susan 48
Sleim, Dan 344
Jno. 344
Pat 344
Sleith, U-Mrs. 314
Slevegg, James 100
Jeremiah 100
Slevin, Ann 554
Bess 554
Cath. 554
Daniel 419
Henry 554
Michael 403
Patrick 308
Thos. 92
Slirney, Patk. 460
Sliven, Ann 186
Sally 175
Susan 175
Silverton, S. 573
Sloan, Alice 311
Belle 209
Betsy 311
Cathe. 540
Eliza 556
Elizabeth 459
Ellen 556
James 246 , 503
John 153
My. 556
Pat. 459
Saml. 207
Sloane, Elizabeth 190
James 191
John 319
Mary 351
Richd. 468
Robert 351 , 421
Sarah 190
Sloaver, Mgt. 244
Sloberdger, John 354
Slottery, Margt. 518
Nelley 518
Sloven, Frederick 457
Slow, Wm. 456
Slowey, H. 527
Slunton, Biddy 151
Mary 151
Sluran, Ann 101
Biddy , 101

Sluran, Cathe. 101
John 101
Mary 101
Michl. 100
Slurry, Michael 357
Smail, A. 47
Ann 426
Ellen 378
Hannah 127
Henry 330
J. 426
Julia 71
Mary 36 , 249
My. 426
Patt 22
Thomas 602
W. 495
Smallen, Ann 102
Anne 155
Betsey 155
Christy 102
Elizabeth 155
Mary-Ann 155
Patt 102
S. 506
William 155
Smalls, Jas. 204
Smallwood, James 233
Mary 233
Smart, Isabella 366
James 231 , 366
Michael 171
R. 554
Smiley, Cath. 426
James 426
Smille, Hugh 339
James 339
Mgt. 339
Wm. 339
Smily, P. 399
R. 397
Thos. 397
U-Mrs. 397
Smith, A. 394 , 573 ,
616 , 620
Adam 74
Agnes 129 , 609
Alex 318
Alex. 536
Alexr. 124 , 596
Alfred 170
Alice 352 , 370
Alley 408
Amy 39
Andr. 129
Andrew 52 , 63 , 74
74 , 169 , 223 ,
237 , 380 , 553 ,
558
Andy 384 , 389
Ann 23 , 24 , 52 ,
59 , 62 , 79 , 83
92 , 101 , 103 ,
148 , 158 , 172 ,
199 , 203 , 221 ,
229 , 230 , 247 ,
254 , 255 , 308 ,
310 , 311 , 323 ,
326 , 354 , 356 ,
358 , 381 , 387 ,
392 , 394 , 422 ,
464 , 511 , 532 ,
558 , 573 , 587 ,
596 , 609 , 619
Ann-Jane 597
Anna 537
Annabella 442
Anne , 27 , 107